MILLENNIUM
YEAR *by* YEAR

DORLING KINDERSLEY
LONDON • NEW YORK • SYDNEY
www.dk.com

A DORLING KINDERSLEY BOOK
www.dk.com

Editor in Chief: Derrik Mercer
Editor: Jerome Burne
Picture Editor: Ruth Darby
Chronology Editors: Hazel Bedford, Henrietta Heald
Assistant Editor: Denis Pitts
Editorial production: Bronwen Lewis (Production Manager), Joan Thomas (Editorial Manager), Christian Danger, Maud Escalona, Laura Hicks, Martine McManus, Francesca Odell, Nathalie Palomba,
Art: Henri Marganne (Manager), Christian Baude
Index: Ian Crane

Conceived and co-ordinated by Jacques Legrand

Published in 1996 by Dorling Kindersley Limited,
9 Henrietta Street, London WC2E 8PS

A CIP catalogue record for this book is available from the British Library.

ISBN 0 7513 0809 9

Revisions to the 1999 edition by
Brown Packaging Books Ltd, London

Colour reproduction by Christian Bocquez, Beauclair, France

Printed and bound in Belgium by Brepols

1000–1200

Politics and Society

Norman England
The Normans conquer Anglo-Saxon England and bring the country into the European feudal system.

Turkish warriors
The Turks become the dominant force in Islam, and inflict a major defeat on the Byzantine empire.

Angkor Wat, Cambodia

Crusades
A succession of crusades is launched to conquer and hold the Holy Land for Christianity.

Americas
Toltec rule collapses in Central America. The Chimu state is founded in Peru.

Cambodia
The rulers of the Khmer empire build the temple complex of Angkor Wat.

African kings
The Hausa kingdoms flourish in West Africa, based on manufacture and trade.

Heian period sculpture, Japan

Technology and Culture

Bayeux tapestry, Normandy

Cathedral building
Europe experiences a wave of cathedral building, a reflection of growing artistic confidence and economic prosperity.

Universities
The first universities are established in Europe, taking their lead from those already set up in the Islamic world.

Love lyrics
Composed and recited by itinerant troubadours, a new form of courtly love poetry is invented in southern France.

East African trade
Kilwa and Gedi, ports on the East African coast, dispatch emissaries to China to develop trading links.

Sung prosperity
Under the Sung dynasty, Chinese art and poetry flourish. Paper money is introduced and stimulates the growth of trade.

Durham Cathedral, England

1200–1400

Black Death
The Black Death ravages Europe and Asia. A form of bubonic plague, it kills many millions.

Rise of the Aztecs
The Aztec empire is established in Central America, centred on Tenochtitlan.

Mongol triumph
Mongol nomad armies overwhelm kingdoms and empires, from China through Asia to Europe.

Maritime traders
The Italian ports of Genoa and Venice achieve wealth and power built on trade.

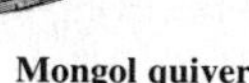

Mongol quiver

Ming China
The Ming dynasty is founded in 1368, replacing the Mongol rule of Kublai Khan and his descendants.

African empire
The Mali empire controls much of West Africa. Its wealth is based on the Saharan gold trade.

Chinese "blue and white" jar

Technology transfer
Some 300 years after its invention in China, gunpowder is first used in Europe. European castle building follows Islamic models.

Easter Island statue

Italian frescoes
The Italian painter Giotto is acclaimed as a major artist; his frescoes exhibit a new, more naturalistic style.

European literature
Dante's *Divine Comedy*, Boccaccio's *Decameron* and Chaucer's *The Canterbury Tales* are written.

Past learning
Classical learning, mostly transmitted through Arabic texts, begins to influence scientific thought in Europe.

Early travellers
Ibn Battuta, from Tangiers, and the Venetian Marco Polo publish accounts of their travels.

Pacific statues
Huge stone statues are erected on Easter Island in the Pacific Ocean.

1400-1500

Inca feather headdress and shirt

Christian victory
The last Muslim ruler is driven from Spain by the Christian monarchs.

Andean empire
Inca power expands through the Andean region.

Henry VII of England

Tudor rule
England is united under the strong rule of Henry VII, who founds the Tudor line.

Ottoman triumph
Constantinople falls to the Ottoman Turks, who make it the capital of their rapidly expanding empire.

Stone city
The power of the stone city of Zimbabwe reaches its height before declining through food shortages.

Russia emerges
The Prince of Muscovy, Ivan the Great, throws off Tartar sovereignty and asserts his independence.

Explorations
Chinese voyages to India and Africa cease by imperial edict. Portuguese and Spanish explorers cross the Atlantic to the Americas.

European printing
A moveable-type printing press is developed in Germany, starting mass production of books.

Renaissance
In Italy, there is an extraordinary flourishing of learning, classical scholarship and the arts.

Navigation
The compass, backstaff and astrolabe are in common use by European sailors.

Human sacrifice
The Aztecs consider human sacrifice essential to propitiate the gods; on one occasion 20,000 are ritually slaughtered.

Literature
Bengali poet Baru Chandidas writes the *Shrikrishnakirtan*, a poem to the Hindu god Krishna.

Michelangelo's *David*

Astrolabe of the type used by Columbus

1500-1600

Religious wars
The Reformation divides Christianity, precipitating religious wars in Europe.

Imported diseases
Venereal disease, probably imported from the New World, ravages Europe. Old World diseases such as smallpox and measles cause havoc in the Americas.

Japan united
Shogun Hideyoshi creates a strong central power, ending an era of civil war.

Islamic rulers
The Ottoman empire is at its peak. The Safavid dynasty inspires a cultural revival in Iran. The Moghul empire is established in India.

Spanish conquest
The Aztec and Inca empires are destroyed by the Spanish *conquistadores*.

African slave trade
The transatlantic slave trade begins, bringing war and depopulation.

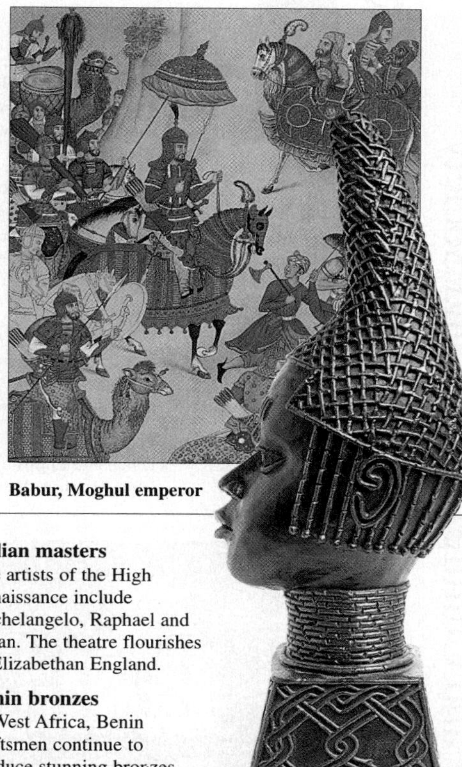

Babur, Moghul emperor

Italian masters
The artists of the High Renaissance include Michelangelo, Raphael and Titian. The theatre flourishes in Elizabethan England.

Benin bronzes
In West Africa, Benin craftsmen continue to produce stunning bronzes.

Mosques
Some of the finest mosques are built in Iran and the Ottoman empire.

Round the world
The earth is circumnavigated for the first time.

Bronze head, Benin, Africa

Exchanges
Old World animals, such as horses and cattle, are brought to the Americas. New World food plants, such as maize and potatoes, reach the Old World.

Iznik tile, Ottoman Turkey

Politics and Society

1600–1700

Oliver Cromwell, England

Newton's telescope

Colonizing America
English colonies are set up in New England and Virginia; the French colonize farther north.

Chinese upheaval
The Ming dynasty is overthrown, and replaced by the northern Manchus.

Germany at war
The Thirty Years' War ravages Germany.

Westerners expelled
The Tokugawa clan wins control of Japan and bans Western influence.

Dutch golden age
Holland's trading prowess brings great wealth. Dutch artists, such as Rembrandt and Vermeer, flourish.

Civil War
In Britain, a series of struggles between the crown and parliament produces a constitutional monarchy.

Explorations
Dutch and English voyagers chart Australasia.

1700–1750

Russia reformed
Reformed by Peter the Great, Russia expands into Siberia and is increasingly influential in Europe.

Colonial growth
British colonies in North America grow in size and wealth. European powers fight over the West Indies.

Moghul decline
The Moghul empire teeters towards collapse, attacked by armies from Iran and the Hindu Marathas.

Trade wars
The struggle between France and Britain is expressed in trade rivalry as well as open warfare.

London painting by Canaletto

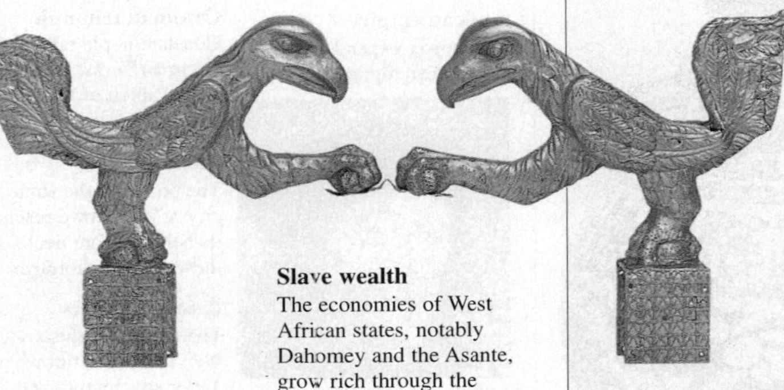

Asante gold, Africa

Slave wealth
The economies of West African states, notably Dahomey and the Asante, grow rich through the transatlantic slave trade.

1750–1800

British power
Military success in the Seven Years' War is followed by dramatic economic expansion.

United States
Colonists in North America declare their independence and win the ensuing war.

Poland divided
Partitions lead to the end of the Polish state, its lands divided up between Austria, Prussia and Russia.

French revolution
Economic collapse and social unrest bring about a revolution that destroys the monarchy and sets up a new republic.

Frederick II of Prussia

South Africa
In southern Africa, Dutch settlers fight with the indigenous Xhosa people over land rights.

British in India
British influence over India increases steadily through trade, treaty and military action.

Europeans in Oceania
The major Pacific islands are visited in Cook's voyages. Australia becomes a British possession and convict colony.

Model of guillotine, France

Technology and Culture

1600–1700

Taj Mahal, Agra, India

Scientific revolution
Western Europe experiences a scientific revolution, with the work of William Harvey, Blaise Pascal, Isaac Newton and others.

Moghul architecture
The Moghul empire in India produces architectural masterpieces such as the mausoleum of the Taj Mahal.

Early opera
In Italy, Monteverdi develops the first operas.

Japanese drama
In Japan, the popular Kabuki theatre replaces the more staid No plays as the main form of dramatic entertainment.

Literary works
In Spain Cervantes publishes *Don Quixote*, in England Milton writes *Paradise Lost*, and Racine and Molière dominate French theatre.

Bracket clock, England

1700–1750

Scientific progress
Edmund Halley accurately predicts the reappearance of comets; Linnaeus proposes a new classification of plants.

Agriculture
Mechanical developments and better understanding of how crops grow stimulate agricultural improvement.

Baroque music
Vivaldi and Scarlatti are leading lights in Italy; J.S. Bach reigns supreme in Germany.

Venetian art
Venetian-born painters Canaletto and Tiepolo achieve fame Europe-wide.

Asante gold
West African craftsmen produce sophisticated gold figurines.

Encyclopedias
In China, a 10,000-chapter encyclopedia is produced, but only 64 copies are published. French writer Diderot produces a best-selling *Encyclopédie*.

Methodist movement
Dissatisfaction with the Church of England leads to John Wesley's "Methodism".

Palace building
New-style palaces are completed in Europe, notably Versailles outside Paris.

Blenheim Palace, England

1750–1800

First iron bridge, England

Industrial Revolution
New sources of power, new industrial processes and improved transport transform Britain's manufacturing output.

Iron bridge
The first cast-iron bridge is built in England, at Coalbrookdale.

Chemistry
Advances in chemistry are made by Lavoisier, Priestley and others.

Self-interest
Adam Smith's *The Wealth of Nations* argues progress is based on self-interest.

Classical music
Composers Mozart and Haydn are active.

Enlightenment
French intellectuals, including Rousseau and Voltaire, encourage a rationalist and humanist view of the world.

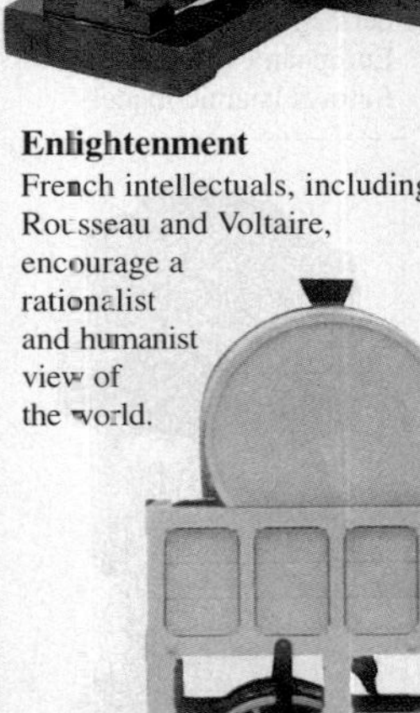

1800–1850

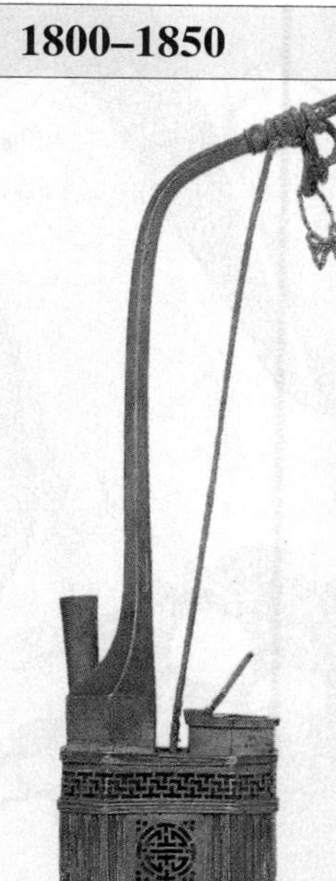
Opium pipe, China

Independence
In Central and South America, the former Spanish and Portuguese colonies win their independence.

Zulu power
The Zulus carve out an empire in southern Africa. Boer settlers from the Cape move into the African heartland.

French emperor
Napoleon Bonaparte crowns himself emperor of France and plunges Europe into war.

Growth of the U.S.
The expansion of the United States continues. The divide between industrial North and slave-owning South is increasingly apparent.

Opium and slaves
European traders force China to import Indian opium. Britain is the prime mover in the outlawing of the slave trade.

Europe in revolt
The revolutions of 1848 are fuelled by nationalist desires and economic frustration.

Romantic movement
The Romantic movement is embodied by poets like Byron and Keats, and artists like Delacroix and Turner.

Japanese prints
In Japan, popular printmaking reaches its peak in the work of Hokusai.

Musical developments
Beethoven and Schubert continue the Viennese tradition; Berlioz exemplifies the French Romanticism.

Steam power
The steam engine revolutionizes transport, providing the power for locomotives and steamships.

Telegraph messages
Samuel Morse devises a code to send messages along telegraph wires.

Exploration
U.S. Army officers Lewis and Clark cross North America.

Science
In Britain, Dalton publishes his table of elements and Faraday invents the dynamo. Darwin prepares his theory of evolution.

1830s train, England

1850–1900

American Civil War
The American Civil War is won by the North; industrial expansion gathers momentum. Native Americans are brutally robbed of their lands.

Europe
Germany and Italy are unified as nation states.

European colonialism
Almost the entire continent of Africa is taken over by European powers. British rule is consolidated in India, the French conquer Indochina.

Japan modernizes
Forced to accept external trade, the country embraces Western ideas and undergoes a rapid industrial transformation.

China in chaos
China is riven by peasant uprisings and aggressive foreign intervention.

Native American headdress

Daguerrotype, early photograph

Berliner's phonograph, 1888

Impressionist revolt
In France, the Impressionists and Post-Impressionists vie with conventional salon art.

Novel geniuses
The novel peaks in the work of Dickens, Flaubert and Tolstoy.

Opera expands
The opera expands in scope through the work of Wagner and Verdi.

Professional sport
Organized sports are developed with formal rules and regulatory bodies.

Engineering
Engineering triumphs include the Suez Canal and the Eiffel Tower.

Medical progress
Major advances in medicine, sanitation and health care start to lower death rates.

Age of inventions
Practical inventions include the telephone, electric light, the gramophone, the internal combustion engine, and the cinema. Photography becomes commonplace.

Statue of Liberty, U.S.

1900–1918

Bristol fighter, 1917

Great War
War breaks out in Europe between the Allies and the Central Powers. The war lasts four years and causes millions of deaths.

Russian revolution
Political frustration and the strains of war lead to a revolution and the emergence of the world's first Communist government.

Suffragettes
Demands for equal rights for women become more vociferous. At the end of the war, women get the vote in Britain and the U.S.

Rise of Japan
Japan defeats Russia in war, establishing itself as a major power.

Chinese republic
The emperor is deposed and a republic is instituted.

Flu epidemic
An influenza epidemic that sweeps the world at the end of the Great War causes more deaths than the war.

Gas respirator from the Great War

Sigmund Freud, founder of psychoanalysis

Psychoanalysis
Sigmund Freud proposes a new interpretation of the workings of the mind.

Polar exploration
The Norwegian Roald Amundsen beats the Englishman Robert Scott to be first man to reach the South Pole.

Relative science
Einstein publishes his theories of relativity. Max Planck invents quantum mechanics.

New writing
Modernism enters literature, especially in the work of James Joyce.

Taking to the air
The first aeroplane takes to the air, wireless radio becomes a new medium of communication, and the automobile becomes a commercial success.

Music
The symphony reaches new heights under Mahler. Avant-garde composers include Stravinsky and Schoenberg.

Artistic rebels
New boundaries are crossed in representational painting with the emergence of fauvism, futurism and cubism.

1918–1945

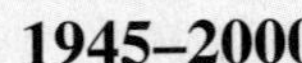

Politics and Society

Soviet propaganda poster

Adolf Hitler, German Nazi leader

Rise of the Nazis
The Nazis assume power in Germany. Their aggressive foreign policy leads to world war and humiliating defeat for their country.

Stalin's power
Under Stalin's brutal leadership the Soviet Union is industrialized, and after the war with Germany, emerges as a superpower.

America triumphant
Rising U.S. prosperity is checked by the Depression of the 1930s, but victory in World War II leaves the United States the world's richest and most powerful country.

Japanese attack
Military success in China encourages a reckless attack on the United States, resulting in military disaster and occupation.

Chinese civil war
The collapse of the old political order produces civil war, compounded by Japanese invasion.

Independence for India
The movement for Indian independence, including Gandhi's campaign of civil disobedience, becomes unstoppable.

Mao Tse-tung, founder of Communist China

Technology and Culture

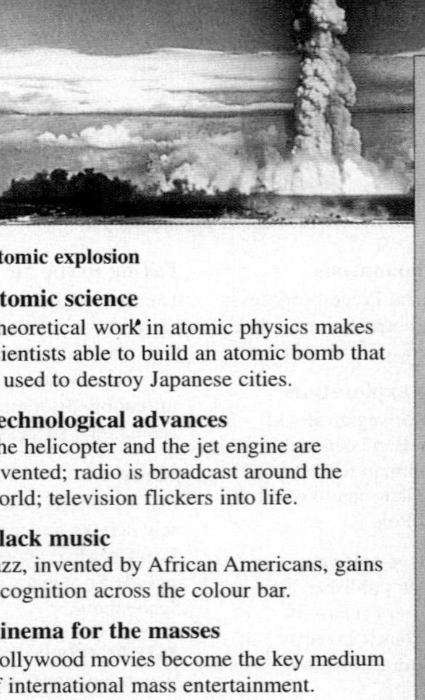

Atomic explosion

Atomic science
Theoretical work in atomic physics makes scientists able to build an atomic bomb that is used to destroy Japanese cities.

Technological advances
The helicopter and the jet engine are invented; radio is broadcast around the world; television flickers into life.

Black music
Jazz, invented by African Americans, gains recognition across the colour bar.

Cinema for the masses
Hollywood movies become the key medium of international mass entertainment.

Modernist art
Modernism triumphs in architecture and the visual arts.

Charlie Chaplin, movie star

1945–2000

Politics and Society

Martin Luther King Jr., Civil Rights leader

Space Shuttle *Atlantis*

Cold War
The United States and the Soviet Union engage in a global contest for political power.

Civil rights
Blacks in the United States win an end to segregation and achieve legal equality

African independence
All European colonial possessions in Africa become independent states.

Soviet breakup
After Gorbachev fails to reform the Soviet Union, the Communist state breaks up.

Middle East
A Jewish state is founded in Palestine; Arab opposition leads to a series of wars. Vast petroleum reserves confer great wealth on some Middle–Eastern states.

Developments in Asia
India gains independence; China is a Communist state; Japan becomes a major economic power.

Feminism
Women achieve greater economic and social freedom, especially in the West.

Pollution threat
Massive population growth and continuing industrialization lead to environmental damage on a global scale.

Technology and Culture

The Beatles, superstars of mass culture

Silicon innovations
The silicon chip makes it possible to produce miniaturized electronic systems; small but powerful computers are developed for business and personal use.

Speed of communications
Satellites help transform communications, allowing near instant international access by voice, television or computer.

Harnessing the atom
Atomic power is used for energy generation, but accidents raise doubts about safety.

Voyages into space
Space exploration puts a man on the moon and probes other planets.

Improvements in agriculture
Dramatic improvements in seeds and fertilizers produce the "Green Revolution", permitting greatly improved yields.

Genetic engineering
Scientists crack the genetic code. New plants and animals can be produced through genetic engineering.

Internet
Computer-based networks spread across the globe; 130 million people use the Internet.

Computer, 1999

MILLENNIUM
YEAR *by* YEAR

1000 YEARS OF WORLD HISTORY

1000 (1000-1014)

Hungary, 25 December 1000. Duke Stephen, in power since 997, is crowned Hungary's first king with regalia sent by Pope Sylvester II.

Balkans, 1001. Basil II, the Byzantine emperor, reembarks upon the conquest of Bulgaria.

Italy, 23 January 1002. The Emperor Otto III dies at Paterno.

Spain, 1002. Mohammed ibn Abu Amir, popularly known as al-Mansur, the chief minister of Caliph Hisham II and effective ruler of the Umayyad caliphate of Cordoba, dies at Medinaceli. He is succeeded by his son Abd al-Malik.

Rome, 12 May 1003. Sylvester II (Gerbert of Aurillac), the first French pope, is dead. Elected in 999, with the backing of Otto III, he encouraged the Holy Roman emperor's ambition to recreate the empire in the West and authorised the title of king for Duke Stephen of Hungary.

Italy, 1004. After the coronation of Henry II as emperor on 14 May, at Pavia, a quarrel develops between the Germans who are accompanying him and the Pavese. This grows into a full-scale battle in which much of the city is burnt and hundreds of citizens are slaughtered.

China, 1006. Granaries for emergency famine relief are set up throughout the country.

Persia, 1008. Al-Hamadhani (Ahmad ibn al-Husayn), the writer who acquired the nickname "the Wonder of the Age", dies at Harat. He invented the literary form known as the *maqamah* – a short anecdote written in rhyming prose, inspired by the Koran.

India, 1008. The armies of the Turkic Ghaznavid people sweep through India from their base in Afghanistan under their ruler Mahmud, defeating the armies of a Hindu confederacy on the plain of Peshawar.

Jerusalem, 1009. The Fatimid Caliph al-Hakim destroys the church of the Holy Sepulchre, apparently in a fit of madness, prompting calls for a Christian crusade to recover the Holy Land.

Ireland, 1014. The Vikings are defeated at the battle of Clontarf by the Irish army of King Brian Boru, who is killed in the battle.

Vikings sail far west

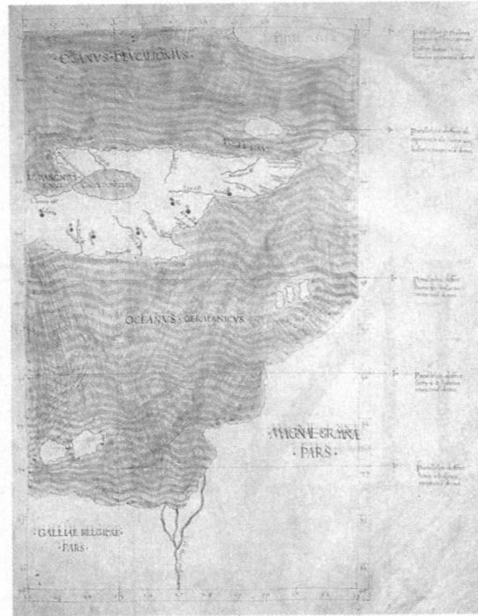

Map of "Thule", possibly Iceland.

Norway c.1000

Tales are spreading that land-hungry Vikings have found a "lush land" after sailing far west across the Atlantic. Until now no-one has explored so far, or returned to tell the tale. The latest expedition has told of a native people with whom it traded goods and milk – from cows it took with it – for furs and skins. The Viking leader, Thorvald, was killed by an arrow in a fight with the natives.

It is almost 20 years ago since Erik the Red used his period of banishment for murder to seek out new land to the north-west. He discovered a good farming country since colonised by 3,000 Vikings and known as "Greenland".

Soon afterwards, in 986, Bjarni Herjolfsson, sailing from Iceland in search of Greenland, was blown too far south and saw a country "well forested with low hills". Some years later Erik's son, Leif, bought Bjarni's ship in Greenland, sailed west and discovered what he called Vinland – "land of wine" – where he stayed through the winter. His brother, Thorvald, repeated the journey in the following year, intending to set up a colony. They spent time inscribing the rocks there as proof that the Vikings had visited.

Thorvald's crew also spent the winter in Vinland before returning with news of his death. Further expeditions seem sure to follow.

Pacific colonised

Pacific Ocean, c.1000

Polynesians have arrived in New Zealand. Their ancestors began to disperse from the eastern islands of south-east Asia in about 1500BC, in the wake of a population explosion caused by the growth of rice cultivation. They had reached Hawaii and Easter Island by AD400. Polynesians are now the most widely-spread race on earth.

A Polynesian statue on Easter Island.

East and West mate in slow chess moves

Chess. Arabs say "Shah mata!" (the king is dead!) on winning.

Madrid, c.1010

East and west may be divided by religious differences, but at least one cultural activity has crossed the great divide between Christianity and Islam more than once. It is a board game which some call *Ya, Shah* (Oh king!: a challenge) and others *chess*. The game might have its origins in ancient Greece, but it has returned to the west in several slow moves from India, where it was known as *shatrandj*, by way of Persia. Two centuries ago Caliph Harun alRashid presented a chessboard to Charlemagne. More recently an Arab scholar, al-Biruni, rediscovered the game in India, much elaborated, with 64 squares. Pieces include an elephant and camels as well as a magic bird called *rukh*.

China gets worst of border peace with northern neighbour

China, 1004

The Song emperor, Zhenzong, has concluded a peace treaty, which is regarded as humiliating by many court officials, with the northern Liao empire of the Khitan nomads.

The emperor had led his army to force the Khitan to abandon land which they had seized in the province of Hopeh. But, well aware of the Khitans' martial prowess, he decided he would rather negotiate than fight. The Khitan Dowager Empress Xiao, an able regent for her young son, was of like mind and, after several skirmishes for honour's sake, envoys were exchanged, and a treaty of "sworn letters" has been agreed which returns Hopeh to the Song and establishes the basis of a lasting peace. But it also stipulates that the Song must pay the Khitans 100,000 ounces of silver and 200,000 bolts of silk every year – a "tribute" which offends many Song officials.

Danes invade England

London, December 1013
Danish forces under King Sweyn are claiming control of the whole of England following the surrender of London. The deposed king of England, Aethelred, is reported to have fled to France to join Queen Emma and their children, who have taken refuge with her brother, the duke of Normandy.

Most of the population, who surrendered rather than resisted, fear that, unlike previous invaders, the Danes will not be prepared to be bought off with bribes. Instead it is thought that King Sweyn plans to consolidate his hold on England as an act of revenge against Aethelred.

The enmity between the two goes back to 1002 when Aethelred, his rule weakened by frequent Viking attacks, ordered the secret St Brice's Day massacre of Danes living in England. Among those murdered was Sweyn's sister, Gunnhild.

A Danish-style tombstone.

Sweyn retaliated by burning homesteads throughout the south for four years before accepting a substantial bribe to withdraw.

The uneasy truce was broken last year when Aethelred persuaded one of Sweyn's top commanders, Thorkell the Tall, to defect. This led to the invasion, with Sweyn landing men on Humberside before marching south.

Irish beat back Viking invaders

Dublin, 1014
Brian Boru, the high king of Ireland and leader of the Dal Cais dynasty, was killed in a vicious all-day battle at Clontarf on Good Friday between two Irish factions, one of them with Viking support. Boru's victorious Munster army has seriously weakened the Norsemen's grip on Ireland. This was the second such victory for Boru. Fifteen years ago, his army defeated the Norsemen occupying Dublin together with Mael Morda, the king of Leinster.

Morda recently formed an alliance with Sitric, the Norse ruler of Dublin. Sitric summoned Sigurd of Orkney, Brodir of Man, and even Thorstein Hallsson of Iceland.

Boru died when Morda broke through his bodyguard and stabbed him. Morda was later tortured to death by the King's furious army.

Kingdom prospers in South India

A statue of Siva seated, from Chola.

Southern India, 1010
Under King Rajaraja of Chola, who extended the Chola domains to all southern India, the Chola empire has become the most powerful and prosperous in India. A Brihadisvara temple 200 feet high has been completed in the capital Thanjavur, a symbol of Chola grandeur.

On Rajaraja's accession in 985, Chola power was in retreat after the initial expansion by Aditya a century earlier. He first turned south, defeating a revived Pandya power and invading Sri Lanka; then east, against the Gangas; finally north, reducing the powerful Vengi state to a mere protectorate. His land conquests complete, he has built a fleet that dominates the Indian Ocean, making Chola rich from Chinese and Near Eastern trade.

A Cholan three-headed brahma.

On death of caliph, Cordoba is jewel in Arab Spain's crown

Cordoba, 1002
Mohammed ibn Abu Amir, known as *al-Mansur* (the Victorious), the dictator of Moslem Spain for the last quarter-century, is dead. Under his rule Spain has reached unprecedented importance, but experts fear that in the power vacuum that now threatens Cordoba, since al-Mansur has left no specific successor, this importance may simply collapse into political in-fighting.

Al-Mansur gained power in 978 when, as chamberlain to the ten-year-old Caliph Hisham II, and backed by the caliph's Basque mother Aurora, he became the effective ruler of the country.

Although al-Mansur ruled as a dictator, he did not abuse his power, but instead worked to increase the influence of his country. Talented and efficient, he expanded Cordoba's power: in the north he took Leon and Compostela away from their Christian rulers, while in the south he expanded the power of Andalucia into western Maghreb.

Al-Mansur's success has not merely been as a conqueror. Cordoba has become a booming city of some 500,000 inhabitants, the largest in western Europe. Its craftsmen are renowned for their work, producing exquisite goods and specialising in textiles, leather and ivory. Streets are clean and safe, and there are many mosques and public baths.

Detail from the front of a Hispano-Arab ivory casket made at Cordoba.

Spain's reputation for learning has also benefited. Hakam II, the father of the young caliph, who died in 978, left an important intellectual legacy. An enthusiastic bibliophile, he collected some 400,000 volumes, a library that covers every aspect of Islamic scholarship, from theology to science. The library is a centre for many scholars, although local Moslem fundamentalists fear that, so wideranging is the collection, many of its works may be heretical. They would purge the library if they could.

1014 (1014-1027)

Russia, 1015. Vladimir, the prince of Kiev, dies. He was converted to Christianity in 988 when he married Anne, the sister of the Eastern Emperor Basil II, thus opening Russia to Byzantine influences.

India, 1015. The Ghaznavid army invades Kashmir, but is forced to retreat.

Britain, 30 November 1016. Edmund Ironside, who succeeded Aethelred as king of England earlier in the year, dies, leaving Canute as unchallenged ruler of England.

Bulgaria, 1018. The Eastern Emperor Basil II completes the conquest of Bulgaria.

India, 1018. Mahmud, leader of the Ghaznavids, sacks Kanauj and breaks the power of the Hindu states.

Sri Lanka, 1018. Rajendra Chola conquers Sri Lanka.

Europe, 1019. England and Scandinavia are unified under the rule of Canute.

France, 1019. Saracens attack the Mediterranean port of Narbonne.

Afghanistan, 1019. Mahmud founds the great mosque at Ghazni, capital of the Ghaznavid domains. His armies now occupy most of northern India.

India, 1021. The Cholas invade Bengal.

Central Asia, 1023. Mahmud and the Ghaznavids turn north and occupy Transoxiana.

North Africa, 1023. Soon after returning from a pilgrimage to Mecca, the Tarsina king of Zanata, a mountain nation on the borders of Morocco and Algeria, dies in battle.

Italy, 1024. Emperor Henry II dies on 13 July; a revolt then breaks out in Lombardy.

India, 1024. The Ghaznavids sack the great Hindu religious centre of Somnath, carrying away vast treasure after slaughtering over 50,000.

Constantinople, 15 December 1025. Basil II is succeeded as emperor by Constantine VIII, his brother and co-ruler.

Persia, 1025. Ferdowski, the author of the *Shahnameh* (Book of Kings), dies at Khurasan. His book charts the history of Persia from its mythical origins up to the Arab conquest.

Syria, 1027. Salih ibn Mirdas, the governor of Aleppo, besieges the city of Marras.

The Emperor Henry, whose majesty is well caught by this later portrait.

Henry crowned as Holy Roman emperor

Rome, 14 February 1014
Yet another German king has travelled to Rome to have himself crowned Holy Roman emperor. With his wife Cunigunde, the daughter of the count of Luxembourg, Henry II was today met on the steps of St Peter's by Pope Benedict VIII, who asked him if he would be a faithful defender of the Church. Henry and his wife were then admitted into the church and anointed. The pope placed in Henry's hand a golden orb surmounted by a cross, symbolic of his rule over the world's empire.

Behind this solemn ceremonial lies the reality of a ruler who faces an endless struggle to contain rebellions and feuds by powerful nobles. Henry, the son of that duke of Bavaria known as the Troublemaker, is pious, well-meaning and in poor health. He was destined for the Church when Otto III died without children. The Bavarians and the Franks called on Henry, who by concessions and favours won the dubious allegiance of Saxons, Thuringians, Swabians and Lotharingians.

Henry came to the throne faced by wars on every frontier. Italy had been lost, Boleslav of Poland was seizing lands in the east, and the count of Flanders was moving on Lotharingia. Henry has responded by seeking the support of the Church. Lavish in his grants of land and titles to bishops and abbots, he seeks to make them servants of the crown.

Turks find a new aggressive leader

Afghanistan, 1024
Mahmud of Ghazni, who defeated his elder brother to seize the throne of Afghanistan, is expanding his empire into Persia and India, raiding from his mountain fastness down into the rich agricultural plain of the Punjab. His conquests are religious as well as territorial, for he is a zealous Moslem and on his forays into India he destroys Hindu temples, carrying off their treasures and forcing their monks to convert to Islam.

His latest campaign in India has taken him to the shores of the Indian Ocean, and to the famous temple of Siva at Somnath in Gujarat where he horrified the Hindus by destroying the temple and carrying away its celebrated golden gates.

Mahmud is also, however, a patron of literature and art. This son of a Turkish slave become king has built a magnificent mosque, the Celestial Bride, at Ghazni, and splendid palaces at Bust and Ghazni, and at his court live the greatest scholars of the age.

Caliph disappears, feared murdered

Cairo, 14 February 1021
Searchers for the missing Fatimid Caliph al-Hakim of Egypt have lost hope of finding their irascible leader alive. Clothes last worn by al-Hakim have been found slashed by a dagger on the Mukattam hills outside the city and it seems almost certain he was murdered, apparently while on a nocturnal walk.

The caliph's sister, Sitt al-Mulk, may have decided to kill her brother to put to an end what many saw as his capricious and cruel rule. He made decrees at whim to ban chess or keep markets open all night, but gained real notoriety for carrying out sudden and brutal executions, and outraged Christians by ordering the demolition of their holiest shrine, the church of the Holy Sepulchre in Jerusalem.

Not everyone has given up hope for Al-Hakim. The Syrian Druze sect believe he is a divine monarch who has simply gone into hiding and is sure to return.

Prisoners blinded as Bulgars are crushed

Bulgaria, 6 October 1014
A sightless army returned from battle today – 15,000 men blinded on the orders of a Byzantine emperor. As the pathetic regiments made their way home, their ruler, Czar Samuel, was so shocked that he died, apparently of apoplexy.

Even the worst excesses of the most evil Caesar could not match the calculated cruelty which took place on the banks of the river Strymon after Basil's forces had surrounded and defeated the Bulgarians. One man in every 100 was left with one eye to guide his pathetic comrades on their long march home to Samuel.

To celebrate his victory and its horrific aftermath, Basil, who is described as a "humane and benevolent" man, has been given the title of *Bulgaroctonus* – slayer of the Bulgars.

For the past 13 years Basil has sought to vanquish Samuel's Bulgarian empire. Once he had secured his eastern borders, the tough and resourceful emperor drew up plans for the attack and led his well-trained armies personally in a series of summer campaigns. His skill was in his ability to divide enemy forces and surround them with fast-moving infantry and cavalry.

Bulgarians cower before Basil.

At the beginning of the war Basil used a soft approach to the Bulgarian chiefs, offering them honours and titles. Believing that they had betrayed him, he began a campaign of unprecedented terror in which massacre became the norm.

Canute unites England and Denmark

England, 1019
Canute is now king of England and Denmark. Three years ago the Danish prince, the son of Swein, was offered the English throne after defeating Edmund Ironside. Now the death of Harald of Denmark has enabled him to unite the two countries. It is the high point of a reign which has been distinguished by skilful statecraft and utter ruthlessness.

Since 995, England under Aethelred had been unstable, liable to frequent Viking incursions. Aethelred ordered every Dane in the country to be killed. At the time of Aethelred's death, in 1016, there were fluctuating alliances between Saxons and Danes, many of whom had intermarried. While Canute's army ravaged the south, Edmund controlled most of the north of England; the treacherous Eadric supported first one, then the other.

Canute defeated Edmund at Ashingdon in Essex, and the two agreed to divide the country. Edmund was murdered soon afterwards, and Canute eliminated potential rivals, including Eadric. In 1017 he married Aethelred's widow, Emma of Normandy. Since then he has espoused Christianity, established equal rights for Danes and Englishmen, and, confident of his position, sent most of his army back to Denmark.

Dual monarch: King Canute.

Indian temple highlights joys – and varieties – of love

The main tower of the temple.

One of the friezes which viewers at ground level are less likely to see.

Central India, c.1020
The stupendous Kandariya Mahedeva Hindu temple at the Chandela capital of Khajuraho is complete. Surpassing the smaller temples built by the Chandela dynasty over the last 100 years, it is the Chandelas' great masterpiece. Built in fine cream-coloured sandstone, its phallic spire rises for 116 feet, though it appears even higher because of the deep basement and the vertical lines on the spire. It is surrounded by lesser spires.

Inside the temple is a *pradaksina*, or walkway, provided with shaded balconies. Outside are the friezes and sculptures. At the lower levels scenes from hunting, warfare and courtly life are depicted. The higher friezes are reserved for representations of gods and goddesses, along with scenes of lovemaking, depicting couples and trios indulging in all the erotic variety which the vivid imagination of the gods has ordained.

Poland becomes independent state

Poland, 1025
Boleslav the Brave is dead, only a few months after being crowned king of Poland. Having received the pope's blessing a year earlier, he had established Poland as a sovereign state independent of the Holy Roman empire. He is succeeded by his son, Mieszko II. When Boleslav became Poland's ruler 33 years ago, he continued the alliance with the empire.

In 1000 the Emperor Otto III came to Gniezno to visit the grave of St Wojciech. But Otto's successor, Henry II, backed by German nobles, and ever anxious to recreate the Frankish kingdom, went to war with Poland.

In successive campaigns against the empire lasting for 14 years (1004-18), Boleslav held his own, occupying parts of Moravia and Bohemia, Lusatia and Milsko. These gains were consolidated in the Peace of Bautzen in 1018. The death of Henry II last year finally allowed full recognition of Poland.

1027 (1027-1050)

Rome, Easter 1027. Conrad II is crowned emperor in the presence of Canute, the king of England and Denmark, and Rudolf III of Burgundy.

Spain, 1028. Sancho III, the Christian king of Navarre, conquers neighbouring Castile.

Afghanistan, 1030. On the death of the great Ghaznavid ruler Mahmud, his son Masud blinds his brother Mohammed and takes the throne. His empire stretches from Persia to the valley of the Ganges.

Syria, 1030. The Byzantine emperor, Romanus III, who acquired the title by marrying Zoe, daughter of Constantine VIII, invades Syria.

Spain, 1031. The deposition of the last Umayyad caliph, Hisham III, brings an end to the caliphate of Cordoba.

France, 2 February 1032. On the death of the childless king of Burgundy, Rudolf III, the emperor, Conrad II, claims the throne, as agreed in the treaty of succession of 1027.

India, 1035. Rajaraja the Great, whose 50-year reign has seen decisive Chola supremacy in the south of India, is dead.

France, 4 June 1039. The Emperor Conrad II, who succeeded Henry II in 1024 and founded the Salian (or Franconian) dynasty, dies.

Central Asia, 1040. Seljuk Turks beat the Ghaznavid ruler Masud, who returns to Ghazni, where he is murdered. His brother Mohammed succeeds.

Italy, c.1040. Guido d'Arezzo, greatest of Europe's musical teachers, dies aged about 50.

North Africa, 1042. The Almoravids, Saharan Moslems inspired by Abdullah ibn Yasin, who preaches holy war and spiritual renewal, invade Morocco.

Italy, 1043. Power in Apulia passes to the Norman brothers William (Iron Arm) and Drogo de Hauteville.

Rome, 1044. The debauched Benedict IX, who was elected pope in 1032, is deposed in favour of Sylvester III.

Rome, May 1045. Having taken back the papal throne by force, Benedict abdicates and sells his office to Gregory VI.

Rome, 1046. The Emperor Henry III forces the abdication of Pope Gregory VI on the grounds of simony, and confirms the depositions of Sylvester III and Benedict IX.

Canute's empire grows

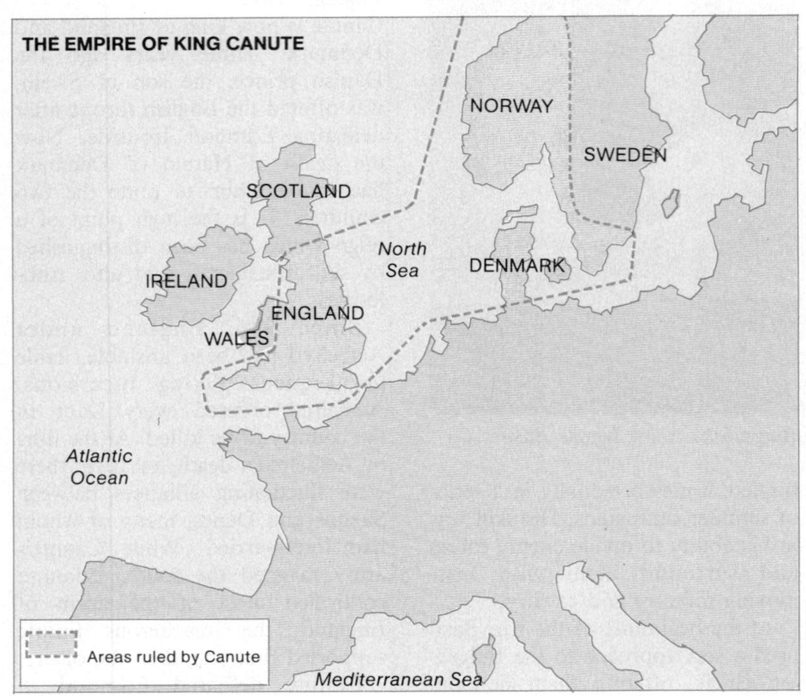

Norway, 1030

Olaf, the former king of Norway, has died at the battle of Stiklestad, his ramshackle forces hopelessly outnumbered by a Norwegian army loyal to Canute. Canute is now master of England, Denmark, Norway and possibly Sweden.

Olaf, who took to the sea aged 12, and fought in Denmark, Sweden, Gotland, Finland, England and France, where he was baptised, returned to Norway to claim the throne 15 years ago.

Within a year Olaf was king of Norway. Although a ruthless warrior, he was an enlightened king, and a firm believer in the law. He not only introduced Christianity to Norway; he created a state church. He fought the Swedes, then married their king's daughter.

But joining the Swedish King Onund in an attack on Denmark was a mistake. Rapidly gaining control of the seas, Canute suborned many of the Norwegian nobles, and landed unopposed in 1028 to claim the throne. When Hakon, made governor of Norway by Canute, died this year, Olaf made his final, ill-fated attempt to reclaim the throne.

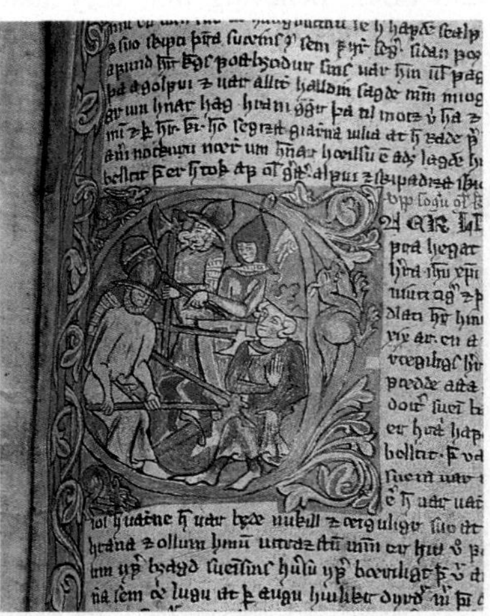

A later view of Olaf's death.

Great master of medicine has died

A later portrait of Avicenna: the Persians revered his vast learning.

Persia, 18 June 1037

Ibn Sina or, as Europeans call him, Avicenna, "the great master", has died at Hamadan and is mourned throughout the Islamic world.

His knowledge in every field of learning was encyclopaedic. He was particularly revered as the greatest modern medical mind through his treatises on the pulse, fevers, symptoms and diagnosis, wounds, fractures, bites, poisons and diarrhoea, among the many conditions listed in his *Canon of Medicine*.

Ibn Sina was also famed as a philosopher, influenced by the Greeks. He believed that human knowledge could be unlimited. He also believed that the saint and the sage could both attain perfect clarity equal to that of the Prophet.

He was born in Alshana, near Bokhara, and spoke Persian. He taught himself medicine. By 16 he had mastered all known science. He wrote his works at night very rapidly, while by day he served several princes as minister. He was often envied and forced to flee and hide, giving medical consultations to earn his living. He spent most of his last years at Isfahan.

Arab philosopher who wrote handbook on India is dead

Ghazni, Afganistan, 1048

Abu Raiham Mohammed al-Biruni, the author of treatises on astronomy, geography, history, chemistry, philosophy and mathematics, is dead. In the roll-call of Islamic thinkers, he is amongst the very first. Al-Biruni was born in 973 in Khwarizm, and became fluent in Arabic and Greek. His brilliance was recognised by Mahmud, the sultan of the Ghaznavids, who devoted his life's energies to expanding his Afghan empire to the Indus. As Mahmud's armies advanced, so al-Biruni followed, learning Sanskrit and studying Indian philosophy for his great work, *Tarikh-ul-Hind*, the acclaimed handbook on India that has become his memorial.

Holy fist-fight greets German ruler

Conrad: the hawkish Emperor.

Rome, Easter 1027
Amid imperial pomp and religious fist-fighting, Conrad, the king of Germany, was crowned emperor here in the presence of two crowned heads, Rudolf of Burgundy and Canute of England. Queen Gisela has been made empress of Rome. Two archbishops (of Milan and Ravenna), who had vied for the honour of leading the king to the altar, exchanged harsh words and even punches outside St Peter's cathedral.

Conrad began his march on Italy a year ago – ostensibly to claim his rightful crown of Lombardy. He came up against stiff opposition from the inhabitants of Pavia, who closed the city gates to his army' and later from Ravenna, where his men hacked down people running to safety. Conrad ordered survivors to parade before him in hair shirts, barefoot, with unsheathed swords hung around their necks, and beg for forgiveness. Much the same ordeal befell the people of Rome today after a riot which followed a dispute between a German and a Roman over the price of a hide.

Pagan is heart of new Burmese empire

A Buddhist temple at Pagan, showing Khmer and Hindu influences.

Burma, 1050
The strictly disciplinarian regime of the new king, Anawrahta, is bringing stability and power to Burma. From its capital, Pagan, the king is extending his empire from as far as the Mons kingdom of Thaton to the Indian Ocean.

Anawrahta has made good economic use of the crossing at Pagan of trade routes to Yunnan, Assam and the Shan States. He is advancing farming techniques, and is in process of strengthening his army by appointing four tough generals. His revolutionary use of elephants adds even greater power to his army.

Conversion to Theravada Buddhism inspired Anawrahta to begin building the Shwezigon pagoda. Worship of many gods was tolerated inside the pagoda. The king said: "Men will not come for the sake of the new faith. Let them come for their old gods and gradually they will be won over."

"World will end" fears grip Christians

Christ: a new earthquake in store?

Tongues of flame – or hellfire?

Burgundy, France, 1033
Panic is spreading through the kingdom this summer. Many people here believe that this year, the thousandth anniversary of the death of Christ, will mark the end of the world. Their belief was nurtured by the famine arising from the torrential thunderstorms which flattened crops in much of France in the spring. Huge crowds are now making public displays of repentance, swearing to keep the peace of God. Thousands more have gone on pilgrimages to the Holy Land.

Similar fears were prevalent 33 years ago on the anniversary of Christ's birth. That year passed without mishap, but the destruction of the Holy Sepulchre in Jerusalem in 1009, by Caliph Hakim, produced a new nervousness.

Radulph Glaber, a Burgundian who now lives in the abbey of Cluny, expressed the feelings of his countrymen when he wrote about the earlier panic which hit the kingdom in the spring: "Men thought that the very laws of nature and the order of the seasons were reversed, that those rules which governed the world were replaced by chaos. They knew then that the end of the world had arrived."

African hilltop town rises on gold trade

Southern Africa, c.1050
The Indian Ocean trade network is bringing riches to the people of the Limpopo river basin in south-east Africa. The most prosperous area is known as Mapungubwe, and trades both with merchants from the coast, and, indirectly, with lands on the other side of the Indian Ocean.

The area has been well-populated for several hundreds of years by farmers of cattle and caprines (goat-like sheep). But they are increasingly reaping the benefits of trade, exporting both rough and finely wrought ivory ware in exchange for large quantities of glass beads, ceramics from the Persian Gulf and other exotic commodities. The people thrive and the towns grow.

A Jewish school: Jewish teaching is now centred on North Africa, Spain and the Rhine. Only one school remains in Babylon, the former centre.

1050 (1050-1065)

Persia, 1052. The Seljuks seize Isfahan.

Italy, 23 June 1053. Pope Leo IX raises an army to expel the Normans from Italy. The papal forces are defeated at Civitate and Leo is captured.

Britain, 1054. Earl Siward of Northumberland leads an army into Scotland in support of Malcolm Canmore, whose father, King Duncan, was murdered by Macbeth, the earl of Moray, who then took the throne. Macbeth is defeated at Dunsinane, near Perth.

Russia, 1054. Iaroslav, the prince of Kiev, dies at Vyshgorod. He took Kiev in 1019, subjugated the Pechenegs and extended his control to the Baltic.

Constantinople, July 1054. The patriarch of Constantinople, Michael Cerularius, is ex-communicated by the papal legate, initiating a schism between the Christian Churches of East and West.

West Africa, 1055. Awdaghost (*in Mauritania*) is seized by Almoravid invaders.

Baghdad, 1055. The Seljuk Toghril-Beg enters Baghdad as the liberator and protector of the Abbasid caliphate against the Shi'ites. He restores the Sunni branch of Islam and instals himself as the temporal master of the caliph.

Germany, 5 October 1056. The German Emperor Henry III dies at Pfalz Bodfeld. As his son, Henry IV, is aged only six, the empress, Agnes of Poitou, becomes regent.

Rome, 1059. Pope Nicholas II issues a decree restricting the right of electing the pope to the cardinals.

France, 1060. Henry, the king of France, is succeeded by his son, Philip, under the guardianship of Baldwin V, the count of Flanders.

North Africa, 1061. After the Almoravid conquest of the Zanata in Morocco, Yusuf ben Tashfin succeeds to the throne.

Morocco/Spain, 1062. Abu Bakr, ibn Yasin's successor, founds Marrakesh and invades Spain.

Portugal, 9 June 1064. Coimbra is captured by Ferdinand, the king of Castile.

Spain, 1065. Ferdinand falls ill while attacking the king of Valencia at Paterna, and dies. His kingdom is divided between his three sons.

Norman pact with pope

Italy, August 1059

The Normans have achieved a vital agreement with their old enemy, the pope. One of their number, Robert Guiscard, has brought off a brilliant diplomatic coup by agreeing the terms of the Treaty of Melfi with Pope Nicholas II. Robert defeated the papal army six years ago at Civitate, but he has chosen the statesmanlike route of a peaceful alliance with the papacy.

In the treaty Robert promises to be faithful to the Catholic Church and to the pope. In return the pope recognises him as duke of Apulia and Calabria, which he has already conquered, and duke of Sicily, which is today occupied by the Saracens.

Pope Nicholas has been under pressure, thanks to continuing quarrels with Byzantium in the east and the military threat from the Arabs in much of the Mediterranean. He is only too thankful to have one less enemy. For Robert it means he can now push on to drive the Saracens from Sicily without the fear that the papal armies will attack his rear.

Roger Guiscard lands in Sicily.

The Normans are descendants of Viking mercenaries – like Robert's father, Tancred of Hauteville – who began to leave Scandinavia some 50 years ago to plunder in France and Italy. A few, like Robert, and William, the duke of Normandy, have now settled down and set up stable governments.

English king exiles his close adviser

Bosham, England, 1051

Under a royal safe-conduct, Godwin, the earl of Wessex, the second most powerful man in England, boarded his ship here – exiled by the king whose accession he had arranged. King Edward had for years been heavily influenced by the ruthless and wealthy earl. The king married Godwin's daughter, Eadgyth, though the marriage has remained childless, and watched helplessly as the earl and his family extended their estates and power in the west.

This power began to wane when Godwin's elder son, Swein, outraged religious feeling by seducing the abbess of Leominster and murdering his cousin.

Then, last year, Godwin went too far. The monks of Christ Church elected a Godwin kinsman as archbishop of Canterbury. The king refused to accept him and appointed a Norman, Robert. This, in turn, infuriated Godwin, who was bitterly opposed to the promotion of Normans in the church. Godwin and his sons mounted an army and prepared to fight near Hereford. The king rallied other earls to his side. Surprised by this royal firmness, outnumbered, and condemned by the church, Godwin chose to flee.

Edward: a later impression.

Chivalry is the code for jousting knights

Europe, c.1065

Improvements in cavalry techniques have led to a major increase in the social status and prestige of mounted warriors. Behind the shift lies the introduction to Europe of the stirrup, from the Orient, in the early 700s; this gave horsemen far greater control, and greatly enhanced the importance of cavalry.

However, it is only recently that full advantage has been taken of the stirrup. It is now possible to deal an enemy a fierce blow with a heavier spear or lance couched under one armpit without falling out of the saddle. But buying all the relevant equipment for this technique, especially protective armour, is a costly business; only wealthy men can really afford to equip themselves or others as knights and hold the tournaments and jousts – essentially training sessions – which have become great social and courtly occasions. Horsemanship – or, as the Normans call it, *chivalrie* – is now a prestigious occupation, and new codes of behaviour are reinforcing the common bonds of the increasingly aristocratic knights.

A Japanese painted wooden statue of the Bodhisattva Jizo – who administers to those in need – dressed as a mendicant.

East-West Church split is threatened

Constantinople, 16 July 1054
Cardinal Humbert, the papal legate, today marched into the cathedral of Saint Sophia here and placed on the altar a bull of excommunication against Michael Cerularius, the patriarch of Constantinople. Local observers see this move as the final gesture of a desperate man who realises that his mission has failed.

Humbert was sent by the pope to try to bring the Eastern Church to heel. Since he became pope, in 1048, Leo XI has aspired to take firm overall control of the Christian Church throughout the world. His ambition takes little account of the prestige and independent behaviour of the Byzantine Church. It also shows little awareness of the deep distrust in the East of the papal alliance with the German emperor.

Patriarch Michael enjoys the support of his people, and the most likely outcome of today's move is the final split between the Eastern and Western arms of the Church. Their differences have been unresolved for some 400 years. Rome believes in the twofold nature of Christ which the East rejects. Rome insists on celibate priests, while the East has continued to allow its clergy to marry. The union of the Churches has depended on both sides turning a blind eye to the reality of the respective practices of East and West.

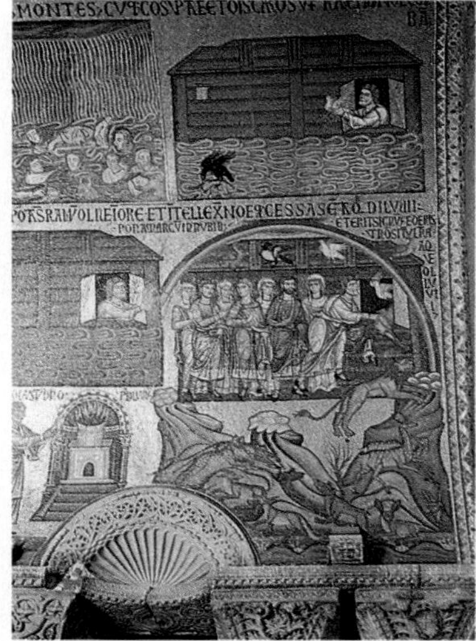

West: Venetian mosaics of Noah.

East: Christ at Constantinople.

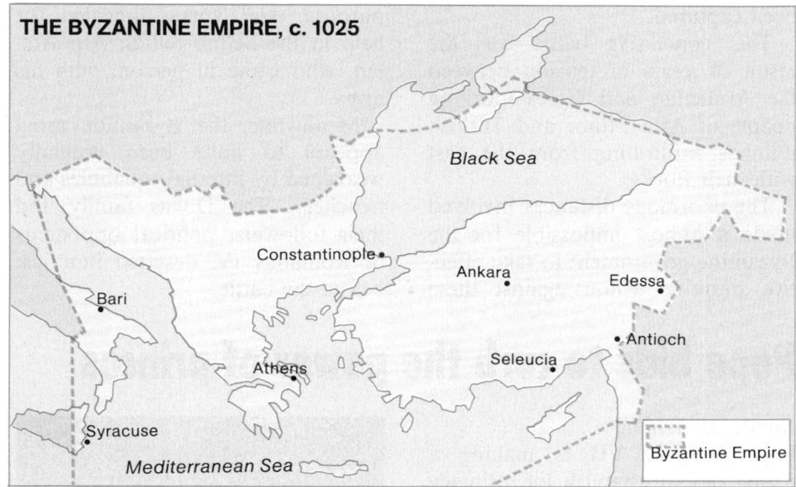

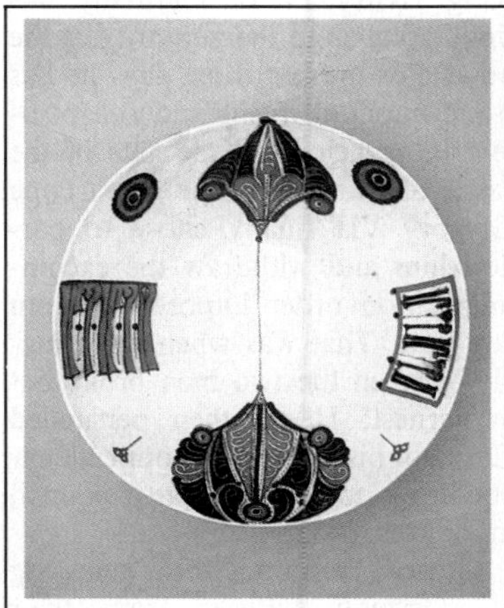

While Christendom is torn between popes, patriarchs and emperors, Islam flourishes. This bowl of sandy earthenware is from Nishapur, in Persia.

Blind hermit poet wrote dark verse

El-Marra, Syria, 1056
After half a century of living in ascetic seclusion, the poet Abu L'Ala al-Ma'arri has died aged 77. Blinded by smallpox at the age of four, the poet refused to compromise his nihilism for money.

Human life and nature were to al-Ma'arri the vanities of the world. He wrote cynically: "Better for Adam and all who issued forth from his loins that he and they never had been created!" The intensely dark, 13,000-verse *Luzumiyyat*, written to glorify God, was al-Ma'arri's antidote to the conventional poets' preoccupation with love, battle and frivolity.

Anarchy spreads through Tunisia

Tunisia, 1057
The decision of the defeated Tunisian ruler al-Mu'izz to retreat into an enclave at al-Mahdiya has left the country in disarray, with large areas controlled by the Banu Hilal. These southern Arabian tribesmen have steadily reduced Tunisia to a state of anarchy since they arrived seven years ago aided by the Cairo caliph, al-Mustanisir.

For al-Mu'izz it represents defeat for his policy of trying to integrate the Banu Hilal. When the tribesmen arrived he gave three daughters to their leaders, but this failed to stop them wiping out his army.

Victories of Spanish King putting the Arabs on the run

Iberia, 1055
Great progress has been made by Ferdinand in his campaign to regain Moslem territories in Spain for the Christians. After a six-month siege the king, who is 40, has just captured Coimbra, which means that he has enough territory under his control in Portugal and the south to exchange his title of "king" for that of "emperor".

Ferdinand's campaign of reconquest got under way when he imposed his authority over the old Leonise empire, ruling Galicia, Leon, Castile and the Rioja. He has not set out to conquer the territories merely by force of arms, preferring to get his way by extracting tribute from them in return for protection. Coimbra, however, resisted his overtures, and it took battering-rams to bring it to its knees. The conduct of the siege could have important consequences for the future. It suggests that if the citizens of a Moslem city surrendered immediately they would be allowed to stay and carry on as normal. If they surrendered during the siege they could depart with their lives and what they could take away with them. But if they went on fighting their city would be stormed and they themselves killed or enslaved.

Ferdinand is also demonstrating that he is not trying to force the Moslems to change their religion. Instead, he is showing himself to be a reconquerer wishing to spread the political power of a Christian community rather than belief in the religion.

A later portrait of King Ferdinand, who is bringing Spain's Moslems under his control.

1065 (1065-1082)

England, 14 October 1066. William of Normandy defeats King Harold at Hastings and becomes king of England.

China, 1067. The poet Wang An-shih campaigns to stem widespread corruption in the administration and the army.

Asia Minor (Anatolia), 1067. The Seljuk Turks take Caesarea in Cappadocia.

England, 1070. The Danish fleet sent against England in 1069 is bribed to depart. This leads to the collapse of the opposition to King William in the fens led by Hereward the Wake.

France, 1071. The death last year of Baldwin VI, the count of Flanders, opens a succession dispute. Baldwin's widow, Richilda, ruling on behalf of his son, is opposed by Robert the Frisian, the son of Baldwin V. Robert defeats Richilda at Cassel and is recognised as count by King Philip.

Italy, 16 April 1071. The Norman Robert Guiscard takes Bari after a three-year siege. Byzantine rule in southern Italy is thus brought to an end after five centuries.

Asia Minor, 1071. The Seljuks defeat the Byzantines under Romanus IV Diogenes at Manzikert. Taken prisoner, Romanus is replaced as emperor by his stepson Michael VII. He is freed and returns home aiming to regain power from Michael, but dies in the ensuing struggle.

Sicily, 10 January 1072. Robert Guiscard and his brother Roger take Palermo.

Spain, 1072. Alfonso VI becomes king of Leon and Castile after the assassination of his brother Sancho. On the death of their father, Ferdinand, in 1065, Alfonso received Leon but lost it to Sancho (who received Castile) shortly afterwards.

Italy, 1073. Robert Guiscard takes Amalfi from Gisulf II of Salerno, securing Norman control of the maritime trade routes, but alienating the pope.

Rome, March 1075. Pope Gregory VII declares that the bishop of Rome is absolute sovereign over the Church.

West Africa, 1077. The nomadic Almoravids seize the kingdom of Ghana.

Italy, 1077. The Emperor Henry IV, excommunicated by Gregory VII, submits to the pope at Canossa.

Byzantines fight Turks, who use stirrups and can shoot with great accuracy.

Turks take Byzantine emperor captive

Eastern Turkey, 26 August 1071
Asia Minor is at the mercy of the Turks after the defeat today of the army of the Byzantine Emperor Romanus IV at Manzikert, north of Lake Van. The emperor himself has been captured.

This conclusive battle was the result of years of tension between the Armenian and Greek-speaking people of Asia Minor and Turkish nomads infiltrating from the east with their flocks.

The enormous distances involved made it almost impossible for the Byzantine government to take effective punitive action against these nomadic bands, and gradually the indigenous population was being forced westward.

Earlier this year, the new emperor resolved to drive the Turks out, and raised a large army for the purpose. The Turks appealed for help to the Seljuk Sultan Alp Arslan, who came in person, with his army.

Meanwhile, the Byzantine army appears to have been crucially weakened by internal squabbles and treachery. The Dukas family and their followers, political opponents of Romanus IV, deserted him just before the battle.

New emperor halts Fujiwara clan rule

Japan, 1068
The hold of the Fujiwara clan over government and imperial throne has been broken with the crowning of Emperor Sanjo II, who is not the son of a Fujiwara mother. The clan have maintained indirect control in Japan for over a century.

As recently as 1062 the Fujiwara appeared to have strengthened their power with a major victory by the Minamoto, a military clan known as the "claws and teeth of the Fujiwara". In a battle which marked the end of nine years of fighting, the Minamoto defeated the rebellious Abe family by destroying their last fortress on the banks of the Kuriyagawa river in the northern province of Mutsu. They were acting on imperial orders.

The Abe resistance was fierce, and the defence was overcome only when the Minamoto general, Yoshiiye, the son of the clan's leader, Yoriyoshi, diverted the water supply and set fire to the stockade.

The Minamoto emerged battle-hardened and politically powerful. But this has not lasted as long as they might have hoped.

Pope bids to curb the power of princes

Rome, April 1075
Pope Gregory VII is making a strong bid to establish the primacy of the papacy and its authority over kings and princes as well as archbishops. *Dictatus Papae* (Sayings of the Pope) contains 27 short and pithy sentences which leave no doubt at all where the ultimate authority lies.

The assertions include: "That he [the pope] alone may use the imperial insignia."; "That he may depose emperors, that he himself may be judged by no one."; "That the pope may absolve subjects of unjust men from their fealty."

Although he has only been pope for two years, Gregory has been a powerful voice in papal reforms for more than 30 years. He was born in Tuscany, as Hildebrand, and became a monk, spending time at Cluny. In 1046 he went into exile with Pope Gregory VI, and every pope since then has followed his advice. Gregory sees the papacy primarily as a governmental institution which must be backed by laws. He has renewed the drive against non-celibate priests and against the sale of church offices. His reforms are likely to renew the smouldering conflict between the papacy and the German emperor.

A later view of the formidable pope.

Barefoot king bows to papal command

Italy, 28 January 1077
King Henry IV of Germany has finally bowed to the authority of the pope. For the last three days he has stood barefoot in the snow, a penitent in sackcloth, at the gate of the castle of Canossa in the Alps. Pope Gregory VII finally chose to pardon him and withdraw the excommunication order imposed on him last year. That was when the struggle between the two men broke out in earnest; Henry then persuaded German bishops to renounce their obedience to the pope at a council in Worms.

Gregory responded by releasing his German subjects from their allegiance to their King. His action served as an excuse for a rebellion by many of the German nobility who were already unhappy about the increase in the king's power since the defeat of the Saxons. They forced Henry to submit to the pope.

New emperor faces foes on all sides

A model of a Byzantine vessel.

Constantinople, 1081
The Eastern Empire has a new emperor: Alexius Comnenus. He comes to the throne beset on all sides by dangers and difficulties.

The Seljuks Turks are established in the Taurus; the Serbs are causing trouble on the Danube and Bulgaria is threatened by the Patzinak nomads. But most serious is the ambition of the Norman Robert Guiscard to invade the empire itself. The Emperor will have to use all his talents as a soldier and diplomat if he is to preserve the empire.

Nomads smash Ghana's empire, and reach Spain

Ghana, 1077
Thousands of Saharan nomads have swept through Ghana, destroying the richest empire in West Africa. The Almoravid conquests began 20 years ago when Abdullah ibn Yasim, preaching holy war and spiritual renewal, united the tribes of the western Sahara and advanced into Morocco with 30,000 zealots.

While one Almoravid army crossed the Straits of Gibraltar into Spain, a second crossed the Sahara into Ghana, occupying its goldmines, making the Almoravids richer than the degenerate sultans they vowed to overthrow, and creating an empire stretching from the Niger to the Ebro in Spain.

William conquers English at Hastings

Hastings, 14 October 1066
Duke William II of Normandy, commanding a mixed force of around 7,000 French, Breton and mercenary soldiers, crushed the army of his rival for the English throne and erstwhile lieutenant, King Harold, on windswept Sussex downland yesterday. The Normans claim that William is the rightful heir to the English throne and that Harold had conceded this.

The battle was a struggle between two opposed styles, mobile French Norman archers against stoical, close-packed ranks of English infantry armed with lances and axes. Yet for much of the day it seemed that the English had the upper hand. They approached through a wood near the top of Senlac Hill, eight miles inland, dismounted and formed up in tight formation on the high ground. William's troops attacked with archers in front followed by armour-clad infantry. They rolled uphill in human waves which broke time and again. William, on horseback, stayed close and so kept control. He was a conspicuous target and had three horses killed under him. As the French front ranks at last panicked and fled, their own knights cut them down. William dismounted , removed his helmet in order to be recognised and, spear in hand, ordered them back into battle.

Many of the English, observing – so they thought – the beginning of a rout, and freed at last from their role as bowmen's targets, ran forward in hot pursuit, only to be hit on both flanks by French cavalry. It was probably the decisive moment of this battle. The French, turning near-disaster to advantage, now used the ploy to encourage the English to break ranks. In the confusion the English leaders were exposed as ready targets. Harold's two brothers were killed in a hail of arrows and spears. Harold himself, despite having lost one eye, fought on magnificently. His body, when recovered, was virtually unidentifiable.

Towards evening, the French continued to squeeze the core of Harold's army until only a few dozen remained standing. These survivors, who knew that all was lost, retreated in good order to make a last stand on ground which gave them the best chance to sell their lives dearly. This was a steep valley cut by ditches and unsuitable for cavalry. William, his lance broken, led a party of men from Boulogne into the enemy redoubt.

The battle provokes many questions about recent events in England. Why did Edward the Confessor, on his deathbed, disinherit his cousin, the duke, and nominate Harold? Why did Harold, after marching to York to defeat the Norwegian King Hardrada at Stamford Bridge only three weeks ago, rush tired troops to Hastings and not wait for reinforcements?

The Bayeux Tapestry (in fact embroidered) tells of the fall of the Anglo-Saxon kingdom. Here, William's ship sails for Pevensey, where the French landed.

The English held off the French on high ground at Senlac Hill for much of the battle, but in the end the Norman attack proved too relentless.

Harold, his two brothers already slain, is struck in the eye by an arrow; the wound was probably fatal, but he fought on with great bravery before dying.

1082 (1082-1087)

Rome, 1083. After two long years of laying siege to Rome, the Emperor Henry IV has finally conquered a part of the city.

Rome, 1084. Having dealt with his rivals in Germany, the Emperor Henry IV again turns his attention to Rome. The Romans submit, although Pope Gregory VII holds out in the Castel Sant'Angelo until rescued by the Norman Robert Guiscard. Meanwhile Henry enthrones an anti-pope, Clement III.

North America, c.1085. Thule Eskimo culture is spreading across all of the North American Arctic area as far as Greenland and Siberia. The Thule Eskimos achieve supremacy by developing basic skills and technologies to a more sophisticated level than that achieved by existing Arctic peoples. They use large *kayaks* (canoes) and *umiaks* (dog sleds) to traverse the continent to hunt whales.

Spain, 25 May 1085. Alfonso VI of Leon takes Toledo, the old capital of Visigothic Spain and the greatest city that the Christians have captured in the reconquest. Alfonso takes the title "Emperor of Toledo". Strategically, the loss of the city is a disaster for the Moslems, penetrating their territorial power bloc.

Italy, 25 May 1085. Pope Gregory VII dies at Salerno. His last words are: "I have loved righteousness and hated iniquity, wherefore I die in exile."

Japan, 1086. Minamoto Yoshiiye suppresses the clans in north-eastern Japan and takes control of the provinces in the region.

Spain, 23 October 1086. Alfonso VI is defeated by the Almoravid Yusuf ibn Tashufin, who has come to the aid of the Arab princes of Spain. Yusuf, who has recently completed the conquest of the Maghreb (in North Africa), rules an empire four times bigger than Spain. After the battle, carts loaded with Christian heads are sent to the chief cities of Spain and the Maghreb to show that the Christians are no longer to be feared.

North Africa, 1087. The Genoese and the Pisans obtain trading privileges in the Zirid emirate as the result of a successful expedition against Mahdia.

Trouble-shooting ruler goes to war

Japan, 1083

Yoshiiye, the warrior leader of the Minamoto clan, who won his spurs in the earlier Nine Years War against the rebellious Abe clan 20 years ago, has set out at the head of another expedition to put down trouble in the north.

This time his opponents are the Kiyowara family who were his allies in the war against the Abes. The emperor rewarded the Kiyowaras for their loyalty, but over the years they have fallen from grace by misruling the province of Matsu.

However, the emperor decided to move against them not so much because of their misrule, but because continuous dynastic squabbles within the clan led to open warfare between its different branches.

So Yoshiiye has been made governor of Matsu with orders to bring peace to the northern provinces. He has taken up his post backed by the prestige and military power of his warrior clan, but so far he has no commission from the court to go to war against the Kiyowaras.

His first efforts, therefore, have been to bring about a truce between the quarrelling factions, and he has had some success in calming the leaders of the factions. But the hotheads among the Kiyowaras are always drawing their swords, and it seems inevitable that Yoshiiye will have to intervene militarily.

Exile completes epic history of China

Silk scroll depicting spring festival celebrations in Sima Guang's time.

China, 1083

The revered statesman-scholar Sima Guang has at last finished his epic history of China. It is called the *Comprehensive Mirror for Aid in Government*, and it has taken him 17 years to fulfil his commission from the Emperor Ying Zong to make "a record of events, of rulers and ministers in successive ages".

Sima Guang was helped by several dedicated assistants whom he urged to consult every type of source for, he argued, official records and histories "are not necessarily to be relied upon and anecdotes are not necessarily without foundation. Make your choice by your own scrutiny".

Ironically, he was able to complete his great work because of a political defeat. A conservative, he was sent into exile when the reformer Wang Anshi came to power, but was allowed to take his library with him. The result of his enforced political idleness and his questing methods is a superb chronicle.

Domesday Book gives William a record of conquered England

England, 1086

Every horse, cow, pig and hen in England is being counted in a massive audit of the nation's wealth being carried out by King William's officials.

The survey, on an unprecedented scale, is expected to take two years to complete and will constitute a comprehensive census of all landholdings and livestock in the kingdom.

The results of the Great Survey, as it is being called in court circles, are being compiled into two volumes, popularly titled the Domesday Book. With information arranged geographically, by shire, hundred and village, the Domesday Book will provide the king with a quick and reliable reference system for levying military taxation. To avoid fraud the king's officials plan to make at least two inspection trips to each shire, using a standard questionnaire to establish the exact state of England's wealth.

Despite his successful conquest of England at the Battle of Hastings 20 years ago, King William believes that he has not yet consolidated his hold on the country or harmonised its feudal system with that of his native Normandy.

The Great Survey will allow him to do both. The terms of the survey overhaul land tenure, with all land in England now deemed to be held directly by the king or by his subjects on his behalf.

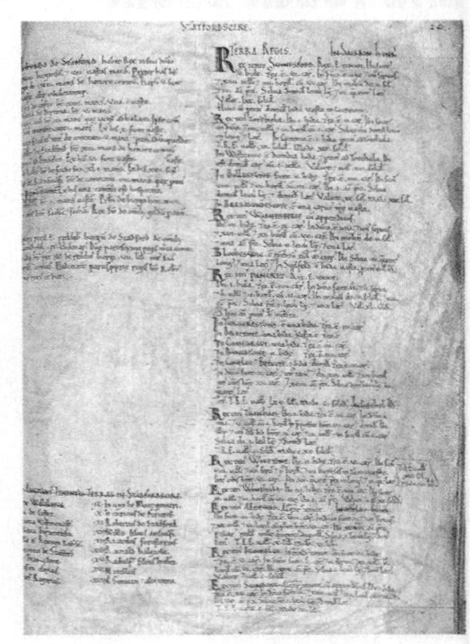

Domesday Book: Staffordshire.

New art favours fabulous monsters

Europe, c.1060-1100

A new style of architecture – Romanesque – now dominates Europe. As the name indicates, it is derived from the round Roman arch, which it repeats in series to divide church naves and abbey cloisters into bays. Half-columns are built against flat wall surfaces, with capitals which are no longer in classical Roman styles.

Very large abbey churches have been built in this style at Rheims and at the great Benedictine abbey at Cluny, which is the largest in Christendom, although the cathedral built at Speyer by the German King Henry IV is the highest, with its nave reaching 107 feet.

Normandy has raised the masterpiece of St Etienne at Caen. The church of Our Lady, crowning the rock of Mont St Michel, is a place of pilgrimage. So is the cathedral of Santiago de Compostela in Spain.

Three great Romanesque cathedrals are being built in England – Winchester, Norwich and Durham. At Durham clusters of columns up the nave alternate with massive piers decorated with carved zig-zag chevrons.

Carved capitals are appearing on church columns and around the arches of Norman churches in England. They take the form of demons, dragons and fabulous monsters, such as centaurs, symbolising drunken lechery, or the basilisk, a mixture of cock and serpent. The crypt at Canterbury is carved with goats and she-devils.

A sanctuary knocker, fashioned as a monstrous head, on the north door of Durham cathedral, a masterpiece of Romanesque architecture.

"The Mouth of Hell", a detail from the grotesque carving of the Last Judgement in the recently built Romanesque abbey at Conques in France.

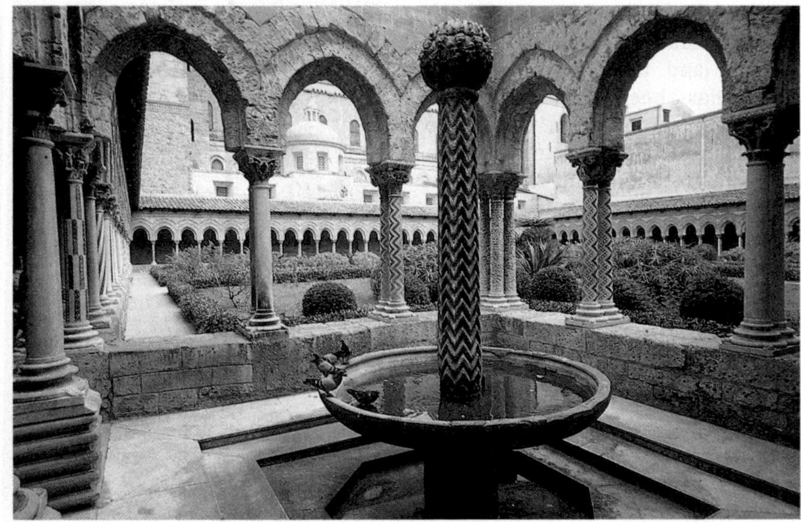

Monreale, in Sicily, where Norman rule has put its mark on architecture.

Romanesque painting: St Matthew.

Rome raped after pope's cry for help

Rome, 1084

A pall of smoke covers Rome and thousands of bodies lie putrefying in the streets after three days in which much of the world's greatest city has been devastated by the Norman army of Robert Guiscard. Pope Gregory is the most hated man in Rome, for it was he who invited the Normans into Rome to protect him against the armies of the Emperor Henry IV – only to see his city destroyed and burnt by the so-called protectors.

Guiscard, the son of a minor Norman landowner, was the scourge of Calabria and had driven the Byzantines out of much of southern Italy before emerging as the most powerful Norman in the country. When Henry had himself crowned emperor he deposed the pope and installed an anti-pope, Clement. Gregory called on Robert for help. Realising that he was outnumbered, Henry left Rome, followed by a terrified Clement. Despite a massive uprising by the Roman citizens, there was no stopping the fury of the Normans.

Christian king wins Moslem Toledo

Spain, 1085

King Alfonso VI of Leon and Castile, the most powerful of Spain's Christian monarchs, has wrested Toledo from its Moslem rulers.

Alfonso inherited Leon in 1065, and fought his brother Sancho for Castile until Sancho's murder in 1072. Alfonso then turned southwards to Toledo, one of the many *taifas* (Moslem petty-states) which followed the break up of the caliphate of Cordoba about 50 years ago. Christian rulers in the north demanded tribute from the taifas, and five years ago, complaining that its tribute was paid in debased coin, Alfonso set out to conquer Toledo.

Alfonso has promised tolerant rule to Toledo's Moslem and Mozarabic (Arabicised Christian) populations. But he has also demanded increased tribute from the taifas, and many are considering an appeal for aid to the Almoravids, the new Berber rulers of North Africa.

1087 (1087-1100)

France/England, 1087. On his death, William the Conqueror is succeeded in Normandy by Robert Curthose and in England by William Rufus.

Malta, 1091. Roger of Sicily, brother of Robert Guiscard, takes control of the island.

France, 1091. William Rufus invades Normandy and gains a foothold in the duchy.

Near East, 1092. The Islamic sect known as the Assassins murder the Seljuk vizier, Nizam al-Mulk.

Rome, 1094. The anti-pope Clement III is deposed. Urban II is installed in Rome.

Venice, 1094. The basilica of St Mark is consecrated.

France, 27 November 1095. Pope Urban II calls for a crusade to free the Holy Places.

Italy, 1096. The world's first university is founded at Salerno.

West Africa, 1097. Umme, the first king of Kanem-Bornu (*in Nigeria and Niger*), who was converted to Islam, dies.

Portugal, 1097. Alfonso VI of Leon gives his son-in-law Henry of Chalon the land between the Minho and Tagus rivers to hold as an hereditary county, known as Portugal.

Near East, 30 June 1097. The Crusaders defeat the Turks at Dorylaeum, opening the way to Asia Minor (Anatolia).

France, 1098. The Cistercian order is founded at Citeaux.

Near East, 1098. The Fatimids recover Jerusalem from the Turks. The Byzantines retake Smyrna, Ephesus and Sardis. The Crusaders take Antioch.

Jerusalem, 15 July 1099. The city falls to the Crusaders.

Near East, 12 August 1099. At Ascalon, the Crusaders defeat al-Afdal, the Fatimid vizier of Egypt, who was bringing an army to relieve Jerusalem.

Italy, 1100. Genoa, Venice and Pisa, whose fleets have helped the Crusaders to capture ports south of Beirut, are rewarded with trading privileges.

Jerusalem, 18 July 1100. On the death of his brother Godfrey of Bouillon, Baldwin becomes king of Jerusalem.

England, 2 August 1100. William Rufus is killed in a hunting accident in the New Forest. He is succeeded by his brother Henry.

"El Cid" triumphs in siege of Valencia

Valencia, Spain, 17 June 1094
The great Arab city of Valencia is in Christian hands today, defeated by starvation after a 20-month siege. The new ruler of the city is a man whom, ironically enough, the Arabs themselves dubbed *el Cid Campeador* (Lord Champion).

El Cid was born Don Rodrigo Diaz de Bivar about 54 years ago, the offspring of a noble Castilian family. He entered the service of King Alfonso VI of Castile and Leon. In 1081 Alfonso banished him for unauthorised raiding and, while nominally still in Alfonso's service, Don Rodrigo in effect became an independent travelling knight, serving both Moslem and Christian masters. He earned the title el Cid (from the Arabic *sayyid*, or *sid*, lord) in the service of the Moslem rulers of Saragossa.

El Cid saw the chance to conquer the Moslem city of Valencia in 1092 when its ruler, al-Kadir, was under threat from the Berber Murabits (Almoravids) from North Africa, who had already conquered much of Moslem Spain. In October 1092 al-Kadir was killed by rebel Valencians with Almoravid backing; but before the Almoravids could seize the city it was besieged by el Cid. Magnanimous in victory, el Cid has promised freedom of worship for his Moslem subjects.

Pope seeks "crusade"

Urban II presides over the Council of Clermont to launch the First Crusade.

Clermont, 27 November 1095
Pope Urban II got a tumultuous reception to his call for a crusade to the Holy Land in a major speech here today. For days it has been known that he was to make an important announcement. The papal throne was set on a platform in an open field, outside the eastern gate of the city, which was packed to capacity.

Pope Urban spoke with great fervour, using all his oratorical skills. He talked movingly of how it was no longer safe for pilgrims to visit the Holy Places in Jerusalem owing to the atrocities and disorganisation of Turkish rule there. He talked of the need to help the Byzantine emperor in the struggle of Christendom against the infidel Moslems.

The response has exceeded the pope's best hopes. So moved was the crowd that cries of "*Deus le vol!*" (God wills it!) punctuated his speech. As soon as he had finished the bishop of Le Puy jumped up and knelt before the throne begging permission to join the crusade. Emissaries from Raymond, the count of Toulouse and St Gilles, offered his services.

Most of the people at Clermont were the poor, and the pope is now seeking more noble support. Each crusader will be expected to wear a red cross sewn onto his coat and to vow to go to Jerusalem.

William, the Norman duke who became king of England, dies

Normandy, 9 September 1087
The king who transformed the face of England in 20 years of repression and reform died today at Rouen. William the Conqueror, aged 60, had gone to Normandy to lead a punitive raid against the French; he was badly hurt when his horse stumbled on the burning cinders of a town which he had sacked. William spent the first years of his reign putting down rebellions by English landowners. Sometimes he was satisfied to seize the land and give it to his Norman retainers; but in Yorkshire the scale of his devastation was so great that the desolation can be seen to this day. To keep the people in subjection, 80 castles have been built throughout the length and breadth of the land. The Conqueror and his queen, Matilda, and two half-brothers came to own a quarter of all the land in England. Another third has been granted to 15 comrades-in-arms from the Battle of Hastings. The rest is in the hands of Norman barons and churchmen.

William retained such English institutions as the sheriffs and shire courts. He improved agriculture and made a wide-ranging record of social and economic life in the *Domesday Book*. The social divisions produced by the conquest are reflected in language: a few craftsmen, such as bakers, smiths, salters and skinners, have kept their Old English names, but butchers, carpenters, grocers and tailors take theirs from French.

A later picture of King William.

Christians take Antioch

Knights of the Order of the Holy Ghost embarking for the Crusade.

Antioch, June 1098

After a bitter five-month siege, the fortress city of Antioch in southern Turkey has fallen to the Crusaders. Today, there is not a Moslem left alive in the city and the air is thick with the stench of corpses rotting in the sun. Antioch is Christian again.

The city was gained by treachery. The Crusaders, led by Frankish and Norman knights, marched across Europe last year to join up with a motley band of Germans, Flamands and other followers of the itinerant monk Peter the Hermit. Crossing the Anatolian plateau in high summer they reached Antioch in October, but winter was coming.

Cold and starvation dashed the enthusiasm aroused by Pope Urban's call for Europe to unite to deliver the Holy Land from the bondage of the Moslem Turks. Desertions increased as reports multiplied that Turkish reinforcements were near. The Crusade looked about to collapse.

But Prince Bohemond, the fair-haired Norman from Taranto, had secretly made a deal with a captain inside the city. After dark Firouz, an Armenian converted to Islam, opened windows in a tower, and the knights climbed in after scaling the walls by ladder.

The Crusaders are supposed to be helping the Byzantine Emperor Alexius Comnenus to regain territory seized by the Turks. But relations are deteriorating: the ambitious Bohemond intends to keep the city he captured and make himself prince of Antioch.

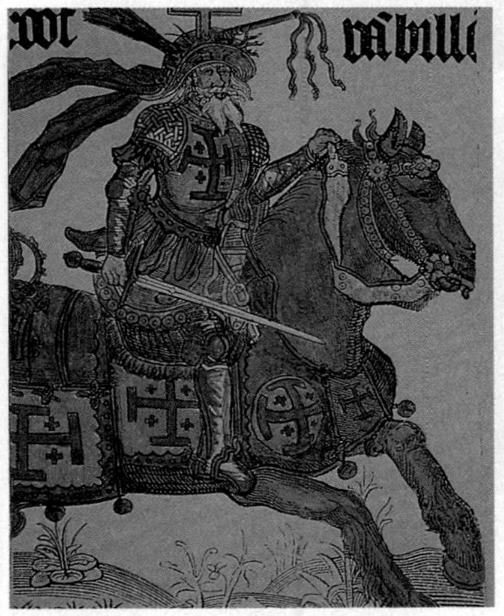

Crusader: Godfrey de Bouillon.

China divided by proposals for reforms

China, 1100

The new emperor, the artistic Huizong, has mounted the throne of a country bitterly divided over the reforms introduced over 30 years ago by the innovator statesman Wang Anshi.

Among his innovations, which shocked the conservatives of the court, were measures to grant low interest loans to peasants, land registration to uncover tax evasion by the rich, the establishment of official pawnshops and grain markets, and fair taxation for property.

The controversy about these reforms has bedevilled China's administration ever since their introduction. Wang Anshi and his chief opponent, the historian Sima Guand, are long dead, but their successors continue the argument. The danger is that it is diverting attention from the growing threat posed by the northern nomads.

Crusaders in Holy City

A later French view of the siege of Jerusalem by the Crusaders.

Jerusalem, 15 July 1099

Late this afternoon the Holy City was restored to Christendom, and the massacres have already begun. When the Moslems and Jews have all been killed, the Crusaders will go to the church of the Holy Sepulchre to give thanks to God and to decide who shall rule Jerusalem. There is some feeling among the Crusaders that Tancred, the nephew of Bohemond the Norman, should not be allowed to keep all the treasure he has looted from the Dome of the Rock mosque.

In the year since they captured the fortress city of Antioch, the Crusaders have passed through Syria and the Lebanon, sometimes making deals with local Arab rulers who were pleased at the prospect of Turkish power being curbed. But in Jerusalem great changes took place during the Crusaders' long march. The Fatimids of Egypt, who lost the city to the Turks, now saw their chance to retake it.

When, on 7 June, the Crusaders arrived outside Jerusalem, they found the Fatimids in possession behind heavily fortified walls. It was another six weeks before the Crusaders had built siege towers and scaled the walls under a storm of fire. In those weeks the knights in their heavy armour suffered greatly from the heat. Now, in the hour of victory, the Crusaders number no more than 12,000 foot soldiers and 1,200 knights, a small force to garrison vast tracts of territory in Asia Minor (Anatolia), Syria and the Holy Land.

The world, centred on Jerusalem.

1100 (1100-1118)

Italy, 1101. Roger of Sicily dies at Mileto in Calabria. As well as holding Sicily and Malta, he had come to dominate southern Italy.

Spain, 1102. The Almoravids' siege of Valencia, which began last year, is lifted by Alfonso VI, who then evacuates and burns the city.

Near East, 1104. The Turks defeat the Latin Crusaders at Harran, allowing the Byzantine forces to advance unopposed. They take Laodicea and places along the coast as far as Tripoli, threatening Antioch. The Latins demand a crusade against Constantinople.

France, 7 August 1106. The Emperor Henry IV dies at Liege after defeating his rebellious son Henry V. Pope Paschal II refuses him a Christian burial, having excommunicated him in 1102.

France, 28 September 1106. King Henry of England defeats his brother Robert at the battle of Tinchebrai and reunites England and Normandy, divided since the death of William the Conqueror.

Japan, 1108. The Taira and Minamoto clans join forces to chastise the *sohei*, warrior monks of the Enryakuji temple on Mount Hiei near Kyoto.

Near East, 1109. Tripoli and Beirut are taken by the Crusaders.

Near East, 1113. The Order of the Knights of the Hospital of St John, founded to take care of pilgrims to the Holy Land, resolves to fight for the defence of the Holy Land.

Spain, 1114. Toledo withstands an attack by the Almoravids. The Almoravid governor of Saragossa attacks Barcelona, but is defeated near Martorell.

Hungary, 1114. Koloman, who conquered Croatia and so brought it within the orbit of Latin Christendom, dies.

France, 1115. Bernard founds the monastery of Clairvaux.

China, 1115. The Jurchen from Manchuria, allied with the Song, overthrow the Khitan Liao, their former masters, and found the Jin dynasty.

Near East, 1118. The Order of the Knights Templar is created to protect the road to Jerusalem.

Spain, 1118. After four years of combat with the Moors, Alfonso, the king of Aragon and Navarre, retakes Saragossa and makes it his capital.

Saragossa falls to conquering Christians

Spain, 18 December 1118

Saragossa has fallen to the Christian King of Aragon, Alfonso (the Battler), in a major blow to Ali ibn-Yusuf, the ruler of Moslem Spain.

The loss of Saragossa is the first serious reversal in the fortunes of the Almoravids, the North African Berber dynasty which was invited to aid the Moslem states of Spain after the fall of Toledo in 1085. Ali's father, Yusuf ibn-Tashufin, defeated Alfonso VI near Badajoz in 1086; he decided to reunite Islamic Spain, taking Valencia – whose conqueror, El Cid, had died in 1099 – in 1102 and the northwestern city of Saragossa in 1110.

But Yusuf was not strong enough to occupy parts resettled by Christians, such as Toledo, before his death in 1106. Alongside this, the Berbers began to prefer Spanish luxuries to battle; disaffection spread among the troops, and it seemed that the Almoravid regime was already beginning to lose its grip.

The regime's unruly soldiers and growing financial difficulties led to widespread disloyalty among the people. This was a key factor in the fall of Saragossa, which will be a boost to the morale of Spain's embattled Christian rulers.

Jin dynasty is founded in China

China, 1115

Akuta, the chieftain of the Jin nomads, has enthroned himself as first emperor of the Jin state, ruling over land seized from the Liao empire. He had previously been employed by the Liao emperor to keep order on his northern frontier, and showed his independence three years ago by refusing to dance for the emperor at a banquet. Akuta launched his warriors against his former master last year, and now the Liao empire is in ruins and the Jin have started a dynasty.

Fast-growing monastic sect builds abbeys in lonely places

France, 1116

A young Burgundian nobleman, Bernard, has just established a new abbey at Clairvaux which is the third daughter monastery of Citeaux, the home of the Cistercian order. As recently as a few years ago the Cistercians seemed to be dwindling in numbers, but the inspired teaching of Bernard and the organising talent of the English abbot, Stephen Harding, have transformed them into the fastest-growing of all of the monastic orders.

The first Cistercian monastery was founded at Citeaux in a desolate swamp some 14 miles from the town of Dijon on Palm Sunday in 1098. That date was also the feast day of St Benedict, which was appropriate since the 21 monks, led by Robert from the Benedictine abbey of Molesme, saw themselves as renewing the Rule of St Benedict.

The monks subject themselves to severe discipline: they eat no meat or fat, and wear no comfortable clothing such as breeches or coats. They observe strict silence while they work; sloth is the great enemy, so all the monks have to do physical labour in addition to their devotions. They choose remote deserted sites and lonely valleys for their abbeys. They will not use slave labour, and they do much of their own farming and are adept at building and civil engineering. They have instituted a system of lay monks. The abbot of the mother house visits once a year. There is a general chapter once a year at Citeaux which is the supreme authority. The thrust of the movement has been a focus on the inner life, to be fostered by the severe discipline and inspired by awe of nature. Bernard is proving one of the most eloquent exponents of it.

He wrote recently: "Believe one who has proved it, you will find among the woods something you never found in books. Stones and trees will teach you a lesson you never heard from masters in the school. Think you that honey cannot be drawn from the rock, and oil from the hardest stone? Do not the mountains drop sweetness, and the hills flow with milk and honey?"

The ruins of the library of Citeaux Abbey from the fifteenth century.

A Cistercian monk in his cowl; breeches and coats are forbidden.

Emperor funds war on all fronts with church treasure

Constantinople, 1118.
The Emperor Alexius Comnenus has died after 37 long years of fighting enemies of Byzantium.

He came to power surrounded by hostile peoples, but he has used every available means to preserve the Empire. He made peace with the Seljuks, established in uncomfortable proximity in the Taurus mountains. He held off the ambitious Robert Guiscard, the Norman Duke of Apulia, by funding rebellion in his enemy's dukedom and by allying with Venice. In 1091 he finally subdued the Patzinak nomads who had threatened Bulgaria. He also had to deal with the Cumans, a tribe in the Ukraine who attacked the Empire in 1114.

He took advantage of civil war among the Seljuks in 1091 to retake some of the lost lands in Asia Minor. Two years before his death he made peace with them, having recovered the Asiatic coastline from Cilicia to Trebizond. Thousands of prisoners returned home. Alexius made himself less popular in his financial dealings. He confiscated Church treasure to fund his military operations and imposed extortionate taxes. But it was this or ruin for the Empire.

Treasures worth fighting for: a mosaic of an earlier emperor.

A detailed miniature from a Byzantine manuscript of three men fishing.

A typical "sweet-embrace" icon.

Mosaic art reaches new heights in today's Byzantium

Constantinople, c.1115
Byzantine art has been enjoying a second golden age under Alexius, the first emperor of the Comnene dynasty. The art of mosaic, along with that of goldsmiths and icon painters, has attained new brilliance, and Byzantine craftsmen are in demand in many lands.

St Mark's basilica in Venice, for instance, is being enriched by Byzantine mosaics, as is the cathedral of Torcello on an island in the Venetian lagoon. Goldsmiths are working on a great treasure for St Mark's, the *Pala d'Oro*, a huge panel of enamelled figures set in a framework of gold and silver adorned with precious stones.

New mosaics are required for Ravenna, and in Sicily at the cathedral of Monreale. The abbot of Monte Cassino has sent to Constantinople for craftsmen to decorate the great monastery, and Salerno cathedral has been supplied with its great bronze doors. The Russians, converted under Vladimir, are building basilicas in Byzantine style at Kiev and Novgorod, both dedicated to St Sophia. Icons, such as the Virgin of Vladimir, are being sent to Russia.

In Daphni, near Athens, a church founded by the emperor has been decorated throughout with the hierarchy of Byzantine sacred portraits, beginning at the dome with Christ Pantocrator.

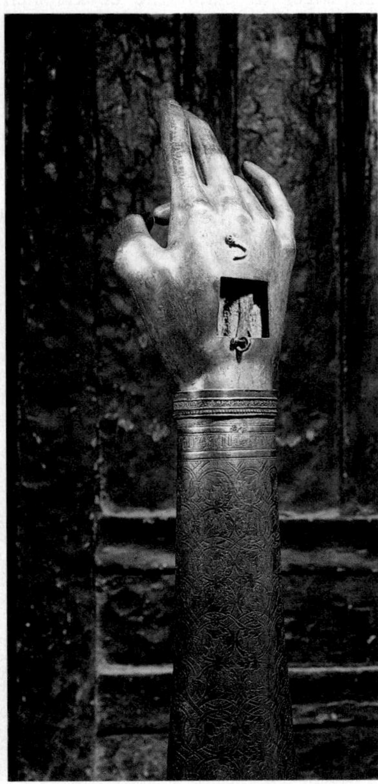

A Byzantine relic of John the Baptist.

Mosaics in the monastery of St Luke ("Hagios Loukas") at Phocis in Greece.

1118 (1118-1130)

France, 1119. Gelasius II, pope since 1118, dies at Cluny. He fled to France during the conflict between the Emperor Henry V and the papacy. He is succeeded by Callixtus II.

Near East, 1123. Fighting in support of the Crusaders, the Venetian fleet defeats the Egyptian fleet off Ascalon.

Aegean, 1125. The Venetians pillage Rhodes, occupy Chios and ravage Samos and Lesbos.

Germany, 1125. The Emperor Henry V dies without an heir. The main candidates to succeed are Frederick of Hohenstaufen, the duke of Swabia, and Lothar of Supplinburg, the duke of Saxony. Lothar is chosen, but civil war ensues.

Mediterranean, 1126. The Venetians occupy the island of Cephalonia. The Emperor John Comnenus restores the trading privileges granted to them by his predecessor Alexius.

Spain, 1126. Alfonso, the king of Aragon and Navarre, launches a raid as far as Granada. Alfonso has been in an almost permanent state of war against the Moslems since succeeding his father, Sancho, in 1104.

France, 1127. The murder of the childless count of Flanders, Charles (the Good), causes a succession dispute. King Louis VI attempts to impose William Clito, son of Robert Curthose of Normandy, but the towns elect Thierry of Alsace.

Italy, 1127. Conrad III, the brother of Frederick of Hohenstaufen, becomes king of Italy.

France, 1128. After the death of William Clito in a civil war, Louis VI agrees to the accession of Thierry of Alsace as count of Flanders.

England, 17 June 1128. Geoffrey V of Anjou, known as Plantagenet, marries Matilda, daughter of Henry, king of England, and widow of the Emperor Henry V.

Portugal, 1128. Afonso Henriques gains control of Portugal by defeating his mother, Teresa, at the battle of Sao Mamede.

France, 1128. Bernard of Clairvaux achieves recognition of the Order of the Knights Templar and drafts its rules.

Hungary, 1128. The Magyars are defeated by the Byzantine Emperor John II on the Danube, near Haram.

Pope and emperor end 50-year dispute over power of Church

Worms, 23 September 1122
A compromise solution to the struggle between the papacy and the German king has emerged at the *diet* (council) here.

The battle has raged since Pope Gregory VII excommunicated Germany's king, Henry IV, in 1076, seeking to impose papal power over kings. Both Henry V, the present king, and his father have on occasion set up an anti-pope and forced the real pope to take refuge in a monastery. Now Pope Callixtus II has persuaded Henry to renounce his right to invest bishops with the ring and crozier and allow their free election. In return the pope will allow the king to be present at the election of bishops and to intervene in disputes, which have occurred regularly over the years.

In practice this solution leaves kings with some influence. However, it goes some way towards establishing the papacy as the supreme Christian authority. It makes a distinction between *temporalia* (temporal power) and *spiritualia* (spiritual power).

A later portrait of Pope Callixtus II.

Pilgrimages establish network of roads and taverns in Europe

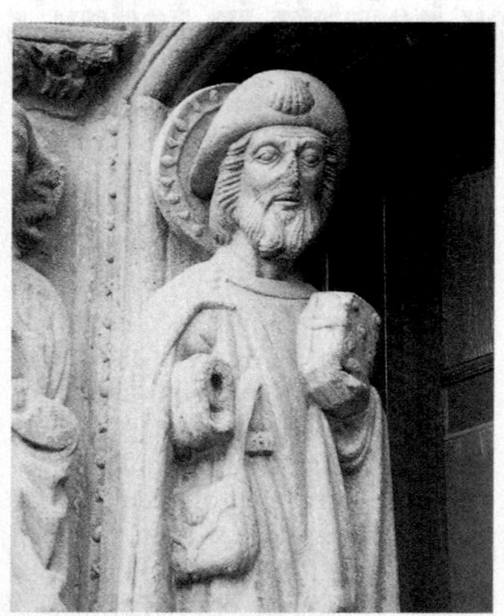
Statue of a pilgrim in the cathedral of St James in Compostela.

Spain, 1126
More than four decades of building reached their climax this year when the new cathedral of St James the Great was completed at Compostela in Spain. It stands on the site of a primitive church, destroyed by the Moslems in 907.

The site of the saint's remains has been among the most important of Christian shrines ever since Gottschalk, the bishop of Puy, came here in 950. Now this magnificent cathedral is bound to increase the flow of pilgrims along the roads of Europe, all eager to claim the cockle-shell badge that indicates their successful visit to St James' shrine. Indeed, many of these roads and the thriving towns that lie along them have developed specifically for the use of pilgrims. Many routes now lead to Compostela, running from Paris, Burgundy, the Auvergne and the south of France. Travellers can follow special guides which list inns, abbeys and churches where they may rest or pray.

It is not only pilgrims who follow the new roads that link Castile to the rest of Europe. Trade has benefited greatly, as has communication, both of information and ideas. And every traveller appreciates the relative safety of these well-maintained routes, on which the bandits who prey on many lesser roads fear to trespass.

Mathematician Umar Khayyam, author of the "Rubaiyat", dies

Eastern Persia, 1126
Future scholars trying to assess the life of the late Umar Khayyam may have to choose between his two lives – as mathematician and poet.

Born at Nishapur, in eastern Persia, Umar Khayyam was for many years best known as a mathematician and astrologer. Among his scientific works is a major treatise on algebra, and he headed a committee of scientists appointed by the *shah* to reform the calendar. However, he also had a second prolific career as a poet and turned out a vast number of *rubaiyats*, quatrains celebrating with a touch of melancholy the pleasures of life. In one he tells an apocryphal story of how wine was first discovered by a king who planted seeds left by a grateful phoenix which he had saved.

A scene from one of the "rubaiyats", in which the poet praises the wilderness.

Fighting monks win pope's approval

Crusading Knights Templars in Jerusalem, with Saracen cavalry outside.

Jerusalem, 1128
Two French knights have gained the pope's approval for their order of chivalry, which will now be officially known as "Knights of the Temple of Solomon of Jerusalem".

Ten years ago Hugh of Payens and Geoffrey of St Omer renounced all worldly ambition and, living as monks, determined to protect and aid Christian pilgrims who travelled to the Holy City. They took their vows of poverty, chastity and obedience before the patriarch in Jerusalem, who gave them a residence near the temple of Solomon. Another task was added – to fight infidels at all times, even though Christians were not threatened. This latter duty was soon to become the Knights Templars' major occupation.

The progress of these crusading Templars was slow. Only last year the two knights had no more than nine supporters, and it was not until Hugh secured an audience with Pope Honorius II that the church council approved the new order. Now, though, the Templars are rapidly gaining popularity throughout the Christian world.

Pioneer of new love poetry dies

Southern France, 1127
The duchy of Aquitaine is mourning the death of its sovereign, Duke William IX. Whatever his knightly achievements, William was best known as the pioneer of a new style of love poetry which has begun to be written in recent years at the courts of southern France, and which is catching on among poets and reciters called *jongleurs*, or minstrels, who wander from court to court to sing or pass on the latest news.

The new poetry is written by *troubadours*, a southern French word meaning inventor (of poetry). It probably began as a means of entertaining the wealthy – and idle – courtiers. The poets sing short, pithy songs of elevated, courtly love and its accompanying moods, which, while aristocratic and feudal in imagery, express universal emotions. They are often addressed to local women, which may explain why they are written in the *langue d'oc*, the language of southern France, and not in Latin.

Minstrels: society's artistic nomads.

New king crowned in Sicily by anti-pope

Palermo, Sicily, 25 December 1130
Amid splendour and pageantry, the Norman Roger II has been crowned king of Sicily and anointed by the special envoy of the anti-pope, Anacletus. The ceremony is of special significance to both Roger, who gains respectability, and Anacletus, who now has an influential supporter in his struggle for the true papacy with Innocent II.

The new king is the son of Roger I, the count of Sicily, who won the island from the Moslems, and Adelaide, who went on to marry Baldwin of Flanders, the king of Jerusalem, in 1113. Roger II fought the Moslems in North Africa in 1123, and claimed his inheritance on the death of his cousin, Duke William of Apulia, in July 1127. He defeated Pope Honorius II at Benevento and became duke of Apulia in August 1128.

Roger II's kingdom stretches from the Abruzzi to Malta and from Tripoli to Kabylia. His court is based on the French feudal system, but his Byzantine administration includes Greeks, Arabs and many other races.

Christ crowns Roger II in Palermo.

Horse soldiers double-cross the Song

China, 1126
The Jin have captured Kaifeng, the capital of the Song dynasty, seized the two Song emperors, Huizong and his son Qinzong, and looted the imperial treasury. The Song offered little resistance to the Jin horsemen, having bought them off with a huge ransom only a few months previously.

The Jin had gratefully accepted five million ounces of gold, 50 million ounces of silver and a million bolts of silk. They had then retired from the gates of the capital, pillaging the countryside as they went. Then they came back, and this time they have taken everything.

A Jin jar decorated with phoenixes.

Drunken sailors put a king on the rocks

England, 25 November 1120
The succession to the throne of England has been thrown into confusion by the death of Henry's only son, drowned in the Channel when drunken seamen drove his boat, the *White Ship*, onto rocks. The prince got away safely, but his boat foundered when he insisted on returning to the wreck to rescue his sister.

Henry now has no legitimate sons to succeed him, and there is speculation that one result of the disaster will be a hasty marriage in the hope of another heir. Meanwhile, one obvious candidate for the throne is his nephew William Clito, whose father lost Normandy to Henry 20 years ago.

Clito is unlikely to find favour with his uncle, however, and the prince's death may provide an opening to another royal nephew, Stephen of Blois, who has already emerged as a great favourite of the king's.

1130 (1130-1148)

North Africa, 1132. The Almohad Abd al-Mu'min is recognised as caliph.

Rome, June 1133. Lothar III of Saxony is crowned emperor by Pope Innocent II.

France, 1 December 1135. Henry, the king of England, dies and the crown passes to his nephew Stephen of Blois. Henry's preferred candidate was his daughter Matilda. Civil war is inevitable.

Germany, 1138. Conrad III of Hohenstaufen succeeds Lothar III on the imperial throne. Civil war erupts when he seizes Saxony and Bavaria.

Poland, 1138. Boleslav III dies after a 36-year rule. He strengthened Poland and expanded his rule to the west and north. His will splits Poland into four principalities.

Rome, April 1139. A Lateran Council settles the Anacletus schism, which arose when rival factions of cardinals elected two popes in 1130.

Portugal, 1139. Afonso defeats the Almoravids at Ourique and assumes the title of king.

Rome, 1143. The Romans declare their independence of the pope.

Jerusalem, 1143. On the death of her husband, Fulk of Anjou, king since 1131, Melisande tries to govern alone.

Portugal, 1143. Afonso of Portugal is recognised as king by Alfonso VII of Castile, and becomes a vassal of the pope.

Near East, 25 December 1144. The taking of the city of Edessa by Zangi (Atabeg of Mosul) leads to calls for another crusade. Zangi has conquered Moslem northern Syria and is at war with Damascus.

North Africa, 1146. Pursuing the "holy war" begun against the Almoravids by his predecessor, ibn Tumart, the Almohad caliph Abd al-Mu'min conquers much of Morocco.

Near East, 14 September 1146. Zangi is murdered. The sultan Nur ad-Din, his son, pursues the conquest of Edessa.

North Africa, 1147. Marrakesh, capital of the Almoravid empire, falls to the Almohads under Abd al-Mu'min.

Greece, 1147. Roger II of Sicily takes Corfu from the Byzantines and pillages Corinth, Athens and Thebes.

Almoravid rule ends in Spain and Africa

An imaginative later view of Moslems before King Roger II of Sicily.

North Africa, April 1147
The Almoravid empire is dead, following the fall of its capital, Marrakesh, to the Almohads.

Originally a Moslem sect, the Almoravids were nomadic Berber tribesmen. About 100 years ago they began to carve an empire covering much of western North Africa, and by 1090, Moslem Spain. But Almoravid strength in Spain was weakened by material luxury, self-interest and financial problems. Christian rulers launched new raids, and revolts in 1144 and 1145 effectively ended Almoravid rule in Moslem Spain.

The Almohads, also in origin a Berber Moslem sect, founded towards 1120 by Ibn-Tumart, steadily eroded Almoravid power in Africa under Ibn-Tumart's successor Abd al-Mu'min. Further expansion seem1inevitable, especially into Spain, where al-Mu'min is already recognised as caliph by some Moslem rulers. To the east, Almohad growth will come up against the Mediterranean's mightiest Christian king, Roger II of Sicily.

Lisbon's Moslems fall to Portuguese

Lisbon, 28 October 1147
The 17-week siege of Lisbon has ended with a peaceful mass evacuation of its Moslem inhabitants after they surrendered to an allied Christian force under Portugal's Afonso Henriques.

With the Moslems having abandoned both shores of the Tagus and been forced to give up bases at Sintra and Palmela, Afonso now controls most of the country's northern and western seaboard from his capital at Coimbra. The Moslems' northern border has been forced back to Evora. Christian forces forecast a Moslem surrender early on after allied troops overran the main Moslem food cache stored in caves, but the defenders held out until English troops finally managed to get a mobile tower up against the walls close enough for a drawbridge to be dropped over the parapet.

Now Afonso's task is to settle his debts with the large combined force of English, Flemish and German Crusaders – 13,000 men in 164 ships – whom he persuaded to help him. Under the alliance terms, which gave the Crusaders the spoils of the city, they can also opt for land in Portugal. The new settlers are being given incentives to stay, including the right to go on enjoying the customs and liberties of their native lands. Several Crusaders have already accepted the offer, with a group of Englishmen settling at Vila Verde.

Church court condemns Abelard, theologian and philosopher

Sens, France, 3 June 1140
Abelard, one of the most famous French philosophers and teachers, was today condemned for heresy by the church court here. He is to appeal to the pope, but there is little hope among his friends that the decision will be overturned.

The critical move was yesterday, when Bernard of Clairvaux persuaded bishops to support the heresy charge. Abelard had hoped to make a laughing stock of Bernard in theological debate. Today he was accused, like a criminal, of heresy, and refused to say anything.

The theological differences are not the root cause of the conflict. It is Abelard's personal style. He is widely loved by his students for his brilliance and willingness to attack orthodox leaders. His personal life has also been highly controversial.

Twenty years ago Abelard, then 40, fell in love with Heloise, a student aged 20, and fathered her child. Her uncle, a canon of Notre Dame cathedral, had Abelard castrated in revenge. Abelard went into the monastery at St Denis and Heloise became a nun. She is now the abbess of the convent of the Paraclete. Their love has survived as a spiritual passion and Abelard writes regular letters to Heloise, "once his wife, now his sister in Christ".

Peter Abelard and his former lover Heloise, now an abbess.

Heart of Mediterranean trade now controlled by the Italians

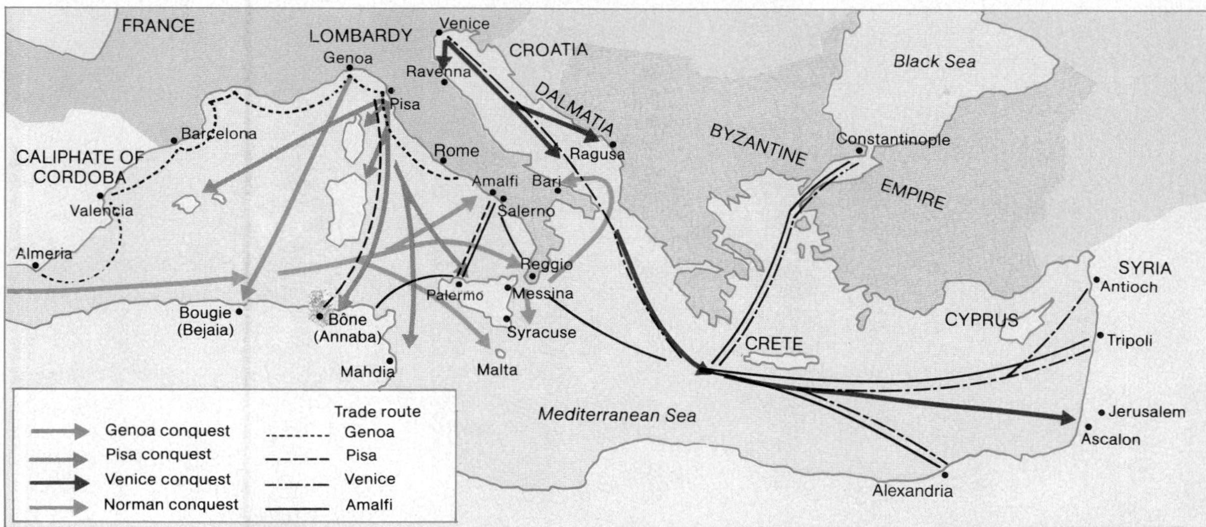

The Mediterranean, c.1140
As Christianity has been driving ever deeper into Moslem lands, control of the sea, and consequently of the world's most important trade routes, has passed into the hands of the Italian coastal cities of Venice, Pisa and Genoa.

The Moslem fleets, which plundered Pisa in 1001 and 1011, and attacked the northern shores of the Mediterranean in 1015, were defeated the following year by the Genoan and Pisan fleets off Sardinia. It was the turning of the tide.

In the western Mediterranean, while the Normans made war o land, the Italians conquered the sea. Pisa and Genoa vied for the cereals, salt, metal, coral and slaves of Corsica and Sardinia, and the grain of Sicily. By the time of the first crusades, when the maritime cities of Genoa, Pisa, Salerno and Amalfi attacked the Tunisian coast, extracting taxes from the emir of Kairouan, Christian fleets dominated the Mediterranean, and all the islands were in Christian hands. The Moslems lacked wood for their ships; their exports of wool and leather were in the hands of Italian merchants.

In the east, the Venetians, privileged traders in Constantinople by courtesy of the Byzantine empire, gradually gained footholds in the markets of Alexandria, Antioch and Tripoli. When the Crusaders invaded the Holy Land, the merchants of Venice, Pisa and Genoa sent relief fleets and were rewarded with quarters, warehouses, markets and churches in conquered towns. In 1123 Venice destroyed the Egyptian fleet off Ascalon, capturing a large merchant convoy and driving the last Moslem ships from the Mediterranean.

The scope of trade has been steadily increasing, with imports of spices, cotton, silk and fabric from the east balanced by exports of wool, flax and hemp cloth as well as older-established provisions like corn, salt, oil and wine. With increasing riches, the towns have cast off feudal ties, and are minting money, fixing tolls and controlling the surrounding country.

Loading up a merchant vessel at a port city, from a French manuscript.

Fine bronzes cast by Igbo in Nigeria

A ritual bronze from the Niger.

River Niger, Africa, c.1139
A remarkable culture is flourishing among the Igbo people of the lower Niger in West Africa. The Igbo have probably been settled in this area for at least 350 years, but appear to have no formal system of government. However, this has not prevented them from developing a high standard of craftsmanship in the working of bronze artefacts, which are the first to be made in this part of the continent.

If the Igbo lack political unity, they are spiritually united by a religious leader called the *Eze Nri*. The Eze Nri may have something to do with a recent tomb which shows the quality of Igbo bronzework. The body, if not the Eze Nri's, is that of some important person who has been buried with slaves.

Among the regalia and ornaments buried with him are a bronze leopard skull, used as the top of a staff, and a finely decorated fly-whisk handle with a figure on horseback. Other items are a copper crown, vessels, armlets and anklets.

Not far from this tomb, a store of ritual objects further displays the astonishing technique of the Igbo metalworkers.

Lincoln ravaged as royals duel for power

England, 1 November 1141
England has fallen into anarchy as Matilda, the daughter of the late King Henry, and her cousin Stephen fight for the throne. At Lincoln, in February, Stephen's cavalry fled in panic when Matilda's forces charged. He was taken prisoner, while Matilda's men, led by the earl of Chester, slaughtered many of the citizens of Lincoln.

Matilda, though disliked for her temper, became *Domina Anglorum* (Lady of the English) and prepared for her coronation. It never came; little more than seven months later her half-brother, the earl of Gloucester, was captured. He was released today in exchange for Stephen, who is now back on the throne. But he is no more popular than Matilda. At one time he was quarrelling with four powerful bishops, including his brother, the Bishop of Winchester. The country seems set for years of turmoil as barons rob and burn not only villages but even abbeys.

1148 (1148-1155)

North Africa, 1148. Roger II of Sicily takes Susa and Sfax in Ifrikiyah (Tunisia).

Near East, June 1149. Nur ad-Din kills Raymond of Poitiers, the prince of Antioch, near Apamea. Last year Raymond urged the leaders of the Second Crusade to join him in an attack on Nur ad-Din, whom he saw as the major threat, but they had preferred instead to attack Damascus.

England, 1149. A university is founded at Oxford.

Germany, 4 March 1152. Frederick (*Barbarossa* – Red Beard), the nephew of Conrad III, who died in February, is chosen as emperor and unites the two factions which emerged after the death of Henry V.

France, 1152. Louis VII secures the dissolution of his marriage with Eleanor of Aquitaine on the grounds of their consanguinity. Eleanor marries Henry of Anjou.

Jerusalem, 31 March 1152. Baldwin III, king of Jerusalem, besieges the citadel and exiles his mother, Melisande, with whom he had been reigning since 1144, to Nablus.

Afghanistan, 1152. Alauddin of Ghur sacks Ghazni and drives out the last Ghaznavid ruler. The empire won by Mahmud, who came to the throne in 998, and his father has therefore vanished after little more than a century.

Near East, 19 August 1153. Ascalon, the last Fatimid possession in Palestine, is taken by Baldwin III.

France, 20 August 1153. Bernard dies at the monastery of Clairvaux, of which he had been abbot since 1115.

England, 1153. The death of King Stephen's son Eustace leads Stephen to recognise Matilda's son, Henry Plantagenet, as heir to the English throne. Henry and his allies do homage to Stephen at Winchester.

Sicily, 26 February 1154. Roger II dies at Palermo. He is succeeded by his youngest son, William (the Bad).

Near East, 23 April 1154. Nur ad-Din seizes Damascus.

England, 25 October 1154. King Stephen dies at Dover.

Rome, 14 December 1154. Nicholas Brakespear, an Englishman, is elected pope. He takes the name Hadrian IV.

The third and highest terrace of Angkor Wat, the spiritual heart of the magnificent Khmer shrine complex.

Stunning temple of Angkor Wat is completed by Khmer king

Cambodia, 1150

The largest and most magnificent Hindu temple in Asia has been completed at Angkor Wat, the Khmer capital. Commissioned by King Suryavarman II as his funeral temple, its size alone makes it a suitable monument for the king who extended the frontiers of the Khmer empire beyond those of any other monarch. The moat encircling the temple and its edifices is 12 miles in circumference.

The grand entrance, over a paved bridge guarded by parapets depicting the part-dragon, part-human Hindu divinities, the Nagas, leads to a magnificent gatehouse, itself one of the grandest Khmer buildings ever erected. It is flanked by galleries, and its triple openings are surmounted by towers.

Beyond the gateway a paved causeway, protected by representations of the Nagas and flanked by two libraries, leads to a raised courtyard surrounded by a gallery. On ground level and gallery level are exquisite reliefs representing the great epics of Hindu mythology: the delights of paradise, the pains of purgatory, the battles of Devas, Asuras and Visnu, the legend of Garuda and Banasura, and Devas and Asuras churning the ocean.

Within the court is a second court, also raised and galleried, the gallery as richly and elaborately sculptured as the outer gallery.

Inside this court is the third, innermost, and highest of the courtyards. Here, standing on a pyramid, is the great temple itself, dedicated to Visnu and marked by five bellshaped towers, one at each corner and one in the centre, over 200 feet high a testimony to man's search for beauty and for God.

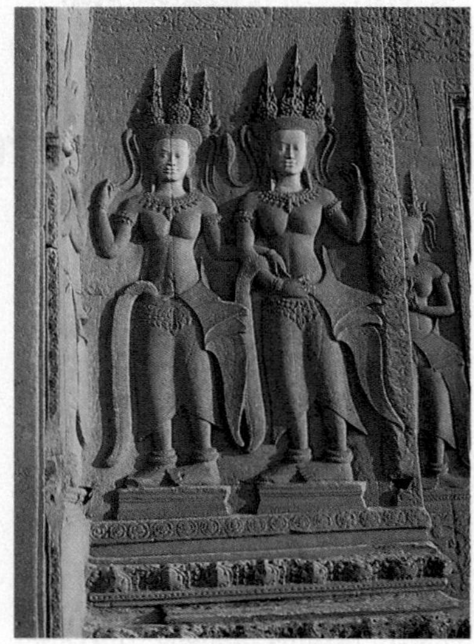

A frieze of dancing female figures.

A many-armed god surrounded by various fabulous animals and demons.

Knights are humiliated

A later view of French and German troops at the ill-fated siege of Damascus.

Damascus, September 1148
The Second Crusade has ended in humiliating failure, and an angry King Conrad of Germany today left the Holy Land, bound for Europe. The other crusading king, Louis VII of France, remains in Jerusalem, putting off the day when he must face the nobles and clerics who had opposed the adventure.

The royal Crusaders attended a great assembly of the Frankish kingdom of Jerusalem in June when it was foolishly decided to attack Damascus. The Frankish barons of northern Syria refused to take part; after all, the emir of Damascus, Unur, was an ally of Palestine against the dangerous ruler of Aleppo, Nur ad-Din.

When they arrived outside Damascus, the Crusaders learned that Unur had appealed to Nur ad-Din, who had despatched a relief force. At the same time Unur was secretly in touch with officials of the court of Jerusalem, and vast sums of money were being paid by him. After only four days the Crusaders abandoned the siege and retreated, harried by Unur's bowmen. The road to Galilee was littered with corpses. The legend of valiant knights from the west lies shattered.

Crusading abbot ends life at monastery

Dijon, 20 August 1153
Abbot Bernard died today, aged 63, in Clairvaux, a few miles from here. He has been a towering church figure for nearly 40 years and is most recently remembered for his preaching of the Second Crusade seven years ago.

Bernard the Cistercian monk.

Bernard came from a noble family and when his mother, of whom he was very fond, died when he was only 17 he decided to become a monk. Four years later he joined the Cistercians and was chosen by them to set up a new abbey when he was still only 25. Clairvaux now has 68 monks and is one of the most celebrated centres of learning.

Bernard's teaching put great emphasis on a severe life style, with the purpose of achieving spiritual marriage with God. In the schism of 1130, when two popes were appointed, he was the principal supporter of Innocent II, who favoured the monastic party. In 1140 he arranged the condemnation of Peter Abelard for heresy at the court in Sens. Abelard had upset the church by his controversial style, but Bernard genuinely believed that his ideas were dangerous.

Empire-building Roger of Sicily is dead

Palermo, February 1154
King Roger of Sicily is dead. The nephew of the great Norman conqueror Robert Guiscard, he made Italy and the Mediterranean his target, and became one of the great rulers of his generation. He is succeeded by his son, William.

Roger inherited control of Sicily from his father, who drove out the Moslems. Recognised by Anacletus II as king of Sicily in 1130, he used it as a base to conquer southern Italy. More recently he invaded Tunisia, capturing several cities, with the apparent intention of establishing an African empire.

In keeping with Norman tradition, Roger established a feudal power structure. But there was a strong Egyptian or Byzantine influence in his highly organised civil service and extravagant court, with rich costumes, a mosaic-encrusted private chapel and, rumour has it, a harem.

Cathedral at Cefalu built by Roger.

Kano walled to keep tribes at bay

Part of the fortification wall around the Hausa city-state of Kano.

Kano, Nigeria, 1150
Tsaraki dan Gijimasu, the ruler of Kano, has completed the city's walls. After five generations of interminable warfare between the Hausa citizens and the surrounding chiefs, the continued existence of the city state is guaranteed.

Kano has been inhabited since the eighth century when iron workings were established. It was not until the 11th century – when Hausa immigrants arrived from the east under their legendary leader, Bayajida, whose seven sons founded the seven city states of Hausa – that the city developed its sophisticated urban civilisation.

Gijimasu (1095-1134), the city's third ruler, began the walls; Tsaraki, his grandson, has completed them, providing the population of aristocrats, merchants, weavers, scholars, smiths and slaves with protection from the barbarians outside the gates.

1155 (1155-1175)

Italy, 1156. Backed by Pope Hadrian, the Byzantines invade Apulia and Sicily revolts. William of Sicily crushes the rebellion and routs the Byzantines at Brindisi. The pope capitulates at Benevento.

Cyprus, 1156. Reginald of Chatillon, the prince of Antioch, sacks Cyprus.

Spain, 1157. On the death of Alfonso VII, the king of Castile and Leon, his realm is divided between his sons, Sancho III and Ferdinand II.

Italy, 1158. The university of Bologna secures its first privileges from the emperor.

Rome, 1159. The election following the death of Pope Hadrian IV produces a schism.

North Africa, 1159. The Arabs retake the lands in Tunisia conquered by Roger of Sicily.

Milan, 1162. The Emperor Frederick seizes and destroys Milan. Its inhabitants are dispersed between four villages.

Italy, 1167. The cities of northern Italy establish the Lombard league in opposition to the Emperor Frederick.

Rome, 1167. Frederick seizes Rome. Pope Alexander III leaves the city.

Egypt, 1169. Saladin becomes vizier of the Fatimid caliphate of Cairo. (Viziers now hold real power, while the caliphs are little more than puppets.)

Italy, 1170. The Lombard league allies itself with the pope and founds a new town in his honour, Alessandria, which gives it command of the routes of western Lombardy.

Constantinople, 1171. The Emperor Manuel Comnenus orders the arrest of all Venetians in the empire and the immediate seizure of their goods and property.

Egypt, 1171. Saladin abolishes the Fatimid caliphate in Cairo and re-establishes Sunnism, thus becoming the effective sovereign of Egypt.

Arabia, 1173. Saladin seizes Aden.

Near East, 1174. Nur ad-Din is succeeded by an 11-year-old child. The struggle over the regency plunges the Moslem world into disunity.

Jerusalem, 1174. On the death of Amaury, the king of Jerusalem, Baldwin IV, aged 13 and a leper, succeeds him. A struggle over the regency ensues.

One thousand Romans die in riot after emperor crowned

Rome, 18 June 1155

A comedy of errors preceded a bloody massacre here today as Hadrian, the English-born pope, crowned the German-born Frederick Barbarossa as emperor.

The comedy involved the ancient custom in which the king holds the stirrups on the pope's horse for as far as he can throw a stone – as a mark of respect for the head of the church. Barbarossa refused what he regarded as an act of vassalage; and Hadrian, in turn, refused to give the king the traditional papal kiss of peace.

Much discussion ensued among the attendant priests and princes and the emperor gave in, duly leading the pope for a short distance and holding his stirrup. Protocol now satisfied, it was the turn of the Roman people to upset the red-bearded king. Their delegation said that they would accept him as emperor – but for 15,000 pounds of silver. Barbarossa refused. "You men of Rome make large demands on our emptied treasury," he said.

When he had arrived at Rome Barbarossa had found the gates of the city closed to him, so he had had to trick his way into the Vatican. A troop of soldiers entered the city by a secret gate and occupied St Peter's. The imperial coronation took place on a Saturday instead of a Sunday – with the soldiers in the congregation whispering their joy rather than shouting it and letting the Romans know what was going on.

But the news got out, and crowds streamed across the Tiber, killing two German guards on St Peter's bridge. Only then did Barbarossa order his army to hack a way out of Rome. At least 1,000 Romans died.

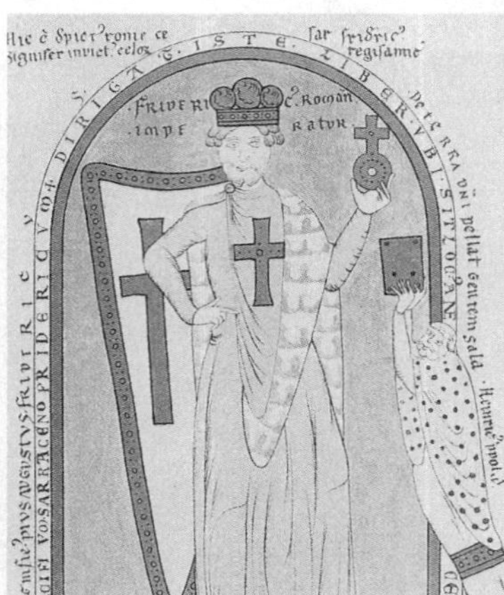

Frederick: the fiery Barbarossa.

Priest who preached poverty is burned

Rome, 1155

An idealistic priest who preached the joys of purity and poverty and created an "alternative Rome" has been sentenced to death and burned for heresy. The ashes of Arnold of Brescia were thrown into the Tiber.

The Arnoldist movement – which stresses apostolic poverty for the clergy and holds sacraments administered by any priest owning worldly goods as invalid – has threatened to split the church since Arnold came to Rome and allied himself with an anti-papal party. His activities have long brought him into conflict with the church. He was banished from Italy and expelled from France before being excommunicated.

Japanese emperor flees his palace disguised as lady-in-waiting

Japan, 1159

The bloody violence which has been raging between the warrior clans of Taira and Minamoto has ended in the defeat of the Minamoto in what has become known as the Heiji Rising, so called from the era-name *Heiji*, which means Times of Peace. At one stage the Minamoto held both the Emperor Nijo and the ex-Emperor Go-Shirakawa prisoner, but the Taira regrouped and the emperor escaped from his palace disguised as a lady-in-waiting. The Taira now attacked the Minamoto stronghold and drove them from the palace.

The Minamoto leader, Yoshitomo, and his three sons fled from the palace under cover of a snowstorm.

The burning of the Sanjo Palace in Kyoto during the Heiji insurrection.

Capital punishment

Japan, 1156

Capital punishment has been reintroduced after 350 years for offences committed by courtiers in the wake of the Hogen disturbances which arose from rivalries within the imperial family and the powerful Fujiwara, Taira and Minamoto families.

The defeated Tameyoshi, the leader of the Minamoto, has already been killed. His son, Yoshimoto, was ordered to kill him, but refused. One of his own officers then killed him, saying that it would be a disgrace for him to die at the hand of a Taira. The officer then took his own life.

Sect takes North Africa

Morocco, 1163

At the end of the reign of Abd al-Mu'min, the Almohads – Berbers from the Atlas mountains – are masters of North Africa. Having supplanted the declining Almoravid dynasty, they have driven the Normans out of Tunisia.

Abd al-Mu'min was the protege of ibn Tumart, a pure Berber from the Anti-Atlas who was head of the al-Muwahhidun Islamic reformist movement. They met in 1117, and Abd al-Mu'min was made a member of the executive body.

Ibn Tumart's death in 1130 was kept secret for three years before Abd al-Mu'min was recognised as his successor. Once anointed, Abd al-Mu'min won the support of the important Zanata Berbers, and in 1145 he won a great victory at Tlemcen over the forces of the Almoravid sovereign, Tashfin ben Ali, who died shortly after the battle.

With the vital Fez route now at his mercy, Abd al-Mu'min took Morocco in 1146 after a nine-month siege. By way of Meknes and Sale he came to the capital, Marrakesh, which fell in 1147. Abd al-Mu'min's next move was against the "infidel" Normans who had captured coastal ports for Roger II of Sicily.

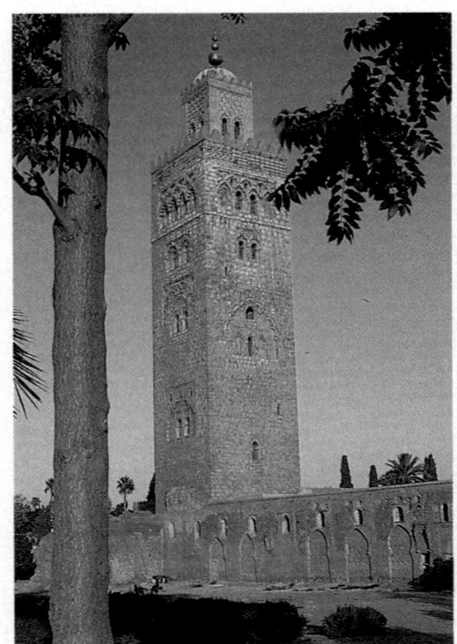
Marrakesh mosque, taken in 1147.

He then recaptured much of the north of Africa, including the important cities of Algiers and Tunis, and went on to conquer Christian strongholds throughout what he and his followers regarded as rightfully their territory in North Africa.

Emperor crushes rebellion of Italian cities

Crema, 3 February 1160

Prisoners, including children, were tied to huge siege machines and hurled at the walls of this northern Italian city during a siege which ended today after six long months of fierce resistance. A furious Emperor Frederick Barbarossa personally ordered the atrocity.

Horror was piled on horror as the German emperor sought to end Crema's status as one of the many powerful independent Italian city states.

Shocked by the sight of the heads of decapitated prisoners being thrown around by Barbarossa's troops, the Cremans retaliated by tearing their prisoners literally limb from limb on the city walls. Barbarossa ordered the mass hanging of prisoners, only to see German soldiers swinging from gallows. It was then that the emperor ordered the child hostages to be brought to the front line.

When Crema finally opened its gates, the inhabitants watched as their city was razed to the ground. Now it is the turn of another defiant city, Milan, Crema's ally, to face Barbarossa's wrath.

Thomas Becket murdered at Canterbury

Becket receives a fatal head wound from the sword of one of his killers.

Canterbury, 29 December 1170

Thomas Becket, the archbishop of Canterbury, was struck down by swords in the north transept of his own cathedral today as he stood by the altar of the Virgin Mary. His killers were four knights of the royal household, who rode here this afternoon and began a violent argument with the 52-year-old prelate.

The archbishop struggled for several minutes with his assailants, while a crowd of his men and townspeople who had come to attend evensong looked on. But when he realised that death was near, he bowed his head and joined his hands in prayer. "I commend myself to God, the Blessed Mary, St Denis and the patron saints of this Church," he said.

The murder comes as the brutal climax to a prolonged quarrel between Thomas and King Henry II. Becket, the London-born son of a Norman merchant, had risen rapidly in the royal service, and when Henry had him installed at Canterbury he believed he was getting a docile cleric. But Becket became a firm upholder of ecclesiastical privileges.

On one occasion Becket, waving his crozier at the king, told him he had no right to judge him. Last June Henry had his son and heir crowned in Westminster abbey by the archbishop of York, assisted by six bishops. Becket denounced the action and excommunicated the bishops.

In his fury the king uttered a fatal cry: "Who will free me from this turbulent priest?" The four knights gave him the answer.

Rich merchant extols virtues of poverty

Lyons, 1175

There is now a flourishing movement here of Waldensians, also called "poor men of Lyons", which is alarming local church leaders. The group lives the life of the early Christians, having given up all possessions in order to help the poor. Members consider that all believers should have the same rights as priests, and feel that the pope and other churchmen have lost touch with the real needs of the poor.

The movement began three years ago when a local money lender, Pierre Valdes, was converted. He was overcome with emotion on hearing a local storyteller talking about the death of St Alexis. He decided to take Christ's words – "Go sell what thou hast and give to the poor ..." – literally. He provided for his family and then used the rest of his wealth for bread and soup for the poor. The money ran out in August 1173. His example, however, attracted a constant flow of other rich converts, so he has been able to continue his work. The poor are pleased, but the Church fears for its authority.

A later image of Pierre Valdes.

1175 (1175-1185)

Constantinople, 1175. The Emperor Manuel Comnenus restores Venice's trading privileges.

Italy, 1176. Defeated at Legnano by the Lombard league, the Emperor Frederick Barbarossa concludes terms with the pope at Agnani.

Asia Minor, 1176. The Seljuk Turks crush the Byzantine army at Myriocephalum.

Near East, 1177. Saladin is defeated by Baldwin IV of Jerusalem at Ramleh.

Rome, March 1179. The Third Lateran Council decrees that a candidate will be elected pope only if he receives two thirds of the cardinals' votes.

Near East, 1180. After a defeat by Saladin last year, Baldwin IV of Jerusalem agrees a truce.

Constantinople, 24 September 1180. Manuel is succeeded as emperor by his 11-year-old son, Alexius II Comnenus, His widow, Maria, is regent.

Rome, 30 August 1181. Pope Alexander III dies. The schism which arose at his election in 1159 has been resolved.

Constantinople, 1182. A revolt led by Andronicus Comnenus against the Empress Maria prompts a massacre of Italians. The Emperor Alexius is forced to sign his mother's death warrant. Andronicus and Alexius rule jointly until Alexius is himself murdered.

Denmark, 1182. Valdemar the Great, king since 1157, dies. He co-operated with the Saxons against the Wends (the Slav peoples of the Baltic).

Near East, 1183. Saladin conquers Syria and becomes sultan.

Germany, 25 June 1183. The peace of Constance ends the conflict between the Emperor Frederick and the Lombard league.

Norway, 15 June 1184. King Magnus V, who had no legal right of inheritance, is defeated by his rival Sverre, who claims to be of royal blood.

Spain/North Africa, 1184. Abu Yusuf Ya'cub al-Mansur succeeds to the Almohad throne.

Italy, 1184. A church council at Verona condemns all heretics. Pope Lucius III and the emperor agree that bishops should excommunicate offenders and that their goods and property should be confiscated.

Toltec empire crumbles

Pyramid in the Mexican city of Tula, surmounted by huge Toltec statues.

Central America, 1175

Famine, fire, anarchy and revolution are steadily destroying not only the Toltec city of Tula, but the whole Toltec civilisation.

Since 1120 the frontiers of the empire have been pushed steadily inwards under the relentless pressure of people moving southwards into Toltec territory, responding themselves to pressure from others behind. Many of these immigrants bear no loyalty to the state, some of them actively supporting the Toltec's rival state, Cholula, which casts covetous eyes at the Toltec's rich cotton lands, and is under the same pressure from the north. Added to this is a new spectre, famine. The result is thousands of refugees pouring into Tula, with insufficient food to feed them. The population is dividing along ethnic lines.

The brief reign of the enlightened Ce Acatl Topiltzin offered hopes of a national revival, that would provide the will and the way to solve the Toltec Empire's problems. Now it seems the renaissance was merely a temporary phenomenon, serving only to delay the inevitable end.

Maya city is sacked, burned, abandoned

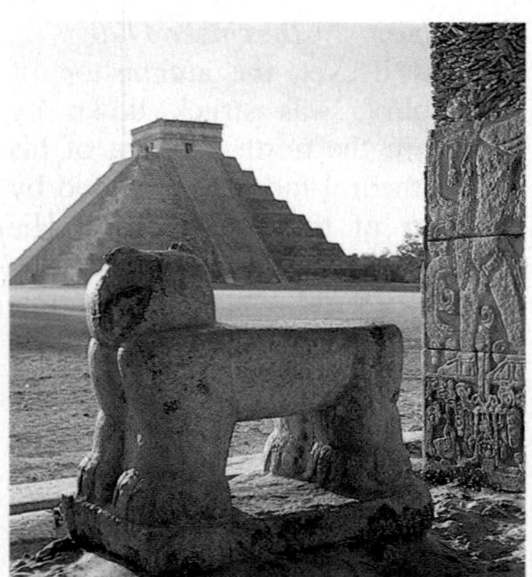

Sacred site at Chichen Itza.

Central America, 1179

As Central America becomes engulfed in anarchy, the Maya city of Chichen Itza has been sacked and burnt by Hunac Ceel, the ruthless and ambitious Mayapan king.

Hunac Ceel's rise epitomises the disorders of the time. First he gained control of his own Mayapan people with cunning and courage, then he formed an alliance with the Izamal state to attack Chichen Itza. Now he has turned on the Izamal.

Chichen Itza, famed as the centre of Maya civilization and re-established by Toltec exiles from Tula 200 years ago, is now deserted. Its great monumental buildings, the Temple of the Jaguars, the Temple of the Warriors, the vast ballcourt, the pyramid-shaped Castillo and the Caracol, the sacred well, are deserted. Those who have survived the sacking have fled south into the wilderness around Lake Peten Itza, where the last survivors of Maya civilization maintain a precarious independence around their new capital, Tayasal.

Church condemns "perfect" heresy

Toulouse, 1179

Cathar leaders here are dismayed at the news from Rome that the Third Lateran Council has banned "dualism" as heresy. The Cathar movement is very strong in the region and particularly in the towns of Toulouse and Albi. It was at Saint-Felix de Caraman, a few miles away, that Cathar beliefs were first formulated by Niketas, a visiting bishop from Constantinople.

Cathars believe there are two principles in the universe, good and evil, spirit and matter. Jesus is pure spirit and man is imperfect. The Old Testament is seen as the work of the devil and many Church rituals are felt to be useless pomp.

It is Cathar practices which have raised most controversy. They make a distinction between the "perfect" and believers. The "perfect" devote themselves to manual labour and live a life of abstinence and fasting. Believers, because they are thought to be saved by the virtue of the "perfect" are given every liberty in their personal lives.

Enemies of the Cathars say that their believers live lives of perpetual debauchery.

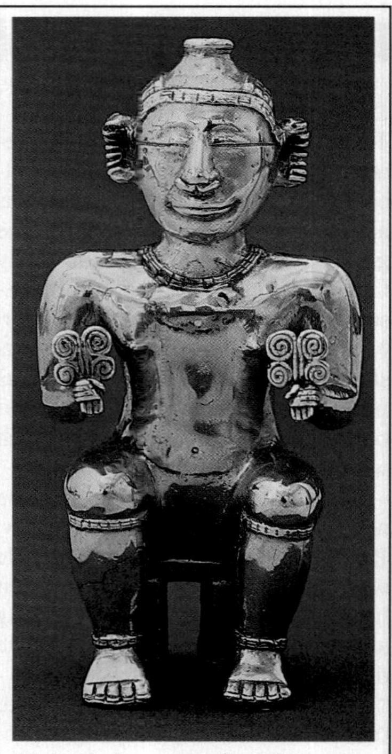

Elaborately worked solid gold seated figure, possibly of a deity, from Quimbaya in Colombia.

Saladin dreams of a "free" Jerusalem

A presumed portrait of Saladin.

Damascus, 1175

A new leader of Islam, Salah ad-Din (or Saladin) has welded the complementary strengths of Egypt and Syria under one command. Such a regional pan-Arab power, combining Egypt's wealth and learning with Syria's army, has serious implications for Christian interests in the Holy Land.

Saladin is a Mesopotamian Kurd and soldier who campaigned with his uncle in Egypt eight years ago. Shirkuh was a general under the Syrian ruler Nur ad-Din. Both leaders died naturally. Saladin, a strong man with a hard line about ridding Palestine of infidels, took command in Egypt after Shirkuh and soon proclaimed himself the actual ruler of Egypt rather than military governor. When Nur died four years ago, Saladin emerged as supreme commander of both countries at the age of 43. Since then he has defeated internal opposition to his role without losing political momentum internationally.

Some observers, noting the benefits to western culture of Arab conquest, including a more flexible number system than the Latin one, as well as opportunities for polygamy among converts, argue that it would not be all loss if Saladin were to realise his dream of "liberating" Jerusalem. This is not a view shared by more devout Christian believers, however.

Beaten emperor bows to power of pope

Venice, March 1177

As thousands watched in St Mark's Square, an emperor kissed the feet of the pope whom he had loathed and fought against for the past 19 years. Frederick Barbarossa has finally succumbed to papal authority and accepted Alexander III as the one and only pontiff.

Frederick had long sought to establish his anti-pope, Victor IV, or the latter's successor, Paschal III, on the papal throne in preference to Alexander. He sought support from King Henry II of England and King Louis VII of France, and succeeded in driving Alexander into exile in Sicily, although he failed in his attempt to win a decisive victory in Italy.

Ten years ago 10,000 knights and mercenaries set out in two columns, beating the Romans at Tusculum and capturing the Vatican after a fierce battle. Paschal was enthroned and victory seemed assured until the German army was decimated by malaria. Two thousand of Frederick's knights are believed to have died; and, with much of Italy uniting against him, Barbarossa fled, disguised as a servant. The indefatigable emperor tried yet another military venture, but has now accepted the right of cardinals to elect the new pope by a two-thirds majority – and not to support pretenders to the Holy See.

The victorious Pope Alexander III.

Five-year-old emperor drowned in battle

A later Japanese screen painting of a cavalryman in the current wars.

Japan, 1185

Antoku, the child-emperor, has perished in a great sea battle between the rival clans of Taira and Minamoto. With him died most of the Taira nobles and Taira power and ambitions. The Tairas, who had charge of the emperor and the regalia, the symbols of imperial legitimacy, had been beaten in a land campaign by the Minamotos acting on the authority of Go-Shirakawa, the "cloistered" emperor.

The Tairas, accomplished seamen, had taken to their ships with the regalia and Antoku, sure that they could defeat the Minamotos in a seafight, especially as they had 400 ships against their enemies' 300. When the fleets met at Dannoura, in the straits between Honshu and Kyushu, it seemed at first as if the Tairas were right to be confident. But when the tide changed and began to rip through the narrow straits, the Minamoto ships gained the advantage. The Taira fleet fell into disorder, its ships were sunk and the child-emperor drowned.

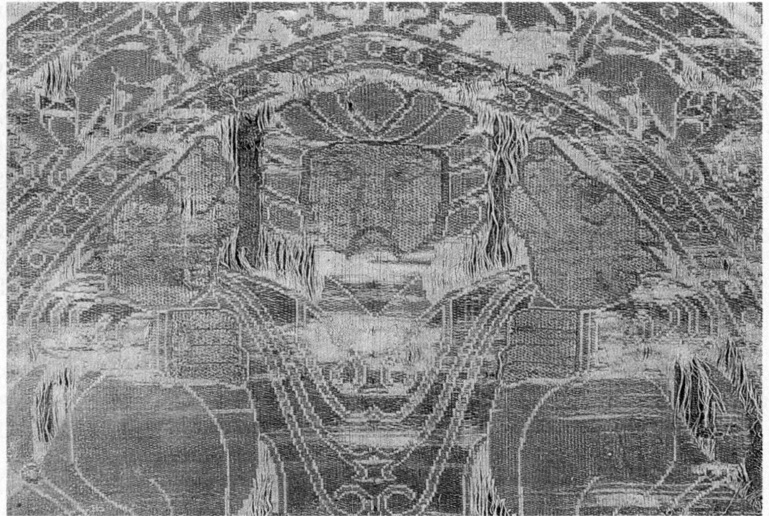

Detail of a Spanish woven silk with gold yarn from the tomb of Bishop Bernard Calvo of Vich, depicting a man apparently strangling two lions.

1185 (1185-1192)

India, 1185. Mohammed of Ghur deposes the Ghaznavids by taking Punjab and Lahore.

Constantinople, 1185. The Emperor Andronicus is killed in a rebellion.

Japan, 1185. Minamoto Yoritomo annihilates the Tairas, establishes himself at Kamakura and sets up a "military government".

Balkans, 1186. The Bulgarians, led by Peter and John Arsen, rebel against the new Byzantine emperor, Isaac II.

Near East, 1187. After his victory at Hittin, Saladin picks off the Frankish garrisons. Soon only Tyre, Tripoli and Antioch still remain unconquered.

France, 21 January 1189. Philip Augustus, Henry II of England and Frederick Barbarossa assemble the troops for the Third Crusade.

France, 1189. Henry II is succeeded as king of England by his son Richard (Lionheart).

Sicily, 1189. William II, king of Sicily since 1166, dies. He fought against the Byzantines until his defeat at Mosinopolis in 1185 and aided the Latins against the Saracens.

Japan, 1189. Having helped his brother Yoritomo in his fight against the Tairas, Minamoto no Yoshitsune becomes the target of Yoritomo's attacks. Defeated, he commits suicide with his family and partisans.

Balkans, 1190. The Emperor Isaac II is vanquished by the Bulgarians at Stara Zagora.

Germany, 1190. The Teutonic Knights are established for the defence of the Holy Land.

Japan, 1191. Shortly after returning from a period of study in China, Eisai founds the Rinzai Zen sect.

Near East, 1191. Richard Lionheart seizes Cyprus. He and Philip Augustus then take Acre. Philip Augustus falls ill and abandons the crusade to return to France. His army remains, led by Hugh of Burgundy.

Rome, 1191. Henry VI, the son of Frederick Barbarossa, is crowned emperor in Rome by Pope Celestine III.

Near East, 1191. Richard Lionheart defeats Saladin at Arsuf.

Near East, 1192. Richard Lionheart seizes Jaffa but is defeated at Jerusalem.

Richard Lionheart is king of England after Henry's death

The effigy of Henry II on his tomb.

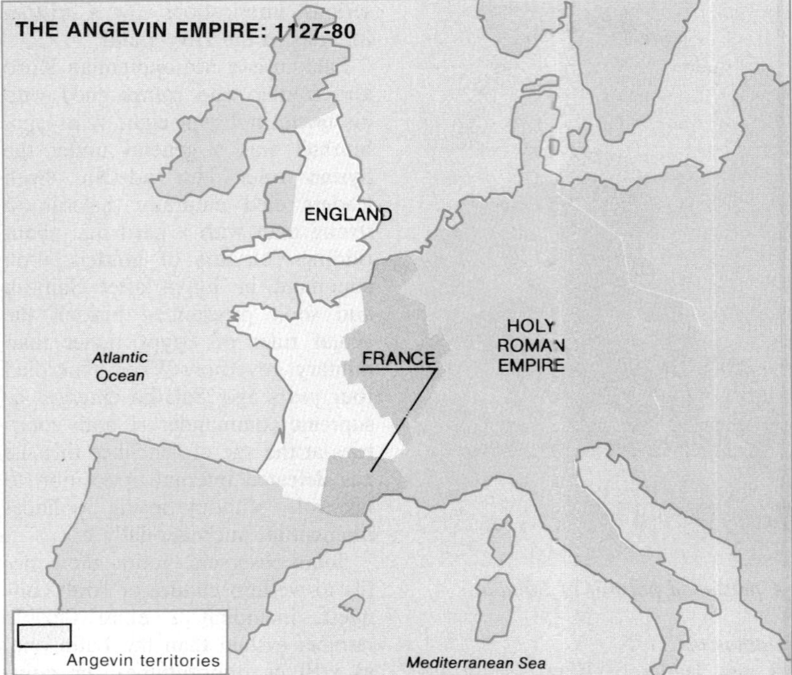

London, 3 September 1189

Richard Lionheart, crowned king of England today, knows little of the country he has inherited. He has spent most of his life in France, as duke of Aquitaine ruling the land of his mother, Eleanor, and fighting his father, Henry II, and his brothers. The old king's dying words to his pugnacious, disloyal son were: "God grant that I may not die till I have had a fitting revenge on you." Richard, aged 32, grew up in an atmosphere of intrigue. Henry had acquired vast territories in France by his marriage, and his sons were never satisfied with their shares. When Richard's elder brother Henry died and he became heir, his father wanted him to leave Aquitaine and come to England.

Richard scornfully refused and another family war, the last in fact, ensued. Richard's first act as king was to release his mother, who had been confined at Winchester for supporting him against her husband. He has been busy raising money for an expedition to Palestine. He can hardly wait to be off crusading once more. The nickname "Lionheart" was given to him in France, as *coeur de lion*, for his military prowess.

Anti-semitic riots spread in England as 500 Jews die at York

York, 17 March 1190

Six months of increasing anti-semitic agitation reached a climax today when more than 500 Jews – men, women and children – were massacred after they had taken refuge in York Castle. The massacre came at the end of a three-day siege of the castle by groups of young men about to depart on a crusade, backed by a number of people deeply indebted to Jewish money-lenders. Some Jews preferred to kill their families, and then themselves, rather than surrender to the mob. Those who did give in, promising to accept baptism if their lives were spared, were killed as soon as they left their sanctuary.

The Jews have never been fully accepted in England, but the uneasy tolerance they usually enjoy was shattered last September. King Richard forbade Jews to attend his coronation feast, but some of their leaders still attempted to enter his palace and offer him gifts. The London mob attacked these and other Jews, burning their houses and killing many of the inhabitants.

Since then the riots have spread through the kingdom, and Jews have been attacked from Durham in the north to Winchester in the south. The riots in Stamford and Newark were especially violent.

Many forces are exploiting the anti-semitic mood. Religious fanatics have convinced the simple-minded that the Jews are responsible for all their problems, and the image of the Jew as a wealthy usurer inevitably makes many people, especially those who use their services, very envious.

Those about to set off on crusades like to whip up their enthusiasm by attacking the Jews, whom they see as enemies of the faith, while those who cannot afford the journey find the vulnerable Jews a far more accessible target than the far-off Saracens.

Jews choose suicide before murder.

Saladin becomes master of the Orient after battle of Hittin

Jerusalem, 2 October 1187
The Christian-Latin kingdom of Palestine is no more. A grand gesture intended to free a beleagured queen caused an entire Christian army to be risked on an impossible march across the waterless, rocky heights of Hittin. It was a doomed expedition, surrounded and chopped to pieces by Saladin in July. As his enemies fell victim to heat exhaustion Saladin set fire to dry scrub and grass surrounding them. For men in chain armour this was torture.

After the inevitable surrender, Christian leaders such as Raymond of Tripoli, who had respected past treaties with Saladin, were treated correctly. Fanatics were executed, one of them (Reginald of Chatillon) by Saladin personally.

In the three months since then, Saladin's army of 30,000 has been able to pick off Christian citadels, from St Jean d'Acre to Beirut, and finally Jerusalem, with calm deliberation. Tripoli, Antioch and the port of Tyre remain in the hands of the Franks, but Saladin is convinced that it is extremely unlikely that the militant Christians will find support now for a costly third crusade.

Salah ad-Din (Saladin): victorious.

Crusade ends in failure for Richard

Acre, 9 October 1192
After 16 months' fighting, Richard Lionheart left Palestine today, with Jerusalem still in Moslem hands. The English king fought valiantly and won battles against Saladin, the sultan of Egypt, but the Christian armies failed to hold on to their gains and Richard quarrelled with his fellow Crusaders.

Richard has made the best of a bad job and patched up a truce with Saladin under which the Christians keep a few coast towns and are promised free access to the church of the Holy Sepulchre in Jerusalem. Unarmed parties from the crusading forces are visiting Jerusalem, but Richard refuses to go.

Crusader king: Richard Lionheart.

Death of Kilwa sultan who won control of gold trade

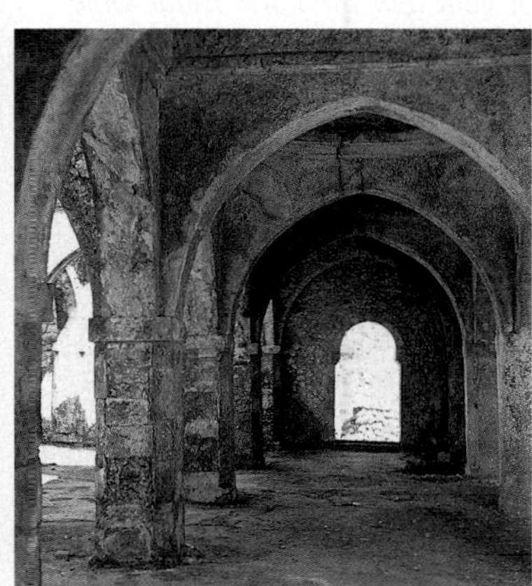

The great mosque of Kilwa.

Kilwa Island, East Africa, 1188
Mourners are gathering from all over Islamic East Africa to pay their last respects to the late Sultan Ali bin Hasan, the architect of modern Kilwa.

The sultan, the first to have his head appear on all Kilwa coinage, was responsible for creating a powerful city-state by uniting Mafia Island, a prosperous trading centre 100 miles south of Zanzibar, with Kilwa Island – well-known for its iron smelting industry and cowrie shell trade – 60 miles further south. A key factor in Kilwa's growing prosperity under Sultan Ali bin Hasan has been its slow but steady annexation of the gold trade from Mogadishu.

Ali bin Hasan and his predecessors started this gradual takeover by encouraging a programme of intermarriage with the Moslems of Mogadishu until the Kilwans had learned enough of Mogadishu's secrets – such as the source of the gold, which was Sofala – to gain control of the gold trade. Much of the prosperity brought by this trade is reflected in Kilwa's elegant and stonebuilt capital, Kilwa Kisiwani.

Frederick Barbarossa drowns during Third Crusade

Asia Minor, 10 June 1190
The drowned body of Emperor Frederick – Barbarossa – was found on a river bank today. He died as he would have wished – on a crusade to save the Latin Kingdom of Jerusalem. His men believe he was thrown from his horse and sunk by his weighty armour.

Frederick's army, near exhaustion after crossing the Taurus mountains, was approaching the port of Seleucia when the emperor died. From the moment they left the Dardanelles straits they had been harried by Turkish tribesmen and suffered badly from hunger and intense heat. Now the commanders, demoralised by the death of their king, have decided to turn back. Barbarossa had organised this third crusade on the orders of Pope Gregory VIII. Jerusalem had fallen to Saladin after the defeat of a previous crusade. Two other kings, Richard "Lionheart" of England and Philip II Augustus of France, are leading their armies to the Holy Land.

A Low German manuscript account of the drowning of the emperor.

The Japanese priest Hoshi, reputedly the incarnation of the deity emerging from his face.

1192 (1192-1202)

India, 1192. After taking Delhi, Mohammed of Ghur instals Qutb-ud-Din Aybak as its first Moslem ruler.

France, 1193. Philip Augustus seizes the Vexin, part of the English territory in France.

Central Europe, 1193. Richard Lionheart is taken prisoner in Vienna and given up to the Emperor Henry VI, of whose rivals – Tancred of Sicily and, within Germany, the Welf faction – he is an ally.

Near East, 1193. The death of Saladin at Damascus sparks off a civil war among his heirs.

Germany, 4 February 1194. Richard Lionheart is freed after paying a large ransom.

France, 1194. Philip Augustus is crushed at Freteval by Richard Lionheart, who re-conquers his French fiefs. They sign the truce of Verneuil.

Sicily, 29 September 1197. The Emperor Henry VI, crowned king at Palermo three years ago, dies at Messina. Henry granted wide concessions to win the pope's cooperation in the preservation of the union of the empire and Sicily.

India, 1197. The celebrated monastery of Nalanda, a centre of Buddhist studies, is destroyed by the Arabs.

Rome, 8 January 1198. On his election as pope, Innocent III calls for a new crusade.

Germany, July 1198. Otto of Brunswick is crowned king by the Welfs. Philip of Swabia, the leader of the Hohenstaufen faction, was elected king by his supporters in March. Civil war is inevitable.

Near East, 1200. Al-Malik al-Adil, who became sultan on the death of his brother Saladin, restores the unity of the Ayyubids' possessions and annexes Mesopotamia.

Peru, c.1200. The city of Cuzco is founded by the Inca leader Manco Capac.

Italy, 1201. Otto IV is recognised as emperor by Pope Innocent III.

Central Asia, 1202. The Tartars are crushed by Ghengis Khan.

France, 1202. The fiefs of King John of England within the jurisdiction of the kingdom of France (Aquitaine, Anjou and Poitou) are confiscated by King Philip, who grants the lands to John's nephew, Arthur of Brittany. In the ensuing war John's army wins a great victory at Mirabeau.

First Andean state established on north-western coast of Peru

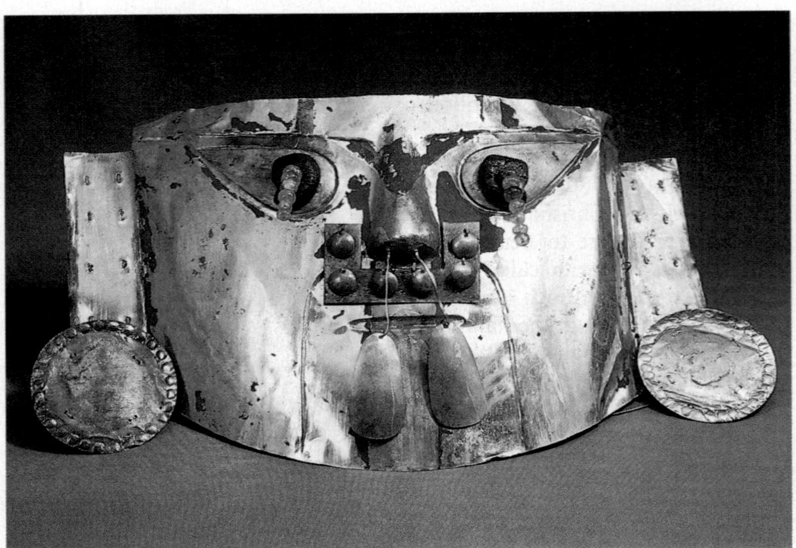

A gold funerary mask from Chimu, with emerald and traces of red colour.

A gold and turquoise ritual knife.

Peru, c.1200

The Peruvian state of Chimu, on the north-western coast of South America, has grown into an empire. Its capital, Chan Chan, in the Chicama valley near Trujillo, dominates the coastal plain from the Andes to the Pacific.

Chan Chan has been steadily expanding since it was founded by Tacayhamo who, according to legend, arrived there on a balsa raft 300 years ago.

The city is divided into ten quadrangles, each one extending over several acres and fortified by ramparts up to 50 feet high. Within the compounds the buildings are laid out according to a single plan, and in addition to the rows of houses there are miniature pyramids, storerooms, irrigated gardens, a public cemetery and stone-lined water reservoirs. For everything except the water reservoirs the building material is the same: rectangular adobe bricks reinforced with sand, gravel and straw.

Each compound is dominated by the fortified palace of the aristocrat who controls the compound. The palace walls are adorned with clay-moulded reliefs of birds, mammals, fish and flowers.

A Chimu breast cover with god-motif.

Japanese warlord rules without rivals

Japan, 21 August 1192

Yoritomo, the warrior head of the Minamoto clan, has today been made *shogun* by the emperor. This is a position of great power, and Yoritomo has established what is virtually a second capital at Kamakura in the lovely bay of Sagami.

With the Taira no longer able to challenge him, Yoritomo has no military or political rivals in Japan, and the ascendancy of the Minamoto is complete.

The shogun is too experienced a soldier to take chances, however, and so he has rewarded his followers with grants of estates at strategic points throughout the country. He is also planning an administrative network which could be the basis for a central government.

Yoritomo, the new "shogun".

Leonard's simple approach to maths

Italy, 1202

Leonardo Fibonacci, known as Leonard of Pisa, has published *Liber Abaci* (The Book of the Abacus), which promises to revolutionise the everyday use of mathematics.

Fibonacci's father, a Pisan merchant, worked in Bugia, in Barbary, where he met daily with Arab mathematicians. As a result of this Leonard learned about the Hindu system of numerals which, by including zero, makes calculations much simpler than by the Roman method.

Liber Abacci offers numbers, fractions, and methods of calculating prices, discounts and percentages.

Chivalrous Saladin dies

A manuscript depicting an imaginary combat between Richard and Saladin.

Damascus, 4 March 1193
Memorial services have been held in the great mosques of Damascus and Cairo following the death of Saladin. During the decade between his forties and fifties he had conquered a world. He had united the heart of Arabia and all but driven Christian fundamentalists out of Palestine.

Perhaps even more importantly, his chivalry won the respect of his opponents. Some were puzzled that a "pagan" (non-Christian) possessed chivalric virtues, wit and style, and suspected that he was a secret convert, knighted by one of his European captives.

Saladin needed no creed. He was that rare combination, a man of action who was mature enough to be generous to those he defeated. His only serious reverse was the unexpected success of the Christians' Third Crusade led by the English king, Richard Lionheart, among others.

This huge operation, launched through Tyre, has already retrieved the ports of Acre and Jaffa. Paradoxically, it seems to some observers that it was Saladin's very success at Hittin that provoked Europe's most powerful leaders into action. So Richard was joined by Frederick Barbarossa of Germany and Philip of France. Some of their allies, including King Guy of Jerusalem, were Saladin's prisoners who broke their word not to fight him again if freed.

CONQUESTS OF SALADIN

Antioch
CYPRUS
Sidon
Damascus
Acre
Jerusalem
Before 1171
Before 1187
Between 1187-89

King killed by an arrow

Two scenes from Richard's life.

King Henry II, Richard's father.

Chalus, France, 6 April 1199
Richard Lionheart, who had not received Holy Communion for seven years, today called one of his chaplains and made his confession. With his soul thus at peace, he directed that his body be embalmed, his brain buried in the abbey of Charroux at Poitiers, his heart in the Norman capital of Rouen, and his corpse laid at the feet of his father in the abbey of Fontevrault. As darkness fell, the brave and often ruthless Richard breathed his last.

For ten years he was king of England, but he spent no more than six months in the country. At the time of his death he was besieging the castle of a disobedient baron when a bolt from a crossbow struck him in the left shoulder. When he tried to pull it out the wood broke, leaving the iron barb embedded. He survived for 11 days.

He almost bankrupted England when, returning from the Third Crusade, he was captured by the duke of Austria, who turned him over to the German Henry VI. A ransom of 150,000 gold marks was demanded. It was never paid in full, but even the first instalment strained the resources of England.

Richard was a favourite of the troubadours, and he himself composed lyrics. He gloried in war; he had little interest in women, but married Berengaria, the daughter of the king of Navarre.

Great Moslem thinker dies in Marrakesh

Marrakesh, 11 December 1198
Ibn Rushd, the greatest Moslem philosopher and scientist of his day, has died in Marrakesh, aged 78. Born at Cordoba in Moorish Spain in 1120, ibn Rushd as a young man rapidly became a favourite of the Almohed caliphs, Abu Ya'qub and his successor Ya'qub al-Munsur, who ruled Moorish Spain.

However, at the height of his powers ibn Rushd found himself briefly out of favour with Caliph Ya'qub al-Munsur and chose self-exile in Marrakesh instead. Observers believe that ibn Rushd was bracketed along with traditionalist philosophers by the caliph, who believed that the traditionalists were opposed to his own philosophical viewpoint and were not being sufficiently dynamic in mobilising Islam against the mounting Christian offensive in Spain. Ibn Rushd chose Marrakesh because the more liberal and open atmosphere was more conducive to the line of thought which he was developing, but after a brief three years in exile he was recalled to Spain by Caliph Ya'qub al Munsur last year.

Among his contemporaries ibn Rushd was considered more than a mere commentator. His view, propounded in his lifetime, was that God made the universe, and it was for physical scientists to explain how it came about.

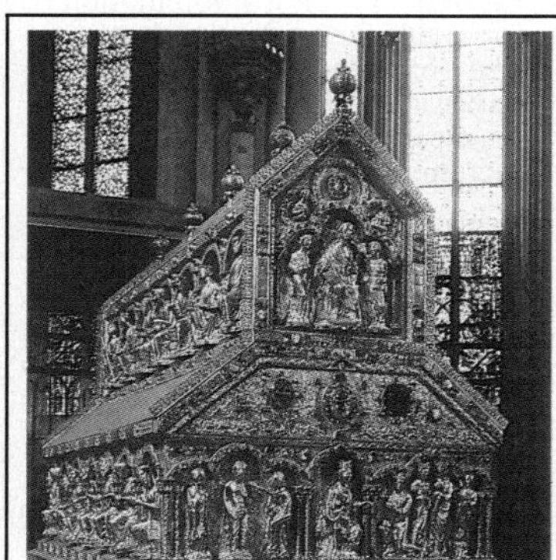

The magnficent gold and enamel Shrine of the Magi in Cologne Cathedral. It was begun by Nicolas Verdun, a master goldsmith and enameller in 1181 and was intended to contain the bones of the three kings, which had been brought to Cologne in 1164.

1202 (1202-1210)

Mediterranean, 1203. The Almohads begin a conquest of the Balearic archipelago.

France, April 1203. Brittany rebels against John, king of England. Last year Arthur of Brittany, arguably the rightful king of England, vanished, believed murdered by John.

France, 1204. Innocent III sends Peter of Castelnau and Armand Amalric, abbot of Citeaux, to wipe out the Cathar heresy in Languedoc.

Constantinople, 1204. The Crusaders seize the city and replace the Byzantine empire with an Eastern Latin empire. The Byzantines hold out in Trebizond, under Alexius Comnenus, and Nicaea.

France, 1204. The whole of the duchy of Normandy, apart from the Channel Islands, is now in French hands.

France, 1205. Anjou is conquered by Philip Augustus.

Greece, 1205. The duchy of Athens is founded by the crusader Othon de la Roche.

Asia Minor, 1206. Theodore Lascaris, son-in-law of the former Emperor Alexius III, is crowned emperor at Nicaea.

India, 1206. After the murder of the last Ghurid sultan, Qutb ud-Din Aybak founds the Moslem dynasty known as "the Slaves".

France, 15 January 1208. Peter of Castelnau is killed by a vassal of Raymond IV of Toulouse. Held responsible, Raymond is excommunicated, and the pope preaches a crusade against the heretics.

Rome, 24 March 1208. King John of England opposes Innocent III on his nomination for archbishop of Canterbury. The pope places England under an interdict, forbidding the clergy to administer the sacraments.

Central Asia, 1208. Ghengis Khan conquers Turkestan.

Rome, November 1209. John of England is excommunicated.

France, 22 July 1209. In the crusade against the Cathars, Simon of Montfort sacks Beziers. Thousands, including many Catholics, are killed.

Rome, 1209. Recognised as emperor after the murder of his rival Philip of Swabia, Otto IV is crowned by the pope.

England, 1209. A group of scholars leaves Oxford as a result of unrest in the town and settles in Cambridge.

Innocent stamps his power on royals

Rome, 1202

Pope Innocent III has crushed the opposition of the German princes in a stinging letter to their leader, the duke of Zahringen. They were protesting at the astonishing increase in the temporal power of the pope during Innocent's four years of office. Innocent asserts that, since it is the pope's duty to crown the German emperor, it is only right that the pope should decide on his fitness for office. Otherwise a pope might have to crown an idiot, a heretic or a pagan.

Innocent has systematically extended the power of the papacy since he became pope in January 1198. He exploited the rapid decline in Germany's power in Italy, which had followed the death of the Emperor Henry VI in 1197. He persuaded Henry's widow, the Empress Constance, to recognise his authority over Sicily.

When Constance died Innocent became sovereign of Sicily and regent of Germany while her son and heir, Frederick II, was a minor. He defeated protesting German nobles, and has since used his moral authority to get his suzerainty recognised by kings as far away as England, Portugal, Poland, Hungary and Denmark.

A later image of ill-named Innocent.

Finest Indian temple yet completed

The Chidanbaram Temple with one of its beehive-shaped gate towers.

Southern India, 1203

The spectacular temple of Nataraja has been completed at Chidambaram. It is the finest temple yet built by the Chola empire, surpassing even the magnificent and beautiful Rajaresvara temple, which was created by the famous Chola emperor, Rajaraja the Great, at Thanjavur in about 1000. The Hindu temple, grand yet simple, is adorned with exquisite sculpture and is almost dwarfed by its four beehive-shaped *gopuras*, or gate towers. No gopuras so large, so intricately carved or so beautifully proportioned have been seen in India before.

Rabbi was doctor and spoke for Jews in sultan's court

Cairo, 13 December 1204

Maimonides, the controversial Jewish lawyer and philosopher, has died, aged 69. Known to Jews as Rabbi Moshe ben Maimon and to Arabs as Abu Imran al-Kutfuni, his rational teaching is seen by fundamentalists as being too unorthodox.

Born in Cordoba, but forced out by the Almohads, Maimonides lived at Fez for ten years, and his family were obliged to convert to Islam. In a *Letter to the Jews of Yemen*, he argued that forced conversion was no sin, if loyalty to Israel was secretly maintained.

In Cairo, he became a doctor in the sultan's court and spokesman for the Jewish community. He wrote the *Mishneh Torah*, summarising Jewish law and ritual, in Hishnaic Hebrew. His most famous work was the *Guide of the Perplexed*, written in 1190 in Arabic but aimed at Jewish intellectuals.

Maimonides justified the concept of the prophet-lawmaker, modelled on Moses, but played down traditional Jewish eschatology and stressed the eternal survival of the human soul.

The character Mahan meets a party of demons who turn his horse into a seven-headed dragon. (Persian miniature.)

Constantinople looted by Crusaders

Constantinople, June 1204

For three days, soldiers wrenched ornate crosses from the high altar, hacked anything of value from the walls, brought mules into the churches to carry the booty away and burnt works of art. A prostitute was enthroned in place of a religious patriarch. The surprise in all this was not the pillage as such, but the professed faith of the pillagers: all claim to be Christians who took religious vows three years ago to join a crusade and respect places of worship.

The vows were discarded on the road to Constantinople, the capital of Byzantium and hub of an empire in the eastern Mediterranean, which is also the seat of the Orthodox Christian Church. The pillage was carried out by Catholic Christians, mostly Frenchmen, with the backing of Venetian entrepreneurs. They did it in the name of religious unity. In fact, it was a short cut to repayment of a loan to fund a fourth crusade to the Holy Land which went very wrong.

Even before the expedition left six years ago, the whole expeditionary force was excommunicated by Pope Innocent III, who had called for a crusade to Palestine. The Venetian doge, Enrico Dandolo, had contracted to supply ships for 30,000 men, but only 10,000 volunteered. Their leader Boniface, the marquess of Montferrat, agreed to seize Constantinople and share the city's wealth "to the honour of God, the pope and empire", and pay the Venetians.

Delacroix's impression of the Crusaders entering the Byzantine capital.

Conquerors scramble to "share out" empire's remnants

"La Serenissima": the "most serene" republic of Venice, happy to reap a crop of territorial spoils from the plundered remains of the Eastern empire.

Constantinople, 1204

After the sack of its capital, the Byzantine empire itself is divided into three parts, like Roman Gaul, as war booty. Twelve Venetian leaders and a dozen non-Venetians representing their accomplices in the Fourth Crusade have formed a commission to allot some of the old empire to the new emperor and other shares to the Venetians and to non-Venetian Crusaders.

By this means, Venice has collected the Adriatic east coast, both shores of the Gulf of Corinth, islands such as Andros, and swathes of Albania.

Many territories "awarded" to the French Boniface and his henchmen – Macedonia, for example – have yet to be conquered. Greeks are no more ready to grovel to new masters than to old ones. Oblivious of that, Boniface and his comrade-in-arms, Baldwin, recently came close to war to establish who has Thessalonica. Whatever the new deal ensures, it is not stability.

Animals "talk back" to Francis

Rome, 1210

Pope Innocent III has approved a new order, the Friars Minor, based on a simple life derived from the gospel. They have given up all their possessions and go around ragged, barefoot and dirty like vagabond beggars, mixing with the poor and helping them. They are 12 in number, like the apostles, and came here with their leader, Francis of Assisi, to plead for papal recognition.

Francis was born in 1181, the son of a wealthy cloth merchant. He became uneasy about the contrast between his riches and the poverty and sickness he saw in the streets. One day he not only gave alms to lepers, but forced himself to kiss one on the lips. The act produced a sudden and profound conversion.

Later he had a second revelation when the crucifix of the church of St Damien spoke to him: "Francis, go and repair my house, which you see is in ruins." He first interpreted this literally and went through the streets begging for stones to rebuild the church. He sold some of his father's cloth to buy more stones.

His father was furious and demanded his money back. Francis gave it to him publicly in front of the bishop's palace. Dramatically, he also took off his clothes and gave them back as well, saying: "Naked I will go to the Lord." He now devotes himself to helping the poor and the sick – and also to animals. He talks to the birds, and they appear to listen to him and talk back.

A later view of St Francis receiving the stigmata by Cima da Conegliano.

1210 (1210-1218)

Germany, December 1212. With papal backing, Frederick II of Hohenstaufen is crowned king of Germany.

England, 15 May 1213. King John submits to the pope, offering to make England and Ireland papal fiefs. Innocent III lifts the interdict of 1208.

France, 12 September 1213. Simon de Montfort defeats Raymond of Toulouse and Peter II of Aragon at Muret.

France, 27 July 1214. John of England is defeated by Philip Augustus of France at the battle of Bouvines.

England, 1214. Oxford University receives its first privileges.

Greece, 1215. Henry of Hainault, the brother of Baldwin IX, whom he succeeded at the head of the Eastern Latin empire, dies at Thessalonica. His title is taken by Peter de Courtenay.

Adriatic, 1215. Theodore Angelus, the despot of Epirus, takes Durazzo and Corfu from the Venetians.

Rome, 1215. At the Fourth Lateran Council, Dominic petitions the pope to found a new order of preachers. The principal mission of the Dominicans will be the conversion of heretics.

Rome, June 1215. Shortly after the sealing of Magna Carta, King John of England approaches the pope to have it annulled.

France, April 1216. Philip Augustus and his son resolve to invade England. Rebellious English barons recently opened negotiations with France for support against their king.

Italy, 16 July 1216. Pope Innocent III dies at Perugia while busy with preparations for the Fifth Crusade. He is succeeded by a Roman noble, Honorius III.

England, 19 October 1216. King John dies at Newark. He is succeeded by his nine-year-old son Henry. William Marshall is made regent.

Europe, 1217. A severe famine affects central and eastern Europe.

England, September 1217. The barons make peace with the new regime.

Asia, 1218. Ghengis Khan occupies Kashgar and the Tarim basin. Korea acknowledges its vassal status.

Moslems crushed in Spanish crusade

Spain, 17 July 1212

Moslem power in Spain is near collapse following the victory today of a huge Christian army over the Almohad Caliph Mohammed an-Nasr, the ruler of an empire stretching from the south of the peninsula to Tripoli in North Africa.

The two armies met at the pass of Las Navas de Tolosa, near the river Guadalquivir between Toledo and Granada, and the odds were stacked from the start against the Almohads. In 1195 Mohammed's father, Abu-Yusuf Yakub, who established Almohad rule in Moslem Spain in the wake of the collapse of the Almoravid dynasty, inflicted a humiliating defeat on King Alfonso VIII of Castile at Alarcos. Exploiting the truce signed after the battle, Alfonso and other Christian rulers set about patching up their quarrels, determined once and for all to end Moslem domination of the peninsula.

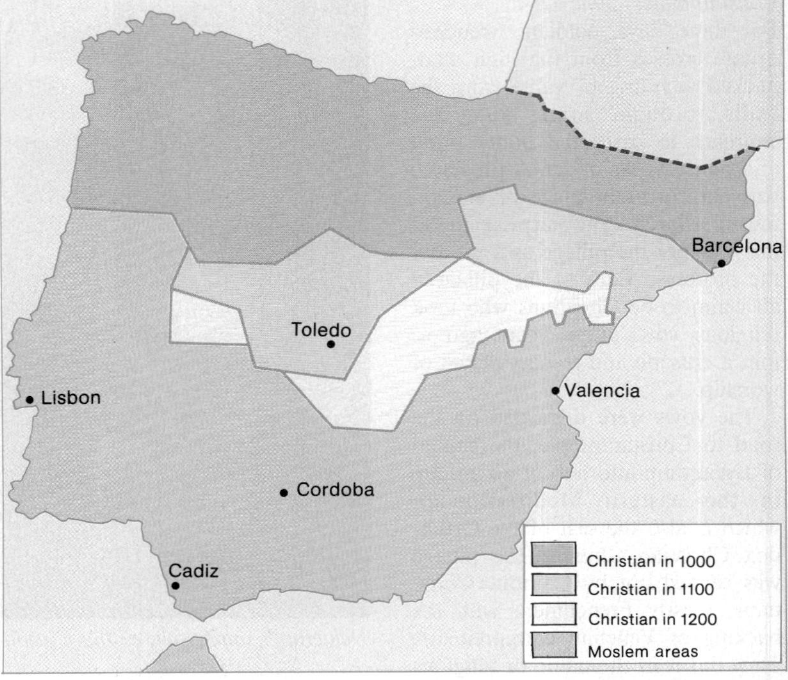

Bishops and archbishops played key roles as mediators, calling for a crusade against the Moslems which gained the official backing of Pope Innocent III and drew supporters from beyond the Pyrenees. Thus it was that the Christian force which advanced from Toledo to meet the caliph included troops from all the Spanish kingdoms, boosted by contingents from France. Provided Christian rulers are not distracted by internal problems, the conquest of Islamic Spain now seems inevitable.

Unknown from northern France is pope's supreme commander

Muret, France, 12 September 1213

The balance of power in southern France altered dramatically today after King Peter of Aragon died in a battlefield skirmish as he tried to lay siege to Simon de Montfort's fortress at Muret.

The shock defeat – Muret was defended by only 30 horsemen and a few foot soldiers – leaves Simon de Montfort in unchallenged control of southern France. King Peter of Aragon had been the southerners' last hope of ousting de Montfort, who they claim had perverted the crusade against the Albigensians – the heretical sect which has gathered much strength in southern France and Italy – for his own self-aggrandisement. Before the campaigns de Montfort was an obscure and minor noble from northern France. Today he is the pope's supreme commander.

A later artist's impression of an episode in the Albigensian Crusade.

In King Peter the southerners believed they had a champion with an impeccable anti-heretical pedigree capable of exposing de Montfort's so-called crusade. Many of the lands seized by de Montfort in his sweep for heretics in the dioceses of Carcassonne and Albi technically came within King Peter's fief.

For a short time it appeared that Pope Innocent III was prepared to back the Catalan king against de Montfort, accusing the latter of killing innocent people. But within a matter of months the pope, under pressure from his southern bishops, who owed their sees to de Montfort, switched sides.

English King John seals Magna Carta

Magna Carta: freedom for whom?

England, 15 June 1215
King John, known as John Lackland, has been forced to make a significant compromise in his struggle with the nobles who threaten his rule. After lengthy negotiations at Runnymede, in Surrey, near London, John today sealed *Magna Carta Libertatum* – the Great Charter of Liberties, which both guarantees to the barons their feudal privileges and promises to maintain the nation's laws.

John's bargaining position has been increasingly undermined by his loss of territories in France and by his highly unpopular attempts to tax those lords and knights who resist joining these costly and unsuccessful campaigns.

Magna Carta is essentially a peace treaty between John and his barons, with a committee of barons to ensure that it is carried out. Central to its 63 clauses are promises to administer an equitable legal system: everyone shall be entitled to the judgement of his peers; corruption will be ended; justice shall be available to all free men.

Mongols capture Beijing

China, 1215
Genghis Khan's Mongol horsemen have taken Beijing. The imperial palace of the Jin emperor is in flames, the city has been razed, and its inhabitants have been butchered in a dreadful orgy of killing which accompanied the Mongol conquest.

The emperor's treasury of gold and precious stones, silver and silk, has been carried away to Genghis where he relaxes near Lake Dolonor, beyond the Great Wall. He was so confident of victory that he did not even deign to appear before Beijing, leaving the conduct of the battle to one of his captains, Muqali.

The fall of Beijing was, indeed, inevitable. When Genghis first mustered his army before the city a year ago, it was powerfully defended, and the Mongol leader cunningly sought easy ransom rather than a hard and expensive victory.

The Jin emperor gave him everything he asked for – treasure, horses, girls, a royal princess for his own bed – and he went away. But the Jin emperor knew that Genghis would be back and in June 1214 he fled from the city. His departure demoralised the citizens, the army mutinied, and when Muqali appeared Beijing was ripe for plucking.

Genghis and his Mongols in battle.

Mongol invaders look west for plunder

Genghis praying to the sun.

China, 1218
Genghis Khan, fretting at the slow business of laying siege to cities, has abandoned his pursuit of the Jin emperor and, leaving his forces in China under the command of Muqali the Jalair, has gone in search of further lands to plunder. He has led his unwashed horsemen, virtually invincible as light cavalry, back to the north, and has swung west towards Turkestan, Transoxiana and Afghanistan. It is a move which bodes ill for the flourishing Moslem states of central Asia, for wherever the Mongols pass they leave nothing but death and destruction.

They emerged from the edge of the Gobi desert, whose harshness may have penetrated their souls, as a feuding federation of tribes. It was Genghis Khan who welded them together into the fearsome fighting force which is now rampaging across Europe and Asia.

Despite their conquest of many cities, and great stretches of China and the mountainous country to the west, the Mongols, unlike previous nomadic invaders, have not settled down and established their own civilisations.

For them cities are not places to be lived in but sources of plunder. Their organisation is purely military. They live and die in the saddle.

Young crusaders defy their king

France, 1212
A crusade of young people, led by Stephen of Cloyes, a 12-year-old shepherd boy, has set out by sea from Marseilles, determined to deliver the Holy Sepulchre from the infidels in Jerusalem.

This "Children's Crusade", as it has been named, is made up of few real children, but takes its title from the Latin word *infans*, literally meaning unable to speak and thus describing a variety of people – landless peasants, poor aristocrats and others – who have no real voice in society, but who have been attracted to the crusade.

King Philip II of France has banned the expedition, but Pope Innocent backs it, and many priests, peasants, women and assorted adventurers have joined in, following their leader, Stephen, who rides in a decorated cart with his bodyguard of young noblemen.

In Marseilles, where the crusaders won more support, they were helped by two merchants, Hugh Ferreus and William of Posqueres (known as William the Pig), who offered them transport.

Major drive against Jews and heresy

Rome, 1215
Major attacks on heresy, Jews and vice, plus moves to strengthen the church, have been announced by the pope in a communique following the Fourth Lateran Council in Rome.

The 1,200-strong council, called by Pope Innocent III, has issued declarations establishing and clarifying the church's teachings on several important issues. Its basic declarations are that:
* Each Mass is a miracle where consecrated bread and wine is miraculously changed into the flesh and blood of Christ whilst retaining the appearance of bread and wine.
* Every Christian must confess and take Communion at least once a year.
* Anyone propagating subversive ideas is automatically a heretic.
* Jews must be kept separate and be identifiable by special clothes.

1218 (1218-1228)

Japan, 1219. The Hojos assume the government at Kamakura after the death of Sanetomo, the third Minamoto shogun.

Egypt, 5 November 1219. The port of Damietta falls to the Crusaders after a siege.

Rome, 22 November 1220. Frederick II is crowned emperor by Pope Honorius III after promising to go to the aid of the Fifth Crusade within nine months.

South-East Asia, 1220. The first Thai kingdom of Sukhothai is established.

Italy, May 1220. Francis of Assisi resigns the leadership of the order which he created.

Italy, 1221. The Emperor Frederick II founds the university of Padua.

Near East, 1221. Sultan Kamil, Saladin's nephew and successor, offers to surrender Palestine to the Crusaders if the Egyptian port of Damietta is restored.

Egypt, 1221. Trapped in the marshes of the Nile delta, the Crusaders are forced to buy retreat by giving up Damietta.

France, 14 July 1223. Philip Augustus is succeeded as king by his son Louis VIII.

India, 1225. Iltutmish, the sultan of Delhi, repulses attacks by the Mongols.

Ethiopia, 1225. Lalibela, the emperor of Ethiopia, dies. He moved the capital from Axum to Lasta (Lalibela) and presided over the building of rock-hewn churches there.

France, 8 November 1226. Louis IX succeeds Louis VIII as king of France. His mother, Queen Blanche of Castile, acts as regent.

Japan, 1227. On his return from a journey to China, the Japanese monk Dogen introduces Zen Buddhism to Japan.

Rome, March 1227. On the death of Honorius III, Ugolini dei Conti, Innocent III's nephew, is elected pope. He takes the name Gregory IX.

North Africa, 1228. Having made himself independent of the Almohads, Abu Zakariyya Yahya founds the Hafsid dynasty and establishes a capital at Tunis.

Spain, 1228. James, who came to the throne of Aragon in 1213 at the age of five, resolves on a major offensive against the Moslems in Majorca.

Wandering Dominic "spoke only to God"

Bologna, 6 August 1221

Dominic, the founder of the monastic order that bears his name and one of the greatest of contemporary evangelists, has died in Bologna after falling ill during a mission in northern Italy. He was 51.

Born in Caleruega, in Castile, in 1170, he joined the church in 1196 and rose rapidly through its hierarchy, travelling widely on church business. This led to his development of an order of wandering preachers, known as the Friars Preacher, who were given papal recognition in 1217. For the next four years, until his death, Dominic devoted himself to expanding the order throughout Europe, spearheading its spread by his own constant journeying.

Dominic's personality was marked by his courage, his devotion to truth, his speedy analysis of every situation and the firmness with which he carried out his decisions. Devoted to the mendicant life, he accepted its privations, indulging in fasts, vigils, corporal penances and much other self-denial. Above all, Dominic was known for his ability to combine his personal religious feelings with an ability to spread the word of God to his fellow men. Absolutely committed to his work, he lived "in imitation of the apostles" and spoke "only of God or with God."

Dominic sees heretical books burnt.

Japanese calligraphy reflects Zen spirit

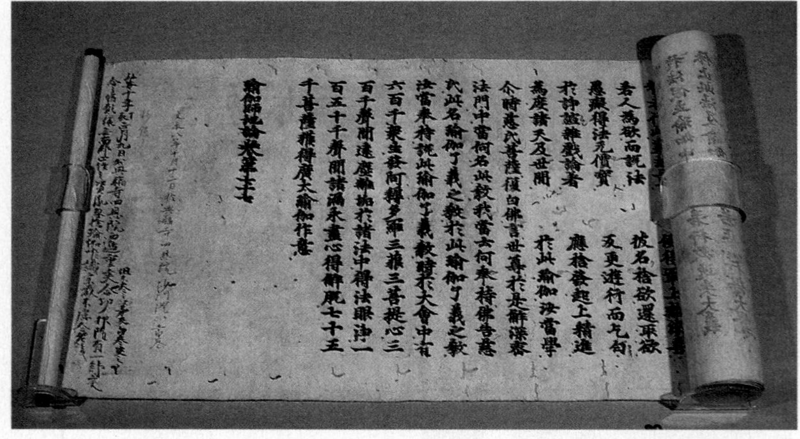

"Doctrine of Stages", by the Yogacara school of Japanese calligraphers.

Japan, c.1228

Calligraphy, the art of beautiful writing which has become such an important part of Japanese art and life, is undergoing a reformation under the influence of Zen culture which is spreading from China.

Zen Buddhism is being adopted by many of the powerful *samurai* warriors, who approve of its arduous mental discipline, and its qualities are being absorbed by artists, poets and calligraphers. Their work now displays the intensity of the Zen spirit, and its vigour is considered to be more important than the traditional skills of elegance and technique.

This new style is said to display both the writer's depth of conviction and his freedom of spirit. It adds a new dimension to the beauty and range of traditional Japanese calligraphy.

Ethiopian churches hewn from rock

Ethiopia, 1220

High in the mountains of Christian Ethiopia, hemmed in on three sides by Moslems, and bounded to the south by pagan tribesmen, a city of churches is being hewn out of raw rock: a symbol of the splendour and permanence of Ethiopia's church and of the dynamism and zeal of the country's rulers, the Zagwe dynasty. For three centuries Ethiopia had been in retreat, first from Moslems, and then, after the Moslems recognised its independence, from pagan Gallas; a few pockets of Christianity survived in the north. By 1150 the Zagwes had reversed the process, regaining control of the Ethiopian Highlands.

A Lalibela church hewn from rock.

Naturally, in a country where religion and national identity are one, political revival was matched by religious revival. Vast monasteries have been established at Tana Qirqos and Debre Libanos, and missionaries, aided by Egyptian Copts such as the saintly Gebre Menfas Qeddus (Servant of the Holy Ghost), are proselytising all over the newly liberated territories.

This city of churches, founded by the present emperor, Lalibela, and named after him, is the culmination of that revival. Here are 12 churches carved by monks out of solid rock. There is a Hill of Calvary, and a church called Golgotha. Running through the middle is a river named the Jordan. Many see this city as a new Jerusalem, and already the common people are calling it the work of angels.

Knight who jousts in dress and blond wig

Jousting knights and spectators.

A knight in full heraldic colours.

Bavaria, 1227

A Bavarian knight, dressed bizarrely in a long blond wig and a woman's dress, has been touring Europe and winning many new supporters for the martial sport of the tournament. Ulrich von Lichtenstein, who claims to be fighting for his own lady and all other women, calls his jousting tour the *Venusfahrt* (Venus tour) and offers a gold ring to anyone who can defeat him. Those who succumb to his lance must pay tribute to his lady. So far, if he can be believed, he has broken 307 spears, given away 271 rings, and dismounted four knights.

Von Lichtenstein's method of publicising his tour may seem extreme, and indeed his descriptions may not be wholly trustworthy, but this type of role-playing is certainly an important element in the growing enthusiasm for jousting among the aristocrats of Europe.

As well as providing excellent practice in the martial arts, and giving successful knights substantial prizes, tournaments offer chances for the upper classes to meet both socially and for political or diplomatic discussions. But tournaments have another task: promoting ceremony, the concept of chivalry and the kind of theatre epitomised by the Venusfahrt.

Von Lichtenstein is hardly the only or, indeed, the first performer of his type. The legend of King Arthur and his Round Table is especially popular, and a number of tournaments take place within an elaborate recreation of Camelot.

Great khan dies in bed

A European view of Genghis Khan's fall from his horse. He never recovered.

China, 1227

Genghis Khan is dead. The Mongol chieftain who carved out the largest empire the world has yet seen has died in his camp in the cool of the foothills of the Linbanshan mountains while his army besieges the Tangut king, Li Xian, in his capital of Ningxia.

The great khan, who had never fully recovered after a fall from his horse while hunting last year, knew death was upon him. He urged his officers to capture Ningxia quickly and, "warned by a dream", he summoned two of his three surviving sons, Ogodei and Toluy, who were campaigning nearby.

He dismissed his officers from his *yurt* where he lay in barbaric splendour and said to his sons: "My children, the end is near for me. Aided by the Eternal Heaven, I have conquered for you an empire so vast that from its centre to its bounds is a year's riding.

"If you would retain it, hold together, act in unison against your enemies, concert to further the fortunes of your followers. One of you must occupy the throne. Ogodei shall be my successor. Respect this choice after my death, and let Jaghatay [his third son], who is not here, make no trouble."

Then, even in great pain, on his deathbed, he outlined to them his plan of action for his last campaign against his old enemy, the Jin emperor. It was a typical Genghis Khan strategy of sweeping cavalry moves combined with the cunning use of the Jin's fearful neighbours.

It was this inflexible spirit which had sustained him through many dangers to become chief of the Mongols and make them the conquerors of the world.

People shudder at his name, for death walked with him. Even now, his corpse brings death, for all those unfortunate enough to meet his cortege on the long road back to Karakorum are killed.

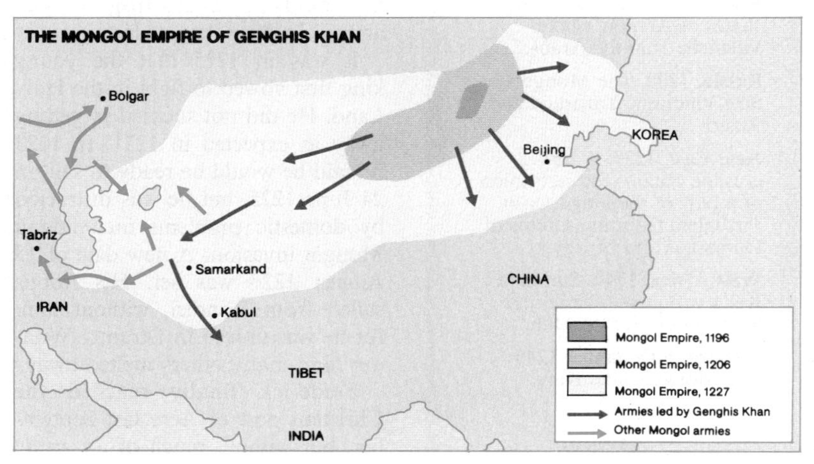

Islamic minaret rises from Hindu ruins

The new minaret in Delhi: the march of Islam continues.

Delhi, 1219

An imposing collection of new buildings is going up in Delhi, built out of material from 27 demolished Hindu temples. The most striking of them is a minaret which is likely to become Asia's tallest building.

Started by Qutb-ud-Din in 1210 and continued under his heir the present Sultan Iltutmish, the project is a tribute to the confidence of the new Islamic regime in northern India, which gained control nearly 40 years ago when the Ghur tribe, originating from a remote part of Afghanistan, seized Punjab, Sind, Bihar and Bengal.

1228 (1228-1242)

Majorca, 1230. Following his capture of Palma, James of Aragon overcomes Moslem resistance on the island.

Spain, 24 September 1230. On the death of Alfonso IX of Leon, Ferdinand III of Castile is accepted as king of Leon, unifying the two kingdoms.

Germany, 1230. The Teutonic Knights are invited into Prussia to help with the forcible conversion of the Prussians and Yatvags.

Switzerland, 1231. The canton of Uri – on the St Gotthard pass, the preferred imperial route across the Alps – is recognised as being under the direct control of the emperor.

Rome, 1233. Pope Gregory IX establishes the Inquisition.

China, 1234. The Mongols take K'aifeng, completing the destruction of the Jin empire.

Germany, 1234. Henry, the vice-regent of the empire, revolts against his father, the Emperor Frederick, and allies with the Lombard League.

Germany, 1235. The vice-regent Henry is deposed and imprisoned by his father.

North Africa, 1235. The Berber kingdom of the Abd al-Wadids is founded at Tlemcen in the Maghreb.

Balkans, 1235. The Bulgarians under John Asen II ally with John III Vatatzes of Nicaea. They conquer Thrace and besiege the city of Constantinople.

Spain, 29 June 1236. Ferdinand III of Castile and Leon takes Cordoba.

Russia, 1237. The Mongols cross the Volga – regarded as the boundary of Europe – and begin to pick off the disunited Russian princes one by one.

Italy, September 1237. The Emperor Frederick defeats the armies of the Lombard League.

Spain, 28 September 1238. James of Aragon retakes Valencia from the Arabs.

Russia, 1238. The Mongols take Vladimir, Yaroslavl and Rostov.

Near East, 1239. A new crusade obtains the restitution of a part of the kingdom of Jerusalem from the sultans of Damascus and of Egypt.

West Africa, 1240. Sundiata Keita conquers Ghana and incorporates it into Mali.

Ukraine, 6 December 1240. The Mongols take Kiev.

King in bloodless coup

A French miniature painter's beautiful, idealised impression of Jerusalem.

Jerusalem, 12 March 1229

Frederick II of Germany – twice excommunicated by the pope for his delayed crusading – has arrived in Jerusalem at last.

It was in 1215 that the young king first vowed to fight in the Holy Land. He did not succeed in getting away as expected in 1221. In 1223 he said he would be ready to sail on 24 June 1225, but he was distracted by domestic problems including a Mongol invasion. A new date of 15 August 1227 was set. His troops sailed from Brindisi, without him, for he was unwell in Otranto. Without him, many others melted away.

Frederick finally reached the Christian port of Acre last September, but without much of an army. However, he had a secret card to play. For more than two years he had been in clandestine diplomatic contact with the sultan of Egypt, al-Kamil. The sultan had been badly shaken by the Crusaders' advance into Egypt during the Fifth Crusade. He was happy to sign a treaty by which he surrendered Bethlehem and Nazareth and a corridor from Jerusalem to the coast as well as most of the city.

A bloodless coup of this sort is a novelty in the history of the Crusades, whose protagonists usually prefer to do things the hard way. It remains to be seen how the Vatican takes the news, for Frederick is still in disgrace, having dared to negotiate with an infidel.

Emperor's men kill pope's sailors

The papacy: imperial enemy.

Tuscany, 3 May 1241

With the red cross of the Crusades on their billowing white sails, a convoy of Genoese ships voyaged into disaster today. Trusting in the emblem of the Crusades to give them immunity, the convoy carried two cardinals and many bishops as well as large sums of money. It was destined for Rome where Pope Gregory IX had called a council seeking support against the Emperor Frederick II.

But the convoy never reached Rome. Off Tuscany it was attacked by a pro-imperial fleet from the rival city of Pisa and overwhelmed. Many Genoese sailors were slaughtered and the churchmen have been thrown into prison. Papacy and emperor have been enemies since soon after Frederick acceded at the age of 18. The emperor's hostages should guarantee the pope's failure to win the support he desperately needs.

The emperor: snub for the Vatican.

Mongols smash Teutonic Knights

Poland, 9 April 1241
Mongol horsemen from the Tartar region have broken an elite force of Teutonic Knights, contemptuously cutting off an ear from each corpse to be bagged and counted later like vermin's tails. Today, it is rumoured, nine bags were collected.

No-one seems sure where this force will strike when it has finished sacking the German city of Liegnitz. Mongol warriors ride four times faster than European heavy cavalry. This team has covered 400 miles from the Vistula River to Germany in a month. The invasion by this so-called "Golden Horde" started 18 years ago when Genghis Khan crushed the Russians at the River Kalka after an expedition through Persia. With Genghis' death in 1227, operations in the west were suspended. But after eight years, Tartar chieftains gathered at Karakorum agreed to ride under the command of Batu Khan, the grandson of Genghis Khan.

The new wave of Mongol attackers entered Russia through the Caucasus, rode north to sack Moscow, but was forced by floods to turn south, away from Novgorod, a trading centre. The Mongols then destroyed Kiev last year, before advancing through Poland to Liegnitz. The momentum of this invasion is such that there is a pervasive fear everywhere in Europe that it will not stop until it reaches the Atlantic. Ruling entire countries through the local aristocracies, now their vassals, the Mongols have created a vast empire which reaches from the Pacific to the Danube.

The skill of its mounted archers is crucial to the Mongol army's success.

First woman Moslem ruler and husband are killed by Turks

India, 13 October 1240
Sultana Raziyya, the first woman to rule a Moslem state, has been killed trying to regain control of Delhi. Turkish-backed Hindu troops murdered the sultana and her husband, Altuniyya, after a surprise attack near Kaithal today.

In 1236 Raziyya assumed this unique role when she succeeded her father Iltutmish to the sultanate of Delhi. The Turks did not share Iltutmish's high opinion of his emancipated daughter. They felt threatened by her popularity and were incensed by her administration.

Raziyya could crush Hindu and Moslem rebellions well enough, but she was no match for her noble Turkish enemies. Early this year they deposed and imprisoned her. The sultana later married her jailer, Altuniyya, and persuaded him and his army to accompany her on the fatal journey to Delhi.

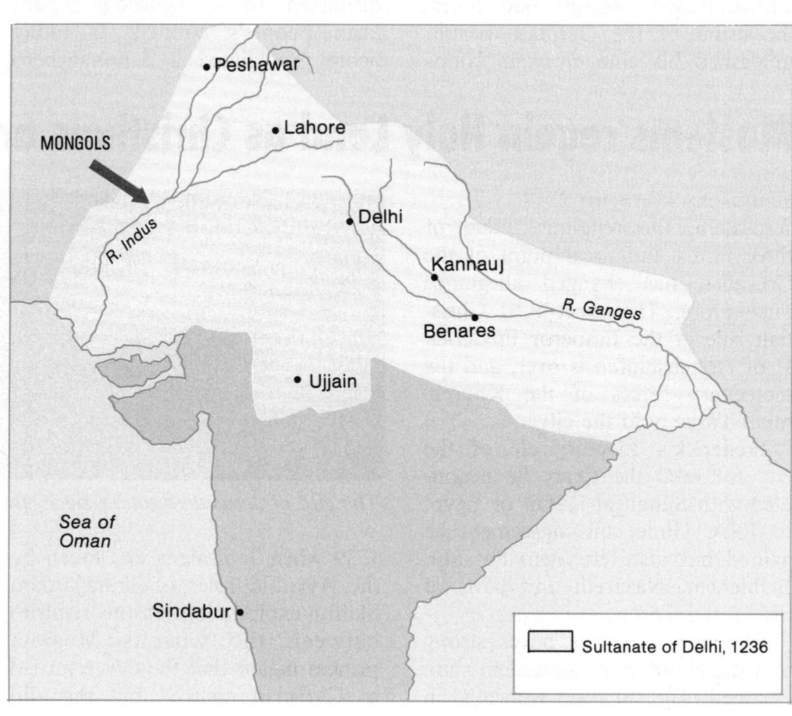

Khan's death saves Europe from horde

Vienna, Spring 1242
The Mongol advance across Europe has been halted, but not by force of arms. During the past winter, indeed, the Hungarian King Bela has been chased across the frozen Danube into Croatia while the main invading army occupied his country with chilling brutality. Winter over, the Mongols were expected to continue west, pushing a shield of prisoners before them if necessary. Instead, news that the great khan, Ogodei, had died in Mongolia started an unsavoury scramble to get home for the pickings.

Death of founder of the Sufi order

India, 1236
One of the world's most well-known ascetics, Khwaja Muinuddin Chishti, the founder of the fast-growing Chishti Sufi order, has died at Ajmir in Rajasthan, aged 97. It was at Ajmir that Chishti preached the mystic Sufi message, propounding a transcendental unity of being. Chishti also developed the nine ascetic rules of his order, requiring disciples to forsake money, never seek help and never possess more worldly goods than were required for a single day. Leading disciples of this mystical Islamic brotherhood want to spread Chishti's message throughout India.

Book of wisdom by master of Sufism

Damascus, 1232-1233
Ibn al-'Arabi has written *The Bezels of Wisdom*, a learned and metaphysical work defining the doctrine of Sufism.

Born in Murcia in 1165, ibn al-'Arabi has spent most of his life reading, meditating and writing. He believes in a God free of all attributes.

The Bezels of Wisdom sets out a Sufist view of the lives of 28 prophets, from Adam to Mahomet. For ibn Taymiyah, the Islamic fundamentalist, every word is a heresy.

1242 (1242-1248)

Balkans, 1242. The Mongols withdraw from Hungary and Dalmatia, cross the Carpathians and return to the lower Volga.

Italy, June 1243. Innocent IV is elected pope in place of Gregory IX, who died almost two years ago.

North Africa, 1244. Seville, Ceuta, Tlemcen and Meknes recognise the suzerainty of Yahya, the Hafsid monarch, over Tunis.

Rome, 1244. The university of Rome is founded.

Near East, 17 October 1244. After sacking Jerusalem, the nomadic Khorezmian Turks join with Egypt to rout the Latins at Gaza.

France, 27 July 1245. A council at Lyons condemns and deposes Frederick II, found guilty of sacrilege and suspected of heresy. The pope calls for a crusade against him.

Germany, 22 May 1246. Henry Raspe, the landgrave of Thuringia, is elected anti-king by the Rhenish prelates.

Germany, 5 August 1246. Conrad IV, the son of Frederick II, is defeated by Henry Raspe at the battle of Nidda.

Greece, 1246. William of Villehardouin succeeds Geoffrey II as ruler of Achaia, one of the Frankish states created after the fall of Constantinople.

Spain, 1246. Seville expels its Tunisian ruler, Abu Zakariyya, who is thought to be too conciliatory towards Christians. Ferdinand III of Castile seizes the opportunity to besiege the city.

Germany, 3 October 1247. On the death of Henry Raspe, Count William of Holland is elected anti-king by the Rhenish prelates.

Italy, 1247. The university of Siena is founded.

France, 1247. Prompted by stories that Jews are ritually murdering Christian children, two Franciscans begin an inquisition in the French diocese of Vienne. Pope Innocent IV disowns them.

Near East, 1247. The Khwarazmian Turks retake Tiberias and Ascalon.

Spain, 23 November 1248. Seville surrenders to Ferdinand III of Castile after a two-year siege. Most of its Moslem inhabitants flee to Granada.

Russian routs Teutonic Knights

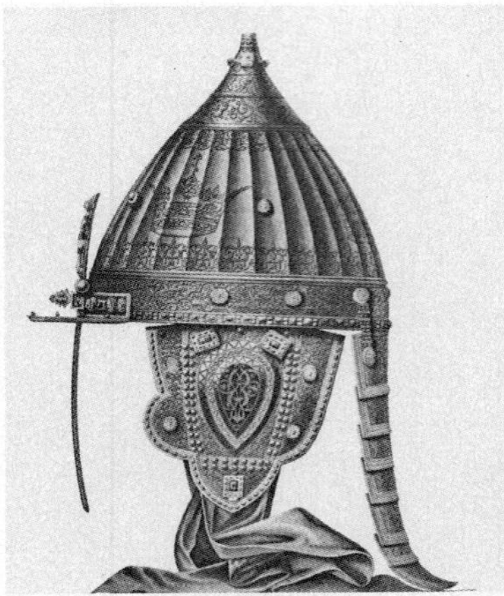

The helmet of Alexander Nevsky.

Alexander Nevsky, the prince of Novgorod and victor over the Teutonic knights. His name comes from his defeat of the Swedes at Neva in 1240.

Lake Peipus, Russia, 5 April 1242
In a dramatic ice-battle Russian troops led by Prince Alexander Nevsky have launched a successful counter-offensive against the Teutonic Knights, bringing to a halt their planned invasion of Russia.

Russian negotiators are forecasting that the routed Germans will be forced to give up all Russian lands that they have seized. The decisive clash between the Novgorod Russians and the Teutonic Knights came on the ice at Lake Peipus, in Livonia, where the German crusaders had concentrated several elite armies.

The turning point in the day-long battle came when Nevsky, whose Russian troops had borne the brunt of the German assault, unleashed his elite *droujina* troops on the German flanks, crushing the enemy into submission. Nevsky, who less than two years ago was dismissed by Novgorod's republican people's council, is today being proclaimed a national hero after agreeing to come out of retirement to lead the counter-attack against the German invaders. In Novgorod, this victory is seen as the end of constant attacks by Catholic crusaders.

Moslems regain Holy Land as Christians are expelled by Turks

Jerusalem, 23 August 1244
Jerusalem, the religious totem of three faiths and focal point of the Crusades, has changed allegiance once more. The short-lived Christian rule of the Emperor Frederick II of Hohenstaufen is over, and the mercenary forces of the Khorezmian Turks hold the city.

The city of Jerusalem under siege, from a French illuminated manuscript.

Frederick's 15-year rule of the city followed the treaty he negotiated with Sultan al-Kamil of Egypt in 1229. Under this agreement he gained not just Jerusalem but also Bethlehem, Nazareth and parts of Sidon and Toron.

Christian rule was never strong and the kingdom of Jerusalem soon declined. The situation worsened in 1239 when Jerusalem was taken by the Ayyubid ruler of Transjordan. Skilful exploitation of the rivalries between the various Moslem princes meant that the city returned to Christian control, but this did not last. King Ayub of Egypt, a signatory to the treaty but still an enemy of Christianity, enlisted the Turks as allies and swept through Palestine. The fall of Jerusalem seals his triumph and that of Islam.

Seljuk army obliterated by Mongols after six-month campaign

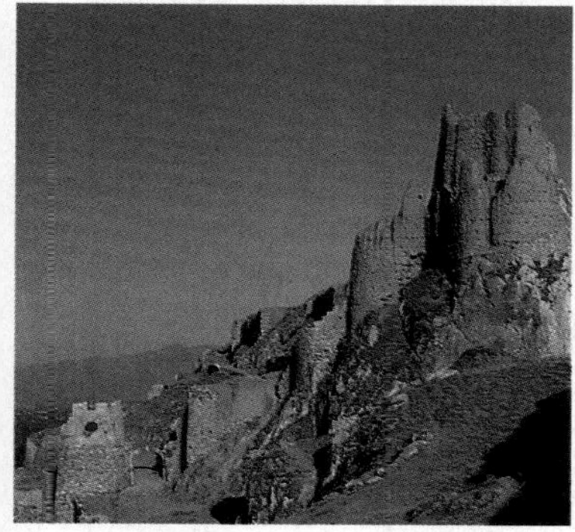
A Seljuk Turkish mountain fortress.

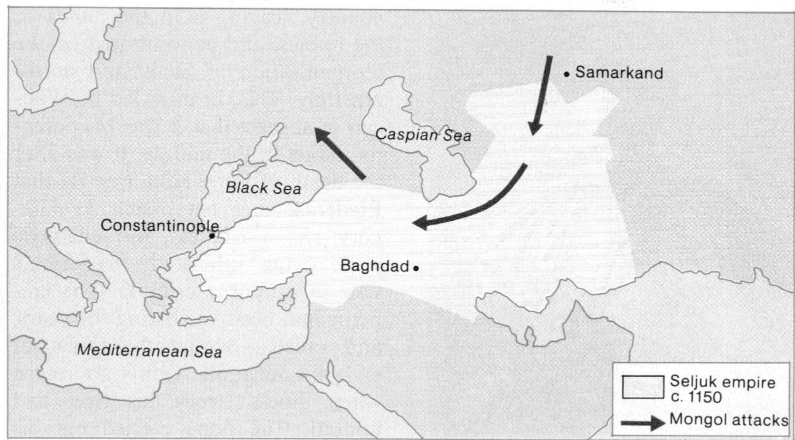

Asia Minor, 26 June 1243
The Seljuk Turkish army has been wiped out by the Mongols. In a campaign which began last winter, the Mongols have advanced from Erzurum to Sivas, sacking this last city ruthlessly in punishment for the resistance that they met.

The Mongols took advantage of internal troubles in the Seljuk state to take Erzurum and managed, largely through treachery, to avoid a siege, which would have been unwise at 3,000 feet in the winter. Well aware of the dangers of Mongol attacks, the Seljuks then tried desperately to rally all possible support around Sivas, where the sultan now went.

They were let down on several sides, including by the Armenians who were already busy trying to make peace with the Mongols, and had no intention of going to war with this terrifying people. It was a sizeable, but ill-assorted army that faced the Mongol leader Bayju and his invading horde.

Finally Bayju adopted the old strategy of a feigned retreat followed by a sudden advance. By this evening, the Seljuk army had been simply obliterated. The sultan and his mother have fled from the victorious Mongols.

Franciscan friars report on Mongols

Kiev, June 1247
An elderly, fat Italian monk who speaks no Oriental languages has returned from an astonishing 3,000-mile mission across some of Asia's harshest terrain, on behalf of Pope Innocent IV, to the great khan, Guyuk.

John of Plato Carpini began his epic journey last year, setting out into the vast steppes with two fellow-monks. They had not travelled far when they met Guyuk's people, the Mongols, and were sent on their way to the city of Karakorum for Guyuk's inauguration as great khan.

The pope's envoys then rode for thousands of miles with very little respite, and little to eat and drink but millet mixed with salt and melted mountain snow – a remarkable achievement for a rather portly 66-year-old friar used to the comforts and luxuries of civilised Italy. John and his companions reached Guyuk on 22 July, just in time for his splendid inauguration at which they were the sole western witnesses.

Guyuk was keen to contact the great priest who rules the west, and sent John back with a letter to the pope in November.

Moslem rebels mix drugs and murder

Syria, c.1245
A rebel Moslem sect from Persia has established new headquarters at Jabal Ansariyah in Syria. Political leaders in the area now live in fear of receiving a "knife on the pillow" warning from the sect, an Isma'ili Moslem breakaway group which carries out ruthless murders for its cause against Islamic orthodoxy. Christians as well as Moslems are now threatened by this fanatical and dangerous sect.

Founded over 200 years ago, the sect was nicknamed the "Hashishin", or "Assassins", because its adherents were rumoured to take the drug hashish. The euphoria induced by the drug was said to give the men such ecstatic visions of eternal bliss that they could not wait to die.

Generals serving the Abbasid caliphs in Baghdad – who claim descent from the family of the Prophet Mohammed – and Seljuk Turkish mercenaries were despatched with ease by Assassin undercover agents planted in camps and cities in Persia. In 1092 the extremists killed their great enemy Nizam al-Mulk, minister to the Seljuk sultans.

The sect's Syrian fortress.

In 1094 Hasan Sabah, the first grand master of the Assassins, captured the Persian fortress of Almut, below the Eldburz mountains at the southern end of the Caspian Sea. From this base Hasan commanded a growing network of guerrilla strongholds all over Persia and Mesopotamia.

Hasan, known as "The Old Man of the Mountain", built a library and encouraged learning amongst his men. The Old Man took Isma'ili free thinking to extremes, saying: "Nothing is true, everything is permitted."

Moslem Spain falls with city of Seville

Spain, 1248
Seville, the last great city in Spain under Moslem rule, has fallen to the army of King Ferdinand III of Castile and Leon. The Christian conquest of the Iberian peninsula is now all but complete.

The defeat of Las Navas de Tolosa in 1212 proved fatal to the Almohad rulers of Spain. In the 1220s ibn Hud overthrew the Almohad governors and set up a regime which, however, had to pay tribute to Ferdinand III, king of Castile from 1217 and of Leon from 1230. Ferdinand demanded Cordoba, the ancient capital of Moslem Spain; ibn Hud refused and Ferdinand captured the city in 1236.

Ibn Hud was ousted by his followers. He had no strong successor, and in 1238 King James of Aragon-Catalonia, Ferdinand's ally against the Moslems who had captured Majorca in 1229, seized Valencia. Also in 1238, the Portuguese took control of all of the Algarve.

Seville's fall leaves the small coastal kingdom of Granada as the only remnant of former Moslem Spain.

A "stave-church" at Borgund, Norway, in the unique Nordic style of Christian architecture. These churches are typically made of rough timber with pyramidal, stacked roofs.

1248 (1248-1258)

Egypt, 1249. Louis IX of France, who left on crusade in June 1248, disembarks in Egypt and takes Damietta before advancing on Cairo.

Finland, 1249. After a century of warfare, Sweden, under Earl Birger, conquers Finland.

Egypt, February 1250. Louis IX is taken prisoner at the battle of al-Mansurah.

Egypt, 1250. The assassination of the last Ayyubid caliph of Egypt marks the takeover of power by the Mamelukes.

Italy, 1250. Following the death of the Emperor Frederick II, rebellions break out in northern Italy against the feudal lords.

Paris, 1252. The secular masters of the university of Paris begin a fight against the mendicant orders.

Italy, 1252. The first gold florin is struck in Florence. The minting of coins was an imperial right, which has been usurped by Florence in the confusion following the death of Frederick II.

Mongolia, 1253. The Franciscan William of Rubruck is sent by Louis IX of France to Mongke, the great khan of Mongolia, to conclude an anti-Moslem alliance.

Asia Minor (Anatolia), 1254. John III Vatatzes, ruler of Nicaea since 1222, dies at Nymphaeum near Smyrna. His alliance with Bulgaria in 1235 won much of Thrace. In 1246 he took Bulgarian territory and deposed Demetrius, the despot of Salonika. The Nicaean empire could claim to be the successor to the Byzantine empire.

West Africa, 1255. Sundiata Keita, the great king of Mali, dies.

Persia, 1256. Hulegu founds the Mongol dynasty of Persia.

Paris, 1258. Robert de Sorbon, Louis IX's chaplain, founds a college for students of theology within the university of Paris.

Baghdad, 10 February 1258. Hulegu seizes Baghdad, bringing an end to the Abbasid caliphate.

England, 1258. Led by Simon de Montfort, the rebellious English barons wrest various concessions, known as the Provisions of Oxford, from Henry III. They include the institution of a parliament meeting three times a year and the presence of a permanent council to advise the king.

Relief at the death of maverick emperor

A later portrait of Frederick II.

Italy, November 1250

The Emperor Frederick II – "The Wonder of the World" – died at Castel Fiorentino, near Lucera, today, leaving to his heirs the task of sorting out a chaotic Europe. In the Vatican there will be sighs of relief, for few emperors have caused as much havoc as this oft-excommunicated maverick of a monarch.

Although king of Germany, Frederick paid scant attention to that country, leaving it in the hands of the nobles, and concentrated on the reorganisation of Sicily and northern Italy. This, in turn, led the Vatican to suspect that it was his potential target in the middle. It was after the death of Pope Honorius III that Frederick met his match in Gregory IX, a ruthless and energetic pope who inherited Frederick's vow to mount a crusade. The emperor had been vacillating for years, and sailed – under the threat of excommunication – only to return when illness struck his fleet and himself. The pope carried out his threat; but, undeterred, Frederick set out once more. Gregory thereupon excommunicated him again – this time for crusading while excommunicated. Frederick negotiated a treaty with the sultan. A third excommunication followed – this time for dealing with an infidel.

Frederick was a scholarly king with a scientific curiosity. One experiment which he conducted involved rearing children in silence in an effort to discover what language was spoken by Adam and Eve.

King's ransom paid for Louis IX of France

Damietta, April 30, 1250

King Louis IX walked to freedom today after handing over the keys of the city of Damietta and a record ransom of one million dinars.

The king, looking tired and ill after his month in captivity, had been taken by his Egyptian captors to the city after ransom terms had been agreed for his release with Turan Shah, Sultan of Egypt, at his royal residence in Fariskur.

The payment of the ransom brings to an end one of the most humiliating episodes in Frankish history. It contrasts strongly with the start of the crusade a year ago when the Frankish army overran Damietta and King Louis was begged by the previous sultan Ayyub to barter Damietta in exchange for Jerusalem. King Louis refused to trade with an infidel.

This position of strength deteriorated in the long drawn-out siege between the two sides outside Damietta. The Franks, through poor intelligence, missed a golden opportunity to exploit disarray in the Egyptian ranks after Ayyub died

King Louis IX faces his captors.

and his successor Turan Shah was still out of the country.

With typhoid reducing the ranks of his army, Louis tried to cut his losses by taking up the old sultan's offer of Damietta for Jerusalem but was turned down and captured.

Death of king who owned gold trade

Timbuktu, 1255

Sundiata Keita, the founder of the empire of Mali, is dead. A Malinke chief who liberated his people from the yoke of Samunguru Kante, king of Sosso, he built an empire stretching from the Atlantic in the west to Gao in the east.

He should never have lived. The Sosso king, fearing the Malinke, killed the 11 heirs to the petty chiefdom, disdaining to kill the twelfth, Sundiata, a sickly, semi-crippled child. Sundiata thrived and escaped to exile. Called back by his people, he united the Malinke against the Sosso, leading them to victory in 1235 at Kirina. Victorious in every campaign, he expanded his kingdom, occupying the entire Ghana Empire by 1240 and all the major caravan entrepots of the southern Sahara by 1250.

His empire is not merely the biggest in Black Africa, but the richest: controlling the copper mines at Takedda, the salt mines at Taghaza and the gold mines at Bure. So rich is Mali, with its "mountains of gold", that the trans-Saharan caravan trade to Morocco is called in Europe "the golden trade of the Moors".

gardoit le main qui issoit hors du
lac qui prist lespee le roy artu.
uant gyfles voit que
faire li couient. si re
uient arriere la ou les
pee estoit si la prent & la recome
ce a resgarder & a plaindre mlt
durement & dist tot en plorant.
ha. espee bone & bele plus que nu
le autre tant est grans damages
de vos. quant vos ne chaes es mains
de preudome. Lors la lance el lac
al plus parfont quil puet. Et main
tenant quele aprocha del aigue.
si vit gyfles une main qui issi del

Part of a French illuminated manuscript of "The Romance of Lancelot", one of many versions of the popular legend of King Arthur and his knights.

Church approves use of torture in hunt for heretics

Rome, 1255
In its constant fight against religious heresy the Roman Inquisition, founded more than 20 years ago, has authorised the use of a terrible new weapon: physical torture. Torture has been common in civil courts for some time, but the church has hitherto resisted its use. Now those accused of heresy who refuse to confess can be tortured until they satisfy the inquisitors.

"The question", as this interrogation is called, is just one part of the well-established inquisitorial process. Once the province of local bishops, the pursuit of heresy is now overseen by Rome itself.

Pairs of inquisitors, invariably Dominicans, tour a country, holding court in a succession of towns. On their arrival they deliver a public sermon on the evils of heresy, then offer a "period of grace" in which heretics can still confess.

Those who do confess gain an automatic pardon, but suspected heretics who still resist are pursued, often with the help of anonymous informers. This is a highly secretive process and the informers need never testify in public. After interrogation, sentence is announced during a second public sermon. Minor offenders receive no more than a penance and a fine; major heretics are imprisoned for life or burnt at the stake. The inquisitors may also impose collective punishments — fasts and pilgrimages.

Heresy: a burning question?

Massacre follows fall of Baghdad

A later Arab picture of Baghdad.

An engraving of a bird's eye view of the city of Baghdad.

Baghdad, February 1258
Baghdad has fallen to the Mongol hordes. Eye-witness accounts of the most appalling massacres have left the Islamic world trembling with shock.

Towards the end of last year Hulegu, the grandson of Ghengis Khan, occupied Persia and came to the outskirts of Baghdad. On 17 January his forces met the army of Caliph al-Musta'sim, the last of the Abbasids. The Mongols won a comprehensive victory, and went on to besiege the capital, Baghdad.

Eye-witnesses say that a thick cloud of dust engulfed the city, accompanied by a mighty rumbling. When the dust cleared, people who had climbed on to roofs and minarets saw the Mongol hordes in their city. When the invaders attacked, there was scarcely any resistance. Then the atrocities began. Those in the garrison who tried to escape were divided among the Mongols to be killed. When the caliph surrendered, on 10 February, Hulegu asked him to order his people out of the city, to lay down their arms. The majority obeyed and, once disarmed, were put to the sword. Three days later Hulegu's army moved into Baghdad, killing all who remained and starting fires. The sacking lasted for 17 days. On 20 February, al-Musta'sim was sewn into a bag and trampled to death by horses.

According to various accounts, the number killed varies between 80,000 and two million. The few who escaped have told their story throughout the Near East, and word has spread of Mongol savagery. Hulegu and his armies have acquired a reputation for invincibility. There is a crisis of morale through the Moslem world as the khan's hordes threaten to move further west.

Ex-monk leads ragged army on rampage

Picardy, France December 1251
This region is being frightened, not to say terrorised, by a ragged army numbering several thousands called *Pastoureaux* (Shepherds). Dressed as shepherds, they march into towns bearing pitchforks, hatchets, daggers and pikes. They beg for food, and if they do not get enough they take it by force.

It all began last Easter when a renegade Hungarian monk, Jacob, began preaching a new crusade. He played on local fears arising from the continued imprisonment of King Louis IX in the Holy Land. People were saying that Mohammed seemed stronger than Christ. Jacob claimed that God was angry at the pride of the nobles and churchmen and had called him to lead a crusade of the lowly. It was to be based on the shepherds, who first brought the glad tidings of the Nativity. He was soon joined by thieves and murderers as well.

The crusaders are supposed to be marching towards the Holy Land, and Jacob has told them that the sea will part for them so that they can walk all the way. Meanwhile they treat him as a messiah. He is said to heal the sick. He claims that their food will never grow less, like the loaves and fishes. He marries followers if they want it, and divorces them too. He even married 11 men to one woman.

Fisherman's son founds new sect

Japan, 1253
Nichiren, a Buddhist monk, has preached a remarkable sermon in which he denounced the traditional Buddhist sects of Jodo and Zen and established his own sect based on the Lotus sutra.

The followers of this fisherman's son are militant and intolerant of other beliefs, which he calls blasphemous. He insists that his disciples strengthen their faith by chanting "*Namu myoho rengekyo*", which means "I take my refuge in the Lotus sutra". His zealotry has already made him many enemies among powerful people.

1258 (1258-1265)

Paris, 1259. By the treaty of Paris, Louis IX cedes the Agenais, Saintonge and parts of Quercy, Limousin and Perigord to Henry III of England. Henry gives up all claims to the Plantagenet fiefs of Normandy, Anjou, Touraine, Maine and Poitou.

Greece, 1259. Intending to conquer Salonika and regain Constantinople, Michael II of Epirus allies with the Frankish prince of Achaia, William of Villehardouin. They are routed by the Nicaean forces at Pelagonia.

West Africa, 1260. Mansa Ule, the king of Mali, who is based at Timbuktu, embarks on a pilgrimage to Mecca.

Italy, 4 September 1260. The Florentine Guelfs, who support papal power, are crushed by the Tuscan Ghibellines, who support the emperor, at the battle of Montaperto.

Italy, 1260. Charles of Anjou, the brother of the king of France, subjugates Piedmont.

Asia Minor (Anatolia), 1261. Michael VIII Palaeologus, proclaimed emperor of Nicaea in 1258, signs a treaty promising the Genoese all the trading privileges within the empire enjoyed by Venice.

Rome, August 1261. Urban IV, the son of a French shoemaker, is elected pope in succession to Alexander IV.

Constantinople, 15 August 1261. Michael VIII Palaeologus seizes Constantinople, putting an end to the Latin empire and restoring the Byzantine empire.

Italy, 1262. Supported by Pope Urban IV, the Guelfs return to power in Tuscany.

Greece, 1262. In return for his freedom, William of Villehardouin, in prison since his abortive attack on Nicaea in 1259, cedes part of Morea (the Peloponnese) around Mistra to Michael VIII Palaeologus.

Rome, 1263. Charles of Anjou – who is being groomed by Urban IV for the role of papal champion against German influence in Italy – is elected senator for life by the Romans.

Italy, 1263. The Venetians defeat the Genoese in a sea battle off Settepozzi.

France, 1264. Arbitrating in the dispute between the English barons and Henry III, Louis IX annuls the Provisions of Oxford, imposed on Henry in 1258.

Glorious cathedrals enhance splendour of European cities

Europe, c.1260

The great surge of Christian faith in this century has found expression in stone cutting, statuary and stained glass, put together to make cathedrals of a new lightness and grace.

It began 100 years ago with the abbey church of St Denis built by Abbot Suger outside Paris. Fifty years ago Bishop Regnault began to raise the two great spires of Chartres which can now be seen for 20 miles. He filled the 160 windows with stained glass, including the great rose window, bathing the interior with blue light. He had the portals decorated with holy statues.

Rheims, where French kings are crowned, has been rebuilt with 550 statues – "the smiling angels". Rose windows like those at Chartres and Rheims have now been added to Notre Dame de Paris.

Meanwhile, in England, King Henry III has begun rebuilding Westminster Abbey with soaring columns, ribbed vaulting, huge windows and flying buttresses. He is employing the French architect Henry of Rheims and plans a rose window copied from St Denis. The new style began in England at Canterbury under the French mason William of Sens, who fell from the scaffolding and was succeeded by William the Englishman. Lincoln, Wells and Salisbury are nearly complete.

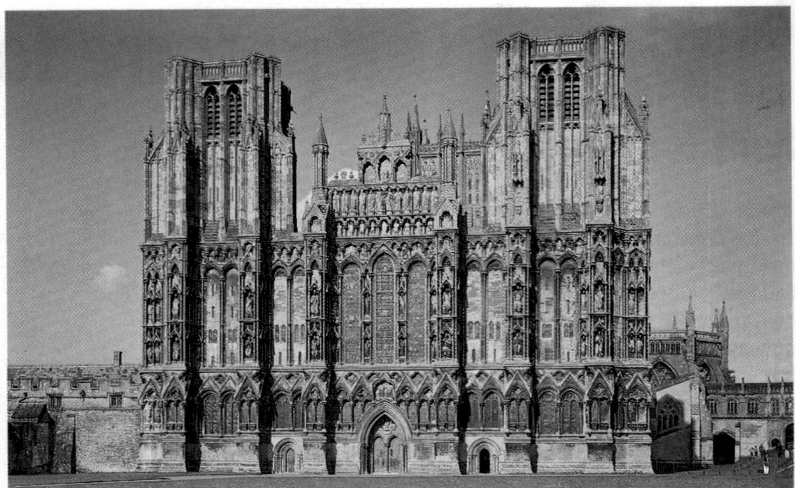

The west front of the spireless cathedral in Wells, Somerset: a magnificent English example of the new soaring, graceful style of church architecture.

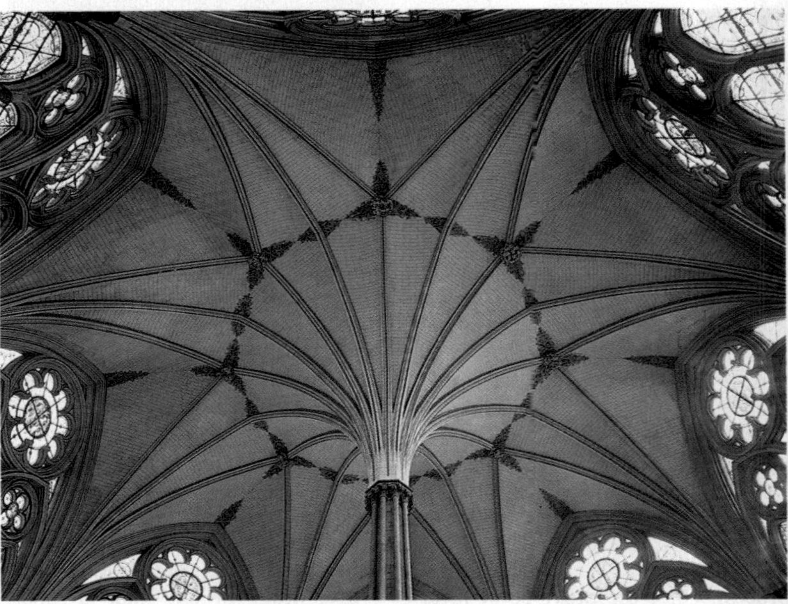

The elegant clustered column in the chapter house of Salisbury Cathedral seems almost too delicate for the glorious vaulted ceiling it supports.

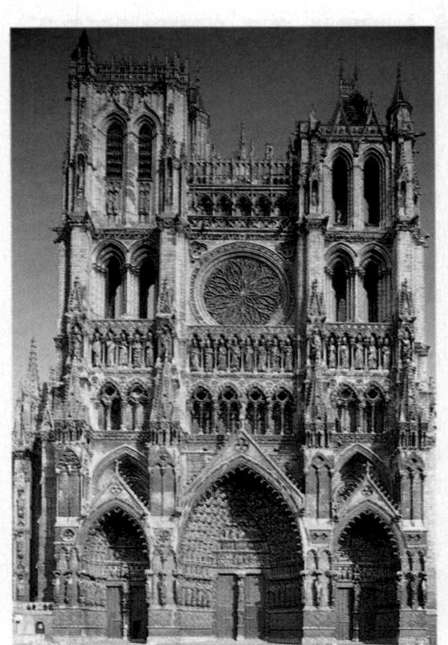

Amiens Cathedral: the west front.

Chartres Cathedral: the rose window.

Bourges Cathedral: the nave.

Kublai Khan heads Mongol empire

China, 1260

Kublai Khan has succeeded his brother Mongke as ruler of the great empire founded by their grandfather, Genghis, the fearsome first great khan of the Mongols.

Like all his family, Kublai is determined on conquest and has chosen his first victim, the remnant of the Song empire in southern China whose fall would bring the whole of China under Mongol rule.

The Mongols look at the great wealth of the Song and lick their lips in anticipation of the plunder, but Kublai is setting about the destruction of the Song with cunning rather than warfare.

He has sent an envoy, Hao Jing, to the Song court, ostensibly to discuss a peaceful settlement. He offered the Song a bargain: if they would acknowledge his reign as the "Son of Heaven" over all China, he would allow them a measure of self rule and the opportunity to benefit from the prosperity which would stem from a tolerant Mongol suzerainty.

Hao Jing embellished this offer by painting a picture of Kublai as a Chinese-style emperor, with Confucian advisers, governing in a civilised fashion.

However, Hao Jing also pointed out that any military resistance would be useless, for nothing could stand against the Mongol army which was now as skilled in siege warfare as it was in the field.

The Song, as aware of Mongol cunning as they are of Mongol ruthlessness, have refused to acknowledge Kublai's claim to be the Son of Heaven and have arrested Hao Jing, a move they will undoubtedly regret.

For the moment, however, the khan remains conciliatory, and is planning to send two more envoys to the Song. He is, in fact, quite unlike his grandfather, for he is an urban man rather than a horseman of the steppes.

He has shown an inclination for scholarship and the arts, and knows that commerce can bring as much profit as pillage. His entourage includes foreign scholars and experts of many races and religions. For all that, he is a Mongol and, like his forefathers, seems likely to wage war ruthlessly to achieve his ends.

Kublai's armies attack a Chinese city in this later painting from India.

Ex-slave army routs Mongols and saves Egypt

Nazareth, September 1260

A new Mongol offensive has been stopped in its tracks by an Arab army led by former Turkish slave mercenaries, the Mamelukes of Egypt. This was more than a military reverse: the mystique of Mongol invincibility has been utterly smashed.

The defeated Asiatic force was under the command of General Hulegu, the brother of the great khan, Mongke. Hulegu traversed the River Oxus on New Year's Day four years ago. It was an eventful trip across southern Asia. The Assassins challenged the Mongols and were wiped out. The Mongols invaded Baghdad next, sacked the city and defied local superstition by murdering the caliph. From Baghdad the invasion moved to the Syrian capital, Damascus, where Christian underdogs cheered foolishly and converted a mosque into a church. Aleppo also fell, and it seemed that Egypt was about to be raped as cruelly as Hungary.

The over-confident Mongols now made a fatal error. Hulegu, responding to word of Mongke's death, withdrew to Azerbaijan with many of his men and still sent the rest forward to crush the Mamelukes. The two forces met on a coast road in Palestine at Ain Jalut, which could mean "Goliath's Eye" or "Goliath's Spring." The Mongol Goliath was defeated by a hard man: Baybars, a product of several slave markets and an experienced assassin. The column commander, Ket Buqa, was last seen riding east, pursued by his bodyguard.

Constantinople falls: Venetian fleet saves some defenders

Constantinople, 15 August 1261

The Latin empire of Constantinople is no more. Michael VIII of Nicaea (Iznik, Turkey) was crowned emperor of Byzantium in the basilica of St Sophia today, his army having captured the city after a lengthy siege.

His agents are believed to have opened a gate from within to admit the Nicaean army. A Venetian fleet has taken off hundreds of women and children who cried for help as their shops and homes burnt behind them. Michael usurped the throne of Nicaea two years ago and made clear his purpose from the outset. The Emperor Baldwin II of Byzantium had assumed that the Nicaeans were the underdogs, and asked for the return of occupied lands. Michael ignored these requests and demanded half the customs dues and half the revenues from the mint. After signing a treaty of alliance with Genoa, Michael surrounded Constantinople. The city held out, although Baldwin was so short of funds that lead had to be stripped from roofs.

The emperor was among the survivors taken off by the Venetian fleet. He was wounded in the arm and leg, and left behind the imperial purple hat decorated with a priceless ruby.

1265 (1265-1281)

Scotland, 1266. Norway cedes the Hebrides and the Isle of Man to Scotland.

Italy, 1266. Charles of Anjou defeats and kills Manfred of Sicily at Benevento. He is invested by Pope Clement IV with the crown of Sicily, and enters Naples.

Near East, 1268. After seizing Caesarea in 1265, the Mameluke sultan, Baybars, takes Jaffa and Antioch.

Italy, 1268. Conradin, the last Hohenstaufen, invades Italy but is defeated by Charles of Anjou at Tagliacozzi.

France, 1270. The bishop of Paris condemns the Averroists – followers of the Moslem scholar Averroes.

Ethiopia, 1270. Yekuno Amlak comes to the throne and founds the Solomonic dynasty with a capital at Ankober.

North Africa, 1270. Louis IX of France dies at Tunis on the way to his second crusade.

Italy, 1270. Charles of Anjou becomes master of Tuscany.

France, 1271. Philip III, the new king of France, inherits Poitou, the Auvergne and the county of Toulouse. Northern and southern France are unified.

Near East, May 1272. The Crusaders, led by Edward of England, reach a truce with Sultan Baybars at Caesarea.

Germany, 1 October 1273. Rudolf of Habsburg, an elderly Swabian count, is elected emperor, putting an end to the great interregnum which began with the death of Conrad IV in 1254.

France, 1274. A general council at Lyons, summoned by Gregory X, regulates the election of the pope by instituting the conclave.

France, 1274. Feeling threatened by Charles of Anjou, Michael Palaeologus makes a submission to the pope at the Council of Lyons. He is granted papal protection.

China, 1275. The Venetian merchant and explorer Marco Polo travels to China.

Central Europe, 1278. Backed by Ladislas of Hungary, the Emperor Rudolph defeats his rival Otokar of Bohemia.

China, 1279. Kublai Khan overcomes the last Song resistance and reunifies China under the Yuan dynasty.

Revolt of English barons ends in failure

Evesham, 4 August 1265
Simon de Montfort, the leader of the dissident barons who tried to curb the powers of King Henry III, died on the battlefield here today. He was beheaded and his body delivered to the monks of Evesham.

Though de Montfort's family was French, he inherited the earldom of Leicester through his mother, and the struggle against the king was in part motivated by a growing dislike of foreign influence, the heavy papal taxation of the church and the extravagance of the king's foreign dependants.

The king, meeting the discontented barons in a parliament at Oxford, made many promises, enshrined in the Provisions of Oxford, but reneged on them. De Montfort called his own parliament, which was notable for including knights and burgesses as well as barons.

De Montfort captured the king and his son, Edward, at the battle of Lewes in 1264, but a year later the barons, perhaps mistrusting his efforts to gain broader popular support, were deserting him. Edward escaped, to lead the victorious army at Evesham.

King Henry III: keeping control.

Typhoon saves Japanese from Mongols

Japan, 1281
Kublai Khan's great invasion fleet has been wrecked by a typhoon on the Japanese coast. The grateful Japanese, who see the hand of God in their deliverance, have named the typhoon *Kamikaze*, the Divine Wind. The Mongol emperor's flotilla of Chinese and Korean ships carried 140,000 troops, and if this army had got safely ashore there is little doubt that it would have conquered Japan despite the bravery of the *samurai* who, banners waving, prepared to meet the invaders.

Thousands of soldiers died when their ships foundered or were driven onto the rocks. The survivors who landed on Tsushima were cut down by the waiting samurai.

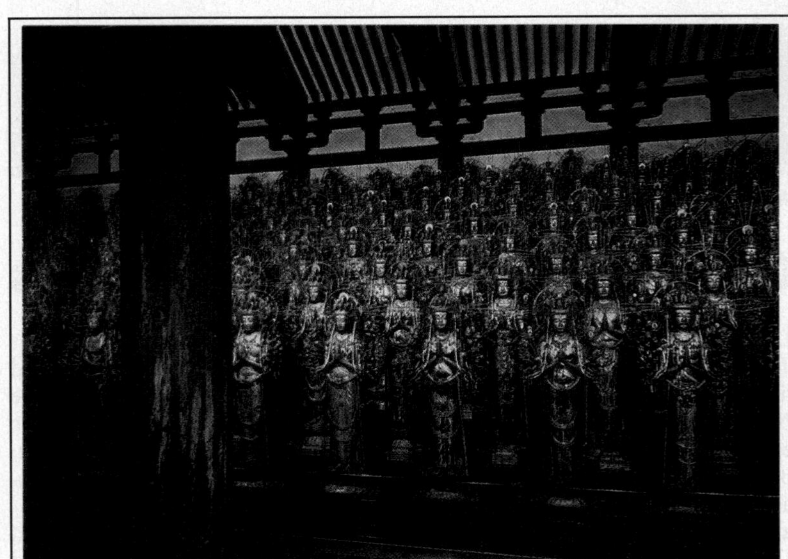

Some of the 1,001 gilded wooden statues of the Japanese deity Kannon in the temple of Sanjusangen-do in Kyoto, founded in 1164.

Man of God dies, admirer of pagans

Rome, 3 January 1274
Thomas Aquinas, the greatest European thinker of recent times, has died at the papal court at the age of 48. His work marks a major watershed in western thought because he succeeded in creating a synthesis of Christian theology and ancient philosophy, in particular that of Aristotle.

Aquinas was born of a noble family at Aquino, near Naples, in 1225 or 1226. He entered the Dominican order, and in 1245 arrived in Paris to study under Albertus Magnus, a fellow Dominican. Albertus had begun an attempt to bring Aristotle – recently available in new Latin translations from Arab sources – into scholasticism, the study of the meaning of Christian teaching. Aquinas studied the philosopher thoroughly when he was back in Italy at the papal court from 1259-68, before four more years in Paris. He returned to Italy in 1272.

A later portrait of Thomas Aquinas.

From around 1260, Aquinas wrote his most monumental works: the *Summa contra Gentiles*, explaining Catholicism, and the unfinished *Summa Theologica*, summing up his whole work. By his profound argument that Aristotelian reason and Christian faith are complementary and confirm each other, Thomas Aquinas has forged a new bond between Christian Europe and one of the great philosophers of its pagan past.

Marco Polo at Kublai Khan's court

China, c.1280
Marco Polo, a young Venetian merchant, has become a favourite of Kublai Khan's at the Mongol emperor's stately capital of Cambuluc where once the Jin dynasty ruled.

Marco Polo arrived with his father and uncle five years ago. It is the older men's second visit. On the first, Kublai entrusted them with a message to the pope, and in 1271 they set out for the east again in the company of two missionaries, taking Marco with them.

The holy men soon abandoned their mission, but the adventurous Venetians eventually arrived at the khan's palace where he has gathered together an international group of advisers and military technicians like the experts in siege warfare whom he has hired from Baghdad.

The khan was much taken by young Marco's wonder at the glories of the capital he had built on the ruins of the city razed by his grandfather, Genghis Khan, and he has employed Marco on a number of diplomatic missions. The Venetian has travelled to India and Persia on Kublai's business and has become fluent in Persian and Mongolian although, curiously, he speaks no Chinese.

A sharp-eyed observer, he is impressed by the efficient Mongol administration with its roads and postal system, its census, markets and paper money, all of which Kublai, a descendant of barbarians, has adopted from the Chinese.

However, of all the wonders of China, nothing has impressed Marco Polo more than Kublai Khan's marble pleasure palace in the city of Shangdu where, it is said, the khan can drink "the milk of paradise".

An imaginative, much later, view of Polo's presentation to Kublai Khan.

Mystics who whirl way to ecstasy

Asia Minor (Anatolia), 1273
The great Persian poet Jalal al-Din al-Rumi, or Mawlana, founder of the so-called "whirling dervishes", has died at the age of about 66. Like most of the best Persian poets, Mawlana was a mystic, and a mystical Islamic fraternity, or *tariqah*, grew up around him at Konya (the ancient city of Iconium).

Members of the order were called Mawlawites after their leader, but the rotating dance that is a key part of their ritual soon earned them the nickname of "whirling dervishes" from outsiders. The hypnotic, whirling dance is in fact a liturgical service, with every gesture carefully and meticulously prescribed; through it, members of the fraternity seek to attain ecstasy and higher truth.

Music and dance are rare in Islamic ritual, but stranger practices than this are found among other of the permanent tariqahs which have grown up in the last hundred years or so, beginning as groups of disciples of some inspiring teacher. The first to appear was the charitable Qadirite sect of Baghdad, founded by Abd-al-Qadir al-Jilani, who died in 1166. This was followed by the Rifa'ites, founded by the Mesopotamian Ahmad al-Rifa'i, who died in 1183. Members of this sect, like those of other fraternities, can do bizarre things such as swallowing glowing coals, live serpents and glass, or passing needles and knives through their bodies.

From an Islamic manuscript: the Dance of the Dervishes.

Reformed womaniser aims to convert the Moslem world

A later image of Raymond Lull.

Majorca, 1270
An extraordinary young man, Raymond Lull, is acquiring quite a reputation amongst the local intelligentsia. He is studying Arabic with a Moorish slave with the intention of going to convert the whole of the Moslem world to his version of Christianity. Meanwhile he is teaching, through stories and song, a new meaning of chivalry to any who come his way.

According to Raymond, it is the duty of the knight to be skilled not only in horse-riding and combat, but also in chivalry. Ethics and science go together in his view. One man in a thousand is chosen to be a knight because he is "the most loyal, the most strong and of most noble courage". It is his duty to defend the people.

Raymond inherited wealth from his father, who helped King James of Aragon to take Majorca from the Moors. He himself was private tutor to the king's son. As a young man he sang in the manner of the troubadours and was renowned as a lover of women. One day in 1263 he looked up from the bed of one of his lovers and saw "the Lord God Jesus hanging upon the cross". Since then he has been devout.

Mameluke Sultan Baybars was a legend in his own lifetime

Damascus, 30 June 1277
Baybars, the sultan of Egypt and victor of Ain Jalut, has died. His name is revered throughout the Near East as the man who defeated the "invincible" Mongols and saved the civilised world from barbarism.

Like his fellow Mamelukes who now hold power in Egypt, Baybars was a slave of Turkish birth. He rose through army ranks to command the Egyptian forces against the advancing Mongols in 1260. At Ain Jalut, near the coast of Palestine, he won a vital victory, claiming the life of the great Mongol general, Ket Buqa, and scattering his army.

Buoyed by his success, Baybars organised the murder of this rival Kutuz and became the army's choice as sultan. He campaigned against the Franks in the Holy Land, capturing Antioch in 1268 and the great fortress of Krak des Chevaliers in 1271. He died in Damascus after a short illness, leaving the Mameluke army the most powerful in the Near East and having prepared his son's succession.

1281 (1281-1294)

Japan, 1281. The Mongols make a second attempt to invade Japan.

Constantinople, 1282. Michael VIII Palaeologus dies. He restored the Byzantine empire, which is now threatened by the Turkish tribes of Asia Minor.

Wales, November 1282. Llywelyn, the prince of Wales, dies near Builth while rebelling against Edward of England, who took Wales in 1277.

Mexico, 1283. The Itza tribe founds the league and city of Mayapan in northern Yucatan.

Prussia, 1283. The Teutonic Knights complete the conquest of Prussia, begun in 1230.

Spain, 1283. Pope Martin IV declares Peter III of Aragon – who has opposed the French in Sicily – deposed, appoints Charles, the count of Valois, in his place and calls for a crusade to conquer Aragon for Charles.

Spain, 4 April 1284. Alfonso X, king of Castile and Leon since 1252, dies at Seville. He protected Moorish and Jewish culture and contributed to the Spanish cultural renaissance.

Mediterranean, 1284. Genoa destroys the Pisan navy at Meloria, off the coast of Italy. Pisa loses its hold on Sardinia. Genoa now rivals Venice.

France, 7 January 1285. Charles of Anjou, the ruler of Naples and Sicily, dies after losing Sicily and failing to realise his hopes of conquest in the east. His heir, Charles (the Lame), is captive in Aragon.

France, 10 May 1285. Philip III is succeeded as king by his son Philip IV (the Fair).

South-East Asia, 1287. Kublai Khan sends an expedition to Burma.

Near East, 29 April 1289. Qala'un, the sultan of Egypt, captures Tripoli, leaving Acre as the only major remaining Christian stronghold.

Portugal, 1290. A university is founded at Lisbon.

Switzerland, 1291. On the death of Rudolf of Habsburg, emperor since 1273, the three Forest Cantons – Uri, Schwyz and Unterwalden – sign a pact.

South-East Asia, 1293. A Mongol expedition to attack Java ends in failure.

France, 1294. War breaks out between Edward of England, also duke of Aquitaine and Gascony, and Philip the Fair.

Waiting for admission to the garden: illustration from the "Roman de la Rose".

Bible of courtly love is brought up to date

Paris, 1281

The *Roman de la Rose*, the bible of "courtly love" for the past 44 years, has recently appeared in a new, revised edition. Its new author, Jean de Meun, has taken Guillaume de Lorris's earlier work and added 18,000 extra lines.

De Meun's lines are a continuation of Lorris' original work, with its allegorical characters and geometrical symbols. The book – "wherein the art of love is fully contained" – still presents lessons in love-making as well as a picture of today's social behaviour. But the new text incorporates major new attitudes. Lorris moved his characters within the closed boundaries of a square orchard, representing a monastic cloister and the life of contemplation lived within it. De Meun sets his story in a circular garden, representing the whole, infinite world.

He has also abandoned Lorris' belief in courtly love: it remains within the poem, but now it is deliberately debunked. Reason and Nature are de Meun's main characters; Lorris concentrated on courtly Joy. De Meun's encyclopaedic technique tries to take in every facet of modern thought.

Mongol conquest to outlast dead leader

Saray, Astrakhan, 1281

The death of the Golden Horde leader, Khan Mangu Temir, is not expected to impede Mongol conquest in central Europe, nor will Temir's successor be more free from the control exercised over all Tartar affairs by the great khan, Kublai Khan, in China.

A half century ago the eldest son of Genghis Khan, named Jochi, became ruler of the most westerly part of the Mongol empire, in the Urals. In 1236 Jochi's second son Batu pillaged eastern Europe on a scale that earned his army the name "the Golden Horde". Legends proliferated about the Mongols, but in fact most of Batu's soldiers were Turks.

The third pillar of this empire comprised compliant Russian princes, including Novgorod's hero Alexander Nevsky. Such vassals, summoned before their Mongol masters, never knew whether they were on their way to execution, or a party.

Carnage in Sicily on Easter Monday

Sicily, 28 April 1282

The whole of Sicily is in rebel hands after nearly a month of uprisings and massacres which have claimed the lives of several thousand French men, women and children. The bloodshed began on Easter Monday outside the church of the Holy Spirit in Palermo. A crowd was waiting to go inside when a group of French officials became insulting towards the local women. When a French sergeant began to molest one woman, her husband drew a knife and stabbed him to death. As the bells began to toll for the Vespers service, the other Sicilians fell upon the Frenchmen and butchered them.

This was the signal which the rebels had been waiting for. For the past 16 years, since Charles of Anjou won control of Sicily from the Hohenstaufen family, the native population has been encouraged to revolt by the Emperor Michael Palaeologus, in Constantinople, and by Pedro III of Aragon, whose wife was a Hohenstaufen. Messengers ran from the church square through Palermo and out into the towns and villages, and the Sicilians rose, killing their French masters and proclaiming themselves independent. Friars were dragged from Dominican and Franciscan monasteries, and were put to death if they could not pronounce the Sicilian word "ciciri". Messina was the last city to hold out, but now the revolt has begun there too, and already the Angevin fleet in the harbour has been destroyed.

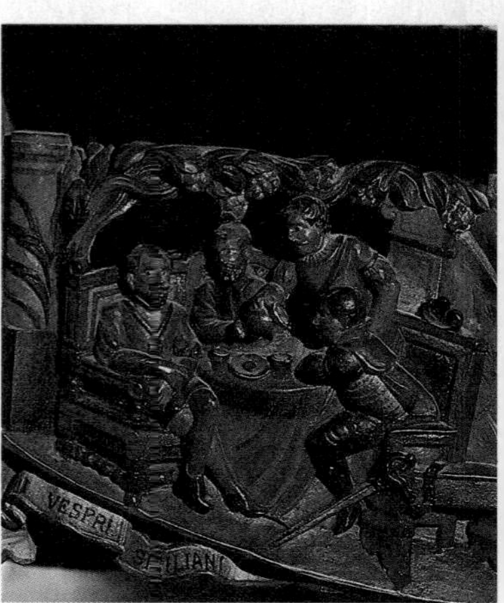

A later Sicilian carving of the rebels plotting the Easter-time massacre.

Bacon's new book queries orthodoxy

Paris, 1292
The English philosopher and man of science Roger Bacon, for many years a controversial figure in academic circles in Paris, is reported to have completed a massive compendium of theological studies which promises to be every bit as challenging as his earlier works.

Bacon was condemned by his superiors in the Franciscan Order for "certain suspect novelties" in his writings, and he spent over ten years in prison. What these novelties were was not made clear, but Bacon has always been dismissive of his contemporaries – St Thomas is "a teacher yet unschooled", another scholar is "an absolute fool", and the Dominicans are the greatest corrupters of biblical texts. Such outspokenness has made him many enemies.

Bacon (who was born near Ilchester around 1214) had a powerful patron in Pope Clement IV. Soon after he moved from Oxford to Paris, the pope wrote to him asking to be sent reports on his scientific studies. Bacon, who argued that there could be no true understanding of religion without a solid grounding in natural science, wrote three major works for the pope and suggested a survey of the whole known world.

Bacon's science, like that of other men of learning, embraced astrology and alchemy. He argued, for example, that since deer, eagles and snakes could prolong their lives by using toads and stones, men should be able to discover an elixir of life. Unfortunately for Bacon, Pope Clement died and he was left without a powerful protector.

A later engraving of the scientist.

Acre falls to Egyptians

Calza's later view of cavalry skirmishes between Crusaders and Moslems.

Acre, 5 May 1291
The last Christian bridgehead into Palestine, the great bastion of Acre, has fallen to a Moslem army after a siege of 53 days. Captive knights and foot soldiers alike are to become slaves, while their women and children are on their way to the Damascus slave market. So plentiful is the supply of Christian captives that girls are selling for a drachma apiece.

A year ago, drunken Italian Crusaders ran wild in Acre, dishonouring a truce which protected everyone including local Moslems. They murdered everyone who even resembled a non-Christian. The Sultan Qalawun of Egypt and his son Ashraf besieged the port with tens of thousands of troops and huge catapults to lob bombs over the walls. Up to 1,000 engineers were assigned to a single strongpoint to undermine it with gunpowder. Clouds of arrows fell continuously, as did their victims.

The defenders, including 1,000 knights and their soldiers, were steadily worn down until they could no longer man the walls. They retreated, setting fire to their own towers as 300 Moslem drummers signalled the final onslaught. On the seaward side of the fortress there was a desperate struggle for places aboard galleys escaping to the island of Cyprus.

England to expel affluent Jews

England, 1290
England's Jewish community, for many years an important part of the national economy, has been expelled from the country. Under law the Jews are the "property" of the sovereign, and now King Edward has chosen to banish them.

Under church law no Christian may operate as a usurer, lending money at interest. The Jews, who are not bound by such restrictions, have filled this necessary role with great skill. The community is small, perhaps 3,000 in all, but it plays a major role in financing the nation.

Now this situation has changed and several explanations for the expulsion have been offered. In the first place there is simple anti-Semitism, which has been increasing. But there are economic reasons too. Regular heavy taxation of the Jews has severely depleted their riches, and the king may well have decided that they were no longer wealthy enough to be worth tolerating. With the Jews gone, he has been able to sell off their confiscated property and, by calling in the debts that they were still owed, boost the royal coffers.

His action may also be justified by the Jews' refusal to comply with the Statute of Jewry of 1275. This abolished usury, offering Jews the chance to become merchants, artisans and even farmers. However, few have chosen to integrate in this way.

Rich European merchants are masters of craft and trade guilds

Europe, c.1290
If you live in a town, have not been born into the aristocracy or the merchant class, and want to get ahead in modern Europe, then make sure that you get into a guild – the new breed of professional society for members with a specific trade or craft.

Failure to join a guild in some towns can be the difference between prosperity and starvation. With the guilds frequently operating monopolies, the real power lies with the masters who run them. This is most pronounced in continental Europe where rich merchants dominate the master class. Acquiring master status requires submission of a masterpiece and payment of a large tax. The price may be high, but masters consider their status a passport to wealth. Guild masters fix prices, dictate standards of quality and decide on the eligibility of members.

In England guild membership, once granted to all free men with a trade, has become steadily harder to obtain. Weavers, especially, are being refused membership, and told to renounce their craft, by merchants worried that too many weavers will create a cheap and plentiful supply of labour likely to force prices down.

Aristocrats of trade: the seal of the Guild of Clothworkers in Bruges.

1294 (1294-1305)

Rome, 23 December 1294. Boniface VIII is made pope in succession to Celestine V, who abdicated after five months.

Sicily, 1296. Frederick, the brother of James, who has renounced the throne, becomes king of Sicily. James succeeded his father, Peter III of Aragon, as king of Sicily in 1285.

Scotland, 1296. The castle of Dunbar surrenders to Edward of England, who invaded Scotland earlier in the year.

India, 1296. Ala-ud-din, sultan of Delhi, founds a dynasty and extends his power over much of India.

Mediterranean, 4 April 1297. The pope gives Corsica and Sardinia to James II, the king of Aragon, as the price of James' giving up his claims to Sicily.

Scotland, 1297. Led by William Wallace, the Scots rebel against the English and defeat them at Stirling.

Portugal, 1297. A treaty is drawn up with Castile defining the Portuguese frontiers.

South-East Asia, 1297. The Burmese become vassals of the Chinese Mongols.

Germany, 2 July 1298. Adolf of Nassau, elected king of Germany in 1292, is defeated and killed near Worms by his rival Albert of Austria.

Florence, 1302. Charles of Valois and his French troops, called in by the pope, connive at the return of the extreme Guelf faction known as the "Blacks", involved in a power struggle with the moderate "Whites". Leading Whites flee.

Flanders, 18 May 1302. The weaver Peter de Coningk leads a massacre of the Flemish oligarchs.

Flanders, 11 July 1302. An army of French knights, led by the count of Artois, is routed by Flemish pikeman.

Sicily, 31 August 1302. Charles of Valois, who invaded in May with papal backing, agrees terms with Frederick, the Aragonese ruler of Sicily, ending the War of the Vespers.

Paris, 20 May 1303. The war between France and England over Gascony is settled by a treaty restoring the pre-war position.

Greece, 1303. Mercenaries employed by the Byzantine emperor, Andronicus II, defeat the Ottomans, but then turn against the empire.

Glass discs offer new eyes for old

The first known picture of spectacles.

Rome, c.1299

It is now possible to correct far-sightedness by wearing specially-made glass discs set in a metal frame. Eye-glasses are thought to have been worn by the Chaldaeans several thousand years ago, and Nero, the Roman emperor was said to have improved his view of the gladiatorial contests by means of a curved, faceted jewel mounted in a ring.

Now a trend seems to be spreading from Italy, where corrective spectacles are being worn. They are making life much easier for both scholars and copyists, allowing them to work in poor light.

Byzantine shock defeat by new arrivals

Byzantine Empire, 1301

Byzantium is still trying to come to terms with the shock defeat of its imperial troops by a group of Ottoman Turkish tribesmen on its eastern border. First reports from the battlefield say that the Turkish attackers were about to raid a valley leading to the port of Nicomedia when they were stopped by imperial forces. The Turks then regrouped and made a swift cavalry charge which broke through Byzantine ranks. Looting is going on in the immediate area, but there has been no further advance on Nicomedia. Byzantium's sense of shock is compounded by its lack of knowledge about its new warlike neighbours under their leader Osman. Of Asian origin, they are descendants of the 400 horsemen who were allowed to settle in northwestern Asia Minor (Anatolia) 60 years ago as a reward for helping the local sultan defeat Mongolian invaders.

Pope held prisoner after French attack

Rome, 7 September 1303

Pope Boniface VIII is tonight a prisoner in his own palace in the hill town of Anagni near here. The palace was attacked at dawn by a band of mercenaries, 300 on horse and over a thousand on foot. They are led by Guillaume de Nogaret, the new minister of the French king, Philip the Fair, and some of the Pope's Italian enemies, notably Sciarra Colonna.

Despite the strong force, the palace's defences held out in the morning. A truce was declared while Boniface considered a demand that he renounce the papacy and hand over all the treasure. He refused.

This evening the attackers broke through, finding Boniface seated on his throne, clutching the papal cross. Colonna wanted to kill him in revenge for his condemnation of his brother, a cardinal. Nogaret insisted on taking him to France as a prisoner. The row began when the French king arrested the bishop of Palmiers and Boniface responded by threatening Philip with excommunication.

A later bust of Pope Boniface VIII.

Drought brings death and destruction to North American towns

Arizona, c.1300

In the Mesa Verde and the Canyon de Chelly the towns and villages hewn out of rock are deserted. So, too, are the great semi-circular dwellings in the Chaco Canyon. The population, Anasazi Indians who have lived here for 1,500 years, have dispersed.

The same has happened in the southwest to the Hohokam Indians, who possessed one of the most sophisticated societies in North America. Their irrigation canals are dry, the mud walls surrounding their towns are crumbling, and their desiccated ball courts (an import from Mexico) are choked with weeds. In the south-east the story is similiar. The multi-room structures around Casas Grandes in Chihuahua, home for the Mogollon Indians since 1060, are dying in the sun. Drought is drying the land, spreading across the North American continent from east to west, and slowly destroying the Pueblo culture.

For 20 years Arizona and New Mexico have experienced climatic change. Rivers have disappeared, crops have failed, towns have declined, and now Navajo and Apache Indians have fallen on the weakened Pueblo peoples, driving them into the desert.

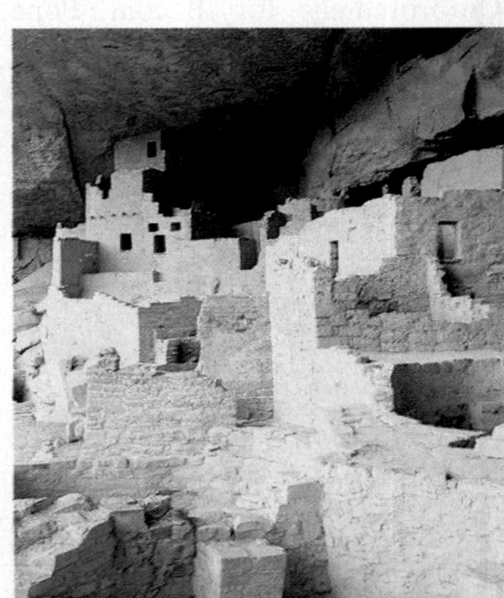

The remains of Pueblo Indian cliff dwellings at Mesa Verde.

Kublai Khan, Asian conqueror, dies

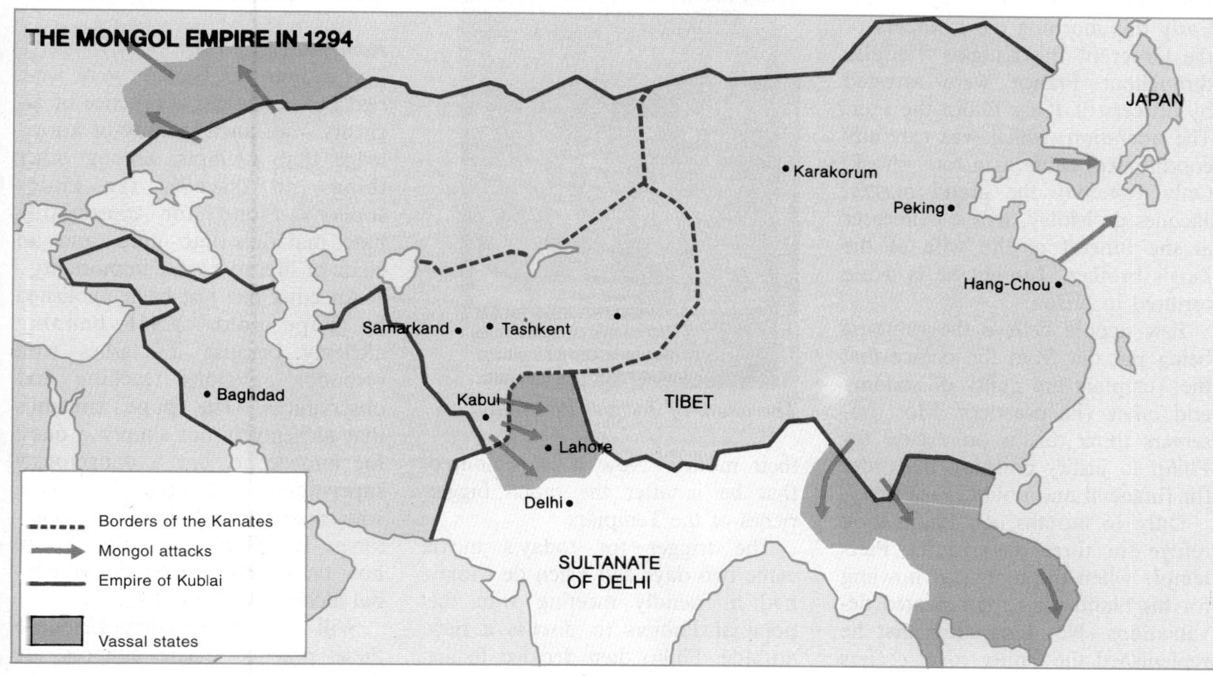

Beijing, 12 February 1294
Kublai Khan, the lord of all the world between the Danube and the East China Sea, is dead. He was 80 and, despite all his great achievements, he died a disappointed man.

The deaths of his favourite son, Zhenjin, and his beloved wife, Chabi, who made important decisions for him as he grew old, turned him into a recluse. He ate and drank to excess and became obese.

His sorrows were political as well as personal. His succession to his dead brother, Mongke, had been fiercely contested by another brother; then his cousins, Khaidu and Nayan, challenged his authority. Nayan was captured and smothered to death in a rolled-up carpet, but Khaidu waged war against the khan for many years. The failure of Kublai's attempts to invade Japan and Java also weighed heavily on him. Yet he conquered all China and established the Yuan dynasty, ruling from a glittering court in Beijing. He became more Chinese than Mongolian. He still hunted like his grandfather, Genghis, but his tent was lined with ermine and sable and so beautifully quilted that not a breath of wind, not a drop of rain, could disturb his comfort. Now, released at last from his luxurious melancholia, he is dead, leaving behind him a vast empire and a court whose brilliance and tolerance, portrayed by Marco Polo, have enthralled the western world.

What must be asked now, as his funeral procession winds its way to his secret grave in the Kentai mountains, is: how long can his empire hold together?

Enlightened rule by Mongol convert

Persia, 1304
The death of Ilkhan Ghazan brings to an end a nine-year reign which proved that the Mongols were capable of enlightened rule. Ghazan will be remembered chiefly for his reforms and his humanity towards his Persian subjects.

As a young prince in Khurasan, Ghazan was influenced by Nawruz, a powerful Mongol emir who persuaded him to convert to Islam. When he became *ilkhan* (subsidiary khan), in 1295, Ghazan and his emirs all became Moslems. Buddhists were ordered out, and Christians and Jews were made second-class citizens. Ilkhan Ghazan's conversion helped to bridge the gulf between the Mongol rulers and their Moslem Persian subjects.

Abroad, however, Ghazan continued the Mongols' feud with the Mamelukes of Egypt, even enlisting the help of the Christian powers of Europe. In 1300 he invaded Syria and drove the Mamelukes back, but was forced to retreat soon afterwards to quell an invasion from the Chaghatai khanate of central Asia.

At home, determined not to tax the peasants out of existence, he regulated the methods of taxation, and had all property registered for assessment. The postal courier system was improved, and the roads made safer. New coinage was introduced, and weights and measures standardised.

Black powder is changing warfare

London, c.1300
A black powder invented in China is likely to revolutionise the nature of warfare for ever. Gunpowder – a mixture of charcoal, sulphur, and saltpetre – is now being made in the west where it is rapidly changing the technology of military strategy. Contrary to popular belief, the inventor of gunpowder was not the celebrated Roger Bacon. Certainly he was aware of it, but so were many before him.

Indeed, as long ago as 1221 there are records of gunpowder arrows and packages being projected in battle, and before that, in the 12th century, descriptions of iron fragmentation bombs.

Gunpowder is now being manufactured on a considerable scale. This, in turn, is hastening the development of large metal-barrelled guns which are making existing weapons of war – such as the trebuchet, ballista and mangonet – completely obsolete. The force of the explosive means that attacks can be made at greater range. And the power of the impact of projectiles means that architects will have to revise their plans for fortifications, setting walls lower and curved to minimise damage. Military technology is changing rapidly with the introduction of gunpowder. Its possibilities in offence and defence seem boundless, and no doubt metallurgists are having to think hard about new ways of containing it within the weaponry now being devised as soldiers will require better protection.

An Italian "bombard": gunpowder has made warfare even deadlier.

1305 (1305-1323)

Rome, 5 August 1305. Bertrand de Got, the archbishop of Bordeaux, is elected pope and takes the name Clement V.

France, 1306. Philip the Fair banishes the Jews and confiscates their property.

Poland, 8 August 1306. Wenceslas III is murdered, a year after succeeding his father, Wenceslas II.

England, 7 July 1307. Edward dies on his way to invade Scotland. He is succeeded by his son Edward II.

Hungary, 1308. Charles Robert of Anjou, the next of kin of Andrew III, who died in 1301, is chosen as king.

Germany, 1 May 1308. King Albert is murdered by his nephew John, refused his share of the Habsburg lands.

Prussia, 1309. The grand master of the Teutonic Order transfers his official residence from Venice to Marienburg.

Rhodes, 1309. The Knights Hospitaller occupy the island.

Greece, 1311. Catalan mercenaries defeat Walter of Brienne, the Frankish duke of Athens, at Cephisus and take possession of the duchy.

France, 6 May 1312. A general council at Vienne abolishes the Order of the Templars, intervenes in the Franciscan dispute about poverty, and condemns the heresy of the Beguines (self-appointed holy beggars).

India, 1312. Ala-ud-din's forces conquer the Deccan.

North Atlantic, 1312. A French ship discovers the uninhabited Canary Islands.

Italy, 24 August 1313. Henry VII, emperor since 1309, dies near Siena. His unfulfilled ambition had been to revive imperial power in Italy.

Scotland, 21 June 1314. The English forces of Edward II suffer a major defeat by the Scots at Bannockburn, confirming Robert the Bruce in power in Scotland.

France, 29 November 1314. Philip the Fair is succeeded by Louis X (the Headstrong).

Ireland, May 1315. Robert the Bruce's brother Edward lands in County Antrim to challenge Anglo-Norman rule in Ireland.

India, 1318. The forces of the Delhi sultanate conquer the kingdom of Maharashtra.

Poland, 1320. Vladyslav, the ruler of Kujavia on the lower Vistula, is crowned king.

Philip of France tortures Knights Templar

Paris, 13 October 1307

Early this morning the members of the Order of the Knights Templar throughout France were arrested by officers of King Philip the Fair. The operation, which was carefully coordinated, came as a total shock. Only yesterday the grand master, Jacques de Molay, was a pallbearer at the funeral of the wife of the king's brother. Tonight he is being tortured in prison.

Few people believe the rumours being put out from the palace that the Templars are guilty of sodomy and other vile practices. Most observers think this is an excuse for Philip to justify crushing the order for financial and political reasons.

Only 16 months ago Philip took refuge for three days in the Paris temple when the mob was howling for his blood after the repeated devaluations. Not long after that he replenished the empty royal coffers by arresting all the Jews and seizing their money. Now it is rumoured that he is after the much bigger riches of the Templars.

The trigger for today's move came two days ago when de Molay had a friendly meeting with the pope at Poitiers to discuss a new crusade. Philip then decided to act immediately.

The death of Jacques de Molay.

Pope cracks down on "elixir" makers

Rome, 1317

The church has become very worried by the extensive practice of alchemy – an ancient body of knowledge that attempts, among other things, to discover the Philosopher's Stone, for transmuting base materials into gold, and an elixir of life, to confer immortality.

An edict has just been published by Pope John XXII banning alchemy because it clashes with orthodox religious teaching and observances. The pope contends that alchemy is not simply a quest for knowledge, but a dangerously superstitious and mystical exercise, with magical and immoral undertones. It will be interesting to see how far his ban affects the influential alchemists themselves.

Will they immediately renounce these practices? The chances are that they will not, whatever the church's official policy. Too many European rulers, eager to fill their coffers – even with fool's gold – will continue to employ them.

Chinese calligrapher and artist is dead

Zhao Mengfu's "Sheep and Goat", showing his mastery of calligraphy.

China, 1322

The celebrated artist and calligrapher Zhao Mengfu has died at the age of 68. Descended from the founder of the Song dynasty, Zhao was prominent as a public figure as well as an artist, holding a government position under Kublai Khan. Zhao's work covers an extraordinary range of styles and subjects, as if in an effort to sum up all the traditional themes of Chinese painting, although his originality means his paintings are rarely merely archaic. His use of colour and space is particularly effective in landscape painting, where he prefers clear brush strokes – not surprising, from the best calligrapher of his time – to washes, giving a realistic effect to scenery. His famous works include *Autumn Colours at the Qiao and Hua Mountains* (1296) and *Water Village* (1302).

Bishop condemns begging sisterhood

West Germany, 1310

The bishop of Mainz has excommunicated Beguine beggars and threatened to evict them from his parishes. This is the second church crackdown on the activities of women who choose to live together in peace and prayer.

The communities are full of single women over thirty. Easily identifiable in black dresses and white veils, they are a familiar sight in the towns of Belgium, northern France and Germany.

Women are committed, after one year's initiation, to stay in the Beguinages for a further six. Some serve their communities by begging; most work in textiles.

The theological independence shown by the sisters in their translations of the Bible and at their street meetings worried the Catholic establishment. One bishop accused them of being idle, gossiping vagabonds who refused to obey men under the pretext that God is best served in freedom.

Swiss foot soldiers rout Habsburgs' army

Switzerland, 15 November 1315
A small army of Swiss footsoldiers at Lake Zug has routed an army which came to the valleys of Schwyz and Unterwalden to subdue the peasant farmers and to bring central Switzerland within the domain of the Habsburg empire. The Habsburgs have long enjoyed manorial rights in these valleys, but have never pressed their claim to political power.

The cantons of Switzerland were becoming increasingly independent; the inhabitants of Schwyz had begun to fortify the entrances to their valley. Conflict was inevitable, especially when a dispute over grazing rights involved the men of Schwyz in attacking an abbey and taking some of the monks hostage.

Leopold, the brother of Frederick of Austria, devised a plan, involving naval forces on Lake Lucerne, to block off Unterwalden and attack Schwyz. However, he did not reckon with the slaughter that followed – mostly of his own force and its noble leaders in the district of Morgarten.

Torrential rain causes famine in England

England, 1316
England is in the grip of famine. The farming economy has been plunged into depression by prolonged rainy spells which have ruined harvests. One in ten of the population is dying of malnutrition or disease. And still the rain is falling.

Bad harvests in recent years have caused hardship not only in England but also throughout northern Europe, where there is not enough to eat if corn crops fail. A wet autumn in 1314 was followed by the miserable summer of 1315. In England only the West Country escaped disaster. On the Bolton Priory estates in the north, wheat yields were a fifth of normal. This year another wet summer has caused unprecedented suffering. On top of bad harvests, there is now a shortage of salt, as salt pans have failed to evaporate, and livestock have been hit by disease. On the Clipstone estate, in Nottinghamshire, half the sheep have died.

Taxes are heavy, in order to finance royal campaigns against the Scots, and the rise in wheat prices – now 26 shillings and eight pence a quarter, compared with last year's already inflated 8/6d – has hit the poor hardest. Alms have been cut. In Berwick, the starving infantry garrison mutinied, and a wheat ship was attacked by a mob in Sandwich.

Calendar of labours (1460): famine means hardship all the year round.

Avignon new home for Pope Clement V

France, 9 March 1309
Pope Clement V arrived in Avignon today to stay at the Dominican priory. Although there has been no indication that this is anything other than a temporary visit, there is a strong chance that the papal court may be set up here.

In his four years' reign, Clement has spent more time in France than in Italy. A lawyer by training, he was elected as a compromise candidate who might hold the peace between King Philip the Fair and the papacy. Philip is still trying to condemn the acts of the last pope, Boniface VIII. Clement is trying to stave off this move, and is also trying to restrain Philip's more recent excesses, such as the arrest and torture of the Knights Templar.

Avignon, en route from Paris to Rome, is an ideal centre for Clement's diplomatic efforts. It is also not too far away from his native Gascony, and there are many abbeys in the hills to provide refuges from the summer heat.

The French-born Pope Clement V.

Divine poet Dante dies alone in exile

From "The Divine Comedy": Dante and the River of Blood in Hell.

Dante Alighieri, lover of Beatrice, as seen by Sandro Botticelli.

Ravenna, Italy, 14 September 1321
Dante Alighieri died peacefully today. He was in the 20th year of his exile from his native Florence, yet his is probably the most illustrious name of all Florence's citizens. He established the Italian language as spoken there as a vehicle for exquisite poetry.

His first collection of poems to his beloved Beatrice was published in his *Vita Nuova* (New Life) when he was 30, after Beatrice's early death in her mid-twenties. He tells us that he first set eyes on her when he was nine years old and nursed a pure passion for her ever afterwards, although both underwent arranged marriages to others.

He promised to say of her "What never yet was said of any woman" in *The Divine Comedy*, in which he voyages in the space of a week in 1300 through all the circles of Hell, or *Inferno*, meeting its famous inmates. Having passed through Purgatory he meets the shade of Beatrice, who conducts the reader through the nine heavens to a vision of the river of light.

1323 (1323-1338)

Avignon, 1323. Pope John XXII clashes with the Franciscans over their belief in the absolute poverty of Christ, which he declares heretical.

Asia Minor (Anatolia), 6 April 1326. Orkhan, the son of Osman, the founder of the Ottoman empire, captures Brusa from the Byzantines and makes it his capital.

Flanders, 24 August 1328. Called in by Louis, the count of Flanders, Philip VI, the new king of France, defeats an army of rebel Flemish artisans and peasants at Mount Cassel.

England, 1330. Edward III takes power. He sends his mother, Isabella, into a nunnery and executes her lover, Roger Mortimer.

Serbia, September 1331. Stephen Urosh IV overthrows his father, Urosh III, who is murdered. Under Urosh III, Serbia has become the leading Balkan power.

Ethiopia, 1332. Ewostatewos founds the Ethiopian monastic movement.

Japan, 1333. After an failed attempt two years ago, the Emperor Godaigo succeeds in overthrowing the Hojo clan and captures Kamakura.

Scotland, 1333. In renewed English forays against the Scots, Philip VI of France supports David Bruce against the English.

Poland, 1333. Casimir III accedes to the throne and abandons the war with the Teutonic Knights which was started by his predecessor Vladyslav.

Japan, 1333. The Ashikaga shogunate is established.

China, 1333. The last five years have seen four successive Mongol emperors, as different Mongol factions vie for power.

England, 1336. Edward III renews his claim to the French throne.

Japan, 1336. The Emperor Godaigo moves his court to Yoshino, south of Kyoto. The Emperor Komyo establishes a court in Kyoto.

India, 1336. The Hindu kingdom of Vijayanagar is founded in southern India.

England, 1337. Edward III begins a war against France by securing allies among the German princes, including Louis of Bavaria. He also withholds wool exports to Flanders in order to stir up unrest there.

English king killed by wife and her lover

England, 21 September 1327
The weak and foolish Edward II, the English king who was forced to abdicate earlier this year, was put to death today in Berkeley Castle, Gloucestershire, where he had been held prisoner. His young son, still a minor, with no real power, was crowned Edward III in January. Edward's fate was sealed a year ago when his wife Isabella and her lover, Roger Mortimer, landed in Essex with a band of foreign mercenaries and marched on London.

Isabella's cause found wide support among the barons and bishops and in the City. The king's favourites, upon whom he lavished lands and lordships, had caused great resentment, and Edward's weakness encouraged dissension, especially after a humiliating defeat by Robert the Bruce in Scotland. Isabella and Mortimer have represented their coup as having the support of parliament and the people. Walter Reynolds, the archbishop of Canterbury, chose the text, "the voice of the people is the voice of God" for his sermon. An orgy of looting has broken out in London.

A later engraving of Edward II.

Giotto, who set painting free, is dead

Florence, 8 January 1337
Giotto, "the principal painter of our time" in the opinion of such poets as Petrarch and Dante, has died aged 70 with his major work, the campanile beside the cathedral here, only just begun. The painter-architect was appointed master of the cathedral works three years ago on his return from Naples where he was working for King Robert.

Giotto was discovered and apprenticed by Cimabue, and as a young man worked on the frescoes that depict the life of St Francis at Assisi. But his masterpiece, the frescoes that completely cover the interior of the Arena Chapel at Padua, changed the whole style of painting and freed it from icon-like formality into something far more naturalistic and dramatic. His crowded scenes, such as "The Adoration of the Kings", depict intensely lifelike figures and animals in bright colours against fragments of architecture and a background of intense blue.

A scene from the life of St Francis: one of Giotto's frescoes at Assisi.

Flemish rebels get English backing

Flanders, 1338
Shrewd economic power-play by the king of England has enabled a Flemish revolt to succeed against this country's French masters. An army of rich and poor led by Jacob van Artevelde, a wealthy burgher of Ghent, is besieging Tournai and has thrown out Louis of Nevers, the count of Flanders, a French ally. The revolt began when Edward III, seeking to force up wool prices, restricted wool exports to Flanders.

The Flemish weavers were badly hit, many of them facing starvation. With memories still fresh of a previous revolt ten years ago – when their peasant army was slaughtered by French cavalry and their leader horrible executed – the weavers prepared to fight back. They found a leader in van Artevelde. The revolt grew as other rich burghers took arms with them.

Edward's lifting of the wool blockade gave both employers and workers a cause to fight for, and van Artevelde, an eloquent and energetic leader, sees his opportunity to unite Flanders under one flag.

At war with France himself, over Philip VI's succession, an alliance with Flanders would be of advantage to Edward and to the Flemish freedom fighters.

Indian ruler shoots victim from cannon

Delhi, 1327
All the inhabitants of Delhi have been forced to leave their homes at a whim of their despotic ruler. The streets of the city are still and silent, and, looking over it, Mohammed bin Tughluq, furious at the citizens for threatening a revolt against him, said "My heart is satisfied, my feelings appeased".

The luckless citizens have been moved to Daulatabad, over 500 miles south, where the emperor is building a new capital. Two citizens unable to comply with the emperor's edict, one a blind man, the other a cripple, have been dispatched in ways much enjoyed by the ruler. One was fired from a cannon and the other had his limbs torn off.

Actors mock their Mongol overlords

Northern China, c.1330
When the Chinese were conquered by the Mongol invaders, and Kublai Khan founded the Yuan dynasty in 1279, they began to develop drama as a means of self-expression. Free of the constraints of Confucianism and censorship, dramatists are learning to explore the stage in a new atmosphere of imaginative invention. Drama grew out of poetry, but music also plays a large part.

Actors and actresses mime, sing, play instruments and dance as much as they speak lines. Music drama is played on several levels at once. There are about 100 Yuan dramatists and hundreds of plays are being performed, especially in the capital Dadu (Beijing). Most of them use legends and popular tales, often introducing satire on the ruling Mongols and their brutal methods. They also depict escapist fantasies of sexual love and the supernatural.

Passages sung by the leading actor or actress are linked by dialogue which narrates the story. On every entrance other characters introduce themselves to the audience, for the style is nonrealistic.

Moslems mourn mystic Indian poet

Delhi, 1325
Amir Khusrau, the "Parrot of India" has died at the age of 95. This great writer, composer and poet to six Delhi sultans was buried close to the grave of his spiritual master, the sainted Chishti Sufi, Nizamuddin Auliya.

Khusrau was the first artist to reflect the absorption of Islam into Indian life by mixing mystic themes and images from both cultures. His poetry and songs gained huge popularity. Khusrau's genius for writing in Persian shows in all his stories, *Laila and Majnun*, *Shirin and Khusrau*, and many more. Khusrau's devotion to the Sufis, a liberal Moslem sect, inspired his best work. The invention of the *sitar* and hypnotic *ragas* (poems of divine belief) were all intended to help Sufis reach mystical rapture.

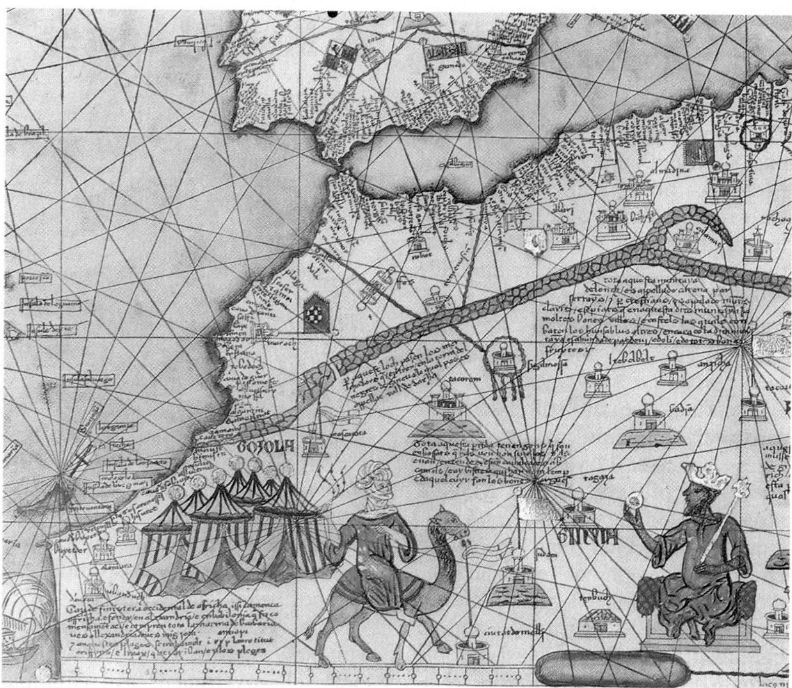

North-western Africa, from a Catalan atlas: Timbuktu is just left of the king.

King of Mali makes pilgrimage to Mecca

Timbuktu, Africa, 1325
Mansa Musa, the emperor of Mali and grandson of the great Suniata Keita, has returned to Timbuktu from his pilgrimage to Mecca. His entourage, preceded by 500 slaves, tailed by 100 camels carrying gold and escorted by 15,000 cavalry, was the most lavish recorded in the annals of the *haj*. Such was Mansa Musa's largesse that his visit caused inflation in Egypt. In Europe it is said that the price of gold is determined by "King Melli".

For most Moslem rulers the haj is more than a mere pilgrimage: it is an exercise in political prestige-building. Mansu Musa's haj is so lacking in political motivations that even the most cynical have been impressed by his sanctity. When he discovered that an audience with the Egyptian Mameluke Sultan al-Malik an Nisran meant kissing the ground in his honour, he refused, saying that he would only kiss the ground in honour of its creator.

Reaching Gao on his return, he has ordered the royal architect, as-Sahali, a Spaniard, to build a new mosque, while at Timbuktu, the main Saharan entrepot for Mali's gold exports, he is continuing the building of the university which is attracting scholars from all over the Moslem world.

Soldier monks beaten by five-foot sword

Japan, 1333
The soldier-monks of Enryakuji, have suffered a humiliating defeat at the hands of the rebels of Rokuhara. The monks, summoned to help the imperial force, marched in great strength from their mountain fastness, certain that the men of Rokuhara would flee.

However, the rebel commanders, knowing that the monks had no cavalry, planned to attack them with mounted archers who would gallop round them shooting arrows "as though at a dog shoot". The monks were so confident that they carried lodging signs to mark the houses which they planned to occupy. But when they reached a temple called the Hall of Eternal Reality the enemy cavalry swirled around them until the monks were utterly exhausted by fighting on foot and weighed down by their heavy armour.

They sought shelter in the temple, but were demoralised by a warrior called Saji Magoro who wielded a five-foot sword. They broke and ran, a defeated rabble.

Mystic heretical theologian is dead

France, March 1327
Meister Eckhart, the celebrated German Dominican mystic, has died in Avignon. It was only last month that he presented himself here to face his critics at the convocation called by Pope John XXII. The pope has condemned 28 of his views in the bull *In agro dominico*.

Eckhart saw the soul as the divine spark which enabled man to know God. To reach God meant turning inwards, doing nothing, owning nothing and knowing nothing. It meant being free of desire, even the desire for sanctity and God. It was the latter which set him apart from many monks who have chosen poverty and self-abnegation. Eckhart also said that the sacraments, though they played a part as preparation, must be cast off if man was to have direct access to God. This was seen as a direct threat to the authority of the church.

Short is beautiful, says thinker Occam

England, 1330
William of Occam, the scholar and philosopher, already established as one of England's most influential and controversial thinkers, has appealed to philosophers, scientists and other scholars to keep their theories as simple and short as possible.

Occam's law of economy (better known as "Occam's Razor") reads: "Entities are not to be multiplied beyond necessity." If, say, an astronomer were to have two explanations for the behaviour of a celestial body, one simple and direct, the other complex and convoluted, he should opt for simplicity, says Occam.

As it happens, this important philosophical rule is not new. The French theologian Durand de Saint-Pourcain has already preached the value of discarding unnecessary intellectual baggage. But it is Occam, who has relentlessly applied his razor to so much woolly thinking, who takes the credit for its widespread application.

1338 (1338-1346)

Asia Minor (Anatolia), 1338. The Ottomans reach the Bosphorus.

Italy, 1339. The Visconti family of Milan, whose power has been growing since the beginning of the century, win a victory over Mastino delle Scala, the ruler of Verona.

Moscow, 1339. Construction begins of a grand ducal palace called the Kremlin.

Flanders, 24 June 1340. The English fleet defeats the French fleet at Sluys, off the Flemish coast. The French fleet is all but destroyed and Edward III gains control of the sea.

France, 1340. Unable any longer to pay their troops, Edward III of England and Philip VI of France agree the truce of Esplechin.

Denmark, 1340. Gerard, the count of Holstein, the leader of the Danish aristocracy, is murdered after governing for eight years. He is succeeded by Waldemar IV.

Spain, 30 October 1340. In alliance with Portugal, Alfonso XI of Castile conquers the Moors at the river Salado. Moslem resistance in Spain has been stiffened by help from the new rulers of Morocco, the Marinids, who first entered the country in 1275.

Brittany, 1341. The death of the duke of Brittany opens a war of succession which draws in both England and France. Edward III supports John de Montfort, the half-brother of the dead duke. Philip VI supports Charles de Blois, the duke's stepfather.

Rome, 1341. Petrarch is crowned poet laureate at the Capitol.

Hungary, 1342. Louis (the Great) succeeds Charles of Anjou as second king of the Angevin dynasty. Charles made a royal monopoly of the Hungarian gold mines and put the monarchy on a sound financial footing.

Avignon, 1344. The Sienese painter Simone Martini dies at the papal court. Among his many great works are the *Maesta* at Siena, inspired by Duccio's, and the fresco of Guidoriccio da Fogliano at the Palazzo Pubblico.

Flanders, 1345. Jacob van Artevelde is murdered in Ghent by a mob in revolt against his dictatorship. Flanders withdraws from active involvement in the war between France and England.

Ivan raked in money for Mongol bosses

Moscow, 1340

They called him *Kalita* (Moneybags) – Ivan, the crafty prince of Moscow, born Ivan Danilovitch, who retired a year ago to a monastery to make his will. His death at the age of 36 ends a remarkable political career in which he manipulated both Russia's absentee Mongol masters and his countrymen's wealth.

The Rus tribes are still a series of separate kingdoms paying Tartar taxes. Just over 12 years ago Prince Alexander of Tver, sick of Mongol atrocities, led his people in a suicidal revolt which Ivan helped to crush. Within three years he was the Tartars' trusted tax collector throughout Rus territory, adding his own percentage. Most people benefited, even if the price of relative peace was Kalita's threats as well as penal taxation. In Rostov, however, plunder very similar to Mongol behaviour occurred.

Moscow: cathedral of the Assumption.

With Kalita's death, Moscow wonders whether his precedent of local self-government will continue under his son, Simeon.

Sultan weds way into power block

Constantinople, 1341

A recent spate of marriage diplomacy – two cleverly arranged marriages in two years – has confirmed the gradual shift of power in the eastern Aegean from the Byzantine empire to Ottoman Turkey.

The main beneficiary of this bout of bloodless diplomacy has been Orkhan, the Ottoman sultan. He now has a secure threshold in Europe by marrying twice over into the Byzantine royal family. Last year he married Theodora, the daughter of Byzantium's new joint Emperor John Cantacuzene, whom he had lent 6,000 troops for his coup. The second marriage was this year when Orkhan's new sister-in-law, Helen, married the other joint emperor and coup victim, John Palaeologus.

Frescoes show "effects of good and bad government" in Italy

Siena, Italy, 1341

The artist Ambrogio Lorenzetti is being widely acclaimed for his magnificent new frescoes commissioned by the city government to decorate the council chamber of its headquarters, the Palazzo Pubblico. Called "Allegory of Good and Bad Government", the frescoes are immediately appealing for their robust naturalism which contrasts with the overworked Byzantine style of Lorenzetti's predecessors, or the strongly derivative style of some of his contemporaries.

The part of the mural showing the effects of good government depicts everyday life in a peaceful city – Siena – with merchants, builders, peasants and other citizens going about their everyday business under the eye of the allegorical figure of Security, one of the first female nudes in Christian art. The figure of Justice will remind the city fathers who use the chamber of the chief role of government, along with the Common Good and the Virtues. Various essential skills and professions are also depicted, such as weaving, agriculture, trade and metalworking. The fresco showing the effects of Bad Government similarly combines allegory and realistic detail, with tyranny, discord, treachery, rape, murder and plunder stalking a ruined landscape.

Lorenzetti's view of the harmonious effects of good government.

"Simple" palace hints at papal austerity

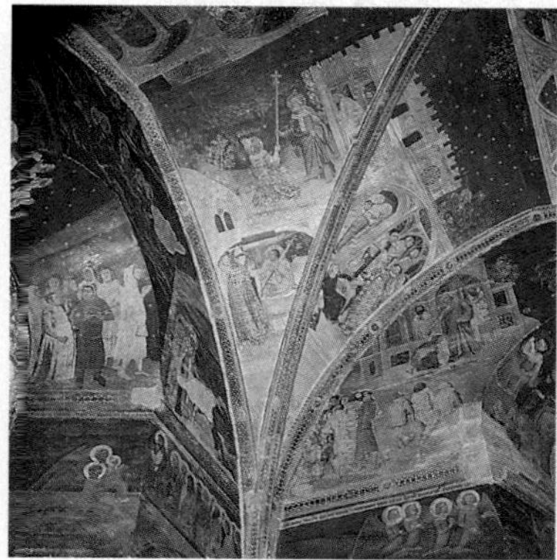
The chapel in the new papal palace.

France, December 1342
The new papal palace at Avignon is nearly complete. Although it is a most imposing building, with four wings built around a cloister, there are no extravagant sculptures. The atmosphere is rather of a monastic simplicity, even austerity. It is in marked contrast to the ornate palaces which many cardinals have built on the north bank of the Rhone, just outside the city.

The style may indicate that Pope Boniface XII, who has already installed himself in the pope's tower, is becoming sensitive to the critics of the papacy. It is now more than 30 years since the papal court first moved here, and the period has been distinguished by lawyer popes adept at running large bureaucracies, collecting huge taxes and otherwise vying with kings for temporal power.

Massive sums have been raised by taxes on bishops and priests and by the ubiquitous tithe. More controversially, there has been a big increase in the sale of church offices and dispensations, through which wealthy people are allowed to breach canon laws, such as those prohibiting the marriage of blood relatives.

Warring Hindu state building new capital

Southern India, 1343
A new capital is being built by Vijayanagara's monarch, Harihara. It will be called Vijayanagar. The collapse of the Delhi sultan's power in southern India around the year 1300 created a litter of petty statelets. Two dominated, the Moslem Deccan and the Hindu Vijayanagara, separated by the Krishna river and regularly at war with each other. Under Harihara (a Hindu convert from Islam, which is unusual), Vijayanagara has become the preeminent power in the south; and in addition to building a new capital, he is clearing forests, irrigating drylands and reforming taxes.

English king bankrupts Italian banks

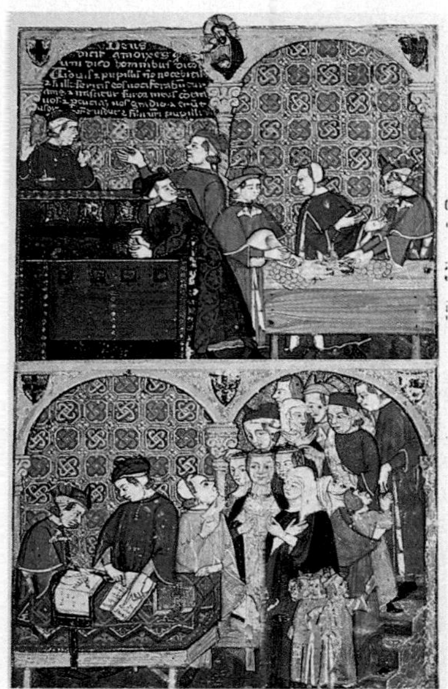
Bankers: counting their losses?

Florence, 1346
The great Italian banking houses are ruined. The bankruptcy of the Peruzzi in 1343 was followed by that of the Acciauoli and Bardi last year. Now the Florentine bankers alone have lost 1.7 million florins. The chief architect of their collapse is Edward III of England.

In Tuscany and Lombardy, bankers have been capitalising on European trade for nearly 100 years. The great Florentine firms are represented throughout Europe. But lending money to kings and princes has proved risky. To finance war against the Scots and French, Edward III has borrowed extensively from the Bardi and Peruzzi banks. He has now repudiated debts of 800,000 florins and imprisoned the banks' agents.

New Aztec capital fulfils old prophecy

A mosaic mask of an Aztec goddess.

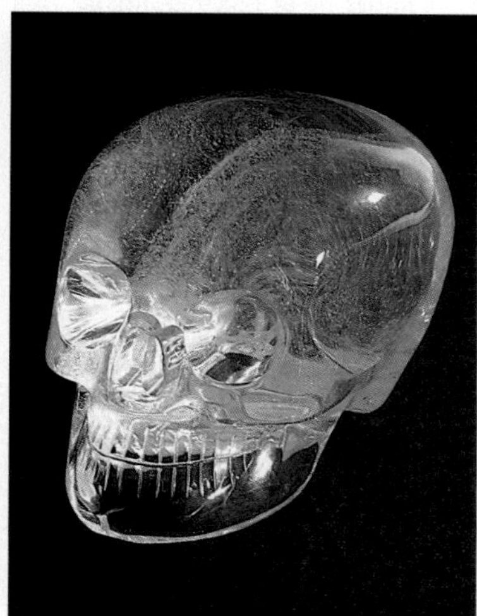
An Aztec skull carved from crystal.

Mexico, c.1345
On a marshy island in the Great Lake a new city is being built by the Aztecs. It is the fulfilment of a tribal prophecy that the Aztecs would found a capital on an island marked by an eagle on a prickly-pear cactus. They have called their city Tenochtitlan, which translates into English as "The Place of the Prickly-Pear Cactus".

The birth of Tenochtitlan marks the end of 200 years of Aztec wanderings through the Valley of Mexico, hiring themselves as mercenaries to the three leading powers in the region: the Tepanec at Atzcapotzalco on the northwestern shores of the Great Lake, the Toltec-derived state of Texcoco east of the lake, and the city-state of Culhuacan to the south. Now, under their priestking, Tenoch, they are a major power, maintaining semi-independence from the Tepanec.

The island city is magnificent, built on a grid and criss-crossed by canals and thoroughfares. Temples abound to the sun god Huitzilopochtli – who must be fed with human sacrifices. The streets are packed with Tenochtitlan's tens of thousands of citizens, the canals crowded with canoes.

The serpent goddess Coatlicue.

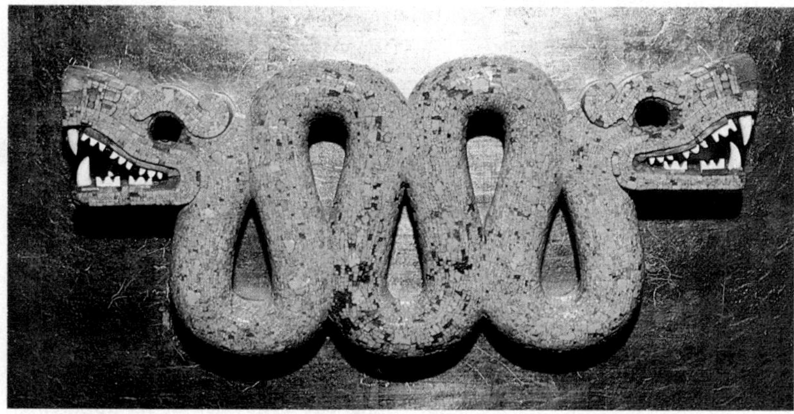
A turquoise and shell chest ornament in the form of a two-headed beast.

1346 (1346-1350)

Germany, 11 July 1346. Charles IV of Luxembourg is elected Holy Roman emperor at the instigation of Pope Clement VI, who has declared Lewis of Bavaria deposed. Most of Germany, however, continues to support Lewis.

France, 3 September 1346. Edward III of England, who invaded Normandy in July, begins the siege of Calais.

Constantinople, 1346. A violent earthquake strikes the Byzantine capital. The eastern arch of St Sophia's crumbles.

India, 1347. Bahman Shah establishes an independent sultanate, based on Bijapur, Bidar and Gulbarga in the Deccan.

Rome, 20 May 1347. The demagogue Cola di Rienzo, whose ambition is to revive Rome's classical role as capital of Italy, is given power by the people and takes the title of tribune.

Europe, September 1347. The Black Death arrives in Greece, Sicily, southern Italy and Livorno.

Germany, October 1347. The Emperor Lewis is killed in an accident, leaving the field clear for his rival, Charles IV.

Europe, January 1348. The Black Death spreads to Pisa, Venice, Avignon and Arles.

Europe, April 1348. The Black Death reaches Toulouse, Lyons and Spain.

Europe, June 1348. The Black Death arrives in England.

Prague, 1348. The Emperor Charles IV, who became king of Bohemia on the death of his father at Crecy, founds the university of Prague.

Europe, 1349. The Black Death comes to Germany and Brittany.

Germany, 1349. William of Occam, the Franciscan philosopher, dies at Munich. His will be best remembered for his law of economy (Occam's razor) in which he exhorted scholars to keep their theories short. He believed in the absolute power of God.

Germany, July/August 1349. Large-scale massacres of Jews occur in Frankfurt, Mainz and Cologne, associated with the activities of the Flagellants. Many survivors flee to Poland.

Avignon, October 1349. Pope Clement VI condemns the Flagellants and forbids their processions.

French beaten at Crecy

The Battle of Crecy: the English longbows (r.) proved decisive.

Crecy, 25 August 1346

Night has fallen on the battle field here, although the cries of the wounded continue to echo through the darkness until they are silenced by the swords and battle-axes of pillaging English footsoldiers. The out-numbered army of Edward III has won a great victory over French chivalry. Philip VI has fled, leaving over 1,500 dead, and the way is open for Edward to advance on Calais.

Two factors gave Edward his victory. The first was French pride and vanity, with Philip's knights ignoring orders and vying with each other to be first to confront the invaders. Confusion reigned in the darkness, and when the first ranks finally came across the English, they turned and ran into their own allies. The second factor was the English longbow. Philip had put great reliance on his 15,000 Genoese crossbowmen and ordered them to attack while he sorted out his divisions.

The Genoese were tired after an all-night march and at first refused to advance. When they finally made their move in a heavy rainstorm, their weapons were almost useless, their bow-strings soaked.

Only then did the English archers take one step forward and begin a rain of arrows on the hapless Genoese who fled into the swords of the French footsoldiers. In the melee that followed, the French presented a perfect target for the English bowmen. The French were already exhausted by the time that they began hand-to-hand combat against the well-prepared English knights and their infantrymen.

Abject burghers beg for mercy from English king

Calais, 3 August 1347

Six burghers of the besieged city of Calais surrendered to the English king, Edward III, today and were on the point of being put to death when Edward's wife, Philippa, sank to her knees, crying: "My dear lord, I ask you in all humility, in the name of the Son of the Blessed Mary and by the love you bear me, to have mercy on these men." The king's heart was softened and he granted her wish.

Calais had been under siege for a year and its citizens were dying of hunger when the governor, Sir Jean Vienne, offered to surrender if the king would spare their lives. Edward agreed on condition that six principal citizens, with heads and feet bare and halters round their necks, delivered the keys of the city and threw themselves on his mercy. Edward rejected all appeals for clemency from his own knights; then Philippa spoke up.

Six citizens of Calais are led to the English (19th-century engraving).

Mystery plague heads west after hitting Russian cities

Crimea, 1347

A new outbreak of plague has hit major cities in the Crimean area of southern Russia and is beginning to take hold in the Mediterranean. Reports state that the epidemic is spreading slowly westwards, engulfing city after city in its apparently unstoppable progress. It has already reached Sicily. The disease appears to be carried by merchant ships, which ply their trade between the Black Sea ports, to which Asian traders bring their goods, and those of the Mediterranean. Whether medicine can halt the epidemic is unknown. What is certain is that trading, upon which so many depend, will continue. First reports of the plague, which has not been seen at this intensity for eight centuries, came in 1345, when it emerged in the cities of the Golden Horde in southern Russia. From there it moved to Armenia and Azerbaijan, Scythia, Byzantium and the Crimea.

Black Death claims third of European population

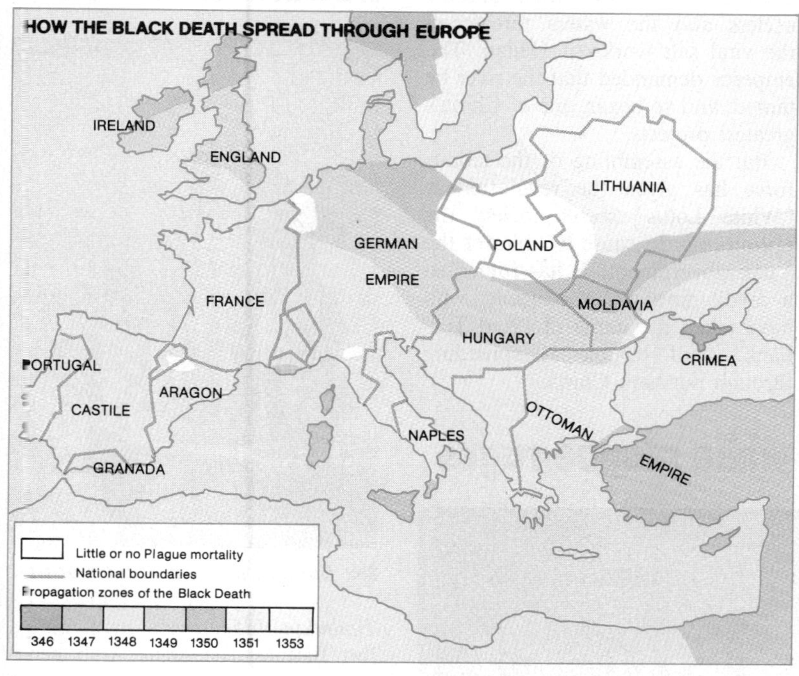

Europe, 1348
Hundreds of thousands of people – men, women and children – are dying in every country in Europe, struck down by an epidemic of an apparently incurable plague which the healthy and afflicted alike call "the Black Death".

Not since the sixth century has such an epidemic attacked Europe. Spreading from Asia, and carried by rat-fleas via the ports of the Black Sea, the plague takes two forms. "Bubonic" plague is seen in the swellings, or buboes, that inflate the lymph nodes at the neck, armpit or groin, while the "pneumonic" plague affects the lungs, and victims choke on their own blood.

The plague has stunned Europe, and everywhere people are desperate for an explanation. Some blame invisible particles carried in the wind, others talk of poisoned wells. Many, inevitably, blame the Jews.

Immediate responses differ widely. Some choose to challenge the plague by bouts of riotous living, others seek protection by barring their doors and living as recluses. Neither method has halted the disease. Others have left home, seeking safety in the remote countryside, but often they too have fallen ill. Attempts to bar villages, towns, even whole cities, to sufferers have all failed. The plague moves on. The outbreak has shattered communities. Families have been set against each other – the well rejecting the sick. Essential services have collapsed; law and order, with so many administrators struck down, barely exist in some areas. A sense of panic pervades Europe and everyone, it appears, is struggling only for his own survival. Properties stand empty, deserted by desperate owners; the sick die alone, for even the most devoted doctors cannot save them; corpses are simply dumped in the street or buried in mass graves. Some depraved creatures, themselves already infected, break into houses and threaten to contaminate all within unless bribed to leave. Agriculture is at a standstill. Crops wither in the fields; cattle wander untended.

Doctors do what they can, but the plague seems irresistible. Even the most expert physicians can do little more than help strengthen people's resolve and build morale. Some recommend the burning of aromatic woods and herbs; others suggest special diets, courses of bleeding, new postures for sleeping and many other remedies. The very rich are trying medicines made of gold and pearls. The terrible truth is that nothing seems to work. Flight is the best option, and if one cannot fly, then all that remains is resignation and prayer.

Flagellant Brethren: whipping up public remorse for the sins of the world.

Flagellants seek to appease angry God

Europe, 1349
Bands of hooded men, wearing white robes marked front and back with a red cross, are moving to and fro across Europe, attempting to atone for the ravages of the Black Death by whipping themselves in ritual public ceremonies.

The Flagellant Brethren, as they are known, believe that the plague is a punishment for human sin, and that by scourging themselves they can show mankind's repentance.

They travel in parties of anything from 50 to 500 men, and are highly organized. Led by a layman – the master – they move from town to town to perform their rituals. Singing hymns and sobbing, the men beat themselves with scourges studded with iron spikes. Blood gushes from their many wounds, and the spikes embed themselves in the torn flesh. The ritual is performed in public twice each day.

Such exhibitions are highly influential. The establishment may criticise their attacks on church corruption and their promotion of a wave of savage anti-Semitism, but the masses worship the flagellants as living martyrs. Their deeds are to be admired and their commands to be carried out.

English king founds new order of chivalry

A funerary badge, including King Edward's new Order of the Garter.

England, 1349
Competition is high among leading knights in the kingdom for invitations from King Edward to join his new Order of the Garter. Just 25 knights and the king are eligible for membership of the new elite order, which meets for the first time on St George's Day. The idea for the order reputedly came after the king, in a much-publicised moment of chivalry, rescued one of the countess of Salisbury's garters at a dance, rebuking onlookers with *Honi soit qui mal y pense* – Shame on whomever thinks this shameful.

1350 (1350-1356)

Spain, 27 March 1350. While besieging Gibraltar, the only city on the Spanish side of the straits still in Marinid (Moslem) control, Alfonso XI of Castile dies of the Black Death. He is succeeded by Pedro (the Cruel).

France, 22 August 1350. John II (the Good) succeeds Philip VI as king of France.

South-East Asia, 1350. Ramadhibodhi, the king of Ayutthaya (Thailand), leads an expedition against Cambodia. Last year he conquered neighbouring Sukhotai and made its king, Lu Thai, a vassal.

France, 1352. John the Good institutes the Order of the Star, in imitation of England's Order of the Garter.

Switzerland, 1353. The free town of Berne joins the league of the three Forest Cantons. This is the latest in a number of recruits, including Lucerne in 1336 and Zurich in 1351.

Asia Minor (Anatolia), 1354. Gallipoli, the key to the Dardanelles, is occupied by the Ottomans, furthering a conflict between John V Palaeologus, the son of the late Emperor Andronicus III, and John Cantacuzene, a former army commander. Both sides have turned to the Turks for help. Cantacuzene was responsible for their entering Europe last year.

Rome, 1355. Arriving in and leaving Rome in one day, Charles IV is crowned emperor by a papal legate. His haste, mocked by the Italians, demonstrates that he has abandoned any pretensions to real imperial authority in Italy.

France, November 1355. Edward III of England resumes the war with France. His son, the Black Prince, begins with a devastating raid in Languedoc.

Balkans, 20 December 1355. Stephen Urosh IV of Serbia dies while marching to attack Constantinople. His reign was one of effective expansion. He maintained his father's control over Bulgaria and conquered Macedonia, Epirus and Thessaly. In 1346 he assumed the title "Emperor of the Serbs".

France, August 1356. Taking advantage of the unrest throughout the French realm, the English organise a great expedition under the Black Prince, who launches a series of raids across Limousin and Berry in south-western France.

Red turbans rebel at taming Yellow River

China, 1351

A peasant revolt has broken out in the province of Huai where the government has sent 20,000 troops and coerced 150,000 men from the surrounding towns as labourers to reroute the mighty Yellow River.

The river has always been unpredictable and seven years ago it went on the rampage, bursting its dykes, flooding 6,000 square miles and inundating 17 walled cities. There was famine and plague. Many refugees turned to banditry.

Then the great river changed its course; the Grand Canal became useless and the waters threatened the vital salt works at Hejian. The emperor demanded that the river be tamed, and so began one of China's greatest projects.

But the assembling of the labour force has given the revolutionary "White Lotus" secret society the opportunity to cause trouble for the Yuan government. It has fomented a revolt among the peasants, who have taken the name of "Red Turbans", and trouble is spreading through northern China.

"Decameron" written while plague rages

A scene from a story in Boccaccio's "Decameron", by Botticelli (1440-1510).

Florence, 1353

Of the many ways of combatting the horrors of the plague, a book might seem the least likely. But the *Decameron*, written by the Florentine author Giovanni Boccaccio, is designed to do just that.

It consists of 100 amusing stories, supposedly told by seven young ladies and three young men taking refuge from the plague in the country, and, according to its author, is meant to console all unhappy lovers. The story-telling takes ten days, hence the name, which in Italian means ten days. But the *Decameron* is not all humour. Boccaccio, who lost his own mother to the plague, watched its ravages in Florence. The book's introduction is one of the finest eyewitness accounts to emerge from this terrible experience.

Boccaccio was born in Tuscany in 1313. His father worked for the bankers Bardi. Despite hopes that he might join either the church or the business world, Boccaccio preferred literature. He has spent many years in Naples, where he moved in court society and launched his literary career.

Moroccan traveller welcomed in Africa

Ibn Battuta, by a much later artist.

Timbuktu, 1352

Ibn Battuta, the great Arab geographer, has arrived in Mali. Born in Tangiers in 1304, he left for Mecca at the age of 21 and travelled through North Africa, Palestine, Persia, southern Russia, India, China, Indonesia, East Africa and Spain before returning to Tangiers.

Part private traveller and part unofficial ambassador for the Moroccan sultan, Abu Inan, ibn Battuta says he is now completing what he calls his last journey. At Sijilmasa, where his caravan set out across the Sahara, he met a man whose brother had given him hospitality in China; at Taghaza he saw the mines where the salt is hewn which, exchanged kilo for kilo for gold, makes Mali so rich; and in the southern sands his caravan almost perished of thirst.

In spite of the food, which he found disgusting, he appears to like the country. "The negroes have an abhorrence of injustice", the roads are safe, the merchants are honest, the women beautiful and "the men possess no sexual jealousy".

German emperor strengthens princely power with Golden Bull

Germany, 10 January 1356

The next king of Germany will be elected by an electoral college of seven, according to a new imperial edict – the Golden Bull – published today and designed to end the succession disputes that have plagued the Holy Roman Empire. Members of the electoral college are the archbishops of Trier, Cologne and Mayence and the rulers of Bohemia, the Rhine Palatinate, Saxe-Wittenburg and Brandenburg. Excluded from the Bull by Emperor Charles IV is the Pope who has frequently repeated his claim that he should be allowed to confirm whoever is elected. Under the Bull the seven electors cannot discuss their choice before casting their votes.

French king is captured

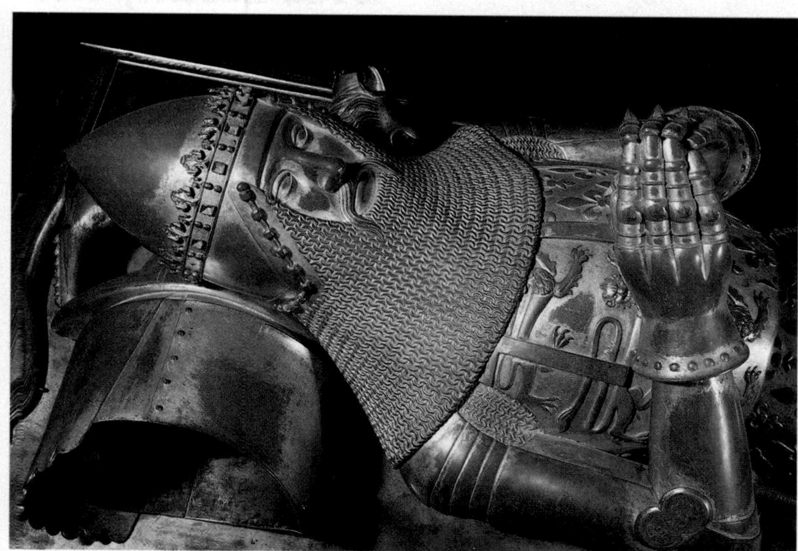
An effigy of the warlike Edward, the Black Prince, victor at Poitiers today.

France, 19 September 1356
The battle was almost won. The inhabitants of Poitiers had closed their gates to the French army and watched from safety as the English began a systematic massacre outside until the French surrendered.

Edward, the Black Prince of England, had fought "like a raging lion" all day and, hearing that victory was certain, he placed his banner on a bush to rally his army. A crimson tent was erected, drinks were brought, and he retired from the field of battle with his lords.

Poitiers: a French manuscript.

It was at that point that a mob of English footsoldiers appeared over a hillock with John the Good, the king of France, in their midst. In the true tradition of chivalry, the king was invited into Edward's tent where the two men drank wine and discussed the battle. At a banquet tonight, the king and most of his captured counts and barons were honoured guests. The victorious Edward refused to be seated in the king's presence, even serving at table as a mark of humility. Tomorrow, after Mass, the prince, his captives, and a mass of booty will leave for London.

Mob kills Roman ruler in woman's dress

Rome, 1354
An innkeeper's son who dreamt of freeing Rome and uniting Italy has been stabbed to death by his former supporters. Cola di Rienzo had succeeded in convening an assembly of the people which elected him tribune and expelled the ruling nobles from the city. Rienzo then went on to challenge papal authority. He was imprisoned, but regained favour and once again ruled Rome. Prison had done much to damage his charisma, however. He emerged fat and flabby, with a huge paunch, his eyes wild and bloodshot from heavy drinking. It did not help his image with the sober Romans that he even washed in wine.

Rienzo: republican dreams.

Rienzo's fate was certain when he introduced tax increases. A mob surrounded the Capitol, calling "death to the tyrant" and stoning Rienzo when he appeared on the balcony and tried to convince them that he, too, was a plebeian. Rienzo tried to escape, using tied tablecloths as a rope. That ruse failed. He put on his helmet and went to meet the crowd, sword in hand, but changed his mind at the last minute, cut off his beard and disguised himself as a woman before the crowd fell on him.

Prague to become "Rome of the North"

Prague, 1350
Prague has been named as the Holy Roman empire's imperial capital and looks like entering on an era of glory. The decision by the Emperor Charles IV is part of his plan to transform the city on the banks of the river Moldau, or Vltava, into the "Rome of the North".

Charles has already founded a university, the first in central Europe. It is composed of four faculties, philosophy, theology, law and medicine. He is also building new churches, including St Vitus', monasteries and fortifications, and spanning the Moldau with a stone bridge which is carrying his name. As a result numerous and famous European artists, architects, sculptors and writers are flocking to Prague, and the cultural boom is being matched by a growth in trade and the increasing importance of artisans' guilds. For some 300 years Prague has been both a busy stone city, where Slavs, Russians, Moslems, Jews and Turks have traded, and a key religious centre.

Cathedral of St. Vitus in Prague.

Heirs of the great khan lose their Persian empire

Persia, c.1353
The Mongols' Persian empire, the *Ilkhanate*, has more or less disintegrated. A succession of short-lived pretenders has merely emphasised the power vacuum that has existed since Abu Said died in 1335 leaving no heir.

After Ghazan died in 1304, his brother Oljeitu ruled for 12 years. Oljeitu could claim two major achievements: he conquered the province of Gilan, on the Caspian coast, the last significant expansion of the Mongol empire; and he left a magnificent memorial in his mausoleum at Sultaniyya, with its remarkable double-skinned dome.

Abu Said, the son of Oljeitu, was only 11 when he came to the throne, and effective rule was in the hands of the leading amir, Chopan. There was fierce rivalry between the Chopanids and the Jalayirids of Mesopotamia, which was to erupt again after Abu Said's death. In 1322 peace was made at last with the Egyptian Mamelukes, and in 1327 Abu Said overthrew and killed Chopan, and took full power himself. The rest of his reign was largely harmonious. There were no serious military rivals to the Mongols, but the Ilkhanate ultimately fell apart for purely dynastic reasons. Arpa Ke'un lasted for only a few months – the first of many distant descendants of Genghis Khan to claim the throne in vain.

1356 (1356-1375)

London, 1358. France and England sign a treaty by which the ransom of John the Good is fixed at four million ecus and extensive French territories are ceded to England.

Balkans, 1358. Lewis of Hungary wins Dalmatia from Venice.

France, 1360. France and England reach accord in the treaty of Bretigny. John the Good is freed from captivity and returns to France.

France, 1363. When John learns that his son Louis of Anjou, whom he had agreed to deliver to the English as a hostage, has escaped, he keeps his word of honour and goes back to London as a prisoner.

Spain, 1363. Backed by Peter IV of Aragon, Henry of Trastamara, the illegitimate half-brother of King Pedro, lays claim to the throne of Castile.

London, 8 April 1364. John the Good dies in captivity at the Tower of London. He is succeeded as king of France by Charles V (the Wise).

Brittany, 12 April 1365. By the treaty of Guerande, the house of Blois cedes its rights in Brittany to John IV de Montfort.

Spain, 1367. Pedro the Cruel, aided by the Black Prince, defeats Henry of Trastamara at Najera.

China, 1368. Zhu Yanzhang captures Dadu (Beijing) from the Mongols and establishes the Ming dynasty, with a capital at Nanjing.

Spain, 28 March 1369. Henry of Trastamara defeats Pedro the Cruel and besieges him in his castle of Montiel. Pedro is captured trying to escape and knifed to death by Henry.

Denmark, 1370. The peace of Stralsund gives trading privileges to the Hanseatic league of German towns.

Balkans, 1371. The Ottoman Turks under Murat defeat the Bulgarian forces at the river Maritza. All Macedonia except Salonika falls to the Turks.

Scotland, 1371. The death of David Bruce brings a new dynasty to the throne: the Stewarts. David's heir is his nephew, Robert II Stewart, the hereditary steward of Scotland.

France, 1372. A Castilian fleet, acting in support of the French, defeats an English fleet off La Rochelle, reversing the effect of Sluys in 1340.

Ships from the Hanseatic league of trading towns in Copenhagen harbour.

German traders unite against competition

Lubeck, 1356

The German Hanseatic towns have formed an association to protect their trading network along the coasts of northern Europe from London in the west to Novgorod in the east. The Hanse is becoming an increasingly important commercial and military power.

German merchants have been extending their trading empire since the 12th century when they established a colony at Wisby on the island of Gotland. Trading with Novgorod and Finland, Wisby then became a link with western Europe, bringing Flanders cloths, salt and beer to the Slavs, and bringing back furs, hides, wax and amber.

Since the last century Hanseatic traders have become established at Lubeck, the focal point of Baltic commerce, Hamburg and Bremen, serving the North Sea and North Atlantic, and at Flanders, dealing with the river-borne commerce of northern Europe. London and Bergen in Norway are more recent additions to this fast-growing trade network.

The newly-formed federation allows competition, but it imposes severe penalties on any member violating a common decision.

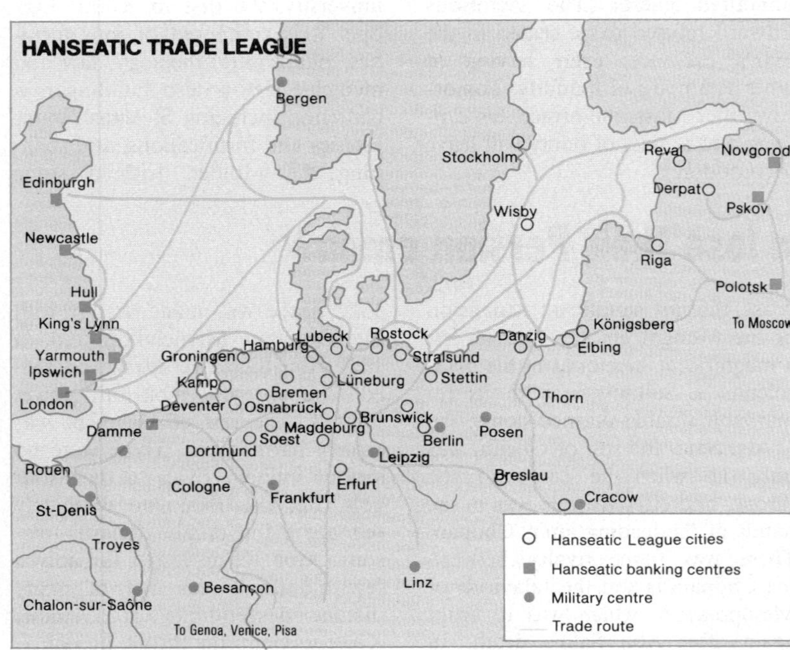

Petrarch, poet who loved classics, dies

A later artist's view of Petrarch.

Arqua, near Padua, 1374

The classical scholar and lyric poet Francesco Petrarca, widely known as Petrarch, has died aged 70 in this small town. Born in Arezzo, the son of a Florentine lawyer, he passed his early life at the papal court at Avignon as a churchman living on benefices from rich patrons.

It was at Avignon in 1327 that he saw Laura, the wife of Hugo de Sade, and conceived a passion for her which he celebrated in Italian lyric poetry, madrigals and sonnets which became famous when collected as his *Canzoniere*. Like Dante's love for Beatrice, Petrarch's for Laura remained pure and distant; she became the mother of 11 children and died in the plague of 1348.

Petrarch wrote his learned works in Latin, including an epic poem in honour of Scipio Africanus and a series of prose biographies of famous Romans, *De Viris Illustribus*. He also wrote a treatise *On the Solitary Life*. He corresponded with his friend Boccaccio, the writer of the *Decameron*.

Petrarch's fame was such that he was an honoured guest at the courts of Europe where his hobby was to search libraries for forgotten Latin manuscripts. In Verona he discovered Cicero's letters, and in Liege some of his orations.

On Easter Day in 1341 he was crowned Poet Laureate on the Capitoline Hill in Rome, the first modern poet to be given the honour by the Senate.

Peasant revolt crushed

The "Jacquerie" rebels are crushed at Meaux: a later French portrayal.

France, June 1358
After three months of terror when rumours of rape, murder – even cannibalism – have spread rapidly through northern France with the speed of the plague, the country's nobles have united to put down a peasant revolt known as the *Jacquerie* with savage ferocity. Towns have been sacked, farmland laid waste and 20,000 rebels killed.

The beginnings of this rebellion are obscure. One report, widely circulated, suggests that peasants killed a knight, roasted him on a spit, gang-raped his wife and forced her to eat some of her husband's flesh. With stories like this circulating from castle to castle, and with peasant mobs roaming freely through the land, fear became the norm.

Noblemen were helpless to act as the mobs broke into their homes, stealing food and wine and burning as the owners trembled behind locked doors. Towns were held hostage, forced to lay on feasts for the growing army of peasants.

Such a feast was taking place in the town of Meaux when two knights with a small army rode into the town and began to slaughter the Jacquerie. Other knights followed suit elsewhere. The revolt was over.

Much of North Africa is ruled from Fez

Morocco, 1358
The death of Abu Inan, the sultan of Morocco, leaves the Marinid dynasty still unsure of the extent of its power, although authority has been reasserted over the Ziyanids at Tlemcen where Arab tribes still block the path to Tunis.

It is exactly a century since the death of the first great Marinid chieftain, Abu Yahya, who led his Berber tribesmen in successful revolt, first against the Ziyanids and then against the Almohad caliphs at Marrakesh. The Marinids then extended their influence under Abu Yahya's brother, Abu Yusuf. He took Marrakesh, defeated the Ziyanids and besieged Tlemcen before occupying the port of Ceuta and invading Spain, where he defeated the Castilians.

From their increasingly splendid headquarters at Fez, the Marinid sultans ruled by a combination of authority and patronage. Provincial governors imposed taxes in the sultan's name, and kept much of the proceeds. Lands and cities were frequently lost and recaptured, but the Marinids' right to the throne has remained unchallenged.

"Holy War" threatens Christian capital

Adrianople, 1361
One of the largest towns in Thrace, Adrianople, has fallen into Ottoman hands, giving the Turks their first major city in Europe and a capital from which to mount their European campaigns.

The fall of Adrianople, coupled with Ottoman control of the Gallipoli peninsula and both sides of the Sea of Marmara, now leaves Constantinople, the Byzantine capital, vulnerable to attack. In Rome the pope has declared that saving Constantinople from the Ottoman Moslems takes priority for crusaders over delivering the Holy Land from infidels. Constantinople is seen as vulnerable following the recent coup in which the Ottoman-backed John Cantacuzene was deposed. Adding to Rome's concern about the Moslem advance west is the frequent Ottoman declaration that it is an Islamic Holy War. One difficulty in ousting the Ottomans from Thrace is lack of support from the Christian peasantry. They have been won over by the Ottomans' low taxes and fairer standards of law and order.

A Turkish Janissary soldier.

Polish hero dies in hunting accident

Poland, 5 November 1370
The Polish King Casimir III, whose reign has been marked by strong economic growth and the advancement of learning, died today in a hunting accident. He was 60. His kingdom was threatened on all sides when he ascended the throne at the age of 30. He repulsed a Mongol invasion, annexed Galicia and created well-defined national frontiers. He encouraged the immigration of Jews to serve as tax-collectors and bankers. He founded the university of Cracow, codified the laws of the land, established a firm, efficient administration and gave peasants the right to migrate from one place to another.

Casimir: firmness and efficiency.

Egyptians release king to life of exile

Armenia, 1375
Life in exile in Europe now awaits the deposed King of Armenia, Leon IV. His Egyptian captors plan to shortly release him from prison in Cairo, where he was taken after his capture at Gaban earlier this year.

The deposed king is expected to take refuge in the Christian courts of Europe where he will try to raise an army. However the Egyptians and their new placeman on the Armenian throne, Achot, an Armenian noble who converted to Islam while in exile in Cairo, believe that the pleas will be politely rejected.

However ex-King Leon will be able to arouse considerable sympathy for the way the Egyptian forces destroyed and ransacked his country, including its once magnificent capital Sis.

1375 (1375-1380)

Flanders, 1375. The English and the French reach a truce at Bruges whereby the English retain only Calais and a coastal strip of Gascony.

Italy, 21 December 1375. The poet Boccaccio, author of the *Decameron*, dies at Certaldo.

Mexico, 1376. Acamapichtli comes to power and establishes Aztec/Mexican dynastic rule.

Rome, January 1377. In fear of losing control of the papal states, Gregory XI, pope since 1370, leaves Avignon and re-establishes the papacy in Rome.

England, 21 June 1377. Edward III is succeeded by his grandson Richard II, who is still a child; effective power rests with the royal council.

England, 1378. The poet William Langland is at work on *Piers Plowman*, an allegory of the soul's journey to find salvation.

Germany, 1378. On his death, the Emperor Charles IV is succeeded in the empire and Bohemia by his son Wenceslas.

Rome, 8 April 1378. The archbishop of Bari becomes Pope Urban VI. Gregory XI died on 27 March, when he was already considering a return to Avignon. The cardinals, under pressure from the Roman mob, hastily elected an Italian pope.

Italy, 20 September 1378. The election of Robert of Geneva as anti-pope by discontented cardinals creates a great schism in the Catholic Church. Robert takes the name Clement VII.

France, 18 December 1378. Charles V denounces the treachery of John IV of Brittany and confiscates his duchy.

Spain, 30 May 1379. Henry II of Trastamara, the king of Castile and Leon, is succeeded by his son John.

Flanders, 1379. Wage earners rebel in Ghent, Bruges and Ypres, but are repressed except in Ghent.

Avignon, 1379. Clement VII sets himself up in Avignon. After his election as anti-pope, both popes resorted to force. Urban VI won the first round, his Italian mercenaries defeating Clement's Bretons, and Clement took ship for Avignon.

Italy, 1380. Venice defeats its long-standing rival Genoa at Chioggia.

Persians conquered by Timur the Lame

Persia, 1379

A Turkoman chieftain called Timur Lenk (Timur the Lame) has led an army from Bokhara, the second city of his homeland of Transoxiana, on a destructive raid on the Persian border town of Urgenj. The attack has sent rumours of conquest rippling across the country from Merv in the north to Shiraz in the south.

The auguries are not good. Timur has a taste for heads – other people's, detached from their bodies – as well as an appetite for territory. Students of the region's geopolitics perceive that the last of the Mongol dynasties are withering away. A power vacuum alongside an expansionist force such as Timur can have only one outcome: occupation. The still unresolved question is: occupation by whom? – for Timur is not the only predator.

In Egypt the Mamelukes are a vibrant economic and military power. To the north the Turkish Ottoman Sultan Bayezid has designs on the remnants of Christian Constantinople. Now Timur adds a third, terrifying, force to destabilise the Near East. The Christian powers of Europe are as uneasy as the Persians. From the days when two rival Christian churches – Rome and Constantinople – had power they have shrunk to a toehold in Asia Minor (Anatolia). Islam is one cause. Another is the greed of Venice and Genoa.

Mongol and Persian warriors.

Moscow prince puts Mongols on the run

Moscow, 8 September 1380

On Curlew Field in Tula province today, exhausted Russian soldiers were treated to the novel sight of an entire "unbeatable" Mongol army galloping at speed – away from them.

The Russian leader, Grand Duke Dmitri, missed the great moment. He was lying under a tree, concussed. The outcome of Dmitri's war of independence against the Tartars was uncertain when the Mongol leader Mamay rode against Russia with 30,000 warriors, including Genoese mercenaries. (Some 34 years ago the Genoese also fought for France at Crecy, against England.)

To win, Mamay had to link with his Lithuanian allies coming the opposite way. Dmitri made a forced march to intercept Mamay, then staked everything on an opposed crossing of the Don river, straight into action. At the battle's climax, Dmitri's secret cavalry reserve swept onto the field to victory.

English surgeon seeks to revise odds against saints and shrines

London, 1376

John Arderne, the English surgeon, has published a lengthy treatise on his most successful operation, the lancing of an anal fistula. He has treated numerous knights, friars, merchants and priests, charging a considerable sum of £40, plus a suit of clothing and an annuity of £40 for as long as the patient survives.

In spite of his successes, he and other surgeons have failed to gain acceptance by physicians, who use elaborate medicines, bleeding and cauterisation to achieve the balance of humours which are believed to mean a healthy body.

Resort to physicians and surgeons is costly and their treatments often unpleasant. Most people rely instead on the healing powers of saints' relics or magic charms. Shrines claim a higher success rate than doctors. Even a specialist like Arderne can offer only a one in two chance of survival.

Arderne learned his surgical skills while serving with Edward the Black Prince during campaigns in France. After the Black Death he went to live in Newark, which had three hospitals and was a noted centre for surgeons.

He sets moral standards for his profession too, saying that surgeons should never be foul-mouthed, never take advantage of female patients, should have a stock of comfortable sayings, but never allow themselves to forget that not every patient can be cured.

A surgeon's clinic, from "Chirurgia" by the Frenchman Guy de Chauliac.

Two popes split church

Clement VII: the French usurper.

Urban VI: spiritual authority.

Rome, 20 September 1378
The Roman Catholic Church was split asunder today following the news that Robert of Geneva, a cousin of the French king, has been elected as Pope Clement VII.

His supporters claim that the election last June of Bartolomeo Prignano, an Italian, as Pope Urban VI was invalid, since the cardinals were acting under fear of the Rome mob. Pope Urban is determined to stay in office. His friends here say that Clement is an antipope illegally elected. They fear that this is a new attempt by the French king to usurp the pope's power. Until last year the papal court had been at Avignon for nearly 70 years, leaving the pope subject to French influence.

The dispute is more complex, however. French cardinals were in a majority at the conclave which elected Urban, but they were divided. Some supported Robert. The rest supported Urban, a man of lowly birth who they hoped would restore some spiritual authority to the papacy.

Since his election Urban has delivered a violent attack on the luxurious life of the cardinals and the sale of church favours. The French cardinals, many still living at Avignon, are understandably annoyed.

The Court of the Lions in the magnificent Alhambra palace in Granada, the seat of Arab rule of Spain. Mohammed V is constructing the Alhambra on the site of earlier Arab buildings on a hill overlooking the city, and work on the court began in 1377. It takes its name from its centrepiece, a fountain supported by 12 marble lions.

English Lollards challenge papal power

A 19th-century engraving of John Wyclif sending out some of his "Lollard" followers to spread his views on reform of church practices.

Lutterworth, England, 1379
John Wyclif, the renowned Oxford scholar, has moved from radical criticism of the church establishment to outright heresy in a series of lectures on the Eucharist. The orthodox view is that at consecration the bread and wine are miraculously changed, but Wyclif insists that they remain bread and wine. So far his views are not widely known beyond the academic community, but word is likely to spread and may well attract hostile attention to the university itself.

Wyclif, once master of Balliol College, is no stranger to controversy. Recently he has launched attacks on papal authority which have been sympathetically received in many quarters. The schism within the church has shocked people at all levels of society, while the English government has, for its own reasons, been willing to criticise the pope's temporal power.

Politically, Wyclif has powerful friends, including the king's uncle John of Gaunt. Their support helped him to weather papal condemnation of a series of errors. It remains to be seen, however, whether they will be as ready to back a declared heretic. Second thoughts may also be prompted by signs that Wyclif's teaching is acquiring elements of social dissent. An attack on papal power easily becomes a critique of state power. Wyclif's followers, known as Lollards, emphasise the importance of ordinary folk reading the Bible for themselves, raising the risk of a doctrinal free-for-all.

Workers take over the city of Florence

Florence, 1378
For over 100 years it has been the wealthy magnates who have ruled this city, but today Florence is in the hands of the Ciompi, the skilled artisans, cloth-workers in particular. If this revolution succeeds, only citizens who have actually worked for a living – either at trades or in business – will be able to hold office in the Florentine commune.

Conflict between the magnates ("The Hats") and the workers ("The Cloaks") had increased markedly in the wake of the Black Death, which considerably lessened the number of men in the cloth industry. In the rioting and burning that turned the tables on the aristocrats, the cry was "Death to the Hats and long live the Cloaks!"

As the inter-communal slanging match grew, the taunts continued. The Hats were given to shouting "Go back to your cloth-making", and "Go and grind the pepper" (to druggists), and one aristocrat lumped the workers together as a crowd of "robbers and traitors and murderers and assassins and gluttons and malefactors".

Such a shouting match had to end in violence. Traders, skilled artisans and the poor joined together to force their way into the palace and take over the city.

1380 (1380-1385)

France, 3 November 1380. Charles VI, who succeeded his father, Charles V, in September, is crowned king.

Paris, 1381. Henry of Langerstein, a German master at the university of Paris, attempts to end the great schism. His arguments are not accepted by Charles VI, who continues to back the anti-pope, and Henry is forced to leave France.

Flanders, May 1382. The rebel leader Philip van Artevelde captures Bruges. Louis de Male, the count of Flanders, appeals for help to Charles VI and Philip of Burgundy.

England, 1382. The Blackfriars council condemns the principal tenets of Lollardy – the teachings of John Wyclif – and takes steps to stamp out heresy within Oxford, so threatening the university's independence. Several of Wyclif's leading followers submit. Wyclif leaves Oxford.

Flanders, 27 November 1382. The French nobility, led by Olivier de Clisson, crush the Flemish rebels. Philip van Artevelde dies in battle at Roosebeke. Ghent, with English support, continues to hold out.

Egypt, 1382. The Mameluke dynasty of the Bahrites is replaced by that of the Burjites.

Paris, January 1383. The Maillotin revolt, which began last year, crumbles after news of the rebel defeat at Roosebeke in Flanders. Its leaders are executed.

Flanders, 1384. Philip II (the Bold), the duke of Burgundy, inherits Flanders, Malines, Antwerp and Artois, becoming count of Flanders.

Holland, 1384. Gerard Groote, founder of the Brethren of Common Life, dies of plague. Not bound by permanent vows, the members of the brethren live together under a rule, holding all things in common and earning their own livelihoods.

England, 31 December 1384. John Wyclif dies at Lutterworth, the parish to which he retired after leaving Oxford.

Italy, 1385. Gian Galeazzo Visconti, who succeeded his father as tyrant of Pavia in 1378, tricks his uncle Bernabo, the ruler of Milan, into captivity and so reunites the Visconti lands – which had been divided between his father and Bernabo.

Venice bolsters trading power by victory in war with Genoa

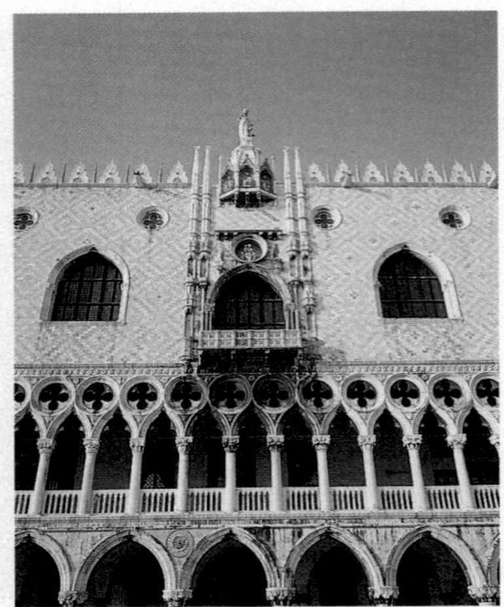

The doge's palace in Venice.

Italy, 1381

The long-running bitter struggle between the republics of Venice and Genoa appears to have been resolved with the outcome of the War of Chioggia and the unconditional surrender of the Genoese force. Although the peace conference held in Turin has left the two exhausted protagonists politically where they were before the fighting, the Venetians have set about making a speedy economic recovery.

The two republics have been squabbling for a hundred years over who is to be the dominant trade power in the region. Venice's wealth has rested on the trade which flows through the city on its way from the east and Constantinople to markets in Europe and northern Italy. In order to protect these routes from piracy, Venetian power has been pushed south and east and ships have even broken into the Black Sea. The Genoese are also great traders and bankers, who import spices from the Far East, trade with Moslem states and have helped to re-establish the Byzantine empire. They were spoiling for a fight with the Venetians, and found one in the Chioggia lagoon in which their fleet was trapped by concrete-filled blockships and sunk by their enemies.

After ecstasy and revelation, leading mystic experiences death

Rome, 29 April 1380

The Christian mystic Catherine of Siena died today, eight days after being paralysed from the waist down by a stroke. She was only 33, but had been in poor health after years of tireless devotion to those in need and to the church, both in her native Siena and elsewhere in Italy. Most recently she had been active in seeking recognition of Pope Urban VI in the face of the breakaway papacy at Avignon. She was perhaps the greatest of the many Christian mystics who have glorified this age of mystical fervour, although mysticism itself is not new. Nor is it confined to Italy: famous mystics include the Germans Hildegard of Bingen (died 1180) and Henry of Suso (died 1365), and Bridget of Sweden (died 1373). England and the Netherlands have also produced eminent mystics, such as Julian of Norwich and John Ruysbroek.

Characteristics of mysticism are the twin experiences of ecstasy and revelation. Divine ecstasy involves a temporary loss of a sense of time and space by mystics in rapture. Divinely-inspired revelations do not necessarily give prophecies of the future; mystics also claim to have visions of contemporary or recent events at a great distance.

HILDEGARDIS a Virgin Prophetess, Abbess of S.t Ruperts Nunnerye. She died at Bingen A° Do: 1180 Aged 82 yeares.

The mystic Hildegard of Bingen.

Cleric turns study of the stars into science instead of prophecy

Astrological aid for sailors.

Paris, 11 July 1382

The death was announced today of the great French cleric, scholar and economist Nicolas Oresme. He was a thrilling preacher, a skilful debater and a subtle thinker, and made many contributions to the development of science, especially astronomy.

Born around 1320, he studied theology at the university of Paris. After various appointments in the church, he became chaplain to King Charles the Wise of France and later became bishop of Lisieux. Oresme was probably the first to think of the heavens as a gigantic clock mechanism. He carried out many mathematical calculations of planetary motions and, in doing so, concluded that the behaviour of the earth in relation to the universe was rather different from that depicted by astrologers. In his *Book on Divinations* he attacked the deterministic belief of astrologers that human actions are guided by the stars, as well as criticising the use of black magic.

One of his major achievements was his book *On the Heavens* in which he questioned Aristotle's view that the stars move around a stationary earth. And one of his most intriguing thoughts was that there may be universes other than our own. It is hardly surprising, therefore, that Oresme's many ideas and speculations have been widely discussed.

English peasants revolt

London, 15 June 1381
The head of the rebel leader Wat Tyler has been displayed on a pole in a London field today, and his followers are making their way home. The king is safe. The peasants' revolt is over.

It has been a bloody but short-lived affair which began – as far as London was concerned – two days ago when Tyler led his mob into the city after tricking his way across the bridge. On their march to London they had taken Maidstone, Rochester and Canterbury and opened the gates of the Marshalsea to free the prisoners. Hundreds of Londoners joined them in widespread looting.

Once in the city, Tyler's "army" marched through Fleet Street, burning shops and breaking into the Temple where legal documents were burnt – a protest against the poll tax which led to this rising. Then the horror began. A judge was beheaded with 18 other leading citizens. The mob vented their fury on the Flemish community, beheading 35 in the street. The archbishop was dragged from the Tower chapel and executed on Tower Hill. His head was set up on London Bridge, his mitre nailed to his skull.

Richard II sails to meet the rebels.

As London burnt around him, Richard II, the king parleyed with the rebel leader, but, angered by Tyler's arrogant attitude, the mayor lunged with his sword. Tyler died soon afterwards, but the king has pardoned his followers.

High taxes provoke uprisings in France

Paris, 1 March 1382
A woman street merchant provoked a major riot today when a tax collector tried to seize her goods. She fought the man off with a cry of "down with taxes". Others took up the chant and, seizing mallets stored in the Hotel de Ville, the mob gave chase to tax-collectors throughout the city. The *Maillotins* thus became one more protest movement against the fierce taxation policies of Charles VI.

Elsewhere the *Tuchins*, peasants and craftsmen driven from the cities by taxation, are a loosely organised group making a living from robbery. Bound together by bloodcurdling oaths, the Tuchins operate in bands of no more than 20. They steal livestock, jewellery and cash, and capture churchmen and nobles for ransom.

Their favourite targets are the English and Gascon *routiers* – plunderers themselves, but vulnerable to attack by the Tuchins who claim patriotic motives. Tuchins are not all peasants. One leader, Pierre de Bres, is connected with many leading families of the Auvergne and Languedoc, and is believed to have joined the anarchic movement after robbing his uncle, a bishop, and discovering his wife having an affair with his squire.

Parisians: up in arms against tax.

Portuguese freedom

The battle of Aljubarrota, as depicted in a later English chronicle.

Portugal, 15 August 1385
The firepower of 300 English archers has won the day in the battle of Aljubarrota and saved Portuguese independence. The army of John of Portugal has scored a decisive victory over that of John of Castile, who has fled to Seville. Now that Portugal is independent of its powerful neighbour, a new age of its history can unfold.

Portugal's affairs have long been bound up with those of Castile, and when King Ferdinand died two years ago Castile's John proclaimed himself king. This led to a popular revolt in favour of another John – the grand master of the Knights of Avis – whom the Castilians decided had to be overthrown. Lisbon was besieged, and only survived because plague hit the Castilian army, killing over 2,000 men and its best commanders. The Portuguese were saved.

But the Castilian king was determined to risk everything on one more battle, and did so at Aljubarrota with a force of some 17,000 men. The Portuguese army was much smaller, but included a company of English archers sent by John of Gaunt who was pursuing his claims to Castile.

Although tired by a 12-mile march, the Castilians were ordered to attack. They came under terrible crossfire from English archers, and those not killed became entangled in a network of wolf-traps and trenches. The battle lasted for less than an hour.

Painter of austere landscapes has died

China, 1385
Ni Zan, currently one of the most revered Chinese artists, has died aged 84. He was born near Suzhou, and his early life was prosperous and comfortable. He knew many artists and scholars, and gained a reputation for being precious and faintly eccentric (he washed constantly) until 1356, when he left his home to live a simple life on a house-boat with his wife. He returned to his old home in old age after his wife's death.

Nearly all his works are small, delicately-toned, intimate and bare of people. There are usually just a few thin trees, a lake and low barren hills. The effect is of an understated, austere beauty.

"Autumn Landscape" (c.1360), typical of Ni Zan's spare beauty.

1385 (1385-1394)

Balkans, 1385. The Ottoman sultan, Murat, takes Sofia.

Balkans, 1386. With the capture of Salonika by Murat, the Byzantine empire is now entirely in Ottoman hands except for Mistra and a small area around Constantinople.

Central Europe, 1386. The Swiss confederation defeats Leopold III, the Habsburg duke of Austria, at Sempach; Leopold is killed in the battle. War broke out last year, prompted partly by Leopold's growing power in Swabia.

Near East, 1387. The Tartar conqueror Tamerlane captures Isfahan and Shiraz and attacks Armenia and Georgia.

England, 1388. A group of Richard II's aristocratic opponents launch an attack on the king's friends and associates. They execute eight and drive others into exile.

Central Europe, 1 April 1389. Albert of Austria signs the treaty of Zurich, recognising recent Swiss conquests and allowing the Swiss to keep all the land they have won.

Asia Minor (Anatolia), 16 September 1389. Bayezid Yilderim succeeds his father, Murat, as sultan of the Ottoman Turks.

Russia, 1389. Dmitri Donsky is succeeded by his son Vasily as Russian leader. In spite of Dmitri's victory against the Mongols in 1380, the Russians are still not free. Tuqtamish, put in charge of the Golden Horde by Tamerlane, has recaptured Moscow and renewed the Tartar yoke.

Japan, 1392. The division between the northern and southern courts ends.

The Baltic, 1392. The Hanse re-establishes its trading rights with Novgorod after a four-year commercial blockade of the city. A simultaneous embargo on trade to the Flemish towns ends, with Philip the Bold renewing the Hanse's privileges.

France, 5 August 1392. Charles VI, the king of France, suffers a second serious attack of madness.

Baghdad, 1393. Tamerlane takes possession of Baghdad.

Asia Minor, 1393. Bayezid overcomes the lesser Turkish dynasties in Asia Minor, paving the way for renewed Ottoman attacks on Europe.

Bulgaria, 1393. Bayezid annexes Bulgaria.

Spanish mobs set Jewish ghettoes ablaze

Barcelona, 9 August 1391

The last four days here have seen the most violent anti-Semitic atrocities in what has been an appalling year for violence against the Jews. On 5 August Castilian sailors set fire to the ghetto, killing 100 Jews. They were joined during the night by a crowd on the rampage, and Jews fled to the royal castle.

The following day the ringleaders were arrested and imprisoned. However, on 7 August the mob freed them. They then besieged the royal castle and forced the Jews to march in procession to be baptised. The 300 who refused were killed on the spot.

This year's violence began when Ferrant Martinez became the temporary administrator of the diocese of Seville. Long known for anti-Semitic sermons, he called this year for the razing of the synagogues and urged the peasants to expel the Jews from their villages. By June, Jews were being killed daily in Seville and mass hysteria was spreading. The Jewish community in Toledo was attacked and there were massacres in Valencia. Some people here think the rise of anti-Semitism dates from the need for the people to blame someone for the bubonic plague.

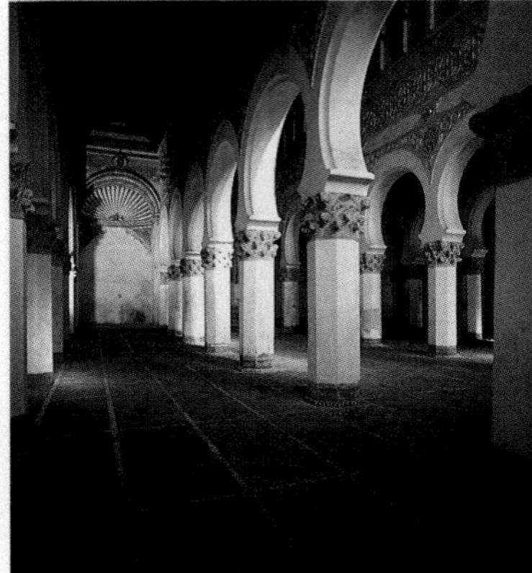

One of the synagogues in Toledo.

Private armies roam and plunder Europe

Paris, c.1391

Great swathes of Europe are being laid waste by armies of freebooting mercenaries who roam free, living off the land, terrorising the townspeople and peasantry, taking hostages for ransom and threatening to destroy the political fabric of much of the continent.

France, divided and made poorer by war and plague, suffers more than most – although German mercenaries operate in Italy, and private armies from Spain are causing havoc in Greece and elsewhere,

In France, the menace come from English *routiers* and French *echorcheurs* who, in the words of a contemporary writer, "resemble the passing of swarms of locusts ... they stripped the land bare and human government proved powerless to restrain them".

And therein lies the dilemma facing Charles VII. With an impoverished treasury, there is no way in which he can mount a royal expedition to clear France of these armies. Even so, most local people prefer to pay their ransom to the freebooters and stay quiet rather than complain and face punishment for the crime of paying it. If legal action is attempted against the leaders, they generally claim that they are men of chivalry and acting on the king's behalf. Pardons are frequent, many bought for cash.

One routier captain who was not pardoned was Merigot Marches who was operating in the south of France – ostensibly in the names of the English king and the counts of Armagnac and Foix. He was tried in Paris and claimed (after torture) that he had sworn loyalty to England.

Knights: chevaliers or charlatans?

Poland grows after a royal marriage

Poland, 1386

A marrige has prepared the way for the union of the Polish and Lithuanian crowns and united the two countries against their common foe, the knights of the Teutonic Order, – the territory-hungry descendants of the Crusaders. At a ceremony in Cracow, Jagello, the 36-year-old grand duke of Lithuania, has married Jadwiga, the Polish queen, who is 12, and been crowned. The marriage ends the long-standing rivalry and means that the Lithuanians adopt Christianity.

Diplomatic manoeuvring over the union has been going on for several years, with Jagello out to save his own position as well as Lithuania's future. He has long wanted to enter the sphere of western civilisation.

Jadwiga, who had hoped to marry an Austrian prince, at first resisted the idea of union with the pagan Jagello. She was finally persuaded by Polish lords and priests to sacrifice herself for Poland's sake. Although she is still so young, her royal dignity, legally equal to that of her husband, is working out well in practice. At the same time Lithuanian nobles are proceeding to adopt the manners and traditions of the Polish aristocracy.

Sergius, the saintly Russian monk, dies

Russia, 1392

The Russian monk Sergius of Radonezh has died at the monastery of the Holy Trinity which he founded at Zagorsk, in central Russia. He was born at Rostov in 1314; civil war forced his parents to flee with him to Radonezh, north-east of Moscow. When he was 20 he and his brother Stephen became hermits in the neighbouring forest, where they eventually attracted followers. By 1354 Sergius led a proper monastic community, and his name spread across northern Russia; directly or indirectly he founded several other monasteries, and intervened to keep peace among quarrelling Russian princes. Renowned for his humility and simplicity, he taught his monks to be selfless.

Warlord who builds piles of heads

Samarkand, Central Asia, 1387

It is less than ten years since Timur the Lame (corrupted in Europe as Tamerlane) began empire-building, but already he has taken control of Persia, a task which took a mere two years, and secured the boundaries of his Transoxianan homeland against the Mongol horde, whose genes he shares.

However, these facts do not convey the bloodthirsty nature of the man. Like Genghis Khan, he offers his adversary a choice of prompt surrender or a bloodbath. Even a hint of token resistance provokes his fury. After capturing one city, Tamerlane ordered that 30,000 of its citizens – not all of them fighters – should be decapitated. He amuses himself by arranging severed heads in great mounds, like melons in a market place.

Tamerlane's war elephants, from a drawing by Raphael (1483-1520).

Physically he is a huge man, with a massive head and a formidable high forehead, his skin fair under his beard. He is devoutly religious. His ethic responds only to physical courage. Possibly this is because of his chronic limp. Some think it was caused by a wound, but others believe that he was born like this. On bad days he cannot ride, but must be carried in a litter. He fights a campaign in advance, sitting immobile over his special chess board, then explodes into action.

It is odd that the man who delights in death takes his advice only from Islam's Sufis, who see God in living things.

Japanese rival courts are reconciled

Japan, 1392

The rival southern and northern courts of the divided imperial family are to be reunited after half a century of strife. Under the terms of the agreement the southern emperor, Go-Kameyama, was to perform a solemn act of abdication in which the imperial regalia held by the south were to be transferred to the north. He has already been betrayed, however, for the regalia have been returned to the north by a small escort of courtiers who carried them to the Tsuchi-mikado palace where the northern emperor, Go-Komatsu, was staying.

This bodes ill for the agreement which had stipulated that the succession was to alternate between the two lines of Japan's imperial family.

A painting from a Kyoto shrine, showing two warriors in close combat.

Serbians crushed by the Ottomans

Serbia, 15 June 1389

Serbia has been crushed by the Ottoman Turks after a battle at Kosovo, when the whole of the Serbian nobility was wiped out. The Turkish conquest is now sweeping rapidly over the Balkans.

Serbia has been the most brilliant, faithful and dangerous of Byzantium's Balkan heirs, but the Ottomans are becoming more bold in their attacks and a menace to both Greek and Slav. Having invaded Bulgaria last year, Sultan Murat turned against the Serbian leader Lazar.

At Kosovo ("field of the blackbirds"), fortune seemed at first to favour the Serbs. The sultan was killed, but led by the heir to the throne, Bayezid, the Ottomans achieved the upper hand. Lazar was taken prisoner and executed with his nobles. One feature of the battle was that the Janissary corps of forcibly recruited Christian boys fought very well for their Turkish rulers.

Koreans end years of Mongol control

Korea, 1392

The dictator Yi Song-gye has deposed King Kongyang and set himself on the throne of Korea, thus establishing a new dynasty untainted by subservience to the once-powerful Mongol empire.

Yi has been able to remove the last vestiges of Mongol rule by enacting a radical programme of land reform which has destroyed the economic power of the aristocratic families. These familes had flourished under the Mongols and Kublai Khan's Yuan dynasty, but now they have been swept away just like the descendants of Kublai. The money from their lands now goes into the treasury of the new dynasty.

A poet who revered God and the vine

Persia, 1389

The poet and Moslem mystic Shams al-Din Mohammed, known as Hafiz, has died at Shiraz, in southern Persia, aged about 70. He is regarded as the greatest master of the Persian *ghazal*, a lyrical short poem characterised by mysticism, richness and subtlety of imagery. Love and wine feature frequently in his work, as in the following lines:

Again the times are out of joint; and again
For wine and the loved one's languid glance I am fain to.

An illustration for a book by Hafiz.

1394 (1394-1400)

Austria, 1394. The Habsburg dukes of Austria agree a 20-year truce with the Swiss confederation, which now comprises eight cantons: Uri, Schwyz, Unterwalden, Glarus, Zug, Berne, Zurich and Lucerne.

Florence, 1394. The English mercenary leader John Hawkwood, whose troops have become a force to be reckoned with in the politics of northern Italy, dies and is buried in an elaborate cathedral tomb.

Avignon, 1394. Benedict XIII succeeds Clement VII as pope.

France, 15 July 1394. Charles VI issues a decree of general expulsion of Jews from France.

Central Asia, 1395. Tamerlane destroys Astrakhan.

Italy, 1395. Gian Galeazzo Visconti buys the title of duke of Milan from King Wenceslas, which gives him the status of a legitimate prince.

Scandinavia, 20 June 1397. The Union of Kalmar unites Denmark, Sweden and Norway under one monarch.

Florence, c.1397. Giovanni de' Medici founds the Medici bank.

Paris, 1398. Earlier attempts to end the schism having failed, owing to the intransigence of the two popes, the university of Paris persuades the French king and clergy to withdraw their obedience from Benedict XIII, thus depriving him of much of his income.

India, 1398. Tamerlane invades India and sacks Delhi.

England, 29 September 1399. Richard II is deposed. His cousin Henry of Lancaster declares himself king under the name Henry IV.

Constantinople, 1399. John II of Boucicaut, the marshal of France, with western troops, holds Constantinople against the Ottomans. The Emperor Manuel II leaves for the west in an attempt to raise further help, leaving his nephew John VII as co-emperor.

Near East, 1400. Tamerlane takes Sivas from the Ottomans and ravages Syria.

Italy, 1400. Gian Galeazzo Visconti takes possession of Perugia, Assisi and Spoleto.

France, 1400. Jean Froissart finishes his *Chronicles*. Their picture of the chivalric world during the second half of the last century is proving immensely influential.

The poet who told Canterbury Tales dies

Chaucer at the court of Edward III, by Ford Madox Brown (1821-93).

London, 25 October 1400

Geoffrey Chaucer, a giant of English poetry, died today with his ambitious poetic cycle *The Canterbury Tales* still incomplete. As England's best-loved writer he is to be buried in Westminster Abbey.

Chaucer came from a well-to-do family of vintners with court connections (his father was deputy butler to the king). Geoffrey received a court education as a page and was put into the service of John of Gaunt.

He fought for England against France, was taken prisoner and later ransomed. He came back enthused by the French fashion for poems of courtly love. He also read in four languages and borrowed tales from Boccaccio.

Chaucer prospered at court, becoming a controller of customs and a magistrate, and was granted a daily jug of wine by Richard II. All this stopped when his patron, John of Gaunt, went to Spain in 1386.

The beginning of the Knight's Tale.

Chaucer was set at leisure. He had just completed *Troilus and Criseyde*, and now turned to his band of Canterbury pilgrims, whom he drew with a mixture of shrewdness and pithy humour.

Constantinople at mercy of Ottomans

Bulgaria, 25 September 1396

A disorganised and ill-led crusade against the Turkish Sultan Bayezid has ended in bloody disaster at Nicopolis. Constantinople is at the Ottomans' mercy.

Following the conquering path of Murad, his predecessor, Bayezid laid siege to Constantinople before capturing Nicopolis, the Bulgarian fortress on the Danube, in 1393, and imprisoning, then killing, the Bulgarian czar.

King Sigismund of Hungary eventually persuaded the French and reluctant vassal forces to join him in a crusade. But the French showed more appetite for pillage and plunder than for military strategy as the allies advanced down the Danube.

Having besieged the Turks in Nicopolis, the allies turned to face the sultan's arriving army. The French advance was brave, but blindly led, and was overwhelmed before the rest of the crusaders' army disintegrated. Bayezid took bloody revenge on his attackers, slaughtering the French captives by the hundred

Marriages put duke on top in Italy

Italy, 1400

Northern Italy is dominated by Gian Galeazzo Visconti, a Lombard noble whose military prowess is outshone by his diplomatic skill and ruthless cunning. Only Florence stands between him and the title "King of Italy".

He inherited the lordships of Pavia and other northern Italian cities, and married Isabel of Valois, the daughter of the king of France. When she died, he married the daughter of his powerful uncle Bernabo, whom he imprisoned to acquire all the Visconti lands.

Having married his daughter to Louis of Orleans, the brother of the king of France, he has made more judicious alliances and, with a minimum of military effort, won control of almost every important city in northern Italy. He is recognised by the Emperor Wenceslas as duke of Milan and Lombardy.

English king abdicates

Richard II hands over his crown and sceptre to Henry, duke of Lancaster.

London, 29 September 1399

The turbulent reign of Richard II came to an ignominious end today in the Tower of London, where the king, under pressure from a delegation of nobles, signed a deed of abdication. Amongst the delegation was Henry, the earl of Hereford and son of John of Gaunt, who promptly claimed the crown for himself. A document of 32 articles accusing Richard of tyrannical rule has been prepared for presentation to parliament. Certainly his claim that the laws of England lay in his mouth, and the wanton luxury of his court, caused great resentment. But the immediate cause of his overthrow was his treatment of Henry of Hereford, whose estates he seized on the death of John of Gaunt.

Henry, who had been living in exile in Paris, set sail for England and landed at Ravenspur in Yorkshire. Richard's armies deserted him and he was brought to London a prisoner. Although his reign ended in disaster, he will be remembered for his courageous handling of the peasants' revolt, when he set himself at the head of the rebels and persuaded them to disband.

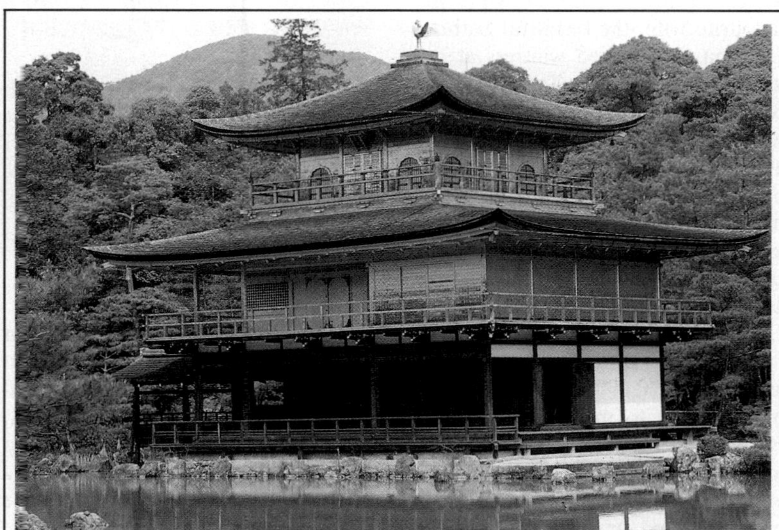

Kinkaku-ji: the Temple of the Golden Pavilion on the outskirts of Kyoto in Japan. It was built by the shogun Yoshimitsu after he had retired.

Ex-monk, first Ming emperor, dies at 70

China, 1398

Zhu Yuanzhang, the peasant who became emperor of China, has died at the age of 70. His rise to supreme power began when he was only 17, when all his family fell victim to the plague and famine. He became a monk in order to survive, but found his real role when he joined the peasant revolutionaries, the Red Turbans.

He rose to power by his military ability and bravery and, switching his forces' attacks from the landowners to overcoming the Mongol Yuan dynasty, he achieved such success that in 1368 he was able to take Beijing and drive the last Yuan emperor back across the Great Wall into the Gobi desert.

He named his own dynasty Ming (Brilliant) and ruled for 30 years. Scarred by the fate of his family, he spent most of his efforts in establishing a stable social and economic order based on agriculture.

He was always concerned with the common man and, even when he grew despotic towards the end of his life, his victims were the nobles rather than the peasants.

It has been suggested that he had been a member of the White Lotus secret society, and, although he denied this, he came to rely on his own web of secret agents and began to look upon any opposition as proof of a conspiracy against him.

He is to be buried in the Purple Mountains outside Nanking, his power base. He leaves this world feared, but respected as the man who reunified China.

A statue on the way to Ming tombs.

Kalmar treaty unites Scandinavian states

Sweden, 20 June 1397

Three Scandinavian kingdoms have come together under a single sovereign with the signing of the Union of Kalmar. Denmark, Sweden and Norway now constitute the second largest accumulation of European territories under one leader, Queen Margaret of Denmark. The three states will have a common foreign policy, and matters of royal succession must be settled by consensus.

The agreement is a triumph for Margaret, an ambitious and skilful politician and gifted diplomat. She became regent of Denmark on the death of her father, and of Norway on the death of her husband. She gained possession of Sweden after deposing King Alfred. Her 15-year-old great-nephew, Duke Erik Vll of Pomerania, has been crowned King of Scandinavia at Kalmar.

Margaret's intention from the beginning has been to provide the union with a suitable male head. But the union also grew to some extent out of a general trend towards the creation of larger political entities such as the formation of Poland-Lithuania and the expansion of Moscow.

Swedish embroidery from Uppsala.

1400 (1400-1410)

South-East Africa, c.1400. A thriving gold trade has been established down the Zambezi valley to the Sofala coast.

Germany, 1400. Wenceslas IV, an indolent drunkard, is deposed as king of the Romans (the title held by emperors not crowned as emperor), though he remains king of Bohemia. The choice of Rupert of the Palatinate to replace him causes a schism when Wenceslas and his supporters refuse to accept the election.

Baghdad, 1401. Tamerlane takes Baghdad for the second time.

England, 1401. A statute is passed authorising the handing over of obdurate heretics to the secular authorities to be burnt.

Asia Minor (Anatolia), 1402. The Ottoman sultan, Bayezid, is defeated by Tamerlane in battle near Angora. Tamerlane captures Smyrna and reaches the Bosphorus. Bayezid is taken prisoner and dies in captivity.

China, 1402. After a long period of civil war, Zhu Di, the uncle of the second Ming emperor, Jianwen, usurps the throne to reign as the Yongle emperor.

North Atlantic, 1402. Henry of Castile sends an expedition to conquer the Canary Islands.

Prague, 1402. The reformer Jan Hus begins to preach in the Bethlehem chapel, founded in 1391 by two laymen as a centre of religious revival.

Japan, 1404. Japan starts to trade with Ming China.

France, 27 April 1404. John (the Fearless) becomes duke of Burgundy.

Florence, 1406. A copy of Ptolemy's *Geography* is brought to Italy from Constantinople and is translated into Latin by James Angelus. Its availability gives an important boost to geographical knowledge in Europe.

Italy, 1407. No longer able to compete effectively with its rival, Venice, Genoa forms its own private banking company of St George.

Paris, 23 November 1407. Louis, the duke of Orleans, is murdered on the instigation of John the Fearless, the duke of Burgundy. With Charles VI prevented from governing by madness, a deadly struggle developed between Louis and John. Their supporters have formed factions known as the Armagnac and Burgundian parties.

Seven years later Delhi still in ruins

Delhi, 1405

The sultanate of Delhi is collapsing. Half a century ago it encompassed almost all India, save the southern tip. Today its capital, Delhi, is still in ruins, too weak to recover from the ravages of Tamerlane the Great seven years earlier.

Rebellions in Gujarat, Jaunpur, the Punjab and the Deccan had already whittled away its territory before Tamerlane's invasion. Corruption, regicide, overtaxation and the vast cost of protecting the Moslem state against its Hindu majority had weakened it from within.

Tamerlane crossed the Indus in December 1398. His pretext was the toleration by Delhi's Moslem rulers of Hindu idolatry. His object was plunder. On 17 December he scattered the sultan's army of 10,000 cavalry, 40,000 infantry and 120 war elephants; the elephants, according to Tamerlane, were "driven off like cows". Next day the city was sacked, Tamerlane leaving behind pillars of skulls.

Since then Mallu, the humiliated sultan, and his sucessor, Mahmud, have regained a fraction of the sultanate, but after the ravages of Tamerlane there seems nothing left with which to rebuild the sultanate.

Deccan art: a female drummer.

Defeated sultan is Tamerlane's footstool

Tamerlane the Great enthroned, from a Moghul manuscript (c.1600).

Angora (Ankara), Turkey, 1402

The great Ottoman leader, Sultan Bayezid, is Tamerlane's prisoner after a quarrel between the two mighty moslem neighbours which, for once, Tamerlane did not initiate. Bayezid rejected an offer of compromise over a border dispute three years ago by questioning Tamerlane's sexual virility. Now the Ottoman sultan is obliged to act as Tamerlane's footstool while his favourite wife, the beautiful Serbian Despina, is a naked waitress at the victor's table. When Tamerlane received Bayezid's insulting letter he was not deflected from his immediate objective: seizure of Syria, including Aleppo and Damascus, destruction of Baghdad, and creation of another of the pyramids of severed human heads which serve as signposts from the Great Wall of China to the borders of Asia Minor.

This year Tamerlane assembled an army of 20,000 men and a team of elephants to move the baggage. By a remarkable bluff he contrived to march into the heart of Anatolia and occupy a position behind his opponent and upstream, across the only water source in that desolate plain, which he diverted. Turkish morale was at rock bottom when the fighting started. Bayezid put Tartar cavalry – of the same blood as Tamerlane – at the front and they promptly changed sides, reducing the Ottoman force by a quarter. Bayezid was still swinging his battle axe like a killing machine when his army collapsed and the Ottoman leader was about to face the ultimate humiliation at the hands of his victor.

A Turkish prisoner, by a later artist.

Timur the Lame is dead

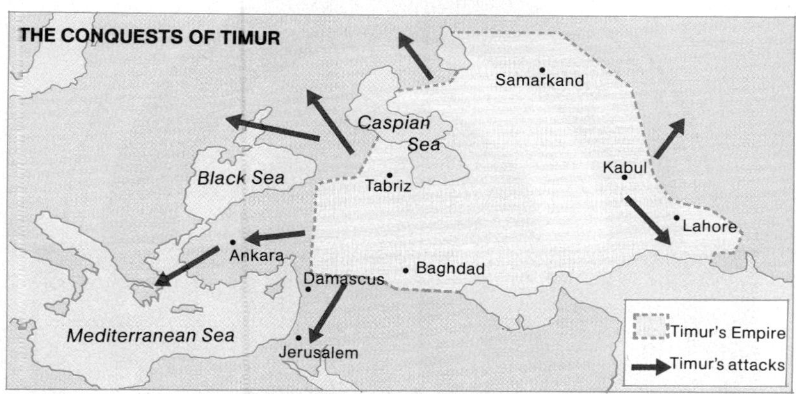

Samarkand, Central Asia 1405
Word has reached the homeland of the great Timur the Lame that he has died during his most ambitious expedition yet.

Having defeated Anatolians, Turks, Persians, Arabs, Mamelukes and Mongols to create an empire stretching from Tartary to India, he wanted to take on the Chinese. In China, the ruling Ming awaited with interest this lost son of Mongolia who now appeared to threaten them from the west.

Timur, known in the west as Tamerlane, was born in Turkestan 69 years ago into the Barlas tribe, a clan originating from Mongolia which had adopted the Islamic religion and the Turkish language. He was a strange human cocktail: a white-haired illiterate who impressed the scholar ibn Khaldun with his wit; a greater tactician than Genghis Khan; a man who made a cult of atrocious cruelty, but who loved philosophy and brooded over chess; a lifelong nomad who was a patron of architecture. He was also a collector: Samarkand is full of elegant loot from Delhi. But he saw little of his treasures; after 1370 he spent most of his next 35 years on the road.

A European view of Tamerlane.

Tamerlane died somewhere in Asia of a fever and "an indiscreet use of iced water". The ruler who dealt deaths of excruciating pain to thousands of innocent people had a peaceful end.

Teutonic Knights defeated by the Poles

Prussia, 15 July 1410
The Poles and Lithuanians have defeated their most powerful and dangerous enemy, the Teutonic Order, at Tannenberg, and ended its two centuries of rule in the region. The battle lasted for a day and resulted in the death of some 200 Teutonic Knights, including their grand master.

Both sides had been preparing for a decisive battle for some time, and had even submitted their cases to public opinion throughout Europe in memoranda sent to several countries, including England. At the same time military preparations were also going on, with the order recruiting Western knights and the Poles enlisting some Czech mercenaries.

When it came to the battle the united Polish and Lithuanian army was larger than the German force, but not as experienced. However, Jagello decided to thrust at the order's capital at Marienburg, and the Polish gentry finally carried the day when the German grand master's charge failed.

Three popes reign in latest church crisis

The three popes. From left to right: Benedict, Gregory and Alexander.

Pisa, August 1409
The Council of Pisa has ended on a sad note, with delegates forced to admit that they have failed. Several hundred bishops, lower churchmen and royal envoys have been meeting here for the last four months seeking to heal the schism in the church. Neither of the two popes (Benedict XIII, based in Avignon, and Gregory XII, the Roman pope) is strong enough to oust the other. The council thought it had found a solution by deposing both popes and electing a Cretan, Petros Philargos, as Pope Alexander V. However, Benedict and Gregory have refused to be ousted, so Alexander is setting up his court here, making three popes in all.

Arab with new historical theory dies

Cairo, 17 March 1406
Abd al-Rahman ibn Mohammed ibn Khaldun, historian, diplomat, judge and administrator, has died aged 74. Born in Tunis into a family of Spanish Arabs, ibn Khaldun held high office in Morocco, Spain and Egypt, invaluable experience for the work for which he is best known: a three-volume history of the Arabs, Persians and Berbers. The first volume is the most famous, because it presents a new theory of historical development taking notice of physical influences, such as climate and geography, as well as moral and intellectual ones. Ibn Khaldun endeavoured to formulate the cycles of national progress and decay, and can be said to have discovered the true scope and nature of history and society.

A pharmacy: the Arabs have excelled in all branches of learning.

1410 (1410-1415)

Italy, May 1410. Following the death of Alexander V at Bologna, John XXIII – said to have poisoned Alexander – is elected pope. His election marks an important stage in the rise of the Medici family, his backers.

Peru, c.1410. Under the leadership of Viracocha Inca, who became ruler of the Incas in 1400, the Inca empire is expanding and the rigidly hierarchical structure of Inca society is growing more formalised.

West Africa, 1410. Kanajejdi, the king of Kano, who introduced iron helmets and quilted horse armour to the Hausa cavalry, dies.

Hungary, July 1411. Sigismund of Hungary, the brother of Wenceslas, is elected Holy Roman emperor. Of the two candidates who were rivals for the title in 1400, Rupert died last year and Wenceslas is retired with a pension.

Portugal, 1411. Aragon and Portugal make peace after some 30 years of wars and truces. John of Portugal, now secure at home, begins a policy of overseas expansion.

England, 20 March 1413. On his death, Henry IV is succeeded by his son Henry V.

Paris, 1413. Demands for reform of finance and justice made by the Paris craftsmen under the patronage of the Burgundian faction result in an ordinance that all officials, both central and local, should be elected. This utopian measure is overturned when the Armagnac faction seizes control of Paris.

England, 1414. Henry V adopts the French claims of Edward III as his own and asserts his right to the inheritance of the Plantagenets.

England, 1414. A Lollard revolt, led by Sir John Oldcastle, discredits the movement by linking it with social radicalism.

Germany, 6 July 1415. Having appeared before the Council of Constance, Jan Hus is convicted of heresy and burnt.

Morocco, 1415. King John of Portugal conquers Ceuta in Morocco. Keen to acquire gold and slaves from Africa, he is also motivated by a dream of allying with Africans against the Moslems of the Maghreb.

East Africa, 1415. An embassy is dispatched from Malindi (Kenya) to China.

Czech reformer is burnt at the stake

Constance, Germany, 6 July 1415
Today Jan Hus, scholar, teacher and popular preacher, was condemned by the Fathers of the Council of Constance as a heretic. He was immediately stripped of his vestments and turned over to the king's men. By order of King Sigismund he was led out of the city to a pyre and offered a last chance to recant. He refused and was burnt to death. He died singing a hymn.

Hus was condemned for his theological ideas just like John Wyclif, the Englishman, some of whose ideas he adopted. But the underlying causes were political. Hus had spoken out strongly against corruption in the church, such as the selling of indulgences and the buying of offices. This made him a popular figure with the discontented poor and a threat to both church and secular leaders. In addition Hus, born of a peasant family in a Bohemian village, was closely identified with Czech nationalism, a clear threat to the German-dominated royal court.

Jan Hus is led to the stake.

Small is beautiful: a miniature entitled January in "Tres Riches Heures".

Miniatures adorn French duke's library

France, 1415
The Limburg brothers are busy preparing a new book, the *Tres Riches Heures* (Very Rich Hours), for the Duc de Berry. It is, as its name suggests, a richly illustrated "book of hours", religious texts and prayers to be read at various set times of the day. It is a masterpiece of miniature painting, and joins other fine books of hours in the duke's well-stocked library.

Peninsula of Malacca converted to Islam by Indonesian prince

Malacca, South Malaya, 1414
Paramesvara, the exiled Indonesian prince who founded a kingdom on the Malaccan peninsula, has been converted to the Moslem faith – but with Paramesvara seeking to counteract the influence of Malacca's ally China, and of her enemy Siam, it is a conversion of convenience. However, for Paramesvara, the prince of Palembang, it has been an epic journey. First he declared Palembang independent from the Hindu kingdom of Majapahit on Java. When Majapahit destroyed Palembang in 1390, he fled to Tumasik on the Malaccan peninsula, and was again pursued. Finally, in 1401, he reached Malacca where, with the help of the Chinese who needed a friendly port in so strategic a place, he established his new state. Malacca has grown prosperous thanks to Arab traders. Paramesvara's shrewd change of faith is likely to increase his country's prosperity considerably.

Krishna is beaten by the god Indra, who rides on the bird-deity Garuda.

Bengali bard sings of the love of Krishna

India, c.1415

The Bengali poet and singer Baru Chandidas has written a beautiful set of songs about Krishna, one of the incarnations of the Hindu god Visnu, whose cult has become very popular in north-eastern India in recent years. Chandidas, a high-caste Brahman, is among the first Bengali writers of Visnuite poetry, and his *Shrikrishnakirtan*, in which he retells the traditional story of the cowherd Krishna and his love for the shepherdess Radha, is unusual in its down-to-earth language. However, Chandidas stresses the importance of human emotion which is free from base desires.

Russian icons, including (bottom right) one of the Holy Trinity.

Calm ecstasy evoked by icon of Trinity

Russia, c.1411

The icon painter Andrei Rublev has confirmed his reputation as the greatest Russian artist of his day with his latest work, *Trinity*, commissioned by the monastery of the Holy Trinity at Zagorsk, near Moscow. Rublev made his name through his work with Theophanes the Greek on the cathedral of the Assumption in Moscow, in 1405, and with Daniel Chorny in Vladimir-Volynsky in 1408. His work is more intimate and realistic in its contemplation of the divine than that of other icon painters, and he makes use of the technique known as *sfumato*, the soft blending of light and shade. The *Trinity*, however, radiates light with an almost total absence of shadow, the rhythmic brushstrokes creating an impression of calm ecstasy in the three finely-drawn angels representing the Holy Trinity itself. It is a wonderfully simple expression of a theologically complex idea.

Lollard coup foiled

England, 13 January 1414

An attempted coup by the heretical Lollard sect has been foiled and 45 of the rebels were executed today. The uprising was led by Sir John Oldcastle, who was sentenced to death for his reformist beliefs last September.

Granted 40 days respite by the king, Henry V, Oldcastle lost no time in forming a last-ditch plan to take power. He escaped from the Tower and gave out word to Lollards across the country. But Henry, alerted to the plot, was waiting for the rebels when they met outside London. Some died in the fighting that followed, and many more were captured. Oldcastle, however, escaped.

African king who gave his army chain mail is dead

Kano, Nigeria, 1410

Kanajeji Sarki, the ruler of Kano, has died after a reign of 20 years. The West African monarch, who gave his soldiers the protection of helmets and chain-mail and introduced war horses protected by quilted body armour, raised the power of Kano to new heights. Two centuries ago Kano was an insignificant city-state, whose writ ran little further than its city walls.

Steadily Kano expanded its territories. By Kanajeji's accession it dominated most of Hausaland (north-western Nigeria). By his death it had surpassed the power of the empire of Mali, dominating West Africa. Not afraid of innovation, he imported chain-mail from Mameluke Egypt, and, recognising the tactical value of the horse, built a superb cavalry, its horses upholstered in quilts. None could withstand them, and Kanajeji's army is now one of most powerful on the whole of the African continent.

1415 (1415-1422)

Spain, 1416. Alfonso V succeeds his father Ferdinand on the throne of Aragon. The election of Ferdinand, the son of John of Castile, in 1412 ended the succession dispute which broke out in 1410 on the death of Martin of Aragon without direct heirs.

France, 1418. John the Fearless of Burgundy, an ally of the English, seizes control of the government in the name of the queen, Isabel of Bavaria. The dauphin Charles escapes from Paris and sets up his base at Bourges, where he takes the title of regent.

Normandy, July 1419. With the exception of Mont St Michel, all of Normandy is now under the control of Henry V of England.

France, 10 September 1419. After a bad-tempered meeting with the dauphin, John the Fearless is murdered at Montereau by supporters of the dauphin. He is succeeded by his son Philip (the Good).

China, 1420. The Yongle emperor moves his main capital to the former Yuan capital Dadu, renaming it Beijing ("northern capital"), the better to defend the country against resurgent Mongol power. Nanjing becomes the secondary capital.

North Atlantic, 1420. Prince Henry of Portugal encourages the settlement of Porto Santo and Madeira.

Florence, 1420. Cosimo (the Elder) becomes manager of the Medici bank.

Paris, 1 December 1420. Henry V makes a triumphant entry into Paris.

Asia Minor (Anatolia), 1421. Murat II succeeds his father, Mahomet, as Ottoman sultan and resumes a policy of expansion.

Central Europe, 1 June 1421. At a meeting at Caslav, the representatives of Bohemia and Moravia renounce the Emperor Sigismund as their king and found a government.

Italy, 1421. As part of his campaign to restore the duchy of Milan, which fragmented into city-states after the death of Gian Galeazzo Visconti in 1402, Filippo Maria Visconti subjugates Genoa.

Flanders, 1421. Gypsies have been recorded as arriving in the city of Bruges. Established in eastern Europe by the end of last century, the gypsies started to move westwards early in the present century.

Church schism is healed at Constance

Martin V: habemus papam.

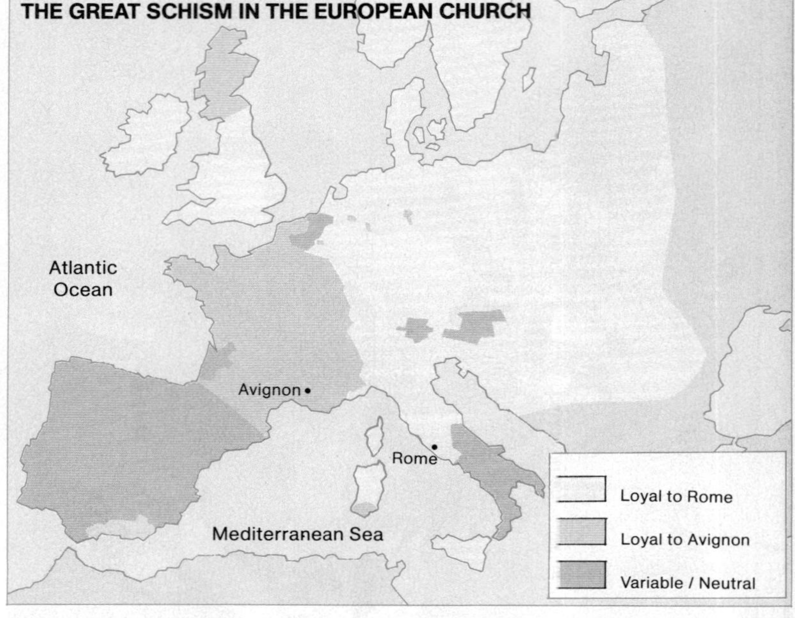

Constance, 11 November 1417

The "Great Schism" in the Christian Church, which began when two rival popes were elected in 1370, is over. Today the Italian Cardinal Oddone Colonna was elected Pope Martin V by the conclave with the support of the major national and clerical factions.

Unlike the ill-fated Council of Pisa, which elected a pope in 1409 and then found that the two existing popes refused to be ousted, the council here started pragmatically. It set out to remove the existing three popes first. The Pisan pope, John XXIII, was the first to fall. He was found guilty by the council in May 1415 of adultery, incest, sodomy, the poisoning of Pope Alexander V and the denial of the immortality of the soul. Gregory XII, the Roman pope, then decided that discretion was the better part of valour, and resigned voluntarily in June. Benedict XIII, the Avignon pope, proved more obdurate, but he was finally deposed on 26 July 1417 as a heretic.

The new pope has no great reputation as a scholar or preacher. Here at Constance, in Germany, he has been seen running with the hare and hunting with the hounds. He is amiable and colourless, perhaps an ideal compromise figure. The key figure in securing unity has been the German King Sigismund, in alliance with England's Henry V, acting for political not theological reasons.

Chinese treasure fleet lands in Africa

China, 1422

Zheng He, the grand eunuch of the Three Treasures, has reached Malindi on the East African coast with his Star Raft, the great fleet sent to spread the Emperor Yunglo's prestige to the west.

This is Zheng He's sixth great expedition and it is no haphazard exploration. The huge treasure ships, with five or six decks, weigh about 1,500 tons each and are provisioned for ocean cruising. They carry a year's supply of grain, herds of pigs and jars of fermenting wine.

They are also equipped with the latest magnetic compasses and are accompanied by auxiliary and store vessels, including horseships for the mounts of the expedition's 27,000 soldiers.

Malindi is a special place for the Chinese, for it is from there that the emperor has been sent giraffes, thought in China to be sacred unicorns. Zheng He ships are filled with porcelain, silks and satins, gold and silver, to trade for lions and rhinos, myrrh and ambergris.

The trade is symbolic as well as profitable, for by accepting the Chinese goods the local chieftains are deemed to have paid homage to the emperor.

Defenestration of Prague Catholics

Prague, 30 July 1419

The conflict between the Czech nation and the Church of Rome has come to a head with an uprising by followers of Jan Hus, the executed reformer. During a mass demonstration in Prague, thousands of Hussites marched on the New Town Hall. After demands for the release of several of their preachers were ignored, the crowd forced its way into the building and threw the Catholic councillors and others whom the Hussites hated out of the windows into the square.

A meeting of townspeople was held and appointed four captains to administer the city. The rising was in protest against the recent pro-Catholic policies of King Wenceslas IV, including the restoration of many churches in Prague and elsewhere to the Catholics.

The king's hard line was prompted by fears of a papal crusade against the country. Now, however, although shocked and frightened by the new Hussite militancy, he is taking no action against it. He has been convinced by his courtiers and members of the conservative Hussite group that, if he does not accept the new pro-Hussite council, the mutiny may even grow.

English win at Agincourt

The film of Shakespeare's "Henry V" evokes the English camp at Agincourt.

France, 25 October 1415

There could have been no greater contrast between these two armies as they awaited battle at Agincourt on the eve of this, St Crispin's Day. The English, numbering 12,000, were well-disciplined and prepared to die, knowing that they were grossly outnumbered by the French. As they lay silent as commanded, their king, Henry V, walked among their lines, talking quietly to archer, footsoldier and knight alike. He had not wanted this battle and had been prepared to strike bargains to avoid it. Half a mile away the French were jubilant, even parading a cart in which they intended to drag the English king through Paris. They had reason: they numbered 60,000. But they had learned little since Crecy, 69 years ago.

This morning Henry attended Mass and, like most of his army, confessed. He donned his armour and a bejewelled helmet and took his position in front of his army as the French began their advance – into a rain of English arrows. The French cavalry panicked, smashing their way through their own infantrymen, causing great breaches in the forward ranks which were quickly filled by English soldiers wielding swords and axes. The battle lasted until four o'clock today, when English victory was assured. A final push by the French forced the English to cut the throats of some 1,000 prisoners.

Mongol power in Persia and Russia slips

Saray, Astrakhan, c.1420

A century of abrasive border disputes in Azerbaijan and Transcaucasia between two expansionist Mongol powers has weakened both to a point where they no longer control events inside their own boundaries. The punch-drunk opponents are the *ilkhans* (subsidiary khans) of Persia and the Golden Horde in Russia and eastern Europe.

Some think that the death of Kublai Khan in 1294 damaged Mongol solidarity. At its peak, the Horde's writ ran from the Danube to the Baltic and from Kiev to the Urals. The Horde's most potent source of wealth, apart from loot and Russian taxation, was the trade link, via Italian middlemen, with Mameluke Egypt. It also controlled trade routes similar to that followed by Marco Polo from Europe across Asia into China.

As Horde domination collapses, the situation is reverting to the position before 1236: semi-independent Turkish nomads, loyal to clan chiefs, roam the steppes. What is new is the identity being forged by Russia.

England and France sign perpetual peace

Philip of Burgundy: co-signatory.

Henry V: chief beneficiary.

France, 21 May 1420

After months of patient negotiation, Henry V, the victor of Agincourt, has brought England and France under one crown. And to cement the agreement, signed with Philip, the duke of Burgundy, the English king is to marry Catherine of Valois, the king of France's daughter. Henry believes that the agreement will bring "perpetual peace" between the two kingdoms. The customs and kingdoms of England and France are to be kept entirely separate, the union of the two crowns to be personal.

The agreement does not tackle the question of succession, however; and no woman can succeed to the French throne. This could prove to be a major stumbling block.

Pleasure-loving sultan broken by battle

Central India, 1420

Sultan Firuz Bahman, ruler of the Deccan (central India), has suffered a crushing defeat at Pangal, north of the River Krishna. The eighth sultan in the powerful Brahmani dynasty, Firuz is unaccustomed to defeat. He came to power in 1397 and immediately established his authority with a thorough-going reorganisation of administration in his lands.

The following year Harihara II, ruler of Vijayanagar (in southern India) tried to invade. Firuz slew the leader's son and, aided by heavy seasonal rains, drove a bedraggled Hindu army back to the south. His own expansionist ambitions were only temporarily halted by an alliance between Vijayanagar, Malwa and Gujarat. In 1406 he defeated his enemies and established his southern border on the river Tungabhadra.

Firuz is not only a war-monger. He has a passion for building and has filled his capital Gulbarga with many splendid edifices, the most remarkable of which is the main mosque, a copy of the one in Cordoba in Spain. He also has a taste for hard drinking, music and women, keeping a huge harem.

But his most recent defeat may change all this. He has returned from the battle a broken-down old man, with little enthusiasm left for his former pleasures.

"Hannya": a demon mask from the Japanese Noh theatre.

1422 (1422-1432)

France, 31 August 1422. Henry V of England, heir designate to the kingdom of France, dies at Vincennes. His heir, Henry VI, is only nine months old.

Constantinople, 6 September 1422. Sultan Murat II ends a vain siege of Constantinople.

France, 30 October 1422. On the death of Charles VI, the dauphin assumes the title king of France, although he controls only Touraine, the Orleanais, Berry, Auvergne and Dauphine.

China, 1424. The Emperor Yongle, who usurped the throne in 1402, dies. His reign is seen as a "second founding" of the Ming dynasty.

Constantinople, 21 July 1425. The Emperor Manuel II dies and is succeeded by his son John VIII Palaeologus. Manuel had ruled only Constantinople itself, while his brothers ruled other fragments of the former Byzantine empire.

Ethiopia, 1427. The Emperor Yeshaq sends envoys to Aragon in Spain to forge an alliance against Islam.

Rheims, 18 July 1429. Charles VII is crowned king of France.

Paris, 26 August 1429. Joan of Arc makes a triumphant entry into Paris.

Greece, 29 March 1430. Sultan Murat II captures the Thessalonica, held by Venice since 1423.

France, 14 July 1430. Joan of Arc, taken prisoner by the Burgundians in May, is handed over to Pierre Cauchon, the bishop of Beauvais.

Bruges, 10 January 1431. Philip the Good, the duke of Burgundy, establishes the Order of the Golden Fleece.

France, 30 May 1431. Joan of Arc is condemned and executed at Rouen.

Central Europe, 1431. The Hussites (followers of Jan Hus) win a series of victories in Bohemia against German armies sent to oppose them. The church council at Basle, which opened in July, resolves to negotiate with them.

Paris, 16 December 1431. Henry VI of England is crowned king of France at Notre Dame by the bishop of Winchester, Henry Beaufort.

Basle, December 1431. Eugenius IV, who succeeded Martin V as pope earlier in the year, declares the Council of Basle dissolved, but the council refuses to obey.

Joan of Arc is victorious at Orleans

Orleans, France, 8 May 1429

In a full suit of armour, a young peasant girl knelt and prayed today as her victorious army celebrated the defeat of the besieging English. Many believe that France owes this critical victory to "voices" heard in her father's garden by the girl, Joan of Arc, since she was 13.

The retreating English army of 5,000, led by the earl of Salisbury, had sought to establish a foothold on the river Loire and open up Anjou to occupation. They had not reckoned with a revitalised, well-disciplined French army, spiritually transformed by Joan's voices.

The voices told Joan that it was the will of heaven that the English should be thrown out of France and that she, Joan, was in some way to be instrumental in their eviction. She must tell the Dauphin that he must be anointed with holy oil at Rheims – after which the English would not be able to stand against him. Four months ago Joan succeeded in reaching the Dauphin near Tours and convinced him of her devoutness and sincerity.

It was indeed a very different army that Joan rode with to Orleans. Whether they viewed the slight young 17-year-old as a mascot, a saint or an inspired leader cannot be said. But this was an elated, ecstatic, crusading army that foreswore swearing and harlots and attended Mass at which they vowed to follow Joan's "voices".

Joan, by a 19th-century artist.

Henry V, English soldier of genius, dies

King Henry V (1387-1422), from a painting in Chichester cathedral.

France, 31 August 1422

Henry V of England has died at the very moment when the crown of France was within his grasp and he was about to realise his ambition to rule over both kingdoms. He is best remembered for his stunning victory at Agincourt, but his reconquest of Normandy was achieved by less spectacular means – the besieging and capturing of castles and walled towns. Last year he married Catherine, the daughter of the imbecile Charles VI of France. He was to have acted as regent and to have succeeded to the throne on Charles' death. Henry's piecemeal conquest of France continued until May this year, when he fell ill. He struggled on for three months until he was too weak to ride his horse. He was 35 and had ruled England for nine years. His son is aged just nine months; this is causing widespread fears of a collapse of English power in France.

Aztecs forge triple alliance in Mexico

Central America, 1428

The Tepanec empire in the Valley of Mexico has been overthrown by a triple alliance of the Aztec island-city of Tenochtitlan, the exiled army of Nezahualcoyotl, the leader of Texcoco, and the disaffected Tepanec city of Tlacopan.

Tepanec tyranny ignited the revolt. The Emperor Maxtla was both cruel and short-sighted, with an unfailing gift for turning friends into enemies. He continued his father's policy of trying to subject Texcoco, his daily atrocities turning the population against him.

At about the same time Tlacopan, overburdened by taxation, revolted against the Tepanecs. Itzcoatl, the Aztec leader, whose militarist island-city has been asserting increasing independence from Tepanec suzerainty, seized the opportunity created by Tepanec weakness to bring the three enemies of the Tepanecs together.

For all three – particularly Tenochtitlan and Texcoco, who are former enemies – it is an alliance of convenience, combining the commercial prosperity of Tlacopan, the prestige of Texcoco and the military might of Tenochtitlan. Nor is there any doubt who has gained the most, and the Aztec state of Tenochtitlan now dominates the Valley of Mexico.

Joan is burnt at stake

Rouen, France, 30 May 1431
After a year of inquisition, torture and imprisonment, Joan of Arc was taken to the stake in the market square here today and burnt to death as a witch. Only two years ago this daughter of a peasant family was acclaimed as the heroine of Orleans. It was then that the French king took note of "voices" heard by Joan that could lead him to drive the English from France.

No one doubts that this was a political trial and execution, or that Charles VII's complacency was one of the main causes of Joan's ordeal. She had played a major role in the attempted recapture of Paris – in which she was wounded – and had fought in minor engagements before being taken prisoner by the Burgundians. They were allied to the English and sold her to the duke of Bedford for 10,000 gold crowns. An English escort took Joan to Rouen, and it was here that she faced the hostile questioning of Bishop Cauchon, a Burgundian, in a secret trial conducted according to the rites of the Inquisition.

Joan conducted her own defence and stressed her purity and her devotion to France, but to no avail. The bishops sentenced her to life imprisonment, but even then they had not finished with her. She resumed the wearing of men's clothing – possibly this was all that she was given. This was taken as evidence of her relapse and she was condemned to the stake. There she asked for a cross to be held before her to see through the flames. Her last word was "Jesus".

Joan the Martyr, from a miniature.

Ruler takes his cut on paradise island

The ruins of Kilwa's 13th-century great mosque; Islam was brought by Arabs.

Kilwa, 1430
The merchant visiting Kilwa who stops to admire its fine buildings, its beautifully dressed and bejewelled inhabitants, its magnificent 100-room stonewall palace or the great mosque being rebuilt with a vaulted dome soon discovers his role in the wealth-creation process that has made the island states of Kilwa the most prosperous in the Indian Ocean.

For whatever he trades, whether he buys or sells, he has to pay his duty to the sultan of Kilwa's treasury. On gold the sultan takes five per cent, on ivory the rate is 14 per cent – one tusk in seven.

It is not only Kilwa that has benefited from 200 years of gold trading. Along the Mozambique coast 37 towns have sprung up. Most of their trade, which Kilwa dominates, is with fellow Moslems from west India. Some is with Europe where there is also huge demand in court circles for spices and slaves. Chinese trade is increasing; Ming emperors have sent two expeditions and another is expected soon.

Tough new armour is developed for Europe's armies

French soldiery in armour.

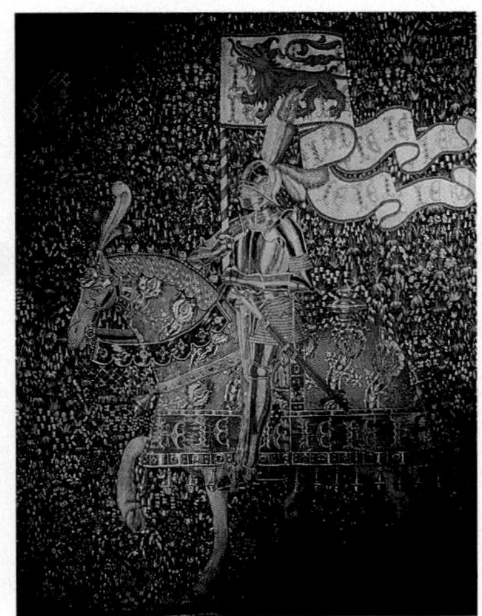

A knight in full military splendour.

Europe, c.1430
Complete suits of armour made of metal plate are now being worn on the battlefield with considerable success. They have been developed to overcome the weakness of chain-mail armour, which provides only limited protection: an arrow or a crossbow bolt can penetrate the openings in chain mail. The new *harnais blanc*, or white armour, as it is called, has been made possible by greater sophistication in metal manufacturing techniques.

Tougher iron and steel are being produced using a new carburising process and blast-furnaces. The white hot plates are then hardened by "quenching" in fluid. Improvements are also taking place in the workshops where the plate is fashioned, so that the armour offers greater resistance to missiles.

Of course, the use of full-plate body armour is not without some drawbacks. It is heavier and more tiring to wear. On the other hand, the incorporation of a lance rest at the side of the breastplate, now standard practice, has made heavy lances easier to handle. Cavalry can now lower their lances from the vertical to the horizontal and take accurate aim while charging at speed towards the enemy.

The Florentine artist Tommaso Masaccio died In 1428, aged 27. He revived Giotto's ideals of expressiveness in art, as in his "Virgin and Child", above.

1432 (1432-1438)

North Atlantic, 1432. The Portuguese discover an archipelago which they name the Azores.

West Africa, 1433. The Tuaregs, desert camel-riders from the north of the continent, capture the city of Timbuktu.

Rome, 31 May 1433. Sigismund is crowned emperor by Pope Eugenius IV, who hopes for his support against the council at Basle.

Switzerland, 30 November 1433. The readiness of the Council of Basle to open negotiations with the Hussites splits the movement between the moderate Utraquists and the radical Taborites.

Bohemia, May 1434. The Taborites are defeated at Lipany by the army of the Emperor Sigismund, with the support of both Catholics and Utraquists.

South-East Asia, 1434. The capital of the Khmer kingdom is moved from Angkor to Phnom Penh.

Florence, 1434. Cosimo de Medici, who was exiled by his enemy Rinaldo d'Albizzi in 1433, returns and seizes power in the city. Although strictly Cosimo remains a private citizen within an independent republic, in effect his power is complete.

France, 19 September 1435. The duke of Bedford, the English lieutenant in France, dies. He had been the one man capable of controlling the factions within the minority government of his nephew Henry VI and his death fuels impatience for the king himself to take power.

France, 21 September 1435. By the treaty of Arras, Philip the Good breaks with the English and recognises Charles VII as the only king of France.

Scandinavia, 1435. Eric of Scandinavia makes peace with the Hanse and restores their privileged position. The Hanse had been drawn into a war between Eric and the count of Holstein over possession of Schleswig.

Bohemia, 5 July 1436. The agreement made with the Hussites in 1433 is confirmed and Sigismund is recognised as king of Bohemia.

West Africa, 1436. The Portuguese, having passed the Saraha coast, begin to explore the Rio de Ouro (the Gold River).

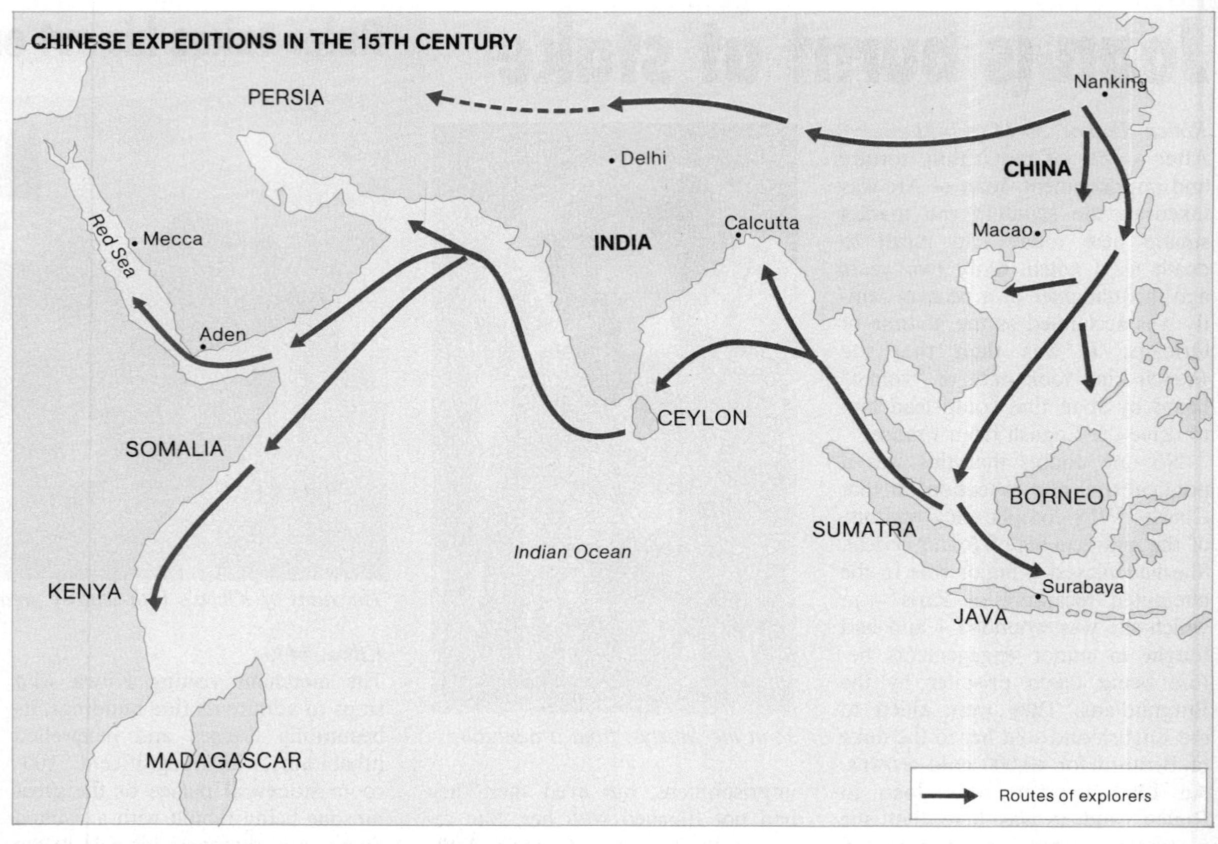

China bans voyages to the west, shuts out rest of world

China, 1433

Zheng He, the eunuch admiral, has returned safely with his fleet for the seventh time. But this will be the last of his voyages to the exotic lands of the west, for the emperor has forbidden him to sail again.

His voyages have always been opposed by the powerful Confucian bureaucrats at court who viewed them as adventures in trade rather than diplomacy and therefore, according to Confucian doctrine, both wasteful and frivolous. When Zheng He's patron, the Emperor Yongle, died, the civil servants persuaded his successor to stop the voyages, but when the latter too died, Zheng He was able to obtain the necessary permission to undertake one last expedition.

He set out with his huge treasure ships two years ago for Arabia and the east coast of Africa, exploring far to the south. He has returned with his ships filled with strange animals, scents and spices, and with much knowledge of the far lands. However, any hopes that he had of being allowed to continue his voyages have been dashed. He is to be honourably retired as military commander of Nanjing.

The civil servants have won such a complete victory that all records of his travels are being expunged and the plans of his ships are to be destroyed. China is shutting itself off from the world.

Empire that bans collections of luxury goods is set to expand

Cuzco, Peru, 1438

Pachacuti, the new ruler of the Incas, has pledged to extend the Incas' territory and build an empire. Already his capital, Cuzco, dominates the Andes. Its stone architecture, going back to 1200, is bleak, unadorned with decoration. The nearest there is to art is the pleating on the thatched roofs. Above the thatches rise the limestone ramparts of the fortress of Saccsailhuaman, a symbol of Inca might.

Pachacuti's Inca administration is well-organised and perfectly capable of expanding into an imperial bureaucracy with power deriving from the emperor, a descendent of Manco Capac, the legendary founder of the dynasty. He is the divine representative of the sun on earth. An hereditary aristocracy takes policy decisions, and local subject aristocracies ("Incas by privilege") carry them out.

Strict rules prohibiting the accumulation of luxury goods discourage both selfishness and crime. The population provides labour in lieu of taxes, with the sick and the old being cared for by the state.

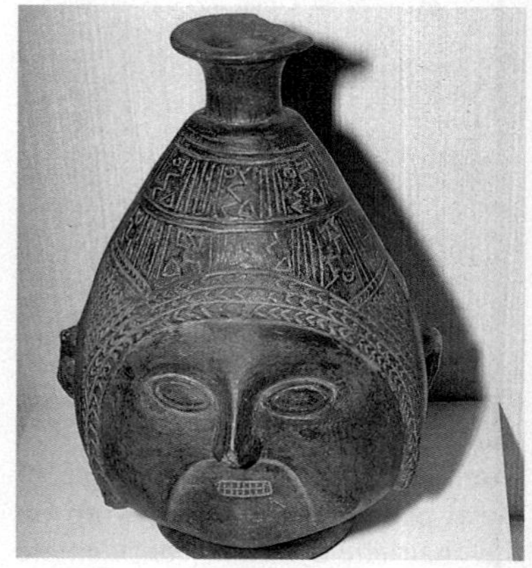

An Inca pot in the form of a head.

Portuguese find new way to the east

Portugal, 1434

One of Henry the Navigator's captains has at last rounded the feared Cape Bojador, on the coast of West Africa, thus fulfilling one of Henry's most fervent ambitions.

The great sailor sent ship after ship out from his palace-observatory at Sagres to sail beyond the sandy bulge of the cape. Not one of them succeeded, and Henry listened patiently to his captains' tales of the dangers of that awful place. But the dangers were in their minds.

They were terrified of the legends of the Sea of Darkness which lay beyond the cape. It was a place where white men turned black and the currents would prevent any ship from returning.

Henry sent Eannes, one of his squires, out to this awesome place last year, but he, like the others, failed to conquer his fears and got no further than the Canaries.

Henry summoned him again this year and, chiding him gently about his fears, sent him out once more. This time the shamefaced Eannes rounded the cape. He found no indication of human habitation there, bringing back only some plants called St Mary's roses.

The importance of his voyage, however, is that he has disproved the belief that ships could not sail the seas beyond Cape Bojador. The way south is now open.

Henry has reacted promptly to Eannes' news. He has sent him to sea again along with another ship commanded by Afonso Baldaya, his cupbearer, with orders to explore beyond the cape.

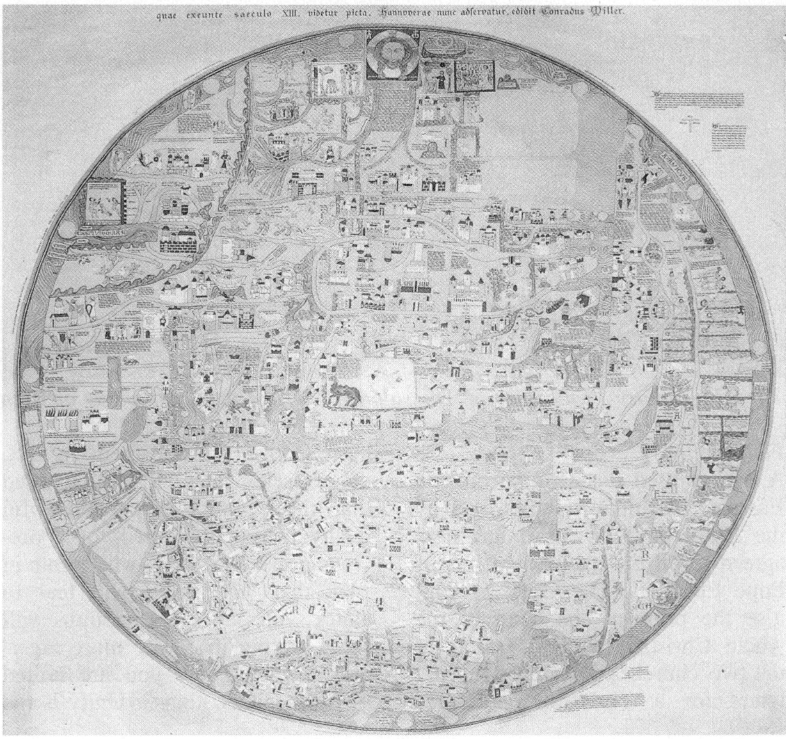

The world according to the 13th-century "Ebsdorf Map"; east is at the top.

Bruges prospers as leading commercial crossroads in Europe

Bruges, Flanders, c.1435

Bruges, the richest commercial staging-post in Europe, has become a world city, prosperous not only in commerce but in the arts, in a new international culture and lifestyle. This is exemplified in the sumptuous court of Philip the Good, the duke of Burgundy.

Developed in the 13th century because of its geographical position between England, France, Italy and the Rhine states, Bruges gave its merchants the chance to become landowners and members of the nobility.

English wool was delivered here so regularly that London ceased to be important to traders in the Hanseatic League. They brought timber, wheat, smoked fish, metals and furs from Germany, Russia and Sweden while spices and oriental products were brought by the Italians, either by sea or up the Rhine. Bruges could export tapestries, cloth and material from Flanders, Brabant and Hainault.

Van Eyck's "Arnolfini Wedding".

In 1336 the Hanseatic League built a factory here, since when international commerce and banking have expanded enormously. The Flanders Council gave foreign merchants significant privileges: import tolls were reduced, accounting methods simplified, and bills of exchange introduced. The Teutonic Knights opened a bank, and papal tithes from all over Europe were banked here.

In 1369 Louis de Male married his daughter to Philip the Bold, the duke of Burgundy, the brother of Charles V of France. The dukes of Burgundy worked to establish Flanders' independence from France, but came into increasing conflict with the English, who were expelled in 1383. Intermittent warfare caused hardship among the native population, who had no share in the trade bonanza.

Today, Philip the Good is the patron of all woodcarvers, metalworkers and artists like Jan van Eyck.

Moslem conqueror of Cyprus is dead

Cairo, 1438

Barsbay al-Zahiri, one of the greatest Mameluke *sultans,* is dead. His 16-year reign has not merely kept a fragile empire intact, but has seen the conquest of Cyprus and considerable commercial success.

When he came to the throne, Frankish corsairs were making damaging attacks on Moslem shipping. Barsbay took reprisals against Frankish traders in Syria, Alexandria and Damietta. But it was the pirates operating out of Cyprus who were causing the damage.

In three expeditions between 1424 and 1426, Barsbay prepared the way for two conclusive battles, one on land, one at sea, which brought Cyprus under effective Mameluke control. King Janus was captured, obliged to pay public homage to the sultan, and reinstated as a vassal ruler.

In the Arabian lands beside the Red Sea, Barsbay ensured that Mameluke influence was not undermined. When Shah Rukh of the Yemen tried to send a *kiswa*, a ceremonial cloth, to Mecca, Barsbay told him that its sacred purpose was the sole prerogative of the sultans of Egypt. He acted with even greater firmness in a dispute over customs dues on ships trading with Jeddah and Mecca. Barsbay's forces occupied both cities and imposed the sultan's own duties. He enforced a royal monopoly to bypass the profiteering Karimi merchants.

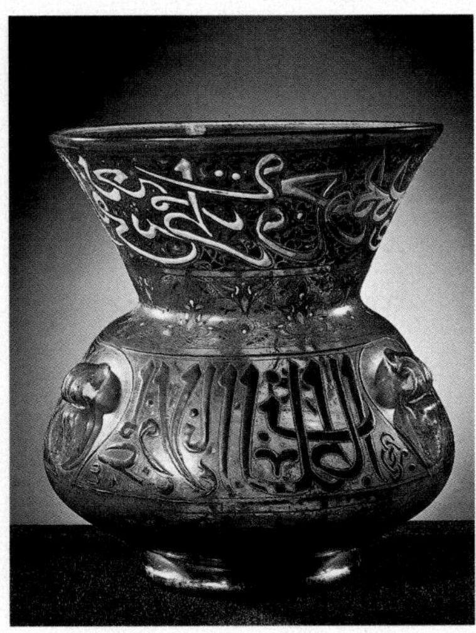

An enamelled glass mosque lamp of the kind used in the 14th century by the Islamic conquerors of Cyprus.

1438 (1438-1440)

Italy, April 1438. Taking advantage of a split in the Council of Basle over the best place to meet a Greek delegation seeking the reunion of the churches, Pope Eugenius invites the Greeks to Ferrara. A minority of the council joins them there, while the majority remains at Basle and declares the pope suspended.

France, 7 July 1438. Charles VII promulgates the Pragmatic Sanction, which limits papal authority over French bishops and gives the king a say in the appointment of prelates.

Scandinavia, 1438. Peasant rebellions and nationalist tensions prompt King Eric to flee from Denmark. He takes refuge on the Swedish island of Gotland, where he turns pirate in order to prey on Baltic shipping.

Italy, 16 January 1439. The church council is transferred from Ferrara to Florence.

Basle, 5 November 1439. The delegates who refused to follow the council to Italy declare Eugenius deposed and elect their own pope. He is a layman, Duke Amadeus VIII of Savoy. Famous for his wisdom and wealth, he adopts the name Felix V.

Germany, 2 February 1440. Frederick III, the senior living Habsburg, is elected emperor. He was chosen on the grounds that he was unlikely to infringe the autonomy of the princes.

Southern Africa, c.1440. The north-east Zimbabwe plateau and trade routes from gold mines to the Sofala coast through the Zambezi valley are now in the control of a great conquerer given the "praise name" of Munhumutapa.

Mexico, 1440. Montezuma becomes ruler of the Aztecs and begins the conquest of tribes outside the valley of Mexico. A triple alliance formed in 1428 between the cities of Tenochtitlan, Texcoco and Tlacopan has led to the final overthrow of Tepanec power in the valley of Mexico. The Aztecs have gradually taken over the area of Tepanec domination.

Italy, 1440. Lorenzo Valla, who has made a scientific study of the Latin language, proves that the Donation of Constantine – made to Pope Sylvester by the Emperor Constantine in 326, and used to justify the pope's authority over the secular rulers of the west – is spurious.

Greek and Roman Churches reach formal agreement to unite

The 13th-century "Epitaphios of Thessaloniki", one of the great works of Byzantine religious textile art.

Florence, 1439

A demoralised delegation from the Eastern (Byzantine) Church, led by the Emperor John VIII, has now agreed to all the major demands of Pope Eugenius. The Greeks recognise the pope as the head of the whole Christian church. Union of the two churches, split on doctrinal issues for a thousand years, has been solemnly proclaimed. In fact, the Greeks have finally realised that they cannot deny the awful reality behind the words of a previous pope, Martin V, who wrote in 1422 that "the Turks will fear to attack you ... and Christians will come to your help with more eagerness if they know you are united with other Christians". Unity is the Greeks' last hope of saving themselves from the Turks. The Greeks have capitulated to the Roman view of the Trinity. Their one real concession is over the marriage of priests which is not mentioned in the agreement. There is no doubt here where the power lies, but whether Greek priests will conform is a more open question.

Matchmaker Warwick, "the father of chivalry", dies in France

France, 31 May 1439

Richard Beauchamp, the earl of Warwick, known as "the father of chivalry", and England's most powerful nobleman, has died at Rouen, where he was resident as lieutenant of France and Normandy. Born in 1381, Beauchamp became the fifth earl of Warwick in 1401. After fighting at the Battle of Shrewsbury, in 1403, he set out in 1408 for the Holy Land and spent six years touring the courts of Europe. On his return he was made captain of Calais by the new king, Henry V, and there organised a *pas d'armes* (a series of formal personal combats, a surrogate for actual war).

The king then sent him as ambassador to the general council at Constance where he met the pope and the emperor and was offered by the latter the heart of St George. Warwick declined and the emperor himself brought the heart to England in 1416. Warwick also helped to arrange Henry's marriage to Catherine, the daughter of the king of France. In 1429 Warwick became guardian of their son, Henry VI, then aged seven – a tribute to his chivalric pre-eminence.

He also accompanied Henry to France for his coronation, and was the English commander at Rouen during the trial of Joan of Arc when a widespread French uprising seemed imminent.

Despot scars his people's faces as slaves

Benin, Nigeria, 1439

Ewuare has taken over the kingdom of Benin, killing the previous incumbent, his own brother, and becoming *oba*. There was heavy fighting, many have been killed, and the capital, Urbini, has been taken by storm.

The coup brings Benin not only a new ruler but a new kind of government. The old constitution, with the power of the ruler limited by the *ozama*, or hereditary chiefs, has been abolished, and Ewuare has ordered all free-born citizens to be scared with facial markings as "slaves of the oba". There is no doubt that Ewuare is making a bid for absolute power.

Already Ewuare has shown himself to be the most energetic ruler the 300-year-old state has known. To offset the power of the ozama, he has established a new order of "town" chiefs directly responsible to him. He has announced that he will be rebuilding the capital, and has already given it a new name, Edo. Finally, he is expanding the army that brought him to power, talking of new conquests beyond Benin's borders.

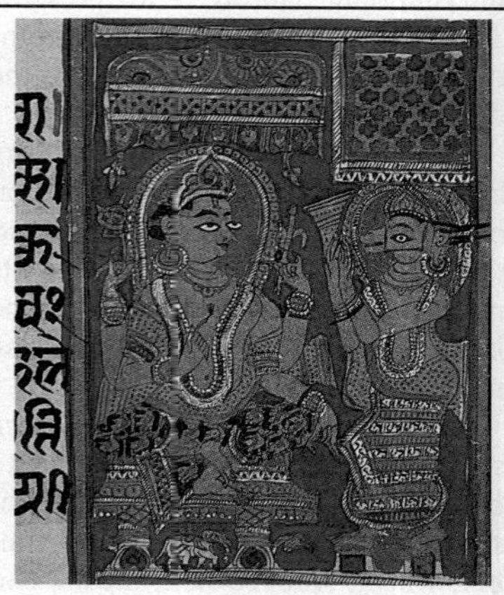

The myth of the birth of Mahavira, founder of Indian Jainism, as seen in Jain scriptures.

Rise of Italian city-states heralds art renaissance

Florence, c. 1440-1450
The cities of northern Italy are in competition not only for wealth and power, but also in an artistic revival in which their richest families vie with one another as patrons of art and learning.

Foremost of them is Florence, whose patron is the banker Cosimo de Medici, the *Pater Patriae* (Father of the Republic). The Florentines at last consecrated their cathedral, Santa Maria dei Fiore, in 1436, on completing the self-supporting octagonal dome designed by Filippo Brunelleschi. The bronze doors of the Baptistry alongside are the life's work of his friend, Lorenzo Ghiberti. The first, with scenes from the New Testament on its bronze panels, was finished in 1424, but the second, Old Testament, door is only just nearing completion, with as many as 100 figures to a panel. Ghiberti is using Brunelleschi's discoveries to give them perspective.

Paolo Uccello is applying the laws of perspective to painting. He has decorated the church of Santa Maria Novella and is now working on a big battlepiece for the Palazzo Medici showing the cavalry charge at San Romano where Florence defeated Siena in 1432. Meanwhile the decorations of the convent of St Mark by its Dominican prior, Fra Angelico, include a remarkable *Annunciation*.

The sculptor Donatello decorated the cathedral facade and campanile with statues and is in great demand in many cities for his bronzes, such as the *David* he cast for the Medicis – the first life-size, naked statue since Roman times. For Padua he did a massive statue of Gattemelata, the soldier of fortune, and the *Miracles of St Anthony* to adorn the high altar.

Arezzo is employing Piero della Francesca on a sequence of frescoes in the church of St Francis. He, too, used perspective in his *Baptism of Christ* beneath a tree set in a receding landscape. Siena is amazed by the precocity of Andrea Mantegna, who began painting a chapel for his master, Squarcione, at the age of 12, as if fully mature. In Venice the Grand Canal has seen the erection of the richest *palazzo* yet, the Ca' d'Oro, painted in gold.

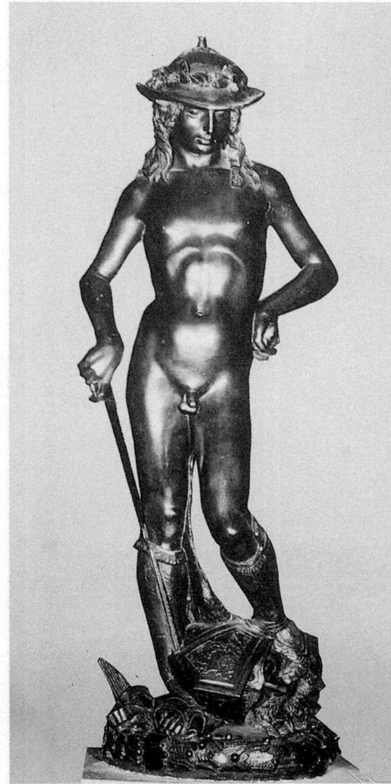

Donatello's bronze, life-size David.

Florence's magnificent cathedral.

The Ca' d'Oro in Venice.

Florence cathedral: ceiling mosaics in Brunelleschi's octagonal dome.

"The Birth" by Fra Angelico in the convent of St Mark in Florence.

1440 (1440-1450)

Portugal, 1441. For the first time, slaves and gold are directly imported from West Africa into Portugal.

Florence, 1441. The Ethiopian Church sends a representative to the Church council. An act of union is signed between the Church of Ethiopia and that of Rome.

Naples, 12 June 1442. Alfonso V of Aragon is crowned king of Naples after conquering the town.

Hungary, 1442. Janos Hunyadi – the general of Vladyslav, the king of Poland and elected ruler of Hungary – wins two victories over the Turks. First he routs Mezid Bey, who had invaded Transylvania; then he overcomes the army sent to avenge the bey's defeat.

Bulgaria, 1444. The Ottomans defeat the Hungarians at Varna on the shores of the Black Sea. This opens their way to Constantinople.

West Africa, 1444. Portuguese explorers reach the mouth of the Senegal and reach Cape Verde.

Poland, 1447. Casimir IV Jagiellonian becomes king of Poland, in succession to his brother Vladyslav III, the king of Poland and Hungary, who vanished in the defeat at Varna.

Milan, 1447. On the death of Filippo Maria Visconti, the last of the male line, a republic is proclaimed by the citizens, who hire Francesco Sforza as their general.

Germany, 1448. Leaving Strasbourg, where he has lived for the past few years, Johannes Gutenberg – who has recently invented moveable printing characters – returns to his native town of Mainz.

Serbia, 19 October 1448. The Hungarian general Janos Hunyadi, who has been the effective ruler of Hungary since the disappearance of Vladyslav at Varna, is defeated by the Ottoman Sultan Murat II at Kosovo.

Constantinople, 6 January 1449. Constantine XI succeeds his brother John VIII Palaeologus as emperor.

Lausanne, 25 April 1449. The rump of the Council of Basle (which was expelled from that city last year) recognises Nicholas V as pope and dissolves itself. Felix V, the pope elected by the council in 1439, abdicates.

"The Adoration of the Lamb", painted for the cathedral of St Bavo, Ghent, was the creation of two van Eycks – Jan and his elder brother, Hubert.

Jan van Eyck, the first oil painter, dies

Bruges, Flanders, 1441

Jan van Eyck, who has died here, took painting an enormous stride forward when he experimented with oil as the medium for his colours. Until then painters had mixed paint with water for frescoes or egg-yolk for tempera. Both Jan and his elder brother Hubert van Eyck painted with oil on wooden panels, which were prepared with plaster and glue. This gave a glowing effect not achieved before.

Their greatest joint work is the altarpiece for the cathedral of Ghent, *The Adoration of the Lamb*, consisting of a landscape and 16 portrait panels, covering over 1,000 square feet, the first oil painting on such a scale. Jan completed the work after Hubert's death in 1426, and settled at Bruges where he developed the new art of secular portrait painting. No-one had seen such realism before – all the wrinkles and warts are rendered so faithfully that the sitters, such as the *Man with Carnations*, seem about to speak.

Jan van Eyck also took delight in his ability to render domestic interiors in gleaming detail. His double portrait *The Arnolfini Marriage* shows the couple in their best robes holding hands. The lady's little terrier stands at her feet and there are oranges scattered by the windowsill. The scene is reflected in miniature in a convex mirror behind the couple, which also shows the painter, who signs himself "Jan van Eyck was here".

Science mourns stargazer khan

Samarkand, Central Asia, 1449

Ulugh Beg, the astronomer khan, is dead, executed on a trumped-up legal charge at the instigation of his own son, Abd al-Latif. Ulugh Beg ruled for only two years after the death of his father, Shah Rukh.

A scientist rather than a warrior, Ulugh Beg faced political chaos on his father's death and had to fight for his inheritance, succeeding in maintaining control of only a part of the empire left by his cruel grandfather, Tamerlane the conqueror.

His reign has now been brought to a swift and shameful end. Abd al-Latif revolted against him, defeated him and has killed him. Abd al-Aziz, the khan's favourite son, has also been put to death.

To murder one's father and brother is regarded as excessive even by Mongol standards, and it is suggested that Abd al-Latif is also not long for this world.

Ulugh Beg was happiest working in his observatory just outside the city of Samarkand where Tamerlane lies in his black onyx tomb. He built a telescope sunk into the hillside to study the stars, and with four other scholars produced a volume of astronomical tables.

These tables, the first since those of Ptolemy, are remarkably accurate. Ulugh Beg was also a patron of architecture and built the beautiful teaching colleges at Samarkand and Bokhara. His death is a great loss to science and the arts.

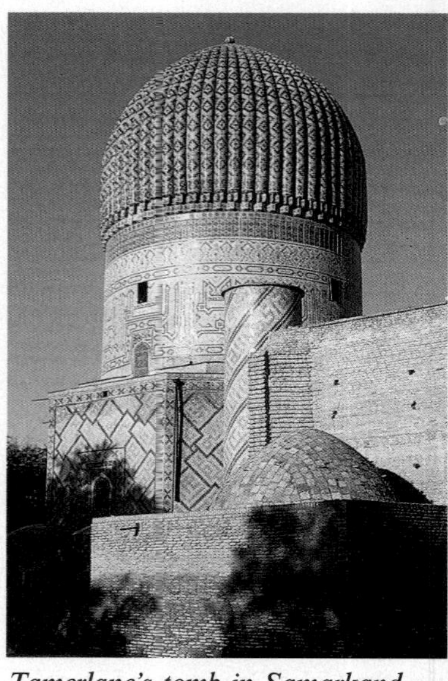

Tamerlane's tomb in Samarkand.

Mongols' victory threatens Beijing

China, 1449

A powerful Chinese army, led by the young emperor, Yingzong, has been ambushed by the Mongol chieftain, Esen. Thousands of men have been killed and the emperor has been captured. It is reported that the Mongols found him seated on a carpet surrounded by the bodies of his slaughtered bodyguard. Now Beijing itself is in danger.

This was a wholly unnecessary affair mounted by the overweening eunuch Wang Jin who, against the advice of court officials, persuaded the emperor to lead the army against the raiding Mongols.

The expedition was a shambles from the start. Wang Jin had no military experience and, brushing aside the protests of officers with long experience of frontier war, he exposed the army to attack in a position where it had neither food nor water.

The disaster is complete. Wang Jin is dead and so are most of the experienced generals. The emperor is held hostage and the road to the capital is open.

Ambassador visits splendid Indian city

Southern India, 1443

The seasoned traveller and Afghan ambassador Abdur Razzaq has had the enviable experience of visiting one of India's greatest cities, Vijayanagar, the capital of the great Hindu empire in the south.

Razzaq was summoned to Vijayanagar by the king while on a mission to Calicut. He was to see a city that was founded over a hundred years ago, in 1336. It lies on the south bank of the Tungabhadra river and is famous across the continent for the grandeur of its buildings, its bazaars teaming with luxurious imported goods and the sheer number of its citizens, enjoying the prosperity.

Early this century, Bukka II, then ruler, embarked on an extensive programme of improvement and expansion. His most remarkable addition to Vijayanagar was a vast dam in the Tungabhadra. Water from the reservoir thus created was brought to the city by acqueduct, over a distance of 15 miles (24km). Razzaq could not but be impressed on this visit.

Albania breaks free from Turks

Kruje, Albania, 28 November 1443

A 38 year-old Albanian noble, taken hostage by the Turks and educated as a Moslem, has led his people in a revolt against their occupiers. George Kastrioti or Skanderbeg (a title he earned at the Turkish court), governor of Albania since 1438, has today proclaimed the restoration of the free principality of Albania.

The son of an Albanian prince, Gjon Kastrioti, Skanderbeg was held as a hostage by the Turks to ensure that his fellow-Albanians would not revolt. A successful career in the Turkish civil service was capped by his appointment as governor of Albania.

Now, it seems, the Turkish plan has backfired. Taking advantage of the Turks' preoccupation with their hostile Hungarian neighbours, Skanderbeg has declared Albania independent, announced himself a Christian, and challenged the occupier to suppress his people. The two-headed eagle of the Kastrioti is flying over the citadel of Kruje and Skanderbeg is a national hero.

State scholars join sons of the nobility at king's Eton College

Eton, 1440

A new school is to be founded at Eton, Buckinghamshire. Eton College is the brainchild of King Henry VI. As well as housing clerks to pray for the king, 25 poor scholars are to be taught grammar there. The school master is also required to teach other applicants on demand.

Education is a fashionable area of concern. Henry's initiative was prompted by William of Wykeham's foundation of Winchester school. Attention is also focussing on the importance of good teachers. Clergymen who set themselves up as schoolmasters may well perform quite adequately, but in the end they lack the real teaching qualifications.

This problem, especially in the important area of the teaching of Latin grammar, was noted last year in a report by William Bingham, who sent in to the King a petition detailing the extent of the problem. He noted that some 70 schools had been forced to close down because of the scarcity of masters, and stressed that without good teachers, the church would be weakened, since no new clergymen would be taught.

He has called for the establishment of a special college, not for the young, but for the training of the teachers who will be sent out to educate them.

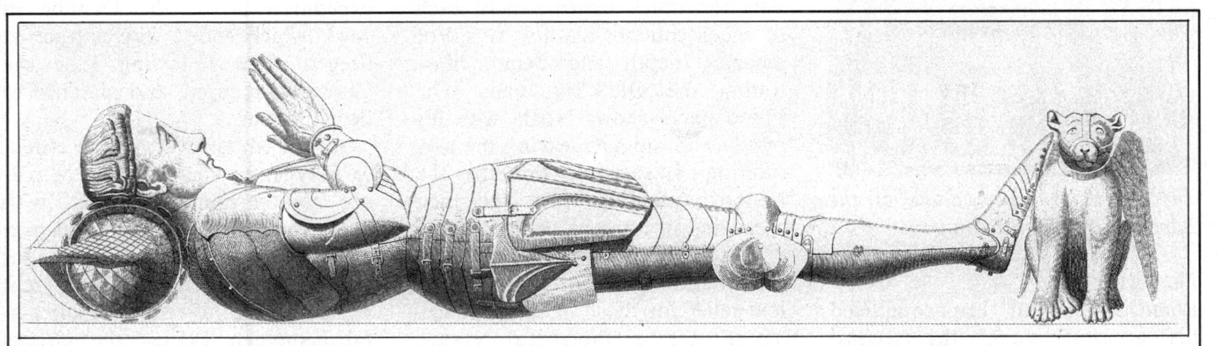

The tomb effigy of Richard Beauchamp, the earl of Warwick, soldier and statesman, who died in 1439.

Black magician and child killer burnt

Gilles de Laval, the seigneur de Rais.

France, 26 October 1440

One of France's most respected and beloved knights was executed today at Nantes. Condemned for the murders of at least 200 children, and for heresy, sodomy, apostasy, sacrilege and violation of clerical immunity, Gilles de Laval, the seigneur de Rais, was garrotted and burnt with his two accomplices.

A man of supposedly unassailable piety, a former commander of Joan of Arc's troops, a marshal of France who boasted a 200-strong retinue, a friend to beggars and patron of the arts, de Rais appeared to embody the chivalric ideal.

But, apparently, behind the goodness lay an inner man as depraved as his external image was pure: a satanist who experimented in alchemy and black magic, and who claimed to model himself on Caligula, the most perverse and cruel of Rome's emperors.

De Rais is alleged to have killed at least 200 children. Some were abducted, and some were sold – often for a dress or a loaf of bread – by impoverished parents. Once entrapped, they were sodomised, then slowly tortured to death. De Rais' real pleasure was watching his victims' slow death agonies.

Throughout his trial de Rais professed devout Christianity. He confessed, and claimed to see his execution as God's fitting punishment.

1450 (1450-1455)

Milan, February 1450. Francesco Sforza, hired as military leader by the republic of Milan, stages a coup and takes the title "Duke of Milan".

South-East Africa, 1450. Mutota, conqueror of the northern Zimbabwe plateau, is succeeded by his son Matope who also takes his father's title of Munhumutupa.

Normandy, 15 April 1450. With a victory over the English at Formigny, the French complete their reconquest of Normandy.

Scandinavia, August 1450. Norway accepts an act of union by which Denmark and Norway will always have the same king. Sweden, meanwhile, is in a state of civil war.

England, 1450. Resentment at Henry VI's incompetent government erupts into open rebellion. Several of the king's advisers are murdered.

Asia Minor (Anatolia), 2 February 1451. Mohammed II succeeds Murad II as sultan of the Ottomans.

Austria, 6 January 1453. Frederick III, crowned Holy Roman emperor last year, confirms privileges granted to Austria in 1359 and raises it to the rank of archduchy.

Constantinople, 29 May 1453. The Ottoman Turks seize the city. The Byzantine empire is at an end.

France, 17 July 1453. France defeats England at Castillon, ending the 100 Years' War.

Burgundy, 17 February 1454. At a grand feast, Philip the Good of Burgundy takes the "vow of the pheasant", by which he swears to fight the Turks.

England, March 1454. The duke of York is appointed protector when Henry VI suffers a mental collapse.

Venice, 18 April 1454. The doge Francesco Foscari signs a treaty with the Ottoman Sultan Mohammed II on terms generous to Venice.

Spain, 21 July 1454. John II, the king of Castile, and Leon, who fought against the Aragonese and the Moors, is succeeded by his son Henry.

Rome, 18 February 1455. The painter Fra Angelico dies.

Rome, 24 March 1455. Pope Calixtus III succeeds Nicholas V, who sent the cardinal Nicholas of Cues on a successful mission to lead reform in Germany.

Zimbabwe is strangled by its own wealth

Part of the massive, abandoned structures of the city of Great Zimbabwe.

Zimbabwe, c.1450

Great Zimbabwe, the African kingdom set in the gold and copper-bearing country between the Zambezi and Limpopo rivers, is slowly dying. In the capital, also called Great Zimbabwe, the streets are deserted and the population dispersed.

For more than 200 years the Zimbabwe state has been growing, its growth reflected in the expansion of its capital city. The city began as a hill fortress built with rough stone walls. It then spread into the valley beneath. The rich lived in homes with elaborate winding walls of stone and clay; outside their gates the poor were huddled in flimsier dwellings made from wattle and daub.

The state expanded; so did the city. The more that Zimbabwe controlled, the richer it became; its subject peoples paying tribute in gold, copper and iron. The very wealth Zimbabwe accumulated is causing her downfall.

The city has attracted so many courtiers, politicians and craftsmen that the surrounding lands are unable to feed them. Thus the city is dying, and with it inevitably the state will die.

Bronze doors are complete after 50 years

The magnificent new doors of the Baptistry by Lorenzo Ghiberti.

Florence, 1452

Lorenzo Ghiberti has completed his greatest work, the second bronze door of the Baptistry of the cathedral of Santa Maria del Fiore, nearly 50 years after he began work on the first door as a young man. Now, at 74, he has surpassed all his previous achievements.

The second door is more ambitious than the first, which depicted the New Testament. This one has only ten much larger panels, each of which contains a whole world of amazing depth and detail, illustrating the Old Testament. The Flood panel shows Noah, with his family and animals leaving the ark, offering a sacrifice beneath the rainbow, planting vines and then sprawling in drunken abandon.

The compositions recede from foreground figures in half-relief to low relief for those in the distance. There are architectural views, mountains, trees and above all people, all in astonishing realism.

Peace-loving ruler preferred poetry

Adrianople, Turkey, 1451

Sultan Murad II has died of apoplexy after a 30-year reign. Under him, the military might of the Ottoman empire has been transformed into an enlightened and civilising force. He is succeeded by his more volatile son, Mohammed II.

Murad, lover of peace, was constantly obliged to make war. He swiftly defeated a pretender to the sultanate in Constantinople and briefly besieged the city, before returning to defeat, then hang, his rebellious younger brother Mustafa, in Anatolia. Mustafa's Karamanian allies were granted vassal status. A treaty was also made with the new emperor, John VIII. In 1430 the city of Salonika, over which Greeks and Turks had been battling for years, was sold by the emperor to the Venetians. Murad won it back, prevented a massacre, and granted the Venetians trading rights throughout his empire.

A 1687 portrait of Murat II.

The Christians of northern Europe, led by Ladislas III of Poland, and inspired by the Hungarian warrior leader Hunyadi, made a daring expedition across the Danube in 1443, which ended with a truce at Szeged. The following year the Christians reneged, and marched to defeat at Varna.

At last Murad was able to retreat to Magnesia, where he built a palace and surrounded himself with poets, mystics, theologians and men of letters, while his son ruled. But two years later Grand Vizier Halil persuaded him to return. A successful campaign against the Greeks was followed in 1448 by defeat of the Hungarians at Kosovo.

Constantinople falls to the Ottomans

Constantinople, last remnant of the Roman empire, falls to the Turks.

Mohammed II, by an Italian artist.

Constantinople, 29 May 1453
Constantinople, the capital of the once-great Byzantine empire, has fallen to the Ottoman invaders. After brave but doomed resistance, the garrison has been overwhelmed, and the head of the Emperor Constantine XI is displayed on the column of the Augusteum.

It is the end of an era. With its soldiers' armaments outdated, its former allies deserting, Constantinople has been in decline for some time. Exploited by the Venetians and Genoese, betrayed by Slav and Byzantine princes, the city was friendless and hopelessly outnumbered by the armies of Sultan Mohammed II.

The siege of Constantinople was the realisation of a long-held ambition. The Ottoman army spent February and March manoeuvring its heavy artillery into position, while several towns on the Sea of Marmara and the Black Sea were overrun. On April 6, the siege began in earnest, the sultan's great cannon directed at the Gate of St Romanus, where the emperor and his Genoese soldiers had mustered.

Initial resistance was strong. A surprise attack was repulsed, and walls damaged by cannon fire were rebuilt. At sea the Turkish fleet suffered a reverse on April 20 when four relief ships battled through to the harbour. Then the sultan decided to transport 72 ships overland from the Bosporus to the Golden Horn, penetrating the harbour defences. A group of captured Venetians were executed in view of the city, so the Greeks did the same with their Ottoman prisoners. The sultan's cannon kept up the bombardment, and the besiegers dug in under the city walls.

Early this morning, the storming of the city began. There was fierce fighting until the Byzantine commander, Giovanni Giustiniani-Longo, left the field to tend his wounds. The emperor was killed in the thick of battle. Then the looting began. People huddled in the church were dragged off to slavery, killed, or assaulted on the altar.

But the sultan curbed some excesses. When the imprisoned Lucas Notaras, grand duke and admiral, was brought before him, Mohammed promised to put him at the head of the city's administration, with the state and court officials.

Defeat ends English rule in France

Charles II of France: the victor.

France, 17 July 1453
The French army of Charles VII defeated the English army at Castillon near Bordeaux today, bringing nearly 100 years of hostilities to a conclusion. Four years ago, Henry VI's armies occupied nearly a third of France; today, as French troops round up English survivors from the battle of Castillon, only Calais remains in English hands. It was the death of the English commander, John Talbot, the earl of Shrewsbury, that made a French victory certain.

Talbot, a general much respected by both sides, had led an expeditionary force which had been welcomed into Bordeaux by its inhabitants, a welcome that began to cool when it became known that three French armies were approaching.

Bordeaux and the walled city of Castillon were threatened with siege; and it was a reluctant Talbot – he had planned to take on all three armies in one battle – who went to Castillon's aid.

Talbot had reckoned with neither the firepower of the 600 cannon that the French brought with them nor the skill of his opponent, Jean Bureau, who succeeded in drawing his enemy between his artillery and the Dordogne river. It was a French cannon ball that killed Talbot's horse, pinning the aged general beneath it. The battle was lost.

Battling Italian city states make peace

Italy, 9 April 1454
As the Habsburg empire continues to grow in strength and France emerges as one of the major European powers, Italy remains fragmented by fierce rivalries between its numerous city states. For the past half century, wars have been frequent and destructive; but now, under a treaty negotiated by Pope Nicholas V and signed at Lodi, peace reigns.

Three bitter rivals – Venice, Milan and Florence – are the signatories, with Rome and Naples likely to join the peace. This newly formed "Italian League" has agreed to recognise and maintain the position of the major states as they exist at the moment. The members have also agreed to protect each other against outside aggression.

Significantly, the League has recognised that there are common interests between its members and that "Italy" is a geographical entity – albeit divided by trade rivalry, countless dialects, the lack of a generally-accepted written Italian language (most business is still conducted in Latin) and the fierce loyalty to city rather than a non-existent Italian state. Trade rivalry is likely to be the most formidable barrier to further agreement.

Blinded prince wins Russian civil war

Novgorod, Russia, 1453
A long-running civil war between Vasily II, the grand prince of Moscow, and his cousin, the "Pretender" Dmitry Shemyaka, has concluded in Shemyaka's death after being exiled and poisoned.

Vasily and Shemyaka had been locked in rivalry for some 20 years. After Vasily was captured by Khan Ulag-Mahmed, the Mongol leader, but freed on payment of a huge ransom, Dmitry began plotting in earnest. Vasily was arrested and blinded, but again freed. This was Dmitry's biggest mistake because his cousin raised an army and one year and one day after being blinded he returned to Moscow in triumph. He is now planning to expand Muscovite territory.

1455 (1455-1468)

England, 22 May 1455. The duke of York, dismissed as protector when Henry VI recovered his senses at the end of last year, defeats the king's forces at St Albans and seizes power in his name.

Hungary, 11 August 1456. John Hunyadi, regent of Hungary since 1446, dies.

Scandinavia, 1457. Christian, already king of Denmark and Norway, becomes king of Sweden.

Hungary, 24 January 1458. Matthias Corvinus, son of John Hunyadi, is elected king.

Bohemia, 2 March 1458. George Podebrad, regent since 1452, is elected king.

Greece, 1458. The Turks occupy Athens.

Naples, 1458. Alfonso V, king of Aragon and Naples, dies, leaving Naples to his bastard son Ferrante. His hereditary kingdoms pass to his brother John II of Navarre.

England, December 1460. The Yorkists are defeated at Wakefield. Richard, the duke of York, is killed in the battle.

Anatolia, 1461. Mohammed II annexes Trebizond, the last fragment of the Byzantine empire.

England, 1461. Edward, the son of Richard, the duke of York, is crowned Edward IV after defeating the Lancastrian forces at the battle of Towton.

Russia, 1462. Ivan III (the Great, succeeds Vasily II as prince of Muscovy.

Florence, 1 August 1464. Piero de Medici succeeds his father Cosimo as ruler of Florence.

Italy, 15 August 1464. Pius II, who became pope in 1458 on the death of Calixtus III, dies at Ancona while laying plans to rescue the Christian East. He is succeeded by Paul II.

France, 18 September 1465. Louis XI, king of France since 1461, signs an agreement with the league of the Public Weal, an anti-royalist alliance of the houses of Brittany, Bourbon, Armagnac and Burgundy.

Prussia, 19 October 1466. The peace of Torun ends a war between the Teutonic knights and their own disaffected subjects, who in 1440 formed the Prussian league, supported by Poland.

Burgundy, 15 June 1467. Philip the Good is succeeded as duke of Burgundy by Charles (the Bold).

Hungarians defeat Ottomans at Belgrade

Belgrade, 14 July 1456

The bloody battle of Belgrade, the Hungarian fortress on the Danube, has ended in a clearcut victory for John Hunyadi over a huge Ottoman army and navy. Sultan Mohammed's first large-scale campaign after the conquest of Constantinople has come badly unstuck after a retreat which degenerated into a rout.

The sultan's campaign was prepared largely in secret and he managed to muster some 150,000 men as well as a fleet of 60 ships to blockade the city. Hunyadi, who heads the Hungarian regency council, gathered an army of only some 60,000 men, mostly volunteers and peasants, and a much smaller fleet.

The Turks also had some 300 siege guns, including 27 giant cannon, and catapults and other weapons which were all entrusted to Italians and Germans. Huge boulders were also hurled at the fortress but were ineffective because of a successful warning system, using bells.

After Hunyadi's navy broke the blockade, his troops relieved the fortress and blunted a series of Turkish attacks. Finally, the siege guns were overrun.

Delicate Ming pottery is export success

Ivory Buddha on turquoise throne.

Elaborately glazed and painted jar.

China, c.1460

The imperial porcelain works at Ching Te Chen are turning out marvels of delicacy and skill for both the domestic market and export to distant lands.

The court takes a keen interest in the blue and white ware developed under Ming rule and paintings are sent from the palace for the potters to copy. Flowers, birds and insects are transferred to cups and vases with incredible delicacy.

Porcelain is only one aspect of Ming craftsmanship. Chinese workers are also carving objects of extraordinary beauty and delicacy, showing a marvellous sensitivity to the texture of ivory, jade, turquoise or other material.

Zara, Ethiopia's reforming emperor, dies

Ethiopia, 1468

Zara Yaqub, the greatest of the Solomonic emperors of Ethiopia, has died. In his reign of 34 years he centralised the imperial bureaucracy, reformed the church and, using his skills in war and peace, brought all the Ethiopian Highlands under his rule. Though Yaqub advocated religious toleration to all Moslems in his empire who posed no threat, Ethiopia under Yaqub became a bulwark against a resurgent Islam, defeating Moslem armies in the Horn of Africa and guaranteeing the freedom of Egypt's Copts. Ethiopian power has thus won the admiration of Christendom. The Pope sent an ambassador, ending centuries of isolation for the mythical kingdom of "Prester John".

Famine hits Aztecs in Central Mexico

Mexico, c.1455

After four years of drought in the Valley of Mexico, the Aztecs are suffering terrible privation. Thousands of people are dying of starvation, their unburied bodies falling prey to vultures and packs of wild boar.

So great is the famine that these once powerful people have been driven to desperate measures to survive. Some have retreated into the forests to try to scrape a living. Others have sold themselves into slavery to the Totonacs from the Gulf Coast area.

The Aztecs have traditionally been hunters, relatively unskilled in agriculture. But the famine has persuaded them to enlist the help of the Texcocans from across the lake in building an aqueduct and irrigation system.

Once-exiled sultan was tolerant ruler

Kashmir, 1467

Zian ul Abidin, the eighth sultan of Kashmir, has died. An exile in his youth from the paranoia of his elder brother, Ali Shah, the previous sultan, he had the unusual distinction of being the prisoner of Tamerlane and surviving.

In his exile Zian ul Abidin's courage, compassion and culture won him the support of Jasrat, the chief of the turbulent Khokar tribe. When Ali Shah tried to seize Zian ul Abidin the Khokar defeated Ali Shah, giving the throne of Kashmir to their young and unusual refugee.

Kashmir was a Moslem state with a Hindu majority. Zian ul Abidin promptly reversed Ali Shah's policy of persecuting Hindus, Brahmans and Buddhists. He founded universities, built bridges, distributed alms, and even restored Hindu temples. He was fluent in Arabic, Persian, Tibetan and Hindu, and the arts and sciences have flourished in his reign. Under Zian ul Abidin, Persian has become the official language of the court.

His subjects loved him, and his delight was to turn war technology into a peaceful art and give them firework displays.

Germans print the Bible

An illustration of Noah's Ark, from a Bible printed at Nuremberg in 1483.

Mainz, Germany, 1468

A German craftsman, writer and inventor, Johann Gutenberg, from Mainz, has died in obscurity. It was Gutenberg who devised a mechanical method of printing – based on the presses already in use for wine and paper-making – and using a revolutionary system of producing metal type-faces. His first publication, in 1455, was a Bible with 42 lines on each page printed in a typeface called "Gothic".

The use of a press for printing was not new – but making type had always involved laborious hours of carving letters from wood; and earlier versions of the Bible had always been handwritten. The new system allowed the printer to make type by pouring molten metal into punchstamped moulds, giving a limitless supply of letters. Gutenberg also developed an oil-based printing ink. Apart from the Bible, Gutenberg's system is in use for publishing religious tracts.

Gutenberg ran into major financial difficulties during the process of invention. He was forced to borrow money heavily, particularly from a rich goldsmith and financier, Johann Fust. The backer became increasingly impatient with the inventor – who was also working on a copperbased system of reproducing etchings on a mass basis – and sued Gutenberg for the return of his 800 guilders. The courts found for Fust and it is he who is making a fortune from sales of the Bible and producing a book of psalms on the Gutenberg system.

Johann Gutenberg, whose invention means that accurate texts can now be produced in great numbers.

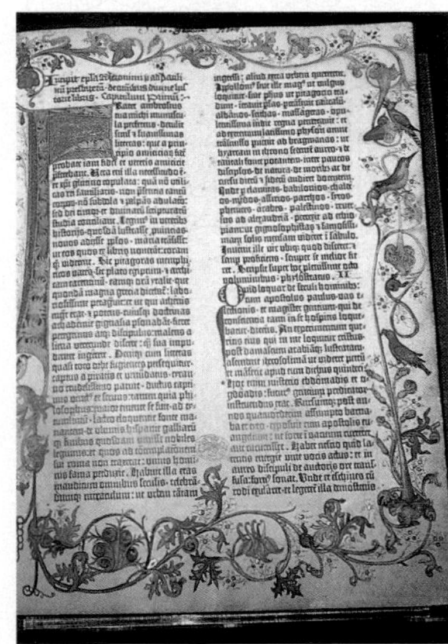

A page of the 42-line Bible printed by Gutenberg at Mainz in 1455; it still has the look of a manuscript.

Explorer-prince dies

This early 15th-century bowl from Valencia shows a Portuguese sailing ship.

Portugal, 13 November 1460

Prince Henry knew the end was near. He granted two islands in the Azores to his nephew and heir Fernando, and assigned the spiritualities of the Madeira islands to the Order of Christ. He provided for Masses to be said for his soul and then made his will. He died today, aged 66, and his remains were taken to the church of St Mary at Lagos. It is said that he remained a virgin throughout his life.

For 40 years Henry, who was the third son of John of Portugual and Philippa, the daughter of England's John of Gaunt, devoted his wealth and his energies to maritime exploration. He grew up at a time when the Moors had at last been driven from Portugal and much of Spain, and the crusading spirit was still vigorous. The navigational enterprises with which he came to be associated began with a crusade against North African Moors.

Though he saw himself as a Christian knight dedicated to the struggle against Islam, his vision carried him beyond old horizons. He brought cartographers from Sicily and elsewhere to train his seamen. He found shipwrights to build craft strong enough to remain at sea in rough weather. Year after year Henry sent expeditions southward along the West African coast. The island groups of Madeira and the Azores became the first overseas colonies claimed by Henry, who dreamed of reaching the legendary Christian kingdom ruled by a priest king, Prester John, which was believed to exist in the heart of Africa. He never found it, but by his death his navigators had explored the coast of Africa as far south as the rugged mountain chain they called Sierra Leone; the Christian message was being carried to the heathen.

Prince Henry (C16th manuscript).

1468 (1468-1477)

Florence, 3 December 1468. Lorenzo (the Magnificent) and his brother Giuliano succeed their father, Piero de Medici, as rulers of Florence.

Scandinavia, 1468. Christian, the king of Scandinavia, cedes Orkney and Shetland to the Scots in pledge for the dowry of his daughter Margaret, who is to marry James III.

Balkans, 1468. The death of Skanderbeg, the "prince" of the Albanians, opens Albania to the Turks.

West Africa, 1468. Sonni Ali, the king of Songhai, drives the Tuaregs out of Timbuktu.

Italy, 9 December 1469. The painter Fra Filippo Lippi dies.

Spain, 1469. Isabella of Castile marries Ferdinand, heir to the throne of Aragon.

England, c.1470. Thomas Malory completes the *Morte d'Arthur*, a retelling of the Arthurian legends.

France, January 1471. Louis XI declares war on Charles the Bold, the duke of Burgundy, and occupies the towns of Picardy.

Anatolia, 1471. Mohammed II conquers the last surviving Turkish emirate, Karamania. All the lands from the Taurus mountains to the Adriatic are now under Ottoman rule.

Germany, 1473. In a bid to acquire the title "King of the Romans", Charles the Bold arranges to meet Frederick III at Trier; but the emperor gives Charles the slip, making him the laughing stock of Europe.

Mexico, 1473. Ayacatl, Aztec ruler since 1468, defeats the neighbouring city of Tlatelolco.

France, 11 June 1474. Louis XI ratifies the "Perpetual Peace", signed by the Habsburgs and the Swiss.

England, 1474. The treaty of Utrecht gives the Hanseatic league (Hanse) generous trading privileges in England.

France, 29 August 1475. Having bought off Edward IV of England, who has been fighting in support of Charles the Bold, Louis XI signs the treaty of Picquigny with him.

France, 1476. The Swiss, now allied with France, open a campaign against Burgundy, seizing the district of Vaud. In response, Charles the Bold seizes Lorraine.

France, January 1477. On the death of Charles the Bold, Louis XI invades Burgundy, Franche-Comte and Artois.

Wolves feed on Charles the Bold

Switzerland, 7 January 1477

Two days after the battle of Nancy, an Italian page has found the body of Charles the Bold, the duke of Burgundy, naked on a frozen pond, half eaten by wolves, his skull cloven by a Swiss battle-axe. The duke was unrecognisable and was identified only by the scars on his body.

Thus ended the career of the turbulent duke who wanted so badly to be a king, a successful general and a conqueror and who failed in all three ambitions. The downfall of this ruthless commander – who modelled himself on Julius Caesar and other great Roman conquerors – began at the battle of Grandson last year, when Swiss pikemen bore down the heavily-armoured Burgundian cavalry. Charles sought revenge for "shameful defeat" by besieging Morat – and was again routed by the Swiss. Half his army died, and Charles fled.

Encouraged by his defeats, Charles' rival, Rene II of Lorraine, reoccupied Nancy and called for Swiss and French help against Burgundy. The army arrived while Charles was besieging the city and, in his third defeat in under a year, the duke lost his life and army.

Death of Bohemian king may start war

Prague, 22 March 1471

Jan Hus may have been burnt at the stake for his heretical beliefs in 1415, but his doctrine – which, among other things, allows for the taking of both wine and bread by the laity at mass – lives on, and has been threatening to bring Bohemia into a major war, with the Ottoman empire prepared to join in.

The Hussites lost a great champion today, however, in the form of George Podebrad, a leading Czech politician who in 1444, at the age of 24, formed a Hussite league – "the Union of Podebrad" – which defied the Catholic party in Prague and the rest of the country. With its backing George made himself master of Prague, driving out the Catholics and restoring the cardinal.

In 1458, Bohemia's young King Ladislas died of plague. George, who had been regent for the last five years, was elected king in his stead. Papal condemnation of George as a heretic in 1466 strengthened his enemies within Bohemia, who also won the support of George's son-in-law Matthias of Hungary. George's party remains in power, but his death may lead to renewed conflict.

Incas extend power over South America

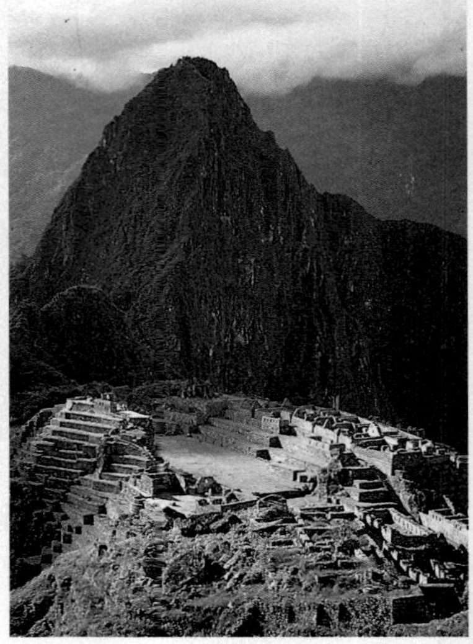

The grassy slopes of Machu Picchu.

Peru, 1470

The Inca army under Topa Inca, son of the great Pachacuti, has overrun the kingdom of Chimor. The Chimu state on the Pacific coast was the most developed in the region. Its defeat by the Incas, bringing to an end eight years of war, has made the Incas the dominant power in South America.

The Inca expansion began 32 years ago when Pachacuti took over the state and, from his capital at Cuzco high in the Andes, built an empire throughout the southern Highlands. Topa Inca has continued his father's policy, leading Inca armies north into the rest of the Andes and west onto the coastal plain. With the inclusion of Chimor in the empire, Inca rule stretches from the Andes to the Pacific.

Inca society could not be more suitable for empire building. It is austere and rigidly, even militaristically, organised. It appears to have little concern for art, except perhaps the art of war. Political and sexual deviance is punished with torture and death by varying methods of execution.

Loyalty to the emperor, the representative of the sun on earth, is absolute. The administrative class of the empire is divided between "Incas by blood", and "Incas by privilege", collaborators drawn from subject peoples. Everything Topa Inca needs to expand his empire is already there.

Mass murderer Prince Dracula dies

Transylvania, 1477

The people of central Europe are sleeping a little easier with the news that its most notorious mass murderer, Vlad the Impaler, has died aged 45 in exile.

Dubbed *Dracula* (from the Rumanian for the Devil), he died after a short campaign to regain his native Wallachia. Crowned Vlad IV there 21 years ago, he was deposed and imprisoned by his Hungarian neighbours. They freed him last year after serving 14 years for conspiring with the Turks to take Hungary, which he coveted and terrorised.

Vlad was at the height of his powers in 1461 when he formed a defensive alliance with the Hungarians and marched across the Danube devastating Turkish Bulgaria and killing 25,000 people by impaling them on stakes. His cruelty and bloodlust – such as forcing children to eat their roasted mothers – was downfall. A Turkish emissary refused to take off his turban, so Vlad had it nailed to his head, thereby angering the Turks.

Dracula before his impaled victims.

Usurper executes king in Wars of Roses

London, 21 May 1471
King Henry VI has died, presumably murdered, in the Tower of London and the usurper Edward IV once more occupies the throne.

Henry's death is the latest episode in the dynastic struggles between the houses of York and Lancaster, or "the Wars of the Roses" as they are called from the emblems of the two sides (the white rose for York, the red for Lancaster). Back in 1454 the Lancastrian Henry VI was stricken with a mental illness and Richard, the duke of York, laid claim to the throne. Richard was killed at the battle of Wakefield in 1460, but his son Edward beat Henry's forces in 1461 and became king as Edward IV.

With French aid, the earl of Warwick and Edward's brother, the duke of Clarence, deposed Edward and restored Henry VI last year. Edward returned with Burgundian backing earlier this year and was reconciled with his brother; he defeated Warwick at Barnet, near London, on 13 April. Warwick died in the battle.

On 3 May, the Lancastrians were trounced at Tewkesbury and Prince Edward, Henry VI's son, was killed. With the death of a dangerous potential rival claimant to the throne, Edward IV had no need to keep the captive Henry VI alive.

Henry VI's widow, Queen Margaret.

Usurper: Edward IV in council.

Venetian Caterina is queen of Cyprus

Cyprus, 1477
Despite the ever-present military threat from the Turks, Cyprus is prospering under Caterina Cornaro, its intellectual Venetian queen. Born in 1454 into a family with financial interests in Cyprus, she was taught by her brothers.

In 1468 she was engaged to King James II of Cyprus. The couple were married in 1472, but James II died just a few months after the wedding. Caterina was entangled in a web of intrigue as she endeavoured to exercise her authority; her young son, King James III, was taken from her by the council of regency, and her cousin and uncle were murdered. In 1474 she regained power for her son, but he died of malaria, leaving her to rule alone.

A later portrait of Caterina.

Plato translated into Latin for Medici

Florence, 1469
As fascination with the ancient world grows among educated Italians, a dedicated priest, Marsilio Ficino, has completed the monumental task of translating the complete works of Plato from Greek into Latin. He is following it up with a substantial philosophical work of his own, *Theologia Platonica de immortalitate animae* (Platonic theology concerning the immortality of the soul), a metaphysical work which argues for the freedom of the soul from the body.

Ficino is a leading member of the Florence-based Platonic Academy founded by Cosimo de Medici, who died three years ago. He saw only the first fruits of Ficino's Plato translation, but his grandson Lorenzo de Medici, the academy's new patron, has continued to fund Ficino's work.

The Platonic Academy, which has no buildings or teachers, consists of a small group of men with a common interest in Plato and respect for Ficino as their mentor. It has exercised a major influence over Italian philosophical thought and has made a significant contribution to intellectual humanism.

A later print of Marsilio Ficino.

Lone Russian merchant arrives in India

Bidar, India, 1470
After an epic journey of 3,000 miles Afanasii Nikitin, a Russian trader, has arrived in Bidar. Leaving his home at Kalinin near Moscow in 1466, he joined an embassy sent by Ivan the Great to Tartary and followed the Volga, past Horde (the summer camp of the Mongol emperor), into the Caspian Sea. They were attacked and imprisoned by Tartar pirates.

Nikitin was released and continued alone. Hugging the shore of the Caspian, he took a boat to Persia, watching the flames from leaking oil deposits as he sailed past Baku. At Chapakur he disembarked and rode south across Persia, through Kashan and Yazd, to Hormuz. There he took a ship, first to Muscat and then India, landing at Chaul, 300 miles south of Bombay. After two months at Junnar he has come to the Moslem state of Bidar. His arrival coincides with a Hindu invasion from Vijayanagar, and the Russian traveller has watched the Moslem army, hundreds of thousands of infantry and cavalry supported by armourplated elephants, march out to battle in barbaric splendour.

Music, maps and posters roll off the new printing presses

Europe, 1477
Gutenberg's movable type printing press has quickly caught on around Europe. Initially printers used the new technology to disseminate a great variety of devotional texts such as Bibles. But the range of printed subjects knows no bounds. In 1472 the first printed music appeared in Bologna, Italy; then followed the printed map; and now a printed poster has rolled off the press of the Englishman William Caxton and advertises the thermal cures at Salisbury.

Caxton is also credited with the first dated book printed in the English language, *Dictes and Sayings of the Philosophers*, which appeared on 18 November of this year. From his printing works and offices in Westminster he is also publishing foreign works. His ambition is to make all kinds of writings widely available, chivalric romances, history, philosophy, and even an encyclopaedia.

1477 (1477-1483)

Flanders, 18 August 1477. Maximilian of Austria, the son of the Emperor Frederick III, marries Mary of Burgundy, the daughter and heir of Charles the Bold. The house of Habsburg is now heir to the duchy of Burgundy, one of the richest states in Europe.

Florence, 1478. Giuliano de Medici is killed as a result of the Pazzi conspiracy against him and his brother Lorenzo.

Spain, 1479. Ferdinand, the husband of Isabella of Castile, succeeds his father, John II, as king of Aragon. Ferdinand and Isabella last year introduced the Inquisition into Spain.

France, 7 August 1479. Maximilian of Austria halts Louis XI's incursions into Burgundian territories.

Milan, 1479. Ludovico Sforza seizes power from his nephew Gian Galeazzo, the youthful grandson of Francesco Sforza.

Russia, 1480. Ivan the Great stops paying tribute money to the Mongols.

Portugal, 1481. John II succeeds his father, Alfonso V, as king of Portugal. His accession gives a boost to voyages of exploration.

Constantinople, 3 May 1481. Mohammed II is succeeded as sultan by his son Bayezid II.

Flanders, 27 March 1482. Mary of Burgundy dies after a hunting accident. Her husband, Maximilian, becomes regent of the Low Countries in the name of their son, Philip.

France, 23 December 1482. Burgundy and Picardy are absorbed into France by the treaty of Arras. Artois becomes the dowry of the two-year-old Margaret of Burgundy, daughter of Mary and Maximilian, who has been promised in marriage to the dauphin. The rest goes to her brother Philip.

England, 9 April 1483. Edward IV dies at Windsor. During his second reign he re-established stability after the upheavals of the Wars of the Roses, but his achievements are threatened by the fact that his heir, Edward V, is aged only 12.

Rome, 9 August 1483. Pope Sixtus IV celebrates the first mass in the Sistine Chapel, which is named after him.

France, 30 August 1483. On the death of Louis XI, Charles VIII is placed under the guardianship of his elder sister, Anne de Beaujeu.

Moneylenders face small farmers' rage

Japan, 1481

Peasant communities throughout the rural areas are rising in violent protest against punitive taxation and the grasping moneylenders who are foreclosing on mortgages and seizing their land.

These moneylenders, who combine usury with brewing *sake*, lend money to the peasants to "tide them over". But natural disasters, wars and predatory landlords have combined to ruin the peasants and whole communities have fallen into the power of the moneylenders.

So the dispossessed farmers are arming themselves and forming bands powerful enough to challenge large armies and to intimidate the ruling classes. The first of their demands is the destruction of the pawnshops.

Rival banking firm plot church stabbing

Florence, 27 April 1478

The palaces of Florence are festooned with corpses of rebels hanged from their windows, following the murder in the cathedral yesterday of Giuliano de Medici and the attempt to assassinate his brother, Lorenzo, joint rulers of the city.

The assassins were members of the rival banking family of Pazzi and their confederates, including the archbishop of Pisa. Francesco Pazzi walked Giuliano de Medici to the cathedral arm-in-arm for High Mass attended by a cardinal from Rome (the pope is believed to have encouraged the conspiracy).

During the Mass the plotters plunged their daggers into Giuliano 19 times while two priests attempted to stab Lorenzo. He escaped, gashed in the neck, and ran to the sacristy for safety. In the stampede from the cathedral the assassins escaped, but the people of Florence turned against the Pazzi and hunted them and their friends down. In the violence which followed there have already been 70 deaths.

Lorenzo de Medici by Vasari.

Death of "Conqueror" sultan leaves great but troubled empire

Ottoman Empire, 1481

The death of Mohammed the Conqueror leaves the Ottoman empire powerful but uncertain. His two sons, Bayezid and Jem Sultan, must fight for the throne, while their subjects grumble about the confiscations and currency debasement that financed Mohammed's wars.

The capture of Constantinople in 1453 earned Mohammed II his title of "Conqueror", and gave him the prestige to dispense with his old adversary, Grand Vizier Halil Pasha. He had previously quelled a revolt among the elite army corps of Janissaries, and bound them closer to him. Mohammed saw himself as *khan*, lord of the nomadic steppes, *ghazi*, fighter for Islam, and *basileus*, emperor of Byzantium. This allowed for religious toleration, but not for the possibility of revolt. He therefore codified Ottoman secular law to apply throughout his lands.

Most of his energies were successfully devoted to warfare, so that by the end of his reign he had taken most of Serbia, Albania, Herzegovina, much of Bosnia and Greece (including Athens and the Peloponnese). Anatolia was subdued, and Venice paid tribute.

Conquering sultan, Mohammed II.

Man seen in terms of Zodiacal symbols, from the guild book of the barber-surgeons of England.

Spain gives up new African territories

Portugal, 4 September 1479

After almost four years of bitter warfare, Spain has agreed to a Portuguese monopoly of trade and navigation along the whole West African coast, and Portugal has acknowleged Spanish rights to the Canary Islands.

The immediate cause of the war had nothing to do with territorial claims overseas. It arose from a dispute over the succession to the throne of Castile. The late king, although known as Henry the Impotent, had in fact fathered a daughter, Joanna, and she laid claim to the throne after marrying her uncle Alfonso of Portugal. The Castilian nobility, however, backed Henry's sister, Isabella.

In the fighting, the Portuguese fared badly at home, but they repeatedly out-fought the Spanish at sea. On the islands, too, they defeated the Spanish everywhere except in the Canaries. This state of affairs explains the terms of the peace treaty signed today at Alcacovas. Isabella, incidentally, is now queen of Castile.

Ferdinand and Isabella unite Spain

King Ferdinand II of Aragon.

Queen Isabella of Castile.

Castile, 1479
The crowns of Castile and Aragon are now united. Isabella of Castile and Ferdinand II of Aragon, who have been married for the last ten years, have joined their countries in what is effectively a federation, and many believe that a powerful new force has been created in today's Europe by this alliance of thrones.

The situation has come about with Ferdinand succeeding to the throne of his father, John II. Isabella on the other hand inherited Castile five years ago when her brother, Henry IV, died.

The couple have since successfully beaten off the Portuguese army of Alfonso V, who has been trying to claim the hand of Joanna, Henry's daughter, and with it the Castilian crown. Ferdinand, aged 27, is fond of women, and of gold and jewels which he not only wears but also adorns the trappings of his horses. He showed great personal courage and endurance during the recent civil war struggles. Isabella, just a year younger, is intelligent, pious and possessed of a great sense of royal dignity.

It is evident that Castile is the dominant partner. Ferdinand is to live in Castile and is not to leave it without his wife's permission. Only Castilians are appointed to the Council of Castile, and Ferdinand is not allowed to wage war without Isabella's advice and, especially, her agreement.

Russian king defies demands of Mongols

Moscow, 1480
Ivan the Great has seen off a Tartar attack and declared the total independence of his state after the Horde's 200-year occupation. The punitive expedition to collect the customary tribute from Ivan was launched by Khan Akhmat, who had intended to join up with a simultaneous Lithuanian incursion.

The Lithuanians never arrived and there was no significant fighting on the banks of the river Ugra. Fed up with waiting, the khan decided to withdraw; it was on the way home that he was assassinated by one of his political opponents. It may be that Muscovite rulers will still have to buy off or repel Tartar invaders but they will no longer accept the patent from the khans.

Ivan has also asserted his rights as titular prince of Novgorod, one of the oldest of Russian towns with wide authority over northern Russia. He has forced Novgorod to renounce relations with Poland and Lithuania. After an attempted revolt he removed 8,000 of the leading families to his own domain and replaced them with merchants from Muscovy.

Ivan III refuses the tribute demanded by the khan, by a 19th-century artist.

Silver pavilion graces shogun's garden

Japan, 1483
The *shogun* (local ruler), Yoshimasa, has indulged his taste for fine architecture by building a magnificent pavilion at his retreat in a scenic area of Kyoto. The *Ginkaku*, or Silver Pavilion, stands on the site of an abandoned monastery.

It gets its name from the shogun's plan to cover it with silver leaf. There, worn out by a lifetime of war and strife, he practises the tea ceremony and welcomes men of taste with whom he discusses his collections of Sung paintings and porcelain. He has ordained that on his death his elegant residence be converted into a temple.

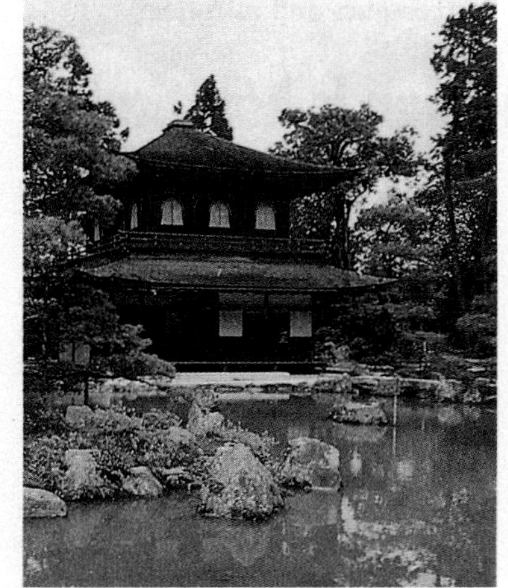
Yoshimasa's silver-plated residence.

Fears for safety of princes in the tower

England, 1483
The two English boy princes, Edward V and Richard of York, have disappeared, and are widely believed to have been murdered on the orders of their uncle and successor Richard III.

The boys were put in the Tower of London before Richard announced his own claim to the throne in June. Rumours almost immediately began to circulate that they were dead. Some stories said they had been drowned in malmsey, stabbed, poisoned or smothered.

Belief in their deaths explains why Richard's opponents, who staged a rebellion this autumn, have had to find another claimant to the throne. Plans to restore Edward V have now been abandoned and the exiled Lancastrian Henry Tudor is the preferred candidate.

The Princes in the Tower, by Sir John Everett Millais (1829-96).

Central Africa, 1484. The Portuguese Diego Cao lands in Angola. Last year he explored the mouth of the river Zaire and set up a stone column marking his arrival.

Rome, 5 December 1484. Pope Innocent VIII issues a bull deploring the spread of witchcraft and heresy generally in Germany, and authorising the Dominican inquisitors to deal with it.

Flanders, June/July 1485. Maximilian takes Bruges and Ghent by siege. Although accepted by Holland, Zeeland and Hainault, Maximilian's claim to authority in the Low Countries as guardian of his son Philip had been rejected by Flanders and Brabant.

England, 22 August 1485. The victory of Henry Tudor (Henry VII) over Richard III at Bosworth establishes the Tudor dynasty.

Central Africa, 1485. Four Portuguese Catholic missionaries arrive in the Kongo kingdom *(Angola)*, south of the mouth of the Zaire river.

Germany, 1486. The Emperor Frederick III has his son Maximilian elected king of the Romans.

Spain, 1 May 1486. The Genoese seaman, Christopher Columbus, persuades Queen Isabella to sponsor his planned expedition to discover a western route to the Indies.

Mexico, 1487. The Great Temple of Tenochtitlan is inaugurated: 20,000 people are ritually sacrificed.

Spain, 1487. Ferdinand and Isabella take possession of Malaga, which until now has been an independent Moslem principality.

Central Europe, 1487. Jacob Fugger, from a rich merchant family in Augsburg, secures the right to mine silver in the Tyrol from Sigismund of the Tyrol.

Flanders, 1488. Maximilian, in Bruges to negotiate with disaffected tradesmen, is trapped by their rising. He is held captive for 11 weeks, and the cities are only brought to negotiate with him by the news that his father, the emperor, is advancing with an army. Maximilian is made to promise that he will give up his regency of the Low Countries.

South Africa, 1488. The Portuguese explorer, Bartholomew Dias, rounds the Cape of Good Hope.

Sailor rounds new Cape

Lisbon, December 1488

A remarkable feat of navigation has been recounted to King John II by the explorer Bartholomew Dias of Portugal, who has returned from a two-year voyage down the West coast of Africa.

Dias sailed so far south that the North Star vanished below the horizon. For 13 days a strong wind carried him out to sea and still further south. When at last he was able to turn back he found the lie of the land was to the east, not the south; Dias had discovered the way round Africa. The explorer continued on his new course to the east and, sighting native herdsmen with cows, went ashore. But Dias was unable to understand the language and the natives were so alarmed at the sight of the ships that they drove their animals inland. Dias has told the king that he named the great cape, with its table-like mountain, the Cape of Storms. But the king wishes it to be known as the Cape of Good Hope, because it gives promise of discovering a sea route to India.

Portuguese calculate latitude by the sun

Lisbon, 1484

The first European manual of navigation and nautical almanac has been prepared by a group of mathematical experts appointed by King John II of Portugal. The king was concerned that his navigators were embarking on long voyages without charts or sailing directions. The dead reckoning method of establishing a position by recording the distance and direction travelled is unreliable, and the North Star is not visible in southern waters.

The king told the mathematicians to devise a method of finding latitude by solar observation. The main problem was that the track followed by the sun in relation to the earth changes from day to day and from year to year. The experts studied a set of tables first worked out by the Jewish astronomer Abraham Zacuto of Salamanca, who had recorded the sun's declination for the years 1473-78.

A simplified version of Zacuto's tables has been produced for seamen. But taking a reading of the sun's position and calculating what is called the "latitude" of a ship from that reading is complicated and a seaman must have a grasp of mathematics and astronomy.

Model of a Portuguese caravel.

Work of cabalistic magician is heretical

Rome, December 1486

A special commission called by Pope Innocent VIII has condemned as heretical part of the latest work of the brilliant 23-year-old philosopher, Pico della Mirandola. His *Conclusiones* comprise 900 propositions about God and man.

He takes a humanist view, writing that "nothing in the world can be found that is more worthy of admiration than man". He suggests Christ did not really descend into hell and that cabalistic magic is the best way of proving the divinity of Christ.

The son of a noble family from Ferrara, he began to study canon law at the age of ten in Bologna and philosophy two years later in Ferrara. He then moved to Perugia to study Hebrew and Arabic and was strongly influenced by Jewish scholars of the *Qabbalah*. He then went to the Sorbonne where he met many humanist philosophers.

Wars of Roses end at Bosworth Field

Henry VII (17th-century print).

England, 22 August 1485

As dawn broke over Redmoor this morning few could have guessed that by noon a new king and dynasty would occupy the throne of England.

On the surface, the odds were against the young exile, Henry Tudor, the heir to the Lancastrian cause, and heavily in favour of King Richard III and the white rose of York. Henry was a complete novice in battle, and led a force of 5,000 men, while the soldierly Richard headed over double that number.

But although Richard's army boasted distinguished commanders of the calibre of the duke of Norfolk, he was beset by men of wavering loyalty, such as the earl of Northumberland and Lord Stanley, who initially held back his troops.

Henry's army, led by the redoutable earl of Oxford, was lighter and more manoeuvrable than Richard's, and contained many expert Welsh, Scottish and French soldiers. In the event, Oxford ably held his own against Norfolk until Richard, frustrated, decided to enter the fray in person at the head of a stupendous cavalry charge. Henry stood his ground, until Stanley finally joined the melee – on Henry's side. Richard, it seems, was forced into a swamp, unhorsed, and hacked to death by Welsh pikemen. His coronet was retrieved and, soon after, was placed on the head of the Tudor prince, henceforth known as King Henry VII.

Aztecs sacrifice 20,000

Mexico, 1487

In the most spectacular sacrificial display ever seen in the Aztec capital, Tenochtitlan, 20,000 people have lost their hearts to Huitzilopochtli, the war god.

The ceremony was supervised by Ahuitzotl, the ruler of the Aztecs. Two queues of 10,000 each, made up of captured rebels from northern Oaxaca, stood on either side of the sacrificial altar in the Great Temple, which Ahuitzotl has restored. Dressed as Huitzilopochtli he tore their hearts out by hand, one by one, and flung them into a gigantic urn where they were burnt to the war god. Exhausted, he retired and his ally, Nezahualpilli, took his place. When he collapsed from exhaustion Ahuitzotl's Aztec councillors continued the work. They retired and lesser notables took up the task in a ritual sacrifice dictated by the belief that only in this way would their god be propitiated.

Huitzilopochtli will not be short of hearts while Ahuitzotl rules. Ahuitzotl has led his army on conquests throughout central America. Wherever he has conquered, his demands for tribute are so unlimited that the defeated have been forced to rebel, increasing the flow of hearts to Huitzilopochtli.

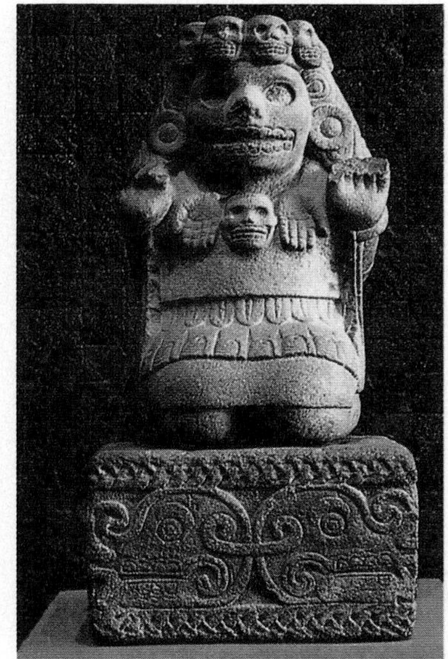

Aztec goddess of life and death.

Book supports witch hunt in Rhineland

Rome, 1486

The publication of an encyclopaedia of witchcraft here confirms that the papacy is lending its support to the growing practice of persecuting and burning witches. For well over a century now Dominican friars have been burning witches, mainly in the villages of the Alps and the Pyrenees. But popes have mostly not seen witches as a real problem, with the exception of Pope John XXII, who lived in personal terror of witches and authorised an inquisition in 1326.

However, two years ago Pope Innocent VIII published a bull deploring the spread of witchcraft in Germany and authorising two Dominicans, Jakob Sprenger and Heinrich Kramer, to stamp it out. They have since been hard at work. Only last year the Como inquisitor burnt 41 witches who had confessed to sex with devils.

Sprenger and Kramer have now published *Malleus Maleficarum* (The Hammer of the Witches). It suggests that witches really do fly, that they can raise hailstorms and hurtful tempests and lightnings, cause sterility and make horses go mad under their riders. Witches are said to eat children, have sex with devils and engage in sexual and cannibalistic orgies. Voluminous evidence of these practices is provided, mostly obtained from torturing suspected witches.

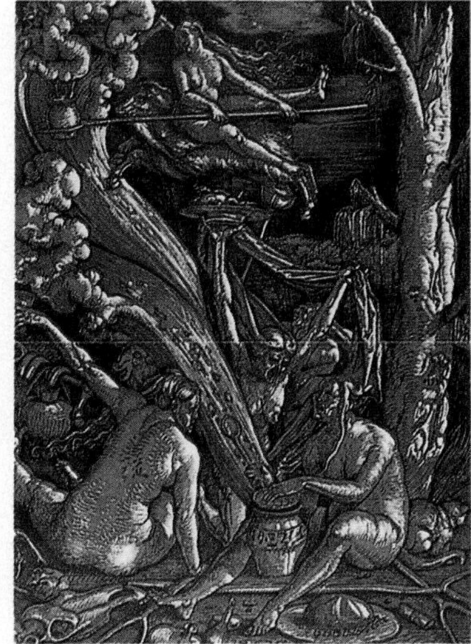

"Witches", a 16th-century woodcut.

Milanese genius is painter and engineer

Designs for war engines by Leonardo; note his right-to-left handwriting.

Milan, 1488

Now in his thirties, an Italian artist, scientist, philosopher and inventor, Leonardo da Vinci, has established himself as a supreme example of the Renaissance ideal of the multi-talented individual. There seems no end to his originality as a thinker – and skill as a craftsman and engineer.

In the six years that he has been living in Milan, Leonardo has accumulated sheet upon sheet of drawings and notes, penned in mirror writing that scans from right to left, the natural way for this left-handed genius.

In these copious notebooks are superb descriptive drawings of the natural world, from flowers in bloom to babies in the womb; advanced geometry and arithmetic; and a prolific array of ingenious mechanical devices. Here can be found a multiple cross-bow gun; a contrivance for repelling enemy scaling ladders during a siege; even an armoured vehicle with firing guns.

For a Milanese castle, Leonardo has designed a forced-air central heating system and an arrangement for pumping water. He also sketches some apparatus to allow one to breathe underwater.

Many of his ideas cannot be realised with existing technology. From watching and drawing birds in flight, he has become fascinated by the possibility of a man-made flying machine and has a similar project for a flying device powered by revolving blade. Leonardo's genius has won him wide admiration.

China's Great Wall to be even greater

China, 1488

The Ming emperors are pressing on with their policy of rebuilding the Great Wall. This work, begun soon after the disastrous battle of Tu-mu in 1449 when the Ming army was slaughtered by the Mongols and the emperor captured, reflects Ming concern with the need for effective defences against the successive waves of barbarians from the north.

The original wall, built out of rammed earth by the Chin dynasty some 1700 years ago, had proved to be no real obstacle to the invaders and for much of its length had eroded into mounds of grassy soil called "earth dragons" by the local people.

Now the Ming emperors, already renowned as great builders, have set armies of labourers to work on a wall which is truly great. When it is finished it will wind across northern China for 1400 miles.

Those parts already completed are faced with brick. The wall is 25 feet high, with a 12-feet wide cobbled road running along the top between guard houses. It seems likely to become one of the greatest man-made structures ever built.

1488 (1488-1492)

Cyprus, 14 March 1489. The purchase of the island by the Venetians from Catherine Cornaro, the last of the Lusignan dynasty of Cyprus, ends several centuries of Frankish sovereignty.

Austria, 6 April 1490. Matthias Corvinus, king of Hungary since 1458, dies in Vienna. In 1479, by the peace of Olomuc, he secured Silesia, Moravia and Lusatia. In two campaigns against the Emperor Frederick III he won control of Vienna, Lower Austria, Styria and Carinthia.

France, September 1490. Maximilian of Austria joins an Anglo-Spanish alliance established last year against France. The English occupy Guingamp and Concarneau; the Spanish occupy Vannes.

Central Asia, 1490. A mausoleum to Tamerlane is erected in Samarkand.

Brittany, 1491. When the French occupy the duchy of Brittany, neither England nor Spain sends help to the Bretons. The proxy marriage between Anne of Brittany and Maximilian of Austria, arranged last year, is annulled and Anne has no choice but to marry Charles VIII, the king of France. The independence of Brittany is effectively ended.

Near East, 1491. The Ottomans and the Mamelukes reach a peace agreement after six years of war. Cilicia in Anatolia is placed under Egyptian control.

Cairo, 1491. The Portuguese envoy Pedro da Covilhao returns to Cairo after an expedition which has taken him as far south as the Sofala coast of south-east Africa and as far east as Calicut in India.

Spain, 2 January 1492. Ferdinand and Isabella take Granada, the last Moslem kingdom in Spain, which had resisted Christian conquest for two centuries.

Milan, January 1492. To pre-empt France's exercising a claim (through marriage) to Milan, and to secure an ally against Naples, Ludovico Sforza renews a Milanese alliance with France.

Spain, 30 March 1492. A royal edict is issued decreeing the expulsion of the Jews.

Rome, 10 August 1492. On the death of Innocent VIII, the Valencian Rodrigo de Borja (Borgia) is elected pope. He takes the name Alexander VI.

Moslem Granada falls to Catholic kings

Granada, 2 January 1492

After a ten-year campaign Granada, the only remaining Moslem state in Spain, has fallen to the Castilian army. The surrender of the city is being hailed by Christians as the "most signal and blessed day there has ever been in Spain". Moslems are describing it as one of the most terrible catastrophes ever to befall Islam.

The war has been directed by Ferdinand and Isabella, the king and queen of Spain, with months of continual skirmishing by the Christian armies eventually wearing down the beleaguered Moslems. The victors are said to have been been extremely generous in victory and virtually all the Moslem petitions were granted. For three years they can emigrate freely, and are allowed to keep all arms except firearms. Their religion is to be free from interference and the Moslems will continue to enjoy their own communal life and maintain their judicial system and local officials.

Throughout Spain and in papal Rome bullfights are being held in celebration and people are rejoicing. Venice and other states are sending more or less sincere messages of congratulation.

All Jews are ordered out of Spain

German anti-Semitic propaganda: Jews ritually killing a Christian boy.

Spain, 30 March 1492

In a mass emigration reminiscent of the Biblical Exodus, the Jews are leaving Spain. But if their forefathers were eager to leave Egypt, these modern Hebrews are going reluctantly, forced to quit by today's edict of expulsion. The 150,000 strong community has just four months to be gone. After years of growing anti-Jewish feeling, the monarchy has decided to end its Jewish problem by expelling them.

Spain's Jews, benefiting for centuries from tolerant Arab rulers, are a highly assimilated group; they operate their own autonomous administrative sytem, the *aljama*, and congregate in special districts, the *juderia*.

Once an integral part of Spanish society and culture, the Jewish situation has declined since Catholic rulers replaced Arab ones. Urban anti-semitism has increased and the state has passed a series of punitive laws restricting Jewish activities. The Inquisition, founded in 1478, has made matters worse, denouncing them as blasphemers and usurers, and encouraging every form of intolerance.

Portuguese envoy arrives in Kongo

Kongo, 1491

A Portuguese embassy to Nazinga Nkuma, the king of the Kongo *(Angola)*, has arrived in Banza, the capital. Its aim is peaceful, to evangelize, not conquer. On Nazinga Nkuma's suggestion, priests, scholars and craftsmen will be left behind when the ambassadors leave.

The embassy is the result of seven years of tentative contact between Portugal and the Kongo. In 1483 Diego Cao, the navigator, came to the mouth of the river Congo, leaving four of his officers to make contact with the king of Kongo. The king already knew of their presence – his subjects had mistaken the Portuguese ships for whales. Diego Cao returned with missionaries in 1485, reaching Banza where they converted the crown prince to Christianity, baptising him Afonso.

Nazinga Nkuma's support for the embassy is essential for its success. The king of Kongo is not like other mortals. He is a *nzambi mpungu*, or superior spirit. Each king marries his sister, so that over generations the heir is descended only from the royal spirit and not from common mortals. There is little doubt that the Portuguese missionaries have their work cut out for them.

New maths signs are a major plus

Germany, 1489

An important development in mathematics has just been introduced in Germany by Johann Widmann. In a recent book Widmann uses the symbols "+" and "−" to denote the operations of addition and subtraction. In doing so, he has not only advanced the operational symbolism of the great Greek mathematician, Diophantus, and the Hindu scholars, but has also greatly simplified matters for fellow mathematicians.

Over the centuries a variety of signs and symbols have been employed, rather idiosyncratically, to denote adding, subtracting and other operations. These have often taken the form of abbreviated words.

Lorenzo de Medici, tyrant and arts patron, dies

Florence c.1490, with the cathedral and, to its right, the Signoria.

Madonna and child, by Filippino Lippi (born c.1457), the son of another celebrated artist, Fra Filippo Lippi (1406-69), and a pupil of Botticelli. His work is full of breadth, strong colours and powerful movement.

Florence, 9 May 1492
Lorenzo de Medici is dead at the age of 44 and the worlds of art and learning mourn the loss of their greatest patron, known everywhere simply as "The Magnificent". He began his rule at the age of 20, with his brother Giuliano, who was murdered by the Pazzi in 1478. Lorenzo showed his nerve and wisdom in pacifying Florence after the crisis and there were no more uprisings.

He was not only a patron of philosophers, he debated with them himself in the Platonic Academy which he maintained. He was the friend of writers like Ficino, the biographer of Plato, and his official poet, Angelo Poliziano, whose poems inspired Botticelli to paint *The Birth of Venus* and *Primavera*; Lorenzo himself was a leading lyric poet in vernacular Tuscan. He delighted in carnivals, for which he wrote songs to be sung in the streets by his own Company of the Star.

Music delighted him – he was taught by the cathedral organist, Antonio Squarcialupi, who often wrote music for Lorenzo's lyrics. He loved antiquities, Greek and Roman busts, cameos, coins, which were collected for him in the Mediterranean. He welcomed scholars to his library of over 1,000 books.

He loved architecture, submitting his own design for the cathedral facade, and commissioned Filippino Lippi to decorate his villa and Andrea del Verrochio to sculpt busts of him and his brother. He also loved women, who found him attractive despite his harsh nasal voice and swarthy complexion. It was said of him: "It would be impossible to find a better tyrant."

A terracotta bust of Lorenzo de Medici by Andrea del Verrocchio.

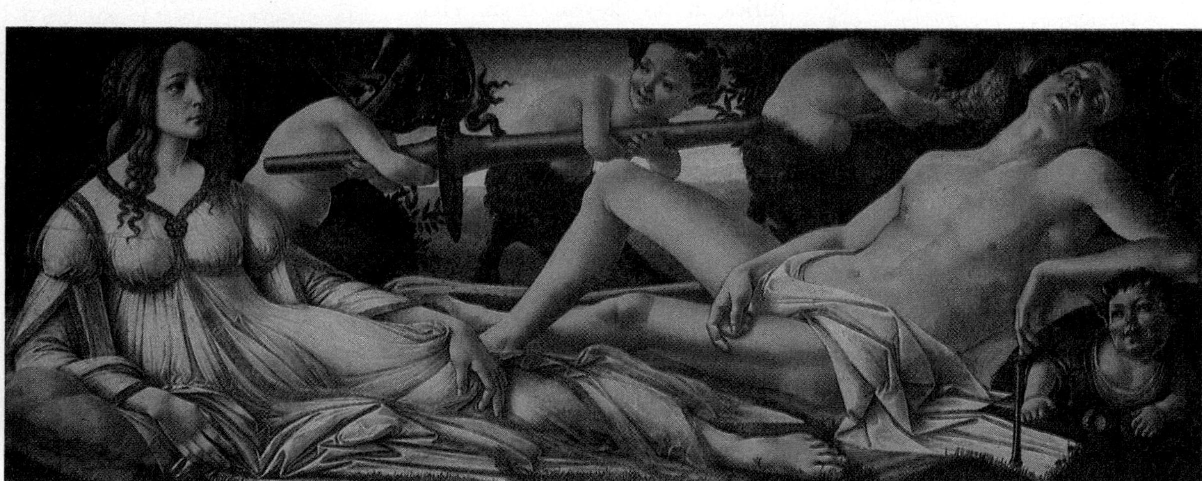

"Venus and Mars", by Sandro Botticelli (b.1440), one of the group of great artists commissioned by Lorenzo.

1492 (1492-1495)

Caribbean, 12 October 1492. Christopher Columbus lands on an island he calls San Salvador *(in the Bahamas).*

Italy, 12 October 1492. The great Tuscan painter Piero della Francesca dies.

Caribbean, 28 October 1492. Columbus arrives in Cuba, believing it to be Japan.

France, 3 November 1492. Learning that Henry VII of England is preparing for war against France, Charles VIII signs the treaty of Etaples: he agrees to pay the money due to England under the treaty of Picquigny of 1475 and promises not to aid any rebels against Henry VII.

Caribbean, 6 December 1492. In search of gold, Columbus lands on an island he calls Hispaniola *(Santo Domingo).*

Spain/France, January 1493. Under the treaty of Barcelona, Charles VIII returns Cerdagne and Roussillon (pledged to Louis XI by John of Aragon in 1462) to Ferdinand of Aragon.

Rome, 4 May 1493. The Spanish-born pope, Alexander VI, decrees that all new lands discovered west of the Azores are Spanish.

Germany, 19 August 1493. Frederick III is succeeded as Holy Roman Emperor by his son Maximilian.

Spain, 29 September 1493. Columbus, who returned to Spain in April, leaves Cadiz on a second voyage of exploration.

Ethiopia, 1494. The Portuguese envoy, Pedro da Covilhao, reaches Ethiopia, where he is detained by the emperor.

Netherlands, 1494. Philip (the Fair), son of the Emperor Maximilian, becomes ruler of the Low Countries.

Rome, 1494. Charles VIII enters Rome with the consent of the pope.

Milan, 1494. Ludovico Sforza, allied with the French king, takes the title duke of Milan.

Florence, 1494. Piero de' Medici is driven out of Florence by the Dominican friar Savonarola, who sets up a form of religious dictatorship.

Caribbean, 5 May 1494. Columbus lands on an island which he names Santa Gloria *(Jamaica).*

Flanders, 11 August 1494. Hans Memling, portrait painter of the nobility, who made a vast fortune from his work, dies at Bruges.

Armies with "French pox" infect Europe

A victim of the new pox, which many believe is a divine punishment.

Europe, 1494

A new, highly contagious disease has arrived in Europe, and cases have been recorded in France, Spain and Italy. Known as "the French pox", it attacks the genitals and according to experts is a punishment for sexual excess, gluttony, drunkenness and a generally dissolute life.

Transmitted through sexual intercourse, it appears as a sore on "the parts of shame" before eroding the palate and uvula, eating away the lips, nose or eyes, then weakening muscles and nerves before bringing its victim to an early and highly painful death. The origin of the pox is unknown – some talk of heavenly influence, others of small, winged worms – but it seems to have spread with increasing speed after the army of Charles VIII of France besieged Naples this year. The siege failed, but the army seems to have infected every country through which it has passed.

Several drugs have been used to combat the pox, but few have helped. The most successful treatment appears to be mercury ointment, already used as a cure for other skin diseases. So terrifying is the disease that numerous charlatans have emerged, all peddling their expensive, but useless, "cures".

Painter of elegant miniatures is dead

One of Bihzad's last works (1493).

Persia, 1494

Bihzad, one of the greatest of Persian painters, has died at the age of around 40. Orphaned early in life, he was brought up by the artist Mirak, and showed natural artistic talent early on. He achieved fame as a painter of miniatures, characterised by the complex and graceful harmony of their composition and by the wonderfully subtle use of the traditional flat, pure colours of Persian miniature painting.

No shortage of suspects in African ruler's murder

West Africa, 1492

Mystery continues to surround the alleged drowning of Sunni Ali, who turned Gao from a small kingdom into one of the largest states in West Africa in his 28-year reign. First allegations, suggesting that Sunni Ali died crossing a Niger tributary, are now thought to be false. New rumours suggest that Mohammed Ture, his nephew and a rival to Sunni Ali's son and successor Baro, was responsible for Ali's death.

There is, however, no shortage of suspects within the huge Songhai empire that Sunni Ali built up from a one-city state by major military conquest, ruthless determination and brilliant administration. Chief among the suspects is the Islamic community in Timbuktu, the scene of Sunni Ali's first conquest, whose mullahs were murdered for defying his authority.

The great mosque of Djenne in Mali was probably begun by a 14th-century Songhai ruler. Made of mud-brick, typical of Mali, it was rebuilt in 1909.

Columbus proves the world is round

Columbus, by Lorenzo Lotto.

Columbus amid the oceans, an imaginative impression by a later engraver.

West Indies, 12 October 1492
Christopher Columbus, who leads the royal Spanish expedition to pioneer a westward route to the Indies, stepped ashore today in a country inhabited by gentle, naked savages. Piously recognising the good fortune in making his long-awaited landfall, he has named this land *San Salvador* or "Saint of Salvation". For years Columbus has believed that the world is round; and today he appears to have proved his point to doubters – including some of his crew – who were convinced that it was flat.

It is 35 days since Columbus and his men last saw land as they sailed over the horizon from the Canaries. The admiral, from Genoa, is a navigator of genius and a shrewd master of men. For nine days he found strong winds to carry him westward. Then, as the ship slowed in a dense swamp of sinister yellow seaweed, the crew became increasingly nervous. The admiral fooled them into believing that they had not run as far west as they thought. As they picked up speed again, so did fears grow that the westerly bearing would take them over the edge of the world to their deaths in a giant abyss. At last, seeing large flocks of migrating birds, Columbus remembered that the Portuguese had discovered the Azores by studying such behaviour. So he changed course to south-west, to the birds' flight line. Only Columbus' calm confidence persuaded the crew to agree to two more days' exploration.

Columbus' fleet of three little ships had weighed anchor just before dawn at Palos in Spain, 71 days ago. His flagship, *Santa Maria*, is 85 feet long and displaces 100 tons; his escorts, *Pinta* and *Nina*, are about 55 tons. The crews have been scraped together from the back streets of Palos and the local prison.

In reality, this voyage began long before they sailed. Columbus, aged 41, first sought backing for his grand obsession in Portugal about eight years ago; then in France and England. He won Spanish support only after fighting the Moors for Spain and promising gold from his expedition to finance another holy war for Christendom. It is still unclear where San Salvador lies. Admiral Columbus believes that it is near Japan.

Compass needle mystery has Columbus looking to the stars

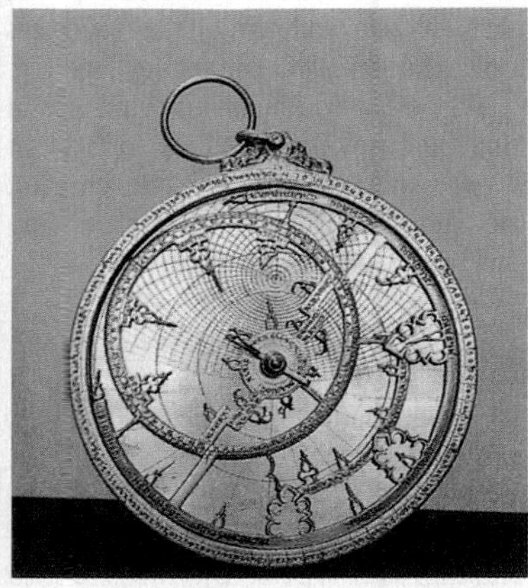
Astrolabe for navigation (c.1300)

Mid-Atlantic, 1492
Four days out of Hiero, the most westerly of the Canary Islands, Christopher Columbus made an alarming discovery. The needle of his compass was pointing markedly west-of-north.

His crew, most of whom were anyway doubting the wisdom of this major expedition, were shaken. If they could not rely on the compass here in mid-ocean, what unimaginable disasters might strike them? Along the Atlantic coast of Europe, mariners have long since noticed that the compass points slightly East of North. It is as if the earth's magnetic fields, instead of being fixed, are subject to fluctuation and variation.

More than ever the fleet of three caravels looks very vulnerable. These small ships, with their triangular lateen sails for tacking and catching light winds, and their squat, square sails for following winds, could be tested to their limits, and beyond. Only Columbus remains confident. His compass may not be trustworthy, but he can still navigate using the Pole Star as his guide.

Spain and Portugal divide up the world

Tordesillas, Spain, 7 June 1494
Under the terms of a treaty signed here today, Spain and Portugal have divided between them all the new lands discovered in the recent voyages of exploration, and any others that may be discovered in the future.

It was Christopher Columbus who stirred things up with his stories about discovering a new world in the West, or maybe a new route to the Indies. Portugal's King John II, who was planning his own expedition to India, became alarmed, the more so when he learned that Ferdinand and Isabella had persuaded Pope Alexander VI to issue a series of bulls giving to Spain all the lands west of the Portuguese Azores discovered, or to be discovered, by Columbus.

John II opened direct negotiations with Ferdinand and Isabella and an imaginary demarcation line has been drawn down the western Atlantic. At this stage of discovery, no-one knows how much land does lie to the west; but Spain would seem to have the best of the deal.

Explorers in search for Prester John

Africa, 1494
The legend of Prester John, a Christian ruler somewhere in eastern Africa, has proved a powerful spur to Portuguese voyages of exploration in this continent. The legend is compounded by the keenness of the kings of Ethiopia to maintain contacts with the Christian west.

Two notable explorers, Pedro de Covilhao and Bartholomew Dias, left Lisbon in 1487 for Africa. While Dias sailed round the Cape of Good Hope, de Covilhao went overland in search of Prester John's mythical connection with the Indian spice trade. After travelling widely in the Levant, the Indian Ocean, the Persian Gulf, the Red Sea and the Gulf of Aden, de Covilhao has now arrived, via Zeila, in Ethiopia.

The Ethiopians are a Christian people. Male children are baptised after 40 days, females after 60. All then take communion.

1495 (1495-1498)

Italy, 31 March 1495. Venice, Milan, Spain, the pope and the emperor set up a holy league against Charles VIII of France, who seized Naples last month.

Lithuania, 1495. The Jews are expelled.

Caribbean, 1495. Columbus orders all Indians over 14 years old in Hispaniola *(Santo Domingo)* to pay tribute money in gold every three years to the king of Spain.

Portugal, 1495. Manuel (the Fortunate) succeeds his uncle John II as king of Portugal.

Europe, 1496. The alliance between the Habsburgs and Castile is strengthened by the marriage of Philip the Fair to Joanna of Castile, daughter of Ferdinand and Isabella.

North America, 24 June 1497. The Italian navigator John Cabot reaches North America after a journey lasting 35 days, and starts to explore the coastline from Cape Breton to Labrador.

South Africa, 1497. On the orders of Manuel, the king of Portugal, Vasco da Gama sets sail for India via the Cape of Good Hope. He rounds the cape on 22 November.

Spain, 1497. The Spanish infante, John of Aragon, the son of Ferdinand and Isabella, dies. He was married to Margaret, the daughter of Maximilian.

Caribbean, 1497. Columbus imposes a system of forced labour on the Indians in Hispaniola *(Santo Domingo).*

Scandinavia, 1497. King John of Denmark invades Sweden and is crowned king, reuniting Norway, Sweden and Denmark under his rule. His father, Christian, the last king to rule all three countries, was expelled from Sweden in 1464.

Russia, 1497. The Pskov charter centralises the administration of Russia.

West Africa, 1497. Askia (Mohammed Towri), the re-organiser of the Songhai empire, completes a four-year pilgrimage to Mecca.

South-East Africa, 25 January 1498. Vasco da Gama reaches Quelimane on the Sofala coast.

France, 8 April 1498. Louis XII succeeds Charles VIII.

Kenya, 14 April 1498. Da Gama arrives at Malindi, after calling at Kilwa and Mombasa.

Florence, 23 May 1498. The preacher Savonarola dies at the stake.

John Cabot returns triumphant after discovery of Labrador

London, 6 August 1497

The Genoese navigator John Cabot has returned in triumph from an expedition across the Atlantic. Henry VII has given him £10 from the Privy Purse, and an annuity of £20. Cabot is planning a large expedition next year.

Though he is Genoese by birth and has Venetian citizenship, Cabot came to England about ten years ago to raise support for a transatlantic crossing, and settled in Bristol. Having set sail from there on 2 May, Cabot's ship *The Matthew* reached America on 24 June, at the coast of Labrador. There Cabot planted the Tudor banner and the standard of St Mark, in contravention of an agreement in 1494 to allow Spain a monopoly of voyages of discovery. The journey took Cabot less time than it had taken Columbus in 1493, and vindicated his decision to explore a more northerly crossing.

"The Cabot brothers leaving Bristol" by Ernest Board (1877-1934). A representative of the city bids farewell to the Genoese navigators before they board their ship, the mainsail of which is emblazoned with the royal coat of arms to show that their mission is officially approved by King Henry VII.

"Tabaco" pipe is good for your health, say American smokers

A later print of American natives smoking their pipes known as "tabacos".

Europe, 1496

Samples of a dried leaf whose fumes are inhaled when burnt are among some of the curiosities brought back from the West Indies by the explorer Christopher Columbus.

His crew were offered the "bewitching vegetable" by natives who use it in ceremonies and believe it possesses unique health-giving properties. According to Romano Pane, a monk travelling with Columbus, the natives dry the vegetable leaf and put it in a small slingshot-shaped pipe, known as a "tabaco". Its two ends are inserted into the nostrils, the leaf is set on fire and the smoke inhaled up the pipe. When exhaling, the smokers look like dragons breathing fire.

The leaf, which is chewable, can also be smoked rolled up tightly in a tube-shape. However, be careful: too much smoke inhaled this way can make you light-headed.

Teeth white, smiles brighter, thanks to Chinese invention

China, 1498

Since earliest times humans have probably wrestled with the irritating problem of food particles left lodged between the teeth. Traditionally, the answer has been some form of toothpick. Now, however, a new idea from China, the toothbrush, seems likely to do the job more effectively. At the same time it imparts a shine to the front surfaces of the teeth. The bristles are mounted at right angles to the handle, allowing one to manoeuvre into every crack and crevice.

Vasco da Gama arrives in India

A portrait of the navigator Vasco da Gama, from a Spanish manuscript.

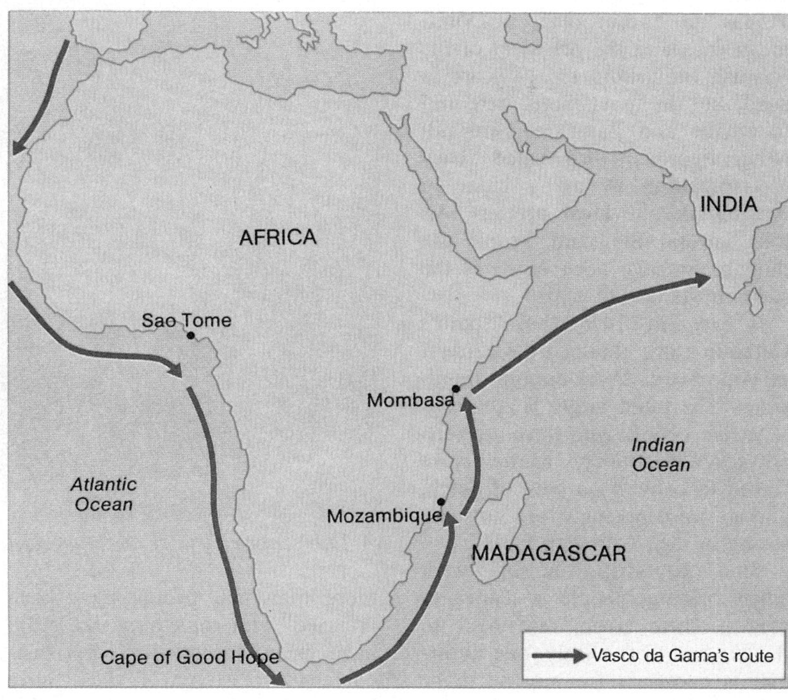

India, 23 May 1498

Almost a year after setting sail from Lisbon, Vasco da Gama has arrived off Calicut, on the Malabar coast, thus becoming the first European to discover a sea route round the Cape of Good Hope to India. During the long voyage he encountered many difficulties and dangers that tested both his seamanship and his qualities as a leader.

Da Gama has four ships with 20 guns and 170 well-armed men, a wise precaution as it turned out, for the Moslem Arab traders, fearing the Christian Portuguese will challenge their monopoly of trade with the Hindus, are already seeking to set the *zamorin*, or king, of Calicut against the newcomers.

When da Gama went ashore he took presents for the king: hats, striped cloth, strings of coral and a case of wash hand-basins. The king scorned them, saying da Gama had claimed he had come from a rich country, but all he had brought were cheap trinkets.

After battling against hurricanes on its way round the Cape, da Gama's expedition met with Moslem hostility at almost every port of call in East Africa. At Mombasa, Moslems pretended to be Christians in order to get on board and prepare for an armed attack on the ships. Da Gama had to bombard Mozambique before he could obtain supplies of fresh water.

At Malindi, however, a friendly welcome awaited the Portuguese and they were able to recruit Ibu Majid, an experienced Gujarati seaman, who piloted them across the Indian Ocean. Da Gama plans to return to Lisbon with half a dozen Indians to show to King Manuel, who funded the expedition.

Pope denounced by "Black Friar"

Florence, 25 December 1497

After six months of silence following his excommunication last June, Girolamo Savonarola today openly defied the Pope. He celebrated Mass three times this morning in the Church of St Mark. For seven years now Florence has been under the spell of this preacher, known as the "Black Friar". He is a short, slender man with a hooked nose, deeply-lined brow and thick lips. But it is his burning grey-green eyes which mesmerise people.

He was born at Ferrara in 1452 and became a Dominican friar. When he became prior at St Mark's he was already known as a prophet. He railed against the corruption of church and secular leaders. He said the art of Florence was immoral and charged Leonardo da Vinci and Botticelli with sodomy, though they were acquitted.

On Good Friday 1492 he revealed his vision of the destruction of Florence by flashes of lightning in a dense black sky. His congregation trembled when he drew vivid pictures of "barbers armed with gigantic razors" invading the city.

In 1494, on a wave of popular frenzy and with the help of the French king, he drove out the ruling Medici family. He has made Florence a puritanical republic, burning "vanities" such as books and pictures. Botticelli has stopped painting nudes and Leonardo has moved to Milan.

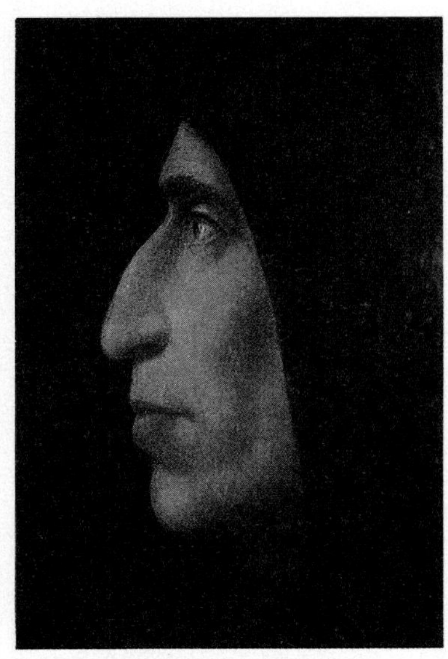
Savonarola, by Fra Bartolomeo.

Exhausted French army limps home after hollow Italian victory

A 19th-century view of the battle.

Italy, 6 July 1495

Exhausted, emaciated and riddled with disease, the army of Charles VIII is limping its way home to France today after being defeated at the battle of Fornovo. It is no more than a shattered shadow of the magnificent army which had paraded through Italy two years before. Both sides – French and Italian – are claiming victory; but if there was one, it was hollow indeed.

The young Charles had dreamed of conquering Naples, and after much dallying and womanising he crossed the Alps and made his way south. His entourage included 50,000 archers, crossbowmen and other footsoldiers, 36 huge cannon, several hundred prostitutes and his own baggage train of bedchamber, chapel, chamberlains, cooks, valets, ushers-at-arms, musicians, jesters, jousters and acrobats.

After much socialising along the route, Charles arrived at a castle near Naples. Heralds were sent forward demanding its surrender – only to return without ears or noses. Charles brought his big guns into play; a massacre followed and Naples fell.

But while the king disported himself there, a rare Swiss and Italian alliance was building up in the north; and it was this alliance that the French met at Fornovo on their return northwards.

1498 (1498-1500)

Spain, 7 June 1498. Columbus leaves on his third voyage of exploration.

Portugal, 1498. All Jews are expelled.

France, 1499. Louis XII repudiates Jeanne of France and marries Anne of Brittany.

England/North America, 1499. Henry VII gives John Cabot a boat to sail to Cathay (northern China). The expedition reconnoitres the coastline from Newfoundland to New England. The boat returns in September without Cabot, who has died on the voyage.

Milan, 1499. Backed by the pope, Venice, Florence and the Swiss cantons, Louis XII of France claims his right of succession to the duchy of Milan. The French, led by the mercenary Trivulzio, seize Milan. The usurper Ludovico Sforza flees.

South America, 1499. The Italian navigator Amerigo Vespucci explores the north-east coastline.

South America, 1499. The Spaniard Yanez Pinzon explores the northern coast of South America from Cape San Augustin to the Orinoco.

Caribbean, September 1499. Columbus puts down a revolt by Spanish settlers and natives against his poor administration in Hispaniola.

Brazil, 1 January 1500. The Portuguese explorer Pedro Alvarez Cabral discovers the coast of Brazil.

East Africa, 1500. Portuguese trading posts are set up along the East African coast.

India, 1500. Cabral creates the first Portuguese trading posts on the west coast of India.

Milan, 1500. The Milanese rebel against the French commander, Trivulzio. Taking advantage of the revolt, Sforza attacks the French at Novara but is deserted by his troops, handed over to the enemy and sent to France as a prisoner.

Russia, 1500. Ivan III annexes Smolensk and Chernigov, thus pushing back the boundary with Lithuania.

North Atlantic, 1500. The Portuguese Gaspard Corte Real explores the southern coast of Labrador and the east coast of Greenland.

West Africa, 1500. Sheikh Masfarma ben Uthman writes a history of Bornu *(northern Nigeria, Niger and Chad).*

Spanish Inquisition continues despite death of Dominican friar

Toledo, 1498

Tomas de Torquemada, a Dominican friar and the president of the Spanish Inquisition for 12 years, is dead. But the inquisitions, here and in Seville and Barcelona, are still being vigorously prosecuted. They are spreading to many cities in Aragon, despite local protests. All told, several thousand people are thought to have been burnt at the stake in the last 20 years.

It was in 1478 that Spain's Catholic kings obtained the consent of Pope Sixtus IV to appoint inquisitors. The main target is *conversos* – Jewish people who have converted to Christianty. Many were forced to convert on pain of death, and so, unsurprisingly, are not very strong in their Christian faith.

The inquisition begins with edicts offering people a chance to confess their errors and also to denounce others. Only one informer is necessary for anyone to be charged. When anyone is convicted they are liable to be "relaxed", which means to be burnt alive; here more than 500 people have been "relaxed" and something like 5,000 have been "reconciled" by their confessions. Many of these have been sentenced to march for six Fridays to the cathedral, whipping themselves in the streets. Such penitents suffer heavy fines, are forbidden to wear anything but the coarsest clothes, and cannot ride horses or bear arms.

Sometimes they are forced to dress only in green, with cloth crosses on their clothes.

A 19th-century view of an "auto-da-fe", one of the Inquisition's show-trials.

Garden is laid out for Zen Meditation

Japan, 1500

A garden of contemplation has been laid out in the grounds of the Zen Buddhist temple of Ryoan-ji in Kyoto, which is not only the capital but also the cultural heart of Japan. The temple was established by the warrior chief Katsumoto after a lifetime of fighting and its garden is a haven of tranquillity. It is oblong and contains 15 rocks of varying sizes arranged in an abstract composition on a bed of carefully raked white sand.

Stones in the garden of Ryoan-ji.

"The Trials of St Antony", by the Netherlandish painter Jerome (Hieronymus) van Aken, known as Bosch from his home town of s'Hertogenbosch. His paintings can be conventional, but some, like this one, are full of bizarre fantasy, with colourful and often horrific imagery.

Cabral claims Brazil for the Portuguese

Brazil, 23 April 1500
A vast territory lying south of the Equator has been claimed for the king of Portugal by the navigator Pedro Alvarez Cabral. He has called it *Vera Cruz*, or True Cross, but already it is becoming known as *Brazil*, after the red-coloured brazil wood which is abundant there.

Cabral had set out for India with a fleet of 13 ships. To avoid the known *doldrums* off the Guinea coast of Africa, he sailed far west and sighted an unfamiliar coastline, with a lofty, circular mountain in the background. Some men appeared on the beach – brown, naked and with bows and arrows.

Cabral's men captured two of them for inspection. They had their lower lips bored and sharpened bones inserted. Next day the natives brought their women to meet the white visitors. The women were also naked and painted with a red dye from the brazil tree.

As is usual on such voyages, Cabral had with him a number of convicts to be used for the more risky operations. He sent two of them to visit the village. They reported that the natives lived in large wooden huts, each with hammocks for 30 or more persons.

Cabral's men paid a number of visits to the land which they had found. Two of his ship's carpenters made a wooden cross which aroused great interest amongst the natives – not because of its shape, or what it represented, but because of the iron tools which the carpenters used. The locals used wedgeshaped stones to cut wood for themselves.

Cabral decided to show the natives the veneration which he and his men had for the Cross; they knelt before it and kissed it. On their final visit to the shore, when the Portuguese landed to collect food and water, as many as 400 natives emerged to watch their new visitors. Some helped to carry wood to the boats and a few ate the food and wine which they were offered. Cabral is now sailing for India, but he will leave a few convicts to study the natives and their land.

Pedro Cabral (a 19th-century print).

Navigator Dias lost in Atlantic storm

Cape of Good Hope, May 1500
Disaster struck Cabral's fleet after it left the newly discovered land of Brazil and set sail across the South Atlantic for India. Cabral had sent one ship back to Portugal to announce his discovery of the new land and was leading the remainder of his fleet across the Atlantic when the tragedy happened.

As it was approaching the Cape of Good Hope, well south of the Tropic of Capricorn, a fierce storm blew up and four ships foundered with all hands, the rest being badly battered and scattered. Among those who perished was Bartholomew Dias, the great Portuguese navigator who, 12 years ago, became the first European to sail round this cape.

That historic voyage was to be the prelude to Vasco da Gama's epoch-making journey to India; in that, too, Dias played an important role. He supervised the construction and fitting-out of da Gama's fleet, and accompanied it on the first stages of its journey. The ships were three-masted, with two square sails on the mainmasts and a triangular one on the mizzen. Much of the equipment Dias had recommended, such as a double set of sails and rigging, was novel at the time, but more recently has been taken for granted.

His brother, Diogo, was among the survivors of the storms which battered Cabral's fleet. Seven ships have managed to limp to a port in Mozambique for repairs.

Almost certainly it is the back-up equipment which has enabled Cabral's battered ships to survive the storm that carried off Dias. While Cabral is at Mozambique, he hopes to make trade agreements which will further entrench Portuguese commercial interests in southern Africa. Trade has always been the spur to the great voyages of discovery undertaken by Portugal and its great rival, Spain, during the second half of this century. But the bravery and skill of men like Dias have also transformed the map of the world.

A later picture of Dias (1450-1500).

Portuguese "carracks" (a type of ship); attributed to Cornelius Anthonizoon.

Husband performs "Caesar" operation

Switzerland, 1500
Reports have reached the medical profession of an adventurous operation performed recently in Sigershauffen, Switzerland. Apparently a pregnant woman, Frau Nufer, was having considerable trouble delivering her child, possibly because of the baby's position or its size relative to her pelvis width.

Fearing for the health of both mother and child, the husband, Jacob Nufer, took the bold step of cutting open the uterus to release the baby.

Legend has it that the great Roman, Julius Caesar, was delivered in this way. The Roman nobility, though, was usually attended by the best physicians and midwives. Jacob Nufer's occupation is that of a sow gelder.

Saxon woman playwright's work is found

Germany, 1500
There is much excitement in literary circles at the recent discovery of works by the tenth-century Saxon canoness Hroswitha of Gandersheim (c.935 to 972). Her writings include six Latin plays which establish her as the first known German woman writer and, more remarkably, the first European playwright since the classical age. Hroswitha's plays (*Abraham, Callimachus, Dulcitius, Gallicanus, Pafnutius* and *Sapientia*) deal chiefly with Christian virgin martyrs, and include some graphic torture scenes similar to those in early accounts of the lives of the saints, as well as moving scenes of the conversion of prostitutes. Her other works include narrative poems and legends of the saints.

1500 (1500-1506)

Spain, 1501. King Ferdinand issues directives to Nicolas de Ovando, his colonial governor in America, sanctioning the system of levying tribute payments from the Indians and using them as forced labour.

Mexico, 1502. Montezuma II becomes chief of the Aztecs.

Spain, 12 February 1502. A royal edict orders the expulsion from Castile of all Moors who have not been baptised as Christians.

Germany, April 1502. A peasants' rebellion breaks out in the bishopric of Speyer. It is known as the "Bundschuh" revolt, after the rebels' symbol of a laced boot.

Persia, 1502. The Shi'ite Shah Ismail founds the Safavid dynasty.

Spain, 20 January 1503. An office is established in Seville to supervise trade with the New World and, in particular, the expenses of Columbus.

Spain, 20 March 1503. The Saragossa Instruction sets out a series of measures intended to encourage the Indians in the New World to adopt a settled way of life and to spread the gospel among them.

Rome, 1 November 1503. Giuliano della Rovere, who takes the name Julius II, is the second pope to be elected in a year. He succeeds Pius III, who became pope on 18 August, on the death of Alexander VI.

East Africa, 1503. The Portuguese levy a tribute from the sultan of Zanzibar.

Balkans, 2 July 1504. Stephen (the Great), prince of Moldavia since 1457, dies. He secured possession of Bessarabia from the Ottomans and, in 1469, repelled a Mongol invasion.

Spain, 7 November 1504. Columbus returns from his fourth voyage, which began on 11 May 1502.

Spain, 26 November 1504. Isabella of Castile dies, leaving her daughter Joanna (the Mad) as heir to the throne of Castile, but effective power remains in the hands of Isabella's husband, Ferdinand.

Afghanistan, 1504. Babur, a descendant of Tamerlane from Turkestan, seizes Kabul.

Sudan, 1504. Funj kings, Moslems possibly of Bornu *(Nigerian)* origin, defeat and replace the Christian kings of Sennar between the Blue Nile and White Nile rivers.

Shi'ism becomes state religion in Persia

Persia, 1502

The conversion of the people of Persia to Shi'ism is being pursued with ruthless dedication. On the orders of Shah Ismail, the new Safavid ruler, Sunni dissenters are being executed.

Shah Ismail came to power last year after routing an Ak-Koyunlu force of 30,000 men at Sharur and marching into Tabriz. The Safavids are natives of Persia and claim to be the descendants of the Prophet Mohammed. Under Khwaja Ali, head of the order from 1391 to 1427, they moved away from Sunnism to militant Shi'ism, based on belief in a line of 12 infallible *imams*, from Ali to Mohammed. A succession of Safavid leaders were killed during the last century, but their propagandists, working from their base in Ardabil, east of Azerbaijan, kept alive a distinctive faith designed to attract non-Ottomans.

To assist the conversion of the Persian people, Shah Ismail has imported *ulama* from Arab lands, Bahrain, Hilla in Mesopotamia, and particularly from Jabal Amil, in Lebanon. Many leading Shi'ite theologians are of Amili origin, notably al-Karaki, the most important religious figure.

Michelangelo's David hewn from marble

Florence, 8 September 1504

A colossus of modern times, a 13-foot-high statue of David, naked, with his sling over his shoulder, by Michelangelo Buonarotti, has been set up in the Piazza della Signoria after a perilous journey of more than 200 yards, suspended by rope from a wooden frame which was winched along over planks.

The sculptor was in Rome, where he carved his widely admired *Pieta* for St Peter's, when he heard that a huge 18-foot block of marble lying in the works yard of the cathedral might be given to him to work on. It had been there since 1464, abandoned because of a gash in the marble. He calculated how to get his *David* out of the block by making a wax scale model. He let no one see it until it was finished.

Everyone is amazed at the faultless proportions and anatomical correctness on such a scale. He has been paid 4,000 crowns by the city, and *David* has established his reputation as a sculptor without rival.

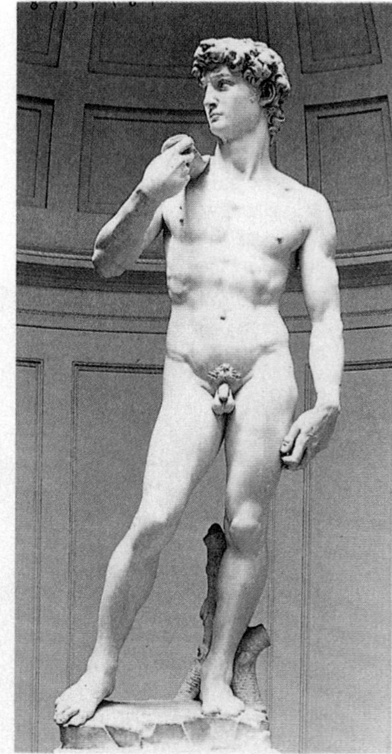

Michelangelo's new statue.

Spring makes timepiece portable

Nuremberg, 1502

Peter Henlein, a German locksmith, has invented a timepiece that can be carried in the hand. About four inches in diameter and three inches in depth, this pocket-size watch is made possible by another innovation, the coiled mainspring.

The flat mainspring is stressed when coiled. Winding it up stores energy in the curved metal. As the coil unwinds, this energy is transmitted to an oscillating section of the watch by means of a mechanism called a verge escapement, a notched gear wheel shaped like a crown, to produce a regular pulse.

Henlein's miniaturisation of the clock is not without its faults, the most serious being that the force of the mainspring is greater when it is fully wound. So time varies.

Explorer tells of cannibals in Brazil

Vespucci, from a 1673 book.

Spain, 1502

Amerigo Vespucci, the Florentine explorer, has returned from his voyage to the New World. Vespucci, whose expedition set off in 1499 to follow the trail of Christopher Columbus, has been sailing down the coast of Brazil to become the first European to see the Rio de la Plata.

Vespucci has written extensively of his experiences, telling of a veritable earthly paradise: a fertile land filled with fruits and wholesome vegetables, swarming with wild animals and exotic birds. But its native population, warlike cannibals who eat their enemies, have lives quite unlike our own.

"Having no laws and no religious faith they live according to nature. There is no possession of private property among them," he wrote. "They have no king, nor do they obey anyone. There is no administration of justice because in their code no-one rules."

They are a brutal people, he adds. The men pierce their lips and cheeks with bones to make themselves look more fierce. In war they slaughter without mercy, and "those who remain on the field bury all the dead of their own side, but they cut up and eat the bodies of their enemies". The survivors are taken as slaves who are frequently offered as sacrifices, providing ritual food for the cannibals.

Death of pope who flaunted his mistress

Rome, 18 August 1503
Romans are rejoicing today following the news of the death of Pope Alexander VI. Rodrigo Borgia was disliked because he was a Spaniard and a libertine. But he was hated because he was a first-rate administrator with enormous energy. He policed Rome and the countryside; he filled the papal treasury by stopping officials from diverting funds and he used the money to help his son, Cesare, to carve out a state in the Romagna, thereby angering nobles whose power he curbed.

Other popes before Alexander have departed from celibacy, but none has so flaunted his reputation as a great lover. He had a portrait of his chief mistress, dressed as the Virgin Mary, painted over the door of his bedchamber.

He publicly acknowledged his three bastards, two of whom have become notorious figures in their own right. His daughter, Lucrezia, had two husbands while still in her teens, although she probably did not have the excessive sex life that Roman gossips suggest. Cesare, his youngest son, must be fearing for his future.

Cesare is a head taller than most tall men, has massive shoulders and blazing blue eyes. He organised *corridas* so that he could show off by beheading a bull with one stroke of his sword. He was ruthless in supporting his father's aims. He lured enemies to the castle of Sinigaglia and had them murdered. He is also said to have had his brother and his sister's second husband killed.

Alexander VI, by Pintoricchio.

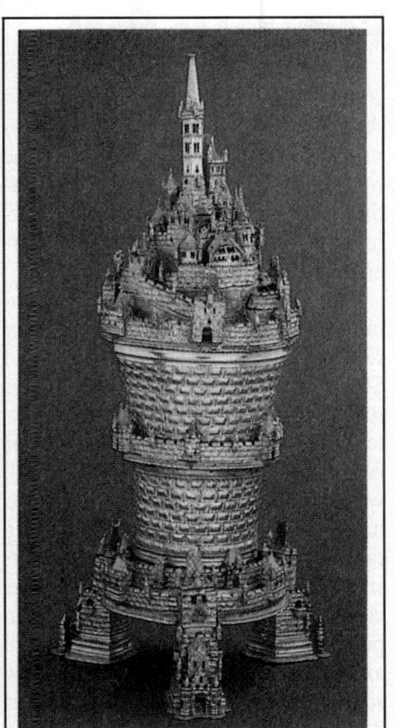

Gold and gilt metal-covered beaker made in the form of a fortress town (German, c.1500).

Moscow breaks up the Golden Horde

Moscow, 1503
Muscovy is politically independent once more, thanks to Ivan III who has consistently refused to pay protection money to Genghis Khan's descendants.

The original Mongolian Golden Horde split into three autonomous *khanates* more than a century ago, but Ahmed, the leader of the core group still known as the Horde, demanded money as recently as 1480. Ivan outmanoeuvred him by negotiating a mutual defence treaty with the Crimean khan and by fighting hard. Ahmed Khan's advance on Moscow in 1472, unsupported by his Lithuanian ally, faded away. A similar assault in 1480 led to a battlefield stalemate after four days. Then Khan Ivak of Western Siberia hit Ahmed's camp and killed him. Muscovy is now ready to expand.

Portuguese punish king for "insolence"

Kilwa, East Africa, 24 July 1505
The Portuguese have inflicted terrible punishment on the African city-state of Kilwa for the insolence of its King Ibrahim and his failure to pay tribute. A German observer with the Portuguese fleet reports that "the heathen" were shot dead, houses were destroyed and "gold, silver, pearls, precious stones and costly clothes" were carried off.

Francisco de Almeida, the Portuguese commander, dropped anchor at Kilwa on his way to India, where he has been made the first viceroy. Ibrahim failed to welcome the Portuguese, offering the excuse that as he left his palace a black tom-cat had crossed his path, which was a bad omen. With that Almeida went on the attack and sacked Mombasa.

King Manuel of Portugal, having found the cost of equipping ships and providing funds for trading too heavy a burden, has made these into commercial operations. Italians and Germans are now partners in the India trade, which also encompasses raids on Moslem city-states in East Africa. The German who saw the sack of Kilwa says that King Manuel has ordered the building of a fort there.

German inventor of the globe is dead

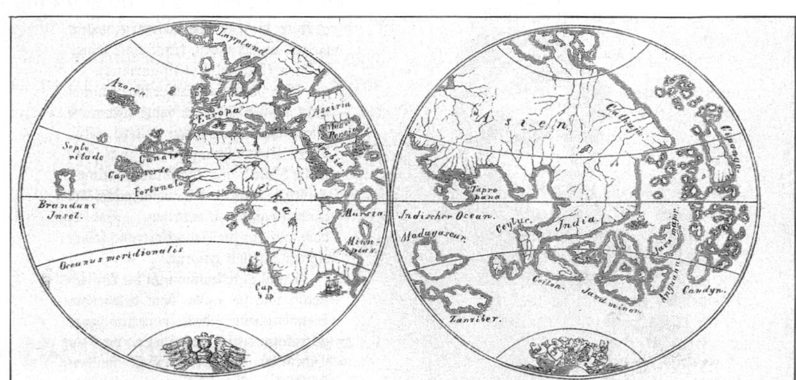

The two hemispheres, after the globe made by Martin Behaim in 1492.

Portugal, 29 July 1506
The great German map-maker Martin Behaim, who constructed the first known globe, has died in Lisbon at the age of 47.

Born into a family of merchants, Behaim spent most of his adult life in Portugal and the Azores. He kept company with all the explorers who came his way, and claimed to have accompanied the navigator Diego Cao on his expedition to Africa in 1485. Later he was captured by English pirates, and held prisoner for several years before being allowed to return to Portugal.

Behaim constructed his famous globe during a visit to Nuremberg in 1492. He drew the outlines of the continents in colour on a surface of fine parchment, probably copying extensively from other maps. The completed work summarised the geographical knowledge of the day.

This colourful tapestry, depicting "wild people" and fantastic animals, was made recently by a craftsman or craftswoman in Switzerland.

1506 (1506-1508)

Spain, 25 September 1506. Philip the Fair dies at Burgos at the age of 28. The son of the Emperor Maximilian, he inherited the Netherlands from his mother, Mary of Burgundy. In 1496 he married Joanna the Mad, the daughter of Ferdinand and Isabella.

Arabia, 1506. The Portuguese Alfonso d'Albuquerque seizes the island of Socotra, the key to the Red Sea.

Rome, 1506. Pope Julius II lays the foundation stone of the basilica of St Peter, the building of which has been entrusted to the architect Bramante. The work is to be financed by the selling of indulgences for the remission of sins.

Rome, 1506. The discovery of the *Laocoon*, a sculpted group from the Hellenic era, causes a great stir. The work is added to the collection of Pope Julius II, who asks Michelangelo to have it restored.

South Atlantic, 1506. The Portuguese Tristan da Cunha discovers an island to which he gives his own name.

Spain, 12 March 1507. Cesare Borgia dies while fighting alongside his brother, the king of Navarre. The son of Pope Alexander VI, Borgia became archbishop of Valence at 16 and cardinal a year later. He was appointed duke of Valence in 1498. In 1502 he had his main enemies murdered.

Italy, 1507. The Genoese rise up against the French forces occupying their city.

Arabia, 1507. Albuquerque takes control of Hormuz, a strategically important position between the Persian Gulf and the Sea of Oman.

Caribbean, 1508. Spain's Sebastian de Ocampo sails around Cuba, proving that it is an island.

North Atlantic, 1508. In search of a north-west passage, Sebastian Cabot reaches Hudson Bay.

Spain, 1508. The Spanish crown is granted rights by the pope to establish and build churches, especially in the Americas.

Rome, 1508. The Fuggers family acquires the right to mint papal currency.

Rome, 1508. Pope Julius II commissions Michelangelo to decorate the ceiling of the Sistine chapel in the Vatican Palace.

Durer studies in Venice and returns to paint Adam and Eve

The young Durer, by himself.

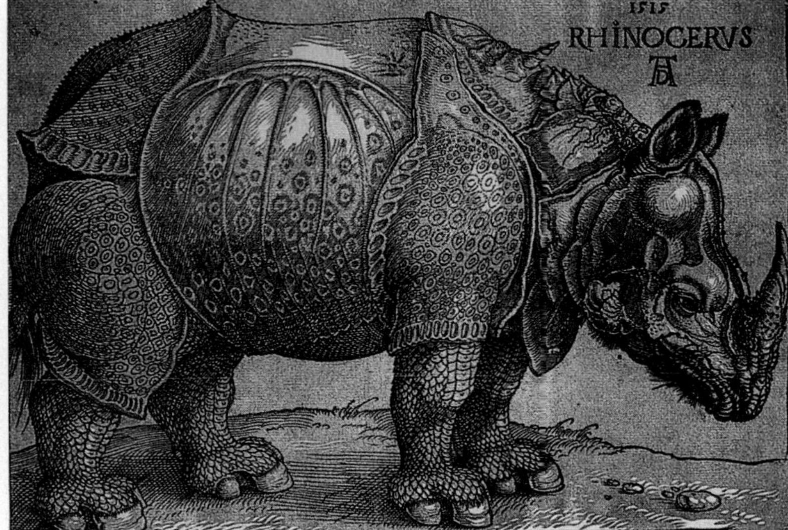

"The Rhinoceros", by Durer, a woodcut engraved from two blocks (1515).

Nuremberg, Germany, 1507

Albrecht Durer, the outstanding German painter and engraver who was born here to a Hungarian goldsmith, has lately returned from a two-year visit to Venice. Having gained a reputation with his popular woodcuts and copperplate engravings, such as *The Apocalypse*, he has turned to oil painting in the Italian manner.

While in Venice he painted a *Feast of the Rose Garlands*, which the doge came to see and which was admired by Giovanni Bellini, the aged Venetian master. Now back at home, he is attempting to render the ideal of human beauty in full length paintings of Adam and Eve – the first full-size nudes to be painted in Germany. These paintings are a contrast to his celebrated engraving of the couple, done a few years ago. Durer's powers of drawing, his studies of mathematics and his theory of art have won him the sort of fame which was unknown for a German artist before his time. People are beginning to speak of a renaissance in the north.

Venice monopolises Mediterranean trade

Carpaccio's "Lion of St Mark", an expression of Venice's civic pride.

Venice, 1507

The island city of Venice, founded more than a thousand years ago, has established itself as the most important centre of Mediterranean trade. Not only do its merchant ships bring in great wealth, but its navy ensures security from the attacks of greedy rivals.

Ideally positioned between western Europe and Asia, its merchants dominate every trade route. Its bankers, insurers and accountants are unrivalled and Venice stands proud, master of Europe's most commercially sophisticated area. Portuguese discoveries in the New World have undoubtedly undermined Venetian power, but the expertise of traders and overall experience has ensured that it continues to dominate the established Oriental routes.

The sought-after spice monopoly has been lost – American silver has given the Portuguese the funds to break it – but the new route round the Cape of Good Hope is simply too time-consuming. Spices do not keep. In any case, no one can rival the Venetian monopoly of Asia's luxury goods.

Indian sultan sinks Portuguese fleet

Bombay, 1508

A Portuguese fleet has been surprised and sunk off Chaul, on the west coast of India, by the Gujaratian and Egyptian navies. The Portuguese viceroy's son, Dom Lourenco, drowned in the battle.

The victory is a triumph for Mahmud Begara, the ageing sultan of Gujarat. A grandson of Ahmed Shah, founder of the state, he has ruled the country for 50 years, extending Gujarat's frontiers to their furthest limits. Tall and martial, with a beard that reaches his waist, he is as proficient at the negotiating table as on the battlefield. A strict Moslem, intolerant of other creeds, he protects himself from poison by daily absorbing small amounts into his system. He is now so impregnated, it is said, that flies die when they settle on him.

His victory has elated Moslems all over India and the Near East, who fear for Islam as it retreats before European expansionism.

Columbus' travels end

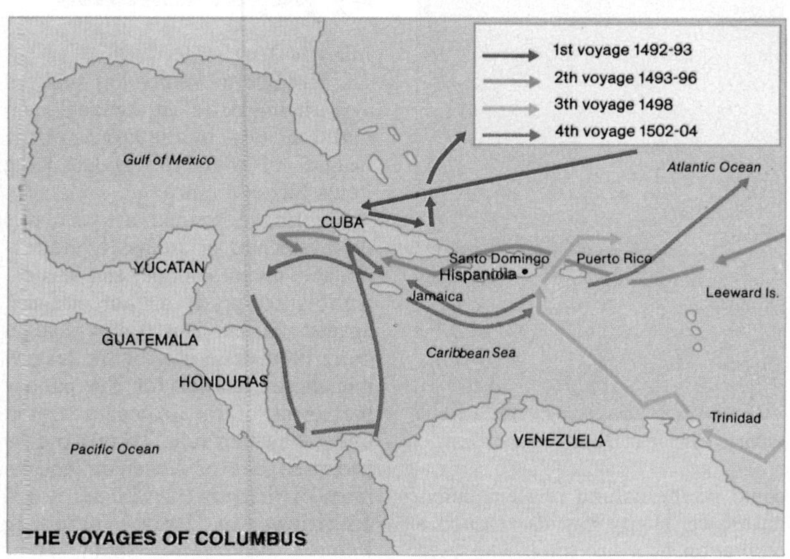

Valladolid, Spain, 21 May 1506
The explorer Columbus died today aged 55, embittered, isolated and still convinced that what he had found in the west was the true Indies, not a place others describe as the "New World." His will, made yesterday, leaves his son the one-tenth share of the wealth generated by his discovery, as promised in his contract with King Ferdinand but still unpaid 14 years later.

Columbus was a great captain, but a poor coloniser. On his first voyage he deposited a small group of settlers at Hispaniola *(Santo Domingo)*. All were soon killed by the natives. In September 1493 he sailed from Cadiz a second time, after only five months in Spain, with 17 ships and 1,200 potential settlers, and returned to the original site of Isabella. There was trouble as soon as the turbulent Spaniards got ashore. Columbus brought this under control and went exploring. He returned to discover his settlers at war with the Indians, who resented demands for food, women and gold. Columbus dealt with the problem by massacring natives. In spite of that, colourful complaints about him came to Madrid from the Spaniards. He would now be fighting on two fronts 3,000 miles apart. While he defended his political corner in Spain, his brother Bartolome built a new settlement, Santo Domingo, which became the empire's regional capital.

By now, with routes established, Spain needed Columbus less. His third voyage ended in 1499, with his return to Spain in irons on the orders of Francisco de Bobadilla, his successor as governor. Columbus' offence was that he had suppressed another rebellion by hanging seven settlers in the street.

Columbus at the Spanish court, by Eugene Deveria (1808-65).

His last voyage ended four years ago, his ships beached and unseaworthy at Santa Gloria *(Jamaica)* and distress signals ignored for a year. Yet not even his worst enemy can diminish his achievements.

He charted about 60 islands, and landed on the shores of Venezuela. He found little gold but much else, including tobacco. His seamanship identified trade winds both ways across the ocean at different latitudes. He was thus, in a sense, the foreigner who put Spain on the map by making the map.

German map calls new world "America"

Lorraine, 1507
A map of the world has just been published which, for the first time, shows the New World to be a distinct continent between Europe and Asia.

It names this continent America, after the Italian explorer Amerigo Vespucci who claims to have discovered the mainland in 1497 – a year before Columbus arrived. In fact, all the indications are that the expedition took place two years later.

The cartographers, Martin Waldseemuller and Matthias Ringmann, seem to have accepted Vespucci's dubious version of events. The truth is, his achievements as an explorer do not compare with those of Columbus, whose log of his expeditions is indisputably genuine in every date recorded. However, Vespucci's accounts of his voyages for Spain and Portugal have earned him a powerful reputation.

He certainly sighted land in several parts of central and south America. On his first expedition, under the leadership of Alonso de Ojeda, he discovered an Indian city built on water and named it Venezuela, or "Little Venice".

The irony of this new map is that – within a year of Columbus' death – it has given the principal credit for the discovery of America to a man whose principal talent seems to have been as a self-publicist.

Spanish settlers make slaves of Indians

Hispaniola, West Indies, 1508
The fortunes of Spanish settlers, once threatened by their failure to find a major supply of gold here *(Santo Domingo)*, have been boosted by a move away from the futile search for precious metal to the cultivation of a profitable cash crop: sugar cane. And they are benefiting from the exploitation of a valuable local commodity: Indian slaves.

Columbus introduced sugar to the Indies on his second voyage in 1493, but his main interest remained the discovery of gold in order to pay off his backers. Hispaniola simply had none to offer and, desperate for funds, Columbus imposed a gold tax, offering the natives copper bracelets for their valuables.

This scheme brought some revenue, but the island was no Eldorado. Today no one expects to find gold here, but the sugar crop is booming, fuelled by slaves working on huge, enclosed estates. Only dwindling manpower threatens profits: of the island's original 250,000 natives, the brutal work has killed off all but 60,000.

Spaniards force Peruvian natives to carry booty in this slightly later print.

1508 (1508-1510)

Baghdad, 1508. The Safavid Shah Ismail seizes Baghdad.

Ethiopia, 1508. Lebna Denguel comes to the throne.

France, 10 December 1508. With the aim of conquering Venice's Italian possessions, the Emperor Maximilian and Louis XII of France, backed by Spain and the pope, form the League of Cambrai.

Rome, January 1509. Pope Julius II instructs Raphael to decorate the *stanze* (chambers) in the Vatican Palace.

England, 22 April 1509. On the death of Henry VII – the first Tudor king and victor of the battle of Bosworth against Richard III – his only surviving son succeeds him as Henry VIII.

Italy, 27 April 1509. Pope Julius II excommunicates the republic of Venice.

Italy, 14 May 1509. A French victory over the Venetians at Agnadello allows the pope to reoccupy the Romagna.

England, 11 June 1509. Henry VIII marries his former sister-in-law Catherine of Aragon, Ferdinand's daughter.

Spain, 1509. A council of the Indies is created to take responsibility for administering Spanish conquests in America.

Brazil, 1509. Diego Alvaros Correa founds the first Portuguese settlement in Brazil, near Porto Seguro.

Ethiopia, 1509. Ethiopia sends Matthew, an Armenian, as ambassador to Portugal.

Caribbean, 1509. Juan Ponce de Leon, a Spanish exile who travelled with Columbus in 1493, seizes control of Puerto Rico.

India, 1509. Krishnadevaraya becomes king of Vijayanager.

Spain, 1510. The importation of African slaves into America is given official authorisation.

Central Asia, 1510. The Safavid Shah Ismail defeats and kills the Ozbeg Mohammed Shaybani and seizes Herat, Bactria and Khiva.

Mexico, c.1510. Two sailors survive a shipwreck on the coast of Yucatan and are captured by Maya peoples. One, Jeronimo de Aguilar, is later rescued by Cortez' expedition. The other, Gonzalo Guerrero, chooses to become assimilated into "Indian" society and helps them to organise resistance to Cortez.

Henry VII, victor of Bosworth Field, dies

England, 22 April 1509

Henry VII, final victor of the Wars of the Roses and head of the House of Tudor, is dead. Since ascending the throne after the defeat of Richard III at Bosworth Field in 1485, and thus ending 30 years of brutal and intermittent civil war, he has brought a period of much needed political stability to his realm.

Such stability has been hard won. Henry faced a number of pretenders to his throne – the most dangerous of which were Perkin Warbeck and Lambert Simnel – but by 1497 he had crushed every rival. Once established, Henry set about ruling his country. He sought to reduce the independence and factiousness of the powerful nobility, not by direct repression, but by building a broad-based body of support among the gentry and by tying the nobles to him financially, using bonds and recognisances. The country has benefited greatly from his reign, though much of the improvement could be the natural result of internal peace. Henry has also earned a reputation as a just king, who used the legal system wisely.

Henry VII: first Tudor monarch.

However, his critics suggest that, especially in his later years, he used the law as much for his own ends as to dispense real justice. He is succeeded by his son who becomes Henry VIII.

Venice is crushed by papal alliance

Italy, 14 May 1509

The republic of Venice has suffered a shattering defeat at Agnadello, in northern Italy, by the armies of the League of Cambrai under King Louis XII of France.

The league, formed last year, was the brainchild of Julius II, the formidable Genoese pope, and was ostensibly set up as a "holy league" against Turks. But Julius had a more immediate use for the league, namely to recover for the papacy the towns of the Romagna region under Venetian rule. To this end he promised bits of Venetian land to most of the powers with territorial ambitions in Italy, including France, the empire, Spain, Hungary, Switzerland and some small Italian states.

But the pope's triumph may turn sour; in crushing Venice he has allowed more powerful states, such as France, to strengthen their footholds in northern Italy.

Eastern economy in decline as a new world beckons traders

Indian Ocean, 1510

The Mameluke dynasty which has ruled Arabia for more than a century, already weakened by a succession of incompetent, corrupt and degenerate sultans, is facing the new and potentially devastating threat of economic decline.

Arab traders have dominated the lucrative routes to the east ever since the eighth century, when they opened up contacts with India. Their ships sail across the Indian Ocean and their caravans bring the goods overland to the great cities of the eastern Mediterranean.

Now that monopoly is in jeopardy. Ever since the Portuguese explorer Vasco da Gama discovered a new route to the Indies, sailing round the Cape of Good Hope, Portugal and other European nations have begun setting up their own trading posts.

Attacks on Moslem shipping in the Red Sea and the Indian Ocean have become increasingly frequent. The Portuguese have set up a trading post in Calicut, on the west coast of India. Sultan Qansawh al-Ghawri has threatened the pope with the destruction of Christian Holy Places, but the Europeans continue to establish themselves as the new spice merchants. Further European exploration has added to Arabia's difficulties, although the explorers have headed west rather than east. The discovery of the New World in 1492 has shifted the centre of world affairs to the west. The Mediterranean, the most westerly area of Arab power, has lost its central role.

A coloured print depicting Arab traders with camels at a desert port.

Safavid artists redesign Persian carpets

A richly-woven Persian carpet showing a leopard attacking a gazelle.

Persia, c.1510

Persian carpet-weaving has recovered from its recent decline and is undergoing a complete revolution under the new Safavid rulers. Leading artists and weavers have gathered in large urban factories to create carpets quite unlike those produced by mediaeval artisans. Each city imposes its own style, but the overall emphasis is on new images. Animal and vegetable motifs predominate, often in combination. Some carpets show landscapes, their stylised contours reflecting current trends in painting.

First African slaves arrive in the Americas

Caribbean, 1510

Cuba is preparing for the first shipment of Negro slaves from Africa to overcome an acute shortage of labour among the native Indians. The Negro slaves from the Guinea coast are being sold to anxious colonists as being capable of doing the work of four Indians.

The importation of slaves plus moves to counter the decline in the Indian population – numbers have slumped in Hispaniola *(Santo Domingo)* alone from 300,000 to just 20,000 since 1492 – should stem settlers' fears that Spain is about to abandon the Americas.

Forthcoming Spanish legislation, prompted by visiting Dominicans appalled at Indian conditions, will regulate the practice of *encomienda*, where Indians are herded into camps for conversion to Christianity and used for forced labour.

Slaves, as depicted on the palace door at Ikere-Ekiti in Nigeria.

Strange breads bring on drugged stupor

Peasants are probably stupefied by a diet of mind-altering foodstuffs.

Europe, c.1510

Ideas are flourishing in studios and workshops, and the shape of the earth seems to change every moment. But how you see the world these days depends above all on what bread you eat.

A shortage of wheat grain means that herbs with odd side-effects are used for breadmaking. Darnel, a grass which causes disorientation, tiredness and nausea, and vetch, which leads to depression, are common adulterants. Poppy, inducing euphoria and sleep, is a common seasoning. Rye bread often contains lysergic acid, a powerful hallucinogen probably responsible for the convulsions and madness called St Vitus' dance. Most of western Europe's poor are in the grip of mind-altering foods such as these.

Japanese pirates pillage eastern Asia

China, c.1510

Japanese pirates, known to the Chinese as *wako*, are once again ravaging China's southern coast, landing to pillage the coastal villages. The pirate ships are often officered by Japanese, but crewed by Chinese, who cut off their pigtails and pretend to be Japanese.

These fake wako are mainly fishermen and sailors who have been deprived of a living by imperial edicts forbidding them to pursue their trades in the belief that if there were no flourishing coastal towns there would be nothing for the pirates to attack.

This absurd policy has created pirates who are more desperate than the Japanese and know where the treasure is hidden. China is not the only country to suffer from the depredations of the seawolves who hunt throughout the Asian seas.

Capital prospers under "benign" king

Vijayanagar, India, 1509

Within nine months of attaining the throne of Vijayanagar, Krishnadevaraya has repulsed an attack on the state by Sultan Mahmud of Bidar, leaving the sultan wounded, defeated an army of his rival, Yusuf Adil Khan, and advanced north into Gulbarga and Bidar. His military prowess, his mercy to his enemies and the benevolence of his rule suggest the beginning of a golden age for Vijayanagar.

Though Krishnadevaraya himself favours Vaishnavism, all Hindu sects are respected equally. Temples are being endowed, the poor are being fed, new lands are being irrigated, and Vijayanagar, the fabulously beautiful capital city, is attracting scholars from all over Hindu India.

1510 (1510-1511)

Italy, 24 February 1510. Pope Julius II lifts the excommunication of Venice, imposed last year, and turns against the king of France.

Switzerland, February 1510. Matthias Schiner, the cardinal bishop of Sion, dissuades the Swiss from forming an alliance with the French against the pope.

Florence, 17 May 1510. The Florentine painter Sandro Botticelli, a pupil of Fra Lippo Lippi, dies. Among his greatest works are *The Birth of Venus* and *Primavera*. He also painted superb portraits and illustrated Dante's *Divine Comedy* with pen drawings.

India, 1510. The Portuguese explorer Alfonso de Albuquerque seizes Goa.

Scotland, 1510. The Scottish theologian John Legrand argues in favour of the use of force to bring about the spiritual conquest of non-Christian races.

Spain, 1511. Diego Columbus, the son of Christopher, recovers the rights over his father's discoveries in America which were confiscated by the Spanish crown, thus restoring his family's fortunes.

North Africa, 1511. A Spanish force occupies the island of Penon, in the bay of Algiers.

Caribbean, 1511. The first African slaves arrive in the New World. This follows the granting of authorisation, in 1503, to Nicolas de Ovando, the Spanish governor of Hispaniola *(Santo Domingo)*, for the introduction to the island of African slaves.

Caribbean, 1511. The Dominican friar Antonio de Montesinos preaches a sermon to the colonists in Hispaniola questioning the religious principles of colonial ventures. He speaks out against the right of conquest, arguing that, because Indians are true men with souls, they should not be subject to enslavement.

Caribbean, 1511. Juan de Esquivel undertakes the conquest of Jamaica.

Caribbean, 1511. Led by Diego Velazquez, the Spanish take control of the island of Cuba by force.

France, 18 October 1511. The chronicler Philippe de Commynes, a former servant of Louis XI, dies. His *Memoires* recount the reigns of Louis XI and Charles VIII.

Warlike Pope set to drive out French

Rome, 5 October 1511

Pope Julius II has now recruited England under Henry VIII as a member of his "Holy League" against France. His main allies are Spain and Venice, but two years ago it was Venice that was the main enemy (for annexing papal provinces on the Adriatic) and France which was his ally. Now he has raised the cry to "clear the Barbarians out of Italy" – meaning the French under Louis XII. They have occupied Milan since 1499, when they captured it from the Sforzas.

A protracted war in Lombardy, the Romagna and the Veneto seems inevitable, now that the papal forces have been joined by Venetian and Spanish troops and Swiss mercenaries.

Julius' strategy is to re-establish the sovereignty of the papacy in all its ancient territories and end the foreign domination of Italy. He is a warlike pope. He is to direct the siege of the fortress of Mirandola in person, helmeted for battle.

Persian empire grows to rival Ottomans

Persia, 1511

The Shi'ite Shah Ismail, who first claimed rule over Persia ten years ago, has conquered Khurasan and killed the Ozbeg Mohammed Shaybani. He has also installed Babur, the descendant of Tamerlane who seized Kabul seven years ago, in Samarkand. As a result of these military successes the Safavid empire now extends from the river Tigris in the west to the river Oxus in the east, where the Ozbeg tribes roam. In the west, this new Persian empire now rivals Ottoman power.

Founded as a religious order by Safi al-Din in 1301, the Safavids established themselves in eastern Azerbaijan over the next 150 years, making alliances, then falling out, with the Ak-Koyunlu, who dominated Persia.

Although three Safavid leaders, Junayd, Haydar and Ali, all died at Ak-Koyunlu hands, Ali's son Ismail eluded them and lived in hiding before leading a successful revolution in 1500. The vital military factor in Shah Ismail's success was the loyalty of the fierce Turcoman tribesmen who became known as the Qizilbash. Having decisively beaten the AkKoyunlu army at Sharur in 1501, Shah Ismail dealt with the remainder at Hamadan in 1503, gaining control of central and

"Night attack", from the "Book of Victory", by the artist Nama Zafa.

southern Persia. In 1504 he subdued the Caspian provinces of Mazandaran and Gurgan, and captured Yazd. Next came the annexation of Diyar Bakr and the pacification of the western frontier. Baghdad was captured in 1508, and thus the conquest of south-western Persia was completed.

Qizilbash influence in government has been reduced by the dismissal of a Turcoman *wakil*, and his replacement by a Persian.

Erasmus censures male stupidity

Paris, 1511

Scholars at the Sorbonne are talking excitedly about a major new contribution to humanist thought. *Praise of Folly*, which has just been published here, is (despite its title) a profoundly serious work, which nevertheless sparkles with wit and imagination. It is written by a 44-year-old Dutchman, Desiderius Erasmus, who is already well known to several French scholars since he is a prolific letter writer.

The central character of *Praise of Folly* is Folly herself, a volatile and ever-changing woman. She delivers a series of homilies against the stupidities of all kinds of men. She even castigates crabbed scholars like Erasmus himself, but her most severe censure she reserves for worldly popes and hypocritical monks. She also shows a sense of humour. "Who would marry," she asks, "if they rationally anticipated the pains and problems?" She thinks a little folly helps to make the world go round.

Erasmus advocates a practical piety which is based on the human spirit rather than religious observances. He thinks that religion is too important to be left to the theologians. Men of letters can purify the scriptures by going back to the ancient sources. They can combine their learning with faith and so achieve mystic unity with God.

He is widely travelled. Recently he spent ten months in Venice as a proof-reader for the printer Aldo Manuzio. Before that he visited scholars in other parts of Italy and in Germany.

Erasmus of Rotterdam, by Durer.

Soft light of Venice produces brilliant paintings

"Concert Champetre", by Giorgio Giorgione, who died this year of plague.

A detail from "The Transfiguration", by Giovanni Bellini (born c.1430).

Venetian crystal reliquary, c.1500.

"Judith", by Giorgione.

"Colleoni", by Andrea Verrocchio.

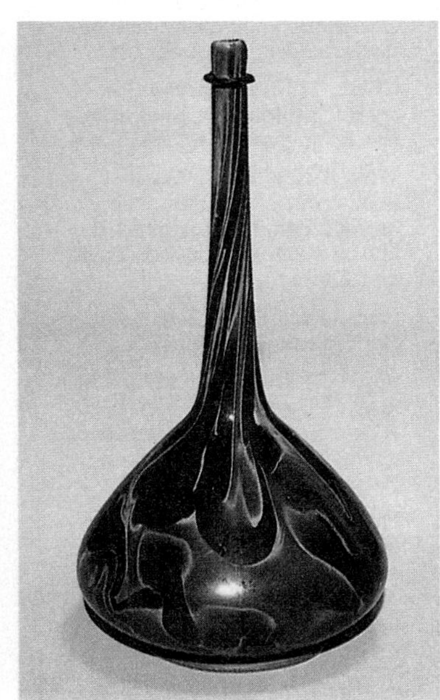
A Chalcedony glass bottle.

Venice, c.1511
Venice, one of the richest of the Italian city states, is flowering with a renaissance like that of Florence 60 years ago. Venetian light, which is softer and more luminous because of its lagoon, affects the character of Venetian painting, which is mainly carried out in oil rather than fresco.

Giovanni Bellini, now in his eighties, is the doyen of Venetian painters. His work for the doge's palace was destroyed by fire, but his portraits of the doges, such as Doge Loredan, are celebrated for their richness of colour glowing as if from within. Bellini is so highly prized that when the Sultan Mohammed invited him to visit Constantinople, having seen some of his portraits belonging to the Venetian ambassador, the Senate would not let Giovanni go. They sent instead his brother, Gentile, who painted the sultan's portrait.

Bellini has introduced a new soft and atmospheric quality to his background landscapes, especially in *The Agony in the Garden* where the hills and sky are suffused with the light of daybreak. He taught this to his pupil Giorgione, who came from Treviso and showed genius at an early age. Besides religious subjects Giorgione produced easel pictures, portraits and landscapes in rich, dark, suggestive colours that combine mystery and romanticism. A good musician, he often introduced music into his pictures, as in his *Concert Champetre.* He died this year of the plague, caught from a Venetian lady with whom he was in love.

One of his assistants, who was also a pupil of Bellini, is Tiziano Vecellio, known as Titian, whose life-size portraits and landscapes with figures show the same romantic character.

Venice has also made a great advance in its long-established craft of glassmaking. The art of making crystal glass which is absolutely clear has been perfected at factories on the island of Murano, where the glass-makers are concentrated by decree. Goblets of elegant lightness, bowls and dishes, many in exquisite colour and worked into bizarre shapes, are being exported all over Europe. The secret of the process is closely guarded.

1511 (1511-1513)

South-East Asia, 1511. The Portuguese secure control of the main strategic positions along the spice route. Alfonso d'Albuquerque occupies Malacca on the Malayan peninsula, while his fleet reaches Amboina on the Moluccan archipelago.

Spain, 22 February 1512. The Italian explorer Amerigo Vespucci, who gave America its name, dies in Seville.

Italy, 11 April 1512. The forces of the Holy League are heavily defeated by the French at the battle of Ravenna.

Italy, 1512. Julius II summons a general council, in opposition to the council called at Pisa by Louis XII, the king of France.

Europe, 1512. The Emperor Maximilian severs his alliance with Louis XII of France.

Spain, 1512. Having seized Pamplona and St Jean Pied de Port, King Ferdinand's army occupies the entire kingdom of Navarre.

Constantinople, 1512. Allied with the Janissaries, Selim, the son of Bayezid II, has his brothers and nephews killed and makes himself Ottoman sultan.

France, 1512. Louis XII imposes a tax on the "new Christians", the converted Jews from the Iberian peninsula.

China, 1512. Peasants in the central province of Szechuan rise up in protest against taxes.

West Africa, 1512. Askia Mohammed the Great, the king of Songhai, conquers the Hausa states of Katsina, Zaria and Kano.

East Africa, 1512. The Portuguese abandon Kilwa.

Spain, 27 December 1512. The laws of Burgos give New World natives legal protection against abuse and authorise Negro slavery.

France, 16 August 1513. The combined forces of Henry VIII of England and the Emperor Maximilian defeat the French at Guinegatte in the "Battle of the Spurs".

Scotland, 9 September 1513. The Scots are defeated by the English at Flodden and James IV of Scotland is killed in the battle. Margaret, the sister of Henry VIII of England, becomes regent for her one-year-old son, James V.

North America, 1513. Juan Ponce de Leon, the former governor of Puerto Rico, claims Florida for Spain.

"Blackmail" charges for St Peter's

Julius' dream for the Piazza di San Pietro: will it ever become real?

Rome, 1513

Pope Julius II, now aged 70, seems determined to go down in history as the man who caused St Peter's basilica to be rebuilt in the finest style of the age. He has already laid the cornerstone, but more money is needed to get the building under way. Nothing but the best is good enough for Julius, and he has been noted during his reign for his patronage of artists like Raphael and Michelangelo.

His financial stewardship is less admired than his taste in art, though. He is relying on the sale of indulgences and the tactics of his envoys in selling them amounts to emotional blackmail, according to his critics. It was Pope Sixtus IV who extended indulgences to loved ones assumed to be suffering from their sins in purgatory in 1476. This year, in efforts to extract money for the rebuilding, papal envoys have been depicting the voices of dead parents wailing in purgatory.

More scandalous still, money is being "diverted" before it reaches Rome. Prince Albert, the archbishop of both Mainz and Magdeburg, is the worst offender. He is deeply in debt to the great German banking house, the Fuggers of Augsburg. He is paying off his debts by selling indulgences.

Florida is claimed for Spanish king

North America, 8 April 1513

Juan Ponce de Leon, the Spaniard whose quest for a fabled Fountain of Youth remains unsuccessful, has discovered a land which he has claimed for the king of Spain.

The new land is believed to be an island. Because of its abundance of flowers, and the proximity of the religious feast of Pasqua de Flores, de Leon has called the territory *Florida*, Spanish for "floral".

De Leon sailed with Christopher Columbus on his second voyage to the New World in 1493. He served on the island of Hispaniola and explored Puerto Rico in 1508, becoming the island's governor in 1509. He was later removed from office through a political dispute.

Governor de Leon: a later print.

Top Hebrew scholar faces heresy charge

Cologne, Germany, 1513

Johann Reuchlin, a noted Hebrew scholar, is to be brought before the court of the inquisition here. The main charge against him, according to the Rhineland inquisitor, Jakob van Hochstraten, is that his latest work, the pamphlet, *Augenspiegel*, is a work of heresy.

The story behind the trial goes back to 1509. In that year Johann Pfefferkorn, a converted Jew, with the help of the Cologne Dominicans, had obtained authorisation from the Emperor Maximilian to destroy all Hebrew books except the Bible. He was frustrated in this by the opposition of the archbishop of Mainz, helped by Reuchlin.

Pfefferkorn then vented his anger against Reuchlin, alleging in print that he had accepted bribes from Jews and that other scholars had written books which Reuchlin claimed as his own. *Augenspiegel*, which argues for the preservation of Jewish literature, was Reuchlin's stinging reply.

Despite the influence of the Cologne Dominicans and the draconian powers of the Inquisition courts, Reuchlin is not without hope. The archbishop of Mainz is still a powerful friend. He is also an internationally known scholar who is particularly respected in Italy.

He first became interested in Hebrew and the Jewish mystical texts of the *Qabbalah* when visiting Pico de la Mirandola in Florence. Reuchlin's most famous work, *On the Rudiments of Hebrew*, shows how the language is essential for Christian theology.

Glories of Josquin and Flemish music

Flanders, c.1512

The current reputation of Flanders as a home of musical excellence is largely due to one man, Josquin des Prez, now in his seventies and almost universally praised as Europe's greatest composer. His music synthesises the polyphony of the Flanders masters Guillaume Dufay (c.1398-1474), Antoine Busnois (c.1430-1492), and, especially, his teacher, the great Johannes Ockeghem (c.1410-1497), with the more harmonic style of Italy, where, like his fellow Fleming, Heinrich Isaac, he is much in demand from major patrons.

Josquin's works include church masses, motets, and songs in German, French and Italian.

Portugal takes Malacca

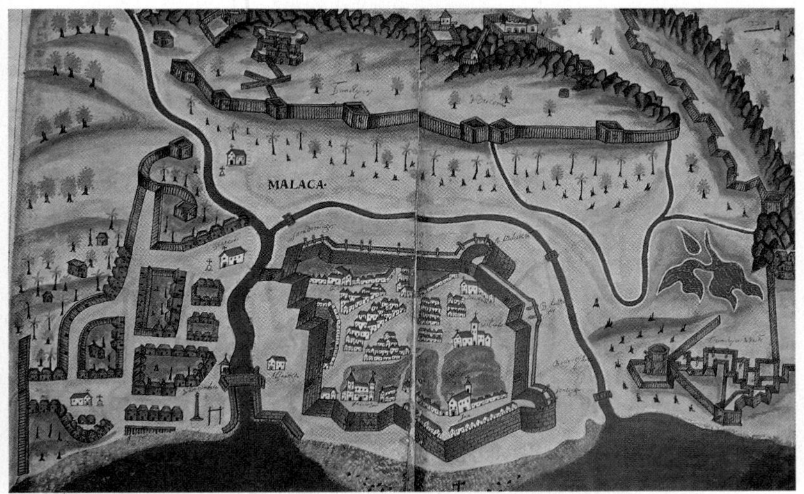

Malacca, whose capture could give Portugal control of the spice trade.

Malacca, 1511
Portugal's potential for dominating the lucrative spice trade with the east has been transformed by the operations of the brilliant naval strategist, Alfonso d'Albuquerque. With his capture of Malacca, which commands the passage from the Indian Ocean to the South China Sea, he has completed a string of naval bases and trading posts running from the Red Sea through Goa in India to the Far East.

The siege of Malacca severely strained his resources in men and ships. Because of the stiff resistance by the defenders and the problems caused by the monsoon he has been obliged to remain in the area for almost a year; during that time Goa, the city built on an island and the centre of a shipbuilding industry, which he captured only last year, almost fell to the Moslem sultan of Bijapur.

A Portuguese accountant who has been assigned to the newly established royal factory at Malacca reports: "Should anyone ask what advantage to his exchequer the king, our lord, can derive from Malacca, there is no doubt that – once the influence is finished that this ex-king of Malacca still exercises – the town is of such importance and profit that it seems to me it has no equal in the world."

The Portuguese are set to begin the regular shipment of Oriental spices to Lisbon. Cargoes will include pepper, cinammon, nutmeg and cloves.

Swiss foot-soldiers rout French at Novara

Novara, Italy, 6 June 1513
France suffered a new and crushing defeat in its struggle with Pope Leo X's Holy League today. Heavily mauled at last year's battle of Ravenna, when honours were declared even, French and Venetian forces have been routed at Novara, near Milan, where Swiss mercenaries under Cardinal Schiner took just an hour to put them to flight.

The defeat, which must surely put an end to French ambitions in Italy, has been compounded by the English invasion of northern France. Landing near Calais, they have already taken the towns of Therouanne and Tournai.

Leo X and nephews, by Raphael.

Spanish explorer discovers "South Sea"

Darien, Panama, 29 September 1513
Vasco Nunez de Balboa, the Spanish explorer, today became the first European to sight what he calls "the South Sea". Balboa and his men travelled from their base in Darien, near the Atlantic Ocean, heading west across the narrow isthmus in a gruelling 25-day journey across 45 miles of near-impenetrable jungle.

On reaching a mountain that overlooked the South Sea, Balboa climbed alone to its peak, where he prayed before calling on his men to join him. He has claimed the new sea, also known as the Pacific Ocean, for Spain.

Balboa (a 19th-century engraving).

As well as natural hazards, Balboa's 190 Spaniards and several hundred Indian slaves have had to fight off hostile natives. Armed with swords, crossbows and arquebuses, and led by a pack of bloodhounds, the expedition fought a pitched battle against them. It was a bloody, unequal struggle, according to witnesses who tell how the big Spanish swords "hewed from one an arm, from another a leg and buttock, and the head from the body at one stroke".

Civil servant's guide to political power

Florence, 1513
In an attempt to regain favour with his former employers, a senior civil servant has written a remarkable study of political power, its uses and abuses. *The Prince*, by Niccolo Machiavelli, is the talk of Florentine political circles.

Machiavelli was 29 when he was appointed secretary to the Council of Ten, the second most important executive tier in the republic. The council handled wars (at a time when war was an almost permanent feature among the Italian city-states) and internal security. The post involved the secretary in frequent visits to Italian and foreign rulers, including the king of France, the pope and Cesare Borgia, upon whom many believe he based the prince in his book.

A later impression of Machiavelli.

When the Medicis returned to Florence in 1512, Machiavelli lost his job and was exiled – urged by the Medicis to devote himself to writing a history of the republic. The secretary had walked the gilt-lined corridors of power, however, and still pined for high office; *The Prince* and three other books, including *Discourses*, are clearly designed to court favour with the Medicis. *The Prince* does not assume that princely rule is any better than popular "democratic" government, but it discusses at length the way in which princely power is gained and, more significantly, it analyses how power is preserved in the volatile climate of Italian politics.

The book does seem to have pleased the Medicis; however, many believe that Machiavelli's approach is too direct and blunt – and obvious in its intent.

1513 (1513-1515)

Indian Ocean, 1513. The Portuguese discover the islands of Mauritius and Reunion uninhabited.

France, 1513. Following the failure of his Italian campaigns, Louis XII is forced to negotiate with Pope Leo X. He also signs a peace treaty with England.

Rome, 1513. The Fuggers bank is asked to sell indulgences to finance the work on the basilica of St Peter.

Europe, 1513. A new edition of Ptolemy's *Geography* shows the newly discovered western lands as two continents, situated between Europe and Asia.

Rome, 11 March 1514. On the death of Bramante, Raphael takes charge of the building of St Peter's.

Persia, August 1514. The Ottomans crush the Safavid Persians at Chaldiran, in the upper basin of the Aras river.

France, 1514. Louis XII marries Mary Tudor, the younger sister of Henry VIII of England.

Central America, 1514. Pedro Arias Davila begins to explore the Pacific coast.

Spain, 1514. New World natives are ordered to convert to Christianity under threat of enslavement or death.

Poland, 1514. The astronomer Nicolas Copernicus returns to his native country after several years studying in Italy, convinced that the earth revolves around the sun – contrary to accepted belief.

France, 1 January 1515. Louis XII is succeeded as king of France by his nephew, Francis, who is determined to prosecute France's claims in Italy.

Vienna, 22 July 1515. The Emperor Maximilian and Vladislav of Bohemia forge an alliance between the Habsburg and Jagiello dynasties. Louis and Anne, the children of Vladislav, will marry Mary and Ferdinand, the grandchildren of Maximilian.

England, 1515. Thomas Wolsey, the archbishop of York, becomes cardinal and lord chancellor. His ambition is to make England the arbiter of European affairs.

England, 1515. Henry VIII decrees a series of measures aimed at protecting peasants from the consequences of enclosure – the practice of dividing up and closing off the common land.

Satire mocks pleasure-seeking monks

Cologne, Germany, 1515

A brilliant new satire, *Epistolae Obscurorum Virorum* (Letters from Obscure Men), has appeared here. It is designed to help the Hebrew scholar Johann Reuchlin in his battle to escape from the clutches of the Inquisition. It is an amusing skit on the Dominican monks, deliberately written in vile Latin.

It is in the form of letters written to monks, teachers and theologians. The letter writer purports to be Ortvinus Gratius, a theologian of the University of Cologne who is one of the principal supporters of the Dominicans in their attempt to convict Reuchlin. The monks are portrayed as having more taste for earthly pleasures than for prayer. They love the wine of the Rhine more than that of the Mass. Their letters are long on coarse pleasantries and short on theological discussion. The title refers to *Letters from Illustrious Men*, written last year by humanists who support Reuchlin's cause.

There is little doubt here that the main author of the satire is Ulrich von Hutten. He comes from a wealthy Franconian noble family. He has never ceased to stress the warrior code of a nobleman of the Holy Roman empire. He is something of a hothead and has long had a reputation for ferocious anti-clericalism. Yet he is also a considerable scholar, having studied both Latin and Greek in Bologna, and is noted for the elegance and eloquence of his Latin poetry and prose.

America seen as two new continents

Europe, 1513

Following lengthy deliberations, cartographers and geographers in Europe have now reached agreement that the newly discovered lands west of the Atlantic Ocean are not in fact Asia.

A new edition of the *Geography* by the Egyptian expert Ptolemy – a popular source since its revival in 1405 – has been published, displaying the land mass as two distinct continents, situated between Europe and Asia.

Christopher Columbus was misled by the Romans' 1,400-year-old calculations, which are now known to have underestimated the circumference of the earth.

Builder of Portugal's Indies empire dies, a disappointed man

A later portrait of Albuquerque, whose service was ill-rewarded.

Goa, India, 16 December 1515

Portugal's greatest naval strategist, Alfonso d'Albuquerque, died at sea near here today, a deeply disappointed man. Despite great services to his country he fell victim to the intrigues of enemies at the Portuguese court. A few days ago he returned from the capture of Ormuz, at the mouth of the Persian Gulf, to be met at the entrance to Goa harbour by a vessel from Lisbon bearing a dispatch dismissing him as the king's viceroy in India. The blow almost certainly hastened his death. He was 62.

Albuquerque was 50 before he made his first expedition to the Indies, but he quickly perceived the need for secure bases, strategically placed to take account of sailing problems caused by seasonal wind and weather changes. Because of its small population – probably not more than a million and a half – Portugal has not been able to colonise the captured territories. Even the garrisons are partly manned by native recruits. Essentially, the system Albuquerque helped to create was to make the Portuguese middlemen in the trade between the east and Europe. It has become an immensely rewarding operation: a trading profit of 800 per cent was reported in 1512.

Priest campaigns against Spanish cruelty

Cuba, 1514

A Spanish missionary, the first priest to be ordained in the New World, has shocked his compatriots with a terrifying account of military atrocities committed during the conquest of Cuba. Bartolomeo de las Casas, who was a member of Panfilo de Narvaez' expedition in 1513, has revealed a nightmarish catalogue of torture and depravity.

His eye-witness report details the wholesale slaughter of the Indian population, sparing neither man, woman nor child. No cruelty seems to have been beyond the Spanish troops, who, as las Casas puts it, were overtaken by the Devil. Babies, torn from the breast, were smashed on rocks; others skewered on pikes. Adults, especially the nobility, were roasted alive on grid irons, or suspended from gibbets, with fires lit beneath them. Friendly Indians were butchered, while any who dared to resist were hunted without mercy by men and savage dogs.

Now las Casas has left Cuba and returned to Spain. He is publicising what he has seen, and is campaigning against the *encomienda* system, under which large estates exploit slave labour.

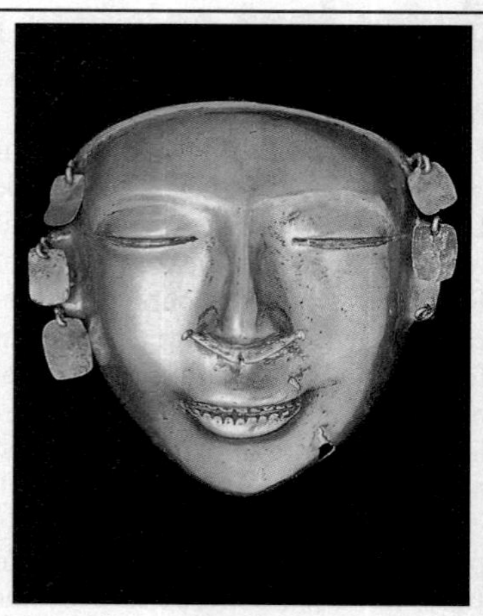

A mask made from gold by a skilled pre-conquest sculptor at Quimbaya in Colombia.

Michelangelo glorifies God and papacy in Rome

Pope Julius II, by Raphael, who has caught his brooding forcefulness.

"The Creation of Adam", by Michelangelo, from the Sistine Chapel ceiling, unveiled last year.

Rome, 20 February 1513
Last month Pope Julius II was given a "Roman triumph" and hailed as "the liberator of Italy". Today he died and, like a prince, has a massive but unfinished tomb sculpted by Michelangelo awaiting him.

One of his first actions on being elected pope in 1503 was to send to Florence for Michelangelo, then 29, to design his tomb, and he resolved to rebuild St Peter's cathedral to make a worthy setting for it. His plan failed. Donato Bramante, who planned the great church, is not long for this world, and scarcely any of it is yet built – though Bramante's classical intentions can be seen in miniature in his Tempietto di San Pietro.

Michelangelo's progress on the tomb was halted by a quarrel. Refused admission to see Julius about obtaining the money he had paid for the marble, the proud sculptor left Rome for Florence and refused entreaties to return. When they were at length reconciled, in 1508, Julius asked him not to resume work on the lavish, three-storey tomb but to paint the ceiling of the Sistine Chapel, begun by Julius' uncle, Pope Sixtus IV. Michelangelo tried hard to escape the task, but Julius could not be defied.

After four years spent lying on his back, working alone behind locked doors, but constantly harassed by Julius demanding that he should work faster, Michelangelo completed his vast design. The ceiling, revealed last year, depicts God's creation of the world.

A powerful portrait of Balthasar Castiglione, by Raphael.

Meanwhile Raphael, Bramante's relative, is painting the pope's apartments with new frescoes and is to be the chief architect of St Peter's. His portrait of Julius II shows what a restless, fiery man was this patron of geniuses.

The Tempietto di San Pietro, by Donato Bramante (born 1444).

1515 (1515-1517)

Switzerland, 29 September 1515. The Swiss confederation signs a perpetual peace treaty with France.

Italy, 14 December 1515. Francis of France makes peace with Pope Leo X. The French king's sole remaining adversary is the Emperor Maximilian.

North Africa, 1515. The Barbarossa brothers, Aruj and Khayr al-Din, instal their fleet at Algiers, presenting a challenge to the Spanish forces occupying the island of Penon.

North Atlantic, 1515. The Spaniard Juan de Bermudez discovers an archipelago which he names the Bermudas.

Cuba, 1515. The Spanish found the city of Havana.

China, 1515. The Confucian scholar Wang Yangming reforms the Chinese state.

South America, 1515. The Spaniard Perez de la Rua discovers the coast of Peru.

Spain, 23 February 1516. The Habsburg Charles I succeeds Ferdinand in Spain.

Italy, 18 August 1516. Francis of France and Pope Leo X sign the Concordat of Bologna regulating the French church.

Baltic, August 1516. Russia and Denmark ally to mount an attack on Poland and Sweden.

Venice, 29 November 1516. The great Venetian painter Giovanni Bellini dies.

Spain, 1516. Cardinal Cisneros, the regent of Spain, bans the importation of African slaves to the Americas.

Portugal, 1516. American territory assigned to Portugal by the treaty of Tordesillas in 1494 is divided into 15 hereditary fiefdoms.

Switzerland, 1516. Ulrich Zwingli, a Zurich priest, denounces the morals of the monks and condemns the luxury of the church and the worship of relics.

Rome, 16 March 1517. The Lateran Council declares null and void the resolutions passed at the council convened at Pisa in 1511 by Louis XII of France and the Emperor Maximilian.

Florence, 26 March 1517. The famous Flemish composer Heinrich Isaac, whose music fuses Flemish, Italian and Germanic styles, dies.

Egypt, 5 July 1517. Sultan Selim makes his entry into Cairo. The Ottomans are masters of Egypt.

Matthias Grunewald completes his Isenheim altarpiece

Isenheim, Germany, 1515

After three years of waiting, the hospital chapel at Isenheim has at last received its altarpiece, and this magnificent creation must stand as one of the contemporary world's finest artistic achievements.

Painted by Mathis Neithardt, known as Matthias Grunewald, the altarpiece has two sides. On weekdays it is a plague altar, devoted to the sick in the care of St Antony. On Sundays it is reversed to reveal four pictures, which can be varied by moveable panels, recounting the story of Christ's life.

Grunewald has been compared to Durer, but while Durer has been influenced by the Italian Renaissance, Grunewald remains rooted in the Middle Ages. The Isenheim Crucifixion, the centrepiece of the altar, stresses this attachment with the intensity of its religious feeling and the wealth of mystical symbolism that runs through the work.

"Nativity and Concert of Angels", by Matthias Grunewald (born 1455).

Sixteen-year-old Habsburg monarch adds Spain to his lands

A marble bas-relief panel from Charles V's palace in Granada in southern Spain, by Juan de Orea.

Spain, 13 March 1516

Charles of Habsburg, aged only 16, was crowned king of Spain today after making a sea voyage around the coast from Brussels. Charles succeeded to the throne on the death of his grandfather, Ferdinand II of Aragon.

The young king has inherited a troubled throne: at least one nobleman, Pedro Giron, is hinting at rebellion, and the young king's North African colonies have been lost in an insurrection. Fortunately, this son of Philip the Fair and Joanna the Mad comes to the throne with experience.

At the age of seven he became the titular ruler of the Netherlands, and was already learning Spanish and the customs of his faraway, future realm from a Spanish teacher, Luis de Vaca. His main teacher was Adrian of Utrecht, a devout ascetic. When Charles' father, Philip, died, Ferdinand locked the unfortunate Joanna away under close watch and assumed the regency. Another important influence in Charles' upbringing was Guillaume de Croy, the lord of Chievres, an ambitious nobleman who would take his bed into the young prince's room "so that he would have someone to talk to when he wakes up".

The young king shows much confidence. At 15 he told his people: "Be good and loyal subjects and I shall be a good prince to you."

French artillery smashes the Swiss

Marignano, 13 September 1515
Two years after the disaster of Novara the French have won a great victory at Marignano, in northern Italy, utterly defeating the Swiss and their leader, Cardinal Matthias Schiner. Now King Francis is marching his victorious troops towards Milan.

Francis has been determined to avenge Novara ever since he succeeded Louis XII earlier this year. An attempt to avoid a fight by offering bribes to the Swiss failed – French kings are renowned as bad payers. Forced to fight, he planned carefully. Treaties were negotiated with England, Venice and Austria, and an army of 40,000 French artillerymen and German light infantry was assembled.

After crossing the Alps and driving the Swiss back into Lombardy, Francis attempted a last-ditch negotiation at Gallarate on 8 September. He demanded the recognition of French claims to Lombardy and Milan and the withdrawal of the Swiss from Italy.

The talks failed and Cardinal Schiner declared: "I want to wash my hands and swim in French blood." Today the armies met at Marignano; the Swiss pikemen fought hard, but French artillery has sealed the victory.

King Francis on horseback, by Francois Clouet (born c.1510).

Ottoman sultan is now head of Islam

Constantinople, 1517
The destruction of the Egyptian Mameluke empire is complete, and the Ottoman sultan, Selim, has returned to Constantinople with the standard and cloak of the prophet. He is now the guardian of the holy places of Mecca, Medina and the pilgrim routes of the Hejaz, and can claim with justification to be the head of Islam.

Victory over the Persians at Chaldiran in 1514 was the first landmark of a period which has seen an extraordinary increase in Ottoman power. Diyar Bakr *(in Turkey)* was occupied the following year; the remaining eastern Anatolian cities over the next two years. Control of the high plateau of eastern Anatolia has given the Ottomans a natural rampart against invasions from the east, as well as the valuable silk routes between Tabriz, Aleppo and Bursa.

Selim beats the Persians (1514).

Meanwhile, the Mamelukes had entered into an uneasy alliance with the Ottomans, to defend themselves against the Portuguese who had destroyed their navy in the Red Sea in 1509.

When Selim invaded Mameluke land in 1516, the Prophet's descendants at Mecca and Kha'ir Beg in Aleppo were ready to go over to the Ottomans. The ageing Mameluke Sultan al-Ghawri nonetheless led his army to defeat at Marj Dabiq.

Tuman Bey proclaimed himself sultan in Cairo, but was defeated and hanged outside the city, leaving Selim master of Syria, Egypt and the Hejaz.

Thomas More writes "Utopia", his vision of the ideal city

Flanders, December 1516
Already it is known as the "golden little book" by the humanists for whom Thomas More, the scholarly lord chancellor of England, wrote it. *Utopia*, published this month at Louvain, is a shrewd, sometimes furious look at European society, an indictment of its harsh rulers, but also a guide – for that is how it is written – to an ideal civilisation.

Utopia is an island – More's title comes from the Greek for no place – somewhere off the New World. Its people are distanced from all the social ills of Europe and live a communal existence, sharing equally in their food, their government, clothes, houses, education and wars.

Only in their marital state is there no sharing. Thomas More is a strict monogamist, and Utopia is a deeply religious community, in which God rewards by an afterlife of immortality. Many see the book as little more than a fantasy, a humourless travelogue of a land which could only exist in the dreams of such an idealist. To some, though, the book is humorous in intent.

Thomas More is a greatly respected lawyer, an under-sheriff of the city of London, much loved by his fellow citizens who regard him as "the fairest of judges, the general patron of the poor". A man of simple tastes, he is noted for his gentle sense of fun and his interest in those around him. He was "born for friendship", according to one witness. More made his name as a writer with his condemnation of the usurper, Richard – "the pestilent serpent" – in a biography.

More's imaginary island of Utopia, somewhere off the New World, whose people live in communal harmony. Is it an idealist vision or a bitter satire on the selfish greed of the Old World?

1517 (1517-1519)

Germany, 31 October 1517. The Augustinian monk Martin Luther publishes 95 theses against the sale of indulgences granting the forgiveness of sins.

Portugal, 1517. The king of Portugal dispatches a first mission to Canton in China.

West Africa, 1517. The explorer Leo Africanus completes an expedition from Morocco to Timbuktu, Gao, Katsina, Kano and Lake Chad.

Mexico, 1517. A Spanish expedition led by Francisco Hernandez de Cordoba lands on the coast of Yucatan.

Netherlands, 1517. The Dutch humanist Erasmus founds at Louvain the College of Three Languages, to teach Latin, Greek and Hebrew.

England, 1517. English sailors complain to King Henry VIII about the growing number of French cod-fishermen in Newfoundland.

Switzerland, 1518. Zwingli receives the support of the Zurich authorities in his attempts to reform the church.

Netherlands, 1518. Erasmus publishes his *Colloquies*, strongly worded attacks on both the reformers and the religious orders.

Germany, 1518. At the diet of Augsburg, Luther refuses to retract his widely-circulated theses on indulgences.

North Africa, 1518. The Spaniards take Tlemcen, and the Barbary pirate Aruj al-Din Barbarossa is killed in the fighting.

Austria, 12 January 1519. Maximilian, Holy Roman emperor since 1493, dies at Wels Castle.

Panama, January 1519. Accused of involvement in a conspiracy, the Spanish explorer, Vasco Nunez de Balboa, is beheaded by order of his father-in-law, Pedro Arias Davila.

North Africa, 1519. The Barbary pirate Khayr al-Din Barbarossa repulses a Spanish offensive on Algiers from the nearby island of Penon.

Mexico, 24 April 1519. Envoys of the Aztec leader, Montezuma II attend the first Easter Mass to be celebrated in Central America.

France, 2 May 1519. Leonardo da Vinci, the Italian painter, sculptor, architect and engineer, dies.

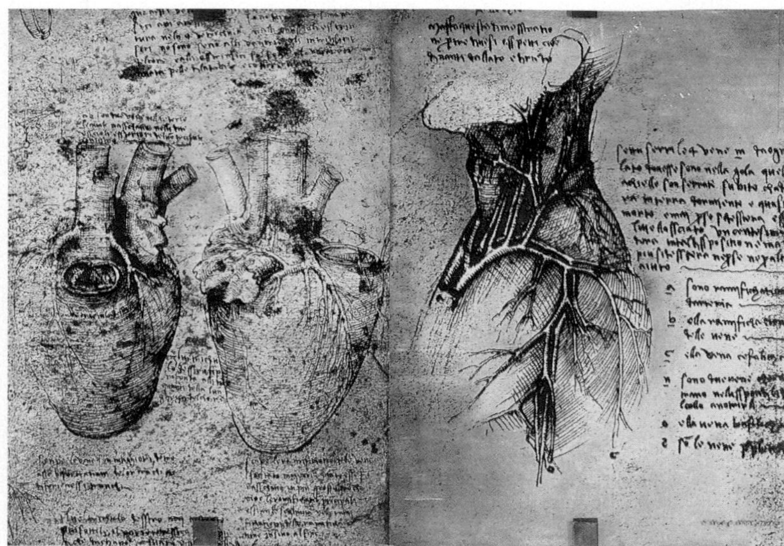

Leonardo's anatomical drawings of the human heart and blood vessels.

"La Gioconda", or "Mona Lisa".

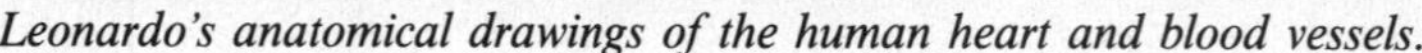

Leonardo da Vinci, painter, theoretician and engineer is dead

Cloux, France, 2 May 1519

Leonardo da Vinci died today at the age of 67. Some say he died in the arms of his last patron, King Francis of France, at whose court he has been an honoured guest for two years. Despite his magnificent achievements one of his last sayings was: "I have not laboured at my art as I should have done."

Leonardo's must be accounted the most curious mind which ever lived. His studies in the sciences as well as in the art of painting and drawing were encyclopaedic. His notebooks are said to be crammed with projects and studies for work, so much of which was left unfinished. Works that were finished have often not lasted because of the experimental methods he used.

Born illegitimate in Vinci in Tuscany, he educated himself and joined the studio of Verrocchio in Florence. At the age of 30 he left for Milan to serve the duke, Ludovico Sforza, as a fortifications engineer. At Milan he painted *The Virgin on the Rocks* and *The Last Supper* in the monastery of Santa Maria delle Grazie. This masterpiece, unfortunately, has already begun to peel.

The same happened to his battle picture for the Palazzo Vecchio in Florence, but not to the portrait of Mona (or Madonna) Lisa, wife of a Florentine merchant. He spent four years on its soft, blurred outlines attempting to paint the inner mystery of a human being. It is doubtful if he was satisfied, for when he went to France he took it with him.

"Portrait of a musician", identity unknown. Painting was just one of Leonardo's vast array of talents; he even learnt to write from right to left, which, because he was left-handed, he found more natural.

Luther nails revolt to castle door

Wittenberg, 31 October 1517

Martin Luther, a 34-year-old professor at the university in this pleasant little town on the banks of the Elbe, has issued a challenge to public debate on this, the eve of All Saints' Day. He has posted a list of 95 theses, mostly attacking the use of indulgences by the church, on the door of Wittenberg church. They are written in Latin and mix fine theological points with an emotional attack on the pope's men.

Luther was deeply shocked earlier this month when he saw the Dominican, Johannes Tetzel, travelling around Germany with a papal bull on a scarlet velvet cushion, auctioning indulgences like a common street pedlar. Even if the money is to be used to build the new Basilica of St Peter's in Rome, this does not justify suggesting to people that they can buy remission from their sins, according to Luther.

In one thesis he asserts that if the pope knew of his preacher's exactions he would rather have St Peter's reduced to ashes than "built with the skin, flesh and bones of his sheep". In another, he asserts that any Christian who is truly repentant is entitled to forgiveness, without any indulgences.

The 95 theses are not especially radical, or different from what many other critics of the church are saying. However, students who have been attending Luther's lectures over the last few years say that he is a most unusual man who is developing a radical theology which could easily bring him into head-on collision with the church.

Unusually for a scholar, he has no sophistication or cunning. He is open about his views and feelings. A big, tough man with disturbing eyes, he is immensely proud of his peasant blood. He is often vulgar, coarse and crude in his language and when he laughs it is long and loud and deeply. He sings tenor and plays the lute.

He was born in 1483, the son of a wealthy copper miner, in Eisleben, in Saxony. He studied nominalist philosophy at the University of Erfurt and after a dramatic experience in a thunderstorm decided to enter a convent of the Austin Friars. He studied St Augustine and fell in love with his work. In 1512, while living at Austin Friars house here, he became a doctor and professor of the university.

His lectures lay great stress on the epistles of St Paul and particularly his view that "the just shall live by faith". Luther argues that priests should not stand between men and the bible, and that faith is a gift from God. Unlike the humanists, he does not think that it can be gained by scholarship.

Portrait by Lucas Cranach of the monk who has angered the Church.

A 19th century view of Luther nailing his theses to the church door.

Sale of indulgences, immediate cause of Luther's stand (19th century print).

Explorer beheaded on treason charge

Panama, 1519

On the orders of his own father-in-law, the famous explorer and *conquistador* Vasco Nunez de Balboa, has been beheaded. Balboa's extraordinary career in Central America began seven years ago, when he fled from his creditors in Spain by stowing away to Santo Domingo.

Hearing from the natives of a gold-rich land washed by an unknown sea, he led 190 men into the swamps and rain-forested hills of the Panama isthmus. On 29 September 1513 he waded into the Pacific Ocean, his sword drawn in a gesture of conquest as the 67 survivors of the expedition sang the *Te Deum*. He had discovered the overland route between America's western and eastern seaboards.

The Spanish governor of Panama, Pedro Arias Davila, promptly betrothed his daughter to this bold adventurer. Father and son-in-law worked together on a series of lucrative gold hunts, but on their first disagreement Davila has had Balboa arrested and executed on a trumped-up conspiracy charge.

Vasco de Balboa: beheaded.

Death – and possible return – of Hindu critic of caste system

India, 1518

Disciples of the outspoken Hindu sage Kabir are claiming that he miraculously returned among them within hours of his death to settle a dispute about how they should pay final homage to him. True or false, the "miracle" is in keeping with Kabir's lifelong attempts to reconcile different views.

Adopted by a Moslem weaver after being abandoned by his Brahman widowed mother on a lotus leaf, Kabir worked tirelessly to reconcile Islam, in which he was brought up, with Hinduism, condemning religious sectarianism and the caste system. Readily accepted by both Islamic and Hindu worshippers, he preached the notion of a monotheistic religion stripped of idols. In Kabir's teachings God was one, whether he was called Rama or Allah.

1519 (1519-1520)

Spain, 28 June 1519. Charles of Spain, the king of the Netherlands and the grandson of the late Emperor Maximilian, is elected Holy Roman emperor and takes the name Charles V. Francis of France and Henry VIII of England were both candidates.

Rome, July 1519. Having implied that the pope is fallible, Martin Luther is summoned to Rome to answer a charge of heresy.

Spain, 20 September 1519. The Portuguese-born sailor Ferdinand Magellan embarks on a voyage to cross the Pacific Ocean and circumnavigate the globe.

Mexico, 1519. The Spanish explorer Hernando Cortes lands at Vera Cruz with a force of over 500. He marches on Tenochtitlan, which the Aztec leader, Montezuma II, surrenders without a fight.

Switzerland, 1519. The Swiss reformer Ulrich Zwingli bans the sale of indulgences in Zurich.

Scandinavia, 6 March 1520. Christian II, crowned king of Norway and Denmark in 1515, becomes king of Sweden.

Spain, May 1520. Angered at the decision Charles, just crowned king of Spain, to leave Spain so soon to be crowned emperor, the "comuneros" (*cities of Castile*) rise up against his Flemish ministers.

Spain, 1520. Chocolate is introduced from Mexico.

China, 1520. A Portuguese ambassador arrives in Beijing.

Portugal, 1520. Portugal sends embassies to Ethiopia and to the Ngola kingdom (*Angola*).

Germany, 1520. Thomas Munzer, a supporter of Luther who has radical political aspirations, begins preaching in Zwickau.

North America, 1520. Having identified the southern coast of the New World, Joao Alvares Fagundes, the Portuguese explorer, attempts to found a colony on Cape Breton island, but the colonists are wiped out by an extremely harsh winter.

Aleala, Spain, 1520. The Complutensian Bible, prepared under the direction of Cardinal Cisneros, is published.
It contains the Old Testament in Hebrew, Latin and Greek, plus the Aramaic Targum of the Pentateuch and the New Testament in Greek and Latin.

Raphael's luminous "Madonna and Child with the Infant Baptist".

Papal court in mourning for Raphael

Rome, 6 April 1520

The papal court has been plunged into grief and mourning by the sudden, early death of Raphael, aged 37. He was friend as well as painter to two popes and was in charge of architectural and decorative work at the Vatican palace. He died of a fever on Good Friday, his birthday, having divided his possessions among his disciples.

Raphael Sanzio, the son of a painter in Urbino, studied so successfully with Perugino that people could not tell his work from that of his master. After studying the work of Leonardo and Michelangelo in Florence, he went to Rome where Julius II appointed him to decorate the Vatican apartments with great semi-circular frescoes, some of biblical scenes, some of classical antiquity, such as the philosophers of the *School of Athens*. He also drew the life-size cartoons for the tapestries to be woven for the Sistine Chapel. His secular portraits were as masterly as his serene Madonnas – that of Pope Julius was so lifelike that people trembled at it and that of Julius' successor, Leo X, was vividly alive. Leo sent Raphael's painting of St Michael casting out Satan to the king of France.

"St Michael and the Devil", c.1505.

Lucrezia Borgia, a father's pawn, dies

Ferrara, 24 June 1519

Lucrezia Borgia, the duchess of Ferrara and daughter of Pope Alexander VI, has died, aged 39, after a life of family intrigue and several broken marriages. Though beautiful and intelligent, she was essentially a pawn in her father's many power games.

Betrothed at the age of 11 to the Spaniard Juan de Centelles, then to the more influential Don Gasparo, the count of Aversa, Lucrezia was eventually married two years later to Giovanni Sforza, the lord of Pesaro. At the age of 18 she left him to make a more politically favourable marriage to Alfonso d'Aragon, the duke of Bisceglie, with whom she fell in love. Two years later, when Pope Alexander was pursuing the French alliance, Alfonso became an embarrassment, and was murdered, probably on the orders of Cesare, Lucrezia's brother.

Never a free agent: the fair Lucrezia.

In 1499 Lucrezia was appointed governor of Spoleto, and later that year was able to buy for 80,000 ducats the castles of the Gaetani family, on the frontier between the Papal States and Naples, after they had been effectively confiscated by the pope. In 1500 Sermoneta was added to her dominions.

In 1501, after some debauched partying involving the pope, Cesare and Lucrezia, she was married for the last time to Alfonso d'Este, the duke of Ferrara. She had already fulfilled her dynastic function by having a son, Rodrigo.

New emperor is elected

Barcelona, 6 July 1519
It took the courier fewer than nine days to ride breakneck from Frankfurt across Europe to the gates of Barcelona to break the news to Charles of Spain that he had won a crucial election and would occupy the imperial throne of the Holy Roman emperor. Charles had successfully bribed the princes of Germany to cast their votes for him.

Few monarchs could move as swiftly as did Charles following the death of Maximilian of Austria in January. Within days of the news reaching the Spanish king, couriers were dispatched urgently to Germany to negotiate with the princes – all seven of whose votes were vital if Charles was to win. It was essential that he could get his bid in before his rivals.

Once the diplomatic work was under way, Charles wrote a courteous note to King Francis of France advising him of his intentions. The king's reply came quickly: "Sire, we are both courting the same lady." There were four candidates in this election: Charles, Francis, Henry VIII of England and Frederick (the Wise), the duke of Saxony. Charles was the favourite, particularly when it was known that he had borrowed freely from the Augsburg banking house of Fuggers, the biggest finance house in Europe (*see below*), who backed him in preference to Francis of France.

Charles of Spain, now the emperor.

Aztec king is captured

The conquest of Mexico: Cortes' army storms the town of Vera Cruz.

Mexico, November 1519
Since the arrival of a Spanish expeditionary force a few days ago, the emperor Montezuma has not been seen. The Spaniards, led by soldier-explorer Hernando Cortes, led Montezuma away after the two leaders had met in the Aztec capital of Tenochtitlan. Nine months of bloody conquest was over.

Cortes had made sure that there would be no retreat when he first landed here in quest of gold. He ordered his 700 men to burn their ships before marching inland to the high plateau of Mexico and Tenochtitlan. It was an ominous act: a decade ago Aztec seers had predicted fire in the night sky as a portent of doom.

After Cortes' sails came into sight Montezuma sent messengers with clothes fit for a god, but Cortes replied with a terrifying show of firepower. Soon he landed and took prisoners in a skirmish at Tabasco. These included a beautiful female slave named Marina, a natural linguist who quickly learned Spanish. Then, with armour, crossbows, firearms, cannon, and horses – all unknown in this country – Cortes burned a steady, bloody road uphill. His route was marked by a massacre at Cholula, but tribes long suppressed by the Aztecs flocked to support him.

Cortes found the capital a "well organised and most orderly" centre where 60,000 people trade goods daily. Alongside such order goes ritual human sacrifice, often of prisoners from tribal wars. The premium placed upon live prisoners for sacrifice later limits the Aztecs' fighting efficiency. Montezuma met Cortes with wary courtesy, his slaves all sweeping the ground before him. Marina (now Cortes' common-law wife) translated.

Montezuma had long suspected that he was being pursued by a Spanish "god", and as the Spaniards gathered round Montezuma, stroking the emperor's arm curiously before taking him by the hand and leading him away, he must have realised that the god had caught up with him. Montezuma has not been seen in public since.

Montezuma comes to meet Cortes.

The bankers who won election for Charles

Augsburg, Germany, 1520
The Fuggers are king-makers; it was their money which bought Charles I of Spain the emperorship and, in return, he has given them the right to exploit silver and mercury deposits in his Central American colonies.

It was 150 years ago that Ulrich Fugger, a poor weaver, settled in Augsburg and set up a small textile business which expanded into an industry exporting fustian and buying Levantine cotton from Venice as well as dealing in spices. The industry was so successful that Ulrich was able to diversify into metals – obtaining, with a Polish partner, a monopoly of silver and copper mines in the Tyrol and much of the rest of eastern Europe.

Ulrich's financial ability was inherited by his sons who have built the House of Fugger into the most wealthy and powerful bank in Europe. Jacob Fugger II is known as "Jacob the Rich", and has the right to mint coinage in Rome as well as controlling the biggest trade network on the continent. Today's bankers are strictly entrepreneurial, with the Fuggers vying with their chief rivals, the Welsers – another German house – for more exploitation in the Americas, their agents acting more like *conquistadores* than businessmen. In the meantime, new and potentially even more powerful banks are developing in Italy, notably in Genoa.

The Fuggers welcome the emperor.

1520 (1520-1521)

Mexico, 20 May 1520. Panfilo de Narvaez, sent to punish Hernando Cortes for insubordination, is defeated by him.

Rome, 15 June 1520. Pope Leo X condemns Luther's 95 theses as "heretical and scandalous".

Mexico, 10 July 1520. Cortes is driven from Tenochtitlan by Cuauhtemoc, the Aztec leader, and retreats to Tlaxcala.

Constantinople, 21 September 1520. Suleiman (the Magnificent), son of Selim, becomes Ottoman sultan.

Germany, October 1520. Luther deepens his rift with Rome by publishing three pamphlets on reform.

Sweden, November 1520. Christian II, the king of the three countries of Scandinavia, has most of his enemies massacred in Stockholm. Gustav Vasa, a survivor, organises a peasant uprising against the Danes.

Pacific, 28 November 1520. Magellan, having discovered a strait at the tip of South America, enters the Pacific.

Germany, January 1521. After publicly burning the papal bull condemning his theses, Luther is excommunicated.

Caribbean, 20 February 1521. Juan Ponce de Leon, the Spanish governor of Puerto Rico, sets out for Florida with 200 prospective colonists.

Spain, 23 April 1521. The *comuneros* (cities of Castile) are crushed by royalist troops at Villalar. Their commander, Juan de Padilla, is executed.

Germany, May 1521. Luther is "kidnapped" for his own safety by the Duke Frederick of Saxony.

France, June 1521. Imperial forces invade Champagne.

France, 26 June 1521. A school of reforming churchmen is established around Guillaume Briconnet, the bishop of Meaux.

Florida, July 1521. The new settlers leave after Ponce de Leon is wounded by natives.

Balkans, August 1521. Ottoman forces take Belgrade.

Mexico, 31 August 1521. Cortes and the Tlaxcalans, who laid siege to Tenochtitlan on 28 April, capture and set fire to the city.

England, 21 October 1521. Henry VIII is named Defender of the Faith by the pope after defending the seven sacraments against Luther.

Portugal becomes Europe's richest state

Shipyards and warehouses are built to cope with Lisbon's booming trade.

Portugal, c.1521

Suddenly, the king of a small country at the south-western corner of Europe has become the continent's wealthiest ruler. Sugar and spice, as well as gold from Guinea, have enabled Manuel of Portugal to build the magnificent monastery of St Jerome at Belem. Learning and artistic expression are being encouraged, and the king is subsidising the famous St Barbara College in Paris as a school for Portuguese students in France.

Sugar from Madeira is sold all over Europe, with England buying 20 tons a year. Spices from the east, shipped round the Cape, are likewise in great demand, since the growth of Turkish power in Anatolia has made the overland route unreliable for traders.

To manage his new-found wealth and his many commercial operations the king relies on Portugal's Jewish community, but now he is under pressure from Spain to expel all Jews. Manuel's stratagem is to tell the Jews that if they merely say that they have converted to Christianity they can stay on with no questions asked. One at least has refused and left; he is Abraham Zacuto, the mathematician whose calculations enabled Portugal to produce Europe's first navigation manual.

Great wealth means exotic windows.

How long the king will remain a *cruzado* multi-millionaire is already a matter for speculation. The first pepper bought in the east for two cruzados for a quintal of 100lb sold in Lisbon for 80. The price has now dropped to 20. And the rising cost of the trading voyages is threatening to exceed returns.

Luther defies both pope and emperor

Worms, Germany, 18 April 1521

Friends of Martin Luther, the radical theologian from Wittenberg, fear for his life tonight. This evening he confronted the young emperor, Charles V, in the *Diet* of Worms, refusing to retract the views which led the pope to excommunicate him last January.

Luther's radical teaching challenges the papal claim to be the sole authority on the scriptures. He questions many of the rights of the priests and rejects the belief that bread and wine become the body and blood of Christ. He affirms Christians' personal right to faith.

The welcome of the German crowd here showed that he has touched a popular chord. The emperor fears that the revolutionary spirit may affect his power. Now that Luther has refused to retract, the diet will certainly denounce him and may even have him executed.

Catholicism adopts new ways in Kongo

Angola, 1521

Bishop Henrique, the son of King Afonso of the Kongo *(Angola)*, has returned to his native land after 13 years in a Portuguese seminary. Portugal's contact with the Kongo goes back to 1482, when its intentions were peaceful, inspired by the desire to convert rather than conquer. Afonso became a Christian and took the throne from his usurping brother, and the Kongo became Portugal's colony.

Traders and opportunists arrived, vast areas have been depopulated by slave traders, white missionaries have behaved like rulers, and presumptions of European superiority have sullied relations between Kongolese and Portuguese. In spite of the hostility of both the Europeans and the indigenous pagans, Bishop Henrique is building a unique African Catholicism, incorporating numerous pagan elements. The Portuguese in Kongo, unable to manipulate it for their own benefit, call it heretical. However, Rome has rejected their accusations, seeing it as eccentric but orthodox.

Chivalry rules "Field of the Cloth of Gold"

A nineteenth-century view of the celebrated meeting of kings.

Guines, France, 24 June 1520
The events of the Field of the Cloth of Gold are over. Henry VIII of England and Francis of France have embraced and parted with tears in their eyes, swearing to build a chapel dedicated to Our Lady of Friendship on the spot where they met. It is not known what the political consequences of this meeting will be. The kings, attended only by their ministers, Wolsey and Bonnivet, met on 7 June and talked for several hours in a tent pitched between their two luxurious camps.

The substance of this talk remains secret, but the feeling in the English camp is that it would be better for Henry to ally himself with the Holy Roman emperor, Charles V rather than Francis. However, Francis owes Henry two million crowns because he is the guarantor of the French debt.

Everything about this encounter has smelt of money. The French pavilions were made of cloth of gold, thus giving the tournament field its name. Henry is said to have spent £15,000 – a seventh of his annual income. His tent was a two-storey palace of wood and glass. Henry appeared as Hercules; the knights jousted and fought on foot. There were banquets and dances. Chivalry ruled the field.

Explorer Magellan dies in tribal skirmish

Portuguese navigator Magellan, killed in the Philippines; from the Farnese palace in Caprarola.

Philippines, 27 April 1521
Having sailed three-quarters of the way round the world across seas hitherto unknown to Europeans, the intrepid navigator Ferdinand Magellan was killed today in a small-time tribal fight on an island in the Philippines. Earlier this month his ships dropped anchor off Cebu, where the local chief agreed to convert to Christianity and then asked Magellan to help him to conquer a tribe on the neighbouring island of Mactan. In fighting on the beach, Magellan was hit in the leg by a poisoned arrow and on his sword arm by a javelin; then, as he covered the retreat of his comrades, he was hacked to pieces with lances and scimitars.

Suleiman the Magnificent seizes Belgrade

Belgrade, August 1521
After a three-week siege Belgrade has fallen to the forces of the Ottoman sultan, Suleiman the Magnificent. The Danube is no longer a reliable line of defence, leaving both Serbia and Hungary exposed to the Ottoman advance.

With Charles V preoccupied by German problems and Luther's revolt, Hungary's pleas for help fell on deaf ears, and the defenders of Belgrade had no answer to the Ottoman mines and cannon bombardment from an island in the Danube.

When the city fell, the Hungarian inhabitants were massacred and the Serbs taken to Istanbul as prisoners. The Venetians are anxiously negotiating peace with Suleiman.

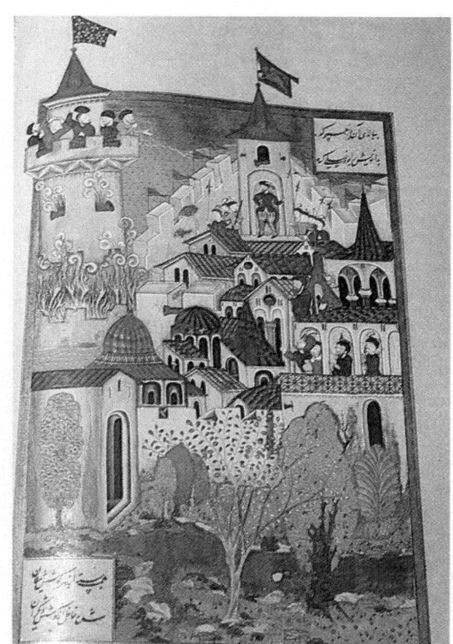

A Turkish view of the Belgrade siege.

Fierce fighting rocks capital of Aztecs

Tenochtitlan, Mexico, 1520
When Montezuma appeared on the roof of his palace with one of his lieutenants, telling his people not to resist the Spaniards, he was greeted with abuse followed by rocks and arrows. The emperor himself was now in irons. His people had scant sympathy for him; they were furious about the latest Spanish atrocity.

The Spaniards had told people to go to a temple courtyard for a religious festival. They then massacred them all without warning. This has unleashed general warfare in which the Mexicans, armed with bows, have besieged their own capital, cutting off the fresh water.

Cortes has been absent throughout, on a campaign to defeat a punitive Spanish column sent after him by the Cuban authorities. There is word that he has won this battle. He left control of the Aztecs to his deputy, Pedro de Alvarado.

A bloody scene as the Spaniards go into action against Montezuma's people.

1521 (1521-1523)

Rome, 9 January 1522. Adrian, the cardinal of Utrecht, succeeds Leo X as pope and takes the name Adrian VI. He plans a programme of church reform to counteract the spread of Lutheranism.

Germany, 24 January 1522. Wittenberg town council issues an order imposing controls on church finances and forms of worship. It provokes an outbreak of iconoclasm (image-smashing) by Luther's supporters.

Mexico, 15 October 1522. Cortes receives letters from the Emperor Charles V promoting him to captain-general and governor of New Spain.

Rhodes, 21 December 1522. Rhodes, formerly the base of the knights of St John of Jerusalem, is conquered by the Ottomans under Suleiman after a six-month siege.

Mexico, 1522. On the ruins of Tenochtitlan, the capital of the Aztec empire, the Spanish found Mexico City. The city is intended to become the capital of New Spain.

Italy, 1522. Defeated by imperial troops at Bicocca, the French are forced to surrender Milan. The imperial army then occupies Genoa, where a doge who supports Charles V is appointed.

Netherlands, 1522. Charles V sets up a state-run inquisition to supplement the long-established papal Inquisition.

South America, 1522. A group of Spanish settlers in Cumana, Venezuela, is massacred by the Indians.

Mexico, 1522. To quell the opposition in the Aztec empire, which they now control, the Spanish launch a series of expeditions against the Zapotec highlanders in the isthmus of Tehuantepec.

Germany, 1522. Luther clashes with the radical reformer Thomas Munzer, who advocates both social and religious reform. Luther, meanwhile, considers religion to be above political and social matters.

Switzerland, 19 January 1523. Ulrich Zwingli publishes his *67 Articles*, the first manifesto of the Zurich Reformation. After giving a summary of the gospel, Zwingli attacks the authority of the pope, transubstantiation and the cult of the saints.

Aztec capital finally falls to the Spanish

A Spanish manuscript showing Montezuma wearing his royal Quezal feathers.

Tenochtitlan, Mexico, 1521

Since the siege of Tenochtitlan last year there has been general warfare in Mexico between Cortes and the Aztecs. Montezuma died in captivity and Cortes returned to lift the siege. As he led his people out, they were ambushed and many were killed. On their way to the coast they wiped out another village and left an epidemic of smallpox.

Now, almost a year later, Cortes has returned, probably with official Spanish blessing. This time there was tougher resistance. The Aztecs have exchanged formal war procedures for guerrilla tactics. This bitter campaign has been fought in boats across lakes and along canals, and ashore among city streets. Aztecs beheaded not only Spanish prisoners but their horses as well, displaying the heads of both on the same rack. After a long siege in which they were deprived of drinking water, the Aztecs surrendered their capital a second time. Now attempts will be made to convert them to Christianity.

Bitter German knights become bandits

Germany, April 1523

The revolt of the small-landowning German knights is over, their forces scattered at Landstuhl, their leaders fled. But a group of Franconian knights including Gotz von Berlichingen have become bandits, terrorising the country near Nuremberg.

Changes in the art of war, with growing emphasis on firearms and artillery, and the use of mercenaries deprived the knights of much of their power. Meanwhile the German princes have been building their political influence through councils and chancelleries.

Knights like Ulrich von Hutten and Franz von Sickingen tried to form a military arm for Luther's revolt against the church, but Luther rejected them.

Von Hutten, leader of the knights' rebellion, is a renowned humanist scholar; but he failed to enlist the support of Luther for a military revolt against the Roman church.

New religious sect retreats from world

Germany, c.1523

As the Lutheran Reformation takes hold, new prophets appear and new religious sects proliferate. The Anabaptists, an unworldly group, are proving more attractive than most.

Anabaptism appears to have started among the Zurich disciples of Zwingli, who had debated the validity of infant baptism. It also owes something to the radical ideas of Carlstadt and Munzer. Led by Conrad Grebel, Balthasar Hubmaier and Felix Mantz, the Anabaptists go further, insisting that only true adult believers should be baptised, and that they should renounce popish worship and political affairs and not bear arms.

The first coherent Anabaptist movements have grown up among the peasantry round Zurich, where they are effectively withdrawing into communities of saints.

Treaty of Moscow ends ten years' war

Moscow, 14 September 1522

The conflict over Lithuanian Smolensk officially ended today with an armistice conceding control of the town to the grand prince of Moscow, Vasily III. The five-year armistice treaty, signed in Moscow today, ends ten years of hostilities between the Muscovites and their Polish-Lithuanian enemies under Sigismund.

The treaty is a triumph for Prince Vasily. His forces – fighting alongside Lithuanian rebels led by Prince Mikhail Glinsky – only gained control of Smolensk eight years ago after two bloody but abortive previous attempts to take it.

Vasily, who styles himself "emperor", now plans to build up Smolensk, strategically placed on the banks of the Dnieper, as the pivot of his western defensive system. The treaty is also a diplomatic coup for Vasily. His defensive alliance in 1514 with Sigismund's western neighbour, the Holy Roman Emperor Maximilian, created papal concern about the conflict and brought pressure from Rome on Sigismund to settle.

Magellan's ship sails round world

Spain, 6 September 1522
Of the fleet of five vessels with which Ferdinand Magellan set sail from Seville three years ago, just one has returned; and of the 265 men aboard, only 15 have survived. But although their leader was not among them, the survivors, and their battered *Vittoria,* have made history by sailing round the world.

Magellan, who planned the expedition for Charles of Spain, was Portuguese, but fell out of favour in Lisbon after years of service in the Indies. He became a Spanish citizen and persuaded Charles that the Portuguese domination of the spice trade with the east, round the Cape of Good Hope, could be broken by ships sailing west to find a passage round South America.

Sailing south-west, Magellan steered clear of the coast of Brazil, where the Portuguese were established. He put in at the River Plate and further south, at Port St Julian. There the expedition encountered a race of primitive giants, whom Magellan named *Patagonians* (Big Feet). Mutiny broke out as the ships sailed deeper into unknown waters. Magellan crushed it and, as is customary, hanged the ringleaders. Further south, on 21 October a year after leaving Seville, Magellan rounded what he called the Cape of the Eleven Thousand Virgins and found himself at the eastern end of the long-sought passage. The channel ran through a maze of reefs, with snow-clad mountains on either side. He lost two ships, one wrecked by the violent winds, the other through desertion. After 38 days he passed a place which, from its many fires, he called Tierra del Fuego, and emerged into the Pacific Ocean. For 98 days the explorers sailed west, running out of food and water and being forced to eat rats.

When they made landfall in the Philippines and Magellan died in a tribal affray, the voyage was still only half completed. Command of the remnants of the fleet fell upon the Spanish navigator, Sebastian del Cano, who set sail with only two ships remaining. In the Moluccas, they traded their merchandise for spices; then, since nobody cared to face the dangers of Magellan's Straits again, they set out across waters where Portuguese merchantmen operated. One ship, the *Trinidad,* was soon seized. Del Cano took the other across the Indian Ocean and round the Cape to Seville and safety with the precious cargo.

A heavenly spirit guides Magellan's ship through the monster-infested seas.

Trip's navigation out by 3,000 miles

Spain, 1522
It is a measure of the achievement of the late Ferdinand Magellan's fleet that when it set out on its epic voyage around the world three years ago there were those who believed that the journey would only take a few days.

Not only did people have no idea of the distance involved, but almost every aspect of the voyage was shrouded in ignorance. In mid-Pacific, for example, an attempt was made to measure the depths of the ocean for the first time. But after paying out a line to 1,300 feet they failed to reach the bottom.

His navigational aids weren't much more use. Although he took 21 quadrants, 18 sandglasses, 23 charts and 37 compass needles by the time he reached the Philippines he was over 3,000 miles away from where he thought he was.

On the plus side he was aided by current developments in naval technology. Ships are now heavier with three or four masts and a variety of square and lateen sails to take advantage of winds from all directions. There have also been improvements in the design of hulls which are built up on a wooden skeleton to which planking is attached, instead of filling-in a framework, making for greater strength and durability.

Leniency sets Spain on path to peace

Spain, 1523
Signs of stability are beginning to return to Spain after three years of civil unrest which severely undermined the authority of its king, the Holy Roman Emperor Charles V. His return to Spain with a general pardon, plus a decision not to withdraw privileges from cities that joined the rebels' *santa junta*, has eased tension.

At one point the Castilian rebels, protesting against both high taxes and top jobs going to Charles' foreign advisers, appeared to have control of Spain, with the revolt spreading to Catalonia and Andalucia. But their junta collapsed after a split between rebel leaders.

Luther translates Bible into German for the common people

Germany, September 1522
Martin Luther, who has been in refuge in the castle here since his denunciation by the *Diet* of Worms last year, has begun his most ambitious work. He is translating the Bible into German. In a few years' time Germans who do not understand Latin will be able to read the Bible and, thanks to the boom in new printing presses, they will be able to buy it relatively cheaply.

Although he is a university professor Luther has always written in plain language. He comes from peasant stock himself, and he makes sure that he is in tune with today's language by listening to the phrases the people use in the marketplace. His Bible is thrilling narrative, not dull theology.

The bottomless pit: woodcut from the first edition of Luther's Bible (1534).

1523 (1523-1524)

Brussels, 1 July 1523. Two of Luther's followers, Augustine monks from Antwerp, are burnt alive.

Switzerland, October 1523. Zurich town council adopts Ulrich Zwingli's programme of Protestant reforms.

Rome, 19 November 1523. Cardinal Giulio de Medici is elected pope and takes the name Clement VII.

Central America, 1523. The Spaniard Pedro de Alvarado undertakes the conquest of Honduras.

Denmark, 1523. Christian II flees the country in the face of the rebellion he provoked. Frederick, the duke of Schleswig-Holstein, is elected king.

South America, 1523. The Spaniard Pascual de Andagoya reaches the southern tip of Colombia.

Spain, 1523. Diego Columbus, the son of Christopher, is stripped of all offices inherited from his father.

France, January 1524. Francis commissions the Florentine navigator Giovanni da Verrazzano to find a north-western route to the Indies.

North America, 1524. The Portuguese Diogo Gomes, in the service of Spain, explores the whole American coastline from Nova Scotia to Florida.

France, 1524. The high constable of Bourbon, who has become Charles V's lieutenant, invades Provence.

Mexico, 1524. Cuauhtemoc, the last Aztec king, who has been held captive for three years, is hanged by the Spanish on a charge of treason.

Switzerland, 1524. Uri, Schwyz and Underwalden, the three former Forest Cantons, remain faithful to Catholicism and make a pact with Austria.

Central America, 1524. In response to an appeal by the Cakchiquel Indians, the Spanish send a new expedition against the Maya into the isthmus of Tehuantepec.

Spain, 1524. Garcia de Loaisa becomes the first president of the Council of the Indies, responsible for administrative, financial and legal matters in Spain's new lands.

Germany, 1524. Martin Luther finally abandons monastic life and vows.

India, 1524. Vasco da Gama becomes viceroy of Goa.

Hero of Swedish independence made king

Sweden, 6 June 1523

The architect of Sweden's independence, Gustav Vasa, has been elected king of Sweden by the *Diet*, the Swedish parliament, in Stockholm today.

King Gustav, who for two years led the successful revolt against the king of Denmark, Christian II, now plans to take Sweden out of the Danish-controlled Kalmar Union which has united Norway, Sweden and Denmark for the last 144 years.

King Gustav is also planning to fill the power vacuum left in the Baltic by Denmark's defeat and its internal problems by building up a strong Swedish fleet of warships to protect its commercial interests.

Internally, King Gustav plans a series of far-reaching reforms to modernise the administration. Brought up at the court of Sten Sture, the old regent of Sweden, he has strong ideas on how the country can be governed more effectively. He plans, wherever possible, to replace nobles in local government with civil servants, answerable and loyal to the crown.

One early task will be to fill vacant bishoprics. The new king has Lutheran leanings and wants candidates who favour church reform. This will be hardest to impose in rural Sweden where Lutheranism is relatively unknown. Here the king, who raised his peasant army at Dalarna to fight the Danes, will be relying on popular support.

A 1560 relief of King Gustav Vasa.

New history records daily life in Egypt

Egypt, 1524

An Egyptian historian, Mohammed ben Iyas, known as ibn Iyas, has published a massive history of his people, detailing the decline of the Mameluke dynasty and early years of rule by the Ottoman Turks.

Ibn Iyas' great work, which is entitled *Bada'i al zuhur fi waka'i al-duhur*, covers Egypt's past from the Pharoahs onwards. The early history is covered quite quickly, but from the Mamelukes onwards ibn Iyas adds more and more detail.

As an intimate of the Egyptian government ibn Iyas is able to offer eye-witness accounts of the more recent events. Among the wealth of fascinating material are his inside reports of court life, revelations of notorious scandals, biographies of the famous, and records of prices and market trends.

Celibate sect stirs church to reform

Italy, c.1524

The work which a new religious order called the Theatines does for the community is changing many ideas within the Church of Rome. The men who founded the new order, Gian Pietro Carafa and Gaetano di Thiene, are dedicated to the relief of human suffering. Formerly leaders of the Oratory of Divine Love, di Thiene and Carafa are attempting to persuade the church – by their own examples – to improve the training of clerics, and argue that priests should live in their parishes.

The Theatines' lives are made up of poverty, celibacy and work in schools, hospitals, orphanages and women's hostels. The puritanism of the order has bred a new kind of bishop to continue the reforms of these saintly founders.

Papacy is back in the Medici family

Rome, 19 November 1523

With a sigh of relief, the College of Cardinals has chosen Giulio de Medici to succeed Adrian VI as pope. He is the second member of his family to assume the papacy.

Adrian VI, who was of Flemish extraction, was an austere and spiritual man, whose pontificate lasted for less than two years. His successor, who has taken the name Clement VII, can be expected to resume the traditions of his cousin, Leo X, a notable patron of artists like Raphael and Michelangelo.

Clement VII, while he will hardly ignore his family interests, is understood to be keen to keep the papacy independent. He also wants to reform the Curia.

Clement VII, depicted by Raphael.

The perfect knight is killed in battle

Spain, 25 April 1524

Pierre du Terrail, the chevalier de Bayard, was known throughout Europe as an exemplar of chivalry and honour. Tonight he is dead – shot in the back by a Spanish *arquebusier* (infantryman armed with a gun) during a battle between his French troops and the imperial army. Refusing to leave the field, he was captured and died in enemy hands. This "fearless and blameless knight" appeared to many as an incarnation of the days of King Arthur's Camelot. He was a saintly figure who scorned money and material comforts and would never abuse a conquered enemy, and his tragic death is widely mourned.

Pizarro's mercenaries thwarted in Peru

What they wanted: ceremonial gold two-spouted huaco (water pot) from Peru.

Panama, 1524

The search for an empire on the South Sea coast by two prominent Spanish citizens of Panama is being temporarily abandoned after becoming bogged down in Peru. The expedition leaders are Francisco Pizarro, a soldier of fortune in the Indies since 1502, and his comrade, Diego de Almagro. The wealthy Pizarro was with Balboa when they discovered the South Sea.

Pizarro says that he will try again. The expedition includes a priest who represents the operation's banker together with a judge, 80 men and four horses.

Two years ago a Spanish sailor, Pascual de Andagoya, safely negotiated this mysterious coast as he searched for an exotic and fabulously rich tribe called the *Viru* or *Peru*.

Andagoya's ships now supply the new expedition, which is encamped at a place known as "Port of Hunger". Nothing of value has been found in the area, but Almagro has lost an eye in a skirmish with local Indians.

Although illiterate and a poor horseman, Pizarro is one of Panama's richest men, a middle-aged bachelor of simple habits. After a lifetime of jungle warfare he is bored without adventure.

His soldiers include some professional mercenaries, hardened by European campaigns, but most are the adventurous younger sons of Spain's grandees. In Spain, an ambitious youngsters will usually get ahead through sword-play or the "right" marriage. Pizaro's adventurous youngsters may find a shortage of suitable brides in the largely Indian inhabited mountains of Peru, however.

Warriors, from a Peruvian cloth.

Italian explores coasts of North America

America, 17 April 1524

Sailing under the French flag, the Italian explorer Giovanni da Verrazzano has landed in the New World (*at Cape Breton*). He first sighted land (*Cape Fear*) on 1 March, and has sailed some 200 miles up and down the coast. As well as seeking a passage through to the Pacific Ocean Verrazzano has explored the fertile terrain and made some contact with the native inhabitants who, he says, "are clad in feathers ... of diverse colours".

Among his discoveries, at the northernmost extent of his voyage, is "a very pleasant place, situated amongst certain little steep hills; from amidst the hills there runs down into the sea a great stream of water" (*New York*). This stream, which he has explored in a small boat, is easily navigable. Its mouth is "very deep, and from the sea to the mouth of same, with the tide, which we found to rise eight feet, any great vessel laden may pass up". Verrazzano began his voyage in the autumn of 1523. Of his four ships, two were lost in a storm. The survivors put into an English port for repairs, then proceeded along the coast of Spain, on which they made a profitable raid.

One ship took the booty back to France while Verrazzano went on to the New World in the other, *La Dauphine*.

Verrazzano, who found a deep river.

Missionaries aim to speed second coming

Spain, 1523

An evangelistic team of Franciscan friars is expected to leave Spain in the next few months to found a Christian mission in Mexico. The proposal has the enthusiastic support of the Spanish king, Charles, and his people. Most devout Christians believe that the second coming cannot happen before the conversion or defeat of all pagans. In the recent past, Islamic heresy has been defeated in Iberia. Spain's discovery of the New World (and more pagans) is seen now as divine intervention. The theory is a particular favourite of the brown friars, who have chosen a team of men known as "The Twelve" to convert the Aztecs to a god of love.

A later image of a friar's attempt to convert an Aztec prince.

1524 (1524-1525)

Persia, 23 May 1524. Shah Ismail dies and is succeeded by his ten-year-old son, Tahmasp.

Egypt, 1524. A rebellion by Ahmed Pasha against Ottoman rule, established in Egypt in 1517, is put down.

Japan, 1524. Hojo Ujitsuna attacks and captures Edo castle. Followers of the Nichiren sect of Buddhism are expelled from Edo.

Germany, 1524. Led by the theologian Thomas Munzer, the peasants in southern Germany rise up and demand the abolition of feudal dues, serfdom and tithes.

Switzerland, 1524. The painter Hans Holbein the Elder dies.

Prussia, 8 April 1525. Albert von Brandenburg, the leader of the Teutonic Order, assumes the title "Duke of Prussia" and passes the first laws of the Protestant church, making Prussia a Protestant state.

Germany, 7 May 1525. The peasants' revolt is quelled. Thomas Munzer, its leader, is imprisoned and beheaded.

Germany, 19 July 1525. The Catholic princes of the north form the Dessau League to fight the Reformation.

Portugal, 21 August 1525. Estavao Gomes returns home after a year's exploration of the east coast of North America. He failed to find a clear waterway through to Asia.

Caribbean, 1525. The Welsers, an Augsburg banking family, establish a commercial and financial agency in Santo Domingo.

Spain, 1525. A conference at Badajoz confirms the 1494 treaty of Tordesillas, by which Spain and Portugal divided up the New World.

Spain, 1525. The last Spanish Moors, working on the great estates of the Valencian plains, are expelled.

Peru, 1525. On the death of the Inca emperor, Huayna Capac, the kingdom is divided between his two sons, Huascar and Atahualpa.

Germany, 30 December 1525. Jacob Fugger II (the Rich), financier to the Emperors Maximilian and Charles V, dies. Based largely on mining and the control of the copper market, the vast Fugger financial empire stretches from Lisbon in Portugal to Cracow in Poland and from the Baltic to the Mediterranean.

Revolt fired by Luther crushed by princes

One of the peasants' protests was against the alleged excesses of the Papacy.

Germany, 7 May 1525
The German peasant revolt has been crushed at Frankenhausen with the massacre of many thousands. German princes have been increasingly worried by the uprisings, which began last year in Bavaria and spread rapidly to Hesse, Franconia, Thuringia, Saxony and the Tyrol. The princes have acted determinedly and today one radical, Thomas Munzer, was beheaded.

The revolt was not a concerted movement so much as a series of local uprisings against oppression by princes, landlords and the church. It was inspired in part by Martin Luther's teachings and by radical Christian communities like the one set up at Allstedt in 1523 based on common ownership.

Some peasant leaders did get as far as drawing up a manifesto at Memmingen. It proposed the abolition of serfdom, the reduction of tithes and the right to choose and expel pastors. It was a programme radical enough to drive the princes to this month's repression.

Luther condemns peasants' uprising

Judgement and execution follow the bloodshed of the rebellion.

Germany, 1525
Martin Luther seems to have turned against the series of peasant uprisings which have been sweeping this country for more than a year. Luther's teachings have been one of the main causes of the revolts. Peasant leaders have been encouraged to call for the right to choose their own pastor, to oppose oppression by landlords and to win back former common land.

Luther supports many of their aims, but he was deeply shocked by a murder at Weinsberg, when peasants speared the count of Helfenstein in front of his wife and child. Luther has denounced them in a four-page tract, *Against the Murdering Thieving Hordes of Peasants*. "You cannot meet a rebel with reason," he wrote. "Your best answer is punch him in the face until he has a bloody nose."

Vasco da Gama, a fighter who won the Indies for Portugal, dies

India, 25 December 1524
Vasco da Gama, recalled from retirement by King John of Portugal to replace an incompetent viceroy in the Indies, died today at Calicut only three months after his arrival. He was 64.

After his epoch-making voyage to India round the Cape of Good Hope almost 30 years ago, da Gama spent five years engaged in trade and armed raids in the Indies. He put down rebellions with unbridled ferocity, on one occasion sailing from Calicut to Cochin "doing all the harm he could on the way to all he found at sea". He discovered the Seychelles Islands and, sailing as admiral of the Indian seas, he discovered and named the Admiralty Islands.

Retiring to Evora, the residence of the Portuguese court, he continued to advise the king on Indian affairs. He was created count of Vidigueira, with special privileges of civil and criminal jurisdiction and church patronage.

Da Gama was born in 1460, the year that Henry the Navigator died. It was Henry's enthusiasm for maritime exploration that gave Portugal the skills and experience vital for da Gama's expedition to discover the sea route to India. Da Gama had already proved himself as a young man fighting in the wars against Castile.

Vasco da Gama (16th century).

French king captured after Pavia disaster

Lannoy's use of the arquebus was the decisive factor in the battle of Pavia.

Italy, 24 February 1525
The French army has been utterly defeated at Pavia in Lombardy. King Francis had his horse shot from under him by an *arquebus* (a kind of gun) and tonight he is being held captive by Lannoy, the viceroy of Naples.

He has certainly lost his war with the Emperor Charles V for supremacy in Europe. The next logical step will be for Charles to force him into signing a humiliating peace treaty.

This disaster for the French began last autumn when Francis, with an army of French and Italian infantry, German and Swiss mercenaries, and a strong train of artillery, laid siege to Pavia.

At first the siege went well; the guns broke down the defences and the king's regiments stormed into the breaches. But Antonio de Leyva, the Spanish governor of the town, had built new fortifications inside the walls, and the French were routed by the defenders.

They retreated to mount a classic siege throughout the winter. Francis, reinforced by Venetian troops, became sure of victory as the town ran short of food and ammunition.

But the imperial forces had been gathering at the nearby town of Lodi, and when they marched on Pavia earlier this month Francis found himself caught between the anvil of Pavia and the hammer of the attacking imperial army.

Pope Clement VII tried to mediate, but failed; battle was joined before first light this morning. At first the French guns gave Francis the advantage, but, believing in chivalry rather than guns, he ordered them to cease fire.

He then led his knights in a disorganised charge without waiting for the infantry. In the shambles that ensued 6,000 French died and their king, fighting on foot, his face bloodied, surrendered his sword.

King Francis: misguided chivalry led to his present captivity.

Pavia marks a change in the face of war

Europe, 1525
The firearms which killed King Francis' horse and destroyed the French army at the battle of Pavia are part of the revolution in military arms and strategy which is rapidly changing warfare in Europe as armies are modernised.

After Pavia, armoured cavalry can no longer be regarded as the rulers of the battlefield. The day of the knight in armour is over. New tactics are already being developed for mounted troops using the new carbines and horse pistols.

Perhaps the greatest changes can be seen in siege warfare where the *trace italienne*, a circuit of low, thick walls punctuated by square bastions, is replacing the high thin walls of the Middle Ages. These new defences, developed in the long-drawn-out Italian wars, are designed to absorb the punishment of the heavy siege guns which are now part of every successful army.

The adoption of this bastion defence is changing the entire pattern of warfare because the cities protected by this method can no longer be taken by the traditional methods of blowing a hole in the walls and pouring infantry through the breach. Now towns have to be encircled by siegeworks and batteries and starved or frightened into submission. Warfare is becoming more and more a matter of engineering and logistics.

No armour for this German soldier.

At sea, too, the advent of the big gun has brought great changes. No longer do ships ram and board each other, but pound each other with formidable arrays of guns firing through ports in the ships' sides. The first such specialised gunship was built in England 12 years ago. It has set a pattern which all maritime nations must follow or face inevitable defeat.

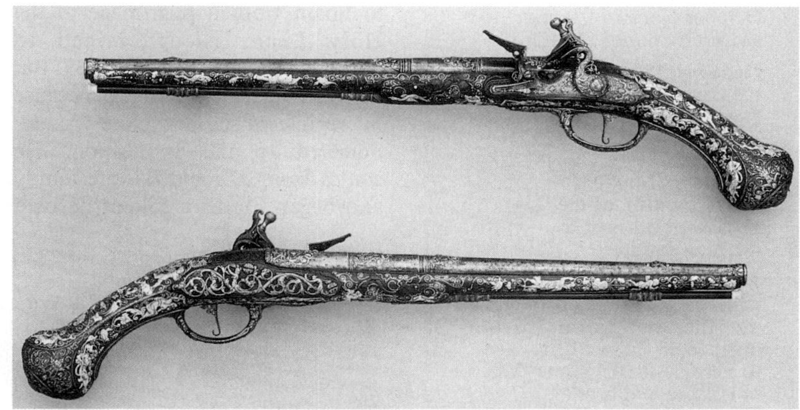
A pair of pistols: beautiful workmanship masks instruments of death.

Swiss rebel against church as a simple service replaces Mass

Zurich, 16 April 1525
This small Swiss town is now the focus of the breakaway movement from the church. Local magistrates have just banned the Roman Mass, and today the radical preacher Ulrich Zwingli held an alternative form of Holy Communion. It was a service of great simplicity with neither music nor singing. Zwingli presided over a table laid with beakers and wooden vessels. He served the congregation first, himself afterwards.

Zwingli was inspired by the humanist Erasmus, and by Luther, but he has proved more radical than either. Although an indifferent preacher with a weak voice, he has acquired a huge following. His tough-minded emphasis on simplicity and independence from Rome have a strong appeal for the mountain peoples of Switzerland.

1525 (1525-1527)

Morocco, 1525. The Sadian dynasty, claiming descent from the Prophet's son-in-law Ali, establish their capital at Marrakesh.

Spain, 14 January 1526. Francis of France, held captive by Charles V for a year, signs the treaty of Madrid. He abandons Burgundy and gives up claims to Flanders, Artois and Tournai. He also renounces all claims to Italy and pardons the rebel high constable of Bourbon.

France, June 1526. King Francis, now released, declares the treaty of Madrid null and void.

Rome, June 1526. Pope Clement VII approves the founding of the Capuchin order by Matteo de Bascio, who aims to revive the Franciscan ideal of saintly poverty.

Caribbean, 26 July 1526. The Spaniard Lucas Vasquez de Ayllon leaves Santo Domingo with several hundred settlers to found a colony in Florida.

Hungary, November 1526. John Zapolyai of Transylvania has himself elected king of Hungary by a section of the nobility. The throne has been left vacant since the death of Lewis II at Mohacs.

Caribbean, November 1526. Settlers from the failed Florida colony organised by Lucas Vasquez de Ayllon return to Santo Domingo without their leader, who died on 18 October – one of the many to succumb on the expedition.

Germany, 1526. In response to the creation of the Catholic Dessau League, Philip, the landgrave of Hesse, and Johann of Saxony establish the League of Torgau. It is later joined by most of the Protestant states in the German empire.

Austria, 1526. In accordance with the 1515 treaty of Vienna, the Hungarian crown – in the absence of a direct heir – goes to Ferdinand, the grand duke of Austria and brother of Charles V. The hereditary territories of Austria and the states of Hungary and Bohemia are thus reunited under the Habsburgs.

France, 1526. Francis of France forms an alliance with the Ottoman sultan, Suleiman the Magnificent, against the Emperor Charles V.

Mexico, 1526. Dominican monks arrive in Mexico.

Ottomans crush Hungarians at Mohacs

Hungary, 29 August 1526

The flower of Hungarian manhood has been destroyed on the battlefield of Mohacs. After one of the bloodiest and most decisive battles of recent times, the young Hungarian king, Lewis II, lies dead with more than 20,000 of his troops, and Europe quivers before the armies of the Ottoman conqueror, Suleiman the Magnificent.

The Christian forces which tried to regroup after the fall of Belgrade in 1521 have since fallen apart. The French king, Francis, captured by the Habsburg emperor, Charles V, at the battle of Pavia in 1525, secretly wrote to propose an alliance with Suleiman. Meanwhile Charles failed to persuade the Protestant *diets* to grant aid for the defence of Hungary against the Turks until a few weeks ago – too late to prevent the slaughter at Mohacs.

Lewis's own forces were weakened by bitter rivalries. No effort was made to hold the line of the river Drava, and the Hungarian nobles rejected all delaying actions which might have enabled reinforcements to arrive. Successive frontal assaults by the Hungarians were met by heavy artillery fire and superior numbers. Any survivors were then massacred.

Suleiman's army at Mohacs.

Suleiman, sultan and conqueror

Ottoman Empire, 1526

The rise of Ottoman power in Europe has been achieved with remarkable speed since Constantinople fell in 1453 to Sultan Mohammed II (ruled 1451-81). He had occupied southern Greece, most of Serbia and the Black Sea coast by 1461, and invaded other Balkan lands in 1463-4. In his war with Venice (1463-79) the Venetians lost several outposts.

Venice reasserted itself in the reign of Sultan Bayezid II (1481-1512). Another war ensued (1499-1503) in which the Turks raided as far as Vicenza and Venice lost more positions. Selim (1512-20) warred mainly in the Near East, but his son Suleiman took Belgrade in 1520, and Rhodes in 1522, and raided Austria and Hungary. After his victory at Mohacs, the Turkish army is just over 100 miles from Vienna.

Suleiman the Magnificent.

Exercises good for the soul, says Basque

Salamanca, 1526

Ignatius Loyola, who has returned to Spain from a pilgrimage to the Holy Land, is determined to become a priest at the age of 33. But he has had to leave Alcala because his regime of self-discipline was denounced to the Inquisition. He comes from a noble Basque family and began life as a soldier devoted to chivalry. Defending Pamplona during the siege of 1521, he was badly wounded in the leg, which left him disabled. During his long convalescence he turned to the life of Jesus and resolved to become a soldier of Christ. Withdrawing to a monastery at Manresa, he subjected himself to prayer, fasting and self-flagellation, only agreeing to break off when his confessor ordered him to eat. He is now writing a book of spiritual exercises designed to break the will by contemplating the agonies of hell and the mercy of Christ.

Suffused with the fire of Divine love.

Glittering court of Margaret of Navarre

France, 1527

Margaret of Navarre, the king's sister, is establishing a brilliant intellectual court at Agen, at the Chateau de Nerac. Having lost her first husband, the duke of Alencon, she has married Henry d'Albret and is therefore queen of Navarre.

Her court is home to writers such as Dolet, Marot and Rabelais. She is a great writer of letters and a poet of merit. Some of her best writing is contained in her short moral tales in the style of Boccaccio's *Decameron*, telling stories which often have erotic themes.

Perhaps more importantly, she is an advocate of religious liberty who gives shelter to clerics who question their church. Under her influence Nerac is becoming an important centre of French reformism.

Guns win priceless gem for Moghuls

Delhi, 21 April 1526

On the field of Panipat, to the north-west of Delhi, the Mongol or Moghul Emperor Babur has annihilated the Indian army of Ibrahim Lodi, the sultan of Delhi. Babur, descended from Genghis Khan and Tamerlane, has known fortune and failure. Thrice king of Ferghana (a tiny portion of Tamerlane's empire) and thrice deposed, he has been both beggar and emperor.

When Safavid power from Persia and Usbeg power from central Asia crushed the remnants of Tamerlane's empire, Babur rallied the Timurid princes and led them to conquests in Afganistan and Samarkand. In 1525 he turned on India, first taking control of the Punjab and then marching on Delhi.

The way was blocked at Panipat, by Sultan Ibrahim's army of 100,000 soldiers and 100 armoured elephants. Babur's army was hardly 12,000 strong. Protected behind a circular barricade of 700 carts, Babur opened up with his artillery, a weapon unknown to the Delhi army. The battle raged until noon, when the Indian army was sufficiently weakened for Babur to deliver the classic rear attack. "That mighty army," Babur later recalled, "in half a day was laid to dust."

With victory secure he sent his beloved son Humayun to Agra to secure the Indian treasury. Humayun returned with a diamond so large that its value would provide "two and a half days' food for the whole world", and offered it to Babur. With the extravagance of a man who has had everything and nothing, he waved it away dismissively. It is called the *Koh-i-Nor* diamond.

The emperor's army attacks a fortified town. From the "Baburnameh" (1590).

First bibles appear in English language

England, 1526

The first translation of the New Testament from its original Greek text into English has begun appearing in England a year after its publication at Worms, in Germany. Its author, William Tyndale, has been working on the project since 1522. The translation means that many more people, readers of English but not Greek, will be able to possess their own copy of the Scriptures.

Tyndale, who was serving as a tutor near Bristol, began his task as a reaction to the ignorance of the local priests and because he believed "that it was impossible to establish the lay people in any truth except when the Scripture were plainly laid before their eyes in their mother tongue, that they might see ... the meaning of the text".

A first-class linguist, Tyndale has drawn on the Greek Testament of Erasmus, published in 1516, for his translation. He has also made it clear, in his translation of certain critical words and passages, that he is seeking to strip away what he sees are the embellishments of Catholicism and lay bare the original text.

It is this rigorous attitude that sent him to Worms to complete his work. Encouraged by Martin Luther, he found a more congenial attitude there than in England. But that same attitude, relished by many readers, may well trouble the authorities.

The first boke of Mo- ses, called Genesis.

The first dayes worke. The seconde dayes worke. The thirde dayes worke.

The fourth dayes worke. The fifth dayes worke. The sixte dayes worke.

The first Chapter.

From a later English Bible.

Moslems conquer Christian Nubia after a seven-year war

Nubia (Sudan), c.1527

The Christian culture of Nubia is dead. Churches where men and women worshipped for a thousand years are empty and crumbling, European travellers report. One, Reubeni, who has visited Soba, the capital of Alwa, found nothing save a few huts. Another, Alvarez, found nothing but ruins.

Christianity came to Nubia from Egypt in the sixth century, just as the two Nubian kingdoms of Maqurra (on the middle Nile) and Alwa (on the upper Nile) were emerging. It became the state religion but never took root amongst the masses. The services were in Greek and incomprehensible. Like Ethiopia, Nubia became isolated from the rest of Christendom by the advance of Islam, but lacked Ethiopia's mountains and sense of national identity. Maqurra fell to Egypt in 1323, and Moslem traders, armies and tribes moved on Alwa.

While Alwa's northern frontiers fell to the Moslems, its southern frontiers crumbled to a new force from further up the Nile, the Funj. Seven years of war against Egypt, with the Funj first allying themselves with Alwa and then turning on it, were the final blow. Crushed by these various pressures the state has succumbed.

1527 (1527-1529)

India, 16 March 1527. The Emperor Babur defeats the Rajputs at the battle of Kanvaha, removing the main Hindu rivals to Moghul power in northern India.

England, 30 April 1527. Henry VIII and King Francis of France sign the treaty of Westminster, a pact against the Emperor Charles V.

Spain, June 1527. Panfilo de Narvaez, with five ships and 600 men, sets out to explore and settle the lands between Florida and Mexico.

Florence, 22 June 1527. The political theorist and historian Niccolo Macchiavelli dies.

Sweden, 1527. Lutheranism in Sweden is sanctioned by the *Diet* of Vasteras, allowing Gustav Vasa to replenish the royal treasury by confiscating the wealth of the church. He uses the opportunity to have a fleet of warships built.

England, 1527. Henry VIII asks the pope to annul his marriage to Catherine of Aragon, who has borne him one surviving daughter but given him no male heirs.

Portugal, 1527. King John III declares his support for the elimination of pirates and French traders in Brazil.

Florida, April 1528. Panfilo de Narvaez lands at Tampa bay with 400 colonists.

Spain, 1528. Having had his power withdrawn in 1526, Hernando Cortes arrives in Spain to plead his cause.

France, 1528. King Francis signs a trade treaty with the Turks.

Spain, 1528. A defence fleet for the Indies is organised.

France, 1528. Paris becomes the capital of France.

Switzerland, 1528. Berne decides in favour of the Reformation and abolishes the Mass.

India, 1528. The Portuguese reach Bengal.

Caribbean, 1528. While on an expedition to Brazil, the Florentine explorer Giovanni Verrazzano is killed by American natives.

Florida, 1528. A few survivors from the expedition led by Panfilo de Narvaez land on a tiny island in the Gulf of Mexico, off the Florida coast. Most of their companions have died from hunger and thirst; Narvaez was lost at sea.

East Africa, 1528. Mombasa revolts against Portuguese rule.

Albrecht Durer, artist and engraver, dies

Durer's "Melencolia" shows his mastery of the art of engraving.

Nuremberg, 1528
Albrecht Durer, who has died here at his home town at the age of 57, was regarded as the Leonardo of the north. A goldsmith's son, he became famous throughout Germany not only as an artist but for his treatises on optics and friendship with such men as Erasmus and Luther.

He met Erasmus on his visit to the Netherlands in 1521 and was disturbed that he did not support Luther openly. He wrote in his journal: "Oh, Erasmus of Rotterdam, where art thou? Defend the truth and earn a martyr's crown!" He drew his portrait in charcoal and Erasmus declared that there was nothing that Durer could not express without the use of colour.

Durer was the greatest master of engraving on wood and metal. He said: "Many a sketch made in a day on half a sheet of paper, or cut on a little piece of wood, has more and better art in it than some great work on which someone has laboured for a year." Some of his greatest works are engravings like *Melencolia* and *The Knight, Death and the Devil*, which he gave to Luther.

"Lot and his daughters".

Features of perfect courtier delineated

Italy, 1528
A book of contemporary etiquette, defining every aspect of a gentleman's life and attitudes, has been published in Venice. As much as any similar compilation, *The Courtier*, by the writer Baldassare Castiglione, epitomises the thinking of modern cultured people.

Castiglione is himself an accomplished courtier, who has drawn on his own experiences in the service of Guidobaldo de Montefeltro, the duke of Urbino, for his work. He is also a veteran of the courts of Popes Leo X and Clement VII. His writing, which takes the form of instructive dialogues, has been further refined by his association with the Medicis and many other important figures.

The Courtier sets out the qualifications for good breeding. It is concerned with neither politics nor morals, but with the lifestyle of an elite, and portrays the cultured courtier as an idealised universal man or woman. It is not wholly original: Castiglione draws openly on Cicero, Plutarch and Livy, and on the opinions of friends such as the humanist Pietro Bembo and Giuliano de Medici.

Castiglione's campaign to remove affectation from well-bred living is having a profound effect on cultured society in Italy, and further afield in France and England.

Meditative soldier dies after revolt

China, 9 January 1529
Wang Yang-ming, the renowned philosopher who preached meditation and intuitive knowledge, has died at the age of 56. A soldier as well as thinker, he died while returning from quashing a revolt by bandits in Gwangxi province.

He made many enemies at court; at one time he was imprisoned, beaten with forty strokes and then banished on the orders of the powerful court eunuch Liu Jin. On his way to exile he found that Liu Jin's agents were following him. Fearing for his life, he left his clothing on a river bank and, tricking them into thinking he had drowned, escaped.

German troops sack and burn Rome

After the city falls, the mercenaries besiege the pope's stronghold.

Polemical engraving by Cranach.

Rome, 6-16 May 1527

Such is the fury of the 15,000 German mercenaries who are sacking Rome, looting, burning and raping in an orgy of destruction, that little can be left of what was once the finest city in the world. The Vatican has been occupied by Lutheran troops, its chapels used as stables and the Raphael paintings in the papal apartments covered with graffiti. As Rome is consumed by the rising flames, Pope Clement VII has beseeched Charles V to call off the men who are destroying the city.

It is too late, however. The commanders of the armies sent to Italy had left before the emperor and pope had signed a truce, and unfortunately one of them (the commander of the Bourbon army) is now dead. The other, Georg von Frunsberg, was badly wounded after telling his men: "I hope soon to make you all rich from the pickings of Rome." The result was inevitable when his unpaid, starving and leaderless army came within sight of the city and its enormous wealth.

It is over a year since the formation of a Holy League by the Treaty of Cognac, under which Rome and Venice allied themselves with the pope to assist the French against Charles V. Few expected the Emperor to take such devastating action against the challenge to his growing power.

Theory seeks to explain why lean-faced men are quick to anger

The four humours: choleric (with lion), sanguine (with ape), phlegmatic (with sheep) and melancholic (with hog). Sound physical and mental health depends on a perfect balance of the humours. From the "Shepherd's Calendar".

Europe, c.1528

For centuries medicine has been dominated by the ancient theory of humours which, through the work of Paracelsus and others, is now coming under attack.

The theory is that the body is composed of four main fluids or humours: blood, phlegm, choler (yellow bile), and melancholy (black bile). In a healthy body, these fluids are in perfect balance; sickness results from losing that equilibrium. In other words, illness is an internal phenomenon.

The humours are also said to affect personality. If a person has an excess of melancholy, he or she will be of a gloomy disposition. Too much blood leads to a "sanguine" or positive character; phlegm is associated with passivity, and choler with quick temper. The humours are also said to influence appearance. Thus, the choleric man is lean faced and hairy.

Medical row drives doctor from city

Basle, 1528

Dr Theophrastus Paracelsus, the town physician of Basle, has been expelled from the city following a dispute with the local magistrates, among them doctors opposed to his medical methods.

Paracelsus, whose real name is Theophrastus Bombastus von Hohenheim, was born the son of a physician, in 1493, in the Swiss canton of Schwyz. He went to Basle university at 16 and later studied alchemy and chemistry with the bishop of Wurzburg. He built up a huge store of facts and learnt medical practice at first hand, acquiring at the same time a deep distrust of traditional methods.

Two years ago he was made town physician at Basle. He taught at the university but, controversially, rejected the writings of earlier physicians such as Galen and Avicenna. Paracelsus also rejects the old notion of the "four humours" of the human body, the balance of which is said to determine illness. He prefers to think in terms of "outside agents" leading to disease, and argues that the body is really a complex chemical factory. To change the progress of a disease people need to change the body's chemical behaviour through specifically-aimed medicines.

However, Paracelsus' teachings, and his reputation for arrogance, have won him many enemies.

Paracelsus wants to bring the principles of alchemy to medicine.

1529 (1529-1530)

Germany, 16 April 1529. After the second Diet of Speyer, 19 reformed states protest against the repeal of an imperial decree – passed in 1526, at the first Diet of Speyer – which allowed each prince to decide the religious allegiance of his state.

Spain, 22 April 1529. The treaty of Saragossa fixes the dividing line between the Portuguese and the Spanish in the Pacific Ocean at 17 degrees east of the Moluccas. The Portuguese have regained control of the archipelago in return for paying compensation to the Emperor Charles V.

India, 6 May 1529. Babur defeats the Afghan chiefs of Bihar and Bengal at the battle of Ghagra. His power now stretches from Kabul in the west to Bengal in the east.

Algeria, 27 May 1529. Khey ad-Din Barbarossa completes his conquest of Algeria in the name of the Ottoman sultan.

Spain, 29 June 1529. The Emperor Charles V and Pope Clement VII sign the treaty of Barcelona, settling their differences.

Spain, 26 July 1529. In Spain to secure the support of Charles V for his proposed expedition to Peru, Ferdinand Pizarro is granted the titles of governor and captain-general of the country he proposes to conquer.

France, 5 August 1529. Louise of Savoy, acting for Francis of France, and Margaret of Austria, representing her nephew Charles V, sign the peace of Cambrai, known as the *Paix des Dames*. Under the treaty, France renounces all its rights in Italy, Flanders and Artois and agrees to pay a ransom of two million crowns. Charles V renounces any claims to Burgundy.

England, 27 August 1529. Henry VIII also accedes to the treaty of Cambrai.

Hungary, 8 September 1529. The Ottoman Sultan Suleiman re-enters Buda and establishes John Zapolyai as the puppet king of Hungary.

Rome, October 1529. Under the influence of the Emperor Charles V, Catherine of Aragon's nephew, Pope Clement VII refuses to grant Henry VIII, the king of England, an annulment of his marriage to Catherine.

England, 17 October 1529. Angered by Thomas Wolsey's failure to secure from the pope an annulment of his marriage, Henry VIII strips him of the office of lord chancellor.

England, 25 October 1529. Thomas More replaces Wolsey as lord chancellor, becoming the first layman to hold the office in living memory. A fierce opponent of Luther he more recently became embroiled in controversy with the Protestant theologian William Tyndale who asserted royal supremacy over the church.

Germany, 1-4 November 1529. On the invitation of Philip of Hesse, the reformers of Wittenberg, Strasbourg and Zurich meet in Marburg to try to resolve the theological differences that divide the German Reformation. Luther, Melanchthon, Oecolampadius and Zwingli fail to reach agreement on the Eucharist.

Japan, 1529. Monks from the Tendai monasteries on Mount Hiei, north-west of Kyoto, sweep down on the city and massacre followers of the Nichiren sect of Buddhism.

England, 3 November 1529. The first Parliament for five years opens. The Commons put forward bills against abuses amongst the clergy and in the church courts.

Ethiopia, 1529. Under the leadership of Ahmad Gran, Moslems launch an attack on Ethiopia from the Red Sea. They win a battle at Shembura Kure and go on to conquer Shoa.

Italy, 24 February 1530. Charles V is crowned Holy Roman emperor by Pope Clement VII at Bologna. Elected on 28 June 1519, Charles was crowned emperor in France on 26 October 1520.

India, 1530. On the death of his father, Babur, Humayun becomes sultan of Delhi.

Brazil, 1530. The Portuguese begin to colonise Brazil.

Malta, 1530. Driven out of Rhodes in 1522 by the Turks, the Knights of St John of Jerusalem are given permission by the Emperor Charles V to settle on the island of Malta.

Silesia, 1530. Georg Bauer, known as Agricola, publishes a work of major importance in the field of mineralogy and mining techniques entitled *De Re Metallica*.

South-East Africa, 1530. Chikuyo, the Munhumutapa or king who has ruled the southern Zambezi escarpment for 30 years, is killed during a civil war.

Florence, 1530. The Medicis are restored to power in Florence by imperial troops.

Italy, 1530. Girolamo Fracastoro gives the name syphilis to the disease the Spanish call *bubas*, which may have been transported to Europe by sailors returning from the New World.

Last thoughts of first Moghul emperor

The dying emperor spends his last days with his son Humayun by his side.

Sakri, India, 1530

Babur, the descendant of Genghis Khan and Tamerlane the Great, who built an empire out of an impoverished central Asian princedom and conquered northern India, is dying. He sits alone in his garden, built to remind him of the pleasures of Kabul, writing his memoirs.

They go back to his childhood when, aged 11, he became king of Ferghana. Three times he lost and won that kingdom. He writes with sadness of tribesmen in 1519 who had never seen guns before, laughing at the noise and confronting them with obscene gestures before being massacred; but he has little sympathy for the supposedly sophisticated societies he conquered.

"Hindustan is a country that has few pleasures to recommend it. The people are not handsome. They have no idea of the charms of friendly society, of mixing frankly together, or of familiar intercourse. They have no genius, no comprehension of mind, no politeness of manner, no kindness of fellow feeling, no ingenuity or mechanical or artistic abilities, no knowledge of design or architecture, no horses, no flesh, no grapes, no melons, no ice, no decent food, baths, no candles, not even a candlestick."

Sometimes he puts aside his manuscript and, drawing hashish smoke into his lungs, allows the memories of bloody battlefields to metamorphose themselves into "wonderful fields of flowers".

He lists with loving detail the flora and fauna of his subject territories, describing parrots, rhinoceroses, the leaves of an apple tree and the changing colours of flocks of geese on the horizon.

His only sadness is his son's sickness. The holy men tell Babur that Humayun will only be cured if he gives up the most valuable thing he possesses. He thinks that this is the *Koh-i-Nor* diamond, not realising it is Babur himself. "What value is worldly wealth, and how can it redeem Humayun? I myself shall be his sacrifice." Babur sits alone in his garden and prepares to die.

Storms and disease end Vienna siege

Vienna, 15 October 1529

Europe can breathe again. The Ottoman armies, which have been encamped beneath the walls of Vienna for nearly three weeks, are heading back towards Belgrade. For once Suleiman has over-reached himself, although bad weather and disease have been the crucial factors rather than any feat of Christian arms.

Two years ago, while the Emperor Charles V was concentrating on his second war in France, his brother Ferdinand defeated the Hungarian nationalist Zapolyai and was crowned king of the part of Hungary that was still in Habsburg hands. Ferdinand was then rash enough to send an envoy to Suleiman demanding the return of fortresses taken by the Ottomans after their victory at Mohacs.

Suleiman, who was now committed to restoring Zapolyai to the Hungarian throne, embarked on his most ambitious campaign to date. His chief problem was to reach Vienna before winter. In the event, he lost a month battling through heavy storms, building bridges across rivers, and leading his troops through treacherous terrain of streams and marshes. Although he left Istanbul on 10 May, he did not arrive in Belgrade until mid-July, reaching Vienna on 27 September.

This time Ferdinand was prepared. In March the German Diet had assembled in Innsbruck and voted 120,000 Rhenish guilders for defence against the Ottoman invader; in May, despite the opposition of Philip of Hesse and other Protestant princes, the Diet of Speyer had promised an army of 16,000 men and 4,000 cavalry. When the first Ottoman troops attacked, they were met by a garrison of seasoned veterans.

Suleiman needed a quick victory, but he did not get it. Wave after wave was beaten back, and no significant breach was ever made in the city walls. The Ottoman army lost horses and men from hunger and disease. Yesterday the sultan gave the order to retreat.

The emperor tramples the Ottomans underfoot, as Suleiman's forces retreat.

Turkish cruelty to Austrian captives.

Divorce row leads to Cardinal's fall

England, October 1529

The man who for the past 15 years has virtually controlled English domestic and foreign policy has been abruptly sacked as lord chancellor by Henry VIII. Thomas Wolsey, cardinal and papal envoy, failed to persuade Rome to allow the king to divorce Catherine of Aragon.

In 20 years of marriage, Catherine had one daughter, five infants who did not survive, and several miscarriages but was unable to produce a male heir. Henry is impatient and is also infatuated with the protestant Anne Boleyn, aged 18, who has a reputation as a flirt.

The king told Wolsey to get Pope Clement VII to annul the marriage to Catherine, who was the widow of Henry's elder brother Arthur. But an earlier pope had issued a special bull which over-rode objections to that marriage on the grounds of the closeness of the relationship. Also Henry's earlier liaison with Anne's elder sister Mary raises the question of a forbidden blood link. For the past two years Wolsey and Henry have been pressurising Rome and the pope has been procrastinating. Catherine is the aunt of the Emperor Charles V, who has the pope in his power after his troops occupied Rome. A furious Henry charged Wolsey with abuse of power and, stripping him of all offices, packed him off to York as archbishop; he is not expected to last.

Defiant princes are dubbed Protestants

Speyer, Germany, 1529

A letter of protest signed by six of Germany's Lutheran princes and the burghers of 14 cities has rejected the findings of the Catholic-dominated Diet of Speyer. The letter, *A Protestation*, for which the signatories have been dubbed "Protestants", is seen as a challenge to the authority of the emperor.

The letter states that "in matters which concern God's honour and salvation and the eternal life of souls, everyone must stand and give account before God for himself". Its message is almost identical to that of the diet three years ago which Charles V swore to overturn.

Church reformers seek to end split

Germany, 4 November 1529

Philip of Hesse has had only partial success in seeking to end the split in the church reform movement. To the amazement of many of their friends, he managed to persuade the two leaders, Martin Luther and Ulrich Zwingli, to meet him in the castle here. Even more surprisingly they signed the "Fifteen Marburg Articles" agreeing on all items of doctrine except the Eucharist.

However, the meeting between the two men was stormy. They remain deeply divided politically. Luther will not move against the emperor; Zwingli is keen for the Swiss to revolt.

Conquest of Peru given royal boost

Toledo, Spain, 26 July 1529

A royal warrant signed today allows the explorer Francisco Pizarro to return to a country which he found three years ago on the Pacific coast south of Panama. The queen's approval (or *capitulacion*) licenses Pizarro to "discover and conquer" Peru, of which he is now Spain's governor. Pizarro has brought back llamas, Peruvian boys to become interpreters, and various artefacts to prove that a highly developed culture exists. First contact with the natives shows them to be friendly. Pizarro's credibility was magnified by the presence at court of the hero of Mexico, Hernando Cortes.

King Henry VIII confers with his lord chancellor, Cardinal Thomas Wolsey; from a painting by Sir John Gilbert (1817-1897).

1530 (1530-1532)

Germany, 25 June 1530. At the Diet of Augsburg, the Lutherans deliver the *Confession*, a detailed statement of their faith prepared by Philip Melanchthon. It is designed to achieve reconciliation with the Catholic Church.

Antwerp, 13 July 1530. The painter Quentin Massys dies. His religious works were in the Flemish tradition of the last century, but his portraits reveal the influence of humanist idealism.

Rome, 8 October 1530. The city is flooded.

Bohemia, 5 January 1531. The Emperor Charles V secures the election of his younger brother Ferdinand as King of the Romans.

Hungary, 31 January 1531. John Zapolyai and Ferdinand of Habsburg, both of whom were crowned king of Hungary in 1526, reach a truce.

England, February 1531. The convocation of the church in England buy a pardon from Henry VIII for their "guilt" under the statute of praemunire (unlawfully exercising spiritual jurisdiction) and recognise him as their supreme head with major qualifications.

Germany, 27 February 1531. German Protestants form the League of Schmalkalden to resist the power of the emperor.

Ethiopia, 1531. Portugal sends troops to assist Ethiopia against the Moslems.

South-East Africa, 1531. The Portuguese begin to trade at the Moslem port of Sena on the lower Zambezi (*Mozambique*).

Florence, 1531. The Emperor Charles V marries his daughter Margaret of Parma to Alessandro de Medici and makes him duke of Florence.

France, 1531. Margaret of Navarre publishes a spiritual handbook entitled *The Mirror of the Sinful Soul*.

France, 1531. Francis of France forms an alliance with John Zapolyai, the king of Hungary.

Brazil, 1531. Martin Alfonso de Sousa, the leader of the first expedition to explore the interior of Brazil, dies during the journey.

Mexico, 1531. Hernando Cortes returns to New Spain as captain-general, having been removed from the governorship two years ago.

Netherlands, 1531. Charles V prohibits the adoption of Protestant doctrines in the Netherlands.

Switzerland, 11 October 1531. During the second civil war between the Protestants and the Catholics, the Protestants are defeated at Kappel. Ulrich Zwingli dies in the battle.

Germany, 24 October 1531. Bavaria, despite being Catholic, joins the League of Schmalkalden.

England, 29 November 1531. Thomas Wolsey, archbishop of York, dies at Leicester while travelling to London to answer a charge of treason.

Portugal, 17 December 1531. An inquisition is established.

England, 16 May 1532. Thomas More resigns as lord chancellor the day after a convocation of the English clergy agrees to seek royal consent before making any decisions.

Germany, 26 May 1532. Francis, the king of France, forges an alliance with Bavaria, Saxony and Hesse against the Habsburg Ferdinand.

Germany, 23 June 1532. The Emperor Charles V signs the peace of Nuremberg with the Protestant princes, who are granted freedom of worship in return for military aid against the Ottoman Turks.

Hungary, August 1532. Suleiman the Magnificent, the Ottoman sultan, who invaded Hungary in June, is defeated at Guns.

France, 1532. A treaty of union ends Brittany's independence.

France, 1532. The writer Francois Rabelais wins instant success with the publication of his first book, *Pantagruel*, a satire of a popular folk tale, which is condemned by the Sorbonne.

Scandinavia, 1532. Christian II of Denmark is taken prisoner after a failed attempt to conquer Norway.

Italy, 1532. *The Prince* by Niccolo Macchiavelli is published posthumously.

Italy, 1532. Ludovico Ariosto completes a revised edition of his epic poem *Orlando Furioso*.

England, 1532. The poetical works of Geoffrey Chaucer are published in a collected edition.

Netherlands, 1532. The painter Jan Gossart, known as Mabuse, dies at Breda. Following his visits to Florence, Rome and Venice, in 1508-9, he developed a passion for Italian art and developed its formal innovations, particularly in his secular works such as *Venus and Cupid* and *Danae*.

Crimea, 1532. Sahib Giray, khan of Kazan since 1523, founds the khanate of Crimea under Ottoman protection.

Protestants seek compromise with church

Augsburg, 25 June 1530
Lutheran Protestants today presented 28 articles of faith to the diet here in an attempt to avoid a split with the Catholic Church. The *Confession of Augsburg* bends over backwards to secure unity. The first 21 articles are points on which both groups are already agreed. The last seven deal with controversial issues like confession and the celibacy of priests, but leave them open as being "under discussion".

The confession is the work of Philip Melanchthon. Luther himself was unable to come since he is still an exile from the empire. While Melanchthon is a loyal disciple, and has not compromised on matters of essential doctrine, he is above all a pacifier who wants to avoid making common cause with the more rebellious Swiss.

The emperor, Charles V, is also keen to achieve unity. He wants the support of German Protestant princes to continue his struggle with the Turks, who last year laid siege to Vienna. Both sides here have been keen to compromise, but close observers see it as window-dressing.

The religious differences remain deep and, though Luther has continually made it clear that he will not go along with armed resistance to the emperor, his battle with the Catholic theologians is as fierce as ever. The Catholics are no less resolute and it can only be a matter of time before the split reopens.

The emperor Charles V rallies Germany's princes at the Diet of Augsburg.

League formed to defend Lutheran Church

Schmalkalden, 27 February 1531
Eight German princes and eleven cities today agreed to form themselves into a league to defend the reformist church of Martin Luther. It is to be called the League of Schmalkalden, after this little town which stands symbolically on the borders of Hesse and Saxony, two of the league's most powerful supporters.

Other members of the league include the duke of Brunswick and Luneburg and the cities of Strasbourg, Ulm, Lubeck, Bremen and Magdeburg. Today they affirmed that "on all occasions that any of us is attacked for the Word of God and the doctrine of the gospel or for any other thing connected therewith, all the others will come to his aid at once".

The princes have political reasons for wanting to resist the power of the emperor. But the key factor was the decision of the Diet of Augsburg last November – when the Catholic militants won the day – which insisted that Lutherans recognise the pope and threatened force if they did not. This united the more moderate Protestants like Luther with the Swiss, who have long been inclined to open revolt.

Ruler seized as Incas are massacred

Lima, Peru, 1532
Over-confident with success in a bitter civil war against his brother, the Inca Atahualpa has gambled with his newly-won empire and lost it. His opponent in a bloody game of chance was Francisco Pizarro, a wily, if illiterate, veteran of many small wars. With only 150 soldiers, including 62 horsemen, and three months' march from any help, Pizarro should have been no match for thousands of Indian soldiers. That is what the Inca himself thought. Atahualpa, who is now a valuable hostage with a fortune in gold to be ransomed, admitted soon after his capture that his plan was to take the Spaniards unawares, sacrifice some of them to the sun god, and castrate the rest for service as eunuchs.

But Pizarro used surprise brilliantly. He occupied, peacefully, some long, low buildings round three sides of a square in the upland valley town of Cajamarca. He invited Atahualpa to meet him. When the Inca came he was handed a Christian prayer book, which he threw down. Pizarro sprang his ambush: two hidden cannon blasted at point blank range into the packed Peruvian ranks, followed by a cavalry charge. Panic did the rest. Pizarro led a squad which snatched Atahualpa from his litter while his soldiers butchered the survivors. In two hours, 7,000 Indians died and their leader became a captive.

These sketches by Felipe Guaman Poma show the cruelty of the conquistadores. On the right, they are seen executing the Inca emperor Atahualpa.

Pizarro's march towards the Inca capital of Cuzco continues. Since the people of Cuzco were subjects of Atahualpa's defeated brother Huascar, they are potential allies, and Pizarro cleverly emulated his former captain, Cortes, in conquering by exploiting a local civil war so as to divide and rule.

Pizarro's campaigning over thousands miles with a small force with no supply lines against apparently overwhelming odds is clearly paying dividends as the remnants of Atahualpa's army limps away from its own tribal territory ahead of the invaders.

New World Indian sees Virgin Mary

Mexico, 13 December 1531
On the morning of 9 December, Juan Diego, an Indian and a devout Catholic, had a vision of the Virgin Mary. She told him to go to the Spanish bishop of Mexico and persuade him to build her a church on Tepeyacac Hill.

Not believing the Indian's story, the bishop refused. When Juan saw the Virgin again that afternoon he begged her to use a Spaniard for her mission. She just assured Juan of her love and concern for his people and asked him to persevere.

On 10 December Diego failed for the second time to convince the bishop. On his way home the Virgin told him to return the next day to collect proof for his story. But Juan's uncle caught the plague that day, 11 December, forcing Juan to stay at home.

On 12 December 1531, the Virgin cured Juan's uncle and simultaneously met Juan at Tepeyacac hill. There she ordered him to pick flowers and carry them to the bishop in his cloak. When Juan opened his cloak, the image of the Virgin was clearly to be seen on the lining and the bishop was finally persuaded to build the church.

Protestant reformer Zwingli dies in battle

Switzerland, 11 October 1531
Ulrich Zwingli, the leader of the Swiss Reformation, has been killed in battle here. He was accompanying the army as a chaplain, but was caught up in the fighting. His body was quartered and burnt.

Zwingli symbolised the new unity of the reformist preachers with the lay power of the cities. In Zurich his reforms of the church service went side by side with a court, jointly administered by magistrates and church elders, which has made church attendance compulsory and punishes adultery.

The churches in Zurich and other Protestant cities, like Berne and Basle, have been freed of Catholic images and the Mass. In their places are a simple service and daily Bible readings. Zwingli blended his religious ideas with appeals to Swiss patriotism in his sermons. He launched the current war on the

Zwingli: patriotic Swiss preacher.

Catholic cantons, but failed to win enough support from other Protestant cities. Some were jealous of Zurich's prestige; others disliked Zwingli's attack on Swiss mercenaries, who are a major export earner for many cities.

Expanding Russia seeks more conquests

Moscow, 1530
As a unified Muscovy continues to confront its Polish and Lithuanian neighbours in the west, its power has increased considerably under the energetic leadership of Vasily III who is assiduously carrying on the work of his father, Ivan the Great, in building the country into a powerful political force in Europe.

Vasily began consolidating his father's work by annexing the two remaining Great Russian territories, Pskov and Ryazan, with little difficulty and no military effort. He appointed a civil servant to run Pskov. He also deprived 300 leading families of their estates, deported them to the interior, and replaced them by an equal number of families from Moscow.

Ryazan was taken over when its grand prince entered into secret negotiations with the Tartars. Determined to add to Ivan's gains in

Vasily: the heir to Ivan the Great.

Lithuanian Russia, Vasily invaded the territory and took Smolensk, the focal point of Muscovy's western defensive system. Vasily's problems on his eastern and southern borders have been eased by the failure of a Tartar invasion.

1532 (1532-1534)

England, 25 January 1533. King Henry VIII secretly marries Anne Boleyn.

England, 30 March 1533. The scholar Thomas Cranmer becomes archbishop of Canterbury. He takes the oath of allegiance to the pope protesting that he is doing so "for form's sake".

England, 1 June 1533. Shortly after the marriage of Henry VIII to Catherine of Aragon has been declared void by Thomas Cranmer – and the marriage to Anne Boleyn valid – the new queen is crowned at Westminster.

Hungary, 22 June 1533. A year after invading Hungary, Suleiman the Magnificent, the sultan of the Ottomans, signs a peace treaty with Ferdinand of Habsburg, the brother of the Emperor Charles V. Hungarian rule remains divided between Ferdinand and the Ottoman puppet John Zapolyai.

England, 11 July 1533. Henry VIII is excommunicated by Pope Clement VII.

Peru, 29 August 1533. On the orders of the governor, Francisco Pizarro, the Inca chief Atahualpa is executed, although he has already paid millions of pounds for his ransom.

Peru, 15 November 1533. Pizarro enters Cuzco.

Russia, 11 December 1533. At the age of three, Ivan IV succeeds his father, Vasily III.

Algeria, 1533. Suleiman the Magnificent appoints Khey ad-Din Barbarossa commander of Algiers with orders to cooperate with the French against the empire.

Germany, 1533. The radical religious sect known as the Anabaptists, which rejects infant baptism, takes power in Munster.

Persia, 13 July 1534. Ottoman armies capture Tabriz in north-western Persia.

North America, 24 July 1534. A French expedition under Jacques Cartier, patronised by King Francis, reaches the estuary of the River of Canada *(St Lawrence)* after a three-month journey from St Malo on the French coast.

North Africa, August 1534. Khey ad-Din Barbarossa wins back Tunis from its Moorish king, an ally of the Spanish.

Paris, 15 August 1534. The Spanish nobleman, ex-soldier and monk Ignatius Loyola vows to found a society in honour of Jesus Christ (the Society of Jesus). In 1521, after an intense religious experience which began his conversion, Loyola went on retreat to Montserrat, in Spain.

France, 5 September 1534. Jacques Cartier returns with furs to Normandy after exploring Prince Edward Island, Chaleur Bay and Gaspe Bay off North America.

North America, September 1534. Cabeza de Vaca, Estevanico (a slave) and two other survivors of the Panfilo de Narvaez expedition of 1527 escape after six years of Indian captivity in south-western North America.

England, November 1534. The Act the Supremacy separates the Church of England from Rome and declares the king to be its supreme head. The Act of Succession vests the succession in the children of Anne Boleyn; severe penalties are prescribed for anyone who opposes Henry VIII's marriage to her or its issue, and the king is given powers to demand an oath of allegiance to the act's provisions.

Baghdad, 31 December 1534. The Ottomans capture Baghdad.

Persia, 1534. Shah Tahmasp executes Husayn Khan, head of the Shamlu tribe, and assumes power in person.

England, 1534. Thomas Cromwell is made principle secretary.

Denmark, 1534. Christian III, a Protestant, becomes king of Denmark after defeating the Catholic supporters of his brother John in a civil war which broke out after the death of their father, Ferdinand, last year.

Florence, 1534. Leaving the Medicis' mortuary chapel at San Lorenzo unfinished, Michelangelo returns to Rome, where he has been commissioned to adorn the Sistine Chapel – whose ceiling he decorated over 20 years ago – with frescoes.

Germany, 1534. Francis of France signs the treaty of Augsburg, an alliance with the Protestant princes against Charles V.

Brazil, 1534. The ambitious scheme of John III, the king of Portugal, to divide the Brazilian coastline into 12 captaincies breaks down. It has been undermined by native attacks and by the reluctance of Portuguese noblemen to assume the necessary responsibilities.

Rome, 1534. On the death of Giulio de Medici (Clement VII), pope since 1523, Alexander Farnese is elected. He takes the name Paul III.

Peru, 1534. The Inca leader Manco Capac II leads an uprising against Pizarro.

Morocco, 1534. Abu Abdullah, the last Nasrid (Moslem) ruler of Granada, in Spain, dies at Fez.

The civilised home life of a Turk, depicted by Eugene Delacroix (1798-1863).

Private wealth, public squalor in the east

Near East, c.1533

The few occidentals who venture through the pirate-infested Mediterranean to what has become known as the "mysterious east" find a very different world awaiting them. Ancient cities like Cairo or Damascus still remain hidden behind their walls, their gates closed to the cries of the *hodja* calling the people to evening prayer from their minarets.

There are no wide streets, only narrow alleys with overhanging buildings which block out the sun; there are no wheeled vehicles, everything being carried on the backs of donkeys or humans. The visitor will find no town halls of the sort he is used to in Europe; the power lies in the sultan's citadel.

The cities are noisy throughout the day with the constant shouts of traders from their tiny booths in narrow covered markets. The visitor will find peace only in the mosques with their wide, cool, peaceful courts. House architecture, too, differs markedly from the west's. The visitor will see little but blank walls and shuttered windows. Elegance and decor are kept for the interior; much of family life takes place around shady courtyards.

Epic poet of bygone heroic age has died

Ferrara, Italy, 6 June 1533

Ludovico Ariosto, the author of the magnificent epic poem *Orlando Furioso*, has died aged 59. The poem, regarded by many as the finest of its era, was first published in 1516 and completed in 1532.

In Ariosto's words, his work celebrates "the ladies, the knights, the battles, the loves, the courtesies and the bold exploits" of a by-gone era: the heroic age of the *Chanson de Roland*, when French might dominated Europe and the noble Roland, Ariosto's Orlando, was a byword for chivalric perfection.

The poem is dedicated to the d'Este family who rule Ferrara and by whom Ariosto was employed as a diplomat, administrator and theatrical producer for 30 years.

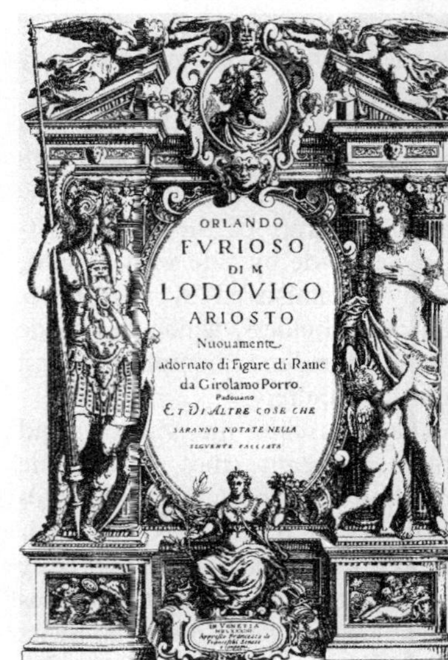

Cover of "Orlando's" 1583 edition.

King defies pope and marries mistress

England, July 1533
The king has had his way and has rid himself of Catherine in order to marry Anne Boleyn. The price has been the repudiation of papal authority in England. Assisted by his new first minister Thomas Cromwell, Henry persuaded parliament to pass a series of measures which make him head of the church in England and allow the archbishop of Canterbury to make all such dispensations as the pope has made in the past.

On the death of Archbishop Warham in January Henry appointed Thomas Cranmer, a favourite of Anne, to Canterbury. Cranmer, though for appearances' sake taking the oath of obedience to Rome, promptly declared Henry's marriage to Catherine invalid and blessed the marriage to Anne.

It was none too soon. Late last year Henry took Anne with him when he visited France's King Francis at Calais. Her suite of rooms adjoined Henry's. When they eventually got back to London Anne was pregnant. She was crowned queen last month and the birth is expected in September. In Rome, Pope Clement has excommunicated Henry.

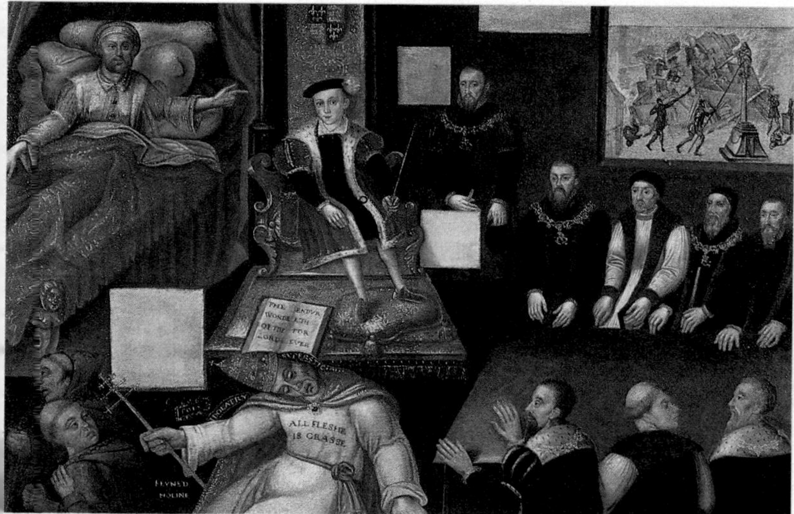

The defeated pope slumps before Henry VIII (in bed) and Edward VI – from a satirical picture (undated) possibly commissioned by the King.

Painter leaves family to work in England

London, 1533
Hans Holbein, the German portrait painter, is back in England, having abandoned his wife and children in Basle, where he normally works. He is busy painting German merchants and has done the portrait of Thomas Cromwell, the king's new favourite and chancellor.

On his previous visit as a young man, in 1526, Master Holbein was the guest of Sir Thomas More, to whom he had introductions from Erasmus, and who is now fallen from favour. His drawing of Sir Thomas among his family was sent to Erasmus, who wrote: "I should scarcely be able to see you better if I were with you."

The picture of *The Ambassadors* from France, standing full length with a strangely distorted skull in front of them, has impressed the king, so that he has begun to patronise the Augsburg-born painter. He has plans for a large mural at his palace at Whitehall, to show him, his parents, Henry VII and Elizabeth of York, and his queen in regal surroundings.

Christina of Denmark, by Holbein.

King becomes head of the English church

England, November 1534
The final break with Rome has been made by parliament. A Succession Act commands allegiance to Anne and her issue and makes it high treason to challenge the king's title to the throne or criticise the marriage. Another measure, the Act of Supremacy, makes the king the supreme head of the Church of England, with full powers to deal with heresies, errors and abuses. No more taxes are to be paid to Rome, and the laws against heresy have been amended to allow criticism of the Catholic Church. A Bible in English is to be published.

What began as a controversy over Henry's matrimonial problems has turned into a political revolution. Not only has England broken with the Catholic Church, but the king's need to carry public opinion with him has caused him increasingly to seek the support of parliament.

England's religious controversies have been taking place against a background of religious revolution in continental Europe. Martin Luther has been preaching against papal indulgences and calling for German control of the German church. In Zurich church reformation is going on; Sweden and Denmark have broken with the pope. But Henry has no fancy for such dissidence. His theology is strictly orthodox. He wrote a book denouncing Luther and his views and for this the pope gave him the title "Defender of the Faith".

Anti-Catholic posters on king's palace

Paris, 18 October 1534
During the night placards violently criticising the Catholic Mass were posted in large numbers in Paris and several provincial towns. Some even appeared on the royal chateau at Blois.

The reaction this Sunday morning has been fierce. A wave of sectarian hatred has engulfed Paris. It is rumoured that the Protestants plan to murder the faithful at Mass. King Francis is expected to take harsh action against reformers.

French Protestant zealots tear down religious images and burn books.

1534 (1534-1536)

Mexico, 17 April 1535. Antonio de Mendoza is appointed the first viceroy of New Spain, assuming power in place of the governor and *audienca* of Mexico.

France, 19 May 1535. Inspired by stories of the wealthy kingdom of Saguenay, the French explorer Jacques Cartier sets out from Brittany on a second trip to North America.

Peru, June 1535. The Spaniard Francisco Pizarro founds the city of Lima.

Germany, June 1535. The town of Munster, the stronghold of the Anabaptists, is taken by an alliance of Protestant and Catholic troops and its inhabitants are massacred.

London, 6 July 1535. After 15 months' imprisonment in the Tower of London, Thomas More is beheaded for refusing to take the oath demanded by the 1534 Act of Succession. John Fisher, the bishop of Rochester, was executed last month for the same reason.

North Africa, July 1535. The Emperor Charles V captures Tunis from Barbarossa.

Canada, 2 October 1535. Having landed in Quebec a month ago, Jacques Cartier reaches a town which he names Montreal.

England, 1535. Henry VIII appoints a commission under his chief minister, Thomas Cromwell, to report on the state of the monasteries.

India, 1535. The Moghul emperor Humayun makes a brilliant raid into Gujarat, storming the fortress of Champener in person.

Spain, 1535. Hernando Pizarro, Francisco's half-brother, gives part of the booty taken from the Incas to Emperor Charles V. Francisco is made governor of New Castile and Diego de Almagro becomes governor of New Toledo.

Mexico, 1535. Spaniards establish a settlement called La Paz on an island off the west coast of Mexico *(Baja California)*. He names the bay between the island and the mainland Santa Cruz.

Mexico, 1535. Augustinian and Franciscan provinces are created in New Spain. The missionaries embark on a campaign against the exploitation of Indians.

South-East Africa, 1535. The Portuguese penetrate the Zambezi valley as far as the Moslem market at Tete. They took Sena, downstream, in 1531.

Milan, 1535. Following the death of Francesco Sforza II, the city is occupied by Charles V.

Britain, 1536. An Act of Union brings together Wales and England under one legal and administrative system. Henceforth Wales will send 24 members to parliament.

England, 1536. Catherine of Aragon, the first wife of Henry VIII, dies. Although she bore the king five children, only one of them, Princess Mary, who was born in 1516, survived infancy.

Switzerland, 21 May 1536. At a meeting of the city council in the cathedral, the Reformation is officially adopted in Geneva. This follows the return of the Protestant convert and reformer William Farel, who had twice been compelled to leave the city.

Switzerland, 1536. The French theologian John Calvin, who was converted to Protestantism several years ago, writes his *Institutes of the Christian Religion*, a full statement of his beliefs, which he dedicates to Francis, the king of France.

London, 19 June 1536. Anne Boleyn, the second wife of King Henry VIII, is beheaded in the Tower of London.

France, 6 July 1536. The explorer, Jacques Cartier lands at St Malo at the end of his second expedition to North America. He returns with none of the gold he expected to find after a harsh winter at Montreal during which 25 of his men died of scurvy.

Germany, 1536. Johann Faust, a physician, astrologist and magician, dies unexpectedly at Breisgau. It is rumoured that his strange disappearance was the work of the Devil.

Italy, 1536. The artist and architect Giulio Romano completes the decorative work on the Palazzo del Te for the Gonzaga dukes of Mantua.

Venice, 1536. Jacopo Sansovino is commissioned to build a library to house the valuable manuscripts rescued from the Turkish invasion by Cardinal Bassarion, as well as the manuscripts left to Venice by Petrarch.

Portugal, 1536. The dramatist Gil Vicente, author of *Auto de Visitacao* and creator of the Portuguese national theatre, dies.

France, 1536. Charles V's troops invade Provence, in pursuit of the army of King Francis, which has attempted to seize Piedmont. They are driven back by Anne of Montmorency, who applies scorched-earth tactics.

North Africa, 1536. The Berber corsair Khey ad-Din Barbarossa reoccupies Bizerta.

Rabelais creates the giant Gargantua

France, 1534

"At the moment of birth he did not yell Waa! Waa! as other children do, but shouted aloud Drink! Drink!" Thus reads the first appearance of the fictional giant Gargantua, the latest creation of the writer Francois Rabelais whose *Pantagruel*, another satirical celebration of gigantic and human appetites, appeared two years ago.

Rabelais is the physician of the municipal hospital at Lyons, and he writes "in moments of relaxation from the solace of the sick", publishing his books under a pseudonym – Alcofribas Nasier, an anagram of his own name.

Rabelais' work mixes fantastic tales with a fictional version of contemporary life. The giant represents everyday humanity, both good and bad, and either way a far cry from the idealised world demanded by the moralists. Above all, man's natural instincts are to be acknowledged. His motto *Fay ce que vouldras* (Do what you like) offers monastic life, with its rules and regulations, a direct challenge.

A Rabelaisian vision of Pantagruel.

Sensual artist Correggio dies, aged 45

Correggio, near Parma, 1534

Antonio Allegri, known by the name of Correggio from this small town of his birth, has died here in his forties, having made the cathedral at nearby Parma one of the wonders of Italy with his paintings. The inside of the dome is a cloud of saints and angels, all seen from directly beneath, escorting the Virgin upwards into heaven. It is as though the dome is lifting off above the spectator's head. Correggio painted much in Parma and other Lombard towns such as Reggio and Bologna. In his last years he painted classical myths such as *Danae* and *Leda* with great sensuality.

Correggio's subtle blend of tones especially suits his pictures of women.

English king executes his second wife

London 19 June 1536

Anne Boleyn, the queen of England, was beheaded in the Tower of London today, a victim of court intrigues and her own arrogance. She used to mock the king, though whether she was guilty of adultery is highly doubtful. She gave Henry a daughter, Elizabeth, but this year she miscarried, and the king decided the marriage was damned. Awaiting execution Anne spoke of her "little neck".

Henry VIII and Anne Boleyn.

Charles V's troops murder 30,000 people

Gulf of Tunis, July 1535
An army of 60,000 allied troops led by Charles V has won a spectacular victory here, taking the city of Tunis and the port of La Goleta and capturing the bulk of Barbarossa's fleet of 80 galleys. Charles has allowed his soldiers five days of pillaging, and 30,000 inhabitants are reported to have been killed.

The emperor chose to invade after Barbarossa's fleet had ravaged southern Italy at the behest of the Turkish sultan. Spanish possession of Tunis would effectively cut off Barbarossa – "the master of Algiers" – from Constantinople. A combined fleet of Spanish and Genoan galleys sailed from Barcelona in April; only Charles and his two commanders, Admiral Andrea Doria and the marquis del Vasco, knew the destination. More ships joined the fleet at Sardinia with 22,000 German and Italian troops.

Charles' shock troops, the formidable *tercio*, were the first to land at La Goleta, followed by artillery and a detachment of cavalry. Barbarossa chose to remain behind the walls, trusting the extreme heat to wear down the enemy.

Allied progress was slow, with many of Charles's soldiers dying of dysentery. Barbarossa had not reckoned with the fire-power of the fleet and land-artillery who pounded the walls for five hours before the infantry broke through. Tunis fell more easily.

Discontent at exile of old African king

West Africa, 1536
Discontent is brewing in Gao, the capital of the vast Songhai empire, at the tyrannical rule of its monarch, Askia Bankouri.

His cruel predecessor, Musa, was assassinated amid general relief three years ago. In 1528 Musa had deposed his infirm and almost blind father, Askia Mohammed, who had founded the current Askia dynasty in 1493. Under Mohammed, peace, order and security reigned in the Songhai empire, and commerce and intellectual life flourished, as did Islam, neglected by his predecessor Sonni Ali, from whose son Mohammed seized the throne.

Mohammed's deposition was a sad affair for the old sovereign, but, given his infirmity, pragmatic for the state. Musa, at least, left him his dignity, whereas Bankouri, Mohammed's nephew, has caused much indignation by having the ex-monarch, now 93, exiled to an island in the river Niger. This is asking for trouble from the old man's other children and Bankouri's position is by no means secure.

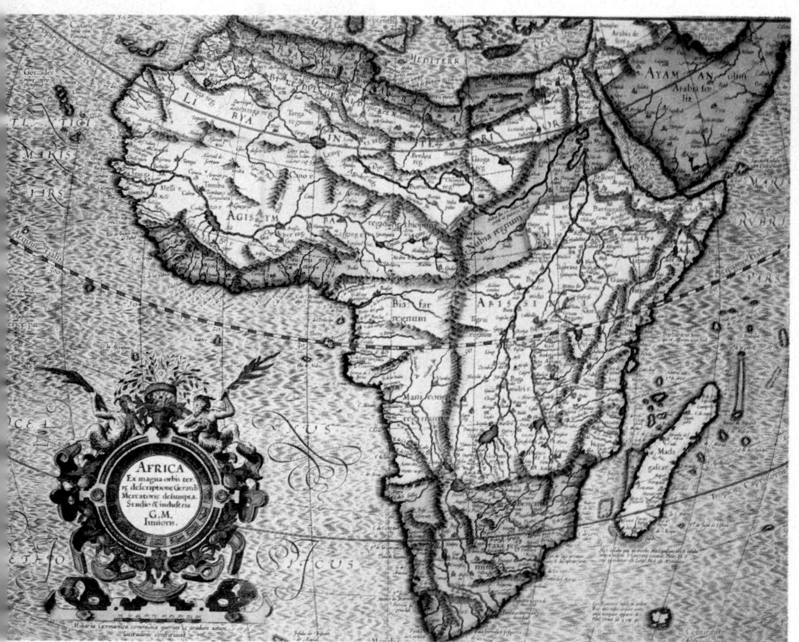

Africa, as shown in the 16th-century Mercator Atlas.

City of polygamy and world rebellion falls

Munster, Germany, 1 July 1535
Anabaptists throughout northern Europe are being forced into hiding as a tidal wave of disgust and repression sweeps Germany, Holland and Switzerland following the liberation of Munster, where Anabaptist revolutionaries had controlled the city for the last two years.

Munster's gates were reopened a week ago by the few citizens who had retained their sanity while millenarian fanatics practised polygamy, seized property, proclaimed world rebellion and threatened to kill anyone unbaptised.

Among the ringleaders seized was John of Leyden. Last August he dismissed the town council and proclaimed himself "King of New Zion" in Munster's marketplace. Leyden held the record for polygamy, taking 16 wives and using the Old Testament to justify his action. Among the 16 was the widow of Jan Matthys, the previous Anabaptist leader, killed last year when he and 20 men tried to take on forces besieging the city.

It was Matthys who ordered that no unbaptised adults should remain within the city. With the only choices being baptism or running the gauntlet of the siege troops, most chose to attend the baptisms in the town's square.

Among those killed last week was the preacher Bernard Rothmann. His questioning of the baptism of infants and promotion of a community of goods among Christians first won the townspeople to the Anabaptist cause two years ago, when some were elected to the city council long before their revolutionary tendencies became apparent.

Cartier searches for riches in Canada

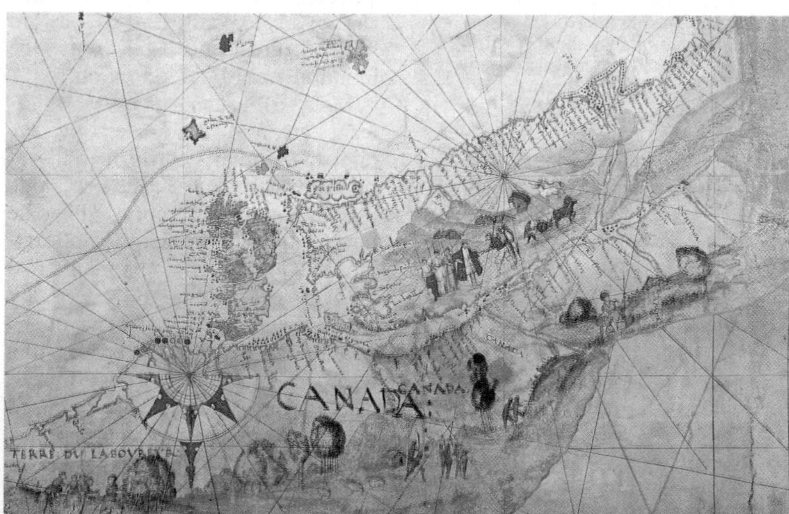

Cartier and his followers are shown in this contemporary map exploring the mouth of the St Lawrence river and having many other adventures.

St Malo, France, 6 July 1536
Jacques Cartier, the explorer, has returned from his second transatlantic expedition, having discovered the great River of Canada *(St Lawrence river)*, which he hopes will open up a huge expanse of North America. With him he has brought Donnaconna, an Iroquois chief, and ten other Iroquois.

It was the desire to find a passage to Asia, and perhaps some gold, which prompted King Francis to commission Cartier on an initial voyage in 1534, in the footsteps of the Florentine explorer Verrazzano. With three ships, Cartier made a circuit of the Labrador coast, and made friendly contact with the Indian natives, bringing two of Donnaconna's sons home with him. Last year he set off on his second voyage, taking the young Indians back. But as they penetrated further upriver, Cartier and his men fell foul of the harsh winter. Several died of scurvy while their ships were locked in ice. It was not until May that they could set sail for France.

1536 (1536-1538)

South America, 1536. Sebastian de Belalcazar is appointed by Francisco Pizarro to organise the province of Quito. He founds the city of Popayan in the north.

South America, 1536. Pedro de Mendoza, the leader of a Spanish expedition founds the city of Santa Maria de Buenos Aires.

France, 14 July 1536. France and Portugal sign the naval treaty of Lyons against Spain.

England, 1536. Henry VIII crushes the "Pilgrimage of Grace", a religious and social rebellion in the northern counties, and orders the dissolution of the monasteries.

South America, 1536. Diego de Almagro, the governor of New Toledo, reaches Chile.

Rome, 2 June 1537. Pope Paul III issues a bull proclaiming Indians to be *veri homines* (real men and women with souls) and banning their enslavement.

England, 24 October 1537. Jane Seymour, the third wife of Henry VIII, dies.

Mexico, 1537. Antonio de Mendoza, the viceroy of New Spain, establishes the territorial limits of the estates distributed to the Spanish conquerors.

Peru, 1537. After rebelling against Pizarro and capturing Cuzco after a siege, Manco Capac II establishes a new Inca state at Vilcabamba.

Europe, 1537. The French and the Turks, who last year formed a military alliance, attack Charles V's forces in Italy and the Mediterranean.

Italy, 1537. Andreas Vesalius, a professor of anatomy at Padua, carries out dissections for the university.

Rome, 1537. Pope Paul III excommunicates the Catholic slave traders.

Hungary, 24 February 1538. Ferdinand of Habsburg and John Zapolyai, the two kings of Hungary, conclude the peace of Grosswardein.

Germany, 10 June 1538. The German Catholic princes form the League of Nuremberg to counteract the Protestant Schmalkaldic league.

France, 1538. By the truce of Nice, King Francis provisionally ends his conflict with the Emperor Charles V.

Europe, 1538. Pope Paul III, Charles V and the Venetian republic form a Holy League against the Turks.

Humans are saved or damned at birth

Basel, Switzerland, 1536
John Calvin, one of the foremost Protestant reformers, has published his personal testament of faith: *The Institutes of the Christian Religion.* Written during his stay in Strasbourg, its aim is to put an end to the divisions between the various strands of Protestantism. Its essential dogma is the omnipotence and omniscience of God.

While Martin Luther, Calvin's predecessor and in many ways his inspiration, concentrated on man and his sins, Calvin turns his attention to God and His awesome power. Calvin's worshippers must adore God; they must also show Him fear. As for sin, Calvin puts forward the doctrine of predestination. God has already chosen the elect: those who will go to heaven. No-one, however devout, can alter the divine decree. What determines whether one is chosen or damned cannot be explained. It is beyond human intelligence, but only the immoral would dare question it.

Man, to Calvin, is an insignificant creature dominated by the taint of original sin which followed the expulsion from Eden. Left alone man is incapable of good; unless he devotes himself to the abject adoration of God he is no more than a prey for every temptation. Only by submitting himself to divine omnipotence can he live a proper life. Such devotion may not lead him to heaven, but should satisfy his need to adore a greater being than his lowly self.

Protestant reformer Calvin stresses the awesome power of God.

"Danae", with Titian's characteristic rich colouring and energetic opulence.

Painter Titian reigns supreme in Europe

Venice, 1538
As a painter, Titian now has no rival in Venice and only one, Michelangelo, in the whole of Italy. He rarely leaves Venice, but this year has gone to Urbino where he is at work on a full-length Venus for the duke. The figure, a courtesan, not a goddess, looks the spectator boldly in the eye, with her little dog asleep beside her and her maids searching in her linen chest. For the duke of Ferrara, Titian painted the sensational *Bacchus and Ariadne*, in which Bacchus leaps through a rich landscape at the head of a train of satyrs and leopards. His portraits are in demand by the doges, the duke of Mantua and the emperor himself.

Humanist Erasmus has died in exile

Freiburg, Germany, 12 July 1536
Desiderius Erasmus, one of the few religious scholars who was as much loved by Catholics as by Protestants, has died here at the age of 69.

Erasmus inspired many to depart from the rigidities of the Roman Church with his emphasis on the value of education and his desire for a Christian renaissance. But he never wished for a complete split with Rome. He remained a Catholic and was recently exiled from Protestant Basle, where he had lived for many years. He believed that man could be helped to be good of his own free will, through diligent reading of the scriptures. His major work was a Greek edition of the New Testament, joined with a Latin translation, which was published in 1517 by his friend Froben, the famous printer.

Born in Rotterdam, Erasmus was widely travelled and corresponded with humanists everywhere, notably with John Colet and Thomas More, the leading English scholars. Although he was a monk for many years his real calling was scholarship. He once taught Greek at Cambridge. Many of his works, like *The Praise of Folly*, are as much critiques of contemporary social life as they are religious.

The theologian and social thinker Erasmus, painted by Hans Holbein.

English king is seizing monastic wealth

Behaviour like this is the king's excuse to scrap monasteries altogether.

England, 1536
The son of a Putney brewer who is now Henry VIII's principle secretary has sent commissioners storming through England interrogating monks, nuns and friars and claiming to have uncovered "profound bawdry, drunken knaves" and whores in feather beds. Thomas Cromwell, a Protestant, often spoken of as a sacreligious ruffian, is seeking excuses for suppressing the monasteries and confiscating their assets. Monastic property is being put up for sale, the proceeds going to the king. Cromwell has boasted that he will make Henry the richest prince in Europe and he may well be right as the King's additional income from the sale of nearly 800 church properties has soared to around £90,000 a year. Most of them have been bought by the gentry via the Court of Augmentations and already plans are in hand to turn many of them into private homes.

Abbots, monks and nuns are being given pensions, but many monks are seeking to supplement their incomes by becoming village priests, and this is causing much clerical unemployment. The dissolutions are said to be causing hardship because the distribution of alms has ceased. This may be one cause of the demonstrations, known as the Pilgrimage of Grace, which are taking place in the north. Others blame the unsettling effects of printing the Bible in English. When bibles were copied by monks with quills and parchment, few people ever read the sacred text. Now the monks have been bypassed by technology.

Ragged explorers were slaves of Indians

Mexico City, 1536
Some call it miraculous, others a sham, but the four emaciated men who have been brought into the city by a slaving party claim that they are all that survives of Panfilo de Narvaez' expedition of 1527, which attempted to penetrate the northern jungles.

Cabeza de Vaca, a Moor called Estevanico and two others allege that they alone escaped as 80 of their companions succumbed to cannibalism and disease. Captured by the Indians, they spent the next six years working as bearers.

Finally they escaped and crossed the country working as *shamans* (quack doctors) They cured sick Indians and attracted large crowds, all desperate to hear the words of the "children of the sun".

Their travels took them all over Mexico, whose southern seacoast, they report, has "the best and all the most opulent countries".

Historian sees Italy as a single country

Florence, 1536
A former diplomat, and councillor to Pope Clement VII has published an important history of "Events in Italy from the Reign of Charles VIII to 1526". Francesco Guicciardini, who was born in Florence in 1483 and rose to become governor of Bologna, retired from public affairs three years ago. Since then he has been writing his History.

Guiccardini is no optimist: he sees man as a weakling, his life determined by chaotic and unforseeable events. The only hope lies in using one's intelligence, even if such efforts are often frustrated.

He despises princes, popes and people equally, although he has earned high honours working for the Medicis and the papacy.

What makes the History unique is its author's view of Italy as a single nation. Where other historians restrict themselves to studying Italy's various provinces, Guiccardini is the first historian to consider Italy as a whole. Wars and diplomacy are not divisive, but simply link one state to another.

Geneva banishes reformer Calvin

Geneva, July 1538
The Protestant reformers John Calvin and William Farel have been expelled from Geneva. The Swiss city may be considered by many as one of the citadels of the Reformed Church, but its council is still unwilling to accept the full force of the Reformation.

Farel, who makes up for his lack of learning with a fiery eloquence, arrived in the city in October 1532. After overcoming initial opposition from the Catholic hierarchy, he set about establishing Protestantism. The more the bishops attacked his preaching, the more the people flocked to hear it. On 21 May 1536 Farel's success was complete: the general council swore solemnly to live according to the word of God.

Calvin began preaching in Geneva in October 1536 and emphasised his own zeal for reform. In 1537 he joined Farel in demanding that every citizen swear to the Confession of Faith, on pain of banishment. The council rejected this reform and the two reformers have been banished themselves.

A new style for city halls in Flanders

The extraordinary town hall at Bruges, by William Callow (1812-1908).

Flanders, c.1537
A new style of architecture, combining the advances of the Italian Renaissance with traditional gothic flamboyance, is to be seen in a number of richly decorated new public buildings in Flanders. Among the principal examples are the Palais de Justice at Michelen, the Stock Exchange at Antwerp and the city hall at Oudenaarde, which was completed in 1525.

1538 (1538-1540)

Peru, July 1538. Diego de Almagro is executed on the orders of Pizarro.

Mediterranean, 1538. Supported by the French, the Ottomans try unsuccessfully to capture the island of Corfu from the Venetians.

Mediterranean, September 1538. The Ottomans defeat the Venetians and their allies under Andrea Doria at Prevesa, securing naval supremacy in the Mediterranean.

India, 1538. Khadim Suleiman Pasha, the Ottoman governor of Egypt, sends a fleet to attack India, but the Turks fail to take Diu in Gujarat and return home.

Arabia, 1538. With the surrender of Basra to the Turks, the Ottoman empire now reaches the Gulf.

Spain, 1 February 1539. The Emperor Charles V and Francis, the king of France, sign the treaty of Toledo.

Germany, 19 April 1539. The Emperor Charles V reaches a truce with the German Protestants at Frankfurt.

Florida, 30 May 1539. The Spanish explorer Hernando de Soto, coming from Cuba, lands 600 troops in search of gold.

Florida, 4 June 1539. Hernando de Soto finds Juan Ortiz, a survivor of the Panfilo de Narvaez voyage of 1527, living with the Indians.

New Mexico, June 1539. The Negro slave Estevanico is murdered by Zuni Indians. Father Marcos, his expedition leader, goes on to find the fabled Seven Golden Cities of Cibola. However, the villages do not contain gold; on the contrary, their Zuni inhabitants live in extreme poverty.

France, 10 August 1539. King Francis orders all legal decisions and documents to be drawn up from now on in French, not Latin. The same decree instructs priests to keep a record of all baptisms and deaths.

Mexico, 1539. Antonio de Mendoza, appointed viceroy of New Spain four years ago, establishes the first printing press in the New World, in Mexico City.

Flanders, 1539. The Emperor Charles V puts down a rebellion in Ghent and strips the town of its privileges. The townspeople had refused to pay taxes to finance the war with Francis of France and had called in vain on the French king for help.

Spain, 1539. Charles V orders the university of Salamanca to suspend all debates and to forbid the publication of all books on the right of conquest.

France, 1539. The edict of Villers Cotterets ends a paralysing strike of the printing industry in Paris and Lyons.

Italy, 27 January 1540. Angela de Medici, who founded the Ursuline order to educate young girls, dies at Brescia.

Mexico, February 1540. Francisco Vasquez de Coronado leaves New Spain with 400 Spaniards and 1,000 Indians on an expedition northwards to find the Seven Golden Cities of Cibola.

India, 17 May 1540. The Afghan chief Sher Khan defeats the Moghul Emperor Humayun at Kanauj. The emperor is forced to flee India and Sher Khan becomes *Sher Shah Suri*, ruler of northern India.

North America, 7 July 1540. Francisco Vasquez de Coronado conquers an Indian *pueblo* in south-western North America, believing it to be one of the Seven Golden Cities of Cibola.

England, 9 July 1540. Henry VIII divorces his fourth wife, Anne of Cleves, the choice of Thomas Cromwell, after only six months of marriage.

England, 28 July 1540. Henry VIII marries Catherine Howard.

London, 23 July 1540. Toppled and discredited by his enemies at court, Thomas Cromwell is beheaded on Tower Hill.

Hungary, July 1540. John Zapolyai, who declared himself king of Hungary in November 1526, dies and is succeeded by his son John Sigmund.

Italy, 28 August, 1540. The painter Francesco Mazzola, known as Parmigiano from his home town of Parma, dies at the age of 37, while still working on his *Madonna with the Long Neck*, which he began in 1534.

Paris, 30 August 1540. The humanist scholar Guillaume Bude dies. His vast learning encompassed languages (including Greek), mathematics, natural sciences, history and theology, and he founded both the College of the Three Languages and the library of Fontainebleau.

North America, August 1540. The Spaniard Hernando de Alvarado forges his way up the Rio Grande in south-western North America to the Indian village of Taos.

North America, August 1540. Hernando de Soto encounters Temple Mound Indian culture at Coosa *(Alabama)*.

Milan, 11 October 1540. The Emperor Charles V puts his son Philip in control of Milan.

Pizarro garrottes former partner in Peru

Diego de Almagro is garrotted and decapitated by Peru's governor Pizarro.

Cuzco, Peru, 1538

Governor Francisco Pizarro rejected pleas for clemency from his former friend and expedition partner, Diego de Almagro, before the 63-year-old Almagro was garrotted. The two men had always disputed the charter which made Pizarro governor. Almagro was also made governor of ill-defined territory beyond Pizarro's. Some years later an Inca rebellion besieged the mountain capital of Cuzco, defended by Pizarro's brothers. Almagro, returning with an embittered force from a fruitless search for gold in Chile, seized Cuzco himself. Internecine warfare followed.

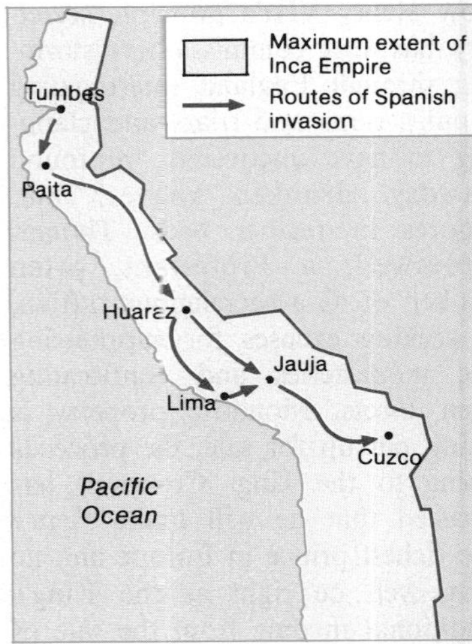

Poet founder of Sikh movement is dead

Punjab, India, 1539

Guru Nanak, poet, mystic and founder of a new faith which discounts both Islam and Hinduism has died.

In 1499, aged 30, Nanak experienced two days of mystical ecstasy. His conclusions are recorded in his *Adi-Granth*. The main emphasis of this religion lays in loving devotion to a wholly spiritual god by divine grace. He has called his followers *Sikhs* – the Punjabi for disciples. On emerging from his vision, the guru declared: "There is no real Hindu and no real Moslem."

Guru Nanak, who founded the Sikh religion after a mystical revelation.

Print makes big impression in Europe

One of Germany's printing presses.

The Byble in Englyshe, that is to saye the content of all the holy scrypture, bothe of ye olde and newe testament, truly translated after the veryte of the Hebrue and Greke textes, by ye dylygent studye of dyuerse excellent learned men, expert in the forsayde tonges.

Prynted by Rychard Grafton & Edward Whitchurch.

Cum privilegio ad imprimendum solum.

A bible with Roman and Gothic type.

Europe, 1539

Fifteen years after the death of Gutenberg there are printing presses in operation in every country in western Christendom: from Sweden in the north to Sicily in the south, and from Spain in the west to Poland and Hungary in the east. The new technology has caught on rapidly and surely.

There have been developments of all kinds, both technical and aesthetic. Initially, the printers followed the old scribes in the type-faces which they used. But soon the possibilities opened up, with metal punch cutters being used to produce distinctive type styles, such as the Roman font which began to supersede the traditional Gothic. Among the purely technical developments to assist the explosive spread of printing has been that of an oil-bound ink – attributed to Gutenberg himself – which clings closely to the metal type and produces a smudge-free impression.

Presses, too, are being improved all the time. The original Gutenberg press was modified so that the screw which forced the paper onto the linked type could be worked with a smaller amount of movement of the bar. This speeds up the printing of each individual sheet.

Few factors in this age of rapid technological advance have had more impact than printing.

Pope approves the Society of Jesus

Rome, 27 September 1540

A papal bull issued here today establishes a new religious order, the Society of Jesus, whose object is "the propagation of the faith". The order began in 1534 in Paris when Ignatius Loyola, a soldier turned priest, and six others took a vow to offer themselves to the pope to be sent wherever he wished to convert infidels, even the Turks.

The new order does not require its members to say the daily office together, like monks, but only to pray silently. Their essential vow is one of total obedience to the pope and to their superior, Loyola, who is to be elected general of the society. His *Spiritual Exercises* are the training for the life of a Jesuit.

Pope Paul III gives his papal bull to Ignatius Loyola, and so founds the Jesuit order.

Monks' treasures seized in royal purge

Monasteries must surrender all their treasures to Henry's commissioners.

England, 23 March 1540

The last of England's big monastic houses, Waltham Abbey in Essex, was seized by the crown today, bringing to a close a four-year campaign that has seen over 550 properties, with their treasure of plate and jewels, pass into the king's possession. The 370 smaller monasteries, which were the first to fall, brought Henry some £32,000 a year, and the 186 bigger ones, which followed, £100,000. But the king will not enjoy the whole of this income.

Henry is giving his supporters gifts of property and putting some other estates up for auction. Family fortunes are being founded on the suppression of the monasteries. A local squire in Sussex, William Cavendish, has already acquired three Hertfordshire manors and reckons that, with luck, he could become a duke in a few years' time. The appropriately-named Sir Richard Rich, who is helping to administer the seized properties, has himself acquired 59 manors, 31 rectories and 28 vicarages. Some of the new rich are founding colleges.

The suppression came about because Henry wanted to lay hands on the wealth, but it is also true that, after his quarrel with Rome, the monasteries were an obstacle to the consolidation of his power over the church. As for the monks, they have lost more than their monasteries: mitred abbots no longer sit in the House of Lords.

The king also wants nuns' wealth.

Artificial limbs help crippled veterans

Paris, 1539

A French army surgeon, Ambroise Pare, has developed an innovation in medical treatment which gives new hope to those unfortunate enough to lose limbs on the battlefield and elsewhere. To replace amputated legs or arms, Pare is fitting ingenious mechanical devices which mimic the movements of the natural limbs. He is not the first to attempt some kind of prosthesis for amputees, but his are the most sophisticated yet developed. One hand has a holder for a pen; another has fingers which move with the aid of tiny cog wheels.

Pare has already gained a reputation in the field for his treatment of gunshot wounds.

1540 (1540-1542)

Flanders, 1540. After putting down a rebellion in the town last year, the Emperor Charles V demands that the aldermen and leaders of the guilds in Ghent come to beg his pardon with nooses around their necks. About 20 of them are executed.

Indian Ocean, 1540. Andriamanelo, the first Merina king of Madagascar, comes to the throne.

South-East Asia, 1540. The Portuguese start to trade with Cochinchina *(Vietnam).*

Germany, c.1540. Maps published by the great cartographer Gerardus Mercator use the word America to describe the new lands discovered by Christopher Columbus – although it is now known that Amerigo Vespucci, after whom the lands were named, was wrongly described as his ship's captain.

France, 17 October 1540. King Francis entrusts the explorer Jacques Cartier with the task of "penetrating further into the country of Canada" in order to find a new route to China.

North America, 19 October 1540. The Spaniard Hernando de Soto is set upon by Choctaw Indians at Mabile *(Mobile, Alabama)*, who kill 18 of his party and injure 170. De Soto claims that his men have killed 2,800 Indians.

France, 14 November 1540. The Italian painter Rosso Fiorentino (Giovanni Battista di Jacopo) dies in Paris. Invited to France by the king in 1532, he supervised the building work on the chateau of Fontainebleau until his death.

North America, 1540. Priests accompanying Hernando de Soto on his expedition conduct the first recorded baptism in the New World: that of an Indian guide.

North America, December 1540. Lopez de Cardenas, an officer in the service of the Spaniard Francisco Vasquez de Coronado, discovers the Grand Canyon.

South America, 12 February 1541. Pedro de Valdivia, a lieutenant of Francisco Pizarro, founds the city of Santiago in Chile.

North America, March 1541. The Spanish suppress an Indian rebellion after a siege of *pueblos* at Tiguex.

North America, 8 May 1541. De Soto reaches a large river which he names Rio de Espiritu Santo *(the Mississippi).*

Peru, 26 June 1541. Francisco Pizarro is assassinated in Lima. Diego el Monzo, the son of Almagro – executed by Pizarro's supporters three years ago – proclaims himself governor.

North America, 23 August 1541. Jacques Cartier lands near Quebec on his third voyage to Canada. His expedition has been commissioned to found a permanent settlement.

Austria, 24 September 1541. The Swiss alchemist and doctor Theophrastus Paracelsus dies in exile in Salzburg.

North America, 1541. Hernando de Soto completes a two-year expedition to explore the lands west of the Mississippi river.

Morocco, 1541. The Portuguese are driven out of Agadir by the Sadian rulers.

Rome, 1541. Ignatius Loyola is elected general of the Jesuits, the religious order which he created.

Hungary, 1541. Ferdinand of Habsburg, the king of Hungary and Bohemia, is defeated at Pest by the Turks, who seize Buda. Hungary becomes a Turkish province.

East Africa, 1541. Francis Xavier, the Spanish Jesuit and companion of Loyola, begins a mission to Mozambique, Malindi and Socotra.

North Africa, 1541. The Emperor Charles V launches an unsuccessful expedition against Algiers.

Hungary, 29 December 1541. Under the treaty of Gyalu, John Zapolyai's widow cedes Hungary to Ferdinand of Habsburg.

England, 13 February 1542. Catherine Howard, Henry VIII's fifth wife, is executed for immoralities committed before she married the king.

Mexico, April 1542. Francisco Vasquez de Coronado returns to Mexico after failing to find in the interior of North America either the fabled Seven Golden Cities of Cibola or another legendary land of fabulous riches called Quivira.

North America, April 1542. Jean Francois de Roberval arrives as governor of Canada at the settlement founded last year by Jacques Cartier, who has now returned to France.

North America, 21 May 1542. De Soto dies on the banks of the Mississippi river.

Rome, 22 May 1542. Pope Paul III summons a general council of the church to meet at the imperial city of Trent. Its purpose is to achieve the reformation of the church, the definition of dogma and the reunion of Christendom.

Europe, 1542. Prompted by the appointment two years ago of Charles V's son Philip to the control of Milan, Francis of France reopens hostilities with the emperor. Charles V has forged an anti-French alliance with Henry VIII of England.

New royal palaces reflect Italian styles

No need for fortifications: Francis' new gallery at Fontainebleau.

France/England, 1540

Spearheaded by the design for the new royal palace at Fontainebleau, an outburst of architectural activity is to be seen in France. Where nobles once built for defence, they are now building for beauty and for comfort. Led by King Francis, with his preference for Italian design, members of the aristocracy are turning their old castles into elegant modern palaces.

The king, who picked up his interest in Italian architecture during his recent campaigns, imported three Italians to work on Fontainebleau. Between them they formed what has been called "The School of Fontainebleau", and their ideas have spread across France, influencing many home-grown architects. And since Fontainebleau was completed, in 1528, the new architecture has spread beyond France to make its impression on builders across the rest of Europe.

Working with the ideas of the Italian Renaissance, architects have begun replacing the old thick walls, small windows and massive towers with elegant new structures which stress the modern role of a nobleman's home.

England, too, has a fine stately home in Hampton Court Palace, built by Cardinal Wolsey and presented by him to Henry VIII in 1526. Unlike many French castles, however, this great house has never been the scene of battle.

The battlements of Hampton Court, near London, are only for decoration.

Amazon named after its women warriors

A golden pectoral ornament of the Tolima culture, c.500-c.1500 AD.

South America, 24 August 1542
Spanish *conquistadores* have sailed the length of the great river which crosses this continent from the Atlantic to the Andes. They have named it the Amazon, after a gang of Indian women who attacked them with bows and arrows on their way homewards.

The 200-strong expedition was led by Gonzalo Pizarro, who set out on Christmas Day 1539 to find the legendary land of El Dorado. It was one of his men, Francisco de Orellana, who ventured onto the river to seek supplies. He built a boat, then sailed it with 57 men – facing danger on the way from Indians and strong rapids. Their journey lasted eight months, by which time Pizarro had returned to the river's mouth.

Francesco Maria Mazzuola's painting of Antea La Bella shows what Italy's smart set is wearing: a silk gown with ruffles, heavy jewellery and fur accessories.

African slave-trade crosses Atlantic

Lisbon, c.1542
It is 108 years since the first slaves were bought by Portuguese traders from African slave dealers and sold in Lisbon. Ten years ago, 800 blacks went to Europe annually. A sharp increase in the trade to American colonies occurred as undermanned plantations sought more labour. The trade measures livestock by the *peca*, or one male slave in peak condition. Two women and a baby make the same unit. From low levels, the trade with America built up about ten years ago to 5,000 pecas from the Kongo alone.

The traffic gives Jesuit and Franciscan missions interesting problems. Africans fit for conversion, the argument goes, must have immortal souls. Having souls they are men, not beasts to be enslaved. Spain's colonial party cites Aristotle's dictum that natives are "slaves by nature".

Pope steps up fight against Protestants

Determined: Titian's recent portrait of the pope and his nephews.

Rome, 21 July 1542
Pope Paul III has today set up a Roman inquisition. Six cardinals have been appointed as inquisitors-general, with powers to imprison on suspicion, to confiscate property and to execute the guilty. The move represents the triumph of the militant party, led by Cardinal Caraffa, which wants to put an end to the attempts of the moderates to conciliate Lutherans and Calvinists. According to Caraffa, "No man is to lower himself by showing toleration towards any sort of heretic, least of all a Calvinist." He wants a purge as fierce as that in Spain towards the end of the last century when many thousands of Jews were killed. Today's Protestants, however, are much more powerful and are likely to resist.

The weavers of Brussels produce finely-worked masterpieces of tapestry. Here, hunters, dogs and other beasts fill an exotic garden.

1542 (1542-1544)

Germany, 26 August 1542. Under the treaty of Nuremberg, the duchy of Lorraine becomes independent of the German empire.

Germany, September 1542. The German craftsman Peter Henlein dies at Nuremberg. He was responsible for inventing a spring to replace the weights in a clock, making possible the production of the first watch.

Peru, September 1542. Diego el Monzo Almagro is defeated at the battle of Chupas and condemned to death by Vaca de Castro, the representative of the Spanish crown.

North America, 28 September 1542. The Spanish explorer Juan Rodriguez Cabrillo enters a harbour *(San Diego)* on the Pacific coast. He is the first European in California.

Spain, 22 November 1542. New laws are passed in Burgos giving protection against enslavement to the Indians in America.

England, 24 November 1542. In a war provoked by Henry VIII's desire to control Scotland, the English inflict a defeat on the Scots at the battle of Solway Moss.

Scotland, 14 December 1542. James V of Scotland dies and is succeeded by his one-year-old daughter, Mary Stuart, whose mother, Mary of Guise, becomes regent.

Switzerland, 1542. Recalled to Geneva, from whence he was expelled three years ago, the Protestant reformer John Calvin begins to implement his original scheme for the creation of a godly government.

India, 1542. The Spanish Jesuit Francis Xavier arrives in Goa on a mission to spread the gospel.

North America, January 1543. Juan Rodriguez Cabrillo dies after exploring the western coast from lower California to the north for 1,000 miles *(Oregon)*.

Germany, 10 February 1543. Johann Mayer, known as Johann Eck, Luther's chief adversary, dies at Ingolstad. A humanist who hoped to see the revival of the Catholic church, Eck was responsible for having Luther excommunicated. He took part in the Diet of Augsburg in 1530 and, in 1537, published a Catholic version of the German translation of the Bible.

Mexico, 14 April 1543. Bartoleme Ferrelo, who took command of the Spanish fleet after the death of Cabrillo in January, returns after discovering and exploring a large bay area *(San Francisco)*.

England, 1 July 1543. England and Scotland sign the peace of Greenwich.

England, 15 July 1543. Henry VIII marries his sixth wife, Catherine Parr.

London, 29 November 1543. The German painter Hans Holbein the Younger dies at the age of 46, while at the height of his career. He settled in England in 1532 and was appointed painter to Henry VIII in 1536. He executed a series of portraits of the great Englishmen of his time.

Scotland, 11 December 1543. The Scottish Parliament repudiates the treaty of Greenwich.

Japan, 1543. A Portuguese ship is wrecked off Tanegashima island. Three matchlock guns on board are bought by the Japanese, who have not seen firearms since the aborted Mongol invasion in the 13th century.

France, 1543. The Berber corsair Khey ad-Din Barbarossa combines forces with the fleet of Francis, the king of France, to bombard, besiege and sack the imperial town of Nice.

England, 1543. Revising the *Bishop's Book* of 1537, which defended Catholic orthodoxy against Protestant innovation, the *King's Book* confirms statutes passed by parliament in May 1539. These maintain key elements of Catholic doctrine, such as the validity of monastic vows, and outlaw any further theological reform.

North America, 1543. Oil is found in the region *(in Texas)* for the first time, by the Spaniard Luis de Moscoso.

Italy, 14 April 1544. A French army defeats the imperial forces of Charles V at the battle of Ceresole, south of Turin.

Scotland, May 1544. The English invade Scotland and attack Edinburgh. They pillage the city but fail to gain a surrender from the Scots.

France, July 1544. In their war with France, the combined forces of the Emperor Charles V and Henry VIII of England take St Dizier and threaten Paris.

France, 14 September 1544. Henry VIII's forces take Boulogne.

France, 19 September 1544. In an effort to restore Catholic unity in Europe, King Francis and the Emperor Charles V sign the treaty of Crespy. Francis promises to support the emperor against the Protestants if they refuse to accept the decisions of the forthcoming Council of Trent; Francis' son will be married to a Habsburg princess.

King's physician was body-snatcher

Andreas Vesalius, the anatomist.

Basle, Switzerland, 1543
A superbly illustrated and printed work on human anatomy has rapidly become required reading among doctors throughout Europe. Called *De humani corporis fabrica libri septem*, this major event in medical publishing is the work of Andreas Vesalius, Charles V's physician, and the anatomical details are based on numerous dissections. Many of these were performed on corpses which had been exhumed or taken from gibbets while he was studying in France.

The book has already created controversy among doctors, who have mostly taken the work of the Greek anatomist, Galen, as definitive in this area. This new study corrects some 200 errors, but Vesalius' methods of obtaining bodies to dissect have offended many. Dissection of human bodies is officially forbidden in any case.

Suleiman assumes power as caliph

Constantinople, 1543
On the death of the last member of the Abbasid family, Suleiman, the Ottoman sultan, has assumed the title of *caliph* – successor to the Prophet Mohammed – which makes him the most powerful of the Moslem sovereigns. He has written to the sherif of Mecca, a direct descendant of the Prophet, to announce that God has put him in charge.

Suleiman's move has been accepted – with some reluctance – by the Islamic community. The sherif has written to the sultan accepting that, "by the grace of God", he does indeed occupy the throne of the sublime sultanate and the dignity of the grand caliphate. But he adds with some subtlety that it is Suleiman's conquests "that have made you first amongst all and the most senior of the sultans of Islam".

The new caliph, Suleiman.

Old adversaries' treaty has secret clause

Crespy, France, 19 September 1544
This small village was the scene today of the signing of a peace treaty between two great adversaries: the emperor, Charles V, and Francis, the king of France. Their countries have been at war for more than 20 years, but France has now agreed to join the emperor in his war against the Turks.

A marriage settlement has been agreed as part of the treaty. Francis' son, the duke of Orleans, is to marry either Charles' daughter Mary, or Anne, the daughter of Ferdinand of Bohemia. In the first case, the dowry would be the Netherlands; in the second, Milan.

In the second part of the agreement, Francis has promised to help the emperor to reform the church and work towards bringing the German Protestants back into the Catholic fold – lending his army for the purpose if necessary. This part has been kept a close secret.

Earth may not be centre of universe

Nicolaus Copernicus, astronomer.

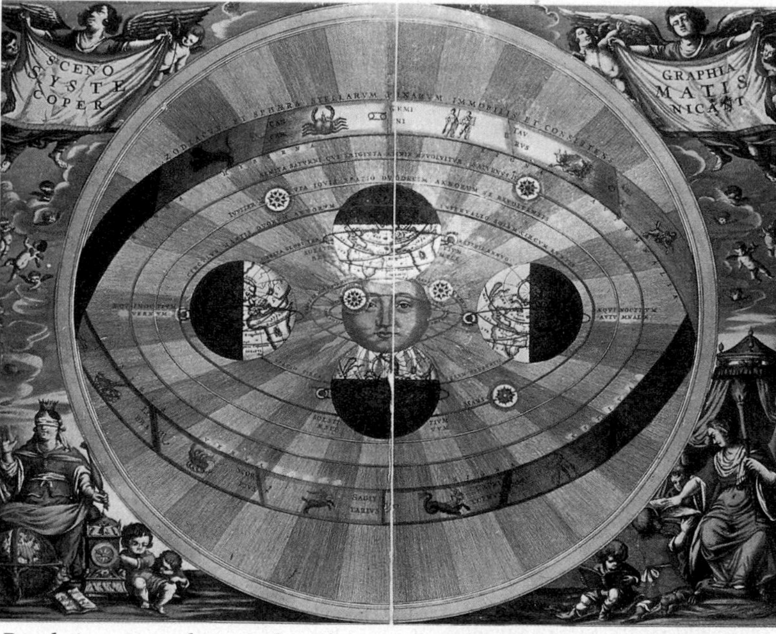

Revolutionary revolutions: the solar system makes Earth just another planet.

East Prussia, 24 May 1543
Today, a new book was brought to its author as he lay dying. The work in question promises to be a major contribution to the science of astronomy, and its author, Nicolaus Copernicus, has suggested a radically different way of seeing the universe and man's place in it.

In the six sections of *On the Revolution of the Heavenly Spheres*, Copernicus proposes a "heliocentric theory" of the universe. He claims that Earth is not, as the influential astronomer Ptolemy had proposed in the second century AD, the centre of all things. The planets do not revolve around us: Earth, like the other planets, revolves around the sun. Indeed, the text argues that even the sun itself is not the true centre of things; this is some distance away. But the heliocentric theory still has a mathematical elegance and cogency that is lacking in Ptolemy and Aristotle.

If Earth is not the centre of the universe then nor, perhaps, are its inhabitants. We should begin to look at ourselves in a slightly different light, not as the trimphant epitome of creation.

Moreover, Copernicus' theory implies that the universe is much bigger than we thought. If Earth orbits the sun we should detect small periodic variations in the positions of the stars. The fact that the stars seem to be static could mean that they are simply too distant for us to detect their variations. Some are saying that perhaps the universe is infinite, with stars going on for ever.

Another effect of the book is to change astronomers' views on falling bodies. In Aristotelian theory, the reason bodies fall to Earth is that Earth is the centre of the universe. Now that Copernicus has destroyed that idea, another explanation will have to be found for why a cannon ball or an autumn leaf falls to the ground.

Japan's "shoguns" get first firearms

Japan, 1543
The gun has arrived in Japan. Two Portuguese adventurers, the first Europeans known to have landed in Japan, brought *arquebuses* with them, and when Tokitaka, the feudal lord of Tanegashima, saw them bring down a duck, he paid a fortune in gold for the guns.

Tokitaka handed them to his chief swordsmith, Yatsuita, and ordered him to copy them. Yatsuita, trading his daughter for lessons from the armourer of another Portuguese ship, has gone into mass production.

Turkish pirates capture and pillage Nice

Nice, France, 1543
Nice has been captured and sacked by the corsair Barbarossa. The town, the gateway to Italy, is on fire and the Turkish pirates are rampaging through the burning ruins, looting and raping. This destruction is in direct contravention of the terms of the surrender agreed when the governor capitulated to the joint French and Turkish forces. Now the French are blaming the Turks while the Turks blame the French.

This alliance against the forces of the Emperor Charles V has never been easy. Dubbed the "impious alliance" by Charles, it has brought Barbarossa's fleet of 100 galleys to the ports of southern France and much unpopularity to King Francis. The corsair – "Chief of the Seas" – has set up his headquarters at Toulon where the inhabitants are humiliated by seeing Moslems pacing the decks of his ships while Christian slaves, Frenchmen among them, are chained to the galleys' oars and rowing benches. The Turks have taken to raiding French villages, carrying off peasants to replace rowers killed by the fever. Christian slaves are sold in the market place and the muezzin calls for Moslem prayer in Christian Toulon.

Explorer dies on Mississippi banks

Mexico, September 1542
The remnants of Hernando de Soto's expedition have landed in Mexico by the Panuco River. They are without their leader, who died on 21 May, aged 46, beside the "great muddy river" *(Mississippi)* that he discovered just over a year ago.

De Soto was an experienced Spanish soldier who made his name with Pizarro's expedition to Peru in 1524. Though he returned to Spain loaded with gold and silver, he grew restless. In 1538, with the blessing of King Charles, he set out from Spain with 600 troops, 200 horses and a pack of bloodhounds, bound for the Americas, once more in search of gold.

Landing on the west coast of Florida in May 1539, de Soto's well-armed force set about subduing the natives, taking prisoners whether they were friendly or not. In August 1540, at Coosa *(Alabama)*, de Soto came across the Indians of the Temple Mound culture. Three months later he met and imprisoned Chief Tuscaloosa, who organised an ambush in which at least 18 Spaniards died, and de Soto claimed to have killed more than 2,000 Indians.

Pressing on through often inhospitable terrain, with hostile Indians, de Soto reached the great muddy river, and spent the next year exploring westwards. After his death, the 332 survivors built a raft and floated down to Mexico.

De Soto: explorer and warrior who sailed the Mississipi last year.

1544 (1544-1546)

England, 1544. Parliament recognises Mary and Elizabeth, the daughters of Henry VIII, as heirs to the throne of England in the event of the king's son, Edward, dying childless.

Peru, 1544. Blasco Nunez de Vela, appointed first viceroy of Peru last year by the Emperor Charles V, arrives in Lima.

Germany, 1544. Denmark and the Netherlands sign the treaty of Speyer, by which the Netherlands are granted full rights of trade and passage in the Baltic.

Germany, 1544. The first Jesuit college in Germany is founded in Cologne.

Denmark, 1544. A major witch-hunt results in the execution of 52 witches in Malmo, Koge and Jutland.

Mozambique, 1544. Portuguese trading posts are opened at the former Moslem port of Quelimane and at Maputo Bay *(Lourenco Marques)*.

Korea, 1544. Chungjong, who came to the throne of Korea in 1506 after a revolt against the cruel ruler Yonsangun, dies. During his reign he used the Confucian scholars in an attempt to curb the power of the great families, but the scholars were defeated.

Scotland, 25 February 1545. The English army receives a set-back at the hands of the Scots at Ancrum Moor.

Italy, 26 August 1545. Pietro Luigi Farnese, the son of Pope Paul III, establishes the duchy of Parma and Piacenza.

Scotland, September 1545. The English again invade Scotland.

France, September 1545. Hans Baldung Grien, the portraitist, engraver and painter of both religious and secular subjects, dies at Strasbourg.

Balkans, November 1545. The Emperor Charles V and Suleiman, the sultan of the Ottomans, reach a truce at Adrianople.

Italy, 13 December 1545. The general council summoned by Pope Paul III in May 1542 opens in the imperial city of Trent. It has been delayed by renewed fighting between France and the empire.

Mexico, 1545. The Spanish missionary Bartolomeo de las Casas takes up his duties as bishop of Chiapas, a position to which he was appointed two years ago. A champion of Indian rights, las Casas is given a hostile reception by the colonists.

India, 1545. Humayun, the Moghul emperor, captures Kandahar.

Germany, 18 February 1546. Martin Luther, dies at his native town of Eisleben.

Scotland, 1 March 1546. The reformer George Wishart, who preached the Lutheran doctrine of justification by faith, is burnt to death on the orders of Cardinal Beaton, the archbishop of St Andrew's.

South America, April 1546. The German explorers Philipp von Hutten and Bartholomew Welser are murdered by the Spanish at Coro.

Scotland, 29 May 1546. Cardinal Beaton, the archbishop of St Andrew's, who is responsible for a sustained persecution of Protestants, is assassinated by a band of conspirators who take possession of his castle. After the death of James V in 1542, Beaton produced a forged will, appointing himself and three others regents of the kingdom. He was arrested, but later became chancellor and promoted a pro-French policy.

France, 7 June 1546. Francis of France and Henry VIII of England sign the peace of Ardres, ending the conflict which began two years ago when Henry launched an invasion of France from Calais. Under the terms of the treaty, Boulogne is to remain in English hands for eight years.

Rome, 7 June 1546. Bent on crushing the independence of the German states and restoring the unity of the church, the Emperor Charles V makes a pact with Pope Paul III, who promises him money and troops in his fight against the Protestants.

Germany, 20 July 1546. Charles V, who has formed an alliance with Maurice of Saxony against the Schmalkalden League of German Protestant princes, outlaws Philip of Hesse and John Frederick, the elector of Saxony.

Paris, 3 August 1546. The printer Etienne Dolet, denounced for printing the works of the humanist reformers such as Erasmus and Melanchthon, is hanged and burnt at the stake for blasphemy, sedition and heresy.

Arabia, 1546. The Ottomans capture Yemen, the gateway to the Red Sea.

Mexico, 1546. The first extractions are made from the silver mine at Zacatecas.

Mexico, 1546. The Spanish gain control of the Maya region after crushing a serious revolt by the Maya people.

India, 1546. The Portuguese rout the Gujarati army at Diu.

Luther, who cracked Catholic unity, dies

Luther's enemies portrayed him as the instrument of, and crowned by, demons.

Eisleben, 18 February 1546

Martin Luther, the founder of the biggest new Protestant church, died here today in this small town in which he was born 63 years ago. His body was broken after years of overwork and illness. His mind, however, was as clear as a bell right to the end. And this man renowned for his violent temper died in a mood of total serenity.

His achievement was vast. Born of peasant stock, he was totally committed to the needs of the ordinary people. His training as a monk and his years as professor at Wittenberg did not diminish this dedication. His great works – a translation of the Bible, a mass, a book of hymns and one of catechisms – were not only written in German; they were written in plain language. Thanks to him, thousands of poor Germans can now read the scriptures. Luther's breach with the Catholic Church became total in 1521 when he was excommunicated. But the rebellious German princes helped him to establish the new church.

The former monk had a happy home life. He married a former nun, Katharina von Bora, in 1525, and fathered six children. Despite his scholarship he was often crude and vulgar and angry, but mostly in the cause of ordinary people, who he felt were exploited and oppressed by church and secular authorities.

He had many enemies. "Dear husband," Katharina once said to him, "you are too rude." "They teach me to be rude," was Luther's reply.

Massacre in France

Provence, France, 20 April 1545

A terrible massacre has been carried out against the Waldensian Protestants who live in this area. Villages have been pillaged, women have been burnt alive in a church, and men rounded up to slave in the galleys. It started with rumours that the Waldensians were plotting sedition, but it seems that the rumours were started deliberately by a local baron, Jean Meynier, who coveted the land of a Waldensian neighbour. The alarmed King Francis gave Meynier the task of stamping out the "sedition". This he has done with great cruelty. He has also seized the land which he coveted.

Smallpox epidemic

Mexico, 1545

An epidemic of smallpox, as devastating as Europe's Black Death, has devastated Mexico's Indian population. The Spaniards have suffered too, but it is the natives who have born the brunt of the disease. More than 800,000 have died.

Smallpox is just one of the diseases which have accompanied European exploration. Others include tetanus, leprosy, typhoid and a variety of intestinal, lung and venereal diseases.

The Indians seem to have no natural defences against these new illnesses which are threatening entire tribes with extinction.

Council to resist Protestant threat

In the chair: Pope Paul III.

The council looks set to confirm the rift between Protestants and Catholics.

Trent, 1546
A general council of the church is meeting in this small town beneath the Alps *(now in Italy)* to discuss Catholic doctrine and reform of the church, in the face of Lutheran ideas. It has been postponed for several years because of the emperor's wars with the French king, now settled. Trent was chosen because, while close to Italy, it lies within the Holy Roman empire and therefore meets the demand that the council should be on German soil.

Pope Paul III summoned the council with the object of debating the doctrinal controversies raised by Protestantism, which has been influential within the Catholic Church. But the Emperor Charles wishes to reconcile the Lutherans, who are dividing Germany, by reforming the church's practices, possibly even permitting the clergy to marry.

The council is being attended by 60 or more Catholic bishops (no Lutheran representatives have yet arrived). So far it has framed decrees which disdain any compromise with the Protestants. For example, it has just decreed that the scriptures are not, as Protestants claim, the only source of divine revelation. Apostolic tradition handed down by the church is also sacred.

The council is now debating the thorny question of justification by faith. There is much disagreement even among Catholics as to whether man may receive grace by his own efforts and good works or, as Luther maintains, by faith alone. There are many shades of opinion among the Augustinians, the Dominicans and the new Jesuit theologians, who stress that man may attract divine mercy by his own efforts. The council has already ruled against Luther's doctrine of original sin.

As the Spanish conquistadores advance deeper into the rain forests of central America, they are sending reports of strange and wonderful beasts. Some, like scaly creatures with humanoid heads, are new discoveries.

Silver vein reflects shepherd's fire

Cuzco, Peru, 1545
While searching for a stray llama, a Quechua Indian named Huallpa was recently stranded high on the slopes of a 14,000-foot mountain at Potosi, a few miles from here. When night fell, he lit a fire to keep warm and ward off evil spirits. Something shone back unnaturally in the firelight. It was a heavy seam of pure silver.

In Inca times a ruler put miners to work on the site to dig gold or silver to decorate Cuzco's sun temple. As they began digging, the hill stirred angrily. Work stopped. Now the Spanish *conquistadores*, hearing of the find, are showing a keen interest in the "silver mountain".

Cannon ball kills Indian reformer

Central India, 1545
Sher Shah Suri, who crushed the Moghul empire in India, completely overhauled the empire's administration, and rebuilt Delhi, is dead – killed by a cannon ball while besieging Kalanjar, the Rajput stronghold.

Originally an Afghan, his grandfather came to India with Sultan Buhlulodi, and his father served Jamal Khan as a cavalry commander. Sher Shah himself served Babur, the Moghul emperor, and then Jalal Khan. Victorious in battle, he first ousted Jalal Khan from Lohani, and then ousted Babur's son, Humayun, from India, becoming emperor himself. Backed by an army of 150,000 horsemen he centralised administration, punished corruption, revalued the coinage and beautified Delhi. Immensely energetic, he followed his motto – "it behoves the great to be always active" – to his last days.

Pride of fleet sinks watched by king

Portsmouth, England, 1545
It was soon after dawn that a fishing boat brought the news that a French fleet had been sighted out in the channel. Portsmouth Harbour became the scene of hectic activity as the British prepared for action. King Henry VIII watched from the shore as his flagship, *Mary Rose*, newly delivered from the builders' yard and the pride of the Royal Navy, was hastily loaded with new cannons and inspected the 400 bowmen in their leathern jackets as they went to their stations. The *Mary Rose* was warped out into the Solent where a stiff wind was blowing up from the Needles Channel. With her sails billowing and her crew scurrying over her decks as they readied themselves for action, she made a stirring sight for the King who watched from Spithead – until, with no warning, a strong gust of wind caused his flagship to heel suddenly. Her newly installed guns broke loose, crashing to her lee side. In less than a minute, *Mary Rose* had disappeared below the white-capped Solent.

1546 (1546-1548)

Italy, January 1547. Gian Luigi Fieschi drowns during a naval attack on Andrea Doria, the doge of Genoa. Fieschi had formed an alliance with Francis, the king of France, and Pietro Luigi Farnese, the duke of Parma and Piacenza, to overthrow the doge, who is supported by Charles V.

England, 21 January 1547. Henry Howard, the earl of Surrey, is executed on a charge of high treason. He was committed to the Tower of London last year after making a series of bitter speeches against the earl of Hertford, who superseded him in command of the English forces in France.

England, 28 January 1547. Henry VIII dies and is succeeded by his nine-year-old son Edward VI, whose mother was Henry's third wife, Jane Seymour.

England, 31 January 1547. Edward VI's uncle, the earl of Hertford, is appointed lord protector and duke of Somerset. He assumes control of the government.

Rome, 25 February 1547. The poetess Vittoria Colonna, marquess of Pescara, who wrote poems in the style of Petrarch, dies. She was the centre of a group of intellectuals and artists and was greatly admired by Michelangelo.

France, 31 March 1547. Francis, king of France since 1515, dies and is succeed by his son Henry II.

Germany, 24 April 1547. Charles V's forces defeat the Protestant League of Schmalkalden at the battle of Muhlberg. Philip of Hesse and John Frederick, the elector of Saxony, are taken prisoner.

Germany, 15 May 1547. Charles V gives control of the electorate of Saxony to Maurice of Saxony, who occupied the region at the end of last year.

Rome, 21 June 1547. The painter Sebastian del Piombo dies. After studying under Giovanni Bellini and Giorgione in Venice, he moved in 1510 to Rome, where he worked with Michelangelo. He painted his masterpiece *The Raising of Lazarus* in 1519.

Scotland, 31 July 1547. The reformer John Knox, a disciple of the Scottish Lutheran George Wishart, is captured by royalist forces at St Andrew's castle after a siege. The castle had been held by Protestants since the assassination of Cardinal Beaton last year.

Scotland, 10 September 1547. The duke of Somerset leads the English forces to a resounding victory over the Scots at Pinkie.

Spain, 2 December 1547. Hernando Cortes, the Spanish conqueror of Mexico, dies.

Russia, 1547. Ivan IV (the Terrible) is crowned first czar of Russia in Moscow. To counter the power of the aristocratic *boyars*, he establishes a special council composed of personally selected advisers.

Scotland, 1547. After his capture at St Andrew's in July, John Knox is exiled and condemned to the French galleys by the regent, Mary of Guise.

Italy, 1547. The Council of Trent is transferred to Bologna.

Afghanistan, 1547. Succession disputes among the successors to Sher Shah Suri have enabled Humayun to oust his Afghan supplanters and regain his Indian lands. He now captures Kabul.

England, 1547. At the instigation of the duke of Somerset, the statute of the Six Articles, a repressive decree of Catholic orthodoxy passed by Henry VIII in 1539, is repealed.

Rome, 1547. Commissioned to direct work on the building of St Peter's basilica, Michelangelo proposes the construction of a huge dome.

Mexico, 1547. Brother Andres de Olmo publishes the first Nahuatl grammar.

Netherlands, 26 June 1548. The administration of the Netherlands is made independent of the German empire.

Germany, 30 June 1548. At the Diet of Augsburg, Schmalkaldic League representatives reluctantly accept an interim agreement with Charles V which has a strongly Catholic bias.

Scotland, 1548. Mary Stuart, the seven-year-old queen of Scotland, is betrothed to Francis, the French dauphin.

England, 1548. The Venetian explorer Sebastian Cabot returns to England – from whence he launched his first expedition to America in 1509 – to seek backing for a project to find a north-west passage to Asia. Cabot has spent recent years in Spain, with whose support he explored the Rio de la Plata and established the first settlement at La Plata. In 1530 he brought gold and silver from the New World to Spain.

Poland, 1548. Sigismund II Augustus succeeds Sigismund I on the throne. His predecessor established serfdom in Poland. In a two-year war with Russia, which ended in 1536, Poland failed to regain Smolensk, lost to the Russians in 1514. Prussia remains a Polish fief.

Angola, 1548. Jesuits begin a mission in the Kongo.

Charles V takes Protestant prince captive

Muhlberg, Germany, 24 April 1547

The outnumbered army of Charles V won a critical battle here today, capturing Prince Frederick of Saxony, who founded the "Schmalkaldic League", a militant Protestant movement in Germany, with Philip of Hesse. Frederick has been sentenced to death after a trial conducted by Charles – although it seems that the death sentence is likely to be commuted to life imprisonment at the imperial pleasure.

This short war should have been won by the Protestants. At the outset, they dominated the Danube, capturing castle after castle as they advanced on the Tyrol. Their plan was to block the passes, ensuring that Italian troops could not get through to join the emperor's force. The plan failed, mainly through lack of organisation. Leading opponents of the emperor – Luther, Henry VIII, Barbarossa and Francis of France – were all dead. Charles' stature had never been higher in Europe and, as reinforcements arrived from the south, he began systematically to take German cities until his armies came to the banks of the Elbe.

Peru is still unruly

Lima, 1548

It is seven years since Francisco Pizarro, the governor of Peru, was assassinated, but the legacy of his murder still undermines attempts to govern Spain's richest colony. It was no accident that wealthy mine-owners, silver millionaires, had private armies to challenge Viceroy Vela, who was killed by them three years ago.

Like many leaders, Pizarro ignored intelligence about threats against him from a faction supporting a lost leader, Diego de Almagro, executed by the Pizarro clan in 1538. On Sunday morning 26 June 1541, the governor's palace at Lima was undefended when 20 of these dispossessed colonists smashed their way in. Pizarro, aged 63, killed one attacker, but was overpowered and killed.

Pastors may marry

Germany, 1548

Churchgoers throughout Germany are rejecting the traditional church service imposed by the settlement this year at Augsburg – the Emperor Charles V's attempt, after his Muhlberg victory, to turn the clock back to the pre-Lutheran era.

The emperor's only concessions to the Protestants – the right of clergy to marry and the use of the cup in the sacrament – are seen as inadequate by most worshippers. They dislike the restored Mass, and those few Catholic pastors willing to serve face open hostility – especially in northern Germany.

With Luther dead and his leading supporters in prison, the emperor had seen the Augsburg resolution as a golden opportunity to return his Protestant subjects to the Catholic fold.

Peking's Forbidden City: A fortress within the city of Peking and the site of the Emperors' Palaces from 1421. Most Chinese people were never allowed to enter the Gates of Heavenly Peace, or even walk near the walls.

Henry VIII dies at 56

England, 28 January 1547
Henry VIII, who died today aged 56, will be remembered for his six marriages and his momentous rupture with Rome, but in his 38-year reign there is much else to add to his reputation. Thomas Linacre, the physician, persuaded him to establish the College of Physicians. He counted Erasmus, the Renaissance scholar, among his friends. Sir Thomas More wrote his *Utopia* while in the king's service.

Henry was masterful and ruthless. He usually got his way in domestic affairs. In foreign affairs he was less successful, and in war with France in 1545 he had the humiliation of seeing his finest ship, the *Mary Rose,* keel over and sink with 500 men on board as 200 French ships were riding up the Solent. That war cost over £2 million and emptied the royal treasury.

His closest collaborators were liable to end up in the Tower. Sir Thomas More was executed for refusing to accept Henry's takeover of the church. Wolsey, sacked for failing to get the pope to sanction Henry's divorce from Catherine of Aragon, died before he could face trial. Thomas Cromwell, who masterminded the suppression of the monasteries, was also executed.

Admired, feared and much married.

Wives, too, were at risk. After Anne Boleyn's execution, Henry married Jane Seymour, who died after giving birth to a son, Edward. Of Anne of Cleves, the king said: "I liked her before I met her. Now I like her less." She was pensioned off and Henry married Catherine Howard, the duke of Norfolk's niece, who was beheaded for immorality. Henry's sixth bride, twice widowed before marrying him, is now a third-time widow.

Great King Francis dies

France, 31 March 1547
Francis, the great king of France, is dead. Aged 53, he was bold, dissolute, talented and unscrupulous, a typical Renaissance monarch. He was the patron of Rabelais; Cellini and Leonardo da Vinci worked at his court; and he built some of the finest chateaux on the Loire.

Despite his brilliance, however, he died a disappointed man. His four wars with the Emperor Charles V for supremacy in Europe ended with his relinquishing his claims to Naples, Flanders and Artois and losing Boulogne to Henry VIII of England, Charles' ally.

His persecution of the Protestants and the massacre of the Waldensians carried out in his name have also left sad marks on his reign, but no-one can deny his personal heroism on the battlefield where he spent much of his time.

He met Henry VIII on the Field of the Cloth of Gold, where these two larger-than-life kings not only conducted affairs of state but wrestled. Francis won. When news of Henry's death reached him at a ball two months ago, he laughed, but when he remembered that Henry had told him "we are both mortal" he grew more serious. That same night he developed a fever. He never recovered.

The late King Francis on horseback.

Ivan IV is the new "Caesar" of Russia

Russia, 16 January 1547
Ivan IV today had himself crowned at a ceremony in the Moscow Kremlin's Assumption cathedral. The new *czar,* which is the Russian form of Caesar, is 17 years of age. He succeeded to the throne when he was three, but the country has been ruled first by his mother, who is rumoured to have been poisoned by the *boyars,* the higher nobility, and then by a regency council.

Last year Ivan declared an end to boyar rule, and he has been taking advice on running Russia from the Metropolitan Archbishop Makary, who is the only man he appears to trust. He has plans to set up a two-chamber body, containing representatives of the gentry and merchants as well as nobles, to act to some extent as a check on the power of the boyar class. Ivan is the first czar to inherit all the Russias, and in theory at least enjoys undisputed sway over these territories. His reign could therefore be crucial to the development of a centralised and unified state in Muscovy.

A woodcut of Russia's new czar.

Diane de Poitiers, the mistress of France's new king, Henry II, painted by Francois Clouet. His cryptic, intellectual style is currently in vogue.

1548 (1548-1551)

England, January 1549. The Act of Uniformity enforces the use of the moderate Protestant prayerbook, *The Book of Common Prayer*, drawn up by Thomas Cranmer.

Bohemia, 14 February 1549. Maximilian II, brother of the Emperor Charles V, is recognised as the future king of Bohemia.

Italy, 14 February 1549. The painter Giovanni Bazzi dies at Siena. A friend of Raphael, he is famed for his frescoes of the life of St Bernard at the monastery of Monte Olivieto Maggiore.

Switzerland, June 1549. John Calvin and the followers of Ulrich Zwingli reach agreement about the Eucharist.

Florida, 26 June 1549. Luis Cancer de Barbastro, a Dominican monk and veteran of missionary activity in Guatemala, is clubbed to death by Indians while praying in Tampa. He had sought to bring the peoples of Florida to obedience by peaceful means.

England, 9 August 1549. England declares war on France.

Italy, 13 September 1549. Pope Paul III closes the first session of the Council of Bologna (Council of Trent).

England, 14 October 1549. Having provoked aristocratic opposition, the duke of Somerset, the lord protector, is committed to the Tower of London.

France, 21 December 1549. Margaret of Navarre, the devotional writer and patron of the French reformers, dies.

Morocco, 1549. The Portuguese are driven out of Arzila, their last stronghold in Morocco.

England, 1549. Sparked by rising prices and the Act of Uniformity, social and religious rebellions break out in various parts of the country. The most serious are in Cornwall and Kett's rebellion in Norfolk.

Japan, 1549. The Jesuit Francis Xavier reaches Japan, and preaches Christianity in Kagoshima.

Brazil, 1549. Appointed the first governor of Brazil by John III, the king of Portugal, Tome de Sousa establishes a capital at Salvador da Bahia de Todos los Santos.

Rome, 7 February 1550. Paul III is succeeded as pope by Julius III, a Roman close to the Farnese family.

France, March 1550. France and England sign the treaty of Boulogne. The English surrender Boulogne for 400,000 crowns and the release of those Protestant Scots, including John Knox, captured by the French at the siege of St Andrew's castle in 1547.

Germany, October 1550. Maurice of Saxony, entrusted with the execution of the decree passed at the Diet of Augsburg two years ago, lays siege to Magdeburg, the centre of the Protestant opposition.

Scotland, 1550. After the signing of the treaty of Boulogne, English troops withdraw from Scotland.

Iceland, 1550. Bishop Arason, who has organised armed opposition to the introduction of Protestantism into Iceland, is condemned and executed by Frederick III, the king of Denmark.

Rome, 1550. A Jesuit college is founded in Rome.

Spain, 1550. Spanish explorers describe great wooden temple mounds built by Indians in south-eastern North America.

Florida, 1550. The Spanish bring the first beef cattle to North America.

West Africa, c.1550. The Nupe defeat the Yoruba of the Oyo kingdom *(in Nigeria).*

West Africa, c.1550. The Manes invade the area of Sierra Leone.

Venice, c.1550. The Flemish composer Adriaan Willaert, the musical director at St Mark's church, is creating a brilliant synthesis of Italian melodic expressiveness and northern European polyphony to produce sumptuous choral sounds, often with instruments added.

Italy, January 1551. The second session of the Council of Trent opens.

Germany, 9 March 1551. Under a Habsburg family treaty, Charles V's son Philip is made the emperor's sole heir.

Austria, 19 July 1551. The treaty of Karlsburg reaffirms Ferdinand of Habsburg's rights to Hungary and Transylvania.

Italy, 1551. Henry II of France resumes the war against the Emperor Charles V and publicly disavows the Council of Trent.

Mexico, 1551. A new law bans Negroes from taking Indian mistresses or carrying firearms. Punishments include whipping, cutting off of ears and imprisonment.

England, 1551. Sir Thomas More's *Utopia* is translated from Latin into English.

Japan, 1551. The Spanish Jesuit Francis Xavier leaves for China after introducing Christianity into Japan. The Jesuit missionaries, two of whom stay behind to help to build up the nucleus of the new church, have come into conflict with the Buddhist priests.

King who kept Poland Catholic has died

Poland, 1 April 1548

Sigismund (the Old), the king who ruled Poland for more than 40 years, has died in Cracow at the age of 81. His reign is widely seen as marking a new peak of Polish civilisation, profoundly influenced by the Italian Renaissance.

Sigismund, who was blessed with a strong character and considerable political perception, governed Lithuania before becoming king in 1507. One of his first tasks was to bring in a programme of financial reforms. On the battlefield he defeated a Russian army under Vasily III. He imposed his rule on Wallachia, and also stamped his authority on East Prussia.

Sigismund was anxious to unite his realm in loyalty to Rome, and enforced strong measures against the Lutherans. He introduced death by burning for importing heretical books and ordered all his subjects attending heretical universities abroad to return home. He also, briefly, brought in a similiar penalty for disobedience. But all such edicts were widely ignored.

Sigismund's monument at Wawel cathedral in Cracow.

Golden Age of Africa excites Europeans

Rome, 1550

An extraordinary book, *The History and Description of Africa and the Notable Things therein contained*, has just been published; it is an account of civilisations of which Europe had heard only rumours.

The author is equally extraordinary. Born in Grenada, a Spanish Moslem, he moved to Morocco, took the name *al-Fasi*, man of Fez, and travelled as far as central Asia and central Africa as a lawyer and accountant. Captured off Tunis by Christian corsairs, he was presented to Leo X in Rome, where he became known as Leo Africanus.

Twice he crossed the Sahara, passing the castle of salt, Teghaza, from where salt was taken to Black Africa and exchanged for gold. He travelled all over the decaying Malian and rising Songhai states.

What excited Europe above all else was his description of Timbuktu. Here was a "stately temple" and a "princely palace", where "the inhabitants are extremely rich" and "of a gentle and cheerful disposition". Here were libraries overflowing with priceless manuscripts, and "doctors, judges, priests and other learned men". Leo Africanus also wrote of "cottages built of chalk", but Europe was too blinded by the streets of gold to notice.

Czar Ivan attacks top Russian aristocracy

Russia, 27 February 1549

Ivan IV today opened a special assembly, known as the *Zemsky Sobor*, given the task of deciding important measures of state policy. This Assembly of the Land is made up of representatives of the *boyars* (the old nobility), the church, merchants, and the new nobility living in the towns and districts.

In a speech to the assembly Czar Ivan harked back to his youth when the boyars plotted against him and his family and dealt harshly with the gentry and the peasants. He warned the boyars that they would be punished if they did not now obey his orders without question, and proposed setting up courts to hear complaints against them.

The czar has also introduced a new code dealing with court procedure and criminal laws. The code is known as the *Sudebnik*, and consists of 100 articles. Capital punishment is prescribed for everyone guilty of armed rebellion and conspiracy against the czar.

Spanish discuss morality of colonisation

Spanish colonists torturing Indian natives; from a later engraving.

Spain, 1550
Sixty years after Columbus landed in the New World and set off a chain of Spanish conquests, a debate is raging among Spanish intellectuals and colonialists. Their argument: is conquest, with its inevitable destruction of Indian culture, morally justified?

The Dominican Bartolomeo de las Casas has stated the case against the conquest, condemning the brutality of Spain's troops. In favour of conquest is Juan Gines de Sepulveda, who justifies Spain's actions by the Biblical text "Go out into the highways and hedges and compel them to come in".

To him the Indians are a barbaric race, certainly not Christians and barely human. "How can we doubt that these people — so uncivilised, contaminated with so many impieties and obscenities — have been justly conquered by such an excellent, pious and most just king?"

Renaissance artists recorded by Vasari

Florence, May 1550
A very popular book of biographies has just been published by Giorgio Vasari, the architect and painter, who was born in Arezzo. Its full title is *The Lives of the Most Excellent Italian Architects, Painters and Sculptors*.

Vasari studied under Michelangelo and became his friend, and the perfection attained by him is the climax of the book. Vasari has travelled Italy collecting memories, anecdotes and written memoirs to illustrate the rebirth of painting, from the time of Cimabue (who died in 1302) and Giotto to the present day. It is the first coherent book of art history and criticism, demonstrating the superiority of the artists of Tuscany.

New tools put nuts and bolts into work

Europe, c.1555
As technology develops, so too do the tools needed to promote it. Nuts and bolts are being used to fasten together materials. To tighten these two elements the spanner has been introduced. Both tools and fasteners are hand-made.

Another recent development is the screw fastener. For a long time pieces of furniture and other wooden objects have been held together by wooden joints. However, these are not adequate when metal has to be held fast to wood. Gunsmiths have found that a nail given a twist before being driven home will hold a gun mechanism tight to the stock. It seemed natural to fix the "screw" with a blade fitting into a slot on the nail head.

Jesuits protect natives from slave traders

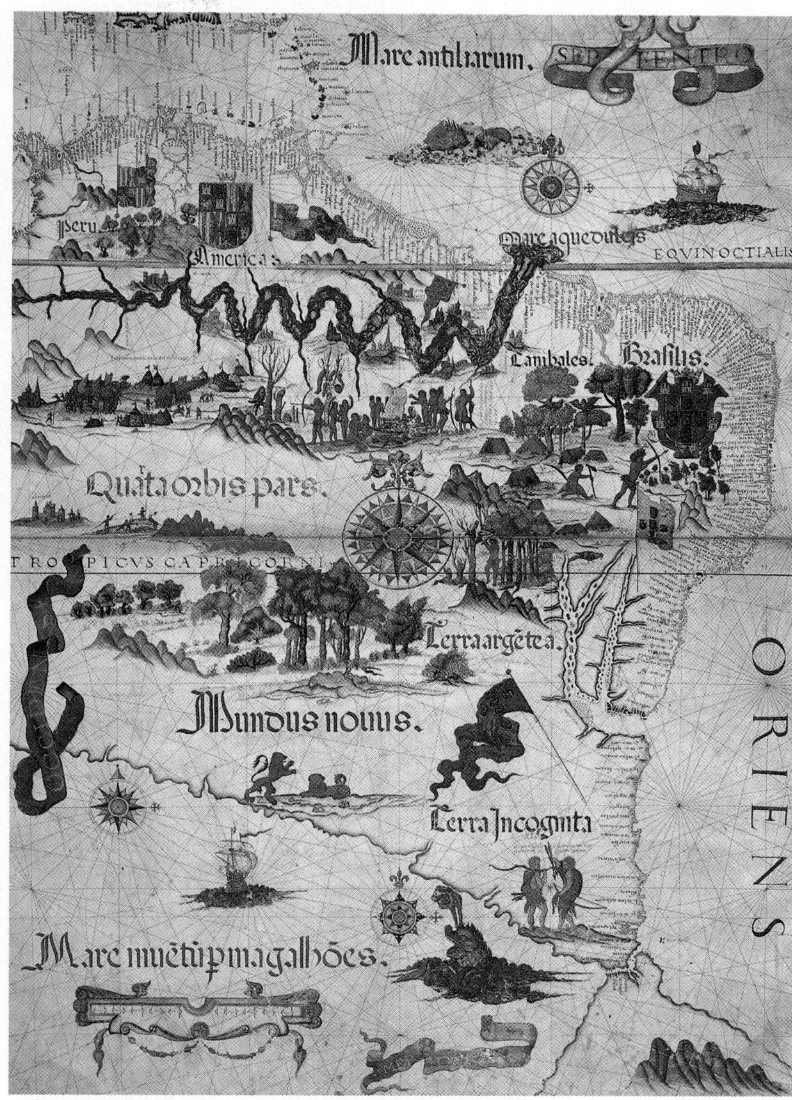

A map of 1558, showing the first phase of the Spanish conquest.

Brazil, c.1551
Jesuit missionaries operating in Brazil have set new standards for the treatment of Indians in the colonies of the New World. While the conquerors have become notorious for their cruelty and exploitation of the native peoples, these missionaries go out of their way to improve the situation and treat the Indians as more than just slaves.

Ever since Manuel de Nobrega, the leader of Brazil's Portuguese Jesuits, founded the country's first archbishopric in the capital, Salvador de Bahia de Todos los Santos, and set up a Jesuit college at Sao Paolo, the order has been closely involved with the Indians.

The Catholic fathers live alongside the Indians, taking direct responsibility for their spiritual and economic welfare. Slavery is official policy, but, while they cannot stand in the way of the exploitation of Indians for work, they do attempt to curb the excesses of the overseers, and cut down on the regular slave raids into the interior.

Ironically, the natives have not responded to their benefactors by embracing their religion. Too many atrocities have been committed in the name of Christ for them to divorce the new faith from the savagery of colonisation which threatens to destroy entire cultures.

Thus the only way in which Christianity can be imposed is by the efforts of the colonial troops. Many more Indians have been converted at the point of a sword than have responded to the kindness of the Jesuits.

1551 (1551-1554)

North Africa, 1551. The Ottomans capture Tripoli.

France, 15 January 1552. Henry II of France and Maurice of Saxony, who has turned against the emperor, sign the treaty of Chambord in opposition to Charles V. Henry promises to provide Maurice with troops and money in return for the formal possession of Metz, Toul and Verdun, which the French captured last year.

England, 22 January 1552. The duke of Somerset, the former lord protector, who played a leading part in the first half of Edward VI's reign, is executed. He was arrested by the duke of Northumberland and tried on trumped-up charges.

England, 24 February 1552. The privileges of the Hanseatic League in England are abolished.

England, March 1552. A new Act of Uniformity imposes an explicitly Protestant prayerbook.

Germany, May 1552. Maurice of Saxony takes Augsburg and almost captures Charles V at Innsbruck.

Germany, 2 August 1552. John Frederick, the elector of Saxony, and Philip of Hesse, taken prisoner by Charles V in 1546, are released.

Germany, 2 August 1552. The treaty of Passau, between Maurice of Saxony and Frederick of Habsburg, who is acting in the name of Charles V, revokes the Augsburg Interim of 1548 and promises religious freedom to the Protestant princes.

China, 3 December 1552. Francis Xavier, the "apostle of the Indies", dies of exhaustion near Canton.

Russia, 1552. Ivan the Terrible conquers the *khanate* of Kazan.

Persian Gulf, 1552. The Ottoman Red Sea fleet attacks the Portuguese stronghold of Hormuz but fails to capture it.

Spain, 1552. The Dominican friar Bartolomeo de las Casas publishes a book entitled *Brief Relations of the Destruction of the Indies*, attacking colonial practices in the New World.

Italy, 1552. The Italian anatomist Bartolommeo Eustachio makes important discoveries regarding the ear and the heart, identifying certain tubes and valves.

France, January 1553. Charles V fails to take Metz.

France, 9 April 1553. Francois Rabelais, whose utopian writings were condemned by Calvin and the doctors of the Sorbonne as licentious and dangerous, dies. His first book, *Pantagruel*, was an immediate success.

England, 1553. A new confession of faith, the Forty-two articles is introduced. It was drawn up by Thomas Cranmer, archbishop of Canterbury, and a committee of six to supplement the new Protestant prayerbook.

England, 6 July 1553. Edward VI dies, having assigned his crown to Lady Jane Grey, the daughter-in-law of the duke of Northumberland, who has her proclaimed queen.

Germany, 9 July 1553. Maurice of Saxony is mortally wounded at Sievershausen while defeating Albert of Brandenburg-Kulmbach.

Italy, 2 August 1553. French forces which have invaded Tuscany are defeated by an imperial army at the battle of Marciano.

England, 3 August 1553. Having thwarted Northumberland's plan to prevent her succession, Mary Tudor, the only surviving child of Henry VIII and Catherine of Aragon, enters London in triumph. She was recently proclaimed queen in Cambridge.

England, 22 August 1553. Arrested and tried for treason, the duke of Northumberland, is executed on the orders of Mary Tudor.

England, September 1553. Protestant bishops are arrested and Roman Catholic bishops restored.

Morocco, 23 September 1553. The Sadians defeat the last of their enemies and establish themselves as rulers of the entire country.

Germany, 16 October 1553. The German painter Lucas Cranach dies. He was closely associated with the reformers, many of whom were the subjects of his portraits. He also painted religious and classical scenes.

Switzerland, 27 October 1553. The Spanish theologian and physician Michael Servetus, who studied medicine in Paris and discovered the pulmonary circulation of the blood, is burnt for heresy. In his writings he denies the Trinity and the divinity of Christ.

Russia, 1553. The English seaman Richard Chancellor, chosen as "pilot-general" of Sir Hugh Willoughby's expedition in search of a north-eastern passage to India, reaches Archangel via the White Sea. He travels overland to Moscow, where he meets the czar.

Netherlands, 1554. Henry II of France invades the Netherlands.

England, February 1554. Sir Thomas Wyatt surrenders to government forces in London after leading a Protestant rebellion in Kent inspired by Queen Mary's proposed marriage to Philip of Spain.

Jesuit gains freedom to preach in Japan

Portuguese merchants accompanied by Jesuit missionaries arrive in Japan.

Japan, 21 November 1551

Francis Xavier, the Jesuit missionary, has sailed for Goa on a Portuguese ship after two years of preaching the gospel to the Japanese. The road was often hard for this son of noble Basque parents.

When Xavier stepped ashore on 15 August 1549 he was initially welcomed by the feudal prince of Satsuma and was given permission to preach in the prince's lands. He made some 150 converts, including the faithful Barnabas who became his servant and guard.

What Xavier did not appreciate was that the prince's indulgence stemmed from the belief that rich Portuguese ships would follow the priest. When they did not materialise the prince issued an edict in the summer of 1550 making it a capital offence for any of his subjects to become a Christian after that date.

Xavier and two companions then set out as wandering missionaries. Poorly clad and with no money, they made their way to the capital, Kyoto, in the bitter winter. Xavier was sometimes forced to hire himself out as a baggage carrier in order to eat. He persevered and, while unsuccessful in Kyoto, won many converts in other parts of Japan.

French troops take German bishoprics

Lorraine, April 1552

Henry II of France has taken up where his father failed and has successfully waged war against the Emperor Charles V. A 35,000-strong French army has marched into Germany, catching the prematurely-aged emperor by surprise and occupying the three bishoprics of Metz, Verdun and Toul which the French intend to annex.

This move is the result of a scheme proposed by Maurice of Saxony who, sensing that Charles' power was failing and the Habsburg family was losing its cohesion, entered into a defensive league with a number of other German princes and Henry in the treaty of Chambord three months ago.

Under the terms of this treaty Henry promised his new allies an army and in return was ceded the bishoprics. Charles did not recognise the importance of this conspiracy. He has been beaten and forced to flee across the Alps.

Ivan the Terrible defeats Mongols

Russia, 1552

In two well-conceived campaigns, supported by excellent artillery, Ivan the Terrible has dealt a devastating blow to the decaying power of the Tartars – Mongol invaders from the east. With a force of some 150,000 men, Ivan has captured Kazan, the Tartar capital on the Volga, after using gunpower to breach the walls. He followed this by conquering Astrakhan, another Mongol stronghold.

These actions have brought the whole Volga basin as far as the Caspian Sea into the Russian empire, thereby opening the way for Russian expansion beyond the Urals and as far as the Pacific Ocean. These new trade routes are also likely to appeal to foreign merchants. The exploits, which were due also in part to Ivan's major reforms of the army, have earned for him the name of *Grozny*, which can be translated as Dread, or Terrible.

Calvin condemns heretic to be burnt

Geneva, 27 October 1553
Michael Servetus, a fugitive from the Spanish Inquisition and author of *On the Errors of the Trinity* (1531), is to die at the stake, on the orders of Geneva's religious leader, John Calvin.

Geneva may be the home of the Reformed Church, but Servetus' attack on the Trinity was intolerable. Calvin's decision was allegedly taken on religious grounds only, but Servetus, a distinguished physician – he discovered pulmonary blood circulation – is one of his severest critics and Calvin had often stated that, were his rival to appear in Geneva, he would be dealt with harshly. Earlier this year Servetus arrived in the city as a refugee and began preaching.

An 18th-century print of Michael Servetus. His anti-trinitarian views brought on him the wrath of Catholic and Reformed Churches alike.

Cranach, Luther's portrait painter, dies

Cranach's "The Stag Hunt of Elector Frederick the Wise" shows his patron engaging in the sport of kings in a richly wooded landscape.

Weimar, Germany, 1553
Lucas Cranach, since Durer's death the leading German painter, has died here aged 81 in the company of his patron, the defeated elector of Saxony, John Frederick. His *Crucifixion* in Weimar church is his masterpiece. Fifty years ago he became court painter to the previous elector, Frederick the Wise, at Wittenberg, where Frederick had founded the famous university.

In later life Cranach was elected burgomaster of Wittenberg, where he and his three painter sons set up a busy workshop, patronised by rich merchants. He brought German landscape into religious painting. His *Rest on the Flight into Egypt* is like a northern forest scene, with angels flying out of the undergrowth. As a portrait painter equal to Durer, he did several portraits of his friend Martin Luther and of Germany's princes, and of the young Charles of Spain before he became emperor. In later years he turned to Venus as his subject and painted a series of erotic nude studies as well as hunting scenes. The most famous is the *Judgement of Paris*.

Harsh city rules silence the dance halls

Geneva, c.1552
The reformer John Calvin, once banished as a religious extremist, is now the unrivalled ruler of Geneva, a city he has re-created in the rigid image of his own Protestant orthodoxy. His *Ecclesiastical Ordinances*, first published in 1541, are fully accepted as the basis of government of both church and state.

The son of a lawyer, and a lawyer himself, Calvin relishes the practical details of government. And, as a religious zealot, he cannot conceive of a government that is anything but subject to the religion of its citizens. The Ordinances have as little time for free will as Calvinism itself, but, like the religion, are firmly stated, clearly laying down what is right and what is wrong. They demand strict moral order and unswerving religious conformism. Within the Genevan republic the laws of church and state are virtually inseparable. Citizenship depends on orthodoxy; perfect orthodoxy includes absolute respect for the state.The Ordinances are administered by several groups of officials, all appointed rather than elected. Pastors deal with religious orthodoxy and elders with public morals. The two groups meet at the weekly consistory and examine the state of Genevan morals. They may summon and punish any alleged sinner. Doctors, appointed by the pastors, deal with secular and spiritual education.

Apart from dealing with such major areas as the regulation of funerals and marriages the Ordinances take in even the trivia. Calvin believes firmly in individual piety. Thus every vestige of one's life must be controlled. Dancing is forbidden, as are the wearing of slashed breeches, the use of folk remedies and many everyday pastimes. The clergy are authorised to visit all parishioners annually, to ensure that they are living properly Christian lives. Yet although not all the rules are petty – Calvin has created an improved city code and sharp practice of every sort is punished – such measures are incidental, ultimately only the spiritual health of the citizens matters.

Dominican tells of destruction of Indians

Spain, 1552
A former colonialist turned Dominican monk has issued a savage condemnation of Spain's regime in the New World and demanded an end to the *encomienda* system, under which the native Indians are enslaved on the great estates.

Bartolomeo de las Casas once ran his own estate, but was so appalled by the excesses of the Spanish forces that he abandoned his holdings and began campaigning for colonial reform. Apart from attacking Spanish cruelty, he has also become an expert on the Indians, citing a mass of evidence to prove that their culture, while neither European nor Christian, is just as complex and sophisticated as their rulers'.

In 1542 he drafted the New Laws, demanding an end to slavery, and Charles V duly backed him up, suspending any new encomienda grants. But those who profited from the system rebelled and the new laws were repealed in 1546. The extraction of labour as a tribute remained forbidden. Now the colonialists may be forced to act themselves. The system generates huge products, but it consumes its own workforce. The brutality of the overseers and the ravages of "European" diseases are decimating the Indians. Soon there may be none left to exploit.

Mexican natives flee from the Spanish; from a contemporary drawing.

1554 (1554-1556)

London, 12 February 1554. Lady Jane Grey – proclaimed queen by her uncle, the duke of Northumberland, last year – is executed in the Tower of London.

England, 25 July 1554. Mary Tudor, the queen of England, marries Philip of Spain, the son and heir of Charles V.

Mexico, 22 September 1554. Francisco Vasquez de Coronado dies. He explored the south-west of North America in the hope of discovering a rich Indian civilisation similar to that of Mexico. He traced the Colorado and Rio Grande rivers and explored widely (*in Arizona, New Mexico, Texas, Oklahoma and Kansas*).

Arabia, 1554. The Ottomans capture Bahrain.

England, 1554. All the religious laws passed under Henry VIII and Edward VI are repealed by parliament. Roman Catholicism is re-established and the authority of the pope is recognised.

France, 1554. The Italian architect and sculptor Sebastiano Serlio dies at Fontainebleau, where he had been involved in work on the chateau. Serlio's architectural treatises helped to spread the ideas of Vitruvius, the Roman expert who flourished during the reign of Augustus, through Europe.

Rome, 1554. The Neapolitan Gian Pietro Caraffa is elected pope and takes the name Paul IV. He succeeds Marcellus II, who was in office for only 21 days. Caraffa is determined to stamp out heresy by any means.

London, 1554. Following Richard Chancellor's visit to Moscow, the Muscovy Company is formed to trade in furs and wood with Russia. The English are now in competition with the German merchants of the Hanseatic League, whose privileges were withdrawn in 1551.

Italy, 1554. Philip of Spain receives the kingdoms of Naples and Sicily and duchy of Milan from his father, Charles V.

Italy, 1554. The duchess of Ferrara, Renee d'Este, is imprisoned for heresy by her husband, the duke d'Este. Renee, the daughter of Louis XII of France, married the duke in 1528. Her support for the Reformation has grown too embarrassing even for the liberal court of France.

West Africa, 1554. Katsina (*in Nigeria*) regains its independence from Songhai.

Italy, April 1555. French forces occupying Siena surrender to an imperial army led by Cosimo de Medici, the duke of Florence, after a 15-month siege.

Scotland, May 1555. John Knox returns to Scotland from Geneva, where he was strongly influenced by Calvin. He begins to preach widely as an advocate of the Calvinist form of Christianity.

Germany, 3 October 1555. The Peace of Augsburg advocates that the religion of a prince should determine the faith of his subjects, thus sanctioning the existence of Lutheran states. It is decided that the imperial chamber should be composed of an equal number of Protestants and Catholics. Calvinists, however, are excluded from the agreement.

England, 16 October 1555. The Protestant bishops Nicholas Ridley and Hugh Latimer are burnt.

Europe, 25 October 1555. Charles V abdicates the sovereignty of the Netherlands to his son Philip.

Near East, 1555. The Ottomans and the Persians sign the peace of Amasya.

Germany, 1555. Philip of Spain renounces his claim to the German throne in favour of Maximilian, the son of Frederick of Habsburg.

Russia, 1555. The English navigator Richard Chancellor makes a second journey to Archangel and Moscow.

India, 1555. The Moghul emperor Humayun, who has recently recovered Kandahar with the help of the Persian Shah Ismail, reoccupies Delhi and Agra after defeating an Afghan claimant to the throne.

Cuba, 1555. The Spanish settlement at Havana is attacked by the French.

North America, 1555. A Basque privateering fleet led by Juan de Erauso and Perez de Hoa raids the French fort at St John's fishery in Newfoundland, capturing it for the Spanish.

South America, 1555. Durand de Villegagnon founds a French colony at Rio de Janeiro.

Ethiopia, 1555. The Emperor Galawdewos is victorious in the Ethiopian-Galla war.

China, 1555. Japanese pirates, who have already launched two attacks on China, besiege Nanjing.

Spain, 16 January 1556. Charles V hands over his remaining Spanish dominions in the Old and New Worlds to his son Philip.

Central Asia, 1556. The Russian army under Ivan IV seizes the *khanate* of Astrakhan, so reaching the Caspian Sea.

Scotland, 1556. Condemned to further exile, John Knox returns to Geneva.

Mary Tudor beheads Lady Jane Grey

Lady Jane Grey is urged to take the crown, by Giovanni Battista (1727-85).

London, 12 February 1554
Lady Jane Grey, queen of England in name only for nine days last year, was executed for treason in the Tower today with her husband.

The order for her execution came directly from Queen Mary Tudor – to whom she surrendered the crown – who feared that the Protestant noblewoman might serve as a rallying point for a rebellion against her own fierce Catholicism.

Jane Grey had successfully proclaimed herself monarch nine days after the duke of Northumberland, John Dudley, had named her, his protegee, as queen. Northumberland was executed immediately. Lady Jane, a granddaughter of Henry VIII, and her husband, Northumberland's son, might have remained alive, but last week 3,000 Kentishmen led by Sir Thomas Wyatt marched unsuccessfully on London to try to stop Queen Mary's marriage to Philip of Spain. Lady Jane had no direct connection with the revolt.

Picaresque novel seen as heretical

Burgos, Spain, 1554
A new sort of novel, known as *picaresque* from its celebration of a hero who is a *picaro*, or wandering rogue, has been published anonymously in Spain. Condemned as immoral, it has been placed on the Index. It is entitled *La Vida de Lazarillo de Tormes y sus Fortunas y Adversidades*.

The picaro is a common character in today's Spain. Often a veteran, he rejects hard work, living on his wits and chancing his luck with every new opportunity.

Reflecting a collapsing society, its citizens overcome by fatalism and a growing insecurity, the book has appalled the authorities, who particularly dislike its vigorous anti-clericalism.

The Frenchman Bernard Palissy has tried for sixteen years to crack the Italian secret of faenza enamel. Unlike the Italians, who favour a pewter solution, he uses a lead-based formula. This is a typical piece of his highly-decorated glazed rustic earthenware from the early 1550s.

Bishops burnt as Mary seeks birthright

England, 1555
Secret meetings of the new English Protestants are taking place in towns and villages in southern England as Catholic Mary's campaign of persecution spreads. Burnings at the stake began last February, the victims including four bishops, one of them a greatly respected friend of the poor, Nicholas Ridley.

Mary has persuaded parliament to abandon the independence of the English church and to submit to papal authority; accordingly, Pope Julius III has appointed Reginald Pole, an Englishman long resident in Italy, archbishop of Canterbury. He has revived the old Catholic services and sacked priests who, under the reforms of Henry VIII and Edward VI, were allowed to marry.

Some observers say that the queen is not directly responsible for the persecutions which have earned her the epithet "Bloody Mary"; still, she has a very personal reason for seeking to restore Catholic authority. When Henry's marriage to Catherine of Aragon was annulled in spite of papal condemnation of the action, Mary became a bastard; she was obliged to make an act of submission acknowledging Henry as "Supreme Head of the Church of England" and affirming that her mother's marriage had been "incestuous and unlawful". If she can restore papal authority over the English church her birth will become legitimate.

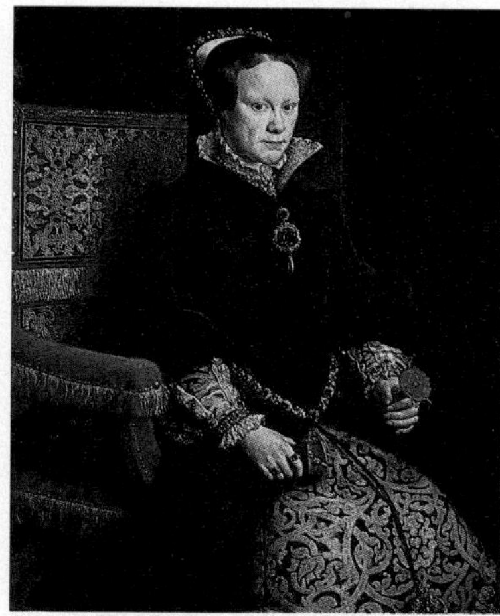
The Catholic Queen Mary: made illegitimate by her father's actions.

From Moorish potters in Spain comes the vivid ceramic technique called majolica, after the island of Majorca. Italian potteries, especially in the Florence area, soon learned how to do the same coloured ornamentation on white enamel. At first the Italians were content to copy the oriental designs favoured by the Moors. Nowadays the preference is for "istorati", illustrations of historical, biblical or mythological themes, such as this plate by F. Xanto from Urbino, showing Actaeon turned into a stag.

Dream dies at Augsburg

Augsburg, 3 October 1555
Catholics and Protestants, who have been meeting in the diet here since last February, today signed a peace treaty that ends the three-year war in Germany. It also represents a clear recognition by the Catholics of co-existence for the new Protestant churches throughout Europe and a recognition by the emperor of the powers and rights of the German princes.

The dream of the emperor, Charles V, was to bring the Protestants back into the Catholic Church and to secure imperial power over both Catholic and Protestant princes in Germany. At the beginning of this year, riven by gout and under attack from the Turks on his eastern flank, he finally admitted that his dream was impossible. He raised his siege of Metz and nominated his brother, Ferdinand, to lead the Diet of Augsburg to find a compromise solution.

The principle established by the peace is *cuius regio, eius religio* (to each kingdom its own religion). In effect, it gives the princes power over the bodies and souls of their subjects. It does not give ordinary people their religious freedom, but at least they can move to adjoining states if their own prince does not permit their religion.

Charles V can also feel satisfied that the peace ensures the continuance of Catholicism in some German principalities. The Catholic princes, driven by different political motives, could never on their own have withstood the surging popularity of Lutheranism.

Local doctor reveals his world prophecies

Salon-de-Provence, 1 March 1555
A French country doctor, astrologer and self-styled prophet has published a book in which he claims to forsee the history of world events for the next 500 years. *Centuries*, by Michel de Nostradame, known as Nostradamus, is a collection of 1,000 quatrains. Each is filled with cryptic and mysterious references which, when deciphered, apparently set out the fate of mankind.

His prophecies are hard to interpret, but they include what readers see as coded references to many European monarchs. Other verses, often almost indecipherable, seem filled with death and disaster and allegedly deal in matters far beyond our own era. That some predictions have already proved accurate has led to *Centuries* being regarded with equal parts of respect and outright fear.

Although critics talk of the occult, and condemn Nostradamus as an agent of the Devil, the prophet, who admits to using deliberately difficult language, stresses his belief in God. All his work, he declares, "has been accomplished through divine power and inspiration".

Nonetheless, Nostradamus is said to have studied the mystical Jewish Qabbalah, the writings of the Sufis and classical Chaldean and Assyrian magic.

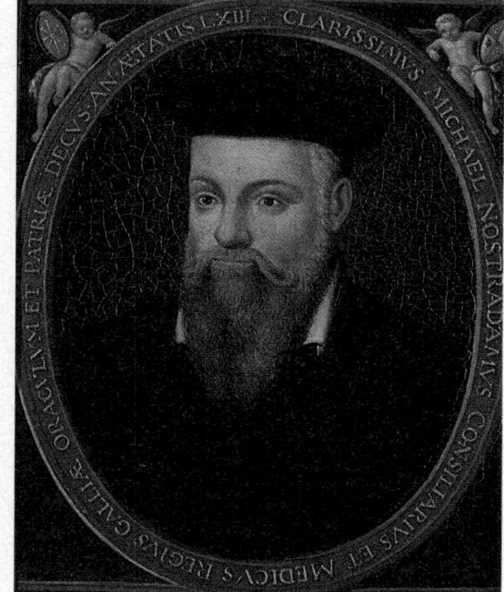

Nostradamus: prophet or crackpot?

Indians' Holy Book

Guatemala, 1555
A survivor of the 1524 Spanish assault on the Qiches tribe at Utatlan city has translated their holy book, *Popol Vuh*, into Roman script.

Until now the book, containing Toltec-Maya Indian theories of evolution, has only been decipherable by high caste members of the Qiches tribe. The *Popol Vuh* tells of past worlds – one where men were made of earth and another where they were made of maize gruel.

1556 (1556-1558)

India, 27 January 1556. The Moghul Emperor Humayan dies after falling from his library roof in Delhi. He is succeeded by his 13-year-old son Akbar.

France, 5 February 1556. Henry II of France and Philip of Spain sign the truce of Vaucelles.

England, 21 March 1556. Thomas Cranmer, the archbishop of Canterbury, is burnt at the stake in Oxford. The English reformer was imprisoned for heresy when Mary Tudor came to the throne.

England, 22 March 1556. Cardinal Reginald Pole, who was a candidate for the papacy in 1549, becomes archbishop of Canterbury.

Rome, 31 July 1556. Ignatius Loyola, the Basque nobleman and former soldier who founded the Society of Jesus, dies.

Spain, October 1556. Charles V resigns the empire to his brother Ferdinand and retires to a remote monastery at Yuste. He is succeeded as king of Spain by his son Philip II.

India, 5 November 1556. The Emperor Akbar defeats the Hindus at Panipat and secures control of the Moghul empire.

Scotland, 10 November 1556. The Englishman Richard Chancellor is drowned off Aberdeenshire on his return from a second voyage to Russia.

Germany, 17 November 1556. Ferdinand founds a military council to govern the German possessions of the Habsburgs.

Florence, 2 January 1557. The painter Jacopo Carrucci, one of the masters of mannerism, dies.

England, 7 June 1557. In support of Philip II of Spain, the husband of Queen Mary, England declares war on France. The war has been provoked by Pope Paul IV, a life-long enemy of Spain.

France, 10 August 1557. French troops, led by the constable, Montmorency, are defeated by the Spanish army of Emmanuel Philibert, the duke of Savoy, at St Quentin. Philip II of Spain promises to construct a magnificent building to commemorate the victory.

France, 1 September 1557. Jacques Cartier, who discovered Canada, dies at St Malo.

Scotland, 3 December 1557. The Protestants are united by a national covenant.

Portugal, 1557. John III, whose son John died in 1554, is succeeded as king of Portugal by his three-year-old grandson Sebastian. Sebastian's grandmother, Catherine of Habsburg, is appointed regent.

Netherlands, 1557. The world commercial centre of Antwerp faces a crisis. As a result of their war debts, the kings of France and Spain find it impossible either to pay the interest on their debts or to repay any borrowed money.

Morocco, 1557. Mohammad al-Mahdi, the effective founder of the Sadian kingdom, is assassinated. During his lifetime, the Sadians secured control of the whole of Morocco and moved their capital from Fez to Marrakesh, causing clashes with the Turks of Algiers.

Italy, 1557. Francis, the duke of Guise, launches an unsuccessful expedition to exercise his rights to the kingdom of Naples.

China, 1557. The Portuguese set up a trading post at Macao.

London, 1557. Sebastian Cabot, the Venetian explorer dies.

Newfoundland, 1557. With the help of an armed escort, the French recover St John's fishery, captured by a Basque fleet two years ago.

Germany, 1557. The first German novel is published: *Der Goldfaden*, by George Wickram.

Switzerland, 9 January 1558. Geneva becomes independent of Berne.

France, 20 January 1558. A French army under Francis, the duke of Guise, takes Calais from the English.

Germany, 14 March 1558. Ferdinand assumes the title of emperor without being crowned by the pope.

Russia, 4 April 1558. Ivan IV grants the merchant Grigory Stoganov the right to use and cultivate the lands in the area of the Kama river and its tributaries.

France, 24 April 1558. Mary, the queen of Scotland, the daughter of James V and Mary of Guise, marries the French dauphin, Francis.

France, 22 June 1558. The French take Thionville.

France, 13 July 1558. The French suffer a resounding defeat at Gravelines by the Spanish army, led by the count of Egmont.

Scotland, 1558. John Knox publishes his *First Blast of the Trumpet against the Monstrous Regiment of Women* attacking female monarchs.

Austria, 1558. The manufacture of firearms begins at Ferlach, Carinthia.

India, 1558. The Moghul Emperor Akbar conquers Gwalior.

Germany, 1558. The Hamburg Exchange is established.

Teenager Akbar wins the Moghul empire

India, 5 November 1556

On the battlefield of Panipat, 60 miles north of Delhi, 13-year-old Akbar, the son of Humayun and grandson of Babur, has gained the Moghul empire – thanks to Bairam Khan, his noble general and guardian.

Humayun regained the empire after the deaths of Sher Shah Suri and the latter's son, Islam Shah, but lived for only a few months to enjoy it before falling to his death down his library stairs.

Hemu, the capable and ambitious Hindu minister of the last Suri sultan, realizing the weakness of an empire ruled by a 13-year-old child, revolted. He took Agra and Delhi and proclaimed himself emperor, or *raja*, Vikramaditya.

Bairam Khan, with a smaller army, met Hemu's forces at Panipat, where Akbar's grandfather, Babur, had won his historic victory 30 years earlier. Victory appeared to be going to Hemu when he was struck by an arrow in the eye. His army, seeing him slumped on his famous war-elephant Hawai, fled. The unconscious Hemu was dragged before Akbar and Bairam and beheaded in front of the victorious Moghul troops. With a love of hunting a paramount factor in his makeup, Akbar shows few signs at this early age of beoming the kind of ruler which the Moghul empire – divided by internal strife and frequent rebellions – urgently needs.

Much will depend on the advice given to him by Bairam Khan in these next few formative years – and whether he will take it.

The founders of the Moghul dynasty, (l. to r.) Babur, Timur and Humayun, with their chief attendants.

First among equals makes maths simpler

London, 1557

A book has just been published, written by an English physician and mathematician, Robert Recorde, which contains a welcome innovation in mathematical notation. In *The Whetstone of Witte*, Recorde proposes the use of the sign "=" to denote "equals". Hitherto mathematicians have been using verbal abbreviations and other short cuts to denote equality, but there has been no consistency. Now they can all employ the same notation. Recorde, a fellow of All Souls' College, Oxford, and the royal physician, also introduced algebra into England.

New empire rises south of the Sahara

Timbuktu, Africa, c.1556

The great empire of Mali is dying. A new empire, the Songhai empire, is taking its place in West Africa. The Malian empire proved too large for its rulers. Its decline was evident by 1433 when it was unable to defend Timbuktu from attack by Tuareg nomads. By 1512 Leo Africanus wrote of the king of Mali being so impoverished that he "cannot even give food to his family".

Over the decades the breakaway state of Songhai, under its ruler Sonni Ali, increased its power, taking Timbuktu from the Tuaregs in 1468. His successor, the philosopher-prince Askia, continued the conquests, extending Songhai's frontiers to the central Sahara in the north, Senegal in the west and Lake Chad in the east. Ten years ago the Songhai army invaded Mali again and, though it has withdrawn, Mali is but a shadow of its ancient glory.

Charles V's final retreat

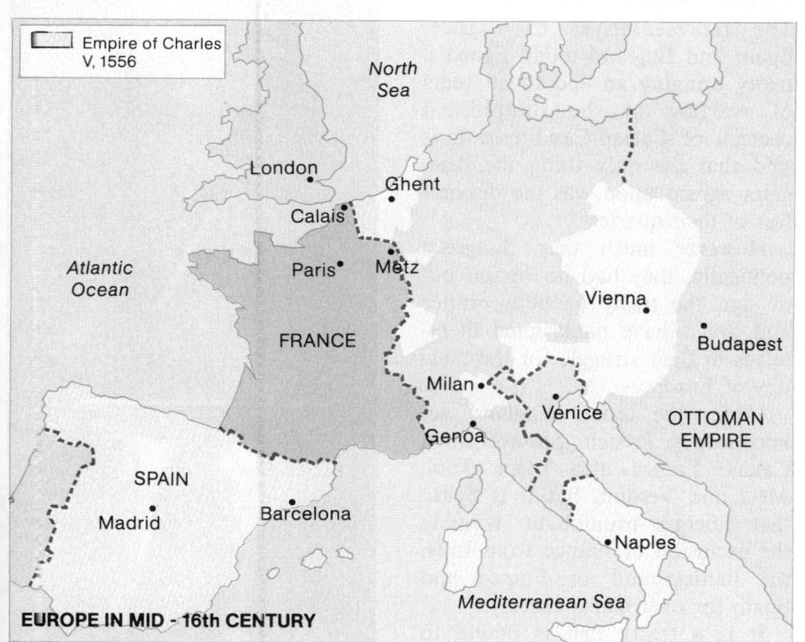

Brussels, 25 October 1556

Dressed entirely in black, except for the red collar of the Order of the Holy Fleece, Charles V, the Holy Roman emperor and king of Spain, Naples and the Netherlands, rode on a gentle mule into the castle here to announce that he had abdicated his empire and kingships and was retreating to a monastery. The 56-year-old emperor, broken in health, handed his kingdoms to his son, Philip, and the empire to his brother, Ferdinand. It was a moving occasion; and as the emperor, his voice breaking with the effort, asked for forgiveness for all past errors, the audience "could not restrain their tears and sobs".

As he drives across the continent to the monastery which he himself has designed, Charles will have much to reflect upon, particularly the state of the Europe which he has bequeathed. He was, by nature, a crusader, who lived for the ideal of a huge campaign to drive the Ottomans from the Holy Lands, yet spent much of his life in a defensive role as the forces of Suleiman the Magnificent continually threatened his realms. To achieve the true crusade he needed a united Europe; but Germany, at the very centre of his empire, was divided by Christian heresy, with its princes using the Reformation to fight for their own independence. Despite his pledge to "exterminate heresy lest it should take root and overturn the state and the social order", Charles was prepared to compromise and accept the alliance of the Protestant princes when central Europe was threatened. Nonetheless, his principal bequest is a divided Germany which threatens to engulf the whole of Europe in a major war.

Charles V, by Van Dyck.

The man who bestrode Europe like a colossus, fighting brilliant battles and travelling huge distances as he sought to hold a great empire together, has one more achievement to reflect upon: it was in his name that Rome was destroyed.

Ignatius Loyola, founder of Jesuits, dies

Rome, 31 July 1556

Ignatius Loyola, the founder and first general of the Society of Jesus, died today, having seen its numbers swell from a handful in 1540 to over 1,000 members. Jesuits prepare themselves by following Loyola's rigorous *Spiritual Exercises*, published in 1548. Subjecting themselves to this ascetic discipline teaches them to master the will and learn total obedience to their superior and to the church. They have to be prepared to believe that what seems black to them is white if the church declares that it is.

One of Loyola's original brethren, Francis Xavier, left for the Indies with three companions in 1541 to carry out their original aim as missionaries. At home and across Europe the society has become a teaching order, starting with schools in the slums of Rome, but now providing education for the best families at Jesuit colleges at the universities such as Padua and Rome. Jesuits are renowned for their teaching methods.

A later French portrait of Ignatius Loyola, Christian soldier supreme.

Bankruptcy looms in Spanish crisis

Spain, June 1557

Philip II of Spain has issued a decree suspending all payments from the Castilian treasury. All outstanding debts are to be consolidated into *juros* – annuities repaying loans out of revenue – at five per cent interest. Though Spain is not technically bankrupt, the move reflects the magnitude of the debts left by the Emperor Charles V.

In the early part of his reign, Charles was able to rely on Italy and the Netherlands to contribute to the fight against heresy in northern Europe, and campaigns against the Turks. But there was a tax revolt in Ghent in 1539, and by 1540 the Spanish viceroy warned that Naples, which had been heavily taxed since 1525, had been virtually bled dry.

The main source of revenue was Castile, followed by Aragon, the church and the South American colonies. But the cost of the emperor's campaigns meant constant new taxes, or other measures like the sale of indulgences by which noblemen became exempt from direct tax. The Cortes and the Spanish Council of Finance voted additional sums. Still Charles needed more, and he turned to German and Italian bankers, at increasingly exorbitant rates of interest.

The Spanish royal family, ostentatiously displaying their enormous wealth.

1558 (1558-1559)

Spain, 21 September 1558. Charles V, Holy Roman emperor between 1519 and 1555, dies. His reign was marked by almost constant wars with France, through which he gained control of Italy under the 1529 peace of Cambrai. Despite his tenacious struggle against the Protestant Schmalkaldic League, Protestantism in Germany won legal recognition under the peace of Augsburg, after Charles had been deserted by his powerful ally Maurice of Saxony.

England, 17 November 1558. Queen Mary, the daughter of Henry VIII and Catherine of Aragon, dies at the age of 42. Her five-year reign saw the restoration of Catholicism as the official state religion and brutal persecution of Protestant "heretics". Mary's half-sister Elizabeth, the daughter of Anne Boleyn, becomes queen.

England, 17 November 1558. Cardinal Reginald Pole, the archbishop of Canterbury, dies a mere 12 hours after Queen Mary, under whom he vigorously championed the restoration of Catholicism. His disapproval of Henry VIII's assumption of supremacy over the English church forced him to leave England in 1532. He was made a cardinal in 1536 and, after Mary's accession, returned to England as papal legate.

England, 20 November 1558. Queen Elizabeth appoints the statesman William Cecil to the post of her chief secretary of state.

Italy, 1558. Ramusio's *Delle Navigationi e Viaggi* is the first narrative of the North American voyages of discovery to be widely circulated in Europe.

Germany, 13 January 1559. The moderate Anabaptist leader Menno Simons dies. By imposing rigid discipline on the sect, he saved Anabaptism from extinction under persecution in northern Europe.

France, 3 April 1559. Philip II of Spain and Henry II of France sign the peace of Cateau-Cambresis, ending the long series of wars between the Habsburg and Valois dynasties. Under the terms of the treaty, France withdraws from Savoy and Piedmont but recovers Calais and retains Metz, Toul and Verdun. In Italy, Spain now controls Sicily, Sardinia, Naples, Milan and the coastal fortresses of Tuscany. The agreement is to be sealed by two dynastic marriages.

England, 8 May 1559. An Act of Supremacy defines Queen Elizabeth as the supreme governor of the Church of England and makes provision for a high commission for the correction of errors and abuses to be set up.

Mexico, 11 June 1559. The Spaniard Tristan de Luna y Arellano sets sail from Vera Cruz at the head of a 1,500-strong expedition, intending to establish a settlement on the gulf coast of Florida.

France, 10 July 1559. Henry II, the king of France, dies after being mortally wounded by Gabriel de Montgomery in a jousting tournament. He is succeeded by his 15-year-old son, Francis II, the husband of Mary Stuart, the queen of Scotland.

Florida, 14 August 1559. Spanish explorer de Luna enters a bay on the gulf coast *(Pensacola).*

England, 1559. The learned theologian Matthew Parker is appointed archbishop of Canterbury. The Anglican service is reintroduced.

Scotland, 1559. Attempts by the regent, Mary of Guise, to suppress Protestant reformers provoke them into open rebellion.

Netherlands, 1559. Margaret of Parma, the sister of Philip II of Spain, becomes regent of the Netherlands.

Scandinavia, 1559. Frederick II, the son of Christian III, becomes king of Denmark and Norway. In alliance with his uncles, the dukes of Holstein, he conquers the peasants' republic of Ditmarsh, located between the Elbe and Eider rivers.

Rome, 1559. Pope Paul IV, who completed the organisation of the Roman Catholic Inquisition and issued a list of prohibited books, dies. He is succeeded by Giovanni Medici, who decides to take the name of Pius IV.

Near East, 1559. With the support of his father, Suleiman the Magnificent, the sultan of the Ottomans, Selim defeats his brother Bayezid at the battle of Konya. Bayezid and his five sons flee to Persia, where they are subsequently executed in return for a large payment made by Suleiman.

France, 1559. A French translation of Plutarch's *Lives* by the humanist Jacques Amyot is published.

Switzerland, 1559. John Calvin and the French Protestant reformer Theodore Beza, who has recently joined him in Geneva, found an academy for the teaching of Calvinist theology.

Germany, 1559. Under the direction of Matthias Flacius, the professor of theology at the newly-founded university of Jena, a group of Lutherans begins work on a church history entitled *The Magdeburg Centuries*.

France is humiliated at peace conference

Cambrai, France, 3 April 1559

The representatives of France, Spain and England today signed a treaty bringing an end to 60 years of warfare at the dilapidated chateau of Cateau-Cambresis. It is said that the only thing the delegates agreed upon was the discomfort of their quarters.

However much they disagreed politically, they had no option but to sign the treaty as both France and Spain have bankrupted themselves in their struggle for the mastery of Europe.

Under the terms, England acknowledges French possession of Calais. France also keeps Toul, Metz and Verdun, but it is Spain that emerges triumphant, winning the exclusion of France from Italy, the battleground of France and Spain for over half a century.

It is a treaty that is bound to cause bitterness among the French who have shed so much blood for so little. Already there is talk of France being humiliated.

Philip II of Spain, by Moro; Spain has won most from the treaty.

King is fatally wounded in tournament

France, 10 July 1559

Henry II has died in agony ten days after he was so terribly wounded at the tournament held to celebrate the Treaty of Cateau-Cambresis and the marriage of his daughter, Elizabeth, to Philip II of Spain.

His death is a story of foolhardiness. Although tired by several passages of arms he insisted on breaking another lance before retiring, and asked Gabriel de Montgomery to oppose him in the lists.

Montgomery begged to be excused and the queen told Henry that he was too tired to joust again. But Henry was adamant. The two men put on their helmets, galloped down the lists, clashed; Montgomery neglected to drop his broken lance and tonight France is ruled by a 15-year-old sickly boy.

Crowds of spectators gathered to watch the jousting at the royal tournament.

Charles V dies in Spanish monastery

The Emperor Charles V at the convent of Yuste, by Alfred Elmore (1815-81).

Yuste, Spain, 21 September 1558
Charles V died today in the monastery in which he had lived out the last three years of his life in solitude. Rejecting a grand funeral, he will be buried in the chapel here under the high altar – "half my body to be placed underneath, the other half outside so that the priest will stand over my head and chest". His last years were spent peacefully enough at Yuste, living in a small villa designed so that he could see the high altar in the monastery from his bed.

After the last rites had been administered, Charles asked for the crucifix which his wife had held on her deathbed and died to the sound of psalms.

Queen dies with Calais engraved on heart

England, 17 November 1558
Mary Tudor was England's first queen regnant. She ascended the throne five years ago with the intention of restoring papal authority over the English church; when she died today, aged 42, she had caused 300 men and women to be burnt at the stake for their Protestant faith.

She lacked experience of governing – her father, Henry VIII, had banished her from his court – and listened to her cousin, Charles V of Spain, who persuaded her to marry his son Philip. The union was unpopular and led to uprisings. When she thought she was pregnant she ordered thanksgiving services in London; but there was no child.

The Spanish connection led to war with France. At Calais the French mounted an unexpected assault on New Year's Day 1558, and captured the town. After 200 years, England's only foothold in Europe was lost. "When I am dead and opened," Mary said, "you shall find Calais engraved on my heart." Philip rarely visited England, yet once again, a few months before her death, Mary said she was pregnant. One of her courtiers sardonically observed that she had better hurry, as it was eight months since she had last seen her husband.

Mary, with Philip II of Spain.

Ivan the Terrible invades Baltic states

Russia, 1558
Ivan the Terrible has sent his troops into Livonia in a lightning strike designed to secure the Baltic region for Muscovy and give it an outlet to the west. Ivan's troops have seized several large towns as well as the coastal fortress of Narva, but disputes in Moscow are beginning to destroy the army's momentum. At the same time the Livonian Order of Knights, still the area's main defence force, is managing to improve its military and diplomatic posture. Riga has put itself under the protection of the Poles, and Sweden and Denmark are looking poised to take over other areas of Estonia and Courland. Livonia is being partitioned.

Ivan may find that he has overreached himself, but the Baltic area would have been a considerable prize. To a backward Russia, with a rudimentary agriculture and little industry, the Baltic and its ports, already important centres of international trade, offer the prospect of benefit from the more advanced countries of the west.

Adventurous goldsmith begins life story

The splendid salt-cellar which Benvenuto Cellini made in about 1540 for King Francis I of France. It is made of gold, enamel and ebony.

Florence, 1558
The goldsmith, sculptor, musician and soldier Benvenuto Cellini has begun what should be a colourful autobiography. Born in 1500, the tempestuous Cellini has served many leading dynasties as artist or soldier in these turbulent times, especially the Medicis in his native Florence. He worked first in Rome, producing jewellery, medals, coins and seals; he moved on to sculpture under the influence of Michelangelo and in around 1540 made the famous gold, ebony and enamel salt cellar for Francis I of France. Another famous sculpture is the Medicis' *Perseus*, made in 1553.

King who saved Ethiopia dies fighting

Ethiopia, 1559
Gelawdewos, who saved his empire first from Ottoman and Somali invaders, and then from Galla from the south, is dead, killed in battle consolidating his empire. His finest hour was in 1540. Almost all of Ethiopia was overrun by the Moslem armies of Almad ibn Ibrahim ("El Gran" – the left-handed). Nine out of ten Ethiopians had renounced their religion. He remained defiantly in the field; and when a Portuguese army sent to assist him was almost wiped out he continued to resist, until in 1543 he brought el Gran to battle at Weyna Dega and killed him.

1559 (1559-1561)

Florida, 1559. De Luna founds a settlement on Mobile Bay (*Alabama*).

Paris, January 1560. The poet Joachim du Bellay dies of apoplexy at the age of 37. He was part of the group of poets known as the *Pleiade* and wrote its manifesto, *The Defence and Illustration of the French Language*.

France, March 1560. In what is known as the "conspiracy of Amboise", a group of Protestants launches an operation to capture the court and topple the Guise family. The Guises are warned, however, and the attempt fails. Several hundred Huguenots are executed and Louis de Bourbon, the duke of Conde, is imprisoned.

India, March 1560. The Moghul Emperor Akbar, now aged 17, dismisses the regent, Bairam Khan, and takes the reins of government into his own hands.

Germany, 19 April 1560. Philip Melanchthon, Luther's close associate, dies at Wittenberg. The main author of the 1530 Augsburg Confession, he was influenced by the humanism of Erasmus. Becoming spiritual leader of the Lutheran Church after Luther's death, he made great efforts to reconcile opposing factions among the reformers.

Sweden, 25 June 1560. Gustav Vasa – whose capture of Stockholm in 1523 drove the Danes from Sweden, thus ending the great Scandinavian union which had existed for 126 years – abdicates. He leaves the foundations of a strong Swedish army and navy and a more settled system of administration.

Scotland, June 1560. The Scottish Parliament accepts a Protestant confession of faith drafted by John Knox which forbids the saying of Mass and renounces the pope's authority in Scotland.

France, 2 July 1560. The Catholic statesman Michel de l'Hopital, who supports a policy of religious toleration towards the Huguenots, is appointed chancellor of France.

France, 6 December 1560. Francis II is succeeded as king of France by his ten-year-old brother Charles IX. The queen mother, Catherine de Medici, the widow of Henry II, becomes regent.

England, c.1560. The English navy is busy building ships on the pattern of Henry VIII's *Henry Grace a Dieu*, nicknamed the "Great Harry", the first four-masted vessel launched in England. The Great Harry is a symbol of the revolution in shipbuilding and navigation which has taken Europeans around the world.

France, 1560. The poet Maurice Sceve, a leader of the *ecole lyonnaise*, which laid the foundations for the *Pleiade* movement, dies.

Moscow, 1560. Construction of the cathedral of the Intercession of the Virgin (St Basil's cathedral) is completed.

Peru, 1560. The Dominican friar Domingo de Santo Tomas writes his *Gramatica y Arte de la lengua general del Peru* and a *Lexicon y Vocabulario*, enabling missionaries to study Quechua, the language of the native Andean peoples.

South-East Africa, 15 March 1561. Father da Silveira, the Portuguese Christian envoy to the Munhumutapa court, is killed at court – probably at the instigation of the Moslem imam.

Caribbean, 9 July 1561. Angel de Villafane and the remnants of the 1559 expedition of Tristan de Luna y Arellano return to Hispaniola *(Santo Domingo)* after failing to establish a colony at Pensacola Bay. Villafane took control of the expedition after de Luna was dismissed for poor leadership.

France, July 1561. Acting on the advice of Michel de l'Hopital, the regent Catherine de Medici sets up talks between the French Catholics and Protestants at Poissy. She consents to an edict giving the Huguenots qualifed toleration.

Scotland, 19 August 1561. Mary, queen of Scots, returns to Scotland following the death of her husband, Francis II of France, last year. The Scottish nobility is bitterly opposed to her Roman Catholicism.

Spain, 23 September 1561. Philip II gives orders that colonising efforts in Florida should be halted.

Netherlands, 1561. In compliance with an undertaking given to the regent, Margaret of Parma, in 1559, Spanish troops leave the Netherlands.

Netherlands, 1561. A papal bull is published proposing the creation of 14 new bishoprics in addition to the four existing ones. This alienates many nobles whose relatives are thus excluded from ecclesiastical sinecures.

Scotland, 1561. The reformer John Knox publishes his *Book of Discipline*, setting out a new Scottish church constitution based on the Calvinist model.

Italy, 1561. A *History of Italy* by the Florentine Francesco Guicciardini is published posthumously. The work completes his *History of Florence*, which was begun in 1508 but was still unfinished at his death.

Lutheran king of Sweden abdicates

Expansionist monarch Gustav Vasa, by Willem Boy (c.1557).

Stockholm, 25 June 1560

Sweden today achieved an orderly handover of power when King Gustav, who has done much to make Sweden a power in its own right, abdicated in favour of his son, Eric, after 43 years on the throne.

King Gustav, an elected monarch, ensured an hereditary succession for his son 15 years ago when he had laws passed establishing that the monarchy would pass through the male line.

The new king, Eric XIV, is expected to continue his father's policy of expanding Sweden's diplomatic and trade links with powers in western and central Europe.

Ever since King Gustav made Sweden independent of Denmark and took it out of the Kalmar Union, Sweden has been conscious that its sea and land routes to the west – the narrow strip of water known as the Oresund, and Norway – remain under Danish control and could ultimately jeopardise its independence.

Before his accession the then prince had already tried to forge one such diplomatic alliance with England by negotiating a marriage with its Queen Elizabeth.

Scottish Parliament bars Roman rituals

Edinburgh, June 1560

A decisive shift of power has taken place in Scotland and, linked as it is to the accession of Queen Elizabeth in England, promises to overturn the old pattern of relations with Europe. At a free Scottish Parliament meeting in Edinburgh, 100 lairds heard a confession of faith drafted by the Calvinist reformer John Knox. This document aims to embrace the "elect of all ages, realms, nations, Jews or Gentiles" and specifically rejects the rituals of Rome and abolishes the pope's authority in Scotland.

This new state of affairs came about after an English army fought alongside the Scots to drive out the French. Such an alliance would have been unthinkable as recently as two years ago, when Catholic Mary was on the throne of England. Even her successor Elizabeth was at first doubtful, not because of popish sympathies – far from it – but because of Knox's pamphlet delivering a blast against the "monstrous regiment" of woman. He has been busy explaining to the English that his fire had been aimed at the pro-French queen mother in Scotland, Mary of Lorraine, who married her daughter Mary to the French dauphin, Francis.

Knox spent two years in irons after being captured by the French. Released after English intervention, he fled to Geneva, where he was inspired by the teachings of Calvin to found the Scottish Kirk.

A later engraving of John Knox, the fiery anti-Catholic Scotsman.

Elizabeth I's church rejects papal power

A 16th-century manuscript illustration of Queen Elizabeth.

England, 1559

After months of parliamentary manoeuvring, and a shake-up of the Privy Council, Elizabeth's secretary of state, William Cecil, has achieved the religious settlement desired by his queen. The church is once more English and papal authority has been firmly repudiated.

Parliament assembled last February after Elizabeth's accession to the throne and in the wake of anti-Roman demonstrations in London and a Twelfth Night court masque, where asses were dressed as bishops. But Cecil's first bills were emasculated in the Lords. Another bill repealing Catholic Mary's heresy laws was also lost.

In the Privy Council, Cecil baited Catholic members until they walked out. He tackled parliament again and got his bills through by agreeing that Elizabeth should be the church's "supreme governor", not "supreme head". The bishops have rejected the settlement and been sacked. Married clergy are returning. Matthew Parker, who was chaplain to Elizabeth's mother, Anne Boleyn, has become archbishop of Canterbury.

French peace talks

France, September 1561

The most eminent Catholic and Calvinist theologians are meeting at Poissy at the instigation of the regent, Catherine de Medici, to try to settle the religious differences which are proving so dangerous to France. On one side there is the brilliant Jesuit, Diego Lainez, and on the other, Calvin's friend, Theodore Beza. But although the debate between these men should be memorable, the differences between both sides are so great there would seem to be little chance of reconciliation.

Catherine de Medici is French regent

France, 1560

Catherine de Medici, the widow of Henry II, has declared herself regent of France in the name of her ten-year-old son, Charles IX. This move puts her in a position of great power and equal danger.

It is an unusual situation for Catherine, for she was virtually ignored during the reign of her husband who was under the thumb of his mistress, Diane de Poitiers. During the short reign of her sickly elder son, Francis II, she was also unable to exert any influence because Francis, although only 16, was of age. Married to Mary, queen of Scots, he came under the control of the ultra-Catholic Guise faction led by Mary's uncles, the duke of Guise and the cardinal of Lorraine.

However, while Catherine may have little experience of power, there is no doubt about her passionate determination to preserve the French monarchy for her sons. Descended from a Florentine family of popes on her father's side and from a noble French family on her mother's, she is a woman to be reckoned with. Her first priority is to gain time to allow a cooling of the religious passions of the Catholics and Protestants which are threatening to tear France apart.

King Francis II, reigned 1559-60.

The colourful domes of the great Russian orthodox cathedral of St. Basil, which was built in the last few years for Ivan, the czar of Russia. Standing next to "Red Square" in the centre of his capital, Moscow, it is a fittingly imposing monument to Ivan's autocratic rule; he is determined not to tolerate any opposition, especially from Russia's feudal aristocracy.

1561 (1561-1564)

Spain, 1561. Madrid becomes the capital of Spain.

France, January 1562. The edict of St Germain supersedes last year's July edict, again giving limited toleration to Huguenots (Protestants) but obliging them to practise their religion outside town walls. Parliament refuses to recognise or register the edict.

France, 8 February 1562. Jean Ribault leaves France at the head of a party of 150 French Huguenots intending to establish a colony in Florida.

France, March 1562. The massacre of an illegal Huguenot congregation at Vassy, by order of Francis, the duke of Guise, sets off a religious war.

Florida, 1 May 1562. Jean Ribault lands on the coast and discovers a waterway which he names the river of May *(St John's river).*

England, 20 September 1562. Queen Elizabeth signs a treaty at Hampton Court with the French Huguenot leader, Louis de Bourbon, the prince of Conde. Under the treaty the English will occupy Le Havre in return for aiding Conde's forces against Catholic troops; Elizabeth will leave Le Havre when Calais has been restored to England.

Venice, 17 December 1562. The Flemish composer Adrian Willaert, who had been chapel master at St Mark's for 35 years and founded a famous choir school, dies. His work synthesises Flemish, French and Italian styles.

West Africa, 1562. The Englishman John Hawkins begins the English slave trade across the Atlantic. He leaves Sierra Leone with a shipment of 300 slaves, sailing to Hispaniola *(Santo Domingo)* in the Caribbean.

Mexico, 1562. In Yucatan, Bishop Diego de Landa orders a large number of Maya manuscripts to be burnt.

Venice, 1562. The painter Paolo Veronese completes his decorations in the Villa Barbaro in Maser – greatly praised as an innovation in Venetian painting.

France, January 1563. The port of Le Havre, occupied by the English under a treaty signed with the prince of Conde last year, is seized by Catholic troops.

France, 19 March 1563. The peace of Amboise brings to an end the war of religion. Although the militant Catholic Francis, the duke of Guise, was assassinated last month and the English allies of the Huguenots defeated, limited toleration is once more granted to the Huguenots.

China, 1563. Ming generals finally manage to gain the upper hand over resurgent Japanese piracy along the south China coast.

Florence, 1563. Cosimo de Medici establishes the Accademia del Disegno, the first academy of art in Europe. Its members, who are governed by formal rules, are drawn mainly from the artists and sculptors of whom Cosimo is already an established patron.

Europe, c.1563. The term "Puritan" is used increasingly to stigmatise those English Protestants who want to purify the church further.

England, 1563. Jean Ribault visits the royal court, bringing his *Whole and True Discoverye of Terra Florida,* the first account of Florida published in English.

England, 1563. The "39 Articles" of the Protestant Church of England are published.

England, 1563. The Statute of Artificers regulates trade and employment contracts and confers on justices of the peace the task of fixing wages in their county.

Spain, 1563. Juan Battista de Toledo begins work in the Escorial palace founded by Philip II of Spain outside Madrid.

Venice, 1563. Veronese paints the *Feast at Cana* for the Benedictine monks of San Giorgio Maggiore.

Russia, 1563. Ivan the Terrible orders the drowning of Jews in the Dvina river.

Scandinavia, 1563. The war of the Three Crowns breaks out between Sweden and Denmark; the latter is supported by Lubeck and Poland.

Paris, 1 January 1564. France adopts 1 January as the start of the year, in accordance with the Julian calendar. The New Year has been on 1 January for most civil purposes until now, but the official year, following a church decree issued 400 years ago, has begun on the day before Easter.

Italy, January 1564. The decrees of the Council of Trent are published. They reaffirm traditional Catholic theology, but propose radical reforms in church organisation, including the education of the clergy.

Netherlands, 22 January 1564. Antoine Granvelle, the adviser of Philip II of Spain and effective governor of the Netherlands since 1559, is recalled to Spain on account of growing unrest against Spanish domination and fierce lobbying against him in Madrid.

Rome, 18 February 1564. The sculptor and painter Michelangelo dies.

Council votes back pope

Trent, Italy, 4 December 1563

News of the severe, perhaps fatal, illness of Pope Pius IV has galvanised the Council of Trent here into action. A series of votes has been carried out rapidly in the last few days emphatically asserting the authority of the head of the Roman Catholic Church so much so that the delegate bishops here express their votes as propositions, which the pope has to approve in order for them to be effective.

The hopes of the reformers here, who hoped to have more power in the hands of the bishops, have been dashed. Pope Pius called the council, the third one here, in the hope of resolving the struggles between Catholics and Protestants, and particularly the bloody war between Catholics and Huguenots. His illness has strengthened the arm of the traditionalists who fear that any weakening in the face of the growing power of the Calvinists in France and the Lutherans in Germany will be fatal.

The council has asserted the importance of the Mass and the authority of tradition and of the bishops. It contradicts the Calvinist assertion of predestination and the idea that ordinary people can interpret the scriptures as well as the clergy. Some ground has been gained by the reformers. Bishops are to be urged to reside in their dioceses. The accumulation of wealth is prohibited. The ordinary clergy are to be properly trained. A new Bible, based on St Jerome's Latin version, is to be produced, which will be the ultimate authority.

The verdict reflects the views of the majority of the 200 delegates, who were Italian, Spanish and French. The Germans, where Protestantism is most powerful, were there as a tiny minority.

One in four dies as plague wracks London

London, 1563

What some call the sweating sickness, others the pestilence, and all know as plague, has hit London again. It is the sixth attack this century. In London more than 17,000 people, one quarter of the population, have died. Plague has become a fact of modern life, finding a welcome in the narrow streets of towns and cities. These "strange and unpredictable diseases which swarm among us", as one writer has it, defeat current medicine.

Every expert holds his own opinion and offers his own cure. The one general belief is that these epidemics reveal a general decline in the world. So random are the outbreaks, so varied those who perish and those who survive, that most observers are sure that the plague is God's work – his punishment for man's sins.

Silver gilt pomander of c.1580, made to carry perfumes to ward off disease.

Murder and rape in French religious wars

The execution of Huguenots: religious civil war seems inevitable in France.

France, 1562
Open warfare of the cruellest kind has broken out between the Catholics and the Huguenot followers of Calvin. Their quarrel has split the country from peasant to nobleman, with Gaspard de Coligny, the admiral of France, leading the Huguenots and the duke of Guise championing the Catholics.

Sadly, the bloodshed stems from an attempt at reconciliation by the regent, Catherine de Medici. After her seizure of power she stopped the persecution of the Calvinists and restored their leaders to influence at court, and in January 1562 her moderate chancellor, Michel de l'Hopital, granted them a degree of freedom of worship. This served only to enrage the fiercely Catholic artisans in Paris and other towns. Led by nobles opposed to religious reform, they began to attack the Huguenots. On 1 March soldiers of the duke of Guise massacred a number of Huguenots as they prayed at Vassy.

The Protestant prince de Conde called the Huguenots to arms, and they retaliated by despoiling churches, murdering priests and raping nuns. They are now in possession of Lyons, Rouen and Orleans, but have been driven out of other towns with great slaughter.

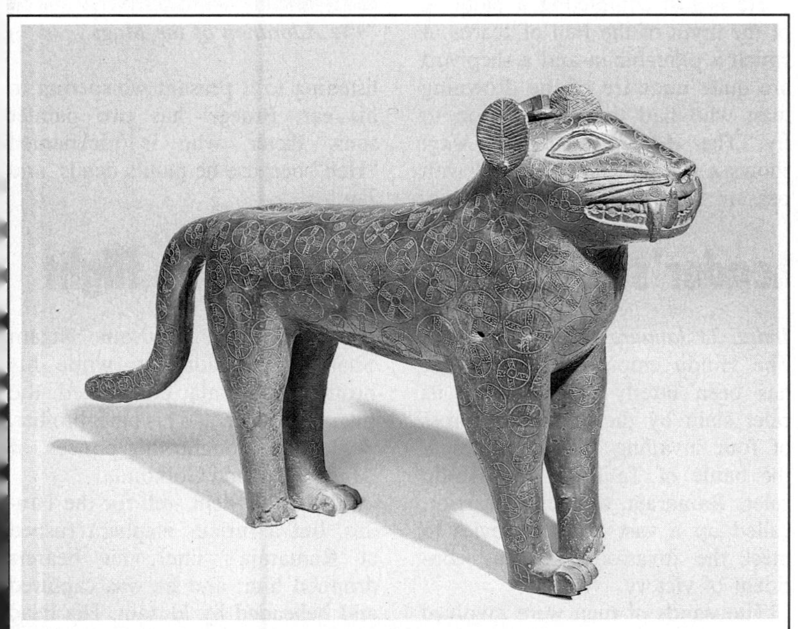

Benin, 16th Century: A brass acquamanile in the shape of a leopard.

Renaissance genius Michelangelo dies

"The Holy Family", by Michelangelo, a great artist, architect and sculptor.

Rome, 18 February 1564
The best all-round artist in Italy, probably the world, Michelangelo Buonarroti, has died at the age of 89. He told his friends on his deathbed that the works he left behind were his sons. His funeral will be in Rome, but Duke Cosimo de Medici plans a tomb for him in Florence.

Twenty years after he finished the ceiling of the Sistine Chapel for Julius II, Pope Clement VII asked him back to paint the wall behind the altar with his giant fresco of *The Last Judgement*, his mightiest composition, teeming with three-dimensional figures in dramatic poses. All his paintings, such as his circular *Holy Family*, are sculptural. His last great frescoes, for a chapel of St Peter and St Paul adjoining the Sistine, were done in his seventies.

Besides having gifts as a poet, Michelangelo was a brilliant architect. He left the design and model for the unfinished dome for St Peter's and his plan for Rome's Capitoline Hill, the Campidoglio. His own dissatisfaction with his work as a sculptor caused him to leave many unfinished statues, like the *Pieta* on which he was working at his death. His friend, Giorgio Vasari, has told how frugally he lived and how he would sculpt through the night by the light of a candle he wore fixed to a paper helmet on his head.

Peace of Amboise follows duke's murder

Amboise, France, 19 March 1563
An edict signed here today has ended the cruel religious war between Catholics and Protestants which has torn France apart for the last year. Catherine de Medici virtually imposed this peace after the murder of the Catholic leader, the duke of Guise, by a Huguenot gentleman a month ago. With the fierce duke removed from the scene, the regent now has unchallenged control of Catholic forces, but, while she believes that France is a Catholic country, she is not a zealot.

There is doubt, however, as to whether this treaty will hold, for it leaves the Catholics angry at the concessions given to the Protestants, while the latter fear that the progress of the new faith has been curbed.

1564 (1564-1566)

Switzerland, 27 May 1564. John Calvin, one of the dominant figures of the Protestant Reformation, dies in Geneva. He is wrapped in a coarse shroud and buried without an address or a hymn.

Florida, 22 June 1564. The Frenchman Rene de Goulaine de Laudonniere lands at Matanzas inlet on the river of May *(St John's river)* with a party of 300 to set up the post of Fort Caroline.

Germany, 25 July 1564. On the death of Ferdinand, who inherited the Holy Roman empire after his brother Charles V abdicated in 1555, his son Maximilian II becomes emperor. Maximilian was named successor two years ago on the understanding that he would remain a Catholic.

Mediterranean, October 1564. The Flemish anatomist Andreas Vesalius dies of hunger and fatigue on an island in the Ionian Sea, where he had been thrown by a storm on a return journey from the Holy Land. Vesalius decided to make the pilgrimage after being accused of vivisection. His great work *De Humani Corporis Fabrica*, published in 1543, greatly advanced the science of biology.

Russia, January 1565. In an increasingly bloody reign of terror, Ivan the Terrible imposes his *oprichina*, a state within the state of Muscovy dominated by a private army called the *oprichniki.*

Brazil, 1 March 1565. A Portuguese colony is established at Rio de Janeiro.

Florida, May 1565. Beset by food shortages and mutinies since he set up Fort Caroline last year, Rene de Goulaine de Laudonniere attacks one of the villages of the Utina tribe. He holds its chief to ransom, hoping that the Indians will pay him with a supply of corn.

Spain, 29 June 1565. Pedro Menendez de Aviles leaves on a mission to Florida to break up the French colony of Fort Caroline.

Florida, 28 August 1565. Long overdue, Jean Ribault arrives at the colony of Fort Caroline with French reinforcements.

Florida, 28 August 1565. Pedro Menendez de Aviles enters the harbour defended by Fort Caroline, which he names San Agostin (St Augustine).

Florida, 13 September 1565. On the verge of attacking Menendez's Spanish settlement at San Agostin, Jean Ribault's fleet is scattered by a devastating storm.

Florida, 20 September 1565. Menendez wipes out the French at Fort Caroline.

Malta, September 1565. The siege of Malta by the Ottoman Turks is finally raised with the arrival of a Spanish relief fleet. The Knights of St John have withstood the Turks assaults since May.

Florida, November 1565. After renaming Fort Caroline as San Mateo, Menendez builds forts along the Indian river, with the help of 500 Negro slaves.

Angola, 1565. King Afonso II of Kongo is assassinated during mass.

India, 1565. Vijayanagar is captured and sacked after being defeated by the united forces of the five Dekhan sultanates at the battle of Talikota.

England, 1565. The English sailor John Hawkins returns from a slaving voyage to America with a shipload of tobacco. Last year he introduced the sweet potato from America into England.

Florida, 1565. Spanish settlers in San Agostin introduce the game of billiards into America.

Pacific, 1565. Arriving from Mexico, the Spaniard Legazpi settles in Cebu in the Philippines and establishes Spanish suzerainty there. He then embarks upon the conquest of the Visayas and the island of Luzon.

Flanders, 1565. Pieter Bruegel *(the Elder)* paints a series of five paintings entitled *The Seasons.*

England, 1565. A statute empowers the Royal College of Physicians in London to carry out dissections of the human body.

Rome, 7 January 1566. Following the death late last year of Pope Pius IV, the grand inquisitor Ghislieri is elected pope and takes the name Pius V.

Scotland, 9 March 1566. The Italian musician David Rizzio, who has become a favourite of Mary, queen of Scots, is murdered at Holyroodhouse in Edinburgh on the instigation of the queen's new husband, the earl of Darnley.

Netherlands, 2 April 1566. Backed up by Calvinist riots, two hundred noblemen petition the regent, Margaret of Parma, to demand the abolition of the Inquisition in the Netherlands. She promises to send a message to Philip II of Spain. The petitioners, led by William of Orange, Egmont and Admiral Hoorne, acquire the nickname of *les gueux*, "the beggars".

France, 25 April 1566. Louise Labe, the so-called "Belle Cordiere", dies. At the age of 16 she joined the royal army as a cavalryman under the name of Captain Loys. She used her knowledge of Greek, Latin, Italian and Spanish to write poetry.

"Children's games", a characteristically rustic, detailed and lively work.

Bruegel celebrates earthy peasant lives

Brussels, 1565

Pieter Bruegel, the genius of Flemish painting, has moved to Brussels from Antwerp and begun a series of detailed paintings of peasant life. He portrays people in a much earthier way than the Italians do, although he studied in Italy after becoming a master painter in the guild at Antwerp.

A brilliant draughtsman, he finds his subjects in the simple routines of haymaking, harvesting, children's games, birds-nesting or hunting in the snow. He likes to illustrate country proverbs, and to show man in harmony with nature.

He is just completing a painting of the myth of the Fall of Icarus in which a ploughman and a shepherd are quite unaware of the drowning man who had the presumption to fly. The *Adoration of the Magi* shows a rough stable crowded with peasant faces and a homely Joseph, listening to a peasant whispering in his ear. Bruegel has two painter sons, Pieter, who is nicknamed "Hell" because he paints devils, and Jan.

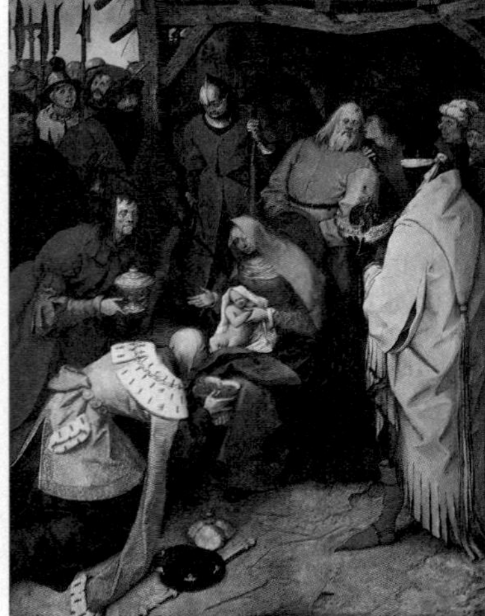

"The Adoration of the Magi".

Leader's head puts Hindu army to flight

India, 23 January 1565

The Hindu empire of Vijayanagar has been utterly defeated and its ruler slain by the combined forces of four invading Moslem states at the battle of Talikota. The Hindu ruler, Ramaraja, a veteran warrior, called up a vast army of levies to meet the invasion and was confident of victory.

Thousands of men were involved on both sides along with war elephants and artillery. Ramaraja, in the centre, faced Husain, Nizam Shah of Ahmadnagar, while his brother Tirumala confronted the ruler of Bijapur, and his other brother, Venkatadri fought the princes of Ahmadabad and Golkonda.

At first all went well for the Hindus, but a furious elephant rushed at Ramaraja's litter; his bearers dropped him; and he was captured and beheaded by Husain. His head was stuck on a long spear and at this gory sight his army fled.

Malta recaptured after falling to Turks

An assault on the Knights of St John during the Turks' failed siege.

Malta, September 1565

After one of the most heroic defensive actions in the history of warfare, the Turks have been repelled from Malta. It is a major setback for Suleiman's hopes of establishing control of the Mediterranean.

The Ottoman fleet having wrecked Philip II's navy and occupied Jerba in 1558, and Turkish corsairs having subsequently established control of most of the North African coast, there seemed little hope for Malta when Turkish ships converged on the island on 18 May. But in Suleiman's absence there was division between Piale Pasha, the head of the navy, and Mustafa Pasha, the land commander. The Knights of St John fought with extraordinary courage, notably in holding the fortress of St Elmo for more than a month with only a few hundred men. When it fell only nine defenders remained alive, and they had claimed the life of Dragut, the leader of the Turkish corsairs.

When a Christian fleet from Sicily arrived to reinforce the Maltese, the Turks were too demoralised to continue. Only a quarter of their forces returned to Istanbul.

Enchanted garden of the duke of Orsini

Italy, 1565

The intellectual duke of Orsini has indulged his taste for the bizarre by having a *sacro bosco* (enchanted garden) laid out around his villa at Bomarzo in Tuscany. Rocks have been transformed into ogres, dragons, nymphs and mermaids, while architectural follies, such as a classical temple, litter the estate.

The architect of the duke's whim is the celebrated Ligorio, who designed the Villa d'Este at Tivoli in 1550 and has also worked at the Vatican for Pope Pius IV. He is one of a group of architects working chiefly in Rome and Tuscany who have achieved notable results in landscape gardening; others are Giovanni Lippi and da Vignola. The gardens at Bomarzo are very different from the sumptuous formality of the Villa d'Este; there, the natural environment is subjected to the rules of formal architectural symmetry. At the Villa Orsini, on the other hand, Ligorio's designs pay respect to the predominantly hilly natural setting.

An ogre's head at Bomarzo.

Spanish wipe out a French settlement

A later, fanciful, impression of Ribault among the natives of Florida.

Florida, October 1565

The French settlement at Fort Caroline has been wiped out, and hundreds have been put to the sword by Spanish troops. The massacre is the culmination of several years of tension between the French and Spanish in the region, exacerbated by religious differences.

Captain Jean Ribault and 150 French Huguenots arrived in Florida in May 1562, but the settlers ran out of food and began to eat each other, and the survivors returned to France. In June last year, Rene de Goulaine de Laudonniere, the captain's second-in-command, established a new settlement at Fort Caroline, on the river of May.

This June, the Spanish commander Pedro Menendez de Aviles set out to destroy the French settlement before reinforcements could arrive. Ribault returned with an auxiliary force on 28 August, just as Menendez entered the harbour, which he named San Agostin. On 13 September Ribault's attempt to attack the Spanish was foiled by a storm, and 200 men were shipwrecked, captured and massacred by the Spanish. Seven days later the Spanish army attacked Fort Caroline.

The attackers showed no mercy, slaughtering 132 people within an hour. Those who surrendered were killed too, including Ribault. Only a few Catholics and some women and children were spared. Menendez has written to his king, justifying the killings as "necessary to the service of God and your majesty". Some were hanged under a placard which read: "I do this not as to Frenchmen, but as to Lutherans."

King's wives hold the key to African gold

Mozambique, 1565

In spite of the assassination of its envoy, the Jesuit Goncola da Silveira, in 1561, by a conspiracy of the king of Munhumutapa and Arab traders, Portugal is continuing to secure its hold on the lower Zambezi area.

So far its occupation has been unprofitable. The gold that brought the Portuguese here remains continually just out of reach the gold traders moving inland whenever the Portuguese approach. Arab traders have allied themselves with the indigenous people to exclude Portuguese traders; and the countryside is unable to feed the local population, let alone provide a surplus for Portugal. Portugal's strength is in its friendship with the king of Munhumutapa's chief wife, the *Mazarira*. Through her the Portuguese are finding a way into the African kingdom. She has moved into the Christian compound at Sena, and she calls herself the Portuguese colonists' "mother". Significantly, the Moslems are represented by the king's second wife.

1566 (1566-1568)

Florida, May 1566. The Spanish fend off an Indian attack on their newly established colony of San Agostin, but lose their supplies and most of their fort to a fire.

London, 7 June 1566. Sir Thomas Gresham lays the foundation stone of the Royal Exchange.

Netherlands, August 1566. A wave of religious iconoclasm hits Flanders, Ghent, Antwerp and the northern provinces. Calvinists attack hundreds of monasteries and churches. The revolt is rooted in hatred of the Inquisition and soaring grain prices.

Japan, 1566. Ieyasu, who formed an alliance with the powerful nobleman Oda Nobunaga in 1562, takes the surname Tokugawa.

Spain, 1566. Prompted by the church, Philip II of Spain takes repressive measures against the *Moriscos* (Moors converted to Christianity). They are forbidden to speak Arabic or to wear their traditional dress.

Netherlands, 1566. With the mediation of William of Orange, the regent, Margaret of Parma, signs a compromise agreement with the Calvinist rebels.

Aegean, 1566. The Turks take possession of the island of Chios.

Florida, 1566. The first Jesuit missionaries arrive in Florida.

France, 1566. The physician and astronomer Nostradamus dies. The publication in 1555 of his *Centuries*, a book of rhymed prophecies that were widely believed, brought him a large popular following.

Venice, 1566. Tintoretto paints a cycle of canvases on the life of St Mark for the Scuola Grande de San Rocco.

Scotland, 9 February 1567. Lord Darnley, husband of Queen Mary, is killed when his house is blown up by gunpowder.

Scotland, 15 May 1567. Mary, queen of Scots, marries the earl of Bothwell, who was acquitted in a mock trial on 12 April for the murder of Lord Darnley.

Scotland, 24 July 1567. Defeated by the Protestant nobility at Carberry Hill, and discredited by the murder of Darnley and her marriage to Bothwell, Mary, queen of Scots, is imprisoned and forced to abdicate in favour of her one-year-old son James VI.

France, 10 November 1567. The 74-year-old constable of Montmorency, one of France's highest nobles, dies during an attack by his Catholic troops on a Huguenot force under Louis de Bourbon, the prince of Conde, at St Denis near Paris.

Netherlands, 1567. Ferdinand, the duke of Alba, Philip II's commander in chief, is sent to the Netherlands to help to crush the Calvinist revolt. He orders the arrest of Counts Egmont and Hoorne, moderate noble leaders, and sets up a new court to try suspected rebels.

Netherlands, 1567. William of Orange, who opposes Philip II's policy of persecution of the Protestants and has tried to secure an agreement to ensure their religious freedom, is deprived of his office of *stadtholder* of Holland, Zeeland and Utrecht.

Japan, 1567. Oda Nobunaga puts down resistance from the Saito family and takes the town of Inabayama (Gifu).

Japan, 1567. The Daibutsuden, a large building in Nara housing the great statue of the Buddha, is burnt down in fighting.

Florida, 2 March 1568. An expedition led by Pardo returns to Santa Elena having charted a route to the Mississippi river.

France, 23 March 1568. Catherine de Medici signs the peace of Longjumeau with the Huguenots, ending the second French war of religion. The 1563 edict of Amboise, which was favourable to the Huguenots, is reimposed.

Florida, 3 May 1568. A French force led by the Catholic soldier Dominique de Corgues avenges the 1565 Spanish massacre of French Huguenots. Having slaughtered hundreds of Spaniards, they burn down the San Mateo fort.

England, 19 May 1568. Defeated by the Protestants at Longside, Mary, queen of Scots, escapes captivity and flees to England, where the Queen imprisons her.

Netherlands, 5 June 1568. Faced with continuing opposition from the province of Groningen, the duke of Alba, the new viceroy, orders the execution in Brussels of 20 noble leaders, including Egmont and Hoorne. He imposes crippling taxation on the rebel province.

Rome, 19 August 1568. Pope Pius V instructs the apostolic nuncio of Spain to set up a commission to deal with the problems of missionaries in America.

Sweden, 30 September 1568. Eric XIV, king of Sweden, is deposed after showing signs of madness. His brother John III becomes king.

Caribbean, 1568. On a slaving voyage to America, the English sailors John Hawkins and Francis Drake are trapped by the Spanish at San Juan de Ulua. Two English ships are lost in the attack.

Akbar trains his soldiers while hunting

"Akbar's remorse on the hunting field": a Moghul manuscript illustration.

Agra, India, 1567

The traditional military training of his Mongol forebears is being used by the ambitious 25-year-old Moghul Emperor Akbar. His army trains as it follows the emperor on his frequent hunting expeditions. It is lean, wholly mounted and capable of great feats of mobility.

Until recently Akbar seemed interested only in hunting, pleasure and military conquest. His dismissal of the worthy regent, Bairam, who had saved his empire, the undoubted enthusiam with which he flung Bairam's son, Adham Khan, over the palace battlements, his opportunist annexation of Malwa, and his designs on the Rajput states, supported this view.

Recently he has mellowed, however. He has become more cultured and his policies are showing tolerance and understanding.

Spanish execute Dutch resistance leader

Brussels, 5 June 1568

The count of Egmont, the former administrator of the Council of the Netherlands and subsequently leader of Dutch resistance to the rule of Spain, was executed today by order of the repressive Court of Unrest, the so-called "Council of Blood".

Egmont was appointed by Philip II in 1556, ruling jointly with the prince of Orange and Philip of Hoorne. In 1563, when Philip II decided to curb the Netherlands' autonomy and to bring the Spanish Inquisition to the country, all three resigned and began challenging Spain. Their stance made them symbols of Dutch resistance, but Egmont has paid the penalty.

Lamoral, count of Egmont.

Revered Suleiman dies

Istanbul, 6 September 1566
Suleiman the Magnificent, the ruler of the Ottoman empire for the past 45 years, is dead. He is succeeded by his eldest surviving son, the incompetent drunkard Selim, all potential rivals having been eliminated by intrigue or murder.

The most powerful influence in the second half of Suleiman's reign was Roxelana, a captive from Galicia who succeeded in replacing the sultan's favourite, Gulbehar, in his affections. After bearing Suleiman a child, Roxelana became in Moslem law his wife, as no sultan's concubine had been for two centuries. In 1541 she again broke new ground by moving, with her 100 ladies-in-waiting, dressmaker and slaves, into the Grand Seraglio, where the sultan governed.

Roxelana is thought to have had a hand in the execution of Suleiman's favourite adviser, Ibrahim. Then she secured the appointment as grand vizier of Rustem Pasha, who had married her daughter by the sultan, Mihrimah. Her next target was the removal of Mustafa, the son of Suleiman and Gulbehar and the sultan's preferred heir.

When Mustafa, the governor of Amasya, grew in reputation and in the affection of the Janissaries, Roxelana and Rustem persuaded Suleiman that he was plotting to overthrow him. Mustafa was murdered on Suleiman's orders.

Suleiman at Qasr-i Shirin in Mesopotamia; C16th painting (detail).

Within three years Roxelana was dead, much mourned by Suleiman, and their two eldest sons, Selim and Bayezid, fought for the succession. When Selim won a battle at Konya in 1559, Bayezid fled to Persia. But Ottoman pressure persuaded the shah to hand him over to the sultan's executioner. Bayezid, like his half-brother, was strangled with a bowstring, as were his five sons, the youngest being aged only three.

Netherland rebels sack, loot churches

A church is ransacked by Calvinists: iconoclasm or simple looting?

Spanish Netherlands, 1566
A bad harvest and the increase in the price of bread have triggered a popular revolt, encouraged by Calvinists and other "heretics", against King Philip II of Spain.

Churches have been ransacked and gold and silver ornaments looted in villages throughout the Low Countries, as magistrates looked on helplessly. Years of smouldering resentment against the Inquisition – pursued with particular vigour in the Netherlands – erupted, to the alarm of Margaret of Parma, governor of the provinces since the departure of Philip to Spain in 1559.

As the rebellion gathered momentum, Margaret turned to Prince William of Orange, a shrewd negotiator, for help. An accord was signed which guaranteed suspension of persecution provided that the people laid down their arms and allowed Catholics to worship unmolested.

This is likely to be a fragile peace, however, as Margaret is using newly-arrived funds from Spain to build up an army.

Rising prices due to Spanish gold flood

Europe, 1568
The relentless and dramatic rise in the cost of living – up 1,000 per cent since the turn of the century – is due to the flood of gold and silver coming in from the New World, according to a French economist.

In a new monetarist treatise, quickly gaining wide acceptance, Jean Bodin points out that "the price of things 50 or 60 years ago was ten times less than at present". Recent research into the money supply shows that coinage in circulation is up by 60 per cent, nearly all of it accounted for by New World silver and gold bullion.

Bodin's theory challenges the conventional belief that food speculators and hoarders are to blame for price inflation by creating artificial scarcities.

British slave-trader escapes Spanish capture in West Indies

London, October 1568
Three English ships commanded by the slave trader John Hawkins have narrowly escaped a Spanish naval ambush in the West Indies. The incident, involving five English ships, has provoked an angry reaction in England, resulting in an undeclared state of war with Spain.

Hawkins, who escaped with his kinsman Francis Drake, is a popular and leading figure in the highly profitable trade of shipping slaves from West Africa to the Spanish West Indies, despite the ban imposed by Madrid. This voyage was Hawkins's third since 1562.

Two of Hawkins' ships were lost in the incident at San Juan de Ulua, which has angered the English crown. While Queen Elizabeth officially disapproves of slave trading, she is known to have invested privately in Hawkins' ventures.

A model of a late 16th-century English galleon, based on the plans of Mathew Baker in his "Elements of Shipwrightery" of c.1585, an important work on shipbuilding which includes many designs for ships.

1568 (1568-1570)

India, 1568. The Moghul Emperor Akbar captures the fortress of Chitor. The Rajput women perform the rite of *jauhar* – immolating themselves on funeral pyres – to save themselves from dishonour.

Japan, 1568. The nobleman Omura Sumitada, who was baptised by the Jesuits in 1562, gives permission for foreign traders to establish posts at a small fishing village called Fukae *(Nagasaki)*.

Peru, 1568. Francisco de Toledo is appointed viceroy of Peru.

Pacific, 1568. The Spanish navigator Alvaro de Mendana explores the Solomon and Ellice islands.

Rome, 1568. Giacomo Barozzi de Vignola, who succeeded Michelangelo as chief architect of St Peter's in 1564, begins work on the church of Jesus. From 1550 to 1555 he built the Villa Giulia for Pope Julius III.

France, 1568. The economist Jean Bodin argues forcefully that there is a relationship between the influx of precious metals from the Americas and the current rise in European prices.

Spain, 1568. John of the Cross founds the first monastery of barefoot Carmelites. Teresa de Avila establishes the order of barefoot Carmelite nuns.

Spain, 1568. Led by Aben Humeya and Aben Aboo, the *Moriscos (Moors converted to Christianity)* in Granada rise up in protest against the campaign of intolerance towards them which began two years ago.

France, 13 March 1569. Royalist forces defeat the Huguenots at the battle of Jarnac. Louis de Bourbon, the prince of Conde, the Huguenot leader, is murdered while crossing the river Charente by the Catholic army of the king's brother, the duke of Anjou.

Poland, 1 July 1569. By the union of Lublin, the grand duchy of Livonia is formally united with Poland. The Jagiellon king, Sigismund II Augustus, now rules over a vast state stretching from the Baltic to the Dniester.

Brussels, 5 September 1569. Pieter Bruegel, the painter of often grotesque and carnivalesque scenes of country life, dies.

India, 1569. Akbar captures the fortress of Ranthambor, bringing independent Rajput power effectively to an end.

North America, 1569. Jesuits work among the Indians, hoping to establish permanent missions *(in Florida, Georgia and South Carolina)*.

Germany, 1569. The Flemish geographer Gerardus Mercator (Gerhard Kremer) publishes a map in the form of a cylindrical projection showing all the lines of longitude as parallel.

Russia, 1569. The Ottomans fail to take Astrakhan despite hauling their ships over land from the Don to the Volga. They retreat with heavy losses and the area remains under Russian control.

Florence, 1569. Cosimo de Medici becomes grand duke of Tuscany.

Scotland, 23 January 1570. James Stewart, the Protestant earl of Moray, who was appointed regent on the abdication of Mary, queen of Scots, is assassinated.

Rome, 25 February 1570. Pope Pius V issues the bull *Regnans in Excelsis* which excommunicates Elizabeth, the queen of England. The pope releases those subjects of Elizabeth who are still loyal to the Church of Rome from all duty of obedience to the English crown.

Moscow, 25 July 1570. Czar Ivan the Terrible attends the public executions of almost all his close advisers and ministers.

France, 8 August 1570. Charles IX signs the treaty of St Germain, ending the third war of religion. The treaty gives the Huguenots a large measure of religious toleration and the security of garrison towns.

Cyprus, August 1570. The Turks overrun Cyprus and expel the Venetian garrison from the island.

Portugal, 20 October 1570. Joao de Barros, author of *Decades*, a history of the Portuguese conquests overseas, dies.

Northern Europe, 2 November 1570. A tidal wave in the North Sea destroys sea walls from Holland to Jutland. Over a thousand people are killed.

Scandinavia, 13 December 1570. The peace of Stettin puts an end to the seven-year war of the Three Crowns between Denmark and Sweden by restoring the prewar frontiers.

South-East Africa, 1570. Portuguese slave trading on the Zambezi leads to the Zimba war among the Chewa to the north.

Spain, 1570. Don John of Austria, the illegitimate son of the Emperor Charles V, harshly suppresses the Morisco uprising.

Russia, 1570. To pre-empt moves by the feudal lords towards independence, Ivan the Terrible orders the savage destruction of Novgorod by the *oprichniki*.

Japan, 1570. Portuguese ships begin trading in Nagasaki.

Mercator publishes new map of world

A 1631 map of the New World according to the great map-maker Mercator.

Duisberg, Germany, 1569

The first comprehensive map of the world has been published in Germany. Its designer, Gerhard Kremer, is a Dutch merchant who fled from the persecution of Protestants in the Netherlands.

Kremer, who is better known by the latinised name Gerardus Mercator (*mercator* means merchant) has developed an advanced system of cylindrical projection. This works outwards from the equator and permits the accurate placing of longitude, latitude, meridians and parallels.

Thus the map is invaluable to sailors, offering a degree of accuracy which has never before been available to navigators.

Spanish king halts Morisco rebellion

Granada, Spain, 1570

After a two-year war marked by appalling cruelties on both sides, Philip II of Spain has crushed the Morisco community of Granada. The Morisco revolt over the right to wear Moorish dress and maintain Moorish customs is at an end. A defeated and sullen population has been dispersed throughout Castile while 50,000 settlers have been brought to Andalucia to fill the gap. Philip's system of government was directly responsible for the outbreak of the revolt. The Moriscos had remained second-class subjects, exploited, hated and feared, and plagued by bandits of their own race. Philip refused to turn a blind eye to their Moorish customs and continue the slow process of assimilation. His half-brother Don John of Austria finally managed to crush them.

Tartar fears unite neighbour states

Lublin, 1 July 1569

Poland and Lithuania have allied themselves to form a vast multilingual union stretching from the Baltic to the Dniester. Under the Union of Lublin the two states have agreed to accept each others' religions and those of West Prussia and of Lithuania's dominions in White Russia and the Ukraine.

It is a remarkable achievement, as this union tolerates not only Jews but all types of Protestantism in officially Catholic Poland, while in Lithuania there is a majority of Orthodox Christians. One reason for the union is the danger to Lithuania from raids of the Crimea Tartars and from Muscovite imperialism. The Lithuanian nobility will now enjoy the enormous political, legal and economic privileges enjoyed by their Polish counterparts in the new union.

Duke crushes revolt in the Netherlands

Ferdinand, the duke of Alba.

Ghent, 5 June 1568

From the moment that 10,000 elite troops of the Spanish king marched through the streets of Ghent in ranks of five, followed by prostitutes in frilly dresses riding donkeys, and a host of camp followers, it was clear that the Calvinist insurrection was finally over. The new military governor of the Spanish Low Countries, the duke of Alba, has pledged himself to bring back the Inquisition and to establish a "new order" for Philip II.

From Alba's first arrival in the Netherlands, in August 1567, the behaviour of his troops underlined the ferocity with which the duke approached his task. Merchants were beaten up, and the population – even good Catholics – insulted in the streets as "traitors" and ' heretics".

Alba's regime rapidly became a dictatorship. He humiliated the civil governor, Margaret of Parma, forcing her to demobilise the army which she had raised to counter an earlier rebellion two years ago, and assuming many of her powers until she left for Italy. A new and sinister form of inquisition – the "Council of Troubles" – was set up and organised the arrests of thousands in spring this year. More than 1,000 alleged heretics were executed and a further 8,000 stripped of their property. In the Calvinist city of Tournai 500 heretical books were seized and burned.

New Spain charts old Mexico history

Mexico, 1569

An impressive new book, almost an encyclopaedia of ancient Mexico, has been published in Spain. Eleven years in the writing, it is entitled *Historia General de las cosas de la Nueva Espana*, otherwise known as the *Calepino*. Its author, the Franciscan monk Bernardino de Sahagun, is being hailed as the foremost historian of the lands which are now known as New Spain.

Sahagun began his career as a missionary to the New World, and has devoted his career to the Colegio de Santiago Tlatelolco, which is dedicated to the education of young Indians.

In parallel to his religious undertakings, Sahagun has developed as an outstanding historian of the native tribes of Mexico. While his central task as a missionary is to wipe out native idolatry and replace it with Christian worship, his natural inclination has been to discover as much as possible about the Indians.

The fruits of these studies are contained in his *Historia*, a work that was begun with aim of giving his fellow-priests as wide as possible a knowledge of the culture with which they deal. It is not the first such history, but Sahagun's research methods make it the most authoritative. He is an expert in native crafts, the best of which he has seen himself, and native language, which he both reads and writes.

Learning local ways: one of de Soto's men who decided to stay in America.

Pope crowns Cosimo de Medici in Tuscany

Florence, 1569

Cosimo de Medici, who has been "head of the government and city of Florence" since 1537, and had established himself at the expense of the emperor Charles V as a major power in Italy, has taken a new title, indicative of his importance as a leader, civic reformer and connoisseur. As from today, when he was crowned by Pope Pius V, he will rule as the first archduke of Tuscany.

Cosimo's road to power has lain in his determination to free Florence from its domination by Charles V. In 1543, when Charles needed funds for his wars in France, he accepted a large payment from Cosimo to withdraw imperial troops from Medici territories. Since then Cosimo has been an independent ruler.

He wrote in 1545: "We are a ruler who accepts the authority of no one apart from God." His career has been concentrated on maintaining Tuscan autonomy. The state may not have expanded its boundaries, but it is far stronger than ever before.

Archduke Cosimo de Medici, painted in 1545 by Bronzino.

Ancient Romans inspire Palladio's villas

Italy, 1570

This year has seen the appearance of a stimulating new work on architecture by the Venetian Andrea di Pietro, known as Palladio. Called the *Four Books of Architecture* it is inspired by the ancient Roman Vitruvius, whose work *De Architectura* Palladio helped to publish in 1556. Palladio describes how he sought out ancient Roman ruins "to find what the whole must have been, and give the design of them". The work is a guide to classical architecture, with sections on orders, materials, cities, churches, and houses (palaces and villas). He uses ancient buildings and his own work as examples.

The classically-inspired symmetry of Palladio can be seen in several fine palaces in the region near Venice, especially in the city of Vicenza. Symmetry is not always possible for Palladio's villas, though, because many of them are essentially grand farmhouses and require various outbuildings.

Classical symmetry: part of the Villa Capra at Vicenza, by Palladio.

1570 (1570-1572)

North America, c.1570. The Iroquois Indians in north-eastern North America form a league of tribes whose aim is to meet and settle their differences peacefully.

Brazil, 1570. A law is passed stating that only those Indians taken prisoner during the course of a "just war", or those suspected of cannibalism, may be enslaved.

Arabia, 1570. The Turks occupy Yemen.

Antwerp, 1570. The first geographical atlas, prepared by Abraham Ortelius, is published.

Spain, 1570. The Council of the Indies passes a law prohibiting *mestizos* (people who are half Indian and half European) from becoming notaries or *caciques* (local rulers).

Netherlands, 1570. The Emperor Maximilian II ennobles the Dutch musician Orlando di Lasso, the composer of many masses and motets. As well as church music, he has written a large number of secular works.

Rome, 1570. Pope Pius V issues instructions that Indians in America should be excluded from the jurisdiction of the Inquisition.

Venice, 1570. The Florentine sculptor and architect Jacopo Sansovino dies.

Palestine, c.1570. The town of Safed, on a mountain in upper Galilee, has become the centre of Jewish mysticism. At the end of last century the community was strengthened by an influx of refugees from Spain. The Sephardic element increased after the Ottoman conquest in 1516. The spiritual flowering of the town has been accompanied by material prosperity: there is a thriving weaving industry and trade in oil, honey, silk and spices.

North America, 2 February 1571. All eight members of a Jesuit mission in Virginia are murdered by Indians who had pretended to be their friends. The killers were led by Don Luis, an Indian who had been converted to Christianity, taken a Spanish name and been a guest at the court of Philip II.

Florence, 13 February 1571. The silversmith and sculptor Benvenuto Cellino, who is famous for his colourful autobiography, dies.

Mediterranean, 20 May 1571. Venice and Spain form a holy league with Pope Pius V to counter Ottoman expansion.

Mediterranean, September 1571. Don John of Austria and the navy of the Holy League defeat the Turks at the Battle of Lepanto, dealing a severe blow to Turkish naval power.

England, 1571. A Catholic plot – masterminded by the Italian banker Roberto Ridolfi, and supported by Spain – to murder Queen Elizabeth and replace her with Mary, queen of Scots, is discovered by William Cecil, Lord Burghley. In Ridolfi's absence abroad, the duke of Norfolk, one of the conspirators, is executed.

Japan, 1571. Oda Nobunaga destroys the rebellious Ikko sect, based near Osaka, and then razes the Enryakuji temple on Mount Hiei, home to a large number of soldier-monks.

Angola, 1571. Portuguese slave trading on the Angola coast leads to the Jaga war in the interior.

Hungary, 1571. Stephen Bathory becomes prince of Transylvania.

Rome, 1571. On the orders of Pope Pius V, an index of prohibited books is drawn up.

Philippines, 1571. The Spaniard Lopez de Legazpi founds the city of Manila.

Mexico, 1571. The Spanish instal an inquisitorial tribunal in Mexico.

Spain, 1571. A doctor called Nicolas Monardes publishes a book praising the medicinal value of tobacco.

England, March 1572. The *Gueux de mer* (Sea Beggars) – Calvinist rebels who fled from the duke of Alba's repression in their native Netherlands – are expelled from English ports. They have harried shipping between Spain and the Netherlands for three years.

Netherlands, 1 April 1572. The Sea Beggars under Guillaume de la Marck land in Holland and capture the small town of Briel.

Netherlands, April 1572. William of Orange returns to the province of Holland, where he is acknowledged as *stadholder* (local official).

Rome, 13 May 1572. Following the death of Pius V, Ugo Buoncompagni of Bologna is elected pope and takes the name Gregory XIII. Pius' six-year papacy marked a decisive stage in the implementation of the Counter-reformation developed at the Council of Trent, with the publication of the Catholic catechism in 1566, the breviary in 1568 and the missal in 1570.

Peru, May 1572. The Spanish capture Vilcabamba, the stronghold of the Inca rebels under Tupac Amaru.

India, 1572. The Moghul Emperor Akbar abolishes the *jizya* tax on non-Moslems.

Ivan the Terrible terrorises feudal lords

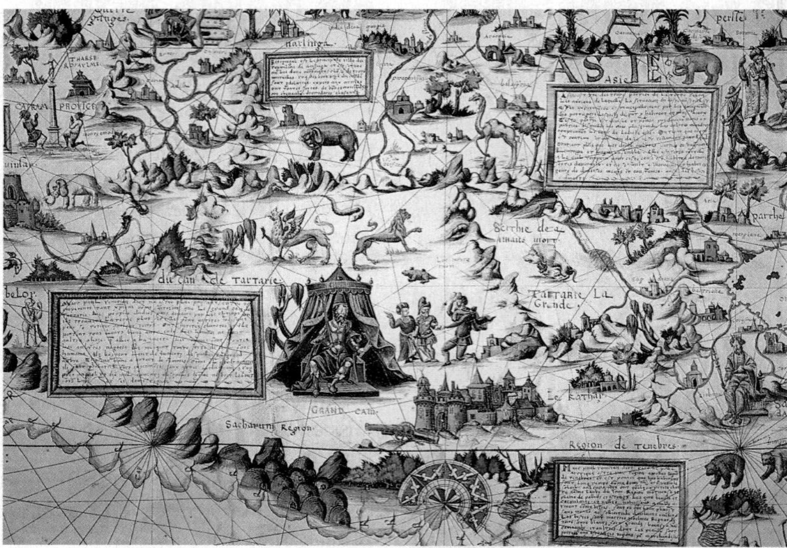

A map of Siberia and northern Asia, after Marco Polo's descriptions.

Russia, 1572

The eight-year reign of terror unleashed by Ivan the Terrible appears to have come to an end with the czar's decision to disband the *oprichnina*, the separate administration and court set up to do his bidding. Years of absurd denunciations, sudden arrests, executions and terror simply for the sake of terror have shattered Muscovite society.

Ivan established the *oprichnina* after a period of bloody infighting with the *boyars*, the aristocratic classes. Determined to eliminate all villains and traitors, and reaffirm his power and the servility of the peasants, he divided Muscovy into two distinct realms. The *oprichnina* was that part which came under his personal rule.

Its main instrument was a select corps of 6,000 oprichniki who wore black uniforms. Their badges were a dog's head and broom, symbols of their doglike devotion to the czar and their role in sweeping away treason from the state. Their atrocities reached their peak two years ago in the sacking of Novgorod after the town was suspected of seeking union with Poland. More than 60,000 people were killed – some by being pushed through holes in the ice – and the town devastated.

Rich gold and enamel ornaments of (from top) the fleece, two stallions and St Michael.

Index to censor books for heresy

Rome, 1571

Pope Pius V has formalised the censorship moves by recent popes in the Congregation of the Index, a tribunal of the Roman *curia* charged with examining books and ensuring that they do not contain any heretical ideas. Pius IV published a list of prohibited books in 1564, but it was Paul IV who brought in the first official Index in 1559. He not only banned middle-ofthe-road works, such as those of Erasmus, he prohibited any bible not in Latin. The puritanical zeal has even led to the painting – over of the nudes in Michelangelo's *Last Judgement* in the Sistine Chapel.

"Sea Beggars" challenge Spanish rule

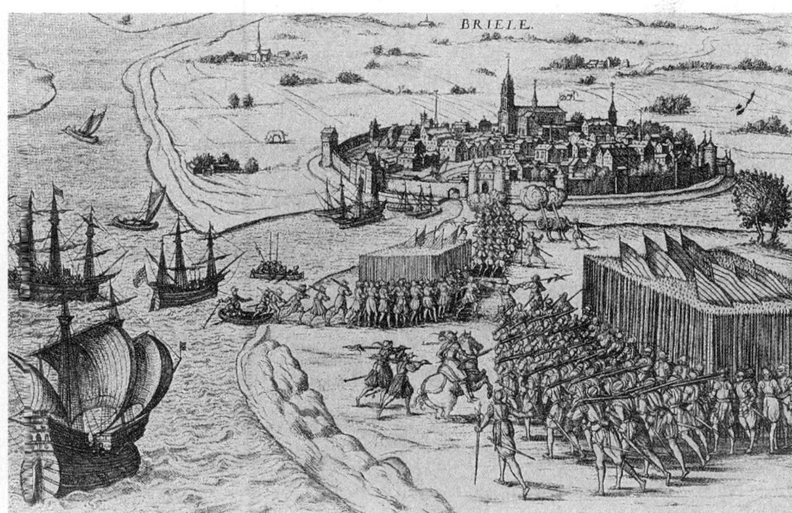

The capture from the Spaniards of Briel by the so-called "Sea Beggars".

Briel, Netherlands, 1 April 1572
A well-organised force of Netherlands privateers and foreign mercenaries – "the Sea Beggars" – has captured this small seaport and set up a bridgehead for the full-scale invasion of the Low Countries. The privateers were licensed by Prince William of Orange who has twice failed to invade the Netherlands.

Despite assurances of their peaceful intentions, the invaders have forced the mayor to swear allegiance and fortify his town against a Spanish counter-attack. Monasteries have been sacked and Catholic nobles removed from the town council. Prince William is counting on support from the artisan classes in their resentment at the hated "tenth penny" tax to be imposed by the tyranical duke of Alba to help a bankrupted Spain and pay his army in the Low Countries.

Bad harvests, famine, floods and mass unemployment have created an ideal climate for a second rebellion. Last month the streets of Ghent were littered with a parody of the Lord's Prayer addressed to the duke:

"Cursed father who in Brussels doth dwell,

"Cursed be thy name in Heaven and in Hell," it began.

The Sea Beggars originally planned to use Dover in England as the base for their operations, but Queen Elizabeth expelled them from the port.

New stock exchange founded in London

London, 1571
The Royal Exchange has been built at Cornhill in the City of London and inaugurated by the queen. It was founded by the businessman and royal agent Sir Thomas Gresham, who worked for many years raising loans in the Low Countries and exporting arms and other goods to Britain. He was a regular visitor to Antwerp's Stock Exchange, and wanted Britain to offer similar trading facilities.

The Royal Exchange is built over piazzas supported by marble pillars. The ground floor is reserved for wholesalers, with retail shops in the gallery above. Merchants are summoned to meetings by bells.

Gresham, by Sir Antonio Moro.

Christians smash Turks in holy war at sea

Christian and Turkish galley fleets clash at the Battle of Lepanto.

Mediterranean Sea, 7 September 1571
It was a spectacle that no survivor of this great sea battle will ever forget. Two great galleys, one flying the pennant of the crucified Christ, the other a huge flag with verses from the Koran, were being rowed directly at each other, gathering speed all the time as the galley-masters whipped their slaves to even greater efforts.

In *La Real*, the Spanish flagship, Don John of Austria drew his sword and braced himself for the inevitable head-on crash as Ali Pasha, the Turkish commander, ordered his men on the *Sultana* to prepare to board. The Cross was meeting the Crescent in what many believe will be the last great encounter between galley fleets.

It was the Turkish invasion of Cyprus by Selim II, Suleiman the Great's successor, that brought the combined fleets of Spain, Venice and Pope Pius V face-to-face with the larger Turkish fleet. Famagusta had fallen, and reports of unbelievable atrocities had incensed the Christians to a crusading fervour as they sailed from Messina.

Pasha's fleet was anchored in the gulf when the Christian fleet hove into sight. The Turks hesitated before moving out to attack in a crescent formation. It was then that *La Real* began her charge forward. The flagships struck so hard that they locked together. Fierce fighting continued for two hours with the fiery young Don John, the son of Charles V, leading his men on to the *Sultana's* foredeck and confronting Ali Pasha in person. The Turkish commander was killed by a bullet from an *arquebus*, his head struck off and presented to Don John.

The Turks have lost 230 galleys in this battle; the Christians, 16. News of the victory will bring great rejoicing throughout the west.

1572 (1572-1573)

Peru, May 1572. Tupac Amaru, the last of the Inca kings, is executed.

Paris, 24 August 1572. In Paris to celebrate the wedding of Marguerite of Valois, the daughter of Catherine de Medici, and the Bourbon Huguenot, Henry of Navarre, thousands of Huguenots are slaughtered with Catherine's connivance.

Paris, 24 August 1572. Among the victims of the massacre is the mathematician and logician Pierre de la Ramee, known as Petrus Ramus. A strong opponent of Aristotelianism, Ramus saw his work condemned by the Sorbonne.

Paris, August 1572. In the aftermath of the massacre, Henry of Navarre renounces the Protestant faith.

Paris, 22 September 1572. The painter Francois Clouet dies. Trained by his father, Jean Clouet, whom he succeeded as court painter, Francois painted four French kings: Francis I, Henry II, Francis II and Charles IX.

Scotland, 24 November 1572. John Knox, the father of the Scottish Reformation, dies in Edinburgh. He was forced to flee to Geneva, where he became a friend and disciple of John Calvin. The rebellion against the Catholic Mary, queen of Scots, in 1559 enabled him to return to Scotland.

Florence, 28 November 1572. The painter Agnolo di Cosimo, known as Bronzino, dies. A pupil of Pontormo, he became the official painter of the grand duchy of Tuscany in 1539. From the second generation of mannerists, he introduced a style of portraiture characterised by cold colours and an icy precision.

India, 1572. The forces of the Moghul Emperor Akbar overrun the fertile region of Gujarat.

Caribbean, 1572. The English sailor Francis Drake launches attacks on Spanish harbours and ambushes and loots Spanish ships.

France, 1572. Henri Etienne publishes his *Thesaurus Linguae Graecae* (Thesaurus of the Greek Language).

Spain, 1572. Sister Teresa of Avila writes the *Book of the Foundations*. She is the prioress at the convent of the Incarnation in Avila, where John of the Cross is the confessor of the Carmelites.

Peru, 1572. Extraction begins from the silver mine of Potosi. Francisco de Toledo, the viceroy, sets up a system by which the miners receive a collective payment in kind, usually of cloth, which is shared out among them by a chief.

Italy, 1572. Woodcuts of bananas and other American fruit trees seen for the first time in Europe appear in Girolamo Benzoni's *Historia del Mundo Nuovo*.

Istanbul, 7 March 1573. Venice concludes a peace with the Turks by which the doge of Venice recognises Turkish possession of Cyprus.

Poland, 11 May 1573. Henry of Anjou, the brother of Charles IX, the king of France, becomes the first elected king of Poland. His election was secured by his mother, Catherine de Medici. In Poland, Henry has to face a hostile nobility which wants to keep effective power.

Rome, 11 May 1573. The architect Giacomo Barozzi da Vignola dies.

Netherlands, December 1573. Recalled to Spain, the duke of Alba is succeeded as viceroy by Luis de Requesens y Zyniga. Brill, Enkhuisen, Flushing, Arnemuide, Veere, Holland and Zeeland are in the hands of the Sea Beggars.

Japan, 1573. The *shogun* Ashikaga Yoshiaki submits to the nobleman Oda Nobunaga, spelling the end of the Muromachi *shogunate*, which was founded in 1335.

South-East Africa, 1573. After punishing Mwenemutapa for the murder, in 1561, of the missionary Father da Silveira, a Portuguese expedition under Francisco Barreto withdraws from the Zambezi valley.

France, 1573. Catherine de Medici makes peace with the Protestants, ending the fourth war of religion, which broke out after the St Bartholomew's Day massacre.

Netherlands, 1573. The Spanish recapture Harlem from the rebels.

North Africa, 1573. The Spaniards, led by Don John of Austria, seize Tunis and Bizerta from the Berbers.

Brazil, 1573. After protests by the colonists at restrictions imposed by a 1570 law, new legislation makes slavery common practice.

England, 1573. Christopher Tye, the organist to the Chapel Royal and composer of some notable church music, dies.

Spain, 1573. Laws are passed barring territorial conquest in the Indies without royal sanction.

Spain, 1573. Sister Teresa of Avila writes her mystical handbook *The Way of Perfection*.

Argentina, 1573. The city of Cordoba is founded.

Venice, 1573. Tintoretto completes his painting of *The Battle of Lepanto* for the chamber of the grand council in the doges' palace.

Drake captures Spanish treasure

London, 1573

Captain Francis Drake is said to be back from his latest raid on the Spanish Main with silver worth £40,000. The government seems pleased with the loot, but Drake must hide like a fugitive. The reason: London wants normal relations with Madrid. A triumphal reception for the man who recruited runaway slaves to ambush bullion convoys ashore at Panama last February is a major embarrassment. So Drake hides, perhaps in Ireland. But is he a pirate?

A later engraving of Drake, whose deeds London covertly approves.

Neither he nor his queen feels bound by a trade treaty of 1494, blessed by the pope, which divides "Latin America" between Spain and Portugal. Queen Elizabeth licensed him as a privateer five years ago. Drake, a fervent Protestant, also has personal motives for his raids. Five years ago his ship *Judith* (50 tons) was part of an English fleet attacked by Spanish sailors while anchored in the Caribbean port of San Juan de Ulua. Drake limped back to England but never forgot Spanish treachery in betraying a local agreement to trade and not fight. He claimed compensation. When none was forthcoming, he recovered the damages himself, with interest. Since then he has become a legend. For his attack on Panama, he sailed last year with two ships which concealed three prefabricated pinnaces, which he reconstructed for raids on Nombre de Dios.

Church design reflects Catholic authority

Rome, 1571

Giacomo Barozzi da Vignola, who took over the direction of the building of St Peter's from Michelangelo, has produced a new design which is being adopted throughout the Catholic world. His impressive church of Jesus has been adopted by the Jesuits as the uniform standard for all churches.

The front view of Giacomo Barozzi da Vignola's church of Jesus.

The essence of the design is that it creates a huge space in the form of a Latin cross. There is an unbroken cornice supporting a lofty barrel vault. The nave is brightly lit by the cupola, in contrast to many existing churches where the light is very dim.

The buildings have been widely admired for their architectural splendour, but the reason for the design is theological rather than aesthetic. It reflects the determination of the papacy to resist reformist and Protestant tendencies and locate the Mass on the high altar.

The centrality of the Mass is reflected in the building. The altar is richly decorated with marble, stucco, fresco and gilded plaster, contrasting with the simple unadorned walls of the nave. The design allows a view of the brightly-lit altar by the maximum number of people. In the centre of it all the priest presides over this colourful ritual, exemplifying the authority of the church

Massacre on St Bartholomew's Day

Coligny is wounded (l.) and assassinated (r.), precipitating the massacre.

Catherine de Medici: the instigator.

Paris, 24 August 1572
A most terrible massacre of Huguenots is taking place in Paris. It started just before dawn this morning, St Bartholomew's Day, when a band of Catholics burst into the house of Gaspard de Coligny, disembowelled him and threw him out of his bedroom window, still alive.

Coligny was the target of an assassin two days ago as he was leaving the Louvre, but the shot only wounded him. It seems that he was marked for death because of his influence over the young Charles IX. The king's mother, Catherine de Medici, fearing that Coligny was pushing the king into war with Spain, conspired with the Catholic leader, Henry of Guise, to have him removed.

When the attempt failed the king swore vengeance on the assassins so, in order to save herself, Catherine convinced him that the Huguenots were about to rebel and begged him to authorise the killing of their leaders by the Guises.

Many of the Huguenots were in Paris celebrating the marriage of their leader, Henry of Navarre, to the king's sister, Margaret. A list of those to be killed was drawn up, headed by Coligny. But once the killing started the people of Paris, apparently overcome by bloodlust, started a general massacre. It is still going on, with men, women and children being slaughtered in their hundreds. There are reports that the killing is spreading to other towns. Henry of Navarre has been spared, but he was arrested at dawn, taken to the king's chamber and forced to abjure Protestantism.

English composers are major force in European music

England, 1573
England has emerged alongside Italy in the front rank of modern European music. Robert White is a name to note among rising young talent, but 35-year-old Thomas Tallis is the most influential figure. He is seeking a royal licence to publish music with a gifted 30-year-old pupil, William Byrd, who, like Tallis, is a Gentleman of London's Chapel Royal. Tallis is regarded as one of Europe's finest composers, although his early work was more old-fashioned than that of Christopher Tye (c.1505-72) and lacked the festal qualities of John Taverner (c.1490-1545), who worked at the new Cardinal College (*now Christ Church*) in Oxford.

But the mature Tallis is master of most forms and styles, from masses and other church music in Latin and English to small-scale instrumental works. A member of the royal household from 1543, he was one of the first to write music for the new Anglican liturgy of 1547-53, and composed for the Catholic Queen Mary in 1553-58. One of his newest pieces is an astonishing motet, *Spem in alium*, written for 40 parts.

Last of the Incas beheaded in Cuzco

Cuzco, May 1572
Tupac Amaru, the last of the Incas, the hereditary sun-kings of Peru, is dead and his kingdom destroyed. Found guilty of opposing the Spanish colonisation of his country and of encouraging paganism, he has been beheaded.

His speedy and, to many eyes, unjust trial and sentence to death shocked Peru. Even the Spaniards appeared to regret the death of this unfortunate man, and many leading clergymen attempted in vain to gain him a reprieve. But Viceroy Francisco de Toledo, determined to stamp out the Incas' power, refused to reverse his decision.

Before his death the Inca, who had been converted to Christianity while in prison, denounced sun-worship and called on his followers to embrace Christ.

The last of the Inca kings, Tupac Amaru, is beheaded in Peru by the Spaniards.

Astronomer shocked by a starry surprise

Copenhagen, 1572
The Danish astronomer Tycho Brahe has sighted a new star in the heavens. On 11 November Brahe observed in the constellation of Cassiopeia a body more brilliant than Venus where no star was supposed to be.

He carried out further research and found that this novel object lies beyond the moon in the realm of what are believed to be "fixed" stars. The scientific community is both intrigued and disquieted by this. It means that the stars are not, as depicted by Aristotle, immutable and eternal. They can come and perhaps go. Together with the Copernican idea now taking hold, that Earth is not the centre of the cosmos, Brahe's sighting shakes still further the concept of celestial stability.

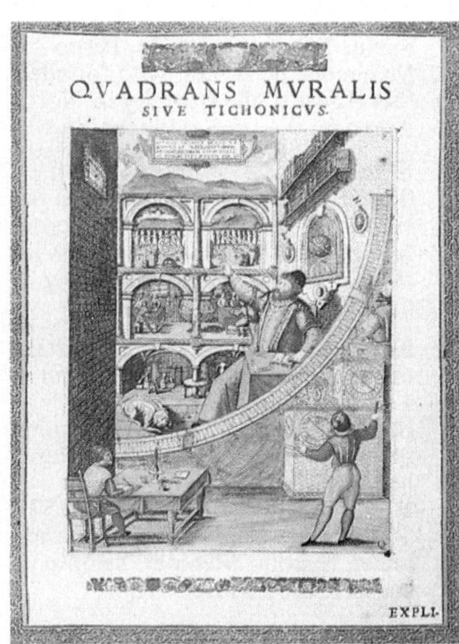

The pioneering Danish astronomer Tycho Brahe in his observatory, from his "Astronomiae Instauratae Mechanicae" of 1599.

1573 (1573-1575)

France, 1574. The duke of Alencon, the youngest son of Catherine de Medici, conspires to kidnap his brother, King Charles IX, but is betrayed by his fellow conspirators.

Mexico, 28 February 1574. On the orders of the Holy Office of the Inquisition, founded in New Spain three years ago, 60 people are scourged and sent to the galleys, seven are imprisoned, and two Englishmen and an Irishman are burnt for heresy.

Netherlands, April 1574. Luis de Requesens y Zuniga, who arrived in Brussels at the end of last year to replace the duke of Alba as governor of the Netherlands, defeats the Protestant rebels at Mook Heide.

France, 30 May 1574. Charles IX dies at the age of 24 after reigning for nearly 14 years. For the first ten years of his reign (1560-70) France was governed by his mother, Catherine de Medici, as regent. She remains a formidable influence. Charles is succeeded as king by his brother Henry III, who is to return from Poland where he was elected king last year.

Netherlands, June 1574. Requesens, the governor of the Netherlands, advises Philip II to grant a general pardon to the Protestant rebels and to abolish the hated "tenth penny" tax imposed by his predecessor, the duke of Alba.

Florence, 27 June 1574. The painter and writer Giorgio Vasari dies. His work includes frescoes for the Vatican of the *Life of Paul III* and the decoration of the Palazzo Vecchio and the Uffizi gallery in Florence. He wrote an account of *The Lives of the Most Eminent Italian Architects, Painters and Sculptors*.

Spain, 7 September 1574. Pedro Menendez de Aviles, who founded San Agostin, the first city in North America, dies in Santander.

Germany, 1574. With the Polish throne left vacant on the return of Henry III to France, the Emperor Maximilian II prepares to press his claims against Stephen Bathory, the prince of Transylvania.

Istanbul, 1574. Selim II, the sultan of the Ottomans, dies after a fall in a Turkish bath. A cultivated patron of arts and sciences despite being dubbed Selim the Drunkard, he largely retired to his harem after the defeat at Lepanto in 1571. State affairs were left to his grand vizier, Sokollu Mehmet. Selim is succeeded by Murad III.

Netherlands, 1574. The university of Leyden is founded.

North Africa, 1574. The Ottomans recapture Tunis and Bizerta and drive the Spanish out of La Goletta. Don John of Austria took Tunis for the Spanish in October last year with an expeditionary force of 20,000 men.

Spain, 1574. The "black code", a series of laws concerning the slavery of Africans in the Americas, is published.

Peru, 1574. A chair is created at the university of Lima for the study of Quechua, the language of the native Andean peoples.

Netherlands, February 1575. The Emperor Maximilian II mediates at a conference at Breda between the governor-general, Requesens, and Protestant representatives from Holland and Zeeland. Requesens agrees to withdraw Spanish troops and officials from the Netherlands.

Spain, 1575. The Spanish state goes bankrupt for the second time.

France, October 1575. Following the outbreak of the fifth war of religion, the Catholic forces under Henry, the duke of Guise, defeat the Protestants at the battle of Dormans.

Poland, 14 December 1575. Supported by the Turks, Stephen Bathory, the prince of Transylvania, is elected king of Poland.

France, 1575. The duke of Alencon forms an alliance against his brother, King Henry III, with the Bourbon Henry of Navarre.

Bohemia, 1575. Rudolf, the son of the Emperor Maximilian II, who was elected king of Hungary in 1572, becomes king of Bohemia.

Rome, 1575. The pope approves the foundation of the Institute of Oratory by Philip Neri.

Peru, 1575. Friar Cristobal de Molina compiles an anthology of *Tales and Ceremonies of the Incas*, a collection of Inca hymns.

Indian Ocean, 1575. Ralambo succeeds to the throne of the Merina kingdom in Madagascar.

Angola, 1575. The Portuguese found the city of Luanda.

England, 1575 Sir Humphrey Gilbert, the MP and explorer, publishes *Discourse to Prove a Passage by the North West to Cathay...* arguing for English colonisation of the far east.

Europe, 1575 The population of Paris is an estimated 300,000 people, compared with London's c.180,000 and Cologne's c.35,000.

Italy, 1575 An outbreak of the plague, which started in Sicily, travels north through the country and reaches as far as Milan.

Europeans face New World inquisitors

Mexico, 28 February 1574

Seventy Englishmen and an Irishman have been sentenced in the greatest trial by the Inquisition since it was officially set up in Spanish America in 1571. The men were all survivors of a slave-trading expedition to the Caribbean under Sir John Hawkins, who was forced to abandon them in 1568. After many tribulations they had mainly ended up as servants to Spanish colonists in Mexico City.

As potential "Lutheran" heretics the men were obvious targets for the zeal of the newly-arrived Inquisitors. They were questioned for months and eventually condemned at a public *auto-da-fe* (act of faith) for offences ranging from heresy to asserting that fornication before marriage was not a sin. Sixty-one men received from 100 to 300 lashes, followed by up to ten years as galley-slaves; seven were ordered to serve in monasteries for five years. Three men, including the Irishman, earned the honour of being the first people to be burnt as heretics in the New World.

Grand mosque at Edirne is completed

Six years in construction, the Selim mosque at Edirne is now complete.

Edirne, Turkey, 1575

The great mosque of Selim is complete, six years after building began. It is probably the finest architectural achievement of Sinan, who was also responsible for the Suleiman mosque in Istanbul.

The dominant feature of the building is the massive central dome. The interior is an octagonal baldachin built within a rectangular enclosure. Sinan may have got this idea from the octagonal mausoleum of Sultan Oljaitu Khodabandah Khan at Sultaniya, in Azerbaijan. The four symmetrical minarets emphasise the centrality of the design.

This magnificent mosque is a supreme expression of the spirit of reason which is sweeping through Ottoman art and architecture.

Polish nobles elect a Frenchman as king

A 1585 tapestry shows a French ballet in honour of Polish ambassadors.

Poland, 1573
In an extraordinary development a devious, egotistical and effeminate Frenchman, Henry of Anjou, has secured the crown of Poland. Henry, whose candidacy was put forward by his mother, Catherine de Medici, was voted king by a majority of some 40,000 Polish nobles and gentry assembled for the election on the Warsaw plain.

The event was precipitated by the death of Sigismund II Augustus, the son of Sigismund the Old. He had no heir, so with him disappeared the Jagiellon dynasty of Poland which had lasted some two centuries. Several footloose young princes ambitious for a crown and a piece of land they could call their own became interested, but by dint of propaganda and persuasion Catherine succeeded in building up a pro-French party among the Polish nobles. At the same time the powers of the Polish crown are being drastically reduced, and Poland is going to be governed by the Senate. Henry may lose interest in Polish power.

Rhyme Thyme comes for Britain's farmers

Suffolk, England, 1573
A Suffolk farmer, Thomas Tusser, has used his gift for verse to sow a rich harvest with the publication of a remarkable work, *Five hundred good points of Husbandry*. It is a book of rhymed proverbs, designed to help Tusser's fellow farmers

Cambridge University educated Tusser has already published his *One hundred good points* in prose, but the poems are more easily remembered. He has advice for every season. When Spring comes, for instance:

Keep threshing for thresher till May be come in,
to have to be sure fresh chaff in thy bin;
And somewhere to scramble for hog and for hen,
and work, when it raineth, for loitering me men.

And the farmer's wife is expected to make "the seede cake, the pasties and furmety pot". So thus ...

Good Ploughmen look weekly of custome and right
for rostmeat on Sundays and Thursdays at night:
Thus doing and keping such custome and guise,
They call thee good huswife, they love thee likewise.

Spanish monarchy plunges into the red

Glory before profit: frescoes illuminate the Escorial, a Spanish royal palace.

Spain, 1575
Imperial Spain, the dominant force in Europe and the New World for nearly a century, is bankrupt. For all its colonies, for all its power and prestige in Europe, years of costly wars – in the Netherlands, against England – have drained what was always a flimsy royal treasury in which apparent glory was set above hard-nosed practical planning.

Some would put the start of the problems as far back as the 1490s when first the Jews and then the Conversos were expelled, seriously depleting the country's merchant class, but the riches of the Americas have never been invested properly.

Philip II, who inherited from his father Charles V a country at the peak of its powers, is an accomplished statesman, but he has let imperial interests override economic ones. The main consequence is that the Spanish crown cannot pay its troops in the Netherlands, so mercenaries frequently mutiny and thus military gains are lost.

Sultan dies after fall in Turkish bath

Istanbul, 1574
Selim the Drunkard is dead. After an undistinguished eight-year rule, the sultan met an ignominious death. He died of a fever after cracking his skull when falling down drunk in a Turkish bath. He is succeeded by his son Murad III.

Selim was short and fat, and no warrior. Nor did he have much appetite for affairs of state, which he left largely in the hands of Sokollu, his grand vizier. He whiled away his time drinking wine in the seraglio, surrounded by flatterers and cronies. Abroad, Ottoman prestige has been badly dented by the empire's defeat at Lepanto in 1571.

Selim II: from a book of poems.

1576

Germany, 19 January 1576. The *meistersinger* Hans Sachs, author of *lieder*, aphorisms and comedies for carnival entertainments, dies in Nuremberg.

France, 6 May 1576. The peace of Chastenoy brings to an end the fifth war of religion. Known as the *Paix de Monsieur* after the duke of Alencon – who gains control of the duchy of Anjou by the treaty – it once again renews promises of religious freedom for the Huguenots.

North America, June 1576. During his first voyage to the American Arctic, in search of a north-west passage to Asia, the Englishman Martin Frobisher explores Labrador and discovers Baffin Island.

Florida, July 1576. On the orders of Hernando de Miranda, the new governor of Florida, the military commander Alonso de Solis raids the village of Oristan. Solis and 26 of his men are killed by Cusabo warriors.

Venice, 27 August 1576. The painter Tiziano Vecelli, known as Titian, dies.

Rome, 21 September 1576. The mathematician Jerome Cardanus dies. In his *Great Art* of 1545 he provided the solution to the cubic equation, which was secretly entrusted to him by the mathematician Tartaglia. Cardanus' keen interest in astrology and magic gave him a reputation as a sorcerer.

Prague, 12 October 1576. Rudolf II, the king of Hungary and Bohemia, succeeds his father, Maximilian II, as Holy Roman emperor. Maximilian died suddenly while preparing to invade Poland.

France, 1576. Following Henry III's acceptance of the humiliating terms of the *Paix de Monsieur*, the majority of French Catholics form themselves into a holy league under Guise leadership.

Japan, 1576. Oda Nobunaga orders building work to begin on a stone castle at Azuchi on the shores of Lake Biwa.

India, 1576. The forces of the Moghul Emperor Akbar conquer Bengal, the richest province of northern India.

India, 1576. Akbar finishes the construction of Fatehpur Sikri, his "City of Victory".

Mexico, 1576. An epidemic of *matlazahuatl* kills 40 per cent of the Indians in New Spain.

Frenchman defends absolute monarchy

Angers, 1576

The new great debate in France after years of civil strife is whether the king, as the Royalist League have long claimed, should have absolute authority.

The leading protagonist for this view is one of France's most influential theoreticians, Jean Bodin, the Angers jurist, who has elaborated his notions of an absolute monarchy in his newly published treatise *Republique* (Six Books of the Commonwealth).

According to Bodin, no state can expect to exist satisfactorily without one single authority formulating, judging and enforcing the laws. Quoting Aristotle and Justinian, he claims that such authority can never be mixed, but has to be united in one person, the king.

In the last resort, Bodin holds, the king is responsible to God for carrying out his duties and administering justice fairly and responsibly. While Bodin does not subscribe to the notion that kings are always appointed by God, his critics claim that unscrupulous monarchs may attempt to misuse his ideas and suggest, they have a divine right to rule.

Plagues kill nine in ten Indians

Mexico, 1576

The number of Indian souls available to Christian salvation has shrunk. This is not because of the enthusiasm with which they have embraced the faith, but a result of epidemics whose appearance in Latin America coincided with the arrival of Europeans.

Colonists worried about native welfare have collated some frightening statistics about mortality in central Mexico. In 1519, there were an estimated 25.2 million Indians, whose life expectancy was good. Then smallpox arrived, followed by measles in 1529. By 1532 the population was down to below 17 million; by 1568 it had dropped below three million. Now a new plague, known as *matlazahuatl,* is wiping out Indians at a rate which could reduce numbers to six figures.

Titian, of the dark red canvases, dies

"The Death of Actaeon" by Titian: rich colours illuminate classical myths.

Venice, 27 August 1576

Venice is in mourning for its "prince among painters", Titian, who has died of the plague. No-one knows his exact age, but he was believed to be over 90. He will be buried in the church of the Frari (Franciscan friars) for which he painted the altar-piece of *The Assumption*, which glows with the red of rubies.

He became the most famous portrait painter in Europe. The dukes Sforza of Milan and Gonzaga of Mantua, Pope Paul III and the kings of France and Spain were among his sitters. Through his friend, the poet Pietro Aretino, he met the Emperor Charles V who sat for him often. He was paid 1,000 gold crowns for each portrait, appointed court painter and made a count. It is said that the emperor even picked up his brush when he dropped it.

Even Michelangelo admired the vibrance of Titian's colour. For Philip of Spain he painted many sumptuous scenes of classical myth with naked goddesses, such as *Diana and Actaeon*. In later years his brush-strokes grew bolder and he often used his fingers.

Titian's "Venus of Urbino" wonderfully expresses his ideal of female beauty.

Seeker after eternal life crowned emperor

Prague, 12 October 1576
The eccentric yet gifted Rudolf II of Habsburg, the archduke of Austria, king of Hungary and Bohemia and one of Europe's great patrons of the arts and sciences, was elected to the throne of the Holy Roman empire today. Despite his encouragement of the astrologers and alchemists – searching at his behest for the elixir for an eternal existence – Rudolf is committed, like Maximilian, his father, to the concept of a single religion.

Maximilian favoured Lutheranism, despite his Catholic upbringing. Rudolf, on the other hand, is a staunch Catholic, and his election has, to some extent, united Protestants – Lutherans, Ultraquists, Calvinists and Bohemian Brethren – within his domain. Like his father before him, Rudolf chose to bend before the winds of change, especially under pressure from the wealthy Protestant nobles. The price of his election was acquiescence to the "Bohemian Confession", a document subscribed to by each of the Protestant churches.

For many, however, the state of the emperor's mind remains a major question mark when it comes to his rule of the empire. Although he has brought great scientists like Kepler to Prague, and commissioned work from artists of the stature of Bassano, Rudolf has likewise surrounded himself with charlatans in his quest for eternal life.

Europeans enjoy peppers and pineapples

Not just food, but art: a 17th-century painting of "Oriental Fruits".

Europe, c.1576
The dinner tables of European society now bear little resemblance to those of even a few decades ago, thanks to the introduction of new delicacies from the New World.

In England the pineapple, a tropical fruit first imported 22 years ago, has become a dessert favourite among top people. In their kitchens spices like red-hot chili peppers and flavourings such as vanilla have also become fashionable. On a less exotic level, maize, the corn grown as animal feed by Indians, is now being successfully cultivated. Some foods are being re-exported, with the Spanish and Portuguese now cultivating American peanuts in parts of Asia.

But the food trade with the Americas is not all one way. Bananas, limes, lemons, oranges, olives, cabbages and lettuces are all being successfully grown in the New World. In the West Indies sugar cane is now a significant crop, while in Florida herds of Spanish cows and pigs are being raised to provide supplies of beef and pork.

Parisian Catholics turn against Huguenots

Paris, 1576
Henry, the duke of Guise, who is known as Henry the Scarred, has formed a Catholic league in Paris in reaction to the edict of Beaulieu which ended the latest round of religious civil war by granting favourable terms to the Huguenots.

These concessions have caused dismay among the Catholic zealots, and the league is receiving much support in the working class districts of Paris and among the fanatical lower orders of the clergy.

It has already become a major political force and Henry is the idol of the back streets of Paris. He has committed the league to the restoration of religious uniformity and has made demands on the new king, Henry III, which are a danger to royal authority.

The king, a foppish young man obsessed with the idea of death, who refused on religious grounds to negotiate a marriage with Queen Elizabeth of England, and helped to instigate the St Bartholomew's Day massacre, is trying to curb the league's power by taking over its leadership and declaring his hostility to the Huguenots.

Capital city built in honour of holy man

Fatehpur Sikri, central India, 1576
A new city has been built at Sikri by the Moghul Emperor Akbar. It is a city on a hill, and crowning the summit are the palace and mosque. The architecture is wholly Indian, drawing on Hindu and Moslem features.

Within Akbar's palace his audience chamber is imperial: Akbar on a pillar, his ministers sitting in a circular gallery, linked by four elegant bridges. His harem of five receding storeys is adorned with delicate stone screens from which ladies can see but not be seen.

It was built in honour of the holy man, Shaikh Salim Chishti, who prophesied the birth of Akbar's sons, Salim (Jahangir), Murad and Daniyal. Following Akbar's defeats of the Rajputs and Gujarat, he has prefixed the name Sikri with Fatehpur (meaning victorious).

Birth of Akbar's son Salim at Fatehpur in 1569, painted c.1590.

Imperial style: part of the palace of the women at Fatehpur Sikri.

1576 (1576-1579)

Persia, 1576. Shah Tahmasp dies after a reign of 52 years and is succeeded by his son Ismail II.

Florida, 1576. 287 colonists are evacuated from the northern settlement of Santa Elena following a siege by Indians.

Spain, 1576. Teresa de Avila is forbidden by the church to found any more Carmelite convents.

Italy, 1576. Dante's *La Vita Nuova* is published posthumously.

London, 1576. The first permanent public theatres, the Theatre and the Curtain, are opened in fields to the north of the city. The old monastery at Blackfriars is also adapted for performances.

Netherlands, November 1576. Spanish troops mutiny and take Antwerp, where they indulge in extortion and robbery.

Netherlands, 8 November 1576. By the pacification of Ghent, the 17 provinces of the Netherlands form a federation to maintain peace, to suppress propaganda against heretics and to keep Spanish and other foreign troops out of the country. Negotiations between William (the Silent), the leader of the rebels, and the states of Brabant were precipitated by the Spanish "fury" of Antwerp.

Florida, December 1576. Nicolas Strozzi, who was in command of a French privateer wrecked north of Santa Elena, tells the Indians that he is an enemy of Spain and builds a fort.

Spain, April 1577. Hernando de Miranda, the former governor of Florida, returns to Spain to face arrest. He is accused of stealing 6,000 ducats before fleeing from his post earlier in the year.

Florida, July 1577. Pedro Menendez Marques arrives in San Agostin to take over as governor and rebuild Santa Elena, which has been destroyed by the Indians.

Netherlands, 23 September 1577. William of Orange makes a triumphant entry into Brussels, where he is appointed lieutenant. Archduke Mathias of Habsburg is nominated governor.

England, October 1577. After a second voyage to America, the Englishman Martin Frobisher returns to Bristol with 200 tons of ore, which he mistakenly believes to be gold.

France, 1577. Marshal Blaise de Montluc, the governor of Aquitaine, dies aged 75. A soldier loyal to the Guise dynasty since the age of 16, Montluc is well known for his *Commentaries*, a work extolling the soldierly qualities of loyalties and uprightness.

Persia, 1577. Shah Ismail II dies and is succeeded by his brother Mohammed.

Ethiopia, 1577. Ethiopia conquers the sultanate of Harrar.

Rome, 1577. Giovanni Pierluigi da Palestrina, the master of music at St Peter's, is told by Pope Gregory XIII to restore the purity of Gregorian chant and to rid sacred music of anything which prevents the words being understood. This is in line with the decisions of the Council of Trent of 1545-63.

Spain, 1577. The painter Domenikos Theotokopoulos, who was born in Crete, moves to Toledo from Venice, where he is believed to have studied under Titian. He is given the name *El Greco* (the Greek).

England, 1577. Francis Drake leaves Portsmouth on a voyage to harass Spanish shipping along the Pacific coast of North America and to circumnavigate the globe.

Spain, September 1578. John of the Cross escapes from a monastery in Toledo where he has been imprisoned since 4 December 1577 by Carmelites hostile to his his proposals for reform. During his imprisonment he wrote 30 stanzas of a *Spiritual Canticle.*

South America, 5 December 1578. After sailing through the straits of Magellan, Francis Drake raids Valparaiso.

Caucasus, 1578. War breaks out between Ottoman Turkey and Safavid Persia as the Ottomans seek to dominate Georgia and other Caucasian principalities.

South-East Africa, 1578. The Portuguese sign a treaty with the Munhumutapa kingdom of the southern Zambezi area.

England, 1578. Martin Frobisher returns empty-handed from his third expedition to North America in search of gold and a passage to India through the northern ice.

France, 1578. Don John of Austria dies of typhus near Namur. After succeeding Requesens as governor of the Netherlands, he resorted to violence when his attempts at negotiation failed. He defeated the army of the estates-general at Gembloux and was last year declared an enemy of the Netherlands. He is succeeded as governor by Alexander Farnese.

Morocco, 1578. The Portuguese are utterly defeated by the Moroccans under Mulai Ahmed al-Mansur at Alcazar-el-Kebir.

Chile, 1578. Santiago is destroyed by an earthquake.

Spain, 1579. John of the Cross becomes rector of the college of Baeza in Andalucia.

Shah of Persia dies after 43-year reign

Persia, 1576

Shah Tahmasp of Persia has died after a 43-year reign. By avoiding pitched battles with the Ottoman army, and by taking decisive action when necessary against the Ozbegs in the east, Tahmasp has kept Persia's boundaries more or less intact, while keeping the peace at home. His two sons, Haydar and Ismail, are rivals for the succession.

In the south-west, Suleiman the Magnificent's forces captured Baghdad in 1534. In the northwest he captured the Safavid capital Tabriz in 1534 and again in 1548, but Tahmasp's scorched earth policy was effective and, after another campaign in 1554, the treaty of Amasya confirmed Ottoman rule over Mesopotamia, while Azerbaijan was to remain Persian. But Tahmasp took the sensible precaution of moving his capital from Tabriz to the more central Qazwin.

In the east, the tyranny of the Qizilbash prompted a section of the native population to seek the help of the Ozbeg ruler, Ubayd Allah, and seize Herat. But when the shah approached, the Ozbegs simply retreated. Khurasan was not threatened again during his reign.

During Tahmasp's rule, slaves from the Caucasus became integrated into the population, while tension between the Turkish military class – the Qizilbash tribesmen – and the Persian bureaucracy was kept well under control.

Frobisher seeks a "north-west passage"

Under fire: Frobisher and his men are attacked near Baffin Island.

London, 1577

The English explorer, Captain Martin Frobisher is preparing for his third voyage in 18 months to find the short, polar way from the North Atlantic to China which learned navigators are convinced must exist as a route known as the "north-west passage".

Last year he sailed into a strait in the far north-west beyond Greenland, convinced that Asia lay to starboard and America to port. He met Asiatic people called Eskimo, and found black ore which an Italian alchemist says conceals gold, although London's goldsmiths do not agree with him.

This year, in a voyage between May and September, Frobisher collected 200 tons of gold ore which the queen had locked up for safekeeping in the Tower of London. As gold fever spreads, there is less interest in the route to Cathay, even though the keepers of the ore protest that they cannot find furnaces hot enough to transmute the ore into gold. Ore apart, the venture has collected only two bewildered Eskimo captives.

Frobisher: seeking polar gold.

Women and children die in Spanish fury

Spanish soldiers portrayed waging brutal war in Harlem, in the Netherlands.

Ghent, 8 November 1576
As Spanish soldiers rampaged through the city of Antwerp, burning, killing and looting – leaving 8,000 dead and 1,000 houses destroyed – Catholic and Protestant leaders of the rebellious Habsburg Netherlands today signed a treaty to be known as the "Pacification of Ghent". Both sides aim to sink their religious differences in the face of the brutality of the Spanish military response to the revolt.

For the past four years, hatred of the Spanish has become universal in this country following the attempt to impose the "tenth penny" tax by Spain's governor, the duke of Alba, and the brutal treatment of rebellious towns during the war of 1572. It was the mutiny four years ago by Spanish soldiers that brought the hatred to boiling point. Thousands of hardened veteran troops expelled their officers and formed their own revolutionary committees. Brutal excesses followed.

Nothing surpassed the brutality seen in Antwerp during the past few days. According to an English observer: "They spared neither age nor sex, time nor place, person nor country, profession nor religion, young nor old, rich nor poor, strong nor feeble, but, without any mercy, did tyrannously triumph."

Children have indeed been killed in their hundreds in Antwerp as what has become known as "The Spanish Fury" continues.

Crusade against Moors crushed in Africa

Morocco, 4 August 1578
King Sebastian of Portugal lies dead on the battlefield of Alcazar-el-Kebir ("Battle of Three Kings"). With him and 8,000 of his soldiers perish improbable dreams of a Christian crusade against the Moors of Africa.

From his early youth, the unstable Sebastian had an obsessive yearning to be Christ's captain against the infidel. In 1576 he found the pretext he needed, when Mulai Mohammed, the sharif of Fez, was deposed by an uncle who was backed by the Ottomans.

Although Philip II of Spain initially refused to help, Sebastian was determined, and in December 1576 asked for Philip's daughter's hand in marriage, and for galleys, men and supplies for a Moroccan campaign. He borrowed money wherever he could, and scraped together an army of adventurers and mercenaries from all over Europe. Out of touch with its fleet, as well as being overcome by the heat, Sebastian's army was outnumbered and crushed. About 15,000 Christians were captured.

Sebastian: defeated holy warrior.

Jewish protege of Sultan dies in Istanbul

Istanbul, 1579
Joseph Nasi, the duke of Naxos, has died in his belvedere palace, having established a Jewish community within the Ottoman court. Nasi was a Portuguese Jew who fled from the Inquisition in his own country, and travelled widely in Europe before finding refuge with the sultan, Suleiman the Magnificent, who valued his intelligence and financial expertise. When Selim became sultan, he put Nasi in charge of Ottoman diplomacy, made him duke of Naxos and, in due course, gave him rights on Tiberias to establish a Jewish colony in Israel.

The first Jew to hold such a powerful position, Nasi became the sworn enemy of Spain and Venice, supporting the rebellion against the Spanish in the Low Countries, and taking Cyprus from the Venetians.

New house on London Bridge was originally built in Holland

London Bridge in the 17th century: a place to live as well as the capital's prime crossing point of the river Thames.

London, 1578
A new and unusual building has appeared among the shops and houses that line London Bridge. It is unusual because it was not built there originally, but in Holland. It was brought over in sections and re-erected. This seems to be the first instance of a pre-fabricated building which makes its name – "Nonsuch House" – particularly apt. It recalls the famous Nonsuch Palace, built in 1538 by Henry VIII, which was also architecturally unique.

Magnificent castle completed in Japan

Japan, 1579
The warlord Oda Nobunaga has built a magnificent castle at Azuchi, overlooking Lake Biwa. Erected as a barrier to invaders from the eastern provinces, it is not only a fortress but also a place of elegance which, as regards architecture, strength, wealth and grandeur, is the equal of anything in Europe. Surrounded by immensely strong stone walls, the castle itself is made entirely of wood and is richly painted in various colours. It is surrounded by exquisite houses decorated with gold, while beneath it a prosperous town is being built to serve the castle's defenders.

1579 (1579-1581)

Netherlands, January 1579. The Union of Arras and the Union of Utrecht finalise the division of the former Netherlands. The United Provinces are formed.

North America, 17 June 1579. The English seaman Francis Drake, who has put in for repairs on the coast of California at a place he calls Drake's Bay *(San Francisco Bay)*, claims the surrounding land for Queen Elizabeth. He names the territory New Albion because its white cliffs and summertime coolness remind him of England.

Florida, August 1579. Pedro Menendez Marques, the Spanish governor of San Agostin, attacks a group of Cusabo tribesmen, killing some 40 Frenchmen from Nicolas Strozzi's party, who are now scattered among the Indians.

Germany, 24 October 1579. Albert V (the Magnanimous), the duke of Bavaria, dies in Munich and is succeeded by William (the Pious), a strong supporter of the Jesuits.

Paris, December 1579. Guillaume du Bartas, a gentleman in the service of the king of Navarre, is enjoying great acclaim for his recent poetical work *La Sepmaine* (The Week), which describes the seven days of creation. It has already been translated into English, German and Spanish.

North America, 1579. Aboard his ship, the *Golden Hind*, docked in Drake's Bay, Francis Drake conducts Protestant services, the first in the New World.

India, 1579. The Emperor Akbar invites the Jesuits of the Portuguese colony of Goa to visit his court.

Madrid, 1579. The Theatre of the Cross is founded.

Rome, 1579. An English college is established for the education of priests and of English people who have remained faithful to the Church of Rome. Seminaries have been banned in England.

Ireland, 1579. The Spanish make an unsuccessful attempt to land in Ireland. The county of Munster rebels against English and Protestant domination.

Istanbul, 1579. The Grand Vizier Sokullo, who engineered the recapture of Tunis and Bizerta from the Spanish, dies. As the sultan, Selim, was preoccupied with pursuing his own pleasure, Sokollu had effectively controlled the Ottoman empire.

England, 1579. The Eastland Company is formed to trade with the Baltic.

Portugal, 1580. Philip II of Spain annexes Portugal, unifying the Iberian peninsula.

France, 13 February 1580. A group of burghers, ordered by Catherine de Medici to suppress a peasant revolt, murders Pommier, the leader of the rebel peasants who for a year have ruled the town of Romans, in the province of Dauphine, in protest at crushing taxes.

Portugal, 10 May 1580. Luis de Camoes, author of *The Lusiads*, an epic account of Portuguese adventures overseas, dies in Lisbon. He spent 17 years in India, the Far East and Africa.

Germany, 25 June 1580. The Formula of Concord agreed between John George, the elector of Brandenburg, Augustus of Saxony, the elector Palatine and 20 other princes, 24 counts and 38 cities brings together most of the German Lutherans.

Florida, 17 July 1580. While inquiring about Nicolas Strozzi at the mouth of St John's river, a French vessel under Gilberto Gil is trapped and destroyed by the Spanish.

Italy, 19 August 1580. The architect Andrea di Pietro, known as Palladio, dies.

England, 26 September 1580. Francis Drake returns to Plymouth at the end of his voyage to circumnavigate the globe.

France, 26 November 1580. The treaty of Fleix is signed by the duke of Anjou, leader of the Catholic forces, and the Protestant King Henry of Navarre. It ends the seventh French war of religion, which broke out last year, maintaining the previous balance between the two factions.

Poland, 1580. The leaders of Poland's Jewish communities create a "council of the four countries" – that is, the four Polish provinces. This new "parliament" will meet annually to discuss Jewish affairs.

India, 1580. The Moghul Emperor Akbar receives three Jesuit missionaries at his court. The Jesuits present him with a copy of the Polyglot Bible of Antwerp. The Flemish engravings introduce the artists in Akbar's court to Renaissance art and the laws of perspective.

Italy, 1580. *Gerusalemme Liberata* (Jerusalem Delivered) by Torquato Tasso is published while the author is in a mental asylum. The epic tells of the triumph of good over evil, symbolised by the capture of Jerusalem by the crusader Godfrey de Bouillon.

London, 1581. The Levant Company is formed to trade with Mediterranean countries.

Low countries divided by Union of Utrecht

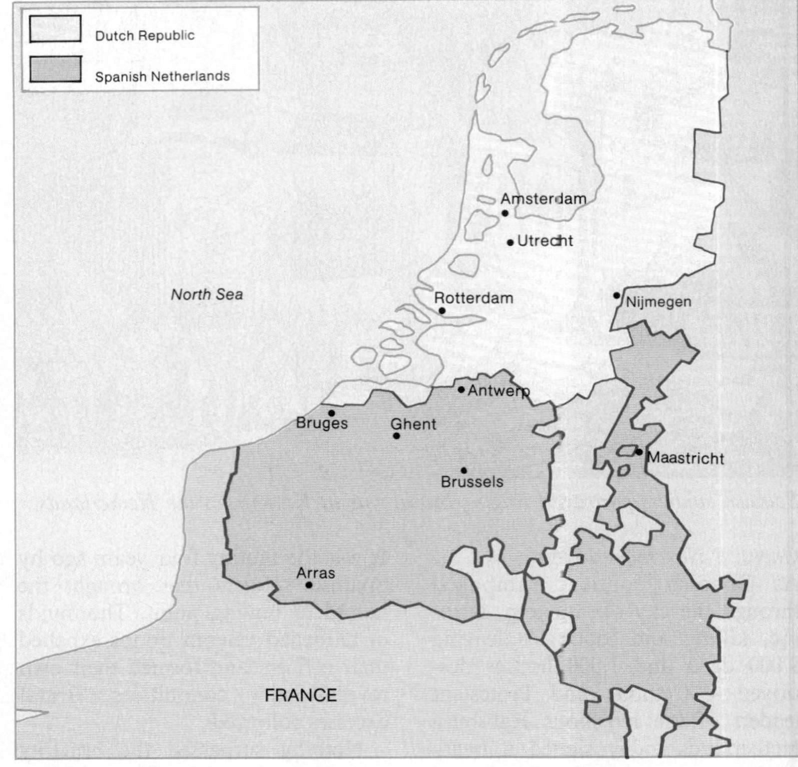

Utrecht, 23 January 1579

Deputies from six provinces of the Habsburg Netherlands met here today to sign an historic agreement which pledges all of them to act together as allies in the event of war.

Even more significant in the treaty was their agreement that each province should be able to govern itself in its own way. For the first time, no mention of the Spanish king's name has been made; nor of the maintenance of the Catholic faith; nor of any question of reconciliation with Spain.

It is doubtful whether the Union of Utrecht will succeed in uniting the Low Countries, however. Earlier this month at Arras the Walloons, the Catholics in the south of the region, joined a union with the states of Hainaut and Artois and opened talks with the Spanish overlord, the duke of Parma, so a new Catholic powerbloc may emerge.

The effect of these separate agreements can only be to split a nation already deeply divided by religious beliefs at a time when Spain is facing new threats from the Turks in the Mediterranean. All hopes that the new Habsburg governor, Don John of Austria, might resolve matters have died with him in a new outbreak of plague.

Tract unites Lutherans against Calvinists

Dresden, Germany, 25 June 1580

James Andreae, the chancellor of the university of Tubingen, has produced a formidable tract of some 17,000 words designed to heal divisions in the Lutheran church. Published today on the jubilee of the Augsburg Confession, it is called the "Formula of Concord". It reaffirms the confession of 1530 as the heart of Lutheran doctrine, after the Bible and the three creeds. It is conciliatory in tone to Catholic, but fiercely attacks Calvinist views of predestination as "all false, horrifying and blasphemous".

Since 1570 Calvinism has spread from Heidelberg to Rhineland, Westphalia and Nassau, the home of the Orange dynasty. Elector Palatine Ludwig has been trying to reverse the trend, and recently expelled over 500 Calvinist leaders. But in Germany they are still a bigger threat to Lutherans than Catholics.

Britain welcomes home pirate Drake

An Indian sets a parrot trap, drawn by one of Drake's companions.

Drake's artist also saw slaves wash gold before handing it to a Spanish overseer.

Plymouth, England, 1580

After a three-year voyage which took him round the world by way of Capes Horn and Good Hope, Francis Drake is back in his native Devon, his ship and men intact, with enough Spanish treasure to reduce taxes for everyone. Spain has demanded his trial for piracy. With an inquiry into his conduct in train, rumours of knighthood are discouraged. Yet as the first captain to sail completely round the globe – Magellan died in the attempt – Drake is a popular, and probably an untouchable, hero.

In 1577, with the queen's backing, Drake sailed with three ships whose crews (along with Spanish intelligence) were misled into believing that they were bound for Alexandria. Instead they sailed west and were becalmed in the doldrums. There was talk of mutiny and at Port Julian, just north of the Magellan Straits, Drake executed his former confidant and fellow commander Thomas Doughty. The expedition's real target was now revealed as Spanish treasure along the Pacific coast.

Drake covered the 300 miles (480km) through the straits without a chart in just 16 days, often piloting the fleet himself in a small sailing boat. Then the fleet was hit by storms. One ship sank without trace; a second returned to England. Drake renamed his craft the *Golden Hind*, and rode out northerly gales which lasted 52 days and drove him far south of Cape Horn. On 1 March 1579 his luck changed. With guns and sailors unmatched in the Pacific, he found the Spanish treasure ship *Cacafuego* and seized 26 tons of silver, 80 pounds of gold, 13 money chests and many jewels.

It was the first of many such operations. He sailed north, claimed "San Francisco" for England and crossed the Pacific in 68 days. His fame preceded him, through Spain's complaints.

Philip II of Spain annexes Portugal

Portugal, 1580

Philip of Spain has annexed Portugal to give his country a new Atlantic seaboard, a fleet to help to protect it, and a second empire stretching from Africa to Brazil, from Calicut to the Moluccas.

After two years of political and diplomatic manoeuvring and, finally, the dispatch of an army to his neighbour, Philip has convened the Cortes at Tomar and taken the oath to observe all the laws and customs of the realm. In turn he was recognised as the lawful king of Portugal.

Portugal's problems arose from King Sebastian's disastrous African crusade when his army was torn to shreds and most of the Portuguese nobility were killed. His throne became vacant and was for a time occupied by his uncle, Cardinal Henry; it was then that Philip made a move.

He announced his claim to succession and, taking advantage of Portugal's bankruptcy, made available liberal supplies of Spanish silver to beat off the claims of his rivals. But because the Portuguese were, by tradition, anti-Spanish, Philip presented Lisbon with an ultimatum. When it was ignored he sent an army under the duke of Alba. For economic reasons Portugal at this moment needs a political connection with Spain, and it could bring benefits.

Philip II of Spain: adding Portugal and its empire to the vast Habsburg dominions spanning the world.

Italian earthquake sets lamps swinging and Galileo thinking

Pisa, Italy, 1581

A 17-year old medical student at Pisa university, named Galileo Galilei, was in the cathedral here when an earthquake rocked the town, causing the great hanging lamps above him to start swinging. Timing the oscillations by means of his own pulse, Galileo found that each lamp always completed an oscillation in a certain time – whatever the range of the swing – which has led him to believe that the regular rhythms he has discovered might be of use in some mechanical device.

Born in 1564, the son of a musician, Galileo looks as if he might abandon his proposed career as a physician in favour of theoretical and experimental science. Between medical lectures, he eavesdropped on a geometry lesson in progress at the university and became so excited by what he learned that he sought lessons under the famous teacher Ostilio Ricci.

His main problem is how to pay for it. He has precious little money to spend on extra tuition. Meanwhile he ponders the mystery of the swinging chandelier.

A later Italian statue of Galileo.

1581 (1581-1582)

Argentina, 1581. Buenos Aires, founded last year by the Spaniard Juan de Garay at the confluence of the Parna and Uruguay rivers, is starting to assume an air of permanence. A previous Spanish colony on the site in 1536 had to be disbanded after attacks by Indians.

France, 1581. Readers of Montaigne's *Essays,* published last year, debate his "scepticism" which leads him to describe all religion as an act of blind faith.

North America, 1581. The first English attempt at establishing a colony here, at Roanoke in Virginia, is reported to be proving successful.

Portugal, April 1581. Philip II, whose troops overran the country last summer on the death of Cardinal Henry, is declared king.

Netherlands, 26 July 1581. The Estates-General (parliament) of the Hague deposes Philip II as ruler of the seven provinces which formed the Union of Utrecht in 1579; by doing so, it declares both independence and war.

North America, 21 August 1581. Francisco Chamuscado, leading a voyage to the Pueblo area in south-western North America, claims it for Spain and gives it the name San Felipe del Nuevo Mexico.

Japan, 1581. Oda Nobunaga attacks Mount Koya, the head-quarters of the Shingon sect of Buddhism.

London, 1581. The English Jesuit Edmund Campion – considered one of the most remarkable members of the "English mission" – is arrested and executed. His fate illustrates the dilemma of those English Catholics who wish to remain loyal to both their faith and the crown.

France, 1581. Merchants from Dieppe, St Malo and Rouen unite to organise a fur-trading expedition up the St Lawrence river in Canada.

Netherlands, 1581. After being named king of the Netherlands by William of Orange, Francis of Valois, the brother of Henry III, attempts to regain Antwerp for the Calvinists.

Russia, February 1582. The Russians heroically resist the siege of Pskov by PolishLithuanian troops.

Rome, February 1582. To ensure that Easter falls on its proper date, Pope Gregory XIII decides to bring back the spring equinox to 21 March by removing ten days – those between 5 and 15 October – from this year's calendar.

Atlantic, 25 July 1582. Philip Strozzi, for whom his cousin Catherine de Medici had secretly promised to obtain the post of viceroy of Brazil, dies during a naval battle off the Azores. He was on his way to Portugal to support the claimaint to the throne in his fight against the Spaniards.

Russia, 10 August 1582. After 25 years of conflict, Russia makes peace with Poland and gives up its claims to the Baltic state of Livonia.

Spain, 4 October 1582. Teresa of Avila, who in 1562 re-established the ancient Carmelite rule for nunneries, dies.

Russia, 1582. A large group of Cossacks, led by Yermak Timofeyevich, invade the Tartar *khanate* of Siberia and capture its capital, Kashlyk.

China, 1582. The statesman Zhang Juzheng dies. For the past ten years he has run the empire, on behalf of the Ming emperor, with a firm hand.

Japan, 1582. Oda Nobunaga, who has reunified the country under his control, is attacked by Akechi Mitsuhide and dies. Akechi subsequently loses a battle with Toyotomi Hideyoshi and is killed.

India, 1582. The Moghul Emperor Akbar attempts a synthesis of the great religions.

Italy, 1582. Giordano Bruno writes a philosophical treatise entitled *The Shadow of Ideas*, a work inspired by Neoplatonism.

China, 1582. The Italian Jesuit Matteo Ricci arrives in Macao and begins an intensive study of the Chinese language and civilisation.

Japan, 1582. Japan, which now has over 150,000 Christians, sends its first ambassador to the Vatican.

Netherlands, 1582. Alexander Farnese, who has been nominated governor of the Spanish Netherlands by Philip II, takes Oudenaarde.

Spain, 1582. Philip II of Spain agrees to give financial support to the Holy League founded in France in 1576 by the duke of Guise in order to help defend the Roman Catholics against the Calvinists.

Europe, 1582. Richard Hakluyt's book *Divers Voyages* gives the English-speaking world a view of the American discoveries.

Istanbul, 1582. On the anniversary of the founding of the famous corps of footsoldiers known as the Janissaries, their recruitment and disciplinary rules are relaxed. In particular, the rule of celibacy is removed.

Church bans reminder of the Inquisition

Act of faith: a 17th-century English engraving of Inqusition "persuasion".

Madrid, 1581

Just over a century after it was founded by a papal bull of 1478, the Spanish Inquisition has found a critic from within the ranks of the Catholic leadership. Although he is a distinguished Jesuit, Juan de Mariana has had his book put on the index of banned works.

Prominent Catholics here do not like being reminded of the early history of this most unusual institution. Although it was set up by order of the pope it was responsible to the Spanish crown. Its first inquisitor-general, the rather shadowy figure of Thomas de Torquemada, was a Dominican friar; but for most of the last century it has been run by Catholic lawyers rather than by the monks themselves.

In the last two decades of the fifteenth century the Inquisition did acquire a fiercesome reputation for the cruel persecution of "deviants" in general and Jews in particular. Some thousands of *Conversos* – Jewish converts to Christianity – were arrested, thrown into jail and sometimes tortured to extract confessions that they were still practising their old faith. They were encouraged to betray their friends and relations. Some thousands were burnt at the stake.

Those days are long past, however. In recent years only three or four people in the whole of Spain have been executed by the Inquisition, generally "Old Christians" who were neither Protestant nor Jewish but did not conform to prevailing views. For instance, people brought before the tribunal have been charged witchcraft, marital misbehaviour and superstition. In rural areas the Inquisition has recently been handing out minor sentences for trivial offences like blaspheming while drunk or using love-potions to seduce the opposite sex. It has also been used to stamp out homosexuality.

Cruel past: sinners go to the stake.

If the Inquisition no longer strikes terror into people's hearts, it is still a powerful force restricting what goes into their minds. It has always been effective as a censor and now it has jumped on de Mariana for daring to remind us of its cruel past.

Akbar attempts to fuse great religions

Fatehpur Sikri, India, 1582
In his new city of Fatehpur Sikri, the illiterate Moghul emperor Akbar sits in his "house of worship" discussing religion with Sunnis, Shi'ites, Hindus, Zoroastrians and Christians. All seek unsuccessfully to monopolise his religious spirit, unaware of his fascination by comparative religion, or his intentions of synthesising the great religions, transforming himself into a deity and saving India from sectarianism.

At first Akbar invited only Moslems, but he was so disappointed by their bigotry that he has renounced orthodoxy and proclaimed his own infallibility. Orthodox Moslems are shocked, but since the failure of their rising in Afghanistan a year ago there is little that they can do. Portuguese Catholics are bitter. Three Jesuits (one a Persian convert from Islam, another a Spaniard and the third an Italian aristocrat) travelled to Akbar's court. They hoped to win him over with their bitter attacks on Islam, but Akbar espouses religious tolerance. The reason behind Akbar's policy is simple: India is divided by different faiths, and only by rising above religions will he be capable of uniting the continent.

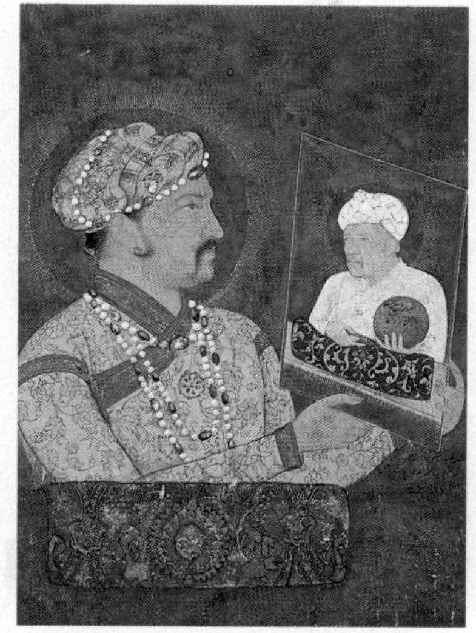
A portrait of Akbar held by his son Salim (Jahangir), painted c.1599.

Cossack firearms defeat Siberian Tartars

Russian guns overcome the Tartars, by the 19th century artist Surikov.

Russia, 1582
The Siberian Tartars have been defeated by Muscovy, their troops unable to withstand withering firepower. Khan Kuchum has been captured and his capital overrun. Yet the organiser of the victory was not the czar but the Stroganovs, a family of immensely rich merchants, and the troops were not Russians but Cossack mercenaries under their ruler Yermak. The Cossacks are roving bands of warriors, as much brigands as regular soldiers. Yermak is a fitting leader, an imposing and energetic warrior whose employers, the Stroganovs, run the north-eastern corner of European Russia as virtually a private kingdom, making a vast fortune from salt and furs.

The larger the kingdom became, the more it has clashed with the Tartars and needed troops. Yermak's 1,500 Cossacks make an ideal private army.

Emperor discovers truth about his tutor

China, 1582
Zhang Juzheng, the most powerful man in China, has died suddenly, only nine days after being granted the title of "Grand Preceptor", an honour that has not been conferred for 200 years. Zhang started his rise to power as tutor to the infant emperor, Wan-li. Working hand in glove with the eunuch Feng Pao, the head of the palace staff, Zhang controlled every action which the emperor took.

Wan-li, who enjoyed the art of calligraphy, simply wrote in royal vermilion what his tutor told him to and took pleasure from his brushwork rather than understanding what the document said. Some attempts were made by court officials to protest to the emperor about Zhang's arrogance, but the protesters were accused of disrespect to the throne and cruelly beaten with jointed whipping clubs.

Zhang and Feng Pao grew fabulously rich through their corruption. When Zhang travelled he did so in a sedan chair, divided into a bedroom and a reception room, which was hauled by 32 bearers. Now he is dead and the emperor is at last learning the truth about his beloved tutor.

Teresa, an ecstatic and mystic nun, dies

Albe de Tormes, 4 October 1582
Teresa of Avila, one of leading reformers of the monastic movement, has died. Her father was a Jewish convert and her mother a Castilian aristocrat. Teresa entered a Carmelite convent at the age of 21. She was shocked by the lack of piety she found, and determined to lead a return to the Palestinian Carmelite tradition of the hermit living in the desert. She first founded the convent of St Joseph of Avila, where she insisted that the main role of the nuns was to pray for souls in danger and intercede for others. Since 1567 she has founded many others, some with the help of John of the Cross, who shared her deep mysticism.

Her best known book is *Castillo Interior*, in which the castle is the soul, which has to go through seven rooms to attain purity. In the final room a divine union is achieved. In contrast with her severe puritanism, her writing is rich with the erotic and sensual experience of the holy. Her asceticism, prayer and piety took her to a state of intensely physical ecstasy of a kind which lesser mortals associate with sexual love.

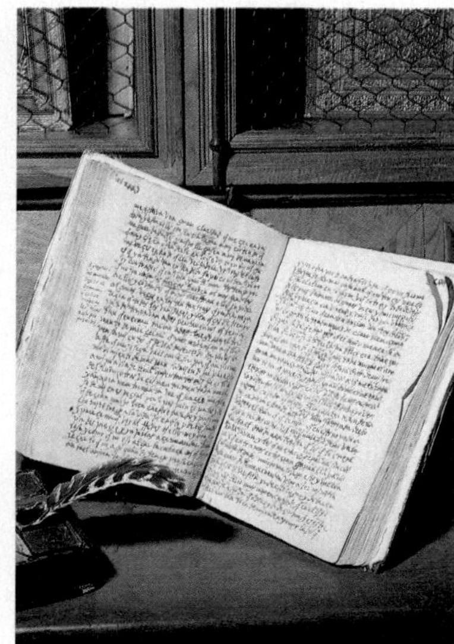
A book written by Teresa.

Ten days vanish with the new calendar

Rome, 15 October 1582
A new era for the Catholic world begins today. As authorised by a papal decree, the Julian calendar, established in 46BC, is to be replaced by a new method of calculation.

It will be named the Gregorian calendar, in honour of Pope Gregory XIII who instituted the reform. Experts have been demanding a replacement for the Julian system, under which calendar time gains one whole day every 128 years, for 300 years. The difference between official time and solar time is currently ten days.

The new system has cut these extra days by making 5 October into 15 October. Accuracy will be maintained by cutting three leap years every 400 years.

1582 (1582-1587)

England, 1582. Robert Browne, a separatist opposed to the Anglican liturgy, flees to Holland.

Netherlands, 1583. Dutch from the seven United Provinces occupy the mouth of the Scheldt, halting any seaborne trade with Antwerp.

North America, 5 August 1583. Claiming the right of first discovery, Sir Humphrey Gilbert takes possession of Newfoundland in the name of Queen Elizabeth.

China, 1583. Yunnan province is invaded by the Burmese.

Atlantic, 1583. On his return journey to England after annexing Newfoundland, Sir Humphrey Gilbert is drowned in a shipwreck.

North America, July 1584. An English expedition organised by Walter Raleigh lands on the south-eastern coast of North America and asserts English authority over an area some 1,800 nautical miles long. Raleigh, who has remained in England, has the permission of Queen Elizabeth to name the area Virginia after the virgin queen.

France, 10 August 1584. The duke of Alencon and Anjou, the younger brother of Henry III, dies, leaving the Valois line without a successor to the throne. According to the rules of succession, the crown should revert to Henry of Navarre, the duke of Bourbon and leader of the Protestants. However, Henry, the Catholic duke of Guise, also stakes a claim.

Milan, 1584. Cardinal Carlo Borromeo, archbishop of Milan, dies after reviving Catholicism in northern Italy.

Poland, 1584. The poet Jan Kochanowski, who translated the psalms, dies at Lublin. He travelled widely in Europe and met leading writers, including the great French poet Pierre de Ronsard. His works have earned him the status of a national poet in his native land.

Rome, 24 April 1585. Felice Peretti is elected pope following the death of Gregory XIII. He takes the name Sixtus V.

North America, 13 July 1585. A group of 108 English colonists, led by Sir Richard Grenville, reaches Roanoke Island. This is the second expedition to North America organised by Sir Walter Raleigh, who was knighted this year.

Netherlands, 17 August 1585 Antwerp capitulates to Alexander Farnese, duke of Parma, the governor of the Netherlands. Farnese has now secured the submission of the southern Netherlands, Flanders and Brabant to the Spanish crown.

Netherlands, August 1585. England concludes an alliance with the United Provinces the treaty of Nonsuch. Robert Dudley, the earl of Leicester, is sent by Queen Elizabeth at the head of an army to support the Netherlands in their war against the Spanish.

Rome, 9 September 1585. Pope Sixtus V deprives Henry of Navarre of his rights to the French crown.

Netherlands, 1 November 1585. Maurice of Nassau, the son of William of Orange, becomes governor of Holland, Zeeland and Utrecht.

France, 27 December 1585. The poet Pierre de Ronsard dies. His work, which was popular with the court of Henry II, reconciles sensuality with faith and enthusiasm for the classics with pride in the French language.

England, 1585. The composer Thomas Tallis dies.

Caribbean, 1 January 1586. Francis Drake, who left England on a new voyage to America last September, makes a surprise attack on the heavily fortified city of San Domingo in Hispaniola, forcing the governor to pay a large ransom.

South America, February 1586. Drake captures Cartagena on the Spanish main by a land and sea attack. He plunders the city and ransoms it for 110,000 ducats.

Virginia, May 1586. The English military leader Ralph Lane heads off an Indian attack, killing Wingina, an Indian chief from Roanoke Island.

Florida, 7 June 1586. Drake burns the Spanish city of San Agostin.

Virginia, 18 June 1586. Francis Drake leaves Roanoke Island on his return journey to England. He has taken aboard Ralph Lane and other surviving English settlers.

Virginia, August 1586. Sir Richard Grenville sets sail from Roanoke, leaving 20 settlers behind.

Japan, 1586. Toyotomi Hideyoshi takes the title of *kampaku* (civil dictator) and takes over the task begun by Oda Nobunaga of uniting Japan under his sway.

Spain, 1586. El Greco paints *The Burial of the Count of Orgaz* for the church of Santo Tome in Toledo. Its typically dramatic, almost feverish, forms and colours confirm his growing reputation.

India, 1586. The Emperor Akbar annexes the kingdom of Kashmir.

Florida, 1587. The Spanish evacuate the northern settlement of Santa Elena.

Protestant rights withdrawn in France

Nemours, France, 7 July 1585
The fearful Henry III has given in to intense Catholic pressure and, in an edict signed here today, has revoked all concessions to the Huguenots and proscribed the "pretended reformed religion".

This edict, which makes another war between the Catholics and Protestants inevitable, was the direct result of the death of the duke of Anjou, the last of the king's brothers. Without an heir, Henry was forced to recognise the Huguenot Henry of Navarre as heir to the throne. This was a shattering blow to the Catholics, and Henry the Scarred of Guise reformed the Catholic League, which had disbanded itself in 1576 rather than allow the king to become its leader.

The league quickly became politically and militarily powerful again. Its leaders replaced royalist commanders with their own men in many towns. The Guise faction then signed a treaty of alliance with King Philip II of Spain, and King Henry, recognising the threat to his throne, has caved in.

Warlord who unified Japan is murdered

Japan, 21 June 1582
Oda Nobunaga, unifier of Japan, was treacherously murdered at dawn this morning at the monastery of Honnoji where he was staying while on his way from his castle at Azuchi to a distant battlefield.

Nobunaga was taken by surprise by a strong force of men belonging to Akechi Mitsuhide with whom he had no quarrel. He and his men fought as valiantly as they always did, but they were overwhelmed and killed. Some reports say that he committed suicide. The monastery was set ablaze and his body has not been recovered. He was 48.

Nobunaga was only 17 when he succeeded to his family's modest feudal barony. Disregarded and forced to fight for his land, he soon proved himself a ruthless warlord, killing his treacherous younger brother and swiftly achieving local ascendancy.

He then embarked on a career of conquest until he could rightly lay claim to being responsible for the reunification of Japan after a century of strife.

Poles elect a Swedish prince to throne

Poland, 19 August 1587
Once more the Polish and Lithuanian nobility have declined to consider a native king, and have opted for a Swede, Sigismund Vasa. The 21-year-old prince was elected by some 15,000 voters who preferred him to the Habsburg Archduke Maximilian. He succeeds Stephen Bathory who has reigned for ten years.

Bathory, who was a Transylvanian prince, will be a hard act to follow. A forceful personality and an experienced soldier, he had set back Moscow's hopes for an outlet to the Baltic and created a big Christian empire in eastern Europe. Yet even before his death it had become clear that the Poles would not support the almost limitless personal ambitions of their king.

Sigismund may find that he has the same problem as his predecessors, namely, failing to banish from his mind the thought of his native country, and this could have a far-reaching effect on both domestic and foreign policy. The Polish king has various powers and prerogatives, but the greatest restriction on his authority is working through parliament.

Sigismund: crossing the Baltic.

The reforming czar who was a monster

Czar Ivan the Terrible: great reformer or deranged monster?

Moscow, 18 March 1584
Czar Ivan the Terrible, a great man who also happened to be a monster, has died at the age of 54 while preparing to play a game of chess. Because his attempted social revolution and his last 25 years of war have brought Muscovy to the verge of anarchy, special guards have surrounded the Kremlin. But the succession appears to have passed easily enough to his son, Fyodor Ivanovitch.

Ivan inherited the throne at the age of three, and when he was 13, in a fit of temper, he had his principal adviser torn apart by dogs. His first wife, one of the Romanovs, was chosen out of 1,500 virgins sent to Moscow from all over Russia. For some 13 years Ivan ruled with a group of good advisers from the clergy and the *boyars*, introducing a new code of law and reforming provincial government.

Ivan was a strong and successful ruler, and the most noteworthy thing about his reign was his policy of extending Muscovy's power and influence. By capturing Kazan and Astrakhan he pushed the borders of Russia eastwards, ambitiously looking towards Cathay and the Pacific. He was denied an outlet to the west by failing to seize the Baltic region, but nevertheless established diplomatic and commercial relations with England. He entered into long and curious negotiations for an English marriage, not shrinking from a union with Queen Elizabeth herself if that were possible. Ivan was almost deranged for the last 25 years of his life.

Spanish agent kills William of Orange

Delft, 10 July 1584
William, the prince of Orange and foremost leader of the Dutch revolt against Spain, was today assassinated by an agent of Philip II. He was shot dead by Balthazar Gerard, a Frenchman, who was posing as a Calvinist refugee.

William of Orange was born in 1533. The governor of Holland, Utrecht and Zeeland, he was appointed to the council of state in 1555 and resigned, with Count Egmont and Philip Hoorne, in 1563, protesting at Spain's growing influence. A Protestant since 1573, William quickly established himself as a leader of the growing revolt against Spain. After the Pacification of Ghent (8 November 1576) the country's seven northern, Protestant, provinces declared themselves the United Provinces of the Netherlands. William was appointed *stadholder*, or chief magistrate.

For a brief period William even won over the southern Catholic provinces, but the scheme collapsed when William's French ally deserted him and the Protestants preferred to stand alone. Until today, he ruled the north alone.

William of Orange holds up the head of the Dutch cow, succoured by Queen Elizabeth, as Philip II sits on it and the duke of Alba milks it.

Elizabeth beheads Mary, queen of Scots

England, 8 February 1587
Proclaiming her Catholicism to the end and raising her voice in Latin to drown the prayers of the English chaplain, Mary, queen of Scots was executed today at Fotheringhay in Northamptonshire. She had been found guilty of joining a conspiracy to murder Elizabeth and promote a Spanish invasion of England.

Mary was sentenced last October, but an anguished Elizabeth repeatedly refused to sign the death warrant. Mary spent almost 20 years as a political refugee in England after her intrigues, her marriages, and the murder of one husband by her next-in-line caused her to be driven from Scotland.

Queen Mary: the Catholic queen driven from her own country.

Poet's heroic death mourned by queen

Sir Philip Sidney: soldier and poet, famed for his selfless courage.

London, 5 November 1586
The queen, the court and the whole city are in deep mourning for Sir Philip Sidney, the poet and soldier, whose body was today brought back from the Netherlands and landed at Tower Hill. At the siege of Zutphen he charged recklessly with 500 English horsemen against 3,000 Spanish cavalry.

Struck in the thigh by a bullet, he managed to ride back to camp where he called for water. But seeing a dying foot-soldier brought in, he handed him the bottle, saying: "Thy necessity is yet greater than mine." After 26 days of suffering, he died of his wound, aged only 32. Elegies for him are being written by poets everywhere.

Decimals invented

Antwerp, 1585
A couple of small pamphlets have just been published with the titles *La Thiende* (The Tenth) and *La Disme* (The Decimal). In them a Flemish mathematician, called Simon Stevin, gives an easy-to-understand account of a system of fractions based on tenths. Stevin says the decimal system beats the present method of counting in twelves. He proposes his way should be in everyday use. Coins could be decimalised, and so, too, could weights and measures. His own career has been impressive. He rose from being a clerk to commissioner of Antwerp's public works.

1587 (1587-1588)

England, 8 February 1587. Mary, queen of Scots, is beheaded at Fotheringhay for complicity in the Babington plot. Its leader, Anthony Babington, and his five associates were executed last year. He had planned to assassinate Queen Elizabeth, free Mary from captivity and rally support among English Roman Catholics for a Spanish invasion force.

Spain, April 1587. Francis Drake attacks and pillages Cadiz and ravages the Spanish coast, destroying naval stores. The incident becomes known as "the Singeing of the King of Spain's Beard".

Virginia, 18 August 1587. The first English child is born in the New World. The daughter of Ananias and Ellinor Dare is named Virginia in honour of both the virgin queen of England and the fledgling colony.

Poland, 19 August 1587. Following the sudden death of Stephen Bathory at the end of last year, Sigismund III, the son of John of Sweden, is cjosen to be the king of Poland.

Virginia, 27 August 1587. Having arrived at Roanoke on 22 July, John White sails for Europe with supplies, leaving his 177 colonists behind. On landing at Roanoke, White's party found no trace of the colonists left behind by Richard Grenville.

England, August 1587. Robert Dudley, the earl of Leicester, returns to England after the failure of his expedition to the Netherlands to aid the Dutch in their revolt against Spain.

France, 20 October 1587. In the eighth war of religion, which began two years ago, Henry of Navarre defeats a Catholic army commanded by the duke of Joyeuse at Coutras. This latest Catholic-Huguenot conflict has developed into a struggle for the French succession between Henry of Guise, King Henry III and Henry of Navarre, known as the War of the Three Henries.

France, 24 October 1587. Henry of Guise forces the Swiss and German troops who are attempting to link up with Henry of Navarre's army at Vimory and Auneau to retreat.

South-East Africa, 1587. The second Zimba war breaks out among the Chewa peoples in Mozambique and Malawi, caused by Portuguese slave trading on the Zambezi.

Japan, 1587. Shimazu Yoshihisa surrenders to Toyotomi Hideyoshi, effectively bringing the whole of Kyushu under Hideyoshi's control.

Italy, 1587. Two banking houses, the Banco di Rialto in Venice and the Tavola in Messina, open.

North America, 1587. Searching for a north-west passage, the English navigator John Davis discovers a strait linking the Atlantic to the Baffin Sea.

Scandinavia, 4 April 1588. On the death of Frederick II, his 11-year-old son Christian IV becomes king of Denmark and Norway and duke of Schleswig-Holstein.

Venice, 19 April 1588. The painter Paolo Caliari, known as Veronese, dies. Veronese made a speciality of great ceremonial compositions with biblical themes, such as *The Marriage at Cana* and *The Feast in the House of Levi*. The latter caused him some trouble with the Inquisition, whose wrath he escaped by claiming the licence granted to poets and madmen.

Paris, 12 May 1588. King Henry III is forced to flee from Paris after Henry of Guise's triumphant entry into the city.

England, 10 September 1588. The Englishman Thomas Cavendish, who set sail from Portsmouth on 21 July 1586, returns home having become the third man to circumnavigate the globe.

England, 15 September 1588. The Spanish Armada – an attempted invasion of England by Philip II – is defeated by the English led by Lord Howard of Effingham.

Persia, 1 October 1588. The feeble Sultan Mohammed Shah, dominated by rival tribal leaders, hands over power to his 17-year-old son Abbas.

France, 23 December 1588. Henry, the duke of Guise, and his brother Cardinal Louis of Guise are assassinated at Blois on the orders of King Henry III.

France, December 1588. King Henry III forms an alliance with Henry of Navarre to defeat the Holy League.

Japan, 1588. Following an anti-Christian edict issued in 1587, some Christians are expelled from Nagasaki.

Rome, 1588. The papal curia is reformed.

Venice, 1588. Tintoretto completes his enormous cycle of paintings on the life of St Mark in the Scuola di San Rocco, begun in 1564.

Spain, 1588. Philip II authorises half-castes in America to become priests – provided that they are legitimate, which is rarely the case.

Spain, 1588. The first complete edition of the works of Teresa of Avila is published.

Court pleads with virgin Queen to marry

Queen Elizabeth: resolved to remain single, despite diplomatic dalliances.

England, 1588
Elizabeth's advisers have never tired of urging her to marry and produce an heir to the throne. Successive parliaments have beseeched God "to incline your Majesty's heart to marriage ... that we may see the fruit and child that may come thereof". Elizabeth accepts that she has a duty to marry, but her courtships have been no more than diplomatic quadrilles with French and Austrian princes.

More than once she has been heard to say that she would "live and die a virgin". London society gossip has it that a physical defect rules out marriage. Be that as it may, she uses her sex and good looks to manipulate her advisers. It is said the relationship between the queen and her secretary of state, William Cecil, is deeply emotional.

From the start, Elizabeth has had to overcome the handicap of being a woman in male-dominated Tudor society. A woman is expected to be an obedient and diligent wife. Sir William Fitzwilliam, the queen's lord deputy in Ireland, speaks of her in the most vulgar terms: "God's wounds, this it is to serve a base, bastard, pissing kitchen woman."

Christians ordered out of Japan

Japan, 25 July 1587
Hideyoshi, the Japanese strongman, has banned Christianity and ordered the Jesuits to leave the country within twenty days. This move has come as a terrible shock to the missionaries, for only yesterday he went on board a Portuguese ship to talk to the vice-provincial, Gaspar Coelho.

He appeared in a friendly mood, but then in the middle of the night a messenger woke Coelho with an angry denunciation from him, accusing the Jesuits of selling Japanese as slaves and smashing Buddhist images. He demanded a reply. Coelho did his best, but was unable to turn aside Hideyoshi's anger.

Two Portuguese priests, as depicted on a Japanese screen in c.1600.

Fireships smash the Spanish Armada

The Armada, possibly by Nicholas Hilliard: the smaller English ships wrought havoc among the Spaniards.

England, 15 September 1588

The ragged remnants of the Armada that was to have humbled the English lie skulking in the harbours of Spain and Portugal today after the most humiliating naval defeat in Spain's history. Outgunned by the English, panicked by their fireships and battered by a raging south-westerly, the scattered fleet sailed north, seeking to escape into the Atlantic round the Orkneys and Shetlands. The disaster would have been even greater had not the pursuing English ships been forced to turn back when they ran out of food and ammunition.

Philip of Spain had intended to teach England a lesson. His colonies and his ships had suffered for years from the raids of Francis Drake, John Hawkins and other English privateers. Whenever the Spanish ambassador protested, Elizabeth was noncommittal and the raids continued. When Elizabeth was told of a huge fleet building up in Philip's ports, she allowed Drake to launch a spoiling operation. With 23 warships he descended on Cadiz, guns blazing, and captured or destroyed 30 ships.

The Armada, commanded by the duke of Medina Sidonia, set sail in May 1588, and was sighted in the English Channel on 20 July. During the night, with the Spanish anchored in close battle formation, the English slipped past to the Spanish rear. The Spanish outnumbered them by two to one, with some ships of 1,000 tons, packed with soldiers with great grappling irons. But the English ships, though small, were highly manoeuvrable and superior in long-range gunfire.

By darting in, releasing their broadsides and escaping before the heavier Spanish cannon could be brought to bear, the English created havoc among the enemy, although they could make no impact on the stout Spanish hulls.

All afternoon and during the night following, the Armada pushed up the Channel, with the English snapping at its flanks. Medina Sidonia was expecting to rendezvous with reinforcements and landing craft from the Spanish Netherlands. They never made it. Patrols of rebel Dutch "sea beggars" saw to that. After a week of running fights, Medina Sidonia anchored off Calais. The English, standing off a mile distant, were ready with fireships, stacked with wood, pitch and explosives. They went in at midnight, the raging forest of fire causing panic aboard the Spanish galleons. Ships collided and sank as anchors were abandoned and cables severed.

Daybreak found the fearsome Armada broken up and drifting. Now the English struck repeatedly. Some ships were sunk, others ran on to sandbanks, the rest fled. All told, the Spanish lost 65 ships and upwards of 10,000 men. The English lost fewer than 100 men and not one ship.

A map by Robert Adam showing the two fleets off the English coast.

French king flees Catholic barricades

Paris, 12 May 1588

Henry III, foiled by the citizens of Paris in his armed attempt to expel the duke of Guise, has been humiliated and forced to flee from the city. A confrontation between the king and the people has been inevitable ever since Guise defied the king's orders and entered the city at the beginning of the month. Rumours swept the streets: the king intended to kill the duke; he was planning another massacre, this time of Catholics; he had hired eight hangmen.

This morning the city woke to the sound of drums as the king's men, supported by the Swiss guards, took up strategic positions. Irate crowds gathered, erected barricades in the streets and stationed *arquebusiers* behind them.

A shot rang out near the Pont St Michel and 60 soldiers died in the ensuing fracas. Milling crowds surrounded groups of isolated troops. Most of these cut-off detachments surrendered to cheering crowds. By nightfall it was obvious that the king's coup had failed.

Sex and war find thoughtful outlet

France, June 1588

The *Essays* of Michel Eyquem, the seigneur of Montaigne, have acquired an avid readership since they appeared in 1580, and a fourth, expanded, edition has just come out. Montaigne was born in 1533 and brought up to speak Latin as his first tongue. After university he was a magistrate in Bordeaux until he sold his post – a common practice – and retired, at 37, to his estate.

Apart from visits abroad in 1580-1 and two terms as mayor of Bordeaux (1581-5), Montaigne has passed his time in his library, where he writes down what he protests are the first thoughts to come into his head. A serene, basically conservative scepticism and tolerance of human diversity lie at the heart of his often profound and always thought-provoking *Essays*. He covers life from sex to war, and concludes that wisdom begins with the study of oneself.

1588 (1588-1590)

Japan, 1588. Toyotomi Hideyoshi institutes a "sword hunt" in order to disarm the peasantry.

France, 5 January 1589. Catherine de Medici dies at Blois. She was born in Florence in 1519 and became queen of France as wife of King Henry II in 1547. Mother of the next three kings – Francis II, Charles IX and Henry III – she dominated French politics from her regency (1560-70) for the young Charles IX until her death.

Moscow, January 1589. Job, the metropolitan of Moscow, is promoted to the newly created post of patriarch by Boris Godunov (who became regent for the incompetent Czar Fyodor after the death of Ivan the Terrible three years ago). The patriarch of Moscow is fifth in rank after that of Jerusalem.

Istanbul, January 1589. The independence of the Russian church is formally ratified by an ecumenical synod.

West Africa, March 1589. A Moroccan army under al-Mansur sets out across the Sahara to invade the kingdom of Songhai.

France, 3 April 1589. King Henry III and King Henry of Navarre are reconciled after sensitive negotiations.

Spain, July 1589. Pedro Menendez Marques persuades the Spanish authorities to agree to his plan to sail from Havana to Virginia and destroy the English settlement.

France, 2 August 1589. Henry III, the last Valois king, dies after being stabbed by Jacques Clement, a fanatical Dominican friar. The Protestant King Henry of Navarre becomes King Henry IV.

France, 21 September 1589. The duke of Mayenne, the brother of Henry of Guise and successor to him as the head of the Catholic League, is defeated at the battle of Arques by Henry IV.

Portugal, 1589. After a failed attempt to reconquer Portugal from the Azores in 1583, Antonio of Crato again lands in the country and marches on Lisbon. In spite of English support he is defeated by the Spaniards.

Portugal, 1589. English merchants are expelled from the kingdom.

Brazil, 1589. A supreme tribunal is created in the capital, Bahia, allowing some administrative arrangements to be transferred from Portugal to Brazil.

France, 14 March 1590. King Henry IV inflicts another defeat on the Catholic League under the duke of Mayenne, at Ivry.

Spain, April 1590. Antonio Perez, a former secretary of state and close adviser to Philip II, escapes from Madrid, where he has been confined for almost a decade, and finds refuge in Aragon. He was arrested in July 1579 after organising the murder of Juan de Escobedo, a councillor of Don John of Austria, who had been threatening to reveal Perez' involvement in political intrigue.

Mexico, 27 July 1590. Castana de Sosa sets out from Nueva Leon with 150 settlers in an unauthorised effort to establish a mining town in New Mexico.

France, September 1590. Alexander Farnese, the duke of Parma – who, as governor of the Spanish Netherlands, captured Antwerp in 1585 – forces King Henry IV to lift the siege of Paris.

France, 1590. Refusing to recognise Henry IV as king, the Catholic party declares the cardinal of Bourbon king under the name of Charles X.

West Africa, 1590. The second Jaga war breaks out in Zaire, caused by Portuguese slave trading on the Angola coast.

Japan, 1590. Toyotomi Hideyoshi completes the political unification of Japan under his rule. His powerful vassal Tokugawa Ieyasu moves his administrative and military base to Edo (*Tokyo*), a strategic position for the domination of the great plain of eastern Japan.

Rome, 1590. Pope Sixtus V, who has worked on the edition of the Vulgate known as the *Sixtus*, declares it the official text for the Catholic Bible. Produced by St Jerome in the fourth century AD, this translation of the Bible was recognised as authentic by the Council of Trent.

Italy, 1590. The composer Claudio Monteverdi publishes a collection of madrigals.

Portugal, 1590. Seeking to attack Spain, an English fleet under the leadership of Francis Drake and Sir John Norris makes an unsuccessful attempt to disembark at Lisbon.

Near East, 1590. Abbas, shah of Persia since 1587, concludes a peace treaty with the Ottoman sultan, Murad III, ending a war which began in 1578. Under the treaty the Turks acquire Georgia, Azerbaijan and Shirwan, thus extending their frontiers to the Caucasus and the Caspian.

India, 1590. Mohammed Quli Qutb Shah, the sultan of Golconda, founds the town of Hyderabad on the banks of the river Musi.

Japanese sword hunt disarms peasants

Hideyoshi: cracking down on civilian sword-bearers (painting on silk).

Japan, 1588

Hideyoshi, the regent of Japan, has ordered a "sword hunt" designed to confiscate the weapons held by civilians. He has cloaked the purpose of the hunt by claiming that the weapons are needed to provide the metal for the Great Image of the Buddha being built for the new Hokoji monastery in Kyoto.

The peasants whose weapons are taken are told their sacrifice will assure them of salvation. But the real reason is to disarm "peasants who keep needless weapons, do not pay their taxes and plot risings against landlords".

In fact, the order is two-edged. It disarms trouble-makers and distinguishes civilians from soldiers. It also provides a way to seize the weapons of the soldier-monks of the turbulent monasteries of Koya-san and Hieizan.

Queen's godson becomes closet inventor

England, 1589

Sir John Harington, the so-called "saucy godson" of Queen Elizabeth, has not wasted his time since his banishment from the court for telling risque stories in front of the ladies.

In the splendid mansion which he has built at Kelston, in Somerset, he has installed what is probably the world's first toilet which can be flushed from an overhead tank. Welcome though such an innovation must be, there is little hope that it will be widely adopted, as human waste will still have to be collected and disposed of manually.

In country districts it can be spread on the land, but in towns it presents a considerable problem. It has to go somewhere, and even a flushing toilet may create health hazards, especially if the waste seeps into rivers and ponds.

Fanatical monk stabs Henry III to death

Paris, 2 August 1589
Henry III, the last of the Valois kings of France, was stabbed to death today by Jacques Clement, a fanatical Dominican monk. So France's bloody religious wars claim one more noble victim. Last December the king had the duke of Guise and his brother, the cardinal of Guise, assassinated.

After these killings the Catholic League declared the Guises' brother, the duke of Mayenne, to be lieutenant-governor of the realm. But Henry will be succeeded by King Henry of Navarre, his ally against the Catholic League, who has a distant claim to the throne, and, more importantly, has his main rival, the ageing cardinal of Bourbon – the league's candidate for the throne – in custody.

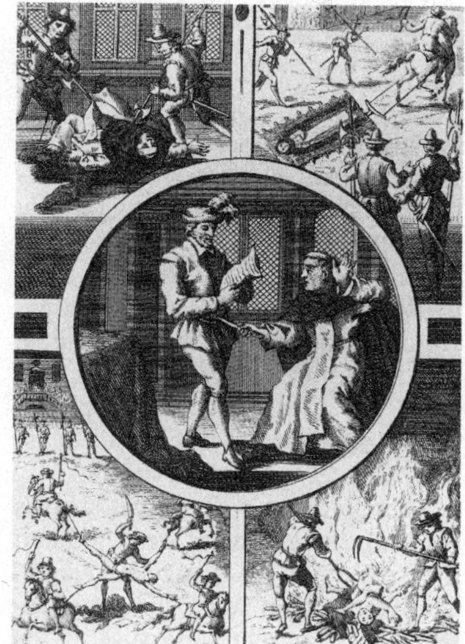

The assassination of Henry III (centre), and the fate of his killer.

Starving Chinese grind stones for bread

China, 1588
Famine and pestilence are sweeping China, and whole provinces are being depopulated as villages are wiped out by hunger and the diseases that come with starvation and foul sanitary conditions.

Drought has brought such famine that people are eating goose droppings and cannibalism is rife. There are unbroken lines of beggars at the gruel kitchens. Children are being abandoned and infants killed. Some peasants, having stripped the countryside of anything growing, are grinding stones into flour.

With their resistance to disease lowered by hunger, the people are falling prey to the diseases that lurk in their filthy homes, especially in the towns where the houses crowd together surrounded by excrement and filth. Epidemics follow one upon the other. "Big Head" fever, in which the head and neck swell up, is currently rampant.

So many people are dying in the southern capital it is said that if you count a bean for every coffin going out of the south gate you will be counting by the pint. In Honan more than half the population has died.

The situation is made worse by the increase in banditry. Starving peasants have become robbers. The rice boats are being attacked on the rivers, and the soldiers sent against the robbers are themselves starving and living off the country. All these factors have led to a catastrophic decline in population.

Amsterdam is refugee capital of Europe

Amsterdam, c.1589
Amsterdam is fast establishing itself as the refugee capital of Europe. Religious toleration was written into the Union of Utrecht (1579), and in return for its generosity the city is gaining an unrivalled access to the world's most profitable trading networks.

Among the most conspicuous refugees are the Sephardic Jews, many of whom are successful merchants. Their forebears were expelled from Spain and then Portugal a century ago, and wandered abroad looking for a permanent home.

Some moved to Moslem countries, where they were tolerated, while others preferred the new Protestant nations of Europe, where the Inquisition, which had spearheaded the persecution of the Jews, was not permitted. Their wealth, their business abilities and their wide-ranging contacts have made them very welcome settlers.

Tree-wielding peasants beat samurai

China, 17 January 1588
Qi Jiguang, the greatest of Ming generals, died today destitute and in disgrace. It was Qi who was given the task of clearing the coast of Japanese pirates who landed in their thousands from fleets of junks and even set up civil administrations complete with courts.

The Ming army had been neglected in the long years of peace. Its weapons were out of date, its supply system non-existent, and the troops had no idea of battlefield tactics. Faced by the fearsome Japanese *samurai* wielding two-edged razorsharp swords, they ran away.

Qi set about rebuilding the army. He recruited peasants for their strength and stolidity, and created a new concept of war. He formed them into squads consisting of lancers, javelin throwers, and strong-armed men carrying bamboo trees complete with their upper branches. Their function was to block the flashing swords of the samurai so that the lancers could deal with them. It was a tactic of beautiful simplicity. Qi's "tree-men" defeated the pirates. Alas, he was implicated in the disgrace of Tutor Zhang and was dismissed by the Emperor Wan-li.

Samurai armour; the helmet dates from 1532, the rest from c.1750.

Tolerant empire thrives under Akbar

Fatehpur Sikri, Central India, 1589
After 33 years as the Moghul emperor, Akbar controls half of India. In battle his army has conquered the Rajputs, Gujarat, Bengal and Kashmir, and is still unbeaten. In his provincial capitals a streamlined bureaucracy collects taxes and rules with moderation. In his empire men of all religions, and of none, are treated with equal respect. His greatest triumph was first the defeat and then the co-option of the Rajputs, India's warriors, who are now the policemen of his empire.

Like his audience chamber in the palace at Fatehpur Sikri – where he sits on a central pillar surrounded by his ministers sitting in a circular gallery – his empire revolves around him. Having elevated himself into demi-god, with Sunni, Shi'ite and Hindu wives, he has succeeded in securing the loyalty of all his subjects. New cities are being built all over India. Akbar's own illiteracy does not stop him founding schools throughout his empire. Assisted by his ministers Raja Todar Mal and Shah Mansur, he has reformed the taxation system and established a new bureaucracy, with 33 grades; officials are being moved every two years so that they have an imperial, rather than a provincial, mentality and cannot develop a local following.

Akbar giving audience, from the work called "Akbarnama", c.1590.

1590 (1590-1591)

Persia, 1590. Abbas, the shah of Persia, who is already responsible for the execution of many important tribal leaders, gives orders for his own father and brothers to be blinded.

Japan, 1590. More christian missionaries arrive in Japan with the returning envoys who were sent to Rome eight years ago.

Rome, 1590. The vast cupola of St Peter's basilica is completed to Michelangelo's designs.

Italy, 1590. The physician and mathematician Giovanni Battista Benedetti dies in Turin. Educated by the mathematician Tartaglia, Benedetti attacked Aristotelian dynamics, arguing that in a vacuum all things should fall at the same time.

Virginia, 17 August 1590. John White, the governor of Roanoke Island, returns to America from Europe to find the settlement mysteriously abandoned. One theory is that the colonists followed the Indians under Chief Manteo to the native village called Croatoan, which would be safer than the original settlement site.

Rome, 27 August 1590. Sixtus V, pope since 1585, dies. An energetic Franciscan of humble origins, he reorganised the papal curia and regularly visited bishops to make sure they were disciplined. In foreign policy he aimed to combat Protestantism and maintain the balance of the Catholic powers.

Rome, 1590. After the death of Sixtus V, two popes rapidly succeed each other on the throne of St Peter. The Roman Cestagna dies on 27 September, after reigning for only 13 days. He is followed by Sfondrati from Milan, who takes the name Gregory XIV.

Germany, 3 February 1591. The German Protestant princes form the League of Torgau to counter the Catholic threat.

Germany, 17 March 1591. The painter Jost Amman, who is also renowned for his wood engravings, is buried at Nuremberg.

West Africa, 25 April 1591. The troops of Ahmad al-Mansur, the sultan of Morocco, led by the Spanish renegade Jaudhar, launch a successful attempt to capture Timbuktu.

Russia, 15 May 1591. The epileptic czarevitch Dimitri Ivanovitch, son of Ivan the Terrible, is assassinated. The regent, Boris Godunov, is suspected of being behind the killing.

Mexico, August 1591. Arrested in New Mexico, Castana de Sosa is brought back to Mexico to face disobedience charges.

Spain, 23 August 1591. The writer and mystic Luis de Leon dies as he is about to be named vicar-general of the Augustinians in Castile. He entered the Augustinian order in 1544 and taught theology at Salamanca, where he was imprisoned by the Inquisition in 1572, accused of heresy. In his work *Of the names of Christ* he defined 13 descriptions attached to the name and person of Jesus.

Rome, August 1591. Pope Gregory XIV dies ten months after his election.

Spain, 1 November 1591. A law is passed integrating the Inca feudal system in Peru into the Spanish system of rule. The king of Spain and his viceroy become the successors of the Inca rulers.

Paris, 15 November 1591. Barnabe Brisson, the president of the Parliament of Paris, is executed by the populist League of Sixteen because he is suspected of being unsympathetic. The killing is part of a reign of terror recently initiated by the league.

Spain, 14 December 1591. The Spanish reformist monk Juan de Yepes, known as John of the Cross, dies at the convent of Ubeda. The author of mystical treatises, he also wrote poems, including the *Spiritual Canticle*, which count among the masterpieces of the age. Up to the end of his life he was a victim of betrayals and persecution.

South-East Asia, 1591. James Lancaster becomes the first Englishman to sail to the East Indies.

Italy, 1591. The Italian traveller Pigafetta publishes an account of customs in the Kongo kingdom (*Angola*) of central Africa.

Spain, 1591. In response to a rebellion over the affair of his adviser Antonio Perez, Philip II enters Aragon with an army and abolishes the province's constitutional privileges. Prosecuted for heresy by the Inquisition at Philip's instigation, Perez was freed by a rioting mob in Saragossa and has now fled the country.

Rome, 1591. Elected pope on the death of Gregory XIV, Facchinetti of Bologna, who took the name Innocent IX, reigns for only two months.

Rome, 1591. Pier Paolo Olivieri begins work on the nave of Sant' Andrea della Valle, a fine monument to the spirit of the Counter-reformation.

Japan, 1591. Sen no Rikyu, the celebrated tea-master who was formerly a favourite of Toyotomi Hideyoshi, is forced to commit suicide by Hideyoshi.

Vatican welcomes Japanese Jesuits

Rome, 1590

Four Japanese Jesuits have set sail for their homeland after spending nearly eight years in Rome. Well-born young men, they were warmly greeted by Philip II in Madrid, and Pope Gregory XIII welcomed them to Rome with a brilliant ceremony. Resplendent in Japanese costume, they rode in procession on fine horses to the Vatican where they kissed the pope's foot and were affectionately embraced by him.

Their mission was a great success for the Jesuits, who were granted the sole right to evangelise Japan. The young men were, however, delayed in their return because of the death of Gregory. It is feared that they may be sailing into danger, for Christianity may have fallen into disfavour during their long absence.

Death of pope who modernised Rome

Rome, 27 August 1590

Pope Sixtus V is dead. In his short reign of only five years he has transformed the appearance of this city. The jumble of old houses has been cleared to make space for broad avenues and squares with splendid vistas. He erected an obelisk in St Peter's Square and built a new aqueduct and many fountains.

He encouraged a revival of art with richly decorated frescoes and sculptures. He had a library and a new palace built in the Vatican. He encouraged cardinals and congregations to rebuild their own churches. He used art and architecture to encourage personal piety and religious mass emotion. He was also politically effective, and resisted the overwhelming power and ambition of Philip II of Spain.

Surgeon who soothed wounds of war dies

An anatomy lesson: Ambroise Pare has won wide respect for his techniques.

France, 20 December 1590

Ambroise Pare, one of the most enterprising and successful of modern surgeons, who has been credited with bringing surgery into a new era, has died in Paris at the age of 89.

A specialist in the treatment of wounds, he made many of his most far-reaching innovations on the battlefields of Europe. A master-surgeon at the age of 36, Pare followed his noble employers onto the battlefield. Here he developed new methods of treating wounds, setting bones and nursing men back to health. His most notable breakthrough was to treat wounds not by cauterising them in boiling oil, as had been traditional, but by tying off arteries and applying soothing lotions.

Between battles Pare kept a shop and wrote a book, *The Method of Treating Wounds*. He never read the classical physicians, but his surgical skills proved his excellence. He became a doctor of medicine in 1554, writing his thesis in French not the usual Latin.

Raleigh's New World colony deserted

Virginia, New England, 1590
Three years ago, English pioneers on the windswept island of Roanoke (*off the coast of what is now North Carolina*) celebrated the birth of the first colonial baby. Since then she and 100 other souls of this little community have vanished, leaving no sign of violence and only one clue to what happened: the word "Croatoan" – the name of an Indian tribe – carved on a post at the entrance to the empty palisade.

The macabre disappearance of Roanoke colony was discovered on 17 August when John White, the governor, returned with two ships. The baby – named Virginia after the infant colony – was his granddaughter.

It is six years since a party of English sailors landed on the neighbouring mainland to claim possession of almost 2,000 miles of American coastline. They were led by Arthur Barlow and Philip Amadas commanding two ships which crossed the Atlantic before stopping at Puerto Rico and Florida.

They were made especially welcome at Roanoke, where Chief Wingina made gifts of meat, fish and other food. As Barlow put it: "We were entertained with all love and kindness and with as much bounty, after their manner, as they could possibly devise. We found the people most gentle, loving and faithful, void of all guile and treason, and such as lived after the manner of the Golden Age."

Two years later the explorer Walter Raleigh was knighted for his initial discovery of the territory, though he ran the Barlow expedition from England for political reasons. He also won royal permission to name the new territory on the eastern seaboard "Virginia" in honour of the "Virgin Queene".

In spite of repeated efforts, the colony has not fared well. Five years ago Sir Richard Greville put 108 settlers ashore without enough food. Their hunger led to hostility with the Indians. After a year, in June 1586, they were rescued by Drake. Greville put another 15 men ashore a few days later. A few months after that, when White put his 100 ashore, there was no sign of Greville's 15 settlers.

Woman and child, by John White.

Native chief, also by White, c.1585.

The native village of Pomiock, a watercolour by John White done in 1587.

Mysterious death of Ivan's last son

Moscow, 15 May 1591
One of Ivan the Terrible's two sons, the nine-year-old epileptic Dimitri, has been found murdered, his throat cut by a gang of hired killers. No arrests have been made, but rumours are widespread that the man responsible for the prince's death is the powerful aristocratic *boyar* Boris Godunov. Godunov has been effectively acting as regent for Czar Fyodor, the younger son of Ivan, an amiable and pious imbecile. Dimitri and his mother, Ivan's seventh and last wife, had been exiled to Uglitch where they may have served as a tool for disaffected boyars anxious to unseat Godunov. The boy was the logical successor to his brother, and this is behind the rumours that Godunov engineered the murder.

Blood flows freely in Angola anarchy

Angola, 1591
Angola is in anarchy. Coastal states are tearing each other apart on the instigation of Catholic missionaries. Portuguese adventurers are using slave warriors to carve out private kingdoms. There is famine, and a new European menace is penetrating deeper into the interior of central Africa: the Atlantic slave trade.

The horrors began in 1561 when Portugal tried to impose its own choice, Affonso, as king of the Kongo. There was a *coup d'etat*; Affonso's brother, Bernardo, took over and some Portuguese were killed. By 1566 Bernardo was dead and the weakened kingdom was invaded by the Jaga, a hard inland people, migrating in their thousands towards the Altantic. No one is in control and missionaries and traders raise mercenary armies. For 30 years the blood has not ceased to flow.

"Rich hill" spawns city of wantonness

Peru, 1591
Potosi, 28 years ago a miserable, windswept hamlet, has burgeoned into an "imperial city" of 130,000 people, bigger than Paris or Madrid. Twelve years ago Judge Matienzo noted the wantonness of the city, with its 34 casinos, 800 gamblers, 120 prostitutes and 14 dance academies as well as 36 lavish churches. The secret of Potosi's wealth is the local silver mountain, the *Cerro Rico*, or rich hill, from which tons of bullion are mined for Spain each year. Some streets are supposedly paved with silver bars and horses shod with the metal. But the mining environment is anything but luxurious: the thin air at an altitude of 14,000 feet, the bitter cold and the notorious roaring wind. The hard work is done almost exclusively by Indians, and the mine-owners are so politically powerful that some are even ready to challenge Madrid's representative in Peru. It is 45 years since Spain's first viceroy, Blasco Nunez Vela, died suppressing the mine-owners' first rebellion.

1591 (1591-1593)

Atlantic, 1591. A Spanish fleet defeats an English fleet off the Azores. Sir Richard Grenville is killed in the heroic fight of the *Revenge*.

England, 1591. The playwright William Shakespeare writes *Henry VI*, an historical drama in three parts, each consisting of five acts. Shakespeare takes his framework from the *Chronicles of England, Scotland and Ireland* by Raphael Holinshed, who died in 1580.

London, 1591. The publication of the second in a series of *Voyages* by Theodor de Bry is a huge success. The book features engravings of Florida Indians based on paintings by Jacques de Magne de Morgues, who lived with the French Huguenots at Fort Caroline until it was destroyed by the Spanish in 1565. He depicts monstrous reptiles, called alligators, and savages with tattoos all over their bodies. There are scenes of terrible executions and barbarous rites.

France, 1591. Francis Viete, a mathematician and privy counsellor to King Henry IV, publishes a treatise on algebra entitled *The Art of Analysis*. His is the first work to use letters to represent mathematical unknowns or indeterminates.

Ireland, 1591. Queen Elizabeth founds Trinity College, Dublin.

Rome, 30 January 1592. Cardinal Ippoliti Aldobrandini is elected pope in succession to Innocent IX and takes the name Clement VIII. He sets about amending the Vulgate Bible, promulgated two years ago by Pope Sixtus V, to produce a definitive version.

Italy, 13 February 1592. The painter Jacopo da Ponte, known as Bassano after his native town, dies. After moving to Venice over 40 years ago, he abandoned the forms and colours of mannerism and painted with a realism in which the effects of light predominate.

Florence, 22 April 1592. The sculptor and architect Bartolomeo Ammannati dies. He worked on the Pitti Palace and conceived the bridge of Santa Trinita and the fountain of Neptune on the Piazza delle Signorie.

France, 13 September 1592. Michel Eyquem de Montaigne dies. From a line of rich merchants, Montaigne studied law and became a member of the Bordeaux parliament. He was deeply affected by the death, in 1563, of his friend Etienne de la Boetie, with whom he was linked by a "marriage of souls". In 1571 he sold his parliamentary seat and retired to Montaigne in the Perigord, where he composed his *Essays*.

Sweden, 27 November 1592. John III, the king of Sweden, dies and is succeeded by his son Sigismund, king of Poland since 1587.

Italy, 3 December 1592. Alexander Farnese, the duke of Parma, who recovered the southern provinces of the Netherlands for the Spanish crown in 1579, dies.

West Africa, 1592. Djouder captures the Songhai capital, Gao.

Korea, 1592. When the government of Korea refuses Toyotomi Hideyoshi's trade terms, the Japanese leader invades Korea and battles with the Korean army with resounding initial successes. The Japanese General Konishi captures the castle at Pusan.

India, 1592. The Emperor Akbar's troops annex Orissa.

France, 1592. A violent peasant rebellion, known as the Revolt of the Croquants, breaks out in south-western France in protest at heavy taxes on the peasantry. It is met with savage repression.

Pacific, 1592. Juan de Fuca claims to have travelled through a north-west passage to the northern Pacific Ocean.

France, 6 February 1593. The classical scholar Jacques Amyot, tutor to the children of Henry II, dies. His translations of *Parallel Lives* and *Moral Works* introduced Plutarch to his contemporaries, in particular Montaigne.

Paris, February 1593. The estates-general, France's parliament, meets for the first time since 1576, under the auspices of the Catholic League, which holds Paris. The assembly – which has hitherto always met in Rheims – calls for a Catholic king of France.

England, 30 June 1593. The dramatist Christopher Marlowe dies in an argument in a tavern at Deptford near London at the age of 29. His rebellious and fevered spirit speaks through his tragedies: *Tamburlaine* (1587), a fierce indictment of ambition; *The Tragedy of Dr Faustus* (1588), in which he affirms his belief in supernatural forces; *The Jew of Malta* (1589), a denunciation of the power of money; and *Edward II* (1592), a tragedy of human impotence.

Milan, 11 July 1593. Giuseppe Arcimboldo, who was court painter to the Emperors Ferdinand and Rudolf II, dies. He is famous for his extraordinary compositions of vegetables, fruits and flowers arranged to resemble human forms.

France, 25 July 1593. King Henry IV abjures Protestantism and becomes a Roman Catholic.

Morocco seeks gold south of the Sahara

Timbuktu, 1592

Morocco, a major power after its army slaughtered 26,000 Portuguese at Alcazar el Kebir, has invaded Songhai. The 4,000-strong Moroccan army of Andalucian mercenaries and Christian renegades, with 8,000 camels, and arms supplied by Elizabeth of England, has crossed the Sahara. Twice it has defeated the Songhai army, first at Tondibi, near the capital Gao, then at Bamba near Timbuktu.

For Morocco's sultan, Mulai Ahmed al-Mansur (the Victorious), the goal is not territory but gold. The first task of his army was to occupy the mines at Taghaza, in the middle of the Sahara, where salt is hewed and traded for gold in Black Africa. On the Moroccans' approach the miners fled and the mine is now closed, a major blow to Moroccan ambition.

In spite of the victories the campaign is a failure. The occupiers are confronted by scorched earth, Gao is deserted, there is no gold to be found, and everywhere Moroccans are being harried by guerrillas.

Venetian Rialto bridge rebuilt in stone

Venice's Rialto bridge over the Grand Canal, by Canaletto (1697-1768).

Venice, 1591

The Rialto bridge, linking the banks of the Grand Canal at the Fondaco dei Tedeschi, has been completed. Functional rather than artistically pleasing, it is a single span, 52 yards long and 24 wide, with two rows of shops dividing it into three corridors.

When the decision was taken to replace the old wooden bridge with one made of stone, a competition was declared which attracted some of Italy's most distinguished architects. Designs were submitted by Michelangelo, Sansovino, Vignola, Scamozzi and Palladio before the job was entrusted to Antonio da Ponte, who had rebuilt the doges' palace.

Armoured ship smashes Japanese fleet

Korea, 1592

An iron-plated and turtle-backed ship developed here heralds a new phase in the history of marine warfare technology. This is the first ship to be build with an "armour" cladding of iron and it was recently used with spectacular success by Admiral Yi-sun-sin in his struggle against the Japanese. Japan's fleet was almost wiped out within a matter of days of the armoured ship's deployment.

The new warship presents a formidable sight, with rows of gleaming spikes, a battering ram at the prow and archery ports for firing arrows.

French king hears Mass for sake of Paris

Paris, 25 July 1593
King Henry IV of France today rejected Protestantism and was received into the Catholic religion. The ceremony took place in the basilica of St Denis and was witnessed by the archbishop of Beaune.

Then, having made his confession and heard Mass, he swore allegiance to the church, reiterated his renunciation of Protestantism, and received absolution. He left the basilica to the cheers of the Parisian crowd which sees in his transformation the promise of an end to the religious wars which have ravaged France for so long.

This is the second time that Henry has abjured his faith; the first time was during the St Bartholomew's Day massacre when he did so to save his life and afterwards recanted. This time it is with the hard-won knowledge that he would never be recognised as the true king of France without becoming a Catholic. As he looked down on the city from the hill of Montmartre today he said: "Paris is worth a Mass."

Henry IV: his rule spells an end to years of French religious strife.

Galileo's thermometer is boon to science

Italy, 1592
The Italian scientist Galileo has invented a device for measuring temperature. It works on a principle known long ago to the Greeks of Alexandria – namely that air expands as it is heated.

Galileo's device has one important feature which sets it above previous attempts. It has a scale etched on it. The "thermometer" consists of a small glass bulb at the top of a thin glass tube containing water. As the air in the bulb is warmed it expands and pushes down on the water in the tube. The level then drops.

With this thermometer the fertile Galileo has given his fellow-scientists a truly scientific measuring instrument.

Galileo's thermometer (model).

Sex scenes arouse trouble for new novel

China, 1593
A long, complex, sophisticated and, some would say, pornographic novel is being passed round the literary world. It is titled *Jin Ping Mei*, or the Plum in the Golden Vase; its author hides his identity under the nom de plume of "The Laughing Scholar of Lan-ling". The book tells the story of a family caught up in the collapse of the Sung dynasty. It is enormously complicated and requires re-reading before its subtle allegories can be fully appreciated.

The anonymous author sets new standards in technical virtuosity, but his explicit descriptions of the sexual act may inhibit a proper critical assessment of his writing.

Queen takes hard line with parliament

England, 27 February 1593
After 35 years on the throne of England, Elizabeth has felt it necessary to remind MPs of her right to "assent to or dissent from anything done in parliament". She has also let it be known that she does not wish MPs to seek to override her in foreign and religious affairs.

The queen has taken action as two new statutes are about to come before MPs. One will heavily increase the fines for Catholics who refuse to attend Church of England services, as required by law; the other will make it a crime to attend Catholic assemblies for worship.

In recent years, Elizabeth, backed by her chief minister Lord Burghley, has found it increasingly difficult to get on with her parliaments. In 1558, on her accession, England was in turmoil after Mary's attempt to reimpose Roman authority over the English church; at the same time the threat of invasion and subjugation by Spain was looming.

There was a dire need for stability and unity, and Elizabeth offered to provide them in co-operation with parliament which gave her support in return. The notion, emerging even under her father Henry VIII, that the sovereign power in the land was the "Monarch-in-Parliament" was strengthened. Now England's newly-prosperous middle classes are represented in parliament and asserting themselves.

William Cecil, Lord Burghley, Elizabeth's secretary of state.

Artist and practical joker dies at court

Man of vegetables: "Summer", from the school of Arcimboldo (1527-93).

Prague, 11 July 1593
Giuseppe Arcimboldo, the master of the revels of Emperor Rudolf and his trusted friend has died at court. He was also known especially for his deceptive portraits. He could paint a collection of books to look like the face of a librarian, and would make up portraits out of animals or a tree-trunk and its branches. He painted one portrait of the emperor himself entirely out of vegetables.

Arcimboldo came from Milan. Rudolf's court is a haven for eccentrics, astrologers and alchemists, as well as astronomers like Johann Kepler and Tycho Brahe.

1593 (1593-1595)

Sweden, 1593. The Diet of Uppsala adopts the Augsburg Confession of 1530, imposing on King Sigismund the continuation of Lutheranism as the state religion.

North America, 1593. A Spanish expedition under Francisco de Levya Bonilla and Antonio Gutierez de Humana to find the "gold mines of Tindan" is massacred by Indians (*in Kansas*).

England, 1593. Parliament passes stringent new legislation aimed at curbing religious dissenters. Protestant separatists who establish self-governing congregations outside the Church of England are to be punished by prison terms as well as fines.

England, 1593. Charged with the authorship of the Marprelate tracts – extreme Puritan attacks on the Anglican bishops – John Penry is convicted of treason and hanged. Penry, a Welsh Puritan, had earlier written three treatises advocating a reform of the Anglican clergy.

England, 1593. Shakespeare writes *Richard III*, *Comedy of Errors* and a collection of erotic poems entitled *Venus and Adonis*.

Rome, 2 February 1594. Giovanni Pierluigi da Palestrina dies and his body is laid in St Peter's basilica. Summoned to Rome in 1551 by Pope Julius II to direct the choir of the Julian chapel, he was successively director of music at the St John Laterano and Great St Mary's churches, and from 1571, at St Peter's. He wrote over 100 masses and 600 motets.

Paris, 22 March 1594. Governor Brissac opens the gates of Paris to Henry IV. The opposition of the Catholic League, whose position was undermined by Henry's conversion to Catholicism last year, is on the brink of collapse.

Venice, 31 May 1594. The painter Jacopo di Robusti, known as Tintoretto, dies. He imitated Titian's use of colour and Michelangelo's drawing technique. A master of perspective, some of his most important work is in the Scuola di San Rocco.

Germany, 24 June 1594. The musician Orlando di Lasso dies. For a long time the master of chapel music at Munich, in the service of the duke of Bavaria, the "Divino Orlando" excelled in motets and songs, in which he combined Flemish and Italian musical traditions.

England, 22 November 1594. Martin Frobisher, the English explorer of North America, who attempted to discover a north-west passage to China, dies of a wound sustained at the siege of Crozon, near the French port of Brest.

Netherlands, 2 December 1594. The influential Flemish geographer and mathematician Gerardus Mercator (Gerhard Kremer) dies.

Central Asia, 1594. The Emperor Akbar's troops take control of Baluchistan and Makran, annexing them to the Moghul empire.

South-East Asia, 1594. The English navigator Sir James Lancaster, a soldier and merchant in the service of Portugal, returns to Europe after a three-year visit to the East Indies.

Netherlands, 1594. The province of Groningen joins the Union of Utrecht.

Hungary, 1594. In a renewed war with Hungary, the Ottoman Turks capture the fortress of Raab.

Florida, 1594. Father Baltasar Lopez holds a mass baptism of 80 Indians to encourage 13 new friars.

England, 1594. Shakespeare writes *Titus Andronicus* and a comedy entitled *The Taming of the Shrew*.

Mexico, 1594. The Mercedarian fathers, members of the Order of Mercy, arrive in Mexico.

Angola, 1594. The Portuguese Furtado de Mendoca is named governor of Sao Paolo of Luanda.

France, 1594. King Henry IV's mistress, Gabrielle d'Estrees, bears him an illegitimate son, Cesar of Bourbon, duke of Vendome.

France, 17 January 1595. Henry IV declares his intention to pursue the war against Spain, which is attempting to enforce the claims of a Spanish pretender to the French throne.

England, 21 February 1595. The Jesuit poet Robert Southwell is hanged for "treason" (i.e., being a Catholic priest) at Tyburn.

Rome, 25 April 1595. Summoned to Rome by Pope Clement VIII to be crowned poet laureate, Torquato Tasso dies at the monastery of Santo' Onofrio before the ceremony can take place. He is the author of the epic masterpiece *Gerusalemme Liberata*.

Rome, 26 May 1595. Philip Neri, the philanthropist and priest who moved to Rome from his native Florence in 1533, dies. In 1564 he founded the Congregation of the Oratory to rededicate the clergy to the service of lay society.

France, 5 June 1595. King Henry IV's army defeats the Spanish at the battle of Fontaine-Francaise and drives them out of Burgundy.

Ireland, 1595. Hugh O'Neill, the earl of Tyrone, who became leader of the O'Neill clan two years ago, has set himself up as the champion of the Catholics and approached Spain for help against the English.

The glowing tones of "St George and the Dragon", by Tintoretto.

Tintoretto, painter of grandeur, is dead

Venice, 31 May 1594

The largest canvas ever painted is the picture of *Paradise*, covering the entire wall of the council chamber in the doges' palace, 84 feet (25.6m) long and 34 feet (10.4m) high. The man who painted it (with assistants), Jacopo Robusti, died today aged 76. He was always known as Tintoretto. His father was a *tintero*, or dyer.

Tintoretto and Paolo Veronese were commissioned to decorate the ceilings and state rooms of the doges' palace with vast and glowing paintings showing the glory of Venice, the queen of the seas. As a youth Tintoretto was dismissed from Titian's workshop for disobedience, although some Titian admirers say it was out of jealousy. His paintings are mystical and often show vivid moments of drama, such as the snatching of the body of St Mark, Venice's patron saint, by night from Alexandria.

Tintoretto worked fast. He decorated the entire Scula di San Rocco in six years and often worked for nothing. He will be buried in the church where his *Last Judgment* 50 feet (15.2m) high, hangs.

Japanese invade Korea

Korea, 1593
The Japanese warlord Hideyoshi's invasion of Korea has become bogged down after a year of fighting and the Japanese army, having lost a third of its strength, is in danger of defeat. The well-prepared invasion opened with a landing at Pusan in May last year. It could have met disaster at the outset, for the Japanese navy failed to rendezvous with the troop convoys, but the Korean ships missed their opportunity to attack.

Troops poured ashore and broke the feeble defence of the Korean army, lopping off 8,000 heads in the first few days. The Japanese then captured Seoul, and the king of Korea fell back to Pyongyang while the Japanese looted his capital. The strong Korean navy had recovered from its surprise, however, and started a damaging series of raids on the Japanese supply ships and troop-carriers. The Korean army's resistance stiffened and the passage of the Japanese through the countryside aroused fierce resistance among the peasants. Guerrilla bands hounded the invaders, more supply ships were sunk and the cruel winter set in. Yet it was the intervention of the Chinese in the early months of this year which proved the turning point. Marching in great strength across the Yalu, they have forced the invaders to evacuate Seoul. The signs are that Hideyoshi is ready to talk peace.

Himeji castle, one of Toyotomi Hideyoshi's strongholds, built in 1577.

Irish uprising threat alarms Elizabeth

Ireland, 30 June 1595
An Irish chief who was made earl of Tyrone for his devoted services to the English cause in Ireland was today officially proclaimed a traitor. It is now known that Hugh O'Neill has been smuggling arms into the country in preparation for an uprising against the introduction of Protestant ways. Another cause of anger among the Catholic Irish has been the arrival in Ulster of Scottish immigrants with their fiercely anti-Catholic Calvinism.

O'Neill, loudly professing loyalty to England, married the daughter of an aristocratic Anglo-Irish family, though the union did not last. He was allowed to raise a force of 600 men, trained by the English. Each year the men were replaced by new recruits, so that when he launched the rebellion this year he had a force of 4,000 musketeers, 1,000 pikemen and 1,000 cavalry.

O'Neill has captured Enniskillen and Monaghan castles and appealed to Philip of Spain for help. But the English have blocked that and fought O'Neill to a stalemate. Now, schools are being opened and Trinity College has been founded – in the hope that education will pacify the Irish.

Europe loses two great masters of music

Composers in sixteenth-century Europe were held in great esteem.

Munich, 14 June 1594
In four months Europe has lost two of its towering musical geniuses. On February 2 Giovanni Pierluigi da Palestrina died; today saw the death of Orlando di Lassus.

Palestrina was born in the town of the same name, near Rome, in about 1525. He worked there until his bishop became Pope Julius III and made him head of music at the Julian Chapel in St Peter's (1551). A series of prestigious posts followed before Palestrina returned to St Peter's in 1571. A prolific composer of mainly sacred works (such as the famous *Papae Marcelli* mass), he was asked in 1577 to revise church plainchant following the Council of Trent's guidelines.

Lassus was born in Flanders in about 1530 and travelled widely. From 1553-55 he was head of music at St John Lateran in Rome (Palestrina succeeded him); he joined the duke of Bavaria's chapel in 1556, heading it from 1563 until his death. Less conservative than Palestrina, his huge output ranges from masses to raucous drinking-songs.

Polish king offered the Swedish throne

Stockholm, 17 November 1593
On the death of John III, the Swedish aristocrats have offered the crown to the king of Poland, Sigismund Vasa. The nobles, who have begun to think of themselves as the historic guardians of Sweden's laws and liberties, have nevertheless staked their claim to a major share in government.

Firmly Lutheran, they are determined to place a curb on Sigismund's Catholicism, as well as imposing new restrictions on the crown. Sigismund has already had to sign the Statutes of Kalmar which were designed to ensure that the union of the crowns should neither endanger the country's independence nor prejudice its faith.

"The horn of Venus", by English alchemist, geographer, mathematician and astronomer John Dee (born 1527). Once in prison for magic, Dee supports efforts to find the north-west passage.

1595 (1595-1596)

North America, 23 September 1595. Having decided that conversion of Indians is preferable to conquest, Spain divides south-eastern North America into mission provinces.

Sweden, October 1595. King Sigismund appoints his Protestant uncle Charles to rule Sweden jointly with the council in his absence from the country.

Hungary, October 1595. Shortly after losing the fortress of Esztergom, the Turkish forces are defeated by a Hungarian offensive, led by Sigismund Bathory, at Giurgiu.

Central Asia, 1595. The Emperor Akbar's troops annex Kandahar. All of India north of the Narbada river, as well as Kandahar, Kabul and Ghazna, now acknowledges Moghul supremacy.

Istanbul, 1595. Mehmet III succeeds Murad III as sultan of the Ottomans. On his accession to the throne he enforces the "law of fratricide", by which a new sultan is obliged to execute his brothers and their male children. Nineteen of Murad III's sons are killed.

Peru, 1595. Luis de Vlasco, the former viceroy of New Spain, is appointed viceroy of Peru.

England, 1595. Shakespeare writes the history play *Richard II* and the black comedy *The Merchant of Venice*.

Pacific, 1595. Having set out from Peru, the Spaniard Mendana de Neyra reaches the Marquesas islands, and then the island of Santa Cruz *(east of the Solomon islands)*, where he meets his death.

South-East Asia, 1595. The Dutch make a voyage round the Cape of Good Hope and across the Indian Ocean to Java. They begin to colonise the East Indies.

South America, 1595. The English navigator Sir Walter Raleigh explores the coast of Trinidad and sails up the Orinoco river.

France, January 1596. The duke of Mayenne, the leader of the Catholic League, surrenders to Henry IV.

Mexico, January 1596. Sebastian Rodriguez Cermeno returns to Mexico after a 22-month sea voyage up the Pacific coast.

Caribbean, January 1596. Sir Francis Drake, the English naval leader and privateer, dies.

France, April 1596. The Spanish capture Calais.

Spain, 1 July 1596. An English fleet under the earl of Essex, Lord Howard of Effingham and Francis Vere captures and sacks Cadiz.

Hungary, September 1596. The Turks, now under the personal leadership of the Ottoman Sultan Mehmet III, defeat the Hungarians at Erlau (*Eger*).

Ukraine, October 1596. The creation of the united Ruthenian church is ratified by the synod of Brest-Litovsk. After a year of negotiation, the Jesuits have managed to unite the Roman Catholic and Orthodox Churches of the Ukraine.

Hungary, October 1596. In spite of a mass desertion by the infantry, the Turks win an astonishing victory at Mezokeresztes. Sultan Mehmet III was personally responsible for turning the tide in the battle, in which 30,000 Hungarians and Germans are reported to have died.

Rome, 1596. Pope Clement VIII absolves Henry IV, the king of France, from his previous excommunication.

France, 1596. France forms an alliance with England and the Netherlands against the Spanish king.

East Africa, 1596. The Portuguese complete the building of Fort Jesus in Mombasa, Kenya.

North America, c.1596. The first wheeled vehicles – wagons, similar to German farm carts – appear in the New World. They are used to haul supplies as the Spanish continue to explore and settle the south-west.

Netherlands, 1596. Albert, the archduke of Austria, is appointed governor of the Netherlands. The third son of the Emperor Maximilian II, Albert was made a cardinal in 1577 and archbishop of Toledo in 1584. In 1594 he became viceroy of Portugal.

France, 1596. The political philosopher Jean Bodin, author of the *Republic* and the famous *Response to the Paradoxes of Malestroit*, dies. Bodin had argued that property and the family form the basis of society and that the best government is absolute monarchy.

England, 1596. *The Faerie Queen*, a seven-volume poem written by Edmund Spenser and dedicated to Queen Elizabeth, is published.

England, 1596. Shakespeare writes the comedy *A Midsummer Night's Dream* and a tragic love story entitled *Romeo and Juliet*.

Austria, 1596. Johann Kepler publishes his *Cosmographical Mystery*, in which he argues that there is a geometrical relationship between the distances of the planets from the sun which can be expressed numerically.

Hundreds burned in German witch hunts

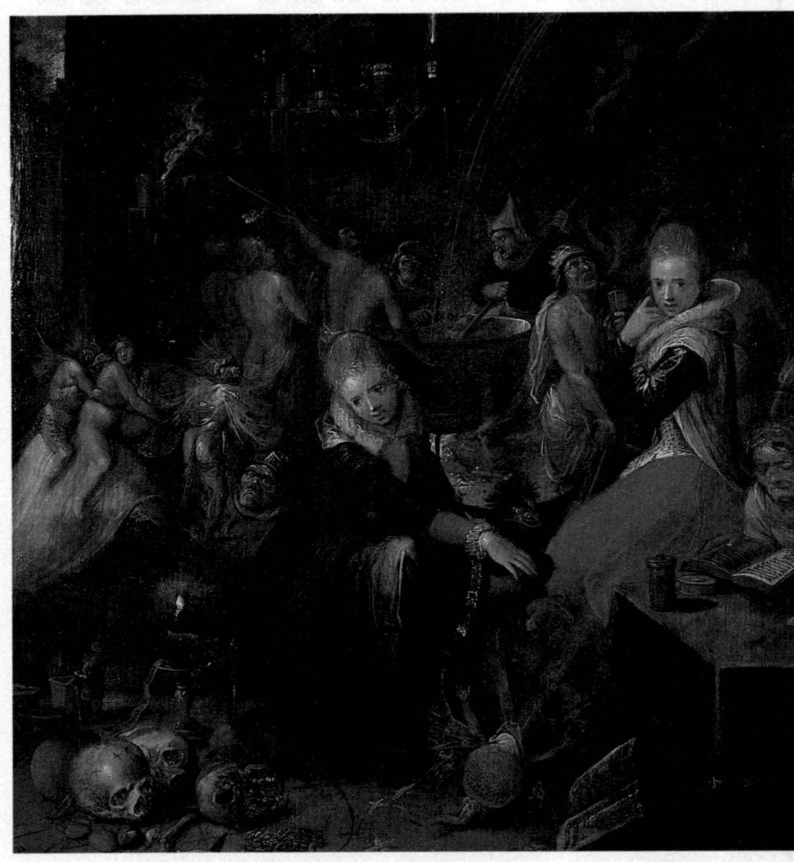

"Witches' Sabbath" (detail), by Frans Francken the Younger (1581-1642).

German states, c.1595

The German states are convulsed with a new epidemic as pervasive, as widespread and as terrifying as the plague: the fear of witchcraft. Unlike the plague, this is a disease of the mind; but while no-one has yet discovered a cure for plague, there is a simple and often used remedy for witchcraft: death.

Germany has been torn by a series of witch-hunts, usually followed by a public trial and then, almost invariably, by the execution of the accused, whose confession has often been extracted through torture. Much of the hysteria has been inspired by the *Malleus Maleficarum* (the Hammer of the Witches), a tract written by the Dominicans Institorus and Sprenger in 1487 and authorised by the pope. Its pages inflame many peasants, fearful of satanic attacks on their crops.

Between 1587 and 1593 the archbishop-elector of Trier burned 368 witches. On a single day in 1589, 133 witches were executed at the convent of Quedlinburg; the list is endless. Church dignitaries are the most ferocious persecutors, but the secular powers are almost as keen. What has sparked off the witch-hunts is debatable. The *Malleus* is notably misogynistic, obsessed with female lust; the majority of the accused are women. The concept of the witches' "Sabbath" or "black mass" is also a potent image.

Newes from Scotland,
Declaring the Damna-
ble life and death of Doctor Fian, *a*
notable Sorcerer, who was burned at
Edenbrough in Ianuary last.
1591.
Which Doctor was regester to the Diuell
that sundry times preached at North Bar-
rick Kirke, to a number of noto-
nous Witches.
With the true examinations of the saide Doctor
and Witches, as they vttered them in the pre-
sence of the Scottish King.
Discouering how they pretended
to bewitch and drowne his Maiestie in the Sea
comming from Denmarke, with such
other wonderfull matters as the like
hath not been heard of at
any time.
Published according to the Scottish Coppie.
AT LONDON
Printed for William
Wright.

From James I's "Daemonologie".

Gothic gives way to Elizabethan style

The new style: Great Bed of Ware, 1580.

England, c.1595
The architecture of England under Elizabeth has swept away the cobwebs of the late Tudor Gothic style, which by the middle of the century had become rather stagnant.

At the root of the new styles lies the continental Renaissance, but via Flanders and France rather than directly from Italy. In 1563 the Fleming Vredeman de Vries published a series of books in which the classical orders of building were extravagantly transformed and adorned with gables and strapwork. This style soon caught on throughout northern Europe, and under its influence English architecture began to acquire great originality, although Italian influence on large houses can be seen in the tendency to build symmetrical frontages. The arrangement of rooms internally is generally similar to that of earlier times, with the great chamber as the ceremonial heart of the house. Among the greatest of the new or rebuilt houses are Longleat (1573), Holdenby (begun 1577), Theobalds (altered 1580s) and Hardwick Hall (early 1590s).

Houses such as these reflect the weath of families prospering from rising prices, royal service and the dissolution of the monasteries. Despite the grandeur, English buildings have come under fire from some critics for being flimsy and two-dimensional compared with those of Henry VIII's day. Windows are, indeed, often flush with walls rather than set deeply into them, pilasters are preferred to columns, and buttresses are rare.

Wollaton Hall, Nottingham (1580-8).

Threatened Portuguese build African base

East Africa, 1596
Shaken by repeated rebellions and the massacre of their small forces at trading stations on the East African coast, the Portuguese have started building a base on Mombasa Island. An Italian military architect has been commissioned, masons are coming from Goa, and labour is being recruited locally for a great castle to be called Fort Jesus.

But the work is proceeding slowly and costs are overrunning to such an extent that Lisbon has begun asking questions about where the money is going. An Augustinian prior and a judge have been appointed to a committee to handle funds, keep signed receipts and buy building materials.

The Portuguese have felt their position on the East African coast to be increasingly under threat after Turkish raiders appeared out of the Red Sea and sailed as far south as Mombasa, where the local ruler welcomed the Turks and turned on the Portuguese. When the Turks withdrew, the Portuguese sacked the town. The Turks returned again a few years later and the pattern of rebellion along the coast was repeated, with only the king of Malindi still loyal to Portugal. That was when Lisbon finally gave heed to the appeals of the local Portuguese for a fortress to be built, with a 100-man garrison.

An African bronze, from Benin, of an armed Portuguese soldier.

Death of Drake, England's great sailor

The Caribbean, 29 January 1596
A lead coffin containing the body of Sir Francis Drake, the scourge of the Spanish Main, was committed to the sea a few miles off Porto Bello, Panama, today. Drake was in his mid-fifties and died of dysentery. In April last year he had sailed from Plymouth (whose MP he had been for a time) on an ill-fated expedition with his old comrade-in-arms Sir John Hawkins. A fleet of 27 ships and 2,500 men could not be concealed from the Spanish enemy who was well prepared wherever the English struck. Hawkins died off Puerto Rico last November.

Sir Francis Drake (c.1585).

Armada disaster and internal revolts push Spain to bankruptcy

Madrid, 29 November 1596
Not for the first time Spain is bankrupt. The richest and most formidable power on earth, with an empire envied by allies and enemies, has admitted that the royal treasury has been drained and the nation's economy ruined. Official reasons given by Philip II for the situation are many. One is the series of wars, and particularly the decision to invade England. Wars have been especially costly, and have weakened the armed forces. Bad weather, poor management and heavy domestic spending have also played their parts as have revolts against the Spanish empire in the New World.

1596 (1596-1597)

Florida, 1596. Over the past two years an estimated 1,500 natives have been converted to Christianity by Spanish Franciscan priests.

Atlantic, 1597. An English expedition to the Azores to intercept a Spanish treasure fleet, led by the earl of Essex ends in failure.

Arctic, 1597. The Dutch explorer Willem Barents dies while on his third voyage to search for a northeast passage to China.

Korea, 1597. The Japanese under Hideyoshi launch a further expedition against Korea, but are expelled by the Chinese.

Switzerland, 1597. The Dutch-born Jesuit Peter Canisius dies at Freiburg. An architect of the Counter-reformation in Germany, Canisius wrote a widely used catechism and founded 13 Jesuit communities.

North America, 1597. Simon Ferdinando, a Portuguese navigator working for the English crown, lands on the coast of Maine looking for treasure.

Spain, 1597. The Spanish lyric poet Fernando de Herrera dies in Seville. The best known of his *canciones* describes the 1571 Battle of Lepanto.

Central Asia, 1597. Abbas, the shah of Persia, drives back the Turkish Ozbegs beyond the Amudarja.

Russia, 1597. Czar Fyodor gives orders that fugitive serfs are to be subjected to ferocious punishments.

North America, 1597. The marquis of la Roche, elected lieutenantgeneral of Canada, founds a colony on Sable Island.

India, 1597. Abul Fazl, the Emperor Akbar's secretary, is hard at work on the *Akbarnama*, a book which is intended to be a comprehensive account of the emperor's reign.

England, 1597. Parliament passes an act allowing sentences of transportation to the colonies for convicted criminals.

England, 1597. Shakespeare writes *Henry IV*, an historical play in two parts, and a comedy entitled *The Merry Wives of Windsor*.

England, 1597. The lawyer and statesman Francis Bacon publishes a first volume of *Essays*.

Lucky victory saves Ottoman empire

Hungary, October 1596

In one fell swoop, Mehmet III, the Ottoman Sultan, has saved a huge swathe of territory for his empire. Threatened by a string of Hungarian military triumphs, his possessions in Macedonia, Bulgaria and Hungary have been secured by a remarkable victory on the Mezo-keresztes plain.

It was a minor earthquake rather than any realisation of danger to his empire that moved the superstitious Sultan to battle. Urged on by his ministers, who feared a revolt by disgruntled janissaries, Mehmet took to the field. The capture of Erlau last month encouraged him to confront the Hungarian forces.

The battle started off badly, when early reverses caused the *sipahis* – the fief-holding backbone of Mehmet's army – simply to walk off the battlefield. The Sultan tried to follow them, but his generals held a council of war to persuade him to stay with the rest of his army. At this point, the over-confident Christians broke rank to plunder the Turkish camp. Mehmet's cavalry charged, killing over 30,000 German and Hungarian troops and taking enormous booty including a hundred cannons.

Mehmet is relieved. He wants to get back to Istanbul, where his mother, the Sultana Valide Baffo, holds the reins of power, keeping him happy with a steady supply of beautiful concubines.

Cowardly victor: Mehmet III.

Danish Astronomer records 777 stars

Denmark, 1597

No fewer than 777 stars have been logged by the Danish astronomer Tycho Brahe in a 20-year career of observing the heavens. Brahe, who was granted the island of Hven in south Denmark by the late King Frederick II to build his observatory, is now the world's foremost astronomer.

As well as noting the stars, he has vastly increased our knowledge of the moon, registered the refraction of light, and perfected a table of correction for the better identification of stars. It is through this table that he has been able to compile his own impressive catalogue of heavenly bodies.

Star gazer: Tycho Brahe (1586).

Dutch explorer dies in Arctic winter

Willem Barents' ship trapped in ice, from an account of the expedition.

Novaya Zemlya, 20 June 1597

An attempt to find a north-east passage to Asia has ended in the death in the Arctic of the Dutch explorer Willem Barents. This was his third attempt to find a route around the north of Russia to China, and the course that he chose took him in a more northerly direction than hitherto. He discovered Spitzbergen and Bear Island before his ship was trapped in ice-floes, forcing him and his men to spend the winter in the Arctic.

The historian of the expedition, Gerrit de Veer, has written a moving description of the men's ordeal by cold and hunger. When it was clear that they were trapped, they built a house from tree-roots. "It froze so hard, that as we put a nayle in our mouths, there would be ice thereon when we took it out again and make the bloud follow,"(*sic*) wrote de Veer.

They were attacked by polar bears and forced to eat foxes as their supplies ran out. They were nearly suffocated by smoke when snow covered their hut.

Despite the intense cold, the 16 survivors managed to celebrate the feast of the Epiphany. "For several days we had not drunke and so that night we made merrie and drunk to the three kings, and therewith had two pounds of meale whereof we made pancakes with oyle and everyman a white biskit which we sopt in wine," wrote de Veer (*sic*).

Akbar orders memoirs of his reign

Punjab, India, 1597

As the century draws to its close, Akbar, the great Moghul emperor, has ordered his historian, Abul Fazl, the son of the unorthodox Moslem mystic Sheikh Mubarak, to write an account of his reign.

None are as well qualified as Abul Fazl for the task. Like his brother Faizi, he is one of Akbar's closest advisers. He is a Moslem freethinker who, like his hero, is not afraid of religious intolerance, and is the proud owner of a library of 24,000 well-used books.

The two books which Abul Fazl is compiling, *The History of Akbar* and *The Laws of Akbar*, seem certain to be two of the most detailed books ever written about a great man.

Researching Akbar's biography Abul Fazl is talking to hundreds of witnesses. Akbar's aunt has recalled the Moghul empire at the time of Humayan, Akbar's father, who lost and regained an empire. Humayan's servants, Jauhar and Bayezid, have added their memories; Bayezid, old and suffering from a stroke is dictating his to Abul Fazl's clerk. Fifteen hundred pages are to be devoted to the minutest details of the emperor's life: what he drank, said and did each day, and which wife he slept with each night. Two clerks are with him wherever he goes, recording his actions for Abul Fazl. Abul Fazl's *Laws of Akbar* is equally weighty, recording the words of Akbar on subjects ranging from philosophy and etymology to cooking recipes and methods of oiling camels.

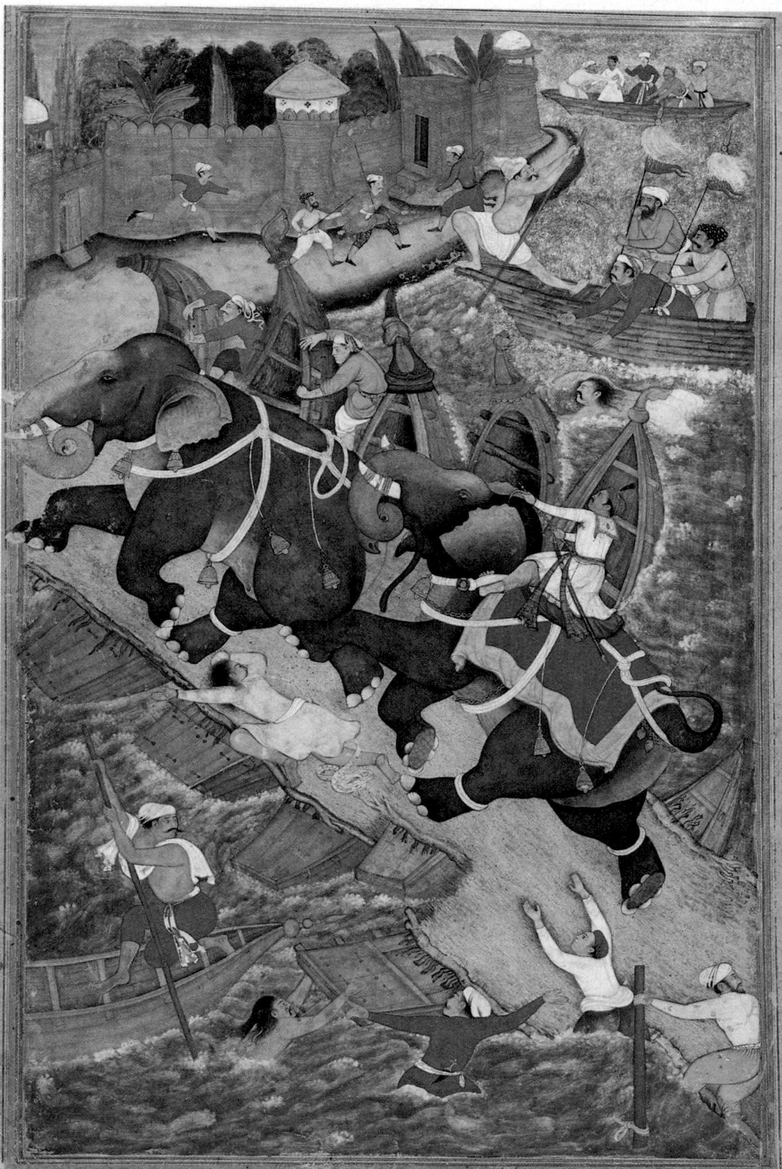

Elephants crossing a pontoon, from Abul Fazl's "The History of Akbar".

Theatres revived after plague threat

London, 1596

The London stage is returning to normal after the recent reopening of the city's theatres, closed in 1593 owing to a plague outbreak. One great figure absent from the revived theatrical scene is the playwright – and spy – Christopher Marlowe, who died in 1593, aged only 29. Apparently, Marlowe met three secret agents at Bull's tavern in Deptford, Kent; a quarrel led to a fight in which he was stabbed above the right eye, dying instantly.

The circles of dark and violent subterfuge in which Marlowe moved are reflected in some of his small output of seven plays, such as *The Jew of Malta*, *The Massacre at Paris* and *Doctor Faustus*.

Until about 50 years ago most plays were on religious themes, but there has since been a shift towards secular themes based on individuals and their motives, often drawn from classical legends, or history, such as Thomas Kyd's *Spanish Tragedy* (1589). The actor-playwright William Shakespeare has emerged as the leading light of the new English drama, working with the new Lord Chamberlain's Company at The Theatre, which was England's first public playhouse, built at Shoreditch in 1576.

Among works written since he came to London around five years ago from his native Stratford are *Henry VI* (in three parts), *Richard III*, *Romeo and Juliet* and *The Taming of the Shrew*.

London's "Swan" Theatre (1596).

Portuguese merchants wary of Dutch rival in East Indies

Holland, 20 August 1597

A Dutch merchant, long resident in Lisbon, has arrived in Holland after a two-year voyage to the Far East Spice Islands that has left the Portuguese fearful for their monopoly of the eastern trade.

Cornelius van Houtman was for many years the prosperous carrier of pepper, nutmeg and other spices from Lisbon to countries of northern Europe. This came to an abrupt end when Philip of Spain claimed the crown of Portugal in 1580 and the two countries were united. He barred the Dutch from Portuguese trade because of their rebellion against his rule in the Netherlands. The Dutch thereupon resolved to get into the eastern trade on their own account.

Houtman was helped on his voyage by a book written by another Dutchman, who had served with the Portuguese East India fleet: Jan Huyghen van Linschoten. On 2 April 1595, Houtman sailed from Holland with four ships; a year later he dropped anchor at Bantam, Java, where the local Portuguese made him welcome. Very soon, though, they became hostile when they realised what the Dutch were about. Houtman outwitted them, persuaded the sultan of Bantam to sign a treaty, and departed with a cargo of spices.

The voyage home was marked by losses of ships and men, but Houtman's tales of rich trading opportunities have fired Amsterdam's merchants with enthusiasm and they are planning to found trading companies, described as *Van Ferne* (of the distant seas).

1597 (1597-1599)

England, 1597. The first crop of domestically-grown tomatoes is produced and eaten.

Mexico, 8 January 1598. Don Juan de Onate sets out on an expedition to New Mexico with some 500 colonists.

Russia, 17 February 1598. Boris Godunov, the *boyar* of Tartar origin, is elected czar in succession to his brother-in-law Fyodor.

France, 13 April 1598. Henry IV, the king of France, promulgates the Edict of Nantes to promote "union, concord and tranquillity" between his Catholic and Huguenot subjects. The edict grants the Huguenots a large measure of religious freedom.

France, 2 May 1598. After three years of declared war, Henry IV signs the treaty of Vervins with Spain, ending Philip II's interference in France. Under the treaty – which is a setback for Habsburg ambitions – Spain keeps the provinces of Flanders, Artois and Charolais, but must leave Picardy.

England, 4 August 1598. William Cecil, chief adviser to Queen Elizabeth on both foreign and domestic matters since her accession in 1558, dies. He was created Baron Burghley in 1571 and lord high treasurer in 1572, and introduced important financial reforms. He built three magnificent mansions: Burghley House at Stamford, Theobalds in Hertfordshire and Cecil House in London.

Ireland, 15 August 1598. Two months after receiving a pardon for his rebellious activities from Elizabeth, the queen of England, Hugh O'Neill, the earl of Tyrone, leads an Irish force to victory over the English at the battle of Yellow Ford.

Madrid, 13 September 1598. Philip II, king of Spain since 1556, dies and is succeeded by his son Philip III.

Sweden, 25 September 1598. Having gained the supported of the Lutheran states against the members of the Swedish council, King Sigismund's uncle Charles inflicts a defeat on his Catholic nephew at Stangebro.

North America, 1598. The marquis de la Roche leaves France with 40 convicts to colonise Sable Island, off Nova Scotia.

Indian Ocean, 1598. The Dutch admiral Wijbrand van Warwijck takes possession of an island which he calls Mauritius, in honour of Maurice of Nassau.

Persia, 1598. Shah Abbas embarks upon an ambition scheme of urbanisation. He plans to make Isfahan one of the most beautiful cities in the world.

China, 1598. The Jesuit Matteo Ricci gains access to the imperial court at Beijing.

Japan, 1598. Toyotomi Hideyoshi, who proclaimed himself civil dictator in 1586, dies after entrusting his son and his dynasty to Tokugawa Ieyasu and four other of his senior councillors.

Korea, 1598. Following the death of Hideyoshi, Japanese troops withdraw from Korea.

West Africa, 1598. The Bambara people, from the Jenne region, overthrow the last of the kings of Mali and found the kingdom of Segu.

Anatolia, 1598. Jelali bands of brigands rise up against Ottoman authority.

England, 1598. Shakespeare writes two comedies: *Much Ado About Nothing* and *As You Like It*, and appears at the Curtain theatre, acting in his friend Ben Jonson's new play *Every Man in His Humour*.

England, 16 January 1599. The poet Edmund Spenser dies. He will be best remembered for his epic work *The Faerie Queen*, written for Queen Elizabeth, in which he sets out to show the ideal gentleman or courtier in action, and for his supreme marriage poem *Epithalamion*, which was written on the occasion of his second marriage.

England, September 1599. Appointed governor-general of Ireland earlier in the year, the earl of Essex returns to England in defiance of Queen Elizabeth's orders. He was sent to Ireland to put down the revolt led by Hugh O'Neill, the earl of Tyrone, with whom he has concluded a truce.

Sweden, November 1599. Sigismund III, king of Poland since 1587 and of Sweden since 1592, is deposed by the Riksdag (the Swedish parliament) because of growing opposition among his Lutheran subjects to his support for the Counter-reformation. His uncle Charles becomes regent.

Poland, 1599. Under the confederation of Vilna, the various branches of the church in Poland unite against the power of the Roman Church.

London, 1599. The actor Richard Burbage pulls down the Shoreditch Playhouse on the south bank of the Thames and begins to build in its place a roofless summer playhouse, the Globe, to seat 1,200 spectators. The Blackfriars theatre, on the north bank, also built by Burbage, is to remain as a winter playhouse. Among Burbage's partners in the new enterprise is the playwright William Shakespeare.

Henry masters France

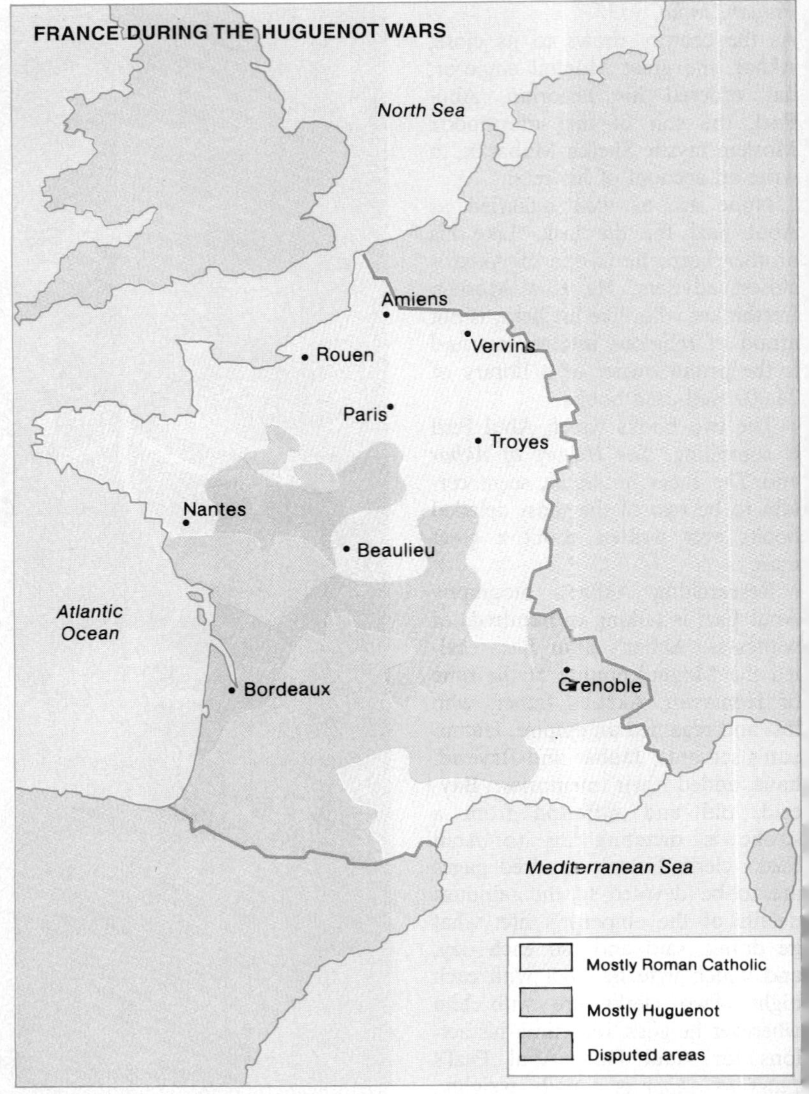

France, 1598

Henry IV can at last call himself king of France. The country is still plagued by brigands to whom warfare has become a way of life, and the religious quarrels are bound to persist, but he has at last brought the long agony of France to an end.

He has done it by diplomacy — his acceptance of the Catholic faith after being the champion of Protestantism for so long was a masterstroke. And he has done it on the battlefield, repelling the Spaniards and quelling the secessionist revolt in Brittany.

He has also won back the support of the Huguenots which he lost when he declared "Paris is worth a Mass". In April he signed the "perpetual and irrevocable" Edict of Nantes which granted Protestants freedom of conscience throughout the kingdom. The edict also restored their old places of worship to them and granted them permission to build new ones. They now have equal civic rights with the Catholics and are allowed access to all public posts.

A full amnesty is granted to all those who took up arms during the wars of religion, and 100 towns are assigned to the Huguenots as "towns of refuge".

The terms of the edict do not please many Catholics, but such is the war-weariness in France that they accepted the edict in return for peace. The following month the ailing King Philip of Spain signed the peace of Vervins and his army marched home. Now France truly belongs to Henry IV.

Irish rout English soldiers at Yellow Ford

Ireland, 15 August 1598
After years of skirmishes and truces between Irish rebels and English soldiers, the Irish have scored a decisive victory at Yellow Ford on the river Callan, near Armagh, Ulster. Last year the English planned a threefold attack on the rebels from Sligo to Westmeath. All three were repulsed and a truce was arranged to last until the middle of this year.

By then the Irish, led by Hugh O'Neill and Red Hugh O'Donnell, were ready. A small garrison on the river Blackwater was under siege and General Sir Nicholas Bagenal set out from Newry with a relief force of 4,000.

O'Neill's men, armed with muskets, sniped at Bagenal's flanks. The force became too scattered for the leading regiment to be given effective support. It was broken up and cut to pieces by cavalry. A rout was avoided, but only about 1,500 of the original 4,000 reached the safety of Armagh. It is a triumph for the Irish, but is certain to enrage Elizabeth who may decide to send more troops.

Boris Godunov elected czar of Russia

Moscow, 17 February 1598
Amid universal rejoicing, Boris Godunov has secured his own coronation as czar. With Fyodor's death the royal house of Russia has been extinguished.

By virtue of the power he has in fact been exercising Godunov was the favoured candidate, but before accepting the throne he insisted upon election by the *Zemsky Sobor*, or Assembly of the Land, drawn from the clergy, the *boyars*, the lesser nobility, officials and merchants.

Godunov is a boyar of Tartar origin who has practically ruled the country for the last 14 years while it has recovered from the disasters of the reign of Ivan the Terrible. He is quite illiterate, but this has not prevented him from directing all correspondence with heads of foreign states and looking like the man running Russia.

He began his career in Ivan's secret police, the *oprichnina*, and succeeded in marrying his sister Irene to Fyodor, thus making himself the new czar's brother-in-law, and indispensable.

Boris Godunov: ruler in effect, and now officially in name.

Catholics crucified on hill in Nagasaki

Nagasaki, 5 February 1597
Twenty-six Christians have been martyred by being crucified upside down on a hill outside Nagasaki on the orders of the Japanese warlord, Hideyoshi. The execution of the seven Franciscans and 19 of their Japanese converts was carried out in the cruellest fashion.

They were condemned to death a month ago in Kyoto and, having first been mutilated, were dragged from city to city in degrading circumstances as a dreadful warning to the Japanese to have nothing further to do with Christianity. Hideyoshi has given no reason for the executions, although he has been surprised by the renewed strength of Christianity in Japan following the return of missionaries after he expelled them in 1587.

What is curious about the executions is that they involved only Franciscans; the strong Jesuit colony was not touched. There is some suspicion of court intrigue behind the martyrdoms. Certainly Christianity in Japan has been dealt a cruel blow.

Spain mourns Philip II

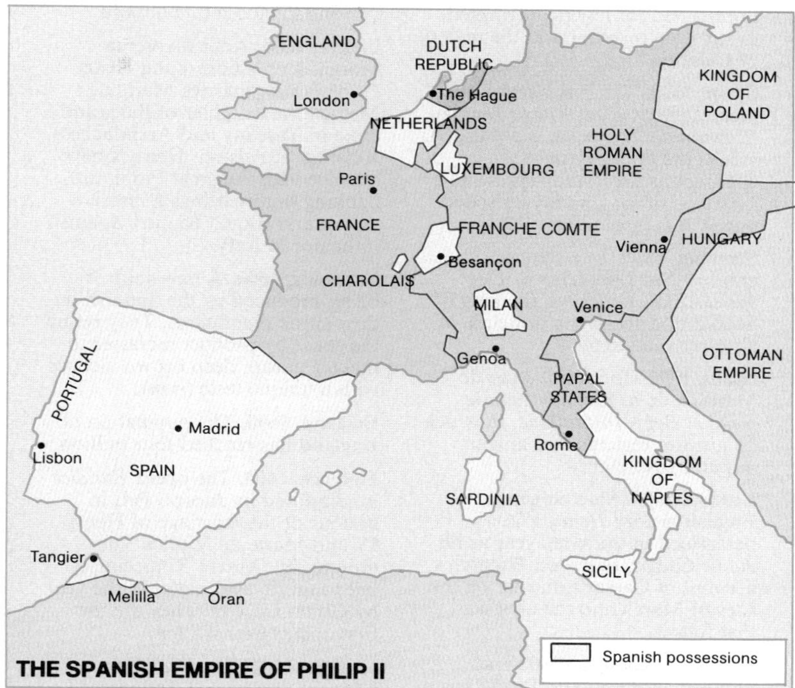

Madrid, 13 September 1598
Philip II of Spain, who has ruled the world's most powerful country for more than 40 years, has died in ulcerous agony in his grim and gloomy Escorial palace outside Madrid. He was 71 and had spent the last few months preparing for his death, ordering black cloth for his own mourning draperies and rehearsing the ritual of extreme unction. Ceaseless prayers will be said in the huge basilica.

Under Philip, Spain became the richest and most formidable nation on earth, and he boasted of ruling the world from the Escorial with pen and paper. But Spain has been in trouble ever since he sent his "Invincible Armada" against the English in 1588. The bid to punish England for its support of Dutch Protestants fighting against Spanish rule, and for plundering Spanish possessions in Mexico and South America, came badly unstuck. Although Spain remained a major power after the defeat, its prestige had been seriously damaged and its naval supremacy lost.

Philip's achievements, however, were many. He and Don John of Austria broke the power of the Turks in the Mediterranean in 1571, and he conquered the Philippines in 1580. But the Netherlands, one of the most valuable possessions in the empire, declared its independence in 1581 and a treaty with France shortly before Philip's death marked Spain's slow retreat from northern Europe.

Philip II: sad end to a reign.

Philip married Queen Mary I of England earlier in his reign, at a time when the English looked upon Spain as their greatest enemy, but deserted her shortly before she died. He regarded himself as a great champion of the Roman Catholic faith and supported the harsh measures of the Inquisition.

1599 (1599-1601)

Naples, 1599. The Dominican monk and Italian philosopher, Tommaso Campanella, is imprisoned for having attempted to stir up a revolution in the region of Calabria.

Spain, 1599. The first part of the picaresque novel of Mateo Aleman, *Guzman de Alfarache*, is published. It tells the life story of the eponymous hero, and represents a new type of long, many-episoded novel. It is instantly popular.

Scotland, 1599. In a treatise entitled *The True Laws of Free Monarchies*, James VI, the king of Scotland, defends the principle of absolute monarchy.

Spain, 1599. The Jesuit Juan de Mariana de la Reina writes *De Rege et Regis Institutione*, in which he justifies regicide and affirms popular sovereignty.

London, 1599. Shakespeare's English history *Henry V* is performed in the same year as his *Julius Caesar*, based on Plutarch's account of Caesar's murder on the Ides of March and the civil war that follow.

Rome, 17 February 1600. The philosopher Giordano Bruno is burnt to death as a heretic after a seven-year trial. Influenced by Neoplatonism, Stoicism and Epicureanism, he believed in a pantheistic system based on Copernican astronomy.

Japan, April 1600. The Englishman William Adams, a navigator in the service of the Dutch, reaches the Japanese port of Bungo. He is thrown into prison as a pirate at the instigation of jealous Portuguese traders.

Madrid, 14 October 1600. The theologian Luis de Molina dies. A disciple of St Thomas Aquinas, Molina is famed for his treatise of 1588 which opposes the Augustinian belief in the complete corruption of human liberty, asserting that free will is total and in accord with divine grace.

Japan, 21 October 1600. Tokugawa Ieyasu defeats his enemies in battle and affirms his position as Japan's most powerful warlord.

Spain, 5 November 1600. King Philip III notifies the Cuban governor Pedro de Valdes of his reservations about missionary and military efforts in Florida.

London, 31 December 1600. The East India Company – "The Governor and Company of Merchants of London trading into the East Indies" – is founded.

London, 1600. Ben Jonson's *Every Man Out of His Humour* is staged for the first time.

Uganda, 1600. The kingdom of Buganda (*near Lake Victoria*) defeats an attack by the neighbouring kingdom of Bunyoro.

France, 1600. After divorcing Margaret of Valois, King Henry IV of France marries Marie de Medici, the daughter of the grand duke of Tuscany and Archduchess Johanna of Austria. Henry's new alliance with the great Florentine banking family brings a massive dowry and should counter Spanish influence in Italy.

Barbados, 1600. A new spirit is being produced by the Spanish on their sugar plantations. They refine the sugar by-product molasses to make a cheap, deep brown alcohol with a unique taste (*rum*).

England, 1600. The population of England has reached four million.

Florence, 1600. The opera *Euridice* is composed by Jacopo Peri in honour of the marriage of Henry IV and Marie de Medici. The libretto, by Ottavio Rinuccini, is put to music again later in the year by Guilio Caccini. They are the first operas ever written.

Canada, 1600. The French found a fur-trading-post at Tadoussac, on the St Lawrence river.

Netherlands, 1600. Maurice of Nassau, the son of and successor to William of Orange, attempts to invade Spanish possessions in the south, having overcome the troops of Archduke Albert of Nieuport.

London, 1600. Shakespeare's new tragedy, *Hamlet*, about a reluctant young revenger caught in a web of intrigue and corruption in the Danish court of Elsinore, opens.

Italy, 1600. The *Rappresentazione di Anima e di Corpo* by the composer Emilio de Cavalieri is performed. It is the first dramatic oratorio.

England, 1600. William Gilbert, doctor to Queen Elizabeth, publishes *De Magnete*, the first treatise establishing a comprehensive theory of terrestrial magnetism. He compares the earth to a magnet and determines the existence of a magnetic field.

Central and South America, 1600. A law is passed in Spanish colonies forbidding whites to enter Indian villages without permission.

France, 1600. A new agricultural treatise by the Protestant Olivier de Serres is gaining influence, especially with the king. It recommends, among other things, crop rotation to make French agriculture more efficient after years of ruinous religious war.

Italy, 1601. A university is founded in Parma.

Portuguese naval mercenaries battle with Indians (late C16th drawing).

East meets west: a Goanese ivory carving of the Holy Trinity.

Goa: Portuguese jewel in the east

Goa, India, c.1600

It has been called Golden Goa – the settlement on India's west coast which is the focus of Portugal's seaborne commercial empire in Asia. Cottons from Gujarat up the coast are traded for pepper in Sumatra; the pepper buys Chinese goods and gold; the Chinese goods are exchanged for Japanese silver. Added to this network is the lucrative export of spices to Europe, also centred on Portuguese Goa.

The Portuguese are very much in the minority, both in Goa itself and as traders. In a population of about 75,000, about 3,000 are pure Portuguese, the rest being Indians, Africans and *Mastizos,* the offspring of Portuguese fathers and Indian women. Women are bought at slave markets; if they can sew, sing, dance and prove they are virgins, they can sell for 30 *cruzados* (a good horse fetches 500 cruzados).

Goa, a city of bazaars and narrow streets, is dominated by churches. The first printing press in Asia is here, and there is a royal hospital where European and Asian medicines come together. A patient will be bled with leeches and then prescribed cow's urine.

All Portuguese are traders, whatever their occupations: officials, including army and naval officers, settlers, even priests. Their activities are outside the official trading system, but they flourish despite opposition from the authorities. Yet Goa's prosperity may not continue much longer; the Dutch and the English are making their presence felt.

Scientific monk burnt alive for heresy

Rome, 17 February 1600

Giordano Bruno, who hoped above all to heal the splits between Protestants and Catholics and the church and science, was burnt alive today. He was first arrested by the Inquisition in Venice in 1592, but freed after he recanted the heresies of which he was accused. However, he withdrew his recantation, and just over a week ago he was expelled from the church as "an impenitent heretic" and sent to a secular court for punishment. Born in Nola, in 1548, he became a Dominican in 1565. He studied the ideas of Copernicus, who argued that the sun is the centre of the universe, not the earth as religious dogma believes. He hoped to reconcile Catholics and Protestants to the new idea of an infinite universe. The church, however, is not prepared to revise its beliefs.

English company to trade with the east

The East Indiamen set sail, hoping to extend Britain's far-flung trade empire.

London, 1 January 1600
Queen Elizabeth granted a charter of incorporation to the East India Company yesterday. This charter gives George Clifford, the earl of Cumberland, and 215 knights, aldermen and merchants the right to trade in the East Indies for 15 years.

The members of the Company have put up £72,000 to finance a large-scale trading expedition, and plans are ready to send out a fleet of five ships to Sumatra and Java to do business in the rich markets of the east. James Lancaster, who returned from a pioneering voyage to Sumatra, Malacca and Ceylon six years ago, has been appointed general of the fleet. John Davis, the great explorer of the Arctic seas, will be pilot-major. Their voyage promises to be in the tradition of the merchant venturers who have carried English trade around the world during the queen's reign.

Persia opens door to English guests

Persia, 1600
A remarkable alliance has developed between Shah Abbas of Persia and a group of English gentlemen adventurers led by the brothers Sir Anthony and Sir Robert Sherley.

Since the Sherleys reached Kazvin in 1598 with 26 followers, and presented gifts of jewels to the shah, they have achieved a favoured position at the Persian court. Sir Anthony returned to England last year as the shah's ambassador, and has been trying to win European support for an alliance against the Turks.

His brother Sir Robert, meanwhile, is putting his knowledge of artillery at the disposal of the Persian army, and helping to reorganise its regiments. As a result of the Sherleys' mission, special privileges have been granted to Christian merchants in Persia. They are free from customs' duties and religious interference.

Japanese military genius wins battle

Japan, 21 October 1600
Tokugawa Ieyasu has won a crushing victory over his enemies in a battle fought in the fog near the village of Sekigehara today. It was a close run thing, for when the fog cleared it could be seen that the forces of Ieyasu's rival for power, Ishida Mitsunari, commanded the high ground and threatened his rear.

Mitsunari had traitors in his ranks, however, and at the height of the battle these traitors, led by a general suborned by Ieyasu, changed sides. Mitsunari's army was routed by four in the afternoon. He has fled from the field where thousands of his men lie dead.

There is no doubt that Ieyasu, who has fought some 50 battles, is a cunning military genius. By winning he has also confirmed his position as the most powerful warlord in Japan. He has already sent out powerful forces in pursuit of his enemies. Their fate is certain.

Tobacco becomes a habit with Europeans

Europe, c.1600
Two products discovered in the New World are now beginning to have an impact on everyday life in Europe.

Tobacco taking – introduced by John Hawkins in 1566 – is now taken for granted. Pipe smokers include princes and peasants. Despite the price – three shillings an ounce – virtually every English pub now provides a communal pipe for its customers.

Less of an indulgence but fast becoming part of Europe's diet are potato tubers. These are now widely grown after being discovered in America, but not, as often claimed, by Sir Walter Raleigh in Virginia. He says he has never been there.

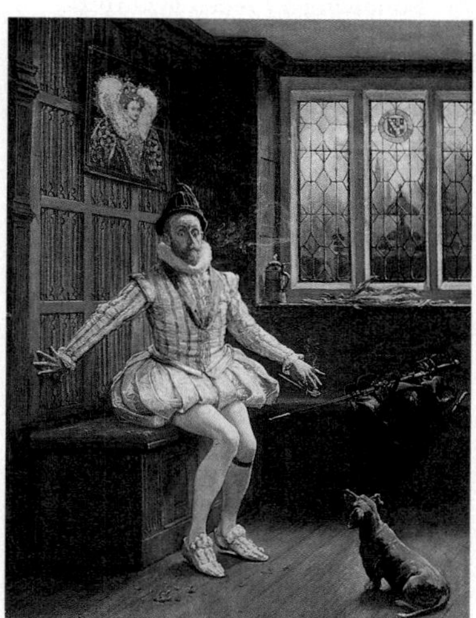

An Englishman experiences his first pipe; from a later painting.

Spanish horses fall into Apache hands

North American Plains, c.1600
Spanish settlers have begun to regret bitterly the day they let security slip and allowed Apache raiders to steal horses during attacks on settlements in the southwestern territories. Since then the Indians have been quick to appreciate the advantages of horsepower in riding and hunting and have started to breed their own horses from captured stock. Stealing horses is now one of their main reasons for raids on Spanish settlements. During the recent Pueblo uprising hundreds of horses were stolen. Some will be kept, but many will be traded for that other commodity the Spanish wish they had never introduced – the gun.

Horror looms out of the darkness. "The Medusa", by the Rome-based artist Michelangelo da Caravaggio, whose strongly-lit, natural looking, dramatic images represent a break with the prevailing mannerist style.

1601 (1601-1603)

France, 17 January 1601. Following a French victory at Chambery, the treaty of Lyons ends a short war between France and Savoy. By the treaty France gains land near the Swiss frontier in return for Saluzzo and French lands beyond the Alps.

London, 25 February 1601. Robert Devereux, the second earl of Essex is beheaded after the failure of a plot he had hatched. Pretending to protect Queen Elizabeth from a Spanish conspiracy, and aided by his own supporters and those of James VI of Scotland, he had attempted to capture London and the Tower.

Prague, 24 October 1601. The astronomer Tycho Brahe dies. He set up an observatory in Prague with the help of the Emperor Rudolf II, and worked there with Johann Kepler. Brahe's greatest contribution to the science of astronomy was that he understood the need for constant observation of the skies and perfected instruments which enabled him to do this with accuracy. He did not believe in the Copernican theory of the universe, which puts the sun at the centre rather than the earth.

New Mexico, 24 November 1601. The governor of Mexico, Juan de Onate, returns to the capital, San Gabriel, after a six-month search for the fabled Quivira (*in Kansas*) – a legendary Indian ruler whose cities are said to be encrusted with gold and precious stones – to find the colony nearly deserted.

India, 1601. The Moghul Emperor Akbar has now absorbed the Dekhan kingdoms of Berar, Ahmadnagar and Khandesh into his kingdom.

London, 1601. Two new plays by William Shakespeare open in London: a comedy, *Twelfth Night*, celebrating the traditionally anarchic festival of 6 January, and *Troilus and Cressida*, a wryly comic tale of the lovesick man and his faithless lover.

Europe, 1601. Germany and France agree to co-operate in the establishment of a new postal service.

Germany, 1601. Many *badestuben* (brothels) are closed by the authorities in an attempt to halt the spread of venereal disease.

England, March 1602. Sir Walter Raleigh sends a final party in search of the Roanoake settlers in Virginia. Using a grant given to Raleigh in 1584, 225 settlers were brought to Roanoke Island between 1585 and 1587, but when the colony was visited again in 1591, no one was there. It is feared that they have died at the hands of Indians or Spaniards.

Rome, 11 March 1602. The composer Emilio di Cavalieri dies. He composed the first dramatic oratorio.

Netherlands, 20 March 1602. The Dutch East India Company is founded.

North America, 16 June 1602. The Englishman Captain Bartholomew Gosnold has given up his colonisation efforts in the north-east of the continent. He left Falmouth on 26 March and has discovered and named Cape Cod, after the fish he found there, and Martha's Vineyard, in honour of his daughter. He is now returning to England.

Paris, 29 July 1602. The duke of Biron is executed for conspiring with Spain and Savoy against the king, Henry IV.

Central America, 14 December 1602. The Spanish merchant and explorer Sebastian Vizcaino, leading an expedition to link up with the navigator Juan de Onate on the Pacific coast, directs his ships into the previously undiscovered Monterey Bay.

Beijing, 1602. The Italian Jesuit missionary Matteo Ricci visits Beijing for the second time and is given permission to stay.

Naples, 1602. Tommaso Campanella, an ex-Dominican friar who led an abortive revolution in southern Italy in 1600, writes *City of the Sun* in prison. It is a fantasy of the ideal city, ruled by priests through scientific magic.

Hungary, 1602. The Counter-reformation gathers force with the persecution of Protestants in Hungary and Bohemia.

South America, 1602. Dutch colonists found a settlement (*in Guiana*) near the estuary of the Essequibo river.

England, 1602. Sir Thomas Bodley opens the Bodleian Library in Oxford.

West Africa, 1603. Idris Aloma, the *mai* (king) of Bornu, dies. During a reign of 33 years he has won many campaigns, thanks to his use of Turkish firearms.

Persia, 1603. Shah Abbas of Persia retakes Tabriz from the Turks.

Canada, 1603. Colonisation of Sable Island has been abandoned. In 1597, 50 petty criminals and their guards were left on the island. They were sending sealskins and oil back to France. However, last year no word was received and when envoys returned to the colony they found that the guards had been killed and then the prisoners had turned on each other. Only 11 survived.

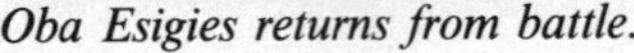

Oba Esigies returns from battle.

Amufi dancers swing from a tree.

Beautiful bronzes created at Benin court

Benin, West Africa, c.1601

Travellers have brought back tales of remarkably advanced bronze and ivory figures sculpted in the kingdom of Benin, in western Nigeria. The kingdom is ruled by the *oba*, who is believed locally to be the reincarnation of the founder of the dynasty in the 13th century.

Carved ivory is reserved for the oba's ornament, and carved tusks decorate the shrines of his ancestors. Ivory leopards, made from five tusks, each with inlaid copper discs as their spots, and bronze heads encased in ring-collars and fantastic helmets, have a style quite new to the European eye.

One traveller reports that at the burial of the oba he saw the grave surrounded by human heads on stakes, belonging to wives and servants who were to accompany the oba to the next world.

A bronze mask from Benin, of the type that has astonished western travellers.

Poor Law offers "whipping for the lazy"

Lazy, good-for-nothing scroungers? "Beggars" (1567) by Bruegel the Elder.

England, 1601
It is being said that parliament's latest bill to reform and extend the Poor Law will give England the best welfare system in Europe. Help for the poor is made a national responsibility, supervised by the Privy Council but administered locally by justices of the peace. The scheme is funded by the levying of rates on better-off households.

Claims that many poor do not want to work are often heard; the new law therefore provides for the whipping of vagrants and beggars, who will be returned to their home villages by the parish constable. Justices of the peace are required to obtain stocks of flax, hemp, wool, thread and other items in order to keep the unemployed usefully occupied. The house of correction awaits anyone who refuses to work.

Elizabeth's reign has been marked by genuine concern for the condition of the poor, partly because it is feared that population growth, economic recession and consequent poverty could lead to widespread unrest.

Wallachia collapses

Wallachia, Balkans, 1601
Michael the Brave, the prince of Wallachia, has been assassinated on the orders of the Habsburg emperor. With his death the independent state of Wallachia collapses.

For the past decade, Wallachia and the neighbouring states of Moldavia and Transylvania have played a crucial role in the balance of power between Austria, Turkey and Poland. No-one played a more delicate balancing act than Michael, who wanted to unite the three small states. He overran Transylvania in 1599, and Moldavia last year, purportedly in the emperor's name. But the emperor did not trust him.

Impostor hanged

Portugal, 7 September 1603
Another pretender to the throne of Portugal – claiming to be the foolhardy King Sebastian who was killed in battle 25 years ago – has been unmasked and executed. Marco Caltizzone, a Calabrian, appeared in Venice and was arrested on the orders of the Spanish ambassador. Like several other such "Sebastians" he was condemned to the galleys, but was later hanged.

The Sebastian phenomenon is the result of the Portuguese having to accept the Castilian king of Spain as their king. Sebastian was king for only a few months before being killed during a disastrous campaign against the Moors.

Dutch join race to trade with the east

Amsterdam, 20 March 1602
The various companies which have been engaging in cut-throat trading competition in the East Indies have today been formed into one corporation. It has been given a monopoly of Dutch trade and navigation east of the Cape of Good Hope and west of the Magellan Straits for an initial period of 21 years.

This Dutch East India Company has also been given sweeping powers. Governed by a court of 17 directors, drawn from the Dutch states, it can conclude treaties, wage defensive war, and build "fortresses and strongholds" in the East Indies. It has thus become a state within a state.

A warship of the Dutch East India Company. High, full-bottomed and manoeuvrable: a queen of the seas.

English navigator builds ships in Japan

Japan, 1601
Will Adams, a Kentish seafarer, is building ships of up to 100 tons for the warlord Ieyasu and teaching his men the skills of long-distance navigation. Adams arrived here as the pilot-major on board a Dutch ship, the *Liefde*, part of a squadron of five trading vessels which were also equipped to destroy their Spanish and Portuguese rivals.

A great storm struck the ships, the *Liefde* was crippled, and many of her crew died. She was towed into Kyushu with barely a score alive. And that was not the end of their privations, for they were denounced as pirates by Jesuit missionaries and threatened with crucifixion. Their lives were saved by Ieyasu, who sent for Adams. The Englishman reached Osaka in May last year along with the *Liefde's* cannons and ammunition which Ieyasu has since put to good use.

Will Adams shows some plans to his employer, the shogun Ieyasu.

Adams has been well treated and is happily employed in his shipbuilding work. It seems unlikely, however, that he will ever see the orchards of Kent again.

True and righteous warrior dies in Africa

Bornu, West Africa, 1603
Idris Aloma, the ruler of Bornu and one of the greatest generals of his generation, is dead. Ascending the throne in 1570, he rebuilt a weak and defenceless state, impoverished by famine, and founded a strong army equipped with firearms. His musketeers and camel-borne troops conquered the So people, the Tuareg and the people of Kano and Kanem, spreading Islam wherever they went. The state they created has surpassed the decaying Songhai empire and become the most powerful in Africa between the Niger and the Nile.

Idris was not only a warrior but also a diplomat and an administrator. Turkey and Morocco paid him their respects. "Truth and righteousness came into their own and shone in Bornu," wrote his chronicler, Ahmad ibn Fartua.

1603 (1603-1605)

Mexico, 21 March 1603. The *San Diego*, one of the navigator Sebastian Vizcaino's ships, returns to Mexico with the first full account of the Pacific coast of Central America.

England, 24 March 1603. Queen Elizabeth dies at Richmond having apparently named James VI of Scotland as her successor.

Canada, April 1603. The French explorer Samuel de Champlain lands in Canada on a mission to study conditions for a possible permanent settlement in New France.

Paris, 20 June 1603. King Henry IV officially reopens work on the Pont Neuf ("New Bridge"). Begun in 1578, building was interrupted by the French wars of religion.

Virginia, 29 July 1603. Bartholomew Gilbert is killed by Indians during a search for the Roanoke colonists, who were last seen in 1587.

India, 30 November 1603. Khwaja Mohammed Baqi Billah, a mystic who has done much to establish the Naqshbandi sufi order in India, has died.

France, 13 December 1603. The celebrated mathematician Francois Viete dies. He was the first person to use alphabetical symbols in algebra.

England, 1603. Puritans led by one Henry Jacob present the *Millenary Petition* (so-called because it was signed by a thousand clergymen) to King James on his first entry to England. It is a moderate plea for church reform, calling for the abandonment of "popish" religious ceremonies, such as the use of the ring in marriage and making the sign of the cross at baptism. The king promises to hold a conference at which it will be discussed.

France, 1603. King Henry IV authorises the Jesuits to resettle in his kingdom.

London, 1603. The city suffers a serious outbreak of the plague.

Morocco, 1603. Ahmed V, or Ahmed al-Mansur, dies. He came to power after his victory over Portuguese invaders in 1578, and was also known as the "Golden" or "Victorious". During his reign Morocco was unified and prospered. He made an alliance with England against Spain, subdued Mauritania, and took possession of the wealthy Songhai empire with its salt mines.

France, 1603. The first beaver skins arrive in the port of La Rochelle from Canada.

Istanbul, 1603. Sultan Mehmet III dies and is succeeded by Sultan Ahmed.

Japan, 1603. A female attendant at the Izumo shrine leads a theatrical performance on a dry river bed. The show includes dancing and comic sketches and is referred to by the audience as *Kabuki*, a term which refers to its unusual or shocking character.

Japan, 1603. Out of the general conflict that followed the death of the civil dictator and prime minister, Hideyoshi (in 1598), Tokugawa Ieyasu has emerged victorious and is now appointed *shogun*. He forms a *bakufu* (military government) in Edo and builds a castle there.

North America, June 1604. The French explorer Pierre du Guast, the sieur du Monts, founds the first French colony in the north-east region, on the St Croix river.

Netherlands, 20 September 1604. After a two-year siege, the Spanish retake Ostend from the Dutch. The Spanish Archduchess Isabella, imitating a chivalric tradition, had vowed that she would not change her blouse until Ostend fell.

Spain, 1604. Mateo Aleman follows up the hugely successful first volume of his gloomy picaresque novel *Guzman de Alfarache* (1599) with a second volume.

France, 1604. The edict of Paulette (after the financier Paulet), a decree of Henry IV, establishes a tax on the hereditary holding of offices, and so institutionalises the sale of government offices.

Rome, 1604. The painter Annibale Carracci puts the finishing touches to the decoration of the gallery in the Farnese palace.

London, 1604. King James describes the habit of tobacco-smoking as "vile and stinking" and "dangerous".

New Spain, 1604. The term "Mexican" appears in print for the first time in *La Gazetta Mexicana*, published by the creole Balbuena.

London, 1604. *Othello, or the Moor of Venice*, a tragedy by Shakespeare on the theme of sexual jealousy, is staged for the first time.

Italy, 1604. Over the past two years the Italian astronomer Galileo has discovered the laws of gravitation and oscillation.

England, 1604. King James dashes Puritan hopes that he would reform the church along lines suggested in last year's Millenary Petition. His only concession has been to authorise a new translation of the Bible.

Canada, 1605. Port Royal is established in Acadia (*Nova Scotia*).

Thousands die in Russian famine

Russia, 1603

Russia is in the grip of a terrible famine which has reduced men to eating grass and birch bark. Some reports talk of cannibalism. The famine is the result of a series of disastrously poor harvests, and it has completed the isolation of Czar Boris Godunov's regime. Whole village populations have disappeared, and a report says that at least 125,000 people have starved to death in Moscow alone.

Government decrees to deal with the problem have been of no avail. The famine has prompted widespread profiteering and a sharp increase in the price of bread. Czar Boris has ordered the distribution of grain to the most needy from the palace granaries. Other relief measures have included a vast building programme in Moscow.

Many landowners, unable to feed their peasants, have driven them from their estates. Another consequence has been the formation of marauding bands of homeless peasants who have been attacking the granaries of the merchants.

Sudden death of Czar Boris Godunov

Moscow, 13 April 1605

Czar Boris Godunov died suddenly today, either from a stroke or, as many suspect, from self-administered poison. He was 53 and had been the ruler of Russia almost since the death of Ivan the Terrible's weak son, Fyodor.

Boris was elected czar in 1598, and in many ways his rule at home and abroad followed the pattern set by Ivan. He was hostile to the *boyars* and more reliant on support from the lesser serving nobility. In foreign relations he pursued Ivan's aggressive policy.

His problems had mounted in recent years, however. To begin with, the land-owning nobles were never reconciled to his election as czar; and, for fear of being poisoned, he maintained six foreign doctors at his court. At the same time there has been famine, epidemics, and a revolt culminating in the appearance of a pretender, a "false Dimitri", named after Ivan's son whom Boris is alleged to have murdered. Even now, this pretender is marching on Moscow.

Mad Spanish knight tilts at windmills

Spain, 1605

A new book by the author Miguel de Cervantes is delighting readers all over his native Spain. The adventures of *Don Quixote de la Mancha* simultaneously poke fun at the traditional tales of chivalry and take a hard look at contemporary Spanish society.

The fictional Don Quixote is a keen consumer of just the sort of stories Cervantes mocks; indeed, too much romance has driven him mad. Accompanied by his squire Sancho Panza, whose earthy common sense contrasts with his master's fantasies, Quixote sets off on his ageing horse Rosinante to roam the world in search of adventure.

In his madness the most ordinary things appear romantic or terrifying. In true chivalric style he has his own fair lady, even if the girl he honours has no idea of his interest. Taking up his lance he tilts at what he thinks are giants, but in reality are only windmills. Quixote searches for fine ideals, but the modern Spain in which he travel proves disappointing. Greed has replaced chivalry, and gold, looted from the New World, has taken the place of the knightly qualities he values.

Title page of the 1612 English translation of Cervantes' masterpiece.

English and Scottish thrones united

England, 24 March 1603
When Queen Elizabeth died at Richmond early this morning, the crowns of England and Scotland became united under her successor, the Scottish King James VI. He will be known, by his wish, as James I of Great Britain – the most powerful Protestant sovereign in Europe.

Elizabeth succeeded to an England riven by religious divisions, at war with France, and heavily in debt to the bankers of Antwerp. After a reign of 45 years she has bequeathed to her successor an exchequer which, for all her parsimony, has been drained by rebellion in Ireland and support for the Protestant revolt against Spain in the Netherlands.

But in her long reign the arts flourished as never before: only last year Shakespeare's drama, *Hamlet*, was performed by the Lord Chamberlain's company of actors.

To her subjects Elizabeth was England personified. As she said before the Armada: "Let tyrants fear. I know I have the body of a weak and feeble woman, but I have the heart and stomach of a king, and a king of England too; and think foul scorn that any prince of Europe should dare invade the borders of my realm."

Her bad habits – swearing, beer-drinking and spitting – did not lose her the affection of those who served her. Her successor, the son of Mary, Queen of Scots, has been welcomed by the English, though some find his brusque manner and Scottish accent disconcerting; and they are none too pleased with his talk of the divine right of kings.

This portrait by Marcus Gheeraerts the Younger captures the stern face of Elizabeth, queen for 45 years.

German maps stars of southern skies

Augsburg, Germany, 1603
Twelve new southern constellations have been mapped out in a groundbreaking astronomical atlas just published by Johann Bayer, a German amateur astronomer. Bayer's *Uranometria*, intended as a popular guide to the heavens, has already been greeted with so much acclaim that Augsburg's city council has decided to reward the 31-year-old bachelor with a 150-gulden honorarium. One of *Uranometria's* key features is the way it maps the stars without relying on verbal descriptions of their locations. Instead, stars are grouped according to their luminosity, with each type of star assigned a Greek letter; the brightest are designated as *alpha* stars.

Golden Temple at Amritsar completed

The Golden Temple at Amritsar: covered in gold leaf, it is the holiest Sikh shrine and represents a shining example of devotional architecture.

Amritsar, India, 1605
The Golden Temple, the great Sikh shrine at Amritsar in the Punjab, is complete. The Sikhs are the followers of Guru Nanak, the Punjabi mystic who rejected both Hindu and Moslem orthodoxies.

The Moghul emperor, Akbar, granted them Amritsar, a waterhole which they renamed the "pool of immortality". There, under the direction of their fourth *guru*, Ram Das, they have built a holy city. The city's architecture, a harmonious mixture of Moslem and Hindu styles, with exquisite ornamentation, centres on the "pool of immortality", surrounded by a finely carved marble balustrade. In the middle of the pool a causeway, also made of marble, leads to a small island.

Here stands the Golden Temple itself, its copper dome, walls and cupolas covered with gold foil that glistens in the Indian sun. The two-storey interior is as memorable as the exterior, displaying some of the most beautiful floral and geometrical motifs in India.

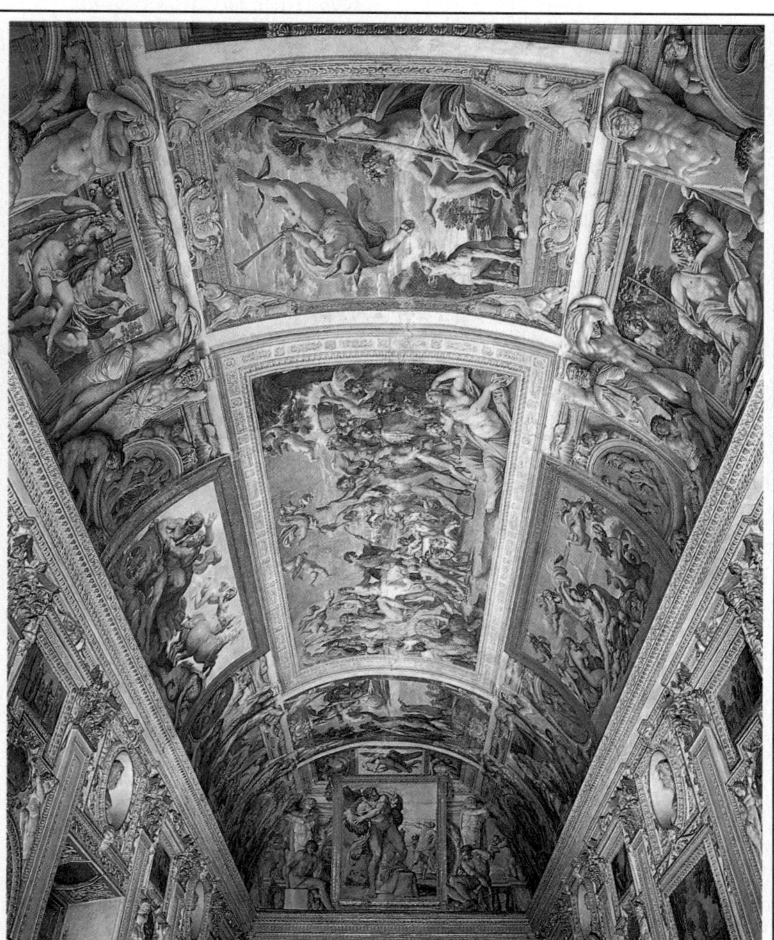
The Bolognese painter Annibale Carracci (born 1560) has recently completed this elaborate ceiling for the Farnese Palace in Rome. Rich in trompe l'oeil (optical illusion) reliefs and full of grand, heroic images, it is acclaimed as his greatest masterpiece so far, ranking with Raphael's frescoes for the papal apartments and Michelangelo's Sistine Chapel.

1605 (1605-1606)

Moscow, 10 June 1605. With Polish support, a Russian who has passed himself off as Prince Dimitri (the supposedly murdered son of Ivan IV) has himself crowned czar.

England, 17 July 1605. George Weymouth returns from the north-eastern coast of America (*Maine*) with glowing reports of agricultural development, notably barley and pea cultivation.

North America, 20 July 1605. The French cartographer and explorer Samuel de Champlain has reached Cape Cod on his second voyage of discovery in search of an ideal location for French settlement in the New World.

London, September 1605. *Eastward Ho* by Ben Jonson and others is published. It satirises the good publicity given to Virginia and the belief that the Roanoke colonists are still alive.

Geneva, 13 October 1605. Theodore Beza, the theologian, pastor and writer, dies. He succeeded Calvin as rector of the Academy of Geneva and wrote poetry, histories, treatises, pamphlets and even a tragedy *Abraham sacrifiant* (1553).

India, 17 October 1605. The Moghul Emperor Akbar the Great dies and is succeeded by Jahangir, his son.

London, 1605. Shakespeare's tragedy *Macbeth*, about the rise to power of a Scottish regicide and his ambitious wife, opens in London.

London, 1605. Ben Jonson's *Volpone, or the Fox*, a black comedy about a wily miser, is staged for the first time.

Germany, 1605. Two hundred and five people convicted of witchcraft have been burnt in the last two years at the abbey of Fulda. Prince Abbot Balthasar von Dernbach supervises the witch-hunts in the area, assisted by his minister Balthasar Ross.

Rome, 1605. Caravaggio's painting *The Death of the Madonna*, commissioned for the Santa Maria della Scala church in Trastevere, is rejected on the grounds of its indecency. The Madonna's body, swollen after death, is that of a poor woman.

America, c.1605. European diseases are decimating the American Indians. Smallpox, measles, dysentery, typhoid and tuberculosis are being passed to Indians at contact points on the coasts of both sub-continents and spread inland by trade and warfare. Alcohol is also reported to be having a disastrous effect on Indian communities.

South-East Asia, 1605. The English sailor John Davis is killed by pirates in the Malacca Straits. When searching for a sea route round the north coast of America in 1587, he discovered a strait linking (*the Baffin Sea to the Atlantic*) in 1592, during an expedition to the southern seas, he discovered islands known as the Malvinas (*Falkland Islands*).

South-East Asia, 1605. The Dutch capture Amboina and take the Moluccas from the Portuguese.

Florida, March 1606. Juan de la Cabezade de Altimirano is the first bishop to visit North America.

Venice, May 1606. Pope Paul V calls on the rulers of the Venetian state to abandon their policy of social and moral control, a power which they took from the church in 1582. They refuse and he places them under an edict.

Russia, 19 May 1606. Vasily Shuisky overthrows the "false Dimitri" to become czar.

Central Europe, 11 November 1606. The treaty of Zsitvatorok puts an end to several years of war between the Ottoman empire and the Habsburgs.

Canada, 14 November 1606. A French performance of *La Theatre de Neptune en la Nouvelle France* in Port Royal is one of the first plays staged in the New World.

England, 20 December 1606. The London Company dispatches the ships *Sarah Constant*, *Discovery* and *Goodspeed*, led by Captain Christopher Newport, to Virginia.

Portugal, 1606. A Dutch fleet blockades the river Tagus.

East Indies, 1606. A Spanish expedition returning from the Philippines recaptures part of the Moluccas from the Dutch. The Dutch attack Malacca with no success.

Germany, 1606. Matthias, the Emperor Rudolf II's brother, has himself recognised as heir.

England, 1606 The Virginia Company is given the task of colonising the area around Florida and Delaware, while the Plymouth Company is to colonise territory inland from Cape Cod Bay.

India, 1606. For two years the Spanish Jesuit Roberto de Nobilis has been preaching in the Dekhan region. He has learnt local dialects adopting the lifestyle of the Brahmins. His lifestyle arouses hostility in his fellow-missionaries.

London, 1606. Shakespeare's *Antony and Cleopatra*, a tale of ill-fated love between the Roman Antony and the queen of the Nile, opens in London.

Plot to blow up parliament is thwarted

The gunpowder plotters seen conspiring, captured and then hanged, drawn and quartered. Finally, their heads are set on poles as a warning to others.

London, November 1605

A Yorkshireman who served with the Spanish forces in the Netherlands after converting to Catholicism has been apprehended in the cellars under the Houses of Parliament with 20 barrels of gunpowder. Under severe torture, Guy Fawkes confessed to plotting to blow up the House of Lords when the king and queen, Prince Henry and members of both houses were assembled for the opening of parliament.

Fawkes at first refused to reveal his accomplices, but King James ordered the torture to continue indefinitely and Fawkes named Robert Catesby, a Warwickshire gentleman and a zealous Catholic, who had been involved in earlier plots against Elizabeth. Catesby and his fellow plotters were to have held a hunting party as a cover for a bid to kidnap the king's daughter Elizabeth once Fawkes had succeeded.

The conspiracy was exposed after Lord Monteagle, a Catholic peer who had declared his loyalty to the king, received an anonymous note urging him to find an excuse to stay away from the opening of Parliament on 5 November, because "God and man" would deliver "a terrible blow". Monteagle showed the note to Lord Salisbury, the king's chief minister, and the cellars were searched. Catesby and three others died resisting arrest. Six more, including Fawkes, await execution.

Breakaway sect plans to leave England

England, 1606

A new sect has emerged from amongst those who have rejected the Church of England but cannot accept orthodox Calvinism. Calling themselves the Baptists, they are led by a former Gainsborough preacher, John Smith, who in turn has broken away from the dissenting Separatists. Facing continuous persecution in England, the sect plans to emigrate to Amsterdam where tolerance is the norm.

Central to Smith's beliefs is his rejection of infant baptism. Since baptism is not simply "washing in water" but also "baptism of the Spirit, the confession of the mouth", how, he asks, can a baby appreciate its importance?

Instead Smith and a hard core of 32 followers believe that adult baptism is a more fitting ceremony. This has caused great controversy, as have the Baptists' refusal to read the Bible in anything but the original Hebrew or Greek and their rejection of the basic Calvinist doctrines of original sin and predestination.

Poisoning suspected in Akbar's death

Bullocks help one of Akbar's sieges.

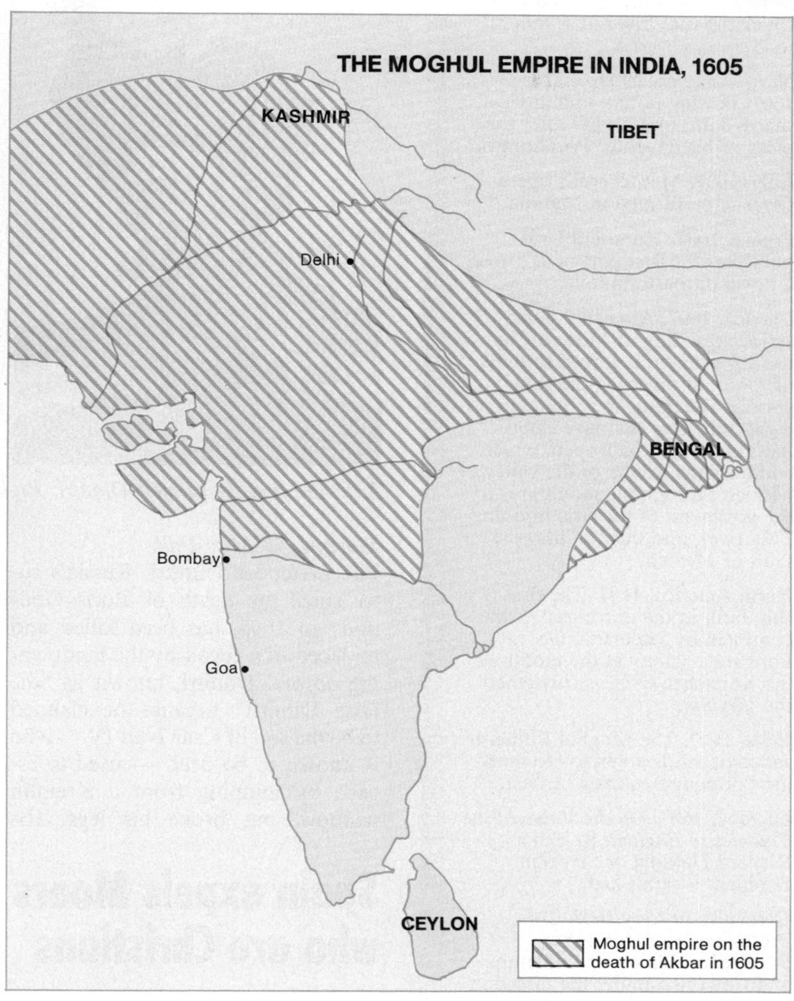

Agra, India, 17 October 1605
Akbar, the greatest of all the Moghul emperors, is dead. He has suffered three weeks of diarrhoea and internal bleeding. Poison is suspected, though the suspects are too numerous to attempt to list.

Illiterate yet noble, capable of immense charm and violent rages, he was every inch an emperor. A Jesuit, who was proud to have been called his friend, described him as "vibrant like the sea reflected in the sun".

As a child he nearly lost his kingdom, but he never lost a battle, and as a man extended his empire by battle after battle until he ruled two-thirds of the subcontinent.

To administer this empire he reformed the bureaucracy, modernised the army and imported technology. He sought to stand above religion. Only in that way could he unite his Hindu, Moslem and Buddhist subjects.

He was both a deist and a mystic, who searched through the traditions of every religion known to him to find truth. He delighted in the fine arts, and in the evenings he loved to have books on history, geography, philosophy and theology read to him.

His only failure appears to have been in his family life. All three of his sons are said to be alcoholics, which bodes ill for India.

"Australia" found in southern seas

North Australia, August 1606
A Portuguese expedition under Luis Vaez Torres believes that it has found a new continent in the southern seas. Ironically the navigator Pero Fernandez de Quiros, whose conviction that there was a southern continent drove the three ships across the Pacific, never saw it. His own ship mutinied and sailed to Mexico. His name for the southern continent remains, however: *La Australia del Espiritu Santo.*

Torres, making his way to the Philippines after his Pacific voyage, may have glimpsed the north coast of Australia (*near Cape York*). Landing on some outlying islands, he found "corpulent and naked" black people and kidnapped some in the interests of research.

Only five months earlier a Dutch vessel, the *Duyfken* (Dove), had reported sailing down the western coast of New Guinea, where some of the crew were killed by "wild, cruel, black savages". It seems likely since Torres' report that New Guinea is the west of this new "Australian" continent.

The discovery of Australia has come as no surprise. There have been numerous rumours of its existence. Marco Polo learnt of it in the 13th century from Chinese traders.

In 1503 a French navigator, Binot Paulmyer, blown off course in the Indian Ocean, landed on a vast land which he was convinced was what is now called Australia. The Dutch historian and geographer Wytfliet estimated in 1597 that this undiscovered continent covered a fifth of the world's entire surface.

Francis Bacon looks at modern learning

England, 1605
A new book has been published by England's leading scientist, Francis Bacon. *The Advancement of Learning*, the first part of which appeared in 1603, is a highly elaborate survey and classification of the various types of knowledge. It is the first of Bacon's works to appear in English rather than Latin.

Bacon's aim is to redefine the whole basis of modern learning. He has divided knowledge into three parts – history, poetry and philosophy – and linked them to three faculties of the mind – memory, imagination and reasoning.

Rejecting the "empirics" – astrologers, magicians and others – who simply heap up unrelated facts, Bacon has attempted to set out what he calls "fixed laws". This system has, he claims, "levelled men's wits", and now anyone can use his laws to explain the occurrence of scientific events.

Habsburgs and Ottomans come to terms

Zsitvatorok, 11 November 1606
In an obscure town on the Hungarian frontier, the Ottoman and Habsburg empires have concluded a peace treaty that promises a new era of stability between two long-standing foes.

Whereas previous treaties have been "graciously accorded by the Sultan" to his "vanquished" rival, the Treaty of Zsitvatorok is between equals. Austria is no longer to pay an annual tribute. A final payment has been agreed, after which the ambassadors of the two great powers will exchange ceremonial gifts every three years.

With the exception of two newly-created provinces and the frontier fortresses of Erlau, Gran and Kanischa, Turkey renounces its claim to Hungarian land. Transylvania, whose prince, Stephen Bocskai, is a party to the treaty, gains considerable autonomy under Turkish rule. The treaty is signed for 20 years.

1606 (1606-1609)

Rome, 1606. The painter Annibale Carracci is overcome by depression and abandons painting almost entirely.

Venice, April 1607. Denied practical support by France and Spain, Pope Paul V is reconciled with Venice, and withdraws the edict of May 1606, in which he objected to the government's control of the moral and social lives of the citizens, formerly the concern of the church.

England, 1 May 1607. *The Gift of God*, funded by Sir Ferdinando Gorges and commanded by George Popham, leaves on a voyage to North America.

Virginia, 24 May 1607. Captain Christopher Newport and 105 followers have founded the colony of Jamestown at the mouth of the James river on the coast of Virginia. They left England last December with 144 colonists.

North America, 15 June 1607. Colonists finish building James Fort in Jamestown, to defend themselves against attacks by the Spanish and Indians.

England, June 1607. Beggars and homeless people around Northampton tear down enclosures recently erected near the town, in protest against the loss of common land. Several protesters are killed; after the actions have been stopped, three people are hanged as an example to the rest.

North America, 14 August 1607. The Popham expedition reaches the Sagadahoc river in the north-east and prepares to settle.

New Mexico, August 1607. Juan de Onate resigns as first Spanish governor here, notifying the viceroy of New Spain that the colony will be abandoned if reinforcements do not arrive by next June.

France, 28 September 1607. Samuel de Champlain and colonists return from Port Royal (*in Nova Scotia*), abandoning the settlement there.

North America, September 1607. Newly-arrived Jamestown colonists have lived on sturgeon and sea crab all summer, and have buried at least 50 people in the last four months, lost to disease and starvation.

Russia, October 1607. A peasant uprising led by Bolotnikov, a former serf who had been captured by Tartars and sold as a slave to the Turks, is put down. Nobles who support the "false Dimitri", ousted by the current czar, initially joined the peasants, but, alarmed by the size of the movement, they betrayed Bolotnikov and he has been imprisoned.

North America, 10 December 1607. John Smith, a founder of the Jamestown colony, heads up Chickahominy river in search of food.

North America, 29 December 1607. Powhatan, the Indian chief, spares John Smith's life after the pleas of his daughter Pocahontas.

Italy, 1607. Monteverdi's opera *Orfeo* is performed in Mantua.

France, 1607. Honore d'Urfe publishes the first part of *L'Astree*, a novel on pastoral love.

Mexico, 1607. After the fourth serious flooding of Mexico City, the government is forced to think of a way of diverting the flood waters. The *desague* is built: an eight-mile long drainage canal, half tunnel and half open, which conducts the waters of the valley of Mexico through the mountains to the northwest of the city, into the Tula river, and then on into the Gulf of Mexico.

North America, 1607. The first ship built in the north-east of the continent by settlers, at George Popham's colony at the mouth of the Kennebec river, is christened the *Virginia*.

India, 1607. The Moghul Emperor Jahangir sends an envoy to meet the Portuguese viceroy in Goa.

England, 1607. *On the Value of the Colonies to England* by either Richard Hakluyt or Sir John Popham, is published.

Germany, 19 May 1608. The Protestant states form the Evangelical Union of Lutherans and Calvinists under the direction of the elector of Brandenburg.

Russia, 1 June 1608. A second "false Dimitri" attempts to usurp the throne, again supported by the Polish who besiege Moscow. He sets up a council in Tushino.

Canada, 7 July 1608. The first French settlement at Quebec is set up by Samuel de Champlain.

England, 1608. The English form an alliance with the United Provinces (*the Netherlands*) against Spain.

South America, 1608. The Jesuit state of Paraguay is founded.

London, 1608. Shakespeare's gory tragedy *Timon of Athens* and Thomas Middleton's lively comedy *A Mad World, My Masters* draw eager audiences.

Chile, 1608. A Spanish royal decree legalises the slavery of Chilean Indians.

Germany, 1609. Regular newspapers are published in Strasbourg and Wolfenbuttel.

Pretender czar killed after window leap

Left: the first counterfeit Dimitri. Right: the second, who waits in the wings.

Moscow, 19 May 1606

The pretender Dimitri, Russia's ruler since the death of Boris Godunov in 1605, has been killed and replaced in a revolt by the landowning *boyars*. Dimitri, known as "the false Dimitri" because he claimed to be the son of Czar Ivan IV — who is known to be dead — tried to escape by jumping from a Kremlin window, but broke his legs. His body was burnt and his ashes shot from a cannon. The pretender's downfall was precipitated by the arrival of his fiancee from Poland with her entourage. This angered Muscovites, who had backed Dimitri to get rid of Godunov, not to instal another czar, unless he was from their own ranks. There are now rumours that another pretender is being groomed for czardom.

Spain expels Moors who are Christians

Spain, 9 April 1609

The *Moriscos*, former Moslems who chose conversion to Christianity as the price of their residence in Spain, are to leave the country. King Philip III, bowing to pressure from his hostile subjects, signed the order for their expulsion today.

Much of the problem springs from the refusal of the Moriscos to assimilate fully into Spanish society. Some may genuinely believe in their new faith, and may have tried to give up their Moorish ways, but the majority of the 300,000-strong community remain essentially Arabs. Their language, society, clothes, customs and even their eating and drinking remain alien to native Spaniards. Few have truly abandoned the Koran. The Moriscos have been pressured to change their ways for a century, for with a large Moslem presence in North Africa, Arabs are seen as a major threat to national security. But still they resist integration.

Calvinists ally with Lutheran rivals

Germany, 19 May 1608

In a rare display of unity, the Protestant princes of Germany – both Calvinist and Lutherans – have formed a union at Anhausen and are now beginning to arm themselves against Catholic aggression following the Habsburg subjugation of the city of Donauworth. The monks there, whose monastery had survived the reformation, had been in conflict with the city's burghers.

The affair was minor, but it was worrying enough to infuriate the Protestant estates which regarded the action as a breach of the Peace of Augsburg. Their protests ended in a walk-out at the imperial diet of Ratisbon (Regensburg) in February this year. Although the new union's membership is confined to six princes – with Saxony and the north-west of Germany staying out – the historic rift between the Lutherans and Calvinists has been hard to hide even in a union of "peace-loving estates".

Earls' flight marks end of Gaelic Ireland

Ireland, 1608
Two fighting earls, Tyrone and Tyrconnel, by turns loyalists and rebels in Catholic Ireland's struggle with the English, have fled to the continent of Europe and been received at the gates of Rome by seven cardinals. The pope has placed a palace at their disposal, but back home they have been declared traitors and their lands in Ulster have been seized for settlement by Protestants from England and Scotland.

After defeat in battle and submission to the English, Tyrone, chief of the O'Neill clan, and Tyrconnel, of the O'Donnells, were pardoned by King James and restored to their lands. But they saw that feudal Ireland with its powerful Gaelic clan chiefs had been abolished and replaced by Englishstyle sheriffs and counties.

Tyrone, now in his mid-sixties, has been a triple renegade, first fighting with the English, then against them, and repeating the apostasy twice more before final defeat. He then found himself in a dispute over his feudal rights and the king invited him to put his case in London. Tyrone, fearing arrest, joined with Tyrconnel to hire a ship and escape abroad with their families and servants.

They planned to go to Spain, but were driven ashore in France. They were not wanted there and became refugees in the Spanish Netherlands. Unwelcome there, too, they went via Lorraine and Switzerland to Italy, finding refuge at last in Rome.

The sculptor Giovanni da Bologna, known as Giambologna, died in August 1608 at the age of 79. His "Rape of the Sabines" in Florence is hailed as the pinnacle of the "Mannerist" style, characterised by powerful figures set in contorted, dramatic poses full of motion and tension.

Netherlands and Spain sign truce

The Hague, 9 April 1609
After 40 years of rebellion and repression, Spain and the Netherlands have finally come to terms. A formal truce has been agreed here after months of negotiation, with envoys from England and France acting as mediators. The truce will last for 12 years but, because of the need to inform troops and ships outside Europe, it will be a year before it takes effect universally.

The truce represents a deal between Spain's governor, Archduke Albert, and his wife, the Infanta Isabella, in the south, and Maurice of Nassau, the leader of the States General of the United Provinces (the formal name for the separatist Netherlands government) in the north. The archduke tried desperately to secure a guarantee of an improvement in conditions for Catholics in the north. With their large merchant fleet, the Dutch, on the other hand, pressed for the right to trade with Spanish colonies.

A clause allows travel and trade between each other's countries, but "as for the places, cities, ports and harbours which he [King Philip III of Spain] holds outside these limits, the States and their subjects cannot engage in any business in them without the permission of the aforesaid king".

Shakespeare's sonnets are literary gems

London, 20 May 1609
The publication today by Thomas Thorpe of William Shakespeare's *Sonnets* has been long awaited. They were written at the time when the plague closed the theatres in 1593-4, and have been circulated privately among friends and intimates of the earl of Southampton, who was the poet's patron.

For the past ten years Shakespeare has been prominent at the Globe theatre on London's Bankside, where he is an actor and a shareholder in Richard Burbage's company, the King's Men, under royal patronage.

Shakespeare acts in his own plays – as Chorus in *Henry V* and Ghost in *Hamlet* – but his leading tragic roles are played by Burbage. Since 1602 they have presented *Hamlet, Prince of Denmark, Othello, Macbeth, King Lear, Antony and Cleopatra* and *Coriolanus*.

King James is very keen on plays, especially on *Macbeth*, which prophesies that his ancestor Banquo will father a line of kings, and deals with witchcraft, of which he has written. The old queen before him so liked the robust character of Falstaff in both parts of *Henry IV* and *Henry V* that she asked for another play to show him in love. This Shakespeare wrote, and presented on St George's Day under the title *The Merry Wives of Windsor*. The company has lately taken over the Blackfriars theatre, which is covered, for the winter seasons.

Portrait by miniaturist Nicholas Hilliard, possibly of Shakespeare.

"God's love for all" says Francois

Paris, 1609
Francois de Sales, the Bishop of Geneva, has published a new book in which he hopes to prove that the intimate love of God, often considered to be the province of priests and clergymen alone, is available to everyone who desires it.

De Sales was born in Savoy in 1567. Since then he has studied in Paris and Padua and has made his way through the church hierarchy to his present eminence.

Inspired by a visit to Paris in 1602, when he met the great representatives of French spirituality, Berulle and marie de l'Incarnation, de Sales has written his "Introduction a la vie devote" (Introduction to a life of devotion).

For de Sales the life of devotion is a life to which anyone may aspire. God does not love only His priests, but all of mankind. Wishing to offer a spiritual life to all, he has reconciled humanism with devotion.

An Indian bronze from Madras, showing the boy Krishna dancing on the snake Kaliya.

1609 (1609-1610)

London, 2 June 1609. The American province of Virginia is granted a new charter, extending its territory "from sea to sea".

France, 25 September 1609. Jacqueline Arnauld, the abbess of the convent of Port Royal, institutes strict enclosure – physical isolation from outsiders – as the first step to achieve a return to stricter monastic standards.

Netherlands, 9 April 1609. A 12-year truce is reached between the Netherlands and Spain, thanks to the mediation of Henry IV.

Bohemia, 9 July 1609. In a "Letter from the Crown", the Emperor Rudolf II grants Bohemia freedom of worship.

Germany, 10 July 1609. In response to the formation of the Protestant Evangelical Union, the Catholic states of the empire set up a league under the leadership of Maximilian of Bavaria.

Rome, 15 July 1609. The artist Annibale Carracci dies. Brought up to be a tailor, he rapidly established himself as a painter. He was influenced primarily by the works of Correggio and Raphael.

Bermuda, 25 July 1609. A hurricane hits a fleet headed for Jamestown, forcing the ship carrying Sir Thomas Gates and Sir Thomas Dale aground in Bermuda.

North America, 13 September 1609. In his second attempt to locate a passage to China, the English navigator Henry Hudson sails his ship, the *Half-Moon*, up the river near Manhattan island, (*the Hudson*) far enough to determine that it does not lead to the Orient. This is a great disappointment to Hudson.

Amsterdam, 1609. The Bank of Amsterdam is founded, modelled on the Rialto in Venice. It has a monopoly over currency exchange and is also a deposit bank. It makes large advances to the Indies Company, and booming sea trade from Dutch ports ensures good revenues.

Russia, 1609. The second "false Dimitri", known as the "bandit of Tushino", calls on Poland for help. The Polish king Sigismund Vasa besieges Smolensk.

Germany, 1609. Regular newspapers are published in Strasbourg and Wolfenbuttel.

England, 1609. Richard Hakluyt publishes *Virginia Richly Valued*, promoting the colony of Virginia.

Spain, 1609. Since the policy of forced conversion has failed, Philip III decides to drive out the *Moriscos* (nominally converted Moslems). They are sent to north-western Africa.

Canada, 1609. Samuel de Champlain sets out on an intrepid voyage of exploration covering the Ottawa river, Georgian Bay and Lake Ontario. He travels by canoe and, while expanding geographical knowledge to a great extent, he is also plunged into the middle of an internecine Indian war.

Spain, 1609. Garcilaso de la Vega, (the Inca) publishes his *Royal Commentaries relating the origins of the Incas.* He was the son of an Inca princess by one of the Spanish conquerors.

Prague, 1609. The German astronomer Johann Kepler provides evidence for the elliptical rotation of the planets round the sun in his *Astronomia Nova.*

Japan, 1609. The Ryuku islands (Okinawa) come under the control of the Shimazu family, the *daimyo* (feudal lords) of Satsuma.

Mexico, 1609. The *caciques* (Indian chiefs) stage an uprising.

Brazil, 1609. Jeronimo de Albuquerque discovers iron mines near the Rio Grande in the north-east of the country.

Beijing, 11 May 1610. The Jesuit Matteo Ricci, who founded the Catholic mission in China, has died.

Russia, July 1610. The Polish king's troops defeat Czar Vasily Shuisky, and proclaim the king's son, Ladislav IV Vasa, czar of Russia.

New Mexico, December 1610. The governor Pedro de Peralta has announced that the small village of Santa Fe is to be the new provincial capital. The first capital was San Gabriel, established in 1599, but Peralta has now decided that this site is too near hostile Indian territory for a governmental seat.

London, 1610. Shakespeare's play *Cymbeline*, based on a semi-historical British king, is staged for the first time.

Netherlands, 1610. The Dutch East India Company introduces the term "share".

London, 1610. Ben Jonson's low-life comedy *The Alchemist*, opens in London.

Madagascar, 1610. Ralambo, the ruler of the Merina kingdom, dies. During his 35-year reign he has greatly extended the kingdom by conquest.

Netherlands, 1610. Protestant theologians take up their positions against the states of Holland: in response to the "Remonstrances" of the Arminians (anti-Calvinists), the Gomarists (Calvinists) draw up their "Counter-Remonstrances".

Galileo's lens shows the way to the stars

Padua, Italy, 1610

Many important discoveries are being made by the Italian scientist Galileo Galilei using the newly-invented telescope. Galileo himself did not invent this remarkable instrument, but he has been responsible for its rapid development. First he built a telescope with a threefold magnifying power; next, 32 times magnification.

He has shown that there are mountains on the moon and he has revealed many stars invisible to the naked eye, proving, for instance, that the Milky Way is a large collection of stars.

When he turned his telescope towards the planet Jupiter, Galileo observed that it is accompanied by four satellites which he has called the "Medicean Stars".

The telescope through which Galileo discovered the four moons of Jupiter.

Young genius defends freedom of seas

Now the open sea is also subject to the pontifications of the lawyers.

The Netherlands, 1609

A one-time child prodigy has published, at the age of 26, a brilliant treatise defending the freedom of the seas. The Dutch theologian and lawyer Hugo Grotius was moved to write *De Mare Liberum* after being retained to defend the Dutch East India Company.

One of the company's captains had captured a rich Portuguese galleon in the Straits of Malacca. The right of a private company to take prizes was strongly disputed, especially by the Portuguese, who claimed that the eastern waters were their private property for trading purposes. Grotius set out to show that the high seas belonged to no one and could not be claimed by any country.

God, argued Grotius, wished human friendships to be engendered by mutual needs, one people supplying the needs of another; and the winds blow to make the oceans navigable. Grotius went to university at 12, accompanied a diplomatic mission to France at 15, at 17 was writing dramas in Latin, and at 20 was appointed historiographer by the States-General.

Jesuit who warned against Sodom dies

Beijing, 11 May 1610
Father Matteo Ricci, the Italian Jesuit who founded the Catholic mission in China and warned the Chinese of "the sins of Sodom", died here today. He arrived in China in 1583, having learnt to speak Chinese in Macao. He believed that if the church was to succeed in the east it would have to adapt to local customs, so he wore a mandarin's robe and took the Chinese name of Li-Mateo.

Ricci was a cartographer and clockmaker as well as a priest, and these skills, along with his profound knowledge of Chinese philosophy, won him permission to live in Beijing in 1601. From then until his death he made important converts and published a number of works which aroused much interest.

He translated the Ten Commandments and the Lord's Prayer into Chinese, and then published his great work, an explanation of Christian doctrine entitled *True Meaning of the Lord of Heaven*. In it he fiercely attacked the "sins of Sodom" which many Chinese practise. "This kind of filthiness," he wrote, "is not even discussed by wise men in the west, for fear of defiling their own mouths." He is to be buried with great honour.

Ricci, the Jesuit evangelist, with Li Paulus, his Chinese colleague.

State extends "as far as eye can see"

Madagascar, 1610
Ralambo, the king of the Andriana, is spreading his domains through the mountains and forests of the Madagascan interior. He has renamed his ever-expanding country *Imerina*, meaning "as far as the eye can see".

Madagascar's cosmopolitan population of Africans, Arabs, Indians and Indonesians looks on him with favour. He has the strength to impose stability – and stability is good for trade.

As well as winning battles Ralambo has established an administration in his state, instituting a poll tax to finance his army, and increasing his country's wealth by raising the production of rice.

Warrior queen dies

Nigeria, 1610
Amina, the Hausa queen, has died after 34 years of a campaign to increase the size of her territory. Amina was 16 when she began the expansion of her ancestral lands, seeking to widen south and west her "empire" to include the mouth of the river Niger. Walled camps increased her military strength, and she was paid for her protection in eunuchs and food. She captured the northern cities of Kano and Katsina and added eastwest trade routes to those through the Sahara. Amina took a lover in every city she captured, but had each one beheaded next morning.

Basilica being built

Mexico, 1609
The construction of a magnificent vaulted basilica has begun near Mexico City, on Tepayac Hill. It will replace the church of the Indians which has housed the image of the Virgin of Guadelupe since 1555. The old adobe-built church marks the place where Juan Diego had a vision of the Virgin 122 years ago. The Holy Mother assured Diego of her love for Indians and sent him to ask the bishop of Mexico to build a church on the hill. Countless pilgrims have travelled there since, and by 1570 they had raised 8,000 *pesos* for the stone temple.

Britain mapped by historian John Speed

John Speed's map of Cornwall, in south-west England, is typical of his work: useful information and views surround a beautifully-drawn, accurate map.

England, 1610
The historian and cartographer John Speed is working on his *Theatre of the Empire of Great Britain*, which will bring together a series of 54 maps of different areas of England and Wales which have already appeared separately over the last four years.

It is the culmination of a career which began as a tailor in London. Speed was admitted to the Merchant Tailors' Company in 1580, but later built himself a house in Moorfields and devoted himself to the study of antiquity.

Speed's historical learning first brought him into contact with the poet Sir Fulke Greville, who became his patron. He also received help from scholars like Sir Robert Cotton and Sir Henry Spelman. Speed is also preparing a *History of Great Britain*, adding valuable material to the established history of the country.

The painter Caravaggio died on 18 July 1610, of malaria, having spent the last four years of his life as a fugitive, wanted for killing a man in a Rome brawl. His later works, such as "Martha Reproving Mary for her Vanity", have a stunning realism and an unusual contemplative stillness.

1610 (1610-1612)

Paris, 14 May 1610. King Henry IV is assassinated by a monk who believes in tyrannicide as a means of putting an end to policies which are against the interests of Catholicism.

North America, 24 May 1610. Sir Thomas Gates institutes "Laws Divine Morall and Martial", a harsh civil code, for Jamestown.

Italy, 18 July 1610. The artist Caravaggio dies of malaria in Porto Ercole aged 36, while waiting for permission from the pope to return to the Papal States. He fled in 1606 having killed an opponent in a duel.

Canada, 3 August 1610. The English navigator Henry Hudson discovers a great bay on the eastern coast of Canada (*Hudson's Bay*).

West Africa, 1610. The Dahomey kingdom is established.

German Empire, 1610. Count Tilly, a French courtier, is appointed Commander in Chief of the Catholic League, formed in 1609.

Virginia, 1610. During a winter of appalling hardship in Jamestown, a man is put to death for eating his wife's body.

France, 1610. Jean Beguin, a French scientist, publishes a chemical recipe book, *Tyrocinium Chymicum*.

Italy, 1610. Using the newly-invented telescope, Galileo observes the moons of Jupiter, and proves Kepler's theories about elliptical planetary rotation.

Portugal, 1610. The king of Portugal withdraws the freedom to trade from the "new Christians", or *Marranos*, converted Spanish Jews.

Rome, 1610. Carlo Borromeo, who was archbishop of Milan, and died in 1584, is canonised.

Paris, 26 January 1611. Maximilien de Bethune, the marquis of Sully, resigns as superintendent of finance and chief minister after disagreements with the regent, Marie de Medici. Concino Concini succeeds him.

Bohemia, 23 May 1611. The Holy Roman Emperor Rudolf II gives up the crown of Bohemia to his brother Matthias.

Virginia, May 1611. Colonists in Jamestown play bowls. This is the first game that settlers in the English colonies have found time for.

North America, 1611. The English navigator and explorer, Henry Hudson, his son and seven sailors are cast adrift in a rowing boat by his crew after a mutiny. They have little chance of survival.

Sweden, 30 October 1611. On the death of Charles IX, the Swedish nobles and the council declare the 16-year-old Gustavus II Adolphus of age, in exchange for a guarantee of their rights.

North America, 13 December 1611. The "Dale Code" codifies two years of harsh laws passed by Dale and others in Virginia.

Russia, 1611. As the Swedes enter Russia, the Poles, pressing home their advantage, occupy Moscow.

Spain, 1611. The Spanish composer Tomas Luis de Victoria dies. He was a profoundly devout man and wrote only religious music.

France, 1611. An assembly of reformed churches is held at Saumur.

Baltic, 1611. War breaks out between Denmark and Sweden. Christian IV of Denmark is determined to gain full power over the Baltic, and he already controls the Sound, without which it is landlocked. Gustavus Adolphus of Sweden has modernised his army, equipping it with units of reindeer-drawn sledges, in addition to the ski-ing units set up in 1567.

France, 1611. In a reversal of Henry IV's policy, Marie de Medici signs a pact with Spain promising that France will not interfere in internal affairs in the empire. To seal the pact, Louis XIII is betrothed to the Habsburg princess, Anne of Austria.

India, 1611. The Dutch found a trading post at Masulipatam on the central eastern coast.

Germany, 1611. The Merchant Adventurers, an English company dealing in foreign trade, sets up a branch in Hamburg.

Rome, 1611. The university of Rome is founded.

England, 1611. A new English translation of the Bible is published. It was authorised by King James in 1604, as a concession to the demands of Protestant clergy for reform.

Italy, 1611. The Italian theologian Marco de Dominis publishes a scientific explanation of the phenomenon of the rainbow.

London, 1611. Shakespeare's play *The Tempest* opens in London. It has a valedictory tone, with the hero, Prospero the magician, abandoning his magic, casting his wand and book of spells into the sea. He is attended to the last by his winged spirit Ariel, and plagued by his earthly servant, the half man, half beast, Caliban.

Germany, 13 June 1612. Matthias II is crowned Holy Roman emperor in succession to Rudolf II.

Monk assassinates "good King Henry"

Paris, 14 May 1610

Henry IV, the king of France, was stabbed to death this afternoon in the Rue de la Ferronnerie by Francois Ravaillac, a fanatical Catholic monk. The king, travelling by carriage from the Louvre to the Arsenal, had dismissed his bodyguard and was accompanied only by a few gentlemen when the carriage was halted in a traffic jam. The crazed assassin leapt onto a wheel and thrust his dagger twice into the king's chest.

The king cried out "I've been stabbed", then collapsed with blood pouring from his mouth. The carriage was then driven to the Louvre and doctors summoned, but Henry the Good was beyond their help. The assassin, a tall, red-haired man, who is believed to have acted because of Henry's proposed war against the Catholic Spanish and Austrian powers, is being examined to see if he belongs to a plot.

The news of Henry's death has caused consternation in Paris. He ruled wisely for over 20 years and his concern for the common people was legendary. The crown now passes to his eight-year-old son, Louis XIII. The king had already made his wife, Marie de Medici, regent in preparation for his absence at war. Now she must rule for their son.

A later engraving of the triumphant Henry IV in ceremonial armour.

Monteverdi makes mark with Vespers

Italy, 1610

A magnificent set of church music published this year and dedicated to Pope Paul V has announced to the music world that it cannot afford to ignore its composer, 43-year-old Claudio Monteverdi.

Born at Cremona in 1567, Monteverdi has been *maestro di cappella* (head of music) at the court of Duke Vincenzo Gonzaga at Mantua since 1601. He has already aroused attention as an advocate of the new, expressive style of music known as the *seconda prattica* (second practice), and as a composer of two operas, *Orfeo* (1607) and *Arianna* (1608), which are the first to show the true potential of this new genre. He has also published five books of madrigals.

At the same time Monteverdi has also shown himself a master of the older style of music, or *prima prattica* (first practice) of Palestrina and earlier composers. Both styles are evident in the *Vespers*, a collection of pieces to be sung at the church's early evening service.

Immoral officials sacked in China

Beijing, 1611

This year's evaluation of the conduct and ability of civil servants has resulted in the sacking of a number of senior officials. So grave were the implications of the evaluation that the Emperor Wan li at first refused to release it, but enemies of the officials censured in the report leaked its details until they became common gossip.

Worse still, fake impeachment papers, spelling out the accusations against corrupt officials, were published in the *Beijing Gazette*, thus compelling the emperor to release the evaluation report.

Seven prominent officials were accused of notorious personal conduct. At the top of the list were Dang Binyin and Gu Zienzhun who were both put on the "inactive list".

This scandal must be seen in the context of the continuing struggle between the eunuch bureaucrats and the reforming Dunglin faction. The Dunglins would seem to have won this round.

Mutineers abandon Henry Hudson to icy waters in rowing boat

London, 1611

The veteran Arctic explorer Henry Hudson was cast adrift in a small boat in Arctic waters together with his teenage son, John, and seven loyal crew members by mutineers, it is being alleged in London. No sign of Hudson has been seen since, and it is almost certain that he and his party froze to death.

Members of the expedition to find a short route (or "North west passage") to the Spice Islands have returned to England. The circumstances of Hudson's loss during a mutiny aboard his ship *Discovery* are now under investigation while the survivors of the trip, drained by famine and sickness, wait in prison.

Hudson sailed from London on 17 April last year. By August he had crossed the Atlantic and found a narrow strait into a great bay which his admirers believe should now bear his name. He spent the next three months charting a watery "labyrinth without end", following creeks and leads that led nowhere. The *Discovery* was too far from open sea to escape the winter ice. On 1 November she was hauled ashore near Moose Fort.

Six months of bitter cold with little food and no work created conditions in which even the smallest quarrel loomed large. Hudson, like Columbus before him, was a remarkable navigator, but a poor leader with little understanding of human nature. He was suspected of distributing rations unequally and favouring the more servile members of the crew. In a series of dangerous changes, he demoted his mate Juet, replaced him with Robert Bylot and, at the end of the winter, as they set sail again, demoted Bylot too. By now almost every man in the expedition was his enemy.

The explorer drifts across the Arctic wastes: a later painting by J Collier.

Authorised version of Bible appears

London, 1611

Robert Barker, the king's printer, has at last brought out the new version of the Bible, authorised and backed by King James himself. It is a folio in black letter with a handsomely engraved title page signed by Cornelius Boel. But it is the majesty and music of the rhythm of the language which critics have been impressed by.

Fifty-four scholars based on the three centres of Oxford, Cambridge and Westminster have worked for seven years to produce the new translation, using much of the original Hebrew and Greek. Their work was reviewed by a committee of 12 before Thomas Bilson and Miles Smith then put the finishing touches to the final version. The unity of style achieved is most impressive. Nobody would guess that this was the work of a committee.

The impetus for the new bible came in January 1604 at a Hampton Court conference. The Bishops' Bible, published in 1568, has not been popular although it is used by many bishops. Many clergy and lay people favour the Geneva Bible. King James, however, thought there were seditious comments in the Geneva version, although he was anxious to have an English bible which was equally grand. He pushed the project ahead, even though many bishops were not very enthusiastic.

THE
HOLY
BIBLE,
Conteyning the Old Testament,
AND THE NEW:
Newly Translated out of the Originall
ANNO DOM. 1611

The handsome title page to Robert Barker's authorised Bible.

King wanted a duel

Stockholm, 16 October 1611

The autocratic and capricious king of Sweden, Charles IX, died here today, a broken old man of 63. His successor, the 16-year-old Gustavus II Adolphus, has inherited a country facing external threat and internal disintegration.

It is seven months since Charles provoked King Christian IV of Denmark into declaring war by Sweden's constant hostility towards Danish ships in the Baltic. Within weeks the Danes had taken the strategic stronghold of Kalmar – infuriating Charles so much that he challenged the Danish king to a duel, an offer scornfully rejected. One serious effect of war with the Danes could be to draw resources from Sweden's Russian front.

Jesuits protect Indians from slavery

Madrid, 1611

About 250,000 Guarani Indians in the Jesuit province of Paraguay will enjoy royal protection from the rigours of slavery thanks to a decree just signed by King Philip III. The lucky natives inhabit a sort of religious Utopia founded by the Order of Jesus seven years ago. All their material and spiritual needs are satisfied, except for the freedom to follow their former, disordered way of life in which work was not a favourite pastime. They now live in a twilight world where all are treated as children.

The Jesuits started their conversion of the Guarani in 1588. Since then the order has built 30 towns, always to the same pattern: a central grassed square is flanked by a church with a tower and three longhouses containing apartments for 100 families or more. The Indians follow a regular day of work, song and prayer. Even the walk to the fields is a religious procession. Jesuits care for their charges like firm, but kindly, parents.

These self-sufficient communities, known as *reducciones*, are efficient enough to export surplus food and draw envious interest from Spanish colonisers dependent on slave labour and cruelty. In Peru's silver mines, for instance, Indians may not leave the workplace except to attend church on Sunday. In the reducciones property is held in common. The crop which the Jesuits harvest with greatest energy is the human soul.

1612 (1612-1614)

Russia, 27 October 1612. The Russians have forced the invading Poles to capitulate. Incensed by Swedish and Polish advances into their lands, the Russian people have organised against them. Kuzma Minin, a merchant, appealed for money and set up a militia. People responded with great generosity and Minin appointed Prince Dimitri Pojarsky, a hero from the siege of Moscow, military leader. With the support of the *Cossacks*, he has finally achieved his aim.

Angola, 1612. The native men and women of Angola are being exported to Brazil as slaves by the Portuguese at a rate of more than 10,000 a year.

North America, 1612. The Dutch send the ships *Tiger* and *Fortune* to trade with Indians on Hudson's river. They build huts and establish a settlement.

Netherlands, 1612. The English Baptist leader John Smith writes *The Retraction of his Errors and the Confirmation of the Truth*, which affirms the beliefs for which he was exiled to the Netherlands but withdraws his condemnation of his opponents, which had been fierce and uncompromising.

Virginia, 1612. Settlers begin to cultivate tobacco plants.

Zaire, c.1612. Kibinda Ilunga, the founder of the Lunda kingdom in southern Zaire, has died.

Antwerp, 1612. Rubens paints his *Descent from the Cross* for Notre Dame cathedral.

India, 1612. The British East India Company defeats the Portuguese off the west coast of India and establishes its first factory at Surat.

Japan, 1612. The silver mint, called *Ginza*, is moved to Edo.

Germany, 1612. Jakob Boehme, a German theosophist and shoemaker, publishes his mystical *Aurora*. It comprises revelations and meditations on God, man and nature, and shows a remarkable familiarity with alchemical writings and the scriptures. It is condemned by the ecclesiastical authorities.

England, 1612. Henry, the prince of Wales, dies of a fever. The eldest son of King James, he was the hope of the English Protestant party because of his violent dislike of popery.

Germany, 1612. Hans Leo Hassler, a German composer, dies. He wrote choral and keyboard works.

South-East Asia, 1612. The East India Company establishes factories at Syriam (*near Rangoon*), Prome and Ava.

France, 11 January 1613. Workers in a sandpit in the Dauphine discover the skeleton of what is alleged to be a 30-foot tall man, the remains, it is thought, of the giant Theotobocus, a legendary Gallic king who fought the Romans.

Scandinavia, 20 January 1613. The peace of Knared ends the war between Sweden and Denmark. They have been fighting since 1611, but the Danish capture of Kalmar has turned the tide firmly in the Danish direction. Sweden gives up Finland, allows Danish merchants to enter Livonia, and gives Denmark Alvsborg as a surety.

Russia, 22 February 1613. Mikhail Romanov is elected czar.

Virginia, 1613. The governor of Virginia rents three acres of land to each colonist, abandoning unsuccessful collectivism.

Spain, 1613. Cervantes publishes his *Novelas Ejemplares*, a collection of short stories which includes amorous exploits and picaresque adventures.

South America, 1613. The Dutch settle in Paramaribo (*on the coast of Guiana*).

Japan, 1613. Date Masamune, the *daimyo* (feudal lord) of Sendai, dispatches a mission to Rome.

Canada, 1613. Samuel de Champlain, the French governor, sails up the Ottawa river and explores lakes Huron and Erie.

Canada, 1613. The Franciscan father Sagard begins to compile his French-Huron dictionary.

France, 1613. Publication of the *Voyages du Sieur Champlain, Saintongeois*, a "faithful Journal of the Observations and Discoveries of New France whilst seeking a northern route to China".

London, 1613. Sir Thomas Overbury is committed to the Tower for refusing a diplomatic appointment abroad. It is concluded that King James wished to put an end to Overbury's influence over Viscount Rochester, who is a favourite of the king's.

Mexico, 1613. Government troops attempt to storm a settlement of runaway slaves in the mountains. The community is led by Yanga, who has lived there for thirty years. Its guerrilla tactics outwit the troops, and the government agrees to treat with Yanga. He and his community remain free, having sworn to cause no more trouble and to help to turn in other runaways.

Spain, 7 April 1614. The Greek painter El Greco dies in Toledo.

Spanish Jesuit champions Indians' rights

Spanish "conquistadores" let their hounds tear native Indians to pieces.

Spain, 1612

A major split between church and state in Spain is threatened as a result of the writings of the Jesuit Francisco Suarez. Prompted by the conquest of America and the subjugation of the natives there, Suarez has championed Indian rights and challenged the divine right of kings.

In *Tractatus de legibus ac de legislatore*, the 64-year-old theologian and philosopher argues that all legislative as well as paternal power is derived from God, and that every law should be His law. Kings, he insists, do not have the same power, and he refutes the patriarchal theory of government. All states, Suarez argues, are the result of a social contract to which the people must give their consent. Indians should be treated no differently.

Suarez is a disciple of Luis Molina, the Jesuit professor of Evora. He adapted Molina's ideas on predestination and free will to the tricky subjects of grace and special election.

Believing that all men are born equal, with an absolutely sufficient grace, Suarez nonetheless argued that a certain elect were granted a special grace to whose influence they would willingly and infallibly yield. This allowed for popes, but not kings.

Musical prince who killed first wife dies

Italy, 8 September 1613

Carlo Gesualdo, the fiery prince of Venosa who had his wife murdered and yet wrote beautiful madrigals and motets, is dead. Gesualdo won notoriety when, in 1590, he caught his wife and her lover *in flagrante* and ordered their deaths. In 1593 he married Leonora d'Este at Ferrara; his musical talent blossomed into genius, and he wrote madrigals and sacred works famed for expressive melodies and unexpected, dissonant harmonies. Eventually he retired to his castle, sunk in melancholy – or remorse? – relieved only by music. He died there today, in his early fifties.

A fresco of Carlo Gesualdo.

Curiosity-collecting emperor is dead

Prague, 1612
Europe is poised for a Habsburg revival following the death this year of Rudolf II, regarded as the most eccentric and ineffective monarch ever to be crowned Holy Roman emperor. In recent years those close to the throne had manoeuvred to strip him of everything but his title. Even before Rudolf died, real power rested with his brother and successor as emperor Matthias, who last year forced Rudolf, aged 59, to abdicate as king of Bohemia in Matthias' favour. Four years ago Matthias awarded himself control of Austria, Hungary and Moravia.

This steady handover of power, fully supported by the rest of the Habsburg family, reflected growing concern about the creeping paralysis that had begun to grip Rudolf. Court circles said that he appeared increasingly shy and unstable, delayed taking decisions and sometimes seemed deranged. In affairs of state he was as likely to take advice from a valet as a minister.

Close friends, however, said that the criticism is unfair and that, after 39 years as emperor, Rudolf was following his inclination towards the arts and science, preferring the company of artists and learned men like astronomers and alchemists to that of courtiers. Rudolf, who preferred Prague to Vienna, also has a passionate interest in things from other countries and built up one of the most outstanding collections of curiosities in Europe.

Matthias: slowly taking control.

Protestants brought in to colonise Ulster

Ireland, 1613
The flight of the earls in 1607 has cleared the way for the systematic colonisation of Ulster by Protestants. Some half a million acres have now been thrown open to settlers, and estates of up to 3,000 acres are being granted to English and Scottish immigrants, who must undertake to build defensible houses. Native Irish who remained loyal to the English during the latest rebellion are also eligible for similar grants.

A parliament has assembled in Dublin to legalise these Ulster "plantations", and the City of London livery companies are now forming an Irish Society to raise capital for the exploitation of timber and fisheries in County Derry. A new city being built will be called Londonderry.

The London companies have undertaken to accept only English and Scots as tenants, but thousands of Irish remain on their holdings and there is little likelihood of their being removed. What is more, these industrious Irish peasants generally outbid the Scot or the Englishman when it comes to paying rent.

A new set of tables makes maths easier

Scotland, 1614
After 20 years of intensive work, the Scottish mathematician John Napier has published a revolutionary book. His 90 pages of tables, called *Mirifici logarithmorum canonis descriptio*, use a complex system of ratios to give "logarithmic" equivalents to numbers. To multiply two or more numbers, you simply look up their logarithms. Add them together and you arrive at the logarithm of the answer. The tables translate it back to the real number. Long division is done by subtracting the logarithms.

Napier's tables look set to be a best seller: astronomers, navigators and scientists are tackling ever more complicated sums.

Sixteen-year-old to rule deserted land

Moscow, 22 February 1613
Russia has put the recent troubles behind it and solved the dynastic problem by electing Mikhail Romanov as czar. He was chosen by the *Zemsky Sobor* – the Assembly of the Land – after much deliberation. The election is not altogether a break with the past for Ivan the Terrible's first wife, Anastasia, had been a member of the Romanov family.

Romanov, who is only 16, has received no training for the monarchy, having been brought up in a monastery. His father, a nobleman who has been patriarch of Moscow, will act as regent. Romanov will be crowned in the Kremlin with all his autocratic prerogatives intact. The Romanovs will ascend the throne amid rejoicing, but they are inheriting a deserted land. Half the villages of Russia are deserted of peo- and, because of the virtual collapse of authority, huge areas are vulnerable to wandering bandits. The treasury, too, is empty, and Romanov has asked another noble family for a loan in cash and kind – fish, salt and grain – to meet the urgent demands of his military and civil officials. And Poles and Swedes still occupy parts of Muscovy.

Passionate religious painter dies in Spain

Toledo, 7 April 1614
Ever since he first arrived in Spain, the painter Domenikos Theotokopoulos, who died today at 73, was known as El Greco, "the Greek". But he was also considered to be a Spanish Catholic religious painter of intense spiritual power.

He was born in Candia, on the island of Crete, and went to Venice to study painting under Titian. Later he met the dean of Toledo who offered him commissions in that city. El Greco arrived in 1567 and remained there for life, mainly painting for its churches. His altarpieces, with their elongated figures, harsh light and cool blues, are highly emotional.

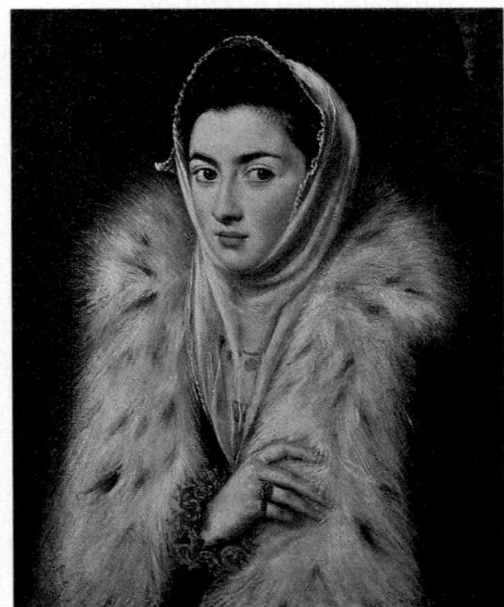
Wide-eyed and beautiful: "Portrait of a Woman in a Fur Cape".

"Christ Driving the Money Changers from the Temple", c.1572.

1614 (1614-1616)

Virginia, 5 April 1614. An Indian princess, Pocahontas, is married to a Jamestown settler. The community hopes it will bring peace between them and the Indians.

France, 15 May 1614. The treaty of St Menehould brings a provisional end to the aristocratic uprising by the prince of Conde and other nobles which broke out in February. Marie de Medici, the queen mother, concedes honours and large pensions to the rebellious nobles in order to prevent an outbreak of civil war. She also agrees to the summoning of the Estates-General.

Amsterdam, 1 October 1614. Adriaen Block returns from North America with maps of the Manhattan coastline.

Germany, 12 November 1614. The treaty of Xanten puts an end to the Julich-Cleves war of succession, following the threat of French and English intervention. Johann Sigismund, the elector of Brandenburg, obtains Cleves and Ravensberg, consolidating his position in the north-east of Germany, while Philippe Louis, the count Palatine of Neubourg, annexes Julich and Berg.

France, 20 November 1614. Louis XIII is declared of age as king.

Russia, 1614. The czar, Mikhail Romanov, defeats the *Cossacks* at Rostokino.

Rome, 1614. Carlo Maderna completes the new facade of St Peter's.

Japan, 1614. The *shogun* Tokugawa Ieyasu issues an edict suppressing Christianity. The churches in Kyoto are to be destroyed and the missionaries are taken into custody. A total of 148 Japanese Christians, including the Christian *daimyo* (feudal lord) Takayama Ukon, are banished overseas, to Manila or to Macao. This action is taken mainly with the military in mind, for it is feared that Christianity will interfere with their loyalty to their overlords.

England 1614. King James asks MPs to grant him benevolences (free gifts to the crown). After the session, all those who spoke out against the king are arrested and thrown into the dungeons of the Tower.

Rome, 1614. The pope pronounces the beatification of St Teresa of Avila.

Denmark, 1614. The Danish East India Company is founded.

Brazil, 1614. The governor of Rio de Janeiro makes legal tender; it may be used to buy things or to pay taxes.

London, 1614. John Webster's revenge tragedy *The Duchess of Malfi* opens in London. The virtuous heroine marries beneath her to her steward, the only good man she can find in her court, but she cannot escape the designs of her wicked brothers.

England, 1614. The mathematician John Napier publishes a series of numbers known as Napierian logarithms.

Paris, 23 February 1615. The Estates-General is dissolved, having been in session since October 1614. It has gained no concessions on taxation from the monarchy.

New France, 28 July 1615. The French explorer Champlain, on his seventh voyage, finds a lake (*Lake Huron*), opening up an easier route inland for fur traders.

France, 1615. Antoine de Montchrestien, a dramatist and economist, writes a treatise on what he terms "political economy". As France, unlike Spain, has no gold supplies, he says it should encourage manufacturing to increase exports and add to gold stocks. He also advocates the creation of more French colonies.

Canada, 1615. Franciscans arrive in Quebec to start missionary work.

India, 1615. The English fleet defeats the Portuguese off Bombay.

France, 1615. In accordance with the provisions of the treaty of Fontainebleau, Louis XIII marries Anne of Austria.

South-East Asia, 1615. The Dutch seize the Moluccas from the Portuguese.

Paris, 1615. At the request of Marie de Medici, Salomon de Brosse begins to build the Luxembourg palace, which, in accordance with the wishes of the queen mother, is to be modelled on the Pitti Palace in Florence where she grew up.

England, 1615. The Merchant Adventurers are granted a monopoly on the export of cloth.

Southern Africa, 1615. Khoisan herders return to the Cape of Good Hope from England. They were taken there a year ago by traders in order to learn the language and culture.

France, May 1616. Conde, who led the aristocratic rebellion in 1614, joins the Royal Council and is entrusted with the government of Bourges.

France, November 1616. Richelieu is called to the King's Council and is made secretary of state for war and foreign affairs.

Lines of battle are drawn up in Europe

Germany, 1614

All Europe is holding its breath as the German princes – Catholics and Protestants alike – prepare for a war which threatens to engulf the whole continent. Battle-lines are now being drawn up and fortunes spent on equipping private armies throughout Germany.

In the mainly Protestant north, whole cities are being ringed with star-shaped walls, bastions and moats; in the Rhineland and Bavaria, great new fortresses pierce the skylines as Catholics brace themselves for war on a scale unprecedented in Europe. Germany, it seems, will be the battlefield should war break out.

Intense diplomatic activity has been taking place, particularly on the part of Prince Christian of Anhalt-Bernburg, the governor of the Protestant Palatinate, who has sought alliances with every other Protestant power to combat a growing Catholic revival since the beginning of this century. Approaches were made to England and France, with little success at first, but King James of England finally agreed to join an alliance with the Protestant Union of six princes and encouraged the union to make similar alliances with the Netherlands and Denmark.

With Louis XIII of France feeling more and more threatened now that the war between Spain and the rebel Dutch has been resumed, the great powers now face one another. On one side – though not necessarily Protestant – France, Holland, Denmark, Sweden, England and Russia in the north and several Italian states in the south are lined up against the Catholic houses of Habsburg and Poland, with Philip IV of Spain prepared to strike at heretics everywhere.

Japan's ruler dies as huge castle falls

Ieyasu's captain, Honda Tadamoto (in horned helmet), at the siege of Osaka.

Japan, 4 June 1615

The colossal fortress of Osaka has fallen to the army of the shogun Ieyasu after a cruel six-month siege, and tonight is burning out of control. Hideyori, the defender of the castle and son of the great dictator Hideyoshi, who built the castle, has commited suicide and his body has vanished in the flames.

Ieyasu, as usual, used cunning as well as force to achieve victory. He fostered dissension among the defenders until they accepted peace proposals in January. But as soon as the treaty was signed, he destroyed the castle's outer defences.

In May he resumed the siege and a desperate struggle ensued until two days ago when the defenders decided to fight a pitched battle outside the castle walls. The result can be seen in the flames. Ieyasu is now master of all Japan.

Englishman reports from Moghul court

Agra, India, 10 January 1615

Sir Thomas Roe, the first English ambassador to India, has been received by the Emperor Jahangir, the dissolute son of Akbar the Great. The Moghul court is magnificent, its daily ceremonies "as regular as a clock that strikes at set hours", according to Roe. At their first meeting Jahangir sat high under a canopy. Two attendants, standing on the heads of wooden elephants, fanned him. Roe refused to perform the standard obeisance of the Moghul court, but greeted Jahangir with a flourish, as he would an European monarch. Of the gifts Roe brought from King James, only two satisfied the emperor: a crate of alcohol and some English miniatures. A globe annoyed him, as he had not known how small the Moghul empire was compared to the rest of the world.

Roe, 35 years old and the Member of Parliament for Tamworth, left England in March 1614, arriving at Surat, on the west coast of India, on 26 September. He is not the first Englishman to be received at the Moghul court. Seven years earlier William Hawkins had negotiated with Jahangir on behalf of the East India Company. Speaking fluent Turkish, he was able to talk and drink with Jahangir, leaving a mixed impression of his countrymen behind him. Roe's mission, though, is likely to be beneficial to both sides. England is a naval power and trading nation. Jahangir requires protection from the Portuguese for his ships carrying pilgrims to Mecca; England requires factories and trading concessions.

A European at the Moghul court.

Comedy and horror lure crowds in London

London, 1 November 1614

Ben Jonson's chronicle of London low life, *Bartholomew Fair*, was performed yesterday with great success at the Hope theatre, and will be repeated tonight before the king at Whitehall. It is the latest hit on the London stage where comedy and a new style of horror plays are drawing enthusiastic audiences.

Jonson's new play is a comedy of knavery, where visitors to a fair at Smithfield are gulled of their money and belongings, whilst also exposing the hypocrisy of certain Puritans. Ben Jonson, once a bricklayer, began to succeed with his play *Every Man in his Humour*, in which Shakespeare acted. Jonson satirised human quirks further in *Volpone* and *The Alchemist*.

John Webster, whose *Duchess of Malfi* was first seen last year, is the poet of horror, providing new ingenuities with each new play. The duchess is killed for marrying her steward after prolonged torments. She finds herself holding a severed hand in the dark. Vittoria, the whore of *The White Devil*, is stabbed to death, while her lover is poisoned by his own helmet and strangled by a "friar" pretending to give him the last rites. Other authors also dwell on horrors: in Cyril Tourneur's *The Revenger's Tragedy*, a lecherous duke is induced to kiss a poisoned skull and dies seeing his bastard copulating with his duchess. Shakespeare's *Titus Andronicus* has a scene where a mother finds that she has eaten her sons in a pie.

Authors often collaborate, so it is hard to be sure who is the author of many plays – Thomas Middleton, Cyril Tourneur, John Marston, George Chapman and Thomas Dekker, besides the ever-popular Beaumont and Fletcher, and even Shakespeare, have put their hands to many between them.

Murder myths spark attacks on Jews

Frankfurt, 28 February 1616

Vincent Fettmilch, the leader of the attack on the city's Jewish ghetto two years ago, was beheaded today, with some of his followers, on the orders of the Emperor Matthias.

The attack, which was simply one more episode in a long history of anti-Semitic violence, was undoubtedly encouraged by charges of ritual murder which have plagued the Jews ever since they set up the Frankfurt ghetto in 1462. The worst example of these charges, which the authorities accept as utterly unfounded, is to be seen in a painting at the city's Bruckenturm Gate. This depicts the supposed martyrdom at Jewish hands of one Simon of Trent in 1474.

Jewish leaders have petitioned for the removal of this painting, but the authorities refused. The mob, believing devoutly the blood libel, is not to lose its symbol, however much the Jews may suffer.

American Indian heroine meets James

London, 1616

An Indian princess has sat with the king of England, James, at a Ben Jonson masque, ten years after becoming a heroine by saving the life of an explorer, John Smith, and aiding the British colony at Jamestown, Virginia, with food and protection. In 1614 Pocahontas married John Rolf from Jamestown and was baptised Rebecca. Her father, the chief of the Algonquin people, had fought the settlers from the start. However, he approved what was obviously a love-match and left his enemies in peace.

Pocahontas pleads for Smith's life.

The architect Mohammed Aga has just completed the magnificent Blue Mosque in Istanbul for Ahmed, the Ottoman sultan, who is content to let his viziers rule while he concentrates on grand artistic projects.

1616 (1616-1618)

New France, 20 January 1616. Wounded in battle with the Iroquois, the French explorer Samuel de Champlain arrives to winter in Huron village.

Italy, February 1616. Galileo is placed under arrest by the Inquisition for his astronomical theories, the most significant of which reaffirms the Copernican concept of the universe, placing the sun, not Earth, at the centre.

Madrid, 23 April 1616. Cervantes, the creator of Don Quixote, dies.

England, 23 April 1616. William Shakespeare dies in his home town of Stratford-on-Avon, four years after returning there from London, where his plays were bringing him increasing fame and success.

Japan, 1 June 1616. The *shogun* Tokugawa Ieyasu dies of an illness. He is succeeded by his son Tokugawa Hidetada.

Arctic, 1616. The British navigator William Baffin, in his search for a north-west passage from the Atlantic to the Pacific, discovers a sound which leads into the Arctic Ocean, to which he gives his name. Following the lack of success of his expedition, Baffin concludes that there is no north-west passage.

South America, 1616. Willem Schouter and Jacob Lemaire discover a new route to the Pacific for Europeans, round a cape south of the Straits of Magellan, which they name Cape Horn.

Virginia, 1616. The population of the colony of Virginia is 351: 205 officials and workers on company land, 81 tenants and 65 women and children.

Brazil, 1616. The Portuguese expel the French from St Louis de Maragnan, ending French efforts to establish an Amazon colony.

South America, 1616. The Dutch found the colony of Guiana.

Istanbul, 1616. Sultan Ahmed's mosque, also known as the "Blue Mosque", is completed.

Poland, 1616. Protestant churches at Poznan are demolished.

Japan, 1616. All Japanese ports except Nagasaki and Hirado are closed to foreigners.

England, January 1617. King James makes his favourite George Villiers earl of Buckingham.

Russia, 9 March 1617. The treaty of Stolbovo ends the occupation of northern Russia by Swedish troops. Sweden also renounces plans for expansion towards the White Sea and in exchange the czar, Mikhail Romanov, gives up Russian access to the Baltic Sea and the towns conquered by Boris Godunov.

France, 24 April 1617. Concino Concini, the favourite of the regent Marie de Medici, is assassinated on the orders of the young Louis XIII, who installs his own favourite Luynes in his place. The queen mother is exiled to Blois, accompanied by Richelieu.

Virginia, May 1617. Captain John Rolfe returns to find that settlers have nearly deserted Jamestown to grow tobacco in the hinterlands.

Rome, 30 August 1617. The Peruvian Rosa de Lima is the first American saint to be canonised.

Lisbon, 25 September 1617. The Spanish Jesuit lawyer and theologian Francisco Suarez dies. At the request of Philip II, he was appointed to the first chair of theology at the university of Coimbra in 1597. His books include *Defensio Fidei* (1613), against King James of England.

Istanbul, 22 December 1617. Mustapha succeeds Sultan Ahmed as ruler of the Ottoman empire.

Virginia, 23 December 1617. The British set up a penal colony.

Spain, 1617. Spain reinforces its alliances against France by signing the treaty of Pavia with Savoy.

West Africa, 1617. The Dutch buy Goree Island, off Cape Verde, from the natives.

Netherlands, 1617. The Dutch mathematician Willebrord Snellius devises a technique of trigonometrical triangulation for surveying and cartography.

Japan, 1617. The ashes of shogun Tokugawa Ieyasu are transferred from Edo to the mausoleum of Nikko.

Geneva, 1617. The theologian John Calvin's collected works are published posthumously.

Germany, 1617. The composer Heinrich Schutz is made *kapellmeister* (head of music) of the elector of Saxony at Dresden.

Persia, 1618. The Ottomans recognise the reconquest of Persia by Shah Abbas.

Sweden, 1617. By the ordinance of Orebro, Catholicism is banned; the move is more aimed against those who want to restore Catholicism than an act of direct religious persecution.

England, 1617. King James makes poet and playwright Ben Jonson England's first "poet laureate".

Hudson's River, 1617. Dutch traders abandon the Fort Nassau settlement, set up in 1614.

Prague, 1617. The Emperor Matthias II makes his cousin Ferdinand king of Bohemia.

Emperor's men thrown through window

Prague, 23 May 1618

Three men were hurled through a window here tonight, giving a new word – "defenestration" – to the language. Two of the men, Martinitz and Slavata, were lieutenants of the Bohemian king, Ferdinand, a fanatical opponent of the Reformation. The third man was their secretary who made the unfortunate mistake of holding on to his employers while the mob vented their fury on them.

Feelings had been running high in the city since Ferdinand's governors refused permission for the building of two Lutheran churches. The Protestant leader, Count Thurn, called a meeting of nobles, gentry and burghers from all over the province, demanding death for the two men.

Martinitz went first, screaming "Jesu, Maria! Help!" as he crashed over the sill. Slavata fought hard and was knocked senseless. One of the rebels looked down from the window and shouted "By God, his Mary has helped!". The victims had landed on a rubbish heap and Martinitz was already stirring. All three men survived. Martinitz has fled and Slavata is being cared for by the Countess Thurn.

The Defenestration of Prague.

Russians lose access to the Baltic Sea

Russia, 9 March 1617

British mediation and a loan have helped secure the peace of Stolbovo today between Russia and Sweden which could now end the years of desultory fighting. For a Russian indemnity of 20,000 silver roubles, Sweden has agreed to evacuate Novgorod and other areas of northern Russia and renounce its claim to the Russian throne. For its part, Sweden will retain the southern coast of Finland and its contact with its Estonian possessions; thus Muscovy is cut off from the Baltic and does not get back towns conquered by Boris Godunov before the Time of the Troubles. Czar Mikhail Romanov's big task now is to clear Russia of the Poles.

Royal Mosque built in Persian capital

Isfahan, 1617

The Royal Mosque, the *Masjid-i-Shah*, the most striking building in the magnificent new capital city of Shah Abbas of Persia, is complete. The mosque is on the south side of the Maydan, the great square at the centre of the city, reached by the wide straight avenue known as the Chahar Bagh. Like the whole city of Isfahan, 24 miles (38km) in circumference and home to a million people, it is an impressive example of imperial town planning. For all its grandeur, the Masjid-i-Shah's floral painted tiles are not as fine as the Timurid mosaics of the neighbouring Friday Mosque.

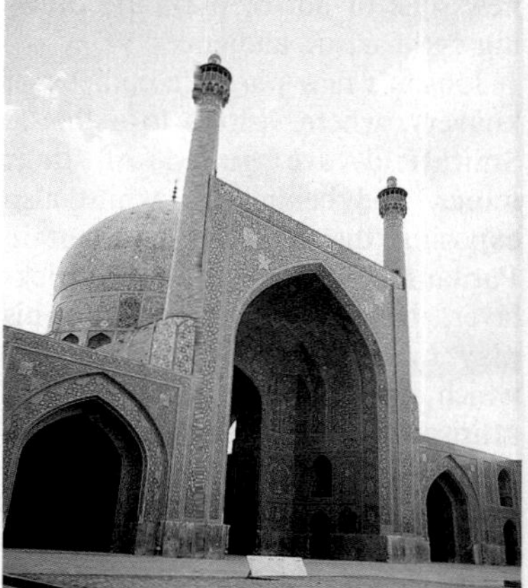

The clean, imposing lines of the Masjid-i-Shah in Isfahan.

Shakespeare shuffles off this mortal coil

England, 25 April 1616
William Shakespeare, the celebrated poet and dramatist, was buried today where he was christened, in Holy Trinity church, Stratford-upon-Avon. He died two days ago, on his 52nd birthday. His father, John Shakespeare, was an alderman of the town; his mother, Mary Arden, was a farmer's daughter from the village of Wilmcote. He went to the local grammar school.

Shakespeare first went to London in the late 1580s and soon made his name as an actor and playwright. After the death of Christopher Marlowe at just 29 in 1593 he emerged as the foremost of London's actor-playwrights, working from 1594 with the new Lord Chamberlain's Company. His "history" plays are mainly from this time. Following the great tragedies and comedies of his middle years, Shakespeare turned to fantastical romance, such as *The Tempest* (1611). The last play in which he had a hand was *King Henry VIII* of 1613.

From about 1610 Shakespeare, an amiable, honest and witty man, established himself as a man of standing in his native Stratford, where he had bought a house, New Place, in 1597 for £60. He is survived by his widow Ann and two daughters.

William Shakespeare: an engraving from the title page of the 1623 edition of his complete works.

Cervantes dies of sudden illness

Spain, 23 April 1616
Miguel de Cervantes Saavedra, the creator of Don Quixote and one of Spain's greatest writers, is dead. He had just completed his latest work, *Persiles y Sigismonde*, when he succumbed to a sudden, fatal illness.

Cervantes was born in 1547, in Alcala, to a noble but impoverished family. He left Spain at the age of 22 and enlisted in the army in Italy; wounded at the battle of Lepanto in 1571, he continued soldiering until in 1575 he was taken prisoner by the Turks. Despite many attempts at escape he spent five years in Algiers before he was ransomed and returned to Madrid. He began writing, but poverty forced him into a variety of temporary jobs.

His first book, *La Galataea*, appeared in 1585, but it was not until the publication of his masterpiece *Don Quixote* in 1605 that he experienced real success, although the playwright Lope de Vega was less than complimentary. So popular was *Don Quixote* that a "second part" appeared, written by an anonymous hack. Cervantes responded last year with a genuine sequel, as popular as the original.

Cervantes also wrote plays, including *La Numancia* and *Los tratos de Argel*. In 1613 he published a set of short stories, which he called *Exemplary novels*.

But it is for the adventures of *Don Quixote*, with its immortal characters of the Don and his squire Sancho Panza, that he will be best remembered.

Miguel de Cervantes, whose death from a sudden illness will long be mourned by all the people of Spain.

Poland to retain disputed province

Russia, 11 December 1618
After the failure of the offensive which brought Polish troops near to Moscow, the two countries have now agreed an armistice. Under the terms of the treaty, Poland will retain the provinces of Smolensk and Seversk. It will recognise the election of Mikhail Romanov to the throne of Russia, but it has not yet renounced a claim to that throne which stemmed originally from the "Time of Troubles" (1604-1613). Poland had Smolensk in its possession at the end of the Troubles and used it as the base for the offensive earlier this year. At one point this caused serious concern to Czar Mikhail who has been grappling with a host of domestic problems which he inherited when he came to the throne five years ago. Somehow Moscow withstood the assault by the Polish forces. The Poles ran short of ammunition and provisions, and withdrew.

Galileo called before the Inquisition

Italy, 26 February 1616
Since 1613, Galileo has been under attack from the theological community for his advocacy of the claim by Copernicus that Earth goes round the sun. The Italian astronomer has observed variations in the way planets move in the sky which have convinced him that Copernicus was right to put the sun at the centre of the planets. The churchmen say that the Copernican system conflicts with holy scriptures, and prefer the ideas of Ptolemy, which make Earth the centre of creation. Infuriated by Galileo's alleged impiety, and his success in communicating widely his novel ideas, his opponents have denounced him to the Inquisition.

Last year he was summoned to Rome and managed to clear his name, but failed to overturn the ruling that the teaching of Copernicanism should be suppressed. Today he was ordered to abandon his views.

A couple relax in a flower garden: a panel of earthenware tile-work decorated with coloured glazes, from a wall of a garden pavilion at Shah Abbas' magnificent royal palace at Isfahan in Persia. The city, an entirely new town, is wealthy enough to support the work of many artists who produce this characteristic style of delicate ornamentation on ceramics.

1618 (1618-1619)

England, 7 January 1618. The statesman Francis Bacon is appointed lord chancellor with the title Lord Verulam.

New England, April 1618. A smallpox epidemic is raging throughout New England, and spreading down the coast as far as Virginia. Indian tribes from the Penobscot River (*in Maine*) to Narrangansett Bay (*in Rhode Island*) are the hardest hit, and have lost up to 90 per cent of their population. At this rate, the disease could wipe out the Indians in the area within three years. One of the latest victims is Chief Powhatan, whose daughter Pocahontas, the wife of a colonist, died of the disease last year in a ship off Gravesend after visiting England.

Brussels, 28 September 1618. The first pawnshop is opened in the Catholic Netherlands. People of modest means can borrow money at a low rate of interest on leaving a security.

England, 29 October 1618. Sir Walter Raleigh is executed to appease Spain.

Virginia, 18 November 1618. The provincial governor, Argall, is recalled after crop failures and his public criticism of Virginia company officials. Sir George Yardley is appointed as the new governor.

Germany, 1618. Since 1611 the ecclesiastical officials of Ellwangen have had some 390 people burnt for witchcraft.

Virginia, 1618. The governor decrees that those who miss church will be jailed "lying neck and heels in the Corps of Gard the night following and be a slave the week following".

Bohemia, 1618. Count Thurn leads Bohemians in a revolt against the pro-Catholic policy of the regents in Prague.

Hungary, 1618. Archduke Ferdinand, made king of Bohemia in 1617, is crowned king of Hungary.

France, 1618. Richelieu is ordered into exile at Avignon for conspiring with the queen mother, Marie de Medici.

Spain, 1618. Lope de Vega publishes his play *Fuente Ovejuna* (Fountain of Rebels), about a fictional village of the same name.

Antwerp, 1618. Flemish artist Anthony van Dyck joins the city's guild of painters.

Brazil, 1618. The *regimento* system is set up: in accordance with the right of discovery, the ownership of mines will revert to the *descobridores*, the men who first discovered the veins of minerals.

Virginia, 1618. Headright laws offer 50 acres per colonist to each investor who pays the cost of the trans-Atlantic passage.

Virginia, 1618. Colonists begin to cultivate wheat.

England, 1618. King James issues a book in favour of games which may be played after church on Sundays. This enrages Puritans.

France, 9 February 1619. Accused of magic and atheism, Lucilio Vanini, who wrote as Giulio Cesare, is burnt alive in Toulouse. His rationalist and naturalist ideas had forced him to leave Naples for England, and England for France. In Paris, his *Amphitheatre of Divine Providence* (1615) and *Secrets of Nature* (1616) attracted the censorship of the Sorbonne.

Germany, 20 March 1619. Holy Roman Emperor Matthias II dies.

Virginia, 14 August 1619. The first general assembly in the provincial capital, Jamestown, has passed a series of stern laws against drinking, gambling, immorality, idleness and "excess in apparell". Settlers have been prohibited from planting mulberry trees, grapes and hemp, all of which could be used to produce intoxicants. Each city, borough or plantation is also required to educate the Indian children.

Bohemia, 26 August 1619. Bohemia has elected a new king, the Protestant Frederick V, the elector of the Palatinate, in preference to the Habsburg Ferdinand, whom the Bohemian estates had "accepted" as king in 1617.

Germany, 28 August 1619. Following the death of the Emperor Matthias II, his cousin Ferdinand, king of Hungary since 1618 and until two days ago king of Bohemia, is unanimously elected emperor as Ferdinand II. Since Bohemia refuses to take an oath of loyalty to the new emperor, he makes an alliance with Duke Maximilian of Bavaria and the Catholic League against Bohemia and the Palatinate.

Virginia, August 1619. A Dutch frigate lands 20 Africans, who are to be indentured servants in the port of Jamestown. This is the first cargo of its kind to arrive in a British North American colony. As the status of slave does not exist in law, the way is open for total exploitation of the labour force.

Virginia, 1619. Some 1,200 new settlers this year bring the population to over 3,000. The newcomers are "choice men, born and bred up to labour and industry", plus 90 women and 100 London slum children.

Indian emperor records animal behaviour

A miniature of a zebra, by Jahangir's favourite painter, Mansur.

Agra, India, 1618

Escaping from the cares of a vast empire and a domineering wife, Jahangir, the Moghul emperor, studies paintings, botany and zoology. Alternatively, at other times, he gets blind drunk. Such contrasts of behaviour run in the family.

Ascending the throne in 1605, after rebelling against his own father, the great Emperor Akbar, Jahangir expanded the empire into the Dekhan and Mewar, but reserved his real passion for nature.

Jahangir keeps a diary which records his love of the natural world. He delights in detailing the mating of two cranes, in dissecting a snake and discovering a rabbit in it, or in finding a meteorite while it was still hot and having swords made out of it.

He has surrounded himself with miniature painters, including the genius of that genre, Mansur, and ordered them to record the natural world around them. Their paintings of turkeys, peacocks, falcons and a hundred other exotic birds are exquisitely coloured and detailed.

A miniature of a dying man, by an unknown artist.

King orders execution of Walter Raleigh

Men whose heads grow beneath their shoulders, as reported by Raleigh.

London, 29 October 1618
After the miserable fiasco of an expedition to South America in pursuit of El Dorado, Sir Walter Raleigh was executed today on the orders of the king. He was 66. He was sent to the Tower of London in 1603 after being accused of plotting against James, but a sentence of death was not carried out and he spent his time writing *A History of the World*.

Two years ago he obtained his liberty by persuading the king that he could find gold in the Orinoco country without clashing with the Spanish. After furious protests from Spain, Raleigh was told that trouble with the Spanish would cost him his life. He reckoned that if he returned with rich booty he would be forgiven by a king in need of funds. But Raleigh fell ill and stayed at Trinidad while the expedition went ahead – and clashed with the Spanish. The dead included his son and several Spaniards; Raleigh returned home, doomed.

Previously, he had been Queen Elizabeth's favourite and she showered him with rewards, including his knighthood. But while he was at sea with an expedition to plunder Spanish galleons she recalled him for seducing one of her maids of honour. Raleigh was sent to the Tower and there married the lady. In the event he turned out to be a good husband and the couple had two sons.

Freethinker burned

France, 9 February 1619
Lucilio Vanini, an Italian freethinker, ex-Carmelite monk and wandering scholar, paid the price today for his unorthodox views. His tongue was cut out, he was strangled at the stake and then burnt to ashes, all on the orders of the Toulouse *Parlement*, which has been trying him since November.

Although faced with the executioner, Vanini proudly proclaimed his belief in a natural morality and his blasphemous view of miracles. He was born near Naples in 1585 and wrote under the name of Giulio Cesare. Many of his works, though admired by scholars from places like the Sorbonne, have been condemned to be burnt. His detractors, however, were not content until they had burnt the man as well.

Dutch statesman goes to block

Holland, 1619
Dutch statesman Jan van Oldenbarneveldt, 72, has been beheaded for treason after a trial on the orders of Prince Maurice of Nassau.

A moderate, Oldenbarneveldt helped secure the Union of Utrecht (1579), an alliance with England and France (1596) and a 12-year truce with Spain (1609). He ensured that Prince Maurice succeeded his murdered father, William the Silent, as stadholder, Dutch leader, in 1585. But the two fell out over the Arminian religious dispute. Maurice opposed the Arminians, who challenged Calvinist beliefs in predestination. Oldenbarneveldt supported the Arminians, and paid for his support with his life.

Blacks and women are sold in America

Jamestown, Virginia, 1619
A consignment of black servants described by Virginians as "twenty negars" has been landed and sold by the captain of a Dutch frigate. They are the first slaves to be delivered to North America, but their local status is unclear. The Normans abolished slavery in England more than six centuries ago. It is uncertain whether the same law holds in a colony 3,000 miles away. Settlers who have acquired these negars believe that they have purchased them outright for life, whereas white servants are free of indentures after five years. In a separate transaction, 90 "willing maidens" were "sold with their consent" at the cost of bringing them here (120 pounds of tobacco) to become brides of settlers.

Black faces, seen in North America for the first time: painting by Van Dyck.

"Pure" Calvinists hammer dissenters

United Provinces, 29 May 1619
The Calvinist synod at Dordrecht has come down firmly in favour of the purest form of Calvinism, reaffirming the belief in absolute predestination.

Many of the followers of Arminius, who maintains God had not wanted Adam to fall from grace, have already been banished from the country. They had been ordered not to preach while they waited their turn to be called before the synod, which began last November.

Prince Maurice of Orange, who called the synod, is against Arminius. The synod president is a stern Calvinist. Politics also played their part. In 1610 the Arminians published a "Remonstrance", which called for religious independence for the Dutch provinces.

Queen Marie leads rebellion against son

France, 1619
The scheming Marie de Medici has emerged from exile in Blois to lead an uprising against her son, Louis XIII. But her campaign has failed to win back the power she enjoyed as regent after the assassination nine years ago of her husband, Henry IV.

Under the influence of her favourite, Concini, she had presided over a period of extravagant misrule. She appeased her nobles by granting them huge pensions, and reversed Henry's foreign policies, striking up alliances with Spain and Austria. But two years ago Louis finally resolved to free himself of his mother's influence. Concini was murdered and Marie was forced to withdraw from the court.

The flamboyant and ambitious Marie de Medici, on horseback, leads a rebellion against her own son; by Theodore Gericault (1791-1824).

1619 (1619-1621)

Russia, 1619. Yeniseysk is founded, as capital of the region of the same name. It is at the heart of the gold-mining region and on the river Yenisei, Russia's eastern frontier.

France, 1619. Louis XIII recalls Richelieu from exile in Avignon to help defuse a rebellion by the queen mother, Marie de Medici.

Madrid, 1619. The Plaza Mayor is completed as part of plans to make Madrid a fitting capital for the Spanish empire. It is a large square, four-storeyed on all sides, with arcaded shops on the ground floor.

Germany, 1619. Johann Kepler, who has demonstrated the truth of the Copernican view of the universe, publishes his *Harmonices Mundi.*

South-East Asia, 1619. The Dutch build a fortress and a colony on the remains of the first settlement, dating from 1596. They call the colony Batavia *Djakarta* after an ancient district in holland.

South America, 1619. The London Amazon Company is created.

London, 1619. William Harvey announces his discovery of the circulation of the blood.

Virginia, 31 January 1620. Leaders of the colony write to the Virginia Company asking for more orphaned apprentices for employment.

France, 10 February 1620. Supporters of Marie de Medici, the queen mother, who has been exiled to Blois, are defeated by the king's troops at Ponts de Ce.

London, 29 June 1620. The crown bans tobacco growing in England, giving the Virginia Company a monopoly in exchange for tax of one shilling per pound of tobacco.

South Africa, July 1620. Two English officers, Captains Shillinge and Fitzherbert, erect the British flag on the shores of Table Bay in the name of King James. But they do not leave a colony to take possession of the Cape. The Cape of Good Hope is valued primarily as a stopping-off post for ships bound to India.

France, 10 August 1620. The king's chief minister, Richelieu, uses his diplomatic tact to persuade Marie de Medici to agree a peace treaty with her son Louis XIII.

England, 16 September 1620. A band of 35 religious dissenters sets sail in the *Mayflower* for Virginia, jubilant at the prospect of practising their brand of worship in the New World without official harrassment.

North America, 11 November 620. After a journey to find the mouth of Hudson's river is aborted because of bad weather, would-be settlers put in at Cape harbour.

North America, 21 November 1620. Leaders of the *Mayflower* expedition gathered in the ship's main cabin today to prepare a social contract designed to bolster unity. The document is meant to placate settlers angered by their arrival on land which has not been granted to them by charter. The "Mayflower Compact" establishes a civil body politic for the new colony that will set up "just and equal laws" based on church covenants.

Mexico, 1620. The population of Mexico has reached 1.2 million.

Netherlands, 1620. Simon Stevin, the mathematician, dies. He taught Maurice of Nassau, and was appointed by him to be engineer in charge of the dykes. He introduced the decimal system for money, weights and measures. Developing Archimedes' theory of physics, he established how to calculate the pressure exerted by a liquid on the sides of a container.

Southern Africa, 1620. The British colony of Saldanha Bay, near the Cape of Good Hope, fails.

England, 1620. Francis Bacon publishes his *Novum Organum*, a scientific treatise promoting his belief that scientific research should be conducted in the interests of humanity.

London, 1620. The poet, physician and musician Thomas Campion dies. He set Latin and English poems to music, as well as his own verses. He leaves several books of "ayres" for the voice, with lute accompaniment.

France, 1620. The province of Bearn becomes part of the kingdom of France. On the basis of a 1617 edict the king reinstates the Catholic religion, using military means to force Protestants to hand back former ecclesiastical property that they had secularised 50 years ago.

Virginia, 1620. The first public library is founded at the site of a proposed college in Henrico. Landowners donate the books for the library.

Japan, 1620. The imperial palace of Katsura is built in Kyoto, on the banks of the Katsura river which supplies the water for the ponds and streams in its gardens.

Rome, 28 January 1621. Pope Paul V dies. He is succeeded by the elderly Cardinal Alessandro Ludovisi from Bologna who will reign as Gregory XV.

Bohemian king has to flee after dinner

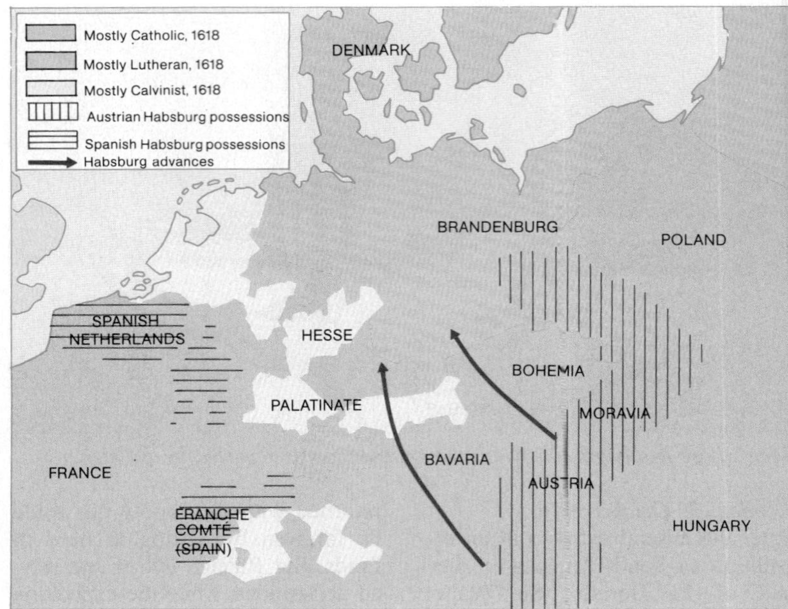

Prague, 8 November 1620
King Frederick of Bohemia and his queen were in high spirits at the dinner table tonight as they entertained the English ambassadors. Although the armies of the fanatically Catholic Emperor Ferdinand II had invaded his country from Austria, Frederick was confident that the enemy's forces were too weak with hunger or wracked with plague to fight. His own army occupied an unassailable position on the White Mountain near Prague.

After dinner, the king rode out to encourage his soldiers. However, he had not reached the city gates when he met the first fugitives. His army had been defeated: the emperor's banner flew over the White Mountain. Frederick's general, Anhalt, entered the city and told the king that the army had become mutinous during a lengthy artillery barrage, and many had refused to fight as they were overwhelmed by Bavarian and Spanish infantry.

As the citizens of Prague closed the gates against the invaders, the king and queen fled in such haste that they almost forgot their youngest prince, although they did remember most of the crown jewels.

Frederick's brief reign as king of Bohemia is over. He had become king in defiance of the emperor; whether the emperor will now allow him to revert to being Elector Palatine Frederick V remains to be seen.

Submarine tested

England, 1620
Cornelius Drebbel, a Dutchman, has just tested an underwater craft on the river Thames. Drebbel's vessels are made of wood with hulls of greased leather. Twelve oarsmen propel the vessels, their oars protruding through tight-fitting flaps covered in grease. The rowers breathe through hollow masts that project above the surface.

There is one snag to Drebbel's design. Under pressure the leather hull and oar openings are not completely watertight. The machine starts to take in water, and slowly but surely, it sinks.

Pope Paul V dies

Rome, 28 January 1621
Pope Paul V died of a stroke today only a few months after the great Catholic victory in the battle of the White Mountain in the war against the Protestants in Germany.

Born Camillo Borghese, in 1552, Paul has dominated the Catholic world in his 16-year reign. He excommunicated the doge of Venice because that state forbade the erection of religious buildings without the permission of Senate. He rebuked King James of England for demanding an oath of allegiance. He also completed the rebuilding of St Peter's.

MPs clash with the English king over punishment powers

Westminster, 18 December 1621
The House of Commons today delivered a sharp rebuff to the king after he had ordered MPs not to "meddle" in affairs of state and claimed the right to punish any MP who commits a "misdemeanour" in parliament. A Commons statement said that "the liberties, franchises, privileges and jurisdictions of parliament" are the birthright of the English people, and every MP must have "freedom from all impeachment and molestation (other than by censure of the House itself)".

James has repeatedly clashed with MPs, and for six years he tried to govern without parliament; but this left him short of funds. Earlier this year, faced with the prospect of war in Europe, he resigned himself to another parliament. MPs were in a determined mood. They curbed the king's power to grant monopolies; they impeached Francis Bacon, the lord chancellor, for accepting bribes; and they set out new guidelines for enforcing the laws affecting religious worship. MPs wanted war with Catholic Spain; James did not, and told them not to meddle in these matters. They made a grant to support the Protestant cause in Europe. James shut down parliament and sent one MP to the Tower.

The king: rebuked by the Commons.

Winter to test "Mayflower" pilgrims

New England, November 1620
After a hazardous voyage across the Atlantic, the *Mayflower*, a 180-ton ship normally used to carry wine, has brought 120 anti-Catholic Puritans to the shores of what they have called "New England". The ship is moored in a harbour now dubbed "New Plymouth" which has become a refuge for the colony.

Danger has stalked the enterprise from the start. A year ago 35 English dissenters, who had lived in exile at Leyden, in Holland, for ten years, persuaded the Virginia Company to agree to a private plantation. They were to cross to England in the *Speedwell* to make convoy with the *Mayflower*, carrying another 66 settlers. After weeks of delay the *Speedwell* was unseaworthy. Everyone crowded aboard the *Mayflower* for a stormy six-week voyage scarred by disease and sudden death. Even as the settlers rowed ashore, Dorothy Bradford, the wife of one of their leaders, fell overboard and was drowned.

Some colonists made it clear that they would obey no law once they landed. The sense of impending lawlessness grew when storms drove the *Mayflower* north of her destination to Indian territory known as Massachusetts. The response of 41 of the settlers was to draft their own "Mayflower Compact": a charter for civilisation rather than anarchy.

A fresh start: a later American tapestry of the landing of the pilgrims.

During the first days ashore, the fitter members carried the ailing majority and built temporary shelters near the beach. Miles Standish, a leading settler, led armed settlers on a reconnaissance of the area. They came under attack from local Indians after interfering with native graves, but frightened the attackers away with gunshot. With winter imminent the settlers must forage for food, including stores of Indian-grown corn. One useful source of food is a breed of bird entirely new to the settlers – the turkey.

England gets its world news on paper

England, 1621
The spread of information to the English public has been greatly increased with the publication this year of a number of newsbooks, or *corantos*, which offer short reports of events happening in a variety of places, often abroad.

These corantos, new editions of which appear every week, originated in Europe, where newsletters of this sort have been published in the Netherlands and Germany for the last couple of years.

Now the system has caught on in Britain, where the first such corantos detailed events in Europe's religious war. The king, under whose authority all printing is carried out, has licensed certain members of the Stationers' Company to issue such pamphlets on a regular basis.

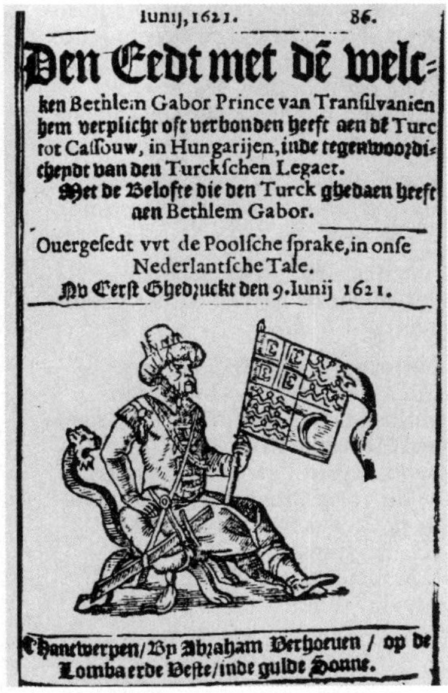
Iunij, 1621. 86.

Den Eedt met dẽ welcken Bethlem Gabor Prince van Transilvanien hem verplicht oft verbonden heeft aen dẽ Turc tot Cassouw, in Hungarijen, inde tegenwoordicheydt van den Turckschen Legaet.

Met de Beloste die den Turck ghedaen heeft aen Bethlem Gabor.

Ouergesedt vvt de Poolsche sprake, in onse Nederlantsche Tale.

Nu Eerst Ghedruckt den 9. Iunij 1621.

Thantwerpen / By Abraham Verhoeuen / op de Lombaerde Veste / inde gulde Sonne.

Page of a Dutch news pamphlet.

Spanish and Dutch renew trade war

Netherlands, 1621
The 12-year truce between Spain and the Netherlands has ended. A renewal of hostilities has become more or less inevitable in recent years as Dutch ships have grown in numbers, trading throughout much of the world and threatening Spain's trade monopoly with its colonial possessions. Apart from their success in trading, the Dutch have waged war with Spanish shipping and settlements on the Pacific.

A major argument at the Spanish court against continuing the truce was the damage that the Dutch were doing to American trade – the Netherlanders have established a "Fort Orange" on Hudson's river in North America. The last straw for the Spanish was the creation of the Dutch West India Company, formed to promote trade – and war – in South America.

1621 (1621-1622)

Germany, 15 February 1621. Michael Praetorius, a leading composer of music for the Lutheran church, dies at the age of 50.

New England, 22 March 1621. The English settlers who arrived in New England in November last year aboard the *Mayflower*, form an alliance with the chief of the Wampanoag Indians.

Madrid, 31 March 1621. King Philip III of Spain dies and is succeeded by his son, who becomes King Philip IV.

Germany, 14 April 1621. The Protestant Union, an alliance of Protestant princes, announces that it is to be dissolved.

New England, 1 June 1621. The *Mayflower* settlers are granted a royal patent, legalising their settlement at New Plymouth, outside Virginia, the area of their original patent.

Netherlands, 3 June 1621. The Dutch found the West India Company. It is granted a monopoly on trade and colonisation in North and South America for a period of 24 years.

Brussels, 13 July 1621. Archduke Albert dies without an heir. This marks the end of the fiction of an independent Catholic Netherlands. Policy towards the Dutch "rebels" is now controlled from Madrid where royal ministers are divided between "doves" and "hawks".

Virginia, July 1621. Sir Edwin Sandys tells colonists that the king has criticised the raising of tobacco in colonies, but settlers refuse to diversify.

Baltic, 16 September 1621. At the head of the most modern army in Europe, the Swedish king, Gustavus Adolphus, seizes Riga from the Poles.

Rome, 17 September 1621. The Catholic theologian Roberto Bellarmine dies. He was a Jesuit cardinal and leading figure in the Counter-Reformation.

England, 21 October 1621. The Privy Council orders all exports from colonies to have customs paid in England.

North America, 25 December 1621. The governor of New Plymouth prevents newcomers from playing cards.

France, December 1621. Albert de Luynes, the commander-in-chief of the king's forces laying siege to Montauban in Provence, has died, and Louis XIII, who is with the soldiers, has failed to secure the surrender of the Protestant town. Huguenots in the region began a rebellion in August.

Virginia, 1621. The first ironworks in the colonies are constructed at Falling Creek.

Angola, 1621. Nzinga, the sister of Ngola Mbandi, the king of Mbundu (*Angola*), is sent as an envoy to Portugal where she is baptised Anne Zingha.

Rome, 1621. The Italian sculptor Giovanni Bernini completes his *Rape of Proserpina*.

England, 1621. Robert Burton publishes *The Anatomy of Melancholy*, a strange book indebted to a huge range of classical and mediaeval writers.

France, 1621. The university of Strasbourg is founded.

Netherlands, 1621. The Dutch composer Jan Sweelinck dies at the age of 59. He composed mainly church music, especially settings of the Psalms, and works for the organ, and developed the fugue.

Alps, 1621. War breaks out between the Swiss League of Grisons and Spain over control of Valtellina.

Germany, 1621. Heidelberg university library is sacked by Count Tilly's Catholic troops.

Virginia, 1621. Elias Legardo settles in Virginia. He is the first Jewish colonial settler in North America.

Germany, 1621. Potatoes are planted in Germany for the first time. They have been brought over from America.

Japan, 1621. The Japanese are forbidden to board foreign vessels or to travel overseas, on pain of death.

London, 1621. John Fletcher's comedy *A Wild Goose Chase* is staged for the first time.

London, 1621. Francis Bacon, Lord Verulam, is accused of accepting bribes from suitors in his court. He is arraigned before fellow peers, fined and imprisoned in the Tower of London. He is also banished from parliament and the court.

Rome, 1621. The papal chancery adopts 1 January as the beginning of the year.

America, 1621. The Scottish settlement in Nova Scotia ("New Scotland") fails.

Germany, 1622. *Apologia pro Galileo*, written by the Italian philosopher Tommaso Campanella in 1616 while in prison, is published in Frankfurt. A defence of the revolutionary astronomer's work, it was first addressed to Galileo himself and Cardinal Bonifacio Gaetani. It is widely circulated here and in Holland.

Thanksgiving feast greets fine harvest

New Plymouth, America, 1621

A year after landing, the Puritan settlement is at peace with the native Indian people thanks to a remarkable pair of English-speaking Indians of the Wampanoag tribe. One, named Tisquantum or "Squanto", was first taken to England in 1605 with Captain Waymouth's expedition.

Squanto recrossed the Atlantic in 1614 to help Captain John Smith, only to be sold as a slave to Spain by the English explorer Thomas Hunt. The Indian escaped and reached England before returning to Massachusetts two years ago.

There were many causes of conflict. Seven years ago some Wampanoags were taken as slaves in an endeavour to reverse the flow of such trade from east to west. There was also the inadvertent desecration of Indian graves when the Puritans first landed. All that seems to be forgotten as both communities come together for a week-long feast of thanksgiving for a bumper harvest of Indian corn. Among the delicacies served at the feast were venison and wild turkey.

A Virginian Indian, by Hollar (1645).

Swedish king digs his way to Riga victory

Poland, 16 September 1621

The astonishing sight of their own king helping to dig assault trenches spurred the Swedish army to victory here today as Riga surrendered after a hard-fought siege. The youthful Swedish king, Gustavus Adolphus, ever at the forefront of his men, came close to death on at least one occasion as his troops advanced under a creeping artillery barrage and stormed the walls.

Two days ago the burghers of Riga parleyed, but angered Gustavus by describing him as "ruling prince in the kingdom of Sweden", rather than "king of Sweden" – their own king, Sigismund, has claimed the Swedish throne. This affront could have meant a full-scale sacking by the Swedish army; Gustavus relented, but is still claiming the city for Sweden.

King Gustavus Adolphus: Sweden's young king, popular for sharing the hardships of his troops.

Woman writes book on sexual equality

France, 1622

The writer Marie le Jars de Gournay has struck a new blow for women's rights with the publication of her book *Egalite des Hommes et des Femmes*. Already established as one of the first successful professional women writers and a staunch defender of women's liberty, de Gournay uses this book to attack the hypocrisy of society's attitude towards her sex. She has been treated with hostility and contempt because of her plain looks and her dogged refusal to play the submissive role expected of her.

The pope skilfully chooses new saints

Now a saint: Teresa of Avila.

Rome, 1622
Pope Gregory XV is proving a skilful politician. His choice of new saints shows careful attention for the temporal needs of the Catholic Church in its struggle against Protestantism, and the spiritual need to encourage the pious life.

Four prominent Jesuits, including their founder, Ignatius Loyola, are among the new saints. It is the Jesuits, above all, who have spearheaded the Catholic fight to regain the religious ground from the Reformation. But the pope has also canonised one of the greatest mystics, Teresa of Avila, who favoured the contemplative life.

Canonised: Jesuit founder Loyola.

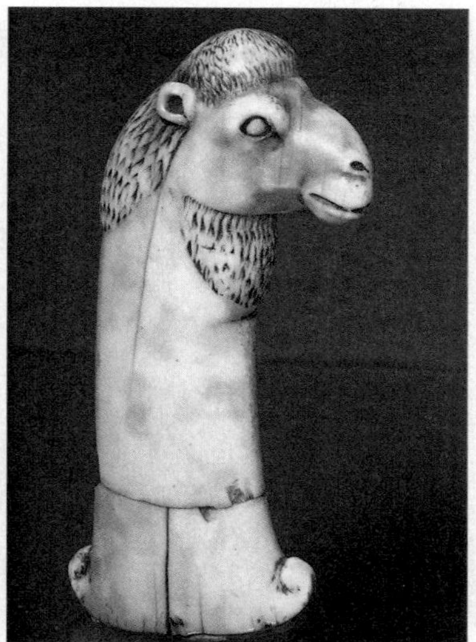
An exquisitely-carved ivory dagger handle in the form of a camel's head; from the British Museum.

A European and his servants, seen through Moghul eyes: a fine example of the new spirit of realism.

Cross-fertilisation of cultures gave birth to this Moghul miniature of the "Nativity" (Bodleian Library).

Realistic and secular Moghul art flourishes under Jahangir

Delhi, 1622
Jahangir, the third Moghul emperor, is proving as great a patron of the arts as his father, Akbar the Great, who extended the empire of the descendants of Tamerlane throughout northern India and Kashmir.

Akbar gathered poets and painters around him, on the model of the Persian court. He recruited Hindu and Moslem painters and set them the task of illustrating the adventures of Amir Hamza, an uncle of the Prophet, in 1,400 painted pages, as well as the Hindu *Mahabharata*, the Book of Wars, in Persian translation.

Jahangir has encouraged portrait painting and pictures of his assembled courtiers as well as nature studies of animals and birds. He is a lover of nature and his favourite painter, Mansur, has produced exquisite paintings of zebras, wild goats, pheasants and turkey cocks. Jahangir has given Mansur the title of *Nadir al-Wasr* – the Wonder of the Age.

Jahangir prides himself on being able to look at any painting and tell immediately whose work it is. When one of his attendants was dying of opium addiction, Jahangir summoned his painters to record the man's emaciated appearance. He had himself painted embracing Shah Abbas of Persia; the Great Moghul is shown surrounded by an enormous gold halo, copied from his European paintings.

One of 1,400 illustrations for the "Romance of Amir Hamza" commissioned by Akbar and finished before 1582 in a mixture of Indian and Persian styles. The epic conflates the Prophet Mohammed's relation with a C9th Moslem hero; in this scene a giant is thrown down a well and beaten by gardeners.

1622 (1622-1623)

India, January 1622. The Moghul Emperor Jahangir's eldest son, the much-loved Prince Khusrau, who led an abortive rebellion against his father in 1606, has died.

London, February 1622. King James dissolves parliament after only two sessions.

Virginia, 22 March 1622. This morning an eight-year peace was shattered by an Indian attack in the James river area which has left 350 colonists dead in their fields and homes. The inhabitants of the port of Jamestown were saved by a warning from Chanco, an Indian who had converted to Christianity and was living on a settler's farm.

Istanbul, 20 May 1622. The 19-year old Ottoman Sultan Osman II is deposed and assassinated by his own guards.

Rome, 22 June 1622. The papal bull *Inscrutabili* founds the Congregation or College of Propaganda.

India, June 1622. The Moghul empire loses Kandahar to the Persians.

America, 5 September 1622. A hurricane has overrun a Spanish fleet bound from Havana to Cadiz, and sunk the prize galleon *Atocha*; 260 passengers were drowned and 200 million pesos went to the bottom with the ship.

France, 18 October 1622. After a hard campaign against the Protestants of southern France, Louis XIII lays siege to Montpellier and forces the duke of Rohan to agree to a peace which reaffirms the Edict of Nantes (a declaration of religious tolerance made at the end of the religious wars in 1598 by Henry IV), but forbids political meetings and leaves the Protestants with Montauban and La Rochelle as their only fortified strongholds.

France, 28 December 1622. Francois de Sales, the bishop of Geneva, a devotional writer and co-founder (with Jeanne de Chantal) of the Order of the Visitation of Our Lady (the Visitandines), dies at Lyons.

England, 30 December 1622. The Council for New England makes Robert Gorges lieutenant-general of New England, granting him 300 square miles on Boston Bay.

France, 1622. The talented French statesman Richelieu, the bishop of Lucon, is recalled to the Royal Council and appointed cardinal.

Netherlands, 1622. The marquis of Spinola, the commander of the Spanish forces, seizes the key fortress town of Bergen op Zoom from the Dutch.

Persian Gulf, 1622. Aided by the English, the Persian ruler Abbas drives the Portuguese out of Hormuz Island.

Hungary, 1622. A peace treaty is signed at Nikolsburg between the Holy Roman emperor and Gabor Bethlen of Transylvania. Bethlen renounces the title of king of Bohemia which he had since 1620.

Naples, 1622. Naples is thrown into turmoil by a series of social disturbances resulting from famine and economic problems.

Paris, 7 February 1623. France, Savoy and Venice sign the treaty of Paris, forming an alliance against Spain.

England, 4 July 1623. The composer William Byrd dies. He will be remembered as one of the greatest masters of polyphony of his day. He composed many works including madrigals, pieces for keyboard, songs and three masses. The masses, written for three, four or five voices, demonstrate the vitality of the art of counterpoint.

Rome, 6 August 1623. On the death of Pope Gregory XV, the Florentine Maffeo Barberini is elected and takes the name Pope Urban VIII. During Gregory's XV's reign, which lasted for two years and five months, the Catholic Counter-reformation made important gains: the spiritual reconquest of Bohemia after the military victory at White Mountain, and the foundation of the Congregation of Propaganda.

North America, 10 September 1623. Lumber and furs are the first cargo to leave New Plymouth for England, on a ship commanded by William Pierce.

North America, 13 December 1623. Colonists at New Plymouth today established the system of trial by 12-man jury in the American colonies. The system was originally instituted in the late 1100s by King Henry II to replace trial by combat or torture, which the defendant had to survive in order to be proved innocent.

Japan, 1623. The English trading station at Hirado is closed due to lack of profits.

New England, 1623. Captain John Mason of Hampshire has established the territory of New Hampshire from land granted to him by King James. Though it is now densely forested and inhabited by wild animals and Indians, Mason dreams of peopling it with farmers and adventurous aristocrats, and of making it an hereditary principality.

Spain, 1623. Diego Velasquez becomes court painter to King Philip IV.

Sultan Osman II is strangled, aged 19

Turkish Janissaries riding camels: a potent force for instability.

Istanbul, 20 May 1622

Sultan Osman II has been deposed and murdered by his own bodyguards, the Janissaries. Osman was 19 and had ruled for four years. It seems that the Janissaries heard of the sultan's plan to raise an alternative army with which to challenge their power. They broke into the harem and called for the reinstatement of the former sultan, the mad Mustapha.

According to various accounts, Dilaver Pasha, the grand vizier, was either executed on Osman's orders, to mollify the Janissaries, or murdered by them, along with the sultan's favourite, Hussein. After Osman had pleaded in vain for his life and throne, he was strangled on the orders of Sultana Valide, Mustapha's mother, who had taken effective control.

The greed and indiscipline of the Janissaries had been an increasing threat since the death of Sultan Ahmed in 1617. When Osman, who had rapidly succeeded Mustapha, led an army against Poland last year, he found the Janissaries unwilling to fight. They blamed him for the campaign's failure.

Tea ceremony intrigues a western guest

Macao, 1622

The western world is due to have a remarkable insight into the unknown way of life of the Japanese when 61-year-old Joao Rodrigues completes his memoirs. Although he is devoting much of the work to Japanese geography, history, politics, government and economy, he is also much concerned with etiquette – in particular the elaborate tea ceremony, about which he has written no fewer than four chapters. As a guest of several leading tea masters during his years in Japan, Rodrigues – exiled during the fierce anti-Christian regime in 1587 – had a rare opportunity to study the teahouses and the ceremony itself.

He stresses the importance that his hosts attached to conforming to nature: "Lack of artificiality is never boring, because experience shows that there is always something new to be found therein."

Christian martyrs beheaded in Japan

Franciscans executed by Hidetada.

Japan, 1622

The persecution of Christians is growing more cruel in Japan. While the last *shogun*, Ieyasu, banned Christianity but carried out no death sentences, his son and successor, Hidetada, is seeking out those Christian missionaries who have gone into hiding and executing them.

Some are beheaded, while others are hung upside down in pits. Great pressure is being put on Japanese who have converted to Christianity in order to make them recant. If they do not, they are tortured hideously and suffer drawn-out, agonising deaths.

This persecution has its roots not only in the opposition of militant Buddhism but also in the fear that the cross is the harbinger of the sword – that where missionaries go, soldiers will follow. It is the policy of the ruling Tokugawa family's military dictatorship to cut off Japan from the western world.

Dutch kill ten rival traders in the East

Indonesia, 1623

In an act of pure savagery, agents of the Dutch East India Company seized English traders at Amboina in Indonesia and tortured them before executing ten, along with ten Japanese and a Portuguese. They were accused of conspiring against the Dutch. Only three years ago, the Dutch gave the English permission to trade in spices at Amboina; they did so well that the Dutch saw their bid to monopolise the trade slipping away.

The perpetrators of the atrocity obviously felt they would be backed by the Dutch governor-general, Jan Pieterszoon Coen, who has acquired a reputation for unbridled ruthlessness since his appointment in 1619. When he founded the new colony at Batavia he razed the old Moslem town and drove out those whom he did not massacre.

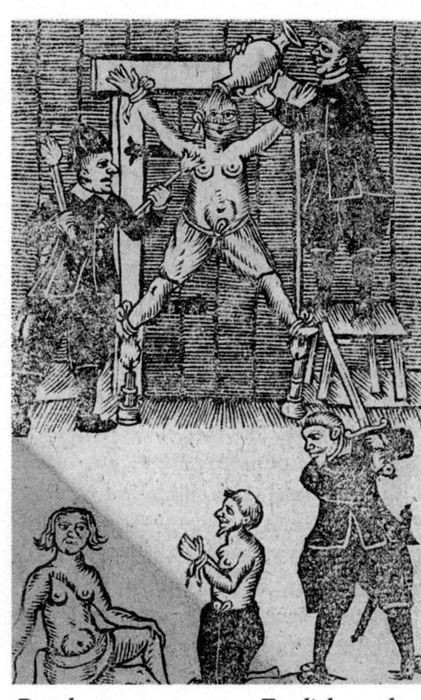

Dutchmen torture an English trader.

Virginia's first settlers face disaster

Catastrophic colony: a map of Virginia, by John Smith, published in 1624.

London, 1623

The troubled Virginia Company headed by Sir Edwin Sandys seems doomed in the light of a recent Royal Commission report on the disasters which have killed around 3,000 settlers in 15 years.

The report provides King James with the pretext to revoke a charter of 1606, and declare Virginia as a royal province. The company's advocates claim that the king is more concerned about the colony's spirit of independence than its viability. Whatever the truth of that, the commission has found that people sent there in efforts to get a colony off the ground are "by sickness of body, famine and massacres dead" or "living in miserable, lamentable necessity".

Tragedies marking the history of the settlement include the failure by settlers to grow their own food despite fertile soil and a good climate. The settlers have been obliged to buy or extort grain, notably local corn, from the Indians. They have expressed their gratitude by killing Indians and burning their crops.

Virtually none of the settlers knew about agriculture before emigrating, though there were several goldsmiths in a territory without gold. Many were gentlemen, good administrators, but ignorant of farming. The working day, for most of them, is four hours. Intrigue and civil disorder provoked hangings and seven years of martial law.

There was just one successful crop, tobacco, which, in 1618, earned £50,000. But even this business suffered when King James denounced smoking as bad for the chest. Worse, the easy profit made from tobacco led to further neglect of basic foodstuffs. Pressure on the local Indians to supply corn at unfair terms provoked a massacre of 347 settlers by a native people who had previously been friendly.

Machine takes the pain out of calculation

Germany, 1623

Although the abacus has been in use for centuries, and William Oughtred's "slide-rule" is growing in popularity, a new step forward in calculation is likely to revolutionise mathematics.

The German Wilhelm Schickard has constructed an ingenious piece of wooden machinery capable of adding and subtracting automatically. Moreover, Schickard's calculating machine can also perform multiplication and division, albeit partly manually. The repercussions of such a device are profound. Human calculators who get tired and need to check their results are looking forward to using this invention.

William Byrd, master of madrigals, dies

England, 4 July 1623

William Byrd, one of Europe's greatest composers, has died at his Essex home, aged 80. Brought up in London, Byrd was taught by that other great master, Thomas Tallis (who died in 1585), and for a time the two men were joint organists of the Chapel Royal.

Byrd's huge output ranged from music for both the Anglican and Catholic churches to songs and instrumental music. He was particularly renowned for his masses and madrigals. These demonstrated a mastery of polyphony which gave him an unsurpassed reputation at home and abroad, is unsurpassed. One contemporary has called him "the father of British music".

1623 (1623-1626)

Paris, 1623. The free-thinker and Huguenot convert to Catholicism Theophile de Viau is sent to prison and his works are banned.

England, 1623. Thomas Weelkes, a famous composer of madrigals, dies aged about 50.

Persia, 1623. The Persian leader Shah Abbas takes Baghdad, Mosul and the whole of Mesopotamia from the Ottomans.

Rome, 1623. Pope Gregory XV clears the Jesuit Roberto de Nobili of corrupting the Catholic faith during his work in India. Nobili adopted local languages and customs and toned down some parts of the Christian message in deference to Hindu sensibilities.

Germany, 1623. The controversial German mystic Jakob Boehme, who came to the attention of the ecclesiastical authoritites in 1612, has published another book entitled *Mysterium Magnum*.

Switzerland, 1623. France withdraws from Valtellina.

Istanbul, 1623. Sultan Mustapha is deposed for a second time and replaced by Murad IV.

London, 1623. Edward Blount and Isaac Jaggard obtain a licence to publish 16 hitherto unprinted plays by Shakespeare on 8 November. Later in the year they publish a folio volume of nearly a thousand pages containing most of the original sixteen plays. Thirty-six pieces in all are brought together in the volume, and they are sold at £ 1 a copy. The plays are listed under three headings: "Comedies", "Histories" and "Tragedies".

Rome, 1623. The Polish poet Maciej Sarbiewski is crowned laureate by the pope.

India, 1623. Tulsi Das, the Hindu poet of the Rama cult, dies. He lived in Benares and will be best remembered for his version of *Ramayana*, the *Ramcharitmanas*.

Mexico, 15 January 1624. The people of Mexico hear at Mass that all churches are to be closed, and that their unpopular viceroy, Diego Carrillo de Mendoza y Pimentel, has been excommunicated as a heretic. A riot erupts and the viceregal palace is burnt and looted. It is the lower ranks of society, free negroes, Indians and *Mestizos*, who begin the riot.

Virginia, 5 March 1624. Class-based legislation is passed, exempting the upper classes from punishment by whipping.

France, 29 April 1624. Louis XIII appoints Cardinal Richelieu chief minister of the Royal Council.

Virginia, 24 May 1624. After years of unprofitable operation, Virginia's charter is revoked and it becomes a royal colony.

Rome, 1624. Pope Urban VIII, angered by tobacco imports from the American colonies, pledges to excommunicate all those who take snuff.

Japan, 1624. The Spanish are forbidden access to any part of the Japanese archipelago.

Caribbean, 1624. The first English settlers arrive in the West Indies, when Sir Thomas Warner occupies the island of St Christopher with a small group of followers.

Germany, 1624. Albrecht von Wallenstein is made duke of Friedland. A Catholic convert of noble Bohemian stock, he has a sizeable army which is now at the service of the emperor.

India, 1624. Bubonic plague, which has been raging through northern and western India for eight years, is at last dying down.

France, 1624. *Croquants* (peasants) in the province of Quercy, oppressed by heavy taxation and the ravages of continuing wars, rebel.

Brussels, 13 January 1625. The painter Jan Bruegel, known as "Velvet" Bruegel, dies. He is best known for his paintings of flowers and his allegorical scenes.

England, 27 March 1625. Prince Charles succeeds to the throne on the death of his father King James.

England, 5 June 1625. The composer Orlando Gibbons dies aged 42. He will be best remembered for his anthems and madrigals.

China, 1625. The first Manchu kings establish their capital at Mukden: their kingdom is a threat to the weakening Ming dynasty which rules China.

Canada, 1625. The Jesuits Lallemand and Brebeuf reach members of Quebec. Previously the Recollect order were the only missionaries operating in Canada.

West Indies, 1625. The Dutch seize San Juan, on Puerto Rico.

London, 1625. The city is ravaged by an attack of the plague.

China, 1625. Private academies throughout the empire are suppressed. They had become centres of opposition to the dominance of the eunuchs and their agents in the increasingly weak Ming dynasty.

North America, 1626. Salem is founded as the capital of Massachusetts.

Viceroy recalled after rioting in Mexico

A seventeenth-century view of Mexico City, by Cristobal de Villalpando.

Mexico, 1624

The viceroy of New Spain has been recalled to Madrid after 70 people died in food riots in which the viceregal palace was burned and looted. The riots were sparked by food shortages after rumours swept the country that the authorities had artifically engineered the situation to force up prices and make a profit. Indians and *Mestizos* – people of mixed Spanish and Indian blood — rampaged through the city, setting fire to government property and destroying 280 shops and stalls before the viceroy's troops finally restored order.

The viceroy has been unpopular ever since he banished the popular archbishop of Mexico from the country after the prelate excommunicated him.

Dutchman writes on the right to war

France, 1625

Hugo Grotius, who gained an international reputation with his treatise on the freedom of the seas, has published another remarkable work, *De Jure Belli ac Pacis* (On the Law of War and Peace). Here he attempts to define relations between the new nation-states of Europe.

He argues that each nation is a sovereign power, subject to no higher authority, but that there is a law of nature, which is derived from custom and experience. To oppose that law is to cast aside the bulwark of peace. Yet a nation that sees its vital interests threatened is right to go to war. Grotius wrote his work in exile in France, where he fled after escaping from prison in Holland. He had published a plea for toleration in religious matters but this displeased the stadholder, Prince Maurice of Nassau.

English king turns down plea for help

Germany, 1623

Bavarian troops led by the imperial commander, the count of Tilly, have completely destroyed the duke of Brunswick's forces at Stadtlohn. Over 15,000 of Brunswick's 21,000 men were killed; now, with Heidelberg and Mannheim firmly in Tilly's hands, the entire northern Palatinate is under the control of the house of Habsburg. News of the defeat has reached the elector Palatine, Frederick V, who has abandoned further military ambitions and asked his father-in-law, King James of England, to mediate.

Although he has offered mediation before, James has turned down the request. His mind is on other things – notably his ambition of a "Spanish match" for his son Prince Charles. The prince has made a secret journey to Madrid to demand a speedy end to negotiations.

King looks to France for Catholic in-laws

The French bride: Henrietta Maria.

The English groom: king Charles.

Paris, 11 May 1625
Charles, the new king of England, has found himself a bride; Henrietta Maria, aged 16, the daughter of Henry IV of France, was married today in Paris, with a French duke acting as proxy for Charles. The terms of the match, initiated by the late King James, include ships for France and the suspension of England's laws against Catholics.

Charles' sister, Elizabeth, made a good Protestant match with the ill-fated Elector Palatine Frederick. To enhance his image as a European peacemaker, King James wanted a suitable Catholic bride for Charles.

Ships traded to win the hand of princess

Paris, 1625
King James of England and Cardinal Richelieu have come to an arrangement under which the English are to lease to the French a warship and seven merchant vessels for use against the rebellious Protestant Huguenots of La Rochelle. The deal, part of the terms of the marriage of James's son, Charles, to the French princess, Henrietta Maria, is not popular in Protestant Britain. But James dislikes those who rebel against kings.

"The Cheat with the Ace of Diamonds", by the French painter Georges de la Tour (born 1593), a master of dramatic lighting effects.

Spanish take crucial city in Netherlands

The key to Breda is handed over to the Spanish forces, ending the long siege.

Netherlands, 2 July 1625
The strategically vital town of Breda surrendered today after nearly a year of siege, and the armies of Spain are poised to overrun the entire Netherlands. Every attempt by English mercenaries – fighting under the banner of the prince of Orange – to break the Spanish siege has been foiled.

So desperate is the plight of the Dutch that their agents have begged France for assistance. Cardinal Richelieu, the French chief minister, has offered a subsidy of a million *livres* on condition that Dutch ships join in a blockade of the Huguenot fortress of La Rochelle which he is besieging. The irony of their navy fighting the Protestant Huguenots is causing great resentment among the Calvinist population of the Netherlands.

Olivares, the chief minister of King Philip IV, is anxious to revert to Philip II's policy of establishing Spanish rule and Catholic supremacy in Europe. The invasion of the Netherlands has created considerable strategic problems for him, however. Spain has to pay heavily to move her troops across Europe from Italy, while her depleted navy has to be deployed in protecting treasure ships in the Atlantic and escorting troopships to Genoa. This has left North Sea and Baltic ports open for Dutch shipping.

Dutch seize Brazilian capital from Spain

Brazil, 10 May 1624
The Dutch have been in revolt against Spanish rule for almost 60 years; now they have taken their fight across the Atlantic and seized the port of Bahia, the capital of Brazil. The Dutch are striking at other American possessions of Philip IV, the King of Spain and Portugal, in an attempt inflict maximum damage on the king's lucrative trade with the colonies.

Had it not been for the rich rewards of trade in the East and West Indies, the Dutch war of independence would have ended years ago. When William of Orange raised the banner of revolt against Spain, only 20 towns with a total population of 75,000 joined him.

In the desperate struggle for survival the Dutch seized any opportunity to trade for profit. They ignored the claims of Spain and Portugal and dealt directly with the colonies. This trade became so large that the king could not make peace, because of what he would lose, and the Dutch would not, because of what they had gained.

1626 (1626-1628)

London, 20 February 1626. John Dowland, the lutenist and composer, was buried today. His early career was overshadowed by his failure to obtain a position in the Queen's Musick in 1594, though he was appointed court lutenist to Christian IV of Denmark in 1598. He finally gained a position in the English court in October 1612.

London, 9 April 1626. The statesman and philosopher Francis Bacon dies of a cold caught while stuffing a fowl with snow to observe the effects of cold in the preservation of meat.

Germany, 27 August 1626. The Danes are crushed by troops of the Catholic League led by Tilly and the imperial army under Wallenstein. This marks the end of Danish intervention in the European wars which have raged since 1618.

North America, September 1626. Following negotiations, a Dutch group led by Peter Minuit agrees to pay the Canarsee Indians the value of 60 *guilders*, or $24, in beads and trinkets, for the 22-square-mile island of Manhattan at the mouth of the river explored by Henry Hudson. The Indians were apparently not interested in being paid in gold or silver.

North America, 15 November 1626. The Pilgrim Fathers, who have settled in New Plymouth, buy out their London investors for £ 1,800.

Naples, 1626. The Spanish painter Jose de Ribera paints the *Drunken Silenus*.

France, 1626. Spurred on by his mistress, the duchess of Chevreuse, Henry de Chalais plots against Cardinal Richelieu. He is executed. Richelieu orders the destruction of all fortified castles, brings the nobles to heel and proclaims an edict forbidding duels.

France, 1626. Food shortages throughout northern France, cause much unrest. Exportation of wheat is forbidden in attempt to improve the situation.

Virginia, 1626. George Sandys, acting as the colony's treasurer, translates Ovid's *Metamorphoses*, the first literary work undertaken in America.

Paris, 1626. Cardinal Richelieu orders the construction of the buildings of the Sorbonne (*University of Paris*).

France, 1626. The poet Theophile de Viau dies at the age of 36.

Rome, 1626. The basilica of St Peter's is consecrated.

Prague, 1626. Adrian de Vries, the Dutch sculptor who worked with bronze, dies and is buried in Prague. He was frequently employed by General Wallenstein, the duke of Friedland and Mecklenburg.

Canada, 25 April 1627. Control of New France passes to the Company of New France (The Hundred Associates); it gains a fur monopoly and land from Florida to the Arctic.

Paris, 22 June 1627. The nobleman Francois de Montmorency Bouteville is beheaded for deliberately flouting King Louis XIII's year-old law banning duels.

Newfoundland, 23 July 1627. Sir George Calvert arrives to develop his 1622 land grant.

France, 27 October 1627. Cardinal Richelieu, Louis XIII's chief minister, lays siege to the Protestant stronghold of La Rochelle.

England, November 1627. King Charles, referring to the tobacco trade, says Virginia is "wholly built on smoke".

Iceland, 1627. Reykjavik, the capital of the island, is attacked by pirates.

China, 1627. Unrest amongst both the military and the peasants bodes ill for the Ming dynasty.

Virginia, 1627. More than 1,500 children who were kidnapped from the streets of London arrived in Virginia this year. It was under King James in 1619 that the practice of exporting orphans began, and since then criminals have been cashing in on this plentiful labour force.

India, 1627. Jahangir, the great Moghul emperor, dies.

Angola, 1627. The queen of Mbundu, Nzinga, is victorious in the year-old war against the Portuguese. She makes her sister queen of the Ndongo, who were previously allies of Portugal.

West Indies, 1627. English settlers arrive on the island of Barbados.

Bohemia, 1627. The kingdom becomes an hereditary possession of the Habsburgs. The Czech nobility emigrate in droves.

London, 1627. Francis Bacon's *New Atlantis*, a philosophical novel concerning the organisation of a city governed by scholars, is published posthumously.

Morocco, 1627. The death of Sultan Zaydan marks the end of the Sadian dynasty.

Virginia, 1627. Despite opposition from the pope and King James, tobacco exports total 500,000 pounds, up from 18,000 in 1617.

Spain to leave the crossroads of Europe

Switzerland, 5 March 1626

The treaty of Monzon between France, Spain and the papacy has settled the long-running dispute over the Alpine valley which has erupted into the forefront of European politics. The treaty restores the *status quo* of 1617 in the area. Spanish forts are to be destroyed, and France is to have the use of the passes in and out of Valtellina which is to be restored to the leaders of three associations of landlords known as the *Grisons*.

The Alpine valley involved lies to the south-east of the Swiss cantons, it has a population of only about 80,000, but has become a crossroads of European politics. Habsburg troops in Italy need a route across the Alps to the Netherlands and Germany, while France wants an Alpine route directly into the Habsburg backyard in Italy.

Chieftain dies of wounds invading China

China, 30 September 1626

Nurhaci, the chieftain of the Manchus, has died in his capital of Shenyang of wounds he received in his failed assault on the strategic Chinese town on Ning-yuan.

Nurhaci welded together the Manchu tribes, the latest of the invaders from the north. He overran the province of Liao-dong, which had formed part of the Chinese cultural area for some 2,000 years, and then prepared to attack the Ming heartland. Much of Nurhaci's military success stemmed from his invention of a system by which his soldiers fought not as tribes but under different coloured banners. He later expanded this system into the civilian administration. Unlike previous invaders from the north, Nurhaci also established himself as ruler of a viable monarchy before attempting his assault on China. This means that his death will not help the disintegrating Ming empire. He is being succeeded by his son, Abahai, a gifted general.

Disgraced eunuch leader hangs himself

China, 1627

Wei Zhong-sian, the most notorious of the eunuchs who have achieved great power under the Ming emperors, has hanged himself to escape the wrath of the new emperor, Zhu Yu-jian. Wei, after a criminal adolescence, voluntarily submitted to emasculation and spent the next 30 years working his way into a position of power in the palace. He succeeded in achieving such dominance over the sickly young Emperor Zhu Yu-jiao that he virtually ran China. When Zhu Yu-jiao died and was succeeded by the 17-year-old Zhu Yu-jian, the new emperor was deluged with accusations about the eunuch's behaviour.

Wei was ordered to leave the capital to take up a minor post. On the way he learned that the emperor had ordered his interrogation. He hanged himself in the city of Fucheng – but he has not been allowed to escape retribution. His body has been dug up, dismembered and put on display.

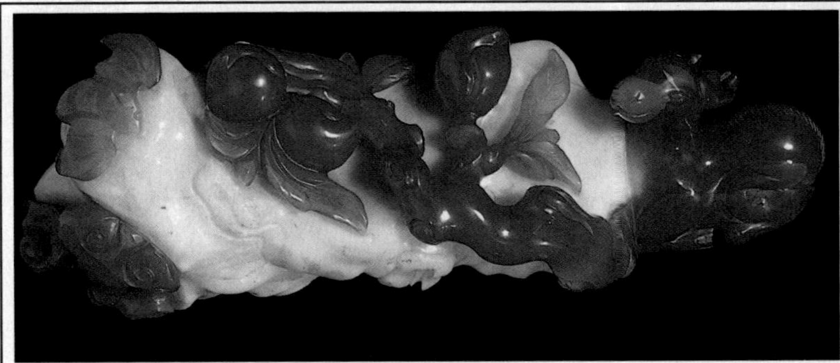

A carnelian and white quartz carving representing the female life force or "Yin" as dark red peaches, encircling its male counterpart or "Yang".

Moghul general bids to topple empress

Lion-hunting, one of the empress Nur Jahan's pastimes.

Agra, India, 1626
As Jahangir, the emperor of India, lies dying, and his wife, Nur Jahan (Light of the World), prepares to secure absolute power, she has tackled a coup mounted by the Moghul Mahabat Khan. His target was not the emperor, but Nur Jahan, who is as adept at killing rivals as she is at killing tigers.

Since 1611, when she married Jahangir, she has dominated the empire. She is the daughter of a Persian adventurer, once beautiful, now merely ambitious. As to her attitude to her husband, she "governs him and winds him up at her pleasure", according to the English ambassador Sir Thomas Roe. As Jahangir withdrew into the natural sciences, she ruled the empire through a triumvirate of herself, her father Itimad-uddaulah, and Jahangir's favourite son, Khurram.

After she had buried her father in a tomb more magnificent than Akbar's, she ran the empire single-handedly from the harem. Public business, reported Roe, "either sleeps or depends on her, who is more inaccessible than a goddess".

Recently she has been preparing for Jahangir's death. His oldest son, Khusrau, she assassinated. His favourite son, Khurram, she has provoked into rebellion. The next in line, the child princes Dara Shukoh and Aurangzeb, she has taken into her care. Mahabat Khan has been jockeying for position since Jahangir fell ill, so she was ready for this attempted coup.

Sexy theatre is sellout on and off stage

Kabuki is emerging from these rowdy popular song and dance performances.

Japan, 1628
Kabuki, a form of entertainment in which comic sketches are performed with dancing and singing, has become increasingly popular with the Japanese, taking the place of the traditional *No* drama which is considered too intellectual.

Okuni, a female attendant at the Shinto Izumo shrine, is generally given credit for developing *Kabuki* out of *No* in 1603 with a performance on the dry bed of the river Kamo-gawa in Kyoto. It was a great success largely because of its sensual dancing and erotic scenes.

It was given the name *Kabuki*, meaning unusual or shocking, and its performances became the scenes of uproar as spectators fought over the entertainers who were prostitutes as well as actresses.

The Tokugawa *shogunate* banned women from appearing in 1629 because it was feared they were corrupting the *samurai* warriors, but their places were immediately taken by young men beautifully made up as women. The authorities remain unhappy about *Kabuki* because these young male entertainers are selling their sexual favours to their admirers, just like their female predecessors.

A scene from a later Kabuki show.

Austrians in revolt after mass hangings

Linz, Austria, 1627
Seventeen Austrian peasants have been led out of Frankenfeld castle and hanged. They have paid the Habsburg price for "heresy". The Austrian overlord did not like their rudness to newly installed Italian Catholic priests in former Protestant churches.

The deaths have angered the Protestant population into revolt. Rebel peasants have put Linz under siege and are pleading for foreign aid. In the neighbouring Habsburg province of Bohemia, however, the Emperor Ferdinand II's avowed determination to "recatholicise" a reluctant Protestant population continues at a furious pace.

Calvinist ministers have been expelled; nobles face a choice between conversion and expulsion; and plans are afoot to proscribe Protestantism completely.

French troops keep Alpine route open

Mantua, Italy, October 1628
Spain has lost a bid to control a vital route through the Alps. A French task force has seen off Spanish troops in a military standoff giving Charles of Gonzaga, the duke of Nevers, the decisive advantage in the struggle for control of Mantua and Montferrat.

The duke of Guastalla, who is backed by Spain's king Philip IV, is expected to leave his strongholds in Montferrat. France is surrounded by Habsburgs in Spain, the Netherlands and the Pyrenees. King Louis and his chief adviser Cardinal Richelieu count this victory as a step forward in their campaign to counteract their growing influence.

The Habsburgs have already established client states in Italy ruled by a member of their family, or failing that, a compliant aristocrat.

1628 (1628-1629)

North America, 7 April 1628. Jonas Michaelius arrives in New Amsterdam as the first Dutch Reformed minister in the colonies.

England, 23 August 1628. George Villiers, the Duke of Buckingham, is assassinated. He was the favourite of King James and then of Charles, and became one of the richest men in England through their favours. He also wielded enormous political influence which made him very unpopular.

North America, 8 September 1628. John Endecott, sailing for the New England Company, arrives with colonists in Salem, the capital of Massachusetts. He is to serve as governor of the colony.

Paris, 16 October 1628. The poet Francois de Malherbe dies. He was granted a pension by King Henry IV and wrote verses in many forms but with little originality.

France, 28 October 1628. After a fifteen-month siege the Huguenot town of La Rochelle surrenders to royal forces.

Virginia, October 1628. Lord Baltimore arrives in Virginia to form a colony. Being a Catholic, he refuses Anglican oaths.

West Indies, 1628. English settlers arrive on the island of Nevis.

France, 1628. A royal decree bars Protestants from settling in New France, sending Huguenots to English colonies.

North America, 1628. The New England Company is established, an English joint-stock venture to promote trade and colonisation in North America. The company is given a patent to land along the coast between the Merrimack and Charles rivers.

France, 1628. The first harbour with locks is built at Le Havre.

France, 1628. *Entretiens spirituels* by Francois de Sales is published posthumously. He was a highly respected bishop of Geneva.

New Hampshire, 1628. American settlers have found a new way of supplementing their meagre livelihoods: gun-running. Selling arms to natives is forbidden, but this has not stopped the new form of trade.

Madrid, 1628. The painter Rubens is sent by the Archduchess Isabel, on a diplomatic mission to Madrid, where he meets Velazquez.

Persia, 19 January 1629. Shah Abbas dies in Isfahan after a reign of 42 years. Of his five sons, two were murdered on their father's orders, two died of natural causes and the last was blinded on his father's orders. He is succeeded by his grandson, Shah Safi.

France, 28 June 1629. An edict of grace is signed, maintaining freedom of worship for Protestants, but depriving them of political privileges (right of assembly) and military privileges (places of safety). After the siege of La Rochelle (1627-1628), the war against the Protestants was carried into Languedoc. The towns were put down one after another.

Canada, 20 July 1629. The English adventurer Sir David Kirke has seized power in Quebec from the destitute French administration of Samuel de Champlain. Kirke had cut off supplies to the French colony, and by the time he reached Quebec the starving settlers were eager to surrender.

New Netherland, 10 September 1629. The Dutch West India Company is acting to colonise its holdings in the New World. A candidate who can round up 50 potential settlers and pay their passages, will be awarded a huge estate, given the title *patroon*, and enjoy privileges similar to those of a feudal baron. Settlers will live and work in conditions of near servitude, and the patroon will have jurisdiction over civil and criminal matters.

Mexico City, September 1629. The city is flooded, with up to six feet of water in some areas. One eye-witness, a Dominican friar, describes the scene as resembling a shipwreck rather than a city. Up to half the population has fled to higher ground outside the city or perished.

Germany, 1629. The Edict of Restitution, promulgated by the Emperor Ferdinand II, restores all ecclesiastical property to those who owned it in 1555. In this way the emperor hopes to recover all German lands lost to Protestantism during the previous 75 years.

North America, 1629. More and more Irish Catholic immigrants have been turning up as servants in the homes of settlers in Virginia, Maryland and Carolina. They are fleeing worsening persecution by the English in their homeland.

London, 1629. The Flemish painter Peter Paul Rubens is appointed envoy to King Charles, who knights him.

New Amsterdam, 1629. Jonas Bronk, a Danish immigrant, has bought 500 acres of land north of New Amsterdam from the Indians. He plans to lease land to farmers for three-year periods, to grow maize and tobacco. Locals are calling the Aquahungtives, Bronk's (*Bronx*) river.

London, 1629. A royal charter is granted to the Guild of Spectacle Makers.

King's ally Buckingham is assassinated

London, 1628

Charles has dissolved the third parliament of his reign, after a year of confrontations and evasions, and embarked on a high-risk strategy of trying to govern (and raise revenue) without parliament. At this crucial period he has lost the court favourite whose counsel has sustained him since his accession three years ago. George Villiers, the duke of Buckingham, was visiting the fleet at Portsmouth when a naval lieutenant who had been refused promotion rushed up and plunged a dagger into his chest. The killing caused rejoicing in the streets.

Charles stubbornly insists on the divine right of kings while practising deception and falsehood, so that he is wholly mistrusted by parliament. Short of money, he tried to pawn the crown jewels in Holland. When that failed he had to recall Parliament. But instead of voting funds for him, MPs raised constitutional questions and drew up a Petition of Right, forbidding taxation without consent of parliament, arbitrary imprisonment, martial law and compulsory billeting of troops in private homes. After much prevarication Charles accepted the petition and MPs grudgingly gave him money.

Buckingham: focus for resentment.

Dutch seize 80 tons of Spanish silver

Cuba, 10 September 1628

Spain's latest bullion cargo – 80 tons of silver and other treasures worth 12 million Dutch *guilders* – has been seized by a veteran seadog named Piet Heyn. Aged 51, Heyn commands a potent fleet formed to carry the Dutch-Spanish war across the Atlantic to colonies and shipping in the New World of the Americas.

Heyn picked up a straggler from a Spanish treasure fleet off Havana, which gave him the intelligence he sought about its movements. He then stalked the Spaniards who fled into a bay, and ran aground on a mud bank. The crews rowed ashore. Without a single shot or any casualty, Heyn moored nearby and crossed in his own cutter to take possession of his prize. He was also able to direct Spanish prisoners to the nearest plantation – ironically, where he had once been held prisoner. A former galley slave of Spain, Heyn treats captives with compassion. Madrid will be less kind to its defeated admiral.

Portugal puts down Mozambique revolt

Mozambique, 1629

After a bloody colonial war in which the Portuguese were nearly driven into the sea by the army of Nyambo Kapararidze, the king of Mozambique (Munhumutapa), the Portuguese have emerged victorious. The defeated Kapararidze has been replaced by a puppet ruler called Mavura, who has signed a treaty turning his kingdom into a Portuguese protectorate.

The war began in late 1628, when the new king, Kapararidze, resentful of Portuguese incursions into his territory, killed the Portuguese ambassador and sacked their trading posts at the instigation of Arab traders who feared competition would break up their monopoly. Four hundred Portuguese were killed before Kapararidze was defeated.

The Portuguese blame the Moslem traders for the conflict, unwilling to recognise the nationalism of the Mozambican populace. Anxious to give credibility to their own prejudices, their first order to the new king is to expel Arab traders.

Spain squanders wealth on a losing war

In Rubens' portrait of Philip IV, the New World holds out the king's helmet. The wealth of Spain's empire lines the pockets of mercenaries and arms dealers.

Spain, 1629

King Philip IV may well be the best horseman in Spain, but he is leaving policy to his closest adviser and favourite, Count Gaspar Olivares. Only four years ago Olivares was able to say "God is Spanish and fights for our nation these days" after a series of victories, including one over an English expeditionary force when it attempted an attack on Cadiz. Now he may not be feeling so optimistic.

The Spanish empire's foundations of sand are beginning to show, as the demoralising effect of a long-running and expensive war in the Netherlands begins to bite. The attempt to bring the Dutch Protestant rebels to heel goes back to the 1560s, with a short break between 1609 and 1621. It is now an almost intolerable strain on Spain's resources in manpower and money.

Spain depends on a steady flow of precious metal from the new world to pay its troops; its empire exists only to fund war. There was a big setback last year, when the Dutch captured an entire treasure fleet in the Caribbean. The proceeds enabled them to launch a major assault in the Netherlands. Meanwhile, Spanish troops mutinied because they not being paid, walking out of the forts as the Dutch took them over.

While Olivares' foreign policies and ostentatious patronage of the arts have helped propel the Spanish kingdom into penury, he has also proposed schemes to raise further income. Noting that Castile alone financed all Spain's wars and supported all her foreign dependencies, he tried to make Aragon, Portugal, Valencia and Catalonia bear their share of the military and financial burden by the "Union of Arms" in 1626. So far he has met outright defiance from the Catalans and limited co-operation from the rest.

Harvey links heart with blood circulation

London, 1628

A small book of only 72 pages recording the results of experiments with animals by an English physician will undoubtedly become an instant medical classic. It is called *Exercitatio Anatomica de Motu Cordis et Sanguinis in Animalibus*, and its author is Dr William Harvey. In it he makes the bold assertion that the blood in our bodies is constantly on the move, driven by the heart, a natural pump.

For centuries the medical profession has believed the theory of Galen, that the function of the heart is that of a natural oven to keep the blood warm, and that blood was not driven in a circulatory system, like water through pipes, but subject to a kind of tidal ebb and flow. Harvey's treatise, though, demonstrates that the heart beats through muscular contraction, squeezing blood out of its interior into arteries through one-way valves. Then it returns the blood back to the heart through the veins. What comes back to the heart is indeed the same blood that left it earlier. It is recycled and not, as has been thought, freshly made.

Born in 1578 in Folkestone, the eldest of seven sons of the mayor of the Kentish town, William Harvey has had a distinguished career. After studies in Padua and the award of the fellowship of the College of Physicians, he has established himself as a brilliant teacher.

A later painting portrays Harvey demonstrating his theory to king Charles.

Persian who drove out Ottomans dies

Kaswin, Persia, 1629

Shah Abbas, the outstanding ruler of the Safavid dynasty, has died. Having inherited a nation in thrall to the Ottomans, he leaves it 42 years later a powerfully centralised empire restored to the boundaries of Shah Ismail I, enjoying internal stability and a flourishing economy.

Born in Herat, where he survived the murderous intentions of his uncle, Ismail II, Abbas became shah in 1587 on the abdication of his father, Mohammed Khudabanda. After a humiliating treaty with the Turks in 1590, he secured his borders against the Ozbegs. He eliminated potential opponents with extreme cruelty – he executed one son and blinded two others for plotting rebellion – or considerable skill, as with the diminishing of the power of Quizilbash tribesmen by forming new crack units of Caucasian slavewarriors. Victory at Sufiyan in 1605 was the greatest of his many triumphs over the Ottomans.

1629 (1629-1631)

Paris, 20 October 1629. The French theologian Cardinal Pierre de Berulle dies. He was the founder of the Congregation of the Oratory (1611), one of the new orders of the Counter-reformation movement.

France, 1629. Marillac, one of Richelieu's chief aides, draws up a series of internal reforms called the *Code Michaud*.

Netherlands, 1629. Albert Gerard is the first to use parentheses and other abbreviations in mathematics.

Australia, 1629. The Dutch sailor Francisco Pelsaert lands on north-western Australia after his ship, the *Batavia*, is wrecked on Morning Reef.

Mozambique, 1629. Munhumutapa state makes its fourth and most humiliating treaty yet with the Portuguese, having been defeated in battle.

Germany, 1629. 274 people convicted of witchcraft are executed in the prince-bishopric of Eichstatt.

Japan, 1629. Female entertainers are banned from appearing in *Kabuki* performances by the Tokugawa *shogunate*. Many of the performers are also prostitutes, and their erotic dancing leads to frequent fights in the audience.

Rome, 1629. The Italian architect Carlo Maderna dies.

Madrid, 1629. Velazquez paints *The Triumph of Bacchus*.

Angola, c.1629. The Portuguese plant the first American crops – maize and cassava – on the Angolan coast.

Massachusetts, 12 June 1630. The flagship of the Massachusetts Bay Company, the *Arbella*, docks in Salem, the first of 11 ships bearing 700 passengers, 60 horses and 40 cows. Led by John Winthrop, who immediately appoints himself governor of the new colony, they are devout Puritans who come to found a new colony and see America as their Promised Land.

Massachusetts, 7 September 1630. Governor John Winthrop and his assistants pass a resolution declaring that Trimontaine, on the Shawmut peninsula, "shall be called Boston". A resolution is passed that Boston will replace Salem as the colony's capital.

North America, 30 September 1630. John Billington is hanged for murder in New Plymouth – the first colonial execution.

Madrid, 5 November 1630. The treaty of Madrid formalises the peace of Susa between England and Spain.

Massachusetts, 9 November 1630. The first ferry route in the colonies opens, from Boston to Charlestown on the Charles River.

France, 10 November 1630. There is a trial of strength between the aggressive, warlike Cardinal Richelieu and Marillac, who is more concerned with domestic than foreign policy, and wishes above all else to keep the people happy by keeping taxes low. It appears at first that Louis XIII has capitulated to the Queen Mother and replaced Richelieu as his chief minister by Marillac. But later in the day the king announces that he will retain Richelieu. Marillac is arrested and Richelieu is left in political control, free to pursue his anti-Habsburg foreign policies.

Germany, 1630. Over the last two years some 124 people have been executed for witchcraft by the Teutonic Order at Mergentheim.

Naples, 1630. Travelling in Italy, Velazquez meets Jose de Ribera (known as the "little Spaniard"), the most prominent painter in the town, who has just finished the *Martyrdom of Saint Bartholomew*.

Geneva, 1630. Agrippa d'Aubigne, born in 1552, dies. He was a Huguenot soldier in the French wars and a poet and historian of note.

Germany, c.1630. In only eight years in the prince-bishopric of Wurzburg, Bishop Philipp Adolf von Ehrenberg has ordered the execution of some 900 people for witchcraft, including his own nephew, 19 priests and several young children.

Sweden, 1630. The king of Sweden, Gustavus Adolphus, invades Pomerania and Mecklenburg to counteract recent German military successes in Europe's long running wars.

Germany, 1630. The astronomer Christophe Scheiner, famous for his observations on sunspots, publishes *Rosa Ursina* in which he explains the apparent deformation of the sun when it sets and demonstrates that it turns on its axis.

Paris, 1630. The Luxembourg Palace, built by Salomon de Brosse for Marie de Medici and including a series of paintings of her life by Rubens, is completed after 15 years.

Denmark, 1630. Anders Christiensen Arrebo, the ex-bishop of Trondheim, who made his name with his translation of the Psalms in 1623, publishes the *Hexaemeron*, an epic work in Danish about the six days of creation.

Mozambique 1631. War breaks out again between Munhumutapa and the Portuguese.

A million feared dead in Italian plague

The survivors struggle to bury the plague dead outside the city walls.

Europe, c.1630

Bubonic plague has hit northern Italy with great ferocity, and the death-toll is rumoured to be approaching one million. Southern France is in the grip of a similar outbreak.

The latest affliction appears to have been brought into Milan by German troops invading Lombardy, perhaps also by French troops moving into Piedmont. The first victim in Milan was a German soldier. For the past three centuries Europe has been affected by plague every ten or 15 years, and doctors, of whom there are between one and ten per 10,000 inhabitants in most European cities, have found no remedy, apart from quarantine. Towns and cities are the worst hit, with poor people suffering the most. At the first hint of plague, the rich flee to the countryside.

Dutch to colonise Portuguese Brazil

Brazil, 1630

The Dutch have captured the sugar capital of Brazil, the port and islands of Recife, which are known as the Brazilian Venice. Though the Dutch were ousted from Bahia after only a year, they are set to get a firm grip on the Portuguese colony's north-eastern region, with its flourishing sugar plantations. Current production is running at some 10,000 tons a year. The Dutch are offering capital to Portuguese planters, and reorganising the slave trade with West Africa to ensure a regular labour supply. About 5,000 new slaves are needed each year.

The port is to be developed on the lines of Amsterdam, with canals and tall town houses. Architects, engineers and artists are coming from Holland. A policy of religious toleration has been introduced, allowing Calvinists, Catholics and Jews to practise their religions without interference.

Astronomer's laws are his monument

Prague, 1630

The German astronomer Johann Kepler, undoubtedly one of the most important scientists of recent years, has died at the age of 59. Kepler started studying theology, but switched to mathematics, teaching the subject at the university at Graz. In his work as assistant to the Danish astronomer Tycho Brahe, and later as astronomer to the emperor Rudolf II, he started to apply the principles of geometry to the movements of the planets, in particular Mars.

Kepler's three famous principles of planetary motion – the laws that govern the paths of planets around the sun – seem certain to ensure his place in astronomical history as they are already being referred to as Kepler's laws. He was an enthusiastic astronomer who spent many hours observing stars and comets, writing up in immense detail his results and theories.

Emperor sacks Wallenstein, the self-made warlord

Bohemia, 13 August 1630

In an extraordinary move, the emperor Frederick II has fired one of his most brilliant military commanders, Albrecht von Wallenstein, the duke of Friedland, and of Mecklenburg and self-styled "General of the Whole Imperial Fleet and Lord of the Ocean and Baltic Sea". The emperor was forced to sack him by pressure from German princes who fear both Wallenstein's power and the power that he created for the emperor.

Wallenstein, born into a minor noble family 47 years ago, is not merely a brilliant and mostly successful warlord; he is an enormously wealthy magnate, the owner of the largest feudal network of land in Bohemia. His early financial success came about through marriage to a wealthy widow. Wallenstein used his wife's fortune and borrowed money to raise an army which he used to help to crush the Bohemian revolt against Habsburg rule headed by Elector Palatine Frederick V, the "winter king" of Bohemia 1619-20. In 1621 Wallenstein became governor of Bohemia and a warlord in his own right, making a fortune out of debasing the coinage and using the profits to buy 60 estates owned by executed and exiled Czech nobles. During the Danish war Wallenstein was made the imperial commander-in-chief, fighting campaigns in northern Germany and Austria.

A later engraving of Wallenstein.

Troops run amok as Magdeburg falls

Death's harvest: men hang from a tree like fruit in a scene of horror engraved by Jacques Callot in 1633.

Germany, 20 March 1631

The whole fury and savagery of war descended on the German town of Magdeburg today. Drunken soldiers of nine nations are reeling among the smouldering ruins, dragging captive women as they seek wine in charred cellars. Bodies are so numerous – estimated at 25,000 – that they are being thrown in wagonloads into the river Elbe. Only 5,000, mostly women, have survived.

Many believe that the people of Magdeburg brought disaster on themselves by refusing to help the Hessian commander, Dietrich von Falkenberg, to prepare his defence against the besieging army of the count of Tilly, the commander of the imperial forces. Even as Tilly began his final assault, they were pleading with the defenders to surrender.

The town fell to a two-pronged attack, and it was then that the horror began. The conquering soldiers, largely Croats and Walloons, ran riot, murdering, raping and looting. A monk herded 500 women into the cathedral for safety. But there was worse to come. Fires – planned by von Falkenberg – spread across the town, fanned by a strong wind. Within minutes, Magdeburg was a roaring furnace, burning soldiers and citizens to death without discrimination.

Holland: land of free expression and religious toleration

Holland, c.1630

"We refuse no honest persons ingress to come and have their residence in this city, provided that such persons behave themselves honestly and submit to all the laws." Thus ran a letter from the magistrates of Leyden, in Holland, to a group of English dissenters seeking refuge in their city, and there is no doubt that of all countries the Dutch republic is the most open and tolerant.

In a Europe torn by feuds and fighting, Holland embraces every variety of freedom. Refugees continue to pour into its cities, especially the capital, Amsterdam, in which 30 per cent of the 100,000 population are immigrants, notably those who have fled from the Catholic southern Netherlands.

Enjoying Holland's freedom of ideas: child musicians, by Jan Molenaer.

Protestants of every country have set up their churches here, and political and intellectual refugees of every persuasion have found the freedom denied to them in their own countries. This influx brings many benefits. Holland can boast more newspapers than the rest of Europe put together; its universities, espcially that of Leyden, are centres of intellectual excellence; literature and painting are flourishing. It is also Europe's trading centre, its wharves crammed with Baltic grain, English textiles, Indian silks and spices, German wine, Scandinavian timber and much more.

1631 (1631-1633)

France, 13 January 1631. Cardinal Richelieu, Louis XIII's chief minister, bent on an aggressive anti-Habsburg foreign policy, signs the treaty of Barwalde with the Lutheran Gustavus Adolphus of Sweden, who is about to plan to launch a military attack on the heartlands of Germany.

Paris, 30 May 1631. *La Gazette de France*, a weekly collection of news and the organ of royal power, is published for the first time by Theophraste Renaudot, under an exclusive royal privilege.

Amsterdam, June 1631. Spurred on by his recent successes, Rembrandt leaves Leyden for Amsterdam, a fashionable centre, where he intends to paint portraits.

Massachusetts, August 1631. The first American-built ship, the 30-ton sloop *Blessing of the Bay*, is launched in Boston harbour. Plentiful timber means that vessels can be built for half the price of those in England, and the colonists hope that this will be the beginning of a profitable new enterprise.

Germany, 17 September 1631. After the Protestant town of Madgeburg had been sacked by the troops of Tilly, the commander of the Catholic League, the elector of Saxony concludes an alliance with Gustavus Adolphus of Sweden, who crushes the Catholic troops at Breitenfeld.

Rome, 1631. Domenico Mazzochi's oratorio *Lamentations of Mary Magdalene* is performed for the first time.

France, 1631. The king's brother, Gaston d'Orleans, and his mother, Marie de Medici, rebel, refusing to be reconciled with the chief minister Cardinal Richelieu. The Queen Mother prefers to take refuge in the Low Countries thus beginning a war between mother and son.

France, 1631. The mathematician, Pierre Vernier invents the "scale" which bears his name and which facilitates the reading of graduations on a sextant. It is an improvement of a device invented by the Spaniard Pedro Nunez for the same purpose.

France, 1631. Pierre Gassendi makes the first observation of the passage of mercury across the sun's disc.

England, 1631. William Oughtred proposes the symbol x for multiplication.

England, 1631. *Love's Cruelty* by playwright James Shirley is first performed.

North America, 1631. Europeans found a settlement in Maryland.

Spain, 1631. The poet and scholar Francisco de Quevedo y Villegas publishes a highly successful expurgated version of his 1627 collection of moral satires, *Dreams*, which was condemned for ridiculing the Holy Scripture.

Amsterdam, 1631. The Czech educational reformer Jan Amos Comenius publishes *The Gates of Language Unlocked*, showing how language is best taught through real things and situations.

Antwerp, 1631. Rubens paints *The Artist with Helen Fourment in the garden*.

Toulouse, France, 30 October 1632. Henry of Montmorency, the governor of the Languedoc, is beheaded for having fomented a conspiracy with the queen mother, Marie de Medici, and Gaston d'Orleans, the king's brother.

New Netherlands, 6 December 1632. The whole colony of Swanadael has been wiped out because of a petty theft. In the autumn an Indian chief stole a Dutch coat of arms made of tin and made a pipe out of it. Settlers reported this to another tribe, who promptly presented them with the chief's head. His tribe took revenge by massacring all but one of the settlers.

Italy, 1632. Galileo publishes his *Dialogue on the the Two Chief World Systems*.

Japan, 1632. Following further executions at Nagasaki and Edo, a thorough search is launched for all remaining Christians in Japan.

Poland, 1632. The treaty of Altmark marks the annexation of the coast of Livonia by Sweden.

India, 1632. The Emperor Shahjahan orders the destruction of Hindu temples. In the Benares district alone, 76 are destroyed.

India, 1632. The Portuguese are forced out of Bengal.

India, 1632. More than a million people have died in a famine in the Dekhan, and some have only survived by cannibalism. The famine was caused by a drought in 1630-1 and excessive rains the following year. It is feared that a plague will follow.

Russia, 1632. One third of the Russian army is now constituted on western lines: troops are recruited locally and mercenaries engaged in the European Protestant countries are hired as officers.

India, 1632. The Emperor Shahjahan has begun the construction of the Taj Mahal in memory of his beloved wife, Mumtaz Mahal, who died last year bearing her fifteenth child.

Cathedral that took 120 years to finish

Bernini's baldacchino in St Peter's.

Rome, 1633

Over 120 years after Pope Julius laid the foundation stone of the new St Peter's, its interior is at last complete. The *baldacchino*, or canopy, marking the site of the supposed grave of St Peter has taken nine years to satisfy its designer, Gianlorenzo Bernini. It consists of four columns, twisted like barley sugar, but made of bronze, supporting an elaborate crown.

It stands at the crossing beneath the huge dome, originally designed by Bramante, but altered by Michelangelo and finished by Giacomo della Porta in 1590. The church was consecrated by Pope Urban VIII in 1626.

English poet nears his final stanza

London, 12 February 1631

A fervent congregation packed St Paul's Cathedral today to hear its dean, the courtly poet John Donne, preach his sermon "Death's Duel" – its subject was death and resurrection. Many felt that the dean's topic was all too personal: he is known to be ill, and it is feared that this could be his final address.

Although Donne's preaching has earned him the title "a second Augustine", it is for his poetry that he is best known. His first works, the *Satires and Elegies*, appeared in the 1590s. These were followed by the *Songs and Sonnets*, written after his marriage in 1601. The *Holy Sonnets*, inspired by the death of his wife, were written around 1610. The *Pseudo-Martyr*, attacking Catholic martyrs, was written in 1610, as was *Biathanatos*, a study of suicide.

John Donne, painted in c.1595.

Death toll mounts as Turk purges traitors

Istanbul, May 1632

The revolt of the Janissaries is over, and the young Sultan Murad IV is embarking on a ruthless purge of traitors. Rejeb Pasha, the Janissaries' choice as grand vizier, has been executed.

Anarchy among the military had been growing under the regency of Murad's mother, Sultana Valide, until there was a general revolt of Janissary garrisons last year. A few weeks ago a mutiny of the household troops brought terror to the Hippodrome for three days. To appease the bloodthirsty soldiers, Murad was obliged to sacrifice to the mob's vengeance his grand vizier, Hafiz Pasha, who was also his brother-in-law, the *mufti* and 15 other court officials.

But divisions grew among the Janissaries while Murad plotted his revenge. Having had the new grand vizier, Rejeb Pasha, strangled and beheaded by eunuchs, he persuaded *sipahis*, janissaries and judges to sign an oath of loyalty and co-operate in a purge on corruption and subversion. Murad is having all suspect traitors rounded up and executed.

Ethiopian leader turns against Rome

An Ethiopian Christ in judgement.

Gondar, Ethiopia, 1632

The dream of Susneyos, of modernising his empire in a generation, has failed. The emperor has abdicated and renounced his Catholicism. Susneyos came to the throne in 1607 with support from the descendants of Portuguese musketeers. Ethiopia, broken by Galla incursions and civil war, could not have been weaker. He proposed an alliance with Philip III of Spain to quash his enemies. In return for Spanish help, Susneyos made Catholicism the state religion.

With his brother, Si'la Christos, he swept tradition aside, imposing European methods of government and importing Jesuit missionaries. The Amhara majority rose up against forced conversion. Three rebellions failed to overthrow Susneyos and his European allies. A fourth has succeeded and forced Susneyos to abdicate. His son, Fasiladas, has become regent and has already promised to expel the Jesuits and restore coptic Christianity.

St George and the dragon.

Boston is capital of Puritan colony

Boston, Massachusetts, 1633

The rolling, wooded countryside of Massachusetts, a self-governing colony rings with the sound of axes to build chapels, homes and even some seagoing ships from an abundance of local timber. It is three years since the Suffolk landowner, John Winthrop, sailed here with the royal charter of government, followed by nearly 1,000 more English Puritans convinced that this rolling, fertile countryside must be the promised land of their Biblical dreams.

Soon after arriving in September, 1630 Winthrop and his assistants passed a resolution declaring that this particularly fine site on the Shawmut peninsula should be the place at which the settlers should build their seat of government. The frame of the governor's house has been moved here together with a church. The site is known by the local Indians as "living fountain" – after a local spring. Winthrop's council has renamed it "Boston" – after the Lincolnshire home town of two settlers, Lady Arabella and Isaac Johnson.

Winthrop's enthusiasm for the settlement is unbounded. "We shall be like a city upon a hill," he proclaimed. "The eyes of all people are on us."

Swedish king dies leading cavalry charge

The heavens open and the cherubs sigh for the late king Gustavus II Adolphus.

Germany, 6 November 1632

Sweden will mourn deeply the death today of the powerful leader who has turned this country from a feudal backwater into a major European power. King Gustavus II Adolphus was killed as he led a cavalry charge into victory in a battle against the forces of Albrecht von Wallenstein at Lutzen near Leipzig. He was only 37.

A huge man, blond and broad-shouldered, Gustavus displayed a remarkable charisma, particularly with the common people. He came to the throne at the age of 16, and it was at this time that he was bullied into signing a charter of accession which allowed only nobles to take high office. Working with his astute chancellor, Axel Oxenstierna, Gustavus was able to surmount this and proceeded to remodel his country in every department. Government was streamlined, its council sitting permanently as a cabinet, making decisions in his absence.

Gustavus was an outstanding statesman and a brilliant military commander. He ensured that his conscript army was paid regularly – a rarity in today's Europe, where most soldiers are expected to live off the land. He built up a large navy to challenge Denmark for the mastery of Baltic.

Artists' guild has admitted woman painter

Haarlem, 1633

A woman has been admitted to the painters' Guild of St Luke here, an extremely rare event. She is Judith Leyster, the daughter of a brewery owner, who showed great talent from an early age as a painter of domestic scenes, still life and portraits. She likes to paint people enjoying themselves, such as *The Serenade* depicting young lovers, *The Jolly Companions* in which a young woman pours wine for her young man who is playing the violin, or *The Jolly Toper*, a man laughing over his glass of wine.

Many of her subjects recall those of Franz Hals, whose pupil she was, and she is quite his equal. While her critics say she imitates him too closely, she has sued Hals for taking one of her apprentices for himself.

Judith Leyster's "Game of Cards": typical of her genre scenes, it shows ordinary people enjoying themselves, painted with warmth and affection.

Japan shuts out rest of the world

Japan, 1633

The persecution of Christians in Japan has been intensified with the issuing of an Exclusion Decree giving orders for the searching out of Christian converts, the arrest of missionaries working underground in Japan and the detention of others being smuggled into Japanese ports. This decree is believed to be aimed at Christianity not as a religion, but because it is the faith of potential invaders of Japan. The Tokugawa *shogunate* fears all foreign influences, and the decree not only attacks Christianity but cuts off Japan from the rest of the world. Nobody is allowed to leave, and all Japanese living abroad are to be put to death if they return.

1633 (1633-1635)

Virginia, 1 February 1633. The tobacco laws are codified, limiting production to reduce dependence on a single-crop economy.

Germany, 1633. During his ten year reign, Bishop Johann Georg II von Dornheim has had 600 people executed for witchcraft in the bishopric of Bamberg, including his own chancellor and one of the burgermeisters. Large numbers of those condemned were poor, elderly women, many of them widows.

Rome, 1633. Bernini finishes the *baldacchino* of St Peter's basilica.

Ontario, 1633. A white man is killed and eaten by the Huron Indians. It is not known whether he was cooked first.

France, 1633. Jacques Callot engraves *Les Miseres de la Guerre*, graphic scenes of suffering in the German wars.

France, 1633. Vincent de Paul and Louis de Marillac found the Order of the Daughters of Charity.

London, 1633. *'Tis pity she's a whore*, a tragedy by John Ford about incest between a brother and sister, is first performed.

India, 1633. The British establish a trading post in Bengal.

Russia, 1633. The Russians lay siege to the town of Smolensk, which is in Polish hands. They make little progress and the new Polish king, Wladyslaw, soon arrives to relieve the town. The king has also obtained the support of the Dnieper *Cossacks*, who have been disillusioned by Moscow's failure to come to their aid during a recent revolt.

Russia, February 1634. The leader of the Russian troops besieging the Polish town of Smolensk accepts an armistice from the Polish king, and the remaining 8,000 Russian men are permitted to retire.

Massachusetts, 4 March 1634. Samuel Cole opens the first tavern in Boston.

Germany, 5-6 September 1634. Imperial and Spanish troops under Archduke Ferdinand inflict a shattering defeat on the Swedes and other Protestant forces near the Bavarian town of Nordlingen. The victory ends Swedish influence in southern Germany.

France, 1634. *Sophonisbe* by Jean Mairet is performed. It is a tragedy which introduces the rule of the three "unities": of time, so that a play may not cover more time in the plot than it takes to perform; of place, so that it is confined to one place; and of action, so that nothing superfluous or irrelevant takes place.

North America, 1634. The French explorer Jean Nicolet crosses a great lake (*Lake Michigan*), wearing a Chinese robe, and enters what he thinks is the Orient. Instead he finds himself in the wilds of the north-west of the American continent, probably the first white man to set foot in the area.

Senegal, 1634. The French establish a settlement at St Louis.

France, 1634. Francois Mansart undertakes the rebuilding of the chateau at Blois, at the request of Gaston d'Orleans, the king's brother.

Spain, 1634. The painter Francisco de Zubaran is called to Madrid by Philip IV to assist in the decoration of the Buen Retiro, under the direction of Velazquez.

China, 1634. English traders establish a factory in Canton.

Japan, 1634. Deshima, a man-made island in Nagasaki harbour, is designated the only place in Japan where foreigners may live. The Dutch move there from Hirado.

North Sea, 1634. A tidal wave destroys Strand Island in the North Sea.

North America, 1634. Maryland is founded by Lord Baltimore.

Paris, 10 February 1635. King Louis XIII grants letters patent to a new French Academy, a group of educated men under Valentin Conrart, whose function, following Italian models, will be to give precise rules to the French language and to compile a dictionary.

France, 19 May 1635. Cardinal Richelieu intervenes in the great conflict in Europe by declaring war on the Habsburgs in Spain.

France, 1635. The French Company of American Islands is founded. The French occupy Guadeloupe.

Maryland, 1635. An Algonquin chief responds to the imposition of English law: "Since you are strangers here, you should rather conform to the customs of our country."

Spain, 1635. The playwright Lope de Vega dies. He is said to have written 1,500 plays, though no record survives of at least half of these. His popular plays were more notable for their entertainment value than their artistic merit.

England, 1635. Rubens finishes *The Apotheosis of James I* which adorns the ceiling of the great Banqueting House in Whitehall.

England, 1635. Anthony Van Dyck paints the *Equestrian Portrait of Charles I* and *Charles I hunting*.

Emperor has treacherous lord killed

Bohemia, 25 February 1634

An Irish captain, Walter Devereux, burst into the bedroom of Albrecht von Wallenstein in his fortress at Eger today and stabbed the famous warlord to death. The assassin was acting on orders from the Emperor Ferdinand II, who had learnt of Wallenstein's secret negotiations with the Swedes and other Protestant enemies.

Wallenstein was fired as imperial commander-in-chief in 1630 for behaving like an independent warlord, although he was recalled in 1632 to fight the Swedes. Latterly he had grown increasingly eccentric and megalomaniacal. He hated loud noises and would order the killing of every dog in any town in which he stopped. Servants – even officers – who talked loudly or shouted near him faced execution. Last month he demanded an oath from his colonels that they be loyal to him alone.

Wallenstein is stabbed to death.

War engulfs Europe as France joins fray

Paris, 19 May 1635

After months of hesitation, Louis XIII finally declared war on Philip IV of Spain today – using the Spanish occupation of the fortress of Trier as his pretext. French intervention means that almost every country in Europe is involved in a complex war which shows no sign of abating even after 17 years.

The greatest fear of the French king's first minister, Cardinal Richelieu, is that the victory by the Emperor Ferdinand II over the Protestant princes of Germany at Nordlingen will lead to the revival of the late Emperor Charles V's dream of universal domination. This fear has involved France in considerable diplomatic activity for several years. In 1631 Richelieu came to the support of Sweden with a financial subsidy; he later succeeded in splitting the emperor's armies by forcing Spain to evacuate a critical transit point for its crack troops, the *tercios*.

The French have now occupied the whole of the duchy of Lorraine and established garrisons in Alsace. France has also signed treaties with Sweden and Holland.

Peacock throne brings misery to millions

Agra, 1635

Shah Jahan, who succeeded to the Moghul empire in 1627 after his father Jahangir's death, is accumulating the largest collection of jewels in the world. The cost in human misery and suffering is stupendous. Millions died in famines between 1630 and 1632 while Shah Jahan emptied his treasury to expand his collection.

His richest jewels are embedded in his "Peacock Throne", so large he can lie in it with ease. Its legs are of gold, and on the twelve pillars of its canopy are portrayed peacocks made of jewels, and trees bearing diamonds, emeralds and rubies on its branches.

Shahjahan sitting regally on the Peacock Throne.

Inquisition tries Galileo

Debate rages fiercely as Galileo's ideas are examined by the cardinals of the Inquisition. The defendant sits in the middle, underneath a huge cross.

Italy, 1633

Once more Galileo, the astronomer who has repeatedly voiced his opposition to the idea (favoured by the church) that the Earth is the centre of the universe, has fallen foul of the ecclesiastical authorities. This time he was called to Rome to stand trial for propounding his ideas in a book, published last year, called *Dialogue concerning the Two Chief World Systems*.

In this work Galileo criticised Aristotle's cosmology with its insistence on the notion that the universe has a central point – namely Earth. He also discussed at length the motion of stars, planets and falling bodies and commented on the periodic nature of sunspots, all of which are inconsistent with a stationary, pivotal Earth.

Sick and ageing, Galileo was forced by the pope to journey to Rome under "suspicion of heresy". After a protracted hearing on 21 June he was finally sentenced, having been found guilty by the Inquisition of teaching the banned Copernican doctrine. He was also ordered to recant, which he did in a carefully-worded formula renouncing his past errors. Although he should have been imprisoned, the pope has commuted his sentence to house arrest.

What has been on trial is not just the astronomical thoughts of one man, but a way of looking at the world that is bound to produce conflict. Galileo is a leading advocate of rational scientific thinking which is opposed to belief, superstition and supposition. For Galileo, numbers are supreme. "The Book of Nature", he contends, is written in mathematical characters. With that single sentence he shows himself to be a founding father of scientific experimental method.

The universe which he sees at the end of his telescope is vastly larger than had previously been conceived. This readiness to accept the value of observable phenomena is critical to the development of new ideas and theories, most of them very unpopular with the large conservative church authorities.

Observing the heavens: should you believe your eyes, or your priest?

Founder urges French: "Settle Quebec"

Quebec, New France, 1635

Over 33 years after he first landed in Quebec, the French soldier-explorer Samuel de Champlain has returned to New France to continue work on the fulfilment of his dream of a flourishing France in the New World. This is de Champlain's first visit to Quebec since it was returned by the English three years ago, after they had forced de Champlain to surrender in 1629.

As the province's founder, one of de Champlain's earliest moves will be to strengthen the French presence by persuading more farmers to settle here. It was lack of settlers, he believes, that made Quebec vulnerable to the English, as French colonists prefer working with the Indians in the fur trade to working the land. Ironically, it was de Champlain's ability to co-operate successfully with the Indians that gave France a foothold in Quebec.

Quebec's founder: de Champlain.

De Champlain's men, outnumbered by the Iroquois, wield their guns.

Statesman takes the helm of Sweden

Sweden, 1633

That Sweden's war effort has not collapsed since King Gustavus Adolphus' early death last year is largely due to one man: his brilliant chancellor Axel Oxenstierna, now effectively regent for the six-year-old Queen Christina.

Oxenstierna became chancellor – chief minister – in 1612. He negotiated peace with Sweden's Baltic neighbours, Denmark, Poland and Russia and, although he tried to prevent his king's entry into the current war, he supported him loyally in his campaigns. Under Gustavus and Oxenstierna Sweden's government and courts were modernised, its education, commerce and industry promoted and immigration encouraged.

A later portrait of Queen Christina.

1635 (1635-1636)

Prague, 30 May 1635. The Emperor Ferdinand II and John George, the elector of Saxony, sign a religious and political settlement known as the peace of Prague.

Armenia, July 1635. The Ottomans capture Yerevan from the Safavid Persians.

Canada, 25 December 1635. Samuel de Champlain, the explorer and founder of New France, dies in Quebec.

Japan, 1635. The *Sankin Kotai* system is introduced whereby all the *daimyo* (feudal lords) are compelled to live in Edo every alternate year, leaving their families there when they return to their provinces. This is to ensure continuing peace by preventing any individual family from building up excessive power.

Japan, 1635. The genre painter Kany Sanarku, the leader of the Kyoto Kano school of painting, dies. After a restless life, he took holy orders in Kyoto. He will be best remembered for his Chinese-style ink paintings.

Istanbul, 1635. The Druse *emir* Fakhr ed-Din and his three children are executed. He had tried to liberate Lebanon from Ottoman occupation.

Netherlands, 1635. The imperial soldier Ottavio Piccolomini, the duke of Amalfi, is sent to aid the Spaniards in the Netherlands to drive out the French. Piccolomini served in Wallenstein's army at Lutzen in 1632, then contributed to his commander's downfall and went on to distinguish himself in the imperial victory at Nordlingen.

England, 1635. In response to a book written by the Dutch philosopher Hugo Grotius in 1625, John Selden writes *Mare Clausum*, in which he claims domination of the seas for England.

China, 1635. A collection of scientific works entitled *Chongzhen Lishu*, jointly edited by Jesuit missionaries and Chinese scholars, is published.

North-central Africa, 1635. Abd el-Krim ben Jame seizes power from his father-in-law Dawud, the last Tunjur sultan in Wadai, and founds a Moslem sultanate in Chad.

Germany, 1635. The famous Jesuit theologian Friedrich von Spee dies. A courageous opponent of the procedure followed in witchcraft trials, he published in 1631 a critique of the subject entitled *Cautio Criminalis*. Von Spee was also a leading poet of his age. Inspired by the Spanish mysticism of John of the Cross, he wrote some fine church hymns and pastoral allegories.

Caribbean, 1635. The French explorers Olive and Duplessis land on Guadeloupe and claim the island for France.

North America, 1635. The charter of the Council for New England, founded in 1620, is returned to the English crown after repeated defiance of its authority by the New England settlers.

Arabia, 1636. The Ottoman Turks are driven out of Yemen by Zaydi *imams*, who establish an independent, theocratic state.

China, 1636. The Manchus, a new power in the north-east of China, adopt the Chinese dynastic name of Qing for their new state.

Netherlands, 1636. The university of Utrecht is founded.

Netherlands, 1636. Antoine van Diemen is appointed governor of the Dutch East Indies.

Ceylon, 1636. A treaty with the king of Kandy allows the Dutch to establish a presence in Ceylon (*Sri Lanka*).

Germany, 1636. After a visit to Venice, the German composer Heinrich Schutz composes his *Kleine geistliche Konzerte*.

Caribbean, 1636. The French take Martinique from the Spanish.

Japan, 1636. Tokugawa Iemitsu prohibits the construction of ocean-going vessels.

North America, 1636. The Puritan John Harvard founds the first American university, at Cambridge, Massachusetts.

North America, 1636. The Dutch are granted the first patents on Long Island.

Germany, 4 October 1636. The Swedes defeat the Saxons at the battle of Wittstock.

France, October 1636. Under the treaty of St Germain-en-Laye, Richelieu hires the services of the Protestant general Bernard of Saxe-Weimar, promising him the duchy of Alsace as a reward. Bernard led the Swedish army to victory at the battle of Lutzen in 1632, but was defeated by imperial forces two years later at Nordlingen.

Paris, December 1636. Pierre Corneille's tragedy *El Cid* is performed on stage for the first time, to great acclaim.

Paris, 1636. On the orders of Richelieu, the Cardinal palace is built and its garden laid out.

Paris, 1636. *Marianne* by Tristan l'Hermite is performed for the first time. A stirring portrayal of passion, its success matches that of *El Cid*.

Velazquez learns new techniques in Italy

Prince Balthasar Carlos on horseback, by Diego Velazquez, c.1635.

Madrid, 1635

A remarkable new picture, by Diego de Velazquez *The Surrender of Breda*, has been installed in the king's new palace of Buen Retiro. People are astonished by its sense of actuality, as if it had been painted on the spot. In fact, Velazquez relied on eye-witnesses.

Breda fell over ten years ago, and both the protagonists in the picture, the Spanish general Spinola and the defeated count of Nassau who is handing him the key to the town, are dead. Breda has since been recaptured by Dutch forces. After a visit to Italy, Velazquez changed to a less formal style of painting and began to employ warmer colouring. King Philip IV has delighted in Velazquez' work ever since he first sat for him when he was 18 and the painter 24.

Velazquez never wearies of using the king as his model. Their friendship is shown by the directness and honesty of the portraits. He has also begun to paint the king's son, Balthasar Carlos, who is only seven, on horseback.

Artist who served Chinese emperors dies

China, 1636

The great statesman and painter Dong Qichang has died aged 82 at his home in the city of Huating. An artist by training, he became renowned as perhaps China's greatest painter and calligrapher since Zhao Mengfu, who died in 1322.

But Dong also pursued a career in government, and in 1594 he became favourite tutor to the imperial heir Zhu Changle. But corrupt officials jealous of his position and integrity led him to retire twice, the second time a dispute over a concubine caused a riot and the burning of his home. At 76 he returned to the Ming court for the last time, retiring at 80 with the high office of president of the Board of Rites.

Arts blossom under authoritarian Charles

Three faces of Charles I, by Carlo Maratti (1625-1713) after van Dyck.

London, 1635

The art collection assembled by England's King Charles over the years is now said to be the finest in Europe. His agents have scoured the continent to bring him the works of Titian, Tintoretto, Raphael and a host of other painters. Poetry and music also enjoy the royal favour. Peter Paul Rubens, who is painting a picture of the king's father, James, ascending into heaven, says Charles is "the most art-loving prince in Europe".

The Rubens is one of three on the ceiling of the Banqueting Hall at Whitehall Palace. The other two portray James as the peacemaker and James linking the crowns of England and Scotland. After these, Rubens will portray Charles as St George slaying the dragon.

While the king enjoys the role of connoisseur of the arts, however, the governance of England is in disarray as he tries to rule without parliament. He is becoming increasingly isolated from the people, making few public appearances, preferring to take part in masques in the Banqueting Hall.

Charles's favourite portrait is at Hampton Court. This 12-foot-high (3.7m) painting shows Charles on horseback, grasping a commander's baton, a long sword on the horse's flank. The king told van Dyck, the painter, that he wished to appear at least six feet tall. Charles is actually five feet four inches.

German war ends: Habsburgs are victors

Prague, 30 May 1635

The war that has devastated Germany came to an end today with the publication of a peace treaty signed by the two leading Protestant electors and Archduke Ferdinand, the emperor's son, who has assumed command of the imperial army. The House of Habsburg has emerged victorious, although the terms of the peace of Prague represent a marked scaling down of Ferdinand II's Catholic zeal.

Under the terms, the dukes of Saxony and Brandenburg retain the ecclesiastical lands which they held in 1627, but their armies will come under imperial command. Calvinists are specifically excluded from the treaty, however, and the empire will continue to wage war on them. As other Lutheran states – Bavaria, Mainz, Cologne and Trier – hasten to add their signatures, the emperor can claim that all the major princes of the empire are united behind him.

It was the battle of Nordlingen, where a combined Austrian and Spanish force defeated the Swedish army, which brought about the ceasefire that led to the treaty.

The peace of Prague may have brought rejoicing to Germany, but other European powers – France and Holland in particular – will be less than joyful at the sight of a united Germany under their old adversary, Ferdinand and his armies.

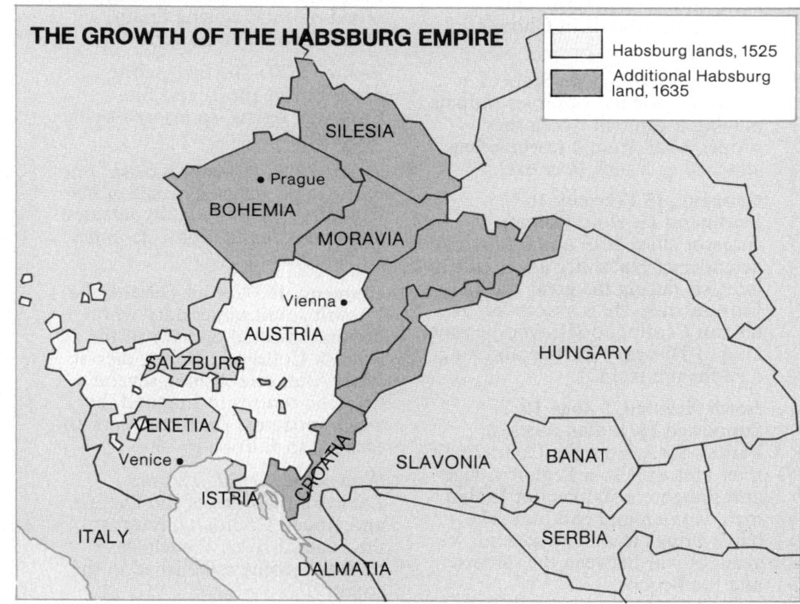

Author who wrote a play a day is dead

De Vega (1562-1635): claimed he could write a play in a day.

Madrid, 1635

This year has seen the death of Spain's most prolific playwright, Lope de Vega, who claimed to have written 1,500 plays as well as six novels, several verse epics and hundreds of sonnets and ballads. His most famous play is *Fuente Ovejuna*, named after a village that rebelled against the Spanish king and queen under the leadership of a young woman.

Lope was notoriously unfaithful to his wife, and had five illegitimate children besides three from his marriage. Despite this he was ordained as a priest and died a poor man, having given most of his large earnings to charity or the church. He claimed he could write a play in a day.

One of his hastily written pieces, *The Mayor of Zalamea*, was rewritten by Pedro Calderon de la Barca. In this play a peasant becomes mayor and defies the class conventions by ordering the execution of the nobleman who has raped his daughter – and is commended by the king for avenging her honour.

Calderon (born 1600): honour comes before class conventions.

1636 (1636-1637)

North America, 1636. Led by the Englishman Roger Williams, the first colonists settle on Rhode Island. A Puritan and champion of religious toleration, Williams, who emigrated to New England in 1630, suffered persecution and banishment for his beliefs. He escaped to the shores of Narragansett Bay and purchased land from the Indians which he has renamed Providence, to mark God's providence to him in his distress.

France, 1636. Following Richelieu's declaration of war on Spain last year, Spanish and Bavarian armies invade France, but are driven back.

Japan, 1636. Ornate buildings are constructed at Nikko to house the remains of Tokugama Ieyasu, the founder of the Tokugama *shogunate*, who died in 1616.

China, 1636. Dong Quichang, the painter and writer on aesthetics, dies. He introduced the distinction between the "northern" and "southern" schools in Chinese painting.

Canada, 1636. Jan de Brebeuf, a Jesuit missionary, observes Indians playing a game in which they propel a ball from a rawhide bag attached to a stick (*lacrosse*).

Germany, 15 February 1637. Ferdinand II, Holy Roman emperor since 1619 and staunch defender of Habsburg and Catholic interests during the great war in Europe, dies. He is succeeded by his son Ferdinand III, who became king of Hungary in 1626 and king of Bohemia in 1627.

North America, 5 June 1637. Supported by Indian allies, a Puritan force from the Connecticut river area attacks a Pequot village and slaughters 500 Pequot Indian men, women and children. The battle brings to an end several years of war between the settlers and the Pequot.

London, 23 July 1637. After a court battle, King Charles hands over the North American colony of Massachusetts to Sir Ferdinando Gorges, one of the founders of the Council of New England.

Scotland, 1637. Religious rebellion threatens, following attempts by King Charles and William Laud, the archbishop of Canterbury, to introduce the English prayerbook and Anglican church practices into Scotland.

France, 1637. An invading Spanish army in the south is repelled by French forces.

France, 1637. The peasant revolutionaries known as the *croquants* stage new uprisings in the regions of Perigord and Rouergue.

France, 1637. The philosopher Rene Descartes publishes his *Discours de la Methode*.

England, 1637. The parliamentarian John Hampden, a cousin of Oliver Cromwell, refuses to pay the assessment of "ship money" levied on his estate in Buckinghamshire. Ship money is a tax imposed by King Charles on maritime towns and shires to meet naval expenses. It was recently extended, however, to inland areas.

England, 1637. The dramatist Ben Jonson dies. He will be best remembered for his four theatrical masterpieces *Volpone*, *The Silent Woman*, *The Alchemist* and *Bartholomew Fair*.

England, 1637. The poet John Milton writes the pastoral elegy *Lycidas*. He is attacked for his outburst against the Laudian clergy.

Portugal, 1637. John, the duke of Braganza, is proclaimed king but, afraid of antagonising Spain, refuses to assume power.

Venice, 1637. The first public opera house, the Teatro San Cassiano, opens, sponsored by the Tron family.

Japan, 1637. Honami Koetsu, one of the most versatile artists of his day, dies. He was equally talented at painting, calligraphy, ceramics and gardening.

Germany, 1637. John Gerard, the English Jesuit missionary who became spiritual director of the English College in Rome, dies at Jena. After establishing several Catholic centres in England, he was imprisoned for three years and escaped to Europe in 1606.

West Africa, 1637. Thomas Lambert, the head of the Dieppe and Rouen Company, returns to the Senegal river. French slave traders become established in the country.

Vietnam, 1637. The Dutch arrive in Hanoi.

Korea, 1637. In response to outside threats, principally from the Manchus, the Korean Yi rulers decide to adopt a closed-border policy. From now on, any relationship with the outside world is punishable by death.

North America, 1637. The English offer a reward for every Indian killed – on production of the victim's scalp.

Brazil, 1637. The Dutchman Maurice of Nassau becomes governor of Brazil.

Netherlands, 1637. The tulip trade collapses after a boom last year which many observers feared had become excessive.

Herons and grass: a Japanese screen by the school of Towaraya Sotatsu.

Japanese calligrapher dies in exile

Japan, 1637

Honami Koetsu, the much admired calligraphist, has died at his village of craftsmen at Takagamine where he lived out his life in exile on the orders of the shogun, Ieyasu.

Koetsu, who came from a family of master swordsmiths, was himself trained in that warlike art before becoming fascinated by the tea ceremony and turning to the design of lacquer ware and ceramics. It was his calligraphy, however, which earned him most fame. Classical in style, his brushwork was soft, full, and sensuous, with a smooth, graceful line.

Some of his best work was done in cooperation with Towaraya Sotatsu, the brilliant designer of fans and screens. Sotatsu would paint a scroll and Koetsu would embellish his exquisite work with a beautifully written poem.

Secrets of Chinese industry revealed

China, 1637

Song Ying-xing, a civil servant from Fen-i district, has published *Tiangong kaiwu* (The Creations of Nature and Man), which explains the latest ideas in agricultural and industrial techniques. The author has taken advantage of the new climate of intellectual enquiry, and his work echoes the realism of contemporary artists, who are painting dogs and horses rather than mythical creatures. *Tiangong kaiwu* describes the growing of grain, manufacture of clothes, use of dyes, salt, sugar and oils, and metalworking techniques. Song Ying-xing writes also of ceramics, paper, ink, yeasts, pearls and gems.

The Gipsy Girl, a recent painting by the Flemish-born artist Frans Hals, who has become renowned for his fine, characterful portraits and rich, lively technique.

Descartes: it's the thought that counts

Paris, 1637
The French mathematician and philosopher Rene Descartes has published a major book, *Discours de la Methode*. It contains a phrase which encapsulates a radically new method of seeking after truth: "I think, therefore I am." Descartes is concerned to break with tradition in more ways than one. His book is written in clear, straightforward French, not Latin, the preferred language of philosophers until now.

Only the existence of the mind cannot be doubted, he argues. We have to begin here as a first principle, and in a framework of scepticism and logic build up to more complex truths. Reason, he argues, reigns supreme. The route to scientific truth is through testing, selecting and setting things in order; not simply accumulating knowledge, but systematising it. From his cornerstone of certainty, Descartes derives a number of basic philosophical ideas such as the existence of God. No imperfect, finite human being, he argues, could have generated the idea of an infinite God. So God must have seeded the notion in us.

An anonymous 17th-century French portrait of Rene Descartes.

Poet who was witty – and fond of a drink

London, 9 August 1637
The funeral of Ben Jonson was held today in Westminster Abbey. King James appointed him to be the first Poet Laureate on a pension of £100, despite the offence the king took years ago at *Eastward Ho!*, which ridiculed his meanness.

Ben Jonson had great classical learning, ready wit and a tendency to drink too much Canary among his friends like Shakespeare, Beaumont and Fletcher. In the middle of a play like *Volpone*, castigating human folly, he was capable of such a lyric as "Drink to me only with thine Eyes". His tombstone bears the simple inscription: "O rare Ben Jonson".

"O rare Ben Jonson": great poet and observer of human foibles.

Spanish woman publishes horror stories

Spain, 1637
The novelist Maria de Zayas y Sotomayor has become the toast of Spain following the publication of her first collection of novels. The stories in *Novelas Amorosas y Exemplares* which have caught the public imagination are deliberately packed with horror and melodrama. All have happy endings and are built around the device of entertaining an elderly lady. The author, a noted scholar, is now working on an equally controversial sequel at her Saragossa home. This time, she says, the stories will have sad endings, but will continue to defend women against male claims of natural superiority and argue for a woman's right to be educated.

Invading allies only 50 miles from Paris

Paris, 8 August 1636
Wracked by internal strife – with peasants rebelling against high taxation – France has been invaded by the armies of Spain, Austria and Bavaria. Spanish troops, led by the count of Olivares, have crossed the border from Flanders and occupied the town of Corbie, 50 miles north of Paris, after an eight-day siege. The whole fate of France depends on the little village of St-Jean-de-Losne which is putting up stiff resistance to Olivares' army.

As advance units of the Bavarian cavalry arrive in the Parisian suburbs, Cardinal Richelieu – who is said to be on the point of a breakdown – is organising defences while King Louis XIII has ridden out at the head of his troops to meet the enemy at Senlis.

Tulip bulbs worth their weight in gold

A fool pays a vast sum for tulip bulbs in this satirical Dutch painting.

Netherlands, 1636
A new obsession has gripped the Dutch: tulipmania, the fanatical collecting and trading of the bulbs of a once-humble flower. In the frenzy of speculation that appears to have overtaken the entire country, single tulip bulbs can fetch 6,000 *florins* each. Critics, who fear the imminent collapse of this inflated market, call it *windhandel* – trading in the wind.

The tulip appeared in Europe around the mid 16th century, imported from Turkey by Ogier Ghislain, the Austrian ambassador. Since then the flower has become increasingly fashionable, although never on the current scale. Today's tulip is a prized commodity, its species classified in a strict hierarchy, its cultivators vying with each other to create ever more exotic varieties, and its buyers apparently undeterred by extravagant prices.

Today's frantic trading was triggered in 1634 when a market in tulip futures was opened to speculate on bulbs not yet reared. In a country devoted to trade, tulips represent the height of showy consumption and a chance to get rich quickly. In the rush to buy the rich pay in cash, the poor in kind; few seem immune from this lust to gamble on nature.

1637 (1637-1639)

Spain, 1637. A religious drama by the prolific Spanish dramatist Pedro Calderon de la Barca, *El Magico Prodigioso*, is performed.

England, 1637. The Puritan pamphleteer, William Prynne, imprisoned and mutilated for seditious writings in 1633, has what is left of his ears cut off in punishment for further publications which he has written while in prison.

Germany, 5 March 1638. France and Sweden sign a pact in Hamburg.

Scotland, March 1638. The Presbyterian opponents of King Charles' religious policy in Scotland sign a national covenant to preserve the purity of the gospel.

Netherlands, 6 May 1638. The theologian Cornelis Jansen, the archbishop of Ypres, dies. After a making a study of St Augustine he wrote *Augustinus*, challenging the doctrine of free will.

France, 14 May 1638. The *abbe* of St Cyran, a leading figure in the Counter-reformation in France, is imprisoned by Richelieu at Vincennes.

North America, 31 May 1638. Disillusioned by the autocratic rule of their leaders in Boston, a group of 100 Puritans, led by Thomas Hooker, a Congregationalist minister, establish a new settlement at Hartford, Connecticut.

Paris, 5 September 1638. Anne of Austria, the wife of King Louis XIII, gives birth to an heir to the throne after 23 years of marriage. He is given the name Louis.

Scotland, November 1638. A general assembly of the Scottish church abolishes the episcopate and defies King Charles' orders to disband.

Germany, 19 December 1638. Bernard of Saxe-Weimar, who has inflicted a defeated on the imperialist forces at Rheinfelden, takes Freiburg and the fortified town of Breisach.

Baghdad, 24 December 1638. The Ottomans under Murad IV recapture Baghdad from Safavid Persia.

Istanbul, 1638. Cyril Lucar, the patriarch of Istanbul, accused of inciting the *Cossacks* against Turkish rule, is put to death on the orders of Murad IV. Lucar's teaching is condemned by a church council at Istanbul because of his Calvinist sympathies.

West Africa, 1638. The French build a slave trading port at St Louis, on the mouth of the Senegal river.

Indian Ocean, 1638. The French take possession of the island of Reunion.

Japan, 1638. The fall of Hara castle brings to an end the Christian rebellion at Shimabara, which began last year. The Japanese are now armed with better guns than the armies of the west.

Japan, 1638. Christians are persecuted throughout Japan. The Japanese are banned from leaving Japan and the country is closed to foreigners. Only the Dutch and the Chinese are permitted to maintain trading posts under guard in a walled compound on the island of Deshima, in Nagasaki harbour.

Paris, 1638. Father Vincent de Paul sets up a charity for orphans, the latest in a series of charitable institutions which he has founded.

England, 1638. John Hampden, who last year refused to pay the "ship money" tax on his property, loses his case but wins a moral victory.

Italy, 1638. Nicolas Poussin paints *The Shepherds of Arcadia*.

North America, 1638. The Swedes and the Finns land in the Delaware estuary and lay the foundations of a colony (New Sweden), with a capital at Christiania.

North America, January 1639. The first printing press in America – at Cambridge, Massachusetts – issues its first volume. It is *Oath of a Free Man*, a broadside lambasting the vow of allegiance that colonists must swear to the English crown.

North America, 24 January 1639. Representatives from three Connecticut towns band together to write the Fundamental Orders, the first constitution in the New World. It establishes a general assembly, the office of governor and the right to tax. It guarantees the political rights of free men, but makes no mention of allegiance to the English crown.

North America, 3 March 1639. The college founded three years ago near the Charles river in Cambridge, Massachusetts, is named Harvard in honour of John Harvard, the Puritan minister who gave it half his fortune.

Near East, May 1639. The treaty of Qasr-i-Shirin establishes peace and a permanent frontier between the Ottoman empire and Safavid Persia. The Ottomans keep Baghdad, Shahrizur, Van and Kars, but renounce all claims to Azerbaijan.

France, 1639. The whole of Normandy is thrown into turmoil by a peasants' revolt.

New prayer book fuels unrest in Scotland

A 19th-century impression of a "Covenanters'" meeting in Edinburgh.

Edinburgh, 1638

The Scottish people have risen in fury over the attempt by King Charles to impose an English-style prayer book on them. Bishops fearing for their lives have fled to England and just one – the bishop of Brechin – read the new book in the kirk. He did so with loaded pistols pointed at his congregation.

Hundreds of thousands of people from all walks of life have subscribed to a "covenant with God" to resist to the death the attempt to destroy their Calvinist traditions. By imposing the prayer book the king hoped to bring Scottish forms of worship to in line with England's. But the people suspected a plot to restore the "popish Anti-christ", especially as some detested rituals, including kneeling when taking communion, and oral confessions, have been reintroduced.

From the start of his reign the king has given offence to the Scots. He threatened the properties of the nobility by revoking all grants of crown lands made in the last 100 years. He ordered the Scottish Archbishop Spottiswood to wear an English surplice for his father's funeral. And Scottish visitors to his court are treated as uncultured roughs. The prayerbook provided the spark that has set off a firestorm of resentment at what Scots see as domination by London.

"Barefoot" peasants rebel in Normandy

France, 1639

A serious rebellion of the *nu pieds*, the barefoot peasants, has broken out in Normandy following the disastrous harvest which has brought hunger to this rich agricultural region. The peasants, enraged by the ever increasing demands of the taxes to pay for the war against Spain, have crushed tax collectors to death under carts with the cry of "Long live the king without the salt tax". Fearful that the urban poor will join the peasants, the authorities have closed many city gates.

Strong forces of the royal army have been ordered to the region, and the headsman's axe is already meting out exemplary punishments. But this seems to be a far more widespread and determined affair than the other peasant revolts which have plagued France for the past ten years, and will not be easily put down.

The peasants are demanding reductions in the new tax demands and amnesty for those taxes, they have been unable to pay because of the bad harvest. They are convinced that not their problems are the fault of the king, but stem solely from his administrators. They have a simple belief that once he is told of their trouble he will protect them against their oppressors. The king appears to have more weighty matters on his mind and is happy to leave the rebellion to his cunning chief minister, Cardinal Richelieu.

Calvinist tendency condemns patriarch

Istanbul, 27 June 1638
The Eastern Orthodox Church today lost one of its most outstanding theologians with the execution of Cyril Lucar, the patriarch of Istanbul. The 66-year-old patriarch was executed on the orders of Sultan Murad after he was accused of inciting the Cossacks to attack the Turkish government.

According to rumours sweeping Istanbul, the accusations were made by the patriarch's enemies, angered by his continuing support for the *Confessio Fidei* that reinterpreted traditional Eastern Orthodox faith in Calvinistic terms. During Lucar's 18 years as patriarch, Rome managed to have him removed from office three times, only to see him reinstated after intervention by Dutch and English envoys.

Lucar's affinity for the reformed churches and distaste for Rome date back to his attendance as a young man at the Synod of Brest-Litovsk in 1596. His pro-Calvinist teachings became famous after he presented his *Codex Alexandrinus* to Charles of England in 1628.

Turks win Baghdad after 15-year war

Baghdad, 1638
Baghdad, occupied for the past 15 years by the Persians, has been regained by the Turks, led personally by Sultan Murad IV. The capture follows a seven-month siege in which the defending Persians had vowed to fight until the last man.

The war between Persia and Turkey sprang from an internal struggle for power between the Ottoman rulers of Baghdad. The *pasha* and the army both claimed power and when, in 1621, a Janissary officer took over, displacing the pasha, he attempted to gain support from Persia to bolster up his position.

The Persians duly moved in, but when the Ottomans agreed to accept him, the Janissary rejected Persia, only to be assassinated, leaving Baghdad in Persian hands.

It has taken five campaigns – dogged by incompetence, bad weather and other commitments – to restore Baghdad to Turkey. Now the city is back in Turkish hands, although Yerevan, which fell to Persia in 1636, is to remain a Persian possession.

Italian-style piazza completed in London

Covent Garden: the piazza and market, painted by John Collet (1725-80).

London, 1638
Inigo Jones, the Surveyor to the Crown, has completed a *piazza* at Covent Garden, just north of the Strand. London's first example of town planning, it is laid out as "an estate for gentlemen" on behalf of its landlord, the earl of Bedford. It is a large square formed by uniform houses built over arcaded *loggias*, in the Italian manner. St Paul's church, like a classical temple of the Tuscan order, stands at one end of the piazza, where a fruit and vegetable market has been opened.

This is the latest of many innovations that Jones has carried out in the capital. The chief of these was the rebuilding of the king's Banqueting House in Whitehall on the Italian model of Andrea Palladio, inspired by Vitruvius' Roman treatise which Jones brought back from Italy. The scale is grandiose and the ceiling panels were commissioned by King Charles from Rubens, who sent them over from Antwerp in 1635. They depict the reign of his father, James, in Olympian style. In the same year Inigo Jones completed a house for the queen, Henrietta Maria, at Greenwich (east of London on the river Thames) in the style of a Palladian villa. Earlier he had built for her the Queen's Chapel in St James' Palace.

He has plans to rebuild Whitehall palace entirely, on as big a scale as Somerset House which he is building for the queen. He began as a stage designer, and his court masques introduced a proscenium arch, a revolving stage, flying scenery and costly costumes of cloth of silver and gold.

One of Jones' costume designs, for a torchbearer in a masque.

British open trading post in eastern India

Madras, August 1639
An English trading post has been established at Madraspattam on the east coast of India. Francis Day, the English merchant who acquired the land from the local ruler, is building warehouses, factories and a fort. The west coast of India has already opened up to English trade following the signing of the Anglo-Portugese treaty of Goa in 1635. With the opening of the east coast the London-registered East India Company will be in a position to expand its trade all over India.

Gujarati bedspread (detail), c.1600.

American settlers massacre whole Indian village in night raid

Connecticut, 5 June 1637
A force of New England settlers, drawn from Massachussetts and Connecticut and backed by their Indian allies, has destroyed a hostile Indian village in bloody revenge for years of raids and murders. Some 500 Pequot men, women and children have been slaughtered. Such a confrontation was always inevitable as nearby Dutch and English settlements grew stronger and threatened the once-powerful Pequots.

While the tribe was able to defend its lucrative trade in shells and beads from Indian rivals, it proved too weak to drive away the settlers. A number of murders of whites by the Pequot tribe have escalated the conflict over the past three years.

The most recent came last month when the Indians killed nine people. Last night's show of strength provided a bloody climax. It is unlikely that the Pequots will threaten the colonists again.

1639 (1639-1641)

France, 21 May 1639. The Italian utopian philosopher Tommaso Campanella dies in the Dominican monastery of St Honore, near Paris. Among his works is an imitation of Plato's *Republic* entitled *Civitas Solis*. Accused of heresy, Campanella was kept imprisoned in a Neapolitan dungeon for 27 years.

England, June 1639. The treaty of Berwick ends the short-lived Bishops' War between England and Scotland. Last year, Scottish nobility and clergy signed a covenant to defend the *kirk* against the imposition of a new prayerbook from London.

France, 18 July 1639. On the death of Bernard of Saxe-Weimar, his army and conquered territories are taken over by France.

Siberia, 1639. After crossing Siberia, a small group of Russians reaches the shores of the Pacific. In recent years the Russians have acquired vast territories in northern Asia. Attracted by easy profit, trappers and traders have moved eastwards, overwhelmed the natives and established Russian rule by building strategically located forts.

France, 1639. The mathematician Gerard Desargues publishes a book entitled *Brouillon Project*, which lays the foundations for analytical geometry.

France, 1639. The mathematician and physicist Blaise Pascal invents a calculating machine.

Spain, 1639. The painter Francisco de Zurbaran is asked to decorate the sacristy of the Hieronymite monastery of Guadeloupe. He is at present at work on a monumental altarpiece for the Carthusians monastery of Jerez de la Frontera.

Danzig, 1639. Martin Opitz von Boberfeld, who during his life was regarded as the greatest German poet, dies. The head of the Silesian school of poetry, he wrote a *Book of German Poetry*, in which he established rules for the "purity" of language, style, verse and rhyme.

Caribbean, 1639. Sugar cane is introduced into Martinique.

Angola, 1639. The Dutch seize the Kongo kingdom from the Portuguese.

Istanbul, February 1640. Ibrahim succeeds Murad IV, sultan of the Ottomans since 1623.

England, 13 April 1640. In order to raise supplies to resume the war against the Scots, King Charles convenes Parliament for the first time since 1629.

England, 4 May 1640. The "Short Parliament" is dissolved after refusing the king money.

Antwerp, 30 May 1640. The great Flemish painter Peter Paul Rubens dies. The dominant figure of contemporary art in northern Europe, Rubens produced over 1,200 works, characterised by dynamic energy, vigorous composition and brilliant colouring.

France, September 1640. *Augustinus*, the great work of Dutch theologian Cornelis Jansen, who died two years ago, is published by his friends.

England, October 1640. After several humiliating defeats of the English by the Scots, the treaty of Ripon ends the second Bishops' War. The Scots keep possession of Northumberland and Durham and are to be paid £ 850 a day until a new English parliament can work out final peace terms.

England, 3 November 1640. Fulfilling his obligations under the treaty of Ripon, King Charles again summons Parliament.

Japan, 1640. In a further step in the persecution of Christians, a board of enquiry called the Examination of Sects is established in Yedo.

Paris, 1640. *Cinna* and *Horace*, two plays by Pierre Corneille, author of *El Cid*, are staged for the first time.

Germany, 1640. Frederick William succeeds his father, George William, elector of Brandenburg since 1619.

India, 1640. The Moghul prince Dara Shikoh, the eldest son of Shahjahan, has the *Upanishads* translated into Persian. Dara Shikoh is deeply imbued with Sufi mysticism and consorts with Hindu philosophers and Christian fathers. His attitude to Islam offends his younger brothers, notably the devout Sunni Aurangzeb.

Rumania, 1640. Peter Moliva, a Moldavian scholar and the metropolitan of Kiev, founds the Basilian Academy, which is modelled on the academy at Kiev. Latin, Greek and the Slav languages are to be taught here, as well as rhetoric, philosophy and poetics.

Finland, 1640. The first Finnish university is founded at Turku by Per Brahe. Lectures are delivered in Finnish. This marks the emergence of an awareness of national identity.

Portugal, 1640. Richelieu supports a revolution which frees the Portuguese from Spanish domination. John IV (the Fortunate) is declared king and founds the Braganza dynasty.

Spain, 1641. An attempted rebellion takes place in Andalucia.

Mass beheadings are shogun's "lesson"

A 17th-century Japanese screen of a Portuguese carrack off Nagasaki.

Japan, 1640

The Japanese have beheaded 61 Portuguese in a ceremonial mass execution at Nagasaki. The Portuguese had arrived as a delegation from their base at Macao in order to plead for the lifting of the ban on trading with Japan.

However, they misjudged the temper of the *Bakufu* Curtain government which is convinced that the Portuguese were responsible for the uprising of the Christian peasantry at Shimabara two years ago. The *shogun* Iemitsu determined to teach the Portuguese a lesson they would not forget and ordered their execution. Thirteen seamen were spared and sent back to Macao to deliver the message.

Spain loses Portugal as Catalans rise up

Barcelona, 6 June 1641

Catalonia is in revolt against Madrid, and in Barcelona the mob have taken over and murdered the viceroy, Santa Coloma. The trouble has been coming on for some 20 years and poses a real problem for the Spanish leadership.

The blame lies in the failure of the count of Olivares to leave the Catalans alone. The principality has been pressed constantly to provide more men and money for the war against the encroaching French, and hatred of Madrid has steadily mounted. The viceroy was unequal to the task of keeping order and was caught and struck down trying to escape from the mob. In Spanish-dominated Portugal, the duke of Braganza has taken advantage of Olivares' preoccupation with the Catalans to enter Lisbon, declare himself King John IV and be crowned in Lisbon Cathedral.

Braganza's rule has been recognised by the Dutch, who have promised to send assistance, and by the French, whose fleet is anchored in the river Tagus. Olivares' only hope is a counter-revolution by an alliance of nobles and Jewish converts to christianity who have been refused any concessions by the Portuguese king for fear of offending the pope. The plot has been discovered, however, and most conspirators arrested.

Dutch rule sea-traders

A Dutch merchant family and a servant: painted cotton from near Madras.

Amsterdam, 1639

New and inexpensive cargo ships, navigational skills and aggressive exploitation of new markets have enabled the Dutch to expand their shipping trade to unprecedented heights world-wide and Amsterdam to become Europe's marine insurance capital.

The long-drawn-out war between the independent Dutch republic and Hapsburg Spain over the Spanish Netherlands has proved only a minor inconvenience. Both sides favour trading with the enemy. The Dutch levy port charges on ships sailing to Spanish territories and use the money to build warships. The Spanish need the grain and naval stores brought by the Dutch from northern Europe. The Dutch have expanded their trading voyages far beyond European coastal waters to the Far East and the Americas. Dutch traders have appeared on the Hudson River, New York, and more trading posts have been established on the Wild Coast at the mouth of the Amazon. The Dutch dominate trade between Brazil and Europe.

Despite their wide-ranging operations the Dutch seem reluctant to establish colonies. Respectable Dutch women, it is said, will not emigrate to tropical countries, and Pieter Both, the governor-general of the East Indies, has advised Dutchmen in those parts to marry "heathen" women.

Japan bans westerners from its mainland

Dejima, Japan, 1641

Japan has now banned all westerners from its mainland in a bid to cut itself off from foreign influences which the shogunate blames for recent uprisings.

The only foreigners allowed to trade with Japan are the Dutch whose mainland trading post at Hirado has just been demolished. Instead the Dutch have been given sole use of Dejima, the 130-acre man-made island in Nagasaki Harbour, originally built for the Portuguese before their expulsion two years ago. The only Japanese allowed on Dejima are male interpreters and courtesans. The Dutch are allowed entry to Japan only on ceremonial occasions.

Parliament plans to stand up to the king

London, 1640

For the second time this year Charles has been forced to call a parliament – and this time MPs are determined not to allow the king to ride rough-shod over them. When the first parliament for 11 years was called last April, Charles tactlessly told the Commons that they would be granted "all their just favours" provided that they voted to give him the money he needed.

The remark was greeted with a buzz of disapproval from MPs, who see their privileges as no more than constitutional rights. Charles did not get his money, and curtly dissolved parliament. But after appealing in vain to the kings of Spain and France, the pope and the City of London, he has been forced to meet MPs once again.

This time they have declared that parliament cannot be dissolved or prorogued without its own consent, and that parliament should meet at least once every three years. Other decisions include one to abolish the hated Star Chamber, which Charles used to punish his critics. It is a measure of the king's sorry plight that he has accepted decisions by MPs which, in effect, say that much of what he has done over the past 11 years has been illegal.

The Orthodox true Minister,
the Seducer and false Prophet.

Pictures from a tract called "A Glasse for the Times", satirising the growing religious and political discontent in England under King Charles.

Expelled Puritans found new colony

Boston, Massachusetts, 1639

A decade after the Massachusetts charter was signed, the Promised Land has expelled its first dissidents. They believe that the Holy Spirit is within each individual, uninfluenced by church ministers. Some even claim that, now they are saved, they are without sin. The ruling Puritans assert that a real Christian must prove himself by religious observance. The breakaway party, led by Anne Hutchinson and others, has bought a large island (some call it "Rhode" island) to start a colony where no-one, except perhaps Catholics, will be unwelcome. It is not the first such quarrel. Last year a Congregationalist minister, Thomas Hooker, went to Connecticut with 100 settlers including some influential merchants. Nearby in what they call "New Haven" are more ex-Bostonians, led away by the Reverend John Davenport from the alleged sinfulness of the New World's first Puritan settlement.

Yet another haven is Maryland, a settlement on the Potomac for Roman Catholics. The first patent was granted to Lord Baltimore (George Calvert) by King Charles. About 250 people, including two Jesuits, sailed from Cowes six years ago. Now there are 2,000.

1641 (1641-1642)

London, 12 May 1641. Impeached for high treason by the Long Parliament (summoned by the king after his defeat in the second Bishops' War), the earl of Strafford, King Charles' chief adviser, is executed.

France, June 1641. France and Portugal form an alliance against Spain.

Portugal, August 1641. Portugal signs a treaty of friendship and commerce with Sweden.

Ireland, October 1641. In protest against despotic treatment and Protestant immigration into Ulster, the Gaelic Irish rebel, slaughtering thousands of English settlers.

London, November 1641. John Pym and other leading Parliamentarians draw up a Grand Remonstrance for King Charles, detailing their position in the struggle against the king's authoritarian rule.

London, 9 December 1641. The great Flemish painter Sir Anthony van Dyck dies.

Massachusetts, December 1641. A woman and a man with "AD" clearly marked on their clothes, have been publically whipped for adultery. This is a relatively lenient punishment – the 1632 law making adultery punishable by death has only recently been abolished.

Naples, 1641. The painter Domenico Zampieri, commonly known as Domenichino, dies in Naples. Born in 1581, he was an assistant of Caracci at the Farnese palace in Rome, where he painted *Woman with a Unicorn*. His masterpiece, *The Last Communion of St Jerome,* hangs in the Vatican palace.

London, 1641. William Laud, the archbishop of Canterbury, is committed to the Tower of London after being impeached for treason by the Long Parliament.

London, 1641. The Star Chamber and the High Commission Court, pillars of the king's autocratic rule, are abolished by the Long Parliament.

Rumania, 1641. Prince Vasile Lupu sets up a printing press in the church of the Three Hierarchs at Jassy, the building of which was completed two years ago. From here the first book printed in Moldavia is issued.

Netherlands, 1641. Cardinal Don Ferdinand, *infante* and governor of the Dutch Netherlands, dies at the age of 32.

Italy, 1641. Claudio Monteverdi composes the opera *Il Ritorno d'Ulisse in Patria* (The Return of Ulysses to his Native Land).

Massachusetts, 1641. The general court of the Massachusetts Bay Colony establishes the *Body of Liberties*, a code of 100 laws.

Japan, 1641. The Japanese order Dutch traders to move from Hirado to the islet of Deshima in Nagasaki harbour, where they are virtually imprisoned and suffer many inconveniences and indignities.

Italy, 1641. Giacomo Torelli revolutionises theatrical tradition by introducing visible scene changes.

Russia, 1641. The Russians capture Azov.

Rome, 8 January 1642. The astronomer and philosopher Galilei Galileo dies. His contribution to science has been immense, including support for the Copernican theory of the universe, an explanation of the composition of the Milky Way, the discovery of Jupiter's satellites, observation of sunspots which enabled him to propose a theory of the sun's rotation and, just before he lost his sight, the discovery of the monthly and annual librations (apparent oscillations) of the moon.

New Netherland, 25 February 1642. Dutch settlers slaughter lower Hudson Valley Indians, who are seeking refuge from Mohawk attacks.

France, 12 September 1642. The marquis of Cinq Mars is beheaded for plotting to assassinate Cardinal Richelieu, the king's chief minister, and for making an illicit treaty with Spain.

France, 4 December 1642. On the death of Richelieu, Cardinal Jules Mazarin becomes chief minister.

Australasia, 1642. A Dutch navigator, Abel Tasman, discovers a large land mass (*New Zealand*) and a small island, Van Diemen's Land (*Tasmania*).

Massachusetts, 1642. An Englishman, Joseph Jencks, arrives in Lynn to set up iron and brass works.

Rome, 1642. Pope Urban VIII bans tobacco as a product of the devil which causes hallucinations and wayward behaviour, upsets relations between men and women and in the end destroys the fabric of society.

West Africa, 1642. The Dutch capture the Portuguese fort of Axim on the Gold Coast.

Rome, 1642. Monteverdi's opera *L'Incoronazione di Poppea* (The Coronation of Poppea) set in ancient Rome is instantly popular.

Few mourners for Cardinal Richelieu

Triple-headed portrait of Cardinal Richelieu by Philippe de Champaigne.

Paris, 4 December 1642

Cardinal Armand du Plessis, the great but unloved duke of Richelieu, died today. He was 57. It is said of him that he converted the absolutist theory of the French monarchy into reality. Although frail in health, he displayed an iron will in carrying out his autocratic policies on behalf of Louis XIII.

Born into a minor aristocratic family, he was destined for the army but gave up his military career to enter the church. Inheriting the family bishopric of Lucon, he prepared himself for politics by working to convert the Huguenots of La Rochelle before moving to Paris. There he began his devious but always logical acquisition of power. He cultivated the queen regent and her Italian favourite, Concini, and almost suffered the same fate as Concini when the young king had him murdered.

He worked his way back into royal favour by acting as mediator between the king and rebellious factions of nobles. Made a member of the Council of State in 1624, he rapidly unseated the chief minister and assumed the position of power which he enjoyed until today.

In his memoirs he said that he promised the king that he would "exalt his name among foreign nations". This he has done, but few are weeping for him today.

Inquisition tries leader of breakaway plot

Mexico, 1642

A minor Spanish nobleman, Don Guillen de Lampart, is being tried by the terrifying methods of the Inquisition. His alleged crime is a plot to declare New Spain an independent kingdom ruled by himself. This is the second time a plot of this sort has emerged from Mexico. An earlier author, some 76 years ago, was Martin Cortez, a member of the explorer's family.

De Lampart, who had suffered under harsh Spanish rule, came to Mexico only two years ago with plans to abolish taxes and slavery, restore the power of religious orders and protect the privileges of ruling colonial families.

Plans of Mexico, Mexico City, and Cuzco City, Peru, taken from Carl Nebel's "Voyage Pittoresque".

Irish rebels kill 10,000 British

Ireland, 1642
Irish rebels have massacred some 10,000 colonists in Ulster and driven the English from the province. With relations between king and parliament in England seemingly heading towards civil war, the Irish have seized their opportunity and a rebel parliament, known as the Catholic Confederacy, has met in Kilkenny.

The rebels have affirmed their loyalty to Charles, preferring him to the militantly Protestant parliament in London. Their demands include freedom of conscience, government by Catholic officials, and restitution of property seized on religious grounds. But the rebels are not united. Most are Anglo-Irish Catholics seeking to protect their religion, while the Old Irish are more interested in recovering confiscated property and preserving the rapidly vanishing Gaelic language and traditions.

Irish soldiers serving with the Spanish have returned home, with France providing arms and money to try to weaken England.

Portugal loses key port to the Dutch

Malacca, South-East Asia, 1641
For six years the Dutch have been blockading the Straits of Malacca, harrying Portuguese shipping, and now at last they have captured Malacca itself, the stronghold that dominates the straits. From the Persian Gulf to Japan the Dutch are picking off Portuguese coastal settlements in their bid to gain control of the lucrative trade in cloves, nutmegs, cinnamon and pepper.

In this struggle, the Dutch have the advantage of a stronger economic base at home to pay for better ships and better trained manpower. Portugal and the Netherlands have roughly equal populations (about 1,500,000), but the Portuguese have for the past 20 years been under Spanish domination and made to serve in the Spanish forces. Dutch commanders are trained professionals, whereas the Portuguese rely on aristocratic and generally incompetent *hidalgos*.

An era ends as Flemish masters die

Marchese Spinola, by van Dyck.

"Samson and Delilah" painted by the Flemish master Peter Paul Rubens.

Endymion Porter by van Dyck.

The Duque de Lerma by Rubens.

Rubens' "Descent from the Cross".

London, 9 December 1641
With the death of Sir Anthony van Dyck, following so soon upon the death of his master, Sir Peter Paul Rubens, in Antwerp last year, an era of supreme Flemish painting has ended. King Charles, who was their patron, knighted them both.

Van Dyck had been his court painter for nine years, painting over 30 portraits of Charles and his queen and especially beautiful studies of their children, full of spirituality along with elegance.

His house at Blackfriars, which the king used to visit by water for sittings, was kept in great style with his own musicians and fools. He was always richly dressed and fascinated women. His fiery English mistress, Margaret Lemon, in a jealous rage once tried to bite off his thumb to prevent his painting. Last year he married a lady-in-waiting.

Rubens lived in even grander style as a diplomat, fluent in six languages, travelling Europe. He was sent to Spain by Isabella, the regent of the Spanish Netherlands, and to England by Philip IV of Spain to negotiate a peace treaty with Charles. Charles, whom he called "the greatest connoisseur in Europe", bought much of his work, as did Philip and Marie de Medici, the queen mother of France, for her palace of the Luxembourg. His vast output of canvases, crowded with nymphs, satyrs and *putti* exhibiting the plumpest of flesh, was the product of a factory of assistants, who painted them from his sketches while he did the finishing touches. His energy was prodigious. "I have never feared to undertake any design however vast," he said. At 53 he gave up court life, retired to his chateau with a wife of 16 and painted landscapes.

1642 (1642-1643)

London, January 1642. King Charles tries to arrest five members of parliament, including John Pym, for treason, but fails.

Nottingham, England, 22 August 1642. The king's declaration of war on Parliament sets off a civil war between royalists (Cavaliers) and Puritans (Roundheads).

England, 1642. Under the command of Oliver Cromwell, six East Anglian counties raise a joint anti-royalist force – the nucleus from which a national parliamentary army could be formed.

Madrid, 14 January 1643. Philip IV dismisses his minister the count of Olivares, who is succeeded by his nephew Don Luis de Haro.

France, 14 May 1643. Louis XIII dies at St Germain. His will provides for a regency council consisting of his widow Anne, his brother Gaston of Orleans, the prince of Conde and Cardinal Jules Mazarin, who will govern during the minority of the four-year-old King Louis XIV.

Paris, 18 May 1643. Queen Anne, the widow of Louis XIII, is granted sole and absolute power as regent by the Paris parliament, overriding the late king's will.

Paris, June 1643. Jean Baptiste Poquelin (Moliere) gives up his law studies and founds the Illustre Theatre with Madelaine Bejart, her brothers Joseph and Louis, Tiberio Fiorelli, known as Scaramouche, and eight other actors.

England, 13 July 1643. The Roundheads (parliamentarians), led by Sir William Waller, are defeated by royalist troops under Lord Wilmot, in the battle of Roundway Down. The vanquished army loses all its ammunition and its cannons.

New Netherland, September 1643. The religious leader Anne Hutchinson is killed with her family in an Indian attack. She and her husband were expelled from the Massachusetts Bay colony by Governor John Winthrop because of their religious beliefs.

England, 25 September 1643. The English Solemn League and Covenant, a national oath to increase the pace of religious reform, guarantees Scottish support of the parliamentary cause in England. The Scots see it as a way to impose Presbyterianism in England and Ireland and to preserve the constitutional liberties won by the Scottish and English Parliaments.

New Haven, November 1643. The General Court, with local deputies, adopts the Frame of Government, with a legal system based on Mosaic law.

Venice, 29 November 1643. The revolutionary composer Claudio Monteverdi dies. He alarmed contemporary critics with his use of unprepared dissonances in madrigals, and went on to develop the new art of opera composition, writing his first, *Ariana*, in 1607. In 1632 Monteverdi became a priest and continued to compose.

Rome, 1643. The Italian composer Girolami Frescobaldi, the organist of St Peter's, dies. He travelled a great deal in the Low Countries and wrote mainly madrigals and pieces for the organ.

France, 1643. Serious rebellions break out in Rouergue, Auvergne and Dauphine. The export of wheat from Brittany and Normandy is banned because of famine in these regions.

England, 1643. Prince Rupert, a leading royalist commander and nephew of the king, captures Bristol. Rupert is the son of Frederick V, the elector Palatine, and Elizabeth of Bohemia (the sister of King Charles). He grew up in exile in the Netherlands and then became a soldier of fortune, enlisting in the royalist cause last year.

Ireland, 1643. James Butler, the duke of Ormonde, who has been put in charge of quelling the Irish rebellion, negotiates a truce.

Amsterdam, 1643. The painter Carel Fabritius leaves Rembrandt's workshop, where he has been a pupil since 1641. His master's influence is evident in Fabritius' recently completed *Raising of Lazarus*.

Amsterdam, 1643. Rembrandt paints a *Self-Portrait* which includes his wife Saskia, who died last year.

North America, 1643. The Puritan colonies of Plymouth, Massachusetts, Connecticut and Newhaven unite to form the dominion of New England.

North America, 1643. On the orders of General Kieft, the Dutch massacre the Algonquin Indians.

Chile, 1643. The city of Santiago is utterly destroyed by an earthquake.

Siberia, 1643. Russian pioneers reach the Amur river.

South Pacific, 1643. The Dutch navigator Tasman discovers the archipelago of Tonga and reaches Fiji and New Guinea.

England, 1643. The fiery Puritan John Milton publishes a pamphlet on *The Doctrine and Discipline of Divorce*. It is a passionate defence of divorce and follows the refusal of his wife, Mary Powell, the daughter of a royalist, to return to him after a visit to her family.

French score first victory for 100 years

The decisive battle of Rocroi, painted by Sauveur Le Conte.

France, 19 May 1643

The duke of Enghien crushed the Spanish army of the Netherlands at Rocroi today, driving its cavalry from the battlefield and slaughtering the *tercios*, the much-feared Spanish infantry.

The impulsive 23-year-old duke, first given the command by Richelieu, his uncle by marriage, played a daring game, leading his horsemen in an attack across the field to cut his way through the centre and drive Don Francisco de Melo's horsemen into the marshes. The tercios, as brave and skilful as ever, alone held their ground. They died where they stood. The importance of this battle cannot be overestimated. It is France's first victory for many years, it has wiped out the cream of the Spanish army and, in Enghien, it has given France a brilliant new commander.

Attack on Jesuits alarms French court

France, 1643

A fierce debate on sacramental practices has opened in the Catholic church with the publication of a defence of the work of the Dutch theologian, Cornelis Jansen.

Written by Antoine Arnaud, it is called *On Frequent Communion* and argues for a return to greater personal holiness. It attacks the Jesuits for their casuistry and has attracted violent opposition from the Society of Jesus. The book is also causing disquiet at court because the rigorous morality of Jansenism reaches outside pure religious debate and extends uncomfortably into public life.

Pope Urban VIII: opposes Arnaud.

Tests show air is not so light after all

Italy, 1643

A pupil of Galileo's, Torricelli, filled with mercury a glass tube sealed at one end. He sealed the other end with his finger, inverted the tube, held the finger-sealed end under mercury in a dish, and removed his finger. The mercury level in the tube fell only slightly, leaving a column around 30 inches high.

Torricelli concluded that air pressing on the mercury in the bowl kept the mercury in the tube up to a height which could be measured.

Civil war clouds loom over England

Strafford's trial and execution.

The royalist William Barnston.

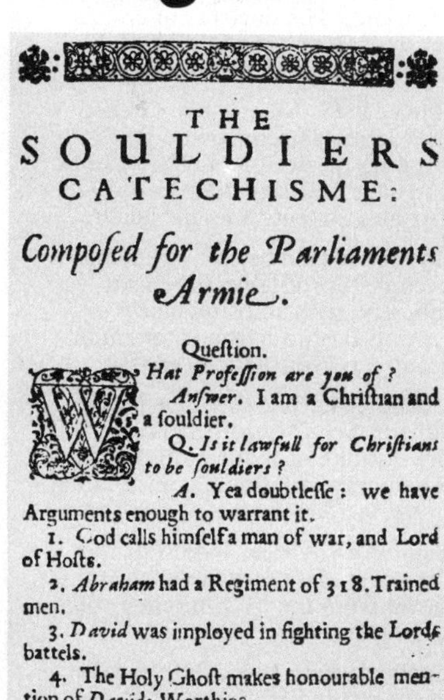
THE
SOULDIERS
CATECHISME:

Composed for the Parliaments Armie.

Queſtion.
W*Hat Profeſſion are you of?*
Anſwer. I am a Chriſtian and a ſouldier.
Q. *Is it lawfull for Chriſtians to be ſouldiers?*
A. Yea doubtleſſe: we have Arguments enough to warrant it.
1. God calls himſelf a man of war, and Lord of Hoſts.
2. *Abraham* had a Regiment of 318. Trained men.
3. *David* was imployed in fighting the Lords battels.
4. The Holy Ghoſt makes honourable mention of *Davids* Worthies.

A 2 5. God

A revolutionary catechism.

England, January 1642
The sands are fast running out for Charles. The king's long-running quarrel with parliament is pulling the country into a civil war that was unthinkable only a few months ago. Embroiled in military operations against Irish rebels, and with Scots enraged by an attempt to impose an English-style prayerbook on them, the king needs money badly. Parliament refuses to give him it until he has redressed their grievances.

Now he has tried to take action against the men he sees as ringleaders. He issued articles of impeachment against five members of the Commons, including John Hampden, a rich landlord who refused to pay a tax he considered unjust, and John Pym, a squire from Somerset. The peers refused to arrest them. When Charles sent a serjeant-at-arms to make the arrests, the Commons procrastinated, saying they would consider the matter. Next day the king turned up with several hundred armed men. But the parliamentarians had taken refuge in the City of London. "The birds have flown," Charles said.

This "Long Parliament" assembled in November 1640 and has been in contention with the king ever since, in an increasingly bitter atmosphere. Last May, the parliament found the earl of Strafford, Charles' chief adviser, guilty of treason. Later it issued a Grand Remonstrance setting out a long list of grievances, intending to curb the king's powers and increase those of the Commons.

Parliament has now passed a Bill to raise a militia and when necessary impose martial law. They have also voted to remove the bishops from the House of Lords. But there are signs that the Commons are wearying. Last autumn attendances began to dwindle and some votes have shown a fine balance of opinion. However, the king's abrasive style is alienating supporters.

Tibetan Buddhism's Mahakala, defender of the faith and fierce assailant of every unbeliever: a painted figure composed of clay, flour, paste and human bones.

Massacres in Brazil

Pernamboco, Brazil, 1643
Portuguese settlers, with the support of the Tupi Indians, have revolted against their Dutch masters. In a series of appalling massacres, the Indians on both sides are suffering much the worst casualties.

The revolt, led by the adventurer Joao Fernandes Vieira, was triggered by settlers' anger at the taxes of the West India Company, and the imposition of Calvinism.

Rebels trapped a Dutch detachment in a fort, released the commander, but killed 200 Indians. The cannibalistic Tapuia Indians, led by the Dutchman Jacob Rabe, have responded with wholesale butchery.

Oliver Cromwell, Puritan leader.

Tibet defies China with golden palace

Lhasa, Tibet, 1643
Perched on a mountain on the roof of the world stands the Palace of Potala, just completed by the fifth Dalai Lama. The Potala, its red mass and golden roofs sharply contrasting with the whiteness of the nearby buildings, is more than the Dalai Lama's winter palace. It is Tibet's largest monastery. Its lines speak a new Tibetan confidence, arrogantly and defiantly standing out on the mountaintop, contemptuous of Moghul and Chinese presumptions of control.

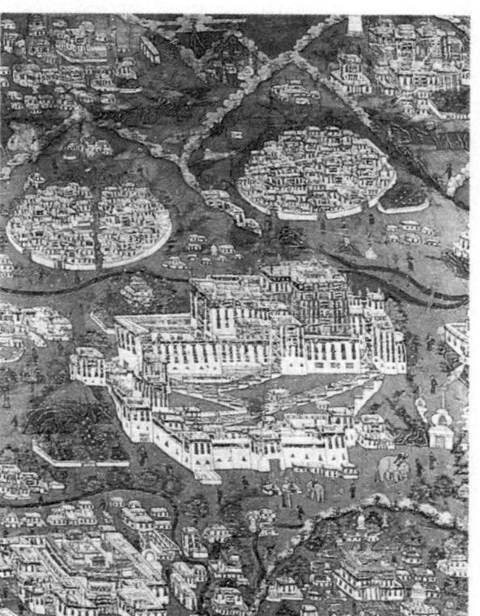
The Dalai Lama's palace at Lhasa.

Philip IV dismisses his right hand man

Madrid, 14 January 1643
The count of Olivares, Spain's dynamic chief minister for more than 20 years, has been dismissed – the victim of intrigues by a handful of disgruntled grandees. The count was the opposite number of the late Cardinal Richelieu, and for years the two men watched each other's every move on Europe's diplomatic chessboard.

Olivares' hectic routine has killed off four of his secretaries during his years in power as the favourite of Philip IV. His mistake was to commit Spain to foreign ventures – such as the bid to reconquer Holland – which were far beyond its powers. Moves to extend Madrid's power over Catalonia and Portugal also led to revolts.

1643 (1643-1648)

Netherlands, 1643. The Dutch artist Adriaan van Ostade, known for his farmyard and low-life scenes, paints the *Slaughtered Pig.*

England, 1643. The Cavaliers (royalists) publish a newsheet, *Mercurius Aulicus*, in Oxford once a week. The Roundheads (parliamentarians) respond with the *Mercurius Britanicus*, published in London.

London, 24 March 1644. Roger Williams, pressed by the New England Confederation, gains a charter for Rhode Island.

England, 2 July 1644. Cromwell crushes the royalists at the battle of Marston Moor, near York, leaving some 4,000 dead, and taking 1,500 prisoners.

Rome, 15 September 1644. Pope Urban VIII dies. He condemned the *Augustinus* of Cornelis Jansen in 1640, and commissioned Bernini to work on the baldachin of St Peter's in 1633.

England, November 1644. The Puritan poet John Milton publishes a pamphlet on the freedom of the press entitled *Areopagitica.*

Germany, 1644. French forces under Turenne defeat the imperial army at Freiburg and capture Mainz and Worms.

Netherlands, 1644. The Flemish surgeon Jan Baptist van Helmont, who discovered carbon dioxide gas, dies. He also identified the role of the gastric juices in digestion.

Rhode Island, 1644. Roger Williams writes *The Bloudy Tenent of Persecution for Cause of Conscience* arguing for religious toleration; the book is burnt publicly in London.

Australia, 1644. The Dutch navigator Tasman compiles a map of the north and west coasts of Australia.

Angola, 1644. Dutch slave traders allied to Queen Nzinga of Angola take Luanda from the Portuguese.

Zimbabwe, 1644. The victors in the Torwa civil war move from Khami to a new hill capital at Danongome.

London, January 1645. William Laud, the archbishop of Canterbury, is executed. He sought to enforce an Anglican liturgy very close to Catholicism, provoking the rebellion of Puritans and Presbyterians.

New Netherlands, 9 August 1645. Settlers gain peace with Indians after the intervention of the Mohawks.

Austria, 1645. Formulated by Gyorgy Rakoczi, the peace of Linz guarantees the religious freedom of the Hungarians.

Paris, 1645. Pierre Gassendi is appointed a professor of the College of France. His doctrine of sensualism and materialism is opposed to influence of Descartes.

Rome, 1645. Athanasius Kircher, the German scientist who is working on deciphering the Coptic language and Egyptian hieroglyphics, invents a magic lantern.

Boston, 1645. The slave trade has become a profitable American industry, with ships regularly leaving Boston harbour for raids along the West African coast.

China, 1645. The German Jesuit Johann Schall becomes director of the institute of mathematics and astronomy in Beijing, contributing to the introduction of Catholicism.

South-East Africa, 1645. For the first time, the Portuguese take slaves from the Mozambique coast to Brazil.

England, June 1646. Oxford falls to the parliamentarians.

Massachusetts, 28 October 1646. John Eliot, a pastor, starts preaching to the Algonquin Indians in their own tongue.

Virginia, October 1646. Chief Necotowance agrees to acknowledge that Indian lands are held by courtesy of the British crown, ending a two-and-a-half year war.

New Netherland, December 1646. The Dutch West India Company's experiment in colonisation, the *patroon* system, fails. Settlers were offered huge areas of land and feudal rights over 50 people if they paid their passages. But it appears that the Dutch are not keen to sell themselves into servitude in a far-flung, uncivilised land.

Virginia, 1646. The colony's first law for the education of the poor is passed, providing for the apprenticeship of poor children.

Massachusetts, 26 May 1647. A new law bans Catholic priests from the colony; the penalty is banishment, or death for a second offence.

Central Asia, 1647. The Moghuls who last year captured the provinces of Balkh and Badakshan in northern Afghanistan from the Ozbegs, are forced to withdraw when their officers prove unwilling to serve in this harsh region and the Ozbegs receive Persian aid.

England, 1647. Convinced that he has been summoned by the Holy Spirit, a shoemaker named George Fox begins preaching. His followers reject the church.

Hungary, 1648. Rakowsky of Transylvania signs a peace treaty with the Habsburgs.

Cromwell routs king's army at Naseby

Royalist troops at Chester in 1646: a stained glass window of 1660.

Naseby, England, 14 June 1645
Charles' royalist forces suffered a crushing defeat today at the hands of the parliamentary army on the outskirts of the village of Naseby, Northamptonshire. The decisive factor was the iron discipline of the cavalry led by Oliver Cromwell.

At the outset the royalists showed their superiority and routed a squadron of parliamentary cavalry. They then made the mistake of setting off in pursuit. Cromwell seized his opportunity and proceeded to overwhelm the rest of the king's army. His Ironsides did not scatter in pursuit of fleeing troops, but remained on the battlefield to grind down the enemy. For practical purposes the war has ended in victory for the parliamentarians.

When, in 1642, Charles set out to achieve by force of arms what he had failed to do by intrigue and bluster, he had the loyalty of rural England. But parliament was backed by the towns, the City of London and, crucially, the navy, which closed the ports to the king and denied him supplies.

Tasman explores the South Seas

South Seas, 1644
Abel Janszoon Tasman, a captain of the Dutch East India Company, has returned from another voyage of exploration in the South Seas. He may not have discovered the fabulous Southern Continent, on which the Company hoped to find treasures equal to those of the new world, but his extensive explorations, notably the circumnavigation of the Southland, have revealed many new territories. Tasman first sighted the Southland on his earlier voyage of 1642-43, naming it Van Diemen's Land, and five days sailing to the east discovered another great island, which he called the Staten Landt.

Czar Alexis brings serfdom to Russia

Russia, 1648
A new and highly repressive civil code is being enacted in Russia. Following the worsening social unrest of the last few years Czar Alexis is preparing to come down hard on those who challenge his authority.

The code will establish the rights of merchants and the prerogatives of landowners. Nobles will be able to bequeath their property and peasants will be legally attached to the land which they cultivate.

Serfs will thus lose virtually all rights and will be no more than items of property, completely subject to the absolute rule of the landowner.

Emperor takes own life

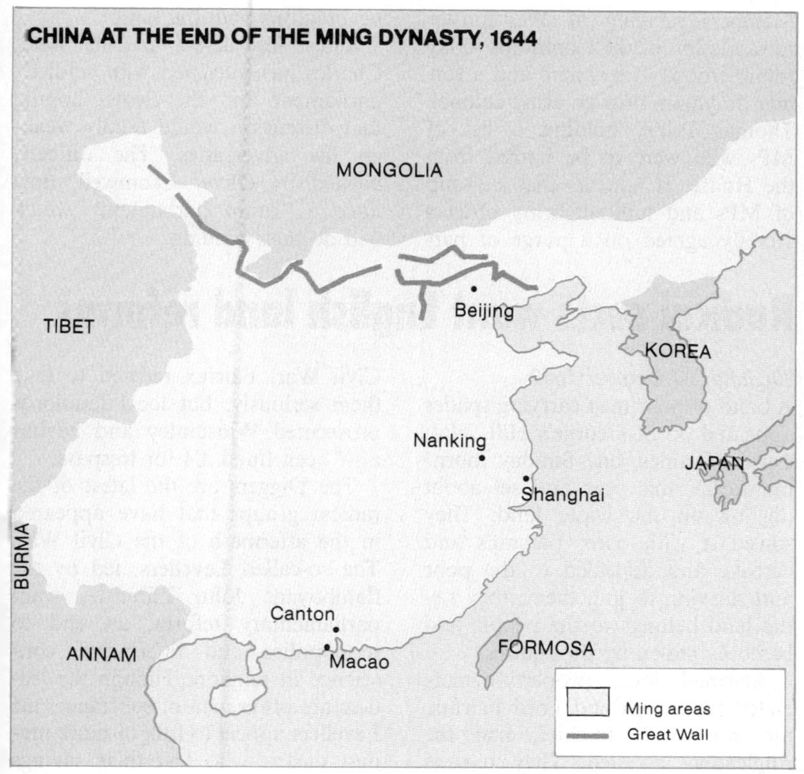

China, 25 April 1644
The Ming Chongzhen emperor hanged himself today in the pavilion of the Imperial Hat and Girdle department in the palace compound. His suicide followed the treachery of the eunuch Cao Huajun who opened the Zhangyi Men gate to the rebel forces of Li Zicheng.

Beijing now belongs to Li, and it seems that the long and glorious history of the Mings is at an end. It has, in fact, been crumbling for a number of years. Peasant uprisings caused by heavy taxation, the Manchu incursions and the breakdown of government were all bringing about the end of the dynasty.

The soldiers have been neither paid nor fed, for the imperial treasury and granaries are empty. Morale no longer exists, one general reporting that "when you whip one soldier, he stands up; but at the same time another is lying down".

In these circumstances it is hardly surprising that many of the emperor's generals and eunuchs have gone over to Li who has proclaimed himself emperor of a new dynasty, the Shun. The presence of these officials has enabled Li to take over the capital in an orderly fashion, though most of his men are more interested in loot than in peaceful administration.

It is doubtful, however, if Li can sustain his claim to be emperor for very long. His motley army is unlikely to be a match for the well-disciplined forces of the Manchu general, Prince Dorgon, who is lurking just north of the Great Wall at Shanhaiguan.

A Ming general, Wu Sangui, is guarding the gate at Shanhaiguan. Li has promised him 40,000 *taels* to join his forces. Much depends on the decision.

A Chinese Ming tapestry embroidered with peonies, phoenixes and rocks.

Descartes thinks; the church worries

The philosopher Rene Descartes.

Paris, 1644
Rene Descartes has extended his reputation throughout Europe and produced more important works to spread his ideas. In his *Meditations* he developed the theme of doubt and scepticism. Indeed, he argued that there may be a great malignant demon which is deceiving humanity into believing things, in which case there is always the secure base of being sure that one does oneself exist.

Although *Meditations* may have enhanced Descartes' reputation, also lead him into dispute and controversy with the church. He has been accused of atheism. Undeterred, he has just brought out his *Principles of Philosophy*. In this book, ranging over physics, chemistry and physiology, he attempts to explain all physical phenomena through one system of mechanical principles. It is small wonder that some authorities are concerned about his rejection of the spiritual in favour of the scientific.

Fishmonger leads uprising in Naples

Naples, July 1647
The rebel who has brought the Spanish government of Naples to its knees is a 27-year-old street-smart illiterate fishmonger from Amalfi, Tommaso Aniello, better known to the crowds as Masaniello.

The new captain-general of the people, as a reluctant viceroy has proclaimed Masaniello, shot to fame on 16 July when he organised the strike in the Piazza del Mercato against the now abolished fruit tax. During the protest Masianello, who once served a jail sentence for smuggling, persuaded the 800-strong crowd to march on the palace, forcing the viceroy to flee. Masaniello's mentor behind the scenes, and the author of the escalating demands for reform, is the veteran radical Giulio Genoino, aged 70.

Masaniello urges on the crowds.

Danish greed loses supremacy in Baltic

The Baltic, 1645
Greed and envy on the part of the Danish king, Christian IV, have forced his country to bow to its Swedish neighbours. Christian had long coveted the German lands now being occupied by Sweden's mercenary armies, and he made the considerable mistake of increasing tolls for ships passing through the Danish Sound. Even though Sweden was exempt from such payments, Christian made life difficult for its ships and increased the toll for ships from any of Sweden's newly-acquired territories.

Two years ago Sweden withdrew an army from Moravia and attacked Denmark. While the Dutch fleet prepared to join them, Swedish troops took Jutland and Skane. Despite a hardfought naval campaign, Denmark can no longer view the Baltic as its private lake.

1648 (1648-1649)

Maryland, 21 January 1648. The first woman lawyer in the colonies, Margaret Brent, has been denied a vote in the Maryland Assembly. She has protested that proceedings were unlawfully conducted without her, since all landowners should be represented.

Netherlands, Janaury 1648. The Dutch and the Spanish sign a peace treaty ending 80 years of war. The seven Dutch provinces are recognised as an independent nation by Spain, which surrenders its rights to the "generality lands" and closes the port of Antwerp.

Britain, March 1648. Royalist uprisings in Wales, Kent and Essex mark the start of a second phase of the Civil War. In December 1647 Charles gained the support of the Scots in return for an agreement to introduce Presbyterianism into England, and this has renewed his strength.

Massachusetts, 13 May 1648. Margaret Jones of Plymouth has been found guilty of witchcraft and sentenced to be hanged by the neck. She is said to have a "malignant touch", causing pain or vomiting, and to administer so-called medicines which brought people closer to death.

England, 19 August 1648. At the end of a two-day battle in Preston, an invading Scottish army led by the duke of Hamilton has been cut off from Scotland and put to flight in a series of running battles.

Paris, 26 August 1648. Parisians rise up in protest at the arrest of Councillor Broussel, who granted them their freedom. The royal family flees to St Germain. This "day of the barricades" marks the start of the so-called *Fronde* uprising (named after a game played by children in the streets of Paris).

England, 6 December 1648. Thomas Pride's purge of parliament arrests or excludes from the Commons, 140 MPs, leaving the "Rump Parliament".

Moscow, 1648. The people of Moscow revolt against heavy taxation.

Paris, 1648. The Royal Academy of Arts is founded.

Naples, 1648. Neapolitan partisans are finally suppressed by the viceroy Arcos and the fleet of Don John of Austria.

Massachusetts, 1648. Trade with the Canaries, Madeira and Spain begins to help the colony out of an economic depression.

Crete, 1648. The Ottoman Turks lay siege to Heraklion in a continuing war with Venice.

England, 1648. The royalist poet Robert Herrick, who was deprived of his living as a clergyman last year by the parliamentarians, publishes *Hesperides, or Works both Human and Divine*, containing many distinctly unpriestly verses.

Muscat, 1648. The Arabs capture Muscat from the Portuguese.

India, 1648. The imperial Moghul court, which was moved from Lahore to Agra in 1598, is now moved to Shahjahanabad (*Delhi*). The building of this new great capital, which includes the Red Fort and the great Friday Mosque, was begun in 1639.

Maryland, 1648. Richard Bennett leads 400-600 Virginians to form the Puritan outpost of Providence (*Annapolis*).

South Africa, 1648. Survivors from the Dutch ship *Haarlem*, which was wrecked in Table Bay last year, find the people and climate of the Cape of Good Hope hospitable.

Angola, 1648. Backed by reinforcements from Brazil, the Portuguese retake Luanda from the Dutch.

England, 1648. The nonconformist George Fox, who started preaching last year, founds the Society of Friends (the Quakers).

Paris, 1648. The painters Louis and Antoine le Nain die. Earlier this year they and their brother Mathieu were received into the French Academy. The subjects of their paintings are quite different from the mythological and allegorial topics currently in vogue. The le Nains paint scenes of humbler life, such as *Boys Playing Cards, The Forge* and *The Peasants' Meal.*

England, 1649. The Diggers, supporters of Gerard Winstanley, denounce property as a tool of slavery and propose a total transformation of society.

Istanbul, 1649. Sultan Ibrahim is deposed and murdered with the connivance of his mother. The seven-year-old Mehmet IV succeeds him.

North America, 1649. The Maryland Assembly passes an act permitting any form of Christian worship in the colony. This religious toleration and the fine position of the colony at the head of Chesapeake Bay attract numerous settlers.

Paris, 1649. Simon Vouet, court painter to king Louis XIII since 1627, dies. His almost classicist style has been enormously influential, and his studio has trained many young artists. His great rival was his former pupil Nicolas Poussin.

Parliament purged to stop deal with king

London, 6 December 1648

Members arriving at Westminster for a session of the Commons today found troops everywhere and a former drayman, now an army colonel, Thomas Pride, holding a list of MPs who were to be barred from the House. It appears that a group of MPs and militant army officers secretly agreed on a purge of parliament, in order to put a stop to negotiations with the king.

Since his defeat in the field, Charles has intrigued with soldiers, parliament and the Scots, hoping that dissension would fatally weaken his adversaries. The officers, backed by Oliver Cromwell, now have a "rump parliament" which will do their bidding.

Radical sects want English land reforms

England, 24 October 1649

A band of poor men carrying spades appeared on St George's Hill, Walton-on-Thames, one Sunday morning earlier this year and set about digging up the waste land. They sowed it with corn, parsnips and carrots, and appealed to the poor and starving to join them; they say the land belongs to the people and has been stolen by the squires.

Alarmed local property-owners called for troops and Lord Fairfax, the commander-in-chief, had the ringleaders arrested. They refused to take off their hats in his presence and one, Gerard Winstanley, said that any rights to common land claimed by lords of manors had ended with the king's defeat in the Civil War. Fairfax refused to take them seriously, but local landlords prosecuted Winstanley and he has now been fined £4 for trespass.

The Diggers are the latest of the radical groups that have appeared in the aftermath of the Civil War. The so-called Levellers, led by the flamboyant John Lilburne, want parliamentary reform, an end to monopolies and liberty of conscience in religion. Though the leaders are often men of substance, the Levellers appeal to folk of more modest means who lost their savings when they lent money to parliament for the war. Another sect, the Ranters, is said to go in for hard drinking and whoring in the name of the Holy Spirit and equality.

A 1647 satire on Levellers, who see all occupations as equal.

Conferences throughout Europe bring peace

Thirty years of war end at Westphalia

Munster, 24 October 1648
Three successive salvos crashed out from 70 cannons on the walls of this city today to announce that peace has come to a war-ravaged Europe after 30 years of bitter conflict in which almost every power became involved both on land and sea. It has taken three years of negotiation in two cities – Munster and Osnabruck – to bring about the signing of the Treaty of Westphalia.

With Swedish troops fighting in Prague – where the war started with a Protestant rebellion against the Catholic Habsburg empire – and the French army winning a succession of victories in Bavaria, Ferdinand III, the emperor, was forced to accede.

The treaty represents failure by the Habsburgs to turn Germany into a Catholic monarchy. It guarantees the full sovereignty of the German states and toleration for all three faiths – Catholicism, Lutheranism and Calvinism – except in the hereditary lands of the Habsburgs. By the terms of the treaty, the Habsburgs recognise the independence of Switzerland and the separation of the United Provinces of the Netherlands from Spain. France has acquired Alsace and other territories as reparation; Sweden has secured Pomerania, giving her dominance in the Baltic.

But now, even as the last shots are being fired in Bohemia, Europe is counting the dreadful cost of the "Thirty Years' War". Whole towns have been razed by siege and fire, some losing as many as 50 per cent of their population from plague borne by countless armies. Over 100,000 mercenary soldiers have to be paid and returned home lest they turn themselves into robber-bands adding even more torment to a war-weary Europe. The high cost of war is certain to cause massive tax demands on both nobles and peasants who are already threatening revolt. It is peace, certainly, but an uneasy peace that reigns in Europe.

Eighty years of war ended by a rumour

Munster, 1648
A rumour carefully planted by Spanish agents has brought about an end to 80 years of war between Spain and the Netherlands. With France making rapid headway in its campaign against Spain in the Low Countries, it was not difficult to persuade the wary Dutch that their French allies were negotiating a separate peace and planning to exchange Catalonia for the Netherlands. Despite strong opposition from the Calvinists of the north, a treaty was drawn up.

Spain – which was anxious to relieve itself of the Netherlands campaign in order to deal with France – has agreed complete independence for the United Provinces. It has also confirmed Dutch conquests in Flanders and Brabant and agreed the Netherlands' right to trade freely in the East and West Indies.

Frederick William, elector of Brandenburg, and his mother Elizabeth Charlotte, painted as "Solomon and Sheba" by Mathias Czwieczek. The elector has gained a number of bishoprics under the Treaty of Westphalia.

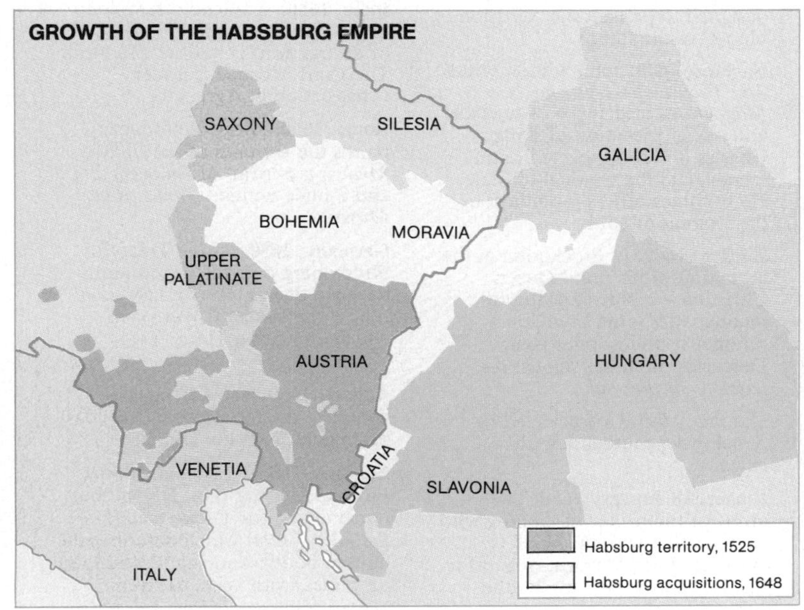

Mad sultan imprisoned and assassinated

Istanbul, 8 August 1648
Ibrahim, the corrupt, worthless and mentally-ill brother of Murad IV, has become the second Ottoman sultan to be deposed and killed. The "mad sultan" was removed from the throne with the consent of his mother, Sultana Valide, then strangled by order of the grand vizier and the *mufti*. His seven-year-old son, Mehmed, has been proclaimed sultan. Ibrahim's mother saved his life when the dying sultan tried to have him killed in 1640. He was reared exclusively in the *seraglio*; weak, vain, greedy and cruel, he spent the next eight years indulging himself and his *harem*, and selling offices.

In 1644 Ibrahim ordered the execution of the grand vizier, Kara Mustapha, who had curbed his worst excesses. The expensive and ill-advised campaign against Venice, which began the next year, turned the Janissaries against him.

Ukrainian Cossacks rise up against Poles

The Ukraine, 1648
A complex conflict has built up in the Ukraine, or Little Russia, between the Poles, the Russians and the *Cossacks*, an intrepid brotherhood that lives for fighting. With fine impartiality the Cossacks have raided in their light vessels for the Holy Roman emperor as far as the coast of Anatolia, marched for the czar of Russia against Poland, and for Poland against Russia. The Cossacks have now risen against their Polish landlords. The revolt is being led by Bogdan Khmelnitski, a well-to-do Cossack who quarrelled with a member of the Polish nobililty over a girl.

Unable to obtain justice from the authorities, he raised the standard. Cossacks are flocking to support Khmelnitski and are being joined by thousands of Orthodox peasants who are banking on the Cossack soldiers freeing them from their Catholic landlords.

1649 (1649-1650)

London, 30 January 1649. King Charles is beheaded. He was brought to trial by the order of the Rump parliament – the MPs who remained after Pride's purge last year – and Thomas Pride signed his death warrant.

Paris, 11 March 1649. The peace of Rueil is signed between the *Frondeurs* (rebels) and the French government and court, bringing to an end the uprising that began last year.

England, March 1649. Parliament abolishes the monarchy and the House of Lords.

England, 19 May 1649. England is declared a "Commonwealth or Free State" by the Rump Parliament, with supreme authority vested in the House of Commons. The executive powers of the monarchy are now assumed by a Council of State composed of 40 members, 31 of whom are MPs.

Ireland, 11 September 1649. On the orders of Cromwell, 1,500 people are massacred at Drogheda. The victims include English royalists, civilians and Catholic priests. This policy of terror is designed to prevent the "effusion of blood" in the future.

England, 1649. John Milton writes *The Tenure of Kings and Magistrates* in defence of regicides and of the execution of King Charles and is appointed Latin secretary to the Council of State. He becomes official apologist of the Commonwealth.

Sweden, 1649. In Stockholm at the invitation of his pupil Queen Christina – a blue-stocking in mathematics – the French rationalist philosopher Rene Descartes publishes his *On the passions of the soul.*

Ukraine, 1649. Cossacks led by Kmelnitsky murder Jewish citizens.

France, 18 January 1650. The arrest of the prince of Conde, who is in conflict with the chief minister, Jules Mazarin, sets off a second *Fronde* uprising by the princes.

Sweden, 11 February 1650. The French philosopher Rene Descartes dies at Queen Christina's palace in Stockholm. At her request he had been rising at five o'clock every morning to give her lessons in philosophy, and the early morning cold gave him a fatal inflammation of the lungs. Descartes will always be associated with the proposition "I think, therefore I am".

Scotland, 3 September 1650. The English under Cromwell defeat a superior Scottish army under David Leslie at the battle of Dunbar. Scotland is subdued.

Connecticut, 29 September 1650. New Netherland governor Peter Stuyvesant signs a border pact with the New England Confederation recognising English claims to much of Long Island, Connecticut.

Netherlands, 6 November 1650. William II of Orange dies of smallpox. Despite the Peace of Westphalia, he had wanted to renew conflict with Spain and had attempted to intervene in the English Civil War on the side of the king, whose daughter Mary he had married in 1641. Towards the end of his life he lost the support of parliament because of his autocratic habits and over-aggressive foreign policies.

Scotland, 19 December 1650. Edinburgh Castle submits to Cromwell.

Michigan, 1650. French Jesuits abandon the last of the Huron missions following the destruction of the Huron population by Iroquois raids.

India, 1650. The British East India Company establishes a trading post at Hughli in Bengal.

India, 1650. A splendid temple to Shiva (the four-armed Hindu god of destruction) is built at Madurai. The Pearl Mosque is under construction at Agra.

Rome, 1650. Diego Velasquez paints the *Gardens of the Villa Medici*, a portrait of *Innocent X* and a nude entitled *Venus at her Mirror.*

Germany, 1650. At the Treaty of Nuremberg detailed negotiations between the Empire and Sweden follow the Peace of Westphalia which ended the Thirty Years War.

Angola, 1650. The Portuguese complete the recapture of the coast of Angola from the Dutch.

England, 1650. The English poet Phineas Fletcher dies. He will be remembered for *Purple Island, or the Isle of Man* which describes the human body as an island, founded on bones, with veins as rivers.

Germany, 1650. The Lutheran theologian Georg Calixtus publishes *Judicium de Controversiis* in an attempt to reconcile Lutherans with Calivinists.

Italy, 1650. The astronomers Fathers Riccioli and Grimaldi publish a map of the moon.

England, 1650. The mystic poet Henry Vaughan publishes *Silex Scintillans*, a collection of religious poems.

East Africa, 1650. The Portuguese are evicted from the Swahili ports on the East African coast by the sultan of Oman.

Moghul splendour in Indian cities

Delhi, 1649

A seventh city is being built in Delhi by the Great Moghul, Shahjahan. It is called Shahjahanabad. It stands on the banks of the river Jumna and a beautiful boulevard, shaded by trees and cooled by water, runs through it. Dominating the city is the Red Fort, a palace, administrative centre, garrison and arsenal all in one building. The Jami Masjid (Friday Mosque) is at the highest point, and the gardens are the most exotic in India.

Work began, after consultations with astrologers, in 1638, and the Red Fort was finished last year. Every month stately pleasure domes and delightful gardens are completed. Shahjahanabad is not the only city built by the Moghuls; each emperor seems obsessed with leaving his mark on the landscape.

Akbar's own ceremonial capital was at Fatehpur Sikri, the home of the holy man Shaikh Salim Chishti, a few miles south of Delhi. Typically of its founder, it celebrated the best in Moslem and Hindu architecture. Equally typically, Akbar never checked the city's water supply and it was abandoned after 14 years. He built a second capital at Agra, downstream from Delhi on the Jumna. His son, Jahangir, preferred Lahore and built his capital there. Now Shahjahan's great capital outshines them all.

View across the courtyard of the mosque Jami Masjid at Shahjahanabad.

Tribes struggle for control of Morocco

Morocco, c.1650

The power of the Sa'di dynasty has waned, and several Berber tribes are vying for supremacy. Since the death of Mawlay Zaydan, in 1627, there has been a sultan of Morocco in name only.

In the Tafilalt, a new family of *sharifs* from the Hijaz is emerging much as the Sa'di did. These are the 'Alawi, who control the main trading routes in the Sahara. But Mulay Mohammed, their sharif, has been unable to conquer Morocco.

In the Fez region, the Dila' fraternity its dominant. The Dila' have spent the last 20 years gradually increasing territory so that they now control central and northern Morocco, with Sultan Mohammed al-Asghar powerless to stop their advance.

Cardinal spirits boy-king out of capital

A later engraving of a Frondist haranguing his fellow-Parisians, urging them to revolt against what is being attacked as the tyranny of Cardinal Mazarin.

Paris, 6 January 1649
Cardinal Jules Mazarin, the chief minister of the crown, has been declared a public enemy by the Paris parliament after spiriting the boy-king, Louis XIV, and his mother, Anne of Austria, out of Paris in the early hours of this morning to escape the clutches of the *Fronde*.

This movement, named after a Parisian street-urchin game, has arisen from a combination of factors: a desire to limit the growing authority of the crown, the ambitions of discontented nobles, and the burden of taxation inflicted on the people by Richelieu and his successor, Mazarin. Trouble broke out last summer when, following the victory at Lens against the Spanish, the regency government felt strong enough to arrest three of its most distinguished critics in parliament.

Paris, as usual, took to the barricades and Mazarin was forced to give in to the demands of parliament to limit the power of the throne. The wily Italian had no intention of keeping his word, however, and made his move last night. He plans to join the duke of Enghien, the Grande Conde, at the head of the royal army to besiege Paris. Meanwhile, the Parisians shout "Murder, murder, murder Mazarin".

Angolan queen at peace with Portuguese

Angola, 1650
After 30 years of fighting between the Mbundu people and the Portugese, the Mbundu leader, Nzinga, the queen of Ndongo and Matamba, has made peace with Portugal.

Succeeding to the throne of Ndongo in 1623 after poisoning her brother, she led her army against the Portuguese, first in alliance with the Jaga people, and later – after she had been driven from Ndongo and re-established herself in Matamba – in alliance with the Dutch. Defiant and cunning, she stole her enemies' tactics, divided Dutch from Portuguese, and ruled both. The cost to Angola, however, has been dire. Tens of thousands have died, hundreds of thousands have been taken into slavery and whole kingdoms depopulated.

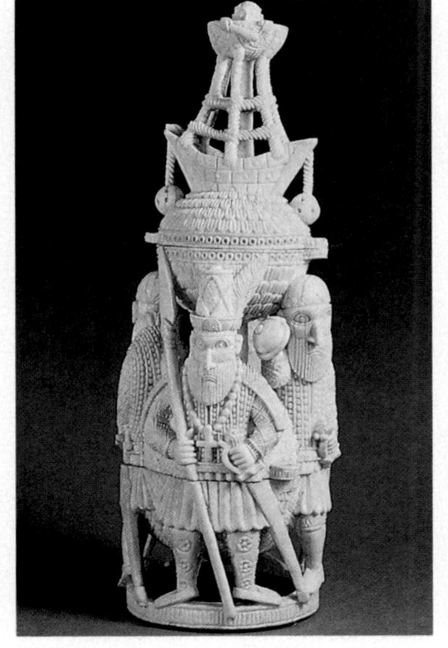

Afro-Portuguese salt cellar, c.1550.

King Charles beheaded

The king meeting his fate, depicted by a slightly later German engraver.

London, 30 January 1649
At two o'clock this afternoon, King Charles stepped onto the scaffold outside the Banqueting Hall in Whitehall. He said that he wanted liberty and freedom for the people as much as anyone, but that "liberty and freedom consists in having of government ... not for having a share in government. A subject and a sovereign are clearly different things". Thereupon he set his head on the block, the hooded executioner brought the axe down and the crowd gave a great groan.

It is almost four years since the royalist forces were decisively defeated at Naseby. In that time the king manoeuvred and intrigued in the vain hope of escaping the consequences of that defeat. He sought the help of the Irish; he promised favours for Roman Catholics if they and the pope would help to restore the monarchy; and he gave himself up to the Scots, believing that they would protect him from the English. But the Scots were sceptical of his promises to establish Presbyterianism and handed him over to the English.

The Rump Parliament set up a High Court of Justice for the sole purpose of condemning Charles as "a tyrant, traitor, murderer and enemy of the people". While soldiers who had forced the trial shouted "Justice! Justice!" as Charles passed by, some of the crowd cried "God save the King!".

Expanding Russia fortifies Siberia

Russia, c.1649
The past ten years have seen a remarkable expansion of Russian territory. Ever since, in 1639, a small detachment reached the Pacific coast and established the city of Okhotsk, the whole of Siberia has fallen to Russian domination.

Most impressive are the series of fortifications that have been built across Siberia. These forts ensure Russia's control of the local population, though the further east one goes in this inhospitable land, the smaller that population becomes. What populace there is can still be exploited, and Russian tax collectors venture deep into the area, even if few colonists are willing to join the natives of Siberia, eking out an existence on the chilly steppes. The *jassak*, a tax payable in furs, a staple of local trading, has augmented the government's coffers.

Siberia may be for the hardy, but its wealth is substantial and more than one fashionable Muscovite owes his family fortune to pioneering journeys into Russia's fruitful eastern territory.

1650 (1650-1652)

France, 1650. Pierre Corneille's *Andromede* is staged for the first time.

Netherlands, 1650. The Dutch poet Joost van den Vondel publishes a *Manuel of Dutch Poetry*. He is a wealthy Amsterdam hosier who writes verse in his spare time.

England, 1650. In his capacity as apologist for the Commonwealth, John Milton writes *Pro Populo Anglicano Defensio* (*In Defence of the English People*).

England, 1650. The non-conformist clergyman Richard Baxter publishes *The Saints' Everlasting Rest.*

England, 1650. England's first coffee house is opened, in Oxford.

England, c.1650. Tea is drunk for the first time in England.

Scotland, 1 January 1651. The executed king's eldest son is crowned Charles II at Scone.

Boston, July 1651. Two leading Baptists, considered ignorant and prejudiced by the city's religious leaders, are arrested for holding an unauthorised religious meeting. One of them, Obadiah Holmes, is whipped in the streets as a deterrent.

England, 3 September 1651. Cromwell defeats Charles II at Worcester.

London, 9 October 1651. Parliament passes a Navigation Act favouring English shipping in an attempt to break the Dutch hold on the carrying trade. Under the terms of the new legislation all goods imported to England must be carried in ships owned by Englishmen or colonials, with crews that are at least half composed of Englishmen.

Massachusetts, 14 October 1651. Laws are passed forbidding the poor to adopt excessive styles of dress.

England, 17 October 1651. The defeated Charles II escapes to France.

Boston, 25 December 1651. The General Court levies a five shilling fine on anyone caught "observing any such day as Christmas".

Paris, December 1651. The king's chief minister, Jules Mazarin, forced to flee from Paris after the city's parliament demanded his dismissal in February, returns to France with 7,000 troops recruited in Germany. He intends to put down the Fronde rebellion led by the prince of Conde.

Virginia, 1651. Anthony Johnson, a free Negro, imports five servants and forms a Negro community on the Pungoteague river.

Virginia, 12 March 1652. The royalist governor of the colony, Sir William Berkeley, submits to warships sent by the English parliament.

South Africa, 8 April 1652. A Dutch expedition to found a military settlement at Table Bay is met by two Khoisan herders who call themselves Harry and Donan and speak English.

Rhode Island, 18 May 1652. A law is passed banning slavery in the colonies, but it causes little stir and seems unlikely to be enforced.

England, 21 June 1652. One of the greatest architects of the day, Inigo Jones, has died. He leaves many varied monuments to his talents: he designed the Queen's House at Greenwich and the Banqueting House at Whitehall; he laid out Lincoln's Inn Fields and Covent Garden; he also staged Ben Jonson's masques for King James, and introduced movable scenery and the proscenium arch.

Massachusetts, 29 June 1652. Under Puritan leadership, convinced of its divine mission, the colony of Massachusetts defies parliament and declares itself an independent commonwealth.

France, 22 July 1652. The Fronde rebels under the prince of Conde narrowly defeat the chief minister Mazarin's loyalist forces at St Martin, near Paris.

Paris, 21 October 1652. On their entry into Paris, which has supported the monarchy against the Fronde rebels, the regent Queen Anne and 14-year-old Louis XIV receive a great welcome.

South-East Africa, 1652. Munhumutapa Manuza dies. Kazuruku Musapa succeeds after a member of the royal family who has become a Dominican declines the throne.

Spain, 1652. The inhabitants of Seville rise in revolt after a decade of economic depression caused by the collapse of American trade and aggravated by an outbreak of the plague in 1649.

France, 1652. The minuet – an elegant dance in three-four time – is all the rage amongst French aristocrats.

England, 1652. In an escalation of the conflict following last year's Navigation Act, England declares war on the Netherlands. The declaration follows an incident in which a Dutch fleet refused to be searched by the British. The Navigation Act was specifically designed to hamper booming Dutch sea trade, and trouble has been brewing ever since it was made law.

New English shipping rules anger Dutch

London, 9 October 1651

The worsening relations between England and the Netherlands received a further setback today with parliament's approval of protective legislation that challenges Dutch mercantile supremacy.

Under the new Navigation Act, goods from Asia, Africa and America can now only be imported into England by English ships. The Act also prohibits goods being imported via another country. This is being interpreted as a thinly-disguised attack on Amsterdam's status as Europe's leading port.

Behind the act lies growing concern in the Council of State and in the City at the state of the English economy, severely depressed for the last three years by plague and harvest failures.

A battle between the English and Dutch fleets, by Isaac Sailmaker.

Dutch seek to avoid absolute monarchy

The Hague, 12 January 1651

With the memory of the late Prince William II of Orange and his attempts to take them once more into a war with Spain still very fresh in their minds, the burghers of all the Netherlands are meeting here in a Grand Assembly to resolve the way in which their country should be governed. William died of smallpox last year at the age of 24, eight days before the birth of a son and heir. It was William II's determination to institute an absolute monarchy, plus concern for the future, that has brought about the constituent assembly of the states that make up the Netherlands.

William's close relationship with the House of Stuart had caused friction between the English Commonwealth and the republican-minded Dutch. To allay fears on both sides, commissioners were exchanged, much to William's fury. The prince's attempts to divide his country by encouraging the Calvinists in the north to join him with France in a campaign against the Spanish was another failure – leading to a royal tour in which the prince harangued officials in the 18 major towns of an unsympathetic Holland. Such was the hostility to this bullying that William, like his father-in-law King Charles, ordered the arrest of six deputies to the States-General. At the same time the city of Antwerp was put under siege by William's cousin, William Frederick, bringing the country close to civil war.

Nasty and brutish life seen by exile

Thomas Hobbes, philosopher of man's fundamental inhumanity.

Paris, 1651
Thomas Hobbes, an English writer living in exile in Paris, has published a new book of political philosophy which casts a grim light on human government.

Leviathan (meaning mortal god) supposes a society where human relations depend entirely on fear. Hobbes sees humanity as locked into a state of permanent war in which "the life of Man is solitary, poor, nasty, brutish and short".

Only the instinct for self-preservation, the fear of violent death, leads us to accept a form of social contract under which individuals give up their natural rights or liberties to society, in other words to the absolute power of the state, or Leviathan as he calls it.

For Hobbes the state is omnipotent and despotic. Its people have not delegated their power, but abandoned it completely.

Dutch settle at the Cape of Good Hope

The Cape, 8 April 1652
A Dutch expeditionary force landed today at the Cape of Good Hope to start building a supply station for mariners making the long five-month voyage from Europe to the East Indies. They were surprised to be met by a couple of local herdsmen, called Harry and Donan, who spoke fluent English.

The Dutch East India Company, which is backing the expedition leader Jacob van Riebeck's team of 90, decided to establish this halfway point between Europe and the East after the crew of a shipwrecked Dutch freighter survived there four years ago by growing their own fruit and vegetables – thereby avoiding scurvy which accounts for many deaths on long voyages.

New light is thrown on life in the womb

England,1651
William Harvey, the physician, has published the fruits of 35 years' research into animal reproduction in *De Generatione Animalium* (On the Generation of Animals). Harvey traces the development of chicken and deer embryos in unprecedented detail.

Harvey concludes that it is not, as has been thought, the mixture of semen and menstrual blood that produces a foetus, but the presence of an egg in the female which contains within itself the substance and power to develop into the animal. He advises midwives that the infant instinctively knows how to be born.

Veto brings political anarchy to Poland

Poland, 1652
At the very worst possible moment Poland is slipping into political anarchy after a deputy of the *Sejm* (parliament) exercised his veto as an individual for the first time. Wladyslaw Sicinski voiced his disagreement with the prolongation of the Sejm after a vote on increased taxes and because he wanted to go home.

The *liberum veto* gives every deputy the right to overturn legislation of which he does not approve. There is now continuous and irresponsible use of the veto at a time of external threats.

John V Casimir, king of Poland.

War, plague and famine ravaged Europe

Europe, c.1650
Three centuries after the Black Death decimated the population of Europe, many countries find themselves in crisis once more. The last century saw a satisfying upturn in the birth rate, with most populations easily making up for the losses of that disastrous era, but now for many nations the best that can be hoped is to resist a decline. Growth is out of the question.

Europe remains vulnerable to a triple threat: war, plague and famine. Some countries, such as England, have remained relatively unscathed. Others, such as Spain and the German states, have been devastated. This century has seen some of the worst plague attacks since the 14th century.

The Thirty Years War was a major factor in the near-destruction of much of the continent. Apart from battlefield deaths, the constant manoeuvring helped to spread disease and laid waste to vast tracts of farmland. Crops have been destroyed, and famine is on the increase. In a grim irony, Europe has passed on its problems to the New World, which it is exploiting, with 95 per cent of the native people killed off by plague.

Two powerful women enemies in France

Paris, 1652
Two passionate, clever and ruthless women who were once friends but are now bitter enemies are the talk of Paris. The first is the queen mother, Anne of Austria, and the other is a beautiful schemer, the duchesse of Chevreuse.

Once they schemed together in an attempt to assassinate Cardinal Richelieu. They failed. Then the queen was accused of treachery and the duchess was exiled. But even in exile she encouraged her admirers to intrigue against Richelieu.

The queen had to endure the cardinal's own schemes against her, following her indiscreet flirtation with the duke of Buckingham, so it might have been expected that when she came to power as regent, the duchess would be welcome at her court. Not so. Now the duchess opposes Mazarin, the queen mother's lover and chief minister, as fiercely as she fought Richelieu.

Much of Europe may still be suffering after the ravages of the Thirty Years War, but this Norwegian family boasts no fewer than 14 children.

1652 (1652-1654)

Barbados, 1652. The governor complains of shortages due to a the parliamentary ban on foreign trade with colonies (Navigation Act).

West Africa, 1652. English royalists destroy a republican settlement on the Gambia river.

Paris, 3 February 1653. Cardinal Jules Mazarin returns to Paris after fleeing from the city two years ago because of the Fronde uprising.

London, 20 April 1653. Cromwell's soldiers throw out the Rump Parliament – MPs who have been governing since Pride's purge in 1648, and who declared the Commonwealth. Cromwell had come to see it as increasingly corrupt and ineffective.

Rome, 31 May 1653. Pope Innocent X condemns the five Jansenist propositions of Nicolas Cornet of the Sorbonne in Paris. Being a puritanical movement calling for moral and doctrinal reform, Jansenism inevitably angers the Roman Catholic authorities, and the pope in particular.

Switzerland, 8 June 1653. The latest in a series of peasant uprisings is violently put down near Berne. The year began with unrest in Lucerne, where peasants demanded reductions in taxes and mortgages and a more stable currency, and the rebellion has spread to neighbouring states.

Sweden, 30 July 1653. Gabriel Naude, the librarian to Cardinal Mazarin, dies while travelling to Stockholm, where he is being exiled because of the Fronde uprising. He is the first theoretician of library organisation and was librarian to Cardinal Richelieu before the latter was replaced by Mazarin. Naude collected some 40,000 books from all over Europe for the *Bibliotheque Mazarine*, and the library was open to all.

New France, 5 November 1653. The Iroquois League has signed a peace treaty with the French. The Iroquois have been waging war against neighbouring tribes for centuries, but most recently have nearly destroyed the Huron Indians, who have been forced to seek refuge with the French settlers.

London, 12 December 1653. The "Barebones Parliament" – which replaced the Rump Parliament – votes for its own dissolution. Composed of religious men hand-picked by Cromwell and the Council of State, it was nicknamed after one of its members, Praise-God Barebone, a sectarian preacher. Alarmed by the intentions of the radical contingent, it is the conservative elements who vote to end the assembly.

London, 16 December 1653. Oliver Cromwell takes on dictatorial powers with the title of "lord protector". The writer John Milton becomes his secretary.

India, 1653. Three sieges of Kandahar, in 1649, 1652 and 1653, have cost the Moghul empire 120m *rupees*, more than half its annual income.

Netherlands, 1653. Johan de Witt becomes councillor pensionary of Holland.

Balkans, 1653. Peasant revolts break out in Croatia.

Hungary, 1653. Apaozai Csere Janos publishes his *Hungarian Encyclopaedia*.

India, 1653. The building of the Taj Mahal is completed.

North Sea, 1653. In the war following the Navigation Act, the English, led by George Monk, defeat the Dutch under Marten Tromp in a battle near Portland. Tromp is killed on the bridge of his ship.

China, 1653. The Dalai Lama holds an investiture for the Manchu dynasty in Beijing.

Russia, 18 January 1654. The Ukraine comes under Russian domination.

London, 15 April 1654. The peace of Westminster puts an end to the war between England and the Netherlands. The Navigation Act that caused the two-year war is retained and England asserts its supremacy over the seas.

Massachusetts, 3 May 1654. The first toll bridge in America is licensed to Richard Thurley at Newbury River. There is a charge for animals but not for humans.

New Amsterdam, 7 September 1654. A group of 23 Sephardic Jews arrives on board the *St Charles*, a French armed vessel. This follows an order given to the 5,000 Jews in Recife, Brazil, that they have three months in which to leave. The order was issued by the Portuguese who took Recife from the Dutch in January.

Maryland, 20 October 1654. Maryland's tolerant Act Concerning Religion, entitling Roman Catholics to the rights of man, has today been replaced by a law taken from the Cromwellian Instrument of Government which states that: "none who profess and exercise the popish religion ... can be protected in this province". The same spirit of intolerance is being fostered by Puritans in Massachusetts.

Germany, 1654. The German musician Samuel Scheidt, renowned for his compositions for the organ, dies.

Oliver Cromwell makes himself protector

London, 16 December 1653

England's outstanding general of the Civil War, Oliver Cromwell, donned a plain black suit today to signify his civilian status when he formally accepted the title of Lord Protector of England from the lord mayor and aldermen of the City of London. After accepting the Great Seal and the Sword of State, he returned to the Banqueting House at Whitehall and three salvos of shots were fired.

For four years the soldiers had struggled to solve the problem of government after the execution of Charles. Last April, Cromwell called in musketeers to send his fellow MPs packing. He formed a parliament of God-fearing men nominated by non conformists churches and army officers; this "Barebones Parliament" muddled along until last week, when it resigned. Now the officers have produced an Instrument of Government; this provides for a lord protector, a council of state and an elected parliament.

Cromwell by the artist Edward Mascall, who worked c.1650-67.

Irish bishop puts a date to the Creation

Armagh, Ireland, 1654

The archbishop of Armagh, James Ussher, has been applying his considerable scholarship to establishing the date of Creation. After years of research that has involved totalling the ages of the Old Testament patriarchs, Ussher concludes that God created the world in the year 4004BC.

John Lightfoot, another scholar, is even more precise. He agrees with 4004BC and gives the date as 26 October – at 9.00am.

Sweden's scholarly queen has abdicated

Uppsala, Sweden, 16 June 1654

Queen Christina, infant monarch, European stateswoman and patron of Descartes, has abdicated the throne of Sweden, to the regret and consternation of her people. She is succeeded by Charles Gustav, her cousin, whom she was once determined to marry. Christina was the only child of Gustavus Adolphus and Princess Maria Eleanora of Brandenburg. She was six when her father died in 1632; until she came of age in 1644, Gustavus' great chancellor, Axel Oxenstierna, ruled as regent. She is an exceptionally gifted young woman, a linguist and a scholar.

In 1648 she was a signatory of the Treaty of Westphalia, which ended 30 years of European war, and confirmed Sweden control of the Baltic. She accelerated the sale of crown lands to pay for her armies, and played off the peasantry against the nobles ensuring Charles Gustav's succession. Her lack of freedom as monarch and a growing sympathy for Catholicism may be reasons for her abdication.

Queen Christina of Sweden: one of Europe's most influential rulers.

Cromwell gives Irish lands to veterans

Ireland, 1653
Cromwell has crushed the Irish rebels and simultaneously solved the problem of paying his soldiers by giving them grants of confiscated land. Those who fought against the English will lose two-thirds of their property; those who did not fight the English but simply failed to show proper regard for them lose one-third. Many landlords have been ordered to remove themselves to remote parts of western Ireland.

At the outset of his campaign to crush the ten-year uprising, Cromwell struck terror into the hearts of the Irish with his capture and sack of Drogheda. His call for the city to surrender and so avoid "an effusion of blood" was rejected. Two costly assaults were necessary before his Ironsides broke through, by which time Cromwell, in a raging fury, was ordering all the enemy to be put to the sword. The spectre of Drogheda's fate was such that other terrified garrisons could hardly wait to surrender and so avoid, as Cromwell put it, "the righteous judgment of God".

Patriarch of Moscow denounced as heretic

Two engraved Russian reliquary crosses picturing Christ and the saints.

Moscow, 1653
Thousands have been killed in a religious rift sparked by moves to change some traditions of the Orthodox Church. The changes have given rise to a new sect, known as the Old Believers, which has separated from the church. The new sect's leader, Avvakum, has been exiled to Siberia and thousands of his followers have been hanged.

Behind the reforms is the Muscovite patriarch Nikon, a peasant turned monk, who believes they are long overdue. The changes are small and largely involve the revision of the liturgy, including such details as the making of the sign of the cross with three fingers instead of with two and the use of the threefold "alleluia".

Nikon is a strongminded and tactless man who is backed by Czar Alexis and who has pursued his reforms with little concern for the simple-minded faithful. It was Avvakum's fierce denouncement of Nikon that led to his exile and the harsh repression by the czar.

An exquisite example of Iranian textile weaving, this silk cloth, with its design of figures in a garden, is from the Safavid era.

Taj Mahal is completed

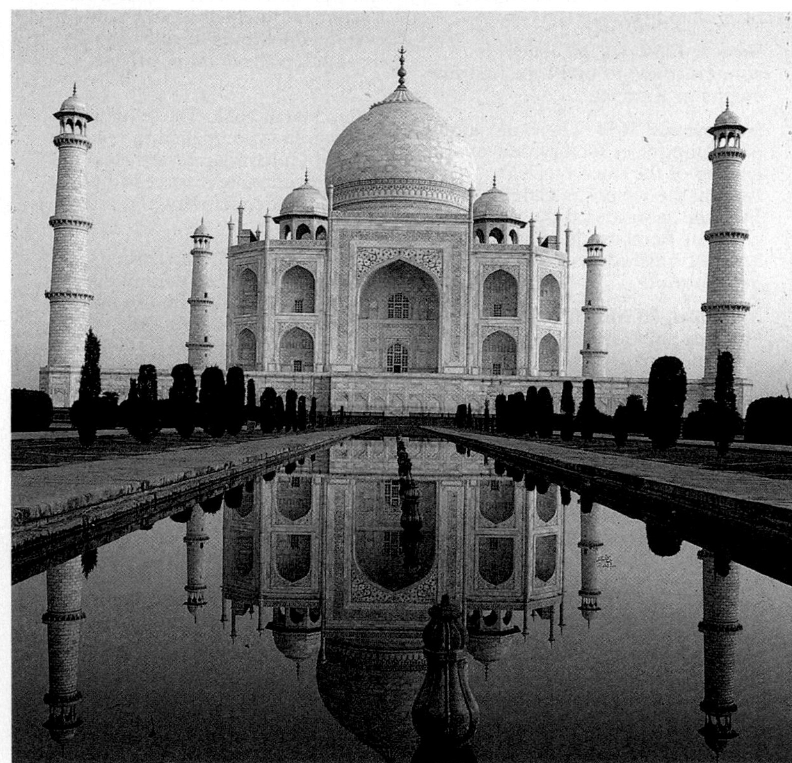

Shahjahan's memorial to his favourite wife: built by the empire's finest craftsmen, the glorious Taj Mahal is a celebration of many national styles.

Agra, India, 1653
The Taj Mahal, emperor Shahjahan's dream in marble to his favourite wife, Mumtaz-i Mahal (Elect of the Palace), is complete. Building started in 1631, two years after Mumtaz-i Mahal died bearing her 14th child. Its designer, the Persian architect Ustad Isa Afandi, gathered together the finest craftsmen of the east. All who visit this magnificent, yet serene, edifice agree it is the greatest architectural masterpiece to emerge from the Moghul building boom.

It reflects the variety of culture in the vast Moghul empire. The architecture comes from Persia, the concept of the ornate garden tomb comes from Afghanistan, the decorative motifs from Shiraz, the dome from Turkey and the use of water as a mirror from Kashmir.

The mausoleum, consisting of three buildings including a mosque, stands with a garden to its south, and sheets of water for its domes and minarets to reflect in. Everything is symmetrical. At its centre is a two-storeyed cube topped by an onion-shaped dome and flanked by domed octagonal wings. Four minarets, surmounted by octagonal kiosks, rise from each corner.

Secret clause lets the Dutch off lightly

London, 15 April 1654
The peace of Westminster which was signed here today brings to an end the short war, fought almost entirely at sea, between England and Holland. Many critics believe that Oliver Cromwell has been too lenient with the Dutch, who have suffered heavily in loss of shipping and trade. Nevertheless the Netherlands will pay reparations for past damages and have agreed to salute English ships in English waters.

The reason for this leniency is contained in secret talks with Holland which have led to the Act of Seclusion under which the House of Orange is barred from the *Stadholderate* and thus unable to ally itself with Charles Stuart. This should ensure that the still-powerful Dutch navy is denied to the Stuarts.

1654 (1654-1656)

France, 1654. An exchange of letters between the scientists Pascal and Fermat gives rise to a theory of probability.

Boston, 1654. Joseph Jencks is commissioned to build the first fire engine in America.

Netherlands, 1654. The explosion of a gunpowder factory destroys a quarter of the town of Delft. Among the victims is Carel Fabritius, considered the most gifted of Rembrandt's pupils. He had just finished painting his *Self-Portrait*.

Maryland, 25 March 1655. Puritans jail Governor Stone after a military victory over Catholic forces.

New Amsterdam, 26 April 1655. The Dutch West India Company rules that Jews must be allowed to stay in the colony.

Boston, 23 May 1655. Joseph Jencks gets a commission to build an engine "for the more speedy cutting of grass".

North America, September 1655. Swedish rule in America comes to an abrupt end when the Dutch capture Fort Christina and retake Fort Casimir from the Swedes.

Morocco, 1655. The Sadi dynasty is overthrown.

Amsterdam, 1655. The architect Jacob van Campen completes the new town hall. It is a grand building in monumental style, with a wealth of decoration, very different from the restrained elegance of the town houses being built elsewhere in the city.

North America, 1655. Women's illiteracy rate in Massachusetts is put at 50 per cent; in New Netherland, 60 per cent and in Virginia, 75 per cent.

Holland, 1655. The Dutch physicist Christiaan Huygens discovers Saturn's fourth satellite and the true nature of its rings.

Paris, 1655. The College of France loses one of its masters: Pierre Gassendi dies. As a philosopher, he criticised the ideas of Rene Descartes and wrote on the moral theories of Epicurus. He was also at the forefront of the developing science of astronomy, counting Galileo and Kepler among his friends.

Sweden, 1655. Christina, the former queen of Sweden, officially becomes a Catholic.

Siberia, 1655. Russians settled in Albazino attempt to penetrate the forests of Manchuria, which are rich in fur-skinned animals.

Virginia, 10 March 1656. Suffrage is extended to all free men, regardless of their religion.

Virginia, 10 March 1656. A plan calls for the seizing of Indian children until conversion, and for a payment to chiefs of one cow for every eight wolves' heads brought in, to teach them about private property.

India, March 1656. The Moghul Aurangzeb is compelled to raise his siege of Golconda; nevertheless the Dekhan sultanate is forced to pay a considerable indemnity and to cede territory.

Boston, July 1656. The first Quakers to enter the colony, Mary Fisher and Ann Austin, are met with strip searches, jail and banishment.

New Haven, 23 July 1656. New Haven becomes the only colony in New England to reject trial by jury.

New Netherlands, 6 September 1656. The Mohawks ask the Dutch to stop selling rum to the Indians.

Maryland, 22 September 1656. The first all-woman jury acquits Judith Cathchpole of murdering her unborn child.

Rome, 16 October 1656. The papal bull *Ad Sacram* of Alexander VII renews the condemnation of the "five propositions" of Jansenism, a reformist, anti-papal creed.

Madrid, 1656. Diego Velazquez paints *Las Meninas* (The Maids of Honour).

Amsterdam, 1656. Rembrandt is declared bankrupt and all his goods are put up for sale.

Massachusetts, 1656. Harvard accepts the Copernican theory of the universe, which places the sun at the centre with Earth and the planets revolving around it.

The Hague, 1656. The prolific and talented Dutch painter Jan van Goyen dies. A landscape artist who perfected the art of conveying subtleties of atmosphere, he has had considerable influence on younger artists.

Sweden, 1656. The Bank of Sweden is founded.

Rome, 1656. The Academy of Painting is founded.

Rumania, 1656. The confederation of Rumanian countries – Wallachia, Moldavia and Transylvania – become an anti-Ottoman coalition.

England, 1656. The writer John Bunyan publishes a vigorous attack on Quakerism, *Some Gospel Truths Opened*.

Ottoman Empire, 1656. An aged Albanian, Koprulu Mehmed, is made grand vizier in Istanbul. He is charged with the re-organisation of the empire and the re-establishment of order.

Manchus push back Russians in Siberia

Czar Alexis Mikhailovitch: the inspiration of Russian expansion.

Siberia, 1655

The almost effortless Russian advance into eastern Siberia has been checked on the banks of the Amur by Manchu warriors despatched by Beijing to avenge the heavy Chinese defeat there three years ago.

The Manchus, then preoccupied with consolidating their conquest of China, failed at the first battle to send sufficient forces, believing that the aggressors troubling their Tartar kinsmen were just tribesmen from the north trying to settle centuries-old squabbles.

Beijing has since woken up to the Russian threat. However, its victory may be late to oust the Russians from their new bases further north along the Pacific.

Jamaica taken by English expedition

Jamaica, 1655

An English army has captured this island and is pursuing the remnants of the Spanish garrison into the jungle. The Spanish viceroy had surrendered before choosing to fight a guerrilla campaign inland. It was the Lord Protector, Oliver Cromwell, who sent the invasion force to the West Indies as part of his "Western design". The intention was to take Santo Domingo. That attempt was vigorously repulsed and the British went on to blunder into Jamaica. The two commanders have returned and been imprisoned in the Tower of London.

Rationalist Spinoza expelled by Jews

Amsterdam, 27 July 1656

Baruch Spinoza, the Jewish philosopher, has been expelled from his home in Amsterdam. His own community refuses to accept the strict rationalism of his beliefs.

Spinoza, a lensmaker by trade, combines orthodox Judaism with the teachings of Galileo and Descartes, to propose a world in which theology and philosophy, faith and reason, are completely separated. To him there is no way of reconciling modern science and the ancient Bible.

Baruch Spinoza: wondering Jew.

Princes act to quell revolt in Rumania

Rumania, 1655

A mutual support pact to guarantee political stability in Rumania has been signed by the region's three main princes, who control Moldavia, Wallachia and Transylvania.

The move is designed to stifle any future revolts and prevent a repeat of the recent disturbances. The princes are reported to be shocked by the strength of the recent peasants' revolt, which was only eventually crushed by brute force and exceptionally repressive measures involving the murder and mutilation of thousands. The authorities blame Serbian and Bulgarian mercenaries who were trying to avoid being treated as serfs by their landowners for starting the uprising.

Portuguese take back Recife from Dutch

Brazil, 1654
With the Dutch distracted by a two-year war against England, the Portuguese saw their chance of regaining the vast sugar-growing area of north-eastern Brazil taken by Dutch colonists almost a quarter of a century ago.

When the Portuguese fleet arrived off the city and port of Recife, the Dutch garrison and burghers, terrified of standing alone without relief from home, capitulated. The territory had been conquered by mercenaries of the Dutch West India Company; so many of these were English that an English Protestant chaplain was stationed in Recife.

Under Governor John Maurits the multi-racial, multi-cultural colony of Dutch and English Protestants, Portuguese Catholics, Jews, Mulattos and black slaves flourished. But after he returned to Holland the colony went into decline, Portuguese planters rebelled and Portuguese from elsewhere in Brazil joined in.

A demonstration of practically nothing

Von Guericke proves his point, as the horses fail to break the sphere.

Germany, 1654
The German experimental scientist Otto von Guericke has just amazed the imperial *Diet* with a flamboyant demonstration. Von Guericke has been experimenting with vacuum pumps and studying the effects of atmospheric pressure.

He has had made two large brass hemispheres which fit snugly together to form a sphere. Before the assembled crowd he pumped air out of the hollow ball. Then he attached teams of eight horses to each side and signalled them to pull.

The strength of the horses failed to tear the hemispheres apart, showing that the atmosphere, while hating a vacuum, exerts considerable pressure.

Portrait painter Rembrandt is bankrupt

Rembrandt's "Scholar at a window": one of the master's later works.

Amsterdam, 1656
Rembrandt van Rijn, for long the most popular portrait painter in Amsterdam and one of the richest, has shocked the city by declaring himself bankrupt. His four-storey house, where he has lived and worked for 20 years, has been put in the name of his son Titus and is up for sale along with his art collection.

Rembrandt, who is 50, first made his name in the city with a group portrait commissioned by Dr Nicholas Tulp, the physician. He was painted giving one of his anatomy lessons, watched by a group of fascinated students. In 1642 he produced an even more dramatic portrait of the militia company of Captain Frans Banning-Cocq, *The Night Watch*. The 18 guards with their pikes are so shrouded in the shadow that Rembrandt loves that, instead of paying them 100 guilders each, it was agreed to vary the sum according to the degree of visibility of each man. Admirers say it makes other militia portraits "look like playing cards".

Of late Rembrandt has given up painting the burghers of Amsterdam for religious subjects and landscapes, and this "personal" work has lost him many patrons. His problems have been compounded by the cost of his collection.

His wife Saskia died in 1642 and under her will he may not marry again or he will forfeit her estate. His present companion, Hendrickje Stoffels, who was once his maid and has borne him a daughter, is taking charge of his affairs jointly with Titus.

Rembrandt's self-portrait, painted late in life, reflects his sadness.

Death of King John IV, who restored independence to Portugal

Lisbon, 6 November 1656
John IV, who regained Portugal's independence after 60 years under Spanish kings, died today, aged 53. In 1580, despite the claims of the House of Braganza, Philip II seized the Portuguese crown for himself. When John succeeded to the dukedom of Braganza in 1630 he set out, with the fervent support of the Portuguese people, to remove the injustice.

On his accession he declared war on Spain, although he was unable to commence military activity until he had found himself an army and navy. He pursued a vigorous diplomatic campaign to have himself recognised as king, which the pope, under Spanish influence, flatly refused. He married, in 1633, Louisa de Guzman, the sister of the Spanish duke of Medina Sidonia. Their son, Alfonso, succeeds.

1656 (1656-1658)

Austria, 1656. The treaty of Konigsberg is forced on the Elector Frederick William of Brandenburg by Charles X of Sweden, following the latter's successful military campaigns last year which culminated in the invasion of Brandenburg. The treaty makes east Prussia into a fief of the Swedish crown and gives Sweden privileged access to the Prussian ports of Memel and Pillau and half the customs revenue. It is a step towards the fulfilment of Sweden's dream of Baltic domination.

Rhode Island, 20 May 1657. The colony becomes the third to defy the British ban on trade with the Dutch.

Massachusetts, 21 May 1657. The colony's governor for 30 years, William Bradford, is dead. He played a major part in the establishment of the colony and was re-elected as governor from 1621 for 30 years.

England, 25 May 1657. In the Humble Petition and Advice, parliament offers the title of, king to Oliver Cromwell, the Lord Protector. He refuses it.

India, August 1657. Over the past year the Moghul Aurangzeb has captured two fortresses in the Dekhan sultanate of Bijapur and ravaged much of the land. It is only by the intervention of his father, Shahjahan, that a complete conquest has been prevented.

England, 1657. John Bunyan, who wrote an attack on the Quakers last year, begins preaching in the Midlands. He rapidly gains a reputation as a powerful speaker and draws large, enthusiastic crowds.

Rhode Island, 1657. Rhode Island is becoming known for its religious tolerance and as a haven for dissenting Puritans, thanks to the efforts of Roger Williams. Williams has been arguing against the involvement of secular authorities in religious affairs since the publication of his book *The Bloudy Tenent of Persecution for the Cause of Conscience Discussed* in 1644. The book was publicly burnt in London on publication.

Aegean Sea, 1657. The Turks take the islands of Tenedos and Lemnos from the Venetians.

West Africa, 1657. The Swedes, who Carolusberg castle, a slave fort, on the Gold Coast two years ago, are driven out by Danes.

England, 1657. The Dutch physicist Christiaan Huygens invents the pendulum clock – using Galileo's observations on the behaviour of oscillating pendulums – and writes the first treatise on probability theory.

Paris, 1657. *Histoire Comique des Etats et Empires de la Lune* is published. The book the work of the fantasist and comic poet Cyrano de Bergerac, is bursting with ideas.

New Amsterdam, 25 January 1658. The governor, Peter Stuyvesant, has prohibited tennis-playing while religious services are being held. The neighbouring colony of Massachusetts has gone even further: during 1655 and 1656 colonists were punished for eavesdropping, scolding, meddling, naughty speeches, profane dancing, making love without the consent of the congregation, playing cards, pulling hair and pushing their wives.

India, 25 June 1658. Aurangzeb proclaims himself emperor of the Moghuls.

New Amsterdam, 12 August 1658. *Ratelwacht*, the first police force in the colony, is formed.

Montreal, August 1658. A French explorer and fur trader, Medard Chouart, the *sieur* des Groseilliers, his brother-in-law Pierre Esprit Radisson and a team of 31 set out from Trois Rivieres on the lower St Lawrence river to explore the southern shores of Lake Superior and the regions south and west of the lake. They hope to establish trading relations with Indians in the area.

South Africa, 1658. Dutch settlers at the Cape of Good Hope begin to import slaves from Madagascar and Java.

Sweden, 1658. The Bank of Sweden produces the first bank notes in the western world.

Maryland, 1658. Conflict between the rebellious Puritan population and the Lord Proprietor has ended with the reinstatement of Lord Baltimore and the restoration of the Religious Toleration Act, repealed by a rebel assembly after an uprising in 1655.

Netherlands, 1658. The naturalist Jan Swammerdam is the first to observe the activities of red blood corpuscles.

Spain, 1658. The Spanish Jesuit writer and philosopher Balthasar Gracian dies. He wrote several works setting out a system of practical ethics, but will be best remembered for his allegorical novel *El Criticon* – a savage's vision of civilisation.

Poland, 1658. The Counter-reformation triumphs, and Protestants are excluded from office.

Ceylon, 1658. The Dutch take Jaffnapatam, Portugal's last possession in Ceylon.

One in two Poles die of war and plague

Poland, 1657

Poland's Golden Age is over and the horrors of more recent history have a new name: "the Deluge". In a very short time invasion, war, plagues, slave raids and mass murders have reduced the population by almost half. Poland's king, John II Casimir, has had a lamentable nine years in power.

Much of the trouble has been due to Poland's neighbours invading the country. After the king failed to reach an agreement with the Cossacks they swore an oath of allegiance to czar Alexis, whose armies promptly invaded the country on two fronts. This alarmed the Swedes, who descended on Poland from Pomerania and Livonia. And these operations provoked the intervention first of Frederick William, the elector of Brandenburg, the heart of the Prussian kingdom, and then this year that of the prince of Transylvania.

The strains of the incessant war have led to all sorts of internal problems. The king has been in continual conflict with the *Sejm* (parliament) over money and constitutional issues. Apart from the sharp reduction in the population, many towns have been destroyed.

Scientist calculates where Jesuits err

Pascal: scientist and theologian.

France, 24 March 1657

A leading French mathematician, as gifted in science as he is in theology, has joined the battles between the Jesuits and the Jansenists of the convent of Port Royal. In 18 polemical letters, *Les provinciales*, Blaise Pascal, writing as "Louis de Montalte", has weighed in against the beliefs of the Jesuit fathers.

Unlike them, Pascal believes firmly that true faith will only appear to the morally upright. His letters blend his own faith, the sophistication of a man of the world and the learning of a genuine genius. He makes the most complex of theological questions seemingly simple, and has attracted a wide audience of "honest men" to whom he has revealed topics once reserved for specialists.

Europeans fight for spoils of Gold Coast

Gold Coast, West Africa, 1657

The Gold Coast is now a battleground between rival European powers. In the latest round the fortress of Carolusberg, which the Dutch took from the Portuguese in 1642, and the Swedes took from the Dutch in 1651, has now been taken by the Danes.

The black populace watches this extraordinary outburst of white tribalism with a defensive self-interest. Politics were simple until 1642. Portugal monopolised power. Now Portuguese, Dutch, Swedes, Danes, English, French and Germans fight for the wealth that can be gained from the gold, cloth, ivory, salt and slave trades.

The profits are enormous. The mines at Mina alone supply one tenth of the world's gold, while since the growth of sugar plantations in the New World there is now more profit from slaves than from gold. Slaves costing 45 *florins* are sold in the Americas for 210 florins. As Europeans fight each other on the coast, anarchy reigns in the interior. Firearms, swapped for gold and slaves, destroy traditional structures and kill thousands. The European powers, as if to protect themselves from the consequences of their own immorality, remain in their coastal forts. These forts frequently change hands and are now so numerous that in some places, like Accra, Komenda and Sekondi, they are even within gunrange of each other.

Saintly favoured son imprisons father

Shahjahan out riding with his son Dara, a favourite but a traitor too.

Aurangzeb, Shahjahan's "most worthy and most saintly son".

Delhi, 25 June 1658

The seemingly "most worthy and saintly" Aurangzeb, the third and favourite son of the Moghul emperor Shahjahan, has imprisoned his father and seized power. Inevitably there have been casualties: two brothers, a son and a nephew are dead. Such is the succession in the Moghul empire.

Shahjahan's illness, which precipitated the crisis, saw Aurangzeb in the Dekhan with a Moghul army. Recognising his three brothers as the three obstacles to the throne, he set out to eliminate them one by one. Unfortunately the three brothers had the same ideas. The oldest, the liberal and honourable Dara, seized Delhi. The second, the dissolute and alcoholic Shuja, the governor of Bengal, went to war against him. The third, Murad, the governor of Gujarat, was tricked into an alliance with Aurangzeb.

Yet more unfortunate for the ambitious brothers, the shah recovered. Shuja continued his advance and was defeated by Dara, who in turn has been defeated by Aurangzeb. Murad has been kidnapped and has disappeared. Finally, Aurangzeb seized his father and imprisoned him in his *harem*.

Rome thrills to Borromini's architecture

Rome, 1657

Francesco Borromini, who worked as a stone carver at St Peter's when he first came to Rome, is winning a reputation as an architect equal to that of his great rival, Bernini. Pope Urban VIII was Bernini's patron. When he died, Innocent X turned to Borromini. Just as Bernini was given St Peter's interior, Borromini was given St John Lateran, which he decorated in Baroque style with giant pilasters and arches. His most original invention was shown in the church of St Charles at the Four Fountains whose walls seem to undulate beneath an oval dome. His St Agnes in the Piazza Navona faces Bernini's fountains.

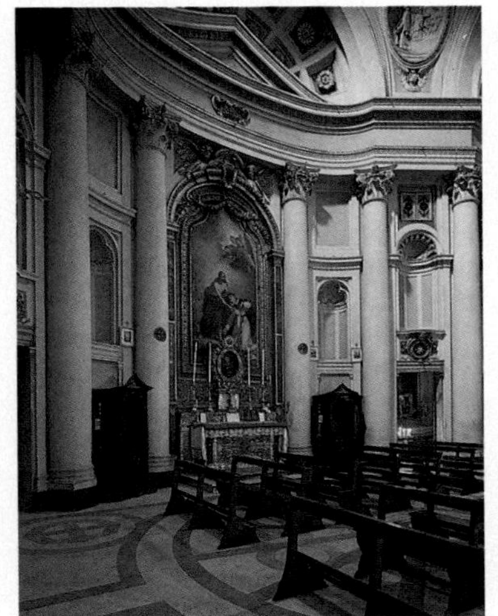

Borromini's church of San Carlo.

Difficult sultan succumbs to Dutch bribes

Traders and natives pursue their business outside a colonial building.

Java, 1657

Despite recurrent difficulties with the sultan of the Mataram empire on Java, the Dutch, established in their fortified town of Batavia, have made no effort to subdue Mataram. Instead they seek to please Sultan Amangkurat by sending him costly gifts, and hope that the rice supplies, on which they depend, will not be interrupted. The sultan rejected a Dutch suggestion that he should encourage overseas trade by his people, saying that they had nothing of their own, everything belonged to him, and it was going to stay that way. He says he is not interested in his people's welfare.

Anglo-French army routs Spaniards

Dunkirk, 25 June 1658

This city has today surrendered to a combined force of English and French troops under the command of Turenne. To the dismay of the French troops, who spilt much blood in the siege, it was promptly handed over to the English under the terms of an agreement between Mazarin and Cromwell.

Mazarin was anxious for English help in the war against Spain and Cromwell was under pressure to halt the attacks on England's east coast sea trade by Dunkirk privateers. The Cardinal was also impressed by the protector's effective army, who have restored England's military reputation in Europe.

The French have not done all the work, however. English troops took part in the rout of the Spanish at the battle of the Dunes 11 days ago. Only a small party of infantry is believed to have escaped.

An ornately-designed German powder flask of stagahorn here mounted in silver gilt.

1658 (1658-1660)

England, 3 September 1658. The Lord Protector, Oliver Cromwell, dies. He has ruled as a benevolent dictator since the dissolution of the Barebones Parliament in 1653, and last year refused the offer of the kingship from parliament.

England, 1658. The poet John Dryden publishes *Heroic Stanzas*, in quatrains, on the death of Oliver Cromwell.

India, 1659. After taking power, the Moghul Emperor Aurangzeb sets about re-establishing order.

Netherlands, 1659. The Dutch-Jewish philosopher and theologian Spinoza identifies God with nature in his *Short Treatise on God, Man and his Well-being*.

Paris, 1659. The first opera in the French language, *Pastorale*, is written by Abbe Pierre Perrin, the librettist, and Robert Cambert. Its performance marks the opening of the Royal Academy of Music in Paris.

Berlin, 1659. The Royal Library is founded.

India, 1659. Sivaji, the Maratha, kills the Moghul general, Afzal Khan, by ripping open his belly with a steel tiger's claw, while embracing him in welcome.

France, 1659. The peace of the Pyrenees is agreed – a Franco-Spanish agreement negotiated by Cardinal Mazarin and Don Luis de Haro, which finally brings the Franco-Spanish War to an end. The treaty is sealed with the arrangement of a marriage between the Spanish King Philip IV's daughter, Maria Theresa, and Louis XIV. The *infanta's* dowry will be paid in full only when she renounces all claims to the Spanish throne.

Italy, 1659. The Sicilian Francisco Procopio perfects the making of icecream.

Netherlands, 1659. The Dutch artist Jan Vermeer paints *Young Girl with Flute*.

England, May 1659. Six months after succeeding his father as lord protector, Richard Cromwell is dismissed by the recalled Rump Parliament, which was thrown out by Oliver Cromwell's troops in 1653. Lacking his father's charisma and will-power, Richard has shown little aptitude for this supremely powerful office.

France, 1659. The dramatist Pierre Corneille returns to the stage with his *Oedipe*.

China, 1659. Father Ferdinand Verbiest, a French missionary, sets out for Beijing.

Netherlands, 1659. A new drama by Joost van den Vondel, *Jephtha*, is performed.

Cambodia, 1659. The English factors of the East India Company's Cambodian factory are forced by an Annamite (*Vietnamese*) invasion to flee the country.

Virginia, 13 March 1660. A statute limits tax on the sale of slaves.

Massachusetts, 1 June 1660. The Quaker Mary Dyer is hanged in Boston. She escaped the noose last year through the intervention of her son, but then disobeyed the authorities by re-entering the colony to spread the doctrines of Quakerism. Unconvinced by her claim of a mission from God, the court ordered her execution.

France, 27 September 1660. The moral leader of the French church, Vincent de Paul, dies. At the age of 25 he was captured by pirates on a sea voyage and sold into slavery in Tunis. He escaped by persuading his master to return to the Christian faith, and landed back in France in 1607. He formed associations for helping the sick, and founded the Congregation of Priests of the Missions, which was sanctioned by Urban VIII in 1632.

England, 1 October 1660. The crown strengthens the Navigation Act, requiring that certain colonial goods are to be shipped only to Britain. Such measures are directed against the Dutch, but they inevitably limit colonial trading outlets and are resented by settlers struggling to establish their communities.

America, 1660. The Narrangansett Indian Passaconaway makes a death-bed speech: "Be careful how you quarrel with the English. Although you may do them much harm, yet assuredly you will all be destroyed and rooted off the earth if you do."

South Africa, 1660. In the Dutch-Khoisan war at the Cape of Good Hope, the Khoisan herders Harry and Donan, who greeted the Dutch settlers when they landed in 1652, are captured and imprisoned on Robben Island.

France, 1660. The artist Nicolas Poussin begins a cycle of paintings for the duke of Richelieu, the *Quatre Saisons* (Four Seasons).

Sweden, 1660. The Swedes mourn the death of Charles X in the course of a new campaign against Denmark. He is succeeded by his young son, Charles XI.

Copenhagen, 1660. Niels Stensen, the Danish anatomist, geologist and theologian, discovers that the heart is a muscle.

East Africa, 1660. The sultan of Oman, supported by the British, takes the port of Mombasa from the Portuguese.

Swedes besiege Danes

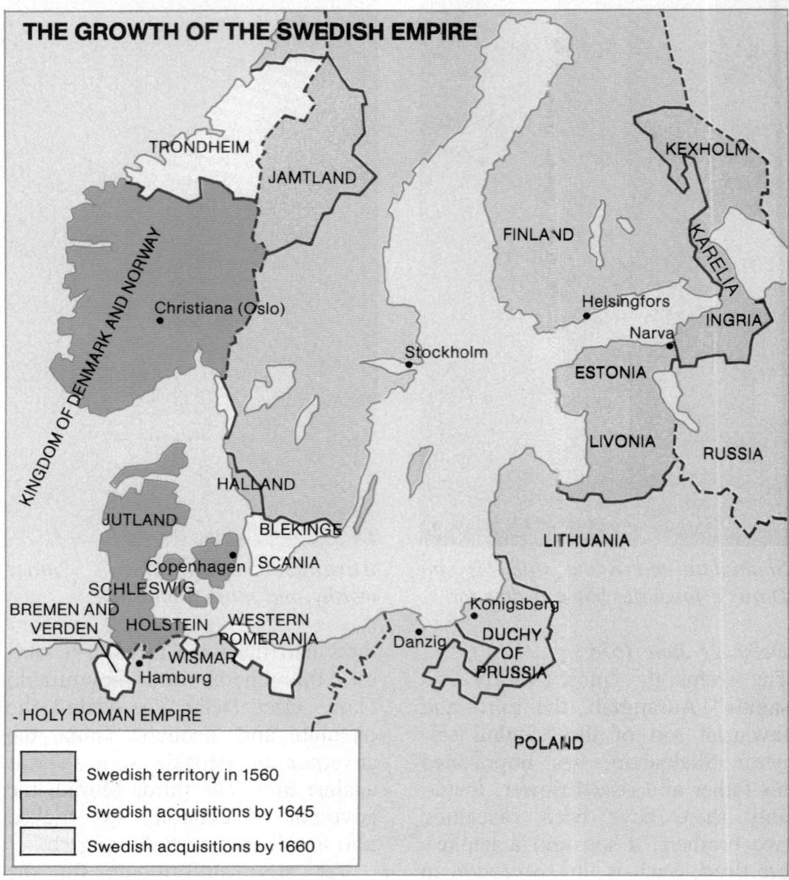

Copenhagen, February 1659

Helped by a Dutch fleet and led by their king, Frederick III, the people of Copenhagen are fighting hard against a Swedish besieging army. The Swedes invaded suddenly last year from the south, taking advantage of the frozen sea in an exceptionally cold winter to move rapidly from island to island, taking Jutland and Zealand before attacking an undefended capital.

The Danes sued for peace and the resulting treaty of Roskilde gave Sweden the islands of Skane, Halland and Blekinge – thus completing her peninsula north of the Baltic Sea – together with the islands of Bornholm and territories in Norway.

It was the aggressive Swedish king, Charles X, who launched this War of the North in 1655. Anxious to protect his empire against a Russian attack, he invaded Poland and took Warsaw.

During this campaign Denmark, encouraged by Holland and Austria, declared war on Sweden. Charles broke off the Polish campaign to turn on Denmark so suddenly. Now, despite the treaty, he has invaded again, determined to occupy the whole of Denmark. Only the courage of Copenhagen can save the Baltic Sea from becoming a "Swedish lake".

Frederick III, leader of the Danes in their struggle against Sweden.

Cromwell, puritan and moralist, dies

The death mask of the Protector.

England, 3 September 1658
All through the night the Lord Protector was restless and he talked much of the grace of God. The last crisis came at three o'clock this Friday afternoon as he slipped into unconsciousness. Oliver Cromwell was in his 60th year and the fifth of his rule over England.

A stern Puritan and an inspiring general, he was respected and feared, but though the private expressions of grief have been many, in public there are none. Nor have the royalists raised their heads. John Thurloe, the head of Cromwell's intelligence service, writes: "There is not a dog that wags his tongue, so great a calm are we in."

Cromwell reshaped the Civil War's New Model Army into a professional force. He set up a militia organised in 12 districts, each under a major-general, to forestall conspiracies and enforce public morals. He wanted to curb drinking and to shut down theatres and whorehouses. He believed in the Bible as the true word of God, to which any man should have access.

The underlying problem of his rule was his dependence on the military and his lack of civilian support. His relations with parliament were uneasy. MPs wanted to be rid of the army, while he knew it was a necessity. They wanted a king, but his conscience could not accept a crown. He is succeeded by his son Richard; few expect him to last.

English to be biggest slavers vows prince

The British flag flies over Fort James at Accra: the Gold Coast is seen as a new source of wealth for the merchants of the expanding empire.

London, 3 October 1660
With the projected foundation of the Royal African Company by Prince Rupert and the equipping of an expedition to wrest control of the Gambia from foreigners, England's invisible earnings will be given a sharp boost. It is Prince Rupert's ambition for England to become the world's leading slave trading nation. The diarist Samuel Pepys, however, offered a share in the venture, politely declined.

Britain's interest in the Gambia began in 1588 when the exiled Portuguese pretender, Antonio, "granted" English merchants trade concessions in the Portuguese colony.

Prince Rupert's interest in the slave trade goes back to the Protectorate, when he led royalist privateers against English shipping on the West African coast. At the head of the Gambia, he was told, there were mountains of unprotected gold and nations of unexploited slaves. French, Dutch, Swedes and English jostle for access, whether their interest is in mining or slave trading, there is money to be made.

Quakers hanged on Boston common

Boston, Mass., 27 October 1659
Two members of the Quaker sect were hanged on Boston common today for preaching their non-violent doctrine in defiance of the Puritan government. A 200-strong guard held the crowd back with long pikes, while drummers drowned the condemned men's parting words. A third prisoner, a woman, was reprieved after being blindfolded with the noose about her neck, in response to her son's pleas. She is banished instead.

The Quakers – Will Robinson, Marmaduke Stevenson and Mary Dyer – have been repeatedly exiled from Massachusetts. They knew that all dissent in Boston is suppressed. Eight years ago, Baptists holding a service in a private house were raided by the sheriff. One of them was publicly whipped. The virus of Puritan intolerance, cultivated in England under Cromwell, has spread to suppress Catholicism in Catholic Maryland by force of arms. As in England, Catholics are fair game, their property pillaged freely.

Franco-Spanish border fixed at Pyrenees

France, 7 November 1659
The Franco-Spanish war is at last at an end. After a series of meetings between Mazarin and de Haro on this island in the Bidassoa river, the peace of the Pyrenees was signed today much to the relief of Europe.

The war had reached a stage where Spain, its treasury empty, and shocked by the defeats of its much-vaunted army at Rocroi, Lens and Dunkirk, could fight no longer. The entry of England into the war, with the Ironsides ranged alongside France's increasingly confident army, was the last straw.

Among the most important of the 124 clauses of the treaty are those restoring Roussillon and Perpignan to France after a century and a half of Spanish rule, thus firmly fixing the Franco-Spanish border at the Pyrenees.

England is to have Dunkirk and Jamaica while the French will gain a series of fortresses in Flanders and Artois. In return the French are to restore Spain's ally, the duke of Lorraine, to most of his duchy. The treaty also stipulates an amnesty for the prince of Conde who, out of pride, fought for Spain. There is also to be a dynastic marriage. Louis XIV is to marry the Spanish princess, Maria Theresa, with a dowry of 500,000 *ecus*.

Theodore van Thulden's allegorical view of the peace of the Pyrenees.

Black-white line is an almond hedge

Cape Town, 6 April 1660
The 12-month South African guerrilla war between Khoisan pastoralists and Dutch settlers is over. The Dutch governor, van Riebeeck, opened peace negotiations today. The two sides are to be separated by a hedge of bitter almonds.

The settlement was founded in 1652 by the Dutch East India Company to provide victuals for their East Indies-bound ships. After five years van Riebeeck, a believer in free enterprise, encouraged company employees to set up their own farms. Africans who tried to thwart them were sent to Robben Island.

Conflict became inevitable: the Khoisans attacked outposts, burned crops and stampeded cattle. The overstretched whites have sued for peace. With the whites hoping to expand their colony and the blacks anxious to win back their land, however, the present compromise is unlikely to last.

1660 (1660-1661)

England, 12 November 1660. John Bunyan, now a Baptist minister, is arrested for preaching other than in a parish church, a practice which local magistrates began to prosecute after the Restoration. He is imprisoned in Bedford county jail.

Copenhagen, 1660. The peace of Copenhagen ends the war between Sweden and Denmark. The Swedes restore the diocese of Trondheim to Norway, and Bornholm to Denmark, but retain Scania and other territories conquered since 1643 on their western borders.

England, 1660. The English political theorist James Harrington publishes his *Political Discourses*. Though a republican, he was a personal attendant of Charles I, and attended him to the scaffold.

Germany, 1660. Friedrich Staedtler founds a pencil factory in Nuremberg.

Germany, 1660. The peace of Oliva ends the war begun in 1655 by Sweden's attack on Poland. The Swedes gain no territory by the treaty, but keep Livonia, and John Casimir, the king of Poland, gives up his claim to the Swedish throne. The treaty also confirms the duchy of Brandenburg's sovereignty over the duchy of Prussia.

France, 1660. The French writer Paul Scarron dies. He earned his living from writing after contracting a disease which ultimately left him paralysed. He wrote sonnets, madrigals, epistles, and satires, but will be best remembered for his realistic novel *Le Roman Comique* (The Comic Novel) which was a reaction against the lengthy, flowery works of such writers as Mlle de Scudery and Honore d'Urfe.

France, 1660. Louis XIV of France marries Maria Teresa, *infanta* of Spain. The musician Francesco Cavalli, who studied under Monteverdi, composes the opera *Serse* in honour of the occasion.

England, 1660. The English writer James Howell publishes *Lexicon Tetraglotten*, an English, French, Italian and Spanish dictionary. Howell was a royalist spy between 1632 and 1642, and was imprisoned by the parliamentarians from 1642 to 1650. At the Restoration, the office of historiographer-royal was created for him.

Netherlands, 1660. Jacob Cats, the Dutch statesman and poet, dies aged 67. Known as "Father Cats", he served twice as ambassador to England, and has spent the last eight years of his life writing his autobiography.

England, 1660. James, the duke of York, becomes Lord High Admiral.

France, 23 April 1661. To fight against Jansenism – a puritanical movement calling for moral and doctrinal reform – a decree from the council orders all members of religious communities to sign a statement conforming to the papal condemnation of the five propositions in Jansen's *Augustinus*.

France, September 1661. Nicolas Fouquet, the superintendent of state finances, is arrested in Nantes at the instigation of Louis XIV. Jean-Baptiste Colbert, who worked for Mazarin until his death earlier this year, and has been agitating for Fouquet's arrest, replaces him.

Italy, 1661. The Italian physiologist Marcello Malpighi observes the flow of blood in the capillaries of a frog's lungs. He confirms William Harvey's theory of the circulation of blood.

Rhode Island, 1661. The Quakers hold their first annual meeting. Also known as the Society of Friends, this newly-emerged sect was founded by George Fox during the Puritan revolution in England. Fox taught that the essence of Christianity was the "inward light" in every man that needs no minister, sacraments or liturgy.

England, 1661. The Irish physicist and chemist Robert Boyle rejects Aristotle's theory of the elements. In his work *The Sceptical Chymist*, he defines simple and primitive bodies and complex bodies. As a physicist, he also improves von Guericke's pump, so that he can demonstrate the necessity of air in respiration and combustion.

Massachusetts, 1661. The first church for the Indians is founded by the pastor John Eliot who began preaching to the Indians in their own language 15 years ago. He also publishes the first bible in the colonies: the New Testament in the Algonquin language.

China, 1661. The Manchu dynasty, which was still being opposed around 1655 by the last Ming partisans, is now recognised throughout China. Shunzhi, the first Manchu ruler, succeeds in the normal way.

Amsterdam, 1661. The brilliant Dutch painter Rembrandt receives his most important commission to date, a gigantic canvas, roughly five and a half yards square: it is to be entitled the *Conspiracy of Claudius Civilus*.

India, 1661. The Portuguese cede the island of Bombay to Charles II as part of the dowry of his queen, Catherine of Braganza. With its fine natural harbour, Bombay has the potential to become a major port for the English, and is their first independent territory in India.

Traveller's gloomy impressions of India

Aurangzeb sits in state surrounded by his courtiers: reports from India tell of a tyrant who puts self-indulgent luxury above the national interest.

Delhi, India, 1660

As the Moghul empire empties its treasury in pursuit of architectural extravagance and aristocratic luxuries, the Indian peasantry, inevitably, pays the price.

The Indo-Persian city of Agra, the Red Fort at Delhi and the Taj Mahal may all be beautiful, but to a French traveller, Francois Bernier, employed in the Moghul court in the final years of Shahjahan and the early years of Aurangzeb, they epitomise tyranny.

It is a tyranny "often so excessive as to deprive the peasant and artisan of the necessaries of life, leaving them to die in misery and exhaustion; a tyranny so excessive men and women prefer to be barren than witness their children die of starvation; a tyranny that drives the farmer from the land, into exile or military service."

Houses fall apart, irrigation canals fall in, there is no will to make repairs. "The country is ruined by the necessity of defraying the cost of the enormous court and army maintained to keep the people in subjection. No adequate idea can be given of how these people suffer. The cudgel and whip compel them to labour for the benefit of their rulers. Ruin and desolation overspread the land," he writes.

Chinese pirate makes base in Taiwan and evicts Dutch

Taiwan, 1661

Koxinga, the son of a Chinese pirate and a Japanese mother, has defeated the Dutch garrison on Taiwan and expelled the Dutch traders from the island.

Athough he was overwhelmingly superior in numbers, Koxinga was unable to storm Fort Zeelandia, a powerful fortress built with bricks imported from Holland. Exasperated by his failure, he wrote to the Dutch commander: "You Dutch people, a few thousand in number, how can you carry on war against us, who are so powerful by our numbers? Really, it is as if you were bereft of your senses."

Eventually he settled down to siege warfare and starved out the defenders. He showed mercy and allowed them to sail away with their possessions. He plans to use Taiwan as a base for an attack on the mainland in the hope of restoring the Mings.

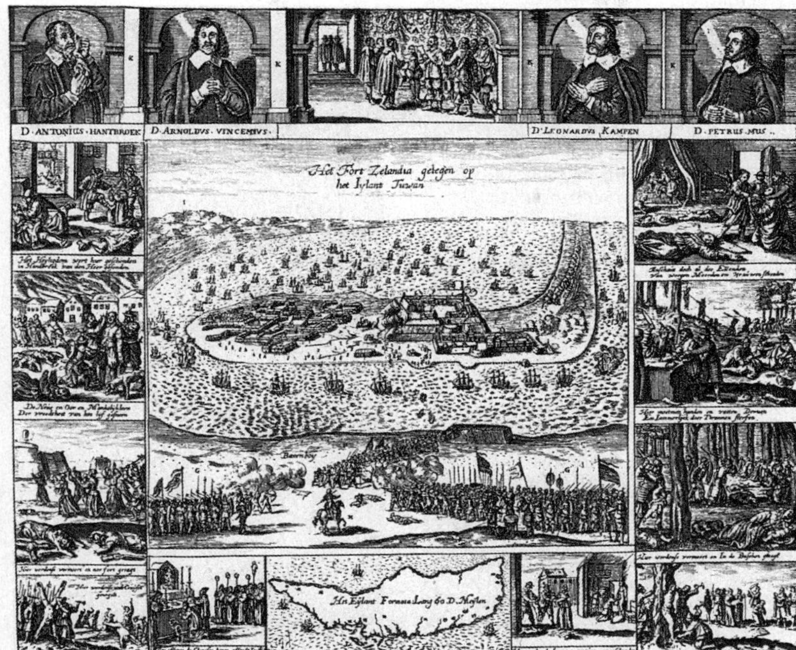

A map of the island of Taiwan, surrounded by pictures which tell the story of Holland's conquest of the island and the colonisation that followed.

Sea trade fuels war on shores of Baltic

Copenhagen, 1660

The conflict between Denmark and Sweden is over, at least for a while. The two countries have signed the Peace of Copenhagen, under which the Danes abandon claims to southern Sweden. This ends the war that began in 1658 with Sweden's attack on Denmark.

As the two countries glower at each other across the narrow sound which allows North Sea traffic to enter and leave the Baltic Sea, the eyes of the Europe are on Sweden and its domination of this inland sea. Charles X is dead, and, as his infant son Charles XI succeeds to the throne, Russia is looking for a foothold on the Baltic coast.

For all the wars that have plagued Europe, the Baltic, like that other inland sea, the Mediterranean, has been a vital route for seaborne trade, especially with the south. From the Levant come the wine, fruit and olive oil that cannot be produced in the north; and the north produces iron, copper and salt-herrings, a vital source of food. The Baltic also supplies the rest of Europe with grain, wood and other naval supplies in great demand. The economic and strategic importance of the Baltic also explains the support of other European states for Denmark when Sweden threatened its neighbour across the sound. The greatest support came from Holland. The Dutch, like other major trading nations, are always anxious lest the narrow, shallow sound which is the only entrance to the Baltic might fall under the control of only one nation.

Charles and the monarchy return to England by popular consent

"The Procession of Charles II" by Dirck Stoop: eleven years after his father was executed by Parliament, the people have called on Charles to restore the Stuart dynasty to its place at the head of English society.

England, 26 May 1660

After eleven years of rule by self-righteous factions in the shadow of the military, England has gained a form of government desired by the vast majority of citizens. Charles II, who landed at Dover today and made a festive journey to London, arrives not as a conqueror, but as a constitutional monarch. The Restoration is the restoration of parliamentary government.

Charles displayed unexpected shrewdness. Cromwell's death had left the nation rudderless. His son Richard was weak and soon gave up. By the end of last year it was recognised that the only solution was restoration. The question was: on what terms?

In Paris, Henrietta Maria, the queen mother, though a Catholic, was intriguing with Calvinists to gain control over her son. But Charles refused to visit her and instead issued a declaration at Breda to the English parliamentarians, saying that he supported liberty of conscience, a general amnesty for past deeds, full arrears of pay for all ranks in the army and full co-operation with parliament. Greatly relieved, MPs accepted these terms and proclaimed Charles king.

Serfs turn robbers under czar's new laws

Russia, 1660

A new danger faces travellers in rural Russia: the rapacious activities of robber bands of renegade serfs who survive by killing and theft. The upsurge of violence in the Russian countryside follows years of famine and plague. Observers also blame the tightening up of the laws on serfdom 12 years ago for making the situation worse.

Under the 1648 Code of Law enacted by Czar Alexis the time limits in which a lord could take legal proceedings to recover a fugitive peasant were abolished so that the right of recovery now lasts for a peasant's life. The code also extends the principle of binding a peasant to land to include the whole family, including sons and nephews. In the past the only person bound had been the head of the household. For heavily taxed peasants living on the edge of bankruptcy, the laws have closed off the last legal means of escape, suddenly making life as a fugitive an attractive alternative.

1661 (1661-1662)

France, 9 March 1661. Cardinal Mazarin, the king's prime minister, dies at Vincennes. Louis XIV confirms his wish to rule personally, without the assistance of a prime minister.

France, 1661. Philip, the duke of Orleans, marries Henrietta Anne, the sister of Charles II, the newly restored English king.

Russia, 1661. The peace of Kardis confirms the preliminary treaty made at Valiesar in 1659 which ended the Northern War between Russia and Sweden (1655-1660). The treaty restores the *status quo* between the two countries, with Russia surrendering all gains it has made in the Baltic provinces.

West Africa, 1661. The English capture Fort James in the Gambia and begin a rapid expansion of the slave trade.

Virginia, 1661. A law is passed which assumes that some Negroes must serve as slaves for life. Previously, Negroes were held for periods of indenture, as many white servants are. Last year the first law acknowledging slavery as an institution was passed, bringing in a tax on tobacco grown with the help of slaves imported by foreigners.

England, 1661. Matthew Locke, who composed the music for Charles II's coronation procession, is appointed composer-in-ordinary to the king.

Netherlands, 1661. The Dutch physicist Christiaan Huygens invents the manometer, an instrument for measuring pressure in gases and liquids.

India, 1661. There is widespread famine in India where there has been scarcely any rain since 1659.

Turkey, 1661. Koprulu Mehmed Koprulu, the grand vizier of Turkey, dies and is succeeded by his son Koprulu Fazil Ahmed.

London, 1661. Sir William d'Avenant, poet and dramatist, opens the Lincoln's Inn Theatre, with Shakespeare's *Hamlet* as the first production.

Tibet, 1661. Two Jesuit missionaries reach the Tibetan capital.

England, 1661. The Dutch artist Peter Lely is made court painter by Charles II. A man of broad sympathies, Lely has also worked for both Charles I and Oliver Cromwell.

France, 1662. Louis XIV, France's "Sun King", draws up plans for a magnificent palace to be built at Versailles, just outside Paris. The palace is to be a sumptuous new residence for the court; Charles Lebrun is the artistic adviser.

England, 1662. Elizabeth of Bohemia, the "Winter Queen", dies in England. The daughter of King James of England and his wife Anne of Denmark, Elizabeth married Frederick V, the elector Palatine, who was elected king of Bohemia in 1618. After the defeat of Bohemian forces at the battle of the White Mountain in 1620, the couple took refuge with Frederick's uncle, Maurice of Nassau. But Frederick died in 1632 and Elizabeth was only rescued from deepening poverty last year by Lord Craven, a former servant and friend, who invited her to England.

England, 1662. The English author Samuel Butler writes the first part of *Hudibras*, a satire on Puritanism which brings him instant popularity.

France, 1662. The dramatist Moliere's new comedy *L'Ecole des femmes* draws the crowds.

London, 1662. The Act of Uniformity is passed, stating that Church services are to be conducted in accordance with the revised prayer book. This is part of the Clarendon Code, a series of measures named after Charles II's chief minister, Edward Hyde, the first earl of Clarendon, aimed at reinstating Anglicanism as the official religion after the Restoration.

England, 1662. *Worthies of England* by the English antiquarian and divine Thomas Fuller, is published one year after his death by his son. It took 20 years to research and write. Fuller was a royalist who wrote several books in defence of the cause and was appointed chaplain to the king in 1660.

London, 1662. Charles II gives a royal charter to the Royal Society, founded to promote scientific knowledge. The society emerged from meetings of scientists and philosophers which were first held in 1645, and was formally established in 1660.

Paris, 1662. Francesco Cavalli's ballet opera *Ercole Amante* is performed in Paris.

England, 1662. An Act of Settlement is passed. A poor law, designed to curb vagrancy, it allows parish overseers to force homeless, unemployed people to return to their native parish.

England, 1662. The hearth tax is introduced, levied at the rate of two shillings per hearth fire. It is an attempt by the government to replace surviving feudal dues with a regular source of revenue, but it proves extremely unpopular.

France, 1662. The marquis de Louvois is appointed secretary of state and minister of war jointly with his father, Michel le Tellier.

Diarist pens attack on London pollution

London Bridge, from Visscher's map of London, originally printed in 1650.

London, 1661

Living in London is unhealthy, especially for the lungs, according to John Evelyn, English country gentleman, author and diarist.

Evelyn has been recording his impressions of places, people and contemporary events in Britain since he was 11. He has also travelled extensively in Europe. Few can match his erudition, and he is an influential figure in his country's cultural, political and religious life.

Now 41, and firmly in favour at the court of King Charles II, Evelyn is directing his energies into social issues. He has been active on a number of royal commissions and makes his views known on important issues of the day.

Pollution is a new crusade for his restless pen. There are, he complains, too many factories burning huge amounts of coal. He calls for various environmental countermeasures, such as the planting of shrubs and trees and the removal of industrial sites to beyond the city limits.

Unfortunately, Evelyn's plan for cleaner, sweeter air seems to be going unheeded. There is, as yet, no prospect of laws being passed to control pollution.

Danish king declares his power absolute

Copenhagen, January 1661

Faced by an angry aristocracy, but backed by the country's burghers and common people, Frederick III of Denmark has declared himself an absolute monarch, "above all human laws and knowing no other superior beings or judge over him ... save God alone".

The Swedish siege of Copenhagen is now two years old. Two days before it began, Frederick called his burghers together and announced far-reaching changes in their status. In the first place, they could control taxation. They could have access to offices of state hitherto reserved for nobility. And they could buy land on an equal footing with nobles who, at that point, were said to be "running like hares", desperate to save their fortunes from the Swedes. The city gates had to be closed to stop them leaving and the country was placed under temporary military control.

Iroquois struggle for fur monopoly

North America, c.1662
The Indian tribes of North America are locked into a relentless war for a highly lucrative prize: the profitable fur trade with France.

Since the start of this century the Huron Indians have built up their own "empire", in which for many years they had a virtual monopoly of the trade. This changed in 1640 when another tribe, the Iroquois, decided to challenge the Huron.

Taking advantage of the war in Europe between France and the Netherlands, the Iroquois enlisted Dutch aid and armaments and began a campaign against their rivals which has proved highly successful. Attempts by a band of missionaries to calm their hostility failed completely – the Iroquois massacred the agents of peace.

In 1649, still on the warpath, they began wiping out Huron villages, killing all in their path. The situation has only stablised with the arrival of Europeans of both sides, determined to end the bloodbath and restore normality.

Mazarin, France's second king, dies

Paris, 10 March 1661
Cardinal Mazarin, who has ruled France virtually as a monarch, died yesterday, and today the 22-year-old king Louis XIV assumed full power over his kingdom. There can be no doubt of his intentions, for he has already given his orders.

Today he told the chancellor: "I request and order you to seal no orders except by my command." And later, when the president of the Assembly of Clergy asked to whom he should apply for the settlement of business, the king replied: "To me, Monsieur the Archbishop, to me."

It is obvious that the king has learnt well under Mazarin and intends to put his lessons to good use in his rule of the powerful nation bequeathed him by Richelieu and Mazarin. His recognition of the debt that he owes to Mazarin, who may have secretly married his mother, is marked by his ordering full mourning for the dead minister.

Popes gild Rome in Baroque style

St Peter's throne, by Bernini: the focus of the great Roman basilica.

Rome, c.1662
Rome has been transformed into a city of elegant splendour under the last three Popes, Urban VIII, Innocent X and Alexander VII. Gianlorenzo Bernini, Europe's leading sculptor and architect, is now creating a new setting for St Peter's with a vast oval piazza surrounded by colonnades which encircle it, he says, "like the mother church embracing the world".

The balustrades above the 60-foot (18m) columns are lined with statues of saints like those on the main facade of St Peter's, which was completed in 1612 by Carlo Maderna, the pioneer of a new, highly decorative style. Inside the church, Bernini has completed an elaborate bronze throne of St Peter.

Bernini's sculpture is also beautifying the city with his fountains, like that of the Triton in the Piazza Barberini, and those in the Piazza Navona whose figures seem as alive as the water that courses among them. His *Ecstasy of St Teresa* in the Cornaro chapel illustrates the harmonious technique, showing the saint elevated at the moment of holy rapture.

This style, which some call "Baroque" (from the Spanish meaning "rough") is spreading throughout the whole of Italy. The Venetian republic has commissioned the church of Santa Maria della Salute to be built at the end of the Grand Canal in thanksgiving for Venice's deliverance from the plague of 1630.

"The Glory of the Barberinis": Cortona's ceiling at the Barberini Palace.

Bernini's "Ecstasy of St Teresa".

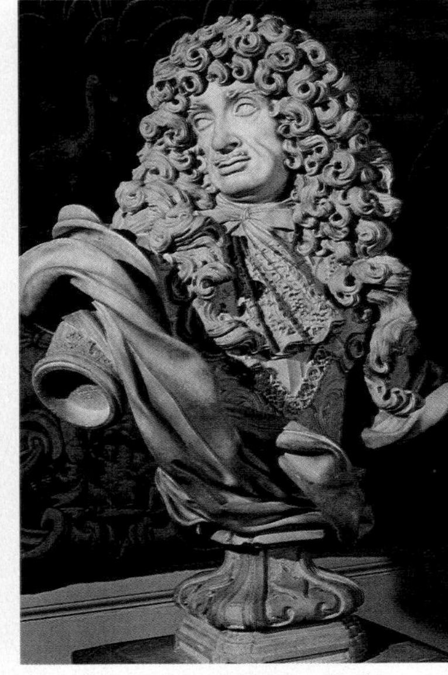
Charles II in marble, by Pelle.

1662 (1662-1664)

London, 3 May 1662. John Winthrop the Younger, the son of the first governor of Massachusetts, has been honoured by being made a fellow of the Royal Society, England's new scientific society. Winthrop has used his election to the society to gain access to the king, who has granted him a new charter uniting the colonies of Connecticut and New Haven.

Paris, 19 August 1662. The French mathematician, theologian and physicist Blaise Pascal dies aged 39. A passionate supporter of the predestinarian Jansenist movement, whose sister was one of the leading membe of the Jansenist Convent at Port Royal, Pascal wrote 18 anonymous pamphlets attacking the Jesuits, prime opponents of Jansenism. When he realised he was dying he asked to be moved to the hospital for incurables so that he could die there in the company of the poor.

England, 12 September 1662. Governor Berkeley of Virginia, in England seeking the revision of the Navigation Acts which severely restrict foreign trade with the colonies, gets a final denial to his appeal.

Amsterdam, 1662. Rembrandt paints *The Syndics*.

France, 1662. England cedes Dunkirk to France for a payment of £ 400,000.

Paris, 1662. Francois, the duke of la Rochefoucauld, publishes his *Memoires*. Destined for an army career, he was involved with the intrigues against Richelieu, which earned him a spell in the Bastille prison in 1637. Hostile to Mazarin, in 1648 he joined in the *Fronde* uprising. Now, re-admitted to favour, he commences a worldly life at court and in the salons.

Japan, 1662. The philosopher Yamaga Soko takes against his masters in a violent way and burns all the books he has written.

China, 1662. The Emperor Kangxi succeeds Shunzhi, who was the first Manchu ruler.

London, 24 March 1663. Charles II awards lands known as Carolina in North America to eight members of the nobility who assisted in his restoration. One of the fortunate is Lord Ashley, who, with the assistance of the philosopher John Locke, has devised a new form of government considered to be one of the most unusual colonial systems so far. It will grant nobility to any person in a position to buy 3,000 acres of land.

England, 8 July 1663. The crown grants Rhode Island a charter guaranteeing freedom of worship.

London, 27 July 1663. Parliament passes a second Navigation Act, requiring all goods for the colonies to travel in British ships from British ports. An extension of the 1651 act, it aims to make England and its colonies less dependent on foreign trade. It is unlikely that the new act will significantly curtail the flourishing smugglers' trade which has developed in response to the earlier restrictions.

Angola, December 1663. The princess dona Ana de Souza dies.

New Netherland, 1663. One Laurens Duyts is sentenced to be flogged and have his right ear cut off for selling his wife.

London, 1663. The Dutch physicist Christiaan Huygens becomes a member of the Royal Society.

North America, 1663. Witches are said to be attempting to undermine the new communities struggling to establish themselves in America. In Connecticut alone, ten offenders have been hanged for "familiarity with the Devil". Strangely, Rhode Island, which is criticised for religious tolerance by the Puritans, has escaped the witches' grasp.

London, 22 March 1664. Charles II has given large tracts of land, from the west of the Connecticut river to the east of Delaware Bay in North America, to his brother James, the duke of York. Much of the land has been claimed by the Dutch, but James has urged the king to help him conquer the New Netherlands, arguing that the continuing presence of Dutch colonists is inhibiting the enforcement of the Navigation Act, which promotes a British monopoly on colonial trade.

New Jersey, 24 June 1664. The area between the Hudson and Delaware rivers is named New Jersey in honour of the new proprietor, Sir George Carteret, the ex-governor of the Isle of Jersey.

Massachusetts, 23 July 1664. Wealthy non-church members get the right to vote.

New Netherlands, July 1664. The Dongan treaty makes the Iroquois subjects of the English king.

Madrid, 27 August 1664. Famous and sought-after in earlier years, the religious painter Francisco Zurbaran dies in poverty and neglect.

France, 1664. Armand de Rance reforms the Trappist order of monks in Soligny, instituting the rule of silence.

New Netherlands, 1664. Horse racing becomes the first organised sport in north America, as Governor Nicolls establishes the Newmarket course at Hempstead plains, Long Island.

Vengeful Russians terrorise Persians

Persia, 1664

In Mazandaran and the Ashurada peninula, by the shores of the Caspian Sea, the populace is living in terror of the notorious robber-baron Stenka Razin and his marauding Cossacks. Their raids have exacerbated Persian fear and loathing of their Russian neighbours.

The present troubles are the result of a diplomatic mission to the Persian court earlier in the year. The mission, which had 800 followers, was a pretext for Russian traders to evade duty on large quantities of merchandise which they had brought with them, and this aroused Persian resentment. When the Russian ambassadors were rudely treated, and one died, Czar Alexis Mikhailovitch sanctioned the Cossack raids in reprisal.

Star wars sentence Jesuit to execution

Looking at an eclipse in China.

Beijing, 1664

Adam Schall, a Jesuit missionary who has spent all his adult life in China, has been condemned to death by dismemberment after being found guilty of accusations made against him by a jealous Chinese astronomer whose calculations he proved to be wrong.

At one stage Schall, who wore the robes of a Chinese scholar and spoke perfect Chinese, was appointed director of the Bureau of Astronomy. But his influence faded, perhaps because he tried too persistently to convert the emperor and his foes. Other missionaries, who thought that he was too Chinese, and jealous Chinese astronomers began to undermine him in Rome and in Beijing.

The Chinese accused him of preparing a Christian revolution and he was found guilty. He is old and ill and it is unlikely that he will be executed, but his lifelong work is certain to be destroyed.

New prayerbook is a must for clergy

England, 1662

A new edition of the Book of Common Prayer, first composed in 1549 by the Protestant martyr Thomas Cranmer, has been issued. As part of the Act of Uniformity, which is designed to restore the Anglican Church to the status it enjoyed before the Commonwealth, the prayerbook is to be imposed on all congregations.

Any clergyman who has not accepted the revised Prayerbook by St Bartholemew's Day (24 August) will forfeit his living. It is expected that a number will still resist, but the bishops, outlawed by Cromwell and restored by King Charles, are determined to reinstitute their authority come what may.

Essays on women's equality published

England, 1662

Women's liberation is the subject of the duchess of Newcastle's latest book, *Orations of Diverse Persons*. The author, better known as the playwright and essayist Margaret Cavendish, concludes that women are the powerful sex, although their domination of men comes through the wiles of love.

Margaret Cavendish was born in 1624, the daughter of Sir Thomas Lucas. She spent two unhappy years at Charles I's court, and in 1645 married Newcastle, a royalist. While they lived in exile in Paris, she wrote poetry, her autobiography, and philosophy. She returned to England after the Restoration to gain a reputation as a popular writer and court eccentric.

Royal Society founded

Leading figures in science, philosophy and the arts are joining the Royal Society: Isaac Newton, Christopher Wren, Robert Boyle and John Locke.

London, 1662
Several groups of scientists have formed a society dedicated to the pursuit of learning. The principal group is that of John Wilkins, which dates back to Oxford in the 1650s and includes such luminaries as John Wallis the mathematician, the chemist and physicist Robert Boyle, the medical researcher Thomas Willis and the great polymath and architect Christopher Wren. These have been joined by people associated with Gresham College and a number of interested and influential royalists.

The society's principal aim is to act as a centre of intellectual debate and excellence, dedicated to scientific enterprise. This will mean, among other things, the financing of buildings, scientific instruments, laboratories and a library. The new Royal Society, as it has been named, levies an annual subscription on its members in order to maintain its independence and to publish a journal called *Philosophical Transactions*.

The society excludes such topics as theology and rhetoric and emphasises instead the "useful arts", such as the work of navigators and engineers, as well as academic scientists. Distinguished contemporary writers, Samuel Pepys among them, are beginning to subscribe. The meetings and lectures are lively and provide a focal point for the most eminent men to air their views, free from any government intervention. In France, a royal academy of sciences may be founded along similar lines.

Gas said to grow when it's on the boil

London, 1662
The Anglo-Irish chemist and physicist Robert Boyle has formulated an important law governing the compression and expansion of gases kept at constant temperatures. The law states that the pressure of a given quantity of gas varies inversely with its volume provided that the temperature is kept constant. Boyle, aged 35, has arrived at this formulation after numerous experiments at Oxford where he has been helped by the inventor Robert Hooke.

However, this is not Boyle's only achievement. He has also shown the crucial role of air in combustion, breathing, the circulation of the blood and the transmission of sound. His is a wide-ranging curiosity. He is concerned about the behaviour of gases and the nature of chemical substances, and also is investigating the freezing of water, the refractive properties of glass and the nature of electricity.

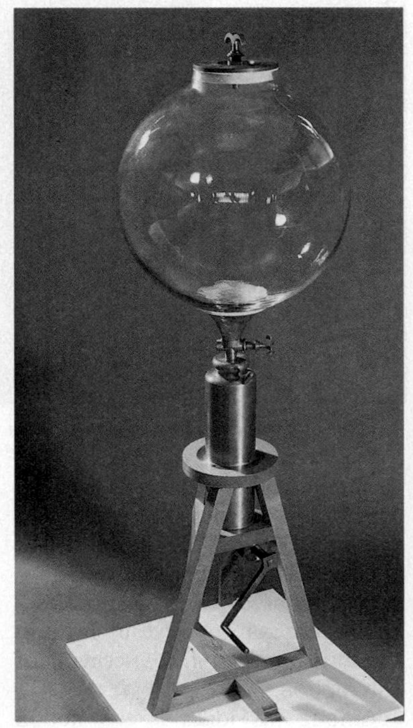

The apparatus used by Boyle and his colleague Robert Hooke.

"Great Elector" has firm hold on Prussia

Prussia, 1663
Frederick William is proving himself to be the "Great Elector" of Brandenburg, which has become the heart of the powerful Prussian kingdom. The elector (ruler) took over his country when he was only 20, and is energetically laying the foundations of what could prove to be military greatness for the region. Frederick has dealt firmly with the *diet*, (parliament), and has taken on himself the responsibility of raising and collecting taxes. This money is being used to build a formidable standing army. He is also improving his country by encouraging industry, building canals and developing a postal system, and he is greatly interested in the arts.

Transvestite highway robber reveals all

London, 1662
Moll Cutpurse died in 1659, aged 75, leaving a full account of her criminal life. The book, published this year, tells how Mary Frith, the cobbler's daughter from the Barbican, became Moll, the famous highway robber.

Always armed and dressed as a man, Moll made an illicit fortune. Jailed only once, for robbing General Fairfax on Hounslow Heath, she escaped by paying a £2,000 bribe. Moll enraged her victims by opening a shop in Fleet Street where they had to pay to recover their own possessions.

Robber Moll in her usual costume.

Nuns of Port Royal defy Louis XIV

Port Royal, France, 26 August 1664
The nuns of the convent of Port Royal, the centre of Jansenist belief, are defying both their king and the pope and refusing to accept the "Formulaire", under which they are to renounce their beliefs. Some have signed the paper, but they have demanded an extra clause, stating the distinction between what they accept as law and what they actually believe.

As Jansenists, the sisters follow the teachings of St Augustine, with their stress on "original sin" and "irresistible grace".

Mother Agnes of Port Royal kneels to pray at the side of another sister.

1664 (1664-1665)

Hungary, 1 August 1664. A Turkish army is defeated at St Gotthard by French and German troops led by the imperial commander Montecuccoli. The battle is hailed as a triumph of Christianity over the infidel.

New Amsterdam, 5 September 1664. After several days of tense negotiation, the Dutch settlement of New Amsterdam has surrendered, without firing a shot, to British forces. The British move was ordered by King Charles II, and took the Dutch quite by surprise. Britain now controls ports from Virginia to Massachusetts, and will be better able to enforce the Navigation Act, which provides for a British monopoly on colonial trade.

Maryland, September 1664. In the latest of a series of laws dealing with slavery, marriages between white women and black men are declared a disgrace to the nation, and the children of such unions are ruled to be slaves.

Carolina, November 1664. Proprietors split the northern part of the colony into the counties of Albemarle and Clarendon.

France, 1664. The French East India Company is founded.

Netherlands, 1664. The Dutch artist Franz Hals paints the *Governors of the Old Men's Home at Haarlem*, a magnificent group portrait.

France, 12 January 1665. The French mathematician Pierre de Fermat dies at Toulouse. He made many discoveries in the theory of numbers, worked out a simple method of quadrating parabolas, and established a method of calculating probabilities.

New York, 11 March 1665. A new legal code is approved for the Dutch and English towns of New York, guaranteeing all Protestants the right to continue their religious observances unhindered.

Spain, 17 September 1665. King Philip IV has just died. Despite his many mistresses and his playboy reputation, it has been said that he laughed only three times in his life. Velazquez, who painted numerous portraits of him, was his only friend. He is succeeded by Charles II, a sickly four-year-old prince, under the regency of Marie-Anne.

Virginia, December 1665. Two actors, brought to trial for frivolity in the first play in the English colonies, *Ye Bare and Ye Cubb*, are acquitted, having performed much of the play to a delighted court.

America, 1665. There are about 75,000 English colonists in the New World, compared with 7,500 French settlers.

Angola, 1665. The Portuguese colonists based in Angola invade the Kongo, but are unable to subdue local resistance.

Paris, 1665. La Rochefoucauld publishes his *Maximes*, which cause a scandal on account of the decidedly pessimistic view of man that they reveal. They condemn the selfish motivation behind passions, feelings and social relationships: "Our virtues are often no more than disguised vices."

Japan, 1665. Yamaga Soko, a controversial leading scholar, publishes a short book, entitled *Essentials of the Sacred Teachings*, which questions accepted interpretations of Confucian thought. As an attack on the ideological foundation of the *shogunate*, the book is banned and Soko is banished from Edo and placed in the custody of the lord of Ako.

Indian Ocean, 1665. The French take Bourbon Island (*Reunion*).

Italy, 1665. The Italian Jesuit and physicist Francesco Grimaldi's *Physicomathesis de Lumine* demonstrating the diffraction of light, is published posthumously. He is also remembered for elaborating on the topography of the moon.

Rome, 1665. The French painter Nicolas Poussin dies in the city where he has spent most of his life. His work has made him a major figure in French classicism.

Portugal, 1665. The Spaniards are crushed at the battle of Montes Claros by the marquis of Marialva.

England, 1665. The scientist Isaac Newton conducts experiments with the force which attracts things to earth.

Netherlands, 1665. The Dutch are at war with Britain for the second time this decade. English attacks on Dutch slave traders in West Africa in 1663, and the taking of New Amsterdam (now renamed New York) last year, have provoked this renewed conflict.

Netherlands, 1665. The Dutch artist Jan Vermeer paints the *Lacemaker* and *Young Woman with Water Jug* in Delft.

England, 1665. The English chemist and physicist Robert Hooke discovers that plants "breathe" and that they contain living cells.

Ethiopia, 1665. Johannes succeeds King Fazilidas.

Italy, 1665. The Italian astronomer Giovanni Cassini determines the periods of Jupiter, Mars and Venus.

England, 1665. Peter Chamberlen, the court physician to Charles II, invents the midwifery forceps.

Spain's playboy king, Philip IV, is dead

Madrid, 17 September 1665

Philip IV, the king who preferred the theatre in Madrid to the theatre of world politics, died today after a 44-year reign during which his country gradually declined.

From the very beginning of his reign Philip handed over power to favourites, the count of Olivares in particular, preferring to spend his time in the company of actresses selected as companions by his agents. While the king thus dallied at court, Olivares committed Spain abroad to tasks beyond her strength and there were frequent setbacks. The Netherlands were never reconquered, Spain lost a war with France, and Catalonia and Portugal both revolted.

Philip, who was 60, had numerous mistresses, by whom he had at least 30 bastards, but the throne passes to his only legitimate son, Charles II, a sickly child.

Philip: mistresses and misfortune.

Priest is lowered into volcano for science

Kircher's picture of the fires that burn deep within the Earth's core.

Germany, 1665

Athanasius Kircher, the gifted and energetic German Jesuit priest and scholar, has had himself lowered into the crater of the volcano Vesuvius in order to observe its features and behaviour in the aftermath of an eruption.

Among his ideas is the notion that Earth has a fiery core. In his geological textbook *The Subterranean World*, Kircher describes our planet in terms of a furnace at the centre with many fire carrying channels spreading outwards to the surface. These are the sources of volcanoes and provide the heat for hot springs. Many people are attracted by these ideas of a hot turbulent core to Earth. Kircher's book looks set to become a standard work of reference.

Executions boost Ottoman fortunes

Ottoman Empire, 1664
After two regicides and several decades of decline, the fortunes of the Ottoman empire have been restored largely through the efforts of successive grand viziers, members of the Koprulu family.

In 1656, after eight years of intrigue following the execution of Sultan Ibrahim, Sultana Turhan, the mother of the boy-sultan, Mehmed IV, called upon the 71-year-old Koprulu Mehmed, an Albanian-born former scullion who had risen to become a governor, to restore order as grand vizier. He accepted on condition that he was given almost absolute power.

Koprulu Mehmed renewed pride and discipline in the army, recaptured Tenedos and Lemnos from the Venetians, suppressed revolts, and had 35,000 executed during his five-year rule. He was succeeded three years ago at his palace, the Bab-i-Ali – now the effective seat of power – by his 26-year-old son, Fazil Ahmed, with the 20-year-old sultan's full consent.

A serpent goblet: a glass bowl surmounts a winged serpent.

Turks halted by Habsburg defences

Austria, 10 August 1664
The Turkish advance into Austria has been halted at St Gotthard, and peace agreed. This effectively renews the treaty of Zsitvatorok, with the Habsburgs paying money to the sultan, evacuating Transylvania and recognising the Ottoman vassal Apafy. The sultan also retains much of northern Hungary, and the newly-conquered stronghold of Neuhausel.

Habsburg incursions into Transylvania triggered this latest conflict three years ago, when Ottoman armies responded by invading Transylvania and Hungary. In June last year, Sultan Mehmed made a rare appearance at the head of his army before returning to the hunting field, leaving Koprulu Fazil Ahmed, his grand vizier, to march on, with the support of Tartars, Wallachians and disgruntled Hungarian peasants, to devastate the territories of Moravia and Silesia.

As Koprulu's armies advanced from Belgrade towards Vienna, the Habsburgs succeeded in persuading their Christian allies to come to their aid. With French and German support, the Austrian general Montecuccoli held the right bank of the Raab. At St Gotthard, French auxiliaries played a crucial role in repelling the superior numbers of the Ottomans, destroying most of their cannon and equipment. The Ottomans remained a threat, however, and Montecuccoli wanted peace.

English name New York

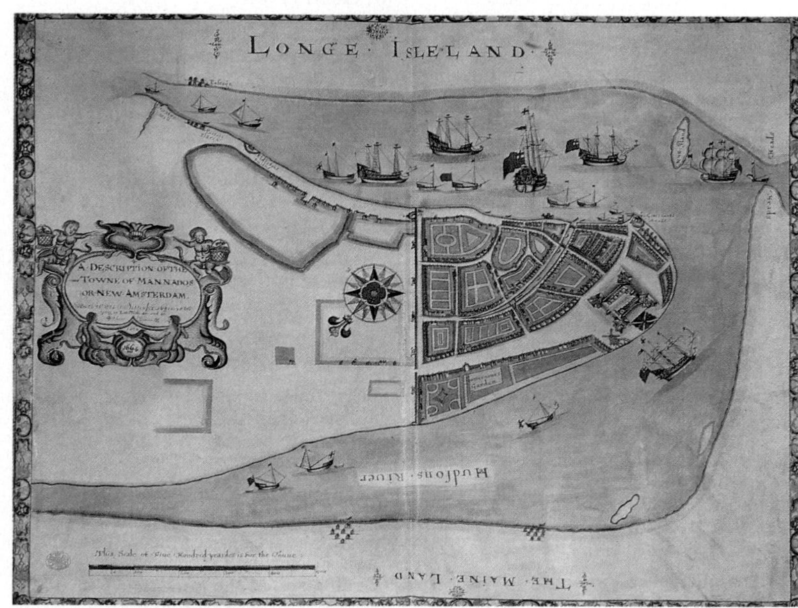

The most recent town plan of Manhattan, Long Island and New York.

Manhattan Island, 2 February 1665
Almost 40 years after the Canarsee Indians sold Manhattan Island to Dutch settlers for $24, the English have established themselves there and today renamed it "New York" after its new proprietor, the king's brother, the duke of York.

The Dutch paid for the island in beads to create a sanctuary for their farmers throughout New England, many under attack by Indians. With deep inlets, fresh water and fertile soil it is a natural fortress, but that was insufficient to keep out the British. A fleet armed with 120 guns and 500 experienced soldiers demanded surrender. Should Governor Peter Stuyvesant have stood his ground? He had just 20 cannon, 250 soldiers and many civilians pleading with him not to fight.

The English commander, Colonel Richard Nicholls, sent a letter promising to recognise human rights and trade with Holland. As tapers smouldered over the cannon, awaiting his order, Stuyvesant walked away saying "I would rather be carried to my grave". England's Charles II, needing a victory for the credibility of the restored monarchy, is reported to be overjoyed at this one.

Londoners flee from the city in panic as plague kills 100,000

London, 28 September 1665
The capital is in the grip of the worst attack of plague since the Black Death two centuries ago, with fears that the death toll could be as high as 100,000.

Official figures put last week's deaths from bubonic plague at 7,000 – the highest since the outbreak began. In July, deaths were averaging 200 a week.

Business has ground to a halt and most of the roads out of London are choked with traffic as people flee the city. Homes affected by the plague have warning red crosses daubed on the doors accompanied by the plea "Lord have mercy upon us". The commonest sound on the streets is the mournful toll of church bells announcing yet another funeral. With graveyards overflowing, corpses are now being laid on top of each other in large plague pits.

Treatment for the sick is almost non-existent because of a shortage of doctors and chemists. In Westminster all the doctors have been killed by the plague. Experts say that victims have only a one in ten chance of recovery. Symptoms usually include sores and enlarged glands, often in the groin. Patients generally run very high fevers accompanied by splitting headaches.

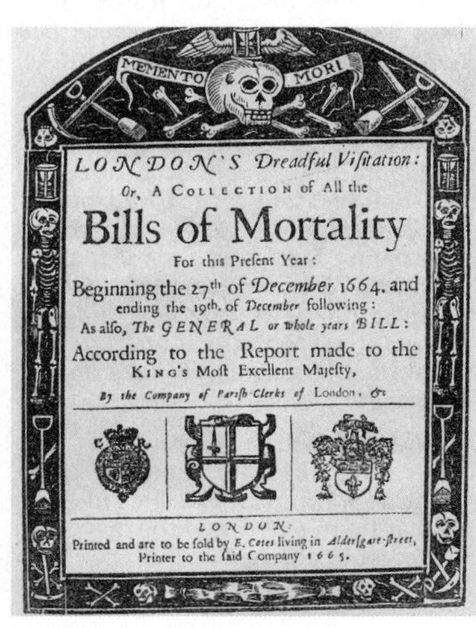

MEMENTO MORI

LONDON'S Dreadful Visitation:
Or, A Collection of All the
Bills of Mortality
For this Present Year:
Beginning the 27th of December 1664. and ending the 19th. of December following:
As also, The GENERAL or whole years BILL:
According to the Report made to the King's Most Excellent Majesty,
By the Company of Parish Clerks of London. &c.

LONDON:
Printed and are to be sold by E. Cotes living in Aldersgate-street, Printer to the said Company 1665.

Counting the corpses in 1664.

1665 (1665-1667)

England, 1665. The Baptist John Bunyan writes *The Holy City* while serving a prison sentence, which began in 1660, for preaching other than in a parish church.

Paris, 20 January 1666. The queen mother is dead. The daughter of Philip III of Spain, she married Louis XIII in 1615. She took part in the plots against Richelieu and was accused of treason for having been in secret correspondence with her brother, the king of Spain. In 1648, on the death of Louis XIII, she became regent, and when her son Louis XIV took power in 1651 she retired to Val de Grace.

India, January 1666. The deposed Moghul Emperor Shahjahan dies. Since 1658 he had been confined by his son Aurangzeb in Agra fort from where he could gaze over the Taj Mahal where his beloved empress lies buried. Shahjahan himself was in revolt against his father from 1624 until he succeeded on his death in 1627.

Anatolia, May 1666. The religious leader Sabbatai Zevi, after a forced conversion to Islam, proclaims himself as the Messiah.

Paris, 4 June 1666. Moliere's *Le Misanthrope* (The Misanthropist) is performed.

Paris, June 1666. Louis XIV restricts the rights of the parliament in Paris.

Italy, 1666. The painter Giovanni Guercino dies in Bologna. He worked for Pope Gregory XV and has lived in Bologna since 1630.

France, 1666. The architect Francois Mansart dies. His buildings are characteristically sophisticated and luxurious; his first masterpiece was the Orleans wing of the *chateau* at Blois, which is unfortunately incomplete. Mansart was notoriously difficult to employ and was dismissed many times in the middle of a project by an infuriated employer. His most complete work is at Maison Lafitte, a country house near Paris.

India, 1666. Sivaji, the leader of the Marathas of western India, has fled in secret from the Emperor Aurangzeb's Moghul court in Agra. After various successful military operations against the Moghuls, Sivaji had been forced to submit and had come to Agra requesting only that Aurangzeb recognise him as an independent prince. When it became clear that the negotiations were not going his way, Sivaji took flight and has returned to his people, bent on revenge.

Spain, 1666. The painter Bartolome Murillo, a protege of Velazquez, finishes a series of 22 great figures of saints for the Capuchin convent.

Southern Africa, 1666. The Dutch take Saldanha Bay, near the Cape of Good Hope.

New Jersey, 1666. The governor, Philip Carteret, lures settlers from New Haven to New Jersey with land grants. Newly arrived colonists form settlements on the model of New England towns.

West Africa, 1666. The Gulf of Guinea is explored for the first time by the French.

Japan, 1666. The master of Japanese pottery, Kakiemon, dies.

Paris, 1666. The English scientist and mathematician, Isaac Newton, develops his differential calculus.

Paris, 1666. Louis XIV's chief minister, Jean-Baptiste Colbert, the marquis de Seignelay, founds the Royal Academy of Sciences.

Rome, 22 May 1667. Pope Alexander VII dies. For much of his rule he was in conflict with the French over the Gallican articles which asserted the king's independent power in temporal affairs. The situation deteriorated to such an extent that the French invaded the papal city of Avignon. Alexander will also be remembered for taking steps to suppress the radical Jansenist movement and employing Bernini to build the colonnade of St Peter's square. He is succeeded by Clement IX.

Virginia, 23 September 1667. A new law passed in Williamsburg bans slaves from obtaining freedom by converting to Christianity.

Paris, 17 November 1667. Jean Racine's tragedy *Andromache* is staged, and praised by Louis XIV.

Rome, 1667. The Italian architect Francesco Borromini commits suicide after finishing the facade of *St Charles of the Four Fountains.*

Lisbon, 1667. King Alfonso VI is deposed. His wife, the Princess of Savoy, has him replaced by his brother. Alfonso is imprisoned in the castle at Sintra, not far from Lisbon.

Germany, 1667. The composer Johann Froberger dies. He was court organist at Vienna for 20 years until 1657 and will be best remembered for his suites for the harpsichord.

Portugal, 1667. The writer Francisco Manuel de Melo dies. In 1640 he abandoned the Spanish language for Portuguese in honour of John, the duke of Braganza who became king of Portugal with the expulsion of Philip IV of Spain from the country. He will perhaps be better remembered for his critical works and his history of the Catalan wars than for his voluminous poetry.

New laws herald golden age for trade

International traders search for profits on Amsterdam's Stock Exchange.

London, c.1666

Bold new attitudes towards finance and commerce are being displayed by City magnates and their representatives in the Restoration parliament. With the granting to the East India Company of full liberty to export ingots to India, a free market in money has, in effect, been created, and a cherished pillar of financial rectitude has gone.

For years the nabobs have been complaining that the potential for trade is enormous but that restrictions on bullion exports have held it back. Now they will have all the funds they need.

It has long been held that the wealth of a nation depends on its possession of precious metals; their export should therefore be curbed, as should all avoidable imports of goods. Now with the emphasis on exploiting the new overseas colonies, bullion is seen as as much a commodity as any other.

Trade has been further boosted by the passing of the Navigation Act prohibiting the import of any goods carried in foreign ships. This has led to a big increase in the merchant marine and produced a formidable challenge to the Dutch domination of overseas commerce.

Despite the success of the Dutch and English East and West India Companies, which operate untrammelled by their home governments, there is no suggestion of free trade. Many still believe that there is a finite amount of world trade and that a country can only expand at the expense of others. Mercantile orthodoxy favours protectionism at home with colonies trading only with the mother country.

Indian textiles and Indian servants: the fruits of an expanding empire.

Fire devastates London

Londoners seek shelter on the river Thames: Stadler's aquatint of 1799.

London, 5 September 1666
At last, after four days and nights, the fire of London has been halted by the duke of York, who brought in naval gunpowder teams to blow up buildings in the path of the flames. Some 400 acres have been razed with 87 churches and over 13,000 houses destroyed. Miraculously, only nine lives were lost.

The fire started during last Sunday night in a baking house in Pudding Lane. When the parish watchman called out Sir Thomas Bloodworth, the lord mayor, he responded irritably: "Pish! A woman might piss it out." He went back to bed. But according to the diarist Samuel Pepys, next day he cried like a fainting woman: "Lord, what can I do? I am spent."

People were desperate to save their goods, even flinging them into the river. Houses were pulled down, but the flames leapt across the gaps. Pepys loaded his iron chests and bags of gold onto a cart and, riding in his nightgown, took them with his wife to Woolwich. People are camping in fields outside the city, covering themselves with a few rags. The king has promised them bread and told them to ignore rumours of a foreign plot.

Firemen use hoses, pumps and leather buckets to battle the fire.

Polish king cedes Ukraine to Russia

Andrusovo, Russia, February 1667
A ten-year war between Russia and Poland is over, with the Polish king, John Casimir V, renouncing his claim to Smolensk, Kiev and a large part of the Ukraine on the left bank of the Dnieper. Lithuania remains in Polish hands. The settlement represents a belated victory for the Ukrainian Cossacks. A campaign against Polish domination from 1648 to 1656 was led by the Cossack Bogdan Khmelnitski, who abandoned the fickle Tartar alliance to put himself under Russian protection in 1654.

Cossack leads peasants' war in Russia

Russia, November 1667
Stenka Razin, the rebel Cossack chieftain to whom the peasantry are now flocking in ever-increasing numbers, has refused to submit in return for a pardon from the czar. Russia is on the verge of civil war.

For the past 20 years, peasants' revolts have broken out sporadically, in protest at price increases in salt and copper, food shortages and the tyranny of serfdom. While bandits roam the countryside, protected by the peasantry, the Cossacks have been plundering the czar's ships on the Volga. Last year the Cossack Vaska Us marched towards Moscow to appeal to the czar, collecting several thousand supporters. He returned after refusing to hand over the rebels.

Stenka Razin has now become the chief rebel, having raided ships, massacred nobles and officers and, in June, taken the fortress of Yaitsk, threatening Astrakhan.

Quaker woman writes treatise on religion

England, 1666
Margaret Fell, a devout widow and mother of nine, has written a book titled *Women's Speaking Justified, Proved and Knowed of the Scriptures*. It explains the revolutionary ideas she shares with her husband-to-be George Fox, the leader of the Society of Friends. Fell's campaign for religious freedom is based on Fox's doctrine that the Christian spirit in people has no need for church services conducted by paid ministers to sustain it.

Fell, who comes from an educated, land-owning family, helped Fox, a Leicestershire cobbler, to develop the political organisation of the Quakers. When Friends were sent to prison she pleaded with Charles II for their release, and in 1663 was sent there herself for refusing to take the Oath of Allegiance.

An uncomplimentary picture of a Quaker meeting by Heemskerk.

Japanese potter sold his ware to the west

Japan, 1666
Sakaida Kakiemon, a master potter, has died at the age of 70. His most oustanding achievement was the development of overglaze enamel-decorated porcelain, in particular the red enamel colour.

Kakiemon won local fame when he presented his gold, silver and coloured enamel to the lord of Nabeshima and became the first Japanese potter to sell his ware to Europeans. It is said that his name was originally Kizaemon, but he was renamed Kakiemon by a nobleman for whom he had made a porcelain ornament in the form of two persimmons, whose Japanese name is *kaki*.

A ceramic dog by Kakiemon, the epitome of the master's style.

1667 (1667-1669)

Netherlands, 31 July 1667. The peace of Breda ends the war between the English and Dutch. Trade laws are modified in favour of the Dutch who also gain possession of Surinam and re cognise English control over New York (which was New Amsterdam), New Jersey and Delaware.

London, 1667. The English chemist Robert Hooke proposes that the weather be recorded systematically.

London, 30 August 1667. Edward Hyde, the first earl of Clarendon, has been dismissed as lord chancellor by Charles II. He had been held largely responsible for the humiliating treaty of Breda signed in July, and this has brought about his downfall. Hyde has played a large part in the formation of colonial policy, favouring a strong crown in the face of colonial ambitions and supporting religious freedom.

Paris, 1667. A new magistracy is created in Paris, that of general lieutenant of the police. The duties are wide-ranging, including security, supervision of customs and censorship of books.

France, 1667. The marquise of Montespan becomes Louis XIV's mistress. Her husband the marquis is thrown into the Bastille.

Italy, 1667. Pietro-Antonio Cesti composes *Il Pomo d'Oro*.

Amsterdam, 1667. The painter Pieter de Hooch comes to live in Amsterdam after a stay in Delft where he met Fabritius and Vermeer. Influenced by the latter, his works reflect the intimacy of comfortable middle-class homes, with welcoming atmospheres.

Amsterdam, 1667. Johann de Witt passes the exclusion act which prevents the prince of Orange from becoming a stadholder (provincial governor).

Russia, 1667. The Cossack Stenka Razin leads a peasant uprising.

The Hague, 23 January 1668. During the War of Devolution, the Triple Alliance is formed between England, Holland and Sweden to defend the Netherlands against the ambitions of the French king, Louis XIV, who is pursuing a claim based on his wife's rights as Spanish *infanta*.

New England, 24 March 1668. Governor Edmund Andros takes personal control of colonial militias to quiet unrest.

Long Island, 25 March 1668. The first American trophy for horse racing is awarded to Captain Sylvester Salisbury.

France, 2 May 1668. The peace of Aix-la-Chapelle ends the War of Devolution.

Massachusetts, 27 May 1668. Thomas Gold, William Turner and John Farnum are the first Baptists to be expelled from the colony.

Maine, 6 July 1668. A convention at York accepts rule by Massachusetts, voting to send deputies to the General Court.

Poland, 16 September 1668. King John Casimir V abdicates. His reign has been one of the darkest periods in Poland's history, with foreign powers threatening partition, and internal strife amongst aristocratic factions.

England, 1668. The poet and essayist John Dryden publishes his *Essay of Dramatick Poesy* in which he attempts to reconcile the traditions of English drama with French classical taste.

North America, 1668. Father Jacques Marquette establishes the first colony in the northern plains.

Germany, 1668. Helvelius publishes his *Cometographia*, a systematic notation of all known comets.

Florida, 1668. The English buccaneer Robert Searles frees Henry Woodward from Spanish captivity.

Lisbon, 1668. The Spanish sign a peace treaty recognising Portuguese independence.

England, 17 August 1669. Three ships under Joseph West sail for Carolina via Barbados, funded by Carolina proprietors in their first sign of willingness to absorb the costs of settlement.

North America, 1669. Exploration of the north-west continues: several Jesuit missionaries have established permanent settlements and the explorer Robert Cavalier, the sieur de la Salle, has entered into friendly relations with the Iroquois. In Virginia, a German adventurer, Johann Lederer, has been granted a permit to explore westwards, and has made three journeys through the passes in the western region of the colony (*into the Blue Ridge Mountains and Kentucky*).

France, 1669. A Turkish ambassador to the court of Louis XIV starts a new trend: coffee-drinking. First drunk as a medicine, it is soon a social habit and is sold by street vendors and in shops and cafes. Both critics and enthusiasts cite the fact that it keeps the drinker awake.

Crete, 1669. The Venetians lose the Mediterranean island of Crete, their last colonial possession, to the Turks.

Massachusetts, 1669. The colony of Plymouth founds the first recorded Sunday School.

Dutch fleet in Thames threatens London

Dutch ships under admiral de Ruyter burn four ships of Britain's fleet as they lie at anchor in the Medway: this attack has badly damaged English pride.

London, 18 June 1667

The Dutch have humiliated the English by breaking through the Chatham defensive chain and sailing up the Thames to sink or burn four ships of the line and tow away the pride of the fleet, the *Royal Charles*.

The English went into the war two and a half years ago cheerfully confident that they could beat the Dutch by seizing their shipping. It did not work. Then England received two heavy blows: the Great Plague was followed by the Great Fire of London, and economic life was crippled. The fateful decision not to assemble a battle fleet for 1667 was taken. Now the price has been paid.

Blind Milton dictated "Paradise Lost"

Satan, Sin and Death: an 18th-century illustration to Paradise Lost.

London, 20 August 1667

John Milton's epic poem, *Paradise Lost*, has been published after much delay. In ten "books" it tells the story of the Fall of Adam and Eve in such a way as to "justify the ways of God to men". Milton has abandoned rhyme, but the sonorous power of his lines is greater than ever. For instance, Satan is thrown out of heaven "sheer o'er the crystal battlements, dropped from the zenith like a falling star".

Milton, who called Cromwell "our chief of men", served as Latin secretary to the Commonwealth, justified the execution of the king and saw his pamphlets burned by the public hangman after the Restoration. Since 1652 he has been quite blind and depends on an amanuensis to take his dictation.

French give nationalist flavour to trade

Paris, 1667

Jean-Baptiste Colbert, the French chief minister, has taken another step on his nationalistic approach to finance. Having already carried out reforms giving Louis XIV power over the conduct of commerce, he has prepared a new tariff which will seriously affect the commerce of English and Dutch merchants who trade with France.

This draper's son has a hard-headed way of dealing with Louis' finances, and his ambition is to make France the wealthiest state in Europe. More money, he says, "will increase the power, the greatness and the affluence of the state".

He does not confine himself to fiscal matters. He seeks also to industrialise France and is putting state capital into many enterprises. Some concerns, especially those dealing with supplies for the army and navy, are being taken over completely by the state. In all this activity Colbert is not neglecting his own finances. Like the late Cardinal Mazarin, his patron, he is amassing a huge personal fortune.

Colbert: his new tariffs will boost France but harm the rest of Europe.

Turks take Crete after 21-year siege

Dutch men-of-war and Turkish galleys mingle off Constantinople: Ottoman power has beaten Venice despite the republic's support from many allies.

Candia, Crete, 27 September 1669

After a 21-year siege, the capital of Crete has fallen to the Ottomans. Koprulu Fazil Ahmed, the grand vizier and supreme commander of the Turkish forces, led his troops into Candia to accept a formal surrender that was agreed 22 days ago.

Spain, Britain, France, the pope, Tuscan and Maltese seamen have all supplied arms, men or provisions to the Venetian garrison. But as the Ottomans intensified their blockade, disagreements with the Venetian commander led to a withdrawal of European forces and made surrender inevitable. In return for Venice's evacuation of the island, the sultan is allowing it to retain some trading privileges.

Japanese force ban on self-burning

Japan, 1668

The Japanese government has acted ruthlessly to stamp out the practise of *junshi*, or self-immolation, in which followers of a dead warlord burn themselves to death. This custom, which came about because it was said that a warrior could not serve two masters and must therefore end his own life when his lord died, was banned five years ago; but it persisted.

Recently a *samurai* attached to the warlord Tadamasa committed junshi. Retribution has been swift. The samurai's two children have been executed and other relatives sent into exile. It is hoped that this exemplary punishment will finish junshi for ever.

Spanish Netherlands fall to French army

Flanders, 1667

A magnificent French army of 70,000 men, the best seen in Europe since Roman times, has advanced into Flanders, taking control of a dozen fortresses with hardly any resistance from the dispirited and outnumbered Spanish army. The French are commanded by the able General Turenne, but Louis XIV is present in all his glory. It is his war, mounted to establish the rights of his Spanish queen and their son to their Spanish inheritance following the death of her father, the late Philip IV.

Born-again London is a thriving capital

London, 1669

Five years after the Great Plague and four after the Fire that burnt it out, London is flourishing as never before. Thriving trade, a burst of new building, improved civic amenities and, above all, an energetic citizenry are combining to make London one of Europe's most influential cities.

The Great Fire may have destroyed much of old London, but it has opened up opportunities for new, exciting development. The Guildhall has been rebuilt under the direction of Sir Christopher Wren, who is also designing a monument to the Fire. London is expanding too. Leicester and Bloomsbury Squares have extended the "West End", while the aristocracy are flocking to St James.

The Fire spurred the growth of better public amenities. Building in brick, rather than wood, means that houses will be cleaner. New laws covering street-cleaning will help limit fresh plague attacks. Perhaps London's most outstanding novelty is the rash of coffee houses, where men gather to talk, to trade and to discuss affairs. The free flow of information to be sampled at every table are enabling the coffee houses to be seen as the best place outside the universities to improve one's learning.

One of the many new coffee houses which have been opening up all over London during the past ten years and which are rapidly becoming social and cultural centres. Here the patrons gather in warm and familiar surroundings to gossip, play cards, read the latest news and drink coffee.

1669 (1669-1670)

India, 18 April 1669. Aurangzeb, the Moghul emperor, gives orders that all recently constructed Hindu temples should be razed to the ground.

England, 31 May 1669. The naval administrator and politician Samuel Pepys makes the last entry in the diary that he began on 1 January 1660.

Amsterdam, 4 October 1669. The Dutch painter Rembrandt van Rijn dies in solitude and poverty, having defied the dictates of fashion to pursue his artistic genius. He survived both his son, Titus, and his mistress, Hendrickje Stoffels, with whom he lived after the death of his wife, Saskia. Among a huge volume of brilliant work, Rembrandt's series of self-portraits, spanning a period of 40 years, stand out as some of his greatest masterpieces.

Rome, 1669. The painter and architect Pietro da Cortona dies. He will be best remembered for his frescoes in the Barberini palace in Rome and the Pitti palace in Florence.

Germany, 1669. The German scientist Johann Becher publishes his *Physica Subterranea*, considering the Mosaic account of Creation in the light of contemporary scientific theories.

Germany, 1669. Hans Grimmelshausen publishes his novel *Simplicissimus*, depicting the sufferings of German peasants at the hands of lawless soldiers who overrun their country.

France, 1669. Jean-Baptiste Colbert, Louis XIV's chief financial adviser, known for the stringency of his protectionist measures, becomes secretary of state for the navy.

Germany, 1669. The German chemist Hennig Brand discovers the element phosphorus by chance while distilling a sample of urine.

Germany, 1669. The *Hanse* (an alliance of towns), which was virtually destroyed by the Thirty Years War, is broken up. Its *diet* meets for the last time.

Poland, 1669. The rebellious French noble, the prince of Conde, has been defeated in his bid for the Polish throne, and cast aside in favour of the Lithuanian Michael Wisnowiecki.

North America, 1669. Robert Cavalier explores the mid-west; he is probably the first white man in this region.

India, 1669. Serious disturbances are caused near the imperial capital Delhi when large numbers of the Hindu Jat peasants rise up against Moghul rule.

Italy, 1669. The Italian physiologist Marcello Malpighi studies the lives and habits of silkworms.

Netherlands, 1669. The architect Pieter Post dies. The city of the Hague owes its town hall to him.

Copenhagen, 1669. The geologist Niels Stensen gives the first specific interpretation of the origin of fossil animals, thus setting out the basis for a chronological geology (stratigraphy). He teaches as an anatomist in Copenhagen.

Copenhagen, 1669. Erasmus Bertelsen Bartholin observes that Iceland spar crystals make rays of light that enter them divide (double refraction).

France, 17 February 1670. A Franco-Bavarian treaty is made for concerted action at the death of either of the monarchs Leopold of Germany or Charles II of Spain.

England, 26 May 1670. A treaty is signed in secret at Dover between Charles II and Louis XIV, ending hostilities between them. Henrietta Anne, the duchess of Orleans, the sister of the English king and sister-in-law of Louis XIV, persuaded Charles to sign the treaty, by which he promises to join a French attack on the Dutch, and to support French claims to the Spanish throne if the Spanish king dies childless. Louis promises money and troops for Charles' personal defence and financial aid during the war with the Dutch.

Spain, 18 July 1670. England and Spain sign the treaty of Madrid, by which the Spanish formally recognise English possessions in the West Indies.

Virginia, 13 October 1670. A law is passed ruling that Negroes who arrive in the colonies as Christians cannot be used as slaves.

Paris, 1670. The central body of the Palace of Versailles is completed.

The Hague, 1670. The Dutch-Jewish philosopher Spinoza publishes his *Tractatus* anonymously. The work promotes democracy as the most natural form of government and is unlikely to be welcomed by the authorities.

Virginia, 1670. Sir William Berkeley estimates that there are 2,000 Negro slaves and 6,000 white servants in an overall population of 40,000.

East Africa, 1670. Oman Arabs raid the east coast as far south as Mozambique.

New Jersey, 1670. An attempt at collecting quitrents – rents due on lands that were originally offered free to encourage settlers – sparks off a rebellion.

Isaac Newton kept his calculus secret

Cambridge, England, 1669

Although only 27 years of age, a Cambridge physicist and mathematician, Isaac Newton, has made some important discoveries. The son of a Lincolnshire yeoman, he recognised early on that he was suited to a life of learning and invention. Even as a student at Cambridge, Newton was quick to respond to the key ideas in contemporary science, being much influenced by Kepler, Galileo and Descartes. He began to think about matter as being composed of particles in motion being held together by various forces. In 1665 the university was closed by plague, giving Newton the opportunity to write up some of the many notes he had compiled. One outcome of this was an essay, *Of Colours*, which later became extended into Book One of *Opticks*.

He has published *On Analysis by Infinite Series*, describing what he terms "fluxions" a mathematical tool for analysing the slopes of curves and the areas bounded by them. Although the concept of fluxions, or calculus as it is also known, has been secret so far, there seems little doubt that from now on it will become widely adopted.

Thoughts on the agony of seeking faith

Paris, 1670

The fragmentary thoughts of the great mathematician and philosopher Blaise Pascal, who died four years ago at the age of 39, were discovered after his death and are now published, incomplete, under the title *Pensees*. They express in masterly language the agony of his search for faith, despite the doubts that his powerful intellect raised to torment him.

He was the son of an able mathematician who educated him personally. By the age of 11 he had worked out for himself most of Euclid's geometry, although his father had not yet taught it to him. He also specialised in the mathematics of probability. His experiments in fluid mechanics proved "Pascal's Principle", that the pressure in a liquid is everywhere equal. In 1641 when still a young man, he invented a calculating machine.

But in 1654 he had a revelation that led him to go into the Jansenite convent at Port Royal and join battle with the Jesuits in his *Lettres Provinciales*.

Miguel March's personification of the liberal arts: gathered in this painting are figures representing the vital branches of learning grammar, logic, rhetoric, music, geometry, arithmetic and astronomy.

Spinoza's world is run on reason

The Hague, 1670
A new philosophical work, the *Tractatus Theologico-politicus* has been published anonymously in The Hague. Its author is thought to be Baruch Spinoza, the Jewish philosopher who in 1656 was exiled from Amsterdam when his own community rejected his rationalist philosophies.

The *Tractatus* aims to prove that states are based in natural rather than religious laws. Natural law guarantees every man his liberty. For security's sake, he has ceded some of that liberty to the state. This gives the ruler, whether the monarch or (as in Holland) the government, as guardian and interpreter of both civil and sacred law, his great powers. Spinoza accepts such power, but trusts authority to rule with justice and wisdom.

China produces exquisite silks

A picture, painted on silk, showing the process of silk manufacturing.

China, c.1670.
Technological advances have put the Chinese at the forefront of the world trade in silk. Shantung, Kwangtung and Chekiang are creating great wealth, and across China, silk is second only to tea in agricultural importance.

Intensive study of silk worms' behaviour has enabled the Chinese to regulate the worms' digestion and control their growth. When a cocoon is spun, the chrysalis is killed by steaming, the cocoon boiled before reeling, then threads spun by a machine worked by a single pedal.

Dutch painters tell the inside story

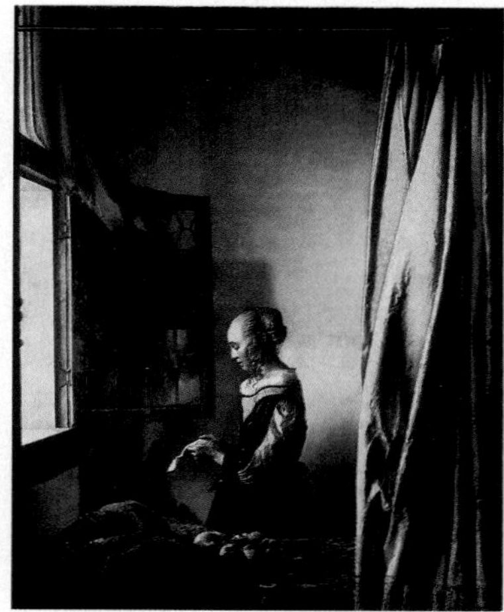
Vermeer's "Girl reading a letter".

"The Beach at Egmond-aan-Zee": a painting by Salomon van Ruysdael.

Delft, 1670
The small town of Delft has gained pre-eminence in Dutch painting. Since Rembrandt's death last year, the two leading Dutch painters both work here – Jan Vermeer and Pieter de Hooch. Both are famed for the richness and serenity of their rendering of domestic interiors of Dutch houses and scenes of domestic life going on within them. What is known as *genre* painting has been raised by them to fine art.

Vermeer was born in Delft and has never left his native town. Most of his pictures show the interior of the house on the main square where both he and his father have dealt in pictures and *objets d'art*. Music is a favourite subject – young women playing guitars, for instance – as is a woman standing at a window to examine a letter or a jewel. His paint gives a translucent glow to every object on the canvas and his colours, especially his blues, are of incomparable richness. His painting of Delft is bathed in a golden calm.

The rich Dutch merchants are enthusiastic picture collectors and this has led to widespread and varied styles of painting. Pieter de Hooch paints many scenes in courtyards or rooms with swaggering soldiers playing cards or drinking with women. Gerard Ter Borch shows the richness of women's apparel. But artists like Nicholas Maes and Gerard Dou have women peeling apples, plucking a duck or playing with children while Steen and Hals portray convivial, sometimes drunken, parties.

"A Wijdship, a keep and other shipping": by Van de Velde the Younger.

Jan Vermeer's painting: "Christ in the house of Mary and Martha".

A painting of "The Backgammon Players" by Dirk Hals.

1670 (1670-1673)

France, 1670. The French occupy Lorraine following the expulsion of the duke of Lorraine for his negotiations with the Dutch.

France, 1670. The astronomer Jan Picard determines the exact length of Earth's radius.

Rome, 1670. Clement X becomes pope in succession to Clement IX, the architect of the reconciliation between the Roman Church and the Jansenists known as the Clementine peace.

Italy, 1670. The Italian physiologist Giovanni Borelli tries to fly using artificial wings. Inspired by Cartesian mechanics, Borelli is the founder of the iatromechanism, which seeks to explain all bodily functions by physical laws.

West Africa, 1670. The French establish a trading post at Offa on the Dahomey coast.

New England, 1670. The English Hudson's Bay Company is formed.

France, 1671. France signs treaties of alliance or neutrality with several German states and the Emperor Leopold.

Hungary, 1671. Following the abolition of the constitution, Hungary becomes a province of Austria.

Angola, 1671. The kingdom of Ndongo is defeated at Ngola by the Portuguese, who annex it to form the Portuguese colony of Angola.

Central America, 1671. Having plundered Cuba, Portobello and Maracaibo, the English buccaneer Captain Henry Morgan sacks and loots the Spanish city of Panama.

Ukraine, October 1671. The Cossack *hetman* Peter Doroszenko is routed by the Poles, who occupy much of the Ukraine. Doroszenko has attempted to make alliances with the Crimean Tartars and the Ottomans to secure Cossack independence from both Poland and Russia.

London, 27 September 1672. The Royal African Company is granted a charter with a monopoly on the slave trade from Morocco to the Cape of Good Hope.

Poland, 18 October 1672. Following several defeats by the Ottomans – who were drawn into the conflict between the Poles and the Cossacks by the Polish occupation of the Ukraine – the Poles are forced to sign the treaty of Buczacz, by which they recognise Peter Dorszenko as sole hetman of the Cossacks and agree to become vassals of the sultan.

Paris, 1672. The German philosopher Wilhelm Leibniz visits Paris on a mission to persuade Louis XIV to conquer Egypt.

Netherlands, 1672. Having declared war on the Dutch, the French cross the Rhine and capture city after city. To halt the invasion the Dutch open dykes, causing extensive flooding.

England, 1672. In support of Louis XIV of France, King Charles II declares war on the Dutch.

New York, 1672. The Dutch regain control of New York from the English. The war of England and France against Holland crossed the Atlantic when 23 Dutch ships arrived in New York harbour on 7 August and attacked the garrison at Fort James.

Morocco, 1672. Mulay Ismail becomes sultan of the Alaouites and sets about uniting Morocco under his rule. He razes part of the old city of Meknes to build a complex of sumptuous palaces.

Netherlands, 1672. The painter Jan Steen returns from Delft to his native town of Leyden. One of the founders of the Leyden Guild, Steen excels at *genre* paintings of social and domestic scenes.

France, 1672. Louis XIV moves the French government from Paris to Versailles.

New Jersey, 1672. Colonists in Elizabethport opposed to the payment of the land taxes known as quitrents form an assembly.

New England, 1672. The Puritan poetess Anne Bradstreet, the first American woman writer, dies. Born in England, she sailed to New England with John Winthrop in 1630. Her first volume of poetry, published in England in 1650, was *The Tenth Muse lately sprung up in America.*

North America, 1 January 1673. A regular mounted mail service begins between New York and Boston. The mail is delivered by a "post road" along which men and horses are posted at intervals.

Paris, 21 February 1673. The great French comic dramatist Moliere is buried in secret.

North America, 11 September 1673. James Needham returns to Virginia after a four-month expedition to the lands to the west (*Tennessee*). He is the first Englishman to penetrate the area.

London, 1673. Parliament passes the Plantation Duty Act, imposing duties on any ship carrying certain products, such as sugar, cotton and tobacco, between colonial ports.

London, 1673. Parliament cuts off funds for England's war against Holland, forcing Charles II to drop the war, rescind religious liberties and accept the Test Act, which is designed to prevent Roman Catholics from holding office.

British slavers promise prompt delivery

London, 27 September 1672

Bulk deliveries of slaves from West Africa are being arranged by the Royal African Company, a new corporation which has just been granted monopoly rights under the English flag to collect slaves from an area that runs from Sallee on the Moroccan coast down to the Cape of Good Hope. With recently-raised capital of £100,000, Royal African promises prompt supply to those prepared to sign contracts for whole cargoes.

A slave between 12 and 40 years old "able to go over the ship's side unaided" will be supplied for £15 per head in Barbados, £16 in Nevis, £17 in Jamaica, and £18 in Virginia.

Philosopher backs natural law

Lund, Sweden, 1672

Natural law, deduced by reason from the evidence of nature, is the true and immutable foundation of the state. Governments may rule, but only in so far as they pass laws that guarantee rights on the basis of this natural law. Thus the theory behind a new book, *On the law and nature of people*, written by the German jurist and philosopher Samuel Pufendorf, the professor of Natural Law at the university of Lund in Sweden. Humans are "social beings" with natural rights and freedoms. It is for governments to ensure that such rights are upheld, he argues.

Samuel Pufendorf: a believer that humans have "natural" rights.

Manchu rule means shaven heads for all

Peking, 1671

These are times of great change in China as the Manchu consolidate their hold over the country. As more and more Chinese come under Manchu rule they are being forced to wear their hair in the Manchu style, with heads shaven except for a pigtail hanging down the back of their necks.

To many loyal supporters of the deposed Mings this is a shameful sign of subservience and many are shaving the whole of their heads in the manner of Buddhist priests rather than submit to the attentions of the Manchu barbers.

Surprisingly, the young emperor Kang-hsi, has allowed the Chinese to resume the practice of binding the feet of young children. On three previous occasions the Manchus had forbidden this strange and cruel practice which leaves women virtually unable to walk. They have now given in to Chinese pressure on this matter as part of the emperor's policy of placation. But he has ruled that the custom must be confined to the Chinese.

Mathematician gets into swing of things

Paris, 1673

The Dutch mathematician, astronomer and physicist Christiaan Huygens has become a founder member of the French Academy of Sciences. The Academy's funding will certainly help his wide-ranging and varied researches. While living in Paris he published a book, *Horologium Oscillatorium*, which deals with the mathematics of pendulum swing and the laws of centrifugal force. Concurrently Huygens has been working on pendulum mechanisms of various kinds. He designed the first practical pendulum clock in 1656, accurate to five minutes a day.

Orangemen murder diplomat brothers

The Hague, 20 August 1672

Johan de Witt, the Grand Pensionary of Holland, a leader of the United Provinces through their years of greatest glory, and his brother Cornelis have been murdered by a mob. Cornelis de Witt was in jail, accused of plotting against William of Orange; his brother was visiting him. As they spoke a mob of Orangemen broke in and literally tore the two to pieces.

Johan de Witt ruled Holland between the death of William II in 1650 and the coming of age of William III in February of this year. It has been a period of unparalleled prosperity, international trade and artistic and intellectual advance.

De Witt backed the merchants and artists, but he was equally devoted to maintaining his own power, scheming ruthlessly to defeat any opposition, notably that of the House of Orange, backed by the Catholic church, the poor and the rural landowners. When William came to power, de Witt was reluctant to give up his authority. But the people, who fear his ties to Louis XIV, rallied to the Orange and showed the intensity of their belief today.

Cornelis and Johan de Witt: two victims of their own ambitions.

King's move sparks fear of popish plots

London, 1672

With England about to go to war with the Dutch yet again, the king has outraged public opinion by issuing a Declaration of Indulgence suspending all penal laws in religious matters. Ostensibly a gesture of toleration, the declaration is intended to favour Roman Catholics.

Charles' arbitrary suspension of statutes is greatly resented, especially as it is becoming known to ministers that the king has made a secret treaty with Louis XIV, promising to become a Catholic in return for French subsidies and troops to keep him on the throne. Parliament is at present in recess, but when MPs reassemble they are certain to force Charles to cancel his Declaration. In the public mind popery, France and arbitrary power are linked together.

King Charles II: his pro-Catholic bias has offended many subjects and parliament demands a climb-down.

Musical world mourns death of Schutz

Dirk Hals: "Elegant figures making music on a terrace by a lake".

Dresden, 6 November 1672

Heinrich Schutz, the first German composer to achieve international fame, has died at the age of 87. As a choirboy at Kassel, Schutz showed early talent, and in 1609 the local ruler gave him money to study music in Venice. Soon after his return, in 1613, he was seconded to the elector of Saxony at Dresden, eventually becoming court *Kapellmeister* (head of music).

Schutz's powerfully expressive music is mostly for the church, and includes oratorical works like passions and motets. One of his few secular works is *Dafne* (1627), the first German opera.

French comedy playwright dies on stage

Jean-Baptiste Poquelin, who is also known as the playwright Moliere.

"Le Bourgeois Gentilhomme", one of Moliere's popular comedies.

Paris, 15 February 1673

Moliere, France's greatest comedian and playwright, died last night of a lung haemorrhage after collapsing on stage during his performance as the hypochondriac in his own *Le Malade Imaginaire*. He was 51. The king is mourning his favourite actor, but Moliere had many enemies at court and in the church who have suffered from his ridicule.

Moliere's real name was Jean-Baptiste Pocquelin. As a young man he joined the large theatrical family of Bejart to form *L'Illustre Theatre*. They failed in Paris and toured France for 13 years of varied fortunes, playing in tennis courts, with Moliere in the lead opposite Madeleine Bejart. In 1658 the King became their patron. They took over the Palais Royal theatre where Moliere created a series of great comedies. *Tartuffe* was banned for years. Moliere married Armande Bejart, a girl of 19 whom some critics alleged was his daughter.

1673 (1673-1676)

Massachusetts, 1673. John Winslow is elected governor of Plymouth, becoming the first native-born colonial governor.

Poland, 20 May 1674. John Sobieski is elected king.

New Jersey, 13 June 1674. Philip Carteret, the governor of New Jersey, launches a campaign to enforce the payment of quitrents, the land taxes which have sparked a rebellion in the colony.

New York, 10 November 1674. All Dutch-held areas of New York are returned to English control by the treaty of Westminster. The Dutch regained the town on 9 August 1672 during the third Anglo-Dutch war.

Canada, 4 December 1674. The fur trader Louis Jolet and the Jesuit Father Jacques Marquette return to Montreal after a 2,500-mile journey exploring the basin of the great river that the Indians call the *Mississippi*.

New England, 1674. George Fox, the founder of the Society of Friends, returns to Rhode Island after a three-year expedition to spread Quaker beliefs in the colonies.

Spain, 1674. A second collection of novels by Maria de Zayas y Sofomayor is published posthumously. As a novelist she wrote sensational melodramatic tales; she also argued for education for women and was an admired playwright and poet.

Paris, 1674. The court and church painter Philippe de Champaigne dies. He painted the Sorbonne chapel, and leaves several portraits of Richelieu and Louis XIII. He was linked with the Jansenists after 1643, and his later serious and austere compositions led him to be considered the most eminent representative of French classicism.

Paris, 1674. Nicolas Boileau publishes *The Poetic Art*, which vigorously champions literary classicism.

Paris, 1674. The philosopher and theologian Nicolas Malebranche publishes *On the search after truth*. He is full of enthusiasm for Descartes' philosophy and develops Cartesianism in a religious sense, linking it with Augustinianism.

France, 1674. French troops conquer Franche-Comte.

India, 1674. Francois Martin founds Pondicherry for the French East India Company.

Iceland, 1674. Hallgrimur Petursson, one of the most important exponents of Icelandic religious poetry, dies.

England, 1674. The chemist John Mayow carries out an experiment placing a lighted candle inside a bell jar under water. In his *Tractatcus quinque Medico-Phisici*, he describes air as consisting of two elements, one inert, the other active. He is the inventor of a real technique for handling gases.

Bulgaria, 1674. Archbishop Peter Parchevitch dies. An ardent patriot who devoted his life to the liberation of his people, he travelled widely in Europe on missions to achieve this goal.

Germany, 28 June 1675. Frederick William, the great elector of Brandenburg, crushes the Swedes.

Germany, 27 July 1675. Turenne, the marshall of France, is killed at Sasbach while fighting the Italian leader Montecuccoli. Turenne recently reconquered Alsace at the battle of Turckheim.

India, 1675. Aurangzeb, the Moghul emperor, executes the ninth Sikh *guru*, Tegh Bahadur, for refusing to accept Islam.

Mali, 1675. Following the troubles in Macina, waves of migrating Fulani arrive in Hodh.

Spain, 1675. King Charles II reaches adulthood, but is sickly and uninterested in affairs of state.

London, 1675. The Greenwich Observatory is established.

Italy, 1675. The town of Messina rises up against the Spanish. Louis XIV sends a fleet which defeats the Spanish, but as soon as the French have left the Spanish return and institute cruel reprisals.

West Indies, 1675. After being knighted by Charles II, the buccaneer Sir Henry Morgan takes up the post of governor of Jamaica.

France, 1675. France comes into conflict with the pope over the previously accepted "king's right" to income from certain bishoprics between the death of one bishop and the appointment of the next.

Paris, 1675. While trying to calculate the speed of light, the Dane Ole Roemer observes eclipses of the satellites of Jupiter.

Netherlands, 1675. The painter Jan Vermeer dies at Delft.

Rome, 1675. The Spanish theologian Miguel de Molinos publishes his *Spiritual Guide*, advocating the suppression of all deliberate acts, giving birth to "quietism".

Massachusetts, 28 August 1676. Metacom, the chief of the Algonquin Wampanoags – known by the English as King Philip – is killed by English soldiers. His death ends a year of fighting between Indians and colonists.

Tax collector's son founds empire in India

Raigarh, India, 6 June 1674

Sivaji, the son of a tax collector, who founded an empire, has crowned himself king. Starting his political career as a bandit, he assembled a private army of Mawali backwoodsmen, and carved an empire for himself in north-west Dekhan. He proved a genius at the profession of arms. By 1657 he was raiding Moghul territory. When Afzal Khan was sent against him, he called for peace talks, then murdered him with hidden "tiger's claws" attached to his fingers. Aware that he could not win directly against the might of the Moghuls, he accepted a peace treaty in 1665, becoming Aurangzeb's vassal and prisoner. After nine months he escaped – by night and on horseback.

For five years he strengthened his position in the Dekhan, building up his Maratha state. Then in 1670 he was at war against the Moghuls again. So decadent have the Moghuls become that they prefer to pay him than fight him. Moghul blackmail money so enriches Sivaji that he can afford to crown himself king, the first king of the Maratha dynasty.

Sivaji: from tax collector to the first of the Maratha monarchs.

A Dekhan papier-mache box, painted, lacquered and fringed with ivory.

Moghul invaders halted at Khyber Pass

Kabul, 1676

A rebellion in Afghanistan led by Akmal Khan, the chief of the Afridis, has almost succeeded in separating Afghanistan from Moghul India. The first attempt to suppress the Afghanis failed in 1672, with 10,000 troops killed and tens of thousands of Afghanis joining the rebellion. A second Moghul attempt in early 1674 was similiarly defeated at the Karapa Pass. The defeats have forced Aurangzeb to come from Delhi and take overall command. In spite of his placing the operational command of his army under his most experienced officer, the Turkish general Agha Khan, his army failed to open a way through the Khyber Pass.

Unable to defeat the Afghans with the weapons of war, he has resorted to the weapons of peace: tribal chiefs have been bribed and religious divisions between Sunnites and Shi'ites inflamed. Now the rebels spend more time fighting each other than the enemy.

Knighted ex-pirate now governs Jamaica

Kingston, Jamaica, 1675
With the kind of pomp and ceremony that attends a royal occasion, a former buccaneer, Henry – now Sir Henry – Morgan, has taken up residence as lieutenant-governor of Jamaica. To the fury of Spain and the surprise of royalist society in London, Morgan was knighted last year by King Charles II and returned in style to the Caribbean where he had previously plundered with great success.

Morgan was born in Glamorgan in Wales in 1635 and went to America as a young man before he was given a command in a fleet led by the privateer Edward Mansfield, raiding Cuba, Nicaragua and settlements along the South American coast. When Mansfield was killed, Morgan took his place. In 1668 Morgan was commissioned by the governor of Jamaica to find out whether Spanish forces were planning to attack British possessions but exceeded his orders by sailing to Portobello in Panama and sacking the city.

There was no stopping Henry Morgan. He went on to attack and burn Maracaibo in Venezuela and crossed the isthmus to sack Panama City. News had not reached him at that point that peace had been made with Spain and that he was in disgrace. That was three years ago, but now, even in his high office, he is still involved in piracy.

Henry Morgan: the pirate chief who is now governor of Jamaica.

Morgan and his buccaneers attack the people of Maracaibo in 1669.

Frederick William crushes the Swedes

The Elector Frederick William of Brandenburg reviews his troops: his attack on Sweden is seen as one more step in his overall plan to unify Prussia.

Brandenburg, 28 June 1675
Frederick William, the elector of Brandenburg, has joined the war between France and Holland which is not only dominating politics in Europe but is also beginning to spread to the New World in the West Indies.

He has come a long way in the thirty-five years since he inherited a scattered group of lands ravaged by the battles of the Thirty Years' War. He consolidated them successfully, and is now a real force to reckon with. Supporting the Dutch, he has conquered their Swedish rivals at the battle of Fehrbellin and gone on to invade Bremen, Verden and Western Pomerania, Sweden's enclaves in north Germany. The elector's intervention may well have changed the course of the war. Observers note that the French seem to be less committed than previously while Frederick William will be encouraged in his greater plan – the unifying of Prussia.

Polish hero is to be the new king

Poland, 20 May 1674
John Sobieski, the architect of Poland's victories against the Turks, the Ukrainian Cossacks and the Swedes, has been elected king. Now Poland's national hero is its monarch too.

The election of a Polish king is a European concern, with all the major powers vying for influence. Sobieski had to defeat three other candidates, none of them Poles. Duke Charles of Lorraine represented Austrian interests, while the duke of Enghien and the prince of Neuberg both favoured France.

Sobieski himself has external sponsors. His marriage to Marie Casimire d'Arquien means that he has ties to Louis XIV, who wants to use Poland in his campaign against Austria. For the Poles what matters is that Sobieski, the victor of Chotin, the battle that smashed the Turks last year, is determined to resist any possibility of selling out their country. For the foreign ambassadors, each pressing his own country's interests, Sobieski is the strongest man available.

Greenwich observatory founded to help navigation at sea

London, 1675
The enterprise and vision of the astronomer John Flamsteed has now been rewarded. He has been arguing that there is a need to establish an observatory to determine the position of the moon and stars in order to give accurate information on longitude at sea for navigational purposes.

Such an observatory has now been built at Greenwich near the river Thames. Flamsteed has had to equip it with instruments, mostly at his own expense. His observatory houses graduated arcs traversed by telescopic lenses for measuring celestial angles, as well as more humble devices such as a quadrant and sextant. He is now at work on a new star catalogue.

Astronomers using a telescope and a sextant at the Greenwich Observatory, where researches should improve the accuracy of international navigation.

1676 (1676-1679)

Virginia, 26 October 1676. Nathaniel Bacon, the leader of an armed rebellion in the colony of Yorktown, dies. The revolt against the forces of Governor William Berkeley was sparked off by the governor's refusal to support Bacon's raids on the Indians.

Paris, 1676. Paul de Gondi, the cardinal de Retz, completes his *Memoirs*. This clergyman without a vocation demonstrated his political ambition as a party leader during the *Fronde* uprising. As a result of the part he played, he was obliged to give up the archbishopric of Paris.

Paris, 1676. Abbot Edme Mariotte studies the compressibility of gases and verifies the laws discovered by Boyle in 1661 expressing the inverse proportionality of volume and pressure at a constant temperature.

Paris, 1676. The artist and art theorist Abraham Bosse dies. A prolific engraver, Bosse was expelled from the Academy following a dispute with le Brun on the subject of perspective.

Ottoman Empire, 1676. Kara Mustapha succeeds his elder brother as grand vizier.

Massachusetts, 1676. The first coffee-house is licensed in Boston.

Paris, 1 January 1677. Racine's tragedy *Phedre* is staged for the first time.

Amsterdam, 21 February 1677. The Dutch-Jewish philosopher Baruch Spinoza dies of phthisis, aggravated by glass dust in his lungs from years of lens grinding. Expelled from the synagogue at the age of 24, he has led an independent life, in 1673 refusing a professorship of philosophy at Heidelberg University in order to retain that independence. The only work he published during his life (the *Tractatus*, 1670) was banned in 1674, by which time Spinoza's ideas on religion were regarded as dangerously subversive.

Virginia, 27 April 1677. Colonel Jeffreys succeeds William Berkeley as governor of Virginia and halts the executions of the followers of the rebel leader Nathaniel Bacon.

West Africa, 30 October 1677. The French take Goree.

England, 15 November 1677. Mary, the daughter of the duke of York and niece of Charles II, marries William of Orange. This marriage puts the seal on Anglo-Dutch rapprochement.

West Africa, 1677. The Dutch forts in Senegal are conquered by the French.

Netherlands, 1677. Spinoza's *Ethics* is published posthumously: it develops a metaphysical system along Euclidian lines from axioms, theorems and definitions. Only God is infinite; there is no notion of free will, we are "free" only in so far as we act in accordance with God.

Paris, 21 April 1678. Richard Simon, the author of a *Critical History of the Old Testament* which was recently published in Amsterdam, is condemned by Bossuet, the leader of the clergy.

England, November 1678. The country is in the grip of anti-Catholic hysteria following the unsolved murder last month of Sir Edmund Godfrey, who testified with Israel Tonge and Titus Oates that Jesuit priests were involved in a "popish plot" to assassinate king Charles II, put the Catholic James, duke of York on the throne and massacre Protestants. Oates may not be the most reliable witness. Expelled from school and colleges, he has also been dismissed from Holy Orders.

North America, 1678. The French explorer Robert Cavalier, the sieur de la Salle, and his chaplain, Father Louis Hennepin, are the first Europeans to see the Niagara Falls.

Paris, 1678. The Dutch mathematician Christiaan Huygens writes his *Treatise on light*.

England, 1678. The promising English composer Henry Purcell composes music for Shakespeare's *Timon of Athens*.

England, 1678. The Baptist preacher John Bunyan publishes his *Pilgrim's Progress*, an account of life as an allegorical journey with much vivid description and realistic narrative.

England, 1678. The poet laureate John Dryden writes a tragedy entitled *All For Love*. Although of Puritan origins, Dryden is now officially recognised.

Netherlands, 1678. Japanese *Chrysanthemums* are cultivated in Holland.

Netherlands, 5 February 1679. France signs a treaty at Nijmegen with the Holy Roman empire.

New England, 10 July 1679. The English crown claims New Hampshire as a royal colony.

India, 1679. Aurangzeb, the Moghul emperor, reimposes the *jizya* tax on non-Moslems, including those in his armies.

North America, 1679. The French explorer Cavalier de la Salle travels in an uncharted region in the northern central part of the continent (*Indiana*).

French playwright puts down pen at 38

This elaborate stage set is for the production of a play at Versailles.

Paris, 2 January 1677

The opening performance of *Phedre* last night at the hotel de Bourgogne was marred for its author, Jean Racine, by the presentation of a rival play of the same name by Pradon, performed by the *Troupe du Roi* backed by the duchess of Bouillon. Racine's play was recognised as a masterpiece, but he declares that he will write no more for the stage, although he is only 38. France's leading tragediennes are in mourning at the news.

Racine's tragedies observe the rules of Aristotle, confining them to one time and place and leaving all physical action to be described by messenger, as in *Phedre*, where the violent death of Hippolytus is the subject of the poetic Recit de Theramene. The only violence on stage is in the declaration of passion in strict metre.

Racine's older rival, Pierre Corneille, compressed the action of *Le Cid* into one day, but was still criticised for being too lax. Like Racine he wrote a *Berenice*, a work about the conflict between love and duty.

A scene from Racine's "Iphigenia" now the playwright has retired.

Huygens suggests light travels in waves

Europe, 1678

An important new scientific work by the Dutchman Christiaan Huygens is said to be near completion. It is titled *Traite de la Lumiere* (Treatise on Light) and contains the idea that light travels in waves.

There have been many theories about the nature of light. The ancient Greeks believed that it originated in objects being viewed. The Platonists believed that light was the fusion of three rays of matte that originated in the sun.

Isaac Newton contends that ligh consists of minute particles of matter that emanate from luminou bodies such as stars and trave through space. The Dutch scientis contends that light consists o waves that travel through the ethe at great speed, in straight lines an with vibrations at right angles t their direction of travel.

Victorious French impose peace treaty

"The Banquet of Peace": an allegorical rendering of the new treaty.

Nijmegen, 5 February 1679
The third Treaty of Nijmegen was signed here today, thus ending the European war which started with the French invasion of the Netherlands seven years ago. The victorious French, intoxicated with pride, are hailing their king as "Louis the Great".

The war has indeed ended on a victorious note for the French. They forced the Dutch to the conference table by capturing Ghent in a surprise attack a year ago, and under the treaty France acquires Franche-Comte from Spain and remains in control of Lorraine. There is also to be a rationalisation of the frontier in Flanders which gives Louis the "duelling-ground" advocated by the renowned military engineer, Vaubin.

So the French may well hail their hero king: but his victory is not as great as it seems. He embarked on this war to crush the Protestant Dutch and seize control of their maritime trade. The war started brilliantly for him, but then the Dutch cut their dykes and, under William of Orange, fought so bravely that Louis was anxious to make peace, his war aims unful filled.

Dissenter publishes pilgrim's tale

Bedford, 1678
A Baptist minister, whose faith has condemned him to more than a dozen years in jail has published a remarkable allegory of the true Christian life. A good deal was written in his prison cell.

The Pilgrim's Progress, by John Bunyan, lays out, in the form of a dream, the journey of Christian from the City of Destruction to the Celestial City. On his way he visits such places as Vanity Fair and the Slough of Despond, and meets Mr Worldly Wiseman, Giant Despair and many other characters.

Bunyan's work, equally popular among the learned and the uneducated, is notable for the clarity of its English, its vivid images and the author's sense of the world.

John Bunyan: a visionary writer.

Moslem zealots rebuffed in African war

Senegal, 1677
The Islamic *jihad* that has swept through the western Sahara since 1673 has collapsed. It began when Moslem zealots, led by the charismatic preacher Awbek ben Ashfaga, invaded Futa Toro and the Wolof states on the river Senegal and "liberated" the Zawaya, agriculturalists who were traditonally prey to the aggression of the Hassani, or warrior class.

Ashfaga assumed the title *Nasir al-Din* (Protector of the Faithful), proclaiming a heady mixture of anti-colonialism, social justice, and Islamic millennialism. Nasir al-Din's first task was to establish an Islamic state and collect the *zakat* (Islamic tax). The collection was his undoing.

Resenting Nasir al-Din's presumption in collecting a tax that only a *caliph* is permitted, many of the Zawaya revolted, and were quickly joined by Hassani opportunists under Hadi, the chief of the Trarza. Though Nasir al-Din thrice defeated them, he was killed in the third battle. Leaderless, the *jihad* is disintegrating, to the relief of established Islamic authority.

Church slams unorthodox bible scholar

Amsterdam, 21 April 1678
A new study of the Old Testament has appeared in Holland, and its author is already facing the wrath of the Catholic Church, which condemns it as impious.

A Critical History of the Old Testament, by the Catholic scholar and priest Richard Simon, submits the texts of Genesis and the Prophets to a searching historical and philological analysis. In it Simon has questioned the very bases of Roman Catholic faith. The church has always emphasised that freedom of research and critical analysis is incompatible with true faith when, like Simon's, it challenges current dogma.

Thus, although Simon's work was undertaken as part of the theological struggle against the Huguenots, it has been condemned by the French theologian Bossuet and placed amongst the forbidden books on the Index. Simon himself has been expelled from his order, the Oratorians.

This illustrated astrological print, among the finest examples of celestial charts and featuring a number of the constellations superimposed upon a view of the globe, is one of 29 views of the heavens in the Harmonica Macrocosmica, a celestial atlas compiled by the monk Andreas Cellarius.

1679 (1679-1681)

India, 1679. The Moghul Emperor Aurangzeb orders the destruction of many Hindu temples.

France, 1679. A study of the basic principles of differential calculus by the mathematician Pierre Fermat is published posthumously.

France, 1679. The Royal Academy of Painting is split by a dispute between the "Poussinists" and the "Rubenists". The latter oppose the rigidity of the Academy's official doctrine, which is based on the ideas of Nicholas Poussin.

Rome, 1679. Alessandro Scarlatti's opera *Gli Equivoci nell'Amore* is performed for the first time.

England, 1679. The astronomer Edmund Halley publishes his *Catalogus stellarum australium*, a catalogue of the stars in the southern hemisphere.

London, May 1679. In spite of King Charles II's opposition, the Act of Habeas Corpus is passed, making it impossible for anyone to be imprisoned without a court appearance.

China, 1679. The Chinese novelist and playwright Li Yu dies. The author of many popular and sometimes licentious novels, he was also a painter and decorative artist. He edited an encyclopaedia of Chinese painting and ran his own theatre company.

India, 1680. The death of Sivaji, the national hero of the Marathas, is followed by clashes between the Great Moghul Aurangzeb and the Marathas' allies the Rajputs.

London, May 1680. An Exclusion Bill, against the succession of James, the duke of York, is passed by the Commons but thrown out by the Lords.

New Mexico, 13 August 1680. The expulsion of the Spanish from Santa Fe by Indians under Chief Pope sets off a war.

England, 25 September 1680. The English satirist Samuel Butler, author of *Hudibras*, dies.

New England, September 1680. The province of New Hampshire is separated from Massachusetts by a Royal Commission.

London, 20 November 1680. John Culpeper, a customs officer from South Carolina, is acquitted of treason after leading the first popular uprising in America – in opposition to the imposition of English trade laws.

England, 30 November 1680. The Dutch painter Peter Lely, who settled in London in 1641 and was employed by Charles I, Cromwell and Charles II, dies. Among his finest works are 13 portraits of the English admirals who fought in the second Dutch war.

France, 1680. The French writer Francois La Rochefoucauld dies.

Paris, 1680. A new theatre, the Comedie Francaise, opens.

Indian Ocean, 1680. The last dodos in Mauritius are killed by English sailors. These large flightless birds were hunted for their meat and plumage.

West Africa, 1680. The Asante kingdom is founded on the Gold Coast.

Poland, 8 January 1681. The treaty of Radzin ends a war which began in 1678 when the Turks under Grand Vizier Kara Mustafa launched a campaign to expel the Russians and Poles from the Ukraine. By the treaty the Turks give up claims to the Ukraine.

England, March 1681. Charles II convenes a parliament in Oxford to debate the exclusion of his Catholic brother James, duke of York, from the succession. A compromise solution fails and the parliament is dissolved after a week.

France, 1681. The building of the canal du Midi, begun in 1664, is completed. The canal, which is more than 120 miles (192km) long, links the gulf of Gascony with the Mediterranean.

Netherlands, 1681. The genre and portrait painter Gerard Terborch dies in Deventer. He specialised in genteel interior scenes and his best compositions rival those of Vermeer.

Netherlands, 1681. Forced to flee France, the rationalist philosopher Pierre Bayle takes refuge in Holland and becomes professor of philosophy at Rotterdam. The son of a Calvinist minister, Bayle converted to Catholicism and then reconverted to Protestantism.

England, 1681. The theologian Thomas Burnet publishes his *Sacred History of the Earth*, developing his fantastic ideas on evolution.

France, 1681. The Benedictine monk Jean Mabillon publishes *De re diplomatica*, which lays the foundation for a science of diplomatics.

Madrid, 1681. The great Spanish dramatic poet Pedro Calderon de la Barca dies. His works include light comedies and many plays of religious inspiration.

China, 1681. The Ch'ing government gains firm control of China after a major civil war between semiautonomous "princes" in the south and south-east of the country.

India, 1681. Akbar, rebel son of the Great Moghul Aurangzeb, flees to the Dekhan. His father uses this as a pretext to invade the region.

Commons try to exclude Catholic heir

Two playing cards illustrating events in the plot against the Protestants.

London, 1680

With public opinion inflamed by lurid stories of popish plots to persecute Protestants and restore the Catholic religion, the House of Commons has set out to secure the exclusion of James, the duke of York, from succession to the throne. James, the brother of Charles II, was forced into exile after he converted to Catholicism and married Mary of Modena, a Catholic princess.

When Charles fell ill recently, James returned from Brussels and MPs made another attempt to push through an Exclusion Bill, only to be frustrated by the Lords. The Exclusionists, or Whigs as they have come to be called, represent the moneyed middle classes; but their willingness to encourage the London mobs in order to put pressure on the king has caused concern. Many Tory peers who were critical of James in the past now support him because they fear the Whigs are undermining the established order. Whigs denounce these Tories as "Papists in disguise".

On one important issue Charles has given way: he has accepted the Habeas Corpus Amendment Act, which makes it impossible for the Crown to imprison anyone without a court appearance.

French sell slaves in the West Indies

Paris, 1679

The French government has set up the "Compagnie francaise d'Afrique". The company's aim is to transport 16,000 slaves to the West Indies in eight years. Since Louis XIII authorised slave-trading in 1642 vast profits have been made providing labour for the coffee, tea and sugar plantations in the New World – in spite of a quarter of each shipment dying en route. The company's main competitor is the British owned Royal Africa Company, which has transported 40,000 slaves to the West Indies since 1674.

The dodo: the last of these large flightless birds has been killed in Mauritius by British sailors.

New high-speed pot piles on pressure

London, 1680

While working here at the Royal Society, the French physicist, Denis Papin, has invented what he calls a "New Digester". This is a cast-iron cooking pot with an air-tight lid which allows the liquids inside to boil at higher than normal temperatures. There is also a safety valve fitted in the lid. Food is cooked, by pressurised steam, in about a quarter of the normal time. The device helps to improve the texture and flavour of meat. He writes in a booklet: "The oldest and hardest Cow-Beef may be made as tender as young choice meat".

Denis Papin: a culinary pioneer.

Prince Akbar loses chance to oust father

Ajmir, India, 27 January 1681

The characteristic of disloyalty, which Aurangzeb, the fanatical Moghul emperor, used so effectively against his father Shahjahan, has been passed on to his favourite son, Akbar. When the Rajputs rebelled against the poll tax, Aurangzeb put Akbar in command of the Moghul army sent to subdue them. So incompetent was Akbar he was relieved of his command.

Smarting under the humiliation, and convinced his father's brutal policy against the Hindu Rajputs threatened the spirit of religious toleration he made an alliance with the Rajputs to overthrow his father. The Rajputs had clashed with Aurangzeb after the death last year of Sivaji, their prime Maratha ally.

Akbar's army, joined by the Rajputs, marched on Ajmir, where Aurangzeb resided. Aurangzeb resorted to the tactic he had used in Afghanistan: guile. He wrote a letter to Akbar implying that father and son were leading the Rajputs into a trap and let it fall into the hands of the Rajputs. By morning Akbar's army had melted away.

Heroic Sivaji, painted c.1700.

Gold brings wealth to Asante kingdom

Ghana, West Africa, 1680

In the forests of West Africa, the Akan petty states are uniting. Rich from the gold and slave trades, supported by a strong army, amd cemented by a common religion, they have become a new regional power. They are the Asantes.

The new Asante kingdom is not based on tribes. It has modern institutions: tax collectors, judges and a bureaucracy. The Asante leader, Osei Tutu, who first brought the Akan states together to free themselves of the domination of their neighbours, the Denkyira, is a first-rate general and politician.

The symbol of the state is the Golden Throne, which is said to have descended from the Asante god on to the lap of Osei Tutu. The Throne, or Stool, is only shown in public on important ceremonial occasions. It not only represents the unity of the Asante, but guarantees their well-being too.

Manchus wipe out Ming resistance

China, 1681

The Manchu emperor, Kangxi has defeated the rebellion of the Three Feudatories, killed its leader, Wu San-kuei, and finally established Manchu rule over the whole of mainland China.

The three feudatories were all former Ming generals who had gone over to the Manchus and put down Ming resistance in South China, where they set up powerful semi-independent states. They demanded huge amounts of money from the government and Wu, who had ordered the strangling of the last Ming emperor in the marketplace at Yunnan, was warlord of a formidable army.

They started their rebellion when Kangxi ordered them to disband their armies since there was no longer any threat from the Ming. But Wu, whose betrayal in opening up the Great Wall to the Manchus led to the downfall of the Ming, now betrayed the Manchus to restore what he had destroyed.

He very nearly succeeded, but a fatal hesitancy in his attack on Beijing allowed Kangxi to gather an army, relying on other former Ming generals who remained loyal to him. Wu was defeated and slain, his body chopped into many pieces. And now the Ch'ing dynasty of the Manchus rules all China.

Bernini, the Roman fountain designer, dies a disappointed man

Rome, 1680

Giovanni Bernini, who left such a mark on Rome with his colonnaded piazza in front of St Peter's, intended to make as a big an impact on Paris; but he has died disappointed in that ambition. In 1665 he was summoned to Paris by Louis XIV to submit designs for the eastern front of the Louvre. However, his flamboyantly curving facades were rejected by the king in favour of the French designers, Le Vau and Perrault. Bernini's last work was the tomb of Pope Alexander VII in St Peter's, where so much of the decoration was his.

Rome's glories: St Peter's, flanked by the Vatican and Bernini's Piazza.

Prince banned from fighting the French

The Netherlands, 1681

A bitter disagreement over foreign policy has arisen between William of Orange and the republic's state leaders. To protect the economy, they have stopped him sending Dutch troops into Europe to quell French hostilities. William, the son-in-law of James, duke of York, who is heir to the English throne, became Dutch leader when John de Witt's regime was overthrown in 1672. For six years he led his country against French attack and occupation. He won limited hereditary power in 1675. An alliance with Spain, Germany and Britain helped him secure the Franco-Dutch Treaty in 1678.

1681 (1681-1683)

France, 1681. Following the occupation of Strasbourg by the armies of Louis XIV, the city is annexed to the French kingdom.

Russia, 1681. As Russia extends its boundaries eastwards, the Tartar lands in the Volga region are confiscated and there are forced conversions to Christianity.

Hungary, 1681. The treaty of Sopron between the Emperor Leopold and the Hungarian nobility restores the Hungarian constitution.

England, 1681. When his protector Lord Shaftesbury is imprisoned for high treason against the Stuarts, the philosopher John Locke, who had retreated to Oxford, is expelled from the university.

England, 1681. The poet John Dryden publishes a fine political satire entitled *Absalom and Achitophel.*

Zimbabwe, c.1681. Changamire Dombo, at the head of an army called the "Rozvi", coming from the eastern Zimbabwe plateau, conquers the Torwa of Butua and makes his capital at Danongombe.

Netherlands, 14 March 1682. The Dutch painter Jacob van Rysdael dies in Haarlem. He excelled in country landscapes and seascapes.

Spain, 3 April 1682. The Spanish painter Bartolome Esteban Murillo dies. He won fame for his cycle of paintings for the Franciscan monastery in Seville and in 1660 become first director of the Academy in Seville. He will be best remembered for his devotional pictures and his genre scenes of peasant children.

North America, 9 April 1682. Having travelled the length of the Mississippi river, the explorer Robert Cavelier, known as La Salle, formally claims possession of the entire Mississippi valley for France. He names the region Louisiana in honour of his king, Louis XIV.

Rome, 11 April 1682. Pope Innocent XI condemns the Declaration of the Four Articles – drawn up by Jacques Benigne Bossuet, the leader of the French clergy – which seeks to reconcile papal authority with Gallican independence.

Hungary, 1682. The Protestant nobleman Imre Tokoly, leader of the revolt against the Emperor Leopold in Hungary and Transylvania which began four years ago, is proclaimed king of Hungary by the Turks.

North America, 1682. Spaniards fleeing the New Mexican Pueblo revolt found the first settlement in Texas.

Ethiopia, 1682. Iyasu (the Great) comes the throne.

Paris, 1682. The English astronomer Edmund Halley observes a comet and plots its orbit.

England, November 1682. After trying unsuccessfully to organise a revolt of radical Whigs following his acquital from prison, the earl of Shaftesbury flees to Holland.

England, 1682. John Bunyan publishes a complex allegorical work entitled *The Holy War.*

England, 1682. Isaac Newton discovers the law of universal gravitation which identifies the nature of the earth's gravity and the pull of the heavenly bodies.

North America, 1682. The English Quaker William Penn founds Philadelphia and the colony of Pennsylvania.

Netherlands, 1682. The French philosopher Pierre Bayle publishes his *Thoughts on the comet* in Rotterdam. On the pretext of challenging superstition, he tackles great metaphysical and theological questions, separating the moral from the religious.

France, 1682. The court of Louis XIV is installed at Versailles.

France, 1682. The Huguenots are excluded from the commercial guilds, financial posts and from the house of the king.

Russia, 1682. Fyodor III dies childless and without naming a successor. The proclamation as czar, of Peter, nine-year-old son of Czar Alexis, is followed by a bloody revolt by the Moscow guard known as the Streltsy. Peter's half-brother Ivan is raised to the throne as co-czar and their elder sister Sophia is appointed regent.

Japan, 1682. The philosopher Yamazaki Ansai dies. Taking his inspiration from the Chinese philosophers of the Song dynasty, he founded thriving schools in Kyoto and Edo (*Tokyo*).

Germany, 1682. *Acta Eruditorum*, the first learned periodical in Germany, begins publication.

West Africa, 1682. Kaladian Coulibaly, king of Segu (*Mali*) since 1652, dies. He made his kingdom into a regional power, guaranteeing the independence of the Bambara.

England, 1683. The Republican politician Algernon Sidney is executed for his alleged involvement in the Rye House Plot against the Stuarts. The duke of Monmouth, illegitimate son of Charles II, also implicated in the plot, is forced into exile.

King's gift aids Quakers' holy experiment

Philadelphia, 31 October 1682

A few days ago the 300-ton *Welcome* arrived here from England. It is perhaps the twentieth ship bearing English Quaker refugees from religious persecution to arrive here in the past year. The difference is that this ship brought with it the 38-year-old English Quaker, William Penn, who is the absolute monarch of this town and the new colony of Pennsylvania which surrounds it.

Penn has been here before. Working with new idealistic settlers in West Jersey he recognised the possibilities. Back in England he used his political skills to persuade King Charles II to give him royal land here to repay debts of £16,000 owed to his father, Admiral Penn.

The Royal Charter of last March gave him absolute powers. But Penn intends this as a "holy experiment" in which "myself and my successors" have "no power of doing mischief" and ensuring that "the will of one man may not hinder the good of a whole country". His cousin, William Markham, has built this town, and won the support of the 2,000 white settlers here with a democratic "frame of government". The Indians, too, have warmed to this Englishman, who is a devoted pacificist.

William Penn negotiates with the Indian natives of Pennsylvania.

Soldiers force conversions in France

Poitiers, 1681

Thousands of Huguenots all over France are being forced to give up their Protestant religion. There has been steadily increasing pressure on them because of the wish of King Louis XIV and some of the Catholic bishops to have a unified France with one religion. The Edict of Nantes of 1598, which gave Huguenots religious freedom, is now being persistently ignored. This town, however, has led the way in Draconian measures. Marillac, the local *intendant*, is using the traditional police practice of quartering soldiers on unruly citizens. These "missionaries in boots" are extracting forcible conversions. But many Huguenots are wealthy merchants and they are emigrating rather than give in.

Louis XIV annexes town of Strasbourg

Strasbourg, 30 September 1681

The independent city of Strasbourg surrendered to Louis XIV's army today under threat of being put to the sword. The citizens, knowing Louis' reputation in these matters, had no option but to open the gates.

Strasbourg thus becomes the latest victim of the French policy of *reunion* under which Louis is using force beneath a cloak of legalism to take advantage of the confusion arising out of the Treaties of Westphalia and Nijmegen. All of Alsace, with the exception of Mulhouse, is now French.

A London lamplighter and his apprentice ply their daily trade.

Sun King's court moves to Versailles

Versailles, 6 May, 1682
King Louis XIV arrived today at his new chateau at Versailles with his family, ministers and court, and announced that from now onwards it would be the seat of French government. He has been making visits for years to inspect the building work that has transformed his father's hunting lodge into the largest palace in Europe.

In 1679 Jules Hardouin Mansart succeeded the original architect Louis le Vau, who had built the central block. He has added two great wings, the southern one for royal princes and their families, the northern one for the courtiers, many hundreds of whom are lodged in the building. With a block for 1,500 servants and stables for the Master of the Horse and the pages, the chateau is a small town with a population of over 2,000 people. There is a service of sedan chairs to carry them from one point to another.

Mansart's new Hall of Mirrors, of immense length, with a ceiling painted by Charles le Brun, is the main assembly point and the scene for the fetes and gambling parties that are a feature of court life. The gardens of formal terraces, ornamental basins of water lined with statuary and 1,500 fountains are the work of Andre le Notre. The tapestries and furnishings of the chateau are all designed by Le Brun and made at the Gobelins factory. The king insists on the strictest etiquette and punctuality throughout the royal day which is regulated by ceremonial – his *lever*, the procession to Mass, reception of ambassadors, his dining in public, his hunting in the afternoons and the evening entertainments, for which he may order the court to appear in new clothes. Many of the nobility fear that they may be ruined by the expense of court life.

Also in residence are Madame de Montespan, who has apartments next to his own, and his new favourite, Madame de Maintenon, who looked after the children whom she had by the king.

Lemonnier's painting of Louis XIV unveiling a new statue at Versailles.

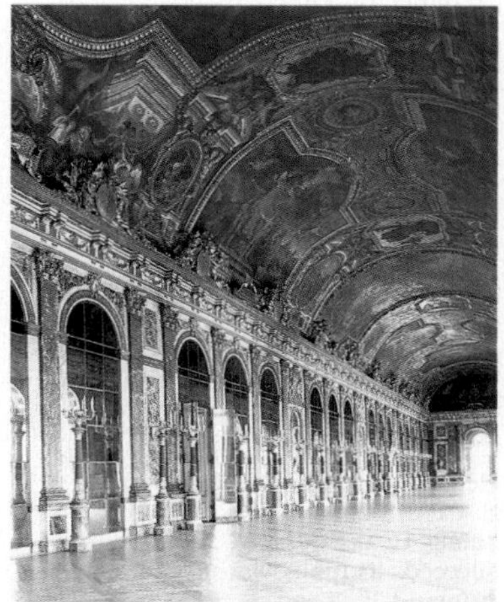
Mansart's "Galerie des Glaces" at Versailles, finished in 1684.

Whigs executed on charge of plotting to murder Charles

London, 1683
The so-called Rye House Plot has the makings of a re-run of the notorious Popish Plot fabricated by Titus Oates five years ago – but with the tables turned. Now it is the Whigs who are the victims of fanciful and often false evidence.

They are said to have plotted to assassinate Charles II and James as they passed Rumbold's Rye House on the London-to-Newmarket road. Prominent Whigs have been executed and others have fled.

Lord Shaftesbury, the former chancellor who intrigued against the Catholic James, escaped to Holland after being accused of treason and died there recently. He played a leading role in the persecution of Catholics after Oates, a sacked navy chaplain, claimed to have discovered a Popish Plot to assassinate Charles II and put James on the throne. Crowds roamed the streets of London threatening Catholics.

The latest purges are not limited to politicians. The City of London, a Whig stronghold, has lost its charter and universities are being brought to heel. John Locke, the philosopher, has left Oxford and fled to Holland, where he goes by the name of Dr Van der Linden, as he works on a book on human understanding.

Russian writer and priest dies at stake

Pustozersk, Russia, 1682
Avvakum, the leader of the a breakaway sect known as the "Old Believers", has been burnt at the stake after spending 15 years in a subterranean prison in the north of Russia. A talented but fanatical priest, he produced a string of sermons and treatises rejecting the influence of the Greek and Latin churches. Avvakum's movement has drawn large numbers of strictly Orthodox Russians, although it has been persecuted by the authorities. Whole groups of its members, even as many as 2,500, have turned to mass suicide by burning, a death preferable to eternal hellfire.

Celebrated landscape painter, Claude Lorrain, dies in Rome

Rome, 23 November, 1682
Claude Lorrain, the greatest of French landscape painters, died today in Rome where he lived and worked from the age of 13. He was 82 and famed for his mastery of light effects. He could even depict the rising or setting sun convincingly illuminating his landscapes.

Lorrain's real name was Gellee, but he was always known after his home province. Like his friend and compatriot Nicolas Poussin, who also spent his life in Rome, Claude liked to sketch direct from nature in the Campagna countryside outside Rome, littered with the remains of Roman architecture. But his ideal mythological landscapes were always imaginary.

Claude Lorrain's "Landscape with the arrival of Aeneas at Pallanteum".

1683 (1683-1685)

Pennsylvania, 23 June 1683. William Penn signs a treaty of peace and brotherhood with the Indians in his new colony.

Vienna, 13 July 1683. Having invaded Austria earlier in the year, the Turks lay siege to Vienna.

Paris, 6 September 1683. Jean Baptiste Colbert, Louis XIV's chief aide, dies. Active in all spheres of public life, Colbert sought to boost the economy by state intervention and to control state spending, but his oppressive taxes provoked public hatred.

Austria, 12 September 1683. A combined Austrian and Polish army, led by Charles of Lorraine and John III Sobieski of Poland, defeats the Turks at Kahlenberg.

New York, November 1683. A Charter of Liberties is enacted, banning taxation without consent.

Serbia, 25 December 1683. On the orders of Sultan Mehmet IV, the grand vizier Kara Mustafa, who led the disastrous Ottoman invasion of Austria, is strangled in Belgrade.

Versailles, 1683. Queen Marie Therese dies. Madame de Maitenon, Louis XIV's new favourite, marries the king in secret.

Iceland, 1683. An Icelandic translation of the Bible by Gudbrandur Thorlaksson is published.

Germany, 1683. The writer Daniel Caspar von Lohenstein, a master of German baroque drama, dies. He leaves unfinished an enormously long novel entitled *Arminius*.

Crimea, 1683. The Tartar chief Murat Giray is exiled by the Ottomans. He had attempted to impose a policy of independence in the Crimea and to replace the "divine law" of Islam with that of Genghis Khan.

West Africa, 1683. Merchants from Brandenburg establish a trading post on the Gold Coast.

China, 1683. Dutch merchants win the right to trade with Canton.

Taiwan, 1683. The Chinese seize the island of Taiwan, destroying the empire of Cheng Ching.

Portugal, 1683. Peter II becomes king of Portugal in succession to his brother Alfonso VI, during whose reign he was regent.

Netherlands, June 1684. A French army under Marshall Crequi seizes Luxembourg.

Germany, August 1684. The Emperor Leopold signs a 20-year truce with Louis XIV of France at Ratisbon, under which France retains control of Strasbourg and Luxembourg.

Paris, 30 September 1684. The tragedian Pierre Corneille, whose *Le Cid* took Paris by storm in 1636, dies.

Paris, 1684. *Nova Methodis pro Maximus et Minimus* by the German philosopher Gottfried Leibnitz, is published in French. In the essay the author sets forth the process which led him to create differential calculus.

South-East Africa, 1684. Changamire Dombo defeats the Portuguese at the battle of Maungwe.

Rome, 1684. Pope Innocent IX forms a Holy League with Venice, Austria and Poland against the Turks.

Netherlands, 1684. Pierre Bayle founds *Nouvelles de la Republique des Lettres*, a review of literary and intellectual life published in Rotterdam but reaching and reporting the whole European "republic of letters".

London, 1684. During an extraordinarily cold winter a "Frost Fair" is held on the frozen Thames. Streets of stalls are set up, meat is roasted on the spit; football, bowls, ninepins, throwing the cock, even foxhunting, are performed on the ice. A novel means of getting about is "sliding with skeetes" (skating).

Japan, 1684. The great Japanese writer Ihara Saikaku composes 23,400 *haikai* verses in a single day and night.

England, 16 February 1685. At the death of Charles II, his brother James II, the duke of York succeeds as the new king of England.

England, July 1685. Defeated by James II's army at Sedgemoor, the duke of Monmouth, illegitimate son of Charles II, is beheaded. Last month Monmouth, who was exiled two years ago after the Rye House Plot, landed at Lyme Regis in Dorset with a small band of men and denounced King James as an usurper.

England, September 1685. Judge George Jeffreys is appointed lord chancellor after presiding over the "bloody assizes" in which about 320 men implicated in the Monmouth rebellion were sentenced to death.

France, 18 October 1685. To force the all French to practise Roman Catholic religion, Louis XIV revokes the 1598 Edict of Nantes, which granted civil liberties and political powers to Protestants.

Scotland, 1685. A rebellion in Scotland on behalf of the duke of Monmouth fails and its leader, the earl of Argyll, is executed.

Emperor Kangxi's tour of Kiang Han in 1699: after Chai Ping Chan.

Enlightened rule of Manchurian emperor

Beijing, 1683

A golden age of culture is blooming under the enlightened reign of Emperor Kangxi. This reign has now lasted for 22 years and has been characterised by the emperor's policy of tolerance towards the Chinese gentry. Although this is partly a question of political prudence, to avert opposition, it also reflects the emperor's own cultural interests. He is a musician, poet, and calligrapher and has a keen interest in the sciences. His patronage has ensured that with the honourable exception of some Ming scholars who have exiled themselves in the south, most of the Chinese scholar officials have transferred their loyalty to the Manchus.

Louis XIV's wife founds poor-girls' school

France, 1684

A year after their secret marriage Francoise de Maitenon and King Louis XIV have founded a girls' school at St Cyr convent. Born in a debtors' prison in 1635, Francoise had a sobering affect on the King. She feared that if he did not mend his extravagant ways he would suffer divine retribution. Francoise met the king when she was nanny to his illegitimate children. When he legitimized them in 1673 he ordered her to bring them to the court and infuriated de Montespan and de Fontanges, his mistresses, when he gave Francoise the estate of Maitenon. After Queen Maria Theresa died, the king made her his morganatic wife.

The royal mistress in a suitably romantic setting: by Casper Netscher.

Protestant churches to be demolished following reversal of Edict of Nantes

Fontainebleau, 18 October 1685
King Louis XIV today revoked the Edict of Nantes, signed by his grandfather in 1598, and granting religious and political freedom to the Huguenots. The move is only the logical extension of the policies of the past four years, during which the Edict has been ignored in practice. Louis is determined to stamp out Protestantism in France.

Nevertheless, today's Edict of Fontainebleau is even more severe than expected. Protestant worship is to be forbidden and the churches demolished. All citizens are being forced into Catholic baptism and marriage. Ministers who refuse to recant are being banished. At the same time the laity are being forbidden to emigrate. The latter measure reflects the king's concern about the economic effects on France of the massive emigration of Huguenots over the past four years. They include many wealthy merchants and skilled craftsmen and countries like England have welcomed their talents.

Many Catholics are rejoicing today. The Edict of Nantes did not abolish the fierce hatred existing between the two religious groups. Louis himself has been as much driven by the desire for political stability as for religious unity. The revolt at La Rochelle in 1628 had convinced him that Protestantism was a political threat to the monarchy while it existed.

Triumphant Catholic zealots demolish the Protestant temple at Charenton.

Luxembourg ceded to France by Spain

Luxembourg, August 1684
Luxembourg, which was occupied by the French army in June, has been ceded to France by Spain in a 20-year truce signed in a Dominican convent in Bavaria. Louis XIV has thus benefited again from the spoiling tactics of his army while the rest of Europe has been occupied with driving the Turks from the gates of Vienna.

The signatories to the Treaty of Ratisbon all had good reasons to sign: Spain because it had been thrashed by the French army; Emperor Leopold because he wished to pursue the Turks and; Louis because the treaty confirmed the gains made by his policy of *reunion*.

James II succeeds debauched Charles

London, 1685
After the amorous and dissolute Charles II, the new king, James II, presents himself as a model of rectitude and frugality. He has called an early parliament, but ensured a subservient one by ordering lord lieutenants to keep out Whigs and make sure Tories are elected.

The Whig cause has been damaged by inept rebellions mounted by the duke of Argyll and the duke of Monmouth, Charles II's illegitimate son. At the "Bloody Assizes" this year Judge Jeffreys sentenced 320 of Monmouth's supporters to be hanged, 841 to be sent as slaves to the plantations, and many more to be flogged.

Vienna siege is lifted

A panoramic view of the Turkish armies during their siege of Vienna.

Vienna, 12 September 1683
Vienna is saved. A 70,000-strong Christian army led by Charles, the duke of Lorraine and King John Sobieski of Poland has routed the vast Ottoman army that has been encamped around the city for the past eight weeks.

Six months ago, Kara Mustafa, the Turkish grand vizier, was in Adrianople, assembling an army of 200,000 men, purportedly to come to the aid of Tekeli in Hungary, and to capture the fortresses of Gyor and Komarom. The real target seems to have been Vienna. There was no effective opposition as Mustafa's forces marched towards Vienna. The siege began on 13 July, and although the Viennese had an advantage in artillery, and the 13,000-strong garrison resisted strongly, it could not have survived much longer.

But Kara Mustafa made fatal errors. He allowed the relief force to cross the Danube, and occupy the Kahlenberg Heights. He then tried to repel the attackers with cavalry alone, and did not commit his main force of janissaries until the initiative had been lost.

Duke of Lorraine defeats the Turks

The Duke of Lorraine, saviour of Vienna from the Ottoman forces.

Hungary, 1685
The Ottoman armies, once threatening Vienna itself, are being driven out of Hungary in a series of defeats inflicted by Imperial troops under Charles, the duke of Lorraine.

Turkish fortunes have been declining since the Ottomans were repulsed at Vienna in 1683. Now the armies of the Holy League, drawn from Venice, Poland, Malta, Tuscany and the papacy, are moving steadily across Hungary.

The Turks are not just suffering military setbacks. Morale in their empire is at an all-time low; the nobility are losing their lands, soldiers go unpaid and the poor have barely enough to eat.

1685 (1685-1688)

Germany, 8 November 1685. Frederick William, elector of Brandenburg, issues the Edict of Potsdam, offering French Huguenots refuge in Brandenburg.

France, 1685. A *code noir* is published defining slaves as chattels with no rights to ownership or justice – though they are allowed to rest on Sundays and be instructed in the Christian religion. The code also specifies punishments for slaves.

South Carolina, 1685. The renunciation of the Edict of Nantes spurs the migration of French Huguenots to South Carolina.

West Africa, 1685. King Wegbaja, who created the kingdom of Dahomey at Abomey, dies and is succeeded by his son Akaba.

South Africa, 1685. French Huguenots begin to settle at the Cape of Good Hope.

China, 1685. Louis XIV, king of France, sends five Jesuits to China, where they found a mission in Peking.

Hungary, 8 July 1686. The Austrians take Buda from the Turks and annex Hungary.

Russia, October 1686. Having joined Pope Innocent XI's Holy League and ensured the safety of Kiev by a treaty with Poland, Russia declares war on the Ottoman empire.

Germany, 1686. The Emperor Leopold breaks the 1684 truce of Ratisbon and joins the League of Augsburg, formed by Sweden and several German states to oppose Louis XIV of France.

India, 1686. The French found Chandernagore.

Bulgaria, 1686. An anti-Turkish conspiracy is uncovered at Tarnovo. The Turks destroy the town.

Moscow, 1686. The Russian painter and engraver Semion Fedorovitch Ouchakov dies. Famous for his decoration of churches, Ouchakov opened an icon workshop in Moscow.

Ireland, January 1687. Richard Talbot, earl of Tyrconnel, is appointed viceroy of Ireland.

North America, 19 March 1687. The French explorer La Salle is murdered by his own men while searching for the mouth of the Mississippi along the coast of the gulf of Mexico.

England, 14 April 1687. Having failed to persuade Parliament to repeal the 1673 Test Act, James II issues a Declaration of Indulgence, granting toleration to both Catholics and non-conformists.

Hungary, 12 August 1687. Charles of Lorraine defeats the Turks at the battle of Mohacs.

India, 1687. The Great Moghul Aurangzeb conquers and annexes the Deccan sultanate of Golconda.

Greece, 1687. The Venetians under Francesco Morosini, who have recently seized parts of Dalmatia and Morea, attack the Turks in Greece. They take Corinth and lay siege to Athens. The Parthenon, converted into a powder magazine by the Turks, is seriously damaged by a Venetian shell.

Istanbul, 1687. With the Ottoman empire in a state of complete anarchy, Sultan Mehmet IV is deposed by the Janissaries. He is succeeded by his younger brother Suleiman II.

England, 1687. The economist Sir William Petty, author of *Political Arithmetic*, a study of the value of comparative statistics, dies. Petty, who also wrote a *Treatise on Taxes* and invented a copying machine and a double-keeled boat, was one of the first members of the Royal Society.

Moscow, 1687. In a gesture of reconciliation between church leaders who are open to western ideas and those who think them dangerous, a Slavono-Greek-Latin academy is established.

Paris, 1687. Francois Fenelon writes his *Treatise on the Education of Girls*, in which he argues that a sound education depends on the fulfilment of a child's natural abilities.

Pennsylvania, 18 February 1688. The radical Protestant sect known as the Mennonites – which evolved out of the Anabaptist movement of last century – is the first religious group in the colonies to condemn slavery.

Hungary, 9 May 1688. The diet of Transylvania accedes to Habsburg domination.

England, 31 August 1688. John Bunyan, author of *The Pilgrim's Progress*, dies.

Serbia, 6 September 1688. Imperial troops defeat the Turks to take Belgrade.

Europe, 1688. Taking advantage of the Emperor Leopold's activities in the Balkans against the Turks, Louis XIV of France begins an undeclared war against the Holy Roman Empire. French forces capture the Palatinate, Trier, Mainz and Cologne and invade Franconia and Swabia.

Versailles, 1688. Jules Hardouin Mansart, chief architect to Louis XIV, constructs the Grand Trianon at the Palace of Versailles.

Emperor's son crowned king of Hungary

Buda, 9 December 1687

The Ottoman empire has suffered a major reverse at the hands of Emperor Leopold I's Habsburg army which has boldly fought its way across the plains to occupy much of Hungary and Transylvania in a campaign lasting more than four years.

The emperor's son, Joseph, was today crowned king of Hungary, putting Austria and Hungary under a Habsburg crown. This has been achieved despite the reluctance of the Magyars now freed of Turkish occupation.

The invasion of Hungary became inevitable when the Turkish army was defeated at Vienna, but remained in strength in Hungary. Leopold's diplomats succeeded in securing a truce with Louis XIV and arranging an alliance with Poland and Venice.

Japanese writer tells passionate stories

Diptych by Kitao Masanobu: "The Autographs of Yoshiwara Beauties".

Japan, 1686

The master of Japanese prose, Ihara Saikaku, has produced a sensational narrative, *Five Women of Pleasure*. It tells of the tragic lives of courtesans in five connected stories, all based on recent events. Like his long narrative, *The Life of a Libertine*, it is a satire and has earned him the rebuke of the moralists. Ihara Saikaku originally practisesed as a poet. Now he is building up a survey of the way society lives today.

Prison critique puts midwife in the dock

London, England, 1687

Elizabeth Cellier, the Catholic midwife who was acquitted of "the Meal Tub plot" in June, is to be tried for her criticism of conditions inside Newgate prison. Many believe that the case has been trumped up to prevent her from being a witness in another case involving allegations of conspiracy to murder the king. Mrs Cellier, a pioneer of midwifery and obstetric skills, was first taken to Newgate after allegations that evidence of a conspiracy to prevent James' accession to the throne had been hidden in her meal tub.

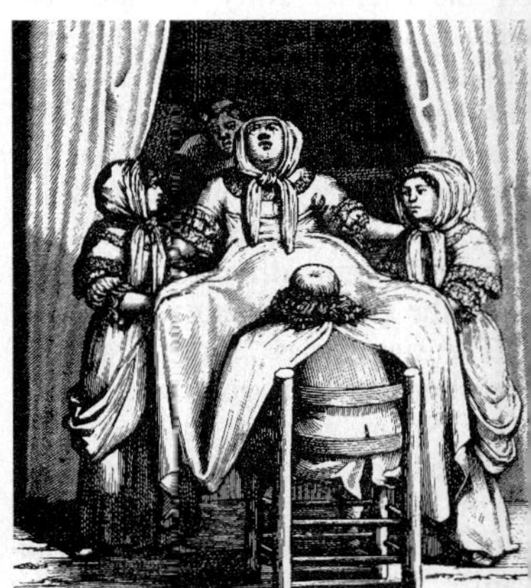

A midwife's profession: obstetrics.

The Universe attracts, says scientist

London, 1687
Two long, hard years of sustained writing effort have culminated in a new book from the mathematician and physicist, Isaac Newton, which is being proclaimed a masterpiece by those fellow-countrymen who are able to understand it. It is called *Philosophiae Naturalis Principia Mathematica*, The Mathematical Principles of Natural Philosophy and consists of three parts. The first part is devoted to the motions of bodies in an unresisting medium – such as planets in orbit round the sun; the second looks at bodies in resisting mediums such as fluids; the third applies these mechanical theories to astronomical problems, and demonstrates what the author calls "the frame of the System of the World".

In the *Principia*, Newton formulates a law of gravitation which is universally applicable. And he supports this gravitational theory with detailed and convincing mathematical proofs, including the use of the calculus. Newton also explicitly defines such concepts as force, momentum and mass and states three laws of motion.

Law one deals with inertia; a body stays at rest unless acted upon by forces. The second law states that the change of motion in a body is in proportion to the force acting on it, and is in a straight line. And the third law states that for every action in nature there is an equal and equivalent reaction.

However, it is the notion of a gravitational force that is capturing everyone's imagination. In Newton's universe, every single piece of matter, from a star to a feather, exerts a force on every other particle. This force is proportional to the product of their masses and inversely proportional to the square of the distance between them.

This universal gravitational law makes sense of the whole structure of the cosmos, and in doing so, produces a unified description of the earth and the heavens.

Newton's reflecting telescope.

A microscope by Christopher Cock.

Isaac Newton: by Antonio Verrio.

A Chinese silver gilt teapot of the late 18th century, with bamboo-shaped spout. This was a rare piece made specifically for the European market.

Negro code to help French sugar slaves

France, 1685
France's negro slaves, whose labour creates the wealth the nation draws from her sugar plantations in the New World, are to be given some respite from the harsh conditions under which they work. The Negro Code is designed to offer them more humane treatment. For the first time they are to receive adequate food, as well as regular time off to cultivate their own crops. But the whip, source of so much cruelty, is to be retained.

Protestants wary of new tolerance by Catholic king

London, 14 April 1687
An ostensible act of reconciliation by James II has been received with great mistrust by his people. The King today issued a Declaration of Indulgence by which all penal laws in matters of religion are suspended. Prominent Dissenters are being released from prison and wooed. But James is a convinced Catholic and he is packing the Privy Council with Catholics. The chief commands of the army and navy have been given to Catholics, and they are being forced on universities. Even the royalist Lord Halifax is hostile. "You are being hugged now only that you may be better squeezed later," he warns English Protestants.

French poets clash over modern arts

Paris, 27 January 1687
The Academie Francaise was the scene of violent dispute between champions of ancient and modern literature today when Charles Perrault read his poem, *Le Siecle de Louis XIV*, which claims that the present age is producing greater literature and art than the age of Augustus or Pericles. He argues that present-day forms surpass the classics. But Nicholas Boileau, the critic and arbiter of French prose style, retorted that the Ancients were the only models to follow.

Charles Perrault: modern is best.

1688 (1688-1690)

France, 26 November 1688. Louis XIV declares war on the Netherlands.

England, 28 December 1688. Invited by seven English lords, William of Orange and his English wife Mary enter London, having landed in England last month. James II, meanwhile, has fled to France.

Ireland, 3 April 1689. After landing in Ireland with troops and money from France's King Louis XIV, James II is acknowledged as king by an Irish Parliament in Dublin.

New England, 19 April 1689. Emboldened by the news of William and Mary's victory in England, the residents of Boston oust their governor Edmund Andros and effectively break up the Dominion of New England.

London, 21 April 1689. William III and Mary II are crowned joint king and queen of England, Scotland and Ireland.

Europe, May 1689. England and the Netherlands join the League of Augsburg.

England, 17 May 1689. Following the decision by Louis XIV to send an expedition to aid James II in Ireland, England declares war on France.

London, 24 May 1689. Parliament passes the Act of Toleration, exempting Protestants dissenting from the Church of England from the penalties of certain laws, as long as they have sworn oaths of allegiance and supremacy. Roman Catholics are specifically excluded from such relief.

Germany, June 1689. The French forces wreak havoc and carry out massacres in the Palatinate.

Scotland, 27 July 1689. The Scottish Jacobites – supporters of the deposed James II – are defeated by government forces at the battle of Killiecrankie.

Ireland, 1 August 1689. A 15-week siege of Londonderry by James II's Irish-French army ends in failure. The Protestants of Londonderry have affirmed their allegiance to William and Mary.

Siberia, 6 September 1689. The Chinese and the Russians sign a treaty at Nerchinsk establishing the boundary between their two countries along the Argun and Gorbitsa rivers and the Stanovoi mountain range.

New York, 14 October 1689. Jacob Leisler, a German-born militia captain, leads a rebellion of supporters of William and Mary against a pro-Jacobite faction and sets up a provisional government.

Russia, 1689. Czar Peter (the Great), who has ruled jointly with his half-brother Ivan V since 1682, launches a successful coup and becomes sole ruler of Russia.

Germany, 1689. The forces of the Grand Alliance, as the Augsburg League has become known, recapture Mainz and Bonn from the French.

North America, 1689. The war of the Grand Alliance spreads to North America, where it is known as King William's war.

London, 1689. Thomas Sydenham, called the "Hippocrates of England", dies. Noted in particular for his invention of laudanum (a medicine with an opium base), Sydenham also wrote a treatise on gout.

Amsterdam, 1689. The Dutch landscape artist Meindert Hobbema paints a masterpiece entitled *The Lane at Middelharnis*.

Ireland, 1690. William III lands in Ireland with an Anglo-Dutch army.

Canada, 11 May 1690. In the first major engagement of King William's war, British troops from Massachusetts, led by Sir William Phips, seize Port Royal in Acadia (*Nova Scotia* and *New Brunswick*) from the French. Their main objective is to take Quebec.

Netherlands, 1 July 1690. Led by Marshal Luxembourg, the French defeat the forces of the Grand Alliance at Fleurus. In addition to England, the Netherlands and the Austrian Habsburgs, the alliance now includes Savoy, Sweden, Spain, the Holy Roman Empire. Bavaria, Saxony and the Palatinate.

England, 1690. French warships decisively defeat an Anglo-Dutch fleet at the battle of Beachy Head.

South-East Africa, 1690. Changamire Dombo's Rozvi army defeats Munhumutapa Nyakunembire.

West Africa, c.1690. The small Aja kingdom of Ouidah (*Whydah*) on the Dahomey coast has become a major port for European ships taking slaves across the Atlantic.

India, 1690. The English found a trading post at Calcutta.

London, 1690. The philosopher John Locke publishes his *Essay concerning Human Understanding* and a *Treatise on Civil Government*.

Paris, 1690. The publication of *Caracteres* by Jean de La Bruyere, a collection of character portraits of men and women of his time, wins the author great acclaim and a number of bitter enemies.

French terror tactics backfire in Germany

Paris, May 1689

A "Grand Alliance" has been formed to counter the war of aggression launched by Louis XIV against the Palatinate states in Germany. The atrocities carried out by French troops on his direct orders have roused hatred for the "Sun King" throughout Europe. Yet instead of forcing the German states to surrender, the burning of their towns has hardened their resolve and the spirit of German nationalism is burning brightly.

Louis started his war with limited objectives: to secure his sister-in-law's claims of succession in the Palatinate, force the appointment of his ally, the Prince of Furstenberg, as Archbishop-Elector of Cologne, and to prevent William of Orange ousting James II of Great Britain.

However, he also had limited resources; the building of Versailles had emptied his treasury. It would have to be a short war. Louis, contemptuous of the Germans, was sure they would quickly capitulate. But the valiant defence of Phillipsberg delayed his offensive and now his enemy, William of Orange, has been welcomed in London and the Grand Alliance formed.

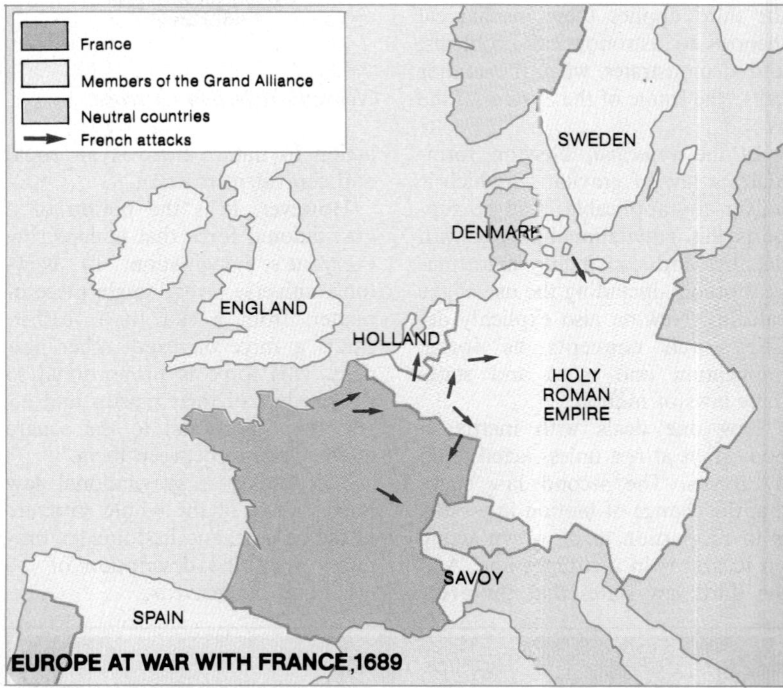

EUROPE AT WAR WITH FRANCE,1689

Ruler who united Prussia is dead

Konigsberg, Prussia, 1688

Frederick William, the Margrave of Brandenberg – but known universally as "The Great Elector" – has died, leaving a united and powerful Prussia. The country that Frederick inherited in 1640 was impoverished by the Thirty Years War, and yet, by shrewd diplomacy, the Elector gained territories, including East Pomerania, and turned a few hundred mercenaries into a standing army of 30,000 highly trained men which is the envy of his European neighbours.

Woman playwright was a former spy

London, 16 April, 1689

Aphra Behn, the first woman in England to be a professional writer is to be honoured by burial in Westminster Abbey. Brought up in Surinam, her best-known work is the story of a West Indian slave *Orinooko*, whom she knew personally. In 1668 Mrs Behn came to England and married a Dutch merchant who soon died. She went to Antwerp as a spy for the king, and then to prison for debt. As a widow she began writing, producing 1‘ plays, several novels and poems.

English exile their Catholic monarch

William of Orange rides into London

London, 28 December 1688
Leading a motley army of Dutch, Germans, French Huguenots, Swedes and Swiss – and reinforced by England's greatest general, John Churchill – William of Orange rode into London today to take over the crown with his English consort Mary. James II had fled and his feared and detested Lord Chancellor, Judge Jeffreys, has been picked up by a mob in east London and imprisoned in the Tower.

James caused dismay when he began putting Catholics in positions of power. Then he ordered his Declaration of Indulgence to be read in churches; seven bishops refused and were put in the Tower. With the birth of a son to James' wife, Mary, a Catholic succession was in prospect. The politicians sent for William and Mary.

James II throws the Great Seal of Parliament into the river Thames.

William of Orange and Queen Mary accept Great Britain's Bill of Rights.

New King agrees to protect freedoms

London, 22 January 1689
England's "Bloodless Revolution" reached its climax today when parliament formally invited William and Mary to become joint sovereigns. The invitation was accompanied by a Declaration of Rights, endorsed by the royal couple, which sets out constitutional guarantees to protect the freedom of the individual and the rights of parliament, in particular to vote taxes and raise an army. The Declaration will be converted into a Bill of Rights to be passed by parliament.

The group of MPs known as "Tories" (who at first had opposed the attempt to exclude James from the throne) joined with their Whig opponents to support his overthrow after being alienated by the arbitrary conduct of James. But some Tories were unhappy with the Whig insistence that James had abdicated and wanted a regency; others wanted Mary alone to be given the crown. But William would have no truck with a regency and Mary said she would not take the throne without her husband.

There is to be no systematic persecution of those who served the Stuart kings. A few are expected to go to gaol, but William insists that mercy can also be a demonstration of strength as well as weakness.

The City of London played a key role in smoothing the transition from the House of Stuart to the House of Orange. William called together members of the Lords, MPs from the time of Charles II, and City merchants to form a kind of pre-parliament convention.

Teenage Czar puts sister in nunnery

Russia, 1689
In a sudden coup, 16-year-old Czar Peter has taken over the country and forced his half-sister Sophia, the regent, to resign and retire to a convent. Her advisers have been arrested. Galitzin has been exiled and Chalitsky, head of the "streltsy" (the palace guard) has been put to death.

For the past seven years Peter has been ostensibly sharing power with his half-brother Ivan. He plotted the coup from a monastery where he had taken refuge, frightened that Sophia planned his execution to ensure Ivan's succession.

Now Peter has appointed a new regent – his mother – and until he reaches adulthood she will effectively rule Russia. Only one thing flaws the new situation: the excitement of events has given Peter what seems a permanent nervous and violent facial twitch.

Russia's new emperor, Czar Peter, who has taken over the country.

Turks rumoured to have poisoned prince

Romania, 1688
Turkish conspirators are suspected of poisoning Serban Cantacuzene, the popular prince of Walachia (*a region of Romania*) who has died suddenly, aged 48. Cantacuzene, a Turkish appointee, was about to march on Istanbul in a bid to drive his former masters back across the Bosporus and out of Europe.

The top-secret venture is believed to have had the moral, if not the practical support of the western powers. Cantacuzene, a cultured aristocrat of Greek descent, is being mourned in Walachia as a progressive leader. In his 11 years as hospador he started maize production, now the country's staple food. His cultural reforms designed to encourage the Romanian language included the creation of the Romanian school in Bucharest and the printing of the Romanian Bible.

Russia and China agree in Siberia

Siberia, 7 September 1689
The Russian and Chinese empires today signed a treaty at the Siberian frontier post of Nerchinsk bringing an end to 20 years of border fighting between Russian cossacks and the Manchu army.

The Russian military exploration of Siberia followed by traders eager to exploit the territory's riches was certain to provoke Chinese suspicion and the Manchus reacted violently to Russian incursion in territory they had already claimed. Four years ago the Manchus destroyed a Russian fort at Albazin on the Amur river and when it was rebuilt they laid siege to it again.

Under the terms of the treaty the boundaries between these two vast empires will lie along the Gorbitsa and Argun rivers thus recognising China's claim to the land north of the Amur.

1690 (1690-1695)

Ireland, 11 July 1690. William III defeats James II at the battle of the Boyne.

Serbia, 8 October 1690. Belgrade is retaken by the Turks.

New York, 26 May 1691. Jacob Leisler, leader of the popular uprising in support of William and Mary's accession to the English throne, is executed for treason.

Ireland, 12 July 1691. William III defeats the allied Irish and French at the battle of Aughrim.

New England, 17 October 1691. Maine and Plymouth are incorporated within Massachusetts.

Ireland, 1691. Limerick, the Jacobite headquarters, surrenders to William III's forces after successfully resisting two sieges. By the peace of Limerick, Catholics are granted a measure of religious toleration, and Jacobite soldiers and civilians remaining in Ireland are granted security of life and property.

Istanbul, 1691. Backed by the vizier Fazil Mustafa Koprulu, Ahmed II succeeds his brother Suleiman II as Ottoman sultan.

London, 1691. The navigator William Dampier publishes his *Voyage around the World*, in which he tells of his expeditions against Spanish trading posts in the Antilles and the Gulf of Mexico.

Scotland, 13 February 1692. On the orders of William III, nearly 40 members of the MacDonald clan are massacred at Glencoe for their Jacobite sympathies and their delay in taking an oath of allegiance.

Netherlands, 3 August 1692. Following their capture of Namur in June, the French forces under Marshal Luxembourg defeat the English at the battle of Steenkerke.

Massachusetts, 1692. Twenty people are executed in Salem for witchcraft.

France, 1692. The French are heavily defeated by a Grand Alliance fleet at La Hogue.

Mexico, 1692. Rioting breaks out in Mexico City, caused by food shortages.

Netherlands, 29 July 1693. The army of the Grand Alliance is crushed by French forces at the battle of Neerwinden.

Versailles, 15 September 1693. Louis XIV repudiates the 1682 Declaration of the Four Articles, which sought to reconcile papal authority with Gallican independence, and attempts to improve relations with the pope.

Germany, 1693. Louis XIV's forces inflict a defeat on Saxony, a member of the Grand Alliance.

New Mexico, 1693. Governor Ponce de Leon completes the reconquest of New Mexico for Spain.

Jamaica, 1693. The English found Kingston.

West Africa, 1693. The French admiral Tourville deals a severe blow to the English navy by capturing 100 ships, almost the entire Smyrna fleet, in the Gulf of Guinea off Lagos.

Japan, 1693. Ihara Saikaku, the great poet and writer of popular fiction, dies in Osaka at the age of 51. He composed hundreds of thousands of *haiku* verses and began a new genre of fiction known as "tales of the floating world".

South-East Africa, 1693. Changamire Dombo expels all the Portuguese from his Rozvi kingdom in Zimbabwe.

France, June 1694. After a desperate struggle with a superior Dutch fleet, the French naval commander Jean Bart recaptures a large flotilla of corn-ships and steers them safely into Dunkirk, breaking the English blockade.

Canada, 23 October 1694. American colonial forces led by Sir William Phips fail in their attempt to seize Quebec, the capital of New France, and withdraw after a two-week siege.

England, 28 December 1694. Queen Mary II dies.

Persia, 1694. Hussein, a devout Shia, becomes shah of Persia.

Aegean, 1694. A Venetian attack on the island of Chios is beaten off by the Turks.

London, 1694. The composer Henry Purcell publishes his *Te Deum for St Cecilia's Day* and *Timon of Athens.*

Paris, 1694. The French Academy publishes its *Dictionnaire*, prepared under the direction of the grammarian Claude Favre de Vaugelas.

Rumania, 1694. Constantin Brancovan founds the Academy of St Sava in Bucharest.

Prussia, 1694. The university of Halle opens. Its patron is the philosopher Christian Thomasius, a fervent patriot who desires to promote the German language in favour of Latin. Jacob Spener, head of the theology faculty, makes the new university a centre of "pietism", a movement opposed to the dogmatism of the established Lutheran church.

India, 1695. The Firangi Mahal school of Moslem learned and holy men is founded.

Exiled English King defeated in Ireland

James II flees after the Battle of the Boyne: painted by Gow in 1888.

Ireland, 1690

The Protestant William has scored a decisive victory over the exiled James II and his Irish, French and English Jacobites. When William arrived James' forces were well dug in on rising ground behind the river Boyne, the only defensive barrier between Belfast and Dublin.

William threw in his forces on 1 July, but kept the untried English regiments in reserve and attacked with his Germans, Danes, Dutch, French Huguenots and Finns. But when hand-to-hand struggles developed, the English were brought in and the Irish, French and Jacobites were broken. James lost 1,600 men killed, wounded or taken prisoner; William lost a third of that number.

Victory on the Boyne has been followed by a brilliant expedition led by John Churchill, who has brought all south-western Ireland under English control, with a swiftly mounted seaborne assault on Cork and Kinsale.

Life on other planets is a possibility

Holland, 1690

Some years ago the Dutch scientist Christiaan Huygens published his ideas on the wave nature of light in his *Traite de la lumiere* (Treatise on Light). But his thoughts have also been taking a philosophical turn, as he contemplates the thought that life exists elsewhere in the universe. The earth is not the central body in the heavens, so why should we assume that we are privileged in being the only planet with life?

Huygens contends that there must be not just life, but other intelligent creatures like ourselves with high levels of intellect. He suggests that there are probably other worlds inhabited by plants and animals very like those on earth. He believes that the inhabitants are probably much like us.

Huygens: the Earth is not alone.

Bank of England formed

Financiers plan the national bank.

London, 1694

Faced with an urgent and recurring need for funds to continue the war with France, William III has adopted the novel idea of setting up a bank which will borrow from the public in order to make loans to the government. Although William takes public credit, the idea is thought to have been inspired by a suggestion of Lord Halifax. Magnates of the City have rushed to subscribe to the new institution, which is being called the Bank of England; the rate of interest, eight per cent, will be secured by trade and beer taxes.

In the past, much of the lending to the state was undertaken by the London goldsmiths, but their greed and appetite for speculation earned them the hostility of the City. Not surprisingly, the goldsmiths opposed the setting up of the Bank, as did the bishops in the House of Lords. The governmnent forced the measure through and within a few months of starting up, the Bank had lent the government the whole of its £1,200,000 authorised capital, though part of it had not been paid up. The shortfall was covered by issuing bills, which the Treasury accepted as cash and were paid out to creditors, who in turn cashed them later at the Bank. So a new phrase is coming into use: *The Bank of England promises to pay.*

So popular has the new institution become that the money was raised within a mere 12 days. There is no pressure to repay the loan, so long as the government continues to guarantee the interest.

The war with France has diverted capital from foreign trade into the manufacture of armaments, smelting and the mining of coal, copper and tin. Numerous joint stock companies have been set up to handle these enterprises.

Albanians throw out Turkish lords

Albania, 1690

Turkey is fast losing control of Albania, the latest Balkan outpost of the weakened Ottoman Empire to succumb to the rising tide of nationalism.

Albanian nationalist rebel forces have seized three key towns – Kamina, Vlore, and the citadel, Medun – as the country slides into open insurrection.

The basis of the fierce anti-Turkish resistance is an unusual coalition of urban Moslems and rural Christians. The Albanian uprising, coupled with the rebellion in neighbouring Montenegro, another Ottoman province, was sparked by the defeat of the Turkish sultan's armies at Vienna.

Banana tree poet had a light touch

Edo (Tokyo), Japan, 1694

Basho, the Zen master and greatest exponent of the poetic form known as the *haiku* has died in Japan. A major literary figure who taught others as well as displayed his own abilities, he leaves a community of 2,000 students.

"Basho" means banana tree and was the name adopted by the poet Matsuo Basho when he moved into a hut beside one to practise Zen and master the new art of the 17-syllable *haiku*.

He became a traveller, taking long journeys throughout Japan and writing travel notebooks in prose and poetry. He strove for "lightness". Now Japan mourns a literary giant.

Portuguese just hang on in Zimbabwe

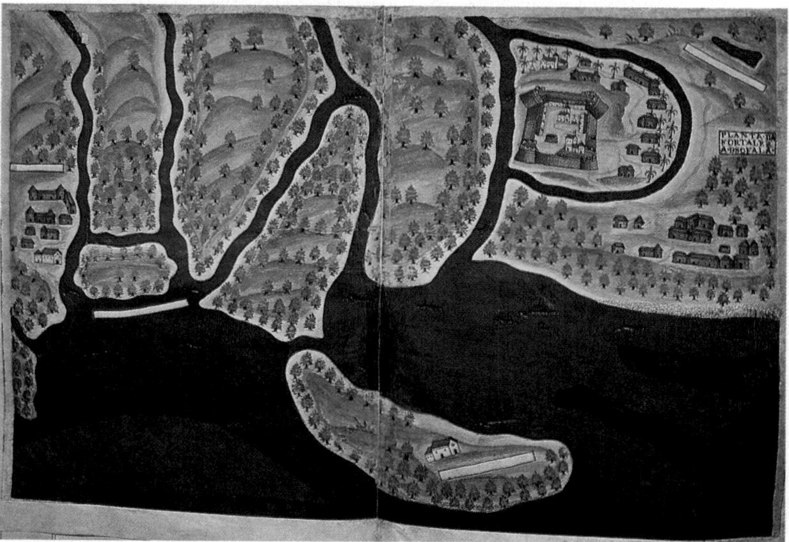

A map of Sofala: one of the East African trading posts set up by Portugal.

Zambezi Valley, East Africa, 1695

Portuguese traders and settlers have survived the onslaught of Changamire Dombo of Zimbabwe, but only just. As the Portuguese barricaded Sena, their last surviving settlement on the Zambezi, news came that Dombo was dead, and his army had withdrawn. Few thoughtful Portuguese are today blaming any but their own people for their predicament.

"The insolence of our people was the cause of these wars, for those who hold power and own African servants commit such excesses that from the scandalized kings and princes breaks forth these disasters," wrote the Portuguese viceroy. Dombo broke away from the Munhumutapa kingdom a generation earlier and it was then that he finally conquered the whole Zimbabwe plateau.

Controlling both the gold and ivory trade he grew rich enough to resist Portuguese pressures to come within their sphere of influence. Observing Portuguese attempts to expel the Moslem traders and dominate the region's commerce, and their economic exploitation of the Africans, Dombo was ready to go to war with Portugal. From the first battle in 1684 Dombo remained undefeated.

"Road on the Dyke" by Meindert Hobbema: a leading pupil of Jacob van Ruisdael. Hobbema's work, as popular in Britain as it is in Holland, concentrates on sunlit, summery representations of nature.

1695 (1695-1698)

France, 4 January 1695. On the death of Marshal Luxembourg, he is succeeded as commander of the French forces by the duke of Villeroi.

Istanbul, 27 January 1695. Mustafa II becomes Ottoman sultan on the death of Ahmed II.

Paris, 13 April 1695. The poet Jean de La Fontaine, author of brilliant collections of *Contes* and *Fables*, dies.

South-East Africa, 1695. Changamire Dombo dies after inflicting a further defeat on the Portuguese.

London, 1695. The architect Sir Christopher Wren designs a hospital for seamen at Greenwich.

London, 1695. *Love for Love*, a comedy by William Congreve, is produced for the first time.

England, April 1695. Censorship of the Press ends with the lapsing of the 1662 Licensing Act.

Brussels, August 1695. The French forces, led by the duke of Villeroi, lay siege to Brussels, which is in the hands of the Grand Alliance, and bombard the city.

Caucasus, 1695. Led by Peter the Great, the Russians lay siege to the Turkish-held city of Azov on the Don river. The siege fails and the Russians suffer heavy casualties.

Netherlands, 1695. Following the defeat of the French forces at the second battle of Namur, Louis XIV enters into secret negotiations with William III of Orange.

London, 10 April 1696. Parliament passes a Navigation Act to tighten its control over colonial trade.

France, 17 April 1696. Madame de Sevigny, famed for her writing of over 1,000 published letters reflecting the history of her time, dies of smallpox.

Caucasus, July 1696. At the second attempt the Russians capture the city of Azov from the Turks after mounting a blockade with their newly built fleet.

Germany, 6 October 1696. Savoy withdraws from the Grand Alliance.

London, 1696. The playwright and architect Sir John Vanbrugh presents his first comedy, *The Relapse*.

Poland, 27 June 1697. Frederick Augustus, elector of Saxony, is elected king of Poland and takes the name Augustus II.

Hungary, 11 September 1697. Imperial troops under the brilliant commander Eugene of Savoy defeat the Turks at the battle of Zenta.

Netherlands, 30 October 1697. The treaty of Ryswick ends the war between France and the Grand Alliance. Louis XIV recognises William III's right to the English throne. France gives up its territories gained in 1688 but retains Alsace and Strasbourg. The treaty also ends King William's War in the colonies, returning to England the territories on Hudson Bay that were seized by French forces.

France, February 1697. Francois Fenelon, who was made archbishop of Cambrai two years ago, publishes his *Explanations of the maxims of the saints*.

France, 1697. Charles Perrault publishes a collection of eight fairy tales entitled *Histoires ou Contes du temps passes*. They include "The Sleeping Beauty", "Red Riding Hood" and "Bluebeard".

Portugal, 1697. The Jesuit Antonio Veira dies. A vigorous opponent of slavery, he sailed up the rivers of Brazil spreading Christianity.

Sweden, 1697. Charles XI, who confiscated large areas of land belonging to the aristocracy and transformed Sweden into an absolute monarchy, dies and is succeeded as king by his son Charles XII.

Siberia, 1697. Continuing their expansion eastwards through the vast territories of Siberia, the Russians reach and conquer the Kamchatka peninsula.

Mongolia, 1697. Western Mongolia is conquered by the Chinese.

West Africa, 1697. Appointed director of the French Senegal Company, Andre Brue attempts to establish trading posts in the valley of the Senegal.

California, 1697. Spanish Jesuits found the first mission in California, at Loreta.

Moscow, 1698. Following a revolt by the Streltsy – the Praetorian guard composed of nobles that was founded by Ivan the Terrible – a thousand of their number are publicly put to death on the orders of Peter the Great.

Moscow, 1698. Peter the Great imposes the use of tobacco on his people.

Persia, 1698. Sent to Persia as a prisoner, the Afghan chieftain Mir Ways beomes a favourite of Shah Hussein.

Vietnam, 1698. The Cambodians evacuate Saigon.

Beijing, 1698. A newly constructed bridge is named after the explorer Marco Polo.

Penal laws oppress the Irish Catholics

Ireland, 1695

A form of racial and religious segregation is being introduced by the Protestant ascendancy in Ireland. The Catholic Irish are allowed to practise their religion, but they are not permitted to vote and are barred from the armed forces. A Protestant may not marry a Catholic and must produce a certificate of religious denomination before marriage. Catholics are not allowed to send their children abroad to be educated as Catholics.

Other measures include a ban on gambling in an attempt to prevent the upper classes losing the family fortunes. All of which measures passed by the minority at the expense of the majority may well satisfy Protestants, but are sure to exacerbate old enmities.

Brazil's gold makes the Portuguese rich

Brazil, 1697

Adventurers of all sorts, the unemployed from all over Brazil and from Portugal, and anyone with an eye to getting rich quick are flocking to the Minas Gerais region here. Gold has been discovered in the river beds and in alluvial deposits in the nearby hills. It is easy to extract and already a number of hopeful miners have made their fortunes. Villages have sprung up overnight and there are now several thousand inhabitants.

Meanwhile, Portugal is tightening its hold on the country. The excitement of finding gold has to be balanced with less romantic endeavours. The governor has just crushed the native black kingdom of Palmares which was threatening sugar and tobacco plantations.

Moghul soldiers are "padded dandies"

The court of Aurangzeb: fountains, elephants, soldiers and splendour.

Dekhan, India, 21 March 1695

The Moghul army of Aurangzeb would be totally unrecognisable to Babur, the empire's founder. Dynamism has given way to decadence; his soldiers, the descendants of the men who had built an empire from central Asia to southern India, are now said to be no more than "padded dandies".

This is the conclusion of Dr Gemelli Careri, a Neapolitan lawyer, received today at the Moghul court, while on a voyage round the world. The bureaucracy is corrupt, the army obese, and the peasants starve to pay for both, he says. The royal encampment has a circumference of 30 miles (48km). Within it are 250 markets and half-a-million soldiers, civil servants and camp followers.

In complete contrast is Aurangzeb himself. He received the Italian at ten o'clock, dressed in simple white cotton, with a white beard and olive skin, "slender and stooping with age". He alone, with his combination of weakness, cruelty and suspicion, holds the empire together; but he cannot live for ever, nor can his empire.

Rebel feminist poet in plague death

Mexico, 1695
The writer, Juana Ines de la Cruz has died at the age of 44 after nursing victims of the recent plague. Four years ago Juana re-affirmed her nun's vows after a row with the Church over her autobiography. In her book she criticises the Inquisition and argues for women's rights and education.

When Juana left the viceroy's court at 18 to join the Order of St Jerome her ambition was to pursue education and avoid marriage. During 21 years of convent life she wrote poems, ballads, comedies and sacramental plays. Juana collected 4,000 books which, until she sold them for charity, formed the largest library in South America.

France gives up the right bank of Rhine

Dignitaries assemble in Paris for the signing of the Peace of Ryswick.

Europe, 1697
With the Grand Alliance of England, Holland, Austria, Spain and Savoy clearly demoralised at the lack of a decisive victory, nine years of war against France has come to an end with the Peace of Ryswick. Although William of Orange's forces had been successful in taking Namur, fighting in the Spanish Netherlands had come to a stalemate. Peace would have been reached earlier had not Louis XIV been so stubborn in his refusal to recognise William as the king of England. Although he had worked hard to split the alliance, it was the cost of fighting on so many fronts that forced him to negotiate.

Under the terms of the treaty, Louis will relinquish his claims to Cologne and the right bank of the Rhine and restore Luxembourg, Mons, Courtrai and Barcelona to Spain; but he will retain Strasbourg and a few towns in Alsace. France will recognise William as king and withdraw support for the Stuarts.

Dom Perignon puts fizz in champagne

Champagne, 1698
France, home of great wines, has a new variety to enjoy: sparkling wine from the abbey of Hautvillers in Champagne. Champagne's "vin gris" is already well known, but the new fizzy version, a white wine made from black grapes, is quite original.

"Vin gris" often fermented in the bottle, thus turning slightly fizzy, but it took the skill of the the abbey's 60-year-old cellarer, Dom Pierre Perignon, to use this fermentation to create the new style of wine. Using a new blend of grapes, he has substituted cork stoppers for the old rag seal and uses strong English glass to withstand the pressure of the sparkling wine.

Critical dictionary looks for tolerance

Holland, 1697
Pierre Bayle, a Huguenot exile from France, has produced a work that is being called "the sceptic's Bible". His *Historical and Critical Dictionary* attacks the dogmas and fallacies of past ages and argues for tolerance and detachment in its series of learned articles. Nothing, says Bayle, is certain and no one person has the monopoly of truth. He even claims that "the grounds of doubt are themselves doubtful." Thoughtful men everywhere are questioning the dogmas of religion and old superstitions, argues Bayle.

Bayle: doubt too is doubtful.

Purcell: writer of first English opera

London, 21 November 1695
Henry Purcell died today at only 36. Purcell was composing by the age of eight, and was organist of Westminster Abbey at 20. As well as church, ceremonial and chamber works he wrote theatre music, including *Dido and Aeneas*, the first true opera in English. He will be buried in Westeminster Abbey.

Rome at odds with Jesuits over Chinese ancestor worship

Beijing, 1697
The success of the Jesuit mission to China is being threatened by a Vatican inquiry into the new line proposed by Monsignor Charles Maigrot, the vicar apostolic of Fukien. Four years ago he instructed his own missionaries to have nothing to do with the cult of Confucius and ancestor worship. Now he is seeking to get the Vatican to impose his views on all missions to China.

The Jesuits have been successful here by arguing that Confucian philosophy does not conflict with Christian laws. They have even lauded the *I Ching* as an excellent book of physics and morality. As a result Emperor Kangxi issued an edict of toleration of Christianity and even allowed a Jesuit house in this Forbidden City.

Oriental Christians are tortured cruelly by their unbelieving enemies.

1698 (1698-1702)

Europe, 11 October 1698. France, England and the Netherlands sign a partition treaty to solve the problem of the Spanish succession after the impending death of the childless King Charles II. Under the treaty, Spanish possessions are to be divided between the dauphin, the electoral prince of Bavaria and the Archduke Charles, son of the Emperor Leopold.

New England, 1 January 1699. The Abenaki Indians and the Massachusetts colonists sign a treaty ending the conflict in New England.

Austria, 26 January 1699. The treaty of Karlowitz ends the war between Austria and the Turks which began in 1683. The Turks cede Transylvania and Hungary to the Austrians, Morea and Dalmatia to Venice and part of the Ukraine to Poland.

Russia, 20 December 1699. Peter the Great sets about reforming the Russian calendar. In August he banned traditional clothing, insisting that his subjects wear European dress.

East Africa, 1699. Fort Jesus (*Mombasa*) and Zanzibar are captured by Omani Arabs.

Philadelphia, 1699. The first clearly reported epidemic of yellow fever in the colonies kills one-sixth of the population.

Europe, 13 March 1700. Following the death of the Elector of Bavaria, a second partition treaty is signed to resolve the Spanish succession. The major share of the Spanish possessions is allocated to Archduke Charles.

Russia, 23 June 1700. Russia signs a truce with the Ottoman empire, halting the war which began in 1695. Russia gives up its Black Sea fleet but retains Azov.

Boston, 24 June 1700. Judge Samuel Sewall writes *The Selling of Joseph*, the first outright appeal for the abolition of slavery to appear in America.

England, 1 July 1700. The English dramatist and poet John Dryden dies. Among the works for which he will be best remembered are the play *All for Love* and the satirical poems *Absalom and Achitophel* and *MacFlecknoe*.

Denmark, 18 August 1700. Having invaded Denmark and captured Copenhagen, Charles XII of Sweden forces Frederick IV of Denmark to sign the peace of Travendal.

Spain, 2 October 1700. Charles II, king of Spain, draws up a will in favour of the Bourbon duke Philip of Anjou, the grandson of Louis XIV of France.

Spain, 1 November 1700. On the death of Charles II, Philip of Anjou comes to the throne as Philip V.

Baltic, November 1700. Charles XII of Sweden defeats the Russian forces besieging the city of Narva.

Boston, 1700. The port of Boston has become the most important colonial centre of the slave trade.

New England, 1700. The first Baptist association in the colonies is founded, on Rhode Island.

Indian Ocean, 1700. English pirates set up a base in Madagascar.

Germany, 18 January 1701. Frederick III, elector of Brandenburg, becomes king of Prussia.

Madrid, 19 February 1701. Philip V makes a ceremonial entry into Madrid.

England, 23 May 1701. Arrested in Boston on a charge of piracy and sent back to England for trial, the Englishman Captain William Kidd is hanged.

London, 12 June 1701. The Act of Establishment excludes Catholics from the English throne.

Michigan, 24 July 1701. Antoine de La Mothe Cadillac establishes a French fort at Detroit.

Netherlands, 7 September 1701. England, Austria and the Netherlands form an alliance against France. The allies are fearful of a union between Spain and France following the choice made by Charles II, the late king of Spain, of a Bourbon as his successor.

Poland, 1701. Having occupied Lithuania and Courland, Charles XII of Sweden invades Poland and seizes Warsaw and Cracow.

London, 11 March 1702. The *Daily Courant*, the first daily newspaper in the world, begins publication.

England, 19 March 1702. On the death of William III of Orange, Anne Stuart, sister of Mary, succeeds to the throne of England, Scotland and Ireland.

Europe, 4 May 1702. To stall the alliance of Spain and France, the Grand Alliance declares war on France.

France, 1702. French Protestants called Camisards – because of the white shirts they wear during night raids to promote recognition – rise up in revolt against persecution following the repeal of the Edict of Nantes in 1695. The Camisards' leaders are Jean Cavalier and Roland Laporte.

Denmark, 1702. King Frederick IV abolishes serfdom.

Catholics excluded from English throne

London, 1701

In a move with far-reaching implications, parliament has passed an Act of Settlement which bars Roman Catholics from the British throne. Any person who inherits the succession and subsequently converts to Rome or marries a Catholic will be declared incapacitated. So Catholics of the House of Orleans who married Stuart princesses are barred. The line of succession, after William and Mary, is her sister Anne and then the Electress Sophia of Hanover, the granddaughter of James I.

William rides high amid the gods.

Riding accident puts Anne on the throne

Anne: a 19th-century portrait.

London, 1702

King William III of England, and as William of Orange ruler of the Netherlands, died today after a fall from his horse while riding at Hampton Court. He will be succeeded by Anne, sister of the late Queen. His death comes only weeks after that of the exiled James II, whom he deposed in the "Glorious Revolution" of 1688.

The English confidently expect the new Queen to rule much as did William. The Dutch, under republican rule once more, face a less predictable future. William's unpopular favourites may well face a backlash, but it is hoped that Heinsius, the former chief minister, will maintain national stability.

Oman Arabs seize Madagascar port

Mombasa, East Africa, 1699

After a three-year siege by the Omanis and their East African allies, Portugal's garrison at Fort Jesus has surrendered. A few enclaves on the Zambezi and Mozambique coast are all that is left in Portuguese possession. Portuguese power had been declining since 1650 when she was evicted from the Arabian Gulf. On the East African coast the indigenous population led by the citystate of Pate, resentful of Portuguese efforts to dominate trade and impose Christianity, allied with Oman and revolted. Portugal's rivals, Holland and England, observe events with interest.

Piratical brethren terrorise Caribbean

Caribbean, 1700

A gang of pirates, known as The Brethren of the Coast, have established themselves in the islands of Jamaica and Hispaniola. Mutineers, escaped prisoners, the riff-raff of every colonial nation – they owe no allegiance to any law, except for that of plunder and gain.

Bloodthirsty and greedy in their dealings with the ships on which they prey, they have their own brutal code. Every man – there are no women – is considered equal. They vote on all matters of policy and share out the spoils and bounties. There are harsh punishments for those who defy the rules.

Czar goes to work in English shipyard

Czar Peter seeks experience among the labourers of the Deptford yard.

Deptford, London, 1698
For three months, workers in the shipyard here have enjoyed the sight of one of the most powerful men in the world wielding a saw or hammer or adze with the best of them. Russia's tall and vigorous czar, Peter the Great, is roving around Europe picking up knowledge and techniques for his drive to westernise his country.

He has become the first czar to cross his frontiers except on a military campaign and is accompanied by a "travelling embassy" of 250 – including priests, officials, dwarfs and bodyguards. After attending a debate in the House of Lords he said: "It is pleasant to learn how the sons of the fatherland tell the truth plainly to the king; we must learn that from the English."

In London Peter lodged in the home of the diarist John Evelyn with 15 other Russians and his coarse habits and drunken horseplay contributed to leaving behind £350 worth of damage to furniture and gardens. Peter also worked as a carpenter in Dutch shipyards and has visited the three Baltic provinces, Prussia, and France.

He has shown interest in government and political ideas, but it is ships, guns, lathes and coins that appear mostly to have caught his attention.

Cutting off their privileges: Czar Peter trims the Boyars' beards.

Seed drill implants fear of job losses

Berkshire, England, 1701
A machine just developed by the English farmer-inventor Jethro Tull of Berkshire has changed the agricultural practices of 10,000 years. No longer is there any need to scatter seed on prepared ground by hand, with all the haphazardness and waste that this implies. Tull has made a seed-sowing machine that delivers the seeds to the soil in straight, even lines. These neat rows of seeds not only produce economies they also make it far easier to keep down the weeds between the growing crops.

Although this new device – and some of Tull's other practical ideas on farm management – seem to benefit the farmer, he is by no means universally popular. Farm labourers fear the machine will put them out of work. Some have even gone on strike against it.

Europe riven by wars

Swedes smash Allies: capture Warsaw

Warsaw, 1702
In a brilliantly fought campaign, the Swedish army of Charles XII has beaten an alliance of Denmark, Poland and Russia and captured Warsaw. The Polish King, Augustus II, has been deposed; Poland, now under a new ruler, Stanislas, has allied itself with Charles against Russia; and Sweden retains her mastery of the Baltic.

Denmark capitulated quickly after Copenhagen was put to siege in 1700; and then Charles led his small army of 10,000 men across Estonia to confront the Russians. Few expected the youthful Swedish king to show such military prowess; but he confirmed his schoolboy studies of his hero, Alexander the Great, with a spectacular victory at Narva against what seemed overwhelming odds.

King Charles XII of Sweden.

Fear of Franco-Spanish union sparks war

Europe, 1702
Had Charles II, the king of Spain, not died childless, Europe would probably have stayed at peace, but now the continent is braced for a major war – this time to stop France and Spain and its colonies uniting under one throne. Even while Charles was dying, every effort was being made to avoid conflict; but because of the complicated series of marriages between the royal families, there was no clear contender for the throne.

France, Britain and Holland negotiated a treaty under which Spanish possessions would be partitioned. Charles rejected this and made a will which made the dauphin's second son, the duke of Anjou, the inheritor. With Charles's death, the French duke is now Philip V of Spain, and England and Holland have declared war.

Ships of the Anglo-Dutch navy destroy the Spanish treasure fleet at Vico.

1702 (1702-1707)

Florida, 1702. A British raid on the Spanish town of St Augustine sets an extension of the European war of the Spanish succession.

Portugal, 27 December 1703. The English diplomat John Methuen negotiates a trade treaty with Portugal.

Poland, 13 April 1703. The forces of Charles XII, king of Sweden, win a victory over the much larger army of Augustus II, king of Poland, at the battle of Pultusk.

Portugal, 1703. Portugal joins the Grand Alliance.

France, 1703. The military engineer Sebastien de Vauban imposes the use of the flintlock rifle by the French army and equips the soldiers with bayonets.

England, 1703. The philosopher Robert Hooke dies. He was the first to use a pendulum to determine the force of acceleration due to gravity.

Russia, 1703. Peter the Great founds St Petersburg.

Massachusetts, 29 February 1704. A French massacre of the Puritan colony at Deerfield intensifies the war, in which the French and their Indian allies have been attacking English settlements throughout New England.

Boston, 24 April 1704. A regular weekly newspaper, the *Boston News-Letter*, begins publication.

Poland, 12 July 1704. Following the deposition of Augustus II, Stanislas Leszczynski, the candidate of Charles XII of Sweden, comes to the throne.

Spain, July 1704. The English, led by John Churchill, duke of Marlborough, seize Gibraltar.

Germany, 13 August 1704. The forces of the Grand Alliance, led by the duke of Marlborough and Eugene of Savoy, defeat the French and the Bavarians at Blenheim.

Newfoundland, 29 August 1704. The English settlement at Bonavista on the east coast is taken by a French and Indian force.

England, 28 October 1704. The philosopher John Locke dies. A staunch defender of liberalism, he aroused the suspicions of the Stuarts and was forced into exile, in France and the Netherlands, until William III came to power.

England, 1704. Isaac Newton's treatise on *Opticks*, presenting his main discoveries concerning light and colour, is published.

Tunisia, 1705. Husayn ibn Ali, bey of the janissaries of Tunis, seizes power in Tunisia, under nominal Turkish sovereignty.

Japan, 1705. The Bakufu government accuses the house of Yodoya, the most prominent in Osaka, of ostentatious luxury and confiscates its entire wealth. In fact, the Yodoya has come to control the finances of many of the *daimyo* of Kyushu and western Honshu, whose huge debts to the Yodoya are cancelled by the confiscation.

England, 1705. The French-born English writer Bernard de Mandeville publishes his *Fable of the Bees*, a charter of utilitarianism in which he argues that the vices of individuals are of benefit to society.

England, 1705. Edmond Halley publishes his *Trajectory of Comets*.

England, 1705. The architect Sir John Vanbrugh builds Blenheim Palace in Oxfordshire.

Austria, 5 May 1705. Leopold, Holy Roman Emperor since 1658, dies and is succeeded by his son Joseph. Leopold tried to transform the Habsburg possessions into a modern state, strengthening the political institutions and re-organising the army and the finances. His struggle against the Turks led to the annexation of Hungary and Transylvania.

Spain, 14 October 1705. The English navy captures Barcelona.

Moscow, 1705. Peter the Great founds Moscow University.

Germany, 9 March 1706. The composer and organist Johann Pachelbel dies at Nuremberg. Highly regarded for the clarity of his polyphony and his well-structured harmonies, Pachelbel wrote motets, magnificats, chorals, variations and preludes.

Spain, 23 May 1706. The English raise a French siege of Barcelona.

Netherlands, 23 May 1706. The French under Villeroi are defeated by the English under Marlborough at Ramillies. The Spanish Netherlands falls to the English.

Spain, October 1706. Having entered Madrid earlier in the year, the Portuguese are driven out by Philip V of Spain.

North America, 1706. Juan de Uribarri claims a vast area in western North America for Spain (*Colorado*).

New Mexico, 1706. The governor of New Mexico, Francisco Cuervo y Valdes, founds an administrative centre for the lower Rio Grande area. He calls it Albuquerque after the viceroy of New Spain.

Persia, 1706. Shah Hussein builds a splendid temple called a *madrasah* at Isfahan.

Britain, 1 May 1707. Scotland is united with England by an Act of Union.

Astronomer claims that comets come back

London, 1705

Comets have been notoriously difficult to study because their appearance is so sudden and short-lived. They have also been surrounded throughout history by superstition and fear. Now, however, the distinguished English astronomer and polymath Edmund Halley has apparently succeeded in computing the motions of comets. He argues that these spectacular objects in the sky follow a regular pattern.

Basing his calculations on Newton's ideas in his remarkable book, *Principia*, Halley concludes that comets travel in elliptical orbits. From this he goes on to suggest that the comets observed in 1531, 1607 and 1682 were, in fact, the same object on its periodic journey through space. He further contends that sightings of a comet in 1305, 1380 and 1456 were again of this same body. Computing the orbit of this comet, he estimates that it will return to the vicinity of Earth in December 1758. Nobody will be completely convinced until and unless Halley's comet makes its predicted reappearance.

Edmund Halley at the age of 80.

English inflict heavy losses on French

John Wooton's painting of Churchill's victory at the Battle of Blenheim.

Blenheim, 13 August 1704

John Churchill, the duke of Marlborough, today inflicted a crushing defeat on the French army, thereby decisively changing the balance of military power in the War of the Spanish Succession. The encounter took place near the Bavarian village of Blenheim, where French forces had assembled on their march to capture Vienna.

Churchill was far to the north in Holland, kept there by the Dutch who feared for their frontiers. They were duped by Churchill, who pretended he was preparing to campaign a few miles up the Rhine at Moselle. Instead, he made a lightning march to the Danube, hundreds of miles distant.

He was joined by Prince Eugene of Savoy and together they attacked the French and Bavarian forces. The enemy losses were 30,000 killed or captured with many more drowned in the Danube. British losses were 670 killed and 1,500 wounded.

England and Scotland are united

London, 1 May 1707
The discovery of 31 dead whales on the sands of Kirkcaldy is seen by many Scots as an evil omen for the union of the English and Scottish parliaments, which comes into effect today. But the opponents of union are far outnumbered by its supporters and those who do not care one way or the other. In the Edinburgh parliament debates some 40 members, a fifth of the House, did not bother to vote on the Union Treaty.

A crucial factor in winning over Scottish opinion was the decision by the London parliament to include in the Treaty a clause which safeguards the privileges of the Presbyterian Church. The Scots will also keep their own legal system. Last-ditch opposition to the Treaty comes from a faction of the Jacobite supporters of the Stuart claim to the English crown, which is widely seen as a lost cause.

Scottish supporters of union are looking forward to an economic boom for Glasgow, strategically placed to exploit the growing Atlantic trade. Scots are already moving south to take up jobs in England's developing industries and Highland regiments are being taken into the British army.

In London the union has been opposed by High Tories who are dismayed by the prospect of a phalanx of rough Scottish Presbyterians taking their seats in the English parliament. But for most English people today is a chance to enjoy an unexpected holiday as Queen Anne rode in state to St Paul's Cathedral for a ceremony of thanksgiving.

The Duke of Queensberry gives a copy of the Act of Union to Queen Anne.

Hungarians resist Austrian rulers' bid to centralise power

Buda, Hungary, 1703
Sixteen years after their country was freed from Turkish occupation, Hungarian peasants have risen against heavy taxation which has been imposed by the Habsburg Empire. Every class has suffered, but the peasants feel themselves particularly hard done by. So fierce is the opposition that the Habsburg army is loth to move in the countryside, confining itself to garrisons and making only sporadic attempts to subdue the rebellion.

Two former Magyar exiles, Francis Rakoczi, a nobleman, and Nicholas Berczenyi have returned to lead the peasants. With much of his army occupied elsewhere, King Leopold is looking to wealthy Hungarian magnates for support.

An armed Hungarian warrior wearing his national costume.

Pamphlet attacks ribald comedies

London, 1707
The latest success of the London theatre, *The Beaux' Stratagem*, has made the name of the young Irish playwright, George Farquhar, following the success of his country comedy, *The Recruiting Officer*. But there has been a reaction against ribald comedies of aristocratic manners like Vanbrugh's *The Relapse* (1696) and William Congreve's *Love for Love* (1695), attacked by Jeremy Collier's pamphlet on stage immorality. Since *The Way of the World*, Congreve has given up the stage.

Farquhar's "Lord Foppington": pictured by Frith in the 19th-century.

Mass suicide by Samurai warriors

Japan, February 1703
Forty-six samurai warriors have become heroes after committing ritual suicide. Their deaths were ordered by the shogun after they raided the home of court official Kira Yoshinaka whom they blamed for the forced suicide of their lord. They cut off Kira's head, presented it to their dead lord's grave and went willingly to their own deaths.

Pope tries to alter Jesuit policy in China

China, 1704
Pope Clement XI has intervened in the bitter doctrinal quarrel between the Jesuits and the other Catholic missionaries in China. He has signed a decree, *Cum Deus Optimus*, in which he condemns the so-called Chinese rites of the Jesuits.

The quarrel arose over the Jesuit willingness to accommodate a measure of Confucian belief in the rites of their Chinese converts. The history of the Jesuits in China has been one of flexibility to the extent of accepting high office under the emperor and has long been the cause of anger among the other orders.

Charles Maigrot, the bishop of Fukien, has become the leader of the opposition to the Jesuits. He is proud of never having frequented the court, that "famous Babylon" and accuses the Jesuits of upholding idolatry in China. A papal legate has now been sent to China to investigate the Chinese rites.

1707 (1707-1711)

Hungary, 1707. The Budapest parliament declares the fall of the Habsburgs and the independence of Hungary.

India, 1707. The great Moghul Aurangzeb dies at the age of 89, having secured control of most of the Indian peninsula. He is succeeded by Bahadur Shah.

France, 1707. *Dime royale*, an attack on the social and economic defects of France by Sebastien de Vauban, is condemned and banned on the orders of Louis XIV.

Britain, March 1708. James Edward Stewart, son of James II and pretender to the British throne, makes an unsuccessful attempt to land in Scotland.

Netherlands, 11 July 1708. The French are defeated at Oudenarde by Marlborough and Eugene of Savoy.

Newfoundland, 21 December 1708. French forces seize control of the eastern shore after winning a victory at St John's.

France, December 1708. After a five-month siege, the city of Lille falls to Grand Alliance forces under Eugene of Savoy.

Mediterranean, 1708. The English capture the islands of Sardinia and Minorca from the French.

India, 1708. The Sikh guru Govind Singh is assassinated.

Russia, 28 June 1709. Charles XII of Sweden, in alliance with the Cossack *hetman* Mazeppa, suffers a terrible defeat by the Russians at the battle of Poltava.

Netherlands, 11 September 1709. After inflicting heavy losses on the enemy, the French forces are defeated by Marlborough and Eugene of Savoy at Malplaquet.

Netherlands, 20 October 1709. Marlborough and Eugene of Savoy take Mons.

Afghanistan, 1709. The Ghilzai chieftain Mir Ways leads an uprising in Khandahar against the Safavid Persian rulers.

Poland, 1709. The Poles rise up against Stanislas Leszczynski, who flees, making way for the return of Augustus II.

Germany, 1709. Giovanni Maria Farina, a Cologne chemist and businessman, makes Eau de Cologne, following a recipe given him by a travelling merchant.

Turkey, 1709. Charles XII of Sweden seeks refuge in Turkey after his defeat at Poltava.

Venice, 1709. The German composer George Frederick Handel wins overnight fame following the triumphant production of his opera *Agrippina*.

Florence, 1709. Bartolomeo Cristofori, the famous maker of harpsichords, invents the pianoforte.

China, 1709. Emperor Kangxi requests the French Jesuits to draw a map of his empire.

Spain, 28 September 1710. Charles III Austrian King of Spain takes Madrid.

Turkey, 30 November 1710. At the instigation of Charles XII of Sweden, Turkey declares war on Russia.

Spain, 10 December 1710. The French defeat the Austrians at Villa Viciosa, forcing Charles III to abandon Madrid and making Philip V Spain's first Bourbon king.

Canada, 1710. A British expedition under Francis Nicholson captures the French stronghold of Port Royal in Acadia (*Nova Scotia* and *New Brunswick*).

Paris, 1710. An income tax known as the "tenth" is introduced.

England, 1710. The philosopher George Berkeley publishes an analysis of sense perceptions entitled *Treatise concerning the principles of human knowledge*.

London, 1710. Coffee-houses in London, which first appeared in the middle of the last century, now number about 2,000.

Vienna, 17 April 1711. On the death of the Emperor Joseph he is succeeded by Charles III, king of Spain, as Charles VI.

Boston, 25 June 1711. With the arrival of 64 British ships, carrying 5,000 troops and 6,000 seamen, preparations begin for an advance on Canada.

Russia, 21 July 1711. By the treaty of Pruth, ending the Russo-Turkish war which began last year, Russia is obliged to return Azov to the Turks.

Afghanistan, 1711. Mir Ways succeeds in defeating the Persian army sent to put down the Ghilzai rebellion and establishes the independence of the Afghan state.

Hungary, 1711. Denied support by France and Russia, the rebels agree peace terms with the Habsburgs.

Germany, 1711. Johann Bottger, who has discovered the secret of manufacturing hard Chinese porcelain, is put in charge of a new porcelain factory in Meissen.

Balkans, 1711. Supported by Venice and Russia, Danilo of Montenegro massacres the Moslems in his country and repels the Turks.

England, 1711. The South Sea Company is incorporated.

Crisis looms at Moghul emperor's death

A final portrait of India's emperor.

Ahmadnagar, India, 3 March 1707
Aurangzeb, the Emperor of India and last of the Great Moghuls, is dead. With him has died the dream of a strong and united India. A devout Moslem, who knew the Koran by heart, his very virtues turned out to be public vices. Out of his religious sincerity came religious intolerance. Hindus and Sikhs were persecuted. The Moghul's most powerful Hindu ally, the Rajputs, became alienated from the state.

His military victories (won more often by guile than by arms) over-extended his empire. His subjects were taxed to starvation to pay for his extravagant campaigns and equally extravagant court. Rarely a year went by without a revolt.

Chinese artist's revolt against tradition

Kiangsi, China, 1707
The painter, poet and calligrapher, Shitao, who renewed the art of Chinese landscape, is dead. He rebelled against the dogma that painters must imitate the style of the old masters and insisted that he would be true to the spirit of his age and his own personality. "Nowadays learned men are like withered bones and dead ashes," he said. "When I am asked if I paint in the style of the southern or the northern school, I say I do not know. I paint in my own style."

His atmospheric paintings show mountain peaks glimpsed through drifting clouds or lashing sheets of rain, rendered in pale washes with accents of dark ink brush-strokes which are allowed to spread and run.

Japanese art reflected the country's political isolation, developing in styles totally different to that of Europe where a more romantic style was flowering. These porcelain figures date from around the year 1700.

Russian winter beats Swedish invaders

Poltava, Russia, 1709
Few campaigns began with such promise for its leader – and none ended in such horror and humiliation. The vanquished invader is the king of Sweden, Charles XII, who has taken refuge in Turkey with the remnants of his once great army. The victors are Czar Peter's generals, who allowed the Swedish king and 10,000 troops to be lured into the depths of the worst winter that even Russia has known in living memory and weakened them to such extent that they were massively defeated at Poltava in June. Charles had not reckoned on a well-trained Russian army; nor on the Russian policy of burning foodstocks as they retreated, avoiding battle where possible. And he had not allowed for the Russian winter.

The Grand Vizier grants an audience to Swedish refugees in Turkey.

Great Sikh guru is killed by Afghan

Dekhan, India, November 1708
Govind Singh, the tenth of the Sikh-gurus, has been assassinated. There seems no doubt his killer, an Afghan, is in the pay of Bahadur Shah, the new Moghul emperor.

Guru Govind was more than a holy man. He was a general who militarized the Sikh movement, and a political leader, who first fought with Bahadur Shah, then turned against him. He will be most remembered as a religious reformer, who did more to shape the Sikh philosophy and identity than anyone since Nanak, who founded the movement 200 years ago.

African kingdoms growing slave rich

Gold Coast, 1708
As tens of thousands of Africans are being forcibly snatched from their villages and cruelly transported to America, the states of West Africa are growing rich from the slave trade.

None have done better than Abomey in Dahomey (Benin), situated between the Ouene and Mono rivers and controlling the slave ports of Allada and Ouidah. Its treasury overflows. It has a fast and efficient army, with many of the soldiers women. When it is not out on slave raids it is fighting the rival Oyo empire.

Marlborough turns tide against French

Netherlands, 11 September 1709
England's greatest general, the duke of Marlborough, today added another victory to his string of successes against the French. After a day's hard pounding at Malplaquet, near Mons, in the Southern Netherlands (Belgium), the French finally retreated. Some critics say the battle was indecisive, but most people believe that after Blenheim, Ramillies, Antwerp, Ostend, Menin and Oudenarde, the French have lost their appetite for doing battle with Marlborough. The duke's triumphs derive from his attention to detail, his care for his soldiers' welfare and his cool head in the heat of battle.

With St Paul's, Wren completes the rebuilding of London after great fire

The north-west view of Sir Christopher Wren's St Paul's cathedral.

London, 1711
The rebuilding of St Paul's cathedral is finished – 38 years after it began and 45 years after it was planned by Sir Christopher Wren when its mediaeval predecessor was destroyed in the Great Fire. Sir Christopher is now all but 80 years old and the last stone above the lantern was laid by his son. He has applied for his back salary of £200 a year; in 1697 parliament said he should be paid only half of it until the building was finished.

London has gained a masterpiece second only to Rome's St Peter's, which has the only larger dome in the world. Wren employed Grinling Gibbons to carve the stalls of the choir and the Huguenot, Jean Tijou, for the sanctuary's wrought-iron gates. But the inside of the dome, which he wanted in mosaic, is to be painted in monochrome by Sir James Thornhill. The cost of the building, £721,552 7s 7d, has been raised mainly by a tax on seacoal. Wren designed 51 of the city churches rebuilt after the Fire. Their towers and steeples surround the great dome with a skyline of ar tectural fantasy. Although Wren has designed other buildings, his plans for radiating streets and vistas came to nothing.

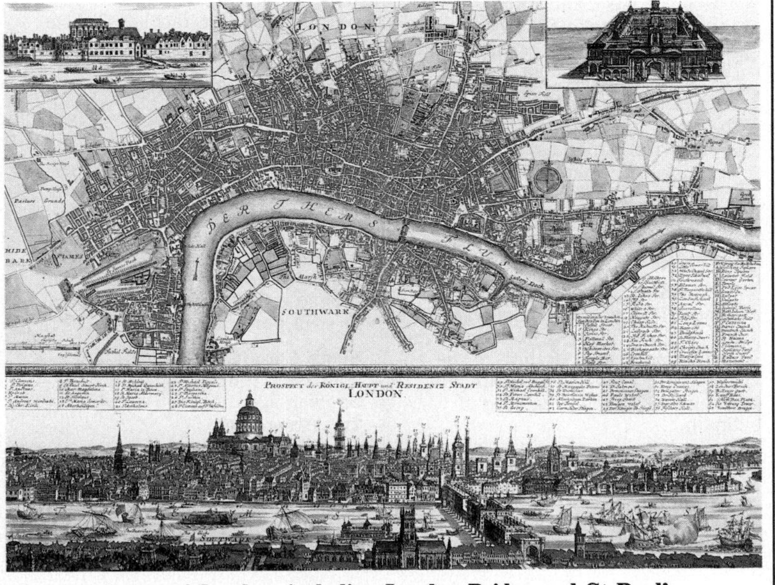

Homanns' map of London, including London Bridge and St Paul's.

1711 (1711-1715)

Carolina, 22 September 1711. Upset by a new wave of settlements, Indians attack colonists on the Roanoke and Chowan rivers, launching the Tuscarora war.

Ottoman Empire, 1711. The Ottoman government chooses a Greek phanariot (resident of Fanar, a suburb of Istanbul) to rule in Moldavia. The Ottomans are worried by Moldavian *rapprochement* with Russia, which is aimed at throwing off the Turkish yoke.

Pennsylvania, 7 June 1712. The assembly bans the importation of slaves into the colony.

New York, 4 July 1712. After one of the first slave uprisings in North America, 12 slaves are executed and six commit suicide before they can be brought to the gallows. Before the militia arrived to arrest them, the slaves killed nine whites.

Pennsylvania, 1712. The colony's Quaker founder, William Penn, suffers a severe stroke. His wife, Hannah, takes over the governing of the colony.

Baltic, 1712. Russians and Danes defeat the Swedes in the Baltic and Scandinavia. Since 1700, in what has become known as the Second Northern War, the Swedish king Charles XII has been fighting to preserve Swedish supremacy in the Baltic. However, after these most recent defeats, it looks as if Charles will be forced to sue for peace.

West Africa, 1712. The Bambara kingdom of Segu is founded upstream from Timbuktu. It is a non-Moslem state which challenges the declining Mali empire to the west.

North Carolina, 23 March 1713. Troops from North and South Carolina capture Fort Nohucke, a Tuscarora base, and force the Indians to negotiate. Fighting broke out in 1711 after the Indians devastated a settlement.

Britain, 26 March 1713. As part of the settlement in Queen Anne's war – the North American extension of the war of Spanish Succession – Britain gains *Asiento*, a contract allowing the South Sea Company to bring 4,800 Negro slaves per year into the Spanish colonies.

Netherlands, 11 April 1713. The treaty of Utrecht ends the war of the Spanish Succession. It confirms the permanent separation of the crowns of France and Spain and recognises Philip V as king of Spain.

Germany, 1713. Emperor Charles VI issues a "pragmatic sanction" settling the succession to the Habsburg lands on his daughter Maria Theresa.

Prussia, 1713. Frederick William succeeds his father Frederick on the throne of Prussia.

South Africa, 1713. The first smallpox epidemic spreads from the sailors at the Cape of Good Hope, killing Khoisan hunters and herders in great numbers.

Netherlands, 1713. Pierre Jurieu, the French Huguenot theologian and polemicist, dies in exile in Rotterdam. He led Calvinist resistance to the rule of Louis XIV.

Russia, 1713. Peter the Great has a naval base built at Tallin in Estonia.

Vietnam, 1713. In a continuing drive against Christianity, French missionaries are expelled from Tongking.

Germany, 6 March 1714. The Holy Roman Empire signs a treaty with France at Rastatt – one of several agreements concluding the war of the Spanish Succession.

Britain, 1 August 1714. On the death of Queen Anne without a direct heir, she is succeeded as monarch of Great Britain and Ireland by George, elector of Hanover since 1698 and great-grandson of James I of England.

Spain, 6 September 1714. King Philip V takes the Italian heiress Elizabeth Farnese as his second wife. The marriage is arranged by Giulio Alberoni, diplomatic agent of the duke of Parma, Elizabeth's father.

France, 1714. The famous keyboard instrumentalist Francois Couperin gives a series of ten concerts entitled *The Joined Tastes*. From a family of musicians, Couperin has been organist in the king's chapel since 1693.

Italy, 1714. The anatomist Bartolommeo Eustachio's *Tabulae anatomicae* is published posthumously. Eustachio died in 1574 and is famous for his discoveries concerning the heart and the ears.

Germany, 1714. The philosopher and mathematician Gottfried Liebniz publishes his *Monadologia*, according to which the universe is made up of "monads", divine mutually isolated creations. Each monad reflects the universe from its own point of view.

South Carolina, 15 April 1715. Yamassee Indians, goaded by Spanish agitation, kill hundreds of English settlers.

South Africa, 1715. Dutch burghers at the Cape of Good Hope elect their own commanders in an attempt to combat cattle rustling by Khoisan herders.

West African king dies courted by Europe

Ghana, West Africa, 1712

Osei Tutu, the founder of the Asante states, has been killed in an ambush. Thirty years ago he had been a penniless refugee, surviving on the largess of the nearby state of Akwamu. He died the ruler of a West African empire.

The Asantes' rulers are immigrants from the south, who settled in the forests only a generation ago. Under Osei Tutu, they forged themselves into a nation, their dominance assured after the defeat of their one-time overlords, the Denkyira, at Feyiase in 1701. Osei Tutu (aided by his powerful high priest, Okomfo Anokye) built an empire by combining war and diplomacy, cementing alliances with marriages, and enriching his people with profits from the gold and slave trades.

European powers, anxious to take a share in the wealth, courted him. Unable to buy slaves with gold (Asante has all the gold it needs), the Europeans bought slaves with guns, thus increasing the Asante's formidible power.

Within a year of Osei Tutu's victory over the Denkyira, Holland sent ambassadors to the Asante capital, Kumasi. Rival European powers, like Britain, unable to extract trading concessions from the Asante, impotently ally themselves with the Asantes' enemies.

Mask of an enemy slain in battle.

A horned and decorated helmet.

Boiling point is a matter of degrees

Holland, 1714

A German-born physicist, working in Holland, Daniel Fahrenheit has made a mercury thermometer that is more accurate than the alcohol-filled instruments currently in use. His thermometer has three fixed points. The lowest – 32 degrees – is the freezing point of a mixture of water, ice and salt. The highest is the boiling point of water at 212 degrees. In between is the temperature of human blood – 98.4 degrees. Fahrenheit is also interested in making precision meteorological instruments, such as barometers. And he discovered that water can remain liquid even below its freezing point and that it boils at different temperatures, according to atmospheric pressure.

British invasion of Canada fails

Quebec, 23 August 1711

Another British attempt to invade Canada has ended in a disaster which the locals here call the "magnificent fiasco". Nine British ships left Boston on July 30, but they got lost in the fog off Egg Island in the Gulf of St Lawrence. Eight of them were blown on to the rocks in a storm. Nearly 1,000 people lost their lives, including 35 women and some drummer boys. Admiral Walker and a few others survived on the remaining ship.

Perhaps Father de la Columbiere, the Montreal priest-in-charge, will be tempted into a repeat of his sermon after the last British effort 20 years ago. Then he claimed that Quebec had been saved by the Virgin Mary.

Treaty of Utrecht reshapes Europe

London, 1713
As the War of Spanish Succession drags to an end on the continent, British politicians are celebrating negotiations which have taken it out of the war. Under the terms of the Treaty of Utrecht, Britain has retained – from Spain – its hold on two great naval bases, Gibraltar and Minorca, and its position in the Mediterranean has been strengthened by a settlement which gives Naples and Reggio to its ally, the Emperor Charles VI. Britain has also gained – from France – sovereignty in Newfoundland, Hudson Bay and St Kitts as well as recognition of the Hanoverian succession in Britain.

The treaty confirms that Spain will be ruled by Philip V, although he has had to secede much of his empire, including Naples, Sardinia and the Netherlands (to Austria) and Sicily (to Savoy). He retains his colonial territories, although Britain has the monopoly of transporting negro slaves to them.

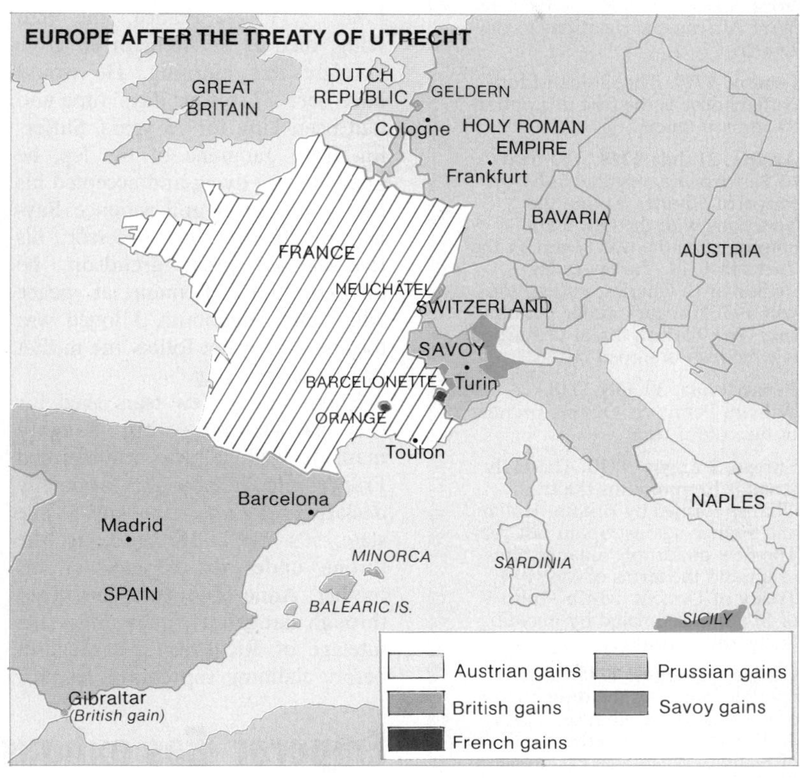

Bull-baiting and cock fighting draw the crowds

England, 1711
Violent sports involving animals have become the norm in England and enthusiasts are flocking to enjoy the twin spectacles of cock-fighting and bull-baiting.

The faint-hearted protest against what they see as the deliberate torture of dumb creatures, but most of the population, from high to low, see no harm in their entertainments.

Cock-fighting offers a chance for its followers to place a bet on one of the two competing birds. Placed in a pit surrounded with shouting spectators and armed with silver spurs they hack and gouge at each other until one is victorious. Wagers can reach twenty guineas and more.

Bull-baiting involves no betting, but simply the setting of dogs on a tethered bull to the amusement of those who watch. Around 30 dogs are used, attacking in twos and threes. Both dogs and bull are likely to be badly injured.

A violin by the master violin-maker Antonio Stradivari of Cremona: a pupil of Amati, his work is gaining an international reputation for unrivalled skill.

New British king cannot speak English

England, 1714
George, the Elector of Hanover, has arrived in London to ascend the British throne, bringing with him two German mistresses, who will be made countesses. He speaks no English and he has a notoriously foul temper and nobody much cares for him, but at least he is a Protestant. Queen Anne, who died at Kensington on 1 August, detested the Hanoverians, but two days before her death she realised that, as the grandson of James I, George would succeed her. The alternative was a Stuart succession which would cause political turmoil – and be bad for business.

Claimant to British throne is defeated

Scotland, September 1715
A disaffected Scottish aristocrat, the Earl of Mar, known as Bobbing John because of his political vacillation, has organised a rebellion in an attempt to put James Stuart, the "Old Pretender", on the throne.

Stuart, the son of James II, believed the British were eager to welcome him, but when he arrived off the Devon coast, as Bolingbroke said, he was "refused even a night's lodging". He went on to Scotland, where 18 Scottish lords rallied to the cause, but English troops, with Dutch allies, put down the rebellion, and a disillusioned Stuart fled to France.

James Stuart: exiled to France.

Berkeley reduces objects to ideas

London, 1713
Few philosophers have made such an instant impact as George Berkeley, the young Irish theologian being introduced to London society by his countryman Jonathan Swift.

Berkeley's arrival coincides with publication of his latest work *Three Dialogues between Hylas and Philonous* in which he propounds his argument that the only things that are real are our ideas of what is presented to our senses.

A graduate of Trinity College Dublin – a haven for independent thinkers – Berkeley developed the metaphysical implications of his theory of perception with the publication three years ago of his *Treatise concerning the Principles of Human Knowledge*.

Berkeley's new principle – in which objects are reduced to ideas – does not mean to question their reality as everyday objects, but tries to bring out their token value. For Berkeley these ideas are part of a system in which God is the creative source.

1715 (1715-1719)

France, September 1715. Following the death of Louis XIV and the accession of his five-year-old grandson, Louis XV, the regency is put in the hands of Philip of Orleans.

Massachusetts, 1715. Three years after the first sperm whale was killed at Nantucket, the whale-oil industry is booming. Nantucket has a fleet of six 30-ton whaling sloops that can cruise for six weeks at a time.

Lousiana, 6 June 1716. The first slaves are brought to French colonial territory in north America, in ships owned by the Company of the West.

Japan, 1716. The famous painter Ogata Koretomi, known as Ogata Korin, dies. Born into a wealthy merchant family, Korin's profligate lifestyle led him into financial difficulties and he was forced to take up painting as a profession. His works are marked by naturalism and an obvious talent for design.

Spain, 1716. The Italian Giulio Alberoni, favourite of King Philip V, becomes prime minister.

France, 1716. Francois Couperin, organist of the king's chapel, publishes *The Art of Playing the Harpsichord*, a treatise on keyboard technique.

Paris, May 1717. On a visit to Europe, Peter the Great of Russia proposes the marriage of his daughter Elizabeth Petrovna to Louis XV of France.

Paris, 4 August 1717. A friendship treaty is signed between Russia and France.

Spain, 1717. A Spanish army is sent to conquer Sardinia on the pretext that a Spanish citizen has been arrested in Italy.

New England, 1717. Colonial ships, now allowed to trade in the West Indies, begin bringing back French molasses, which they use to distil cheap rum in New England.

Vienna, 1717. The Schonbrunn Palace, built on the model of the Palace of Versailles, is completed. Intended as a place of leisure, its size and splendour serve to illustrate the magnificence of the imperial power.

Netherlands, 1717. A triple alliance, directed against Spain, is signed in The Hague by France, England and Holland. This is a response to Spanish expansionist ambitions: Philip V, as Louis XIV's grandson, wishes to gain the French crown, and his wife Elizabeth Farnese wants her children to inherit familial lands in Italy.

China, 1717. The painter and art theoretician Che-t'ao dies.

West Africa, 1717. Prussia sells its West African slave stations to the Dutch.

London, 1717. The Golden Lion coffee house is the first in London to admit women.

Austria, 21 July 1718. The treaty of Passarowitz, negotiated by the Emperor Charles VI and the Venetians with the Ottoman empire, ends the war begun by the Turks in 1714. Turkey cedes Temesvar to Charles, putting the whole of Hungary under Habsburg rule. The Turkish threat to Europe is effectively stamped out.

Pennsylvania, 30 July 1718. William Penn, the Quaker founder of the colony, dies.

Europe, 2 August 1718. The Holy Roman Empire joins the triple alliance formed by Britain, Holland and France against Spain last year. The new quadruple alliance aims to uphold the terms of the 1713 Treaty of Utrecht, which Philip V of Spain has violated by invading Sicily and Sardinia.

Europe, 24 August 1718. In the conflict following the drawing up of the quadruple alliance, Victor Amadeus of Savoy cedes the island of Sicily to Austria in exchange for Sardinia.

Virginia, 22 November 1718. The infamous pirate Edward Teach, known as Blackbeard because of an immense beard which he tied with ribbons, is killed by an English naval officer. A reward of £100 pounds had been offered by the government of Virginia for his capture.

Louisiana, November 1718. Governor Bienville founds a new city at the mouth of the Mississippi river, calling it New Orleans in honour of the French regent, the duke of Orleans.

Norway, 11 December 1718. Sweden's king, Charles XII, dies in battle at Frederikshald (*Halden*). He came to power in 1697 and has spent almost his entire reign engaged in the Second Northern War. Most recently he had been defeated by Russia and sued for peace, but then marched on Norway. He was killed by a musket shot fired from the fortress of Frederikshald.

Spain, 9 January 1719. In escalation of the conflict caused by the Spanish occupation of Sardinia and Sicily, and the drawing up of the quadruple alliance, Philip V of Spain declares war on France.

Prussia, 22 March 1719. Frederick William abolishes serfdom on crown property.

Dying Sun King was "punished by God"

St Germain, 1 September 1715

Louis XIV of France, the Sun King, died at St Germain en Laye at eight this morning. He would have been 77 in four days' time and had been king for 73 years. Suffering from gangrene of the leg, he knew he was dying and accepted his fate with courage and patience. Saying goodbye to his successor, his five-year-old great grandson, he advised him: "Remain at peace with your neighbours. I loved war too much. Do not follow me in that or in overspending."

There will be few tears shed for this hard-working, but haughty man. It was he who transformed France into an absolute monarchy declaring: *L'Etat, c'est moi* ("The state, it's me"). He came to the throne under the regency of his mother, Anne of Austria, and lived through dangerous times under the tutelage of Richelieu and Mazarin before claiming supreme power for himself. The last years of this brilliant monarch have been darkened by defeat, a bankrupt economy and family deaths. He died believing he was being punished by God for the terror he had inflicted on Europe.

Louis poses as a Roman noble.

Emperor dies exhausted for China's sake

Beijing, 23 December 1717

The Emperor Kangxi called his many sons and his officials to the Eastern chamber of the Jianjing palace today and delivered a valedictory edict in preparation for his death. He said he would rather they listen to his words than those of an anonymous scholar.

The emperor, who is nearly 70 and has reigned for over 50 years, was in a reflective, sad mood, recalling the days of his youth when he was strong and talking about the burdens of ruling China: "Bowing down in service and wearing oneself out ... I exhaust myself for the country's sake."

He told them that the art of ruling was to be "always diligent and always careful, and maintain the balance between leniency and strictness, between principle and expediency ... that's all there is to it". Finally, he told them: "I've revealed my entrails and shown my guts, there's nothing left within me to reveal. I will say no more."

Workers constructing a dyke during the reign of Emperor Kangxi.

Turks lose Belgrade

Belgrade, 22 August 1717
Austrian forces today occupied the strategically important city of Belgrade, ending the Turkish military revival in the Balkans. As victorious troops of the Imperial House of Habsburg marched into the devastated city 60,000 Moslems, including 20,000 Turkish soldiers, were allowed to leave.

The Turks, who had supplies for another six months, decided to surrender after their relief force camped outside the city was slaughtered in a dawn raid a week ago by Imperialist troops led by Prince Eugene of Savoy.

The August 16 raid was a dramatic triumph for Prince Eugene who appeared to stand little chance of winning this battle. His siege army, ravaged by dysentery and raked by deadly artillery fire from the Turkish relief force on a plateau to the east, was thought to be trapped and on the verge of destruction. Prince Eugene left 10,000 men to watch Belgrade while, under cover of fog, 60,000 Imperial troops fortified by wine and beer overran the Turks.

In Vienna, Prince Eugene is now being hailed as the architect of the Imperial success. His victory against a much larger Turkish force in Hungary last year, plus the shrewd treaty with England to safeguard the empire's Italian flank from a Franco-Spanish attack, are now regarded as having laid foundations for the Imperial success.

Inefficient French seek German help

Louisiana, December 1719
French Louisiana, so inefficient that it must import its food from France, has recruited German farmers to raise agricultural output. The first of the new breed of colonists disembarked at Ship Island, near Biloxi last month.

The Germans are sturdy Rhinelanders and tough hill farmers from Switzerland, all hungry for land and sanctuary from Europe's endless wars. Formerly, only French settlers were accepted in Louisiana. Now the Germans are said to be "just the colonists we need", though they have much to learn.

A great German thinker is dead

Hanover, 14 November 1716
Gottfried Wilhelm Leibnitz, the German philosopher who dedicated his life to the spread of scientific discoveries for the benefit of all mankind, has died. He was 70.

To further his belief Leibnitz tried to construct a universal language and develop a system of logic through which any controversy could be solved. Central to his theories was the idea of "monads": indivisible substances on which all things are based.

Cristofori's "piano e forte" catches on

Two young ladies play a new tune.

Europe, c.1715
Musicians are taking an increasing interest in the instrument invented around 20 years ago by the Florentine keyboard maker Bartolomeo Cristofori (born 1655). He calls his invention a *gravicembalo col piano e forte* or "harpsichord with soft and loud"; it differs from normal harpsichords in that when the keys are pressed the strings are struck rather than plucked. The mechanism of what is becoming known as the "piano e forte" or "forte-piano" allows the struck string to resonate, giving the instrument a much greater range of loudness or softness.

Blood curdling rituals bind freemasons

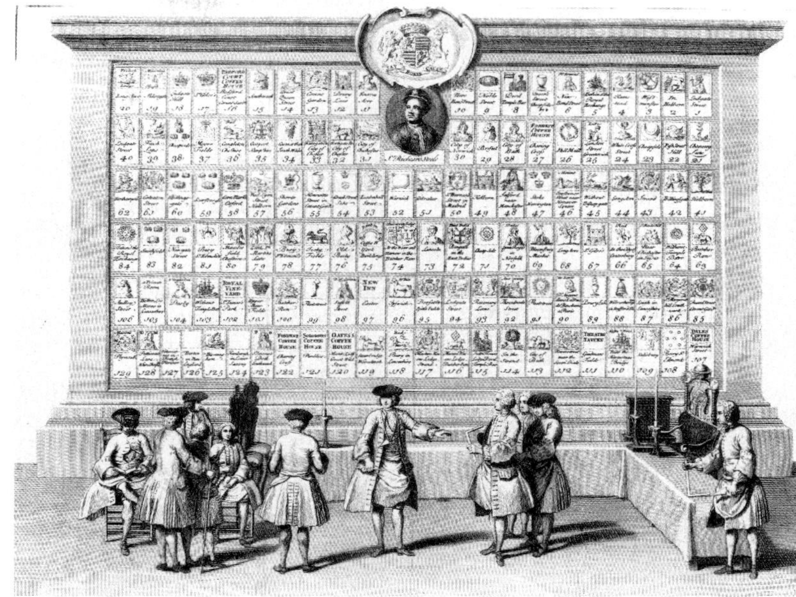

Masons meet under posters displaying the names of their many "lodges".

London, 4 June 1717
A secret society, which claims to date back to the beginning of time, has established itself in London. Freemasonry, as the society is known, has been growing for a number of years. Now the first Grand Lodge, or headquarters, has been set up at the Goose and Gridiron tavern in Covent Garden.

The Craft, as it is known, allegedly began with the sons of Adam, and its more immediate roots lie with Hiram, master-mason of Solomon's Temple, who it is said was killed for refusing to reveal masonic secrets. England's first freemasons, who appear to number around 1,300, were a trade guild like many others, and their lodges or local assemblies developed to meet the needs of workers whose jobs kept them moving from place to place.

Today's society includes few working masons. The old craft guild was gradually diluted by outsiders and now members join for the social and professional benefits. None the less freemasonry is highly secretive, with elaborate rituals, a blood-curdling initiation ceremony and a secret handclasp – the "Masonic Word" – by which members may recognise each other.

A view of the Schonbrunn Palace in Vienna: completed in 1717 the palace is designed as a place of enjoyment and relaxation, but its vast dimensions and superb furnishings make it a symbol of imperial might.

1719 (1719-1722)

South Carolina, November 1719. Colonists overthrow British proprietors.

Texas, 1720. Two years of hostilities between French and Spanish troops in Florida and Texas – caused by the war of the Quadruple Alliance in Europe – are over. Spanish possession of Texas has been confirmed.

Netherlands, 17 February 1720. Spain signs the treaty of The Hague with the Quadruple Alliance (Britain, Holland, France and the Holy Roman Empire), ending the war begun in 1718. Philip V of Spain agrees to evacuate Sardinia and Sicily, the invasions of which started the conflict. He exiles his chief minister Alberoni, whom he holds responsible for the war.

Sweden, 20 February 1720. Queen Ulrika Eleonora, Charles XII's younger sister, abdicates in favour of her consort, Frederick of Hesse-Kessel.

Paris, 24 March 1720. Banking establishments close in the wake of financial crisis.

West Africa, c.1720. Biton Mamari Kouloubali makes himself leader of the kingdom of Segu (*Mali*). Mamari was elected head of the *ton-den* brotherhood and began to conscript young Bambara into it destroying its previously egalitarian nature. He is establishing the *ton-den*, and himself, as the dominant powers in the community.

North America, 1720. Population of the British colonies now stands at 474,000. Boston is the largest city at 12,000; Philadelphia has an estimated 10,000 and New York some 7,000 inhabitants.

Central America, 1720. The English colony of Honduras is established.

Austria, 1720. The Pragmatic Sanction – issued by Emperor Charles V in 1713, settling succession to the Habsburg lands on his eldest daughter Maria Theresa – is slowly recognised by the Habsburg states.

Russia, 25 January 1721. The Holy Synod replaces the Patriarchate of Moscow and steps are taken against the sect of the Old Believers. They object to the 1667 revision of Russian church ritual and liturgy in accordance with Greek practice, and are regarded as schismatics by the Orthodox church.

Germany, 24 March 1721. The supremely talented musician Johann Sebastian Bach publishes the *Six Brandenburg Concertos*.

England, 3 April 1721. Following the collapse of the South Sea Scheme, the ambitious Whig politician Robert Walpole is made Chancellor of the Exchequer in the hope that he will restore financial order.

Rome, 8 May 1721. After the death of Clement XI on 19 March, Michelangelo dei Conti is elected pope and takes the name of Innocent XIII. He was secretary of state for Clement XI and has been elected after a long contentious conclave as a man of diplomatic tact and political acumen.

France, 18 July 1721. The painter Antoine Watteau dies of tuberculosis from which he had suffered all his life. Watteau will be best remembered for the palace-garden landscapes that form the typical background to many of his pictures.

Sweden, 30 August 1721. The peace of Nystad ends the Second Northern War – between Sweden and Russia – which began in 1700. Sweden cedes Livonia, Estonia, part of Karelia and Ingermanland to Russia and retains Finland. This marks a considerable increase in Russian power in the Baltic.

Greenland, 1721. Led by the Norwegian minister Hans Egede, the Protestant mission of Godthaab is established with the aim of converting the Eskimos.

New Orleans, 1721. A group of women taken from a house of correction in France arrives to relieve the shortage of females in the colony. Many are married almost immediately after arrival, and the rest parcelled out to various French settlements to appease lonely bachelors.

Massachusetts, 1721. During an outbreak of smallpox Dr Zabdiel Boylston of Boston experiments with innoculation at the prompting of Reverend Cotton Mather. Mather heard of the technique from his African slave Onesimus. Opponents to innoculation believe it has caused the disease to spread more rapidly, though all but six of the 240 Boylston innoculated have survived.

France, 25 October 1722. Louis XV is crowned at Rheims.

Austria, 19 December 1722. Charles V creates the Ostend Company, an association of Flemish merchants trading with the east. This is a result of the transfer of the Spanish Netherlands to Austria under the Treaty of Utrecht of 1713. Both Britain and Holland object to the foundation of the Company seeing it as a threat to their own trading ventures.

Sweden's dream of Baltic power is dead

Stockholm, 21 January 1720

The last line of an epigram by the Swedish poet Carl Cederhielm says it all: "...and Sweden's clock has moved from XII to I..." he wrote as Sweden signed the Treaty of Stockholm, losing its empire and its control of the Baltic Sea. The "XII" referred to the late King Charles – killed while laying siege to Fredrikshald – whose impetuous advance into Russia in mid-winter impoverished his country, leaving it vulnerable. After the defeat of the Swedish army at Poltava, Prussia and Hanover joined the alliance of Denmark, Poland and Russia against Sweden. The greatest threat came from Russia whose raiding parties had already reached Stockholm.

This fear that created intense diplomatic activity, particularly by Britain – anxious to secure supplies of spars and hemp for her navy – and France, Sweden's long-time ally.

Sweden has lost her Baltic states to Prussia and Hanover and a once-great power has settled for a minor role on the world stage.

Tale of castaway Crusoe proves popular

London, 25 April, 1719

A book purporting to tell "The Strange Surprising Adventures of Robinson Crusoe of York, Mariner" is being read eagerly by people who take it to be a true account of shipwreck. It is only some half-dozen years since the Scottish castaway, Alexander Selkirk, got home after four years in solitude on the Pacific island of Juan Fernandez.

Robinson Crusoe claims to have exceeded this, having been marooned 28 years. But after 15 of these he discovered a creature he calls Friday to be sharing his island. Daniel Defoe, former editor of *The Review* and author of many political pamphlets, is the transcriber – or author? – of these remarkable adventures.

Daniel Defoe's Robinson Crusoe.

Letters from a Persian lost in Paris

A Persian prince out hawking.

Amsterdam, 1721

Letters have been published anonymously here and in Cologne purporting to be from a Persian living in Paris, satirizing French society. They are in fact the work of the Baron de Montesquieu.

The *Lettres Persanes* represent a correspondence between two brothers, Rica, in Venice, Usbek, in Paris, and their relatives in Isfahan. Usbek writes from Paris about his puzzlement at the role of that "magician", the Pope, and the political system which allows him such extraordinary influence.

Montesquieu, who is 32, is a member of the Academy of Science, and a writer of exceptional wit and perception.

Financial panic in Paris

"The Bubbler's Medley": a satirical print mocking the South Sea Bubble.

London, 1720
Financial scandals have erupted in London and Paris in the wake of an orgy of speculation by gullible investors tempted by promises of vast fortunes. The man who started it all is John Law, a Scottish exile who gained the confidence of the French Regent, the Duc d'Orleans. Law was allowed to launch a note-issuing Banque Royale, a trading company, the Compagnie des Indies, and to collect some land taxes. He promised to pay off the national debt by encouraging the public to exchange their government bonds for shares in his India company.

That gave ideas to Robert Harley, who had earlier founded the South Sea Company. Investors rushed to turn in their government bonds in exchange for South Sea stock. In six months the shares rose from 150 to 1,000. John Windham, a Norfolk squire, wrote to his brother: "I grow rich so fast I like stock jobbing above all things."

All England seemed to join in. Hundreds of other companies were launched, with bizarre promises – to drain bogs in Ireland, to get gold from sea water, to collect hair for wig-making, to organise funerals. When the South Sea Company accused some of its rivals of dishonesty, the public lost confidence and began selling. Within weeks, South Sea shares had plunged to 180. Windham now wrote: "Almost all one knows or sees are upon the very Brink of Destruction."

The story was much the same in Paris. The India Company's shares slumped and panic-stricken Parisiens besieged the Banque Royale; but Law had fled.

Persian capital falls to the Afghans

Isfahan, 12 October 1722
Shah Sultan Husayn has surrendered the Persian capital to Afghan rebels after a seven-month siege, in which more than 80,000 people have died of famine.

The fall of Isfahan represents the collapse of the Safawid dynasty, defeated with remarkable ease by a modest tribal army, but crucially undermined by its own weaknesses. Since the death of Shah Abbas II in 1666, Persia has lacked a strong ruler.

Sultan Husayn, shah since 1694, is a weak man, dominated by mullahs whose determination to force Shi'ite Islam on a reluctant population has encouraged rebellion. Mahmud, the leader of the Sunnis of Afghanistan, now enjoys tenuous control of Persia.

Silk cloth: a youth drinking wine.

Spanish defeat at hands of Triple Alliance

Madrid, 26 January 1720
Guilio Alberoni, the devious cardinal of Madrid, was ordered out of Spain today – bringing to an end a short and bloody attempt to restore his country's Mediterranean empire and crush Habsburg power in Italy. British troops have occupied Vigo, Spanish troops are to evacuate Sardinia and Sicily and Philip V has acceded to the Treaty of Utrecht.

Alberoni organised a futile attempt at invading England by the pretender, James III – foiled by storms off Finisterre – and also intrigued to start an abortive rebellion in Brittany.

Pacific island discovered on Easter day

Chile, 1722
Admiral Jacob Roggeveen, a Dutch navigator, has discovered a strange, lonely Pacific island inhabited by primitive sun worshippers. They call it "Rapa Nui" but Roggeveen, noting the festival on which he landed there, has renamed it "Easter Island". As well as natives it is populated by hundreds of extraordinary statues, long-eared icons up to 32 feet (9.75m) tall.

The strange statues that have been found by Roggeveen on Easter Island.

1722 (1722-1727)

New England, 1722. The English parliament bans trade with Canada.

France, 22 February 1723. Louis XV comes of age.

Russia, 12 September 1723. The treaty of St Petersburg puts an end to the Russo-Persian war which began last year when Peter the Great, made anxious by a Turkish push towards the Caspian Sea, launched an offensive. By the treaty Russia gains control of the coastal areas between Derbent and Resht on the Caspian Sea and the shah receives a loan of Russian troops for domestic peace-keeping.

England, 2 October 1723. The English block Austrian trading activity by passing a law against trade with the Ostend Company of merchants.

Prussia, 10 October 1723. The treaty of Charlottenburg is signed between Britain and Prussia. Britain is seeking Prussian friendship in the face of the Emperor Charles VI's promotion of the Ostend Company.

Philadelphia, October 1723. Benjamin Franklin, 17-year-old publisher of an irreverent weekly, the *New England Courant*, leaves Boston for Philadelphia following a fight with his brother. Franklin writes satirical pieces under the pseudonym Silence Dogood.

West Africa, c.1723. King Agaja of the Dahomey kingdon at Abomey invades the kingdom of Allada. Allada, founded about 150 years ago, was once the most powerful kingdom of the Aja peoples.

Germany, 1724. Johann Sebastian Bach's *St John Passion* is performed on Good Friday in Leipzig.

Rome, 29 May 1724. The new pope, Benedict XIII, a very old man, allows Cardinal Niccolo Coscia to rule in his place.

London, 27 December 1724. Thomas Guy, a well-known philanthropist and bookseller, dies. Two years ago he began the construction of a new hospital on a site opposite St Thomas', and the building is now complete. His will provides for a vast number of people, both known and unknown to him, as well as leaving sufficient funds for the running of the new hospital.

Austria, 1724. Commercial differences between England and Austria are resolved. The Ostend Company of Flemish merchants is put into liquidation.

Louisana, 1724. The Black Code makes it legal for slave owners to cut off runaways' ears, hamstring and brand them. It also bars Jews and Catholics from the colony.

France, 1724. The famously talented keyboard instrumentalist Francois Couperin completes his second collection of *Royal Concerts*.

Russia, 8 February 1725. Peter the Great dies in St Petersburg. He is succeeded by his wife Catherine.

Spain, 2 March 1725. The architect Jose Benito de Churriguera dies. One of his finest works is the high altar in San Esteban, Salamanca.

Austria, 30 April 1725. Philip V of Spain and the Emperor Charles VI sign the treaty of Vienna ending Spanish and imperial adhesion to the Quadruple Alliance. Philip guarantees the Pragmatic Sanction – allowing for the succession of the emperor's daughter on his death – and receives a promise of support in the recovery of Gibraltar and Minorca, though this does not extend to military aid. Spain appears to have gained little, but the Spanish negotiator Ripperda's claims of secret clauses are worrying Britain and France.

France, 15 August 1725. Louis XV marries Maria Leszczynska, daughter of the deposed Polish king, Stanislav Leszczynski, by proxy in Strasbourg.

Naples, 22 October 1725. The composer Alessandro Scarlatti dies. He wrote many operas, among them – *The Triumph of Liberty* (1707), *Tigrone* (1715), *The Triumph of Honour* (1718) and *Griselda* (1721).

Netherlands, 1725. The composer Antonio Vivaldi publishes *The Four Seasons*.

Southern Africa, c.1725. Langa, the ancestor chief of Ngwane, Swazi and Hlubi nations, dies. Langa was tributary to the Tembe kingdom at Maputo Bay.

South America, 1725. Montevideo is founded.

Naples, 1725. The Italian philosopher Giambattista Vico publishes *Principles of a New Science*.

France, 12 June 1726. Louis XV's tutor, Fleury, becomes prime minister following the fall from grace of the duke of Bourbon. His dangerous foreign policies threatened to involve France in a war with Spain and Austria.

Russia, 16 August 1726. Russia becomes an ally of Austria and recognises the Pragmatic Sanction guaranteeing the succession of Emperor Charles VI's eldest daughter, Maria Theresa.

Ottoman Empire, 1727. The Ottomans and Persians form an alliance against Russia.

Czar Peter the Great's reforms: a commoner may rise to noble rank

Peter the Great's new palace of Petrodvorets in the city of St Petersburg.

St Petersburg, 24 January 1722

Czar Peter – "the Great" – has transformed Russia and set her on the path to becoming a great European power. His dazzling reforms over the past 30 years were capped today by the introduction of a "Table of Ranks" which will give the country a well-organised military and civil service. From now on a commoner can climb on merit to the highest positions.

Peter's other reforms include the abolition of the old *duma* of the Moscow aristocracy, the reorganisation of the government, and major financial changes including the introduction of a poll tax. His social revolution has included the shaven chin and the short coat of the western European – anyone appearing at the gates of a city wearing a long Russian robe is made to kneel while the coat is cut to the knee.

For most of his reign Russia has been at war and he has constructed a formidable military machine with an army of some 200,000 men. His most cherished project was the building of a fleet and Russia is now one of the sea powers of Europe. He is renowned for his cruelty but he has remodelled the calendar, simplified the alphabet, and founded the first Russian newspaper.

Czar Peter as a ship's carpenter.

King of Spain in sudden abdication shock

Spain, 10 January 1724

The courts of Europe are in a state of shock at the announcement by King Philip V of Spain that he has abdicated in favour of his eldest son, Louis. The move remained a well-kept secret, although Philip apparently had been planning it for more than three years. His motive is uncertain, but it is thought he has been concerned about the fits of depression that have been afflicting him. He was the first Bourbon king of Spain and under his autocratic rule, administration became more efficient, feudalism was destroyed and power was concentrated in the crown.

Regent dies after seven years of pleasure

Paris, 2 December 1723

Philippe, the duke of Orleans, has died of apoplexy just nine months after giving up the regency of France when Louis XV celebrated his thirteenth birthday and came of age. Philippe, who did a deal with the *Parlement* to ensure that he became regent against the wishes of the late Louis XIV, had shown soldierly qualities in the war against Spain and could have had an outstanding career.

Instead, he gave himself over to pleasure. His rakish friends turned the seven years of his regency into a disorderly reaction against the sad, stiff austerity which characterised the last years of his uncle Louis XIV's long reign.

The new young king: Louis XV, a teenage monarch for France.

Discoverer of life-giving forces has died

Holland, 1723

The death has been announced of Antoni van Leeuwenhoek, the remarkable self-taught scientist who has done so much to advance the practice and technique of microscopy. In 1671, when Leeuwenhoek was 39 years old, he constructed a simple microscope, having ground the lens by hand himself. His crucial discovery was in 1674 when he found that the moving objects he saw through his microscopes were minute organisms such as bacteria and protozoa. In 1677 a medical student called Johan Ham told him that he had seen tiny animals in human seminal fluid. Leeuwenhoek identified these spermatozoa as a normal component of semen and went on to postulate that it is they that fertilise the egg.

Bering in the Arctic

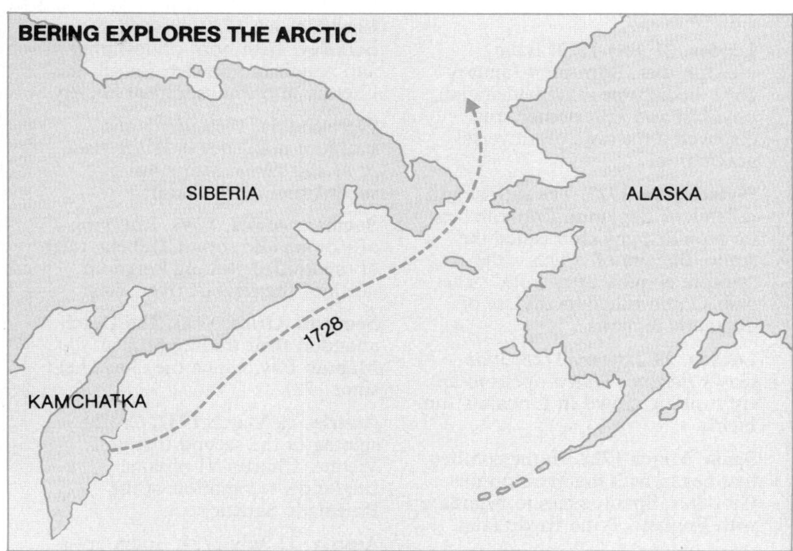

Moscow, 1725

Vitus Bering, a Danish sailor exploring the oceans for Peter the Great, the czar of Russia, has discovered previously unknown straits separating Russia from the American continent. Czar Peter had commissioned Bering to find out exactly where Siberia meets Alaska. Bering had already distinguished himself in the czar's service in the wars against Sweden.

Bering's small expedition set out last year, overland from St Petersburg to a small port in Kamchatka. There a ship was built and set out along the shore of the Kamchatka peninsula. The leader and his 33 men moved northwards up the Siberian coast towards the north-eastern corner of Asia. Bering found that there is no strip of land between Siberia and America. His vessel passed through the straits into a new northern ocean before being forced to turn back.

Russia has three czars in two years

St Petersburg, 1727

In just two years Russia, the largest empire in the world, has had three rulers. After Peter the Great's death in 1725, power passed to his widow Catherine. Bawdy, kindly and a great brandy-drinker, she was also illiterate and left the affairs of state to Prince Alexander Menshikov, a close aide of the former czar.

Catherine has now died and has been succeeded by Peter the Great's 12-year-old grandson, also Peter, who is spending much of his time on extended hunting expeditions and precocious flirtation, not least with his voluptuous aunt, Elizabeth. Menshikov had secured the betrothal of his daughter to young Peter, but his overbearing ways upset his prospective son-in-law; he has been exiled to Siberia.

Polemicist Swift takes Gulliver to Lilliput and beyond

London, 28 October 1726

A small book of *Travels into Several Remote Nations of the World* by a ship's captain, Lemuel Gulliver, is being eagerly bought and discussed with great amazement. Gulliver describes his voyages to Lilliput, an island off the Indies, where the people look human but are six inches tall, then to Brobdingnag, where they are as tall as church steeples. He next finds himself taken up into a flying island called Laputa, and finally reaches a land governed by horses of wisdom who employ as their beasts the Yahoos, who resemble gross and violent human creatures.

Wherever Gulliver goes to explore human civilisation, it is made to appear ridiculous, barbarous and disgusting, and it is generally thought that the satirical Irish dean, Dr Jonathan Swift, is the true author of these *Travels*.

Gulliver exhibited to the Brobdingnagians: a 19th-century illustration.

1727 (1727-1733)

Spain, March 1727. Spain breaks the terms of the treaty of Utrecht, invades Gibraltar and attacks the English.

London, 31 July 1727. Isaac Newton dies. Born on 4 January 1642, he became a mathematician, physicist and astronomer, and discovered the laws of universal gravitation.

Philadelphia, 1727. The satirist and polemicist Benjamin Franklin sets up a philosophy club called the Junto, the aim of which is the "sincere enquiry after truth". The club's main rule bars the use of dogmatic remarks.

London, 29 January 1728. John Gay's *Beggar's Opera* opens to an enthusiastic crowd in Lincoln's Inn Fields.

Spain, March 1728. In the conflict that began with the invasion of Gibraltar, Spain agrees to negotiate with England at the Pardo talks.

Germany, 23 December 1728. Prussia signs the treaty of Berlin with the Emperor Charles VI, guaranteeing the Pragmatic Sanction.

Madrid, 1728. The first masonic lodge in Madrid is presided over by the duke of Wharton, a Roman Catholic agent of the Pretender. The lodge is attended only by Englishmen.

Germany, 15 April 1729. Johann Sebastian Bach's *St Matthew's Passion* is performed on the evening of Good Friday, conducted by the composer.

Spain, 9 November 1729. In signing the treaty of Seville, Spain renounces its right to Gibraltar, which remains in English hands. All English economic privileges in the Spanish American colonies are retained.

Louisiana, 28 November 1729. Natchez Indians massacre most of the 300 French soldiers and settlers in Fort Rosalie, in the most vicious attack yet in the Louisiana colony. It was triggered by the demand that the Natchez give up their sacred burial ground and temple.

Russia, 29 January 1730. Peter II, czar since 1727, dies of smallpox and is succeeded by Anna Ivanova, daughter of Czar Ivan V. In 1728, Peter moved his court from St Petersburg to Moscow.

England 15 May 1730. Following the resignation of Lord Townshend, Robert Walpole becomes the sole minister in the English cabinet.

Louisana, December 1730. In retribution for last year's attack on Fort Rosalie, French soldiers take prisoner Sun, chief of the Natchez Indians.

Africa, 1730. The Portuguese finally lose Mombasa to the native power of the Omani.

Rhode Island, 1730. George Berkeley, Irish-born philosopher and Anglican minister, founds the Literary and Philosophical Society.

Pennsylvania, 1730. Benjamin Franklin publishes *A Witch Trial at Mount Holly*, satirising superstition of witchcraft.

Southern Africa, 1730. Tau, king of Rolong and son of Thibela, ruler of the unified Rolong kingdom north of the Orange river, dies.

Southern Africa, 1730. The Dutch abandon their trading post in Maputo Bay, which they have held since 1721.

Austria, 16 March 1731. On the signing of the second treaty of Vienna, Charles VI obtains England's recognition of the Pragmatic Sanction.

Austria, 22 July 1731. Spain gives its adherence to the Anglo-Austrian agreements and signs the third treaty of Vienna.

West Africa, 1731. The slave trading kingdom of Dahomey at Abomey, after defeats in battle, accepts the suzerainty of the Oyo empire (the Yoruba people).

Persia, 1731. Tasmasp II, shah for less than a year, is deposed by his brother-in-law Nadir Kuli. Tasmasp's eight-month-old son, Abbas, is elevated to the throne as a puppet.

Caribbean, 1731. Robert Jenkins, master of the *Rebecca*, sailing from Jamaica with sugar and other commodities for London, has his ear cut off by Spanish coast guards. After prolonged torture of Jenkins and his men, during which the Spaniards repeatedly asked for money, they sliced off his ear with a cutlass and told him to carry it home to the king.

Germany, 11 January 1732. The German Diet meets in Ratisbon (*Regensburg*) and guarantees the implementation of the Pragmatic Sanction which allows for the succession of Maria Theresa, Emperor Charles VI's daughter.

Pennsylvania, May 1732. The *Philadelphia Zeitung*, the first foreign language newspaper in British colonies, is published by Benjamin Franklin.

London, 7 December 1732. The Covent Garden theatre opens.

London, 1732. A law is passed prohibiting the export of American hats to England. Designed to protect English hat makers, the law is seen as another example of the so-called mercantile system which seems to benefit the mother country only.

Queen is power behind unpopular throne

London, 1727

Coffee house gossip has it that the power behind the throne of the new English king, George II, is Caroline, his cultured and determined wife. She likes to get away from her husband and spend time talking politics with Sir Robert Walpole, the prime minister. When George I died in June, in a carriage driving to Hanover, Caroline intervened to stop her husband sacking Walpole.

George II has been described as a humourless, choleric, conceited bore and womaniser. A man of routine and a penny-pincher (he counts his money, coin by coin, daily), he was banned from Court when he was prince of Wales after he quarrelled with his father over who should be godfather to his children. Now he threatens to ban his son Frederick from Court for intriguing with opposition politicians.

George II: Britain's new king, but as yet little loved by his peoples.

Encyclopaedia of 10,000 chapters finished

Beijing, 1728

A remarkable encyclopaedia of Chinese knowledge has just been published. Entitled "Collection of texts and illustrations old and new" it consists of no fewer than 10,000 chapters with a table of contents of 40 chapters and is so large only 64 copies have been printed. It was originally the work of the scholar Chen Menglei, who was brought back from exile by Emperor Kangxi and appointed tutor to Prince Yinzhe who became his patron and funded his work. When the emperor died, however, Chen again fell out of favour and the work was completed by Jiang Tingxi, a scholar who was appointed Grand Secretary this year.

"A scene from the Beggar's Opera" by William Hogarth: a painter and engraver, Hogarth is already well-known for his portraits, but he is fast establishing a new genre, that of what he calls "pictured morality".

Sultan's fall ends the "Tulip Period"

Istanbul, 1730
The abdication of Sultan Ahmed III and the execution of his Grand Vizier brings to an end the Tulip Age, in which the traditional Ottoman ethos of authority and militarism has given way to a more European culture exalting peace, beauty, literature and the arts.

Treaties in 1712 and 1713 secured the frontier with Russia, but gains by the Ottomans in Greece at Venetian expense were balanced by reverses in northern Europe; these culminated in the Treaty of Passarowitz in 1718, which gave Hungary and Serbia back to the Austrians.

The Sultan was now able to indulge his passion for building, music and books. He moved his summer court to the "Sweet Waters of Europe", at the head of the Golden Horn, where he diverted streams to make marble-lined canals, lakes, and fountains watering gardens. He built a summer palace at Sa'adabad, modelled on the French chateau of Marly. The high point of the year was the Tulip Fete, in the spring, when the Sultan would receive homage among spectacular tulip displays, multicoloured lamps and singing birds. Ahmet Nedim was the outstanding poet in a court where literature flourished, and artists were allowed to represent the human form.

A significant tool of the new enlightenment was a printing press brought from Paris by the Turkish ambassador in 1727.

Dancers and singers entertain sultan Ahmed III in a break from the hunt.

Russian friendship treaty with China

Kyakhta, 14 June 1730
Russia and China have signed an important friendship and trading treaty in this border town south of Lake Baikal.

The new treaty confirms the boundaries agreed 41 years ago at Nerchinsk, when the Chinese Emperor Kangxi was mustering his forces on the border in response to Cossack incursions. Communication between the two nations had been non-existent until that point, when Jesuit priests installed in Beijing acted as intermediaries. The Russians, who had wanted to make the Amur river the frontier, agreed then not to venture beyond the Stanovoi mountains.

Today's pact, concluded in Latin, with official copies in Manchu and Russian, provides for regular merchant caravans to Peking. It also gives the Russians the opportunity to import textiles, tea, pottery, tobacco and ink from China, chiefly through Kyakhta.

Hand-picked debtors form a new colony

New England, 1732
England's thirteenth American colony has been founded by hand-picked debtors rescued from jail by their new governor, General James Oglethorpe MP. The general has acknowledged his royal charter by naming the colony "Georgia", after King George II. Its purpose is to remove debtors from prison and to create a buffer between hostile Spanish Florida and English Carolina. In Georgia, hard liquor and slavery are prohibited.

Corsican bandits rise up against Genoa

Genoa, 1729
The Genoan Republic has been shaken by a rebellion against the old order. For generations this maritime city state has been governed by a clique of top families ruling colonies with scant regard to local rights. Corsicans, for whom banditry is a "profession of honour", have united, surprisingly, to resist Genoan domination. Separated by sea from the mainland, they might yet be blockaded into submission.

Sealed alcohol is key to new thermometer

France, 1730
Thermometers have been in use for about 100 years now, but so far they have not embodied scales that all scientists accept as universal. Fahrenheit's linear scale with its fixed points has attracted a lot of attention. But a Fahrenheit thermometer is only accurate if the diameter of the inside of the tube is perfectly regular along its length.

A French naturalist and physicist Rene Antoine Ferchault de Reaumur has now attempted to meet this difficulty by constructing a hermetically-sealed thermometer using alcohol. In this a single degree of temperature is determined by volume as a fraction of the alcohol sealed in the tube.

Reaumur and his assistant work on constructing the new thermometer.

Compulsory military service in Prussia

Berlin, 1732
Frederick William I, the "Sergeant King", has introduced compulsory military service in Prussia, creating the fourth biggest army in Europe after the French, Russian and Austrian.

The permanent nucleus is provided by the peasantry. Every male is eligible for conscription from the age of 18. Each noble family sends one of its sons for training as an officer. Volunteers are recruited from abroad to swell the ranks.

The pride of the army is the infantry, under Prince Leopold of Anhalt. It has become a model of discipline, marching with great precision and outdoing others with its rapidity of fire.

Prussia's "Sergeant King".

1733 (1733-1739)

France, 10 October 1733. France declares war on Austria over the question of Polish succession following the death of Augustus II. Augustus III, supported by Austria, Saxony and Russia, has been elected in preference to Stanislav Leszczynski, the candidate supported by France.

France, 17 November 1733. The controller general, Orry, imposes the tenth emergency tax – repealed during the regency – to cover the cost of the war of declared on 10 October.

Japan, 1733. A large-scale food riot takes place in Edo (*Tokyo*) when some 1,700 people attack a rice store in protest against exorbitant prices. Such riots are becoming increasingly common, the earliest similar disturbance having occurred in Nagasaki in 1713.

Austria, 1 January 1734. The War of Polish Succession escalates when Emperor Charles, in an alliance with Russia and Saxony, declares war on France.

Poland, 9 March 1734. The Russians takes Danzig (*Gdansk*).

West Africa, 1734. The Sultan of Bornu becomes overlord of Kano following the war which began in 1731 in northern Nigeria.

France, 23 August 1735. Rameau has his opera *Les Indes galantes* performed.

France, 5 October 1735. France and Austria begin secret talks to settle the Polish question.

Germany 17 January 1736. The architect Matthaus Poppelmann (born in Herford in 1662) dies. He created the Zwinger complex in Dresden – one of the masterpieces of contemporary architecture in Saxony.

North America, 6 February 1736. The young Anglican preacher John Wesley lands in Georgia.

Austria, 12 February 1736. Maria Theresa of Austria, heir to the imperial throne by the provisions of the Pragmatic Sanction, marries Francois-Stephane of Lorraine.

Austria, 13 April 1736. Franco-Austrian talks on Poland and Lorraine are resumed following the conflict which broke out over the question of Polish succession in 1733. Augustus III is to remain on the Polish throne.

Austria, 21 April 1736. Prince Eugene of Savoy – a great general and military tactician – dies. He was commissioned by the Emperor Leopold and went on to a glorious military career, famously co-operating with the duke of Marlborough to win a decisive victory at Blenheim in 1704.

Netherlands, 16 September 1736. The German physicist Daniel Fahrenheit dies. Though not the first to use mercury as a thermometric substance, he is responsible for making mercury thermometers popular. He also devised the temperature scale using the temperatures of melting ice and salt, and the healthy human body, as his fixed points.

Ottoman Empire, 1736. Discovering that France is seeking Turkish aid in the war of Polish Succession, Russia declares war and sends troops into Turkish territory to the north of the Black Sea. The Ottomans inflict heavy losses on the invaders and force them to retreat to the Ukraine.

Austria, January 1737. Austria comes to the aid of her ally Russia, declaring war on the Ottoman empire.

Italy, 18 December 1737. The master violin maker Antonio Stradivarius dies in Cremona.

Scotland, 1737. A mob breaks into Edinburgh jail and hangs an English soldier, Captain Porteous. He was responsible for the shooting of several citizens six weeks ago at a riot which broke out following the execution of a popular smuggler called Wilson.

Austria, 2 May 1738. After three years of difficult negotiations, the fourth treaty of Vienna is signed, putting an end to the conflict caused by the question of Polish succession after the death of Augustus II.

Sweden, 1738. The "Hat" party is born during campaigning for the general election; they champion the French connection and advocate war with Russia. Their opponents, the "Caps" are led by Arvid Horn

India, 20 March 1739. Nadir Shah of Persia occupies Delhi and takes possession of the Peacock throne.

Austria, 23 September 1739. Having lost Belgrade to the Turks, Austria enters into negotiations and signs the treaty of Belgrade.

Russia, 3 October 1739. Having lost the support of Austria, Russia decides to make peace with the Turks and relinquishes all her conquests except Azov by the treaty of Nissa. The three-year conflict is over.

England, 19 October 1739. England goes to war with Spain over borderlines in Florida and the mistreatment inflicted on British subjects. A British sailor, Robert Jenkins, attends a sitting of parliament exhibiting his ear which was cut off by Spanish coast guards. The conflict becomes known as "the war of Jenkin's ear".

Quarrels over the Polish throne

A snuffbox portrait of Stanislas Leszczynski: twice king, twice deposed.

Poland, 1733

After February's death of Augustus II, King of Poland since 1697 and elector of Saxony since 1694, the country, as ever the volatile centre of contesting international interests, has been plunged into a new crisis. The succession has excited new rivalries between the great powers, each backing its own candidate. The controversy remains limited to diplomatic manoeuvring, but the sabre-rattling may escalate into all-out war.

Affairs are further complicated by the nature of Augustus II's rule. By no means a clear-cut candidate himself, he was elected in 1697 against the interests of France, whose preference, the Prince of Conti, arrived too late in Danzig to put himself forward. Thus Augustus was duly elected, backed by the German sovereigns. The new king showed little interest in Poland, spending most of his time at the sumptuous electoral court of Dresden. In response to his lengthy absences the Swedes demanded a proper ruler and in 1704 forced the election of Stanislas Leszczynski. He ruled for five years until the Russians, who occupied Poland, deposed him and returned Augustus to the throne.

France, Spain, Sardinia, and the bulk of the Polish nobility all back the return of Leszczynski, now the father-in-law of Louis XV and he was elected in September. The election failed to last. Russia backs Augustus' son, as does Austria.

With the support of the the Lithuanian nobility, who are equally in favour of maintaining the ruling family, and judicious bribing of the electors, Leszczynski's victory has been annulled. Augustus III replaced him in October and Leszczynski has fled to Danzig.

Moghul empire mocked by its old enemy

Delhi, India 1737

Beyond the city walls a Marathan army – the Hindu enemy of the Moghuls – camps is at its leisure. So weak has the Moghul empire become that they have no effective army to march against them. For the Marathas of central India, it is merely a political demonstration; but for the Moghul monarch, Mohammed Shah, it is a personal humiliation. "I am resolved to tell the emperor the truth, to prove that I am yet in Hindustan, and to show him flames and Marathas at the gates of his capital," proclaimed the Maratha leader, Baji Rao Peshwa.

As Moghul power has declined, so Maratha power has grown. For years they fought a guerrilla war against the Moghul Empire. In 1720 Mohammed Shah, sought to co-opt them by giving them the tax revenues of the Dekhan province.

With their new wealth they became masters of Gujarat, Malwa and Bundelkhand; and Moghul armies sent against them have all been defeated. They are now the most powerful force in India.

Botanist Linnaeus classifies plants

Sweden, 1737
With the increase in world trade, new plants and animals are constantly being discovered, and with them comes the problem of how to classify the natural world. Carl von Linne – better known as Linnaeus – has for many years been working on a system of classification.

Linnaeus bases his classification on a so-called "binominal" system. That is, he puts organisms into both species and genera. And he has devised a way of temporarily classifying recently discovered plants and animals until they can be permanently arranged in the system. This year saw the publication of *Genera Plantarum*, said to be a milestone in systematic botany.

The Swedish naturalist Linnaeus.

Nadir Shah, pictured as Persian troops destroy Moghul forces at Delhi.

Nadir Shah takes the Peacock Throne

Delhi, India, 20 March 1739
Nadir Shah, the most successful warrior Persia has ever produced, has entered Delhi in triumph. His entry, with the Moghul emperor Mohammed Shah a virtual prisoner, is the culmination of ten years of war. Born in 1688 in Kubkan, he first served the declining Safavid dynasty. He pacified Khurasan, defeated the Afghans who were occupying central Iran, drove back the Ottomans, besieged Baghdad and conquered Transcaucasia.

On 8 March 1736 he crowned himself shah, then invaded Afghanistan. Three years later, after defeating the Moghuls at Karnal near Panipat, he controls Delhi. The Moghuls, weakened by attacks from their Hindu enemy, the Marathas, were no match for the Persians.

Russia intervenes in the Balkans

Belgrade, 23 September 1739
Russian soldiers have occupied the Walachian town of Iasi within hours of the signing of the new three-way Treaty of Belgrade between the Russian, Austrian and Turkish empires.

The Russian advance, seen as evidence of Czarina Anna Ivanovna's ambitions in the Balkans, came as Belgrade was rocked by a series of controlled explosions as departing Austrian troops demolished fortifications put up 22 years ago when they captured Belgrade.

The new Treaty – signed at six o'clock this morning after 34 days of intensive diplomatic negotiations – hands Belgrade back to the Turks and ends the latest conflict between the Austrian and Turkish empires. Ironically the conflict might never have started had Russia not invoked a military assistance agreement with Austria when Russian troops seized the Turkish town of Azov in the Crimea three years ago.

Under the new Treaty the Austrians lose all the gains made in 1718 and are forced back to the borders defined in the the Treaty of Carlowitz 40 years ago. Western Walachia, Serbia and Banat all return to Ottoman control. The fortress of Azov is to be razed to the ground and the area around it declared a neutral zone between Russia and Turkey.

Spanish slice off an English ear

Havana, 9 April 1739
The British trading brig, *Rebecca* was sailing past this Caribbean port today when a Spanish coastguard schooner ordered her to heave to.

The Spanish demanded heavy duties on *Rebecca's* cargo of sugar and rum. The British master, Robert Jenkins refused to pay. The Spanish tortured Jenkins and his crew. When Jenkins continued to refuse payment, the Spanish sliced off his ear with a cutlass, handed it to him and told him to give it to his King. An angry Jenkins is returning to England – where he will seek the ear of Prime Minister Walpole.

Anglican priest John Wesley founds a "Methodist" movement

London, May 1739
This month sees the first anniversary of the conversion of a young Anglican priest, John Wesley, and people are talking of a new religious movement. Wesley recalls a specific time – a quarter to one – when he felt his "heart strangely warmed" by a feeling of contact with God. Since then he has moved around the country preaching in the open air to workers and peasants, rather as evangelist preachers such as Howell Harris are doing in Wales. Wesley and his brother Charles formed a Holy Club at Oxford in 1729. They were derisively called "Methodists" because of their studious and logical approach.

John Wesley, founder of Methodism, preaches from his father's tomb.

1739 (1739-1742)

England, 7 April 1739. The famous robber and smuggler Dick Turpin is executed; his body is seized by a mob and taken to York for burial. The son of an innkeeper, Turpin gained a name as a young man for atrocious robberies. Later he formed a partnership with the highwayman Tom King, whom he shot and killed by accident while trying to save him from arrest. Turpin was traced by clues left by the dying King.

England, 1739. The 28-year-old philosopher David Hume publishes his *Treatise of Human Nature*. Hume opposes the commonly accepted ideas on the absolute power of reason and follows John Locke and George Berkeley in claiming that knowledge comes from experience. This empiricist position finds little favour with his educated audience.

South America, 1739. The Spaniards establish New Granada as an independent viceroyalty, encompassing all territories between the Amazon and the Orinoco.

Colorado, 1739. French explorers Pierre and Paul Mallet arrive in New Orleans after a nine-month trek across the Great Plains during which they discovered a mountain range known to the Indians as the Rockies.

Netherlands, 1739. Voltaire publishes the *Anti-Machiavelli*, written by Frederick of Prussia, in Amsterdam.

Massachusetts, January 1740. Some 50 slaves are hanged after the exposure of alleged plans for an insurrection.

Florida, January 1740. Georgia's Governor Oglethorpe, taking advantage of the protection of some friendly Indians, invades Florida, capturing Forts Picolata and San Francisco de Pupo.

Prussia, 31 May 1740. Frederick William dies and is succeeded by his son Frederick II.

Russia, 17 October 1740. The empress Anna Ivanovna dies and is succeeded by Ivan IV.

Austria, 19 October 1740. The Emperor Charles VI dies. The succession rights of his daughter Maria Theresa, established by the 1718 Pragmatic Sanction, are challenged by Frederick II of Prussia.

Prussia, 16 December 1740. Frederick II invades Silesia starting yet another war in a Europe already beset by conflict.

Paris, 1740. The still-life and genre artist Jean Baptiste Chardin paints *Grace before a Meal*.

South Carolina, 1740. The assembly makes it illegal to teach Negroes to write or to hire them as scribes.

Britain, June 1741. The British prime minister Robert Walpole suffers an election setback as a result of opposition from the self-styled "patriots" to his foreign policy.

Vienna, 28 July 1741. The Italian violinist and composer Antonio Vivaldi dies. He won fame for the 12 concertos of *L'Estro Armonico*, which appeared in 1712. *The Seasons*, completed in 1725, was also enormously popular.

Sweden, August 1741. Sweden declares war on Russia, counting on support from France and intending to co-operate with the Russian czarevina Elizabeth, who is planning a coup d'etat in St Petersburg. The Swedes hope to take advantage of the fact that Russia is at war with Turkey.

Russia, 26 November 1741. In a palace rebellion, the czarevina Elizabeth overthrows Ivan VI and his mother, the regent Anne Leopoldovna. This puts an end to the German influence in Russia, which had been encouraged by the regent.

New York, 31 December 1741. Following a series of arson attacks in New York City, 29 slaves are executed – 11 are burned at the stake and 18 are hanged.

France, 1741. Maurice Quentin-Latour presents his *Portrait of the President of Rieux* to the Salon. Marivaux publishes his novel *The Life of Marianna*.

Pennsylvania, 1741. Scots-Irish presbyterian immigrants are arriving in the colonies in droves, driven out of the Irish province of Ulster by renewed religious persecution.

India, 1741. The Marathas threaten Pondicherry and Madras.

Germany, 24 January 1742. Charles Albert, elector of Bavaria is elected Holy Roman Emperor as Charles VII.

England, 25 January 1742. The astronomer Edmund Halley dies at Greenwich.

Britain, February 1742. Robert Walpole, Britain's first prime minister, resigns and is replaced by John Carteret.

Alaska, 9 August 1742. The remaining 31 members of Vitus Bering's expedition set off from their marooned ship on a timber raft, hoping to make it back to Russia. The Dutch navigator Bering, who was employed by the Russians to explore the lands east of Siberia, died of scurvy last year.

War drags on over imperial succession

Vienna, 1742

In the two years since Charles VI of Austria died, much of Europe has become embroiled in a ragged, sprawling war, in which almost everybody has changed sides at least once. Ostensibly the war concerns the Austrian succession; in fact, the dispute is seen as a chance to break up the Austrian empire.

For years Emperor Charles VI sought backing for something he called the Pragmatic Sanction; it was a decision to leave the crown to his daughter Maria Theresa. This did not suit Charles Albert of Bavaria; he claimed the throne because he had married a niece of Charles VI. Frederick of Prussia, seeing Maria Theresa preoccupied with the succession, marched into Silesia and offered to support her if she would cede the territory to him. Maria Theresa refused and sent her troops against him, only to have them shattered by the Prussians.

France then intervened with a plan. She would support Frederick provided he gave up part of his Silesian gains to Augustus of Saxony. The Bavarian Charles Albert would receive most of the Austrian empire, but Sardinia and Spain would share the spoils in Italy. France itself would get whatever it could take from the Dutch.

Britain and Hanover joined the war on the side of Maria Theresa, but took care not to offend Frederick in case he should decide to invade Hanover. Maria Theresa recruited an army from her Hungarian subjects and invaded Bohemia, where her rival, Charles Albert, had been proclaimed Austrian emperor in Prague.

Encouraged by Britain, who promised subsidies, she offered Frederick a deal. He was only too glad to accept; his troops were weary and his war chest was running out. Britain now offered to send a force to the Netherlands to join Austrian troops there and, with the Dutch, invade France. The Dutch refused to play. The war drags on.

Intellectual son replaces Prussian king

Berlin, 1740

The scholarly new king of Prussia, Frederick II, has brought a new style to the throne, in sharp contrast with his stern and soldierly father, Frederick William.

He is now free to indulge his taste for French literature and music composition at his home in Rheinsberg Castle. He has surrounded himself with intellectuals like Jordan of Geneva and devotes his free time to the study of Bayle and Racine. He exchanges letters with Voltaire and has published his first book, *The Anti-Machiavelli*, expressing the conviction that a King should serve his State.

Scholar king: Frederick II.

Dozens are slain in slave rebellion

Charleston, South Carolina, 1739

America has experienced its first slave revolt, a chilling affair which started when a group of blacks left their plantation to walk to Spanish Florida in search of freedom.

Embittered by years of harsh treatment, the rebels set out to kill every white man they met on the road. By the time they were finally surrounded, 21 people had been murdered. White settlers massacred the entire group of 44 men in revenge.

Soon other blacks revolted. At Stono River, a rebel called Cato and his men killed 30 whites. Slave-oriented South Carolina is getting nervous that the violent rebellion may continue to spread.

European music and art are flowering in harmony

Painting: visions of the grand and lowly

Canaletto's "Thames and the City of London from Richmond House".

Europe, 1742

One of Italy's most celebrated painters, Canaletto, moved to Rome this year from his native Venice with a reputation as one of the best of modern painters from one of the greatest centres of painting. Born Giovanni Antonio Canal in 1698, he is famed in particular for his views of Venice and other cities, highly atmospheric in their quiet colours and their exactness of detail and perspective.

Influenced by Canaletto, but more fanciful and impressionistic, are the townscapes of his fellow Venetian Francesco Guardi (born 1712). Another Venetian, Pietro Longhi (born 1702), depicts everyday life with charm and attention to detail. The works of these men stand in contrast to the art of the most spectacular of Venetian painters, Gian Battista Tiepolo (born 1696). He combines panache and grandeur with vibrancy and an exquisite lightness of touch.

The elaborate pastoral fantasies of Antoine Watteau (1684-1721) are in contrast to the intimate realism of Jean-Baptiste Chardin (born 1699). Real life also provides subjects for England's William Hogarth (born 1697), who specialises in earthy social satire.

Watteau's "The Masked Party": typical of the artist's pastoral fantasies.

Music: the school of 1685 leads the field

Europe, 1742

"The sublime, the grand, and the tender, adapted to the most elevated, majestic and moving words". Thus wrote a Dublin music critic following the first performance of the oratorio *Messiah* by George Frederic Handel on 13 April this year. Handel was born in Saxony in 1685 and worked in Hamburg and Italy; he settled in London after his employer, the elector of Hanover, became King George I in 1714. He has written much for royal occasions, from the *Water Music* for a boating party to *Zadok the Priest* for George II's coronation in 1727. He has also written chamber music and about 40 Italian operas. Italian opera has become less popular recently, and Handel has turned to odes and oratorios such as *Alexander's Feast* (1736), *Israel in Egypt* (1739) and, of course, *Messiah.*

Of equally towering stature is another Saxon who has stayed closer to his roots. Also born in 1685, Johann Sebastian Bach has been head of music at Leipzig since 1723. His duties centre around the city's two main churches and his output includes motets, cantatas and two oratorio-like "passions", derived from the gospels of St John (1724) and St Matthew (1727). His instrumental music includes many organ works, and the six *Brandenburg Concertos* (c.1720). Italian music is mourning the loss last year of Antonio Vivaldi (born 1678), the great Venetian priest-composer. He is renowned for his nearly 400 concertos, some of which Bach arranged and over half of which are for violin; his Opus 8 includes the set known as *The Four Seasons.* Italy's greatest living composer is probably Domenico Scarlatti, a friend of Handel and also born in 1685. His father, Alessandro (1659-1725), was important for his operas; Domenico, a composer at the Spanish court, is famed for his brilliant keyboard music.

Opera is the chief activity of the French composer Jean-Philippe Rameau (born 1683). He brings to his operas a wide range of moods and expressiveness together with richly coloured orchestration.

George Frederic Handel: oratorios, odes and music for royal occasions.

Alessandro Scarlatti: renowned for his operatic compositions.

Johann Sebastian Bach: cantatas, concertos and gospel passions.

1742 (1742-1745)

Ireland, 13 April 1742. The *Messiah* by the German-English composer George Frederick Handel is performed for the first time, in Dublin.

Germany, 11 June 1742. Maria Theresa of Austria and Frederick II of Prussia sign the peace of Breslau, which recognises Frederick's claim to Silesia.

Rome, 11 July 1742. A papal bull is issued condemning the actions of the Jesuits in China.

Peru, 1742. The Indians rise up in rebellion.

London, 1742. The poet Edward Young publishes his *Night Thoughts on Life, Death and Immortality*.

France, 29 January 1743. Cardinal Fleury dies. He became tutor to the future Louis XV in 1714 and replaced the duke of Bourbon as prime minister in 1726, at the age of 73. A convinced pacifist, Fleury supported the alliance with England. He brought France into the war of Polish succession only with the greatest reluctance.

Pennsylvania, January 1743. The printing magnate Benjamin Franklin sells his businesses to his partner, intending to devote his life to science, in particular the study of electricity.

Germany, 27 June 1743. An army of British infantry, led by King George II in person, destroy the French cavalry at Dettingen in Bavaria.

Sweden, 17 August 1743. By the treaty of Abo (*Turku*), Sweden cedes south-east Finland to Russia and accepts the Empress Elizabeth's choice of a successor: Adolf Frederick of Holstein-Gottorp. This ends a disastrous war with Russia in which Sweden had intended to help the empress take the throne. In the event, the Swedish army was hopelessly disorganised and Elizabeth herself seized power in a palace revolution.

France, 28 October 1743. Louis XV of France and Philip V of Spain forge a defensive and offensive alliance at Fontainebleau. This pact between the two Bourbon lines is known as the Second Family Compact.

New England, 1743. The American Philosophical Society is founded.

New Jersey, 1743. John Woolman, an itinerant Quaker clergyman, begins preaching about the evils of slavery.

Naples, 1744. The Italian philosopher Giambattista Vico, author of *Scienza Nova*, dies. He argued that the historical method is no less exact that the scientific.

London, 30 May 1744. The great satirical poet Alexander Pope dies. Among his masterpieces are *The Rape of the Lock* and the *Dunciad*.

Bohemia, September 1744. Having invaded Bohemia last month, Frederick II of Prussia takes Prague.

Paris, 8 December 1744. The beautiful and intelligent Madame de Pompadour comes into favour with King Louis XV.

East Africa, 1744. Mohammed ben Uthman al-Mazrui, who came to power as governor of Mombasa in 1739, declares himself independent from Oman.

Europe, 8 January 1745. England, Austria, Saxony and the Netherlands form an alliance against Russia.

Germany, January 1745. Charles Albert, elector of Bavaria, who was elected Holy Roman emperor in 1742 as Charles II, dies.

Germany, 22 April 1745. Maria Theresa of Austria and Maximilian Joseph, elector of Bavaria and son of the Emperor Charles VII, sign the peace of Fussen, restoring the status quo existing before the war of the Austrian Succession.

Netherlands, 11 May 1745. The French under Marshal Saxe defeat an Anglo-Dutch-Hanoverian army at the battle of Fontenoy.

Canada, 16 June 1745. After a six-week siege, the French fort of Louisbourg on Cape Breton Island falls to British colonial forces from New England. This intensifies hostilities in what is known as King George's war, an extension of the European war of the Austrian Succession.

New England, August 1745. The French and their Indian allies carry out a series of raids on English settlements.

Germany, 25 December 1745. By the treaty of Dresden, Frederick II of Prussia recognises Francis, duke of Lorraine and husband of Maria Theresa of Austria, as Holy Roman emperor. Frederick's control of Silesia is also recognised under the treaty.

England, December 1745. Having advanced as far south as Derby, Charles Edward Stuart, the young pretender, is forced to retreat.

England, 1745. The painter William Hogarth completes *Marriage a la Mode*. Like his earlier *Rake's Progress*, the work is a moral narrative – a series of scenes exposing the follies and vices of his age. This new genre is a departure from the small portrait groups, known as conversation pieces, which Hogarth favoured in the 1720s.

Enslaved Peruvians rise up against Spain

Peru, 1742

The native Indians of Peru, enslaved by their Spanish conquerors for the past two hundred years, have risen up in a rebellion. Slaves across the vice royalty have thrown away their shackles and united in a series of attacks on their hated masters.

The rebellion is led by Juan Santos, an Indian from the Huarochiri region. Taking up the old Inca tradition he has proclaimed himself emperor and taken the name Atahualpa II. This is a deliberate tribute to Atahualpa I, "the last of the Incas", whose execution by the Spaniards in 1533 inaugurated the enslavement and exploitation of his people. Over the past two centuries the once-thriving Indians have lost some nine-tenths of their population.

The brutality of their conquerors, the hardships they endure in the mines and the destruction brought by European diseases against which their bodies have no defence have all combined to destroy a once-proud civilization.

Santos' forces have proved surprisingly successful. Drawing on widespread support, his army has moved across the country's central plateau, defeating the Spanish in a number of battles. The Indians have reached Lima, the capital, where they are challenging the aristocracy, Spain's native allies.

Strict new faith attracts Arab rulers

Arabia, c.1744

The sheikh and emir of the Ibn Saud family of central Arabia have sworn reciprocal loyalty and adopted the fundamentalist Islamic doctrine of Wahhabism. They have created the first legally instituted Wahhabi state.

A jurist from Najd, Mohammed ibn Abd al-Wahhab, wanted to redefine Islam to make it distinct from Iranian Shi'ism and what was seen as the decadent Sunnism of the Ottomans. Insisting that faith must be inseparable from religious practice, he emphasises the absolute unity of Allah at the expense of all other forms of belief which might dilute the faith. The visiting of tombs and veneration of saints are therefore completely forbidden.

Wahhabism relies on the view of nature put forward in the Koran, and condemns any innovation that embroiders or departs from that original teaching. It is the ultimate fundamentalism, excluding any possibility of polytheism, and creating a uniquely Arab Moslem movement.

The renowned mirror room at the Amalienburg in Munich: this ornate, heavily decorated style, known as Rococo, was built by Francois Cuvillies; the stucco, a vital characteristic of the design, is by J B Zimmerman.

England's Prime Minister resigns

London, February 1742
Sir Robert Walpole, the Norfolk squire who who headed the British government for 20 years, has fought his last battle in the House of Commons – and lost. His opponents, failing to defeat him over his conduct of the war with Spain, manoeuvred to gain control of the Parliamentary Committee on Elections, a body which hears petitions for unseating MPs guilty of corrupt practices. When one of his supporters was voted down Walpole knew his days were numbered and resigned. Nominally a Whig, his practices seemed distant from principles of the Revolution of 1688.

Officially he was simply First Lord of the Treasury, but in time, as he gained the confidence of both the king and the House of Commons, he came to be known as Prime Minister. His reputation was established by his skilful handling of the the South Sea Bubble financial crisis. From then on, he clung to two principles: sound finance at home and freedom from the intrigues and wars on the continent.

When a sea captain, Robert Jenkins, told MPs how a Spanish officer had cut off his ear with a cutlass while searching his ship in 1739, public indignation boiled over and Walpole was forced to declare war on Spain.

Prime Minister Walpole addresses his cabinet: a picture by Joseph Goupy.

Papal Bull against Jesuit toleration of Chinese ways

Rome, 11 July 1742
Pope Benedict XIV has issued a stern papal bull *ex quo singulari* designed to put an end once and for all to the bitter Chinese Rites controversy. He has forbidden the Jesuits in China to continue with their policy of allowing their converts to include Confucian traditions in their Christian observances.

The Jesuits had ignored a previous attempt by Pope Clement XI to curb the practise of Chinese Rites under which they accepted ancestor worship and even domestic idols. But they cannot argue against this ruling.

It remains to be seen what effect it has on the Confucian-Christian symbiosis and the position of the Jesuits in China. The Jesuits fear with some justice that it will jeopardise not only their position but that of the whole Christian community in China.

The Chinese authorities are known to feel affronted by the pope's edict. The Jesuits had persuaded the emperor to issue a statement on the meaning on the rites which was in their favour. Now he has lost face and the results for the mission will certainly be embarrassing if not positively dangerous.

Poet and satirist Alexander Pope dies

London, 30 May 1744
The death has been announced of that master of the heroic couplet, the English poet and satirist, Alexander Pope. He was 56.

Pope was born into a Catholic family and was brought up in Windsor Forest without formal education. He moved in London's literary circles from the age of 15, and became friends with Tories like Swift, Oxford and Bolingbroke.

In the intensely political atmosphere of the time, Pope rapidly won recognition with his *Essay on Criticism* and his mock-epic *The Rape of the Lock.*

His translations of *The Iliad* and *The Odyssey* brought him financial stability. Later, in *The Dunciad*, he bitterly satirised the literary critics of the day.

The late Alexander Pope: master of wit, satire and the heroic couplet.

Irish and Scottish exodus to America

Philadelphia, c.1742
A flood of immigrants is arriving in the American colonies from the Irish province of Ulster. If present trends continue, they will be turning up at the rate of 10,000 a year by the end of the decade. Fortunately America has always offered a traditional refuge to the persecuted of other lands, whether on religious or political grounds.

Most of these newcomers are descendants of Presbyterians from lowland Scotland who settled in Ulster to safeguard English Protestant interests there. The renewal of religious persecution has meant that, increasingly, these so-called Scots-Irish are looking to the colonies as a refuge.

East India traders are braced for war

India, 1743
The tentacles of the European war have reached as far as India as British and French ready themselves to fight for national supremacy on the sub-continent. As news of the war arrived here last year, the British East India Company was much stronger commercially than its French equivalent, although it was prepared to accept a local agreement of neutrality. French and British fleets are in the vicinity, however, and fighting seems certain.

Both sides are courting Indian princes as allies, although French missionary zeal is not helping their cause. The British prefer to leave Hindu customs well alone and concern themselves solely with trade.

1745 (1745-1750)

Scotland, September 1745. Charles Edward Stuart, grandson of James II and pretender to the British throne, defeats a government army at the battle of Prestonpans. The "young pretender" – son of James Edward Stuart, the "old pretender" – landed in Scotland two months ago and rallied some of the Highland chiefs and other Jacobites against King George II.

Europe, 1745. Ewald von Kleist, a German, and the Dutchman Petrus van Musschenbroek independently invent the Leyden jar. This is a glass vessel, partially filled with water and with a nail projecting from a cork stopper, which can store electricity.

Scotland, 17 January 1746. Charles Edward Stuart, the young pretender, defeats the government forces at the battle of Falkirk.

Brussels, 21 February 1746. Following their defeat of the Austrian allies at Fontenoy last year, French troops occupy Brussels.

England, 1 April 1746. George Frederick Handel presents his oratorio *Judas Maccabeus*.

Scotland, 27 April 1746. The young pretender Charles Edward Stuart is defeated by King George II's army at the battle of Culloden and goes into hiding in the Highlands.

Austria, 2 June 1746. Austria forms an alliance with Russia against Prussia and the Ottomans.

Spain, 9 July 1746. On the death of Philip V, his son Ferdinand VI comes to the throne.

India, 20 October 1746. Following the spread the war of the Austrian Succession to India, Joseph Francois Dupleix, the French colonial governor, takes Madras.

France, 1746. The philosopher Etienne Condillac publishes an *Essay on the Origin of Human Knowledge*.

France, 1746. Denis Diderot's recently published *Philosophic Thoughts* is burnt by the parliament of Paris.

New Jersey, 1746. Princeton University is founded.

Persia, 10 June 1747. The Persian ruler Nadir Shah is assassinated at Fathabad. After defeating the Afghan invaders in 1729, Nadir restored Tahmasp to the throne and went on to defeat the Ottomans in the west. Proclaimed shah himself in 1736, Nadir conquered Afghanistan and launched a campaign against India which culminated in 1739 in the sack of Delhi.

Afghanistan, June 1747. After the death of Nadir Shah, Afghanistan becomes independent of Persia.

Netherlands, 2 July 1747. Marshal Saxe leads the French forces to victory over an Anglo-Dutch force under the duke of Cumberland at the battle of Lauffeld.

Netherlands, 16 September 1747. The capture of Bergen-op-Zoom consolidates the French occupation of Austrian Flanders.

Netherlands, 1747. The republic of the United Provinces is overthrown and the title of *stadtholder* (governor) is reinstated. William of Nassau, prince of Orange – grand-nephew of William III of England – is made hereditary *stadtholder*.

Beijing, 1747. The summer palace of the Emperor Qian Long is decorated and furnished in western style.

Pennsylvania, 26 August 1748. The first Lutheran synod is founded in the colonies, in Philadelphia.

France, 18 October 1748. The peace of Aix-la-Chapelle ends the war of the Austrian succession, giving general recognition to the Pragmatic Sanction and the Prussian conquest of Silesia.

England, 1748. The philosopher David Hume publishes his *Enquiry Concerning Human Understanding*.

France, 1748. The philosopher Julien Lamettrie publishes his materialistic work *The Man Machine*.

England, 1748. Samuel Richardson, author of *Pamela*, publishes the last part of his seven-volume novel *Clarissa*, again written in epistolary form. The novel is described as showing the "distresses that may attend the misconduct both of parents and children, in relation to marriage".

Pennsylvania, 1749. The university of Pennsylvania is founded in Philadelphia.

Canada, 1749. Some 2,500 settlers sent by Lord Halifax to consolidate the British hold on Nova Scotia found the town of Halifax.

France, 1749. Georges Louis Buffon publishes the first three volumes of a great *Natural History*, the prospectus of which he issued last year.

Spain, 1749. A lodge of freemasons is established at Cadiz, with over 800 members.

England, 1749. Henry Fielding publishes Tom Jones, a comic novel of manners designed, like his *Joseph Andrews*, as a reaction to the moral conventionality of Samuel Richardson.

France, 1750. The philosopher Jean-Jacques Rousseau publishes a *Discourse on the Sciences and the Arts*.

Lost Roman city emerging from grave

Later excavations reveal the city emerging from the ashes at Pompeii.

Naples, 1748

An entire city which suffocated to death in AD 79 under a pall of volcanic ash and sulphur fumes from Mount Vesuvius is being brought to light near Naples in a state of extraordinary preservation.

The excavations began on the orders of King Charles III. The ruins were revealed by tunnelling many years ago, but their scale was unknown. Streets of houses lie buried alongside two theatres, a forum, temples and baths. Skeletons of the inhabitants lie where they succumbed. An inscription has identified the site as Pompeii.

Wall painting of houses, Pompeii.

Slave-rich African state beaten in battle

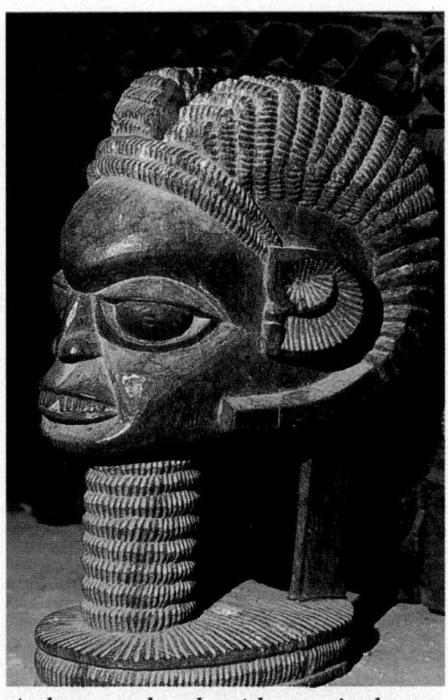

A human head with ram's horns, made of carved wood, from the shrine of the King of Oyo, in eastern Yorubaland, Nigeria.

West Africa, 1747

Half a century of war between the states of Dahomey and Oyo is over, with Dahomey defeated. Dahomey was a state whose enormous wealth was derived from the slave trade with Europe.

First she took control of the hinterland and then of the coast, where tens of thousands were shipped to the New World. Oyo's strength was in her cavalry. Envious of Dahomey's wealth, she invaded the country in 1698, defeating all who confronted her.

Dahomey reverted to guerrilla warfare and threw out the invader in the 1730s, only to be subjected to the Oyo cavalry again in 1738. After nine more years of guerrilla war, Dahomey has accepted defeat. None are more relieved than the slavers, who need a stable environment in which to conduct their business.

Bonnie Prince defeated

The Duke of Cumberland leading British troops to victory at Culloden.

Scotland, 1746

Disguised as a woman and with a price of £30,000 on his head, Bonnie Prince Charlie, the Young Pretender, is believed to be hiding in a cave in the Scottish Highlands after the defeat of his Jacobite force by British troops at Culloden. He intends to lie low until a French ship comes to his rescue.

When he arrived off Inverness-shire aboard a French brig last year, Scottish clan chiefs tried to persuade him to drop the idea of staging a rebellion to regain the English crown for the Stuarts. He went ahead and raised a force of 2,000 men. He defeated a detachment of dragoons and, seizing Edinburgh (but not its castle), he had his father proclaimed James VIII of Scotland.

Although the promised French assistance never arrived, he pushed on south. By the time he had reached Derby and looted the city, the English had put two new armies in the field. Then, as he retreated north, the desertions began.

Charles, still only 25, grew up believing the people of Scotland and England were ready to welcome a Stuart. But few of his supporters cared to run risks for him. The Highlanders who joined him at the start soon dropped out; for them, war was merely an excuse for brigandage. Charles, educated in Rome, speaks English, French and Italian, but his letters in English are barely literate.

Prince Charles Stuart, by Blanchet.

Lead piping shown to damage your health

New York City, 1750

Lead piping in common use in plumbing, may be a health hazard according to an American doctor, Thomas Cadwalader, who has just published a work entitled "An Essay on the West-India Dry-Gripes".

In it, Cadwalader describes a case of gripes apparently brought on by a patient drinking rum. The rum had, it transpires, been distilled through lead pipes. Although Cadwalader himself does not attribute the poisoning to the lead, that is indeed the obvious inference. Lead is known to have toxic properties. Now these may be felt even through pipes such as those that bring us our water.

The peace treaty that pleases no one

Aix-la-Chapelle, 18 October 1748

The War of the Austrian Succession has at last been brought to an end with all the adversaries in a state of exhaustion. The war ended not with a great victory, but with the realisation that it could not be allowed to continue.

Under the terms of the treaty signed here today the courageous Maria Theresa was confirmed as the legitimate occupant of the Habsburg throne and her husband, Francis of Lorraine, was elected to the imperial throne.

In return, however, she has been forced reluctantly to abandon Silesia to King Frederick of Prussia. Frederick is, in fact, the only contestant in this land-grabbing war to be happy with the treaty. The others get less than they wanted.

England and France will exchange colonial outposts. France has agreed to evacuate the Austrian Netherlands, much to the disgust of Marshal Saxe who has spent so much time and trouble conquering them for Louis XV. Spain has failed to regain Gibraltar and Minorca from the English. The treaty has thus failed to settle the causes of Europe's bloody feuds.

Maria Theresa, Empress of Austria.

Europe's cities: full of muck and money

Gin Lane, an unsavoury corner of London, by William Hogarth.

Europe, c.1750

Europe, for so long dominated by the countryside, a society of landowners, farmers and peasants, is undergoing a radical change. The town has replaced the village as the centre of daily life for an increasing number of people, and the great cities are expanding as never before.

London and Paris, always important for their commerce, have developed into teeming urban centres, their growing populations each numbering half-a-million souls already. Such expansion is seen everywhere and while the cities still hold less people than the country, the urban minority is increasingly influential and important.

Thriving, energetic, never resting by day or night, the cities reflect the emergence of an affluent middle class whose lives are based not on land-owning but on trade. The old aristocrats appreciate the change and many have added a sumptuous town house to their rural acres.

Such luxury is restricted. The poor, abandoning their cottages for the city life, are crowded into insanitary tenements, crushed hugger-mugger along the narrow, dirty streets. Visionary architects are imposing more ordered design on city centres, with spacious boulevards and fine new buildings, but the masses remain trapped in squalor.

Cities are prosperous and an enterprising man may make his fortune, but they are dangerous too. Traffic threatens pedestrians by day and thieves lurk in the dark streets by night. London, where pavements offer refuge from the carts and coaches and where streetlights illuminate at least the major roads, has set an example to its peers.

1750 (1750-1751)

Venice, 17 January 1750. The composer Tomaso Albinoni dies aged 79. He wrote operas, cantatas, sonatas, concertos and other works, characterised by distinct melodies.

Portugal, 31 July 1750. John V dies and is succeeded as king by his son Joseph Emanuel, who appoints Sebastiao Jose de Carvalho e Mello, marquis of Pombal, as his chief minister. Pombal immediately deprives the Inquisition of its rights.

India, 1750. By his victory at the battle of Tanjore, Joseph Dupleix, the French governor of Pondicherry, wins control of the Carnatic region in southern India.

London, c.1750. A works for the manufacture of bone china is established at Stratford-le-Bow.

Venice, 1750. The painter Giambattista Tiepolo completes his frescoed ceiling in the Palazzo Labia, the culmination of a series of works devoted to the story of Antony and Cleopatra.

Tibet, 1750. The Tibetans rebel against China.

Canada, 1750. British forces attempt to conquer Acadia (*Nova Scotia* and *New Brunswick*).

North America, c.1750. The population of the colonies passes the one-million mark.

Canada, January 1751. France and England conclude a provisional agreement over Acadia.

Britain, 20 March 1751. Frederick Louis, prince of Wales, dies.

India, November 1751. The French siege of Arcot, which was captured by Robert Clive in September with 210 men, is lifted after 53 days.

France, 1751. Voltaire publishes *Le Siecle de Louis XIV*.

England, 1751. The Englishman John Burton suggests that common puerperal or childbed fever may be caused by those who attend the patient. It is, he believes, their carelessness that produces the disease.

Denmark, 1751. Count Johann Bernstorff, the former Danish envoy in Germany and France, becomes foreign minister.

Germany, 1751. Johann Albrecht Bengel, the architect of the German Protestant evangelical movement known as pietism, dies.

Death comes to composer J S Bach

Leipzig, 28 July 1750

Earlier this month Johann Sebastian Bach, ill and blind despite two eye operations, began to dictate an organ piece, the last of a series he was revising. The 65-year-old composer decided to change the title to *Before thy Throne*. Days later he was dead.

Bach sometimes got into trouble when he put creative impulses before official duties. But few denied his genius; he was famed as Europe's greatest organist and only Handel matches his mastery of fugue and counterpoint. He wrote almost every type of music except opera, of which his employers, for the past 27 years the Protestant city of Leipzig, disapproved.

Bach's two wives (the first died in 1720), bore seven and 13 children respectively. His eldest sons, Wilhelm Friedemann (born 1710) and Carl Philipp Emanuel (born 1714) are both distinguished composers. Emanuel is harpsichordist to Frederick II of Prussia, whose chief relaxation is music (he plays the flute and composes). Three years ago J S Bach visited his son and family at Frederick's palace in Potsdam. As well as trying out a new "pianoforte" – he was unenthusiastic – Bach was given a theme by the king himself to improvise upon. The royal tune was used for a set of pieces dedicated to Frederick called a *Musical Offering*.

Maestro: Johann Sebastian Bach.

Military hero leaves nothing to chance

Punishments in the German army, an engraving by von Fleming, 1726.

Paris, 1750

That great soldier, Maurice, the Count of Saxony, better known as Marshal Saxe, has died, loaded with honours, at the age of 54. The natural son of Augustus II of Saxony and Countess Maria Aurora Konigsmark, he divided his life between equal pleasures: making war and making love. His long love affair with the actress Adrienne Lecouvreur was especially notorious.

Fighting under a number of flags, he eventually became Marshal General of France, capturing Prague and winning the Battle of Fontenoy for Louis XV. Saxe was a handsome man and a thinking soldier, leader of a new breed of commanders who revolutionised warfare. He called for the institution of universal military service and conscription to replace the old armies of the criminals and the dispossessed.

He also argued that no army should field more than 46,000 soldiers, for "multitudes serve only to perplex and embarrass" and he advocated the use of mobile units of infantry and cavalry. But, above all he insisted that "war should be made so as to leave nothing to chance."

The Female Soldier parades on stage

London, 1750

Publicity for the biography, *The Female Soldier*, has drawn a big crowd to Sadlers Wells theatre to watch Hannah Snell perform military drill in full dress uniform.

In 1723 Snell, a single mother from Worcester, posed as a man and joined the Army to look for her sailor husband. After marching to Carlisle she deserted her foot regiment and joined a Marines' ship bound for India. When shot at Pondicherry by the French, she maintained her disguise by finding a woman to remove the bullet. On reaching Portugal, after more adventures in two more ships, she heard that her missing husband had been executed in Italy.

Brilliant victory for Clive in south India

India, 5 November 1751

After a 53-day siege, British-led troops have brilliantly beaten off a superior French-led force at Arcot, the capital of the Carnatic, India's south-eastern coastal region.

British and Indian troops led by Robert Clive, 26, seized Arcot on 12 September as part of the struggle for control of southern India between the British and French East India companies, which first flared up in 1744. So far, the French and their allies have had the upper hand, but their failure at Arcot has turned the tables. In the British camp the talk is only of Clive, the former East India Company clerk who only took up soldiery with the company's army three years ago.

The Encyclopaedia will explain existence

Paris, April 1751

The first volume of the *Encyclopedie*, or National Dictionary of the Arts, Sciences and Professions, appears this month. Published by Le Breton it will be sold by subscription and the complete work will comprise eight illustrated volumes, making up 280 books.

The original idea came from England, where Chambers' *Cyclopedia* appeared in 1723. The *Encyclopedie* was to be a simple translation but its editor-in-chief Denis Diderot, hired by the publishers whose scheme it is, rejected that idea.

Instead he has set out to create an entirely original work, a grand plan that, on completion, will provide a rational explanation for every aspect of existence.

Diderot is backed by two formidable men: Jean d'Alembert, one of France's most gifted mathematicians, and the wealthy, hard-working Louis de Jaucourt. He has also enlisted many leading intellectuals as contributors. Montesquieu writes on politics, Buffon on nature, Turgot on economics, d'Holbach on mathematics, while Voltaire and Rousseau will each write on philosophy.

Denis Diderot, painted by Greuze.

Complaints box at shogun's castle gate

Eighteenth-century Japanese scroll showing a domestic scene, with animals.

Japan, 1751

The shogun Tokugawa Yoshimune who has controlled Japan for the last 29 years, has died at the age of 67. A forceful and capable man, he used the practical experience he gained as a feudal ruler drastically, but quietly, to redress some of the worst injustices of shogun rule.

One of his innovations was to put a *meyasubako*, a complaints box, at a gate of his castle in which the people could deposit suggestions for his personal attention, bypassing the bureaucracy.

He was a frugal man who wore plain clothes and lived on brown rice and vegetables. He had the luxurious apartment of the shogun torn down and lived in a bare anteroom. His spartan life helped him to understand his people's problems and formed the basis of his reforms.

Enclosures improve English farming in agricultural revolution

Catalogue of Fruits, Furber, 1732.

Eighteenth-century drill plough, with seed and manure hopper.

Britain, c.1750

Encouraged by various acts of Parliament, the enclosure system is taking hold of English farming. The system of open farms is giving way to enclosed fields. Small landowners are yielding reluctantly to larger estates, and there have been many complaints.

Enclosure is having profound effects on agricultural techniques. In the first place, farmers can now practise farming on a larger scale, introduce mechanisation and institute extensive land drainage schemes. They can also carry out a certain amount of stock-breeding. And devote some of their time to scientific experiments with both plants and animals.

Using Jethro Tull's straight-line drilling of wheat and roots, allowing a horse-drawn hoe to cultivate the space between the rows, means that the spoil can be constantly tilled. Seed drills are now in widespread use. So, too, is the Rotherham triangular plough which replaces large teams of oxen attended by two horses and one man. There is also a great deal of attention being paid to the relationship between crop and animal. Rotating crops means that the two forms of farming can be complementary.

Farmers are also having to respond to increasingly diverse demands from the market place. As industry develops so too does the need for raw materials: animal fats for soap; hides for leather goods; bones for glue. Only by turning to labour-saving devices and techniques can these demands be met. Truly we are witnessing the onset of a massive "agricultural revolution", although like any revolution, the changes are disturbing to many vested interests, not least the tenant farmers whose livelihoods have been sacrificed to the demands of a new world.

Temple of Heaven

Beijing, 1751

Work has been completed on restoring the Hall of Prayer for Good Harvests in the Temple of Heaven. The round hall, which rests on a triple-layered marble terrace, is 30 metres across and has a roof shaped in three cones covered by brilliant blue tiles. It is surmounted by a golden sphere. Perhaps the most remarkable fact about this beautiful building is that it is made entirely of wood, yet not one nail has been used in its construction.

It is here that the emperor comes to give homage to the heavens and to make sacrifices and pray for a good harvest. It is set in a large park forbidden to the people.

The Temple of Heaven, in Beijing.

1751 (1751-1754)

Paris, 1751. The Sorbonne condemns 14 propositions on evolution in Georges Buffon's *Natural History*. To avoid theological controversy, Buffon signs a declaration abandoning anything in his work that might be contrary to the account of Earth's origins given in Genesis.

Netherlands, 1751. On the death of the *stadtholder* William IV of Orange-Nassau, his widow Anne becomes regent for the three-year-old heir, William.

England, 1751. The philosopher David Hume publishes *An Enquiry Concerning the Principles of Morals*.

England, 1751. The poet Thomas Gray composes his *Elegy written in a Country Churchyard*.

England, 1751. The Scottish writer Tobias Smollett publishes a second novel, entitled *Peregrine Pickle*. His first novel, *Roderick Random*, appeared in 1748.

Paris, February 1752. The parliament of Paris condemns the *Encyclopedie*, edited by Denis Diderot, the first volume of which appeared last year.

Philadelphia, June 1752. In his book *Experiments and Observations in Electricity*, Benjamin Franklin concludes that lightning is identical with electricity produced by friction.

North America, July 1752. The French overrun the English trading post of Pickawillany in an effort to re-establish control over the Ohio river valley region.

India, July 1752. The English go on the attack. Robert Clive takes Trichinopoly and forces the French commander Bussy to evacuate Aurangabad.

India, 1752. Ahmed Shah Durrani, the ruler of Afghanistan, captures Lahore after a four-month siege.

Sudan, 1752. Abu al-Qasim, sultan of Darfur, dies in battle during a war with the sultanate of Kordofan, whose troops are led by the Funj general Abu al-Kaylak. The influence of the Darfur sultanate, which dates from the 1630s, stretches from Bornu around Lake Chad in the west to Kordofan near the Nile in the east.

South-East Africa, 1752. The Portuguese south-east African coastal settlements of Mozambique island, Zambezi prazos and Sofala are placed under the governor at Mozambique; they are no longer subordinate to the Portuguese colony of Goa in India.

Britain, 1752. The Gregorian calendar is adopted. The eleven days between 2 and 14 September are omitted.

Austria, January 1753. Count Anton Kaunitz, the former Austrian ambassador in Paris, is appointed chancellor by the Empress Maria Theresa.

London, June 1753. A conference is held with the aim of ending the Anglo-French conflict over India.

Paris, 25 August 1753. On becoming a member of the French Academy, the naturalist Georges Buffon delivers a *Discours sur le style*.

North America, 12 December 1753. George Washington, adjutant of Virginia, delivers an ultimatum to the French forces at Fort Le Boeuf, south of Lake Erie, reiterating Britain's claim to the entire Ohio river valley.

England, 1753. The home of John Kay, who invented the flying shuttle in 1733, is destroyed by a riot.

England, 1753. Samuel Richardson publishes a third novel, *Sir Charles Grandison*, which is designed to portray the perfect gentleman.

London, 1753. The British Museum is founded.

Britain, 6 March 1754. On the death of Henry Pelham, he is succeeded as prime minister by his brother Thomas, duke of Newcastle. Since November last year the brothers have headed the so-called "broad-bottomed" administration comprised of many political factions.

North America, 17 April 1754. The site of a British fort at the fork of the Allegheny and Monongahela rivers in the Ohio river valley is captured by the French. Militiamen under George Washington had been sent to build the fort by Robert Dinwiddie, governor of Virginia, in order to protect the region from French seizure.

New York, July 1754. At the Albany Congress, which brings together delegates from the 13 British colonies, Benjamin Franklin calls for the establishment of a common council of defence to fight the French and the Indians.

North America, 3 July 1754. British forces under George Washington are defeated by the French near Fort Necessity in the Ohio river valley.

Spain, 1754. Spain signs a concordat with Pope Benedict XIV by which the Spanish church becomes virtually independent of Rome and is placed under the control of the Spanish government.

England, 1754. The Society for the Encouragement of Arts, Manufacture and Commerce (*Royal Society of Arts*) is established.

Alexander and Campaspe in the Studio of Apelles, painting by Tiepolo.

Tiepolo's figures are floating in space

Wurzburg, Germany 1752

The flamboyant Venetian painter, Giovanni Battista Tiepolo, has been brought to Wurzburg to decorate the new residence of the Prince-Bishop. Amid its fantastic white and gold rococo interiors he has produced luminous frescoes of the life of the Turkish ruler Barbarossa. To decorate the great staircase he has brought together an amazingly heterogeneous gathering of the races, costumes, animals, plants and flowers of the known world, as well as crowds of gods and allegorical figures floating in space.

Tiepolo has already decorated many of the *palazzi* of Venice, Milan, Bergamo, Udine and villas at Vicenza, as well as painting single portraits. His *Alexander and Campaspe in the Studio of Apelles* is actually a picture of himself in his studio with his wife as his model.

Rioters attack shuttle inventor's house

Bury, England, 1753

Shuttle inventor John Kay has fled to Paris after making a narrow escape from a violent mob that stormed his home in Bury. The rioters blame Kay and his labour-saving invention, the flying shuttle, which has doubled mill operatives' output and halved manpower requirements, for putting jobs in jeopardy and making their work more monotonous.

Kay, who patented the shuttle 20 years ago, chose exile in France because he fears he can no longer get fair treatment in this country. He is disgruntled with mill owners who have refused to pay patent royalties and have banded together into a Shuttle Club to help pay the costs of numerous legal actions for patent infringement. Kay has won most of these cases, but has been ruined financially by legal costs. Kay claims to have many more inventions like the flying shuttle, but will not release them until the royalty situation is resolved.

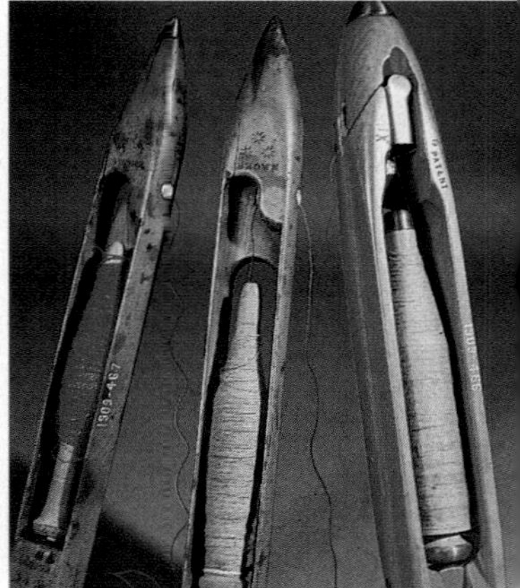

Flying shuttles. Kay's on right.

Dalai Lama accepts authority of Beijing

Tibet, 1751
The Dalai Lama has been forced to acknowledge that he is the vassal of the Emperor of China after an abortive revolt by the Tibetans against Chinese rule. Two commissioners and many Chinese were killed in the revolt, but it was easily put down by a Chinese expedition.

Emperor Qianlong has heaped honours on the Dalai Lama, making him head, both spiritual and temporal, of Tibet and putting the Ministerial Council under his command; but there is no doubt who rules in Lhasa now.

A Tibetan bronze statuette of the supreme Adi-Buddha, with his female counterpart, the Sakti.

Royal approval for female "quack"

Germany, 1754
Germany's first woman medical doctor, Dorothea Erxleben, has graduated from Halle University with King Frederick's approval. Dr Erxleben, a widow of 39, interrupted her studies 12 years ago to nurse her father, get married and produce four children.

After being accused of practising "quack" medicine among the poor, she returned to University. Her book, *Rational Thoughts on Education of the Fair Sex* was published in 1749.

Franklin calls for union in America

Join, or Die. First American political cartoon. Pennsylvania Gazette, 1754.

Albany, New York, 10 July 1754
A call for the "voluntary union" of the 13 British colonies in North America was greeted enthusiastically today at a conference which included the chiefs of the six Iroquois nations. The proposal came from 48-year-old Benjamin Franklin, the proprietor of the *Pennsylvania Gazette*, whose plan is backed by the British government which sees the union as a way to control and pacify the Indians.

The new government would be administered by a president-general – to be appointed by the crown – and a general council of delegates from the colonies. It would have exclusive control of Indian affairs, regulating Indian trade and buying Indian land for the crown. It would also construct forts and pay troops to man them.

A less successful aspect of the conference was the dissatisfaction shown by the Indian delegates who complained about the removal of William Johnson, a representative of the crown who not only spoke several Indian languages but knew about their affairs and had their interests at heart.

"Machiavellian" chancellor for Empress

Vienna, January 1753
Prince Wenzel Anton von Kaunitz, a Machiavellian dandy with a wealth of cunning and ruthlessness hidden behind his fashionable frills and lace, has been appointed chancellor of Austria by the Empress Maria Theresa. Once destined for the church, this well-born aristocrat has served the empress well, first as minister to Turin, then in negotiating the Treaty of Aix-la-Chapelle and for the last three years as ambassador to Paris.

He became a close intimate of Madame de Pompadour, the mistress of Louis XV, and told a friend "I am here for only two things: for the interests of my queen, and these I serve well; for my pleasures, and on this score I need consult no one but myself...I have two persons to manage, the king and his mistress. I am getting along well with both".

Count Wenzel Anton von Kaunitz.

There are now signs that he will attempt to bring about a revolution in European diplomacy by persuading Maria Theresa that Prussia, not France, is Austria's enemy.

Outcry greets new calendar in Britain

London, 1752
The British Parliament has approved a switch from the Julian to the Gregorian calendar, but the people are furious. "Give us back our 11 days!" is the popular cry.

Since 1582, when Pope Gregory promulgated a new, more accurate calendar to replace that introduced by Julius Caesar in 45BC, Britain has lagged 11 days behind the Catholic and, later, Protestant countries which adopted the Gregorian year.

The change was the work of the astronomer, George Parker, earl of Macclesfield, and the bill was introduced in the House of Lords by Lord Chesterfield.

Franklin flies a kite in a thunderstorm

Franklin's experiment. Lithograph.

Philadelphia, 1752
During a recent thunderstorm Benjamin Franklin, the American statesman and inventor, flew a kite with a metal top. From this hung a key on a thread. As soon as lightning flashed in the sky, he held out his hand near the key and observed sparks streaming across to his fist and thence down his body to earth. He says that the damp thread had acted as a conductor of electricity.

Franklin believes that it may be possible to fix metal strips to buildings to conduct the flashes to earth, thus reducing and possibly even eliminating the risk of fire.

1754 (1754-1756)

India, 1754. Joseph Dupleix, governor-general of the French possessions in India since 1741, is recalled to France after a brilliant colonial career. His departure leaves British prestige in India firmly established.

England, 1754. The novelist Henry Fielding dies. He will be best remembered for his epic novel *Tom Jones*, which appeared in 1749. Fielding began his writing career as a playwright, but in 1740, with the appearance of Samuel Richardson's *Pamela* – whose prudery and sentimentalism Fielding found highly amusing – he began a parody of the book. This became his first novel, *The Adventures of Joseph Andrews and his friend Mr Abraham Adams*.

Scotland, 1754. The Scottish philosopher David Hume begins publication of a monumental *History of England*.

France, 1754. The French philosopher Jean-Jacques Rousseau publishes his *Discourse Upon the Origin and Foundation of the Inequality Among Mankind*.

France, 1754. Pierre Louis Moreau de Maupertuis, the mathematician and scholar, publishes his *Essai sur la Formation des Corps Organises*, where, for the first time, the idea of evolution of the species is stated in philosophical terms.

Moscow, 12 January 1755. The first Russian university opens in Moscow. The great scientist Mikhail Lomonosov played an important part in its founding.

Paris, 10 February 1755. The philosopher Baron de Montesquieu dies. His first great literary success was *Lettres Persanes*, published in 1721, which included a satire of French society. His most influential work was *De l'Esprit des Lois*, of which 22 editions were published in the two years following its first appearance in 1748.

England, 15 April 1755. Samuel Johnson's *Dictionary of the English Language* is published. The product of eight years' work, the *Dictionary*, which is both useful and entertaining, provides excellent definitions of the actual senses of words employed by the "best authors", without tracing their historical growth. Johnson believes that the English language reached almost its fullest development in the days of Shakespeare, Bacon and Spenser.

France, 26 May 1755. The bandit and outlaw Louis Mandrin is executed in Grenoble.

Britain, 8 July 1755. As their land dispute in North America intensifies, Britain breaks off diplomatic relations with France.

North America, July 1755. George Washington takes command of the British forces after their defeat by the French at the battle of the Wilderness, near Fort Duquesne (*Pittsburgh*). The British commander, Edward Braddock, was fatally wounded during the battle.

North America, 8 September 1755. British forces under William Johnson defeat the French and the Indians at the battle of Lake George.

Canada, 24 October 1755. A British expedition against French-held Fort Niagara ends in failure.

Lisbon, November 1755. More than 10,000 people die in an earthquake.

Canada, November 1755. The British admiral Edward Hawk takes possession of 300 French merchant ships.

South Africa, 1755. The first outbreak of smallpox in Cape Town spreads rapidly inland. Brought by sailors, it proves fatal to many Khoisan hunters and herders.

Corsica, 1755. The Corsican patriot Pasquale Paoli is appointed commander of an uprising against Genoese rule.

Canada, 1755. The British expel about 7,000 Acadians (*people from Nova Scotia and New Brunswick*) for refusing to take an oath of loyalty to Britain.

North America, 1755. The first regular passenger ship service begins between Britain and the colonies.

Burma, 1755. King Alaungpaya founds a new capital at Rangoon.

London, 16 January 1756. King George II and Frederick II of Prussia sign the treaty of Westminster, an agreement to secure the neutrality of the German states in the Anglo-French struggle developing in Europe.

India, 21 April 1756. Ali Vardi Khan, the ruler of Bengal, dies.

North America, 1756. A stage-coach line opens between Philadelphia and New York. By travelling at 18 hours a day, the distance can be covered in three days.

North America, 1756. The College of New Jersey is moved from Newark to Princeton.

Tunisia, 1756. Tunis is seized by troops led by the *bey* of Algiers.

France, 1756. The publication of Voltaire's *Essay on Universal History* confirms his reputation as a fine historian.

Quake brings fire and floods to Lisbon

An engraving of the Lisbon earthquake, from Le Monde Illustre.

Lisbon, November 1755

A terrible earthquake has devastated Lisbon, killing more than 10,000 people and reducing three-quarters of all buildings to heaps of rubble. Plans are already being drawn up for a completely new city to be designed by the military engineer Manuel de Maia. The earthquake struck Lisbon on All Saints' Day, when the churches were full, and lasted some nine minutes. One result was that the waters of the river Tagus receded, piled up and then came rolling back into the city to flood a huge area. This was followed by a great fire which raged for six days. Lisbon was a wealthy city with a population of about a quarter of a million.

Statue illustrates empiricist's theory

Paris, 1754

If you find a Parisian staring at a statue it is probably because he is musing over the latest philosophical theory put forward by the influential empiricist Etienne Bonnot, the abbot of Condillac.

Bonnot, in his recently published *Treatise des Sensations*, argues that the source of all our knowledge is our senses, which we transform into knowledge by the processes of attention, memory and reflection.

Take the statue. Bonnot invites readers to imagine it as first having only one sense, smell for example, and then another, perhaps taste, until it has all the senses. Try to imagine, he says, the statue's mental state at each stage. By combining the different sensations it would arrive at "judgements" in much the same way as humans reason, because the basis of our reasoning is our senses. This idea that reasoning is deductive challenges the traditional Cartesian view that man is endowed by God with knowledge of the basic principles of life.

Divine right's noble sceptic dies in Paris

France, 10 February 1755

The philosopher Baron de Montesquieu, renowned for his challenge to the divine right of kings, has died. Born in 1689, his most famous work *De l'Esprit des Lois* – The Spirit of Law – first appeared anonymously in 1748. Although banned by the Catholic Church, it ran through 22 editions in two years.

In his challenge to the divine right de Montesquieu based the authority of law on human reason and argued that it varied from country to country according to differences in climate, religion, customs and past history. A constitution good for one nation may be bad for another.

He admired the constitution of Britain where he spent two years believing that the English attitude to religion, commerce and liberty are the result of their cold climate which makes men impatient with tyranny. "Servitude always begins with sleepiness," wrote the baron whose other work included satires of French society.

British routed by French in North America

North America, 13 July 1755

British attempts to end French expansion in North America have been dealt a serious blow with the latest French victory in the Ohio river valley, the focal point of recent Anglo-French clashes.

Early this month a British and colonial force was sent to recapture Fort Duquesne (*Pittsburgh*), a former British base which the French seized last year. On 9 July, seven miles south of the fort, French and Indian troops ambushed the British, killing or wounding almost two-thirds of the 1,000-strong force. The British commander, General Edward Braddock, was fatally wounded, and died today.

Command of the British forces has now fallen to Braddock's 23-year-old aide, Lieutenant-Colonel George Washington, who distinguished himself during the battle and retreat (he had two horses shot from under him and four bullet holes in his coat). Last year the governor of Virginia sparked off the present conflict when he sent Washington to scout and later eliminate French forts encroaching on land claimed by British colonies.

France's Indian hero beaten by peace

Pondicherry, India, 1754

The marquis of Dupleix, the formidable governor of France's Indian enclave, has been sacrificed in the cause of European peace. Even his enemies, the British, admire his audacity. With meagre resources, he almost took control of southern India.

The Marquis of Dupleix.

From 1742, when France and Britain went to war, he made up for his lack of French soldiers with astute diplomacy (turning Indian princes from overlords into dependants) and bold strategy, building up a trained Sepoy army and taking Madras in 1746. Britain recaptured it with reinforcements, but it was not until Robert Clive was given command of the British forces that Dupleix found himself against an opponent of equal skill. Clive's capture in September 1751 of Arcot, which he held for 50 days, wrecked Dupleix' strategy. Unable to gain victory on the cheap, France has opted for peace.

Cultured mistress enrages the people

Mme de Pompadour, by Boucher.

France, 1755

Public protest is building up the folly and extravagance of Louis XV and his beautiful mistress Madame de Pompadour. They are bleeding France's economy by their lavish spending on the arts, fine houses and court entertainments.

Pompadour seduced the King in 1745 when she appeared at the dauphin's marriage ball dressed as the goddess Diana. Lonely after the death of his favourite, the duchess of Chateauroux, the king rapidly installed Pompadour at Versailles. In September, that year he formally presented his new mistress to the queen.

Born Jeanne Poisson in 1721, the daughter of a clerk, and educated by her mother's lover, Pompadour is an intelligent woman, well-read, charming and musical. She became patron to Voltaire, Montesquieu and Rousseau, and is said to be unfailingly loyal to her family and friends who helped her to reach such an influential position.

Comfort and light: new priorities in French interior decor

Candelabrum, by Claude Duvivier.

Louis XV's roll-top desk by J F Oeben, completed later by J H Riesener.

Paris, 1754

The change from the style of Louis XIV to Louis XV is a change from the formal and stately to the elegant and human. It can be seen in the Place de la Concorde, laid out this year with modest facades and ornamental gardens by the royal architect, Jacques Ange Gabriel. The traditional formal gardens are giving way under English influence to a natural style, as at Bellevue.

In the salons, the centre of social life, the taste is for amusing decoration, based on imaginary beasts, foliage, shepherdesses, *Chinoiserie* and *singerie* – decorative panels featuring monkeys. Chairs have become lighter and markedly more curved in appearance. They are also more comfortable. Tapestries take the paintings of artists such as Boucher as their subjects. In carpets the fashion is for the Savonnerie factory's medallions of flowers and acanthus leaves. A new type of room is in vogue – the *boudoir*, where ladies receive friends while conducting their toilette at the dressing table.

There is a demand for *ebenistes* to provide veneers and marquetry and *ormolu* mounts at the corners and edges of furniture. Gilded bronze decorations riot over the curved surfaces of commodes. One of the most elaborate pieces is a bureau, now being constructed for Louis XV, by Jean Francois Oeben.

1756 (1756-1759)

Versailles, 1 May 1756. The Austrian chancellor, Kaunitz, signs a treaty of alliance with France.

Mediterranean, June 1756. The British-held island of Minorca is taken by the French.

India, June 1756. Sirajuddaula, the new ruler of Bengal, captures Calcutta. Many of the British residents who surrender are allowed by Sirajuddaula's agents to die in a "black hole".

New England, 14 August 1756. Soon after arriving in America to command the French forces, Louis Montcalm de St Veran takes Fort Oswego from the British.

Germany, 29 August 1756. Frederick II of Prussia invades Saxony, setting off a war in Europe. Prussia is allied with Britain against Austria and France.

New England, 31 August 1756. The British at Fort William Henry surrender to Louis Montcalm.

Britain, November 1756. On the resignation of the duke of Newcastle as prime minister, William Pitt is appointed secretary of state and takes charge of the war against France.

Paris, 5 January 1757. Robert Francois Damiens makes an unsuccessful attempt to assassinate King Louis XV.

India, 28 January 1757. Ahmed Shah, the first king of Afghanistan, occupies Delhi and annexes the Punjab.

Austria, 2 February 1757. Austria, already allied with France, forms an offensive alliance with Russia against Prussia.

India, 22 June 1757. After retaking Calcutta and seizing the French station at Chandernagore, Robert Clive, leading the British East India Company's forces, defeats the ruler of Bengal's much larger army at Plassey, 100 miles up the Hooghly from Calcutta.

Bohemia, June 1757. After suffering a defeat by the Austrians at Kolin, the Prussians are forced to lift a siege of Prague and evacuate Bohemia, which they invaded earlier in the year.

Germany, 30 August 1757. Having invaded eastern Prussia, the Russians defeat the Prussians at Gross-Jagersdorf.

Germany, September 1757. The Swedes, who are in alliance with Austria, France and Russia, invade the province of Pomerania.

Germany, 16 October 1757. The Austrians reach Berlin.

Germany, 5 November 1757. The Prussians, led by Frederick II, defeat a Franco-Austrian force at Rossbach.

Germany, 6 December 1757. The Prussians inflict another defeat on the Austrians, at Leuthen.

Morocco, 1757. Mulay Mohammed III ben Abdullah comes to the throne and sets about re-establishing the economy and the army, which have been in disarray since the death of Mulay Ismail in 1727.

France, 1757. Denis Diderot presents a "bourgeois drama" entitled *The Test of Virtue*.

Germany, 23 June 1758. British and Hanoverian armies defeat the French at Krefeld.

New England, 8 July 1758. A British attack on Fort Carillon at Ticonderoga (in *New York state*) is foiled by the French.

Canada, 26 July 1758. British forces under James Wolfe capture Fort Louisbourg on Cape Breton Island from the French. The fort was taken by the British in 1745, but returned to the French three years later by the treaty of Aix-la-Chapelle.

Germany, 25 August 1758. The Prussians defeat an invading Russian force at the battle of Zorndorf.

Portugal, September 1758. A plot by a group of nobles against the king and Pombal, known as the conspiracy of the Tavora, is uncovered. Its leaders are tortured and executed.

North America, 25 November 1758. After losing Louisbourg and Fort Frontenac to the British, the French are forced to evacuate Fort Duquesne (*Pittsburgh*), which the British rename Fort Pitt.

Senegal, December 1758. Having taken St Louis from the French in April, the British seize the island of Goree.

India, 1758. The Maratha leader Raghunath Rao occupies Lahore.

France, 1758. Jean-Jacques Rousseau publishes his *Lettre a d'Alembert*.

Paris, 1758. *On the Mind*, a statement of militant atheism by the philosopher Claude Helvetius, is denounced by the Sorbonne and publicly burnt on the orders of the parliament of Paris.

India, 1759. Ahmed Shah Durrani, the king of Afghanistan, invades India for the second time.

England, 1759. The publication of *Rasselas, Prince of Abyssinia* by Samuel Johnson popularises the romantic view of Ethiopia.

London, 1759. The British Museum, which was founded six years ago, opens its doors to the public.

"Messiah" composer has died aged 74

London, 14 April 1759

George Frideric Handel, the towering figure in English musical life for over 30 years, died today. He will be buried in Westminster Abbey.

Handel, like Bach (whom he never met), was born in 1685 in eastern Germany; otherwise their careers ran different courses. For example, Bach remained in Germany, whereas Handel travelled to Italy and settled in England, becoming a British citizen in 1727. Bach wrote almost nothing for the stage; Handel composed about 40 operas and slightly fewer oratorios, including *Messiah* (1742).

Handel wrote much for royal occasions, such as the *Water Music* and music for the 1727 coronation. The story goes that George II was so moved by the *Hallelujah* chorus in *Messiah* that he stood up; the audience felt that it had to follow the king, and a tradition was born.

Handel's monument (1784).

Scarlatti, composer-royal, dies in Spain

Scarlatti; an anonymous portrait.

Madrid, 23 July 1757

Domenico Scarlatti has died agec 71. Born in Naples, he was the sor of the composer Alessandro Scar latti (1660-1725) and one of th great trio of composers (with Bach and Handel) born in 1685.

Scarlatti was made organist anc composer to the Neapolitan cour when just 15 years old. He worke at Rome from 1707 to 1719, an after a time in Sicily became com poser to King John V of Portugal he taught the king's gifted daughte and went with her to Spain whe she married the Spanish crow prince in 1729. This fame rests o hundreds of keyboard sonatas mainly written for the princess which show a brilliant range o imagination and technique.

Swiss mathematician works on calculus

Berlin, 1755

Not only does the Swiss scientist Leonhard Euler find time to teach and carry out research at the university here, he also has written hundreds of books on topics as varied as artillery and ballistics, shipbuilding and navigation, astronomical orbits and many aspects of applied technology and engineering.

An important work is his recen *Institutiones Calculi Differentialis* which shows him to be one of th most significant mathematical inno vators after Isaac Newton. Thi book details Euler's many discov eries in the fields of both ordinar and partial differential equation which are useful in problems c mechanics.

New pact links France and Austria

Versailles, 1 May 1756
Chancellor Kaunitz of Austria succeeded today in bringing about what is being called a "diplomatic revolution" with the signing of a treaty between those traditional enemies, France and Austria.

The treaty is especially advantageous to the Austrians, for it contains an undertaking by each country to protect the other, with a promise of military aid, in the event of aggression and Austria is under threat from the Prussians.

Kaunitz must thank his friend Madame de Pompadour for her help in bringing off this coup by persuading her lover, King Louis, to end the old enmity. There were other potent forces at work as well, for this year has seen a dramatic upset in the alliances which have governed Europe for so long.

The Anglo-Austrian alliance has died because both countries were disillusioned with it. Britain had already signed a treaty with Russia, and in January the Hanoverian King George II of Britain signed the convention of Westminster with Frederick of Prussia under which they agreed to guarantee the security of Silesia and Hanover.

With France and Britain already fighting in India and America, the Westminster treaty made Louis and his advisers much more receptive to the proposals from Vienna.

The Anglo-Prussian agreement has also disturbed the Russians and, despite the St Petersburg treaty, the indications are that they will now seek better relations with Austria and France.

Louis XV, the king of France.

Frederick II, the king of Prussia.

British Museum opens to the public

An engraving of the garden front of the British Museum, c.1800.

London, 1759
The British Museum has opened in Bloomsbury. It is to be a "general repository for all arts and sciences" and will be open "for public use to all posterity". It is Britain's first great public assembly of antiquities and will be administered by a number of trustees, drawn from the church and state.

The museum's exhibits are based upon the collections of Sir Hans Sloane, the physician and antiquary, and those of the first and second earls of Oxford. King George has donated the Old Royal Library, built up by successive monarchs over 300 years.

Plans for the museum began after Sloane's death in 1753. A lottery, provided for by the British Museum Act of 1753, raised £300,000 – sufficient to buy the Sloane and Oxford collections and to buy and then expand Montagu House in Great Russell Street to house them.

Reform is bringing Portugal up to date

Lisbon, 1759
The marquis of Pombal, Portugal's all-powerful prime minister, has set about dismantling the country's system of privilege and laying the foundations of a new order. Encouraged by King Joseph, he has introduced a remarkable series of reforms which have already earned him the nickname of the "Portuguese Richelieu".

Pombal has been particularly tough on the Jesuits, who had exercised control not only of the royal conscience and of the souls of the Brazilian Indians but also of education. He has expelled them and closed convents. His educational reforms intend to turn Coimbra into Portugal's greatest and richest university. Pombal is also working towards creating a wealthy mercantile class with, behind it, the phalanx of officials necessary to carry on administration and trade. Portugal's alliance with Britain has continued, despite resentment at London's stranglehold on the country's trade.

Agriculture is key to national wealth

An allegory of a farmworker.

Paris, 1758
A nation's prosperity is solely dependent on its ability to increase its levels of agricultural production, according to a new group of Parisian economists, the Physiocrats.

Their leader, Dr Francois Quesnay, a physician with a passion for economics, has set out France's national income and expenditure in terms of agricultural goods in his new book *Tableau Economique*.

Quesnay, who regards agricultural production as the only true form of wealth creation, says that money is not true wealth and commerce is only a minor source of prosperity. His group, which takes its name from physiocracy – control by nature – wants the state to intervene less in agriculture, lower taxes and lift out-dated guild regulations which hamper production.

Japanese lacquer work: cobweb and insect design.

1759 (1759-1761)

Paris, 8 March 1759. For the second time, the parliament of Paris condemns the *Encyclopedie* edited by Denis Diderot.

West Indies, 23 April 1759. The English seize Basse-Terre and Guadeloupe in the Antilles from the French.

Canada, 25 July 1759. British forces under the leadership of John Prideaux defeat the French at Fort Niagara; Prideaux is killed in the battle.

New England, 26 July 1759. Outnumbered French defenders blow up Fort Carillon at Ticonderoga and flee before an attacking British force.

Canada, 31 July 1759. In the face of a British attack on Crown Point, the French blow up Fort St Frederic.

Germany, 1 August 1759. British and Hanoverian armies defeat the French at battle of Minden.

Spain, 10 August 1759. On the death of Ferdinand VI, he is succeeded as king of Spain by his half-brother Charles III.

Prussia, 12 August 1759. The Austro-Russian coalition wins a resounding victory over Frederick II at Kunersdorf.

Portugal, September 1759. The marquis of Pombal, the prime minister of Portugal, gives orders for the Jesuits to be expelled from the country. This is a direct result of last year's Tavora conspiracy, in which some Jesuits were involved.

Canada, 18 September 1759. Quebec surrenders to the British after a battle which saw the deaths of both James Wolfe and Louis Montcalm, the British and French commanders.

France, 1759. Voltaire publishes a short story entitled *Candide*, a satire on the philosophy that "all is for the best in the best of all possible worlds".

India, 22 January 1760. British forces under Eyre Coote win a decisive victory over the French, led by the count of Lally, at Wandiwash in southern India.

South Carolina, 16 February 1760. Cherokee Indians held hostage at Fort St George are killed in revenge for Indian attacks on frontier settlements.

Netherlands, April 1760. Peace talks begun at The Hague to end the conflict between the European powers break down.

Quebec, 28 April 1760. French forces besieging Quebec defeat the British under James Murray in the second battle on the Plains of Abraham. The British retreat into the city.

Germany, 23 June 1760. The Austrians defeat the Prussians at Landshut.

South Carolina, 7 August 1760. The British garrison of Fort Loudon is overrun by Cherokee Indians after it was forced by starvation to surrender.

Germany, 15 August 1760. Frederick II defeats the Austrians at the battle of Liegnitz.

Quebec, 8 September 1760. The French surrender the city of Montreal to the British.

Britain, 25 October 1760. On the death of his grandfather George II, George III comes to the throne.

Germany, 3 November 1760. Following the Russian capture of Berlin, his capital, Frederick II of Prussia defeats the Austrians at the battle of Torgau.

North America, 29 November 1760. Major Robert Rogers takes possession of Detroit on behalf of Britain.

North America, 1760. People of African descent are said to constitute 30 per cent of the population of the 13 British colonies in North America.

France, 1760. Jean-Jacques Rousseau publishes *Julie ou la Nouvelle Heloise.*

China, 1760. Canton becomes the only port in China authorised to trade with other countries.

Italy, 1760. The great comic dramatist Carlo Goldoni presents a new play entitled *The Tyrants.*

Scotland, 1760. The poet James Macpherson publishes *Ossian*, allegedly a collection of fragments of ancient poetry translated from the Gaelic. In fact, the author is Macpherson himself.

England, 1760. Josiah Wedgwood establishes a pottery works at Etruria in Staffordshire.

England, 1760. The Irish-born clergyman Laurence Sterne publishes the first two volumes of an eccentric novel entitled *Tristram Shandy.*

India, January 1761. The Moghul emperor and his Maratha allies are defeated by the Afghan leader, Ahmed Shah Durrani, at the battle of Panipat. There is no longer an Indian army able to resist British penetration seriously.

France, 8 June 1761. After the failure of peace talks with the French, the English capture Belle Ile sur Mer.

Britain, October 1761. William Pitt, finding himself isolated in the cabinet over war policy, resigns as secretary of state.

Royal desire for peace defeats Pitt

London, 1761

William Pitt, who came to power at the lowest ebb in Britan's fortunes and transformed the French war, has been forced to resign. He saw that Spain was about to join France and he wished to anticipate the blow with an ultimatum. But the king, George III, who said the war was "bloody and expensive", wanted peace and the Cabinet deserted Pitt.

Yet only months ago they were loud in his praise. Four years ago, a string of British defeats had culminated in the failure at Minorca, for which Admiral Byng was shot after a court-martial. Pitt shifted the war from Europe, where France was stronger, to the high seas and the colonies, where Britain had the advantage. The French were defeated by Wolfe in Canada, by Clive in India, and by Hawke and other admirals in the West Indies and West Africa.

Though Pitt is out of office, the Spanish will yet be faced with the consequences of his policies. The expeditionary forces which he raised are now poised to seize the Spanish colonies of the Philippines, Florida, Cuba and a string of islands in the Caribbean.

Chairing the member: an English scene by William Hogarth, c.1754.

Berlin burnt and pillaged by Russians

Berlin, 9 October 1760

A combined force of Russians and Austrians entered Berlin today, and the soldiers are busy pillaging the royal palaces of Charlottenburg and Schonhausen. The occupiers have also demanded the payment of a "war tribute" by the city.

The ordinary people, fearing for their lives, are cowering behind locked doors, but so far the enemy soldiers are too preoccupied with filling their knapsacks with royal treasures to undertake serious looting in the city.

It seems, in fact, that the Russians and Austrians are engaged in a secondary operation and are not here in great numbers. Rumours are spreading that King Frederic is already hurrying to the relief c the city with his formidable army.

However, while he will certain be able to throw the invaders out c Berlin, the war is going badly fo him. Prussia is exhausted by it, h soldiers have suffered great loss and much of his artillery has bee captured or destroyed.

Frederick, renowned as a mil tary leader, almost abandoned th fight last year after the Kunersdo defeat. He contemplated suici and wrote: "I believe everything lost; I shall not survive the collap of my fatherland." But he continu to fight and two months ago d feated the Austrians at Liegnitz.

Battle of Quebec: French expelled

Quebec, September 1759
In a carefully planned and brilliantly executed combined operation, British troops have scaled the allegedly "impossible" Heights of Abraham and driven the French and their allies from Quebec. Few thought that such an attack was possible, and the defenders of Quebec themselves were so confident that they made little effort to harass the British fleet under Vice-Admiral Charles Saunders as it weaved its way through the treacherous currents of the St Lawrence River – without the help of charts – with 8,500 war-seasoned soldiers. A previous British attack had ended in disaster 48 years before, and it was not until the British were encamped on the opposite bank that the French became concerned.

Even so, the French commander, marquis of Montcalm, remained confident that no army could scale the huge cliffs surrounding his city. He had not reckoned with James Wolfe, a youthful brigadier-general who had been chosen especially for this role. After weeks of deliberation, Wolfe chose to lead his men in a surprise attack involving a silent approach by flat-bottomed boats and a dangerous climb in darkness.

By dawn, the British Redcoats were lined up to attack. Montcalm chose to leave his fortress and attack at once, but British firepower won the day. Montcalm and Wolfe were both mortally injured, but the dying Wolfe, hearing of his victory, said: "Now, God be praised, I will die in peace."

The death of General Montcalm near Quebec; an engraving by Watteau.

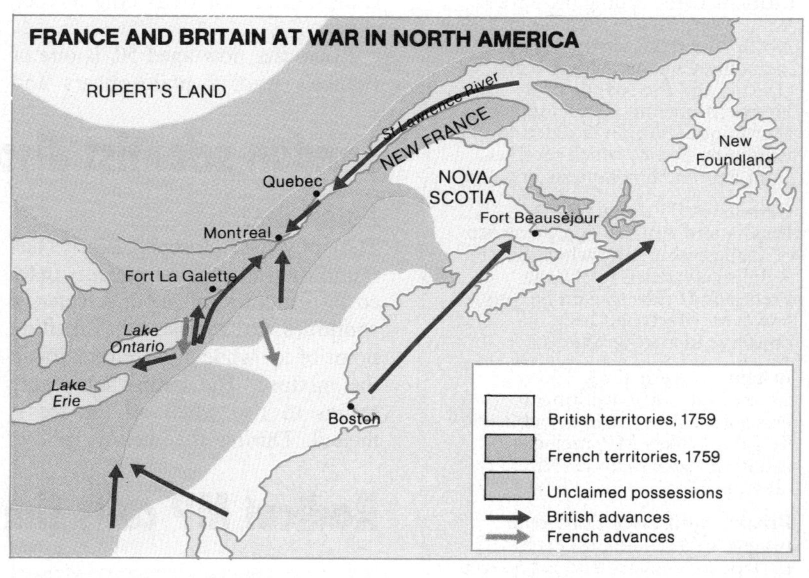

Thousands die as Moslems defeat Hindus at Panipat

Panipat, India, 22 January 1761
After a terrible eight-hour battle, in which the fate of India lay in the balance, the Afghan army of Ahmed Shah Durrani has annihilated the Marathas.

Since 1748, when Nadir Shah of Persia died, apportioning to his son Durrani his eastern conquests, India has been a battleground between the Moslem Afghans and the Hindu Marathas, the Moghuls' allies. In October 1760 Durrani challenged the Marathas to battle. The Marathas opted for positional warfare, building a fortified camp at Panipat. It proved their undoing. The 300,000 soldiers and camp followers ran out of food and were forced to fight. Durrani, with only 80,000, staked everything on the outcome. "The Marathas are the thorn of Hindustan," he said. "By one effort we get this thorn out of our sides for ever."

For six hours the advantage was with the Hindus. An unexpected charge by Durrani's cavalry, in which the Maratha leader's son, Viswas Rao, was wounded, turned the tide. "As if by enchantment, the whole Marathan army turned their backs and fled at full speed, leaving the field of battle covered with heaps of dead," one eye-witness reported. As many as 200,000 Marathas may have perished in those eight frightful hours. But the blood-letting has weakened both sides, with the British poised to benefit.

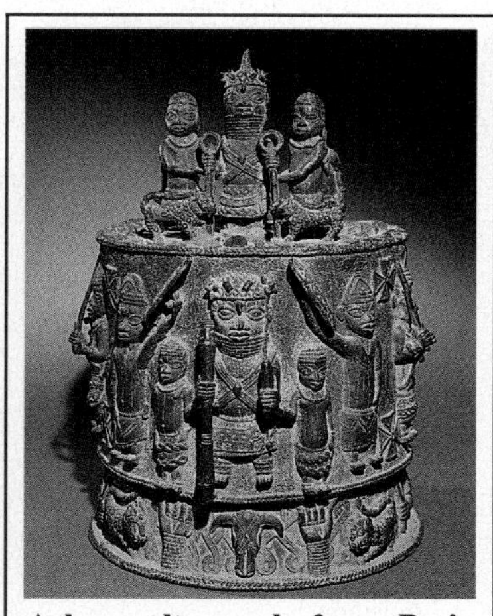

A brass altar made for a Benin king after 1750.

Lay preachers raise question of dissension for Methodists

Bristol, England, 1760
John Wesley has taken a decisive stand against Methodists separating from the Church of England at the annual conference here. He led the conference in disavowing lay preachers who have been administering the sacraments and who have taken out licences as dissenting ministers to legalise their positions. He said that he would never ordain a separate ministry.

The pressure for separation has been building up for several years now. The strength of the Methodists is outside the church; initially it was in large outdoor meetings, but as the movement has grown around one hundred chapels have been built. Most of their meetings are deliberately held at different times from church services, but in many parishes the clergy remain hostile to Methodism.

Unlike Wesley, most Methodist preachers are tradesmen and craftsmen who have no loyalty to the established church. Only the immense prestige of Wesley has avoided a split.

John Wesley: wants to avoid split.

1761 (1761-1763)

Paris, 1761. The parliament of Paris condemns the Society of Jesus following a court case against the Jesuit priest Antoine de Valette, the leader of the order's French houses in South America.

Spain, 1761. Spain is drawn into the war of European powers by the so-called third Family Compact, which makes its foreign policy subservient to that of France. This treaty of mutual assistance involving all the ruling Bourbon dynasties was drawn up by the duke of Choiseul, Louis XV's chief minister.

India, 1761. British forces under Eyre Coote seize Pondicherry from the French.

England, 1761. The writer Samuel Richardson dies. His *Pamela*, which appeared in 1740, is regarded as the first modern novel.

Britain, 2 January 1762. Britain declares war on Spain.

Russia, 5 January 1762. The Czarina Elizabeth dies and is succeeded on the throne by her nephew Peter III, the maternal grandson of Peter the Great.

West Indies, 5 February 1762. Martinique, a major French base in the Lesser Antilles, surrenders to the British.

Germany, May 1762. Frederick II of Prussia signs a peace treaty with Sweden.

Britain, 29 May 1762. Lord Bute, a close adviser of George III and a believer in the supremacy of the royal prerogative, becomes prime minister.

Russia, July 1762. Peter III is assassinated with the complicity of his wife, Catherine, who succeeds him on the throne as Catherine II. During his brief reign, Peter gave his support to Frederick II, restoring eastern Prussia to him.

Germany, 21 July 1762. Frederick II defeats the Austrians at Berkersdorf in Silesia.

West Indies, 12 August 1762. The British capture Cuba from Spain after a two-month siege.

Philippines, 5 October 1762. A British fleet bombards and captures the Spanish-held city of Manila.

Austria, 5 October 1762. The opera *Orpheus and Eurydice* by Christoph Gluck is staged for the first time.

Austria, 24 November 1762. Austria signs a truce with Frederick II of Prussia.

North America, 3 December 1762. France cedes to Spain all lands west of the Mississippi – the territory known as Upper Louisiana.

Portugal, December 1762. With British support, the Portuguese repel an invasion by French and Spanish forces.

France, 1762. Charles Emmanuel of Savoy issues two edicts giving freedom to serfs.

France, 1762. Jean-Jacques Rousseau publishes *Le Contrat Social* (The Social Contract), which contains the opening sentence "Man is born free, yet everywhere he is in chains" and the slogan "liberty, equality, fraternity". He also publishes *Emile*, in novel form, which outrages church and state with its unorthodox views on monarchy and religion and causes him to flee into exile in Switzerland.

Versailles, 1762. The architect Jacques Ange Gabriel begins work on the Petit Trianon.

Rome, 1762. Construction of the Trevi fountain, the work of the architect Niccolo Salvi, is completed.

Paris, 10 February 1763. By the treaty of Paris, ending the Seven Years War, France loses all its North American territories, including Canada, except New Orleans and the islands of St Pierre, Miquelon, Guadeloupe and Martinique. Florida is ceded to Britain by Spain, which receives from Britain all conquests in Cuba.

Germany, 15 February 1763. Prussia and Austria sign the peace of Hubertusburg, by which Silesia is definitely ceded to Prussia. Frederick II fails to gain Saxony, however, which had been his objective in starting the war.

Britain, 23 April 1763. Today's issue of the anti-government newspaper *North Briton*, published by John Wilkes MP, includes insulting remarks about King George III.

Britain, April 1763. Lord Bute resigns after leading an extremely unpopular ministry and is replaced as prime minister by George Grenville.

North America, 7 May 1763. Pontiac, the chief of the Ottawa Indians, begins an all-out war on British garrisons in the region west of Niagara.

Lithuania, September 1763. Russian troops invade Polish territory.

Poland, 5 October 1763. Frederick Augustus II, the elector of Saxony and king of Poland, dies.

North America, October 1763. A large area on the Canadian border which is claimed by both New Hampshire and New York is given the name Verd-mont, meaning green mountain.

Illegal "Social Contract" is published

France, 1762

A new philosophical treatise – *Le Contrat Social* by Jean-Jacques Rousseau – has been published in Holland. Like others of Rousseau's works it is officially banned in France, but what is proving to be a major addition to our knowledge of human relations has been widely, if illicitly, circulated.

Le Contrat Social, Rousseau's political testimony, advocates universal justice through equality before the law, as well as a fairer distribution of wealth. He believes that government is essentially a contract between the rulers and the ruled.

Under the "general will" of the people, they consent to turn over power to their governors to be exercised for the common good. The community is greater than the individual, but as such the community is responsible for well-being of each citizen.

Rousseau, now aged 50, is one of France's leading philosophers and contributor to the *Encyclopedie*. His *Emile* also appeared this year and his influential *Discourse on the origins of inequality* was published in 1755.

Jean-Jacques Rousseau, the writer.

London scientist discovers hidden heat

London, 1762

The physicist Joseph Black has found that, if a thermometer is placed in a mixture of ice and water, it continues to register the melting point of ice while any ice remains in the mixture. The temperature only begins to rise when all the ice is melted. During the melting phase, Black concludes, it is as if heat is passing steadily into the mixture of ice and water without affecting the thermometer. It is hidden or "latent" heat. Further experiments with latent heat show how this hidden form of energy may be measured. These findings may also aid the development of steam engines.

Radical MP calls the king a prostitute

John Wilkes, MP and journalist.

London, 23 April 1763

John Wilkes, the radical MP for Aylesbury, a member of the Hellfire Club and the publisher of the scurrilous anti-government newspaper – *North Briton*, has made his most outrageous attack on the government yet.

Today's edition of *North Briton*, number 45, contains outspoken criticisms not only of the prime minister, Lord Bute, but also of the king. Condemning Bute as incompetent, Wilkes, a fervent democrat, suggests that the king, by supporting him, has drawn the monarchy into "prostitution". This affront has reached far beyond its target and it seems impossible that Wilkes will go unpunished.

Coup d'etat brings Czarina Catherine to Russian throne

Catherine the Great of Russia.

St Petersburg, Russia, 1762

The Czarina, Catherine, has seized power in a *coup d'etat* staged by her lover, Gregori Orlov, a fiery lieutenant of the St Petersburg garrison, by whom she had a child last April. She was wildly cheered by the soldiery when she arrived in the capital. They kissed her hand and called her "little mother".

Four days after the coup her husband, Peter III, died in a scuffle during dinner. His guard, another Orlov brother, Alexis, says he cannot recall what happened. Peter was universally detested. After the death of his mother, Czarina Elizabeth, he continued drinking and whoring, while Catherine, in black, spent hours kneeling by the coffin. Peter offended the church by shouting and putting his tongue out at the priest during divine service. He took the soldiers out of the uniforms given to them by Peter the Great.

Indians leave trail of death along the Canadian frontier

America, 7 May 1763

Four Indian tribes – the Shawnees, Delawares, Chippawas and Ottawa – have laid siege to the British stronghold of Fort Detroit in the Great Lakes region in an uprising by the native American people in which hundreds of British redcoats have lost their lives. The Indian leader, Pontiac, an Ottawa, has destroyed several British outposts and crushed expeditions with great ruthlessness.

It was a Delaware wise man calling for a return to the old Indian customs and a rejection of the white man who inspired the uprising of the tribes. Pontiac, concerned at the loss to his people of tribal lands and the valuable fur industry, brought the tribal chiefs together and announced a plan to drive the British out. He planned a surprise attack on Fort Detroit, but the plan was exposed, giving the British time to build new fortifications.

Chief Pontiac: a later engraving.

Paris treaty ends war

A contemporary cartoon of the signing of the Treaty of Paris, 1763.

Paris, 10 February 1763

Seven long, bloody and financially exhausting years of war ended today with the signing of the Treaty of Paris. Although it does not meet Pitt's demands, the treaty secures a great deal of land for Britain's burgeoning empire.

Among its provisions, France cedes Canada to Britian and relinquishes its Indian possessions except for Pondicherry and four small trading posts. Britain also gets Florida from Spain and, in compensation, France has given Spain the Louisiana territory west of the Mississippi.

Other provisions return Minorca to Britain, and there is an exchange of islands in the West Indies. Britain is to restore Havana and Manila to Spain and adjustments are made in African colonies.

The treaty, hammered out over two years of negotiations, should prove to be of great value to Britain but, while it is being received thankfully in France, it must surely mean the end of France's colonial ambitions in the New World.

Britain and France have also withdrawn from the war in Europe, and it is expected that Prussia and Austria will make peace within the next few days. The war will end in a triumph for Frederick of Prussia. So often near defeat, his right to Silesia now seems about to be recognised and he is confirmed as a hero in the eyes of the Germans.

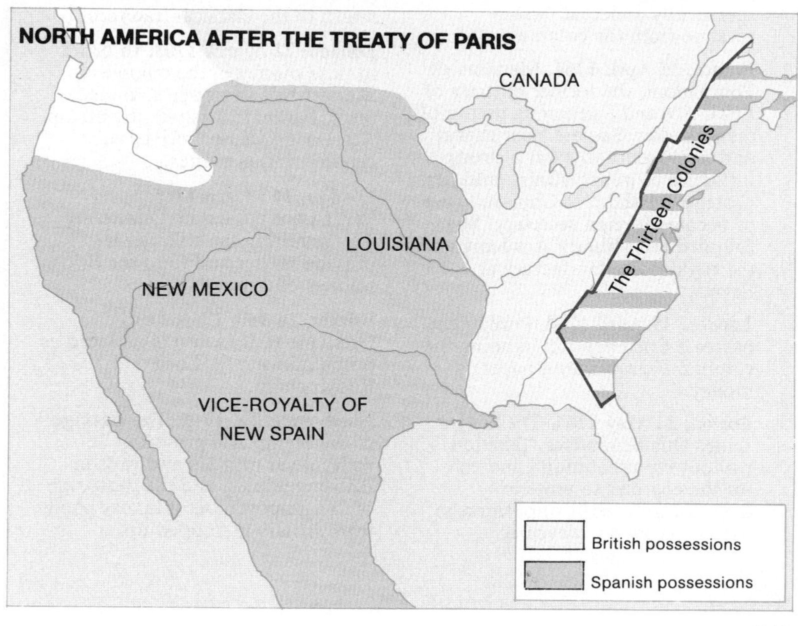

Mystic made Hindu-Moslem split deeper

Delhi, 1762

Shah Wali-Allah, the great Indian Moslem philosopher and mystic, has died. A man who sensed that he was living at the end of an age, he revitalised Islam in India.

His father, a religious official at the Moghul court, abandoned the luxury of court life and founded a religious school. Wali-Allah himself studied in Mecca. Troubled by the disorders of the times he evolved a new philosophy, based on Sunni Islam.

The worship of saints at shrines was to be given less emphasis. Moslems should become more exclusive, mixing less with Hindus, and should work to make their society more perfect in anticipation of the heavenly life to come. He leaves a stronger Moslem India behind.

1763 (1763-1765)

North America, November 1763. The Ottawa Chief Pontiac, who has inflicted several defeats on the British in the Great Lakes region, lifts a six-month siege of Fort Detroit after failing to gain French support for his rebellion.

North America, 1763. Two English surveyors, Charles Mason and Jeremiah Dixon, begin to survey a boundary line between the two colonies of Pennsylvania and Maryland.

North America, 1763. The British prohibit settlements in the entire region west of the Appalachian mountains.

New England, 1763. The Touro synagogue, the first major centre of Jewish culture in America, opens at Newport, Rhode Island.

Britain, 1763. Arrested on a general warrant of seditious libel, John Wilkes, the publisher of the newspaper *North Briton*, is discharged on the ground that his arrest infringes his privileges as a member of Parliament.

Russia, 1763. Catherine II appoints a commission to determine the future of the Russian nobility.

France, 1763. The group of French economic and political thinkers known as the Physiocrats begins publication of a newspaper entitled *La Gazette du Commerce*.

Iraq, 1763. The port of Bassora becomes the pivot of trade with Britain.

Britain, 19 January 1764. John Wilkes MP is expelled from the House of Commons and outlawed.

North America, February 1764. A French trading post is established at St Louis on the west bank of the Mississippi river, not far below the mouth of the Missouri.

London, 5 April 1764. Parliament passes a Sugar Act, its first law specifically aimed at raising revenue from the colonies.

France, 15 April 1764. Madame de Pompadour, the former mistress of Louis XV and a generous patron of the arts, dies. She used her charm and intelligence to exert a strong influence in public affairs, and her protege, the duke of Choiseul, rose to become foreign secretary. She founded the Military Academy and the royal porcelain factory at Sevres.

London, 19 April 1764. Parliament passes a Currency Act banning the colonies from printing paper money.

Boston, 24 May 1764. The lawyer James Otis denounces "taxation without representation" and calls for the colonies to unite in demonstrating their opposition to Britain's new tax measures.

Boston, August 1764. City merchants organise a boycott of luxury goods from Britain, inaugurating a policy of non-importation.

Poland, 6 September 1764. The pretender Stanislas Poniatowski, a favourite of Catherine II of Russia, becomes king of Poland.

India, 22 October 1764. The British defeat the Moghul emperor and the ruler of Oudh at Buxar, making themselves masters of Bengal, the richest province of India.

France, November 1764. King Louis XV officially dissolves the Jesuit order.

North America, November 1764. Allies of the Ottawa Indian Chief Pontiac reach a peace agreement with the British, but Pontiac himself is not among them.

Paris, 1764. Julie de Lespinasse opens a literary salon which attracts politicians, wits and artists.

England, 1764. The painter and engraver William Hogarth dies. One of his favourite subjects in later life was political caricature.

Russia, 1764. Catherine II orders further exploration of Alaska, the territory across the sea from the north-eastern tip of Siberia.

St Petersburg, 1764. The French architect Jean Baptiste Vallin de La Motte begins construction of Gostiny Dvor to house Catherine II's art collection.

Florida, 1764. The British farmer John Bartram discovers vast groves of wild oranges in Florida.

France, 1764. Voltaire publishes his *Dictionnaire Philosophique*.

Dresden, 1764. The German archaeologist Johann Joachim Winckelmann publishes *The Art of Antiquity*, in which he defends the return to the classical tradition.

London, 22 March 1765. In order to raise money in the colonies to support British troops stationed there, Parliament passes the Stamp Act, taxing stamps affixed to certain printed matter.

London, 24 March 1765. Parliament passes the Quartering Act, requiring the colonies to provide shelter and food for British soldiers and their horses.

Britain, 16 July 1765. Lord Grenville resigns and is replaced as prime minister by Lord Rockingham.

North America, 1765. The passage of the Stamp Act provokes widespread protests and riots in British colonies, and the campaign of non-importation of luxury goods from Britain is stepped up.

The Rake's Progress: Orgies, part of the series by William Hogarth.

London's sardonic chronicler is dead

London, 1764

William Hogarth, the engraver and painter, is dead. He was 67. Hogarth, the son of a modest but educated family, was an outstanding satirist of modern manners, using his art to create visual stories deliberately designed to have the same effect as a stage play.

Such series as *The Harlot's Progress* (1731), *The Rake's Progress* (1735) and *Marriage a la Mode* (1745) have made him the unrivalled, if sardonic, chronicler of fashionable London. *Gin Lane*, *Beer Street* and the *Four Stages of Cruelty* (all 1751) show the city's darker side with their depictions of poverty and decay.

A successful man who profoundly influenced his contemporaries, Hogarth was one of the first popular engravers to profit from his art. From 1735, in what was known as Hogarth's Act, artists held copyright in their own works, and piracy, from which Hogarth had suffered greatly, was made illegal.

Philosopher lobbies for justice and truth

Paris, 9 March 1765

Voltaire's influence and talent for satire has cleared the name of Jean Calas, executed three years ago for murdering his son Marc-Antoine.

Marc-Antoine was found dead in Jean's house in Toulouse. Rumour had it that the father, a staunch Calvinist, had killed the son because he intended to join the Catholic church. Jean insisted he was innocent, but was tortured on the wheel and executed in 1762.

Calas' sons brought the case to Voltaire's attention. He wrote a series of articles proving Marc-Antoine's suicide and the judges' pro-Catholic bias. The case was reopened and today the judges unanimously declared the case null and void.

Voltaire, the poet and philosopher.

Stamp tax inspires American rebellion

Boston, 25 August 1765
A mob sacked and burned the home of the Massachusetts governor, Thomas Hutchinson, tonight – furious at his support for the Stamp Act which has led to widespread opposition throughout the American colonies. In Boston, an effigy of the former prime minister, George Greville, hangs from the gallows, and serious rioting is reported in New York City.

The Stamp Act was imposed by Parliament to pay for British troops in North America. Like last year's Sugar Act – which gives British planters a monopoly of the American trade and restricts imports of foreign goods into the colonies – it has been denounced by speakers at public assemblies. The phrase "No taxation without representation", coined by James Otis, the Boston politician, is a familiar cry everywhere. With the British treasury running a high deficit following the Indian and French wars in America, the Stamp Act calls for revenue to be raised by affixing stamps to such printed matter as newspapers, pamphlets, legal documents like mortgages, deeds, licences and other items such as playing cards.

Parliamentary support for the act is by no means unanimous. The former prime minister, Pitt, believes that it was a mistake and that trade with the colonies is bound to suffer.

A Tory stamp agent is strung up on a liberty pole in an anti-Stamp Act demonstration in 1765; an engraving by John Trumbull, 1795.

Parisian salons turn from wit to politics

The first lecture at Madame Geoffrin's, on Voltaire, painted by Lemonnier.

Paris, c.1764
Literary and intellectual culture, always central to fashionable Parisian life, has established itself in a new world, that of the *salon*. Writers and artists once attended the royal court, but those days are gone. The new "monarchs" of the intellectual world are smart women, and the salons, held regularly in their own homes, are the new court.

Not only artists, writers and thinkers frequent the salons. Politicians mingle with the intellectuals, and eligible visiting foreigners are often invited.

The salons began some sixty years ago. At first they celebrated wit for its own sake, but these days the gatherings are more serious. Ladies such as Mlle de Lespinasse, Mme du Tencin and Mme Necker concentrate on politics. Mme du Deffand and Mme Geoffrin the "mother of the *Encyclopedie*", play host to the *philosophes*.

Voltaire's composer friend has died

Paris, 12 September 1764
The greatest French composer of the day, Jean-Philippe Rameau, died today, shortly before his 81st birthday. Born in Dijon, Rameau worked there as well as at Avignon, Clermont and Lyons before settling in Paris in 1722.

He soon became prominent as a musical theorist and composer of keyboard music and cantatas. In 1733 his first opera, *Hippolyte et Aricie*, caused excitement and some bewilderment by its unusual expressiveness and rich orchestral sounds, and it was for the stage that Rameau wrote much of his finest music.

Rameau was a friend of many of today's intellectuals, including Voltaire, and became more interested in musical theory in his later years. He was involved in several theoretical disputes, for example with Rousseau and Diderot.

Marquis calls for an end to torture

Italy, 1764
The guiding principles of law in most European countries have been challenged in a remarkable book by the 25-year-old marquis of Beccaria. *Of Crimes and Punishment* seems destined to become a seminal work, typical of the current trend for scientific enquiry.

Beccaria owes much to predecessors like Rousseau and Montesquieu, and he revels in the pure exercise of the intellect. Applying his rational analysis to contemporary law, he argues that executions, torture and retributive punishments are barbaric and useless.

Everyone should be equal before the law, argues Beccaria, and people should not suffer for their religious beliefs.

Although Beccaria is enthusiastically received by the Paris encyclopaedists, sceptics accuse him of trickery or plagiarism.

Archaeologist puts Greek art in vogue

Pompeian Room, Packington Hall.

Rome, 1764
A German cobbler's son is bringing order into the study of the art of the ancient world with a mighty reference work which seems set to stimulate the enthusiasm for all things Greek that is sweeping Europe

Johann Joachim Winckelmann arrived in Rome in 1755 as librarian to two cardinals. He visited Naples and the sites of Herculaneum and Paestum and managed to inspect the king's private collection amassed from these sites and from Pompeii. He has now published his *History of the Art of Antiquity* which classifies Egyptian, Persian, Etruscan and Greek art and sculpture. He writes rapturously of the Greek ideal of male beauty in sculpture as "noble and serene".

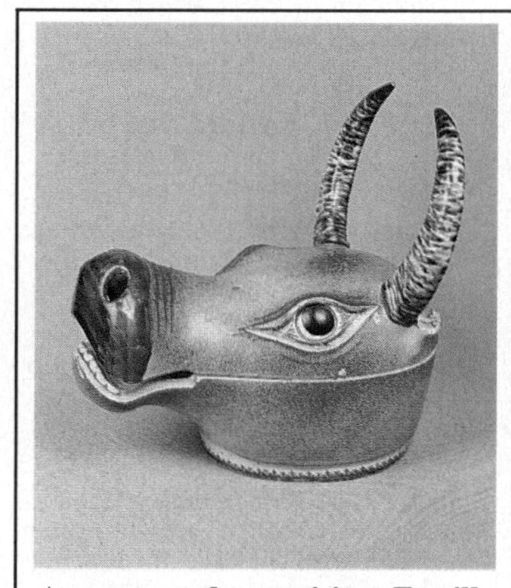

A rare and exquisite Famille Rose ox-head tureen, probably late 18th-century Qianlong porcelain. The top half of the head forms a detachable cover.

1765 (1765-1767)

India, 12 August 1765. Robert Clive receives revenue authority over Bengal from the Moghul emperor.

Austria, 18 August 1765. The Emperor Francis dies and his wife, Maria Theresa, retires from public life. Their eldest son becomes emperor as Josef II.

France, December 1765. On the death of the dauphin, his son Louis becomes heir to the throne.

St Petersburg, 1765. The Russian scholar and writer Mikhail Lomonosov dies. Known for his work in chemistry, electricity, mechanics and history, Lomonosov was instrumental in the founding of Moscow university in 1755.

South Atlantic, 1765. A British colony is established on the western of the two main islands in the Malouines (*Falkland Islands*). The first permanent settlement in the islands was created last year by the French.

Austria, 1765. When the Emperor Josef II cedes to the state the large private fortune bequeathed to him by his father, his mother, Maria Theresa, reassumes power and makes Josef co-regent.

England, 1765. James Watt refines and improves the steam engine invented by Thomas Newcomen by making the first engine with a separate condenser.

Denmark, January 1766. Christian II succeeds his father, Frederick V, as king.

France, 23 February 1766. The former king of Poland, Stanislas Leczinsky, the father-in-law of Louis XV and duke of Lorraine since 1737, dies in a fire at his palace in Luneville. His death heralds the end of Lorraine's nominal independence; the duchy now comes under French control.

Versailles, 3 March 1766. The parliament of Paris, which had pledged its support to its counterpart in Brittany, backs down at the Seance de la Flagellation, presided over by Louis XV, which repudiates the Brittany parliament.

London, 4 March 1766. Parliament repeals last year's Stamp Act, the cause of bitter and violent opposition in the colonies.

Louisiana, 5 March 1766. Antonio de Ulloa, the first Spanish governor of Louisiana, arrives in New Orleans.

Spain, June 1766. Charles III makes the count of Aranda prime minister with the task of restoring order after uprisings against his Italian advisers allegedly perpetrated by the Jesuits.

Canada, 24 July 1766. The Ottawa chief, Pontiac, signs a peace agreement with William Johnson, the superintendent of Indian affairs, at Fort Ontario, ending his three-year rebellion.

London, August 1766. Charles Townshend becomes chancellor of the exchequer in a new ministry headed by Lord Grafton and Lord Chatham (William Pitt).

New York, 19 December 1766. Thomas Gage, the commander in chief of the British forces, closes the New York Assembly, which has resolutely refused to comply with the controversial Quartering Act.

France, 1766. Louis de Bougainville embarks on a voyage to circumnavigate the world.

Philadelphia, 1766. Benjamin Franklin invents bifocal spectacles.

Philadelphia, 1766. Southwark theatre, the first building in the colonies designed expressly for the staging of drama, opens.

France, 1766. Gribeauval, a military engineer, initiates a reform of the French artillery.

Russia, 1766. Catherine II confirms the privileges of the nobility.

Germany, 1766. Frederick II sets up the Bank of Berlin.

England, 1766. The Irish writer Oliver Goldsmith publishes his novel *The Vicar of Wakefield.*

England, 1766. The architect Robert Adam builds a Neoclassical hall at Luton Hoo, near Bedford.

Germany, 1766. Gotthold Lessing publishes *Laokoon*, a work of aesthetics concerning the relationship between poetry and painting.

St Petersburg, 1766. The French sculptor Etienne Falconet is commissioned by Catherine II to produce an equestrian statue of Peter the Great for St Petersburg.

India, February 1767. Robert Clive, the British governor of the East India Company, is recalled.

Spain, 27 February 1767. The new prime minister, Aranda, expels the Jesuits from the country.

London, June 1767. Parliament passes the Townshend Acts, spearheaded by Charles Townshend, the chancellor of the exchequer, imposing new taxes on the colonies and suspending the New York Assembly until it complies with the Quartering Act.

Russia, 1767. Catherine II gathers a great commission, composed of a representative of all social classes except the serfs, with the aim of drawing up a code of reforms.

Indians riot as Jesuits are ordered home

An engraving of Spanish settlers putting natives to work in the New World.

Mexico City, 25 June 1767

It is now a year to the day since the papal order expelling the Jesuits from New Spain (*Mexico*). Several hundred are still here, waiting for ships back to Europe. Others are coming in from outlying parts, surrounded by soldiers and mostly kept away from the towns.

The Jesuits had established a moral and intellectual leadership here which was popular with both the Creole elite and the Indians. Their expulsion has led to many Indian uprisings which have been brutally put down. Ringleaders have been shot and their heads placed on pikes. Others have been whipped for days on end.

The viceroy is now trying to get the Jesuits out as quietly as possible since every time they are seen the Indians flock to their carriages and kiss their hands.

Burmese invaders destroy Thai capital

Thailand, 1767

Ayutthaya, the Thai capital, has fallen to Burmese invaders after a bitter and bloody two-year siege. Until 1752 Burma embroiled in continual civil war was no threat to its neighbours. But King Alaungpaya united the country, extending its frontiers to their former limits.

Although his 1760 invasion failed, his son's 1764 invasion has succeeded. First he took Chieng-mai; the Thai army was predictably defeated, and now his troops control the capital city.

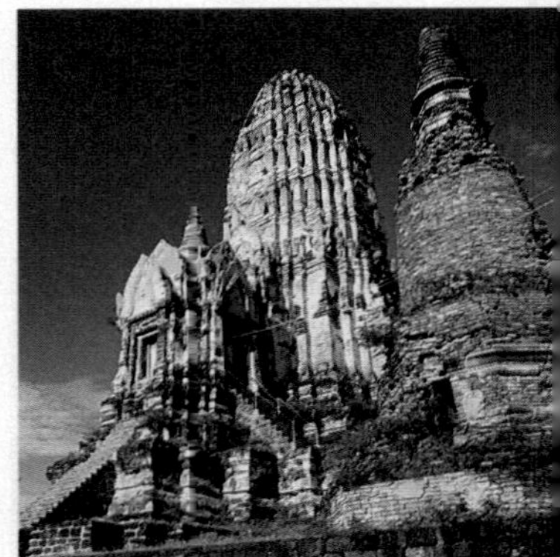

The ruins of Ayutthaya.

Composer dies, leaving 6,000 works

Hamburg, 25 June 1767

Georg Philipp Telemann has died aged 86. Born in Magdeburg, he could play four instruments by the age of ten and went on to become a universally acclaimed composer.

He wrote over 6,000 works – five times more than Bach – which range from opera to occasional music. Much of this vast output i[s] rather superficial, but there are als[o] hundreds of works of substance i[n] Telemann's fluent, elegant styl[e]. From 1721 he worked mainly a[s] music director of the city of Hamburg. He refused a similar post [a]t Leipzig in 1723, and the job went t[o] the city's third choice: J S Bach.

Emperor gives Clive power in Bengal

Clive receives the "diwani" of Bengal from the Moghul empire.

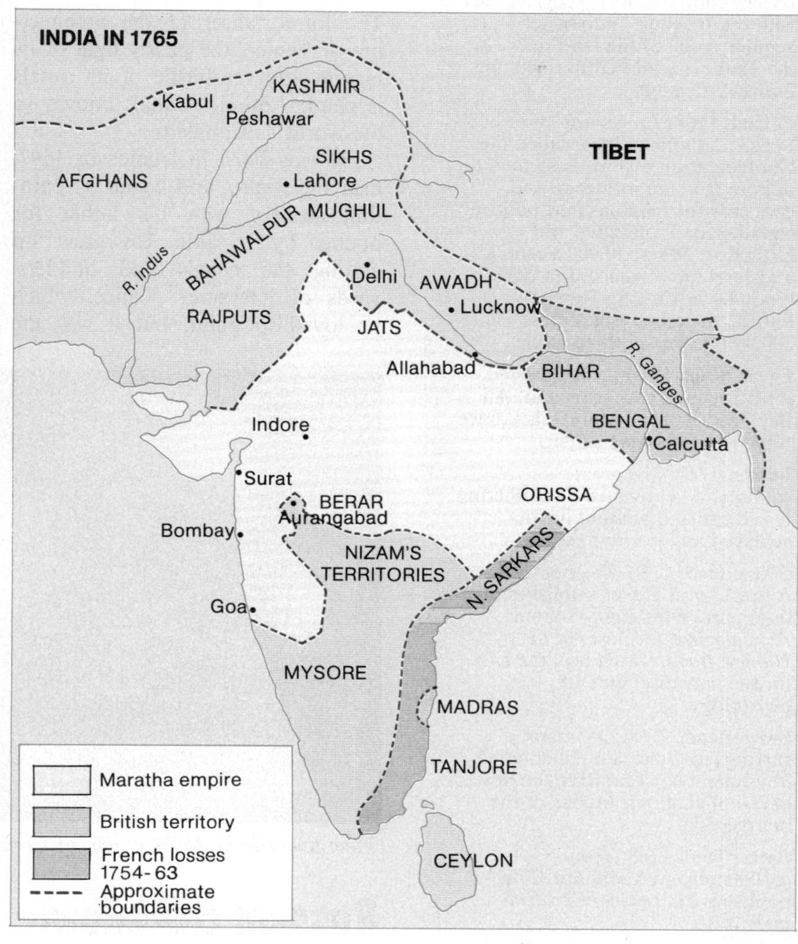

Bengal, India 1765

As the Moghul empire disintegrates and the French, British and a dozen Indian princes battle for the remains, Emperor Shah Alam has granted the British East India Company the *diwani* (revenue authority) of Bengal.

In 1756 the Moghul ruler of Bengal, where the British had established factories and trading posts, died. His grandson, Siraj-ud-Daula succeeded and went to war against the British and captured Calcutta, where 123 British prisoners died, incarcerated in the "Black Hole".

The company's administrator, Robert Clive, defeated first Siraj's allies, the French, and then Siraj, replacing him with the more pliable Mir Jafar. Clive left India in 1760.

Mir Jafar was soon overthrown by his son-in-law, the ambitious, able, and thoroughly anti-British, Mir Kasim, who hated the company for milking Bengal dry. War came in 1763 and Mir Kasim was beaten in five battles, the last of them at Baksar on 22 October 1764. Shah Alam, the Moghul emperor, wavered during the conflict, but with the British so victorious he came out in support of them.

In his new agreement, essentially a recognition of what is already a fact of arms, the emperor has given to Clive and the company total authority in Bengal. The result, many fear, will be anarchy, corruption and extortion as never before.

Clive himself is extremely happy and sees no cause for alarm. Unlike so many he has yet to make his Indian fortune. The *diwani* of Bengal should change that.

Inflammable air is discovered in water

London, 1766

The English chemist Henry Cavendish has discovered what he calls "inflammable air". It is the gas that with oxygen forms water, hence the term "hydrogen" as it has been called. Cavendish has made this important discovery through meticulous experimentation and observation. He has taken dilute acids and studied their action on zinc, iron and tin. In this way he finds that he obtains his "inflammable air" – a gas that burns very readily.

Cavendish has also determined the density of this colourless, odourless and tasteless substance. He also finds that when air is decomposed into oxygen and nitrogen there is a small residue remaining and the air may contain other, inert gases, yet to be identified.

Equipment used by Cavendish.

Empress calls for a modernised Russia

St Petersburg, 1767

Greatly influenced by the liberal ideas currently spreading through western Europe, the Czarina or Empress Catherine has appointed a high-powered commission of 564 deputies to make recommendations for the modernisation of the Russian state. The commission has been furnished with a lengthy set of instructions written by Catherine herself.

The deputies represent landowners, burghers, administrators, Cossacks and ethnic minorities (but not the church or serfs). They have been told to prepare a new code of laws, to recommend limiting landowners' powers over their serfs and to draw up a scheme for comprehensive education. Some western ideas, however, are not entirely to her taste. For instance, the English model for the division of powers into the executive, the legislature and the judiciary will be reworked and applied to make liberal despotism work more efficiently.

English in, French out, on German stage

Hamburg, 1767

A leading German drama critic, Gotthold Ephraim Lessing, has just produced a most successful comedy called *Minna von Barnhelm*. Lessing has frequently attacked the dominant influence of French classical dramatists in Germany and championed Shakespeare in their place as a model for less artificial drama. In this comedy there are real, living characters, Minna and her impossibly high-minded fiance, a Prussian officer with exaggerated ideas of honour. She cures him of his pride by being equally standoffish and inhuman.

The Hamburgers want to make their theatre a national theatre and have entrusted Lessing with the task. His work *Hamburgische Dramaturgie* or commentaries on dramatic theory and opposition to the style of Corneille and Voltaire are increasing his reputation which began with *Laokoon*, a treatise on art and poetry, which he published last year.

1767 (1767-1769)

New England, 28 October 1767. Boston leads a revival of the boycott of British goods.

Denmark, 1767. Christian VII, who was crowned king last year, extends his power over Schleswig and Holstein.

England, 1767. The chemist Joseph Priestley publishes the *History and Present State of Electricity*.

England, 1767. Laurence Sterne finishes *Tristram Shandy*, a long digressive comic novel which has been coming out in parts since 1760 and has delighted readers with its eccentricity and waywardness.

France, 1767. Georges Louis Leclerc Buffon publishes the last part of a 15-volume *Natural History*. The early volumes, which began to appear in 1749, caused a scandal by challenging certain ideas about the animal evolution.

Austria, 1767. The German musician Christoph Willibald von Gluck composes the opera *Alcestis*.

Austria, 1767. The Emperor Joseph II demands control over papal texts.

Boston, February 1768. Samuel Adams, the first American leader to deny the authority of the British Parliament over the colonies, calls for united action to oppose the Townshend Acts.

London, 10 May 1768. The imprisonment of the journalist John Wilkes as an outlaw provokes outbreaks of violence. Wilkes was recently returned to Parliament as member for Middlesex.

Corsica, 15 May 1768. By the treaty of Versailles, France purchases the island of Corsica from Genoa.

France, 16 September 1768. Rene-Nicolas de Maupeou is appointed chancellor in place of Guillaume de Lamoignon.

Boston, 1 October 1768. Lord Hillsborough, British secretary of state for the colonies, sends two regiments to Boston to quell unrest provoked by the Townshend Acts.

New Orleans, 28 October 1768. Germans and Acadians join French Creoles in an armed revolt aginst the Spanish governor, Antonio de Ulloa.

New York, 30 October 1768. Wesley Chapel, the first Methodist church in the colonies, is dedicated in New York City.

Istanbul, October 1768. Mustafa II, the Ottoman sultan, declares war on Russia, which has violated the 1711 treaty of Pruth by occupying Poland.

New York, 5 November 1768. William Johnson, the northern Indian commissioner, signs a treaty with the Iroquois Indians to acquire much of the land between the Tennessee and Ohio rivers for future settlement.

Poland, 1768. An organisation of Polish Catholic nobles, called the Confederation of Bar, is formed to oppose Russian influence and demands for religious and political equality for Protestants and Orthodox. When 20,000 Catholics and Jews are massacred in cold blood by advancing Russian armies, the rebels kill almost 200,000 people in three weeks.

Egypt, 1768. Having slaughtered the other beys two years ago, Ali Bey, leader of the Mamelukes since 1763, is proclaimed sultan.

Russia, 1768. The great commission convened by Catherine II is dismissed without having achieved any positive results.

Switzerland, 1768. The botanist Albrecht von Haller publishes the final part of his eight-volume *Physiological Elements of the Human Body*, which lays the bais for the new discipline of physiology.

Switzerland, 1768. Democratic stirrings in Geneva are embodied in a liberal edict limiting the power of the oligarchy is favour of the bourgeoisie.

Switzerland, 1768. The mathematician Leonhard Euler publishes his *Institiones calculi integralis*.

New England, 1768. The assembly of representatives in Massachusetts issues a petition in an attempt to organise a convention in Boston of all the colonies.

London, 1768. The Royal Academy of Arts is founded. The portrait painter Joshua Reynolds becomes its first president.

England, 1768. The English naval officer James Cook leaves Southampton aboard the *Endeavour* on a voyage to the Pacific.

England, 1768. Richard Arkwright perfects a spinning frame and sets up a mill in Nottingham driven by horses.

Spain, 1768. Charles III orders the distribution of common lands.

Corsica, 1769. After holding out against the French, who acquired Corsica from Genoa last year, the Corsican patriot Pasquale Paoli is overpowered and flees to England.

California, 1769. The Spanish begin to settle in California, establishing a mission at San Diego.

Canaletto dies in his beloved Venice

Venice, 20 April, 1768

The immortaliser of the architecture of Venice, the pearly light of its lagoon and the bustle of its canals is dead: Antonio Canal, known to the world as Canaletto.

He was born in Venice in 1697, near the Rialto, and began by painting scenery with his father for operas by Vivaldi. He grew up among the canals and builders' yards of backstage Venice, which he loved to paint, but it was the detailed and accurate views of the delicate architecture of St Mark's square and the Grand Canal which sold to the visiting noblemen doing the Grand Tour. An Englishman, Joseph Smith, banker, collector and English consul in the city, commissioned no fewer than 50 works for himself and many more for English visitors. In 1746 Canaletto went to England to paint the Thames and country houses, his only subjects other than his beloved Venice.

View towards St Mark's, one of Canaletto's many paintings of Venice.

Russian crackdown outrages the Poles

Poland, 1768

As many as 200,000 people have died in three weeks of bitter fighting which followed a Russian crackdown on Polish moves for greater political and religious freedom.

A tidal wave of anti-Russian anger swept Poland after the ruthless suppression of the *Seym* (parliament) by Russian grenadiers and the deportation of deputies and bishops. A group of squires had met in Bar, in the east, to proclaim a confederation of Catholic Christians to resist Orthodox Russia.

The Empress Catherine had one of her ex-lovers, Stanislaus Poniatowski, elected king while Russian troops stood by. But Stanislaus turned out to be a reformer and Prince Nikolai Repnin arrived from St Petersburg to impose Catherine's orders, followed by the Czarina's troops moved in. The latest bloodshed was sparked by a massacre of 20,000 Catholics and Jews.

Chemist publishes electrical history

Leeds, England, 1767

The British chemist Joseph Priest ley, who combines scientific re search with a ministry in the Pres byterian faith, has produced an im portant new book. *The History an Present State of Electricity, with Or ginal Experiments* is really an exten sion of the author's deep interest i education. He wrote this book i order to encourage others to ex plore the nature of electricity.

He has for instance looked at th capacity of different substances t conduct electricity, ranging each i a table of comparative conduc tivity. He is the first researcher notice the distinctive flash mark left when a spark discharges on metal surface, or, as they are no called, "Priestley's Rings". H most remarkable discovery, how ever, owes something to Newto Priestley has found that there is a inverse square law governing th force between electrical charges.

Radical Russian journal attacks serfdom

Moscow, 1769
A group of spirited young writers encouraged by Empress Catherine to launch literary journals on the model of Addison and Steele's *The Spectator* in England, seem to have got out of hand. Nikolai Novikov, who is 25, started *The Drone* and, despite his reputation as a moderate, promptly began attacking existing social conditions, including serfdom. The radical Aleksander Radishchev, a disciple of Rousseau, is writing a journal of a journey from St Petersburg to Moscow, in which he plans to attack both serfdom and autocracy. Novikov expects that his *Drone* will soon be banned.

Russian porcelain figures.

Corsican freedom fighter sent into exile

Tuscany, Italy, 1769
General Pasquale Paoli, the Corsican independence leader, and 300 of his supporters have landed in Tuscany after their crushing defeat by French forces.

The 44-year-old Paoli, who welded Corsica's warring clans into a nationalist front, is reported to be contemplating exile in England. A trained soldier and self-taught classicist, he admires the British system of government. Many of the institutions he set up during Corsica's brief independence were based on British models. For the French, who bought Corsica from the Genoese a year ago for two million livres, Paoli's choice of the traditional enemy, England, means that the threat of a nationalist revival cannot be ruled out.

English troops "show the flag" in Boston

British troops land at Boston, 1768. An engraving by Paul Revere.

Boston, 1 October, 1768
Watched by a sullen crowd, British troops landed in force here today and marched through the main street to the crash of drums and the sound of fifes. Men-of-war of the Royal Navy remained anchored offshore as the two infantry regiments – clearly determined on a show of strength – pitched their tents close to the centre of town.

Two other regiments have been ordered to Boston from Halifax by order of the secretary of state for the colonies after reports that the colony of Massachusetts, deeply resentful of the new Stamp Acts, was "teetering on the brink of anarchy". The disembarkation was made peacefully, however, and the army was greeted by Tory sympathisers and British officials who applauded General Thomas Gage, the commander of the British forces when he spoke of the "treasonable and desperate resolves" of the opposition leaders.

However, many moderate colonists view the billeting of troops on them in peacetime as a provocation.

London's greatest artists flock to join the Royal Academy

London, 10 December 1768
King George III today signed the founding document for the Royal Academy of Arts and declared himself its "patron, protector and supporter". Joshua Reynolds, who was elected its president, said: "One advantage, I venture to affirm, we shall have in our academy which no other nation can boast – we shall have nothing to unlearn."

He intends to give regular discourses on the Rules of Art to the students of the RA School, the first art school to be set up, in Somerset House. Beginning next year there will be an annual exhibition of the 40 Academicians' work. Among the founding RAs is Thomas Gainsborough, the Suffolk portrait painter, who has set up his studio in the fashionable world of Bath. Reynolds himself paints the cream of society in London at more than 100 guineas a portrait. Their rivalry is becoming acute. Reynolds has pointedly referred to Gainsborough as "the greatest landscape painter of the day".

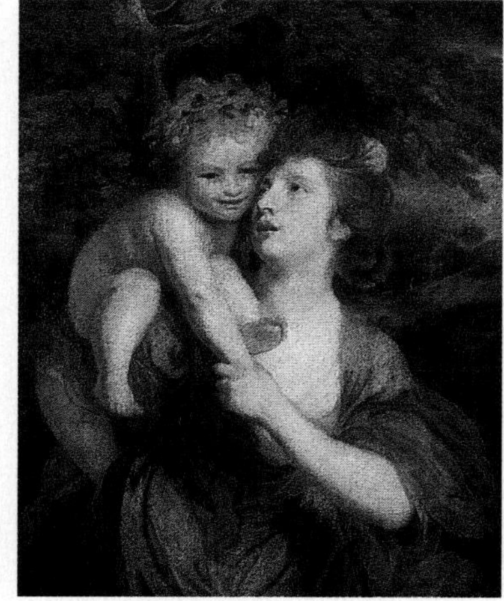
Mrs Hartley, one of the greatest paintings of Sir Joshua Reynolds.

Jane, Lady Whichcote, painted by Thomas Gainsborough.

Gainsborough often combines landscape with portrait painting, posing sitters against their country houses or out walking. Reynolds sticks to studio portraits in the grand manner, but excels at tender paintings of children. He wants to raise the status of painters and start a literary club with such distinguished members as Dr Johnson, Goldsmith, Boswell, Sheridan and David Garrick as members.

Outstanding atlas by Jesuits in China

China, 1769
The Jesuits, still pursuing a "flexible" attitude to their mission in China despite the disapproval of Rome, have produced an atlas of great accuracy. Called the "Qianlong Atlas" after the emperor, it is far superior to any European atlas.

From their arrival in China some 200 years ago, the Jesuits have been active in scientific work, especially astronomy and mathematics, seeing this as a way to lead the court towards Christianity.

This policy brought them into conflict with Chinese astronomers who became jealous when the Jesuits proved their calculations to be incorrect. But under the liberal patronage of the Manchu emperors Kangxi and now Qianlong, the Jesuits have prospered scientifically, even if such successes have not been accompanied by similar advances in their missionary work.

1769 (1769-1770)

North America, 20 April 1769. The Ottawa Chief Pontiac, who led a rebellion against the British from 1763 to 1766, is murdered by an Indian in Cahokia. It is rumoured that the British had him assassinated.

Rome, 17 May 1769. Giovanni Vicenzo Ganganelli is elected pope and takes the name Clement XIV. He succeeds Clement XIII, pope since 1758, who was elected through the efforts of the Jesuits but proved too weak to save them.

Virginia, May 1769. The House of Burgesses condemns the policies of London. Dissolved by the governor of Virginia, the House decides to boycott British merchandise.

Pacific, 17 June 1769. The English navigator James Cook observes the planet Venus from the island of Tahiti.

Pacific, September 1769. The Cook expedition circumnavigates New Zealand.

North Carolina, 7 November 1769. North Carolina joins South Carolina in adopting the Virginia Association's ban on trade with Britain pending the repeal of the Townshend Acts.

North America, 1769. The explorer Daniel Boone penetrates the fabled territory west of the Blue Mountains which the Iroquois Indians call Kentake (*Kentucky*).

Virginia, 1769. Thomas Jefferson, the scientist and free-thinker who was recently elected to the House of Burgesses, calls for the emancipation of slaves.

Ottoman Empire, 1769. Continuing their war against the Turks, which began last year, the Russians rout the main enemy army along the Dniester river and overrun Moldavia and Wallachia.

India, 1769. The French East India Company is dissolved.

Sweden, 1769. The "Hats" and the "Caps", the two major factions in the Stockholm government, come into conflict with King Adolphus Frederick.

North America, 1769. Virginia's boycott of British goods is joined by Maryland, South Carolina, North Carolina, Delaware and Connecticut.

France, 1769. Denis Diderot writes *D'Alembert's Dream*, a bold philosophical essay in which the author puts forward his materialist conception of the universe.

France, 1769. The French nobleman Louis Antoine de Bougainville completes a two-year voyage around the world. Seeking new lands for France, he explored Tahiti, Samoa and the New Hebrides.

London, 1769. John Wilkes – released after imprisonment as an outlaw last year – is twice re-elected as an MP, but Parliament, despite pro-Wilkes riots, declares his election void.

New York, 19 January 1770. A group of New Yorkers called the Sons of Liberty engage British troops in a pitched battle in New York city over British demands for compliance with the Quartering Act.

Britain, January 1770. Lord North, who is in favour of King George III wielding personal power, succeeds Lord Grafton as prime minister.

Boston, 5 March 1770. In what immediately becomes known as the Boston Massacre, British soldiers open fire on demonstrators, killing five.

London, 12 April 1770. Parliament repeals all the duties on the colonies imposed by Charles Townshend except the tea tax.

Pacific, 19 April 1770. The British expedition led by James Cook sights the east coast of Australia.

France, 16 May 1770. The dauphin Louis marries Marie Antoinette of Austria, the daughter of Maria Theresa.

Aegean, 6 July 1770. The entire Ottoman fleet is destroyed by the Russians at the battle of Cesme.

Ottoman Empire, August 1770. The Russians defeat a Turkish-Tartar army attempting to retake Moldavia and force it to retreat.

France, 7 December 1770. A disciplinary edict issued by Louis XV leads to the mass resignation of all members of the parliament of Paris, who are joined by certain members of the provincial parliaments.

Boston, 12 December 1770. The British soldiers responsible for the massacre in March are acquitted on murder charges.

France, 24 December 1770. Etienne Choiseul – who has controlled France's foreign policy, army and navy for over a decade since his appointment as foreign minister through the influence of Madame de Pompadour – falls from power. It is believed that his dismissal may have been caused by the hostility of Louis XV's new mistress Madame du Barry.

India, 1770. During a great famine in Bengal which began last year the population has been reduced from 29 million to 19 million.

Paris, 1770. The first public restaurant opens in Paris.

London, 1770. John Wilkes is elected lord mayor of London.

"Spinning Jenny" for the textile industry

Revolutionising the textile industry: Hargreaves' spinning jenny.

Yorkshire, England, 1769

The latest innovation in the textile industry comes from James Hargreaves who, for the past five years or so, has been working on his "spinning jenny". It consists of eight spindles – though this number will probably soon be increased to 16 and even more – all of which hold spinning yarn simultaneously. Thus, a single operator can handle far more thread than on a single spindle. Another inventor, Richard Arkwright, has just developed a water-powered loom called the water frame. Used in conjunction with Hargreaves' jenny, and other devices which are being developed, these technological innovations seem certain to transform working conditions and productivity in the textile industry.

Pragmatist North is new British premier

London, 1770

George III's new prime minister believes in letting sleeping dogs lie. An Old Etonian, Lord North is a classical scholar who did the grand tour after Oxford and speaks German, French and Italian. He has no new policies for home affairs, believing prudent housekeeping is all the country needs. Taxes will be held down because he fears that raising them would alarm the squires. In the Commons he intends to proceed with the measures that were in hand under his predecessor, the Duke of Grafton.

In foreign affairs he intends to stay out of Europe's quarrels; as to the colonies he will act with what is called quiet firmness. He is seeking a compromise with the Spanish, who have thrown the British out of the Falkland Islands. He has decided to retain the tea duty in the North American colonies and to present a Boston Ports bill.

A less than flattering cartoon of the Prime Minister, Lord North.

Russians destroy the Ottoman fleet

Mediterranean, July 1770
Military commentators are speaking of recent events in the eastern Mediterranean as a momentous turning point in the Ottoman empire's history. Two fleets of Russian warships, one commanded by a Scotsman, Admiral John Elphinstone, the other by a Russian, sailed from the Baltic down the Atlantic and into the Mediterranean, where they joined battle with the Turks off the island of Chios. In the engagement that followed, the Turkish fleet was annihilated.

On land, Russian armies have swept through the Turkish province of Moldavia and, with their capture of Bucharest, have been hailed by Christians as liberators from the Moslems.

The Turks said that they went to war because they were alarmed by Russian thrusts into Poland. But, in the wake of Russia's new successes, other great powers apart from the Turks are now wondering whether the ambitious and military-minded Empress Catherine will be content with her conquests.

Horror at German's mechanistic vision

London, 1770
Europe's religious and political establishment, including Voltaire, has been scandalised by the publication of the *System of Nature*, by the German-born writer Paul-Henri Dietrich, baron of Holbach.

The book has been published here under the pseudonym Mirabaud, because of French prejudice against the atheistic opinions of Holbach and his ally, Diderot. It is the most eloquent explanation yet of a godless, mechanistic philosophy of the world.

In *System of Nature*, Holbach argues that man is simply a physical being, organised to feel and think; that the soul is just the body considered relative to some of its functions; that morality is based on the need for reciprocal conduct to ensure social cohesion; and that evil arises simply from a mistaken vision of future happiness, which can be corrected by education.

Boucher's nude goddesses and cherubs delight French court

Spring, by Fragonard.

Feminine voluptuousness: Diana After the Hunt, by Francois Boucher, with buxom, semi-naked women masquerading as goddesses appealing directly and unashamedly to the viewer's sensuality.

Autumn, by Fragonard.

Sugary sexuality: Psyche crowning love, by Jean-Baptiste Greuze whose sentimental portrayals of young love have proved predictably popular.

Paris, 1770
French painting under Louis XV has shed many of its inhibitions. Francois Boucher, who died this year, appealed unashamedly to sensuality, filling his canvases with rosy-pink naked female forms disguised as goddesses, above all Venus – *The Birth of Venus, Venus after the Hunt, The Triumph of Venus* – invariably surrounded by cascades of fat-cheeked cherubs.

The lightness and artificiality of his charming compositions made ideal tapestries. He also made exquisite portraits of his discerning patron, the king's favourite, Madame de Pompadour.

Boucher's most brilliant pupil is Jean-Honore Fragonard, whose pictures idealise the life of pleasure and high fashion at court, exemplified by the inviting pose of the young girls in *The Swing, The Stolen Kiss* or *The Stolen Shift* and other playfully erotic subjects, saved from giving offence by their charm.

Uninterested in today's fashionable world are France's two *genre* painters, Chardin and Greuze, both baptised Jean-Baptiste. Chardin, the master of still-life, loves to paint food, children at play and scenes of everyday life and domestic toil, giving his works a soft-edged serenity. Greuze's sweet, sugary paintings of slightly wanton-looking young girl models are highly popular.

Sublime serenity: Boy Playing Cards, painted by Chardin.

1770 (1770-1772)

Denmark, 1770. With King Christian VII reduced to an imbecile condition by debauchery, his physician Johann Struensee – reputedly the lover of Queen Caroline Matilda – seizes power. Struensee replaces as leader Johann Bernstorff, who in 1767 negotiated with Catherine the Great of Russia a treaty whereby Denmark acquired the long-disputed lands of Holstein-Gottorp.

Greece, 1770. At the instigation of Russian agents, the inhabitants of the Peloponnese rise up against Ottoman rule. The revolt is put down by the Turks with Albanian support.

Austria, 1770. While peasant revolts rage in Bohemia, the Empress Maria Theresa publishes a new penal code.

North America, 1770. The campaign of non-importation of British goods is eased following the recent repeal of the Townshend duties.

England, 1770. The renowned portrait painter Thomas Gainsborough paints the *Blue Boy*.

England, 1770. The American-born artist Benjamin West paints *The Death of General Wolfe*, in which he defies precedent by depicting an event from recent history in contemporary costume.

South Atlantic, January 1771. Spain recognises British claims to a part of West Falkland in the Malvinas (Falkland Islands). A British colony was established on the islands in 1765, a year after the French founded the first settlement there. In 1766 Spain purchased the Malvinas from France and at first raised objections to the British colony.

Sweden, 12 February 1771. Gustavus III succeeds his father Adolphus Frederick as king.

North Carolina, May 1771. William Tryon, governor of North Carolina, puts down a group called the Regulators, who have been in rebellion against the Eastern elite in the colony since 1764.

England, July 1771. The poet Thomas Gray, author of the *Ode on a Distant Prospect of Eton College* and *Elegy in a Country Churchyard* dies. The latter was written at Stoke Poges, where his mother is buried and where he is to be buried beside her. In 1757, Gray refused the poet laureateship.

England, 17 August 1771. The Birmingham scientist Joseph Priestley discovers that oxygen is released from growing plants.

California, September 1771. Franciscans have founded three more permanent missions in California.

Scotland, 17 September 1771. The Scottish novelist Tobias Smollett dies. In 1741 he sailed as ship's surgeon on the expedition to Cartagena and described his experiences in the picaresque novel *Roderick Random*. This was followed by *Peregrine Pickle*, and *Humphrey Clinker*, which was published this year.

Crimea, 1771. Pursuing their war with the Turks, the Russians conquer the Crimea.

England, 1771. Captain James Cooke completes a voyage of exploration during which he circumnavigated New Zealand and took possession of the east coast of Australia for Britain. He returned home by way of Java and the Cape of Good Hope.

England, 1771. Richard Arkwright, the inventor of the spinning frame, opens England's first spinning factory, driven by water power, at Cromford in Derbyshire.

Scotland, 1771. A three-volume dictionary of arts and sciences edited by William Smellie and entitled the *Encyclopaedia Britannica* is published.

France, 1771. Nicolas Maupeou, who succeeded his father as chancellor of France in 1768, abolishes the parliaments and establishes new courts, incurring great unpopularity.

France, 1771. Gaspard Monge invents analytical geometry.

France, 1771. The chemist Antoine Lavoisier, a member of the French Academy, analyses the composition of the air.

Germany, 1771. Maximilian Joseph of Bavaria conducts a census of his kingdom's population.

Austria, 1771. Austria and the Turks sign a defence alliance against the Russians.

New England, 10 June 1772. Patriots led by Abraham Whipple seize and destroy the British customs boat *Gaspee* after it has run aground near Providence, Rhode Island.

England, 22 June 1772. During the case of James Somersett, a black slave – one of over 10,000 in England – who had escaped from his master, the lord chief justice Lord Mansfield declares that slavery is illegal on English soil.

Britain, July 1772. A crisis in the British banking system causes a reduction of credit in the colonies; as merchants begin selling off inventories, panic ensues.

St Petersburg, 5 August 1772. Russia, Prussia and Austria sign a treaty agreeing on the partition of Poland.

Poland stripped of a third of its lands

Poland, 5 August 1772

In a shameless act of brigandage, three East European monarchs have carved up the sovereign kingdom of Poland and seized one-third of its territory and about half its population.

Frederick II of Prussia had long coveted the wedge of territory known as West Prussia that separates Brandenburg from East Prussia. Catherine of Russia wants to see a weak Poland and to expand Russian power at the expense of Turkey. But Catherine's successes in the recent war with Turkey caused near panic in Austria.

Frederick calculated, rightly, that he could gain his ends by appealing to the greed of his fellow potentates. Catherine could take the slice of eastern Poland known as White Russia and calm Austrian fears by pulling out of the buffer territory of Danubian Turkey. The Austrians could have Silesia as a consolation prize for Frederick getting his hands on the most valuable of the spoils, economically and strategically: the maritime palatinate of West Prussia.

Stanislaw Poniatowski: Poland's last king. Will there be another?

Radical reform of French judicial system

Paris, 23 February 1771

Chancellor Rene-Nicolas Maupeou has today introduced a radical reform of France's legal system which is being seen in many quarters, not least in the nobility, as an attack on the law itself.

The Paris parlement which is recognised as being too large, slow and costly, has been broken up with new courts established at a number of cities to hear the civil and criminal cases previously dealt with by the Paris parlement.

Paris itself is restricted to judging cases concerning the Crown and the peers of the realm. The reform also abolishes the right to buy and sell judicial posts and bans all charges on litigants. The argument now rages: is the reform an act of despotism or progress?

Japanese anatomy

Japan, 1771

Scholars have taken part in the first scientific dissection ever held in Japan. Normally such tasks are left to men of the *eta*, an unclean caste who work as butchers and tanners.

Armed with a Dutch book on anatomy, the scholars were allowed to attend the opening of the executed body of a notorious woman criminal, "Old Mother Green Tea".

They found that her organs were exactly as described in the book. One of the scholars, Sugita Gempaku, has written an account of the dissection in which he points out that the Chinese had no names for many of the body's parts. He is now translating the Dutch book.

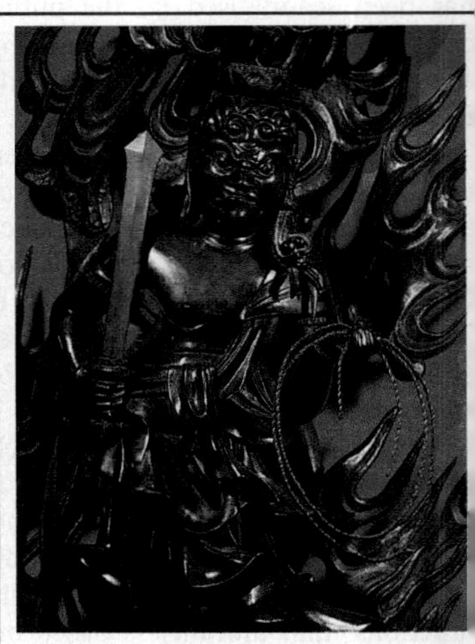

A figure from Japanese mythology: Fudo the Immovable. Detail from bronze figure of the 18th century.

British map the Great Southern Continent

Captain Cook lands at the amazingly lush anchorage he calls Botany Bay.

Portsmouth, England, 1770

After three years' sailing round the world, HMS *Endeavour* has come home. The crew of sailors and scientists under Captain James Cook, searching for the Great Southern Continent, visited Tahiti, discovered New Zealand and mapped the east coast of Australia, the first Europeans to see it.

They reached Tahiti, via Cape Horn, in April 1769. There they found an innocent Arcadia, its people the epitome of Jean-Jacques Rousseau's *Noble Savage*. "Upon the whole," wrote Cook, "these people seem to enjoy liberty in its fullest extent." When the crew sailed off three months later, leaving behind a respect for private property and several cases of venereal disease, the islanders begged them to stay.

From Tahiti the *Endeavour* sailed south, reaching New Zealand in September. Seven months later, on 19 April 1770, they sighted Australia. The crew's first hint of land had come three days earlier when they saw a butterfly.

Cook made his way up the eastern coast to a natural anchorage. "The country this morn rose in gentle sloping hills which had the appearance of the highest fertility, every hill seemed clothed with trees of no mean size," wrote Joseph Banks, the ship's scientist. So verdant is the coastline the crew call the anchorage Botany Bay.

Marathas install puppet emperor in Delhi

Delhi, 12 April 1771

Shah Alam, the Moghul emperor in exile under British protection in Allahabad, has been restored to the throne in Delhi. For this he must thank the Marathas and their leader, Mahadaji Sindhia, the kingmaker of India.

Driven from his capital by Rohilla Afghans, Shah Alam lived for years on British promises of support, which came to nothing. Realising the British preferred a weak Moghul emperor in exile to a strong one in Delhi, he played the Marathan card, and played it well. The Marathas, who came from the north-west quarter of the Dekhan Peninsula, are the warriors of India. Though defeated at Panipat in 1761, they have used the intervening decade to retrench. All those years they remained faithful to the emperor. When Shah Alam was threatened by revolts they crushed them. For the ruler in Allahabad they were a natural ally.

On 10 February the Marathas drove the Afghans out of Delhi and installed Shah Alam's son in temporary authority. Today, the emperor himself left Allahabad for Delhi, to the extreme discomfiture of the British.

An Indian prince entertains British officers at his house in Delhi. c.1820.

Columns of a young French genius revolutionise the art of war

France, 1771

The Count of Guibert, a military genius at the age of 28, has set out his revolutionary ideas in a book, the *Essai de Tactique* which seems destined to become the bible of officers who are pursuing new lines of military strategy.

Guibert, a fervent admirer of Frederick the Great, has produced what amounts to a formula for winning battles. He dismisses the old concept of the firing line as the main formation in battle and advocates the use of swift-moving columns.

A villager is recruited into the army. Painting by Jean-Baptiste Greuze.

These, he argues, will enable armies to manoeuvre freely on the battlefield instead of being tied to prepared positions. And, knowing his soldiers, he insists that their movements must be simple and easily learnt. He believes such columns will inevitably defeat any troops that are formed into line and thus can only change their position slowly. He also advocates the use of the column for its shock effect in attack. His proposals extend into all branches of warfare with new rules for cavalry, light infantry and even the baggage train.

Poor peasants' fury at ban on serfdom

Turin, 19 December 1771

Charles Emmanuel III has decided to make another attempt at abolishing serfdom in Savoy in a bid to improve the position of the rural classes and do away with feudalism. But the result is an outcry from his poorer peasants who have joined up with the nobles to oppose him.

For the second time in ten years he decreed that peasants could be released from Crown lands, and the nobles compensated through a fund raised from taxes and property sales. The idea has turned sour on Charles because the proposed changes will largely benefit the more prosperous peasants, the middle class and those who can afford to buy land.

1772 (1772-1773)

Denmark, 1772. Johann Friedrich Struensee is hung, drawn and quartered after the discovery of his affair with Caroline Matilda, the young queen. Struensee, who took power in Denmark in 1770 after obtaining the dismissal of the prime minister, Bernstorff, decreed the freedom of the Press, religious tolerance and the abolition of torture. His authoritarianism, however, won him numerous enemies.

India, 1772. The Englishman Warren Hastings, who has been a member of council in Calcutta and Madras, is appointed governor of Bengal.

England, 1772. James Cook embarks on a second voyage to the Pacific.

Scotland, 1772. The Scottish physician and botanist Daniel Rutherford establishes a distinction between "noxious air" (nitrogen) and carbon dioxide.

Russia, 1772. Catherine II abolishes the privileges of the Cossacks.

Portugal, 1772. The marquis of Pombal, the prime minister, introduces the teaching of exact sciences at the university of Coimbra. He has made important reforms in the army, agriculture and commerce.

France, 1772. *On Man* by the philosopher Claude Helvetius is published posthumously.

France, 1772. Denis Diderot publishes the *Supplement to Bougainville's Voyage*, the last section of the *Encyclopedie*.

Germany, 1772. The poet and dramatist Johann Wolfgang Goethe finishes his play *Gotz von Berlichingen*.

Germany, 1772. Christoph Martin Wieland publishes a political novel entitled *The Gilded Mirror*.

Sweden, 19 August 1772. Gustavus III, who became king of Sweden last year, destroys the rule of the parties in a bloodless military coup and re-establishes an absolute monarchy.

Mexico, 22 August 1772. The provinces of northern Mexico (including Texas) are separated from the rest of the country under a new authority as the Provincias Internas.

New England, 2 November 1772. In the face of a growing number of clashes between the English authorities and the settlers over the imposition of customs measures, radical Americans set up Committees of Correspondence.

Antarctica, 17 January 1773. Captain James Cook is the first person to cross the Antarctic Circle.

London, 10 May 1773. To keep the troubled East India Company afloat, Parliament passes the Tea Act. The Act allows the company to export tea directly to the colonies and keeps the Townshend duty of threepence a pound on tea.

London, 1 September 1773. Phillis Wheatley, a 20-year-old Negro slave from Boston, publishes a collection of poetry, *Poems on Various Subjects, Religious and Moral*, in London. The book had been rejected by American publishing houses.

Russia, September 1773. An army of Cossacks, led by Yemelyan Pugachev, besiege the towns of Orenburg and Kazan. Pugachev claims to be the deposed Czar Peter III, who was killed in the coup of 1762.

Istanbul, December 1773. Abdul-hamid succeeds his father, Mustafa III, as sultan of the Ottomans.

Rumania, 1773. Attempts to end the Russo-Turkish war at the peace congress of Bucharest end in failure.

Rome, 1773. Pope Clement XIV suppresses the Jesuit order.

India, 1773. Under a Regulating Act the British Parliament attempts to control the East India Company. Warren Hastings is made governor-general with super-intending authority over the presidencies of Madras and Bombay as well as Calcutta. The crown asserts the right to set up a supreme court in Calcutta.

Afghanistan, 1773. On the death of Ahmad Shah Durrani, he is succeeded by his son Timur Shah.

England, 1773. Robert Clive, suspected of embezzlement during his time in India, is acquitted on account of services rendered to the nation.

England, 1773. Work begins on the first iron bridge, at Coalbrookdale on the river Severn.

England, 1773. The brothers Robert and James Adam publish their *Works of Architecture*, the manifesto of the Neoclassical movement.

England, 1773. *She Stoops to Conquer* by Oliver Goldsmith is performed for the first time.

St Petersburg, 1773. The French writer Denis Diderot arrives in St Petersburg at the invitation of Catherine the Great.

Spain, 1773. The prime minister Pedro Aranda falls from power and is sent to France as ambassador.

Near East, 1773. Revolts in Egypt and Syria against Turkish rule are put down.

Spain pressurizes Pope to ban Jesuits

Rome, 21 July, 1773

Pope Clement XIV has issued a bull, *Dominus ac Remptor Noster*, abolishing the Society of Jesus. Clement was once a fervent admirer of the Jesuits and dedicated one of his first books to their founder. However, he has given in to the pressure from the kings of Spain and France. Vatican sources say that he sent a draft of the bull to the Spanish embassy for approval.

Their strongly argued theological views have sometimes made enemies for the Jesuits in Rome, but it is their activities overseas which have led to today's move. In China the row over the Chinese rites reflected fears that the Jesuits had gone too far in trying to secure *rapprochement* with Confucianism.

In New Spain (*Mexico*) their success brought their downfall. They had established an intellectual, moral and political leadership; they also won the admiration of Creole leaders and the love of the Indians whose material lot they helped to better. This was all too much for the king of Spain who saw them as a threat to authority.

Pope Clement XIV, former admirer, now scourge of the Jesuits.

Four scientists all discover noxious air

Europe, 1772

A new gas, "phlogisticated" air, or "nitrogen", as it is generally called, has been "discovered" independentley by four chemists. A Scot, Daniel Rutherford, who calls it "noxious" air; a Swede, Carl Scheele; and two English chemists Joseph Priestly and Henry Cavendish. Rutherford's technique for isolating this gas is noteworthy. He obtains nitrogen by subtracting from air those components easily removed by combustion or respiration.

Island totem: this grotesque but powerful figure carved out of wood represents Ku, the war god of the Hawaiian islands.

Battle symbol: this feather image of Ku, also known as Kakailimokum is carried into battle to strike fear into the enemy.

Encyclopedia infuriates church and state

Turning the cloth for Gobelins Tapestries: illustration from Encyclopedie.

France, 1772

The *Encyclopedie*, promoter of the latest intellectual ideas, is coming under increasingly severe attacks from the Establishment here. The government resents its criticism of despotism and intolerance, the Roman Catholic church condemns its denial of organised religion.

The *Encyclopedie* has been forbidden to Catholic readers since it was placed on the Roman Index in 1759. Those who read or own it face automatic excommunication. Much of this hostility stems from the publication in 1758 of "On the Mind" by Claude-Adrien Helvetius, an enthusiastic encyclopedist. The book denied the existence of God and infuriated the authorities by stating that all men are equal. Unsurprisingly it has been banned and burnt.

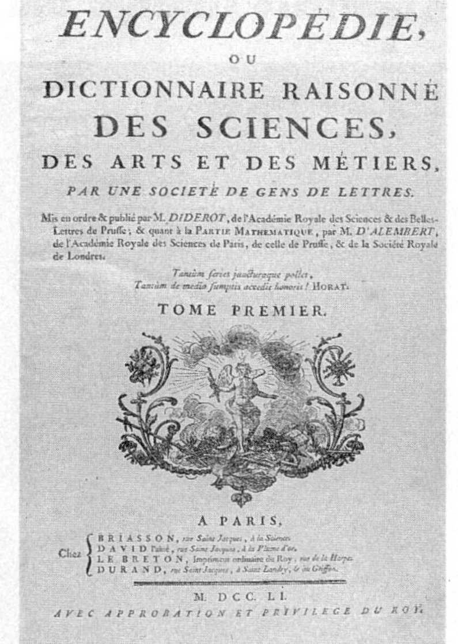

ENCYCLOPÉDIE,
OU
DICTIONNAIRE RAISONNÉ
DES SCIENCES,
DES ARTS ET DES MÉTIERS,
PAR UNE SOCIETÉ DE GENS DE LETTRES.

Mis en ordre & publié par M. *DIDEROT*, de l'Académie Royale des Sciences & des Belles-Lettres de Prusse; & quant à la PARTIE MATHEMATIQUE, par M. *D'ALEMBERT*, de l'Académie Royale des Sciences de Paris, de celle de Prusse, & de la Société Royale de Londres.

Tantùm series juncturaque pollet,
Tantùm de medio sumptis accedit honoris! HORAT.

TOME PREMIER.

A PARIS,
Chez BRIASSON, *rue Saint Jacques, à la Science.*
DAVID l'aîné, *rue Saint Jacques, à la Plume d'or.*
LE BRETON, Imprimeur ordinaire du Roy, *rue de la Harpe.*
DURAND, *rue Saint Jacques, à Saint Landry, & au Griffon.*

M. DCC. LI.
AVEC APPROBATION ET PRIVILEGE DU ROY.

The Encyclopedie, of Diderot and d'Alembert. The title page.

Egyptian leader mortally wounded

Cairo, 8 May, 1773

Ali Bey, the increasingly autocratic ruler of Egypt since 1760, has died, a week after being wounded in a battle with rebels led by Abu'l-Dhahab. In a tempestuous reign, he was the first sheikh of the mamelukes, or former soldier-slaves, to challenge Ottoman authority. Installed as the premier bey in Egypt in 1760 by Abd al-Rahman Kahya, leader of the Qazdughliyya clan, Ali Bey began rapidly to eliminate opponents.

Abd al-Rahman Kahye was banished to the Hijaz, then Salih Bey exiled to Gaza. His commander Husayn Bey Kashkash deserted to Cairo, to build his own faction. Briefly isolated and banished to Syria, Ali Bey returned, reconciled with Salih Bey, to defeat his enemies. Kashkash and his ally Khalil Bey were defeated and put to death, then Salih Bey was assassinated.

Ali Bey put mamelukes in powerful posts instead of Ottomans. But when he attempted the conquest of Syria, he overreached himself, and his forces, led by Abu'l-Dhahab, rebuilt the Ottoman alliance.

East India Company gets opium monopoly

Calcutta, 1773

The British-owned East India Company has obtained a monopoly of the production and sale of opium in Bengal, where "Patna" and "Benares", the two most popular forms of opium in China, are grown.

British and Portuguese merchants have been exporting opium to China for 50 years. Until recently, however, profits were small. The East India Company used cotton as a staple to exchange for China tea, and cotton was where the profits were to be found.

Yet with ever-rising demand from the millions of customers, opium has taken over from cotton as the staple crop for export. Thousands of tons are shipped yearly to China. The Emperor of China may have banned opium, but the market remains. Shipping is left to "private traders", who run the contraband up the Canton River to Whampoa where it is distributed.

Workers in an opium den cut up balls of the drug to mix with tobacco.

American colonies defy British ruling

Boston, Mass., November 1772

Radical American colonists, infuriated by what they see as attacks on their liberties, are banding together to defy the British crown. Colonists in Massachusetts and Virginia, are forming "committees of correspondence", expressly designed to safeguard colonial rights.

The depth of feeling was made absolutely clear when a British schooner, commanded by lieutenant William Dudingstone, was burned to the waterline by American patriots after it had seized local fishing boats and their cargoes.

A furious British Government demanded that the culprits should be brought to England for trial, but the chief justice of Rhode Island, Stephen Hopkins, refused to sanction their arrest. Now the British have stated that colonial judges should be paid by the Crown and not dependent on colonial salaries.

Swedish sovereign stages coup d'etat

Stockholm, 19 August 1772

In less than an hour, Gustav III, backed by a handful of Guards officers of the Stockholm garrison, today staged a *coup d'etat* that has been hailed by cheering crowds as a blow for freedom. The king says he acted to establish himself as a constitutional monarch and to curb the extremes of Parliament.

When Gustav succeeded to the throne last year he sought to set up a government of national reconciliation between the rival parties: the self-proclaimed party of the people, the Caps – the pacifist "nightcaps" as their opponents dub them – and their opponents, the Hats, named for the tricorn hats worn by army officers. But the dominant Caps refused to co-operate, preferring tc pursue extremist policies while the country's economy declined. Gustav had no option but to make his move.

1773 (1773-1775)

Boston, 16 December 1773. Patriots board three British tea ships anchored in Boston harbour, hack open all the tea chests and throw their contents into the harbour.

England, 4 April 1774. The playwright and novelist Oliver Goldsmith dies.

France, 10 May 1774. Louis XV dies and is succeeded as king by his grandson Louis XVI.

London, 20 May 1774. Parliament passes the Coercive Acts to punish the American colonists for their increasingly belligerent and anti-British behaviour. Among other things, the Acts close the port of Boston and reduce the power of the Massachusetts legislature.

London, 20 May 1774. Parliament passes the Quebec Act, enlarging the boundaries of Quebec to include French-speaking settlements (*in Ohio and Illinois*).

Ottoman Empire, June 1774. The Russians defeat the Turks in a battle near Shumla, almost wiping out the Turkish army.

London, 2 June 1774. Parliament reactivates the Quartering Act of 1765, requiring that all colonies provide housing for British troops.

France, 12 June 1774. Louis XVI ends the exile of the duke of Choiseul, a former minister of Louis XV famous for his reformist policies, which the king had condemned in 1770.

France, 20 July 1774. Louis XVI reshuffles his council, appointing the count of Maurepas minister of state and the count of Vergennes foreign secretary.

Russia, July 1774. The Cossack leader Yemelyan Pugachev captures Kazan, to which he laid siege last year.

Ottoman Empire, 16 July 1774. The Russians and the Turks sign the treaty of Kuchuk-Kainardji, ending their six-year war. Moldavia and Wallachia are returned to Turkish control and the Crimea becomes independent. Russia gains control of much of the northern Black Sea coast.

France, 13 September 1774. Turgot, the new controller of finances, urges the king to restore the free circulation of grain in the kingdom.

Russia, September 1774. The Cossack rebels led by Yemelyan Pugachev are decisively defeated by Catherine the Great's forces, ending their year-long revolt.

Philadelphia, 26 October 1774. A congress of colonial leaders criticises British influence in the colonies and affirms their right to "life, liberty and property".

Paris, 12 November 1774. Louis XIV recalls the magistrates who were exiled by Maupeou in 1771 and re-establishes parliament. Maupeou himself was dismissed as chancellor in August.

Virginia, 1 December 1774. George Washington signs the Fairfax Resolves, which bar the importation of slaves and threaten to halt all colonial exports to Britain.

New Hampshire, 14 December 1774. In the first military action by colonists against the forces of the crown, the lawyer John Sullivan and a group of militia capture Fort William and Mary and seize gunpowder and weapons.

Italy, 1774. The anatomist Anne Manzolini dies. She became professor of anatomy at the university of Bologna in 1760 and was an expert in making anatomical models from wax.

Italy, 1774. Charles III, king of the Two Sicilies, commissions Luigi Vanvitelli to build a palace at Caserta in Campania to rival that of Versailles.

Germany, 1774. Goethe's *The Sorrows of Young Werther* inspires a wave of hopeless passion among the book's admirers.

Austria, 1774. The physician Franz Mesmer uses hypnotism for therapeutic purposes. Immediately his name is perpetuated as the terms "mesmerism" and "mesmerise" are coined.

Austria, 1774. Maria Theresa grants religious tolerance to the non-Catholics of Hungary.

Austria, 1774. The composer Wolfgang Amadeus Mozart writes his *Mass in F Major*.

Paris, 1774. The German composer Gluck stages his first French opera *Iphigenia in Aulis* and the equally successful *Orpheus*.

France, 1774. The painter Jacques Louis David is awarded the Prix de Rome for his work *Artiochus et Stratonice*.

England, 1774. The German-born English astronomer William Herschel builds a great telescope.

England, 1775. Captain James Cook returns home after completing his second voyage of exploration. He circumnavigated Antarctica, discovered the South Sandwich Islands and annexed South Georgia, where he reported the presence of large herds of seals.

England, 1775. The engineer James Watt sells his first steam engine, to the industrialist John Wilkinson.

Brazil, 1775. The church of Notre Dame is constructed in Rio de Janeiro.

Cossack rebel betrayed and executed

Moscow, 21 January 1775

A disgruntled army deserter, who claimed to be the husband of the Empress Catherine and stirred up a peasant rebellion, has been captured, brought to Moscow in a cage and executed. At the start, the Cossack Emelian Pugachev had a price of 500 roubles on his head. Within weeks, as the rebels captured forts on the Volga and the Ural, and were joined by Moslem Bashkirs, the reward soared to 28,000 roubles. Pugachev was exploiting the genuine grievances of the serfs, whose conditions have worsened under Catherine. But his own Don Cossacks became disillusioned with him and handed him over to government forces.

Pugachev, the Russian Pretender, is brought to Moscow in a cage.

Chemists change old beliefs in England

Experiment with a Pump, painting by Joseph Wright (1734-97) of Derby.

England, 1775

Recent chemistry research is drastically altering many long-held beliefs. In England, Joseph Black has discovered that the air contained in some medical substances differs from that in the atmosphere. Henry Cavendish has studied "inflammable air" – hydrogen – which he adds to the two types of air or "gases" identified by Black.

But Joseph Priestley has identified and described seven individual gases: oxygen; hydrogen chloride; ammonia; nitric oxide; nitrous oxide; nitrogen peroxide and sulphur dioxide. Priestley's work gives a tremendous boost to the developmen[t] of chemical investigation. Studie[s] of oxygen, for example, show i[t] greatly facilitates combustion.

Frenchman Henri Lavoisier' studies of water show it to be reducible to two gases. Water, then, i[s] no longer a prime element.

These developments are accom[panied] by major breakthroughs i[n] other scientific fields. Last year th[e] German-born English astronome[r] William Herschel built a powerfu[l] new telescope, while this year Sco[t]tish engineer James Watt sold hi[s] first engine powered by steam to th[e] industrialist John Wilkinson.

A tea party at Boston

Destruction of the tea cargoes in Boston harbour by colonists.

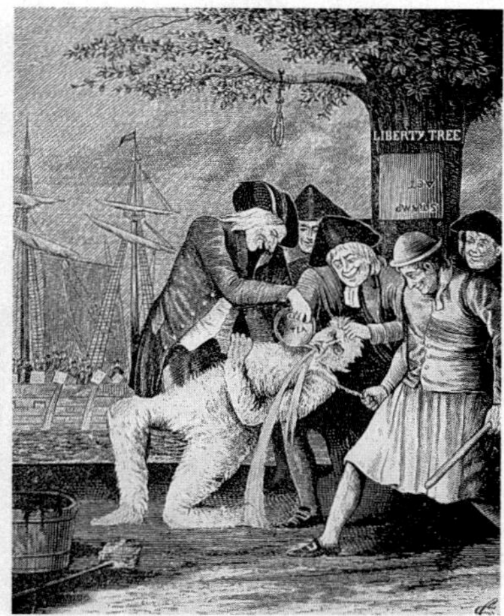

A Boston tax collector tarred and feathered. British cartoon, 1774.

Boston, Mass., 16 December 1773
Brandishing axes and whooping like Indians, their faces disguised with bronze paint, a thousand patriots ran from the Old South Meeting House here tonight and boarded three British ships loaded with tea. The crews were unharmed; but, within a matter of minutes, the *Dartmouth*, the *Eleanor* and the *Beaver* had been stripped of their cargo and hundreds of tea-chests had been emptied into the harbour.

As the sea-level fell, leaving the tea piled up on the beaches "like haystacks" – according to witnesses – no one can doubt that the tide of revolution is close at hand. As Bostonians wait for a British reaction, their leaders see this display of rebellion as the beginning of a major campaign for colonial freedom. Josiah Quincy, a patriot leader, saw it leading to "the most trying and terrific struggle this country ever saw" and even the moderate John Adams clearly sees it as an epoch in history. "The people should never rise," he said, "without doing something to be remembered, something notable and striking. This destruction of the tea is so bold, so daring, so firm, intrepid and inflexible, and it must have important consequences."

As tidings of what is already becoming known as the "Boston Tea Party" spreads through the North American colonies and fast ships race to England with the news, war now seems inevitable with settlers and established colonists vowing never to pay British taxes.

The duty was imposed to capitalise on a massive "mountain" of tea which has piled up in London – threatening the East India Company with bankruptcy.

A tax of three pence a pound on her tea

There was an old lady lived over the sea,
And she was an Island Queen;
Her daughter lived off in a new country,
With an ocean of water between,
The old lady's pockets were full of gold,
And never contented was she,
So she called on her daughter to pay her a tax
Of three pence a pound on her tea
Of three pence a pound on her tea

The tea was conveyed to the daughter's door,
All down by the ocean's side;
And the bouncing girl poured out every pound
In the dark and boiling tide.
And then she called out to the Island Queen,
"Oh Mother, dear Mother," quoth she,
"Your tea you may have when 'tis steeped enough,
But never a tax from me".

Colonists will ban tea and make war

Philadelphia, 5 September 1774
In a new act of defiance against the hated Tea Bill, delegates from all 13 colonies are meeting here today in what has already been dubbed a "continental congress" – called by the florid-faced and raucous rebel from Boston, Sam Adams. The delegates are meeting in secret, but is believed they will introduce measures to ban the consumption of tea throughout the colonies.

In several northern states, the "Sons of Liberty" are attempting to enforce an embargo of everything British. Some traders have been tarred and feathered; and others have had their homes burned. An ominous sign is the raising and training of independent companies of militiamen in every county. The colonies are preparing for war.

Turks humiliated in treaty with Russia

Ottoman empire, 16 July 1774
Russia's expansion at the expense of the Ottoman empire received a boost today when the Russians and Turks signed the treaty of Kuchuk-Kainardji, ending a six-year war between the two empires.

The treaty gives Russia lands and ports around the northern Black Sea coast, breaking the Turkish control of the sea. Russia has forced the Turks to recognise the independence of the Crimea, formerly controlled by the sultan, although he remains caliph (spiritual leader) of Crimean Moslems.

The Russians have also secured the right to build and protect an Orthodox church in Istanbul. This neatly furnishes them with a pretext for future interference in Turkish internal affairs.

Goethe inspires wave of suicides

Lotte and Werther. An illustration from Goethe's controversial novel.

Frankfurt, 1774
Every author yearns to write a book that will truly move the public but few can have achieved so frightening a success as has Johann Wolfgang Goethe, a young poet whose autobiographical novel, *The Sorrows of Young Werther*, has triggered a wave of suicides throughout Europe.

The story is simple: a sensitive artist, at odds with society, falls in love with a girl who is engaged to someone else. It ends tragically and draws unshamedly on Goethe's own passion for Charlotte Buff, a friend's fiancee.

The mix of Werther's rejection of the pains of real life and his glorification of the mystical force of nature seems to have captured young Europe's imagination. Often the identification is harmless – teasets with scenes from the novel are highly popular, men ape Werther's blue coats and yellow breeches – but copying Werther's suicide sets a grimmer tone.

1775 (1775-1776)

London, 9 February 1775. Parliament declares Massachusetts to be in a state of rebellion.

Massachusetts, 21 February 1775. As the conflict with Britain worsens, the committee of public safety votes to buy military equipment for 15,000 men.

Pennsylvania, February 1775. Thomas Paine, who arrived last year from England, at the urging of Benjamin Franklin, founds the *Pennsylvania Magazine.*

Paris, 23 February 1775. Beaumarchais' new comedy, *The Barber of Seville*, is a great success.

London, 22 March 1775. The statesman Edmund Burke makes a speech in the House of Commons urging the government to adopt a policy of reconciliation with America.

London, 13 April 1775. Lord North extends the New England Restraining Act to South Carolina, Virginia, Pennsylvania, Maryland and New Jersey. The act forbids trade with any country other than Britain and Ireland, and will be bitterly resented.

Massachusetts, 14 April 1775. General Gage gets orders to use force to implement coercive acts and halt colonial military build up.

Philadelphia, 14 April 1775. Benjamin Franklin and Dr Benjamin Rush form the Society for the Relief of Free Negroes Unlawfully Held in Bondage, the first colonial anti-slavery group.

Massachusetts, April 1775. Fighting breaks out between English and American troops – the Lexington massacre in Massachusetts is followed by more bloody outbreaks at Concord.

France, 28 April 1775. Jacques Necker, a Genevan banker, publishes a book on the grain trade and laws, attacking the finance minister Turgot's reformist policies.

North Carolina, 20 May 1775. Mecklenburg is the first colony to declare its independence.

Massachusetts, 12 June 1775. General Gage, imposing martial law, proclaims all armed colonists traitors and offers pardons to those who swear allegiance to the crown.

Massachusetts, 17 June 1775. British troops led by General William Howe defeat colonists at the battle of Bunker Hill. They take the stronghold overlooking the Charleston peninsula and Boston, but it is a costly victory.

Boston, 26 June 1775. George Washington of Virginia arrives to assume command of the continental army.

France, 21 July 1775. Malesherbes, whose remonstrances against royal abuses in 1771 led to banishment from court, but who was recalled with the accession of Louis XVI, is appointed secretary of state to the royal household.

London, 23 August 1775. King George III rejects an offer of peace, declaring that the colonies are in open rebellion against the crown.

Philadelphia, 13 October 1775. Congress bars Negroes from the continental army.

France, 27 October 1775. The count of St Germain, an ardent supporter of the enlightened Prussian king Frederick II's military strategy, is appointed secretary of state for war.

Virginia, 17 November 1775. Governor Dunmore offers freedom to slaves who join the loyalist army, thus losing the support of most planters, who see slaves as vital to their livelihood.

Massachusetts, 31 December 1775. Fearing the response to Lord Dunmore's offer to slaves, George Washington orders recruiting officers to accept free Negroes in the army.

Ethiopia, 1775. James Bruce returns to Britain from a pioneer British exploration of Ethiopia and the Blue Nile to contribute to cartography and trade intelligence of the area.

France, 1775. Bread shortages and a poor harvest, cause violent unrest to break out in the Champagne, Brie and Paris regions. This so-called "flour war" compromises finance minister Turgot's reform plans.

Austria, 1775. The Empress Maria Theresa's foreign policies ensure the Turkish surrender of the province of Bukovina, north of Transylvania. At home she issues a patent abolishing the corvee (tenants' obligation to work for landlords so many days a year) in Bohemia and the Austrian states.

Russia, 1775. Catherine II introduces major administrative reforms by which Russia is divided into 50 governments, which are then subdivided into districts. She gives assurances guaranteeing the freedom of trade and industry.

Palestine, 1775. Abul-Dhahab of Egypt invades Palestine on behalf of his Ottoman masters.

Lisbon, 1775. Lisbon's Comercio Square is opened, following the rebuilding of the Portuguese capital after the earthquake of 1755.

France, 1776. The marquis of Abbans experiments with a steam-powered boat on the river Saone.

Watt puts power of steam into industry

The steam-engine, important invention of James Watt, of Glasgow.

Birmingham, England, 1776
Steam-engine technology has made some crucial strides. The latest innovations come from James Watt, a former instrument maker in Glasgow University. When he was asked to repair a demonstration model of Thomas Newcomen's steam-pumping engine, Watt thought of ways in which this basic machine, first constructed in 1712 for use in the mines, could be improved.

One was the notion that the steam condenser could be kept separate from the cylinder, thereby lessening steam and fuel consumption.

In order to finance the development of his ideas, Watt has entered into a partnership with Matthew Boulton, owner of an engineering works at Soho near Birmingham.

From the outset, industrialists such as Cornish mine owners have been interested in using their engines for pumping purposes.

One effective innovation developed by Watt is the automatic regulator which maintains a constant speed in the engine shaft. In this way the straight-line pumping action of the piston is converted into a smooth and regular circular motion.

Spain rejigs South American policy

Peru, 1776
A new administrative system has been imposed on the viceroyalty of Peru by Spain. In an attempt to counter native independence movements in the New World, and to beat off British interests in the area, the new autonomous viceroyalty of La Plata has been created. Centred on Buenos Aires, the viceroyalty will be well equipped to protect the southern mainland. The estuary of the river Plata offers both access to the interior, and a port for ships patrolling the southern sea routes.

The new system is bound to benefit the economy and Buenos Aires, already a thriving centre, appears to be set upon a period of unprecedented prosperity.

The serene luxury of India's royalty is captured in this painting of a prince and his mistress.

War flares in America

The Battle of Bunker Hill, 17 June 1775. Painting by Charles McBarron.

Charlestown, Mass., 17 June 1775
British soldiers are in control of the key strategic hills overlooking the Charlestown peninsula and Boston, but their success has been bought at a high price. Some 1,000 British soldiers were killed in the battle for Bunker Hill – three times the casualties borne by the defeated Americans. And there is no sign that this British victory has quenched the spirit of the rebellious colonists.

It is barely three months since the first shot was fired in what has become the Americans' war for their independence from British rule. No one knows who fired that first shot. It could have been one of General Thomas Gage's British redcoats; or a "Minuteman" – a greenjacketed American patriot. The Patriots had been warned that the British were marching by a Boston dentist and engraver, Paul Revere – a "Son of Liberty" whose society had been preparing for just such a British move for several months. A single lantern hanging in a church tower was the signal for Revere to ride the 20 miles to warn that the British were coming to seize a Patriot arsenal. The British redcoats were forced to retreat to Boston where they were then besieged. British plans to counter-attack by seizing the hills were discovered by the colonists who were waiting for the redcoats. British reinforcements eventually won the day, but the war is far from over.

Scottish traveller returns from Ethiopia

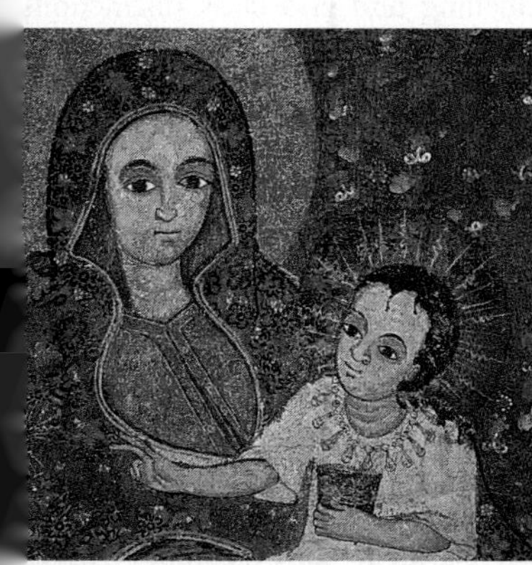

Virgin and Child, painted on cloth. Eighteenth-century Coptic art from Gondar, in Ethiopia.

London, 1775
A Scottish laird, James Bruce, has arrived in London claiming to have discovered the source of the river Nile. Reaching the Ethiopian capital, Gondar, in 1769, he befriended Ras Michael, the power behind the throne, who flayed and stuffed his enemies. Bruce stayed two years, and visited Lake Tana, but travel was limited due to civil war.

"Africa is, indeed, coming into fashion," announced essayist and traveller Horace Walpole, but lexicographer Dr Samuel Johnson, whose opinion is always to be noted, thinks the man a fraud.

Self-interest seen as the basis of wealth

London, 1776
A comprehensive analysis of the economic forces that shape society has been published by the Scottish academic Adam Smith. *An Inquiry into the Nature and Causes of the Wealth of Nations* suggests that economies are built on individual self-interest, and should not be constrained by the state.

Born in Kirkcaldy and Oxford-educated, Smith holds the chair of Moral Philosophy at Glasgow University. In 1763 he acted as tutor and companion to the Duke of Buccleuch on a continental tour. He studied European economies, and in Paris, met a group of thinkers and writers known as the Physiocrats, who see agriculture as the basis of all wealth. The *Wealth of Nations*, which has taken ten years to write, is the result.

In a work that is both learned and popular, Smith insists that people conduct business to advance themselves. When they have the freedom to do this, the results are of general benefit. Capital gives rise to profit, which provides jobs.

Adam Smith, writer-philosopher.

Architectural revolution sweeps England

London, 1775
In their illustrated catalogue, *Works in Architecture of Robert and James Adam*, these Scottish brothers claim "to have brought about a kind of revolution in the whole system" of English architecture and decoration. In the year since it appeared it has been copied by decorators everywhere and has quite eclipsed the Palladian style.

An Adam house is conceived as a whole, its rooms of varying shapes with their plasterwork, mantelpieces, furniture, even doorknobs and candlesticks contributing to the total effect. Externally the houses are adorned with stucco, for which the Adams hold a patent. Inside, the low-relief plasterwork is based on playful motifs such as griffins, sphinxes, swags, Grecian urns and coiled-leaf motifs on friezes and frames for mirrors and fireplaces.

The Adams style is seen at its best in London houses such as Ken Wood, Osterley Park, and Syon House. But their speculative Adelphi Terrace in the Strand nearly bankrupted them.

Carved and gilded pier glass, by Robert Adam. Osterley House, Middx.

Etruscan Room, by Robert Adam. Home House, Portman Sq, London.

1776 (1776-1777)

France, 1 March 1776. The French minister for foreign affairs, Charles Gravier, the count of Vergennes, advises his Spanish counterpart, Geronimo de Grimaldi, to support the American rebels against the English.

Boston, 26 March 1776. British troops and loyalist families evacuate Boston following the American capture of the strategic fortification of Dorchester Heights.

Denmark, April 1776. A provisional treaty of exchange is signed at Copenhagen. Russia cedes claims to Holstein.

France, 12 May 1776. Louis XVI dismisses Turgot.

New England, 7 June 1776. A vote on a resolution for independence is taken. It is carried by twelve colonies. New York is the only colony which does not vote.

Philadelphia, 4 July 1776. The American colonies declare themselves independent.

New York, 10 July 1776. Patriots and soldiers pull down a statue of George III in New York City in celebration of the declaration of independence on 4 July.

France, 19 August 1776. Louis XVI restores forced labour which was abolished by the ex-finance minister, Turgot.

Philadelphia, 9 September 1776. Congress resolves that the name of the colonies should be changed from United Colonies to United States.

Tanzania, 14 September 1776. The French make a treaty with the Kilwa sultanate to supply slaves for sugar plantations in Ile de France (*Mauritius*) and the Reunion islands.

United States, 3 October 1776. Congress borrows five million dollars to halt the rapid depreciation of paper currency, which is being printed to finance the revolution.

France, 22 October 1776. The bailiff Taboureau des Reaux becomes finance minister, in place of Turgot.

West Indies, 16 November 1776. Cannon fire on the Dutch island of St Eustatius is the first salute to the new American republic.

Paris, 31 December 1776. The American Benjamin Franklin arrives in Paris to negotiate for French aid for American rebels.

Naples, 1776. The chief minister, Bernardo Tannucci, who has been legal adviser to the crown for 20 years, is forced to retire. Tannucci reformed the brutal Neapolitan legal code and restricted the feudal privileges of the nobility.

Britain, 1776. Edward Gibbon publishes the first of what are planned to be several volumes of his *Decline and Fall of the Roman Empire*. Readers are scandalised by his treatment of Christianity as the chief cause of Rome's decline.

Senegal, 1776. The Tukulor chiefs seize power. They are led by Suleiman Bal who replaces the worship of local spirits with Islam.

Spain, 1776. Charles III appoints the reformist Floridablanca as his prime minister.

England, 1776. The explorer James Cook embarks on his third major voyage, hoping to find a north-west passage connecting the north Atlantic Ocean with the north Pacific Ocean.

London, 1776. The official royal architect, William Chambers, is commissioned to build Somerset House.

Vienna, 1776. The composer Wolfgang Amadeus Mozart composes his *Serenade in D* for the marriage of Elizabeth Haffner.

Central America, 1776. Guatemala Nueva (*New Guatemala*) is founded.

Paris, 1 January 1777. The *Journal de Paris*, the first French daily, hits the streets.

New Jersey, 3 January 1777. American troops under Washington defeat the British at Princeton.

Paris, 13 February 1777. The marquis de Sade is arrested. He was condemned to death in 1772 for various crimes, but escaped from prison before the sentence could be carried out.

Portugal, 24 February 1777. King Joseph dies and is succeeded by his daughter, Maria of Braganza. The prime minister, the marquis of Pombal, is dismissed by the queen mother, Marianna Victoria. Pombal used the power which he gained following his masterful handling of the 1755 earthquake disaster in Lisbon to reduce the tyranny of the church, expelling the Jesuits in 1759 and breaking the Inquisition.

Britain, February 1777. The Habeas Corpus Act, which says that people must be formally charged after they have been arrested, is suspended.

New England, 13 March 1777. Congress orders its European envoys to appeal to high-ranking foreign officers to send troops to reinforce the American army.

France, 29 June 1777. Following the dismissal of Taboureau des Reaux, Necker is made director general of finance.

Pamphlet hits at English king's cruelty

Philadelphia, 9 January 1776

The author of an anonymous pamphlet, *Common Sense*, which calls for complete independence of the American colonies from Britain is now known to be Thomas Paine, a former English customs officer and the editor of the *Pennsylvania Magazine*. More than 120,000 copies have been sold – although keeping the price low to attract potential readers has left Paine in debt.

Common Sense is a powerful polemic against King George III – "the pride of tyrants" – who, says Paine, "trampled nature and conscience beneath his feet and by a steady and constitutional spirit of insolence and cruelty procured for himself an universal hatred. It is now the interest of America to provide for herself."

Paine argues that the longer the colonies wait for independence, the harder it will be to accomplish while politicians are divided.

"Let the names of Whig and Tory be extinct," writes Paine. "Let none other be heard among us, than those of a good citizen; an open and resolute friend; and a virtuous supporter of the Rights of Mankind, and of the Free and Independent States of America."

Mad Tom, or The Man of Rights: Thomas Paine, in a 1791 cartoon.

Austrian emperor abolishes torture

Vienna, Austria, 2 January 1776

A series of sweeping legal reforms including the abolition of the death penalty, torture and the crime of witchcraft was announced today by the Emperor Josef II.

The Habsburg emperor, elected last year, also announced the appointment of law reform commissions to bring in the changes and create new criminal and civil codes.

Until now Austrian law has been a mixture of Roman, Saxon and Swabian codes mixed with imperial edicts and overlaid with municipal and local laws. The Emperor Josef is keen to see changes that reflect the rationalist enlightenment spirit of the times and to abolish laws based on superstition and fanaticism. Along with witchcraft, intermarriage between Christians and non-Christians and apostasy – desertion of the faith – are to be abolished as crimes.

The emperor wants the commissions to abolish unnecessary torture such as the rack and breaking a man on the wheel, but to keep flogging, branding and the stocks. The reforms are expected to outlaw duelling and end class distinctions with aristocrats liable to the same punishments as serfs.

French reformer ousted by aristocrats

Versailles, 12 May 1776

The struggle to set France on the road to reform received a major setback today with the dismissal of Robert Turgot as the king's comptroller-general after less than two years in office.

His removal is a major victory for the court establishment opposed to his reform package, the Six Edicts. Opposition centred on the proposed abolition of the *corvee*, the labour tax on the peasantry, and its replacement by a tax on all landowners without any exemption for the privileged classes. Also included in the package was a proposal to abolish tithes paid to the church. But Turgot's major achievements – opening up the grain trade and reducing state debt – are unlikely to be repealed.

American independence is declared

Philadelphia, 4 July 1776
In the words of John Adams, a delegate from Massachusetts, this was the "most memorable epoch in the history of America". He spoke as fellow delegates from 12 of the 13 colonies approved a moving document which declares these colonies independent from Great Britain. Only New York has abstained, but is expected to approve shortly.

The Declaration of Independence was drafted by a committee which included John Adams and Benjamin Franklin, and the text was written by a delegate from Virginia, Thomas Jefferson, chosen for his masterly prose style. "We hold these truths to be self-evident, that all men are created equal, that they are endowed by their creator with certain unalienable rights, that among these are life, liberty and the pursuit of happiness," it proclaims. It continues with a firm condemnation of King George III: "... the history of the present King of Great Britain is a history of repeated injuries and usurpations, all having in direct object the establishment of an absolute tyranny over these States," and goes on to outline injustices.

The declaration lists some 26 examples of British tyranny which range from the king's obstruction of justice to the cutting off of American trade with the rest of the world, the waging of war on the colonies and the quartering of armed troops on the colonial peoples. No one can doubt the power and sincerity of this document, least of all the British Parliament which has been "petitioned for redress in the most humble terms" yet "only answered by repeated injury". King George III is seen as "unfit to be the ruler of a free people".

And as the bells ring out in this town tonight and the king's statues are toppled to the ground, John Adams sums up the feeling of the people about this first day. "It ought to be solemnised with pomp and parade, with shows, games, sports, guns, bells, bonfires and illuminations, from one end of this continent to the other, from this day forward for ever more," he said.

The Declaration of Independence, from the painting by John Trumbull.

Independence marchers: The Spirit of '76, painted by A M Willard.

Mercenary troops too drunk to fight

New Jersey, 26 December 1776
Hessian mercenary troops slept off the Christmas festivities today – unaware that an American division was preparing a "near-impossible" attack which involved the crossing by 2,400 men of the icy Delaware river in small boats in complete darkness. General George Washington, the American commander-in-chief, supervised the entire operation from the river bank. He had guessed well: the Hessian commander, Johann Rall, was sound asleep, dead drunk, when Washington's men stormed his camp and routed his men.

Rall had dismissed intelligence reports that the Americans might attack. "Let them come," he said. "We will go at them with bayonets."; but, before his men could fix their bayonets, they were overwhelmed. A hundred Hessians – including their commander – were killed and 900 taken prisoner.

"I have never seen Washington so determined as he is now," wrote one of his colonels. "The Americans are ready to suffer any hardship and die rather than give up their liberty."

For the Americans, it was a brilliant victory which may turn the entire course of the struggle. It was sweet revenge, too. Two weeks ago, General Washington was forced to retreat across the same river, pursued by Lord Cornwallis' twelve regiments.

Ruthless dictator Pombal spearheads major shake-up in Brazil

Brazil, 1777
"Energetic ... of iron will ... vindictive ... frightfully cruel": these are just some of the epithets chosen to describe the marquis of Pombal, Portugal's dictator in Brazil since 1751. Yet for all the fear and loathing he inspires, he is also an effective, respected ruler.

Backed by vigorous administrators, Pombal has revolutionised Brazilian government, crushing his opponents and ousting foreign interests, while vastly expanding the profits which Portugal takes from this wealthy colony.

Ruthlessly enforced fiscal policies have combined to reorganise public services, reform industry and agriculture, outlaw Jesuit influence and abolish slavery.

Play pits nature's storm and stress against reason's cold logic

Frankfurt am Main, 2 July 1777
Sturm und Drang (Storm and Stress) is the title of a new play by Friedrich Maximilian Klinger. Judging by its reception, when it stunned much of the first-might audience with its flouting of theatrical conventions, Klinger's title could not be more apt.

Ostensibly the tale of two Scottish families embroiled in the American War of Independence, the play celebrates the idea of "genius", setting the "storm and stress" of nature above the logic of reason.

Klinger rejects the sophistication of the Enlightenment, substituting the primitive energies of a rural culture, preferring the spontaneity of "natural man" to the artificial manners of his urban cousin.

General George Washington, the American commander-in-chief; a portrait after Charles Peale.

1777 (1777-1779)

New York, 7 July 1777. American troops give up Fort Ticonderoga, a huge complex of fortifications on Lake Champlain, to the British.

New England, 27 July 1777. The marquis of Lafayette arrives to help the rebels. He is accompanied by other European officers, including Kalb, a German in the service of the king of France.

New England, 26 September 1777. British troops launch a major offensive and capture Philadelphia.

New England, 17 October 1777. The British troops from Canada are defeated at Saratoga.

New England, 15 November 1777. Congress adopts the Articles of the Confederation, codifying the division of power between the states and the centralised government, and submits it for the approval of the States.

US, 23 December 1777. A plot to overthrow General Washington, the head of the continental army, is discovered, and the leader executed.

Germany, 30 December 1777. Maximilian III of Bavaria dies. He is succeeded by Charles Theodore, the elector Palatine.

Britain, 1777. The philanthropist John Howard publishes *The State of the Prisons in England and Wales*, calling for wholesale reform of the penal system.

France, 1777. The French chemist Antoine de Lavoisier perfects his theory of combustion.

Paris, 17 December 1777. Louis XVI recognises the independence of the American colonies and agrees to negotiate with them.

France, 6 February 1778. France signs a trade agreement with the United States by which it agrees to enter the war against Britain. The treaty is the result of lengthy negotiations led by Benjamin Franklin, who is now seen as the permanent ambassador at Versailles.

France, 30 May 1778. The writer and philosopher Voltaire dies at the age of 84.

New England, 28 June 1778. Retreating British troops are attacked from the rear at the battle of Monmouth, but the action is bungled by the American commander and only the arrival of Washington's main force prevents defeat. The British withdraw and arrive in New York by nightfall.

France, 2 July 1778. Jean-Jacques Rousseau, the Genevan political philosopher, dies insane after a sudden attack of thrombosis. Among his greatest works is the novel *Emile*, setting out his theories on education.

France, 10 July 1778. In support of the American rebels, Louis XVI declares war on England.

France, 31 July 1778. Denis Diderot dies of apoplexy. A prolific and radical writer, Diderot will be best remembered for the *Encyclopedie* which he edited, enlisting the greatest French writers to help him to transform Ephraim Chambers' original edition.

New England, August 1778. The French fleet gives up the idea of attacking New York and runs aground off Newport.

New England, 29 December 1778. The British take the American revolution southwards and capture Savannah, the capital of Georgia.

Paris, December 1778. King Louis XVI issues a loan of 80 million livres in an attempt to reduce the nation's deficit, which is being increased by France's aid to the rebels in America.

Paris, 1778. The composer Wolfgang Amadeus Mozart visits Paris and gives a performance of *Les Petits Riens*.

Britain, 1778. John Hunter, an Anglo-Scottish physician, establishes that tooth decay begins on the surface of teeth, not in the interior. He contends that decay is more likely at those sites where food particles are lodged.

South Africa, 1778. Governor von Plettenburg of the Dutch Cape Colony places a beacon on Fish river, and claims the river as the colony's eastern frontier. Dutch settlers known as Boers had been trying to set up cattle ranches in the area west of Fish river known as Suurveld (sour-grass country), already occupied by Khoisan and Xhosa cattle herders.

Italy, 1778. A new opera house, called La Scala, is inaugurated in Milan.

Bavaria, 1779. The crisis of the Bavarian succession, following the death of Maximilian II, escalates. Charles Theodore, the elector of the Palatinate, who succeeded as elector of Bavaria, ceded part of the territory to the Emperor Josef II in order to gain imperial recognition of his succession. This has angered Prussia and Saxony who have now invaded Bohemia in protest at Austrian expansion.

England, 1779. Thomas Chippendale, the well-known English cabinet-maker, dies. He is known for his use of the new wood, mahogany, in classically designed chairs, and for his much-consulted book of designs, *The Gentleman and Cabinet Maker's Directory*.

British troops defeated at Saratoga

"The Surrender of Burgoyne at Saratoga" (1817-1821) by John Trumbull.

Saratoga, 17 October 1777

Watched by its American opponents, a humiliated British army lined up in the town square here today to pile up its arms. General John Burgoyne solemnly handed his sword in surrender to a jubilant Horatio Gates, the American commander whose army had foiled constant British attempts to drive a wedge between the Patriot armies in the northern and middle states.

Gates had demanded an unconditional surrender, but agreed after negotiation to a "convention" which granted a free passage home for the British on their promise that they would not fight again on American soil.

The surrender was a gentlemanly affair. Towering over Gates, who looked up at the English general through thick pebble-lensed spectacles, Burgoyne said: "The fortune of war, General Gates, has made me your prisoner." Gates replied: "I shall always be ready to bear testimony that it has not been through any fault of your excellency."

In recent days, no less than seven British generals have been captured with 300 officers and nearly 6,000 men.

Swiss banker helps with French finances

Paris, June 1777

The wealthy Swiss banker Jacques Necker has been put in charge of the purse strings of France. King Louis XVI appointed the 45-year-old financier, whose fortune comes from speculation in East India Company shares, as his next comptroller-general on the advice of his chief courtier, Maurepas. It is felt to be time that France had a more stable financial policy; Necker will be the third finance minister in barely 18 months.

Necker, a prominent figure in French society, is a technician rather than a politician, and is unlikely to introduce any radical measures like Turgot's, although some administrative reforms are promised.

Jacques Necker, the Swiss banker who holds the French purse strings.

First iron bridge across the Severn

Shropshire, England, 1779
Work has been completed on the world's first cast-iron bridge. It has been built across the river Severn, in an industrial area of the English Midlands. The engineer responsible for the bridge is Abraham Darby, whose father and grandfather were both pioneers in the ironwork industry locally.

The new bridge has a span of almost 33 yards, and a rise of over 15 yards consisting of five huge cast-iron ribs. The weight of iron in the precisely engineered, interlocking structure is calculated as 378 tons, ten hundredweight.

Other engineers, inspired by Darby's example, are busy drawing up plans for similar projects in other parts of the country.

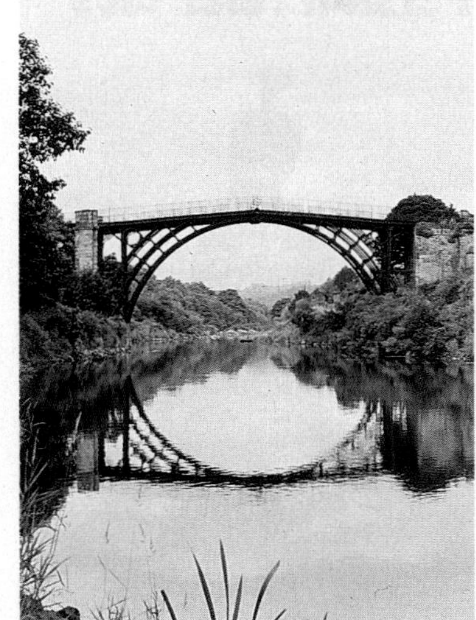
The iron bridge over the river Severn, at Coalbrookdale, in Shropshire.

Rebel genius was legend in own lifetime

Paris, 30 May 1778
One of the greatest Frenchmen of the century, Francois Marie Arouet, known to millions throughout Europe by his pen name "Monsieur de Voltaire", has died in Paris.

The prolific 84-year-old writer and philosopher, a legendary figure in his own lifetime, died – with an irony which he would have appreciated – as a result of his own triumph. Returning to Paris two weeks ago from self-imposed exile in Switzerland for the opening of his latest play, he was overwhelmed by the immense crowd that turned out to greet him. For two days Voltaire delightedly shook everyone's hand – a ceremony so exhausting that he never recovered from it.

Voltaire was a lifelong rebel against virtually every kind of authority, using his brilliant gifts as a writer, his enormous reputation and his wealth – earned from slave trade investments and army contracting – to wage constant war against injustice and oppression.

Dangerous, amusing and courageous, the friend of four kings, he was imprisoned twice in the Bastille and lived most of his life in exile.

Piranesi's macabre visions of Rome better than the reality

Rome, 9 November 1778
After a lifetime creating the dramatic architectural engravings of ancient Rome that are familiar throughout Europe, Giovanni Battista Piranesi has died, satisfied that his work will preserve for posterity the ruined splendours of his adopted city. Trained as an architect in Venice, he put his work into drawing buildings, not erecting them.

His first published etchings, *Carceri*, were of prisons. These vast, vaulted spaces, steeped in macabre gloom, were entirely imaginary, like so many of his architectural studies. His *Views of Rome, Ancient and Modern* seemed to show the ruins by moonlight and festoon them with sinister vegetation. Tourists, lured to Rome by his poetic visions in dramatic lighting, were often disappointed in the reality. However, his work appealed greatly to the new taste for the picturesque and romantic which is spreading fast.

The ruins of the Julia fountain, Rome; an engraving by the Venetian architect Giovanni Battista Piranesi.

Fossil studies show a new animal world

A Brazilian Red Curlew, from Buffon's "Histoire Naturelle".
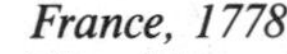

France, 1778
The idea of a natural order of things, conforming neatly to biological classifications, has been challenged by Georges Buffon, the superintendent of the Paris observatory. Buffon believes that the study of fossils shows the properties and appearances of various species changing as a result of environmental conditions.

Buffon is the author of a 36-volume *Histoire Naturelle* which brings together the knowledge of astronomers, mathematicians, geologists and naturalists. In it he opposes Linnaeus' theories of classification and advocates organised study of the behaviour and reproduction of animals.

"Life and movement," writes Buffon, "instead of being a metaphysical degree of existence, are physical properties of matter." He believes observation of animals will establish the reasons for migration and other phenomena of the natural world.

1779 (1779-1780)

England, 15 January 1779. The actor David Garrick dies aged 61. He retired as joint manager of the Drury Lane theatre three years ago. Since his debut as Richard III at Goodman's Fields in 1741 he has been acclaimed as the greatest actor ever. He "improved" many of Shakespeare's plays, cutting the duel in *Hamlet* to leave Laertes on the throne.

US, 25 February 1779. American troops recapture the fort at Vincennes, forcing the British to surrender.

France, February 1779. Lafayette returns from America and asks the king for more money for the revolutionaries.

Russia, 31 March 1779. Russia and Turkey sign a treaty by which they promise to take no military action in the Crimea.

Spain, 12 April 1779. By a secret treaty signed at Aranjuez, Spain is guaranteed a number of advantages if it joins with France in supporting the American rebels.

France, 27 April 1779. On the advice of Necker, the comptroller-general, a provincial assembly is created in the Dauphine to reduce the powers of the bailiffs and allow nobles to take part in regional administration.

Prussia, 13 May 1779. The treaty of Teschen, Silesia, ends the war of the Bavarian succession which started in 1778. The new king of Bavaria, Charles Theodore, placated Josef II by ceding lower Bavaria to Austria, whereupon Frederick II of Prussia invaded Bohemia, angered by the Austrian expansion. By the treaty, Austria relinquishes its claim to all but a narrow strip of Bavarian land along the Inn river, while Frederick II gives up his claim to Bohemia. The sovereignty of Charles Theodore, the elector of the Palatinate, is confirmed.

France, 10 August 1779. Louis XVI frees the last remaining serfs on royal land.

England, 23 September 1779. American privateers fighting for the cause of the American revolution capture a British warship, the *Serapis*, after a great naval battle off the English coast.

South Africa, 1779. The Orange river is traced from the southern African interior down to its mouth on the Atlantic by H J Wikar, a Swedish explorer. The Dutch settlers call the river "Orange" in honour of the ruling house of their native land, but the native Sotho people of the upper river call it *Ntshu*, meaning black, river.

Russia, 1779. A decree is issued to ensure freedom of enterprise.

England, 1779. By combining the spinning jenny and the water frame, the Lancashire weaver Samuel Crompton invents the spinning-mule. Making use of the spindle-carriage, this can produce thread suitable for making fine muslins which up to now have only been available as imports.

Netherlands, 1779. A deputation of Dutch settlers, calling themselves patriots and inspired by the American revolution, arrives in the Netherlands from Cape Town, vainly seeking representative government and a written constitution.

Paris, 1779. Christoph Willibald Gluck's new opera, *Iphigenie en Aulide*, is a great success.

Venice, 1779. The sculptor Antonio Canova produces *Daedalus and Icarus*, his first Neoclassical work.

West Africa, 1779. Britain abandons the Senegambia crown colony, withdrawing to the mouth of the Gambia river and leaving the wider Senegal area to the French.

Antilles, 1779. The British capture the island of St Lucia and force the French fleet led by Admiral d'Estaing to withdraw to Martinique.

France, January 1780. The finance minister, Necker, starts reforming the king's household in an attempt to improve the kingdom's disastrous financial situation.

Austria, 1780. The Empress Maria Theresa, who has ruled as co-regent with her son Josef II since 1765, dies. Her rule has been characterised by domestic reform, of the army, the church and the administration.

New Spain, 1780. Martial law (*estado de guerra*) is declared in New Spain (*Mexico*).

Britain, 1780. All colonial territories are placed under the secretary of state for war, and the post of secretary for colonies is abolished. This establishes a military administration pattern in place of the civilian, trade-orientated administration which existed previously.

Uganda, 1780. King Kyambugu of Buganda dies, having ruled since 1763. Under Kyambugu, Buganda has developed a strong economy based on bananas, and has strengthened its army in order to open up trade routes with the east coast through Kenya.

India, 1780. India's first newspaper, the *Bengal Gazette*, edited by James Hickey, is published.

Just and modest Persian ruler dies

Karim Khan Zand, the regent of Persia; a French engraving.

Shiraz, Persia, 1779

Karim Khan Zand, the regent of Persia and the country's undisputed ruler for 20 years, has died. Seeing himself as a representative of the people rather than the founder of a dynasty, he refused the title of "shah" (keeping the nominal shah in comfortable seclusion at Abadeh), and called himself *wakil*, or regent.

Ignoring military adventures – making himself an exception among eastern potentates – he set a standard in justice and efficient administration unknown before his regency.

So anxious was Kharim Khan for his subjects to be happy that he paid musicians to play to them. He encouraged trade with the British, granting them a trading post at Bushire.

He made his capital in the city of Shiraz, where he built the magnificent mosque of Masjid-i Wakil.

Austrians mourn death of empress

Vienna, 29 November 1780

Maria Theresa, the Habsburg empress, archduchess of Austria and queen of Bohemia and Hungary, died today at the age of 63 after a long and tempestuous reign of 40 years.

Warm-hearted, pious and simple, the mother of 16 children by Francis of Lorraine, she was also an inspiring leader of her people in times of war. Her courage and tenacity in the war to secure her succession when she was only 23 won the hearts of her people and the admiration of the rest of Europe.

She worked on affairs of state, and especially on educational reforms, almost until the moment she died. Sitting up in a chair, she signed many documents and comforted her children who gathered round her. She refused sedatives, saying: "I wish to see death coming." All Austria mourns her passing.

Maria Theresa, empress of Austria for 40 years, in her maturity.

Louis XVI abolishes serfdom and torture

Paris, 1780

Legalised torture, known as "preliminary questioning", has been outlawed on the orders of King Louis XVI. This reform, a year after the king's decision to end serfdom – still thriving on feudal rural estates – convinces traditionalists at court that Louis must be watched. They see the king as unduly influenced by liberal thinkers such as Malesherbes, the chancellor, a censor who relaxed censorship. There are rumours that the next step will be equal rights for Protestants.

The liberals argue that the king is too timid towards opponents of liberalisation. The aristocrats, for all their rigidity, must accept the necessity for change.

Cook dies in Hawaii

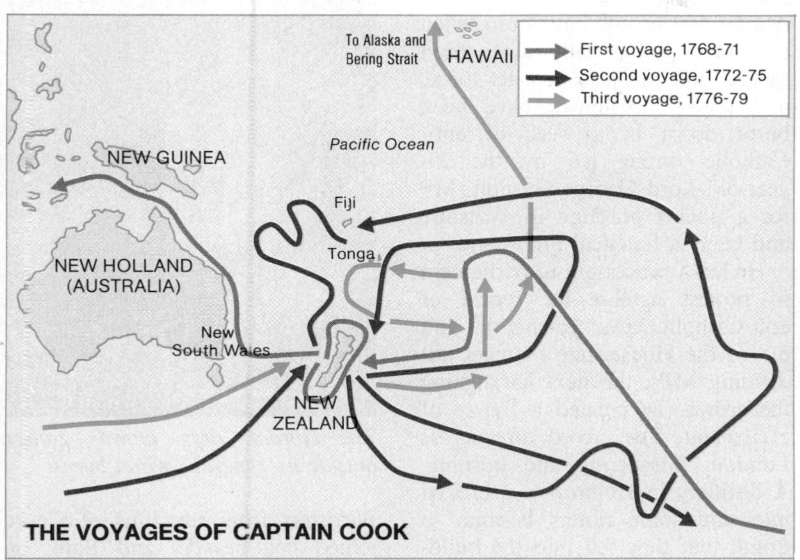

Night dance by women in Hapaee, from Hodges' "Journal of Captain Cook".

Hawaii, 14 February 1779
Captain James Cook, the bluff Yorkshire collier master who rose through the ranks in the Royal Navy and added an entire hemisphere to Europe's knowledge of the world, is dead. He has been killed in an unnecessary skirmish in Hawaii on his third great voyage of discovery in the Pacific Ocean.

On his first voyage he visited Tahiti, charted New Zealand and surveyed the eastern coast of Australia. On his second he reached Antarctica and discovered New Caledonia, and on his third he sailed to Alaska in search of the north-west passage between the Pacific and Atlantic.

Unable to find the passage, he made for Hawaii to survey and refit. The local people, who knew Cook from an earlier visit, had mixed feelings. A local chief was abused by sailors and Cook's ship's cutter was stolen. Cook landed with 12 marines to take a hostage. The islanders, undeterred by firearms, which they had never experienced, attacked. Cook fell. The greatest explorer of the day lies dead.

Captain James Cook, the explorer.

Galvani's frogs and the body electric

Galvani's anatomical experiments; a contemporary copperplate engraving.

Rome, 1780
A strange and accidentally-produced effect has led to a fascinating theory about electricity in animal bodies. The 43-year-old Italian anatomist and physicist Luigi Galvani had laid out the spinal cord and lower limbs of a frog and was noting the responses which occurred when he applied a conductor from a static electricity machine. Galvani noticed that the frog's limbs would contract even when they were detached from the electricity machine. Indeed, they would twitch when some distance away from it.

From this Galvani suggests that an electric current passes through the frog itself when it is touched by a metal conductor. And the frog's nerves and muscles themselves seem to be charged with electricity of animal origin.

Conserve Mexico's past, urges Jesuit

Italy, 1780
A 59-year-old Jesuit priest, Clavijero, born in Mexico but exiled to Italy in 1767, has produced a major history of his country, the *Historia Antigua de Mexico*. Unlike previous historians, Clavijero has produced not simply a chronicle, but a wide-ranging study of many aspects of Mexican culture.

As a Jesuit, Clavijero is as keen to refute the beliefs of the Enlightenment as he is to chart Mexican history. As he puts it, the book's aim is "to serve my country and to restore to its true splendour the truth now obscured by the unbelievable rabble of modern writers."

In addition to religion, Clavijero is as fascinated by the physical side of Mexico as he is by its history and culture. He stresses the need for conservation, proposing a national museum and imploring his countrymen to preserve, while still possible, such remnants of Mexican architecture as have survived the Spanish conquest.

Home rule calls get louder in Ireland

Dublin, April 1780
Encouraged by mounting discontent among Protestants as well as in the Catholic majority in the country, Henry Grattan, the Irish nationalist leader, has moved a series of resolutions in the Dublin parliament calling for home rule for Ireland. The resolutions have been defeated by the dutiful backbenchers of the lord lieutenant, London's representative, but the feeling is widespread that something must be done to settle Irish affairs.

Grattan is a moderate, and loyal to the British connection, but he is in danger of being outflanked. Already, Irish magistrates are refusing to punish military deserters under the British Mutiny Act. The Irish have been greatly influenced by the defiant example of the American colonies, where many Irishmen have settled. At the same time, while they sympathise with the American rebels, Catholic and Protestant Irish are also volunteering to fight them.

1780 (1780-1781)

Russia, 28 February 1780. Czarina Catherine II appeals to European countries that are neutral in the American Revolution to unite against Britain in a league of armed neutrality. This is in protest at the fact that the British navy is attacking ships indiscriminately, whether they are involved in the conflict or not. The league threatens to declare war if this practice is not stopped.

Gibraltar, February 1780. The squadron of the British Admiral Rodney forces the Spaniards to lift their siege of Gibraltar.

France, 2 May 1780. Following Lafayette's latest departure for America, Louis XVI sends 6,000 men to New England under the command of Rochambeau to reinforce the revolutionary force.

Madrid, 11 May 1780. Negotiations begin between Spain and the American revolutionaries. France has been pressurising Spain to give support to the rebels' cause.

South Carolina, 12 May 1780. Five thousand American troops surrender Charleston to Major Benjamin Lincoln.

Russia, June 1780. Czarina Catherine II and the Emperor Josef II meet on the River Dnieper and then at St Petersburg to discuss new conquests in the Ottoman empire.

France, July 1780. The assembly of the clergy votes for a free donation of 30 million livres to help the nation's finances.

France, 24 August 1780. Louis XVI abolishes the "preliminary question", or torture, used to get suspects to confess.

France, 30 August 1780. Acting on the finance minister Necker's advice, the king announces a reorganisation of the prison system in a bid to improve conditions in jails.

India, September 1780. Under attack by the *nawab* (ruler) of Arcot – who is supported by the British – the Moslem ruler of Mysore, Haidar Ali, allies himself with the Marathas and retaliates fiercely. He launches an attack on the British coastal region of the Carnatic and the Marathas threaten Madras, where the East India Company has its headquarters. British soldiers relieve Madras and the Marathas withdraw to make a separate peace.

New England, October 1780. Considering himself unjustly treated, the American general Benedict Arnold betrays his country by giving the British the opportunity to capture West Point.

France, October 1780. Antoine de Sartine, the minister of the navy, is publicly disgraced after being accused by the finance minister, Necker, of being responsible for his ministry's vast debts of 20 million livres.

Britain, 20 November 1780. Britain declares war on Holland, one of the members of the League of Armed Neutrality. The Dutch had been supplying French and Spanish arms to the American rebels through their West Indian base.

France, 23 December 1780. The Upper Council is reshuffled as France battles with a deepening financial crisis.

New York, 1780. The Iroquois, who have occupied the valleys of the Mohawk river in central New York for generations, are devastated by American troops. In just over a month the Americans destroy their homes, barns, storehouses and cultivation. Most of the Indians flee. Washington ordered the offensive to discourage the Indians from attacking while the Americans are engaged in the war with Britain.

Mozambique, 1781. The Portuguese take the fort they call Lourenco Marques back from Austria, and resume control of Maputo Bay trade. This includes the slave trade from the southern Mozambique coast to Brazil, the French Indian Ocean islands and Arabia.

South Africa, 1781. The Suurveld war (eastern Cape frontier war) which began in 1779, ends. The war was provoked by Boer ranchers to take away land from the Khoisan and Xhosa peoples in the Suurveld area around Fish river. The conflict began with Boers shooting at Africans who scrambled for tobacco thrown on the ground before them – and it has been a success for the Boers.

Paris, 1781. The marquis of Condorcet, a brilliant mathematician and radical thinker, publishes his *Reflections on Negro Slavery*, contributing to the growing debate on the slave trade.

Austria, 1781. The Emperor Josef II publishes the Edict of Toleration for Protestants and Orthodox Christians.

England, 1781. Illiterate children in Gloucester are the first in the country to attend a Sunday school, established by the Christian educationalist Robert Raikes. They learn the catechism, and how to read and write.

India, 1781. The governor general, Warren Hastings, founds the Calcutta Madrassah, a college designed to foster Arabic studies.

Anti-Catholic rioters devastate London

London, June 1780

Almost 500 people have been killed or injured, five jails have been sacked and the prisoners let loose, and scores of houses have been burnt down in a week of anti-Catholic rioting led by the 29-year-old Lord George Gordon, MP for a pocket borough in Wiltshire and lately a fanatical Protestant.

He led a procession to parliament to protest against the repeal of anti-Catholic laws. Racing in and out of the House, one moment addressing MPs, the next haranguing the crowd, he created a frenzy of excitement. The crowd tore across London, plundering and burning. A distillery in Holborn was broken into and some rioters became so drunk that they fell into the buildings which they had fired.

At last the king and the Privy Council ordered troops to open fire.

The Gordon riots: crowds gather outside as Newgate prison burns.

Barristers from the Inns of Court joined coal-heavers and Bank of England clerks using bullets made from melted-down ink wells in suppressing the riot.

Sumo wrestling becomes public spectacle

Japan, 1780

The ancient sport of *sumo* wrestling, originally performed at shrines and temples as part of religious festivals, has become a public spectacle, with wrestlers taking part in competitions lasting for ten fine days, with rain stopping the bouts.

The wrestlers, who are paid for their performances, are easily recognised by their bulk which they use to force their opponents out of the small, circular ring. They are ranked according to their prowess and there is much ritual surrounding the short sharp bouts. The wrestlers arouse great passions among their followers, who include normally demure women as well as men. The *shogun* himself attends the bouts.

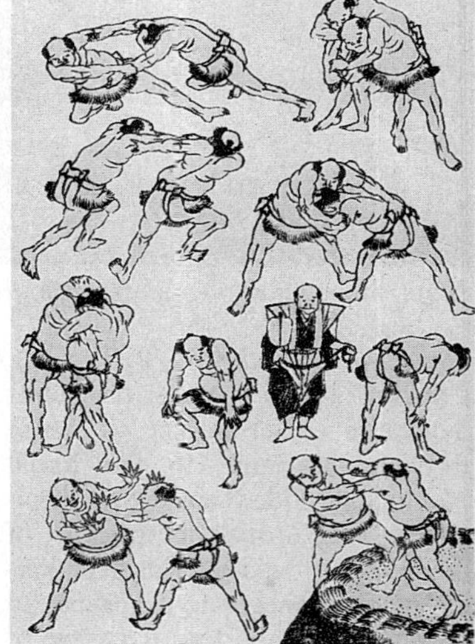

Wrestling positions, by Hokusai.

Land-hungry Boers massacre tribesmen

Cape Town, 6 June 1781

For the third time in three years, Xhosa Blacks have been massacred by Boers. The motive is land. Throughout the century Dutch *trekboers*, or frontiersmen, have expanded eastwards. Against the sedentary Khoisan they encountered little resistance, the Khoisan "selling" their land for liquor and tobacco, and being either driven off or turned into slaves. The Xhosa are more nomadic and present a more difficult problem.

The settlers have solved it by forming commandos under the dynamic Adriaan van Jaarsveld. The Dutch authorities in Cape Town are disgusted by his activities; van Jaarsveld usually asks the Blacks to leave the land before he shoots them.

100,000 African slaves a year traded for tobacco and rum

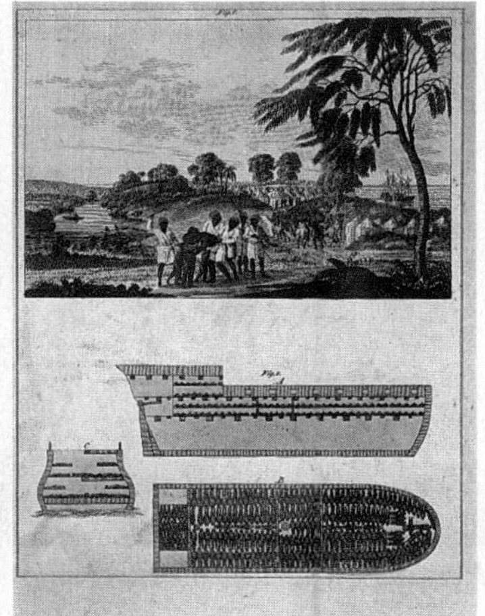

Slaves are captured and taken by ship (cross-sections).

Cruel treatment of slaves in the West Indies; an engraving by a British artist, representing a growing humanitarian backlash against slavery.

Atlantic Ocean, 1780

Among the crews of the slavers trading between Europe, Africa and the Americas, it is the infamous middle passage that is most dreaded. A ship puts in at Liverpool with a cargo of cotton, sugar or tobacco and, after loading a variety of trade goods, including textiles, hardware, spirits and trinkets, sets sail for West Africa. On the Gold Coast and the Niger delta, the African middleman waits with slaves from many sources. The ship's captain may spend up to two months bargaining with the local potentate. One king told a slaver that he found no demand for tankards, yellow beads and the like.

Once the deal has been made the shackled slaves are put on board, packed side-by-side and end-to-end like logs. Then begins the fearful journey across the Atlantic, the stench of bodies rising through the battened hatches, the cries of men, women and children making an unholy counterpoint to the creak and slap of mast and sail. At last, at Charleston or some such port in the New World, the slaves who have survived are unloaded and sold. Cotton, tobacco and other produce are loaded and the grim triangular voyage resumes. For Britain, France and other European countries it is a profitable trade. It extends from the southern states of North America, across the Caribbean and into Portuguese Brazil. Its apologists point out that the tropics are the white man's grave, the indigenous American Indian is dying from European diseases, and only the African can resist tropical diseases. Some 100,000 slaves are now shipped across the Atlantic each year, but criticism of the trade is mounting in England especially.

TO BE SOLD *by* William Yeomans, (*in Charles Town Merchant*,) a parcel of good Plantation Slaves. Encouragement will be given by taking Rice in Payment, or any Time Credit, Security to be given if required There's likewiſe to be ſold, very good Trooping ſaddles and Furniture, choice Barbados and Boſton Rum, alſo Cordial Waters and Limejuice, as well as a parcel of extraordinary Indian trading Goods, and many of other ſorts ſuitable for the Seaſon.

A notice of sale of slaves, from the "Charleston Gazette", 1744.

Marquis wins allies for colonists' cause

Philadephia, 1780

The marquis of Lafayette has returned from a brief visit to Paris where he succeeded in persuading the French government to send reinforcements of troops and ships to aid General George Washington's Patriot army. Lafayette, a 23-year-old enthusiast for the American War of Independence, came here in 1777 as a volunteer. He is a close friend of General Washington.

He fought at Brandywine, when Washington's army was outmanoeuvred by Howe's British divisions, and at Valley Forge, where the American army came close to total defeat during the worst winter in living memory. It was the plight of the troops that persuaded the aristocratic Frenchman to use his influence in Paris to aid Washington. With a French fleet threatening British reinforcements and Cornwallis' army hard pressed by General Greene's brilliant hit-and-run tactics, the advantage appears to have shifted to Washington.

New power rises to rule lands of Nile

Uganda, 1780

A new power is emerging in central Africa: Buganda. From their tiny state on the north-western edge of Lake Victoria the Baganda rose from total obscurity in the 17th century, conquering territory after territory. In the last 30 years, under their Kings Suna and Mutesa, the pace of conquest has increased. With the defeat of their main rivals, the Banyoro, and the annexation of the remnants of their Kitara empire, Buganda now dominates the lands at the source of the Nile.

One reason for their success has been the efficient centralisation of the state by King Suna, who replaced hereditary positions with royal appointments. Another is the effectiveness of the Buganda army.

Some observers, however, attribute every success to the fruitfulness of the banana, the Buganda staple diet. Baganda, they claim, have so much free time on their hands that they have little to do but go to war.

Passionate young Mozart makes a break for artistic freedom

Vienna, June 1781

Wolfgang Amadeus Mozart, the 25-year-old composer and former child prodigy, has been dismissed from the service of the prince-archbishop of Salzburg. He plans to earn his living as a freelance performer and composer in Vienna, abandoning the secure, if demeaning, world of noble patronage.

For Mozart, though, his position at Salzburg had become intolerable. From 1777 to 1779, on leave from Salzburg, he had travelled to Germany and Paris (where his mother died) in an unsuccessful attempt to find a post suited to his huge talents. In March this year he was summoned to join his archbishop in Vienna at festivities for the new emperor, Josef II. Mozart was placed at table below the valets, and forbidden to play for the emperor.

Mozart's frustration came to a head and he asked for his discharge. He was refused, but on 9 June he saw the archbishop's chief steward and at last won his release, with, as he wrote to his father Leopold, "a kick up the backside." His Salzburg job will go to Michael Haydn, younger brother of Josef.

Wolfgang Amadeus Mozart.

1781 (1781-1782)

Paris, 19 January 1781. Continuing his major reform programme, Necker sets up the Hospital Administration.

West Indies, 3 February 1781. During the war declared by the British on the Dutch last year, the British capture the Dutch Island of St Eustatius.

Paris, 19 February 1781. Necker publishes his *Compte-rendu*, a report to the king for the year 1781. It shows the state of the kingdom's finances in detail and is a big success, even persuading the people that Necker has achieved a surplus. But financiers accuse the minister of cooking the books by leaving out arrears and the nation's special expenses.

United States, 2 March 1781. Maryland is the last state in the union to ratify the Articles of Confederation.

France, 19 May 1781. After having sought the position of minister of state in vain, Necker foresees his fall from grace and submits his resignation. His departure shakes financiers' confidence in the *Bourse* (the French stock exchange).

Russia, May 1781. An exchange of letters between Czarina Catherine II and the Emperor Josef II establishes a defensive alliance between their two countries against the Ottoman empire.

Prussia, May 1781. Prussia joins the League of Armed Neutrality formed by European countries that are not involved in the American revolution in order to protest against indiscriminate British naval attacks.

India, 1 July 1781. In the second Mysore war, Haidar Ali, the Moslem ruler of the southern Indian state of Mysore, is defeated at Porto Novo in the Carnatic by the British.

California, 4 September 1781. The Spanish name a tiny village near San Gabriel, Los Angeles.

North America, 19 October 1781. French and American allies defeat the British at Yorktown during the American War of Independence.

Austrian Netherlands, November 1781. The Emperor Josef II ends the "barrier" regime which was introduced at the time of the Treaty of Utrecht in 1713. He orders the destruction of all fortified towns in the Austrian Low Countries.

France, 1781. Jean-Jacques Rousseau's *Confessions* – a book of startling frankness – is published posthumously. Rousseau died insane in 1778. His last published works was *Lettres de la Montagne*, written in exile in Switzerland.

France, 22 October 1781. Louis Joseph, the son of Louis XVI and Marie Antoinette, is born.

London, 27 February 1782. Parliament rejects Lord North's ministry, voting to abandon further prosecution of the American war.

Ireland, March 1782. Legislative independence is granted to the Irish parliament following the plea by Henry Grattan at last month's Convention of Dungannon.

Britain, 19 March 1782. Lord Rockingham replaces Lord North, who resigned as prime minister on 11 March. William Pitt the Younger demands parliamentary reform.

Paris, 10 April 1782. Pierre Choderlos publishes *Les Liaisons Dangereuses*, which immediately causes a scandal.

West Indies, 12 April 1782. The British and the French fight a naval battle in the Saints Passage.

France, 7 May 1782. Peace negotiations are begun between France and Britain.

Vienna, 16 July 1782. Mozart's opera *Abduction from the Seraglio*, telling the tale of an escape from a Turkish harem, is performed for the first time.

Gibraltar, 13 September 1782. The British fortress in Gibraltar comes under attack by the French and Spanish, allies in the American War of Independence. Despite their new secret weapon – the floating battery – the allies are defeated and abandon ship, leaving many wounded men to burn to death in vessels pumped full of red-hot shot.

Prussia, 1782. The Academy of Berlin awards a prize to a treatise *On the Universality of the French Language* by Antoine Rivarol.

Russia, 1782. The architect Giacomo Quarenghi completes the theatre of the Hermitage at St Petersburg.

Britain, 1782. A bill introduced by the duke of Montrose repeals the act forbidding the wearing of Scottish kilts or other garments. The act was passed by the Hanoverian government in 1747 following the suppression of the Stuart rebellion.

India, 1782. Haidar Ali, the Moslem ruler of Mysore, dies while engaged in the second Mysore war with the British. His son Tipu Sahib takes command, but military aid promised by the French arrives too late and Mysore is defeated.

USA, 1782. Thomas Jefferson writes in his *Notes on Virginia* of the British empire: "The sun of her glory is fast descending the horizon."

Part-time astronomer spots new planet

Germany, 1782

A young German organist with a spare-time interest in mathematics and astronomy has just made an extraordinary discovery. On 13 March this year William Herschel was observing a small group of stars in the constellation of Gemini when he noticed that one of these "stars" had some peculiar features.

It has soon become apparent to astronomers that Herschel has seen a new planet in our solar system. Including Earth, there have been six known planets since ancient times. This new seventh one is the outermost planet so far – twice as far from the sun as Saturn. Now a suitable name is being sought for it. The favourite candidate is Uranus – the oldest of all the classical gods.

Herschel's telescope; an engraving.

Herschel is no novice astronomer. As an expert lens-grinder, who works with his sister Caroline, he has already built the largest telescope yet assembled.

36,000-volume anthology copied by hand

China, 1782

A mammoth book collection made up of 36,000 volumes has been completed on the orders of the Emperor Qianlong. The *Sigu Kuanshu*, or Complete Collection of the Four Treasuries of Literature, is so big that only seven hand-written copies have been made, and it is unlikely that it will be printed. There is a dark side to this huge project: its compilation was used to destroy thousands of "subversive" books and all favourable references to the Manchus have been cut out. Worse still, some authors have been executed and their families are being persecuted.

Author of hit play told to write no more

Mannheim, Germany 14 Jan 1782

A first play by a young army officer of 22, Friedrich von Schiller, had a huge success at the national theatre here last night. It is a revolutionary work.

Schiller was forced to become an army surgeon like his father by the tyrannical Duke Karl Eugen of Wurttemberg. He spent a reluctant four years at cadet school and as a surgeon in Stuttgart, writing his play which was published last year at his own expense. He attended the performance in Mannheim without leave. The duke has placed him under arrest and ordered him to write nothing but medical works in future.

Friedrich von Schiller, the writer.

The play, *Die Rauber* (The Robbers), is a fiery justification of rebellion against political tyranny in the strongest language. Schiller is one of the *Sturm und Drang* (Storm and Stress) writers, like Goethe. In his tale of two brothers, it is the outlawed one who leads a robber band in the forest, who turns out to be the noble idealist. Schiller plans to resign and flee to Mannheim.

Boy sailor tells of war

The battle of the Saints, 12 April 1782: a painting by Thomas Whitcombe.

Aboard HMS Goliath, 1782
A boy of 12, Midshipman Jimmy Gardner, one of several aboard British warships in action against the French during the American war, has described how he missed by inches a cannon ball that knocked the speaking trumpet out of the first lieutenant's hand. Another ball went through a fellow midshipman, pulling out his stomach, which stuck on the side of a launch. The ship's butcher tried to scrape it off, saying: "Who the devil would have thought the fellow's paunch would have stuck so?"

Another boy, aged 11, wrote to his mother after joining his ship at Spithead: "I am very happy and as comfortable as at home, and like it of all things. I have not yet gone higher than the maintop. Pray tell Patty I do not sleep in a hammock but a cot ..." This agreeable picture does not reflect the generality of life aboard ship. British crews are recruited from convicts and debtors, press-ganged or lured by bounties.

As one officer has written: "In a man-of-war, you have the collected filth of gaols. There is not a vice committed on shore, but is practised here."

British shipping technology is inferior to France's, though two recent inventions are now being copied by other countries: copper sheathing, which has reduced the fouling of ships' bottoms by weeds and barnacles, and the carronade, a short-barrelled large-calibre gun which is very effective at short range. Britain has now become the world's strongest naval power, with 174 ships of the line and 294 smaller vessels.

"The Merry Ship's Crew": a cartoon satirising brutal naval discipline.

Britain loses America

American victory: the British surrender to George Washington at Yorktown.

Virginia, 19 October 1781
Charles Cornwallis, the portly British commander-in-chief, could not bring himself to watch the surrender of his army here at Yorktown today. He pleaded ill-health and sent a subordinate officer to hand his sword to the American victors. No-one doubts now that Britain must lose its 13 American colonies and that the Americans have gained their independence after five years of fighting.

As a band played a tune with the ironic – though appropriate – title of *The World Turned Upside Down*, American troops watched with quiet satisfaction as British soldiers marched out of their encampment, their bright red coats contrasting vividly with the victors' tattered clothing. Many of the British soldiers appeared to be drunk. "Their step was irregular, and their ranks frequently broken," reported one American. "They were disorderly and unsoldierly." When ordered to surrender their weapons, many of the British soldiers started throwing their weapons on the pile with violence, as if to make them useless.

General George Washington, the American commander-in-chief, watched the surrender with his French ally the marquis of Lafayette, whose French and American troops had stormed British fortifications to find a "surprisingly weak and confused resistance". Washington, who had been planning an attack on New York, turned his army rapidly towards Yorktown when he learnt that French warships were off Chesapeake Bay, cutting off any chance of British reinforcements.

Kant says intuition comes before reason

Konigsberg, Germany, 1781
Immanuel Kant, the professor of mathematics at the university here, has produced a new book which promises to be the talk of philosophers all over Europe. He has grappled with the problem facing scientists ever since Descartes and Leibniz asserted the primacy of thinking over sensory experience.

Kant, in *Critique of Pure Reason*, suggests a synthesis between the analytical and the experimental. He suggests that theories are validated by reference to time and space, which are known only by intuition and sensory experience.

His father was a saddler and his early life was dominated by poverty and puritanism. He was destined for theology, but since joining the university in 1740 he has devoted himself to physics, mathematics and philosophy. He is only a little over five feet tall, has a deformed right shoulder and has never been further than 40 miles from here. He is widely read, however, and is a lively talker whom others travel a long way to hear.

1782 (1782-1784)

Ohio, 10 November 1782. American troops devastate the British-backed Shawnee Indians. One thousand Kentucky riflemen fire unremittingly on the Indians and destroy their food supply.

Paris, 30 November 1782. After several months of negotiations – from which the French are pointedly excluded – a preliminary peace treaty is drawn up to end the war between Britain and the United States.

Virginia, 1782. Legislation makes it legal for any man "to emancipate and set free his slaves".

Britain, 20 January 1783. Britain signs peace agreements with France and Spain, who allied against it in the American War of Independence.

London, 4 February 1783. Britain officially proclaims an end to the hostilities in America.

France, 23 February 1783. Ever deeper in financial crisis, Louis XVI creates a committee of finance. He appoints Charles Vergennes as its head.

Europe, February 1783. Spain, Sweden and Denmark recognise the independence of the United States of America.

Philadelphia, 11 April 1783. After receiving a copy of the provisional treaty on 13 March, Congress proclaims a formal end to hostilities with Britain.

Britain, April 1783. The Whig leader Charles Fox forms an alliance with Lord North, under whom he has previously refused to serve, in order to bring about the downfall of Shelburne's government. William Portland is prime minister.

Russia, 3 May 1783. Catherine II, thought of as an enlightened ruler by all of Europe, officially introduces serfdom in the Ukraine.

France, 4 June 1783. The Montgolfier brothers, Joseph Michel and Jacques Etienne, launch the first hot air balloon. Fascinated by the aeronautical ideas of a 14th-century Augustinian monk, Albert of Saxony, and the 17th-century Jesuit priest Francesco de Luna, they construct a balloon which takes off when a cauldron of paper is lit beneath it.

France, 3 September 1783. The Treaty of Paris formally ends the American Revolution. Britain recognises American independence, the Spanish regain Florida and Minorca from Britain, and France gets Senegal and Tobago. The United States are granted fishing rights off the British-Canadian coast, and they undertake to protect former loyalists.

Massachusetts, October 1783. A Negro woman is discharged from the army having served for three years under the name of Robert Shirtliffe.

Britain, 19 December 1783. Following the fall of the Fox-North alliance under Portland, which came to power in April, William Pitt the Younger becomes the youngest-ever prime minister at the age of 24.

USA, December 1783. It is estimated that up to 100,000 loyalists will have left the United States by the end of this year, following the defeat of the British. Some have returned to England, but the majority have settled in Nova Scotia and Canada, where land grants are being made available to the newly-arriving settlers.

Spain, 1783. The jurist and economist Pedro Campomans, the procurator of the Council of Castile since 1762, becomes president of the council.

Paris, 1783. Jean le Rond d'Alembert, the mathematician and philosopher, dies. With Diderot he was joint founder of the influential, but controversial, *Encyclopedie*.

New York, 1783. A 25-year-old graduate, Noah Webster, publishes *The American-Spelling Book*, the first acknowledgement that American spelling may differ from that which had been used previously by the English.

Angola, 1783. The Portuguese build a fort at Cabinda on the north side of the Congo river.

Maryland, 1783. The state prohibits the slave trade, which has now been banned in all northern US states.

Spain, 1783. The financier Francois de Cabarrus founds the San Carlos Bank.

Austria, 1783. Josef II continues the reorganisation of the church and takes action against the sects. He also makes a number of economic changes, abolishing private tolls and making the regulations for the sale of manufactured goods more flexible.

France, 1783. The chemist Antoine Laurent Lavoisier creates water from hydrogen and oxygen.

Prussia, 1783. The philosopher Immanuel Kant publishes *Prolegomena to any Future Metaphysic.*

Bohemia (*Czechoslovakia*), **1783.** Peasant revolts break out following land reforms.

Austria, 1783. Mozart completes his *Symphony in C Major.*

Pitt is prime minister at the age of 24

London, 19 December 1783

A young man whose health was so delicate as a child that he was educated at home has become Britain's prime minister at the age of 24. George III's appointment of William Pitt, only two years an MP, was ridiculed by the Commons as "a boyish prank". But the old politicians had discredited themselves with their intrigues and squabbles in the wake of the American war. Pitt, meanwhile, had relentlessly harried the old guard for incompetence and corruption. Why, he asked, was Lord North claiming £1,300 for stationery? Pitt intends to appeal to the country over the head of the Commons, which he says is unrepresentative.

The Bottomless Pitt; a cartoon of William Pitt the Younger, 1792.

Mob attacks the "patriots" in Holland

Holland, 1783

Sporadic riots and incitements to rebellion are commonplace in Dutch cities, as the *stadholder* (provincial governor) enlists the support of the mob against the militant "patriots" of the bourgeoisie.

An anonymous pamphlet published two years ago, entitled *To the Netherlands People*, is at the root of the present troubles. It urged people to take to the streets to protest about their grievances, to demand a free press, and to arm themselves. It was immediately banned by the government.

The pamphlet's author was Baron Joan Derk van der Capellen tot den Pol, a regent who sought to represent small traders, artisans, craftsmen, merchants and shopkeepers. Like other bourgeois agitators, he derided the government for social and moral decadence.

The "patriot regents" like van der Capellen enjoy the support of the Free Corps militia, while the stadholder relies on the mob's jealousy. Recently, mobs have attacked rich burghers and their homes, while the Free Corps has intensified policing in cities like Rotterdam.

Female black poet has died in America

Boston, Massachusetts, 1784

The Afro-American poet Phillis Wheatley, who encouraged her readers to trust in God, has died in poverty and debt. Phillis was eight when she arrived in Boston from Senegal. She was bought by the Wheatleys, a kind couple who gave her a good education.

In 1773 her book, *Poems on Various Subjects, Religious and Moral,* was published. Five years later, after a successful trip to England, Phillis' luck ran out. The Wheatleys died. She married badly, her husband went to prison, her children died and she lost touch with all her literary friends.

A posthumous study of Raja Goman Singh, ruler of Kotah in Rajasthan, who died in 1771. He is shown indulging in the sport of kings, shooting one of the lions which abound in Rajasthan.

United States of America recognised

Paris, 4 September 1783

Two years after the surrender of Cornwallis and his force of 7,000 soldiers at Yorktown, Virginia, the British have formally recognised the independence of 13 ex-colonies now known as the "United States of America". The new nation, which declared independence seven years ago, covers an area lying between British Canada and Spanish Florida, from the Atlantic to the Mississippi river.

This was a quarrel in which Britain had no friends except, at last, in secret diplomacy, its American "enemies". The French fleet helped to win the War of Independence from 1778 and provided a base for diplomacy to end the conflict. Spain, Holland and Russia all sided with the ragged rebels who routed a regular army. Peace talks began two years ago. The writer Benjamin Franklin – a friend of many British politicians – was prominent in the American team.

The Americans suspected that their claim to lands in the west, between the Allegheny mountains and the Mississippi river, would be blocked by French and Spanish ambitions. A separate pact was discreetly reached with London: Britain also did not wish to see Latin or French America grow. The agreement that Britain would support the States did not take immediate effect, but it strengthened the Americans' hand in relation to their allies. Yesterday's Treaty of Paris between France and Britain, confirmed the earlier arrangement between the States and Britain. The last sticking points were American debts to Britain, and assets taken from Americans loyal to England.

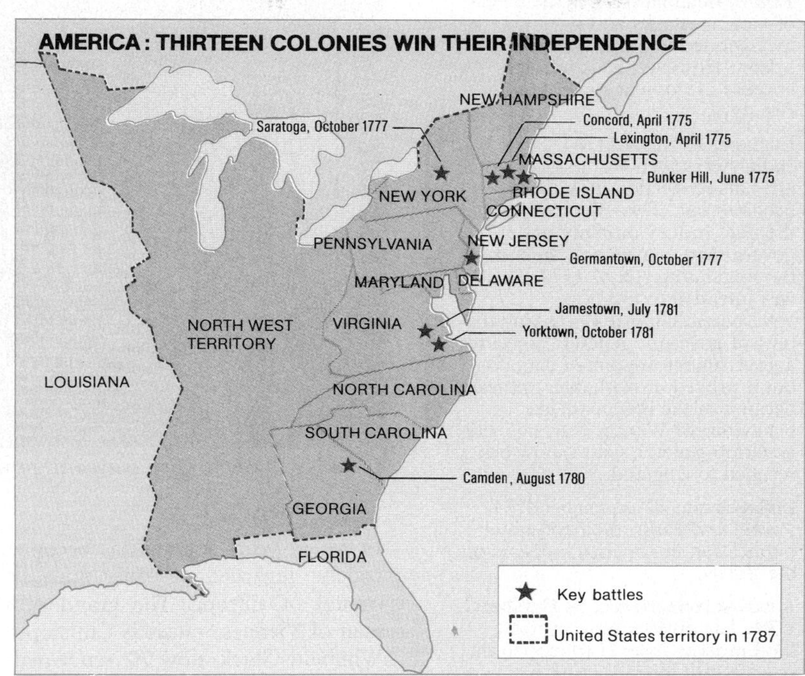

A Dutch cartoon displays Britain's misery in symbolic detail. Britain, in the form of a cow, stands helplessly while the American Congress chops off her horns. Holland gleefully milks her, while France and Spain wait to be fed. In the background, a British warship, rudderless and stripped of its guns, has run aground at Philadelphia while American militiamen sleep. At right, the royal British lion lies prostrate, oblivious to the monkey on its back and the Briton in mourning, praying for her rejuvenation.

A huge new base is planned in Crimea

Crimea, 1784

Czarina Catherine has commissioned huge new fortifications to be built in the Crimea, following her annexation of the territory. A vast base is planned, and will be named by combining the Russian forms of two words, the Latin *augustus* and the Greek *polis*: together they make the "Russified" name of Sevastopol.

The Crimea was formerly ruled by a feeble *khan*, nominally under Ottoman protection. The Czarina, who has long dreamed of a vast empire in the south, told her ex-lover and court favourite, Prince Grigori Potemkin, to settle the matter. He chose an outbreak of unrest, which he had probably instigated, as an excuse to intervene and humiliate the sultan of Turkey. A delighted Catherine has rewarded him with the gift of substantial estates in the region.

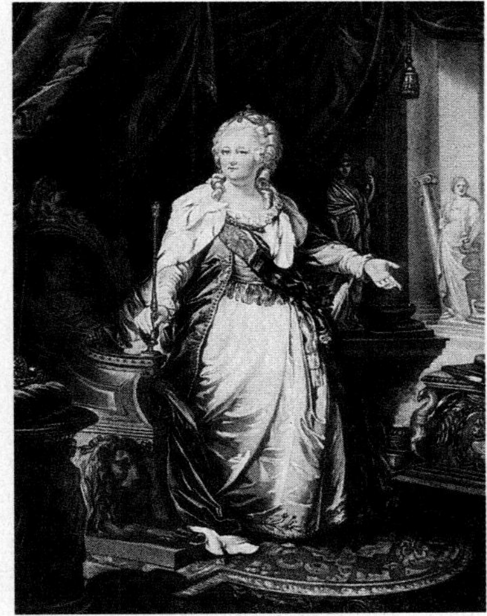

Catherine the Great, the Czarina of Russia, scourge of the Ottomans.

Army service brings freedom for slaves

Virginia, USA, 1782

Up to 10,000 negroes have won freedom from slavery in the past seven years by serving in the continental army or colonial militias. On practical as well as moral grounds, Thomas Jefferson has recently urged the state legislature to permit all slaveholders to free their slaves.

Most of the former slaves served as privates in the army or seamen in the navy. Many of them, according to Jefferson and those who favour freeing them, saw heavy combat and fought with conspicuous bravery. In the navy, they enjoyed greater freedom.

The records of one Connecticut regiment show 48 negroes adopting names befitting their new situation: names like Pomp and Jeffrey Liberty, Dick, Prinnis, Cuff, Ned and Jube Freedom.

Death for Peruvian hero and his family

Cuzco, Peru, 1783

A brief revolt against Spanish tyranny has ended with a macabre execution of the Inca leader Tupac Amaru II and his family in the main square of Cuzco. Tupac's wife and sons were tortured to death as he watched. His tongue was cut out; his limbs were pulled four ways by horses and he was then beheaded. Parts of the dismembered body were exhibited around the country. Tupac's "crime" was to insist that Spain kept laws promising protection for Indians.

Last year he appeared on a white horse to lead his rebellion. As thousands followed, he ordered the execution of a senior colonial official. He freed all slaves and abolished forced labour and taxation. As the Spanish plan the murder of all his relations, his cousin Diego has become the new rebel leader.

1784

Istanbul, 8 January 1784. Vergennes, the French secretary of state for foreign affairs, intervenes to settle the long conflict over the Crimea between the Ottoman empire and Russia. Last year Russia took over the Crimea, claiming that it was simply restoring order. This enraged the Turks who signed a treaty with Russia in 1779 agreeing that neither side would take military action in the region. The Turks have now been persuaded to accept the inevitable.

France, 18 January 1784. Appointed finance minister on 3 November 1783, Charles Alexandre de Calonne joins the council and is appointed minister of state.

New York, 22 February 1784. Captain John Green sails for China on a voyage which marks the beginning of American trade with China.

India, 11 March 1784. Tipu Sahib, the *sultan* of Mysore and Haidar Ali's son, signs the treaty of Mangalore with the English, ending the second war of Mysore. Both parties surrender their respective conquests.

Britain, 25 March 1784. Following the rejection of William Pitt's bill on India – aimed at bringing the East India Company under government control – parliament is dissolved.

Maryland, 23 April 1784. A congressional land ordinance drafted by Thomas Jefferson names ten new states to be created from land ceded to the government by New York, Connecticut and Virginia.

Paris, 27 April 1784. Beaumarchais' *The Marriage of Figaro* opens at the Comedie Francaise theatre. The play has been the talk of Paris for four years while the dramatist submitted it to censor after censor, repeatedly being refused permission for its performance. Louis XVI has condemned it as "unperformable" and ordered it to be banned – probably on account of its subversive morals, as it tells the tale of a handsome valet outwitting his master.

Britain, 18 May 1784. In the elections following the dissolving of parliament in March, Pitt is returned with an increased majority.

France, 20 May 1784. The peace of Versailles between England and Holland ends the hostilities that erupted when Britain discovered that the Dutch were supplying arms to American rebels. Holland cedes Negapatam on the south-east coast of India.

Paris, May 1784. After the performance of *The Marriage of Figaro*, Beaumarchais is the object of violent attacks and is incarcerated in Saint Lazare prison. However, he is released because of popular pressure after five days.

England, 13 August 1784. Pitt's India Act, which was passed soon after his re-election in May, becomes law. This effectively puts the East India Company under government control and amends the Regulating Act of 1773. This was intended to impose government control by making the post of governor general subject to a government-appointed council, but it proved unworkable, not least because of the independent behaviour of Warren Hastings, the governor general, who is now being recalled to England.

Philadelphia, 21 September 1784. *Packet and Daily*, the first daily publication in America, appears on the streets.

Austrian Netherlands, 18 October 1784. The unilateral decision by the Emperor Josef II to reopen the river Escaut to traffic causes disagreement between Austria and Britain.

England, 13 December 1784. The lexicographer, poet and critic Samuel Johnson dies aged 75. He spent many years writing hack work for London's literary magazines to fend off encroaching poverty; but from 1762, a crown pension of £300 a year enabled him to take his place in high society and give free reign to his versatile genius. His remarkable dictionary, which took him eight years to compile, will probably be long remembered.

Paris, December 1784. Jacques Necker violently criticises the financial management and performance of his successor, Charles Calonne, in a treatise entitled *De l'Administration des Finances de la France.*

Austria, 1784. Josef II alters the ecclesiastical structure of his states and orders the destruction of theological works.

USA, 1784. Ethan Allen publishes publishes *Reason, the Only Oracle of Man* – believed to be the first anti-Christian book published in America.

Alaska, 1784. The Russians found their first colony in North America, on the island of Kodiak, in the Gulf of Alaska. Up to now the island has been inhabited only by a large number of bears and a small group of Eskimos – American observers are still puzzling over possible motives for the Russian settlement.

Vienna dominates Europe's musical scene

Chamber music is often played at private salons; an 18th-century painting.

Vienna, 1784

In recent years Vienna has become widely regarded as the musical capital of Europe. The grand old man of Viennese music is Christoph Willibald Gluck, now 70, renowned throughout Europe as the man who reformed opera. In his operas, which include *Orpheus and Eurydice* (1762), the Bohemian-born composer strove to make the music more relevant to the drama.

Gluck is now more or less retired, and Austria's senior active composer is Franz Joseph Haydn, aged 52, the music director to Prince Esterhazy. Haydn has brought to the symphony and string quartet a range of expressiveness that has made him famous as far away as France and Spain.

A good friend of Haydn's, but 34 years his junior, is Wolfgang Amadeus Mozart. Mozart has become renowned for his piano playing, usually in his own concertos. He is also writing string quartets, and is planning more operas following the success of *Die Entfuhrung aus dem Serail* two years ago.

Joseph Haydn, the composer, painted by Christian Ludwig Seehas.

Austrian ruler grants freedom of worship

Vienna, 1784

Freedom of worship is to be allowed in the Holy Roman empire as part of as wide-ranging shake-up of religious laws by the Emperor Josef II. His latest edict promoting religious tolerance grants freedom of conscience and worship to both the Protestant and Eastern Orthodox Churches. Civil marriage, divorce and freemasonry are to be recognised. Jews will no longer be barred from the university.

The Roman Catholic Church remains the official church, but now comes under state control with bishops expected to swear an oath of loyalty to the emperor. He will also be responsible for determining new religious laws, ceremonial procedures, and diocesan and parish boundaries. Priests will not be allowed to publish papal bulls without his consent. Monasteries which are not devoted to education, the care of children or the sick are to be closed. All pilgrimages and processions are banned.

The moves are part of a flood of reforms introduced by the emperor when he became sole ruler four years ago after his mother's death.

Treaty leaves Britain ruling the waves

London, 20 May 1784
The Royal Navy's victory over the French at the battle of the Saints two years ago gave Britain command of the sea, but was too late to save the American colonies. It has, however, enabled the British to gain advantages elsewhere.

When the Dutch made the hostile gesture of proclaiming armed neutrality during the American war, the British seized practically the whole of the Dutch merchant marine. In the peace treaty with the Dutch, signed today, Britain has annexed Negapatam, near Madras, and forced the Dutch to concede freedom of navigation in the Dutch East Indies.

These gains give Britain security of communications with India and beyond to Canton in China – vital to Britain's trade and prosperity in Asia. But some in Britain already have their eyes on the Dutch base in Ceylon.

Mesmer's magnetism falls out of favour

Salon and clients of Franz Mesmer, the doctor and alternative therapist.

Paris, 1784
The methods of Franz Mesmer, the German doctor who has become a favourite with fashionable society here, have been condemned by a committee of the Academy of Sciences. Mesmer works around a tub containing magnetised rods in fluid. The clients hold hands and the doctor presides dressed in lilac silk and waving an iron wand.

Such theatricality did not impress the committee, which included the American ambassador, Benjamin Franklin, no mean scientist himself. Members said that the animal magnetism, which Mesmer believes is the healing force, had no effect on them or other subjects.

They said that the convulsions experienced by his patients were produced by the imagination. Mesmer made his name in Vienna by curing a friend of Mozart's of blindness, but was forced to leave in 1778 by rumours spread by rivals. The committee has now demolished his theory, but ex-patients still claim that the tub therapy made them feel much better.

Magic touch or animal magnetism? A caricature of Doctor Mesmer.

Money problems rob puddler of payment

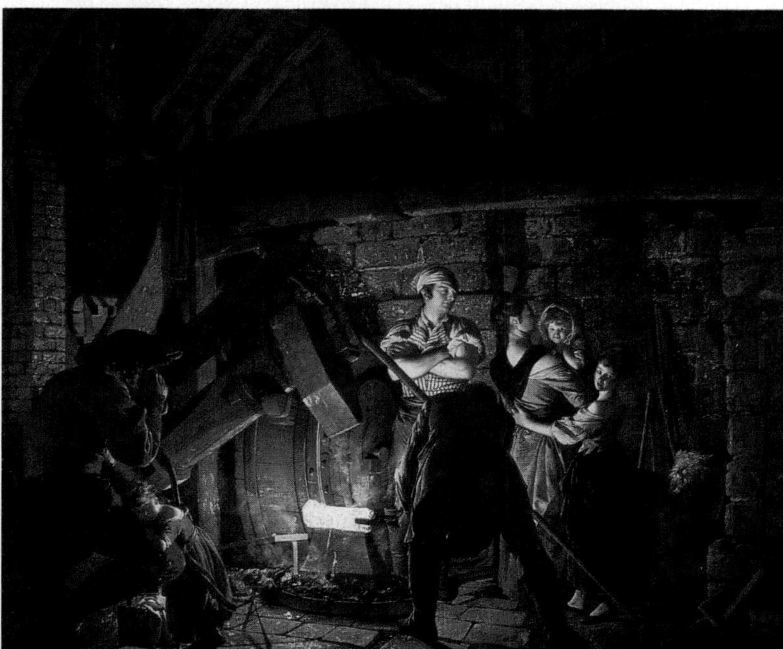

The iron forge at Broadlands, Hampshire; by Joseph Wright of Derby.

Britain, 1784
Henry Cort, a British inventor and industrialist, and creator of what he calls "puddling", a revolutionary new process for manufacturing quality cast iron, has lost his patents to this most valuable discovery. Beset by financial problems Cort has become unable to keep the process to himself. Now every ironmaster will be able to experiment with Cort's discovery.

Cort's loss is definitely the industry's gain. Despite years of gradual improvements in the manufacturing processes, cast iron has always remained too brittle. "Puddling" has changed that for good.

The technique involves refining pig iron over a coal fire, pouring the molten metal into a furnace to eliminate impurities, then making the molten metal into sheets.

Cort's method has three chief advantages. It uses coal, not expensive charcoal. It uses British pig iron and turns this into a substance that rivals high quality Swedish metal. And it makes iron in one continuous process from puddling – that is, melting and stirring – through to hammering and rolling.

Poor children sent to Sunday school

Gloucester, 1784
Two years ago Robert Raikes, the editor of the *Gloucester Journal*, hired four women and set up a Sunday school for 90 poor children. Now his supporters claim that there are no fewer than a quarter of a million children in such schools all over the country.

Raikes did not invent the Sunday school, but he has given it a new thrust and much publicity through his own paper and through his articles for *The Gentleman's Magazine*. An Anglican and a committed penal reformer, he sees the Sunday school as a means of teaching the illiterate to read and write in an age when many of the young are working in factories. "The aim of the Sunday School," he says, "is the reformation of Society."

Methodists have taken up the idea with enthusiasm. John Wesley called it "one of the noblest institutions which have been seen in Europe for some centuries". Mrs Sarah Trimmer, who has set up one of the best-known schools in Brentford, just north of London, has called upon all upper-class young ladies to come to the schools and exercise a civilising influence upon the children. She has written her own books to teach them, and *History of the Robins* is now a bestseller.

1784 (1784-1786)

USA, 1784. The effects of an economic depression begin to be felt.

France, 7 January 1785. The Frenchman Jean Blanchard and the Englishman John Jeffries succeed in the first hot air balloon crossing of the Channel.

Paris, 14 April 1785. Calonne, the controller-general of finance, restructures the French India Company.

France, 17 July 1785. By order of the council, the importation of goods from Britain is strictly limited.

France, 1 August 1785. By agreement with the king, Jean Francois de la Perouse travels to the Pacific with the aim of developing the fur trade with China and Japan.

Paris, 8 November 1785. The treaty of Fontainebleau is signed under French supervision between the Emperor Joseph II and the Dutch. This settles a conflict which arose when the Habsburgs tried to open the Scheldt river to Austrian shipping, in contravention of the treaty of Munster (1648). The Dutch refused to give up their monopoly on the Scheldt trade and appealed to France for support. By the treaty Austria receives territory in Brabant and Limburg and complete control of the Scheldt above Sanftingen, plus 10 million florins in exchange for surrendering claims to Maastricht.

Britain, 1785. The reverend James Wilmot of Warwickshire claims that the dramatic works of William Shakespeare were actually written by Francis Bacon, Viscount St Albans.

Prussia, 1785. The philosopher Immanuel Kant publishes *Fundamental Principles of the Metaphysics of Ethics.*

Britain, 1785. Amid allegations of partiality and high-handedness, Warren Hastings, governor general of India, resigns his post and returns to Britain.

New York, 1785. The state makes slavery illegal.

Netherlands, 1785. The monopoly of the Dutch East India Company is ended.

Britain, 1785. The poet William Cowper publishes *The Task*, a work concerning nature and religion, written at the suggestion of Lady Austen.

France, 1785. The French astronomer Pierre Simon de Laplace advances a new theory on the rings around Saturn. He believes that there are many narrow rings or ringlets around the planet, and that each one is solid.

Paris, 1785. The painter Louis David's latest work, *Oath of the Horatii*, a classical piece inspired by the discovery of the ruins of Pompeii and Herculaneum, is highly praised in Paris. His austere rendering of the tragic tale from antiquity is heralded as a new manifestation of the classical school.

Virginia, 16 January 1786. The Council of Virginia guarantees religious freedom.

Vienna, 1786. Mozart's opera *The Marriage of Figaro* – based on the play by Beaumarchais – opens in Vienna. The story of the valet Figaro denying his master the feudal *droit de seigneur* of a night with his servant's new wife gives the piece a subversive flavour that delights the crowd.

Sweden, 1786. The chemist Carl Scheele dies in Stockholm. He discovered numerous acids and elements such as chlorine, oxygen, barium and manganese. In 1777 he demonstrated that the atmosphere consists mainly of two gases, one supporting combustion and the other preventing it.

Europe, 1786. The count of Mirabeau, the well-known soldier, returns from fighting in the American War of Independence and tours Europe.

Britain, 1786. The prime minister, William Pitt, introduces a new "sinking fund", into which a million pounds' worth of government revenue per year is to be paid to reduce the national debt. Walpole first established a sinking fund in 1717, but it was undermined when the money was used for other purposes. Pitt is appointing independent commissioners to ensure that his fund is put to its intended use.

Sicily, 1786. Marchese Domenico Caracciolo becomes the prime minister of Ferdinand IV of Naples, the king of the two Sicilies, and assumes the title of viceroy. His attempts at political and social reform on the island come up against the apathy of the central government and the opposition of the Sicilian nobility.

Sweden, 1786. King Gustavus III founds the Academy of Eighteen in Stockholm, based on the Prussian and French models. On his visits to Paris he attends meetings of the Academie Francaise, but he is more interested in art and literature than in the ideas of the philosophers.

Austria, 1786. The Emperor Joseph II issues a decree abolishing the guilds and continues his ecclesiastical reforms, advising the Catholic Church to conduct mass in the vernacular.

Hot air balloons take off all over Europe

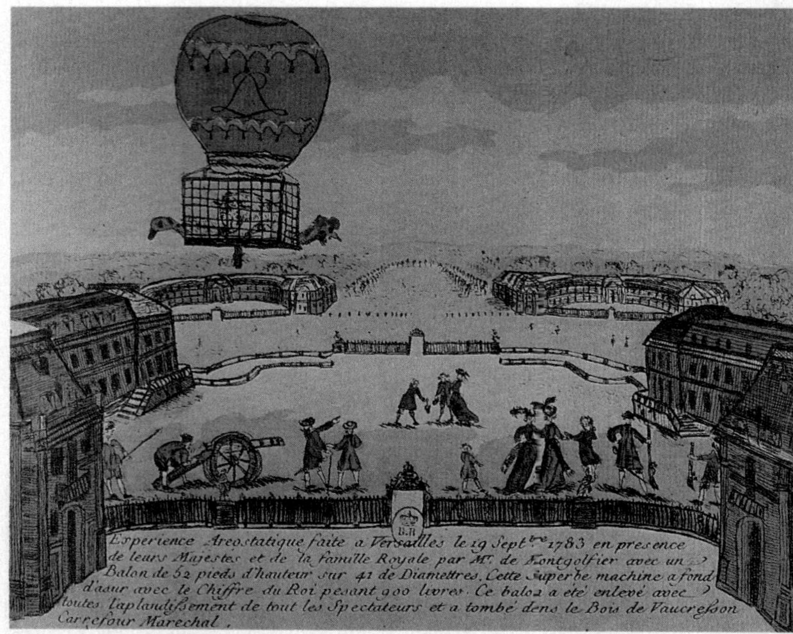

Montgolfier's balloon takes off at Versailles in front of King Louis XVI.

London, 15 September 1784

Floating several hundred yards above the city, to the acclamation of the prince of Wales and 150,000 onlookers, Vincent Lunardi, the secretary to the Neapolitan ambassador, has become England's first human hot-air balloonist.

Lunardi's ascent, accompanied by a cat, a dog and a picnic hamper, was the latest adventure in a craze which has swept Europe in the past year. The first balloonists were the brothers Etienne and Joseph Montgolfier who, in June last year at Annonay, launched a canvas globe of glued paper filled with inflammable gas obtained by burning wet straw. The vessel rose 950 metres, and remained airborne for ten minutes.

Three months later, the Montgolfier brothers launched the first passengers when a rooster, a duck and a sheep took off in *Martial* in front of King Louis XVI and his court at Versailles. This craft, carrying almost two hundredweight more than its own weight, rose 480 metres and landed over a mile away. The rooster broke its skull, but the sheep survived to become part of Marie Antoinette's menagerie.

Vincent Lunardi's balloon, exhibited at the Pantheon in 1784.

Industry steams ahead

Britain, c.1786
In the decade since James Watt constructed his famous engine, industry has benefited enormously from the refinements in steam technology. Steam is proving to be the driving force of an industrial revolution. For the first time man has harnessed a reliable source of energy that relies neither on muscles nor on the wind.

Steam engines are suited to water pumping. This means that it is possible to mine deeper and deeper coal seams to extract the necessary fuel to power the factories that more and more can be seen as the prime source of national wealth. And it is steam power that drives the hoisting gear to lift the coal out of the ground.

Steam engines are being used in blast furnaces, too, where they produce a blast strong enough to burn coke instead of expensive and limited charcoal. This makes for all-year-round production, with the furnaces running continuously.

In other industrial processes steam has become indispensable. It drives spinning and weaving machines, paper mills, breweries and flour mills. Indeed, steam has made possible the development of industries such as these on a large scale. It has been the vehicle of mass production; the cottage industry is a thing of the past.

What is happening in Britain is that steam has changed industry from a wood and water occupation to a coal and iron enterprise. No longer is the muscle of the horse or the drive of the watermill or windmill enough to meet the growing needs of the manufacturer. An average windmill will only generate five or ten horsepower, the largest 30 horsepower. With steam those figures look trivial: 300 horsepower is not uncommon. Small wonder that Boulton and Watt alone are said to have manufactured around 500 steam engines. And there is no sign of any shortage of clients.

James Watt, the industrial pioneer who invented the steam engine.

French chemist turns dry gas into water

Lavoisier with his combustion apparatus for converting gases into water.

France, 1785
The chemist Antoine Laurent Lavoisier has succeeded in burning substantial amounts of dry gases to obtain water, using a combustion apparatus. He concluded that the weight of the water was equal to the sum of the weights of the two gases from which it was made. He then went on to declare that water is not, as had been thought, a simple substance, but a mixture of gases, namely oxygen and hydrogen.

Lavoisier is acknowledged as foremost among today's chemists. Born into an aristocratic family in 1743, he made himself even richer by investing in a company that was used by the government to collect its taxes. He has used these profits to construct a large laboratory.

Like a number of scientists Lavoisier has considered the theories of combustion by "phlogiston", but this discovery, among other experiments, suggests they are false.

Astronomer foresees black stars in space

England, 1784
An English astronomer has calculated that a star as dense as the sun, but with a radius 500 times larger, would have sufficient gravity to stop light itself from being emitted and would thus be invisible. John Michell's theory argues that the velocity of light particles might be reduced by powerful gravitational fields so they could not travel through space.

Marie Antoinette: victim of a necklace

Paris, 1785
Queen Marie Antoinette has become involved in an extraordinary and complex affair over a diamond necklace consisting of 647 stones and worth a fortune. And, with her extravagant court expenditures already contributing to the French state's huge debt, it has done no good to her and her husband King Louis XVI's public standing.

The queen's passion for diamonds brought her into a scandal involving Cardinal Rohan, who was acquitted on all counts at his trial. The accusation that she was having a sexual relationship with the cardinal is unjust, but it has discredited the monarchy and increased its general unpopularity.

An extravagant and unpopular queen: Marie Antoinette.

Archery art: a Chinese painting on silk from the late 18th century.

1786 (1786-1787)

Morocco, 11 July 1786. Morocco agrees to stop attacking American ships in the Mediterranean for a payment of $10,000.

Egypt, July 1786. The Ottoman sultan, Abdul Hamid, sends an expeditionary force of 1,500 men to Alexandria. They occupy the delta and drive out the *bey*, who takes refuge in upper Egypt and starts a civil war. The sultan blames him for having signed an agreement with France in 1785 guaranteeing safe passage for merchandise travelling from Suez to Alexandria.

Savoy, 8 August 1786. Jacques Balmat and Dr Michel-Gabriel Baccard become the first to climb Mont Blanc.

Prussia, 17 August 1786. Frederick II (the Great), king of Prussia since 1740, dies and is succeeded by Frederick William II. Frederick the Great used his genius as a military commander to make Prussia into a great power. After coming to power he seized Silesia from Austria, and during the Seven Years War (1756-63) he prevented Austria, in alliance with Russia and France, from regaining the province. In 1772 he agreed a partition of Poland with Austria and Russia.

Versailles, 20 August 1786. In order to bypass parliamentary opposition, the French finance minister Charles Calonne advises King Louis XVI to convoke an assembly of notables to agree on a plan of financial reform, including more equitable taxation.

Germany, 25 August 1786. A group of German bishops who support the Holy Roman Emperor Josef II in his campaign to curtail papal influence draw up a document entitled the Punctuation of Ems, which amounts almost to a declaration of independence from the papacy.

Virginia, 9 September 1786. George Washington calls for the abolition of slavery.

Maryland, 11 September 1786. The Convention of Annapolis opens with the aim of revising the articles of confederation of 1776.

India, 12 September 1786. Lord Cornwallis – the British general who distinguished himself in the American Revolution, despite being compelled to surrender at Yorktown – is appointed governor general of India.

London, 26 September 1786. France and Britain sign a trade agreement.

Netherlands, 1786. The recently formed Dutch Patriot Party, which represents French influence, deprives the *stadholder* William V of the command of his army.

Massachusetts, 26 December 1786. Daniel Shays, a veteran of the revolutionary war, leads a rebellion of 1,200 farmers protesting about seizures of farms, livestock and household goods for non-payment of debts.

Italy, 1786. Leopold, the grand duke of Tuscany, brother of the Emperor Josef II, proposes a programme of ecclesiastical reform strongly influenced by Jansenism. The grand duke pursues his reformist policies by abolishing torture and the death sentence.

Paris, 1786. Supporters and opponents of a planned reform of the French judicial system clash after the Paris parliament sentences three peasants from Chaumont to death for murder.

France, 1786. The botanist Vilmorin introduces cultivation of sugar-beet to France.

Scotland, 1786. Robert Burns, an impoverished Scottish farmer, publishes *Poems Chiefly in the Scottish Dialect*, including the "Address to a Mouse".

Britain, 1786. The English naval officer Captain Arthur Phillip is put in command of a fleet whose purpose is to establish a penal settlement in Australia. He is also offered the governorship of New South Wales.

France, 11 January 1787. The signature of a Franco-Russian trade agreement opens up new opportunities for French traders in the Baltic and the Black Sea.

Japan, 1787. Matsudaira Sadanobu is appointed chief senior councillor and launches a far-reaching programme of bureaucratic reforms. He purges the government ranks of supporters of his predecessor Tanuma Ogitsugu.

Japan, 1787. Serious rice riots break out in Edo (*Tokyo*) following several years of famine and rising prices. Five thousand people go on the rampage, smashing rice shops and homes of rich merchants.

India, 1787. The East India Company signs a treaty whereby it gains substantial control over the revenues and the army of the ruler of the Carnatic region in southern India.

South-East Asia, 1787. Following the signature of a friendship treaty between Vietnam and France, Count Thomas de Conway, the French governor of Pondicherry, sends troops to Vietnam to restore King Nguyen Anh to the throne.

Scotland, 1787. The Scottish engineer William Symington patents an engine for road locomotion.

Mont Blanc conquered by Swiss hunter

Jacques Balmart and Michel-Gabriel Paccard, descending from Mont Blanc.

Chamonix, France, 1786

Two Frenchmen, a hunter and a doctor, have become the first climbers to reach the summit of Mont Blanc, at 15,782 feet the highest peak in Europe.

Not long ago mountains were thought unfit places for civilised people, who drew blinds on windows of carriages traversing Alpine passes. Lately the enthusiasm for nature of writers such as Rousseau and scientists including the Geneva naturalist de Saussure has changed popular opinion.

De Saussure offered a reward to the first person to reach the summit. The feat was accomplished jointly by Jacques Balmart and Michel-Gabriel Paccard.

Small farmers rebel at harsh debt laws

Massachusetts, 25 January 1787

Months of discontent boiled over into full-scale rebellion here today as an army of small farmers fought its way to the courthouse and federal arsenal at Springfield seeking weapons. The farmers were confronted by artillery and fled across the snow after one volley was fired. Their reluctant leader, Daniel Shays, has fled to Vermont, and militiamen are searching out his lieutenants, who face the death penalty.

The cause of the revolt was the harsh law of indebtedness. With trade at a near standstill and a heavy poll-tax imposed to pay off war-debts, the farmers, unable to sell their produce, faced eviction and prison as tradesmen demanded payment. The farmers' revolt has succeeded in creating public awareness, and new legislation is likely to exempt household goods and tools from seizure for debt.

Ottoman troops land in Egypt

Alexandria, Egypt, 1786

Ottoman troops have landed in Egypt to reassert Turkish control over the Mameluke *beys*, or princes, who rule in the sultan's name but act like independent sovereigns.

Since the death of Ali Bey the Great in 1773, Egypt has been ruled – or rather misruled – by two Mameluke strongmen, Murad Bey and Ibrahim Bey who not only oppress their subjects with high prices, famine and corruption, but hold their lives cheap. As one European resident remarked: "Death may prove the consequence of the slightest indiscretion".

Both Britain and France have interests in Egypt and the *beys'* foreign policy has been to play one off against the other. It is this independence in foreign affairs has given the Ottoman sultan, nominal master of the *beys*, one pretext for trying to reimpose his control over his unruly governors.

Frederick the Great dies

Potsdam, 17 August 1786

The flute-playing aesthete who became King Frederick the Great of Prussia loathed the sight of military uniform when he succeeded his father, Frederick William. Later he took to wearing a shabby blue tunic – torn with bullet holes and spattered with snuff – and it became his exclusive dress. He was wearing it when he took the military review in a rainstorm that led to his final illness. He died today, aged 74.

Frederick leaves a state that has become feared throughout Europe. Its territory has expanded from under 46,000 to over 71,000 square miles, and the population has grown from 2.2 to 5.8 million. It has a standing army of 200,000, strictly disciplined and ready for action in war and peace – Frederick thought nothing of attacking without a declaration of war. He kept some of his wars going with subsidies from the British.

Frederick's early interest in literature and music angered his father, and the boy learned to dissemble. At 21 he was married to Elizabeth, the duke of Brunswick's daughter. But he hardly ever went near his wife, and there were no children. Almost certainly the marriage was not consummated.

A so-called "enlightened despot", Frederick abolished torture, except for mass murder, lese-majeste and treason. He cultivated Voltaire, although he annoyed him by asking him to rewrite bad poetry. Frederick kept a pair of whippets, which slept on his bed.

Frederick the Great: aesthete.

French struggle with looming bankruptcy

Paris, 20 August 1786

France is heading for bankruptcy unless a universal land tax, payable by everyone, is brought in immediately, the comptroller-general, Calonne, warned today as he introduced a package of reforms to save the French economy. His proposals include moves to protect free trade and creating provincial assemblies.

Since taking over in 1783 he has been alarmed by rising debt interest on loans taken out by his predecessor, Necker, and continuing court extravagance. National debt at £800 million now exceeds the annual budget of £550 million.

Alexandre de Calonne: financier.

Breech-loading gun invented in London

London, 1786

A London gunsmith, Henry Nock, is promoting his new invention, a development of the musket, known as the "breech-loader", which is bound to revolutionise weapons technology. By loading the musket through the breech the shot and powder can be put in quickly at the rear of the barrel, not dropped down through the bore, as has been the old, cumbersome method.

The musket has been in use for over 250 years, and in that time it has incorporated many improvements. There has been the introduction of lighter, more manageable weapons, and mechanisms such as the flintlock and wheellock have made firing more effective.

Mendelssohn, the "court Jew", has died

Berlin, 4 January 1786

Moses Mendelssohn, the philosopher who became known as "the German Socrates" and a leading figure in the Jewish community in Germany, has died. He was 56.

Mendelssohn was introduced to the court of Frederick II by the pro-Semitic playwright Gottfried Lessing, who used him as a model for his character "Nathan the Wise" in his play of that name.

Frederick freed Mendelssohn from the usual restrictions on Jewish life in 1763, from when, as the "court Jew", he was a leader of Germany's intelligentsia.

Moses Mendelssohn: philosopher.

Shogun blamed for famine and epidemics

Japan, 1786

Tanuma Ogitsugu, who rose up through the bureaucratic ranks to become chief official of the last two *shoguns*, has been stripped of office and disgraced by the powerful relatives of the new, infant, shogun. Tanuma, a controversial figure who concentrated on increasing the profitability of the shogun's lands, is now being accused of everything that is wrong with Japan, including natural disasters, volcanic eruptions, famines and epidemics.

Catherine the Great's magnificent neo-classical palace at Tsarskoie Selo, built between 1786 and 1796. The empress herself preferred a more severe style, in keeping with her image as an absolute monarch, and had no hesitation in treating her architects like serfs.

1787 ⇒

Ukraine. The Emperor Josef II and Catherine II of Russia meet to discuss plans for the reconquest of Istanbul.

Versailles, 13 February. Charles Vergennes, the minister of foreign affairs, dies and is replaced by the count of Montmorin.

Versailles, 22 February. At the opening session of the Assembly of Notables, the finance minister, Calonne, admits that there is a national deficit estimated at 112 million livres (£ 800 million).

Versailles, 8 April. Calonne resigns under pressure from the Notables. He is replaced by Lomenie de Brienne.

Prague, 20 April. Ardent supporters of the papacy invade Prague cathedral and stone the insignia of Scipione dei Ricci, the councillor of Grand Duke Leopold of Tuscany, sounding the deathknell for Jansenist reform.

Italy, 23 April. Tuscan bishops meet to discuss the Jansenist theories put forward by Grand Duke Leopold and his adviser Scipione dei Ricci.

Britain, May. Warren Hastings, who was made the first governor general of India in 1774 and returned to England in 1785, is impeached for corruption.

USA, 25 May. A convention to draw up the constitution for the United States of America, presided over by George Washington, opens in Philadelphia.

Versailles, June. Lomenie de Brienne, the new French finance minister, replaces forced labour with a tax and allows the free circulation of grain.

Spain, 8 July. At the instigation of his minister Floridablanca, King Charles III decrees the setting up of a ministerial council known as a *junta*. This is an attempt to modernise central government by creating a link between separate ministerial departments.

USA, 13 July. Congress adopts the North-west treaty regulating future colonisation of the lands between the Ohio, the Great Lakes, the Appalachians and the Mississippi. It provides a framework for the incorporation of new states into the Union.

Paris, 30 July. After having demanded a meeting of the Estates-General, parliament refuses to approve a new land tax.

Ottoman Empire, 13 August. Following Catherine II's rejection of their ultimatum calling for an end to the Russian protectorate in the Crimea, the Ottomans declare war on Russia.

Versailles, 27 August. The council of ministers is reshuffled. The count of la Luzerne is appointed minister of the navy and the count of Brienne, Lomenie's brother, becomes minister of war.

Versailles, 30 August. Louis XVI decrees the parliament's exile.

Netherlands. The Prussians intervene to support the *stadholder* William V in his struggle with the Dutch Patriot Party.

Europe. Britain, Prussia and the Netherlands form an alliance against France and Austria.

Austria. The Emperor Josef II promulgates the Josephine code, guaranteeing the equality of all his subjects before the law.

England. *Thoughts and Sentiments on Slavery* by Ottobah Cugoana, a Fante freed slave living in England, is published. It calls on the British government to send its navy to the West Indies to suppress slave trading.

England. Following the pioneering anti-slavery work of Granville Sharp, the Committee for the Abolition of the Slave Trade is formed by the Rev Thomas Clarkson, with William Wilberforce as its parliamentary representative.

West Africa. Freed slave settlers from England land on the Sierra Leone estuary to found a "Province of Freedom". They elect James Weaver as their governor on the basis of a constitution drawn up by Granville Sharp.

Crimea. The Russian politician Grigori Potemkin, a favourite of Catherine II, erects sham villages to impress his monarch during a royal tour. Potemkin was responsible for annexing the Crimea in 1783 and developing a Black Sea fleet.

Prague. *Don Giovanni*, an opera by the Austrian composer Wolfgang Amadeus Mozart, is performed for the first time. Mozart's *The Marriage of Figaro* caused great excitement when it appeared last year.

Vienna. Christoph Willibald Gluck, the doyen of Viennese composers who spearheaded important reforms in the art of opera, dies. His greatest operatic success was *Iphigenie en Tauride*, which appeared in 1779.

Germany. The dramatist Johann Schiller completes a play in blank verse entitled *Don Carlos*. Parts of the play, along with many of Schiller's poems, first appeared in the author's own theatrical journal, which he began publishing two years ago.

Europe's youth takes to the East

A somewhat romanticised impression of the Ottoman sultan's harem.

Istanbul

The Grand Tour, the "finishing school" for the wealthy young men of Britain, has extended itself eastwards into the Orient.

Until a few years ago, the Grand Tour meant Italy and France. Better roads, a romantic youth and peace has opened up the Ottoman empire to rich young travellers.

Young men – and, increasingly, women – on tour now take in Greece, for a touch of antiquity, and sail through the Dardanelles to Istanbul, with its splendid Ottoman palaces. Here they buy their first Oriental prop, a *hookah*. From there – with the assistance of a local guide to interpret the many splendours of the east – the traveller rides at leisure through Anatolia to Aleppo, where he or she turns right for the Holy Land. Such places as Jerusalem, Bethlehem and Damascus are all available to the ambitious traveller. Such tours are now regarded as part of an education. Like the Arab geographers, the English regard travel as good for the character.

Eunuch and Lady of the harem.

Colony of freed slaves founded in Africa

West Africa, 10 May

Three British transport ships have anchored on the Sierra Leone river. They are carrying 411 immigrants, four-fifths black men and one-fifth white women, sent to colonise the territory.

The colonists include freed slaves, negro loyalists, who supported Britain in the American War of Independence, and the black poor of London, former domestic servants and the victims of London society's frequent changes in fashion. They have called their settlement Granville Town, after Granville Sharp, their patron.

The settlement comes as the morality of the slave trade is being increasingly questioned in Britain. The Rev John Newton, the rector of St Mary Woolnoth and a former slaver, and Ottobah Cugoana and Olaudah Equiano, former slaves, have just published their memoirs and a committee has been formed in London, led by Thomas Clarkson, Granville Sharp, Samuel Hoare and William Wilberforce, to further the cause of abolition.

India corruption charges

Warren Hastings: castigated by the eloquence of the MP, Edmund Burke.

London, 3 April

Warren Hastings, the governor general of Bengal and effective ruler of British India, is to be impeached by parliament.

The 22 articles of impeachment – including violation of treaties, the sale of states, the stealing of treasure, fraud, corruption and judicial murder – were accepted after a brilliant speech by Edmund Burke, an MP who had himself invested heavily in the East India Company. Whigs are united against Hastings, while Tories are happy to sacrifice him for the well-being of the coalition government.

Hastings has many friends – the tens of thousands of Indians who benefited from his reforms – but none can influence events in the Commons. When Hastings took over as governor general of Bengal in 1772, the taxation system was oppressive and the administration corrupt, while fortunes were being made by company servants.

"We now arm you with full powers," the directors wrote to Hastings, "to make a complete reformation." Taxation was reformed. Customs duties were levied at a uniform rate for British and Indian, and the most corrupt of the Company's officials were dismissed.

In Hastings' favour were his energy, his ability to command and his personal honesty. Against him were his arrogance, his ability to make enemies and his high handedness. For every 10,000 Indians he won as friends, he made ten members of the administration enemies. Amongst them none is more venomous than Sir Philip Francis, the former member of British India's ruling council who briefed Burke.

Hastings, by George Romney.

Russian Czarina fooled by fake buildings

Crimea

Czarina Catherine the Great has made a triumphal progress down the river Dnieper, climaxing her voyage by opening Russia's new naval base at Sevastopol. Particularly gratifying were the many fine buildings along the river bank. But rumour has it that they are merely facades, set up by her lover and adviser Field-Marshal Potemkin, and will be dismantled later. Fakes or not, the czarina was greeted in the Crimea by an old lover, Poniatowski, now king of Poland, and the Emperor Josef II of Austria.

A lengthy round of banquets and parades led up to the ceremonial opening of the new base, where 40 warships lay at anchor. A medal marking the journey shows the bust of Potemkin wearing Roman armour; on the reverse is a map of the route.

The royal sledge of Catherine the Great, the Czarina of Russia.

Ex-slave calls for trade not terror

London

A former slave has added his voice to the growing outcry against the slave trade in the West Indies. Ottobah Cugoano, a freed slave who has just published his memoirs, wants the British government to despatch a fleet to the West Indies immediately to stop slaving.

Cugoano, transported from Africa to America as a child and freed when he became a servant in England, is from the small but growing community of poor blacks who have joined forces with the anti-slave trade campaigner Thomas Clarkson and his parliamentary spokesman, William Wilberforce.

Cugoano says that England will benefit if it stops treating Africans as a human merchandise and starts seeing them as potential customers.

A slave executed by the Dutch.

Giant "wonder boat" is made of iron

London

John Wilkinson, the English industrialist and ironmaster of Staffordshire, is well known for his innovative uses for iron. His latest venture is causing a sensation.

Wilkinson has built a 70-foot-long barge – called *Trial* – with an iron hull. The iron ship was designed specifically to transport the heavy ordinance which Wilkinson is contracted to manufacture for the government. It breaks with centuries of traditional wood-based technology and opens up greater possibilities for both shipbuilding and the British iron industry.

Trial is not the very first iron-hulled boat, but it is by far the biggest.

1787 (1787-1788)

Versailles, 4 September 1787. Louis XVI recalls parliament.

USA, 17 September 1787. The Philadelphia Convention publishes a constitution for the USA.

Versailles, 29 November 1787. Louis XVI promulgates an edict of tolerance, granting civil status to Protestants.

Australia, January 1788. A British fleet led by Captain Arthur Phillip arrives in Botany Bay and hoists the British flag at Port Jackson in Sydney cove. Apart from officials, marines and 579 convicts, the ships carry agricultural implements, seeds, animals and provisions.

Paris, January 1788. The mathematician Joseph Lagrange publishes his *Analytical Mechanics*, a vast synthesis of all the major advances in mechanics.

Versailles, 17 January 1788. Enraged by a charge of despotism, Louis XVI summons a delegation from the Paris parliament to explain its condemnation of the system of sealed orders, which allows the king arbitrarily to imprison unruly subjects.

Normandy, 20 January 1788. After a dispute over the abuse of justice, Normandy's parliament acquits three peasants from Chaumont who had been sentenced for a murder committed in 1783.

Paris, 20 January 1788. Antoine Rivarol publishes a *Little Almanac of Great Men*, a scathing satire of pillars of the establishment.

Paris, 29 January 1788. Parliament approves the king's decree granting civil status to Protestants, without guaranteeing either their freedom of religion or their access to office.

Paris, February 1788. Lomenie de Brienne, the finance minister, is suspected of an anti-parliamentary plot.

France, 17 February 1788. The painter Maurice Quentin de la Tour dies. He was a brilliant portraitist whose works include paintings of major figures of the court and the world of arts.

Paris, 19 February 1788. Abbot Gregoire, Jean Pierre Brissot and the marquis of Lafayette found the Society of Friends of the Blacks to fight against the slave trade.

Versailles, 19 February 1788. Summoned by Louis XVI, a delegation from the Brittany parliament is severely reprimanded for having given its support to the principle of the equality of all the nation's parliaments.

Paris, March 1788. Bernardin de St Pierre publishes another volume of his *Studies of Nature*; the first three volumes appeared in 1784.

Australia, 15 March 1788. In command of two frigates, *La Boussole* and *L'Astrolabe*, the Frenchman la Perouse sails east from Botany Bay for the last lap of his voyage around the world.

USA, 21 March 1788. Almost the entire city of New Orleans is destroyed by fire.

Versailles, 16 April 1788. Louis XVI ends the exile of his unruly cousin, the duke of Orleans, allowing him to return to Paris.

Paris, 16 April 1788. Georges Louis Buffon, author of a 36-volume *Natural History*, dies.

Versailles, 1 May 1788. On the orders of the lord chancellor, Lamoignon, parliament is stripped of all its legislative and judicial powers, which are given to two newly-formed bodies.

Paris, 8 May 1788. After barricading themselves inside the law courts for a night, the councillors Goislard de Montsabert and Duval d'Epremesnil, who had written parliamentary decrees criticising the reforms of the Brienne ministry, are arrested on the orders of Louis XVI.

France, 31 May 1788. Provincial parliaments revolt against judicial reforms.

Brittany, 3 June 1788. Magistrates in Rennes opposed to reforms win a reprieve from threatened exile after a riot in their support.

France, 7 June 1788. Street fighting erupts in Grenoble when royal troops try to break up an illegal meeting of magistrates, called to oppose Lamoignon's judicial reforms.

USA, 21 June 1788. The American constitution comes into force, ratified by nine states.

Finland, 21 June 1788. King Gustavus III of Sweden launches an invasion of Russian Finland without having declared war.

Paris, 28 June 1788. The German musician Jean Vogel, the composer of many famous operas, dies.

Black Sea, June 1788. The Russian Black Sea fleet, commanded by the American naval hero John Paul Jones, defeats the Ottomans in two naval battles near the mouth of the Dnieper river. Earlier in the year, the Russians repelled an Ottoman attempt to seize the Crimea and invaded Moldavia.

Paris, June 1788. *Voyage of the Young Anarcharsis to Greece* by Jean Jacques Barthelemy is published. Based on the fictitious journey of a young Scythian to the Athens of Demosthenes' day, the book brings the Orient and antiquity back into fashion.

French financial reforms blocked by fear

Paris, September 1787

As France plunges further into chaos with food riots on the streets, diehard conservatives appear to have won their campaign to prevent King Louis XVI's advisers bringing in reforms to save the French economy, now close to bankruptcy. Martial law has been imposed by troops under Marshal Biron in response to the riots and to wall posters lampooning the king and his ministers.

The sole glimmer of hope is that the Parisian parliament – exiled two months ago – has been recalled. It will support new loans, provided that the reform edicts are withdrawn and a meeting of the Estates-General – representatives of the clergy, nobility and bourgeoisie – is called.

The deal puts an end to the reforms first proposed by Calonne, comptroller-general, who resigned in April. His successor, Lomenie de Brienne, the archbishop of Toulouse, who opposed the reforms out of office, adopted them only to run into similar opposition from entrenched interests in the aristocracy and the provincial parliaments.

The Parisian rejection of the reform package is seen as a guarantee that other provincial parliaments will follow suit.

Congress plans to colonise Indian lands

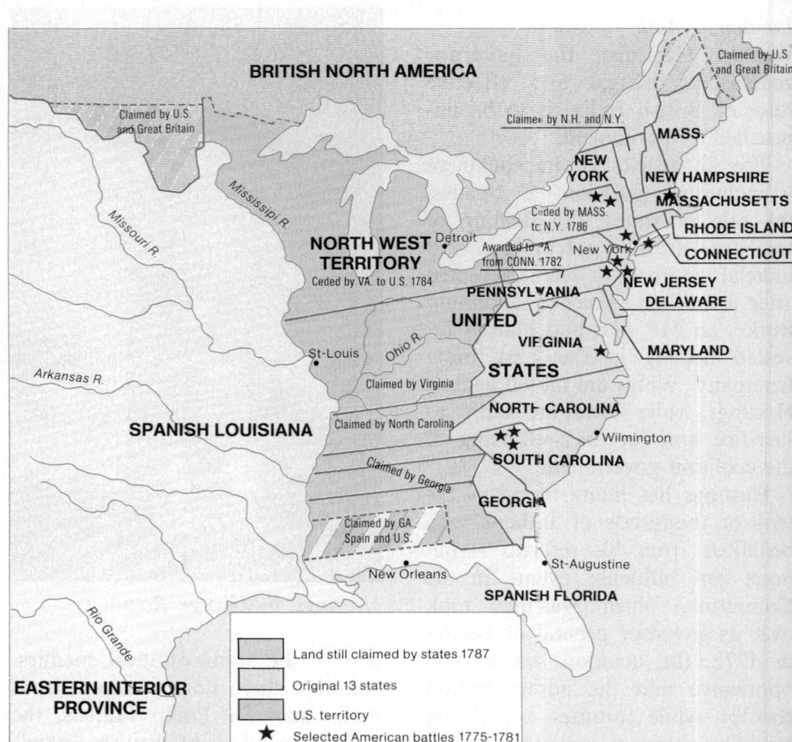

Washington, 1787

Only 11 years after the US declared itself free from colonial rule, the US Congress has approved a measure to extend its territory north-west by colonising former Indian territory. The US now comprises 13 former English colonies on the Atlantic coast. The new Northwest Ordinance provides for up to five new states across the Ohio.

Indian rights and land are protected from invasion unless Congress authorises a "just and lawful war"; yet the new governor is to create townships in places where "the Indian titles shall have been extinguished". The decree does not recognise the vital differences of perception of land ownership between the native population – who exist in a philosophical relationship with the land – and settlers who seek to own parts of it exclusively. Voters in the new territory must be adult, free males owning 200 acres. The governor has 1,000 acres of freehold land; judges have 500.

United States constitution approved

Philadelphia, 17 September 1787
Thirty-nine delegates, representing 12 of the 13 states, approved a constitution for the United States of America today and then adjourned, in the words of the chairman, George Washington, "to the City Tavern, dined together and took a cordial leave of each other". Delegates will take the draft document to their individual states for ratification, after which America will have one supreme law. Only tiny Rhode Island seems likely to dissent.

During weeks of what has been described as "occasionally tumultuous" debate, the major task facing the delegates was the framing of a federal system in which each state would be adequately represented.

George Washington accepts the Consititution of the United States.

Central to the constitution is the concept of the "separation of powers", designed as a system of checks and balances on the executive, the legislature and the judiciary.

All legislative power will be vested in a congress consisting of a senate and a house of representatives, the numbers of representatives based on the taxed populations of the various states. The legislatures of each state will elect two senators to the other house.

The role of the president will be crucial. He will serve for a four-year renewable term and have the right of veto, which Congress can annul by a two-thirds majority. He can be arraigned by the House of Representatives and judged by the Senate and removed from office on conviction for treason, bribery or other "crimes and misdemeanors".

Some southern states are worried that they will be at a numerical disadvantage, although it was a southern delegate, James Madison, who brought them round. "As we are laying the foundations for a great empire here," he told the conference, "we ought to take a permanent view of the subject."

"The Times" hits the London streets

London, 1 January 1788
In a bid to recapture readers, the fledgling *Daily Universal Register* was relaunched today as *The Times*. Its owner, the bookseller turned publisher John Walter, claims that the new title is more easily identified than the *Register*, which he says was easily confused with both the *Annual Register* and *Harris' Register of Covent Garden Ladies*. However, many readers believe that the change of title and the forthcoming redesign of the paper, scheduled for March, are intended to stave off competition from the *World and Fashionable Advertiser*, launched last year. *The Times* has added arts and literature coverage – the *Advertiser's* main features – to its normal diet of parliamentary and city news. Politically *The Times* promises it will have "two faces like Janus: with one it will smile on the friends of Old England, with the other it will frown upon her enemies".

THE TIMES
OR DAILY UNIVERSAL REGISTER

The new face of "The Times".

Orange family back in Low Countries

Netherlands, 1787
William V of Orange is back in power, the Patriotic movement having fallen victim to powerful foreign alliances as well as its own internal weaknesses and contradictions.

For five years, the democratic Patriots have been gaining ground, winning control of town governments in Utrecht and Holland, with the support of the local Free Corps militia. But their support springs mainly from the lower middle-classes, disillusioned by Holland's economic decline compared with France and Britain. They have never won over the peasants, aristocrats or richest merchants.

The democrats' crucial mistake was to turn against the urban regents, who appealed to William for help. When his brother-in-law, the king of Prussia, lent an army, the "revolution" collapsed, and more than 5,000 eminent Patriots went into exile, many in France.

Cartwright's rival to the hand loom

Derbyshire, England, 1787
A visit by an English clergyman to a Derbyshire cotton mill has led to a new development in weaving technology. Edmund Cartwright, having looked round Richard Arkwright's spinning mills, has patented a machine for weaving.

Until now, the weaving process has been carried out on hand looms and has thus lagged behind other branches of the industry which are rapidly being mechanised.

Cartwright's new steam-driven loom, although needing further improvements, is operating in his own factory in Doncaster, Yorkshire. Unfortunately the power loom's future seems insecure. For one thing, Cartwright himself is reported to have money troubles which could slow down its development. And some people, particularly the weavers, remain unconvinced of the need for the change from manual to machine working.

Bach's son is dead

Hamburg, 14 December 1788
The pioneering composer Carl Philipp Emanuel Bach has died aged 74. The second son of J S Bach, he worked for the Prussian crown prince (later Frederick II) from 1738 until 1767, when Frederick, himself a flautist and composer, agreed to let him succeed Telemann (C P E Bach's godfather) as Hamburg's music director. In the city's less conservative atmosphere Bach wrote his most adventurous music, including keyboard works, oratorios and symphonies, often in a passionate, expressive style.

Fundamentalists threaten sultanate

Arabia, 1788
'Abd al-'Aziz has secured the recognition of his son Amir Saud as heir to his Arabian empire. Loyal to the rigorous Islamic fundamentalism of Mohammed ibn 'Abd al-Wahhab, the Saudis are a growing threat to Ottoman influence. The Wahhabi state was established in the Najd plateau over 40 years ago, annexed Riyadh in 1773, and gained control of Jabal Shammar last year. It now threatens the tribal territory of al-Ahsa in the east, the Hijaz to the west, and the Muntafiq on the fringe of Mesopotamia.

1788

Paris, 6 July. Ten thousand troops are called out as unrest mounts in the poorer districts.

France, 13 July. A devastating tornado wipes out crops and causes severe damage to buildings across the country.

Paris, 15 July. Louis XVI jails 12 Breton deputies who protested to him about the judicial reforms ordered by the lord chancellor, Lamoignon, in May.

Paris, 19 July. Prices plunge on the Paris stock exchange.

South-East Asia, 20 July. Thomas de Conway, the governor of the French colony of Pondicherry, abandons plans to send troops to place King Nhuyen Anh back on the throne of Vietnam.

India, August. Tipu Sahib, the sultan of Mysore – who supports France's campaign to prevent Britain from dominating India – sends three ambassadors to France.

England, 2 August. The painter Thomas Gainsborough dies at the age of 61. As well as being a fine landscape artist, Gainsborough was a rival of Sir Joshua Reynolds as the most admired portrait painter of the age, notably for his portrait of the actress Sarah Siddons.

Versailles, 8 August. In an attempt to ward off economic crisis, Louis XVI decrees that the Estates-General will meet on 1 May 1789.

Versailles, 16 August. Having failed to persuade the financiers to provide new funds for the treasury, Lomenie de Brienne, the finance minister, declares the French state bankrupt.

Versailles, 25 August. In an attempt to save France from total economic collapse, Louis XVI recalls Jacques Necker, the Genevaborn Protestant banker, who was disgraced in 1783, to replace Brienne as finance minister.

Paris, 29 August. Eight people are killed in riots following the news of Brienne's resignation.

Paris, 12 September. The jailed Breton nobles, who have become symbolic victims of despotism and the abuse of royal power, are released at Necker's request.

USA, 13 September. New York is declared the federal capital of the USA and the seat of Congress.

The Hague, 15 September. An alliance signed by Britain, Prussia and the Netherlands on 13 August in Berlin is ratified.

Versailles, 19 September. Charles de Barentin becomes lord chancellor, replacing Lamoignon, who has been forced to resign.

Versailles, 23 September. Louis XVI announces that the judicial reforms have been dropped and the traditional roles of the parliaments restored.

Paris, 24 September. The parliament of Paris reassembles in triumph.

Poland, 6 October. The Polish *Diet*, which has effected important administrative reforms since being forced to accept the partition of Poland in 1772, decides to hold a four-year session.

Prussia, October. The Frenchman Jean Blanchard invents a flying ship equipped with six paddles hooked up to a hot-air balloon.

Spain, 14 December. Charles III, king of Spain since 1759, dies and is succeeded by his son Charles IV.

Australia. The British expedition led by Captain Arthur Phillip establishes an agricultural settlement at Parramatta, upriver from Sydney.

Prussia. King Frederick William II issues a "religious edict" abrogating all freedom of worship. The freedom of the press is also abolished.

Ottoman Empire. Continuing their war with the Ottomans, the Russians massacre the captured Turkish inhabitants of several towns in Moldavia and along the Black Sea.

Ottoman Empire. Ali of Teleben, an Albanian nobleman, seizes the town of Yanina and proclaims himself *pasha* of all Albanian territories.

Denmark. Serfdom is abolished.

England. The historian Edward Gibbon completes his *Decline and Fall of the Roman Empire.*

England. The philosopher Jeremy Bentham publishes his *Introduction to the principles of morals and legislation.*

England. The African Association is founded to promote a "legitimate" trade to replace the slave trade.

France. The astronomer Nicole-Reine Lepaute dies. From 1759 she was employed by Lalande, the director of the Paris observatory. Among her works are a monograph on the transit of Venus, published in 1761, and calculations for the sun, moon and planets.

Christianity aided Rome's breakdown

London

It is 24 years since Edward Gibbon, "musing on the ruins of the Capitol at Rome", had the idea of writing a history of the *Decline and Fall of the Roman Empire*. Now his great work, whose early volumes sold so quickly, has been completed with a fifth and sixth volume, with which the diminutive author (who is below five foot in height) has ended his labours.

They bring the history, which began in AD 180 with the death of Marcus Aurelius, down to 1453, the fall of Constantinople and the end of the Eastern empire, and includes Mohammed, Saladin, Genghis Khan and Tamerlane. Gibbon blames the decline of Rome on the loss of its old military virtues and the rise of Christianity. But this in turn helped to civilise the barbarian invaders. "We cannot determine to what height the human species may aspire in their advance towards perfection, but it may be presumed that no people will relapse into their original barbarism."

Human behaviour has universal laws

Konigsberg, East Prussia

Konigsberg's world-famous professor of philosophy, Immanuel Kant, has just published his second *Critique*, on moral philosophy. Seven years ago, in his *Critique of Pure Reason*, Kant argued that our knowledge of the physical world does not arise purely through sense-impressions, as David Hume, the Scottish sceptical philosopher, claimed. Experience is made possible by universal patterns or "categories" of space, time, unity and causality, all based on first principles and imposed on our perceptions by the mind.

Now, in the *Critique of Practical Reason*, Kant argues that our moral duties arise likewise from the mind and its awareness of being under obligation, a concept that he calls "the categorical imperative". Reason demands that we act in such a way that our maxims of conduct could serve as universal laws. Kant, a bachelor who has never left Konigsberg, lives to a strict timetable, beginning his studies at 5am.

Written rules for ancient game of cricket

Classy sport: a game of cricket at Kenfield Hall near Canterbury in Kent.

London

The game of cricket, long popular in English villages and recently taken up by the aristocracy, has been given a written set of rules by the Marylebone Cricket Club in London. Played with bats and balls (now of fixed size) on village greens, cricket satisfies the upper class passions for fresh air, exercise and gambling.

Typically, a prominent landowner will recruit villagers to do battle with rivals, and enjoy a wager on the result. British colonies are also learning the game.

King who brought Spain up to date dies

King Charles III of Spain.

Madrid
The best king Spain has had for many decades, Charles III, has died after taking to his bed with a cold, which developed into high fever. He had ruled Spain for nearly 30 years with an enlightened policy of of material and cultural progress, and many of his reforms should prove to be of outstanding value.

Charles was the king of Naples and brother of the late Spanish king when he took over at the age of 43, after quickly renouncing his Italian kingdom for that of Spain. He proved to be a monarch who governed truly. Upright, inflexible, but at the same time reasonable, he carried out his kingly duties with mechanical exactitude.

His blind spot was that his foreign policy was often dictated by prejudice, such as the hatred of Great Britain which led him to take part unwisely in the American War of Independence, an adventure whose outcome might cause serious damage to the Spanish empire. Charles had also set his heart on taking Gibraltar from the British and laid siege to the rock, but he was unsuccessful. But under the Treaty of Versailles Spain won back Minorca and Florida.

People's vote in Estates-General raised

The Third Estate, burdened by the privileged clergy and aristocracy.

Versailles, 26 December
King Louis XVI has given in to the increasingly urgent demands of the bourgeoisie and has doubled the representation of the Third Estate at the meeting of the Estates-General planned for next May – the first time it will convene for 174 years.

The Third Estate, speaking for some 24 million people out of a total population of 25 million, will therefore equal the First Estate, the nobility, and the Second Estate, the clergy, when they discuss the urgent reforms needed to cope with France's desperate economic crisis.

The added power of the Third Estate may not, however, be reflected in the proceedings, for the king, at the urging of the nobility, has not so far agreed to holding joint debates or permitting a free vote.

English convict ship arrives in Australia

Sailors and marines from HMS Endeavour raise the flag at Sydney Cove.

Sydney, Australia, 26 January
A British convoy, including six transport ships carrying 730 convicts, has landed at Port Jackson. The commander, Arthur Phillip, describes the bay as "the finest harbour in the world". One cove, a quarter of a mile across and half a mile deep, he has called Sydney.

The convoy sailed from England 36 weeks ago. Before Phillip took command many convicts were suffering from smallpox and venereal disease. Although Phillip dramatically improved their conditions, 48 died during the passage.

Of the convicts, 570 were men and 160 women. The youngest was John Hudson, a nine-year-old chimney sweep. The oldest was Dorothy Handland, an 88-year-old rag dealer. Phillip was taking convicts to Australia because he refused to take slaves.

Their first landfall was six days ago at Botany Bay. Phillip found the bay unsuitable for colonisation and sailed round the coast to Sydney, where the second-in-command of the expedition, Captain John Hunter, described the land as resembling a deer park.

While the rest of the convoy waited in Botany Bay they encountered two French ships, commanded by la Perouse, on a world voyage. They also came upon Sydney's indigenous people who waved their fists at the intruders and shouted "*Warra-warra!*" – Go away!

Englishman reports on poverty in France

France
Reports of the misery of the French peasantry are reaching England via the pen of Arthur Young, a traveller and agriculturalist. They echo the dispatches of British diplomats, who sense revolution in the air.

Last year, Young wrote from the Dordogne of "many beggars ... country girls and women without shoes or stockings ... a poverty that strikes at the root of national prosperity". This year his travels took him through Brittany, where he saw primitive husbandry, wild people, mud houses and broken pavements. "Who is this Mons de Chateaubriand, the owner, that has nerves strung for a residence amidst such filth and poverty?" asked Young. In Montauban, he saw similar deprivation and misery.

On 17 April, from the British Embassy in Paris, one diplomat wrote to the Foreign Office of "disgrace and difficulties ... an entire revolution looked forward to with the greatest eagerness".

On 2 July, an envoy who had dismissed rumours of unrest two months earlier wrote: "The spirit of resistance is making hasty strides throughout the kingdom ... some of the regiments have already shown great reluctance to act against their fellow-citizens."

1789 ⇒

Poland, 19 January. The *Diet* suppresses the permanent council and takes over all its powers.

France, January. To avert a major famine, the finance minister Necker imports thousands of tons of grain and flour.

France, January. Electoral rules for the meeting of the Estates-General are published. Third Estate patriots in Brittany and Provence condemn them as unfair and demand equal representation with the other two orders (the nobles and the church).

Sweden, 20 February. King Gustavus III imposes an Act of Union and Security on the Riksdag, establishing despotism.

London, February. King George III regains his sanity after three months of madness, during which the Pitt government framed a bill providing for a regency regulated by Parliament.

Provence, February. Honore Gabriel Riqueti, the count of Mirabeau, is excluded from the order of the nobility after speaking out in favour of the Third Estate.

France, February. Pierre Lavoisier completes his *Elementary Treatise on Chemistry*.

USA, 4 March. The first Congress meets in New York.

Poland, March. The Diet imposes a tax of ten per cent on revenue from lands and 20 per cent on ecclesiastical property.

Istanbul, 7 April. Selim III succeeds his uncle Abdul Hamid as Ottoman sultan.

Pacific, 28 April. After a mutiny provoked by his harsh treatment, the British sailor William Bligh, the commander of the *Bounty*, is cast adrift near the Friendly Islands in a small open boat with 18 men.

USA, 30 April. George Washington is inaugurated as the first president of the USA.

France, April. Members of the Third Estate condemn the heavy tax burden on the poor and demand a constitution which would limit arbitrary royal power.

Paris, April. The Academy of Sciences publishes *Annals of Chemistry*, a compendium of major new discoveries in chemistry and related subjects.

Paris, 28 April. Three hundred people are killed when troops open fire on rioters at the Reveillon wallpaper factory. The riot started after news of a proposed pay cut at the factory.

Paris, 30 April. Two men sentenced to death for their part in the Reveillon riot are hanged.

Marseilles, 30 April. Rioters seize control of the city's three forts, killing one of their commanders.

Versailles, 5 May. The Estates-General is formally opened by Louis XVI.

Versailles, 11 May. Debate at the Estates-General is deadlocked by the Third Estate's refusal to comply with the proposed voting system.

Versailles, 22 May. The nobility follows the example of the clergy by giving up its fiscal privileges.

Prussia, May. The foreign minister, Herzberg, puts forward a plan to destroy Russian influence in Poland.

Austrian Netherlands, May. Weary of the rule of the Habsburg Emperor Josef II, Belgians call for a national monarchy.

Austria, May. The states of Styria and Carniola rise up against the Emperor Josef II.

France, 4 June. The dauphin Louis dies of consumption at the age of seven.

South-East Asia, 14 June. Captain William Bligh, cast adrift in April by his mutinous sailors on the *Bounty*, arrives at Timor, near Java, having sailed his small boat for more than 3,500 miles.

Versailles, 17 June. The Third Estate assembly changes its name to the National Assembly.

Austrian Netherlands, 18 June. Following the refusal of the Belgian states to pay taxes – to block increasingly unpopular decrees by the Emperor Josef II – Austrian troops occupy Brussels.

Versailles, 19 June. The chamber of the clergy votes for union with the Third Estate.

Versailles, 20 June. Following the closure of the Estates chamber by the king, the National Assembly deputies are sworn in at a meeting on the tennis courts of the Jeu de Paume.

Versailles, 27 June. Louis XVI caves in and calls on his "faithful clergy and loyal nobility" to meet jointly with the Third Estate. A group of 47 nobles joins the National Assembly.

Paris, 30 June. A mob attacks the Abbaye prison and frees a group of mutinous French Guards, who have allied with the lower middle classes.

Berlin. The composer Mozart visits Berlin in the hope of gaining a post at court. He is commissioned to write a series of string quartets for the Prussian king, who is a fine cellist.

Frenchmen compile lists of grievances

The French king, Louis XVI, distributing gifts amongst the poor.

France, March

Insufficient food, high taxes, an interfering government, overmighty noblemen and, priests who enrich themselves without labour – these are some of the complaints being listed in France's *Cahiers de doleances* or Books of Grievances.

The books were established by the Estates-General, France's legislative assembly, in 1484, and every tax-paying Frenchman over 25 is eligible to register his complaints with his parish assembly or, if a townsman, with his corporation. Once collected, the local lists are collated and the major points finally presented to the king.

This year's books centre on economics. The Third Estate deplores the heavy burden of taxes faced by the poorest citizens and condemns the activities of government tax collectors who are accused of systematic, gross corruption.

In the towns the professional guilds are under fire for their economic monopolies, while the rural areas concentrate on the nobility's maintenance of defunct feudal rights.

Marie Antoinette, Austrian-born queen of France, at Versailles.

Most important of all are the political demands. The books call for a constitution limiting royal power and establishing equality and the rights to property and individual freedoms.

Radical reforms to boost taxes in Japan

Japan

A radical reform programme, known as the Kansei reforms, has been carried out by the *shogunate* in an attempt to rectify a huge drop in revenue and a steep rise in inflation. The reforms are not only economic. They are also aimed at the widespread bureaucratic corruption which is weakening the administration of the government. In the countryside, the reforms are aimed at restoring tax farming and the building up of rice reserves to cope with the series of famines and natural disasters which plagues the country. Monetary reform has also been carried out, with the reminting of silver coins and a revaluation of the gold currency.

French bourgeoisie demand to be heard

Ceremonial costumes of (l. to r.) clergy, nobility and commons.

Versailles, 5 May
The king is to address the Estates-General today when it meets for the first time since 1614. The people of France care little for the ceremony. They are demanding bread and reform from the Third Estate, which represent them in the legislature.

Much is expected of this meeting. The Books of Grievances, open to every Frenchman, are full and the members of the Third Estate, whose numbers have been doubled, are fully aware of the hopes resting on their shoulders.

Abbe Sieyes summed up these hopes in his pamphlet, *What is the Third Estate?* Answering his own question, he replied: "Everything," adding: "What does it ask? To be something."

All now rests on the king. Advised by his finance minister, the Swiss banker, Necker, he must today address himself to the aspirations of his people.

Washington elected first US president

New York City, 30 April
Looking tired and gaunt, George Washington took the oath of office as the first president of the United States today before a joint session of Congress and swore to "preserve, protect and defend the Constitution".

The 57-year-old Virginia landowner was clearly over awed by the solemnity of the occasion. One senator said that the great war hero seemed "agitated and embarrassed more than he ever was by the leveled cannon or pointed musket".

Washington's election was never in doubt. Members of the electoral college were unanimous in casting their votes for the hero of Yorktown, and today, as he drove from his home at nearby Mount Vernon, his coach was surrounded by well-wishers whenever it stopped. Despite his large land-holdings, Washington is said to be "cash-poor" and needed to borrow money to pay the expenses of this inauguration. He took his oath wearing a simple worsted suit and white silk stockings. The only trace of former military glory was his dress sword. One of his first executive decisions was to appoint the experienced Thomas Jefferson to take charge of foreign affairs. John Adams will be Washington's vice-president.

Washington, by James Peale (elder).

Third Estate swears oath in tennis court

Versailles, 20 June
The representatives of the Third Estate, and those members of the clergy who joined with them three days ago in proclaiming themselves the National Assembly, arrived at the Menus Plaisirs hall this morning only to find it locked against them on the king's orders, ostensibly for "cleaning".

Amid the ensuing uproar, Dr Joseph Guillotin, one of the deputies from Paris, suggested they should meet in the nearby tennis courts of the Jeu de Paume.

They hurried off to this large, bare building with its blue ceiling picked out with golden fleurs de lys and there, with a bench as a desk, they held their meeting while an enthusiastic crowd outside shouted *"Vive l'Assemblee!"* At first there was talk of withdrawing to Paris to "seek the protection of the people", but Jean Joseph Mounier demanded that they must take an oath "never to separate and to meet whenever circumstances demand, until the Constitution of the Kingdom has been firmly established and consolidated".

The delegates went forward one by one to take the oath before the astronomer Jean-Sylvain Bailly, the elected senior member of the Third Estate.

Only one member, Martin d'Auch, refused to sign the oath and, despite cries of protest, was allowed to register his opposition "out of respect for the liberty which all members of the Assembly enjoy".

The Tennis Court Oath, painted by Jacques-Louis David (1748-1825).

Brazil's revolutionary "dentist" arrested

Minas Gerais, Brazil, 10 May
The Portuguese authorities have acted decisively to nip the conspiracy for an independent Brazil in the bud. Today they arrested all the key figures including the leader, Jose Joaquim da Silva, a sub-lieutenant of the dragoons. He is known as *Tiradentes* (the Dentist) because of his knowledge of dentistry.

The would-be revolutionaries were betrayed – although they had failed to agree about anything important. They include idealistic poets and priests who want a new republic as well as landlords and businessmen who are upset because Portugal has drained off the profit from the gold mines.

A Brazilian negro with a brightly coloured tropical bird.

1789 ⇒

Versailles, 9 July. The National Assembly declares itself the Constituent Assembly and sets about preparing a French constitution.

Paris, 12 July. Louis XVI's dismissal of Necker, the highly popular finance minister, fuels the violence in Paris, which is on fire after two days of non-stop rioting.

Paris, 14 July. The Bastille is seized by the people of Paris.

Paris, 15 July. The electors of Paris set up a "Commune" led by Bailly, who is elected mayor of Paris, and Lafayette, who becomes head of the National Guard.

Versailles, 16 July. Louis XVI recalls Necker.

Versailles, 16 July. The court nobility begins to emigrate from France.

Paris, 18 July. Camille Desmoulins publishes the first republican manifesto of the revolution, *La France Libre*.

Versailles, 20 July. Robespierre, a deputy from Arras, backs the revolutionaries.

Paris, 21 July. The Comedie Francaise is to reopen as the Theatre of the Nation.

Paris, 22 July. Bertier, the bailiff of Paris, and his father-in-law, the financier Foulon, are murdered by the mob.

New York City, 27 July. The department of foreign affairs, the first executive agency in the USA, is set up, with Thomas Jefferson at its head.

France, July. A "Great Fear" sweeps through the provinces and the revolution spreads to the provincial towns.

Paris, July. The botanist Antoine Laurent de Jussieu completes his *Genera Plantarum*, a classification of the vegetable world.

Versailles, August. The National Assembly is rocked by a provincial arson campaign and tax boycott.

Germany, August. Influenced by events in France, peasants in the Rhineland rise up in revolt against the nobles' privileges.

New York City, 2 August. A US war department is created, with Henry Knox at its head.

Versailles, 4 August. The Constituent Assembly abolishes the privileges of the nobility, destroying the social structures of the Ancien Regime.

Versailles, 26 August. The Constituent Assembly approves the final version of the Declaration of Human Rights.

France, 26 August. Miners in the Pyrenees rise up in protest against their working conditions.

Paris, August. Jacques Louis David completes his painting *Brutus*, a homage to republican self-sacrifice.

New York City, 2 September. A treasury department, headed by Alexander Hamilton, is created.

Orleans, 13 September. Guardsmen open fire on rioters trying to loot bakeries, killing 90.

Paris, 16 September. Jean-Paul Marat sets up a new newspaper, *L'Ami du Peuple*.

New York City, 24 September. Congress passes the Federal Judiciary Act, creating circuit courts, district courts and a Supreme Court.

New York City, 25 September. Congress proposes 12 amendments to the constitution known as the Bill of Rights.

New York City, 29 September. Congress votes to create a US army.

Paris, 7 October. After a march by the women of Paris to Versailles to demand bread, the royal family is forced to return to Paris, where they take refuge in the Tuileries.

Serbia, 9 October. Having invaded Serbia in the spring, Austrian troops defeat the Ottomans to take Belgrade.

Versailles, 10 October. Louis XVI is named "King of the French" by the Assembly.

Versailles, 10 October. The Paris deputy Joseph Guillotin, a professor of anatomy, says that the most humane way of carrying out a death sentence is decapitation by a single blow of the blade.

Paris, 12 October. The Constituent Assembly transfers from Versailles to Paris.

Paris, 21 October. The deputies impose martial law after the brutal killing of a baker accused of hoarding bread.

Austrian Netherlands, 24 October. The insurgents proclaim independence and strip the Emperor Josef II of his sovereignty over the country.

Germany, 24 October. The author Georges Francois Mareschal dies at Triesdorf in Bavaria. He was known as the "father of puns" for his habit of playing on the meaning of words.

Paris, 29 October. The Assembly approves a decree known as the "silver marc", by which only the rich will be allowed to vote.

Tension in Paris as king sends in troops

Versailles, July

Only a few days after bowing to the pressure of public opinion and summoning his "faithful clergy and loyal nobility" to meet jointly with the Third Estate, Louis XVI has ordered the old marshal de Broglie with 30,000 troops to "defend Paris from unrest". There is no doubt among the deputies of the Third Estate, however, that the king has declared war on them and means to put down their constitutional rebellion by using the army.

It is a move which is full of danger; there is great unrest in the provinces and Paris is as explosive as a powder keg.

French declare everyone has equal rights

Paris, 26 August

The Assembly has today approved the Declaration of the Rights of Man. This document, which states that "men are born and remain free and with equal rights", is based on the theories of the philosopher Rousseau and on the American Declaration of Independence.

It is not, however, merely a pious declaration, but aims to be a workable political document embodying the freedoms long denied to the French under the rule of the divine right of absolute monarchy. It specifies that the "free communication of thoughts is one of the most precious rights of man". From today the French may think, speak and write freely.

Not all the delegates are convinced of the wisdom of the declaration. One, Malouet argued: "Why should we carry men up to the top of a mountain and thence show them the full extent of their rights since we are forced to make them descend again, and assign them limits?"

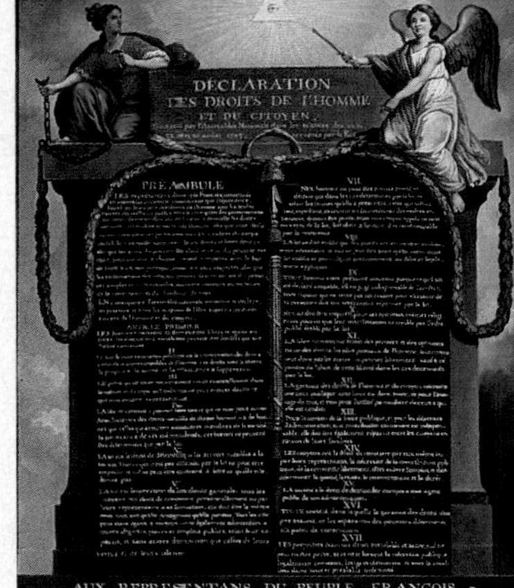

Declaration of the Rights of Man.

Frank confession of insane French writer

Rousseau: confessing all.

Paris

"I desire to set before my fellows the likeness of a man in all the truth of nature, and that man myself." So wrote Jean-Jacques Rousseau at the opening of the *Confession* which he began during his exile in England. The second volume ha only now appeared, 11 years afte he died insane.

In it the author of *The Socia Contract* writes of his innermos feelings with unprecedented frankness. "I am not made like any o those I have seen. This is what have done, what I have thought what I was. I have told the goo and the bad with equal frankness."

Rousseau confesses to his man passions for women – and their for him – to his cold decision t place his illegitimate children in foundling hospital, and to friendships that ended in bitter quarrels and reveals his continual suspicion of conspiracies against him. He ends with his books publicly burn his house stoned, himself expelled.

Parisian mob storms the Bastille

Paris, 14 July

The people of Paris today stormed the Bastille, the grim prison which was the symbol of absolute monarchy. The dramas started at dawn with the looting of the Invalides prison by the mob in search of arms to fight an expected attack by soldiers loyal to the king.

The mob found 32,000 rifles, but no ammunition. A rumour spread that ammunition was stored at the Bastille. The mob rushed there.

The prison was armed with cannon and guarded by 80 soldiers unfit for front-line duty reinforced by 30 Swiss Guards. The crowd, many of them furniture makers armed with their tools, milled around, frightened by the cannons.

A message was sent to the Assembly which despatched a delegation to negotiate with the Bastille's governor, Bernard de Launay. He promptly invited the envoys into the prison for lunch. When they did not return the mob became angry, believing they had been arrested.

A second delegation was then sent in, only to re-emerge to say that the governor refused to surrender. The spokesman added, however, that the cannon were unloaded and that de Launay had promised not to fire if they did not attack. But by now the crowd was in no mood to listen to reason.

The cry went up: " We want the Bastille! Down with the army!" The army in fact showed no desire to intervene, withdrawing to the Champ de Mars. Suddenly a group of youths climbed on to a perfumier's shop built against the prison wall and dropped into the courtyard. They let the drawbridge fall with a crash, killing one of the crowd. The mob rushed into the courtyard. There was a volley of shots. Men fell. A howl of rage went up and the fire was returned.

The fighting raged on into the afternoon until cannon were dragged through the streets to blow down the gates. De Launay surrendered before they could fire; his severed head was later paraded by the mob. There were only seven prisoners in the whole prison, but that was unimportant. An ancient symbol of royal tyranny had fallen.

A crude but vivid view of the siege by Cholat, who was in the crowd.

A surrender note is pushed through.

Feudal privileges to vanish in France

Paris, 5 August

In an amazing all-night sitting the National Assembly has done away with the social structure and feudal rights of the old regime. The delegates had spent the day discussing with much trepidation the reports of turmoil in the provinces where peasants are revolting against their landlords. They seemed fearful, unable to make decisions.

Suddenly, at eight o'clock in the evening, the viscount of Noailles rose. The thing that drove peasants to sack country houses, he said, was the heavy burden of lordly rights and dues. They must be swept away.

The Assembly reacted with astonishment at first and then with wild enthusiasm. Everybody seemed to forget that Noailles was so poor that he was known as "Landless John" and had no rights to give away. It did not matter. A wild enthusiasm seized the Assembly, with delegates eager to give away not only their own rights but also those of other people.

The bishop of Chartres relinquished sporting rights at which the duke of Chatelet muttered: "Ah! The bishop is taking away my game; I'll take something from him." So he declared the end of tithes and was greeted with acclamation.

By eight o'clock this morning some 30 decrees had been made law. An astonishing social revolution had been accomplished in the course of one extraordinary night.

The snakes of privilege are crushed.

African kingdom that grew rich from trade in slaves and cloth

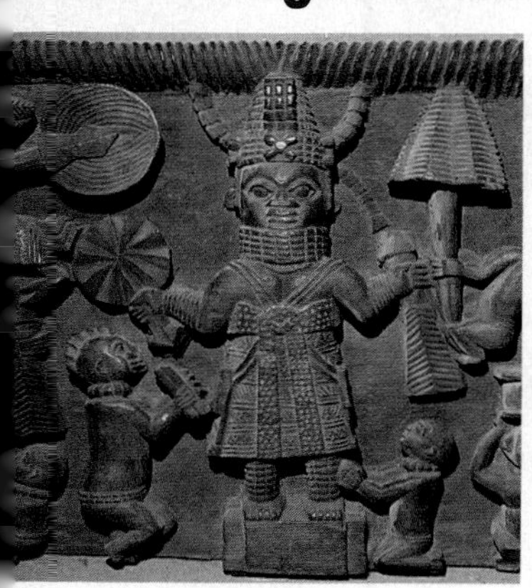

An Oyo chief from Eastern Yoruland, Nigeria. Note the umbrella: symbol of state.

West Africa

The West African slave state of Oyo *(south-western Nigeria)* is mourning the death of its ruler, Abiodun. He came to power 15 years ago by a *coup d'etat*, centralised the administration and weakened the Oyo oligarchies. Under him Oyo grew rich on trade in cloth, manufactured goods and slaves; Porto Novo, in particular, exported tens of thousands of the latter. Its revenues, like those of all the slave ports, went straight to Abiodun's exchequer. Oyo became widely known and the English moralist, Dr Samuel Johnson, pronounced that it contained 6,600 towns and villages. How long this age of prosperity can continue is uncertain. The Oyo army is no longer the unbeatable force of a generation ago.

Wars and political upheavals in the north have made it difficult for its cavalry (the most powerful arm of the forces) to obtain mounts. The state has been increasingly relying on Dahomeyan soldiers to hold down insurrections. The revolt of the Egba people has still not been suppressed. Most significantly of all, an Oyo army was defeated by an army from Borgu in 1783.

1789 (1789-1790)

Black Sea, October 1789. The Russian general Suvorov takes Ochakov, the port at the mouth of the Bug, from the Ottomans.

France, 2 November 1789. All church property is nationalised.

Paris, 12 November 1789. The Assembly decrees that the towns and rural parishes will from now on have elected local councils.

Netherlands, 18 December 1789. Belgian patriots, who recently proclaimed the independence of Belgium, win a victory over the invading Austrians at Turnhout.

France, 1 December 1789. A mutiny of sailors in Toulon sets off a crisis in the French navy.

France, 13 December 1789. The National Guard is created.

France, 19 December 1789. Four hundred million francs' worth of government bonds, known as *assignats*, are issued to help to repay the national debt.

France, 24 December 1789. Protestants are given the vote on the same basis as Catholics.

North Pacific, 1789. A Spanish squadron lands at Nootka Sound, a small natural harbour (*off Vancouver Island*) in Canada, claiming it for Spain. A British trading settlement was established on the sound after its discovery by James Cook in 1778.

West Africa, 1789. The "Province of Freedom" formed two years ago in Sierra Leone collapses as settlers scatter after an attack by the local Temne ruler, "King Jimmy". The freed slaves had incautiously allied with local European slave traders against King Jimmy.

West Africa, 1789. King Abiodun, the great ruler of the Oyo state (*South-western Nigeria*) among the Yoruba people, dies. Oyo has never recovered from its defeat in 1783 by the army of Borgu from the north, and Abiodun's son Awole inherits a weakened kingdom.

India, 1789. Tipu Sahib, the sultan of Mysore, attacks Travancore, an ally of the East India Company in southern India.

USA, 1789. *The Power of Sympathy, or the Triumph of Nature* by William Hill – whose purpose is to "expose the dangerous consequences of seduction" – is the first novel published in the USA.

Ukraine, 1789. Polish nobles blame Russian infiltrators for new unrest among peasants in the Ukraine.

Paris, 21 January 1790. Dr Guillotin proposes a new method of execution: a machine designed to cut off the condemned person's head as painlessly as possible.

Paris, 25 January 1790. Maximilien de Robespierre's demand for universal suffrage is greeted by jeers in the Assembly.

Paris, 13 February 1790. The Assembly bans monastic vows and abolishes contemplative religious orders.

Paris, 19 February 1790. The marquis of Favras is hanged for his part in a plot to help the king escape and to kill Lafayette and Bailly.

Vienna, 20 February 1790. The Emperor Josef II, an embodiment of enlightened despotism, dies at the age of 48. He is succeeded by his brother Leopold, the grand duke of Tuscany.

Avignon, 22 February 1790. The papal consuls resign their positions in Avignon, ending the pope's secular power there. Tithes and feudal rights have already been abolished in the city.

France, 26 February 1790. France is divided into 83 departments.

Paris, 8 March 1790. The Assembly votes in favour of the continuation of slavery in France's colonies.

Paris, 15 March 1790. Jean Paul Rabaut St Etienne, a Protestant, is elected president of the Assembly.

Paris, 21 March 1790. Having banned sealed royal orders and ruled in favour of the equality of death duties, the Assembly abolishes the salt tax, dealing a final death-blow to the abuses of the Ancien Regime.

Paris, 31 March 1790. Robespierre is elected president of the Jacobin Club.

Algiers, 4 April 1790. A 100-year-old peace treaty between France and Algiers is renewed.

Paris, 7 April 1790. The publication of the *Red Book* listing gifts given by Louis XVI reveals that his secret expenses have totalled 228 million francs since the start of his reign. The destination of much of this money is unclear.

France, 17 April 1790. The government bonds known as assignats become legal tender.

Philadelphia, 21 April 1790. Twenty thousand people attend the funeral of the scientist and statesman Benjamin Franklin, who died on 17 April at the age of 84. The inventor of the life-saving lightning conductor, Franklin combined a fascination with new ideas and a determination to pursue Puritan aims to benefit the common good.

West Indies, 3 May 1790. Port Louis, the capital of Tobago, is destroyed by fire.

Satire bites as France allows free speech

From the shop floor to the streets, the press now shapes public opinion.

Paris, 1789

Political discussion is raging in France as never before, fuelled by a rash of new newspapers and political clubs, all dedicated to dissecting the ever-shifting world of governmental affairs and offering a mix of biting satire and hardhitting criticism.

The latest newspaper to appear is *L'Ami du Peuple*, published by Jean-Paul Marat, an ambitious radical whose book *Chains of Slavery* appeared in England in 177 and who clashed with the authori ties earlier this year for the anti royalist content of his pamphle *Offerings to the Motherland*.

But Marat is only the most re cent of many. The new mood o open discussion emerged in Jul last year when the government re laxed its usual censorship, callin for the public to express opinion on the forthcoming meeting of th Estates-General.

Bastille Day celebrations in France

The Altar of the Fatherland (centre) is the focal point for the ceremony.

Paris, 14 July 1790

About 300,000 people flocked to the Champ de Mars today on the first anniversary of the storming of the Bastille for a ceremony dubbed "The Festival of Federation". Un daunted by torrential rain the watched as the king and othe swore to maintain the constitutio in a celebration of national unity.

Enlightened ruler whose reforms failed

Vienna, 20 February 1790
The emperor Josef II, the Habsburg empire's most ambitious reformer, died today a disappointed man as discontent, generated by his reforms, continued to spark protests and unrest throughout the Holy Roman empire. The emperor, who was 48, had been ill for some time.

During the last few months of his ten-year rule he had become aware of the growing resistance to his reforms, and anticipating his death had written his own epitaph: "Here lies Josef II, who was unfortunate in all his enterprises."

His brother Leopold, recalled from Tuscany, inherits most of these enterprises. One of his first moves will be to decide whether to end Austrian involvement in the unpopular Ottoman war, which has placed a heavy tax burden on Habsburg subjects. Josef's attempts to bring Hungary more directly under Viennese control has already been thwarted, and Leopold will have to accept coronation in Hungary.

Leopold is unlikely to undo other key reforms. The decision to make German the official language, despite its unpopularity in Hungary and Flanders, the abolition of most monasteries, the narrowing of church power, naturally unpopular with prelates, and the introduction of the secret police, who are hated by civil servants, will all remain.

Ironically the Emperor Josef, a follower of the Enlightenment, believed that all his reforms would enhance the dignity of the individual and thus benefit his people.

Enlightened despot: the late Holy Roman Emperor Josef II.

French clergy's property is nationalised

Fate worse than death: caricature from 1789 on clergy's loss of property.

Paris, 22 July 1790
The king reluctantly promulgated the Civil Constitution of the Clergy today. Under this decree, passed after months of intense debate, the clergy's property will be nationalised, and the state will employ priests as it does civil servants.

The constitution also reorganises the geography of the church, cutting the number of dioceses from 139 to 83, with each diocese conforming to the map of the civil departments. The "profane and scandalous" Concordat with Rome has been abolished because, according to the politician the count of Mirabeau, it was concluded "between an immoral pope and a despot, without the knowledge of church or empire", in order to divide the rights and the gold of Frenchmen between two usurpers.

The pope, who was not consulted over the reforms, is unlikely to be pleased by the new constitution: it recognises his supremacy over the Roman Catholic church, but removes the French clergy from his jurisdiction.

European's diaries tell of flourishing slave society in Surinam

London, 1790
When the Scottish-Dutch soldier John Stedman first stepped ashore in Dutch Guiana (*Surinam*) more than 20 years ago he saw "a beautiful negro maid". She was weighed down with chains. Her only other dress was "a rag round her loins which was like her skin cut and carved by the lash of the whip in the most shocking manner". The girl's crime was to fail to please her owner in a trivial domestic task.

Stedman fought an army of runaway slaves who began to massacre whites. Yet he never lost respect for "my brother the negro". After a life of adventure he has settled in England where he has written a journal of a five-year campaign against the rebels. It is an intimate account of a slave-owning society from within. Stedman is not opposed to slavery as such, only to the unnecessary excesses of those abusing the system. These include overgrown widows, stale beauties and over-aged maids" who torture young slave women to death. The jealousy is overtly sexual. Stedman claims that many of the white men in this and similar colonies are frequently exhausted by their relations with "uninhibited" black women. He also admires the skill and courage of blacks as jungle fighters. It is only with the aid of "slaves in red coats" (soldiers) that white rule survives.

Skinning a snake in Dutch Guiana.

One casualty of a slave revolt.

No matter what it is, it won't go away

Paris, 1789
A new book by the French chemist Antoine Lavoisier contains many new ideas on the properties and behaviour of matter. Called an *Elementary Treatise on Chemistry,* it describes most of the discoveries of the age and is the first to provide a complete list of known elements.

Explicit reference is made to an important principle that others such as Black and Cavendish have stated implicitly. It is the Law of Conservation of Matter. In a passage on fermentation, Lavoisier declares that in the laboratory and in nature matter is always conserved: the same amount exists after a chemical process as before.

1790 ⇒

France, 10 May. At Montauban, in the south, Catholics and aristocrats clash with Protestants and members of the National Guard, leaving five dead and 16 others injured. When 55 patriots are thrown into jail, Protestants begin to flee from the town.

Paris, 21 May. Paris is divided into 48 zones.

Paris, 22 May. A law is passed whereby the Assembly and the king will share the right to declare war.

France, 29 May. The patriots imprisoned at Montauban are freed.

West Indies, 9 June. Civil war breaks out in Martinique between white settlers and Blacks campaigning for equality.

Avignon, 12 June. Avignon breaks its ties with Vatican and seeks union with France.

France, 15 June. Called out in support of patriots, Protestant militiamen massacre about 300 Catholic "aristocrats" in Nimes.

Paris, 19 June. The Assembly passes a law abolishing the hereditary nobility.

Paris, 3 July. The marquis of Condorcet proposes giving civil rights to women.

Baltic, 9 July. Pursuing their war with Russia, which broke out two years ago, the Swedes win the great naval battle of Svensksund, sinking or capturing a third of the Russian fleet.

France, 12 July. The Assembly approves a Civil Constitution providing for the election of priests and bishops.

Paris, 14 July. A huge celebration of the Federation – a nationwide bond of mutual help and brotherhood, adopted by the Assembly on 7 June – is held on the Champ de Mars.

Paris, 23 July. A letter from Pope Pius VI dated 10 July condemns the proposed new Civil Constitution for the French church. It arrives the day after the king approves the proposals.

Lyons, 26 July. An attempt at a counter-revolution is put down by the National Guard.

Prussia, 27 July. Prussia and Austria sign the treaty of Reichenbach, giving Austria a free hand to take action against the Belgians.

Paris, 28 July. The Assembly refuses the Emperor Leopold II the right of passage over French territory to put down the Belgian insurrection, breaking the 1775 alliance between Vienna and Paris.

USA, 1 August. The first census taken in the USA reveals a propulation of nearly four million.

Sweden, 24 August. The treaty of Varala ends the war between Sweden and Russia and returns to the *status quo.*

Paris, 26 August. The Assembly refuses to help Spain in its conflict with Britain over Nootka Sound, breaking the "Family Compact" between the Bourbons of France and Spain.

France, 31 August. A revolt of soldiers in the Chateauvieux garrison at Nancy is put down with the loss of over 300 lives.

West Indies, August. An attempt by planters in Santo Domingo to win independence from France ends in failure.

Paris, 2 September. Forty-five thousand people march in protest at the massacre of mutineers in Nancy.

Paris, 4 September. Jacques Necker is forced to resign as finance minister.

France, 17 September. Sailors mutiny in the port of Brest.

North Pacific, October. Britain and Spain reach agreement on navigation of the North Pacific and the use of Nootka Sound, ending their year-long dispute.

England, October. The politician and philosopher Edmund Burke publishes his *Reflections on the Revolution in France.*

France, 21 October. The tricolour is chosen as the national flag of France.

Paris, 27 October. The Assembly adopts the decimal system for weights and measures.

Netherlands, 22 November. The Austrians start to reconquer the rebellious Belgian states.

Paris, 27 November. The Assembly forces priests to swear allegiance to the church's Civil Constitution.

The Hague, 10 December. Having completed the reconquest of the rebel Belgian states with his capture of Brussels a week ago, the Emperor Leopold II signs a treaty guaranteeing the restoration of Belgian national institutions.

Rhode Island, 21 December. Samuel Slater opens first cotton mill in the USA. The mill has 250 spindles powered by water and operated by children. Slater learnt textile manufacture as an apprentice to a partner of Richard Arkwright, inventor of the water frame.

Ottoman Empire, 22 December. The Russians take Ismail in Bessarabia (*Romania*).

"Canal mania" boosts English trade

The Grand Junction Canal disappears into a tunnel at Blisworth.

England, c.1790

The growing number of people who have lost patience with goods disappearing in the post, and who fear threats to the parcel service on the thief-infested roads, are turning to a safer alternative. The canal system, which will soon link most of the great navigable rivers, carries an increasing weight of general merchandise as well as the bulk loads of coal and timber associated with narrow boats. So popular are the new waterways that wits have coined a new phrase, "Canal Mania".

On one canal the general merchandise moved from Liverpool to Wigan between 1786 and 1787 increased from 3,836 tons to 4,610 tons. Almost 4,000 miles of waterway have been created over the last 30 years, costing £11 million.

But if canal transport is safe, it is slow compared with most land routes. Travelling from London to Glasgow, using successive teams of horses on improved roads, takes only 63 hours. Merchants use slow pack horses less and carriers' wagons more. Another innovation is the commercial traveller with his samples and order book instead of a complete consignment of goods for sale. Yet the high cost of Royal Mail services, often inflated by private tolls on what were public roads, means that modern times have not touched many communities. Some villages are unfamiliar with the potato, sugar and cotton.

Monarch sends impostor to pay tribute

Annam

The king of Annam (Vietnam), Nguyen Hue has recognized Chinese suzerainty over his country by making the long journey to Beijing to present tribute to the emperor, Qianlong. Hue, who was invited to China "to come and be transformed", is being received favourably by the Chinese, following their traditional policy of managing tributary states on "an equal basis of benevolence." On learning that Hue was accompanied by his son, the emperor praised the son for his loyalty and made him crown prince. Yet there is a doubt about Hue's visit. It is said that, reluctant to leave his throne to the mercy of his enemies, he has sent a double to Beijing in his place.

Qianlong, the Emperor of China who established suzerainty over Annam.

London orphans work in MP's mill

London
The new breed of man who is taking up the reins of power in Britain is epitomised by the arrival in the House of Commons of Robert Peel, the third son of a Lancashire mill-master, a self-made man and now head of one of the wealthiest "new money" families in the land.

The Peels were yeoman farmers settled near Blackburn and, like many of their kind, began to feel the pressures generated by large-scale agriculture and industrialisation. Robert's father mortaged their land and with a brother-in-law and a local publican opened a factory for calico printing, to which were later added spinning and weaving, operated by James Hargreaves' spinning jenny.

The enterprise prospered, but the local handloom weavers resented the new technology and wrecked the machines. The Peels moved to Burton-on-Trent and built three new mills and a canal. In response to a growing labour shortage in the region, the Peels hit on the novel idea of recruiting stray children found on the London streets and putting them to work in the mills. Robert, deciding to go into politics, bought himself a pocket borough at Tamworth, Staffordshire.

Revolution fever spreads to Geneva

Geneva
The poor townspeople and the peasants in rural Geneva have been infected with the new freedoms achieved across the border in France. They have now found a leader to press their new-found aspirations for political rights and a national assembly. Jacques Grenos is an aristocrat, but he developed an antagonism to his own class after his exile following the counter-revolution of 1782.

Before 1782 the bourgeois party which Grenos supported had been winning increasing power. In that year France, Zurich and Bern intervened to restore power to the aristocrats. Opponents were banished or went into voluntary exile.

Neither the townspeople nor the peasants have any political rights, and the former group have been increasingly disaffected since 1782 when efforts to improve their lot were reversed. Many of those who live in towns are educated and have been inspired by the French Revolution.

Grenos hopes to capitalise on this. He has a hard task. The aristocrats and the bourgeois are already seeking to compromise on some of their ancient disagreements and to unite against the new threat.

Burke stirs up anti-revolutionary feelings

A cartoonist's view of Burke's attack on revolutionary sympathisers.

London, October
The first denunciation of the French Revolution has come from Edmund Burke, the English Whig parliamentarian. His *Reflections on the Revolution in France*, just published, condemns its philosophical basis as false. Burke does not accept Rousseau's doctrine of a social contract or of the "natural rights" of man in a state of nature. The "real rights of men", he says, "apply only in a civil society ruled by law from which man obtains his right to justice and to his property, inheritance and the fruits of his industry. The state ought not to be considered as nothing better than a partnership agreement in a trade of pepper and coffee, calico and tobacco, to be taken up or dissolved by the fancy of the parties," as the French have torn up their constitution.

For Burke, human society evolves by a slow process like the British constitution, "adapted over the centuries to fit the nature of English society". Britain's "Glorious Revolution" of 100 years ago did not overturn the social order. Burke foresees that the consequences will be bloodshed, civil war and tyranny: "Some popular general will establish a military dictatorship in place of anarchy."

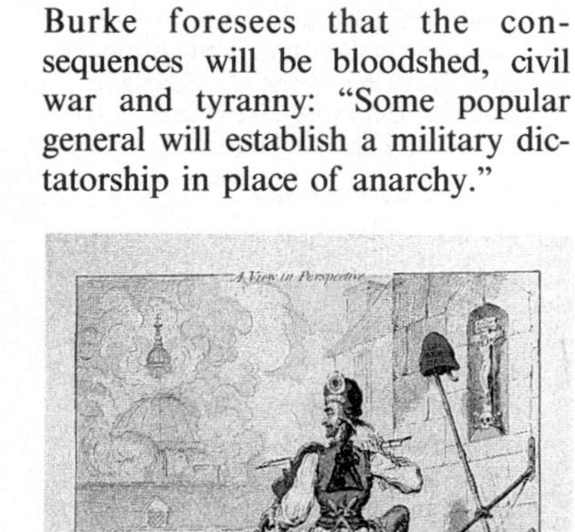

"The Zenith of French Glory": a British view of the Revolution.

Russian gentleman's pamphlet on the evils of serfdom

The Grand Place, and its shops, in the centre of Moscow (in 1795).

St Petersburg
A wealthy Russian belonging to the landed gentry has been sentenced to death for sedition after he published a book recounting the evils of serfdom and proposing its gradual abolition. Alexander Radishchev was sent by the government to study at the university of Leipzig; on his return he became a civil servant. But the Pugachev revolt of 1773-4, in which landlords were massacred, made him aware of the sufferings of the Russian peasants.

In his book *Journey from St Petersburg to Moscow,* he argues that exploitation of the peasants discourages effort and holds down production. The peasant must work six days for his master and only on the seventh day can he plough land for himself. Such a system is counter-productive: "Everything we do for our own sake, everything we do without compulsion, we do carefully, industriously and well. On the other hand, all that we do not do for our own advantage we do carelessly and lazily." Radishchev's radical notions, though they have upset the czarina, may not prove fatal, after all; she is now talking of simply sending him to Siberia.

1790 (1790-1791)

Paris, December 1790. Louis XVI seeks help from Frederick William II of Prussia, asking him to set up a "European congress backed by armed forces".

Southern Africa, 1790. Zwide succeeds his father, Yaka, as chief of the militaristic Ndwandwe chiefdom, centred on the Pongola river. Once subjects of the Tembe kingdom at Maputo Bay, paying tribute in ivory and cattle, the Ndwandwe took advantage of the Tembe's involvement in civil war to build up power by attacking their neighbours.

Austria, 1790. Mozart completes a new opera, a sexual comedy entitled *Cosi fan tutte*. The opera was ordered by the late Emperor Josef II, to whom Mozart was chamber musician.

Paris, 13 January 1791. The Assembly introduces a universal tax on rent and property values.

France, 16 January 1791. A national police force known as the *gendarmerie* is created.

France, 20 January 1791. Talleyrand, who has taken the oath of allegiance to the church's civil constitution – of which he was the main author – is forced to resign as bishop of Autun.

France, January 1791. The requirement to swear allegiance to the church's civil constitution stirs up a widespread rebellion among priests.

France, 2 February 1791. The first bishops are elected under the new civil constitution.

Paris, 14 February 1791. The expedition to circumnavigate the globe led by the famous French explorer la Perouse is pronounced lost. Both his ships, *L'Astrolabe* and *La Boussole*, are believed to have sunk in the Pacific.

France, 19 February 1791. The king's aunts, Adelaide and Victoire, leave the country and seek refuge abroad.

Germany, 23 February 1791. The prince of Conde arrives in Worms to set up an army of exiles.

Philadelphia, 25 February 1791. President Washington signs a bill creating the Bank of the United States.

West Indies, 26 February 1791. The leaders of a Mulatto uprising in Santo Domingo are executed.

Paris, 28 February 1791. After putting down a people's uprising in Vincennes, Lafayette rushes back to Paris to disarm revolutionary plotters.

USA, 4 March 1791. Vermont becomes the 14th state of the Union.

London, 13 March 1791. Thomas Paine, a firm supporter of the French Revolution, publishes the second part of his *Rights of Man*, in which he rejects the arguments in Edmund Burke's *Reflections on the Revolution in France*.

Britain, 21 March 1791. Britain reaches an agreement with Prussia to oppose the expansionist ambitions of Russia.

Paris, 23 March 1791. Etta Palm, a Dutch champion of women's rights, sets up a group of women's clubs called the Confederation of the Friends of Truth. The Friends aim to give assistance to the poor, visit the sick and handicapped and take care of children's education.

Paris, 2 April 1791. Mirabeau, who has proved himself a highly influential force in the Assembly, dies. Poisoning is suspected.

Rome, 13 April 1791. Pope Pius VI threatens to suspend all priests who have sworn allegiance to the French church's civil constitution unless they recant within 40 days.

Paris, 18 April 1791. National Guardsmen prevent Louis XVI and his family from leaving Paris.

Poland, 3 May 1791. Stanislas II Augustus Poniatowski, the king of Poland, creates a constitution for his country providing for an hereditary monarchy and the separation of executive, legislative and judicial powers.

Paris, 16 May 1791. Maximilien de Robespierre, an increasingly influential figure on the extreme left of the Assembly, persuades the deputies to vote against seeking their own re-election.

Paris, 26 May 1791. The Assembly forces Louis XVI to hand over all the assets of the crown to the nation.

Paris, 30 May 1791. Robespierre calls for the abolition of the death penalty.

Paris, 1 June 1791. The Assembly abolishes all forms of torture.

Paris, 14 June 1791. The le Chapelier law bans strikes and abolishes all workers' associations.

France, 25 June 1791. The royal family return to Paris after their attempt to flee ended with the arrest at Varennes.

Paris, 25 June 1791. The Assembly temporarily suspends Louis XVI's powers.

France, 26 June 1791. News of the king's attempted escape sets off serious unrest in the Lyons region.

Brussels, 29 June 1791. The count of Provence, the brother of Louis XVI, arrives in Brussels after successfully fleeing from Paris.

William Blake: poet of revolutionary age

"Glad Days": from "Songs of Innocence" by William Blake.

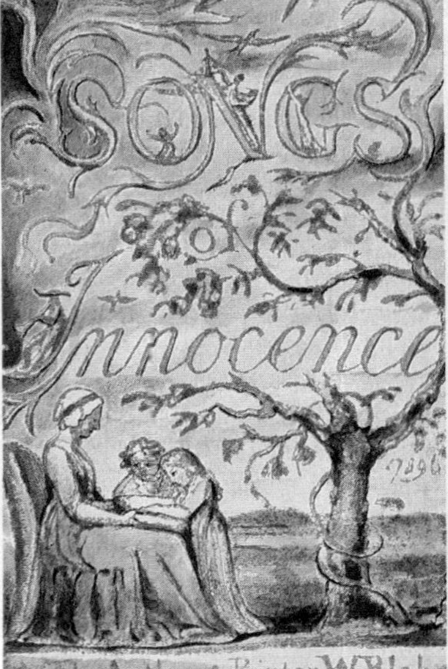

Title page from William Blake's "Songs of Innocence".

London, 1790

William Blake, an engraver, of Poland Street, Soho, has invented a method of "illuminated printing" for his book of poems, *Songs of Innocence*. Words and images are combined on a single plate, resembling mediaeval illuminated manuscript. Each volume is finished by hand in full colour and no two are the same.

The poems concern man's childlike capacity for joy, spoiled by the "mind-forged manacles" put on him by society and religion. "How can the bird that is born for joy sit in a cage and sing?" Blake calls himself a "Son of Liberty" and openly wears the red revolutionary bonnet in the streets. He has written and printed, but not yet published, *The French Revolution*, a dramatised debate between king, nobles and commons.

His mystical work, *The Marriage of Heaven and Hell*, denies the separate existence of God and the soul of man. "The road of excess leads to the palace of wisdom", runs one of his "Proverbs of Hell".

"Semaphore" helps fast communication

Paris, 2 March 1791

A new system of rapid communication was unveiled today, and the transfer of information will never be the same again. Created by the engineer Claude Chappe, the optical telegraph is a truly revolutionary invention.

The device is simple: machines equipped with mobile arms are sited on towers built on open ground. The arms may be moved into 196 positions, 92 of which represent the signs used in transmitting a message. The system of signs is known as "semaphore".

The operator need only consult a codebook before sending information on to the next tower where it can be read by another operator, armed with a telescope, and duly passed on once more.

Armed for communication: Claude Chappe's original optical telegraph.

Paine's "Rights of Man" backs revolution

Thomas Paine, as seen by contemporary political cartoonist Cruikshank.

London, March 1791
Many writers have challenged Edmund Burke's anti-Revolution pamphlet, *Reflections on the Revolution in France*, but the most outspoken response has come from Thomas Paine, a Norfolk man who played a part in the American Revolution. *The Rights of Man* which he has written is dedicated to George Washington. It accuses Burke of outrageous abuse on the French Revolution and the principles of liberty". Paine's tract explains the origins of the revolution in the ideas of Montesquieu, Rousseau and others and describes the Rights of Man as essentially that men are born free and equal in their rights to liberty, property, security and resistance of oppression.

"Man has no property in man," he says, "There is a dawn of reason rising on the world."

Slavery bill vetoed

London, 18 April 1791
After a speech of four hours in the House of Commons today, William Wilberforce moved that the import of African slaves into British colonies should be banned. He lost the vote by 163 to 88, but intends to keep the anti-slavery campaign going. Wilberforce, the son of a rich merchant family from Yorkshire, believes that his cause has been harmed by the abortive rebellion of slaves in the French colony of Santo Domingo, where many white slave owners have been killed.

Aztec art is dug up

Mexico, 1790
Drainage work in Mexico City has uncovered two massive pieces of pre-Spanish conquest Aztec sculpture. The first is already becoming known as the "Stone of the Sun", a circular object with an agonised face, tongue protruding. The second is an elaborate block weighing many tons, representing the goddess Quoatlicue or another named Teoyamiqui. The block has clawed feet and tusks. Both are housed in the university. The round stone might be a calendar.

Louis XVI's flight fails

Exposed: the fleeing French royal family is arrested at Varennes.

Varennes, 21 June 1791
The French royal family have been arrested at Varennes as they attempted to flee in disguise to Metz to join the army of the marquis of Bouille. The attempt was well planned by the count of Fersen, the Swedish officer who is believed to be the queen's lover. Dressed as a hackney driver, he smuggled the royal family out of the Tuileries.

They intended to head east towards the village of Pont de Sommeville where they would be met by the young duke of Choiseul and his hussars. But they were delayed and the villagers became suspicious of the soldiers, who had to hide in the woods and got lost.

The king, disguised as a valet, drove on and reached Varennes, 142 miles from Paris, where he was recognised by a horseman sent in search of him by Lafayette, the commander of the National Guard. The fugitives were escorted to the shop of the local prosecutor, a grocer named Sauce, where they were arrested. They are now on their way back to Paris.

Polish liberals oust Russia's old regime

Warsaw, 3 May 1791
Taking advantage of Russia's preoccupation with war with the Ottoman empire a group of Polish patriots today staged a *coup d'etat* to throw off the Russian yoke and introduce a new constitution to rid the country of its out-dated and anarchical customs. The patriots' leader, Hugo Kollontaj, acted when opponents of reform in the parliament were away.

Class distinctions are abolished and the special privileges of the gentry, including land ownership and access to state and church offices, are opened to townsmen. Plans are being made to abolish serfdom. But the Czarina Catherine is none too pleased at the course of events.

King splits Canada up into two parts

London, 19 June 1791
King George III today signed the Constitution Act, granting equal rights to the French and English inhabitants of Canada. The region is split into two provinces, each with its own representative assembly. In Quebec province there will be a huge French majority. French is recognised, with English, as the official language and full rights are granted to Roman Catholics.

Some see the measures as gratitude to the French for their loyalty during the American War of Independence. Others think that Britain has realised that British Canada cannot survive with a large disaffected French population in the north and a new republic to the south.

1791 ⇒

Pacific, June. The French navigator Etienne Marchand takes possession of the Marquesas Islands for France and renames them the Revolution Isles.

Paris, June. The publication of *The Spirit of the Revolution* by Louis Antoine de St Just, an ardent supporter of Robespierre, is a great success.

Italy, 6 July. At Padua, the Emperor Leopold II calls on the monarchs of Europe to join him in demanding the king of France's freedom.

England, 14 July. Celebrations to mark the anniversary of the fall of the Bastille cause a riot in Birmingham. A banquet given by the pro-liberal chemist Joseph Priestley is broken up by a mob incited by Anglican clergymen.

Paris, 15 July. The Assembly decrees that Louis XVI was not responsible for his own actions in fleeing and that he can only be put on trial after his abdication.

Paris, 16 July. Louis XVI is suspended from office until he agrees to ratify the constitution.

Paris, 16 July. A major split opens up in the Jacobin Club over the future of the monarchy.

Paris, 17 July. A republican demonstration on the Champ de Mars calling for the deposition of the king ends in bloodshed when the National Guard opens fire on the crowd, killing dozens.

Paris, 24 July. On the instigation of Robespierre, all Jacobins opposed to the principles of the Revolution – known as Feuillants – are expelled from the society.

Vienna, 25 July. Chancellor Kaunitz opens talks with Prussia aimed at setting up a European congress opposed to the French revolution.

Ottoman empire, 4 August. Austria and the Ottoman empire sign the peace of Sistova, by which Belgrade is returned to the Ottomans.

West Indies, 12 August. Black slaves on the island of Santo Domingo rise up against their white masters.

Prussia, 27 August. The Emperor Leopold II and Frederick William II of Prussia issue a joint declaration at Pillnitz in support of the French monarchy.

Paris, 8 September. The Salon opens at the Louvre palace. 247 artists, including 19 women, exhibit their works.

France, 9 September. Royalists take control of Arles and barricade themselves inside the town.

Paris, 14 September. Louis XVI solemnly swears his allegiance to the French constitution.

France, 14 September. Avignon and the papal state of the Comtat Venaissin are formally joined to France.

France, 27 September. Jews in France are granted French citizenship.

Paris, 30 September. During its final session, the Assembly decrees a general amnesty for all those sentenced for rioting since 1788.

Paris, September. The author Olympe de Gouges publishes a declaration of the rights of women.

Paris, 1 October. The National Legislative Assembly holds its first meeting. It comprises 745 deputies: on the right are 264 Feuillants; on the left 136 Jacobins, led by Condorcet and Brissot; and 345 independents.

Paris, 8 October. Lafayette resigns his post as commander of the National Guard in Paris.

Belfast, 14 October. The Protestant lawyer Theobald Wolfe Tone sets up the Belfast Society of United Irishmen, calling for the emancipation of Catholics – who are denied the right to vote – and parliamentary reform.

Avignon, 17 October. Sixty-one prisoners – arrested in August when the patriots took control of Avignon – are massacred in reprisal for the murder of the patriot secretary of the commune, Lescuyer.

West Indies, 19 October. An alliance is signed between the leaders of the Mulatto revolt in Santo Domingo and the royalist commanders who protect the white planters in west of the island.

Paris, October. The marquis de Sade publishes a work of fiction entitled *Justine or the Misfortunes of Virtue*, in which virtue is punished and vice triumphs. It was written during his imprisonment in the Bastille.

USA, 4 November. US troops under Arthur St Clair, the governor of the Northwest Territory, suffer a humiliating defeat in a battle with Ohio Indians under Chief Little Turtle.

France, 4 November. The marquis of Hericy and 84 other noblemen involved in a royalist plot are arrested in Caen.

India, 6 November. The French colony of Chandernagore promulgates its own constitution.

Dublin, 6 November. The Dublin Society of United Irishmen is set up.

Europeans intend to restore French king

Royal solidarity: the emperor, the king of Prussia and the elector of Saxony.

Pillnitz, Prussia, 27 August

The sovereigns of Europe, in a gesture of support for their cousin Louis XVI, have declared that royal authority should be restored in France.

Meeting at Pillnitz in Prussia, Leopold II of Austria and Frederick William II of Prussia have invited the rest of Europe's rulers to join in their attack on the revol utionary government.

The first response of France' Constituent Assembly was to pre pare for war with Europe, but cool er heads have realised that the De claration of Pillnitz is only a diplo matic move, designed to pressuris the Assembly and bolster the hope of the French king.

Rebel slaves take part of Santo Domingo

Santo Domingo, 24 August

The black slaves of France's colony of Santo Domingo, "the pearl of the Antilles", have risen in a bloody revolt against their masters, the *grands blancs*, or rich plantation owners. A French expeditionary force is heading for the island.

Whites have died and the canefields have been burnt in the fertile Plaine du Nord area. The revolt has been directly inspired by the Revolution in France. In May the National Assembly decided to give the vote to the *gens de couleur*, the colony's Mulattoes and free Blacks. The planters, while demanding colonial autonomy, refused to comply, and a major controversy began.

Taking advantage of the confusion, some 100,000 of the island's half a million slaves chose to revolt on 12 August. Driving the White from their plantations, they hav destroyed the sugar and coffe crops and are currently in contro of part of the island.

Toussaint-Louverture: rebel leader.

French revolution fires Irish rebels

Dublin, December
Wolfe Tone, a young Protestant lawyer fired by the ideas of the French Revolution, has helped to found a society of United Irishmen to fight for social, political and economic rights for all Irish, Catholic and Protestant. Its supporters, largely Dublin and Belfast middle class, have been deeply impressed by the all-men-are-created-equal slogan of the Americans and the cries of "Liberty, Equality, Fraternity" heard in Paris.

London has been seeking to respond to Irish Catholic grievances. Catholics now hold the franchise on equal terms with the Protestants; they can serve on juries and be given junior commissioned ranks in the army. But the Anglo-Irish governing class refuses to agree to complete equality for Catholics for fear of losing its ascendancy.

Whatever happens, the United Irishmen are not interested in mere reforms; they want complete independence for Ireland. They are allied with agrarian terrorists and Tone plans a secret trip to Paris to persuade the French to send troops to support an Irish rebellion. In response the Protestants in Ulster have formed an Orange Society to fight for their interests.

An Irish rebel: a follower of the United Irishmen leader, Wolfe Tone.

King signs constitution

The nation gives the king a constitution as clergy and nobles scrutinise it.

Paris, 4 September
King Louis XVI today approved France's first constitution. It was finally agreed yesterday after two years of work by the Assembly. The constitution embodies all the laws passed since that fateful day in 1789 when the Third Estate met in the royal tennis court at Versailles.

With his own hand Louis has, in fact, signed the death sentence of the absolute monarchy. France retains a monarchy, but it is a figurehead institution. The only power left to the king is to hold up for three years decrees issued by the Assembly. He has become, in effect, a civil servant of the state, with a salary of 50 million livres. He has even had the right to declare war and conclude international treaties taken away from him.

Power now rests with the Legislative Assembly, made up of 745 deputies elected for two years by 50,000 electors who are themselves to be appointed by "active" citizens paying an annual tax equal to at least three days' work. The king, despite his reservations on the viability of the constitution, has agreed to accept it before the Assembly.

Jews and actors better off in France

Paris
The social and economic impact of the Revolution is being felt in every aspect of life. Actors, Jews and Protestants now officially enjoy full civil rights, although some actors still find it difficult to get married in church, while Jews and Protestants still suffer from traditional prejudice.

Civil marriage has been introduced, and there is much agitation for a law allowing divorce. Socially, although gambling and the theatre are flourishing, people are more discreet in dress and manners.

The ending of feudal rights also ended feudal responsibilities, so another law had to be introduced for the state to take over the feeding of abandoned children, formerly the responsibility of the lord on whose land they were found. Perhaps the most popular of the reforms is the abolition of the "sealed orders" by which the king could consign anyone to prison.

Economically, abolition of both the salt tax and the Paris city toll has been heartily approved by the populace, but the cutting of the customs tariffs which have protected French industries has aroused much opposition.

Mozart dies of a fever, aged only 35

Vienna, 5 December
Last December, Mozart saw Haydn off on his long journey to London; fearing that his elderly friend would not survive the trip he wept and said: "We shall never meet again!" His prophecy proved sadly right; but today it was Mozart who died, of a fever, aged only 35.

In spite of his early death, no musician can challenge Mozart's greatness. A child prodigy, he astonished audiences in Vienna, Paris and London; he wrote the first of his symphonies at nine and his first opera at 12. Frustrated by the limited opportunities of his native Salzburg, Mozart settled in Vienna in 1781, married in 1782 and gained a minor court post in 1787. Despite often living beyond his means and borrowing money, Mozart earned a good living from teaching and composing, especially piano concertos and operas (including *The Marriage of Figaro* (1786), *Don Giovanni* (1787) and *The Magic Flute* (1791)). He leaves a requiem mass unfinished.

Wolfgang Amadeus Mozart.

Writer jailed for warning on Russia

Japan
The military commentator Hayashi Shihei has been arrested for publishing a book in which he warns of the dangers of a Russian invasion and advocates the development of Japan's northern defences.

He had great difficulty in raising the money to print the book and knew that it would cause trouble, for in the preface he wrote: "I realise that I have gone far beyond my station and that I shall not escape punishment. But it is his words and not the author which matter."

When his arrest was ordered for spreading false information and criticising official policies, he recited an epigram: "Will this head fly or won't it? Spring will soon be here." We shall see. Meanwhile he is locked up in Edo prison, awaiting trial.

1791 (1791-1792)

Paris, 11 November 1791. Using one of his few remaining powers, Louis XVI vetoes decrees ordering French emigres, including his own brother, to return to France.

China, 21 November 1791. The French navigator Etienne Marchand sets a new record for a crossing of the Pacific Ocean, completing the journey in 60 days.

Paris, 28 November 1791. Maximilien Robespierre is elected president of the Jacobin Club.

USA, 15 December 1791. Virginia is the tenth state to approve the ten amendments to the constitution known collectively as the Bill of Rights. As three-quarters of the states have now ratified the amendments, they become law.

Paris, 19 December 1791. Louis XVI vetoes a decree imposing punitive measures on priests who refuse to swear allegiance to the church's civil constitution.

Paris, 1791. The Dutch feminist Etta Palm leads a women's delegation to the Assembly and makes a speech calling for women's rights in education, politics, law and employment.

Japan, 1791. The famous author Santo Kyoden is sentenced to 50 days' house arrest in handcuffs for the publication of three risque books which have fallen foul of new censorship regulations. The books have been banned and the publisher heavily fined.

West Africa, 1791. Uthman dan Fodio – a scholar and poet in the Arabic and Fula languages, who has became an itinerant missionary preaching strict Islamic doctrine – is appointed tutor to the Gobir royal family in Niger. After taking up his new job, he has visions under the influence of Sufism and becomes an influential figure at the Gobir court.

West Africa, 1791. King Pepple of Bonny seizes control of slave trading at New Calabar (*Nigeria*) from his base in the Niger delta, establishing a prosperous coastal trade.

Australia, 1791. The third British fleet to arrive in Australia since 1788 increases the number of convicts and civilians in the new settlement at Sydney, putting extra pressure on supplies, already low as a result of crop failure from drought and inappropriate farming techniques.

England, 1791. The Sierra Leone Company is founded to promote "legitimate" trade to replace the slave trade in Sierra Leone.

England, 1791. The Scottish author James Boswell writes a biographical masterpiece entitled *Life of Samuel Johnson.*

Paris, January 1792. A split in the Jacobins between Robespierre and the Girondin party, led by Brissot – who favours war with the other European powers – is confirmed.

Ottoman Empire, 9 January 1792. The Ottomans sign a treaty with the Russians at Jassy ending their five-year war. Moldavia is returned to the Ottomans, but the Russians retain Ochakov and all the conquered lands between the Bug and Dniester rivers. Under the treaty Sultan Selim III also formally recognises the Russian annexation of the Crimea, achieved in 1783.

Paris, 24 January 1792. Five days of looting ends in a riot as the cost of living soars.

London, 25 January 1792. A political society modelled on the French Jacobins is set up. It is called the London Corresponding Society.

West Indies, 28 January 1792. The rebellious slaves in Santo Domingo launch an attack on the city of the Cap.

Vienna, 7 February 1792. Austria and Prussia sign a new military convention against France.

Vienna, 7 February 1792. The Italian composer Domenico Cimarosa presents his comic opera *The Secret Marriage* to great acclaim.

London, 23 February 1792. Sir Joshua Reynolds, the first president of the Royal Academy and one of the most brilliant portrait painters of his day, dies.

Strasbourg, 1 March 1792. Leopold II dies and is succeeded as emperor by his son Francis II.

Paris, 5 March 1792. The Sorbonne and the faculties of theology are banned.

Paris, 20 March 1792. The Legislative Assembly approves the use of the guillotine.

Paris, 23 March 1792 A ministry dominated by Girodins is formed.

Paris, 24 March 1792. Political rights are granted to free coloured men in the colonies.

Sweden, 29 March 1792. Gustavus III, king of Sweden since 1771, dies from wounds sustained in an attack by a nobleman, Ankaestrom, on 16 March at a masked ball. He was one of the firmest backers of the restoration of absolute monarchy in France.

USA, 2 April 1792. The first silver dollar is struck.

England, 1792. The chemist William Murdoch perfects a technique for the use of gas lighting.

Sloth, rudeness and high spirits recalled

London, 1791

Since the death of Dr Samuel Johnson seven years ago there has been a rush of memoirs about him. Now comes the long-awaited two-volume *Life of Johnson* by his Scots companion, James Boswell.

Boswell met Johnson in 1763 when the doctor was 54, his wife was dead, his *Dictionary* completed. He was already devoting most of his energy to conversation. Boswell made a habit of taking notes of Johnson's talk "of extraordinary vigour and vivacity" as soon as he left his presence.

In 1785 he published his journal of their entertaining *Tour to the Hebrides* when Johnson was 60, which had great success. He leaves out nothing – as well as the sayings, Johnson's slovenly dress, ungainly movements, uncouth eating habits, Lichfield accent, and mixture of melancholy, sloth, rudeness and high spirits contribute to an unforgettable likeness. "He will be seen as he really was," he writes.

Goldsmith, Boswell and Johnson at the Mitre Tavern, London.

Englishman offers to be French gaoler

London, 1791

An English philosopher has amiably offered to go to France, establish a model prison and himself be "gratuitously the gaoler thereof". He is Jeremy Bentham, the author of the newly published *Panopticon*, advocating penal reform.

Bentham was born in 1748; happy and hardworking, unmarried and unimaginative, his passions for friends, music and animals were extremely mild. In 1768 he came upon the formula "the greatest happiness of the greatest number". It has remained the rock of his philosophical principles. People, he believes, should not be punished on the basis of some principle of right or wrong; punishment should depend on the effects which both crime and punishment have on society: on "the greatest number".

States vote for Bill of Rights

Virginia, 15 December 1791

Ten vital amendments to the US Constitution, known as the Bill of Rights, have been ratified by three-quarters of the states and become law. Their acceptance is seen as a personal triumph for James Madison and his supporters, the anti-Federalists, who fear that the original constitution provides insufficient guarantees of rights for the states and individual citizens against central government.

Eight of the amendments protect the rights of individuals: the first guaranteeing freedom of religion, speech, assembly and redress. The second gives citizens the right to bear arms. Others include the right to protection "against unreasonable searches and seizures", the "right to a speedy public trail" and "the right to trail by jury".

Sultan forced to cede Crimea to Russia

A cartoon expressing Europe's attentiveness to Russian expansion.

Jassy, Moldavia, 8 January 1792
After years of procrastination, the Ottoman sultan has finally bowed to the inevitable and accepted Russia's annexation of the Crimea and suzerainty over Georgia.

Fearing that the Czarina Catherine was planning a partition of the Ottoman empire, the sultan declared war on Russia, but the Russians won victory after victory, culminating in the massacre of the Ottoman army at Mashin on 4 April last year; the outcome is the treaty of Jassy, signed today.

Catherine has vastly increased her territories on the Black Sea, thereby causing concern to the British, who see the weakening of the Ottoman positions in the region as a looming threat to British Mediterranean interests. Some observers claim that Catherine dreams of recreating a Byzantine empire based on Constantinople.

Court martial for "Bounty" mutineers

Portsmouth, 1792
The court martial of the ten recaptured *Bounty* mutineers is set to commence on 12 August on board *HMS Duke* here. The ten, who face hanging if convicted, are charged with mutiny and desertion.

The prosecution witnesses will be led by the master of *HMS Bounty*, Captain William Bligh, who was cast adrift with 18 others in a 23-foot longboat on 28 April last year after the *Bounty* had anchored off the Friendly Isles.

In a remarkable feat of seamanship, Bligh's castaways, equipped with food but no maps, managed to sail 3,500 miles to Timor, in the Dutch West Indies, in just 47 days. Bligh and 12 survivors reached England late last year.

The ten mutineers were all captured on Tahiti. Another 12 and the ringleader, Fletcher Christian, plus three taken against their will, are missing, presumed to have settled somewhere in the South Seas.

The mutiny started after the *Bounty's* crew had spent six months in Tahiti collecting 1,000 breadfruit trees to ship to the West Indies. Some of the crew had formed attachments to Tahitian women and wanted to stay. The defence will argue that Bligh was a harsh and sadistic master.

Later portrayal of Bligh taking breadfruit trees aboard HMS Bounty.

War looms as new regime is sworn in

Paris, 23 March 1792
The Girondins, the group of moderates whose leaders were deputies for the Gironde, have brought about the downfall of the Feuillants' government, itself composed of moderate Jacobins, and have been summoned by the king to form a new administration.

Brissot, the Girondin leader, will not join the government: he needs to keep his seat in the Assembly. At stake is the question of war with Austria. The Girondins are in favour of war, but the situation has been thrown into confusion by the unexpected death of Leopold II of Austria, the brother of the queen.

It was Leopold who instigated the Declaration of Pillnitz inviting the European powers to join forces against the French revolutionaries. It seems now that the Girondins and the king are allied in their determination to go to war with the queen's relations.

Authoritarian Swedish king is killed

Stockholm, 29 March 1792
Sweden's formidable king for two decades, Gustavus III, died from his wounds today – two weeks after being shot while attending a masquerade at the opera. He was the victim of a plot conceived by his enemies who ranged from civil servants of noble birth to army officers cherishing grudges from Swedish defeats in wars against the Russians.

Gustavus, who was 46, spent a long period in France before coming to the throne, and one of his first acts was to impose a new constitution suppressing political parties and reducing the powers of the *Riksdag*, the Swedish parliament. He went on to rule as an enlightened despot. Gustavus introduced currency reform, reorganised Swedish defences and also tried, unsuccessfully, to tackle increasing alcoholism by centralising all output of spirits in crown distilleries. But his war with Russia created huge inflation which fed the conspiracy on the part of his many enemies.

Gustavus III, King of Sweden.

First silver dollar minted in America

Philadelphia, 2 April 1792
The newly independent United States of America now has its own coinage, the dollar. The first coins, bearing the head of an eagle, have been struck by the Philadelphia mint on the authority of the Bank of the United States, established by Congress last December.

Gold dollars have 24.75 grains of gold, and silver ones contain 371.25 grains of fine metal, roughly in line with the market ratio for the price of the two metals. However, sceptics warn that there could be difficult times ahead if the two metals fail to hold the same price ratio.

The "hard-money" men behind the US constitution prefer coins to paper money, which is easy to debase and has colonial overtones.

1792 ⇒

Europe, 20 April. Following Chancellor Kaunitz's refusal to dissolve the congress of European sovereigns, the French Legislative Assembly approves by a huge majority the king's proposal to declare war on Austria. Louis XVI's plan to attack his own nephew, the Emperor Francis II, violates the alliance that has linked France and Austria since 1756.

USA, 22 April. President Washington proclaims American neutrality in the war in Europe.

France, 29 April. The Jacobins regain control of Avignon.

New York City, 17 May. A group of 24 merchants and brokers creates the New York stock exchange, on Wall Street.

Poland, 18 May. Russian troops invade Poland.

Paris, 27 May. The Assembly orders the deportation of all priests who refuse to swear allegiance to the church's civil constitution.

Paris, 15 June. In a government reshuffle, moderate Feuillants take power at the expense of the Girondin group known as the Brissotins (followers of Brissot).

Paris, 20 June. A huge mob overruns the Tuileries during a march by the Brissotins to demand that the royal veto of the latest decrees be withdrawn and their ministers recalled.

Paris, 29 June. Lafayette makes an unsuccessful attempt to mobilise the National Guard to break up the Jacobin Club by force.

Germany, 14 July. At Koblenz, the duke of Brunswick, the commander-in-chief of the Prussian army, publishes a manifesto threatening Parisians with exemplary revenge if they do not submit to their monarch.

Poland, 24 July. By approving the confederation formed at Targowica by Polish nobles who support Russia, Stanislas II Augustus Poniatowski, the king of Poland, yields to Catherine II of Russia. This marks the death of the Polish constitution.

Paris, 10 August. The *sans-culottes* seize the Tuileries. The king is taken prisoner and suspended from office.

Paris, 11 August. A revolutionary commune is formed. Antoine Santerre is made head of the National Guard. The Assembly appoints a provisional executive council of six members, including Georges Danton and Jean Marie Roland, and calls a national convention.

Netherlands, 19 August. Lafayette is arrested by the Austrians. The fall of the Tuileries marked the final split between Lafayette and the revolution: the commander of the northern army was asked to hand over power to Dumouriez and chose to desert rather than face the guillotine, crossing the border into the Netherlands.

Paris, 25 August. Du Rozoy, the director of the *Gazette du Paris*, who had been charged with collecting funds for emigres and trying to start a civil war, is the first journalist to be guillotined. All monarchist newspapers have already been banned and their printing presses seized.

France, 26 August. The fortified town of Longwy surrenders to the Prussians.

Paris, 31 August. The Assembly cancels a decree, passed yesterday, that the rebel commune formed on 10 August is illegal.

France, 2 September. Verdun surrenders to the Prussians.

Paris, 2 September. More than 1,100 die as a wave of massacres spreads to the jails of Paris. Many of the killers are tradesmen living near the prisons and the majority of their victims are common criminals.

Paris, 5 September. The Paris deputies, including Robespierre and Danton, are elected to the National Convention.

Paris, 8 September. Bigot de Sainte Croix, the new foreign minister, orders the invasion of Savoy.

Paris, 17 September. The crown jewels are stolen.

Paris, 19 September. Thomas Paine arrives in Paris after fleeing from England, where he faces treason charges for views expressed in his *Rights of Man*, a defence of the French Revolution.

Paris, 20 September. The Assembly legalises divorce.

China. The British king, George III, sends Lord Macartney as a special envoy to the Qing court, but his mission to regularise diplomatic and commercial relations between the two countries achieves little success.

India. Ranjit Singh becomes king of the Sikhs at the age of 12.

Australia. Captain Arthur Phillip, the founder of the first British settlement in Australia in 1788, returns to England. Since the settlement was established, shortages of food and equipment, and conflicts among the settlers and between whites and aborigines, have been common.

The man who lost America saves India

A mechanical growling tiger devouring a British redcoat, made for Tipu.

Southern India, 16 March

Charles, Lord Cornwallis, the man who lost British America, has saved British India. Tipu Sahib of Mysore, who fought three wars against the British, has surrendered. The victors, British, Maratha and Hyderabadi, are to take half his lands.

To the British, Tipu was a man without honour who milked his peasants dry and trained British boy hostages as Hindu dancing girls. Cornwallis' methods were the antithesis of Tipu's. In February 1791 he hanged nine British soldiers for looting. Tipu himself gives the appearance of accepting the terms; but already he has told his advisers he sees the arrangement as only temporary.

Guillotine sharpens up executioner's act

Paris, 25 April

The first execution to be carried out by the supposedly scientific means of the *guillotine* has been carried out on a convicted highwayman, Joseph Pelletier. A large crowd watched as the weighted blade, guided by upright runners, neatly removed the criminal's head.

Named after its inventor, the anatomist Dr Joseph Guillotin, who first demonstrated it to the Constituent Assembly in 1789, the aim of the machine is to replace archaic and brutal forms of execution with a quick, clean death.

In Guillotin's view the murderer, for all his or her criminality, is still a human being, and should be respected as such.

Dr Joseph Guillotin: humanitarian.

Scottish look-alike coast in Pacific

North Pacific, 20 July

Extract from a letter from a British seaman aboard *HMS Discovery* which is exploring the north-west American coast: "We have now reached a latitude level with Newfoundland, exploring the inlets between a large island and the mainland which is dominated by a huge range of snowcapped mountains covered with pine forests."

"Today we were visited by natives in canoes who traded otter skins and salmon for our buttons and beads. Captain Vancouver is due to meet the Spanish Commissioner here shortly to ensure there is no repetition of the Spanish seizing of our small post at Nootka Sound. This beautiful country reminds us of Scotland and looks ideal for British settlement."

Hardliners now firmly in control of revolution

Tuileries seized: king at mercy of mob

Paris: the revolutionary mob breaks into the royal wine cellar.

Paris, 20 June
This day, the anniversary of the Tennis Court Oath and the king's abortive flight to Varennes, has seen the most extraordinary events yet in the French Revolution.

A huge mob armed with all kinds of weapons first invaded the Assembly, where they demonstrated for three hours demanding the removal of the king's right of veto, and then marched on the Tuileries palace.

The people found the king in an anteroom whose door they smashed down with pikes. Then they made the man who was once their absolute ruler stand on a bench while they harangued him, chanting together "No aristocrats! No veto! No priests!".

They did little physical damage to the palace, but they humiliated the king, forcing him to put on that mark of revolutionary fervour, a Phrygian cap, and making him toast his visitors. He did so, saying: "People of Paris, I drink to your health and to that of the French nation." But, despite his bravery, he is now powerless.

Revolution threatened by foreign powers

Paris, 25 July
Fears of intervention by foreign powers in French affairs are growing following the publication in Germany, of a violently worded manifesto in which the duke of Brunswick threatens "exemplary punishment" to France if the slightest harm befalls the French royal family. Paris, he says, will be destroyed, and the revolutionaries punished "in a suitable manner".

The manifesto is believed to have been written not by the duke, but by a French emigre, the marquis of Limon. The threat follows the events of last month when the mob forced its way into the Tuileries palace and humiliated the king, forcing him to wear a Phrygian cap and drink to the French nation.

However, the manifesto has probably done more harm than good to the king at a time when there is an increasing clamour for him to be deposed. With his assertion that the aim of the war is to "put an end to attacks against the throne", the duke has given ammunition to those who argue that the European powers are preparing to invade France in Louis' interests.

French soldiers rally to the Revolution: an opponent's view.

Red caps all the rage for revolutionaries

France
The true revolutionary is not just an activist, but a fashion-plate too. As the revolution advances, so too do its symbols, many of them manifested in the clothes one wears.

The red woollen "Phrygian" cap, symbolising the caps worn by ancient slaves, is especially popular, as are cockades in the national colours of red, white and blue.

Clothing that deliberately reverses current aristocratic fashions is especially favoured. Many revolutionaries sport the baggy trousers that mock the tight breeches (*culottes*) of the nobility.

Voltaire is given a Phrygian cap.

Priests and prisoners torn to pieces

A prisoner before a "court" of drunken revolutionaries, 2-3 September.

Paris, 4 September
For three days now the people of Paris have been swept up in bloody communal madness. Incensed by rumours of treason and fear of the advancing Prussian troops, groups of them are invading the prisons, dragging prisoners from their cells, subjecting them to travesties of trials and cruelly butchering them.

The original idea was to purge the nation of the priests and royalists who had not yet been put to death by the courts. But in the frenzy of killing, ordinary criminals are being hacked to death.

Today it was the turn of an almshouse containing prostitutes, madwomen and young orphaned girls. The killers, soaked in blood, spared none of them. At the Abbaye prison the queen's friend Madame de Lamballe was killed, and her head cut off and stuck on a pike. It was then paraded before the Temple where the king and queen are imprisoned.

1792 ⇒

France, 20 September. The French army under Kellerman defeats the Prussians under the duke of Brunswick at Valmy.

Paris, 21 September. At its first public meeting the National Convention decrees the abolition of the monarchy.

France, 22 September. The French republic is proclaimed. The Convention decides that all official rulings will from now on be dated from Year I of the French republic.

France, 24 September. Revolutionary troops march into Chambery, completing their conquest of Savoy.

USA, 29 September. Despite widespread protests in Pennsylvania and the South, President Washington says that he plans strictly to enforce the whisky excise tax introduced last year.

France, 29 September. Revolutionary troops take Nice.

Rhineland, 30 September. The French army of the Rhine, led by General Custine, seizes Speyer before making for Worms.

Germany, 5 October. French troops take Worms.

France, 7 October. The Austrians lift a siege of Lille.

Paris, 9 October. The Prussians leave Verdun.

Paris, 11 October. Santerre, the commander of the National Guard, resigns following a mutiny of guardsmen.

Germany, 21 October. The French army of the Rhine under Custine takes Mainz.

Germany, 23 October. The Society of German Friends of Liberty and Equality, modelled on the Jacobin Club, is established in Mainz.

Netherlands, 27 October. French forces led by General Dumouriez invade the Austrian Netherlands and march on Mons.

Switzerland, 30 October. French troops seize Basle. A republic is immediately proclaimed.

Netherlands, 6 November. The French under Dumouriez inflict a crushing defeat on the Austrians at Jemappes.

Netherlands, 14 November. Having entered Belgium on 27 October, defeated the Prussians at Jemappes and captured Mons, the French commander Dumouriez enters Brussels.

Spain, 22 November. Manuel Godoy, who recently replaced Aranda as prime minister, orders the arrest of French clergymen who have sought refuge in Spain.

France, 27 November. The former duchy of Saxony beomes the French department of Mont Blanc.

Netherlands, 28 November. A French army under General Miranda marches into Liege.

Netherlands, 29 November. The French take Antwerp.

France, 1 December. A revolt in the Beauce region is put down.

Germany, 2 December. The Prussians drive the French troops out of Frankfurt 40 days after they marched into the city.

Netherlands, 2 December. Namur surrenders to the French.

USA, 5 December. George Washington is re-elected president.

Netherlands, 7 December. French troops put down a demonstration in Brussels calling for the independence of Belgium.

Paris, 11 December. Louis XVI appears for the first time before the Convention, to hear the charges against him.

London, 13 December. Parliament votes to support William Pitt's war preparations against France.

West Indies, 13 December. The colonial assembly of Martinique declares war on the French republic.

Naples, 17 December. A French fleet arrives in Naples to force Ferdinand IV, the king of the Two Sicilies, to recognise the ambassador of the French republic.

Spain, 28 December. Spain offers to maintain its neutrality in the European war provided that the French royal family is freed.

West Indies, 29 December. An uprising in favour of the French republic breaks out in Guadeloupe.

Poland, December. The Prussians occupy the towns of Torun and Danzig, and Little Poland.

England. The exceptionally gifted singer Elizabeth Ann Sheridan, the first wife of the playwright Richard Brinsley Sheridan, dies.

Strasbourg. Rouget de Lisle writes the words and music for a *Chant de guerre pour l'armee du Rhin* (the *Marseillaise*).

West Africa. Freetown, Sierra Leone, is founded by 1,190 freed slaves who have landed from England.

England. *A Vindication of the Rights of Women* by Mary Wollstonecraft is published.

English workers read radical pamphlets

England

Inspired by the French Revolution, reformers in England have begun to publish pamphlets advocating manhood suffrage, annual parliaments, cheaper government and fairer land and legal systems.

Most influential is the Corresponding Society of London, led by a shoemaker, Thomas Hardy. It began with small meetings at the Bell Inn, near Covent Garden, often discussing ideas put forward in pamphlets from an intellectual elite calling themselves the Society for Constitutional Information. Whereas the latter charges its members five guineas a year, the Corresponding Society charges only a penny a week. Its numbers have grown since January from nine to 650, corresponding with groups in Manchester, Sheffield, Leeds and Norwich. In November it sent a delegation to the National Convention in Paris.

An "Address to the People" in August promised lower taxes, better education, prison reform and provision for the poor and old.

King promotes his queen's "companion"

Madrid

King Charles IV has appointed a new first secretary, the handsome duke of Alcudia, better known as Manual Godoy, who is also the queen's companion – and the Spanish people do not like it. Godoy, aged 35, has risen rapidly in military rank and government position over the past three years and was ennobled because he has enjoyed the protection of Maria Luisa.

This is a feature of aristocratic life in Madrid. Charles is said to be aware of the relationship and taking it for granted. But the lower classes of Madrid, as well as some of the nobles, are scandalised.

King Charles IV and Queen Maria Luisa of Spain.

Men furious at call for women's rights

England

Male opinion is up in arms following the publication of an essay which seriously questions the dominance of men in society. Challengingly entitled *A Vindication of the Rights of Women*, its author is 33-year-old Mary Wollstonecraft, a leading English radical.

She dismisses the notion, promoted by Rousseau, that women are inferior to men. She argues for equal opportunities in education and employment for women and men, and calls for female companionship with men on equal terms.

Mary was born near London of Irish parents; her father was a drunkard and wife-beater who squandered a fortune. She was largely self-taught and in 1782 started a school which failed. By 1790, while working for a London publisher, she was part of a radical group which included Tom Paine. Her works include *Thoughts on the Education of Daughters* (1787) and an essay on the French Revolution.

Radical: Mary Wollstonecraft.

French Revolution saved

The Battle of Valmy, where France's new army saved the revolution.

Valmy, France, 20 September
The French Revolution has been saved on a fog-shrouded plateau at Valmy where the duke of Brunswick's well-trained soldiers were turned back today by the untried army of the new France supported by cannons which once belonged to the king.

It is true that the Prussians were ravaged by dysentery, but as they marched towards Paris they expected to find a people ready to surrender. Instead they found 50,000 Frenchmen ready to stand and fight, roaring "Long live the nation". It was not much of a battle, confined mostly to an exchange of cannon fire which killed 200 French and 300 Prussian soldiers, but the Prussians had no heart for it. "We won't be able to beat them here," said Brunswick, and ordered a humiliating retreat.

"You'll see how these little cocks will strut now," said one dispirited Prussian. "We have lost more than a battle." At the windmill headquarters of the victorious French generals, Dumouriez and Kellerman, the battle is being called the "miracle of Valmy".

Royalty abolished and republic declared

Paris, 21 September
The monarchy was formally abolished at the first session of the National Convention meeting at the Manege in Paris today. There was some legalistic hesitation, but Collot d'Herbois, the leader of the Paris delegates, argued that it was a matter which could not be postponed "without being unfaithful to the wishes of the nation".

Another delegate then launched a virulent attack on the concept of royalty, demanding the destruction of "this magic talisman ... kings are morally what monsters are physically". Although some preached caution, all objections were swept aside amid great excitement.

A decree was then passed unanimously declaring royalty abolished in France. There were scenes of great enthusiasm and couriers were despatched all over the country with the news. However, no mention was made of the establishment of a republic, which must now be inevitable.

Planting the Tree of Liberty: a painting by the le Sueur brothers.

Colony of freed slaves has second start

West Africa
A second group of black settlers has arrived at Sierra Leone. The colonists will take over this outpost of progress from the survivors of the first group of 411 colonists who arrived three years earlier and have been decimated by hunger, disease and war. The old colonists were idealistic. Their settlement was self-governing and they elected their own governor, Richard Weaver.

The new colonists are mostly from Nova Scotia and New Brunswick, black slaves who escaped from American owners and came to England after the War of Independence. The settlement is no longer self-governing, but financed and controlled by the British-owned Sierra Leone Company.

The newcomers are as idealistic as the original colonists and, since the early attempts at agriculture have failed, they are concentrating on trade, hoping to prove to neighbouring African rulers that slavery is not the only profitable trade.

France's long-trousered revolutionaries

Paris
To be called a *sans-culotte*, a man without breeches, used to be an insult in Paris. Now it is a name worn with pride by the extreme republicans and nobody dares to treat them with contempt.

Instead of breeches, they wear simple trousers held up by braces, short jackets called *carmagnoles*, a scarves at their open necks and the symbols of revolution, the red woollen Phrygian, or "liberty", caps on their heads. There are women sans-culottes who wear long skirts and are more fearsome than the men.

Both sexes are well armed with captured swords and most of them carry pikes, many of which have borne the heads of butchered aristocrats. They have abandoned all forms of polite behaviour, using *Citoyen* instead of *Monsieur* and have become a power in the streets of Paris.

A sans-culotte: one of the vanguard of the French Revolution.

Russians breach Japanese seclusion

Japan
An expedition sent by Catherine the Great has arrived at Nemuro Bay, Hokkaido. Commanded by Adam Laxman, the Russians are using the return of a number of Japanese castaways as a pretext for their landing.

Laxman asked permission to travel to the capital, Edo, asking to be regarded as "neighbouring allies" not as "antagonistic and infidel adversaries". Among the castaways he has brought home is Daikokuya Kodayu, who was blown onto the Aleutians ten years ago and was taken to St Petersburg where he had an audience with the czarina. It is doubtful that he will be as well received in Edo, for he has broken the *shogunate's* rule of seclusion forbidding anyone to leave Japan.

1793 ⇒

Paris, 21 January. Louis XVI is guillotined.

France, 21 January. The county of Nice is annexed to France.

Poland, 23 January. Prussia and Russia agree on a second partition of Poland.

Ottoman Empire, January. The sultan, Selim III, introduces a new administrative regime and reorganises the Ottoman army on the European model.

Ireland, January. Catholics are given the vote.

France, 1 February. France declares war on Britain and the Netherlands.

France, 14 February. The principality of Monaco is annexed to France.

Indian Ocean, 25 February. An anti-royalist riot breaks out in Ile de France (*Mauritius*) following the proclamation of the French republic on the island.

Europe, February. Britain, Austria, Prussia, Spain, the Netherlands, Sardinia, Tuscany and Naples form a coalition against France.

Corsica, February. A conflict develops between Pascal Paoli, who seeks Corsican independence from France, and the Francophile Napoleon Bonaparte.

Netherlands, 5 March. Austrian troops crush the French to recapture Liege.

France, 7 March. France declares war on Spain.

France, 11 March. A rebellion against the republic breaks out in the Vendee.

Netherlands, 18 March. Having entered Breda on 25 February, the French commander Dumouriez is heavily defeated by the Austrians under Frederick of Saxe-Coburg at Neerwinden.

Germany, 20 March. French troops annex the German duchy of Zweibrucken.

France, 20 March. The rebellious Vendeans inflict a defeat on a French revolutionary army.

Europe, 25 March. By the treaty of London, Russia joins the coalition against France.

Netherlands, 4 April. Dumouriez, the commander-inchief of the French armies, defects to the Austrians.

Paris, 5 April. Elected president of the Jacobin Club, Jean-Paul Marat orders the arrest of counter-revolutionaries and the ousting of the main Girondin deputies.

Paris, 6 April. The Convention sets up a Committee of Public Safety.

West Indies, 14 April. The British seize control of Tobago.

West Indies, 14 April. A royalist rebellion in Santo Domingo is crushed by French republican troops.

France, 20 April. Spanish troops lay siege to Perpignan.

USA, 21 April. The US government officially proclaims its neutrality in the European conflict.

Paris, 23 April. The Convention decrees stringent new measures against priests who refuse to swear allegiance to the church's civil constitution.

Paris, 24 April. The revolutionary tribunal acquits Marat of despotism.

Paris, 24 April. The republican General Miranda is arrested because of his links with Dumouriez.

India, 27 April. The British orientalist Sir William Jones, who introduced eastern thought and literature, especially Sanskrit, to the west, dies in Calcutta.

France, 9 May. General Dampierre, the commander of the French army in northern France, is mortally wounded during an Austrian offensive at Valenciennes.

Paris, 10 May. Claire Lacombe sets up the Society of Revolutionary Republican Women.

North Atlantic, 24 May. The British recapture the archipelago of St Pierre and Miquelon off Newfoundland, dealing a blow to the French cod-fishing fleet.

France, 30 May. Girondins seize power from Jacobins in Lyons.

Paris, 2 June. After three days of street demonstrations, the moderate Girondins are ousted from the Convention by Jacobins.

France, 6 June. Marseilles, Nimes and Toulon rebel against the Convention.

France, 9 June. The royalist Vendean army captures Saumur.

West Indies, 20 June. The city of the Cap in Santo Domingo is destroyed after an attempted royalist uprising.

India, 24 June. A British squadron blockades Pondicherry.

Paris, 25 June. The extremist Enrages group, led by Jacques Roux, presents the Convention with a petition attacking the constitution.

France, 30 June. Saumur is recaptured by republican troops.

Cotton-cleaning machine does work of 50

Whitney's cotton gin: boosting production in America for British mills.

South Carolina
American production of cotton is set to increase dramatically thanks to a new invention which can clean in a day as much raw cotton as 50 men. Eli Whitney's saw-gin solves the problem of cleaning seeds from green seed cotton, the crop grown in the inland Carolinas by farmers keen to supply the fast-growing English cotton industry. Until Whitney unveiled his machine the whole process was done by hand.

Whitney, a Yale graduate who came south to teach mechanics, stands to make a fortune from his invention. The legislature of South Carolina has already bought the patent rights for statewide use for 50,000 dollars. Whitney shares royalties with the backer who put up the stake to build his first gin, so called from an archaic abbreviation of "engine".

The gin has a cylinder equipped with teeth projecting through strips of metal. These draw in the cotton fibre leaving the seeds behind. A second roller, fitted with brushes to free the teeth from the lint, revolves in the opposite direction. The gin can be powered by hand, by a horse or by water. Whitney got his idea for it after realising that there was a fortune to be made from automating the cleaning of cotton.

Counter-revolution begins in France

Vendee, France, 14 March
Counter-revolutionaries, under the charasmatic leadership of Jacques Cathelineau, a cart driver and door-to-door salesmen, have seized Chemille and are taking over the Vendee, (western France). The rebels talk of restoring the monarchy and the church, and are united by a religious vervour fed by the Church.

Today in the town's church the Abbot Barbotin, one of the most virulent opponents of the revolutionaries in Paris, came out of hiding and sung a Te Deum. The humble Cathelineau acted as his server. The capture of Chemille is not the peasant army's first victory. Two days ago they bested a republican force sent against them at Saint Florent. Cathelineau and his Catholic peasant followers have no doubt of the outcome of their revolt. When his wife – who has more doubt – pleaded with him to stay at home and support his family, he replied "God, for whom I am going to fight will take care of you".

Cathelineau: counter-revolutionary.

French cut off the head of their king

Paris, 21 January
King Louis XVI of France went to the guillotine in the Place de la Revolution this morning. The blade fell on his neck and the royal head tumbled into the basket just before 10.30 on this cold, grey day.

Louis Capet, as he was called by his judges in the Assembly, met his death calmly. He left for the scaffold in a large green coach with his priest, Edgeworth de Firmont, and surrounded by a strong escort of National Guardsmen. Drummers marched in front of the carriage, beating loudly to drown any cries of support for the doomed monarch. But there was hardly a sound in Paris. Every shop was closed and there was a stillness in the city despite the curious crowds that hurried to the bloody spectacle.

The scaffold, where the executioner, Sansom, waited, was surrounded by armed men. No chance was taken of a Royalist rescue. As the coach arrived the king commended his priest to the guards: "Take care that after my death no insult be offered to him."

Sansom's assistants reached out to grab him. He shook them off and prepared himself for death, untying his neckcloth and opening his shirt. Then, despite his protests, his hands were tied. He climbed the steps on the arm of his priest and turned to address the crowd. Immediately, the drums were ordered to beat, and only those close to him heard his last words: "I die innocent of all the crimes laid to my charge; I pardon those who have occasioned my death; and I pray to God that the blood you are going to shed may never be visited on France."

There was an awful silence as his severed head was shown to the crowd. A shout of *"Vive la République"* was then taken up by a thousand voices. Then there was silence again as the people realised what they had done. They had given the counter-revolutionaries their greatest martyr.

Royal victim: the execution of Louis XVI at the Place de la Revolution.

Regicide: Philippe Egalite, ex-duke of Orleans, by Cruikshank.

France discharges its women-at-arms

France
The women of France, who have fought with conspicuous bravery in the nation's cause, are to be deprived of their right to enlist in the army. Scandalised by the very idea of women as soldiers, the Convention has today decreed that women may no longer join up.

Many women enlisted in 1792, and such heroines as the young Fernig sisters, Reine Chapuy, Rose Bouillon and Catherine Pochetat have distinguished themselves with bravery the equal of any man's. Often dressed only in rags, they fought in the front ranks of such battles as Valmy and Jemappes.

To their fury, such valour counts for nothing now. All the deputies will offer in compensation are five *sous* for every league the women must travel to return home. Such tiny sums are unlikely to last very long, and many women fear a future in which they have neither job nor income. In any case, the women fought as much for glory as for cash, and they regret deeply being deprived of the excitement of military life. The world of family life holds little appeal to those for whom the army is a way of life.

Revolutionary women soldiers in France are now to be disbanded.

Turkish sultan's "New Order" ignored

Ottoman Empire
A call for 12,000 volunteers to join the *Nizam-i-Jedid*, the New Order, of Sultan Selim III has been virtually ignored – an indication of the difficulty the sultan is having in carrying through his reforms.

In an effort to stem the decline in Ottoman power, Selim, with the support of 'Abdullah Effendi, the chief judge of the council, has reorganised his council, relieving the grand vizier of some administrative duties, and is reforming provincial government. Most crucially, he is trying to reform the army. With the help of European advisers, he has achieved better artillery training and equipment. But streamlining the Janissary corps is proving more difficult.

A Turkish Janissary, a major obstacle to reform.

Poland partitioned for the second time

Warsaw, 23 January
Czarina Catherine of Russia and the treacherous King Frederick William II of Prussia have agreed on a second partition of Poland. Catherine gets most of Lithuania and the western Ukraine (total population, three million). Prussia gets Danzig, Thorn and western Poland almost to the gates of Warsaw (total population, one million).

Frederick had signed a treaty agreeing to aid the Poles if Russia attacked. But when the blow fell, the Poles found that Frederick had gone over to the enemy. The Polish parliament, with Russian troops outside the building, have formally endorsed the annexation.

1793 ⇒

France, June. Outlawed by Pascale Paoli last month, Napoleon Bonaparte and his family are exiled from Corsica and forced to seek refuge on the French mainland.

France, 1 July. The Convention dissolves Corsica's primary assembly and splits the island into two departments to reduce Pascale Paoli's influence.

India, 11 July. A British expeditionary force lands near Pondicherry, which is defended by French troops.

Paris, 13 July. Jean-Paul Marat is assassinated by Charlotte Corday.

France, 14 July. Jacques Cathelineau, the commander of the Catholic and royalist army of the Vendee, dies after being wounded during the siege of Nantes.

France, 16 July. Joseph Chalier, the leader of the Jacobins of Lyons, is executed.

Paris, 17 July. Pascale Paoli is declared a traitor to the French republic.

Paris, 17 July. Charlotte Corday is guillotined.

Paris, 22 July. Custine, the commander of the northern army, is arrested.

Germany, 23 July. The French garrison at Mainz capitulates to the Prussians and is allowed to leave the city.

Paris, 27 July. Robespierre becomes a member of the Committee of Public Safety.

France, 28 July. Valenciennes surrenders to the allied troops led by the duke of York.

Paris, 1 August. The Convention decrees the total "destruction" of the rebellious Vendee.

France, 14 August. Republican troops lay siege to Lyons.

India, 23 August. When news of the fall and execution of Louis XVI reaches Pondicherry, the French surrender the port to the British forces who have been besieging it since 24 June.

France, 25 August. Republican forces capture Marseilles.

France, 28 August. The Federalists of Provence hand Toulon over to the British.

Paris, 28 August. General Custine is guillotined.

West Indies, 29 August. Slavery is abolished in Santo Domingo.

Philadelphia, August. In the worst health disaster ever to strike an American city, over 4,000 have died in a epidemic of yellow fever.

Netherlands, 8 September. French troops under General Houchard defeat an AngloHanoverian army under the duke of York at Hondschoote.

Paris, 17 September. The Convention passes an "anti-suspect" law by which all enemies of the revolution will be arrested and held until the war is over.

USA, 18 September. In Washington DC, President Washington lays the foundation stone of the Capitol, the intended seat of the US government.

France, 9 October. The rebellious Jacobins in Lyons capitulate to the republican army after 60 days of fighting.

India, 10 October. Lord Cornwallis leaves India after greatly strengthening British administration in India. He has made a firm distinction between the commercial and administrative functions of the East India Company, Europeanised the administration and settled the revenue and land system of Bengal.

Paris, 10 October. An emergency government is formed.

France, 16 October. The French defeat the Austrians at Wattignies, forcing the Austrians to lift the siege of Maubeuge.

Paris, 16 October. Marie Antoinette is guillotined.

France, 17 October. The Catholic and royalist Vendean army is defeated by the republicans at Cholet.

France, 17 October. The French India Company goes into liquidation.

Paris, 31 October. Jacques Brissot and 20 other Girondins are guillotined.

Germany. Friedrich Schiller publishes a *History of the Thirty Years War*.

Germany. The philosopher Johann Gottfried Herder starts publishing his *Letters for the Advancement of Humanity*.

North America. Sir Alexander MacKenzie become the first white man to cross the North American continent, finishing his journey by canoeing down the Bella Coola river in Oregon territory to the Pacific.

Japan. Matsudaira Sadanobu resigns from the office of chief senior councillor, which he has held since 1787, and goes into retirement. His departure follows a clash with the emperor and growing disaffection with his authoritarian style.

Twenty-one moderates are executed

Paris, 31 October

It took five carts to bring the 21 moderate Girondin leaders to the scaffold today, and, even as they came close to the guillotine, they were singing the *Marseillaise*.

Many in the crowd wept, but there was no unrest. The Girondins knew all through their week-long trial before a revolutionary tribunal that their fate had been decided. To let them live would be an admission that a mistake had been made; and, such is the fear spreading through Paris, not one lawyer could be found to defend them.

The Girondins had been voted out of office in June when a mob of *sans-culottes* had threatened to over-run the Convention. Had it not been for legal difficulties, they would certainly have been executed long before now. The insurrection which brought about the arrest of the Girondins began late on 31 May when a secretly organised committee of Marat and the Montagnards called the people of Paris "to arms!".

Despite a powerful speech by the radical Jacobin Robespierre, the Convention resisted demands for a purge and immediate sentences. When members reassembled on the following morning, they found cannons levelled at the Palais National and troops preparing to arrest the "traitors".

Charlotte Corday stabs Marat in bath

Charlotte Corday is arrested after assassinating Jean-Paul Marat.

Paris, 13 July

Jean-Paul Marat, the founder of *L'Ami du Peuple*, deputy for Paris and sans-culotte supreme, is dead. Working as usual in his daily bath, where he nursed a persistent skin disease, he was stabbed to death by Charlotte Corday, the daughter of an impoverished aristocrat and a staunch royalist.

Corday appeared at Marat's apartment at 20, rue de Cordeliers, and gained admission to his rooms by claiming to have details of a group of Girondin conspirators in the Calvados.

As Marat listened to her story she pulled a kitchen knife from her bodice and stabbed him in the chest. He died almost immediately. Corday, who lives in Caen with her aunt, and is closely involved with the same Girondin whom she pretended to betray, arrived in Paris two days ago, determined to murder the man whom she saw as an enemy of the human race. She had planned to kill him at the Bastille Day parade, but, when the planned festivities were cancelled, was forced to attack him in his home.

When the police arrived on the scene she offered no resistance, but stood calmly at the window observing the mob which had gathered, and awaiting her arrest

Chinese reject western barbarians

Chinese Emperor Qianlong meets the British ambassador, Lord Macartney.

Canton, October
Lord Macartney's mission to persuade the Chinese to lift trade restrictions on British merchants trading with Canton has failed.

The elaborate 95-man mission, costing £78,000, has been told that the celestial empire of the Emperor Qianlong, son of heaven, has not "the slightest need" for manufactured goods from England. The emperor has also rejected requests for a British ambassador – the first from the west – to be stationed at his court.

The East India Company, which financed the mission, hoped that a permanent ambassador could persuade the emperor to lift trade barriers. All exports from China, including high-demand items such as tea and silk, have to be paid for in silver. British exports to China bear high import duties plus the cost of bribes to officials.

The Macartney mission was politely received and the Irish peer was allowed into the imperial presence without having to knock his head nine times on the floor, as is customary. However, it was made clear that there was no place for a "barbarian from the western ocean", however eminent, in China.

All natives corrupt, says departing ruler

The Bengal Levee: Lord Cornwallis holding a reception in Calcutta.

Calcutta
After seven years as governor general of Bengal, Charles, Lord Cornwallis, is leaving India. He came here fresh from his surrender at Yorktown (for which, surprisingly, no one blamed him), and took on the job out of a sense of duty. He continued the reforms begun by Warren Hastings and completed the transformation of British India into the most powerful state in the sub-continent.

Unlike Clive or Hastings, his rank and reputation placed him above faction. Further, he had the supreme confidence of William Pitt, the British prime minister. Thus he was able to reform British India, essentially by separating the commercial elements of the Company from the administrative. Bribery is no longer normal practice.

In wars against Tipu Sahib he was applauded for his humanity and moral courage; but his "Europeanisation" of the civil service ("Every native in India, I verily believe, is corrupt") has caused much resentment, and his system of land taxation, creating a new revenue collecting class, the *zamindars*, is adding to the heavy weight of the already burdened peasantry.

A Georgian dandy or "macaroni": a victim of fashion from the tight buckled shoes and elaborate garters to the baroque wig and face-powder. By the end of the century men's fashions were more elaborate than women's.

The rise of Robespierre: a change in the mood of the revolution

Paris, 27 August
An ambitious young left-wing lawyer, Maximilien Robespierre, has been elected – "against my inclination" – to the Committee of Public Safety, a move which may well change the direction of the French Revolution. Robespierre, who is regarded by many as "incorruptible", had little influence at the Convention while it was dominated by the moderate Girondins; but now, invited to join the committee by left-wing friends, his political skills and deep respect for the law are certain to stand him in good stead at a time when lawlessness, with the sans-culottes mobilised throughout France, threatens to rip the country to shreds.

At first sight, 32-year-old Robespierre is not an engaging figure. He is small, thin and vain, with thick, carefully brushed hair and a pock-marked skin of a greenish pallor. He is a nervous man, highly strung, who bites his nails, pushes his tinted spectacles on to a bulging brow when he speaks and utters a rare, hollow laugh when required.

Robespierre has proved himself to be a hard-working and competitive advocate – although his soft voice usually failed him whenever as a deputy to the National Assembly, his left-wing views were shouted down. When he spoke to the masses, however, he was more successful. He wanted bigger audiences at the Assembly. "Under the eyes of so many witnesses, neither corruption, intrigue nor perfidy would dare show themselves," he claimed.

Maximilien Robespierre, the "uncorruptible" politician.

1793 ⇒

Paris, 3 November. Olympe de Gouges, the feminist who once tried to defend Louis XVI, is executed.

Paris, 6 November. Philippe of Orleans, the cousin of Louis XVI, is executed.

Paris, 8 November. Madame Roland, the muse of the Girondins, is executed.

France, 10 November. The Girondin Jean Marie Roland commits suicide in Rouen after his wife's death.

Paris, 16 November. General Houchard is executed for having held talks with the enemy.

Paris, 18 November. The National Art Museum at the Louvre palace opens.

Paris, 24 November. The Convention approves the new revolutionary calendar.

New York, 25 November. In one of a series of Negro uprisings, slaves in Albany, New York state, cause huge damage to the city by arson.

France, 30 November. The French general Lazare Hoche is defeated by the Prussians at Kaiserslautern in Alsace as he attempts to break the siege of Landau.

Paris, 4 December. A new war government takes office.

Paris, 5 December. Camille Desmoulins launches a newspaper, *Le Vieux Cordelier*, to campaign against the Terror.

Paris, 8 December. Madame du Barry, the former mistress of Louis XVI, is guillotined.

France, 12 December. Republican troops under Marceau and Kleber crush the Vendeans at Le Mans.

France, 19 December. French troops recapture Toulon from the British.

France, 24 December. After a further defeat, at Savenay, the Vendean army is dispersed.

Paris, 25 December. Robespierre gives his support to the Terror policy.

France, 26 December. French troops under Lazare Hoche defeat the Austrians at Geisberg, relieving the threat to Strasbourg.

USA, 31 December. Thomas Jefferson resigns as secretary of state and retires from public life.

New symbols for new names of the months: Ventose (l.) represents what used to be February, Thermidor (c.) is July and Frimaire (r.) is November; the months of the calendar are now symbolised by the climate and seasons.

Revolutionary calendar wipes out the past and renames months

France, 24 November

The revolution has brought many great changes, but none so far has touched the very time in which people live. Now that too must change. Today the Convention has initiated a new calendar, based on a scheme proposed by a committee including the mathematician Charles Romme and the dramatist Fabre d'Eglantine.

From today the traditional calendar – "a monument of slavery" – is to be abandoned. In its place comes a "natural" calendar. There will be 12 months, each of 30 days, with names reflecting changes in the climate – *Pluviose, Nivose* – or seasons – *Germinal, Floreal.* The five spare days, the *sans-culottides* will be holidays. Weeks, or *decadis*, will now last for ten days; days are renamed *primidi, duodi*, and so on Religious holidays are gone: there is no Christmas now, and saints' days will be renamed for plants, tools or animals.

Citizens of France are equal so long as they are not women

Paris, November

Olympe de Gouges and Manon Roland have mounted the scaffold, Theroigne de Mericourt has apparently lost her sanity and the Republican Women's clubs have been banned – this has been a devastating month for France's women, whose role in the Revolution has been as vital as that of any man.

Women's contribution to the revolution cannot be over-stressed. They included intellectuals like Roland, who dominated the Girondins, the feminist de Gouges, founder of the notorious Club des Tricoteuses, and the former courtesan Theroigne, whose Revolutionary Republican Women was only one of the clubs she founded.

Just as important were the anonymous market-women, fishwives and whores, who were among the most militant and implacable of the Revolution's pioneers. It was a woman, dressed fittingly as an Amazon, who led the atack on the Bastille. Equally momentous was the women's march on Versailles in October 1789. Demanding to know why the King had deserted his city in its crisis, they set in motion events that ended in the King's execution. Of all the revolutionaries, the women of France have seemed least restrained, and it is this overthrowing of the ultimate law – of male superiority – that has led to this month's backlash.

Women patriots: their clubs, which preached revolution, have been banned.

"Woman is born free and her rights are the same as those of a man ... All citizens, be they men or women, must be equally eligible for all public offices, positions and jobs, according to their capacity and without any other criteria" – so said the *Declaration of the Rights of Women*, by Olympe de Gouges which was published in 1791.

Now, it seems, such feminism has outlived its usefulness. The Revolution still proclaims the "Rights of Man" but today it ignores those of women.

Jefferson resigns office

Virginia, 31 December
Thomas Jefferson, the author of the Declaration of Independence, has resigned as secretary of state and retired to his Virginia farm despite fervent pleas by the president. Jefferson, a former ambassador to Paris, is said to be disillusioned by Congress's refusal to impeach his arch-enemy, Alexander Hamilton, the secretary of the treasury, for financial impropriety.

The two men have been adversaries since the framing of the Constitution, Hamilton advocating a strong central government while Jefferson preferred to see greater power in the individual states.

Jefferson was a firm opponent of the "Hamiltonian System" under which the treasury assumed Revolutionary War debts, issued new bonds and established a Bank of the United States.

Although Jefferson has confided to his friend James Madison that "the motion of my blood no longer keeps time with the tumult of the world", few believe that this distinguished reformer – for all that he owns slaves – will be able to resist a return to public life.

Thomas Jefferson, one of the founding fathers of the USA.

European monarchs unite against France

Europe, September
The whole of Europe has united against revolutionary France. With the signing of a treaty with Britain by Portugal – the last nation to join the counter-revolutionary Convention – the republic faces a ring of hostile monarchies.

Ever since the Declaration of Pillnitz in 1791, when Austria and Prussia called for an alliance against France, Europe's governments have been moving towards a unanimous position. Co-ordinated by Britain's prime minister, Grenville, state after state has joined the Convention. Members now include Austria, Russia, Sardinia, Spain, Naples, Prussia and Portugal.

Nonetheless, the alliance remains flimsy at heart. Its members have called for France to restore the monarchy and return her conquests, but have signed no general agreement. There is no real leader, and each state thinks first of itself.

Bombardment of the crowned heads of Europe with revolutionary ideas!

Terror is firmly on the agenda in France

Sans-culottes, "refreshing after the fatigues of the day": an English view.

Paris
Suddenly, no-one is safe from the guillotine. A legalised reign of terror has set neighbour against neighbour, and no more than a hint, a whisper or a rumour of anti-revolutionary thought may bring a suspect to the guillotine. Revolutionary committees are working with extraordinary zeal to seek out those who, "by their behaviour, their relationships or what they have written have shown themselves to be supporters of tyranny". The entire city of Lyons has suffered under draconian laws for not supporting the revolution. The guillotine was so busy there that firing squads were called in to shoot 59 "suspects". Here in Paris, the Protestant minister and ardent defender of religious freedom, Rabaut St Etienne, was beheaded for his moderation; so, too, was Olympe de Gouges, a feminist lawyer who had tried to defend Louis XVI. The Girondist poet Mme Roland looked at the statue overlooking the scaffold and said: "O Liberty, what crimes are committed in thy name!"

Wages and prices fixed in economic crisis

Paris, 29 September
The levels of prices and wages are to be fixed as part of an all-out attempt to tackle the economic crisis that is plaguing France.

Under the Convention's General Maximum Law, prices will be fixed by individual departments, and are to be pegged at no more than 30 per cent more than those of 1790, irrespective of inflation. Wages will be permitted to rise by up to 50 per cent of the 1790 levels.

The move follows a summer of agitation as the demands of a war economy channelled foodstuffs to the troops and the towns, robbing the peasants of what they feel is rightfully theirs. At the same time, the people of Paris had been demanding higher wages.

The French peasant: the success of the revolution depends on him; only stable prices can secure his support.

1793 (1793-1794)

South Africa, 1793. The second Suurveld war, which began in 1789, comes to an end. The war was provoked by the Xhosa chief Ndlambe's attempt to regain control of Suurveld (*Eastern Cape Frontier*). Under the peace agreement, the Boers have to concede to Ndlambe, but they blame their Dutch magistrates for the defeat.

North Atlantic, 1793. A British attempt to colonise the Cape Verde Islands, begun last year, ends in failure.

Paris, 11 January 1794. Lamourette, bishop of Lyons since April 1791, who was taken prisoner by republican troops on 29 September 1793 during the siege of Lyons, is tried and guillotined.

Paris, 13 January 1794. The poet and musician Fabre d'Eglantine, a Dantonist opponent of the Terror, is arrested on charges of involvement in a financial scandal concerning the India Company, which compromises several prominent people. Fabre signed a fake decree ordering the liquidation of the company, to his own benefit.

France, 28 January 1794. Henri la Rochejaquelein, leader of the revolt in the Vendee, is killed by two isolated republican soldiers on a road near Nouaille in Maine et Loire.

France, January 1794. Republican troops under General Turreau embark on a systematic destruction of the Vendee region.

Paris, 4 February 1794. The Convention issues a decree abolishing slavery throughout the French colonies.

Paris, 10 February 1794. Jacques Roux, one of the leaders of the Enrages, the most extreme political group to emerge from the sansculottists, commits suicide in jail.

Mediterranean, 27 February 1794. Austria and Russia reach agreement on the sharing out of Venetian possessions in the Mediterranean.

Corsica, February 1794. Pascal Paoli, the patriotic leader who has now become governor of Corsica, seeks British help to maintain the autonomy of the Corsican republic, threatened by the Jacobin faction on the island. A nationalist assembly proclaims George III, the British king, as the island's sovereign.

Paris, 13 March 1794. Following a call for an insurrection by the extremist Cordeliers, Jacques Hebert, the editor of *Le Pere Duchesne* – who has come to dominate the Cordelier Club – and leading Hebertists are arrested.

West Indies, 23 March 1794. The British recapture Martinique, from which they were expelled last year by the French.

Poland, March 1794. Tadeusz Kosciuszko – who became leader of a group of exiled Polish patriots after the partition of Poland by Prussia and Russia last year – arrives in Krakow, wins the support of dissident Polish officers and proclaims a provisional constitution giving him dictatorial powers.

Paris, 24 March 1794. The extremist Jacques Hebert and leading Hebertists are guillotined for treason.

Paris, 27 March 1794. The *sans-culotte* "revolutionary army" is dissolved on the orders of the Convention.

Scandinavia, 27 March 1794. The Scandinavian states create a league of armed neutrality.

Paris, 28 March 1794. The Paris Commune is reorganised. The Hebertists are replaced by supporters of Robespierre.

France, 29 March 1794. Marie Jean Condorcet, the philosopher and mathematician who became president of the Legislative Assembly in 1792, is found dead in his cell in the town formerly known as Bourg la Reine. Condorcet, who was condemned for his Brissotin sympathies and went into hiding for several months before being recognised and arrested, is believed to have committed suicide.

Paris, 31 March 1794. Georges Jacques Danton and a group of his friends, including Camille Desmoulins, are arrested on charges of having connived with the foreign monarchs who are in league against the French republic. They are also accused of being accomplices of Fabre d'Eglantine in the India Company scandal.

Poland, 4 April 1794. At Raclawice, the Polish insurgents under the leadership of Tadeusz Kosciuszko inflict a defeat on a superior Russian army.

Indian Ocean, 1794. The Ile de France (*Mauritius*) ignores the French Convention's declaration of the abolition of slavery.

Southern Africa, 1794. The Maputo kingdom is victorious in the Tembe civil war, which has been raging around Maputo Bay for the past half-century. Maputo power, however, is limited to the bay and to trade with Portuguese ships, while the hinterland that stretches into South Africa (*Natal*) and Swaziland is left open to new militaristic powers, notably the Ndwandwe and Mthewa chiefdoms.

"Infernal columns" crush French revolt

Vendee, January 1794

General Turreau, the head of the Army of the West, calls it "a military stroll" but the peasants of the Vendee, whose revolt he is systematically wiping out, prefer another name: they call his troops, who pillage and massacre without restraint, the "infernal columns".

The revolt collapsed after last month's defeat at Savenay and many peasants were summarily executed by firing squads. Now Turreau, leading 12 columns of "Blue" troops, has set out to obliterate every remaining sign of resistance and impose a bloody "peace" on the area. His generals have been ordered to follow his scorched earth strategy without mercy.

"All brigands who are found with arms in their hands or are convicted of having taken up arms will be bayoneted to death. You will act in the same way with women, girls and children who are in the same category. All of the villages, towns, crops and everything else that can possibly burn will be consigned to the flames."

Total power of revolutionary government

Paris, 19 April 1794

Who governs France today? The answer is clear to everyone, the "Committee of Public Safety", in which almost total authority is invested. Headed by Robespierre, it has taken over responsibility for almost every political decision made in France. Although it is nominally answerable to the Convention, few delegates would dare to question the Committee, whose Revolutionary Tribunal is almost daily sending moderates to the guillotine.

The Committee has dismissed ministers, and its latest move is to order that all charged with conspiracy must be tried by the Paris Revolutionary Tribunal. It has given itself powers of arrest and has even formed its own police.

British gold driven off Indian warpath

Philadelphia, 19 November 1794

Britain is to withdraw its support for the Indians and to evacuate its posts in America's Northwest Territory by 1 June 1796. This is the central point in a treaty that has been negotiated between the two countries by the British prime minister, Grenville, and the US chief justice, John Jay.

Other provisions include the settling of outstanding US debts to Britain and the payment by the British of damages claimed by America.

Britain's encouragement of Indian attacks on American settlers, and its desire to make the territories into an Indian client state, has led to much bad feeling between the two countries. President Washington barely managed to stop Congress declaring war. Not until last August, when Major General Wayne roundly defeated the British-backed Indians at the battle of Fallen Timbers, destroyed their villages and built Fort Wayne, did Britain's government realise the need to change its policy. The more militant Americans still oppose a treaty, but war does seem to have been averted.

Animal forms not fixed, says radical

London, 1794

The English physician and radical freethinker Erasmus Darwin believes that animal species evolve over time. His new book *Zoonomia* posits a theory of evolution based on adaptability and competition.

Species, claims Darwin, evolve through both the inheritance of acquired characteristics and the preferential survival of those competing species that are best suited – or adapted – to the prevailing conditions.

Although he has yet to produce any convincing proof, Darwin contends that all life forms descend from a single source, and that all organisms are evolving to some higher level.

Revolution celebrated in arts and crafts

Post-revolutionary playing cards, without kings and queens.

A revolutionary tobacco box.

Racine replaces the King of Clubs.

Paris, 1794

Artists and craftsmen are serving the revolution by turning out images of its leaders and great events. Popular prints portray the Fall of the Bastille, or the execution of the king or Marie Antoinette. Female images of Liberty and the red Phrygian "Cap of Liberty" decorate plates, porcelain and snuff and tobacco boxes.

Jacques Louis David has been made official painter to the Convention (to which he is a deputy). He paints heroes and martyrs of the revolution, such as Joseph Bara, the boy who was killed for shouting "*Vive La Republique!*" instead of "*Vive le Roi!*", and the famous *Assassination of Marat*. David had visited Marat, who worked in his bath because of a skin complaint, the day before Charlotte Corday killed him.

At the Louvre, now a museum, the erotic paintings of the royalist era by Boucher and Fragonard have been removed from public view. "Art must educate the people," rules David.

Since 1792 it is illegal to use royal insignia, so all packs of playing cards have been redesigned. The King, Queen and Jack are now symbolic figures, like *Prosperity*, *Modesty* and *Justice*, or are replaced by Racine, Voltaire and Rousseau.

Slavery abolished in all French territories

Paris, 4 February 1794

As the three black delegates from Santo Domingo watched from their seats in the Assembly, the Convention voted today to abolish slavery throughout the territories of the republic and to confer French citizenship on every former slave. Then the Domingans were led to the Tribunal where the president embraced them as the Convention rose in a standing ovation.

The abolition was proposed in Paris by the deputies Levasseur, Danton and Lacroix, but it was events in Santo Domingo that inspired the Convention's move.

In 1792, a year after the outbreak of the slave revolt, two civil commissioners – Sonthonax and Polverel – were sent to administer the island. In August 1793 they freed all of the 500,000 slaves. This humanitarian act had its political side. As long as the revolt continued it was impossible for France, at war with Spain and Britain, to defend its colony. Loyal freedmen were naturally better patriots than rebellious slaves. Now the Convention hopes that France's example will stimulate Britain's slaves to rise in their turn, thus helping to undermine Britain's war effort. Danton, a fervent abolitionist, voiced his hopes for the effects of such an uprising. "Today," he declared, "Pitt died."

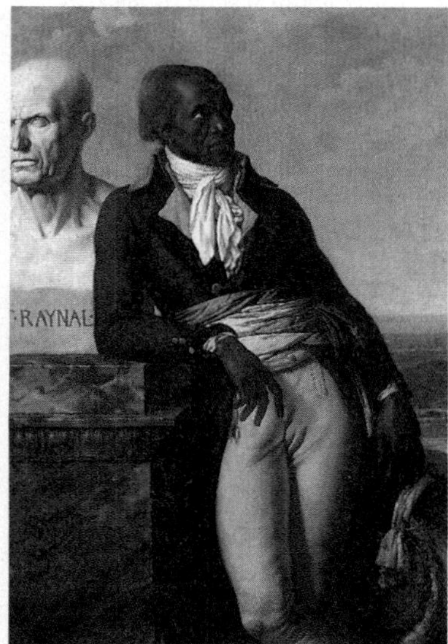

Belley: Santo Domingo's deputy.

Republicans recapture city from British

Toulon, France, 19 December 1793

Toulon, France's premier naval base, has been recaptured by the republicans. For three months it had been a royalist stronghold, and played host to the British fleet.

The republican army's attack began five days ago. On the third day a young artillery captain called Bonaparte saw a weakness in the royalist Aiguillette redoubt. General Dugommier's forces stormed it. The next day the British fleet sailed off, burning the French fleet on the way out. Today the republicans marched into the city.

Toulon went royalist in September after Toulon republicans had killed 17 people and been driven out of the city. The loss to the navy is enormous; ships, stores, arsenal and cargo vessels have been destroyed. The entire French fleet must be rebuilt.

The British fleet, under Admiral Hood, in Toulon harbour.

1794 ⇒

Paris, 5 April. Georges Jacques Danton and several of his supporters, including Camille Desmoulins, are guillotined.

Italy, 18 April. Napoleon Bonaparte, appointed a general in the French army in February, captures the port of Oneglia, a Piedmontese enclave on Genoan territory.

Poland, 19 April. Tadeusz Kosciuszko, the Polish rebel leader, enters Warsaw, which has been in revolt for two days against Russian occupation. The Russians withdraw from the city.

Netherlands, 19 April. Britain, Prussia and the Netherlands sign a treaty against France in The Hague.

Paris, 22 April. Chretien Malesherbes, a former minister under Louis XVI, is executed along with the Assembly members Thouret, le Chapelier and Duval d'Epremesnil.

Poland, 23 April. Kosciuszko enters Vilna, which was seized by the Jacobins yesterday.

France, 30 April. Landrecies in northern France surrenders to the Austrians.

Spain, 1 May. French troops enter Spanish Catalonia.

Paris, 7 May. On the insistence of Maximilien Robespierre, the Convention approves a decree recognising "the existence of a Supreme Being and the immortality of the soul".

Paris, 8 May. The famous chemist Antoine Lavoisier, who discovered the composition of water, is executed.

Paris, 10 May. Elisabeth, the sister of Louis XVI, is beheaded.

France, 17 May. General Moreau captures Tourcoing, opening up the route to Belgium for the French army.

Indian Ocean, 17 May. The British capture the island of Mahe from the French, securing control of the Seychelles archipelago.

Corsica, 22 May. British forces supporting Paoli Pascal capture Bastia.

Paris, 24 May. Robespierre survives an assassination attempt by Cecile Renault, a 25-year-old stationer's daughter. It is the second attack on his life in two days.

France, 29 March. The Austrians and the Piedmontese sign a mutual defence treaty at Valenciennes.

Spain, 31 May. The French invasion of Catalonia sparks off anti-French rioting.

Paris, 1 June. The Mars military academy is founded.

Paris, 4 June. Robespierre is unanimously elected president of the Convention.

West Indies, 4 June. British troops capture Port au Prince, the administrative capital of Santo Domingo, after a five-day siege.

West Indies, 7 June. After proclaiming the abolition of slavery, Victor Hugues, the envoy from the French Convention, recaptures Guadeloupe, which was taken by the British earlier in the year.

Paris, 8 June. Robespierre presides over the celebration of the Supreme Being held on the Champ de Mars.

Paris, 10 June. A law is passed establishing the regime known as the Great Terror. In future there will be no preliminary questioning of defendants or witnesses in trials if the revolutionary tribunal states it has enough factual or "moral" proof. Defence lawyers are banned and juries will have to choose between two verdicts: acquittal or death.

Poland, 15 June. The Prussian army defeats the French, who leave Warsaw.

Netherlands, 26 June. After seizing Charleroi, the French under General Jean Jourdan defeat the Austrians, led by Frederick of Saxe-Coburg, at Fleurus and force them to retreat.

Netherlands, 1 July. The French expel the Austrians from Ostend.

Brussels, 8 July. French troops capture Brussels.

France, 15 July. Landrecies, one of the last French strongholds to be held by the enemy, is liberated.

Paris, 27 July. The Convention orders the arrest of Robespierre and his followers. The Commune declares itself in revolt and hands them over.

Britain. The distinguished English silversmith Hester Bateman dies. On the death of her husband in 1760, she took over his work in gold and silver and registered her own hallmark. Her shop, which became very profitable, was known for its elegant domestic silver, especially coffee- and teapots, spoons and other tableware.

Britain. The novelist Mrs (Ann) Radcliffe publishes *The Mysteries of Udolfo*, a fantastic tale of horror, calculated to send shivers down her readers' genteel spines.

Supreme Being celebrated by Robespierre

The Festival of the Supreme Being: an idealised interpretation.

Paris, 8 June

Despite fears that revolutionary France would become an atheistical society, the entire country today celebrated what has been termed "The Supreme Being and Nature". From early morning, the residents of this city were decorating their houses with flowers and leaves and making their way through the Tuileries to join a procession led by Maximilien Robespierre himself, carrying an ear of wheat.

As the whole of France celebrates Robespierre's discovery of a supreme being, many are concerned about the Catholic undertones of the festival or fear that the "supreme being" they are feasting may turn out to be Robespierre himself.

Savage sentences stir Scots to fury

Scotland

Rumours of revolution are sweeping Scotland, where economic and political grievances have been fuelled by indignation at the savage sentences handed down to dissenters. Parliament has suspended *Habeas Corpus* to allow political suspects to be held without trial.

The most potent symbol of repression is the Scottish judge Lord Braxfield. Holding the constitution to be perfect, he has therefore found anyone proposing change to be an enemy of the state. Last year he sentenced Thomas Muir, a lawyer and the founder of Scottish Friends of the People, to 14 years' transportation for sedition, and the leading unitarian Thomas Palmer to seven years transportation.

While Palmer's pamphlet condemning the war with France is circulating, Muir is understood to be in Paris, forging links with Irish republicans.

Arrests after a secret convention in Edinburgh were followed by transportation and one death sentence – in contrast to the acquittal of alleged agitators in England on similar charges.

Revolutionary court guillotines Danton

Paris, 5 April

At his own request, the head of Georges Jacques Danton, once the favourite of the *Sans-culottes*, was held up to a hushed crowd here today. With his colleague, Camille Desmoulins, and other moderate "Indulgents", Danton was tried by a revolutionary court on charges of corruption and having former contacts with royalty. Most observers believe that the flimsy evidence produced was fabricated and that the court was acting under instructions from Robespierre.

Danton's eloquence was clearly swaying the crowd. The chairman took advantage of an interruption by him to order the defendants out of court, and the death sentence followed almost immediately. Danton was defiant to the end. "Take us to the guillotine now!" he shouted. Desmoulins pleaded with the crowd to save them.

The Indulgents' real offence was to speak out against the revolutionary committees, which they regarded as dictatorial, and to demand the return of the Convention. Such talk – especially by such popular figures as Danton – is regarded as treason by Robespierre.

Georges Jacques Danton, executed for his eloquence and moderation.

French get Austrian army on the run

The battle of Fleurus, where France stopped the Austrian army.

Fleurus, France, 26 June

As hot-air balloons hovered overhead and French generals rallied their men to ever-greater feats of valour, the Austrian army under the prince of Saxe-Coburg was forced to retreat today at the village of Fleurus, near the Belgian border. The 185,000-strong Austrian army had been pursuing a successful campaign through Belgium this summer until 13 May, when it was defeated at Tourcoing. Now the defeat at Fleurus should ensure that Saxe-Coburg's ambitions will be brought to a halt.

The battle raged for 14 hours, as 80,000 Frenchmen struggled to hold back the Austrians. Bravery apart, their victory was helped by a tactical blunder. At one crucial moment a simple flanking movement might have trapped the French, but it never came.

Colour blindness described by victim

London

Some people cannot distinguish between the colours red and green. They have a form of "colour blindness". One such individual is the British chemist and physicist John Dalton, who has just described the condition in some detail in *Extraordinary Facts Relating to the Vision of Colours*.

Being colour blind, however, has not incapacitated Dalton, who has made major contributions to the understanding of meteorology and the nature of gases. He is best known for his atomic theory – that all elements are really composed of indestructible atomic particles.

John Dalton, the scientist.

France's army invades Piedmont

Northern Italy, April

Faced by an alliance of European monarchs and fearing that Piedmont, lying in the foothills of the Alps between France and Italy, will be used as a base to attack France, the French have launched a military offensive "in support of Piedmont's revolutionaries".

The offensive was due to coincide with a Jacobin rising in Turin, Nice and the main towns, but the conspiracy has been discovered. Of the conspirators, 48 have been arrested, and three executed. Piedmont is anxiously soliciting a defence treaty with Austria. Such setbacks have not stopped the French, however, whose general, Bonaparte, has just captured Oneglia.

New Prussian code is aimed at radicals

Berlin

A definitive code of Prussian law, which has just come into effect, seeks to regulate the mutual relations of citizens and also their relations with the state. It lays down the powers of the king to levy taxes without seeking public consent. It re-defines the king's rights as duties. The lawyers who drafted the code wished to establish the judiciary as an independent mediator between the state and the people, but the king would have none of it.

The code defines the rights of citizens according to their estates: noblemen, burghers and peasants. The universities are free from censorship, but private citizens face severe penalties if they criticise political conditions and spread ideas likely to cause unrest. The monarchs of Europe are looking over their shoulders at France.

A Prussian officer.

1794 (1794-1795)

Paris, 28 July 1794. Robespierre and 21 of his companions are guillotined.

Paris, 2 August 1794. The painter David, once a fervent supporter of Robespierre, is arrested.

Paris, 2 August 1794. James Monroe, a Francophile and a partisan of the revolution, takes up his post as American ambassador in Paris.

France, 20 August 1794. Having been arrested on 9 August on suspicion of being a Robespierrist, General Bonaparte is released at the request of the commander-in-chief of the forces in the Alps and Italy in order to reinforce the Army of Italy's general staff.

USA, 20 August 1794. The revolutionary General "Mad Anthony" Wayne defeats the Ohio Indians at the battle of Fallen Timbers in the Northwest Territory, ending Indian resistance in the area.

Corsica, 21 August 1794. Bombarded by Captain Nelson's artillery at sea, and harassed on land by Pascal Paoli's Corsican nationalists, the French finally give the island up to the British.

Russia, 28 September 1794. The Anglo-Russian-Austrian alliance of St Petersburg is signed, directed against the French.

Poland, 10 October 1794. The Russian General Alexander Vasilyevich Suvorov crushes the rebel Polish army at Maciejowice. The injured Polish leader, Kosciuszko, is taken prisoner.

London, 17 October 1794. The British prime minister, William Pitt, cuts finances for Prussian troops. He holds Prussia responsible for the recent defeats suffered by antiFrench forces in Germany.

Germany, 23 October 1794. The French General Jourdan takes Koblenz.

Netherlands, 25 October 1794. Prussia denounces the treaty of the Hague, signed between Britain, Prussia and Holland in April, and withdraws its troops from the Netherlands.

Paris, 3 November 1794. After the intervention of the American ambassador James Monroe, Thomas Paine, the revolutionary writer who is an elected deputy of the Convention, is released from jail. He was imprisoned early this year having offended the Robespierre faction.

Poland, 4 November 1794. The rebel Polish army is beaten and massacred by the Russians at Praga.

London, 6 November 1794. Thomas Hardy, the leader of the radical Corresponding Society, who was charged with treason last month, is acquitted.

Poland, 9 November 1794. The Russians enter Warsaw, having successfully put down the Polish uprising led by Kosciuszko.

Britain, 11 November 1794. As part of a round of public order measures prompted by a fear of Jacobin activity, the British government suspends the ancient act of Habeas Corpus, which protects citizens against arbitrary arrest.

Philadelphia, November 1794. The uprising of the "whisky rebels" comes to an end. The dispute began in June when farmers in western Pennsylvania and throughout the Appalachians refused to pay the federal excise tax on whisky. The rebellion disintegrated when President Washington personally took the field with a force of 12,500 militiamen.

Paris, 26 December 1794. The painter David is granted a provisional release pending trial. He was imprisoned as an associate of Robespierre's.

Netherlands, 27 December 1794. Following the collapse of the treaty of The Hague, French forces invade Holland.

France, 31 December 1794. France signs an armistice with the Austrians.

Persia, 1794. The brutal and ambitious chieftain Aga Mohammed overthrows the Send dynasty, which has dominated Persia since 1750, and establishes the Kajar dynasty.

Paris, 1794. Claire Lacombe, known as "Red Rosa", is arrested while trying to leave Paris.

Germany, 1795. The writer Jean Paul Richter, who prefers to be known by his first names only, publishes a new novel, *Hesperus of Forty-five Days from the Post to the Dog*.

Britain, 1795. Having completed his composition of *The Marriage of Heaven and Hell*, the visionary poet William Blake goes on to write *The Book of Los*.

Nigeria, 1795. Sultan Agwaragi of Katsina defeats the sultan of Gobir, Bawa Jan Gwarzo, in battle near Kiawa and kills him.

Germany, 1795. The writer Friedrich Schiller – a trained army surgeon who is now honorary professor of history at the university of Jena – writes his *Letters concerning the aesthetic education of mankind*.

The Terror's creator dies

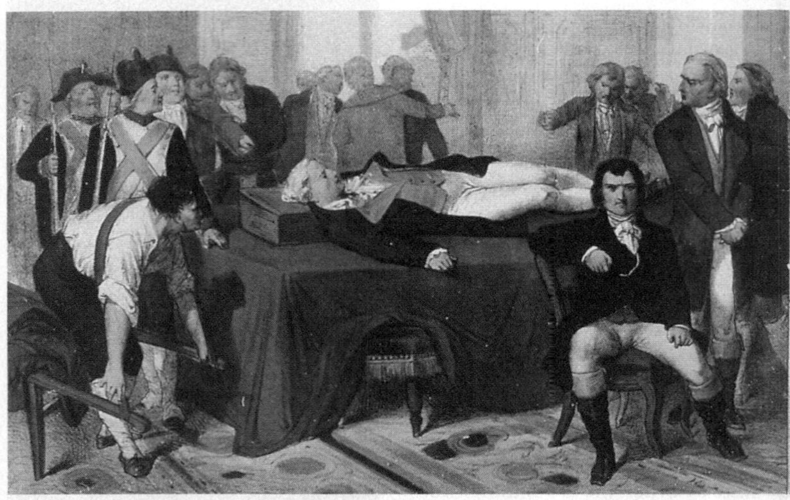

Robespierre, the "People's Friend", awaits the tumbril, his jaw broken.

Paris, 28 July 1794

Paris turned on the "incorruptible" Robespierre today, and jeered as the architect of terror and 21 of his allies were brought by tumbril to the guillotine which they had used so effectively to paralyse this country with fear.

Few expected such a dramatic turn in revolutionary events, but a conspiracy of deputies to the Convention – including many alleged supporters of the "tyrant Robespierre" – had been braced for this moment. They had filled the Convention with allies who cheered as Billaud Varenne, himself a member of the Committee of Public Safety, began a speech which turned many moderate supporters of Robespierre against their leader.

Robespierre, the incorruptible.

Fighting broke out in the Convention, and as Robespierre appeal- to the Montagnards for help, they turned their faces away from him. Finally, two deputies called for Robespierre's arrest, but such was his reputation that the ushers refused to take him and the others to the cells; nor would the turnkeys lock them in that night. In an ensuing scuffle, Robespierre was shot in the chin and could only nod when the death sentence was passed on him. Robespierre and the others could last night have turned Paris into a bloodbath, but, strangely, the army they mobilised was impotent to act.

Russia crushes patriotic Polish uprising

Warsaw, November 1794

Warsaw once again lies helpless beneath the Russian heel after a glorious and doomed eight-month uprising led by the Polish patriot Tadeusz Kosciuszko, a hero of victorious battles in the American and French revolutionary wars. Last April, when the Poles rose against the second partition of their country, they drove the Russians from Warsaw and repulsed Frederick William of Prussia. Catherine sent in her greatest general, Alexander Suvorov, who overwhelmed the Polish forces and slaughtered 6,000 civilians trapped against the banks of the Vistula.

Bloody Terror is ended

Victims of the revolution, after the revolutionaries turned on their own.

Paris, August 1794

The reign of Terror is over. With Robespierre and his allies dead, the Convention is in control of the revolution once again and, as the prison gates are opened to release thousands of political detainees, France has begun a bizarre headcount of those who have perished since last September when the real Terror began.

No-one will ever know the exact numbers who were brought to the guillotine after summary trials by revolutionary tribunals, but at least 25,000 people were beheaded – most of them for alleged treason or rebellion – often on the flimsiest evidence. The merest hint of royalist sympathies or counter-revolutionary activity could bring a citizen before the dreaded tribunals. The Terror was an ideal opportunity for paying off old scores.

Paris recorded 2,639 executions. Outside the capital, it was the west of France and the Rhone Valley that suffered the most. In Loire Inferieure no fewer than 3,548 people were to face the guillotine's blade.

At the height of the Terror, the prison population of Paris alone soared to more than 8,000 and new prisons had to be opened to hold the flood of prisoners.

Scanty fashions all the rage in France

Paris, December 1794

It may be Paris in the depth of winter, but the capital's fashionable young women, barely clothed in draperies of sheer gauze, put many onlookers in mind of classical Athens.

Known as the "Wonderful Women", these exquisites, dedicated to the display of "insolent luxury amidst public wretchedness", wear their dresses with fans in the belts, purses at the bosoms and blond wigs on their heads. They are followed by their "handkerchief bearers", enraptured young men.

Radical chic: French "Incroyables".

Cruelty of Persia's castrated monarch

Shah Aga Mohammed Khan.

Persia, 1794

Aga Mohammed, the *khan* of the Kajars, has completed the liquidation of the old Zand dynasty and cemented his reputation as the cruellest Persian ruler.

Castrated at the age of five by Adil Shah, Aga Mohammed, the eldest son of Mohammed Husein Khan, became the candidate for the throne of Persia on the death of Karim Khan, the regent, in 1779. After a prolonged struggle for power he took control, and in 1786 he moved the capital from Shiraz to Tehran, nearer his home base among the Kajar tribesmen.

He then set about subduing the southern half of the country, culminating in the destruction of Kerman, the headquarters of Lutf Ali Khan, the son of Kharim Khan and heir to the Zand dynasty.

Lutf Ali was wounded, captured, blinded and finally strangled in Tehran. The women of Kerman were raped, killed or sold into slavery. From the men Aga Mohammed demanded 20,000 pairs of eyes, which were duly delivered to him.

"Rosa" fires Paris

Paris, 1794

Claire Lacombe, known as "Red Rosa", has been arrested for inciting women's desire for suffrage. The 29-year-old actress, a heroine of the storming of the Tuileries two years ago, was leaving Paris for the theatre in Dunkirk when she was stopped by the National Guard and taken to the Bastille.

Rosa blatantly ignored Robespierre's ban on meetings of her Revolutionary Republican Women. Associated with the leftwing Enrages, the society was an organisation of women workers determined to petition for women's right to vote and participate in the Revolutionary Committee.

French Revolution finds echoes in Europe

Europe, 1794

The French Revolution has galvanised Europe. Paris is the centre of political activity, attracting foreign intellectuals and publishing newspapers in English and French. But the Terror's victims have included the German Anacharsis Cloots, executed with the Hebertists, and the English radical Thomas Paine, in prison since December 1794.

British radicals are highly sympathetic, but the government remains vehemently anti-French. In Corsica the revolutionary ideas of Buonarotti have been rejected in favour of British rule by viceroy.

In the Habsburg empire there have been Jacobin conspiracies in Vienna and Hungary, but the Brabant revolution has been crushed. In Italy, Masonic lodges have become revolutionary cells, while in Holland rebels have linked up with invading French forces.

Hot Scot rocks are moving very slowly

Edinburgh, 1795

What is the nature of the forces that shape our earth? In a two-volume work, *Theory of the Earth,* published this year, the scientist James Hutton draws on extensive observations of the countryside of his native Scotland and sees features that lead him to claim that geological forces act extremely slowly over time. For example, Hutton says that stratified rocks were deposited as sediments of former seas. And if the strata are distorted from their regular horizontal layers, he says that this is because of movements in the earth's crust due to internal heat.

1795 ⇒

Brittany, 3 January. *Chouans* (royalists) and republicans agree to a ceasefire.

Russia, 3 January. Russia and Austria hold a secret meeting to draw up plans for the partition of Poland.

Amsterdam, 19 January. French forces led by General Pichegru enter Amsterdam after a vicious winter campaign. The *stadholder*, William V, flees as the Batavian patriots greet their "liberators".

Netherlands, 23 January. French republican forces take the entire Dutch fleet while it lies ice-bound off Texel.

France, 31 January. Violent rioting is sparked off in Rennes by food shortages. General Hoche calls in the army.

France, 3 February. Four *sans-culottes* are attacked by "reactionaries" in Lyons, marking a change in public mood towards the activists and their supporters.

France, 9 February. France and the grand duchy of Tuscany sign a peace treaty affirming Tuscany's neutrality.

France, 14 February. Joseph Fernex, a judge of the Revolutionary Committee who has been in prison since the overthrow of Robespierre, is killed and thrown into the river Rhone in broad daylight by "reactionaries".

France, 21 February. The convention approves a decree restoring freedom of worship.

Paris, 27 February. After clashes between "reactionaries" and Jacobins in the theatres, they are closed indefinitely.

Paris, 3 March. The *Bourse* (stock exchange) is reopened.

Paris, 25 March. Food stocks reach an all-time low. Only enough wheat for 115 days is left in the warehouses.

Paris, 1 April. A mob breaks into the convention screaming "We want bread!". But the protest fails to develop into a full-scale uprising, and the hungry men and women are rounded up by a unit of bayonet-wielding grenadiers. Martial law is declared.

Basel, 5 April. France and Prussia sign the treaty of Basle ending hostilities between the two countries.

Paris, 10 April. The Convention takes harsh measures following the protests of 1 April. It also takes the opportunity to root out *Thermidorians* (reformed Robespierrists) whom it suspects of trying to slow down the forces of reaction.

Paris, 12 April. Almost a year after his mysterious death in a prison cell, the philosopher Condorcet is honoured by the Assembly, though he died an outlaw.

Brittany, 20 April. The *Chouans* (royalists) agree to recognise the republic and not to take up arms against it again.

Paris, 26 April. Officially sanctioning the collapse of paper money, the Convention annuls the decree forbidding gold and silver trading.

France, 4 May. Thousands of rioters enter jails in Lyons and massacre 99 Jacobin prisoners.

France, 8 May. Hearing of his appointment in the west, General Bonaparte leaves for Paris in order to obtain a different posting.

France, 16 May. The French impose a treaty on The Hague, recognising the Batavian republic.

Budapest, 20 May. Ignac Martinovics, the head of the Jacobin movement in Hungary, is executed, dashing the hopes of Hungarian revolutionaries.

Paris, 23 May. After four days of rioting and violence, a *sans-culotte* uprising is suppressed. It began when rioters demonstrating against a severe bread shortage broke into the Conventiony. By yesterday the army had been called in and today the Saint Antoine district capitulated.

France, May. The White Terror, so called to differentiate it from Robespierre's Red Terror, sweeps across France, with all who are suspected as "terrorists" or political militants standing to lose their lives at the hands of the "reactionaries".

Marseilles, 5 June. Southern royalists calling themselves the Company of the Sun kill 700 defenceless "terrorists" in the prison of Saint Jean fort.

Luxembourg, 7 June. The duchy of Luxembourg, an Austrian possession for the last 82 years, surrenders to the French.

Paris, 8 June. The young *dauphin*, Louis, a prisoner in the Temple for three years, dies.

Paris, 15 June. General Napoleon Bonaparte has himself put on sick leave, having not received the posting he wanted from his superiors.

Paris, June. The writer Madame de Stael, daughter of the financier Necker, returns to Paris and reopens her salon. She declares herself a supporter of the republic.

Britain takes Cape Colony from the Dutch

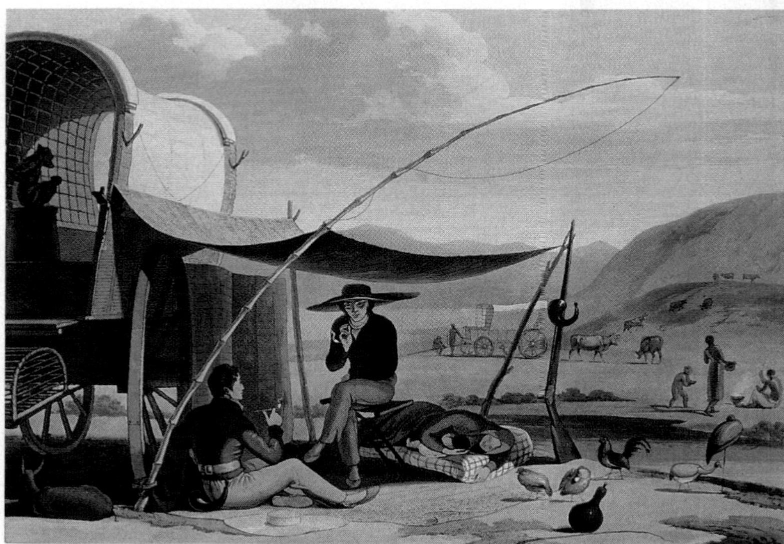

Boer farmers, who see themselves as Africans and resent the British presence.

Cape Town, South Africa

As the revolutionary Boers were declaring for liberty, equality and fraternity, British troops landed in Cape Town and took the colony from the Dutch. The British are now blockading the revolutionary republics into submission.

The Boer colony has been steadily expanding northwards, attacking and killing native Africans who got in the way. Holland opposed these methods. The Boers responded by driving out Dutch officials, sporting the revolutionary cockade and declaring republics.

It is unlikely, though, that the revolutionary ideas will benefit Africans. Indeed, one reason that the Boers declared their republics was to be able to attack their neighbours undisturbed.

France takes firm measure with measures

Paris

One of the important scientific outcomes of the French Revolution is the introduction of a new system of weights and measures. From now on there will be one system to replace the confusing variations from region to region. It will, it is declared, be a system "for all time, for all people".

The system is named *metric* after the Greek word for measure. The standard measure of length is the *metre*, which is one ten-millionth of the distance from the north pole to the equator. The system works in multiples of ten; thus, a *centimetre* is a hundredth of a metre, while a *millimetre* is a thousandth. The closest metric equivalent of the English mile is the *kilometre*. The new units of weight are based on the *gramme*, which is the weight of one cubic centimetre of water at a temperature of four degrees *centigrade* – another metric innovation to measure temperatures.

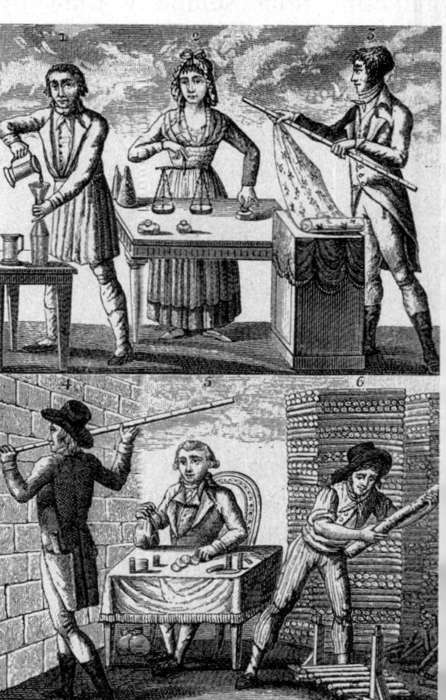

French propaganda prints herald the recently approved metric system; it is based on units of ten, to be universally applied "for all time, for all people" to calculate weights, volumes and distances in the new France.

Uprising in Paris put down by troops

Paris, 23 May
With the rallying cry of "Bread or Death!" thousands of revolutionary sans-culottes swarmed into the streets, smashing the gates of the Assembly, killing a deputy, Feraud, and brandishing his severed head on a pike before the president of the Convention, Boissy d'Anglas. Many rioters are women who spend hours queuing for the meagre bread ration of two ounces per person.

In the chaos that followed, Montagnard deputies formed themselves into an executive committee and, for a few hours, it seemed that the Robespierrists could be back in power. By nightfall, however, most of the sans-culottes had gone home, giving the Convention time to call in the regular army. As soldiers and insurgents faced each other today, the mob succeeded in freeing Feraud's killers. Nonetheless, as artillery faced the barricades, the sans-culottes were forced to surrender.

Sans-culottes rioting for bread.

New Dutch republic submits to France

French cavalry charging Dutch warships over the ice last winter.

The Hague, 16 May
The French republic has formally recognised the Batavian republic – the former United Provinces of Holland, which were occupied by French troops last year after the Dutch navy became trapped in ice.

The French move follows a popular uprising in the Provinces in which the stadholder (head of state) was driven out of office and a revolutionary constitution, based on the French model, adopted. The Dutch will pay dearly for their freedom, however. The new republic has to cede Dutch Flanders, Maastricht and Venlo to France, and pay 100 million florins as war compensation. It also accepts the installation of a French base at Flushing and has agreed to form an alliance with France against Austria and Germany.

The two republics may share revolutionary zeal, but there is no doubt who is the master.

Clay reclaims Wedgwood, master potter

Britain, 3 January
Josiah Wedgwood died today at Etruria, near Stoke-on-Trent, where he built what is now the biggest pottery in the world. He was 64. His success came after a difficult boyhood. The 13th son of a potter, he began work aged eight on the death of his father. He soon became an expert "thrower", but smallpox at 15 left him weak, so much so that his elder brother refused to take him into the firm. He concentrated on design and technique, producing the superb *Queen's Ware*, setting new higher quality standards, which made him world famous.

A Portland vase, by Wedgwood.

James Boswell, a British man of letters

London, 19 May
James Boswell, Dr Johnson's biographer, has died four years after publishing the long-awaited *Life*. It was an immediate success, and a second edition came out in 1793.

Boswell began keeping "an exact journal" from the age of 18 and put his best literary talents into it. He would often sit up all night recording his conversations as well as his sexual adventures. His irresistible good humour made him welcome amongst London's greatest wits – Goldsmith, Burke, Reynolds and Wilkes. His other works include an *Account of Corsica* and the famous *Tour to the Hebrides*.

France approves a new constitution

Paris, 23 September
A new French constitution was ratified today after a referendum in which over a million French people voted in favour and fewer than 50,000 against. Only an eighth of the eligible population voted.

The constitution drops universal suffrage and replaces it with a two-tier system based on property ownership. Male taxpayers and army veterans of 21 or over and born in France – about five million people – will be eligible to vote in elections to local electoral assemblies in the French *departements*. The members of these assemblies – about 30,000 citizens – must be 25 or over with an income equal to 200 workdays a year. In the second tier of voting, the assemblies will elect members of a two-chamber national legislature. executive will consist of a five-man Directory with wide powers. The constitution contains many checks to block any attempt to set up a dictatorship.

Worker unrest now comes to England

London, 29 June
Fearful of an outbreak of rioting, the government today deployed a large force of cavalry and guards in Lambeth, south London, where a mass meeting was held to demand manhood suffrage and annual parliaments and to protest against "the cruel and unnecessary war" against revolutionary France. Some 10,000 people (the organisers say 100,000) endorsed a loyal address to the king before dispersing peacefully.

Many radical societies, inspired by events in France, have been formed in London and the provinces, but it is the hardship caused by war that has given the radical movement a sharper edge. Exports have collapsed and many workers are in dire straits. In Norwich, 25,000 of the city's 40,000 population are on poor relief.

Politics do not rule all hearts, though. One activist, Henry Redhead Yorke, was sent to prison for conspiracy; there he met and married the governor's daughter and abandoned his radical views.

1795 (1795-1796)

Paris, 7 July 1795. At the Convention Thomas Paine defends the principle of universal suffrage which the deputies have decided to abandon in the next constitution.

France, 21 July 1795. Royalists are defeated at Quiberon, on the north-west coast. In alliance with the English, French emigres had planned an invasion of the mainland, but underestimated the powers of the republican army.

Basle, 22 July 1795. France and Spain sign a peace treaty following the fall of Bilbao and Vittoria.

Paris, 4 August 1795. The artist David is acquitted on charges relating to his friendship with Robespierre, who fell dramatically from a position of almost supreme power and was executed last year.

France, 15 August 1795. The Convention creates a new monetary unit, the *franc*.

Prussia, August 1795. Prussia joins the talks between Russia and Austria on the partition of Poland.

South Africa, 16 September 1795. Following the royal Dutch government's overthrow by France and the local Jacobins, the *stadholder*, William V, invites England to seize the Dutch colonial domain. England begins with Cape Town.

Netherlands, 29 September 1795. The government of the Batavian republic puts the stadholder William V on trial on a charge of high treason.

Paris, September 1795. The marquis de Sade publishes a new novel, *Aline and Valcour*, the story of an incestuous father thwarted by a double child swop, and of the dangers encountered by his virtuous wife during a voyage round the world.

Paris, 15 October 1795. An attempted armed takeover of the Convention by wealthy Parisians is put down, but only with heavy military intervention. From now on the Convention will have to take the army into account. One among the officers who attracted much attention was a young general, Napoleon Bonaparte.

Paris, 16 October 1795. Bonaparte is promoted to major-general.

Poland, 24 October 1795. The third partition of Poland is agreed between Russia, Prussia and Austria.

Paris, 31 October 1795. The Executive Directory, which replaces the Convention, is appointed. It consists of five Directors, nominated by the Council of Five Hundred and elected by the Council of Ancients.

Poland, 25 November 1795. King Stanislas abdicates following the partition of his country.

France, 17 December 1795. The British fleet, abandoned by the count of Artois, the pretender to the French throne, leaves the Ile d'Yeu.

Paris, 9 March 1796. Bonaparte marries Josephine de Beauharnais.

Santo Domingo, 31 March 1796. A coup by a mulatto general fails.

Italy, 11 April 1796. Bonaparte starts the Italian campaign at the head of 40,000 men.

Italy, 15 April 1796. The last Austrian corps in the Apennines surrenders at Dego.

Italy, 22 April 1796. Bonaparte wins the battles of Montenotte, Millesimo, Dego and Mondovi between 13 and 22 April.

Piedmont, 28 April 1796. Bonaparte concludes a treaty in Cherasco with the king of Piedmont and Sardinia. He has exceeded his instructions from Paris in the signing of this treaty.

Paris, 10 May 1796. A plot by the *Communes*, led by Francois Babeuf, to overthrow the Directory is uncovered and the leaders are arrested.

Italy, 10 May 1796. Bonaparte wins a brilliant victory against the Austrians at Lodi bridge.

Italy, 12 May 1796. Lombardian patriots rise up against the French and almost take Milan.

Milan, 15 May 1796. Bonaparte enters the Lombardian capital of Milan in triumph.

Paris, 15 May 1796. The treaty between France and Piedmont-Sardinia is signed, ceding Savoy and Nice to the French republic.

Italy, 23 May 1796. The people of Pavia massacre the French soldiers who sought refuge in the citadel.

USA, 1 June 1796. The Southwest Territory becomes the sixteenth state, known as Tennessee.

Italy, 5 June 1796. Bonaparte signs an armistice with the kingdom of Naples.

Italy, 23 June 1796. The pope, Pius VI, signs an armistice with Bonaparte in Bologna.

Elba, 9 July 1796. British forces take Elba as a Mediterranean base, having lost Leghorn to the French.

Philadelphia, 17 September 1796. President Washington makes his farewell address after 20 years as president.

Spain, 5 October 1796. Spain declares war on Britain.

Russia, 7 November 1796. Czarina Catherine II (the Great) dies.

French rout Austrians in battle for bridge

French troops crossing the river Alpone to take the Austrians from the rear.

Italy, 17 November 1796

The brilliant Napoleon Bonaparte, still only 27, scored another crushing victory in northern Italy today, where he has been campaigning since April. He as driven the Austrians back to Arcole after three days of heavy fighting for the bridge over the Alpone river.

The battle was brought about by the advance of the Austrian General Alvinczy and 50,000 troops transferred after the French retreat in Germany. At the beginning of the month he defeated the tired troops of Massena at Bassano, and then beat Augereau at Caldiso. Suddenly the whole French position in Italy was in danger. Napoleon met Alvinczy at Arcole, and both armies fought for two days over difficult, swampy ground until Napoleon showed his tactical genius by moving his men across the river on pontoon bridges and taking the Austrians in the rear.

Massena is now pursuing the Austrians through Arcole, and Augereau is harassing their flank. In three days of fighting the Austrians have lost 7,000 men and 11 cannons. The French have also taken heavy punishment, and sorely need rest and supplies. Bonaparte told them: "You have won battles without guns, crossed rivers without bridges, made forced marches without boots, encamped without food."

Theory links liberty with obeying laws

Jena, Germany, 1796

Man cannot achieve real freedom without a rational legal system, according to a new theory developed by the philosopher Johann Gottlieb Fichte, a disciple of Kant.

In his just-published *Foundation of the Study of Human Knowledge*, Fichte, a 34-year-old professor, explains that since man is forced to live in society, laws naturally arise from the social relationships that exist between men.

When these laws are guaranteed by the state then they form a protective framework that allows the individual to fulfil himself, argues Fichte. His new theory is a marked about-turn. Three years ago he was violently hostile to the state.

French astronomer makes stars clearer

Paris, 1796

The French mathematician, astronomer and physicist Pierre-Simon de Laplace has finally crowned his life's work on the structure and evolution of the solar system with a popular book.

Laplace's recently-published *Exposition du systeme du monde* is a beautifully written work on celestial mechanics. He is able to account for all the planets' deviations: why, for example, Jupiter's orbit seems continually to be getting smaller while that of Saturn is expanding. Another intriguing idea concerns planetary formation. The solar system, he argues, is formed out of a cooling, contracting mass of gas – the *nebula* hypothesis.

Despotic czarina leaves a stronger Russia

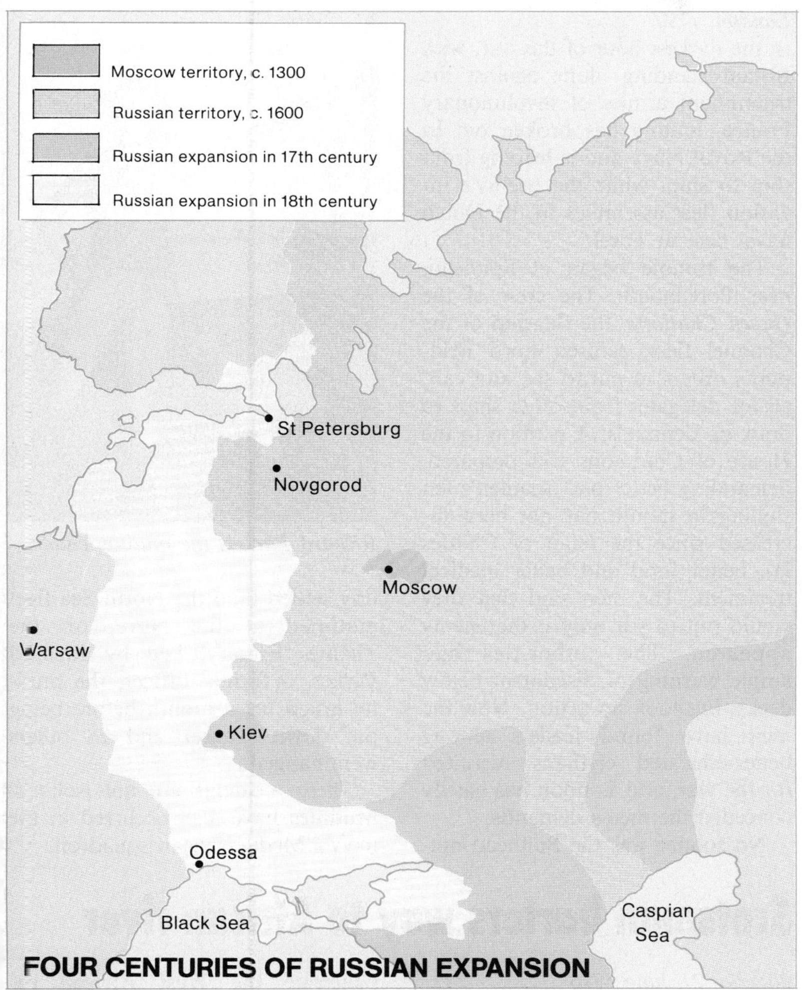

Czarskoye Selo, 7 November 1796
Her court is riddled with corruption, scoundrels are promoted to the nobility, and injustice is rampant. Yet the czarina, who died today aged 67 at Czarskoye Selo (the Czar's Village), near St Petersburg, has become universally known as Catherine the Great.

She had not a drop of Russian blood. Born at Stettin, Pomerania, the daughter of the prince of Anhalt-Zerbst, she was taken to Russia at the age of 15 to become the bride of the mentally subnormal Grand Duke Peter. She endured 17 wretched years until, on Peter's succession to the throne, she arranged for his assassination by one of her lovers.

As czarina she was more Russian than the Russians whom she ruled. She said: "All I wish is that this country, in which God has cast me, should prosper." She said serfdom was against God's law, but under her serfdom flourished. She pushed the empire's boundaries to the Dniester in the west and the Black Sea in the south. In her will she advised her successors to avoid consulting "Germans of both sexes".

Robbie Burns, poet

Dumfries, Scotland, 21 July 1796
Scotland's bard, the poet Robert Burns, died today, aged 37, after months of failing health. Through hundreds of poems and folksongs, such as *Auld Lang Syne, The Highland Lassie* and the *Jolly Beggars*, he captured the soul of Scotland.

Yet Burns was 25 before he burst upon a startled world with a small book of poems that instantly sold out. The eldest son of a poor peasant farmer, Burns used the funds from his second book to buy a farm. Through contacts in Edinburgh society, which briefly lionised him, he obtained a job as an excise official in south-west Scotland.

Polish cake carved into three pieces

Warsaw, 1795
A bankrupt Englishman is the last foreign diplomat in Warsaw, the capital of a country that has ceased to exist. He has 300 refugees in the embassy and has written to London asking for money, but the British are too concerned about the victories of France's revolutionary armies to bother about a faraway land of which few people have heard. After crushing the Polish uprising last year, Russia, Prussia and Austria, which had twice before annexed large areas of Poland, decided to finish the job. The Prussians pushed their frontier further east to take in Warsaw; the Austrians seized the Cracow region; the Russians took the rest, which was greater than Prussian and Austrian gains combined. The three powers agreed to suppress the name of Poland "forever".

Lotus cult is focus for Chinese rebels

China, 1796
The White Lotus Society, an ascetic creed which believes that a "future Buddha" will usher in an era of peace and plenty, has risen in revolt against the government. Trouble has been brewing for some time, due to government oppression, and the White Lotus rebellion is spreading rapidly through the countryside.

The society is famous for driving the Mongols out of China in the 14th century, and its adherents have lost none of their ferocity in war. Its teachings are spread from village to village by missionaries and its members are protected by local defence associations. It is these which have taken up arms against rapacious local officials and, basing themselves in fortified mountain villages, are raiding valley towns for supplies and recruits.

Milkmaid clue to smallpox prevention

London, 1796
Smallpox – which has killed millions over the centuries – could be eradicated, thanks to the work of an English country doctor, Edward Jenner of Gloucestershire.

Jenner noticed while still a student that milkmaids who had contracted a disease called cowpox, which also causes blistering of cows' udders, did not catch smallpox. So now Jenner has taken some of the fluid from a cowpox blister and scratched it into the skin of an eight-year-old boy named James Phipps. A single blister rose up on the spot but, amazingly, young James has not caught smallpox even though he has been in close contact with other children suffering from the disease. Jenner has thus found a way of preparing the body in advance to cope with an infection.

The wonders of the smallpox vaccine, as seen by the Anti-Vaccine Society.

1796 (1796-1797)

Ireland, 24 December 1796. A storm breaks up the French fleet which was bound for Ireland to help the nationalists in their fight against the British.

Italy, 14 January 1797. Bonaparte crushes Alvinczy's army at Rivoli.

Italy, 16 January 1797. The main body of Provera's Austrian army surrenders to Bonaparte at La Favorite.

Italy, 20 January 1797. In accordance with a treaty signed with Bonaparte, the Polish general, Dobrowski, calls all Polish patriots to arms, to form a legion with him in Italy in support of the French.

Italy, 2 February 1797. Bonaparte takes Mantua from the Austrians, opening up the road to Vienna.

Italy, 9 February 1797. Bonaparte moves into the Vatican states and occupies Ancona, with a view to forcing Pius VI to negotiate.

Portugal, 14 February 1797. The Spanish fleet, which is allied to France, is defeated by the British just off the Cape of St Vincent.

Italy, 19 February 1797. Bonaparte signs the treaty of Tolentino with Pope Pius VI.

Paris, 2 March 1797. The Directory authorises vessels of war to board and seize neutral vessels, particularly if the ships involved are American.

England, 2 March 1797. Horace Walpole, who set the fashion for "Gothick" romance in *The Castle of Otranto*, dies. He lived in a "Gothick" castle which he had built at Strawberry Hill near London in reaction to the prevailing Classical style of country houses.

USA, 4 March 1797. Vice-president John Adams, elected president on 7 December to replace George Washington, is sworn in.

London, 18 March 1797. Chateaubriand brings out his *Historic Essay on Revolutions*, which is instantly popular among the emigres of the upper classes.

Paris, 20 March 1797. On the eve of the polls, the Directory passes a law requiring all voters to swear commitment to the republic and the constitution.

Italy, 27 March 1797. The constitution of the Cispadian republic is promulgated at Bologna.

Austria, 31 March 1797. Bonaparte makes peace proposals to Archduke Charles of Austria.

Paris, 4 April 1797. Election results show that the French people are now predominantly right-wing reactionaries rather than revolutionaries.

Austria, 7 April 1797. In the absence of news about the French campaign in Germany, Bonaparte signs an armistice with the Austrian envoys in Judenburg.

Britain, 15 April 1797. The British fleet mutinies at Spithead.

Verona, 17 April 1797. On Easter Sunday several hundred French soldiers are massacred by locals.

Verona, 27 April 1797. The revolt of the people of Verona and Venice, as a reaction against French taxes, is violently crushed and the *doge* removed from office.

Paris, 30 April 1797. The Directory ratifies the Leoben agreement between Austria and France, which Bonaparte signed on 18 April though he had no authority to do so.

Britain, 2 May 1797. The naval mutiny spreads from Spithead to the North Sea fleet.

Venice, 12 May 1797. The Grand Council replaces the doge by with a democratic republic.

Philadelphia, 15 May 1797. President Adams calls Congress into a special session, hoping to resolve the crisis with France.

India, 15 May 1797. An alliance between France and Mysore is made in Seringapatam.

Paris, 26 May 1797. The trial of Babeuf and his followers, for conspiracy to overthrown the government, comes to an end. Babeuf is sentenced to death.

Italy, 14 June 1797. A 22-man government appointed by Bonaparte takes up its duties in Genoa, marking the birth of the Ligurian republic.

Persia, 17 June 1797. The *shah*, Aga Mohammed, is assassinated. He is succeeded by his nephew Fath Ali.

Italy, 9 July 1797. The Cisalpine republic is founded in Milan, combining Lombardy and the Cispadian republic.

Britain, 9 July 1797. Edmund Burke, foremost political philosopher of the day, dies aged 68. He defended constitutional government against the French revolutionaries, but advocated conciliation with the American colonists before the War of Independence.

Mediterranean, 28 August 1797. The USA agrees to pay tribute to Tunis in an effort to halt piracy against American ships.

France, 22 September 1797. General Pichegru, convicted of treason because of his royalist sympathies, leaves France for Guyana where he is to be imprisoned.

Mutiny sweeps through British navy

London, 1797

In the darkest hour of the war, with Britain standing alone against the triumphant armies of revolutionary France, mutiny has broken out in the Royal Navy and is leaping from ship to ship, while the enemy's invasion fleet assembles in the Dutch naval base at Texel.

Richard Parker, the mutiny leader.

The trouble began at Spithead, near Portsmouth. The crew of the *Queen Charlotte,* the flagship of the Channel fleet, refused Lord Bridport's orders to put to sea and called for delegates from other ships to draw up demands. A petition to the House of Commons was prepared, demanding better pay (seamen's ten shillings a month has not been increased since the reign of Charles II), better food and better medical treatment. The men said that they would put to sea only if the enemy appeared. The authorities had ample warning of discontent below decks, but took no action. Now the men have found leaders among better-educated civilians recruited for the war, and London has hastily conceded the men's demands.

No sooner was the Spithead mutiny settled than the North Sea fleet mutinied at the Nore, on the Thames Estuary. Led by Richard Parker, a former officer, the mutiny lasted for a month before being put down. Parker and 28 others were hanged.

These incidents are not isolated. Mutinies have also occurred in the navy's Mediterranean squadron.

Scotsman barters way to African river

Nigeria, 21 June 1796

By reaching the majestic Niger river at Segu, Mungo Park, a 24-year-old Scottish doctor, has discovered one of the secrets of mysterious Africa. He reports that the river is as broad as the Thames at Westminster and flows eastwards. He marked his discovery by drinking the river water and thanking God. Park is the first European to penetrate the West African interior; he has done it alone, and has learnt to live on native food and without western luxuries.

His instruments consisted of a pocket sextant, compass and thermometer. He paid for his food and shelter with beads, amber and tobacco, but was ultimately reduced to selling the buttons off his rags. His story should be a bestseller.

Park's first sight of what he called the "glittering" Niger (later portrayal).

Lucknow prospers under Asaf-ud-Daula

The royal family of Oudh, painted in Lucknow by Tilly Kettle, in foreground.

Lucknow, India, September 1797
Asaf-ud-Daula, the monarch of Oudh, is transforming Lucknow into the new cultural capital of northern India. Palaces, mosques and schools are being built. The finest poets, painters, musicians and architects of Moslem India have gathered here; so have travellers, adventurers, merchants and confidence tricksters.

Already Lucknow has surpassed Delhi in splendour, drawing into it such poets as Mirza Rafi, known as *Sauda*, Mir Taqi (*Mir*) and Mir Ghulam Hasan – the finest Indian and Persian poets of the age. Poets are not the only ones to be tempted by the wealth of Oudh. Shi'ite scholars from Persia, painters from India and Europe, actors, musicians and Moghul princes flock to the city. Asaf-ud-Daula, who is bored by the bread-and-butter of statecraft, collects such people as other Indian princes collect jewels.

Yet behind the luxury and pomp of Lucknow there is little substance. The economy of Oudh is firmly in the hands of the British-owned East India Company. The more Asaf-ud-Daula has to rely on the military might of the British, and the more Oudh's treasury becomes indebted to the British, the more extravagantly Asaf-ud-Daula embellishes Lucknow, in splendid defiance.

Man demonstrates "parachute" device

Paris, 22 October 1797
From now on, stricken aeronauts whose hot-air balloons fail them will enjoy a way of escape, thanks to the pioneering efforts of the physicist Andre Jacques Garnerin, who today demonstrated his revolutionary *parachute* in the Monceau park.

Supported by one such device, made of 36 tapered strips of material sewn together to form a spherical "skullcap" eight metres in diameter, Garnerin dropped from a balloon 3,050 feet above the park. The folded parachute was attached to the gondola, and crowds watched as Garnerin cut the cord that attached him to the balloon and then, as the parachute unfolded above him, floated safely to earth.

Garnerin descends with his parachute above the environs of Paris.

France extends rule over Italian republics

Milan, 9 July 1797
Napoleon sat his horse for three hours in the burning sun today as the birth of his Cisalpine republic was celebrated in grand operatic – some would say musical comedy – style in the streets of Milan.

Cisalpine consists of two of his previous statelets, the Transpadian and Cispadian, and includes Modena, whose duke has been deposed. It follows Napoleon's policy of imposing his version of the French Revolution on states he has conquered on behalf of France. His victories and the flood of indemnities and loot he sends back to Paris have made him enormously popular. There are those, however, who fear that the little general is becoming over-ambitious.

He has set up what can only be called a court at the chateau of Montebello, a few miles from Milan and he and his wife, Josephine, are behaving like royalty. They are surrounded by his family, his generals and brilliantly uniformed *aides de camp*.

Napoleon receives the nobility of Lombardy and the envoys of kings at his chateau. He basks in his glory and disposes of states like an emperor.

New republics, established by French arms, sprout throughout Italy.

Bonaparte's hand is seen in Paris coup

Paris, 4 September 1797
A *coup d'etat* led by the hulking General Augereau has swept away the royalist faction which, largely financed by the British, had made much ground in last spring's elections.

Primed with champagne, Augereau announced: "I have come here to kill the Royalists." When some of the deputies protested "in the name of the law", one of his officers replied: "The sword is the law."

However, while Augereau is the very visible arm of the coup, there is little doubt that Bonaparte, safely out of the way in Italy, has a powerful hand in it. He despises Augereau, but uses him.

It was Bonaparte who wrote to the Directory: "If you need force, call on the armies!"

English missionary team arrives in Tahiti

Tahiti, 1797
Thirty-nine English missionaries have landed in Tahiti. The party of four ministers, carpenters, weavers, bricklayers and even shopkeepers is being financed by the Presbyterian London Missionary Society.

The near-Arcadian paradise that Captain Cook found has disappeared within a decade. Firearms, venereal diseases, rum and infanticide have decimated the population. The staunch lower-middle-class Protestants who sailed halfway round the world on *The Duff* have no illusions about Arcadia. Guilt, hard work and public decency must be implanted in the islanders. The missionaries themselves observe such principles remorselesssly.

Ironically, they forgot to add a day when they passed the date line. Thus they observe a sober and silent sabbath every Saturday.

1797 (1797-1798)

Paris, 26 October 1797. The Directory ratifies the treaty of Campo Formio, signed by Bonaparte and the Austrians on 18 October.

USA, 4 November 1797. Congress agrees to pay a yearly tribute to Tripoli in a deal similar to that concluded last year with the *bey* of Algiers. This is the USA's only way of protecting its shipping.

Prussia, 16 November 1797. King Frederick William II dies and is succeeded by his son Frederick William III.

Germany, 1 December 1797. Bonaparte signs a convention with Austria at Rastatt, agreeing to a simultaneous evacuation of Mainz and Venice.

Paris, 12 January 1798. Bonaparte presents his plans for the invasion of England to the Directory.

Paris, 18 January 1798. Increasing pressure on British trade, the Directory passes a law authorising the seizure of any neutral vessel carrying British goods.

Switzerland, 24 January 1798. The people of Vaud, in the west, proclaim the republic of Leman, in defiance of authorities in Berne.

Rome, 15 February 1798. The republic of Rome is proclaimed by the French.

Rome, 24 February 1798. The French army rises up against its new chief, Berthier. The people of Rome seize the opportunity to revolt against the occupation.

Paris, 5 March 1798. Having shelved plans for the invasion of England, on Bonaparte's advice, the Directory accepts the idea of invading Egypt and puts Bonaparte in charge of the project.

Switzerland, 6 March 1798. French troops seize Berne, under the pretext of helping Vaudois patriots to remain independent.

Indian Ocean, 4 April 1798. French soldiers are under siege in their barracks in the Ile de France (*Mauritius*). Taking advantage of military unrest, the white and mulatto populations of the island have staged an uprising against slavery. The soldiers are trying to negotiate a surrender and are asking to be returned to France.

Switzerland, 12 April 1798. Deputies from 12 cantons proclaim a Swiss republic at Aarau.

Austria, 29 April 1798. Haydn's oratorio *The Creation* is first performed. Inspired by his hearing of Handel's oratorios in England, Haydn sets a text derived from Milton and James Thomson. It is scored for full orchestra, large choir and three soloists, and is a great success.

Caribbean, 2 May 1798. The black general Toussaint L'Ouverture forces the British forces to agree to evacuate the part of Santo Domingo still in their possession.

Ireland, 23 May 1798. Believing that a French invasion is imminent, the Irish nationalists rise up against British occupation.

Malta, 11 June 1798. The island surrenders to Bonaparte.

Ireland, 21 June 1798. British forces suppress an uprising by Irish patriots at Vinegar Hill near Wexford.

Egypt, 29 June 1798. The first French frigate to arrive at Alexandria learns that Nelson's fleet put in the previous day in search of the French.

Egypt, 1 July 1798. Napoleon Bonaparte takes Alexandria.

Egypt, 7 July 1798. Bonaparte's army begins its march towards Cairo.

Philadelphia, 11 July 1798. As the possibility of war with France grows, Congress passes the Sedition Act, aimed at curbing internal dissent. French negotiators are trying to intimidate the American envoys, and war at sea has already broken out, though it is undeclared. Under the Sedition Act American citizens may be imprisoned for obstructing the imposition of federal law or for seditious writings.

Russia, 21 July 1798. Czar Paul sends his army to help Austrian troops in their struggles with France.

France, 1798. The American engineer Robert Fulton invents the first submarine. He arrived in France two years ago and submitted his plans to the Directory. Now the *Nautilus* has taken to the water in a successful demonstration. However, naval officers are not convinced.

England, 1798. William Wordsworth and Samuel Taylor Coleridge publish the *Lyrical Ballads*, a joint collection of poetry. The volume marks a significant departure from current poetic conventions and is a celebration of the imagination and creative originality. Coleridge, in particular, reacts against the poetic dictates of the 18th century, revitalising his language by a skilful use of archaic diction, while Wordsworth is striving to transform everyday reality and to describe a mystical union of man with nature.

Austria, 1798. Ludwig van Beethoven presents his piano sonata, opus 13, known as the *Pathetique*.

Smuggler gangs bring home the brandy

Revenue men often ambush smugglers in the most picturesque surroundings.

England, c.1798

The coasts of Britain, from the North Sea round to Devon and Cornwall, are under siege from a widespread and highly successful variety of seaborne rogue: the smuggler, a breed that has grown in numbers and in profits over the last hundred years.

In 1782 the Customs Board reported ruefully on "the enormous increase of smuggling, the outrages with which it is carried on, the mischiefs it occasions to the country, the discouragement it creates to all fair traders, and the prodigious loss the Revenue sustains by it". There is no sign that the situation has improved.

Smuggling, the illegal duty-free importation of various goods – particularly rum, brandy and tea – all of which attract heavy taxes, began about a century ago. Faced with the sharp increases in duty that helped to finance the wars of William III, many of those living along the coasts saw the chance to make large profits by bringing in goods duty free.

Although the volume of goods smuggled in has certainly increased, the technique remains much the same. A ship anchors out at sea, dispatching a small boat to alert those waiting on shore. Once contact has been made, more small boats ferry the contraband ashore.

Smuggling is highly profitable. One Devonshire captain, Harry Carter, is said to make £1,000 profit a week. It also requires experts – even on a calm day, off-loading is a dangerous, skilful task, and smugglers are also outstanding seamen. The Revenue opposes the gangs as best it can, but its numbers are small, and few men will testify against hard-bitten smugglers who have no qualms in killing those who get in their way and who have many friends in high places.

Austria surrenders to Bonaparte in Italy

Campo Formio, 18 October 1797
Bonaparte has today signed a peace treaty with Austria after five months of hard bargaining. Given that the Austrians were driven to accept his proposals of peace by the threat his army posed to Vienna, they have come well out of the negotiations. Austria cedes Belgium to France, but no decision has been made about the left bank of the Rhine. Vienna also cedes Lombardy to the Cisalpine republic, receiving in return Venice and mainland territory as far as the Adige.

Bonaparte has behaved in his new customary high-handed fashion, for in giving up Venice he acted in contradiction to the government's orders. But he seems not to care for the politicians in Paris. A threat of resignation always brings them to heel. It is evident that he is prepared to trade territory – which he can always recapture – in return for fame in France as both conqueror and peacemaker.

One image of Bonaparte.

Immoral and mystical Prussian king dies

Berlin, 16 November 1797
The imposing Brandenburg Gate in Berlin is a memorial not to King Frederick William II but to his first mistress, Wilhelmine Enke, the daughter of a horn-player in the royal orchestra, whom he took to his bed when she was 16. She it was who discovered the architect Langhans and won him royal support. When Frederick William died here today, aged 53, after a long illness, Wilhelmine was at his bedside.

After the disciplined regime of his uncle Frederick the Great, Frederick William's reign was a period of moral ambiguity. The arts flourished, and Immanuel Kant's *Critique of Pure Reason* was hailed as the masterpiece it is; but Kant was forbidden to write on Christianity. The king was recruited by the Rosicrucians, who claimed to possess occult powers. Besides Wilhelmine, the king had many other mistresses and two royal and two morganatic marriages.

King Frederick William of Prussia.

Lead balls reveal density of planet Earth

London, 1798
The latest achievement of the distinguished scientist Henry Cavendish is an experiment which claims to reveal the weight and density of the planet Earth itself. The "Cavendish Experiment" consists of a horizontal rod with a lead ball at either end, suspended in the centre from a fine wire or fibre. Two large lead spheres are then moved near to the lead balls, producing a gravitational attraction.

This gravitational force is calculated from the amount the rod turns. From this figure Cavendish has sought to work out the mass of Earth. When divided by Earth's volume, this figure yields a value for Earth's density.

Temperature drives the ocean currents

United States, 1798
An American scientist, Benjamin Thompson, has shown in an essay, *On the Propagation of Heat in Fluids*, that water heated by the sun in northerly latitudes becomes denser and descends to the ocean bed. There it spreads out towards the equator and forms a countercurrent that drives back up from the tropics in a northerly direction. Thus water is constantly warming, cooling, rising and descending in a massive circulatory cycle. Thompson also argues that heat is transferred to and from the atmosphere with important consequences for climate as well as ocean currents.

Scientist claims animals do not evolve

Paris, 1798
An argument is brewing over the idea that life-forms on earth have evolved over time. Many biologists hold that view, but Georges Cuvier, a French zoologist and academician, has this year argued for the comparison of the features of one creature with those of another rather than the study of changes over a period of time. As a result of his studies, Cuvier is convinced that the anatomical differences that characterise animals are evidence that evolution did, and does, *not* take place. Each animal species, says Cuvier, is so well coordinated in form and function that it could not survive any significant changes in its bodily makeup. This means, he claims, that each creature is now the same as when it was created.

Explorer's African trip ends in failure

Zambia, 18 October 1798
A gallant attempt by the Portuguese geographer Francisco Maria de Lacerda to cross the continent of Africa has failed. He has died, halfway through his journey, in the central African Lunda kingdom.

Since the British occupied Cape Town, Portugal has feared that they will expand north, driving a wedge between Portugal's colonies of Angola and Mozambique. Last year Portuguese traders made contact with King Kazembe of Luanda. Lacerda, the governor of Mozambique's Rivers province, saw this as the opportunity to unite the two colonies. The expedition was a disaster. War, fever, dysentery and desertions took their toll, Lacerda dying today outside Kazembe's court. The survivors have been unable to make any agreement with Kazembe. One of Portugal's greatest explorers lies dead; his efforts have come to naught.

"The British Menagerie", a 1796 cartoon depicting the powers of Europe fed by Pitt with Britain's gold, including: 1, the Austrian leopard; 2, the Prussian eagle; 3, the (royal) French cock; 4, the Russian bear; 5, the Sardinian hedgehog; 8, the Neapolitan bat; 9, the Dutch frog; 10, the Swedish pig; 11, what the artist dubs the "whore of Babylon" – the Pope.

1798 (1798-1799)

Egypt, 23 July 1798. General Bonaparte enters Cairo which his troops occupied two days ago.

Egypt, 1 August 1798. The French navy is destroyed by Nelson at Aboukir. The French army is virtually imprisoned in Egypt.

France, 6 August 1798. Unaware that the Irish rebels have been defeated, a French expeditionary force sets sail for Ireland to help them in their fight against the British.

Ireland, 27 August 1798. After defeating several British contingents, the French General Humbert proclaims an Irish republic.

Malta, 2 September 1798. The Maltese people revolt against French occupation, forcing the French troops to take refuge in the citadel of Valetta.

Ottoman Empire, 9 September 1798. The Ottoman empire declares war on France because of its occupation of Egypt.

Ireland, 15 September 1798. The French force under General Humbert surrenders to General Cornwallis at Ballynamuck. This is the end of the attempted French invasion of Ireland.

Egypt, 22 October 1798. An uprising by the people of Cairo is brutally suppressed by French soldiers of occupation.

Caribbean, 22 October 1798. The black General Toussaint L'ouverture's supporters drive the French government's last agent off the island of Santo Domingo.

Mediterranean, 27 October 1798. Having taken the island of Zante on 25 October, the Russians now take Cephalonia. Of the other Ionian islands, only Corfu remains in French hands.

Luxembourg, 30 October 1798. A Belgian peasants' revolt against conscription into the French army is put down.

Greece, 5 November 1798. The Russo-Ottoman fleet begins a blockade of Corfu, which is held by the French.

Indian Ocean, 7 November 1798. The Ile de France (*Mauritius*) is in the hands of its settlers who have occupied the capital and dissolved the colonial assembly.

Ireland, 19 November 1798. In prison awaiting execution, the Irish nationalist leader Wolfe Tone commits suicide.

Italy, 22 November 1798. The Austrian-led Neapolitan army attacks the republic of Rome, defended by the French General Championnet.

Italy, 27 November 1798. The Neapolitan army of Ferdinand IV, the king of Naples and Sicily, who was forced to sign a peace treaty with France two years ago, occupies Rome.

Egypt, 7 December 1798. French troops capture Suez.

Rome, 14 December 1798. The French re-occupy the city after it is abandoned by the Neapolitans.

London, 29 December 1798. A second military alliance against France is formed by Britain, Austria, Russia, Naples and Portugal. The first coalition collapsed when the Austrians signed the treaty of Campo Formio with France. Now plans are being made to challenge France in the Netherlands, Italy and Brittany.

Mozambique, 1798. The Portuguese reoccupy the fort of Lourenco Marques at Maputo Bay and re-establish trade with the local Maputo kingdom in ivory and slaves.

Britain, 1798. Thomas Robert Malthus publishes his *Essay on the Principle of Population as it Affects the Future Improvements of Society* in which he asserts that populations inevitably increase more rapidly than food supplies.

Austria, 1798. Haydn composes his *Missa in Angustiis*, a brilliant, austerely powerful work. Shortly before its first performance the news arrived of Nelson's victory in Egypt; it has since been dubbed the *Nelson Mass*.

Italy, 23 January 1799. French troops take Naples after fierce street fighting.

Italy, 26 January 1799. As agreed with the French, the radicals of Naples proclaim the Parthenopian republic.

Botswana, 1799. Kora (Khoisan herders and hunters) from the south attack Kanye, the capital of the Ngwaketse kingdom, which is rich in hunting goods and cattle as well as copper. The Kora were leading Griqua and Boers north along the trade routes into the Kalahari. The attack is repulsed.

Philadelphia, 1799. In the first organised labour action in the United States, the Federal Society of Cordwainers (shoemakers) wins a nine-day strike.

Japan, 1799. Following unrest fomented by the Ainu people, the whole of Ezo (*Hokkaido*) is placed under the direct control of the *shogun* at Edo.

Germany, 1799. The well-known writer Friedrich Schiller concludes his dramatic trilogy *Wallenstein*, about the famous general of the Thirty Years War.

Population growth is threat to humans

England, 1798

The greatest threat to humanity, according to Thomas Malthus, the economist and Anglican minister, is the fact that population growth is bound to outstrip any increases in food production. The population of Europe has risen from from 66 million in 1700 to 180 million.

In his *Essay on the Principle of Population*, originally published anonymously, Malthus asserts: "Population, when unchecked, increases in a geometrical ratio. Subsistence increases only in an arithmetical ratio." He cites as an example the United States of America, where the population has doubled in 25 years. While that figure might go on doubling every 25 years, the food supply could not do more than increase by a similar amount each 25 years, he says.

Applying his theory to England, Malthus argues that the poor laws, which now provide £4,000,000 a year, tend to increase population without increasing the food for its support. "Dependent poverty ought to be held disgraceful," he writes, since it diminishes "both the power and will to save". Instead he advocates the abolition of parish laws, incentives for agriculture, and workhouses for those in distress.

Thomas Robert Malthus.

New coalition formed against Bonaparte

A French cartoonist's view of the effects of British military expenditure: Britannia (l.) armed to the teeth and (r.) ruined as a result.

Europe, 1799

Since last December Britain has been putting together a formidable new coalition to fight France. Czar Paul of Russia has agreed to join the Anglo-Austrian alliance and is preparing to send an army into Italy to attack Bonaparte's puppet states.

The Russians have also promised to join Britain in an invasion of Holland and to send an expeditionary force to Brittany. In return the British have agreed to pay £225,000 plus £75,000 a month towards the costs of the war.

Turkey, Portugal and the kingdom of Naples and Sicily complete this second coalition. It is a considerable diplomatic and military achievement.

Bonaparte's army has conquered Egypt

The battle of the Pyramids, where Napoleon crushed the Egyptian Mamelukes.

Cairo, 21 July 1798
Bonaparte is the master of Egypt. His tired, thirsty men, grilled by the desert sun, today faced the glittering array of the Mameluke warriors and pummelled them into bloody defeat.

They met at Giza by the pyramids of the pharaohs. Some 50,000 men waited for the French. The entire Mameluke cavalry, mounted on the finest Arab horses, were drawn up on the left bank of the Nile, with the morning sunshine shining on their spears and jewelled scimitars.

Bonaparte ordered his divisions to form squares and place their cannon at the corners. Then they waited for the enemy cavalry. On came the Mamelukes with the utmost courage. The guns tore great holes in their ranks and the volley fire of muskets tumbled horses and riders.

The carnage continued for most of the day until 2,000 Mamelukes lay on the battlefield. Murad, their leader, was gravely wounded. At last he gave the order to retreat and burnt his boats to prevent the French from pursuing him across the Nile. Tonight the desert is lit by fires as French soldiers strip the richly-clad bodies of the Mamelukes. And Cairo is Bonaparte's.

Nelson smashes French navy off Aboukir

Aboukir, Egypt, 1 August 1798
In an all night battle, the French Mediterranean Fleet has been almost completely destroyed by a British naval squadron commanded by Lord Nelson. Napoleon and his armies are literally trapped in Egypt.

Nelson had been searching for the French fleet since May, and found them at anchor. He formed his ships into two files, one led by HMS *Goliath* attacking the enemy centre, the other, with Nelson's *Vanguard* leading, savaging the French flanks. Five French ships were sunk with 4,000 men. Two were captured; and two frigates managed to escape.

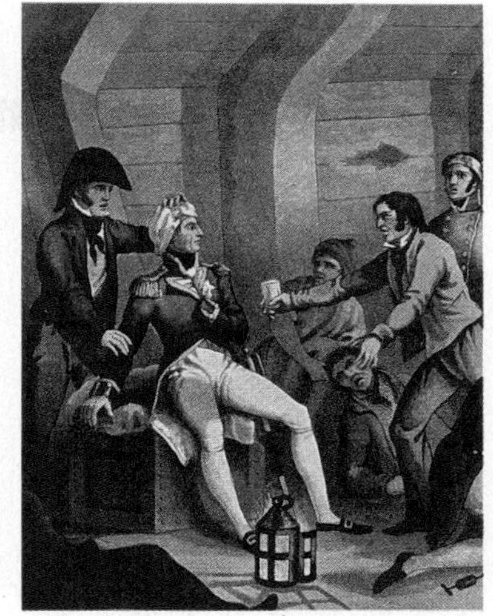

Nelson, wounded in the battle.

Parisians see looted Italian art treasures

The spoils of war arrive at the Festival of Arts and Sciences in Paris.

Paris, 28 July 1798
"To the victor the spoils" runs the saying, and a triumphant France, after winning its campaign in Italy, is showing itself a firm believer in the old proverb.

The fruits of two years' systematic ransacking of the art treasures of Italy were paraded through the Champ de Mars today, as part of the annual celebrations of the revolution. It was an exhibition worthy of a Roman triumph. Every piece has been selected by a seven-man artistic commission.

Some French artists have argued against the army's looting of so many treasures, but the crowds were ecstatic as 29 floats moved by, crammed with sculptures like the *Apollo Belvedere*, the *Laocoon* and the horses of St Mark's, and paintings that included Raphael's *Transfiguration* and Correggio's *Virgin with St Jerome*. Carriages packed with medals, books, precious manuscripts and much more were followed by loot of a different type: bears from Switzerland, lions and camels from Africa and other exotic beasts.

Raphael's "Transfiguration".

US Navy scores victory over the French

Nevis, West Indies, 9 February 1799
A US Navy frigate, the recently-commissioned *Constellation*, won a significant duel with the French *Insurgente* – giving the new and untried US Navy first blood in its sea war with France. In an engagement fought in gale force conditions, Captain Thomas Truxton was chasing the French ship which lost its maintop in a squall. The French ship tried to grapple with the *Constellation*, but Truxton held off and raked her with gunfire until she struck her colours. A prize crew is bringing *Insurgente* into St Kitts with 173 prisoners.

Since the capture of one of its schooners by a French ship off Guadeloupe, the United States has stepped up its naval building programme, concentrating on fast frigates like the *Constellation*, one of five ships that patrol the Caribbean to protect American shipping from French interference.

1799 ⇒

India, 3 February. British troops enter Mysore in order to subjugate Tipu Sahib, with whom Bonaparte is trying to establish contact.

Egypt, 10 February. Bonaparte leaves Cairo for Syria, at the head of 13,000 men.

Palestine, 24 February. Bonaparte's army occupies Gaza.

Greece, 3 March. The last French garrison in the Ionian isles surrenders to Russo-Ottoman troops who have invaded the island of Corfu.

Palestine, 7 March. Napoleon captures Jaffa where his men massacre more than two thousand Albanian prisoners.

Germany, 25 March. French troops are defeated by Archduke Charles of Saxe-Weimar at Stokach.

Italy, 27 March. Austrian troops move into Verona having defeated the French at Legnano, near Milan.

Palestine, March. Soldiers in the French garrison at Jaffa are dying of bubonic plague at the rate of 30 a day.

Germany, 23 April. The conference at Rastatt between Austria and France collapses after a renewal of hostilities between the two countries. The conference was set up after the treaty of Campo Formio to supervise Prussian cession of lands on the left bank of the Rhine to France.

Italy, 29 April. The anti-French coalition army enters Milan.

India, 4 May. Tipu Sahib, the ruler of Mysore, dies fighting the British under the command of the governor, the marquis of Wellesley.

Palestine, 17 May. Bonaparte lifts the siege of Acre after failing to take the city.

France, 18 May. The great comic playwright Pierre de Beaumarchais dies of apoplexy. He returned to Paris in 1796 from exile in England and Holland, having lost his vast fortune in the revolution. The two plays which established him as a comic genius are *The Barber of Seville* and *The Marriage of Figaro*.

Spain, 5 June. The naturalist and explorer Alexander von Humboldt sets sail for America, planning to explore Venezuela, Colombia and Peru.

Paris, 18 June. The legislative councils force the resignation of the Directory as dissent grows among the elected deputies, triggered by the worsening military situation.

Britain, 12 July. The Combination Act is passed, forbidding the forming of an association by two or more people with the purpose of obtaining wage increases or improved conditions of work. The measure is prompted largely by fear of revolutionary ideas spreading from France.

Egypt, 17 July. Ottoman forces, convoyed by a British fleet, capture Aboukir from the French.

Egypt, 19 July. A stone bearing ancient Egyptian hieroglyphics and *demotic* (ancient Egyptian script) and Greek is found near the town of Rosetta on the west bank of the Bolbitic arm of the Nile. The discovery is greeted with great excitement by archaeologists who may be nearer to deciphering hieroglyphics.

Egypt, 25 July. Bonaparte defeats the Ottomans at Aboukir on his way back from Syria.

Italy, 30 July. The French garrison in Mantua surrenders to the Austrians.

France, August. Royalist uprisings break out across France.

Egypt, 23 August. Napoleon sails for France.

France, 29 August. Pope Pius VI dies in Valence.

Netherlands, 31 August. The fleet of the Batavian republic, moored at Texel, surrenders without a fight to General Abercrombie's British forces.

France, 15 September. Two hundred royalist leaders from Brittany, Anjou, Maine and the Vendee hold a council of war with a view to resuming hostilities against the French republic.

Netherlands, 19 September. The French repulse Anglo-Russian forces at Bergen in the continuing war over the Batavian republic.

France, 9 October. After avoiding a British squadron off Toulouse, Napoleon comes ashore at Saint Raphael.

Netherlands, 18 October. British and French generals sign an accord at Alkmaar concerning the withdrawal of Anglo-Russian troops from the Batavian republic.

Paris, 13 December. Having seized power in a military coup last month, Bonaparte has himself elected first consul.

Philadelphia, 14 December. The retired president, George Washington, dies. His last words are " 'tis well".

Austria. Haydn composes his *Theresienmesse* (Theresa Mass), named after the consort of the Emperor Francis II.

Chinese emperor dies; courtier follows

Kirghiz tribesmen present the Emperor Qianlong with a horse, by the Jesuit Castiglione, who painted for the court in a westernised Chinese style.

Beijing, 7 February

The Emperor Qianlong has died after ruling China for over 60 years. He officially retired three years ago in order not to rule longer than his grandfather, but it was a retirement in name only and he continued to exercise supreme power.

This meant that his favourite courtier, Heshen, also continued in power. Few men in China's long history have been as corrupt or as hated as Heshen. His power has been limited only by the emperor and there has been no limit to his greed.

His corruption has been one of the factors in the oppression and decay which marked the last years of Qianlong's rule. One of Heshen's favourite bribes was a pill made of a pearl encased in gold. He took one every morning believing they sharpened his powers of memory. There were always men ready to provide him with this luxurious tonic. But, although his behaviour was notorious, few officials dared to attempt to curb him, and those who did found themselves defeated by Heshen's cunning. His enemies bided their time. They knew that the heir to the throne, Jiaqing hated Heshen. They were right. Heshen has been "allowed" to commit suicide and join his master in death.

A robe of belonging to one of Qianlong's concubines.

Workers' associations banned in Britain

London

Beset by the continuing war with revolutionary France, the prime minister, William Pitt, and his cabinet have become alarmed at the growth of militancy and the spread of subversion among skilled workers. Pitt has responded with a series of tough measures.

He has cracked down on strikers with the Combination Act, which allows workers accused of forming trades unions to be given a summary trial by a justice of the peace. Radical groups in what are known as Corresponding Societies in London and the provinces have been banned and their leaders arrested. Among them are cotton spinners, shoemakers, printers and clerks.

The press has also been curbed. The authorities must be given a copy of every issue of a newspaper together with particulars of the printer, publisher and proprietor. These measure follow a report by an MPs committee investigating subversive activities.

George Washington, first president of US

Philadelphia, 14 December
The United States mourned its first president today. Courtrooms and churches were draped in black and citizens wore black crepe in memory of George Washington, who died today after a brief illness. Full mourning dress was worn in Congress and already plans are being made to build a "grand marble monument at a new city named after Washington under which, with the permission of his lady, the body of the general should be deposited".

George Washington came from a wealthy Virginia family and saw action in the French and Indian wars before leaving the British army with the rank of colonel. He was a strong political supporter of the independence movement and was elected commander-in-chief at the second Continental Congress. His principal task then was to mould 16,000 volunteers into a cohesive fighting force, which was finally victorious against the British. As president, he tried always to remain above political factions, but became identified with federalism.

General George Washington.

Coup in Paris: Bonaparte seizes power

Bonaparte's coup of 9 November (18 Brumaire in the revolutionary calendar).

Paris, 9 November
Bonaparte has ousted the French government and the fate of the republic is now in his hands.

It was a *coup* that almost failed. Plotting with Emmanuel Sieyes, a member of the Directory who wanted the constitution overhauled, Napoleon, supported by his generals, yesterday had himself voted commander of the troops in Paris. Today, however, he got a hostile reception from the neo-Jacobins in the legislature, the Council of Five Hundred, at Saint Cloud and was spat upon.

The scuffle saved the coup. It was claimed that he had been attacked with a knife. His soldiers, incensed, marched into the council chamber. And tonight Bonaparte, Sieyes and Duclos rule as consuls.

British kill their main Indian adversary

Tipu Sahib, the sultan of Mysore.

Southern India, 4 May
Tipu Sahib, the warrior of Mysore and bulwark of resistance to British expansion in India, has been killed. Since his defeat by Cornwallis in 1784, Tipu, the most powerful ruler in southern India, had been preparing for war. Britain's conflict with revolutionary France provided him with the opportunity. He planted a tree of liberty and made a secret alliance with France, whose army was in Egypt.

The British governor-general, the marquis of Wellesley, brought 4,000 reinforcements to India and made a pre-emptive attack on Tipu, besieging his capital, Seringapatam. Today, assisted by the treachery of one of Tipu's commanders, he stormed the city with 5,000 troops. Tipu fought to the end, despite four wounds. "He had the appearance of dignity or perhaps sternness in his countenance, which denoted him above the common order of people," a British officer said. As for his tree of liberty, it has been hacked down.

Printing techniques take a leap forward

Europe
Literacy is on the march, and ever more books are in production. To meet the new demand, printing techniques, for many years little advanced from their 15th-century origins, have been developing fast. In Germany Alois Senefelder has invented lithography, a method of printing pictures without engraving them first. In France the Didot family have created stereotypy, making it possible to keep and re-use typographic characters.

Postal service, the sole link to civilisation in some parts of the West, is expanding as fast as the frontier it serves. Mail carriers now travel on 16,000 miles of postal roads, a six-fold increase over the last 10 years. The postmen who began to appear on a full-time basis in 1794, are paid by the piece, generally two cents per letter.

1799 (1799-1801)

Spain, 1799. The court painter Francisco Goya publishes *Los Caprichos*, a series of etchings which express his criticisms of a corrupt establishment. He withdraws them shortly after publication, fearing the Inquisition.

France, 1 February 1800. The new constitution, with Napoleon Bonaparte as first consul, is accepted by a referendum.

Brittany, 14 February 1800. The Chouan (*royalist*) leader Georges Cadoudal surrenders. The other leaders laid down their arms last month.

Rome, 14 March 1800. Pope Pius VII is elected to succeed Pius VI who died in 1799.

Egypt, 20 March 1800. Kleber, the French chief commander in Egypt, defeats the *grand vizier*, Ibrahim Bey, at Heliopolis.

Italy, 6 April 1800. The Austrians launch an offensive against the French.

Philadelphia, 7 May 1800. Congress divides the Northwest Territory into two parts, with the border between them running north from the junction of the Ohio and Kentucky rivers. The western part will be known as the Indiana Territory while the eastern sector keeps the name of the Northwest Territory.

Italy, 2 June 1800. Having crossed the St Bernard pass on 23 May, in response to the Austrian offensive, Bonaparte seizes Milan.

Egypt, 14 June 1800. The French commander, Kleber, is killed.

Italy, 17 June 1800. Having defeated the Austrians at Montebello and Marengo, Bonaparte signs an agreement by which the Austrian General Melas cedes the whole of Italy as far as the river Mincio to him. He then reconstitutes the Cisalpine republic.

Paris, 30 September 1800. The treaty of Morfontaine is signed, ending the undeclared but bloody naval war between American and France, waged mainly in the Indian Ocean. France will lift its embargo on American ships and the USA will return captured warships.

France, 1 October 1800. There are rumours that King Charles IV of Spain has signed a secret treaty with Bonaparte returning Louisiana to the French.

Virginia, 30 October 1800. The leaders of a planned slave revolt involving more than a thousand Negroes are hanged. Though the revolt was called off at the last minute, the conspiracy was betrayed to the authorities and more than 25 people are now dead.

Europe, 22 November 1800. Fighting breaks out again between the Austrians and the French.

Austria, 3 December 1800. The French General Moreau is victorious against the Austrians at Hohenlinden.

Europe, 16 December 1800. Russia, which had withdrawn from the field of battle in 1799, is the moving spirit behind a league of neutral Baltic nations which is anti-British in stance.

Paris, 24 December 1800. An attempt to assassinate Napoleon Bonaparte fails.

Philadelphia, 1800. William Young makes shoes designed specifically for the right and left feet.

India, 1800. The British compel the *nizam* of Hyderabad to accept the status of protectorate.

Washington DC, 1800. This year's census puts the nation's population at 5.3 million, an increase of more than 30 per cent in the last decade.

Germany, 1800. The poet who uses the pen name "Novalis" publishes verses called the *Hymns of the Night* in the final issue of the periodical *Athenaeum*.

India, 1800. Nana Fadnavis, the brilliant Maratha minister, dies.

Germany, 1800. The prolific dramatist and poet Johann Goethe publishes his *Ballads and Romances*.

South Africa, 1800. Dingiswayo seizes the chieftainship of the Mthethwa from his brother. The Mthethwa are a small clan on the Mfolozi river (*northern Natal*), but in Dingiswayo, who already has a considerable reputation as a hunter and warrior, is determined that his kingdom should rival the powerful Ndwandwe kingdom of King Zwide. Dingiswayo allies with the Maputo of Laurenco Marques (Maputo) against the Ndwandwe, with the aim of controlling ivory supplies from the interior to Portuguese ships.

Germany, 1800. The philosopher J G Fichte publishes *The Exclusive Commercial State*. Friedrich Schelling publishes his *System of Transcendental Idealism*.

Sierra Leone, 1800. Asante settlers arrive in Sierra Leone having been deported as rebels from Jamaica. They had been living independently in the mountain interior as freemen, and were known locally as *maroons*.

Washington DC, 4 March 1801. The House of Representatives chooses Thomas Jefferson as the new president and Aaron Burr as vice-president after the two men receive exactly the same number of votes in the electoral college.

British ready to buy all the tea in China

Filling tea chests in a British-owned factory on the Chinese coast.

Canton, China, c.1800

Tea from China has become the British national drink, accounting for five per cent of the average London worker's household budget. The British government also has a vested interest through 100 per cent excise duties on tea imports.

The tea trade is conducted entirely through the East India Company, which now invests £4 million a year in this one commodity. A triangular trading system involves the shipping from Calcutta to Canton, of raw Indian cotton, the profits from which are used to buy the tea, which is sold in London to help reduce the Company's increasing debts. This combination of consumer demand and economic necessity ensures that trade with China continues, despite diplomatic ructions like the *kowtow* affair, in which British ambassadors were reluctant to bow before the emperor.

Tea in the garden: tea is now the most popular drink in Britain.

Volta makes electrifying discovery

Rome, 1800

The inventor Alessandro Volta has made an apparatus for producing a continuous flow of electricity – an electric "battery". The principle is that if two different metals are immersed in a solution of acid, alkali or salt, an electric current will flow along a wire linking the plates. Suitable metals, Volta finds, are zinc, copper or silver. If pairs of these are placed in layers with brine-soaked paper or flannel between each pair, then a "Voltaic pile" is created. Each pair or cell is linked to the next to produce a combined electrical output. Volta's equipment is the first method yet devised for giving a steady current.

Volta shows his battery to Bonaparte

US president moves house to Washington

Washington DC, the new federal capital of the United States of America.

United States, 1800
On lush farmland close to the Potomac river, workmen are putting the final touches to a two-storeyed house that will shortly become the executive mansion for President John Adams and his wife Abigail, the "First Lady". Several hundred acres of the state of Maryland have been set aside for the building of a fine city which is to be the federal capital, in what is known as the District of Columbia, to be named "Washington". Congress approved the site – which will be free from partisan state pressures – and a distinguished French architect, Pierre Charles l'Enfant, has been commissioned to create a city with wide boulevards, fine buildings and wide vistas. More like Paris than Paris itself, some hope.

Dublin parliament votes to dissolve itself

Dublin, 5 February 1800
William Pitt reckons that he is well on the way to solving the Irish problem once and for all. As Britain's prime minister, he saw that there could be no peace so long as the Irish remained disaffected second class citizens in their own country. His policy of reconciliation took a big step forward today when the Dublin parliament resolved to dissolve itself and to unite with Westminster, as Scotland did a century ago.

To the Catholic majority in Ireland, Pitt argued, that since their emancipation would be seen as a threat to the Protestant ascendency, reform would always be blocked.

William Pitt, uniting the kingdom.

To the Protestants, he argued that union with Britain would make the Catholics a minority and therefore less of a threat to their position in Ireland.

These arguments were reinforced by a blatant appeal to the cupidity of the Protestants controlling the Dublin parliament.

MPs were promised peerages, jobs and hard cash – £7,000 for each seat. As the debate continued, the son of Lord Cornwallis, the viceroy, was asked who would succeed his father as ruler of Ireland if the proposed union and Catholic emancipation were rejected. Mindful of French attempts to stir up revolution in Ireland, he replied "Bonaparte".

Pius VII signs concordat with Bonaparte

Two princes: Caesar's and God's.

Paris, 15 July 1801
A concordat was finally signed today by Pope Pius VII and Napoleon after prolonged and troublesome negotiations. It is popular with no-one. In the end it was imposed by the pope on a reluctant anti-Napoleonic church and by Napoleon on a reluctant anticlerical government.

The agreement recognises Catholicism as the religion of "the great majority" of the French people, but makes no claim for the restitution of church property. Its importance to Napoleon, who is cynical about religion, is that it restores religious peace to France.

Water splits in face of electric charge

London, 1800
Within weeks of Volta's invention of the electric cell, the new device has been put to use by two chemists, William Nicholson and Anthony Carlisle. They have made their own "battery" and, with it, separated water into its constituent gases, oxygen and hydrogen. When the leads from their battery were placed in water, the two scientists observed that they broke up the fluid by a process of "electrolysis". At the ends of the wire they noticed bubbles, indicating the liberation of the two gases.

Prolific Chinese go forth and multiply

The Pingzimen, one of the western gates into the Chinese capital, Beijing.

China, c.1800
The population of China is exploding at an alarming rate. In the century of internal peace that lasted until the outbreak of the White Lotus revolt four years ago, the population doubled from some 150 million to over 300 million. The increase continues, with natural disasters having little effect.

The result has been ever more pressure upon land even in the agriculturally marginal border regions. Refugees from poor harvests are moving into new areas and setting off intense competition for land, with consequent tensions. New kinds of economic and political growth are essential to absorb the fecund people of China.

1801 (1801-1802)

France, 9 February 1801. The peace of Luneville puts an end to the war with Austria in Bonaparte's favour. This leaves Britain as the only survivor of the second coalition against France.

Egypt, 6 March 1801. British troops land in Egypt, which is currently in the hands of the French.

Spain, 21 March 1801. France signs the treaty of Aranjuez with Spain. The duchy of Tuscany is transformed into the kingdom of Etruria and the American territory of Louisiana is returned to France.

Italy, 28 March 1801. France signs the treaty of Florence with King Ferdinand of Naples and Sicily. The island of Elba is ceded to France and the ports of the kingdom are closed to British trade. Otranto and Brindisi on the Adriatic are provisionally manned by a French garrison.

Denmark, 2 April 1801. The British bombard the port of Copenhagen, hastening the break-up of the neutral alliance against Britain. Its main moving spirit, Czar Paul of Russia, was assassinated on 23 March. He is succeeded by his son Alexander.

Tripoli (Libya), 14 May 1801. *Pasha* Yusuf Karamanli declares war on the United States.

Tripoli, 17 July 1801. A US fleet arrives to blockade Tripoli, following Pasha Yusuf Karamanli's declaration of war in May when a demand for more tribute, to protect US ships from piracy, was refused.

Malta, 1 August 1801. The US schooner *Enterprise* captures the barbary corsair *Tripoli*, heaves its 14 guns into the sea and chops off its mast.

Egypt, 2 September 1801. The French under General Menou begin to leave Egypt following the arrival of British troops in March. France lost Cairo on 28 June and Alexandria on 30 August.

Spain, 29 September 1801. The treaty of Madrid puts an end to the "War of the Oranges" between Spain and Portugal. The Portuguese agree to French demands that they should not allow English naval vessels to enter their ports. Spain acquires the frontier town of Olivenza. During the fighting Britain has taken possession of Madeira and the Portuguese trading posts in India.

Netherlands, 6 October 1801. Bonaparte imposes a new constitution on Holland.

France, 8 October 1801. France signs a treaty with Russia, a culmination of the improvement in relations detectable since 1800.

New York, 16 November 1801. The *New York Evening Post*, published by Alexander Hamilton and John Jay, appears on the streets.

Japan, 1801. Ino Tadataka, an astronomer and surveyor, ordered by the *shogun* to undertake a geographical survey of the whole of Japan, heads north to start work in Ezo (Hokkaido).

India, 1801. Ranjit Singh, the leader of the Sikhs, defeats the Bhangis.

Britain, 1801. The first census shows a population of 10.4 million.

Persia, 1801. The British sign a trade treaty with the *shah*.

Germany, 1801. Friedrich Schiller's new play *The Maid of Orleans* opens.

USA, 1801. The American inventor Evans exhibits his steam-driven vehicle in the streets of Philadelphia.

Vienna, 1801. Ludwig van Beethoven writes a sonata (Opus 27, number 2) which is nicknamed "Moonlight".

Germany, 1801. Inspired by William Herschel's discovery of a type of radiation beyond the red end of the spectrum (*infrared radiation*), the German John Ritter looks for something similar beyond the violet. He thus discovers ultraviolet radiation.

France, 18 January 1802. Bonaparte gets rid of all members of the Tribunate who are opposed to him.

Italy, 26 January 1802. Bonaparte is elected president of the Italian republic, the new name given to the Cisalpine republic.

France, 27 March 1802. Bonaparte signs the peace of Amiens.

France, 20 May 1802. Slavery and the slave trade are restored in the colonies.

France, 2 August 1802. Bonaparte is proclaimed consul for life by a plebiscite.

China, 1802. Over the last three years, during a revolt fomented by the secret White Lotus society, anti-Manchu supporters have been savagely repressed.

Mexico, 1802. Mexico's first archaeologist, Antonio de Leon y Gama, dies. He will be best remembered for his book describing the statue of Coatlicue, the mother goddess, and the Stone of the Sun, found in Mexico City during sewerage excavations.

Italy, 1802. The writer Ugo Foscolo publishes *The Last Letters of Jacopo Ortis*, an epistolary novel lamenting the Austrian occupation of Venice.

British navy opens Baltic to its shipping

The battle of Copenhagen, where Nelson sank the neutral Danish fleet.

Copenhagen, 2 April 1801

A defiant gesture by the British admiral, Horatio Nelson, has sunk the Danish fleet, ensuring that the Baltic Sea will remain open to British shipping.

Vice-admiral Nelson was leading a squadron through shoal waters under heavy fire from Danish shore batteries when signals went up from the commander-in-chief, Sir Hyde Parker, ordering him to withdraw. On the quarter-deck of *HMS Elephant*, Nelson said "Damn me if I do!" and placed his telescope to his blind eye. Although Nelson has gone ashore to explain his action to his "brother Danes", Britain is bound to suffer international disapprobation for this surprise attack on a neutral country, even one so blatantly pro-French.

Ailing king forces William Pitt to resign

London, 14 March 1801

After 17 years as Prime Minister, William Pitt has been forced to resign by the king's stubborn refusal to accept Catholic emancipation. His successor is Henry Addington, the speaker of the House of Commons, an old friend of Pitt's. He has said that he will work for peace with France and do nothing about Catholic emancipation. Pitt offered his resignation last month, but stayed on when George III was stricken by another bout of insanity, apparently brought on by the Irish question. Pitt, having achieved the union of the London and Dublin parliaments, had moved on to what he saw as the necessary sequel: Catholic emancipation. When this was put to the king he was enraged. Pitt says that he will never again raise the subject with the king.

Country united after 30 years of struggle

Hue, Annam (Vietnam), 1802

Nguyen Anh, the Emperor of Annam (*Vietnam*) has reunited his country after some 30 years of dynastic struggle and civil war. The emperor, who is a great organiser as well as a soldier, now rules from his palace in this pleasant city built astride the Perfumed River.

However, while Nguyen Anh rules Annam he has to recognise the suzerainty of China under the tributary system. For the Chinese it is an economical way of dealing with a border country without actually having to occupy it.

Another important influence on Nguyen Anh is that of the French missionary Pigneau de Behaine who helped the emperor in his struggle for power. Nguyen Anh has now given the French missionaries free rein to preach the Catholic gospel in his country.

Britain critical of treaty with French

Amiens, 25 March 1802
The treaty signed here today by Britain and France has brought peace to the world, but at a cost not appreciated by most Britons. In the general exchange of territory Britain retains Ceylon and Trinidad but relinquishes Malta, the Cape and Egypt and most of its maritime conquests.

France, on the other hand, gives little except Naples and a guarantee of integrity for Portugal. What disturbs the British, however, is Bonaparte's refusal to lift the trade prohibitions imposed during the war; the Continent remains closed to British trade. There is much criticism of "this frail and deceptive truce" throughout Britain.

Czar Paul is killed in his bedchamber

Paul I, son of Catherine the Great.

St Petersburg, 23 March 1801
At two, o'clock this morning, after a night of carousing, a party of guards officers went over to the St Michael Palace and, breaking into the royal bedchamber, strangled the mentally unstable Czar Paul. One of the assassins, Nikolai Zubov, then awakened Paul's son, Alexander, to tell him that he was the new czar. Paul hated his mother Catherine, and decreed that no woman should ever again rule Russia. He went to war against France, then changed sides to ally himself with Bonaparte. He lost popular support by repealing Catherine's law exempting the free classes from corporal punishment.

People vote Napoleon Consul for Life

Paris, 2 August 1802
The senate proclaimed Napoleon Bonaparte "Consul for Life" today following a plebiscite in which three and a half million Frenchmen voted in favour of the proposal and a mere eight thousand people voted against.

Napoleon (the name was used for the first time in the wording of the plebiscite) now assumes almost regal powers. A new constitution is about to be announced which will confer on him the royal prerogatives of pardoning the condemned and naming his own successor. Power will be further concentrated in his hands by the extension of the powers of the senate in which decrees will replace the debates of the other assemblies.

The overwhelming vote in favour of Napoleon certainly reflects the nostalgia for the past which is replacing the revolutionary fervour of the day ten years ago when the monarchy was abolished.

Sensing this reaction, Louis XVIII had written from exile asking Napoleon to restore the monarchy. He was sharply rebuffed. Napoleon replied: "You must not expect to return to France. It would mean marching over a hundred thousand corpses."

The concordat with Rome and the peace of Amiens increased Napoleon's own popularity, and he used it to "purify" the Tribunate and the Legislative Assembly by removing his opponents when their appointments came up for renewal. The senate, in a spirit of self-preservation, then voted to extend his term as first consul for a further ten years. It was not enough for Napoleon. He ordered the plebiscite which has made him Consul for Life. Curiously, and most significantly, many of the "No" votes were cast by the army.

Napoleon Bonaparte, voted by over three million Frenchmen "Consul for Life".

Goya's "La Maja Desnuda". Born in 1746, Goya spent his early years first in Zaragossa and then in Madrid, where he settled, after a tour of Italy, in 1775. In spite of his liberal and republican sympathies, he became a court painter in 1786, and the first court painter in 1786. Some of his finest paintings have been of the Spanish royal family. He hears no acclaim, however. A severe illness in 1792 has left him stone deaf.

Painting with light

London, 1802
Recently it was seen that certain compounds of silver nitrates can be used to preserve an image. Working with such light sensitive papers Thomas Wedgwood, the son of the famous English pottery innovator, and the chemist Humphrey Davy have now succeeded in taking light pictures or photographs. They have produced pictures of natural objects such as leaves and insect wings by putting them on chemically-treated paper and exposing them to sunlight. These images only last for a short time; they need further chemical treatment to "fix" them.

1802 (1802-1803)

Italy, 11 September 1802. Piedmont is annexed by France.

Russia, 20 September 1802. The reformist Czar Alexander, who came to power last year, grants the senate legislative and judicial rights. Educated by the Swiss rationalist Jean Francois de Laharpe, he also grants an amnesty to all political prisoners and exiles.

Louisiana, 16 October 1802. In breach of the 1795 treaty of San Lorenzo – establishing the 31st parallel as a border between America and Spain in North America – Spain closes New Orleans to US cargo.

India, 31 December 1802. The Maratha Peshwa Baji Rao signs the treaty of Bassein with Lord Wellesley, giving the British mastery of central India.

USA, 1802. All states north of the Mason-Dixon line (between Pennsylvania and Delaware in the north and Maryland and West Virginia in the south) except for New Jersey have now passed anti-slavery laws calling for gradual emancipation.

Vienna, 1802. The composer Ludwig van Beethoven realises that he is going irreversibly deaf. However his new, second symphony reveals little of his personal anguish.

Switzerland, 19 February 1803. Bonaparte imposes the Act of Mediation which restores almost in full the thirteen cantons as they were before 1798, less Geneva and Mulhouse. Six new cantons are created. The constitution is a federal one, the cantons having a federal *diet* for external affairs.

USA, 1 March 1803. Ohio is the seventeenth state to join the union.

Britain, 15 March 1803. Britain contravenes the terms of the treaty of Amiens by demanding the right to remain on the island of Malta for ten years. By the treaty, signed on 25 March 1802 with Bonaparte, Britain agreed to give up all her overseas conquests.

France, 12 April 1803. The ban on workers' meetings is renewed. The same law sets up factory chambers to regulate trademarks.

France, 14 April 1803. The Bank of France is granted the privilege of issuing paper money for a period of 15 years, valid only in Paris.

Louisiana, 19 April 1803. The Spanish reopen New Orleans to American merchants.

Netherlands, 26 April 1803. In contravention of last year's treaty of Amiens, Bonaparte occupies Flushing and Dutch Brabant. Worried by this move, the British issue an ultimatum.

Netherlands, 12 May 1803. Napoleon withdraws from Flushing and Dutch Brabant.

France, 18 May 1803. Following Bonaparte's continued military activities in Italy, the Netherlands, Switzerland and Germany, the British government makes a formal break with the treaty of Amiens and declares war on France.

Germany, May 1803. The French General Mortier occupies the kingdom of Hanover, a personal possession of the king of England.

Europe, 5 June 1803. Czar Alexander proposes that he should mediate between the French and the British, but without success.

France, 20 June 1803. British imports are banned.

Ireland, 23 July 1803. Irish patriots rebel against union with Britain, which was established by law on 1 January 1801.

Caribbean, 29 August 1803. General Dessalines proclaims the independence of Haiti at the western end of the island of Santo Domingo.

Pittsburgh, 31 August 1803. Captain Meriwether Lewis leaves Pittsburgh on what is rumoured to be the first government-sponsored exploration of far western country.

India, 14 September 1803. General Lake, after defeating the Marathas beneath the city walls, captures Delhi for the British. The Maratha confederacy is the last remaining obstacle to the British East India Company's control of southern and eastern India.

India, 23 September 1803. Sir Arthur Wellesley achieves a notable victory over the Marathas at Assaye in the Dekhan.

Europe, 27 September 1803. France and the Helvetian republic sign a treaty of military alliance.

France, 2 December 1803. An army prepares itself to invade England at a camp in Boulogne.

USA, 20 December 1803. The United States buys the Louisiana territory from France.

Russia, 1803. Czar Alexander invades southern Georgia and occupies eastern Alaska.

Antilles, 1803. Britain occupies the islands of St Lucia and Tobago, and Dutch Guiana.

Brazil, 1803. Over the past 45 years, a total of 642,000 slaves have been taken from the ports of Luanda and Benguela on the Angolan coast to the Portuguese colony of Brazil.

Honolulu, 1803. Richard Cleveland and William Shaler introduce horses to the Hawaiian islands.

British factory workers helped by new law

The evils of child labour, as seen by the cartoonist, George Cruikshank.

London, 1802

In an unprecedented step to regulate life in the new factories the British Parliament is to introduce a ban on pauper apprentices working more than a 12-hour day.

The forthcoming Health and Morals of Apprentices Act follows growing concern that pauper children from London sent to work in mills and factories in the north are being exploited and made to work at night. Until now the factories that have sprung up to house the new cotton and wool processing machines have been unregulated. These factories have provided a welcome outlet for the London Poo[r] Law authorities. By sending thei[r] charges north they have been abl[e] to claim that they have discharge[d] successfully their duty of not allowing paupers, or their offspring, t[o] become a burden on the paris[h] rates.

However, reformers led by Si[r] Robert Peel, the bill's proposer, ar[e] concerned that this wholesale extension of Poor Law practice ha[s] meant that large numbers of children are now working in place[s] without their parents or other relatives to supervise their physical o[r] moral welfare.

Colours of rainbow can be measured

London, 1803

Light, says the English doctor and physicist Thomas Young, consists not of particles but of waves. This is the conclusion he arrives at after experimenting with light, proclaiming a principle of "interference". If light is shone onto a screen in which there are two pinholes set close to each other, the light beams produced will spread apart and overlap. In these areas of overlap, he says, there are bands of light and dark which are due to one wave interfering with the other, similar to the effect of two ripples merging on a pond. Young goes on to give an approximate wavelength to the seven colours in the spectrum: red, orange, yellow, green, blue, indigo, violet.

German cathedral sold to a butcher

Bavaria, Germany, 1803

Friesing cathederal has been sold t[o] a butcher. Dozens of ecclesiastica[l] states, prince-bishoprics, electorates and imperial abbeys, and hundreds of monasteries, have bee[n] secularised. All over German[y] churches have been vandalised.

The Catholic Church is the bigg[est] loser in Germany's reorgan[i]sation, agreed by the leaders of Ge[r]many's states meeting in Ratisbon.

The Ratisbon meeting was prompted by Napoleon's conquest of th[e] left bank of the Rhine, which co[n]centrated the mind of Germany[']s statesmen on the need to mode[r]nise. Prussia, Bavaria, Bade[n] Wurttemberg and HesseDarmsta[dt] now dominate the informal c[on]federation.

US doubles its land area

Paris, 20 December 1803
The greatest land sale in history was concluded here today after months of negotiation between French and US diplomats. With the "Louisiana Purchase" the United States of America has literally doubled in size overnight – acquiring from France the whole of the Mississippi Valley as far as the Rocky Mountains, an area of 828,000 square miles. The price was high – 15 million dollars – but both the vendor, Napoleon Bonaparte, and the purchaser, the Congress of the United States, are delighted with the deal.

Napoleon wanted to sell this former Spanish territory. He had relinquished his former ambition (with Talleyrand) of creating a colonial empire in the West Indies and North America. US hostility to France was growing, and war with Britain seemed imminent.

President Jefferson wanted the land, and dispatched a special envoy, James Monroe, to assist in negotiations. Only Spain – concerned at the breaking of a French pledge never to sell the land – has objected. Whether the land-sale is constitutionally correct is a matter of doubt. Napoleon and Jefferson do not seem to be concerned.

Robert Livingstone, who bought Louisiana for the United States.

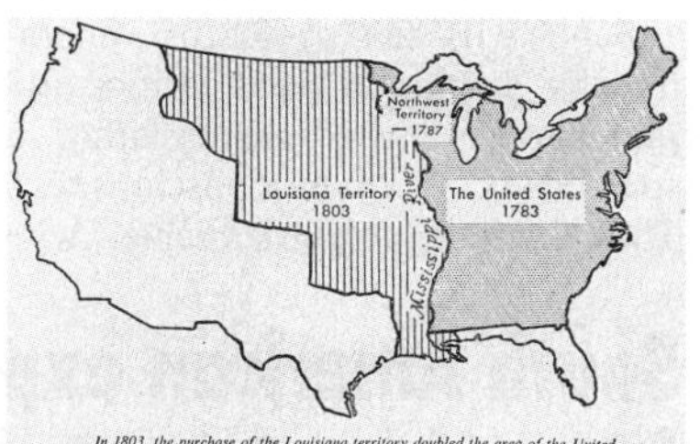

The Mississippi river, once the frontier of the US, now divides it in two.

Irish rebellion against Britain fails

Lord Kilwarden, who was killed by Irish rebels led by Thomas Emmet.

Dublin, 24 July 1803
Late yesterday, Thomas Emmet donned his uniform of green coat, white breeches and cocked hat and led a chanting crowd of rebels to attack Dublin Castle. On the way they encountered Lord Kilwarden, the Lord Chief Justice and, dragging him from his carriage, stabbed and clubbed him to death with their pikes. But that act of brutality was the limit of the latest uprising against British rule, and Emmet has fled into the Wicklow mountains.

Emmet, the son of a physician to the British viceroy, is described in a Wanted notice as having "an ugly, sour countenance and dirty brown complexion". He studied at Trinity College, but soon fell under the influence of the United Irishmen who led the 1798 rebellion.

In Paris, Emmet met Napoleon and, believing that a French invasion of England was imminent, returned to Dublin to plan rebellion. But he was forced into premature action when his Patrick Street arms cache blew up. His movement was riddled with British spies.

New music hits Europe's capitals

Vienna, 1803
Joseph Haydn, Europe's greatest living composer, has had a visiting card printed with the first line of one of his songs: "Gone is all my strength, old and weak am I." Haydn, now 71, is exhausted by the effort of writing his great works of the last few years, which include six masses and two oratorios, *The Creation* (1798) and *The Seasons* (1801). This year he embarked on a string quartet, but so far has been unable to finish it.

At the same time, one of Haydn's ex-pupils, Ludwig van Beethoven, aged 32, has become renowned, though partly for his rebellious temperament. He moved from Bonn to Vienna in 1792 and made his name as a fine pianist and a composer of talent. Last year was a time of crisis for Beethoven, who realised that he was going deaf. But his second symphony, written at about that time, reveals little anguish, and he is now working on a third, which is on a grander scale than any previous symphony.

Ailing genius, Joseph Haydn.

Slavery divides north and south in US

Virginia, 1802
The question of slavery is dominating every federal issue discussed in the United States today. It is 35 years since two surveyors, Charles Mason and Jeremiah Dixon, drew a line – at that time to define a border between Pennsylvania and Maryland – which has become a critical demarcation line between the slave-owning south and the liberal-minded northern states.

The knowledge that their brothers north of the Mason-Dixon line are free has been enough to foment a series of uprisings by slaves in several southern states. In North Carolina, 15 slaves have been executed after an alleged conspiracy to overthrow their masters.

Briton puts forward radical social theory

London, 1802
Jeremy Bentham, the philosopher and political writer, has put forward the idea that the object of all legislation should be "the greatest happiness for the greatest number". Bentham trained as a lawyer and has now become the exponent of utilitarianism in his *Introduction to the Principles of Morals and Legislation*. Bentham's conclusions are that mankind is governed by two sovereign motives, pain and pleasure, and the principle of utility recognises this state of affairs. The fame of the *principles* is spreading widely. He has been made a French citizen and his advice is respectfully received in many other countries of Europe and in America.

1803 (1803-1805)

Germany, 1803. The writer Johann von Herder dies. A friend to the young Goethe, Herder conveyed his own enthusiasm for folk-songs, ballads and the works of Shakespeare to a whole generation of writers who formed the *Sturm und Drang* movement, making a break with the age of reason and creating a new movement, the Romantic movement.

Britain, 1803. Henry Shrapnel's fragmentary shell, which he invented in 1784, is adopted by the British army.

Britain, 1803. The painter J M W Turner is elected the youngest Royal Academician at the age of 27. The son of a Covent Garden barber, he has been studying with the Royal Academy since the age of 14. This year he showed *Calais Pier*. Many dismiss his modern art as decadent and unrealistic.

Caribbean, January 1804. Haiti, occupying the western half of the island of Santo Domingo, becomes the first negro republic. It has declared itself independent after 11 years bitter fighting.

France, 28 February 1804. Following the discovery of a royalist plot to assassinate Napoleon Bonaparte, two senior officers, Generals Pichegru and Moreau, are arrested.

Serbia, February 1804. Karageorges (Black George) leads a Serbian revolt against the Ottoman yoke.

France, 21 March 1804. Napoleon Bonaparte promulgates a civil code unifying legal practices across France. A compromise between the old regime and the egalitarian principles of the revolution, it protects the rights of property ownership above all else.

India, April 1804. War breaks out between the Maratha leader, Holkar, and the East India Company.

USA, 14 May 1804. The explorers Meriwether Lewis and William Clark set off on a journey to reach the Pacific.

New Jersey, 12 July 1804. The former treasury secretary, Alexander Hamilton, dies from wounds inflicted in a duel yesterday with his political opponent Aaron Burr.

Austria, 10 August 1804. Fearing that the new modernised configuration of Germany, put into effect after the French occupation of the left bank of the Rhine, no longer guarantees his heir the title of emperor of the Holy Roman empire, Francis II proclaims himself hereditary emperor of Austria, with the name Francis I.

France, 16 September 1804. The physicist Joseph Gay-Lussac sets an altitude record of 22.942 feet (7.016 metres) during an ascent in a balloon with the aim of measuring the possible modifications of the composition of air.

Caribbean, October 1804. Jacques Dessalines, from Guinea, is proclaimed Emperor Jacques of Haiti following the declaration of independence in January.

France, 6 November 1804. A plebiscite ratifies the nomination of Bonaparte as hereditary emperor.

Europe, 6 November 1804. Austria and Russia sign a secret agreement against France.

Paris, 2 December 1804. Napoleon Bonaparte crowns himself emperor of France. He is known henceforth just as Napoleon.

Germany, 1804. Following Napoleon's coronation as emperor, Ludwig van Beethoven cancels the planned dedication of his *Third Symphony* and names it *Eroica.*

Denmark, 1804. King Frederick VI abolishes serfdom in his states.

Japan, 1804. Nicholas Rezanov, the Russian ambassador to Japan, reaches Nagasaki with the permit given to the Russian Lieutenant Adam Laxman in 1792 and requests permission to trade. After waiting six months, he is told that permission is not granted.

England, 1804. The poet William Blake publishes *Jerusalem*, a stirring religious and patriotic piece.

Chad, 1804. Uthman dan Fodio leads his people, the Fulani, in a *jihad* (holy war) against the majority Hausa people and founds the Sokoto *caliphate.*

France, 1804. Charles Nicolas Appert publishes his process for the preserving of food which he invented in 1795.

England, 1804. Richard Trevithick constructs the first steam engine to run on a "railway", called the *Penn-y-Daran.*

China, 1804. The major rebellion stirred up by the White Lotus secret society in 1796 against the Manchu goverment is finally put down. The Qing dynasty survives but is much weakened.

Europe, 8 January 1805. France and Spain sign an agreement fixing the naval aid which the latter must supply to France in their joint war with Britain.

Italy, 17 March 1805. The Italian republic is established as the kingdom of Italy, with Napoleon as its sovereign. An hereditary kingdom, Italy nevertheless remains independent.

German artists and thinkers go romantic

Great romantics: Friedrich von Schelling, Novalis and Friedrich Schiller.

Weimar, 18 March 1804

Friedrich Schiller's drama *William Tell* was given here last night to great enthusiasm. It turns the story of the 14th-century Swiss patriot, who was forced to shoot an apple from his son's head, into the symbol of a people's struggle for freedom. It is theatrically more effective than Schiller's recent poetic historical dramas, *Wallenstein, Maria Stuart* and *The Maid of Orleans.*

Schiller is the object of veneration by Romantic poets, critics and philosophers who are creating a specifically German consciousness. They include Johann Fichte, who introduced the concept of the *ego*, or self-conscious self; Friedrich von Schelling, who deifies nature as the "world soul"; and Novalis, the Romantic poet.

The brothers von Schlegel jointly edit the influential *Athenaeum.* One of them, August, translates the plays of Shakespeare in such a way that they are now regarded as German classics. Clemens Brentano and Achim von Arnim are compiling authentic folkpoems to be called *Des Knaben Wunderhorn.* Ernst Hoffmann writes tales of the utmost fantasy. The Romantic cult is spreading all over Germany.

South American expedition is remarkable for seeking knowledge not conquests

Paris, 1804

A German explorer and scientist, Alexander von Humboldt, has published a remarkable treatise based on his recent four-year adventure in South America. With the French naturalist Aime Bonpland he identified the convergence of the Amazon and Orinoco rivers, climbed the Peruvian Andes and studied an ocean current which seems certain to bear his name.

Scientific acumen accompanied physical boldness. His discoveries include the precise relationship between altitude and temperature; the influence of meteor showers; the use of isotherms in making maps, and measurement of the way the earth's magnetic field varies between the poles and the equator.

Humboldt on the Orinoco river.

Some authorities already believe that Humboldt's great work – *Travels to the Equinoctial Regions of the New Continent during the years 1799 to 1804* – will lay the foundations for future physical geographic and meteorological research. Yet before his voyage there was little to suggest that this assessor of mines in Berlin would be one of the new breed of explorers: people who do not pillage but acquire knowledge instead.

Napoleon crowns himself emperor

The emperor distributes eagles to his regiments on the Champ de Mars in Paris.

Paris, 2 December 1804

Napoleon crowned himself emperor of France in a magnificent ceremony in Notre Dame today. Pope Pius VII had been persuaded to conduct the ceremony, and he anointed the Corsican general; but Napoleon placed two golden laurel wreaths on his own head and then crowned his wife, Josephine.

This was not a spontaneous insult to the pope, as some spectators thought, but had been arranged with the *Curia* after long discussions about the ceremony. There can, however, be no misunderstandings about its meaning.

Charlemagne had also crowned himself. Napoleon sees himself in the same mould and the pope, the head of Catholic Christendom, had travelled from Rome to bless a self-made emperor.

It was in this fashion that monarchy returned to France almost 11 years after Louis XVI's gory head was shown to the crowd in the Place de la Revolution.

Americans launch night attack on Tripoli

Tripoli (Libya), 5 September 1804

A daring attack in February led by a young lieutenant, Stephen Decatur, succeeded in burning the captured US frigate *Philadelphia*, ensuring that it would never be used by the piratical *pasha* who has been holding *Philadelphia's* captain and crew hostage. The British admiral, Lord Nelson, described Decatur's action as "the most daring act of the age".

Decatur attacked by night; today, also under cover of darkness, Commodore Edward Preble took a leaf out of Sir Francis Drake's book and sent a fireboat, loaded with gunpowder, into Tripoli harbour to destroy the pasha's fleet after a day of bombardment. The ship was spotted by enemy gunners and blown up. It was to gain the release of the *Philadelphia's* captain and crew that Preble, aboard the 44-gun *Constitution*, has been battering Tripoli throughout the day. The United States has been paying substantial "protection money" to the pasha after attacks on US merchant shipping.

The burning US frigate "Philadelphia" lights up Tripoli harbour.

British supremacy is expanded in India

Calcutta, India, 1805

Lord Wellesley, the governor-general of Bengal and the man who turned the British presence in India into an empire, has been recalled. An energetic imperialist, his skills at defeating the French and their Indian allies by force, and the Indian princes by shackling them with treaties, are no longer required.

He arrived in India at a time of crisis. Bonaparte in Egypt threatened British India from without, and Tipu of Mysore from within. First Wellesley marched south, defeated Tipu and annexed the Carnatic. Next he turned on the lesser princes, provoking one against another, then "guaranteeing" the independence of both with troops.

Only in 1802 did he take on the still formidable Marathas. Exploiting divisions in the Maratha leadership, he imposed a treaty depriving them of their homeland. Then he provoked them to war; his brother Sir Arthur Wellesley defeated them at Assaye and Argaon. Thus is Britain building an empire here.

The English in the Orient.

France unified by a single set of laws

Paris, 21 March 1804

A new legal framework, known to some as the "Napoleonic Code", has been approved after a four-year debate. Almost 16 years after the Revolution, the civil code gives France its first coherent set of laws concerning property, the family and individual freedom.

The code emerged from 84 wearing sessions of the State Council. Napoleon presided at 36 of these, all concerned with the family and property. The authority of husbands and fathers is stronger, but the rights of illegitimate children are reduced. Women have no legal equality and colonial slavery is re-introduced. For men, however, the code enshrines the principle that all individuals are equal before the law; all enjoy freedom to work and to dissent from religious dogma.

Doctor knocks out wife for surgery

Japan, 1805

Hanaoka Seishu, a doctor in Kii province, has carried out an operation on a patient under a general anaesthetic for the first time in the history of medicine. His patient is his own wife and the operation, for breast cancer, is claimed to be a success.

The doctor has succeeded in preparing an anaesthetic substance after 20 years of experimentation. He calls it *mafutsusan*; it is a mixture of six crude drugs, including datura and aconite, listed in the traditional Chinese pharmacopoeia.

As he prepares to use his discovery in other operations, students are coming from all over the country to learn about his new techniques. His motto is: "Elucidate the principles of life, unite internal medicine with surgery."

1805 (1805-1806)

Europe, 11 April 1805. Britain and Russia sign an agreement of St Petersburg directed against France, thus inaugurating the third coalition. Sweden, already linked with Russia by an alliance signed in January, and the kingdom of Piedmont-Sardinia, are also members.

Virginia, 1 May 1805. A law is passed by the state leglislature requiring all freed slaves to leave the state, or risk either imprisonment or deportation.

Italy, 28 May 1805. Napoleon is crowned in Milan and appoints his stepson, Eugene de Beauharnais, as viceroy.

Tripoli, 4 June 1805. Yusuf Karamanli, *pasha* of Tripoli, signs a peace treaty with the United States ending the war which he declared in May 1801. He has been forced to surrender by the US fleet patrolling outside his harbour and by that fact that his rebellious brother Hamed has been installed, with US backing, in the eastern city of Derna.

Genoa, 10 June 1805. The Constitutional Assembly ratifies the annexation of Liguria to the French empire.

Ohio, 4 July 1805. A final treaty is between the United States government and the indigenous Indians for the purchase of Cleveland.

Louisiana, 25 July 1805. Leading US politician, Aaron Burr visits New Orleans as he allegedly develops plans to establish a country separate from the United States with New Orleans as its capital.

Europe, 9 August 1805. Austria joins Britain, Russia, Sweden and the kingdom of Piedmont-Sardinia in the third coalition against France.

Europe, 25 August 1805. Napoleon signs a treaty of alliance with Bavaria at Bogenhausen. In exchange for aid in the form of troops, the elector of Bavaria is maintained on the throne.

Bavaria, 8 October 1805. In a major battle the outnumbered French army of Napoleon defeats the invading Austrian army at Ulm and halt them.

Prussia, 3 November 1805. Coerced by Russia, Prussia joins the third coalition against France by a sectret treaty signed at Potsdam.

Pacific Ocean, 7 November 1805. The expedition led by Meriwether Lewis and William Clark has reached the Pacific coastline after a journey of nearly 4,000 miles which has taken 18 months. Many hope this will open a new era of westward expansion for the USA.

Austria, 14 November 1805. The French army enters the city of Vienna.

Austria, 2 December 1805. Napoleon defeats the combined Austrian and Russian armies at the battle of Austerlitz.

Austria, 26 December 1805. Austria signs the peace of Pressburg with France, abandoning the third coalition.

Italy, 27 December 1805. Napoleon proclaims the deposition of the House of Naples and forces the king to flee.

France, 31 December 1805. The republican calendar introduced after the French Revolution is abandoned in favour of the Gregorian one.

China, 1805. Several Roman Catholic priests are deported when a map of north China by the Italian priest Adeodato is discovered, ready to be sent to Rome.

Mexico, 1805. The first Mexican daily paper, *El Diario de Mexico*, is published.

France, 1805. Joseph Jacquard introduces the first weaving looms, thus enabling unskilled workers to produce beautiful and intricate patterns.

Britain, 23 January 1806. The prime minister, William Pitt, dies. The government is led by Lord Grenville and Charles James Fox.

France, 13 February 1806. Napoleon breaks with Pius VII after reservations expressed by the pope about the "imperial cathchism" which makes Napoleon "God's minister on earth".

Europe, 15 February 1806. The treaty of Paris is signed by France and Prussia, forcing the latter to accept the closing of its ports to British goods. Britain declares war on Prussia.

Spanish America, February 1806. The revolutionary Francisco Miranda – who has plans for a new great nation of South America – returns from Europe and attempts a coup in Venezuela which fails through lack of popular support.

San Francisco, 5 April 1806. Spanish authorities agree to sell supplies to Russian-American colonists who come down from Alaska in search of provisions. This is a complete reversal of policy and follows months of hard negotiating by the Russian representative, Nicholas Rezanov. He returns to his people not only with the agreement but also with a bride, the daughter of the Spanish commander of San Francisco.

French troops massing to invade England

Britain's answer to Napoleon's Grand Army, as George Cruikshank saw it.

Boulogne, August 1805

Napoleon is encamped here, waiting for Admiral Villeneuve to arrive with his fleet to cover the crossing of the Channel. Napoleon's orders are: "Let us be masters of the Straits for six hours, and we shall be masters of the world." He has assembled 2,343 ships and barges that can hold 167,590 men, but he will need calm weather over a number of tides before he can get his soldiers across, even without the attentions of the Royal Navy. He plans a lightning strike at London. But time is running out, and the only sails he can see are those of British frigates.

Explorers battle across Missouri to Pacific

Columbia River, 7 November 1805

After a hazardous 18-month journey across 4,000 miles of the unmapped plains, forests, mountains and deserts of North America, a United States government expedition is standing on the shores of the blue Pacific. The 28-man (and one woman) "Corps of Discovery" has been led by Captain Meriwether Lewis, President Jefferson's secretary and a veteran of several Indian wars, and Captain William Clark. Its mission is to survey the newly-purchased Louisiana territory.

The woman – who carried her baby son all the way – is a 16-year-old Shoshone Indian *squaw* called Sacajawea who is married to the expedition's interpreter, Toussaint Charbonneau. At one point, Sacajawea saved Lewis' life when he was threatened by an Indian chief.

The explorers left St Louis and journeyed up the Missouri River in six canoes and two longboats, sending back plant, animal and mineral specimens. They wintered in

Lewis and Clark on the Columbia.

Dakota before crossing Montana where they first saw the Rocky Mountains.

On the other side of the Continental Divide, they were met by Sacajawea's tribe who sold them horses for the long trek through the Bitterroot Mountains. The last leg of the journey, down the dangerous rapids of the Clearwater and Snake rivers in canoes, brought them to the Columbia river and the sea.

French lose at Trafalgar

The mortal wounding of Admiral Nelson, on the main deck of "HMS Victory".

Falmouth, 5 November 1805
The schooner *Pickle* sailed into the harbour here, bearing news of a great British naval victory off Cape Trafalgar. Twenty French and Spanish ships have been taken or sunk and Britain is safe from the invasion which Napoleon has been preparing. British joy will be tempered, however, by news of the death of Admiral Nelson, who was shot by a French sniper in the thick of the battle as his flagship, *HMS Victory*, came to grips with the French *Redoutable*.

The battle took place on 21 October. The combined fleets of France and Spain had been blockaded in Cadiz and it was a reluctant French admiral, Villeneuve, who sailed out on Napoleon's orders, hoping to avoid combat and unaware of the size of Nelson's fleet. Nelson divided his 27 ships into two columns to attack the rear of the enemy line, and as his fleet advanced in light winds, the admiral signalled: "England expects that every man will do his duty." Losses were heavy on both sides, but it was Nelson who carried the day.

Nelson's death will be mourned throughout Britain. His successes had made him one of the most popular men in the country with a public prepared to forgive his adulterous caperings with the voluptuous Emma, Lady Hamilton. His last words were: "Thank God I have done my duty."

French win at Austerlitz

Austerlitz, 2 December 1805
Napoleon crushed a numerically superior alliance of Russians and Austrians in a decisive battle here today, the first anniversary of his coronation as emperor of France.

Not for the first time, he started the battle in a precarious position. Outnumbered, he had to force a battle before the full weight of the allies could be brought to bear.

He pretended to retreat and gave an impression of weakness. Czar Alexander was taken in by this ruse and at daybreak advanced in extended line against the French massed behind the Goldbach brook, west of Austerlitz. The czar's plan was to turn the French right wing and cut off their retreat to Vienna. Napoleon allowed the allies to come on, with Davout holding fast on the right wing. The movement down the heights of Pratzen weakened the allies' centre where, suddenly, Napoleon ordered Soult to storm the heights.

There was a desperate fight between the Russian Imperial Guard and the French Guards until the Russians gave way. The allies were split in two and broke in utter rout, leaving 26,000 men dead and Napoleon as master of the battlefield.

Napoleon surveys the field of victory after the Russian and Austrian defeat.

Cape Town seized

Cape Town, 10 January 1806
Cape Colony surrendered today to the invading British naval and military force led by Admiral Popham and Sir David Baird. There was little resistance from the meagre local forces assembled by the Dutch governor, General J W Janssens, who answers to Napoleon's puppet government in Holland.

The British first captured the Cape in 1795, but they found it a troublesome possession. The Boers and Xhosa Africans fought on the frontiers. The Boers, originally Dutch, had no love for the French, but they appeared to like the British even less. They rebelled in 1801 and in 1802 Britain gave up the Cape in the treaty of Amiens.

New ruler for Egypt

Cairo, 3 August 1805
Mohammed Ali, an Albanian former tobacco merchant, is the new ruler of Egypt. Khurshid Pasha, the former viceroy, has accepted the inevitable, and evacuated the citadel where he has been holding out since 14 May.

Seven years ago Mohammed Ali was recruited by the Ottomans to serve against Napoleon. At the head of a group of Albanian clansmen, he profited from the power struggle between Mamelukes and Ottomans. In 1803 he supported the Mamelukes, then last year switched to the Sultan's side. With Khurshid's administration accused of corruption, sultan Selim III turned to Ali to restore order.

Slave emperor of Caribbean state dies

Haiti, 1806
Jean-Jacques Dessalines, the slave who became emperor of Haiti, the Carribean's first independent state, has died. He was 48 years old. Born in Guinea, he came to the rich sugar-producing French colony of Haiti on a slave ship, and took the name of his owner, Dessalines, as his own.

When Haiti's free negroes, and then her slaves – their expectations inflated by the slogan *liberte, equalite et fraternite* – revolted in 1891 under Toussaint L'Ouverture, he rose to become second-in-command. For seven years the two men led the slave army, first against the French, then against the Spanish and British, defeating all of them. When Napoleon re-imposed slavery in 1800 and sent a military expedition to retake Haiti, L'Ouverture and Dessalines took to the field again. L'Ouverture was captured and died in a French prison in 1803 and Dessalines took control of the army. He renewed the war with vigour and cruelty, and drove the French Army from the country in October.

On 1 January 1804 he declared Haiti independent and then, on 8 October, he crowned himself emperor. Now unrestrained by the magnamnity and statesmanship of L'Ouverture, he gave his cruelty free reign. Hundreds were brutally killed and tortured. Indeed he proved so oppressive a tyrant that his leading general, Henri Christophe, ended up assassinating him. Christophe has now taken over control of the unhappy country.

1806 (1806-1807)

France, 10 May 1806. The university of France is founded.

Britain, 16 May 1806. Advised by Charles Fox, the foreign secretary, the cabinet decrees a blockade of the European coast from Brest to Hamburg.

Netherlands, 5 June 1806. The Batavian republic is established as the kingdom of Holland under Louis Bonaparte, the Emperor Napoleon's younger brother.

Germany, 12 July 1806. The confederation of the Rhine is established.

Germany, 1 August 1806. Napoleon gives notice to the Emperor Francis II of the end of the Holy Roman empire.

Germany, 6 August 1806. The Holy Roman Emperor Francis II accepts Napoleon's ultimatum and abdicates.

Spanish America, 12 August 1806. A British expeditionary force which took Buenos Aires in June, meeting little resistance, is forced to capitulate by a local army.

France, 22 August 1806. Jean Honore Fragonard, the painter of the erotic coquetry of the court of Louis XVI and Marie Antoinette, dies. He fell from favour with the revolution, was forced to give up his rooms in the Louvre and ended his days in poverty and obscurity.

London, 27 August 1806. US negotiators open talks with Lord Holland with a view to ending naval hostilities.

Britain, 13 September 1806. The death of the foreign secretary, Fox, interrupts Lord Yarmouth's mission, entrusted to him in March, to negotiate peace with France.

France, 21 November 1806. Napoleon promulgates the Berlin decree which declares the British Isles to be in a state of blockade and orders the confiscation of British merchandise in French territory, the imprisonment of British subjects, and the closure of all French ports to ships coming from Britain or British territories.

France, 10 December 1806. The Grand Sanhedrin, an official institution of the Jewish community, is created. This comes after the meeting of 111 representatives of the Jewish communities of France and Italy, which took place on 30 May in Paris. It marks the recognition of the French character of the empire's Jews.

Ottoman Empire, December 1806. Following a declaration of war by the Ottomans on Russia, the Russians occupy Baku, on the Caspian Sea.

Britain, 1806. Admiral Francis Beaufort perfects a graduated scale for measuring wind speed.

Haiti, 1806. The Emperor Jacques, who came to power two years ago, is assassinated following a rule of extreme barbarity during which he contrived the murder of almost the entire white population.

South Africa, 1806. Cape Colony is surrendered once again by Holland to Britain. The colony reverted to the Batavian republic (Napoleonic Holland) in 1803 under the treaty of Amiens of the previous year. After war resumed, the British first landed at Cape Town in July 1805, but have now returned in force.

India, 1806. Ranjit Singh, the Sikh leader, takes Lahore.

Paris, 4 January 1807. Napoleon visits the studio of the painter Louis David, who has just finished his monumental composition *The Coronation of the Emperor*, started on 21 December 1805.

London, 7 January 1807. Responding to the Emperor Napoleon's Berlin Decree, blockading the British Isles, a British order in council closes the coastal waters of France and its allies to all commercial shipping.

Britain, 25 March 1807. Parliament passes an act abolishing the slave trade. A resolution for the abolition of slavery was first brought before parliament in 1789.

Ottoman Empire, 25 May 1807. A revolt by the Janissaries (foot soldiers recruited from slaves) leads to the deposition of Selim III and to his replacement by Mustapha IV.

Russia, 25 June 1807. At the Tilsit convention Napoleon and the Russian Czar Alexander agree an end to hostilities between their two countries.

Spanish America, 5 July 1807. Having taken Montevideo on 3 February, the British fail in their attempt to re-take Buenos Aires.

Prussia, July 1807. The ministers Gneisenau and Scharnhorst reorganise the Prussian army.

England, 1807. Charles Lamb publishes his *Tales from Shakespeare*, written by him and his sister Mary. Lamb is guardian to his sister who stabbed their mother in a fit of insanity.

China, 1807. Robert Morrison, of the London Missionary Society, the first Protestant missionary to China, arrives in Guangzhou.

Japan, 1807. Russian ships attack Japanese settlements in the north in reprisal for the treatment of the expedition of the ambassador, Nicholas Rezanov, in 1804.

Utamaro, painter of the "floating world"

Utamaro's exquisite print "Lovers on a Balcony" from "Poems of the Pillow".

Edo (Tokyo), 31 October 1806

The death occurred today of the foremost painter of the "Floating World" school in Japan, Kitagawa Utamaro. His prints were published under such titles as *The Seven Beauties of the Gay Quarter, Ten Types of Feminine Demeanour* and *Women in Love*. His subjects were the famous beauties among the courtesans and tea-house girls of the Yoshiwara pleasure district.

He idealised the sitters, but subtle variations of detail conveyed feminine characteristics such as fickleness, conceit or petulance. In 1804 he portrayed the wife and concubines of *shogun* Toyotomi Hideyoshi and was imprisoned for "insult". He was kept in handcuffs for 50 days and painted no more.

Utamaro's "Three Girls Paddling".

New Reforms for beaten Prussia

Berlin, 1807

Shattered by Napoleon's defeat of his army at Jena, and with his kingdom cut to a mere half of its former size, Frederick William III of Prussia has turned to the outspoken and resolute Baron Heinrich von Stein for salvation.

Stein is pushing through a big reform programme, which includes the abolition of serfdom and all class distinctions in state employment. Local self-government will be introduced. Queen Louise, the real power behind the throne, is backing Scharnhorst and Gneisenau in reorganising the army.

Locals expel British from Buenos Aires

Buenos Aires, 1807

Creole irregulars defending thei[r] Argentian capital have inflicte[d] two successive defeats on British in[-] vaders. In June last year Britis[h] forces launched from South Afric[a] a successful but unauthorised sur[-] prise attack with 1,200 men to seiz[e] a virtually undefended Buenc[s] Aires. Two months later, a French[-] man led a locally-raised militia t[o] defeat the invaders. On 3 Februar[y] this year a new British expeditio[n] took Montevideo, then crossed th[e] river Plate to reoccupy Buenc[s] Aires. Again the invaders wer[e] trapped and disarmed.

Napoleon crushes Prussian army at Jena

Jena, Germany, 14 October 1806
Napoleon's lightning offensive in Germany has met with two spectacular victories against the Prussians on the same day, one here at Jena under Napoleon himself and the other a few miles to the north, at Auerstadt, where the main Prussian army was routed by a French force under General Davout, who performed so well at the battle of Austerlitz last December.

Napoleon was faced with his usual problem of crushing one ally, the Prussians, before the other, the Russians, arrived. Thinking that the main Prussian force was at Jena, he occupied the heights overlooking the Prussian camp and sent his men rushing down on the enemy, driving them from the field.

Meanwhile, Davout with only 26,000 men was engaging the duke of Brunswick with 70,000 men. The duke was mortally wounded and his troops, retreating in disorder, became entangled with their defeated comrades fleeing from Jena. The result was utter confusion and rout. Tonight the ever-victorious Davout is leading his troops on to Berlin.

Napoleon's victory at Jena, where French columns savaged the Prussian army.

Sudden collapse of British government

London, March 1807
The so-called "Ministry of All the Talents", a coalition of British political parties in the Commons formed to prosecute the war against France, has collapsed. Lord Grenville formed the government after the death of Pitt last year, and at once found himself confronted by the Irish question. A young Catholic merchant, James Ryan, presenting to parliament a petition for Catholic emancipation, found himself rebuffed and joined the agitation by Catholics in Ireland.

Grenville decided to grasp the nettle. He persuaded George III to agree to allow Catholics to join the army in mainland Britain (as they could already in Ireland). But when they came to draft the bill, Grenville and his ministers put in a clause allowing Catholics to become generals and admirals. George said he wanted to hear no more about Catholic relief and Grenville's government resigned.

Reforming sultan is deposed in Istanbul

Istanbul, 29 May 1807
Selim III, the reforming sultan, has been deposed in favour of his cousin, Mustapha IV. The New Order has been disbanded, leaving the militarist Janissaries and reactionary *'ulema* (council) back in control. The reaction is hardly surprising, since two years ago Selim's support for Serbian rebels against their tyrannical Janissary masters was followed by a Janissaries' revolt. The Sultan was forced to suspend his proposed general levy for the New Order, and install the *agha* of the Janissaries as *grand vizier*.

The catalyst this time was an order to the Yamaks, levies in the Bosporus region, to adopt new Europeanstyle uniforms. When they refused, they were joined by Janissaries. With the support of the *chief mufti*, rebels rounded up and killed noted reformers. His deposition proclaimed, Selim tried to drink poison, but his successor dashed the cup from his lips.

Britain abolishes trade in human flesh

London, 25 March 1807
The royal assent today for the act to abolish the slave trade marks the successful conclusion of a twenty year struggle by one man. William Wilberforce, the 47-year-old independent MP for Yorkshire, took up the anti-slavery cause in 1787. He had been converted to evangelical Christianity in 1785. His mentor told him told him to focus on the plight of the slaves: "If you carry this point in your whole life, that life will be far better spent than in being prime minister many years."

William Wilberforce: freer of slaves.

Wilberforce moved the first abolition bill in May 1789. But, despite the growing evidence of deaths and ill-treatment of negroes on ships from Africa to the Americas, there were repeated delays in the Commons and the Lords. The West Indian sugar lobby combined with the admirals who saw negro slaves as a "nursery of seamen" and won support from landed gentry afraid of revolutionary movements. But Wilberforce won his majority through moral argument.

Napoleon and czar agree to divide Europe

Tilsit, Russia 7 July 1807
Czar Alexander, whose army was slaughtered by the French last month at Friedland, today met his conqueror, Napoleon, and at once fell under the spell of the French dictator. Napoleon offered him a partnership: let us divide Europe between ourselves, Napoleon said. Russia will be free to attack Finland, Sweden and Turkey. France gets the rest of Europe, including a puppet duchy of Warsaw. But Napoleon's real aim is to isolate Britain. During their talks aboard a raft on the river Niemen, the czar agreed to join Napoleon's policy of barring British goods from Europe. The czar also secretly promised to declare war on Britain.

It is said that Alexander, brooding on his defeat at the hands of Napoleon, blames the British for their failure to open a second front in Europe. "Why do you not send your militia?" he demanded angrily of Leveson-Gower, the British ambassador.

Isolating Britain at Tilsit: the Emperor Napoleon and the queen of Prussia.

1807 (1807-1808)

Virginia, 3 August 1807. Treason proceedings begin against Aaron Burr. He is accused of being involved in a plot for the secession of New England.

France, 18 August 1807. The abolition of the Tribunate leaves the Emperor Napoleon as sole ruler.

Virginia, 1 September 1807. A jury acquit Aaron Burr, the former vice-president, of treason.

Prussia, September 1807. Dismissed on 3 January by Frederick William III, Heinrich von Stein is recalled after the intervention of the queen, with the implicit agreement of Napoleon, who sees in his abilities as an organiser the guarantee that Prussia's war debts will be paid.

Prussia, 9 October 1807. Heinrich von Stein begins a process of reform designed to turn Prussia into a modern state. These include the abolition of serfdom and the privileges of the nobility.

Denmark, 30 October 1807. Having been forced to adhere to the continental blockade of the British isles (initiated by Napoleon), Denmark suffers a British bombardment on Copenhagen and forms an alliance with France.

Europe, 7 November 1807. After the Tilsit convention in July of this year, the Anglo-Russian alliance – at the heart of the third coalition against France – is broken.

Britain, 11 November 1807. Britain extends its blockade to the Russian seaboard following the collapse of the third coalition, and threatens neutral countries with reprisals if they refuse to undergo verification of their merchandise.

USA, 22 December 1807. Congress passes the Embargo Act, which halts all trading completely and is immediately effective. Trade, not only with Britain and France but with the whole world, is banned, both import and export. The president hopes that this will force Britain and France to reconsider their harassment of US ships. The act is viewed by merchants, sailors and producers with dismay.

USA, 1 January 1808. The law banning the import of slaves comes into effect, but is widely ignored.

Europe, 21 February 1808. Russia occupies Finland, which is under Swedish domination.

France, 1 March 1808. Napoleon creates an imperial nobility.

Spain, 18 March 1808. Following the French invasion, public fury is such that the king is obliged to arrest the prime minister, Godoy.

Prussia, 16 April 1808. German patriots found the *Tugendbund*, a cultural and scientific association directed against Napoleon.

France, 17 April 1808. The Emperor Napoleon orders the confiscation of all US ships putting in at French ports, saying that he is simply helping the US government to enforce its Embargo Act prohibiting US trade anywhere in the world.

France, April 1808. Admiral Sebastiani, the commander of the French fleet in the eastern Mediterranean, is recalled. His withdrawal leaves the field open for the British against the Ottomans.

Spain, 2 May 1808. The people of Madrid rise up against the army of Napoleon.

Spain, 6 May 1808. Negotiations between the Spanish rulers and Napoleon end in the former forced abdications.

Spain, 6 June 1808. On hearing of Napoleon's decision to appoint his brother, Joseph, king of Spain, a *junta* that has withdrawn to Seville declares war on France.

Spain, 22 July 1808. Whilst Joseph Napoleon enters Madrid on 20 July, Spanish patriots under General Francisco Javier Castanos surround the French army under General Dupont and force it to surrender at Bailen in Andalucia.

Ottoman Empire, 28 July 1808. Sultan Mustapha IV is deposed and his cousin Mahmud II is put on the throne.

Spanish America, July 1808. Following the capture of the revolutionary Francisco Miranda during an attempted coup in Venezuela, one of his followers, Simon Bolivar, seizes power in Caracas.

London, 1808. The building of the Bank of England is completed. It is designed by the architect John Soane and was started in 1788.

Washington DC, 1808. Negroes are declared competent witnesses in all court cases.

West Africa, 1808. Britain's Royal Navy starts anti-slavery patrols along the West African coast to arrest slave ships and set slaves free in the newly proclaimed crown colony of Sierra Leone. The British Parliament had passed an act in 1807 banning slave trading from 1 March 1808.

Germany, 1808. Goethe, who accepted the Legion of Honour from Napoleon on 2 October, publishes the first part of his *Faust*. Inspired by his love for Minna Herzlieb he also writes *Deep Understandings*.

Navies have no use for submarines

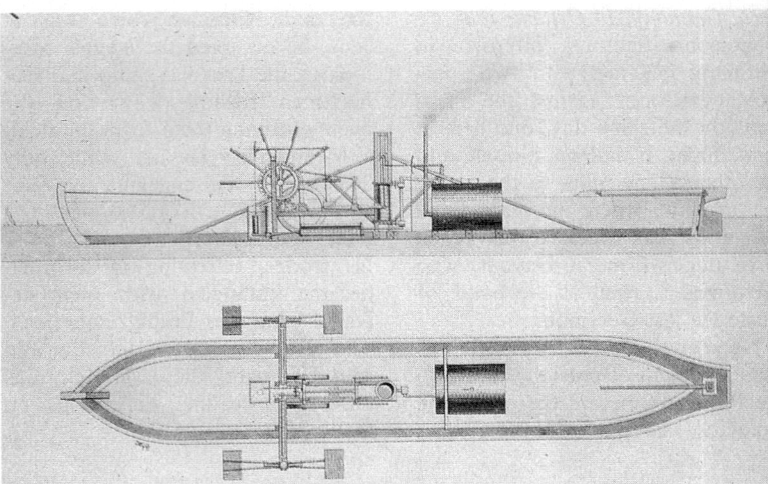

Fulton's "submarine", or submersible warship: an experiment that failed.

Connecticut, September 1807

Despite considerable interest from the navies of three countries, Robert Fulton, the distinguished inventor and artist, has failed to convince them that his latest invention – the *submarine* or submersible warship – has any practical value in sea warfare.

Fulton, whose steamships ply on many rivers in the USA, tried first in France, where Napoleon gave him a substantial grant to develop *Nautilus*, a craft made from iron ribs with copper sheathing. This craft was powered by sail on the surface and by a hand-cranked propeller below the waves. The warhead was an explosive charge fixed to the hull of an enemy ship by a screw device. It worked in an experiment, but *Nautilus* could not keep up with British warships. Fulton took his invention to England and sank another ship. The navy was not impressed. Now he is trying to get a congressional grant for a bigger submarine.

Another new weapon: the torpedo.

A touch of Paradis

Vienna, 1808

Vienna's young musical talent is flourishing at the new Theresia von Paradis Institute. Paradis, aged 49, gives her students much of the wide musical education she herself received from such distinguished musicians as Kozeluch and Salieri.

Despite being blind, Paradis is a gifted singer, concert pianist, organist and composer. Her *Cantata on the death of Louis XVI* was one of the many works she wrote using a device invented by Riedinger. Her artistic interpretation impressed Mozart so much that he wrote for her the piano concerto number 18 in B flat.

Anti-Slavery patrol

Freetown, 1808

Britain's decision to prohibit its citizens from slave trading has given rise to a new naval patrol. The squadron has about six small obsolete ships based at Freetown, Sierra Leone, to patrol 3,000 miles (4,800km) of coastline and arrest the biggest maritime trade out of Africa. A court at Freetown prosecutes crews carrying slaves.

Not all slaves win freedom as a result. Slavers often dump their human cargo overboard to dispose of the evidence. If the system is imperfect, it is still a triumph for the campaign led by Wilberforce against slavery in England.

US bans all trade with rest of world

Washington, 22 December 1807

After months of mercantile harassment by the British and French navies, the US Congress today voted to ban all trading with the rest of the world. No American ship can sail to any foreign port and all exports from America are prohibited. President Jefferson believes that these economic sanctions will force the British and French to rescind orders in council and decrees against neutral trade.

The US public is furious at what it terms the latest British outrage. The frigate USS *Chesapeake* refused an order to stop from *HMS Leopard* which opened fire without warning, killing 21 of her crew. Chesapeake's captain was forced to allow his ship to be boarded and three British seamen and a US citizen were impressed into the king's service.

British in Lisbon to harass French

Lisbon, 1 August 1808

A British military force led by Sir Arthur Wellesley has landed at Lisbon to help Portuguese and Spanish resistance to Napoleon. It has promptly routed the French Marshal Junot at Vimeiro. The action is seen as heralding the start of a Peninsula War which could tie down thousands of Napoleon's troops in the region.

The British landing must come as shock to the French leader, who has been counting on Spain to give him with ships, troops and cash. Spain had been forced to deny harbours to the British, and Portugal should have followed suit under threat of occupation. But Napoleon scattered his armies in attempts to capture and close Spanish-held ports, leaving Lisbon open to British ships and allowing Wellesley to land without opposition.

Importation of slaves in US is banned

Washington DC, 2 March 1807

The importation of slaves from Africa into the United States will be illegal from next January under an act passed by Congress today. Anyone who knowingly buys an illegally imported slave faces a penalty of $500, and equipping a ship for the slave trade is punishable with a $20,000 fine.

It was President Jefferson who insisted that the act should be placed in the statute book. The president has been a long-time opponent of slavery, and fought unsuccessfully with southern delegates to introduce anti-slavery statements in his first draft of the Declaration of Independence

There has been little opposition to the move. The United States has more than enough slaves at present. But what looks like a coming boom in the cotton industry could create a substantial demand by the southern states. Some unscrupulous owners are already talking about "slave-breeding farms".

Establishing ownership: branding.

Locomotive inventor mounts London show

Richard Trevithick's "steam circus".

London, 1808

Richard Trevithick, the inventor of a locomotive steam engine, has exhibited his latest engine in London. The engine, known as the "catch-me-who-can", can be seen on the New Road as the centre piece of a "steam circus" on which the public may ride for a charge of a shilling.

Trevithick's first locomotive – known as "the puffing devil" – was completed in 1801 at his home town, Redruth, in Cornwall. A second followed in 1803, but the delicate engineering suffered on the rough roads, and his experiments in "steam-carriages" had to be abandoned. His first locomotive to run on tracks was completed in 1804. It could run at five miles per hour for nine and a half miles, pulling ten tons of iron, 70 men and five wagons. But this, too, was used mainly as a stationary machine. The problems were with the track; the engine was blameless.

Napoleon blockades British commerce

George Cruikshank's view of the continental blockade; a starving Europe.

Paris, 1807

The "Continental System", Napoleon's boycott of British goods, is beginning to bite. When he issued his famous Berlin Decree last November, in which he declared "the British Isles are in a state of blockade" and British goods ordered to be seized, he was greeted with derision. Cartoons showed Boney blockading the moon.

Now, however, the treaty of Tilsit has forced Russia and Prussia into the system and their ports are closed to British trade. Napoleon is sure that his boycott will ruin Britain and force it to sue for peace.

He has told his brother, King Louis of Holland: "I mean to conquer the sea by land", and writes of Britain's vessels "laden with useless wealth wandering around the high seas, where they claim to rule as sole masters, seeking in vain ... for a port to receive them". The boycott has indeed had a serious effect on British trade this year, but such is the cunning of British smugglers and the greed of French officials that great holes are being torn in the blockade and Europe is overflowing with British goods.

Atoms all arranged on Dalton's table

London, 1808

The British scientist John Dalton has succeeded in devising chemical symbols for the various elements, such as oxygen and gold. He has drawn up a list of atomic weights and arranged them in a table. He has formulated the theory that a chemical combination of elements occurs according to certain laws governing the ratio of these atomic weights: the *Law of Multiple Proportions* and the *Law of Constant Composition*.

All these ideas are expounded in his *New System of Chemical Philosophy* which shows Dalton to be a unique thinker.

1808 (1808-1809)

Portugal, 30 August 1808. Having landed in Portugal at the beginning of the month, British troops force the French to surrender.

Algeria, 27 August 1808. The British bombard Algiers.

Europe, 14 October 1808. During their meeting at Erfurt which finishes today, Napoleon and the Russian Czar Alexander renew the treaty of Tilsit which both countries have broken since it was made last year.

Prussia, 24 November 1808. Napoleon obtains the dismissal of the minister Stein whom he suspects of organising an anti-French uprising.

Spain, 4 December 1808. Napoleon conquers Madrid, having put down the resistance in Somosierra last month.

Washington DC, 7 December 1808. James Madison is elected president in succession to Thomas Jefferson.

Vienna, 22 December 1808. Beethoven gives the first performance of his fifth and sixth symphonies, in a long, under-rehearsed and ill-received concert.

Serbia, December 1808. The popular leader Karageorges (Black George) is recognised as hereditary prince of the Serbs by an assembly of his people.

China, 1808. British forces occupy Macao.

Japan, 1808. Mamiya Rinzo explores Sakhalin and discovers that it is an island.

Britain, 1808. The Englishman Humphry Davy uses the newly-invented voltaic pile to isolate barium. In this same year he also succeeds in isolating strontium, calcium, magnesium and boron.

India, 1808. Holkar, the Maratha leader, has become insane.

France, 28 January 1809. Having plotted against the emperor with Fouche, Talleyrand falls into disgrace. Stripped of every position he holds, he places himself at the service of Metternich, the Austrian ambassador to Paris.

Persia, 12 March 1809. Britain signs a treaty with Persia, forcing the French out of the country.

Europe, 10 April 1809. Austria declares war on France and her forces enter Bavaria.

India, April 1809. The treaty of Amritsar is signed. The British agree to give Ranjit Singh, the ruler of the Sikhs, a free hand to the west of the river Sutlej in return for his giving them a free hand to the east.

Portugal, 12 May 1809. The second British landing is led by Viscount Wellington.

New York, 8 June 1809. The revolutionary writer Thomas Paine dies. He was born in 1737 in England and came to America in 1774. After playing a leading role in the American Revolution, Paine became involved in French politics and was elected a deputy in the Convention. In an abrupt but not unusual fall from favour, Paine was imprisoned for 11 months, and then restored to his seat in the Convention. He eventually became disillusioned with French politics and returned to the US in 1802.

North America, 2 July 1809. The government of the Western Territory announces that the famous Shawnee Indian Chief Tecumseh and his brother (the Prophet) have launched a campaign to unite the 10,000 Indians who live in the area west of the Mississippi river. The aim of this confederation is to halt American expansion in their lands.

Washington DC, 9 August 1809. President Madison reinstates the embargo on British trade following Britain's refusal to revoke the orders in council that justify harassment of American shipping.

Rome, 20 August 1809. Pope Pius VII, who was arrested on 6 July on the orders of the emperor for having excommunicated him on 12 June, is moved to Savona from Grenoble.

Spain, 28 July 1809. An inconclusive battle is fought between the French and the Anglo-Spanish forces at Talavera.

Rome, 20 August 1809. General Malet organises his first plot against the Emperor Napoleon, which comes to nothing.

Netherlands, 30 September 1809. A British army that landed at Walcheren on 30 July is forced to set sail again.

Russia, 17 September 1809. The signing of the peace treaty of Hamina guarantees Russia's jurisdiction over Finland.

Britain, 1809. The painter Turner exhibits *London Seen from Greenwich.*

Spain, 1809. The novelist Alessandro Manzoni brings out *Urania.*

France, 1809. The scholar Lamarck edits his *Zoological Philosophy* in which he explains his theory about the origin and evolution of species.

Prussia, 1809. The *Tugendbund*, a cultural and scientific association directed against Napoleon, is dissolved by the king.

France honours artist of the revolution

David's vast canvas "The Sabine Women": three yards high and five yards wide.

Paris, 1808

Jacques Louis David, the artist most closely linked with the revolution and now official painter to Napoleon, has been awarded the Legion of Honour. David's many admirers welcome this fitting tribute to the foremost painter of the last two decades.

David learnt his art in Italy and his style has a conspicuously classical bent, to be seen in such works as *The Oath of the Horatii*, the painting that brought him his first real celebrity in 1785, the propagandist *Lictors Bringing to Brutus the Bodies of His Sons* (1789) and his masterpiece, *The Death of Marat* (1793).

With the fall of Robespierre in 1794 David himself faced trial, but escaped death despite a spell in jail. In 1799 his giant canvas *Les Sabines* attracted the attention of Bonaparte and David, an admirer, became a government painter once more. His latest painting is of Napoleon's coronation in 1804.

Haydn, master of symphony, dies

Vienna, 31 May 1809

As French armies bombarded the Austrian capital, Joseph Haydn died peacefully today, aged 77. Haydn wrote hundreds of fine works and will be revered as the person who brought the symphony and string quartet to the highest level of sophistication.

He wrote the last 12 of his over 100 symphonies for visits to London and crowned his career with six magnificent masses and two oratorios, including *The Creation.* "Papa" Haydn was a close friend of Mozart, and was devastated by his early death. Mozart summed him up perfectly: "There is no one who can do it all – to joke and to terrify, to evoke laughter and profound sentiment – and all equally well: except Joseph Haydn."

Family is dead in idealist's society

France, 1808

The family as we know it is dead. Instead, we should all live in co-operative groups of 100 families each, working together in agricultural communities.

Such is the view of Charles Fourier, the social reformer and mathematician. Fourier, whose theories appear in his book *Theory of Four Movements*, calls the philosophy *Fourierism.* The communities are *phalansteres*, a word combining *phalange*, meaning phalanx or tightly linked formation, with the final *stere* of *monastere*.

These communities are to share all profits, with the largest share going to the labourers. Women are to be completely equal, and it seems that free love will be taking the place of marriage.

Napoleon arrests insubordinate pope

Pius VII, the defiant pope.

Rome, 6 July 1809
Pope Pius VII and his secretary, Cardinal Pacca, were arrested today on the orders of the French general, Radet, and sent to Grenoble. This act is the result of the pope's continued defiance of Napoleon which dates from the emperor's coronation at which the pope officiated, but gained nothing.

Humiliated, he determined to make no more concessions. He refused to allow the Papal ports to become part of Napoleon's system of boycott against Britain. Napoleon replied by occupying Rome.

The pope shut himself up in his residence. Two months ago, when Napoleon annexed the Papal States to his empire, Pius issued a bull of excommunication against "the despoilers of the church".

He was careful not to name Napoleon, but when the emperor received the text of the bull shortly before the battle of Wagram, he wrote: "He is a madman who should be shut up. Arrest Pacca and other followers of the pope." It may be that he did not intend the pope to be arrested, but it is done now and Pius is to be interned.

Chinese writer tells of his floating life

China, 1809
Shen Fu, a government clerk of no great ability or status, has written a charming book which is enjoying a great success. Called *Six Records of a Floating Life,* it tells the story of his marriage to his childhood sweetheart, Yun.

It is essentially a love story although, in Chinese fashion, his married life is interspersed with affairs with courtesans and with his wife's attempts to find him a concubine. It explains much about Chinese married life to a western reader. Shen Fu emerges from the book as a dreamer, capable of crippling self-deception, forced by his education to be a scholar-administrator, but unable on a number of occasions to provide for his family.

He would have been better off if he had taken a higher-paid job with a more lowly status, but he could not bring himself to do this. This, his voyage through life, reflects only too accurately many of the ills plaguing China today.

The floating state: the emperor's gardens, Beijing, seen by William Alexander.

Retreating British thwart French in Spain

Corunna, where General Sir John Moore saved the British army in the Peninsula.

Paris, 17 January 1809
The failure of Marshal Soult to smash the redcoats at the Spanish port of Corunna and prevent them embarking has wrecked Napoleon's plans for the conquest of the Peninsula, and should give the shattered Spanish armies time to reorganise. After this failure to defeat the British army, Napoleon has put off his planned invasion of Portugal and Andalucia and left Madrid for Paris. The setback for France is all the more remarkable as Napoleon was in Madrid with some 75,000 men after accepting its surrender. He assumed that Sir John Moore, who replaced Sir Arthur Wellesley at the head of the British troops, would retreat to Lisbon, which the French had targeted for capture, and pursued him. Moore took 12 days to reach Corunna, making marches of 17 hours a day in rugged country covered with snow and cut up by torrents and defiles. But some 6,000 of his men dropped out, wearied by the perpetual marching and the absence of any battle.

At Corunna, as embarkation began, Moore pulled the army together and the infantry repulsed Marshal Soult's assault. Moore was hit by grape-shot while applauding his men going into action and died that night. As French guns on the heights re-opened fire on the harbour he was hastily buried in a grave dug by soldiers of the 9th Foot, with his cloak around him.

Unused organs wither, says scientist

Paris, 1809
The evolutionist Jean Baptiste Lamarck has given a clear statement of his views on how animals evolve. There are, he says, two basic laws governing the way organisms develop on their way to a higher stage. The first is that organs are improved with repeated use and weakened by disuse, even to the point of disappearing altogether. The giraffe owes its long neck to frequent stretching in order to eat from higher branches, and the snake has lost its presumed original four legs through lack of use. The second law is that these environmentally-determined changes acquired in an individual animal's lifetime are passed on to its offspring.

Jean Baptiste Lamarck: evolutionist.

1809 (1809-1811)

Europe, 14 October 1809. Austria signs the peace of Schonbrunn, ceding its Illyrian provinces to France.

Spanish America, 6 November 1809. The British are authorised to trade in Buenos Aires.

France, 16 December 1809. The Emperor Napoleon divorces Josephine on the grounds that she has not given him a son.

Britain, 1809. Walter Scott founds the *Quarterly Review*, designed to challenge Whig reformist doctrines.

Russia, 4 February 1810. Czar Alexander refuses Napoleon the hand of his sister Anna, aged 15.

Italy, 17 February 1810. France annexes the papal states.

Netherlands, 9 July 1810. Following the abdication of Louis Bonaparte, in disagreement with his brother about the usefulness of the blockade, the kingdom of Holland is annexed and divided into seven departments.

Mexico, 16 September 1810. A parish priest, Hidalgo, launches an appeal for Mexican independence.

Germany, September 1810. Courses begin at the university of Berlin, founded on 16 August 1809. Its first rector is the philosopher Fichte.

Washington DC, 27 October 1810. President Madison orders the annexation of the western part of West Florida following a rebellion of settlers in the area against the Spanish authorities. Troops are being sent to enforce the claim.

USA, 2 November 1810. President Madison, elected on 4 March 1809, re-establishes freedom of trade with France, having been assured that European ports will be opened to American shipping.

Sweden, 17 November 1810. Sweden declares war on Britain.

Indian Ocean, 3 December 1810. The British seize the islands of Reunion and Maurice following the battle of Grand Port in August. They undertake to respect the languages, laws and customs of the inhabitants.

Germany, 13 December 1810. The North Sea coastline of the duchy of Oldenburg is annexed by the French empire.

Britain, 15 December 1810. The writer Mrs Sarah Trimmer dies aged 69. A friend of Samuel Johnson, she was influential in setting up some of the earliest schools for the education of the poor. She published several educational books and also edited two magazines, *The Family Magazine* and *Guardian of Education*.

Russia, 31 December 1810. Czar Alexander breaks the Continental System of blockades, opening Russian ports to trade with neutral countries, and at the same time banning French imports in the Russian empire.

Britain, 1810. Walter Scott, a most popular writer of romantic verse, including *The Lay of the Last Minstrel* and *Marmion*, publishes *The Lady of the Lake*.

Germany, 1810. Franz Gall and Johann Spurzheim publish a four-volume work on the anatomy of the nervous system. They introduce the idea that various mental processes are localised in different regions of the brain. Gall also invents *phrenology*, a method of determining personality and intelligence by studying bumps on the skull.

Honolulu, 1810. The island of Hawaii is unified by King Kamhameha the Great.

Washington DC, 1810. The population of the US has risen by 36.4 per cent in the last decade, according to a census which puts the population at 7.2 million.

Madagascar, 1810. King Nampoina dies, having ruled since 1782. He is succeeded by King Radama.

Ghana, 1810. In retaliation against local traders who are allied with their enemies the Asante, the Fante people attack the coastal ports of Accra and Elmina.

France, 1810. Napoleon has Madame de Stael's manuscript *Concerning Germany* destroyed.

France, 1811. The banker James de Rothschild establishes a branch in Paris.

Venezuela, 1811. A congress proclaims Venezuela's independence and sets up a republican constitution. Simon Bolivar is a popular leader of the movement, as is the veteran revolutionary Francisco Miranda.

Indian Ocean, 1811. The British finally end French power in the area by taking the Seychelles, Mauritius and Madagascar.

China, 1811. A revolt by the Celestial Order (Tianlijiao) sect breaks out in the provinces of Shandong and the Hebei.

China, 1811. After the banning of Christian preaching in 1810, steps are taken against foreign missionaries and converted Chinese.

Haiti, 1811. Henri Christophe, an ex-slave, is crowned King Henri in the northern part of Haiti. The south falls to an educated Mulatto, Alexandre Pieton.

False freedom cloaks French occupations

Paris, 1810

The French Empire is at its zenith. Most of Europe lies under Napoleon's heel. Everywhere, liberty, equality and fraternity, the ideals of the revolution, have given way to repression of the cruellest nature.

A formidable secret police force, far more efficient than anything possessed by the beheaded "tyrant" Louis XVI, enforces a savage penal code in France. The old punishments of branding and the *carcan* or iron collar, have been revived. State prisons have just been re-established. A general controls the press. Napoleon's court is as lavish as that which was "swept away for ever" in 1793.

In the occupied territories, the fearsome effect of Napoleon's hegemony is even more obvious. His soldiers arrive preaching the "enlightened" law of the *Code Napoleon* and enforce it by the bayonet.

Such oppression breeds reaction. Spain will never forget the *dos de Mayo* when French soldiers slaughtered the people of Madrid. Andreas Hofer, the Tyrolean patriot, has been executed, but remains a hero. Napoleon told his brother recently: "Abroad and at home, I reign through the fear I inspire."

Napoleon seen through British eyes.

Bags of rice bran get Japanese clean

A bath-house, or "uya", for Japanese women at Edo, the capital of Japan.

Japan, c.1810

Bath houses are becoming increasingly popular in Japan. There are 600 in the capital, Edo, alone. Originally these public establishments were places of ill-repute, more used for illicit sex than bathing, but they have developed into an important public service, as only the largest of town houses have bathrooms.

In the early days of the bath houses it was customary for men and women to bathe together, but decorum was ensured by the lack of lighting and the wearing of loin cloths by the men and underskirts by the women. Today, separate facilities are provided for each sex.

Soap is expensive, so bags of rice bran are used for the preliminary wash. Towels are strangely skimpy and bathers dress while still damp. The Japanese insist that this keeps them cool.

Metternich aims for new power balance

Vienna, 8 October 1809
Prince von Metternich has been appointed Austrian foreign minister by Francis in the hope that something can salvaged from the country's series of military defeats at the hands of Napoleon. The shrewd 36-year-old nobleman has served as Austrian minister in France and is thought to be a good judge of Napoleon and his plans.

Metternich is a committed anti-revolutionary. He was forced to flee three times himself before the advancing revolution – from Strasburg, then from Mainz, and from the Netherlands when Napoleon invaded. He has long been working for an effective alliance of Austria, Prussia and Britain to counter the French.

He failed to persuade Frederick William III of Prussia to join Austria in the 1805 war. But in his new position he will be well placed to achieve his aims.

Metternich: conservative diplomat.

Canoe of silver for barbarian of genius

Madagascar, 1810
Despite the death of the Malagasy King Nampoina there is optimism here that the strong centralised kingdom which he created will survive. Nampoina (the Desired One) seized power from in 1783. He has been buried with high honours in a silver canoe. He was called by visiting Frenchmen a "barbarian of genius". He took land from the ruling families and redistributed it to the needy. He created a society where everyone worked. He used forced labour for public works and ensured that the lazy were beaten. He has carefully suppressed his other sons so that his favourite, Radama, is the unchallenged successor.

New Moslem ruler emerges in Nigeria

Nigeria, c.1811
Virtually the whole of northern Nigeria is now controlled by a strong Moslem ruler, Uthman dan Fodio. The last decade has seen an amazing transformation in the fortunes of the minority Fulani people at the expense of the Hausa majority. It has been achieved by Uthman, who is the son of an Imam, and also a religious teacher. But in 1802 the new Hausa king, Yunfa, banned the wearing of the turban and the veil in a bid to stop Moslem conversions. Uthman then had a series of visions urging him to restore the faith by *jihad* (holy war). He stirred the scattered Fulani leaders to combine in a successful war.

Chinese pirate fleet led by women

Guangzhou, China, 20 April 1810
Zheng Yi Sao, the "dragon lady" of the South China Sea and leader of the area's feared confederation of pirates, surrendered today to governor-general Bai Ling. Zheng, a former prostitute, replaced her late husband Zheng Yi as pirate supremo when he died in 1807. For three years, backed by her lover and adopted son Zhang Bao, Zheng Yi Sao has dominated an empire of 1800 junks and 70,000 men and women. Her negotiating skills, as much as the fleet's unassailable power, have made her a great, if criminal, leader. It is those same skills that have created from her surrender a new victory. No pirate is to be punished – all will be pardoned – and Zheng and some of her senior commanders are to be given highranking positions in the state's military.

Independence movement born in Mexico

Mexico: cursed by the extremes of Spanish wealth and Indian poverty.

Mexico, 16 September 1810
Revolution has broken out here, inspired by the battlecry of the parish priest of the village of Dolores, a man demoted by his church but loved by his parishioners.

A follower of French philosophy, especially that of Rousseau, Father Miguel Hidalgo de Costilla has always sided with the underdogs of society, the Indians and the peasants. He has also been plotting against the authorities.

Hearing that the plot had been discovered and that the government was about to arrest him, Hidalgo chose this morning's sermon to act. After distributing weapons to his trusted supporters, he addressed a large crowd gathered at the church.

"My children, this day comes to us a new dispensation. Are you ready to receive it? Will you be free? Long live our Lady of Guadalupe, down with bad government! Death to the Spaniards!"

This *grito de Dolores*, or warcry of Dolores, set a great march in motion. It appears that as many as ten thousand Indians and a number of peasants have taken to the roads, a rag-tag but enthusiastic army. They have camped out for the night, but are heading for the city, their parish priest at their head.

Italian chemist describes nature of gases

Turin, Italy, 1811
A professor of physics at Turin university, Amadeo Avogadro, has proposed a new law governing the nature of gases. The hypothesis is that, under the same pressure and at the same temperature, equal volumes of different gases contain an equal number of molecules.

This is a controversial statement because it implies that atoms of the same element can become bound together in molecules – a completely novel concept.

1811 (1811-1812)

New Orleans, 10 January 1811. An uprising of over 400 slaves is put down. Sixty-six Negroes are either killed in the fighting or executed and their heads strung up along the road to the plantation where the uprising began.

Washington DC, 15 January 1811. In a secret session, Congress plans to annex Spanish East Florida.

USA, 2 February 1811. President Madison sends Britain an ultimatum, demanding that it revoke its orders in council of 1807 which justify British harassment of US shipping.

Briain, 5 February 1811. The Regency Act is passed, authorising George, the prince of Wales, to exercise the powers of regency in the place of his father, George III, who is insane.

Austria, 15 March 1811. The wave of financial speculation due to the Continental System of blockades, and inflation caused by soaring military expenditure, bankrupts the state.

Britain, 10 May 1811. With the country in the grip of economic crisis, the government is forced to adopt paper money as currency.

Virginia, 16 May 1811. Acting in response to instructions calling for the vindication of "the injured honor of our Navy", Commodore John Rodgers of the warship *President* attacks the British sloop *Little Belt* by night, killing nine and wounding 23.

Vienna, May 1811. Ludwig van Beethoven performs his fifth piano concerto, nicknamed *The Emperor*.

Spain, 28 June 1811. While the French commander Massena is defeated by Wellington at Fuentes de Onoro on 3 May, his compatriot Suchet takes the fortress of Tarragona.

Mexico, 30 July 1811. The parish priest Hidalgo, who called for Mexican independence last year, is executed, having been tried by the court of the Inquisition.

Prussia, 14 September 1811. By adopting an edict concerning the regularisation of relations between peasants and the nobility, Prussia abolishes the feudal system.

Europe, 17 October 1811. Prussia and Russia sign a military convention for joint action in the event of an invasion by France.

Washington DC, 4 November 1811. The 12th Congress convenes. It is Republican and dominated by a new breed of nationalistic, expansion-orientated "war-hawks".

Mississippi, 16 December 1811. A catastrophic earthquake hits the Mississippi valley.

Egypt, 1811. The Ottoman sultan concedes supreme authority in Egypt to Mohammed Ali, an Albanian tobacco merchant who entered Ottoman service leading Albanian troops in the war against the French.

Japan, 1811. Following the Russian raids of 1807, the Japanese capture the Russian LieutenantCommander Golovnin and his subordinates and take them to imprisonment in Matsumae.

Prussia, 24 February 1812. France and Prussia sign a military convention by which Prussia grants French troops all the quartering and provisioning facilities it needs on the way to Russia, as well as sending it a corps of 20,000 men.

Austria, 4 March 1812. Napoleon signs a military convention with Metternich similar to that concluded with Prussia. The Austrian corps is to be 30,000 strong.

Venezuela, 12 March 1812. An earthquake wreaks havoc in the capital, Caracas, and other republican territories. Royalist clergy proclaim the disaster as divine vengeance on the revolutionaries.

New Orleans, 4 April 1812. The territory of Orleans becomes the 18th state and will be known as Louisiana.

Finland, 9 April 1812. Russia and Sweden sign a treaty of alliance at Abo. Sweden cedes Finland to Russia and agrees to supply 30,000 men to co-operate with Russian forces. Russia agrees to help Sweden annex Norway.

France, 9 May 1812. Rejecting proposals by the Russian Czar Alexander questioning the policy of the continental blockade, Napoleon breaks relations with Russia.

Germany, 1812. The idealist philosopher Hegel publishes the first volume of his *Science of Logic*.

France, 1812. The naturalist Georges Cuvier publishes the first volume of *Researches on the Bones of Fossil Vertebrates*.

South Africa, 1812. During the fourth Cape Eastern Frontier War, the British under Colonel Graham support the land-hungry Boer ranchers and expel 22,000 Khoisan and Xhosa eastwards across Fish river. They then set up a line of forts along the river.

Mexico, 1812. Worried by the growing independence movement, the viceroy, Venegas, suspends ecclesiastical immunity, requisitions Mexico City University and the convents for quartering troops, and suspends the exemption from military service for students.

Regent replaces Britain's insane monarch

London, 5 February 1811

The prince of Wales was today appointed prince regent and effective king of England as his father, King George III, slipped further into madness.

Under the Regency Act – approved by a special commission because of the king's insanity – the prince regent's powers are severely limited. For the first 12 months he can make no long-lasting changes that the king might object to on his recovery. Consequently, the prince regent cannot grant peerages pensions, or deal in the king's property.

The care of the king has been entrusted to his wife, Queen Charlotte. The 73-year-old monarch, who lost his sight last year and has a history of mental illness, became so chronically depressed after the death of his favourite daughter Amelia last autumn that he was unable to transact official business. The 49-year-old prince regent is the complete opposite of his father, with whom he clashed over his flamboyant lifestyle, his womanising, his excessive habits and his Whig politics.

Keeping up with the regent, a dedicated and time-consuming vocation.

Followers of "Ned Ludd" smash machines

Nottingham, 1811

They move about in bands at night, masked and sworn to secrecy, smashing up the new machinery which is taking over in the textile industry. Their leader is a mysterious Ned Ludd of Sherwood Forest, who has been likened to the legendary Robin Hood as a friend of the poor and discontented.

The hardships caused by the long war with France have been greatly increased by the new technology, which is displacing the old handicraft methods of producing stockings and lace. The high levels of productivity achieved by the new knitting frames have reduced the demand for labour, so even those craftsmen who keep their jobs suffer wage cuts.

The Luddites are well-organised and have public opinion on their side. They have been reported in action as far north as Yorkshire and Lancashire.

Grimm Brothers collect German folklore

The Young Giant and the Tailor.

Kassel, 1812

A book of folk-tales entitled *Kinder und Hausmarchen* has caused enormous interest in Germany. The tales have been collected mainly in this area by Jakob and Wilhelm Grimm. They contain no fairies, but plenty of magic, enchanted princes and princesses, witches and cruel stepmothers, stupid giants and helpful dwarfs. Some stories are similar to the eight published by Charles Perrault in Paris as *Tales of Mother Goose* in 1797. *Aschputtel* by the Grimms is Perrault's *Cinderella*, but he did not have *Snowwhite* or *Rapunzel*.

American troops beat Shawnee Indians

Indiana, 7 November 1811

As European settlers continue to press westwards, a major confrontation with the native Indian people was inevitable. It came today at Tippecanoe where an army of 1,000 soldiers – said to be the equal in quality to the finest in the US – came face with the combined tribes of the Shawnee people.

Rebuffed in territorial demands by the governor, Harrison, the Indian leader, Tecumseh, rode to the south to unite the other tribes. Harrison chose to anticipate the chief and marched into Indian territory. The Shawnees attacked as soldiers slept and battle raged at close range – often hand-to-hand – throughout the night until a series of charges drove the Indians off. Harrison's men have marched on the Indian town of Prophetstown and razed it to the ground. Many believe that Harrison's victory was by no means as decisive as he would care to claim. The Shawnees were beaten, but not vanquished. It is believed that they were inspired by British agents.

US troops bayonet charge Shawnee Indians during the battle of Tippecanoe.

Things happen like this – probably

Paris, France, 1812

The French mathematician Pierre Simon de Laplace, has published a philosophical essay, *A Theoretical Analysis of Probabilities*.

Imagine this game of chance between two players. They each toss a coin. For every head, player A pays player B £1, and vice-versa for every tail. What is the probability that a player will be ruined?

Such questions have obsessed de Laplace for years. He has studied not only games of chance, like dice, cards and roulette wheels, but also the physical world.

Probability, de Laplace asserts, can be applied to the chances of having twins, the drift of smoke from a chimney, the eventual fate of the universe itself.

US declares war on Great Britain

Baltimore, 19 June 1812

American ships sailed from Chesapeake Bay today bearing giant flags proclaiming "Free Trade and Sailors' Rights". The United States of America is at war with its former colonial master, Great Britain. There are several reasons: the first is the frustration felt by the Americans at the trade restrictions imposed by Britain in retaliation for Napoleon's decree declaring Britain to be under blockade. The second is the way in which British ships are stopping American ships and "pressing" alleged British deserters, many of them US seamen, into service with the Royal Navy. Britain's relations with hostile Indians in the northwest of America are another factor.

Egyptian "pasha" destroys Mamelukes

Mohammed Ali's treacherous massacre of the Mameluke rebels in Cairo castle. By ending their threat to his rule, he can modernise Egypt.

Cairo, 1 March 1811

Leaders of the Mameluke dynasty were shot down here today in an act of treachery by Mohammed Ali, Egypt's ruler. Those who remained in their Upper Egypt homeland are being hunted down, and their homes destroyed.

Mohammed Ali, who always saw the Mamelukes as the single greatest threat to his rule, has avoided confrontation for several years, while taking comfort from a continuing feud between the two main houses of the Mamelukes, which sufficiently diverted their energies from taking over the throne.

The Egyptian leader is known for both his subtlety and his ruthlessness. He planned each of his moves. At first he appeared to be offering an olive branch when he invited the Mameluke leaders to a ceremony in Cairo's citadel to invest Ahmed Tusun Pasha, Mohammed Ali's son, as leader of an expedition against the Wahhabis in the Arabian peninsula. But the Egyptian ruler's assassins were waiting for them.

There followed a massacre, as Mohammed Ali's black slaves poured down bullets from the citadel's walls on the Albanian slaves, castrated in boyhood, who once served Egypt as her finest soldiers and now oppress her with their decadence.

Crazed businessman murders British PM

London, 11 May 1812

Towards five o'clock in the evening Spencer Perceval, the prime minister, was passing through the lobby of the House of Commons when a man rushed up brandishing a pistol. He fired one shot. The bullet struck Perceval in the breast and entered his heart. He died soon afterwards.

The assassin, it was learned, is a businessman, John Bellingham, who has been ruined by the war. It seems that for some time he has been besieging government offices vainly seeking redress. Though he is undoubtedly insane, he will be sentenced to death.

John Bellingham shoots Spencer Perceval in the House of Commons.

1812 (1812-1813)

Ottoman Empire, 28 May 1812. The Ottomans sign a peace treaty with Russia at Bucharest whereby Russia acquires Bessarabia (*Romania*) and the Ottoman-Russian border is set along the Pruth river.

Britain, 9 June 1812. Following the assassination of the prime minister, Spencer Perceval, Lord Liverpool forms a new ministry.

USA, 19 June 1812. Prompted by British interference with US shipping and the press-ganging of US sailors, the USA declares war on Britain.

Russia, 24 June 1812. Napoleon, at the head of the *Grand Armee*, crosses the Nieman and begins his invasion of Russia.

Poland, 28 June 1812. Napoleon captures Vilna, the capital of Russian Poland.

London, 29 June 1812. Mrs Sarah Siddons, the queen of the English stage, gives her last performance, as Lady Macbeth.

Sweden, 18 July 1812. Britain signs the treaty of Orebro, making peace with Russia and Sweden.

Spain, 22 July 1812. British forces under the duke of Wellington defeat the French at Salamanca.

Venezuela, 26 July 1812. Francisco Miranda the commander of the Venezuelan revolutionary army, surrenders to the Spanish, who have regained control of the country after the creation of an independent *junta* in 1810.

Spain, 12 August 1812. The British commander Wellington occupies Madrid, forcing Joseph Bonaparte, the king of Spain, to abandon the city.

Russia, 18 August 1812. Napoleon enters Smolensk.

North America, August 1812. General William Hull, the governor of Michigan, loses his battle plans to the British, who go on to capture Fort Detroit. Hull's campaign was intended as the first of two pincer movements designed to knock Canada out of the war.

Russia, 14 September 1812. Having forced the Russians to retreat after the battle of Borodino earlier in the month, Napoleon enters Moscow, which has been set on fire by its fleeing inhabitants.

Canada, 16 October 1812. British forces defeat US forces at Queenstown, near Niagara Falls. The Americans were attempting to cross the Niagara river and eliminate Canada from the war.

Russia, 18 October 1812. Murat, the king of the Two Sicilies, commanding Napoleon's cavalry, is defeated by Russia at Vinkovo.

Russia, 19 October 1812. After failing to persuade Czar Alexander to come to terms, Napoleon begins a retreat from Moscow.

Spain, 2 November 1812. Joseph Bonaparte reoccupies Madrid after the British fail to take Burgos, to which they laid siege in September.

Canada, 23 November 1812. Demoralised by a tactical error which resulted in two of their own columns fighting each other, the US forces abandon their Canada campaign and retreat to winter quarters in New York state.

Russia, 28 November 1812. The survivors of the *Grand Armee* cross the Beresina.

USA, 2 December 1812. James Madison is re-elected president.

Russia, 5 December 1812. Napoleon decides to return to Paris to put down a rumoured plot against him and raise a new army.

Prussia, 20 December 1812. The remnants of the *Grand Armee* reach eastern Prussia.

Lithuania, 30 December 1812. Having deserted the French after the catastrophic invasion of Russia, Prussia signs a treaty of neutrality with Russia at Tauroggen.

East Africa, 1812. The people of Lamu defeat the army of Mombasa and Pate at the battle of Shela. Lamu becomes independent of Pate.

Germany, 1812. The folklore experts Jakob and Wilhelm Grimm publish a volume of *Fairy Tales*.

England, 1812. Lord Byron publishes his *Childe Harold's Pilgrimage*, a poetical account of the author's grand tour of Europe.

Canada, 22 January 1813. British forces under Henry Proctor defeat a US contingent planning an attack on Fort Detroit.

France, 25 January 1813. Napoleon forces Pope Pius VII to sign a second concordat and sanction the 1809 French annexation of the papal states.

Austria, 30 January 1813. Austria signs an armistice treaty with Russia.

Prussia, 3 February 1813. Frederick William III of Prussia calls all his people to arms.

Poland, 18 February 1813. Czar Alexander enters Warsaw at the head of his army.

South America, 24 February 1813. The British ship *Peacock* is sunk by an American ship off the coast of Guiana.

Prussia, 27 February 1813. Frederick William III signs an offensive and defensive alliance with Russia at Kalisz.

Wellington captures Madrid for Britain

Madrid, 12 August 1812

Viscount Wellington is winning significant victories against the French and today entered Madrid with 28,000 troops to be greeted with great enthusiasm. Joseph Bonaparte, Napoleon's brother, has evacuated the Spanish capital, and everywhere in Spain guerrilla forces have taken new heart.

The British general's offensive to clear the Peninsula has gone on for more than a year. At Salamanca last month, a mass of British cavalry fell upon 40,000 French troops who were beaten in some 40 minutes. "There was no mistake," Wellington said. "Everything went as it should. There never was an army so beaten in so short a time."

The Peninsular War, seen in all its horrors, through the eyes of Goya.

The ripples of this first British and Spanish victory in open battle continue spreading. In Britain criticism of the long war is stilled. Wellington may still find it impossible to corner the French army in the north of Spain. But the pattern of the campaign is now of a French withdrawal northwards, which would free much of southern Spain.

Lord Elgin's Greek marbles go on display

Part of the Parthenon frieze which was taken to Britain by Lord Elgin.

London, 1812

The British public is to be allowed to see the controversial Greek antiquities shipped back from Athens over the past decade by the Scottish peer Lord Elgin. With the arrival this year of the last 80 cases, the collection, which has been assembled in a private house in Park Lane, is now complete.

The removal of the marbles – priceless relics of the Parthenon and other ancient Hellenic monuments – has cost Lord Elgin his reputation. The former British ambassador to the Ottoman empire is now branded a vandal and a thief.

In his defence the art-loving peer claims that the Turkish authorities allowed him to remove parts of the monuments although he originally only sought permission for his draughtsmen to take casts and make drawings. Only when he saw the damage done by the Turks did he decide to remove them, he says.

Russian winter drives out Napoleon

Russia, 29 November 1812

The remnants of Napoleon's *Grand Armee* crossed the Beresina yesterday with the rearguard holding off the Russians. Fifty thousand men got across before General Eble set fire to the two makeshift bridges which he had thrown across the river. He delayed destroying the bridges for two hours after his deadline, but thousands of stragglers were left behind to be killed or captured. The great army which crossed into Russia on 24 June is no more. Today its survivors face a new peril: the Russian winter.

Marshal Ney wrote a hurried letter to his wife in which he described the horrors of the French retreat. "The army marches covered in great snowflakes. The stragglers fall to the lances of the Cossacks. As for me, I cover the retreat. Behind files the army in broken ranks. It is a mob without purpose, famished, feverish.

"The Grand Army is surrounded by the Russians on the banks of the Beresina. It is necessary to construct a bridge. At the order of General Eble three hundred sappers hurl themselves into the icy water with a sublime devotion.

"The crossing begins and the Russian shells fall into the middle of this crowded mass, jostling and pushing – a dreadful sight. General Famine and General Winter, rather than the Russian bullets, have conquered the Grand Army."

The disintegration of the army started the moment that Napoleon ordered the retreat from burnt-out Moscow on 19 October. His army was still 100,000 strong, but it was encumbered by its loot, its sick and wounded – and its 600 guns.

There is no food. Bands of Cossacks and partisans cut down foraging parties unprotected by the cavalry whose horses have died. Thousands of men are killed in running battles. Ney's rearguard has 800 men left out of 8,000. Now men are staggering through the snow, dying where they fall. Only Napoleon still eats well. He always has white bread, beef and mutton, and rice and beans or lentils, his favourite vegetables. He has Chambertin to drink and his linen is fresh. Even so, not one murmur is heard against him from the troops.

Invading Russia, the eternal problem, seen by cartoonist George Cruikshank.

The burning of Moscow by Russian patriotic incendiaries in September 1812.

Authoress exposes pride and prejudice

London, 29 January 1813

A new novel "by a Lady" entitled *Pride and Prejudice* (Egerton, 18 shillings) is attracting the attention of discriminating readers who believe it to be the work of the same Lady as *Sense and Sensibility*, published two years ago. Reviewers call it "a blend of instruction and moral entertainment".

It is the story of Elizabeth Bennet, one of the many daughters of a foolish, husband-hunting mother, and her gradual admission of love for the haughty, aristocratic Mr Darcy. The insight and tart precision of the character-drawing, especially of foolish or disagreeable people, such as Lady Catherine de Bourgh and the toady Mr Collins, cause some to call the nameless author the pioneer of "the modern novel", though others find her tame compared to romantic melodrama.

Some profess to know that the author is a spinster, Jane Austen, who lives in Hampshire.

Jane Austen, the 38-year-old who is said to be the anonymous author.

Russia and the Ottomans agree treaty

Bucharest, 28 May 1812

A peace of sorts has been reached in the six-year on-again, off-again war between Russia and the Ottoman. The treaty was signed here today after mediation by the British envoy, Stratford Canning.

The Russians had for years been clawing at the Ottoman empire's frontiers in Anatolia, but then in 1806, alarmed by growing French influence in the Balkans, they invaded the Rumanian principalities. They were not, however, left free to exploit their gains. Hearing of Napoleon's plans to invade Russia, Moscow hastily came to terms with the Ottomans, retaining Bessarabia, but surrendering the Principalities and Serbia.

Argentina fails to spread revolution

Buenos Airies, Argentina, 1812

Argentina has failed to spread its revolution to Uruguay, Paraguay and Bolivia. An army under Manuel Belgrano sent to liberate Paraguay has been defeated.

A Spanish colony since the 16th century, the Argentinians gained national confidence in 1806 and 1807 when they drove two British expeditions out of the country. In 1810 the country refused to accept Napoleon's brother, Joseph Bonaparte, as king of Spain, and established a junta, dominated by Mariano Moreno and Manuel Belgrano. Morena is now dead and Belgrano defeated. For Argentinia's revolutionaries, who aim for a free continent, it is a bitter blow.

1813 ⇒

Sweden, 3 March. Britain signs a treaty with Sweden guaranteeing not to oppose the union of Norway with Sweden. Under the treaty Britain pays Sweden a subsidy in return for its providing the allies with an army of 30,000 men commanded by the regent, Prince Bernadotte.

Germany, 4 March. The Russians reach Berlin. The French garrison evacuates the city without a fight.

Germany, 18 March. Russian troops occupy Hamburg and, on the 27 March Dresden, the capital of Saxony.

Rome, 24 March. Pope Pius VII revokes the concordat signed with Napoleon in January at Fontainebleau.

Prussia, 27 March. King Frederick William III declares war on France.

North America, 15 April. US troops under James Wilkinson seize the Spanish-held city of Mobile (*in Alabama*).

Canada, 27 April. US troops capture York (*now Toronto*), the seat of government in Ontario, from the British.

Germany, 2 May. Napoleon defeats a Russian and Prussian army at Grossgorschen near Lutzen.

USA, 9 May. US troops under William Harrison break a ten-day British siege of Fort Meigs in Ohio.

Germany, 18 May. Swedish troops land in Pomerania.

Paris, 20 May. Panic breaks out on the stock exchange.

Germany, 20 May. Napoleon engages the allies at Bautzen.

USA, 27 May. US troops under Winfield Scott take control of Lake Ontario after dislodging the British from three forts in the area.

Germany, 4 June. Worn out by recent defeats, the allies sign a 40-day armistice with Napoleon at Pleischwitz. Despite heavy losses, Napoleon's troops have succeed in pushing the allied armies back to Silesia.

Spain, 12 June. Madrid is evacuated by the French.

Germany, 15 June. At Reichenbach, Britain signs conventions with Prussia and Russia, establishing a new coalition.

Spain, 21 June. French forces under Jourdan are defeated by the British under Wellington at the battle of Vittoria. Joseph Bonaparte, the king of Spain, flees to France.

Germany, 27 June. Russia, Prussia and Austria sign the treaty of Reichenbach, agreeing that the duchy of Warsaw should be abolished, the Illyrian provinces restored to Austria and French conquests in northern Germany relinquished. If France refuses to accept these terms, Austria will declare war.

India, 1 July. The East India Company's monopoly of trade in India is abolished.

Prague, 15 July. Representatives of Napoleon and the allies meet in Prague to discuss peace.

Austria, 12 August. Austria declares war on France.

Britain, 14 August. The US ship *Argus*, which has captured 27 ships in the Channel over the past few months, is taken and boarded by the British.

Germany, 17 August. Prussia, Russia and Sweden sign the protocol of Trachenberg, agreeing on an offensive against Napoleon.

Ottoman Empire, August. Taking advantage of the war in Europe, the Ottoman forces occupy Serbia and destroy the forces of Karageorges, the Serbian independence leader.

South America, August. While the Spanish are busy reconquering Chile, Simon Bolivar reoccupies Venezuela and its capital, Caracas.

Germany, 23 August. French forces under Oudinot are defeated at Gross-Beeren by the Swedes led by Prince Bernadotte.

Germany, 27 August. Napoleon defeats the main allied army under Schwarzenberg at Dresden.

Germany, 29 August. French forces under Macdonald are defeated by Blucher at Katzbach.

North America, 30 August. In revenge for white encroachment on their land, Creek Indians raid Fort Mims (*in Alabama*) and massacre over 500 whites.

Germany, 30 August. French forces under Vandamme are defeated by the allies at Kulm.

South Africa. A Griqua republic is proclaimed at Klaarwater *(Griquatown)* on the north side of the Orange river. The Griqua are people of Khoisan and Boer ancestry, who settled as horsemen, ranchers and hunters north of Cape Colony.

Italy. Gioacchino Rossini's opera *Tancred* opens in Venice to great acclaim.

England. Eight editions of *The Giaour*, a poem by Lord Byron, are sold out in a year.

Europe is now Napoleon's family business

Paris

Napoleon may be a great general and ruler of the "Grand Empire" but he is still a Corsican at heart and in family matters he behaves like one. His brothers and sisters expect to share in his good fortune and he has not disappointed them. He has loaded them with honours and turned the ruling of Europe into a family business.

He made his elder brother, Joseph, king of Naples in 1806 and, although Joseph proved highly inefficient, made him king of Spain instead two years later. The crown of Naples was simply transferred to Marshal Murat who had married Napoleon's sister, Caroline.

Another brother, Louis, was made king of Holland in 1806 after reluctantly marrying Hortense Beauharnais, Josephine's daughter by her first husband. But he only lasted for four years, Napoleon forcing him to abdicate when he objected to the ruinous effect of the Continental System (forbidding trade with Britain) on Holland.

Jerome, the youngest brother, was made king of Westphalia in 1807 and has pretensions to a military career. Only Lucien of the brothers has no title. He fled from Napoleon and is interned in England. Elisa, the most intelligent of the Bonaparte sisters, married Felix Bacciochi, an infantry captain, and was made princess of Lucca and Piombino in 1805 and duchess of Tuscany in 1809. Napoleon, it seems, is creating his own dynasty. But how long will it last?

Caroline Murat, the queen of Naples (left) and Elisa Bonaparte, (right), sister of Napoleon.

Lucien Bonaparte (left), and Joseph Bonaparte, the king of Spain (right), Napoleon's brothers.

Imperial ties: Jerome Bonaparte (left) and Louis Bonaparte (right).

James Gillray's Napoleon: a "little Corsican gardener" planting his garden.

Britain moves to curb the power of the East India Company

Calcutta, India
As the expansionist policy of Lord Wellesley is brought to a halt, the British government has drastically curtailed the powers of the East India Company and its *nabobs*, ending their monopoly of trade.

Reform is long overdue. The Company's policies are confusing and contradictory. In the south, Sir Thomas Munro is deliberately bypassing the indigenous aristocracy to better the lot of the cultivators. In the west, Mountstuart Elphinstone is strengthening the aristocracy and rejecting the "levelling" tendencies of Munro. In the north, the landlords are permitted to exploit the peasants at their will. Everywhere the peasants, unable to pay taxes with cash, are taking out mortgages on their land which they can never repay, creating a new landless class. Worse, the Company's treaties with one native prince after another, stationing troops in the prince's domains, are institutionalising misrule.

The last days of the nabobs, the English who made their fortune in India.

Italy trying to wriggle out from under the imperial thumb

Italy
There is turmoil throughout the country as the Italians attempt to escape from the collapsing "Grand Empire" of Napoleon. Austria, once more allied with Prussia, is threatening to invade, while the forces of Europe gather for a climactic battle in Germany.

The Italians are not inclined to die for Napoleon any more. They fought bravely in Russia, and less than one in eight survived the horrors of the retreat from Moscow.

Economically, the country is groaning under the system of tariffs imposed by the French. Imports of machinery have been discouraged so that Italy cannot compete with French manufacturers and serves only as a supplier of food.

The blockade has had a devastating effect on the ports. Genoa has been ruined. Milan is being swept by a wave of bankruptcies. And all the time the kingdom has to contribute two and a half million *lire* a month to the empire. As the war returns to Italian soil so the protests of the businessmen grow louder.

The church also has a quarrel with Napoleon for, despite his attempts to appease the clerics, they will not forgive him for abducting the pope from Rome.

Then there is Marshal Murat, the king of Naples, the dashing cavalryman who is married to Napoleon's sister, Caroline. He is with Napoleon in Germany, but the emperor does not trust him – and with good cause, for he has already tried to make a deal with the allies to preserve his kingdom.

Above all there is the rising tide of nationalism and secret societies such as the *Carbonari* who are fighting for Italy's independence.

A village in Italy, by Gianbattista Cimaroli: ruins, peasants and cattle.

Wellington lances Napoleon's dream of Spanish glory

Spain, July
After five years of bloody conflict the Peninsular War appears to be over with the beaten French army continuing to retreat across the Pyrenees. This is the end of Napoleon's "Grand Design". The emperor's "Spanish ulcer" – Lord Wellington's military skill and constant guerrilla activity – has reversed his great achievements.

Wellington, the Anglo-Irish aristocrat who learned his skills in India, tied down vastly superior French forces. After victories he has often retreated, compelling the badly-mauled French to stagger along in pursuit until they finally arrived once again in front of carefully prepared and disciplined defences. Wellington has been coordinating the activities of some 200,000 British and Spanish troops extending from Catalonia through central Spain to the Portuguese border. Wellington has benefitted from Spanish priests supplying him with intelligence about the French army. He said: "The French never did or said a single thing I did not know, and they never suspected it."

Lord Wellington: his soldiers referred to him as "Old Nosey".

Thus last month he cornered the French at Vittoria. The enormous booty included five million dollars, of which only about $100,000 has reached Wellington's military chest. The campaign has a catastrophe for Napoleon, and now he faces a grand European alliance.

1813 (1813-1814)

Germany, 6 September 1813. While attempting to take Berlin, French forces under Marshal Ney are defeated by the Prussians under Bulow at Dennewitz.

Germany, 9 September 1813. Russia, Prussia and Austria sign the treaty of Teplitz, an alliance guaranteeing mutual assistance against Napoleon.

Canada, 10 September 1813. The British fleet on Lake Erie is destroyed by American warships.

Germany, 3 October 1813. Prussian troops cross the Elbe.

China, 8 October 1813. With the help of palace eunuchs, members of the millennial religious sects calling themselves the Eight Trigrams are thwarted in their attempt to seize the Forbidden City in Beijing. This violence coincides with disturbances in Shandong and Henan by associated sectarians.

France, 8 October 1813. Having liberated Spain from French occupation, British troops under Wellington invade southern France.

Germany, 8 October 1813. By the treaty of Ried, signed by Austria and Bavaria, Bavaria withdraws from the Confederation of the Rhine and joins the allies against Napoleon.

Germany, 19 October 1813. After defeating Napoleon in a three-day battle near Leipzig, the allies storm Leipzig, capturing the king of Saxony and forcing the king of Westphalia to flee.

Austria, October 1813. Driven out of Serbia by the Ottomans, Karageorges, the leader of the Serbian independence movement, takes refuge in Austria, where he is imprisoned.

Ottoman Empire, 28 October 1813. British troops occupy Ragusa (Dubrovnik).

North America, 3 November 1813. In retaliation for the attack by Creek Indians on Fort Mims in August, US troops destroy the Indian village of Tallushatchee in the Mississippi valley.

Mexico, 6 November 1813. Jose Maria Morelos proclaims Mexican independence from Spain at the congress of Chilpancingo.

Florida, 9 November 1813. US troops under Andrew Jackson kill almost 300 Indians in an attack on the village of Talladega.

Paris, 15 November 1813. Napoleon returns to Paris after seeing his meagre troops cross the Rhine between 2 and 4 November. Of an army 450,000-strong at the start of the autumn, there are no more than 50,000 survivors.

Netherlands, 15 November 1813. The Dutch rise up against the French, expelling French officials.

USA, 16 November 1813. The British announce a blockade of Long Island Sound, leaving only the New England coast open to shipping.

Germany, 1 December 1813. Napoleon rejects the peace terms offered by the allies at Frankfurt on 9 November.

France, 11 December 1813. By the treaty of Valencay, Napoleon recognises his prisoner Ferdinand VII as king of Spain and releases him.

USA, 17 December 1813. An embargo banning trade with Britain comes into effect. It is aimed at New England merchants who have been supplying the British in Canada.

North America, 23 December 1813. US troops under Ferdinand Claiborne take Escanachaha, the so-called "holy city" of the Creek nation, driving the death toll higher in the Indian war.

France, 31 December 1813. During New Year's Eve the Prussian forces under Blucher cross the Rhine, beginning the allied invasion of France.

Britain, 31 December 1813. The foreign secretary, Lord Castlereagh, is sent to Germany with full powers to give assistance to the allies.

Russia, 1813. Under the terms of the treaty of Gulistan, Russia receives control of the Caucasus region from Persia.

Colombia, 1813. Colombia declares itself independent of Spain.

Italy, 11 January 1814. The king of Naples, Joachim Murat, enters into an alliance with the Austrians – whom last year he crushed at Dresden – and decides to occupy central Italy.

Scandinavia, 14 January 1814. Under the treaty of Kiel, Bernadotte, the prince regent of Sweden and marshal of the northern armies against Napoleon, forces Denmark to surrender Norway to him.

France, 1 February 1814. After defeating Blucher at Brienne on 29 January, Napoleon is defeated at La Rothiere.

France, 14 February 1814. Napoleon wins his fourth victory in four days over Blucher, at Vauchamps.

France, February 1814. At the conference of Chatillon-sur-Seine, the allies offer to return France to its 1792 borders, but Napoleon rejects the proposal.

British outgunned by the US Navy

Lake Erie, USA, 10 September 1813
The Royal Navy suffered a humiliating defeat here today when a British fleet struck its colours in surrender to US warships after a long and bloody battle. British victory looked certain when the US flagship, *Lawrence*, hauled down her ensign, but two Royal Naval frigates, *Detroit* and *Queen Charlotte*, collided and became entangled, giving the Americans an easy target. With his masts shot away, it was the British captain's turn to admit defeat.

There will be grim faces when the news reaches the Admiralty in London. The Royal Navy has suffered a string of defeats in single ship actions, with superior US gunnery and seamanship playing a decisive role. The roles were reversed, however, off Cape Anne where *HMS Shannon* beat the equally matched *USS Chesapeake* in a classic duel at sea.

US Navy Commander Oliver Perry directs the battle from a rowing-boat.

Exiled hero fights way back to Venezuela

Caracas, October 1813
After leading 500 guerrillas on a forced march through jungle and swamps, the Venezuelan patriot Simon Bolivar has entered Caracas in triumph. With the flight of the Spanish garrison, Bolivar is hailed as "the Liberator" by the city where he was born 30 years ago.

The son of an affluent family, he studied revolution in Europe before practising it at home. Exiled to neighbouring Colombia after a failed coup last year, he rapidly became a general. As his latest success demonstrates, he is a master of irregular warfare.

What is still uncertain is how completely he will consolidate his hold on Venezuela. A Spanish attempt to restore the *status quo* is a near-certainty. If it should happen Venezuelan national solidarity would be severely tested.

Asteroid's orbit is calculated success

Germany, 1813
Karl Friedrich Gauss, one of the greatest mathematicians of all time, has shown his gratitude to the duke of Brunswick for giving him financial support for his higher studies by performing a remarkable calculation which has defeated all the other mathematicians of the day. Astronomers had discovered the asteroid *Ceres* as it approached the sun, but had been quite unable to work out its orbit. Using his method of calculation, and only three observations, Gauss has been able to describe the asteroid's orbit and enable astronomers to locate *Ceres* with complete accuracy.

Allies defeat Napoleon

The battle of Leipzig, where Napoleon lost 60,000 out of his 190,000 men.

Leipzig, Saxony, 19 October 1813
Napoleon has been totally defeated in a battle which has raged for three days of slaughter. The French, 190,000 strong, faced 320,000 Russians, Prussians, Swedes and Austrians financed by Britain.

Despite the numerical advantage of the allies in this "Battle of the Nations", Napoleon had the best of the first day's fighting, but he lost too many men and waited in vain for the reinforcements to launch a decisive attack. He could have retreated then and saved his army, but chose to stay and fight it out. The turning point came when the Saxons, fighting as allies of the French, changed sides in the middle of the battle.

Yesterday the French were driven off the battlefield into the city. There was only one way of escape, the Lindenau bridge. The survivors poured across this today until it was blown up, the rearguard sacrificed. In the end it was a rout and Napoleon lost 60,000 men. The question being asked now is: how long can he continue the struggle?

Mexico declares it is independent

Chilpancingo, Mexico, 1814
After 300 years of smouldering resentment, Mexican nationalists have asserted their country's independence from Spain as Spain itself is relieved from domination by Napoleonic France. Although the new Spanish king, Ferdinand – who has been installed in place of Bonaparte's brother, Joseph – is acting like a dictator, his small army has failed to quell the Mexican insurgents.

Four years ago a priest, Father Miguel Hidalgo y Costilla, preached revolution to Indian peasants and fomented a wave of violence. Hidalgo was executed a year later, but his death inspired a new generation of Mexican patriots. Their new constitution creates a republic and abolishes class distinction as well as slavery.

House of Orange returns to Holland

The Hague, 2 December 1813
Orange cockades were everywhere to be seen today as the rule of the House of Orange was formally restored to this country. The prince, who landed at Scheveningen two days ago, was proclaimed William I, sovereign prince of the Netherlands. The end of French rule became inevitable after Napoleon's defeat at Leipzig. On 12 November Cossack troops moved in and the French military and officials began to leave. The people of Amsterdam revolted on 15 November and formed a provisional government, headed by a former official of King Louis Napoleon. Two days later the revolt spread here and the leaders, who had stood aloof from French rule, called for a return of the Orange dynasty. The prince was waiting in the wings.

Marquis dies but his "sadism" lives on

France, 2 December 1814
Donatien-Alphonse-Francois, the marquis de Sade, died today, still an inmate of the asylum at Charenton where he has been held for the past 13 years. He was 74 a philosopher, and erotic novelist, whose taste for pain as the basis of sexual pleasure will link his name with this particular sexual perversion.

The inventor of sadism: a later view.

Debt-ridden and dogged by scandals that arose from satisfying his sexual tastes, de Sade's life was typical of many aristocrats of the *ancien regime*. It was his writings that raised him above the commonplace debauchee.

His novels, a mix of philosophy and pornography, always emphasising the cruel side of sex, include *Justine* (1791) and *Juliette* (1798). Most notorious of all is the *120 Days of Sodom* (1784), a catalogue of sexual excess, written while he was jailed in the Bastille. De Sade had no illusions as to his character. All his portraits have been destroyed and in his will he hopes that "my memory will be effaced from the mind of men".

"Puffing billy" steams on smooth rails

Northumberland, England, 1814
George Stephenson, the engineer, has just built his first locomotive at the Killingworth colliery in Northumberland. The train is superior to others in many respects. Unlike existing colliery trains, it does not run on notched rails that engage in toothed wheels. Stephenson's rails are smooth, but they are effective even when the coal is being hauled up and down gradients.

It is more powerful than the existing engines designed by Richard Trevithick and John Blenkinsop. It had pulled a load of 30 tons of coal up an incline of one in 450 at a steady speed of four miles per hour. Its inventor is now working on improvements in the engine and boiler springing.

Stephenson has a vision of a country criss-crossed by these new "iron horses", or "puffing billies" as this first train is known, and is looking for financial support.

George Stephenson's "puffing billy", or "iron horse"; a later print.

1814 ⇒

France, 9 March. The four allied powers – Austria, Russia, Prussia and Britain – sign the treaty of Chaumont, negotiated by the British foreign secretary, Lord Castlereagh. Under the terms of the treaty, each ally will supply 150,000 troops to defeat Napoleon and Britain will provide a subsidy of £ 5 million.

France, 10 March. Napoleon is defeated by a combined allied army at the battle of Laon.

France, 12 March. Led by the duke of Wellington, British forces occupy Bordeaux.

France, 21 March. After failing to get the better of Blucher's troops, Napoleon is defeated at Arcis-sur-Aube by an Austrian army under the command of Schwarzenberg.

North America, 27 March. US troops under General Andrew Jackson inflict a crushing defeat on the Creek Indians at Horseshoe Bend (*in eastern Alabama*). More than 800 Indians lose their lives in the battle.

Paris, 30 March. Paris – encircled, poorly defended and flooded with refugees – surrenders to the allies.

Paris, 31 March. Czar Alexander and Frederick William III of Prussia enter Paris in triumph.

France, 6 April. Granted the sovereignty of the island of Elba and a pension from the French government, Napoleon abdicates at Fontainebleau. He is allowed to retain the title of emperor.

USA, 14 April. The Embargo and Non-Importation Acts, banning trade with Britain, are repealed.

Italy, 28 April. After rising up against the French earlier in the month, Milan is occupied by the Austrians.

France, 2 May. Having disembarked at Calais on 24 April, Louis XVIII issues the proclamation of St Ouen, making known his intention to govern as a constitutional monarch.

Paris, 3 May. Louis XVIII enters Paris.

Mediterranean, 4 May. Napoleon disembarks at Portoferraio on the island of Elba.

Spain, 4 May. King Ferdinand VII abolishes the 1812 constitution.

Norway, 17 May. A new constitution is adopted, providing for a single-chamber national assembly and denying the king an absolute veto and the right to dissolve parliament.

Italy, 20 May. Victor Emmanuel, the king of Piedmont, enters Turin.

Rome, 24 May. Pope Pius VII, who was exiled to France after Napoleon's annexation of the papal states, returns to Rome.

Paris, 30 May. The treaty of Paris returns France to its 1792 frontiers. It is agreed that the final settlement of Europe will be made at a congress to be held in Vienna.

France, 14 June. Louis XVIII grants a constitutional charter providing for an hereditary monarch, a chamber of peers nominated by the king and a chamber of elected deputies.

Canada, 5 July. US troops under Jacob Brown defeat a superior British force at Chippewa.

USA, 22 July. Five Indian tribes in Ohio make peace with the USA and declare war on the British.

Britain, 25 July. The engineer George Stephenson tests his first steam locomotive, at Killingworth colliery.

Canada, 25 July. British and US forces fight each other to a standstill at Lundy's Lane, in one of the bloodiest battles of their war which broke out in 1812.

North America, 9 August. By the treaty of Fort Jackson, ending the Creek war, the Creek Indians are forced to cede 23 million acres (*half of Alabama and part of southern Georgia*) to the whites.

USA, 25 August. The British capture and burn down much of Washington, DC, including the White House, causing President Madison to flee.

USA, 11 September. US forces led by Thomas Macdonough rout the British fleet on Lake Champlain.

USA, 13 September. British troops make an unsuccessful attack on Baltimore. During the battle, the American Francis Scott Key composes a patriotic song entitled "The Star-Spangled Banner".

New York City, October. *Fulton*, the world's first steam-engined warship, is launched.

Vienna, 1 November. A congress composed of representatives of almost all the countries of Europe opens.

Canada, 5 November. Having decided to abandon the Niagara frontier, the Americans blow up Fort Erie.

Florida, 7 November. Andrew Jackson attacks and captures Pensacola, defeating the Spanish and driving out a British force.

British army burns down the White House

Revenge for 1776: a British cartoon on the sack of Washington.

Washington, DC, 25 August

This fine capital city is a smouldering ruin tonight, burned by a British invading army which landed in Chesapeake Bay six days ago and marched unopposed to the banks of the Potomac river. The White House is a charred hulk, the House of Representatives and the Library of Congress totally gutted, as are many other fine buildings.

With only 500 militiamen to defend Washington against 4,000 infantrymen – fresh from campaigning in France – the militiamen had little chance. They assembled across the Eladensburg Bridge over the River Potomac, but fled in the face of a British assault supported by volleys of Gongrave rockets. President Madison, who had placed far too much confidence in the abilities of both his militia and himself was forced to flee, but his wife Dolly, watched the capital blazing from the safety of a friend's house in Virginia. She has rescued the life sized portrait of George Washington and the original Declaration of Independence.

Napoleon's fall allows writer back

Paris

Now that Napoleon has abdicated, the political thinker and writer Germaine de Stael is back in Paris. The emperor banned her from her native France in 1804 after she turned her salon into a centre of opposition against him. As First Consul, in 1799, he snubbed the erudite de Stael by discarding her advice and opinions.

He could not stomach her view that ideas and feelings are inseparable and was infuriated by her romantic novelel *Delphine*. She was exiled at the age of 38, and spent some of the time under house arrest at her estate by Lake Geneva. There she always kept her salon open to Europeans wishing to plot against the emperor.

"Australia" is new name for new land

Sydney, Australia, 18 July

The Great Southern Continent ha been given a name, *Terra Australis*. The man who named it, Captai Matthew Flinders, died today, 2 hours after the publication of hi book *A Voyage to Terra Australis*.

Flinders, born in 1774, went t seas after reading *Robinson Cruso* when young. In September 1795 h arrived at Port Jackson on the *Rel ance*, and with the ship's surgeon George Bass, began the first majc survey of the continent's coast, cor tinuing it in 1799 in command c first the *Norfolk* and then the *Investigator*. Captured by the French, h spent seven years as a prisoner i Mauritius. It broke his health, an it is a miracle that he lived lon enough to complete his book.

Allies enter Paris and oust Napoleon

Paris, 6 April

Napoleon, faced with an impossible military situation and a revolt by his war-weary marshals, abdicated today at Fontainebleau Palace with the bitter comment: "You wish for repose. All right, you shall have it."

His downfall has been inevitable since his crushing defeat at the "Battle of the Nations" six months ago. He employed his military genius to inflict a series of stinging reverses on the allies as they advanced into France, but with each battle his army grew weaker. On 11 March he wrote: "The Young Guard melts away like snow." Murat abandoned him. Talleyrand betrayed him. His brother, Joseph, tried to organise an address from the Council of State and the National Guard in favour of peace.

Napoleon refused the first allied peace proposals, which would have allowed France to retain her "natural boundaries", sure that he could still defeat them. But as they advanced to Paris so their terms hardened. By 19 March they were demanding that France must accept its "prerevolutionary limits", a price which would have wiped out all the gains the revolution had made. Napoleon refused and decided on one last gamble. He left Paris uncovered, certain that its garrison and people could hold out for months, and withdrew to the east where he planned to attack the allied lines of communication, thus forcing them to withdraw. Unwisely he wrote about this plan to his wife. The courier carrying the letter to her was captured.

The first reaction of the allies on reading this letter was to pursue Napoleon, but Czar Alexander persuaded them to hurry on to Paris where Marmont and Mortier had barely 20,000 men to guard the capital. The French were beaten at La Fere-Champenoise on 25 March, and five days later fought the last battle at Montmartre. That night Marmont surrendered Paris. Napoleon talked of marching on the capital, but two days ago Ney told him: "The army will not march". Napoleon made one last effort to have his son recognised as his successor. But the victors refused. Tonight they have it; the senate has voted for the recall of Louis XVIII and Napoleon has been banished to Elba.

Russians in Paris, collecting souveniers of their travels in western Europe.

The Grand Army bids farewell to the "little corporal" who brought it glory.

Turncoat diplomat finds new role

Paris

The elegant, crippled, devious Talleyrand has been made foreign minister by the restored Louis XVIII as a reward for his successful negotiations with the victorious allies. He is thus restored to the position in which he served Napoleon.

Napoleon had no illusions about him. On one famous occasion when Napoleon got wind of a plot between Talleyrand and Fouche, the police minister, the emperor berated him for half an hour, calling him a thief, a coward and a traitor.

Talleyrand remained impassive and the infuriated "Boney" taunted him with his lameness and his wife's affairs. Then, losing all control, he told him that he was nothing but "shit in a silk stocking". Talleyrand did nothing. When asked why, languidly replied: "I did think of doing so, but I was too lazy." He was, in fact, biding his time, and remained at Napoleon's court in the empty position of vice-grand elector.

He was already convinced that Napoleon was over-ambitious and destined for disaster, and made little secret of the fact that he was preparing for that day. His opportunity came with the allies' advance on Paris. It was he who persuaded the senate to depose the emperor. It was at his house that the czar stayed. And it was he who persuaded the czar to reinstate the Bourbons on the French throne.

Talleyrand: the French diplomat who ended upon the winning side.

The Treaty of Paris rolls back French border to pre-war lines

Paris, 30 May

Talleyrand has obtained relatively favourable peace terms from the victorious allies. In the Treaty of Paris signed today, France, as expected, must generally return to the frontiers of 1792 but will be allowed to keep certain areas of Belgium, Savoy, Alsace and the Rhineland. Britain will keep Malta, but will return all France's captured overseas territories except Tobago, St Lucia and Mauritius. France will pay no indemnity and suffer no humiliation.

The treaty consists of six sections which contain a number of secret clauses. It is said that these entail the transfer of Norway to Bernadotte's rule and the takeover of Belgium by Holland. Northern Italy will be shared by Austria and Piedmont. The treaty also calls for a congress to be held in Vienna "to establish a genuine and durable system to preserve the balance of power in Europe" on the basis of the Paris agreements.

France must be grateful indeed today for Talleyrand's diplomatic skills.

1814 (1814-1815)

USA, 13 December 1814. General Andrew Jackson, who made his reputation fighting Indians, proclaims martial law in New Orleans as British forces disembark at Lake Borne, 40 miles east of the city.

USA, 23 December 1814. Andrew Jackson halts a British advance on New Orleans.

Netherlands, 24 December 1814. British and US representatives sign a treaty in Ghent ending their war. Territory seized by Britain will be returned to the USA. It will take at least a month for the news to reach America.

Paraguay, 1814. Jose Francia becomes dictator of Paraguay, which declared its independence three years ago.

Rome, 1814. Pope Pius VII restores the Inquisition and the Jesuit order.

Denmark, 1814. The grammarian Kristian Rask writes a paper demonstrating the relationship between Icelandic and Slavonic languages and Greek and Latin. He is the first person to suggest the existence of an original Indo-European language.

Spain, 1814. Francisco Goya paints the *Dos de Mayo* and the *Tres de Mayo*, which celebrate the uprising of the citizens of Madrid against French occupation in 1808.

Britain, 1814. *Waverley*, a novel about the Jacobite rebellion of 1745, is a best-seller, but its authorship is a mystery.

London, 1814. The Marylebone Cricket Club plays its first match at Lord's cricket ground.

London, 1814. *The Times* is the first newspaper to be printed on steam presses.

London, 1814. Dulwich Picture Gallery, the first art collection accessible to the public, is opened.

Connecticut, 5 January 1815. Federalists from all over New England draw up the Hartford Convention, demanding several important changes to the US Constitution.

USA, 8 January 1815. The US forces under Andrew Jackson defeat the British at the battle of New Orleans.

USA, 11 February 1815. News of the treaty of Ghent, ending their war with Britain, finally reaches the Americans.

New Zealand, 24 February 1815. The Reverend Samuel Marsden is the first European to purchase land in New Zealand from the Nga-Puhi tribe. He intends use the land to establish a Church Missionary Society station.

France, 1 March 1815. Returning from Elba, Napoleon lands at Cannes with a force of 1,500 men and marches on Paris.

Mediterranean, 3 March 1815. Angered by the resumption of piracy in the Mediterranean, the US Congress authorises hostilities against the *bey* of Algiers.

Netherlands, 13 March 1815. Louis XVIII, the king of France, flees to Ghent.

Paris, 20 March 1815. Napoleon enters Paris.

Vienna, 25 March 1815. Britain, Austria, Prussia and Russia conclude a new alliance against Napoleon.

Austria, 10 April 1815. Austria declares war on Joachim Murat, the king of Naples, who has again given his support to Napoleon.

France, 23 April 1815. An act is passed re-establishing the constitutional charter granted by Louis XVIII last June, but making the chamber of peers hereditary.

Italy, 3 May 1815. Murat, the king of Naples, is defeated by an Austrian army at Tolentino.

Italy, 20 May 1815. Abandoned by his generals, who sign the Casa Lanza Convention with Britain and Austria, Murat leaves Naples and flees to France.

Prussia, 22 May 1815. King Frederick William III publishes an edict renewing the promises of the 1810 constitution.

France, 1 June 1815. Napoleon swears an oath of fidelity to the constitution.

Italy, 3 June 1815. Murat is replaced by the former king of Naples, Ferdinand IV.

Vienna, 9 June 1815. Britain, Russia, Prussia, Austria, France, Sweden and Portugal sign the Act of the Congress of Vienna, establishing a comprehensive peace in Europe.

Vienna, 9 June 1815. An act is passed creating a German confederation, comprising 39 states, to replace the old Holy Roman empire.

Netherlands, 9 June 1815. By the treaty of Vienna, Belgium and Holland are united to form the kingdom of the Netherlands.

Netherlands, 16 June 1815. Napoleon defeats the Prussians under Blucher at the battle of Ligny.

Egypt, 1815. A revolt by the Albanian regiments in Egypt compels the governor, Mohammed Ali, to flood Cairo. The revolt is suppressed and the mutinous troops sent to upper Egypt.

Imperial eagle returns to his empire

Paris, 20 March 1815

In astonishing scenes of enthusiasm Napoleon was today reinstalled in the Tuileries which Louis XVIII had left in a great hurry last night. It is a year since Paris capitulated to the allies and it has taken the emperor just three weeks to reach Paris after landing at Golfe Juan, Cannes, with a handful of men.

British fears that Elba was too close to the mainland as a place of confinement for Napoleon have now been realised. Yet, when he set out on his march north through the Alps, he gathered little support. It was not until he reached Grenoble and the soldiers posted to stop him fell in behind him that his return to glory seemed possible.

Regiments sent to oppose him went over to him. Marshal Ney, who had promised the king that he would take Napoleon to Paris in an iron cage, embraced him with all the old fervour.

Napoleon marched north, gathering men all the way, and today the "Eagle" returned to his eyrie. War with the allies must follow.

British army is repulsed at New Orleans

The death of Major-General Sir Edward Pakenham at New Orleans.

New Orleans, 8 January 1815

A hastily improvised rag-tag army of militiamen, volunteers, Negro troops and local French-led pirates has inflicted a massive defeat on 8,000 veteran British troops – and saved New Orleans. The fiery Major-general Andrew Jackson, a Tennessee lawyer and former commander of his state militia, was in a position to choose the killing field – a narrow strip of land which the British had to traverse. As the British commander, Major-General Sir Edward Pakenham, the duke of Wellington's brother-in-law, assembled his army, the Americans dug ditches, stacked cotton bales and placed artillery batteries to cover their flanks.

Wave after wave of red-coated infantrymen was repulsed with huge losses from the defenders' concentrated musket fire, grapeshot and cannon-balls. General Pakenham was killed as he tried to rally his troops; his second in command, General Gibbs, died later. More than 2,000 British troops died, against 45 Americans.

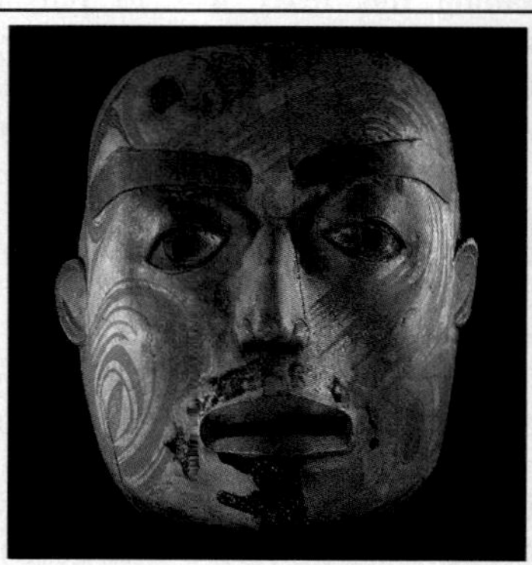

The art of the American Indians: the mask of a man from the north-western coast of America.

Map of Europe is redrawn in Vienna

The duke of Wellington, whose advance into France ended the war.

Vienna, 9 June 1815
The Congress of Vienna has remade Europe after the devastation inflicted by Napoleon. The "Final Act" signed today after nine months of negotiations confirms the territorial arrangements of the Treaty of Paris and, among other measures, creates a German confederation to replace the Holy Roman empire.

The Swiss Confederation is re-established with a guarantee of permanent neutrality. The legitimate dynasties are restored in Spain, Naples, Modena, Piedmont and Tuscany. Prussia benefits hugely, getting Posen, Danzig, a slice of Saxony, Westphalia and the former Swedish territories in Pomerania.

The congress also dealt with non-territorial matters, establishing the principle of free navigation on the Rhine and the Meuse, condemning but not abolishing the slave trade and extending the rights of the Jews. Another aspect of its work has been the establishment of an internationally recognised system of diplomacy in which ambassadorial precedence and the rights of diplomats are recognised.

It has been an exhausting time for the delegates, not only because of the amount of work they have accomplished but also because of the glittering social life surrounding the congress. Czar Alexander, convinced that he was responsible for the downfall of Napoleon, has been the dominant figure in the dazzling crowd of monarchs and statesmen. Emperor Francis of Austria has entertained 216 chiefs of mission and has been so lavish with his hospitality that his treasury has suffered severely.

His court's festival committee arranged a rich programme of events for his guests. There were balls, concerts, sleigh and skating parties, hunts, horse-shows and galas. There was a choice of dinner parties every night and the whole city was filled with diplomatic and sexual intrigue.

Most of the decisions have been taken by the four leading allies – Austria, Britain, Russia and Prussia – but Talleyrand has served his new master, King Louis, with great adroitness, weaving his way through the quarrels and the bargaining to France's advantage.

There was a considerable *frisson* when the news arrived of Napoleon's return from Elba. The congress reacted by declaring: "Napoleon Bonaparte has placed himself outside the pale of civil and social relations and, as the enemy and disturber of the peace of the world, has exposed himself to public indictment." Then the delegates went on dancing – as well as intriguing and settling the future of Europe.

Deep breaths greet the new stethoscope

Paris, 1815
A chance observation of a children's game has led to a revolution in medical diagnosis. The French physician, Rene Laennec, is said to have been walking in the courtyard of the Louvre when he saw some children bending over long hollow pieces of wood. Some were listening at one end while, at the other end, their friends were flicking pins to produce a tiny sound. From this Laennec went on to devise what he calls a *stethoscope* (from the Greek word meaning *chest*). It is simply a sheet of paper rolled into a tube and tied with a string. Placed on the chest, this concentrates and transmits the sounds made in a patient's lung. Now its inventor has made a wooden version of the device.

Boers rebel against British authority

Cape Town, South Africa, 1815
Although British troops have managed to suppress a rebellion by up-country Boer farmers, the final act – a bungled execution in which the hangman's rope broke – has not done much to help British prestige in the province. Britain is anxious to improve the lot of the black population; the Boers less so.

The insurrection originated in Britain's abolition of the slave trade in 1808, creating a labour shortage; the spread of the Boers into the interior; and the embracing of revolutionary ideals by white society after the French Revolution. The spark was the killing of Frederick Bezuidenhout, shot by British-officered Black Redcoats while resisting arrest.

Fortunately for Britain the rebels failed to gain the support of the majority of Boers, while the Blacks, inevitably, took the side of Britain. Even more fortunately, in spite of the disgraceful scenes at the execution, none but the most incorrigible see the rebels as martyrs.

Spain puts down American uprising

Mexico City, 1815
All over Spain's central and south American empire, her troops are putting down revolts. The wave of nationalist revolutions began in 1809 with an uprising in Chuquisaca, Bolivia, which was rapidly suppressed. Another in Chile led by Bernardo O'Higgins and Juan Martinez de Rozas was defeated by Spain, although a bloodless coup has gained independence for Paraguay.

The most serious revolt was in Mexico. A rebellion by Indians in 1810, led by a priest, Miguel Hidalgo, was crushed at Calderon Bridge in January 1811, and Hidalgo excecuted. A second revolt, led by another priest, Jose Maria Morelos, declared a republic and abolished slavery and judicial torture, before the Spanish under General de Iturbide broke through the rebel lines around Mexico City and defeated them. Morelos, like Hidalgo, has since been executed.

1815 (1815-1816)

Netherlands, 18 June 1815. Napoleon is decisively defeated by the British and the Prussians at the Battle of Waterloo.

Paris, 22 June 1815. Napoleon abdicates for the second time following the refusal of the parliamentary chambers to co-operate with him.

Algiers, 30 June 1815. Faced with a US threat to bomb Algiers, the *bey* agrees to cease piracy and release US prisoners.

Paris, 7 July 1815. The victorious allies enter Paris.

Paris, 8 July 1815. Louis XVIII returns to Paris.

France, 17 July 1815. After a futile attempt to escape to America, Napoleon surrenders to the British at Rochefort.

France, July 1815. Catholic royalists in southern France begin a campaign of reprisals, known as the White Terror, against supposed Bonapartists and revolutionaries; part of the garrison at Nimes is massacred.

North Africa, 5 August 1815. The US naval hero Stephen Decatur neutralises the Barbary pirates by persuading the bey of Tripoli to agree to similar terms to those accepted by the bey of Algiers.

Switzerland, 7 August 1815. The 22 cantons adopt a federal treaty which guarantees each of them its own constitution and territory. They are all authorised to sign agreements with foreign powers to supply contingents of troops.

France, 22 August 1815. The reactionary ultra-royalists win a large majority in the first parliamentary elections.

Netherlands, 24 August 1815. William, the new king of the Netherlands, grants a moderately liberal constitution.

Europe, 26 September 1815. At the instigation of Czar Alexander, Russia, Austria and Prussia sign a holy alliance, by which they agree to act towards each other and towards their subjects in accordance with Christian principles.

France, 26 September 1815. The duke of Richelieu, an opponent of the Ultra-royalists, is made prime minister and minister of foreign affairs.

France, 7 October 1815. Marshal Ney is condemned to death and shot for having left the service of the king and joined Napoleon's army.

South Atlantic, 17 October 1815. Napoleon arrives on the island of St Helena, where he has been banished by the allies.

Britain, 5 November 1815. Britain signs a treaty assuming a protectorate over the Ionian islands.

Paris, 20 November 1815. A second treaty of Paris puts an end to the war between France and the allies, reduces France to its 1789 frontiers and creates an organisation charged with the collective security of Europe.

Europe, 20 November 1815. Britain, Austria, Prussia and Russia renew their quadruple alliance, agreeing to maintain the exclusion of the Bonaparte dynasty from France for 20 years.

Poland, November 1815. The grand duchy of Warsaw – which was annexed to the Russian empire by the treaty of Vienna – is organised as the autonomous kingdom of Poland and given its own constitution by Czar Alexander.

South Africa, 1815. Five Boers are publicly hanged at Slagter's Nek, in the Eastern Cape Frontier, for rebellion against the British. The revolt was sparked by Boer anger at the British courts' willingness to hear cases brought by Khoisan labourers against their Boer masters. The Boers failed to get the Xhosa chiefdoms across the border to join them in their struggle.

Ottoman Empire, December 1815. Milos Obrenovic, a former pig farmer who made his fortune and led a rebellion, is recognised by the Ottomans as leader of the Serbs, for whom he obtains freedom of worship and a certain degree of autonomy.

Europe, 1815. The Holy Alliance formed in August is joined by most of the other European states, except Britain, the Ottoman empire and the papal states.

Scandinavia, 1815. Sweden and Norway ratify an act of union.

Germany, 1815. The German jurist Friedrich Karl von Savigny publishes his *History of Roman Law in the Middle Ages*.

Germany, 1815. The philosopher and critic Friedrich von Schlegel publishes a *History of Literature*.

China, 1815. Chinese officials execute the French missionary Jean Gabriel Taurin Dufresse.

China, 7 February 1816. The Chinese authorities at Changsha (*Hunan*) execute the Italian missionary Giovanni Lantrua of Triora.

Portugal, March 1816. John VI succeeds his mother, Maria of Braganza, on the throne. He has been emperor of Brazil since 1807, when he fled from Portugal to escape Napoleon's army.

Czar invokes religion in "Holy Alliance"

Paris, 26 September 1815

The Orthodox Czar Alexander, deeply influenced by the mystical beliefs of Baroness von Krudener, has formed a holy alliance with his more conservative allies, the Lutheran king of Prussia and the Catholic emperor of Austria.

The three powers have agreed that "the precepts of Justice, Christian Charity and Peace must have an immediate influence on the Councils of Princes and guide all their steps".

The czar expects Europe's monarchs to join his alliance with the exception of the sultan – barred because he is not a Christian. The pope refuses to associate with heretics, and the prince regent has constitutional objections but agrees with their "sacred maxims".

Europe's statesmen, fearing the might of Russia and its influence on Europe, are less kind to the idea. Metternich calls it a "loud-sounding nothing", and according to Castlereagh it is "a piece of sublime mysticism and nonsense".

The czar, author of the "Holy Alliance": sacred truth or nonsense?

Britain's corn law halts grain imports

The price of victory: high-priced corn, hungry bellies and popular discontent.

London, 23 March 1815

The free-traders have been defeated in the long-running controversy over the import of corn. In a move to protect the agriculture industry, Parliament has passed an act permitting the import of foreign corn free of duty only when the domestic price is 80 shillings a quarter.

A corn law passed in 1804 was seen as a selfish measure by landlords in Parliament to hold on to the high prices caused by war and bad harvests. But Napoleon's defeat and the end of the economic blockade, followed by good harvests, brought the price of home-grown corn tumbling down.

The economist the Rev Thomas Malthus, who recently argued that poverty is inevitable because populations increase faster than food supplies, supported protection because, he told MPs, Britain should not depend on foreign corn. Another economist, David Ricardo, spoke for free trade, saying that Britain should use its wealth and population to encourage enterprise and competition.

Crushing British victory at Waterloo

The Battle of Waterloo, where the duke of Wellington and his British Redcoats finally defeated Napoleon.

Waterloo, 18 June 1815

Napoleon has suffered a catastrophic defeat here today at the hands of the duke of Wellington (previously Sir Arthur Wellesley) and Blucher. The French army has been routed. Napoleon, defeated, and exhausted, has fled the field.

Wellington was dancing at the duchess of Richmond's ball in Brussels three nights ago when he realised that the French were about to attack. "Napoleon has humbugged me, by God!" he cried, and set his "infamous army" in motion.

Napoleon's plan was to destroy Blucher before turning on Wellington, but he succeeded only in delaying the Prussians. Wellington, on his horse, Copenhagen, coolly directed his soldiers in the face of the French cannonade. The battle raged with terrible ferocity all day. One whole British regiment died as it stood in square. Marshal Ney had five horses shot under him.

The end came late in the day when Napoleon at last unleashed the formidable Imperial Guard. The British infantry poured shot into them at close range. They wavered, broke and ran. At that moment Blucher arrived. The day was won but, as Wellington said, it was "the nearest run thing you ever saw".

John VI is crowned king of Brazil

John VI, the new king of Brazil.

Brazil, January 1816

Dom Joao, the former prince regent of Portugal and head of the House of Braganza, has declared himself King John VI of Brazil and Portugal. The king and his family fled from Portugal in 1807, when Napoleon's French troops invaded.

The arrival of the royal family has been a great boon to Brazil. The economy has surged ahead, and cultural and intellectual links with Europe have been strengthened. A flood of immigrants, mainly professionals, continues to arrive. King John rules as an enlightened despot backed by Brazilian nobility.

Social and political order are guaranteed, although there is a growing movement for independence from Portugal.

Davy lights way for safer coalmines

London, 1815

Following a horrific disaster which killed 92 Durham miners, the leading scientist, Humphry Davy, has been asked to find a way of preventing lethal sparks which can turn a mass of "fire-damp" – methane gas – into a lethal underground explosion.

He has come up with a safety lamp in which the flame is enclosed in a wire-mesh cylinder to prevent the explosion of air and fire-damp mixture. The presence of fire-damp actually augments the flame in this gauze-covered lantern, thus warning of danger.

Napoleon settles into exile on the island of St Helena

St Helena, 1815

Napoleon, who was depressed by the volcanic mass of this island when he arrived on *HMS Northumberland* after his defeat at Waterloo, has settled into a pavilion in the garden of a house called "The Briars", the home of William Balcombe, the agent of the East India Company. As it will only house a few people he is relieved of the quarrelling antics of his mini-court, and his tedium is relieved by his friendship with Betsy, the 14-year-old tomboy daughter of the Balcombes. Napoleon, who grew up in a large and noisy family, takes much pleasure in teaching Betsy French, and this odd couple enjoy a friendship uninhibited by ceremony. When he teased her about English roast beef she retaliated by producing a cartoon of a Frenchman with a frog jumping down his throat. She saddened Napoleon when she showed him an ingenious toy which made "Boney" climb a ladder and then fall onto St Helena. Her mother was furious and shut her in the cellar. Napoleon fed her sweets through her "prison" bars.

Such is the life of the former emperor in his own far-away prison. He refuses to accept official invitations because they are addressed to "General Bonaparte", but enjoys talking to the islanders on his long rides and walks.

Napoleon on "HMS Bellerophon", observed by crowds at Plymouth on his way to the island of St Helena.

1816 (1816-1817)

India, 2 March 1816. Gurkha tribesmen in Nepal sign a peace treaty with the British, ending their year-long war.

South America, 9 July 1816. The United Provinces of Rio de la Plata (*Argentina*) declare independence.

Florida, 27 July 1816. Fort Apalachicola, which was occupied by runaway slaves after being abandoned by the British, is destroyed and 270 of its occupants killed after a ten-day siege by US troops.

China, 28 August 1816. A mission led by Lord Amherst, which left Britain on 8 February, arrives in Beijing.

France, 5 September 1816. King Louis XVIII dissolves the chamber of deputies, which has become too reactionary and independent, challenging his authority by opposing the initiatives of his chief minister, the duke of Richelieu.

France, 4 October 1816. Moderate royalists and liberals, supporters of Richelieu, win a majority over the Ultra-royalists in an election.

Germany, 5 November 1816. The *Diet* of the German Confederation, created by the 1815 treaty of Vienna, meets for the first time, at Frankfurt.

London, 2 December 1816. Rioting breaks out at Spa Fields during a mass meeting to promote demands for parliamentary reform.

USA, 4 December 1816. James Monroe, who served as secretary of state under his President, Madison, is elected to succeed him.

USA, 11 December 1816. Indiana becomes the 19th state in the union.

USA, 28 December 1816. The Presbyterian clergyman Robert Finley establishes the American Colonization Society, aimed at recolonising American Negroes in Africa.

India, 1816. The ruler of the Himalayan border state of Sikkim signs a treaty accepting British control of its relationship with other Indian states.

Japan, 1816. British ships reach the Ryukyu islands (*Okinawa*) and Uraga Bay near Edo (*Tokyo*) seeking trade. Their overtures are rebuffed, but increase the government's awareness of western pressures on Japan to open the country to foreign business.

Ghana, 1816. The Reverend Philip Quaque, the first Anglican African clergyman, dies. He was a key figure in the cultural development of the Anglo-African coastal elite of trading and professional families.

South-East Asia, 1816. The island of Java is restored to Dutch control.

Russia, 1816. A group of Russian Guards officers founds the Union of Salvation to promote the establishment of constitutional government and to abolish serfdom.

Netherlands, 1816. The British engineer John Cockerill takes over the factory founded by his father at Seraing, near Liege, in 1807, and starts to manufacture steam engines.

France, 1816. A new science of "comparative anatomy" is born with the publication of Georges Cuvier's book on classifying the animal kingdom. Cuvier is also a clever palaeontologist, able to "reconstruct" whole skeletons of long-dead animals from just a few bones.

Germany, 1816. The linguist Franz Bopp publishes a study of the *System of Conjugation in Sanskrit*, in which he seeks to trace the common origin of Sanskrit, Persian, Greek and Latin.

England, 1816. The anonymous author of *Pride and Prejudice* and *Mansfield Park* publishes another novel, *Emma*.

Ottoman Empire, 1817. Karageorges returns to Serbia from exile in Austria. Karageorges, the former leader of the Serbian independence movement, hopes to overthrow the increasingly unpopular Serbian leader, Milos Obrenovic, but is assassinated on the orders of his rival.

West Africa, 1817. Uthman dan Fodio, the scholar-warrior and instigator of the Islamic reformation of the Hausa states, dies.

Madagascar, 1817. Radama, the king of the Merina, who has embarked on a major expansion of his kingdom with the aim of dominating the whole island, signs a treaty of alliance with the British, who have promised military aid. The British see the Merina as effective agents for suppressing the slave trade from coastal areas into the Indian Ocean.

Hawaii, 1817. Russian fur traders who have abused the hospitality of the Hawaiian Islands for over a dozen years are banished by King Kamehameha.

USA, 1817. Construction begins on the Erie canal, designed to link the Great Lakes with the Atlantic.

Germany, 1817. Georg Hegel, who became professor of philosophy at Heidelberg university last year, publishes his *Encyclopaedia of the Philosophical Sciences*.

Unbending envoy wrecks trade prospects

Beijing, 29 August 1816

Lord Amherst's mission to Beijing, to establish better conditions for British traders in China, ended in farcical failure today.

The emperor Jiaqing agreed to receive Amherst only on condition that the English lord would perform the ritual of *kowtow*, kneeling three times and knocking his head on the ground nine times. But Amherst would only bend a knee, bow his head three times and repeat the performance three times.

This was accepted by the Chinese officials, who reported that the barbarian was learning how to *kowtow*. The emperor then agreed to an immediate audience. But when Amherst arrived, exhausted by his journey, and officials tried to hustle him to the palace, he insisted on resting and waiting for his credentials.

The emperor, told he was ill, reacted furiously: "China is the universal overlord. How can she willingly submit to this kind of insult and insolence?" Amherst's "tributes" have been rejected, his mission expelled.

The Chinese port of Canton, the entrepot for all trade coming into China.

Britain defeats Gurkhas, but only just

Nepal, 2 March 1816

The British army has won a decisive victory over Gurkha tribesmen – despite being pinned down for days in the Kathmandu Valley. It was an ill-deserved victory, however, with the war-seasoned British troops outnumbering the hill people by three to one. Only shrewd generalship by the British commander, Sir David Ochterlony, saved the day for Britain.

War became inevitable two years ago when Gurkhas seized the hill states of Simla, Garwhal and Kumaon and descended on British-controlled Oudh. Fighting began again last year with Ochterlony taking Kathmandu by an indirect approach. The fighting ability of the Gurkhas has gained much respect from the British, who see them as "good losers" and have allowed them semi-independence.

First black Anglican priest is dead

West Africa, 1816

Philip Quaque, Africa's first Anglican clergyman, has died aged 75. In his own terms, he was a failure. To the hundreds of Mulatto children whom he educated, he was an outstanding success. Sent to England to be educated and ordained, he returned to the Gold Coast with his English wife in 1765, fluent in Christian values but unable to speak his own language.

A victim of two cultures, only after his wife died and he "went native" did he find happiness – and a truly African Christianity.

France's King Louis XVIII dissolves the incredible chamber

Louis XVIII, burdened by the extremism of his own supporters.

Paris, 5 September 1816
King Louis has today signed a decree dissolving the Chamber of Deputies, an elected body of men so royalist that Louis himself called it "the Incredible Chamber".

The young and zealous royalists, elected under a widened franchise last year, have proved an embarrassment to the government, many of whom served under Napoleon. Swiftly getting themselves dubbed "the Ultra-royalists", they forced the government to accept a number of repressive measures.

Under this "White Terror" the army and the administration have been purged. Many who supported Napoleon during the "Hundred Days" have been exiled and some, like the gallant Marshal Ney, have been shot.

Louis has been forced to act against the royalists, but in doing so he has affirmed the power of the crown over the electorate.

England's romantic movement puts passion back into poetry

London, 1816
The last 12 months have been rich in Romantic poetry, with publications by Samuel Taylor Coleridge, Percy Bysshe Shelley and Lord Byron and the first sonnet of a 21-year-old newcomer, John Keats.

Coleridge first amazed his readers with the haunted vision of *The Rime of the Ancient Mariner* in 1798. The fragmentary poems he now publishes were written soon afterwards. *Kubla Khan*, considered his finest poem so far, was composed under the influence of opium and written down on waking – until interrupted half way through. The solitary remorseful wanderer is a favourite theme of the Romantics, and in *Alastor (or the spirit of Solitude)* Shelley hurls the Poet through ocean, precipice and torrent on a quest for the ideal that ends in death. Lord Byron, who has left the scandals which he caused in London society for further travels, has added a new canto to the autobiographical picturesque travelogue *Childe Harold's Pilgrimage* which made him famous overnight in 1812. In it he visits the field of last year's great battle, Waterloo. Keats' Romantic sonnet, *On First Looking into Chapman's Homer*, is in *The Examiner*, where Shelley's work first appeared.

Three poets of the English Romantic school: (left to right) John Keats, Percy Bysshe Shelley and Lord Byron.

Protesters stone British prince regent

London, 28 January 1817
As the prince regent was passing through St James' Park after the opening of parliament, he was stoned and greeted with a tirade of abuse. The *Kendal Chronicle* reports: "Gravel, stones, and other things were thrown at the Royal carriage," by the mob, "accompanied by the most foul, shocking, insulting and blasphemous language." Windows in the royal carriage were broken and there are reports that an air gun was fired at the prince.

Cabinet ministers are linking the attack to agitators who have been holding meetings in London and the provinces to demand votes for all men over 18, and no property qualifications for MPs, only "talent and virtue". During a meeting at Spa Fields, Clerkenwell, a mob broke into a gun shop, seized arms and went on to appeal to soldiers in the Tower of London to join the uprising. That "uprising", like the others, petered out. Now the government is using the outbreaks of discontent, caused by post-war hardships, as justification for a crackdown on dissent.

Briton expounds economic theory

London, 1817
David Ricardo, who made his fortune on the Stock Exchange and retired at the age of 27, has published a treatise on pay, profits and taxation in Britain in which he lays down the Iron Law of Wages, arguing that attempts to improve the real incomes of workers are bound to fail, because wages inevitably settle at about the subsistence level. In international trade he claims that exchange rates reflect values that would be accepted if trade were conducted by barter.

Ricardo, of Dutch-Jewish parents, broke with his family and adopted the Christian faith when he married a Quaker. He took up the study of economics after reading Adam Smith's *Wealth of Nations*.In his latest book, Ricardo says that taxes are not always paid by those on whom they are levied. A tax on farm produce, for example, falls on the consumer; a tax on wages is paid by the employer but the consumer pays the tax on profits.

Fundamentalist Islamic reformer who built up African empire

Nigeria, 1817
All over the savannalands of West Africa, Moslem fundamentalists are mourning the death of Uthman dan Fodio, the preacher and reformer, whose armies swept through Hausaland. Less fundamentalist Moslems are greeting his death with relief. Born into the devoutly Moslem Banu Al clan in 1754, from the age of 20 he called for reformation. All over the Hausa states he gathered disciples.

Faced with the hostility of the sultan of Gobir he proclaimed holy war in 1804, defeating Gobir four years later. Soon the green flag of Islam was flying all over Hausaland, and his son, Mohammed Bello was proclaimed the precursor of the *Mahdi*, the Expected One. By 1812 his state was so large that it was divided, his brother, Abdullah, administering the west, and his son the east, persecuting secularism and superstition everywhere. Content with his achievements he retired to a life of contemplation, writing over 100 theological works before his death.

1817 (1817-1818)

Britain, March 1817. In response to the riot at Spa Fields in London last year, a series of Coercion Acts are passed; these include the temporary suspension of habeas corpus and an extension of the 1798 act against seditious meetings.

Britain, March 1817. A delegation of Manchester spinners and weavers – called blanketeers on account of the blankets they carry – attempts to march to London to present its economic and political grievances to the prince regent. The march is halted by troops and its leaders are imprisoned.

Mexico, 5 April 1817. An expedition organised in Britain and the USA under Francisco Xavier Mina lands on the Gulf coast with the aim of overthrowing the royalist Spanish regime.

Maryland, 7 April 1817. Some 200 Negro slaves in Maryland riot, attacking Whites.

Germany, 18 October 1817. At the festival of Wartburg – organised by Jena university students to celebrate both the 300th anniversary of the Reformation and the battle of Leipzig – reactionary texts and military effigies are burnt. The university of Jena has become the centre of a liberal movement spearheaded by new student societies known as the *Burschenschaften*.

Ottoman Empire, 5 November 1817. Serbia is granted partial autonomy by the Ottomans.

Colombia, November 1817. Pola Salavarreta is captured and shot as a republican agent in the public square in Bogota. While working as a seamstress in the houses of Spanish royalist women, she passed on the information which she heard to Colombian rebels.

Mexico, 11 November 1817. Xavier Mina, defeated in his attempt to overthrow the royalist regime, is executed.

USA, 10 December 1817. Mississippi becomes the 20th state in the union.

USA, December 1817. A war starts in earnest between US troops and Seminole Indians, who last year refused to leave land between Georgia and Florida.

Australia, 1817. The Australian pioneer and wool merchant Elizabeth Macarthur retires from the management of Elizabeth Farm, the first great Australian estate. After taking over the business from her husband in 1809, she built up the merino flocks and travelled throughout Australia, expanding sales into the British market and establishing New South Wales as a major wool-producing area.

South America, 1817. Following his victories over the Spanish in Rio de la Plata (*Argentina*), General Jose de San Martin embarks on a campaign to liberate Chile.

England, 1817. The "romantic" poet John Keats publishes his first anthology of poems.

England, 1817. Lord Byron publishes his tragic poem *Manfred*.

Washington, DC, 1 January 1818. President Monroe gives the first public reception at the new White House, his official residence, rebuilt after being burnt down by the British in 1814.

New York City, 5 January 1818. The first regularly scheduled transatlantic service, between New York and Liverpool, begins.

Sweden, 5 February 1818. Jean-Baptiste Bernadotte, prince royal since 1810, succeeds Charles XIII as king, taking the name Charles XIV.

Florida, April 1818. Andrew Jackson, officially acting against the Seminole Indians, takes the Spanish fort of St Mark's, before capturing a Seminole stronghold in central Florida.

Germany, 26 May 1818. Bavaria adopts a constitution granting extensive powers to the king and nobility and giving the latter exclusive right of entry to the "first" chamber. A "second" chamber, more open to other classes, is created.

Prussia, 26 May 1818. A bill presented by the economist and councillor Karl Maaseen is adopted. It abolishes customs procedures within Prussia and lifts trade restrictions.

India, 2 June 1818. The Marathas are conquered by the British army and their empire is annexed to British India.

Florida, May 1818. Andrew Jackson recaptures the Spanish fort of Pensacola and sets up a military government.

India, June 1818. The Pindaris, freebooters who have ravaged much of central India since 1806, have finally been brought to heel.

Germany, 22 August 1818. Baden adopts a constitution similar to that of Bavaria.

USA, 23 August 1818. The first steamship service on the Great Lakes opens.

North America, 19 October 1818. Following the cession by Quapaw Indians of holdings in Arkansas to the USA, the Chickasaw Indians sell all their lands north of the southern boundary of Tennesseee to the government.

New architecture blooms in Britain

John Nash's Royal Pavilion in Brighton: built for the Prince Regent.

Cruikshank's mockery of Nash's architecture: "Nashional Taste".

London, 1818

A great new thoroughfare called Regent Street is being driven through the centre of London by the Prince Regent's architect and surveyor-general, John Nash. Now Nash is rebuilding the exterior of the Royal Pavilion in Brighton.

Regent Street will connect the prince's residence at Carlton House with Regent's Park (formerly Marylebone Park) which Nash is adorning with lakes and villas according to the principles of the new picturesque architecture.

He plans to surround the open space with terraces of houses sharing long stucco facades, which the tenants will be obliged to renew every year, named after royal titles, such as Cumberland, Hanover and York. A new Regent's Canal is being driven through the park. In the central part of Regent Street above Piccadilly Circus Nash has inserted a curve, known as the Quadrant, adorned with projecting colonnades, to break the straight line. At the top of the street he has placed the circular colonnade and spire of All Souls' church.

The Royal Pavilion at Brighton is even more spectacular. The Chinese-style interior is being kept, but the old neo-classical exterior is being completely transformed into a Moghul emperor's palace, with onion-shaped domes, tentshaped roofs, and pseudo-Moslem pinnacles and minarets.

A regent's extravaganza: the Music Room in the Royal Pavilion, Brighton.

Army of the mountains defeats Spanish

Chile, 12 February 1817
The "Army of the Andes", recruited by Jose de San Martin, the liberator of Argentina, and led by the redoubtable Bernardo O'Higgins, has struck a blow for Chilean independence. A surprise attack has routed the Spanish at Chacabuco. Now O'Higgins and his army are marching on Santiago.

The preparations for the advance go back to 1811 when San Martin established himself at Mendoza in western Argentinia and built an army. In 1814, after the disasterous battle of Ranagua re-established Spanish royalist authority in Chile, O'Higgins joined him.

The victory was as notable for its logistics as for the course of the battle itself. A force of 5,400 men marched 200 miles across mountain passes almost 13,000 feet (3,937 metres) above sea level. The crossing took a month, but the four columns met at exactly the appointed place and time. With that degree of precision, the success at Chacabuco was almost a foregone conclusion.

General Bernardo O'Higgins: hero of the "Army of the Andes".

British army defeats Maratha alliance

Bombay, 2 June 1818
After a six-month campaign by 100,000 British Indian troops, the Marathas have been crushed and their domains annexed. The final obstacle to British hegemony over India has been overcome.

The Marathas have plundered central India since 1812, even attacking the Bombay Presidency, or district. Lacking unity, they proved easy victims to Governor General Lord Hastings' tactics of "divide and rule". Hastings' first move was diplomatic, isolating the most ambitious of the Maratha leaders, Sindia, by treaty. Next he broke the most anarchic elements, the Pindaris. Then he turned on the Maratha head, the *Pewsha*, provoking him into hostilities before he was ready. This left only the Pewsha's rival, Holkar, whose army he annihilated at Mahidpur on 21 December 1817. Britain is now truly master of India.

The household of an Indian monarch: courtiers, servants and hangers-on.

Mary Shelley's "Frankenstein" published

London, 1818
An extraordinary Gothic novel has appeared from the pen of Mary Wollstonecraft Shelley, the wife of the poet and daughter of the atheist William Godwin. *Frankenstein* is the story of a monster – man-made and mis-shapen – which turns on its creator when he gives it the the spark of life.

The tale was the result of a competition between the authoress, Shelley and their friend Lord Byron at Lake Geneva in 1816 for each to write a ghost story during a cold spell. The poets gave up when the weather improved, but Mrs Shelley completed hers which came to her one night in a trance.

"I saw the dull yellow eye of the creature open; it breathed hard."

Ottoman empire defeats the Wahhabis

Arabia, 1818
With the fall of the Saudi capital of Dariyya, the last of the Wahhabi fortresses has fallen to the Ottomans. The *emir*, Abdallah ibn Saud, has been executed in Istanbul. The campaign against the Wahhabi empire began in 1811 when an expedition set out from Cairo under Ahmed Tusun Pasha, the son of Mohammed Ali, Egypt's ruler. The aim was to reclaim control of Mecca, Medina and the Hijaz, essential if the sultan was to be the true *caliph* and guardian of the sacred places of Islam. Tusun's forces recaptured Yanbu, Medina and Mecca, then agreed to a truce which ensured the free passage of pilgrims. When Tusun died in 1816, Ibrahim Pasha took over command, and advanced into the Saudi heartland of Najd until the last fortress fell.

Parkinson names a nervous disease

London, 1817
The distressing disease known as "shaking palsy" which can affect both men and women in late adult life – and sometimes earlier – has been described in detail by the English surgeon James Parkinson. "Parkinson's Disease", as the condition is now being termed, is a relatively common malady, although no-one, including Parkinson himself, has been able to trace its cause.

It is certainly a nervous disorder. Over the course of ten to 20 years, an individual progressively acquires a number of striking symptoms. Body movements are a mixture of rigidity and tremor – *paralysis agitans*, to use the Latin name.

Ultimately, these symptoms become so severe that sufferers may lose balance frequently and fall over. Speech becomes poorly articulated and manual skills – such as writing – are gradually lost.

Atoms are weighed in Swedish kitchen

Stockholm, 1818
Atoms – nature's building blocks – are small. Typically an atom will measure no more than 300 millionths of an inch in diameter. This means that, if its nucleus or central particle, were the size of an orange, it would be half a mile across.

So it is remarkable that the Swedish chemist and academician, Jons Jacob Berzelius, has been able to determine the weights of different atoms. He has published a table of relative proportions and weights in which oxygen – with a value of 100 – is the standard. In addition, Berzelius had drawn up tables for the molecular weights of over 2,000 compounds which he has studied for over a decade.

His achievement is all the more noteworthy given his working conditions. He has made his discoveries in his spare time – improvising equipment from his own kitchen.

1818 (1818-1819)

North America, 20 October 1818. Britain and the USA agree that the western border between Canada and the USA should be the 49th parallel.

Europe, 15 November 1818. The Quadruple Alliance between Britain, Russia, Austria and Prussia is renewed as a precaution against another possible revolution in France.

France, 30 November 1818. In accordance with an agreement reached at the congress of Aix-la-Chapelle earlier in the month, the last foreign troops leave France. The congress also settled the question of France's war indemnity payments and agreed to admit France to the alliance of European powers.

USA, 3 December 1818. Illinois, including Chicago, becomes the 21st state in the union.

France, December 1818. The prime minister, the duke of Richelieu, retires and is replaced by the marquis of Dessoles. Elie Decazes becomes minister of the interior.

South Africa, 1818. Faced with a threat to their capital in the Pongola valley, the Ndwandwe defeat the Mthethwa under the great warrior Dingiswayo at the battle of Mbuzi Hill. Dingiswayo is found demented in defeat and executed by the ruthless Ndwandwe leader Zwide. One of Dingiswayo's chiefs – Shaka of the Zulu clan – escapes back to his own people to build them up and fight another day.

Prague, 1818. The National Museum of Prague is founded.

Germany, 1818. The philosopher Arthur Schopenhauer publishes *The World as Will and Idea.*

Italy, 1818. The poet Giacomo Leopardi publishes *First Love.*

Germany, 20 January 1819. Karl von Stein founds the Society of Earlier German History.

North America, 22 February 1819. The US foreign minister, John Quincy Adams, signs a treaty with his Spanish counterpart, Luis de Onis, by which eastern Florida is ceded to the USA. The border of western Florida is fixed at the Mississippi.

Germany, 23 March 1819. The dramatist August Kotzebue is stabbed to death by a Jena student for having ridiculed the nationalist *Burschenschaft* movement and spying for the Czar of Russia.

Germany, April 1819. The economist Georg Friederich List founds an association of German industrialists to fight for the abolition of tariff barriers within the German Confederation.

Hawaii, 8 May 1819. Kamehameha, the Lonely One, the first chief of a united Hawaiian people, dies.

Bohemia, 1 August 1819. Prince Metternich and Karl Hardenberg, the chief ministers of Austria and Prussia, finalise the details of the secret convention of Teplitz, which introduces reactionary policies throughout the German Confederation.

Bohemia, August 1819. A series of decrees is issued at Carlsbad to check revolutionary and liberal movements in Germany.

USA, 14 December 1819. Alabama becomes the 22nd state of the union.

South-East Asia, 1819. The Englishman Sir Thomas Stamford Raffles occupies Singapore, which has been bought from the *rajah* of Johore by the East India Company.

South Africa, 1819. The British are victorious in the fifth Suurveld (*Eastern Cape Frontier*) war and imprison the enemy leader, the Xhosa prophet Makhanda, on Robben Island. After defeating the major chief of western Xhosa, Ngqika, Makhanda crossed into Cape Colony "to chase the white men to the sea that cast them up".

South Africa, 1819. The Zulus under Shaka defeat the Ndwandwe at the battle of Mhlatuze river and emerge as the dominant military power in the Natal region.

USA, 1819. Financial panic caused by runaway depreciation and speculation following the war of 1812 touches off a depression.

France, 1819. The adoption of the three *de Serre* laws relaxes restrictions on the press. Censorship and prior consent are abolished, the number of violation laws is reduced, and provision is made for any dispute concerning the press to be resolved by a jury.

France, 1819. The doctor Rene Laennec publishes his treatise *On Medical Auscultation*, describing the uses of the *stethoscope*, his invention.

Germany, 1819. Friedrich Jahn, who in 1811 founded the *Turnplatz*, the first open-air gymnasium, is arrested and the *Turnplatz* closed. Jahn played a leading part in the formation of the student patriotric societies known as the *Burschenschaften*, and is accused of being involved in subversive activities.

Scotland, 1819. The Scottish industrialists Thomas Hancock and Charles Macintosh perfect a process for manufacturing waterproof material.

United States takes over Spanish Florida

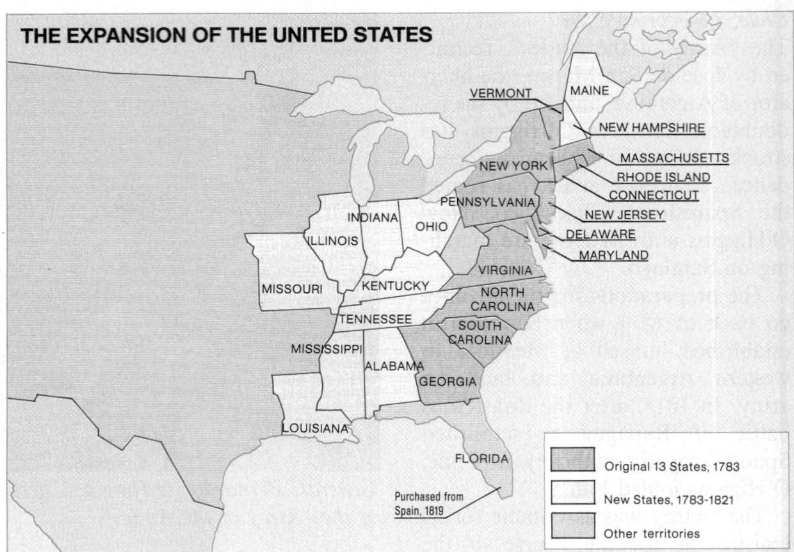

Washington DC, 22 February 1819
A private war fought by General Andrew Jackson, the hero of New Orleans, has brought all Florida under United States rule.

Congress has long claimed Florida as its own and today, in a treaty signed between the secretary of state John Quincy Adams, and his Spanish counterpart, Spain relinquishes claims to all its colonies east of the Mississippi. Jackson launched his invasion last year, after being ordered to suppress the Seminole Indians on the border. With an army of 1,000 men from his home state of Tennessee, supplemented by the Georgia militia and friendly Indians, Jackson pushed on southwards, executing several Indian chiefs and two white sympathisers, both British, before taking Pensacola and establishing military rule. Jackson faces a congressional inquiry, but few believe that he will be censured.

New alliance ties up Europe's loose ends

Aix-la-Chapelle, 21 Nov 1818
The Quadruple Alliance today completed its deliberations in the first congress of a series designed to discuss measures that would be "most salutary for the repose and prosperity of the nations and for maintaining the peace of Europe".

The congress tidied up much of the debris of the Napoleonic years. It agreed to Wellington's suggestion that the occupation troops should be withdrawn from France, and cut France's war indemnity. France is also to be admitted to the newly-constituted Quintuple Alliance. The congress also confirmed the decision taken at the Congress of Vienna extending the civil rights of German Jews, the slave trade was discussed and measures for Napoleon's security on St Helena, approved. Lord Castlereagh, Britain's foreign secretary, has played a major role in the congress, but there are signs that he is already becoming disillusioned with the system of congresses, he has warned the others that Britain will not take part in interfering, unasked, in the internal affairs of other states.

Louis XVIII: the main beneficiary of the Quadruple Alliance.

African military genius expands empire

Southern Africa, 1819
The greatest military genius Africa has yet known, Shaka, the chief of the Zulus, is building an empire.

Shaka's childhood was a psychological disaster. The product of incest, he was driven with his mother from his home and hounded and despised by all who came into contact with him. Burning with revenge, he took to the profession of arms. He proved so brilliant that by 1816 he had returned to his Zulu clan as their chief. His genius lies in his attention to detail. He banned clumsy sandels so his barefoot army runs at 50 miles per day. Unaware of his two contemporary geniuses, he synthesised the Napoleonic column and the Wellingtonian square, creating horns, and can thus attack his enemies on three sides at once.

He has also introduced a new weapon, the short-handled stabbing spear, and a tough new shield made of cow-hide, to protect his soldiers from the long-handled throwing spears of his enemies.

Spanish artist suffers black nightmares

Vision of age and death: Francisco Jose de Goya's "Old Women".

Germany cracks down on revolutionaries

August von Kotzebue, the czar's spy, murdered by radical students.

Karlsbad, Bohemia, August 1819
Austria's Prince Metternich has persuaded ministers of the German states, meeting at Karlsbad, to adopt sweeping repressive powers to ban political meetings, impose press censorship and investigate the educational system.

The crackdown follows the stabbing to death by students of a minor author, Kotzebue, who topped up his income by sending the czar reports on student agitators. Student associations have been calling for a "true" German fatherland and protesting against foreign influences and Jews, who are now prominent in German literary circles. The students wear beards and long hair; they are confused romantics, but to the conservative Metternich they threaten revolution.

Red tide predicts Hawaiian king's death

Honolulu, 8 May 1819
Kamehameha ("the Lonely One"), who united the islands of Hawaii, died today. His death was predicted two days ago after an ominous red tide flowed into Honolulu harbour.

Innovative and ambitious, from his first contact with Europeans he was determined to exploit western technology to build his kingdom. "As savage a looking face as I ever saw" was how Cook's Lieutenant King described him, adding, "he was good natured & humourous, although his manner shewed somewhat an overbearing spirit".

Demanding payment for port facilities with firearms, and using renegade seamen as military advisers, he conquered one island after another. His greatest gift was patience. When his invasion fleet bound for Kauai was wrecked he spent 13 years rebuilding it before trying again. The threat was sufficient to secure Kauai's obedience.

The victory, without a shot fired, was his greatest triumph. "Endless is the good I leave you to enjoy" were his last words.

Madrid, December 1819
Francisco Goya, who has survived a dangerous illness, is covering the walls of his house, the *Quinta del Sordo* (Villa of the Deaf), with horrific "black paintings". One shows Death awaiting two old women, obscene in their youthful dresses and make-up. Another shows Saturn devouring his two sons. A third portrays Goya's rescue from his deathbed by his doctor. The doctor holds him upright to take a draught of medicine while, in the shadows ghoulish faces watch.

Goya's dark imagination dates from the illness that left him deaf in 1792. He went on to create his etchings *Los Caprichos* and *The Disasters of War*.

Scottish author's "Ivanhoe" starts trend for historical novels

Edinburgh, December 1819
A romantic novel of adventure, *Ivanhoe*, has sold out its first edition here within a fortnight. As with the *Waverley* novels, of which *The Bride of Lammermoor* is just out, no author is named. All are believed to be the work of the Edinburgh advocate Walter Scott, Scotland's most famous living poet since *The Lay of the Last Minstrel.* Novels like *Waverley, Rob Roy, The Heart of Midlothian* and *Old Mortality* show resemblances to Scott's historical poems. *Ivanhoe* leaves Jacobite Scotland for the mediaeval England of Richard the Lionheart, romance and chivalry.

1819 (1819-1820)

South America, 17 December 1819. At the congress of Angostura, the republic of Great Colombia – consisting of New Granada, Venezuela and Quito – is established. Simon Bolivar is made president and military dictator.

Britain, 1819. After the Peterloo Massacre, the government issues the Six Laws, banning any meeting of 50 or more people and any flag-bearing procession, authorising the arrest of anyone carrying a firearm and imposing a new tax on newspapers.

Spain, January 1820. A mutiny of troops in Cadiz sets off other revolts in northern Spain against King Ferdinand VII's anti-liberal policies and incompetent government.

Britain, 29 January 1820. George – prince regent since 1811, when his father, George III, was pronounced terminally insane – becomes king on his father's death.

New York, 6 February 1820. The ship *Mayflower of Liberia* leaves New York harbour for Sierra Leone in West Africa with 86 free Negroes aboard.

France, 14 February 1820. The duke of Berry, the nephew of the king, is assassinated by a fanatic. Elie Decazes is held indirectly responsible for the crime by the royalists and is forced to resign from the government.

China, 18 February 1820. Chinese officials at Wuchang strangle the French missionary Jean Francois Regis Clet.

Spain, 7 March 1820. To quell the mounting tide of revolt in Spain, King Ferdinand VII restores the constitution of 1812, which he abolished on coming to the throne in 1814.

USA, 9 March 1820. Congress passes the Land Act, paving the way for westward expansion by rich land speculators.

USA, 15 March 1820. Congress reaches a compromise on the slavery issue by admitting Maine to the union as a free state and Missouri as a slave state.

Europe, 28 March 1820. Louis XVIII of France and king William of the Netherlands sign a treaty fixing the frontier between their two countries at the 1790 border.

Hawaii, 30 March 1820. The first American missionaries arrive in Honolulu from New England.

Britain, 1 May 1820. The militant radicals involved in the Cato Street conspiracy to kill the prime minister and other members of the cabinet are executed. Their leader, Arthur Thistlewood, is suspected of being a police informer.

USA, 15 May 1820. Congress designates the slave trade a form of piracy.

Vienna, 24 May 1820. The Final Act of the Congress of Vienna is passed, authorising the German confederation to intervene in the affairs of member states threatened by internal unrest.

Germany, 20 July 1820. The German Confederation accepts the Final Act agreed at the Congress of Vienna.

Portugal, 29 August 1820. Encouraged by the revolution in Spain, the Portuguese army rebels at Oporto.

USA, 26 September 1820. The legendary frontiersman Daniel Boone dies.

USA, September 1820. Washington Irving publishes *The Sketch-book*, a collection of fanciful tales, including *Rip Van Winkle* and *The Legend of Sleepy Hollow*.

Germany, 19 November 1820. At the congress of Troppau, convened by Czar Alexander to discuss the rebellions in Spain, Portugal and Naples. Austria, Russia and Prussia sign the Troppau protocol, promising united action if national revolutions appear to threaten international order. Britain refuses to agree to the proposal.

USA, 6 December 1820. James Monroe is re-elected president in a landslide victory.

Portugal, 1820. The Portuguese rebels succeed in driving out the regency established in 1807 during King John VI's period in Brazil.

Africa, c.1820. Successful new crops are being introduced for cultivation on plantations – cloves into Zanzibar and cotton into Angola. Both crops are for export rather than local consumption, and their success depends on promoting the internal African slave trade for labour.

Africa, 1820. The Egyptian *pasha* Mohammed Ali conquers the Sudan and the region of Kordofan.

England, 1820. The poet Shelley publishes *Prometheus Unbound*.

England, 1820. Keats publishes a volume of odes and ballads which puts him in the first rank of contemporary poets.

Russia, 1820. Pushkin's romantic epic *Russlan and Ludmilla* is published.

France, 1820. Alphonse de Lamartine publishes his *Poetical Meditations*.

France, 1820. The doctors Pierre Joseph Pelletier and Joseph Bienaime Caventou discover quinine.

Simon Bolivar is "liberator" of Colombia

Colombia, 17 December 1819

Simon Bolivar, already liberator of his native Venezuela, has brought independence to another Spanish colony. The republic of Colombia, formerly a part of New Granada, was proclaimed today. A constitution has been adopted and Bolivar will be the first president.

Bolivar's plans for Colombia stalled in July 1817 when he was forced pitch camp on the island of Angostura on the Orinoco river. Faced by the ruthless Spanish general Morillo he was unable to advance his cause until he enrolled 6,000 English and Irish fighters, veterans of the war against Napoleon.

These troops, and Bolivar's promises of land and cattle, persuaded the *llaneros*, the people of the great plains. In February 1819 Bolivar was given dictatorial powers by a congress called at Angostura. He crossed the Andes in May and began a hard-hitting campaign. Caught by surprise, the Spanish lost a series of short, sharp battles until the decisive encounter at Boyaca on 7 August. This victory opened the way to Bogota, Colombia's capital, and Bolivar entered the city three days later.

Simon Bolivar, the "liberator" of Venezuela and Colombia.

Mounted businessmen kill demonstrators

The Manchester Yeomanry in St Peter's Fields: their glorious "Peterloo".

Manchester, 16 August 1819

More than 60,000 men, women and children turned up at St Peter's Fields, Manchester, today to hear the pugnacious radical farmer, Henry Hunt, deliver a speech demanding parliamentary reform and repeal of the Corn Laws. The crowd was orderly – families had brought picnic lunches – but when Hunt began to speak a force of Manchester Yeomanry appeared. The mounted yeomanry are undisciplined local businessmen, and they were soon laying about right and left with their sabres, crying "Have at them!". Magistrates, fearful of radical gatherings, had issued warrants for Hunt's arrest. Nine men and two women were killed and 600 injured in what is already called the "Peterloo" massacre.

Farmer George, Britain's mad king, dies

Windsor, 29 January 1820
After the death of his favourite daughter Amelia, George III's insanity became permanent and when he died today at Windsor Castle, after years of seclusion, the 81-year-old king was blind as well as mad.

He had lived through a tumultuous period in Britain's history. An empire was lost in America, another was founded in India and Australia and, alone among the European powers, Britain had remained steadfast throughout the Napoleonic Wars. If the king's stubbornness lost the American colonies, it gave stiffening to the wars with France.

A conscientious, family-loving man, George was not much liked by his people when he came to the throne; but, as he became better known, affection grew. He liked going into the country and talking about such homely matters as making apple dumplings, so that he became known as Farmer George.

George III, the farmer king who lost one empire but gained others.

George asked Lord Bute "to save a great deal of trouble" and find him a wife. The marriage to Charlotte Sophia of Mecklenburg lasted for almost 60 years, until her death two years ago.

Plot to blow up the British cabinet foiled

Cato Street: the escape of the radical conspirators over the rooftops.

London, 23 February 1820
An estate agent turned revolutionary was seized today with a score of his followers and a cache of arms in a loft in Cato Street, off the Edgware Road. Arthur Thistlewood, last in the public eye when he called for an uprising at a Spa Fields meeting, came out of prison last year and set about plotting to blow up the cabinet while they took dinner in Grosvenor Square. Thistlewood was greatly helped by a certain Mr Edwards, who provided pistols, grenades, powder and ball and gave the place and date of the dinner.

Edwards was really a police informer, so the "horrid conspiracy" was broken. Now the government claims its repressive measures have been justified and has called an election.

Uneasy deal over slave states in US

Washington, DC, 15 March 1820
After a noisy, rancorous all-night debate, Congress has accepted a compromise solution to the slavery argument which is threatening to tear these United States apart. Until now, slave and non-slave states have been equal in number, but, with the application by nonslave Maine for statehood, the balance will be upset.

The compromise was proposed by a senator from Illinois. It allows Maine to be admitted as a "free" state, with Missouri to join the union as a slave-state. It also calls for slavery to be totally prohibited north of a line in the Louisiana Purchase area.

Despite this uneasy agreement, the question of Missouri's admission and the opposition to slavery by the northern states threaten to provoke a major political upheaval, with the political divisions between north and south ever widening.

A slave gang in chains, passing the Capitol in Washington, DC.

Steamship crosses the Atlantic in 26 days

Liverpool, England, 20 June 1819
The steamship *Savannah* arrived here today – 27 days after she left Savannah, Georgia. Although she was aided by sail, *Savannah* is the first ship to cross the Atlantic partly by steam power. When she left her home port, dubious onlookers described her as a "steam coffin", but it is her captain, Moses Rogers, who has the last laugh.

Steam power has been harnessed to open up the vast open spaces of North America to exploration. The United States War Department has commissioned five steampowered paddle-boats to survey the Missouri river. The first of these, the *Independence*, travelled 200 miles upstream to the settlement of Franklin in May to unload sugar, flour and whisky. Three other ships were less successful, their deep draughts unsuitable for the numerous Missouri mudbanks.

The most successful exploration trip was made by the *Western Engineer*, which has reached Council Bluffs with a team of leading US scientists and artists. *Western Engineer* is "dragon shaped" with a raised head that snorts steam and draws only 20 inches. She can travel at three miles per hour.

The steamship "Savannah", arriving at Liverpool after crossing the Atlantic.

1820 (1820-1821)

Southern Africa, 1820. Southern Africa is thrown into turmoil by the great Mfecane wars. Since the defeat of the previously all-powerful Ndwandwe army by the Zulus at Mhlatuze last year, there has been a chain reaction of defeated armies fleeing and attacking rival chiefdoms. While the Zulus are subduing people to the south, remnants of the Ndwandwe army have formed raiding parties, know as *Ngoni*, as far as Maputo Bay in Mozambique.

Japan, 1820. Following increasing incursions by foreign ships into Japanese waters, a special commissioner is appointed to build up coastal defences, especially around Edo (*Tokyo*).

Russia, 1820. A mutiny by the Semonovsky regiment induces Czar Alexander to halt his programme of social and political reforms.

USA, 1820. The population of the USA reaches almost ten million.

China, 3 February 1821. Following the death of the Emperor Jiaqing last year, Daoguang comes to the throne.

Rome, 23 February, 1821 The poet John Keats has died of consumption after the publication last year of *Ode to a Nightingale*.

Mexico, 24 February 1821. General Agustin de Iturbide proclaims Mexican independence, declaring that the government should be a constitutional monarchy under Ferdinand VII of Spain or another European king.

Greece, February 1821. Archbishop Germanos of Patras calls for a Greek uprising against the Ottomans.

Ottoman Empire, March 1821. The Greek nationalist leader Alexander Ypsilanti invades Moldavia with a battalion, seizes its capital, Jassy, and occupies Bucharest.

Italy, March 1821. An Austrian army overthrows the revolutionary government installed last July by Guglielmo Pepe and restores King Ferdinand to the throne.

Italy, March 1821. King Victor Emmanuel of Piedmont, who has refused to accept a constitution, is forced to abdicate in favour of his brother Charles Felix. In Charles Felix' absence, Charles Albert of Savoy becomes regent and proclaims the Spanish constitution.

Italy, 8 April 1821. A combined Austrian and Sardinian army defeats the Pietmontese army at the battle of Novara, returning Piedmont to Sardinian rule.

Greece, April 1821. The Ottomans begin a campaign of repression following a Greek massacre of Turks in the Peloponnese.

South Atlantic, 5 May 1821. Napoleon dies on the island of St Helena.

Germany, 12 May 1821. The congress of Laibach, which opened in July, comes to an end. In spite of British opposition, the congress authorised Austria to put down the rebellions in Naples and Piedmont.

Switzerland, May 1821. The cantons expel liberal Italians who had taken refuge in Switzerland after the defeat of their movements in Piedmont and Naples.

Berlin, 10 June 1821. The German composer Carl Maria von Weber triumphs with his opera *Der Freischutz*.

Ottoman Empire, 19 June 1821. Greek troops under Alexander Ypsilanti are heavily defeated by the Ottomans at the battle of Dragasani, west of Bucharest.

Florida, 17 July 1821. Andrew Jackson becomes governor of Florida.

Peru, July 1821. Peru declares itself independent of Spain.

Russia, 4 September 1821. Czar Alexander declares that Russian influence in North America extends as far south as Oregon and closes Alaskan waters to foreigners.

Central America, 15 September 1821. San Salvador proclaims its independence and becomes a member of the United Provinces of Central America.

China, 23 September 1821. Terranova, a sailor on the US ship *Emily*, is executed by the Chinese for the death of a Chinese.

Greece, 5 October 1821. Greek rebels capture Tripolitza, the main Turkish fort in the Peloponnese.

England, October 1821. Thomas de Quincey publishes his *Confessions of an English Opium Eater*.

China, 15 December 1821. A Chinese is killed in an attack on the landing party from *HMS Topaze* at Linding; the surrender of British sailors for punishment is refused.

Central America, December 1821. Panama declares itself independent of Spain and unites with Colombia.

Germany, 1821. The philosopher Georg Hegel publishes *The Philosophy of Right*.

USA, 1821. The USA's first natural gas well is tapped at Fredonia, New York state.

USA, 1821. The distinguished soldier Davy Crockett – who claims to have killed 105 bears in seven months in the western Tennessee wilderness – is elected as a state legislator in Tennessee.

Detail from "Landscape: Noon", usually referred to as "The Hay Wain".

John Constable portrays idyll of rural life

London, 1821

John Constable is showing a large six-foot landscape at the Royal Academy summer exhibition at Somerset House this year. Entitled *"Landscape: Noon"*, it shows an empty hay wain fording the river Stour in Suffolk beside a lowly rural cottage. The scene is painted with freshness and captures the light of an overcast midday sky, but it has not been noticed as much as the fashionable "history" paintings that make up much of the exhibition, nor has it been sold. Constable spends the summer sketching in Suffolk around East Bergholt, where his father, a wealthy corn merchant, owned several mills.

Like J M W Turner, he was trained at the Royal Academy schools, but whereas Turner was elected an RA in 1802 at the age of only 26, Constable is still only an Associate at 45. He was married recently and moved to Hampstead where he turns his outdoor sketches into large easel paintings.

Britain tightens its grip on West Africa

West Africa, 15 January 1821

The West African enclave of the Gold Coast, formerly administered by British merchants, becomes a crown colony today.

The official reason is to provide Britain with a secure base for its anti-slavery patrols. The real reason is fear of growing French influence in Senegal, and the news that the US will be establishing a home for liberated slaves (*in Liberia*). Britain, with a colony for former slaves in Sierra Leone, a second colony on the river Gambia, and numerous coastal trading forts, is determined to contain the new arrivals and dominate trade in the interior. Whether it will succeed, given both the competition from France and the USA and the cost, is open to question.

Secret societies in Neapolitan rising

Ferdinand, the king of Naples, a bulwark against reforms.

Naples, 2 July 1820

An unexpected revolt by two military garrisons outside Naples has put pressure on King Ferdinand to bring in constitutional reforms similar to the concessions made in Spain after the uprising there last January.

The rebel officers under General Pepe wanted the restored royal house limited to a constitutional monarchy, administrative reforms to lower taxes and a more vigorous attack on feudalism.

The officers from the Nola and Capua garrisons also resent serving under an Austrian commander. Many belong to the *Carbonari* – charcoal burners – the Masonic-style secret societies that now flourish in Italy. The Neapolitan Carbonari are mainly affluent republican sympathisers, but without any clearly defined leadership.

Asian poet dies

Annam (Vietnam), 1820

Nguyen Du, the author of the verse novel *The History of Kieu*, a celebration of filial piety, and the finest contemporary practitioner of classical Chinese poetry, has died. A mandarin, born in Ha-Tinh, he served the Le dynasty, but refused to serve the Tay-Son emperor and was exiled, when he wrote his most exquisite poetry. He returned to public office under Gia-Long, but in his heart remained a poet – the greatest Annam has produced.

Napoleon dies of boredom and ill-health

St Helena, 5 May 1821

Napoleon is dead. At two this afternoon he muttered: *"France. Armee. Tete d'armee. Josephine"*, and then fell into a coma. His household gathered round him and watched him die peacefully as the sun slipped into the sea.

He was 51 and had spent the last six years like a caged lion, suffering the petty indignities heaped on him by the British governor, Sir Hudson Lowe, who was ever fearful that "General Bonaparte" would escape. Napoleon took a certain delight in taunting Lowe, but as he grew ill Lowe's treatment of him became vindictive.

His approaching end became apparent last October when he fainted, and his vomiting and lack of appetite weakened him. He told his faithful court chamberlain Montholon: "There is no more oil in the lamp." Now, the light of this military genius has gone out on a lump of volcanic rock far from the battlefields of Europe which he ruled with such mastery and the courts where he made and unmade kings.

Napoleon: the British claim he died naturally, the French are unsure.

George's embarrassing queen has died

London, 7 August 1821

She was a queen who was vilified, persecuted and humiliated by her husband, George IV; but she was loved by the people, and when she died today, aged 53, the City of London decided to pay tribute to her. But George said Caroline's cortege would not pass through the City, even if he had to call out the Life Guards to stop it.

When George first set eyes on Caroline of Brunswick he had to drink a dram of brandy to recover. They had one child and then separated. For the rest of her life he tried to prevent her seeing her daughter. He ordered the passage in the Prayerbook which prays for "our Gracious Queen" to be removed. On coronation day last month, Caroline was barred from Westminster Abbey. The next evening she was taken ill at Drury Lane and died a week later. George is now free to dally with Lady Jersey and with Mrs Fitzherbert, whom he married secretly years ago.

Caroline with an admirer, Bergami; her husband publicly vilified her.

Electric motor built by English inventor

London, 1821

The enthusiastic young scientist Michael Faraday has already been at the centre of important discoveries in the field of chemistry. Now, turning his attention to electricity, he is making practical use of two recent discoveries and has created an electric motor.

Oersted, a contemporary scientist, has discovered that a flow of electricity through a wire produces a magnetic field around it. Ampere too, has shown that this field is magnetic. Now Faraday has built a device – little more than a scientific toy at the moment – which uses electricity to produce rotary motion.

This impressive demonstration of electro-magnetic rotation is a tribute to the hands-on skill and intellectual power of Faraday, who was once laboratory assistant to the great Humphry Davy. Davy had been so impressed by Faraday's letter of application that he offered him the job on the spot – he had just fired Faraday's predecessor.

Faraday: a scientist and inventor.

Greek independence movement born out of spontaneous revolts

Greece, 1821

The Ottoman empire's centuries-old domination of Greece is beginning to crumble as a spontaneous wave of nationalist revolts sweeps the country.

The signal for the uprising appears to have been a proclamation by the metropolitan of Patras on 25 March that Greeks should no longer acknowledge Ottoman rule.

Among the first Ottoman strongholds to fall were the Morean fortresses, temporarily undermanned with most of the Ottoman garrison away in Albania trying to suppress the breakaway movement there. Key ports around the Greek coast are now in nationalist hands after attacks by Greek privateers. Among the islands held by the rebels are Psara and Spetsai – where a wealthy widow has paid to blockade the local gulf. In Hydra, as in many other parts of Greece, shipowners have organised and funded the revolt.

1821 (1821-1823)

Japan, 1821. Ino Tadataka's map of the whole of Japan, based on accurate surveying, is finally finished. It was begun on the *shogun's* orders in 1801 and completed after Tadataka's death in 1818 by his followers.

Greece, 13 January 1822. At Epidaurus, nationalist rebels proclaim the independence of Greece and draw up a constitution.

Aegean, April 1822. The Ottomans massacre thousands of Greek insurgents on the island of Chios.

South America, 24 May 1822. Antonio Jose de Sucre, a lieutenant of Simon Bolivar, defeats the Spanish royalist forces at the battle of Pichincha, securing the independence of Quito (*Ecuador*).

South America, 29 May 1822. The provinces of Quito unite with Colombia.

Mediterranean, 19 June 1822. A Ottoman fleet is destroyed by the Greeks under Constantine Kanaris.

Spain, 30 June 1822. King Ferdinand VII is taken prisoner by the rebels led by Rafael Riego.

Mexico, 21 July 1822. General Agustin de Iturbide has himself crowned emperor of Mexico.

Greece, July 1822. Following the invasion of Greece by a large Ottoman army, the Greek government flees to the islands.

Portugal, September 1822. A liberal constitution similar to Spain's is adopted.

Brazil, September 1822. Brazil declares its independence from Portugal.

Italy, 20 October 1822. A congress opens in Verona to discuss the revolutions in Spain, Greece, Italy and South America. It is attended by Austria, Prussia, France, Russia and Britain.

Brazil, October 1822. Dom Pedro, the son of King John VI of Portugal, is proclaimed emperor of Brazil.

USA, 12 December 1822. The USA grants formal recognition to Mexico's new revolutionary government, headed by Agustin de Iturbide. In June President Monroe extended diplomatic recognition to Great Colombia.

Italy, 14 December 1822. The congress of Verona closes. In spite of British opposition, France has been authorised to intervene militarily in Spain to quell revolt and restore Ferdinand VII to the throne.

Crete, 1822. A rebellion in Crete, set off last year by the Greek War of Independence, is brutally put down by the Ottomans, with the aid of Egyptian reinforcements.

South Africa, 1822. The Mfecane wars spread west over the Drakensberg mountain escarpment onto the South Africa plateau. The Khumalo, led by Mzilikazi, a brilliant young general, have fled from Zulu assaults to confront the Pedi peoples of the Transvaal, who name the attackers *Ndebele*. Another small army has fled from the Zulus to attack the Sotho peoples of South Africa and Lesotho, provoking the rise of numerous competing Sotho armies.

California, 1822. California becomes part of the republic of Mexico.

West Africa, 1822. Encouraged and financed by the American Colonization Society ,a group of white clergymen and businessmen in the USA, the American Colonisation Society, freed African Americans found a small settlement on the West African coast. The new colony becomes known as Liberia.

Ottoman Empire, 1822. The city of Janina in north-west Greece capitulates to the Ottomans after a two-year siege. Its leader, Ali Pasha, is put to death.

Italy, 8 July 1828. The poet Percy Bysshe Shelley is drowned.

Russia, 1822. Pushkin's narrative poem *The Fountain of Bakhchisarai* is published.

Vienna, 1822. Franz Liszt, aged 11, makes his debut as a pianist.

USA, 23 January 1823. The USA gives formal recognition to Argentina and Chile.

Greece, January 1823. Having failed to take the key fortress of Missolonghi at the entrance to the Gulf of Corinth, the Ottomans are forced to withdraw.

Mexico, 19 March 1823. Agustin de Iturbide, who become emperor last year, is forced to abdicate following an uprising led by Antonio de Santa Anna.

Spain, April 1823. French forces led by Louis de Bourbon, the duke of Angouleme, cross the Pyrenees into Spain and march to Madrid. The rebels holding King Ferdinand VII are driven south to Cadiz, taking the king with them.

Prussia, 5 June 1823. Eight provincial assemblies in which the landed gentry hold the greatest powers are created. The reform is intended to reduce differences between the conservative, Protestant agricultural east and the more advanced, liberal and Catholic regimes in the west.

Britain, 1823. At a football game at Rugby school, William Ellis picks up the ball and runs with it, inventing a new game – rugby.

"Independence or death" cries emperor

Brazil, where the poor and barefoot take on the burden of independence.

Brazil, 12 October 1822

Dom Pedro, the 24-year-old son and heir to King John VI, today declared himself constitutional emperor of Brazil. He has been regent for the last 18 months, since his father finally gave in to demands that he return to Portugal.

Once seen as a dissolute young man, Pedro has come to symbolise the nation's hopes for independence in the face of Lisbon's efforts to reduce Brazil once again to the status of a dependent colony. He has refused an order to join his father in Lisbon, promising instead to remain in Rio de Janeiro. He has appointed a leading campaigner for independence as his chief adviser and in May accepted the title of "Perpetual Protector and Defender of Brazil".

Last month Portugal annulled all his acts. His response was simple: "The hour has come! Independence or death!"

Hero of Peruvian freedom has resigned

Lima, Peru, 27 July 1822

Jose de San Martin, the figurehead of the struggle for South American independence, has resigned from his post as protector of Peru. Faced by increasing dissatisfaction he will quit politics and may well leave the country he fought so valiantly for.

San Martin entered Lima on 9 July 1821 and took the title "Protector of Peruvian Freedom". His brief rule has been precarious and unhappy. Of all South America's colonies, Peru, with its rigid class system bolstered by slave labour, was least ripe for a republican government. Indeed, San Martin suggested that a European prince should be imported to establish a monarchy. It appears that San Martin's decision was influenced by yesterday's meeting with Simon Bolivar, the Colombian leader and a fellow freemason, at Guayaquil. Whether San Martin had already chosen to resign, or if Bolivar's refusal to back his regime with cash or troops left him with no alternative, is debatable. Either way, he left the meeting abruptly, returning to Lima. There, declaring himself no longer useful, he resigned.

Tobacco is becoming fashionable again in England, despite the complaint by Dr Johnson over a generation ago that the habit far from creating placcid tranquility is anti-social and barbarous.

"Hands off", US warns Europe

Washington, DC, 2 December 1823

The United States has sent a "hands off" warning to any European country contemplating future colonisation anywhere in the Americas – North *or* South. The declaration, by President James Monroe in his annual message to Congress, follows a rumour, picked up in London by US diplomats, that European powers were planning the reconquest of the Spanish American republics which had declared their independence from Spain.

The "Monroe Doctrine" declares that the United States' political system is essentially different from those in Europe; and that any attempt by a European country to extend its influence in America will be regarded as dangerous to America's peace and security.

James Monroe: the fifth president of the United States, in Washington.

French fear Spain's radical government

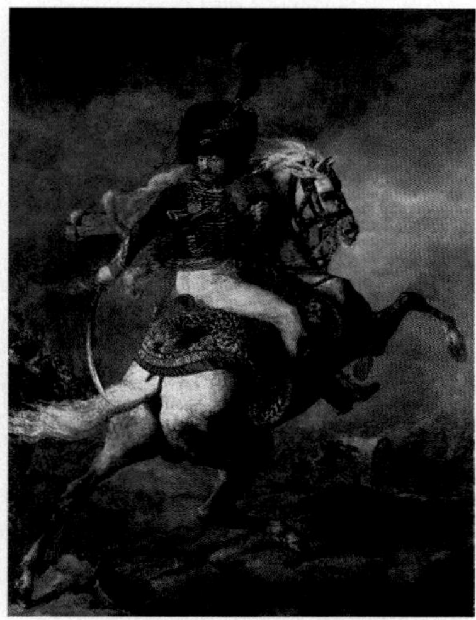

A French Hussar officer: the perfect vehicle for counter-revolution.

Paris, 25 December 1822

The French government today declared its intention of acting alone to overturn the revolution in Spain. Chateaubriand, the impetuous foreign minister, is already planning to get together an army of 100,000 men to march on Madrid and restore King Ferdinand VII to power. Since the revolution of 1820 Spain has been governed by the so-called "jail birds", the persecuted liberals of the 1812 movement.

For the past year France, Russia, Austria and Britain have been squabbling with each other about what to do about Spain. All of them fear the spread of revolution to their monarchies. But Britain particularly will be furious if today's move leads to restoring Spanish power in South America.

US founds African home for freed slaves

Montserrado, West Africa, 1822

An advance party of freed American slaves is building the first homes for a settlement at the mouth of the Sewa river as part of a plan to establish a Negro homeland for ex-slaves and their descendants in West Africa. The ex-slaves are the first of 6,000 that the American Colonization Society hopes will settle here.

The settlement's director is a white American, Jehudi Ashmun, who started the society over five years ago to raise funds to buy slaves their freedom and pay for their passage to Africa. Contributions have come from the society's branches in every state, churches and state legislatures opposed to slavery. West Africa was chosen for the new homeland as the first generation American slaves are thought to have come from here.

A miniature mask, made by the Dan people near the Sewa river.

British foreign minister commits suicide

Robert Stewart, Lord Castlereagh.

England, 12 August 1822

Lord Castlereagh, Britain's foreign secretary, who was due to leave for a summit meeting of European powers at Verona, was found dead today at his country home in Kent. His health had been deteriorating for some time and his doctor, concerned about his patient's mental stability, had removed all the razors. A penknife, however, had been overlooked and with it Castlereagh cut his throat.

Castlereagh's greatest achievement was the peace settlement after the Napoleonic Wars and the creation of a concert of European powers through regular consultation. He opposed the Russian "doctrine" of military intervention to preserve the status quo.

Cannibals forgiven by African statesman

Cape Town, South Africa, 1822

As anarchy reigns in the no-man's-land between Shaka's Zulu empire in the north and the British empire in the south, one man, Moshoeshoe, the chief of the Mokoteli, stands firm in defence of civilised values.

Refugees, driven out by the two empires, are competing for land. One tribe after another – the Hlubi, the Khumalo, the Ngwaneni – achieved temporary dominance only to be crushed. The final horror is the emergence of the *makhwata* (lean ones), men so hungry that they have taken to cannibalism. One victim was Moshoeshoe's own grandfather. With a magnanimity rarely equalled he has first defeated them and then – calling them the "living souls of my grandfather" – given them cattle to discourage their appalling practice.

Alas, Shaka, instead of saluting his statesmanship, sees him as a rival, and is sending his warriors to punish for him for his presumption in acting as peacemaker. There seems to be little chance of relief for the people of southern Africa.

Mr Macintosh invents a waterproof fabric

Manchester, 1823

The latest – and perhaps the most suitable – fashion being worn in Manchester is the Macintosh. It is a raincoat made of a layer of rubber sandwiched between two layers of cloth. The material was invented by Charles Macintosh, a chemist.

The material does have some disadvantages. It tends to become brittle in cold weather and can smell pungently in the heat of summer. And the work-force in Macintosh's Manchester factory tends to be inept in making the material to the owner's prescription.

Macintosh, who began his working life in a counting house, has made several notable industrial contributions in the manufacture of dyes, bleaching powder and other commercial chemicals.

1823 (1823-1824)

South Africa, June 1823. Sotho Mfecane raiders are defeated by the Tswana people at the battle of Dithakong. The Tswana victory stops the further invasion of Sebetweane's Kololo, who were rushing to join the attack, and turns the Kololo northwards to invade Botswana instead.

Central America, 1 July 1823. Guatemala, San Salvador, Nicaragua, Honduras and Costa Rica declare themselves sovereign states within the confederated United Provinces of Central America.

Britain, 14 July 1823. King Kamehameha II and Queen Kamamalu of the Hawaiian Islands die of measles during a visit to Britain.

Mexico, 20 August 1823. Mexico recognises the independence of the United Provinces of Central America.

Rome, 28 August 1823. Leo XII becomes pope in succession to Pius VII, who died a week ago.

Spain, 31 August 1823. The Spanish revolutionary forces under Rafael Riego are defeated by the French at the battle of Trocadero.

Spain, 23 September 1823. Cadiz falls to the French. Ferdinand VII, who was taken there by the rebels, is handed over to the victors and restored to the throne.

USA, 7 November 1823. John Quincy Adams, the US secretary of state, rejects a British offer to form an alliance to thwart possible intervention by the Holy Alliance in Latin America.

India, 1823. In spite of the failure of his mission to China, Lord Amherst is appointed governor general of India.

Britain, 1823. Robert Peel, the home secretary, institutes wide-ranging reforms of the criminal law and prison system.

France, 1823. Nicephore Niepce discovers the principle of photography.

South-East Asia, February 1824. Following the Burmese occupation of Assam and Manipur in north-eastern India, war breaks out between Britain and Burma.

USA, 17 April 1824. The USA signs a treaty with Russia settling their border dispute.

Burma, 11 May 1824. British naval forces under Sir Archibald Campbell seize Rangoon.

France, 6 June 1824. The foreign minister, Chateaubriand, is abruptly dismissed after a bitter disagreement with the prime minister, Villele, especially over the issue of Greece.

Britain, 6 June 1824. A law is passed recognising the right to strike.

Mexico, 19 July 1824. Returning secretly from exile, Agustin de Iturbide, the former president, is arrested and shot.

USA, 4 August 1824. The USA gives formal diplomatic recognition to the newly independent nation of Brazil.

France, 15 August 1824. Censorship is reimposed.

France, 16 September 1824. Louis XVIII dies and the count of Artois, his brother and the leader of the Ultra-royalists, succeeds him as Charles X.

Rhode Island, October 1824. A mob of more than 400 whites riots and attack Negro residents of Providence in a protest against their employment.

USA, 1 December 1824. No clear winner emerges from a bitterly fought presidential election.

Peru, December 1824. Following the defeat of the Spanish by independence fighters under Antonio de Sucre at the battle of Ayacucho, the Spanish are forced to agree to the withdrawal of the royalist troops remaining in Peru. Peruvian independence is secured.

North America, 1824. An expedition led by the explorer William Ashley discovers a huge salt lake west of the Rocky Mountains.

Greece, 1824. Mohammed Ali, the Albanian-born governor of Egypt, intervenes in the Greek War of Independence on the side of the Ottomans.

USA, 1824. An American invention makes it possible to harvest at three times the previous speed. Drawn by a two-horse team, Cyrus McCormick's reaper-harvester is an improvement on Patrick Bell's, which is pushed from behind.

California, 1824. The constitution of the United Mexican states is adopted, giving California territorial status.

Hawaii, 1824. The dowager Queen Kaahumanu becomes regent for her young brother Kauikeaouli.

France, 1824. The painter Delacroix exhibits *The Massacre at Shios* at the Paris Salon.

Vienna, 1824. Ludwig van Beethoven composes his ninth symphony.

London, 1824. The National Gallery opens.

Britain, 1824. The Society for the Prevention of Cruelty to Animals is founded.

British use steamboat to seize Rangoon

British troops storming one of Rangoon's principal stockades.

Rangoon, Burma, 11 May 1824

A task force of 11,000 British troops has captured Rangoon as a retaliatory first step against the king of Burma's invasion of the British Indian possession of Shahpuri in February.

The British commander-in-chief, Sir Archibald Campbell, is under orders from Lord Amherst, the governor general, to occupy all of Burma and depose the king. Sir Archibald, whose task force took Rangoon after a 400-mile river journey, plans to leave 3,500 men to garrison Rangoon before proceeding up the Irrawaddy to attack this mountainous kingdom's other main cities. However, the task force is locked in Rangoon until the end of the year as the monsoons, expected any day now, make the river impassable for six months. Included in the flotilla is the first steamboat to be used by Britain in war.

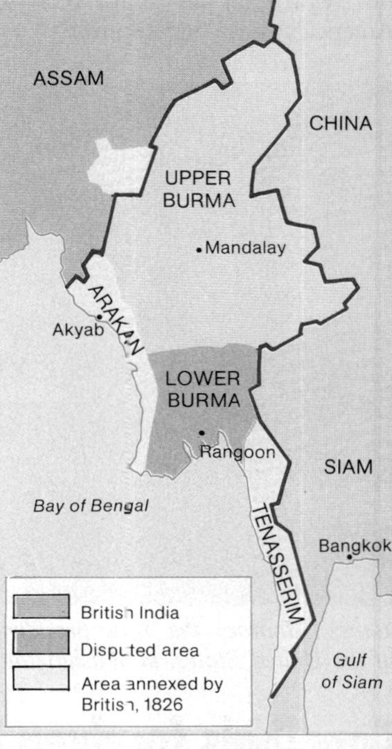

Steam engine study generates new law

Paris, 1824

A former officer, Sadi Carnot, has long been fascinated by scientific and technical ideas and turned his attention to improving the design of steam engines. France, he felt, was lagging behind in this area which has brought such wealth to Britain and the United States.

His interest is in the theoretical use of steam as a driving force. Now he has published an essay showing how the motive power of a steam engine is produced when the heat drops from the temperature in the boiler to the cooler condenser.

The efficiency of engines, Carnot concludes, depends on the temperatures of its hottest and coolest parts – and not on the energy source that drives the machine.

The "Carnot cycle", as it is called, is not therefore just about steam power, but abut energy movement in particular. His conclusions form a law of *thermodynamics*.

Britain recognises workers' right to strike

Britain, 1824
This year workers are once more allowed to form trades unions, and to strike, thanks to the repeal of the controversial Combination Laws of 1799 and 1800.

The change in the law was the result of a campaign by the activist Francis Place and the radical politician Joseph Hume. A parliamentary committee appointed to inquire into the Combination Laws was packed by Hume, and its recommendation for repeal was accepted by parliament. But Place was the inspiration. Unlike some of his associates, Place is not a political extremist, but a self-made businessman – refused work in 1793 after organising a strike – who has managed to support a wife and ten children from his tailor's shop.

He seeks reform, not revolution, and one of the keys to his success has been his ability to work with people from different classes, like Joseph Hume and the political economist J R McCulloch. Above all he has shown himself to be a brilliant manager of committees.

Cartoon politics: George IV, as Coriolanus, addresses the workers.

Louis XVIII, a good king of France

Paris, 16 September 1824
Louis XVIII, who died today after a long illness, leaves a strong, peaceful and prosperous France. This was quite an achievement for a man who was not a particularly strong personality and who came to power when France had suffered the shattering defeat of Waterloo.

Louis XVIII was the brother of Louis XVI, but he managed to escape the guillotine by fleeing to Brussels in 1791. As the revolution spread he moved first to Brunswick and then to Warsaw, until he finally went to England in 1807. In 1814, when the defeat of Napoleon seemed certain, he went to Ghent and made a shrewd compromise with the wily and opportunist French foreign minister, Talleyrand.

Talleyrand promised to restore the monarchy; Louis agreed to preserve the parliament.

Irish campaign for Catholic civil rights

Dublin, 10 May 1823
A 48-year-old Irish barrister, Daniel O'Connell, believes that he can pressure the British into granting full civic rights to Catholics by forming a mass movement based on an alliance between the Catholic middle class, the priesthood, peasants and moderate Protestants.

Earlier Catholic activist groups have been largely composed of lawyers, businessmen and landlords. With his Catholic Association, O'Connell intends to pitch his appeal right across the spectrum, from the rich, who will subscribe £1 a month or more, to the poorest, who will pay a penny a month. The funds will be used for both eduational purposes and political campaigning. O'Connell intends to take up Catholic grievances over rents, tithes, and the administration of justice.

Mexico is to become a federal republic

Mexico City, now the capital of Antonio de Santa Anna's new federal republic.

Mexico City, 1824
Mexico has declared itself a constitutional republic after 14 years of war and anarchy. The republic is to be federal, on US lines, and General Guadalupe Victoria has been appointed president.

Mexico gained its independence from Spain in 1821. The following year General Agustin de Iturbide, the Mexican conservative who had put down the radical nationalist revolt against Spain in 1815, seized power and declared himself emperor. His rule lasted for only ten months; then General Antonio de Santa Anna overthrew him and made way for the new republic.

Even then conflict amongst the Mexican republicans did not come to an end. Conservatives advocated a centralised state and radicals a federal state, each group identified with a different brand of freemasonry. The radicals appear to have won. To sooth the centralists' wounded feelings, President Victoria has recognised the special position of the Catholic Church, a key conservative demand.

Britain's Lord Byron becomes Greek hero

Byron, dressed as a Greek soldier.

Missolonghi, Greece, 19 April 1824
Lord Byron, who died of marsh fever here today, is being mourned as a national hero in Greece. He arrived in the Ionian islands last August and spent £4,000 on equipping a fleet to sail here to join the insurgents. In a poem written on his 36th birthday he foresaw his death.

Byron's poetry was mostly written in foreign lands. He first visited Greece on the Grand Tour when he was 22, and emulated Leander by swimming the Hellespont. From this eastern journey he produced the early cantos of *Childe Harold's Pilgrimage* and awoke "to find myself famous" as the archetypal Romantic figure, pale, sated with sensuality and suffering yet scornful of fate. After his marriage ended he left England in 1816 amid an aura of scandal. His years in Italy produced *Don Juan*, his long, relaxed, conversational poem.

His death removes the third English romantic poet abroad. Keats died in Rome in 1821, in his middle twenties, and Shelley was drowned the following year, aged 30.

1824 (1824-1826)

Australia, 1824. A penal colony is founded in Brisbane.

USA, 9 February 1825. John Quincy Adams, the former secretary of state, is elected president, ending a two-month impasse over the choice of the new head of state. The other main contender was Andrew Jackson.

Greece, February 1825. Egyptian troops led by Ibrahim Pasha, disembark in the Peloponnese and take the port of Pylos.

West Indies, 17 March 1825. The Spanish party on the island of Santo Domingo proclaims its independence in the name of the Dominican Republic.

France, 28 April 1825. The chamber of deputies adopts a law indemnifying emigres for loss of property damaged in the revolution.

Portugal, August 1825. Portugal recognises the independence of Brazil.

USA, 25 October 1825. The Erie Canal, linking the Great Lakes with New York City via the Hudson river, is completed.

Russia, 1 December 1825. Czar Alexander dies and there is confusion about the succession. His brother Constantine has secretly renounced his claims in favour of the youngest brother, Nicholas, who refuses to believe in the arrangement until he has secured a further renunciation.

USA, 12 December 1825. With the demise of the Federalist Party at the recent election, the rival Democratic-Republican Party splits into two factions in Congress.

USA, 25 December 1825. The USA signs a trade treaty with the Central American Federation.

Russia, 26 December 1825. The Northern Society – which is campaigning for representative government, the abolition of serfdom and social reforms – launches a disorganised revolt, which is immediately crushed by Nicholas, who has now accepted his succession as czar.

USA, December 1825. The Creek Indians sign a treaty ceding all their remaining land to the state of Georgia.

South America, 1825. Bolivia and Uruguay declare themselves independent of respectively, Peru and Brazil.

Japan, 1825. After further encroachments on the Japanese coast by British and American ships, the *shogun's* government issues an edict calling for the expulsion of all foreign ships from Japanese waters.

Caucasus, 1825. Persia rejects the 1813 treaty of Gulistan, which ceded the Caucasus region to Russia, and attempts to retake Georgia.

Sudan, 1825. Uthman Bey, the commander-in-chief of the Egyptian forces in Sudan, builds a citadel at Khartoum as the capital for Egyptian rule of the upper Nile.

India, 1825. A college is founded in Delhi to act as a channel for western learning in northern India.

England, 1825. *The Diary of Samuel Pepys*, which was left, with his library, to his Cambridge college, Magdalene, has been deciphered by John Smith and is published.

USA, 1825. Guided by visions, Joseph Smith publishes his *Book of Mormon* and founds the first Mormon church, at Fayette, New York state. He claims to be restoring the ancient, primitive Christian religion.

USA, 1825. On the death of her husband, Rebecca Webb Lukens takes over his boiler-plate mill in Pennsylvania, becoming the first woman manager in the iron industry.

France, 1825. Henri de Saint-Simon, the founder of a new system of social philosophy, dies. He argued for a reorganisation of society which would give the controlling share in government to industrialists and scientists instead of the military and property-owning classes.

Italy, 1825. Alessandro Manzoni publishes an historical novel entitled *I Promessi Sposi*, a Milanese story of the 17th century.

Denmark, 1825. The chemist Hans Christian Oersted isolates aluminium by reducing aluminium chloride with potassium.

South-East Asia, 1825. The aristocracy of the ancient kingdom of Java, led by Prince Diponegoro, rise up against the Dutch colonists.

Boston, 13 February 1826. The American Society for the Promotion of Temperance is formed.

India, February 1826. The British sign a peace treaty at Yandaboo with the king of Ava, bringing an end to a war that has raged since 1824. The Burmese cede the territories of Arakan and Tenasserim, agree to pay an indemnity of £ 1 million, conclude a commercial treaty and admit a British resident.

Portugal, 18 March 1826. King Pedro of Brazil inherits the Portuguese throne as Pedro IV on the death of his father, John VI.

Peruvians drive out Spanish rulers

Lima, Peru, 1825

The Spanish army in Peru has capitulated and 23,000 Spanish troops are to be withdrawn. The Spanish had little choice after their defeat by Antonio de Sucre at Ayacucho on 9 December. The independence of Peru is thus assured.

Peru had originally declared its independence in 1821, proclaimed by San Martin who asumed supreme authority. Factional quarrels weakened the new republic, San Martin was overthrown and Simon Bolivar took over the government. Taking advantage of the disorders, Spain counter-attacked.

Supported by Colombian reinforcements under de Sucre, Bolivar defeated the Spanish at Junin on 24 August 1824 and then returned to Lima. De Sucre took command and it was his army of 5,800 men that defeated the 9,300 Spanish troops at Ayacucho, ensuring their capitulation.

Antonio de Sucre: liberator of Peru.

Bolivia attains independence

Simon Bolivar, the scourge of Spain and now the liberator of Bolivia.

Bolivia, 1825

Another part of Spain's South American colonies has gained its independence. Upper Peru, among the most barren and remote areas of the continent, is to become the nation of Bolivia, named in honour of Simon Bolivar, the architect of South American freedom. Bolivar has also drawn up the Constitution.

For all its aspirations Bolivia is less a coherent state than a name. A vast territory of arid mountains and dense jungles, it lacks social, political or geographical cohesion. Its Indians are impoverished and the jungles virtually uninhabited. The ruling class lacks the ability to rule.

The former valuable trade route from Lima to Buenos Aires, which passed through the capital of La Paz, and in many ways justified the colony's existence, has been abandoned. Mining, once a vital industry, is no longer viable.

Sudan falls to brutal Egyptian invaders

Sudan, 1825

Mohammed Ali, the rough visionary who dragged Egypt into the 19th century with sheer will-power, has conquered the Sudan. Whether there is anything left there worth holding on to is debatable.

His motives are simple: to deny the Mameluke rebels (who previously effectively controlled all of Egypt) the sanctuary of Dongola, to milch the country of all the slaves and gold, and to divert his army from plotting at home. The army has obeyed his orders to the letter. Since they crossed the frontier in 1820, the brutality of the troops, commanded by Mohammed Ali's son, Ismail Pasha, has guaranteed Sudanese resistance. The Mamelukes of Dongola fled before him, but the Shayqiyya of the Nile fought and were massacred. Kordofan fell in 1821.

West African army defeats the British

Gold Coast, 22 January 1824
A British force has been wiped out by an Asante army under Osei Bonsu, with the British commander, Sir Charles MacCarthy, committing suicide. By coincidence, Osei Bonsu died of natural causes on the same day. The background to the British defeat is the refusal of the coastal Fante tribe to accept Asante domination. In this they were encouraged by the British who wrongly see Asantes as slave-traders and regard their hegemony as a threat to the standard policy of "divide and rule".

The major mistake of the British was to underestimate the strength of the Asantes under Osei Bonsu, who had ended the anarchy in the kingdom and centralised the state.

The defeat is the first serious defeat of a major colonial power by an indigenous African army. To recover their lost prestige, the British must now either mount a major expedition against the Asante or make peace.

A brass cast of an Asante family pounding "fu-fu", the staple diet in their region in Africa.

World's first steam railway is opened

The opening of George Stephenson's Stockton to Darlington railway.

England, 27 September 1825
There were scenes of wild enthusiasm here today when the Stockton to Darlington railway opened to traffic. It is the first railway in the world designed for steam locomotives. Parliament approved the building of the line in 1821, but it was only after the company acquired the services of a young engineer, George Stephenson, that the decision was made to go for steam. Stephenson's locomotive weighs eight tons and can run at speeds of between 12 and 16 miles an hour. It is not only the engine that is crucial. Stephenson has found that even quite small hills can reduce hauling power by 50 per cent. So he surveyed the route himself. He also pushed for malleable iron rails, much more suitable for locomotives than the cast-iron used for most of the present crude tramways.

Ottoman sultan annihilates Janissaries

Istanbul, 16 June 1826
The Janissary corps, once the elite of the Ottoman army, but lately a corrupt, anarchic force posing the crucial obstacle to reform, has been annihilated by Sultan Mahmud II.

Unlike his ill-fated reforming predecessor Selim III, Mahmud secretly built up a new force, with powerful artillery, to resist the inevitable Janissary mutiny. When the Janissaries marched on the capital yesterday, Mahmud's guns moved them down outside the *seraglio*, then bombarded them to destruction when they sheltered in Istanbul's Hippodrome.

The slaughter complete, Mahmud has abolished the Janissary corps, destroyed its standard, and proscribed its name. Thus, the feudal Ottoman empire is dead.

The Janissaries: against reform.

"Romantic" composer Weber dies at 39

London, 5 June 1826
German music has lost one of its pioneering figures with the death today from consumption of Carl Maria von Weber. He was 39. Weber, a cousin of Mozart's wife, championed a new emotional and "Romantic" style, which found its greatest expression in his German operas, especially *Der Freischutz* (1821) and *Euryanthe* (1823). The former won Weber international fame and he was invited to write an opera for London. He gave the first performance of this work, *Oberon*, at Covent Garden in June; it was a great success, but the effort dealt the final blow to Weber's health.

Czar's troops stop December coup plot

St Petersburg, 18 December 1825
After a day of mutinous turmoil, with soldiers and sailors breaking ranks and shouting for political reforms, the new czar, Nicholas, is tonight personally interrogating the plotters, who include princes from famous families, the Obolenskis and the Trubetskis among them.

The plotters, inspired by the open societies of western Europe, had become disillusioned with the repressive Alexander, and after his death they refused to take the oath to Nicholas, who sat on his horse amid the surging mob, for several hours before giving the order to open fire. In southern Russia, a mutiny collapsed after the fiasco in the capital was reported.

Czar Nicholas, who had little difficulty crushing the Decembrists.

Brothers go to war

Lisbon, May 1826
Civil war has broken out here after a constitutional battle between two brothers. Before his death, King John VI of Portugal had recognised Brazil as an independent country. His eldest son, Pedro, ruled in Rio. Before he made his move, Pedro issued a parliamentary charter for Portugal and then renounced his throne in favour of his seven-year-old daughter, Maria – provided she married his brother, Dom Miguel, who would have to abide by the new constitution. Dom Miguel accepted the conditions – only to reject parliamentary government once he was in power.

1826 (1826-1828)

St Petersburg, 4 April 1826. Russia and Britain sign the protocol of St Petersburg, agreeing to mediate between the Ottomans and the Greeks with the aim of achieving complete autonomy for Greece under Ottoman suzerainty.

Greece, 23 April 1826. Missolonghi falls to Egyptian forces under Ibrahim Pasha.

USA, 26 April 1826. The USA signs a treaty of friendship and commerce with Denmark.

USA, 2 May 1826. The USA extends diplomatic recognition to Peru.

Portugal, 2 May 1826. Pedro IV waives the right of accession to Portuguese throne; Maria is to become queen provided she marries Dom Miguel, his brother.

Panama, June 1826. Simon Bolivar convenes a congress of Latin American states to promote continental cooperation, but only Peru, Colombia, Mexico and the Central American Confederation attend.

USA, 4 July 1826. On the 50th anniversary of the signing of the Declaration of Independence, two American founding fathers and former presidents, John Adams and Thomas Jefferson, die.

Caucasus, 26 September 1826. The Persian cavalry is routed by the Russians at the battle of Ganja as their war over possession of the Caucasus intensifies.

USA, 7 October 1826. The first railway in the USA opens at Quincy, Massachusetts.

California, 27 November 1826. An expedition led by the 25-year-old fur trapper Jebediah Smith reaches San Diego, becoming the first Americans to cross the south-western part of the continent.

South-East Asia, 1826. Penang, Malacca and Singapore are united to form the Straits Settlements.

Russia, 1826. Czar Nicholas re-establishes the Third Section, Russia's secret police, which was abolished by Alexander.

USA, 1826. James Fenimore Cooper, the first major US novelist, publishes *The Last of the Mohicans*, a frontier story set in America's recent past.

Peru, 26 January 1827. Peru ends union with Colombia and declares itself independent.

Switzerland, 12 February 1827. The Swiss educationalist Johann Pestalozzi dies. He argued that the development of human nature should depend upon natural laws and that all knowledge is acquired by observation.

New Orleans, February 1827. Students from Paris introduce a new *Mardi Gras* (Shrove Tuesday) celebration in New Orleans, supplementing the traditional masked balls.

Vienna, 26 March 1827. The composer Ludwig van Beethoven dies.

Greece, 11 April 1827. Ioannes Capo d'Istrias is elected president of the Greek national assembly.

Greece, 5 June 1827. Athens falls to the Ottomans.

London, 6 July 1827. France, Britain and Russia sign the treaty of London, threatening to use force if the Ottoman empire does not agree to an armistice with Greece.

Britain, 8 August 1827. George Canning, who succeeded Lord Liverpool as Tory prime minister in February, dies. During a political career spanning more than 30 years, Canning promoted liberal policies at home and abroad.

Ottoman Empire, August 1827. In response to a joint demand by France, Britain and Russia, the Ottomans refuse to accept an armistice in their war with Greece.

Mediterranean, 20 October 1827. British, French and Russian forces destroys the Ottoman-Egyptian fleet at the battle of Navarino.

China, 8 November 1827. The *Canton Register*, the first English-language newspaper in the Far East, begins publication in Guangzhou.

Armenia, 1827. Russia seizes Yerevan from Persia.

USA, 1827. Chief Red Bird, the leader of an Indian uprising against continued intrusion by whites into tribal lands in Michigan territory, is captured and held prisoner by Lewis Cass, the governor of Michigan, putting an end to the so-called Winnebago war.

England, 1827. In his *New System of Chemical Philosophy*, John Dalton presents the first formulation of atomic theory.

England, 1827. A fundamentalist Christian sect known as the Plymouth Brethren is founded.

Scotland, 1827. The poet and Edinburgh advocate Sir Walter Scott admits that he is the author of the extremely popular *Waverley* novels.

South Africa, 1828. In Cape Colony the British abolish the labour laws of 1809-23 which tie Khoisan (Hottentot) servants to European masters as "apprentices", creating a labour crisis for poorer, especially Boer, white farmers.

Owen's followers fail to live in Harmony

Indiana, 26 May 1827

An attempt to create an idealistic, socialist community in the United States ended in failure today when the British philanthropist Robert Owen admitted that his commune on the banks of the Wabash at Posey County was near to collapse from internal anarchy.

The Welsh-born, self-made mill-owner – whose humane treatment of his employees in Britain had made him noted as a reformer and educationalist – bought 30,000 acres of Indiana and founded a "model" village which he named New Harmony. Nine hundred disciples – many of them intellectuals – followed him there, pledging to make "an empire of good sense". All property was to be held in common and there was to be "absolute freedom of action for the individual" and equality of the sexes. Chores were to be shared. Owen did the baking; the community suffered communal indigestion. But Owen overlooked human greed and jealousy, and has lost four-fifths of his fortune.

Quadrille dancing at Owen's earlier community in New Lanark, Scotland.

World mourns Beethoven, giant of music

Vienna, 29 March 1827

Ten thousand mourners turned out today for the funeral of Ludwig van Beethoven, who died three days ago aged 56 after months of illness. Among the pallbearers was the composer Franz Schubert; a funeral oration was written by the poet Franz Grillparzer. The occasion was a tribute to the stature of the man who altered the face of music, from the symphonies, concertos, quartets and sonatas of the 1800s to the glorious *Missa Solemnis* (1823), the *Choral Symphony* (1824) with its huge setting of Schiller's *Ode to Joy*, and the extraordinary vision of his last string quartets (1825-26).

Beethoven had aristocratic patrons but, unlike his teacher Haydn, and Mozart, was never employed by the nobility. He helped to usher in a new age of the independent artist as a hero greater than anyone eminent by birth alone. It is wrong to say that he "improved" on his predecessors, but he fashioned their musical legacy into something different, not "better", but more monumental, and more personally emotional.

Beethoven, for whom the act of composition was always a struggle.

Ottoman fleet destroyed

Navarino, 20 October 1827
The fragile peace in the Mediterranean was shattered today when the Ottoman and Egyptian fleets were destroyed by a combined fleet of British, French and Russian ships sent to guarantee Greek independence.

Over 50 Ottoman and Egyptian ships were sunk in the Bay of Navarino. They are reported to have opened fire first as the fleet sent by the three great powers entered the bay. The British, French and Russian ships were all at battle stations but under orders not to fire first.

Admiral Codrington, the fleet's commander, was told before he set sail to enforce "a pacific blockade" to maintain the uneasy armistice between the Greek nationalists and the Ottomans in the Peloponnese.

Why the admirals went beyond the spirit of the treaty agreed by the great powers in London last year not to take part in hostilities is certain to be the subject of an inquiry. In a pre-battle briefing Admiral Codrington is reported to have told his captains that, despite the treaty the British ambassador in Istanbul Stratford Canning, the brother of the late premier, believed that "cannon-shot would be the final arbiter" in settling Greek claims for independence.

The British lion watches as the Russian bear prepares to consume Turkey.

Current laws for electricity found

Europe, 1827
In his book *The Galvanic Circuit* the German physicist Georg Ohm has introduced a new law concerning the flow of electric current. Ohm's Law says that the amount of current is directly proportional to the potential difference or voltage, and inversely proportional to the resistance of the material through which it is flowing.

Meanwhile, in France, Andre Marie Ampere has discovered another law based on his observations of electric currents and magnetism. This gives a quantitative statement of the relationship between a magnetic field and the electric current that produces it.

Vital forces are put on the run by urea

Berlin, 1828
Although many people are clinging to the age-old belief that there is a "vital force" which distinguishes all matter taken from living creatures, science has now come up with an organic substance which has been synthesised from inorganic chemicals – a worrying development for the "vitalists".

The animal product is urea – the substance secreted in urine as an end-product of protein breakdown. Starting with ammonium cyanate, Friedrich Wohler, a chemistry teacher from the Berlin technical school, has succeeded in producing an entirely artificial synthetic version of the substance.

Ambitious Czar has his eyes on Armenia

St Petersburg, 1828
For Czar Nicholas, who began his reign by crushing an army mutiny, war with the sprawling Ottoman empire seemed a good way to keep his soldiers occupied. He has used the Greeks' struggle to throw off the Ottoman yoke as the pretext for going to war; but his ambitions extend from the Balkans to Asia.

In the Caucasus, at the eastern end of the Black Sea, Nicholas has just forced Persia to cede a substantial slice of Armenia, including Yerevan and the port of Baku. The czar is determined to seize the rest of Armenia from Turkey.

Meanwhile, he is consolidating Russia's grip on Siberia right through to the Bering Strait. A new governor-general has reorganised the administration, and agreements have been made with the United States and Britain settling the frontier of Alaska. Britain and France are none too pleased at Russia's expansionism, but there is little that they can do except seek to curb the czar's ambitions to seize a warm-water port in the Balkans.

A Persian warrior on horseback.

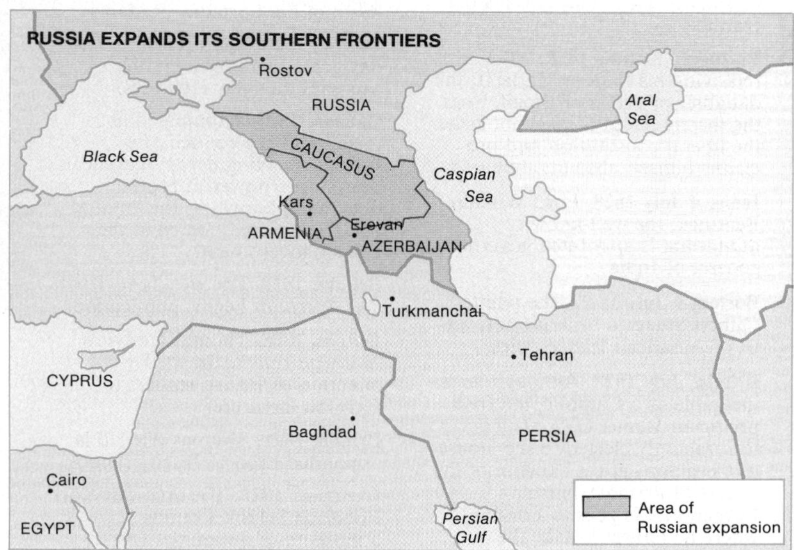

British PM quits after 15 years in office

London, February 1827
They said of Lord Liverpool, who has resigned as prime minister after a paralytic stroke, that he lacked vision but was a good chairman of committees. He entered the Commons when he was 20, waited a year before making his maiden speech, and became prime minister 21 years later, remaining in office for 15 years, a record exceeded only by Pitt and Walpole.

In the years of privation and unrest after the the Napoleonic Wars, Liverpool's government responded with repression, but public hostility was directed at his more colourful colleagues, Castlereagh and Sidmouth, rather than at him. He wanted to modify the Corn Laws, which were causing hardship.

Last December he began to feel that he could no longer face the burdens of office. "The government," he said, "hangs by a thread." He was married twice and has no children. Aged of 57, he lingers on, barely conscious.

1828 (1828-1829)

Britain, 25 January 1828. The duke of Wellington and Robert Peel form a Tory government.

Persia, 22 February 1828. Following the Russian capture of Tehran, Persia and Russia sign the treaty of Turkmanshai, ending their two-year war. Russia acquires part of Armenia, including Yereivan.

USA, 21 April 1828. *The American Dictionary of the English Language*, compiled by the editor and grammarian Noah Webster, is published.

Russia, 26 April 1828. In support of the Greek struggle for independence, Russia declares war on the Ottoman empire.

Washington, DC, 19 May 1828. President Adams signs a tariff bill imposing high duties on a wide range of manufactured goods.

Washington, DC, 24 May 1828. Congress passes the Reciprocity Act, calling for the elimination of discriminatory duties on goods imported from reciprocating nations.

Ottoman Empire, 8 June 1828. Pursuing their war with the Ottomans, the Russians cross the Danube.

Portugal, 30 June 1828. After removing his fiancee Maria II, the daughter of Pedro of Brazil, from the throne, Dom Miguel abolishes the liberal constitution and proclaims himself absolute monarch.

India, 4 July 1828. Lord William Bentinck, the well-known utilitarian, is appointed governor general of India.

Boston, 9 July 1828. The painter Gilbert Stuart, a brilliant portraitist of American leaders, dies.

Britain, July 1828. Although he is ineligible as a Catholic, the Irish politician Daniel O'Connell is triumphantly elected to the House of Commons at the expense of the liberal Protestant minister Fitzgerald. He goes to London, where he refuses to take the anti-papist oath of 1692, and his election is declared null and void.

Egypt, August 1828. The Egyptian pasha Mohammed Ali signs an agreement with Britain and France providing for the evacuation of Egyptian forces from Greece.

South Africa, 22 September 1828. The Zulu leader Shaka the Great is assassinated by his brothers Dingane and Mhlangane, who become joint kings. After his mother's death in 1827, Shaka became mentally unbalanced and started arbitrary executions. Zulu conquests reached a peak in the Natal area, with a double victory over the last Ndwandwe remnants in the north in 1826 and 1828.

Germany, 24 September 1828. Several German states found the commercial Union of Central Germany, after signing a customs agreement with Prussia and undertaking never to enter into any other such alliance.

Ottoman Empire, 12 October 1828. The Russians take Varna.

Vienna, 19 November 1828. The composer Franz Schubert dies.

USA, 3 December 1828. Backed by the fledgling Democratic Party, Andrew Jackson is elected president, defeating his long-time rival John Quincy Adams, the sitting president.

North America, 20 December 1828. Cherokee Indians cede their traditional lands in Arkansas territory to the USA and agree to migrate to lands west of the Mississippi river.

India, 1828. *Brahmo Samaj* is founded by Ram Mohan Roay in Calcutta. Its aim is to meet European criticisms of Hinduism by restoring Hindu worship to its early purity.

Madagascar, 1828. Queen Ranavalona becomes queen on the death of her husband, Radama.

Pacific, 1828. The French navigator Dumont d'Urville occupies the New Hebrides.

Canada, 1828. Nominated as a member of the council, the French-speaking deputy Papineau draws up a powerful protest document, known as the "ninety-two resolutions", aimed at the British government.

Britain, 1828. The weekly review *The Spectator* begins publication.

Britain, 1828. Thomas Carlyle's *Essay on Goethe* draws the attention of British readers to German literature.

Britain, 1828. Thomas Arnold is appointed head of Rugby school.

Germany, 1828. The architect Karl Friedrich Schinkel builds a museum of antiquities (*the Pergamon Museum*) in Berlin.

Germany, 1828. The *Memoirs* of the Italian adventurer Giovanni Casanova, who died in 1798, are published in many volumes.

London, 22 March 1829. At an ambassadorial conference, agreement is reached on the boundaries of an independent Greece.

Rome, 31 March 1829. Pius VIII becomes pope in succession to Leo XII, who died on 10 February. The new pope is opposed to the liberalism and the secret societies of Italian democrats.

London, 13 April 1829. The Catholic Emancipation Act becomes law.

Uruguay born of Argentina-Brazil rivalry

Uruguay, 1828

Territories along the eastern bank of the Rio de la Plata, formerly known in Brazil as the *banda oriental*, are to gain independent statehood. The new country is to be known as the republic of Uruguay.

The banda oriental has for many years been a focus of rivalries between Brazil and neighbouring Argentina, who took over the competition previously waged by their former colonial masters Portugal and Spain. Once part of the Spanish vice royalty of Rio de la Plata, the territory was annexed to Brazil by Portugal in 1776. When an Uruguayan independence movement emerged in 1825 it was funded by Argentina. Diplomatic rivalry developed into war and only mediation by Britain separated the rivals. Trade routes, threatened by the clash, were reopened and the disputed territory was removed from both spheres of influence as newly independent Uruguay, a buffer between two regional powers.

Schubert, master of the song, dies at 31

Vienna, 21 November 1828

Last year the composer Franz Schubert helped to bear the coffin at the funeral of his hero, Beethoven. No one could have imagined that today, less than two years later, Schubert himself would be laid to rest. He died two days ago, aged just 31, on the brink of great fame. He had been ill for some time.

Despite his early death, Schubert will surely be remembered for a long list of extraordinary masterpieces. His symphonies (especially the last two, one of which is incomplete) and chamber music wonderfully demonstrate his profound, lyrical expressiveness. But he was renowned in his lifetime above all for his vast output of over 600 songs, or *lieder*, which have established the *lied* as a major art form.

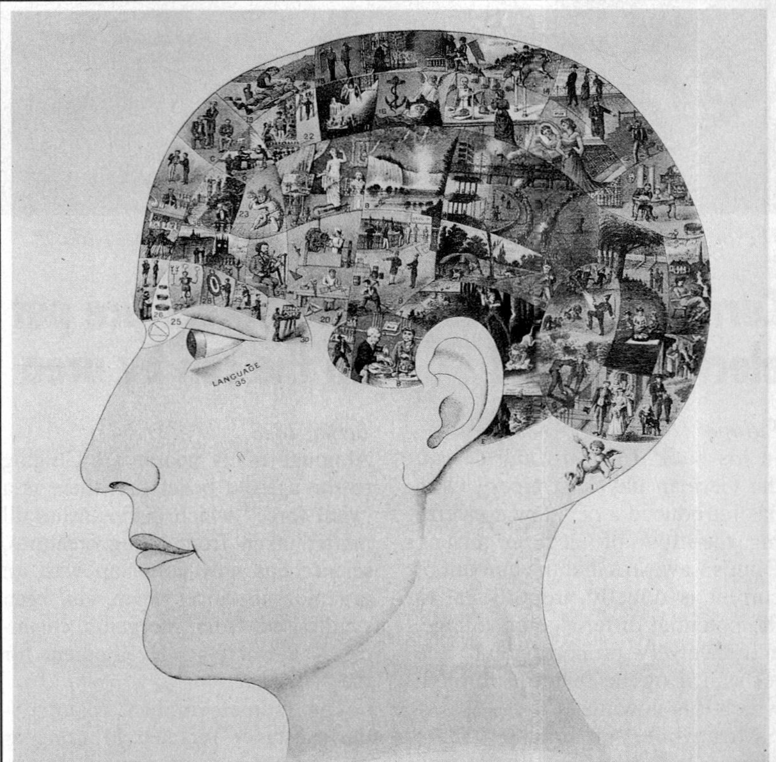

"Phrenology": the new science that claims to determine a man's morality, instincts, talents and intelligence by the shape of his head. It was invented by Franz Josef Gall, an Austrian living in Paris; his book "The Functions of the Brain", published in 1808, defined each part of the brain and established its potential. Criminologists find it fascinating.

British Catholics allowed to run for office

Fears of popery: Catholic clergy using the head of Robert Peel, a leading MP in the House of Commons, to batter down English Protestant institutions.

London, 13 April 1829
With the prime minister, the duke of Wellington, fighting every inch of the way against an evasive king and the intrigues of Protestant hard-liners, the Catholic Emancipation Bill has at long last become law. From today, Catholics can hold all public offices except those of regent, lord chancellor, and lord lieutenant of Ireland. It is being said that nobody but the "Iron Duke" could have done it.

After the success of O'Connell's Catholic Association in mobilising Irish opinion, the duke and his ally in the Commons, Robert Peel, agreed that emancipation was the only way of averting civil war in Ireland. The duke was ferociously attacked by the fanatical earl of Winchilsea, who accused him of introducing "popery into every department of the state". The duke responded with a challenge and they met in Battersea Fields one morning last month. The duke fired wide; the earl fired into the air and promptly apologised for his intemperate language.

Police force formed to stop city crime

London, 1829
Alarmed by the increase in crime in London, the British parliament has passed an act to create a police force for the metropolis. The measure was introduced by Robert Peel, the home secretary, who based his proposals on his experience of law enforcement in Ireland.

Though everyone agreed that the widespread robbery and violence called for tough action, Peel's plan has been attacked as an insidious attempt to enslave the people. But Peel claimed that an estimated one person in every 22 is involved in criminal activities. Besides, the new force will be answerable to parliament through him. But will the Peelers, as they are already being called, simply drive the criminals elsewhere?

Peeler and suspect: for many the police were seen more as a force for repression than protection.

US workers' movement grows in strength

New York, 1829
The newly-formed Workingmen's Party has polled 30 per cent of votes in the election here – confirming the emergence of a labour movement in the United States.

Craftsmen and artisans, alarmed at their declining status as *entrepreneurs* drove small shops out of business, were the impetus behind last year's creation of the Philadelphia Workingmen's Party. The "Workies" are campaigning for the reduction of the working day to ten hours, the abolition of imprisonment for debt, curbs on banks and other monopolies, free education for all, free public land, and liens on buildings to prevent cheating by corrupt contractors.

US bosses are alarmed by the involvement of foreigners like Robert Owen and Fanny Wright, whom they blame for the discontent.

German general's logic ends in total war

Berlin, 1829
A German general who fought at the Battle of Waterloo and with the Russians against Napoleon's *Grand Armee* has expounded the concept of total war in an analysis of the factors making for success in battle. In his massive work *Vom Kriege*, Karl von Clausewitz stresses the importance of chance and psychological factors, neither of which can be precisely calculated.

Strategy, therefore, should not be concerned solely with the enemy's armed forces, but should also embrace his resources and his will to fight. This means that enemy civilians and their property should be attacked. After all, he says, war is simply the continuation of diplomacy by other means.

Clausewitz, who comes from a family of Polish settlers in Prussia, joined the army at the age of 12 and saw his first battle a year later. He caught the eye of Gerhard von Scharnhorst, the director of the Berlin military academy, who introduced him at court; there Clausewitz met and married Countess Marie von Bruhl and later became *aide* to the crown prince.

Karl von Clausewitz, who served in the Prussian and Russian armies.

Britain stamps on Indian widow-burners

Bengal, 1829
Suttee, the practice whereby a Hindu widow burns herself on her husband's funeral pyre, has been abolished in British India.

Evangelicals, utilitarians and other advocates of western values have applauded the decision. "Old India hands", who have a deep respect for Indian cultures, regard it as arrogant, insensitive and potentially dangerous. Typically, the administrative class feels caught in a dilemma: a dilemma as old as Pontius Pilate's.

The practice varies throughout Hindu India. In Bengal suttee is rarely voluntary and widows are dragged screaming to pyres by sons anxious to avoid supporting aged relatives. In the martial areas, suttee is not only voluntary but attains a certain savage nobility.

Every Englishman in India has his suttee horror story. Some, like Charles Harding of the Bengal civil service, risked riot to resue widows. Interestingly the best argument against suttee was put by Akbar the Great 200 years ago. "It is a strange commentary on the magnanimity of men that they should seek deliverance through the self-sacrifice of their wives," he said.

1829 (1829-1830)

Ottoman Empire, 11 June 1829. The Russians under General Diebitsch defeat the Ottomans at the battle of Kulevcha, opening up a route to the Balkan mountains.

France, 8 August 1829. King Charles X appoints the prince of Polignac, an Ultra-royalist, to replace his chief minister Martignac, a moderate, who was dismissed two days ago.

Ottoman Empire, 14 September 1829. Following Russian victories at Silistria and Adrianople, Sultan Mahmud II signs a peace treaty with Czar Nicholas at Adrianople. He recognises Greek independence and accepts the terms of the London agreements of November 1828 and March 1829, which established the borders of Greece. Russia receives Moldavia and Wallachia from Turkey.

Mexico, 2 December 1829. President Guerrero exempts Texas from the Mexican prohibition of slavery, revising a decree issued in September.

Argentina, 8 December 1829. The provincial leader and federalist Juan Manuel de Rosas becomes governor of Buenos Aires. Since independence in 1816, numerous rebellions in the provinces have reduced Argentina to a state of anarchy.

Maryland, 22 December 1829. The Baltimore and Ohio Railroad Company opens the first passenger railway line.

Netherlands, 1829. The two Belgian parties, the Catholics and the liberals, form a united front against King William, who is becoming increasingly autocratic. Angered by a concordat signed with the pope two years ago and by harsh press restrictions, the opposition demands non-intervention by the state in church affairs and freedom of education and the press.

France, 1829. The Paris professor Louis Braille, himself blind since the age of three, invents a reading system for the blind.

France, 1829. Victor Hugo publishes a collection of poems entitled *Les Orientales*.

Netherlands, 1829. The Belgian statistican and astronomer Adolphe Quetelet carries out the first statistical analysis of a census.

Berlin, 1829. On Good Friday, Felix Mendelssohn and the choirs of the Berlin Academy perform Johann Sebastian Bach's *St Matthew Passion*, which has lain forgotten for 100 years.

London, 1829. The first Boat Race between Oxford and Cambridge universities takes place on the Thames.

London, 1829. The first horse-drawn omnibuses appear on the streets of London.

Europe, 1829. A passion for the waltz, a dance which made its appearance at the end of the last century, spreads through Europe.

England, 7 January 1830. Sir Thomas Lawrence, the president of the Royal Academy and the leading portrait painter during the regency, dies.

London, 3 February 1830. At a London conference, Britain, France and Russian guarantee Greek independence.

Ottoman Empire, 5 February 1830. Milos Obrenovic has himself declared hereditary prince of Serbia.

Paris, 18 March 1830. Following criticism of his policies, Charles X dissolves the chamber of deputies.

Chile, 17 April 1830. The conservative party under Diego Portales, supported by the upper classes and the clergy, victorious in a civil war with the pro-democratic liberal party.

Colombia, April 1830. Following the separation of Venezuela and Quito (*Ecuador*) from Colombia, Simon Bolivar abdicates as dictator of Colombia.

Ecuador, 13 May 1830. The republic of Ecuador is created, with Juan Flores as president.

Washington, DC, 28 May 1830. The Indian Removal Act, giving Indians perpetual title to western lands, is passed.

Britain, 26 June 1830. On the death of George IV, he is succeeded as king by his brother William IV.

Algiers, 5 July 1830. A French expeditionary force captures Algiers and deposes the *bey*.

Uruguay, 18 July 1830. Uruguay adopts a liberal constitution.

USA, 1830. The latest census records the population of the USA as nearly 13 million.

France, 1830. The philosopher Auguste Comte begins publishing his *Course of Positive Philosophy*.

Italy, 1830. The French writer Stendhal (the pseudonym of Marie-Henri Beyle) publishes a novel entitled *Le Rouge et le Noir*.

England, 1830. The critic and essayist William Hazlitt, the author of *A View of the English Stage* and *The Spirit of the Age*, dies.

England, 1830. William Cobbett, a leader of the reform movement, publishes *Rural Rides*, a survey of England, in which he christens London "the Great Wen".

Treaty preserves Ottoman empire

Adrianople, 14 September 1829

The Ottoman empire, reeling from a succession of defeats at Russian hands, remains intact under the terms of a treaty concluded here today. The Russians, it seems, shrank from marching on Istanbul for fear of destroying the empire and precipitating a European war.

Under the treaty the Ottomans retain a nominal title over the Balkan principalities of Wallachia and Moldavia, which pay a fixed tribute. But Ottoman fortresses have been evacuated, their subjects withdrawn, and native governors appointed for life. Russian influence is now paramount in these areas.

In the wake of the Greeks' successful fight for independence, the treaty represents a major shift of power. Although the Ottomans can hardly complain, other European powers, notably Britain, are anxious at the growing power of Russia, which is perceived as a threat to Mediterranean interests.

Map swap brings torture and deaths

Japan, 30 December 1829

The German scientist Philipp von Siebold sailed from Japan today under orders never to return after being found guilty of exchanging forbidden maps with his Japanese friend. He was lucky to escape so lightly. His friend did not.

The case started a year ago when the ship which was to carry Siebold home was blown ashore and had to be unloaded. When the cargo was examined the prohibited articles were found; they pointed directly to the brilliant mapmaker Takahashi Kageyasu who was already under suspicion for his friendship with Siebold.

Takahashi was tortured, and when he died in prison after months of interrogation his body was pickled so that sentence could be passed on him. When he was found guilty, his head was chopped off. Siebold suffered terribly from the thought that he had brought such pain to his friend and attempted suicide. It is believed, however, that he has made copies of the maps.

Farewell to the clef by Rossini the chef

Gioacchino Rossini: composer of some of Italy's finest comic operas.

Paris, 1829

Gioacchino Rossini has announced that *William Tell*, recently premiered here to rapturous acclaim, will be the last work from his pen.

Rossini's 39 operas, renowned for their characterisation, brilliant, subtle scoring and winning melodies, are adored in Paris (his home since 1824), London and Vienna (Beethoven admired *The Barber of Seville* of 1816), but the hectic world of Italian opera has left Rossini, aged 37, exhausted. He can now pursue his other pleasures. Rossini is a celebrated gourmet and wit. A tenor, whose high notes he thought merely showy, called on him. "Tell him to leave his C sharp on the coat rack," he said.

A dance craze hits Europe, the waltz: a reaction to the formality of the 18th-century minuet.

Indian tribes exiled to western America

Washington, DC, 28 May 1830
America's native people – the Indian tribes who roamed the prairies and woodlands of this country long before the white man came – are likely to be swept westwards, away from the populated areas. Under the Indian Removal Act signed today by President Andrew Jackson, the tribes will receive perpetual title to lands in the west, financial assistance and a government guarantee of security.

Debate in Congress was fierce and lengthy. Many representatives thought the bill was inhumane.

A Creek Indian chief, promised land "as long as the grass grows".

Supporters claimed that it was the only way to save the Indians from extinction. For President Jackson the bill represents a singular personal triumph. He has never hidden his ambition to drive the Indians westwards. Last year, he urged the Creek tribe to cede its land and go west.

"Your white brothers will have no claim on the land and you can live on it, you and all your children, as long as the grass grows or the water runs in peace and plenty. It will be yours for ever," he told the chiefs. Indians are resentful as well as sceptical. They are aware that much of their tribal land covers valuable mineral deposits, and it will immediately leap in value as developers move in. Cherokees in Georgia are planning legal action to safeguard their gold.

The "Jupiter" and the "North Star", two of the steam engines on the Liverpool to Manchester run.

Train accident kills top Tory as Britain goes mad about railways

Liverpool, 15 September 1830
William Huskisson, a Liverpool MP and former cabinet minister, died today after falling under a train making its inaugural run from Liverpool to Manchester on the first railway line built primarily to carry passengers.

The opening of the Liverpool and Manchester Railway is the latest development in an industry which promises to revolutionise transport. Enthusiasm for railways has grown steadily since the turn of the century. By 1812 there were 150 miles (240km) of track in South Wales alone, carrying coal; by 1821, 19 railway acts had been passed.

The man behind the railway boom is 49-year-old George Stephenson, engineer of the Stockton to Darlington Railway. This was opened in 1825 primarily to carry coal, but became the world's first steam railway to carry passengers. Stephenson is not only engineer of the Liverpool to Manchester line but designer of the "Rocket" engine which won a competition last year for the best steam locomotive. It was the "Rocket" that crushed Huskisson to death.

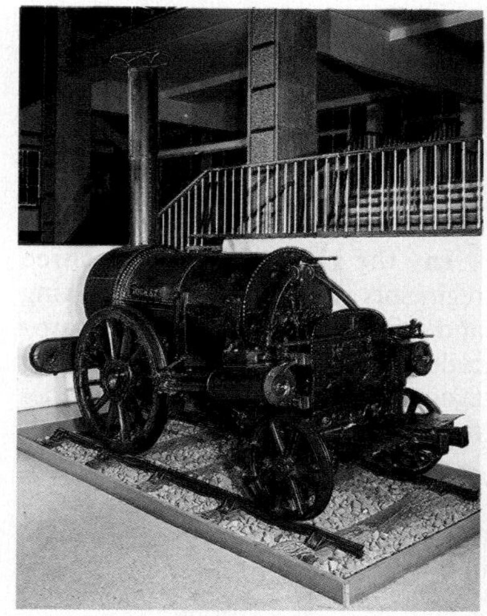

George Stephenson's famous Rocket.

The accident occurred as Huskisson, a distinguished Tory reformer, was crossing the tracks after greeting the duke of Wellington who, as prime minister, insisted on his resignation from the cabinet two years ago. He lost his balance as he was clambering out of the path of the oncoming train.

George Stephenson, the engineer.

His death may fuel safety fears, but new lines are planned from Bristol to London, Liverpool to Birmingham and Newcastle to Carlisle.

French expeditionary force seizes Algiers jewel collection

Algiers, 5 July 1830
A French expeditionary force today captured the fortress at Algiers giving France a much sought foothold in North Africa. In Paris the conquest may help to restore the fortunes of the embattled royalist Polignac ministry, which has been desperate for a foreign policy success as it goes to the polls.

French troops have also seized the priceless collection of jewels assembled by the now deposed *Dey* of Algiers.

Algiers: France's imperial rival, Britain, happily awaits the French defeat.

1830 ⇒

France, 26 July. King Charles X issues five ordinances limiting political and civil rights.

Paris, 29 July. Led by the marquis of Lafayette, liberals opposed to the king's ordinances seize Paris.

France, 2 August. Charles X abdicates.

France, 7 August. Louis Philippe, the Bourbon duke of Orleans, is proclaimed king of the French by the liberals.

Netherlands, August. Belgian resentment at forced union with the Dutch bursts into open rebellion in Brussels and throughout the provinces.

Netherlands, 4 October. A provisional government formed a week ago proclaims Belgian independence.

Netherlands, 27 October. The Dutch bombard the Belgian city of Antwerp.

USA, 5 October. Following diplomatic negotiations, President Jackson opens trade with the British West Indies.

London, 4 November. A conference of European powers to settle the Belgian question opens.

Britain, 16 November. The resignation of the duke of Wellington as prime minister ends nearly half a century of continuous Tory rule. He is replaced by the Whig leader, Earl Grey.

Poland, 29 November. Ten days after announcement of the mobilisation of young Poles in the Russian army to deal with the revolutionary threat in France and Belgium, an anti-Russian insurrection breaks out in Warsaw.

Britain, November. Violent riots by farmworkers in the south of England are harshly repressed by the army. "Bloody assizes" condemn nine workers to the gallows. Nearly 500 are deported and hundreds are imprisoned.

South America, 10 December. Simon Bolivar, the liberator of the Americas, dies.

North America, 13 December. Captain Black, a British naval officer, lands at Fort Astoria in Oregon and raises the Union Jack.

North America. The first wagon train to cross the Rocky Mountains, led by Jedediah Smith, reaches the Upper Wind river in Western Frontier territory.

Uprising calls upon king to abdicate

Paris at the barricades, where republicans and radicals have held their ground against royalist troops.

Paris, 30 July

The French capital is again in the grip of revolutionary fervour, with barricades on the streets and republicans claiming that King Charles will be forced to abdicate within days, and a republic proclaimed.

In the last 24 hours three regiments have deserted the king and joined rebel forces on the barricades as the three-day-old protest against a series of repressive decrees turns into open insurrection. The 73-year-old king, the brother of Louis XVI, who was beheaded in the revolution, is thought to be preparing to flee to Scotland which he knows well. He was in exile there for 25 years until the restoration of the monarchy in 1815. His loss of control started at the beginning of July when the opposition won an overwhelming election victory against the reactionary Polignac ministry. The king's decision four days ago to stage a royal *coup d'etat* by disbanding the new radical and republican Chamber before it had even met and imposing censorship sparked off the uprising.

The insurgents – workers, students and petty bourgeois citizens alienated by the disbanding of the National Guard – split into two factions. One wants to replace King Charles by a republic, the other wants a limited constitutional monarchy with the duke of Orleans, Louis Philippe, as the new king.

Street fighting in Paris: a characteristic feature of the French Republican tradition since 1789.

Hero of South American liberation dies

Colombia, 10 December

Simon Bolivar, the patriot and revolutionary hero of South America's wars of independence, died today aged 47. He helped create Bolivia, Chile, Peru, Colombia and Venezuela, but has died a disillusioned man. "America," he said on his deathbed, "is ungovernable. Those who have served the revolution have ploughed the sea."

Born into a wealthy Creole family in Venezuela, Bolivar travelled widely in Europe and was influenced both by the French Revolution and by Napoleon, his lifelong hero. A self-proclaimed "man of destiny", he vowed in 1805 to liberate Venezuela from the Spanish. Despite exile and hardship he succeeded, and went on to help other colonies to gain statehood. Bolivar's tragedy was that having destroyed Spanish rule, he failed to replace it with an adequate form of government. The people proved less idealistic than their liberators and the champion of equality was forced by circumstances into despotism and dictatorship.

Burmese sacred goose, engraved in gold and studded with rubies.

Britons washed by tidal wave for reform

London
The general election, caused by the death of George IV in June, is taking place in a highly-charged atmosphere, with the threat of violence; just as the campaign opened, news came from France of the Paris mob bringing down the Bourbons and of the Citizen King, Louis Philippe ascending the throne.

At election meetings up and down the country, the people, egged on by radical agitators, are demanding parliamentary reform. They are calling for an extension of the vote, the abolition of "pocket boroughs" (controlled by single landowners) and "rotten boroughs" (controlled by a handful of voters) and an end to bribery at elections. Some even want a secret ballot.

When the new Commons meets, the Tories will have about 30 fewer seats. Tories and Whigs alike accept that electoral reform will have to be tackled. But if the Duke of Wellington remains prime minister he could prove an obstacle. It is said that he believes that reform would be pushed to such lengths as to rob the upper classes "of the political influence which they derive from their property – and possibly eventually of the property itself".

The dilemma of reform: four interpretations, from reactionary to radical.

Wagons cross Rockies

The first wagon train crosses the Rocky Mountains on its way west.

California, September
After an ordeal by bitter cold at high altitudes and scorching heat in the Californian desert, the first covered wagons have arrived here from the east. Although the settlers were close to starvation and few of the farm animals they brought with them survived the journey, this sun-rich western seaboard with its lush, fertile land has been opened to land traffic at last. Until now, travellers have either had to travel by land, risking disease and bandits in Panama or Mexico, or around Cape Horn at a huge cost.

The settlers used the southern route across the Continental Divide – using a route discovered by fur trappers in 1812, and plotted by Jebediah Smith, the legendary "mountain man" who lost an ear and was nearly killed by a savage grizzly bear when he came this way three years ago.

America is learning more and more about its vastness from adventurers like Smith and Jim Bridger, a fur trader who reported finding a huge salt lake west of the Rockies and Henry Ashley who is advertising for "mountain men" to travel to the source of the Missouri river and develop the fur trade.

The spectre of cholera haunts Europe

Europe
Cholera, unknown in Europe until 1817, is spreading westwards from Asia. Already Russian cities such as Moscow and St Petersburg have had their populations decimated – the majority of the victims from the urban poor.

In St Petersburg the epidemic caused panic among the wealthy, who fled the city. The fearful epidemic has now reached Poland, and is soon expected in western Europe.

European doctors, who wait for its arrival with trepidation, know no cure. Optimists speak of the benefits of bismuth, chlorine, quinine and steam baths. Experts are silent. Asians have suffered from cholera from at least the ninth century, when the symptoms were described in a Tibetan Sanskrit manuscript. In the common delta of the Ganges and Brahmaputra rivers thousands die every year from the disease.

What Europeans find particularly shocking are cholera's symptoms: debilitating dehydration caused by unstoppable diarrhea and vomiting. Cramp sets into muscles, the tongue becomes dry, the lips blue, the voice hoarse and the skin cold and clammy. In short, it should be a savage's, rather than a European's disease.

King Cholera, who has killed more people than any general could boast of and, like war, always discriminates against the poor and helpless.

1830 (1830-1832)

South-East Asia, 1830. Prince Diponegoro, the leader of an uprising against the Dutch colonists in Java, is captured and exiled to Macassar.

South-East Asia, 1830. Johannes van den Bosch, the Dutch governor general of the East Indies, institutes a system whereby the native population is forced to share one-fifth of its land and harvests with the government.

England, 1830. The scientist Michael Faraday discovers the phenomenon of electromagnetic induction.

Boston, Mass., 1 January 1831. William Lloyd Garrison publishes the first edition of a journal entitled *The Liberator*, calling for the complete and immediate emancipation of all the slaves in the USA.

London, 20 January 1831. The London conference of European powers signs a protocol delineating the boundaries of Belgium and Holland and establishing Belgium as a neutral state under the permanent guarantee of the powers.

Poland, January 1831. Following the Polish *diet's* proclamation of the end of the Russian succession to its throne, war breaks out between Poland and Russia.

Belgium, 3 February 1831. The duke of Nemours, the second son of Louis Philippe, rejects the offer of the Belgian throne under pressure from Britain.

Poland, 25 February 1831. The Poles halt the Russian advance at the battle of Grochow.

France, March 1831. The exiled Italian republican activist Giuseppe Mazzini founds a revolutionary society called Young Italy, with the aim of uniting Italy through a general uprising and elevating Italian patriotism by moral fervour.

Brazil, 7 April 1831. Under pressure from both the army and the people, the unpopular Emperor Pedro abdicates in favour of his five-year-old son.

India, 6 May 1831. The Sikh forces of Ranjit Singh suffer a defeat at Balakot in an attempt to establish a Moslem state by holy war in north-western India.

Poland, 26 May 1831. The Russians defeat the Poles under Jan Skrzynecki at the battle of Ostrolenska.

Belgium, 4 June 1831. The Belgians elect Leopold of Saxe-Coburg king, three months after the national congress had confered the regency on its president, Baron Erasme Surlet de Chokier.

Philadelphia, 11 June 1831. The Convention of the People of Colour, the first such convention ever for free Negroes, opens.

Netherlands, 26 June 1831. King William rejects the "Eighteen Articles" drawn up at the London conference to regulate the separation of Belgium and the Netherlands.

Virginia, 21 August 1831. The radical Negro preacher Nat Turner leads a band of slaves in revolt on a large plantation, killing 57 whites.

Belgium, August 1831. Breaking off the armistice, King William of the Netherlands launches an invasion of Belgium but is obliged to retreat under pressure from the European powers.

Poland, September 1831. Russian forces seize Warsaw, crushing the Polish rebels with whom they have been at war since January.

Netherlands, 15 October 1831. King William refuses to accept the "Twenty-Four", Articles, drawn up by the London conference on terms more favourable to the Netherlands than previous proposals.

Britain, 31 October 1831. Two days of rioting in Bristol, caused by parliament's rejection of the Reform Bill, comes to an end.

India, October 1831. William Bentinck, the governor general of India, meets Ranjit Singh, the ruler of the Punjab, at Lahore, in order to sign a commercial treaty.

Southern Africa, 1831. Soshangane and his Shangane people, who have retreated north from the Zulu threat around Maputo Bay in Mozambique, win a civil war among the *Ngoni* on the Save river. Other *Ngoni* flee inland to launch raids on the Zimbabwe plateau, spreading the Mfecane wars towards the Zambezi.

USA, 1831. The physicist Joseph Henry invents the first electromagnetic motor and first telegraph.

New York City, 1831. Edgar Allan Poe, dismissed from West Point military academy for "gross neglect of duty" and "disobedience of orders", publishes his *Poems*.

New York City, 1831. Two Swiss cafe owners, John and Peter Delmonico, open a European-style dining room called a *restaurant*.

Paris, 1831. The Barbizon school of artists, who paint from nature, gives its first exhibition at the Paris Salon.

Italy, 22 February 1832. Louis Philippe sends French troops to the port of Ancona on the Adriatic to counter ever-increasing Austrian influence in the region.

Belgium wins independence from Dutch

Brussels, 20 December 1830

Three and a half million Belgian citizens rejoiced today as the Dutch King, William, conceded defeat and allowed them their independence. Resentment had smouldered for years since the treaty of 1815 which created the kingdom of the United Netherlands. The Belgians, who make up the majority of the population, were angered at the favouritism shown to the Dutch.

There were serious religious differences between the Catholic Belgians and their Protestant neighbours; when the cost of living soared, the Belgian workers, inspired by the July revolution in Paris, built barricades in the streets of Brussels. Although reluctant at first, the middle classes joined in. The demand was for administrative separation of the two provinces. King William refused and ordered Dutch troops into Brussels. Every attempt to repress the rebellion failed and, despite a plea from the Dutch king to the czar of Russia for assistance, the army has been forced to withdraw.

Divine revelation inspires new US church

Ohio, January 1831

Joseph Smith was only 15 and living in New York when the "revelation" came to him. He was woken, he said, by a vision of God, who told him that all existing religions were fraudulent and that Smith had been chosen to found the one true church. That was 17 years ago. Smith founded his church and faced persecution in New York. Now he and 70 of his followers, who call themselves Mormons, have arrived in the township of Kirtland to build a new Zion. Whether they will escape religious opposition – even here in the wilderness – is doubtful. They are hard-working, thrifty people who may find it hard to cope with the lawlessness of the west, in spite of the great trust they place in Smith's re-written Bible, the *Book of Mormon*.

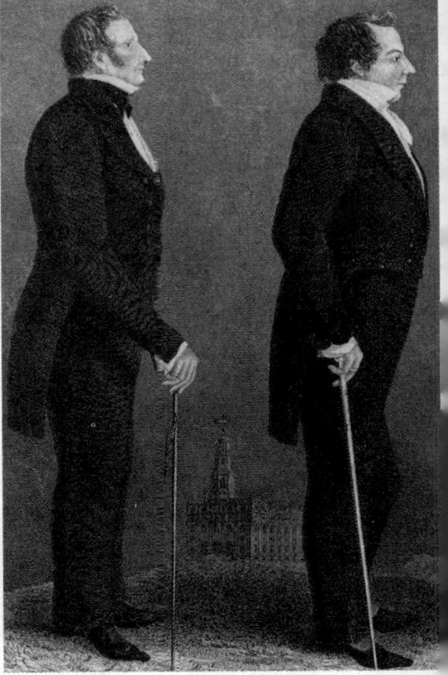

Joseph Smith (right) and his brother Hyrum: founders of a new church.

European settlers kill Tasmanian natives

Tasmania, Australia, 1830

A new sport has become fashionable in Tasmania and is spreading through Australia: "Abo hunting". In Tasmania's largest "hunt" so far, a line of beaters spread across the island to push the Aborigines into the muzzles of huntsmen's guns. Bitter experience has made Aboriginal people wise to the tactics and, to the disappointment of the "sportsmen", only one was caught.

What good this will do to their longterm survival is uncertain. Many who escape the huntsmen succumb to smallpox, venereal diseases, alcoholism and hopelessness. The government discourages the practice. Indeed, Arthur Phillip, New South Wales' first governor and lately, Tasmania's lieutenant governor, Thomas Davey, have been threatening "Abo hunters" with the death penalty; but witnesses for the prosecution rarely come forward, and dead men cannot speak from the witness box.

Australia's attitude to the Aboriginal people is ambivalent. To the educated administrators they are "noble savage", "mild and cheerful", according to Captain Cook with "unusual grace and elegance" (said Sir George Grey). To the uneducated settlers they are vermin to be subdued and slaughtered.

England: slow pace of reform brings riots

Riots in Bristol: Third Dragoon Guards charge protesters calling for reform.

London, 1831
Three attempts to push through an electoral reform bill have been frustrated by Tories and backwoodsmen peers, and protest meetings, leading to widespread riots, are taking place in provincial towns.

A mood of angry frustration began to build up late last year after the prime minister, the duke of Wellington, said that the present system was perfect and would not be changed. But the injustices have been repeatedly pointed out: some hamlets have two MPs, many industrial towns have none.

Wellington was defeated and Earl Grey formed a Whig ministry. The first reform bill was thrown out in April, the second in October and the third has run into stiff opposition in the House of Lords; Grey is talking of resigning. The situation may be saved, however, by the king. William IV is threatening to create an army of new peers ready to vote for the measure and override the opposition.

"Young Italy" founded by exiled patriot

Marseilles, 1831
Giuseppe Mazzini, the 26-year-old Italian who founded a secret society called the *Carbonari*, and has been exiled for a year, has formed a new group with other expatriate Italians here. It is called *La Giovine Italia* (Young Italy) and aims for nothing less than the liberation of the Italian states and their unification into a free independent republic.

Mazzini is certainly bold and ambitious. He wrote an open letter to Charles Albert, the king of Piedmont, asking to be put at the head of a liberation movement, and for a new constitution and the expulsion of the Austrians from Lombardy.

The Young Italy group, which comprises people of all social classes, combines revolutionary tactics with an emphasis on education and belief in God, duty and sacrifice.

Giuseppe Mazzini, Italian patriot.

Mazzini is against both popes and kings, and thinks that Italy can only be saved and unified by a combined effort: the people and God working together.

Russia puts down chaotic Polish uprising

Warsaw, September 1831
After nine months of heroic but muddled rebellion, the Poles have once more been crushed by the Russians. Polish universities have been shut down and Polish students told to go to St Petersburg to study. Russian instead of Polish must be used in the administration.

The uprising began in the officers' training school and was soon joined by most army regiments and large numbers of civilians. But appeals for help from western governments went unanswered. Party squabbles broke out in the Polish parliament and when rioting erupted in Warsaw Russian troops were able to suppress the rebellion with little trouble. Some 10,000 Polish activists and intellectuals have fled to the West.

A Polish patriot, in an era when patriotism alone was not enough.

Bloody deaths end US slaves' rebellion

Virginia, USA, 11 November 1831
A huge crowd gathered in Jerusalem, Virginia today to watch the hanging of Nat Turner, a radical preacher and literate slave who was the leader of a slave revolt in which 57 white people were killed. Turner believed himself to be a divine instrument to lead his people out of bondage, and incited a group of fellow slaves to kill whites.

A posse of more than 2,000 armed men – together with troops and sailors – hunted the rebels down, killing many innocent black people in the process. Turner managed to escape and remained at large until his recapture. While he was at large he wrote an autobiography, *The Confessions of Nat Turner*, which has been edited and published in Baltimore. The rebellion has led to fears of a mass insurrection. Extra security is being imposed throughout the south, with many slaves finding themselves manacled at night.

The capture of Nat Turner, the leader of the slave revolt.

Thesis and antithesis resolved for Hegel

Berlin, Prussia, 1831
Georg Wilhelm Friedrich Hegel, the most outstanding German philosopher since Kant, has died in a cholera epidemic.

His system of thought was summed up in his final work, the *Encyclopaedia of Philosophical Science*, covering logic, nature and mind. He claimed it included all knowledge. Hegel is best known for his "dialectical logic" in which thought proceeds from thesis to its denial, antithesis, and thence to synthesis, a combining of opposing ideas. This in turn provides a new thesis and the process starts again until it reaches an absolute, free of self-contradiction.

Hegel's political philosophy sees the state as a kind of super-individual with a reason and will superior to that of the people who compose it.

1832 (1832-1833)

USA, 25 January 1832. The immediate abolition of slavery is rejected by the Virginia Assembly.

Paris, 18 May 1832. The novel *Indiana* is published by George Sand, the pen name of Amandine Aurore Lucie Dupin. The 28-year-old Sand left her husband last year and came to Paris to make a living out of writing.

London, 4 June 1832. A bill of parliamentary reform is passed giving the vote to men of substantial property.

New York City, June 1832. Some 4,000 people die in a cholera epidemic.

Germany, 5 July 1832. Following the Hambach festival of South German Democrats, where revolt against Austrian rule was advocated, the government takes steps to curtail the freedom of the press and to limit the formation of unions and public meetings.

Minnesota, 13 July 1832. An expedition led by Henry Schoolcraft discovers the source of the Mississippi river.

Vienna, 22 July 1832. The duke of Reichstadt dies. Born the king of Rome, the son of the Emperor Napoleon I and Marie-Louise of Austria, he was known as Napoleon II during the hundred days between Napoleon I's escape from Elba and his defeat at Waterloo in June 1815.

Greece, 8 August 1832. The Greek national assembly elects Prince Otto, the second son of the king of Bavaria, king of Greece.

North America, August 1832. Chief Black Hawk and his tribe are massacred by US troops at the battle of Bad Axe, waged at the junction of the Mississippi and Bad Axe rivers (in Michigan).

North America, 21 September 1832. The Sauk Chief Keokuk, a rival of Chief Black Hawk who was defeated last month at the battle of Bad Axe, signs an agreement giving up his tribe's claims to lands east of the Mississippi river.

Britain, 21 September 1832. Sir Walter Scott, the most popular writer in Britain today, dies. As a poet he is best loved for *Marmion*, *Young Lochinvar* and *The Lay of the Last Minstrel*, but he will also be remembered for the *Waverley* novels.

Missouri, October 1832. The artist George Catlin returns from a voyage up the Missouri river with sensational pictures of Indian life. On a voyage of over 2,000 miles Catlin befriended Sioux and Mandan tribes and was rewarded by permission to record sacred rituals as well as daily life.

Washington, DC, 5 December 1832. President Jackson is re-elected.

Ottoman Empire, 21 December 1832. Russia offers military assistance to the Ottoman Sultan Mahmud II in his war with the *pasha* of Egypt, Mohammed Ali, whose troops have just taken control of Konya. Hostilities broke out earlier this year when the Ottomans refused to give Egypt Syria, which they had promised in return for military aid during the Greek War of Independence. The pasha's troops are now some 50 miles from Istanbul.

France, December 1832. Now that the Society of Friends of the People is being dissolved, another society closely linked to the working class, comprising three sections and recruiting about six thousand members, appears: the Society of the Rights of Man.

Algeria, 1832. Having been proclaimed *bey* by local chiefs, following his victories against the French, Abd al-Kader is now recognised as *emir* of Mascara.

London, 1832. William Wilkins designs the National Gallery in Trafalgar Square to house the Angerstein collection and other gifts.

Berlin, 22 March 1833. A customs treaty (*Zollverein*) is signed between Bavaria, Wurttemberg, Prussia and Hesse-Darmstadt, notably excluding Austria.

Texas, 3 April 1833. American settlers adjourn a three-day meeting, having agreed to make Texas independent of Mexico.

Germany, 4 April 1833. A liberal student uprising against Frankfurt police is brutally suppressed.

Piedmont, April 1833. The Italian radical Giuseppe Mazzini organises an anti-government plot which is discovered by the army. Mazzini's aim is the unification of Italy under a republican form of government. Following discovery of the plot, Mazzini flees and is sentenced to death in his absence.

Ottoman Empire, 4 May 1833. The treaty of Kutahya between the Ottoman Sultan Mahmud II and the Egyptian Pasha Mohammed Ali gives Egypt sovereignty over Syria and Cilicia and brings at least a temporary truce in the war between the two nations which began last year.

Britain, 15 May 1833. The actor Edmund Kean dies aged 45. Hailed by some as the greatest English actor since David Garrick, his delivery was described by the writer William Hazlitt as "like reading Shakespeare by flashes of lightning".

Twelve-hour day for Britain's teenagers

Children in a rope factory: in theory they will receive some education.

London, 1833

Tougher laws to prevent the exploitation of children in textile factories have been passed by the British Parliament. The new legislation closes loopholes in previous Factory Acts and limits the maximum number of hours that those aged between 12 and 18 can work to 12 hours a day.

The new act prohibits children aged nine to 13 from working more than nine hours a day and reaffirms the ban on under-nines working. No-one under 18 can work nights any longer, and one and a half hours have to be allowed in each day's shift for meal breaks.

The legislation does not apply to silk factories. Enforcement provisions in the new act allow four inspectors to be appointed to prevent employers evading the law.

Until now employers have bee able blatantly to disregard th limits on ages and hours, safe in th knowledge that there was no one t present evidence against them.

Employers are also to be mad more responsible for the welfare o any children in their employ, pro viding those aged nine to 13 with a least two hours' schooling a day.

The new legislation follow increased concern about condition in the recently opened textile mil that now employ over 100,00 Lord Ashley, the son of the earl o Shaftesbury, decided to champio the act after visiting Lancashire an seeing so many young peop severely crippled by working con ditions that their distorted limb looked "just like a crooke alphabet".

Success for symphony inspired by Italy

London, 14 May 1833

A London audience was last night delighted to hear the new *Italian Symphony* conducted by its composer, the 24-year-old German Felix Mendelssohn-Bartholdy.

Inspired by a trip to Italy two years ago, the symphony is the latest in a series of astonishingly mature and beautiful works by the young composer, who has been hailed as the greatest prodigy since Mozart. One was an octet for strings, written when Mendelssohn was just 16 and had already composed many apprentice works, including symphonies, operas and concertos. The octet was followed by the lovely overture to Shakespeare's *A Midsummer Night's Dream* the following year.

Felix Mendelssohn-Bartholdy: t young composer of mature music.

More Britons to vote

The Great Reform banquet at the Guildhall marks the passing of the Act.

London, 4 June 1832
Against a background of violent public disorders in London and the provinces, and under pressure from King William IV, the Lords today abandoned its stubborn opposition to parliamentary reform and passed an act that will give the vote to the small property owners and tenant farmers of middle classes. Now one in five adult males will have the vote – twice as many as before.

In declining rural areas, 56 "Rotten Boroughs" of fewer than 2,000 inhabitants have lost their representation entirely, and another 30 have lost one of their two MPs; their seats will be transferred to Manchester, Birmingham and other expanding industrial towns, some of which have been without MPs. The bill would have passed the Lords last year had it not been for the solid resistance of the 21 bishops.

In the long-running controversy over increased representation, Tories have accused Whigs of stirring up the people and risking revolution. The Whig cabinet, all but four of whose members are in the Lords, argues that prudent concessions to popular feeling are necessary in order to ensure stability and protect property.

Lord Grey's Whig cabinet resigned last month when King William refused to create 50 peers to get the bill passed; he stuck at 20 peers. But the Tories were unable to form a government and Grey was back within a week, with the king promising 50 peers. They were not needed; the Lords caved in.

Goethe's lovers inspire his poetry

Weimar, 22 March 1832
The great genius of German letters, Johann Wolfgang von Goethe, is dead. Poet, dramatist, scientist and court councillor to the duke of Weimar, he had been fully occupied in all these fields until his death at the age of 82, uttering as his last words "*Mehr licht!*" (more light).

It appears that he had finished his masterpiece, *Faust*, on which he had worked for most of his life. He published the first part in 1808 and its greatness was immediately recognised. The second part is his legacy.

Goethe's many love affairs inspired his outpouring of lyric poetry, the simplest and best Romantic poems in German, such as *Roslein*. His loves ranged from a parson's daughter to a society beauty, from a baron's wife to a humble village girl who bore him many children before he married her. Even in his seventies he was inspired by a new love, Ulrike von Leventzow, then 18. He is to be buried beside Schiller, his friend and rival.

Goethe: poet, dramatist, romantic.

Greatest happiness advocate has died

Bentham: the preserved body.

London, 1832
Jeremy Bentham, a leading English thinker behind legal, parliamentary and social reform advocated by a group of "Benthamites" including Edwin Chadwick, James Mill and the latter's son John Stuart Mill, has died, bequeathing his body to University College, London, which he founded "to provide higher education without religious bias".

His principle of "utility" was that men pursue pleasure and avoid pain and should be governed to produce "the greatest happiness of the greatest number". Trained as a lawyer, he advocated reform of the law, the penal system, public health, the Poor Law administration and suffrage. His plan for a model prison was rejected.

Papal bull condemns free-thinking press

Rome, 15 August 1832
Pope Gregory XVI has demolished the hopes of the new liberal Catholics in France led by Lamennais. In a papal bull, *Mirai Vos*, issued today he condemns the freedom of the press and other freedoms which Lamenais has been espousing in his Paris newspaper *L'Avenir*.

Under the slogan "God and liberty – unite them", Lamennais has been working for four freedoms: freedom of the press through the abolition of censorship; freedom of education through ending the monopoly of the state-controlled Napoleonic university; freedom of association for both workers and religious communities; and freedom of worship, including the right of individual churches to discipline their members.

He came to Rome in March to plead his cause in person, but the pope gave him only a 15-minute audience. Today the pope has declared that the church does not need reforming at all.

Spaniards rise up against heir to throne

Madrid, September 1833
Isabella has become queen of Spain and sparked off a savage civil war over the succession which threatens to ravage the countryside. She has succeeded her father Ferdinand VII against the wishes of the *Carlists*, a political group demanding that the throne is given to his brother Don Carlos. Isabella is backed by the liberals, the supporters of the democratic constitution that Ferdinand choose to repeal during a disastrous reign when Spain lost all her overseas possessions except Puerto Rica, Cuba, the Philippines, the island of Guam and a few outposts in Africa.

The sudden outbreak of a dynastic war among the semi-guerrilla Carlists, liberals and other groups is creating widespread disorder.

1833 (1833-1834)

Ottoman Empire, 8 July 1833. The Ottomans sign the treaty of Unkiar-Skelessi with Russia, secretly granting Russian ships the right, in time of war, to close the Dardanelles straits.

London, July 1833. In order to enforce laws passed in 1802 and 1819 for the protection of child labour, an act is passed ensuring the appointment of factory inspectors.

New York City, 1 September 1833. Benjamin Day launches the *New York Sun* newspaper, price one cent. Packed with human interest stories and selling at a price that everyone can afford, the paper aims for a mass market. Editors of quality papers are sceptical about its chances of survival.

Washington, DC, 26 September 1833. President Jackson has government funds withdrawn from the Second Bank of the United States in the belief that it is controlled by his enemies in Congress and is out to oust him from office.

Spain, 29 September 1833. Civil war breaks out between the *Carlists* (supporters of Don Carlos, the pretender to the throne) and the supporters of Queen Isabella, who succeeded on her father's death.

Germany, September 1833. Russia, Prussia and Austria hold the semi-secret convention of Munchengratz, at which they agree concerted foreign policies. They support Don Carlos against Queen Isabella in Spain – France and Britain support the queen.

Britain, October 1833. Robert Owen presides over a conference of the *National Equitable Labour Exchange* which decides to set up a workers' trade union comprising all types of trade. The Union will be called the *National Consolidated Trades Union.*

Alabama, 13 December 1833. The people of Alabama witness the most spectacular part of a meteor shower that is visible across the North American continent. Known as the Leonid shower, it can be seen every year, but this year is the most dramatic so far on record.

Philadelphia, December 1833. Women led by Lucretia Mott found the Female Anti-Slavery Society, having discovered that women are banned from the American Anti-Slavery Society.

Mexico, 1833. General Santa Anna is elected president of the republic. Santa Anna supported General Iturbide, who was inspired by Napoleon's example to declare himself emperor in 1822, but was instrumental in his overthrow the following year.

Britain, 1833. A sermon given by the young John Keble, entitled *National Apostasy*, gives rise to the Oxford Movement which calls for the Church of England to reassert itself as a divine society with unquestioned authority. Members are disquieted by the liberalism they perceive in the 1829 Catholic Emancipation Act and the 1832 Reform Act.

South Atlantic, 1833. A British gunboat claims the Falkland islands as crown territory. In 1820, the Argentinians had claimed to succeed Spain in possession of the islands, which are also known as the Lalvinas, but Britain has now taken them without a fight.

Japan, 1833. Following the second poor harvest in a row there is famine throughout the country and the starving populace riots in several towns, smashing the houses of wealthy merchants.

Britain, 1833. The physicist Michael Faraday makes significant progress in his experiments aimed at the identification of electricity from different sources.

New York City, 1833. The Irish actor Tyrone Power makes his debut on the American stage.

Greece, 1833. Following the declaration of national independence last year, the Greek Church decides to sever its links with Istanbul.

Vatican, 1833. Pope Gregory XVI organises evangelistic missions to the South Sea Islands.

France, 1833. The historian Jules Michelet begins to publish the first volumes of his *Histoire de France.*

USA, 1833. Samuel Colt develops a new firearm – the revolver. This is a pistol with revolving chambers which allows several shots to be fired without reloading.

Germany, 1833. The physicist Carl Gauss invents the electromagnetic telegraph which is able to send messages over long distances by means of electric pulses passed along wires.

Honolulu, 1833. Kauikeaouli comes of age and is crowned King Kamehameha III.

Algeria, 26 February 1834. Without consulting the French government, General Desmichels signs a treaty with the *emir* of Mascara, Abd al-Kader, recognising him as commander of the faithful and his sovereignty over the *beylik* of Oran.

Savoy, February 1834. Revolutionary groups led by Giuseppe Mazzini and the Genoan Ramorino infiltrate the Annemasse area with the aim of seizing power, but they are soon dispersed by peasants.

Japanese artists Hokusai and Hiroshige make for Mount Fuji and Tokaido

Katsushika Hokusai's "Mount Fuji in clear weather", one of 36 views of the volcanic mountain by Japan's first painter to create landscape paintings.

Edo, Japan, 1833

Ando Hiroshige has completed his set of woodblock colour prints entitled *Fifty-Three Stages on the Tokaido*, the main highway between Edo and Kyoto, which his senior, Hokusai, also painted on a sketching journey made 20 years ago. These are considered Hiroshige's finest work to date.

Hiroshige inherited from his father the post of warden of the Edo fire brigade. He had to carry out these duties until he could pass them on to his own son and concentrate entirely on his own art. The pure landscape is a new departure in Japanese prints. Until now figure studies, of the girls of the pleasure district, or of actors or *Samurai*, have been preferred.

The great pioneer of landscape painting is Katsushika Hokusai, 30 years older than Hiroshige. Although over 70, he is now completing his most ambitious work, an illustrated book of *Thirty-Six Views of Mount Fuji*. He writes, "Of all I drew before the age of 70 there is nothing of any great note. At 73 I finally learned something of the true quality of birds, insects, fishes, grasses and trees. At 80 I shall have made some progress."

Hiroshige lacks Hokusai's versatility and his powerful realism, but he is admired for his relaxed human touch.

One of the stages on the Tokaido, the road between Edo and Kyoto, by Ando Hiroshige, a follower of the Japanese landscape painter Katsushika Hokusai.

Egypt asserts itself against Ottomans

Ottoman Empire, 3 May 1833

Mohammed Ali, the viceroy of Egypt, has consolidated the gains made by his son Ibrahim in campaigns against his Ottoman "masters". The convention of Kutahya confirms his acquisition of the *pashalik* of Acre, and he now controls Palestine, Syria and mountain passes on the Turkish frontier.

Hostilities began last year when the sultan, jealous of any overmighty vassal, declared Mohammed Ali an outlaw and sent an army against him. Ibrahim, having occupied Gaza, Jerusalem, Acre, Jaffa and Damascus, defeated the Ottoman army at Beilan, then, even more crushingly, at Konya in December.

With Ibrahim poised to attack Istanbul, the great powers intervened. A Russian force of 6,000 landed in the Bosporus and, to ensure its withdrawal, the British and French persuaded the sultan to concede Mohammed Ali's demands.

Mohammed Ali: the ruler of Egypt.

Oxford dons seek a different church

Oxford, England, 14 July 1833

In a sermon at St Mary's here today which kept the whole congregation wide awake, John Keble called for a radical transformation of the Church of England. He called for a revival of liturgical ceremonial, the introduction of religious communities, and a greater social awareness through the church establishing up settlements in poor areas.

All told, it represents a move back towards Catholicism which will produce fierce opposition. But Keble and two other fellows of Oxford's Oriel College, John Newman and Edward Pusey, are a determined group. More is likely to be heard of them.

Analytical engine is calculating marvel

England, 1833

There is a growing need for more and more calculations. Armies of clerks do them at present, but the English inventor Charles Babbage has the visionary idea of a machine for doing any calculations that its operator can specify.

It consists of thousands of cogs and gearwheels that form the heart of the "analytical engine", carrying out the arithmetical functions. In order to instruct the machine in what it has to do, there is a programme incorporated in a punched card. This technique has been used in the textile industry, in the Jacquard loom which has punched cards to vary the patterns.

Frenchman teaches the blind to read

Paris, 1833

Louis Braille, the blind inventor who teaches at the National Institute for Blind Children in Paris, is developing and improving his new form of writing which will enable blind people to read.

He first started working on this unseen writing in 1824, aged 15. He has even adapted it to musical notation. In 1829, when only 20 years old, he published a treatise announcing his invention. Now he is developing it with further elaborations. Already hundreds of blind children in Paris are learning to read books, and many are now capable of sitting standard academic examinations.

Braille himself was blinded at the age of three; yet he is an accomplished cellist and organist, as well as inventor.

A blind ballad seller in London.

From Bengal to Bristol: story of a genius

Bristol, 27 September 1833

Ram Moham Roy, the Indian utilitarian philosopher, has died. For a man dedicated to bridging east and west, who spoke ten languages, Stapleton, near Bristol, was as likely a deathplace as any other.

Born in 1770, he left his home in protest at a relation's death by *suttee* (widow-burning). Studying Buddhist, Hindu, Moslem, Hebrew, Greek and Christian texts, he devoted his life to the search for universal truths.

Nor were his concerns purely religious. He founded India's first newspaper (publishing Bengali, Persian and English editions), established secondary schools and rose to the highest position an Indian could hold in the Bengal Civil Service.

London in 1833, looking west over Westminster, Chelsea, Kensington and Paddington, from the painter's platform on the roof of the Colosseum in Regent's Park. The market gardens of Shepherd's Bush and Chiswick beyond the suburbs of west London can be seen in the distance.

1834 ⇒

London, 22 April. Britain, Spain, France and Portugal form a quadruple alliance, prompted by last year's Munchengratz convention at which Russia, Prussia and Austria met. The four countries pledge to work together to guarantee Belgium's independence and to support Queen Isabella's claim to the Spanish throne against *Carlist* opposition. Meanwhile the civil war in Spain continues.

India, 6 May. Sikhs led by the Punjab ruler Ranjit Singh capture Peshawar, the Muslim city in north-west India.

Portugal, 24 May. King Miguel finally capitulates to his brother, Pedro, the emperor of Brazil, who restores his 15-yearold daughter Maria II da Gloria to her rightful position as queen of Portugal.

Washington, DC, 20 June. Congress passes a law making all land west of the Mississippi river – other than the states of Missouri and Louisiana and the Territory of Arkansas – Indian country.

New York City, 4 July. The Annual Convention of People of Color sets 4 July as a day of prayer and contemplation of the Negro condition.

China, 15 July. Following the recent abolition of the East India Company's trade monopoly, Lord Napier arrives at Macao as the first British chief superintendent of trade.

London, 1 August. Slavery is abolished throughout the British empire.

London, 2 August. The *South Australia Association* gains a charter to found a colony.

London, 14 August. The Poor Law Amendment Act is passed, establishing a system of workhouses.

China, 11 October. Lord Napier, the British chief superintendent of trade, who has failed in his negotiations with the Chinese, dies in Macao.

Philadelphia, October. A town meeting condemns race riots that erupted this summer in the city's Negro areas. The riots began when nearly 500 unemployed Whites entered the area intending to drive the Negroes out of town. Compensation will be paid to the Negro residents.

Britain, 27 December. The much-loved essayist and poet Charles Lamb dies. Writing under the pseudonym "Elia" he had his first success in 1807 with the *Tales from Shakespeare* which he wrote with his sister Mary.

Britain. The Whig prime minister, Lord Grey, resigns because of cabinet disagreements over his Irish policy. He is replaced by Robert Peel.

France. The prolific novelist Honore de Balzac publishes *Eugenie Grandet*.

South Africa. News of the British abolition of slavery reaches white Boer farmers in Cape Colony. Aghast at this loss of labour, many begin to move north in search of land outside British control.

London. The French wax-modeller Marie Tussaud establishes a permanent exhibition of her figures of famous people in Baker Street. A friend of Napoleon's ex-wife Josephine, Mme Tussaud emigrated to Britain in 1802.

Japan. A new senior councillor, Mizuno Tadakuni, is appointed and initiates reforms to cope with a financial crisis in the *shogun*'s government and the growing unrest caused by famine.

Britain. Six farm workers from the village of Tolpuddle in Dorset are sentenced to seven years' transportation to Australia for setting up a local trade union, a branch of the Friendly Society of Agricultural Labourers. The severity of the sentence causes huge public outcry and the six are hailed as the Tolpuddle Martyrs.

Persia. The Persian army seizes the town of Serakhs in Afghanistan while the British and Russians reach an agreement on the limits of their mutual zones of influence in the area.

Russia. Alexander Pushkin publishes a novella entitled *The Queen of Spades*.

Russia. Nikolai Gogol publishes *Taras Bulba*. This colourful and dramatic tale is a hymn to the Cossack people whose primitive, wild nature is exalted by Gogol.

Mexico. The president, General Santa Anna, launches a campaign to eliminate the vice-president, Gomez Farias, and assume a position of sole power.

Britain. The popular writer Bulwer Lytton publishes a new historical novel, *The Last Days of Pompeii*.

South Africa. Dutchspeaking Griqua hunting parties raid the Mfecane war areas to the north of their settlements for labour and cattle. They suffer a disastrous defeat at the hands of the Ndebele of Mzilikazi in the Pretoria region of the Transvaal, but do not give up their ambitions of northwards expansion.

Republican rising is crushed in France

Paris, April

Yet another insurrection against the Bourbon monarchy of Louis Philippe and his banking and factory-owning allies has been crushed. As usual the forces of "order" left their traditional trail of blood, killing hundreds of men, women and children in the Parisian working-class districts of the Cloitre Saint-Merri and Rue Transnonain.

This time the rebels were silk-workers from Paris and Lyons. Few save the leaders, such as Auguste Blanqui of the secret Society of the Rights of Man, are able to articulate their demands. Hungry men know more what they are opposing than what they want. The origins of the uprising are in the deplorable conditions of the French proletariat.

Trades unions are illegal, strikes forbidden, factory acts ignored and factory workers forced to carry the hated *livrets* (workbooks) listing all previous employers.

Further, the "July Revolution" of Louis Philippe, establishing a government committed to abolishing the peerage and extending the franchise, has created rising expectations among the poor that cannot be fulfilled: hence the piles of pathetic corpses in the Rue Transnonain.

Outcry greets harsh workhouse plans

Britain's new workhouses: "uninviting places of wholesome restraint".

London

Traditional poor law relief in Britain is to be abolished as a wages supplement and replaced by a system of workhouses, according to a new Poor Law report just published. The report, which proposes changes to the original Elizabethan legislation, has been condemned by every national newspaper as harsh and uncaring. Opponents fear that its central proposal – the establishment of workhouses – will destroy family life among the poor.

The report, which took two years to complete, advocates an end to the system of wage supplements and subsidies awarded to the low-paid according to family size. Instead, able-bodied men and women who want assistance will have to live and work in workhouses. According to one of the report's authors, these should be "uninviting places of wholesome restraint". A typical workhouse will separate husbands from wives and parents from children, restrict visitors and enforce silence at meal times. Tasks will include stonebreaking, bone-grinding and the hand-grinding of corn.

The report claims the workhouse will be preferable to the present system of outdoor relief which now costs over £8 million a year. This relief, however, will still be available to the old and the sick.

Slavery abolished in British colonies

London, 1 August

By today, Emancipation Day in the British empire, three-quarters of a million slaves have been set free. The man responsible for their emancipation, the philanthropist and campaigner Thomas Buxton, who took over the leadership of the Emancipation Party in the House of Commons from William Wilberforce in 1824, celebrated the success of his life's work quietly at his house in Spitalfields. Fellow campaigners presented him with two handsome pieces of plate.

The trade in slaves had been prohibited in Britain in 1807. Slowly and reluctantly other countries followed suit. Napoleon abolished the trade during the Hundred Days, but Bourbon France continued it until 1819. Spain abolished it in 1820 (getting £400,000 compensation from Britain), Portugal in 1830 (getting £300,000).

Inevitably the next stage was the abolition of slavery itself. The plantation-owners had dominated the unreformed parliaments before 1832, but with the passing of the Reform Act the emancipators had a sudden majority. Within a year the Emancipation Act was passed, with the slave-owners receiving £20 million in compensation.

Every slave in Britain's colonies is now free, although, to offset the dangers of a shortage of labour in the West Indies, field slaves will be "apprenticed" to their former masters until 1840 and domestic slaves until 1838.

Antigua: a plantation owner watches his black overseer supervising his slaves.

New scheme unites Germany's states

Germany

Seventeen states, with a population of more than 20 million, have formed a customs union, the *Zollverein*, under Prussian leadership. The architects of the scheme hope that it will prepare the way for German leadership of the civilised world.

Prussia's economic development was hampered until recently by 67 different tariffs and 13 non-Prussian enclaves, each with a different fiscal system. When Prussia abolished internal customs duties in 1818, a number of small states opted to be absorbed. Other German states formed their own unions in 1828, but have now decided to come under the Prussian umbrella.

The *Zollverein* is the brainchild of the economist Friedrich List, who returned last year from exile in the United States. Although the maritime cities remain independent, the rest of Germany may be further unified by a railway system radiating from Berlin.

Grain harvester to revolutionise farming

Virginia, USA, 21 June

Cyrus Hall McCormick has invented an automatic grain-reaping machine, which will reduce labour and agricultural coats and multiple the US agricultural industry's productivity. Its components include a reel to gather grain, a vibrating blade to cut it and a platform on which the cut grain is collected. His father, a blacksmith, had tried for years to make such a machine and Cyrus spent more time in his father's workshop than in school.

Midwifery advances in South America

Rio de Janeiro

New obstetrics practices from Europe are dramatically reducing the city's infant mortality rate. Marie Durocher, the first woman obstetrician to qualify in Rio, is using methods developed by midwives at La Maternite hospital in Paris and Geissen in Germany. She believes in the minimum of intervention in normal childbirth, and takes full advantage of modern monitoring and measuring instruments. The fact that these improvements are coming from France and Germany, not from Britain, is largely due to their governments' sponsorship of midwifery training.

Tussaud's waxworks find London home

Madame Tussaud's waxworks.

London, December

Madame Marie Tussaud, the 73-year-old wax modeller, who attended the guillotine to take death masks from the severed heads during the French Revolution, is to establish a permanent exhibition site in Baker Street for her waxwork gallery of heroes, rogues, victims and confidence tricksters. Apprenticed to her uncle Dr Curtius, who owned a waxworks in the Palais Royal, Paris, she was imprisoned herself in the Revolution, but only for a short time. She came in England with her two children in 1800, and since then has been touring the country with her representations of Marie Antoinette, Napoleon, Sir Walter Scott and scores more.

The Palace of Westmister, the residence of English kings from Edward the Confessor to Henry VIII and seat of parliament, burning down in 1832.

1834 (1834-1835)

India, 1834. The British depose the *rajah* of Coorg because of his cruelty.

China, 1 January 1835. The *Society for the Diffusion of Useful Knowledge* meets for the first time. It is organised by foreign merchants and missionaries in Canton (Guangzhou).

Washington, DC, January 1835. Congress allocates surplus revenue as the government makes the final payment on the national debt.

Vienna, 2 March 1835. The Austrian Emperor Francis dies and is succeeded by his son Ferdinand in order to preserve the principle of hereditary succession. Mentally subnormal, Ferdinand is to be assisted by a regency council dominated by the conservative Prince Metternich.

Ottoman Empire, 24 March 1835. Sultan Mahmud II grants Britain complete freedom to trade in silk in Syria. But, following the Ottoman-Egyptian war which ended in 1833, Syria is now in the hands of Mohammed Ali, the *pasha* of Egypt, and he refuses to implement the arrangement.

USA, March 1835. The writer Edgar Allan Poe publishes a short story entitled *Berenice* in the *Southern Literary Messenger*.

London, 18 April 1835. William Lamb, Lord Melbourne, becomes prime minister following the resignation of Robert Peel.

Paris, 25 April 1835. France authorises the payment of American claims for damages incurred during the Napoleonic wars.

Belgium, 5 May 1835. The Brussels-Malines railway line is opened, providing the first passenger service in mainland Europe.

Algeria, 28 May 1835. The *emir* of Mascara, Abd al-Kader, attacks French troops in the Macta pass and defeats them.

France, 9 July 1835. The St Etienne-Lyons railway opens as a passenger service for the first time.

New York City, 25 August 1835. The popular *New York Sun* newspaper reaches a nationwide audience following the publication of an article claiming that vegetation grows on the moon.

USA, August 1835. The Anti-Slavery Society distributes 75,000 anti-slavery leaflets by mail to the south, to the fury of slave-owners.

Britain, 9 September 1835. The Municipal Corporations Act is passed, reforming city and town government in line with the shift in population brought on by industrial developments.

Italy, 26 September 1835. Donizetti's opera *Lucy of Lammermoor* is performed for the first time.

France, September 1835. The government takes steps to strengthen court procedures and punish offences committed by the press more severely in order to combat republicanism.

Mozambique, 19 November 1835. The Ngoni army of Zwangendaba crosses the Zambezi northwards during an eclipse of the sun. After four years of raiding on the Zimbabwe plateau, Zwangendaba is now taking his army north to spread the Mfecane wars to eastern Zambia and Malawi. He leaves some Ngoni raiders behind in Zimbabwe, notably those led by his niece Nyamazana.

Bavaria, 7 December 1835. The first German railway between Nuremberg and Furth passes into private ownership.

Texas, 20 December 1835. Leaders of the Texan secession movement issue a declaration of independence from the dictatorship of the Mexican President Santa Anna, and officially proclaim the creation of the republic of Texas. Full-scale civil war erupts.

Florida, 28 December 1835. Over one hundred US troops are massacred by Seminole Indians resisting attempts to drive them out of Florida.

New Orleans, December 1835. Residents ride in steam-driven streetcars on the New Orleans and Carrollton Railroad as the line puts its horses out to pasture.

Germany, 1835. Georg Buchner, a doctor and a poet, publishes a play based on the French Revolution entitled *The Death of Danton*.

France, 1835. The poet and dramatist Alfred de Musset writes *May Night* and publishes his *Confession of a Child of the Century*.

Britain, 1835. The young writer Charles Dickens publishes a collection of his journalistic pieces under the title *Sketches by Boz*, receiving £150 for the copyright.

Russia, 1835. Nikolai Gogol publishes his *Diary of a Madman*, inspired by the German Romantic movement.

Germany, 1835. The theologian and writer David Strauss publishes his *Life of Jesus* which is violently attacked by the religious authorities and involves him in legal proceedings. In it he interprets the New Testament as a product of communal Christian spirit rather than a divine revelation.

The noble savage, the object of Protestant endeavour: natives from New Guinea

Protestants come to save Samoans' souls

Samoa, 1835

The most important event on the island this year has been the arrival of the first Protestant missionary. The Rev Peter Turner, a Wesleyan, has already had substantial success in converting Tongans living here, and is beginning to make an impression on the native Samoans.

The Protestant missions can be dated back to the end of the 18th century when the London Missionary Society set up pioneering missions at Tonga and Tahiti. They did not stay long, but several other groups made efforts on other islands in the following years. The breakthrough came in 1811 when the Rev Samuel Marsden resumed the Tahitian mission. In 1814 he established the New Zealand mission at the Bay of the Islands.

Marsden had a genius for organisation. He treated missionary work as if it were a military campaign dividing the South Seas into evangelistic compartments. He stopped the doctrinal differences of Church of England, Wesleyans and others splintering the efforts. How long the united effort will last is in doubt, however. Squabbles have recently broken out between the two missions on Tonga.

Poet who dreamed on opium has died

London, 25 July 1834

Samuel Taylor Coleridge, who died today, owed his high reputation in an age of poets to a single period of intense inspiration in 1797-98 in which he wrote *The Ancient Mariner, Kubla Khan* and *Christabel.* By 1802 he was mourning the loss of his poetic response to nature in an *Ode to Dejection*. It also ended his close collaboration with Wordsworth. Together they had rejected the artifice of 18th-century poetry in their joint book, *Lyrical Ballads*, which began the Romantic movement in poetry in 1798. Coleridge, who suffered endless financial problems, became a critic and journalist. He spent his life struggling against an addiction to opium, prescribed for rheumatic pain. Under its influence he "dreamed" of Xanadu.

Fall of Oyo empire splits West Africa

West Africa, 1835

The empire of Oyo, one of the grea[t] empires of West Africa, is breakin[g] up. Its capital, Oyo, is deserted. The Oyo cavalry swept across th[e] West African savannalands to[wards] the end of the last century and built a nation that grew ric[h] from the slave trade.

Over a generations ago, under it[s] ruler, Alafin, Oyo reached it[s] zenith. From his death the stat[e] went into steady decline, weakene[d] by internal discord and foreign in[vasions], mainly by the Fulani.

Driven from their lands the Oy[o] people moved south, colonising th[e] forest lands of the Egda and the [...] peoples, where their distinctiv[e] double-ended *gangans*, or talkin[g] drums, have been adopted by th[e] indigenous people.

Mr Gordon Bennett founds newspaper

New York City, 6 May 1835
A revolutionary new penny newspaper, the *New York Herald*, came onto the streets today and achieved instant success for its editor and proprietor, Gordon Bennett. The Scottish-born journalist has managed to launch the *Herald* despite lack of funds or party support.

The new paper owes its success to its comprehensive coverage of local news – presented in a piquant, highly individual style – and the fiercely independent editorials, most of them written by Bennett himself.

Gordon Bennett: newspaper owner.

Infernal machine fails to kill French king

Failed assassins: Fieschi, Morey and Pepin on their way to the guillotine.

Paris, 28 July 1835
King Louis Philippe narrowly escaped assassination on a Parisian boulevard today as a hail of bullets intended for him killed 18 bystanders and wounded many others. The assassination attempt happened on the Boulevard du Temples as the king and his sons were on their way to review troops. The king's sons all escaped unhurt. Among those who died were members of the court and some National Guardsmen.

Hundreds of bullets were fired at the king's party by an infernal machine, as police are calling it, devised by a republican sympathiser named as Giuseppe Maria Fieschi. The 45-year-old Corsican had rigged together 25 guns, linking their firing pins so that they could be fired simultaneously.

Police have also arrested two of Fieschi's alleged accomplices, Pierre Morey and Pierre Pepin, both members of the extreme republican group, the Society for the Rights of Man, which has advocated violence.

Fieschi, a smalltime crook who has served ten years for theft, made contact with the society recently. He claims to have worked as a secret agent for the government, infiltrating the Bonapartist movement under a false name.

Today's assassination attempt will almost certainly strengthen the hand of those in government who want to curb the incitements to violence that have appeared of late in the republican press.

Corporations take over British towns

London, 9 September 1835
The old rough and ready methods of running municipal affairs, by means of borough oligarchies or parish meetings, are being swept away and replaced by elected municipal councils. The Municipal Reform Act applies to two million people in 178 boroughs in the thriving industrial and commercial areas of the country.

The new councils will be elected on a much wider franchise than the parliamentary one. All rate-paying householders of three years' standing will have the vote; this effectively transfers municipal power from Tory lawyers, Anglican clergy and factotums of the aristocracy to shopkeepers, businessmen and Non-conformists. Some better-off members of the working class will become voters.

The new councils will take over the work of the Improvement Commissions which have been set up on the initiative of public-spirited citizens, who obtained their powers by private acts of parliament. The commissioners widen streets, improve water supplies and provide other amenities. In Manchester, the Police Commissioners have built a gas works and acquired fire engines. But critics of these "cursed improvements" say that the gas works should be sold to a private firm.

Romantic composer dies aged only 33

Paris, 23 September 1835
Once, playing through a piece of music to a friend, the Italian composer Vincenzo Bellini said: "If I could write one melody as beautiful as this, I would not mind dying young." Bellini did write many beautiful melodies, and today he died, of consumption, aged only 33.

Slight, languid and with swathes of curls, Bellini cut a romantic figure and attracted many admirers in Paris, where he spent a number of years. His operas, such as *Norma*, *I Puritani* and *La Sonnambula* allow the singers to display amazing feats of vocal acrobatics, but Bellini also pioneered an expressive, romantic style with rich, long, poetic melodies.

Vincenzo Bellini, the genius and consumptive, who died today aged 33.

Fairy story ends unhappily ever after

Copenhagen, 1835
A little book of *Tales Told for Children* has been published by Hans Christian Andersen, who began life as the son of a poor cobbler, tried to become an actor, and won himself an education at Copenhagen university and a royal pension on which he travelled around Europe. He has already published poems, plays and a novel.

His fairy stories include *The Tinderbox*, *The Princess and the Pea*, *Little Claus and Big Claus* and *Little Ida's Flowers*. They are founded on folk tales which he heard as a boy. He intends to publish many more. In spite of their frequently unhappy endings, these tales are in great demand.

Tommelise sitting desolately on a water lily leaf, from "Thumbelina".

1835 (1835-1836)

Argentina, 1835. Juan Manuel de Rosas, the governor of Buenos Aires, assumes dictatorial powers and embarks on a reign of terror.

Venezuela, 20 January 1836. The United States and Venezuela complete a treaty of peace, amity, commerce and navigation.

Algeria, 25 January 1836. In the long conflict between Algerians and French colonists, the French governor general, Clauzel, drives the resistance leader, *Emir* Abd al-Kader, out of the Tafna gorges.

Texas, 24 February 1836. Mexico's dictator, General Santa Anna, with 5,000 soldiers, lays siege to the fortified mission station, the Alamo, defended by 187 Texans.

Paris, 29 February 1836. Meyerbeer's opera *Les Huguenots* is performed for the first time.

Texas, 6 March 1836. The Alamo fort falls to Mexican troops.

Texas, 27 March 1836. The Mexican army massacres Texan rebels at Gohad.

Algeria, March 1836. The Algerian resistance leader Abd al-Kader occupies the capital, Mascara.

Texas, 21 April 1836. Texan troops led by General Sam Houston inflict a crushing defeat on the Mexicans at San Jacinto, taking General Santa Anna, prisoner.

Washington, DC, 26 May 1836. A resolution is passed stating that Congress has no authority over state slavery laws.

Arkansas, 15 June 1836. Arkansas becomes the 25th state of the USA.

London, 16 June 1836. The London Working Men's Association is founded.

Paris, 1 July 1836. Alfred de Musset publishes his play *Never Swear to Anything* in the magazine *La Revue des Deux Mondes*. It is a minor masterpiece on a light theme, full of freshness and youth, with a cast of worldly characters delightfully drawn from the society of his day.

Algeria, 6 July 1836. The French General Bugeaud wins a victory against Abd al-Kader's forces beside the Sikkak river.

Texas, September 1836. A referendum calls for annexation by the United States.

Texas, 22 October 1836. General Sam Houston is sworn in as president of the Texas republic.

Strasbourg, 30 0ctober 1836. King Louis Philippe pardons Prince Louis Napoleon Bonaparte, following his attempt to persuade the local garrison to rebel against the government, and banishes him to America.

South Africa, 1836. Following the end of the sixth Eastern Cape Frontier War last year, Boers are disappointed when the British government hands back captured land to the Xhosa, with whom it makes friendship treaties. The Boers had joined the war in an attempt to gain land outside British domination following the abolition of slavery, but Christian missionaries had informed the government of the settlers' motives. The Boers are now *trekking* north to join hunters and raiders beyond the Orange and Vaal rivers.

Britain, 1836. Joanna Baillie, a 74-year-old Scottish poetess and dramatist, publishes a three-volume collection of her works.

USA, 1836. Oliver Wendell Holmes's *Poems* are published.

New York City, 1836. The New York Women's Anti-Slavery Society bans Negroes from membership.

USA, 1836. The radical writer Ralph Waldo Emerson publishes *Nature*, a collection of his lectures which develop the theory of the individual's potential for divinity.

Czechoslovakia, 1836. The historian Frantisek Palacky publishes his history of the Czech nation in Bohemia and Moldavia up to 1526.

France, 1836. The Schneider brothers, Eugene and Adolphe, buy the metalworking factory at Le Creusot, the royal foundry started by Louis XVI.

Germany, 1836. The League of the Just is founded, following in the steps of the League of the Reprobates, formed in Paris in 1832. It brings together apprentices and journeymen with the admirable aim of freeing Germany from oppression and humankind from slavery.

USA, 1836. James Madison, who was the fourth president of the USA, dies in Virginia.

Zimbabwe, 1836. The Rozvi kingdom, which has ruled Zimbabwe since about 1681, suffers a serious defeat at the hands of Nyamazana, a woman general who stayed behind after the main Ngoni force moved north last year. Nyamazana was determined to crush the Rozvi and she has lead an assault on the rocky citadel of Manyanga. Some say that she has had the last *mambo*, or king, Chirisamhuru II, skinned alive.

Britain, 1836. Parliament passes the Locomotive Act limiting the speed of all trains to five miles per hour, with a person carrying a red flag walking in front on the steam engine.

Boers "trek" out of South African cape

South Africa, 1836

A people is on the move. From all over Cape Colony wagons drawn by oxen, escorted by armed outriders, move north-eastwards. Ten thousand Boers are trekking to new lands beyond the reach of the British crown because they feel that they are being discriminated against. For a brief moment, inspired by the ideals of the French Revolution, they established republics, but Britain soon crushed them.

Complaints against Britain's utilitarian colonial policy are endless. West Indian slave-owners, who are British, received full compensation for the emancipation of their slaves. Dutch Boer slave-owners received one-fifth. Land on which Boers had shed their blood is denied them and handed back to Blacks. British principles that all races should be treated as equal before the law have been twisted to favour the Blacks, it is said.

The road across the high *veldt* and over the Drakensberg Mountains is hard, and for the stubborn Boers it will seem very long indeed.

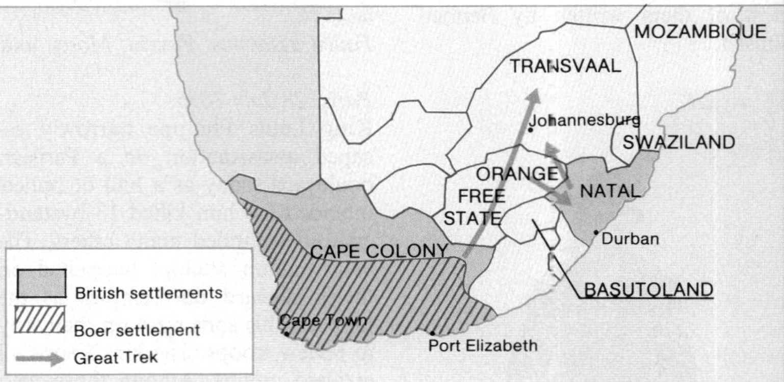

US president survives assassination bid

Washington, DC, 30 January 1835

A madman armed with two pistols took aim at President Andrew Jackson from a distance of six feet in the Capitol rotunda today. Both weapons misfired and Jackson was unhurt.

The fiery president is no stranger to gunplay. When he took office three years ago he was carrying two bullets in his body. One in his arm, the legacy of a gunfight 20 years earlier, was removed shortly after. The other, received from a duel over a gambling debt, stays lodged near his heart. Jackson killed his opponent, aiming deliberately at the groin.

This was the first-ever assassination attempt on a United States president in office. The assailant, a house painter called Richard Lawrence, claims to be the rightful heir to the British throne.

Despite Jackson's avowed hatred of the British and his controversial Indian policies, no political motive is suspected.

The Arc de Triomphe: Paris' great celebration of Napoleonic splendour.

Mexico takes Texan fort

The fall of the Alamo: a later, romanticised version of the Texans' battle.

San Antonio, Texas, 6 March 1836
After 12 days of bombardment, 5,000 Mexican troops stormed a former Spanish mission called the Alamo here today, taking no prisoners and slaughtering the 187 Texan defenders to the last man. The Mexican general, Antonio Lopez de Santa Anna, tonight gave orders to have the Texan bodies piled up and burned like cordwood as an example to other rebellious Texans – but already the call is echoing throughout the state of Texas "Remember the Alamo!".

Santa Anna, a vain, ambitious and devious blusterer, had marched into Texas when American settlers declared themselves independent and elected their own president, David Burnet. Surprised at the size of Santa Anna's army, the Texan Colonels William B Travis and James Bowie retreated to the Alamo – despite orders from their commander, the tough and doughty General Sam Houston, to withdraw from a defenceless position.

Once he had surrounded the mission, Santa Anna demanded an unconditional surrender from the Texans who replied with a single cannon shot.

The Mexican general hoisted a red flag – the traditional symbol that there would be no quarter given – and ate and drank well in a shady garden as his artillery pounded the mission into a ruin. Some reports suggest that more than 1,000 Mexican infantrymen were killed or wounded when they finally advanced; but it took them less than an hour to massacre the defenders.

Colonel Travis lay dead, rifle in hand; Colonel Bowie – who had won fame from his exploits with the Bowie knife – was bayoneted to death; the body of Colonel Davy Crockett, the legendary frontiersman who had arrived in Texas only two weeks earlier, was found badly mutilated.

The only survivors were women who had sheltered in the sacristy below the mission. Santa Anna told one of them, Susanna Dickinson, a blacksmith's wife, to pass the message to other Texans that fighting was hopeless.

The Tennessee-born frontiersman Davy Crockett, with his hunting dogs.

British naturalist ends southern survey

London, 1836
HMS Beagle, a ten-gun brig of 235 tons, has reached port safely after completing a memorable five-year voyage of survey of South America and its islands under the command of Captain Robert Fitzroy.

One of the most remarkable aspects of the voyage of the *Beagle* was the work carried out by Charles Darwin, a young naturalist who sailed at the invitation of the captain and was on the ship's books for victuals, but got no pay.

He is well satisfied, however, by the wonders he has seen and by his collections of animals, birds and plants which are his to dispose of as he wishes.

He left England as an apprentice scientist and has returned a successful collector, an expert geologist and with a wide knowledge of nature acquired at first hand in many wild parts of the world. His letters home speak of being so excited by his work he "could literally hardly sleep at nights". He was especially interested at the way in which related but different species inhabit the various islands of the Galapagos off the coast of Ecuador.

Charles Darwin: naval naturalist.

Algerians resist French expansion

Algeria, 28 May 1835
Algerian tribesmen, who united together to resist the French invaders in a holy war in November 1832, have defeated French troops in the Macta Pass. It is not their first victory, but Algerian victoriesare rare on the open battlefield. Their leader is the Emir, Adl-el-Kader, who has been fighting the French relentlessly since 1831. Since the French occupation of the coast he has continued the war in the interior, and refuses to surrender.

Editor calls for unity among Slavs

Zagreb, 1836
The literary review, *Danica Illirska* is no longer to be written in the Zagreb dialect, understood only by Croats, but in a language which can be read by Serbs as well. Its editor, Ljudevit Gaj, seees cultural rebirth as closely linked to a political awakening in south-east Europe. He has published a *Manifesto of the Illyrian Movement* in his review, calling on Southern Slavs to unite as Illyrians, to end their domination by other races.

No creed or church for writer's religion

Concord, Massachussetts, 1836
Ralph Waldo Emerson's book *Nature* has inspired his friends and disciples, such as Henry Thoreau, to form a discussion group, the Transcendental Club, which meets in Concord, a town founded by Emerson's ancestors.

Emerson gave up his ministry in the Unitarian Church four years ago, after a visit to England where he met and discoursed with Wordsworth, Coleridge and Thomas Carlyle. He finds God in nature, and revelations of the divine in man's intuitions which transcend the experiences of the senses.

Transcendentalism is a religion without a creed or a church. Emerson teaches individual effort and a life of "plain living and high thinking". He writes: "A man should learn to detect and watch that gleam of light that flashes across his mind from within ... We are ashamed of that divine idea which each of us represents ... Trust thyself".

1836 (1836-1837)

California, 3 November 1836. Californian rebels proclaim the territory's freedom from Mexico.

Austria, 6 November 1836. Charles X of France dies in exile at Gorz. His regime was toppled in 1830 in the *Trois Glorieuses* (three glorious days of revolution).

Britain, 7 November 1836. The British aeronaut Charles Green leaves London in the *Royal Vauxhall* balloon, crosses the channel and lands near Nassau in Germany after a journey covering 480 miles and lasting 18 hours.

Michigan, 26 January 1837. Michigan becomes the 26th state to join the union.

Washington, DC, 3 March 1837. On his last day in office, President Jackson recognises the Lone Star republic of Texas.

Japan, 27 March 1837. Oshio Heihachiro, a constable and philosopher in Osaka who led an abortive peasant uprising in protest against the lack of famine relief, commits suicide.

Britain, 20 June 1837. On the death of her uncle, William IV, Princess Victoria becomes queen of Great Britain and Ireland.

Britain, July 1837. The Birmingham Political Union, led by Thomas Attwood, the banker and MP, organises a demonstration that brings together 50,000 people in favour of a programme of political reform, demanding above all universal suffrage.

Washington, DC, 25 August 1837. The government notifies the republic of Texas that it will not be admitted to the union.

Dakota, August 1837. Fifteen thousand Indians in the Mandan, Hidatsa and Arikara tribes, who live on the Missouri river, die of smallpox. The epidemic is thought to have been started by an American Fur Company steamboat that came up the river in June.

New Mexico, 12 September 1837. Mexican troops crush the revolt that broke out on 25 August.

Washington, DC, 12 October 1837. Congress authorises the issue of $10 million in short-term government notes in an attempt to stem the financial panic that is sweeping the country.

Algeria, 13 October 1837. In the second war of Abd al-Kader, the town of Constantine is taken by General Valee, who guarantees French sovereignty over the province of Constantine.

Florida, 21 October 1837. Under a flag of truce and during peace talks, US troops seize the Indian Seminole Chief Osceola.

St Louis, 7 November 1837. Elijah Parish Lovejoy, the editor of the *St Louis Observer*, is killed by a pro-slavery mob. Lovejoy had been campaigning for the abolition of slavery for many years despite violent popular opposition.

South Africa, November 1837. After an eight-day running battle with Boers and Griqua people in the Marico plains, the Ndebele army strikes camp and marches northwards to find a new home.

Argentina, November 1837. Tenskwatawa, the "Shawnee Prophet", dies in exile. He spent his life working with his brother Tecumseh to unite Shawnee Indians against encroachment by white settlers of Indian lands.

Florida, 25 December 1837. US troops rout Seminole Indians at Lake Okeechobee.

Sicily, 1837. Riots break out in Messina, Syracuse and Catania due to rumours suggesting that cholera, which is claiming many victims, is being caused by poisonous powders distributed by the government.

Afghanistan, 1837. A British envoy, Alexander Burnes, conducts a "commercial mission" to Kabul as concern mounts about growing Russian influence in the area.

Switzerland, 1837. The Italian revolutionary Giuseppe Mazzini is prevented from leaving for Britain because of his political activities.

USA, 1837. In the autumn, Sioux Indians give up their traditional lands east of the Mississippi river.

Britain, 1837. The first measure favourable to the Irish Catholics is obtained by Daniel O'Connell, the Irish nationalist MP who was enabled to take his seat by the Roman Catholic Relief Act of 1829. From now on they will no longer have to pay a tithe to the Anglican Church.

Sierra Leone, 1837. The first groundnuts exported from Sierra Leone go down well with consumers in America and Europe, who call them peanuts.

Afghanistan, 1837. Moving in from India, the British prevent the Persians from occupying the town of Herat and the surrounding region.

Germany, 1837. The philosopher Georg Hegel's *Lessons on the Philosophy of History* is published posthumously.

Britain, 1837. The Scottish historian Thomas Carlyle publishes a *History of the French Revolution*.

Moscow, 1837. John Field, the Irish composer of nocturnes, dies in Moscow aged 55.

Macadamising engineer dies on the road

John McAdam: the "colossus" of the new transport era of turnpikes.

Dumfriesshire, 26 November 1836
John McAdam, who gave his name to a process of road improvement, has died on the road from Scotland, aged 80. He helped to develop the mailcoach network which has increased national prosperity.

A banker's son from Ayr, John McAdam bought an estate in Ayrshire where he was magistrate, deputy county lieutenant and road trustee, and constantly experimented with new road surfaces.

As agent for revictualling the navy in western ports in 1798, he transferred his Scottish experiments to Falmouth, and proved the effectiveness of a raised surface of broken stone, with drains on either side. After being made surveyor-general of Bristol roads in 1815, he wrote two books on road-building.

Parliament adopted his technique for road-surfacing in major towns, and in 1827 he became general surveyor of roads. His son James accepted the knighthood which his father had declined, and is now chief trustee and surveyor of metropolitan and turnpike roads.

Roads not controlled by trusts have been slow to improve, but that may change as a result of last year's General Highway Act, which gave parish ratepayers the right to appoint surveyors and levy rates.

The forge at Creusot in France, painted by Theodore Chasseriau. A century earlier, travellers like Defoe and Young had marvelled at the scale of the new industrial enterprises. By 1836 they had become the norm.

Getting the message gets easier – with Pitman's shorthand and Morse's code

Building telegraph lines in the USA.

Britain and US, 1836
A communications revolution is under way in Britain and the US as resourceful inventors devise speed-writing systems and ways of sending messages over long distances.

In Bath, Isaac Pitman, a former textile mill clerk turned schoolteacher, has invented what he calls a Stenographic Sound Hand, based on the phonetic principle, or the sounds of vowels and consonants, rather than the conventional spelling of words.

Straight lines and shallow curves are used for consonants, and sounds are paired: a light slanted line stands for P and a heavier one for the deeper sound B. For vowels, dots and dashes are placed against the consonant strokes.

This invention enables speeches delivered at 50 words a minute and more to be written down.

In the US, Samuel Morse turned from portrait painting to telegraphy after a shipboard conversation on signalling gave him an idea, which he jotted down:

1) An apparatus to send signals by opening and closing an electric circuit;
2) A receiver to record the signals as dots and spaces on a tape;
3) A code to turn the dots and spaces into letters and numbers.

Morse spent a great deal of effort trying to turn this brilliantly simple idea into a complicated means by which the government could send messages in secret code.

When he realised that the dots and spaces could be heard as dots and dashes, he knew that he had hit on a revolutionary method of public communication.

In another area of communication inventions William Cooke and Charles Wheatstone are working in London on a "telegraph" system for sending signals by wires alongside railways.

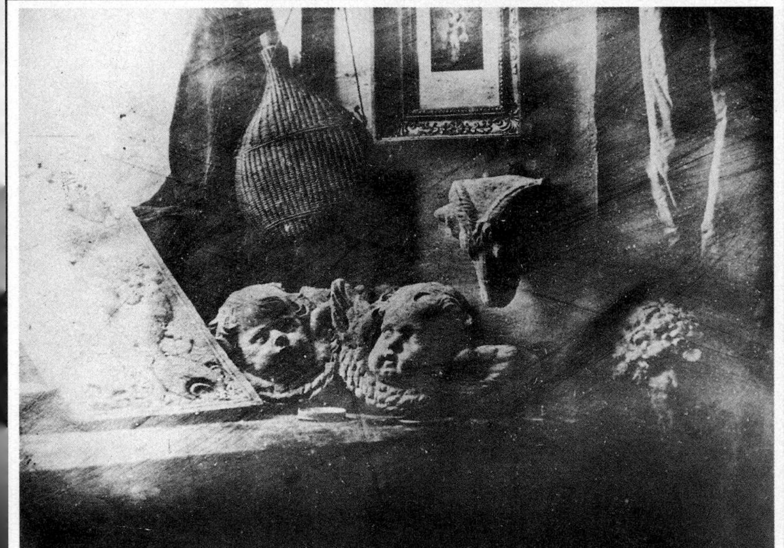
France, 1837: the earliest photographic image by Louis Daguerre, who has captured light and dark on copper plate and reproduced them.

"Little Magician" elected US president

Washington, DC, 7 December 1836
Martin van Buren, a New York lawyer known universally as "The Little Magician" – largely for his skill in political manipulation – was elected president of the United States today, the first president not to bear a British family name.

The former vice-president has pledged himself to support the policies of his predecessor, Andrew Jackson, although he is distrusted by both slave-states and abolitionists, having courted both.

It was as secretary of state that van Buren made his name as an outstanding negotiator. He brought about an end to the dispute between Britain and the United States over West Indian trade and secured a financial agreement with France.

Van Buren, the eighth US president.

British put down rebellions in Canada

York (Toronto), 14 December 1837
Although British troops have successfully quelled two rebellions that threatened to wreck this fast-growing colony, anti-government hostility continues to fester and there is an increasing danger of intervention by the United States.

The most serious uprising was led by Louis-Joseph Papineau, the Speaker of the Lower Canada Assembly, who has fled to the USA after agitating for an armed uprising. Twelve of his supporters have been executed. In Upper Canada, the second revolt was led by a Scottish-born journalist and political agitator, William Lyon Mackenzie, whose Radical Reformers were seeking a greater level of democracy in Canada. The uprising was put down quickly, although Mackenzie, with several followers, has established a government-in-exile in the USA.

London is placing high hopes in the newly-appointed governor general, the reformist Lord Durham, who is on his way here with "dictatorial powers".

Boer trekkers reach their promised land

Natal, South Africa, June 1837
Thousands of Boer *trekkers* have crossed the Drakensberg Mountains and settled in Natal. To the Dutch-speaking pioneers, coming out of the mountains, the rich and verdant pastures of Natal are like the Promised Land.

Here, in the no-man's-land between the British and Zulu empires, settlements are being built and the burgher democracy of the early Boers is being re-established. A constitution has been drawn up, and a governor, Piet Retief, has been elected. The state is to be known as the Free Province of New Holland.

Princess Victoria is new British queen

London, June 1837
With the death of William IV, the crown passes to his niece, Victoria, aged 18; she is without experience of public affairs, but is dutiful and self-possessed. At her first Privy Council meeting officials presented documents naming her Alexandrina Victoria. She told them to cross out the Alexandrina.

She then told her mother, Princess Victoria of Saxe-Coburg, that the latter no longer exercised any authority; she instructed her mother's secretary, Sir John Conroy, to stay out of London; and her uncle by marriage, Leopold of Belgium, was told to go home.

1837 (1837-1838)

Germany, 1837. Hanover becomes separate from Britain with the accession of Queen Victoria. Governed by Salic law, which forbids succession through the female line, Hanover is now ruled by Victoria's uncle, Ernest Augustus.

London, 1837. The architect Sir John Soane, who designed the Bank of England, dies aged 84. He bequeathes his house in Lincoln's Inn Fields to the nation.

Germany, 1837. The educationalist Friedrich Frobel sets up the first *kindergarten* in the world, at Blankenburg, in Thuringia.

Canada, 1837. The speaker of the Lower Canada Assembly, Louis-Joseph Papineau, leads a rebellion by French-Canadians against the proposed union of the British provinces of Upper and Lower Canada. A similar rebellion in Upper Canada is led by the Scottish journalist and political activist William Lyon Mackenzie.

Russia, 1837. The novelist and poet Alexander Pushkin dies of a wound received in a duel fought to defend his wife's honour. Unpopular and widely misunderstood in his liberal beliefs, Pushkin was forced into the duel by enemies at court. He leaves a large body of work, much of it influenced by Russian folktales.

England, 1837. The painter John Constable dies aged 61. He was highly acclaimed during his lifetime and will be remembered above all for his landscapes, among the best of which are *Valley Farm*, *Cornfield* and *Hay Wain*.

Austria, 6 January 1838. The first rail link, between Vienna and Wagram via Florisdorf, is opened.

South Africa, 6 February 1838. Having failed to obtain land by trickery from the Zulus, the Boer leader Piet Retief is executed as a witch by the chief Dingane.

China, 24 February 1838. The Medical Missionary Society is formally instituted.

Iowa, 4 July, 1838. The Territory of Iowa is established and Robert Lucas is appointed governor.

Ottoman Empire, 16 August 1838. The *Porte* (Ottoman government) signs a trade treaty with Britain which provides for the abolition of commercial monopolies throughout the empire, including Egypt. The Egyptian *pasha*, Mohammed Ali, who is hostile to this agreement, takes up arms.

Ohio, 30 October 1838. Oberlin College becomes the nation's first institution of higher education to admit women on an equal basis with men.

Britain, 1 November 1838. Lord Durham, the governor general of British North America, returns home after mediating between English and French speakers.

China, 12 December 1838. A riot breaks out when British and American opium traders drive away Chinese officials intending to execute a native opium dealer in front of the foreign factories.

China, 31 December 1838. Lin Zexu is appointed imperial commissioner "to investigate and manage maritime affairs" and deal with the opium problem in the province of Canton (Guangzhou).

Canada, 1838. Robert Nelson, a survivor of the insurrection led by Papineau, decides to continue the armed struggle to the bitter end and declares himself president of the republic of Lower Canada. Having taken the town of Napierville, which he makes his provisional capital, he is forced to flee from the advance of the British army under John Colborne.

Mexico, 1838. King Louis Philippe demands 600,000 *pesos* from the Mexican republic in compensation for damage suffered by French nationals in Mexico. The demand is prompted by the complaint of a French pastrycook that his shop has been looted by Mexican soldiers. French ships take a fortress near Vera Cruz, and General Santa Anna comes out of retirement and joins the fighting with no authority. The conflict, which soon becomes known as the Pastry War, is settled when the president, Anastasio Bustamante, agrees to pay the compensation.

Philadelphia, 1838. The abolitionist Robert Purvis is made president of the now formally established Underground Railroad, a network of contacts which helps fugitive slaves to escape their owners.

USA, 1838. The writer James Fenimore Cooper turns to social criticism in his new work *The American Democrat*.

Italy, 1838. The French and Austrian expeditionary forces leave the cities of Ancona and Bologna in the papal states, to which they were summoned in 1832 to keep order.

Britain, 1838. The novelist Charles Dickens begins to publish a new work, *Nicholas Nickleby*, in serial form.

Guatemala, 1838. The government of Mariano Galvez falls from power. Galvez came to power in 1831 and has been responsible for introducing liberal reforms. Since 1837 the country has been badly affected by a cholera epidemic and an Indian uprising.

British steamships start Atlantic service

Isambard Kingdom Brunel's steamship "Great Western" crossing the Atlantic.

New York, 1838

The 703-ton *Sirius* has become the first ship to cross the Atlantic entirely under steam, and has beaten by a few hours the 15-day crossing record set recently by the *Great Western*. A transatlantic passenger service is now established.

The *Great Western*, a wooden paddle vessel 236 feet long and 35 feet wide, is far bigger than any previous steamship. Built by Paterson of Bristol, powered by Maudslay and Field, the brainchild of the great civil engineer Isambard Kingdom Brunel, the builder of bridges and railways, the *Great Western* has proved the viability of Brunel's theories on screw propulsion. The *Sirius* was of more modest origin – built for service in the Irish Sea. Chartered by the British and American Steam Navigation Company, she sailed from London to New York via Cork with 40 passengers. When fuel ran out just short of the American coast, the captain, determined not to resort to sail, insisted on feeding spars into the furnace. The vessel made it just in time to avert a mutiny.

The *Sirius* did, however, introduce one potentially important technical innovation: a condenser to recover fresh water used in the boiler.

Hindu thugs strangling a traveller: worshippers of Kali, the goddess of destruction, they would waylay travellers, steal from them and kill them according to ancient rites. They were not suppressed until 1837.

Briton writes with a social conscience

London, 1837

A new serial by the author of *The Posthumous Papers of the Pickwick Club*, which began last year and multiplied its sales a hundredfold, is appearing in monthly parts. The new novel, *Oliver Twist*, is the story of an orphan boy in a workhouse who falls into the company of criminals and pickpockets. It is shrouded in an atmosphere of evil far removed from the genial world of Mr Pickwick.

The hardships of Oliver reflect something of those of the author, Charles Dickens, in his own childhood, part of which he spent in a blacking factory while his father was in Marshalsea prison for debt.

Prolific author: Charles Dickens.

Convicts in Tasmania, Australia, made to walk 30 miles carrying 56lb weights.

Report claims convicts corrupted settlers

New South Wales, 1838

News of the evidence given before the House of Commons committee on the transportation of convicts is causing much anger here. Settlers, according to the evidence, have been "demoralised" and "corrupted" by transportation and the assignment of convict labour to free farmers. The settlers had prepared themselves for the end of the assignment system and, probably, of the increasingly unpopular dumping of Britain's unwanted convicts in Australia, but they had not expected to be insulted as well.

Much of the trouble stems from the fact that those convicts who will not or cannot work for the free colonists are held by the government in penal settlements where they are ruled by fear of the cat o' nine tails. In 1837 more than a quarter of a million lashes were laid on the bleeding backs of convicts. Another aspect of life in Australia which is causing much concern is the treatment of the Aboriginal population. Often hunted for sport, the Aborigines are being driven off their tribal lands and, when they resist, are herded into settlements where they exist on government handouts and die of drink and disease.

This is a great land, but much needs to be done before it can attract the free immigrants it so desperately needs.

The icy continent attracts explorers

London, 1838

The hitherto unexplored continent of ice which surrounds the south pole (*Antarctica*) is attracting expeditions from the United States, France and Britain. The interest is mainly scientific, though some of the voyages combine whaling and sealing with exploration.

Captain Cook's great voyage of 1774 destroyed myths about a southern continent which was actually habitable. Later James Weddell found an open sea route deep into the ice.

Liberal deals with rebels shock MPs

Canada, 1838

Despite the draconian powers which he has been given to put down Canadian rebellions, the new governor general, Lord Durham – "Radical Jack" – has shocked parliament and the prime minister by his liberal approach.

Lord Durham chose 24 June – Queen Victoria's coronation day – to announce an amnesty for all but 24 French-Canadian rebels. Until now, uprisings in the province have been dealt with harshly. In London, the prime minister, Lord Melbourne, has dissociated himself from Durham's moderation.

People's charter demands change

London, 8 May 1838

Demands for "one man, one vote" elections, secret ballots and an end to conditions that prevent working men from becoming MPs have been put forward in a radical reforming People's Charter.

Also included in the six-point charter are demands for annual elections, equal electoral districts, salaries for MPs and abolition of the property qualification for parliamentary candidates.

The charter, published by the London Working Men's Association, has been endorsed by the radical Birmingham Union and the *Northern Star* newspaper.

Treaties have pushed America's Indians west across Mississippi

Western America, 1838

Already it is being called the "trail of tears" as thousands of American Indians are forcibly moved from eastern states to reservations in the far west. Under the Indian treaties, only successful Indian farmers are allowed to stay east of the Mississippi; the rest are being "persuaded" by chiefs, many of whom were made drunk by federal commissioners, to sign assents.

Numbers are being drastically reduced by disease and the Indians are being systematically robbed by officials. The survivors are so poor that they cannot hope to buy the equipment needed to till the soil in their new homelands, and starvation threatens.

Indian country: romanticised image of a Sioux Council by George Catlin.

1838 (1838-1839)

Germany, 1838. Mathias Jakob Schleiden, the professor of botany at Jena university, defines the cellular structure of vegetables.

France, 1838. The palaeontologist Boucher de Perthes discovers roughly-chipped flint instruments in the area around Abbeville.

USA, 1838. The American David Bruce builds the first automatic device for printing characters, at the rate of 100 per hour.

Pennsylvania, 12 January 1839. Anthracite coal is used for the first time in iron smelting.

Near East, 16 January 1839. The strategic important port of Aden is annexed to British India. This follows mistreatment of the crew of a wrecked British ship in 1837 and the sultan's failure to sell the town to the British as restitution, as his father had promised.

China, 24 March 1839. The commissioner Lin Zexu blockades foreign factories to force foreign merchants to surrender their opium stocks which are to be destroyed.

London, 19 April 1839. The treaty of London, signed by Britain, France, Prussia, Austria and Russia, finally guarantees the independence and neutrality of Belgium. It also closes the Scheldt river and establishes Luxembourg as an independent grand duchy.

Ottoman Empire, 24 June 1839. The sultan, Mahmud II, launches another offensive against Mohammed Ali, the *pasha* of Egypt.

Ottoman Empire, July 1839. Following the death of Sultan Mahmud II, his son Mahmud Abdul-Medjid succeeds to the throne.

London, 5 August 1839. News of the Chinese suppression of the opium trade at Canton (Guangzhou) reaches London.

China, 23 August 1839. In the continuing hostilities over the opium trade, British ships assemble off Hong Kong.

China, 4 September 1839. Following the evacuation of Canton by British traders, the destruction of confiscated opium, the stoppage of foreign trade as well as the denial of food and water to the British, British naval forces fire the first shots in the as yet undeclared Opium War.

London, 1 October 1839. The British government decides to send a punitive naval expedition to China.

China, 3 November 1839. British and Chinese forces clash near the Bogue forts at the mouth of the Pearl River.

Ottoman Empire, 3 November 1839. Sultan Mahmud Abdul-Medjid promulgates an imperial charter, the *Tanzimat*, which confirms the equality of all citizens of the empire, guarantees freedom and individual property and promises reforms of the tax system.

Algeria, 3 November 1839. Following an expedition by the French General Valee into the Hamza territory in October, the *emir*, Abd al-Kader, launches his horsemen against the Mitidja plantations and resumes hostilities with France.

Paris, 24 November 1839. The composer Hector Berlioz stages his opera *Romeo and Juliet.*

Russia, 1839. Czar Nicholas unites the Uniate Church with the Russian Orthodox Church.

Russia, 1839. A Russian military expedition in central Asia fails to take the oasis town of Khiva.

France, 1839. The republican theoretician Louis Blanc publishes a treatise, *The Organisation of Labour*, and founds *The Review of Progress*.

Britain, 1839. The painter J M W Turner presents the Royal Academy with five oil paintings including *The "Fighting Temeraire" Tugged to her Last Berth to be Broken Up*.

Philadelphia, 1839. Edgar Allan Poe publishes his first book of stories, *Tales of the Grotesque and Arabesque*, which lives up to its title.

Britain, 1839. Parliament passes the Infant Custody Act, giving divorced or separated mothers access to their children.

Mississippi, 1839. For the first time in the United States, women are given legal control over their property.

USA, 1839. The American Charles Page, a professor in Washington, builds the first electric locomotive.

Afghanistan, 1839. The British army deposes the emir of Kabul, Dost Mohammed Khan, and starts an Afghan war. The British are anxious about the growth of Russian influence in the area and intend to replace Dost Mohammed with a former emir who is more sympathetic to their wishes to protect the northern approaches to India.

Britain, 1839. The Anti-Corn Law League is established in Manchester by Richard Cobden and John Bright to petition for the repeal of duties on imported grain.

USA, 1839. Charles Goodyear discovers how to vulcanise rubber.

Boers kill 3,000 Zulu at Blood River

Natal, South Africa, 1838

A new leader skilful in war has emerged amongst the Boer *trekkers* of Natal: Andries Pretorius. For two years Boers have been settling in the Zulus' rich pastureland of Natal. Inevitably, the Zulu army of King Dingane came down on them. Piet Retief, the original leader, was killed, and the Boers were only saved by Pretorius who quickly raised a 500-man *commando* and stopped 10,000 Zulu at the Blood River, killing 3,000.

An austere nationalist, committed to Boer independence, Pretorius is expanding his commando, and fully expects to use it again.

Zulu soldiers: undefeated until now.

Sikh state mourns leader Ranjit Singh

Ranjit Singh: the great Sikh leader.

Amritsar, India, June 1839

The Sikhs are mourning the death of their *maharajah*, Ranjit Singh. Ranjit Singh has done more for the Sikh nation than any ruler for 200 years. Succeeding to power in Lahore in 1799, he defeated one rival after another, marching into Amritsar, the Sikhs' sacred capital, in 1802. Having united the Sihks, he created a French-trained army and extended Sikh power to the borders of British India and Afghanistan.

"He is almost the first inquisitive Indian I have seen," one Frenchman who knew him wrote. "He asks a hundred thousand questions, about India, the British, Europe, Bonaparte, the world in general and the next."

Anti-Corn Law protest movement grows

Manchester, 1839

The "bread stealers" and "foot-pad aristocrats" in the British parliament have come under renewed attack in the wake of the recent bad harvests that have sent the price of corn soaring. The landowners, who have a majority in parliament, are resisting efforts to repeal the Corn Laws, which allow corn imports only when the price has reached a certain figure; at one time it was 80 shillings a quarter.

The renewed agitation has led to the launching of an anti-corn law league by a group of Lancashire manufacturers. The leading figures are Richard Cobden, who made his fortune as a calico printer, and John Bright, a Quaker textile manufacturer with powerful oratorical gifts. They rouse their audiences with a wealth of colourful abuse directed at landowners, because, as Cobden admits, people come to meetings not to learn, but to be "excited, flattered and pleased".

Free trade is the basis of the campaign. Imports of corn, it is argued, would be paid for by increased exports of textiles and other manufactured goods. But protectionists say that the campaigners want cheap bread in order to cut wages.

New breakthrough captures images

Paris, 19 August 1839

The French government today published details of a new invention, the *Daguerrotype*, by which exact images are produced through a lens on a copper plate by the action of light alone. With similar developments of *photogenic* images announced earlier this year in Britain, it appears that a major new art form is being born.

Louis Daguerre, a scene-painter who presents the Diorama in Paris, discovered the effect when tracing images thrown on a screen by a *camera obscura*. In 1837 he captured the interior view of his studio on a copper plate coated with silver iodide and exposed to the light through the lens. He sold the rights in the process to the government in return for a life annuity. His book on the process he uses is a best-seller. "One can make the most detailed views in a few minutes without any knowledge of chemistry," he claims.

In England, the Royal Society has awarded its gold medal to William Henry Fox Talbot, an English scientist who published an account of his alternative process of 'photogenic drawing" earlier this year after hearing of Daguerre's experiments. He began experimenting because of his inability to draw the landscapes of his holiday travels. He discovered how to make paper sensitive to light by soaking it in silver chloride. On exposure to light this turns dark, creating a "negative" impression. From the negative he can make any number of positive prints. His results, though, are less sharply detailed than Daguerre's, and require people to sit still for many minutes.

A summer's afternon at Lacock Abbey, by William Henry Fox Talbot, who experimented with photography because of his inability to draw landscapes.

The Tuileries and apartments of King Louis Philippe, by Louis Daguerre: the first photograph of Paris, taken from the left bank of the Seine.

British march into "soft" Afghanistan

Afghanistan, April 1839

The 5,000-strong British army that has just occupied Kandahar on its way to Kabul is finding that – so far – its invasion of Afghanistan is an easy matter.

There is little resistance; the 12,000 camp followers march without danger, and it will be months before winter.

The force, sent to instal the unpopular *Shah* Suja as emir and forestall Russian efforts to win influence in Afghanistan and thus threaten India, has the enthusiastic backing of Lords Palmerston and Melbourne and all but one of the British cabinet.

The exception is the duke of Wellington. The problem, the duke says, is not getting into Afghanistan; it is getting out.

Guns force British radicals to back off

London, July 1839

The threat of an armed working-class revolt and a general strike organised by the Chartists is now receding following army intervention. The credit for calling the Chartists' bluff is being given to the commander of the northern district, Sir Charles Napier.

His decision to opt for a show of force by stationing troops in key northern cities and then inviting Chartist leaders to a demonstration of how artillery fire could disperse a mob is thought to have dissuaded the Chartists from violence. Prior to the demonstration they had been advocating revolutionary tactics.

Jamaican riots bring down government

London, 1839

A rebellion by former slave-owning sugar planters in Jamaica has succeeded in temporarily bringing down the British government. Despite getting £20,000,000 in compensation following the abolition of slavery, the colonists are facing serious economic difficulties as world sugar prices fall. British demands for better conditions in Jamaica's Negro jails led to the island's legislature refusing to govern. With Tories in parliament refusing to support the suspension of the Jamaican constitution, the queen called on Robert Peel to form a new government.

Peel agreed, but insisted that some of the Whig ladies in the queen's household should be replaced by Tories. The young queen refused, and Lord Melbourne is back at 10 Downing Street.

Destruction of opium crop is ordered

Canton, June 1839

Lin Zexu, the imperial envoy sent to Canton to put an end to the opium trade, has ordered the destruction of 20,283 chests of opium worth 12 million dollars surrendered on his orders by British merchants.

The opium is to be destroyed in public, and trenches have already been dug so that the drug, imported from India, will drain away. The Chinese decision to stop the opium trade comes from the emperor who has been advised that the drug "utterly ruins the minds and morals of the people, it is a dreadful calamity". It is also draining wealth from the country, with huge profits in silver going to the merchants.

At the heart of the trouble, however, lies not only the opium trade but also the whole question of the opening up of China to the west.

1839 (1839-1840)

Guatemala, 1839. The Indian leader Rafael Carrera seizes power. Last year the liberal government of Mariano Galvez fell following a revolt led by Carrera and the unrest caused by an epidemic of cholera.

Paris, 1839. Frederic Chopin publishes his 24 preludes, written last winter on the island of Majorca where he was staying with his lover, the novelist George Sand. They are dedicated to the piano-maker, Camille Pleyel, a friend of the composer.

Britain, 1839. Lord Durham, who served as governor general in Canada last year, publishes a report recommending that a firm stand be taken against the French-speakers and that Canada be given a responsible, independent government.

USA, 1839. Henry Wadsworth Longfellow's *Voices of the Night*, his first book of poems, is published and goes down well with the critics.

Germany, 1839. The Leipzig publisher and bookseller Karl Baedeker starts to publish travel guides for Europe.

London, 10 February 1840. Queen Victoria marries her first cousin, Prince Albert of Saxe-Coburg-Gotha.

Canada, 10 February 1840. Following the Durham report of 1938, in which union was recommended, an act is passed uniting the British provinces of Upper and Lower Canada.

France, 1 March 1840. The Soult administration resigns. It is replaced by a team headed by Adolphe Thiers.

Illinois, 10 May 1840. The Mormon leader Joseph Smith moves his band of followers to the Commerce Purchase in Illinois in order to escape the hostilities they experienced in Missouri.

China, June 1840. The formal beginning of the Opium War is declared.

Prussia, June 1840. On the death of Frederick William III, his son Frederick William IV succeeds to the throne. Welcomed by liberals for his "Romantic" reputation, he quickly disappoints them and comes under the influence of an effective, conservative court clique.

China, 5 July 1840. British naval forces bombard Dinghai on Zhoushan Island and occupy it.

China, 15 August 1840. The British plenipotentiary arrives at the Beihe in north China to force the Qing court in nearby Beijing into negotiations concerning the Opium War.

Connecticut, August 1840. A Spanish slave ship, the *Amistad*, arrives in Connecticut with 53 Africans in command. Slaves on board the ship rebelled while the ship was *en voyage* from one Cuban port to another, killing the captain and all but two of the crew. Spain is expected to demand extradition of the rebels.

China, 11 September 1840. Chinese officials strangle the French missionary Jean-Gabriel Perboyre at Wuchang.

China, 28 September 1840. Lin Zexu, the imperial commissioner whose hard line sparked off the opium war, is dismissed and replaced by Qishan.

Ottoman Empire, 6 October 1840. France, Britain and Russia enter the war between the Ottoman empire and Egypt on the side of the Ottomans. They occupy the Syro-Palestinian coastline to cut the Egyptian *pasha* Mohammed Ali, off from the route to Anatolia.

Netherlands, 10 October 1840. Following the abdication of King William , who refused to submit to the rules of the constitution, his son William II succeeds to the throne.

France, 29 October 1840. Adolphe Thiers resigns in the wake of the treaty of London which confirmed the existence of Belgium. He is replaced by Soult and Guizot, who has been ambassador to London since March.

Egypt, 4 November 1840. A British fleet bombards the ports of Beirut and Acre.

Washington, DC, 2 December 1840. William Henry Harrison is elected president of the United States, having won the hearts of the electorate with his "Log Cabin and Hard Cider" campaign emphasising his links with the common people.

Prussia, 4 December 1840. The Army adopts the artillery shell developed in 1836/7 by the gunsmith Nicholas Dreyse which combines the fuse, charge and projectile stages.

Paris, 15 December 1840. The ashes of the Emperor Napoleon I are buried at Les Invalides.

Britain, 1840. The Anglo-Canadian shipowner Samuel Cunard founds the first regular steamship line from Liverpool to Boston and New York.

Baltimore, 1840. Baltimore College of Dental Surgery, the first dental college in the country, is founded.

Britain, 1840. Sir Rowland Hill's proposals for a system of penny postage are implemented, despite bureaucratic opposition.

First commercial telegraph service

Wheatstone's telegraph receiver.

London, 1839

William IV has just granted a patent to William Fothegill Cooke and Professor Charles Wheatstone of King's College, London for an electric telegraph ("writing at a distance") system. It consists of fire wires connected to five needles, any two of which can be moved simultaneously to indicate a letter on a diagram. With electricity running along the wires, these signals are transmitted very quickly. The military will almost certainly take an interest in telegraphy, So, too, will the expanding railway networks.

Ndebele cross the Limpopo River

Zimbabwe, 1840

The army of the Ndebele has marched 300 miles (480km) north to the Zimbabwe grasslands since their defeat by white Boers trekkers in 1837. Their leader Mzilikazi, has gone further, taking a scouting party to survey the land as far as the Zambezi. Now he has returned to his Ndebele people and settled around Bulawayo.

After putting done a coup by one of his own generals, Kaliphi Gundwane, who had made Mzilikazi's own son king, he has strengthened his state by marrying Nyamazuma, the female general of the Ngoni people, who conquered the Bulawayo area just before the Ndebele arrived.

French king resists feeble coup effort

Boulogne, 6 August 1840

France has shrugged off the second attempted coup by Bonapartists in four years with its ringleader, Louis Napoleon, in jail today after staging an attempted invasion remarkable only for its ineptitude. Napoleon's latest attempt to emulate his late uncle and become leader of France started at 4.30 this morning and ended 210 minutes later with the 32-year-old pretender rescued by his capturers as he and five of his men half-drowned in the Boulogne surf. The death toll among the invaders is put at 45.

The 50-strong invasion force, dressed as members of the 40th Regiment, landed outside Boulogne after sailing overnight from London in the steamer *Edinburgh Castle*.

Napoleon intended to win over the Boulogne garrison while a sympathiser was in charge, rally the townspeople and then march on Paris to depose the king. Napoleon's plans misfired when his sympathiser was replaced on duty by a commander loyal to the king. Behind the invasion was the imminent arrival of the late emperor's ashes from St Helena. Napoleon is outraged that the regime which displaced his uncle is now making political capital from his remains.

Victoria and Albert: their seriousness after the extravagances of George III's sons made them popular with the people, though not with the aristocracy.

Britain claims New Zealand as colony

New Zealand, 6 February 1840

Captain Hobson of the Royal Navy today signed the Treaty of Waitangi with the Maori chiefs. Under this treaty New Zealand now becomes British, but the Maoris are guaranteed the rights to all their lands. If any of them wishes to sell this lands he must first offer them to the British government so that he will not be cheated. The Maoris are also promised full protection as British subjects.

Rarely has the annexation of a country been undertaken so reluctantly. The government's hand was forced by French plans to send settlers to New Zealand and by increasing concern at the treatment of the warlike but naive Maoris by landsharks, adventurers and escaped convicts from Australia.

These men have set up trading posts where they sell the Maoris guns and rotgut alcohol. One of their most profitable items of trade is preserved Maori heads which are sold at a high price in Europe. The situation has been further complicated by the formation of a private jointstock company headed by Gibbon Wakefield, who has already played a large part in the development of Canada and Australia. The government's orders to Captain Hobson note that the annexation is "fraught with calamity to a numerous and independent people".

There are already signs that many Maoris object to the terms of the Treaty of Waitangi.

The signing of the Treaty of Waitangi, which annexed New Zealand to Britain.

Canada is awarded independence by British statute

London, 23 July 1840

Canada is to be a self-governing union under a statute published by the British government today. The momentous decision follows the *Report on the Affairs of British North America* by Charles Buller, the chief secretary to the former governor general, Lord Durham.

The principal reason for the government's move is the fear of US expansion northwards, which is why responsibility for foreign affairs will remain with London.

The statute allows for the union of Lower and Upper Canada to be governed by a cabinet of colonists with a governor general as chief executive.

Buller's report recommended that the French-speaking Canadians should be harassed into abandoning their language – and that their minority status should be perpetuated.

Great powers recognise Egypt's new ruler

London, 15 July 1840

The great powers have recognised the right of Mohammed Ali and his heirs to the *pashalik* of Egypt. Only the French were not party to this agreement, and their support is encouraging Ali to insist on holding on to all his gains in Syria and Palestine. This latest concession to the Egyptian ruler, which further fragments the Ottoman empire, was precipitated by another disastrous campaign by the sultan, whose forces invaded Syria last summer. Within a week the Ottomans were defeated at Nezib, and the sultan died before the news reached Istanbul. The appointment of a new *grand vizier* has prompted the Ottoman admiral, his political rival, to surrender his fleet to Mohammed Ali.

Mohammed Ali Pasha, with his French and British military advisers.

Property is theft says socialist

Paris, 1840

A new book, *What is Property?*, has caused a sensation. "Property", says its 31-year-old author, Pierre-Joseph Proudhon, "is theft." All over France men of property are demanding that it be banned.

Proudhon is no parlour socialist. The son of a drunken tavern keeper, he was herding cows in the Jura at the age of nine. The experience made a profound impression on him, and much of his vision of an ideal society comes from the Jura.

He won a scholarship to college, taught himself Latin, Greek and Hebrew, and came under the influence of the French utopian socialist Charles Fourier. A second scholarship took him to Paris where he has devoted the last two years to writing his book.

Men, he says, are dehumanised not merely by capitalism, but by large-scale production. He advocates a society of peasants and craftsmen, where the individual would remain in control of his own means of production and of his destiny.

Stamps devised as payment for mail

"Penny Black", the first postal stamp.

London, 1840

The reformer Rowland Hill has taken advantage of the evolving rail network and growing literacy to create a universal, cheap postal system in Britain. For just a penny a letter weighing half an ounce may be sent anywhere in the realm. Payment is by purchase from a post office of an adhesive tag bearing the queen's head (a "stamp") which is attached to the envelope.

1840 (1840-1841)

China, 1840. The mandarin Lin Zexu – dismissed when the harshness of his measures sparked off the Opium War – is recalled following British successes along the coasts of the province of Canton (Guangzhou). The war continues.

France, 1840. The essayist Alexis de Tocqueville publishes *Democracy in America*, a work of penetrating analysis that brings him almost instant fame.

USA, 1840. It is estimated that approximately 93 per cent of northern free Negroes are disenfranchised.

France, 1840. The historian Augustin Thierry brings out his *Accounts of Merovingian Times*, an evocative description of sixth-century Gaul.

USA, 1840. A census shows that the population has grown by a third over the last decade to just over 17 million.

Britain, 1840. The first episodes from a new novel, *The Old Curiosity Shop*, by the popular novelist Charles Dickens appear.

Germany, 1840. The chemist Justus von Liebig publishes *Organic Chemistry Applied to Agriculture and Physiology*, one of the earliest works of agricultural chemistry.

France, 7 January 1841. After three failures that affected him deeply, the writer Victor Hugo is elected a member of the Academie Francaise.

China, 20 January 1841. Following lengthy negotiations between British and Qing representatives concerning the conflict known as the Opium War, spurred on by a British attack on the Bogue forts, the draft convention of Chuanbi is concluded. Among other things, the Chinese negotiators agree to pay indemnities and cede the island of Hong Kong to Britain.

China, 29 January 1841. British ships occupy the Chinese island of Hong Kong and continue their attacks along the coast to Amoy, Ningbo and Shanghai, seeking to impose the lucrative opium trade on unwilling imperial authorities.

China, 25 February 1841. A proclamation is issued by the Chinese offering rewards for British heads.

China, 26 February 1841. British forces capture the Bogue batteries.

Washington, DC, 9 March 1841. The rebel slaves who seized a Spanish slave ship two years ago are freed by the Supreme Court, despite Spanish demands for extradition. They now plan to raise money to return to Africa.

Washington, DC, 4 April 1841. President William Harrison, aged 68, becomes the first US president to die in office, just a month after being sworn in. He developed pneumonia soon after a bitterly cold inauguration day on which he refused to wear a hat or overcoat, made a two-hour speech and went to three inauguration balls. Vice-president John Tyler becomes acting president.

Washington, DC, 9 April 1841. Acting president John Tyler is confirmed as president after appealing to Congress to grant him full powers. The US constitution is unclear on who succeeds presidents who die in office.

London, 30 April 1841. The British cabinet decides to dismiss Charles Elliot and appoint Colonel Sir Henry Pottinger as the new plenipotentiary to China.

USA, April 1841. Edgar Allan Poe's new book, *The Murders in the Rue Morgue*, makes a new kind of story popular – the detective story.

China, 27 May 1841. Local Qing officials agree to "ransom" the city of Canton (Guangzhou) with six million silver dollars. The rejection by both sides of the Chuanbi convention has led to renewed conflict, culminating in a full-scale attack by British forces under General Gough on Canton.

China, 30 May 1841. A massive force of rural dwellers attacks British forces near the village of Sanyuanli, just north of Canton. The villagers are incensed by the violent behaviour of the British troops who have been raping the local women and violating graves.

London, 13 July 1841. The Straits Convention is signed by the leading European powers. In a deal largely the work of Britain's foreign secretary, Lord Palmerston, the powers agree that the Bosporus and the Dardanelles should be closed to warships of all nations while the Ottoman empire is at peace.

Germany, 1841. The philosopher and moralist Ludwig Feuerbach publishes a radical book entitled *The Essence of Christianity* which sees religion merely as a consciousness of the infinite, and God merely as an outward projection of the human being's inner nature.

Germany, 1841. The economist Friedrich List publishes *The National System of Political Economy* arguing that tarriffs are essential during the shift from an agrarian to a manufacturing economy. The book is widely read and influential.

Treaty closes Dardanelles to all warships

The Dardanelles, 13 July 1841

The straits between the Aegean and the Sea of Marmara are closed to all foreign warships as long as the Ottoman empire is at peace, under the terms of the Straits Convention signed today by Britain, Russia, France, Austria and Prussia.

This agreement brings to an end an unusual arrangement between Russia and the Ottoman empire dating back to the treaty of Unkiar Skelessi in 1833. That treaty supposedly provided for mutual support in the event of an attack, but a secret clause absolved the Ottoman empire of the need to come to Russia's aid provided that the Dardanelles were closed to foreign warships, while allowing the Russians free passage from the Black Sea. Austria and Russia agreed later the same year to take common action to protect the Ottoman empire.

But Britain was suspicious of Czar Nicholas' intentions towards the declining Ottoman empire. "Russia ... perhaps thinks it better to take the place by sap than by storm," said Palmerston in March 1834.

Anxiety over the Ottoman empire's future was increased by its defeat in June 1839 by Mohammed Ali of Egypt at the battle of Nezib. France, Russia and Britain all compete with each other for influence. This latest treaty is of clearest benefit to Britain, which has acquired the protectorate of Aden.

Violinist with devilish reputation dies

Niccolo Paganini, the violin master.

Nice, 27 May 1840

There were things which Niccolo Paganini did on the violin which, so the rumour goes, only the Devil could have taught him. He would stop in mid-performance, cut three strings from his violin and perform amazing feats of musical wizardry on the remaining string. Tall, gaunt and forbidding, with a weakness for women and gambling, the Italian relished his devilish reputation. He amassed wealth and an army of toadies, but was generous to genuine admirers like Berlioz and Liszt. A romantic showman and virtuoso legend, Paganini died today of consumption. He was 58.

Charles Barry's new Houses of Parliament: originally a Classicist, he built the Travellers' Club in Pall Mall in Italianate style, and Parliament in Gothic style. Whatever the style, there was always grandeur of outline.

White men explore Australian interior

Australia, 7 July 1840
Edward Eyre, the pioneer of the overland droving routes for sheep and cattle, walked into Albany in Western Australia with his faithful Aborigine, Wylie, today at the end of a year-long journey of exploration from Adelaide across the Nullarbor Plain around the Great Australian Bight.

Eyre had been given up for dead and indeed came close to death from hunger and thirst. His friend and overseer, John Baxter, was murdered by two Aborigines who stole Eyre's water, leaving him to exist off dew mopped up with a sponge.

"Three days had passed since we left the last water," said Eyre, "six hundred miles had to be crossed before we could find help and I knew not one drop of water had been left us by the murderers."

The story of his expedition is typical of those men who are opening up this vast land. He tells of uncharted mountain ranges, of limitless inland seas too salty to drink, of privation and dying horse.

Sometimes Aborigines appeared out of the vast emptiness to help them to find water. At other times they gnawed the roots of eucalyptus trees to assuage their thirst. Ironically, Eyre and Wylie arrived in Albany in a rainstorm. Tonight Wylie is with his people and Eyre is celebrating with a hot brandy and a bath after a year of privation.

Fleet shells China as opium row grows

The British ship "Nemesis" bombarding Chinese junks in Anson's Bay.

China, 5 July 1840
British warships of the "Eastern Expedition" bombarded the island of Zhoushan at the entrance to Hangchow Bay today and landed troops to occupy the island. Tonight the British flag flies over the Chinese city of Dinghai. The origins of this "Opium War" can be traced to the Chinese seizure and destruction of 20,000 chests of opium belonging to British traders last year. Relations worsened when the British refused to hand over sailors who killed a Chinese peasant in a brawl.

The Chinese retaliated by ordering a boycott of British ships, and the traders retired to the barren island of Hong Kong where they have been living in conditions of some hardship. The proposal to send an expedition has not met with universal approval. William Gladstone argued in the House of Commons: "A war more unjust in its origin, a war more calculated to cover this country with permanent disgrace, I do not know. The British flag is hoisted to protect an infamous traffic."

This war is about more than opium, however. It is designed to force China to open its ports to British ships with consular rights for the traders. Britain has gathered a considerable force to fight the war, with 4,000 British and Indian troops carried in a score of warships and transports led by the 74-gun *Wellesley*. The Chinese appear to have no answer to the firepower of the British guns and rockets.

Teetotaller starts a travel business

Loughborough, 5 July 1841
Thomas Cook, a wood-turner and pillar of the temperance movement, has chanced on a new scheme that could revolutionise the way that England takes its pleasures. Hoping to attract a large crowd to a temperance meeting in Loughborough, he arranged with the Midland Counties Railway to run a special excursion train from Leicester.

This was the first time such a "special" had been run for the public. So popular was Cook's idea, and so extensive the requests that he organise further trains, that he intends to expand his scheme.

Slaves who killed their captors freed

Washington, 9 March 1841
The trial of the African mutineer Cinque and his 52 fellow slaves ended here today. Swayed by the defence counsel, John Quincy Adams, the court found all the defendants not guilty and ordered their freedom. Two years ago the Negroes seized the Spanish slave ship on which they were held as it sailed around Cuba. They killed the captain and most of the crew before sailing north and landing in Connecticut. Spain has demanded their extradition, but today's verdict will make that impossible.

Sultan moves from Muscat to Africa

Zanzibar, 1840
Sayyid Said, sultan of Muscat, and head of a rich trading empire based on his sultanate in the Persian Gulf, is moving the centre of his operations to this East African island.

Africa has been Muscat's biggest growth area for 20 years. As Muscat trade grew, so did the number of Swahili ports under Muscat control. By 1837 the sultan had taken control of Mombasa and secured commercial treaties with Britain, France and the USA. The take over met with little resistance and is now accepted by both the local people and the foreign powers.

War breaks out again as Afghans resist British domination

Kabul, December 1841
As the first snowflakes float down on Kabul, the British army of occupation realises that all is not as it should be. There has been an insurrection in the city; British officials are being assassinated; worse, the elderly and gout-ridden British commander, General Elphinstone (who served bravely at Waterloo but has seen no active service since), is incapable of decisiveness.

Few worry, though. The camp, on low-lying ground overlooked by hills and two miles from the supply depot, is large enough for a racecourse and polo field, and everyone is expected to be thoroughly entertained over Christmas.

Afghan artillery dragged onto high ground to bombard the British camp.

1841 (1841-1842)

London, 28 August 1841. The Conservative leader Sir Robert Peel succeeds the Whig Lord (William) Melbourne as Prime Minister. This will be his second period in office. He has announced that his policy will be to reduce import duties in the cause of free trade.

Ohio, August 1841. Streets fight in Cincinnatti develop into a five-day anti-Negro riot.

China, August 1841. British forces, at war with China, who Britain is forcing to buy Indian cultivated opium, move along the coast, reoccupy Zhoushan island and enter the Yangze river. The troops are supported by a fleet of 16 warships.

Germany, 4 September 1841. The liberal democrat Hoffman von Fallersleben composes new words to the tune of Haydn's Austrian *Imperial Hymn*. The text, beginning *"Deutschland, Deutschland uber alles"* (Germany, Germany, above all), is a plea, not for German superiority, but for national unification.

Europe, 19 September 1841. The first railway line to cross a frontier is completed between Strasbourg and Basle.

USA, November 1841. As the conquest of the west continues, a group of 130 colonists crosses the Rocky mountains at South Pass and arrives at Walla Walla in Oregon after a 2,000-mile trek.

Afghanistan, December 1841. As attacks on occupying British troops mount, the puppet Afghan ruler, Shah Shuja al-Mulk, installed in Kabul is assassinated. His murder is followed by that of the British resident in Afghanistan, Sir Alexander Burnes.

Russia, 1841. M Y Lermontov, author of *A Hero of Our Time*, is killed in a duel.

South-East Asia, 1841. The sultan of Brunei, in northern Borneo, gives British interests influence over Sarawak, in return for support against enemy attacks. James Brooke, the British representative, becomes *rajah* of the region.

Germany, 1841. The philosopher Arthur Schopenhauer publishes *The Two Fundamental Problems of Ethics*.

Germany, 1841. At Leipzig, Felix Mendelssohn conducts the premiere of Robert Schumann's first symphony, the *Spring Symphony*.

Italy, 1841. The *Stabat Mater*, a sacred work by Gioacchino Rossini, is published. The first piece Rossini has produced since he retired in 1829, it was written before 1837, when he was in Paris.

Britain, 1841. The Miners' Association of Great Britain and Ireland is formed. It aims to represent and mobilise around 200,000 mineworkers.

Britain, 1841. The National Charter Association is created to press for the demands of the People's Charter through peaceful means. It has 282 branches by the end of the year.

Britain, 1841. The Scottish philosopher Thomas Carlyle publishes his *On Heroes and Hero-worship*.

London, 1841. The journalists Henry Mayhew and Mark Lemon launch a new satirical magazine, *Punch*.

Central America, 1841. The state of El Salvador declares its independence, effectively ending the Confederation of Central American States set up in 1823. Nicaragua and Costa Rica withdrew in 1838, followed in 1839 by Guatemala and Honduras.

USA, 1841. In a good year for American literature, the poet Henry Wadsworth Longfellow publishes his second book of poetry, *Ballads and Other Poems*; the novelist James Fenimore Cooper writes *The Deerslayer* and the radical Ralph Waldo Emerson publishes *Essays, First Series*.

West Africa, 1841. A large British force under a Royal Navy captain and a black African chaplain, Samuel Crowther, enters the Niger delta to set up an "African Civilisation Society" with missionary and commercial aims. The expedition is a failure owing to the many deaths from fever.

North Africa, 1841. A French expeditionary force under Thomas Bugeaud, which arrived in Algeria last year to launch a concerted campaign against Abd al-Kader, drives the Algerian resistance leader into Morocco, where he enlists Moroccan support.

Afghanistan, 6 January 1842. A 16,500-strong Anglo-Indian force under Lord Auckland is massacred while retreating from Kabul.

Britain, May 1842. Parliament rejects a new Chartist petition, for which Feargus O'Connor has collected three million signatures.

North America, 9 August 1842. The Webster-Ashburton treaty is signed by Britain and the USA, fixing the border between the state of Maine in the USA and New Brunswick in Canada.

China, 29 August 1842. Britain's opium war with China is over. Britain and China sign the treaty of Nanjing, ceding Hong Kong island to Britain and opening five ports to foreign trade.

Wagons cross Rockies via Oregon Trail

Settlers going west across the continent: a wagon train on the Oregon Trail.

Oregon Territory, November 1841
The lure of fertile valleys, ripe for grain harvests and orchards, the salmon-rich Columbia river and a warm moist climate has brought the first wagon train over the Rocky Mountains to Oregon Territory. This was no easy journey for the men, women and children who brought their covered wagons – "prairie schooners" – from the arid frontier states of Iowa and Missouri in search of wood, water and game.

The trail to Oregon is littered with furniture, discarded to lighten the load as the settlers blazed the trail westwards. Every night they parked their wagons in a ring against hostile Indians, and sang hymns to drown the howls of prairie wolves.

As they began the climb over the mountain range, the pioneers suffered terrible hardship from hunger as they left the known route and moved north. There was worse to come as they crossed the Wyoming Basin where alkali made the water almost undrinkable, killing many of the animals that accompanied the wagon train

Even as they reached Oregon, the newcomers could not be sure whose country they were in. Britain and the United States are still discussing territorial rights and the border with Canada has yet to be resolved, with Britain threatening war if the United States annexes Oregon.

Sums are solved by calculating machine

England, 1842
Ada, Lady Lovelace, the mathematician has translated and annotated a paper by Menabrea on the *difference machine*, a machine that can think mathematically. Ada, the daughter of Lord Byron, the poet, has as good a grasp of symbolic logic as her friend and fellow mathematician, Charles Babbage, the inventor of the calculator.

Now the government is paying Babbage to develop an advanced "analytical engine" while Ada, who has a household and three children to support, works on a secret gambling system.

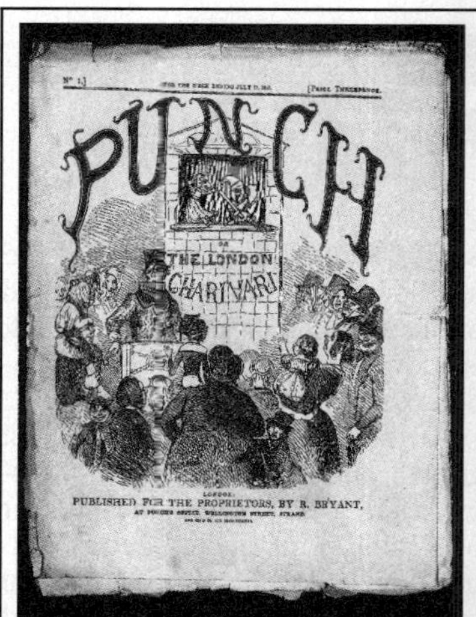

PUNCH

THE LONDON CHARIVARI

"Punch": the first issue of the satirical magazine published in 1841, disrespectful of authority and always banging its drum.

British guns force China to open up

China, 29 August 1842
The Opium War, which has lasted for two years of often intense fighting, ended today with the signing of the Treaty of Nanjing and complete success for the British. The treaty, forced on the Chinese after by the fall of Chin-kiang and the threat of a massive bombardment of Nanjing by British warships in the Yangze, opens with a call for "peace and friendship" between the two countries, but the terms are a total humiliation for the Chinese.

Over the next four years they must pay $21,000,000 which, includes the cost of the opium whose destruction started the war. More importantly the ports of Canton, Amoy, Foochow, Ningbo and Shanghai are to be opened to British trade and Britain will have consular rights in these ports. The island of Hong Kong is to be ceded "in perpetuity to Her Britannic Majesty, her heirs and successors". All British subjects and Chinese friends of Britain held in prison are to be released. This treaty promises to be a turning point in China's relations with the west. Curiously, no mention is made in it of the opium trade.

The signing of the Treaty of Nanjing, forced on China after the bombardment of the city by the Royal Navy.

British besieged by Boer trekkers in Port Natal

South Africa, June 1842
British troops, who marched into Port Natal (*Durban*) in May to cut off the inland Boer republic from the sea, are under siege. Two riders have broken through the Boer lines to call for reinforcements from Cape Colony.

Meanwhile Boer settlements, subject to the republic of Natalia, are proliferating in the interior. The Winburg colony, south of the Vaal river, and the Potchefstroom colony north of the Vaal, are typical representatives of the mixture of democracy and authoritarianism. Winburg is run by a democracy of white Boer men.

The governing body is the *volksraad*, people's council. Potchefstroom's system of government is the opposite. It is subject to the patriachy of Hendrik Potgieter. Women are silent, and Potgieter regularly defers his decisions to the Almighty.

US and Britain agree on Canadian border

Washington, 9 August 1842
The United States and Britain today signed a treaty settling several outstanding issues concerning the US-Canadian border.

The treaty agreed by Lord Ashburton and the US secretary of state, Daniel Webster, gives 5,000 square miles of disputed territory on the Maine border to the Canadian province of New Brunswick and 7,000 square miles to Maine. The treaty also settles how the border is mapped and marked.

Violent Chartist protests shake Britain

The Charter: a special delivery.

London, 1842
Riots and strikes have broken out in northern England in protest against reductions in wages. The riots, which started in Lancashire when strikers pulled the plugs out of factory boilers, have now spread to Glasgow and the Midlands.

The authorities blame the Chartists for stirring up the unrest after their three-million-signature petition demanding universal suffrage was rejected by the Commons in May. In Staffordshire 54 Chartists have been sentenced to transportation. Among the agitators tried was the petition organiser, Feargus O'Connor, who was acquitted on a technicality.

Britain stages bloody retreat from Kabul

Afghanistan, January 1842
A lone rider is sighted by a British sentry at Jalalabad, on the road to Kabul. His name is Dr Bryden. He tells the horrified officers that he is the sole survivor of the expeditionary army sent into Afghanistan.

First the Afghans cut the British camp off from its supply depot two miles away; then they attacked it; the camp was indefensible and soon the British General Elphinstone was asking for terms. The Afghans gave him none, except to leave their country. So the 15,000 British soldiers began their retreat. Officers abandoned their men, thousands were slaughtered by Afghans, thousands more just lay down in the snow and died.

Afghans slaughtering British troops during the terrible retreat from Kabul.

1842 (1842-1843)

St Petersburg, 9 December 1842. Mikhail Glinka's opera *Russlan and Ludmilla*, based on a story by Pushkin, is performed for the first time. It confirms Glinka's reputation as Russia's leading composer.

Britain, 1842. In the budget the prime minister, Robert Peel proposes lowering tariffs on about 450 types of merchandise. To compensate for the loss in revenue he plans to tax incomes of over £150 a year.

Britain, 1842. Lord Ashley's Mines Act, prohibiting the employment underground of women, girls, and children under ten years old, comes into force.

Ireland, 1842. The Irish poet Thomas Osborne Davis, with John Dillon and Charles Duffy, founds the *Nation*, the newspaper of the Young Ireland party. The paper aims "to direct the popular mind to the great end of nationality".

China, 1842. The scholar Wei Yuan publishes the *Shengwuji*, a work which stresses the need for military and political reform in China.

Serbia, 1842. Prince Michael Obrenovic, the son of Prince Milos Obrenovic and Serbia's ruling prince (under Ottoman suzerainty) since 1839, abdicates. The Serbian Senate sends for Alexander Karageorge, in exile in Russia, to replace him. The Ottomans accept the senate's choice, but insists that Karageorge is not an hereditary prince.

Russia, 1842. The novelist Nikolai Gogol publishes *Dead Souls*, a sombre portrayal of Russian life under serfdom.

Britain, 5 April 1843. Queen Victoria proclaims Hong Kong a British crown colony.

China, 26 June 1843. Britain and China sign a protocol to the Treaty of Nanjing which defines the legal status of merchandise.

Spain, July 1843. General Baldomero Espartero, who was made regent two years ago, is forced into exile as the result of an uprising backed by the former regent Maria Cristina. General Manuel Narvaez, the leader of the moderate faction, succeeds him. He plans to reinstate the Spanish monarchy with full powers.

France, 26 August 1843. The democratic newspaper *La Reforme* is founded.

Switzerland, August 1843. The anti-clerical majority in the Swiss Federal Diet approve the closure of all monasteries. The Catholic cantons of Lucerne, Freibourg and Zug appeal to France, Piedmont and Austria to help them to obtain a postponement of the decision.

Greece, September 1843. King Otto yields to popular demands for a Greek constitution.

France, September 1843. Queen Victoria of Britain visits France and meets King Louis Philippe.

China, 8 October 1843. Britain and China sign a diplomatic treaty determining the rights of British consuls and nationals on Chinese territory.

China, 17 November 1843. The port of Shanghai opens for foreign trade in accordance with the terms of the Treaty of Nanjing.

China, 1 December 1843. Opium smoking, the cause of the Opium War with Britain, is again banned by imperial edict.

South Africa, 1843. Britain declares the former Boer republic of Natalia to be the British colony of Natal, subject to the governor of Cape Colony. Some Boers remain, but most retreat across the Drakensberg Mountains to the Orange and Vaal countries of the plateau. The dream of the independent Boer state, with a sea coast and international recognition, is lost.

Italy, 1843. Vincenzo Gioberti publishes, in exile, a manifesto called *On the moral and political primacy of the Italians*. It calls for a united Italy under papal rule.

India, 1843. British troops under Sir Charles Napier and Sir Hugh Gough capture the Sind region after a campaign much lacking in strategy and skill.

St Petersburg, 1843. Czar Nicholas decides to send Admiral Putyatin to Japan in an attempt to open up the country. For financial reasons the expedition is postponed.

Afghanistan, 1843. Dost Mohammed is restored to the leadership of Afghanistan after the British defeat two years ago. Deposed and imprisoned by the British in 1839, he escaped and attempted to restore his regime, but was deported to India.

Milan, 1843. Giuseppe Verdi's new opera *I Lombardi*, set during the Crusades, is an immediate success. Its reception follows the success of the biblical opera *Nabucco*, which was premiered in Milan last year.

Britain, 1843. The political philosopher and utilitarian John Stuart Mill publishes his *Psychology as an independent science* and the *System of inductive and deductive logic*.

Britain, 1843. Michael Faraday establishes a general theory of electrolysis; his fellow physicist James Joule formulates the principle of the equivalence of forms of energy.

"The Fighting Temeraire" by J M W Turner, with clouds of scarlet.

Critic defends painter said to be mad

London, 15 May 1843

A passionate defence of the work of J M W Turner as superior to the Old Masters, *Modern Painters*, has been published by "A Graduate of Oxford". He has been identified as the precocious 24-year-old John Ruskin, the son of a sherry merchant who buys paintings for his son.

The violence of colour and vagueness of form in Turner's recent paintings has led some critics to suggest that he is mad. At last year's Royal Academy he exhibited a picture of a snowstorm at sea, noting: "The author was in this storm." He made the sailors lash him to the mast so that he could draw it. The painting shows a steamer in a vortex of churning foam and driving spray. It was dismissed by one critic as "soapsuds and whitewash".

Turner's painting of *The Fighting Temeraire*, a veteran ship of the Battle of Trafalgar being towed up the Thames by a steam tug under a symbolic sunset, was the sensation of the Royal Academy exhibition four years ago. "No man had hitherto painted clouds scarlet," writes Ruskin.

Greek king becomes constitutional ruler

Otto: now a constitutional monarch.

Greece, September 1843

A popular revolt has forced King Otto of Greece to agree to a constitutional monarchy, under which a Greek oligarchy will take the place of his own Bavarian line.

The second son of King Ludwig of Bavaria, Otto was made king of Greece by the great powers in 1832 and subsequently confirmed by the Greek National Assembly. He instituted a new legal code and organised a regular army, but he was a Roman Catholic in an Eastern Orthodox country, and his autocratic rule and high taxation made him unpopular.

When he failed in 1841 to regain Crete from the Ottomans he lost the support of the British as well as that of his own people.

Britain extends its rule across three continents

Ireland: opponents of union arrested

Dublin, 1843
British authorities have strengthened their hold on Ireland. Following year of mass meetings in all of the Irish provinces outside Ulster, Daniel O'Connell and eight other nationalists have been arrested and charged with conspiracy to change the government, laws and constitution by "intimidation and the demonstration of great physical force".

Until the defeat of the Whig government two years ago, O'Connell and his colleagues, as Westminster MPs, sought reform by supporting the Whigs. When Peel's Tories took office, O'Connell went home to start a grass-roots campaign for repeal of the union with Britain. Within months the Repeal Association had organised over 40 mass meetings and was collecting £700 a week in subscriptions, with money coming from Irish communities in the United States. O'Connell became increasingly defiant; he talked of the association setting up its own courts of justice and a national assembly to form a *de facto* government.

The British in India, and their wives: Indians carying them ashore at Madras.

India: rough justice for annexed Sind

Karachi, India, 1843
Sind has joined British India. It has become a province. In February an agreement forced on the Sind leaders resulted in the British residency at Hyderabad being attacked. Anxious to impose his will, the British commander, Sir Hugh Gough, marched straight into Sind with 3,000 men and with will and firepower defeated a Sind army of 20,000 at Miani. Six *emirs* were captured. Only one, Sher Mohammed, held out until he was defeated in one of Gough's blind and furious battles.

In spite of cabinet disapproval of extensions of empire, Sind has been annexed. Amongst those most resentful are the *sepoys* (soldiers), who fear that all India will soon be British. Some, no longer entitled to overseas allowances for being in Sind, are refusing service there.

Natal taken; Hong Kong is now colony

London, December 1843
Satisfaction and dismay greet the imperial balance sheet this year. Believers in the "Forward Policy", who are to be found in the war office and the colonial office, are pleased to see new red spaces on the world map: Natal, in South Africa, and Hong Kong, off the south-eastern coast of China.

Their opponents, who prefer influence to rule, regard colonies as a burdensome expense and see themselves as consolidators, are horrified. In neither case was annexation justified, they argue. In Natal a perfectly respectable Boer republic had been established and would have been left in peace if it had not been for the Evangelical lobby's claims that Blacks were being maltreated. In Hong Kong a useful military offshore base on the mouth of the Canton river, which had served well in the Opium War, has been turned into a colony. Further, the Anglo-Chinese agreement, signed at Nanjing, awarded Britain the expense of a colony and gave her rivals the benefit of the five new "Treaty Ports".

Law to stop British scandal of women and children in mines

London, 1842
Women, girls and children under ten are no longer to be allowed to work underground in coal mines following new legislation just approved by the British Parliament.

The Mines Act implements the principal recommendations of the commission appointed two years ago to investigate the scandal of conditions in Britain's coalmines. It found that children, sometimes as young as five, are employed underground to haul trucks in passages too narrow for men.

Others spend their entire day hunched down in dark, confined spaces operating ventilating shafts while women and girls are being harnessed like horse and made to pull coal trucks.

The new act provides for inspectors to enforce the law. It comes at a difficult time for Sir Robert Peel's new ministry, which is reluctant to alienate industrialists at a time of adverse trade figures.

Children, some only five years old, hauling trucks in coalmines: now to be a thing of the past.

Homeopathist dies, apothecaries' bane

Paris, 2 July 1843
Samuel Hahnemann, the founder of the controversial new medical practice of *homeopathy*, died here today aged 88. He was hounded by the medical establishment, particularly the apothecaries, and had to leave Leipzig, where he had studied medicine and done most of his formative work, in 1821. Patients, however, loved him and he secured the patronage of royalty. He then lived at Cothen as the guest of the archduke, before moving here in 1835.

Hahnemann's system is based on what he termed the "law of similars". Diseases can be cured by drugs which produce similar symptoms in the healthy, and only minute doses are needed, much less than those usually prescribed.

1843 (1843-1844)

Britain, 1843. Charles Dickens publishes his novel *A Christmas Carol.*

Britain, 1843. The writer Thomas Macaulay, who achieved great popularity last year with *Lays of Ancient Rome*, publishes his collected *Critical and Historical Essays* in three volumes.

Britain, 1843. The weekly periodical *The Economist* begins publication.

Germany, 1843. Richard Wagner is given a conducting post at the Dresden opera following the success of *The Flying Dutchman*. However, it was less successful than his opera *Rienzi* of last year, possibly owing to its various structural innovations.

Denmark, 1843. The physicist Georg Ohm formulates the law of sonic vibrations.

China, 1843. Wei Yuan publishes his geography of foreign countries, *Haiguo Tuzhi*, in 50 chapters, providing a rather simplistic view of the non-Chinese world.

West Africa, 6 March 1844. The British governor of the Gold Coast (*Ghana*) forts, taken over from British traders last year, makes a "bond" with the various Fante states of the coast. It includes an alliance against other European powers on the coast and against inland Asante power, and gives Britain judicial rights over Fante people who come to the forts.

Sweden, 8 March 1844. Charles XIV, king since 1818, dies and is succeeded by his son, Oscar.

Spain, 13 May 1844. The regent Manuel Narvaez establishes a paramilitary police force called the *Guardia Civil*, aimed mainly at maintaining public order.

Washington, DC, 24 May 1844. The inventor Samuel Morse taps out the first telegraph message between two cities, to a friend in Baltimore, 40 miles away.

USA, 27 June 1844. Joseph Smith, the leader of the Mormon sect, and his brother Hyrum are killed by a mob in Carthage, Illinois, where they had been held on a charge of riot. This follows months of tension between the Mormons, who settled at Nauvoo, Illinois, in 1839, and locals who had come to resent and suspect Mormon political and economic power.

Prussia, June 1844. Weavers in Silesia rebel in protest at lower pay for hand-loom workers imposed by employers who have gone over to mechanical weaving. The revolt is bloodily suppressed.

Morocco, 1 July 1844. A French squadron under the duke of Joinville bombards Tangiers.

China, 3 July 1844. China and the USA sign the treaty of Wanghiya, giving US nationals similar rights to those granted to Britain by last year's protocol to the treaty of Nanjing. It also gives the USA access to the five ports now open to international trade.

Italy, 25 July 1844. The Bondiero brothers are shot for fomenting a revolt in Calabria.

USA, 8 August 1844. Brigham Young is chosen to head the Mormon church in succession to Joseph Smith.

Morocco, 14 August 1844. France's Marshal Bugeaud attacks and defeats the army of Abd al-Kader, the Algerian resistance leader, and his Moroccan supporters at the Isly river.

Morocco, 10 September 1844. France and Morocco sign the treaty of Tangiers, ending their conflict. France agrees to withdraw from Morocco.

Italy, 1844. King Charles Albert of Piedmont orders the foundation of teacher training colleges in a move to reduce the influence of the Jesuits. This is the latest in a series of liberal measures which began with the introduction of a civil code in 1837 and, two years later, a penal code establishing the principle of equality before the law.

Serbia, 1844. Prince Alexander Karageorge embarks upon a policy of land reform.

Japan, 1844. The *shogun* refuses a demand by King William II of the Netherlands that Japanese ports be opened to foreign vessels for trade and provisioning.

West Indies, 1844. The Dominican Republic secedes from Haiti.

Denmark, 1844 *The Concept of Anguish*, by the philosopher Soren Kierkegaard, appears. It follows the publication last year of *Either/Or, Fear and Trembling* and *Repetition.*

Germany, 1844. Heinrich Heine publishes *New Poems*, an anthology, and *Germany, Winter Story.*

Atlantic, 1844. The iron-hulled *Great Britain*, designed by the engineer Isambard Kingdom Brunel, becomes the largest steamship to cross the Atlantic.

Britain, 1844. The historian Thomas Carlyle publishes the essay *Past and Present.*

Britain, 1844. J M W Turner paints his dramatically atmospheric *Rain, Steam and Speed.*

Italy, 1844. Verdi's operas *Ernani*, based on Hugo, and *I due Foscari*, based on Byron, receive their first performances in Venice and Rome respectively.

Emperor's decree bans opium smoking

Imperial propaganda: a wife chops up her addicted husband's opium pipe.

China, 1 December 1843

The emperor has once again banned opium smoking in his unavailing struggle against the drug. It is doomed to have as little effect as his other measures, as his people have an insatiable appetite for it, an appetite which British traders are only too willing to feed.

The East India Company, anxious not to jeopardise its legal trade in tea, auctions its Indian opium to private traders in Calcutta. The "country traders" then ship the drug to China in specially built and heavily armed opium clippers.

Unloaded onto fortified receiving ships moored off the southern coast, the illicit cargoes are transferred to multi-oared "fast crabs" and "scrambling dragons" crewed by fierce Chinese pirates.

They run the opium past bribed officials and it is fed into the smuggling networks run by gangsters and secret societies like the *Triads*. The addicts are of all classes, but bureaucrats and soldiers seem especially vulnerable.

Commissioner Lin, whose burning of British traders' opium sparked the Opium War, has even written to Queen Victoria demanding that she ban the trade which, he said, "is repugnant to human feeling and at variance with the Way of Heaven". To no avail. The profitable trade goes on.

French book stars "Three Musketeers"

Alexandre Dumas: a relentless writer, after an idle and irregular youth.

Paris, 1844

The prolific Alexandre Dumas, who has already had ten years of success with his historical plays, has turned his hand to novels of adventure with *Les Trois Mousquetaires* and *Le Comte de Monte Cristo*. In the first, the three musketeers of the title, Athos, Porthos and Aramis, are joined by the young D'Artagnan in a series of adventures in the service of the queen, Anne of Austria, against Cardinal Richelieu, the mentor of King Louis XIII. Dumas has many collaborators – some say as many as 90 – who feed him with historical material for his newspaper serials or *feuilletons*. The output under his name includes four other books this year alone.

French guns defeat the Moroccan cavalry

Oujda, Morocco, 14 August 1844

French troops pacifying the Algerian-Moroccan border have crossed the frontier into independent Morocco and defeated the Moroccan cavalry in the Isly valley.

The decision to attack is certain to have repercussions in Paris where King Louis Philippe and his government had given the veteran campaigner, Marshal Bugeaud, express orders not to cross the Moroccan border.

French troops using scorched earth tactics have now advanced about 40 miles into Morocco, but do not appear to be following up their victory with an advance on Fez, the capital. Marshal Bugeaud ordered his men to attack in the early hours of this morning after the duke of Joinville's fleet had shelled Moroccan ports yesterday.

Bugeaud's troops stormed across the valley of the Isly and engaged the Moroccan cavalry, which was forced to surrender by noon.

A post-battle statement by Marshal Bugeaud, who has made his men more mobile by lightening their equipment, celebrated the "glory of arms" and put the losses for each side at 800 Moroccans and 27 Frenchmen killed.

Britain creates new colonies in Africa

West Africa, c.1844

The European powers are turning the old bottlenecks of the Atlantic slave trade into colonies. Forts such as St Louis, Bissau, Christiansborg and Rufisque, each owned by a rival trading power, have become miniature city-states, producing a population of Mulattoes who act as middlemen between the European traders and the Africans in the interior. Until recently the boundaries of the city-states never went beyond the fort gates.

The Gold Coast typifies the development. The British, taking advantage of the fear that the coastal Fante people have of the neighbouring Asante empire, have formed a "bond" with the Fantes, extending British jurisdiction over 100 miles (160km) into the interior.

Mormon leader is murdered by mob

Carthage, Illinois, 27 June 1844

Mormon leader Joseph Smith and his brother Hyrum were dragged from their prison cell tonight by a mob of 200 and lynched – despite an assurance of safety by the state governor. The Mormon community had been split by a controversy over polygamy – which the Smiths sanction – and the brothers were jailed for destroying the offices and press of a rival Mormon newspaper, the *Expositor*, which opposed their views.

Martial law was declared when the crowd surrounding the jailhouse heard that the Smiths were about to be freed. The guards were powerless to hold off the mob whose leaders proclaimed that "as law could not reach them, powder and shot should".

Isambard Kingdom Brunel's "Great Britain": the most powerful ship afloat. Her launch on 19 July 1843 marked another first for Britain.

Cooperative and ten-hour movements help improve the lot of British workers

Workers of Lancashire unite: the dividend from the "Co-op" awaits you.

England, 21 December 1844

A group of unemployed workers in the Lancashire mill-town of Rochdale has hit upon an ingenious scheme for helping others while helping oneself. For the past six months members have been meeting in the Weavers' Arms and today they opened for business in a small shop in Toad (T'owd) Lane.

At present stocks are limited to a few essentials such as sacks of flour, but expansion is expected to be swift. Already, the Rochdale Pioneers, as they call themselves, have almost 50 members. Items are sold at regular market prices, but customers, who join the Pioneers for a shilling membership fee, receive a share or dividend of the profits. Thus thrift is encouraged and everyone is part of the business.

The idea of self-help is catching on among the working classes. In London, a drapery shop assistant is one of a dozen young men who have formed a club for the spiritual improvement of employees in the drapery and other trades. It is to be called the Young Men's Christian Association. The lot of the mill worker has greatly improved in recent years. The law now forbids anyone under 18 years to work more than twelve hours a day, and there is even talk of restricting teenagers to a ten-hour day.

Children under thirteen are already restricted to a 48-hour week and must attend school for two hours a day.

Frederick Engels: socialist thinker.

1844 (1844-1846)

China, 14 December 1844. The Qing court issues an edict relaxing a ban on the Catholic Church.

Germany, 1844. Mendelssohn's violin concerto in E minor is performed for the first time, in Leipzig, to great acclaim.

Brussels, 1 February 1845. The German political philosopher and dissident Karl Marx settles in the Belgian capital after being expelled from France.

USA, 4 March 1845. The Democrat James Polk is sworn in as 11th president following his landslide election victory last November. He is a supporter of further US expansion westwards.

New Zealand, 11 March 1845. Seven hundred Maoris led by their chief, Hone-Heke, burn the small town of Kororareka in protest at the settlement of Maori land by Europeans, in breach of the 1840 Treaty of Waitangi.

North America, 28 March 1845. Mexico severs relations with the USA following the US Senate's ratification of the annexation of Texas on 1 March.

Switzerland, 31 March 1845. Religious strife continues between anti-clerical radicals and the Catholic cantons. The radicals fail to seize the Catholic canton of Lucerne in their second organised attack in four months.

China, 25 July 1845. China grants Belgium equal trading rights with Britain, France and the USA.

Algeria, 8 September 1845. A French column surrenders at Sidi Brahim in the continuing Algerian war.

Germany, 21 October 1845. Wagner's new opera *Tannhauser* is given a mixed reception at its premiere.

Switzerland, 11 December 1845. In response to the armed band organised by the liberal cantons, the seven Catholic cantons – Uri, Schweitz, Unterwalden, Lucerne, Zug, Freiburg and Valais – form the *Sonderbund* to protect their interests.

Britain, 20 December 1845. Robert Peel returns to office as prime minister two weeks after resigning. This follows the failure of the Whig leader, Lord John Russell, to form a government, as invited to do after announcing his support for a repeal of the Corn Laws.

USA, 29 December 1845. Texas joins the United States of America and becomes the 38th state in the union.

India, December 1845. The British army in India embark on the conquest of Kashmir and the Punjab.

Britain, 1845. John Henry Newman, aged 44, a leading force in the Oxford Movement since 1833, converts to Roman Catholicism.

Britain, 1845. Parliament passes an law permitting Jews to stand for elections.

Britain, 1845. The politician and writer Benjamin Disraeli, the head of the "Young England" group of young Tories, publishes *Sybil*, his second political novel. His first, *Coningsby*, appeared last year.

Germany, 1845. Friedrich Engels publishes his *Condition of the Working Classes in England.*

Britain, 1845. The Scottish engineer R W Thompson patents an air-filled tyre for use on the *coupe*, a new two-seater convertible carriage for town use.

Poland, 1845. As part of their campaign for greater Russification, the Russians abolish the Polish penal code and impose the Russian one instead.

China, 1845. The boundaries of the British concession at Shanghai are fixed; Hong Kong becomes linked to Britain by a regular shipping line.

France, 1845. Prosper Merimee publishes the novel *Carmen*, set in Spain.

Peru, 1845. Ramon Castillo seizes power in a *coup d'etat* and establishes a reformist dictatorship.

USA, 1845. The author Edgar Allan Poe publishes his *Tales of Mystery and Imagination.*

Ireland, 1845. Blight strikes the potato, the staple food of the Irish countryside, making much of this year's crop inedible. The prospect of serious famine looms.

Sierra Leone, 1845. William Ferguson becomes Britain's first black colonial governor. Sierra Leone has a growing western-educated commercial, clerical and official class, and Forah Bay College, founded in 1827 for the education of clergymen, was Africa's first Christian college.

Germany, 1845. Robert Schumann's piano concerto in A minor appears. It is based on an earlier *Fantasy* written for his wife Clara, a fine composer and brilliant virtuoso pianist, in 1841.

India, January 1846. After several battles in a war with the Sikhs which began last year, the British break up the Sikh forces at Sobraon.

Madagascar, 1846. In protest at a government order making all foreigners subject to the native law, the French and British bombard Tamatave.

Maoris protest against foreign colonists

A Maori war dance; now the Maoris are really fighting, to protect their lands.

New Zealand, 11 March 1845

Hona-Heke, a Maori tribal chieftain, today led his warriors in an attack on the small town of Kororareka. The town was set on fire and a number of people were hurt in the fighting between Maoris and settlers. This attack, one of a number since the Treaty of Waitangi, five years ago, under which the Maoris ceded sovereignty but not land, is a direct result of Maori accusations that settlers are cheating them out of their birthrights. The settlers also have grounds for complaint because they fall foul of complicated tribal customs when they try to buy land from the Maoris. The situation is becoming increasingly dangerous, and the government will have to take strong action to prevent a bloodbath.

Religious fighting flares in Switzerland

Lucerne, December 1844

Theological debate has turned into armed clashes here in the last month or two. Earlier this year the Great Council of Lucerne invited the Jesuits to take all the theological teaching. This provoked an angry response from the Protestants which has now turned into actual fighting. Fuel to the flames of the old religious differences has been added by their new revolutionary fervour. Lucerne has now joined with six other Catholic cantons to form a defensive alliance called the *Sonderbund.*

Controversial composer stages new opera

Wagner: divisive genius.

Dresden, 21 October 1845

Excitement mixed with bewilderment greeted last night's premiere of the opera *Tannhauser* by Richard Wagner, at 33 the joint director of music at court here.

The work, set in the Middle Ages, is novel in that the music is more continuous and seamless than in operas based on the traditional pattern of arias and choruses – a departure already evident in his *Flying Dutchman* of two years ago. Wagner's music arouses either fanaticism or loathing, but he is used to controversy. In 1839 he had to slip out of Riga to avoid creditors, and he is involved in German patriotic movements. On top of this, he makes no secret of his contempt for Jews and all things Jewish.

Samurai preparing for war with West

Feudal Japan: soon to disappear.

Japan, 1844

Wide-ranging reforms instituted in the face of fierce opposition by Mizuno Tadakuni, the chief *shogunate* councillor, are changing the face of Japan. He has rooted out corrupt officials, and ordered the *samurai* to practise their martial arts in anticipation of an attack from western ships. He has also made urbanised peasants return to the land, to ensure food supplies, and has set about restoring the country's economy.

Potato blight forces Irish to seek refuge

Dublin, 1845

There have been over 20 largescale failures of the potato crop in Ireland in the past century, but this year's is without precedent. It has been caused by the blight which has ravaged crops in America appearing without warning in Britain and Ireland. The gravity of the situation can scarcely be exaggerated; over four million people in Ireland and two million in Britain live almost wholly on potatoes. Until well into July the Irish crop appeared to be very good. Then the hot, dry weather changed abruptly to chilling rain and fog. The first warning of trouble came from the Isle of Wight, which reported that potatoes were being destroyed by a mysterious distemper.

Before the authorities had quite grasped what was happening, Ireland was being devastated. When first lifted the potatoes appeared healthy, but within a few days they became a stinking putrefying mess. The scale of the famine has overwhelmed the authorities; the British have no machinery for dealing with disaster on such a scale. Besides, attitudes towards relief are much influenced by free trade notions, so that corn continues to be exported while the Irish starve.

Public works schemes have been hastily devised, and soon 750,000 people will be employed on relief work, which means that some three million people are being supported by public funds. Even that is insufficient; Irish families are emigrating in tens of thousands, even though the voyage to America is almost as deadly as the famine – about one person in every six dies at sea. In their sufferings the Irish have, perhaps inevitably, blamed the disaster on "English oppression", a charge that has caused resentment in London where it is pointed out that the British government has provided more than £8 million for relief.

The potato famine: four million Irish people live purely on potatoes.

Texas joins rest of the United States

Washington, 29 December 1845

The vast republic of Texas became the 38th state in the union today – annexed peacefully after an almost unanimous vote in favour by its citizens. The ten-year-old republic has long been coveted by both the United States and Mexico, and an American diplomat, John Slidell, has been dispatched to Mexico City to smooth Mexican resentment. Texas was formerly a Mexican province and fought a bitter war before declaring its independence in 1836.

Since then the republic has lived through a series of upheavals. Its first president, Sam Houston, sought political stability, peaceful relations with the Indian tribes and ultimately to join the union.

His successor, Mirabeau Lamar, took a different policy line altogether. He saw Texas as a permanent republic and established diplomatic relations with Britain and France. Unlike Houston, Lamar saw the Indians as a threat and began a series of aggressive campaigns against them.

Houston was re-elected president of Texas three years ago and found the republic seriously in debt. Annexation became inevitable and it was Britain and France who acted as the intermediaries with Mexico.

China relaxes ban on Catholic Church

China, 24 October 1844

The French, following British and US tactics in their determination to open up China to western trade, have today signed a treaty with the Chinese at Whampoa which will have far-reaching effects.

It opens up Chinese ports to French ships on a "most-favoured nation" basis, and gives France consular rights for its citizens, so Frenchmen will be above Chinese law, answerable to French law.

Where the Whampoa treaty differs from the British Nanjing treaty and the American Wanghiya treaty is in granting toleration of Roman Catholicism and giving the French the right to build Catholic churches in the treaty ports.

Sikhs humbled as Britain sells off Kashmir for £1 million

A village in the Punjab, the Sikh heartland, still Sikh after the treaty.

Kashmir, 1846

Kashmir has been forcibly separated from the Sikh domain by the British and sold to the neighbouring *rajah* of Jammu for £1 million.

The Kashmir settlement is just part of the treaty which Britain is forcing on the Sikhs after defeating them at Sobraon in January. In addition the Sikhs are paying an indemnity to Britain of half a million pounds, half the price of Kashmir.

British moves against the Sikhs have been inevitable since 1839 when Ranjit Singh died and the Sikh territories degenerated into anarchy. For Britain the final straw came last December when Sikhs raiders attacked British troops. Now Britain is dictating the terms, which the Sikhs have no choice but to agree to.

1846 (1846-1847)

Poland, March 1846. The Russians and the Austrians occupy the free republic of Cracow, ending a pro-independence revolt that began last month in nearby Galicia, the part of Poland that is under Austrian rule.

USA, March 1846. As tension grows between the USA and Mexico, President Polk orders the US army under Zachary Taylor to the Rio Grande river.

USA, 13 May 1846. The USA declares war on Mexico.

Britain, 25 June 1846. The highly unpopular Corn Laws, which imposed duties on imported grain, are repealed.

USA, 15 June 1846. Britain signs a treaty with the USA agreeing to end its joint occupation of Oregon Territory. All the land west of the Rocky Mountains and south of the 49th parallel now belongs to the USA.

Rome, 16 June 1846. Giovanni Maria Mastai Ferretti succeeds Gregory XVI as pope and takes the name of Pius IX.

Britain, 29 June 1846. Bitterly opposed to the repeal of the Corn Law, the protectionist wing of the Tory Party, led by Benjamin Disraeli, mount a revolt against Robert Peel's Tory government, forcing Peel to resign as prime minister.

California, 7 July 1846. A US navy squadron sails into Monterey and formally claims California for the USA.

Denmark, 8 July 1846. King Christian VIII lays claim, under the Danish succession law, to the independent duchies of Schleswig and Holstein.

Rome, 16 July 1846. Pope Pius IX orders an amnesty for political prisoners.

USA, 16 October 1846. The dentist William Morton carries out the first surgical operation under local anaesthetic, using sulphuric ether.

Spain, October 1846. The affair of the "Spanish marriages" severely damages Franco-British relations. Queen Isabella II marries her cousin Francis, the duke of Cadiz; her sister Louisa marries the duke of Montpensier, the son of Louis Philippe of France. Both marriages breaks agreements made between France and Britain, which has pressed the claim of another of Isabella's suitors, Prince Leopold of Saxe-Coburg.

Poland, 6 November 1846. Following the March uprising, the small republic of Cracow is annexed to Austrian-controlled Galicia, losing its independence.

Mexico, 16 November 1846. After defeating a large Mexican force at Monterey in September, General Zachary Taylor takes Saltillo.

California, 6 December 1846. A pro-Mexican revolt in California is put down by US troops.

Paris, 6 December 1846. Hector Berlioz cantata *The Damnation of Faust* is performed for the first time.

Panama, 12 December 1846. The USA and Colombia sign an agreement granting the USA transit rights on the narrow isthmus of Panama between the Atlantic and Pacific Oceans.

New Mexico, 25 December 1846. US troops defeat the Mexicans near Las Cruces, virtually completing the conquest of New Mexico.

USA, 28 December 1846. Iowa is admitted as the 29th non-slave state in the union.

Japan, 1846. Commodore Biddle arrives in Japan on an official mission from the US government. He enters Edo (*Tokyo*) Bay with two vessels and asks for the opening of trade relations between the USA and Japan. The Japanese refuse.

Portugal, 1846. Following the publication of a public health order ordering Portuguese peasants to be clean and decreeing that cemeteries must in future be sited outside large centres of population, peasants led by priests of the Minho region rise up and overthrow the dictatorial government of Costa Cabral.

Paris, 1846. A new brass reed-instrument known as a saxophone, one of a range of improved instruments invented by the Belgian Adolphe Saxe, makes its appearance.

California, 13 January 1847. The final surrender of pro-Mexico resisters in California to the US ends 25 years of Mexican rule.

France, 28 January 1847. During a period of severe depression and unemployment, disturbances break out among agricultural workers in central France, provoked by food shortages.

Canada, January 1847. Lord Elgin, a liberal and friend of Robert Peel, is made governor general of Canada. On his arrival, Queen Victoria announces an amnesty for those convicted all after the uprisings of 1837-38.

Prussia, 3 February 1847. King Frederick William IV convenes a new assembly which brings together delegates from all the Prussian provinces but is given no effective power over legislation or the budget.

Prime minister falls as free traders win

London, 25 June 1846

After a five-month debate in the House of Commons, the free-traders carried the day with a vote to repeal the hated Corn Laws. All duties on imported wheat, oats and barley are reduced to a nominal one shilling a quarter until full repeal in three years' time.

But within hours the protectionists had wreaked revenge on the prime minister, Sir Robert Peel. The Tory landowners on his own backbenches had never looked on Peel, a manufacturer's son, as a genuine Tory, and his conversion to free trade was taken as the ultimate betrayal. A bill to use coercion against Irish nationalists is coming up and the landowners, who had never been against coercion for Ireland, say they will vote against it.

Sir Robert Peel: the ex PM.

Peel's decision to tackle the Corn Laws was given an added urgency last year, with the failure of the potato crop in Ireland. But he could not get the solid support of the cabinet and resigned last December. Within a fortnight he was again prime minister, the Whigs having been unable to agree among themselves as to who would be in the cabinet.

The fight was now within Peel's own party. Protectionists, who control a number of family seats in the Commons, gave orders for Peelites to resign. Peel argued that since repeal was necessary for the well-being of the people the party should support him – in vain. The landowners took their revenge – and split the Tory party.

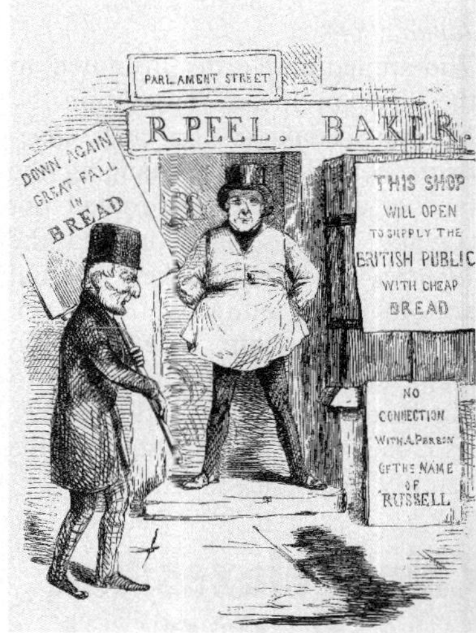

Sir Robert Peel's cheap bread shop.

New planet is found in the solar system

England, 1846

There is another planet in our solar system, discovered after something of a scientific race. The joint winners are the brilliant student John Couch Adams from Cambridge and the equally clever French astronomer Urbain Le Verrier. The planet has been named Neptune.

It all began years ago when astronomers noticed that there was something amiss in the orbit of the planet Uranus. It simply did not behave as it should, unless – and this was the intriguing thought – there were yet another planet further out producing perturbations and distortions in its motions. This prompted a lot of intense mathematical work to calculate the mass, distance and orbital velocity of this mysterious "planet X". Adams in Cambridge came up with an idea as to where the planet might be in 1845.

Simultaneously Le Verrier was independently arriving at the same position as Adams for the as yet unseen planet. He then contacted J G Galle at the Berlin Observatory who on 23 September of this year came up with the first sighting, less than one degree from the calculated, predicted position.

US and Mexico fight over California

Mexico, 13 May 1846
Although Congress in Washington only made a formal declaration of war today, full-scale fighting between the US army and Mexican troops has been under way on either side of the Rio Grande for several days. It was when the news reached Washington last night that Mexican forces had crossed the river and killed and captured US troopers that Congress went to war. "Mexico has ... shed American blood upon the American soil," declared the Democratic President James Knox Polk.

Despite his ringing denunciation of Mexico, few doubt that Polk has deliberately baited Mexico into conflict – with New Mexico and California as the prize. The US wants to buy both territories – with "money no object" for California – but the Mexicans have spurned offers and refused to talk money. The disputed Rio Grande was the excuse for the war, although Polk's justification is that Britain and France – both extending their Pacific ambitions – have covetous eyes on harbours in California.

As General Zachary Taylor – "Old Rough and Ready" – is reporting success by his 2,200 strong army against 6,000 Mexican troops massed on the border, the US is divided over the declaration of war. Texas and the southern states are delighted and have furnished more than 49,000 volunteers. The original colonies are less eager and have supplied only 14,000 men. Abolitionists see this as a war of conquest by the slave lobby.

The battle of Palo Alto on 8 May: 2,200 US troops defeated 6,000 Mexicans.

Nonsense verses set readers guessing

London, 1846
A new kind of verse is sweeping like wildfire through the adults of the country – the limerick:

There was an old man of Peru
Who watched his wife making a stew
Till one day, by mistake,
In a stove she did bake
That unfortunate man of Peru.

There are great numbers of Unfortunate Old Men, or Young Persons, in *A Book of Nonsense*, just published. Eccentric drawings illustrate the plight of the Young Person of Crete (whose toilette was far from complete), the Young Lady (whose bonnet Came untied when the birds sate upon it). The author, on the title page tells us:

There was an old Derry down Derry,
Who loved to see little folks merry,
So he made them a book
And with laughter they shook
At the fun of that Derry down Derry.

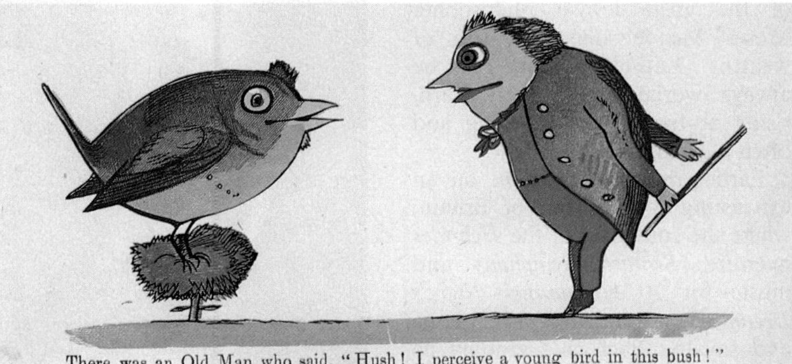

There was an Old Man who said, "Hush! I perceive a young bird in this bush!"
When they said, "Is it small?" he replied, "Not at all!
It is four times as big as the bush!"

The old man who said "Hush!", from "A Book of Nonsense".

French fugitive is hiding in London

London, 27 May 1846
Louis Napoleon, the nephew of Napoleon Bonaparte and claimant to the French throne, has been spotted in Piccadilly, having escaped from the chateau at Ham, near Amiens, where he has been imprisoned for the past six years.

He was seen by Lord Malmesbury, who reported the fact to a French Embassy attache at dinner this evening. "I never saw a man look so frightened," said Lord Malmesbury as the attache rushed out of the room.

Louis Napoleon is the son of Napoleon's brother, Louis Bonaparte of Holland, and Hortense Beauharnais, the emperor's stepdaughter. As a young man he travelled throughout Europe and lived in Italy, Bavaria, Switzerland and London. In 1836 and 1840 he failed in attempts to lead Bonapartist revolts against the July monarchy.

The government of Louis Philippe is understandably nervous about him, for the name of Napoleon still stirs the French.

Faraday reveals electrical secrets

London, 1846
Having established himself as a leading experimentalist of the day with his development of the principle of the electric motor, Michael Faraday has now offered a further intriguing contribution to our understanding of the mysterious forms of energy that hold together all matter. In a Royal Institution lecture in London, Faraday discussed "Thoughts on Ray Vibrations" and described the magnetic and electrical forces holding together atoms, suggesting that these might serve to transmit light. Faraday seems to be suggesting that we might even unify all the forces of nature into just one.

Faraday, the inventor and scientist.

War starts over axe in south Africa

South Africa, 1846
After ten years of uneasy peace, war between British and Xhosa has broken out once more on the Cape eastern frontier. The stealing of an axe by a Xhosa man, and a botched attempt by his comrades to rescue him, set off the war.

The British have kept the peace by making treaties with Xhosa chiefs across the frontier. But from 1844 British administrators began to bend before the pressure of white sheep farmers, seeking more land for expensive merino sheep imported from Europe.

1847 (1847-1848)

Mexico, 23 February 1847. US troops under Zachary Taylor rout General Santa Anna's Mexican army at the battle of Buena Vista.

Mexico, 9 March 1847. In the first large-scale US amphibious operation, General Winfield Scott lands thousands of troops on the beaches south of Vera Cruz.

Mexico, 29 March 1847. US troops under Winfield Scott take possession of the Mexican stronghold at Vera Cruz.

Rome, March 1847. Pope Pius IX passes a liberal law on the press which entrusts censorship to a lay committee.

Mexico, 18 April 1847. US forces defeat a large Mexican army under Santa Anna at Cerro Gordo in one of the bloodiest battles of the war.

Washington, DC, 1 May 1847. The Smithsonian Institution for the increase and diffusion of learning, headed by the Princeton physicist Joseph Henry, is dedicated.

Philadelphia, 7 May 1847. The American Medical Association is founded.

Britain, 8 June 1847. An act is passed limiting the working day of women and children aged 13 to 18 to 10 hours.

Rome, June 1847. Pope Pius IX creates a council of ministers and a civil guard.

Britain, June 1847. In London, Karl Marx, Friedrich Engels and Stefan Born found the Communist League.

Utah, 24 July 1847. A group of Mormons led by Brigham Young founds a settlement on the banks of the Great Salt Lake.

Italy, August 1847. Austrian troops occupy the town of Ferrara in an attempt to check the introduction of liberal measures.

Germany, 12 September 1847. The radical and middle-class opposition, meeting at Offenburg, adopts a liberal and democratic reform programme which includes abolition of privileges, freedom of the press and equal voting rights.

Mexico City, 14 September 1847. A US army storms and captures Mexico City, putting an end to the Mexican war.

France, 19 September 1847. Francois Guizot becomes prime minister.

Morocco, 23 October 1847. Having lost the support of the sultan of Morocco, the Algerian resistance leader Abd al-Kader surrenders to the French.

Oregon, 29 November 1847. Cayuse Indians massacre 14 members of an Oregon mission.

Britain, 8 December 1847. An international convention of the Communist League adopts Karl Marx's principles of the overthrow of the middle classes and the dictatorship of the proletariat.

Italy, December 1847. Austrian troops are withdrawn from Ferrara.

Canada, December 1847. Following the victory of the reformists in a general election, Lord Elgin, the governor general, proclaims the birth of a parliamentary system.

Austria, 1847. The physician Ignaz Semmelweis discovers that the high mortality rate in newborn infants is due to infections.

South Africa, 1847. The British are victorious over the Xhosa people in the War of the Axe, which broke out last year as a result of moves by British sheep farmers to acquire more land.

West Africa, 1847. Liberia, the state founded by the American slave-trade abolitionists, proclaims its independence.

France, 1847. Reform "banquets" calling for measures such as universal suffrage and parliamentary reform are held throughout the country.

Britain, 1847. Among the new novels published this year are *Vanity Fair* by William Thackeray, *Wuthering Heights* by Emily Bronte, *Jane Eyre* by Charlotte Bronte and *Dombey and Son* by Charles Dickens.

Milan, 3 January 1848. Clashes occur during an anti-Austrian demonstration organised by the liberals.

India, 12 January 1848. The earl of Dalhousie, the young and gifted British minister, is appointed governor general of India.

Sicily, 12 January 1848. Following the outbreak of a revolutionary movement, Sicily proclaims a provisional independent government.

Paris, 14 January 1848. The prime minister, Guizot bans a reform banquet which was due to be held in Paris next month.

Denmark, 20 January 1848. Frederick VII succeeds his father, Christian VIII, as king.

Naples, 27 January 1848. The people of Naples rise up and demand a constitution.

Naples, 10 February 1848. King Ferdinand II promulgates a new constitution.

Tuscany, 17 February 1848. The duke of Tuscany promulgates a constitution.

Brighter future for surgery and childbirth

Massachusetts General Hospital: a tooth extracted under anaesthetic.

Boston, Massachusetts, 1847

Two recent advances in medical techniques hold out the hope that in future surgical operations will be almost painless and childbirth much safer. At Massachusetts General Hospital, in Boston, the US dentist William Morton has used the gas *ether* for the first general anaesthetic in the west; though some claim that the US surgeon Crawford Young has been using ether for anaesthesia for several years.

A patient had a neck tumour removed, and came round afterwards having felt no pain. So complete is the loss of sensation that Morton's technique could even be used for limb amputation.

Meanwhile, in Vienna, Dr Ignaz Semmelweiss, a Hungarian, has discovered the cause of puerperal or "childbed" fever, the scourge of maternity wards: careless students – careless because they come straight into the wards from the dissecting room without washing their hands. From now on, washing hands in a solution of chlorinated lime is the rule. Already mortality rates are plummeting.

Mendelssohn dies of a stroke at 38

Leipzig, 4 November 1847

Felix Mendelssohn-Bartholdy died today after his second stroke in six months, aged just 38. The grandson of the great Jewish philosopher Moses Mendelssohn and son of wealthy Lutheran converts, he always worked punishingly hard, rising at five in the morning and often working into the night.

Earlier this year he went on an exhausting concert tour of Britain, where the composer of the *Hebrides* overture, *Scottish Symphony* and music for *A Midsummer Night's Dream* was popular with public and royalty. Back in Germany he learnt of the death of his sister Fanny, herself a fine musician, and his health finally gave way.

Mendelssohn: popular composer.

Gold sends people rushing to California

Sutter's Mill, where the gold was found.

Los Angeles, February 1847
Six years after a prospector, Francisco Lopez, found traces of gold in the roots of a newly-dug onion, the world is waking to the news that there is gold in plenty in the streambeds of California. A gold rush is starting as farmers from across the country mortgage their property, clerks leave their desks – even ministers quit their pulpits – as they head for California.

The popular song is "I'm off for Sacramento with my washbowl on my knee". However, many believe that news of the gold finds is being deliberately fostered by a government anxious to encourage population growth in the Mexican-owned state.

Free Blacks declare their independence

Liberia, West Africa, 1847
A new state has been born: Liberia, a nation built by freed slaves. Founded by the United States as places to absorb both its surplus Black population and its freed slaves, the settlements of Liberia, Grand Bassa and Mississippi are aggressively colonial. Now, under the leadership of a prominent merchant, Joseph Roberts, they have proclaimed themselves a republic, but the United States has yet to recognise it.

US infantrymen storm Mexico City

Mexico City, 12 October 1847
After a day-long artillery bombardment, US infantrymen stormed the Mexican capital today: a major victory in the two year war over the sovereignty of Texas. Santa Anna, the Mexican commander, is in full flight with the remnants of his army, and General Winfield "Old Fuss and Feathers" Scott watched in full dress uniform as the union flag was hoisted over the National Palace. The battle cost more than 1,000 American lives.

Swiss army crushes Catholic alliance

Geneva, 29 November 1847
After a civil war lasting for less than a month, a defensive alliance of seven conservative Catholic cantons in Switzerland has been broken up. The defeated cantons, centred on Lake Lucerne, had reacted against the anti-clerical policies, including the closure of monasteries, of the radical federal government. The Swiss Catholics had powerful friends in France and Austria, but the federal government moved fast and the rebels surrendered within a month – too quickly for their allies to intervene. Jesuits, who allegedly organised the uprising, are being expelled.

New Indo-Chinese ruler faces threat

Annam (Vietnam), 1847
Tu Duc, the head of the Nguyen dynasty, has succeeded to the throne of Annam. He rules the biggest and most powerful state in the Indo-Chinese peninsula. Forces are gathering, however, which seem to be beyond his comprehension and threaten the survival of his regime. He has closed his mind to any modernisation and does not recognise the decline of Vietnamese influence in Cambodia. He also refuses to open up his country to western trade despite the clear indication of the Opium War in China that the west is prepared to open Asian markets by force.

Sharp social satires and romantic tales flourish in vintage era of English novels

(Left to right) Currer, Ellis and Acton Bell, alias the Brontes, with their alcoholic brother Branwell, who provided them with their best plots.

London, 21 December 1847
It has been an exciting year for novel readers in England. Early in the year William Makepeace Thackeray, already noticed for his *Punch* series on "The Snobs of England", began publication of *Vanity Fair*. Its monthly parts in yellow paper covers are keenly awaited for the latest doings of Miss Becky Sharp, clawing her way up the social ladder with "only herself and her own wits to trust to", or the latest tearful episode of her rival, "that little pink-faced chit", Miss Amelia Sedley. "Some people consider fairs immoral altogether: very likely they are right. Vanity Fair is not a moral place, certainly, nor a merry one, though very noisy," writes the author, who invites us to "step in for half an hour and look at the performances: some scenes of high life and some of very middling indeed".

This is far from the style of *Jane Eyre* by a new author, Currer Bell, whose reception in October has called for a second edition, published today. It tells the story of a plain and independent-minded governess, Jane Eyre, and her growing fascination for her employer, the dark tormented – and married – Mr Rochester.

Even more passions are unlocked in *Wuthering Heights*, set in the wild Yorkshire moors. The violence of Heathcliff makes havoc of other people's lives in an electric atmosphere described with great power by Ellis - Bell. It is published with *Agnes Grey*, a comparatively plain tale by Acton Bell. Some believe that all three Bells are the same author.

Tancred, the third novel of Mr Disraeli's trilogy, is a satire about religious issues, following *Coningsby*, which dealt with the ruling class, and *Sybil*, which contrasted England's "Two Nations", the rich and the poor, so feelingly.

William Makepeace Thackeray, a satirist on Victorian values.

1848 ⇒

France, 23 February. Following the outbreak of fighting between demonstrators and troops in Paris, Guizot is replaced as prime minister.

France, 24 February. Louis Philippe abdicates and a republic is proclaimed.

France, 27 February. The government, which yesterday recognised the right to work, creates national workshops to relieve unemployment.

Austria, 13 March. The chancellor, Prince Metternich, resigns following demonstrations in Vienna.

Rome, 14 March. Pope Pius IV grants a constitution.

Prussia, 17 March. With the outbreak of a revolt in Berlin, Frederick William IV grants a constitution.

Milan, 22 March. Joseph Radetszky's 20,000 Austrians are driven out of Milan by a popular uprising.

Venice, 22 March. The Venetians proclaim their independence and create a provisional government.

Hungary, 23 March. Hungary proclaims its independence of Austria.

Italy, 23 March. Charles Albert of Piedmont declares war on Austria and attacks Austrian forces in Lombardy.

Italy, 8 April. The Austrians are defeated by the Piedmontese at Gioto.

Sicily, 13 April. Sicily declares itself independent of Naples.

Rome, 26 April. Pope Pius IX condemns the Italian nationalist movement.

Denmark, 2 May. Prussia invades Denmark over the Schleswig-Holstein question.

Paris, 4 May. The constituent assembly elected last month holds its opening session. In the elections the moderate republicans won a large majority over the socialists and the monarchists.

Poland, 7 May. Prussian troops suppress Warsaw uprising.

Paris, 15 May. Demonstrators invade the assembly and proclaim it dissolved. The revolt is put down by the National Guard.

Naples, 15 May. The revolt in Naples collapses.

Italy, 29 May. The Austrians defeat a Tuscan army at Curtatone.

Marx calls Europe's workers to revolt

1848, the year of revolution: barricades against a Baroque background at Michaelerplatz in Vienna, 26 May.

Brussels
An obscure German-Jewish journalist living in exile in Belgium has cooperated with a German textile manufacturer's son settled in England to publish a ringing call to working men to rise up in rebellion and smash the capitalist system.

Karl Marx' family converted to Christianity and he was sent to a Protestant high school in Trier; it was under police surveillance because it was suspected of employing liberal teachers. All his life Marx has never been short of adversaries, be they police spies or fellow socialists. Only when he met Friedrich Engels did he find a good friend – who could also relieve his poverty.

Last year Marx and Engels joined a secret society of exiled German workers, the League of the Just, for which they wrote a pamphlet. "All history has hitherto been a history of class struggles," this *Communist Manifesto* proclaimed. But now the proletariat has taken the stage fo the final struggle to end the clas system for ever. "Workers of th world, unite!" cry Marx and Engels. "You have nothing to lose bu your chains."

The manifesto came out at th beginning of the year. Since then revolution has erupted in France Italy, Austria and Germany. These revolutionaries were not inspire by Marx and Engels; the author believe that others will be.

Flames of revolution burn capitalist power bases

Italy: states expel Austrian rulers

Milan, March

Stirred by the news of revolution in Vienna and the flight of Prince Metternich, the people of Milan have risen in revolt against their hated Austrian masters. After five days of street fighting, the military governor, Marshal Radetsky, judging his force of 10,000 men to be too small to put down the rising, retreated to the Quadrilateral system of fortresses, last used in the Napoleonic Wars.

A provisional Italian government has been proclaimed, and now the people of Venice have risen, driven out the Austrians and proclaimed the republic of St Mark. As far south as Naples and Rome volunteers are clamouring to join the war and calling on the liberal Pope Pius IX to back them.

After some hesitation, Charles Albert, the king of Sardinia, who defused the revolutionary mood at home by granting a constitution, has been compelled by popular clamour to declare war on Austria. He has arrived at Cremona, in Lombardy, with 70,000 men, but his heart is not in it; too many of the Italian patriots are republicans and he fears revolution more than he detests Austria.

The Tuileries stormed: the art was saved, but the hall of state destroyed.

France: monarchy falls, republic declared

Paris, 24 February

The political storm that followed the government's ban on a "democratic banquet" planned by young radicals has blown up into full scale revolution and sent Louis Philippe, France's king for the past 18 years, fleeing into exile in England.

As the storm developed, the king sacked his prime minister, Francois Guizot, who had been resisting reforms. It was too late. Today the king escaped down the Champs Elysees as the Paris mob, armed with weapons seized from gunsmiths' shops, began pillaging his palace, before going on to take over the Prefecture of Police and the Post Office.

A brawling crowd which invaded the Chamber of Deputies was invited to agree to the formation of a provisional government. This "government" took over the Hotel de Ville and proclaimed a republic, with a promise to reduce working hours and guarantee jobs for the unemployed.

Germany makes U-turn on reforms

Berlin, 21 March

After a week of violent disorder in Berlin, with soldiers and citizens fighting running battles, the erratic King Frederick William IV has made a dramatic change of policy and assumed the role of reformer, promising a free press, a new Prussian constitution, a meeting of the *Landtag* to draw up an electoral law – and, boldest of all, a pan-German parliament.

This last move is a calculated appeal to German nationalist sentiment. The liberal movement in the German lands certainly demands curbs on arbitrary power and wants popular participation in government. But it also seeks the unification of the German people.

The king's action has set off a chain reaction of liberal promises in other German states. Much of the agitation is conducted by middle-class intellectuals and merchants. But a deepening economic crisis and widespread unemployment have pushed workers into action; as repression has eased, trade unions have appeared. In Berlin an attempt has been made, through the Central Committee of Working Men, to establish an all-German trade union centre.

Hungary: rebellion against Habsburgs

Hungary, 31 March

The Emperor Ferdinand has approved the March Laws, passed 16 days ago by the Hungarian *Diet*, which sweep away many feudal legacies and give substantial autonomy to a government in Budapest.

Rebellion against Habsburg rule in Hungary has been led by Lajos Kossuth, a radical patriotic pamphleteer released seven years ago from imprisonment for treason. Kossuth galvanised the diet earlier this month with his call for tax reform and national representation.

The Hungarian rebels have been peaceful, and have not sought separation from the Austrian empire.

Austria: riots oust Chancellor Metternich

Vienna, 13 March

Metternich, chancellor of Austria since 1821, has been forced to resign, the sacrificial victim of a reform movement which has taken its inspiration from the revolt in Paris and led to riots in Vienna and the provinces.

Pressure has built up rapidly in the past two weeks, with an industrial crisis in Vienna, petitions from students and the bourgeoisie, and intense political intrigue. Peaceful demonstrators have clashed with troops, and unrest is spreading.

Metternich's own vanity has been his downfall, since he has claimed personal responsibility for various decrees that have made him a symbol of repression.

Prince Metternich: diplomat.

England: collapse of Chartist idealism

London, 10 April

A threatened confrontation between the Chartists and the military was averted today when Chartist leaders decided not to lead a mass march on parliament to present their million-signature petition. The climb-down came after a surprisingly small crowd of Chartists had gathered on Kennington Common in south London.

The police, backed up by armed troops, warned the Chartists that the procession would not be allowed to reach Westminster. After speeches the crowd dispersed, and the petition was delivered by three black cabs.

1848 ⇒

Prague, 17 June. The Austrian General Alfred Windischgratz crushes a Czech uprising in Prague.

France, 24 June. The national workshops are disbanded by the assembly.

Paris, 26 June. Another revolt in Paris is bloodily put down by Louis Cavaignac.

Germany, 27 June. Heinrich von Gagern, the president of the German national assembly, orders the formation of a provisional central government.

Prague, 17 June. A pan-Slav congress, led by Frantisek Palacky, demands the transformation of the Austrian empire into a federation of peoples with equal rights.

Italy, 25 July. The Piedmontese army is defeated by the Austrians at Custoza.

Italy, 9 August. Piedmont signs an truce with Austria agreeing to abandon Lombardy and Venice.

Vienna, 12 August. The Emperor Ferdinand, who fled to Innsbruck on 17 May, returns to Vienna.

Italy, 26 August. Having continued to resist since the signing of the armistice, Giuseppe Garibaldi and his volunteers are defeated by the Austrians at Morazzone.

Scandinavia, 26 August. Denmark and Prussia sign a truce at Malmo, both agreeing to evacuate the duchies of Schleswig and Holstein.

Vienna, 7 September. The constituent assembly of Vienna, which opened on 22 July, abolishes serfdom.

Hungary, 24 September. Lajos Kossuth is proclaimed president of the committee for national defence.

Switzerland, September. A federal constitution is adopted, replacing the pact of 1815. An executive federal council and two legislative assemblies are created.

Persia, September. Mohammed, Shah of Persia since 1834, dies and is succeeded by his son Nasir al-Din.

Hungary, October. Joseph Jellacic, commander of the imperial forces operating against the Hungarians, is driven out of Hungary.

Vienna, 31 October. Prince Alfred Windischgratz forces Vienna to surrender after a third uprising.

Mexico cedes Texas and California to US

Don Pio Pico, the last Mexican governor of California, with his wife and nieces.

Vera Cruz, Mexico, 2 February
After over two years of fighting, in which nearly 13,000 US soldiers lost their lives, Mexico has finally collapsed. Under a treaty signed here today, Mexico surrenders Texas, New Mexico and California to the USA in return for a payment of $15 million. The acquisition of these territories increases the size of the USA by a third.

The Mexicans were anxious to save their own country from US occupation, and with their war chest empty they were desperate for the money. Although Generals Winfield "Old Fuss and Feathers" Scott and Zachary "Old Rough and Ready" Taylor are being hailed as the victors, the unsung hero is a State Department clerk, Nicholas Trist.

He was dispatched to Mexico by President Polk with orders to negotiate a peace. Months passed without progress. Polk ordered Trist to return, but the clerk ignored the order and went through the final battles with General Scott until the moment was right. Although at first sight Trist described Scott as "the greatest imbecile I have ever had anything to do with", the two ended the war as close friends.

Prussia in border war with Denmark

Schleswig and Holstein, April
Prussian troops have moved into the disputed duchies of Schleswig and Holstein and are fighting the Danish army on behalf of the rebellious German citizens, who wish to escape from the detested Danish rule.

The duchies have been a source of controversy for many years. Holstein's population is essentially German, and as such part of the German Confederation of States, but its hereditary ruler, the duke, is also king of Denmark. He also rules Schleswig, which is divided between Germans in the south and Danes in the north. Since it is not part of the Confederation, Denmark claims it as an absolute possession. The issue is further complicated by dynastic difficulties. The Danish crown passes through the female line, whereas the duchies themselves recognise only the Salic law, which demands male inheritance. Under this law the German dukes of Augustenburg claim that they have a greater right to rule.

Schleswig and Holstein have also become the focus of European interests. Prussia backs its German cousins, but Britain and France back Denmark, hoping to preserve the balance of power in the face of an expanding Germany.

Women fight for votes and equal status

Seneca Falls, 21 July
The first-ever all-women convention on women's rights ended here today with demands for universal suffrage and an end to religious and social discrimination against women. The convention – attended by 300 delegates who packed the Wesleyan chapel – was organised by the radical and feminist antislavery campaigners Lucrecia Mott and Elizabeth Stanton.

Basing their ideas on the Declaration of Independence, the delegates resolved to fight for the vote and to gain legal equality in marriage, education and work. Elizabeth Stanton worked on the Married Women's Property Act – allowing divorced women to keep some of their possessions – which was passed this year by New York.

Amelia Jenks Bloomer, wearing the costume named after her.

Call for state to regulate economy

London
A new book by the philosopher John Stuart Mill, *The Principles of Political Economy*, has cast a fresh light on Britain in the age of the "industrial revolution".

Mill, a former civil servant and politician, and the owner of the *London Review*, is a follower of Jeremy Bentham's "utilitarian" philosophy. He has also taken up and developed the economic ideas of Adam Smith, Ricardo and Malthus. A firm believer in social welfare, he suggests that economic policy should be dictated by government legislation. To ensure that this happens, he wishes to see government interference in an increasingly wide sphere of activities.

Revolutionaries face pro-establishment backlash

Italy: Austrian break-out defeats rebels

Italy, 25 July
The Italian nationalists, seeking to throw off their Austrian oppressors, reckoned without the 84-year-old Marshal Josef Radetsky. He has spent the last four months reorganising his forces in the Quadrilateral fortress complex hinged on Verona. He disregarded orders from Vienna to seek an armistice, ignored political concessions his government had made under British pressure, and two days ago came out fighting.

At the village of Custoza, 11 miles from Verona, he routed the army of King Charles Albert of Sardinia, who is now in full retreat. The outcome seems in little doubt. In a few days the king will be forced to surrender and Austrian rule will have been restored.

The Austrians charging at Custoza.

Germany: a constitutional assembly

Frankfurt, 18 May
The all-German parliament which has assembled here to draw up a constitution for a united Germany has over 200 lawyers and magistrates, 100 university teachers and one peasant. Its president, Baron Heinrich von Gagern from Hesse, favours Prussia's King Frederick as leader of the new Germany, with Austria and her emperor having only associate membership. Doubtless Frederick William would like to become *Kaiser* (Caesar), but he is not likely to accept, partly for fear of upsetting the Austrians, but also because his divine right will not allow him to accept a crown from commoners. Still, this gathering of middle-class intellectuals, assisted by the token peasant, will keep talking.

France: left-wingers are suppressed

Paris, 26 June
The radicals of the February revolution, who promised welfare services and jobs for all, have been crushed in four days of bloody battles in the streets of Paris. Some 10,000 people are believed to have died, and 3,000 more have since been shot without trial. Thousands more are to be transported.

After last April's elections, liberal republicans formed the majority in the assembly. Moderate socialists remained in the government, but the militants set out to exploit the workshops, which had been created to provide jobs for men thrown out of work by the economic crisis.

The workshops were soon overwhelmed by provincials streaming into Paris. In addition, the militants were using the workshops to recruit a revolutionary army. On Wednesday 21 June the workshops were shut down and the men told to go back to the provinces or join the army.

The workers of Paris took to the barricades. Alphonse Lamartine, the radical poet who headed the government, resigned after handing over to the minister of war, General Louis Cavaignac, who went into action with a ferocity that has sent shock waves across Europe and turned the tide of revolution into reaction. In London, the crushing of the radicals has been received with satisfaction by businessmen who had been alarmed at threats made by Lamartine and other ministers to nationalise the railways.

British investors are the biggest shareholders in the railways, but when they complained to Palmerston, the foreign secretary, he told them they must accept the risks of investing in foreign countries.

General Louis Cavaignac (left) crushing the Paris uprising.

Austrian emperor flees democratic Vienna

Ferdinand, the mentally retarded emperor of Austria.

Vienna, 17 May
Popular pressure for democratic reform has persuaded the Emperor Ferdinand to flee to Innsbruck, having already conceded constituent power to an elected chamber. There has been a fundamental shift of power in European politics.

Metternich's resignation two months ago was followed by the emperor promising a constitution, freedom of the press and the formation of a council of ministers. Encouraged thereto by events in France, Italy and Germany, the imperial government granted Hungary an autonomous constitution, and published its own two weeks later. Eight days ago, all Austria's citizens were given the vote.

Ireland: Tipperary insurrection fails

Tipperary, 29 July
Irish hopes of a nationalist uprising have been dashed with the arrest of a second key figure in the radical Young Ireland movement. Police arrested William Smith O'Brien after a skirmish in a cabbage patch in Tipperary as he and his supporters protested against the sentencing of another Irish Confederation member, the journalist John Michel, to 14 years in prison and transportation for advocating a rent strike. The rebels, who planned to declare an Irish republic, expected more support from the peasantry whose main preoccupation is surviving the famine.

French colonies get the right to vote

St Louis, West Africa
In the Senegalese towns of St Louis and Goree, France's Mulatto people are celebrating. News has just come by ship that the republican government in Paris has given them the vote. From now on they will be returning a representative to the National Assembly, like any *departement* in mainland France.

Since the French Revolution the inhabitants have been *citoyens* in theory. Yet it was not until a few months ago, when the republicans took power in France, that slavery was abolished. Now the people will by law have the same rights as any other Frenchmen.

1848 (1848-1849)

USA, 7 November 1848. Zachary Taylor, the former commander who distinguished himself in the war against Mexico, is elected president.

France, 12 November 1848. A new constitution comes into force, providing for a single assembly of 750 representatives elected for three years by universal suffrage, and for a president of the republic, elected for a single term of four years.

Italy, November 1848. Following the assassination of Pellegrino Rossi, the prime minister of the papal states, Pope Pius IX flees to Gaeta.

Austria, 2 December 1848. The Emperor Ferdinand abdicates in favour of his nephew Franz Josef.

Prussia, 5 December 1848. King Frederick William IV dissolves the national assembly and grants a new constitution.

France, 10 December 1848. Louis Napoleon is elected president of the French republic by a huge majority.

Hungary, 15 December 1848. The Austrian army, led by Prince Alfred Windischgratz, invades Hungary.

USA, 1848. The Declaration of Sentiments and Resolutions at the Seneca Falls Convention begins the women's rights movement in America.

Tanzania, 1848. Zwangendaba, the Ngoni chief who led his people on a 2,000-mile migration from Natal to the Fipa plateau in western Tanzania, dies. After his death, his people begin to break up into five smaller chiefdoms.

China, 1848. Xu Jiyu's geography of the world, *Yinghuan Zhilue*, is completed.

England, 1848. A group of English painters, led by John Everett Millais, William Holman Hunt and Dante Gabriel Rossetti, founds the Pre-Raphaelite Brotherhood. The members aspire to bring a new moral seriousness to painting, to study directly from nature and to develop an iconography to express new ideas.

Hungary, 5 January 1849. Budapest surrenders to the Austrians.

Rome, 9 February 1849. Giuseppe Manzini proclaims the Roman republic.

India, 21 February 1849. The Sikh forces are decisively defeated by the British at the battle of Gujerat.

Revolt in Europe: victory or defeat?

The siege of Vienna in October before Austrian troops crushed the unrest.

Austria: emperor is forced to abdicate

Vienna, 2 December 1848

The Emperor Ferdinand has abdicated in favour of his 18-year-old nephew Franz Josef. The move was engineered by Prince Felix Schwarzenberg, who has become the most powerful man in Austria since the sudden resignation of the Austrian foreign minister and arch-conservative, Prince Metternich.

He is determined to put down the unrest, disorder and anarchy which has surfaced in Austria's imperial territories. The remnants of any radical dissent in this city were therefore ruthlessly stamped out by Prince Alfred Windischgratz, the Austrian military commander, when his troops marched in five weeks ago to end a siege of this city.

Schwarzenberg, a more moderate conservative than Metternich, has since formed a ministry of able men and presented a reconstruction programme to the *Reichstag*, which is still working towards the establishment of a federal, democratic constitution.

Italy: pope flees from the Vatican

Rome, 27 November 1848

Alarmed by the activities of revolutionary clubs and the spreading disorder in Rome, Pope Pius IX has fled to the seaport village of Gaeta, in the kingdom of Naples, where he is brooding on the assassination of Count Pellegrino Rossi, the man whom he chose to form a constitutional government, and having second thoughts about his support for reform in the papal states. A republic has been proclaimed in Rome; *Pio Nono,* as he is known, has appealed to Catholic monarchs to restore him to his temporal power in the eternal city.

Germany: emperor exiles assembly

Prussia, 5 December 1848

The king no longer fears the reformmers, radicals and revolutionaries who have dominated the Prussian Assembly since it first met last May against a background of social unrest and the threat of insurrection. During the summer months the assembly was voting reforms right and left, and Frederick William IV did nothing. But when it set out to sack army officers considered to be hostile to democratic aspirations, the king sent the army onto the streets to crush dissent. Then he told the assembly to leave Berlin and meet in the provinces.

France: Bonaparte elected president

Paris, 11 December 1848

The year that opened with the overthrow of the monarchy and the proclamation of a republic is closing with the election of a prince-president who dreams of donning the mantle of his famous uncle and becoming emperor of a Bonapartist France.

During his years of exile, Prince Louis Napoleon gained the reputation of an adventurer and a political buffoon. He staged an abortive *coup* at Strasbourg and another at Boulogne, for which he was sentenced to life imprisonment. Having escaped to England, he returned to France last February and, despite the laws against Bonapartes in politics, was elected to the National Assembly. In the presidential election he was opposed by two left-wingers and a right-wing republican, General Louis Cavaignac. The leftwingers together received fewer than half a million votes. Cavaignac received a million and a half. But Louis Napoleon scooped up five and a half million, from workers and peasants as well as the bourgeoisie and upper-class conservatives, all of whom quite evidently judged him by his name rather than his achievements, which are non-existent.

Prince Louis Napoleon, who dream of following in his uncle's footsteps.

America's master of macabre dies

Baltimore, USA, 3 October 1849
In an ending that could have come out of one of his own horror stories, the poet and storyteller Edgar Allan Poe died today, aged 40. Four days ago he was found drunk and delirious. He was taken to hospital, but never recovered.

Born in Boston and educated in England, he dropped out of university, rose to the rank of sergeant-major in the US Army, and was expelled from military school for deliberate neglect of duty. Already he had published his first poems.

He quickly gained success with his fantastic and frightening tales, but what money he made went on alcohol and opium. Impoverished and addicted, he attempted suicide last year. Now he has found the peace that he searched for through opium.

Famous composer dies an imbecile

Bergamo, 1848
Bergamo's most famous native composer, Gaetano Donizetti, has died aged only 51, paralysed and an imbecile. His first international success was the opera *L'Elisir d'Amore* in 1832, followed by *Lucia di Lammermoor*, whose virtuoso mad scene caused a sensation at Naples in 1835. In 1843 Paris acclaimed his *Don Pasquale*.

Gaetano Donizetti, who died mad: his late operas were failures.

The Sikhs become part of British India

Artillery shelling the Delhi gate at Multan, the heart of the Sikh revolt.

Amritsar, India, 21 February 1849
The powerful Sikh army has been shattered by the British at Gujerat. Since 1846, when British troops defeated the Sikhs and imposed a treaty on them, British policy has been to maintain the Sikh state as a buffer between Afghanistan and British India.

Complaining of British interference in their affairs, the Sikhs revolted again last year, this time in support of Diwan Mulraj, the governor of Multan, who killed two British officers sent to Multan to instal his rival.

In September a pro-British Sikh force under Sher Singh, sent to confront the rebels, went over to them. Then, on 10 October, the governor general of India, the earl of Dalhousie, declared: "Unwarned by precedent, uninfluenced by example, the Sikh nation has called for war, and on my word, they shall have it with a vengeance."

Command was given to Sir Hugh Gough, as energetic as he is unintelligent. Fortunately for the British soldiers they survived his disastrous generalship at two battles (at Ramnagar and Chillianwalla), and have now won the third at Gujerat.

The Sikh lands are no longer a buffer between Afghanistan and British India. The Sikhs can no longer claim to be the great warriors of India. By the fortunes of war, they are now part of British India.

Austria opens war against Hungary

Hungary, 3 October 1848
After the euphoria of the spring revolution, Hungary is running into trouble. Beleaguered in the south by Slav armies, it now faces the wrath of the empire, which declared war in the aftermath of the murder of the imperial high commissioner by a Hungarian mob ten days ago.

Hungary's struggle for independence from the Austrians inspired nationalist movements among its neighbours Transylvania, Carinthia and Croatia, who all owe historical allegiance to the crown of St Stephen, but when these movements turned to the newly independent government in Budapest for recognition they were denied. In assemblies at Karlowitz, Blassendorf and Zagreb they proclaimed their autonomy and abolished feudal rights. Their declarations were endorsed by the government in Vienna. Hungary was isolated.

Lajos Kossuth, the Hungarian nationalist who inspired the *diet* in March, took charge of the recruitment of a Hungarian defence force, while across the frontier Josef Jellacic, a Croatian nobleman and general in the Austrian army, was given dictatorial powers by the Zagreb assembly. After its victory against the Italians the imperial government has repealed the March Hungarian independence laws.

Libreville, a city for freed French slaves

West Central Africa, 1849
As France takes on the work of suppressing the slave trade in its territories it is building a new city for freed slaves on the Atlantic coast and calling it Libreville.

Inland from Libreville, in the Gabon grasslands, there is anarchy as slave-traders and ivory-traders fight for the vast profits that are available, and firearms foment the ambitions of petty potentates. On the coast, however, protected by the frigates of France's anti-slavery patrol, all is in order, and France hopes that Libreville will soon grow into a major centre for French trade with Central Africa.

Cholera linked to polluted water supply

God's gift of water: a London pump, supervised by "King Cholera".

London, 1849
Only now do we know what causes cholera – and it is not carried on the air. The English doctor John Snow contends that there is an infectious organism in polluted drinking water that carries the illness. Fatality rates are far higher in those areas supplied by water from parts of the Thames most contaminated by human waste.

This was convincingly demonstrated when the handle was removed from the water pump in Broad Street – a particularly cholera-prone corner of the city – and illness and death in the neighbourhood dropped dramatically. Snow argues for killing germs by boiling all drinking water.

1849 ⇒

Hungary, 26 February. The Austrians under Windischgratz defeat the Hungarians at Kapolna.

Austria, 1 March. The Kremsier constitution, drawn up by the Austrian *Reichstag*, provides for a decentralised, federal form of government.

Austria, 4 March. The Austrian prime minister Felix Schwarzenberg promulgates his own constitution, providing for a highly centralised system.

Austria, 7 March. The Austrian Reichstag is dissolved.

Italy, 23 March. The Austrians under Marshal Radetsky crush the army of Charles Albert of Sardinia at Novara.

Italy, 24 March. Charles Albert of Sardinia abdicates in favour of the duke of Savoy, Victor Emmanuel II.

Germany, 27 March. Meeting at Frankfurt, the national assembly adopts a constitution which creates a federal state under an hereditary "Emperor of the Germans".

Germany, 4 April. Frederick William IV of Prussia, who was elected "Emperor of the Germans" on 28 March, rejects the imperial crown.

Hungary, 14 April. After retaking Budapest and defeating the Austrians at Godollo, the Hungarians hold a congress at Debrecen and declare Hungary independent of Austria.

Italy, 25 April. Asked by Pope Pius IX to intervene against the Roman republic, a French expeditionary force lands at Civitavecchia.

Rome, 30 April. The republican patriot and guerrilla leader Giuseppe Garibaldi repulses a French attack on Rome.

Russia, 1 May. The Russians and the Ottomans sign the convention of Balta-Liman, agreeing on joint supervision of the Danubian principalities for seven years.

Germany, 8 May. The Prussians suppress a revolt at Dresden.

New York City, 10 May. At least 20 die in anti-British riots provoked by Irish gangs.

Sicily, 15 May. Neapolitan troops enter Palermo, completing their reconquest of Sicily.

Italy, 25 May. Having subjugated Leghorn, the Austrians enter Florence.

Germany, 26 May. Prussia, Saxony and Hanover accept a draft constitution providing for a union of non-Habsburg Germany under the leadership of Prussia.

France, 26 May. The French National Assembly is dissolved.

Hungary, May. The Emperor Franz Josef appeals to Czar Nicholas for help in putting down the Hungarian insurrection.

Denmark, 5 June. A liberal constitution is introduced.

Germany, 18 June. The German National Assembly, which has moved to Stuttgart, is broken up by government troops.

Rome, 4 July. French troops under the command of General Oudinot occupy the city after a siege.

Germany, 23 July. Rebels in Baden capitulate to the Prussians.

Italy, 28 July. The Austrians restore Leopold, the grand duke of Tuscany, who fled to Gaeta in February.

Egypt, 2 August. Mohammed Ali, ruler of Egypt from 1805 to 1848, dies. Apart from his military successes, he laid the foundations of a modern administrative and educational system and revolutionised the Egyptian economy.

Italy, 6 August. Following the signature of the Vignale armistice by Victor Emmanuel II, the new king of Piedmont, Sardinia, the Austrians and the Piedmontese agree on the peace of Milan.

Hungary, 9 August. The Hungarians are defeated by a Russian army at Temesvar.

Hungary, 13 August. The Hungarian general Arthur von Gorgey surrenders to the Austrians at Vilagos.

China, 22 August. The Portuguese governor of Macao, Amaral, is assassinated because of his anti-Chinese policies.

Italy, 22 August. Venice surrenders to the Austrians.

Austria, 27 August. Austria rejects a Prussian scheme of union.

Baltimore, 7 October. The poet and horror-story writer Edgar Allan Poe dies at the age of 40.

Indian Ocean. French merchants on the island of Reunion, desperate for labour on the sugar estates, found a "free labour emigration scheme". This is a ploy to get slave labour from Zanzibar and East Africa without offending the French or British navies.

USA. Associated Press, a cooperative venture organised to distribute telegraphic news to the daily press, begins operation.

Gold rush prospectors flood California

Dreams of wealth and riches: panning for gold in northern California.

San Francisco, California
The greatest-ever gold rush is under way and this once peaceful sun-blessed state will never be the same again. Thousands of gold-hungry prospectors are flooding into California from all points of the globe following a major find by a Swiss settler, J A Sutter.

Within the US alone more than 80,000 people have headed west, and the nation's unexplored heartland is criss-crossed with trails. More still are sailing here via Cape Horn or crossing the Panama Isthmus. Others are arriving from Australia and China, and the harbour here is a forest of clipper masts as hundreds pour ashore clutching picks and pans and high hopes.

Fortunes are being made – so much so that Congress has agreed to the minting of a gold dollar and a $20 "double eagle". They are being lost, too, in the plethora of gambling houses which have mushroomed, along with saloons and brothels, in San Francisco which has grown from a village to a city of 25,000 in a few months. Traders are making the real fortunes, with apples fetching $5 each, eggs at $10 a dozen and a small whisky selling for a pinch of gold-dust.

Frenchman measures the speed of light

France
A French physicist has claimed this year that light travels at the speed of 186,000 miles – or 300,000 kilometres – a second. The true nature of light – that form of energy that makes visible those objects that produce or reflect it – has long been something of a mystery.

Current opinion seems to be in favour of a wave theory, though there are still those who cling to the notion that this energy consists of particles. Whatever light consists of, we do know that it travels extremely quickly – a flash of lightning is seen much earlier than the accompanying rumble of thunder – just how quickly has now been determined with some accuracy by the experiments of Armand Hyppolyte-Louis Fizeau. He already has another claim to fame: like Doppler, he has also explained the so-called "red shift" in light coming from stars.

Revolutions that came from nowhere

Europe

Now it's over, shaken statesmen and briefly triumphant revolutionaries alike are asking how it could have happened. At the start of 1848 Europe seemed stable and secure within the framework of the settlement bequeathed by the Congress of Vienna more than 30 years before. Yet within weeks the established order had been shaken to its foundations, pope and princes were fleeing in fear of their lives and revolutionary regimes were proclaiming liberal constitutions.

Then, as suddenly as it had erupted, the storm began to abate, authority recovered its nerve, and today the revolutionaries are on the run. But the *status quo ante* has not been completely restored. The constitutions that promised universal suffrage, a free press, the right to work and much else have generally been thrown aside, but monarchies are no longer quite so absolute, and the abolition of the feudal system by the revolutionary assemblies is a gain that reactionary forces dare not touch.

The revolutions were made not by the masses but by intellectuals inspired by the ideas of the French Revolution of 1789 and by nationalist aspirations. Their rhetoric terrified rulers haunted by the spectre of Jacobinism, but the fabric of society was not about to be torn apart. Extremists were were soon marginalised and conservatives grasped the reins. In France, the republican constitution survives, but only just. Louis Napoleon is clearly plotting a *coup d'etat*.

Giuseppe Garibaldi, who defended Rome against the besieging French.

The fall of revolutionary Rome: French troops enter the city.

In Hungary, the bid for independence from Austria under Lajos Kossuth, has been crushed with the help of Russian troops. In Vienna, the imbecile Emperor Ferdinand has been replaced by his 18-year-old nephew Franz Josef, the democratic *Reichstag* has been dissolved and a new constitution, with a limited franchise, proclaimed. But even this does not satisfy the prime minister, Prince Felix Schwarzenberg, who requires a centralised state with ministers responsible not to the Reichstag but to the emperor. Austrian power is restored in Lombardy and Venetia, but in Piedmont Victor Emmanuel II remains a constitutional monarch. His kingdom has become the refuge for Italian patriots and liberals.

Elsewhere, political refugees choose England. Louis Philippe was followed by Prince Metternich, who has bought a house at Richmond. Now, Louis Blanc and other socialists have arrived. Lord Palmerston has told Blanc that he can use the state papers in the British Museum for his projected history of the French Revolution.

Chopin, pianist and composing genius

Paris, 17 October

Frederic Chopin, the great Polish composer who wrote almost exclusively for the piano, died today from consumption. He was 38, and had lived in Paris since first arriving there in 1831. The city took the great pianist, whose father was French, to its heart, and he made many influential friends. He wrote some of his best music while living with the woman novelist George Sand for nine years. Their traumatic break-up two years ago hastened his decline, as did his exhausting trip to Britain last year. He found the English hard to fathom. "What a queer lot," he wrote. "May God have pity on them."

Frederic Chopin, Polish composer.

Russia puts down Hungarian uprising

Budapest, 6 August

A Hungarian uprising was crushed by Russian troops at Temesvar today. The Russians acted on behalf of their ally Austria, which occupies much of Hungary. Responding to the spirit of independence that inflamed much of Europe last year, a lawyer, Lajos Kossuth, demanded a British-style constitution. This failed and he declared unilateral independence on 14 April. The uprising was defeated from within, by dissident Croats who aided Austria, as well as through external force. Kossuth is alive, but seems doomed to spend the rest of his life in exile.

Hokusai, versatile painter of Buddhas, landscapes and animals

Edo, Japan, 10 May

Katsushika Hokusai, who called himself "the old man mad about painting", has died at the age of 89, asking for "yet another decade".

In younger days he used to give public exhibitions of his powers, painting pictures of Buddhas and mythological figures in Zen temples which were over 2,000 square feet in size. His celebrated series, the *Thirty-Six Views of Mount Fuji*, includes the bold "breaking wave" which hangs suspended, frozen in motion, above the distant peak of Mount Fuji.

He wrote: "At the age of 90 I shall have penetrated even further the deeper meaning of things. At 100 I shall be truly marvellous."

"The wave", by Hokusai, a painter who sought "the deeper meaning of things".

1849 (1849-1851)

Greece, January 1850. Britain orders a blockade of the Greek coast following an attack on Dom Pacifico, a Moorish Jew.

China, 9 March 1850. The Daoguang emperor's fourth son, Yizhu, ascends the throne in succession to his father, who died last month.

France, March 1850. A law – proposed by the liberal Catholic deputy Falloux – is passed extending the influence of the church over education by allowing state funds to be used for the foundation and continuance of church schools.

Italy, 9 April 1850. Giuseppe Siccardi, the minister of justice in Piedmont, Sardinia, introduces a law curbing the powers of the Catholic Church.

USA, 19 April 1850. The USA and Britain sign the Clayton-Bulwer treaty, which pledges both countries to a protective role in Central America and ensures the neutrality of the prospective Panama Isthmus canal.

Germany, April 1850. At Erfurt, an assembly of German states – excluding, among others, Saxony, Hanover, Wurttemberg and Bavaria – accepts the Prussian scheme for German union, which Austria strongly opposes.

Rome, April 1850. Pope Pius IX returns to Rome.

Palestine, 28 May 1850. France reaffirms its right to the Holy Places.

France, 31 May 1850. A new electoral law abolishes universal suffrage.

Germany, May 1850. The Austrian premier Felix Schwarzenberg revives the *diet* of Frankfurt and invites the German states to discuss a revision of the old German Confederation.

Berlin, 2 July 1850. Denmark and Prussia sign a peace treaty by which Prussia agrees to withdraw from Schleswig and Holstein.

USA, 10 July 1850. Millard Fillmore is sworn in as president following the death yesterday of Zachary Taylor.

Persia, 19 July 1850. Sayyid Ali Mohammed – known as the *Bab* (gateway) – the founder of *Babism*, a new Islamic mystical movement, is executed on the orders of *Shah* Nasir al-Din.

China, July 1850. Groups of pseudo-Christian God-Worshippers gather at Jintian, in Guangxi province, to stage a revolt.

Germany, 28 August 1850. Franz Liszt conducts the first performance of *Lohengrin*, an opera by his friend Richard Wagner. Wagner, who took an active part in the Dresden uprising of 1849, has fled fled Germany to escape arrest.

Australia, August 1850. The British parliament passes the Australian Colonies Government Act, giving the colonies self-government.

London, August 1850. At a conference in London, Denmark obtains a guarantee of its territorial integrity from the great European powers and from Sweden.

USA, 9 September 1850. California becomes the 31st state in the union.

Germany, September 1850. A revolt in Hesse-Cassel, supported by the Prussians, is opposed by the Austrians, bringing Prussia and Austria to the brink of war.

Italy, 11 October 1850. On the request of Victor Emmanuel II, Massimo d'Azeglio forms a government in Piedmont. Count Camillo Cavour is appointed minister of agriculture.

China, 22 November 1850. Lin Zexu, who was appointed imperial commissioner last month by the Qing court to deal with the God-Worshippers, dies.

Germany, 29 November 1850. By the convention of Olmutz, imposed by Austria, Prussia agrees to abandon the Erfurt Union and acknowledge Austrian superiority within the German Confederation.

West Africa, 1850. Denmark sells off its Gold Coast (*Ghana*) possessions to Britain and withdraws from African colonisation.

Britain, 1850. The pope decides to divide England into Roman Catholic dioceses and restore a regular Catholic hierarchy in the country.

Britain, 1850. Proposed by William Ewart, an act is passed authorising the establishment of public libraries.

Paris, 1850. Gustave Courbet attracts attention with his *The Stone Breakers* and *The Burial at Ornans* at the Paris Salon and sets himself up as the leader of the Realist school of painting.

USA, 1850. Nathaniel Hawthorne, known for his tales of Puritan life, publishes *The Scarlet Letter*, a novel of adultery set in 17th-century Boston. It is an instant bestseller.

Britain, 1851. The great English painter J M W Turner dies.

Rail revolution is transforming the world

Europe and North America, 1850

The spread of railways promises an economic and social revolution. In Britain, where the phenomenon began, an express train can travel the 175 miles from London to Exeter in less than seven hours – three times as quickly as a stagecoach, and at less cost.

Although a Jesuit missionary in Beijing built the first self-propelled steam vehicle at the end of the 17th century, it was the Stockton and Darlington Railway of 1825 which got British railways started. The Liverpool and Manchester in 1830 was followed in 1836 by the London and Greenwich, the first passenger service to London. By the time of the Great Western Railway in 1841, linking London and Bristol, there were more than 1,300 miles of track in Britain.

In continental Europe state planning made progress slower. By 1841, when the first international line, from Strasbourg to Basle, was completed, France had 350 miles of railway. In Austria and Germany the first steam railways began operating 15 years ago. Russia will be transformed by the 404-mile Moscow to St Petersburg link, now being built.

In the United States the Baltimore and Ohio Railroad in 1830 was the inspiration. By 1840 there were 2,800 miles of track. Here and in Canada the railroad is the means of opening up new territory.

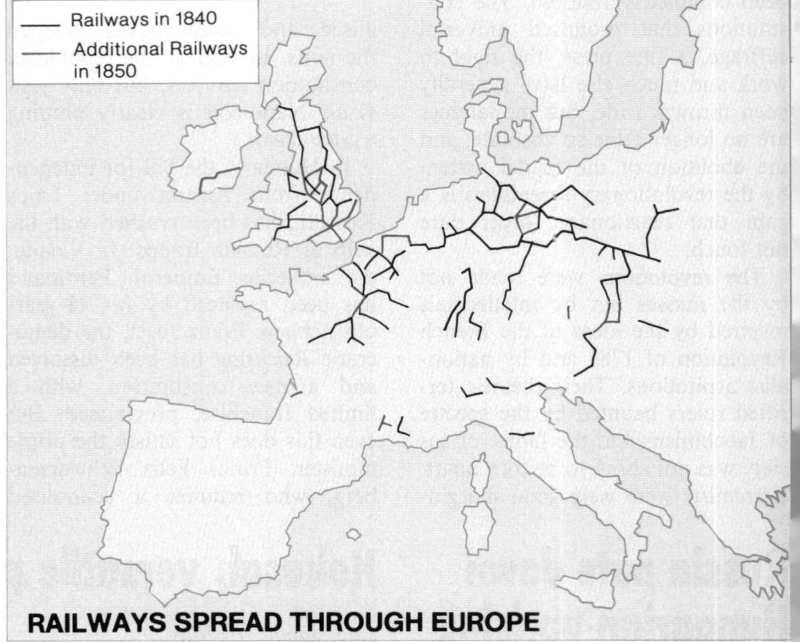

RAILWAYS SPREAD THROUGH EUROPE

Britain blockades Greece for dubious debt

Greece, 1850

As relations with France collapse, and an impotent but ostensibly independent Greek government is forced to look on, British ships are blockading the coast of Greece today. Yet this was no major international incident, rather a case of grossly inflated nationalism.

A Portuguese money-lender, one Dom Pacifico, had his house pillaged during a riot in Athens. Born in Gibraltar, he claims British citizenship and has demanded massive compensation from Greece and called on Britain to back his claim. The prime minister, Palmerston, already infuriated by Greece's failure to pay outstanding debts to far more credible British citizens, ordered the blockade. Although Russia and France are Britain's co-guarantors of Greek independence, he neglected to consult them.

Now Palmerston faces hostility at home and abroad. The opposition have capitalised on his blunder, while France, with whom he has reluctantly negotiated, has withdrawn its ambassador.

More colonies key to ending slavery

London, 1850
Ending the slave trade is proving to be more difficult than the philanthropic lobby in London had realised: no sooner has it been stopped in one place than it starts up again in another place.

The establishment of a separate administration for the Gold Coast, and the purchase from Denmark of her forts on the coast, was supposed to have effectively stopped the trade in the area. So it has. Instead the trade has increased in nearby Dahomey and Lagos, which are independent states. Indeed, the recent civil wars amongst the Yoruba has increased the supply of slaves. The only answer of the well-intentioned philanthropic gentlemen in London is to call for yet further colonial expansion.

Everything linked by new theory

Glasgow, Scotland, 1850
All theories dealing with matter and energy can be united into one theory of everything, according to William Thompson, Glasgow university's professor of physics. Thomson, who regards all forms of energy as interrelated, has formulated a second law governing the movement of heat – thermodynamics. At its simplest this states that heat cannot of itself pass from a cold body to a warm one; in other words the direction of naturally occurring processes is irreversible.

Two literary giants close their books

London and Paris, 1850
Two great writers disappeared from the European literary scene this year. In England, William Wordsworth, the poet laureate, died aged 80. As a young man he was a revolutionary in politics and literature, throwing over artifice for simplicity.

In middle age his work deteriorated sadly, but his early poems, to daffodils, the rainbow, a daisy, cuckoo, skylark or the sleeping city of London, contain great passages and lines familiar to many.

In Paris, Honore de Balzac, who attempted to paint a complete picture of French society in his novel sequence *La Comedie Humaine*, died aged 51. His formidable energy turned out 85 novels in 20 years, inventing 2,000 characters.

Wordsworth, romantic reactionary.

College is founded for women in London

London, 1849
With the opening this year of Queen's College, women finally have the opportunity of a university education. John Maurice, the principal, is for the first time training women to teach girls mathematics, classics and sport.

The well-known academic and Christian socialist shares his views on educational equality with Mrs E Reid who has decided to open her house in Bedford Square for lectures to women. Two star students at Queen's are Frances Buss, who combines her studies with teaching at her mother's school, the North London Collegiate, and Dorothea Beale, who hopes to become head of Cheltenham Ladies College.

Funding for the new college came from the combined efforts of The Governesses' Benevolent Association and Miss Murray, one of Queen Victoria's maids of honour. They began raising money two years ago after the Taunton commission had criticised the education of girls as dreary and superficial.

Australians join in great rush for gold

Australian gold miners. The first finds were kept secret by the government.

Sydney, May 1851
A California-style gold rush has started in Australia after the discovery of the metal in New South Wales.

The town of Bathurst is besieged by treasure hunters with tools for digging and panning. The most gullible come with just a hoe, believing that two days' work in the Blue Mountains goldfields will make them rich for life.

The man who started the rush is Edward Hargraves, a veteran of the gold fever in California two years ago. He says the first clue was a similarity to the California terrain in the geological structure of the land around Summer Hill Creek. He said: "I took a panful of earth which I washed in the water hole. The first trial produced a small piece of gold. "Here it is," I exclaimed. Then I washed five panfuls in succession, obtaining gold from all but one."

Using the most basic of equipment, some prospectors are earning as much as £8 a day in the goldfields, and the government is considering the introduction of a strict licensing system.

Austria and Prussia avoid going to war

Olmutz, 29 November 1850
Prince Felix Schwarzenberg has won a major diplomatic victory for Austria here in the negotiations with the Prussians. Earlier this month both powers sent troops into Hesse and it appeared that a full-scale war was imminent. There was a strong lobby in Prussia which wanted to fight, but King Frederick William IV has opted for caution.

He decided that territorial gains in Hesse were not worth fighting for because of the danger of shattering the traditional conservative alliance of Austria and Prussia against liberal forces.

The Vulture, from "Birds of America", by American painter-naturalist, John James Audubon, who died in 1851.

1851 (1851-1852)

China, January 1851. Hong Xiuquan, the leader of the God-worshippers, plans to declare himself heavenly king and set up a "heavenly kingdom of great peace" in Guangxi province.

Britain, February 1851. Lord John Russell, the prime minister, introduces an Ecclesiastical Titles Bill to curb attempts to restore a Catholic hierarchy in Britain.

Germany, March 1851. At a conference of German states in Dresden, it is decided to re-establish the German Confederation in its original form.

Spain, 16 March 1851. Spain signs a concordat with Pope Pius IX recognising the Catholic religion as the sole authorised faith and giving the church wide control over education and censorship.

Vietnam, 21 March 1851. Christian priests are put to death by the Emperor Tu Duc.

Britain, 6 April 1851. The Anglican prelate Henry Manning is converted to Roman Catholicism.

London, 1 May 1851. The Great Exhibition opens.

Portugal, 15 May 1851. On his return from England, where he went into exile in 1847, John Saldanha founds a monarchist party with the support of the middle classes.

Argentina, 25 May 1851. Jose Justo de Urquiza leads a rebellion against the authoritarian policies of his former ally, the absolute ruler Juan Manuel de Rosas.

Denmark, 5 June 1851. Frederick VII of Denmark, who has no heir, agrees with the Russian Czar Nicholas that he will choose a successor from a family which is loyal to Denmark and not suspected of having Prussian sympathies, namely the Sonderburg-Glucksburgs.

Uruguay, June 1851. Manuel Oribe, the leader of the *blanco* faction in Uruguay, which is supported by Rosas of Argentina, is forced to abandon an eight-year siege of Montevideo.

Australia, 1 July 1851. Victoria is separated from New South Wales and becomes a distinct colony.

Britain, 22 August 1851. A US yacht, *America*, wins a 60-mile race round the Isle of Wight to capture the Royal Yacht Squadron cup. The prize is dubbed the America's Cup.

Cuba, 1 September 1851. The Venezuelan-born Narciso Lopez is garrotted for leading an invasion force into Cuba with the aim of overthrowing the Spanish. Fifty others, mostly Americans, have also been executed for the revolt.

Germany, 7 September 1851. Prussia scores a diplomatic success by persuading Hanover, a city which has until now been a supporter of Austria, to become a member of the customs union.

China, 11 September 1851. The *Taipings* break out of the Qing military blockade and begin their march northwards into central China.

Ottoman Empire, October 1851. Czar Nicholas insists that Greek Orthodox monks must be allowed to maintain authority over the Holy Places in Palestine, bringing Russia into conflict with France over protection of the region.

France, 2 December 1851. Louis Napoleon Bonaparte, the president, overthrows the legislative assembly in a *coup d'etat* and dissolves the constitution.

France, 14 December 1851. In a plebiscite, French voters endorse Louis Napoleon's right to draw up a new constitution.

Britain, 19 December 1851. Lord Palmerston is dismissed as foreign secretary for recognising, without consulting his colleagues, the overthrow of the French republic by Louis Napoleon.

Austria, 31 December 1851. The abolition of the 1849 Austrian constitution leads to increased centralisation of imperial power.

USA, 1851. The painter John James Audubon – acclaimed for his dramatic pictures of birds and other wildlife – dies.

USA, 1851. A Young Men's Christian Association is founded for the first time in the United States in Cleveland, Ohio.

USA, 1851. The ex-whaler Hermann Melville publishes *Moby Dick*, a novel about a prolonged and obsessive hunt for a deadly great white whale.

Italy, 1851. Giuseppe Verdi's opera *Rigoletto* is performed for the first time.

Britain, 1851. William Newton and William Allen found the Amalgamated Society of Engineers. It soon has 11,000 members in Lancashire and the London area.

Britain, 1851. The critic and art theorist John Ruskin, a champion of the Pre-Raphaelites, publishes *The Stones of Venice*, in which he advocates a revival of the Gothic style.

Britain, 1852. William Holman Hunt, who co-founded the Pre-Raphaelite Brotherhood in 1848, paints *The Light of the World*.

London, 1852. Isambard Kingdom Brunel engineers Paddington railway station.

Bonaparte coup supported by plebiscite

Prince Louis Napoleon rides through Paris after his popular coup d'etat.

Paris, 19 December 1851

A huge majority of the people of France have endorsed by plebiscite the new constitution introduced by Louis Napoleon after his coup of 2 December. Leading republicans have been arrested.

Once elected president of the Second Republic in 1848 – after years of exile and failed attempts to claim the throne – Louis Napoleon was on a collision course with the assembly, with which he was obliged to share power. The constitution only granted the president a four-year term.

Although Louis approved conservative measures, including a limit on the franchise, to appease the majority in the assembly, he longed to put his own vision into practice. Last year he delivered a speech to the assembly outlining schemes for building railways, road, harbours and canals, for introducing agricultural machinery, establishing model farms, improving cultivation, cattlebreeding, sanitation, drains and street widening. He also proposed reintroducing universal suffrage.

Thwarted by the assembly, Louis appeared as the people's champion. Brief fighting in Paris and other cities was the only resistance to his assumption of power.

Slavery issue divides American states

New York, 1851

Bitter divisions over slavery surfaced again at the annual convention of the Anti-Slavery Society. At the heart of the debate was whether the United States should split in two with the pro-slavery southern states allowed to go their own way. Opposing this view, the Negro leader Frederick Douglass declared that the US constitition implied the eventual ending of slavery, and called for political action to end slavery in all states. Until now an uneasy peace has prevailed between northern and southern states. A series of bills last year covering slavery and other laws in new states such as California represented a temporary compromise.

THE LAND OF LIBERTY.

American hypocriscy, by "Punch".

Britain stars in "great exhibition"

London, 1 May 1851
Millions of visitors, including many from overseas, are expected to flock to the world's largest exhibition, which was opened today by Queen Victoria in London's Hyde Park.

Staged inside a giant iron and glass conservatory which has been dubbed the Crystal Palace, the Great Exhibition of the Works of Industry of all Nations is designed to pay tribute to the industrial advances that have given Britain unprecedented prosperity and economic mastery in the first half of this century.

The 13,000 exhibits from around the world are housed inside an 1,848-foot long, 408-foot-wide and 66-foot high glasshouse with 108-foot-high transepts. Designed by Joseph Paxton, the building won the Great Exhibition design competition against 254 international entries. It is an immensely magnified version of the Lily House at the duke of Devonshire's Chatsworth House, where Paxton was head gardener. The prefabricated structure took 17 weeks to erect and used a million feet of glass. The main focus of attention is the Machinery Court showing Jacquard looms, De La Rue's envelope machine and a pioneer reaping machine from America. The queen showed interest in the medalmaking machine and the electric telegraph, using the latter to send messages to Edinburgh and Manchester.

The Great Exhibition, at the Crystal Palace, Hyde Park; the world's largest exhibition, it has gathered together the "Works of Industry of all Nations".

Promises of heaven by teacher stir up rebellion in China

China, 25 September 1851
The followers of Hong Xiuquan, meeting in great numbers in the mountain town of Jintian, today announced that he had been chosen by God to be the heavenly king of their movement, the *Taiping tien-kuo* or heavenly kingdom of great peace.

Hong is a schoolteacher-mystic who, influenced by Protestant Christian tracts, believes himself to be the younger brother of Jesus Christ. Passionately dedicated to his beliefs, he has found zealous disciples among disaffected people in China. He appeals to all types, poor miners and charcoal burners, landlords and scholars, deserters from the increasingly corrupt army and peasants ruined by the inefficiency and greed of the Manchus.

The Taipings, as they call themselves, proclaim that "our heavenly king has received the Divine commission to exterminate the Manchus, to exterminate all idolaters generally, and to possess the the empire as its true sovereign".

Converts are flocking to join the Taipings who are now some 10,000 strong. Their discipline and dedication makes them a formidable enemy for the Manchu army, weakened as it is by opium smoking. They look for nothing less than a heavenly kingdom on earth.

Giuseppe Verdi, whose opera "Rigoletto" premiered in 1851.

Population soars in European countries

Europe, 1852
Figures released over the last two years show that populations in Europe have soared, despite emigration to the United States; the figures below are in millions.

Country	c.1800	c.1850
Austria	14.0	17.5
Britain	15.7	27.4
France	27.4	35.8
Germany	23.0	33.4
Hungary	5.0	13.2
Italy	17.2	24.4
Russia	40.0	68.5
Spain	10.5	15.5

Americans invent machines for sewing

USA, 1851
Spinning and weaving have been mechanised. Now it is the turn of sewing. Three American inventors have come up with a machine for sewing. Elias Howe from Boston has developed a machine that will sew seven times faster than by hand. Simultaneously Walter Hunt of New York and Isaac Merritt Singer, a mechanic from Pittsburgh, have been working on their own versions. Of them all, that of Singer is proving the most successful. This machine powered by a treadle, produces a lock stitch. A toothed wheel moves on the fabric between stitches, with a small foot-like presser holding it down.

Singer making final adjustments to his newly-invented sewing machine.

1852

France, 14 January. A new constitution, providing for a senate, council of state and legislative assembly, is adopted.

South Africa, 17 January. At the Sand River convention, the British recognise the independence of the Transvaal Boers.

France, 22 January. Louis Napoleon issues a decree banning the Orleans family from France.

Argentina, 3 February. In alliance with Uruguay and Brazil, Justo de Urquiza defeats the dictator Juan Manuel de Rosas at the battle of Caseros.

France, 17 February. Press censorship is introduced.

Britain, 27 February. Lord Derby forms a Conservative minority government following the resignation of Lord John Russell, Whig prime minister since July 1846.

China, 28 April. Having broken the siege of Yongan, the rebel God-Worshippers known as the Taipings arrive at Guilin, the capital of Guangxi province.

Italy, 6 May. Leopold II, the grand duke of Tuscany, abolishes the Tuscan constitution.

London, 8 May. Britain, France, Russia, Austria, Prussia and Sweden sign a protocol confirming the agreement signed in Warsaw in 1851 between Denmark and Czar Nicholas guaranteeing the integrity of Denmark. Prince Christian von Glucksburg is to be the next king of Denmark.

China, 10 June. Feng Yunshan – the close friend, principal lieutenant and first convert of Hong Xiuquan, the leader of the God-Worshippers – is killed in battle at the age of 30.

France, July. The poet and novelist Theophile Gautier publishes a collection of poems entitled *Emaux et Camees.*

Channel Islands, August. Choosing to go into exile following Louis Napoleon's *coup*, the French writer Victor Hugo settles in Jersey.

Britain, 14 September. Arthur Wellesley, the duke of Wellington, the great soldier and statesman, dies.

France, 24 September. Henri Giffard makes the first flight in his newly invented steam-driven balloon.

USA, 2 November. The Democrat Franklin Pierce wins a landslide victory in the presidential election, defeating the Whig candidate, General Winfield Scott.

Italy, 4 November. Count Camillo Cavour becomes prime minister of Piedmont.

China, 12 November. Zhang Luoxing, the leader of a group of Nian bandits in northern China, starts an uprising in Bozhou.

France, 2 December. Louis Napoleon is proclaimed emperor as Napoleon III.

France, 9 December. The poet Charles Leconte de Lisle publishes his *Poemes Antiques.*

Britain, 29 December. Lord Aberdeen, the former foreign secretary, forms a Peelite-Whig coalition government. Aberdeen resigned with Peel over the Corn Laws in 1846 and succeeded him as leader of the Peelites.

Burma, December. Britain annexes the kingdom of Pegu in southern Burma, ending the second Anglo-Burmese war, which broke out in April.

New Zealand. A new constitution is promulgated, providing for the division of the country into six provinces, each to be governed by a superintendent and an elected district council.

Angola. Swahili traders from Zanzibar reach Benguela, having crossed the African continent.

USA. Henry Wells and William G Fargo, the founders of the American Express Company, which serves the eastern USA, establish a new company to provide a mail service in the western half of the country.

France. The physicist Leon Foucault invents the gyroscope, which, whatever its position, continues to move in the same direction. Foucault has also determined the speed of light and proved by means of a freely suspended pendulum that the earth rotates.

France. The philosopher and sociologist Auguste Comte publishes his *Catechisme positiviste.*

France. Two new banks, the Credit Foncier and the Credit Mobilier, are founded.

Russia. The writer Ivan Turgenev publishes his *Sportsman's Sketches,* impressions of peasant life, which is interpreted by the government as an attack on serfdom.

Russia. The novelist and playwright Nikolai Gogol dies. He will be best remembered for his comic drama *The Inspector-General* and the novel *Dead Souls.*

Britain. Alfred Tennyson writes an *Ode on the Death of the Duke of Wellington.*

Britain. Karl Marx, the Hegelian philosopher, publishes *The 18th Brumaire of Louis Napoleon Bonaparte.*

Wellington, England's soldier-statesman

Wellington's funeral car, epitomising the pomp which he said he despised.

London, 14 September

The duke of Wellington, the victor of Waterloo and a former prime minister of Britain, died today, aged 83. He will be given a state funeral. For almost half a century "the Iron Duke" personified strength of will and public spirit. Although a rather delicate boy, whose greatest love was playing the violin, Arthur Wellesley, the third son of an Irish peer, became a disciplinarian who transformed the British army from, in his words, "the scum of the earth" into "worthy fellows". He served in India and distinguished himself in Spain before vanquishing Napoleon at Waterloo.

His new career in politics after Waterloo suffered from his trenchant opposition to electoral reform, but it was impossible to form a Tory government without him. In 1848 he came out of retirement to organise a military force against the Chartists. In later life, his advice was still sought. The problem of birds fouling the Crystal Palace stumped all except him. "Sparrow hawks, Ma'am," he said to the queen. He was right – as usual.

After years working in the railway engine workshops at the Gare de l'Ouest, in Paris, Henri Giffard, an impoverished railway mechanic, makes the first steered flight over Paris in a balloon, watched by tens of thousands. The balloon is powered by a simple steam engine 18 feet (six metres) below the balloon. A triangular sail acts as a rudder. In spite of adverse and changing winds, Giffard is able to steer the machine with relative ease. Giffard is acclaimed by Paris and urged to build another. But the poor mechanic has been almost ruined by the cost of his invention, and claims that he has no hope of building another such flying machine.

A Bonaparte is back on French throne

Paris, 2 December
A Bonaparte is once again emperor of France. With a flourish of glory reminiscent of his famous uncle, Louis Napoleon today elevated himself from president to emperor, restoring the house of Bonaparte after a 38-year interval.

The bachelor emperor, who styles himself Napoleon III on the grounds that Napoleon I had abdicated in favour of his son, now has to guarantee the hereditary succession that he persuaded Frenchmen to approve by an overwhelming majority in a referendum two weeks ago. The favourite to become the empress is Eugenie de Montijo, the daughter of a Spanish aristocrat who fought with the French.

The 44-year-old emperor is still largely an unknown quantity in the country which has just elected him. Since his return from exile four years ago he has out-manoeuvred his opponents, jailing thousands while at the same time gaining massive popular support with his programme of tax and welfare reforms to benefit the French working man. Foreign anxieties about the return of a Bonaparte have been eased by his Bordeaux declaration that "the empire means peace".

Napoleon III, emulating his uncle.

"Uncle Tom's Cabin" rocks US slave trade

The book that moved a nation.

New York City
A small and simple book by a novice writer is stirring the conscience of America more than a thousand speeches by a thousand anti-slavery politicians. The book is called *Uncle Tom's Cabin, or, Life Among the Lowly*, and it is written by 39-year-old Harriet Beecher Stowe of Maine.

It is the story of a devoutly religious black slave who selflessly rescues a white child – but then finds himself sold to a sadistic master, Simon Legree, who is so unhinged by Tom's goodness that he has him flogged to death.

Uncle Tom first appeared as a serial in the *National Era* magazine, and has sold 300,000 copies as a book. The pro-slavery lobby has been forced to issue a reply, a collection of essays *In Defence of Slavery*.

Bon Marche, a French retailing revolution

Paris
The Bon Marche, a small shop in Paris, in recent years has greatly expanded the amount of goods it carries and looks set to change radically the way that Parisians do their shopping. The store's founder, Aristide Boucicaut, has swept aside old restrictive practices and given shoppers wide choice under one roof, low and fixed prices, and the right to return goods. Staff have been encouraged by receiving commission on sales.

Row splits churches in Jesus' birthplace

Palestine, December
A dispute over the holy shrines of Bethlehem has brought Russia and France to the brink of war. Czar Nicholas has refused to recognise the Emperor Napoleon III's claim to have the right to protect Roman Catholics there, and has mobilised troops on the Danube and put the fleet at Sevastopol on stand-by.

For 100 years the Greek Orthodox Church, with Russian support, has argued its right to protect Christian shrines in Palestine. Now Napoleon, fresh from his success in restoring the pope to Rome, has pressured the Ottomans to recognise French rights over the Catholics in the area, and the French hold the key to the manger.

Russian satirist joins dead souls

Moscow
Nikolai Vasilievich Gogol, one of Russia's most popular novelist, dramatists and satirists, has died. A former civil servant and history lecturer, his *Inspector-General*, a satire on the corruption, vanity and ignorance of Russia's civil servants, came out in 1836, and his best-selling *Dead Souls*, a comedy on a small landowners attempts to gain compensation payments through the purchase of dead serfs, appeared the next year.

Like most of Russia's intelligensia, he left the country as soon as he could afford to, living in Rome from 1836 to 1846, before returning to Moscow as the grand old man of Russian literature.

Newspaper man is ruler of Piedmont

Count Cavour, the liberal statesman.

Turin, 4 November
Count Camillo Cavour, aged 42, is the new prime minister of Piedmont. He has widespread support from the anti-clerical left wing in parliament. At the same time because of his aristocratic connections and his diplomatic skills, he commands the respect of the conservatives. Political commentators here think that he is the ideal man to resolve the rumbling differences between King Victor Emmanuel and the parliament.

Cavour is a liberal by conviction. Because of that he abandoned his army career and visited Britain to study scientific farming and the parliamentary system. In 1847 he founded *Il Risorgimento*,, a newspaper which became a fierce advocate of a liberal but monarchical Italy. He entered politics two years later, and rapidly rose to cabinet rank.

Babis persecuted throughout Persia

Tehran, 15 September
A wave of persecution has broken on Shi'ite Islam's newest sect, the Babis, since four Babis failed to assassinate Shah Nasir al-Din as he went hunting a month ago. Today has been the bloodiest of all, with 28 senior Babi holy men killed, each assigned to a different class in the population, so that all Persia would have blood on their hands. Their fortitude in death probably won more converts than ten years of proselytizing. The movement, which condemns Persia's political and religious establishments as corrupt, first appeared 50 years ago, but grew rapidly after 1842 when a 24-year-old Seyyid Ali Mohammed, proclaimed himself *Bab*, Gate to God. He was imprisoned in 1847 and executed in 1850. The movement still grows, mounting revolts in 1847, 1850 and this year.

1853 ⇒

Rome, 19 January. Giuseppe Verdi's opera *Il Trovatore* is performed for the first time.

France, 30 January. Napoleon III marries Eugenie Maria de Montijo, a Spanish countess.

Italy, 6 February. An uprising inspired by Giuseppe Mazzini in Milan, which is under the rule of the Austrian military dictator, Radetsky, ends in failure.

Germany, 19 February. Austria and Prussia sign a 12-year commercial treaty.

Russia, February. Russia proposes to Britain that the two countries share out what remains of the Ottoman empire.

Istanbul, February. Czar Nicholas sends his envoy, Alexander Menshikov, to Istanbul to secure concessions from the Ottomans in the matter of the Holy Places and conclude a treaty recognising a Russian protectorate over Orthodox churches in the Ottoman empire.

Balkans, 3 March. Having been forced to withdraw from Montenegro, which they invaded last year, the Ottomans sign a peace treaty with Prince Danilo of Montenegro. Danilo, who came to power last year on the death of his uncle, Prince-bishop Peter II, has embarked on a campaign to secularise the Montenegrin government.

China, 19 March. *Taiping* forces capture the large city of Nanjing on the lower Yangzi river.

Germany, 4 April. The customs union signed by the various German states is extended for a further 12 years. Austria remains excluded.

Netherlands, 20 April. The decision to introduce a Catholic hierarchy in the Calvinist Netherlands brings about the downfall of the liberal prime minister, Johann Rudolph Thorbeke.

China, May. Taiping forces launch an abortive expedition to capture the Qing capital of Beijing.

Istanbul, May. The Russian ambassador Menshikov returns home after failing to reach a settlement with the Ottomans on the issue of the Holy Places.

Mediterranean, June. After the failure of further diplomatic initiatives, fleets from France and Britain – which oppose Russia's position in the dispute over the Holy Places – assemble at Besika Bay off the Dardanelles.

Balkans, 2 July. Czar Nicholas sends his troops to invade the Danubian principalities of Moldavia and Wallachia.

Connecticut, 4 July. In a protest at the requirement that women cover their legs, Amelia Jenks Bloomer, an advocate of women's rights, gives a speech wearing a pair of Turkish-style pantaloons under a short skirt.

Japan, July. A US squadron under Commodore Matthew Perry arrives off Edo (*Tokyo*) and demands that Japan opens up for trade with the outside world.

Japan, 8 August. A Russian expedition under Putyatin arrives in Nagasaki harbour seeking to open trade relations with Japan.

China, 7 September. The "Small Sword" society, led by Liu Lichuan, occupies Shanghai.

Mediterranean, 23 September. The British fleet is ordered to Istanbul.

Ottoman Empire, 4 October. Following Russia's refusal to withdraw from the Danubian principalities, the Ottomans declares war on Russia.

Balkans, 23 October. Led by Omar Pasha, the Ottomans cross the Danube into Wallachia.

India. India's first railway, linking Bombay to Thana, opens.

Pacific. The island of New Caledonia, off eastern Australia, is annexed by the French.

West Africa. Britain gives its Gold Coast (*Ghana*) colony a legislative council.

New York City. The German-born piano-maker Heinrich Steinweg (Steinway) opens a piano factory.

New Orleans. Eleven thousand people die in a yellow fever epidemic.

France. Joseph Gobineau writes an *Essay on the Inequality of Human Races*, in which he develops his theory of the superiority of the Germanic race, on the basis of physical criteria.

Switzerland. The German composer Richard Wagner, in exile in Zurich, completes the text for *Nibelung's Ring*, a cycle of operas on the Nordic and Germanic sagas.

Germany. Franz Liszt, who has settled in Weimar, composes his sonata in B minor.

Italy. *La Dame aux Camellias*, a novel by Alexandre Dumas (*fils*), serves as the basis for Verdi's opera *La Traviata*, which is given its first performance in Venice this year.

Britain. Among this year's new novels are *Cranford* by Mrs Elizabeth Gaskell and *The Heir of Redclyffe* by Charlotte M Yonge.

Election breaks up painting brotherhood

Holman Hunt's "Our English Coast" (strayed sheep): Hunt shared a studio with Rossetti and was one of the founders of the brotherhood.

London

The election of John Millais as an associate of the Royal Academy has finally broken up the Pre-Raphaelite Brotherhood of controversial young rebel artists. Dante Gabriel Rossetti has declared that he will no longer exhibit. William Holman Hunt, the third founder, is leaving to paint in the Holy Land.

The brotherhood was founded in secret in 1848, when all three were students at the Royal Academy. They set aside tradition to paint directly and truthfully from nature, as Ruskin advocates. Pictures with the initials "PRB" appeared at the academy in 1849. In 1850 the aims of the group leaked out and the members abused for insulting the name of Raphael. Dickens, in his magazine *Household Words*, described Millais' painting of *Christ in the House of His Parents* as "a hideous, wrynecked, blubbering, red-headed boy" and his mother as looking like "a monster in the lowest gin-shop in Europe". Queen Victoria sent for the painting to see it for herself Millais caused a sensation with his *Ophelia*, drowning beneath the willow tree. His model, Elizabeth Siddall, caught cold posing in a bath in his studio. This year *The Order of Release* had police protection.

"Ophelia" by Millais. Elizabeth Siddall, the model for this picture, epitomised pre-Raphaelite beauty for the Brotherhood, who saw her as their own Ophelia.

US threatens "shogun"

Captain Perry meeting representatives of the emperor on 14 July.

Japan, 8 July

Commodore Matthew Perry of the United States Navy today anchored his fleet of four ships in Edo (*Tokyo*) Bay almost within sight of the Japanese capital. The "black ships", which include the powerful steam frigates *Mississippi* and *Susquehanna*, have thrown the Japanese authorities into complete panic.

They have ordered Perry to take his ships to Nagasaki, the only port open to foreigners, but he has refused. He carries with him a letter from President Millard Fillmore and he intends to see that it is delivered to the seat of power. The letter requests that shipwrecked US sailors should be treated more kindly than they have been; that US ships should be allowed to coal and provision, and that one or more ports be opened to US trade.

The Japanese, mindful of the defeat of the Chinese in the Opium War with the British, will be well aware of the threat behind these requests. They must fight, or end two and a half centuries of isolation.

Argentina split on new constitution

Argentina, 25 May

Argentina adopted a new constitution today, developed by last year's constitutional convention in Santa Fe, but Buenos Aires, the nation's most important province, is refusing to join the new confederation. Buenos Aires' independent stand is an extension of long-term rivalries. Under its governor, Rosas, the province has dominated the rest of Argentina since 1829 and Rosas himself has enjoyed an unprecedented degree of support from all sections of society.

Only the army showed itself dissatisfied, and in May 1851 General Justo de Urquiza proclaimed a revolt against the "despot". Backed by Brazil, his forces defeated Rosas' troops at Caseros. Urquiza then set up the Santa Fe convention. Today's constitution is the result.

Russia furious at rebuff by Ottomans

Istanbul, May

Prince Menshikov, the Russian ambassador, has left the city in high dudgeon after the *sultan* rejected as "inadmissible" his demand that Russia be given a protectorate over all Orthodox Christians under Ottoman rule. The demand followed the French success last year in gaining control of the shrine at Bethlehem.

Before he departed, the Russian blamed the British ambassador, Lord Stratford de Redcliffe, for the Ottoman refusal. Stratford, no friend of the French, had no objection to the Russians supervising the Holy Places, but he drew the line at the Russians' further claim to have rights over any Christians in the Ottoman empire. An angry Menshikov accused Stratford of "trampling over the czar and his church".

Ten Commandments delight Chinese rebel

Nanjing, April

Sir George Bonham, the governor of Hong Kong, has had an interview with Wei Changhui, the "northern king" of the Taiping rebels who have set up their Heavenly Capital in the city.

The interview went badly at first, with Wei lecturing Sir George on the need for the whole world to obey the Taiping leader, Hong Xuiquan, the "heavenly king." It took a turn for the better when Wei asked Sir George if he knew the "heavenly rules" and, with an inspired guess, the governor recited the Ten Commandments. Wei was delighted and cried: "The same as ourselves!" The mystical Hong, deeply influenced by the teachings of Protestant missionaries, has imposed an absolute discipline on Nanjing.

Opium, alcohol and tobacco are forbidden, and nobody is allowed to wear the Manchu pigtail. Prostitution has been outlawed and so has the crippling binding of women's feet. Rape is punishable by death and women are treated as the equals of men. It is the combination of such discipline with fervent faith which has allowed the Taipings to defeat the imperial armies.

Taiping rebels, who seized the Yochow arsenal and stormed Nanjing.

Bavarian sells brown jeans to US miners

San Francisco

At least one *entrepreneur* is making his fortune from the Californian gold rush. Levi Strauss, a Bavarian tailor, saw the miners' need for strong durable trousers and has created what have become known as "jeans" – from the French *genes* – made from durable twilled cotton with ample pockets for the miners' tools. The original jeans were brown in colour, but Strauss is experimenting with a blue indigo-based dye, a cheaper colouring – which might be appreciated by the less successful miners. Strauss is just one of many traders who are thriving in this boom city. Fresh fruit, chocolates and other luxuries sell at premium prices here and on the goldfields.

Gold miners at the Last Chance mine in California wearing the Bavarian tailor Levi Strauss' new twilled cotton trousers nicknamed "jeans".

1853 (1853-1855)

Portugal, 15 November 1853. On the death of Queen Maria II, she is succeeded by her son Pedro V.

Black Sea, 30 November 1853. A Russian naval squadron bombards and destroys an Ottoman fleet at Sinope.

Black Sea, 3 January 1854. The British and French fleets enter the Black Sea to protect Ottoman coasts and shipping.

South Africa, 23 February 1854. At the convention of Bloemfontein, the British recognise the independence of the Orange Free State.

South Africa, February 1854. Following the British annexation of the territories north of the Orange river, inhabited by Africans and Boers, the Boer leader Andreas Pretorius instigates a revolt and forces the British back.

Europe, 12 March 1854. Britain and France form an alliance with the Ottoman empire.

Europe, 28 March 1854. Britain and France declare war on Russia.

Japan, 31 March 1854. The USA and Japan sign the treaty of Kanagawa, opening the ports of Shimoda and Hakodate to American trade.

Washington, DC, 31 March 1854. The USA and Britain sign a Reciprocity Treaty, agreeing on North American fishing rights and abolishing certain import duties.

Greece, 26 May 1854. Franco-British forces occupy the port of Piraeus to prevent the Greeks from joining Russia against the Turks.

USA, 30 May 1854. The Kansas-Nebraska Act, allowing settlers of the newly created territories of Kansas and Nebraska to choose between free land and slavery, is passed. The Missouri Compromise of 1820, which banned slavery north of the southern boundary line of Missouri, is repealed.

Austria, 14 June 1854. Austria, which has formed a defensive alliance with Prussia against Russia, signs a treaty with the Ottomans agreeing to occupy the principalities of Moldavia and Wallachia.

China, 17 June 1854. The "Red Turban" revolt breaks out in Guangdong province.

Spain, 28 June 1854. A liberal revolt led by Leopoldo O'Donnell and Balsomero Espartero overthrows the government and ousts the authoritarian Regent Maria Christina. Her daughter, Isabella, II, succeeds to the throne.

Egypt, July 1854. Abbas, khedive of Egypt, is murdered near Cairo.

Balkans, August 1854. The Russians evacuate Moldavia and Wallachia, which are occupied by the Austrians.

Crimea, 14 September 1854. Having abandoned the Black Sea port of Varna last week, the allies land at Eupatoria on the west coast of the Crimea.

Japan, 14 October 1854. Under the Nagasaki treaty, the British are awarded most-favoured-nation status and the right to refuel at Nagasaki and Hakodate.

Crimea, 20 September 1854. The allies defeat an inferior Russian force at the battle of Alma.

Crimea, 17 October 1854. The allies lay siege to the Russian naval base of Sevastopol.

Crimea, 25 October 1854. The allies win another victory over the Russians, at Balaclava.

Crimea, 5 November 1854. The Russians are defeated by the allies at the battle of Inkerman.

Egypt, 30 November 1854. The Frenchman Ferdinand de Lesseps obtains from Said Pasha a 99-year concession to build a canal linking the Red Sea to the Mediterranean.

USA, 1854. Kansas and Nebraska are admitted to the union.

USA, 1854. Two Boston gunsmiths, Horace Smith and Daniel Wesson, develop a new revolver.

USA, 1854. Groups opposed to the Kansas-Nebraska Act coalesce to form the Republican Party.

India, 1854. India's first cotton mill is established, in Bombay.

India, 1854. A new government-sponsored grant-in-aid system encourages a rapid growth in the number of Christian schools.

Angola, 1854. The British explorer David Livingstone arrives in Luanda after a journey from Bechuanaland (*Botswana*) and Cape Colony.

West Africa, 1854. For the first time, quinine is used successfully to treat malaria.

France, 1854. Gerard de Nerval publishes a collection of short stories entitled *Les Filles du feu*, with an appendix including the 12 sonnets *Les Chimeres*.

France, 1854. The French scientist Henri Sainte-Claire Deville synthesises aluminium for the first time.

Austria, 1854. The Semmering railway, the first mountain railway in the world, opens in eastern central Austria.

Britain, 1854. Lord Tennyson, the poet laureate, writes *The Charge of the Light Brigade*, a poem based on the battle of Balaclava.

Russia wipes out Ottoman war fleet

Turkey: Russia's Christmas meal?

Istanbul, 30 November 1853
The Ottomans have been at war with Russia for the past seven weeks, but they believed that they had an understanding that military operations during the winter would be strictly defensive. Today they discovered how mistaken they were. The Russians seized their chance, swooped on the Ottoman fleet in the Black Sea harbour of Sinope, on the north coast of Turkey, and annihilated it, drowning 4,000 Ottoman sailors. The attack has caused indignation in London; the government has ordered a naval squadron to join the French in a foray into the Black Sea.

Pacifist joins "underground railroad"

Concord, Massachussetts, 1854
The abolitionist lobby has found a major champion in Henry David Thoreau, one of America's most remarkable thinkers, who is writing and lecturing against slavery throughout the northern states – and working with others to help runaway slaves on what is known as the "underground railroad". Ten years ago the philosopher and poet forsook the urban life and built a one-roomed hut in the wood near Concord, vowing to live a life of complete self-sufficiency.

He described his experience in his book *Walden, or Life in the Woods*. His stay was interrupted when he was jailed for refusing to pay tax on the grounds that it supported the Mexican War and a government that allowed slavery.

Brazilians find railway is just the ticket

San Paulo, Brazil, 1854
Brazil's first railway has opened between nearby Guanabara Bay and the Serra do Mar. The milage is minute by North American standards, but its construction was an epic – thousands of labourers, most of them ex-slaves, hacking their way over mountains that have been called "a wall without gates", to the coffee plantations in the interior. The line does not only bring coffee to the coast, but people to the interior. New townships are growing all along the line.

Brazil's economy *is* coffee. Federal taxes vary as its prices goes up and down. Until now coffee has come to the coast by expensive mule trains. The railway, built with mostly British capital, will significantly lower production costs.

Virgin Mary free of original sin – pope

Rome, December 8, 1854
In a bull, *Ineffabilis Deus*, issued here today Pope Pius IX proclaimed the total sinlessness of the Virgin Mary. The bull declares: "From the first moment of her conception the Blessed Virgin Mary was, by the singular grace and privilege of Almighty God, and in view of the merits of Jesus Christ, Saviour of mankind, kept free from all stain of original sin." This finally ends a controversy which has raged for centuries. The idea of Mary as a sinless "new Eve" dates back to the seventh century.

In the 12th century the French theologians argued that since Mary was conceived in the natural way she could not be free of the stain of original sin. However, by the 16th century the doctrine of the Immaculate Conception was firmly established.

Blunder wipes out Light Brigade

Crimea, Russia, 25 October 1854
As night fell in Balaclava the British were both celebrating victory and mourning one of the most brave and foolhardy actions in their military history. As a result of a confusion over orders, a brigade of light cavalry charged one and a half miles (2.4 kilometres) down a narrow valley directly into the mouths of Russian guns with artillery batteries raking them from either side as well.

William Howard Russell of *The Times* of London has described the final moments thus: "They swept proudly past, glittering in the morning sun in all the pride and splendour of war ... At the distance of 1,200 yards the whole line of the enemy belched forth, from thirty iron mouths, a flood of smoke and flame, through which hissed the deadly balls. Their flight was marked by instant gaps in our ranks, by dead men and horses, by steeds flying wounded or riderless across the plain." Of the 607 who rode out, only 198 returned. Although the charge itself had no military value, the poorly provisioned British won the battle against much stronger Russian forces. It was the second victory since Britain, France, the Ottoman empire and Sardinia landed here six weeks ago to attack the giant Russian Black Sea naval base at Sevastopol.

It is a war that has happened almost by default. Lord Aberdeen, the British prime minister, wants to make peace as soon as possible, but he has in his cabinet a war party, led by Lord Palmerston and Lord John Russell, and in France's Napoleon III an ally who counts on military glory to bolster his regime.

The ostensible cause of the war was a dispute between Russia, France and the Ottomans about the rights of protection of Christian shrines in the Ottoman-controlled Holy Land. When the Ottomans refused Russia's demands, Russia marched into Ottoman territories across the Danube. Britain was prompted to issue an ultimatum to the czar to withdraw – not out of concern for shrines but out of alarm at the prospect of a Russian occupation of Istanbul and a consequent threat to British communications with India.

Roger Fenton's photograph of British soldiers resting in the Crimea.

"The thin red line": the 93rd Sutherland Highlanders at Balaclava.

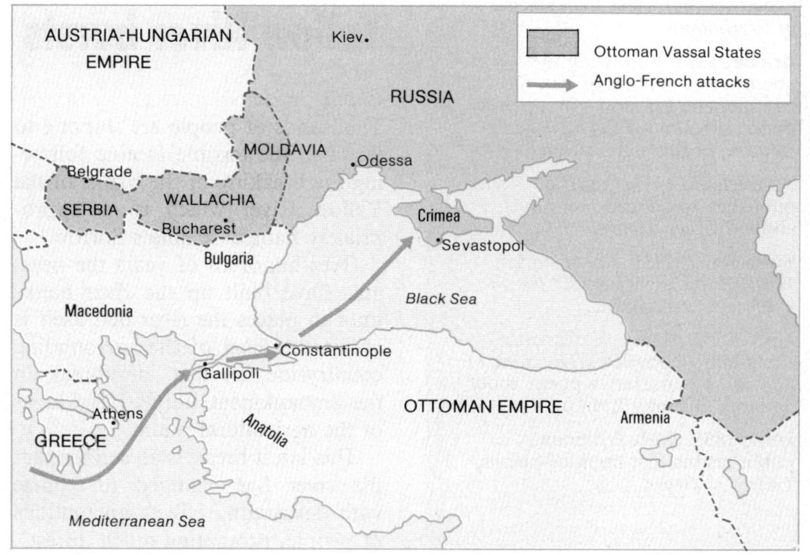

English nurse gives hope to the injured

Scutari, Crimea, 7 November 1854
A team of nurses led by Florence Nightingale has set to work with scrubbing brushes to clean up Scutari hospital. Doctors obstinately refused Nightingale's help until casualties from the battle of Inkerman spilled into their rat-infested corridors.

They resented interference from the trained outsider who was given £30,000 and a brief from Sidney Herbert, the secretary of state for war, to take complete charge of nursing British soldiers in the Crimea. By keeping army officials at bay and her nurses sober Florence turned Scutari into a highly effective hospital.

Nightingale, loaded with problems of administration and supply, always took her turn at nursing, and in the darkness of every night carried her lamp through the wards giving comfort and advice to her patients.

Florence Nightingale at Scutari.

Canal for Suez strip

Egypt, 1855
Work will begin shortly on a 100-mile (160-kilometre) canal connecting the Mediterranean at Port Said with the Red Sea at Suez. The canal will cut by almost a half the journey from London to Bombay. The accession of the pro-European Said Pasha to the throne of Egypt has created the opportunity for Ferdinand de Lesseps, a persuasive 49-year-old French viscount and engineer, to begin the ambitious project.

1855 (1855-1856)

Italy, 26 January 1855. Count Camillo Cavour, the prime minister of Piedmont, takes Piedmont into the Crimean War alongside the allies. He agrees to send 15,000 men to the Crimea.

Panama, 28 January 1855. The 47-mile Panama railway, linking the Atlantic and Pacific across the isthmus of Panama, is completed.

Britain, February 1855. Following the fall of Lord Aberdeen's coalition as a result of mis-management of the Crimean War, Lord Palmerston forms a Liberal administration.

Japan, February 1855. Russia and Japan sign a treaty of friendship at Shimoda.

Russia, 2 March 1855. On the death of Czar Nicholas, he is succeeded by his son Alexander II.

Afghanistan, 30 March 1855. Dost Mohammed of Afghanistan signs the treaty of Peshawar with Britain, ending 12 years of war.

Britain, 31 March 1855. The novelist Charlotte Bronte dies. She revealed in a note to the second edition of *Wuthering Heights* that its author, "Ellis Bell", was her sister Emily, "Acton Bell", the author of *Agnes Grey*, was her sister Anne and "Currer Bell", the author of *Jane Eyre*, was herself.

Paris, 14 May 1855. The Italian revolutionary Pianori is executed after attempting to assassinate Napoleon III.

Italy, 29 May 1855. Cavour abolishes all religious orders and convents in Piedmont which are not dedicated to preaching, education or helping the sick.

China, 31 May 1855. The Mongol prince Senggelinqin, the commander of the Qing imperial forces, captures the *Taiping* leader Li Kaifeng at Chiping in Shandong. This marks the end of the Taiping expedition to take Beijing.

USA, 4 July 1855. New York becomes the 13th state to ban the production or sale of alcoholic beverages.

Austria, 18 August 1855. The cardinal-archbishop of Vienna signs a concordat with the pope giving the Catholic church control of education, censorship and matrimonial law.

China, 7 September 1855. The Moslem leader Du Wenxin occupies the town of Dali in Yunnan province.

Crimea, 10 September 1855. Sevastopol, under siege for nearly a year, capitulates to the allies.

China, 24 September 1855. Zhang Xinmei of the Miao people rises in rebellion in Guizhou province.

Denmark, 11 November 1855. The philosopher Soren Kierkegaard dies. In his best known-work, *Concluding Unscientific Postscript*, he put forward the theory that subjectivity is truth. He attacked system-building in philosophy, arguing that existence is too varied to be incorporated into a particular system.

Hungary, 19 November 1855. The poet and playwright Michael Vorosmarty, who was inspired by popular folktales, dies. In 1840 he wrote the Hungarian national song *Szozat*, and he was a member of the 1848 national assembly.

Sweden, 21 November 1855. Sweden concludes a treaty of alliance with Britain and France against Russia.

Caucasus, 27 November 1855. The Russians take the town of Kars from the Ottomans after a siege.

Japan, December 1855. Much of Edo (*Tokyo*) is destroyed by the great Ansei earthquake. Many people lose their lives in the resulting fires.

Ethiopia, 1855. Ras Kass, who has reunified Gojjam, Begember, Tigrai and Shoa by conquest, crowns himself Emperor Tewodros (Theodore) II.

West Africa, 1855. The French annex Walo on the Senegal river, one of the Wallof kingdoms – the first inland colonial possession of a European power in West Africa.

India, 1855. India's first jute-spinning mill is set up, in Serampore.

Germany, 1855. Gustav Freytag publishes *Debit and Credit*, a monumental novel about German commercial life.

England, 1855. Robert Browning publishes *Men and Women*, a collection of love poems.

England, 1855. Herbert Spencer, the sociologist and philosopher of evolution, publishes his *Principles of Psychology*.

Britain, 1855. Following the abolition of the Stamp Tax on newspapers, London's first penny paper, the *Daily Telegraph and Courier*, begins publication.

Switzerland, 1855. Gottfried Keller publishes an educational novel entitled *Green Henry*.

Switzerland, 1855. The historian Jacob Burckhardt issues *Cicerone*, a guide to Italian art.

USA, 1855. Henry Wadsworth Longfellow completes *The Song of Hiawatha*, a narrative poem about a young Ojibway Indian.

USA, 1855. Walt Whitman publishes his first book of poems, *Leaves of Grass*.

Thundering waterfall named after queen

Stampeding buffalo at Victoria Falls: a romantic view by Thomas Baines.

Africa, 17 November 1855

A breathtaking waterfall at least 1,000 yards (914m) wide and 100 feet (30m) deep, and thought to be the largest in the world, has been reported in southern Africa by the explorer and missionary David Livingstone.

The 42-year-old Scot, keen to arouse British public interest in this previously unexplored area, has renamed the waterfall on the Zambezi "the Falls of Victoria" in honour of the queen. In doing so, he follows the precedent of his friend, Sebetwane, the leader of the Kololo, who renamed it Mosioatunya ("the smoke that thunders"). The original local name is Shongwenamutitma ("the boiling pot").

A native of the Zambezi by Baines.

Famine in China as Yellow River bursts

China, 1855

Thousands of people are starving to death in the terrible famine following the breaking of the banks of the Yellow River which is so appropriately named "China's Sorrow".

Over hundreds of years the peasants have built up the river banks until in places the river bed itself is above the level of the surrounding countryside, so that any break in the embankment floods large areas of the agricultural plain.

This latest break is so serious that the river has changed its course with devastating effects on millions of people, prompting much unrest.

Rioting miners are acquitted by court

Melbourne, 22 February 1855

Thirteen gold diggers have been acquitted of rioting and manslaughter after last December's fighting at the Eureka gold mine where 5 soldiers and 30 miners were killed. The diggers were demanding the right to the vote and to land ownership, and an end to their licence fee.

The diggers built defences, after taking over the town, "constructed of piles of slabs", according to one eyewitness. Troops cleared them with little difficulty. Now, by treating the rioters with leniency the government has averted a major radical confrontation.

Mexican ruler falls after years of strife

Mexico City, 1855
General Lopez de Santa Anna, Mexico's "president for life", has been deposed. He was ousted by a consortium of liberals who backed a liberal manifesto known as the Ayutla plan. He is to be replaced by General Juan Alvarez.

The story of Santa Anna is the story of modern Mexico. Born in 1797, he fought with Iturbide to rid Mexico of the Spanish, but overthrew him in 1822 to become president himself in 1833. Though he was forever losing battles he never accepted he had lost a war. Defeated by Texas rebels in 1836, he was imprisoned for eight months; defeated again by the French at Vera Cruz, he lost a leg; and twice defeated by the United States between 1846 and 1848, he became a symbol of Mexican independence. Twice president and twice exiled, he returned to his country from exile in Venezuala to take power again after the conservative revolution of 1853.

A courageous soldier rather than a thoughtful statesman, his political conservatism, presumption of royalty (he took on the title "His Most Supreme Highness") and financial recklessness alienated Mexico's liberals, who, led by the fiery Juan Alvarez, have overthrown him and sent him into exile for the third time. Liberals hope that his overthrow will open up the country to new ideas – and new liberties.

Fallen dictator: Santa Anna.

France and Britain capture Sevastopol

Corporal Philip Smith winning the Victoria Cross at Sevastopol.

Sevastopol, 10 September 1855
After a 12-month campaign marked by muddle, incompetence and querulousness on the part of all the military commanders, friend and foe alike, British and French forces have captured the Sevastopol naval base of the Russian Black Sea fleet. France's General Pelissier was so delighted he embraced General Sir James Simpson and kissed him. "It was a great occasion," Simpson said. "I couldna' resist him."

Many observers believe that the base should have been taken a year ago when the combined allied land and sea forces first arrived. The Russian commander, Menshikov, had failed to construct proper defence works, but French troops arrived late and British and French commanders disagreed over the timing of attacks. The British spent a bitter winter without adequate protection and on one occasion the Light Brigade attacked the wrong guns. For the final assault, Simpson sent his least experienced troops into action. Not surprisingly, Pelissier was relieved at the result.

Disease is spread by germs in the air

Paris, 1856
What actually causes disease to spread? For a long time now, the prevailing theory has been that poisonous vapours – miasmas – are to blame. But now a French chemist of humble origins and relatively little formal training has demonstrated that infection is the work of tiny living organisms.

Louis Pasteur has carried out many experiments on fermentation and on the putrefaction and souring of food. He concludes that germs in the air are responsible.

He has gone on to argue that disease, too, is caused by microorganisms. Agents such as bacteria are the mysterious carriers of infection.

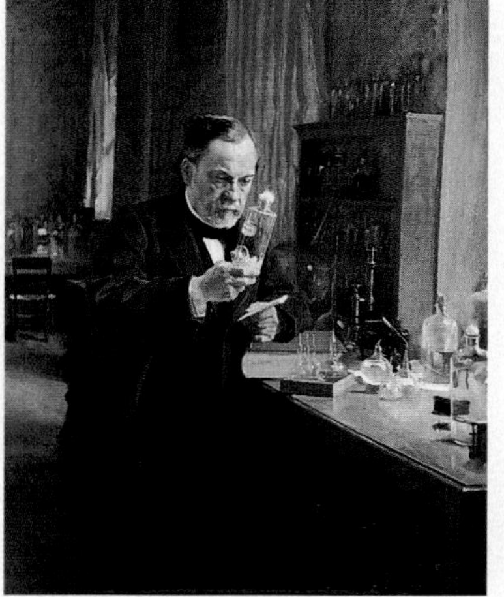
Louis Pasteur, who discovered that the vehicles of infection are tiny living organisms called bacteria.

Piedmontese swell anti-Russian army

Turin, 26 January 1855
Piedmont-Sardinia is sending an expeditionary force of 15,000 men to help Britain in the Crimean War against the Russians. King Victor Emmanuel is hoping to get some military glory for himself from the move. He also hopes to distract attention from the real problems in Lombardy, where the Austrians have been confiscating the possessions of Piedmontese citizens.

The prime minister Cavour, is believed to be unhappy at the move. However, he is himself fighting to stay in office. He walks a tightrope, seeking to maintain the support of parliament, with its powerful liberals, without arousing too much anger amongst the conservatives who surround the king and would like to oust Cavour.

Heaven and Earth society is defeated

Shanghai, 17 February 1855
The army of the "Small Sword" secret society which has occupied Shanghai for the past two years was defeated today by imperial Chinese forces with the aid of French marines. The Small Sword leader, Liu Lichuan, a former interpreter for the British, part-doctor and part-sorcerer, was captured and immediately beheaded.

The Small Swords, one of the many societies of southern China, is a branch of the *Triads*, or Heaven and Earth Society, and draws its membership mainly from unemployed sailors and artisans.

Denouncing corrupt officials and harsh taxes, Liu's red-sashed fighters seized the walled city of Shanghai in September 1853, but carefully avoided the westerners' settlements outside the city.

The imperial forces caused the westerners more trouble than the Small Swords, and after an Englishwoman was insulted the celebrated Battle of Muddy Flat was fought between European volunteers, supported by British and US seamen, and the Chinese army. Most of the few casualties were caused when the British and Americans shot at each other.

1856 (1856-1857)

Japan, January 1856. Japan has now signed treaties of peace and friendship with the USA, Russia, Britain, France and the Netherlands.

Germany, 17 February 1856. Heinrich Heine, Germany's foremost lyric poet, dies.

Ottoman Empire, 19 Februry 1856. The Ottoman sultan, Abdul Mejid, issues a reform edict guaranteeing his Christian subjects security of life and property and the power to exercise freedom of conscience. The civil power of the heads of the Christian churches is abolished and civil offices are made open to all.

China, 28 February 1856. The Honghao rebellion, in Guizhou province led by Xu Tingjie, is put down.

China, 29 February 1856. The French Catholic missionary Auguste Chapdelaine, who has entered the country illegally, is beheaded.

Paris, 30 March 1856. Britain, France, Russia, the Ottoman empire, Piedmont, Austria and Prussia sign the treaty of Paris, ending the Crimean War and securing the neutrality of the Black Sea.

Europe, 15 April 1856. Austria, France and Britain agree to joint action in defence of Ottoman independence and integrity.

South Africa, 12 July 1856. Natal is made a British colony, after being part of Cape Colony.

Japan, August 1856. Townsend Harris arrives in Shimoda from the USA as the first foreign consul in Japan. He immediately encounters bureaucratic obstruction.

Switzerland, September 1856. An attempted royalist coup in the canton of Neuchatel, which proclaimed itself a republic in 1848, ends in failure.

Spain, 25 October 1856. The liberal Leopoldo O'Donnell, who replaced Baldomero Espartero as premier in July, is dismissed by Isabella II, who appoints Ramon Narvaez to head a more authoritarian regime.

China, October 1856. *Arrow*, a ship flying the British flag, is boarded at Guangzhou (*Canton*), by Chinese officers who arrest the entire crew on suspicion of piracy.

South-East Asia, October 1856. Siam (*Thailand*) signs a treaty with France which guarantees its frontiers.

Britain, 1 November 1856. In response to a Persian invasion of Afghanistan with the object of capturing Herat, Britain – which last year signed a treaty with the Afghans – declares war on Persia.

USA, 4 November 1856. At his fourth attempt James Buchanan, a Democrat, is victorious in the presidential election.

South Africa, December 1856. Western Transvaal Boers adopt US-style constitution for a South African Republic, with a capital at Pretoria. Eastern and northern Transvaalers still refuse to join.

India, 1856. The British annex the kingdom of Awadh in northern India. This is the most recent in a series of annexations since 1848, which has included the states of Satara, Jhansi and Nagpur.

Germany, 1856. At Neanderthal, near Dusseldorf, the remains of a *homo sapiens*, probably dating from 70,000 BC, are discovered.

Germany, 1856. The physicist Hermann von Helmholtz publishes his *Handbook of Physiological Optics*.

France, 1856. The political scientist and politician Alexis de Tocqueville publishes *The Old Regime and the Revolution*, in which he seeks to show the continuity of political behaviour and attitudes that makes post-revolutionary French society as prepared to accept despotism as that of the old regime.

Egypt, 1856. The first railway line in Africa, between Alexandria and Cairo, is inaugurated.

Britain, 1856. The first limited liability companies in Britain are formed.

Persia, January 1857. The British seize the port of Bushire on the Persian Gulf.

Vienna, 24 January 1857. A conference in Vienna introduces the silver standard in Austria and the countries of the customs union.

Greece, 28 February 1857. French and British naval forces end their occupation of the port of Piraeus, which began in May 1854.

China, 3 March 1857. Using the pretexts of the assassination of the French missionary Chapdelaine and the seizure of the *Arrow* last October, France and Britain declare war on China.

Balkans, March 1857. The Austrians evacuate Moldavia and Wallachia, and elections are held in the principalities to settle the question of their union. Widespread corruption results in a defeat for the unionists.

West Africa, 20 April 1857. Al-Hajj Umar, the Tukulor Moslem leader who in 1852 declared a *jihad* (holy war), continues his campaign of conquest by laying siege to the French fort of Medine built two years earlier on the Senegal river.

Bloodshed grows as Chinese rebels split

Nanjing, November 1856
The *Taiping* movement, the Heavenly Kingdom of Great Peace, which at one stage threatened to destroy the Qing dynasty, is tearing itself apart with a great bloodletting brought about by the rivalry between its leaders.

The killing started in September when Yang Xuijing, the "eastern king" who wielded power in Nanjing, made his bid to take over the movement from its founder, the "heavenly king", Hong Xiuquan who was growing increasingly remote from reality. Hong was not so remote that he could not smell out a plot and he summoned the other leaders to his aid. Yang and thousands of his followers were killed by the troops of Wei Changhui, the northern king. Then Shi Dagai, the "assistant king", and the Taipings' best general, fled in fear and his family was slaughtered. Wei then challenged for supreme leadership of the Taipings, but the heavenly king has had him executed and has sent his head, pickled in brine, to Shi Dagai.

A treaty to "civilise" Ottoman empire

Istanbul, 1856
A wide-ranging charter of reform for the Ottoman empire has been incorporated into the treaty of Paris. But Lord Stratford de Redcliffe, its chief instigator, is furious that the great powers have made no commitment to enforce it.

Carefully framed to ensure the empire's acceptance as a civilised western state, the charter emphasised the free and equal status of all Ottoman citizens, regardless of religion, race or language, for the purposes of taxation, education, the law and eligibility for public office. It also outlined financial and monetary measures, aid for commerce and agriculture, and the building of roads and canals.

Sultan Abdul Mejid: reformer.

But the parties to the treaty specifically refused "to interfere either collectively or individually in the relations of the sultan with his subjects or in the internal administration of the empire". Lord Stratford de Redcliffe, who worked hard to convince the sultan of the need for reform, is now extremely sceptical about the charter's value.

US adventurer seizes power in Nicaragua

Granada, Nicaragua, May 1856
With a small mercenary army of no more than 250 men an American has seized this country and declared himself president. William Walker, a stocky, retiring man whose mild manner belies an adventurous past, has been recognised by the United States government.

This is the second attempt by Walker, a failed lawyer and journalist, to establish a puppet republic. His previous effort – in Lower California – ended in disaster. This time he has the backing of Cornelius Vanderbilt who plans to expand his transport empire here. Despite his mild manner, Walker appears to have impressed the Nicaraguan people as a man of action. One of his first moves this month was to make General Corral, the former dictator, his secretary for war. Soon after, Corral was led in front of a firing squad and shot for conspiring to take his country back.

Walker has grandiose plans for a trans-ocean canal and for the eventual unification of the whole of Central America. He also plans to introduce African slaves into his new and somewhat dubious "republic".

Crimean War ends with neutral Black Sea

Peace celebrations in London's Hyde Park mark the end of the Crimea war.

Paris, 30 March 1856

The Russian delegate to the Paris peace conference, Count Orlov, today agreed to the demilitarisation of the Black Sea as a prime condition for ending the Crimean War. The Czar will have to demolish four naval bases, including Sevastopol, and to withdraw his fleet from the area. Russia also renounced its claim to give protection to the Ottoman empire Christians. Lord Palmerston, who took over as British prime minister at a low point in the war, wished to impose even tougher terms on the Russians, but Napoleon III was trying to use the peace conference to liquidate the settlement imposed on France at the Congress of Vienna after Waterloo.

Palmerston decided that a relatively soft peace would be better than risking that. The queen was disappointed, but he told her that Britain could not continue the war alone.

French writer faces obscenity charges

Paris, 25 June 1857

Gustave Flaubert, one of France's rising literary stars, and a self-proclaimed "thinker and demoraliser", went on trial today. His new novel, *Madame Bovary,* was charged under French law as "an outrage against moral standards". But despite the prosecution's singling out of a number of passages as "immoral", the book as a whole was not found obscene and Flaubert has been acquitted.

The book is a study of the adulteries and eventual suicide of the wife of a provincial doctor. What shocks Flaubert's accusers is a plot that they claim belittles marriage at the expense of the charm of illicit love. In fact, Flaubert is more subtle. His book, with its attack on self-delusion, undermines not morality, but all human hope.

Kiwis "capable of ruling themselves"

New Zealand, 1856

New Zealand is to become self-governing. Already Canada, New South Wales, Victoria, South Australia and Tasmania are self-governing, as Britain realises that it can run its white empire far more efficiently through indirect rule, so long as Blacks cannot vote.

For half a century after Captain Cook's arrival, New Zealand had no status. For years the indigenous Maoris were persecuted by white settlers without any restraint; in 1836 there were even suggestions that France would take over the islands. In 1840 New Zealand was annexed to the crown, but the Maoris were still alienated and rebelled in 1845. It is their defeat that has made the steps to self-government so easy. There is no-one to protest.

Pro-slavery gang attacks abolitionists

Kansas Territory, 1856

As the fierce dispute between pro- and anti-slavers brings more and more bloodshed to Kansas, Governor Daniel Woodson – a pro-slaver – has declared the territory to be in a state of insurrection.

The blame for what has become a guerrilla war, with heavy casualties reported on both sides, is being laid at the door of John Brown, a fiery abolitionist from Connecticut, whose followers are alleged to have slaughtered five settlers on the Missouri border. Brown is crusading to keep Kansas from becoming a slave state. In retaliation, 300 pro-slavery men attacked Brown's stronghold at Osawatomie, but were driven off successfully by Brown and his 40 supporters.

John Brown: fiery abolitionist.

Xhosa slaughter cattle to fulfil prophecy

South Africa, October 1856

Cattle are being slaughtered by the thousand throughout Xhosaland following a 16-year-old's vision.

Nongquause, the 16-year-old, is the niece of the Xhosa's chief spiritual diviner. In her vision she was told that the Xhosa had to purify themselves: they had to kill all their cattle, cease planting crops and destroy all grain. Then the Xhosa dead would rise again, a great wind would sweep the white men into the sea, and food would become plentiful. News of the vision spread like wildfire. Thousands believe her.

The Xhosa have suffered one defeat after another at the hands of the white men. They are desperate, but they have been encouraged by rumours of British defeats on the Black Sea. Famine and depopulation are inevitable; this is a prospect which excites the land hunger of whites.

Syphilis kills Schumann in mental asylum

Bonn, 29 July 1856

Robert Schumann died today in a mental asylum near Bonn, where he had been placed at his own request four years ago. He was 46.

The man regarded as the champion of musical romanticism was tended at the end by his wife Clara, one of the greatest pianists of her day, and friends including Johannes Brahms, a talented young composer. Mental illness ran in the family, but Schumann probably caught syphilis before his marriage and over his last 15 years he grew increasingly withdrawn, unbalanced, and unable to work. Early in 1852 he had wild hallucinations of Hell and on 27 February he threw himself into the Rhine, celebrated in his *Rhenish Symphony*. He was rescued, but his mind was lost.

Robert Schumann and wife Clara: loyal to the final hours.

1857 ⇒

India, 10 May. *Sepoys* in the Bengal army at Meerut in northern India mutiny against their British officers.

India, 11 May. The Indian mutineers seize Delhi.

Switzerland, 26 May. Frederick IV of Prussia renounces his right of sovereignty over the canton of Neuchatel.

Britain, 25 June. Albert, the husband of Queen Victoria, is made prince consort.

Italy, 29 June. The patriot Giuseppe Mazzini, who has already provoked risings in Milan and Mantua, makes a vain attempt to mount a rebellion in Genoa.

Japan, June. The American consul Townsend Harris secures agreement from Japan on a trade treaty with the USA.

India, July. Over 200 Britons are massacred in Cawnpore.

Italy, 1 August. The republican lawyer Daniele Manin founds a national association for the unification of Italy under the king of Piedmont. Giuseppe Garibaldi is appointed vice-president.

Europe, August. France, Russia, Prussia and Piedmont break off diplomatic relations with the Ottoman empire over the issue of the union of Moldavia and Wallachia.

Tunisia, 10 September. In an effort to modernise Tunisia, the *bey*, Mohammed, grants a charter guaranteeing the equal treatment of Moslems and Jews.

India, 20 September. The British recapture Delhi.

India, 25 September. British forces under General Havelock arrive to relieve the British Residency in Lucknow, which has been under siege by mutineers since July.

Cochin China, (Vietnam), September. The French occupy Da Nang and Saigon.

Balkans, September. Following the annulment of the corrupt elections held in March, new elections in Moldavia and Wallachia result in a victory for the unionists.

Spain, 25 October. The liberal Leopoldo O'Donnell again replaces General Narvaez in power.

India. Universities are founded in Calcutta, Madras and Bombay.

US stock market bust follows boom

New York City, 8 August

The booming, bustling USA felt the first chill of economic depression today as one of the country's biggest finance houses, the Ohio Life Insurance and Trust Company, collapsed with huge liabilities. Most banks in this city have been forced to suspend all large payments.

As panic spread through the financial markets today, news came that several western railroads were plunging into bankruptcy, together with a number of other speculative enterprises. Over-speculation in railroad securities has led to the failure of 4,932 companies nationwide. Despite gloom on the New York Stock Exchange, America remains very much a boom country with Pennsylvania, at the heart of a coalfield 12 times larger than any in Europe, and vast agricultural production, fuelling an ever-expanding economy.

What makes a sun?

Kirchhoff: spectrum analyser.

Germany

A German scientist, Gustav Kirchhoff, has discovered a method of identifying the chemical composition of the sun, stars, and all the planets in the firmament.

After years of research he realised that when light passes through a gas or any heated material, only certain wavelengths are absorbed and emitted. Thus, by studying the spectrum of emissions, he can reveal its chemical composition.

Britain aids Afghans as Persians strike

Persian horseman: a mid 19th century hand-painted ceramic tile.

Persia, March

Persia, defeated by a British-Indian expedition led by Sir James Outram, has sued for peace. The second Persian campaign in Afghanistan in 20 years has ended, as before, with recognition of Afghan boundaries and the complete evacuation of Afghan territory. After 12 years of hostilities, the British and the Afghans made peace two years ago by the treaty of Peshawar. So when the Persians invaded Afghanistan in another attempt to capture Herat – they had tried in 1836, with Russian help – the British came to the Afghans' aid, just as they had done before. On 1 November last year, Britain declared war on Persia, and on 1 January seized the port of Bushire on the Persian gulf. The rapid end to the war gives Dost Mohammed the opportunity to try to unite Afghanistan, with its independent local rulers, under his kingship.

"The Gleaners", by Jean-Francois Millet. Born a peasant, he painted in poverty until exhibiting his first painting of rural life, "The Winnower", in 1848. He moved to Paris, became a friend of Theodore Rousseau, and continued painting serious and romantic rural scenes – including "The Bottlers" – celebrating the virtues of honest labour.

India rises up against "insensitive" British rulers

May: regiment mutinies and takes Delhi

Indian mutineers defending their position: a British caricature.

Delhi, 11 May

Thousands of Indian troops in Meerut have mutinied, killed their officers and marched on Delhi. Discontent has been growing in the Indian Army. Hindus resent the increasing dominance of Britain in India; Victorian military efficiency threatens the *caste* system and pay has not kept up with expectations. Nor is the discontent confined to the military; it can be found in the villages. Old India, with its priests and its princes, fears for its future in an entirely British India.

Two weeks ago, 85 men of the Third Cavalry regiment refused to handle new cartridges, which they claim contains cow and pig fat (thus offending both Hindus and Moslems). They were court martialled two days ago. The next day, while the European officers were attending church service, the convicted men's comrades rose in arms and liberated them.

Incredible as it sounds, the British had 24 hours' warning of the mutiny. Lieutenant Hugh Gough, warned by an Indian officer, told both his colonel and his brigadier, but such was their over-confidence that they "treated the communication with contempt, reproving me for listening to such idle words".

Joined by other regiments, the troops have captured Delhi, where they have killed every Briton they could find, and are holding the Moghul emperor prisoner.

September: British forces storm capital

Delhi, 21 September

Delhi has been retaken. The capital of India and heart of the Mutiny fell after a week's street fighting. It is being looted tonight.

Delhi was taken by the rebels on the second day of the Mutiny, the Sepoys proclaiming the somewhat uncomfortable Moghul emperor, Bahadur Shah, sovereign of India.

Delhi in the insurgents' hands directly threatened British India. The city meant more than prestige; it meant legitimacy. By June, troops had been gathered from Burma, the Punjab and southern India (which has remained quiet). A Sepoy army sent to intercept them was defeated at Badli-ki-Serai, and the British established themselves on a ridge to the north-west of the city. They were unable to surround Delhi, and there were times when it seemed they were being besieged.

On 14 September, strengthened by reinforcements, the British stormed the city. Two columns burst through breaches in the walls, a third flowed through the Kashmir gate, where four Victoria Crosses were earned during its blowing up. Twelve hundred British were killed. Street fighting, from one barricade to the next, continued for a week. Then, suddenly, resistance evaporated. Delhi is now in the hands of the British again; tonight it lies under a pall of smoke.

One against many: a British view.

Britons chopped up and thrown down well

Cawnpore, India, 15 July

The mutilated bodies of 200 British men, women and children have been found in a well. The victims, discovered by General Havelock's column which came in to the city this morning, had been killed only last night. Sepoy riflemen refused to do the deed, which was done by the town's butchers instead.

Cawnpore joined the Mutiny on 4 June, its troops following Nana Sahib, a disaffected landlord. For three weeks, loyalists under 70-year-old General Hugh Wheeler held out against the mutineers. Most were massacred after surrendering. The survivors were the ones massacred yesterday. "The pavement was swimming in blood, and fragments of ladies' and children's dresses were floating on it," said one eyewitness.

The British are disgusted. Rumours, without foundation, that the women and children were raped before being butchered spread through the British Army. Indian prisoners cannot expect much mercy from the revengeful British.

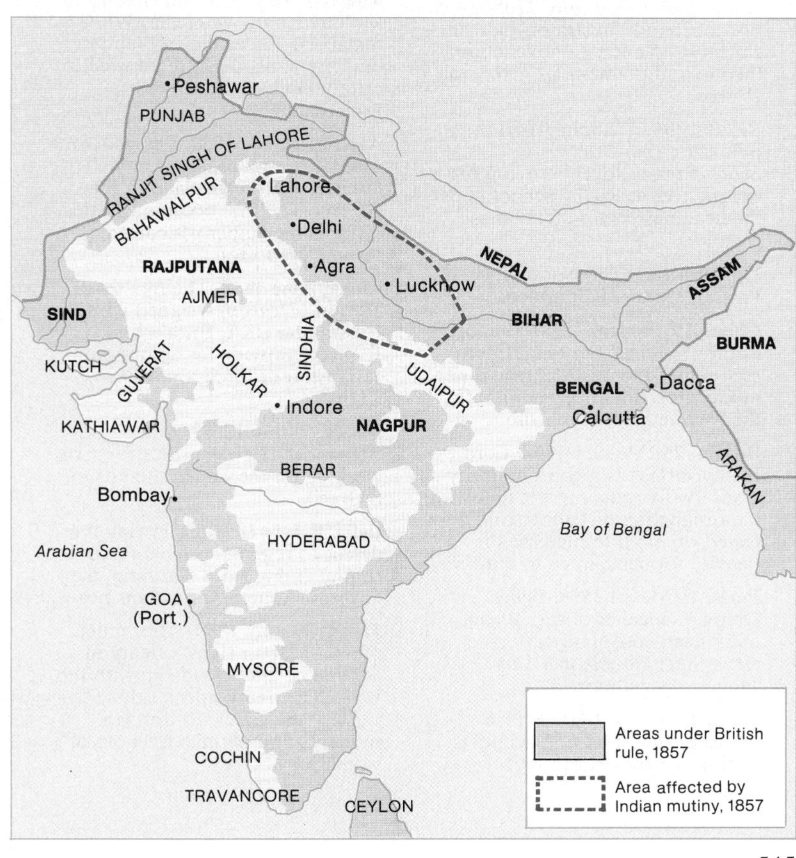

1857 (1857-1858)

Russia, 2 December 1857. Committees of aristocrats are set up with the aim of abolishing serfdom.

China, 29 December 1857. Guangzhou (*Canton*) falls to an Anglo-French force after heavy bombardment.

USA, 29 December 1857. William Walker, the renegade former leader of Nicaragua, is arrested and reprimanded for his exploits. Walker was extradited to the USA following his ejection by Central American troops after a failed attempt to regain power in Nicaragua.

Mexico, 1857. The adoption of a federal constitution and other political and religious reforms leads to a civil war between conservatives and liberals.

Spain, 1857. The Spanish heroine Agostina, known as *La Saragossa*, dies. She won fame for her bravery in the defence of Saragossa against the French invaders in 1808 and became a symbol of national pride, courage and liberty.

USA, 1857. The periodical *Atlantic Monthly* begins publication.

New York City, 1857. The first passenger elevator, invented by Elisha Otis, is installed in a New York department store.

France, 1857. Charles Baudelaire begins the Symbolist movement in France with his collection of poems *Les Fleurs du Mal*.

Britain, 1857. Anthony Trollope, a post office administrator, publishes *Barchester Towers*, a novel about the life and politics of a cathedral close.

Britain, 1857. Thomas Hughes publishes *Tom Brown's Schooldays*, a novel based on his experiences at Rugby school under the headmastership of Thomas Arnold.

London, 1857. The National Portrait Gallery is founded.

China, 19 January 1858. The forces of the "Sparks from the Lantern" sect, under Liu Yishun, take Sinan in Guizhou province, setting off the "White Signal" rebellion.

Britain, 25 February 1858. Lord Derby forms his second minority Conservative government following the resignation of Palmerston, defeated on a bill to increase the penalty for conspiracy to murder.

Paris, 13 March 1858. Felice Orsini, the leader of the Italian republican conspiracy to assassinate Napoleon III in January, is guillotined.

India, 21 March 1858. British forces lift the siege of Lucknow, ending the Indian Mutiny.

China, 31 March 1858. The Chinese agree to negotiate with the British and the French, who have ravaged Canton. They receive four envoys, including representatives from the USA and Russia.

India, 10 April 1858. Ye Mingchen, the governor general of the Chinese provinces of Guangzhou (*Canton*) and Guangxi, dies a prisoner in Calcutta. He was arrested by British and French forces in January after the fall of Guangzhou.

Mexico, 4 May 1858. The liberal government led by Benito Juarez establishes a capital at Vera Cruz. The conservatives, meanwhile, who control the army and are supported by the upper classes and the church, are ruling from Mexico City under the leadership of Miguel Miramon.

USA, 11 May 1858. Minnesota becomes the 32nd state.

China, 20 May 1858. British and French forces attack and take the Dagu forts near Tianjin, in northern China, in order to force an agreement to the demands made on the Qing court by the foreign powers.

China, 28 May 1858. By the treaty of Aigun, China recognises the territory north of the Amur river as Russian.

Paris, May 1858. At a conference to discuss the future of the Balkan principalities, it is decided to create a common organisation to deal with the army, law and finance in Moldavia and Wallachia. While remaining under the suzerainty of the Ottomans, they are allowed to call themselves the United Principalities.

Algeria, 2 June 1858. The governor general is replaced by a French minister with responsibility for Algeria. The first occupant of this office is the emperor's cousin, Jerome Napoleon.

China, June 1858. The treaties of Tianjin (*Tientsin*) – signed with Russia, the USA, Britain and France – provide for aggressive expansion of foreign power in China.

Russia, 2 July 1858. Czar Alexander II gives orders for serfs working on the imperial lands to be freed.

India, 8 July 1858. Following the defeat of remaining rebel forces in central India, Lord Canning, the governor general, proclaims peace.

Japan, 29 July 1858. After much pressure Japan signs a treaty of commerce and friendship with the USA. The treaty opens Edo (*Tokyo*) and Osaka to foreign residents and permits freedom of worship.

Livingstone pleads for missions to Africa

Cambridge, October 1857

He is short, shy and a poor speaker. His face is etched with exposure to the African sun. He speaks slowly, with a Lanarkshire accent, frequently halting to find words as if unfamiliar with the English language after 16 years in the African bush. He is a man who positively hates publicity. But that is the one thing that David Livingstone, explorer extraordinary, cannot avoid. And he knows it. So with the same humble aplomb which won over African natives David Livingstone, who returned in December, is winning over English society, using his status as a national hero to raise funds for more missions to Africa.

Dr Livingstone reading the Bible.

The Livingstone message, addressed in private to the queen and to well-heeled audiences everywhere, is that Central Africa's salvation depends on three vital Cs – Civilisation, Commerce and Christianity. By direct trading and providing the cloth and guns that Central Africa wants Britain can end the Portuguese-run goods-for-slaves trade. The task of opening up the interior will last beyond Livingstone's lifetime, and he plans to appeal to Cambridge students to take up the missionary challenge.

Benito Juarez, Mexico's new president

Mexico, October 1857

Benito Juarez was sworn in today as Mexico's new president, although he faces sustained opposition from an establishment backed by General Santa Anna.

The ceremony marks the climax of the 51-year-old populist's remarkable rise to power. Born into a poor Indian family, orphaned at the age of three, Juarez seemed condemned to a life of rural hardship. His chance employment as the servant of a Franciscan lay brother changed his life. He gained an education and by 1831 had begun work as a legal clerk. His practice concentrated on helping poor Indians, and the campaigning lawyer gradually evolved a substantial political power base.

He served in the national congress during the war with the United States and then, between 1847 and 1852, as governor of Oaxaca. He proved an outstanding official, boosting the state economy and attacking corrupt officials.

Banished by Santa Anna in 1853, Juarez returned in 1855 to begin a new campaign that has climaxed in today's presidency.

The largest ship afloat: Isambard Kingdom Brunel's "Great Eastern", crossing the Atlantic Ocean on her maiden voyage to New York.

British reopen Opium War with China

China, January 1857
Hostilities have broken out again between Britain and China. The ostensible reason for the renewal of the Opium War, which was supposedly ended by the treaty in 1842, was the boarding of the British registered ship *Arrow* by Chinese officials who arrested the Chinese crew and are said to have hauled down the British ensign.

The facts of the incident remain obscure, but it roused British anger and – given Palmerston's belief that "such half-barbarian countries as China ... need a dressing down every ten years or so" – war became inevitable.

Relations with the Chinese, who believe that it is the British who are the barbarians, have been fragile ever since the Nanjing treaty was signed. The British have tried to capitalise on the trade concessions in the treaty, while the Chinese have done their best to prevent the despised intruders from gaining any further advantages.

Given this situation, it is not surprising that tensions have mounted in the treaty ports. There have been anti-foreign riots in Canton where European trading factories have been burnt down and threatening posters put up by secret societies.

One of these threatened: "If we do not completely exterminate you pigs and dogs, we will not be manly Chinese". With the British also displaying their contempt for the Chinese it was inevitable that war would erupt again.

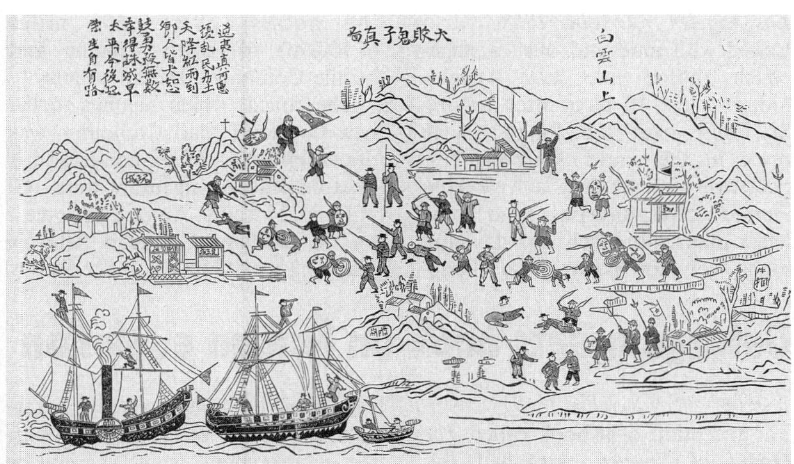

A Chinese representation of British invaders – and Chinese resisting them.

Virgin Mary appears in Lourdes grotto

Lourdes, 15 February 1858
The small French town of Lourdes is eagerly discussing the claims of a 14-year-old peasant girl who says that for the last four days a lady "surrounded with light" has appeared before her in a cave.

Bernadette Soubirous, who referred to the vision as *Acquero* (The Thing), had gone into the grotto while her sister and another girl collected firewood. They returned to find her on her knees.

She told them: "I saw a young girl in white with a yellow rose on each foot. She was not bigger than me. She made a little bow and I saw a rosary hanging on her arm. She made the sign of the cross and was surrounded with light."

Artistic view of Bernadette's vision.

Assassin's bomb fails to kill Napoleon III

Italian republican Felice Orsini's attempted assassination of the emperor.

Paris, 14 January 1858
Emperor Napoleon and Empress Eugenie today escaped unhurt after an Italian assassin threw a bomb at their carriage as they drove to the Paris Opera. However, eight bystanders were killed and up to 100 people injured.

Police have named the assassin as Felice Orsini, an Italian republican sympathiser. He told them that he regarded the emperor as a traitor to the Italian cause. This is thought to be a reference to the emperor's support for the Italian *Carbonari*, which he supported as a private citizen. The emperor's uncle, Napoleon I, is still remembered in Italy as the country's liberator.

The attempted assassination has triggered a clampdown on republicans in France, with hundreds of arrests, and a wave of anti-British sentiment. A police raid has discovered papers showing that Orsini plotted the assassination with Italian republicans based in London, where they made the bomb.

Indian rebels surrender Lucknow fortress

Lucknow, India, 22 March 1858
British troops have entered Lucknow for the third time in a year. This city has been a weathercock of the Mutiny. For 87 days the residency had been under siege. Reinforcements came in September but were too few and the city endured three more weeks of fighting.

Even after the relief, Lucknow remained a rebel stronghold, and though one rebel centre after another fell to the British, the city remained with the *Sepoys*.

In the end the British, under Sir Colin Campbell, used 25,000 troops and 80 artillery pieces to subdue the Sepoy army. The collapse of the Sepoys yesterday, after two weeks fighting a battle of manoeuvre outside the city, took even the British generals by surprise.

Only *The Times'* correspondent, William Howard Russell, rose to the occasion, giving a first-hand account of the final assault.

"The Sepoys, dismayed by the fierce onslaught, abandoned their positions; and as they fled, with Brasyer's Sikhs and the Tenth regiment in fast pursuit, they rushed in such confusion through the detached houses that a universal panic was created. Some were shut up, or secreted themselves in recesses, and in the many mysterious apartments of an eastern palace; but all who were found in arms were shot down or bayoneted on the spot," he wrote.

With the final fall of Lucknow, the Indian Mutiny can now be said to be over, but not forgotten. The two sides have competed with each other in atrocities. The horrifying memories, on both sides, will be remembered in India for a long time to come.

1858 (1858-1859)

Atlantic, 2 September 1858. The first transatlantic telegraph cable – running from the USA to Britain via Newfoundland – breaks down only 28 days after going into operation.

Prussia, October 1858. Frederick William IV, who has suffered a stroke, relinquishes power and his brother William becomes regent.

India, 1 November 1858. Queen Victoria is proclaimed ruler of India. The East India Company is abolished and the administration of India is transferred to the crown.

Prussia, 23 November 1858. The liberals win a majority in the elections to the Prussian ruling assembly.

Balkans, November 1858. The great European powers recognise the independence of Montenegro, which recently repulsed an Ottoman invasion.

Serbia, November 1858. Prince Alexander Karageorge, unpopular because of his servile policies towards Austria and his authoritarian internal rule, is deposed by the *diet*. He flees and takes refuge with the Ottomans.

Britain, 1858. Lionel de Rothschild becomes the first Jew to be admitted as an MP to the House of Commons. Although he was elected in 1847, and five times re-elected, he was not allowed to take his seat until the introduction of a new form of oath which omitted the words "on the truth faith of a Christian".

New York City, 1858. The Irish immigrant John Stephens founds an Irish revolutionary society whose members are known as the *Fenians* or the Brotherhood.

France, 1858. The *Bibliotheque Nationale* (National Library) opens.

Germany, 1858. The physicist Julius Plucker discovers cathode rays and the deflection produced upon them by magnetic fields.

London, 1858. The London news agency Reuter's acquires its first newspaper client, the London *Morning Advertiser*. Since its founding in 1851 by Paul Julius Reuter, a bank clerk, the Reuter's Telegraph Company has provided a commercial news service to banks, brokerage houses and leading business firms.

France, 19 January 1859. Following the secret meeting between Napoleon III and Count Cavour at Plombieres last July, France and Piedmont sign a treaty of alliance.

Serbia, January 1859. Following the deposition of Prince Alexander Karageorge, Milos Obrenovic, the 79-year-old former ruler of Serbia, is restored to power.

USA, 14 February 1859. Oregon becomes the USA's 33rd state.

Cochin China, (Vietnam), 17 February 1859. In revenge for the massacre of missionaries by the Emperor Annam Tu Duc, the French Admiral Rigault de Genouilly occupies Saigon.

Russia, 3 March 1859. Russia signs a secret treaty with France guaranteeing its neutrality in the event of an Austro-Franco war.

France, 17 April 1859. Napoleon III grants an amnesty for political prisoners.

China, 22 April 1859. Hong Rengan, the cousin of Hong Xiuquan, a leader of the God-Worshippers, arrives in Nanjing and sets out to introduce a reform package.

Egypt, 25 April 1859. Work begins on the building of the Suez Canal.

Italy, 26 April 1859. Count Cavour rejects an Austrian ultimatum to Piedmont to disarm.

Italy, 29 April 1859. Austrian troops invade Piedmont.

France, 3 May 1859. France declares war on Austria.

Italy, May 1859. Revolutions instigated by the National Society – which is campaigning for a unified Italy under the king of Piedmont – break out in Tuscany, Modena and Parma.

China, May 1859. Lan Chaogui and other members of the Incense Burners' League rebel at Daguan and Zhaotong in Yunnan province.

Italy, 4 June 1859. Piedmont and France crush Austria at Magenta.

Britain, 18 June 1859. Lord Palmerston forms his second Liberal ministry following the defeat of the Conservatives on an electoral reform bill.

Italy, 24 June 1859. The French and Piedmontese defeat the Austrians at Solferino.

China, 25 June 1859. British and French warships again attack the Dagu forts, but are defeated by the Chinese garrison. They are saved by the timely intervention of US naval forces.

Italy, June 1859. Rebellions break out in the papal states of Ravenna, Ferrara and Bologna.

USA, 1 July 1859. John Wise, an aeronaut, and three others are the first to transport mail by balloon. Their machine, *Atlantic*, covers the 812 miles between St Louis, Missouri, and Henderson, New York state, in 19 hours 40 minutes.

Italy, 11 July 1859. Napoleon III and Franz Josef of Austria reach peace terms at Villafranca.

Coach crosses US in 20 days non-stop

The Overland Mail Company's coach passing Mount Shasta, California.

Los Angeles, 7 October 1858

Caked with mud and dust, a stage-coach rattled into Los Angeles today – just 20 days after leaving St Louis over the longest stage route in the world. Carrying five passengers – including a *New York Herald* correspondent – and some letter mail, the coach ran day and night, non-stop (apart from changing horses) over 2,600 miles (4,160km) of deserts, plains and hostile Comanche Indian country.

The coach, which belongs to the new Overland Mail Company, was drawn by teams of six horses and is capable of covering more than 100 miles in 24 hours. Among the investors is William G Fargo, who is planning a national mail service.

Outrage greets book on human evolution

London, 30 November 1859

The reception of a book called *The Origin of Species*, published this week but already sold out, has been a mixture of amazement and violent rebuttal. In it Charles Darwin advances the theory that species evolve into other species by mutations from a common ancestor. The mechanism of "evolution" is by variations in individuals being selected by the pressures to survive in the environment: some variations flourish, others perish.

"Natural Selection" was the subject of two papers jointly delivered to the Linnaean Society last July by Darwin and Alfred Russel Wallace, who had arrived independently at the same conclusions.

Indian art: a fish seller and sweetmeat maker with their customers, by Shiva Dayal Lal, one of India's finest painters, from Patna, Bihar.

Secret deal on the liberation of Italy

Plombieres, 21 July 1858
Count Cavour, the prime minister of Piedmont-Sardinia, had a secret meeting with the Emperor Napoleon III here today. The emperor took time of from his numerous mistress and the two talked for several hours and then went for a three hour drive together in the Vosges forest. Napoleon took the reins himself.

Apparently Napoleon has agreed to help Piedmont to rid Italy of the Austrians. Cavour is planning to incite the people of Massa and Carrara to ask for the protection of Napoleon. This, they expect, will cause the duke of Modena to react aggressively with Austria's help. Then France can move its troops in to protect the people.

In return, Napoleon wants Nice and Savoy. An even bigger potential stumbling block is that he wants his cousin, Prince Napoleon, to marry Clotilde, the young daughter of King Victor Emmanuel, a suggestion which will not be welcome.

Women campaign to end US slavery

Men, women and children are auctioned in Charleston, South Carolina.

United States, 1859
Three years after the publication of Harriet Beecher Stowe's *Uncle Tom's Cabin*, women – former slaves among them – are in the forefront of the campaign for the abolition of slavery. Apart from lecturing throughout the country, often risking violence at the hands of fanatical pro-slavers, they are playing an important role in supporting the clandestine "underground railroad" to the north for runaway slaves.

Sojourner Truth was born a slave and belonged to several owners before she fled to New York where she wrote her autobiography, *The Narrative of Sojourner Truth.* Now she travels throughout the west, giving dramatic talks on slavery and the suffrage issue. Another former slave, Harriet Tubman, escaped when she was due to be sold to the deep south. She has helped more than 300 fugitives to reach the northern states and Canada, using routes that are changed frequently and demanding strict discipline – often at pistol point – from the escapees.

Sojourner Truth: abolitionist.

Carnage as Austrians retreat in Italy

Solferino, 24 June 1859
The small northern Italian village of Solferino is tonight in French hands amid shocking scenes of carnage and suffering unrivalled since the Crimean War. Total casualties in the battle – the latest in the conflict between French-backed Piedmont and Austria – are estimated at over 40,000 after barely nine hours of fighting, much of it grim hand-to-hand combat.

With the Austrians retreating into the Quadrilateral, the impregnable defensive box formed by four fortified cities on the Mantuan plain, the conflict is at stalemate, with Piedmont no closer to gaining Lombardy or Venetia in its bid to unite Italy, which would relieve it of the need to cede Savoy to France under the deal agreed with Napoleon III. Many of the 22,500 Austrian casualties came as French shells rained relentlessly down on the town that Emperor Franz Josef, aged 29, fighting his first battle, had selected as the starting point for a counter-offensive. Many of the 17,500 French casualties died as they charged *en masse* up the hill.

A captured Austrian cavalryman.

Self-help is solution for Samuel Smiles

London, 1859
The Industrial Revolution may be a matter of worry for many people, but the author and reformer Samuel Smiles has used it as the backdrop for his new book of social improvement, *Self-Help.*

Smiles, whose own jobs have included surgeon, newspaper editor and railway administrator, has produced a paean to industry, thrift and self-improvement. The individual is responsible for the success or failure of his own life; Smiles deplores "over-government".

Smiles has certainly touched a chord, even if his critics decry the book as the embodiment of smug middle-class individualism, claiming that such efforts are beyond society's many unfortunates.

Samuel Smiles: prophet of self-help.

Sydney is a cesspit, says British writer

New South Wales, October 1858
Parts of the city of Sydney are denounced by a sociologist as "social cesspools" of vice, misery and poverty, peopled by a "vicious and filthy humanity". The British-born William Jevons, writing in the *Sydney Morning Herald,* said that the muddy, narrow streets were devoid of gutters or sewers, and lined by dilapidated cottages with no sanitation. He asserted that both ground and air were poisoned by the cottagers' "foul drainings" which soaked into foundations and ran under other people's doors. He called on the council to clean up these slums.

1859 (1859-1860)

Italy, 12 July 1859. Count Cavour resigns as prime minister of Piedmont in protest at the peace terms concluded yesterday by France and Austria.

Italy, August 1859. Parma, Modena, Tuscany and Romagna form a military alliance and demand union with Piedmont under King Victor Emmanuel.

Serbia, September 1859. On the death of Milos Obrenovic, he is replaced as Serbian leader by his son Michael.

China, October 1859. The rebel Incense Burners' League occupies Yunlian and Gaoxian in Sichuan province.

Switzerland, 11 November 1859. In confirmation of their preliminary negotiations at Villafranca in July, France and Piedmont sign a peace treaty with their defeated enemy, Austria, at Zurich. Lombardy is ceded to Piedmont.

Argentina, 11 November 1859. The city of Buenos Aires is compelled to rejoin the Argentine Federation, from which it broke away in 1853.

Britain, November 1859. Charles Darwin publishes his *Origin of Species by Means of Natural Selection.*

Australia, 1859. Queensland is established as a separate colony, with its capital at Brisbane.

India, 1859. The first power-loom is set up in India.

Massachusetts, 1859. The Massachusetts Institute of Technology is founded at Cambridge.

Russia, 1859. Ivan Goncharov publishes a novel on the delights of indolence entitled *Oblomov.*

Britain, 1859. John Stuart Mill publishes his essay *On Liberty*, stating the principle that individual freedom should be complete provided that it does not interfere with the liberty of others.

England, 1859. Karl Marx, in exile in London, publishes his *Critique of Political Economy*, putting forward a "materialist" interpretation of history.

Britain, 1859. Edward Fitzgerald publishes his verse translation of the *Rubaiyat of Omar Khayyam*, the mediaeval Persian poet and philosopher of resignation.

France, 1859. The naturalist Felix-Archimede Pouchet publishes *Heterogenie*, in which he gives details of his theory of the spontaneous generation of life from non-living matter.

France, 1859. Eugene Delacroix, the leader of the Romantic school of painting, completes his *Jacob and the Angel.*

France, 1859. Charles Gounod's opera *Faust* is performed for the first time. Among this year's other premieres is *Orpheus in the Underworld*, an operetta by Jacques Offenbach.

Germany, 1859. Richard Wagner completes his opera *Tristan and Isolde*.

USA, 10 January 1860. In the first big factory accident, 77 people are killed when a textile factory building collapses in Lawrence, Massachusetts.

Piedmont, 21 January 1860. Count Camillo Cavour becomes prime minister again, with the intention of uniting the duchies of Parma, Modena, Romagna and Tuscany. Referendums will be held in March.

Britain, 23 January 1860. Richard Cobden, one of the leaders of the movement to repeal the Corn Laws, negotiates a commercial treaty with France aimed at reducing customs duties on over 40 articles.

Prussia, February 1860. General Albert von Roon, who was appointed minister of war in December, puts forward proposals for reform of the army.

USA, 6 March 1860. The Republican politician Abraham Lincoln makes a campaign speech defending the right to strike.

Japan, 24 March 1860. Ii Naosuke, the *shogunal* councillor who signed the treaty of trade and friendship with the USA in 1858, is cut down and mortally wounded while on his way to an audience with the emperor. Anti-foreign extremists hold Ii Naosuke responsible for the current liberal foreign policy in Japan.

Italy, 24 March 1860. France signs a treaty with Piedmont at Turin. Piedmont is to annex central Italy, while France is promised Nice and Savoy.

Italy, March 1860. Tuscany, Parma, Modena and Romagna vote in favour of union with Piedmont.

Russia, 1860. The port of Vladivostok is founded on the coast of the Sea of Japan.

Russia, 1860. *The Tempest*, by Alexander Ostrovsky, Russia's leading playwright, is performed for the first time.

Britain, 1860. George Eliot (a pseudonym of Mary Ann Evans) publishes *The Mill on the Floss*, following the success of *Adam Bede* last year.

Britain, 1860. Wilkie Collins publishes *The Woman in White*, a new kind of novel – detective fiction.

First oil well yields 25 barrels per day

Pennsylvania, 28 August 1859

They have known about oil for the past 300 years in America. It seeped from the ground then, and was used firstly as a medicine to cure blindness, rheumatism, coughs, colds, sprains and baldness. In those early days it was skimmed from creeks in its crudest form and proved invaluable for lighting – even though it gave off a smelly, powerful odour. A chemist succeeded in distilling the crude oil into a satisfactory lighting fuel.

But it was in 1833 that the true value of oil as an industrial lubricant was realised, and there was a case for major exploitation. Edwin Drake, a former railroad conductor, has done exactly that, employing techniques used in drilling salt wells and boring down 69 feet to produce a steady flow of 25 barrels of oil daily which he is marketing for heating and lighting. With industry expanding rapidly, speculators are watching Drake's operation with more than usual interest and, already, other prospectors are at work in the Allegheny valley and elsewhere.

Drake (in top hat) and his oil well.

English craze for everything mediaeval

James Archer's Death of Arthur, where neo-Gothic and pre-Raphaelite meet.

London, 1859

Alfred Tennyson, Britain's poet laureate since 1850, has published the first instalment of a long poem on the legend of King Arthur, *The Idylls of the King*. Since he wrote *Maud*, *In Memoriam* and *The Charge of the Light Brigade*, he is the most-read English poet of the time. He published *Morte d'Arthur* and *Sir Galahad* in 1842. Now he adds *The Coming of Arthur* and other idylls. *The Holy Grail* and others are still to come. The Arthurian legend dominates literature. Matthew Arnold's *Tristram and Iseult* and William Morris' *Defence of Guenevere* have come out recently. Morris and Rossetti decorated the Oxford Union debating hall with Arthurian murals last year. Pugin's Gothic revival in architecture is part of the current mediaevalist craze.

Chinese rebels defeated

Shanghai, 19 August 1860
The *Taiping* rebel army has today been halted at the gates of Shanghai by a combined force of British, Indian and French troops. The Taipings, ravaging the land as they advanced, tried to buy off the "foreign devils" by offering them trading rights in their captured cities, but the British and French commanders promised the terrified inhabitants that they would protect the city against massacre and pillage, and they have kept their word.

This is a serious setback for the Taipings who had broken out of Nanjing under their brilliant new general, Li Xiucheng, the "loyal king", and shattered the besieging imperial army. Their long rebellion may now be sliding into defeat. The irony of today's clash is that in the north the British and French are preparing to advance on Beijing.

Taiping rebels under Li Xiucheng attacking Shanghai, by land and sea.

Peru grows wealthy on bird droppings

Peru, 1860
Peru, whose economy in recent years has been devastated by political upheaval, has found a new deliverer. But the agent of national wealth is not men, but birds, or, more precisely, bird-droppings.

Guano, as the Peruvians call it, has long been collected by the Indians, who gather it from the coast where it is deposited by millions of seabirds. They take it inland where it provides a rich fertiliser. Early colonisers, intent on gold, ignored this less romantic treasure, but recent scientific research has shown how very valuable guano is.

Now the Peruvian government has declared the exploitation of guano as a national monopoly. An extensive trade has been established with Europe, where the benefits of so rich a fertiliser are in great demand.

Fighter for slaves freedom hanged

Charleston, Virginia, 2 Dec 1859
Henry Wadsworth Longfellow summed up the feelings of many of his fellow-Americans. "This is sowing the wind to reap the whirlwind which will soon come," he said. He was referring to the hanging today of John Brown, a 59-year-old fanatical abolitionist, for treason, murder and conspiring with slaves.

Brown had planned to seize the arsenal at Harper's Ferry and turn the town into a base for an uprising by slaves. The plan succeeded, but the arsenal was recaptured soon afterwards by a force of marines led by Captain Robert E Lee. During his trial Brown refused to answer questions, saying that God had given him a mission to free slaves.

Many believe that John Brown was insane. The governor of Virginia has received 17 affidavits to that effect.

Japan's nationalists murder foreigners

Japan, 1860
Fanatical Japanese nationalists in the capital, Edo (*Tokyo*), have begun a campaign of assassination against foreigners. A Russian officer and two sailors were among the first to be killed. They were followed by two Dutchmen and Henry Heusken, the Dutch-born secretary and interpreter for Townsend Harris, the US consul.

Heusken, who had helped several foreign envoys in their negotiations with the Japanese authorities, was one of the most respected members of the foreign community. The presence of the increasing number of foreign diplomats in Edo has given the assassins a choice of targets, and their reign of terror has caused the envoys to absent themselves discreetly from the capital.

Only Townsend Harris, the US representative, a wealthy New York banker who gained his knowledge of the east by shipping cargo in his own boats, has stayed at his post. He has acquired considerable prestige among the Japanese by his courage in refusing to run away from the killers.

A drunken foreign sailor served saki.

Gold transforms southeastern Australia

Victoria, Australia, 1860
Gold fever has gripped Victoria and transformed the colony's economy. In ten years the mines at Ballarat and Bendigo have produced eight million ounces, and the population of Victoria colony has risen from 77,345 to 540,322.

Thousands of new immigrants, have flocked to the fields. Many are from California, whence they have brought the latest mining skills. Others have come from Ireland and have brought radical and anti-British traditions with them. Another large group comes from Germany, and the thousands of Chinese cause deep resentment in the white working class.

The wave of people with their accompanying skills has created new industries in Victoria, while the new-found gold has provided much-needed capital. A decade ago the colony exported only sheep. Now it also exports gold.

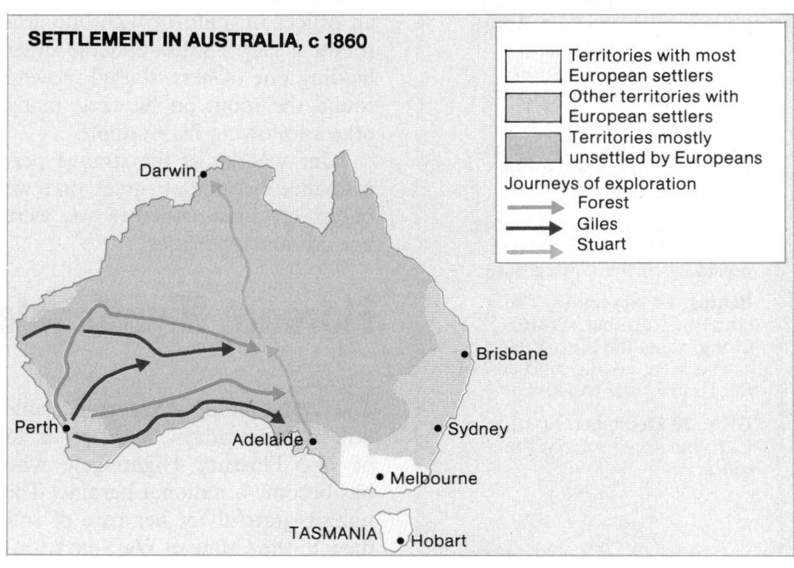

1860 ⇒

Italy, 11 May. Garibaldi lands at Marsala in Sicily.

China, June. The American F T Ward enlists foreigners in a volunteer corps to defend Shanghai against *Taiping* rebels.

China, 19 August. British and French regular forces defeat Li Xiucheng's Taiping troops near Shanghai.

China, 21 August. Anglo-French forces take the Dagu forts in northern China, defeating the Qing defenders.

Honduras, 12 September. The American William Walker, the one-time ruler of Nicaragua, is executed by firing squad.

Italy, 18 September. Piedmontese troops move into the papal states to forestall Garibaldi. They defeat the papal troops at Castelfidardo.

Germany, 21 September. Arthur Schopenhauer, the most influential philosopher since Hegel, dies aged 72.

China, 21 September. Fighting continues in the second Opium War. AngloFrench forces defeat Qing troops at Baliqiao, on the road to Beijing.

China, 22 September. The Xianfeng Emperor flees from Beijing to Jehol.

Beijing, 13 October. Anglo-French troops occupy Beijing after several days spent looting the Summer Palace.

Beijing, 20 October. The Summer Palace is burnt to the ground.

Austria, 20 October. The October *Diploma* sets up a federal constitution for the empire. This is very unpopular with the Hungarians.

Beijing, 25 October. Following the signing of the Sino-British convention of Beijing yesterday, today the Sino-French convention is signed. The war is over.

Italy, 5 November. The papal states vote to unite with the Piedmontese monarchy.

Washington, DC, 6 November. Abraham Lincoln is elected president of the United States.

Beijing, 14 November. The emperor's brother, Prince Gong, signs the Sino-Russian convention, ceding land east of the Ussuri river to Russia.

USA, 20 December. South Carolina secedes from the union.

Postman gallops 2,000 miles in 11 days

Sacramento, Cal., 13 April
The first Pony Express clattered into town today bringing 49 letters and three newspapers posted in St Joseph, Missouri, 11 days ago. Hundreds cheered as young Tom Hamilton galloped up to the post office and handed over the mail satchel. The new mail service – which involves a run across 1,966 miles (3,145km) of desolate prairie with risks from hostile Indians and flash floods in the mountains – has been organised by the Central Overland Company which bought 500 horses and advertised for "skinny, expert riders willing to risk death daily". Each horse is galloped at speed for about 12 miles (19km) before the horseman changes mounts.

The first Pony Express rider arrives in California to a hero's welcome.

US customs amaze Japanese envoy

San Francisco, 18 May
The first Japanese envoys to the United States have seen many amazing sights since they arrived, but none has astonished them more than the scene they witnessed tonight after a dinner given for them Secretary of State Lewis Cass.

Vice-ambassador Muragaki recalls: "The music commenced and an officer in uniform with one arm round a lady's waist and the other holding one of hers, started moving round the room on his toes, many others following his example ...

"Our wonder at the strange performance became so great that we began to doubt whether we were not on another planet."

The Japanese envoys in Washington.

Thousand redshirt rebels in Sicily

Genoa, 6 May
The Italian republican and international revolutionary, Guiseppe Garibaldi, sailed from here today with a force of a thousand redshirts aboard two small steamers. They plan to liberate first Sicily and then Naples in the name of a united Italy. Garibaldi began gathering his force in the hope of stopping the ceding of his native Nice to France, but he realised that he could not get the support of Piedmont's King Victor Emmanuel. The king is likely to support his bid for a united Italy, however.

Giuseppe Garibaldi was born in 1807 and as a young man became a supporter of Mazzini's Young Italy movement. He was forced to flee to South America in 1834 and won military fame in battles against the Argentinians In 1848 he returned to Italy and organised the defence of the Roman republic against the French. He was forced into a courageous retreat and exile. He has become the symbol of Italian liberation, and launched a guerrilla attack on Lake Como last year.

Giuseppe Garibaldi in old age.

Florence Nightingale brings nurses and midwives more respect

England
The ambition of every respectable little girl nowadays, it seems, is to be like Florence Nightingale who has become a national heroine. The public, grateful for her care of soldiers in the Crimean War, have funded the Nightingale Nurse Training School at St Thomas' Hospital in London where a selected few will study, fully paid, for one year. Florence Nightingale has been dedicated to the reform of hospitals since she left her rich upper-class family to train as a nurse at Kaiserwerth Institute near Dusseldorf. Now aged 40, still full of determination, she plans to open another school next year. This time it will be for midwifery nurses at King's College Hospital, also in London.

Beijing falls to Allies

The Summer Palace, with the Bridge of Marble in the foreground, looted today.

Beijing, 6 October
The Franco-British expeditionary force has today captured Beijing, and tonight the troops are looting the fabulous Summer Palace of China's emperor.

Rarely can an army have captured so rich a prize. The emperor left behind all his treasure when he fled. There is so much that the French and British envoys, Baron Gros and Lord Elgin, have appointed commissioners from each army to divide up the spoils equally.

Lord Elgin chose the emperor's jade baton for Queen Victoria, and a similar one was found for the emperor of France. Every soldier is to get his share.

At first sentries kept the troops away from the 200 richly furnished buildings of the palace, but when the soldiers learnt that peasants had climbed the walls to steal what they could, they brushed the sentries aside and stormed the buildings.

English, French, Scots and Sikhs are staggering out of the palace, their arms filled with silks and brocades and their pockets with jewels. Some are cavorting in the gowns of the emperor's concubines.

They are smashing the furniture to get at the jewels set into the woodwork. Snuff boxes, pearl necklaces, and golden table sets are stuffed into sacks. One officer has acquired a priceless black jade chess set. Now we hear that Lord Elgin is considering burning the palace in revenge for the killing of 20 allied prisoners.

Lord Elgin's new Chinese marbles, a trinket from his travels.

Abraham Lincoln elected US president

Washington, 20 December
After a bitterly fought campaign, Abraham Lincoln, a former frontier shopkeeper and postmaster who became a successful lawyer in Illinois, was elected president today. The United States, already severely divided over the issues of slavery and the right of states to secede from the union, is braced for civil war. South Carolina has already seceded from the union, and six other southern states are threatening to follow suit before Lincoln takes office next year.

A tall, gangling conservative, noted for his dry wit and folksy wisdom, Lincoln won the election on an anti-slavery platform. "I believe this government cannot endure permanently, half slave and half free," he has said, although he admits freely that he sees no way of solving the problem. His only hope of saving national unity lies with more moderate southern leaders like Jefferson Davis who are prepared to give the new administration a fair chance. The moderates are heavily outnumbered, however, by slave-owning planters.

Abraham Lincoln: 16th president.

China succumbs to British trade demands

Beijing, 24 October
Lord Elgin, escorted by British soldiers, marched through the deserted Chinese capital today to the Hall of Rites where the defeated Chinese, cowed by the burning of the Summer Palace, signed a treaty acceding to Britain's demands.

The terms are similar to those of the "treaty of peace, friendship and commerce" signed at Tianjin two years ago. It was the breaking of this treaty, when the Chinese refused to allow foreign diplomats to establish their embassies in Beijing, which led to the Anglo-French occupation of the capital. Under the terms 11 more ports, including Shanghai, the gateway to the Yangzi, are to be opened to foreign trade, and diplomats will be allowed to live in Beijing. China is also to pay an indemnity and cede part of Kowloon to Britain. Lord Elgin was met by 500 *mandarins* led by Prince Gong, half-brother of the emperor.

Bare-fist fighting is loser as marathon battle ends in stalemate

England, April
A bare-knuckled boxing match between the champions of England and the US ended in a draw this month after two hours and 20 minutes. Yet in one sense the marathon battle may yet prove conclusive: it seems increasingly likely that it will have been the last bout of its kind.

The possibly historic encounter occurred when Sayers, the English champion for the past three years, met Heenan, the best heavyweight in the United States, at Farnborough in Hampshire. The stakes were £200 a side. In a gruelling encounter, the much lighter Sayers suffered a torn tendon while his opponent was virtually blinded by facial swelling. Members of Parliament and famous authors watched the match, which was staged in secret because of police disapproval.

Bare-knuckled prize-fighting became an international sport 50 years ago, but now appals many of its original aristocratic promoters. Poorly-trained and ill-rewarded fighters often fall into penury and drunkenness. But the introduction of skintight gloves has helped to reduce injuries.

A pugilist, posing for the canvas.

1861

Prussia, 2 January. On the death of Frederick William IV, William succeeds to the throne.

USA, 8 February. Following the example of South Carolina, other slave states secede from the union and form the Confederate States of America.

Prussia, 8 February. The Progressive Party is set up with the aim of unifying Germany under Prussian leadership.

Italy, 18 February. Following the capture of Gaeta by Piedmontese troops four days ago, King Victor Emmanuel II of Sardinia is proclaimed as "king of Italy". King Francis II of Naples takes refuge in Rome which is still held by France. Austria holds Venetia.

Austria, 26 February. The February Patent establishes a federal constitution.

Russia, 3 March. Serfs are emancipated by Alexander II as part of a programme of westernisation.

Washington, DC, 4 March. Lincoln is sworn in as president.

New Zealand, 19 March. An uneasy truce brings an end to fighting between the Maoris and British settlers sparked off in 1859 by a dispute over a land purchase near the Waitari river.

South Carolina, 14 April. Fort Sumter in Charleston port falls to Confederate troops.

Britain, 13 May. The government declares its neutrality in the American Civil War.

Italy, 6 June. Count Camillo di Cavour, the prime minister who worked to unify Italy, dies.

Ottoman Empire, 21 July. Sultan Abdul Mejid dies and is succeeded by Abdul Aziz.

Virginia, 21 July. The first thrust by union forces towards the confederate capital of Richmond is repulsed at Bull Run.

Washington, DC, 22 July. The senate passes the Crittenden Resolution, stating the war's main purpose as the preservation of the union, not the abolition of slavery.

Washington, DC, 5 August. President Lincoln makes the first nationwide income tax law, in an attempt to fund the civil war.

Washington, DC, 16 August. President Lincoln bars all commerce with the confederate states.

Austria, 21 August. Following the February Patent, establishing a federal constitution, the Hungarian *Diet* is dissolved and replaced by Austrian imperial commissioners.

Tientsin, China, 2 September. A new commercial treaty is signed by representatives of China and Prussia, opening up China to further Prussian commercial penetration.

Frankfurt, 26 October. The German professor of physics, Johann Philipp Reiss, presents a telephone to the Society of Physics.

South Carolina, 7 November. Union cannons pound confederate troops into submission in Port Royal, the second major victory for the union in a blockade of less than two months.

Portugal, 11 November. King Pedro V dies in a typhoid epidemic. He is succeeded by his brother Luis.

China, 2 December. Following the death of the Xianfeng emperor on 22 August, and the accession of Zaichun on 11 November, the two empresses dowager, Ci'an and Cixi, become regents.

Britain, 14 December. The prince consort, Albert, dies of typhoid, to the great sorrow of Queen Victoria.

Rumania, 23 December. The European powers recognise the principality of Rumania (Moldavia and Wallachia) which is ruled by Prince Alexander Cuza.

China, December. The *Shanghai xinbao* (New Shanghai Paper) is a new weekly.

Britain. The popular novelist Charles Dickens publishes the first episodes of *Great Expectations* in the journal *All the Year Round*. It is the story of Pip, a village boy, brought up by his overbearing sister and her gentle husband, Joe Gargery the blacksmith.

Nigeria. The British establish a protectorate over the port of Lagos.

Germany. Johannes Brahms composes his first piano concerto.

Britain. The feminist Maria Rye publishes the *Emigration of Educated Women* outlining her plans to find unemployed women positions in Australia and Canada.

France. The *velocipede* is invented – a two-wheeled vehicle which the rider sits astride and propels with his feet.

Madagascar. Queen Ranavalona's successor, Radama II, tries to impose a policy of westernisation, but comes up against opposition from the small elite that governs the country.

West Africa. The Tukulor leader, Al-Hajj Umar, who has been waging a *jihad* (holy war) since 1852, destroys and occupies the Bambara kingdom of Segu.

France extends rule in Cochin China

Cochin China (Vietnam), 25 Feb

A French force of some 3,000 men under Admiral Charner has taken the forts guarding Saigon and relieved 900 French and Spanish troops blockaded in the city by 20,000 Annamese regulars commanded by General Nguyen Tri Phuong. There was some stiff fighting, but the French are now in command of the countryside in the vicinity of Saigon. They have thus extended their influence in Cochin China without setting out on any well planned imperialist venture.

Admiral Charner's orders were merely to relieve the garrison and consolidate the points already occupied by the French who were originally sent to Cochin China with some Spanish troops to protect persecuted Catholic missionaries. The appointment of M Chasseloup-Laubat as minister of marine and colonies may well bring a more aggressive approach to the spread of French influence in Cochin China, with a demand for French sovereignty over the newly-occupied south-east Asian territories.

The emperor and his ministers.

Victor Emmanuel II, the first king of Italy

Garibaldi, fitting the king's boot.

Turin, 17 March

Victor Emmanuel II, the king of Piedmont-Sardinia, was recognised as king of the new united Italy by the parliament here today. Victor Emmanuel – the cavalier king, as he is known – has been popular; but his position as monarch of all Italy is owed to the diplomatic and political skills of his prime minister, Cavour. The critical events were last year. The success of Garibaldi's revolutionary army was ensured in the south and he was ready to march on Rome. He wanted a united republican Italy. Four days after Garibaldi's army entered Naples Cavour invaded the papal states, ostensibly to prevent revolution there.

There was no justification in law and Napoleon publicly condemned the act. Privately, though, Napoleon supported Cavour and sent only a small French force to Italy. After his military victory Cavour arranged plebiscites by secret ballot in Naples and Sicily which brought massive majorities for a united Italy under Victor Emmanuel.

Imbecile gives a clue to map of the brain

France, April

They called the patient "Tan". It was the only word that he knew. A surgeon, Pierre-Paul Broca, conducted a *post mortem* which revealed that Tan's brain was degenerate in the frontal region. Broca believes that language seems to be placed in the frontal area of the brain; presumably processes like movement, emotion and memory are situated elsewhere.

It's civil war in the US

Fort Sumter, Virginia, 15 April
With the high society of Charleston, the women in ball-gowns, their men in evening dress, watching from the waterfront, the first shots in this civil war two nights ago could well have been no more than a distant fireworks display. Few could accept that these were the first blasts of a conflict which threatens to rip the country apart.

With the confederacy of seven rebel southern states established under its president, Jefferson Davis, President Lincoln, determined to maintain the union, ordered union forces to relieve the federal garrison at Fort Sumter. But today, after a massive bombardment, the union commander surrendered and marched his men out with colours flying.

In Washington, President Lincoln called for 75,000 volunteers to fight forces "too powerful to be suppressed by the ordinary course of judicial proceedings". A senator summed it up as a "war of sentiment and opinion by one form of society against another form of society".

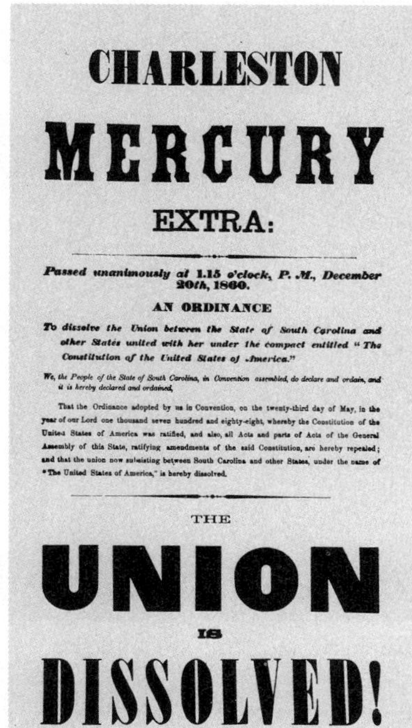
CHARLESTON

MERCURY

EXTRA:

Passed unanimously at 1.15 o'clock, P. M., December 20th, 1860.

AN ORDINANCE

To dissolve the Union between the State of South Carolina and other States united with her under the compact entitled "The Constitution of the United States of America."

We, the People of the State of South Carolina, in Convention assembled, do declare and ordain, and it is hereby declared and ordained,

That the Ordinance adopted by us in Convention, on the twenty-third day of May, in the year of our Lord one thousand seven hundred and eighty-eight, whereby the Constitution of the United States of America was ratified, and also, all Acts and parts of Acts of the General Assembly of this State, ratifying amendments of the said Constitution, are hereby repealed; and that the union now subsisting between South Carolina and other States, under the name of "The United States of America," is hereby dissolved.

THE

UNION

IS

DISSOLVED!

A South Carolina newspaper announces the first state to break from the Union last December, on the issue of slavery and state's rights.

Mexico promises to pay foreign debts

Mexico, 31 October
Representatives of the governments of Spain, France and Great Britain met in London today to sign an agreement under which they hope to regain the substantial loans each country has made to Mexico.

Under the convention of London the countries will occupy the Mexican coast until the debts, some of them 50 years old, are repaid in full. They will occupy the customs house at Vera Cruz and seize all customs receipts for themselves. There is no question of interfering in Mexican politics, or attempting to take over Mexican territory. They say: "The parties bind themselves not to seek for themselves any acquisition of territory, or any peculiar advantage, and not to impair the right of the Mexican nation to choose and freely to constitute the form of its own government."

Britain and Spain may well be sincere in their promises, but observers fear that France, whose president Louis Napoleon yearns to emulate his famous uncle, may have thoughts of actual conquest.

Czar Alexander frees twenty million serfs

St Petersburg, 3 March
For half a century Russia's leaders agreed that serfdom was evil – but that nothing could be done about it without risking the stability of society. When Alexander II came to the throne he said: "It is better to abolish serfdom from above than to wait until the serfs begin to liberate themselves from below." Today, the sixth anniversary of his accession, he issued an edict freeing 20 million serfs – one third of the population – and granting them the right to own the land they cultivate. But the serfs have to pay for their land, partly to the government and partly to their former landlord, so the effect of freedom may not be too great in practice.

Australian gold diggers attack Chinese

Victoria, 15 July
Three thousand goldminers, many armed, have driven thousands of Chinese immigrants from their camp at Lambing Flat, Victoria, Australia. And when police intervened, they threw them out as well.

There is a growing fear among uneducated whites that the large numbers of Chinese immigrants could undercut white labour. The first riot took place last December when 500 Chinese were driven out. The riots a fortnight ago were worse. The tiny police force stood by as Chinese gold diggers were burnt out of their homes. Yesterday the police finally moved and arrested three men for taking part in the attacks, or "roll-ups", as they are known locally. By evening the jail had been stormed, the three prisoners "liberated", and the ineffectual police force driven away. Needless to say there was not a Chinaman in sight in the camp.

The government's response has been remarkably speedy. In addition to the expected military column that is being assembled to restore order, the premier, Charles Cowper, has made it clear that he will be putting bills before parliament both to ensure gold diggers' safety standards and to limit Chinese immigration.

Nervous crown in new-look Indian policy

The ruins of the East India Company's India: skeletons of sepoys at Lucknow.

Delhi, India
The old paternal Englishman, with his *hookah*, his Indian mistress, and his languid Orientalism, no longer rules India. In a series of reforms following the suppression of the Mutiny, the old East India Company's governing powers have been taken over by the crown and the Indian Army has been reorganised.

The changeover from company to crown is hardly noticed. Little has changed except the letterheadings. Changes to the Indian Army have been more drastic. One third of the army (the Bengali regiments) took part in the Mutiny. The Company's European troops are to be disbanded. Every Indian brigade is to have a British battalion in it; Indian regiments are to be deprived of artillery.

Other changes have been somewhat less dramatic. Finances have been put in order without oppressing the peasantry. Indian princes have become more tightly bound to the crown, and Indians are being treated like subjects.

The Indian middle class, which remained loyal to Britain during the Mutiny, is taking on a greater role, but so great is the fear that the British now have of the Indians that the latter are being denied political responsibility.

1862 ⇒

Mexico, February. An accord is reached with the British and the Spanish, who agree to re-embark their troops at Vera Cruz. They moved in following president Benito Juarez' declaration of a two-year moratorium on the payment of foreign debts last year.

London, 29 March. A world trade exhibition opens.

Cochin China, (Vietnam), 13 April. France and Annam sign the treaty of Saigon by which France annexes Cochin China.

Nashville, Tennessee, 15 April. Nashville is the first confederate capital to fall to union forces.

Mexico, 5 May. French troops are defeated at Puebla. Napoleon III maintained an army in Mexico following the withdrawal of Spanish and British troops, and plans to establish a Mexican empire.

East Africa, 16 May. The Moslem Chief Al Hajj Umar continues his *jihad* (holy war) conquests by taking the Peul kingdom of Masina.

Virginia, 2 June. General Robert E Lee assumes command of the confederate armies of North Virginia.

China, 3 June. Rebels led by Lan Chaogui (of the Incense Burners' League) move from Sichuan to Shaanxi province.

Japan, 25 June. An imperial decree announces the expulsion of foreigners despite the advice of the *shogun*.

China, 29 June. Following a Moslem-Han Chinese massacre, in which thousands are killed, Moslems attack the city of Xi'an (*Shaanxi*).

Japan, 14 September. A merchant by the name of Richardson is killed in a *samurai* attack on a party of Britons in Yokohama.

USA, 22 September. In a deliberate attempt to cause social chaos in the rebellious southern states, President Abraham Lincoln proclaims the freedom of slaves in the confederate states as from 1 January 1863.

Greece, 26 October. King Otto is deposed and returns to his native Bavaria.

Indiana, 4 November. Richard Gatling patents a gun that fires hundreds of rounds a minute by using a cluster of rotating barrels.

Blood and iron – the ultimate arbiters

Berlin, 24 September

Otto von Bismarck, the *junker's* son from Brandenburg, has become minister-president of Prussia with the task of rescuing the king from his quarrel with the liberal majority in the House of Deputies. The deputies rejected a bill put forward by King William to expand the army; when the king persisted, they threw out the budget.

Bismarck's solution is to tell the deputies that he does not need their vote in order to continue collecting taxes. The deputies strongly disagree, but there seems to be nothing that they can do about it – particularly since Bismarck has accused them of being wealthy aristocrats not representative of the people.

When he addressed the deputies' budget commission he largely disregarded finance and concentrated on foreign affairs. Speaking as the former Prussian envoy to the assembly of German states at Frankfurt, he said: "Germans do not look at Prussia's liberalism but at her power. Prussia must keep her power together for the auspicious moment. The great questions of the age are not settled by speeches and majority votes, but by iron and blood."

Bismarck: the "Iron Chancellor".

A Chinese girl seated looking out of a window, by Lam Qua, who was trained in western painting styles by the Irish artist, George Chinnery, in China, lived in Hong Kong, and made his living selling Chinese scenes.

Les Miserables is a big hit in Paris

Paris, 30 June

The latest novel by Victor Hugo, published in Paris today, is an epic story of tortured conscience and remorse. Critics suggest that *Les Miserables* will be one of the author's major successes. In this densely plotted detective story, Jean Viljean, a thief dodging the police, moves to a small town, changes his name and reforms. He flourishes and becomes the mayor. Then he learns that a prisoner is on trial at the local assizes as the wanted criminal Viljean. He confesses after an anguished struggle with his conscience. Imprisoned, he escapes and is presumed dead. *Les Miserables* shows a huge range of genius.

Hugo: author and revolutionary.

Steeled for speed

Liverpool, England

Ships are increasingly benefitting from the latest technology which enables thin steel plates to be used in their design and manufacture. The first such vessel, a small paddle steamer, is now being built here; it is claimed that it will set new speed records when it goes into service next year. The *Banshee* is a 189-foot-long, 27-foot beam craft built by a Liverpool firm to ply between Dublin and North Wales, although its owners have not ruled out a trans-Atlantic voyage for their 16-knot steamer. Its 350-horsepower engine is being built by the Greenwich firm of John Penn.

French march on Mexico City is halted

A Mexican cattle herdsman: tough, independent and willing to fight.

Mexico, 5 May
Mexican troops led by General Ignacio Zaragoza have won a significant victory over invading French forces at Puebla. The French, under General Charles Latrille, had expected an easy, if not an unopposed, march from the coast to Mexico City. Their hopes have been severely confounded.

Far from the special *Te Deum* which Latrille had promised his troops that a grateful clergy would offer, the French were met at Puebla with a stern defence. Attacking recklessly, they used up half their ammunition within two hours. Zaragoza commanded his troops with a mix of caution and audacity and the French assault was repulsed with great success.

The day's decisive moment came when the youthful Brigadier-General Porfirio Diaz inspired his men to fight off a determined attack on the right flank.

US immigrants find haven of opportunity

The new railways are bringing thousands of hopeful immigrants out west.

New York City
Despite the civil war, great waves of immigrants are continuing to arrive in the United States. With the burgeoning steamship and railway companies in cut-throat competition for trade, it is possible today to get from Liverpool to New York and Chicago for as little as $35. "Agents", armed with enticingly adjectival pamphlets, are scouring Europe for potential customers.

The great bulk of newcomers are from the British Isles, many from the north of England and Scotland finding ready employment in the prospering armament factories in the north. With landlords "consolidating" small farms in Ireland and memories of the potato famine still fresh in their minds, it is the Irish who make up almost 80 per cent of immigrants.

For many, the lure is the fertile farm country of the west, and the Homestead Act, passed this year, offers every head of a family a 160-acre farm free of charge.

Death toll mounts in US

Union troops storming Confederate positions at the battle of Antietam.

Fredericksburg, 13 December
This once-pleasant town in Virginia, with its wide, tree-lined streets and white "colonial" houses is a smouldering ruin tonight after a day-long battle in which union troops failed to take a strategically important – though impregnable – ridge, Marye's Heights. Watching the bloody repulse of the doomed frontal attack by General Burnside's northern army, General Robert E Lee told an aide: "It is well that war is so terrible – we should grow too fond of it."

No-one can be fond of this war which is taking a terrible toll of human life as north and south are locked in mortal combat. At the end of it all, the battle of Marye's Heights may not prove to be significant; but it typifies the difference in military style between commanders. Heavily outnumbered, Lee, a cavalryman, relies on the manouvrability of his armies and his own capacity for quick thinking in battle. Union commanders like Burnside and Ulysses S Grant look to superior fire-power and text-book outflanking movements.

The casualty lists are horrific. In the battle of Antietam in September, no fewer than 23,500 soldiers were killed in one day of fighting in Maryland.

Garibaldi's men march to conquer Rome

Calabria, 28 August
Garibaldi has landed here in southern Italy with an army which he hopes will march to take over the papal states. He still dreams of establishing Rome as the capital of the new united Italy. Pope Pius IX is equally determined to stop him. He has refused to recognise the new Italian state and ordered Catholics not to vote in the parliamentary elections. King Victor Emmanuel has privately encouraged Garibaldi, but it is doubtful if he will help when it comes to the crunch. He depends on the support of France, and Napoleon III is unlikely to be prepared to risk challenging the authority of the pope.

Garibaldi: warrior and visionary.

1862 (1862-1863)

China, 1862. *Taiping* rebels approach Shanghai and come into conflict with Chinese regional armies, western-led forces such as the Ever-Victorious Army, and British and French regular forces garrisoned around Shanghai.

Virginia, 1862. The confederate army manufactures a balloon from silk dresses.

Austria, 1862. The musicologist Ludwig Kochel publishes a chronological catalogue of the musical works of Wolfgang Amadeus Mozart.

USA, 1862. John D Rockefeller invests $4,000 in his first oil refinery.

London, 1862. The Albert Memorial is designed by Gilbert Scott to be placed opposite the Royal Albert Hall, which is now being built.

Red Sea, 1862. As a response to the British presence in Aden, Napoleon III purchases Obock on the African coast of the Gulf of Aden.

France, 1862. Gustave Flaubert publishes *Salammbo*, an exotic tale somewhat buried in historical detail.

Nevada, 1862. Samuel Clemens becomes a reporter, using the pen name, "Mark Twain".

Paris, 1862. The actress Sarah Bernhardt makes her debut as Iphigenie with the Comedie Francaise.

Washington, DC, 1 January 1863. President Abraham Lincoln signs the Emancipation Act, proclaiming all slaves in the confederate states free.

Egypt, 30 January 1863. Ismail succeeds Said as khedive of Egypt.

Poland, February 1863. Polish nationalists rise up in revolt against Russian rule. The rebellion was prompted by a new law conscripting almost the entire young population of Poland.

Prussia, 8 February 1863. In order to combat the revolt in Poland, the Prussian prime minister, Otto von Bismarck, signs the convention of Alvensleben with Russia, which makes provision for reciprocal military assistance against the rebels.

Washington, DC, 3 March 1863. President Lincoln signs the Conscription Act, compelling US citizens to report for duty in the civil war, or pay $300. Thus he hopes to bolster the troops and top up the coffers.

Kansas, 3 March 1863. Congress provides for the forcible removal of all Indians from the state of Kansas.

China, 25 March 1863. Charles George Gordon takes over command of the Ever-Victorious Army following the death of F T Ward last September in battle near Shanghai with *Taiping* rebels.

Denmark, 30 March 1863. King Frederick VII separates Schleswig from Holstein and incorporates it into his states.

Greece, 30 March 1863. William, the prince of Denmark, is recognised as king of Greece.

Virginia, 10 May 1863. The confederate General Thomas Jonathan "Stonewall" Jackson, dies of wounds received in battle at Chancellorsville four days ago.

Mexico, May 1863. Mexican troops led by Jesus Gonzalez Ortega surrender Puebla after two months of resistance against French forces. Reinforcements have arrived from France since the Mexican victory in Puebla in 1861.

New Zealand, May 1863. Fighting between Maoris and British settlers breaks out in Taranaki. Conflict erupted in 1859 over a controversial land purchase and the 1861 truce has failed to maintain peace.

France, 1863. Alphonse Beau de Rochas, an engineer, perfects the theory of the four-stroke combustion engine.

Uganda, 1863. J H Speke and J Grant establish that the source of the river Nile is Lake Victoria.

Germany, 1863. The first socialist organisation – the German General Workers' Association – is formed under the influence of Ferdinand Lassalle who worked with Marx during the 1848-9 revolution trying to launch socialism in the Rhineland.

Russia, 1863. In the continuing programme of westernisation undertaken by Alexander II, academic freedom is restored to the universities and secondary education is made available to all who pass the necessary exams.

Britain, 1863. The scientist Thomas Andrews discovers a technique for liquefying gases.

India, 1863. Satyendra Nath Tagore is the first Indian to enter the Indian Civil Service.

Britain, 1863. The Football Association outlaws handling the ball, thus distinguishing soccer from rugby.

West Africa, 1863. The French establish a protectorate over the kingdom of Porto Novo in Dahomey.

Sierra Leone, 1863. The first elections to the legislative council are held.

America's slaves win their freedom

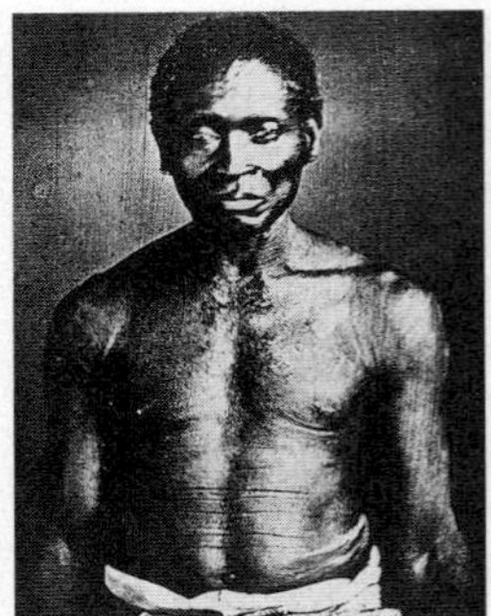
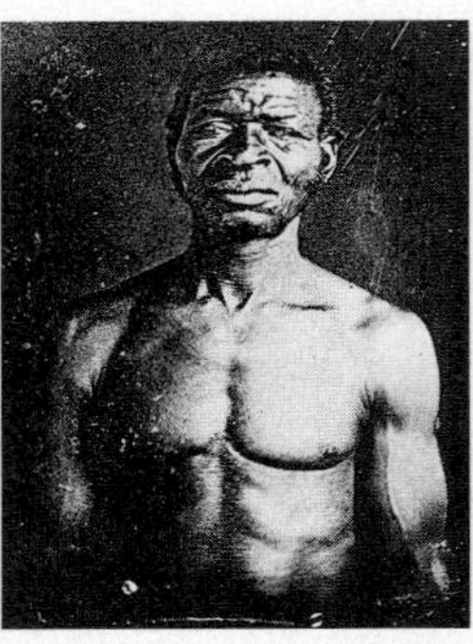
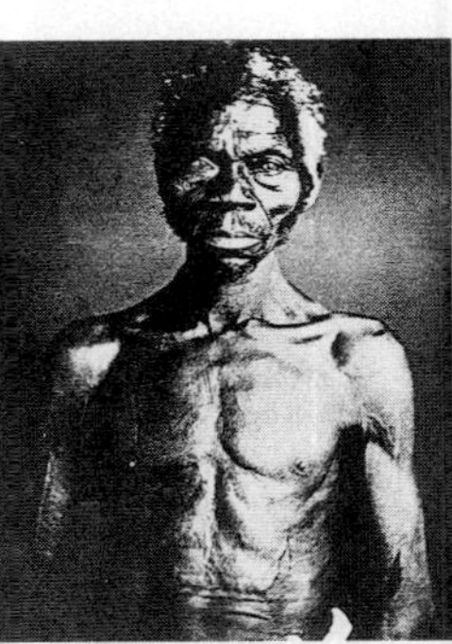

Three faces of slavery: an unknown slave; Renty (born in the Congo); and Jack (who was a slave driver from Guinea); all three from South Carolina.

Washington, 1 January 1863
Huge crowds of freed slaves and joyful abolitionists besieged newspaper offices as they awaited copies of the Emancipation Proclamation – freeing all slaves in the confederate states – which was signed today by President Lincoln. The proclamation honours a pledge made by the president last year. As free Negroes filled churches and held candle-lit vigils throughout the north, Lincoln said: "The old south must be destroyed and replaced by new propositions and ideas." The proclamation issue has dominated Lincoln's re-election campaign, with northern Democrats claiming that "two or three million semi-savages" would overrun the north. Already, two all-Negro army units are being formed.

Explorer crosses Australia, south to north

A township sends off an earlier expedition under Captain Sturt in 1844.

Melbourne, November 1862
A lone man, John King, has come from the outback with a harrowing tale. One of a party led by Robert O'Hara Burke and W J Wills that set out across Australia from south to north in August 1860, he is the only survivor.

Burke was impatient and overconfident. He set out with Wills, King, a man called Grey and a train of Afghani camels, not waiting for his baggage. They crossed the Great Dividing Range and followed the Flinders river to the Gulf of Carpentaria, which they reached in February 1861. The return was terrible; Grey died, and the surviving three arrived at their base camp at Cooper's Creek nearly dead. Brahe, a member of the expedition who had stayed four months at base, had left the camp only seven hours earlier.

The three trekked on across the Stoney Desert, making for Mount Hopeless, 150 miles away. Soon Wills and Burke were dead. King only lived to tell the tale because he was rescued by Aborigines.

Quality of happiness counts, says Mill

London, 1862
England's most celebrated philosopher, John Stuart Mill, was brought up by his father, James Mill, on Jeremy Bentham's principle that "the greatest happiness of the greatest number" should govern human affairs and legislation and refined it in *Utilitarianism*, published last year. Bentham did not distinguish between qualities of pleasure; Mill states: "It is better to be a human being dissatisfied than a pig satisfied. And better to be Socrates dissatisfied than a fool satisfied." He argues that general rules of conduct should have priority over single acts; for example, keeping promises or telling the truth, even if at times it seems better not to.

Mill learnt Greek from the age of three, logic at 12 and political economy at 13. He published his *System of Logic*, treating inductive reasoning, in 1843 and his *Principles of Political Economy* in 1848. *On Liberty* followed in 1859.

Krupp uses new process for steelmaking

England, 1862
It is the American William Kelly who is credited with the technique of making steel by blowing air through or over the hot metal. But the English inventor Henry Bessemer is the first to find a method of cheap mass-production.

The Bessemer furnace or converter rapidly produces purified ingots – hardened by the right amount of carbon – in great quantity for use in forging or rolling mills. World steel production is soaring. Among the customers for the Bessemer process is the German industrialist Alfred Krupp who is rolling massive ingots into armoured plate for naval vessels. Krupp, who built up his father's small iron forge into one of the biggest foundry in Europe, has been manufacturing armaments since 1847. Other applications include railway lines and locomotives and structural engineering.

Krupp's enormous output is making him a steel magnate of awesome proportions.

Outraged critics damn erotic French art

Paris, 1863
Edouard Manet's painting, *Dejeuner sur l'Herbe*, outraged the crowds at the Salon des Refuses after it was rejected by the Salon itself. People jeered at the indecency of a nude woman picnicking casually with men fully clothed in modern dress. "This is a young man's practical joke and not worth exhibiting ... Unfortunately the nude hasn't a decent figure and one cannot think of anything uglier than the man who has not even taken his cap off." Jean-Auguste Ingres, the *doyen* of French classical painters, who is 83, is showing nudity on a far more lavish scale in his erotic fantasy, *The Turkish Bath* – indolent females abandoned to the music and incense of the bathhouse. This is the final version of a painting done for a Turkish count whose wife disliked it.

Eugene Delacroix, who died on 13 August, was Ingres' rival but shared his taste for the exotic. On a visit to North Africa he painted *Algerian Women* reclining in a harem.

Pain and pleasure: Delacroix's fantasy of the erotic and exotic Orient, which tells far more about the European psyche than about the Orient.

Profusion and pleasure: Ingres' Turkish bath, an Oriental fantasy.

Pastoralism and pleasure: Edouard Manet's Dejeuner sur l'Herbe, the picture that outraged Paris, and brought the erotic home.

1863 (1863-1864)

Virginia, 3 June 1863. Setting out with 75,000 confederate troops, General Robert E Lee begins a second attempt to invade the union states.

West Virginia, 20 June 1863. West Virginia is the 35th state to join the union.

Japan, 24 June 1863. After protracted negotiations, the government pays substantial indemnity for the murder of a British merchant last September and the threat of war is averted. But on the same day batteries in the Choshu domain near Shimonoseki open fire on a US ship.

Mississippi, 4 July 1863. Confederate forces under General Joseph Pemberton surrender unconditionally to federal troops which have besieged Vicksburg since May. Now that the union troops have control of this strategic town, the confederacy is effectively split in two.

Greece, 13 July 1863. Prince William of Denmark is recognised by Britain, France and Russia as King George of Greece.

Cambodia, 11 August 1863. The French establish a protectorate in Cambodia.

Japan, 15 August 1863. A British naval squadron bombards Kagoshima, the capital of the Satsuma domain, as punishment for the murder of Richardson last September.

Germany, 1 September 1863. A meeting of German princes in Frankfurt aimed at reforming the German Confederation breaks up following Prussia's refusal to co-operate.

Germany, 1 October 1863. The German *diet* decides to take federal action against Denmark following the Danish annexation of Schleswig earlier this year.

Washington, DC, 3 October 1863. President Lincoln declares the last Thursday in November a national holiday of thanksgiving.

France, 18 October 1863. A photographer by the name of Nadar takes the first aerial photographs from his balloon *The Giant*. But the trip ends in mishap near Hanover, with Nadar breaking a leg.

Ionian Sea, 14 November 1863. Britain cedes the Ionian Islands to Greece.

Denmark, 15 November 1863. Following the death of Frederick VII, who left no issue, Christian IX comes to the throne.

France, 23 November 1863. Louis Thiers forms a Third Party in opposition to Napoleon III.

China, November 1863. Li Hongzhang's Huai army attacks the *Taiping* stronghold of Suzhou, backed by General Gordon's Ever-Victorious Army.

China, 6 December 1863. Taiping leaders defending Suzhou (*Jiangsu*) handed the city over to the Qing military commander Cheng Xueqi two days ago on the understanding that they would be given high military commissions in the Qing army. But today Li Hongzhang and Cheng have had them executed instead. In view of this treachery, Gordon threatens to leave the Ever-Victorious Army.

Britain, 23 December 1863. William Makepeace Thackeray dies aged 52. The author of *Vanity Fair*, *Henry Esmond* and many other works, he was the country's most popular novelist after Charles Dickens.

Germany, 24 December 1863. Following the Danish annexation of Schleswig earlier this year, Saxon and Hanoverian forces move into Holstein.

France, 1863. The French theologian and philosopher Ernest Renan publishes his *Life of Jesus* in which he treats his subject as an ordinary man and scandalises the devout.

Russia, 13 January 1864. A law is passed which provides for the institution of *zemstvos* – regional assemblies elected by three bodies of electors the landowners, town-dwellers and the peasants.

China, January 1864. As part of a programme of military modernisation, Li Hongzhang orders the Scotsman S Halliday Macartney to purchase mechanical equipment for the Suzhou arsenal.

Virginia, 4 April 1864. Lieutenant-General Ulysses S Grant receives his commission to command the federal troops, and plans a consolidated strike against confederate troops in a bid to end the fighting.

Colorado, 1864. The gold rush dries up as many lodes run out.

Geneva, 1864. A multilateral agreement on the Red Cross – a voluntary relief society dedicated to the care of those wounded in war – is signed at the Geneva convention. This is largely the work of Henri Dunant, a Swiss humanitarian who organised emergency aid for French and Austrian wounded soldiers at the battle of Solferino in June 1859.

France, 1864. The engineer Pierre Martin perfects William Siemens' furnace – the new open-hearth process. He re-uses heat from the gases generated in the furnace to weld steel.

Underground railway opens in London

London, 10 January 1863

After three years of painstaking work, disturbing the growing network of sewers and gas mains, London now has the world's first underground railway. Aimed at relieving the city's congested roads, the line runs from Paddington to Farringdon Street. There are five intermediate stations, with Euston and King's Cross both being served.

The Metropolitan Railway was built by a method called "cut and cover". First, a trench was dug, often in an existing street then the side walls and arched roof were put into place. With the outside filled in, the street could be paved over once again.

Ordinary steam locomotives are being used. The railway company is trying to dispel public fears about breathing in sulphurous fumes by claiming that they are beneficial. There is, however, concern for the foundations of nearby houses.

The first underground passengers going to a banquet to celebrate the opening.

Mercenaries defeat the Chinese rebels

Soochow, December 1863

The Ever-Victorious Army, whipped into fighting shape by Major "Chinese" Gordon, has been in the vanguard of Viceroy Li Hongzhang's offensive, which has just led to the capture of this important city from the Taipings.

Originally commanded by an American adventurer, Fred Ward, who was killed in a reckless charge, the Ever-Victorious was taken over by another American, Burgevine, who, after a quarrel over money, deserted to the Taipings. In 1863 he later surrendered to the Imperial army and was expelled from China.

Major Gordon, authorised by the British Army to take service with the Chinese, then took command and turned it from an ill-disciplined mercenary force into a well-trained army of conscripts. At last living up to its name, it has won a series of victories against the Taipings. Viceroy Li thinks highly of Gordon: "What a sight to see this splendid Englishman fight."

New equations held to be "great guns"

London, 1863

In a direct line of descent from Faraday, Ampere and Thomson comes the brilliant work of James Clerk Maxwell. Maxwell's theory is that electric and magnetic fields are both aspects of one and the same force – electromagnetism. His superb mathematical equations take us one convincing step nearer to a unification of all the forces in nature. Maxwell himself holds them to be "great guns".

Important, too, are Maxwell's predictions that there are probably other forms of electromagnetic radiation at other wavelengths as yet undetected.

Confederates routed at Gettysburg

Lee: a compassionate commander.

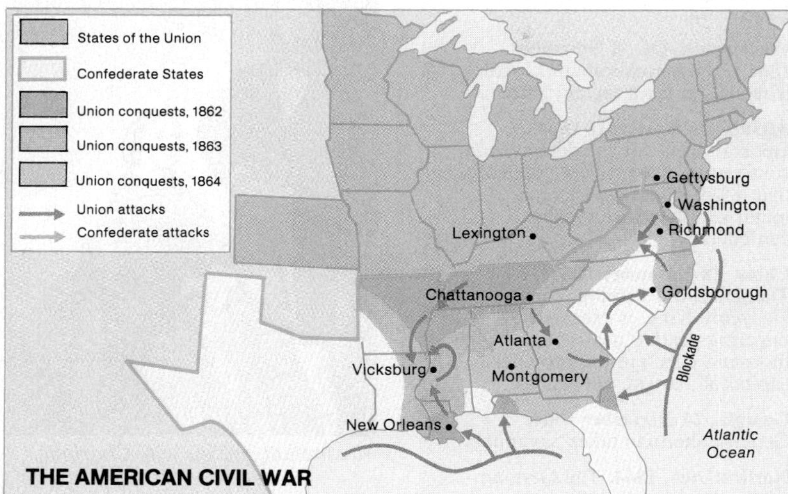

Gettysburg, Penn., 3 July 1863
With battle-flags flying and the sun glinting on thousands of bayonets and swords, a mile-long battle line of confederate troops advanced over open terrain – to be torn to shreds by union shells and bullets. A few rebel soldiers reached the union lines only to be killed or captured. As survivors struggled back, their general, Robert E Lee kept repeating: "It's all my fault."

The bloodiest battle so far in this civil war is over and more than 40,000 bodies litter the cornfields and orchards around this small Pennsylvania township. The battle reached its crescendo today as both sides fought a massive artillery duel which preceded Lee's attack. The union army has finally scored a major victory against General Lee whose superior tactics with inferior numbers have tormented the north since the war started.

Relying heavily on his tried and trusted colleague, General Thomas "Stonewall" Jackson – killed at the battle of Chancellorsville in May – Lee had won several critical engagements against the union. As Jackson succeeded in pinning down a superior force in the Shenandoah valley, Lee's army held back an attempt to capture the confederate capital, Richmond, and later forced the union to retreat back to Washington at the battle of Bull Run. More success followed at Fredericksburg, where the northern commander was forced to withdraw.

Lee's only real mistake was to invade Pennsylvania. The result was today's awesome debacle.

Union soldiers pose for the camera.

Government by and for the people, US president pledges

Gettysburg, 20 November 1863
Fifteen thousand people gathered on the site of the battlefield today to dedicate a cemetery for the nation's war dead today. They heard a thunderous two-hour oration by the scholar and lecturer Edward Everett, but, surprisingly, few of them caught many of the words spoken by President Lincoln who followed. And yet the *Chicago Tribune* – whose reporter took a shorthand note – has said that Lincoln's short address will "live among the annals of man".

The president reminded his audience of the very nature of this country. "Four score and seven years ago, our fathers brought forth upon this continent a new nation, conceived in liberty and dedicated to the proposition that all men are created equal," he began. "Now we are engaged in a great civil war, testing whether that nation – or any nation so conceived and so dedicated – can long endure."

In his high-pitched voice, Lincoln told the crowd "that the dead shall not have died in vain", and that "this Nation under God shall have a new birth of freedom and that government of the people, by the people and for the people shall not perish from the earth".

Leader of "superior" Moslem sect dies

Timbuktu, West Africa, 1864
Al-Hajj Umar, the warrior and religious leader, has been killed attempting to break out of Hamdullahi in Massina where he was besieged by Fulani and Tuareg rebels. He was 70 years old.

Umar, an imposing man of magnetic personality, was a fervent supporter of the Tijanniya sect of Sufism which claimed superiority over all other Moslems and promised its followers favoured treatment on the Day of Judgement. He was imprisoned for his beliefs and exiled from a number of West African states, but acquired guns and warriors and grew powerful enough to launch a *jihad* (holy war) in which he fought the French and established the *Caliphate* of Tukolor.

Al-Hajj Umar comes from a line of Islamic reformers who have swept out of the Sahara, and established empires dedicated to reasserting the Koran, which have rarely lasted beyond the lifetime of the founder.

Four nations shell Japan back into world

Japan, September 1864
After bombarding Japanese defences on the Straits of Shimonoseki and Kagoshima, the navies of four countries have opened up Japan to foreign trade. The navies, from Britain, France, Holland and the USA, only acted after the emperor, against the advice of his *shogun* (chief minister), informed western diplomats that Japan would be reverting to her traditional policy of isolation. They refused to discuss the idea. After a day's bombardment, marines landed and spiked Japan's shore guns. On both land and sea Japanese tactics and equipment proved inadequate, and Japanese modernists are already urging Japan to learn from westerners, and beat them at their own game.

British, French and Dutch "barbarians" arrive at Yokohama.

1864 (1864-1865)

Mexico, 10 April 1864. The Austrian Archduke Maximilian is appointed emperor of Mexico with the backing of the French army.

USA, 19 May 1864. Nathaniel Hawthorne, the leading American novelist and short story writer, dies aged 59. His most famous work is *The Scarlet Letter*, telling the tragic tale of a convicted adulteress forced to wear a symbol of her sin.

China, 31 May 1864. The Ever-Victorious Army, composed of foreign-trained soldiers fighting against the *Taiping* rebels, is disbanded.

China, 1 June 1864. The Taiping ruler and self-styled "younger brother of Jesus", Hong Xiuquan, kills himself.

China, 3 June 1864. A Moslem rebellion breaks out at Kucha, in Chinese Turkestan.

Washington, DC, 7 June 1864. The Republicans nominate President Lincoln for a second term.

China, 15 July 1864. A Moslem rebellion breaks out at Urumchi, in Chinese Turkestan, following that which erupted last month at Kucha.

China, 19 July 1864. Nanjing has fallen to Hunan (imperial) forces which mounted a fierce attack on the Taiping-held city 14 days ago. Some 100,000 Taipings either commit suicide or are killed by Qing troops. This marks the end of the Taiping rebellion.

Alabama, 5 August 1864. A federal fleet takes Mobile Bay for the union, despite the fact that the harbour is mined.

China, 7 August 1864. The Taiping commander Li Xiucheng is executed in Nanjing, aged 41, having written his own account of the Taiping rebellion for the imperial leader Zeng Guofan.

Italy, 15 September 1864. The French government signs a convention with the Italian minister Minghetti, planning the departure of French troops from Rome between now and 1866, the date by which the pope should have formed an army. The king of Italy, Victor Emmanuel II, undertakes not to interfere and to move the capital from Turin to Florence.

Spain, September 1864. The regent Queen Maria Christina, returns to Spain, after ten years in exile.

Virginia, 22 October 1864. Confederate troops are swept out of the Shenandoah valley.

China, 25 October 1864. Hong Tianguifu, the Taiping leader known as the Young Heavenly King, who escaped from Nanjing when it fell to imperial forces, is captured at Shicheng, Jiangxi.

Vienna, 30 October 1864. By the peace of Vienna, Denmark gives up Schleswig, Holstein and Lauenburg.

Washington, DC, 8 November 1864. President Abraham Lincoln is re-elected for a second term.

Atlanta, 16 November 1864. General Sherman wreaks havoc in confederate Atlanta, determined that it will no longer serve as a major supply centre for the confederacy.

China, 18 November 1864. Hong Tianguifu, the Taiping Young Heavenly King, is executed by lingering death ("death of a thousand cuts") in the provincial capital of Jiangxi. He was 15.

Georgia, 24 December 1864. General Sherman takes Savannah.

North Africa, 1864. The German soldier Gerhard Rohlfs explores the central Sahara.

Britain, 1864. John Henry Newman writes an *Apologia pro Vita Sua*, defending his conversion to the Church of Rome.

Britain, 1864. The poet Alfred Lord Tennyson publishes *Enoch Arden*.

Zambia, 1864. The Lozi people of the upper Zambezi flood-plain revolt against the rule of the Kololo – migrants from the south.

Nigeria, 1864. Ex-slave Samuel Crowther becomes the first black African Anglican bishop of the Niger river area.

China, January 1865. Buzurg Khan – a descendant of a former ruling house of Kashgar – Ya'qub Beg, his chief of staff, and other Moslems enter Chinese Turkestan from Kokand. Buzurg Khan declares himself king of Kashgar.

China, January 1865. The Chinese government borrows £1,430,000 from Britain, beginning its national debt.

North Carolina, 22 February 1865. Wilmington, the last open confederate port, falls to union forces.

Washington, DC, 2 March 1865. President Lincoln rejects the confederate General Lee's plea for peace talks, demanding unconditional surrender.

China, March 1865. Tuoming declares himself "pure and true king" at Urumchi.

Ethiopia, 1865. The ambitious Christian Emperor Tewodros (Theodore) II, who came to the throne in 1855 after overthrowing the prince of Tigre, fails to capture the Amharic state of Shoa of King Menelik II.

Archduke crowned Mexico's king

Maximilian and his wife Charlotte.

Mexico, 10 April 1864

Maximilian, the archduke of Austria and brother of the Emperor Franz Josef, has been appointed emperor of Mexico. The move comes as part of France's attempt to establish a Catholic empire in the country and has been inspired by the ambitions of Napoleon III.

Maximilian was formerly the governor of Lombardy-Venetia, but was removed from office in 1859, blamed for Austria's failure to retain Lombardy against a Piedmontese-French attack. Since then he has lived in his castle at Trieste, busying himself with his hobby, botany.

Shy mathematician invents a wonderland

Oxford, 1865

Charles Lutwidge Dodgson, a brilliant if retiring lecturer in mathematics at Christ Church, Oxford, writing under the pseudonym "Lewis Carroll", has produced a new children's book which promises to delight every reader.

Alice's Adventures in Wonderland originated during a boat trip down the river Thames three years ago. To amuse the three Liddell children, the daughters of the Dean of Christ Church, Dodgson created "Alice", named for ten-year-old Alice Liddell, who so enjoyed the tale that she persuaded Dodgson to write it down. Now the shy don has published it as a book.

Alice and Humpty Dumpty.

Reactionary pope attacks liberal beliefs

Pope Pius IX: keeping rationalism, pantheism and liberalism at bay.

Rome, 8 December 1864

Pope Pius IX today launched a two-pronged attack on liberal and radical opinions which is quite astonishing in its comprehensive character. First there is the encyclical *Quanta Cura*, an assertion of the distinction between true religion and false beliefs and a condemnation of socialism and communism. Then there is the *Syllabus Errorum*, or Syllabus of Errors.

The latter contains no fewer than 80 propositions. It condemns pantheism, naturalism and rationalism. It condemns those who deny the miracles. It condemns divorce and any interference in marriage by civil magistrates.

Southern city is destroyed in a firestorm

Union troops outside Petersburg, where they were thrown back last June.

Atlanta, Georgia, 15 Nov 1864
Puffing his ever-present cigar, General William Sherman, the eccentric union commander, watched tonight as his troops turned this city into an inferno. Determined to prevent Atlanta's further use as a confederate supply base, Sherman had tents, wagons and bedding piled up at the local railroad depot and put a torch to them. A firestorm ensued, destroying hotels, theatres, stores, fire stations and the local jail. Little of Atlanta remains.

It took five months of bitter fighting for Sherman to take Atlanta. He wasted no time in ordering the residents to evacuate the city. When civic leaders protested, he told them: "You might as well appeal against the thunderstorm as against the terrible hardships of war."

Though Sherman is idolised by his troops, his ruthlessness has made him unpopular even in the north, where newspapers have questioned his sanity. He is a brilliant tactician, however, and highly regarded by President Lincoln.

Sherman: authoritarian and cruel.

Marx sets up international socialist club

London, 28 September 1864
The First International Workingmen's Association has been established by Karl Marx with the aim of coordinating the efforts of workers in various countries to achieve socialism.

The formation of the First International was prompted by two French delegates who wanted to marshal support for the Polish rebels. Many of the leading figures are foreign exiles settled in London, including Mikhail Bakunin, the Russian revolutionary anarchist, who does not share the pure socialist ideals of Marx and Engels.

Although conservatives are alarmed, the movement does not involve English trade unionists in any active commitment other than general sympathy with the socialist cause. Union officials take little part in meetings and, although there has been local terrorism, the larger associations have specifically repudiated the use of violent or criminal methods.

Suicide of mystic rebel

Nanjing, June 1864
Hong Xiuquan, "heavenly king" of the Taiping rebels, at last realising that defeat was inevitable, has poisoned himself by eating gold leaf. He has been buried in the garden of his palace, and the trees above his grave are macabrely decorated with the bodies of his wives who have hanged themselves in grief at his death.

With death and disaster all around him, he retreated into unreality. He told his starving people they should eat "sweet dew" and, as his defeated troops retreated, he occupied himself with issuing decrees prescribing the method of execution to be imposed on those who did not use the word "heavenly" in documents. When the "loyal king" urged him to flee Nanjing, the "heavenly capital", he replied that he had nothing to fear because he was "the sole lord of ten thousand nations". When at last reality intruded he said that he had failed his heavenly Father and his brother, Jesus Christ, and swallowed his golden poison. This was the man who came near to toppling the Manchus from the throne of China, whose movement has maintained a separate kingdom for 15 years.

Meanwhile, the "loyal king", Li Xiucheng, is fighting on, desperately trying to drive the imperial forces from the walls of Nanjing. But miners are already burrowing under those walls. The end is very near, and a great slaughter is feared when the city falls.

Prussia beats Denmark in a land dispute

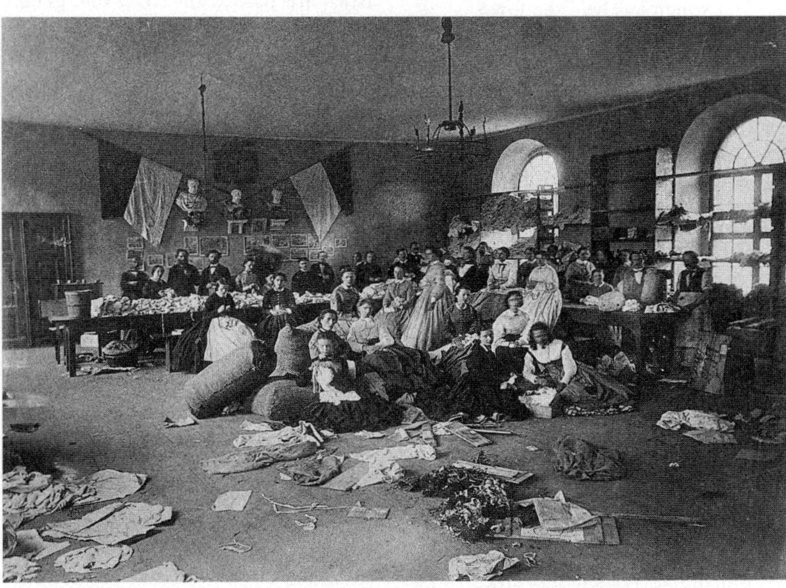
Gearing Prussia for total war: officers' wives making bandages.

Berlin, August 1864
Bismarck has had his first war. The duchies of Schleswig and Holstein are largely German, though they have been ruled since the Middle Ages by the king of Denmark as duke. On the death of the Danish king, a German, Frederick, the prince of Augustenburg, laid claim to the duchies and won the support of Prussia and the German states.

The dispute found the European powers in disarray. Russia was preoccupied with a Polish uprising. Napoleon III was fobbed off with vague promises of rearranging European frontiers in France's favour, Austria was coaxed into supporting a Prussian war against Denmark, and in Britain Palmerston was unable to persuade parliament to take a tough stand.

Bismarck seized his opportunity, sent in Prussian troops, which easily defeated Denmark, and forced the new King Christian to renounce his claim to the duchies. Bismarck's successful war has been applauded by many of his liberal critics in the House of Deputies.

1865 ⇒

USA, 3 March. The Bureau of Freed Slaves is created to offer education, medical care and financial assistance to former slaves.

Virginia, 5 April. Union troops leave the confederate capital, Richmond, a smouldering ruin.

Virginia, 9 April. The confederate General Robert E Lee surrenders.

Washington, DC, 15 April. President Lincoln is killed by an assassin's bullet.

Virginia, 27 April. John Wilkes Booth, the accused assassin of President Lincoln, is shot dead.

Illinois, 4 May. The president is buried in Springfield, where he married and started his legal career.

Virginia, 22 May. Jefferson Davis, the former president of the defeated confederacy, is imprisoned, having been discovered disguised as a woman.

China, 4 July. Qing forces take Qianxi from the White Signal sect which has held the town since 1859.

Washington, DC, 8 July. Four of the conspirators convicted of President Lincoln's assassination are hanged today. Another three will serve life prison sentences.

China, 7 August. In the continuing Moslem rebellion in Chinese Turkestan, Ya'qub Beg captures the oasis towns of Kucha and Aksu and takes the ruler Burhanuddin prisoner.

Germany, 14 August. A convention signed at Gastein between Prussia and Austria allots Schleswig to Prussia and Holstein to Austria.

New Zealand, 2 September. Fighting stops between the British settlers and the *Kingitanga* – a Maori unity movement seeking to prevent individual chiefs selling land.

China, 7 September. Ya'qub Beg's rebel Moslem forces capture Kashgar, slaughtering some 4,000 Han Chinese. Ya'qub assumes the leadership of the Moslem rebellion in the Kashgar area.

Ireland, 15 September. The English authorities arrest *Fenian* leaders who are preparing an uprising.

London. William Booth founds a militarist Christian evangelist movement known as the Christian Revival Association.

Undertakers find doctor was a woman

London, 25 July

Who would have thought that Dr James Barry, a senior inspector-general and a very superior sort of man, would turn out to be a woman?

After her death this morning undertakers discovered Barry's 70-year-old female form hidden under copious nightclothes and blankets. It is thought that Barry – with her red hair and high cheekbones – was the granddaughter of a Scottish earl. It was her love for a military surgeon that made her join the army in male disguise – and the life certainly suited her.

She spent 45 years, from the age of 18, travelling the world and working her way up through the medical ranks, ending as a skilled physician at the top of her profession.

Austrian abbot discovers heredity laws

Austria

Watching an Austrian monk pottering in his monastery garden, one would hardly think that important scientific discoveries might be afoot. Gregor Mendel is no ordinary monk, however. He is a skilled and intelligent botanist and plant breeder who has been thinking hard about the way in which characteristics are passed on from one generation to another.

For his experiments he uses the humble garden pea. By crossbreeding different varieties, he can trace in the ensuing hybrids features such as height, colour, shape, flower position and pod forms.

From the data gleaned through these observations, Mendel has formulated certain laws governing patterns of inheritance, using statistical methods. Now this popular, devout man has given mathematical form to the shape of inheritance. And, perhaps, not only in plants.

Gregor Mendel, scientific monk.

When put to the test Mendelism may well be applicable to all biological organisms – humans included. So far, however, the scientific community wants nothing to do with Mendel's ideas.

British artist scales "unclimbable" peak

Whymper's party descend the peak.

Milan, Italy

A British party led by Edward Whymper, an artist, has conquered the Matterhorn, the mountain that towers 14,780 feet over Switzerland and Italy. The triumph was short-lived – four members fell to their deaths on the way down.

An 1861 entry in a hotel register reads "Edward Whymper – *en route* for the Matterhorn". He came to the Alps to sketch the scenery before developing an obsession with the peak which has defeated him on seven attempts. As the British party searches for its dead, a rival Italian team is still making an ascent of the mountain which many thought unclimbable.

Unplayable opera is a great success

Wagner: his work as loved as hated.

Munich

Tristan und Isolde, an opera or "music drama" by Richard Wagner, has been given an enthusiastic premiere here – at the second attempt.

In Vienna the piece was abandoned as unplayable after 77 rehearsals. Its chromatic harmonies have been compared to "a perfumed fog shot through with lightning". Nietzsche said: "Wagner's art is diseased; he has made music sick."

The opera is based on Arthurian legend. Tristan, conveying Isolde to marry King Mark, falls in love with her on the voyage. He dies at their reunion and Isolde literally dies of love in the concluding *Liebestod*. Wagner is believed to have been inspired by his love for Mathilde Wesendonck, the wife of his patron.

Tristan and Isolde prepare to die.

Confederates surrender

The surrender of General Robert E Lee at the Appomattox Court House.

Appomattox, Virginia, 9 April
General Robert E Lee shook hands with his opponent, General Ulysses S Grant, in the courtroom here today and formally surrendered his exhausted confederate army to the federal commander-in-chief. The civil war, which set brother against brother in cruel, costly conflict and has taken more than half a million lives, is effectively over.

The contrast between the two generals could not have been more marked. Lee was resplendent in his full-dress uniform as he sat and waited for the victor who arrived in a rumpled tunic, his mud-spattered trousers tucked into muddy boots.

Lee and his 27,000 men had fought to the very end, trying to reach a railway which could take them south to unite with General Johnson in North Carolina. They were blocked by cavalry and infantry, and when Grant's well-fed army closed the trap, Lee sent a note asking for terms. Grant lived up to his nickname – gained in an earlier battle – of "Unconditional Surrender". Lee agreed, but told an *aide*: "I would rather die a thousand deaths."

Grant has allowed Lee's men to keep their small-arms and horses and to be paroled without punishment – on condition that they do not take up arms again against the north.

As Lee stood waiting for his horse, he struck his fist repeatedly into his palm in despair as federal troops began to hand out rations to the army he had just surrendered. The confederate soldiers were beaten and starving; they wept as their general rode away.

US president murdered

Washington, DC, 15 April
The president of the United States, Abraham Lincoln, died early today from an assassin's bullet, fired as he watched a play in a Washington theatre last night. His secretary of state, William Seward, is critically ill from stab wounds received in a separate incident. Tonight, as a nationwide hunt is under way for Lincoln's assassin, John Wilkes Booth, a failed actor, police and federal agents are investigating the possibility that the president was the victim of a confederate conspiracy seeking revenge.

Just after 10 pm Booth entered Box Seven of Ford's Theatre and shot the president in the back of the head with a single bullet. The audience was laughing; few heard the shot. Slashing at an army officer who rushed him, Booth jumped on to the stage and shouted: "*Sic semper tyrannis!* (Thus always to tyrants) – the South is avenged!" The president was carried to a cheap lodging house opposite the theatre, where a doctor said that he had been mortally wounded and could not possibly survive.

Before he went to watch the performance of *Our American Cousin* with Mrs Lincoln, the president told friends he had dreamt the previous night that he was moving with great rapidity towards a dark and undefined shore. It was a dream that he had dreamt on the eve of every major battle in the civil war. Earlier yesterday Booth, the son of a well-known actor, boasted in a bar that he would be the most famous man in America; as his victim lay mortally wounded, drifting rapidly towards that unknown shore, the US is preparing to mourn its 16th president.

Lincoln assassinated by John Wilkes Booth in Ford's Theatre, Washington.

Russian boundaries expand to the south

Central Asia
Russia's expansion southwards has taken another step forward this year with the occupation of the great city of Tashkent in Turkestan and the addition of new frontier lands to the Romanov domains.

The Russian conquests stretch about 700 miles from the Aral Sea in the west to the Kirghiz mountains in the east, and are mainly at the expense of Khokand, one of three states on the northern borders of Persia and Afghanistan. Russia's current thrust into central Asia began in around 1840, when its frontier was marked by the Ural river, 1,000 miles north of Tashkent. As well as hoping to expand their own influence, the Russians have been determined to counter British activity in the region, a resolve heightened since Russia's Crimean defeat. There are commercial motives, too: the civil war in America means that Turkestan is currently the only place from which Russian factories can obtain cotton.

Napoleon and Bismarck agree neutrality

Biarritz, France, 4 October
Bismarck has arrived at Biarritz to bathe in the invigorating waters of the Bay of Biscay – and to bamboozle Napoleon III into remaining neutral while Prussia goes to war with Austria over the Schleswig and Holstein duchies.

Just three months ago, Bismarck persuaded Austria to make a deal over the duchies: Austria would take over Holstein, with Prussia having Schleswig. The arrangement effectively isolated Austria because it was made behind the back of the German Assembly at Frankfurt.

Now Bismarck tells Napoleon that, if he stays neutral, Prussia will back his territorial ambitions; not with regard to German territory, of course, but to French-speaking parts of Belgium, perhaps. Nothing is being written down; they are statesmen and men of honour, surely. Napoleon's family are delighted with the wily Prussian. "A really great man," one observer says. "Full of *esprit*."

1865 (1865-1866)

China, 8 October 1865. The White Signal sect rebels take Guangshun and Dingfan (*Guizhou*).

Britain, 18 October 1865. Lord Palmerston dies.

Britain, October 1865. The practice of transporting criminals to Australia is abolished.

New Zealand, October 1865. Wellington is established as the capital of New Zealand.

Japan, November 1865. The *shogun*, Tyemochi, persuades the emperor to renew trading relations with the west.

Sweden, 7 December 1865. In a reform of the constitution, a two-chamber parliament is created, but the members will only be elected by ten per cent of the population.

Belgium, 10 December 1865. Leopold II succeeds his father Leopold.

Washington, DC, 18 December 1865. The 13th Amendment to the US Constitution abolishes slavery.

Hungary, December 1865. Austria incorporates Transylvania into Hungary.

Paris, 1865. Edouard Manet's painting *Olympia*, echoing Titian's Venus but showing a very worldly model in the same pose, causes a scandal at the Salon des Refuses where works rejected by the Salon of the Academy are exhibited.

Tennessee, 1865. A secret society is formed in Tennessee. Members, mostly Confederate veterans, ride at night in hooded white robes and there are fears that they intend to act against freed Negroes. However, the founders claim that the *Ku Klux Klan*, as it is known, is a harmless fraternity.

India, 1865. Bombay enjoys a cotton boom because of the US falling production during the civil war.

Paraguay, 1865. Under its ambitious dictator, President Francisco Solano Lopez, Paraguay is at war with a triple alliance composed of Brazil, Argentina and Uruguay following a dispute about Brazilian intervention in Uruguay last year.

Peru, 14 January 1866. Following last year's treaty ending the war with Spain, Peruvian resentment is such that General Mariano Ignacio Prado takes control and declares war once again.

Mexico, 12 February 1866. Invoking the Monroe Doctrine, (a US declaration warning European powers against further colonisation in the Americas) the USA calls for the withdrawal of French troops from Mexico.

Rumania, 24 February 1866. Wealthy landowners angered by land reforms overthrow their ruler, Prince Cuza. Bismarck and Napoleon III choose as his replacement Karl Friedrich, the cousin of the king of Prussia, who alters his name to Carol.

Chile, 31 March 1866. President Jose Joaquin Perez sides with Peru in the war against Spain.

New York City, 10 May 1866. At the first post-war meeting of the National Women's Rights Convention, a unanimous vote confirms the organisation of the American Equal Rights Association.

Egypt, 21 May 1866. The Ottoman sultan grants the right of primogeniture to Ismail of Egypt.

Germany, 8 June 1866. Prussia annexes Holstein, which came under Austrian rule by the convention of Gastein last year.

Austria, 12 June 1866. Austria signs a secret treaty with France as conflict with Prussia escalates.

Germany, 16 June 1866. Having declared the German Confederation dissolved two days ago, Prussia invades Saxony, Hanover and Hesse.

Italy, 20 June 1866. Prussia's ally, Italy, declares war on Austria.

Italy, 24 June 1866. The Austrian armies, led by Grand Duke Albert, defeat the Italian forces of Marquis Alfonso de la Marmora at the battle of Cuseozza.

Bohemia, 3 July 1866. Prussian troops defeat Austrians in Sadowa.

Austria, 4 July 1866. Austria cedes Venetia to Napoleon III.

Spain, 1866. General Juan Prim y Prats fails in his attempt to overthrow the government of Queen Isabella II.

Central Asia, 1866. The Russians continue the occupation of Chinese Turkestan (which began last year), and of Tashkent, the capital of the *khanate* of Kokand. They claim to be protecting themselves against the Moslem revolt in this area.

Rome, 1866. The Norwegian playwright Henrik Ibsen publishes *Brand*, an austerely puritan work.

England, 1866. Algernon Charles Swinburne publishes the first volume of *Poems and Ballads*.

Bohemia, 1866. The Bohemian composer Bedrich Smetana composes a new opera, *The Bartered Bride*.

Japan, 1866. Fukuzawa Yukichi publishes *Conditions in the West*, based on his own observations. The first edition of 150,000 is a sell-out.

"Pam" is dead after a mutton breakfast

London, 18 October 1865

Palmerston was staying at Brocket, his wife's house in Hertfordshire, when he was stricken by a violent fever. His doctors expected him to die in the night; remarkably, he appeared to recover and ate a hearty breakfast of mutton chops washed down with port. During the following night he became weak and died today at 10.45 am, two days before his 81st birthday.

When "Pam", as he was known, was born on 20 October 1784, the population of Britain was about nine million, of whom 80 per cent worked in agriculture; today it is 29 million, of whom 60 per cent work in industry.

He was secretary for war, foreign secretary and finally prime minister during an era when Britain was the richest and most powerful nation on earth. He encouraged reform abroad because he opposed absolutism; at home he opposed reform, believing that the British system, as it stood, was the best in the world.

Palmerston: British is best.

Victoria, who never liked him, wrote in her diary: "Strange and solemn to think of that strong, determined man – gone!" On the Stock Exchange Consols fell by a quarter per cent.

Fast-sailing clippers shrink the world

London, 6 September 1866

Thousands of Londoners lined the banks of the Thames today to watch the conclusion of a remarkable race by clippers bringing tea from China. Five of these great ships left Foochow in China within two days of each other last May. Three of them – *Taiping, Ariel* and *Sericaa* – arrived within two hours of each other. The other two are due within two days. This new breed of fast, elegant sailing-ship emerged from America, developed from privateers used in the slave trade, where speed was essential to outrun naval patrols.

Although American-built clippers like the *James Baines*, achieved remarkable records, British ships, with their streamlined hulls and huge sail areas, are putting up stiff competition in maritime trading.

A clipper on the tea-run from China: the fastest sailing ships afloat.

Prussia crushes Austria

Kaiser William, rallying his Prussian troops during the battle of Sadowa.

Sadowa, Bohemia, 3 July 1866
It was a decisive victory for Prussia and a personal triumph for the master of military strategy, Field Marshal Helmut von Moltke. In one day's fighting at Sadowa, 65 miles east of Prague, the Austrians lost 24,000 men killed or wounded and 13,000 taken prisoner. Prussian losses numbered 9,000.

This is the war that Bismarck has been looking for. He picked a quarrel with Austria over Schleswig-Holstein, and when the German princes backed Austria he took that as a declaration of war. Using the new railways, Moltke quickly deployed a main force of 250,000 men along a 270-mile (432km) front. The Prussians were equipped with the superior breech-loading rifle, while the Austrians still used the muzzle-loaded gun.

Thanks to Moltke, Prussia has defeated not only Austria but also her six German allies: Hanover, Nassau, Bavaria, Frankfurt, Hesse-Kassel and Saxony. Moltke has shaped the Prussian army into a formidable war machine, based on compulsory military service in peacetime. When war came, he had a huge reserve of trained men that he could call up.

Prussia takes control of her neighbours

Berlin, 1866
Austria's decisive defeat by the Prussian army in the Seven Weeks' War has changed the political map of Germany. The battle of Sadowa signified the end of Austrian dominance of the German states, but Bismarck, shrewdly judging that a humiliated Austria would attract sympathy, will be lenient.

The only territorial sacrifice demanded is the ceding of Venetia to Italy. The Italians made a poor showing in the field, but as useful allies of Prussia they have to be rewarded. Venetia represents an important step towards the unification of Italy.

Bismarck will not immediately exert to the full Prussia's new-found hegemony, but five of the six German states which sided with Austria in the war – Hanover, Nassau, Bavaria, Hesse-Kassel and Frankfurt – are being annexed. Saxony alone escapes.

Swede makes highly explosive discovery

Stockholm, 1866
The Swedish government has refused permission to Alfred Nobel to rebuild his factory after a serious explosion.

Some politicians have called him a "mad scientist", but Nobel, who was manufacturing liquid nitroglycerin, a powerful explosive compound, at the time of the blast which killed his brother and four workers, is persisting. He is determined to perfect his *dynamit* and make it safe to handle.

Negroes promised full civil rights

Washington, 6 April 1866
It took a civil war to achieve the historic Civil Rights Act which passed through Congress today. It means that Negroes and "anyone born in the United States" is a citizen of this country. The only exceptions are non-taxpaying American Indians.

Despite an attempt at a veto by President Andrew Johnson, the southern-born president who succeeded after Lincoln's assassination, the act gives people "of every race and color" all privileges to make contracts, hold property and testify in court.

Negroes may be equal in northern states; but a secret society, the Ku Klux Klan, dedicated to white supremacy, is thriving in the former rebel states. With other clandestine societies, the Klan ("the invisible empire of the south"), is conducting a terror campaign against "unruly" Negroes.

Back from Africa a slave ship captured

Havana, Cuba, 1866
A slave ship has been captured by Cuba. The slaves in it are to be returned to West Africa. With the Spanish authorities in Cuba and the newly-independent South American states acting against the slave-traders, and the United States executing captains of ships engaged in the trade, the Atlantic trade in human cargo can be said finally to be suppressed.

It has taken a long time. Since 1804, when the Danes declared the trade illegal, one country after another renounced it. The shipments did not come to an end, however, in spite of the Royal Navy's anti-slavery patrols. There were even larger profits to be made from the illegal trade than from the legal one and conditions on the voyages were far worse. Only British and US pressure on South America, the source of demand, has brought the trade in humans to an end.

Three and a half lines recipe for divorce

Love and marriage, a wood block print by the Japanese artist, Kiyonaga.

Japan, 1866
It takes just three and a half lines of writing for a man to divorce his wife in Japan. These lines, known as *mikudari-san*, are in a set form giving the woman permission to leave the house and to form any other liaison she wishes. The husband is supposed, legally, to refund her dowry, but usually there is little left. However, if she reports that she is pregnant within three months of being given her *mikudari-san* he must provide for the child.

It is typical of the relative status of men and women in Japan that women have no similar rights of divorce. All that they can do to escape from an unhappy marriage is take refuge in a temple.

1866 (1866-1867)

Britain, 1866. A committee presents the first petition for women's suffrage to parliament, through John Stuart Mill.

Russia, 1866. An attempt is made on the life of the czar, Alexander II. Fearful of the spread of atheism and socialism, he begins to slow down his programme of westernisation.

Crete, 1866. Christians on the island rebel against Ottoman rule when the *Porte* (Ottoman government) fails to implement promised reforms. The rebels force an entire Ottoman army to surrender on the plain of Apokoronas and in revenge the Ottomans attack a fortified monastery killing hundreds of refugees.

Russia, 1866. Fyodor Dostoyevsky publishes an epic novel, *Crime and Punishment*, which brings him instant popularity.

France, 17 January 1867. Jean Auguste Ingres, the foremost classical painter in France since David, dies aged 87.

Japan, 3 February 1867. The Emperor Komei dies. He is succeeded by his 15-year-old son Mutsuhito.

Germany, 24 February 1867. The parliament of the North German Confederation is opened. The crown of Prussia controls the league and represents the confederation internationally. An imperial *diet*, elected by universal male suffrage, will meet in Berlin to make federal laws. Count Bismarck becomes chancellor of the confederation.

Mexico, February 1867. French troops depart for France, without the Emperor Maximilian, who refuses to leave.

Paris, 1 April 1867. The Paris World Fair is opened. The occasion is marked by the demonstration of the first hydraulic lift by the engineer Edoux, and by the first viewing in the west of Japanese art.

Virginia, 11 May 1867. The former confederate president, Jefferson Davis, walks out of a courtroom a free man, after two years in prison. But he still faces charges of treason and involvement in the assassination of President Lincoln.

Luxembourg, 11 May 1867. The Luxembourg problem is settled by the treaty of London. Napoleon III had hoped to annex the grand duchy, which was under Dutch authority, as payment for services rendered to Bismarck and the Italians. However, in the face of the hostility of the other powers, he is forced to accept a collective guarantee of the independence and neutrality of the country.

Mexico, 19 June 1867. The Emperor Maximilian, placed on the Mexican throne, and then abandoned by Napoleon III, is seized by the republican President Benito Juarez' supporters and executed.

Canada, 1 July 1867. Four provinces have united to form the Canadian Federation: Quebec, Ontario, Nova Scotia and New Brunswick.

China, 5 July 1867. The revolt of the "night-bird bandits" (salt smugglers) erupts in Cangzhou, Yanshan, Bazhou and other parts of Zhili province.

China, 20 July 1867. Qing (imperial) troops in Guizhou under Can Yuying inflict a decisive defeat on the Miao rebels, killing 20,000 and capturing the former *Taiping* military commander Tao Xinchun.

Russia, 26 July 1867. Russia forms the governor-generalship of Turkestan, having moved into the area to prevent Moslem rebel incursions into their territory.

Europe, 1867. Europe suffers an economic crisis which is exacerbated by poor crops.

Crete, 1867. Ottoman troops leave, having destroyed property in the White Mountains in retaliation for the Cretan uprising last year.

Paraguay, 1867. Brazilian troops acting for the triple alliance of Brazil, Uruguay and Argentina, sack the Paraguayan capital of Asuncion. The Paraguayan leader Lopez, who declared war on Brazil in 1864, flees to the mountains with a guerrilla force.

India, 1867. A college designed to train Moslems to sustain Islamic society outside the framework of the colonial state has been founded at Deoband, north-east of Delhi.

Moscow, 1867. The Moscow Slavonic Ethnographic Exhibition is held, celebrating Russia's historic mission to free the Slavs from Ottoman and Habsburg domination. It is greeted with enthusiasm by the ruling classes.

France, 1867. Emile Zola publishes the novel *Therese Raquin* in the new "realist" style of fiction.

France, 1867. Gautier, Verlaine and Baudelaire form an association which calls itself *The Parnassians* to promote art for art's sake.

Norway, 1867. The first performance of *Peer Gynt* makes the reputation of the Norwegian playwright Henrik Ibsen.

Paris, 1867. The poet Charles Baudelaire, whose greatest work is the volume *Les Fleurs du Mal*, published in 1857, dies aged 46.

Britain gives Canada dominion status

London, 1 July 1867

Canada has moved one step further on the road to self-government following the passing of the British North American Act. Four Canadian provinces will become part of a federation to be called a "dominion". Although Britain will maintain control of foreign policy, the act effectively shows up its current lack of interest in colonial administration. As the provinces have matured over this century, they have tended to move away politically and economically from Britain. Canadians have not benefited from Britain's free trade policies and want to negotiate their own trade agreements. Hostility between English and French-speaking Canada has led to the belief that federation might help to harmonise relations.

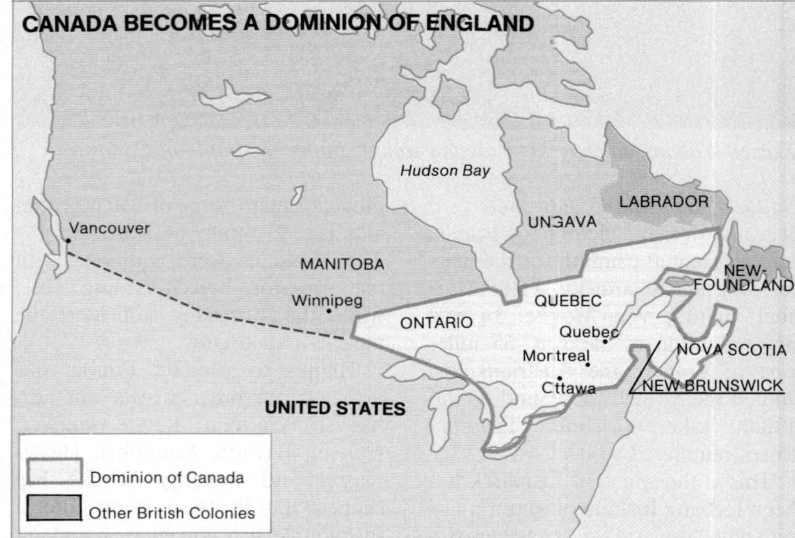

Telegraph cable stretches across Atlantic

London, 27 July 1866

Communication with the United States is no longer subject to the hazards of a sea voyage, thanks to the successful laying of a transatlantic underwater cable. Since 1856 numerous attempts have failed, notably the 1857 effort which relayed the message "Glory to God in the highest, and on earth peace, good will to men". Shortly after, the cable broke. The electric telegraph was invented over 30 years ago with the need for a fast exchange of information about the movements of trains. Its potential was soon recognised by journalists. The service improved with Samuel Morse's code and the enterprise of Paul Reuter who set up the first international news agency in 1851 (using pigeon post where the lines were incomplete). In cities the telegraph ended the isolation of police precincts and fire brigades. The same medium informed the British public of the horrors in the Crimea. The 2,500-mile-long transatlantic cable, running from Newfoundland to Ireland, owes its success to the perseverance of C W Field, a one-time clerk who used his fortune from paper distribution, and government grants from both sides of the Atlantic to fund the venture.

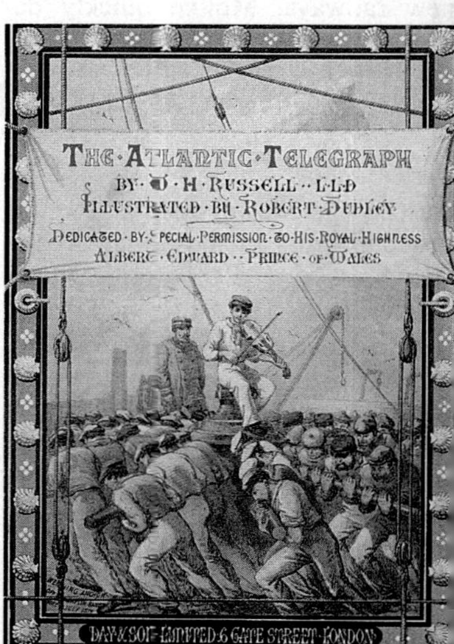

Cable ship weighing anchor.

Mexican emperor killed

The ghost of the hapless Maximilian, playing Banquo to Napoleon's Macbeth, haunts the French emperor while the statesmen of Europe look on.

Querataro, Mexico, 19 June 1867
Maximilian, the emperor of Mexico, was executed today on the orders of the republican president, Benito Juarez. Maximilian was crowned three years ago, as a figurehead for Napoleon III's ambitions to establish a Catholic empire in Mexico. Now, abandoned by France, he has paid the penalty for Napoleon's imperial dreams.

Maximilian's brief rule, during which, surprisingly perhaps, he managed to set up a stable government, followed the invasion of Mexico by France, Spain and Britain, pursuing their debts. Spain and Britain abandoned the scheme, but France stayed, flouting the promises of the convention of London, which justified the invasion but denied any ideas of colonial expansion. Faced by increased pressure from the United States, Napoleon gave up his plans, and with them his emperor. Alone, the hapless Maximilian, an involuntary ruler at best, could only await his fate.

Hungary and Austria agree joint rule

Vienna, 15 March 1867
Austria and Hungary have buried the hatchet at last with the *Ausgleich* uniting the two countries under one monarch, with shared foreign, defence and financial commitments, but separate parliaments. The Slavs resent Hungary's privileged position.

The Austro-Hungarian *rapprochement* was made possible by the emergence of moderate Hungarian leaders like Deak and Andrassy. Deak in particular, though he held fast to the April Laws rescinded by the emperor and had advocated passive resistance in the 1850s, always believed in Habsburg legitimacy. Since December 1864 he had been involved in covert negotiations instigated by the Emperor Franz Josef.

A few months ago, Andrassy persuaded Franz Josef to drop federalism; the Saxon Count Beust joined the government, and the pro-Slav prime minister Belcredi resigned. Beust took over, secured a majority in the *Reichsrath*, and carried through the *Ausgleich*, which he hopes will modernise the empire.

Franz Josef, the emperor of Austria.

Russia sells Alaskan wasteland to US

Washington, 9 April 1867
By a single vote, the United States Senate agreed today to buy Alaska from Russia for $7.2 million – so bringing to an end one of the most bitter campaigns to be fought by the government since the end of the war. Opponents of the measure claimed that the purchase of an "utterly useless land of perpetual snow" was an insane investment. Journalists have suggested that the vast expanse of land in the Arctic Circle should be named "Icebergia" or "Polaria".

For years William Seward, the secretary of the interior, has been urging Congress to buy the land, and he claims that – at two cents an acre – the country has got a bargain on its hands. Alaska's furs, minerals and fisheries will be of "untold value" in future years, he says, and the territory is worth seven times what the US is paying for it.

A US cartoon derides William Seward for buying Alaska.

Lister's sterile surgery is a life-saver

Glasgow, 1867
Eleven-year-old James Greenlees fell while he was playing and broke his leg. It was a compound fracture, and when James was brought into the Royal Infirmary here, Professor Joseph Lister cleaned the wound thoroughly and swabbed it with a coal-tar product called carbolic acid. Six weeks later young James went home, his leg perfectly healed.

James is just one example cited by Lister in his frequent lectures on the need for cleanliness in surgery. Heavily influenced by the work of Louis Pasteur on germs and disease, the Scots surgeon has surprised his colleagues by his high rate of success in combating "hospital disease" – often fatal and generally caused by unclean surgical instruments and unsterile dressings. Many patients die unneccessarily – even though the original operation was a success – from blood poisoning which causes wounds to fester.

Although the introduction of his antiseptic system is likely to prove a major breakthrough in modern medicine, Lister is also well known for his research on blood coagulation and the various causes of inflammation.

1867 (1867-1868)

Britain, 15 August 1867. Parliament passes a Reform Act – spearheaded by Benjamin Disraeli, the chancellor of the exchequer – which adds nearly one million more voters to the electorate by enfranchising most male urban ratepayers.

China, 16 August 1867. Imperial Qing forces capture a stronghold of the Miao rebels near Weining.

Austria, August 1867. Napoleon III of France and Franz Josef of Austria meet in Salzburg with the aim of strengthening their ties against Prussia.

Britain, August 1867. Britain sends a military expedition to Ethiopia to force the emperor, Tewodros (Theodore) II, to release British officials held since 1864, when Britain failed to offer expected aid in escalating conflicts with the Turks. The mission is headed by Sir Robert Napier, commander-in-chief of the Bombay army.

Britain, September 1867. Karl Marx publishes the first volume of *Das Kapital*.

Austria, October 1867. The continuing dispute between Austria and Hungary is resolved by the *Augsleich* (Compromise), creating two theoretically separate countries under one monarch.

Italy, 3 November 1867. Giuseppe Garibaldi, who launched a march on Rome last month, is defeated by papal and French troops at the battle of Mentana. Garibaldi is captured, and Pope Pius IX is granted French support for a further three years.

Japan, 9 November 1867. The last *shogun*, Tokugawa Keiki, resigns in favour of the Meiji emperor Mutsuhito. Before his resignation he had become a virtual prisoner in his palace at Kyoto.

Austria, 1 December 1867. Johanns Brahms' *German Requiem* is performed for the first time.

New York City, 2 December 1867. The popular English novelist Charles Dickens gives readings around the city, drawing large crowds.

Britain, 13 December 1867. The Irish republican movement known as the *Fenian* Brotherhood launches a bombing campaign in London. Another attack in Manchester on 18 September, also ended in failure.

Austria, 21 December 1867. A new, more liberal, constitution is adopted.

New York City, December 1867. Cornelius Vanderbilt takes control of the New York Central Railroad by outmanoeuvring rival stock-holders.

Austria, 1867. Johann Strauss composes the *Blue Danube* waltz.

New York City, 1 January 1868. Susan B Anthony begins publication of a weekly Suffragist journal called *The Revolution*.

Japan, 3 January 1868. The Emperor Mutsuhito announces that the office of shogun has been abolished and assumes direct control of Japan.

China, 5 January 1868. The Eastern Nian rebels are annihilated by imperial Qing forces near Yangzhou and Lai Wenguang is captured.

China, 7 January 1868. The revolt of the "night-bird bandits", which began in July last year, is put down.

Britain, 25 February 1868. Ill induces the resignation of Lord Derby. He is succeeded as Conservative prime minister by Benjamin Disraeli.

Madagascar, March 1868. Rasoherina is succeeded as queen by Ranavalona II, who is married to Rainilaiarivony, the chief minister and effective ruler of the country.

Japan, 6 April 1868. The Charter Oath establishes the broad principles of the new government, including the convocation of an assembly and pursuit of knowledge in the interests of the nation.

Ethiopia, 13 April 1868. Following his defeat by the British under Sir Robert Napier at the battle of Aroge, the Emperor Tewodros (Theodore) II commits suicide.

USA, 26 May 1868. President Andrew Johnson is acquitted of all charges of impeachment.

Germany, 21 June 1868. Richard Wagner's comic opera *The Mastersingers of Nuremberg* is performed for the first time.

France, June 1868. Following the enactment of a liberal press law last month, the law governing public meetings is made less stringent.

Serbia, June 1868. Having rid the country of Ottoman troops, Prince Michael Obrenovic is murdered by conspirators seeking the restoration of Alexander Karageorgevitch. The assembly nominates his 14-year-old cousin Milan Obrenovic to succeed him, with Jovan Ristic as regent.

USA, June 1868. The first patent is granted for a typewriter.

USA, 25 July 1868. President Johnson signs an act officially creating the territory of Wyoming.

USA, 28 July 1868. A treaty is signed granting unrestricted Chinese immigration into the USA.

US president just escapes impeachment

Washington, 26 May 1868

By a single vote, the Senate failed to impeach the president of the United States today. Andrew Johnson, the man who succeeded after Lincoln's assassination, has continued to anger Congress by his refusal to accept the First Reconstruction Act which divided the southern states into military districts subject to military commanders.

The articles of impeachment were mostly concerned with Johnson's dismissal of his secretary of state, Edwin Stanton, but several dealt with speeches – said to be inflammatory – made by Johnson on a national tour. The most serious charge suggested that the president was involved in the conspiracy to murder Lincoln.

Johnson and a blindfolded Justice.

Garibaldi captured in bid to take Rome

Rome, November 1867

Garibaldi's irregular army was defeated for the second time this month and he himself has been captured. His dream of annexing the papal states for Italy and making Rome the capital has once again been frustrated.

After the first defeat he reconstituted his army and attacked at Mentana. However, the French had sent a large force to help the pope. They were equipped with a new rifle, the *chassepot*, which loads at the breach and has twice the range of a conventional rifle. They easily defeated Garibaldi. The once proud leader has been humiliated. No longer a threat, he will be allowed to return to Caprera.

Britain dithers over self-rule for blacks

Gold Coast (Ghana), 1868

The Gold Coast is 4,000 mile (6,400 kilometres) from London Messages from London take a long time to get there, if they arrive at all. In 1865 a select committee of the House of Commons urged the British governor "to encourage in the natives the exercise of those qualities which may render it poss ible for us more and more to trans fer to them the administration" Yet, three years later, after an in digenous Fante confederation had been formed for the express pur pose of ruling themselves, the Brit ish administration is opposing it doing all that it can to drive a wedge between the young intellec tuals and the traditional chiefs.

New Russian novel tells of holy fool

St Petersburg, Russia, 1868

Fyodor Dostoyevsky, who had such success with his novel *Crime and Punishment* here two years ago, has followed it with another extraordinary story, *The Idiot*. Whereas the first was a psychological study of a nihilist and murderer, Raskolnikov, the hero of the second, Prince Myshkin, is of outstanding goodness, simplicity and moral radiance, drawing, everyone to him. Yet his influence leads to tragedy and his return to idiocy One of the stories Myshkin tells so compellingly is of the sensations o a man who lived through the las minutes leading up to his execution

This is exactly what the autho must have experienced when con demned to death as a dissident in 1849. Reprieved from the firin squad when all was ready, he wa sent to hard labour in Siberia, abo which he wrote the moving boo *The House of the Dead*.

Teenage emperor's coup in Japan

Japan, 3 January 1868
The youthful Emperor Meiji, supported by the most powerful feudal lords of Japan, has today seized power from the shoguns who have ruled Japan for the last 700 years.

For all that time the emperors have been powerless, cut off from the world, their only function being to carry out certain religious rites while their country was ruled by the shoguns as hereditary *de facto* chief ministers.

The shoguns have been acknowledged as the real rulers of Japan by the great powers, and international negotiations have been conducted in their names and not those of the unknown men living in seclusion at Kyoto. Now all that has been changed by the proclamation "Restoration of Imperial Government". The great powers will now have to deal with the 16-year-old emperor and his advisers from the Chosu and Satsuma clans who have forced the resignation of the Tokugawa shogun, Keiki, whose family have been shoguns for 200 years.

Japan's relations with the west lie at the heart of this astonishing development. The failure of the shogunate can be traced back to the treaty made with Townsend Harris, the US consul, in 1858 which gave the Americans farreaching concessions.

In order to safeguard himself from criticism, the shogun took the unprecedented step of asking the emperor to sign the treaty. This not only gave the impression that all treaties not signed by the emperor were invalid but, when he refused to sign the Harris treaty, sparked off fierce opposition to "the barbarians".

The Choshus and the Satsumas clashed with the western navies and were quickly defeated. However, their defeat convinced them of the impossibility of opposing western power, and by buying western arms and adopting western methods they have been able to overcome the demoralised shogunate. The way is now open for a new, western-influenced era in Japan.

A village in Japan, still unprepared for the arrival of the outside world.

Emperor Meiji, in his "hif" robes.

Workers will take over, says Marx

London, 14 September 1867
Capitalism will collapse from its own contradictions, and be followed by a dictatorship of the proletariat. This is historically inevitable, according to Karl Marx, a German-Jewish philosopher, newspaper columnist and member of numerous revolutionary movements, in his newly-published tome *Das Kapital*.

Marx was expelled from France and Germany for his revolutionary activities. For the last 18 years he has lived in London, spending many hours in the reading room of the British Museum. The most moving passages of *Das Kapital* are those setting out the facts of the misery experienced by the British working class.

Marx turns a lot of conventional thinking upside down. He argues that economic conditions determine men's thoughts, opposing Utopians who consider that great thoughts change social conditions. "The handmill gives you society with the feudal lord; the steammill, society with the industrial capitalist," he wrote in an earlier work.

Marx, with his friend Friedrich Engels, was the author of the *Communist Manifesto*. Its closing words – "the proletarians have nothing to lose but their chains. They have a world to win. Working men of all countries, unite!" – are intended to be a future rallying cry.

Karl Marx: a scientific socialist.

Irish bombs rock England, killing twelve

London, 13 December 1867
A barrel of gunpower was used to demolish the outer wall of Clerkenwell prison today in a bid by bombers to rescue an Irish prisoner. They not only brought down the wall but also wrecked a row of houses opposite, killed 12 people and injured 120 others. They failed to release their man.

The bombers are known to belong to the Fenian Brotherhood, a secret society named after a legendary band of warriors who roamed Ireland defending it against foreigners. The present-day Fenians, who were launched in the United States, have mounted a number of attacks on British property, usually without success.

Fenianism: an English view.

Secret society plans to topple the Sultan

Constantinople, 1867
A group of young middle-class intellectuals has formed a secret society to promote democracy. Through literature and journalism, the members hope to undermine the sultan's autocratic rule. The Young Turks, as they are called, became a coherent force two years ago at a picnic in the forest of Belgrade when they formed a "patriotic alliance" to pursue democratic ideals. Among their leaders are Ibrahim Shinasi, a poet and newspaper editor, Ziya Pasha, who has recently moved to Paris, and Namik Kemal, a radical essayist and devout Moslem.

1868 (1868-1869)

USA, 28 July 1868. The 14th Amendment to the constitution, giving full US citizenship to Negroes, is passed.

China, 16 August 1868. The western Nian bandits are wiped out by Qing troops near Chiping in Shandong province.

Austria, 22 August 1868. Annoyed at the minor role accorded the Czechs by the Austro-Hungarian *Augsleich*, or compromise, of last October, the Czech deputies withdraw from the parliament.

China, 22 August 1868. Some 10,000 people plunder and destroy the missionary residence of the China Inland Mission.

Spain, September 1868. Queen Isabella II is forced to flee to France after a liberal uprising.

San Francisco, 21 October 1868. An earthquake causes $3 million worth of damage.

Japan, October 1868. Edo is renamed Tokyo, and the new era is named *Meiji*.

USA, 3 November 1868. General Ulysses S Grant, a Republican who was in ultimate command of all union armies during the civil war, is elected president.

Japan, 6 November 1868. The last supporters of the Tokugawa family, led by Shogun Yoshinobu, are defeated at Wakamatsu.

USA, 6 November 1868. The Oglala Sioux Indians led by Chief Red Cloud sign a peace treaty with General William Sherman of the US government at Fort Laramie, Wyoming. The pact ends two years of fighting between gold miners and the Sioux.

China, 9 November 1868. A British naval force captures China's first naval steamship, the *Tianji*, construction of which was completed in July.

USA, 27 November 1868. The US Seventh Cavalry under George A Custer defeats a combined force of Arapaho and Cheyenne Indians led by Chief Black Kettle on the Washita river, east of the Texas Panhandle.

Britain, 9 December 1868. William Ewart Gladstone, who succeeded Earl Russell as Liberal leader last year, forms a ministry, following a Liberal general election victory.

China, December 1868. Ya'qub Beg, the leader of the independent Moslem state of Kashgaria, opens relations with Britain and Russia.

West Africa, 1868. The Fante confederation – an alliance of Fante rulers and the coastal trading/professional elite – is established to provide for defence and create a modern state.

Swaziland, 1868. King Mswati, the founder of the state of Swaziland, dies.

USA, 1868. *Little Women* by Louisa May Alcott – a novel about four teenage sisters growing up in a Victorian New England village – is a bestseller.

USA, 1868. The world's first railway dining car, invented by George Mortimer Pullman, comes into service.

Britain, 1868. The Trades Union Congress is founded.

Britain, 1868. Charles Darwin publishes *The variation of animals and plants under domestication.*

Britain, 1868. William Morris publishes *The Earthly Paradise*, a long poem based on Chaucer, alternating mediaeval tales with those of ancient Greece.

Britain, 1868. Wilkie Collins publishes *The Moonstone*, the first detective novel in English.

Germany, 1868. The historians Ranke, Sybel, Burckhardt and Mommsen publish *The Foundations of Historical Science.*

France, 1868. Edouard Manet paints a portrait of Emile Zola.

France, 20 February 1969. The poet Paul Verlaine publishes *Les fetes galantes.*

USA, 27 February 1869. The 15th Amendment, requiring all Southern states to allow Negroes to vote, is passed.

Japan, April 1869. The emperor moves from Kyoto to Tokyo and takes the old shogunal castle as his palace.

Europe, 10 May 1869. France signs a secret treaty against Prussia with Austria and Italy.

Spain, June 1869. A new constitution, providing for the continuance of monarchical government, is adopted. Francisco Serrano, the leader of last year's revolt, becomes regent, and Juan Prim is made chief minister.

Germany, 1869. Wilhelm Liebknecht founds the Social Democratic Workers' Party.

India, 1869. Mirza Asadullah, who wrote under the pseudonym "Ghalib", dies. He was the leading Urdu and Persian poet of the age and the last poet laureate of the Moghul emperors.

Britain, 1869. Robert Browning publishes an epic poem, *The Ring and the Book*, based on the story of a murder by an Italian count.

France, 1869. Jules Verne writes in instalments a story of an imaginary voyage in a steel submarine, *Twenty Thousand Leagues Under the Sea.*

Paraguay in ruins as its capital falls

Asuncion, Paraguay, January 1869

Asuncion, Paraguay's capital, has fallen to the armies of Brazil, Argentina and Uruguay. Though Paraguay's dictator-president, Francisco Lopez, escaped the Triple Alliance's encirclement of the city, his dream of a new South American empire lie smouldering in the sacked city. After four years of war Paraguay is almost destroyed. Nearly two-thirds of the adult population has died or disappeared, and most of the country is under enemy occupation.

The war started over Lopez' attempts to force a pro-Paraguayan president on Uruguay. Brazil intervened in support of the legitimate president, and Lopez declared war on it. Soon his megalomania dominated strategy. He declared war on Argentina for refusing to allow his troops passage through the country, and declared war on Uruguay just to add to his enemies.

Naturally Brazil, Argentina and Uruguay came together in a triple alliance, formed on 1 May 1865. A few months later Brazil's navy had sunk the Paraguayan navy in the Parana river. By 1867 the alliance's land forces under the Argentinian General Bartolome Mitre were advancing deep into Paraguay's territory. The country is now paying the price for its president's ambitions almost total devastation.

Spain's rebel generals oust the queen

Spain, 28 September 1868

The defeat of the loyal government troops at Alcolea has compelled Queen Isabella to abandon her summer residence in the Basque country to seek refuge in France. Spain is now in the hands of rebel generals.

Corruption and inefficiency had undermined popular support for Isabella so that when a coalition of liberal generals and urban radicals led a rising, local revolutionary *juntas* lent a hand. Generals Francisco Serrano of the Liberal Union and Juan Prim of the Progresistas are committed to universal suffrage and a free press. All they need is a new monarch.

Isabella, the deposed queen of Spain making way for liberalism.

Chinese army wipes out rebels in north

China, 16 August 1868

The Chinese imperial army has today wiped out the last of the Nian rebels who have plagued the northern part of the country for the past 15 years. During this period, while the best of the imperial forces were occupied with the *Taiping* rebellion, the peasant Nians, specialising in guerrilla warfare led by mobile cavalry, carried on a robbers' war against the authorities.

Commanded by a former salt smuggler, Zhang Luo-xing, and based on the White Lotus secret society, the Nians allied themselves to the Taipings and grew rich on ransom, plunder and protection rackets. They sheltered the remnants of the Taipings, but once the battlehardened imperial army had finished slaughtering the Taipings the Nians' turn came.

Their cavalry was confined by massive dykes built round their base areas where the earth was "scorched" to deny them supplies. They managed to break out and split into two groups, but the eastern group was annihilated last January and the western group met its end at Shandong in a fierce battle today. This is not the end of China's troubles. There are uprisings among Moslems in Yunnan the north-west and Turkestan.

King Ludwig builds castles in the air

Ludwig's fantasy, the Persian Peacock Throne at Linderhof Castle, Bavaria.

Munich, Bavaria, 1869

King Ludwig II has begun construction of Linderhof castle, modelled on the Trianon palace at Versailles. Like all his building projects, it is fantastic and costly. His most outlandish castle is to be Neuschwanstein, perched on a crag in the Bavarian mountains like a fairy-tale castle and decorated with scenes from Wagnerian operas.

Wagner is the king's other craze. He invited the composer to Munich when he ascended the throne at the age of 18, gave him a villa and a princely salary and offered to build him a theatre. But Wagner's interference in politics and his scandalous affair with Cosima von Bulow, the wife of the conductor and Liszt's daughter, caused Ludwig to banish him to Lake Lucerne.

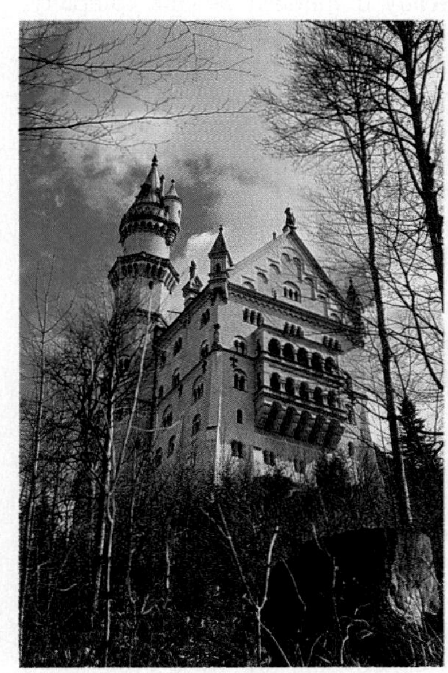

Neuschwanstein: Ludwig's folly.

Russian count writes of war and peace

St Petersburg, 1869

The work that has occupied Count Leo Tolstoy for seven years is at last finished. *War and Peace* is the most ambitious and possibly the greatest novel yet written. It presents a gradually unfolding panorama of Russia from 1805 to 1814, depicting its struggle with Napoleon's armies and moving from defeat to deliverance.

Against this background the novel traces the fortunes of great families such as the Rostovs and Bolkonskys, and of peasants, of town and country, war and peace. Individuals like Natasha, Andrei and Pierre grow older and wiser through their experiences. The author believes that chance, not choice, determines human afffairs.

His vivid descriptions of battle and army life reflect his first-hand experience as a battery commander at the siege of Sevastopol during the Crimean War.

Leader's defeat ends Maori guerrilla war

New Zealand, 14 March 1869

With the defeat of the Maori guerrilla leader Titokowaru in the extreme south of South Island, the third Maori rebellion in 15 years appears to have been put down.

The rebellion was a blow to the governor, Sir George Grey, who had recognised the justice of the Maoris' claims to their land. In 1863 a militant Maori leader, Rewi Maniapoto, emerged, and urged Maoris to kill Europeans. On 15 April 1863 his followers killed eight British soldiers near New Plymouth in North Island. By June there was a fullscale war in North Island. On South Island the British disarmed all Maoris and demanded that they take an oath of allegiance or leave the British zone. Then they concentrated on North Island. Soon they had ten infantry regiments ploughing their way through the Maori lands.

Behind them came 3,000 armed settlers, recruited from the unemployed in the Australian goldfields to establish fortified settlements in the new lands.

By 1864 it looked as if they had won. Then the Maoris turned to guerrilla warfare, which spread through both islands. For five long years the two sides' atrocities have sapped the country. Now, with Titokowaru's defeat, peace may come to both peoples.

British trades unions split over report

British trades unions: the emblem of the London Society of Compositors.

Manchester, England, 1868

The first meeting of delegates from trade unions throughout Britain is being held here to decide a common front against a forthcoming Royal Commission report, which is likely to recommend only partial legalisation of unions.

The first Trades Union Congress is split between those who want to stay outside the law and the powerful London Trades Council which wants to accept the Royal Commission's minority report. It recommends legalising unions and making union activities legal provided that they are inside the common law. The issue is likely to be debated further at a second Trades Union Congress next year.

Elementary table

St Petersburg, Russia, 1869

Scientists have made notable attempts to classify elements. The latest system to date has been devised by a Russian chemist, Dimitri Ivanovich Mendeleyev, professor of chemistry at St Petersburg University for the last three years. In his periodic table all the elements are arranged in order of increasing atomic weights. Their properties are grouped so that, at a glance, the chemist can take in the nature of a given element, such as its hardness, colour and stability. One new element he discovered has even been named after him: "mendelevium".

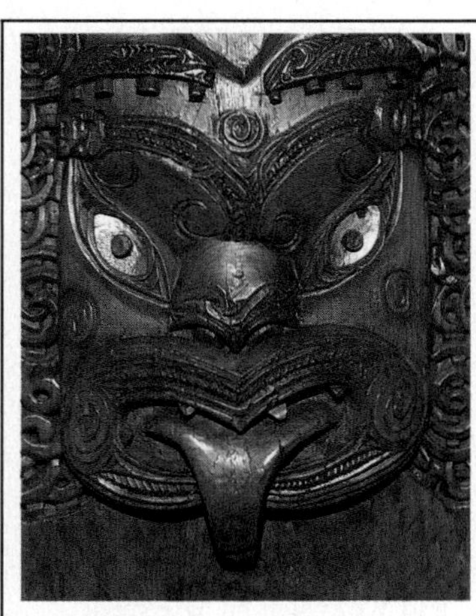

Maori art: an ancestor's face, carved on a plank lining the inside of a tribal meeting house.

1869 (1869-1870)

Britain, July 1869. Parliament passes a bill disestablishing and partly disendowing the Anglican Church in Ireland.

China, September 1869. Ding Baozhen, the governor of Shandong, executes An Dehai, the favourite eunuch of the Empress Dowager Cixi, for corruption. His action severely curbs eunuch power.

Egypt, 17 November 1869. The Suez Canal opens.

France, 17 November 1869. Gustav Flaubert's novel *L'Education Sentimentale* is published.

Canada, November 1869. The Hudson's Bay Company signs an agreement with Britain handing over to Canada the north-western regions between Ontario and the Rocky mountains for $1.5 million.

Canada, November 1869. French-Indian rebels in western Canada set up a provisional government at Fort Garry (*Winnipeg*), with Louis Riel as president.

Rome, 8 December 1869. Pope Pius IX opens the Vatican Council, the first general council of the Catholic Church since that of Trent over 300 years ago.

USA, 10 December 1869. Women in the territory of Wyoming are given the vote.

USA, 1869. Horatio Alger publishes *Luck and Pluck*, a series of wildly popular rags-to-riches novels.

Spain, 1869. Prince Leopold of Hohenzollern-Sigmaringen is offered the Spanish crown.

France, 2 January 1870. Emile Ollivier, a leader of the radical liberal party, is appointed prime minister by Napoleon III.

USA, 10 January 1870. John D Rockefeller and his brother William found the Standard Oil Company of Ohio.

Paris, 12 January 1870. Over 100,000 people demonstrate against the empire at the funeral of the republican journalist Victor Noir, who was murdered by Pierre Bonaparte, a cousin of Napoleon III.

Japan, January 1870. Japan's first telegraph line is established, between Tokyo and Yokohama.

Europe, 2 February 1870. The press agencies Havas, Reuter and Wolff sign an agreement whereby, between them, they can cover the whole world.

Scramble for South African gold and gems

Diamond mining: "white diggers" and black labourers near Klipdrift.

Southern Africa, 1869

Since diamonds were found near the lower Vaal river in 1867, and gold was found at Tati and Botswana this year, thousands of prospectors – many of them veterans of the Californian and Australian gold rushes – have streamed northwards across across the Vaal and Limpopo rivers in search of riches. The first diamonds were found around Hopetown; more were found near Klipdrift on the north bank of the Vaal. The area is claimed by the Boer republics (the Orange Free State and Transvaal), two African peoples (the Griquas and the Tlhapings) and the British. Gold came two years later the biggest find was at Tati, which is already dominated by one company, the London and Limpopo, which has its own steam engine. The prospectors call themselves "diggers", after the Australian term. They don't actually do any of the digging, though. That is done by the thousands of blacks who have migrated to the mines and form Africa's first industrial proletariat.

Drive for womens' rights grows in Britain

A woman's role: a post-Mill view.

England, 1869

John Stuart Mill, the political philosopher of Utilitarianism, has published a new book which should add to the current debate on women's rights. *The Subjection of Women*, heavily influenced by his late wife Harriet, demands the emancipation of women and acknowledges their complete equality with men.

Mill has been a consistent campaigner for feminism. During debates on the 1867 Reform Bill he claimed that the vote, even for a minority of women, would benefit all: "They would no longer be classed with children and lunatics, as incapable of taking care of themselves or others, and needing that everything should done for them."

Mill's efforts are part of a growing movement. This year's Married Women's Property Act has made it possible for women to own property. A women's suffrage committee was founded in 1866. The Ladies' Discussion Society, founded in 1865, is one of a number of such groups; and the *Englishwoman's Review* has since 1857 come out unequivocally for women's rights.

Morris designs for individual homes

Burne-Jones and William Morris.

London, 1869

A revolution in home decoration is being inspired by William Morris and his firm of craftsmen, Morris Marshall, Faulkner and Co, which he founded with Dante Gabriel Rossetti, Edward Burne-Jones Ford Madox Brown and the architect Philip Webb who designed the Red House in Bexleyheath, Kent for Morris. It is dedicated to personal design, not mass production.

"Have nothing in your house that you do not know to be useful and believe to be beautiful," is the motto of Morris, an all-rounder who is a painter, glass-stainer and poet, the author of *The Earthly Paradise*. He has now begun designing wallpaper and tapestry.

Morris' "St Catherine", in silk.

US joined east to west

Promontory, Utah, 10 May 1869
As bands played and several thousand railwaymen cheered, the governor of California aimed a mighty sledgehammer blow at the ceremonial golden spike that finally completed the world's longest railroad. Governor Sandford missed, but nonetheless the telegraphs flashed the message to the whole of America that its east and west had been joined by 1,776 miles (2,841 kilometres) of steel track.

After three years of intensive stripping of forests, bridging, tunnelling and earth moving, the Union Pacific line has met the Central Pacific line here in Utah. The plan was for a decorous ceremony, with company directors, engineers and politicians attending from both directions. By the time that the Union Pacific train came roaring in three days late – it had become stuck in prairie floods – Promontory was inhabited almost exclusively by the working crews and their camp-followers – gamblers, whores, saloon-keepers and moneylenders. Both companies had every reason to race. The government was paying $16,000 for every mile of track they laid – more for mountainous areas.

The Central Pacific's and Union Pacific's chief engineers shake hands.

Canal opened at Suez

The thousands of labourers who excavated the Suez Canal watch its opening.

Suez, Egypt, 17 November 1869
Three months after the waters of the Mediterranean and the Red Sea met in the Bitter Lakes, a procession of vessels representing all the rulers of Europe is making its way along the Suez Canal which was opened officially today.

Built in spite of British opposition and costing the French-backed Suez Canal Company 400 million francs, 100 times its initial estimate, the 26-foot-deep canal has made use of several lakes to avoid the need for locks. There are bays every 16 miles (25.6 kilometres) for ships to pass. Work on the project, headed by Ferdinand de Lesseps, began over ten years ago. Until 1866, progress was slow with the use of forced labour, but speeded up when machinery took over.

In Britain there are many who fear that the canal will reduce its influence in the Near East and thus open up India, the lynchpin of the empire, to unwelcome outsiders. But commercial opinion largely favours the benefits that should ensue from the new sea passage.

Britain severs Irish Church from state

Disraeli and "Victorian Morality" watch as Gladstone erodes the foundations of the Irish Church.

London, July 1869
Having been swept to power with a Commons majority of 112 for his Liberals, William Gladstone, the prime minister, seized his opportunity and produced a bill to sever the Church of Ireland's link with the state. The bill sailed through the Commons with what Disraeli called a mechanical majority, and even the peers have not dared to oppose it. Apparently the queen, at Gladstone's suggestion, told the archbishop of Canterbury that the bill ought not to be defeated.

The church claims descent from Ireland's patron saint Patrick, but since the time of Henry VIII it has been unpopular because of pressure to follow the reformed Church of England.

Canada: rebels fear British immigrants

Ottawa, October 1869
A rebellion in western Canada has caught the government off guard and turned much of that remote region into a breakaway republic run by mixed-race (mainly French-Indian) rebels known as *Metis*.

The Metis were satisfied with the *laissez-faire* administration of the Hudson's Bay Company. Impending transfer of its territory to the federal state aroused fears of British immigration into a region to be renamed Manitoba. The rebels are led by a Montreal law student, Louis Riel, aged 25. They have now seized the big settlement of Fort Garry and want to negotiate acceptable terms for union with Canada. As tension mounts, force is as likely as diplomacy.

Berlioz, the titan of French music, dies

Paris, 8 March 1869
Hector Berlioz, the composer who could not play a single instrument properly but was one of music's most original geniuses, died today at the age of 65. Emotionally volatile, urbane, witty and extravagant, with deepset eyes, hooked nose and "an enormous umbrella of hair", the composer of the *Fantastic Symphony* and the massive *Requiem Mass* was a major figure in French musical life. But his own music was too advanced for Parisian taste – it was thought bizarre, or simply "wrong" – and he was forced to earn a living from journalism. He had a small, ardent following, though, and other great musicians, such as Wagner, recognised his unique and grand vision.

1870 (1870-1871)

France, 20 April 1870. A new liberal constitution, introduced by a decree of the senate, gives both the legislative assembly and the senate the right to initiate legislation and to amend bills proposed by the government.

India, April 1870. A political association known as the Poona Sarvajanik Sabha is founded in western India.

France, 8 May 1870. A plebiscite gives overwhelming endorsement to the constitutional changes proposed on 20 April.

China, 21 June 1870. A Chinese mob attacks a Roman Catholic orphanage in Tianjin accused of kidnapping and using children for devilish magic. Twenty-four foreigners are killed, including French and Belgian nuns, as well as the French consul.

Spain, 12 July 1870. Prince Leopold of Hohenzollern-Sigmaringen withdraws his acceptance of the Spanish throne, announced just over a week ago.

Prussia, 14 July 1870. Otto von Bismarck, the prime minister of Prussia, publishes a doctored version of the Ems telegram – a communication between himself and King William of Prussia about the Spanish succession – which is extremely insulting to the French.

France, 19 July 1870. France declares war on Prussia.

New York City, 24 July 1870. The first transcontinental through train arrives from San Francisco.

Britain, 1 August 1870. An Irish Land Act provides tenant farmers with compensation for eviction.

France, 18 August 1870. Prussian forces defeat the French at the battle of Gravelotte.

France, 1 September 1870. The French are decisively defeated by the Prussians at Sedan.

France, 2 September 1870. Napoleon III capitulates to the Prussians at Sedan.

Paris, 4 September 1870. A republic is proclaimed and a government of national defence formed.

Australia, 6 September 1870. The last British troops to serve in Australia are withdrawn.

Paris, 19 September 1870. The Prussians lay siege to Paris.

Rome, 20 September 1870. Taking advantage of the French defeat at Sedan, Italian forces enter Rome and expel the papal troops.

France, 28 September 1870. Strasbourg, under siege since August, surrenders to the Prussians.

Rome, 2 October 1870. In a plebiscite the papal states vote in favour of union with Italy. The capital of Italy is moved from Florence to Rome.

France, 27 October 1870. Metz surrenders to the Prussians.

Spain, 16 November 1870. Amadeus of Savoy, the son of Victor Emmanuel II of Italy, accepts the Spanish crown.

Germany, November 1870. The south German states of Wurttemberg and Bavaria ally with the North German Confederation, ensuring Prussian political hegemony.

USA, 12 December 1870. Joseph H Rainey becomes the first Negro member of the House of Representatives. The Rev Hiram R Revels became the first Negro member of the Senate in February.

Spain, 30 December 1870. The premier Juan Prim is assassinated.

Ireland, 1870. Isaac Butt, a Protestant lawyer from Dublin, sets up the Home Government Association, to spearhead the movement for Irish home rule.

Britain, 1870. An Education Act introduced by the Liberal MP William Forster makes elementary education available to all children between the ages of five and 13.

Venezuela, 1870. After a period of civil war, the liberal leader General Guzman Blanco wins power from the conservative federalists.

Central Africa, 1870. Swahili slave trader, Tippu Tib, sets himself up as ruler west of Lake Tanganyika.

Turkey, 1870. The German archaeologist Heinrich Schliemann begins excavations at Hissarlik, believed to be the site of Troy.

Britain, 1870. Dante Gabriel Rossetti publishes his *Poems* after the manuscript has been retrieved from the coffin of his wife, Lizzie (Elizabeth Siddall), where he placed it in grief at her death.

Paris, 8 January 1871. Prussian troops begin to bombard Paris.

France, 18 January 1871. William of Prussia is proclaimed German emperor (*kaiser*) at Versailles.

France, 28 January 1871. Beset by famine and surrounded by Prussian troops, Paris surrenders. During the siege, balloons were used to maintain contact with the rest of the country.

France, 26 February 1871. France and Prussia sign a preliminary peace treaty at Versailles.

France, February 1871. Elections are held for a national assembly which meets at Bordeaux and elects Louis Adolphe Thiers prime minister.

General is the pawn in China power game

Kashgar, China, 8 November 1870

The Turkic General Ya'qub Beg unified the many-headed Moslem revolt against Chinese repression today when he accepted the surrender of his rival, Tuoming, the self-appointed "pure and true king", at Urumchi in Chinese Turkestan. Now all the rebels will fight under Ya'qub Beg's banner.

This development takes place against a background of intense rivalry between Russia and Britain in this region. Czarist forces are continuing their advance into central Asia, and their probing towards the Indian frontier is causing the British much anxiety.

The British therefore look to Ya'qub Beg's newly-founded *emirate* of Kashgaria as a buffer state between India and Russia. Contact has been established between Ya'qub and Lord Mayo, the viceroy of India, who has sent a member of his staff to Kashgaria. So, without realising it, Ya'qub Beg is now a player in the "great game".

Pope declared source of infallible truths

Pius IX: the infallible pope.

Rome, 18 July 1870

The Vatican General Council meeting here today passed a major new constitutional dogma by an overwhelming majority. The dogma, *Pastor Aeternus*, declares that the pope, when he speaks as "Shepherd and Teacher of all Christians", enjoys infallibility in defining doctrine on faith and morals. His definitions are "unalterable in themselves and not by virtue of the assent of the church".

It represents a triumph for the conservative views of Pope Pius IX and a defeat for the liberal Catholic scholars, who have argued that history and science are disciplines in their own right, and that Catholics should learn from them. From now on the Vatican can be expected to be less tolerant of dissent.

Novelist's death hastened by overwork

Rochester, Kent, 9 June 1870

The sudden death has occurred of Charles Dickens at his home, Gadshill, which he bought in 1856, having coveted it as the son of a poor clerk in the navy yard at Chatham. He was 58; his death was hastened by his strenuous programme of public readings from his novels which he acted to the full.

Dickens first won recognition with his newspaper sketches of London life signed "Boz". He married his editor's daughter, Catherine Hogarth, but they separated after the birth of ten children. His readers waited eagerly for each part of his current novel. The death of Little Nell in *The Old Curiosity Shop* caused nationwide grief.

Charles Dickens at a public reading

Germany crushes France at Sedan

Napoleon III surrenders to Kaiser William after the battle of Sedan.

Sedan, 2 September 1870

A shattered Emperor Louis Napoleon, frequently in tears, surrendered his sword to William, kaiser (or king) of Prussia today after 44 days of warfare that have devastated France and confirmed newly-unified Germany as the most powerful new nation in Europe.

The beginning of the end came yesterday when Prussian troops encircled the emperor's relief force at Sedan as it tried to reach Metz, where the main French force has been penned in. The emperor, looking pale and dogged by illness, ended the squabbling among his generals and ordered the white flag to be raised. It was his reluctant acceptance that his 235,000-strong French army had been out-manoeuvred, outnumbered and outgunned by a 380,000-strong Prussian force. Only the hastily assembled National Guard now stands between the Prussians and Paris.

The surrender were negotiated this morning at a poignant meeting in a tiny weaver's cottage between the emperor and the architect of his downfall, the Prussian prime minister Bismarck, who has used the war to bring the Rhineland states into a German confederation.

It was Bismarck's decision to publish a provocative version of the Prussian response to French complaints over the nomination of a German prince for the Spanish throne that first inflamed French public opinion and forced a reluctant Napoleon to declare war, even though he knew that his army was weak. Tonight he is paying the price – as prisoner of the Prussians in the comfort of the royal apartments at Wilhelmshohe castle.

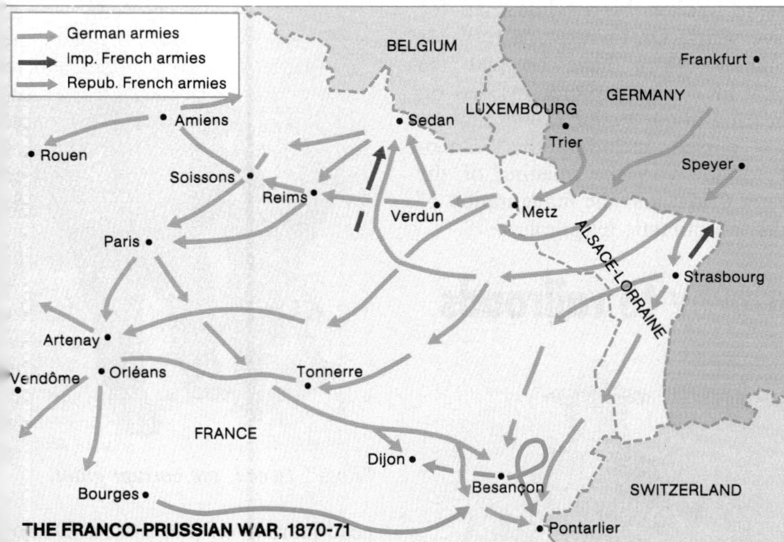

rance declared a republic once more

ᵓaris, 4 September 1870

ᶠrance is once again a republic, vith revolutionary crowds roaming he streets following the collapse of he 20-year-old second empire fter Napoleon III's defeat by the russians at Sedan.

The new republic was declared oday by the emperor's opponents n the legislative body, anxious to ead off a revolutionary movement rom the extreme left. A provisional overnment of national defence has lso been established under the military governor of Paris to combat e Prussian threat. Meanwhile the mpress Eugenie and the prince nperial have fled to England.

The guilty men, French and Prussian: a Republican view.

Germany proclaims empire in France

Versailles, 18 January 1871

Amidst the glittering splendour of Louis XIV's hall of mirrors in the Palace of Versailles, Bismarck today realised his long-cherished dream. His Prussian king, William, became emperor of a new German *reich*, and Bismarck himself became the first chancellor.

The *venue* for the ceremony was a humiliation for the French, but the choice had much to do with a desire to impress the numerous German princes, who had to be cajoled into joining the reich and giving up some of their petty privileges. The crushing defeat of France, and the capture of Napoleon III at Sedan, by Germans who had accepted the Prussian military system stirred German public opinion; the princes had to give way.

William, Europe's new emperor.

Victor Emmanuel makes Rome his capital

Rome, 20 September 1870

The army of Victor Emmanuel II entered Rome today and declared its intention of making it the capital of Italy. Garibaldi made several attempts to take Rome with his people's army, the last being in 1867, but he was defeated by the French. Success this time had more to do with the absence of the French than with the prowess of the Italian army. Napoleon III withdrew his forces from Rome to help him in his war with the Prussians. Earlier this month the Prussians routed the French at Sedan and Napoleon was himself taken prisoner. For the first time Italy was free to move on the papal states without having to fight the French.

There was little resistance. The walls were shelled, and a breach made at Porta Pia. Only a few lives were lost.

1871 ⇒

Paris, 1 March. German troops enter Paris.

London, 13 March. Britain, Russia, Germany, France, Austria, Turkey and Italy agree to abrogate the 1856 Treaty of Paris, ending Black Sea neutrality.

Paris, 18 March. The National Guard, which has been united under a central committee, takes over the Hotel de Ville.

France, 22 March. Following the proclamation of the Lyons *Commune* yesterday, a commune is declared at Marseilles.

Paris, 28 March. The Paris Commune is declared.

Germany, 14 April. The imperial constitution is adopted, providing for the election of a parliament of 382 members, the *Reichstag*.

Germany, 10 May. France and Prussia sign a peace treaty at Frankfurt.

Rome, 13 May. Victor Emmanuel II, the king of Italy, issues the Law of Guarantees, assuring the pope that the Vatican remains outside Italian jurisdiction and granting him freedom in the exercise of his spiritual ministry.

Paris, 28 May. The Paris Commune is suppressed by troops from Versailles after a week of fighting. The Lyons and Marseilles Communes have already collapsed.

China, 3 June. London is connected with Shanghai by undersea electric cable via San Francisco.

Japan, 27 June. A new system of currency is established, based on the yen.

Britain, 29 June. The unions are granted legal status under the Trades Union Act.

China, 4 July. Russian troops occupy the Ili area of Chinese Turkestan.

Germany, 8 July. Bismarck launches a cultural struggle, the *Kulturkampf*, against the Catholic Church by abolishing the Catholic department for spiritual affairs.

New York City, 12 July. Fighting between Scots-Irish Presbyterians and Irish Catholics during a Scots-Irish parade leaves 31 civilians and two policemen dead.

New York City, 30 July. An explosion on the Staten Island ferry kills 72 and injures 135.

US newsman discovers African explorer

"Dr Livingstone, I presume?" "You have brought me new life."

Ujiji, Central Africa, 13 November

Britain's most famous explorer, David Livingstone, has been found alive at Ujiji in Central Africa after being feared dead for the past four years. An expedition led by a *New York Herald* journalist, Henry Morton Stanley, traced Dr Livingstone, frail and short of supplies, to the edge of Lake Tanganyika.

Mr Stanley's greeting: "Dr Livingstone, I presume?" were the first words the 58-year-old explorer has heard spoken by a white man for five years. Dr Livingstone told Mr Stanley: "You have brought me new life." The explorer insisted on hearing about major events that he has missed, including the Franco-Prussian War, the opening of the Suez Canal and the inauguration of the transatlantic telegraph.

Law makes Indian land prey to railroads

Washington, DC, 3 March

After decades of wrangling about the rights of the native Indian population and their legal relationship to the American government, legislation was introduced today that formally ends the idea that the Indians are inhabitants of a separate state. It has been thus since the British signed a treaty at Fort Stanwix in 1768 which recognised the "Indian Nation".

Under the Indian Appropriations Bill, all Indians will be considered as "individuals" and treated as such. They will be designated "wards" or government charges.

One reason for the new approach to the Indian problem is that the Indians do not have the same concept of sovereignty as "European" Americans. A chief may sign a treaty, but the extent of his authority is rarely agreed upon by his own people. And when Indians sign treaties, neither they nor the government knows for sure to whom the rules apply. Hence the "individuality" accorded these highly individual people. Little is said in the bill, however, about the rights of railroad owners to slice great parcels of land off the reservations. The new bill, indeed, allows the government freedom to do that with the stroke of a pen.

Indians: now to be "individuals".

US party boss faces huge fraud charge

New York City, December

The law has finally caught up with William "Boss" Tweed, the corrupt czar of Tammany Hall – but not before he and his cronies had managed to salt away an estimated $100 million from bribes, graft and swindles on a gargantuan scale.

Tweed, a former saddler and bookkeeper, rose through the political ranks to become an alderman of the city and quickly showed a marked talent for corruption. He formed a ring of equally corrupt associates – who quickly became known as "the forty thieves" – and set out to use Tammany Hall, the headquarters of the state's Democratic Party, to become the virtual dictator of the party.

"Boss" Tweed, the corrupt giant.

He secured membership of key boards and "placed" members of his ring in strategic positions where they could extort bribes and commissions from almost anyone who sought a city hall permit. Bogus citizenships were issued by the thousand – all at a cost – and rigged elections were the norm.

When Tweed tried to tighten his grip on New York with a new "city charter", the press, notably in cartoons by Thomas Nast in *Harper's Weekly*, turned its attention to the "forty thieves". The *New York Times* came into possession of evidence of the mass swindling. A committee of 70 eminent citizens was formed and even the corrupt police were forced to move.

Communards and French army tear Paris in half

Radicals proclaim commune in Paris

Paris, 28 March

It was quite a spectacle they put on outside the Hotel de Ville today. On a platform draped with scarlet cloth a group of men wearing red scarves stood to attention as units of the National Guard marched past. The parade came to a close with massive salvos of cannon-fire, and a man wearing a Phrygian cap, the symbol of revolution and liberty, began to speak, but his words were lost in the chants of *"Vive la Commune"*.

So the power of the people was asserted and the Commune of Paris proclaimed after a lost war. The marching and cheering and singing of the *Marseillaise* continued into the night. The National Guard, a locally-raised militia heavily infiltrated by left-wing elements, had made a poor showing during the four-month German siege of the city; now it was glowing with triumph. The government, led by Louis Adolphe Thiers and lodged at Versailles, was impotent. "I have got four men and a child," Thiers said when asked for reinforcements to crush the commune. The regular army has been reduced to a single division and the supposedly reliable elements of the National Guard have disintegrated.

Most of the *Communards* who took over the Hotel de Ville are writers, painters and assorted intellectuals, clerks and petty tradesmen, with a handful of workers. Vaguely inspired by slogans from France's past revolutions, they have no clear idea of what they want to achieve, other than somehow erasing the stain of defeat.

A month ago, National Guardsmen raided artillery parks in Paris and removed some 200 cannon to the heights of Montmartre. A detachment of regular troops sent to recover the guns arrived without horses to tow them away; was set on by Guardsmen and two generals were lynched. A wealthy Parisian woman, told that the Commune had banned night work for bakers, commented: "The Communards have decreed that Paris shall eat stale bread."

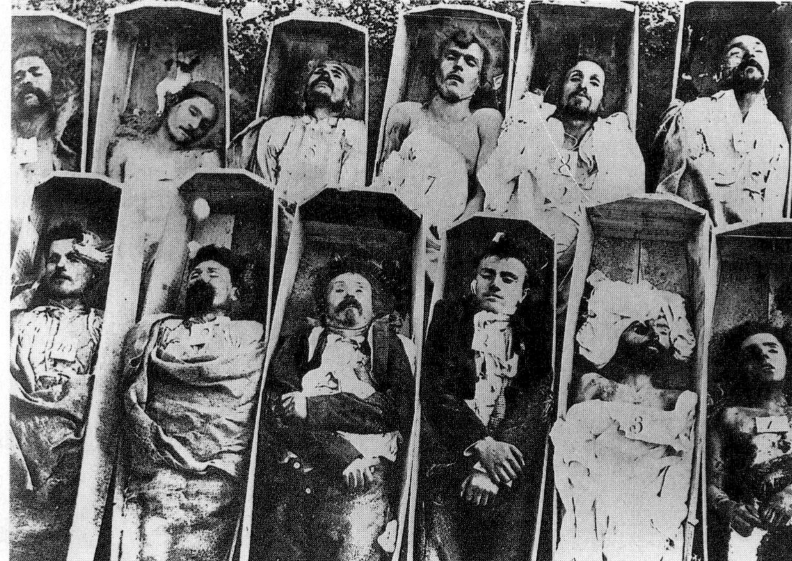

A few of the Communards who died in Paris. "They were madmen" said the painter Renoir, "but they had a flame within them that will never die."

Barricades at Port Maillot, stormed by Versailles troops early in the assault.

France concedes victory to the Prussians

Frankfurt, 10 May

A peace treaty formalising the end of hostilities between France and Germany was signed here today. It confirms the agreement reached by the two sides after Paris fell to Prussian troops in March.

Under the treaty France finally surrenders to Germany all of the border province of Alsace and most of neighbouring Lorraine. It was this demand that had prolonged the war. France also has to pay an indemnity of five billion francs to Germany, with a German army of occupation remaining in France until the indemnity – equivalent to the amount Napoleon I imposed on Prussia in 1807 – is paid. The handing over of Alsace and Lorraine without a popular vote has led to a protest by the British prime minister Gladstone, who claims that the people should have been consulted.

The treaty, which places no limit on France's armed forces or foreign policy, reflects a strategic gamble on the part of Prussia's prime minister, Bismarck, who believes that France has already been sufficiently isolated and humbled by the catastrophic defeat at Sedan.

Paris commune is bloodily crushed

Paris, July

The commune is dead, drowned in blood. The communards, who had withstood Prussian and French besiegers for nine months, fought their last fight amid the graves and headstones of Pere Lachaise cemetery. Most communard prisoners taken are being shot. They expected no better.

The all-out assault on the city began by chance on 21 May, when one of the giant forts defending the western approach to the city was found to have been abandoned – which says much about the inefficiency and incompetence of the commune's leaders. Versailles troops poured in and during the following week, *La Semaine Sanglante*, Paris was taken, *boulevard* by *boulevard*, barricade by barricade, body by body.

The *forces d'ordre* came in through the predominately middle class west, where they were greeted as liberators. Soon they captured the city centre, though the *hotel de ville* and many other public buildings were burnt down by arsonists. South of the Seine the French army encountered strong resistence around Les Gobelins and the Jardin des Plantes. North, particularly in the working class areas, the resistence was even greater. Some of the most ferocious fighting came from Louise Michel's women's battalion around Place Blanche and Pigalle. Realising the French army's tactic of outflanking through the side streets, she had most of her battalion on her northern flank. Gradually the women retreated, the streets of Montmartre littered with their corpses, until they joined the men of Belleville for a last heroic stand in the cemetery.

Between 20,000 and 25,000 people were killed in fighting or are being executed in "retaliation" for the killing of the Archbishop of Paris. Whether these troops will be as successful in killing the myth of the commune in less certain. For Paris has become a place of horror and heroism – the stuff that legends are made of.

1871 (1871-1872)

France, 31 August 1871. Louis Adolphe Thiers is elected president of the republic.

Japan, August 1871. Feudal domains are abolished and prefectures are created as the new units of local administration.

Brazil, 28 September 1871. The Rio Branco law, stipulating that children born to slaves are free, is passed.

Japan, 8 October 1871. The tenets of equality in taxation laws and compulsory, fee-paying education are laid down. A modern postal system is introduced.

Chicago, 9 October 1871. A great fire kills 300 people, makes 90,000 homeless and causes $200 million worth of damage.

Los Angeles, 24 October 1871. Nineteen Chinese are killed in anti-Chinese riots.

South Africa, 27 October 1871. Britain annexes the diamond region of Griqualand West.

Austria, October 1871. The Emperor Franz Josef rejects Bohemian demands for a position similar to that of Hungary in the Dual Monarchy.

France, 23 November 1871. The Chinese imperial commissioner, Chonghou, apologises to President Thiers for the Tianjin massacre of June 1870.

Germany, 4 December 1871. The *mark* becomes the unit of currency.

South Africa, 3 November 1871. Cape Colony takes over the government of Lesotho (Basutoland).

Europe, 1871. The Mont Cenis tunnel, the first great Alpine tunnel, connecting France and Italy, is completed.

France, 1871. Following the defeat of the Paris *Communards*, Elizabeth Dimitrieva, a Russian-French socialist who organised the Women's Union for the Defence of Paris as a branch of the Socialist International, escapes to Russia.

France, 1871. The electrical engineer Zenobe-Theophile Gramme gives a demonstration of his invention, the continuous-current dynamo.

Switzerland, 1871. The French mountaineer Henriette d'Angeville, the first woman to organise and undertake her own climb of Mont Blanc, dies in Lausanne.

Russia, 1871. Count Dimitri Tolstoy, the minister of education, reorganises the educational system in order to combat materialism and revive classical education.

USA, 1871. The National Association of Professional Baseball Players is founded.

Britain, 1871. James McNeil Whistler paints *Arrangement in Grey and Black – the Artist's Mother* and Sir John Millais exhibits *The Boyhood of Raleigh*.

Britain, 1871. Lewis Carroll publishes *Through the Looking Glass*, a sequel to *Alice in Wonderland*; and Edward Lear follows up his *Book of Nonsense* with *Nonsense Songs and Stories*.

Britain, 1871. Charles Darwin publishes *The Descent of Man*, which expounds his theory of natural selection.

London, 1871. Having left Paris because of the Franco-Prussian War, the French impressionist Claude Monet paints the Thames and its bridges.

Belgium, 25 January 1872. Henry, the count of Chambord, a claimant to the French throne, makes a speech in Antwerp rejecting a call for a "revolutionary monarchy" in France.

Bay of Bengal, 8 February 1872. Lord Mayo, the viceroy of India, is murdered by a Moslem fanatic while visiting a penal colony on the Andaman Islands.

West Africa, 6 April 1872. The British take over the Dutch forts in Gold Coast (*Ghana*).

China, 12 May 1872. The Miao rebellion is finally suppressed with the capture of its main leader, Zhang Xiumei.

Germany, 22 May 1872. The foundation stone is laid for the Bayreuth festival theatre in Bavaria, intended specifically for performances of Wagner's works.

Spain, May 1872. Don Carlos, a claimant to the throne, enters Navarre, but is driven back beyond the frontier by General Moriones.

France, May 1872. Marshal Bazaine, who surrendered to the Prussians at Metz, is sentenced to 20 years' imprisonment for treason.

France, June 1872. An agreement over war indemnities is signed with Germany at Versailles. They are to be paid in stages and the French government may settle the debt in advance and thus speed up the departure of Prussian troops.

Germany, 4 July 1872. A law is promulgated as part of the *Kulturkampf* banning all religious assemblies, particularly Jesuit ones.

Britain, 18 July 1872. The Ballot Act is passed providing for secret ballots at elections.

South Africa, July 1872. Thomas Burgers, a Dutch minister from the Cape, is Transvaal's new president.

Britain, 1872. Samuel Butler writes *Erewhon*, a Utopian satire on religious traditions and morals.

Telegraph to link Australia to the world

Adelaide, 23 November 1872

Australia's isolation from the rest of the world is about to end following the construction of an overland telegraph line linking south Australia with Darwin in the north. In November the new telegraph will be connected to a new undersea cable from Darwin to Java that will link Australia into the fast-growing transoceanic telegraph network.

The owners of the international cable, the British Australian Telegraph Company had made the completion of the Overland Telegraph a precondition of the Darwin-Java cable. The final join in the cable, nearly 2,000 miles (3,200 kilometres) long, was made today at Frew's Pond after work on the northern section of the line had been constantly interrupted by floods.

The route for the north-south cable which cost £120,000, follows that opened by John M'Dowall Stuart's third and successful nine-month expedition ten years ago when he became the first explorer to cross the Australian continent from sea to sea.

Ku Klux Klan, US racist club, suppressed

A Klan warning, directed as much at northern "carpet baggers" as Negroes.

Washington, August 1871

The civil war may have finished six years ago with slavery abolished, but many Negroes in the former slave states of the south remain in constant fear of the burning cross of the *Ku Klux Klan*, the hooded white terror organisation pledged to white supremacy. Former slaves who dare to tread the same sidewalk as white men are liable to be seized to face a secret court of hooded men and to be flogged – and often lynched from the nearest tree – if the "court" so decides.

In Florida alone, 153 Negroes were killed in a single parish this year; over 300 were murdered in the countryside near New Orleans.

Few doubt that the Klansmen are ardent former confederates, resentful in defeat and frustrated by the lack of subservient labour, and northerners have become increasingly angry at the idea that the south is robbing them of their success. The result is a bill before Congress which outlaws the Klan and other secret societies and allows for the suppression of violence by military force.

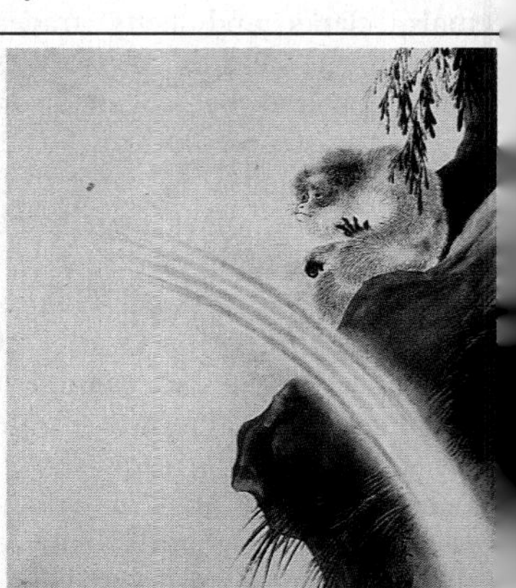

"Monkey and Rainbow", one of a series of exquisite and restrained watercolours by the 64-year-old Japanese artist Shibato Junzo Zeshin.

Bismarck launches attack on Catholics

Berlin, 14 May 1872

Bismarck has become embroiled in a struggle with the Roman Catholic Church – and found his own weapons turned against him. The conflict of beliefs, or *Kulturkampf*, stems from the Vatican Council of two years back, when it was decreed that when the pope speaks on matters of religious faith he is infallible and has to be obeyed by all Catholics. Distinguished German Catholics, some employed by state universities, objected; they were excommunicated and the Vatican called on the government to dismiss them.

Bismarck responded by pointing to the constitution, which guarantees civil and political rights irrespective of religious belief. Now he has published a set of laws which forbid the church to intervene in affairs of state, forbid the clergy to discuss politics in the pulpit and exclude the church from the state education system. The church is defending itself by pleading for the right to worship as conscience and reason dictate.

Bismarck: "Iron Chancellor".

Indian nationalist has killed the viceroy

Port Blair, India, 8 February 1872

The viceroy of India, Lord Mayo, has been assassinated, struck down by a lone Indian nationalist while inspecting a penal settlement. A moderate conservative in the House of Commons, Mayo was conciliatory by nature. He disliked military intervention and sought to support rather than undermine states like Afghanistan, which he saw as "outworks of our empire" against Russia.

He was a promoter of education for the Moslem people, and ally of the princes; but he failed to understand the increasing alienation of the urban middle class intelligentsia from British rule, and he has paid for it with his life.

French author looks into a bright future

One man's journey of imagination.

Paris, 1872

Lovers of "scientific" adventure have been eagerly reading *Le Temps* newspaper which carries regular instalments of Jules Verne's latest *voyage imaginaire*, entitled *Around the World in 80 Days*. This latest journey remains on the surface of the earth – or just above it – unlike his *Journey to the Centre of the Earth* or *Twenty Thousand Leagues under the Sea*.

It begins in London's Reform Club when a gentleman called Phileas Fogg makes a wager with his companions at the card table that he can circle the globe and be back in 80 days exactly. His stratagems include crossing the Alps in a balloon. Eighty days is of course an impossible time for such a voyage.

Marie Celeste mysteriously abandoned

Atlantic Ocean, 4 December 1872

She lay lifeless in the Atlantic swells, her sails flapping idly, and failed to respond to signals from the British freighter that spotted her. They made out her name as *Marie Celeste*, but saw no sign of life on her. The British crew were even more mystified when they boarded her and found her crewless. The cabin in her saloon was laid for tea. There was no sign of mayhem. Her cargo of 1,700 barrels of alcohol was intact.

The maritime world is completely baffled and theories abound in every seafarer's tavern. Some say the crew had got to the cargo, killed the captain in a drunken orgy and escaped on a southbound ship. Some talk of a sea-monster. Others think it was pirates ... but teetotal pirates? It seems unlikely that the mystery will ever be solved.

Verdi's Egyptian opera opens in Cairo

The libretto and music for Guiseppe Verdi's grand but taut opera, "Aida".

Cairo, 25 December 1871

The delayed first performance of Giuseppe Verdi's new opera, *Aida*, took place last night at the Italian Theatre, Cairo, built to mark the opening of the Suez Canal. It was to have opened the theatre last year, but the siege of Paris prevented the scenery arriving. The *khedive*, Ismail Pasha, Egypt's ruler, suggested the story.

The plot is about Aida, who is the slave of Amneris, the Pharaoh's daughter, and their rivalry for the love of Radames, the captain of the guard. The opera ends with Aida sharing the fate of Radames when he is entombed alive. "Celeste Aida" and the triumphal march are two of the opera's hits.

Edgar Degas' "Dance Studio at Rue le Peletier". Born in 1834 to a wealthy Parisian family, he studied at the Ecole des Beaux-Arts, learning his superb draughtsmanship from Jean Auguste Ingres. After three years in Rome he took to painting historical scenes, but after meeting Edouard Manet he began to paint contemporary themes, particularly ballet, the circus, cafes and horse races. He has been praised for his spontaneity, a quality which he rejects: "No art was ever less spontaneous than mine."

1872 (1872-1874)

Germany, September 1872. The emperors of Germany, Austria-Hungary and Russia form an alliance in Berlin.

USA, 5 November 1872. Ulysses S Grant is elected for a second term as president.

New York City, 19 November 1872. William "Boss" Tweed, the former head of Tammany Hall, the city's Democratic organisation, is jailed for fraud and corruption.

China, 26 December 1872. Du Wenxiu, the leader of the Moslem rebellion in Yunnan province, is executed, having surrendered to Qing troops at Dali.

South Africa, December 1872. Responsible government is established at Cape Colony, with John Molteno as the first prime minister.

Germany, 1872. The philosopher Friedrich Nietzsche publishes *The Birth of Tragedy*, dedicated to Richard Wagner, whose operas he regards as the true successors to Greek tragedy.

France, 1872. Georges Bizet composes the incidental music for Alphonse Daudet's play *L'Arlesienne*.

Hawaii, 8 January 1873. Prince William Lunalilo becomes the first elected monarch of Hawaii.

Britain, 9 January 1873. Napoleon III of France dies at Chislehurst, Kent, where he had withdrawn following his imprisonment at Wilhelmshohe, near Kassel, immediately after his surrender to the Prussians at Sedan.

Japan, January 1873. The imperial army is reorganised and modernised on European lines.

China, January 1873. Qing forces carry out a large-scale massacre of Moslems at Dali.

Spain, 11 February 1873. Amadeus abdicates after a two-year reign as king of Spain, and the first Spanish republic is proclaimed.

Southern Africa, 30 April 1873. The Scottish missionary and explorer David Livingstone dies near Lake Bangweulu (*in Zambia*). From the age of ten to 24 he had worked in a cotton factory. He was ordained under the London Missionary Society aged 27-years-old. He discovered Victoria Falls aged 41, and Lake Nyasa aged 46. He died aged 60.

France, 24 May 1873. President Thiers resigns and the right-wing monarchist candidate Marshal Marie Edme MacMahon is elected president.

China, 29 May 1873. The last remnants of the Yunnan Moslem rebellion are defeated.

Germany, May 1873. New laws against religious education bring seminaries under state control. The Catholic opposition takes shape, particularly in Silesia, Poland and the Rhineland, where ecclesiastical dignitaries are threatened with internment.

China, 29 June 1873. The US, British, Dutch, French, Japanese and Russian ministers are received in audience by the emperor and present their credentials.

Germany, 9 July 1873. The *Reichstag* passes a law which pegs the value of the *mark* to gold.

San Francisco, 1 August 1873. The first cable car service begins operation.

France, 16 September 1873. The last German troops leave France.

China, 12 November 1873. The Gansu Moslem rebellion ends with Zuo Zongtang's capture of Suzhou in Gansu province. His troops slaughter many thousands of Moslems.

Central Asia, 6 December 1873. Ya'qub Beg formally accepts the title of *emir khan* from the sultan of Turkey. From now on he is called Emir Mohammed Ya'qub Khan of Kashgaria.

Central Asia, 11 December 1873. Ya'qub of Kashgar receives Sir Douglas Forsyth, a British envoy sent from India, and expresses warm friendship for Britain.

USA, 14 December 1873. The Swiss-born naturalist Louis Agassiz, author of four volumes of a *Natural History of the United States*, dies at Cambridge, Massachusetts.

Bolivia, 1873. A peace treaty is signed at La Paz fixing the frontier between Chile and Argentina along the ridge of the Andes *cordillera*.

West Africa, 1873. Asante forces defeat the British at Assin Nyankumasi in the Gold Coast (*Ghana*).

Central Asia, 1873. The Russian General Skobelev captures the oasis of Khiva, the capital of the khanate of Khiva, to the south of the Aral Sea in Uzbekistan.

Brussels, 1873. The French poet Paul Verlaine is sentenced to two years' hard labour for shooting his friend and fellow-poet Arthur Rimbaud in the wrist. Rimbaud published this year a prose volume entitled *Une Saison en Enfer*.

France, 1873. The novelist Jules Verne publishes *Around the World in 80 Days*.

Britain, 1873. The Custody of Infants Acts is passed, extending the access of separated or divorced women to their children.

Bank failures and bad harvests hit US

New York, 1873

It has been a bad year for the United States of America. The country has been hit badly by not only natural disasters but also several man-made financial catastrophes. Drought has afflicted mid-western states, where unnaturally high rainfall in the 1860's brought illadvised settlement, and trains are being halted by the grease of millions of crushed grasshoppers on the tracks. In September, panic on the New York Stock Exchange left many ruined in its wake.

Over-speculation, believed to be at the root of the turmoil in New York, has also caused several national banks to collapse. As the demand for gold as a monetary unit goes up, the supply of the metal is now insufficient to meet the needs of the world's burgeoning economies.

Japan invaded Formosa to get at China

Formosa, October 1874

The Japanese are to withdraw the expeditionary force sent to Formosa (*Taiwan*) to punish the Formosans for the murder of 54 shipwrecked fishermen from the Ryukyu Islands four years ago. The truth of the matter is that the Japanese care little for the fate of the fishermen, but care a lot for ownership of the Ryukyus – foggy, remote islands which pay tribute to Beijing but fell under the control of a Japanese warlord 200 years ago. Now it seems that the Japanese have tricked the Chinese into acknowledging Japan's sovereignty over the islands, for, in order to stop the occupation of Formosa the Chinese have agreed to indemnify Japan for the murder of the fishermen. They have bought off the Japanese, but have succeeded only in whetting Japan's appetite.

The new Remington typewriter, produced by the famous gunsmiths of New York state. The first practical typewriter was invented by Christopher Latham Sholes in 1867. His second model a year later wrote faster than a pen. It was still cumbersome, and it was not until he signed a contract with the Remington company that he was able to produce a machine for the mass market. Its components are a cylinder, with line-spacing and carriage return mechanisms, and typebars so arranged as to strike the paper through an inked ribbon at a common centre. One of Remington's first customers for the machine is Mark Twain, the novelist.

Three emperors in pact

Three emperors: Czar Alexander, Kaiser William and Emperor Franz Joseph.

Berlin, 7 September 1872
After his victory in the Franco-Prussian war, Bismarck – rewarded by a grateful Kaiser William with the title of prince – looked for some means by which Germany could guard itself against a revanchist France. He has now persuaded Franz Josef of Austria and Alexander of Russia to affirm their solidarity with William in the preservation of peace in Europe. The fine-sounding *Dreikaiserbund* – the League of the Three Emperors – has yet to face its first test, but many observers believe this will have nothing to do with the French.

The real trouble spot is seen as the Balkans, where both Russia and Austria have long had designs on pieces of the increasingly feeble Ottoman empire. Bismarck could not remain indifferent to a big power struggle there.

Conscription swells European armies

Europe, c.1872
In much of Europe, with the exception of Britain, the professional armies which fought other people's wars for the last century are being diluted by conscripts. "National service", first introduced in Prussia in 1814, is now a fact of life for young men in France and Austria-Hungary and probably soon will be in Russia. Most states opt for a period of between one and three years in uniform, but the process is beset by doubts. The French President Louis Adolphe Thiers, with the *commune* in mind, describes it as "putting a rifle on the shoulder of every socialist". Yet the French working man, far from seeking a military life, dodges the draft in his thousands, occasionally using self-mutilation or assuming gender changes if other ploys fail. In Germany, fewer recruits are selected from politically unreliable states than from more conservative areas.

Despite such snags, the size of armies is growing apace. Some observers wonder if a part-civilian army will blur the distinction made between combatants and unarmed civilians in any future conflict.

A soldier's farewell to his family.

Spain's king quits; republic declared

Amadeus, who failed to establish himself as a constitutional monarch.

Madrid, 11 February 1873
Spain's unpopular King Amadeus has abdicated and the Cortes (parliament) has decided that the country must become a republic. Amadeus has reigned for four years, and throughout this time his regime has been beset by difficulties, largely caused by quarrelling among several political parties.

Over the last year ministry has succeeded ministry as parties split up, which has made stable government impossible. There has been non-stop opposition to any policy from the *Carlists*, culminating in another full-scale revolt which has effectively ended the democratic monarchy. Amadeus decided to step down after an attack on the army by the Radicals, and deputies voted in a republic.

Russian anarchist clashes with Marx

The Hague, Netherlands, 1872
Mikhail Bakunin, a turbulent, free-wheeling anarchist who for a quarter of a century has sought to ferment unrest in much of Europe, is no longer a member of the First International Workingmen's Association, the organisation created eight years ago by Karl Marx to coordinate socialist struggles.

Bakunin, an advocate of terrorism who claims that "the passion for destruction is also a constructive passion", was once a Russian army officer. He has been sentenced to death twice, and spent six years in a Russian prison before escaping – with such ease that suspicions that he was a czarist agent were rife – from exile in Siberia.

Marx, whose overriding concern is to set up mass socialist parties, has waged a vitriolic personal campaign aimed at reducing anarchist influence in the International. By meeting here, far from Bakunin's bastions of support in Spain, Italy and Switzerland, Marx' followers obtained Bakunin's expulsion.

Bakunin: prophet of anarchy.

"Blackbirding" – kidnapping of near-slave workers – banned

Brisbane, 1874
Ross Lewin, the greatest "blackbirder" of them all, is dead. He was shot in the back by a native as he walked towards his veranda. The native, whose cousin Lewin had shot for banana-stealing, had been hiding for three days in a coconut palm waiting for his opportunity. "Blackbirding" is the practice of recruiting South Sea Islanders, particularly the Kanakas, for work on the sugar plantations in Australia. The first 67 arrived on the schooner *Black Dog* in 1863. By 1867 Ross Lewin was advertising "the best and most serviceable natives to be had in the islands at £7 a head".

Ostensibly the natives were on contracts. Actually they were kidnapped and frequently brutally treated. Planters like Robert Towns argued that the Kanakas were well suited to the work and that he was avoiding "the inhumanity of driving to the exposed labour of field work the less tropically hardy European women and children". Public opinion and the law have now stopped the trade.

1874 (1874-1875)

Spain, January 1874. On the retirement of Emilio Castelar – made head of government last September during *Carlist* risings – a military *coup* puts Marshal Francisco Serrano back in power.

Vietnam, 31 January 1874. France signs a treaty with the Emperor Tu Duc which acknowledges a French protectorate over Cochin China.

Britain, February 1874. Following the defeat of Gladstone's Liberals in a general election, Disraeli forms his second Tory ministry.

Hawaii, 12 February 1874. On the death of King Lunalilo after one year's reign, rioting breaks out among islanders who support the claim to the throne of Queen Emma, the widow of King Kamehameha IV. The other claimant is Prince David Kala-kaua, whom Lunalilo defeated in a bitter election fight for the crown.

Gold Coast (Ghana), 14 March 1874. After suffering a defeat by the British in January, the Asantehene, king of Asante, signs a treaty with Btitish representatives at Cape Coast ending the Anglo-Asante war.

Japan, 13 April 1874. Eto de Hizen, a *samurai* of the Satsuma clan, is beheaded for rebelling against the imperial decision not to invade Korea, which had refused to receive missions from Japan.

Switzerland, April 1874. The Swiss Constitution is revised to increase the powers of the federal government, especially in military affairs. The principle of referendum is adopted for national legislation.

France, April 1874. The novelist Gustave Flaubert publishes *The Temptation of St Antony*.

Britain, 30 August 1874. The Factory Act limits the working week to 56.5 hours.

Switzerland, 9 October 1874. A treaty is signed in Berne by 22 countries establishing a Universal Postal Union.

Italy, October 1874. France recalls the ship *Orenoque*, which has been moored off Civitavecchia since 1870 ready to receive the pope should he be forced to leave Rome. The pope is waging an uncompromising battle against the Italian government and calling on Catholics not to participate in politics.

Pacific, October 1874. Britain annexes the Fiji Islands.

USA, 18 November 1874. The national Women's Christian Temperance Union is founded.

Spain, 29 December 1874. The *infante*, Don Alfonso, is declared king of Spain, ending the dictatorship of Francisco Serrano.

Sudan, 1874. General Charles Gordon succeeds Sir Samuel Baker as governor general of Sudan in the service of Egypt. Baker completed the conquest of the upper Nile region as far as Bunyoro (*Uganda*) and began the suppression of the slave trade.

Sudan, 1874. Zubair Pasha, a former slave-trader in the Sudan, conquers Darfur on behalf of the *khedive* of Egypt.

China, 1874. The rickshaw is introduced.

Germany, 1874. Wilhelm Wundt publishes his *Physiological Psychology*.

Spain, 1874. The writer Pedro Antonio de Alarcon publishes a short picaresque tale called *The Three-Cornered Hat*.

USA, 1874. Mark Twain publishes *The Gilded Age*, a novel satirising unbridled materialism.

China, January 1875. The Tongzhi emperor dies at the age of 18. The Empress Dowager Cixi (Ziaoqin) adopts her nephew Zaitian, the late emperor's cousin, and makes him successor to the throne. The two empress dowagers become co-regents for the second time.

France, 30 January 1875. France adopts a republican constitution under which legislative power will be exercised by two chambers: the Chamber of Deputies and the Senate. Executive power will reside with a president, elected for a period of seven years.

Rome, 5 February 1875. Pope Pius IX issues an encyclical denouncing Bismarck's laws and the *Kulturkampf*.

Germany, 6 February 1875. Civil marriage is made obligatory.

China, 21 February 1875. The murder of the British legation official Augustus Raymond Margary near the border with Burma by native bandits heightens Anglo-Chinese tensions.

China, 25 February 1875. The Guangxu emperor formally ascends the throne.

USA, 1 March 1875. Congress passes the Civil Rights Act, guaranteeing equal rights in transport, theatres and inns and on juries.

Hawaii, 18 March 1875. Hawaii signs a treaty giving exclusive trading rights with the islands to the USA.

China, 27 March 1875. The widow of the Tongzhi emperor, who died in January, commits suicide.

USA, 1875. Thomas Adams of Brooklyn, New York, manufactures the first chewing gum.

Rejected Paris painters put on show

Monet's impression of fog – "Try to forget what objects you have before you."

Paris, 15 April 1874

A group of artists who have been regularly rejected by the prestigious Salon, the arbitrator of taste, has put on its own exhibition as an independent group in a former photography studio on the Boulevard des Capucines. It is attracting incomprehension and ridicule. The group includes Claude Monet, Pierre-Auguste Renoir, Camille Pissarro, Edgar Degas and Paul Cezanne – 39 painters in all. Their aim is to capture light as it is directly perceived by the eye reflected from objects in particular conditions, rather than the objects themselves. They use short brushstrokes of pure colour and high tone, even in shadows, that blend when seen from a distance. Claude Monet declares that he seeks to capture "the most fleeting effects". He paints from a boat on the Seine.

Outraged spectators object to the formlessness and vagueness of the paintings, which appear to be unfinished. Monet's *Impression: Sunrise* has been seized on by Louis Leroy the critic of *Le Charivari*, to call the group "Impressionists" – a term of abuse. "Wallpaper in its embryonic state is more finished than that seascape," he writes.

Monet's impression of a poppy field – "Paint it as it looks to you."

British make peace with Asante ruler

West Africa, 14 February 1874
After two years of war, the British and the Asante have made peace. Technically, the British, under Sir Garnet Wolseley, won a battle, but neither side can claim to have won the war. At Fomena, Kofi Karikari, the Asante ruler, and Wolseley signed a peace treaty under which the Asante relinquish claims to the coastal states, which become British possessions.

War became inevitable after the Dutch evacuated their coastal forts. The Asante claimed one, Elmina, and the British took it. The Asante advanced and Wolseley's column of British and local troops marched to relieve it. The Asante withdrew, not because they were overawed by Wolseley, but because they were suffering from smallpox.

"The army of a civilised nation need not have been ashamed of a retreat conducted with such skill and such success," said Wolseley's secretary, Mr H Brackenbury. Since then Wolseley has taken the Asante capital (which was not defended), but failed to destroy their army.

A cartoon entitled "The British Lion Aroused" shows how the Asante war was seen by a jingoistic press.

"Editors" are hired just to go to jail

Japan, 1875
A struggle has developed in Japan between the Meiji government and the nation's press following the passing of a press law which gives the government extensive powers of control over the newspapers. Any editor criticising government policy is liable to a fine and imprisonment. The editors have retaliated by hiring "prison editors" whose sole function is to pay the fine and serve the jail sentence while the real editor produces the paper.

While this ploy is causing much amusement among the populace, the government is not amused and is already planning swingeing new laws which will entail the closing down of the papers as well as fines and jail for the "prison editors". The authorities also plan to make newspapers deposit large sums of money which will be forfeited whenever they break the law.

Turkestan falls to Russian invaders

Central Asia, 1874
Ya'qub Beg, the ruler of Kashgar and a thorn in Russia's side for over 20 years, has yielded at last. Russia is now master of all Turkestan.

In 1852 Ya'qub Beg commanded the Khokand fortress of Ak-Mesjid against the invading Russians, and inflicted heavy losses on them before being bombarded into submission.

The past decade has seen a remorseless Russian advance into Turkestan. Since the fall of Tashkent in 1865, Bokhara has accepted Russian protection.

Ya'qub Beg, who founded the autocratic state of Kashgaria in eastern Turkestan, cultivated both the British and the Ottomans. He had coins minted in honour of the *sultan*, and an Ottoman military commission came to Kashgar to train Beg's army, secretly supplied with British arms.

Novelist politician back at Britain's helm

Benjamin Disraeli: 32 years an MP.

London, 18 February 1874
At 70, Benjamin Disraeli has found the time and the energy to carry on a romantic correspondence with two sisters, Lady Bradford and Lady Chesterfield, reorganise the Conservative Party, and win a resounding victory over his old adversary, Gladstone, to become prime minister for the second time.

Six years ago, when he first took office, he said: "I have climbed to the top of the greasy pole." He lasted only a matter of weeks, and though he continued as Conservative leader he devoted far more time than his rivals approved of to writing another novel, the three-volume political comedy *Lothair*.

Englishmen now ask: Anyone for tennis?

England, February 1874
A new game has been patented in England and its inventor, Major Wingfield, expects that this popular descendant of "real tennis" will establish itself as a firm favourite.

Lawn tennis, or *Sphairistike*, (from the Greek for playing ball), has been played before, but the major has set down formal rules. He first introduced the game last year, at a house party, and the rigours of its hour-glass shaped court proved no barrier to players of either sex. Indeed, heartier sportsmen have already condemned Sphairistike as too soft and social – for ladies only.

Tennis players, by Horace Cauty: a new ball-game for the middle classes.

Sultan bankrupt after a spending spree

Istanbul, October 1875
The Ottoman government's creditors are to receive only half the interest due to them, the remainder to be replaced over the next five years by bonds carrying five per cent interest. In other words, the *Porte* is bankrupt again.

Responsibility for the latest financial *debacle* rests squarely with Sultan Abdul Aziz, who, since the death of Ali Pasha in 1871, has appointed six different *Grand Viziers* in three years and paid no attention to any of them. Returning from a European tour, he embarked on lavish palace entertainments and a massive programme of building warships and railroads. When state money ran out, he spent his own, and he repaid his loans by simply borrowing more.

1875 (1875-1876)

Germany, 8 April 1875. The publication in the Berlin *Post* of the article "Is War in Sight?", which expresses concern over recent French military measures, provokes panic in France.

Kentucky, 17 May 1875. The first Kentucky Derby – a horse race – is run at Louisville.

Germany, May 1875. Bismarck abolishes all Catholic orders and congregations.

Germany, May 1875. The Social Democratic Party is founded.

Germany, May 1875. Britain and Russian intervene to prevent war between France and Germany.

France, 3 June 1875. The composer Georges Bizet dies after the "failure" of his opera, *Carmen*, described by critics as obscene.

France, 16 July 1875. The new French Constitution is finalised.

Balkans, 29 July 1875. The peasants of the two mountain provinces of Bosnia and Herzegovina rebel against the Ottomans and put up resistance to the Ottoman army. The Bosnians wish to join Serbia, whereas the Herzegovinians prefer to be integrated into Montenegro.

Southeast Africa, July 1875. In an arbitration award, France assigns the southern shore of Delagoa Bay to Portugal, rejecting British claims.

Balkans, 16 September 1875. Following the uprising in Bosnia and Herzegovina, Bulgarian patriots under the leadership of Khristo Botev, the president of the revolutionary committee, trigger off a rebellion in Stara Zagora.

USA, 30 October 1875. Mary Baker Eddy publishes *Science and Health with Key to the Scriptures*, arguing that illness is illusory and laying the basis for Christian Science.

Egypt, 27 November 1875. Britain buys Suez Canal Company shares.

New York City, November 1875. The Russian theosophist Helena Petrovna Blavatsky founds the American branch of the Theosophical Society, whose beliefs are based on universal brotherhood.

Dakota, November 1875. War breaks out between the Sioux Indians of the Black Hills and white prospectors.

Russia, 1875. Count Leo Tolstoy publishes a new novel, *Anna Karenina*, about a sophisticated lady, unfulfilled by Russian polite society, who takes a lover, with tradic results. On the title page he put the quotation: "Vengeance is mine, I shall repay". His own marriage had never been happy.

Britain, 1875. The Public Health Act and the Artisans' Dwellings Act, which deals with the problems of housing the poor, are passed.

Hungary, 1875. Kalman Tisza forms the Liberal Party and becomes prime minister after the new party wins a large majority in an election.

Britain, 1875. The Conspiracy and Protection of Property Act legalises peaceful picketing.

Central Africa, 1875. The British explorer Verney Cameron is the first European to cross Africa from Zanzibar to Benguela in Angola.

Switzerland, 1875. The French geographer Elisee Reclus publishes the first volume of a vast *Universal Geography*.

France, 1875. The International Bureau of Weights and Measures in created.

India, 1875. Aligarh College is founded by Saiyid Ahmad Khan to build a bridge between Indian Moslems and western civilisation.

India, 1875. The *Arya Samaj* is founded by Swami Dayananda Saraswati to oppose Brahmanism and return Hinduism to the simplicity of Vedic ritual on the one hand and to oppose Islam and Christianity on the other.

New Zealand, 1875. New Zealand is brought under one government following the abolition of provincial councils.

East Africa, c.1875. The *kabaka* of Buganda, Mutesa reverses his pro-Islam policy, which he sees threatening his authority, and develops his policy of playing missionaries off against each other.

London, 1875. Sultan Sayyid Bargash of Zanzibar makes a state visit to London and meets Queen Victoria at Windsor.

Germany, January 1876. The imperial *Reichsbank* opens.

Korea, February 1876. Japan recognises Korean independence.

Italy, 25 March 1876. Led by Agostino Depretis, the progressive party forms a government and embarks on a far-reaching programme of reform.

USA, 1876. Mark Twain publishes *The Adventures of Tom Sawyer*, a novel based on his own childhood.

USA, 1876. John Harvey Kellogg, a Seventh Day Adventist, begins developing new types of flaked cereals. These, Kellogg claims, if included in a vegetarian diet, will help to curb sex drive.

USA, 1876. Henry J Heinz begins bottling and marketing tomato ketchup.

Horse buying stirs war scare in Berlin

Berlin, May 1875

Rumours that French agents are travelling through Germany buying up horses has set off a war scare in Berlin. Chancellor Bismarck has banned the export of horses, and the press is filled with excited articles asking whether war with France is imminent. It is widely known that France's rapid recovery from the defeat of 1871 has aroused fears in Germany that the old enemy might be plotting a war of revenge. This has led to suggestions in some quarters that Germany should launch a preventive war.

Some observers even suspect Bismarck himself of starting the war scare in order to stir up feeling against France.

Trucanini, Aboriginal queen, has died

Hobart, 11 May 1876

Huge crowds gathered in Hobart, Tasmania, today for the funeral of Trucanini, known as the Queen of the Aborigines, the last of her line. She was in her sixties.

Trucanini, 4ft 3in tall, saw her mother stabbed to death by white men; at 16 she was raped by white convicts. She took to hanging about work camps, selling herself for a handful of tea and sugar. Then she met a house-builder, a white man, whom she helped to record tribal customs. Last week she cried out "Rowra [the evil spirit] catch me!" and fell senseless. The coffin lowered into her grave was empty; fearing body-snatchers, the authorities buried her elsewhere.

Captain swims from England to France

Webb arriving to a hero's welcome at Calais, after swimming the Channel.

Calais, 25 August 1875

At 10.40 this morning, an Englishman, Captain Matthew Webb walked onto the beach here: the first man to have swum the English Channel. He had been in the water for 22 hours and had swum through the night a distance of 40 miles (64 kilometres). His body was covered by porpoise grease to keep out the cold. He was fed with cod-liver oil beef-tea, brandy, coffee and stron[g] old ale by accompanying boats.

Webb, now 27, learnt to swim i[n] a local river when he was eight. H[e] saved his brother from drowning [a] year later. Last year he won a meda[l] for jumping overboard from a Cun[ard] ship to try to save a seaman fro[m] drowning.

Britain snaps up shares in Suez Canal

Cairo, 27 November 1875
Britain has bought nearly half the shares in the Suez Canal for £4 million from the *khedive* (ruler) of Egypt. Disraeli, the British prime minister, is relieved to have prevented the French from wholly owning the canal. When the Suez Canal was built six years ago by French enterprise and French money, the then British prime minister, Gladstone, refused to take any interest. Now British ships account for four-fifths of the canal's traffic.

Twelve days ago Disraeli learned that the *khedive*, who held 177,000 of the 400,000 shares but was on the verge of bankruptcy, wanted to sell, or at least arrange a mortgage to a French syndicate. The British agent in Egypt asked for a suspension of negotiations while Lord Derby, the British foreign secretary, exerted pressure on his French opposite number, the duke of Decazes. The French syndicate, without government help, pulled out, and Britain, with the financial help of Baron Lionel de Rothschild, was able to buy the shares.

Tenniel's anti-Semitic view of Disraeli's purchase of the Suez Canal.

Japan fakes military attack on Korea

Korea, 1876
Japan is determined to open up the "hermit kingdom" of Korea, just as Japan was opened up by the arrival of Commodore Perry's "black ships"; it is now using the same tactics of threat and bluff that the western powers used against it.

Rebuffed by the Koreans in their attempts to negotiate a treaty which would have destroyed Korea's isolation, the Japanese have sent warships to survey the Korean coast, braving the fire of coastal guns. At the same time they have warned the Koreans that the ships are preparing the way for the landing of an expeditionary force.

The bluff seems to have worked. The Chinese, who claim suzerainty over Korea and have been recently forced to agree to concessions in the Ryukyu Islands following the Japanese attack on Formosa, have told the Koreans to accept the Japanese diplomatic mission.

Yoshitaka's painting of the Japanese cabinet planing the invasion of Korea.

Composer of Carmen dies as opera flops

France, 3 June 1875
Last night, an opera singer in Paris was stricken with such terrible foreboding that she fainted when she left the stage. The opera was *Carmen*, and its composer, Georges Bizet, was hours from death after a massive heart attack. He was 37.

Three months ago to the day, the Paris premiere of *Carmen*, Bizet's most mature work to date, caused a scandal at the Opera Comique. Its Spanish setting of thieves, gypsies and cigarmakers and its tragic ending were thought "obscene", its music "Wagnerian" and tuneless. Bizet was mortified. Never a very well man, he fell ill with quinsy, rheumatism and, finally, two heart attacks.

Painted in her finest role as Carmen is the opera singer Emma Calve.

Germany's socialists unite in one group

Gotha, Germany, May 1875
Spurred on by Germany's galloping industrialisation and recent political unification, the two main strands of its rising workers' movement united with the foundation of the Social Democratic Party at a unity congress here this month.

The new party's programme combines the democratic socialist ideas of the late Ferdinand Lassalle with the revolutionary communist ideology of Karl Marx. Lassalle thought that workers could own the means of production after a fair electoral system was introduced. Marx believes that the state must be overthrown first. The party's demands include freedom of the press, adult enfranchisement, free and compulsory education and a single progressive income tax. It also seeks the prohibition of work on Sunday and "all forms of labour by women which are dangerous to health or morality".

August Bebel, German leftist leader.

"I promise liberal rule," says Mexico's new leader, Diaz

Mexico, November 1876
Mexico has a new leader. Porfirio Diaz, aged 46, has been elected president in a ballot that followed his army's occupation of Mexico City earlier this month. He promises to restore the liberal constitution of 1857.

Diaz was born in Oaxaca, the son of poor Indians. At the age of 17 he planned initially to enter the priesthood, but chose the army instead. After a year's service he turned to law and joined the Liberal movement. In 1855 he fought for Benito Juarez' guerrillas in the civil war against Santa Anna and then against the French invaders. In January 1861 he led Juarez' troops into Mexico City, ready to welcome his triumphant leader. Only when Diaz found Juarez disappointing as a ruler did the two fall out.

In 1871 Diaz attempted to defeat Juarez at the polls. Defeated himself, he led a rebellion; it failed, but after Juarez died in 1872 and was succeeded by Lerdo de Tejada, Diaz retreated to Texas, where he developed his plans to take power.

1876

Balkans, June. The Ottomans embark on largescale massacres to put down a rebellion in Bulgaria.

Balkans, 30 June. Serbia declares war on the Ottomans.

Balkans, 1 July. Montenegro declares war on the Turks.

Bohemia, 8 July. Andrassy and Gorchakov, the Austrian and Russian foreign ministers, meet at Reichstadt to agree on the future of the Balkan states on the conclusion of the current conflict.

USA, 1 August. Colorado becomes the 38th state in the union.

Serbia, 9 August. Having invaded Serbia, the Turks defeat the Serbs at Aleksinac.

Ottoman Empire, 31 August. Abdul Hamid III becomes sultan following the deposition of Murat V, who succeeded Abdul Aziz, himself deposed in May by the *grand vizier* Midhat Pasha.

Serbia, 1 September. The Ottomans inflict another, decisive defeat on the Serbs at Aleksinac.

Brussels, 12 September. Leopold II of the Belgians forms the International African Association to coordinate the activities of European explorers in Central Africa.

Balkans, 31 October. Under pressure from Russia, the Ottomans agree to an armistice with Serbia and Montenegro.

Ottoman Empire, 23 December. Midhat Pasha, the grand vizier, introduces a liberal constitution.

India. Surendranath Banerjea founds the Indian Association, the leading Indian political association of Bengal.

China. The ShanghaiWusong railway, which was opened in April by Jardine Matheson & Co to serve the foreign mercantile community, is purchased by the Chinese authorities and dismantled.

Ethiopia. The Ethiopians inflict two defeats on the Egyptians near Gura, forcing Egypt to relinquish claims to the whole Nile basin up to Lake Victoria.

Germany. The engineer Nikolaus Otto builds an internal-combustion engine.

Germany. The Bayreuth theatre opens with the first complete performance of Richard Wagner's *Ring* cycle.

Call for help is heard down a wire

Bell: demonstrating his telephone.

Philadelphia

Alexander Graham Bell, the Scottish-American inventor and pioneer of mechanical methods of teaching deaf children, was about to test a new device which transmitted his voice over a distance along a wire. It was then that he spilt battery acid on his leg. He used his "electric speech machine" to call his assistant. "Watson, come here, I need you" were the first words to be spoken on what has quickly become known as the *telephone*.

The message is generated by a vibrating diaphragm that is activated by the voice to a receiver that amplifies the voice. It was developed from a form of deaf-aid.

Bell has demonstrated the system at the Centennial exhibition here, reciting "To be, or not to be" over 150 yards of wire to an excited emperor of Brazil who shouted "I hear! I hear!".

Born in Edinburgh, Bell was educated in London before emigrating to Canada and, later, the USA.

Bulgarian atrocities outrage the British

London, September

Though crippled by an attack of lumbago, Gladstone dashed off in four days a pamphlet, *The Bulgarian Horrors and the Question of the East*, which has become a runaway best seller. The Liberal opposition leader is incensed by the attitude of indifference adopted by Disraeli, the prime minister, towards the sufferings of the Bulgarians.

More than 12,000 men, women and children were massacred by Ottoman irregulars when the Bulgarians rose against their oppressors last May. Disraeli refused to intervene because, he said, Britain should support the Ottoman empire as a barrier to Russian ambitions in the eastern Mediterranean.

Gladstone, however, proclaims it to be a profoundly moral issue. The Ottomans are the "great anti-human species of humanity" who have violated "the purity of matron, of maiden and of child". He addressed a meeting at Blackheath in pouring rain and called on the Russians to drive the Ottomans out of Bulgaria. Referring to Disraeli, he told a friend that the Jews had always been against Christians. Disraeli, for his part, says that Gladstone is playing party politics and is worse than any Bulgarian horror.

Punch's cartoon of Britain's "naivete" in allying with Russia in response to the Ottoman's atrocities.

Queensland's law bids to keep it white

Queensland, Australia

As thousands of Chinese labourers pour into northern Queensland, where gold has been discovered on the Palmer River, the government of Queensland has given in to the agitation for a "white Australia for white Australians". It has passed the Goldfields Amendment Bill imposing a heavy tax on Chinese immigrants to the minefields (repayable only when they leave), and a licence fee six times what white men pay. The Chinese government has protested and the governor of Queensland has already said he will reject the bill on the grounds that it is offensive to British subjects.

The arrival of the Chinese has provoked a violent backlash from the white working class, who fear being undercut by cheap labour. Chinese labourers have been lynched (one unfortunate was nailed to a tree by his ears), and the goldmining centre of Cooktown – where Chinese outnumber white by seven to one – was burnt down by a white mob.

Scientist sees secrets of the mind by looking you in the face

Rome

Is there such a thing as the "criminal face"? Or "criminal build"? Is the wrongdoer, in fact, a product of the environment or of heredity?

Cesare Lombroso, the Italian anthropologist, is convinced not only that criminals are born with the "mark of Cain" but that it is possible to see criminality in their physical features. He believes that the criminal type has certain physical abnormalities or *stigmata*. These might be seen, for example, in a certain pattern of lumps on the skull that mark out an individual as irredemeably immoral. Lombroso also cites such areas as nose and brow as important in criminal identification.

Not everyone likes Lombroso's ideas. Although his name is becoming widely known, his eccentric views are confined to a minority. Just what physical features have to do with a crime is not made clear.

Cesare Lombroso: criminologist.

Indians wipe out General Custer's troops

The last stand of Custer and 265 of the Seventh Cavalry at Little Big Horn.

Little Big Horn, Dakota, 25 June
The buckskin-clad General George A Custer expected to find no more than a handful of Sioux Indians as he led his force of 265 troopers of the Seventh Cavalry along the Little Big Horn river. Instead, as the cavalrymen rounded a bend, they found an entire army of Sioux, Cheyennes and Crows prepared to fight. With more Indians behind him, Custer had little choice but to raise his sword and order his men to charge. Within less than an hour, the general was dead and so was every one of his men. Custer's body was found on the pinnacle of a hill where he made his last stand, the flag of the Seventh Cavalry still flying over him.

George Custer: the civil war hero.

So desperate was the army's plight that Custer's men shot their horses for cover and formed a square from which they took a heavy toll of the Indians. With no hope of relief, they were overwhelmed. Custer's force was a key element in a campaign to force the Indians to leave the plains and return to their reservations. They have been forced to leave the reservations by the threat of starvation.

Sultan agrees to liberty and equality

Istanbul, December
Abdul Hamid II has become the new sultan, subject to a constitution largely drawn up by the Young Ottomans, or Young Turks. His grand vizier is Midhat Pasha, one of the most influential advocates of liberty, equality and ministerial responsibility. Six months ago Sultan Abdul Aziz yielded to the demands of army and people, abdicating in favour of his nephew Murat V, backed by the democratic campaigners. But Murat proved mentally unstable, and Midhat was authorised to approach Abdul Hamid, Murat's younger brother.

The Ottoman sultan Abdul Hamid.

India has new empress

London, April
After a good deal of ill-tempered resistance from the Liberal opposition, Queen Victoria has received the title she greatly desired and is now empress of India. Some objected to the title because "emperor" supposedly has "bad associations" with Continental despots. But Disraeli told MPs that "the amplification of titles" was often necessary in order to catch "the imagination of nations". He said the title was being anxiously awaited by the people of India; it would demonstrate to the world Britain's commitment to India at a time when Russia had advanced to within a few days' march of the frontiers.

After the king of Prussia became the German *kaiser* (emperor), Victoria said to Lord Ponsonby, her secretary: "I am an empress and in common conversation am sometimes called empress of India. Why have I never officially assumed this title?" She argued that the title would once and for all settle questions of precedence with other European monarchs. Lord Ponsonby, discussing the question with his wife, quoted Dr Johnson, who had asked: "Who comes first, a louse or a flea?"

"New crowns for old ones", an anti-semitic jibe at Disraeli by Tenniel.

Triumph for Wagner at his own festival

Bayreuth theatre, Wagner's "total art work" for music, drama and dance.

Bayreuth, Bavaria, August
A huge banquet for 500 people has ended what has been called the musical event of the decade: the first performance together, over three days, of all four operas in Wagner's massive *Ring* epic, in the new opera house he has had built for his own works. It is a triumph for Wagner's unabashed belief in his own genius. Building on the opera house began years ago, with money raised by subscription and by donations from the eccentric King Ludwig II of Bavaria, always willing to spend more than his ministers like on palaces and Wagner. The festival was attended by 4,000 people, including the emperors of Germany and Brazil as well as King Ludwig. Among the 60 correspondents were two from New York, reporting via the new transatlantic cable.

1877 (1877-1878)

India, 1 January 1877. Queen Victoria is formally proclaimed queen-empress of India.

New York City, 4 January 1877. Cornelius Vanderbilt, who rose from poor agrarian roots to amass $100 million in shipping and railways, dies at the age of 83.

Balkans, 15 January 1877. Russia and Austria sign an agreement at Budapest whereby Austria agrees to remain neutral in a war between Russia and the Ottoman empire. The two powers reject the idea of a Slav state in the Balkans.

USA, 3 March 1877. Rutherford B Hayes, the Republican governor of Ohio, is elected president, his election confirmed by an electoral commission after disputed elections the previous November.

Ottoman Empire, 17 March 1877. The first session of parliament under the new constitution opens.

London, 31 March 1877. An international conference on the Balkans adopts a protocol demanding that the Ottomans introduce reforms which benefit the Ottoman Christians.

Russia, 24 April 1877. Following an Ottoman refusal to introduce reforms, Russia declares war on the Ottoman empire.

USA, 1 May 1877. President Hayes withdraws all federal troops from the south, ending what has become known as Radical Reconstruction in the aftermath of the civil war.

Nebraska, 6 May 1877. Chief Crazy Horse and his Sioux Indians give themselves up to US troops, abandoning claims to Nebraska.

France, May 1877. Following the crisis of *Seize Mai* (16 May), when President MacMahon forced Jules Simon, the republican prime minister, to resign, the duke of Broglie forms a pro-monarchist government.

Balkans, May 1877. Rumania enters the Russo-Ottoman war on the Russian side and proclaims its independence. Russian and Rumanian troops lay siege to the Bulgarian town of Plevna.

Boston, 1 August 1877. The Bell Telephone Company, headed by Alexander Graham Bell, is incorporated.

Australia, 20 August 1877. Sir Arthur Kennedy, the new governor of Queensland, gives his assent to a bill drastically cutting Chinese immigration into Queensland after the previous governor refused to pass it.

Britain, 23 August 1877. The Merchandise Marks Act obliges exporters to indicate the place of manufacture of their goods.

Utah, 29 August 1877 The Mormon leader Brigham Young dies.

France, October 1877. Despite losing a few seats to the monarchists, the republicans maintain a large majority in a general election and their share of the vote increases.

Caucasus, 18 November 1877. The Russians attack and capture the Ottoman fortress of Kars.

France, 13 December 1877. After two failed attempts by President MacMahon to sustain a royalist ministry, Jules Dufaure forms a republican government.

Balkans, December 1877. Ottoman forces at the Bulgarian town of Plevna, besieged by Russian and Rumanian troops since May, finally surrender.

Central Asia, 1877. Ya'qub Beg, who founded the independent state of Kashgaria in 1866, and sucessfully resisted Russia's ambitions in central Asia for years, is murdered. The Chinese have used the occassion to embark on the reconquest of Chinese Turkestan.

Paris, 1877. A sculpture, exhibited anonymously at the presigious Paris salon causes outrage. The naked figure of a young male is so lifelike that it is rumoured to have been cast from a living model. According to those who claim to know, the man responsible is a former mason, Auguste Rodin.

Italy, 1877. The Depretis government passes the Coppino Act, which makes elementary education free and compulsory for all.

France, 1877. The French inventor, Georges Leclanche, makes an electric battery.

Washington, DC, 1877. A new newspaper, the *Washington Post* appears in Washington.

Italy, 9 January 1878. King Victor Emmanuel II of Italy dies. He is succeeded to the throne by his son, Umberto.

Ottoman Empire, 31 January 1878. Having captured Plevna, Plovdiv and Adrianople, Russian troops are closing in on Istanbul. The Turks open truce negotiations at Adrianople.

Rome, 7 February 1878. Pope Pius IX dies and is succeeded by the cardinal, Gioacchino Pecci, who takes the name Leo XIII.

Ottoman Empire, 15 February 1878. A British fleet arrives at Istanbul in support of the faltering Ottoman empire. An earlier decision to send a fleet was reversed in January.

Judges free Russian populist agitators

Moscow, 23 January 1878

The sensational trial of 193 populist revolutionaries, most of them students, ended in anti-climax today when more than 100 of them were set free and the rest were given light sentences. In an earlier attempt to suppress the Populist movement, 770 people were arrested and 215 imprisoned, including Prince Peter Kropotkin.

Czar Alexander lost his enthusiasm for reform after university students from well-off families adopted the rhetoric of socialism and revolution and one of them made a clumsy attempt to assassinate him. Five years ago he ordered home all the young girls who had gone to Switzerland to study. They returned with heads full of anarchist notions and enthusiastically joined young men in donning peasant clothes and "going to the people" to spread revolution. More recently the activities of these young idealists has taken a sinister turn. It is believed that some have formed a secret terrorist society called the "People's Will".

Contraceptive campaigner acquitted

England, 1877

A couple who faced imprisonment and heavy fines for distributing a pamphlet giving instructions on family planning have been acquitted on appeal. Even so, the pamphlet was described as "indecent, lewd and obscene" when Annie Besant and Charles Bradlaugh faced the judges in court.

Due to publicity from the trial large numbers of the offending manual, *Fruits of Philosophy,* have sold to poor women desperate for relief from continual pregnancies. But the promotion of the revised edition of Dr Knowlton's book, first published in America in the 1840s, has brought nothing but hardship to Annie Besant.

Annie Besant: family planner.

Since her name has been linked to birth control she has been ostracised by society. She lost custody of her daughter because the judge feared that she might contaminate the child with her ideas, and the suffragette movement gave her no support for fear of jeopardising its case for enfranchisement of women in Britain.

Machine can reproduce the human voice

Edison: phonograph inventor.

USA, 1877

Thomas Alva Edison, the inventor advanced to a horn-shaped device and solemnly spoke five historic words. "Mary had a little lamb", he intoned. Edison rewound a foil covered cylinder and placed a needle in a groove. The machine played his voice saying "Mary had a little lamb".

Edison's *phonograph* consists of a diaphragm attached to a stylus which etches the grooves. The cylinder is turned by hand. A second needle picks up the signal, and the recorded voice played back.

Samurai defence of rights fails

Japan, 24 September 1877

The *samurai* rebellion which erupted in Satsuma last January is over, crushed by the regular army, and its leader, Saigo Takamori, has committed suicide on the battlefield.

Saigo resigned from the government when it decided not to invade Korea, and became the leader of some 40,000 disaffected samurai frustrated at being deprived of a foreign war.

Their disaffection stems from the fact that these once fearsome warriors have been overtaken by the march of events, and their revolt was a last desperate effort to stave off the inevitable.

They had been forbidden to wear their distinctive dress or carry swords, and the new, western-style army threatened their status as a military elite.

What drove them to rebellion, however, was the financial hardship they were suffering because the government had assumed responsibility for their stipends – and cut them to the bone. They had become low grade civil servants.

Samurai, Japan's knights errant, defeated by firearms and technology.

Violent railroad strike paralyses US

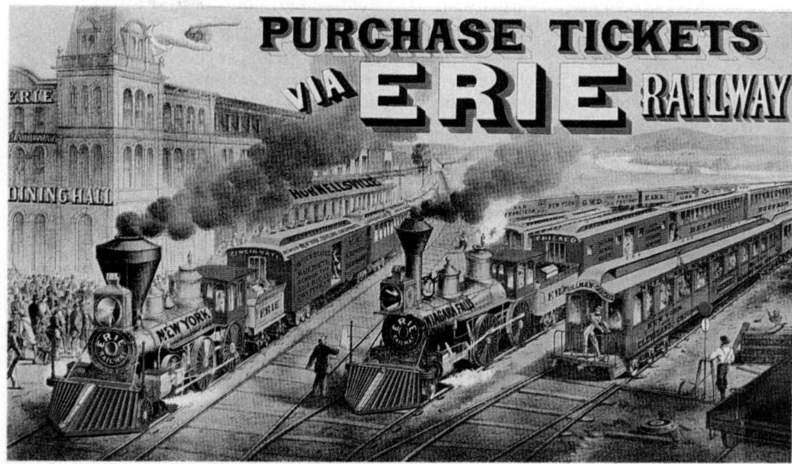

A poster for the Erie railway, famous for its "beautiful scenery".

Chicago, 26 July 1877

Nineteen people were killed here today when police and cavalry charged striking railwaymen. The growing violence follows the killing of nine men and boys in Baltimore last week when soldiers fired on a crowd marching on the railroad station. This first national strike by railway employees – angered by a ten per cent wage cut — has halted all throughline services and now threatens to bring the country's trade to a standstill.

In Pittsburgh, a mob set fire to the Pennsylvania Roailroad yards, burning some 2,000 carriages and trucks, a rail depot and a grain elevator.

Some observers are insisting that the strike is the work of foreign agitators and linked to what they regard as "communistic ideas". In some parts of Pennsylvania, the militia is reported to side openly with the strikers and has refused to move against them.

The strikers refute any political motive. They argue that a brakeman's rate of pay for a 12-hour-day is $1.75 and that this is the second wage-cut in four years.

Boer fury as British take over republic

South Africa, 12 April 1877

Britain has annexed the South African republic (Transvaal), to a wave of Boer resentment. The state treasury is bankrupt after false hopes of prosperity based on gold, and expensive warfare against the blacks. At the Sand River Convention in 1852 Britain recognised the republic. Now, claiming that the republic is unable to defend itself against its black neighbours, and that its existence constituted a danger to "Her Majesty's subjects and possessions in South Africa", it has torn up the treaty.

The Boers' response, taking their lead from the ousted president, Thomas Burgers, is non-violent resistance. One of Transvaal's most respected leaders, Paul Kruger, a veteran of the Boer treks, is going to London to present their case.

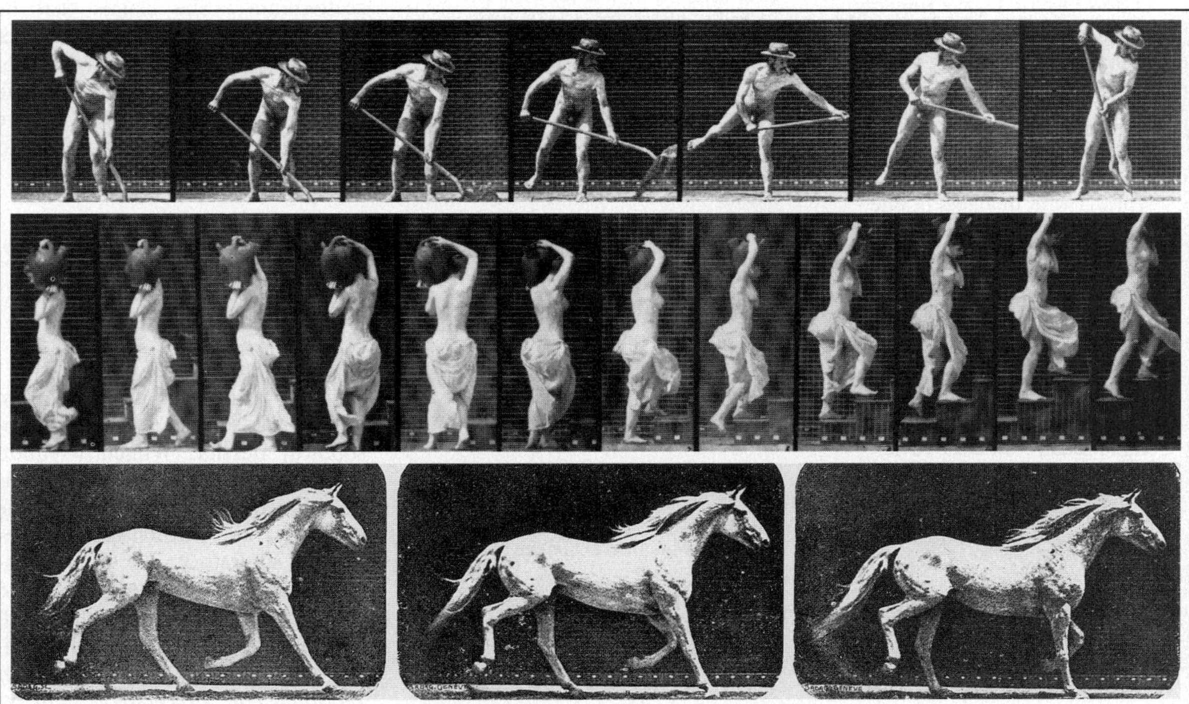

The British-born photographer Edward Muybridge's pioneer studies of limbs in motion, using a fast camera shutter, a revolutionary technique which he developed in the USA between 1872 and 1877.

1878 (1878-1879)

Rome, 20 February 1878. Pope Leo XIII opens negotiations with the German government aimed at ending the *Kulturkampf*.

Ottoman Empire, 3 March 1878. Russia and the Ottomans sign the treaty of San Stefano, granting independence to Serbia, Montenegro and Rumania. Bulgaria becomes an autonomous state under Russian authority, and Bosnia and Herzegovina are granted reforms.

Germany, 24 May 1878. The *reichstag* rejects Bismarck's proposal to introduce repressive legislation following an attempt on the *kaiser's* life by a radical named Emil Hodel.

Germany, 2 June 1878. The kaiser is badly wounded in an assassination attempt, by another radical student, Karl Nobling.

Cyprus, 4 June 1878. Britain and the Ottoman empire sign a secret agreement by which Britain is allowed to occupy Cyprus in return for protecting the empire against Russian advances in Anatolia.

Germany, 30 June 1878. The Conservatives make substantial electoral gains at the expense of the National Liberals.

Germany, 13 July 1878. At the congress of Berlin, Britain, Russia, Austria, Germany, France, Italy and the Ottoman empire reach agreement on the future of the Balkan states superseding the terms of the treaty of San Stefano.

New York City, 15 October 1878. Thomas Alva Edison founds the Edison Electric Light Company.

Germany, 19 October 1878. Bismarck passes an anti-socialist law placing many restraints on socialist meetings and banning trade union activities.

London, 26 November 1878. The American artist James McNeill Whistler wins damages of one farthing in a libel action against the critic John Ruskin, who, on seeing *Nocturne in Black and Gold: The Falling Rocket*, accused Whistler of "flinging a pot of paint in the public's face".

USA, November 1878. An epidemic of yellow fever in the Gouth has claimed 14,000 lives.

Afghanistan, November 1878. Following the refusal of the *emir*, Sher Ali, to receive a British mission in Kabul, after a Russian one is received, the British invade Afghanistan.

China, 1878. The Qing reconquest of Chinese Turkestan is completed.

India, 1878. Over five million people have died of famine in the Dekhan area in the past two years.

Britain, 1878. The laws governing female and child labour are consolidated in the Factory Act.

Britain, 1878. Arthur Sullivan and W S Gilbert collaborate to produce the light opera *HMS Pinafore*.

Germany, 1878. The chemist Adolf von Baeyer successfully carries out the synthesis of indigo.

France, 1878. The first sleeping bag is made, commissioned by the Scottish writer Robert Louis Stevenson for his journey across the Cevennes mountains.

Madagascar, 1878. On establishing closer relations with Britain, Queen Ranavalona II seizes lands belonging to Jean Laborde, the French consul, and then occupies the Sambirano coast, which is under French protection.

France, 30 January 1879. Following large republican gains in elections to the senate, President MacMahon resigns and the conservative republican Jules Grevy is elected to succeed him.

Uganda, 17 February 1879. The White Fathers – the Society of Missionaries of Our Lady of Africa, which was founded in Algiers in 1868 – arrive in Entebbe.

East China Sea, 25 March 1879. Japan invades the kingdom of the Liuqiu (*Ryukyu*) Islands, hitherto a vassal of China.

Afghanistan, May 1879. By the treaty of Gandamak the emir of Afghanistan hands over territories to the British, permits the establishment of a British resident in Kabul and agrees to conduct foreign relations on British advice.

South Africa, 1 June 1879. Prince Louis Napoleon, the son of the former emperor, Napoleon III, dies in combat against the Zulu during an ambush.

Egypt, June 1879. Following the deterioration of relations between the French and British authorities, Ismail Pasha abdicates, to be succeeded by his son Tawfiq.

Belgium, 1 July 1879. The Liberal government brings primary education under state control.

Germany, 1879. The socialist August Bebel publishes the highly acclaimed *Women and Socialism*.

Paris, 1879. The first European telephone exchange is opened.

Russia, 1879. Tchaikovsky completes his opera *Eugene Onegin*.

India, 1879. Ghulam Ahmad of Qadian in Punjab begins preaching a heterodox form of the Moslem religion. His followers are known as the *Ahmadiyya*.

British outrage at Russo-Turkish treaty

Ottoman Empire, March 1878

The treaty of San Stefano on 3 March, which ended the war between Russia and the Ottoman empire, has aroused furious reaction from the other great powers. The chief bone of contention is the enlargement of a Russianised Bulgaria; it now includes much of Thrace and Macedonia, with ports in the Black Sea and the Aegean.

Russia, after aiding and abetting abortive risings against the Ottomans in Serbia and Montenegro, invaded the Ottoman empire last April, but met stiff resistance before the fortress of Plevna fell in December. British support for the Ottomans was equivocal until the Russians stood at the gates of Istanbul. The arrival of a British fleet in the Bosporus persuaded the czar to make peace. The terms of the treaty, in which the Ottomans made enormous concessions to Russia's Slav allies in Montenegro and Bulgaria, were such that the Ottomans may have believed all along that it would not last. Britain and Russia are on the brink of war.

Doll's bid for freedom causes scandal

Copenhagen, 29 December 1879

Shock and scandal surround the latest play by Henrik Ibsen, the Norwegian author of *Peer Gynt*, who lives abroad in Italy. Just published here and performed for the first time last night, *A Doll's House* ends with a bank manager's wife deserting her husband and children for no better reason than to assert her freedom.

"It's your fault that I have made nothing of my life," Nora tells Torwald, her husband, who has shown her every indulgence as his "little songbird", "little squirrel" or "little scatterbrain". She claims that he has made her into a doll, just as her father did. When he accuses her of failing in her sacred duty as a wife and mother she replies "I have another duty – to myself" and slams the door.

Ibsen: playwright of pessimism.

Pyschology is now a German science

Leipzig, Germany, 1879

Psychology has for centuries been less of a science than a philosophical pursuit. Wilhelm Wundt, a professor at the university here, is determined to change all that. He has set up the world's first psychological laboratory. He uses scientific methods to explore people and their attitudes; how they feel, generate ideas and experience sensations. His *The Principles of Physiological Psychology* conveys his belief that we will understand behaviour by seeing it as the outcome of the workings of the brain.

Sultan stamps on Ottoman assembly

Istanbul, January 1878

The Ottoman parliament, which is less than a year old, has been dissolved for the second time after bringing charges against three of the sultan's ministers in connection with the recently-concluded truce with Russia.

Although not free of official pressure, the elected parliament represents a cross-section of Christians, Jews, Turks and Arabs, and has proved willing to criticise the government. The sultan, however seems autocratically inclined, and has banished dissenters.

Powers divide Balkans

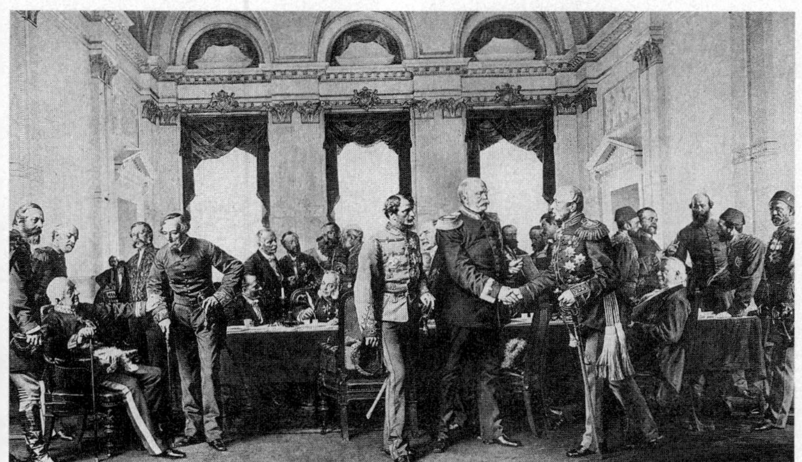
The statesmen of Europe, dominated by Bismarck (centre), divide the Balkans.

Berlin, 13 July 1878
The dismemberment of the Ottoman empire was taken a stage further today when the Congress of Berlin gave the Caucasus to Russia, and Bosnia and Herzegovina to Austria, and confirmed Britain's right to occupy Cyprus. Bulgaria becomes an autonomous principality and Roumelia, including Macedonia and Albania, though still nominally Ottoman, is to have a Christian governor. The Russians have given an undertaking not to fortify Batum.

It could have been worse. Russia used the protection of Christians as a pretext for going to war against the Ottomans; the real motive was pan-Slav aggrandisement and the two-year conflict was ended last March by a treaty that created a Bulgaria which incorporated Macedonia and extended to the Aegean Sea. The Ottomans were required to pay a huge indemnity.

The treaty, signed at San Stefano, near Istanbul, caused misgivings in Austria, where the Bulgarian annexations were seen as a threat, and in Britain, which saw Bulgaria as offering Russia overland access to the Mediterranean. Thus Disraeli went to Berlin determined to rein in Russia's pan-Slav intrigues. He kept a special train waiting and, when Russia proved intransigent, threatened to quit. Bismarck, who was certain Disraeli was in earnest, put pressure on the Russians.

William Booth recruits Christian soldiers

A Salvation Army preacher among "fallen women" in Whitechapel.

London, 1878
Its motto is "Through Blood and Fire", its leaders are generals and its favourite hymn, trumpeted by bands that would not look out of place on the parade ground, is "Onward Christian Soldiers". The Salvation Army, founded this year in London's poor quarter of Whitechapel by a former Methodist minister, is showing that Jesus too needs his troops.

"General" William Booth, aged 49, opened the Christian Mission, the forerunner of the Army, in 1864. It preaches two ideas: that the unconverted face eternal damnation, and that the lot of society's poorest must be improved. The Army is devoted to both causes.

Bismarck curbs German Socialist Party

Berlin, 19 October 1878
Two attempts on the life of the kaiser in the space of one month have been seized on by Bismarck as pretexts for a determined assault on Germany's Socialist Party.

When a half-witted tinker from Leipzig attacked the kaiser, Bismarck blamed it on socialist ideas and presented the reichstag with a bill curbing socialist activities. It was voted down 251-57. A few days later a Dr Karl Nobling seriously wounded the kaiser.

This time Bismarck was ready. Neither of the would-be assassins had anything to do with the socialists, but Bismarck dissolved the reichstag and orchestrated a furious anti-socialist press campaign. He counted on killing two birds with his one stone. He hoped to win a conservative majority and rid himself of dependence on the liberals, and to demolish the socialist vote, which has risen from just over 100,000 to almost 500,000 in six years.

The election result was a disappointment. The socialists did lose a few seats, but the liberals remain powerful. Today, however, when the new reichstag met, liberals joined conservatives to pass the bill banning socialist meetings and publications.

Balkan deal crowns career of Disraeli

Disraeli's triumph after the Congress in Berlin: together Britain and Russia will share the Balkan element of a somewhat scrawny Turkey (Ottomans).

London, July 1878
Declaring that he had brought back "peace with honour", Disraeli drove past cheering crowds to today on his return from the Berlin Congress where his reception had been scarcely less enthusiastic, with Bismarck hailing him as *"Der alte Jude, das ist der Mann"*. (This old Jew, he's a real man.)

It was a remarkable achievement for a man from a Jewish family whose first success came with a novel describing the deep social divisions in Britain – *Two Nations*. He made three unsuccessful attempts to enter parliament before becoming an MP in 1837. A Tory reformer, he added a million town workers to the electorate in 1867 with the Reform Act while promoting empire abroad – making Victoria empress of India and buying into the Suez Canal which his great Liberal rival Gladstone consistently ignored.

His flamboyance in speech and dress made him a favourite of the queen, but, already an earl, he has refused a dukedom, saying he wants only the Garter. But at 73 his health is poor. In Berlin he was taken ill and was too sick to attend the farewell banquet.

1879

South Africa, 4 July. British troops defeat the Zulus in the battle of Ulundi, later capturing their king, Cetewayo.

Germany, 4 August. A law is passed making Alsace Lorraine a *reichsland* (territory) of the empire.

Vienna, 12 August. A coalition cabinet, made up of Austrians, Czechs and Poles, is set up under the leadership of Edward von Taaffe.

Germany, 15 August. The Czar Alexander II sends a letter of complaint to Kaiser William about Bismarck's diplomacy during the Berlin Congress last year.

Ireland, 18 August. Michael Davitt founds the Irish Land League calling for the land to be returned to the Irish people. Charles Parnell, leader of the Irish party in the House of Commons is invited to be president.

Afghanistan, 3 September. Sir Pierre Cavagnari, the British envoy in Kabul, is murdered, disrupting the peace brought by the treaty of Gandamak in May.

China, 2 October. The Qing envoy Chonghou signs the treaty of Livadia, concerning Russia's return of the Ili region in Chinese Turkestan to China, without government approval. Russia annexed the area in 1871 during Moslem unrest.

Germany, 7 October. A dual alliance is formed with Austria following months of tension between Germany and Russia. The allies agree to come to each other's aid in the event of Russian aggression.

Chile, 8 October. The Peruvian iron-clad battleship *Huascar* is destroyed by the Chileans off Antofagasta in the conflict over nitrate-rich land in the Atacama desert which began earlier this year.

Idaho, October. War with the Indians in the north-west ends with the capture of 388 Indians.

Kabul, October. Following the murder of the British envoy in Kabul last month, the British move into the city forcing the *emir* Yakub Khan, to flee.

Peru, 17 December. Chilean troops take Lima.

Russia The author Fyodor Dostoyevsky publishes the first part of *The Brothers Karamazov*.

"Degenerate" painter of fleshy nudes wins social success

"Le Moulin de la Galette" by Renoir: he speaks of his "rainbow palette".

Renoir's "decomposing flesh".

"Black is the queen of colours."

Paris

For the first time a painting by Pierre Auguste Renoir has been hung at the Salon. It is a glamorous portrait of Madame Charpentier, the hostess of a celebrated literary salon, dressed by Worth, in her Japanese drawing room with her two pretty children. It is likely to win Renoir more commissions.

Until now he has exhibited with the Impressionists. At their first exhibition in 1874 he showed *La Loge*, in which the woman in the theatre box is dressed in striking black and white stripes, echoing her escort. "Black is the queen of colours," according to Renoir, who finds subtle tones within it. In 1876 he showed *Le Moulin de la Galette*, an animated panorama of the crowd under the trees at the Montmartre pleasure resort.

He has been sternly criticised for his nudes. "Try to explain to M Renoir that a woman's body is not a heap of decomposing flesh with green and mauve patches of putrefaction," sneered *Le Figaro*. He has also been called "degenerate".

Edison develops incandescent lightbulb

Edison's light bulb. Originally a railroad newsboy, he has invented an automatic telegraphy repeater, a megaphone and a phonograph.

New York City

When an electric current flows through wire it generates heat – and light. This has been known for a long time. In Newcastle, in England, Joseph Swan developed a filament lamp – but it has taken the inventive Thomas Edison to use the glowing wire principle to make an electric light-bulb that burns for at least 13 hours.

Spurred on by Swan's success, Edison has made a bulb that he plans to produce on a mass scale. It consists of a filament of sewing thread converted to carbon by baking – an arrangement the inventor finally came to after trying thousands of possible materials.

Edison is now experimenting with paper filaments and claiming precedence over Swan in his patent applications. A battle in the courts is likely to ensue.

Missionaries used as insurance policy

East Africa, 17 February

Five years ago Buganda seemed threatened by the Moslem *sultanate* of Zanzibar; its *kabaka* (king), Mutesa invited Moslem holy men to his court Two years ago it felt threatened by Egypt. Mutesa invited Anglican missionaries from Britain. Now, feeling threatened by the penetration of British influence up the Nile, he has invited Catholic White Fathers, from France.

He keeps them all at court, always ensuring that no one group dominates, and uses them to offset the traditional power of the chiefs "I am called Mutesa," he once said "which means reformer, benefactor. I want history to say of me one day that if I had not been given that name at birth, posterity would give it to me at my death."

Zulus butcher Britons

King Cetewayo of the Zulus, who rejected Frere's ultimatums.

Napoleon III's son, the prince imperial, a British officer, killed by Zulus.

South Africa, 22 January

Zulu *impis* (regiments) have attacked the invading British army's main base at Isandhlwana, and killed 1,600 imperial troops, half of them British. Today's Zulu victory over white colonisers is triumph of African resistance.

War between the British and Zulu has been inevitable for two years, since the British governor-general Sir Bartle Frere took such a hostile attitude to the Zulus. Frere considered the Zulus' militarised society to be the most serious threat to the British empire in South Africa. Last summer he asked London for reinforcements, saying "the peace of South Africa for many years to come seems to me to depend on your taking steps to put a final end to Zulu pretensions". He was refused them. Ignoring the wishes of the British government he sent ultimatiums to the Zulu king, Cetewayo, demanding that he end the ban on marriages in his army – an action that would wreck the entire Zulu sociomilitary structure. Cetewayo refused.

So ten days ago Frere sent a column into Zululand under the command of Lord Chelmsford. The Zulus let it come deep into their territory, then lured the main force away by a feint. With astonishing speed the *impis* descended on the undefended camp.

The waggons had not even been *laagered* (formed into a defensive ring) – a mistake that no *Voortrekker* (Boer pioneer) would have made. British prestige has been severely dented.

Irish peasants boycott Captain Boycott

County Mayo, Ireland

Lord Erne's land agent, Captain Charles Cunningham Boycott, earned a reputation for ruthlessness in evicting tenants unable to pay. The usual response of a desperate people was rick-burning or cattle-maiming. But Charles Parnell, the Irish nationalist leader, said that anyone renting a farm from which a poor tenant had been evicted should be isolated "as if he were a leper of old". Everyone promptly refused to work for Boycott, deliver goods to him or buy his produce. In desperation, Boycott sent to Protestant Ulster for help, which only served to publicise his plight. Now others will be given the Boycott treatment.

"No rint" (rent), the agricultural equivalent of the industrial strike.

Boers assert their independence again

South Africa, 16 December

The Transvaal is in revolt. Today, the anniversary of the Boer stand against the Zulu at Blood River, a day packed with symbolism, the old Boer republic of Transvaal is reasserting its independence. Already Boers and British are fighting at Potchefstroom.

The last few years have seen a reawakening of Afrikaaner nationalism. Inspired by Calvinist revivalism and German nationalism, thinkers like Stephen du Toit and political leaders like Paul Kruger have inspired men to dream of nationhood again. Most important of all, the Boers assert that southern Africa is their country and was built with their blood. "Weep Afrikaaners! Here lie your flesh and blood! Martyred in the cruellest fashion!" wrote du Toit in his *History of our land in the dialect of our people*, published two years ago.

In London the Liberal cabinet under Mr Gladstone – unlike Mr Disraeli's cabinet – want neither the cost of a colony nor the cost of a war.

China devastated by terrifying famine

Street scene in China: a travelling cook, a fortune-teller and a barber.

China

Millions of people are dying in one of the most terrible famines ever visited on this troubled country. So great is the people's hunger that cannibalism is rife. There has been drought for three years now. The crops have failed. The fields have turned to dust. Even the thatch from roofs has been eaten. Great stretches of farmland lie unploughed, as bare as winter. The farmers are selling their daughters into prostitution and their sons into slavery. Disease rages everywhere.

Hundreds have become bandits and the government has reacted harshly, executing them by starvation in the "sorrow cage". Good work is being done by the missionaries, but the disaster is too vast. Hunger triumphs.

Austria signs defence deal with Germany

Vienna, 7 October

Austria's occupation of Bosnia and Herzegovina, endorsed at the Congress of Berlin last year, has become extremely unpopular, and Count Andrassy, the foreign minister, who wanted the occupation, is being forced to resign. His last act was the signing of the Dual Alliance with Bismarck of Germany. The Austrians are anxious to preserve the *status quo* in Europe and see the alliance as protection against a Russian attack. As for Bismarck, he embraces Austria to prevent its being taken up by France, which he fears may be plotting war to avenge the defeat of 1871. All European powers, fearing war, are seeking "insurance" treaties.

1880 (1880-1881)

China, 19 February 1880. The court renounces the treaty of Livadia, concerning Russia's return of the Ili region in Chinese Turkestan, signed by the envoy Chonghou without government consent last year. China demands re-negotiation and mobilises an army along the Russian border.

Washington, DC, 8 March 1880. President Hayes declares that the United States will have jurisdiction over any canal built across the isthmus of Panama.

Paris, 27 March 1880. On the first day of its release, the publisher Charpentier sells 55,000 copies of Emile Zola's new novel *Nana*.

Britain, 15 April 1880. Following a Liberal election victory, William Gladstone takes over from Benjamin Disraeli, the Earl of Beaconsfield, as prime minister.

Tahiti, 29 June 1880. France annexes Tahiti.

Chile, June 1880. In the continuing war between Chile, Peru and Bolivia, disputing ownership of the nitrate-rich Atacama desert, Chile moves north and takes the towns of Arica and Tacna.

Morocco, 3 July 1880. The Madrid conference on Morocco ends having guaranteed all European powers in Morocco the status of most-favoured nation, thus establishing an open-door policy.

France, 11 July 1880. Amnesty is granted to the political prisoners sentenced for having taken part in the *commune* of 1871.

Germany, 14 July 1880. Chancellor Bismarck puts an end to the *Kulturkampf* – his anti-Catholic policy.

St Petersburg, 30 July 1880. A Chinese imperial commissioner, Zeng Jize, arrives to re-negotiate the treaty of Livadia.

Afghanistan, 1 August 1880. Sir Frederick Roberts frees the British garrison of Kandahar.

China, 12 August 1880. Chonghou, who signed the now annulled treaty of Livadia with Russia, without government authority, is released from jail where he had been awaiting decapitation.

France, 23 September 1880. Jules Ferry, the education minister in Charles de Freycinet's cabinet, succeeds him as prime minister.

Congo, 1 October 1880. The Afro-French explorer Pierre de Brazza-Savorgnan makes a treaty with the Kongo kingdom founding Brazzaville as the basis for a French colony.

North Africa, 1880. The French explorer Paul Flatters leads an expedition into the Sahara.

New Jersey, 2 November 1880. The suffragettes Susan B Anthony and Elizabeth Cady Stanton attempt to vote in the national election, but are stopped by a polling booth inspector.

Washington, DC, 2 November 1880. James A Garfield is elected Republican president.

New York City, 8 November 1880. The French actress Sarah Bernhardt makes her American debut.

Japan, December 1880. The liberal Itagaki Taisuke sets up the country's first political party.

Afghanistan, 1880. The conflict with Britain ends with the accession of Abdur Rahman Khan, the grandson of the kingdom's founder, Dost Mohammed, who supports British interests.

London, 1880. A newly-elected MP, Charles Bradlaugh, is banned from the House of Commons following controversy over his taking of the oath. An atheist, Bradlaugh initially refused to take the oath and though he later agreed to do so, conservatives objected that it would not bind him.

Sudan, 1880. The German explorer Wilhelm Junker sets off on an expedition to the Uele River.

USA, 1880. The author and soldier Lew Wallace's religious novel *Ben Hur* is a best seller.

Switzerland, 1880. Johanna Spyri publishes *Heidi* – a moving tale of a little girl forced to leave the mountains for the city.

Switzerland, 1880. The nine mile long St-Gotthard tunnel, linking the upper Reuss and Tessin valleys, is completed.

South Africa, December 1880. The Boers declare war on the British and drive them out of the Transvaal. The uprising is led by Petrus Joubert, Paul Kruger and Marthinus Pretorius.

USA, 1880. A census shows the population to have grown by more than 11.5 million in the past decade to 50 million.

St Petersburg, 31 January 1881. The funeral cortege of the novelist Fyodor Dostoyevsky, who died on 28 January, is followed by 30,000 people. His greatest works are *Crime and Punishment*, *The Idiot* and *The Brothers Karamazov*.

Paris, 10 February 1881. Jacques Offenbach's fanciful opera *The Tales of Hoffman* is produced posthumously.

Sahara, 16 February 1881. The French expedition of Paul Flatter's is massacred by Tuareg nomads.

British force lifts siege of Kandahar

Kandahar, 1 August 1880

The siege of the garrison at Kandahar was lifted today after a spectacular march by a relief force from Kabul which has routed the Afghan rebels and restored British authority in the southern part of Afghanistan.

The 10,000-strong relief force under General Sir Frederick Roberts covered the 313 miles (500km) in just 23 days, surprising the rebels under Ayub Khan, the son of the deposed pro-Russian *emir* of Kabul. Khan had laid siege to Kandahar after taking Maiwand in July.

Britain now plans to unite the province of Kandahar with Kabul under its new pro-British *emir*, Abdur Rahman. Kandahar's British-installed ruler, Sher Ali Khan is to retire to India.

Major White winning the VC today.

Cold meats get frosty welcome in England

London, February 1880

Housewives are giving a frosty welcome to the first supplies of chilled meat to arrive from Australia. Even though Australian frozen beef sells for less than threepence per pound, compared to as much as a shilling per pound for home-produced beef, many complain that refrigerated meat looks limp when it is thawed and is difficult to cook – a complaint levied against the first imports of chilled American beef six years ago. Traditional butchers are refusing to handle the imported beef saying that they do not want to be "hardbeef mashers". Importers are therefore setting up their own outlets, mainly on market stalls.

The resistance has surprised importers who see refrigeration as the key to bringing cheap and plentiful supplies of meat from South America and Australia without spoiling. The *Glasgow Herald* agricultural correspondent believes that some sections of the trade are sidestepping this hostility by passing off foreign meat as home-produce.

"Soul of French youth" freed from Jesuits

Jules Ferry: educating the French.

Paris, 30 March 1880

The French republican government today pushed through a new law expelling the Jesuits from France. The driving force behind it is Jules Ferry, the minister of public instructions, who is determined to build up a public education system which is free from church domination. His principal target is the Jesuits. "It is from them that we wish to tear away the soul of the youth of France," he said.

Ferry plans even more far-reaching reforms. He wants to make primary education free. He wants to open separate schools for girls and to introduce the teaching of technology and modern languages.

Kansas becomes first US state to go dry

Driving men to drink: US women's holy war against intemperance.

Kansas, 1880

Singing joyful hymns and waving banners of thanksgiving, thousands of long-suffering housewives marched through the towns and villages of Kansas today as the doors slammed shut on the state's saloons and hard drinking men came face-to-face with soft sarsaparilla.

After a lengthy and raucous campaign by the Women's National Christian Temperance Union and the Prohibition Party, Governor John St John has forced a bill through the state legislature outlawing the sale and consumption of alcohol. Until now, officials have refused to shut down illegal saloons – often for fear of physical reprisals by the drinkers within.

Prohibition represents a major victory for the women – angered by the high level of drunkenness and violence associated with alcohol – and indicates the new political muscle enjoyed by the temperance movement. They are certain now to make this a nationwide struggle, campaigning in every local, state and federal campaign, with the wealthy "booze lobby" bracing itself for the fight.

Argentinian troops crush Indian rebels

Patagonia, Argentina, 1880

Patagonia's Indians have been utterly crushed by Argentinian troops. Patagonia will now be opened for stock-raising, land speculation, railways and eventual colonisation by Argentina's newly-arrived Spanish, Italian and German immigrants.

For years the provinces south and west of Buenos Aires have been the victims of Indian raids, the Indians killing settlers' cattle with *bolas* (ropes with weights that entangle cattle's legs).

The campaign against them was organised by General Julio Argentino Roca, war minister until this year, and now president. He drew the Indians into the Rio Negro valley where, using modern military technology, he annihilated them.

Chinese negotiator may lose his head

China, March 1880

Chonghou, the Chinese statesman who so unwisely signed the treaty of Livadia with Russia without telling Beijing of its terms, has been sentenced to death by beheading while the government frantically tries to renegotiate the treaty and hotheads demand war with Russia.

Chonghou, a pleasant nobleman without too many brains, certainly allowed the Russians to foist terms on him which involved the cession of a large part of the strategic territory of Ili whose return he was supposed to negotiate.

However, execution seems an excessive punishment for diplomatic naivete, and pleas for his reprieve are arriving from all over the world. Even Queen Victoria has asked the dowager empress to spare him.

Ned Kelly, outlaw who wore steel armour

Melbourne, 11 November 1880

Edward "Ned" Kelly, Australia's most notorious bushranger, whose outlaw gang has terrorised the state of Victoria for the past two years, was hanged today at Melbourne jail. His last words were "Such is life". He was 25 years old.

Kelly came from an Irish convict family: his father had been transported to Tasmania in 1842. Scraping a living like most of his peers, he began his criminal career when he shot a certain Constable Fitzpatrick who had attempted to arrest his father for horse-stealing. It is also thought that Ned resented Fitzpatrick's pursuit of his sister and his ill-treatment of their mother. With three friends he fled to the bush, pursued by four policemen to Stringybark Creek. A shoot-out followed and the outlaw killed three policemen. A reward was offered for Kelly, alive or dead.

The gang's exploits polarised society. The upper classes condemned him as a killer, his fellow-poor saw him as a folk-hero, a latter-day Robin Hood determined to avenge the wrongs done to his family.

The last stand of Ned Kelly, the 25-year-old Australian bushranger.

Kelly was captured on 28 June, after a gunfight in the town of Glenrowan. Then, even his home-made armour failed to save him, although he survived to face trial.

US book tells story of Indian sorrow

"Move on!": Harper's comment on the American Indians' lack of franchise.

New York City, 1881

A bitter indictment of the US government's treatment of the country's Indian population is stirring the consciences of thoughtful Americans. It comes in *A Century of Dishonour*, a ruthlessly researched book by Helen Hunt Jackson, a poet and storyteller, and tells a sad story of broken promises, cancelled treaties, enforced migration and countless massacres.

Although the native Americans lived in relative harmony with the white settlers for two centuries, it was the relentless push westwards across prairies and plains that brought death, disease and the white man's whiskey to these once-free people.

1881 (1881-1882)

St Petersburg, 24 February 1881. The treaty of St Petersburg is signed, replacing the treaty of Livadia. China regains a large strip of territory in Chinese Turkestan and Russia is granted the right to establish consulates in Turfan and Suzhou (*Gansu*).

Transvaal, 27 February 1881. British troops are defeated by the Boers at Majuba Hill, on the border of British Natal.

St Petersburg, 13 March 1881. Czar Alexander II is assassinated.

Russia, 28 March 1881. The composer Modest Petrovitch Mussorgsky dies of alcoholic epilepsy. He will be best remembered for his opera *Boris Godunov*, first performed at St Petersburg in 1874.

Russia, 3 April 1881. The revolutionary Sofya Perovskaya is hanged for her part in the assassination of the czar.

Ireland, 7 April 1881. The Land Act is passed, outlawing Michael Davitt's Irish Land League but accepting its programme. The new law is likely to meet opposition from both the English landowners and the Irish tenants.

Britain, 19 April 1881. On the death of Disraeli, Robert Gascoyne Cecil, Lord Salisbury, is chosen as leader of the Conservative Party.

Germany, 18 June 1881. The emperors of Germany, Austria and Russia sign a secret treaty guaranteeing the neutrality of the three signatories should one of them enter into conflict with a fourth power. A further agreement provides for Austria's annexation of Bosnia and Herzegovina.

Austria, 28 June 1881. A secret agreement is made with King Milan of Serbia, who undertakes to ban all Serbian propaganda in Austria in return for a vague promise that Austria will recognise his rights over the Vardar valley.

Greece, 2 July 1881. The Graeco-Turkish Commission, set up by the Berlin Congress to define the frontier between the two countries, accords to Greece the Volos, Larisa and Trikkala districts to the north. The town of Ioannina is restored to the Ottomans.

Washington, DC, 2 July 1881. President Garfield is seriously injured by an assassin's bullets.

New Mexico, 4 July 1881. The outlaw William H Bonney, alias Billy the Kid, is shot dead.

Canada, 20 July 1881. The Sioux Chief Sitting Bull, a fugitive for five years since he masterminded the massacre of General Custer and his men at Little Big Horn, gives himself up to the army.

Transvaal, 3 August 1881. At the Pretoria convention Britain recognises Transvaal's self-government.

New York City, 4 September 1881. The Edison electric lighting system for the city goes into operation as a generator serving 85 paying customers is switched on.

Boston, 22 October 1881. The Boston Symphony Orchestra gives its first concert.

Vienna, 8 December 1881. A fire breaks out in the opera house during a performance of Offenbach's *The Tales of Hoffman*. Four hundred spectators die.

Sudan, 1881. Mohammed Ahmed ibn Abdallah proclaims himself *al-Mahdi* (the expected guide) and calls for a holy war against the Europeans and the Egyptians.

Vietnam, 1881. France declares its sovereignty over Vietnam and sends troops down the Red River to occupy Tonkin in the north.

Colorado, 1881. The first geological survey of the Grand Canyon is completed.

Germany, 1881. Doctor Karl Eberth discovers the typhoid bacillus.

USA, 1881. The ethnologist Lewis Henry Morgan dies. He will be remembered as the founder of scientific anthropology, and for his work on kinship systems and theories of social evolution.

Berlin, 1881. The first electric tramway, invented by Werner von Siemens, opens in Berlin.

Central Africa (in Zaire), 1881. Henry Morton Stanley founds Leopoldville on the Congo river on behalf of the International African Association, a private company founded by King Leopold of the Belgians in 1876.

France, 1881. The chemist Louis Pasteur experiments with the anthrax vaccine on sheep.

Boston, 1881. Publishers are forced to withdraw the new edition of Walt Whitman's volume of poetry, *Leaves of Grass*, in response to charges of indecency.

France, 1881. The novelist Gustave Flaubert's *Bouvard and Pecuchet* is published posthumously.

South Africa, 1881. The gun war fought by Cape Colony in an attempt to disarm armed horsemen of Lesotho comes to an end. They will keep their guns but must register them and pay compensation.

Serbia, 6 January 1882. Milan of Serbia declares himself king.

Washington, DC, 25 February 1882. The Reapportionment Act expands the size of the House of Representatives from 293 to 325.

New goods are "puffed" by advertisers

Advertising hoardings at Charing Cross Railway Station in London.

Au Bon Marche: Parisian big store.

Sex and class, a new media tactic.

An advertisement for bustles, USA.

London and New York, c.1881
As ever more commodities emerge from the factories of the "industrial revolution", a new phenomenon is developing: advertising, designed to ensure that no potential customer misses the chance to buy. Manufacturers have used advertising for many years, but in the last decade the profession has moved far from the corrupt hucksterism that typified early practitioners.

The advertising agency, once no more than a wholesaler of newspaper space, now provides specialist services for the advertiser and has become a staple of modern commerce. Firms such as America's N W Ayer & Sons and J Walter Thompson, and their English peers, have revolutionised the way manufacturers are able to present their goods to the consuming world.

Health cures, new foods and inventions of every type are "puffed" as critics have it, by advertisements in newspapers or on hoardings in the streets. The new department stores – Whiteley's in London, Macy's in New York – are equally keen on touting their wares.

Shot US president dies

New York City, 20 September 1881
Less than a day after the death of President James Garfield from an assassin's bullet, his vice-president, Chester Alan Arthur, took the oath of office in the early hours of this morning.

Garfield had been president for less than four months when, on 2 July, he was shot in the back and arm as he walked through a railroad waiting room in Washington. The president, who was rushed back to the White House, was heard to say as the shots were fired: "My God! What is this?"

His assailant, Charles Guiteau, a disappointed office seeker, will now face a murder charge, even though President Garfield eventually died of blood poisoning – possibly caused by the use of unsterile surgical instruments.

Arthur, who had originally supported President Grant for a third term, but fought on the Garfield ticket, represents the extreme right wing – the "Stalwarts" – of the Republican Party. He had been at odds with Garfield during the latter's short presidency.

These conservatives have been locked in a bitter feud with the "Half-breeds", moderate republicans who favour a conciliatory policy towards the south and a reformed civil service which bans "spoils of office". The Stalwarts face defeat. When holding the smoking pistol, the assassin is said to have shouted: "I am a Stalwart and now Arthur is president." Memories of Lincoln's murder are fresh in many minds.

Crowds outside the New York Herald office read the bulletins on Garfield's condition: "The president was somewhat restless and vomited several times during the night."

Russian czar murdered

St Petersburg, 13 March 1881
The czar was returning to the Winter Palace after a military parade when a bomb was thrown at his carriage. Uninjured, he stepped out and was standing in the road asking questions when another bomb was thrown, killing him.

Two years ago, members of a terrorist society known as the People's Will condemned Alexander II to death for failing to summon a constituent assembly. A terrorist got a job in the Winter Palace, smuggled dynamite in and kept it under his pillow. He blew up the room where the czar was to receive a Bulgarian prince. Neither was in the room. Other terrorists placed mines under railway tracks to blow up the royal train. They failed. Today's assassination would also have failed if the czar had not stood around asking questions.

After his death, the public (and the assassins) learnt that, before the military parade, the czar had agreed to reforms.

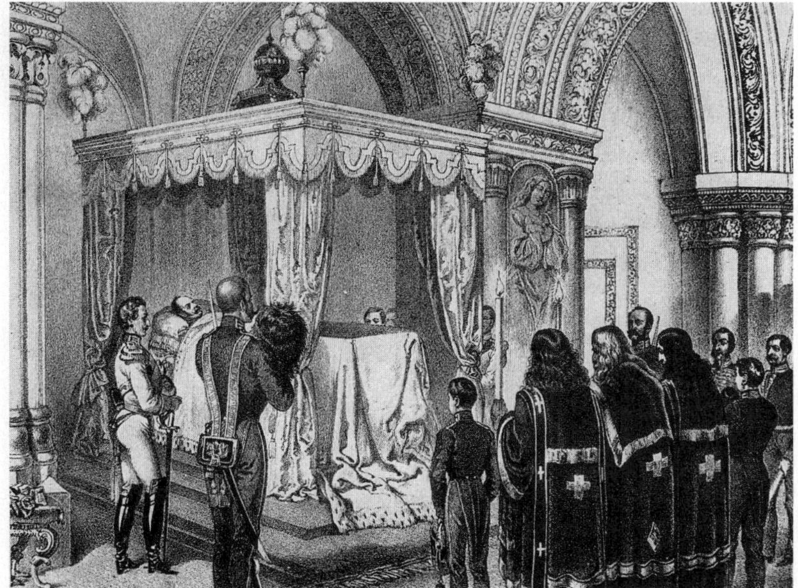
Alexander II, the assassinated czar, lying in state in the Winter Palace.

Boers defeat the British at Majuba Hill

South Africa, 27 February 1881
A British force of 359 men has been annihilated by the Boers, with its commander, Sir George Colley, shot through the forehead.

The force, part of a 1,500-strong column, marched into the Transvaal after the country had declared itself a republic last December. There has long been tension between British and Boer settlers – and it has not been ended by the Great Boer Trek of the 1830's.

General Colley, a practitioner of the "forward" school of imperialism, had come to South Africa during the Zulu War, and was transferred to India where he was instrumental in sending British troops into Afghanistan after the destruction of the British legation in Kabul. In 1880 he was back in South Africa. Arrogant and over-confident, he suffered reverses at Laing's Neck and Ingogo, but pressed on. Then, on Majuba Hill, where Colley had established himself, what was left of his force was overwhelmed. The British forces are now in a state of acute shock.

Highlanders fleeing Majuba Hill.

Tunisia becomes French protectorate

Tunisia, 12 May 1881
The treaty of Bardo has made Tunisia a French protectorate. The French invaded three weeks ago when the Tunisian first minister decided to sweep away various privileges which gave them effective economic control. French influence over Tunisian affairs, like Britain's dominance of Egypt, has increased as the Ottoman empire and its neighbouring powers have declined into actual, or effective, bankruptcy. However, the new treaty only gives France a veto over diplomatic manoeuvres. It leaves the government to Tunisia's own *bey* and his people.

China brings home its polluted students

China, 1882
The government has recalled its educational mission to the United States, and the students who were sent there to "learn the superior barbarian techniques to control the barbarians" are being treated more like outcasts than future leaders of a modernised China. They are housed in filthy lodgings in Shanghai and watched by the secret police. Their "crime" is that they have been exposed to excessive "spiritual pollution" by taking too enthusiastically to the American way of life.

1882 (1882-1883)

Massachusetts, 24 March 1882. The poet Henry Wadsworth Longfellow dies aged 85. His best loved work is the *The Song of Hiawatha* which recounts Indian legends.

Missouri, 3 April 1882. The bank robber and train hijacker Jesse James is shot dead by a cousin seeking the $10,000 dollar reward offered by the authorities.

Indochina (Vietnam), 25 April 1882. Commander Henri Riviere seizes the citadel of Hanoi. This is seen as a serious act of provocation at a time when France and China are in the process of negotiating a common protectorate in the region.

New England, 27 April 1882. Ralph Waldo Emerson, essayist, poet and leading transcendentalist, dies. He first came to public attention with the publication of his essay *Nature* in 1836.

Ireland, 2 May 1882. An informal agreement is made at Kilmainham between the nationalist Charles Parnell and the British government. The government agrees to make further concessions to tenants, and Parnell is released from jail having promised to call a halt to the campaign of violent protest.

Ireland, 6 May 1882. On the evening of his arrival in Dublin, the new secretary of state for Ireland, Lord Frederick Cavendish, is assassinated in Phoenix Park, along with his assistant, Burke, by members of a secret society known as the Invincibles. The Kilmainham agreement is broken.

Italy, 20 May 1882. Italy joins the Austro-German alliance.

Washington, DC, 22 May 1882. The United States signs a treaty with Korea, recognising Korean independence from China, Russia and Japan.

Egypt, 11 July 1882. A British fleet bombards Alexandria in retribution for nationalist violence in which 50 Europeans have died.

Korea, 23 July 1882. A pro-Chinese conservative *coup d'etat* occurs in Korea, directed against Japanese influence. The *Taewongun*, (regent), Yi Si-eung, seizes power.

Germany, 26 July 1882. Richard Wagner's new opera *Parsifal* is performed in Bayreuth to great acclaim.

Washington, DC, 3 August 1882. Congress passes the Immigration Act to control the influx of foreign workers to the United States. In particular the new act bans convicts, lunatics and idiots from entering America and bans Chinese emigration for ten years.

Austria, 1 September 1882. The German National Association is founded. It calls for an aggressive pan-German policy and for workers to be incorporated into cooperatives.

New York City, 5 September 1882. Thirty thousand workers join the first Labor Day march.

New York City, 6 November 1882. The actress Lillie Langtry makes her debut on the American stage.

Boston, 11 December 1882. The Bijou theatre is lit with 650 bulbs as Gilbert and Sullivan's operetta *Iolanthe* becomes the first electrically illuminated theatrical production in the country.

Britain, 1882. The second Married Women's Property Act is passed, whereby women are allowed to own property in their own right after marriage. Previously all property passed to the husband.

Amsterdam, 1882. A Dutch doctor, Aletta Jacobs, establishes the world's first birth control clinic.

Italy, 1882. An independent workers' party is formed at the instigation of the Milan Workers' Circle.

India, 1882. The viceroy, Lord Ripon, forms a commission to examine the state of Indian education.

India, 1882. Bankim Chandra Chatterji's historical novel, *Anandamath* is published. It contains the hymn *Bande Mataram* (Hail to the Mother).

Germany, 1882. The composer Johannes Brahms completes his second piano concerto.

Egypt, January 1883. Britain unilaterally abolishes its joint rule with France over Egypt. The general consul for Great Britain now has almost unlimited power.

Tunisia, 11 February 1883. France sets up a general secretariat whose job is to control the *bey's* ministers.

France, 19 February 1883. Villiers de l'Isle-Adam publishes his *Cruel Tales*, short stories that show a significant debt to the American writer Edgar Allan Poe.

New York City, 26 March 1883. Mrs Alva Vanderbilt throws the world's most expensive party, spending $75,000 on food and entertainments at a costume ball.

South West Africa (Namibia), 24 April 1883. Germans settle the port of Angra Pequena which they rename Luderitz Bay.

Madagascar, May 1883. French warships blockade the island and occupy the port of Majunga. But the prime minister, Rainilaiarivony refuses to capitulate.

Chinese immigration barred for a decade

Red gentleman to yellow gentleman: "Pale face 'fraid you crowd him out, as he did me."

Whites welcome: going to America.

Washington, 1882

California needed cheap Chinese labour to dig its gold. It even imported shiploads of coolies to shift millions of tons of earth and rock to build its rail link to the east. Now – with 150,000 Chinese living in California alone – the white working class fear their labour will be undercut and have forced Congress to ban Chinese immigration for the next ten years.

Led by an Irish agitator, Denis Kearney, the anti-Chinese movement gathered strength during the '70s and was taken up by the Californian Workingmen's Party. The Chinese are accused of working long hours at low rates of pay with the clear intention of returning home with their savings. The reluctance of the Chinese to change their customs and adapt to western ways has created a serious outbreak of racial prejudice which is being fanned by the agitators.

The writer Robert Louis Stevenson has defended the Chinese workers. "They could work better and cheaper in half a hundred industries and hence there was no calumny too idle for the Caucasians to repeat and even to believe", he wrote in *Across the Plains*.

Scientist finds cause of tuberculosis

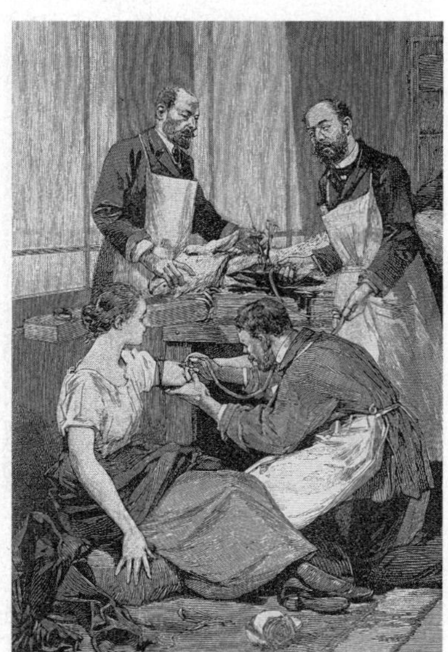
Robert Koch's treatment for tuberculosis, drawing blood from a goat and transferring it to the patient.

Berlin, 1882

It is seven years since Robert Koch identified the anthrax bacillus and performed what was thought to be a "miracle cure" on a dairy-maid for whom there had been no hope.

Now, with government support Koch has established a laboratory in Berlin where he has succeeded in identifying another killer germ – the tubercle bacillus which causes the lung disease which has wiped out thousands, particularly in the kind of damp, airless slum conditions which have become endemic in industrial countries.

Although many medical traditionalists are prepared to scoff at this new science of "bacteriology" Koch and men like Louis Pasteur in Paris are convinced that it will make marked inroads in the treatment of illness.

No shortage of millionaires in America

Rockefeller, only 42 years old.

New York City, 2 January 1882
In an almost unprecedented atmosphere of secrecy and intrigue, control of the entire US oil industry has passed into the hands of just nine men. A "trust" agreement signed here makes John D Rockefeller the most powerful man in the United States outside the White House. Rockefeller's Standard Oil already dominates the industry, and under this agreement shareholders have transferred their shares "in trust" to Rockefeller, his brother William and seven others – giving them power to create or dissolve corporations in any state and allocate funds of more than $70 million.

There is no shortage of millionaires in this free-wheeling, Devil-take-the-hindmost land. When the late Cornelius Vanderbilt sneezed, they said, New York shuddered; such was the power of the financial wizard who started life running a small sailing ferry between Manhattan and Staten Island and amassed $100 million from his railway and shipping empire.

Vanderbilt left the bulk of his money to his family. In contrast, Scots-born Andrew Carnegie, the steel magnate from Pittsburg, describes himself as a "distributor of wealth for the improvement of mankind" and will devote his fortune to education and scientific research.

Valhalla greets Jew-hating genius

Venice, 13 February 1883
Richard Wagner, the man who revolutionised European music, died today from a long-standing heart complaint. He was 69.

Wagner attracted either near-religious worship or near-animal loathing. But no-one disputes his profound influence on the whole language of music: harmony, form and orchestration have been transformed by the series of operas that ended last July with the mystical, sublime *Parsifal*, based, like many of his works, on Germanic legend.

Wagner was an outrageous egotist, even building an opera house for his own works. He knew he was a musical genius and thought he was a literary one too, writing his own libretti and churning out long, turgid tracts on many subjects. Jews, for example, he called "former cannibals, educated to be society's business leaders" who had corrupted "Aryan" purity.

Dreams and nightmares: Richard Wagner at home in the Villa Wahnfried.

Britain bombards Egypt

Conquerors of Egypt: Highlanders posing by the Sphinx at Giza.

Egypt, 13 September 1882
The British expeditionary force under Sir Garnet Wolseley today met Arabi Pasha's army at Tel el-Kebir and totally defeated it, driving the Egyptians from the field and restoring the power of the spineless and pro-British ruler, the *Khedive* Tewfik.

The battle follows on the events of June when British ships bombarded Alexandria after the mob massacred 50 Europeans in the anarchy sweeping Egypt. The shelling led to riots and Arabi was transformed from a mutinous officer into a nationalist hero.

Fears for the safety of the Suez Canal and anger at the atrocities of the rebels led to the despatch of the expeditionary force to the Canal Zone. The soldiers have admirably fulfilled their mission, but their victory can only lead to increased British involvement in Egyptian affairs, a development not desired by the prime minister William Gladstone.

Hush-hush defence accord is signed

Berlin, 20 May 1882
The treaty signed today between Germany, Austria-Hungary and Italy is officially secret, but it has for some time been the subject of speculation in the chancelleries of Europe. It is an extension of an earlier secret treaty between Germany and Austria-Hungary.

The new pact is essentially a defensive alliance directed against France. The three powers are seeking to safeguard conquests made in recent years: Austria-Hungary's in the Balkans, Germany's in Alsace and Lorraine, and Italy's takeover of the papal states. Italy has another grievance against France: for occupying the Ottoman province of Tunis last year and declaring a protectorate.

Jews flee from Russian pogroms

St Petersburg, May 1882
The assassination of Alexander II last year was blamed on the Jews by people in high places with strongly anti-Semitic views, and the slander was given official endorsement by the new czar, Alexander III, who issued a *ukase* forbidding Jews to settle in rural areas, even within the permitted zone of residence, the Pale of Settlement.

The inevitable consequence has been a series of violent *pogroms* which have now lasted for over twelve months and taken the lives of many innocent Jews. Large numbers of Jews are being forced into ghettoes in Moscow and St Petersburg. Others are fleeing even further afield – to western Europe and the United States.

1883 (1883-1884)

New York, 25 May 1883. Brooklyn Bridge, designed by John A Roebling to link New York City and Brooklyn, is opened.

Tunisia, 8 June 1883. A convention specifies the details of the treaty of Bardo of 1881 which establishes a French protectorate over Tunis.

Madagascar, July 1883. Queen Ranavalona II dies and is succeeded by her cousin who becomes Queen Ranavalona III and also marries the country's prime minister Rainilaiarivony, himself a widower.

Indochina (Vietnam), 25 August 1883. While fighting continues with the French, a treaty is signed at Hue recognising Tonkin, Annam and Cochin China as French protectorates. This has been rejected by the Chinese, however, who regard the territory as a vassal state.

Indochina (Vietnam), 3 September 1883. Liu Yongfa's Chinese Black Flag irregulars and Vietnamese forces fight against the French in a bloody and costly battle near Hanoi.

Chile, 20 October 1883. The treaty of Ancon finally ends the war between Chile, Peru and Bolivia for land in the Atacama desert which is rich in nitrates. By the treaty Peru cedes Tarapaca to Chile and Chile also keeps Tacna and Arica for a period of ten years.

Vienna, 30 October 1883. Within the framework of the triple Alliance, Austria and Rumania sign their own secret alliance.

Germany, 1883. Johannes Brahms, the composer, completes his third symphony.

France, 1883. The artist Pierre Auguste Renoir completes his painting *Dancing in the Country*.

Bulgaria, 1883. The *sobranie* (upper parliamentary house) calls unanimously for Prince Alexander of Battenberg to restore the Turnovo constitution, which was suspended on 1 July 1881 when the prince was given full powers for seven years.

Wisconsin, 1883. James and William Horlick sell a new milk drink called Horlick's Malted Milk.

Spain, 1883. The architect Antonio Gaudi begins work on the church of the Holy Family in Barcelona.

USA, 1883. The growing influence of anarchism in the American workers' movement, brought over by European emmigres is illustrated by the formation of the revolutionary anarchist International Working People's Association in Chicago.

USA, 1883. In Chicago, William le Baron Jenney constructs the Home Insurance Building, the first "skyscraper" to have a facade which is disconnected from the building's skeleton.

Egypt, 1883. The fundementalist leader the *Mahdi* defeats the Egyptian army under General William Hicks and occupies Darfur and Bahr al Ghazal.

France, 1883. The French painter Edouard Manet dies. He hit the headlines in 1863 when his *Dejeuner sur l'herbe* caused a scandal when it was exhibited at the Salon des Refuses.

Switzerland, 1883. The Emancipation of Labour Group is founded by the Russian revolutionary Vera Zasulich.

India, 1883. The storm of protest raised by the European community in India against the Ilbert Bill of 1882, which proposes that Europeans should be open to trial by Indian judges, continues.

France, 19 January 1884. The French composer Jules Massenet meets fresh success with his new opera *Manon*.

Central Asia, 31 January 1884. Russian troops seize the town of Merv in Turkmenistan near the disputed area of Afghan border territory, alarming the British.

London, January 1884. A group of socialists founds the Fabian Society, named after the Roman general Fabius Cunctator who used delaying tactics to defeat his enemies.

Sudan, 18 February 1884. General Gordon, sent by the British government to evacuate Khartoum, decides to stay there.

Central Africa, February 1884. Britain signs a pact with Portugal over the control of the Congo estuary in an attempt to prevent King Leopold extending his empire in the region.

Washington, DC, 6 March 1884. Some 100 suffragists, led Susan B Anthony, present President Arthur with a demand that he voice public support for female suffrage.

Paris, 13 March 1884. A new Arab review, *The Indissoluble Link*, is published, aimed at thwarting British policy in the east by developing a pan-Arab, rather than pan-Islamic, consciousness.

France, 21 March 1884. The Waldeck-Rousseau law grants official status to professional and trades unions.

Chile, 4 April 1884. By the treaty of Valparaiso, Bolivia grants Chile the right to control Antofagasta including the Atacama desert.

Karl Marx, sower of socialist seeds, dies

London, 17 March 1883

Karl Marx, the revolutionary thinker who died on 14 March aged 64, was buried today at Highgate in London, where he has lived since his expulsions from Prussia and Paris in 1849. His friend and collaborator, Friedrich Engels, described him at the funeral as "the best-hated and most calumniated man of his time", but asserted that he died "mourned by millions of revolutionary fellow-workers".

Marx and Engels together drew up the *Communist Manifesto* in January 1848 for the Communist League of London, ending with its famous call to workers of all lands to unite. Later that year Marx took part in the revolutionary events in Cologne and made his only public speech at a street demonstration.

In London he, his wife Jenny and their children lived in poverty in two rooms in Soho while Marx studied economic history in the British Museum. He published *Das Kapital*, volume I, in 1867. He was the leading member of the First International Working Men's Association. Engels is editing the rest of *Das Kapital*.

Karl Marx: Hegelian philosopher.

Nietzsche's Zarathustra speaks out

Nietzsche: prophet of the superman.

Basle, Switzerland, 1883

Friedrich Nietzsche, the German philosopher who is a professor here, has published the first part of his major work of philosophical mysticism, *Also Sprach Zarathustra* (Thus Spake Zarathustra) in which he presents his idea of an *Ubermensch*: "I teach you the Superman. Man is something to be surpassed."

In a previous book he declared that "God is dead"; he considers that Christianity is played out and claims that "morality is the herd instinct in the individual". He shows the greatest contempt for the herd who, he fears, will trample individual excellence underfoot. Hence the idea of a race of Supermen, beyond good and evil.

Darkness at noon after volcano erupts

Krakatoa, Java, 28 August 1883

Over 30,000 people are feared dead after the volcano at Krakatoa erupted, triggering a tidal wave 120 feet (36.5 metres) high that has flooded homes in the nearby coastal towns of Java and Sumatra. Rescue efforts are being hampered by a thick cloud of black volcanic ash 17 miles (27 kilometres) high that has blotted out the sun and plunged the region into darkness for the last two and a half days. The volcano's most violent eruption yesterday could allegedly be heard 2,200 miles (3,520 kilometres) away in Australia.

Bolivia loses her coastline to Chile

South America, 1883
The War of the Pacific, waged between Chile and the allies Peru and Bolivia since 1879, is over and Chile has won. Chile has occupied much territory, including Lima, and defeated every allied campaign.

Under the peace Chile is to retain the mineral-rich areas it has seized from Peru, as well as the littoral that served as Bolivia's narrow connection to the sea. In return Chile will build a railway for the now land-locked Bolivians. The war began in 1879 following disagreements over national boundaries and the taxation by Bolivia of Chilean nitrate firms operated under Bolivian jurisdiction. When these taxes were raised and the Chileans refused to pay, the firms were seized. Chilean troops occupied the town of Antofagasta.

When Peru attempted to mediate the Chileans rejected its efforts, pointing out that Peru and Bolivia were allies under a treaty of 1873. Chile's demands that the treaty should be scrapped were ignored and war was declared.

Chilean gunners mounting heavy coastal guns during the War of the Pacific.

India worries over Russian advances

Persia, February 1884
The vaguely defined frontiers between Russia, Persia and Afghanistan to the east of the Caspian Sea have been causing concern in London and New Delhi, where officials fear continuing Russian pressure could pose a threat to India.

The Russians have just taken over a place called Merv and, though travellers say that it is no more than a mudhut village with an oasis, it is only 12 days' march from Herat in Afghanistan. The Indian government is urging London to get "a clear understanding" with the Russians as to the exact frontier line in the region. The Russians are proving evasive; worse still, they have forced the *shah* of Persia to accept a Cossack brigade to "defend" the frontier region.

Huckleberry Finn, tale of runaway boys

USA, 1884
The publication of *The Adventures of Huckleberry Finn* confirms the arrival of a major literary talent in Mark Twain, the pen name of Samuel Clemens, a lawyer's son. This latest book is a companion to *The Adventures of Tom Sawyer*, published nine years ago. Both tell of childhood adventures on the banks of the Mississippi, and are drawn from Twain's own life.

A journalist and travel writer, Twain has a growing international reputation. Four years ago he published *The Prince and the Pauper*, an adventure story that was also a socio-political allegory.

Buffalo Bill's Wild West

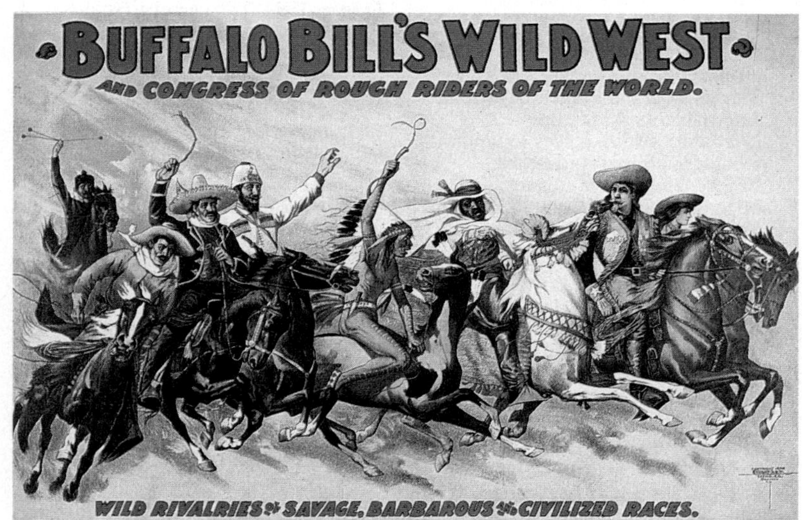

America's new mythology: a poster for William Cody's famous Wild West show.

Jesse James and the Younger gang.

William Bonney: "Billy the Kid".

Omaha, Nebraska, 17 May 1883
A new kind of circus came to town today – with gun-toting cowboys, heavily war-painted Red Indians, a herd of buffalo and a buckskin-clad sharpshooting colonel with shoulder-length hair by the name of Buffalo Bill. His real name is William Cody; he is a former cavalry scout, and his "Wild West Show" is aimed at re-creating America's pioneering days with fake gun-duels and stagecoach hold-ups.

Yet the show is not doing too well, perhaps because people in these parts don't really see why they should part with money when the real thing is still going on.

The west is still wild, with legendary heroes like Marshal Wyatt Earp, noted for his shootout at Tombstone's OK Corral in 1881 and Sheriff "Wild Bill" Hickok who was shot in the back in a saloon clutching a poker hand 1876. The villains are equally legendary. The New York-born "Billy the Kid" (William Bonney) murdered 21 men before he was shot down in 1881; Jesse James, the bankrobber, was shot in the back in 1882 as he dusted a picture in his mother's home.

1884 (1884-1885)

South-West Africa, 24 April 1884. Bismarck cables Cape Town that South West Africa is now a German colony.

China, 11 May 1884. Li Hongzhang signs a convention in Tianjin with the French negotiator Fournier over Indochina (*Vietnam*). China agrees to recognise all past and future Franco-Vietnamese treaties, to open Yunnan and Guangxi to French trade and to withdraw its troops to the Chinese frontier.

New York City, 10 May 1884. Theodore Roosevelt, the 25-year-old legislator renowned for his attacks on government corruption, is retiring from politics following the sudden deaths of his wife and mother. He plans to hunt buffalo in Dakota.

Indochina, 23 June 1884. Unaware of the Li-Fournier convention, Chinese forces defeat the French at Bacle and force them to retreat.

Equatorial Africa, 11 July 1884. Germans begin to sign up Cameroons chiefs as subjects.

Indochina, 12 July 1884. The French government sends an ultimatum to China demanding observation of the Li-Fournier convention and payment of an indemnity of 250 million francs. The *Zongli* Yamen refuses payment but withdraws Chinese troops from Indochina.

Formosa (Taiwan), 5 August 1884. French naval forces bombard Jilong because of the Chinese refusal to pay an indemnity for their non-observance of the Li-Fournier treaty.

China, 23 August 1884. French warships attack Fuzhou, sink or disable all seven warships of the Fujian fleet and destroy the French-built Fuzhou dockyard.

China, 26 October 1884. The court declares war on France.

Zurich, October 1884. Engels publishes *The Origin of the Family, Private Property and the State*.

Berlin, 15 November 1884. An international conference on the Congo question is organised by the German chancellor, Bismarck.

China, 17 November 1884. Chinese Turkestan is given provincial status, re-named Xinjiang (New Frontier).

Korea, 6 December 1884. Following a *coup d'etat* by pro-Japanese radicals three days ago, Yuan Shikai yesterday led some 2,000 Qing troops stationed in Seoul and Korean forces in an attack on the royal palace. The Japanese are defeated and withdraw from Seoul.

London, 1884. Maxim invents a new weapon, the machine gun.

France, 1884. The chemist Hilaire Bernigaud, the count of Chardonnet, patents artificial silk.

Bohemia, 1884. The composer Bedrich Smetana dies in an asylum. He is the founder of Czech nationalism in music.

London, 1884. The Reform Act introduced by Gladstone's government allows householders in the counties to vote and increases the total electorate from three to five million. By a separate act parliamentary seats are redistributed so that representation corresponds to population.

Central Africa (Zaire), 1884. Henry Morton Stanley leaves the Congo area 40 trading posts having set up on behalf of King Leopold of the Belgian's company, now called the International Association for the Congo.

Missouri, 1884. Mark Twain publishes *The Adventures of Huckleberry Finn*, the tale of an orphan and a runaway slave's journeys on the Mississippi River.

New York City, 1884. Lewis E Waterman has developed the first ink-storing pen fit for manufacture.

France, 1884. Divorce is reintroduced and can be obtained on the grounds of cruelty or injury. Financial maintenance and custody are to be awarded to the successful petitioner of a divorce. This gives women the means to keep their families which they have not previously enjoyed.

East Africa, 1884. The German Karl Peters founds the Society for German Colonisation and sets off on a journey along the coast of Tanganyika.

South Africa, 1884. The first black Southern African newspaper, *Imvo zabaNshundu* (The Voice of the Black People), is founded in Xhosa.

New York City, 1884. The surgeon William Stewart Halsted discovers that injected cocaine is an effective anaesthetic.

South Africa, 1884. The Tembu National Church, the first black church in Southern Africa, is founded.

Austria, 1884. The composer Anton Bruckner composes his seventh symphony which is a huge popular success.

East Africa, 17 February 1885. Germany establishes a protectorate over the Tanganyika coast.

Berlin, 25 February 1885. The Berlin Act is passed, summing up the agreements over West Africa at last year's Berlin's conference.

Horseless carriage frightens the cattle

Karl Benz's rival, Gottlieb Daimler, driven in his vehicle by his son, Adolf.

Mannheim, Germany, 1885

In the quiet and dusty lanes around this city, a noisy threat has emerged which could change the traditional, peaceful rural way of life for ever. At nearly eight miles (13 kilometres) an hour, young Karl Benz's "horseless carriage" is frightening the cattle and worrying the horse-trade.

The first such carriage devised by Nicholas-Joseph Cugnot in 1769, was steam-driven, but Benz is exploiting petrol and has created an internal combustion engine with the pulling power of one horse. The engine has electric ignition and is sited at the rear of the vehicle. The machine is capable of variable forward speeds through a system of pulleys with power transmitted by means of a drive belt. The single front wheel makes for easier steering than on horse-drawn vehicles, but it must be said that Benz's machine is not entirely reliable. It breaks down; knowing that rivals like Gottlieb Daimler are working on their own designs, Benz is anxious to ensure that it does not.

Newsman exposes underage vice scandal

London, 1885

William Stead, the 36-year-old editor of the *Pall Mall Gazette* and self-appointed "trumpeter in ordinary of the Salvation Army", has published a horrifying revelation of Britain's white-slave trade. Now he faces a trial for publishing obscene material.

"A maiden tribute of modern Babylon" details a ghastly catalogue of degradation and exploitation. Stead mingled with prostitutes and took down their stories. Particularly shocking was his purchase for £5 of a girl of only thirteen.

Stead's pamphlet has excited much interest, even if his critics do dismiss him as a sex-obsessed puritan, an exploiter himself who uses sensation to sell his magazine.

Journalist as prisoner: a protest.

France blasts ships in surprise attack

Fuzhou, China, 23 August 1884
The French fleet which has been moored in the harbour here for over a month treacherously opened fire today, sinking 11 Chinese ships, destroying the dockyard which had been built with French help and killing some 3,000 people.

This attack follows the French bombardment of Jilong in Formosa earlier this month and is part of the French pressure on China to fulfil the terms of the Li-Fournier convention under which the Chinese agreed to withdraw from Annam (*northern Vietnam*) in exchange for a French promise not to invade South China. A clash between French troops and Chinese units not yet ordered to withdraw has given the French the opportunity to demand further concessions.

Germans expand African "empire"

Africa, 1884
German colonial expansion continues with the foundation of the Society for German Colonisation, by Karl Peters, a pastor's son. Peters is travelling along the East African coast persuading local chieftains to accept the society's protection.

Bismarck, the German chancellor, has encouraged merchants to found colonies. Adolf Luderitz, from Bremen, who acquired land round the bay of Angra Pequena in South West Africa. Britain recognised German South West Africa on 22 June, after Germany made threats over Egypt.

In July, Togo and Cameroon, acquired by the Hamburg merchant and shipper Adolf Woermann, were also made German colonies.

Chinese foil Japanese coup in Korea

Seoul, 6 December 1884
Chinese troops stationed in the Korean capital today seized the royal palace following an attempt by pro-Japanese radicals to mount a coup d'etat.

The coup was instigated by the Japanese minister to Korea, Takezoe Shinichiro, who led 200 Japanese soldiers in defence of the palace. The coup failed and the Japanese were defeated.

It was a minor incident in terms of casualties, but it reflects Japan's determination to exert its growing power in Korea, for so long a Chinese vassal state. Korea's strategic geographic position between China and Japan is rapidly turning it into the cockpit of Asia.

Georges Seurat's "Bathers at Asnieres". Seurat seeks to go beyond the fleeting images of the Impressionists to a more timeless image, combining naturalism with formality. Earlier works had been exhibited in the Salon in 1883, but the Salon rejected Seurat's bathers the following year as superficial. Outraged fellow artists acclaim it as a masterpiece. Now Seurat is calling his minute brush-stokes, almost dots, "pointillism".

Europe shares out Africa

The Congress of Berlin, where the nations of Europe cut the African cake.

Berlin, 26 February 1885
Delegates from 15 nations, meeting in Berlin with Bismarck in the chair, have agreed on the partition of Central and East Africa. Though Germany and France have gained substantial areas, by far the biggest prize has been taken, not by one country, but by one man: King Leopold II of the Belgians has been given possession of 900,000 square miles (2.3 million square kilometres) of the Congo basin.

Leopold used intrigue, bluff and downright humbug. Stanley, the explorer who has first-hand knowledge of the Congo, attended the conference as an adviser to the US delegation; in fact, he is in Leopold's employ. When delegates expressed doubt about giving in to him, Leopold threatened to abandon development of the Congo and wreck its settlements. At the same time, Leopold presented himself as a high-minded philanthropist who wanted to help the black man with his International Association for the Exploration and Civilisation of Central Africa.

But the decisive factor was Bismarck's determination to keep Britain out of the Congo basin. The British are not worried; when their options on various pieces of Africa have been closed they will control twice as much as that of France and Germany combined.

Congo is king's prize in African carve-up

Brussels, 1 August 1884
King Leopold II of Belgium formally proclaimed his "Congo Free State" today, following the concession to him by other European powers at Berlin last February.

His interest in the Congo dates from 1876, inspired by the travel narrative of H M Stanley, who described the river as "the great highway of commerce to broad Africa". Leopold recruited Stanley to open up the river basin for his company. In five years Stanley has founded 40 trading stations.

Under the Berlin agreement, the Congo basin is meant to be a free trade area, but Leopold has no intention of losing his profitable monopoly of the highway.

Stanley, journalist and explorer.

1885 (1885-1886)

Washington, DC, 4 March 1885. Grover Cleveland, Democrat, is inaugurated as president.

Indochina (Vietnam), 29 March 1885. Yesterday Qing troops under Feng Zicai attacked French forces at Langson on the Vietnamese side of the border, seriously wounding General Francois de Negrier. Today Langson has fallen to Feng.

Afghanistan, 30 March 1885. Russian troops inflict a crushing defeat on Afghan forces at Ak Teppe, despite orders not to fight. The British, Russians and Afghans are now seeking a settlement.

Paris, 30 March 1885. Jules Ferry's cabinet resigns following the loss of Langson to the Chinese.

Korea, 18 April 1885. The Sino-Japanese Li-Ito treaty is signed. Both powers withdraw their troops, which have been fighting since 1884, and undertake to work in concert in all new actions.

Central Africa (Zaire), 30 April 1885. Leopold II of the Belgians proclaims himself sovereign of the Congo Free State.

Paris, 1 June 1885. Victor Hugo, the famous novelist and poet who died on 22 May, is given a state funeral. His greatest work is without doubt *Les Miserables*.

Nigeria, 5 June 1885. Following the signature of the Anglo-Sokoto treaty on the first of this month, a British protectorate is established over the Niger districts.

China, 9 June 1885. The French minister Patenotre and Li Hongzhang sign the Sino-French treaty on Indochina in Tianjin. It reaffirms the French protectorate over Indochina and settles border and trade regulations.

New York City, 19 June 1885. The Statue of Liberty arrives from France.

Sudan, 22 June 1885. The religious leader the *Mahdi* (Mohammed Ahmad ben Abdullah) a *faqir* (fakir) from Dongola, dies. He proclaimed himself *al-Mahdi* (the expected guide) on 19 June 1881 and led his people in war against the British.

Washington, DC, 1 July 1885. The US cancels an 1871 treaty with Canada, terminating reciprocal fishing rights.

New York, 23 July 1885. Ulysses S Grant, the former president dies aged 63 leaving nothing but his memoirs.

Ireland, 14 August 1885. The new British government establishes close relations with Charles Parnell and passes the Land Act providing large state loans for Irish peasants to buy lands from the English landowners.

Bulgaria, 17 September 1885. A rebellion in eastern Rumelia allows Alexander of Battenberg, the prince of Bulgaria, to annex the region.

Southern Africa, 30 September 1885. The British divide the Bechuanaland protectorate (*Botswana*) from Bechuanaland colony.

Bulgaria, 17 November 1885. The Serbian army, with Russian support, invades Bulgaria following the announcement of its union with Rumelia. The Serbs are defeated at Slivnitsa, 25 miles outside Sofia.

Spain, 25 November 1885. On the death of Alfonso XII, his widow Maria Cristina comes to the throne in the name of the child she is carrying, due to be born in May.

Burma, November 1885. The British seize the capital, Mandalay.

Madagascar, 17 December 1885. By a treaty signed in Tamatave, France acquires the protectorate of Madagascar, which it is to represent in all foreign relations.

USA, 1885. Robert Louis Stevenson publishes *Dr Jekyll and Mr Hyde*, a chilling novel dealing with the question of evil.

Germany, 1885. The engineer Gottlieb Daimler invents the first motorcycle.

New Zealand, 1885. The American Mary Leavitt, an envoy of the Women's Christian Temperance Union of the United States, visits New Zealand and founds 15 branches of the organisation. In the US it has acquired a distinctly feminist character, concerning itself mainly with the issue of women's suffrage.

India, 1885. Bharatendu Harischandra, the father of modern Hindi, dies.

Paris, 1885. European vineyards are being destroyed by a plant louse called *phylloxera vasatrix*, brought over in American vines. The louse eats away at the roots of the vines and is devastating the European wine trade.

Germany, 1885. Johannes Brahms composes his fourth symphony, a tragic work whose unusual finale wins a mixed reception.

Washington, DC, 1885. The veterinarian Daniel Elmer Salmon describes salmonella bacteria which he believes causes food poisoning.

New York City, 1885. Gilbert and Sullivan's new musical *The Mikado* is given its American premiere, directed by Richard D'Oyly Carte.

Bulgaria, 3 March 1886. Bulgaria and Serbia sign the peace of Bucharest which maintains the *status quo* between the two countries.

British troops on the road to Mandalay

Rangoon, Burma, November 1885
An expeditionary force of 10,000 soldiers of the British Indian Army is marching up the Irrawaddy valley to head off French intervention in Upper Burma. Lower Burma, administered from Rangoon, is British as a result of campaigns in 1824 and 1852. Upper Burma, formerly a friendly independent state, is now ruled by young King Thibaw, who massacred 80 relatives on his coronation six years ago. Thibaw encouraged overtures by France, which itself occupies much of Indochina by force of arms, relying on Foreign Legion mercenaries. British traders in Rangoon protested about the likely loss of trade and influence. It is now likely that Upper Burma, a kingdom larger than Britain with a population of four million, will be brought under tighter control and possibly annexed. King Thibaw's army is no match for the British.

Frenchman inoculates child against rabies

Pasteur with English children whom he is inoculating against rabies.

Paris, 1885
A nine-year-old boy's life has been saved after he was bitten by a rabid dog. Until now rabies was regarded as incurable. Even though doctors had predicted certain death for the boy, Joseph Meister, he was taken to the surgery of Dr Louis Pasteur, a doctor who has been experimenting with a vaccine made from a weakened strain of rabies virus developed from dog saliva.

Young Joseph made an amazing recovery, and, within days, Dr Pasteur found his surgery besieged by crowds of optimistic victims of dog bites.

Pasteur, who pioneered the technique of heating milk to kill germs which is now named after him, has become something of a national hero after devising new methods for the treatment of anthrax and cholera.

Ramakrishna, India's saintly holy man

India, 1886
India is mourning the death at the age of 50 of Shri Ramakrishna, one of the saintliest of all its religious leaders.

The son of a village priest in Bengal, Ramakrishna went into his first mystical trance at the age of seven, and was installed as a priest in Calcutta with his brother when only 16. His utter devotion to the search for God brought him further mystical experiences, and, in due course, followers from the educated middle classes, who helped to propagate his simple, rustic holiness.

Guerrilla leader who fought French in Senegal is dead

Senegal, West Africa, 1886
Lat Dyor, the ruler of Kayor, who waged a four-year guerrilla war against the French in Senegal, has been killed. He fell in battle, dying with his men at N'Dekete.

He first became ruler of Kayor in 1862, but was driven out by French forces and fled to the Senegalese Moslem leader, Maba Diakhou Ba, who was fighting a holy war against the French. Lat Dyor became a Moslem and, when Diakhou died, led the resistance, until coming to terms with the French in 1871. He was reinstated as king, and soon controlled all western Senegal.

When France began building a railway into the interior to open up the area for trade, groundnut cultivation and French administrators, Lat Dyor recognised the danger to independent Africa and began a guerrilla war, tying down thousands of French troops.

Lat Dyor's death and defeat will not bring the war to an end – too many of his followers are still fighting – but it will take the railway further towards the river Niger.

Nationalist party is formed in India

Bombay, India, 28 December 1885
As British troops occupy Upper Burma, and the British empire takes control of more territory than ever before, Indian nationalists have met to form a new political movement. They are calling the movement the Indian National Congress. Since the founding of universities at Bombay, Calcutta and Madras in 1857, a middle class has emerged, resentful at being treated by Englishmen as racially inferior and being denied political responsibility. Congress' resolutions could not be more moderate: the British administration should be responsible to the House of Commons, and there should be elected representatives on the legislative councils and equality of opportunity in the Indian Civil Service. The British should watch them: over half of them are lawyers.

Dervishes spear Gordon in Khartoum

Khartoum, 26 January 1885
General Gordon is dead, killed by a Dervish spear today on the steps of his office and beheaded, while the relief force fights its way up the Nile against fierce opposition from the Mahdi's fanatics.

"Chinese" Gordon, who made his name fighting the *Taiping* rebels, had been sent to Khartoum to evacuate the Anglo-Egyptian forces from the Sudan where they were in danger of being overrun by the all-conquering forces of Mohammed Ahmad, hailed by his Moslem followers as the Mahdi or "divinely guided one".

Gordon, however, was a mystic and a puritan, as much a zealot as the Mahdi, and when he arrived in Khartoum he saw it as his duty to defeat the Dervishes.

He asked for reinforcements from a government whose instructions expressly refused him a free hand. Gordon's will was pitted against Gladstone's determination not to be involved in fresh colonial adventures.

Lord Randolph Churchill took up Gordon's cause in the House of Commons as the Mahdi's forces closed on Khartoum. "Are they to remain indifferent," he asked, "to the fate of the one man on whom they have counted to extricate them from their dilemmas, to leave him to shift for himself, and not to make a single effort on his behalf?"

The public responded to the call. Gordon was a true British hero, a man of action who fought against slavery and for the children of the poor. Eventually, last September, the government gave in and General Sir Garnet Wolseley was sent to Cairo to raise a rescue force.

Ten thousand men were assembled with speed, but their progress against the Mahdi's forces along uncharted reaches of the Nile has been painfully slow. Sir Herbert Stewart took his Camel Corps in a dash across a loop in the Nile. He died in a desperate battle in which a British square was broken by the people they call "fuzzy wuzzies". But the survivors pressed on. They are within two days of Khartoum, but too late: Gordon is dead and the Mahdi is master of the Sudan.

An earlier British success against Mahdi forces at Tamanieb last year.

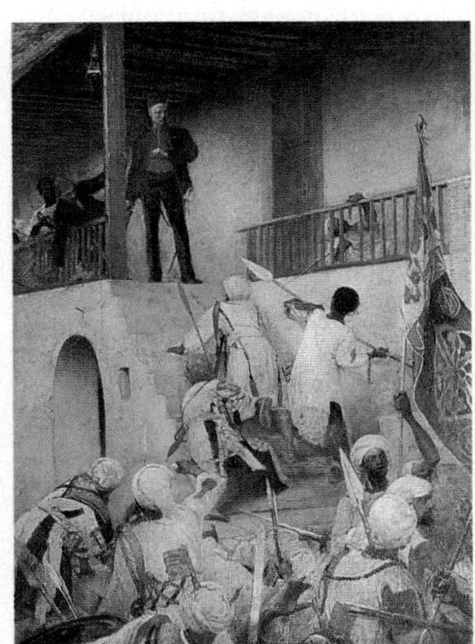
The death of Gordon at Khartoum.

Waves in the ether

Germany, 1885
It was James Clerk Maxwell who, 20 years ago, put forward a theory that an unknown form of radiation exists that can travel at the speed of light through space. Now Heinrich Hertz, a German physicist, has demonstrated the existence of this radiation.

His experiment consists of a battery generating electric sparks between two metal balls. A yard or so away Hertz holds up a wire loop with two more metal balls at the ends, separated by a small gap. Whenever the first sparks appear, so do others which jump across the second "spark gap".

Henry James, promising young novelist

James, a middle-aged young man.

London, 1886
A select public is appreciative of the subtle technique of Henry James, the American novelist who has adopted England as his home and lives off Piccadilly, dining out in London literary circles. His work contrasts European and US culture and attitudes, the Americans being shown as raw, innocent and narrow but possessing a free spirit and zest for life. The flirtatious heroine of *Daisy Miller* was declared to be "a libel on American womanhood". *Portrait of a Lady* also showed the American woman abroad, but *The Bostonians* returns to the society of James' youth.

1886 (1886-1887)

USA, 1 May 1886. Over 100,000 workers across the country strike for an eight-hour day.

Chicago, 5 May 1886. A bomb explodes on the fourth day of the general strike.

Bavaria, 10 June 1886. The minister of foreign affairs, Count Krafft von Crailsheim, dismisses Ludwig II, who has gone mad. The king's uncle, Leopold, is appointed prince regent.

Bavaria, 13 June 1886. The mad King Ludwig II drowns himself and his private doctor in the Starnberger See near Schloss Berg.

Greece, June 1886. The European powers organise a blockade of the Greek coast in order to prevent an attack on Turkey. Greece is demanding compensation for the Bulgarian union with eastern Rumelia, but the Ottomans are not co-operating.

London, 10 July 1886. A British royal charter is given to the Royal Niger Company to colonise Nigeria.

Burma, 24 July 1886. Following the British conquest of Upper Burma, the Chinese negotiator Yihuang and the British representative N O'Conor sign a convention relating to Burma and Tibet. China recognises British rule in Burma and Britain allows the continuation of Burmese tribute to China. Britain also agrees not to press the opening of Tibet.

Britain, 26 July 1886. William Gladstone is replaced by Lord Salisbury as prime minister, following his election defeat.

Arizona, 4 September 1886. The Apache leader Geronimo surrenders to General Nelson A Miles after a decade of guerrilla fighting designed to deter settlers in New Mexico and Arizona.

Bulgaria, 4 September 1886. Alexander of Battenberg, the prince of Bulgaria, abdicates, following the pro-Russian *coup d'etat* staged by the Sofia regiment last month.

South Africa, 20 September 1886. The city of Johannesburg is founded.

Germany, November 1886. Karl Benz patents the first motor car.

India, December 1886. Saiyid Ahmed Khan founds the Moslem Education conference, in part to prepare Moslems for life in a world dominated by the west and in part to prevent them from joining the Indian National Congress.

Atlanta, 1886. A pharmacist, Dr Pemberton, produces a non-alcoholic fizzy drink made from coca leaves, water and sugar, called Coca Cola.

London, 1886. A new speaker to the House of Commons, Peel, insists that Charles Bradlaugh, an admitted atheist MP who has been banned from the House of Commons since his election in 1880, be allowed to take his seat in the House.

Britain, 1886. A law is passed allowing women to assume sole guardianship of their children on the deaths of their husbands.

Germany, 14 January 1887. The *reichstag* is dissolved by Bismarck as a result of its refusal to vote for the military budget.

New Zealand, 20 January 1887. New Zealand annexes the Kermadec islands.

Honolulu, 20 January 1887. A renewal of the reciprocity treaty between the Hawaiian kingdom and the United States contains an amendment granting America exclusive rights to a coaling station in Pearl Harbor.

Washington, DC, 8 February 1887. An act is passed allowing the president to override Indian governments and sell traditional, communally-owned tribal lands to private owners.

Russia, 27 February 1887. The composer Alexander Borodin dies. He was the illegitimate son of a Georgian prince and was a notable scientist as well as a composer. One of the group of nationalist composers known as "the five", he leaves the unfinished opera *Prince Igor* which he has been working on since 1869.

Germany, 11 March 1887. Following the victory of the conservative cartel on 21 February, the second seven-year military law is passed.

London, 26 May 1887. A British royal charter is given to the Imperial British East Africa Company to colonise Kenya and Uganda.

Mediterranean, May 1887. Concerned about developments in the Balkans, Britain aims to stabilise relations with the Mediterranean countries and counter Russian designs on the area. Having exchanged secret letters with Italy guaranteeing the *status quo* in the Mediterranean and the Black Sea, Britain makes similar agreements with Austria and Spain.

London, 20 June 1887. Queen Victoria meets Annie Oakley, the famous American markswoman who can slice a playing card in two at thirty paces sideways on.

Honolulu, 7 July 1887. Revolution is threatened after King Kalakaua is identified as the ringleader in an opium bribery case.

The Irish question brings down Gladstone

London, 8 June 1886

The Irish question has brought down yet another British government. William Gladstone became prime minister only six months ago, with a 335-249 majority over the Conservatives, but dependent on Parnell's 86 Irish votes for an overall Commons majority.

Gladstone's Irish Home Rule Bill proposed a parliament and cabinet in Dublin, but with defence, foreign affairs, currency, customs and the post office remaining at Westminster. The bill was defeated 343-313, with almost a hundred Liberals deserting to the Conservatives. Influential Liberals had refused to join the cabinet because of the Irish issue. One was Lord Hartington, whose brother, Lord Frederick Cavendish, was murdered in Dublin in 1882.

Gladstone: three times PM.

Liszt, genius, showman, lover, is dead

Liszt, who gave piano concerts from the age of 12, with family and friends.

Bayreuth, Bavaria, 31 July 1886

Franz Liszt, the greatest pianist of his day and one of Europe's greatest musical pioneers, died today aged 74. In Paris, about 1830, he was impressed by Paganini's virtuoso fireworks and by the musical poetry of Chopin. Flamboyant, vain, often arrogant, but also generous and kindly, Liszt was a great showman. He was the first to give solo piano recitals and would appear in all his many medals, throwing his gloves to the floor and tossing back his mane of hair before lunging at the keyboard. He had a long affair with a married countess (one daughter later ran off with Wagner) and another with a Polish princess.

He worked for a time in Weimar, promoting advanced composers such as Wagner, Schumann and Berlioz as well as his own extraordinary, forward-looking works. In later life he took minor holy orders and lived mainly in his native Hungary, but travelled, composed and taught right up to his death.

Liberty enlightens the world at New York

"Give me your tired, poor, huddled masses yearning to breath free."

New York, 28 October 1886
An imposing 300-foot high statue commemorating the friendship between the peoples of France and the United States was dedicated today by President Cleveland on Liberty Island at the entrance to New York harbour.

The statue of a woman holding a torch in her raised right hand and holding a tablet with the date of 4 July 1776 in her left is the brainchild of the French historian Edouard de Laboulaye. He proposed it after the American Civil War and funds poured in from all over France. The 225-ton structure made of hand-hammered copper sheets on a steel frame was assembled in France and then dismantled and shipped to America.

Canadian-Pacific railway crosses country

Canada, 7 November 1886
Five years ahead of schedule Mr Donald A Smith drove in the last spike today, and the Canadian Pacific railway is finished. Taking in 25 million acres of land, and financed with a government loan of $25 million, this magnificent feat of civil engineering is seen as the centrepiece of Canada's development.

It has already been of use, even before all the track was fully linked. Three years ago half-breed settlers in the north-west, fearing the effect on their lives of the rapidly expanding immigrant population, staged a rebellion against the authorities in Ottawa.

They drove off a small force of police, but the militia, carried swiftly along the new tracks, crushed the rebels completely.

Settlers on the Canadian-Pacific.

Western fancy dress ball shocks Japanese

Tokyo, April 1887
A fancy dress ball held earlier this month in the *Rokumeikan*, the pavilion built in the western style by the government, has shocked Tokyo, and the prime minister, Ito and his cabinet are being severely criticised for attending the event.

Ito argues that the social functions held in the pavilion bring the Japanese and the foreign community into a closer understanding and will help in the negotiations for the revision of Japan's unequal treaties with the west. However, while most Japanese will listen politely to western music and talks on cooking and dressmaking, the sight of a leading official wearing fancy dress and dancing with a foreign woman is deemed degrading.

Even the interest in all things western and the hope of revising the treaties does not compensate for such a severe assault on Japan's ingrained sensibilities.

US union clashes kill 13

An impression of events in Chicago just before the bomb was thrown.

Chicago, 1886
An anarchist bomb that killed seven police and strikers and injured 60 more has seriously damaged the US's fast-growing trade union movement. Fears of an international conspiracy are rife, and membership of the "Knights of Labour", which had reached 750,000 in five years, is dwindling rapidly.

At a time of comparative prosperity, the Knights and socialist unions struck for an eight-hour day. On 3 May police killed six strikers at a harvester factory. On the following day, an anarchist – a member of the "Black International" movement led by a German, Johann Most – threw the bomb. The perpetrator was never found; but a judge ruled that those who incited the bombing were equally guilty, and sentenced seven men to death. One committed suicide, four were executed and the other two had their sentences commuted.

Despite popular revulsion against the wholly innocent Knights of Labour, at least one trade union organisation appears to be gathering strength in the United States. The American Federation of Labour (AFL) which was founded this year in New York, is the brainchild of the London-born Samuel Gompers, a former worker in an insanitary East Side cigar factory. The AFL is determinedly divorced from independent political action and aims to become a national federation of craft unions contending for the immediate objective of shorter hours and better wages. It will rely on salaried organisers and its own labour press to keep solidarity among its workers and, unlike the idealistic "Knights", it accepts capitalism as a reality.

Justice crushing the Chicago Seven, sentenced to death for incitement.

1887 (1887-1888)

China, September 1887. Towards the end of the month the Yellow River bursts its southern banks at Zhengzhou (Henan) causing disastrous flooding over a large area.

India, 1 October 1887. Baluchistan, an area crucial to the British north-west frontier, is declared British territory and united with India.

France, October 1887. In order to sanction its policy of alliance with Germany, France breaks the Franco-Italian trade agreement and begins a price war. It is intensified by the new Italian prime minister, Francesco Crispi, who was appointed on 1 August, a few days after the death of Agostino Depretis.

Louisiana, 23 November 1887. At least 20 Negro workers are killed by members of the sheriff's posse as more violence erupts in the sugar cane workers' strike in Thibodaux.

France, 2 December 1887. President Jules Grevy resigns following the discovery of an illicit trade in medals organised by his son-in-law. He is replaced by Marie-Francois Sadi Carnot.

Germany, 1887. The biologist August Weismann perfects the chromosome theory of heredity.

Nigeria, 1887. Britain establishes its protectorate over the country on the initiative of George Taubman Goldie, the founder of the Royal Nigeria Company.

USA, 1887. The physicist Albert Michelson repeats an experiment that he had already carried out in 1881 to prove that "absolute space" does not exist. As he finds no evidence of the motion of the earth relative to ether, he states that the speed of light is the same in any given space, whatever the speed of the light source, the observer or the length of the wave.

Italy, 1887. Giuseppe Verdi completes his opera *Otello*.

Russia, 1887. Tchaikovsky composes his ballet *Swan Lake*.

India, 1887. The Parsi magnate J N Tata opens his Empress cotton mill at Nagpur. This is a major step forward for the Indian textile industry.

Congo Free State (Zaire), 1887. Tippu Tib, a Swahili slave-merchant, is made governor of the Stanley Falls district on behalf of the Belgian king, Leopold II.

France, 1887. Tolbert Lanston invents the monotype, a typesetting machine.

East Africa, 1887. King Lobengula of the Ndebele signs a treaty of friendship with Transvaal Boers.

France, 1887. The engineer Gustave Zede draws up the plans for the "Gymnote", a submarine weighing 30 tons, which travels at a speed of five knots underwater and seven on the surface.

Germany, 9 March 1888. The Emperor William dies and his only son, the crown prince, succeeds him as Frederick III.

South-East Asia, 17 March 1888. Britain establishes a protectorate over Sarawak in the Malayan archipelago.

South-East Asia, 12 May 1888. Britain establishes a protectorate over North Borneo.

Brazil, 13 May 1888. Slavery is abolished, despite fierce resistance by the planters, thanks to the efforts of two societies founded in Rio de Janeiro in 1880, the *Sociedade Brasileira contra a Escradidao* and the *Associacao Central Emancipacionista*.

Germany, 15 June 1888. On the death of Frederick III at Potsdam after a three-month reign, his son succeeds as Emperor William II.

Britain, 1888. After founding the Scottish Miners' Union, the miner James Keir Hardie decides to stand for election, breaking away from the Liberals to found the Scottish Labour Party, which includes both radicals and socialists. His election manifesto gives priority to demands for an eight-hour day and the need for working-class MPs.

Italy, 1888. The Crispi government reforms local and departmental administration. From now on the presidents of the departmental assemblies and the mayors of the largest communes are to be chosen by election.

Greenland, 1888. The Norwegian explorer Fridtjof Nansen crosses Greenland from east to west.

China, 1888. Earthquakes in Zhili and Shandong, and floods in Henan, Shandong and Zhili, result in the deaths of some 3.5 million people.

East Africa, 1888. The British East Africa Company, headed by Sir William MacKinnon, is granted a charter to develop British territory in the region.

USA, 1888. George Eastman perfects the first Kodak camera.

USA, 1888. Gunpowder is replaced by guncotton or nitrocellulose, a new explosive which burns more slowly but releases more hot gases and so is more powerful.

USA, 1888. Congress adopts the Allotment Act which makes provision for the dividing up of Indian reservations.

London rocked by "Bloody Sunday" riots

London, 13 November 1887

Two people have been fatally wounded and over 100 injured around Trafalgar Square after police and troops clashed with protesters demanding the removal of the ban on open-air meetings in the square and the release of the MP William O'Brien, a leading figure in the Irish rent strike. Several hundred people have been arrested, including two MPs. The worst of the clashes came as the police, heavily outnumbered, staged baton charges to disperse demonstrators trying to get into the square from Holborn, the Strand and Parliament Street. Eventually troops on horseback cleared the square. Had they failed, a magistrate was ready to read the Riot Act. Blame for the incident is being aimed at the commissioner of police, Sir Charles Warren, who imposed the ban on meetings.

New work for the anti-Wagner brahmins

Brahms who symbolised tradition as opposed to radical Wagner.

Vienna, 1887

A concerto for violin and cello has ben completed this year by the great German composer Brahms. His supporters, known as Brahmins, regard him as the standard-bearer of traditional music against the iconoclasm of Wagner.

In 1853 when he was 20 Brahms met the composer Schuman who wrote in his diary, "Brahms to see me (a genius)". Born in Hamburg, where, as a ten-year-old prodigy, he played in dockland brothels to boost the family income, Brahms settled in Vienna in the mid 1860s. The *German Requiem* of 1868 made him famous, but awed by Beethoven's, Brahms waited until 1876 to write his first symphony. A series of masterpieces followed, including three more symphonies and the second piano concerto.

Light travels fast, report scientists

USA, 1887

Using a sensitive optical instrument – the Michelson interferometer – two American scientists have succeeded in doing what many scientists have thought impossible: measuring the speed of light. The instrument compares the paths of two light beams moving at right-angles towards each other.

The velocity of light is 186,329 miles (299,835 kilometres) per second, and this speed is constant and unchangeable throughout the universe.

Fellow scientists have described the discovery as "perhaps the most important negative finding in the history of science".

Bismarck stirs spy furore in Lorraine

Paris, 30 April 1887

When the police commissioner, Guillaume Schnaebele, was arrested by the Germans and accused of spying, the French detected the hand of their old enemy Bismarck, and hotheads in the government wanted to go to war. President Jules Grevy, however, sent the Germans evidence that Schnaebele had actually been invited to cross into the German territory of Lorraine and promised safe conduct. Today after mounting tension and reports of German mobilisation, the Germans admitted that they had tricked Schnaebele, and, released him. The French believe that Bismarck was testing their nerve.

Victoria enjoys Jubilee

Queen Victoria accepting congratulations on her Jubilee from the court.

London, 1887

For the splendid Jubilee Thanksgiving Service in Westminster Abbey, attended by over 50 royal highnesses and hundreds of lesser potentates, Queen Victoria refused to wear a crown and robes of state. She insisted on a bonnet of white lace trimmed with diamonds.

After the service, during which the choir sang her husband's hymn, *Gotha*, 30,000 children gathered in Hyde Park and were given bun, milk and Jubilee mugs. In the East End, where she opened the People's Palace, the queen was puzzled by "a horrid noise". She was told it was "booing", but it was only from socialists and Irish. After weeks of parades, presentations and parties, Victoria wrote in her diary: "Never, never, can I forget this brilliant year, so full of marvellous kindness, loyalty and devotion of so many millions."

She has seen her people fashion the greatest empire in the history of the world. She has given her name to an age when Britain became the world's workshop and the British the umpire of world affairs, building railways, populating remote lands, curbing savage potentates and bestowing the *Pax Britannica*.

As the year drew to a close, it became apparent that the queen would not be returning to the old seclusion, so disliked by her subjects, into which she had retreated after her husband Albert's death.

Rhodes diamond empire

Cecil Rhodes the empire-builder.

Kimberley, South Africa, 1887

Here, in the boom town that Anthony Trollope called "the ugliest place in the world", the bitterest financial battle in the history of Black Africa has been fought and won by the millionaire Cecil Rhodes. "Some people have a fancy for this, and some for that," the loser, Barney Barnato, told Rhodes. "You've a fancy for making an empire."

The rush for diamonds began after a rich find was made in an area of seven square miles in 1871. There were soon 3,600 small claims. Within 16 years the diamond field was dominated by two companies, Barney's Central Company and Cecil Rhodes' De Beers. Between them, in no-man's-land, stood a third company, the French Company. Which ever of the two capitalists controlled the French Company would control Kimberley, and thus control the world's diamond market. With money advanced by Rothchild's Bank in London, Rhodes won.

Rhodes denies that his motive is greed. He needs the profits from the Kimberley diamonds to finance a white man's homeland in southern Africa, one to be as loyal to the diamonds in the crown as to those in the ground. Both Rhodes' colleagues and enemies are sceptical.

The Kimberley diamond mine, 400 feet (130 metres) deep. Once Kimberley was divided into small claim; now it is dominated by one man.

Nationalist music flourishes in Russia

Rimsky-Korsakov, who was a naval officer before turning to music.

Russia, 1888

Two new works by Nikolai Rimsky-Korsakov, *Capriccio Espagnol* and *Sheherezade*, prove how Russian nationalist music has flourished in recent decades. Glinka (1804-57) led the way, and his protege, Balakirev, now aged 51, led a group known as "The Five". The towering genius of Mussorgsky (1839-81), an alcoholic and ex-army officer, contrasted with the lyricism of Borodin (1833-87), the bastard son of a prince and also a great chemist. Rimsky, now aged 44, an ex-naval officer, and Cesar Cui, now aged 53, completed the quintet.

Bulgaria frustrates Russian intrigues

Bulgaria, 1887

Prince Ferdinand of Coburg has been elected ruler of Bulgaria, and recognised by Britain. His accession confirms Bulgaria's independence from Russia and the Ottoman empire. Since the Treaty of Berlin nine years ago, North and South Bulgaria have come together in a surge of nationalist pride, frustrating Russian intrigue, beating off a Serbian invasion and winning the acceptance of the Ottoman sultan.

When Russia kidnapped the Bulgarian Prince Alexander and tried to postpone elections, it only increased popular support for the rebel leader Stambulov, who has become an effective dictator.

Having ruled successfully in conjunction with the three regents appointed by Alexander as his successors, Stambulov has defied the Russians, who have broken off diplomatic relations. Sultan Abdul Hamid, in spite of Russian overtures, has refused to invoke his sovereign right of entry.

Britain now sees Bulgaria as a bulwark against Russian expansionism, hails Stambulov as the "Bulgarian Bismarck", and welcomes Ferdinand of Coburg, a relation of Queen Victoria.

1888 (1888-1889)

Britain, 6 August 1888. The Local Government Act establishes elected county councils.

Ottoman Empire, August 1888. A railway line is opened between Hungary and Istanbul.

Zimbabwe, 30 October 1888. Lobengula, the king of the Matabele, agrees to the Rudd Concession, which grants exclusive mineral rights in Matabeleland and Mashonaland to a syndicate headed by Cecil Rhodes.

Ottoman Empire. A German bank is granted the concession to start the Berlin-to-Baghdad railway.

Russia, October 1888. Russia acquires a large loan from France in order to finance industrial expansion.

USA, 6 November 1888. Benjamin Harrison, a Republican and the grandson of a former president, wins the presidential election, defeating Grover Cleveland, the present Democratic incumbent of the White House.

China, November 1888. The first railway in China, from Tanghshan to Tianjin, is opened.

East Africa, December 1888. The British agree to mount a naval blockade to help the Germans crush Moslem resistance on the German East African coast.

South Africa, 1888. Paul Kruger is re-elected president of the Transvaal.

Germany, 1888. The physicist Heinrich Hertz discovers electromagnetic waves.

Russia, 1888. The composer Tchaikovsky completes his fifth symphony.

France, 1888. The Dutch artist Vincent van Gogh moves to Arles, Provence, where he paints *Sunflowers*, *The Drawbridge*, *Yellow Chair and Pipe* and *The Cafe Terrace*.

West Africa, 10 January 1889. France declares a protectorate over the Ivory Coast.

France, 27 January 1889. General Georges Boulanger, the former war minister who has become the rallying force for disaffected radicals, fails in his attempt to provoke a "crisis" in Paris.

Austria, 30 January 1889. Archduke Rudolf, the liberal crown prince of the Austrian empire, commits suicide with his mistress, Marie Vetsera, at Mayerling. Archduke Franz Ferdinand, the emperor's nephew, becomes the heir.

Japan, 11 February 1889. A new constitution, which safeguards the powers of the emperor, is promulgated.

Britain, February 1889. Richard Pigott, an Irish journalist, admits forging politically damaging letter purporting to be from Charles Parnell, the leader of the Irish home rule group of MPs.

USA, 2 March 1889. Kansas becomes the first state to pass a law regulating trusts.

USA, 2 March 1889. Congress proclaims the entire Bering Sea, an important seal-breeding area, to be under US control.

Serbia, 6 March 1889. After a series of political mistakes and financial extravagances, Milan Obrenovic abdicates in favour of his 12-year-old son, Alexander.

Ethiopia, 10 March 1889. Following the death of John IV in battle against the Mahdists, Menelik, king of Shoa, proclaims himself emperor of Ethiopia.

USA, 1 May 1889. Asa Briggs Candler of Atlanta buys the rights to a local drink, Coca-Cola.

Britain, 31 May 1889. The Naval Defence Act is passed to meet the growing sea power of Russia and France.

Pennsylvania, 31 May 1889. Johnstown, in south-central Pennsylvania, is washed off the map by a flood. Deaths are estimated at about 2,000.

Germany, May 1889. Bismarck clashes with Kaiser William II over the handling of a strike of 90,000 miners in the Ruhr district. The chancellor wants to send in the army, but the kaiser is in favour of compromise.

Pacific, 14 June 1889. Following a conflict between Germany and the USA over the control of the Samoan Islands, Germany, the USA and Britain sign a treaty guaranteeing the independence and neutrality of the islands under the surveillance of the three powers, and the return of Chief Malietoa.

France, 17 July 1889. A law is passed banning multiple candidacies at elections.

London, 19 August 1889. A strike by 30,000 London dockers begins.

Germany, August 1889. The Social Democrats set up a miners' union.

South Africa, 1889. A chamber of mines is founded to provide a regular labour supply for the gold mines of Witwatersrand.

Britain, 1889. The Irish writer and socialist George Bernard Shaw edits a collection of *Fabian Essays* for the Fabian Society.

Ethiopia 1889. The Italians claim that the treaty of Ucciali with Emperor Menelik recognises Italian paramountcy over Ethiopia.

Thespian sex with servant causes outrage

Strindberg: accused of threatening the moral values of Swedish society.

Stockholm, 1888

A new play just published by August Strindberg, *Miss Julie*, the theme of which is a sexual liaison between a young lady of good birth and her father's valet, is causing the usual scandal that attaches to the author. Last year in *The Father* he dramatised the in-fighting of a marriage – thought to reflect his own to his actress wife, Siri von Essen, who is to play Miss Julie in a forthcoming production.

"No uglier, more revolting scene has ever been presented in a Danish theatre," was one Copenhagen review. Strindberg himself is the son of a housemaid and has written the story of his unhappy childhood in *A Servant's Son*.

Coca-Cola cures hysteria in the female

Atlanta, Georgia, 1889

Dr John Styth Pemberton, an Atlanta pharmacist, puzzled for weeks before coming up with a name for the fizzy drink which he had invented. It started life as "French wine of Coca – an ideal Nerve Tonic and Stimulant". Apart from being too long, it was hardly likely to attract thirsty teetotallers.

Pemberton repaired to his laboratory, removed the alcohol from the liquid and added caffeine-rich essence of cola nut. The resulting drink still did not go very well; despite claims that Pemberton's drink cures everything from head colds to "hysteria in the female", only 13 glasses a day were sold at the pharmacy as it competed with products like "Imperial Inca Cola" and "Coca Coffee".

It was Pemberton's book-keeper, Frank Robinson, who came up with the name. He called it "Coca-Cola" and designed a logo which was printed for the first time this year in the *Atlanta Journal*.

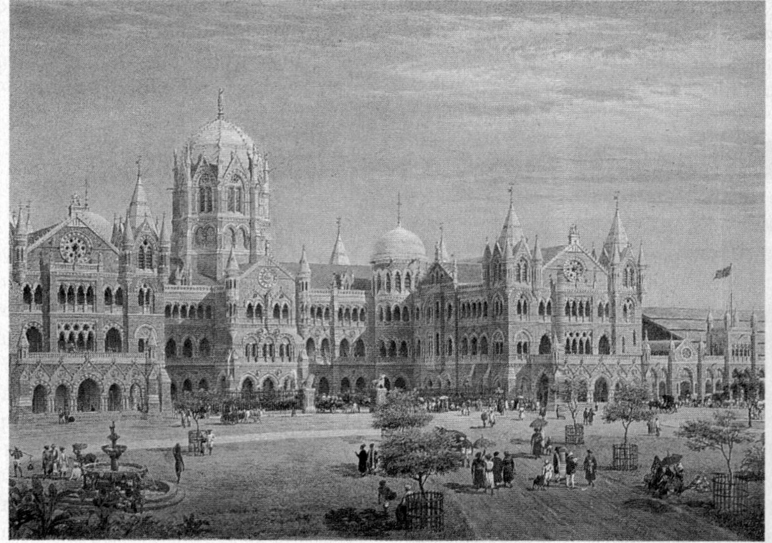

The British "raj" at its most vulgar and splendid: the Indian Peninsular Railway Terminus at Bombay, a brutal synthesis of Norman, Perpendicular and Moghul styles held together by cold steel. The terminus has been hailed as a symbol of the enduring quality of British rule in India.

Austria's archduke dies in suicide pact

Vienna, 30 January 1889
Archduke Rudolf, the crown prince of Austria, committed suicide today with his 17-year-old mistress, Baroness Marie Vetsara, at the hunting lodge of Mayerling.

Rudolf, unhappy in his arranged marriage to Stephanie, the daughter of the king of the Belgians, and unable to marry the lovely Marie, was also frustrated by his father's refusal to listen to his liberal plans for the future of the empire.

It is believed that his profound depression over these matters led to his shooting Marie and then turning the gun on himself. But already rumours are rife that he was murdered to prevent his succession to the throne.

Marie Vetsara, wearing the clothes that she always wore at Mayerling.

Scots writer seeks South Sea warmth

Robert Louis Stevenson and family, with islanders and a naval brass band.

Samoa, December 1889
Robert Louis Stevenson has arrived here after 18 months spent sailing across the South Sea by way of the Marquesas, Tahiti and the Gilbert Islands. With his American wife, Fanny, and his stepson, Lloyd Osbourne, he has decided to build a home among the forested hills. He is delighted with the islanders.

Stevenson has suffered from lung trouble, thought to be tuberculosis, since his youth in Edinburgh and has travelled frequently in search of a kinder climate. He is more famous in the US than in his own country. *Dr Jekyll and Mr Hyde*, his story exploring a man's double identity, one half good, the other evil, has had a great success on the New York stage. He returned to the subject of a man possessed by evil in *The Master of Ballantrae*, which he finished in Tahiti. His adventure stories *Treasure island* and *Kidnapped*, originally written as serials for a boys' paper, are now achieving popularity as novels.

Guns win mining rights

Bulawayo, 30 October 1888
Lobengula, the chief or king of the Matabele people, today signed an agreement with Cecil Rhodes' partner, Charles Rudd, giving mineral rights in Matabeleland and Mashonaland.

In return for this, Rudd has promised to give Lobengula 1,000 Martin-Henry breech-loading rifles, ammunition, a gunboat to patrol the Zambezi river and a monthly rent of $200.

This "Rudd Concession" is not all that it seems, however, for one of its terms grants the concessionaires "full power to do all things that they may deem necessary to win and procure the minerals". There seems little doubt that Rhodes will interpret that clause in the widest possible sense.

It means that Lobengula, who made the concession in the hope of preserving his land against the depredations of the aggressive colonialists, has, in fact, opened it up to them.

The chief was led into this decision by three of his senior chiefs who were bribed by the white men. He took their advice rather than that of the young men who wanted to fight any incursion by the would-be colonisers.

Lobengula certainly has no illusions about the British. He asks: "Did you ever see a chameleon catch a fly? The chameleon gets behind the fly and remains motionless for some time, then he advances very slowly and gently, first putting one leg and then another."

"At last, when well within reach, he darts his tongue and the fly disappears. England is the chameleon and I am that fly."

Cecil Rhodes: the empire-builder.

Lobengula: the king of the Matabele.

British footballers form players' league

London, September 1888
In a major expansion of the fixture list, football clubs in the north and midlands of England have decided to play matches under a league system. The new system is intended to generate more interest in the game and guarantee regular matches for the increasing number of professional players. Clubs in the league have agreed to play each other twice in the season, once at each ground, and have guaranteed – subject to penalties – to field their best teams in each match.

The additional games will allow clubs to spend more on players. Recently clubs have begun to pay wages and expenses to key players so that they can afford time off work to train for important games. The new league plans to be independent of the Football Association, the game's governing body.

1889 (1889-1890)

London, 14 September 1889. The London dock strike, which has ended today, has given rise to a widespread movement of international solidarity.

Washington, DC, 2 October 1889. The first International Conference of American States, organised by the secretary of state, James Blaine, opens.

Germany, 20 October 1889. Gerhardt Hauptmann presents his play *Before Dawn*, introducing a new theatrical realism into Germany.

South Africa, 29 October 1889. Britain grants a charter to the British South Africa Company, under Cecil Rhodes, to colonise Bechuanaland and other parts of southern Africa.

Istanbul, 29 October 1889. Britain, Germany, France, Austria, Spain, Italy, the Netherlands, Russia and the Ottoman empire sign a convention declaring the Suez Canal neutral and open to all ships in wartime as well as peacetime.

USA, 11 November 1889. The territories of Washington, Montana and North and South Dakota are admitted to the union as states.

Brazil, November 1889. following the deposition of the Emperor Pedro II in an army *coup*, a republic is proclaimed and a provisional government is set up.

Britain, 12 December 1889. Robert Browning, the author of *The Pied Piper of Hamelin* and *The Ring and the Book*, dies. In 1846 he married Elizabeth Barrett, whose *Sonnets* and *Aurora Leigh* were reckoned superior to her husband's work.

Chicago, December 1889. Construction of the Auditorium Building, designed by Louis Sullivan and Dankmar Adler, is completed. The ten-storey opera auditorium is topped by a 17-storey tower.

Sudan, 1889. The American explorer Henry Stanley leads an expedition to "rescue" Emin Pasha, the German-born governor of Egyptian Equatorial Sudan, reputed to be trapped in the province by enemies. The true purpose of the mission, largely financed by Leopold of the Belgians, is to stake a claim of an outlet to the upper Nile for the Congo state.

Crete, 1889. The Ottomans put down a Greek-backed rebellion in the island.

France, 1889. The company formed to build a canal through the isthmus of Panama, headed by Ferdinand de Lesseps, collapses as a result of corruption and mismanagement.

France, 1889. The philosopher Henri Bergson publishes *Time and Free Will: an Essay on the Immediate Data of Conscience.*

Italy, 1889. Gabriele d'Annunzio publishes *The Child of Pleasure*, the first volume of his *Romances of the Rose.*

Paris, 1889. Gustave Eiffel builds the Eiffel Tower.

Germany, 1889. The American markswoman Annie Oakley, touring Europe with the Buffalo Bill Wild West Show, proves her prowess by shooting a cigar from Kaiser William II's mouth.

USA, 31 January 1890. John Duke of North Carolina combines five of the largest tobacco manufacturers in the USA to form the American Tobacco Company.

USA, 18 February 1890. The National American Women's Suffrage Association is formed.

Germany, 20 February 1890. In the legislative elections, the Conservatives lose a third of their seats to the Liberals, the Social Democrats and, in particular, the Catholic Centre Party.

Germany, February 1890. In a growing rift between Bismarck and William II, the chancellor refuses to sign the kaiser's proclamation proposing an international conference on social questions.

Germany, 27 March 1890. Germany decides not to renew the Reinsurance Treaty concluded with Russia in June 1887. Under the treaty the two powers agreed to remain neutral in any conflict other than an Austro-Russian or Franco-German dispute.

Berlin, March 1890. The first international conference on job protection is held.

USA, 2 May 1890. The federal territory of Oklahoma, formerly known as the Indian Territory, is created.

Italy, 17 May 1890. The composer Pietro Mascagni wins fame with his one-act opera *Cavalleria Rusticana.*

Ethiopia, May 1890. The Italians proclaim a protectorate over the Red Sea coast (*Eritrea*).

Australia, 1890. Responsible government is established in Western Australia.

Germany, 1890. The bacteriologist Emil von Behring discovers the diphtheria and tetanus viruses.

Germany, 1890. The poet Stefan George founds a poetical journal called *Blatter fur die Kunst.*

Spain, 1890. Universal suffrage is adopted.

Armed uprising forces king to abdicate

Brazil, 16 November 1889

The 49-year rule of Pedro II, during which Brazil has enjoyed an unprecedented degree of stability and progress, is over. The emperor has abdicated following a military coup and will leave for Europe.

Pedro's rule has been characterised by his intelligence, backed by appointing excellent advisers. He balanced the country's warring interest groups and maintained good relations abroad. The economy prospered and Pedro helped to open up the country with railways and other forms of communication. For all his popularity, he became increasingly isolated from Brazil's most powerful groups: the army, which felt it would receive greater powers under a republic, and the emergent middle class. The turning point came with his abolition of slavery.

The landowners resented the lack of compensation, while the middle class wanted the process to go much faster. Pedro, ever liberal, refused to suppress his opponents: now they have chosen to usurp his power.

Satirical Mexican engravers beat censor

Posada's "Calavera" of the Cyclists: a relief engraving on type metal.

Mexico, 1889

Despite attempts by successive governments to censor them, Mexican artists are creating a lively tradition of satirical illustrations, best seen in the current crop of cheap new illustrated papers and popular broadsides known as *calaveras* and *corridas*.

Foremost among these satirists is Jose Guadalupe Posada, a 37-year-old lithographer whose work has been appearing since 1871. Posada mixes his undoubted graphical ability with telling satires on government and society, all of which are released by the Arroyo publishing house.

Capitalising on new technology, he has extended his skills to every type of printing and is responsible for the new technique of etching on zinc. Posada's output of illustrations easily exceeds 10,000.

Briton turns economics into a science

Cambridge, 1890

Alfred Marshall, the professor of political economy at the university here, has just published the first volume of a massive work, *Principles of Economics*, which goes a long way towards establishing economics as a science. Marshall's first discipline was mathematics and he was elected to a fellowship in that subject at St John's College in 1865. Two years later he began to apply his scientific mind to economics.

Marshall has introduced new concepts such as elasticity and welfare economics, and shows how they can be measured. He believes that the theory is now well established and that further progress will come from practical applications.

Popular French leader flees the country

Boulanger presents his credentials while assorted politicians dance to his tune.

Paris, 8 April 1889
General Georges Boulanger, with his blond beard and white horse, captured the imagination of many Frenchmen bored with grey politicians, but now he has fled to Belgium to avoid arrest on charges of attempting to overthrow the state.

Support for this former minister of war came from the discontented of all classes. He cultivated the private soldier and ignored the generals. He connived with every opposition party, accepting vast sums from the royalists while preaching radicalism. Even his vanity and ambition appealed to voters sickened by the scandals and squabbles that tarnish the reputations of more moderate politicians. He became "the man on the white horse" and, although the prime minister, Floquet, told him "at your age, General, Napoleon was dead" he posed a severe threat to the third republic. No longer. His flight must shatter his charisma and his power.

Eiffel's towering achievement stuns Paris

Paris, 1889
Parisians are divided over the world's tallest building, bestowed on their city to commemorate this year's centennial of the French Revolution. No-one doubts that the Eiffel Tower, the new 984-foot (289-metre)-high landmark alongside the Seine, is a unique technological masterpiece. It is its aesthetic value that is is in doubt. Artists and writers, including Dumas and Maupassant, have signed a protest comparing the tower to a "gigantic black factory chimney" and labelling it "a dishonour to the city".

The controversy has confirmed the wrought-iron open-latticework tower as the city's most popular tourist attraction. One of its main draws is the glass-cage lifts that travel on a curve on each of the four semicircular arches at the base.

Eiffel, with his engineer, above Paris.

Tourists benefit Gustave Eiffel, who designed the competition-winning monument. Under the rules he gets the profits from the tower for the next 20 years.

The white man rushes for Indian lands

Oklahoma, 22 April 1889
At noon precisely, a government official raised his gun and fired a single shot. The great race for land was on as thousands of settlers headed west into territory that was once home to 75,000 Indians. They swarmed over the border in covered wagons, carriages, hacks, on horseback, on bicycles and on foot.

It is estimated that more than 200,000 people had crossed over the state borders from Texas and Kansas by nightfall and that almost every one of the two million acres of the Oklahoma district had been claimed and settled.

President Harrison has finally succumbed to pressure from the US's "Boomers" – railroad executives and real-estate agents, together with farmers seeking their 160 acres of free land.

The idea of the land race was to ensure fair play. Law enforcement officers have been hard pressed to ensure that "sooners" who tried to beat the gun have not snatched up the prime plots.

Now, as neighbour fights neighbour over water-rights and rich "cattle barons" are using hired gunmen to oust homesteaders, many dreams are fast becoming nightmares for Oklahoma's new settlers, and the land is no more than a fading memory for the Indians who have moved on westwards.

Dockers' victory is union breakthrough

London, 14 September 1889
Striking dock workers today claimed victory in a month-long dispute after the employers conceded the strikers' main demand for sixpence an hour – the docker's tanner.

The strike victory is a major breakthrough for the new unionism espoused by the dockers' leaders Ben Tillett, John Burns and Tom Mann, all active socialists. Their strategy of persuading 10,000 men to come out together, ignore trade differences and take political action through marches and protests followed the pattern set by the gasworkers in their recent dispute.

Marching for the docker's tanner.

Despite the damage to trade, the strike has had massive public support. Over £50,000 has been contributed to the strike fund, allowing the men to draw strike pay, while the employers have found blackleg labour scarce. Even the City has backed the dockers in their fight against casualisation, which is seen as unfairly penalising men who want to do an honest day's work.

Germans gain from Bismarck's social laws

Berlin, 22 June 1889
Bismarck's welfare programme for workers was completed today when the *reichstag* passed his bill to provide old age pensions and disability insurance. In the past six years accident and health insurance schemes have been established, with employers contributing one-third of the cost and employees two-thirds.

Initially, Bismarck wanted to set up a central government department to administer all welfare schemes, so that the workers would see who was really helping them and become loyal supporters of the *reich*, instead of falling prey to the socialists. But the Catholic Centre Party was opposed to the growth of big government, and the Liberals disliked welfare legislation because it smacked of socialism and undermined the self-reliance of the workers, so schemes are being administered at local level. Bismarck thinks that his welfare schemes have failed. The workers' lot may be eased, but they still support the socialists.

1890 (1890-1891)

Berlin, 1 July 1890. Germany and Britain sign the Heligoland treaty, by which Germany gives up claims in East Africa, including Zanzibar, in return for the British island of Heligoland, off the Elbe estuary.

Washington, DC, 2 July 1890. The Sherman Anti-Trust Act, banning trade monopolies, is passed.

Brussels, 2 July 1890. An International Convention for the Suppression of the African Slave Trade is signed.

USA, 10 July 1890. Wyoming becomes the 44th state in the union.

South Africa, 17 July 1890. Cecil Rhodes becomes prime minister of Cape Colony.

France, 5 August 1890. Britain signs an agreement with France recognising Madagascar as a French protectorate, in exchange for the recognition of Zanzibar as a British protectorate. In West Africa, France gives up the lower Niger and retains the desert territories of the Sahara.

New York City, 6 August 1890. New York introduces a new form of capital punishment: the electric chair.

Mashonaland (Zimbabwe), 12 September 1890. The British South Africa Company founds the town of Salisbury (*Harare*), at the end of a pioneer march from South Africa.

Germany, 30 September 1890. The anti-socialist laws are revoked. The free unions combine to form the General Commission of German Unions.

Russia, 4 November 1890. Alexander Borodin's opera *Prince Igor* is performed for the first time.

Algeria, 12 November 1890. In an address to a gathering of naval officers, Cardinal Charles Lavigerie urges all French citizens to support the republican regime.

South Dakota, December 1890. The US Seventh Cavalry kills 153 Minneconjou Sioux at Wounded Knee.

Britain, December 1890. Charles Parnell is forced to resign as leader of the Irish party at Westminster after being cited as co-respondent in the O'Shea divorce case.

USA, 1890. The posthumous publication of Emily Dickinson's *Poems* wins her a reputation as the first lady of American verse. She died in 1886 after living as a recluse for 25 years and keeping her talent hidden throughout her life.

USA, 1890. The Harvard professor William James, the brother of the novelist Henry James, publishes *The Principles of Psychology*.

New York City, 1890. The McLeod American Pneumatic Company instals a system of air circulation which provides warmth in winter and cool air in summer.

New York City, 1890. The National Carbon Company markets the first commercial dry-cell batteries under the brand name "Ever Ready".

Britain, 1890. Construction is completed of a railway bridge – described by the poet and artist William Morris as "the supremest specimen of all ugliness" – across the Firth of Forth in Scotland. At 1,700 feet, its span is the longest so far in the world.

Britain, 1890. The mathematician John Venn produces a diagram which facilitates work on sets.

Hawaii, 29 January 1891. Following the death of her brother King Dalakaua, Princess Liliuokalani is proclaimed queen.

Brazil, 24 February 1891. A constitution similar to that of the USA is adopted.

New Orleans, 14 March 1891. A mob breaks into a New Orleans prison and executes 11 reputed Mafia members suspected of killing the city's police chief.

New York City, 4 April 1891. Edwin Booth, America's greatest actor, retires after a performance of Hamlet.

Ethiopia, 15 April 1891. Britain signs a second treaty with Italy, supplementing one signed last month, recognising borders of a would-be Italian protectorate over Ethiopia.

France, 1 May 1891. Troops open fire on a crowd of demonstrating workers at Fourmies, killing women and children.

Germany, 6 May 1891. The triple alliance between Germany, Austria and Italy is renewed.

China, 13 May 1891. In the belief that the missionaries were kidnapping children, a mob destroys the Catholic mission premises at Wuhu in Anhui province and attacks various Protestant missions.

Rome, 15 May 1891. Pope Leo XIII publishes an encyclical on the condition of workers, applying Christian principles to relations between capital and labour.

Zaire, May 1891. Fearing British annexation from the south, Belgian forces attack the Garenganze kingdom in the copper-rich province of Katanga.

Zimbabwe, 10 June 1891. Dr Leander Starr Jameson, a friend of Cecil Rhodes, becomes administrator of the British South Africa Company's territories.

Young kaiser dismisses old Bismarck

Berlin, 18 March 1890

When the crown prince became Kaiser William II at the age of 29 he said of his chancellor: "I shall let the old man snuffle on for six months, then I shall rule myself." In fact, Bismarck survived for a year and a half.

He treated the young kaiser with contempt, remaining at his country retreat, riding, reminiscing over enormous dinners about his past triumphs, and rarely visiting Berlin. He lost support in the *reichstag* and tried to inveigle William into staging a coup to govern without popularly-elected deputies. The kaiser, seeking popularity by backing labour reforms, said he would not start by shooting Germans. Bismarck invoked a "red scare", talking of strikes and civil war.

"Dropping the Pilot", by John Tenniel.

The end came when the kaiser called at the ministry for a frank talk and found Bismarck still in bed. William, a wilful young man, self-conscious because of his withered left arm, demanded the old man's resignation. Bismarck spent three days composing a letter full of self-justification. The new chancellor is Count von Caprivi.

Congress bans unfair trade agreements

"The Menace of the Hour": George Luks' protest at growing monopolies.

Washington, 2 July 1890

With more than 90 per cent of the US's oil industry in the hands of the Rockefeller family, and sugar, wheat and alcohol prices governed by equally mysterious "trusts", the US government was forced to act today against the monopolies and cartels which threaten the entire economic structure of the country.

A judge, Mr Justice Harlan, summed up the feelings of millions of Americans. "The nation had been rid of human slavery," he said, "but the conviction was universal tha the country was in real danger from another kind of slavery, namely the slavery that would result from the aggregation of capital in the hands of a few." Today's Anti-Trust Ac forbids "trusts" or similar con spiracies which restrain trade among the states, and declare attempts to monopolise commerce to be illegal. Whether or not the ac will work is doubtful; some believe that it will help those who seek to evade the law.

Indians butchered at Wounded Knee

South Dakota, December 1890

The United States Seventh Cavalry has called it a battle, but few believe that the Sioux Chief Bigfoot's few half-starved braves were capable of serious resistance to heavily armed soldiers with artillery support. It was a massacre which left 153 Sioux, half of them women and children, dead in the Dakota snow.

It was a vision of an Indian holy man, Wovoka, which brought the rival Sioux tribes together. The holy man had predicted that if his people fasted and danced in a circle around a sacred tree, their dead brothers would rise again and lead them to good hunting grounds. Worried that the Ghost Dance religion would bind tribes that had warred for centuries, the 5,000 cavalry moved into the reservation.

An attempt by Sioux police, loyal to the government, to arrest Chief Sitting Bull, a firm believer in the Ghost Dance, ended in the shooting of that veteran leader. Hearing of this, Chief Big Foot moved 350 of his people through the snow to their old camp on the Cheyenne river. The Sioux refused to hand over their weapons. The army opened fire with four cannons on a distant hillside, accounting for most of the women and children. Army casualties are said to be 25.

The burial of the dead, after another "victory" by the Seventh Cavalry.

Queen Victoria gives kaiser a mountain

Berlin, 1 July 1890

The colonial rivalry between Germany and Britain in East Africa and the naval rivalry between the two powers in the North Sea have been resolved. Britain is to have the island of Zanzibar and the East African interior north of it as far as the Congo; Germany is to have all the interior to the south, and the island of Heligoland in the North Sea.

As a special concession to Queen Victoria, the East African border will be additionally redrawn to give Germany Mount Kilimanjaro. The queen was anxious for this since the kaiser, her grandson William, had no mountains in Africa. The German chancellor, von Caprivi, is jubilant. In return for the loss of its economic influence in Zanzibar, Germany has gained a colony, a naval base, a possible ally against France and Russia – and an extinct volcano.

Van Gogh, beset by gloom, kills himself

The face of suffering: a self-portrait, after he had sliced off part of his ear.

Auvers-sur-Oise, 29 July 1890

A Dutch painter called Vincent van Gogh died here in France today, after shooting himself in the chest two days ago. He had been living under the supervision of Dr Paul Gachet, an amateur painter, after being released from a mental hospital at St Remy, Provence. His brother, Theo van Gogh, who is an art dealer with the firm of Goupil et Cie, reports his last words as "the sadness will never end".

A few days ago he completed an ominous painting of a wheatfield under threatening skies, in which lurid golden corn is overhung by blue cloud and black low-flying crows. In Arles, two winters ago, he shared a house with Paul Gauguin, another painter, but after a quarrel in which he threatened him with a razor, van Gogh cut off part of his own ear and nearly died as a result.

He showed two pictures at the Salon des Independants – *Irises* and *Starry Night* – causing bewilderment. He has only sold one painting – at a gallery in Brussels. A recent article in the *Mercure de France*, however, suggests that one day his mystical and original art may become fashionable, although it seems unlikely today.

Troops open fire on striking French miners, killing two children

Fourmies, 1 May 1891

Nine factory workers, including two children, died and about 60 more were injured today when French troops opened fire on strikers from the Sans Pareille factory in the streets of Fourmies. The incident, the most violent so far in the French workers' campaign for an eight-hour day, has sparked widespread protests among workers in northern France.

In many places the dead are already being honoured as martyrs in the worldwide workers' movement for a shorter working week. The killings are likely to harden support for left-wing candidates at the next general election. Among those standing is Paul Lafargue, Karl Marx' son-in-law.

1891 (1891-1892)

Mozambique, 1st June 1891. Portugal and Britain sign an agreement settling their territorial disputes around Lake Malawi.

Britain, June 1891. Edward, the prince of Wales, the eldest son of Queen Victoria, causes a scandal by appearing as a prosecution witness in the Tranby Croft case, about gambling irregularities. Edward, the leader of the rich and sophisticated "Marlborough House set", has been virtually excluded by his mother from royal political responsibilities.

Southern Africa, 31 July 1891. Britain declares territories north of the Zambezi, up to the Congo basin, to be within its sphere of influence.

Russia, July 1891. a French squadron visits Kronstadt, and France and Russia open negotiations on an alliance.

Russia, 27 August 1891. France and Russia sign an *entente* by which each power agrees to consult the other if threatened by outside aggression.

Chile, 19 September, 1891. Jose Manuel Balmaceda, who was elected president of Chile in 1886, commits suicide after the defeat of his forces in a civil war.

Brussels, 30 September 1891. General Georges Boulanger, who attempted to lead a radical uprising in Paris in 1889, commits suicide.

Germany, October 1891. The Social Democratic Party adopts a Marxist programme at its Erfurt conference.

Britain, October 1891. At their party conference in Newcastle, the Liberals adopt a new programme which, as well as Irish home rule, includes disestablishment of the Welsh and Scottish churches, extension of the Employers' Liability Act, restriction on working hours and the abolition of plural voting.

Germany, 14 December 1891. The illustrated magazine *Berliner Illustrierte* begins publication.

Congo (Zaire), 20 December 1891. Belgian Congo forces kill Msiri, the king of the Garenganze kingdom which controls the copper mines of Katanga.

China, December 1891. The government puts down an uprising in Manchuria by the Golden Elixir Sect which began last month. The rebels employed both anti-Qing and anti-foreign slogans and attacked foreign churches.

Russia, 1891. Work starts on the building of a Trans-Siberian railway which will link the Ural mountains with the port of Vladivostok.

Russia, 1891. Thousands of Jews are evicted from Moscow and forced into ghettoes.

USA, 1891. A new slide fastener known as a "zipper" is patented.

USA, 1891. Herman Melville, the author of *Moby Dick* and other classic novels, dies.

USA, 1891. William Burroughs is granted a patent for an "adding machine".

Germany, 1891. Frank Wedekind's play *The Awakening of Spring*, dealing with the sexual awakening of three adolescents, provokes a scandal.

Germany, 1891. Edmund Husserl publishes *The Philosophy of Arithmetic*.

Germany, 1891. The Norwegian playwright Henrik Ibsen completes his *Hedda Gabler*.

Britain, 1891. Oscar Wilde publishes a novel entitled *The Picture of Dorian Gray*.

Britain, 1891. Arthur Conan Doyle publishes *The Adventures of Sherlock Holmes*.

Britain, 1891. The novelist Thomas Hardy publishes *Tess of the d'Urbervilles*.

France, 1891. Jean Rey and Jules Carpentier invent the periscope, making submarine navigation possible.

New York City, 1 January 1892. An office is opened on Ellis Island to cope with the vast flood of immigrants to the USA, many of them fleeing from political and racial persecution in Russia and Central Europe.

Egypt, 7 January 1892. Abbas Hilmi succeeds his father, the weak and pro-British Tewfik, as *khedive* of Egypt.

Germany, 1 February 1892. Georg von Caprivi, who succeeded Bismarck as chancellor, signs commercial treaties with Austria, Italy, Belgium and Switzerland.

Rome, 16 February 1892. Pope Leo XIII publishes an encyclical encouraging French Catholics to support the French republic.

Italy, 21 May 1892. The composer Ruggiero Leoncavallo presents his opera *I Pagliacci*.

Nebraska, 4 July 1892. The People's Party, formed as an alliance of farmers, holds its first national convention.

USA, July 1892. Federal troops are sent in to break up a miners' strike in Idaho, caused by a 15 per cent cut in wages.

Russia, 17 August 1892. Russia signs a military convention with France.

All the world is Sarah Bernhardt's stage

Paris, 1891

Sarah Bernhardt has set off on the most ambitious of her world tours, including South America and Australia in her itinerary. The French actress' first visit to London in 1879 with the Comedie Francaise was marked by her triumph as Racine's Phedre. Besides this role, audiences clamour to see her as Marguerite Gautier in *La Dame aux Camellias*, dramatised from his novel by Alexandre Dumas the younger.

In the last decade she has scored her greatest triumphs in melodramas written for her by Victorien Sardou: *Fedora, La Tosca* and last year *Cleopatre*.

Sarah Bernhardt, aged 33, in 1876.

Walt Whitman, bearded bard of US life

Whitman: the poet of the New World.

New York City, 26 March 1892

Few writers have managed to capture the exuberance of this fast-growing young country more than Walt Whitman, the poet, who died here today aged 73. Whitman had been a newspaperman until he published a set of mystical, sensual poems under the title *Leaves of Grass*. Although intellectuals like Thoreau and Emerson hailed it as a work of genius, the book fell like a lead weight from the press. Few readers could understand it, and many of those who could were shocked by the homosexual undertones. But in poems like *Song of the Broadaxe* Whitman expressed the United States as it is, vibrant and burgeoning.

Tempestuous poet dies after leg cut off

Marseilles, 10 November 1891

The death of Arthur Rimbaud here at the age of 37, after the amputation of a leg, brings his precocious and scandalous career to an end. He ran away from his birthplace, Charleville, to Paris at 15 and again at 16, when he stayed with the symbolist poet, Paul Verlaine. Later Verlaine left his wife to live with Rimbaud in London. Theirs was a stormy relationship and during one of Rimbaud's attempts to leave, Verlaine shot him, wounding him in the wrist, and was imprisoned. It was from this phase of his life that Rimbaud distilled his magical prose poems, *Les Illuminations*.

Arthur Rimbaud: an unpoetic death.

US sky "scraped" by lofty buildings

St Louis, Missouri, 1891
Louis Sullivan, an architect from Boston, has put up buildings as many as ten storeys high by using a new method of construction made possible by the use of special steel girders. The new Wainwright Building is supported by a frame of beams moulded in the shape of a capital "I" and made of Bessemer steel from Pittsburgh. In theory there is no limit to the height such buildings may reach in future, now that mechanical lifts are available.

Unlike architects who imitate the motifs of the classical styles, Sullivan has made the steel skeleton of his building manifest and refuses to disguise it with applied decoration. "Form follows function" is his dictum. It enables him to provide large uninterrupted floor areas and admit more light to the interior. Functionalism is the creed of a new generation of architects.

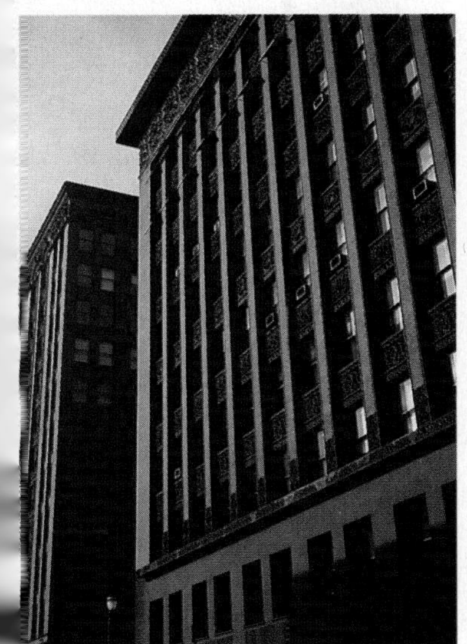

St Louis' new Wainwright Building.

Civilised world faces growing poverty

Newport, Rhode Island, 1891
In one world – the home of the Vanderbilt family in Newport – dinner guests were handed silver trowels and invited to dig in a sandbox for rubies and sapphires, and a man called Harry Lehr threw a party for 100 dogs, with stewed liver on the menu and diamond-studded collars as presents.

In the other world – the teeming, overcrowded tenements and foul dark alleys of the Lower East Side of New York City – children are working up to 16 hours a day in grimy sweat-shops.

Never has the contrast between monumental wealth and abject poverty been more stark. The great American dream has become a grey nightmare for millions. In Europe, too, the great industrial revolution may have created huge private wealth, but the accompanying public squalor and misery is a tragic feature of the Victorian era.

In New York, Jacob Riis, a Danish immigrant to America, has touched the conscience of New York's middle class with a book, *How the Other Half Lives,* in which he paints a grim picture of slum life. The tenements, he says, are "hotbeds of epidemics" and "nurseries of pauperism and crime" that breed "40,000 human wrecks" each year. It has had the same effect on the US's conscience as William Booth's *In Darkest England, and the Way Out* on the English conscience.

Despite the miserable conditions that await them, immigrants are pouring into New York at the rate of 3,000 a week; their numbers are swollen by disillusioned pioneers returning to the city after being bankrupted ("In God we trusted: in Kansas we busted") by mortgage sharks and deflation. Across the Atlantic, the newly-formed London County Council is tackling the archaic system of sewage and reforming the education, housing and hospital systems; even so the *Pall Mall Gazette* reports that one in four Londoners is living in abject poverty; yet more immigrants arrive from eastern Europe each year.

One of Jacob Riis' photographs portraying slum dwellers in New York City.

Public disinfectors, employed by local authorities in their war against lice and fleas among the urban poor.

Back-to-back slums in Yorkshire.

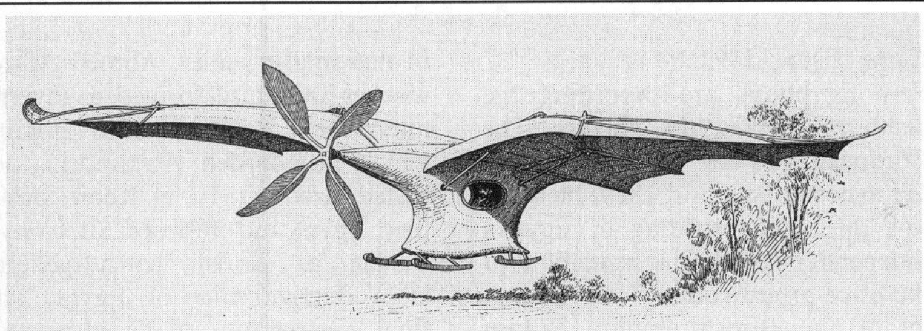

A flying machine, designed by Clement Ader and powered by a steam-driven propeller, has risen four feet above the ground and flown 180 feet. It weighs 150 pounds and is called "Eole" – the Greek god of the winds.

Social Democrats bring Marx to Germany

Erfurt, October 1891
After a heated debate at its Erfurt conference, the German Social Democratic Party adopted Karl Marx' doctrine of the class war and the transformation of society by the socialisation of the means of production and exchange. The conference, the first to be held in Germany since the lifting of Bismarck's anti-socialist laws, heard demands by young activists for the rejection of bourgeois parliamentary activity in favour of revolutionary campaigning in the streets. But moderates argued that the party must also appeal to the middle classes. August Bebel, the Prussian soldier's son who founded the party 21 years ago, said that they would fight for socialism inside and outside parliament.

1892 (1892-1893)

Britain, 18 August 1892. William Ewart Gladstone forms his fourth Liberal government, following his defeat of Lord Salisbury's Tories in a general election.

Italy, August 1892. The Congress of Italian Workers splits into two factions, the socialists and the anarchists.

South Africa, September 1892. A railway from Cape Colony through the Orange Free State to Johannesburg is completed.

Russia, September 1892. Sergei de Witte is appointed minister of finance.

Britain, 6 October 1892. Alfred, Lord Tennyson, poet laureate since 1850, dies. Among his greatest works are *In Memoriam* and *The Idylls of the King*.

USA, 8 November 1892. The Democrat Grover Cleveland is re-elected president, defeating Benjamin Harrison for the Republicans.

France, November 1892. A parliamentary investigation begins into the collapse of the Panama Company in 1889 and the activities of Ferdinand de Lesseps and his associates.

West Africa, 3 December 1892. Following their occupation of the capital, Abomey, the French impose a protectorate on Dahomey (*Benin*).

Russia, 18 December 1892. Tchaikovsky's ballet *The Nutcracker* is performed for the first time.

Russia, 1892. Russia is devastated by a severe famine, which began last year.

Belgium, 1892. The play *Pelleas and Melisande* by Maurice Maeterlinck receives its premier.

Germany, 1892. Count Alfred von Schlieffen, the chief of the German general staff, devises a plan for offensive military action based on the premise that, in any future war, Germany would have to fight both France and Russia. The plan provides for a swift "knock-out blow" against France, while maintaining a defensive position against Russia.

Germany, 1892. The militant social democrat Clara Zetkin founds the socialist women's paper *Equality*.

Germany, 1892. The engineer Rudolf Diesel patents the first internal combustion engine.

Germany, 1892. The playwright Gerhardt Hauptmann, who won fame in 1889 with *Before Dawn*, causes another stir with his *The Weavers*, a compassionate dramatisation of the Silesian weavers' revolt of 1844.

India, 1892. The Indian Councils Act allows for the election of Indians to the provincial and central legislative councils of British India on a limited franchise.

Pacific, 1892. Britain proclaims a protectorate over the Gilbert and Ellice Islands.

New York City, 1892. Jose Marti founds the Cuban Revolutionary Party while in exile in the USA.

New York City, 1892. *Vogue* magazine begins publication.

New York City, 1892. Thomson-Houston Electric and Edison General Electric merge to form the General Electric Company.

Britain, 13 January 1893. The Independent Labour Party, founded by James Keir Hardie, who was elected to parliament last year, holds its first meeting.

Hawaii, January 1893. Queen Liliuokalani is deposed and the Hawaiian islands are declared a republic.

China, January 1893. Rebuilding of the Summer Palace, destroyed by the British in 1860, is completed.

Italy, 9 February 1893. Giuseppe Verdi's opera *Falstaff* receives its premiere.

USA, 27 March 1893. The American Bell Telephone Company makes the first long-distance telephone call – to its branch office in New York.

Germany, 1893. Germany signs trade treaties with Spain, Rumania and Serbia.

USA, 1893. The Anti-Saloon League is founded in Ohio to promote prohibition of alcohol.

USA, 1893. As a result of a stock-market crash, 600 banks, 74 railways and 15,000 commercial businesses collapse.

Chicago, 1893. Swami Vivekenada, who has founded a mission in India to preach the modern Hindu message of Ramakrishna, makes a great impact at the World Conference of Religions.

Chicago, 1893. The first self-service restaurant in the USA opens.

Britain, 1893. The idealist philosopher Francis Bradley publishes *Appearance and Reality*.

Italy, 1893. Giacomo Puccini's opera *Manon Lescaut* achieves a great success.

Britain, 1893. The Irish writer Oscar Wilde completes two plays, *Lady Windermere's Fan* and *Salome*, the latter in French.

Hundreds wounded in Japan poll violence

Japan, 15 February 1892

Twenty-five people have been killed and some 400 wounded in violence at today's general election, the bloodiest in Japan's history. The violence stems directly from the feudal lords' determination to retain power and to strengthen their representation in the *diet* at the expense of the popular parties. The violence became inevitable when Shinagawa Yajiro, the ruthless home minister, ordered the police to support the government's candidates; where the voters could not be bribed, they were beaten.

Even these strongarm tactics do not seem to have been sufficient, however. The indications are that the popular parties have won.

Toulouse-Lautrec, artist of Paris clubland

Lautrec, by himself, "en Japonais": a fashionable Parisian fantasy.

Toulouse-Lautrec's poster of the Moulin Rouge star May Belfort.

Paris, 1893

Striking posters advertising the cabarets and dance halls of Montmartre appearing in Paris are the work of an equally striking and unusual artist, Henri de Toulouse-Lautrec, the scion of an ancient and noble family. His eccentric appearance – accidents to his legs in childhood have left him with the stature of a dwarf – is a familiar sight at the Moulin Rouge, the leading new resort of Montmartre night-life. He takes as his subjects the *declasse* cabaret performers and can-can dancers, such as La Goulue and Yvette Guilbert, Jane Avril, May Belfort and Aristide Bruant.

Toulouse-Lautrec shows them in the full vigour of their performances, making no concession to beauty. His bold use of line and space convey the *louche* atmosphere of Paris by night.

Britain's Egyptian puppet ruler has died

Cairo, Egypt, 1892

Few Egyptians are mourning the death of Tewfik, the *khedive*. The European powers' replacement for the deposed Ismail in 1879, he oversaw the steady eroding of Egypt's independence and the reduction of the once-proud country into a chattel of the British empire. Within months of his accession the European powers had secured complete control of Egypt's finances. When Egyptian officers led by a new kind of nationalist leader, Ahmed Arabi, rose in 1881 and formed a government, Tewfik appealed to Britain, which bombarded Alexandria, defeated Arabi at Tel el Kebir, occupied Egypt and imposed Sir Evelyn Baring as British consul-general and effective ruler of Egypt. The final destruction of its independence came in 1888, when the Suez Canal was "internationalised" under British control – without a protest from Tewfik.

A cloth cap in the House of Commons

Capitalism frightened by a shadow.

London, 3 August 1892
The new MP for the docklands constituency of West Ham shocked the frock-coated Tories and Liberals when he arrived at Westminster today in a two-horse brake to the strains of the *Marseillaise* played on a cornet. James Keir Hardie was wearing yellow tweed trousers, a serge jacket and a cloth cap.

Hardie was elected as an independent MP, but campaigned as a socialist, and there is talk now of forming a Labour Party to champion the working-class cause.

Hardie started work in the mines at the age of ten, educated himself at night school, and, joining a trade union, campaigned for socialism for the workers.

Hardie: Britain's first socialist MP.

France destroys the Dahomey kingdom

West Africa, 17 November 1892
As France steadily extends its control over the interior of West Africa, French troops are marching into Abomey, the capital of Dahomey. Since French-led Senegalese troops came into the country in May, it has taken them six months to subject the kingdom. Five times the Dahomeyan army threw itself against them. It was a bitter and well-fought campaign, and many died on both sides.

The war was forced on Dahomey by France, which created "protectorates" amongst Dahomey's subject kingdoms, then provoked Dahomey into trying to reassert its control over them. Behanzin, the king of Dahomey, heard of the French declaration of war in April. His reply was defiant and dignified: "I would like to know how many villages in France I, king of Dahomey, have destroyed."

Behanzin, the king of Dahomey, who fought the French invaders with all the noblity of a "civilised" monarch.

France is determined to hold on to the kingdom, to provide its rapidly-growing empire in the interior with an outlet to the sea on the south coast of West Africa. That empire is expanding year by year. Since 1883, when French troops occupied Bamako on the river Niger, columns have been spreading out eastwards. Last year they reached Bissandugan, on the frontier of Guinea, Segou, further downstream on the Niger, and Nioro, on the edge of the Sahara desert. Their next stop, French officers boast, will be Timbuktu.

Private eyes break up US strike action

The Pinkerton Agency's ominous "private eye" logo and motto.

Pinkerton (centre), Lincoln's exbodyguard and the founder of the firm.

Pittsburgh, 1892
In the most violent strike in American history, armed and club-wielding private detectives fought a daylong battle with steel workers in Pittsburgh, leaving scores of dead and injured outside the gates of the Carnegie Company's Homestead works.

The detectives – industry's latest anti-strike weapon – belong to the company formed by Allan T Pinkerton, a civil war veteran. Although they were hired by the Carnegie Company's president, Henry Frick, heavy criticism is being aimed at Andrew Carnegie, the company's founder, who refused to talk to union officials and left for his native Scotland.

At a time when much of the industrial United States is being rocked by union activity, with the constant threat of strikes, the employment of "private armies" is seen as an ominous turn. In previous disputes, the police and national guard – and sometimes the army – have been called in, often with loss of life on both sides. In many cities, however, the police are demoralised by their poor payrates, and the volunteer national guardsmen are reluctant to fight.

Although many capitalists, like the banker Henry Clews, claim that strikes are treasonable, the unions insist that if capitalists can combine in so-called "trusts", labour should also be able to unite.

In 100 years the buffalo population of the US has been reduced from 20 million to 1,000. As recently as the mid-1860s there were 13 million. The slaughter began in earnest with the transcontinental railway boom, which started in 1867. Professional buffalo hunters, providing meat for railway construction workers, were followed by "sportsmen". In 1873 alone, three million were killed. Yet old Indians can still remember riding all day in a straight line, and never coming to the end of a herd of buffalo.

1893 (1893-1894)

Hawaii, 13 April 1893. US troops are ordered to leave Hawaiian soil, ending a protectorate established four months ago, when Queen Liliuokalani was deposed.

Serbia, 14 April 1893. Alexander, the son of Milan Obrenovic, who abdicated in 1889, stages a *coup d'etat* and abolishes the regency.

Belgium, 18 April 1893. Plural and universal male suffrage is introduced.

South Africa, 22 April 1893. Paul Kruger is re-elected president of the South African republic (Transvaal).

South Africa, 12 May 1893. Responsible government is introduced in Natal.

New York City, 24 May 1893. The Czech composer Antonin Dvorak completes his symphony *From the New World.*

Germany, 13 July 1893. A bill is passed substantially increasing the size of the German army and reducing military service in the infantry from three to two years.

Zimbabwe, July 1893. After a Matabele (*Ndebele*) raid on Mashona in the north of the country, troops of the British South Africa Company invade Matabeleland.

Greece, 6 August 1893. The Corinth canal opens.

Philadelphia, 31 August 1893. The anarchist Emma Goldman is arrested on a charge of incitement to riot.

USA, 18 September 1893. The Great Northern Railway, the northernmost transcontinental route operating between the Mississippi river and the Pacific Ocean, is completed.

Britain, September 1893. An Irish Home Rule Bill, introduced by Gladstone, is passed by the House of Commons but rejected by the House of Lords.

South-East Asia, 3 October 1893. Siam (*Thailand*) gives up all its territory east of the Mekong to France and recognises Laos as a French protectorate.

Austria, 29 October 1893. Count Eduard von Taaffe, the prime minister of Austria, resigns following the defeat of his bill providing for the introduction of universal manhood suffrage.

Russia, October 1893. Peter Tchaikovsky's sixth symphony, the *Pathetique*, is performed for the first time.

Zimbabwe, 4 November 1893. Having defeated the Matabele in battle, the British occupy Bulawayo, the capital of Matabeleland.

West Africa, 12 December 1893. Advancing down the Niger valley from Kayes in Senegal, the French take Timbuktu, the capital of Mali.

Russia, 27 December 1893. Russia and France reach an *entente* agreeing on mutual aid in the event of war with Germany.

Italy, 1893. The Italian Socialist Party is founded in Reggio nell'Emilia. In Sicily, the socialist leaders organise networks (*fasci*) of workers.

France, 4 January 1894. The French government ratifies the Franco-Russian military convention.

Germany, 10 February 1894. Germany signs a commercial treaty with Russia.

Africa, 15 March 1894. Germany and France sign a pact agreeing on their respective zones of influences in tropical Africa, around Cameroon and along the Chari river.

Korea, 17 March 1894. The nationalist *Tonghak* (Eastern Learning) rebellion breaks out. Chinese and Japanese troops are sent to Korea.

Britain, March 1894. Gladstone resigns as Liberal prime minister following the failure of his attempt to establish Irish home rule. He is succeeded by the Liberal imperialist Lord Rosebery.

East Africa, 11 Avril 1894. Britain declares a protectorate over Uganda.

Washington, DC, 1 May 1894. Jacob Coxey, who led a march of 100,000 jobless to the capital to demand economic reform, is arrested.

Armenia, 1894. In order to suppress a revolutionary movement for Armenian independence, the Ottoman Sultan Abdul Hamid II orders Turkish and Kurdish troops to embark on systematic massacres of Armenians.

Britain, 1894. Sir William Harcourt, the chancellor of the exchequer, introduces death duties.

Britain, 1894. Sidney and Beatrice Webb publish *The History of Trade Unionism*.

Britain, 1894. Rudyard Kipling publishes *The Jungle Book*, a collection of animal stories.

Germany, 1894. German landowners, angered by the concessions made to industry by the chancellor, Caprivi, at the expense of agriculture, form the Agrarian League.

Italy, 1894. Gabriele d'Annunzio publishes *Triumph of Death*, the third in his series of *Romances of the Rose*.

Prick with a needle cures many ills

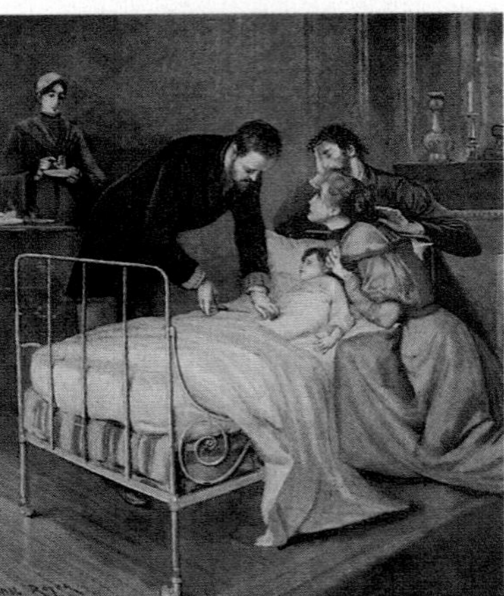

Dr Emile Roux, the bacteriologist, immunising against diphtheria.

London, 1894

Vaccines such as those developed by Jenner and Pasteur work by activating the body's natural defence mechanisms. A person is injected with a weakened or "attenuated" strain of what would otherwise be a dangerous, even deadly, microorganism. This stimulates the immune system to produce specialist blood cells to fight any future infection.

This principle is now being widely applied to protect people against all sorts of infections. Emile Roux, a French bacteriologist, together with the Swiss Alexandre Yersin, has shown that the symptoms of diphtheria, like those of tetanus, are due to a toxin produced by the diphtheria bacterium. Now a diphtheria antitoxin is likely to become available which will immunise the recipient against the disease.

Tchaikovsky dies, the rumours begin

St Petersburg, 6 November 1893

Nine days after the premiere of his anguished sixth symphony, Peter Ilyich Tchaikovsky has died after drinking unboiled water infected with cholera. He was 53.

That, at least, is the official story. But Tchaikovsky, the composer of six symphonies, four concertos and the ballets *Swan Lake*, *The Sleeping Beauty* and *The Nutcracker*, was at the height of his fame (which included receiving a doctorate from Cambridge university) and there were apparently fears in high places that his homosexuality would become public knowledge and embarrass the Russian court. There is talk that he was "tried" by a "court of honour" of his old school, found "guilty" of dishonourable conduct and "sentenced" to commit suicide.

Peter Tchaikovsky, the introspective composer and temperamental genius.

Australian journalist sets sail for Utopia

Australia, 16 July 1893

"Come together in all unselfishness, to trust each other and be free! To live simply, to work hardly, to win not the gold that poisons, but the home life that saves." Thus the stirring words of William Lane, the liberal journalist who has set sail with 220 followers, all trade unionists and teetotallers, to establish a settlement of "New Australia" in the South American land of Paraguay.

Lane began calling for volunteers to join him in the creation of an ideal commonwealth in 1889. A[s an] active unionist, he chose only those of like enthusiasms, each of whom had to put up £60 in cash. Given the high standards of his recruits, it seems that Lane's dream may well become fact. Critics regret only that so motivated a party should be removed from Australia, but Lane is convinced that his dreams would fail in "worn out" Australia.

"The world will be changed if we succeed," he says confidently. "And we shall succeed. We cannot help succeeding."

Panama bribes scandal rocks France

An excavator at work on the unsuccessful attempt to build the Panama Canal.

Paris, June 1893
Frenchmen with a little money to invest could not resist the Panama Canal project when they heard that Ferdinand de Lesseps, the genius of Suez, was the construction engineer. Millions of francs were borrowed from thousands of small savers for a 40-mile seaway to link the Atlantic and Pacific Oceans.

But Panama was not a sea-level Suez and de Lesseps had not reckoned with having to build locks. A combination of extravagance on a grand scale and shady financiers linked to shadier politicians led to bankruptcy in 1889. Although the government tried to hush up the scandal, it finally came into the open when de Lesseps and his associates went on trial for corruption; they were sentenced, but the sentence was "set aside". Work on the canal is to go ahead under new management. But prospects are not promising: in eight years, over 22,000 workers died from malaria and yellow fever.

Red planet is alive, claims astronomer

Arizona, 1894
Is there life on Mars? According to at least one wealthy astronomer, the red planet is populated by a race of intelligent beings. Percival Lowell, who has built his own observatory in Arizona specifically to study Mars, says that it is a drying, dying planet: its water resources are desperately scarce. So the Martians have built an intricate system of waterways to carry the precious liquid from the north and south poles.

Through the telescope one can see these "canals", though Lowell concedes that they may be belts of vegetation. He is not the first to suggest that there is life on Mars. Over a decade ago Schiaparelli also claimed the existence of canals, as did Secchi even earlier.

A celebration of life in the New World

New York, 17 December 1893
The Bohemian composer Antonin Dvorak scored a major triumph last night with the premiere of his new symphony, entitled *From the New World*, at Carnegie Hall.

In this work Dvorak says that he has tried to reproduce "the spirit of Negro and Indian melodies", and refers to the spirituals "Swing low, sweet chariot" and "Goin' home". Otherwise, however, this beautiful symphony is as Czech as Dvorak himself. Dvorak, aged 52, a butcher's son whose chief passion, next to music, is trains, came to public notice when Brahms recommended some of his piano pieces to a publisher in 1876. Dvorak never looked back, and last year he was invited to be head of a new National Conservatory of Music in New York.

Women get the vote in New Zealand

New Zealand, 19 September 1893
At 11.45 this morning the governor put his signature to the Electoral Act making this country the first to allow the female vote. A petition signed by a third of the women here persuaded the House of Representatives to pass the act, first mooted eight years ago by the Women's Christian Temperance Union. The head of the union's franchise department, Katharine Sheppard, had petitioned for the reform three times in the last three years. The number of women's signatures she collected rose each time by 10,000, until a record list of 31,872 names finally swayed the House. Despite an unscrupulous liquor trade lobby, New Zealand women won the first victory for the WCTU in its world suffrage campaign.

US takes over the Hawaiian islands

Honolulu, 17 January 1893
Grass-skirted Hawaiian islanders watched with bemusement today as US marines landed from the *USS Boston* and took up combat positions around the capital. Within hours, however, the marines, now garlanded with flowers, were relaxing under the Pacific sun with the local female populance, and the first stage of the annexation of Hawaii by the US was complete.

It is 40 years since Commander Matthew Perry predicted the rise of Japan as a world power and foresaw the need for a US base in the Far East; six years ago King Kamehameha III ceded Pearl Harbor on the island of Oahu to the United States government. The new ruler, Queen Liliuokalani, has been much concerned at American influence, and was looking for the return of autocracy. Her attitude, combined with pressure from sugar plantation owners on the islands to sell behind the newly-imposed US tariff wall, brought about demands for annexation. The queen has been deposed.

A traditional Hawaiian feather cape.

Norwegian paints his moment of torment

Munch's shrill "Scream", which has pierced Berlin's art establishment.

Berlin, 1893
Edvard Munch, the 30-year-old Norwegian painter, was ordered to remove his 50 paintings from an exhibition by the Berlin Artists' Union last year. As a result of the furore several of its members, headed by Max Liebermann, are leaving to form a Berlin *Sezession*.

Munch has an ambitious plan to assemble a "Frieze of Life" – paintings on the theme of "the poetry of life, love and death". One of these is *The Scream*, a lurid evocation of fear and horror. Munch was crossing a bridge by a *fjord* under the sunset when, he says: "I sensed a scream passing through nature. I seemed to hear the scream. I painted the clouds as actual blood."

1894 (1894-1895)

France, 24 June 1894. President Marie Francois Sadi-Carnot is fatally stabbed by Santo Caserio, an Italian anarchist.

France, 27 June 1894. Jean Casimir Perier is elected president of the French Republic.

Korea, June 1894. Troops from both China and Japan arrive in Korea in response to a plea for help from the monarchy, which is faced by a rebellion by the *Tonghak* society in the south of the country.

Hawaii, 4 July 1894. Having seized power, Judge Sanford B Dole proclaims the republic of Hawaii and issues a new constitution.

Ethiopia, 17 July 1894. The Italians take Kassala on the Eritrean/Sudanese border from the *Mahdists*.

France, 22 July 1894. The first automobile race takes place, between Paris and Rouen.

Korea, 23 July 1894. Japanese troops take over the Korean imperial palace, carry off Queen Min and her children to the Japanese legation, and attack the Chinese offices.

Korea, 25 July 1894. Japanese forces attack and sink the British steamer *Kowshing* carrying Chinese reinforcements to Korea.

Korea, 1 August 1894. War is formally declared between Japan and China.

USA, 27 August 1894. The Wilson-Gorman Tariff Act, introducing an income tax, becomes law.

South Africa, August 1894. Cecil Rhodes, newly-appointed minister of native affairs in the Cape government, introduces a "native policy" to attract Afrikaaner support in the Boer republics. It includes the removal of the right to vote from African landholders.

France, 15 October 1894. Captain Alfred Dreyfus, a Jewish army officer, is arrested for betraying military secrets to Germany.

Germany, 26 October 1894. Count von Caprivi is dismissed and replaced as chancellor by Prince Chlodwig von Hohenlohe-Schillingsfurst.

Russia, 1 November 1894. Alexander III dies and is succeeded as czar by his son Nicholas II.

China, 21 November 1894. Japan defeat China at Port Arthur (*Lushun*).

Washington, DC, 22 November 1894. The USA and Japan sign a commercial treaty.

Hawaii, 24 November 1894. Sun Yat-sen organises the Revive China Society in Honolulu.

Madagascar, 12 December 1894. Following increasing conflict between French settlers and the Hova government under the prime minister, Rainilairanivony, the French occupy Tamatava.

Chicago, 14 December 1894. Eugene Debs, the president of the American Railway Union, is jailed for six months for ignoring an injunction to end the Pullman railway strike, which began in July.

France, 1894. The sculptor Auguste Rodin completes his monumental group *The Burghers of Calais*.

France, 1894. Gustav Lanson publishes his *History of French Literature*.

France, 1894. The brothers Charles and Emile Pathe open the first French phonograph factory.

Hawaii, 16 January 1895. The former queen, Liliuokalani, believed to be plotting a violent overthrow of the republic, is jailed for treason.

France, 17 January 1895. Felix Faure is elected president following the resignation of Jean Casimir Perier.

China, 12 February 1895. Following a humiliating Chinese defeat on land and at sea by the Japanese at the battle of Weihaiwei, the Qing naval commander Ding Rucheng commits suicide.

Cuba, February 1895. Prompted by Spain's failure to carry out economic and political reforms, a newly formed revolutionary movement begins waging a guerrilla war against Spain with the aim of achieving Cuban independence.

Japan, 17 April 1895. China and Japan sign the peace treaty of Shimonoseki. China recognises the independence of Korea and cedes Formosa (*Taiwan*), the Pescadores Islands and the Liaodong peninsula to Japan.

Japan, 23 April 1895. Russia, France and Germany intervene in the settlement between China and Japan, forcing Japan to return the Liaodong peninsula to China.

Washington, DC, 20 May 1895. The Supreme Court rules that the income tax introduced last year is unconstitutional.

Germany, 21 June 1895. The Kiel Canal, connecting the Baltic with the North Sea, opens.

Madagascar, 1895. A French force of 15,000 troops under Jacques Duchesne lands at Majunga.

British gun down Matabele warriors

Zimbabwe, January 1894

Frederick Selous, the white hunter famous throughout Southern Africa, has written to his mother in England: "The campaign has gone through in the most wonderfully lucky way for our side." He was writing from Bulawayo, the *kraal* of the once-powerful Matabele chief, Lobengula, who has fled into the bush.

Dr Jameson, Cecil Rhodes' administrator of Mashonaland, had been looking for a pretext for war. His opportunity came with a raid by Lobengula's *impis* in July 1893 on Mashona people working for white settlers.

He seized the opportunity to declare war. British South Africa Company troops invaded from the west, while British government troops dawdled in the south. Bulawayo was seized and burnt. Matabeleland is now a white colony – and its land and cattle are being parcelled out among the settlers, thus strenthening further the hold of whites in Southern Africa.

Matabele warriors, mown down by the British South African Company.

Italian anarchist stabs French president

Lyons, 24 June 1894

President Sadi Carnot was stabbed to death here today by a young Italian workman who cried "*Vive l'anarchie*" as he plunged a knife into the president's body.

M Carnot, visiting Lyons for the *Exposition*, had given orders for people to be allowed to approach his open carriage as he drove through the streets, so when his murderer pushed through the crowd with his knife hidden in a newspaper the guards allowed him to pass, thinking that he carried a bouquet of flowers.

The assassin, a baker's apprentice called Santo Caserio, made no attempt to escape. He comes from Milan, the home of political turbulence, and belongs to a Swiss anarchist group called "Hearts of Oak", one of hundreds of anarchist groups that have sprung up in Europe, particularly in Italy and Spain, in this angry decade.

Seaside resort has a towering attraction

The new tower at Blackpool.

Blackpool, 18 September 1894

The Lancashire town of Blackpool has already established itself as a popular place for mill workers from northern England to celebrate their "Wakes Week" holiday by the sea. Today the town opened a new attraction, destined to bring even more holiday-makers to what is becoming a prime example of the new-style seaside resorts opened up by the railway boom.

The Blackpool Tower, a 500-foot (152-metre) replica of Paris' Eiffel Tower, is unrivalled in Britain and joins the town's three piers, music-halls, aquaria, ballrooms and this year's other addition, the Grand Theatre.

Irish wit jailed for his homosexuality

London, May 1895
Until this month Oscar Wilde was the toast of the stage, with his two wittiest comedies running simultaneously in London theatres. In January Charles Hawtrey opened in *An Ideal Husband* at the Theatre Royal, Haymarket; in February *The Importance of Being Earnest* was put on by George Alexander at the St James' to even greater admiration. All that is over.

Wilde's name has been removed from the theatres, posters and bills. After two sensational trials the portly poet and aesthete has been delivered to Reading jail to wear convict stripes for two years.

His dramatic downfall began with his friendship with Lord Alfred Douglas, the son of the Marquess of Queensberry; the latter accused Wilde of being a sodomite by inscribing the word (misspelt) on his card and pinning it up at his club. Wilde's suit for criminal libel collapsed and he was urged to flee the country by his friends. Instead he awaited arrest at the Cadogan hotel, confident that he would win.

The Importance of Being Earnest shows, he said, that we should treat trivial things seriously and serious things "with sincere and studied triviality". Well may he reflect on that during his two years of hard labour. "The truth is rarely pure and never simple," he also said. Never more so than in his case.

Wilde and Lord Alfred Douglas: a "sincere and studied triviality".

Japan the victor in anti-Chinese war

The battle of the Yalu estuary, where the Japanese navy sank the Chinese fleet, on 17 September 1894.

Japan, 17 April 1895
The Chinese statesman Li Hongzhang, nursing the wounds inflicted by a Japanese fanatic, today signed the treaty of Shimonoseki ending China's disastrous war with Japan.

The Japanese, who had destroyed the Chinese fleet and inflicted humiliating defeats on China's corrupt and badly-led army, were able to impose harsh conditions. China is to pay a huge indemnity and to cede the Pescadores Islands, Formosa and the Liaodong Peninsula to Japan. Four new treaty ports will be opened to Japanese trade and industry which will be exempt from Chinese taxation, and Korea's independence will be recognised by China but not by Japan. It was rivalry over Korea that led to the war. The immediate causes were the assassination of a pro-Japanese Korean politician in Shanghai and an uprising in Korea which gave the Japanese an excuse to send in troops. Hostilities opened without war being declared when the Japanese sank a Chinese troopship and machine-gunned the survivors.

Debussy's "Faun" panned as formless

Paris, 1894
The 32-year-old composer Claude Debussy is at the centre of a musical controversy following the premiere this year of his symphonic poem *Prelude a l'apres-midi d'un faune* (The afternoon of a faun).

The work is a dreamy, highly evocative piece of a quite novel character. Its fluidity and sensuous orchestral sounds have led to it being derided by some critics as "formless" and "tuneless". It betrays Debussy's interest in the exotic and atmospheric gamelan music of the East Indies, which he heard at the Paris international exhibition of 1889.

Last year Debussy produced a string quartet which anticipates the style of the *Prelude*. He is working on an opera based on the recent play *Pelleas and Melisande* by the Belgian Maurice Maeterlinck.

French "spy" captain gets life sentence

France, 22 December 1894
Captain Alfred Dreyfus, an artillery officer attached to the general staff, was today found guilty of spying for Germany. He was sentenced to life imprisonment on Devil's Island off French Guiana.

This affair started when a French agent found evidence of treachery in the German embassy. Suspicion fell on Dreyfus. He was ordered to take a handwriting test; his hand shook and he was arrested.

He is an unlikely spy. Aged 33, he is nondescript in appearance, noteworthy only for the rimless *pince-nez* he effects. He is not liked by his fellow officers who find him a cold fish. But he has been punctilious in his duties, and he has no money troubles, as his father is a wealthy textile manufacturer.

He is, however, a Jew and therefore a natural target of suspicion for the militant Catholics who dominate the officer corps. There are already disturbing signs of an outbreak of anti-Semitism. But is Dreyfus guilty? There are worrying aspects to his court martial at which he protested his innocence. The evidence was thin and his lawyers were barred from the court.

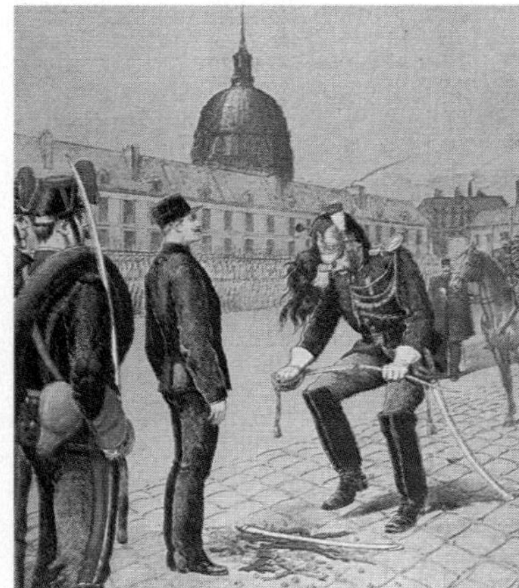

The degrading of the French Jew Alfred Dreyfus, convicted of spying.

1895 (1895-1896)

Britain, 25 June 1895. Following the fall of Lord Rosebery's Liberal government, Lord Salisbury forms his third ministry, a Conservative-Liberal Unionist coalition. Joseph Chamberlain is appointed colonial secretary.

Central America, June 1895. Nicaragua, Honduras and El Salvador conclude a treaty of union at Amapala.

South Africa, 8 July 1895. The opening of the Delagoa Bay railway – from Johannesburg and Pretoria to Maputo Bay – gives the Transvaal access to the sea independent of the British colonies.

Balkans, 15 July 1895. Stephen Stambulov, who was dismissed as Bulgarian prime minister last year, is murdered by Macedonian rebels.

China, 1 August 1895. The people of Gutian in Fujian province destroy churches and kill more than ten British and Australian missionaries, including women and children.

Britain, 5 August 1895. During a visit by Kaiser William II to Britain, Lord Salisbury, the prime minister, suggests the partition of the Ottoman empire as a solution to the troubles of the Near East.

USA, 26 August 1895. A hydroelectric plant, designed by Nikola Tesla and built by Westinghouse, opens at Niagara Falls.

Madagascar, 30 September 1895. Tananarive, the island's capital, surrenders to the French.

Madagascar, October 1895. France rejects an offer by Queen Ranavalona to accept a French protectorate over Madagascar on condition that she remains queen.

China, October 1895. Having launched an unsuccessful attempt at a revolution in Guangzhou, Sun Yat-sen flees to Hong Kong.

Germany, 5 November 1895. *Till Eulenspiegel* by Richard Strauss receives its premiere.

Germany, 27 November 1895. The Association of Industrialists is formed.

China, 30 November 1895. China concludes a secret treaty with Russia, allowing Russia to build the Trans-Siberian railway through Manchuria to the Russian Pacific port of Vladivostok.

South Africa, 29 December 1895. Leander Starr Jameson, an agent of the British South Africa Company, invades the Boer republic of Transvaal at the head of 470 men.

Ottoman Empire, December 1895. Britain intervenes to stop massacres of Armenians by Turks and Kurds.

China, 1895. Serious anti-Christian riots occur in Sichuan province.

Vienna, 1895. In collaboration with Joseph Breuner, Sigmund Freud publishes *Studies in Hysteria.*

France, 1895. French trade unionists combine to form the *Confederation Generale du Travail* (CGT).

France, 1895. Armand Peugeot perfects a petrol-driven engine and founds the Peugeot automobile company.

France, 1895. Emile Durkheim publishes *The Rules of Sociological Method.*

Britain, 1895. *The Time Machine*, a scientific novel by H G Wells, is a huge success.

Britain, 1895. Thomas Hardy completes his fourth novel, *Jude the Obscure*. It follows *The Return of the Native* (1878), *The Mayor of Casterbridge* (1886) and *Tess of the D'Urbervilles* (1891).

South Africa, 2 January 1896. Following his defeat yesterday by the Boers at Krugersdorp, Jameson surrenders at Doorn Kop.

Germany, 3 January 1896. Kaiser William II sends a telegram to Paul Kruger, the South African president, congratulating him on the suppression of Jameson. The telegram causes a storm of indignation in Britain, who sees in it an attempt by Germany to expand her influence in Africa.

USA, 4 January 1896. Utah becomes the 45th state in the union.

South Africa, 6 January 1896. Cecil Rhodes is forced to resign as prime minister of Cape Colony because of his implication in the Jameson raid.

South-East Asia, 15 January 1896. Britain and France sign an agreement on their respective spheres of influence in south-east Asia. Both countries guarantee the independence of Siam (*Thailand*) and the French protectorate over Laos is recognised.

Balkans, 19 February 1896. At the instigation of Nicholas II, the new czar of Russia, Ferdinand, the prince of Bulgaria, is recognised by the powers.

Crete, February 1896. A Christian rebellion against Ottoman rule breaks out in the island.

Ethiopia, 1 March 1896. The Italians are decisively defeated by the Ethiopians under Menelik at the battle of Adowa.

China, 27 March 1896. The Chinese diplomat Li Hongzhang leaves Shanghai on a goodwill tour of Russia, Germany, France, Britain and the USA.

Designer socialist against ugliness

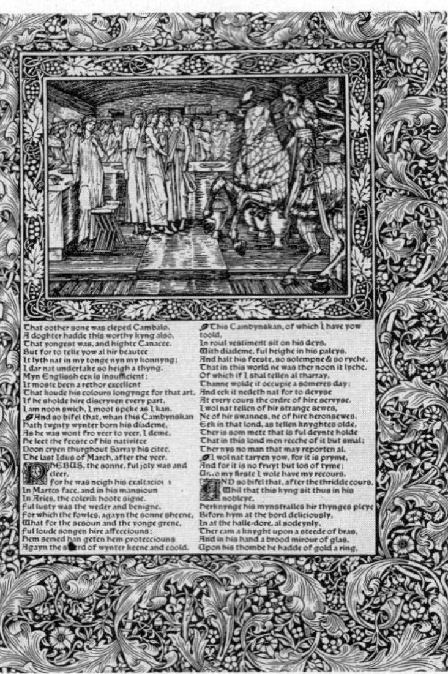
That oother sone was cleped Cambalo.
A doghter hadde this worthy kyng also,
That yongest was, and highte Canacee.
But for to telle yow al hir beautee
It lyth nat in my tonge nyn my konnyng;
I dar nat undertake so heigh a thyng.
Myn Englissh eek is insufficient;
It moste been a rethor excellent
That koude his colours longynge for that art,
If he sholde hire discryven every part.
I am noon swich, I moot speke as I kan.
And so bifel that, whan this Cambynskan
Hath twenty wynter born his diademe,
As he was wont fro yeer to yeer, I deme,
He leet the feeste of his nativitee
Doon cryen thurghout Sarray his citee,
The last Idus of March, after the yeer.
PHEBUS, the sonne, ful joly was and cleer,
For he was neigh his exaltacioun
In Martes face, and in his mansioun
In Aries, the colerik hoote signe.
Ful lusty was the weder and benigne,
For which the fowles, agayn the sonne sheene,
What for the seesoun and the yonge grene,
Ful loude songen hire affeccioun;
Hem semed han geten hem proteccioun
Agayn the swerd of wynter keene and coold.
This Cambynskan, of which I have yow toold,
In roial vestiment sit on his deys,
With diademe, ful heighe in his paleys,
And halt his feeste, so solempne & so ryche,
That in this world ne was ther noon it lyche.
Of which if I shal tellen al tharray,
Thanne wolde it occupie a someres day;
And eek it nedeth nat for to devyse
At every cours the ordre of hire servyse.
I wol nat tellen of hir strange sewes,
Ne of hir swannes, ne of hire heronsewes.
Eek in that lond, as tellen knyghtes olde,
Ther is som mete that is ful deynte holde
That in this lond men recche of it but smal;
Ther nys no man that may reporten al.
I wol nat taryen yow, for it is pryme,
And for it is no fruyt but los of tyme;
Unto my firste I wole have my recours.
AND so bifel that, after the thridde cours,
Whil that this kyng sit thus in his nobleye,
Herknynge his mynstralles hir thynges pleye
Biforn hym at the bord deliciously,
In at the halle-dore, al sodeynly,
Ther cam a knyght upon a steede of bras,
And in his hand a brood mirour of glas.
Upon his thombe he hadde of gold a ring,

A page from William Morris' intricately-designed Kelmscott Chaucer.

London, 3 October 1896

William Morris, who spent his life resisting the materialism and ugliness of industrial society, died today and is to be buried at Kelmscott, Oxfordshire, which gave its name to his press. He devoted his last years to producing beautifully handprinted editions of classics, such as the Kelmscott Chaucer, in his own type fonts.

Morris and Co moved to Merton, Surrey, where it produces tapestries designed by Edward Burne-Jones. Since the 1880s Morris had preached socialism, founding the Socialist League. *News from Nowhere* described his vision of a rural Utopia. His regret was that working men could not afford his firm's goods.

William Morris' and Edward Burne-Jones' Merton Abbey tapestry.

X-rays to reveal the naked truth

Germany, 1895

A chance observation during a physics experiment has lead to an important discovery: a new form of radiation. The German scientist Wilhelm Roentgen calls it simply "X-rays". But whatever the rays' nature they have one astonishing property: they allow one to see through objects. While passing a current through a cathode tube, Roentgen noticed that rays were given off that passed through everyday materials such as paper, wood and aluminium.

This opens up an exciting prospect for doctors. Might it not be possible to use X-rays to see through flesh and study, say, broken bones?

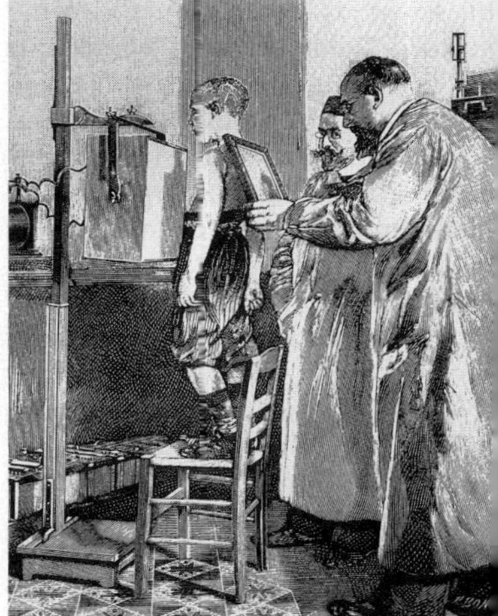

Preparing a patient for an X-ray.

Venezuela sparks international row

Washington, DC, 17 December 189

Relations between the US and Britain have fallen to their lowest since the 1812 war following an ultimatum today by President Clevelan over the long-simmering Britis Guiana-Venezuela border dispute.

In a surprise move the presiden announced a US commission to de cide the borderline. The US, h said, is prepared to impose the com mission's findings on Britain b force if necessary. Venezuela re cently granted a US syndicate cor cessionary rights over some of th disputed territory.

British hand seen in Transvaal raid

Dr Jameson, taken prisoner by the Boers after the failure of his uprising.

Johannesburg, January 1896
A foolhardy and criminal attempt to overthrow the Transvaal regime of Paul Kruger, the Boer leader, has been humiliatingly crushed by a force of Boer commandos.

The *Uitlanders* – foreign businessmen, engineers and speculators, drawn to Johannesburg by goldmining operations – have talked frequently of rebelling against Kruger's persecutions. At the end of last year, Dr Jameson, who works for Cecil Rhodes, decided to help things along by invading the Transvaal with 470 mounted men. The Uitlanders did not rebel and Jameson's men were taken prisoner. Did Rhodes, the mining tycoon who is prime minister of Cape Colony, know that Jameson was planning the raid? And did Joseph Chamberlain, the colonial secretary in London, also know? Despite denials, suspicion remains.

Shah is killed by Islamic extremist

Tehran, Persia, 1896
Naser al-Din, the *shah* of Persia, has been assassinated. He was shot at point-blank range by a man handing him a petition at the shrine of Shah Abdul-Azim, four miles (6.4 kilometres) south of Tehran.

For a decade the country has complained as the shah sold European companies concession after concession to finance his extravagances, accusing him of selling the country. A concession for a monopoly of the sale of tobacco provoked riots, but its cancellation left Persia with a debt of £3,500,000, for which the state's customs receipts were pledged.

The assassination is the work of Islamic fundamentalists, who have strong links with both Persia's *mullahs* and Jamal al-Din Afghani, the preacher and revolutionary who calls for pan-Islamic unity.

The assassination of Shah Naser al-Din by a pan-Islamic revolutionary.

British housewives are cooking with gas

Britain, c.1895
Gas for heating, lighting and cooking is becoming daily more popular. Economical and convenient, its use among all classes has rocketed since the invention of the gas mantle and the slot meter.

Although several large cities like London, Sheffield, Bristol, Liverpool and Newcastle are still dependent on private companies, more than 150 municipal authorities now control their own gas supplies. Having invested in gas, these corporations have checked the spread of electricity by successfully lobbying for limits on operating licences.

On top of commercial and municipal use, the slot meter, pioneered in Liverpool, then London, has introduced tens of thousands of households to gas within the last three years.

Lighting, too, has been revolutionised by the Welsbach incandescent gas mantle, which intensifies lighting by passing a jet through a chemically treated fabric. Gas mantle sales have risen from 20,000 to 300,000 in two years.

Turks kill Armenians

Istanbul, 29 August 1896
The Ottoman authorities have reacted with the utmost ferocity to the seizure of the Ottoman bank in Istanbul by Armenian revolutionaries. At least 3,000 people have been massacred and killings are still taking place after three days.

The Armenians rose against Ottoman rule two years ago, hoping to attract attention to their plight and gain sympathy in Britain and elsewhere, as had happened to the Bulgarians when Ottoman massacres began. The uprising was put down with great brutality by Turkish troops and Kurdish irregulars.

Britain took the lead in setting up an inquiry into the apparent butchery and put pressure on the sultan to introduce reforms and reconcile the Armenians to Ottoman rule. The sultan has promised reforms, but has done nothing – or, worse, launched more massacres.

In October last year, he accepted a joint British-French-Russian plan and simultaneously began killing Armenians throughout Anatolia. About 200,000 people are believed to have been killed. Because of its efforts on behalf of the Armenians, Britain risks losing the favoured position it has enjoyed for over 40 years at the sultan's court.

The Germans are already intriguing to take Britain's place, encouraging the sultan in his stubbornness and manoeuvring for railway concessions.

Abdul Hamid, the Ottoman sultan: the "butcher" of the Armenians.

Three black kings see a white queen

Windsor, 20 November 1895
Three African kings – Khama, Sebele and Bathoen – met a single British queen today. At a reception at Windsor Castle, Queen Victoria presented each with a personally-inscribed Bible. The kings, all from Botswana, travelled here in an attempt to challenge Britain's decision to amalgamate their country with the British South Africa Company's territory.

They are paying their own way and, accompanied only by the Rev W C Willoughby of the London Missionary Society, have undertaken a substantial tour of the country. King Khama has proved a particularly effective orator whose impassioned delivery is in no way diminished by his interpreter.

The visit has proved popular, and public opinion is in the kings' favour. However Cecil Rhodes, the territory's founder, is determined to annex Botswana, and is working hard to this end.

Engels, salesman of communism, dies

London, 5 August 1895
Friedrich Engels, the immigrant businessman who, with the socialist Karl Marx, founded the political philosophy known as "Communism" is dead. He was 74.

While Marx was undoubtedly the better theoretician, Engels, with his experience in business as a partner in the Manchester textile firm of Ermen and Engels, was communism's exemplary salesman. Without his laudatory reviews, few readers would have noticed Marx' seminal work, *Das Kapital*.

Engels developed his political sensibilities in Germany where, in 1842, he discovered the radical theories of communism. He moved to England that year, believing that there he could best combine business with the pursuit of politics. He met Marx after submitting an article to his magazine, and in 1848 the two men crowned their relationship with the *Communist Manifesto*, the basis of their ideology.

1896 (1896-1897)

India, 15 April 1896. In a further example of growing nationalism in western India, the Maharashtrian leader, Tilak, launches a Shivaji festival, following his successful Ganpati festival a few years ago.

Ottoman Empire, April 1896. To pacify the Internal Macedonian Revolutionary Organisation, founded in 1893, the Ottoman Sultan Abdul Hamid II promises reforms in Macedonia.

Moscow, 3 June 1896. In Moscow for the coronation of Czar Nicholas II, the Chinese envoy Li Hongzhang signs a secret treaty of alliance with Russia.

Germany, 1 July 1896. A Civil Law Code is enacted by the *reichstag*.

Madagascar, 6 August 1896. Madagascar is proclaimed a French colony.

Canada, 12 August 1896. Gold is discovered on a creek off the Klondike river in Yakon Territory.

Zanzibar, August 1896. Sultan Khaled, who seized control of Zanzibar over the head of the British-favoured candidate Seyyid Hamoud, surrenders to the British after a bombardment of his palace. Seyyid Hamoud becomes sultan and recognises the British protectorate set up on 4 November 1890.

Sudan, 21 September 1896. Herbert Kitchener, who took control of the Anglo-Egyptian army in March with the object of reconquering the Sudan, seizes the town of Dongola.

Tunisia, 28 September 1896. France and Italy sign a convention by which Italy recognises the French protectorate over Tunisia and the status of Italian residents in Tunis is resolved.

Zimbabwe, 13 October 1896. Cecil Rhodes makes peace with the Matabele chiefs who revolted against his rule.

London, 23 October 1896. Kidnapped and detained in the Chinese legation in London, awaiting secret transfer back to China for execution, the Chinese revolutionary Sun Yat-sen is released through the intervention of his former teacher, Dr Cantlie.

Ethiopia, 26 October 1896. The Italians and the Ethiopians sign the treaty of Addis Ababa by which Italy recognises the independence of Ethiopia and retains only the colony of Eritrea.

USA, 3 November 1896. William McKinley, former Republican governor of Ohio, is elected president.

Persia, 1896. Following the assassination of *Shah* Nasir al-Din, he is succeeded by his son Muzaffar al-Din.

USA, 1896. *The Red Badge of Courage*, a second novel by Stephen Crane, about the American civil war, is published.

France, 1896. The Hungarian Jewish writer Theodor Herzl publishes *The Jewish State*, in which he advocates the formation of a Jewish state to solve the Jewish Question.

France, 1896. The physicist Henri Becquerel identifies the radio-activity of uranium.

Germany, 1896. The satirical newspaper *Simplicissimus* is founded by Albert Langen and the cartoonist Thomas Heine.

Spain, 1896. The novelist Vicente Blasco Ibanez publishes *Tierras Malditas*.

Britain, 1896. A new newspaper, the *Daily Mail*, begins publication.

New Orleans, 26 January 1897. Prostitution is legalised in an area on the edge of the French Quarter which is becoming known as "Storyville".

Crete, 10 February 1897. Following Crete's proclamation of union with Greece four days ago, the Greeks send ships and troops to the island.

Madagascar, 28 February 1897. The Malagasy monarchy is abolished.

Crete, 18 March 1897. The powers announce a blockade of the island.

Zanzibar, 6 April 1897. Sultan Seyyid Hamoud abolishes slavery.

Greece, 7 April 1897. War breaks out between Greece and the Ottoman empire.

St Petersburg, 30 April 1897. Russia and Austria reach an agreement to maintain the *status quo* in the Balkans.

Britain, 14 May 1897. The Italian physicist Guglielmo Marconi makes the first communication by wireless telegraphy.

Greece, 19 May 1897. Having suffered several defeats by the Ottomans and been forced to withdraw from Crete, the Greeks sign an armistice at Thessaly, ending their month-old war.

France, May 1897. The writer Andre Gide publishes *The Fruits of the Earth*.

Britain, 22 June 1897. Queen Victoria celebrates her Diamond Jubilee.

Germany, June 1897. Admiral Alfred von Tirpitz is appointed secretary of state for the navy.

Uganda, 6 July 1897. Following the arrest by the British of some of his chiefs, who were planning a revolt against Protestant power, *Kabaka* Mwanga flees.

Queen Victoria celebrates 60 years' reign

London, July 1897

The queen has taken up with great enthusiasm the suggestion by her colonial secretary, Joseph Chamberlain, that her Diamond Jubilee celebrations could be highlighted by a full-scale conference of prime ministers of all the colonies and representatives of India and the dependencies.

An informal gathering on these lines was held at the time of the Golden Jubilee. Now, ten years on, the imperial vision has gained a stronger hold on the public imagination, largely due to the efforts of Mr Chamberlain, who says that the empire must unite if it is to survive in the face of the growing power of Germany and other rivals. The colonial premiers applauded his call for closer political, military and commercial links, but, jealous of their own self-government, rejected his suggestion for a federal council for the empire.

Queen Victoria arrives at St Paul's Cathedral to celebrate her Diamond Jubilee

Audiences flock to moving picture shows

New York City, Autumn 1896

People in the front row of a theatre here are ducking in their seats as a huge wave threatens to engulf them – but they stay dry. What they have been watching is the latest craze in entertainment.

It is the moving picture show, or "flickers", the result of almost simultaneous inventions by Thomas Edison in America and the Lumiere brothers, Auguste and Louis, in France. Several vaudeville theatres in New York are now equipped with the Edison "Vitascope" system and, between comedy turns, dancers and ballads, show hand-tinted scenes including an umbrella dance, a burlesque boxing match and that wave breaking on a New Jersey pier.

The Lumiere "Cinematograph" opened in June, showing six short films made by the brothers, and the American "Biograph" offers *Rip Van Winkle* and a spectacular railway journey shot in Wales. In Britain, enthusiastic "producers" centred in Hove, Sussex, are also making short "flickers".

Pere Ubu gives much calculated offence

Paris, 1896

Uproar engulfed the Theatre de l'Oeuvre at the premiere of *Ubu Roi*, a fantastic play by Alfred Jarry which offends all the traditional rules of playwriting and good taste. It centres on the grotesque character of Pere Ubu, bloated to pumpkinlike proportions and equally gross in his speech and behaviour. He opens the play by advancing to the footlights and hissing a swear word in the audience's face. There are many more obscenities in this celebration of absurdity. Pere Ubu and his wife Mere Ubu lead a cast of unlikely characters such as the king and queen of Poland and a single person carrying a banner inscribed "Whole Polish Army".

"Big Sword" gang broken up after clash

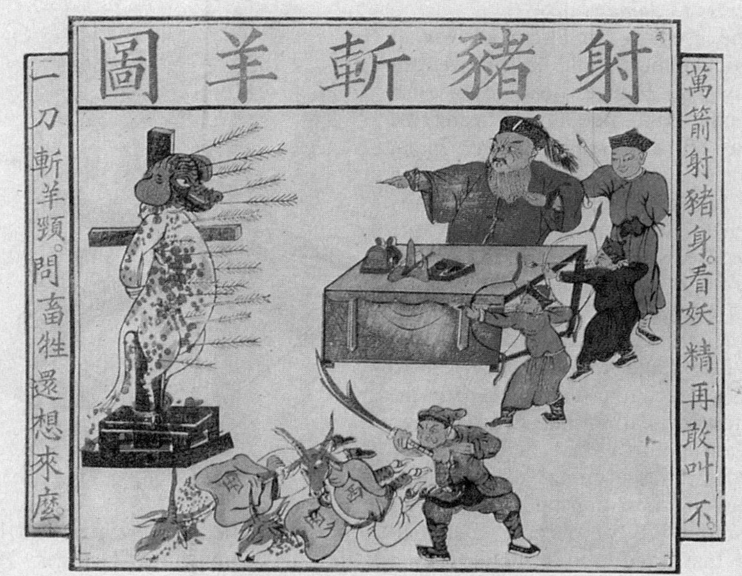

The crucifixion of Christ. The word "Jesus", in Chinese, means pig.

China, 1 July 1896

The troublesome Big Sword Society which has been raiding Catholic missions and the homes of their converts in Jiangsu was broken up by the authorities today. Thirteen members of the band led by Peng Guilin have been arrested following a clash between the society and troops cooperating with the local militia.

The origins of the Big Swords are lost in antiquity, but they emerged in the last few years as a self-protection organisation when troops were withdrawn from the coastal areas to fight in the Sino-Japanese war and banditry became rampant. The bandits were well-armed, so the Big Swords concentrated on learning martial arts and bolstered their fighting techniques with charms and incantations which were reputed to make them invulnerable to swords.

This combination of boxing skill and magic protection became known as the Armour of the Golden Bell. The Big Swords enjoyed considerable success against the bandits, but fell foul of the authorities when they turned on the Christians in a quarrel which had its origins in a feudal dispute over land.

German air pioneer dies in his own glider

Germany, 1896

Otto Lilienthal, one of the great pioneers of aviation, has made his last, tragic flight. News has come from Stolln, near Rhinow, in Germany, that his latest machine, a glider, has crashed, killing the man who had made over 2,000 flights.

Lilienthal had a passion for flying. He designed and flew monoplane and biplane gliders of all kinds, which he launched from an artificial hill near Lichterfelde. He also explored the possibilities – as Leonardo da Vinci had done centuries earlier – of aeroplanes with flapping wings. Lilienthal did much to popularise gliding as a European sport.

Otto Lilienthal flying in one of his unique gliders, near Lichterfelde.

Ethiopia routs Italians

Ethiopia, 1 March 1896

In the worst disaster to befall a European army in Africa, 100,000 Ethiopian troops have destroyed an Italian army at Adowa, in Tigre province, leaving over 7,000 dead.

The war was hardly necessary. But Crispi, the Italian prime minister, faced with economic depression and anarchy at home, was resolved on foreign conquest – and conquest on the cheap.

He despatched to Eritrea the elderly General Baratieri, a fellow veteran of Garibaldi's Thousand, to take charge of an inadequate army of 16,000. Recklessly provoking Ethiopia by occupying northern Tigre, Baratieri lingered in Tigre for a year, giving Menelik time to gether his army of 100,000 – 80,000 with Italian rifles.

Last night Menelik drew the Italians out of their prepared positions. Their advance was chaotic. Orders were misunderstood, brigades became separated, and one by one the Ethiopians wiped them out. The result will shock Europe. More Italians have died here than in the entire Italian *Risorgimento*.

Menelik, who has united Ethiopia, commanding his army at Adowa.

Athens hosts the revived Olympic Games

The start of the Olympic 100 metre race, won by Burke (USA) in red shorts.

Athens, April 1896

After a gap of over 1,500 years the Olympic Games are being revived here in modern style. The original games were first held on the plains of Olympia, near here, in 776BC, in honour of the god Zeus. They included athletics, games and contests of choral poetry and dance. They were held every four years until AD393.

The new games focus on athletics and sports. They have been revived by Baron Pierre de Coubertin, a strong advocate of physical education in France. He began working on the idea in 1892 at a meeting of the French Athletic Sports Union. Two years later he won the unanimous support of an international athletics congress in Paris.

Coubertin is not just interested in physical prowess. He hopes that the big nations will fight each other in the games instead of rushing into wars of national prestige.

1897 (1897-1898)

Boston, 1 September 1897. An underground railway system comes into operation.

China, 14 November 1897. Using the murder of two German Catholic missionaries in Shandong province on 1 November as a pretext, German naval forces occupy Kiaochow Bay, with a view to developing it and the village of Qingdao into a German naval base.

Spain, 25 November 1897. On the return to power of the liberal statesman Praxedes Sagasta, the Madrid government adopts a conciliatory attitude towards the rebels in Cuba.

Austria, 28 November 1897. Casimir von Badeni is forced to resign following his unpopular decision to give the Czech and Moravian languages equality with German for judicial and administrative purposes.

Istanbul, 4 December 1897. The Greeks and the Ottomans sign a peace treaty.

China, 15 December 1897. Russian warships enter Port Arthur (*Lushun*) on the Liaodong peninsula.

France, 28 December 1897. The playwright Edmond Rostand makes his name with *Cyrano de Bergerac.*

Sweden, 1897. The Swedish engineer Salomon Andree and his two companions are lost in an attempt to cross the north polar region by balloon.

Egypt, 1897. Mohammed Abduk publishes his *Epistle*, a modern interpretation of Islam.

India, 1897. Serious risings break out on the North-West Frontier against British rule.

Switzerland, 1897. Theodor Herzl convenes the first Zionist Congress at Basle.

Britain, 1897. The physicist Joseph John Thomson discovers that atoms include very small negatively-charged particles called electrons.

New York City, 1 January 1898. The boroughs of Brooklyn, Queen's, Richmond, Manhattan and the Bronx unite to form Greater New York.

Cuba, 15 February 1898. The US warship *Maine* blows up in Havana harbour – Spanish sabotage is suspected.

China, 6 March 1898. Germany signs a convention with China by which it acquires "leased territories".

India, 27 March 1898. The lawyer and educational reformer Saiyid Ahmed Khan, the greatest Indian Moslem of the century, dies.

Germany, 28 March 1898. An act is passed providing for a substantial expansion of the German navy.

USA, 25 April 1898. The USA declares war on Spain.

Germany, 30 April 1898. Admiral von Tirpitz founds the German Navy League.

Philippines, 1 May 1898. US forces under George Dewey destroy the Spanish fleet in Manila Bay.

Britain, 19 May 1898. The great Liberal statesman William Ewart Gladstone dies.

Italy, May 1898. Following a riot caused by the economic situation and the defeat in Ethiopia, a state of siege is proclaimed in Milan.

China, 1898. Britain obtains the New Territories of Hong Kong under a 99-year lease. In addition, Britain obtains Weihaiwei on the Shandong peninsula as a leased territory. France acquires Guangzhouwan in Guangdong province under a similar lease arrangement.

China, 1898. Devastating floods caused by breaks in the Yellow River banks in Shandong are followed by prolonged and severe drought in northern China. This conjunction of natural disasters and foreign aggression contributes to the rise of the violent anti-foreign *Boxer* movement.

West Africa, 1898. Samori Toure, who retreated west in 1894 to set up a new Mandingo kingdom in the Ivory Coast/Gold Coast hinterland, is captured by the French and exiled to Gabon.

France, 1898. The sculptor Auguste Rodin unveils his *Monument to Balzac.*

France, 1898. The social scientist Emile Durkheim founds a learned journal called *L'Annee Sociologique.*

France, 1898. Oscar Wilde publishes *The Ballad of Reading Gaol* while living in Paris under the name of Sebastian Melmoth.

Britain, 1898. H G Wells publishes *The War of the Worlds.*

Spain, 1898. Miguel de Unamuno, Jose Ortegay Gasset and Jose Martinez Rui, known as Azorin, call for an intellectual and moral renaissance in Spain.

Moscow, 1898. Fyodor Chaliapin, the Russian bass, makes his first appearance as "Boris Godunov".

USA, 1898. The novelist Henry James publishes *The Turn of the Screw.*

USA, 1898. Caleb Bradham of North Carolina begins marketing Pepsi-Cola.

J'Accuse! Emile Zola pleads for Dreyfus

Paris, 13 January 1898

The seething cauldron known as the Dreyfus Affair boiled over today with France's leading novelist, Emile Zola, publicly accusing the war office of judicial crime. In an open letter headlined *J'Accuse* in *L'Aurore*, Zola indicts the army general staff for anti-Semitism and for the way it has covered up the wrongful conviction for treason of Alfred Dreyfus, a Jewish officer, now serving life on Devil's Island.

Zola's attack, which may lead to his prosecution, was sparked by the latest farcical episode two days ago when Commandant Ferdinand Esterhazy was acquitted after requesting a court-martial. Esterhazy's handwriting was recently identified as that found on a note from a French officer to the military *attache* at the German embassy. Less than four years ago the handwriting was identified as Dreyfus' and led to his conviction. Georges Picquart, the intelligence chief who made the Esterhazy connection, has since been posted to Africa.

Zola: a sword for a pen.

Crete rises up against its Ottoman rulers

Crete, Summer 1897

After months of fighting between Christians and Moslems all over the island, Crete has won the approval of the great powers for its declaration of autonomy. Greek forces have left the island, but an Ottoman army remains.

Last September a package of reforms was agreed; since then Crete's Ottoman rulers have been dragging their feet, and the *Ethnike Hetaeria* secret society has been agitating for a Greek-led rebellion.

The arrival of a Greek expeditionary force in February brought renewed clashes and massacres, but an international fleet blockaded the coast while Greece and the Ottomans were forced to come to terms.

In 1896 gold nuggets were found in Yukon Territory, on Klondike Creek, a tributary of the River Yukon in north-western Canada. Now miners are pouring up the Yukon trail from California. Typical of the adventurers is 20-year-old Jack London – a runaway, sailor, socialist, drunk and tramp; hardly the sort of settler that Canada would wish to encourage.

Chinese lands grabbed

China, 15 December 1897
Chinese fears that their country will be "sliced up like a melon" by the great powers were justified today when the Russian fleet sailed into the ice-free naval base of Port Arthur on the Liaodong Peninsula. The Russians are using the pretext of protecting China, and forcing the Germans to withdraw from Kiaochow which they seized after the murders of two German missionaries.

The rivalry to slice the melon intensified after China's defeat in the war with Japan revealed all its weaknesses. Russia, France and Germany intervened when they learnt that Japan was to receive the Liaodong Peninsula under the treaty of Shimonoseki, and forced China to "retrocede" it. The powers have used threats, loans at exorbitant rates and huge bribes to obtain pieces of Chinese territory and trade. The Russians bribed Li Hongzhang, the emperor's envoy, with three million *roubles* to sign a deal enabling them to extend the Trans-Siberian Railway through northern Manchuria, giving them a shorter route to Vladivostok. France has forced concessions in Indochina and Britain is enlarging its Hong Kong colony. Soon the melon will have no pips left.

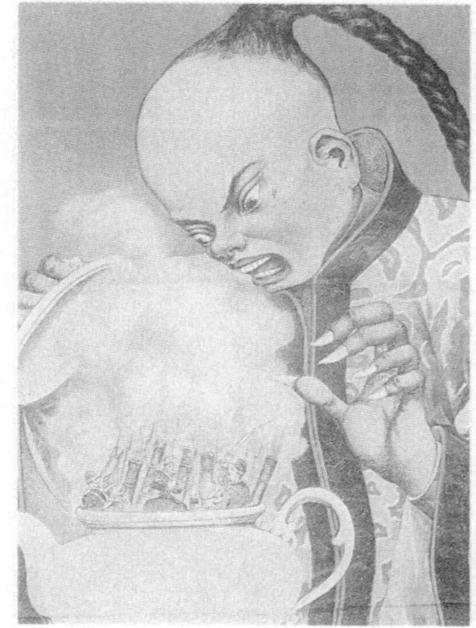
A Russian cartoon of Chinese reaction to increasing western penetration.

FOREIGN POWERS IN CHINA

RUSSIA
MANCHURIA
OUTER MONGOLIA
XINJIANG
INNER MONGOLIA
Beijing
Port Arthur (Russ.)
KOREA
SHANTUNG
Weihai (Brit.)
Quingdao (Ger.)
TIBET
Shanghai
TAIWAN (Jap.)
Macao (Port.)
Hong Kong

Spheres of interest or influence
Russian
British
French
Japanese
German
No dominant foreign influence
Foreign ports

World Zionist Congress spearheads push for a Jewish homeland

Switzerland, 31 August 1897
Leaders of the world's Jewish community met today in Basle to discuss their hopes for the establishment of a Jewish state in Palestine.

More than 200 delegates attended, embracing every variety of Jewish thought. They came primarily from the poorer communities of central and eastern Europe and Russia, where the Zionist dream has flourished most dramatically.

They heard the Zionist leader Theodor Herzl, the author of *The Jewish State* (1896), declare: "We want to lay the foundation stone for the house which will become the refuge of the Jewish nation."

The three-day congress then agreed the "Basle programme", stating: "Zionism aspires to create a publicly guaranteed homeland for the Jewish people in the land of Israel."

"Decadent" artist dies a Roman Catholic

London, 1898
Aubrey Beardsley, the leading visual exponent of the "decadent" wing of *art nouveau* has died of consumption, aged 26. Daubed in his lifetime a force of evil, he died a convert to Roman Catholicism.

He stood for the new century which he never saw, and his graphic style questioned old assumptions and old philosophies. As his illustrations for the quarterly, *The Yellow Book* and *The Savoy*, he was not frightened to shock. His drawings for Oscar Wilde's banned play *Salome* caused scandal because of their eroticism, and this attained pornographic proportions in *Lysistrata*.

Like so many British artists he received more acclaim from abroad than from home. In Germany and Austria, where Gustav Klimt uses the *art nouveau* style, which they call *Jugendstil*, he is rated one who has captured the spirit of an age without god – though he found that God in the end.

William de Morgan's peacock plate.

Beardsley's magnetically evil Isolde.

A poster for Job cigarette papers.

Gustav Klimt's painting "The Kiss".

1898

China, 11 June. The Guangxu emperor issues a decree instigating a period of reform and self-strengthening.

Nigeria, 14 June. Britain and France conclude the Niger convention, settling one African dispute which is bringing them to the brink of war.

Pacific, 20 June. The US Navy seizes the island of Guam.

Sudan, 10 July. French troops under Jean-Baptiste Marchand occupy Fashoda on the Nile.

Cuba, 17 July. US forces capture Santiago.

Puerto Rico, 28 July. The island surrenders to the USA.

Hawaii, 12 August. The sovereignty of the republic of Hawaii is transferred to the USA.

Philippines, 13 August. Manila, the capital of the Philippines, falls to the US.

Europe, 30 August. Britain and Germany agree to share in a loan to the bankrupt Portuguese government, for which the Portuguese colonies in Africa will be treated as security.

Sudan, 2 September. Sir Herbert Kitchener leads the British to victory over the *Mahdists* at Omdurman and takes Khartoum.

Switzerland, 10 September. Elizabeth, the empress of Austria, is assassinated by the Italian anarchist Luigi Luccheni at Geneva.

Sudan, 19 September. British troops under Kitchener reach Fashoda.

China, 21 September. The Empress Dowager Cixi carries out a *coup d'e'etat* when a plot by the emperor and the radical reformers against her is discovered. This ends the "Hundred Days" of reform.

Ottoman Empire, October. Kaiser William II visits Palestine and Syria and assures the Ottoman sultan, Abdul Hamid II, of his support.

Sudan, 3 November. Following an acute crisis in Anglo-French relations, the French evacuate Fashoda.

Crete, 6 November. The Ottomans evacuate the island.

Paris, 10 December. The USA and Spain sign a treaty ending their war in the Caribbean and the Pacific. The USA acquires Cuba, Puerto Rico, Guam and, for a $20 million indemnity, the Philippines.

Spain loses its colonies

The blowing-up of the "Maine" in Havana harbour, on 15 February.

Paris, 10 December

In March, a photographer sent to Cuba to take pictures of Cuban insurgents fighting for their liberty sent a cable to his editor. EVERYTHING QUIET STOP NO TROUBLE HERE, he reported.

The reply came from the publisher of the *New York Journal.* PLEASE REMAIN STOP YOU FURNISH THE PICTURES AND I WILL FURNISH THE WAR – HEARST. In three weeks the US was at war with Spain.

From the moment that Cuban colonists rose up against their masters in Madrid, William Randolph Hearst's *Journal* and its bitter rival, the *New York World* had been feeding and fomenting public feeling with stories of atrocities and brutality in Spanish concentration camps.

Despite the sincere reluctance of President McKinley, jingoism by Congress and people was a major factor in the declaration of war; when the *USS Maine* was blown up by a Spanish mine in Havana harbour with the loss of 252 men, the US was gripped by war hysteria. Washington's "hawks" had their way and Congress dispatched an ill-equipped invasion force to Cuba. The bellicose under-secretary for the navy, Theodore Roosevelt, made a name for himself, perhaps for foolhardiness, by leading his horseless "Rough Riders" in a near-suicidal charge up a hill at Santiago with 1,000 casualties.

McKinley versus Alfonso of Spain.

A peace treaty was signed today. Spain has ceded Cuba, Puerto Rico, Guam and the Phillipines to the US for 20 million dollars. The secretary of state, John Hay, has called it "a splendid little war".

Married team finds glowing radium

Paris

Pierre and Marie Curie have identified the components of radium. The two scientists, Pierre Curie and Marie Sklodowska met in the spring of 1894 and were married the next year. For three years they have endured poverty to have time to develop their researches. Their first achievement was the discovery of a highly radioactive and dangerous element, which they called *polonium*, after Marie's native country, Poland. Since then the two scientists have continued their work and have now discovered another, more important, radioactive material in nature *–radium.* They detected it when they were extracting pure substances from ore. The Curies plan to study its radioactive properties in detail, including its effect on living tissue.

Britain wants pacts with US, Germany

Birmingham, Britain, 13 May

In a speech that has caused a sensation in foreign capitals, Joseph Chamberlain, the colonial secretary, told his Birmingham constituents that Britain could no longer live in splendid isolation, "envied by all and suspected by all". All the powerful states of Europe had made alliances and Britain must follow suit. He was critical of Russia for breaking its pledges of peace, saying: "Who sups with the devil must have a very long spoon."

Mr Chamberlain made it clear that he favoured pacts with Germany and the United States. His speech was received with derision in the German press, denounced in St Petersburg, scorned by his own prime minister, and welcomed only by some leading US journals.

Russian Seagull soars to dizzy heights after first flop

Moscow, 17 October

Anton Chekhov, who made his name with one-act farces, vowed that he would never write again for the stage after his first full-length play, *The Seagull*, was hissed in St Petersburg two years ago. Though described as a comedy, it centres on a young would-be playwright, Konstantin, and a young would-be actress, Nina, both of whom come to unhappy ends.

The new Moscow Art Theatre, dedicated to natural acting by its founder, Konstantin Stanislavsky persuaded Chekhov to allow another production, which has triumphed as a new natural kind of drama. "There's no use being theatrical," Chekhov told his actors, "these are simple ordinary people."

Reforms crushed by Chinese empress

China, 21 September
The Empress Dowager Cixi, the power behind the young emperor's throne, moved ruthlessly today to stamp out the reform movement threatening to sweep aside the old, corrupt Manchu bureaucracy. The reformers, led by the scholar Kang Youwei, had gained the confidence of Emperor Guangxu in the crisis following China's defeat by Japan and the subsequent scramble for concessions by the great powers.

Kang Youwei urged the emperor "to adopt the purpose of Peter the Great of Russia as our purpose, and to take the Meiji Reform of Japan as the model for our reform".

Guangxu, impressed by the reformers' writings, summoned Kang to an audience on 11 June and began to issue decrees based on his proposals. In 103 days he issued 110 edicts ordering the remaking of China. This period is famous as the "Hundred Days of Reform".

The Manchu officials did their best to stem the flood; then, panicking, urged Cixi, "the Old Buddha", to take action. She, with all the accumulated cunning of 40 years in power in China, bided her time.

The moment came when the reformers, worried by their lack of military support, enlisted a sympathetic general, Yuan Shikai. But he betrayed them. Cixi staged a palace coup. The emperor has been made prisoner. Kang has fled. Six other reformers await execution.

Cixi, China's dowager empress: the power behind the imperial throne.

Mahdists lose in Sudan

British Redcoats resist the first Mahdist attack of the battle, at 6.30am.

Khartoum, Sudan, 2 September
An Anglo-Egyptian force commanded by General Sir Herbert Kitchener today defeated a massive army of dervishes in a pitched battle outside Omdurman, killing at least 10,000. Of the 26,000 half-British and half-Egyptian army, only 500 have been killed. Gordon of Khartoum, the military misfit with passions for the bible and teenage boys, killed by dervishes 14 years ago, has been avenged.

The battle began when dervishes attacked the Anglo-Egyptian encampment at Egeiga, four miles from Khartoum. They fought with savage and noble courage, falling in lines to Kitchener's Maxim guns. Then Kitchener ordered a counter-attack towards Omdurman and nearly lost the day when dervishes charged his rear. Only the equally noble and savage courage of the Sudanese Brigade saved the day. The battle ended in a cloud of dust, blinding all combatants, as the 21st Lancers – against all the rules of war – charged over open ground in a frontal attack on dervishes holding broken land. If the large dervish force there did not happen to be leaving (so the Lancers charged into nothing), they would have been slaughtered. As it was the dervish rearguard sniped off 25 per cent of them. Gordon would *not* have approved. He would probably have sent the Lancer's commander home. He would have disapproved even less of a young officer named Winston Churchill who claimed that he led the charge. He would have probably have had him shot. "I think we have given them a good dusting," said Kitchener, forgetting he was nearly overrun from behind.

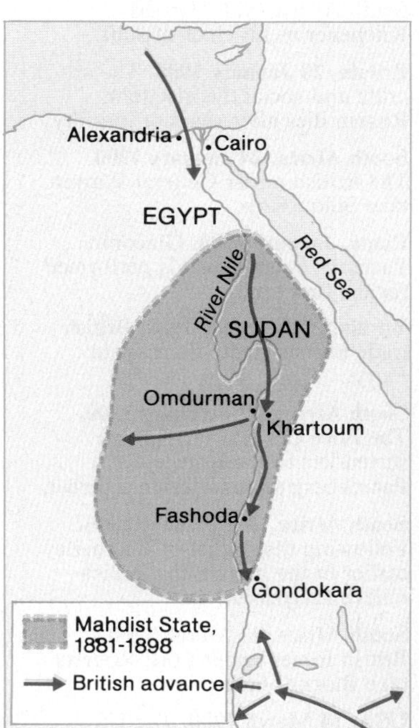

French army forced out of Fashoda as Britain claims Nile

Southern Sudan, November
A French force of several hundred Senegalese troops under six white officers, are to evacuate their fort at Fashoda on the upper Nile. The French, under Captain Jean-Baptiste Marchand arrived there after an epic journey across the continent from Brazzaville, long after the dervishes had driven Britain out of the Sudan. The French came into a pagan area which the Moslem dervishes made no effort to occupy. Since then General Kitchener has defeated the Mahdists and advanced down the Nile, backed by an army of 25,000. Kitchener – who had no intention of allowing the headwaters of the Nile to go to a rival power – treated them with extreme courtesy, then hoisted the British and Egyptian flags and told them to clear off. The affair had the makings of a major international incident, but the French foreign minister, Theophile Delcasse, has accepted the local inbalance of power, averting a possible war.

Kitchener, as seen through French eyes: "the pacifier of Africa".

Matabeles revolt against Rhodes' dream

Zimbabwe, April 27
The revolts and risings by Africans which have rocked the white colony of "Rhodesia" for the past two years are over. The revolt of the old Ndebele kingdom was crushed in six months of 1896; but since then numerous small shona chiefdoms have risen. Now, with the execution of two priests who inspired the shona, the whites think they have crushed the spirit of rebellion. Nonetheless, the blacks hold the names of the two priests, Chimurensa and his female collegue, Nehanda, sacred.

1899 (1899-1900)

Sudan, 19 January 1899. Britian and Egypt establish condominium over Sudan.

Philippines, 4 February 1899. Fighting breaks out between US forces and Philippine rebels, who have proclaimed an independent republic.

France, 18 February 1899. Emile Loubet is elected president following the death of Felix Faure.

Sudan, 21 March 1899. Britain and France sign a convention ending the Fashoda crisis.

South Africa, 24 March 1899. *Uitlanders* (foreigners) attracted into the country by gold petition Queen Victoria to redress their numerous grievances.

Crete, March 1899. Prince George of Greece is appointed high commissioner of the island.

South Africa, 5 June 1899. Talks at Bloemfontein between Alfred Milner, the high commissioner in South Africa, and President Kruger break down over the issue of granting the vote to Uitlanders.

East Africa, 15 June 1899. By a victory at Isangi, east of Lake Kivu, Germany takes control of the lakeside kingdom of Rwanda.

The Hague, 29 July 1899. A peace conference attended by representatives from 26 states decides to set up a permanent international court of arbitration.

France, 7 August 1899. The guilt of Captain Alfred Dreyfus, condemned and deported for treason in 1894, is confirmed by a court martial at Rennes.

USA, 6 September 1899. The secretary of state, John Hay, embarks on an "open door" policy towards China, urging the European powers and Japan to respect the territorial integrity of China and pursue a policy of free trade with the country.

Somalia, September 1899. Mohammed ben Abdullah, a Somali chief known as the Mad *Mullah*, proclaims himself *mahdi* and declares a *jihad* (holy war) on the British and the Italians.

South Africa, 12 October 1899. War breaks out between the British and Boers from the Transvaal and Orange Free State.

South Africa, 15 October 1899. The Boers, who surrounded Mafeking two days ago, lay siege to Kimberley.

Moscow, 27 October 1899. *Uncle Vanya* by Anton Chekhov is performed for the first time, at the Art Theatre.

South Africa, 2 November 1899. The Boers under Piet Joubert lay siege to Ladysmith.

Washington, DC, 2 December 1899. The USA, Germany and Britain sign a treaty agreeing that the Pacific Samoan Islands will be divided between the USA and Germany.

South Africa, 11 December 1899. The Boers under Piet Cronje defeat the British at Magersfontein.

South Africa, 15 December 1899. British forces under Sir Redvers Buller are defeated by the Boers at the battle of Colenso.

Britain, 1899. Edward Elgar's *Enigma Variations* is performed for the first time.

Nigeria, 1 January 1900. Nigeria becomes a British protectorate.

New York City, 2 January 1900. The first electric omnibus goes into operation.

South Africa, 10 January 1900. Lord (Frederick) Roberts replaces Sir Redvers Buller as commander-in-chief of the British forces in South Africa, with Herbert Kitchener as his chief-of-staff.

Britain, 20 January 1900. The art critic and social theorist John Ruskin dies after years of insanity.

South Africa, 24 January 1900. The British under General Warren take Spion Kop.

Rome, January 1900. Giacomo Puccini's opera *Tosca* is performed for the first time.

Britain, 27 February 1900. British trade unions create the Labour Party.

South Africa, 27 February 1900. The Boer General Piet Cronje surrenders to the British at Paardeberg after suffering a defeat.

South Africa, 28 February 1900. Following their relief of Kimberley earlier in the month, the British relieve Ladysmith.

South Africa, 13 March 1900. British forces under Lord Roberts take Bloemfontein.

USA, 14 March 1900. The US dollar goes onto the gold standard.

Crete, 19 March 1900. The British archaeologist Sir Arthur Evans begins excavations at the palace of Knossos.

Brussels, 4 April 1900. Jean-Baptiste Sipido, a 16-year-old anarchist, attempts to assassinate the prince of Wales.

South Africa, 9 April 1900. The Boers defeat the British at Kroonstadt.

Paris, 14 April 1900. The World Exhibition opens.

Pacific, 19 May 1900. Britain annexes the Friendly Islands (*Tonga*).

Britain takes over control of Nigeria

A king receives his new masters.

Lagos, 1 January 1900

Britain's Colonial Office today gains control of all three parts of Nigeria. Since the Lagos colony was founded on the coast 40 years ago, British power has been moving inland. This power has been largely in the form of a private company, the Royal Niger Company, which was given the right to rule by the Crown in a charter of 1886. Now that the company has staked claims as far north as the Hausa (Fulani) kingdoms, the Colonial Office feels the time is ripe to take charge of administration and to leave the business of commerce and profit-making to the company. So from today, northern Nigeria joins southern Nigeria and Lagos under Whitehall control.

Ugandan kings deported to Seychelles

Kampala, Uganda, 1899

British officials have exiled the two most powerful local kings to the Seychelles in the hope of establishing peace in this country which has been scarred by wars for most of the last decade.

Although Britain established the protectorate of Uganda in 1894, old rivalries soon broke out. Mwanga is *kabaka*, or king, of the Baganda and Kabarega rules their traditional rivals, the Banyoro. As well as ancient tensions there are conflicts between Protestant and Catholic converts and with Moslems who have the support of many of Britain's Sudanese troops. Mwanga declared himself a Moslem in his final abortive bid for power.

US split over war in the Philippines

Armour from the Philippines.

Washington, DC, 24 Nov 1899

After nine months of fierce jungle fighting, US troops completed the capture of Luzon, the biggest island in the Philippines, today. But fighting is far from over for the Americans in a country which favours guerrilla warfare.

The Philippines were surrendered to the United States by Spain under last year's treaty of Paris. President McKinley has vowed to "uplift and Christianise" the Filipino people – despite the fact that they have been Christians for centuries.

The US is deeply divided over the war, with influential politicians of both parties joining with trade unionists and industrialists to campaign against what they see as "new imperialism". Mark Twain has suggested that "the Stars and Stripes should be replaced by the skull and crossbones".

France finally grants pardon to Dreyfus

Paris, 19 September 1899

Alfred Dreyfus, the Jewish officer who claims that he was wrongly convicted of espionage, was today formally pardoned by the French government in a bid to end the bitter controversy over injustice and anti-Semitism that continues to threaten France's political stability. The move is a major rebuff for the army and its allies in the church and on the right.

In June the army, faced with growing public pressure to acquit Dreyfus, staged a retrial, reconvicting the 40-year-old Jewish captain of treason and sentencing him to ten years. The decision, against the weight of evidence and with many officers blatantly perjuring themselves to cover up corruption at the original hearing, convinced the government that the army will never give Dreyfus a fair trial. Dreyfus now wants his name cleared of spying for Germany.

Zola stoking the flames, as seen by the Italian newspaper "Il Papagallo".

Priest finds Chinese treasure trove

Beijing, 2 July 1899

A Daoist priest has discovered an amazing array of Buddhist paintings and sculptures in caves at Dunhuang in Gansu. Dunhuang is at the eastern end of the Silk Road, one of the great trade routes that crossed central Asia. Manuscript evidence reveals that the first cave was carved in 366, and that over the next thousand years more than a thousand caves were cut into the hillside, stretching to an area of over 30 miles (48 kilometres).

The paintings show how the Chinese had mastered the Indian styles even at this early date. Figures of the Buddha dominate, showing him as a preacher and also in some of his early incarnations, such as a golden gazelle. Some of the ceilings pay homage to other religions as well, and one has Buddhist, Hindu and Daoist figures together.

The new finds are of immense importance to scholars because the ninth-century persecution led to the destruction of most Buddhist art in China. There are also full versions of Chinese texts of the Tang dynasty, which have hitherto been known to scholars only as fragments.

One of the exquisite Chinese paintings found in the Dunhuang caves.

Boers score successes

Boer General Joubert with his staff occupying Newcastle in Natal.

Capetown, 16 December 1899

At the end of a black week for the British in South Africa, almost 2,000 men and 12 heavy guns have been lost in battles with the Boer forces. A despondent Sir Redvers Buller, the commander-in-chief who arrived with reinforcements from England, cabled the cabinet in London saying he wanted to surrender. He has been replaced by Lord Roberts.

The British were outnumbered when war began last October with the Boers invading Cape Colony; they had 15,000 regulars in South Africa, with 10,000 due from India, to face the Boers' 50,000 mounted infantry. The Boers were also superior in field tactics and the gathering of intelligence. Within weeks they had all the British forces besieged in Ladysmith, Kimberley and Mafeking.

This was when the Boers made a strategic mistake. If they had contained the British in the three towns and sent their main force into the Cape, they would have had virtually the whole country under their control and deprived the British of their supply port and naval base.

Instead, the Boers – who went to war to rid themselves of British influence in the Transvaal and Orange Free State – may be wasting their strength on mounting full-scale sieges. They have 10,000 men around strategically unimportant Mafeking, for instance.

Enigmatic theme in Elgar's variations

London, June 1899

The finest English composer since Purcell – that is the verdict on Edward Elgar since this month's premiere of his *Enigma Variations*. In this work a theme (Elgar says it "goes with" a well-known tune – hence the enigma) is varied 14 times, sketching his wife, friends and himself in music. Elgar, aged 42, is a Catholic organist's son from Worcestershire. In him the tree of British music, which has produced Arthur Sullivan, Hubert Parry and Charles Stanford, seems at last to have borne the fruits of greatness.

Class struggle is all, says Red Rosa

Berlin, 18 April 1899

Rosa Luxembourg, a 28-year-old Polish-born Marxist, emerged as a leading anti-revisionist force in the Social Democratic Party today.

Her vehement attack on Eduard Bernstein, who argues that the conditions of the workers have improved, so reforms must come from within the system, stressed that parliament is a bourgeois sham and reaffirmed the need for revolution.

"Bloody Rosa", who is German through a marriage of convenience, also emphasised the internationalist nature of Marxism.

1900

South Africa, 20 May. The British relieve Mafeking.

China, 21 May. Russia annexes Manchuria.

South Africa, 29 May. Britain annexes the Orange Free State.

China, 17 June. In response to the growing *Boxer* threat, the allied troops of Britain, Germany, France, Russia, the USA, Italy, Austria and Japan capture the Dagu forts.

China, 20 June. Dong Fuxiang's Gansu troops and the Boxers begin attacks on the legations, churches and other foreign establishments.

Philippines, 21 June. Arthur MacArthur, the US military governor, grants an amnesty to the Filipino rebels.

Britain, 29 June. The *Dictionary of National Biography* is completed.

Paris, 19 July. The *Metro* underground railway opens.

Italy, 30 July. King Umberto is shot dead by an anarchist. Victor Emmanuel III succeeds.

USA, 10 August. The USA wins the first International Lawn Tennis Trophy, established by Dwight F Davis.

China, 14 August. The allies enter Beijing and end the siege of the legations.

Germany, 25 August. The philosopher Friedrich Nietzsche dies after 12 years of insanity.

South Africa, 1 September. The British annex the Boer republic of the Transvaal.

Britain, 17 October. Lord Salisbury's Tory government is re-elected.

Europe, 20 October. Britain and Germany sign a pact to continue the open-door policy towards China.

USA, 6 November. The Republican President William McKinley is re-elected.

Canada, 8 November. Liberals under Sir Wilfrid Laurier win the general election.

Britain, 22 November. Arthur Sullivan, the composer of the famous Savoy operas with librettos by W S Gilbert, dies.

Paris, 9 December. *Nocturnes* by Claude Debussy is performed for the first time.

Paris, 30 November. The Irish writer Oscar Wilde dies.

India. The famine and the epidemic of bubonic plague, which have ravaged India for the past four years, abate.

New century opens in optimistic glow

The "Dawn of the Century" march.

London, 1 January

The first chime of midnight echoed down the length of Whitehall and deafening cheers rocked Trafalgar Square as a hundred thousand raucous Londoners went joyfully crazy as they sang, danced and kissed their way into the new century.

They had good reason: had not the 19th century belonged to Britain? Had not the *Pax Britannica* brought peace and stability to huge areas of the world? And, after all, Britain had been both the strongest power on this globe economically and the most stable politically.

But as rockets crashed out and countless bands played *Auld Lang Syne*, it was a good time to reflect. Britain is truly *Great* Britain today, but how much longer can it wear that mantle? It is the head of a great empire – but a savage war in South Africa has done much to shatter what had become national complacency.

Economically, Britain is being overtaken by Germany and the United States – both of whom possess greater manpower and mineral resources.

The mood in the streets last night was one of sublime optimism. More thoughtful Britons tempered that glow in the knowledge that Britain is slowing down, becoming smug, indeed. Where are the giants of the Industrial Revolution, men like Stephenson and Brunel, and the inventive geniuses like Arkwright? And could any wealthy and civilised nation truly rejoice and ignore the conditions of overcrowding and poverty that are only just beginning to touch middle-class consciences?

Count flies up in a motorised balloon

Count von Zeppelin's airship, on its maiden flight over Lake Constance.

Friedrichshafen, 2 July

A ship that flies was launched into the sky over Lake Constance today. The 420-foot craft, "airship" *LZ1*, has been invented by Count Ferdinand Zeppelin, aged 62, who retired from the army ten years ago. Zeppelin made balloon ascents in 1863 as a military observer during the American Civil War. His craft is a cigar-shaped frame lifted by gas. A 16hp engine linked to two propellers makes it independent of wind and provides a top speed of 20 mph (32kph). A sliding weight on the keel adjusts pitch and two rudders ensure horizontal control. Crew and passengers occupy two chambers in the keel.

The craft has taken ten years to design. Some problems of control were evident during today's first outing from a floating hangar on the lake near Friedrichshafen. But Zeppelin will assuredly get public support and funding. The count's basic idea of lighter-than-air flight is more rational in the light of experience than plans to build a machine which must overcome its own weight by forward speed and lift from wing surfaces.

Doctor tells us what our dreams mean

Vienna, 14 October

"Dreams are most profound when they seem most crazy." So declares Sigmund Freud, the Austrian psychologist, in a major work just published, *Die Traumdeutung*, or "The Interpretation of Dreams".

Freud believes that dreams are "the royal road to the unconscious" and contain disguised symbols for the repressed desires of the dreamer censored to an acceptable form. He analyses universal dream imagery. Walls which one climbs represent a man or a woman, according to the smoothness of the surface. Parents appear disguised as kings and queens, birth is represented by water – falling into it, or saving someone from it – and death by setting out on a journey. The majority of images are sexual symbols.

Freud: exploring the unconscious.

Mafeking siege lifted

Long Tom, a Boer heavy gun, trained on the besieged British troops at Mafeking.

London, 20 May
As it happened, Queen Victoria was visiting Wellington College in Berkshire. As she drove up, a banner was raised in greeting, bearing the words "Queen of Mafeking". The whole school was "quite mad with delight", she recorded in her diary. As for Londoners, she said, the goings-on were "indescribable".

Throughout the land, the news of the relief of Mafeking, after a siege of 217 days, has been received with a wild excitement that betrays the sense of relief felt by the British people after months of military reverses. Now they hope that, with Lord Roberts, the hero of Afghanistan, in command in South Africa, the Boers are in for a drubbing.

Mafeking is a small town on the railway from Kimberley to Rhodesia. It is of no strategic importance in the war, but Colonel Robert Baden-Powell, the cavalry officer, the commander of the British force there, tied up a Boer force of 10,000 by holding out. He organised teams of sappers to dig trenches and throw up earthworks, and kept outposts in touch with his HQ by using the town's schoolboys as runners, whom he called Boy Scouts. He sent out messages telling the folk at home that morale was high among soldiers and citizens.

Not everyone has been impressed by Baden-Powell's heroics. Colonel Sir Herbert Plumer, who commands the Rhodesian detachment, has remarked that it is an odd sort of cavalry officer who, at the first whiff of battle, begins digging trenches and eating his horses.

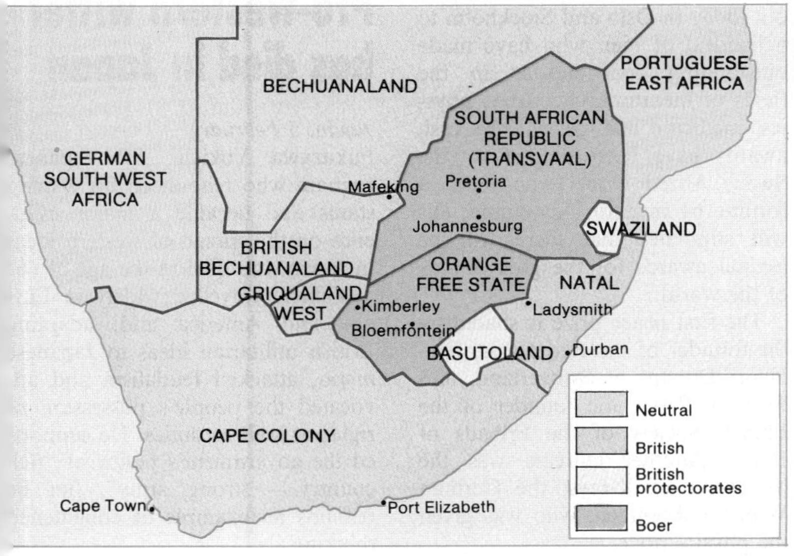

Allies march on Beijing

China, 14 August
The eight-nation allied relief force fought its way into Beijing in the early hours of this morning and lifted the siege of the legations, driving away the Boxers and the regular troops who have besieged the diplomatic quarter and the Beitang cathedral for the past two months.

The defenders have shown the utmost bravery, beating off repeated attacks while suffering from hunger and living in the most appalling conditions. It is unlikely, however, that they would have survived if it had not been for the restraining hand of Ronglu, the Chinese commander, who refused to allow the besiegers to use artillery which would have blown the legations apart.

Ronglu is convinced that the decision by Cixi, the empress dowager, to declare war on the "foreign devils" will prove disastrous for China. There seems little doubt that he is right. His army has vanished and Cixi, along with her nephew, the emperor – whom she keeps a captive – has fled, allegedly disguised as a peasant. Allied soldiers are already looting.

The trouble started with the wave of xenophobia which swept China after the defeat by Japan and the foreign scramble for concessions. From it emerged the society of Righteous and Harmonious Fists, who became known as the Boxers. Like their predecessors, the Big Swords, they practise martial arts and believe themselves immune from harm on the battlefield.

The explosion came last May when the Boxers massacred Chinese converts and isolated foreigners, burnt churches and destroyed the railway line between Beijing and Tientsin. Cixi was caught up in the tension. The German minister was murdered and foreign retribution became inevitable.

Allied troops battle against Boxers while relieving the legations at Beijing.

Theory says energy comes in tiny packets

Germany
A profound and disturbing idea has just been put forward that upsets the picture of the material world according to Isaac Newton that has been popular for centuries. The revolutionary theory comes from a 42-year-old German physicist, Max Planck. Planck, having studied a source of radiation known as a blackbody, has concluded that energy is emitted not in waves but in tiny packets, or *quanta*. Thus light consists of streams of packets called *photons*.

This new *quantum* theory explains phenomena such as absorption and radiation at the atomic level more convincingly than conventional theories. And Planck has also been able to describe quanta in precise mathematical terms.

1901

Australia, 1 January. The Commonwealth of Australia comes into being.

Britain, 22 January. Queen Victoria dies and is succeeded by her son Edward VII.

Italy, 27 January. The composer Giuseppe Verdi dies.

Moscow, 31 January. Anton Chekhov's play *Three Sisters* is performed for the first time.

India, 12 February. The viceroy, Lord Curzon, creates the North-West Frontier province between Afghanistan and the Punjab.

Germany, 6 March. An anarchist makes an attempt on the life of Kaiser William II.

USA, 31 March. The first Mercedes motor car is built.

Venezuela, 9 August. Colombian troops invade Venezuela.

Detroit, 21 August. The Cadillac motor company is founded.

Britain, 4 September. In the Taff Vale railway case, the House of Lords rules that trade unions are liable for the financial losses of companies affected by industrial action.

China, 7 September. The *Boxer* Protocol is signed by China and the foreign powers, ending the Boxer rebellion.

France, 9 September. The painter Henri de Toulouse-Lautrec dies at the age of 36.

USA, 14 September. President William McKinley dies after being shot by an anarchist.

West Africa, 25 September. Britain annexes the Asante kingdom as part of the Gold Coast (*Ghana*).

China, 16 October. Russia signs a new agreement with China over Manchuria.

USA, 24 October. George Eastman sets up the Eastman Kodak camera company.

South Africa, October. Boer commandos invade Cape Colony, coming within 50 miles of Cape Town.

USA, 18 November. Britain and the USA sign the Hay-Pauncefote treaty, agreeing terms for a canal through Central America.

USA, 2 December. King Camp Gillette announces plans to market a disposable razor.

Britain, 11 December. Guglielmo Marconi sends the first wireless message across the Atlantic.

Polish anarchist assassinates president

President McKinley: a photograph taken 15 minutes before he was shot.

Washington, 14 September

President William McKinley, who established the United States as a world power with an overseas empire, died today after being shot by a Polish anarchist in Buffalo, New York. He is succeeded by the vice-president, Theodore Roosevelt, aged 42, already famous as a man of letters, soldier and statesman.

McKinley had served only six months of a second term; his administration has seen the highest tariffs in American history and the growth of expansionist policies. In 1898 Hawaii was annexed. In the Spanish-American War – when Roosevelt won glory commanding a volunteer force – the US acquired the Philippines, Puerto Rico and Guam.

"Teddy" Roosevelt becomes the youngest US president. Identified with the reform wing of the Republican Party, he sees his task as serving as the moral leader of the American people and safeguarding the nation against special interests.

Great minds deserve a prize, says Swede

Alfred Nobel, whose dynamite fortune will be used to further peace.

Oslo, 10 December

The first Nobel prizes were handed out today in Oslo and Stockholm to a handful of men who have made outstanding contributions in the fields of literature, chemistry, physics, medicine and peace. The cash awards have been funded by the Swede Alfred Nobel who made a fortune by inventing dynamite. His will stipulates that there will be annual awards for the great minds of the world.

The first peace prize is shared by the founder of the Red Cross, Jean Henri Dunant of Switzerland, and Frederic Passy, the founder of the French Society of the Friends of Peace. Another laureate was the discoverer of X-rays, the German Wilhelm Roentgen, who was given the physics prize.

Red radicals storm Russian cathedral

St Petersburg, 17 March

Mass was beginning in the great Kazan cathedral with its 96 Corinthian columns when several hundred students came tearing down the Nevsky Prospekt. They burst in, jeering and throwing stones at the precious *icon* of the Virgin of Kazan.

The students were eventually driven into the street, where they handed out leaflets calling for the overthrow of the czar. Two regiments of mounted Cossacks appeared and in a series of charges rounded up over 800 demonstrators.

Violent street demonstrations have occurred in Odessa, Kharkov and Kiev, and in Moscow, where the writer Leo Tolstoy joined factory workers and students in setting up barricades.

Cossacks clear Moscow barricades.

Pro-western writer has died in Japan

Japan, 3 February

Fukuzawa Yukichi, the Japanese *samurai* who renounced his warrior status and became a major influence on the spread of western ideas in Japan, has died at the age of 66.

Yukichi travelled widely in Europe and America and, adapting British utilitarian ideas to Japanese *mores*, attacked feudalism and advocated the people's possession of rights as well as duties. He supported the government's policy of "rich country – strong army", but he remains an example of enlightened thinking.

Australia becomes commonwealth

Melbourne, 1 January
After more than 50 years of debate and false starts the six separate states of Australia, including Tasmania, are united in a federal commonwealth constitution. Local pride and political jealousies repeatedly blocked moves towards unity, but external pressures did much to overcome parish-pump sentiment.

Notable among such pressures were fears from 1883 onward that Germany might colonise New Guinea and that France coveted the New Hebrides. Equally potent was the fear of Asian migration into Australia's remote northern territories. No unified defence policy existed for either contingency.

Even after the British Parliament had been presented with Australia's agreed proposals, Western Australia tried to amend them. There is still no agreement about the site for a federal capital except that it will be in New South Wales some 100 miles (160 kilometres) from Sydney. The first parliament, however, will meet in Melbourne later this year.

Australia proclaims whites-only policy

Australia
One of the first acts of the new Australian government has been to pass a law restricting the immigration of non-whites. The Federal Immigration Restriction Act prohibits the permanent settlement of any coloured person but allows students, officials and businessmen to enjoy temporary residence. Chinese immigration during the gold rush 50 years ago, which provoked riots, and a local shipping firm's attempt to replace white crews with cheap Chinese labour prompted the move.

There is also an underlying anxiety for Australia's cultural identity if massive immigration occurred from Asia or Polynesia. Some advocates of the new law think that a multiracial society would result in 'mongrelisation", although white migration represents the genetically mixed stock of Celtic Ireland and Anglo-Saxon England. Aborigines are not discussed.

End of an era as Queen Victoria dies

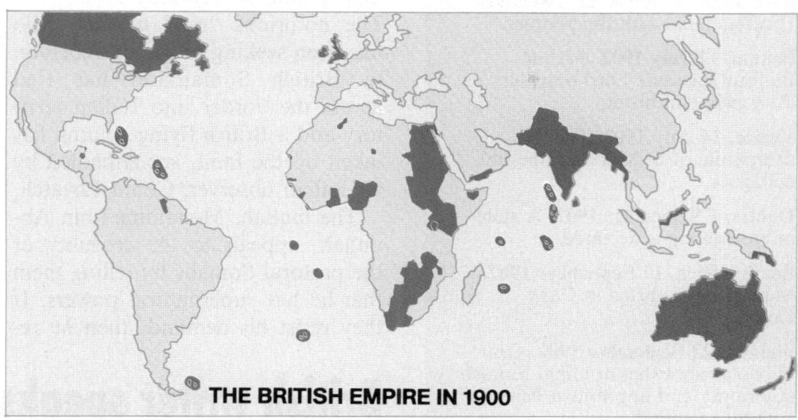

Victoria at her Diamond Jubilee.

Isle of Wight, Britain, 22 January
In recent months she left her chair only once without help, and then it was to pin a medal on a hospital patient. She was 81; her eyesight was failing and she suffered much from insomnia. The news filled her with sorrow. Her son Alfred ("poor, dear Affie") died, the king of Italy was assassinated, and a grandson, Prince Christian of Schleswig-Holstein, died of fever in South Africa. The war in South Africa overshadowed the last years of her eventful reign. Her 63 years on the throne had seen times of hardship and danger, but nothing quite like that war against a foe small in numbers but able to humiliate the greatest power on earth. It was like a portent. Victoria, the daughter of the impoverished duke of Kent, had seen her island people carry her power to the far corners of the world. They had made new countries, drawn new frontiers, and enjoyed wealth beyond the dreams of avarice. But now there were other runners in the race, bigger and potentially more powerful.

In the early years of her reign Victoria was supported by the dearly-loved Prince Albert, the husband from Germany. For many years she had mourned his death, but she had borne nine children and, as they married into other royal families, she became known as the "grandmother of Europe". This evening, soon after six o'clock, with her children and grandchildren at her bedside, her grandson the German kaiser among them, she passed into history.

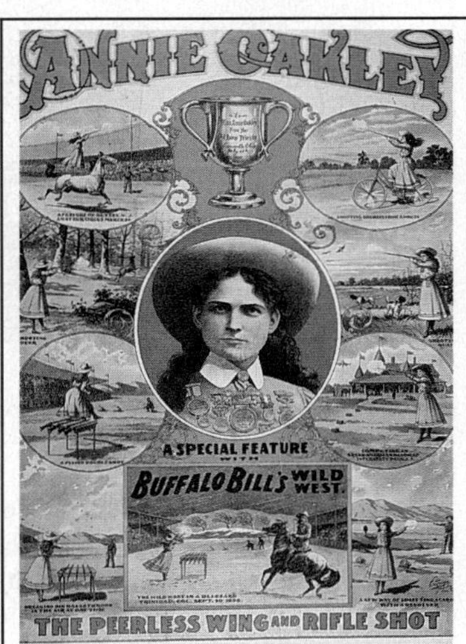

Annie Oakley, the last of the great North America frontier myths, now in show business.

Wireless message spans Atlantic Ocean

Guglielmo Marconi, whose messages in morse code can now cross the Atlantic.

Newfoundland, 11 December
Guglielmo Marconi, the 27-year-old Italian inventor, has finally confounded the sceptics who have sneered at his attempts at wireless transmission. At St John's here he has just received a message tapped out in morse code on the other side of the Atlantic in Poldhu, in Cornwall, England.

It is an even more impressive feat than his reports from mid-Atlantic on the yacht race two years ago. Marconi's invention owes a lot to the time he spent working in England, first with Sir Oliver Lodge and then with Sir William Preece, the chief engineer of the Post Office.

But it has been Marconi who pushed ahead with practical applications, first using balloons and kites to get his aerials to greater heights in order to transmit over huge distances.

1902 (1902-1903)

London, 30 January 1902. Britain and Japan sign a treaty agreeing to respect each other's interests in China and Korea.

Berlin, 15 February 1902. The Berlin underground railway opens.

Spain, 20 February 1902. About 500 die in Barcelona strike clashes.

USA, 22 February 1902. The Yellow Fever Commission announces that the disease is carried by mosquitoes.

Britain, 26 February 1902. Lord Rosebery, the former Liberal prime minister, forms the Liberal League, splitting the Liberal Party.

Russia, February 1902. More than 30,000 students strike in protest at government attempts to curb the activities of student organisations.

South Africa, 26 March 1902. The British colonial statesman Cecil Rhodes dies.

USA, 7 April 1902. The Texas Oil Company (Texaco) is founded.

China, 8 April 1902. Russia signs a treaty with China over Manchuria, promising to withdraw its troops.

London, 9 April 1902. The Underground Electric Railways Company is incorporated.

Russia, 15 April 1902. Sipyagin, the head of the secret police, is killed by socialist revolutionaries.

Dublin, 16 April 1902. At a rally in Phoenix Park, 20,000 people protest at the British government's plans to impose tough new laws in Ireland.

Martinique, 8 May 1902. An eruption of Mount Pele wipes out the whole town of St Pierre.

London, 29 May 1902. The London School of Economics and Political Science opens.

Spain, 30 May 1902. King Alfonso XIII suspends the Madrid *Cortes* amid growing unrest.

South Africa, 31 May 1902. The Boers surrender to the British and sign the peace of Vereeniging, ending the Boer war and recognising British sovereignty.

Britain, 18 June 1902. The satirist Samuel Butler dies.

Europe, 23 June 1902. The triple alliance of Germany, Austria and Italy is renewed for 12 years.

USA, 28 June 1902. The USA pays France $40,000 for the rights to the Panama Canal.

Vienna, 29 June 1902. The French car maker Marcel Renault wins the first Paris-Vienna motor race.

USA, 1 July 1902. The Philippine Government Act, under which Filipinos will be ruled by a US presidential commission, is passed.

Russia, 3 July 1902. To avoid the spread of riots, in which thousands have already died, Czar Nicholas II offers talks with the people.

Britain, 12 July 1902. Arthur Balfour succeeds Lord Salisbury as Tory prime minister.

Venice, 14 July 1902. The campanile of St Mark's cathedral collapses.

Dublin, 1 September 1902. A state of emergency is declared.

South Africa, 17 September 1902. Martial law is lifted in Cape Colony.

Finland, 22 September 1902. Czar Nicholas abolishes nominal Finnish autonomy and appoints a Russian governor general.

France, 29 September 1902. The writer Emile Zola, the author of *Germinal* and *Therese Raquin* and valiant champion of Captain Dreyfus, dies.

Zimbabwe, 6 October 1902. A railway link between Bulawayo and Salisbury is completed.

Belgium, 15 November 1902. The anarchist Gennaro Rubino makes an attempt on the life of King Leopold II.

Germany, 22 November 1902. The steel magnate Friedrich Krupp, head of Germany's largest manufacturing firm and the richest man in the country, dies.

Vienna, 1 December 1902. Austria and Russia agree on joint supervision in Macedonia.

Venezuela, 9 December 1902. British and German warships seize the Venezuelan navy, demanding settlement of compensation claims arising from President Cipriano Castro's 1899 coup.

Egypt, 10 December 1902. The massive Nile dam at Aswan is completed.

Britain, 18 December 1902. The new Education Act puts elementary and secondary education in the hands of borough and county councils.

Britain, 1902. Beatrix Potter publishes *The Tale of Peter Rabbit*.

Britain, 1902. Among this year's new novels are *Anna of the Five Towns* by Arnold Bennett and *Heart of Darkness* by Joseph Conrad.

India, 1 January 1903. A mighty *durbar* is held in the old Moghul capital of Delhi to proclaim Edward VII king-emperor of India.

Central America, 22 January 1903. The US and Colombia sign a treaty to allow the construction of the Panama Canal.

British forces advance on Somali mullah

Somaliland, 24 February 1903
The notorious "mad *mullah*" who has been seeking to stir up rebellion in British Somaliland has fled across the border into Italian territory and a British flying column has taken up the hunt, accompanied by an Italian observer, Count Lovateli.

The mullah, Mohammed bin Abdullah, appeals to the credulity of the pastoral Somalis by telling them that he has supernatural powers. If they resist his demands then he returns with a raiding party to rob and kill. When he is on the run, as he is now, he is liable to vanish into the bush and lie low for months.

The British column includes detachments of the Punjab Mounted Infantry and the Camel Corps. A transport docked at the Indian Ocean port of Obbia recently with 600 camels, but many more are needed, and ports up and down the coast are being scoured for the animals at any price.

British writer speaks with imperial voice

Kipling: spokesman for (and critic of) Britain's empire in the east.

London, 1902
Rudyard Kipling, the poet of empire, has written more for children than for adults in recent years: this year the *Just So Stories*, telling how the camel got his hump and other matters, last year *Kim*, the brilliant evocation of British and native India as he knew it in boyhood. Before that came *Stalky and Co*, based on his schooldays, and in 1894-5 the two *Jungle Books*.

Kipling found himself famous at 25 for his *Plain Tales from the Hills* and *Barrack Room Ballads* – the lore of the private soldier east of Suez, who knew the road to Mandalay and the worth of Gunga Din.

A train arrives at a station platform – a symbol of expanding horizons and the modern world. Two brothers, Auguste and Louis Jean Lumiere, 33 years old and 31 years old, by taking one photograph after another extremely fast, and running the developed film through a projector at the same speed onto a screen, relive the movement of the train as it comes into the station. Many watching this extraordinary moving photography are impressed. Others find it jerky and say it gives them headaches. All agree it is quite unique. No one has seen anything like it before.

Slavery and atrocities revealed in Congo

London, 15 April 1903
Britain's consul in the Congo Free State, Roger Casement, is preparing an analysis of the barbarities inflicted on Blacks by the Belgian administration of King Leopold II.

Villagers are being intimidated by threats to their families into making arduous, dangerous trips into the forest to collect a high quota of raw, wild rubber. For this service they are paid nothing. While they are away for days at a time, working without food or shelter, becoming the prey of wild animals, their families are hostages to "sentinels" licensed to impose virtually any punishment for any "crime" they identify. Communities which do not deliver a set quota, or argue, are attacked by paramilitaries or regular troops who hack off the hands of dead victims.

King Leopold is blamed. He has dishonoured international guarantees, using the Congo as a personal estate a million miles square, to be squeezed for the last *sou*. Funds raised by such cruelty are used by the king to build increasingly preposterous buildings in Belgium, a modest nation which detests his architectural taste as much as his inhumanity.

King Leopold: the man accused of cruel exploitation in the Congo.

Ford has vision of cheap cars for all

Ford in his first car, the quadricycle.

The price of the new mobility.

Detroit, 1903
Despite being turned down by the banking house of Morgan – which dismissed the idea of workers owning their own motor cars as "ridiculous" – a farmer's son, Henry Ford, has managed to raise $28,000 from local investors to rent a shed and build automobiles in Detroit. Although he has managed to sell seven models of his first design, an eight-horsepower car with two cylinders, Ford has not lost sight of his dream – a low cost automobile available to all – and is seeking a strong cheap metal.

With more than 50 automobile companies already in production in America and others joining the race, Ford faces stiff competition. But not all of the others see a mass market as Henry Ford does.

US-backed rebels take power in Panama

Panama, 6 November 1903
A small group of railroad workers, barmen and militiamen, supported by the fire brigade and US adventurers, has overthrown Colombia's rule in the Panama Isthmus and proclaimed Panama a republic. To no great surprise, the US government, whose cruiser *Nashville* is lying off shore to deter Colombian troops from landing, has recognised the republic.

The *coup* was no more of a surprise than was the US state department's somewhat hasty recognition. Three months ago the Colombian Congress rejected a treaty for a canal to be built across the isthmus from the Atlantic to the Pacific, which would reduce the USA's shipping costs from the east coast to the west coast by millions of dollars. Needless to say, the new *junta* in Panama is extremely enthusiastic for the canal. Indeed the leader of the coup is none other than Philippe Jean Bunasu-Varilla, the canal's foremost advocate, who will be leaving for Washington in a few days to complete the arrangements.

Britain clinches Pacific deal with Japan

Tokyo, 30 January 1902
The Japanese government today welcomed the signing of the Anglo-Japanese alliance which recognises the special interests of Britain in China and Japan in Korea and provides for each country to safeguard the other's interests.

There is also a secret naval codicil which is believed to provide for an exchange of facilities and an agreement for both countries to maintain large naval forces in Far Eastern waters. Perhaps the most pleasing aspect of the treaty from the Japanese point of view is that Japan has become the ally of one of the most powerful European states.

The Anglo-Japanese agreement, seen from Paris: a debauched King Edward charmed by a geisha "girl".

Britain blockades debtor Venezuela

Venezuela, 31 December 1902
The navies of Great Britain, Germany and Italy have set up a blockade of the coastline of Venezuela. Their action follows the refusal of Venezuela to compensate European nationals who have been injured in a recent series of rebellions. They are also acting to force Venezuela to repay its outstanding debts.

Britain's argument with Venezuela dates back to 1896, when both nations were involved in a major wrangle over the boundaries of British Guiana. Only the notably pro-Venezuelan stance of the US president, Cleveland, restrained the British. Now Venezuela has appealed to the new president, Roosevelt, but he is determined to keep out of the controversy.

African workers found churches

South Africa, 1903
New politico-religious movements are emerging amongst the black migrant labourers of South Africa. Identifying themselves as Africans rather than as members of tribes, they have established native congresses and black churches.

The native congresses associate themselves with the Pan-African movement in the New World. The black churches, which broke away from white Protestant missionary organisations, have united, calling themselves the Ethiopian Church (Ethiopia being the word for Africa in the Bible). They, too, have a black American link with the African Methodist Episcopal Church – the biggest black church in the USA.

1903 (1903-1904)

Washington, DC, 13 February 1903. Britain, Germany and Italy sign a treaty agreeing to lift the blockade of Venezuela.

Balkans, 23 February 1903. The Ottoman Sultan Abdul Hamid II accepts Russian and Austrian proposals for reforms in Macedonia, in order to quell a rebellion there.

USA, 3 March 1903. A bill is passed curbing immigration and banning "undesirables".

Russia, 12 March 1903. Czar Nicholas II issues a manifesto conceding important reforms, including the freedom of religion.

Nigeria, 15 March 1903. Following the fall of Kano last month, troops of the West African Frontier Force, led by British officers, take Sokoto. The sultan flees.

France, 18 March 1903. The religious orders are dissolved.

Finland, 26 March 1903. The czar appoints the Russian general Bobrikov virtual dictator of Finland.

Balkans, 14 April 1903. Bulgarians kill 165 people in a Moslem village near Monastir in Macedonia.

Balkans, 16 April 1903. In the latest act of Jewish persecution, peasants in Kishinev, in Bessarabia, massacre scores of Jews.

Britain, 21 May 1903. Joseph Chamberlain, the colonial secretary, founds the Tariff League to promote a preferential trading system within the empire.

Serbia, 11 June 1903. King Alexander and Queen Draga are murdered by disaffected army officers and Prince Peter Karageorgevich is proclaimed king.

Germany, 16 June 1903. The socialists make large gains in elections to the *reichstag*.

Britain, 17 July 1903. The American painter James McNeill Whistler dies.

France, 19 July 1903. Maurice Garin wins the first Tour de France bicycle race.

Rome, 20 July 1903. Pope Leo XIII, who worked throughout his 25-year reign to unite Christendom and reduce class warfare, dies.

Rome, 4 August 1903. Giuseppe Sarto, the patriarch of Venice, becomes Pope Pius X.

Switzerland, 19 August 1903. Delegates to the sixth Zionist Congress in Basle clash over proposals to set up a Jewish state in Uganda.

Britain, 22 August 1903. Lord Salisbury, who was Conservative prime minister three times, dies.

Britain, 17 September 1903. Joseph Chamberlain resigns as colonial secretary to have greater freedom to promote preferential trade with the empire.

USA, 21 September 1903. *Kit Carson*, the first Wild West movie, opens.

Balkans, September 1903. The Ottomans have massacred 50,000 Bulgarians in the region of Monastir.

Britain, 10 October 1903. Emmeline Pankhurst founds the Women's Social and Political Union.

Germany, 1 November 1903. The historian Theodor Mommsen dies.

France, 12 November 1903. The painter Camille Pissarro dies.

Russia, 17 November 1903. Vladimir Lenin splits the Social Democratic Labour Party, leading a majority breakaway group, the *Bolsheviks*.

Central America, November 1903. Panama declares itself independent of Colombia.

USA, 17 December 1903. Wilbur and Orville Wright fly a heavier-than-air flying machine at Kitty Hawk, North Carolina.

Korea, December 1903. Japan lands marines at Mok-Pho to deal with rioting Korean labourers.

South-West Africa, 11 January 1904. Rebellious Herero massacre 123 German soldiers and male settlers near Okahandja, the seat of the Herero chief, Samuel Maharero.

Moscow, 17 January 1904. *The Cherry Orchard*, a play by Anton Chekhov, receives its premiere.

Cuba, 5 February 1904. America ends its occupation of Cuba.

China, 8 February 1904. Provoked by Russian penetration of northern Korea and failure to withdraw from Manchuria, war breaks out between Japan and Russia with a Japanese attack on Port Arthur (*Lushun*).

Germany, 8 March 1904. The reichstag lifts its ban on Jesuits.

Tibet, 31 March 1904. British forces under Macdonald kill some 300 Tibetans attempting to halt a British mission to Tibet.

Europe, 8 April 1904. France and Britain sign an *entente cordiale* settling their colonial disputes in North Africa.

Britain, 22 April 1904. A bill is passed legalising peaceful picketing during strikes.

Britain, 26 April 1904. George Bernard Shaw's play *Candida* is performed for the first time.

Rivals wreck Madam Butterfly premiere

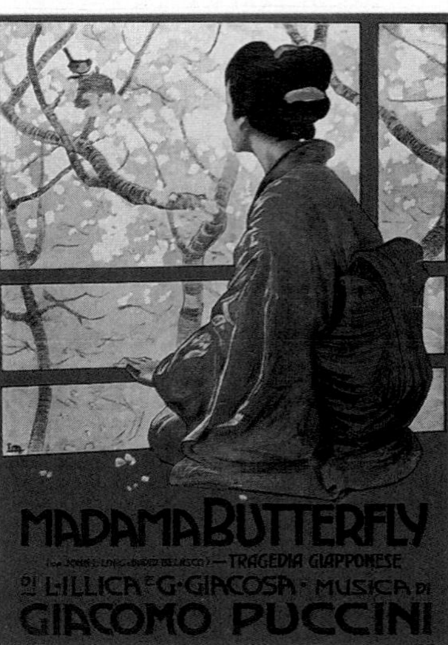

"Madam Butterfly": a tragic opera by Puccini on Japan, America, and the price paid when east meets west.

Milan, 18 February 1904
Jeering, whistling and general uproar greeted last night's premiere of the opera *Madam Butterfly* by the Italian composer Giacomo Puccini.

He has withdrawn the work, a tragic love tale set in Japan, for revision. However, the fiasco seems to have been caused by Puccini's rivals, who tried to ruin the first performance of his hugely successful *Tosca* in Rome four years ago.

Puccini, whose family have been musicians since 1712, is the greatest of the new generation of composers writing "realist" operas, often with contemporary, unheroic people and violent emotions on stage. He was born in 1858; his first big success was *La Boheme*, whose 1896 premiere was conducted by the brilliant young Italian, Arturo Toscanini.

Stockbroker who painted idyllic island life

Atuaha, Marquesas Is, 8 May 1903
Paul Gauguin, the French painter who has lived in the South Seas since 1891, died here today of syphilis, aged 54. He was under a prison sentence for defamation of the administration and the church. He gave up a successful stockbroking career on the Paris *Bourse* when he was 35 to concentrate on painting, at which he was self-taught.

He met Pissarro and Cezanne, and was influenced by the impressionists, before breaking from them. At 43 he finally abandoned his family and went to Tahiti in search of primitive culture.

Giving up naturalism completely, he aimed at expressing intense emotion with areas of deep, flat colour as in *The Watching Spirit of the Dead*, which shows his 13-year-old native wife who believed that such spirits entered houses in darkness. He exhibited in Paris in 1893 but sold little. He returned to Tahiti, moving to the Marquesas in 1901.

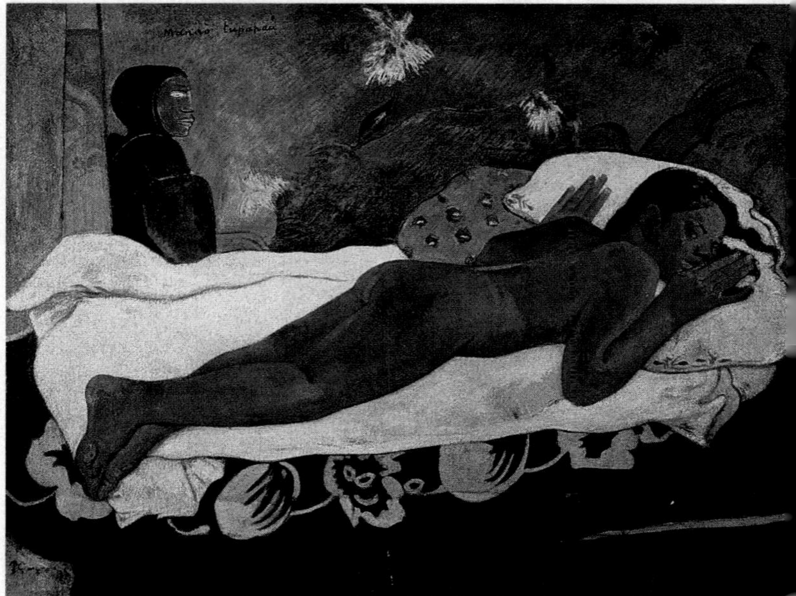

Paul Gauguin's painting "Manao Tupapau": the spirit of the dead keeps watch

Turks kill 50,000 Bulgarian civilians

Sofia, Bulgaria, 8 September 1903
Another massacre of civilians by Ottomans has reportedly taken 50,000 Bulgarian lives. The worst butchery seems to have happened at the village of Monastir, politically part of Serbia but ethnically Bulgar and near the border with Bulgarian Macedonia. Women and children were among those slaughtered by a punitive expedition.

The reason for such savagery is a Bulgarian plan to launch a general uprising against Ottoman rule. The rebellion was due to start on 31 August, but the Ottomans got word of it and swamped Macedonia with 300,000 troops. The last similar event occurred in April 1876 when 12,000 Christian Bulgars were exterminated by the Islamic Ottoman government.

Ottoman troops killing Bulgarians.

A week ago Macedonian terrorists blew up a Hungarian ship, killing 29 passengers and crew, in an apparent effort to internationalise the crisis provoked by Ottoman dictatorship. Such repression is perilous for the peace of Europe generally because of the number of great powers which may be drawn into defending client Balkan states.

"Bolsheviks" split Russian socialists

London, 17 November 1903
Vladimir Lenin, a Russian professional revolutionary, has emerged as leader of the *Bolshevik* group following the split at a congress today of the Russian Social Democratic Party. Lenin had found himself in a minority at the congress, but a walkout by a disgruntled group of Jewish Social Democrats played into his hands and gave him a slight majority. The *Bolsheviks* (majority) are seeking to overturn Russia with a single centralised party of professional revolutionaries. The opposing *Mensheviks* (minority) are led by Yuly Martov and advocate a broad proletarian party. They also fear that Lenin favours the suppression of free intra-party debate and is in favour of a one-man dictatorship.

Marie Curie is first woman Nobel winner

Paris, 10 December 1903
Marie Curie, aged 33, has become the first female winner of the Nobel prize. She has won it jointly with her husband and a colleague for the discovery of radiation. But it was Madame Curie who did most of the pioneering work, discovering first *polonium* (named after her native Poland), then *radium*.

Her father was a teacher of physics in Warsaw, but after he lost his savings through bad investment she had to work as a governess and did not begin scientific work until she came here. She hopes that radiation will play an important part in the treatment of some diseases.

Marie Curie, Nobel prize winner and discoverer of polonium and radium.

Brothers take to the air

North Carolina, 17 December 1903
It lasted for only 12 seconds, and the fragile machine in which he rode rose a scant ten feet above the ground and covered barely 120 feet (37 metres) from start to finish, but today, on the sand dunes near Kitty Hawk, North Carolina, man has taken wings and made his first-ever powered flight.

The brothers Orville and Wilbur Wright, bicycle mechanics from Dayton, Ohio, have been moving steadily towards today's flights since 1899 when they began looking into hitherto unsuccessful attempts to fly. After experimenting with gliders they realised that the secret lay in rigid, airworthy wings. After exhaustive testing of every part of their proposed flying machine, the Wrights came to Kitty Hawk. With Orville lying face down in a cradle slung beneath the wings, and the elder brother, Wilbur, running alongside, *Flyer I*, powered by its 12 mph engine, moved along the runners that supported it, and then, as the wind caught it, the flying machine gently rose upwards into the wind.

The Wrights made three further flights before their machine, called *Flyer*, was damaged by a sudden gust. The longest lasted for 59 seconds and covered 852 feet.

Orville Wright's first successful flight from Kitty Hawk, North Carolina.

Women form political pressure group

Manchester, 1903
Emmeline Pankhurst has formed a militant Women's Social and Political Union to rival the National Union of Women's Suffrage started six years ago by Millicent Fawcett. Pankhurst and her followers, many of whom are local women mill workers, impatient for the vote, feel that drastic action is now necessary to change electoral law in this country. "Action not Words" is their motto.

The first parliamentary debate on women's suffrage was over 36 years ago and, apart from Mrs Pankhurst's achievement of gaining the right for all women to participate in local elections, polite demonstrations of women's views have had no effect in getting them national voting power.

Emmeline Pankhurst: the leader of the new ultra-militant suffragettes.

1904 (1904-1905)

Bohemia, 1 May 1904. The Czech composer Antonin Dvorak dies.

Britain, 4 May 1904. Charles Rolls and Henry Royce sign an agreement to build motor cars.

Britain, 9 May 1904. The British explorer Sir Henry Stanley dies.

New York City, 15 June 1904. About 1,000 die when the paddle-steamer *General Slocum* catches fire in New York harbour.

South America, 15 June 1904. Britain and Brazil sign an arbitration convention to settle the disputed border of British Guiana.

Finland, 23 June 1904. The Russian governor general, Bobrikov, is assassinated.

China, 24 June 1904. Japanese forces inflict a major defeat on the Russians at Telissu.

Austria, 3 July 1904. The Hungarian-born Zionist Theodor Herzl dies.

Switzerland, 14 July 1904. Paul Kruger, four times president of the Transvaal republic, dies in exile in Geneva.

Russia, 15 July 1904. The playwright Anton Chekhov dies.

Russia, 28 July 1904. Viacheslav Plehve, the minister of the interior, is assassinated.

France, 29 July 1904. France severs diplomatic links with the Vatican.

Tibet, 4 August 1904. Following the arrival in Lhasa of British troops led by the explorer Francis Younghusband, the Dalai Lama flees to Urga.

France, 25 August 1904. The painter Henri Fantin-Latour dies.

Tibet, 7 September 1904. On behalf of Britain, Francis Younghusband signs a treaty with Tibet by which Tibet agrees not to cede territory to any foreign power.

Belgium, September 1904. Leopold II, the king of the Belgians, appoints an international commission to investigate conditions in the Congo Free State.

Morocco, 3 October 1904. France and Spain sign an agreement on Morocco by which the northern part of the country is recognised as a Spanish zone of influence.

North Sea, 22 October 1904. Ships of the Russian Baltic fleet torpedo and sink two British trawlers off the Dogger Bank.

New York City, 27 October 1904. The underground railway opens.

USA, 8 November 1904. The Republican Theodore Roosevelt is returned to power in the presidential election.

China, 5 December 1904. The Japanese destroy the Russian fleet at Port Arthur (*Lushun*).

Stockholm, 10 December 1904. The Russian physiologist Ivan Pavlov wins a Nobel prize for his work on the digestive system.

London, 13 December 1904. London's first electric underground train goes into operation.

Russia, 26 December 1904. Czar Nicholas II issues a decree offering liberal reforms, but warns that strikes and riots must stop.

Britain, 27 December 1904. James Barrie's play *Peter Pan* opens.

Russia, 1 January 1905. The Trans-Siberian railway officially opens.

China, 2 January 1905. The Russians surrender to the Japanese at Port Arthur.

St Petersburg, 22 January 1905. The czar's troops shoot dead more than 500 strikers on "Bloody Sunday".

USA, 7 February 1905. The states of Oklahoma and New Mexico are admitted to the union.

Russia, 13 February 1905. The Japanese lay siege to Vladivostok.

Moscow, 17 February 1905. Grand Duke Sergei, the uncle of Czar Nicholas II, is assassinated.

Russia, 9 March 1905. Found culpable by an international commission for the Dogger Bank incident, Russia agrees to pay Britain £65,000 compensation.

China, 10 March 1905. The Japanese defeat the Russians at Mukden after a ten-day battle.

France, 24 March 1905. Jules Verne, the inventor of the scientific novel, dies.

India, 4 April 1905. An earthquake in Lahore kills more than 10,000.

France, April 1905. The psychologist Alfred Binet invents intelligence tests.

Warsaw, 1 May 1905. Troops fire on May Day demonstrators, killing 100.

Switzerland, 6 May 1905. Seven eastern European socialist parties form a new group in Geneva.

Sea of Japan, 28 May 1905. The Japanese annihilate the Russian fleet in the strait of Tsushima.

Norway, 7 June 1905. Norway declares independence from Sweden.

Athens, 13 June 1905. The prime minister, Delyannis, is assassinated outside the Greek parliament.

Britain, June 1905. The Automobile Association is founded.

Irish writer is the toast of London stage

GBS, the Irish playwright, as seen in a later poster for "Great Catherine".

London, November, 1905

Major Barbara, the third play by George Bernard Shaw to be presented at the Court theatre this year, has confirmed his dominance among contemporary playwrights. In March his Irish comedy, *John Bull's Other Island*, made the king laugh so much that he broke his chair. In October came *Man and Superman*, introducing the Shavian philosophy of creative evolution.

Shaw had been better known as a journalist, critic and Fabian socialist than a playwright until Harley Granville-Barker began presenting seasons of his plays at the Court last year. *Major Barbara* contrasts different ways of dealing with poverty – "the worst of crimes".

Auguste Rodin: thinking man's sculptor

Rodin's "The Thinker", one of a series of sculptures for his "Gates of Hell".

Rodin's nude, the "Age of Bronze", the sculpture that so shocked.

Paris, 1904

France's greatest sculptor, Auguste Rodin, has unveiled a bronze entitled *Le Penseur* (The Thinker) which has all his power and ruggedness but less than his usual provocation. It is intended for the central position in his massive 20-foot (six-metre) *Gates of Hell*, which is planned to rival Ghiberti's *Gates of Paradise* in Florence.

Rodin's career began with an outcry at his *Age of Bronze*, exhibited in 1877, a figure that was so lifelike that it was rumoured to have been cast from a living model. There were some objections to his group *The Burghers of Calais* from the town council which commissioned it, to his commemorative bust of Victor Hugo, and above all to his monument to Balzac, whose massive head was shown impressionistically emerging from the dressing-gown which he wore for writing. It was compared to "a toad in a sack".

In 1898 *The Kiss* was declared unfit for public exhibition at the Chicago World's Fair. Like *The Thinker*, this was intended for the *Gates of Hell* but executed as a separate sculpture.

Impressive Trans-Siberian railway opens

Siberia, 21 July 1904
The Trans-Siberian railway, a major new trading route linking Russia and China, has been completed. It is a feat of engineering and human endurance in one of the most inhospitable climates in the world.

The first stretch of the line was built in 1878 between Perm and Ekaterinburg, on the eastern slope of the Urals. This was extended to Tyumen, beside tributaries of the Ob, across the plains to Omsk, then Irkutsk, and round Lake Baikal to Chita and Vladivostok. The Chinese agreed in 1896 to extend the line across Manchuria.

Chiefly in order to bring tea, silk and cotton from China, and grain and cattle from Siberia, Russian workers braved temperatures as low as minus 85 degrees fahrenheit, and snowstorms.

Convicts who worked on the Trans-Siberian railway posing near Nertschinsk.

British army tangles with Tibetan troops

New Delhi, 6 May 1904
In the latest clash between a column of British-led Indian troops and Tibetan militia, at Gyangtse, on the road to Lhasa, 190 Tibetans died. The battle was similar to one in March, when 300 of the Dalai Lama's men were mown down by British Maxim guns and mountain artillery. The column fighting its way into Tibet is escorting Colonel Sir Francis Younghusband on his mission to persuade the Dalai Lama, a "living god", to stop supporting Russian intrigue on the north flank of India.

The Dalai Lama flees British troops.

Meddling kaiser provokes Morocco crisis

Tangier, Morocco, 31 March 1905
In a surprise visit, Kaiser William II has interrupted a Mediterranean cruise to speak up for Moroccan independence. His intervention will cause much consternation among the British, French and Spanish, who have privately agreed to the partition of Morocco. Germany has not previously declared any interest in Morocco, but Kaiser Willliam has been determined to increase his country's maritime influence. Now he proclaims "great and growing interests in Morocco", and insists that the *sultan* should be free to deal equally with all foreign powers.

Russian navy is crippled

The Russian flagship "Petro Pavlovsk", sunk by Japanese ships on 13 April.

Port Arthur, 9 February 1904
Russian and Japanese rivalry over Manchuria erupted into war here last night when the Japanese made a surprise attack on the Russian fleet lying at anchor in this heavily fortified naval stronghold.

As has become usual with the Japanese, they made no declaration of war but sent nine destroyers of Admiral Togo's main fleet at full speed under cover of darkness to launch their torpedoes at the fully-illuminated Russian ships whose officers were attending a ball given by the admiral's wife. Two of the destroyers collided on the way in, but the others executed a classic torpedo attack and escaped before the Russians could man their gun batteries. The Russians are lucky in that only three of the torpedoes exploded, but it is two of their best battleships, the *Czarevitch* and *Retvizan*, along with the cruiser *Pallada*, which have been hit and put out of action.

The Russians have always been convinced of their superiority over the Japanese "monkeys" and believe that they can beat them by "throwing our caps at them". It will not be so easy. Togo is now cruising off Port Arthur in his modern ships, tempting the Russians to sally out to fight. It is an invitation that they may well refuse.

The Japanese emperor as a hawk, with the Russian bear at his mercy.

"Extermination" order shocks Germany

Namibia, November 1905
An insurrection by the Herero people in which 123 European colonists were killed last year has led to an unprecedented campaign of revenge by German troops.

Repression began immediately, with German soldiers driving 5,000 people into the desert where most of them died of thirst. For the German commander, Lothar von Trotha, negotiation with surviving Hereros was out of the question. "Every Herero with or without a rifle, with or without cattle, shall be shot," he ordered, and he then signed his decree as "the great general of the most powerful emperor, von Trotha".

Von Trotha has been recalled after a national outcry, but three out of every four Hereros are dead.

1905

Odessa, Russia, 3 July. Czarist troops kill 6,000 demonstrators to restore order in Odessa. Unrest, for long underground, is coming to the surface. A general strike is declared in St Petersburg.

South Africa, 4 July. Dutch-speaking Boers protest that the new electoral laws imposed by the British favour the English-speakers, and are an example of how Boers are discriminated against.

Russia, 8 July. The crew of the battleship *Potemkin* surrender to the Rumanians, who say they will not be extradited because the mutiny was a political act.

London, 10 July. Puccini's opera *Madame Butterfly* is performed for the first time in Britain at Covent Garden.

USA, 16 July. Commander Peary sets sail on his second expedition to the North Pole.

Finland, 24 July. The German Kaiser, Wilhelm II and Russia's Czar Nicholas II conclude the treaty of Bjoerkoe.

Russia, 31 July. The Russian governor of Sakhalin Island, off the Siberian coast, surrenders to Japanese forces.

German East Africa, July. Coastal peasants rebel, destroying cotton fields that German colonists forced them to plant.

Russia, 19 August. In a step towards constitutional monarchy, the Duma (a representative assembly) is established.

USA, 29 August. Russian and Japanese delegates agree peace terms. An armistice is arranged for August 31.

Russia, 2 September. The worst famine since 1891 is reported.

Central Asia, 5 September. Hundreds die in battles between Moslem Tartars and Christian Armenians.

USA, 5 September. The war fought in Korea and Manchuria between Russia and Japan ends today with the signing of a peace treaty at Portsmouth, New Hampshire.

London, 19 September. The Irish doctor, Thomas John Barnardo, who set up over 112 homes for deprived children, died today.

Stockholm, 25 September. The terms of Norway's independence from Sweden are announced.

USA, 5 October. The Wright brothers, Orville and Wilbur, make the longest flight yet of 38 minutes and three seconds.

Britain, 13 October. The greatest actor of the day, Sir Henry Irving, dies aged 67.

Britain, 14 October. The suffragettes Christabel Pankhurst and Annie Kenney opt to go to prison rather than pay a fine for assaulting a policeman at a political meeting in Manchester.

Sweden, 27 October. King Oscar II formally abdicates the crown of Norway.

Russia, 30 October. Czar Nicholas II issues an imperial manifesto that transforms the country from an absolute autocracy to a semi-constitutional monarchy in an attempt to quell mounting unrest.

London, 1 November. Police close George Bernard Shaw's new play, *Mrs Warren's Profession*, because of its portrayal of prostitution.

Russia, 8 November. 1,000 Jews are killed in a pogrom in Odessa when a mob of 50,000 goes on the rampage shooting and stabbing Jewish men, women and children.

Poland, 12 November. Martial law is declared in Russian-occupied Poland.

Norway, 18 November. Prince Charles of Denmark accepts the Norwegian throne, taking the name Haakon VII.

Vienna, 28 November. Universal suffrage is granted.

London, 5 December. Sir Henry Campbell-Bannerman, the Liberal leader, accepts King Edward VII's commission to form a new government following the resignation of Arthur Balfour, the Tory premier.

France, 6 December. A law is passed separating the state and the church.

Alaska, 6 December. The Norwegian explorer Roald Amundsen completes a two and a half year journey across the American Arctic coast from the Atlantic to the Pacific.

Russia, 7 December. Revolutionaries occupy the fortress at Kiev in the Ukraine.

Germany, 9 December. Richard Strauss's opera *Salome*, based on Oscar Wilde's play, has its first performance.

British East Africa (Kenya), 19 December. The Nandi resistance leader Koitalel is assassinated by a British officer in a drive to put down native opposition to colonisation.

Moscow, 30 December. Government forces crush an uprising by students and workers after a week of street fighting.

Austria, December. The publication of *Three Essays on the Theory of Sexuality* by the psycho-analyst Sigmund Freud sparks off fierce controversy.

"Fauvists" make artistic splash in Paris

Paris, 1 October

A room at the *Salon d'Automne* is astonishing visitors to the exhibition. Gathered in it are a group of painters who have freed colour from any connection with the way it occurs in life, applying it quite arbitrarily as decoration, straight from the tube.

A critic, Louis Vauxcelles, compared them to wild beasts – *Les Fauves* – and they have adopted the nickname. Their leader, Henri Matisse, shows a portrait of his wife with a green stripe down her nose. Andre Derain paints the trunks of trees bright crimson. Others in the group include Maurice Vlaminck, Georges Rouault, Georges Braque and Raoul Dufy.

Matisse, by Andre Derain: the two men are founders of Fauvism.

The vast soundscapes of modern music

Strauss and Salome: a satirical caricature of modern musical tastes.

Vienna

The monumental seventh symphony by Gustav Mahler was heard for the first time this year, and confirms that music is vaster, more complex and more emotionally charged than ever before. Wagner started it, and Bruckner, Richard Strauss (no relation of Johann) and Mahler have followed. The huge, noble symphonic canvases of the pious, unprepossessing, ill-tailored Professor Bruckner (who died in 1896) have been likened to cathedrals of sound. Strauss, 40, has recently turned more to opera after a string of brilliant, opulently scored orchestral pieces such as *Till Eulenspiegel*, *Don Juan* and *Don Quixote*. He caused a scandal with his "obscene" and "blasphemous" opera *Salome*, inspired by Oscar Wilde's work, last year. Mahler, 47, is the director of the Vienna Opera. But the genius once referred to as "that Jew" had to be baptised a catholic before he could gain the post in this anti-semitic city.

Russian navy wiped out

The Russian battleship Navarin, sunk by the Japanese fleet at Tsushima.

Tsushima, 28 May
The Russian Baltic Fleet has been annihilated in a single day after sailing for eight months halfway round the world to meet Admiral Togo's warships in the Straits of Tsushima.

The Russian fleet's voyage, planned to link up with the ships at Port Arthur and sweep the Japanese from the eastern seas, was a tale of misfortune. It opened fire on a British herring fleet in the North Sea in the belief that the fishing boats were Japanese torpedo boats.

Then it took so long, with its poorly trained crews laboriously refuelling from German-chartered colliers, that Port Arthur and its ships fell to the Japanese before Admiral Rozhdestvenski reached the eastern waters. He was ordered to sail for Vladivostok but this meant passing through the narrow straits between Korea and Japan, waters dominated by Admiral Togo's modern battle fleet.

The Russians, with their crews debilitated and their ships fouled by the long voyage, did not stand a chance. Ambushed by Togo, they were battered and disorganised within an hour. The battleship *Oslyaba* was the first victim, followed by the flagship *Suvorov*. Then the *Alexander III* went down with all hands. Ship followed ship to the bottom until the survivors surrendered. A few small ships have got away, but the fleet and Russia's hopes of winning the war have been wiped out.

Russia is defeated: a moth-eaten bear and his Japanese keeper.

Physicist believes everything is relative

Germany
This year has seen the publication of several key papers by Dr Albert Einstein, the German physicist who, since the age of 12, has been determined to solve "the riddle of the world". He asserts that light consists of individual quanta – *photons* – that can behave both as waves and particles. This is revolutionary stuff. So, too, is the view of mass and energy which we must regard as one and the same.

A further stunning idea is the concept of relativity. Embracing time, space and motion, this states that there are no absolute motions in the universe.

Navy mutineers throw officers overboard

Odessa, Russia, 27 June
Russian sailors have thrown their officers overboard and seized control of the battleship *Potemkin* in the most dramatic outbreak of unrest yet against the czar and his regime. The city of Odessa is in the grip of a general strike, with shootings and explosions.

The *Potemkin*, the most powerful battleship in the Black Sea, was keeping an eye on street rioters when one of the sailors complained about bad food, and was shot by the first lieutenant. The crew immediately mutinied. To cries of "liberty, liberty!" they threw the captain and several other officers overboard, and hoisted the red flag. The remaining eight officers joined the mutiny.

It appears that the crew of two torpedo boats may have joined in. A steamer laden with coal was seized and the fuel transferred to the *Potemkin*. The authorities are on the verge of panic, with no apparent means of controlling the Odessa populace who are in open revolt. Buildings along the waterfront are ablaze.

This latest revolt is by far the most serious yet, coming four days after Czar Nicholas repudiated his earlier promise to give Russia an elected assembly. In the wake of the catastrophic defeat of the Manchurian army by the Japanese at Mukden, there has been growing discontent over the war. Two provincial governors were assassinated last month before the Russian navy was annihilated by the Japanese at Tsushima.

The main squadron of Russia's Black Sea fleet is expected to steam to Odessa to crush the mutiny; but the fact that it happened at all suggests the Czarist regime's authority is now precarious indeed.

Flattery at its most outrageous: "Liberty" kissing Czar Nicholas.

India's viceroy quits in defence quarrel

Delhi, India, 20 August
Lord Curzon, the viceroy of India, has resigned. A believer in the "forward" school of imperialism, his stewardship of India was brilliant, ostentatious and tactless. His pedestal was high, his fall is long.

His very arrogance ensured his fall. Not only did he alienate the army with his determination to protect the Indian peasantry from the brutality of the soldiery, but he alienated the commander-in-chief, Lord Kitchener. He blocked Kitchener's reforms and insisted on Kitchener's subordination to him. Kitchener refused to work under Curzon and offered his resignation. Curzon was powerful, but not popular, and had little chance against the hero of South Africa and the Sudan. In the end it was Curzon who resigned.

Though his foreign policy, which included crude displays of might in the Persian Gulf, displayed all the arrogance of a world power unsure of its own supremacy, his internal reforms will not be forgotten. He changed the taxation laws for the benefit of the peasantry and protected cultivators from eviction for debt.

Curzon: brilliant, but tactless.

1906 (1906-1907)

London, 7 February 1906. The Liberals win a landslide victory in the general election. The Labour Representation Committee, led by James Keir Hardie, also makes substantial gains.

Tahiti, 8 February 1906. A typhoon kills over 10,000 people.

Britain, 10 February 1906. *HMS Dreadnought*, the most powerful warship in the world, is launched.

Rome, 11 February 1906. Pope Pius X condemns the separation of the French church from the state.

London, 12 February 1906. Keir Hardie is elected leader of the new Labour Party in the House of Commons.

Nigeria, 20 February 1906. British troops arrive to quell protests by the Tiv people against Moslem Hausa rule.

USA, 23 February 1906. Johann Koch of Chicago, alias "Bluebeard", who is said to have murdered at least one of his 50 wives, is executed.

Natal, 5 March 1906. British troops kill 60 Zulu in fierce clashes against the poll tax.

Finland, 7 March 1906. Suffrage is extended to all tax-paying men and women over 24.

Britain, 8 March 1906. A government publication out today states that the empire occupies one-fifth of the land-surface of the globe and has a population of 400,000,000.

Russia, 20 March 1906. Army officers are massacred in a mutiny in Sevastopol in the Crimea.

Paris, 22 March 1906. England win the first rugby international against France by 35 to eight.

New York, 28 March 1906. The State Meteorological Office says that the science of forecasting the weather is "within our grasp".

Spain, 31 March 1906. A conference on Morocco closes in Algeciras having upheld French hegemony under the sultan.

Italy, 7 April 1906. Mount Vesuvius erupts, destroying the town of Ottaiano.

Britain, 17 April 1906. The Labour Party calls for female suffrage.

France, 19 April 1906. The nobel prize-winning physicist Pierre Curie dies aged 47.

San Francisco, 18 April 1906. A major earthquake destroys most of the city.

Tibet, 27 April 1906. China reluctantly grants Britain control of Tibet, following the occupation of the capital Lhasa by British troops.

St Petersbury, 24 May 1906. Czar Nicholas II concedes universal suffrage but refuses to grant amnesty for political prisoners as suggested by the Duma.

Norway, 28 May 1906. The playwright Henrik Ibsen dies aged 78. Among his most controversial works are *A Doll's House*, *Ghosts* and *Hedda Gabler*.

Europe, 6 June 1906. Italy re-affirms its alliance with the Austro-Hungarian and German empires.

France, 27 June 1906. The first circuit motor race held at Le Mans is won by the Hungarian, Ferenc Szisz in a Renault.

London, 7 July 1906. Seven balloons take part in Britain's first hot-air balloon race.

France, 12 July 1906. Captain Alfred Dreyfus is rehabilitated having been publicly disgraced 11 years ago on charges of espionage and treason.

Guatemala, 20 July 1906. A treaty ends the war between Guatemala on the one side and El Salvador and Honduras on the other. Guatemala invaded both its neighbours in May but was defeated six days ago.

Russia, 21 July 1906. The Duma is dissolved and martial law is declared.

Cuba, 28 September 1906. The American war secretary William Taft declares himself provisional governor of Cuba following the resignation of President Palma, under threat from rebel forces.

Russia, 2 November 1906. The Jewish revolutionary Leon Trotsky is exiled for life to Siberia.

Belgium, 9 November 1906. Prince Albert is declared successor to Leopold as king of the Congo.

Japan, 15 November 1906. The world's biggest battleship the *Satsuma* is launched.

South Africa, 12 December 1906. The Transvaal is given autonomy with white male suffrage.

New Hebrides, 1906. French and British residents agree to set up a joint administration.

China, 1 January 1907. Four million people are starving owing to heavy rains and crop failure.

German East Africa, 16 January 1907. The great rebel leader Abdallah Mapanda, who has been at the head of maji-maji (*magic water*) uprisings since July 1905 is run to ground by the Germans.

Tehran, 19 January 1907. Mohammed Ali Mirza is crowned Shah of Persia. He is intent on a programme of liberalisation.

Moslems form political league in India

Dacca, India, 31 December 1906
India's middle-class Moslems have scorned the predominantly Hindu Congress Party, and formed a Moslem League. Within a day of its foundation Congress leaders are calling it a British inspiration and accusing it of sectarianism. The League repeats Sir Syed Ahmed Khan's accusation: "The Congress is no more than civil war without the use of guns". However, the Moslem League is British-inspired. Its paymaster, the Aga Khan, told Moslem leader Mohsinul-Mulk "not to move before finding out if the step has the full approval of the government privately".

Whether, as Congress says, it is simply a policy of divide and rule, is less certain. The new century has seen an upsurge in pan-Islamic consciousness, with India's Moslems identifying with Afghans, Turks and Egyptians. A moderate League could act as a safety-valve.

War secretary Taft sends troops into Cuba

Havana, Cuba, 6 October 1906
A thousand US troops have landed at Havana and will proceed to Camp Columbia tomorrow by trolley car. They are the first of 5,500 troops who will be coming in to suppress the liberal and anti-Yankee revolt of Jose Gomez at the request of ousted president Estrada Palma; though officially they will be in Cuba to supervise the disarming of both sides. Effective power in the country is now in the hands of US war secretary William Howard Taft, who declared himself provisional governor last week.

Painter who sought cone and sphere dies

Aix-en-Provence, 22 October 1906
Paul Cezanne has died at the age of 67 after being caught in a rainstorm on a painting expedition. He was just beginning to be recognised as one of the greatest modern French painters after a large exhibition devoted to his work two years ago.

In recent years his favourite subject has been Mont Sainte Victoire near here. Last year he finished his monumental *Grandes Baigneuses* after seven years' work. Cezanne's aim was to render space and volume ever more subtly through colour alone. Painters, he says, should "look for the cone, the sphere and the cylinder in nature".

He exhibited originally with the Impressionists, but he said that he wanted to make Impressionism "something solid and durable like the art of the museums". After the death of his banker father he became rich and lived as a recluse in the family mansion near Aix.

Cezanne's "Grandes Baigneuses": "something solid and durable", as he wanted.

Earthquake turns San Francisco to rubble

The ruins of San Francisco's Sacramento Street, looking towards the sea.

San Francisco, 19 April 1906
More than a thousand people are thought to have been killed in the massive earthquake which reduced downtown San Francisco to rubble yesterday. Shock waves are still hitting the city and an even bigger problem is the raging fires, which are now threatening the fashionable residential area of Nob Hill. Firemen are hampered by the destruction of the water mains in the first tremor and are using dynamite to try to control the fire.

Thousands slept last night in the parks. Thousands more fled, filling all available ferries and trains. Sadly, the lawless minority of this former gold-rush town tried to exploit the chaos. Martial law has been declared and the army has been moved in to help the police. Several looters have already been shot down on the streets.

Drooling dogs reveal our hidden reflexes

Moscow, 1907
A dog will lick its lips and salivate when presented with its bowl of food. It will salivate, too, if a bell is rung just before you hand it the bowl. It will even salivate on hearing the customary bell, even if you do not give it any food at all. These observations by the Russian medical researcher Ivan Pavlov have led to a new theory about what he calls "conditioned reflexes" – that is, conditioned by a stimulus such as the bell.

Pavlov has done many experiments on the salivation of animals at feeding time and produced detailed descriptions of what stimulus produces the strongest and most durable effect. He has also investigated how these reflexes are acquired and how, sometimes, they appear to be lost.

Animals, Pavlov says, need to form conditioned relexes in order to survive in a changing, predictable environment. His experiments are confined to dogs and monkeys, but there is no doubt in Pavlov's mind that humans, too, form these conditioned reflexes.

Ivan Pavlov: a student of behaviour.

Russian parliament urges disobedience

Russia, 31 July 1906
Do not give a *kopek* to the throne or a soldier to the army. That is the advice issued in the name of the imperial *Duma*, Russia's first democratic institution, which was dissolved 10 days ago by the prime minister Peter Stolypin.

It is just over two months since the duma was opened by the czar. Since then unrest has continued, with a vicious *pogrom* aimed at the Jews, and mutinies among the soldiery.

The duma, which had limited power over financial and other matters, was never respected by the government, and is now seen to have been a sop to an angry populace. When it was dissolved, nearly 200 leftist deputies fled to Finland to avoid the Russian police.

Today's manifesto from the duma warns that it may not reassemble for at least seven months, during which time the government can be expected to act arbitrarily. Meanwhile, government concern centres on disaffection in the military, and security after the assassination of General Kozlov.

The opening session of the Russian Duma, dissolved ten days ago.

Landslide victory in British elections

David Lloyd George, one of the members of the new Liberal cabinet.

London, 7 February 1906
After ten years in opposition, the Liberals have scored a stunning election victory in Britain over the Conservatives. They have 375 seats to the Conservatives' 157. The growing strength of the six-year-old Labour Party is reflected in its 54 seats. Liberals and Labour made an electoral pact giving Labour a free run in what were considered winnable Conservative-held seats; in return, Labour would not contest Liberal seats.

The Conservatives went into the election deeply divided over tariff reform, and the vagaries of the electoral system worked against them. They polled over 2,460,000 votes, only about 100,000 behind the Liberals, but secured 218 fewer MPs. Over 500,000 votes went to Labour. But it is the Irish Nationalists who are heavily over-represented: for a mere 35,109 votes they have 83 MPs.

Tehran rocked by revolution threat

Tehran, June 1906
The Persian capital is in ferment. Most merchants and artisans are on strike, with bazaars closed and rioters running amok. A large number of the merchants and other protesters demanding legal reforms have taken sanctuary in Qum.

The prime minister's attempt to expel two influential preachers was the catalyst for this latest revolt. It echoes the actions of a rebel group which took refuge in various sanctuaries last December in protest at the punishment of merchants accused of raising the price of sugar.

That earlier revolt was stalled when Shah Muzaffar-al-Din promised legal reforms. When nothing was done, there was a groundswell of unrest on which revolutionary secret societies could capitalise.

1907 (1907-1908)

Washington, DC, 26 February 1907. President Roosevelt puts the US army in charge of building the Panama Canal.

London, 8 March 1907. Keir Hardie's Women's Enfranchisement bill is defeated.

Finland, 15 March 1907. The first women are elected to parliament.

South West Africa, 31 March 1907. The Germans end the state of emergency as all the Nama (*Hottentots*), except those led by Simon Koper, have been defeated.

Russia, 3 April 1907. Twenty million people are starving in the worst famine on record.

China, 15 April 1907. Japan hands Manchuria back to China under the terms of the treaty of Portsmouth which ended the Russo-Japanese war.

British East Africa, 16 May 1907. Nairobi is chosen as the capital of British East Africa (*Kenya*) because of its central location on the Mombasa-Uganda railway line.

London, 18 May 1907. Mrs Ramsay MacDonald chairs the Women's Labour League's first conference.

London, 10 June 1907. J M Synge's play *The Playboy of the Western World* is performed for the first time.

France, 10 June 1907. The cinematographers Auguste and Louis Lumiere invent a simple form of colour photography which they believe will make moving pictures in colour commonplace.

Russia, 16 June 1907. Russia's second *duma* is dissolved with the prime minister, Peter Stolypin, accusing 55 socialist members of plotting against the czar.

South Africa, 1 July 1907. The Orange River colony gains autonomy as the Orange Free State.

Korea, 19 July 1907. The emperor abdicates and is succeeded by the crown prince.

Casablanca, 4 August 1907. French troops arrive in Casablanca to avenge the murder of nine Europeans by Moorish extremists.

St Petersburg, 20 August 1907. The trial opens of the 18 revolutionaries accused of plotting to assassinate Czar Nicholas II.

Britain, 31 August 1907. An agreement with Russia is signed defining spheres of influence in Persia and policies in Tibet and Afghanistan.

Norway, 4 September 1907. The Norwegian composer Edvard Grieg dies aged 64. His incidental music for Ibsen's *Peer Gynt* is a classic.

The Hague, 7 September 1907. The peace conference, determining the conventions of war, rules that all powers must give notice of war.

India, 4 October 1907. Nationalist Riots rage in Calcutta following the visit of the Independent Labour Party MP Keir Hardie who accused the British government of running India "like the czar runs Russia".

Russia, 14 October 1907. A third duma, or parliament – conservative, royalist and pro-Stolypin – meets.

The Hague, 18 October 1907. A secret proposal for an international court of justice, drawn up at the peace conference, is made public.

Brussels, 28 November 1907. King Leopold transfers the kingdom of the Congo to the state.

London, 29 November 1907. King Edward VII appoints 87-year-old Florence Nightingale to the Order of Merit.

Sweden, 8 December 1907. King Oscar II dies and is replaced by Gustavus V.

Stockholm, 10 December 1907. Rudyard Kipling wins the Nobel prize for literature.

Natal, 12 December 1907. Dinizulu, the king of the Zulus and the rebel leader, surrenders to government troops.

Addis Ababa, 1907. The Emperor Menelik is paralysed by a stroke and Ras Tasamma becomes regent.

South Africa, 1907. White miners strike to preserve a job colour bar, reserving skilled jobs for whites only, after mines begin employing African and Chinese workers as operators of new mechanical drills.

Norway, 1907. Parliamentary suffrage is granted to women in a certain income bracket.

France, 1907. The philosopher Henri Bergson publishes his most significant work to date – *Creative Evolution*.

Transvaal, 30 January 1908. Mohandas Gandhi, the leader of the Indian protest against new laws requiring Asiatics to register, is released from prison.

Lisbon, 1 February 1908. King Carlos and Crown Prince Luiz are assassinated following last month's failed revolution. Don Manuel is to succeed the king.

Lisbon, 3 February 1908. The dictator Joao Franco and his cabinet resign following the king's assassination.

Russia, 8 February 1908. Czar Nicholas II orders troops to the Persian border following Turkish incursions into Persia.

Marxist writer's fame spreads to France

Paris, 1907

Literary circles in Paris are acclaiming a new talent whose works have just been translated from their native Russian. Maxim Gorky (born Alexei Peshkov) wrote his play *The Lower Depths* in 1902, and his novel *Mother* last year. Now both have appeared in France.

Gorky, whose pseudonym comes from the Russian word for "bitter", is deeply involved in his country's revolutionary movement. He has been a Marxist since 1899, and all his works, commencing with the short story *Chelkash* (1895), reflect his sympathies for Russia's exploited and poverty-stricken underclass. Now he is being compared to Tolstoy himself.

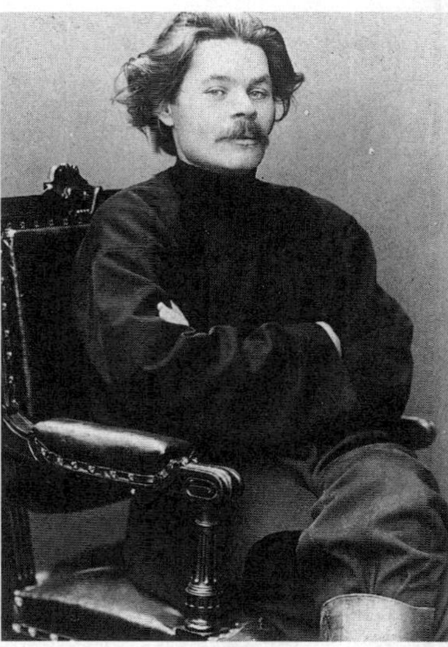

Maxim Gorky: revolutionary writer.

Spanish painter breaks all the rules

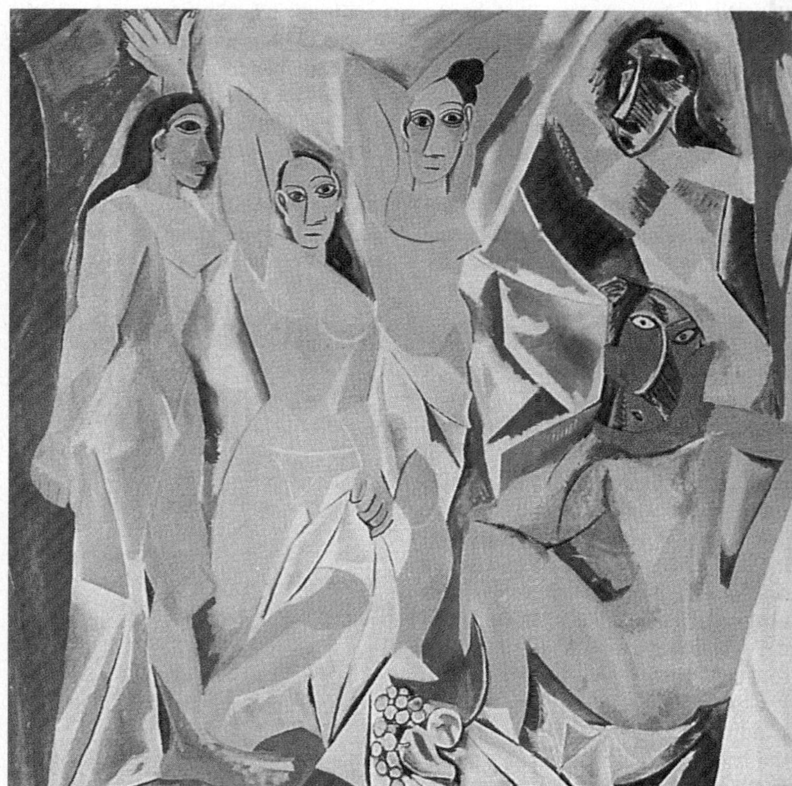

Picasso's "Les Demoiselles d'Avignon": new perspectives, new dimensions.

Paris, 3 July 1907

Pablo Picasso, a Spanish painter of 26 who moved to Paris in 1900 from Barcelona, has astonished his fellow-painters in Montmartre with his latest work, called *Les Demoiselles d'Avignon*.

It depicts three female figures posing like goddesses in an old master "Judgement of Paris" for two mystery spectators in African totem masks. The title refers to a brothel in Barcelona. The geometrical distortion of the forms, the multiple viewpoints and the flatness of the picture-plane made Guillaume Apollinaire declare: "It's a revolution!"

Women in court for staging votes protest

London, 14 February 1907
A record number of 57 suffragettes were sent to Holloway prison today after clashes with the police. Last night mounted officers rode into a deputation from the Women's Social and Political Union, on their way to parliament to demand the vote. A five-hour struggle ended with 15 women reaching the House of Commons. They, too, were arrested. In court, one defendant, Christabel Pankhurst said: "The women who asked for votes were in danger of their lives. We do not come here in any way to excuse our conduct. We feel yesterday was a great day for our movement."

The women had set up their own "parliament" in a London hall and the idea of the march was to present a petition to its all-male counterpart at Westminster. The women set off at dusk and were very soon under attack from mounted police. Some had their clothes ripped and their bodies bruised, but still they fought their way through to the House of Commons where they tried to hold a meeting.

Police expel demonstrating suffragettes from the Houses of Parliament.

Indian congress suspended after clashes

Surat, India, 27 December 1907
The Congress Party of India was rent today by recriminations and violence. In the specially built pavilion in the French Gardens, decorated with scrolls and bunting, the 600 delegates have been fighting furiously with sticks, stones and fists. One British observer, Henry Newinson, said he had "caught glimpses of the Indian National Congress dissolving in chaos." The split is clear-cut between moderates and radicals. The Congress establishment leaders are middle class. They seek a franchise, but a limited franchise; they call for self-government, but set no date. They urge the "Indianisation" of the civil service to ensure their place in it.

The radicals despise such attitudes. Led by Bal Gangadhar Tilak, they want Congress to become a mass movement, fighting the British with civil disobedience to win their freedom.

Transvaal Indians refuse to toe the line

Johannesburg, 22 March 1907
Transvaal's Indian community has chosen an unusual form of protest against a humiliating law which requires them to carry residence permits at all times.

Led by Mohandas Gandhi, a lawyer who has stated that "India's honour is in our keeping", they are practising *satyagraha* or non-violent non-cooperation. This means inviting, rather than causing, suffering in order to redress the wrongs they are facing. Gandhi has been aware of South Africa's deep-rooted racism ever since he was thrown out of a first-class train compartment soon after arrival 13 years ago. Now he aims to "root out the disease and suffer hardships in the process".

With the Permit Offices due to open soon, Gandhi, who has chosen a self-sufficiency lifestyle on a farm near Durban, is preparing for the next phase of the confrontation.

The longest and most gruelling motor race ever held, from Beijing to Paris, ended on 10 August. The winner was Prince Borghese of Italy, who confronted on his 8,000 mile, 62-day journey – deserts, swamps, mountains, a bushfire, and a Belgian policeman who stopped him for speeding.

Atlantic liners battle for speed record

The "Lusitania" arrives in New York after her record-breaking crossing.

Sandy Hook, 11 October 1907
The German-held record for the fastest-ever transatlantic crossing was cut by several hours today as the British luxury liner *Lusitania* steamed into Sandy Hook, New Jersey, after crossing from Queenstown, near Cork, in four days, 19 hours and 52 minutes.

The Cunard-owned *Lusitania*, carrying 1,200 passengers and 650 crew, averaged just over 24 knots, one knot faster than the previous record, held by the German-owned *Deutschland*.

British hopes are high that the record could be lowered further. Recent developments with turbines have produced speeds as high as 34.5 knots.

US clamps down on Japanese immigration

Washington, 24 February 1908
The Japanese government has formally agreed to limit emigration to the US. It reflects a stiffening in the US positon following the gentleman's agreement reached between President Theodore Roosevelt and the Japanese last year, to discourage "emigration of its subjects of the labouring classes". It was the influx of Chinese coolies following the Californian gold rush which finally caused the US to abandon its open-door immigration policy.

Immigration restrictions were introduced in 1882, 1890 and 1902, and as a result the Chinese population is falling from its peak of 107,000. The flood of Japanese immigrants is much more recent and in 1900 there were only 25,000 in the whole country.

1908 (1908-1909)

South West Africa, March 1908. The final battles of the German-Nama war are fought as Simon Koper retreats with his followers into the British territory of Bechuanaland (*Botswana*).

London, 12 April 1908. Herbert Asquith becomes the Liberal prime minister after the resignation of Sir Henry Campbell-Bannerman.

Algeria, 16 April 1908. The French Foreign Legion put Moorish bandits to flight following raids on French outposts on the border.

Washington, DC, 22 May 1908. The Wright brothers patent their "flying machine".

Uganda, 23 May 1908. 4,000 have died in famine in the Usoga region.

Russia, 21 June 1908. The Russian nationalist composer Nikolai Rimsky-Korsakov dies aged 64.

Ottoman Empire, 24 July 1908. The success of the Young Turks' revolution, which began on 3 July, forces Sultan Abdul Hamid II to restore the constitution.

Cuba, 1 August 1908. The US supervises elections.

USA, 12 August 1908. Ford's first Model T is produced in Detroit – "a motor car for the multitude".

Morocco, 23 August 1908. The sultan, Abd-el Aziz, flees after his defeat by Mulai Hafid, who declares himself sultan.

Switzerland, 29 September 1908. The international conference on workers' protection bans night shifts for children under 14.

Bulgaria, 5 October 1908. Prince Ferdinand declares Bulgaria independent of the Ottomans.

Crete, 6 October 1908. Crete declares its independence from the Ottomans and union with Greece.

Balkans, 7 October 1908. Austria annexes Bosnia-Herzegovina. Though formally part of the Ottoman empire, the territory's predominantly Serbo-Croat population favours union with Serbia. Austria's unilateral move shocks other European powers.

Malta, 9 October 1908. A Royal Navy fleet sails for the Aegean as the Balkan crisis worsens.

London, 12 October 1908. Russia persuades Britain to participate in a congress on the Balkan situation.

London, 21 October 1908. The prime minister, Herbert Asquith, announces emergency measures to reduce unemployment.

London, 24 October 1908. The suffragette Emmeline Pankhurst and her daughter Christabel are jailed after a sensational trial in which two cabinet ministers are called as witnesses for the defence.

Washington, DC, 3 November 1908. William Howard Taft, the Republican candidate, is elected 27th president of the USA.

Australia, 12 November 1908. Andrew Fisher becomes the new Labour prime minister.

Balkans, 15 November 1908. Austria sends troops to the Serbian frontier.

Panama, 15 November 1908. The US President Roosevelt visits the city of Panama – the first president to travel abroad during his term of office.

Berlin, 17 November 1908. The kaiser endorses a retraction of his interview with *The Daily Telegraph* in which he expressed anti-British sentiments.

London, 28 November 1908. The Court of Appeal rules that unions cannot put their funds to political use. Many Labour MPs depend on sponsorship by the unions.

China, 2 December 1908. The child Emperor Puyi succeeds to the throne as Xuantong.

Vienna, 9 December 1908. Austria and Turkey resume talks aimed at easing the Balkan crisis.

Stockholm, 10 December 1908. Professor Ernest Rutherford wins a Nobel prize for his work on radioactivity and the atom.

Italy, 28 December 1908. The most violent earthquake ever recorded in Europe has devastated Messina.

Britain, 1908. Edward Elgar's first symphony is performed over 100 times.

Britain, 1908. Kenneth Grahame publishes a delightful children's book – *The Wind in the Willows*.

Britain, 1908. E M Forster publishes *A Room with a View*.

London, 1 January 1909. Astronomers sight what may be a planet beyond Neptune.

London, 1 January 1909. Men and women over 70 draw their first old-age pensions.

India, 5 January 1909. Hindus and Moslems riot in Calcutta.

Balkans, 12 January 1909. The Ottoman empire accepts Austria's offer of 2.5 million Turkish pounds for BosniaHerzegovina.

Cuba, 27 January 1909. The US governor leaves the island as Jose Gomez is sworn in as president of the republic.

Morocco, 9 February 1909. A Franco-German agreement recognises French hegemony.

Balkans, 24 February 1909. Serbia demands that Austria cede Bosnia-Herzegovina to it.

US temperance campaign shuts saloons

New York, 1 February 1909

Trouble is fermenting throughout the United States as war is waged on alcohol by an abstinent army of prohibition campaigners.

The successes of the movement, with women at the helm, include a ban on saloons in 315 townships in New York state, 57 of Ohio's 66 counties and 48 towns in Colorado. In Tennessee it is now an offence to manufacture or sell liquor.

One temperance crusader is Mrs Carrie Nation who, with her 500-strong army, has organised raids on saloons leaving chaos behind. She has vowed not to rest while "there are yet some hell-holes here". The liquor lobby argues that prohibition leads to fraud, secret drinking and drug abuse.

Carrie Nation waging intemperate war against alcohol in Kansas City.

Artists celebrate age of speed and steel

Paris, 1909

A new outrageous way of viewing the infant century has shocked Italy. "The splendour of the world has been enriched with a new form of beauty, the beauty of speed," says the *Futurist Manifesto of Poetry*, which was published in *Le Figaro* by the Italian-born poet Filippo Marinetti.

The new technological century has presented new challenges, he writes. Painters and poets must reject both the stifling oppression of tradition and the pessimism of the *fin de siecle*. The alternative is to be buried beneath the weight of history. "Set fire to the libraries! Flood the museums!" he urged in his manifesto. "An automobile, its bonnet writhing with metal tubes, is more beautiful than classical sculpture!"

Even in conventional society futurism is the vogue. Futurist histories foretelling the unlikely shape of things to come are published yearly – though none envisage a world quite like that of the dynamic Marinetti.

Elgar symphony gets a warm welcome

Elgar, the leading figure in the English musical renaissance.

Britain, 31 December 1908

The long-awaited first symphony by Sir Edward Elgar arrived this month to wild acclaim. Elgar is now at the height of his prestige, which began with the *Enigma Variations* in 1899. The oratorio *The Dream of Gerontius* followed, then the overture *Cockaigne*, an evocation of London, and four superb *Pomp and Circumstance* marches. King Edward VII suggested putting words to the great tune in No 1: "Land of Hope and Glory" is now almost a second national anthem. The oratorios *The Apostles* and *The Kingdom* and the lovely *Introduction and Allegro* are the other main works of the Worcester man who was knighted in 1904.

Black boxer wins a world fight title

Jack Johnson (right), the new heavyweight world champion.

Sydney, 4 December 1908

The American fighter Jack Johnson made boxing history today when he knocked out the reigning champion, Tommy Burns, to become the first Black to hold the heavyweight championship of the world.

The Texas-born Johnson's victory over Burns, a Canadian, returns the title to the USA after just two years. Americans have now held the title all but four times in its 26-year history. Johnson, aged 30, is the fifth American to become world champion.

For the giant nicknamed Li'l Artha, the championship is the key that should finally give him control of his career. He will no longer have to tolerate being discriminated against by the US white boxing establishment which has persistently denied him purses and opportunities since he turned professional 11 years ago. Now the worried US boxing establishment is pinning its hopes on bringing the former world champion James J Jeffries out of retirement to challenge Johnson as its "Great White Hope".

Empress dies and new era begins

China, 15 November 1908

The Empress Dowager Cixi, who once claimed to have more power than Queen Victoria, died today of an attack of dysentery after eating a huge helping of her favourite dish of clotted cream and crab-apples. She was 73 years old. Commonly known in her later years as the "Old Buddha", this remarkable woman began her long reign as the power behind the Qing throne as the beautiful young concubine of the Xianfeng emperor.

She was made empress when she bore him a son in 1856, and from that moment on has controlled the destinies of China. Ruthless and reactionary, she had kept the Guangxu emperor, who was both her nephew and adopted son, prisoner ever since his flirtation with the reform movement ten years ago. He died the day before her and she just had time to designate a new emperor, the two-year-old Puyi, whose weak and reactionary father, Prince Chun, will be regent.

Two sovereigns lying in state: the empress dowager and the emperor.

Kaiser's loose talk infuriates British

Berlin, 31 October 1908

Not for the first time, the kaiser's free-wheeling approach to foreign affairs has caused consternation in the chancelleries of Europe; on this occasion, though, he has excelled himself. He chose to give an interview to a British newspaper in order to "have a go" at Britain.

He told *The Daily Telegraph* that during the Boer War, Germany, Russia and France held secret talks on finding a way to "humiliate England to the dust". He also claimed that most Germans of the middle and lower classes were "anti-British." German newspapers describe the interview as a "catastrophe". The chancellor, Prince von Bulow – to whom, under German rules, the interview had to be submitted – is being strongly criticised in the press for allowing it to be published without having read it first.

Leopold loses his heart of darkness

Congo, 15 November 1908

The Congo Free State has been nationalised by the Belgian government. King Leopold of the Belgians, who personally owns the colony, has received 50 million Belgian *francs* in compensation.

The take-over follows a ten-year campaign by missionaries, traders and Mr Roger Casement, the British consul in Boma, the Free State capital, against the atrocities committed in King Leopold's name. Hostages are shot or mutilated when rubber quotas are not reached, villages are razed to make way for rubber plantations, forced labour has become the norm. According to Casement, up to 100,000 natives are slaughtered yearly.

Leopold remains unaffected by the outcry. The atrocities are "sad, but one cannot accomplish a great work without doing some evil".

Parisian artists applaud amateur painter

Paris, May 1908

A banquet was given by Pablo Picasso in his studio at the Bateau Lavoir, Montmartre, in honour of Henri Rousseau, the primitive painter – known as *Le Douanier* because he was in the customs service until he retired to concentrate on painting. Self-taught, he used to exhibit at the Salon des Independants to general merriment. Now the meticulous and dreamlike clarity of his jungles, populated with tigers and monkeys, have won the respect of the most *avant-garde* painter of the day. "We are the two greatest artists of the age, you in the Egyptian manner, I in the modern," said Picasso to Rousseau, who is extremely innocent.

Henri Rousseau's "Tropical storm with Tiger", making a virtue of naiveie.

Nationalists turn to terror tactics

London, 1909

A new form of revolt has grown up in India: terrorism. Its roots are in the *thuggees* who worshipped Kali, the goddess of destruction, and in the European anarchist movements. In their boldest move so far they have shot Sir Curzon Wyllie, here in the very heart of the empire. In spite of a spate of killings all over India, Lord Minto, the viceroy, is not going to be diverted from his policy of liberalisation, even though the London Cabinet has vetoed his appointments of Indians to the Viceroy's Council.

1909 (1909-1910)

Balkans, 8 March 1909. The Balkan crisis worsens as Austria rejects Russian mediation in its dispute with Serbia.

Ireland, 24 March 1909. The Irish playwright J M Synge dies aged 37. His greatest work is the comedy *The Playboy of the Western World.*

Balkans, 28 March 1909. The European powers agree a formula for Serbia to renounce claims to Bosnia-Herzegovina.

North Pole, 6 April 1909. Commander Robert E Peary of the United States Navy is the first person to reach the North Pole.

Britain, 10 April 1909. The poet and literary critic Algernon Charles Swinburne dies aged 72.

Persia, 10 April 1909. British forces land at Tabriz as fear of famine causes widespread unrest.

Bulgaria, 19 April 1909. The Ottoman empire recognises Bulgarian independence.

Ottoman Empire, 23 April 1909. Moslem fanatics backed by the *sultan* have massacred at least 30,000 Armenians in the last week.

Bulgaria, 27 April 1909. Germany, Austria and Italy recognise the independence of Bulgaria.

Ottoman Empire, 2 May 1909. The new sultan, Mehmet V, promises liberty, equality and justice.

Paris, 7 June 1909. France joins the arms race with a government announcement that it will spend £120 million on new ships.

South Africa, 12 June 1909. Natal votes for union with South Africa.

Congo (Zaire), 12 June 1909. Belgian and British troops clash over the border of Congo and Northern Rhodesia (*Zambia*).

Persia, 26 June 1909. Mohammed Ali Shah annuls a new law which promised elections, and defers the promised constitution.

Persia, 13 July 1909. Nationalists opposed to the *shah* take Tehran.

Persia, 16 July 1909. The 12-year-old crown prince, Sultan Ahmed Mirza, is proclaimed shah.

Paris, 21 July 1909. The cabinet, led by Georges Clemenceau, resigns following a dramatic debate on the state of the navy.

Spain, 1 August 1909. An anti-government revolt in Catalonia leaves up to 1,000 dead.

Britain, 2 August 1909. Czar Nicholas II visits his uncle King Edward VII.

London, 7 September 1909. Lord Northcliffe, the owner of *The Times*, claims that Germany is preparing for war with Britain.

Geneva, 13 September 1909. The Congress of Egyptian Youth demands British withdrawal from Egypt.

Spain, 26 September 1909. The government announces that the Moors in Morocco have been defeated.

London, 28 September 1909. It is confirmed in the House of Commons that imprisoned suffragettes are being force-fed.

Spain, 13 October 1909. The anarchist Francisco Ferrer is executed by a firing-squad following the *Semana Tragica* – a week of rioting in Barcelona.

Brussels, 28 October 1909. The government announces major liberal reforms in the Congo.

Hawaii, 14 November 1909. The US president, William Taft, announces that a naval base will be built at Pearl Harbor to protect the US from a Japanese attack.

New York City, 28 November 1909. Sergei Rachmaninov gives the world premiere of his third piano concerto.

Russia, 29 November 1909. Maxim Gorky is expelled from the Revolutionary Party for his "*bourgeois*" high living on Capri.

London, 30 November 1909. The Lords reject Lloyd George's People's Budget. A general election will be held in the new year.

London, 3 December 1909. King Edward VII dissolves parliament. Taxes on beer, spirits, tobacco and cars are lifted because the budget has not been passed.

London, 7 December 1909. The South Africa Act, bringing together the Cape of Good Hope, Natal, Transvaal and Orange Free State, is given the royal assent, as promised by the British at the end of the Boer War.

London, 10 December 1909. The Liberal Herbert Asquith puts Irish Home Rule and abolition of the Lords' veto at the centre of the liberal's election campaign.

Belgium, 17 December 1909. King Leopold II dies aged 74.

Nicaragua, 21 December 1909. Dr Jose Madriz is elected to succeed President Jose Zelaya who was ousted by Americans on December 16.

Britain, 1909. H G Wells' *Ann Veronica*, the story of an independent woman, is banned by many libraries.

Africa, 15 January 1910. France reorganises French Congo as French Equatorial Africa.

Persia, 31 January 1910. Russia and Britain decide to intervene as political unrest sweeps the country.

"People's Budget" squeezes rich Britons

London, 29 April 1909

Britain was today presented with the most radical budget in its history and asked to pay for more dreadnoughts and the new old-age pensions. By introducing what he called the "People's Budget", David Lloyd George, the chancellor of the exchequer, stirred up a hornets' nest of opposition. But he described his policy as "Liberalism, not lunacy".

Among proposals for raising an extra £16 million in revenue is a new "supertax" of sixpence in the pound to be levied on the 10,000 people with incomes over £5,000 a year. The standard rate of tax on earned income stays at ninepence in the pound up to £2,000 and one shilling above that level. There will be increases in the "luxury" taxes on alcohol, tobacco and petrol.

The budget was bitterly attacked by the Tory opposition and it will be opposed in both Houses. The Opposition is arguing that the taxes will hit the propertied classes on whom, it claims, the prosperity of the country depends.

A conservative poster attacking Lloyd George's radical "People's budget".

Japanese Bismarck is assassinated

Harbin, 26 October 1909

Prince Ito Hirobumi, renowned as the "Japanese Bismarck", was assassinated here today, shot down by a Korean nationalist. He had given up his post as Japanese minister-resident in Korea earlier this month and had travelled to Harbin to reassure the Russians about Japan's intentions towards Korea.

Prince Ito, who was 72, visited England in secret in 1863 and returned the next year to mediate between Britain and Japan after the bombardment of Shimonoseki.

From then on he played a leading role in building Japan into a world power. He helped to frame the constitution and became Japan's first prime minister. His final task was to bring Korea under Japanese control, a task for which he paid with his life.

Peary's Pole rival cooked the books

Copenhagen, 21 December 1909

A committee appointed by the university here today pronounced that it was Commander Robert Peary of the United States Navy who got to the North Pole first. He sailed to Greenland in the *Roosevelt* and got to the pole last April after a 90-mile (144-kilometre) trek lasting 36 days. It was his sixth attempt. The committee dismissed the claim of a Brooklyn doctor, Frederick Cook, who went with Peary on an earlier attempt. Cook said that he reached the pole a year earlier accompanied by two Eskimos. They testified that he had turned back when 20 miles (32 kilometres) from his target. The committee also ruled that Cook's documents lacked the vital observations proving that he had reached the precise geographical position of the pole.

Frenchman flies across English Channel

Louis Bleriot, with admirers, and the plane in which he flew the Channel.

Dover, 25 July 1909

Louis Bleriot, the 37-year-old French aviator, made history today with a 43-minute flight from Sangatte, near Calais, to Dover Castle, and won the £1,000 prize offered by the *Daily Mail* to the first flyer to cross the English Channel, a feat previously the monopoly of the birds.

A French destroyer stood by in mid-Channel, but Bleriot's flight, which has been put off for five days as he waited for ideal weather conditions, went without a hitch. His 24-horsepower monoplane, its three-cylinder engine driving a single propeller, made a perfect flight at an average speed of 40 miles per hour (64 kilometres per hour).

His fellow-aviators warned Bleriot that cross-Channel winds could bring him down, but he remained confident that he could do it in his monoplane, convinced that a biplane could not have made so successful a flight.

Radio call captures suspected murderer

London, 31 July 1910

Nine years after Marconi demonstrated the use of wireless across the Atlantic, the system has been used to detain two much-wanted fugitives from justice. An American, Dr Harvey Crippen, has been arrested on board the liner *Montrose* off Canada for the murder of his wife, Bella, whose dismembered body was found in London. Two days after the discovery, Crippen and his mistress, Ethel le Neve, sailed for Quebec.

Miss le Neve was disguised as Crippen's "son" but the ship's master, Henry Kendall, got suspicious when he saw them holding hands. Kendall had read newspaper stories of the search for the pair and sent radio signals about his passengers to London. Chief Inspector Walter Dew of Scotland Yard then crossed the Atlantic on board the speedier *Laurentic* and boarded the *Montrose* disguised as the St Lawrence pilot. When he was arrested, Crippen said: "Thank God it's all over. The suspense has been too great. I could not stand it any longer."

The arrest of Dr Harvey Crippen and Ethel le Neve on the "Montrose".

Young Turks topple tyrannical sultan

The sultan's palace is stormed by troops of the "Young Turks".

Istanbul, 27 April 1909

The tyranny of Abdul Hamid is over. The parliament he set up under pressure last summer has voted to depose him and instal his brother Mahmud Reshad.

An uprising by Islamic zealots supported by the Sultan has been suppressed, and a handful of troops in the palace garrison loyal to the Sultan overcome. The troops of the Young Turks, committed to the enactment of democratic reforms, are in control.

The seeds of the Sultan's downfall were sown in Paris in 1907 when the exiled reformers decided to build support in the army. They moved their headquarters to Salonica, and, led by Majors Niazi Bey and Enver Bey, recruited among dissident minorities in Macedonia and Armenia, and among the discontented troops in Arabia.

By last summer they had persuaded most of the Turkish army to pledge loyalty to the constitution that Abdul Hamid had introduced in 1876, suspended in 1878 and continued to flout ever since.

Ballet takes a step forward in Paris

Paris, 18 May 1909

The *Ballets Russes*, presented by Sergei Diaghilev at the Theatre du Chatelet, made a sensational debut last night, amazing an audience used to the conventions of Paris ballet by the free expressiveness of their dancing.

The excitement of the choreography by Michel Fokine in the Polovtsian dances from *Prince Igor* with the exotic decor of Alexandre Benois and rich costumes by Leon Bakst, above all the dazzling steps of Tamara Karsavina and Vaslav Nijinsky, the leading dancers, have never been combined before into a single spectacle like this.

Nijinsky, who danced the poet in *Les Sylphides* to the music of Chopin, was described by a critic as "the power of youth, drunk with rhythm, terrifying in his energy". "I do not follow fashion," said Diaghilev, "I create it."

Collector's item: the programme for Sergei Diaghilev's dazzling ballet.

Mark Twain, US storyteller supreme, dies

Redding, Conn., 21 April 1910

"Mark Twain" was the cry leadsmen used sounding the depth of the river when it was two fathoms deep when Samuel Clemens was a boy on the Mississippi. At the age of 18 he contributed humorous pieces to the *Hannibal Journal*, which he and his brother set up in Missouri. At 22 he learned from a steamboat captain the trade of a Mississippi pilot. It was his reminiscences of his boyhood in the person of Tom Sawyer or Huckleberry Finn, that made him a national character, in drooping moustache and bowler hat, beloved for his pithy aphorisms. One was that "reports of my death have been greatly exaggerated" – not this time, alas.

1910 (1910-1911)

Africa, 7 February 1910. Belgium, Britain and Germany fix the frontiers of Congo, Uganda and German East Africa respectively.

London, 14 February 1910. Tories and Liberals tie in the general election but the Liberals remain in power, supported by Labour MPs.

Tibet, 23 February 1910. The Dalai Lama flees to India as Chinese troops invade Lhasa. He returned from exile in Beijing only two months ago having fled in 1904 when British troops invaded.

Berlin, 6 March 1910. Socialists are shot and sabred during a suffrage demonstration.

China, 10 March 1910. Slavery is abolished.

Italy, 27 March 1910. Mount Etna erupts.

Australia, 13 April 1910. The Liberal prime minister Alfred Drakin loses to Andrew Fisher's Labour party in federal elections.

London, 14 April 1910. The House of Commons votes for bill to abolish the Lords' power to veto bills.

Ottoman Empire, 25 April 1910. Turkish troops battle with Albanian rebels.

London, 7 May 1910. King George V succeeds the throne following Edward VII's death from pneumonia yesterday.

London, 20 May 1910. Halley's comet today passes within 13 million miles of the earth.

London, 1 June 1910. Captain Robert Falcon Scott sets out on a journey to conquer the South Pole.

Russia, 3 June 1910. The Duma is to abolish Finnish autonomy.

Germany, 22 June 1910. Nobel prize winner, Dr Paul Ehrlich, puts forward a new drug for syphilis, known as salvarsan.

South Africa, 1 July 1910. The Union of South Africa, formed on 31 May, becomes a dominion of the British empire.

Far East, 4 July 1910. Russia acknowledges Japan's occupation of Korea in return for a free hand in Manchuria.

Ottoman Empire, 27 July 1910. Turkey threatens Greece with war if it accepts Cretan representatives in the Greek parliament.

London, 13 August 1910. The nursing pioneer Florence Nightingale dies aged 90.

New Jersey, 27 August 1910. Thomas Edison demonstrates talking motion pictures.

Balkans, 28 August 1910. Montenegro declares its full independence from the Ottoman empire under King Nicholas.

France, 2 September 1910. The painter Henri "le Douanier" Rousseau dies aged 76.

South Africa, 15 September 1910. Afrikaner nationalists win the first parliamentary elections.

South Africa, 19 September 1910. Although the prime minister Louis Botha loses his seat in the election, his National Party decide he should remain as leader.

Britain, 12 October 1910. Ralph Vaughan Williams' first symphony, "*A Sea Symphony*" is performed for the first time.

Portugal, 17 October 1910. The provisional government banishes the royal family and abolishes the nobility.

Britain, 20 October 1910. The liner *Olympic* is launched, the largest vessel afloat.

Switzerland, 30 October 1910. Henri Dunant, founder of the Red Cross, dies aged 82.

Portugal, 9 November 1910. The republic is recognised by Britain, France, Germany, Russia, Spain, Norway and Belgium.

Britain, 11 November 1910. The prime minister, Herbert Asquith, asks King George V to create enough liberal peers to allow the passage of the Lords reform bill.

London, 18 November 1910. Asquith the prime minister, announces that the king will dissolve parliament and this year's second general election will be held before Christmas.

London, 23 November 1910. Dr Crippen is hanged for the murder of his wife.

Germany, November 1910. A Russo-German convention is signed at Potsda.

Morocco, 3 December 1910. France takes the port of Agadir.

London, 20 December 1910. Liberals and Tories tie in the general election and the Liberal Herbert Asquith remains in power with the backing of 42 Labour MPs and 84 Irish nationalists.

Britain, 1910. Bertrand Russell and A N Whitehead publish *Principia Mathematica*.

Nicaragua, 2 January 1911. The American President Taft acknowledges the government of Jose Estrada and orders the withdrawal of troops.

Germany, 26 January 1911. Richard Strauss's new opera *Der Rosenkavalier* opens to great acclaim in Dresden.

Britain, 6 February 1911. The Labour Party elect Ramsay MacDonald as its chairman.

Spectacular Firebird sets Paris alight

The design for the second scene of Stravinsky's ballet "The Firebird".

Paris, 25 June 1910

Diaghilev's Russian Ballet has again astonished Paris with a spectacular new ballet to an old Russian fairy tale, *The Firebird*. Richly designed in oriental splendour by the painter, Natalia Goncharova, the Firebird wore a head-dress and costume of peacock feathers. Tamara Karsavina glided over the stage on point throughout. But the real sensation was the music, specially commissioned from a young Russian composer of 28, Igor Stravinsky.

A student of Rimsky-Korsakov, at whose country house the score was composed, he out-glitters even his master's music.

Eccentric Tolstoy dies in a railway station

Astopovo, Ryazan, 20 Nov 1910

Peasants are flocking to the little railway station at Astopovo, where the author Leo Tolstoy died today after a secret flight from his family estate at Yasnaya Polyana accompanied by his daughter Tatiana. At the age of 82 he was seeking to live as a hermit, free of land he inherited as a count but which made a mockery of his later beliefs.

After his conversion in 1879, related in *A Confession*, he rejected the Orthodox Church, which excommunicated him for his attacks in his last novel, *Resurrection*. He lived as a peasant working in the fields, but his wife, Sofya, refused to turn ascetic with him. He died refusing to see her.

Tolstoy, and his gipsy sister-in-law, Sasha, at his home, Yasnaya Polyana.

Fear of revolution returns to Mexico

Mexico, 18 November 1910
After thirty years of comparatively stable government under president Porfirio Diaz, Mexico is once again facing the convulsions of a revolution. Francesco Madero Jr, who calls himself a liberal and a reformer, today proclaimed an uprising against the authorities.

Earlier this year Madero challenged Diaz in the election. His reform platform faced a campaign filled with corruption and dirty tricks. Arrested at one stage for simply gathering a crowd, his defeat was ensured by systematic fraud at the polls.

Diaz himself, a former general, was seen as Mexico's saviour when he seized power in 1876. He did modernise his country, but his economic policies proved unpopular. He sided openly with the rich, neglecting the major problems of poverty and land reform.

After his defeat Madero retreated to San Antonio, Texas, where, on 7 October, he declared himself the provisional president. Although today's revolution seems somewhat muted – there has been but a single skirmish – Madero has gained important backers, notably Pancho Villa and Emiliano Zapata.

Art and revolution, insurgent Mexicans call for land and liberty.

Suffragette hunger strikers force-fed

Liverpool, January 1910
Suffragettes on hunger strike in prison are being tortured by force feeding. Lady Constance Lytton, who is in Walton jail, under an assumed name, told visitors she was allowed only four days without food before doctors began this violent treatment on her.

Everyday she refuses to eat, a steel gag is pushed into her mouth and her jaws are fastened wide apart. A four-foot (1.2 metres) tube is pushed down her throat and liquidised food poured through it into her stomach. Her body promptly rejects the food making the whole cruel process pointless.

The Asquith Government is under pressure now to find a humane way of dealing with Mrs Pankhurst's militants. It wants to keep them alive, in or out of prison, without condoning their actions or giving way to their demands for female suffrage.

Suffragettes being force fed in prison.

Korea bows to new Japanese masters

Tokyo, 29 August 1910
Japan has achieved its ambition of annexing Korea. By a treaty made public today the Japanese have acquired sovereignty over Korea and its citizens are to be subject to Japanese law. The law is to be administered by the army and there is no doubt that it will make every effort to stamp out Korean nationalism.

It was an expression of this nationalism, the murder of Prince Ito, which led directly to the annexation. The Japanese installed Terauchi Masatake as minister-resident in Seoul and backed him with troops.

Terauchi rapidly assumed control of every aspect of Korean public life and the Korean king was at his mercy. Within a month Terauchi was able to agree to "Korea's request for annexation". The treaty was signed by Terauchi and the Korean king a week ago.

Revolutionaries oust Portuguese monarch

King Manuel's last Sunday as a monarch, before being toppled by a coup.

Lisbon, 4 October 1910
A republican-led coup has ended the short reign of Manuel II, who escaped from his bombarded palace today.

Coming to the throne less than three years ago, after his father and elder brother were assassinated by anarchists, Manuel sought political unity in Portugal by bringing all the main parties into government, but intense divisions between monarchists and republicans thwarted any prospect of success.

Although the coup had been anticipated, few of the troops brought in to defend the 19-year-old king proved reliable.

Italian army seizes Tripoli from the Turks

Tripoli, Libya, 20 October 1911
An Italian expeditionary force of 9,000 infantry landed here this morning. Four thousand more landed in Libya's second city, Benghazi, after a prolonged naval bombardment through the night.

The Turkish garrisons put up fierce resistence, though outnumbered and outgunned; and in Tripoli the army managed to escape into the desert, from where they are harassing the Italians. Since Italy's humiliating defeat by the Ethiopians at Adowa in 1896, it has coveted this Turkish colony, and in 1900 gained French recognition that it lay within its sphere of influence.

Three weeks ago Italy declared war on Turkey. Today's landings will raise Italian pride, and reestablish Italy as a colonial power after the disaster at Adowa.

1911 (1911-1912)

Norway, 17 March 1911. Anna Rogstadt takes her seat as the country's first woman MP.

Morocco, 30 March 1911. The sultan asks for French help to put down the uprising that began last October.

Mexico, 15 April 1911. American troops begin fighting rebels led by Francisco Madero.

Mexico, 20 April 1911. Madero refuses to agree a ceasefire until President Diaz resigns.

Paris, 23 April 1911. The cabinet agrees to send reinforcements to put down the Moroccan uprising.

Portugal, 30 April 1911. Women get the vote.

London, 4 May 1911. Lloyd George reveals the Liberal government's insurance bill designed to deal with sickness and unemployment.

Austria, 18 May 1911. The great composer Gustav Mahler dies at the age of 50. He will be best remembered for the songsymphony *Das Lied von der Erde*.

Britain, 30 May 1911. The British writer and Sir Arthur Sullivan's librettist Sir William Schwenk Gilbert dies aged 75.

Mexico, 7 June 1911. A huge earthquake rocks Mexico City.

Britain, 14 June 1911. The seamen's union in Liverpool calls for a national strike.

Morocco, 16 June 1911. The French army occupies Fez.

Morocco, 1 July 1911. Kaiser Wilhelm II dispatches a German gunboat to the Moroccan port of Agadir, to the alarm of the French.

Balkans, 5 July 1911. 10,000 Montenegran troops have been mobilised on the Albanian border.

Lisbon, 5 July 1911. A revolt against the republic is put down after street fighting in the capital.

North Africa, 3 August 1911. Aeroplanes are put to military use when Italians reconnoitre Turkish lines near Tripoli.

London, 10 August 1911. The House of Lords gives up its right of veto, accepting the Liberal government's parliament bill. The bill follows a general election and a threat by King George V to create sufficient peers to pass it.

London, 18 August 1911. The Official Secrets Bill gets royal assent.

Paris, 22 August 1911. Leonardo da Vinci's masterpiece the *Mona Lisa* is stolen from the Louvre.

Portugal, 24 August 1911. Manoel Jose de Arriaga is elected first president of the republic.

China, 4 September 1911. Flooding along the Yangzi river kills 100,000 people.

Paris, 7 September 1911. The poet Guillaume Apollinaire is arrested, and later released, for the theft of the *Mona Lisa*.

Russia, 19 September 1911. Czar Nicholas II appoints Vladimir Kokovstev as premier in succession to Stolypin.

Berlin, 23 September 1911. France and Germany settle the Moroccan dispute.

Mexico, 2 October 1911. Francisco Madero is elected president.

Portugal, 3 October 1911. Royalists are beaten by republican troops in battle at Oporto.

Britain, 23 October 1911. Winston Churchill is appointed First Lord of the Admiralty.

Mexico City, 24 October 1911. Rebel supporters of Emiliano Zapato carry out raids around the capital.

North Africa, 1 November 1911. Italians carry out the first aerial bombing on Tanguira oasis in Tripolitania.

China, 2 November 1911. Hankou is burnt by imperial troops.

Egypt, 2 November 1911. Martial law is proclaimed following widespread Moslem unrest.

North Africa, 5 November 1911. Italy announces the annexation of Tripolitania, Libya and Cyrenaica.

China, 10 November 1911. Imperial troops massacre republicans at Nanjing.

Britain, 13 November 1911. Andrew Bonar Law becomes leader of the Tory party, succeeding Arthur James Balfour.

Russia, 6 December 1911. Mongolia is declared a Russian protectorate.

China, 6 December 1911. The regent Prince Chun resigns.

India, 12 December 1911. George V is crowned emperor of India and founds New Delhi to replace Calcutta as the Indian capital.

China, 29 December 1911. Dr Sun Yat-sen, leader of the Chinese revolution, becomes provisional president of the Chinese republic.

London, December 1911. The National Insurance Bill, providing for unemployment and sickness insurance, is passed.

Paris, 1911. Vaslav Nijinsky dances the lead role of Petrushka in Stravinsky's new ballet.

China, 1 January 1912. The republic of China is officially proclaimed.

Insurgents expel Mexico's hated dictator

Pancho Villa and his guerrilla officers, during the advance on Mexico City.

Mexico, 25 May 1911

Porfirio Diaz, the Mexican president since 1876, resigned today, victim of a popular revolution that has been brewing since last October, when the liberal reformer Francisco Madero declared him an "illegal" president, and called on the people to overthrow his rule.

Since then Madero and his allies, the guerrilla bands led by Emiliano Zapata and Pancho Villa, have advanced steadily towards power. Madero, temporarily exiled to Texas, first demanded an uprising on 20 November, but few Mexicans responded. The situation changed when on 14 February this year Madero returned to Mexico to take the head of the guerrilla forces. Softened by years of power, Diaz's Federal troops could put up no real resistance to the uprising.

Aged generals, an ill-disciplined soldiery and an overall lack of strategy all combined to help the rebels. On 10 May the federal commander at Ciudad Juarez, where Madero had launched his first attacks, surrendered. From thereon the revolution gained momentum and the veteran president's support rapidly collapsed.

Diaz accepted a plan whereby he would resign and an interim president, who would immediately hold a general election, would be appointed. As guerrilla troops marched into Mexico City, Diaz was already en route for Paris.

Russian minister is murdered at opera

Kiev, 18 September 1911

Russia's premier, Peter Stolypin, died today after having been shot down at close range a week ago at the opera. Stolypin, who was 49, had made many enemies through his hard-line policies. The assassination was watched by Czar Nicholas II and his two daughters who were sitting in a box.

The assassin, Mordkha Bogrov is a socialist lawyer, as well as a police informer, and he entered the opera house without difficulty. He is also a Jew and there is considerable unease that the murder could create conditions for a retaliatory pogrom.

US senators to be directly elected

Washington, 12 June 1911

Proposals which will take America nearer the historic ideal of government by the people and for the people were agreed here today. They provide for the Senate, the upper house of the Congress, to be elected by direct popular vote.

At present the senators, two from each state, are chosen by a vote of each state's legislature. This means the choice is dominated by the local party machines which are in power at the time of the election every four years. If, as expected, the proposals pass into law, senators will be elected for six-year terms.

Five-year-old emperor losing power

Beijing, 30 October 1911
Revolution is sweeping across China and in a desperate attempt to stem the tide the reactionary but weak ruling Manchu clique headed by the Regent, Prince Chun, has today established a constitutional government and a cabinet of commoners. Acting in the name of his son, the five-year-old Emperor Puyi, the prince, who is incapable of handling the explosive political situation, has summoned the man he hates most, General Yuan Shikai, to be prime minister.

It was Yuan who betrayed Chun's reforming brother, the Guangxu emperor, and in revenge Chun had him removed from office in the most insulting manner, claiming that he had a bad leg which made him hobble and so made it unseemly for him to be seen at court.

Yuan retired to his estates but retained the loyalty of the troops of his well-trained Northern army and they will not move against the rebels without him. But he is returning Chun's insult, claiming that his leg is too bad for him to obey the Prince's summons.

He can be seen pottering about wearing a cotton smock and straw hat in the mild autumn weather. He fishes for carp, but his real quarry is power on his own terms and he seems likely to get it.

The rebellion which started prematurely when a store of explosives blew up in Hankou on 9 October, forcing the rebels into action, caught everyone by surprise. Dr Sun Yat-sen, the revolutionary leader, was in Denver on a fund-raising tour and learned of it from the American newspapers. The explosion enabled the government to arrest some of the rebel leaders, but the uprising took on a momentum of its own, with mutinous troops forcing unwilling officers to lead them.

Fanned by popular discontent, the movement is spreading rapidly through the western and southern provinces. Unless Yuan and his men march soon, there is little doubt that the long reign of the Manchus will be ended.

Dr Sun Yat-sen and his wife, with pro-Republican officers of the Canton Army.

Scientist sees huge power within the nucleus of an atom

Manchester, 1911
Ernest Rutherford, the outstanding physicist has shown that the atom is like a miniature solar system. At its centre is a nucleus around which revolve other particles – its "planets". Within these atomic nuclei are unimaginably powerful forces.

The nucleus occupies less than one thousand million millionth of the atomic volume. Alpha particles cannot be deflected by powerful electric forces, yet they can be turned round by a thin gold foil. "It was," says Rutherford "as if you had fired a 15-inch shell at paper and it had bounced back."

US Democrat wins, thanks to split vote

Washington DC, 5 November 1912
Democrat candidate Woodrow Wilson, the former president of Princeton College and the man called "the schoolmaster in politics", has won the presidency with only 6.2 million votes. The win is a result of a split vote amongst his opponents, with Republican outgoing President Taft receiving 3.5 million votes, the former Republican president and now Progressive Party leader, Theodore Roosevelt, receiving four million votes, and the socialist Eugene Debs receiving almost a million votes.

Woodrow Wilson on the campaign trail, keeping to the rails.

Norwegian beats Briton to South Pole

South Pole, 14 December 1911
Norway has won the race to the South Pole. In a message from Antarctica, explorer Roald Amundsen confirmed that his team had beaten their British challengers, led by Captain Robert Scott, in a competition that dates back to the beginning of the century.

"Everything went like a dance," said a jubilant Amundsen, although the 2,000-mile (3,200 kilometres) trek at a height of 10,000 feet (3,084 metres) above sea level, was full of hardships. Spurning the motorised transports used by the British, the Norwegians owe much of their success to the resilience of the dogs who pulled their sledges.

As for Scott, who has not been heard from since he set out for the Pole in November, Amundsen too knows nothing. However, he agrees that it is "extremely likely" that the British team will reach the Pole.

Captain Roald Amundsen, who beat the British team to the South Pole.

Riots ravage strike bound Britain

Liverpool, 8 August 1911
Violence flared in the streets of this seaport city today as the rest of the country was being brought to a virtual standstill by a nationwide strike. Two men were shot dead when troops opened fire on rioters; and police with military escorts are using armoured vehicles to patrol the city. Warships are anchored in the Mersey where a queue of merchant ships are waiting to unload.

Liverpool is badly affected; but more than 50,000 armed troops have arrived in London where the strike – by stevedores, railwaymen and other transport workers – is threatening a nationwide famine.

Labour leader Keir Hardie told strikers: "The masters show you no mercy. They starve you, they sweat you, they oppress you. Pay them back in their own coin."

1912 (1912-1913)

USA, 6 January 1912. New Mexico becomes the 47th state.

France, 13 January 1912. Raymond Poincare forms a coalition government.

South Pole, 17 January 1912. The British explorer Robert Scott reaches the south pole to discover that his Norwegian rival, Roald Amundsen, has beaten him to it.

Britain, 10 February 1912. Lord (Joseph) Lister, the pioneer of antiseptics, dies.

USA, 14 February 1912. Arizona becomes the 48th state.

China, 15 February 1912. Yuan Shikai takes over from Sun Yat-sen as provisional president of the republic of China.

USA, 28 February 1912. Albert Berry makes the world's first parachute jump from an aeroplane.

London, 7 March 1912. Henri Semiet makes the first Paris-London non-stop flight.

Morocco, 30 March 1912. By the treaty of Fez, Morocco becomes a French protectorate.

Britain, 13 April 1912. The Royal Flying Corps is set up.

Paris, 1 May 1912. *L'Apres-midi d'un Faune*, a ballet created by the Russian dancer Vaslav Nijinsky, receives its premiere.

Rhodes, 4 May 1912. The Italians occupy the Ottoman island.

Russia, 5 May 1912. The first issue of the *Bolshevik* newspaper *Pravda* appears.

Sweden, 14 May 1912. The playwright August Strindberg dies.

Balkans, 29 May 1912. Greece signs an anti-Ottoman alliance with Bulgaria.

Paris, 8 June 1912. The Ballets Russes give the first complete performance of Ravel's ballet *Daphnis et Chloe*.

Los Angeles, 8 June 1912. Carl Laemmie founds Universal Studios.

Balkans, 2 July 1912. Serbia joins the Greek-Bulgarian alliance against the Ottoman empire.

Britain, 22 July 1912. The admiralty recalls British warships from the Mediterranean to the North Sea to counter the growing German naval threat.

Europe, 1 August 1912. An air-mail service begins between London and Paris.

Albania, 3 August 1912. The Ottomans grant Albania limited autonomy.

Far East, 7 August 1912. Russia and Japan reach agreement on their spheres of influence in Mongolia and Manchuria.

Morocco, 11 August 1912. Sultan Mulai Hafid abdicates.

France, 14 August 1912. The composer Jules Massenet dies.

Britain, 1 September 1912. The composer Samuel Coleridge-Taylor dies.

USA, 23 September 1912. Mack Sennett releases the first *Keystone Cops* film.

Balkans, 8 October 1912. Montenegro declares war on the Ottoman empire.

Balkans, 14 October 1912. The Ottomans invade Serbia.

Switzerland, 18 October 1912. The Ottoman empire and Italy sign a treaty at Ouchy whereby the Ottomans cede Tripoli and Cyrenaica to Italy.

Turkey, 19 October 1912. The allied Balkan armies invade Turkey.

Balkans, 23 October 1912. The Greeks rout the Ottomans at Sarandaporos.

Germany, 25 October 1912. Richard Strauss' opera *Ariadne auf Naxos* receives its premiere.

Balkans, 1 November 1912. The Greeks occupy Samothrace.

Balkans, 8 November 1912. The Greeks capture Salonika.

Balkans, 18 November 1912. The Serbs take Monastir.

Morocco, 27 November 1912. France and Spain sign a treaty outlining their respective spheres of influence in Morocco.

Albania, 28 November 1912. Albania declares independence.

Balkans, 4 December 1912. The Ottomans conclude an armistice with Bulgaria and Serbia. Greece refrains from signing.

Europe, 5 December 1912. Germany, Austria and Italy renew their triple alliance for six years.

South Africa, 20 December 1912. Louis Botha forms a new cabinet.

Switzerland, 1912. Carl Gustav Jung publishes his *Theory of Psychoanalysis*.

Britain, 1912. George and Weedon Grossmith publish *The Diary of a Nobody*.

France, 17 January 1913. Raymond Poincare is elected president.

Turkey, 23 January 1913. The extreme nationalist Young Turks, led by Enver Bey, stage a *coup d'etat*, overthrowing the Ottoman *grand vizier*, Kiamil Pasha.

Britain, 31 January 1913. The House of Lords rejects a bill for Irish Home Rule.

Ottomans reel under Balkan offensive

Balkans, 31 October 1912

The Ottoman empire's centuries-old domination of the Balkans is coming to a violent and bloody end as the sultan's troops retreat in disorder, pursued by triumphant Bulgarian and Serbian forces. There are reports in the Bulgarian capital, Sofia, that the Ottoman minister of war, Nazim Pasha, has been shot and hundreds of officers are to be punished for their incompetence.

The Ottoman *debacle* comes only two weeks after the outbreak of hostilities. Serbia and Bulgaria have been spoiling for a fight for some time, and saw their chance when the sultan became embroiled in a fight with an Italian force in Libya. They sent a stiff note to Istanbul demanding immediate autonomy for Macedonia, which shares frontiers with Greece, Serbia and Bulgaria, and, counting on a less than satisfactory reply from the Ottomans, ordered a general mobilisation.

The sultan also mobilised and told his men that "not an inch of the sacred soil soaked with the blood of your ancestors" was to be given up to the enemy. The enemy, however, which consists of Bulgaria, Serbia, Greece and Montenegro – all once under Ottoman domination – considers the soil to belong to it. If it were simply a question of subject peoples fighting for their freedom, the rest of Europe would stand by and applaud. But the crumbling Ottoman empire offers rich pickings to tempt the great powers. More than once Russian czars have intrigued to lay their hands on Ottoman provinces, a process viewed with apprehension in the Austro-Hungarian capital of Vienna. Now the Italians, arriving late at the feast, are seeking to fashion an empire for themselves out of the Ottomans' North African provinces. They lost out to the French in Tunis, but have struck first in Libya.

The Ottoman army in retreat, followed by Bulgarian troops.

Ulster loyalists rally to fight Home Rule

Belfast, 28 September 1912

While the Westminster parliament again discusses government plans to grant home rule to Ireland, the Protestant minority in the north of that country has put on a menacing show of armed force to back a "covenant" signed by 471,414 people. Seven days of marches and drum beats ended with a parade by riflemen who were addressed by their leader, Sir Edward Carson, the barrister who led the prosecution of the playwright Oscar Wilde for immoral practices in 1895. The Liberal government has other weighty opponents to Home Rule. F E Smith, the Conservative spokesman on Ireland, told the rally to use "permissible resistance" against the "technical law" on this issue. Many senior soldiers, including the influential Anglo-Irish General Sir Henry Wilson, agree.

Edward Carson: a Unionist who is playing the "Orange card".

Chinese emperor forced to resign

Beijing, 12 February 1912
The Manchu dynasty fell today after 267 years when the weeping Empress Dowager Longyu, the widow of the Guangxu emperor, read out an edict of abdication on behalf of the boy-emperor, Puyi.

The edict designates the strongman General Yuan Shikai as the new ruler of China and the republican leader, Dr Sun Yat-sen, has agreed to step down as president of the republic in favour of Yuan in order to avoid civil war.

It is a decision which Dr Sun may soon regret, for the general is cast in a dictatorial mould.

Puyi, his father and young brother.

"Unsinkable" liner sinks: 1,500 missing

The last moments of the "Titanic" in the Atlantic: an artist's impression.

Newfoundland, 15 April 1912
A frantic sea-search is under way in icy Atlantic waters for survivors of the supposedly "unsinkable" luxury liner *Titanic* which sank last night after hitting an iceberg. Of the 2,340 passengers and crew, more than 1,500 are believed to have perished – which makes this the greatest-ever sea disaster.

The *Titanic*, the pride of the White Star Line, was on her maiden voyage, and her captain was said to be aiming to break all records for an Atlantic crossing as he ignored iceberg warnings and ploughed at speed towards New York. Her designers claimed that she could never sink because she was built with 16 water-tight compartments; this is why she was equipped with a minimum of lifeboats. She sank within hours – and the first lifeboat to get away was almost empty and occupied by directors of the line and their friends.

Initial reports suggest that first-class passengers were given priority and that many of those who went down with the *Titanic* were women and children immigrants on cheap "steerage" passages. There was heroism, too, from wealthy men, like John Jacob Astor who stayed behind after ensuring that his bride was safe in a lifeboat; and from the ship's band, which played hymns as the ship sank under it.

South Africa gets a national congress

South Africa, 12 January 1912
Representatives from dozens of provincial congresses and of South Africa's kings and tribal chiefs are meeting at Bloemfontein to unite in a South African native national congress. They are calling for better education, racial equality and national independence. The meeting was called by Pixley Seme, a New York- and Oxford-educated barrister, who pronounced: "The brighter day is rising upon Africa. Already I seem to see her chains dissolve, her desert plains red with harvest, her Abyssinia and her Zululand the seats of science and religion, reflecting the glory of the rising sun from the spires of her churches and universities."

Significantly, the day's meeting opened with prayers by a minister of the African Methodist Episcopal Church, which is strongly influenced by Negro Protestant churches in the USA. The new president, John Langalibalele Dube, was educated there and is a disciple of the ex-slave Booker T Washington. The vice-president, Walter Rubusana, the only black member of the Cape legislature, has a degree from McKinley university in the USA. These men are modernisers, not traditionalists – a novel threat to white power.

Continents drifting, says latest theory

Germany, 1912
The world's continents are constantly on the move, says the German geologist Aldred Wegener in his new theory of "Continental Drift". Once there was just one supercontinent on this planet; this broke up and the pieces slid around over millions of years until they took up their present positions. The rate is very slow: no quicker than human fingernails grow. This theory explains why the eastern coast of South America neatly fits that of western Africa. The Himalayas were formed by the Indian land-mass or "plate" driving up into the bottom end of Asia. Wegener has observed tiny continental movements we could all see.

World naval arms race speeds up

London, 22 July 1912
Britain is being asked to spend a record £45 million to build warships, including four dreadnoughts, eight cruisers, 20 destroyers and several submarines. The proposal comes from the first lord of the admiralty, Winston Churchill.

Meanwhile, British battleships are being withdrawn from the Mediterranean to patrol the North Sea. These moves follow the breakdown of talks with Germany to limit big shipbuilding programmes by both countries. The Germans have offered a mutual guarantee of neutrality to reduce the risk of war by accident, started by allies of either party. Britain, tied to France and Russia, says "No".

Decathlon star stripped of Olympic gold

Jim Thorpe: minor pro, major star.

Geneva, 27 January 1913
Jim Thorpe, whose stunning decathlon and pentathlon victories at last year's Stockholm Olympic Games won him the accolade of "the greatest athlete in the world", was today stripped of both his titles by the Olympic Committee.

Under the Olympic rules, no professional may compete in the strictly amateur games. When a newspaper revealed that Thorpe had received $25 a week to play minor league baseball in North Carolina, he was branded a professional and declared ineligible for olympic competition. Thorpe's name has been removed from the record books, even though the runners-up in both events have refused to claim his medals, in respect for a man more professional than the amateurs.

1913 (1913-1914)

New York City, 2 February 1913. Grand Central Station, the world's largest railway station, opens.

Antarctic, 10 February 1913. The British explorer Robert Scott and two of his companions, who were attempting to return from the south pole, are found dead.

Mexico, 23 February 1913. Francisco Madero, who was deposed as president last week by Victoriano Huerta, is shot dead.

USA, 25 February 1913. Federal income tax is introduced.

Balkans, 6 March 1913. In a resumption of hostilities, the Greeks take Janina, capturing 32,000 Turks.

Australia, 12 March 1913. Canberra becomes the federal capital.

Greece, 20 March 1913. Following the assassination of King George, his eldest son Constantine, the duke of Sparta, becomes king.

Balkans, 26 March 1913. The allies take Adrianople after a 155-day siege.

Britain, 3 April 1913. The suffragette leader Emmeline Pankhurst is jailed for three years for inciting arson.

China, 8 April 1913. China's first parliament opens in Beijing.

USA, 14 April 1913. Dr Harry Plotz discovers a typhus vaccine.

Berlin, 18 April 1913. Professor Behring makes a new serum for diphtheria.

Balkans, 22 April 1913. Scutari falls to the Montenegrins after a six-month siege.

The Hague, 26 April 1913. The International Women's Peace Conference opens.

Paris, 29 May 1913. *The Rite of Spring*, a ballet by Igor Stravinsky, receives its premiere.

London, 30 May 1913. The Ottomans sign a peace treaty with the Balkan League, ending their war.

Germany, 6 June 1913. A bill is passed providing for a large increase in the German army.

Turkey, 11 June 1913. Mahmud Shevket Pasha, the new *grand vizier*, is assassinated.

Britain, 13 June 1913. David Lloyd George, the chancellor of the exchequer, and other ministers are exonerated of illegally dealing in shares of the Marconi company.

Balkans, 24 June 1913. Greece and Serbia break their alliance with Bulgaria over a border dispute.

Norway, 29 June 1913. Women get equal electoral rights to men.

Balkans, 30 June 1913. Bulgaria attacks Serbia and Greece.

Balkans, 1 July 1913. Greece and Serbia declare war on Bulgaria.

China, 8 July 1913. China agrees to grant Mongolian independence.

London, 8 July 1913. The suffragette Sylvia Pankhurst is sentenced to three months in jail.

Balkans, 11 July 1913. Rumania declares war on Bulgaria and invades.

London, 15 July 1913. The House of Lords again rejects an Irish Home Rule bill.

London, 16 July 1913. Robert Bridges becomes poet laureate.

Balkans, 10 August 1913. The treaty of Bucharest ends the second Balkan war.

China, 1 September 1913. A "second revolution", staged by the nationalist *Guomindang* and other forces in reaction to Yuan Shikai's anti-democratic forces, ends.

Balkans, 21 September 1913. Turkey and Bulgaria settle their frontier dispute; Turkey keeps Adrianople.

Tunis, 23 September 1913. Frenchman Roland Garros completes the first flight over the Mediterranean.

Panama, 10 October 1913. The Panama Canal is opened.

Mexico, 11 October 1913. President Huerta declares himself dictator.

Mexico, 15 November 1913. The rebel Pancho Villa takes Ciudad Juarez.

France, 1913. Marcel Proust publishes the first volume of a novel entitled *A la Recherche du Temps Perdu.*

France, 1913. Henri Alain Fournier publishes his novel *Le Grand Meaulnes.*

Britain, 1913. Parliament passes the "Cat and Mouse" Act, allowing the temporary release from prison of suffragette hunger-strikers whose health is in danger.

German East Africa, 2 February 1914. A 900-mile railway opens from Lake Tanganyika to Dar-es-Salaam.

Paris, 16 March 1914. Madame Caillaux, the wife of the French finance minister, shoots dead Gaston Calmette, the editor of *Le Figaro*, which has attacked her husband's plans to tax the rich.

London, 13 April 1914. *Pygmalion*, a play by George Bernard Shaw, receives its premiere.

Mexico, 21 April 1914. US troops opposed to President Huerta land and seize Vera Cruz.

Ford unveils moving car assembly line

Ford's Model T assembly line at Detriot: a completely new production process.

Detroit, 7 October 1913

Henry Ford, the one-time inventor whose automobiles are revolutionising the American way of life, has launched a new production process that is intended to alter the whole face of car manufacture and go a long way towards meeting the ever-expanding demand for new cars.

Ford's Model T, "the motor car for the multitude", appeared in 1908, the product of an "assembly line" using mass-produced precision parts. Now the car they call the "Tin Lizzie" will be put together on a 250-foot-long moving assembly line. Each worker will be assigned a specific task and will perform it over and over again as car after car rolls slowly by on the line.

It is estimated that the new system will mean that a new chassis can be assembled in just two man-hours, a huge increase over the former schedule of 14 man-hours. It will take only three man-hours to produce a complete new car; Ford aims to produce 250,000 next year.

Indian poet and teacher wins Nobel prize

Stockholm, 1 December 1913

The Nobel prize for literature has been awarded to the Indian poet Rabindranath Tagore – the first time that the prize has gone to an Asian. Educated India has gone wild with excitement at this recognition of Indian culture in the west. The poet said: "I shall never have any peace again."

Tagore comes from a cultured and talented Bengali family. He won fame at 20 with his first volume of Bengali poems. He also translates his poetry into English. Last year he published *Gitanjali* (Song Offerings) on the death of his wife and three children. He has founded a centre of Indian culture at Shantiniketan near Bolpur.

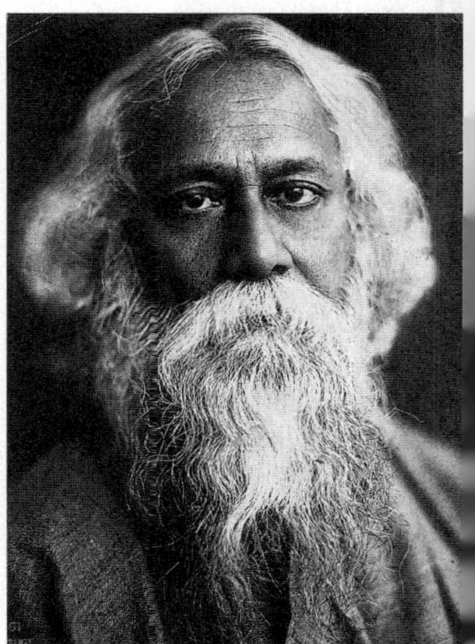

Indian poet. Rabindranath Tagore.

Treaty ends Balkan war

Bucharest, 10 August 1913
After their successful war against the Ottoman empire, the four Balkan allies, Bulgaria, Serbia, Greece and Montenegro, quarrelled among themselves over the spoils: Macedonia. Their brief war – Bulgaria against the others – came to an end today with a treaty signed in the Rumanian capital, Bucharest.

The Ottomans had surrendered Macedonia on the understanding that it would become a new and independent state, Albania. That did not suit Serbia and Montenegro. Serbia and Greece then plotted to carve up Macedonia between them and Bulgaria promptly attacked. Under the Bucharest treaty, almost all the territory claimed by Bulgaria in Macedonia and Thrace goes to Serbia and Greece. Serbia and Montenegro are doubled in size and Rumania, which stopped the war by invading Bulgaria, helps itself to a slice of Bulgarian territory.

In this murderous game of Balkan musical chairs, Serbia seems never to miss out. Diplomatic observers fear that the Serbs will ask for even more and that there will be yet another crisis in Europe.

Macedonian rebels fighting the Ottomans, in control of the route to Salonika.

Mystery man assassinates king of Greece

Salonika, 18 March 1913
King George of Greece was assassinated here this afternoon. As the 68-year-old monarch took his regular afternoon walk through the town where he has lived for the past five months, the assassin, Alexander Schinas, shot him through the heart. The king collapsed and died in the arms of an *aide*.

Schinas admits to no motive, and has revealed nothing about himself other than his name. His victim, who was within a few days of completing 50 years as king, will be succeeded by his son, crown prince Constantine.

King George: assassin's victim.

US marines snatch Mexican seaport

Mexico, 21 April 1914
Three thousand United States marines seized the port of Vera Cruz today. The seaborne attack has so far cost the marines four dead and twenty wounded; the Mexican garrison is believed to have lost at least 200 men.

The Americans have given no specific reason for the landing, but it is presumed that President Wilson wishes to prevent supplies of arms from reaching General Huerta from Germany. Wilson opposes the Huerta regime, and backs instead the revolutionary forces that are fighting to unseat him.

"Rite of Spring" outrages audience

Paris, 30 May 1913
Bewilderment, shock, outrage: these were the reactions of the Paris audience at last night's premiere of the ballet *The Rite of Spring* by the Russian composer Igor Stravinsky. Stravinsky's supporters, led by Debussy, appealed for silence as the jeering and cat-calling greeted the pounding, discordant evocation of primaeval Russia. The uproar actually started *before* the curtain rose on the production by Diaghilev's Ballets Russes. Stravinsky has already provided Diaghilev with two works, *The Firebird* (1910) and *Petrushka* (1911).

Natal riots follow Gandhi jailing

South Africa, 25 November 1913
Two Indians were killed and 20 injured when Natal police fired into a crowd demonstrating against the jailing of Mohandas Gandhi, the British-educated lawyer who organised an ambulance corps in the Boer War and who is leading the non-violent passive resistance campaign against racial inequality.

Gandhi refused to pay a fine for defying a law prohibiting Indians from Natal entering the Transvaal. He led 2,500 Indians into the Transvaal, where they were violently arrested. Riots have been daily occurrences since then, but these are the first deaths.

Suffragette movement mourns its first martyr, Emily Davison

Britain, June 14 1913
A suffragette heroine was given a martyr's funeral today. Tens of thousands lined the streets of London to watch as militant women took Emily Davison to her last resting place in her beloved Northumberland. Flanked by a bodyguard of suffragettes dressed in white with black sashes, the coffin was drawn on an open carriage by four black horses and followed by vehicles bearing hundreds of wreaths from all over the world. The funeral procession was over two miles long.

Miss Davison, who had been imprisoned and force-fed on many occasions, died when she ran in front of the king's horse in the Derby horse race ten days ago.

Emily Davison, killed under King Edward's horse, Anmer, at the Derby.

1914 ⇒

London, 15 June. Britain and Germany sign an agreement settling their differences over the Baghdad railway.

Balkans, 28 June. Archduke Franz Ferdinand is assassinated at Sarajevo.

Vienna, 23 July. Austria issues a drastic ultimatum to Serbia.

Vienna, 28 July. Austria declares war on Serbia.

Mexico, July. President Huerta is expelled from office and civil war breaks out between Venustiano Carranza, the rebel leader, and his lieutenant Pancho Villa.

Berlin, 1 August. Kaiser William II declares war on his cousin Czar Nicholas II.

Luxembourg, 2 August. Germany invades Luxembourg.

Berlin, 3 August. Germany declares war on France.

Belgium, 4 August. The Germans invade Belgium.

Europe, 4 August. Britain and Belgium declare war on Germany.

Turkey, 5 August. The Ottomans close the Dardanelles.

Vienna, 6 August. Austria declares war on Russia.

Serbia, 6 August. Serbia declares war on Germany.

Europe, 12 August. Britain and France declare war on Austria.

Belgium, 16 August. Liege falls to the Germans.

France, 17 August. A British expeditionary force lands.

Belgium, 20 August. German troops take Brussels.

Rome, 20 August. Pope Pius X dies.

Japan, 23 August. Having issued an ultimatum to Germany, Japan declares war and attacks the German fortified port of Qingdao on Chinese territory.

Belgium, 23 August. The British are forced to retreat after bitter fighting with the Germans around Mons.

France, 26 August. The prime minister, Rene Viviani, forms a coalition government of national unity.

North Sea, 28 August. The British sink three German cruisers and two destroyers off Heligoland Bight, opening the war at sea.

Japan. Nine million people are reported to be starving.

Archduke's murder unsettles Europe

Sarajevo, Bosnia, 28 June

Archduke Franz Ferdinand, the heir to the Austro-Hungarian empire, and his morganatic wife, the duchess of Hohenburg, were assassinated here today by a Serbian nationalist. It was the 14th anniversary of their marriage.

The killer, Gavril Princip, darted out of the crowd as the car carrying the royal couple slowed to change direction. His first bullet struck the archduke in the neck, the second hit the duchess who had flung herself in front of her husband. She died almost immediately, the archduke ten minutes later. The murders were evidently part of a concerted plot. Earlier, the couple were on the way to the town hall of this capital of Bosnia when a bomb was thrown into their car. The archduke picked it up and threw it into the road where it exploded, wounding those in a following car.

The implications of this outrage are dangerous in the extreme. The killer, seized by the police, has told them that he wanted to take revenge for the oppression of the Serbian people. He is believed to have been helped by a secret society of Serbian officers known as the "Black Hand". There can be no doubt that the Austrians will make drastic demands on what the Austrian foreign minister, count von Berchtold, calls the "Serbian wasp's nest". But the Serbs, backed by Russia, are in no mood to be bullied by the Austrians.

An artist's impression of the assassination of Franz Ferdinand at Sarajevo.

Blacks protest over white land grab

London, 26 June

A black South African delegation, led by John Dube, the president of the South African Native National Congress, saw the colonial secretary, Lewis Harcourt, today. The delegation came to protest at the Native Land Act, passed last year. The act gives all but seven per cent of South Africa's land to Whites. Even in the poor and scattered "scheduled areas" Blacks may not actually own the land. Blacks living on white farms have to give 90 days labour to the farmer every year or be expelled to the reserve. In the Orange Free State, Africans are being defined "squatters" and driven to the reserves by force. The Blacks, with no economic base, are forced to work as migrant labourers.

The visit shows the confidence that the rapidly growing South African Native National Congress has acquired after campaigns against racial discrimination and landlessness and has been warmly welcomed by the British Labour Party. The colonial office has been less welcoming. Mr Harcourt, a Liberal, has told the delegates that they should be grateful for the act, since it stops the Whites taking *all* the land and the Blacks being reduced to the plight of their fellows in the Congo.

Ulster on the brink of war crisis

Belfast, 25 February

Civil war in Ireland seems imminent as an English-led Ulster Volunteer Force of 100,000 armed men puts on public shows of strength applauded by members of the establishment. In Tyrone, 12 infantry companies performed a tactical exercise under the eyes of their commander, Sir George Richardson. Such displays have not yet achieved their political aim – to frighten the British government into excluding Ulster from the Irish Home Rule Bill – but Sir George urges his men to attack more.

Europe stumbles into war as diplomats holiday

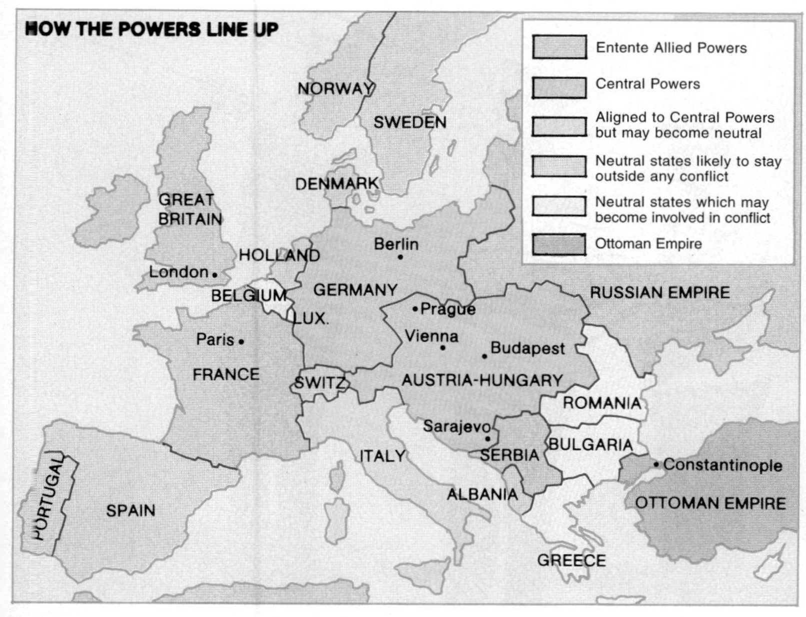

Volunteers from neutral USA rush to sign up in Paris for the duration.

Balkan crisis destroys precarious balance

London, 4 August
Britain declared war on Germany today and all the carefully constructed checks and balances of European diplomacy came tumbling down into catastrophe.

Few people foresaw the impending disaster. The German kaiser had talked of giving Austria full support, but had then left for his customary yachting holiday in Norway. General von Moltke, the German army commander, was taking the cure at a foreign *spa*. The French president was on a state visit to Russia. The Serbian prime minister was in the country, preparing an election campaign.

Austria's ultimatum to Serbia brought Russia in as Serbia's ally. Germany came in as Austria's ally, and France as Russia's ally. Britain might well have stayed out of it had not Germany invaded Belgium in an attempt to outflank France.

Now – as the British foreign secretary, Sir Edward Grey, put it – the lamps have gone out all over Europe, while trains are moving millions of men to the two fronts. In the east, Russia has struck at East Prussia and Galicia; German and Austrian forces have answered with a thrust into Poland. In the west, von Moltke is drawing the French army into a "revolving door" that will take the Germans to Paris. The British Army is preparing to go to France. The shots at Sarajevo are echoing round the world.

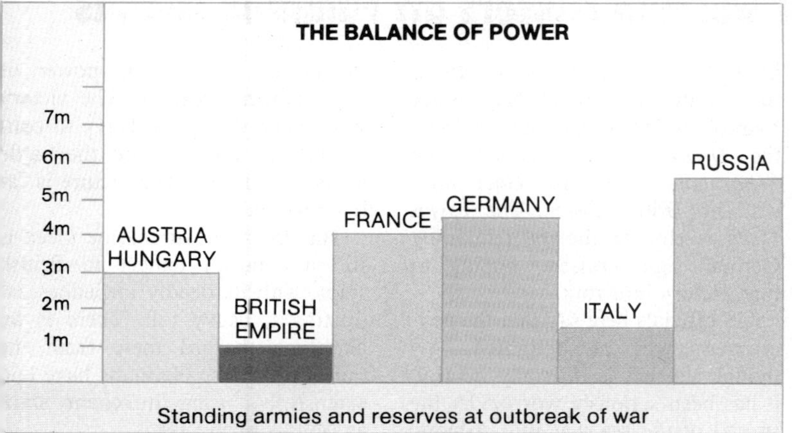

Crowds cheer as volunteers rush to arms

London, 11 August
The tremendous enthusiasm which brought cheering crowds surging through London to sing the national anthem outside Buckingham Palace when war was declared has not abated.

Young men, anxious not to miss the war which is confidently expected to be over by Christmas, form long queues outside the recruiting offices. Farm boys, City workers, peers and dustmen are leaving their jobs to "serve King and Country".

There is a feeling of embarking on a great adventure amongst these young men. Many are schoolboys who give false ages. Friends join in groups, anxious to fight together. They think nothing of the hardships and dangers that they will face, and see war not only as a patriotic duty but also as a holiday from a humdrum workaday existence.

This same enthusiasm is being seen throughout the empire. Australia, Canada and New Zealand have offered to send contingents to the help of the Mother Country, and the men of the colonies are making their way in from remote outposts to join up.

Meanwhile, the professionals, the men of the Regular and Territorial Armies, marching in field uniform through the streets to join the British Expeditionary Force, are being given emotional farewells by their families and by total strangers who shower them with cigarettes and sweets.

Many of these men have seen the face of battle before, however, and their attitude is more workmanlike than emotional. Sir Edward Grey, the foreign secretary, is another professional who views the war realistically. "The lamps are going out all over Europe," he said to a friend. "We shall not see them lit again in our lifetime."

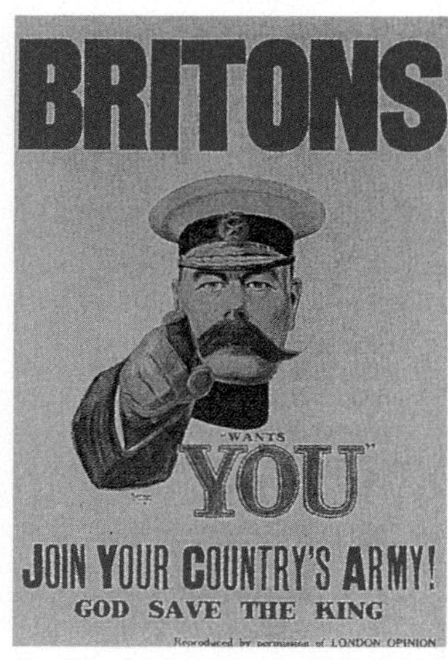

Feeding the front line: a 1915 British Army recruiting poster.

1914

Russia, 31 August. St Petersburg is renamed Petrograd.

Ottoman Empire, 2 September. A general mobilisation of Ottoman forces is ordered.

Rome, 3 September. Giacomo della Chiesa is elected pope as Benedict XV.

London, 4 September. Britain, Russia and France agree not to make separate peaces.

Western Front, 5 September. The Germans take Rheims.

Western Front, 14 September. The Allies drive back the Germans on the Marne, relieving the threat to Paris.

Eastern Front, 14 September. The Russians are forced to retreat from East Prussia after the battle of the Masurian Lakes.

Pacific, 26 September. The Australians take the port of Friedrich Wilhelmshafen in German New Guinea.

Hungary, 27 September. The Russians invade Hungary.

Western Front, 9 October. The Germans take Antwerp.

Western Front, 14 October. French and British troops occupy Ypres. The Belgian government flees to France.

Western Front, 15 October. Having captured Ghent and Bruges, the Germans take Ostend.

Egypt, 22 October. Britain orders all foreign vessels out of the Suez Canal.

Black Sea, 28 October. Turkey attacks Russian ports.

Eastern Front, 1 November. Paul von Hindenburg becomes German commander-in-chief.

Ottoman Empire, 4 November. The Russians invade Armenia.

Europe, 5 November. Britain and France declare war on the Ottomans, following Russia.

Cyprus, 5 November. Britain annexes Cyprus.

China, 7 November. The German fortified port city of Qingdao falls to the Japanese.

Indian Ocean, 10 November. Australians sink the German cruiser *Emden* off Sumatra.

Istanbul, 14 November. The sultan declares a *jihad* (holy war) on the Allies.

Poland, 6 December. The Germans capture Lodz.

Egypt, 16 December. Britain declares Egypt a protectorate.

Germany routs Russia at Tannenberg

Petrograd, 31 August
The myth of the Russian steamroller that was to flatten the German forces on the eastern front has been cruelly shattered in four days of fighting at Tannenberg, on the East Prussian border.

Some 300,000 men took part in the battle, with white-bloused Russian infantrymen being mown down as they charged German machine-gun posts. The German artillery was vastly superior to the Russians', and German supplies, brought up on the strategic railway system, simply overwhelmed the czarist forces. In the Russian capital, now renamed "Petrograd" to be rid of the Germanic St Petersburg, the defeat has been acknowledged with unusual candour.

The Russians sent two armies into East Prussia under the command of Generals Alexander Samsonov and Pavel Rennenkampf. Initially their advance went unchecked, but then two new generals took over the German defences – Erich von Ludendorff and Paul von Hindenburg, Prussian regular soldiers, born in Poznan. They adopted a plan submitted by a Colonel Max Hoffmann, based on his knowledge of a bitter feud between Rennenkampf and Samsonov.

The Germans concentrated their attacks on Samsonov's army at Tannenberg, taking 100,000 Russian prisoners. Rennenkampf made no move to come to the aid of his fellow general. Samsonov, after his crushing defeat, was filled with shame and shot himself. Soon it will be Rennenkampf's turn to face the Germans.

The czar with his army commander, Grand Duke Nicholas, in August 1914.

Russian prisoners of war, taken into Germany after the battle of Tannenberg.

British navy sinks four German cruisers off Falkland Islands

South Atlantic, 11 December
Britain once again rules the waves everywhere except the North Sea and the Baltic. The war at sea, which has been raging for three months now, took a decisive turn last night, with the German and British fleets concluding a running battle that has taken them a long way from home.

The decisive encounter was fought off the Falkland Islands, when under cover of nightfall, the two fleets came within six miles (9.6 kilometres) of each other. In a fierce battle the Royal Navy sank four of the finest German cruisers, the *Dresden*, the *Nurnberg*, the *Scharnhorst* and the *Gneisenau*, with no British losses. The Royal Navy is chasing the the remaining German light cruisers, hoping to turn victory into rout.

US officials here say that the government will be delighted. Although the US is officially neutral, it has been seriously worried by the spread of the sea war into Atlantic waters and by the fire-power of some modern cruisers. The victory will enable the Royal Navy to concentrate its resources on the battle in the North Sea. The picture is far less rosy there.

The German submarine fleet is still a constant danger to British ships, with its deadly torpedoes extracting a heavy toll. There is an additional hazard there from the mines which the Germans have laid extensively, using merchant ships as well as navy vessels.

Germans overcome Belgian defences

Belgian refugees, with what few possessions they can take, pouring westwards on the unarmed road of flight.

THE WESTERN FRONT
German "Schlieffen Plan" to encircle Paris
Actual route of German armies
Allied counter-offensives
HOLLAND
Ostend
Antwerp
Ghent
Calais
Brussels
BELGIUM
Liège
Lille
Mons
ARTOIS
R. Sambre
ARDENNES
R. Moselle
R. Somme
Amiens
Dieppe
LUXEM.
Compiègne
Soissons
Verdun
Rheims
LORRAINE
GERMANY
R. Oise
R. Seine
Paris
R. Marne
R. Meuse
Nancy
FRANCE
ALSACE

Belgium, 10 October
Antwerp capitulated to the Germans today after a gallant battle in which the Belgian army, only six divisions strong, was led with much bravery by King Albert. The effort of the Belgians, reinforced by a brigade of British marines and two brigades of naval volunteers sent by Mr Churchill, the First Lord of the Admiralty, has considerably upset the German Schlieffen Plan for the invasion of France.

A *sortie* by the king yesterday threatened the Germans' communications and forced them to deal with Antwerp before resuming their drive into France. They attacked Antwerp on 28 September, reducing its fortifications with huge siege guns until the garrison could no longer hold out.

King Albert and his government have sailed to England to carry on the war, and the Belgian Field Army has escaped down the Flanders coast under the cover of two British divisions landed at Ostend and Zeebrugge in an attempt to save Antwerp. It is too late for that and Belgium must be considered lost to the enemy which invaded so treacherously. But the courage of "Little Belgium" lives on in Allied propaganda, which speaks of a war "in defence of small nations".

The war in Europe begins to involve each side's colonies

Africa and Asia, December
On 12 August Regimental Sergeant-Major Alhaji Grunshi, advancing into German Togoland, was the first British empire soldier to fire on a German. Two weeks later New Zealand troops occupied the German colony of Samoa in the Pacific.

Other campaigns outside Europe have not gone so well for Britain. A South African advance into German South-West Africa was dislocated by a rebellion of pro-German Boers. In German East Africa the British are unable to subdue Colonel von Lettow Vorbeck's Tanganyikan troops in spite of reinforcements from India. One Indian Army amphibious assault on the German port of Tanga was ignominiously repulsed by a swarm of bees.

The entry of the Ottoman empire into the war in November added new problems for Britain. William Wassmus, a German agent in Istanbul, has made contact with pan-Islamic revolutionaries and Indian nationalists, and is calling for a holy war against the British empire. Britain has made Egypt, constitutionally part of the Ottoman empire, a protectorate – to the disgust of Egyptian nationalists. Pro-Ottoman Senussi tribesmen are raiding its frontier from the safety of neutral Italian Libya. In south Arabia, Britons and Ottomans are unable to dislodge each other from Aden and Yemen respectively. In Somaliland Mohammed bin Abdullah, the so-called "Mad Mullah", has renewed his campaign against the British.

New machines rain death from the sky

Paris, 16 December
As the big battalions fight a war of attrition on the western front, aerial combat in the skies above – where individual fighter-pilots fight one-to-one battles under almost mediaeval rules of chivalry – is forcing strategists to reappraise their ideas of what is possible.

Initially only reconnaissance missions were flown, but soon airmen of both sides were using grenades and hand-held bombs against the men in the trenches. One aircraft has already shot down another, and over Rheims yesterday a British pilot fired his revolver to dissuade a German aviator from dropping a bomb on the city. With an eye on the Germans' superior airship technology, strategists speculate as to what will happen if a Zeppelin bombs central London and whether it will cause mass panic. Another risk of what some call "air power" is the insertion behind the lines of spies and assassins. A picture is emerging of warfare without rules.

Optimism turns to jingoism in Britain

London, 31 December
They said that the war would be over by Christmas. But Christmas has come and gone and optimism has been replaced by jingoism as the stern-faced Lord Kitchener urges the country's youth to arms on thousands of posters. A popular music hall song tells young men "We don't want to lose you, but we think you ought to go", and recruiting centres offer the king's shilling (for signing up) and a shilling a day pay to volunteers. Britons at home had their first taste of war this month when three German warships shelled Scarborough and other seaside towns in the north-east, killing 100 civilians and injuring a further 200.

Anti-German feeling is rife and hundreds of suspected "spies" have been rounded up under the emergency Defence of the Realm Act (DORA) which gives the authorities almost unlimited powers. London's Olympia exhibition centre has become a concentration camp.

1915 (1915-1916)

Italy, 13 January 1915. An earthquake kills 29,000 in central Italy.

North Sea, 24 January 1915. British warships sink the German battle cruiser *Blucher.*

China, January 1915. Seeking to extend its influence in China, Japan makes "21 demands" which severely undermine Chinese sovereignty.

Britain, 2 February 1915. The Germans announce a submarine blockade of the British Isles.

Germany, 1 March 1915. Britain begins a blockade of German ports.

New York City, March 1915. D W Griffith's epic film *The Birth of a Nation* opens.

Western Front, 5 April 1915. The French begin a broad offensive from the Meuse to the Moselle.

Western Front, 22 April 1915. The British launch a new offensive at Ypres.

London, 25 April 1915. Italy signs a secret treaty with Britain, France and Russia agreeing to enter the war on their side in return for territorial gains.

Turkey, 26 April 1915. Allied forces establish themselves along the Gallipoli peninsula.

Russia, 30 April 1915. The Germans invade the Russian Baltic provinces.

South-West Africa, 9 May 1915. German forces surrender to General Louis Botha's South Africans.

Italy, 23 May 1915. Italy declares war on Austria.

Britain, 25 May 1915. Herbert Asquith forms a wartime coalition.

Italy, 25 May 1915. The Austrians bomb Venice.

Eastern Front, 4 June 1915. Austro-German troops recapture Przemysl from the Russians.

Albania, 11 June 1915. Serbian troops invade Albania and take Tirana.

Eastern Front, 23 June 1915. The Austrians retake Lemberg, the capital of Galicia, which they lost to the Russians last year.

Eastern Front, 5 August 1915. The Austro-Germans take Warsaw.

Italy, 21 August 1915. Italy declares war on the Ottoman empire.

Eastern Front, 30 August 1915. The great Russian fortress of Brest-Litovsk falls to the Germans.

Poland, 1 September 1915. Following the partition of Poland by Germany and Austria, Josef Pilsudski forms a movement for a free Poland.

Petrograd, 5 September 1915. Czar Nicholas II takes personal command of the Russian army.

Bulgaria, 6 September 1915. Bulgaria signs a military convention with Germany and Austria.

Eastern Front, 19 September 1915. The Germans take Vilna.

Greece, 23 September 1915. King Constantine gives the order for the Greek army to mobilise in aid of Serbia against the Bulgarians.

Western Front, 26 September 1915. French and British troops launch two great offensives, in Champagne and Flanders.

Balkans, 8 October 1915. Russia opens hostilities against Bulgaria.

Serbia, 9 October 1915. Belgrade falls to the Austro-Germans.

Brussels, 12 October 1915. The British nurse Edith Cavell is executed by a German firing squad for treason.

Balkans, 14 October 1915. Bulgaria and Serbia declare war on one another.

Balkans, 16 October 1915. The allies blockade Bulgarian ports.

Europe, 19 October 1915. Russia and Italy follow Britain and France in declaring war on Bulgaria.

Britain, 23 October 1915. The great cricketer W G Grace dies.

Paris, 29 October 1915. The socialist Aristide Briand becomes prime minister after the resignation of Rene Viviani.

Paris, 14 November 1915. Tomas Masaryk, a leader of the Czech nationalist movement, issues a manifesto calling for the establishment of a Czech national council.

Germany, 12 December 1915. Hugo Junkers completes the first all-metal aeroplane.

Western Front, December 1915. Joseph Joffre is appointed commander of the French forces, Douglas Haig of the British forces.

Britain, 1915. Among this year's novels are *Victory* by Joseph Conrad and *Of Human Bondage* by W Somerset Maugham. The poet Rupert Brooke died on active service en route to the Dardanelles.

Germany, 1915. Albert Einstein propounds a new theory of gravity.

Central Asia, 17 January 1916. The Russians launch an offensive against the Ottomans.

Britain, 27 January 1916. Military conscription is introduced.

West Africa, 28 January 1916. British and Belgian troops take Yaounde, the capital of the German Cameroons.

Sub sinks "Lusitania"

The sinking of the "Lusitania", as seen by the German painter Claus Bergen.

Cork, 8 May 1915

More than 1,400 men, women and children are thought to have drowned yesterday when the *Lusitania* was torpedoed without warning by a German submarine. It happened within sight of the coast here, just eight miles (13 kilometres) off the Old Head of Kinsale. The liner was on the last stage of a return voyage from New York to Liverpool.

One passenger, Ernest Cowper, a Canadian journalist, actually saw the submarine's conning tower and the track of the first torpedo which struck at 2.12 pm. There was a loud explosion and pieces of the hull flew into the air. Seconds later came a second torpedo and the ship, one of Cunard's two finest ocean liners, sank in 21 minutes. There were 1,978 people on board. According to the survivors, at least five of those who drowned were women with babies in their arms.

Amongst the casualties were 128 Americans, including friends of President Woodrow Wilson and the millionaire yachtsman Alfred Vanderbilt.

The former president, Theodore Roosevelt, has already condemned the sinking as "an act of piracy". It will almost certainly lead to calls for President Wilson to abandon his policy of neutrality in the war. Today, however, the state department in Washington would go no further than to say that it viewed the incident "most seriously".

Japan issues "21 demands" to China

Beijing, 18 January 1915

The Japanese minister in Beijing has today presented 21 demands to President Yuan Shikai. The demands are so far-reaching and so severe that if Yuan accepts them China will become virtually a Japanese protectorate.

Notable among the demands are that China should cede Japan all German rights in Shandong; that Japan should supply weapons and advisers to the Chinese army, and that it should have have joint responsibility for the policing of important places in China.

Charlie Chaplin, the clown from Lambeth, in "The Tramp", which came to the cinemas in 1915.

Allies retreat from Gallipoli debacle

Australian infantry assaulting an Ottoman position at Gallipoli three days ago.

Aegean Sea
Suvla Bay
Anzac landing
Anzac Cove
△ Conquered forts ▲ Forts
● Mines ✸ Battles
Allied offensives
Allied positions
Turkish positions
Cape Helles
Dardanelles
Kum Kale

Turkey, 20 December 1915
The ill-fated attempt to force open the Dardanelles and capture Istanbul was abandoned today after ten months of bad luck and indecisiveness – and extraordinary heroism by Britons, Australians and New Zealanders who fought Ottoman troops, flies, fever, malaria, and the incompetence of their commanders. It is sad to reflect that the most skilful operation of the whole campaign was the evacuation, carried out under the muzzles of the Ottoman guns without a life being lost.

The saddest thing of all is that the plan to knock the Ottoman empire out of the war might well have succeeded, but the landings were not made until two months after the navy had first bombarded the Dardanelles forts and then lost six ships in a minefield. All the advantages of surprise were lost, so that when the troops did storm ashore they were mown down by the entrenched Ottoman troops. The tally for Gallipoli is 25,000 dead, 76,000 wounded, 13,000 missing and 96,000 sick.

Germany advances on eastern and Balkan fronts

Berlin, October 1915
The outstanding field commander in Germany's operations in eastern Europe is without question General August von Mackensen. After a string of victories in Poland and Galicia, he assumed command of a German-Austrian force on the Balkan front and has given the Serbs a severe drubbing. Belgrade was taken after fierce house-to-house fighting, and the railway through Greece to the port of Salonika has been cut, thus disrupting the Serbs' links with the Allied force recently landed there. Informed military observers expect Serbia to be overrun within weeks.

Von Mackensen commanded the force that captured the Russian fortress of Brest-Litovsk last August, after a 120-mile thrust from Warsaw in a month. It seems that the Russians' morale never recovered from the smashing defeats they suffered at Tannenberg and the Masurian Lakes early in the war. Von Mackensen was there, too.

Radicals take over Indian Congress

India, 1916
A year after the death of Gopal Krishna Gokhale, the father of Indian nationalism and India's "First Moderate", the Congress Party has been taken over by radicals. The arguments of 1907 between moderates and radicals are being rehashed, though this time a third force exists: a middle way, led by the Indian lawyer who led the civil disobedience campaign in South Africa, Mohandas Gandhi.

The death of Gokhale, a secular liberal who was trusted by Moslems, was the biggest blow that Congress has suffered. Even his radical opponent Bal Gangadhar Tilak praised him: "This diamond of India, this jewel of Maharashtra, this prince of workers, is taking eternal rest on the funeral grounds. Look at him and emulate him." Congress will become more militant under Tilak, taking advantage of Britain's wartime difficulties.

Poison gas: this war's horrific weapon

France, 22 April 1915
The Germans have introduced an horrific new weapon to the war. As dusk fell today Allied troops holding the line north of Ypres were enveloped in a swirling greenish-yellow cloud of poison gas released from the German trenches.

The gas, thought to be chlorine, choked and blinded the defenders, and they were swiftly overrun by German troops wearing gas masks who tore a four-mile gap in the defences until they were stopped by soldiers untouched by the gas. Allied troops have no protection against this weapon, which spreads panic among the bravest.

German soldiers wearing gas masks await an attack near Chemin des Dames.

Botha rounds up the Boer rebels

South Africa, February 1915
The pro-German Boer rebellion, centred on the western Transvaal and led by five Afrikaner Boer War generals, has collapsed.

The rebellion was a disaster. One general was shot at a roadblock by policemen who thought that he was a bandit. Another was drowned swimming the Vaal river on his way to German South-West Africa after his commando unit had been scattered at Rustenburg. The third escaped to Mozambique while the fourth has been captured. The fifth was routed with his commando at Mushroom Valley in November. Altogether, 4,000 Boers have been taken prisoner.

Most Boers either support Britain or remain neutral. Indeed, the 40,000-strong South African army that is advancing into German South-West Africa is led by the rebel leaders' fellow ex-Boer War generals, Smuts and Botha.

1916 (1916-1917)

Western Front, 21 February 1916. The Germans launch a major assault on the Verdun forts.

Britain, 28 February 1916. The novelist Henry James dies.

Central Asia, 2 March 1916. The Russians take Bitlis in Turkestan.

Germany, 9 March 1916. Germany declares war on Portugal.

Europe, 9 March 1916. Britain and France sign the Sykes-Picot agreement, specifying plans for the future division of Asiatic Turkey.

Mexico, 31 March 1916. Sent in retaliation for Pancho Villa's raid into the USA, in which 18 Americans died, US troops under John Pershing rout Villa's forces.

Turkey, 14 April 1916. The Allies bomb Istanbul.

East Africa, 17 April 1916. The Boer leader Jan Smuts leads an anti-German drive from Kenya.

Dublin, 25 April 1916. A revolt breaks out against British rule.

Ottoman Empire, 29 April 1916. British troops surrender to the Ottomans at Kut-el-Amara in Iraq after a siege of 143 days.

Dublin, 12 May 1916. James Connolly is the last of the seven rebels who signed the proclamation of an Irish republic during the Easter Rising to be executed.

Britain, 6 June 1916. Lord Kitchener dies when the cruiser *HMS Hampshire* is sunk by a mine off the Orkney Islands.

China, 6 June 1916. President Yuan Shikai dies.

Arabia, 21 June 1916. Hussein, the *grand sherif* of Mecca, declares war on the Ottoman empire with the aim of achieving Arabia's independence from Britain.

Eastern Front, 23 June 1916. A Russian offensive under Alexei Brusilov has resulted in the capture of most of Galicia.

Western Front, 24 June 1916. The Germans begin a new Verdun offensive.

Western Front, 1 July 1916. The British and French launch a major offensive on the Somme.

Petrograd, 6 July 1916. Russia and Japan sign a peace treaty.

Dublin, 3 August 1916. The former diplomat Roger Casement, famous for exposing slavery in the Congo, is sentenced to death for his part in the Easter Rising.

Egypt, 5 August 1916. The British defeat the Ottomans in a naval battle off Port Said.

Persia, 7 August 1916. Persia forms an alliance with Britain and Russia.

Italian Front, 9 August 1916. Italian troops take Gorizia.

Germany, 24 August 1916. The socialist Karl Liebknecht is jailed for his part in peace protests.

Germany, 27 August 1916. Paul von Hindenburg becomes chief of the German general staff.

Italy, 27 August 1916. Italy declares war on Germany.

Balkans, 27 August 1916. Rumania declares war on Austria; Germany declares war on Rumania.

Balkans, 10 September 1916. The Allies launch an offensive in Salonika.

Western Front, September 1916. Tanks are used for the first time in battle, by the Allies on the Somme.

Prague, 16 September 1916. A provisional government of "Czechoslovakia" is recognised by France and Britain.

Balkans, 27 September 1916. Greece declares war on Bulgaria, which declared war on Rumania earlier in the month.

Greece, 9 October 1916. Spiridion Lambros takes over as prime minister.

Greece, 17 October 1916. Having occupied Athens, the Allies recognise the pro-Allied rebel government of Eleutherios Venizelos, opposed to Lambros.

Western Front, 24 October 1916. French troops break German lines along a four-mile front as the second battle of Verdun opens.

Berlin, 5 November 1916. The Central Powers, Germany and Austria, proclaim the independence of Poland.

USA, 7 November 1916. Jeannette Rankin of Montana becomes the first woman member of the United States Congress.

USA, 11 November 1916. Woodrow Wilson is re-elected president.

Austria, 21 November 1916. Franz Josef, ruler of the Austro-Hungarian empire since 1848, dies.

Vienna, 6 December 1916. The Czech nationalist Tomas Masaryk is sentenced to death for treason in his absence.

Britain, 7 December 1916. David Lloyd George succeeds Herbert Asquith as prime minister.

Petrograd, 30 December 1916. Gregory Rasputin, the infamous Siberian "seer" and "miracle worker", is murdered.

Petrograd, 9 January 1917. Dimitri Golitzin becomes prime minister, succeeding Alexander Trepov who resigned in the face of strikes, food shortages and anti-war protests.

No sex in women's battalion of death

Moscow, 1917

Although British women are playing a vital wartime role – as ambulance drivers, nurses and auxiliaries on the western front, and in industry at home – few have taken part in actual combat. With the formation of a "Women's Battalion of Death" in Russia, that situation may well be changed. The suffragette leader, Mrs Emmeline Pankhurst, who wants to negotiate women's war work in return for the vote, and is on a visit to Russia, is said to be "delighted" with the idea.

Two 1,000-strong battalions are being trained at a women's institute near here. Almost all the women are under 35 and represent most social groups. The army is providing male instructors.

Discipline is strict. Yashka Bochkareva, the commander, cashiered 80 girls in the first two days, and uses face-slapping to punish recruits who flirt with instructors. She has decreed that sex will be outlawed for the duration.

It was that last stricture that caused a mutiny. Incited by Bolsheviks, volunteers demanded a "soldiers' committee". Bochkareva has refused and is now left with only 300 of the original women.

Irish patriots stage uprising at Easter

Dublin, 1 May 1916

An Irish republican leader waited politely in a queue for stamps in the General Post Office here – before drawing a pistol and telling the startled counter-clerk that an Irish republic had been declared. Within hours Dublin was ablaze, as well-armed British troops – many of them Irish veterans from the war in France – blasted republican strongpoints, including the post office, with heavy artillery. It has taken a week to put down the insurrection – and Dubliners have jeered prisoners as they are being marched to internment. About 450 rebels are dead and 2,000 captured, with 100 soldiers dead or injured.

China challenges would-be emperor

Beijing, 6 June 1916

Yuan Shikai, the first president of the Chinese republic, died today at the age of 56 bitterly regretting that he had never achieved his ambition of proclaiming himself emperor and founding a new imperial dynasty. At first he denied this ambition, claiming in 1912: "Ignorant people are fabricating rumours to delude the masses, with alarming reminders of the story of Napoleon". Two years later, however, he announced the formation of a new Chinese empire. His plan was foiled by the men of his own Northern Army. They would have a dictator, but not an emperor and, revealed as a buffoon, he had to withdraw.

Thousands die in North Sea naval clash

London, 31 May 1916

Both the British and the German navies are claiming victory today in what sailors are already calling "the greatest naval battle in history", off Jutland. The Royal Navy, commanded by Lord Jellicoe ("the only man who could have lost the war in an afternoon") says it has driven the German fleet off the seas. But Berlin claims that British sea power has been destroyed.

Britain has lost seven ships and nearly 7,000 men, the Germans three ships and over 2,500 men, and have retreated to their ports. The sea is awash with bodies; one passing steamer counted over 500.

Action stations at Jutland.

Trench war deadlocked despite Somme bloodshed

British troops going "over the top" in one of the fruitless assaults in the Battle of the Somme in which half a million British troops died.

Western Front, 1 January 1917
The terrible slaughter of 1916 has been brought to an end by the onset of winter, with little accomplished. The Allies failed bloodily to make their "great breakout" on the Somme, despite the introduction of the tank, and lost over half a million men; 60,000 Britons perished on the first day alone at the Somme. The Germans also lost half a million, notably in the "mincing machine" of Verdun.

Now the men of both sides have again settled into the routine of the trenches where, except for snipers' bullets and random shells, they are reasonably safe. But the trenches have their own particular horrors. Hugely fat lice, killed by running a candle flame along the seams of a shirt, are everywhere. So are the rats which feed off the bodies of the dead. The trenches also breed their own diseases. There is trench foot, a rotting of the foot caused by standing in deep mud and water; trench fever which spreads like wildfire; and a sickness which is only now being recognised as shellshock. Sufferers become hysterical and disorientated. Some refuse to obey orders; many have been courtmartialled for cowardice. Now they are treated with more sympathy.

The trench dwellers lead a life of dirt, danger and monotony. From "stand-to" at dawn, their days follow a regular pattern of digging, wiring, and short periods keeping watch from the "firing step". The boredom is so intense that there is never any shortage of volunteers for raiding parties on the enemy lines. Small groups of men armed with knives, clubs, sharpened entrenching tools and grenades slip through the barbed wire and go looking for trouble in no-man's-land.

Perhaps the moment that the men wait for most eagerly – apart from going to the rear – is mail call, when the letters arrive from home. Then these hardened, dirty soldiers find a quiet corner in the trench to read and reread those precious few lines from wives and sweethearts.

It is an extraordinary life: just a day's travel away from the delights of London, but it might just as well be on the moon. No-one who has served in the trenches will ever be the same again. Certainly, the soldier writing his letter home in the corner of a revetment will never be able to tell his story of fear and death, bravery and comradeship. Perhaps, paradoxically, that will be the task of the poets.

The rest of the world is up in arms

London, 1 January 1917
The war is truly a world war. In East Africa, von Lettow Vorbeck continues his brilliant campaign against the British. In Egypt, British and Ottoman troops are entrenched in stalemate, fighting for control of the Suez Canal. In Mesopotamia, British troops are pushing up the Tigris towards Baghdad after their defeat at Kut by the Ottomans in 1916. In Persia, William Wassmus, the German agent, leads a pan-Islamic army pledged to overthrow the pro-British government. Rarely are white troops to be seen: most of the fighting is done by and against brown-skinned people.

1917 (1917-1918)

Berlin, 1 February 1917. Germany announces a resumption of unrestricted submarine warfare.

Washington, DC, 2 March 1917. Congress passes the Jones Act, making Puerto Rico a US territory.

Ottoman Empire, 11 March 1917. The British enter Baghdad.

Petrograd, 12 March 1917. The *duma* ignores Czar Nicholas II's decree ordering its suspension and sets up a provisional government.

Russia, 16 March 1917. Czar Nicholas II abdicates.

Ottoman Empire, 27 March 1917. The Ottomans are heavily defeated by the British near Gaza.

USA, 1 April 1917. The ragtime musician Scott Joplin dies.

Washington, DC, 6 April 1917. President Wilson signs a declaration taking the USA into the war.

Western Front, 16 April 1917. Allied troops launch an offensive against the Germans manning the Hindenburg Line.

Petrograd, 17 April 1917. On his return to Russia with the other Bolshevik leaders, Vladimir Lenin publishes demands for the transfer of power to workers' *soviets*.

Western Front, 3 May 1917. The battle of Arras ends following the Canadian capture of Vimy ridge.

Italy, 3 June 1917. Italy declares Albania a protectorate.

Brazil, 4 June 1917. Brazil declares war on Germany and seizes all German ships in its ports.

Western Front, 8 June 1917. The British capture the Messines ridge.

Greece, 12 June 1917. The pro-German King Constantine, who has dismissed the pro-Allies Venizelos government, is forced to abdicate by the Allies.

Petrograd, 16 June 1917. The pan-Russian Congress of Soviets opens.

Western Front, 27 June 1917. The first US troops land in France.

Ukraine, 29 June 1917. The Ukraine declares its independence.

Berlin, 14 July 1917. Georg Michaelis succeeds Theobald von Bethmann-Hollweg as chancellor.

Finland, 14 July 1917. Finland proclaims its independence.

Russia, 16 July 1917. The provisional government crushes a *Bolshevik* uprising; its leader, Vladimir Lenin, flees.

Portugal, 17 July 1917. Pilgrims flock to Fatima, where visions of the Virgin Mary have been seen.

Petrograd, 22 July 1917. Alexander Kerensky is appointed prime minister.

Paris, 25 July 1917. Mata Hari, a glamorous Dutch dancer, is sentenced to death for spying.

China, 14 August 1917. War is declared on Germany and Austria.

Rome, 14 August 1917. After a failed peace bid last year, Pope Benedict XV sends another peace plan to the major powers.

Western Front, 20 August 1917. The French break the German lines at Verdun on an 11-mile front.

China, 10 September 1917. Sun Yat-sen sets up the republic of China military government in Guangzhou, in opposition to the Beijing government.

Petrograd, 15 September 1917. Kerensky proclaims Russia a republic.

Poland, 15 September 1917. Germany and Austria cede administrative and legislative power to the provisional government.

Russia, 17 September 1917. The Germans drive the Russians out of the Baltic port of Riga.

France, 26 September 1917. The painter Edgar Degas dies.

Western Front, 6 November 1917. Canadian troops capture the village of Passchendaele, ending the third battle of Ypres.

Petrograd, 7 November 1917. Kerensky and the provisional government are ousted in a Bolshevik coup.

Britain, 9 November 1917. Arthur Balfour, the foreign secretary, unveils plans for a Jewish national homeland in Palestine.

Russia, 16 November 1917. Bolshevik troops take Moscow.

France, 17 November 1917. The sculptor Auguste Rodin dies.

Palestine, 18 November 1917. British troops capture Jaffa.

USA, 7 December 1917. The USA declares war on Austria.

Portugal, 12 December 1917. Pro-German army officers under Sidonio Paes oust President Bernardino Machado in a *coup*.

Britain, 17 December 1917. Elizabeth Garrett Anderson, the first British woman doctor, dies.

Russia, 22 December 1917. The Bolsheviks open peace talks with Germany and Austria.

France, 14 January 1918. The ex-prime minister Joseph Caillaux, who advocated a negotiated peace with Germany, is jailed for treason.

Russia, 28 January 1918. Lenin creates a Red Army and the *Cheka*, a security police force.

US troops arrive to fight European war

US "doughboys" arriving in Britain on their way to the western front.

France, 27 June 1917

The first American troops to fight alongside the Allies were given a heroes' welcome as their ships tied up in French ports this morning.

Because of the submarine menace the troops' landing site had been kept a closely guarded secret, but by the time that the first US Marines had lined up to take their first salute on French soil a huge crowd had gathered to cheer them enthusiastically. With the arrival of each successive ship the crowd grew larger and the cheering louder in the brilliant summer sunshine.

The Marines are commanded by Major-General John Pershing, a much-decorated veteran of the Mexican and Filipino wars, who will be independent of the Anglo-French command. They are the vanguard of a US expeditionary force expected to number several hundred thousand men.

Apart from the Marines, an elite fighting force, many of the US troops to arrive will be conscripts fresh from training camp. Since the US entered the war 11 weeks ago urgent measures have been taken to augment their regular 128,000-strong army. Moves include the passing of the Selective Service Act, allowing all men aged between 21 and 30 to be drafted into the army.

Britain rejoices at Jerusalem capture

Jerusalem, 9 December 1917

The Ottoman commander of the Holy City has surrendered to General Edmund Allenby. The news has been welcomed by Jewish leaders and celebrated in London, where church bells rang out for the first time since war began.

The fall of Jerusalem is the culmination of an inspired campaign against the Ottomans which began nearly six weeks ago with the capture of Beersheba.

Guards have been placed over Christian holy places, and Moslems from the Indian Army are guarding Moslem shrines. Martial law is expected to be declared.

The power of the tank: a new weapon of war, but undervalued by traditional commanders.

Bolsheviks stage bloodless coup

Outside the Winter Palace: crowds scatter at the first burst of gunfire.

Revolutionary trio: Lenin, with Stalin and Trotsky alongside.

Petrograd, 7 November 1917

An ormolu mantelpiece clock in the Winter Palace stopped at ten minutes past two this morning. That was the moment when a party of "Red Guards", followed by an unruly mob, burst into the room and seized members of the provisional government. The cabinet ministers narrowly escaped being lynched by the mob before they were carted off to the Peter and Paul fortress. The total casualties in this seizure of power by a group of political conspirators known as Bolsheviks was three officer cadets wounded.

The leader of the Bolsheviks is a former law student, Vladimir Lenin, who only a few months ago was living in exile in Switzerland, virtually unknown outside the unholy circle of police agents and revolutionary visionaries. But the Germans knew him and sent him back to Russia in a sealed train: a troublemaker who they hoped would knock his country out of the war. That was after the February Revolution, when liberals and moderate socialists finally got rid of czarist autocracy following months of military defeats. In the euphoria of those days there was no sympathy for the Bolsheviks, and Lenin fled to Finland to escape arrest. But the people were war-weary and hungry, and the provisional government, led by Alexander Kerensky, had only rhetoric to offer.

The coup was masterminded by Leon Trotsky, once Lenin's bitter critic but now his closest comrade. Trotsky got the Petrograd Soviet, or revolutionary assembly, to vote for action, and sent armed squads to take railway stations, the telephone exchange and other key points. When the cruiser *Aurora* came up the Neva and fired a blank shell outside the Winter Palace, it was pretty well all over.

Palestine should be homeland for Jews, say British rulers

Palestine, 9 November 1917

Palestine as a permanent homeland for the Jewish people is the declared aim of the British government. The foreign secretary, Arthur Balfour, has conveyed a declaration of intent to Baron Rothschild, the representative of the Zionists.

The War Cabinet, under David Lloyd George, believes that Zionist support will help the war effort, particularly the campaign against the Ottomans. Arabs outnumber Jews ten to one in the Holy Land, but, under leaders like Dr Chaim Weizmann, Zionists can be expected to try to build up their numbers.

Australian cavalry conquers Jericho

Jericho, 21 February 1918

Australian cavalry rode triumphantly through the rain into Jericho this morning. The Ottomans have lost their advance base for the defence of Palestine. Five miles (eight kilometres) from the river Jordan, Jericho is a strategically important supply route, linked to the Hedfaz railway. Now it can help the Allied forces under General Allenby in his advance north towards Syria.

U-boats blast US and neutral ships

Washington, 26 February 1917

News of the sinking of the Cunard liner *Laconia* reached Capitol Hill today at the very moment that Congress was debating measures to deal with the growing menace in the Atlantic of German submarines. Earlier this month a US ship, the *Housatonic*, was sunk, making a total of 134 neutral ships destroyed by the Germans in the last three weeks.

President Woodrow Wilson was asking Congress to authorise the arming of US vessels to "protect our ships and our people in their legitimate pursuits on the sea". Already the US Navy is mounting naval patrols in the Atlantic to protect US shipping.

Germany penetrates deep into Italy

Northern Italy, 31 October 1917

The Italian army has been shattered by a surprise German onslaught, and is retreating in disarray towards the Piave river, a mere 15 miles (24 kilometres) from Venice.

The Italian Second Army, which had held off the Austrians comfortably through 1916, and captured the stronghold of Monte Santo only two months ago, had seemed well entrenched in the mountains around Caporetto and Udine.

But a German gas attack, followed by a furious creeping barrage from artillery, made the Italians suddenly vulnerable. When German and Austrian troops made light of the rain and snow to punch through their most northerly postions, the defenders lost heart. Italian losses have been high, with 10,000 dead and 30,000 wounded.

Of greater strategic significance is the capture of nearly 300,000 troops, armour and ammunition, and the total collapse of morale. Throughout northern Italy, soldiers are throwing away their weapons and fleeing. Although military police have set up roadblocks, and field courts-martial are common, it is estimated that half a million may have deserted.

As German and Austrian forces advance from the mountains across the river Tagliamento, General Cadorna, the Italian commander-in-chief, has been obliged to retreat to the river Piave, where he is desperately trying to establish a new line of defence.

The home front: a British woman munitions worker filling shells. Industry has been surprised by female efficiency; some factories are more than twice as productive as when staffed by men.

1918

Britain, 6 February. Married women over 30 win the vote.

Russia, 20 February. On the breakdown of peace talks, the Germans resume attacks on the Russians.

Estonia, 24 February. Estonia declares its independence.

Britain, 26 February. The Labour Party adopts a constitution aiming for common ownership and state control.

Russia, 3 March. Russia signs a peace treaty with Germany at Brest-Litovsk.

Russia, 5 March. The capital is moved from Petrograd to Moscow.

Western Front, 21 March. The Germans launch a great offensive on the Somme.

Western Front, 26 March. Ferdinand Foch is appointed commander-in-chief of the allied forces in France.

Britain, 1 April. The Royal Air Force is formed.

Far East, 6 April. US, British and Japanese troops land at Vladivostok.

Western Front, 23 April. British forces raid the Belgian port of Zeebrugge.

Rumania, 7 May. Rumania forms alliance with Germany and Austria.

Ireland, 19 May. Five hundred *Sinn Fein* members, including Eamon de Valera, are jailed.

Russia, 26 May. Armenia and Georgia declares independence.

Russia, 10 July. A provisional government of Siberia is set up.

Russia, 16 July. The former Czar Nicholas II and his family are massacred in a cellar at Ekaterinburg.

Western Front, 18 July. Allied forces launch a counter-offensive on the Marne.

Germany, 29 July. Germany severs diplomatic relations with the Ottoman empire.

Russia, 2 August. A British-led force lands at Archangel to support the White Russian opposition to the Bolsheviks.

Western Front, 8 August. The German line collapses as Allied forces go into action near Amiens.

USA, 15 August. The USA severs relations with Russia.

Western Front, 3 September. German forces begin a retreat to the Siegfried Line.

US launches post-war peace plan

Woodrow Wilson: 14 points for a brave new liberal world.

Washington, DC, 9 January

A liberal vision of a post-war world free of restrictions, enjoying open diplomacy and free trade and encouraging national self-determination was disclosed by President Wilson to Congress today.

The 14-point Wilson Plan, as it is being called, is based on proposals which the president put to the recent inter-Allied conference which failed to agree any post-war aims. Many of the points have also been put forward by a secret policy group in New York, known as the "Inquiry" and led by a young journalist, Walter Lippmann.

The president's aim in publishing the plan is to turn the German people against their government and push the Allied governments into granting liberal peace terms.

Specific proposals for post-war Europe include Germany evacuating occupied territories in Russia, Belgium and France as well as returning Alsace-Lorraine to France. The problem of the Balkan states, still ruled by the now politically unstable Habsburg and Ottoman empires, is solved by granting these states autonomous development. A novel feature of the plan is the formation of an association of nations to guarantee independence and national integrity.

Russia signs peace deal

Brest-Litovsk, 3 March

The four-month-old Bolshevik regime today put its seal on a peace treaty with Germany that requires Russia to give up 26 per cent of its population, 27 per cent of its own area, three-quarters of its iron and steel output, 26 per cent of its rail network, and to surrender Poland and the Baltic states. The Ukraine becomes an independent state. And the Bolsheviks have agreed to pay 3,000 million *roubles* in reparations. The surrender has angered Russia's western allies, who will now be faced with massive German reinforcements brought from Russia to the western front. The *pince-nez*-wearing people's commissar for foreign affairs, Leon Trotsky, bamboozled the Germans for nine weeks with neither-war-nor-peace talk, hoping that revolution would spread to Germany.

That did not happen. German forces thrust deep into Russia and Lenin ordered peace at any price, before the Germans overthrew his shaky Bolshevik regime.

The Bolsheviks came to power last November with the popular slogan "Peace, land, bread – and all power to the *Soviets*". The people have now got their peace – and they must pay the price in land and bread.

Czar and household slaughtered in cellar

The czar and family at Czarskoe Selo before being taken to Ekaterinburg.

Ekaterinburg, 16 July

The deposed Czar Nicholas II and his family arrived in this small town in the Urals a few weeks ago when local Bolsheviks dragged them from a train that was taking them from Tobolsk to Ufa. Scarcely had they arrived in Ekaterinburg than the local Bolshevik-dominated soviet began expressing fears that they could be liberated by advancing anti-Bolshevik "White Guards" and Czechs.

The local branch of Lenin's secret police, the *Cheka*, took over guard duties at the house where the Romanovs were being held. Today the family were taken into the cellar, where the ex-czar, his wife, the invalid czarevitch and the four daughters were shot and bayoneted to death. And to make sure that nobody survived to bear witness, the family physician, valet, cook, parlourmaid and dog were killed. The bodies were burnt and thrown into a pit.

The Bolshevik leadership in Moscow has put it about that the massacre was a local decision; the truth, it seems, is that Moscow saw the Romanovs as a possible rallying force for anti-Bolshevik groups and let it be known that the liquidation of the family would not be unwelcome.

Allies smash through German lines

Western Front, 30 September

The German army is falling back all along the line under the hammering of 200 Allied divisions in the offensive launched at dawn four days ago. Von Ludendorff, the German commander, has described 8 August as the "black day of the German army", but today's news is even more significant.

The Germans, who came so close to success in the spring, are now avoiding battle wherever possible, making a stand only to cover the retreat as British, French and the fresh, confident Americans drive on from the Scheldt in the north to Sedan at the southern end of the western front.

King Albert's 28 Belgian divisions are in the forefront of the advance in Flanders, liberating their country which was occupied by the Germans in the first days of the war, four long years ago.

Tanks and planes are being used in large numbers and the stalemate of the trench lines has been broken. The British left wing is almost through the last defences of the Hindenburg Line, and the Allies will soon be where they have always wanted to be – in open country, fighting a war of mobility.

German morale is cracking everywhere, and all along the ruptured front pockets of soldiers are being found hiding in shellholes and ruined buildings. They offer no resistance, and are throwing down their weapons and equipment; everything, in fact, except a small sack containing a few necessities – bread, soap and razor – for the prison camp. It is pointed out that many of these Germans belong to low-grade units; it is expected that Ludendorff, employing a system of elastic defence, will allow the Allied offensive to tire before putting in his reserve fighting divisions.

However, the evidence coming from the battlefield is of a German army emaciated by four years of bloodshed, and with its morale sapped by news of unrest at home, unable to cope with the fierce determination of the British and French and the keenness of the Americans.

That eagerness brings its own problems, for the Americans, with an untried war machine, and short of artillery, are apt to rush in where more experienced soldiers fear to tread. But they mean to win.

Autumn offensive: British troops move into no-man's-land near Bellicourt.

Number One Squadron of the new Royal Air Force, formed on 1 April.

British major helps to free Damascus from Turkish rule

Damascus, 1 October

Major T E Lawrence, known as Lawrence of Arabia, has led a triumphant Arab army into Damascus just ahead of General Allenby's army of Palestine. Horsemen cavort in the streets as the greatest city in the Arab world celebrates its liberation from the Ottoman yoke.

Alongside Lawrence is *Emir* Feisal, the son of *Sherif* Hussein, who now expects to be crowned king of Syria. Starting in the Hejaz several months ago, they have built an Arab army and led it across the desert, through skirmishes with Ottoman troops, Lawrence's tactical skill and Feisal's charismatic leadership proving a potent combination.

The only Ottoman troops left in the city now are the wounded, left behind in hospitals in appalling conditions. Although the tribesmen and Syrian townspeople have much to celebrate, there is concern at the possible breakdown of law and order. Allenby's first task will be to instal a military government in Damascus to prevent wholesale slaughter as a vengeful populace seeks out those who collaborated with the Ottomans. Thereafter, the French will take over Syria while Allenby moves on to join French forces in the advance on Beirut.

Lawrence of Arabia: an incorrigible romantic in an unromantic war.

Civil war threatens Russian Bolsheviks

Moscow, 26 June

Lenin's Bolshevik regime is beset on all sides. In the south, General Anton Denikin has seized large parts of the Caucasus and the Ukraine; in the north, bands of anti-Bolsheviks roam at will; Czech former prisoners of war, now organised in the Czech Legion, have taken Omsk on the Trans-Siberian Railway. Over 100 British marines have landed at Murmansk to keep the port out of German hands. Trotsky, desperately seeking to create a Red Army, offers recruits 150 roubles (£2) a month.

1918

Bulgaria, 30 September. Bulgaria surrenders.

Bulgaria, 4 October. King Ferdinand abdicates in favour of his son Boris.

Near East, 7 October. British forces take Beirut and Sidon.

Czechoslovakia, 15 October. The republic of Czechoslovakia is proclaimed.

Hungary, 17 October. Hungary declares independence from Austria.

Italy, 30 October. The Austrian army completes its evacuation of Italian territory.

Ottoman Empire, 31 October. The Ottomans surrender to the Allies. The Dardanelles are reopened to Allied shipping.

Vienna, 3 November. Austria signs an armistice.

Germany, 7 November. Socialists under Kurt Eisner declare a republic in Bavaria.

Germany, 9 November. Kaiser William II abdicates and a republic is declared.

Austria, 11 November. The Emperor Karl abdicates and a republic is declared.

France, 11 November. Germany agrees to an armistice at Compiegne.

Prague, 14 November. Tomas Masaryk is elected the first president of Czechoslovakia.

Warsaw, 14 November. Josef Pilsudski becomes president of Poland with dictatorial powers.

Britain, 21 November. The German High Seas fleet surrenders to the British.

Denmark, 1 December. Denmark grants independence to Iceland.

Portugal, 15 December. President Sidonio Paes is assassinated.

Britain, 28 December. Lloyd George's coalition government is returned to power in the first election in which women were allowed to vote. Countess Markievicz, a *Sinn Fein* candidate, is the first woman to be elected to Parliament, though like all *Sinn Feiners* she refuses to take her seat.

France, December. The province of Alsace-Lorraine is reincorporated into France.

Britain. Marie Stopes' book *Married Love* causes controversy by mentioning birth control.

Western Front. The poet Wilfred Owen is killed in action.

Armistice: Europe sighs with relief

Western Front, 15 November

Along the western front, from the Channel to the Swiss border, men are slowly becoming accustomed to an eerie, unfamiliar sound. It is the sound of silence. After four years and 14 weeks, the crash of artillery, the thump of the howitzer and the scream of the *minenwerfer* are no longer heard. Peace has come to a war-weary Europe, received with delirious relief by the victors and with bitterness by the defeated.

The end, when it came, took many by surprise. In mid October, Foch, the Allied commander, was asking for reinforcements for a November offensive and the Americans had their sights on campaigns in 1919. But behind the German lines there was a sense of desperation. Von Ludendorff, once the hero of the hour, was replaced by the levelheaded General Groener who told the kaiser either to shoot himself or abdicate.

By the end of last month, with their army reeling under the Allied blows, the Germans were in no position to haggle over the armistice terms. Shortly before dawn, in a railway carriage in the forest of Compiegne, Foch and the British Admiral Wemyss received a German delegation, including two generals and a Catholic politician. Six hours later, at 11am on the 11th day of the 11th month, the armistice took effect. The terms are hard,

The day the world stopped fighting: "The nightmare is over," said George V.

Germany surrendering 5,000 heavy guns, 30,000 machine guns, 2,000 warplanes, all its U-boats, 150,000 wagons and 5,000 trucks.

The German navy will be interned in British waters. The Allied blockade of Germany will remain in force to ensure that the Germans keep their word. When Germany first sought an armistice it undertook to end submarine warfare, but the U-boats continued to attack, sinking a transport, with the loss of 600 lives, and a British cruiser. In Britain, the firing of "maroons" told people that peace had come and the whole country became, as one commentator said, "like a giant school let loose".

Boy Scouts cycled through the streets sounding the "all clear" on bugles. Factories shut down, munitions workers danced with servicemen, fireworks spluttered and paper boys raced along waving special editions. Wartime licensing laws were ignored and pubs stayed open until they ran out of beer.

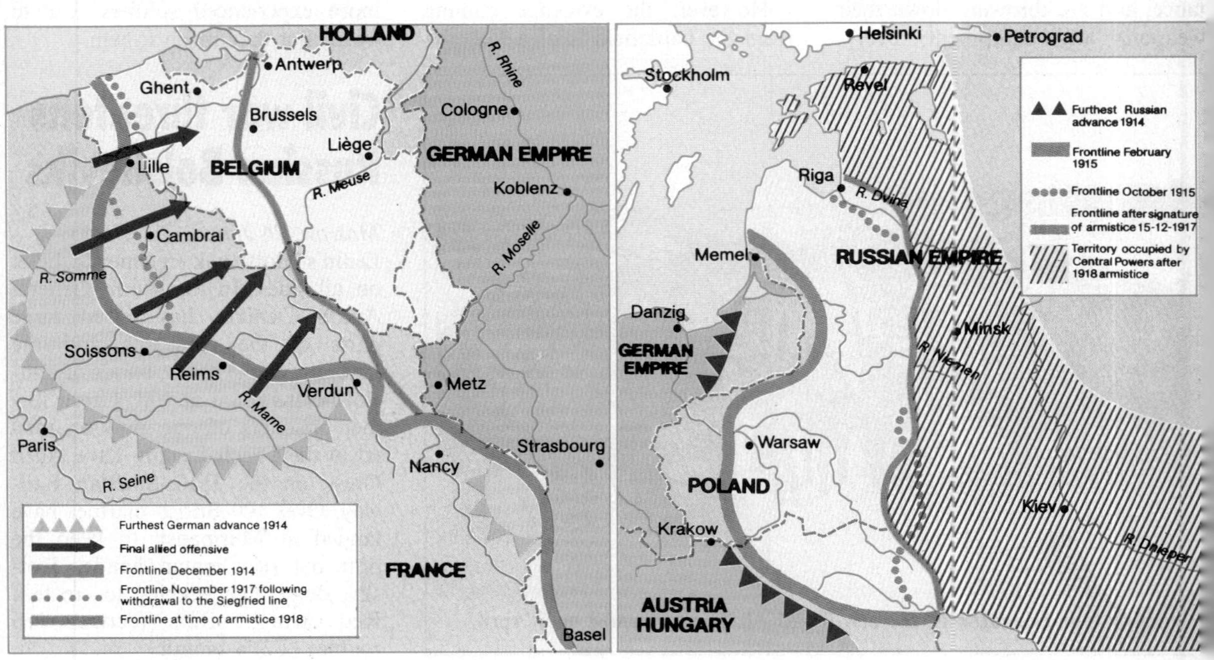

Defeated Germany plunges into chaos

Berlin, 30 November
The order and discipline for which the Germans were known, and even respected, throughout Europe vanished virtually overnight in the wake of defeat in war. The kaiser has fled to Holland, angry political agitators roam the streets, sailors have mutinied and dishevelled, disillusioned soldiers are seizing their command posts.

The Social Democrats are led by Friedrich Ebert, aged 47, a trade union boss and former saddlemaker who is attempting to restore order. Ebert told the *reichstag* that a republic had been proclaimed and that arms were being distributed to soldiers' and workers' councils. But he has appointed a tough-minded Socialist, Gustav Noske, as his minister of defence. Noske has gone to work with a loyal general, Wilhelm Groener, to form volunteer units of loyal anti-revolutionary soldiers.

Ebert and Noske are being fiercely denounced by extreme left-wingers like Karl Liebknecht and Rosa Luxembourg, who have formed the revolutionary Spartacus League and are calling for "a free socialist republic". In reaction to this left-wing ferment, far-right factions in the army are talking of "dealing" with such people as Liebknecht and Luxembourg.

Habsburg empire breaks into pieces

Vienna, 30 November
With the break-up of the Habsburg empire following the end of the World War, four "new" nations have come into being – Austria, Hungary, Czechoslovakia and one yet to be named. Their roots go back into Europe's pre-history.

Austria is now a republic and has kicked out Karl, the last Habsburg emperor. Czechoslovakia is led by the popular Tomas Masaryk. The Hungarians, or Magyars, who have enjoyed equality with Austria in the empire, have a government headed by the liberal aristocrat Michael Karolyi. The as yet unnamed country is a confederation of South Slavic peoples, including Serbs, and will be ruled by King Peter who led Serbia to victory.

Peace comes to the far-flung frontiers

Africa and Asia, 30 November
General von Lettow Vorbeck heard of the armistice on a bicycle, leading his undefeated 250 German and 1,750 African troops to invade Rhodesia. For four years they have held down over 130,000 Allied troops.

In Istanbul news of the armistice came after the Ottoman collapse in Palestine and Mesopotamia. General von Papen, the deputy commander in the Near East, was as shocked by the encouragement of soldiers' councils by his senior, von Sanders, as by the armistice.

Von Hentig, who for four years raised anti-British revolts in Persia, Afghanistan and China, heard the news in Shanghai. He is to be repatriated via the US, and thus will have circumnavigated the globe.

Spanish flu claims more lives than war

The World
The Great War is estimated to have claimed ten million lives. But a disastrous pandemic of a type of influenza called "Spanish flu" has already this year exceeded that figure. Doctors believe that the death-toll worldwide over the coming year could reach a staggering 20 million.

This virulent strain of influenza is itself dangerous, but it is the added risk of bacterial infection in the lungs which causes complications such as lethal pneumonia. So far, attempts to develop a vaccine to combat this mass epidemic have been unsuccessful.

The tag "Spanish Flu" may be a misnomer. No-one is sure where it originated. So far the greatest suffering has been in India and China where millions have already died. But now the menace is spreading to America and Europe.

Already in Britain the signs are being felt: absences from work are escalating and essential services such as the London central telegraph office are being hit as people sign off sick.

Ten million dead, a generation lost: world counts cost of its first total war

Paul Nash's "The Menin Road", as bitter a poem on canvas as Owen's on paper; with form, like no-man's-land reduced to its most naked.

31 December
"Blow out, you bugles, over the rich dead!" wrote Rupert Brooke, and Laurence Binyon echoed, in consolation: "They shall not grow old, as we that are left grow old." But that was said before the enormity of the casualties could be guessed at – over ten million dead, in war cemeteries lining the battlefields like serried battalions of crosses, or in unmarked graves at the bottom of the sea. In sheer total of dead, wounded and missing, Russia leads the list, followed by Germany and Austria-Hungary, France and then Britain and its empire with one million. Britain gave 767,000 dead and the empire 200,000 more.

The cost was a Lost Generation, and none were more aware of it than the writers on both sides. "What passing bells for these who die as cattle?" asked Wilfred Owen. Those who died, either in action or on active service, included Brooke, who came to stand for his generation cut off in the bud of promise, Edward Thomas, Isaac Rosenberg, and Owen, killed a week before the armistice on the western front. His poems, written in the trenches, begin with the words: "My subject is war and the pity of war. The poetry is in the pity."

Some of the survivors, like Siegfried Sassoon, have already made public the uncomfortable view that the lost generation had been sacrificed by incompetent commanders, careless of the lives of those who had to do the dying. Sassoon threw his Military Cross into the river Mersey in protest at the slaughter. His reward for such sanity was to be despatched to a mental hospital, diagnosed as shell-shocked.

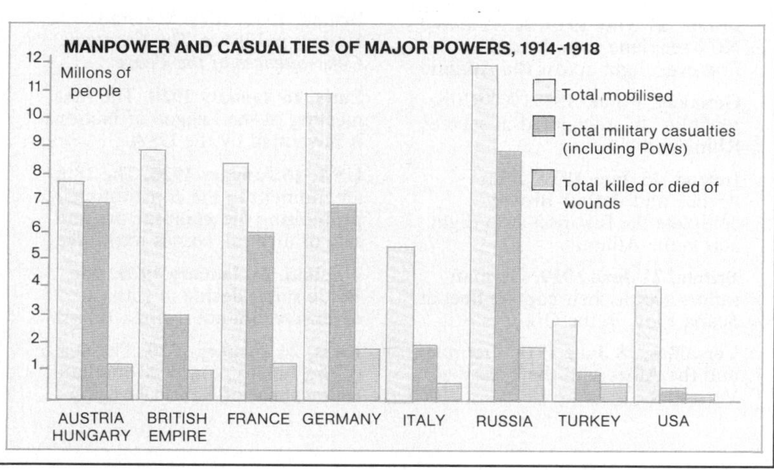

1919 (1919-1920)

London, 13 January 1919. Sir Satyendra Prassano Sinha becomes the first Indian peer and thus a member of the House of Lords.

Berlin, 16 January 1919. Rosa Luxembourg and Karl Liebknecht, the leaders of the Spartacist uprising, are murdered by German soldiers.

Versailles, 18 January 1919. Peace conference opens.

Dublin, 21 January 1919. An unofficial Irish "parliament", formed by 25 Westminster *Sinn Fein* MPs who refuse to attend the Commons, holds its first meeting.

Hungary, 20 February 1919. Bela Kun leads a communist revolt.

Germany, 22 February 1919. After the murder of the Bavarian prime minister, Kurt Eisner, a *soviet* republic is declared in Bavaria.

Russia, 3 March 1919. Bolshevik leaders establish the Communist International (Comintern) as a vehicle for world revolution.

Europe, 11 March 1919. The Allies reach agreement to supply famine-hit Germany with food relief.

Italy, 23 March 1919. Benito Mussolini founds a party, the Fasci di Combattimento, to fight both liberalism and communism.

Hungary, 26 March 1919. The former president Michael Karolyi is arrested by the communists.

Versailles, 4 April 1919. The Allies sign an agreement with Germany making Danzig a "free city".

Ireland, 5 April 1919. Eamon de Valera becomes Sinn Fein's president.

Mexico, 10 April 1919. The rebel leader Emiliano Zapata is killed by government troops.

Germany, 2 May 1919. Berlin government troops enter Munich to overthrow the fledgling soviet regime in Bavaria.

Afghanistan, 24 May 1919. Having defeated Afghan raiders in a clash on the Indian border, the British bomb Jalalabad and Kabul.

Lisbon, 27 May 1919. A US Navy NC4 seaplane completes the first-ever flight across the Atlantic.

Germany, 1 June 1919. A "Rhine republic" is proclaimed in several Rhineland cities.

Ireland, 15 June 1919. John Alcock and Arthur Brown complete the first non-stop flight across the Atlantic.

Britain, 21 June 1919. German sailors scuttle their captive fleet at Scapa Flow in the Orkneys.

Versailles, 28 June 1919. Germany and the Allies sign the Treaty of Versailles.

Britain, 13 July 1919. The British airship *R-34* completes the first two-way crossing of the Atlantic.

Germany, July 1919. A republic is declared at Weimar and a new constitution adopted.

Hungary, 4 August 1919. Rumanian troops enter Budapest, ending Bela Kun's 133-day-old communist republic.

Britain, 19 August 1919. A bill disestablishing the church in Wales becomes law.

Europe, 25 August 1919. The world's first scheduled international daily air service begins between London and Paris.

South Africa, 3 September 1919. Jan Smuts becomes prime minister following the death of Louis Botha.

France, 10 September 1919. Austria signs the treaty of St Germain with the Allies.

Ireland, 11 September 1919. The *Dail Eireann*, or Irish parliament, is declared illegal by the British government.

Italy, 23 September 1919. The poet-aviator Gabriele d'Annunzio occupies the city of Fiume.

Egypt, 19 November 1919. Britain grants Egypt a constitution.

Washington, DC, 19 November 1919. The US Senate votes against ratifying the Versailles Treaty.

France, 27 November 1919. Bulgaria signs the treaty of Neuilly, recognising the independence of Yugoslavia.

London, 1 December 1919. Lady (Nancy) Astor becomes the first woman MP to take her seat in the House of Commons.

London, 22 December 1919. David Lloyd George, the prime minister, announces plans for the partition of Ireland.

China, 1919. China refuses to sign the Treaty of Versailles, which has produced widespread anti-western sentiments in China and awakened interest in Marxism.

Britain, 1919. John Maynard Keynes publishes *The Economic Consequences of the Peace.*

Paris, 16 January 1920. The first meeting of the League of Nations is boycotted by the USA.

USA, 16 January 1920. The 18th amendment to the constitution, prohibiting the manufacture and sale of alcohol, comes into force.

Helsinki, 21 January 1920. The Baltic states decide to form a defensive alliance against Russia.

Paris, 24 January 1920. The death of the Italian painter Modigliani follows that of Renoir last year.

Berlin routs confused communist uprising

Berlin, 12 January 1919

The communist uprising in Berlin has been crushed by troops loyal to the government after a week of bitter street fighting.

The revolt by the Spartacists, who take their name from the last slaves to revolt against the Romans, began to collapse yesterday as 3,000 *Freikorps* men marched into the capital to reinforce the Freikorps forces already in the city, government troops and members of the Socialist People's Militia. By this morning the Spartacists, whose call to the workers to take up arms against the troops has been ignored, had faded away. The whereabouts of their leaders, the revolutionaries "Red Rosa" Luxembourg and Karl Liebknecht, a former *reichstag* deputy, is not known. They led the occupation of a number of public buildings after the government refused to bow to their demands for the formation of a true socialist republic – the same as the Bolsheviks have set up in Russia.

A Spartacist attempt to occupy the war office failed after the under-secretary of state told the leader of the raiding party that he needed proper written authority to do so. Much of the fighting has been confused, with men on both sides occupying barricades. Hundreds of bodies are still lying in the streets, according to eye-witnesses.

Right-wing Freikorps forces at the barricades behind newspaper bundles.

Beijing students in "sell-out" protest

Beijing, 4 May 1919

Some 3,000 student demonstrators assembled at the Gate of Heavenly Peace today to protest against the decision taken by the Allies at Versailles to give defeated Germany's rights in Shandong to Japan rather than return them to China. The students, believing that the minister of communications had sold out to the Japanese, sacked his house. Thirty-two were arrested, but the protest continues, drawing strength from the reformist faculty of Beijing university.

Eclipse test proves Einstein is right

London, 1919

A scientific expedition to the Gulf of Guinea has taken photographs during a total eclipse, verifying one of this century's most important scientific theories. The team was from the Royal Society of London and the theory is that of relativity as propounded by Albert Einstein. According to Einstein, gravity is not, as Newton said, a force but a curved field in space-time. This can only be proved by measuring the deflection of starlight during a total eclipse of the sun.

League of Nations formed to stop war

Paris, 14 February, 1919
Delegates from 27 nations at the peace conference here today voted to set up a league of nations to try to prevent war. Much remains to be done before it becomes a reality, but today's vote demonstrates that the US president, Woodrow Wilson, is winning support for his belief that "the conscience of the world" is ready for such a move.

The league's charter is to be incorporated in the peace treaty with Germany being debated here. But there are still deep divisions between the hawks, like the French, who want to make Germany pay, and the doves, like Wilson, who argue for a "just peace".

An English scientist has split the atom

Manchester, 1919
Experiments at Manchester university have culminated in a process for "splitting" atoms. Professor Rutherford has fired alpha particles through hydrogen gas and dislodged the nuclei of some of the hydrogen atoms. He has also managed to knock hydrogen nuclei – H-particles – out of the nuclei of boron, fluorine, sodium, aluminium, phosphorus and nitrogen. He names these H-particles *protons*. They seem to be the indivisible building blocks of the nuclei of all elements.

Aviators pioneer new routes round world

Alcock and Brown's Vickers-Vimy biplane taking off from Newfoundland.

Australia, 10 December 1919
The flying Smith brothers arrived in Australia today and claimed the £10,000 prize offered by the Australian government for the first flight to arrive from Britain in under 30 days. Their trip brings to a climax a year of massive advances in international aviation.

In February fare-paying passengers were carried between London and Paris for the first time when a Farman F60 Goliath took three and a half hours to make the journey. A month later, on 27 March, the Atlantic was bridged by a US Navy NC4 seaplane, whose pilots Lieutenant-Commander Read and Lieutenant Stone flew 3,150 nautical miles in 44 hours. This involved three stages, the longest spanning the 1,200 miles between Newfoundland and the Azores.

On 15 June the Anglo-Irish team of Captain John Alcock and Lieutenant Arthur Whitten Brown went one step further. Despite atrocious weather conditions their Vickers-Vimy biplane flew the Atlantic non-stop, landing successfully in an Irish peat bog. They completed the 1,900-mile flight from Newfoundland in 16 hours and 12 minutes.

Aircraft are not the only means of airborne travel. The British airship *R-34* made the first two-way trip over the Atlantic in July. The leisurely *dirigible* took four days to reach New York, slightly longer than a fast liner.

Germany forced to pay cost of peace

Versailles, 28 June 1919
For five months the victors of the Great War had laboured to produce a peace settlement and for two months the vanquished had refused to accept the terms. Today, at ten minutes to four in the afternoon, the German delegation finally bowed to threats of military occupation and signed a peace treaty. The news was signalled by gunfire and greeted by cheers from crowds outside the Palace of Versailles.

The peace terms had caused anguish and division amongst the allies. The French had led those arguing for a tough line, urging that Germany be partitioned. Lloyd George, the British prime minister, had promised to "squeeze the German lemon until the pips squeak", but even he is now wondering whether the final terms might be too harsh. "We shall have to fight another war all over again at three times the cost," he said.

Under the treaty Germany has to make a provisional compensation payment of 20 billion gold marks – with further reparations to be decided later. Territory lived in by seven million people is to be surrendered; the Rhineland is to be demilitarized; and the Saar controlled by the new League of Nations. The German cabinet resigned and although the majority of the National Assembly voted to accept the terms, the bitterness remains.

Amritsar massacre stalls reform plans

Delhi, 1919
Emergency war regulations have been imposed by the British authorities and proposals for provincial self-government shelved. Britain's dilemma over India was sharpened in April when Gurkha troops, commanded by Brigadier Dyer, killed 379 unarmed demonstrators at Amritsar, the holy city of the Sikhs. Dyer's order to open fire has been condemned, but the emergency powers which prompted the demonstration have been toughened, diluting the impact of plans to "Indianise" the army and civil service.

Dixieland jazzmen take syncopation to every nation

London, 7 April 1919
Jazz, now the rage in America, has arrived in Europe with the "Original Dixieland Jazz Band". Its tour has reached the London Palladium. Jazz began in New Orleans with its marching funeral bands and its "cornet kings". Many black musicians left the city with the closing of its red light district of Storyville two years ago. White jazz is known as "Dixieland", and the "ODJB" was formed by white New Orleans musicians in Chicago. It is led by Nick La Rocca, a cornettist and the composer of *Tiger Rag*, which nightly brings audiences to their feet stamping and clapping.

Nick La Rocca's all-white band, spreading jazz where black men fear to tread.

1920

Russia, 20 February. The Red Army captures Archangel.

Germany, 24 February. The National Socialist Workers' Party, led by Adolf Hitler, publishes a programme for a third *reich.*

Hungary, 29 February. The monarchy is restored, with Miklos Horthy as regent.

Syria, 8 March. Syria proclaims its independence from the Ottoman empire, with *Emir* Feisal, hero of the Arab Revolt, as king.

Turkey, 16 March. Allied troops occupy Istanbul.

Ireland, 26 March. Eight hundred special constables, the "Black and Tans", arrive from England to put down the republican revolt in the South of the country, where public order is rapidly deteriorating.

Budapest, 28 March. The Hungarian parliament is dissolved and the regent, Miklos Horthy, becomes dictator.

Germany, 6 April. French troops occupy Frankfurt.

Turkey, 23 April. Turkish nationalists set up a provisional government at Ankara, with Mustapha Kemal as president.

Ukraine, 7 May. Polish troops seize Kiev from the Red Army.

Persia, 19 May. The Red Army invades northern Persia.

Mexico, 22 May. President Venustiano Carranza is murdered by rebels under Rodolfo Herrera.

Czechoslovakia, 27 May. Tomas Masaryk is elected president; Eduard Benes is foreign minister.

Poland, 28 May. War is declared between Poland and Russia.

Spain, 1 June. The Spanish Communist Party is founded.

Versailles, 4 June. The treaty of Trianon cuts Hungary to a quarter of its former size.

Geneva, 13 June. The International Feminist Congress opens.

The Hague, 16 June. The League of Nations Permanent Court of Justice opens.

Mexico, 8 July. The guerrilla leader Pancho Villa surrenders to the Mexican government.

Syria, 24 July. A French expeditionary force occupies Damascus and the port of Aleppo. Emir Feisal, installed in Damascus by the British three months ago, flees.

London, 31 July. The Communist Party of Great Britain is founded.

France, 10 August. The Ottoman empire signs a peace treaty with the allies at Sevres, confirming the loss to it of 80 per cent of its land.

Geneva, 11 August. The first ecumenical conference is held, bringing together European, US and Eastern churches.

Poland, 16 August. As Russian troops close on Warsaw, US warships are sent to Danzig (*Gdansk*).

Poland, 23 August. With the support of British airmen, the Poles repel the Russian advance on Warsaw.

Near East, 1 September. France proclaims the creation of the state of Lebanon, with the seat of government at Beirut.

India, 10 September. The Indian National Congress votes to adopt Mohandas Gandhi's programme of non-violent non-cooperation with the Indian government.

Latvia, 6 October. Poland and Russia sign an armistice at Riga.

Britain, 7 October. The first 100 women are admitted to Oxford university to study for full degrees.

Russia, 14 October. The *Soviet* government recognises the independence of Finland.

Ireland, October. Riots erupt across the country following the death of the hunger striker Tomas MacSwiney, lord mayor of Cork.

USA, 2 November. Warren Harding, the Republican candidate, is elected president.

Geneva, 13 November. The first full session of the League of Nations opens, attended by 5,000 representatives from 41 countries worldwide.

Dublin, 21 November. Fourteen British officers and officials are killed in their beds by IRA members, setting off a day of violence and killing in Ireland.

Norway, 10 December. Woodrow Wilson, the former US president, is awarded the Nobel peace prize.

Ireland, 11 December. Martial law is declared.

Geneva, 15 December. China and Austria are admitted to the League of Nations.

Geneva, 18 December. Britain and France reach agreement on the frontiers of Syria and Palestine.

London, 23 December. The Government of Ireland Act, providing for the partition of Ireland between south and north, becomes law.

Italy, 31 December. Gabriele d'Annunzio hands over Fiume to Italy.

Somaliland, December. The Somali guerrilla leader Mohammed bin Abdullah (the "Mad *Mullah*") is killed by a chance bomb.

French troops occupy German Ruhr zone

A French tank in the streets of Frankfurt – "making the Germans pay".

Essen, Germany, 7 April

The risk of a dangerous international confrontation increased today when French troops were attacked by angry mobs as they advanced into the major cities of the Ruhr to counter a German breach of the Treaty of Versailles.

A number of people have been killed in skirmishes between German nationalists and French Moroccan soldiers. Student leaders are reported to have climbed onto motor cars to harangue the mobs.

The swift and decisive French move, which began with occupying Frankfurt yesterday, came after German forces had moved into the area in an attempt to block plans by armed communists to seize control of the industrial centre.

The German move, taking its troop levels in the neutral zone above the 40,000 threshold permitted by the Treaty of Versailles, has raised French fears that Germany plans to reoccupy the area. To defuse the situation the German government has sent a telegram to the Allies insisting that the communist threat in the area has become so serious that it could not wait any longer for permission to enter the Ruhr on a temporary basis.

America spurns the League of Nations

Washington, 19 March

President Woodrow Wilson's vision of a league of nations to end wars received a major setback today when the Senate refused to support US membership. Most of the opposition related to Article Ten, under which the US would have to go to war if another member were attacked. But there was also hostility to the voting rules which would give Britain and the dominions six votes.

There has been a long fight over the proposals. A Republican senator, Henry Cabot Lodge, had worked out a compromise solution acceptable to most senators, but Wilson, incapacitated by a stroke, refused to support it.

Mary Pickford, "the World's Sweetheart", founder of United Artists, with Douglas Fairbanks, Charlie Chaplin, D W Griffith.

Victorious allies redraw the map of the world as peace deals carve up empires

Sevres, France, 10 August
The final piece of the jigsaw of the post-war world was completed here today with former territories of the Ottoman empire divided amongst the victorious allies. Peace treaties earlier this year had already redrawn the map of Europe with that at St Germain creating Yugoslavia and Czechoslovakia; it also gave Galicia to Poland, Transylvania to Romania, and Istria, Trentino and South Tyrol to Italy. Agreement at Neuilly saw Greece and Yugoslavia acquire parts of Bulgaria. League of Nations mandates for the future of German colonies have also been agreed.

East Africa goes to Britain; most of the Cameroons to France, which shares Togoland with Britain; the Samoan Islands to New Zealand; and South-West Africa to South Africa. Germany itself was dealt with by the Treaty of Versailles in 1919 which gave territory to France, Denmark, Poland and Lithuania.

Russia's Red Army defeats the Whites

Moscow, 16 November
The bloody and chaotic civil war which has wracked Russia since the October Revolution is effectively over. Bolshevism has triumphed. The last of the "White" generals, Baron Wrangel – who supported the provisional government – has been beaten by Leon Trotsky's Red Army in the Crimea and evacuated with his men to Turkey.

The war has raged with varying fortunes since the winter of 1917-18. At one time communist rule was confined to an area similiar in size to that of the grand princes of Muscovy in the 15th century. The tide turned after Trotsky managed to whip the Red Army into shape, and Allied troops from Britain, Japan, the United States and some other countries had left. The Bolsheviks now control nearly all the former Russian empire with the exception of Poland, Finland, Bessarabia and the Baltic states.

The ultimate Red victory was due to the failure of the Whites to organise the peasants and to unify their aspirations. They also failed to work together. Lenin is now in charge of a poor, battered, starving, bankrupt country. Russia will need time to recover from its wounds.

Brave new world: Lenin addressing the Russian masses while Trotsky looks on.

US drinkers despair as prohibition bites

New York State troopers seizing booze, struggling to enforce the unenforceable.

Washington, DC, 16 January
The United States, the home of the mint julep, the gin sling and plain corn whiskey, has gone permanently on the wagon. And that's official. At one minute past midnight this morning the prohibition of the sale and consumption of alcohol became law, sanctioned under the Volstead Act, which was ratified in January 1919.

The temperance campaigners of the Anti-Saloon League, whose fight against the "demon drink" finds its roots in the sermonising of such 17th-century Puritan divines as Cotton Mather, and in the 19th-century campaigning of Carrie Nation, are jubilant. Their prime motivation has always been to preserve Christianity, even if the hard-headed businessmen whose votes in Congress actually made the law possible were more influenced by fears of the effect of too much liquor on their workforces. Stocks of alcohol have been seized, and a 1,500-strong body of enforcement agents is ensuring that the law sticks.

For those for whom drinking is no more than an admirable social pleasure, prohibition is one more example of the puritanism that has always been central to American life, running paradoxically hand-in-hand with a society that boasts of its devotion to freedom.

Gandhi formulates non-violent plan

Calcutta, September
The Indian National Congress has voted for Mohandas Gandhi's programme of non-cooperation with the British government. The programme, Gandhi told Congress, would win "complete responsible government" within a year.

Mr Gandhi's second victory is in persuading the predominately Hindu Congress Party to work with the Moslem *Khilafatist* movement. Indeed, Gandhi seems to be the only Indian leader capable of uniting the two communities.

An English concert is heard in Europe

Britain, 15 June
The voice of the singer Dame Nellie Melba was heard all over Europe by listeners who have wireless sets. Her voice could even be heard by radio enthusiasts in Newfoundland. It came from a concert promoted by the *Daily Mail* and broadcast by Marconi from its transmitter at Writtle, Chelmsford. The Marconi company obtained a licence for experimental broadcasts last year, but now there are complaints that the new medium should not be used merely for entertainment.

1921 (1921-1922)

Dublin, 22 January 1921. British tanks are sent into Dublin.

Russia, 5 February 1921. Anti-Soviet sailors mutiny at Kronstadt naval base outside Petrograd.

South Africa, 8 February 1921. Jan Smuts is elected prime minister.

Russia, 8 February 1921. Prince Peter Kropotkin, anarchist, dies.

Delhi, 9 February 1921. The new Indian Central Legislature opens.

Paris, 19 February 1921. France signs a military and economic pact with Poland.

Moscow, 26 February 1921. The Soviet government signs treaties respecting the territorial integrity of Persia and Afghanistan.

Germany, 8 March 1921. On account of Germany's failure to give a satisfactory response to demands for war reparations, Allied troops occupy Ruhr towns.

Moscow, 12 March 1921. Lenin announces that state planning of the economy will end and free enterprise will be permitted.

Russia, 17 March 1921. The anti-Bolshevik rebellion in Kronstadt is crushed by Red Army troops.

London, 17 March 1921. Marie Stopes opens Britain's first birth-control clinic.

Britain, 21 March 1921. Austen Chamberlain succeeds Andrew Bonar Law as Conservative leader.

China, 10 April 1921. Sun Yat-sen is elected president.

Sweden, 8 May 1921. Capital punishment is abolished.

Germany, 11 May 1921. Germany finally agrees to pay the war reparations demanded by the Allies.

Egypt, 23 May 1921. British troops are sent in to quell nationalist rioting in Alexandria.

Belfast, 22 June 1921. King George V opens the new Northern Ireland Parliament.

USA, 2 July 1921. President Harding signs a peace decree, formally ending the war with Germany and Austria.

China, 10 July 1921. Mongolia declares its independence as a people's republic, becoming the world's second communist state.

Ireland, 22 July 1921. Eamon de Valera, the president of *Sinn Fein*, agrees to a truce with the British government.

China, 23 July 1921. The first congress of the Chinese Communist Party is held in Shanghai.

Italy, 2 August 1921. The opera singer Enrico Caruso dies.

Ottoman Empire, 5 August 1921. Mustapha Kemal is appointed virtual ruler in the face of a Greek advance.

Baghdad, 23 August 1921. *Emir* Feisal is crowned king of Iraq.

India, 25 August 1921. Over 1,000 people die in riots on the Malabar coast.

Baltic, 22 September 1921. The Baltic states of Latvia, Lithuania and Estonia join the League of Nations.

Czechoslovakia, 26 September 1921. Eduard Benes becomes prime minister.

Berlin, 22 October 1921. The German government resigns as an economic crisis deepens.

Hungary, 25 October 1921. The ex-Emperor Karl is defeated in battle while attempting to regain the Hungarian throne.

Japan, 5 November 1921. Crown Prince Hirohito is made regent on the assassination of the prime minister, Takashi Hara Kei, the head of the first parliamentary government.

India, 17 November 1921. Riots break out in Bombay when Mohandas Gandhi, leader of the Indian Congress Party, burns foreign cloth during a visit by the prince of Wales.

Belfast, 21 November 1921. Troops are sent in to restore order as rioting breaks out in east Belfast.

Kabul, 22 November 1921. Britain signs a treaty recognising the independence of Afghanistan.

Ireland, 6 December 1921. An Anglo-Irish treaty is signed granting 26 counties of Ireland dominion status within the British empire as the Irish Free State.

Washington, DC, 13 December 1921. Britain, France, Japan and the USA sign a treaty aimed at controlling the naval build-up in the Pacific.

Britain, 1921. The novelist D H Lawrence publishes *Women in Love*, a sequel to *The Rainbow*, all copies of which were destroyed for obscenity in 1915.

Britain, 1921. Agatha Christie publishes her first detective novel, *The Mysterious Affair at Styles*.

South Atlantic, 5 January 1922. The British polar explorer Ernest Shackleton dies on the island of South Georgia.

Dublin, 21 January 1922. The *Dail Eireann* approves the treaty with Britain setting up the Irish Free State.

Rome, 22 January 1922. Pope Benedict XV dies.

Frontiers agreed in the Near East

Cairo, March 1921
The spoils of the Ottoman empire have finally been divided up, to the satisfaction of all save those who live there. At a conference chaired by the British colonial secretary, Mr Winston Churchill, and attended by such stars of British Near Eastern policy as T E Lawrence, Arnold Wilson, Sir Percy Cox and Miss Gertrude Bell, France's claims to Lebanon and Syria have been recognised. Iraq is to have Feisal (who led the Arab Revolt, and was expelled from Syria, where he had made himself monarch) as king; Palestine, with its mixture of Arabs, Christians and Jews, is to come under British control.

Whirling blades lift off helicopter

Paris, 18 February 1921
After a decade of experiments a gyroplane, or helicopter, has finally taken off. It is a triumph for its designer, Etienne Oehmichen, who has told the French Academy of Sciences how he built the machine with a light 25 hp motor, the whole structure weighing only 220 pounds (100 kilos). In theory, he says, an 8.5 hp motor can lift 297 pounds (135 kilos).

Other gyroplanes have been built, but they were powered by heavy and cumbersome motors and were only able to hover a few inches above the ground. Oehmichen can lift his machine; however, he has yet to stabilise it.

Italian Fascist chief calls himself "Duce"

Rome, 7 November 1921
A balding, heavily-jowled former editor, Benito Mussolini, declared himself *Il Duce* (the leader) of Italy's Fascists today and told businessmen that they could trust him and his followers to smash communism in the country.

Mussolini, a wartime corporal, has succeeded in uniting right-wing groups into a single force, and his blackshirted Fascists have been hired by businessmen to break up strikes and political meetings.

A one-time ardent socialist himself – he edited the party's paper, *Avanti*, before he was expelled – Mussolini formed his *Fasci di Combattimento* movement in Milan two years ago. Now it has 35 deputies in parliament.

Benito Mussolini: self-styled duce and bulwark against communism.

Spanish are driven from Morocco's Rif

Morocco, 19 September 1921
The Rif is declaring itself a republic. Since July, when 5,000 Rif tribesmen under Abd el Krim and his brother Mhamed inflicted a devastating defeat on a Spanish army at Anual, killing its general, Manuel Silvestre, the Spanish have been driven from all their Moroccan colony except for Tetuan, Chaoun and the coastal enclave of Melilla. The head of the new state is Abd el Krim himself, who has successfully united all the Rif clans against the Spanish. When the war is over he plans to hand over authority to Mhamed, his younger brother.

The el Krim brothers are no simple Berber tribesmen. Abd was educated at the university of Fez and has edited a Spanish Moroccan newspaper; Mhamed is a qualified engineer from the university of Madrid. Now they are Arab heroes, examples to all the oppressed people of the Moslem world, according to the Algerian writer Messali Hadj.

Bolsheviks appeal for aid as famine grips

Furlongs to furrows: a former racecourse is ploughed up to plant food.

Moscow, 4 August 1921
Russia is starving to death. No one can count the victims, but some seven million people may have died from hunger and disease since the Bolshevik Revolution. Vladimir Lenin, the Soviet leader, has admitted that not since 1891 has there been anything like it, and has appealed to the world community.

The worst-hit area is the huge Volga region east of Moscow where people are eating clay and twigs and cannibalism has appeared. Millions of peasants have slaughtered their starving cattle and are fleeing from the area and heading towards the towns to find food. Last year's drought, which wiped out the harvest, is the immediate cause of the famine, but the effects of the revolution and the civil war have also played a part. There are peasant disturbances, banditry and highway robberies. Lenin has been forced to make a strategic retreat from Marxism and has introduced a "New Economic Policy" restoring private trade and ending the arbitrary seizure of food from the peasants. But it has come too late to deal with the famine.

The United States has responded to Lenin's appeal and 800,000 tons of food are on the way. Food trains should soon reach the Ukraine.

Britain agrees Irish Free State package

London, 7 December 1921
Irish aspirations have at last won expression in a treaty creating an Irish Free State. It incorporates all of Ireland except six northern counties which stay with the UK. This effort to satisfy conflicting wishes of the Catholic majority and the descendants of the Protestants who settled three centuries ago contains an important ambiguity. The partition line is subject to a boundary commission report. Also, a council of Ireland is to discuss eventual reunification, though in time the Catholic birthrate could yield a voting majority in the north.

Insulin brings new hope to diabetics

Toronto, Ontario, 1921
A cure for diabetes is in sight. Drs Frederick Banting and Charles Best, working in Toronto, Canada, have succeeded in isolating the natural chemical – insulin – in which diabetics are deficient. With too little or no insulin produced by the pancreas, a person cannot regulate the amount of glucose (sugar) in the blood.

Banting and Best have experimented with insulin production in laboratory animals, and the chemical which they have obtained has a pronounced therapeutic effect on diabetes in other animals.

Germany agrees to pay war reparations

Berlin, 11 May 1921
The risk of a major international crisis over Germany's war debt has been narrowly averted at the last minute today, with the German government agreeing to pay the unpopular war reparations in full.

With only a few hours to go before the expiry of an Allied ultimatum to pay or face reoccupation, right-wing ministers in the coalition government withdrew their threats to resign if reparations were paid. Their resignations would almost certainly have brought the Weimar government down, precipitating a political crisis.

Anticipating a German refusal to pay, an advance Allied force of British, Belgian and French troops crossed the Ruhr eight weeks ago. The French government, which has spearheaded Allied demands that the Germans pay for war damage, has since mobilised its army for a further advance into the Ruhr.

Under the reparations deal Germany must pay £10 billion in gold over the next 42 years plus a 12.5 per cent tax levied on its exports.

US forced to set immigration quotas as unemployment soars

Washington, 19 May 1921
New immigration laws announced today lay down quotas limiting the yearly influx to three per cent of each nationality in the US in 1910. This ingenious proposal will favour groups from Britain, Ireland, Germany and Scandinavia, but severely restrict the newer waves from southern Europe and the Orient which have been flooding in much more recently.

Three groups have backed the measures. Organised labour is worried about unemployment; social reformers feel that the problem of the city slums will not be solved if tides of poor illiterates are not curbed; a third group thinks that any nonNordic race is inferior – it wants an absolute ban on Japanese immigration.

Immigration officers on Ellis Island sifting the tired and huddled masses.

Gandhi is jailed for sedition in India

Allahabad, India, 18 March 1922
Mohandas Gandhi, the Congress leader, has been sentenced to six years' imprisonment for sedition. Dressed in a simple loin-cloth and shawl, the British-trained barrister, the veteran of non-violent campaigns in both South Africa and India, pleaded guilty to all charges. Preaching disaffection, he told the judge, has "become almost a passion with me". He would "submit cheerfully to the highest penalty that could be inflicted".

He accepted responsibility for the violent riots in Malabar, Bombay and Chauri-Chaura, but would not renounce his policy of non-cooperation. Non-violence was the first and last article of his faith.

1922 (1922-1923)

Rome, 12 February 1922. Achille Ratti, the archbishop of Milan, is elected pope as Pius XI.

India, 13 February 1922. The Indian National Congress suspends its civil disobedience campaign.

The Hague, 15 February 1922. The Permanent International Court of Justice opens.

Italy, 5 March 1922. Fiume surrenders to the Fascists.

Egypt, 16 March 1922. Egypt formally declares independence under King Fuad.

China, May 1922. Peng Pai, a member of the Chinese Communist Party, begins to organise peasants for revolution in Haifeng, in Guangdong province.

Ireland, 16 June 1922. The pro-treaty party wins the first election in the Irish Free State.

London, 22 June 1922. Sir Henry Wilson, the former chief of the imperial general staff, is shot dead by IRA gunmen.

Berlin, 24 June 1922. Walther Rathenau, the foreign minister, is shot – extreme right-wing nationalists are suspected.

Dublin, 13 July 1922. The Irish Army Council is formed under the leadership of Michael Collins.

Ireland, 21 July 1922. Free State troops capture Waterford and Limerick from anti-Treaty rebels.

Paris, 24 July 1922. The League of Nations Council approves the British mandate in Palestine and the French mandate in Syria.

Italy, 4 August 1922. Mussolini's Fascists, who have already taken Bologna and the areas around Modena and Ferrara, take Milan.

Britain, 13 August 1922. Lord Northcliffe, the pioneer of popular newspapers, dies.

Ireland, 22 August 1922. The Irish nationalist leader Michael Collins is killed during an ambush in Cork. His death follows that of Arthur Griffith, the president of the *Dail Eireann*, last week.

Turkey, 29 August 1922. The Ottomans launch a major offensive against the Greeks to recover land lost after the Great War.

Balkans, August 1922. Rumania, Yugoslavia and Czechoslovakia sign a mutual defence agreement, establishing the "Little *Entente*".

Greece, 9 September 1922. The Greeks are ousted from Smyrna, ending their presence on the eastern Aegean seaboard.

Greece, 26 September 1922. Following the Greek defeat in Turkey, Constantine abdicates. He is succeeded by George II.

Turkey, 11 October 1922. The Ottomans and the Allies sign the treaty of Mudania, recognising Ottoman occupation of eastern Thrace.

London, 11 October 1922. Britain signs a treaty of alliance with Iraq.

Turkey, 15 October 1922. The Greeks sign the Mudania treaty and begin to evacuate Thrace.

Italy, 30 October 1922. Benito Mussolini becomes dictator.

Ottoman Empire, 1 November 1922. Mustapha Kemal abolishes the *sultanate*.

Berlin, 14 November 1922. Joseph Wirth resigns as chancellor over the economic crisis.

London, 14 November 1922. The newly-formed British Broadcasting Company makes its first regular news broadcast by wireless.

Britain, 16 November 1922. The Tories, led by Andrew Bonar Law, win an overall majority of 75 in a general election.

Britain, 21 November 1922. James Ramsay MacDonald is elected leader of the Labour Party.

Berlin, 22 November 1922. Wilhelm Cuno becomes chancellor.

Ottoman Empire, 24 November 1922. Ex-Sultan Abdul Majid II is installed as *caliph*.

Egypt, 26 November 1922. The archaeologists Howard Carter and the earl of Carnarvon uncover the treasures of the Pharoah Tutankhamun, buried 3,000 years ago, near Luxor.

Ireland, 5 December 1922. The Irish Free State is officially proclaimed.

Stockholm, 10 December 1922. The Danish physicist Niels Bohr wins the Nobel prize for physics for his work on atomic structure.

Russia, 30 December 1922. Soviet Russia is renamed the Union of Soviet Socialist Republics (USSR).

Paris, 1922. The bookseller Sylvia Beach brings out a limited edition of a novel by James Joyce entitled *Ulysses*, banned in the USA and Britain for obscenity.

China, 1 January 1923. The Haifeng Federation of Peasant Unions is inaugurated by Peng Pai.

Germany, 11 January 1923. In response to the German default in payment of reparations, French and Belgian troops occupy Essen.

China, 26 January 1923. A policy of cooperation (united front) between Chinese nationalists and communists is announced.

Germany, 27 January 1923. The National Socialist (*Nazi*) Party holds its first rally in Munich.

Broadcasting station opens in London

Lauritz Melchior, the Wagnerian tenor, broadcasting on 2LO from London.

London, 15 November 1922
The London broadcasting station, 2LO, went on the air yesterday for the first time as the British Broadcasting Company. A news bulletin was read by Arthur Burrows of the Marconi company from Marconi House in the Strand.

The Marconi company had been putting out weekly trial broadcasts since May, as had another station at Writtle, Chelmsford, run by Captain Peter Eckersley. Now the General Post Office (GPO) has decreed the formation of a single British Broadcasting Company as a consortium of wireless equipment manufacturers, to avoid the confusion that has arisen in America, where there are 500 rival stations. Today the BBC opens transmissions from Manchester and Birmingham. It hopes soon to broadcast for four hours a day, with news, talks and concerts.

John Reith, an engineer from Aberdeen, has been appointed general manager of the company, which is to be financed by the sale by the GPO of ten-shilling licences for the right to operate a receiver. For those who do not feel up to making their own crystal set, with "cat's whisker", the BBC offers sets at between £2 to £4, including headphones.

Beijing falls as war lords clash in China

Beijing, 28 April 1922
The Manchurian warlord Zhang Zuolin has been decisively beaten in battle today by his rival, Wu Peifu, and his army is retreating north in disorder leaving Wu Peifu firmly in control of Beijing.

In the chaos that rules in China this is more than just another fracas between warlords, for Wu Peifu is allied to Dr Sun Yat-sen who has returned from exile in Japan and set up his power base in the south, especially in the Guangzhou (Canton) area. An additional complication is that Zhang is paid by the Japanese while Wu Peifu is the pawn of Britain and the United States.

Modern art arrives in South America

Sao Paulo, Brazil, February 1922
A deliberately outrageous exhibition of contemporary Brazilian art has shocked Brazil's conservatives. The exhibition is the centrepiece for Sao Paulo's Modern Art Week, a festival of art exhibitions, concerts and poetry readings – which few Brazilians understand. Many of the paintings – if they can be called that – are by women, for example Anita Malfatti and Tarsila do Amaral, who take their Dadaist and Cubist perspectives from Paris and their revolutionary politics from Mexico. Needless to say, thanks to the wealth of their parents, they can afford to visit both places.

Mussolini marches into power in Italy

Rome, 30 October 1922
Singing the anthem *Giovinezza* (*Youth*), 30,000 blackshirted members of Benito Mussolini's Fascist movement marched from Naples to Rome today to force the government to resign and make way for their leader as dictator of Italy. Soon afterwards *Il Duce* himself arrived in an open car provided by King Victor Emmanuel – who has long feared a communist revolution in Italy.

The weak government was helpless, especially when it became clear that the Fascists would hold the balance of power. The sight of so many young men in Fascist uniforms was enough to make deputies surrender.

"Blackshirts" have carried on a vicious street war with communists and socialists for the past three years; now their leader proposes to introduce a new electoral law which limits the voters' choice to Fascist candidates. He has already threatened a ruthless campaign to extinguish left-wing parties – several of whose leaders have already fled. Mussolini proposes a corporate state in which private enterprise and state-managed industry could co-exist, with labour courts taking the place of strikes and lock-outs.

He is also going to institute a welfare programme with old age pensions and holidays provided for workers, if they are Fascists. As Mussolini stood with the king on the balcony of the Quirinal palace tonight, he brandished the party symbol – an axe surrounded by a bundle of rods. It is called a *fasces* and was once carried before the magistrates of ancient Rome.

Marching on Rome: Mussolini and his Fascist leaders – who came by car.

Family planning pioneer awarded libel damages

London, 1923
The ethics of sex education and contraception were brought into question during the recent nine-day libel case between Dr Marie Stopes and Dr Halliday Sutherland. She objected to his allegations that her birth control campaign encourages women's immorality and that she uses the poor as guinea pigs for her contraceptive experiments. Dr Stopes won and was awarded £100 in damages – despite a ruthless cross-examination by the defence and a summing-up from the judge which described as "obscene" her book *Married Love*. Her first clinic opened last year.

The birth control pioneer Marie Stopes and her three-month-old son.

British coalition government breaks up

London, 19 October 1922
David Lloyd George, Britain's prime minister for the past six years, was driven to Buckingham Palace today to tender his resignation to the king. The coalition government collapsed when Tories, meeting in the Carlton Club, voted by 187 to 87 to withdraw support for the fiery Welshman, who had wanted a vote to prolong the coalition and instead found himself with one to end it.

With most of his cabinet resigning around him, Lloyd George had no alternative but to resign. His principal supporter is Austen Chamberlain, the leader of the Tory Party, but he, too, has been ousted – disowned by his former supporters. Many Conservatives have long distrusted Lloyd George and his idiosyncratic style of government. Stanley Baldwin, the president of the board of trade, is an arch-enemy, and it was his speech at the Carlton Club that swayed many MPs and peers against the coalition. Lloyd George, he said, was threatening to split the Tory Party – just as he had almost wrecked the Liberals when he split with Asquith.

The king has invited Andrew Bonar Law to form a new government. He has agreed, but insists on a Tory vote of confidence.

David Lloyd George, the Welsh wizard who is running out of party tricks.

Joyce and Eliot give new life to words

London, 1 October 1922
A new literary magazine, *The Criterion*, contains a long poem by its editor, the American T S Eliot (who works in a City bank), entitled *The Waste Land*. It has been greeted as "incomprehensible" and "a literary game" because of its many allusions to other poets, like Dante and Shakespeare, and to the *Upanishads* alongside Cockneyisms, the whole calling up a spiritual desert.

Another obscure publication this year is the novel *Ulysses*, banned from Britain and the US for "immorality" — 500 copies were destroyed by the US Post Office. Its author, James Joyce, is a Dubliner; he has lived abroad since 1904, but his book is impregnated with his native city. The events of the *Odyssey* are paralleled by the doings of Leopold Bloom on a single June day in 1904. The characters' thoughts occur in "interior monologues" like Mrs Bloom's long soliloquy which closes the book.

Roentgen, X-ray pioneer, has died

Germany, 1923
The death has been announced, at the age of 77, of Wilhelm Roentgen, the German scientist and medical researcher who received the first Nobel prize for physics in 1901. Roentgen's name is synonymous with the now widespread use of so-called X-rays to examine the internal state of a body without the need for surgical intervention. These rays enable the doctor to study broken bones (which are denser than soft tissue) and patches of infection in the lungs, for instance.

1923 (1923-1924)

USSR, 9 March 1923. Vladimir Lenin retires from the Bolshevik leadership after a stroke.

India, 24 March 1923. The salt tax is restored.

Paris, 26 March 1923. The French actress Sarah Bernhardt dies.

Germany, 31 March 1923. Rioting Germans at the Krupps work at Essen in the French-occupied Ruhr are shot by French troops.

Paris, 13 April 1923. Madame Alfred Mortier is the first woman admitted to the Academie Francaise.

London, 28 April 1923. The Empire Stadium at Wembley stages its first sporting spectacular – the FA Cup Final.

Britain, 8 May 1923. Jack Hobbs, the Surrey and England batsman, scores his 100th century in first-class cricket.

Britain, 21 May 1923. Stanley Baldwin becomes Conservative prime minister on the resignation of Andrew Bonar Law.

France, 26 May 1923. The first 24-hour Le Mans Grand Prix is won by the Frenchmen Lagache and Leonard.

Britain, 7 June 1923. The Federation of British Industries is granted a royal charter.

Bulgaria, 9 June 1923. Alexander Stambouliski, the leader of the Peasant Party, is replaced as prime minister by Alexander Zankoff in an army *coup d'etat*.

Germany, 22 June 1923. The *mark* is trading at 622,000 to the pound sterling, having lost nearly half its remaining value since the start of the month.

Britain, 6 July 1923. Suzanne Lenglen of France wins the ladies' singles tennis championship at Wimbledon for the fifth successive year.

London, 18 July 1923. The Matrimonial Causes Bill, allowing wives to divorce their husbands for adultery, becomes law.

Mexico, 20 July 1923. Pancho Villa, the revolutionary turned rancher, is shot dead by gunmen.

Switzerland, 24 July 1923. Turkey, Greece and the Allies sign the treaty of Lausanne, whereby Armenia and territories in the Aegean lost after the Great War are restored to Turkey.

USA, 2 August 1923. Vice-president Calvin Coolidge succeeds to the presidency following the sudden death of Warren Harding.

Berlin, 12 August 1923. Chancellor Cuno resigns as the German economy collapses. Gustav Stresemann takes over.

Spain, 13 September 1923. Army officers led by Miguel Primo de Rivera and backed by King Alfonso XIII seize power.

Geneva, 10 September 1923. The Irish Free State is admitted to the League of Nations.

Germany, 26 September 1923. President Friedrich Ebert declares a state of emergency throughout the country.

Palestine, 29 September 1923. The British mandate officially begins.

Germany, 30 September 1923. Dr von Karr, the newly appointed dictator of Bavaria, imposes martial law on the province.

Rhodesia, 10 October 1923. Rhodesia (*Zimbabwe*), previously British South African Company administered, becomes a self-governing British colony.

Turkey, 12 October 1923. The Turkish capital is moved from Istanbul to Ankara.

Germany, 13 October 1923. With the approval of the *reichstag*, the government assumes dictatorial powers.

Germany, 20 October 1923. Bavaria breaks off relations with the *reich*.

Germany, 21 October 1923. A republic is declared in the Rhineland.

Germany, 27 October 1923. French troops occupy the Rhineland areas of Bonn and Wiesbaden.

Turkey, 29 October 1923. Mustapha Kemal proclaims Turkey a republic and himself its first president.

USA, October 1923. Albert Fall, the secretary of the interior, is implicated in the Teapot Dome oilfield-leasing scandal.

Berlin, 15 November 1923. A loaf of bread costs 200 billion marks.

Britain, 25 November 1923. The first transatlantic wireless broadcast to the USA is made.

Berlin, 29 November 1923. Dr Wilhelm Marx succeeds Stresemann as chancellor.

Stockholm, 10 December 1923. The Irish poet W B Yeats wins the Nobel prize for literature.

Britain, 11 December 1923. A general election results in a hung parliament.

Germany, 9 January 1924. Herr Heinz, the leader of the "Rhineland republic", is assassinated.

China, 20 January 1924. The first congress of the *Guomindang* (Nationalist Party) approves the "united front" of communists and nationalists.

Earthquake razes Tokyo

Tokyo in ruins, following the worst earthquake that Japan has ever experienced.

Tokyo, 1 September 1923

The Japanese capital, Tokyo, was devastated today by the worse earthquake that Japan has ever experienced. Half a million of Tokyo's houses have been destroyed, a million of its people made homeless, and 132,807 killed.

Towns and cities for hundreds of miles around have been levelled, including Yokohama, while the Fukuro, Chiyo and Takimi rivers have burst their banks, bringing the total number of dead to over 300,000, with 2.5 million homeless. In Tokyo – where martial law has been declared – and Yokohama essential services such as water and hospitals no longer exist, and there are fears of cholera and starvation.

Ku Klux Klan claims a million members

Baltimore, 30 June 1923

The Ku Klux Klan, notorious for its white hoods and flaming torches carried through the night to harass Negroes, Jews, Catholics and even any foreigners, now claims one million members. Its strength lies in the south; it was founded after the Negro slaves won their freedom in the civil war. It soon degenerated into anti-Negro terrorism and was disbanded in 1869. Revived in 1915, it has gradually widened its targets to include anyone who is not white and Protestant. The new imperial wizard is a dentist, Hiram Evans, who even opposes foreign alliances.

A Ku Klux Klan get-together in Georgia, articulating "poor white" fears.

Germany groans under crippling inflation

Clerks picking up their firms' wages from a Berlin bank in laundry baskets.

Berlin, 15 November 1923

In a desperate effort to rescue the country from raging inflation, the *Reichsbank* has invented a new German mark. It is to be called a *rentenmark* and will be tied to the country's real estate. Each rentenmark will be worth a trillion existing marks.

Since the beginning of the year inflation has spiralled out of control. In January a loaf of bread cost 250 marks – still high, compared with 63 *pfennigs* in 1918 – and by July it had reached 3,465. By this month the cost of the loaf had soared to 201,000,000,000 marks. A US dollar is worth four trillion marks – if you can find anyone who will sell a dollar. The pound sterling buys 20 trillion marks.

In effect, German money is now worthless; barter is increasingly being adopted for trading goods and services, and middle-class families who kept their wealth in banks have been wiped out.

The government cannot escape blame. When French and Belgian troops occupied the Ruhr in order to enforce war reparations, the Germans encouraged resistance and printed marks in limitless numbers to finance the fight, though industry was crippled and unable to produce the wealth.

Chinese gang seize 300 train hostages

China, 6 May 1923

Bandits swooped on the luxurious "Blue Express" at Lincheng last night. They killed an American who resisted, derailed the train, and then marched some 300 hostages, including a number of wealthy foreigners, to their impregnable hideout on top of Mount Baozigu.

The bandits, numbering around 1,000, are ex-soldiers from the disbanded army of a defeated warlord. They made an extraordinary sight hustling their captives away. They had looted the train, even taking mattresses from the sleeping berths. One man had a brassiere tied round his waist, using the cups to carry his loot. Their demands are awaited.

National hero leads Turkish republic

Turkey, 29 October 1923

Turkey, once the figurehead of the Ottoman empire, was proclaimed a republic today. Mustapha Kemal, under whose astute military leadership the Turks successfully expelled a Greek invasion, and who fought successfully for Turkish territory at the Lausanne conference, is to be the first president.

The Ottoman empire, which backed Germany in the Great War, was deprived of 80 per cent of its possessions in 1920. In his unyielding struggle to hold on to territories in which Turks formed a majority, the new president established himself as a national hero. His new post comes as a fitting reward.

Greece deposes its king, democratically

Athens, 25 March 1924

King George II of Greece was deposed today, voted out of office by the nation's parliament. Few were surprised: so unpopular was the king that he was forced to flee into exile last year, making his home in Rumania, the country of his wife, Queen Elizabeth.

George is the fourth successive Greek monarch to gain and then prematurely lose power since 1913, when George I was assassinated. The pro-German Constantine was forced to abdicate in 1917, and Alexander died of a monkey bite. Monarchy as an institution may well not survive in Greece. The people are determinedly republican at the moment, and crowds celebrated in the streets as they heard the news of George's deposition.

A referendum on the monarchy will follow soon, and the whole population will be given the chance to decide whether it wants yet more kings. Given the current mood, it seems unlikely. In the meantime Admiral Konduriotis is acting as regent.

Agitator starts revolution in beer cellar

Munich, 12 November 1923

A gang of men wearing brown shirts burst into a *bierkeller* (beer-cellar) here today. Its leader, a man with a toothbrush moustache, leapt on to a chair and fired a shot into the air. "The national revolution has begun!" he shouted.

The man has been identified as Adolf Hitler, the leader of the National Socialist (or *Nazi*) Party which is demanding dictatorship for the whole of Germany. In his harangue to an eager crowd Hitler called on people to march with him to Berlin.

He produced as his star supporter a somewhat reluctant Field-Marshal Erich von Ludendorff, the war hero.

Hitler, on parade before his bierkeller coup, with his "flag of blood".

"Element Mecanique" by Fernand Leger: an example of the abstract art which is developing, of which Pablo Picasso is a leading proponent.

1924 (1924-1925)

Moscow, 22 January 1924. A council is appointed to succeed Lenin: Gregory Zinoviev, Leon Kamenev and Joseph Stalin.

USSR, 26 January 1924. Petrograd is renamed Leningrad.

Rome, 27 January 1924. Mussolini signs a pact with Yugoslavia, annexing the free city of Fiume.

Rome, 27 January 1924. Mussolini dissolves the chamber of deputies.

Britain, 1 February 1924. Britain recognises the USSR.

India, 4 February 1924. Mohandas Gandhi is released from prison.

Italy, 7 February 1924. Italy recognises the USSR.

New York City, 12 February 1924. *Rhapsody in Blue* for jazz band and piano, by George Gershwin, is performed for the first time.

Ankara, 3 March 1924. Mustapha Kemal, Turkey's secular nationalist leader, who saved Turkey from Greek invasion, abolishes the *caliphate*.

Cairo, 15 March 1924. The first Egyptian parliament is opened.

Washington, DC, 28 March 1924. Harry Daugherty, the attorney-general, resigns in the Teapot Dome oilfield-leasing scandal.

Britain, March 1924. The airline Imperial Airways begins operation.

Germany, 1 April 1924. Adolf Hitler is jailed for five years for his abortive Munich beer-hall *putsch*.

Hollywood, USA, 16 April 1924. The new Metro-Goldwyn-Mayer film corporation is formed by merger.

Germany, 16 April 1924. Germany agrees to a new war reparations plan, drawn up by the American banker Charles Dawes.

Italy, 17 April 1924. Mussolini's fascist party wins a sweeping electoral victory.

Britain, 23 April 1924. King George V opens the British Empire Exhibition at Wembley Stadium.

April, 24 April 1924. Britain recognises the Greek republic.

India, April 1924. An epidemic of plague has claimed 25,000 victims.

Berlin, 6 June 1924. The *reichstag* votes in favour of the Dawes plan.

France, 13 June 1924. Gaston Doumergue is elected president.

South Africa, 17 June 1924. Jan Smuts loses his seat as nationalists win the general election.

Paris, July 1924. At the Olympic Games, Harold Abrahams and Eric Liddell triumph for Britain; while Paavo Nurmi, the "Flying Finn", wins five golds.

Germany, 17 August 1924. Following the signature by Germany and the Allies of the protocol on German war reparations, French and Belgian troops withdraw from the Ruhr.

USSR, 16 September 1924. The government quells a revolt in the southern republic of Georgia.

Britain, 9 October 1924. The minority Labour government falls after losing a vote of censure.

France, 12 October 1924. The author Anatole France dies.

Arabia, 20 October 1924. Having forced the abdication of Hussein, king of the Arabs since 1916, Wahabi forces under ibn Saud enter Mecca.

London, 24 October 1924. The foreign office publishes the "Zinoviev letter", allegedly from Moscow, urging a revolution in Britain.

France, 28 October 1924. France recognises the USSR.

Britain, 31 October 1924. The Tories win a huge victory in a general election following the scare over the Zinoviev letter.

USA, 4 November 1924. Calvin Coolidge is returned to the presidency.

Rome, 12 November 1924. Mussolini opens Italy's new one-chamber parliament.

Cairo, 19 November 1924. Sir Lee Stack, the governor general of the Sudan, is shot dead by Egyptians.

Cairo, 24 November 1924. Zaghlol Pasha resigns as prime minister after refusing to apologise to Britain for the death of Stack.

Moscow, 26 November 1924. A special session of the Communist Party called by Stalin, Zinoviev and Kamenev denounces Trotsky.

Germany, 20 December 1924. Adolf Hitler is freed on parole after serving just eight months of his jail term for treason.

Albania, 24 December 1924. Albania is declared a republic.

Britain, 1924. The novelist E M Forster publishes *A Passage to India*.

Norway, 1 January 1925. The capital, Christiania, is renamed Oslo.

Rome, 5 January 1925. Having assumed full dictatorial powers, Mussolini forms a new cabinet.

Germany, 15 January 1925. Hans Luther, an independent, becomes chancellor.

Turkey, 30 January 1925. Constantine II, the Greek Orthodox patriarch, is expelled from Istanbul.

Socialist government comes to Britain

Ramsay MacDonald, the new Labour prime minister, with his supporters.

London, 22 January 1924

James Ramsay MacDonald, a weaver's son from Scotland, emerged through the gates of Buckingham Palace today as the first Labour prime minister of Great Britain. MacDonald will head a minority government which will depend on Liberal MPs for support. Few believe that any of Labour's socialist policies can be implemented.

MacDonald has named mass unemployment as his government's principal target. An ambitious slum-clearance and house-building programme will also be introduced.

The new prime minister has been forced to deliver powerful lectures to left-wingers in the Labour Party, many of whom were prepared to oppose his decision to accept power on these terms. Some of them were demanding salary cuts for cabinet members. MacDonald dismissed the notion. He had good reason to: unlike previous prime ministers, he and his family are poor, and when the MacDonalds moved into 10 Downing Street tonight they had no more than a few scraps of furniture. "We are camping out in one room while the country's destiny is being decided in the cabinet room next door," his daughter told friends. The ministry of works is helping out.

Gandhi goes on a hunger strike

Allahabad, 18 September 1924

Mohandas Gandhi, serving six years' imprisonment for sedition, is to fast for 21 days. He calls the fast "an effective prayer to Hindus and Moslems not to commit suicide".

The announcement comes after days of communal rioting between the two communities. Hundreds have been killed and driven from their homes. Even as he spoke, Moslems and Hindus were being killed in Kohat. A pacifist and believer in universal toleration, he speaks sadly of his "unbearable hopelessness".

Big socialist murals brighten Mexico

Mexico City, 1924

The public buildings of Mexico City are being transformed by the Mexican artist Diego Rivera, lately returned from painting in Paris. A massive man, over six feet, weighing 21 stone, he works on a massive scale in fresco. His murals commissioned for the new ministry of education cover over 1,900 square yards with scenes of peasants and revolutionaries. His best-known mural, *The Distribution of Land to the Peasants*, is inspired, like all his work, by passionate Socialism.

Lenin, Soviet Russia's founder, dies

Moscow, 21 January 1924
The middle-class lawyer who made a revolution on behalf of workers and peasants died today after a series of debilitating strokes. Vladimir Ilyich Ulyanov, who called himself Lenin, was 54.

His death sets the stage for a power struggle in the six-year-old Soviet state. Leon Trotsky, the spellbinding visionary who created the Red Army, is mistrusted for his very brilliance. The Communist Party general secretary, Joseph Stalin, seems certain to make a bid for power, even though Lenin warned against his bullying ways.

Lenin, the third of five sons of a schools' director in Simbirsk, on the Volga, took up revolution after his brother Alexander was executed for his part in the attempted assassination of Czar Alexander III. Exiled to Siberia for subversive activities, Lenin met and married Krupskaya, an idealistic social worker. They lived abroad for much of their life. In London, Lenin spent his time studying in the British Museum library. After the 1917 seizure of power, he nationalised all business and industry, shops, banks and agriculture. In the summer of 1921, when the Russian economy had ground to a halt, Lenin produced the New Economic Policy, allowing private trade in goods and farm produce; rationing was abandoned and workers were paid by results. He denied that he was giving up socialism. "It's two steps forward, one step back," he said.

Russians queuing for hours outside the Kremlin, to file past the body of Lenin, the father of the Russian revolution.

China's nationalists seek Russian help

China, 20 January 1924
Sun Yat-sen's Nationalist Party, or *Guomindang*, opened its first congress at Guangzhou (Canton) today. Dr Sun, disappointed by the warlords and refused support by the western powers, has turned to the Soviet Union for help.

The Bolsheviks have sent one of their top agents, Michael Borodin, to advise Dr Sun, and such is his influence that he is reputed to have drafted the Guomindang's constitution. Among the moves agreed is that the Chinese Communist Party will join the Nationalists to form a "united front".

Winter sports get Olympic treatment

Chamonix, 31 January 1924
The first series of winter sports competitions sanctioned by the International Olympic Committee finished here, in this French Alpine resort, today.

So great was the opposition to the committee's decision that the week-long contests have yet to be given the official title of "Olympic Games", but every sport drew top-class performances from the competing teams. Sportsmen, and a few women, from 18 nations took part, notably the Norwegian Thorleif Haug, the master of cross-country ski-ing and the Finn Clas Thunberg, an outstanding skater.

Gold medallist Tullin Thams ski-jumping in the Chamonix games.

Italian Fascists kill Socialist opponent

Rome, 10 June 1924
Few people dare to speak their minds freely in Mussolini's Italy. One man did last week: a deputy in the Chamber, Giacomo Matteotti, who denounced the Fascists and the atmosphere of terror in which they conducted the elections. He gave details of the extent of the frauds used to obtain huge Fascist majorities, and demanded that the elections be declared void. At the end of a passionate speech he told deputies: "And now get ready for my funeral." He knew. He was abducted in the street today, and is assumed to have been murdered.

Britain plans naval base in Far East

Singapore, 19 March 1925
Britain is to reinforce its network of strategic links with the empire with the establishment of a major new naval base at Singapore.

The proposed £400,000 base, incorporating a huge floating dock seized from Germany, will serve as a vital supply and maintenance centre for the Royal Navy in the Far East, securing vital links with Hong Kong and other British possessions in the Pacific.

Many MPs, led by the Labour Party leader Ramsay MacDonald, are concerned that Japan will see the new base as a threat.

Soldier's tale is a musical milestone

Vienna, 1925
Alban Berg, the Austrian composer, has opened new musical horizons with his latest opera *Wozzeck*, premiered this year in Berlin. The three-act tale of a soldier's downfall shows just how expressive the new "dissonant" music can be. It is a powerful work, with styles ranging from cafe music to crunching counterpoint, and passages harking back to Mahler. Berg, like his fellow-Austrian Anton von Webern, is an old pupil of Arnold Schoenberg, the man who pioneered "atonal" music – music without keys – in 1908.

1925 (1925-1926)

Germany, 14 February 1925. The state of emergency and ban on the *Nazi* Party is lifted in Bavaria.

Austria, 2 March 1925. A new currency is introduced, the *schilling*.

China, 12 March 1925. On the death of Sun Yat-sen, Chiang Kai-shek becomes leader of the *Guomindang* (Nationalist Party).

Austria, 30 March 1925. Rudolf Steiner, the founder of "anthroposophy", dies.

Australia, 8 April 1925. The government announces a scheme to encourage large-scale immigration.

Britain, 14 April 1925. The American-born painter John Singer Sargent dies.

Turkey, 16 April 1925. A Kurdish uprising against the government of Mustapha Kemal is quelled.

Morocco, 23 April 1925. Troops of the rebel Rif leader Abd el Krim enter French Morocco.

Germany, 25 April 1925. Paul von Hindenburg becomes Germany's first directly elected president.

Britain, 28 April 1925. Winston Churchill, chancellor, puts Britain on the gold standard.

Britain, 30 April 1925. The Distillers whisky group is formed.

Paris, April 1925. The Exposition des Arts Decoratifs reflects the growing popularity of "Art Deco".

Cyprus, 1 May 1925. The island becomes a British colony.

South Africa, 8 May 1925. Afrikaans is made an official language of the Union.

China, 30 May 1925. British police kill demonstrators protesting at working conditions in Japanese-owned factories in Shanghai's international settlement.

Detroit, 6 June 1925. Walter P Chrysler founds the Chrysler Motor Company.

Greece, 25 June 1925. General Theodoros Pangalos seizes power in a *coup d'etat*.

South Africa, 29 June 1925. A law is passed further excluding Blacks, Coloureds (people of mixed race) and Indians from all skilled jobs.

China, June 1925. The "30 May incident" leads to protests in Hankou and Guangzhou – foreign troops kill more demonstrators.

China, 1 July 1925. The Nationalists begin a "northern expedition" to reunify China.

Britain, 31 July 1925. The government agrees to pay a subsidy to coal-mine owners in order to end a month-long strike in the pits.

Washington, DC, 8 August 1925. The first national congress of the Ku Klux Klan opens.

Britain, 18 August 1925. The Surrey batsman Jack Hobbs surpasses W G Grace's record of 126 centuries in top-class cricket.

Rome, 20 August 1925. Rome's first underground rail line opens.

China, 7 September 1925. Anti-British rioters are shot in Shanghai.

Switzerland, 16 October 1925. Germany signs a mutual security pact with Britain, France, Belgium and Italy at Locarno. The pact also affirms the postwar frontiers set out in the Versailles Treaty and accepts Rhineland demilitarisation.

Paris, 28 October 1925. Paul Painleve forms a left-wing cabinet.

Persia, 31 October 1925. Reza Khan deposes *Shah* Ahmed Mirza, ending the Kajar dynasty.

USSR, 6 November 1925. Kliment Voroshilov is chosen to succeed Trotsky as head of the Red Army.

Germany, 9 November 1925. The Nazi *Schutzstaffel* (Protection Squad), or SS, is founded.

Paris, 14 November 1925. The first Surrealist exhibition opens. Artists exhibiting include Max Ernst, Paul Klee, Joan Miro and Picasso.

Paris, 28 November 1925. Following the resignation of Paul Painleve, Aristide Briand forms his eighth ministry.

London, 3 December 1925. Stanley Baldwin, the prime minister, signs an agreement fixing the frontier between Northern Ireland and the Irish Free State.

Stockholm, 10 December 1925. The Irish writer G B Shaw wins the Nobel prize for literature.

California, 12 December 1925. The first "motel" in the USA opens in San Luis Obispo.

USSR, 21 December 1925. *Battleship Potemkin*, a film by Sergei Eisenstein, opens.

Britain, 1925. The "Charleston", the dance that scandalised America, takes Britain by storm.

London, 1925. A surgeon, Henry Souttar, performs the first surgical operation inside the heart.

Germany, 6 January 1926. The airline *Lufthansa* is founded.

Paris, 12 January 1926. The Pasteur Institute announces the discovery of an anti-tetanus serum.

Berlin, 10 January 1926. Fritz Lang's film *Metropolis* opens.

Germany, 30 January 1926. British troops end a seven-year occupation of the Rhineland.

Three million dead in Chinese famine

China, 1925

Famine, the perennial scourge of China, is once again ravaging this vast country which is in turn both bountiful and cruel. This year it is Szechuan's turn to suffer. The crops have failed in the rich plain along the capricious Yangzi, and some three million people have already starved to death.

The villages present dreadful scenes, with bodies lying unburied in the streets, torn by dogs and crows and, sometimes, with pieces hacked off them by starving relatives turned cannibal. Many once prosperous communities are deserted. Their inhabitants have fled in a great migration to the virgin lands of Manchuria in search of food and security – for it is not only the failure of their crops which has brought death to them, but also the anarchy which covers the land.

Rival armies march across the fields, destroying, looting and killing. Peasants turned brigands take what is left. The misery of the innocent people is heartbreaking to see.

Genesis view triumphs in "monkey trial"

Scopes arriving at the Tennessee court room with Clarence Darrow (right).

Dayton, Tennessee, 21 July 1925

The "monkey trial", which has brought the world's press crowding into the tiny courtroom here, ended today with victory for the religious fundamentalists. A biology teacher, John Scopes, was found guilty of teaching evolution in a state school and fined $100. He is expected to appeal to the state's supreme court.

Scopes was accused of violating a law passed by the Tennessee legislature earlier this year banning the teaching of theories denying the divine creation of man as told in the Bible. The indictment charged that he "did teach thereof that man has descended from a lower order of animals".

The trial was a battle royal. Prosecuting was William Jennings Bryan, a spell-binding orator and former Democratic candidate for president. Leading for the defence was Clarence Darrow of Chicago, one of the finest lawyers in the country. Outside the court hundreds of fundamentalists cheered, sang hymns and prayed for a favourable verdict.

Bryan ridiculed Darwin's theory of human descent from monkeys. Darrow challenged him. "The creation might have been going on for a long time?" he asked. "It might have continued for millions of years," Bryan admitted. But the judge stressed that the schoolroom was the place in which to teach discipline, restraint and character, not to violate the laws. At one point he himself read the creation story from Genesis. On another occasion he adjourned the court after gales of laughter had greeted Bryan's attempts to advocate biblical truth.

Trotsky falls from grace

Commissar of War, Leon Trotsky, addressing Red soldiers before being ousted.

Moscow, 16 January 1925
Leon Trotsky, who played a leading role in organising and carrying out the Bolshevik Revolution, has been ousted from leadership in the Soviet Communist Party by Joseph Stalin, his deadly rival. Trotsky has been sacked as commissar for war and is effectively under house arrest. The *Cheka* security police, which are under Stalin's control, have rounded up hundreds of Trotsky's allies and bundled them off into exile in remote areas of Russia.

Trotsky's position in the ruling *Politburo* has been growing steadily weaker since the death of Lenin last year, and he is the first major victim of the power struggle that followed. It is inconceivable that he will ever be able to make a comeback.

Trotsky, an intellectual who has lived most of his life outside Russia, has emerged as too individualistic and restless to be a good politician. He has certainly proved himself to be no match at all for Stalin, the Georgian who became the party secretary in 1922 and had consolidated his grasp on the party apparatus before Lenin's death.

In the inter-party struggle Stalin cleverly allied himself with the leading Bolsheviks Zinoviev and Kamenev to defeat Trotsky, using the slogan of "building socialism at first in one country" to counter Trotsky's call for "permanent revolution".

Hitler tells his tale in "Mein Kampf"

Munich, Germany, 1925
Adolf Hitler, whose *putsch* with Field-Marshal von Ludendorff ended ignominiously in 1923, has written a book. Most was written in the Landsberg fortress, dictated to his cellmate Rudolph Hess.

It is not easy to read. Like James Joyce's *Ulysses*, it needs to be read twice. Hitler writes of the cleansing nature of war, blames Germany's defeat on Jews and communists, and glorifies Germany's ancient myths. The book is called *Four and a Half Years of Struggle against Lies, Stupidity and Cowardice*. Friends suggested he shorten the title to *Mein Kampf* (My Struggle).

Ibn Saud proclaims rule from Riyadh

Mecca, 8 January 1926
All the *sheikhs*, merchant princes and *imams* of the Hejaz gathered in the Grand Mosque today to witness a ceremony honouring Abdul Aziz ibn Saud as king of the Hejaz – which he proposes to rename Saudi Arabia.

Having set out from exile in Kuwait 24 years ago to capture his home city of Riyadh, ibn Saud reached the pinnacle of power last month when he arrived in Jeddah in triumph to accept the city's surrender. His traditional enemy, Hussein, the sheikh of Mecca, had already abdicated, and was followed into exile by his son Ali.

Jazz Age inhabits a nightmare castle and a sanatorium with art deco style

Novelists of the 1920s: F Scott Fitzgerald, Franz Kafka and E M Forster.

The distinctive tone of the Twenties can now be heard in its literature. F Scott Fitzgerald has become a symbol of what he christened "the Jazz Age", which "raced along under its own power served by great filling stations full of money". *The Great Gatsby* is about an American dream soured by money. A fellow American, Ernest Hemingway, has cultivated the style of a camera shutter, deliberately withholding warmth in his novel of Americans in Europe, *The Sun Also Rises*.

The European novel has also changed. Works of Franz Kafka, an insurance official in Prague, have been published posthumously against his instructions. They take their readers into a waking nightmare in *The Trial* and *The Castle*, symbols of an alienating and hostile system. Thomas Mann has set *The Magic Mountain* in a sanatorium, his characters decaying as the world outside goes mad.

In *A Passage to India*, the English novelist E M Forster has discomfited many by describing Anglo-Indian relations very differently from Kipling. The new voice of Virginia Woolf seeks to capture consciousness, inner and outer, in a myriad of facets, *Mrs Dalloway* being her boldest experiment so far.

In the visual arts, too, there is a distinctive Twenties style, christened "Art Deco", or International Style. France's ultra-modern architect Le Corbusier designed the Pavilion of New Spirit for the 1925 Paris Exhibition, a year that saw two major exhibitions characterising the era, the Exposition des Arts Decoratifs, celebrating Art Deco, and an extraordinary exhibition of the new surrealism.

A dining room in the Art Deco style: note the curved "ocean liner" lines, the rich and luxurious colours, and the Pharaonic-Hollywood ambience.

1926 (1926-1927)

Geneva, 13 March 1926. Germany is refused a permanent place on the League of Nations council.

Britain, 13 March 1926. Alan Cobham ends a 16,000-mile return flight from London to Cape Town.

Italy, 7 April 1926. Benito Mussolini survives a third attempt on his life.

India, 24 April 1926. The first Hindu-Moslem riots for many years break out in Calcutta.

Berlin, 24 April 1926. Germany signs a friendship treaty with the USSR.

Persia, 25 April 1926. Ali Reza Khan Pahlavi is crowned *shah*.

Britain, 1 May 1926. A national coal strike over proposed pay cuts and longer working hours begins.

India, 2 May 1926. Indian women are granted the right to stand for election to public office.

Britain, 3 May 1926. The first general strike in British history begins after the Trades Union Congress votes to back the miners.

Britain, 12 May 1926. The TUC calls off the general strike.

Poland, 13 May 1926. Josef Pilsudski takes control after leading a military *coup*.

Alaska, 13 May 1926. An international team of flyers completes the first-ever trip over the north pole in an airship.

Germany, 17 May 1926. The Center Party candidate Wilhelm Marx becomes chancellor again.

Britain, 20 May 1926. The miners resolve to fight on alone.

Morocco, 26 May 1926. The rebel leader Abd el Krim surrenders to a French-led force.

Portugal, 28 May 1926. General Manuel Gomes da Costa seizes power in a *coup d'etat*.

London, 8 June 1926. The soprano Nellie Melba gives her farewell performance at Covent Garden.

Geneva, 10 June 1926. Brazil leaves the League of Nations.

Britain, 25 June 1926. The American Bobby Jones becomes the first amateur since 1897 to win the Open Golf Championship.

Canada, 28 June 1926. The Liberal prime minister William Mackenzie King and his cabinet resign in the wake of a customs scandal.

Portugal, 9 July. General de Costa, who seized power in May, is overthrown by General Carmona.

Britain, 6 August 1926. Gertrude Ederle from the USA becomes the first woman ever to swim the Channel, cutting more than two hours off the record time.

Greece, 22 August 1926. A coup led by Georgios Condylis overthrows the regime of Theodoros Pangalos.

USA, 23 August 1926. The Italian-born film star Rudolf Valentino dies.

Germany, 29 August 1926. A *Nazi* Party rally is held at Nuremberg.

Spain, 7 September 1926. Spain leaves the League of Nations after being denied a permanent seat on the council.

Geneva, 8 September 1926. The League of Nations votes to admit Germany as a member.

Canada, 25 September 1926. Mackenzie King's Liberals are returned to power in an election.

London, 1 October 1926. Alan Cobham completes a record 28,000-mile round trip to Australia by air.

Italy, 7 October 1926. The Fascist Party is decreed the party of the state. Mussolini assumes total power and bans all opposition.

Britain, 14 October 1926. A A Milne publishes *Winnie-the-Pooh*, a book for children.

Moscow, 23 October 1926. Leon Trotsky and Gregory Zinoviev are expelled from the Communist Party central committee.

USA, 31 October 1926. The Hungarian-born escape artist Harry Houdini dies.

Britain, 2 November 1926. Imperial Chemical Industries (ICI) is formed.

South-East Asia, 12 November 1926. Nationalists in the island of Java launch a rebellion against Dutch rule.

Britain, 19 November 1926. Miners end their six-month pit strike, agreeing to work longer hours.

Italy, 15 December 1926. The Roman *fasces*, the symbol of authority and origin of the word "fascist", is adopted as the national emblem.

Japan, 25 December 1926. Hirohito ascends the throne on the death of his father, the Emperor Yoshihito.

Dublin, 1926. A fight breaks out on stage during a performance of Sean O'Casey's *The Plough and the Stars*, about the Easter Rising.

Britain, 1 January 1927. The British Broadcasting Corporation comes into being.

India, 8 January 1927. The first scheduled London-Delhi flight arrives.

Britain, 4 February 1927. Malcolm Campbell sets a world land-speed record of 174.224 mph in his car, *Bluebird*.

Old empire turns into commonwealth

London, 20 November 1926

The greatest empire that there has ever been today acquired an extra title. An imperial conference in London, taking note of the self-reliance acquired by the self-governing dominions during the war, decided that Canada, Australia, New Zealand, South Africa and Newfoundland should have equal status with Britain as members of the British Commonwealth of Nations. Each dominion will acknowledge George V as its king. His title is now "George V, by the Grace of God, of Great Britain, Ireland and the British Dominions beyond the Seas, King, Defender of the Faith, Emperor of India".

The empire, including colonies and protectorates in Africa, the South Pacific and the South Atlantic, represents one-fifth of the land area of the entire globe. The first colony was Newfoundland, acquired in 1583.

Moralists attack degenerate new fashions

Causing a flap: Charlestoning.

Causing more flaps: Oxford bags.

Rome, 1926

Catholic bishops in Italy are banbing scantily-dressed women from church and criticising women's new involvement in sport as "incompatible" with a woman's dignity.

Outrage at women's fashions and manners is not confined to bishops. Traditionalists claim that women's morals decline as their hemlines rise. Many find men's fashions no less ridiculous, particularly the acres of flannel called "Oxford bags" which young men wear.

Not so George Bernard Shaw. In England he is encouraging wearers of short, light dresses, saying that they are for "real human beings" rather than "upholstered Victorian angels". But doctors warn that fashion slaves of the current Art Deco-style boyish look are weakening their health by obsessive dieting. Others believe that dances like the "Charleston" can cause complications in future childbirth.

The trend for rich modern women to live frivolous lives of parties and wild American dancing puts them at risk, too. Dr J S Russel told the institute of hygiene this year that women are turning to drink and drugs in a desperate bid to cope with their hectic lives.

Strike paralyses Britain's industry

England, 20 May 1926
Despite a resolution by the Trades Union Congress to call off the general strike which has threatened to paralyse the country, Britain's miners – feeling "deserted" by their brother trades unionists – vowed at a delegate conference to continue industrial action; but the national strike has failed.

The trades unions had neither the will nor the cash to support it, particularly when 5,500 trains were running – many of them driven by eager volunteers – and troops were unloading food at London Docks and delivering it throughout London.

Many believed that the general strike would be a signal for violent social upheaval, but there was little sign of this during the nine days in which only one newspaper was published – the *British Gazette*, edited by Winston Churchill – and the BBC fought off attempts at government control of its news.

Some trains were derailed, and public vehicles were driven off the road in Glasgow where looting took place. For thousands of undergraduates and railway enthusiasts, it was a time to put on official armbands and drive trains, buses and lorries, breaking the law with abandon.

Moving images are sent by wireless

Baird with the two ventriloquist's dolls were the first images to be televised.

London, 27 January 1926
The transmission of moving images by wireless was demonstrated in London today by John Logie Baird, a Scottish engineer of 38. He calls the process "television".

Before an audience at the Royal Institution he managed to project flickering and indistinct pictures of two ventriloquist's dolls on to a screen with the aid of an electrical camera which converts the image into electronic signals. These are transmitted by wireless and recreated through a cathode-ray tube by a 240-line scanning process.

The result is far from equal to film images on a cinema screen, but Mr Baird, who gave up his job with a Clyde Valley electric power company in order to concentrate on his research, believes that one day there will be a television screen in every home.

Savage race riots break out in India

Calcutta, 24 April 1926
The brief unity of Hindus and Moslems that Gandhi brought about after the war is over. Gandhi's dream of the two communities united in the struggle for nationhood is spattered with blood. Already 151 have died here in the worst communal riots within memory. Many of the bodies are horribly mutilated. The rioting started over a rumour – that two Moslems had been beaten to death by Hindus – which turned out to be untrue.

Rockets penetrate upper atmosphere

USA, c.1926
The rocket is emerging as a scientific tool for exploring space, and the father of modern rocketry is undoubtedly the American professor of physics at Clark university, Robert Goddard.

Goddard's rockets are designed to study the upper atmosphere about a mile above Earth. From the Russian Tsiolkovsky, Goddard borrowed the idea of multi-stage vehicles which discard successive spent-fuel units. He is experimenting with a variety of solid and liquid fuels.

Final blink for once-reviled eye of "Impressionist" founder

Giverny, Normandy, 6 Dec 1926
Claude Monet has died, aged 86, at the house where he had lived for 40 years, with its garden and lilyponds which he so often painted.

He was the first "Impressionist" – the name was derived from one of his works, *Impression – Sunrise* – and the last survivor of the group that exhibited to incomprehension and ridicule from 1874 to 1886. His huge output includes series of paintings done under varying light conditions of haystacks, poplars, Rouen cathedral, the steamy Gare St Lazare, and the Thames. Monet worked on several paintings at once, changing them with the weather. "My strong point is knowing when to stop," he said. "Only an eye," Cezanne said of him, "but my God, what an eye!"

Monet's "Gare St Lazare", painted shortly before his battle with blindness.

Revolt threatens to engulf Austria

Vienna, 15 July 1927
Eighty-nine people have died in rioting that engulfed Austria's capital, Vienna, today. As armed police fired on crowds of workers, the ministry of justice was set on fire and many shops were looted and burnt. The trouble began when three members of the right-wing *Kampfer* party were acquitted of last January's murder of two communists, killed during a political *fracas*. Left-wing orators urged the revenge murders of judges, juries and the middle class. The enraged masses duly took to the streets.

The *Volkswehr* reserve, called out by Chancellor Siegel, refused to defend law and order, but the police proved loyal to the authorities.

1927 (1927-1928)

Paris, 6 February 1927. Yehudi Menuhin, a ten-year-old violinist of Russian-Jewish parentage, causes a sensation with his playing.

Lisbon, 9 February 1927. Antonio Carmona, who seized power in a *coup* last year, puts down an attempted revolution.

China, 21 March 1927. The victorious Nationalist army of Chiang Kai-shek enters Shanghai.

Britain, 26 March 1927. The Gaumont-British Film Corporation is founded.

Florida, 29 March 1927. A Briton, Henry Segrave, sets a new world land-speed record of 203.841 mph.

Paris, 7 April 1927. Abel Gance's film *Napoleon* has its premiere.

Cardiff, 21 April 1927. The National Museum of Wales opens.

China, April 1927. Chiang Kai-shek carries out a coup against left-wing elements, killing trade union activists and communists, leading to the break-up of the united front. The communists are driven into the rural areas.

Canberra, 9 May 1927. The new Australian Parliament House is opened by the duke of York.

Saudi Arabia, 20 May 1927. Britain signs the treaty of Jeddah, recognising the independence of Saudi Arabia.

Britain, 24 May 1927. Britain severs diplomatic relations with the USSR amid accusations of espionage and subversion throughout the British empire.

Czechoslovakia, 27 May 1927. Tomas Masaryk is re-elected president.

South-East Asia, 4 June 1927. Ahmed Sukarno founds the Indonesian Nationalist Party.

USSR, 9 June 1927. The Russians execute 20 people accused of being British spies.

Britain, 14 June 1927. The writer Jerome K Jerome, the author of *Three Men in a Boat*, dies.

Britain, 23 June 1927. Parliament passes the Trade Disputes Act, making sympathetic strikes illegal.

Britain, 30 June 1927. The US team wins the first Ryder Cup professional golf tournament.

Dublin, 10 July 1927. Kevin O'Higgins, the vice-president of the Irish Free State, is shot dead.

Vienna, 15 July 1927. Government troops put down communist riots and strikes provoked by the acquittal of nationalists for political murder.

Romania, 21 July 1927. Prince Mihail, aged five, succeeds King Ferdinand.

China, August 1927. Ye Ting and He Long lead a communist uprising in Nanchang, in Jiangxi province, holding the city for a few days.

France, 14 September 1927. The American dancer Isadora Duncan is strangled when her shawl is caught in a car wheel.

Geneva, 15 September 1927. Canada is elected to the League of Nations council.

Germany, 16 September 1927. President von Hindenburg repudiates German responsibility for the Great War.

China, 19 September 1927. The "autumn harvest uprising" which began earlier in the month, under the leadership of Mao Zedong (Tse-tung), suffers a serious defeat.

Ireland, 20 September 1927. President William Cosgrave wins his second Irish Free State general election in three months with an effective majority of six.

Moscow, 1 October 1927. The USSR signs a non-aggression pact with Persia.

Iraq, 15 October 1927. Iraq's first oil strike is made at Kirkuk.

Norway, 17 October 1927. The first Labour government is elected.

China, October 1927. Remnants of Mao's uprising move to the Jinggang mountains in Jiangxi province and set up the first revolutionary base there.

France, 18 November 1927. Jules Rimet, the head of the International Football Association, announces the creation of a "World Cup".

London, 23 November 1927. Stanley Baldwin, the prime minister, refuses to meet 200 unemployed miners who have walked from the Rhondda Valley.

Berlin, 23 November 1927. Germany and Poland sign a trade pact.

Britain, 25 November 1927. A commission is set up to study the working of the constitution granted to India after the Great War.

China, 15 December 1927. Russians are expelled from Shanghai following an attempted communist coup in Guangzhou.

London, 15 December 1927. The House of Commons rejects a revised Book of Common Prayer.

New York City, December 1927. Florenz Ziegfeld's *Showboat* opens, with music by Jerome Kern.

London, 6 January 1928. Fourteen people die as the Thames bursts its banks, flooding low-lying areas including the palace of Westminster.

Talking movies enthral cinema audiences

Al Jolson in "The Jazz Singer", the first "talkie" that cinema-goers have heard.

New York, 6 October 1927
The first spoken voice in a feature film, that of Al Jolson in *The Jazz Singer*, brought the audience to its feet applauding when it was shown today. In the middle of a night club sequence, Jolson suddenly spoke: "Wait a minute, wait a minute," he said. "You ain't heard nothin' yet!" In another part of the film he sits at the piano exchanging lines with his mother between verses of *Blue Skies*.

Jolson had ad-libbed during the shooting of the two music sequences and the producers left it in. Synchronised music in film has been possible since Warner Brothers bought the "Vitaphone" system last year, using it first with John Barrymore's *Don Juan*, but no-one had spoken spontaneously to audiences before in a realistic way. Crowds are flocking to hear it.

Fox have been developing a rival sound system called "Movietone" for shorts since early this year. In June they showed the reception for Charles Lindbergh by President Coolidge and a speech by Mussolini. These had such effect that Fox are setting up Movietone News to make regular sound newsreels.

The industry is faced with costly reinvestment in sound studios and theatres, and many predict that sound will only be popular briefly. Charlie Chaplin discounts it.

Pioneer of African education has died

New York, 30 July 1927
James Kwegyir Aggrey, Africa's most influential scholar and educationalist, died here today aged 52. Born in the Gold Coast and educated in missionary schools, he sailed to the USA in 1898, attended Livingstone college in North Carolina, stayed on the faculty, and studied at Columbia university, New York. In 1920 and again in 1924 he toured Africa for the Phelps-Stokes commissions into African education. His great work on the history of Africa remains incomplete.

Scientists ask what can the matter be

Germany, 1927
The German Werner Heisenberg has just developed his "Uncertainty Principle" – that there is no certainty in the way an electron revolves around the atomic nucleus. Its path is totally unpredictable.

Another uncomfortable notion has been put forward by Paul Dirac in Cambridge. He reckons that the negatively-charged electron has a positive equivalent – a "positron". Thus, here is a particle with an "anti-particle" having directly opposite properties.

Left purged in China

Generalissimo Chiang Kai-shek addresses the "People's Political Council".

China, 12 April 1927
General Chiang Kai-shek, who took over the Nationalist movement on the death of Sun Yat-sen two years ago, carried out a bloody purge of leftists in Shanghai today. He pre-empted Communist moves to take over the movement by hiring Du Yuesheng, a powerful gangster. Du's gunmen, disguised as workmen, raided the homes of Communists and took them away to be executed while Nationalist army units disarmed the Communist military force, the Workers' Inspection Corps, and shot its leaders. There was further bloodshed when machine guns opened fire on people demonstrating outside Chiang's headquarters.

While all this was going on Chiang was in Nanjing where he had gone to supervise a similar purge of leftists in preparation for establishing a new conservative-dominated Nationalist government there. He intends to destroy the Communists.

Solo flyer crosses Atlantic at 110 mph

Paris, 21 May 1927
Charles Lindbergh has touched down at Le Bourget airport after a solo flight of 3,600 miles across the Atlantic. His Ryan NYP monoplane, the *Spirit of St Louis*, was greeted by a crowd of 100,000. Backed by a consortium of St Louis businessmen, and regarded as an outsider, he took off from Roosevelt Field, Long Island, at dawn yesterday. Thousands watched him fly northwest to Newfoundland and then, at 7.15pm, west across the ocean. He came in to Paris 27 hours later. He is a shy midwesterner, now richer by $25,000 prize money; the main question he was asked was how he answered calls of nature. The reply: into a bottle.

Crowds greet the "Spirit of St Louis" at Croydon Airport on 29 May.

Stalin sends his opponents into exile

Moscow, 16 January 1928
Joseph Stalin has cracked down on his defeated political rivals and sent many of them into exile in Siberia. His security police, the *OGPU*, have rounded up some 30 leading Bolsheviks, including Leon Trotsky and Stalin's closest allies, among them Zinoviev and Kamenev. His chief opponents have been banished for alleged "counter-revolution." His triumph over his former comrades, whom he has consistently outmanoeuvred, is nearly complete.

The crackdown comes at a time of grave social crisis which Trotsky, among others, had predicted. With the short-fall in the government's purchases of peasants' grain, there are several cities and towns facing famine. Meanwhile there are virtually no consumer goods to be had in the nation's shops, and Soviet exports are negligible.

Bushwhackers get their own flying doctor

Queensland, Australia, 1928
A unique new medical service aimed at getting doctors to the most remote parts of the Australian bush has already saved several lives and is to be extended throughout the country. Since May, Dr St Vincent Walsh and his pilot have flown thousands of miles in their de Havilland aircraft, touching down on hastily improvised airstrips and caring for a variety of medical and surgical problems – including childbirth.

The service is the brainchild of John Flynn, the superintendent of the Queensland Presbyterian Mission, who borrowed the plane from a local flying club and arranged for the installation of "pedal-powered" wireless sets in distant mission stations.

Frenchman ends his search for times past

Paris, 1927
Although he died five years ago, still hard at work revising his immense novel, even Marcel Proust's search for "lost time" has come to an end this year with the publication of the last part of *A la Recherche du Temps Perdu*, entitled *Le Temps Retrouve* – Time Recaptured. No recluse ever devoted his life more singly to a work of art, working by night in his corklined apartment, conjuring out of memory a whole lifetime spent among the *Beau Monde* – artists, hostesses, courtesans. "The true paradises," he writes, "are the paradises one has lost."

Duke Ellington (centre), jazz's foremost composer and the bestknown black American jazz player in the US, with his 11-piece band. The Duke has now taken up residence at Harlem's Cotton Club, and his music is being played on the wireless and phonograph all over the United States.

1928 (1928-1929)

Britain, 15 February 1928. The *Oxford English Dictionary* is completed after 70 years' work.

Near East, 20 February 1928. Britain recognises the independence of Transjordan.

Near East, 3 March 1928. British planes strafe Wahabi tribesmen from Saudi Arabia who have launched a huge raid aimed at Kuwait and the Iraq frontier.

Malta, 12 March 1928. The British colony of Malta becomes a dominion.

China, March 1928. Anticommunist forces destroy the Haifeng and Lufeng soviet governments set up in Guangdong province by Peng Pai.

China, 7 April 1928. Nationalist troops launch an offensive with the ultimate aim of capturing Beijing.

Turkey, 9 April 1928. Islam is abolished as the state religion.

China, 3 May 1928. Seeking to impede Chiang Kai-shek's drive for national reunification, Japanese forces clash with Nationalists at Ji'nan in Shandong province.

London, 7 May. Women over 21 win equal suffrage in British elections.

China, 11 May 1928. The Japanese win control of the stricken provincial capital of Shandong after three days of savage fighting.

New York City, 16 May 1928. Share prices plunge as panic selling hits Wall Street.

China, 4 June 1928. Fearing that he is no longer willing to be a Japanese puppet, the Japanese murder the warlord Zhang Zuolin.

China, 8 June 1928. Beijing is taken by Nationalists, who have set up a government in Nanjing.

Germany, 28 June 1928. The Socialist Hermann Muller succeeds Wilhelm Marx as chancellor.

China, 28 June 1928. The name of the old capital is changed from Beijing (northern capital) to Beiping (northern peace).

Mexico City, 17 July 1928. President Alvaro Obregon is assassinated at a lunch to celebrate his election earlier this month.

Egypt, 19 July 1928. Having dismissed the prime minister, Nahas Pasha, King Fuad ends parliamentary government in Egypt and makes himself dictator.

Japan, 22 July 1928. Japan breaks off relations with China.

Britain, 27 July 1928. Randall Davidson resigns as archbishop of Canterbury following the House of Commons' second rejection of the revised Book of Common Prayer.

Yugoslavia, 1 August 1928. Croatian deputies set up a separatist parliament in Zagreb.

Albania, 25 August 1928. President Ahmed Zog declares Albania a kingdom and himself king.

Paris, 27 August 1928. Delegates of 15 nations sign the Kellogg-Briand pact, outlawing war.

Berlin, 31 August 1928. Bertolt Brecht's *Threepenny Opera* is performed for the first time.

Moscow, 6 September 1928. The USSR signs the Kellogg-Briand pact.

Rome, 20 September 1928. The Grand Fascist Council becomes the supreme legislative body in Italy.

USSR, 1 October 1928. Joseph Stalin issues a five-year economic plan to industrialise the USSR.

China, 6 October 1928. A new Chinese constitution is promulgated. Chiang Kai-shek becomes president of the republic.

USA, 6 November 1928. The Republican Herbert C Hoover is elected president.

Japan, 10 November 1928. The 27-year-old Emperor Hirohito is crowned.

Paris, 11 November 1928. Raymond Poincare forms a cabinet which excludes Radical Socialists.

Mexico, 30 November 1928. Emilio Portes Gil is sworn in as president.

Russia, November 1928. Stalin continues to arrest and exile hundreds of Trotsky's supporters.

Afghanistan, 17 December 1928. King Amanullah and Queen Suriya take refuge in a fort outside Kabul as a revolt against reform breaks out in the capital and Jalalabad.

China, 20 December 1928. Britain signs a tariff pact with China, recognising Chiang Kai-shek.

Britain, 1928. The novelist Evelyn Waugh publishes *Decline and Fall.*

Yugoslavia, 6 January 1929. King Alexander dissolves parliament, abolishes the constitution and establishes a dictatorship.

Afghanistan, 14 January 1929. King Amanullah abdicates in favour of his brother Inayatullah.

Moscow, 16 January 1929. Nikolai Bukharin resigns as head of the Comintern.

Afghanistan, 17 January 1929. King Inayatullah abdicates in favour of the rebel chief Bacha-i-Sachao, who leads a coup.

USSR, 23 January 1929. The OGPU, the secret police, arrest 400 Trotskyists for an alleged plot to start a civil war.

Stalin prescribes five-year economic plan

Moscow, 1 October 1928

Joseph Stalin's first Five-Year Plan went into operation today hurling the whole of the USSR into a gigantic struggle to build socialism. Over the next few years Stalin intends to transform the face of the nation and lay the foundations of a modern industrial society very quickly. A country standing only a decade earlier on the brink of dissolution is about to be put in the very forefront of world economic development.

The plan is a six-volume work which has taken two years' study. Class A industries – coal, iron, oil, steel and machine-building – are scheduled to triple their output. Class B industries, which turn out consumer goods, are to double their output. The plan is to be achieved through the ruthless accumulation of capital, the ploughing back of surplus and the limitation of personal consumption and amenities. A major programme of heavy industrial development, with huge ironworks, blast furnaces, oil refineries and tractor factories, is planned. The plan goes hand in hand with a revolution in the countryside – the collectivisation of agriculture, which could easily prove to be the biggest event in all Russian history.

The key question is: will the USSR's mainly peasant population put its back into the plan?

Stalin, the Bolshevik whom Lenin so distrusted, transforming the USSR.

Woman says she is late czar's daughter

New York City, 6 February 1928

A mysterious young woman, calling herself Anastasia Chaikovsky and claiming to be the youngest daughter of the murdered Russian czar, reached New York today.

Mrs Chaikovsky held a press conference on the liner *Berengaria* and told reporters that she is here to have her jaw reset – it was broken by a Bolshevik soldier, she said. She was welcomed by the son of the czar's doctor, who was killed in the cellar with the royal family. Mr Gleb Botkin greeted her grandly as "Your Highness" and declared that she was certainly the grand duchess with whom he had played as a child. He denied that the public were being hoaxed. Rumours have persisted of survivors from the Bolshevik carnage at Ekaterinburg in 1918, and of the crown jewels' continued existence. Even so, Anastasia will not find it easy to prove her claim to royal blood.

Mouse called Mickey steams into action

New York, 19 September 1928

A mouse with big boots and ears like black ping-pong bats made his bow today in *Steamboat Willie*, the first animated cartoon to have a sound track. His perky and impudent voice was supplied by his creator, Walt Disney, who hurriedly added voices at the last moment to keep abreast of feature films. The drawing is the work of his animator partner, Ubbe Iwerks. Disney's wife supplied the name "Mickey". The idea was Disney's.

A star is born: Mickey Mouse at the helm in "Steamboat Willie".

Chiang launches attack

China, 7 April 1928

General Chiang Kai-shek has launched a massive assault on the northern warlords. The objectives of this Northern Expedition, first planned by the late Sun Yat-sen, are to drive the warlords out of Beijing, crush their power and unite China under a Nationalist government.

Chiang, who returned to lead the Nationalists recently after a tactical "retirement", commands an army of nearly a million men against the smaller but still formidable forces of the Japanese puppet, Zhang Zuolin. One of the dangers that Chiang faces is of Japanese intervention on behalf of their client warlord. It is difficult to gauge how the offensive is progressing, for Chiang has refused to allow foreign observers to accompany his troops, no doubt to conceal his secrets from Japan.

While Chiang concentrates his efforts on the warlords, his other enemies, the Communists, are retreating to the mountains to lick their wounds following the debacle of the "Autumn Harvest" uprising.

Free India report is for Hindus only

New Delhi, 15 August 1928

As India steadily becomes less governable, a report is out drafting the constitutional framework of a free India. The report, by the Congress leader, Motilal Nehru, calls for universal suffrage, a two-chamber parliament and dominion status. Unfortunately it represents the aspirations of only one community, the Hindu majority. For a moment, in 1927, it looked as if Hindus and Moslems would agree to a proposed constitution, but any concession to one community was rejected by the other. The old cycle of minority Moslem and majority Hindu fears has triumphed once again.

Mouldy dish may be health breakthrough

London, 30 September 1928

A substance that appears to kill bacteria responsible for many human infectious illnesses has been discovered, by a combination of chance and shrewd observation, by a British scientist. Professor Alexander Fleming of Queen Mary's hospital in London seems to have stumbled on an important find with many potential applications.

He had left a dish of staphylococcus bacteria on his laboratory bench. When he looked at it next, a mould had contaminated the sample. However, around the mould were patches that were completely clear of staphylococcus. The inference is that the mould – which Fleming later identified as *Penicillium notatum* – kills other kinds of infectious micro-organisms too, so this could form the basis for new kinds of "antibiotic" agents.

However, the germ-killing agent has to be isolated. Then it has to be cleared for use on humans. This may take several years.

Brisbane welcomes cross-Pacific flyer

Brisbane, Australia, 9 June 1928

Half the population of Brisbane welcomed Charles Kingsford Smith and his co-pilot, C T P Ulm, after their 7,000-mile (11,200-kilometre) non-stop flight in a Fokker tri-motored aircraft, the *Southern Cross*, from California across the Pacific. The 83-hour journey is the longest flight ever made over water.

"Smithy" served in the Royal Flying Corps in the Great War, winning the Military Cross, and then took up stunt-flying. In 1927 "Smithy" and Ulm made a round-Australia flight in less than half the previous record time, giving the two the experience needed for their epic trans-Pacific flight.

Violins open up on Valentine's Day

Chicago, 14 February 1929

Chicago shuddered today as news spread of one of the worst-ever outbreaks of homicidal gangland warfare. In what seems to have been a premeditated attack, seven members of George "Bugsy" Moran's gang, assembled in a garage at 2122 N Clark Street, were machine-gunned to death by five assailants, all dressed as police officers.

Investigators attribute the killings, which the press have christened "the St Valentine's Day Massacre" and which stem from rivalry over the lucrative market in bootleg liquor, to the gang of Al "Scarface" Capone, who is fighting for supremacy among Chicago's mobsters.

Mexican president killed by fanatic

Mexico City, July 1928

Alvaro Obregon, who first served as Mexico's president from 1920 to 1924, following one of the bloodiest decades in his country's history, is dead. He was assassinated today by a religious fanatic, just weeks after he was re-elected to the presidency. It was hoped that he might continue his successful social and economic reforms. A follower of Madero's revolution of 1911, Obregon, then a general, had led the troops of Mexico's north-west. He challenged Huerta's *coup d'etat* of 1913, siding instead with the "first chief" Carranza. When in 1920 Carranza denied him a spell as president, Obregon organised his own coup.

Hirohito aged 27, Japan's emperor in the steps of his "heavenly and imperial ancestors".

1929 (1929-1930)

Vatican, 11 February 1929. The Vatican state comes into being.

Germany, 15 February 1929. Over three million are now out of work.

Paris, 21 February 1929. The exiled Leon Trotsky, Stalin's most feared opponent, is refused asylum.

Beiping (Beijing), 2 March 1929. Martial law is declared after a mutiny is crushed among Nationalist troops.

Washington, DC, 4 March 1929. Herbert Hoover is inaugurated as president.

Mexico, 8 March 1929. Catholic rebels take the town of Juarez.

France, 20 March 1929. The French commander Marshal Ferdinand Foch dies aged 68.

Italy, 25 March 1929. Mussolini's "single party" government claims it has won 99 per cent of the votes in the general election.

Germany, 4 April 1929. The engineer Karl Benz, the builder of the first internal-combustion motor car, dies aged 84.

USA, 6 April 1929. President Hoover sends warplanes to the Arizona-Mexico border following the deaths of American troops in cross-fire between Mexican rebels and government troops.

Monte Carlo, 14 April 1929. The first Monaco Grand Prix is won by Williams of Britain in a Bugatti.

Rome, 20 April 1929. King Victor Emmanuel III and Mussolini open the first all-Fascist parliament.

Berlin, 3 May 1929. The city is declared to be in a state of siege as civil unrest escalates.

Bombay, 5 May 1929. A curfew is imposed in a bid to quell new Hindu-Moslem riots.

London, 10 May 1929. King George V dissolves parliament and election campaigning begins.

USA, 16 May 1929. The Academy of Motion Picture Arts and Sciences gives its first awards.

India, 27 May 1929. The nationalist Pandit Nehru calls for rebellion if India does not get dominion status by the year's end.

Britain, 31 May 1929. Thirteen women are elected as MPs. The Tories win most votes but Labour most seats.

London, 7 June 1929. Ramsay MacDonald forms Britain's second Labour government.

China, 13 June 1929. Soviet troops cross into China in retaliation for raids on Russian consulates.

Tokyo, 26 June 1929. The government ratifies the Kellogg-Briand pact banning war, the last of the signatories to do so.

Britain, 11 July 1929. Leon Trotsky is refused asylum.

Russia, 17 July 1929. Russia breaks off relations with China and begins to mobilise on the border.

Italy, 19 August 1929. Sergei Diaghilev, the founder of the Ballets Russes, dies aged 57.

India, 21 August 1929. Mahatma Gandhi is elected president of the Indian National Congress, but refuses to accept the post.

Jerusalem, 25 August 1929. The British declare martial law as Arabs and Jews continue fighting.

Geneva, 5 September 1929. Aristide Briand, the French prime minister, proposes a united states of Europe.

China, 9 September 1929. Heavy fighting between Chinese and Soviet troops is reported along the Manchurian border.

South America, 16 September 1929. Bolivia and Paraguay sign a peace treaty to end their ten-month-old border dispute.

Berlin, 22 September 1929. Communists and Nazis are involved in armed street confrontations.

Belgrade, 3 October 1929. Yugoslavia is declared the official name of the Kingdom of Serbs, Croats and Slovenes.

Kabul, 17 October 1929. The Afghan national assembly elects the rebel leader Nadir Khan king.

New York City, 24 October 1929. The stock exchange crashes.

Germany, 8 December 1929. Hitler's *Nazi*, or National Socialist, Party, wins Bavarian municipal elections.

Lahore, 22 December 1929. The All-India National Congress demands independence.

Russia, 22 December 1929. The Sino-Soviet border dispute over the eastern railway ends with both sides agreeing to withdraw troops.

Cairo, 11 January 1930. A new Egyptian parliament opens after 18 months of rule by royal decree. The majority of the deputies are nationalists, supporting the Waft party.

China, 13 January 1930. Two million have died of starvation and famine threatens millions more.

Spain, 29 January 1930. The dictator General Primo de Rivera resigns.

London, 31 January 1930. The Five Power Naval Conference, between Britain, the US, Italy, France and Japan, aimed at curbing the arms race, opens.

Stalin declares all farms are collectives

Soviet peasants making a "spontaneous" demonstration against kulaks.

Soviet Union, 5 January 1930
Tens of thousands of government agents have been sent to the countryside to persuade rich peasants, or *kulaks*, to join collective farms.

Encouraged by the initial success of collective farms, and spurred on by the threat of famine, Stalin has decided that the nation's agriculture should be turned into a cooperative system. Under the scheme, every poor farmer who turns his land over to collective ownership will be allowed to own a house, garden, stable and one car for his family. He will also be allowed to keep any income from the sale of garden vegetables.

Stalin's reconstruction of the country's agricultural system promises to be a social revolution. It will also enable him to strengthen party control over the traditionally independent peasantry.

Woman minister in new Labour cabinet

London, 7 June 1929
Britain is to get its first woman cabinet minister. Margaret Bondfield is to become minister of labour, a key job in the light of the lengthening dole queues. Hers is the most exciting appointment in the government list announced today by the Labour Party leader, Ramsay MacDonald.

This is only Britain's second Labour government, and like the first one it has no overall majority in the House of Commons, so MacDonald is concerned to present a moderate image. Most appointments go to those on the right of the party, and left-wing socialist measures are unlikely.

On foreign affairs, moves to resume diplomatic relations with the Soviets are in train and there will be vigorous pursuit of disarmament. The government will be helped because the Conservatives and Liberals hate each other more than they hate Labour. Another first was chalked up by the new prime minister. He presented his new team in front of film cameras invited into the Downing Street garden.

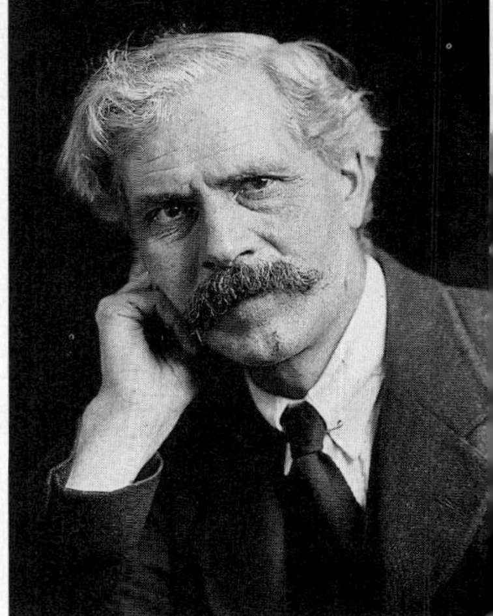

Ramsay MacDonald: the Labour PM courting a moderate image.

Financial panic as Wall Street dives

New York's Wall Street on the morning of the Great Crash.

A victim of the Crash: "Brother can you spare me a thousand dimes?"

New York City, 24 October 1929

The show-business weekly *Variety* summed it up in a headline. WALL STREET LAYS AN EGG, it proclaimed, as millions of shares became worthless in a matter of hours and panic-stricken brokers fought each other at the Stock Exchange counters. Their orders were to "sell at any price" – but there were few prepared to buy worthless pieces of paper today.

President Hoover's belief that the participation by millions of small investors – farmers, bus drivers, road-sweepers, chorus girls and housewives among them – was "the final triumph over poverty" has been proved disastrously wrong. Soon after Wall Street opened for trade this morning, brisk selling caused the value of shares to fall. With the ticker tapes unable to cope with the volume of traffic, they fell further, and as worried investors throughout the country added their orders to sell, the market plummeted until at 11.30 it was in total chaos.

As leading bankers held an emergency meeting today at the offices of J P Morgan and Co, the market rallied at the hope of intervention. The bankers' injection of $25 million into the market did ease matters, but not for the thousands of small investors who fought with riot police as they struggled to get to their brokers and sell.

The bankers tried hard to soothe and smooth things over. "A minor adjustment," said one. "A little distress selling," declared another. Eleven suicides in New York alone tell another story.

New plan to rejig German war debts

The Hague, 8 June 1929

Financial reparations imposed on Germany to compensate the Allies for debts incurred to the USA during the Great War seem to have been rescheduled. Under a provisional agreement, Germany is no longer required to reconstruct France's war-damaged provinces.

The Young Plan, named after its American author Owen Young, removes controls over the German economy. Nevertheless, Germany must repay £1.65 billion over the next 40 years, including £2 million a year which Britain still insists must be repaid to cover its American debt. Militant Germans, including the Nazis, are demonstrating against such payments.

Germany – chained and bound by the fetters of the Young Plan.

Fairbanks presents first Academy Awards

Hollywood, 16 May 1929

The film industry's first awards for outstanding achievement by actors, directors, producers and technicians were presented last night. The award is symbolised by a 12inch (0.3 metre) -tall model of a naked man plated in gold. The awards were given by the Academy of Motion Picture Arts and Sciences formed in 1927 by producers like Louis B Mayer of MGM as "an alliance of the creative elite of Hollywood".

The academy president, Douglas Fairbanks jnr, gave statuettes to Janet Gaynor and Emil Jannings, the directors Frank Borsage and Lewis Milestone, the screenwriter Ben Hecht and the producer Jack Warner. The awards will be annual.

Janet Gaynor: first award-winner.

Britain keeps order in Palestine riots

Palestine, 31 August 1929

British troops stepped in today as Arabs and Jews continued to clash in the sultry summer heat. Outbreaks of rioting have been suppressed for the moment, but a large force of Arabs is said to be massing across the Syrian border. Spotter aircraft are shadowing their movements. The worst riots came in Safed last Thursday, when armed Arabs killed eight Jews and then burnt whole streets of houses. The cause of the riots is unknown, although many see it as stemming from Arab hostility to Jewish access to the Wailing Wall, a Jewish monument isolated in the heart of Arab Jerusalem.

Fascist-papal pact

Vatican City, 11 February 1929

The Vatican state came into being at noon with a treaty designed to end the church's six decades of hostility with the Italian state.

The 27-point agreement, signed by Mussolini and Cardinal Gaspari, Pope Pius XI's representative, emphasises the sanctity of marriage, recognises Roman Catholicism as the state religion and makes Catholic education obligatory in schools.

The Vatican, which gets a 1,750 million *lire* lump sum settlement, is guaranteed certain civil immunities and promised specific services by the state.

1930 (1930-1931)

USA, 18 February 1930. A new planet discovered beyond Neptune by the astronomer Clyde Tombaugh is named Pluto.

London, 22 February 1930. Press baron Lord Beaverbrook launches the United Empire Party to promote imperial preference.

Russia, 24 February 1930. A report claims that 40 *kulaks* (rich peasants) a day are being murdered by Stalin's agents.

Italy, 2 March 1930. The controversial novelist D H Lawrence, author of *Sons and Lovers* and *Women in Love* dies of tuberculosis at the age of 44.

Britain, 19 March 1930. Arthur James Balfour, the conservative prime minister from 1902-05, dies.

Britain, 21 April 1930. Robert Bridges, poet laureate since 1913, dies aged 85.

London, 21 April 1930. The London Naval Treaty, limiting the great powers' navies, is signed.

China, 23 April 1930. The nationalist General Chiang Kai-shek battles with the northern warlord General Yan Xishan.

Britain, 9 May 1930. John Masefield is appointed poet laureate.

South Africa, 19 May 1930. White women are given the vote.

London, 22 May 1930. Talks between Labour and Liberal leaders over electoral reform break down. The informal pact between the two parties is over.

London, 29 May 1930. The BBC forms its own permanent symphony orchestra under the directorship of Adrian Boult.

India, 31 May 1930. New measures are introduced to curb civil disobedience, following the arrest of Gandhi on 5 May and the consequent civil unrest.

Baghdad, 30 June 1930. Britain recognises Iraqi independence.

Germany, 30 June 1930. France pulls the last of its troops out of the Rhineland, five years before the date set by the Versailles Treaty.

Britain, 7 July 1930. The writer Sir Arthur Conan Doyle, the creator of Sherlock Holmes, dies aged 81.

China, 10 July 1930. Communist armies unite to attack Hankow.

Egypt, 22 July 1930. British battleships sail for Egypt to deal with nationalist anti-British riots.

Uruguay, 30 July 1930. Uruguay win football's first World Cup.

London, 7 August 1930. Two million people are unemployed.

Central Asia, 12 August 1930. The Turkish and Persian armies launch an offensive on Kurdish rebels.

Australia, 18 August 1930. The two halves of the new Sydney Harbour Bridge are joined.

Peru, 25 August 1930. President Augusto Leguia resigns after a coup.

Beiping (Beijing), 2 September 1930. General Yen Hsi-chan forms a rebel government.

Argentina, 6 September 1930. The radical president Hipolito Irigoyen is overthrown by army officers led by General Uriburu.

Germany, 15 September 1930. The *Nazi* leader Adolf Hitler is barred as an Austrian citizen from taking his seat in the *reichstag.*

Athens, 5 October 1930. A congress between the Balkan states opens, aimed at promoting cooperation.

Berlin, 13 October 1930. There is uproar in the reichstag when Nazi deputies turn up in uniform, which is illegal for civilians.

France, 16 October 1930. A line of defences known as the Maginot Line is to be built along France's frontier with Germany.

Ankara, 30 October 1930. Turkey and Greece sign a treaty of friendship.

Brazil, 1 November 1930. President Vargas dissolves the congress.

Addis Ababa, 2 November 1930. Ras Tafari is crowned Emperor Haile Selassie of Ethiopia.

China, 5 November 1930. An "encirclement campaign" by Nationalist government forces against areas of Hunan, Hubei and Jiangxi begins.

Austria, 9 November 1930. The Socialists are victorious in elections to the Austrian parliament.

Japan, 14 November 1930. The prime minister, Hamagushi, is shot dead by a right-wing militant.

Germany, 30 November 1930. The Nazis are victorious in municipal elections in Bremen.

Iraq, 6 January 1931. A royal palace dating from 550BC is found at the site of the city of Ur.

London, 23 January 1931. The Russian ballerina Anna Pavlova dies aged 49.

London, 26 January 1931. Winston Churchill resigns from Baldwin's shadow cabinet after disagreeing with the policy of conciliation with Indian nationalism.

India, 26 January 1931. Mahatma Gandhi, the Indian nationalist leader, is released from prison.

Woman flies from England to Australia

Darwin, Australia, 24 April 1930
Record crowds were here this afternoon to cheer the arrival of Amy Johnson. At 3.55 pm, after circling the aerodrome, she landed her plane smoothly to become the first woman ever to fly solo from England to Australia.

Amy Johnson's adventure began with crossing the English Channel in thick fog. Violent storms twice made her lose control of her de Havilland Moth and forced her to land – once in a Near Eastern Desert, and again between Java and Sourabaya. She finished her epic journey in 19 days, despite delays in Rangoon and Bangkok to repair damage to the plane.

Amy Johnson, on the Tiger Moth that took her to Australia.

British report recommends federal India

London, 23 June 1930
The Simon Commission has recommended a federal India. Such a federation, the former Liberal home secretary believes, will safeguard the many different Indias: Hindu India, Moslem India, Sikh India, Anglo-India and the India of the princes. State elections (outside the princely states) will be direct, federal elections will be indirect. That Britain is prepared to consider self-rule for India is seen as a victory for one man, though like the rest of the Congress Party he boycotted the commission: "this one-time Inner Temple lawyer, now turned seditious fakir", as the report's bitterest critic, Winston Churchill, calls Gandhi.

Plan for Palestine angers the Zionists

Palestine, 20 October 1930
Zionist leaders today condemned Britain's latest plan for Palestine as a charter for the control of immigration to what the world's Jews still see as their "promised land". Dr Chaim Weizmann, the president of the Jewish Agency, has threatened to resign in protest against the terms of the White Paper. Ramsay MacDonald, the British prime minister, claims the plan will give more self-government to both Jews and Arabs. He says that in accordance with the League of Nations' mandate, it favours neither group. Zionists contend that the plan reverses the Balfour Declaration of 1917, in which Jews were promised a national home in Palestine.

Twin threat to power of Chiang Kai-shek

China, 23 April 1930
Two powerful challenges, from the right and the left, emerged this week to challenge General Chiang Kai-shek's long struggle to bring the whole of China under the rule of his Nationalist Party.

The aggressive northern warlord Yan Xishan has mounted a surprise "punitive expedition" and driven Chiang's men back to the southern bank of the Yellow River. Nationalist sources, however, claim that the warlord's advance has been halted and that Chiang is preparing a counter-offensive.

A far more serious long-term threat to Nationalist rule is posed by the growing power of the Communists. Bloodily and treacherously purged from the Nationalist party, they have retreated to a base in Jiangxi province where they have established a communist state and built up an army of 10,000 dedicated men and women.

Gandhi marches in defiance of salt laws

Dandi, India, 6 April 1930
Mahatma Gandhi has reached the sea, after a 300-mile (480-kilometre), 25-day journey from his *ashram* near Ahmedabad. Thousands followed him, prepared to defy the British salt tax and "break the mournful monotony of compulsory peace that is choking the heart of the nation for want of free vent". To India's millions of nationalists the salt tax of one *rupee* per 82 pounds (40 kilos) is an effective poll tax, burdening the poorest, and a symbol of foreign oppression.

At 5.30 this morning Gandhi walked down to the shore and symbolically picked up a piece of crystallised seasalt, thus breaking the salt laws. His thousands of followers did likewise. They had wanted to work the saltflats, encrusted with salt at every high tide, but the police forestalled them by stirring the salt deposits in the mud. Many have been arrested, including Ram Das, Gandhi's son, charged with selling salt illegally. So far no policeman has dared arrest the father.

Defying the salt laws: Gandhi and his followers on the road to Dandi.

Hitler is runner-up in German elections

Young Nazis "encouraging" support during the election campaign.

Berlin, 15 September 1930
The unexpected success of extreme right-wing National Socialist candidates in the Reichstag elections sent shock waves through the Berlin *Bourse* today, with shares falling as much as 20 points. The Nazis, as they are known, gained 107 seats to become the second largest party after the Socialists. In the old Reichstag they had only 12 deputies. Their vote went up from 800,000 in 1928 to 6,409,000, only 2,000,000 behind the Socialists. Adolf Hitler, the Nazi leader, played on voters' fears of economic chaos and social disorder. The world economic crisis has meant soaring unemployment and widespread hardship, and the powerful Communist Party has instigated violent street demonstrations in the hope of starting revolution. In the election campaign, Hitler made furious speeches denouncing Jews and Bolsheviks as the cause of the nation's problems and promising to make Germany great again.

Army coup in Brazil ousts ruling clique

Rio de Janeiro, 26 October 1930
The Brazilian *coup d'etat* was formally completed today with the appointment of Dr Gertuilo Vargas as new provisional president.

He was chosen by a *junta* of army officers who overthrew the government of President Luis and his elected successor, Dr Julio Prestes, during a three-week uprising which enjoyed some popular support. The greatest number of casualties – 27 dead – occurred when the revolutionaries shot at a German liner as it left Rio.

The old regime had held power for 40 years. Its sudden disappearance has taken foreign governments by surprise. The US, a staunch supporter of the Luis regime, now wonders whether the change threatens a lucrative export market for American goods as well as its primary source of coffee.

Dr Vargas, Brazil's new strongman.

Stars are twinkling in daylight (by radio)

United States, 1931
A new kind of astronomy has been born with a "radio-telescope" developed by the American Karl Jansky. Working at the Bell Telephone laboratories, Jansky has discovered that the stars in our galaxy – the Milky Way – emit not only light but radio waves. He has studied this radiation emanating from the constellation of Sagittarius, towards the centre of the galaxy.

This is an important development because it enables astronomers to observe the heavens in broad daylight.

Weimar star Marlene Dietrich, breaking into the English-speaking market with Josef von Sternberg's cinematic masterpiece, "The Blue Angel".

1931 (1931-1932)

Spain, 18 February 1931. Martial law is re-imposed as King Alfonso struggles to retain power.

Germany, 24 February 1931. Almost five million people are unemployed.

London, 28 February 1931. Oswald Mosley forms the New Party, dedicated to parliamentary reform.

Washington, DC, 3 March 1931. "The Star Spangled Banner" becomes the US national anthem.

India, 4 March 1931. The viceroy agrees to end the government's salt monopoly in return for an end to civil disobedience.

London, 16 March 1931. The minority Labour government is defeated in the Commons over a clause in the Electoral Reform Bill.

Spain, 12 April 1931. Election results show that republicans have swept the polls in most cities.

Spain, 14 April 1931. King Alfonso XIII abdicates.

Turkey, 20 April 1931. The Republican People's Party of Mustapha Kemal wins by a landslide in the national elections.

China, 30 April 1931. Rebels under General Chen Jitang split with Chiang Kai-shek and take control of Guangzhou (*Canton*).

New York City, 1 May 1931. President Hoover opens the 1,245 foot, 120-floor Empire State Building.

Vienna, 11 May 1931. The bankruptcy of Credit-Anstalt begins European financial collapse.

Rome, 31 May 1931. The pope denounces Mussolini's Fascists following attacks on priests and church property.

Chicago, 12 June 1931. Al Capone and 68 henchmen are charged with breach of prohibition laws.

China, 17 June 1931. The British arrest Nguyen Ai Quoc, also known as Ho Chi Minh, founder of the Indochinese Communist Party.

Washington, DC, 22 June 1931. The President Herbert Hoover proposes that all war debts should be suspended for a year, in order to revitalise world trade.

Germany, 13 July 1931. All banks close until 5 August following the collapse of the *Danatbank*.

China, 17 July 1931. Rebels launch a drive on Tientsin.

London, 22 July 1931. Britain, the US and France renew recent credits for Germany for three months, to help Germany through financial difficulties.

China, 3 August 1931. Hundreds die when a dam on the river Yangzi bursts during a typhoon.

Cuba, 10 August 1931. President Machado declares martial law to quell a rebellion.

China, 18 September 1931. Japanese troops occupy Shenyang in Manchuria.

London, 24 August 1931. An all-party national government is formed to cope with the financial emergency that defeated the Labour government. Ramsay MacDonald remains prime minister.

Belgrade, 2 September 1931. King Alexander ends his dictatorship.

Austria, 13 September 1931. A *coup d'etat* by the Fascist Heimwehr (*national guard*) fails.

London, 15 September 1931. Gandhi demands Indian independence at a conference.

London, 23 September 1931. The Stock Exchange re-opens after closing for two days when Britain abandoned the gold standard.

Copenhagen, 28 September 1931. Denmark abandons the gold standard. Norway, Sweden and Egypt did so yesterday.

London, 6 October 1931. A general election is called for 27 October.

Britain, 28 October 1931. The National government stays in power after the largest election landslide in history.

China, 7 November 1931. The Chinese Soviet Republic is established, with Ruijin (*Jiangxi*) as its capital.

Germany, 15 November 1931. The *Nazi* Party wins elections in the state of Hesse.

China, 27 November 1931. Mao Zedong is appointed chairman of the central executive committee of the Chinese Soviet Republic.

London, 1 December 1931. The conference on India ends in failure.

Spain, 10 December 1931. Senor Nicetor Alcala Zamora is elected as Spain's first constitutional president by the national assembly. Manuel Azana is prime minister.

Tokyo, 11 December 1931. Japan abandons the gold standard.

India, 4 January 1932. Gandhi is arrested and the Indian National Congress outlawed.

China, 31 January 1932. Japanese forces take Shanghai in the war that began with the invasion of Manchuria.

China, 19 February 1932. The Japanese government has established a puppet regime in occupied Manchuria.

Berlin, 25 February 1932. Hitler is granted German citizenship.

Pound devalued as Britain faces crisis

London, 20 September 1931

The pound is poised to take a nose-dive on the foreign exchanges tomorrow after the government's shock announcement that it is abandoning the gold standard because of heavy pressure on the nation's gold reserves. A 30 per cent devaluation is expected to take the pound from $4.86 to around $3.50.

The National government, formed a month ago by Ramsay MacDonald, the Labour prime minister, promised then to take all necessary steps to restore confidence in sterling. But the cuts in unemployment pay and other economies proved inadequate in the face of the financial crisis sweeping the world.

The Labour government collapsed when the cabinet could not agree on spending cuts. The king asked MacDonald to head an all-party cabinet; he has four Labour ministers, four Tory and two Liberal. But Labour back-benchers, almost to a man, have denounced him as a traitor.

"Poison" fears for wonder racehorse

San Francisco, April 1932

Forensic scientists are to examine the stomach contents of Phar Lap, after an autopsy has revealed that the champion Australian racehorse may have been poisoned.

A close check is also being made on all visitors to Phar Lap's stable at Menlo Park outside San Francisco where the horse collapsed and died after making a sensational debut in America two weeks ago.

Phar Lap was resting at the stables while a contract was being negotiated with Hollywood's MGM studio for the racehorse to star in a series of short films.

America like Australia, had taken Phar Lap to its heart after the horse had won Mexico's prestige *Agua Caliente* Handicap after giving the leaders ten lengths' start before storming to the front with half a mile to go. In Australia, where flags are flying at half-mast for Phar Lap, newspaper placards are carrying the news with the words "He's Dead".

Devastating quake hits New Zealand

The morning after: the British Insurance Company's offices in Napier.

Hawke's Bay, 3 February 1932

At least 256 people have died and thousands have been injured and made homeless by an earthquake that struck Hawke's Bay's two main centres, Napier and Hastings, early today. A fire that followed the 'quake swept through both towns and also destroyed several other centres. The force of the earthquake – New Zealand's worst – has destroyed landmarks, with chunks of coastline falling into the sea. Napier's Bluff Hill, a substantial suburban promontory, has crumbled and disintegrated.

A wide stretch of water, Ahuriri Lagoon, has been emptied by the 'quake's upthrust, creating 9,000 acres of land in a day.

Republicans force out Spanish king

Alfonso XIII, Spain's unlucky monarch, deposed by the republicans.

Madrid, 14 April 1931

With the abdication today of King Alfonso, Spain has been declared a republic and is again thrown into political turmoil. The king's downfall follows the collapse last year of the military dictatorship of General Miguel Primo de Rivera and last week's elections when the republicans swept the polls in most Spanish cities and won a huge majority in the *Cortes* (parliament).

As they celebrated victory the Republicans made it clear that it was a question of either the king's abdication or civil war. In a dramatic ceremony in the Royal Palace he signed a renunciation document, and then stood up and told the country's leading politicians: "I believe I have conscientiously served my country. Such has been my intention. At this moment I feel more a Spaniard than ever."

During his reign King Alfonso has survived several attempts on his life by anarchists, including a bomb attack on his wedding day when he was driving with his bride in an open carriage. In 1923 the army seized control with his full approval and he counted the brilliant General Primo de Rivera as his friend.

The general's resignation led to some fierce street battles between the police and students throughout Spain, and the veteran General Berenguer, appointed prime minister to see through the crisis, was unable to fill his cabinet.

Atoms smashed to pieces by scientists

Cambridge, 1932

With a £1,000 grant from their university and the backing of Lord Rutherford, two Cambridge physicists have built a machine for smashing atoms.

John Cockroft and a young Irishman, Ernest Walton, have designed and constructed a machine for accelerating elementary particles up to high speeds, using the kicking force of 800,000 volts of electricity.

In April this year, they trained a high energy beam of protons – constituents of the atomic nucleus – on to a target of lithium and transmuted the lithium atoms into those of helium. This is the first time such a transformation has been achieved.

Royal Navy mutiny against pay cuts

Scotland, 30 September 1931

The Royal Navy has mutinied. The mutiny – involving 12,000 naval ratings on 15 ships of the Atlantic Fleet at their Invergordon base on the Cromarty Firth – is the seamen's response to the government's tough new measures to combat the international crisis and prevent the country "living beyond its means". These include the 25 per cent cut in servicemen's pay which sparked off the mutiny.

The mutineers, led by Able Seaman Len Wincott, occupied a shore canteen and held a mass meeting on a nearby recreation field. The atmosphere, however, is closer to a peaceful strike than a mutiny. Though there are firearms on the ships, the ratings have not broken into the magazines, and the only violence has been an officer being hit on the head by a beer glass. The men have now returned to their ships, singing "The more we are together, the merrier we will be".

Protests against the economic measures are not confined to the navy. Government employees, who will all suffer cuts, have been marching the streets in protest all month. Reaction amongst the unemployed has been even stronger, with rioters in the streets demanding a full restoration of the "dole".

Japanese launch attack in Manchuria

Manchuria, 18 September 1931

Japanese troops, sent to Manchuria to guard the South Manchurian railway which Japan has turned into a huge military-industrial complex, today launched a surprise attack on the Chinese garrison at Mukden. The local Japanese commander used the pretext of a bomb explosion on the railway line to attack the Chinese garrison. He seems to have acted on his own initiative.

Between 70 and 80 Chinese soldiers have been killed, and the city has been overrun without any resistance being offered. The governor of Manchuria apparently ordered his men not to shoot because he believes that the attack is designed to provoke an incident which will provide the Japanese with an excuse to seize Manchuria. To outsiders, however, it appears that the ultranationalist Japanese officer corps intends to annex Manchuria as the first stage in the occupation of all China, with or without pretext. General Chiang Kai-shek is understood to be placing his faith in an appeal to the League of Nations rather than fight the Japanese.

Might and money: Japanese militarism suckling Japanese capitalism.

Light goes out for legendary inventor

Edison: the inventor of the lightbulb, phonograph and ticker-tape machine.

New Jersey, 21 October 1931

America dipped its lights for a minute tonight in honour of the man who gave it the electric light-bulb. Thomas Alva Edison, perhaps the most prolific inventor in history, has died at the age of 84. His was an extraordinary career, a huge catalogue of nearly 1,300 inventions. His energy was equally tireless. "To stop is to rust," he once said – 3,500 crammed notebooks bear testimony. To him the world owes the lightbulb, the phonograph, ticker-tape machines and much of the technology of moving pictures. He gave this insight into the workings of the creative mind: "Genius," he said, "is one per cent inspiration and 99 per cent perspiration."

Huxley's vision of a Brave New World

London, 1932

Critics are hailing *Brave New World*, a vision of the future as a sanitised playground for carefully indoctrinated inhuman beings, as one of the most important novels since the Great War.

Aldous Huxley, the grandson of the scientist T H Huxley and author of satires on contemporary life, envisages a Utopia in which babies are fertilised in laboratory bottles, children are made to conform by "sleep-learning", sterile adults indulge in safe promiscuous sex and a mildly stimulating drug called "soma" is passed around at parties. The "Feelies" have overtaken the movies. The burden of the nightmare is that the idea of human progress through scientific advance will turn out to be an illusion.

1932 (1932-1933)

China, 9 March 1932. Puyi, the last emperor of China, is installed as head of the Japanese puppet state of Manchukuo (*Manchuria*).

Australia, 18 March 1932. Sydney Harbour Bridge is opened, the world's longest single-span bridge.

Ireland, 29 March 1932. Eamon de Valera, the hard-line republican leader of the *Fianna Fail* Party, will head the new government.

Germany, 10 April 1932. Paul von Hindenburg wins the presidency against Adolf Hitler after a second ballot to secure a majority.

Berlin, 24 April 1932. The *Nazis* lead in four state elections. In the Prussian state parliament their seats rise from six to 162.

China, 5 May 1932. Japanese troops withdraw from Shanghai after an armistice is signed.

France, 6 May 1932. President Paul Doumer is assassinated.

Japan, 15 May 1932. Militarists assassinate the prime minister, Ki Inukai.

Austria, 20 May 1932. Engelbert Dollfuss, the Christian Socialist leader, is appointed chancellor to succeed Karl Buresch who failed to form a government.

Athens, 25 May 1932. A new government is formed with Andreas Papanastasiou as prime minister, following the resignation of Eleutherios Venizelos on 21 May.

Berlin, 31 May 1932. President Hindenburg invites Franz von Papen to form a government.

Berlin, 1 June 1932. Franz von Papen forms a cabinet that excludes the Nazis.

Bangkok, 29 June 1932. The Siamese army seizes power in a *coup* against the monarchy.

USA, 2 July 1932. Franklin D Roosevelt wins the Democratic nomination for president.

Lisbon, 5 July 1932. Antonio de Oliveira Salazar is appointed Fascist prime minister.

Switzerland, 9 July 1932. The allies vote to ease Germany's economic crisis by suspending the repayments of war debts.

Switzerland, 11 July 1932. The World Bank calls for a return to the gold standard.

Berlin, 26 July 1932. The war minister, Kurt von Schleicher, says that Germany is ready to rearm.

Germany, 31 July 1932. The National Socialists (Nazis) are now the biggest party in the *reichstag* following the general election, but without an overall majority.

Berlin, 13 August 1932. Adolf Hitler refuses to serve as vice-chancellor under von Papen.

Berlin, 30 August 1932. The Nazi Hermann Goering is elected president of the reichstag.

Madrid, 9 September 1932. The government acknowledges the autonomy of Catalonia.

India, 24 September 1932. The Poona Pact is signed, extending the voting rights of Untouchables. Gandhi, who has risked unpopularity for supporting the Untouchables' cause, ends his prison fast.

Britain, 28 September 1932. Four Liberal ministers resign in protest against the National government's trade policies.

China, 6 October 1932. With the help of Germany military advisers, Chiang Kai-shek launches a campaign to isolate rebel territories held by both the warlords and the Red Army.

USSR, 9 October 1932. Joseph Stalin expels two leading Bolsheviks, Gregori Zinoviev and Leon Kamenev, from the Communist Party and exiles them to Siberia.

Berlin, 14 October 1932. The government unveils plans for direct presidential rule in the state of Prussia.

Berlin, 16 October 1932. Albert Einstein puts the earth's age at ten billion years.

London, 30 October 1932. Hunger marchers, protesting at unemployment, fight pitched street battles with police.

USA, 8 November 1932. Franklin D Roosevelt defeats the sitting Republican president, Herbert Hoover, in the presidential elections.

Berlin, 17 November 1932. The prime minister, von Papen, resigns after failing to form a government.

Berlin, 21 November 1932. Hitler refuses the chancellorship if it means combining with other parties as Hindenburg wants.

Germany, 24 November 1932. The Nationalists take seats from the Nazis in the election.

Berlin, 2 December 1932. General Kurt von Schleicher is appointed chancellor.

Britain, 25 December 1932. King George V makes the first royal Christmas Day broadcast to the empire.

Dublin, 2 January 1933. The *Dail* is dissolved; de Valera calls an election for 24 January.

Berlin, 28 January 1933. Amidst growing violence General von Schleicher resigns as chancellor.

Martial law in Spain as anarchy brews

Madrid, 10 January 1933

Spain is rapidly descending into violent anarchy and the government is poised to declare martial law. The trouble is being caused by the Anarchists, who have been joined by the Anarcho-Syndicalists and the Communists, and a general strike is in the offing.

In the southern provinces, where the turmoil is at its worst, there is already undeclared martial law. A number of people in Seville have been wounded in exchanges of gunfire, and there have been several bomb explosions. In Barcelona bombs have killed five people in the last few days. An Anarcho-Syndicalist manifesto has called on opponents of the government to disrupt telephone, telegraph and railway lines. Given the situation, the prime minister, Manual Azana, is not expected to survive in office.

Australian leader is forced from office

Sydney, 13 May 1932

In an unprecedented constitutional move, John Lang, the prime minister of New South Wales, has been dismissed by the state governor, Sir Philip Game. Lang, a militant socialist, led the 1925-27 Labour government of New South Wales, which restored the 44-hour week, introduced free secondary education and brought in child endowment and widows' pensions. Re-elected in 1930, he promised to be equally radical, but his plan to limit the effects of the Depression by withholding interest on British loans provoked strong opposition. The strongest comes from the neo-fascist New Guard, which has promised to stamp out "the bushfire of Langism".

India: favour for one alienates other

New Delhi, India, 16 August 1932

Electoral arrangements for the provincial legislatures of India have just been published. The plan is known as the "Communal Award", but it appears that only one community has got any awards – the Moslems, who now have control of Bengal and Punjab. The new provincial legislatures are Britain's main hope for legitimacy as the pro-Congress Hindu majority continues its policy of non-cooperation. But fear by Moslems of Hindus, and fear by Britain of Congress, have weighted the reforms in the Moslems' favour. Indeed, the Moslems and the princes are Britain's only allies in India, but the more it relies upon them, the more militant the Hindu majority becomes.

"King Kong", Hollywood's version of "Beauty and the Beast": the story of a prehistoric monster, captured, displayed and humiliated, yet refusing to submit to the outrages inflicted on him – until face to face with Beauty.

Japan quits the League

Japan's Manchurian candidate, Puyi, ready to serve his masters.

Wondering why? A victim of Japanese bombing and his daughter.

Japan, 25 February 1933

Japan withdrew from the League of Nations this afternoon in response to a vote condemning the invasion of Manchuria. The league unanimously resolved that the Japanese should evacuate Manchuria and allow an autonomous government to be set up.

The split has been on the cards ever since Japanese troops attacked the Chinese garrison at Mukden in September 1931. American mediation secured a temporary cease-fire, but within a few weeks the Japanese had advanced again and captured Shanghai. British, Italian and French forces became involved, in an attempt to protect foreign nationals.

Having installed Puyi, the last emperor of China, as head of the puppet state of Manchuria, Japan pursued its war with China, claiming that the Nationalist government of Chiang Kai-shek had no sovereign rights over the area.

"Japan has left the League of Nations with a heavy heart," said Mr Matsuoka, the chief Japanese delegate, who was outvoted 42-1, with the Siamese abstaining. Dr Yen, the Chinese delegate, thanked the league for its "courageous verdict".

Dark days of Depression

London: hunger marchers from the north, charged by mounted police.

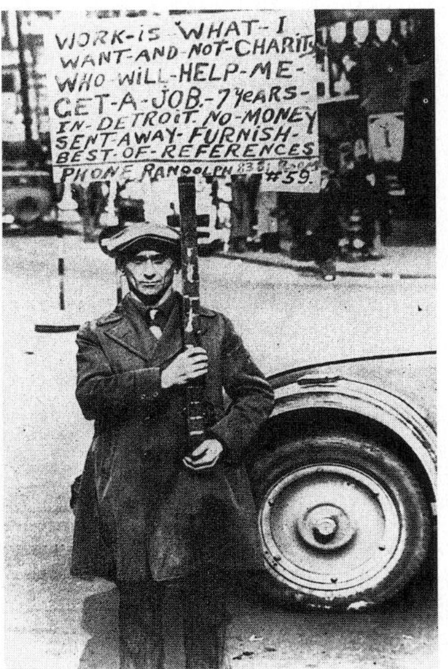

USA: an unemployed man, fighting the stigma of the unemployable.

The World, 1932

In Britain, ironically enough, they are singing "The sun has got his hat on" as the country lurches into deep industrial depression. In America, where unemployed executives and skilled workers begged on street corners, the smash hit song is more to the point. "Buddy, can you spare a dime?" it asks.

Throughout the western world unemployment has soared. More than two million Britons are out of work, relying on the "dole" money of 29s 3d a week to live. The industrial north is hardest hit, with factories, mills and docks lying idle.

Although men have marched to London from Lancashire to protest, and food riots have taken place in London, Bristol and Liverpool, the bulk of unemployed appear to have accepted their lot with sullen stoicism. They have even accepted a means test, allowing a tribunal to cut their meagre dole on the slightest suspicion of extra earnings.

In America, some 14 million are unemployed and a young British student, Alistair Cooke, has written of well-dressed men who had told their wives they were looking for night work, begging for dimes.

American hopes are pinned on a presidential candidate, Franklin Roosevelt. Britain has discarded a much-divided Labour government; in Germany, five million unemployed look to Adolf Hitler's Nazi party to solve their problems.

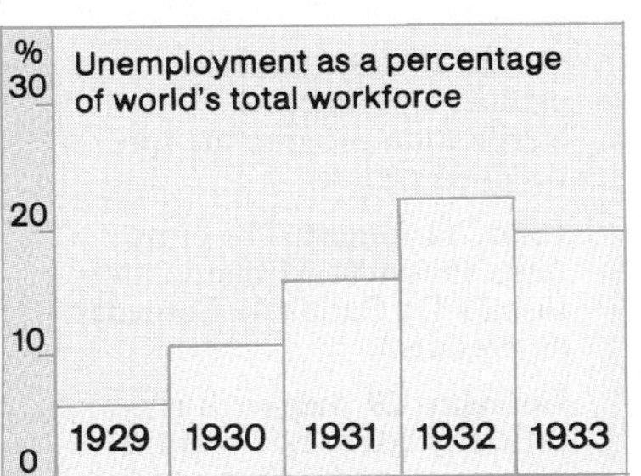

Stalin purges close colleagues of Lenin

Moscow, 9 October 1932

Joseph Stalin has stepped up his purge of the Old Bolsheviks and has expelled two close colleagues of Lenin from the Communist party. Lev Kamenev and Gregory Zinoviev, who shared power with Stalin after Lenin's death have lost their party cards and been sent into exile in Siberia. Nearly 20 other leading Communist officials have also been caught up in the crackdown. They have all been accused of trying to restore capitalism, and more significantly, of receiving documents from a "counter-revolutionary group". This is seen as a reference to a journal written by the exiled Leon Trotsky, whose strident criticisms of Stalin's authoritarian rule could produce a ferocious backlash.

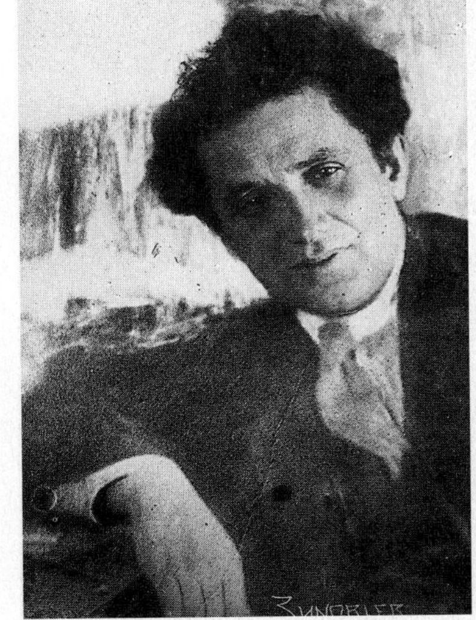

Zinoviev, chairman of the Communist International – ousted.

"Bodyline" bowling is just not cricket

Adelaide, January 1933

A total break in cricket relations between England and Australia is now threatened, following a cabled demand by Australia's Cricket Board of Control to the MCC for a ban on bodyline bowling, which has marred the first three Tests.

The potentially dangerous technique, developed by England's Harold Larwood, of bowling very fast short-pitched deliveries on the leg side is a "menace" and "unsportsmanlike", the Australian board says. It warns that "unless stopped at once it is likely to upset friendly relations existing between Australia and England".

Australian tempers flared during the latest Test at Adelaide when rising balls from Larwood knocked out one Australian batsman and thumped the Australian captain, Billy Woodfull, close to the heart.

1933

Germany, 30 January. Adolf Hitler becomes chancellor.

Germany, 28 February. The communist playwright Bertolt Brecht goes into voluntary exile in protest against the Nazis.

Berlin, 28 February. The *reichstag* burns down.

Germany, 9 March. Nazis occupy the Bavarian state parliament and expel deputies.

Germany, 15 March. Hitler declares the Third *Reich*.

Germany, 20 March. The Nazis open a concentration camp at Dachau, near Munich.

Berlin, 28 March. Hitler orders a boycott of Jews and Jewish shops.

London, 29 March. The Commons approves a plan for a federal constitution in India.

Washington, DC, 30 April. The US comes off the gold standard to prevent a drain on gold stocks.

Berlin, 5 May. Hitler proposes "eugenic laws" to ban mixed Jewish and Aryan marriages and to begin sterilisation.

Britain, 24 May. The TUC calls for a boycott of Germany to protest against Hitler.

Madrid, 8 June. Manuel Azana is dismissed as premier.

Vienna, 19 June. The prime minister, Engelbert Dollfuss, bans all Nazi organisations.

Rome, 15 July. The Rome pact is signed by Britain, France, Italy and Germany binding them to nonaggression.

Berlin, 25 July. Hitler's cabinet announces a sterilisation programme for disabled people.

Cuba, 12 August. The army ousts President Machado and installs Dr Carlos de Cespedes as president.

Germany, 29 August. It is officially confirmed that the Nazis are sending Jews to concentration camps.

Baghdad, 18 September. King Ghazi is crowned following the death of his father King Feisal on 8 September.

Berlin, 14 October. The Nazi government announces its withdrawal from the League of Nations.

Kabul, 8 November. King Nadir Shah is assassinated; his son Zahir Shah succeeds.

USA, 5 December. Fourteen years of prohibition come to an end.

New York is shocked by Marxist mural

Diego Rivera: a detail from his mural "The city of Tenochtitlan".

New York, 13 May

A mural by the Mexican revolutionary painter, Diego Rivera, for the Rockefeller Center has so shocked New York Society that Nelson Rockefeller has destroyed it. Called *Man at the Crossroads*, it is provocatively Marxist, with portraits of Marx, Lenin and Trotsky.

Mexico's muralists emerged from the Mexican revolution. "The Revolution revealed Mexico to us," said the painter Octavio Paz. "Or better, it gave us eyes to see it." Mexico had a long Indian tradition of mural painting. Rivera saw his first Indian murals at Chichen Itza, in the Temple of the Jaguars, on his return to Mexico after a successful career as a Cubist painter in Paris. Soon, like his fellow revolutionaries, he was heavily romanticising Mexico's Indians, seeing them as Mexico's proletariat.

With his fellow revolutionary muralists, Jose Orozco and David Siqueiros – *Los Tres Grandes* – he daubed Mexico City in bright murals, depicting man at the centre of an Indian universe. One, Orozco's *Christ destroying his cross*, was so defaced by angry Catholics that it had to be repainted. Rivera's early murals, such as his *Creation*, were allegorical. It was not until 1926 that they took on the political and epic qualities that have so outraged New York Society.

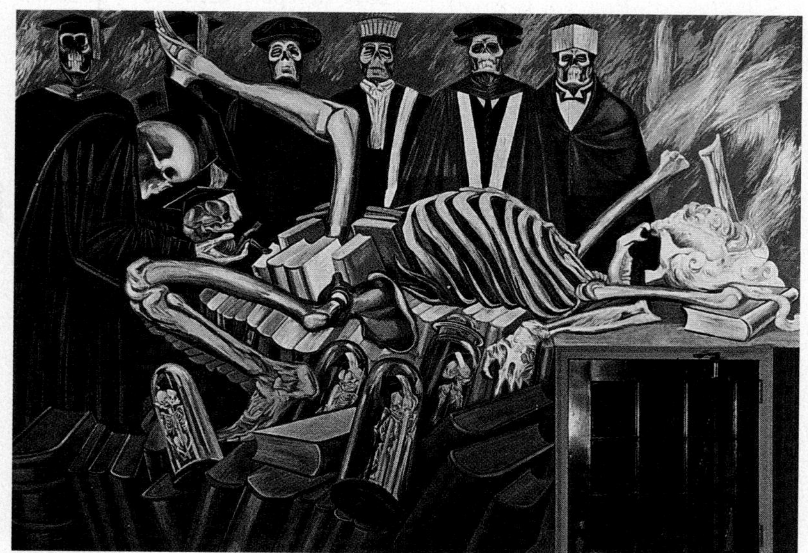

Mexican Marxist Jose Clement Orozco's mural "Gods of the Modern World".

FDR: 100 days of war on Depression

Washington, 16 June

No one really believed that this shy, crippled patrician, the very epitome of American wealth, could take hold of the failing economy of this country and shake it so violently. President Franklin Delano Roosevelt has done just that.

Today he persuaded the US Congress to pass an act – the National Industrial Recovery Act – which would have been considered unthinkable in a capitalist society six months ago, before he became president. The act gives him power not merely to control industry but to bring unions and bosses together, shorten working hours, fix wages and regulate production.

Roosevelt made it clear that he was prepared to adopt near-dictatorial powers to save the country. He closed the banks, allowing federal aid only to the efficient; now he is bailing out farmers and homeowners who are behind with their mortgages. Three billion dollars are being ploughed into public works programmes throughout the states. The Tennessee Valley Authority will bring water and forests to the dustbowl, and a civilian "conservation corps" will employ young people to plant trees. A million new jobs will be created.

"What we need is another pump": a comment on the New Deal.

Unlike others, this president confides in the people in regular "fireside chats" on the radio which are listened to by millions. With supreme confidence, he has repealed prohibition laws. "I think this would be a good time for a beer," he told Congress; back at work, Americans drank his health.

Terror and oppression launch Hitler's new age

Hitler becomes chancellor in new coalition

Berlin, 30 January

Adolf Hitler, a rabble-rousing Jew-baiting demagogue who has never held public office, today became chancellor of Germany. President Paul von Hindenburg, who had earlier dismissed Hitler as "that Bavarian corporal" who would make the country a dictatorship, finally gave way to pressures from bankers, high army officers and right-wing politicians, who were crying for order and discipline.

Three chancellors in as many years failed to secure a stable majority in the reichstag and were obliged to rule by presidential decree, while unemployment soared to six million and Hitler's Nazis and Communists fought bloody street battles.

The right-wing Nationalists in the cabinet, including Franz von Papen, the vice-chancellor, are confident they will soon tame Hitler and his wild men in brown uniforms with swastika armbands. Others are not so sure. Hitler's speeches, in which he denounces Jews, Bolsheviks, capitalists and the Versailles peace treaty, bring his audiences to their feet baying *"Sieg Heil! Sieg Heil!"* and stabbing the air with Nazi salutes.

Hitler at a Brownshirt rally.

Reichstag is funeral pyre of democracy

Berlin, 28 February

All legal guarantees of personal liberty, freedom of speech and the right of assembly were wiped out today by an official decree issued in the wake of last night's devastating reichstag fire. For many Berliners the gutted, smoke-blackened building represents the funeral pyre of German democracy.

The fire has been blamed on a simple-minded Dutch Communist, Marinus van der Lubbe, who was picked up by police in the reichstag grounds. But some observers accuse the Nazis of having a hand in the affair. Certainly Adolf Hitler, who became chancellor a month ago seems delighted. "This is a God-given signal," he cried as he watched the building burn.

Within hours he had pressured President Hindenburg into giving him dictatorial powers. Now he no longer needs the votes of the deputies in the reichstag, where his Nazis did not have a majority. In the run-up to the election, to be held next month, Nazi Storm Troopers, now enrolled as special police, are arresting socialists and communists and suppressing opposition newspapers. The radio has become a Nazi propaganda vehicle controlled by Dr Goebbels.

The forces of order surveying Germany's gutted democracy.

Germany is swept by a wave of tyranny

Nazi students feeding a bonfire of liberal and intellectual "vanities".

Berlin, 23 March

Against a background of mounting Nazi violence throughout Germany, the reichstag today voted to give Hitler, rather than the president, full powers to rule by decree. In spite of the intimidation practised during the election campaign, the Nazis, with 17,277,180 votes (44 per cent) failed to gain a reichstag majority. Hitler solved the problem by having Communist and Socialist deputies arrested.

The Nazi campaign of terror against Jews is being stepped up. Jewish-owned shops are being shut down, Jewish professors are being thrown out of universities, and school textbooks are to be rewritten to include "racial science". A three-times-married mother of 11 children, Gertrud Scholtz-Klink, has been appointed National Women's Leader to mobilise German women to serve the state.

Officials of trade unions and employers' organisations are being sacked and replaced by Nazis. The Boy Scouts are being dissolved and replaced by a Hitler Youth organisation run by the anti-Semite Baldur von Schirach.

Ich bin Jude aber ich will mich nicht über die Nazis beschweren

Translated – "I am a Jew but I will never complain about the Nazis."

"Urban debauchery," by Otto Dix, one of first artists to flee from Hitler.

1934 (1934-1935)

Germany, 10 January 1934. The alleged Reichstag arsonist Marinus van der Lubbe is guillotined.

Britain, 21 January 1934. The British Union of Fascists, led by Sir Oswald Mosley, holds its biggest rally ever in Birmingham.

Berlin, 26 January 1934. Germany signs a ten-year non-aggression pact with Poland.

Belgium, 17 February 1934. King Albert dies in a climbing accident near Namur; his son succeeds as Leopold III.

Austria, 17 February 1934. A Socialist uprising is bloodily suppressed.

Nicaragua, 22 February 1934. National Guardsmen gun down General Augusto Sandino.

Britain, 23 February 1934. Sir Edward Elgar, Master of the King's Musick since 1924, dies aged 76.

China, 28 February 1934. The ex-emperor Puyi accepts the throne of Japanese-occupied Manchukuo (*Manchuria*).

Madrid, 25 April 1934. Martial law is declared as the government resigns.

Rome, 29 April 1934. The Italian parliament votes to remove its last remaining powers.

Vienna, 30 April 1934. The Chancellor Engelbert Dollfuss is made dictator of a rump parliament which then votes itself out of existence.

Near East, 6 May 1934. Saudi Arabian forces capture the Yemeni city of Hodeida.

Saudi Arabia, 13 May 1934. Saudi Arabia signs a truce with Yemen in Jeddah.

Bulgaria, 19 May 1934. Fascists seize power in a coup aided by King Boris.

Louisiana, 23 May 1934. The famous outlaws Bonnie and Clyde are killed in a police ambush.

Czechoslovakia, 24 May 1934. Tomas Mazaryk is elected president for the fourth time.

Britain, 25 May 1934. The composer Gustav Holst, who made his name with the suite *The Planets*, dies aged 59.

Eastern Europe, 8 June 1934. Poland, Rumania and the USSR sign a pact guaranteeing their present frontiers.

Saudi Arabia, 27 June 1934. King ibn Saud and the Imam of Yemen sign a peace treaty to end the "Desert War".

Germany, 30 June 1934. In the "Night of the Long Knives" Hitler purges the Fascist Party.

Berlin, 3 July 1934. The Vice-chancellor von Papen, resigns.

Berlin, 13 July 1934. Hitler justifies the "Night of the Long Knives", claiming that the SA were plotting to overthrow him.

Germany, 13 July 1934. Heinrich Himmler is appointed head of the concentration camps.

Vienna, 26 July 1934. The government orders the round-up of Austrian Nazis following the murder of Chancellor Dollfuss.

Vienna, 29 July 1934. Dr Kurt von Schuschnigg is appointed chancellor.

Berlin, 2 August 1934. Hitler assumes the title "Fuhrer" on the death of Hindenburg.

Germany, 4 September 1934. 750,000 attend the opening of the Nazi party conference.

Spain, 8 October 1934. Martial law is declared following a bid to declare Catalonia independent.

Yugoslavia, 11 October 1934. Anti-Italian and anti-Hungarian riots follow the assassination of King Alexander in Marseilles two days ago. His ten-year-old son Peter will succeed.

Ankara, 25 November 1934. Mustapha Kemal tells Turks to adopt a surname by 1 January 1935. His will be "*Ataturk*", Father of The Turks.

Egypt, 30 November 1934. A royal decree annuls the constitution and dissolves the Egyptian parliament.

USSR, 1 December 1934. Stalin's aide Sergei Kirov is murdered.

Ethiopia, 5 December 1934. Ethiopian and Italian troops clash at Wal-Wal, over 20 miles inside southeastern Ethiopia.

Turkey, 14 December 1934. Women get the vote.

Tehran, 27 December 1934. The government declares that Persia will now be known as Iran.

USSR, 29 December 1934. More than 100 people have been executed following the murder of Stalin's aide Sergei Kirov.

North Africa, 1 January 1935. The Italian colonies of Cyrenaica, Tripoli and Fezzan are merged under the name of Libya.

Africa, 15 January 1935. Mussolini unites Eritrea and Somaliland as Italian East Africa.

Rome, 24 January 1935. Mussolini dismisses the entire cabinet.

Italy, 23 February 1935. Troops set sail for Ethiopia as the border dispute over the Italian post at Wal-Wal inside Ethiopia escalates.

Purge follows murder of Stalin associate

One of Stalin's party "purge committees", rooting out "Trotskyists".

Leningrad, December 1934

The bloody reprisals following the murder of Sergei Kirov, a rising star in the Communist Party, have led to speculation that Joseph Stalin is once again embarking on a policy of terror.

More than 100 people have been hastily implicated, tried and executed. Zinoviev and Kamenev, former comrades of Lenin, have been sent into internal exile. However, it is rumoured that Stalin himself ordered the assassination, carried out by an obscure dissident.

Stalin claimed recently there was "nothing to prove and no one left to beat"; the civil war against the peasants was over and most of the industrial targets of the first Five-Year Plan had been met. However, this month's events suggest he has declared war on the party that gave him his ladder to power.

Encircled Chinese communists break out

China, 16 October 1934

China's Communists under their general, the ex-warlord, ex-opium addict Zhu De, have began to break out of their Jiangxi Soviet Republic through Chiang Kai-shek's encircling forces. Columns of troops, carrying rifles, hoes and sowing machines, pour westwards. Chiang, who failed to take Jiangxi by storm in four campaigns, has adopted new tactics, surrounding the Red enclave with a network of barbed wire and blockhouses. Nearly half a million men and 400 modern aircraft have been used against the communists, and the innocent peasants caught up in this ruthless war have suffered terribly.

One 10,000-strong force under Fang Zhihmin tried to break out earlier this summer but it was wiped out and Fang's head was put on display in Nanchang. Now Zhu De and his political mentor Mao Zedong have set out with 80,000 troops, accompanied by 20,000 non-combatants, to march eastwards to safety, although no one knows where. All that is certain is that it will be a very long march.

On the march: Mao Zedong, political mentor of China's Reds.

Long knives buried in Brownshirt backs

Munich, 30 June 1934
Lurid stories of perversion and debauchery are being passed on after the massacre, in the early hours this morning, of hundreds – some say thousands – of senior Nazi Storm Troopers. Among the dead is Ernst Roehm, one of Hitler's closest comrades from the earliest days of the National Socialist Party. He was dragged from his bed and shot in a lakeside hotel outside Munich. In another room, Obergruppenfuhrer Edmund Heines was found in bed with a youth. Hitler was on hand to make sure no one was overlooked. Hitler claims he has foiled a plot to overthrow him, but the more generally accepted story is that the army threatened to take over unless he got rid of his Brownshirt thugs and stopped talk of socialist revolution. Whatever the truth, the "Night of the Long Knives", has crushed the Brownshirts and established the supremacy of the Blackshirts, or SS.

Unrest in Spain as Catalonians rebel

Half a million demonstrating in Barcelona for a "free Catalonia".

Madrid, 8 October 1934
Despite martial law fierce fighting is taking place throughout Spain as workers stage a series of strikes and riots with Catalonia bidding to set up its own government. The trouble has been triggered by the new right-wing government in Madrid introducing three ministers from the staunchly Catholic "Popular Action".

In Catalonia the situation was relieved with the arrival by sea from Morocco of a battalion of the Spanish Foreign Legion which marched from the harbour to the sound of bugles and drums. Rifle and machine-gun fire can be heard from many quarters of Madrid. The army garrison has been mobilised to relieve the exhausted civil guard. The home of the prime minister, Lerroux, has been fired at.

Some 8,000 monarchist officers who were retired at the time of the abdication of King Alfonso have been invited over the radio to resume service with the colours.

Briton invents aeroplane tracking device

Slough, England, 1935
A new device for tracking enemy aircraft has been developed at a government research station here. It bounces radio off flying objects.

"Radar" is the brainchild of Robert Watson-Watt and his colleague, A F Wilkins, who recalled a Post Office engineer reporting in 1931 that passing aircraft distorted radio reception.

The idea was put to the test on 26 February when a BBC transmitter at Daventry detected a bomber at 10,000 feet from a distance of eight miles (13 kilometres).

Austrian dictator dies in failed Nazi coup

Homage to Dollfuss, his coffin guarded by members of his old regiment.

Vienna, 25 July 1934
Over 150 Austrian Nazis are under arrest tonight after an unsuccessful coup d'etat, during which the Chancellor, Engelbert Dollfuss, was shot in the throat and left for four hours to bleed to death in his office. It is widely believed that Hitler was behind the plot.

The Nazi gang, dressed in army and police uniforms, broke into the Chancellery around noon. When it was apparent the coup was going to fail, they took other ministers as hostages and tried to negotiate safe conduct to the German border. A promise was given and then retracted when it was found that Dollfuss was dead. Three police and two Nazis died in a three-hour battle for the radio station

Six months ago, Dollfuss, a devout Catholic and violently anti-socialist, used the army to crush the Schutzbund, the socialist defence force established in the big housing estates outside Vienna. The workers held out for five days. Dollfuss suspended the constitution and intended ruling by decree in order to check the growing strength of the Austrian Nazis. He sought the backing of Mussolini in resisting German pressures.

Last Chinese emperor is Manchuria's first

Manchuria, 1 March 1934
Puyi, once the boy emperor of China, now the puppet of Japan, was installed today as emperor of conquered Manchuria, renamed Manchukuo by the Japanese.

The ceremony took place amid scenes of high nostalgia. The streets were thronged with bemedalled soldiers, Mongol horsemen, painted geishas and Lama priests. Chinese nobles paid homage in splendid robes hidden since the revolution.

At his first court Puyi, now using the title Kangte, announced: "The empire of Japan, in the name of righteousness and justice, assisted the establishment of this state. Armed hostilities have ceased. The country is bathed in the radiance of the sun and moon."

Puyi: last emperor no more.

1935

Bangkok, 2 March. King Prajadhipok abdicates when his government rejects plans for more democracy in Siam.

Switzerland, 7 March. Nine-year-old Prince Ananda, now in Europe, is crowned king of Siam.

USSR, 9 March. Nikita Khrushchev is elected chief of the Communist party.

Berlin, 11 March. The German air force, or *Luftwaffe* is officially created in a proclamation by Hermann Goering.

Greece, 12 March. The former president Eleutherios Venizelos fails in an attempted coup.

Britain, 18 March. Britain protests at Germany's introduction of conscription.

Moscow, 31 March. Anthony Eden, the Lord Privy Seal, meets Maxim Litvinov, the Soviet foreign minister for talks on the international situation.

Danzig, 7 April. The Nazi party wins 60 per cent of the vote in the free city.

Italy, 14 April. France, Britain and Italy agree to form a united front against German rearmament.

Geneva, 17 April. The League of Nations condemns Hitler's reintroduction of conscription.

Paris, 2 May. France and the USSR sign a mutual defence pact in case of attack.

Britain, 19 May. The soldier and writer Colonel Thomas Edward Lawrence dies aged 46 in a motor bicycle accident.

London, 22 May. The government announces plans to treble the size of the air force in the next two years.

Rome, 24 May. Pope Pius XI condemns the Nazi sterilisation of 56,244 "inferior" German citizens.

Paris, 4 June. Pierre Laval becomes prime minister.

Britain, 7 June. Stanley Baldwin becomes prime minister again following the resignation of Ramsay MacDonald for health reasons.

Argentina, 12 June. Bolivia and Paraguay sign an armistice to end their three-year-old war over the disputed Chaco area.

Paris, 19 June. French anger mounts following the Anglo-German naval deal signed yesterday which allows Germany to build up its navy again, albeit limited to one third of the tonnage of the Royal Navy.

Moscow, 9 July. Engineers on the underground railway discover Ivan the Terrible's torture chamber.

Britain, 29 July. T E Lawrence's *Seven Pillars of Wisdom* is published posthumously.

Washington, DC, 14 August. President Roosevelt signs the Social Security Bill, introducing welfare for the old, sick and unemployed.

Germany, 15 August. On Hitler's orders the *swastika* becomes the national flag.

Ethiopia, 25 August. The country is put on a war footing in anticipation of an Italian invasion.

Mexico, 1 September. It is announced that women workers are to be given the vote.

Utah, 3 September. Sir Malcolm Campbell sets a new land speed record of 301.337 mph.

Philippines, 15 September. Manuel Quezon is elected president in the first elections since the US granted a new constitution.

Ethiopia, 3 October. Mussolini's Fascist troops march into Ethiopia.

Britain, 8 October. Clement Richard Attlee is elected stop-gap leader of the Labour party.

Ethiopia, 8 November. The Italians complete their occupation of Tigre province, seizing the provincial capital, Makale.

Britain, 16 November. The National government, now Tory in all but name, is back in power with a huge majority.

Italy, 18 November. Economic sanctions are imposed on Italy by the League of Nations.

Greece, 25 November. King George II returns to his country after 12 years in exile, restored to his throne by a referendum.

China, 26 November. Japanese troops march into Beiping (*Beijing*) to support a coup in Tokyo which has set up the so-called autonomous state of Hebei province in the north.

Cairo, 12 December. King Fuad restores Egypt's 1923 parliamentary constitution.

Czechoslovakia, 18 December. Eduard Benes, the chosen successor to Masaryk, who resigned four days ago because of old age, is elected president.

Britain, 18 December. Sir Samuel Hoare, the foreign secretary, resigns following an agreement he made with the French prime minister, Pierre Laval to appease Mussolini. The prime minister, Stanley Baldwin, demanded apology or resignation.

London, 22 December. Anthony Eden is appointed foreign secretary.

Mao's troops end long march into history

China, 20 October

At the end of a march which has lasted a year and covered 6,000 miles (9,600 kilometres) the battered, emaciated survivors of the Communists' First Front Army have at last reached the comparative safety of Yan'an in the wilds of northwest China.

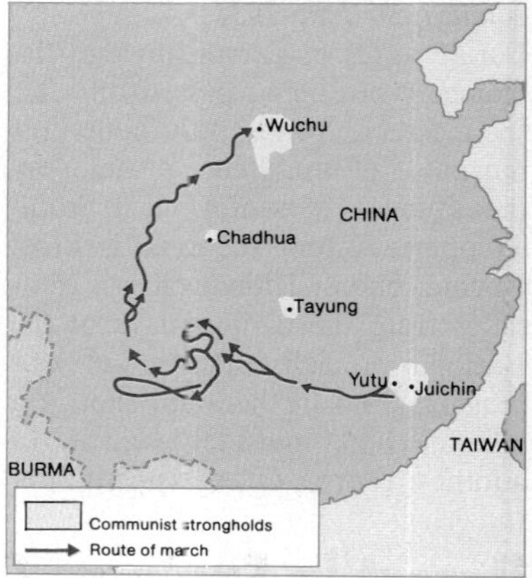

The long march has already become a legend. The Communists, forced out of their "soviet state" of Jiangxi, have passed through 11 provinces, crossed 18 mountain ranges and 24 major rivers and broken through ten encircling armies. They fought all the way. Of the 100,000 that set out only 10,000 footsore survivors have reached safety.

There are many stories of bravery against impossible odds, none more remarkable than that of the 30 volunteers who captured the Luding bridge over the Dadu river gorge in the teeth of murderous machine-gun fire. The march has established Mao Zedong as the undisputed leader of the China's communists. He awaits the arrival of stragglers from other communist forces and plans to rebuild the Red Army on the battle-hardened, dedicated cadres of the Long March.

China caves in to Japanese ultimatum

Japanese soldiers being blessed by the emperor before departing for China.

China, 18 June

The government of China caved in today to a Japanese ultimatum and agreed to remove a division of troops from the north and to dismiss Song Zheyuan, the governor of Chahar and one of the few Chinese commanders to put up a successful resistance to the Japanese during the aggression of 1933.

The Chiang Kai-shek government has also agreed to replace loyalist government officials with puppets who can be trusted to do the bidding of the Japanese. The excuse for this humiliating agreement was the arrest of three Japanese secret agents. The Japanese pretended outrage at this treatment of their "civilian officials" and demanded a more "friendly" attitude from the Chinese.

Chiang, busy fighting the Communists, was forced to give in, but he will lose much political and military influence in northern China.

Britain to increase spending on arms

London, 4 March

In a major reversal of rearmament policy Britain today announced new expansion plans for its army, navy and air force. The plans, in a defence white paper, are to demonstrate that Britain does not take lightly Germany's continuing rearmament.

The white paper calls for an enlarged fleet, improved defences for warships against air attack, more aircraft for the RAF and new coastal and anti-aircraft defences. The emphasis on air defence follows fears that Britain is an easy target for cross-Channel air raids.

Explaining the government's policy shift Stanley Baldwin said: "Our attempt to lead the world towards disarmament by unilateral example has failed." German rearmament now threatened to put peace at peril. Despite claims by Germany's leaders that they wanted peace, Britain could not ignore the way Germany's forces are constantly being mobilised, he added.

Britain's new stance on the eve of an important Anglo-German meeting in Berlin is a victory for those in the government who believe in the healing effects of the drums of war now beginning to sound more loudly across Europe. At the Berlin meeting they want Hitler left in no doubt about how strongly Britain feels about German rearmament.

A Conservative poster for the National Government in the 1935 British general election.

Fascist troops march into Ethiopia

Ethiopia, 3 October

Mussolini's Fascist troops marched into Ethiopia today – and as the war-drums called Emperor Haile Selassie's people to fight, the League of Nations in Geneva was facing its greatest test since it was formed in 1919. Mussolini has long coveted Ethiopia, the only independent black state to survive the scramble for Africa, which inflicted such a humiliating defeat on Italy at Adowa in 1896, which he is determined to avenge.

Although the Ethiopians are resisting strongly, in spite of being attacked by gas, the real question is whether or not the league has any teeth to counter aggression. Ethiopia has cabled the league, claiming that the first bombs on the country struck a hospital bearing the Red Cross. Neither Britain nor France – the most interested of the world powers – seem anxious to intervene. Between them, they can close the Suez Canal to Italian troopships, but France is treatybound with Italy not to oppose the invasion, and Britain's Foreign Secretary, Sir Samuel Hoare, does not want to alienate Mussolini and drive him into the arms of Hitler. Although many Members of Parliament are pleading for sanctions against Italy, he has made it clear that he will seek a "breathing space" before taking steps.

For millions of Britons who have enjoyed a sweltering summer, events in Ethiopia are little more than a sideshow; the US, impotent because it is outside the League, can do nothing except except express outrage. But some observers see ominous overtones as a well-armed European power vents its power against a near-primitive African nation. In every town and village in Italy, 40 million people were ordered to gather to listen to Mussolini defy any move by the League of Nations. "We will answer with our discipline and our abstemiousness and our spirit of sacrifice," he told his captive radio audience.

Hoping for another Adowa, Ethiopia's army awaits the Italian invader.

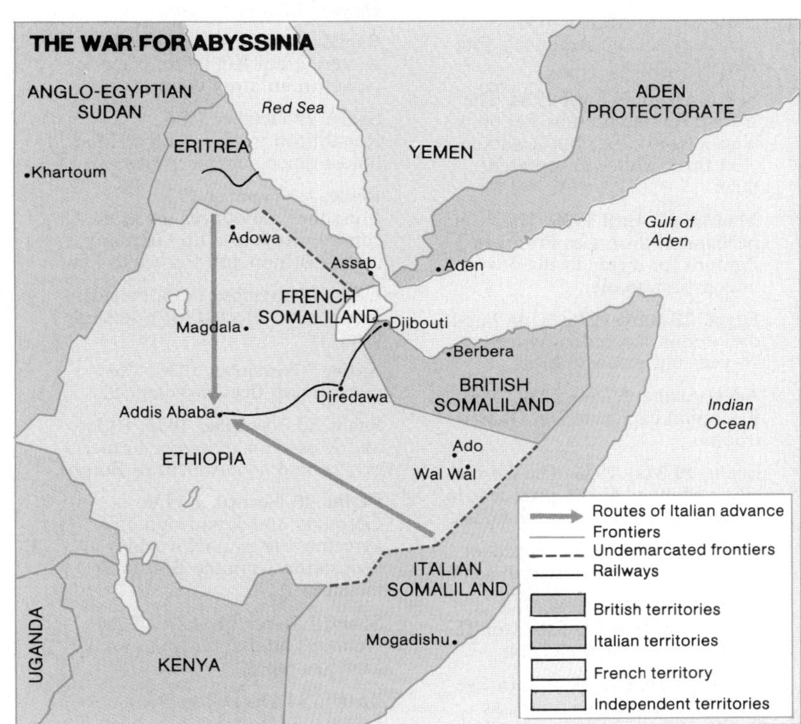

War between Bolivia and Paraguay claims 35,000 victims

Paraguay, 12 June

Urged on by the United States and a confederation of five South American states, the warring nations of Bolivia and Paraguay accepted a truce here today, bringing to a halt the three-year long Chaco War.

The war, which has claimed 35,000 victims, has been fought over the ownership of the *Chaco Boreal*, a wasteland of some 100,000 square miles west of the Paraguay river, the subject of a dispute between Paraguay and Bolivia since 1825.

Bolivia, deprived of its coastal territories since the war of the Pacific, wanted to use the Chaco as a shipping route for its oil exports. It also hoped to exploit the oil reserves of the Chaco itself.

Bolivian troops invaded in 1928, but a Pan-American conference averted outright war. Skirmishes continued until 1932 when Paraguay launched a major offensive, and formally declared war in May 1933. The Bolivian army, larger and better trained, fought back successfully, but in 1934 the Paraguayan offensive reversed the position, capturing much Bolivian land.

This tit-for-tat sequence came to an end today when the two sides, wearied by war, accepted the ceasefire.

1936 (1936-1937)

Britain, 21 January 1936. Edward VIII is proclaimed king following the death of his father George V yesterday.

India, 8 February 1936. Jawaharlal Nehru is elected president of the Indian National Congress.

Paraguay, 18 February 1936. President Eusebio Ayala resigns following yesterday's coup by military rebels.

Washington, DC, 29 February 1936. President Roosevelt signs the second neutrality bill, banning loans to countries at war.

Rhineland, 7 March 1936. German troops march into the Rhineland, in defiance of the treaties of Versailles and Locarno.

Paraguay, 11 March 1936. Paraguay sets up America's first Fascist regime.

South Africa, 7 April 1936. The Native Representation Act bans blacks from office but lets them elect three whites to represent them.

Madrid, 17 April 1936. The parliament dismisses President Zamora for trying to dissolve it unconstitutionally.

Egypt, 28 April 1936. King Fuad dies and is succeeded by the 16-year-old Prince Farouk.

Addis Ababa, 5 May 1936. The Ethiopian capital falls to Italian troops.

Spain, 10 May 1936. The *Cortes* elects Manuel Azana president in succession to the ousted Zamora.

Bolivia, 17 May 1936. President Tejada Sorzano is ousted in a coup.

Belgium, 24 May 1936. The *Rexists*, Belgian Fascists, win 21 seats in the general election.

France, 8 June 1936. Within five days of sweeping to power as leader of a socialist popular front coalition, Leon Blum ends the strikes that have crippled France.

Palestine, 21 June 1936. British planes go into action against Palestinian Arabs who have ambushed British troops.

Spanish Morocco, 17 July 1936. General Franco heads an uprising against the government in Melilla.

Spain, 19 July 1936. General Franco lands in Cadiz heading rebel Spanish foreign legionnaries.

Spain, 24 July 1936. The government appeals for foreign help in the civil war.

Berlin, 1 August 1936. Adolf Hitler opens the Berlin Olympics.

Spain, 19 August 1936. The writer Federico Garcia Lorca dies shortly after his arrest, aged 37.

Egypt, 26 August 1936. An Anglo-Egyptian treaty ends the British protectorate over Egypt and gives Britain control of the Suez Canal for 20 years.

Spain, 29 August 1936. Following the rebels' capture of Badajoz, Spain is divided in half, with the nationalists holding the southwest and the north and the government controlling Madrid.

Spain, 17 September 1936. Franco's troops take Maqueda, between Toledo and Madrid.

Spain, 28 September 1936. Franco is made head of the rebel forces.

London, 11 October 1936. 100,000 people barricade East London streets to prevent a march of Oswald Mosley's Fascists.

Baghdad, 29 October 1936. Pro-western Iraqi Kemalists come to power in an army coup.

Spain, 29 October 1936. Republican troops south of Madrid hold Franco's forces at bay.

Rome, 1 November 1936. Mussolini announces the anti-communist Axis with Germany, urging Britain and France to join.

USA, 3 November 1936. President Roosevelt is elected for a second term.

Spain, 7 November 1936. The government flees to Valencia.

Spain, 18 November 1936. Hitler and Mussolini recognise Franco's provisional government in Burgos.

Berlin, 25 November 1936. Germany and Japan sign an agreement to protect world civilisation from the Bolshevik menace.

Spain, 1 December 1936. 5,000 Germans land at Cadiz to join Franco's rebels.

Britain, 11 December 1936. Edward VIII makes his abdication speech.

Britain, 12 December 1936. Prince Albert is proclaimed king as George VI.

Britain, 1936. Among the great writers who died this year are Rudyard Kipling, A E Housman and G K Chesterton.

Britain, 1 January 1937. The Public Order Act comes into force banning political uniforms and sounding the death-knell for Oswald Mosley's British Union of Fascists.

Berlin, 7 January 1937. Hitler agrees to support a non-intervention pact on Spain if all other powers do likewise.

Moscow, 17 January 1937. The USSR refuses to halt aid to the republican rebels in Spain.

Colonialism in Africa: contrasting views

On the top of the pile: French colonialism, through German eyes.

THE EMPIRE STANDS FOR PEACE!
WE ALL WANT PEACE FOR OURSELVES AND OUR CHILDREN, SO DO THE FATHERS AND MOTHERS OF EVERY COUNTRY IN THE EMPIRE OVERSEAS.
The best guarantee of peace we can give the world is a united and prosperous British Empire. Every man and woman can help to provide that guarantee by buying Empire produce.
● ASK FIRST FOR HOME PRODUCE
● ASK NEXT FOR THE PRODUCE OF THE EMPIRE OVERSEAS

On top of the world: British colonialism, through British eyes.

Southern Africa, January 1936

As arrangements are made for Britain's African colonies to join in the celebrations for the accession of King Edward VIII, there are sharp differences of opinion about whether colonial rule is benefiting or exploiting the native populations. Men like Sir Charles Rey, the UK's resident commissioner in Bechuanaland, fume at what he calls "the rotten socialist dogs at home" for misguidedly claiming that the military brutally overawe the natives. Instead, as the accession celebrations approach, he revels in the idea of "wild savages and civilised beings, drawn together at the insistance of a single white officer in common loyalty to the head of this vast Empire of ours".

A less rosy view, supporting the idea that Africa is being raped by Europe, is taken by Major Trevor, director of public works in Northern Rhodesia for 40 years, who claims that "the only reason that takes any white man, other than a traveller or missionary, to a tropical dependency is to exploit cheap land, cheap labour and new mines".

Negro upstages Nazis at Berlin Games

Jesse Owens: leaping into history.

Berlin, 16 August 1936

The Black American athletics star Jesse Owens has shattered two worldclass sprint records – and the Nazi regime's hopes of turning the 11th Olympic Games into a showcase for its dogma of Aryan supremacy. Owens, who won four gold medals in the 100 metres, 200 metres, 400-metres relay and the long jump, was the undisputed star of the games which closed today with a host of records by 5,000 athletes from 53 nations. Just as notable was Owens' upstaging of the Nazi leader Adolf Hitler who had intended to greet winners. The thought of publicly congratulating a Negro was too humiliating, and after Owens' second win Hitler stormed out of the stadium.

Show trial purge of 17 "Trotskyists"

Moscow, 29 January 1937
Joseph Stalin, bidding to extend his phenomenal power over the Soviet people, scored a notable success today with death sentences meted out to 13 of the 17 party members on trial for treason and lengthy prison terms for the others.

The trial was little more than an obscene farce, with ludicrous confessions abounding. The accused readily admitted to plotting with the exiled Leon Trotsky against Stalin. In the custody of the *NKVD*, Stalin's secret police, they had been processed through a mixture of ill-treatment, threats for the safety of their families and pleas for party loyalty.

Crisis in Palestine as riots continue

Palestine, 25 May 1936
A force of 300 Arabs attacked the Jewish colony of Mesha last night, writing another, bloodier than ever chapter in the story of murder and rioting that has dominated recent Palestinian history.

In six weeks of civil strife between Arabs and Jews, 11 people have died and 50 have been wounded. Both sides blame Britain. Jews are demanding that the authorities suppress Arab violence; Arabs wish to see an end to Jewish immigration and land-buying.

Trouble has flared in Gaza and a general strike has been called in Nablus by Arab leaders. A curfew has been established in a number of places.

Civil war erupts in Spain

Defending the republic: Spanish men and women rally to the call.

Madrid, 31 July 1936
Spain is in the grip of bloody civil war, with the shaky Republican government being challenged by Nationalist rebels centred on the army. The war is being waged with the utmost ferocity, and atrocities are being carried out by both sides.

The war erupted a fortnight ago when the army rose against the new government of Jose Giral, a leftwing Republican, who promised to step up revolutionary experiments in collectivisation. General Franco, one of the rebel leaders, warned Madrid in a telegram sent from the headquarters of his African army in Morocco: "The Spanish Restoration Movement will triumph very shortly, and we will demand explanations of your conduct."

Franco will have difficulty ferrying his men across the Straits of Gibraltar and has turned to Italy and Germany for help. At the same time, however, several areas have already fallen to the rebels, mainly around the conservative towns of Leon and Old Castile.

This is a deeply rooted and complex conflict involving struggles between workers and employers, landowners and peasants, Catholics and secularists, regionalists and centralists. It might also be seen as an ideological class war between the forces of reform and reaction.

The Nationalists appear to share the single basic aim of smashing the republic, whereas the Republicans are divided between those fighting to defend the constitution and those who see the war as a launchpad for social revolution.

King quits, putting love before duty

London, 11 December 1936
Broadcasting from Windsor Castle tonight, King Edward VIII announced his abdication of the throne, a burden he found it impossible to carry, he said, "without the help and support of the woman I love". He added: "The decision has been mine and mine alone. The other person most concerned has tried to persuade me to take a different course."

The king's wish to marry the twice-divorced Mrs Simpson (born Wallis Warfield of Baltimore) has been the talk of the European and American press for two years. But Britain has only just learned of it because of self-censorship by Fleet Street. Tomorrow Albert, the duke of York, will be proclaimed King George VI in his brother's place.

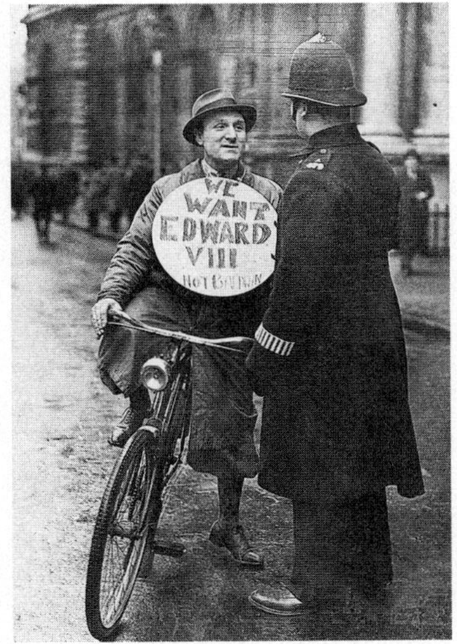

"On your bike": a pro-king demonstrator moved on in Whitehall.

Right-wing army coup bid fails in Tokyo

Tokyo, 29 February 1936
The attempt by a group of young right-wing officers to overthrow the government, which has paralysed Tokyo for the last four days, has collapsed with the surrender of its leader, Captain Teruzo Ando.

Troops led by the ultra-nationalist officers occupied the government quarter while teams of assassins murdered leading politicians who were thought to be too liberal. They had intended to kill the prime minister but were foiled by the Imperial Guard. While there is relief that the attempted *coup* has failed there is much worry here that the plotters represent a strong element in the army and navy.

It is composed of politically active junior officers who belong to a secret society called the *Sakura-kai*, or Cherry Society, who advocate the uncompromising worship of the emperor, military conquests and the domination of the Pacific.

Chinese leader mysteriously kidnapped

China, 12 December 1936
The Chinese Generalissimo Chiang Kai-shek was kidnapped today, the "Double Twelfth", at Xian, the headquarters of the "Young Marshal", Zhang Xueliang, The town was woken by the sound of a furiously beaten gong and gunfire as troops of Zhang's Northeastern Army rounded up Chiang's staff.

Chiang himself escaped in his pyjamas, but was captured on a nearby mountainside. His feet were bleeding so he was carried down on the back of his captor, Sun Mingchiu, commander of Chang's bodyguard. The generalissimo is now housed in "new quarters" at Zhang's own headquarters.

This mysterious incident has its origins in Chiang's determination to continue fighting the Communists against the wishes of Zhang and a number of other generals who want him to lead a united China in war against the Japanese.

1937 (1937-1938)

Spain, 8 February 1937. Malaga falls to Franco, aided by 15,000 Italians.

Spain, 22 February 1937. Britain, France, Germany, Italy, Portugal and the USSR agree to a cordon around Spain to enforce the arms ban agreed on the 16 February.

China, 23 February 1937. Chiang Kai-shek, the head of the Chinese government, rejects Communist suggestions that they and the Nationalists should join forces to fight against the Japanese invaders.

Spain, 26 February 1937. Portugal and the USSR withdraw from the Spanish cordon pact.

India, 1 April 1937. The Indian constitution comes into being under the Government of India Act. Burma is separated.

Spain, 27 April 1937. Guernica is destroyed by the German air force.

Washington, DC, 7 May 1937. An enquiry begins into the Hindenburg disaster.

London, 12 May 1937. King George VI and Queen Elizabeth are crowned.

Spain, 16 May 1937. The prime minister Largo Caballero resigns.

Spain, 18 May 1937. Franco is checked at Guadalajara.

Britain, 28 May 1937. Neville Chamberlain becomes prime minister following Stanley Baldwin's retirement.

Spain, 31 May 1937. Italy and Germany withdraw from the Spanish non-intervention cordon.

France, 3 June 1937. The ex-king Edward VIII, now the duke of Windsor, marries Mrs Simpson.

USSR, 12 June 1937. Eight top generals are executed as Stalin's purge extends to the Red Army.

Spain, 19 June 1937. Bilbao falls to Franco's rebels.

Paris, 21 June 1937. Leon Blum's Popular Front ministry resigns.

London, 7 July 1937. The British government announces plans to partition Palestine.

China, 7 July 1937. Japanese soldiers in night manoeuvres outside their designated area attack Wanping at the southern end of the bridge near Beiping (*Beijing*).

Eire, 21 July 1937. Eamon de Valera is re-elected president.

Germany, 1 August 1937. A new concentration camp has been opened at Buchenwald.

China, 8 August 1937. The Japanese occupy Beiping (*Beijing*).

Baghdad, 12 August 1937. General Bakr Sidki Pasha, Iraq's dictator, is assassinated.

China, 14 August 1937. Hundreds are reported dead in a Japanese bombing raid on Shanghai.

Germany, 5 September 1937. The biggest-ever Nazi rally marks the opening of the Nazi congress in Nuremberg.

China, 25 September 1937. The Japanese bomb the Chinese Nationalist capital Nanjing.

Geneva, 28 September 1937. The League of Nations condemns the Japanese invasion of China.

China, 25 September 1937. Chinese troops defeat the Japanese at Pingxingguan (*Shanxi*).

China, 29 September 1937. Chiang Kai-shek, the Chinese leader, comes to an agreement with his Communist rival Mao Zedong in the face of the full-scale Japanese assault on their country.

Palestine, 20 October 1937. The British authorities limit Jewish immigration.

Spain, 21 October 1937. Gijon, the last Republican stronghold in northern Spain, surrenders to Franco.

Moscow, 21 October 1937. Sixty two are executed in Stalin's latest purges.

Italy, 6 November 1937. Italy joins the anti-communist pact between Germany and Japan.

China, 9 November 1937. The Japanese take Shanghai.

Spain, 28 November 1937. Franco tells the government to surrender by 12 December or face a massive offensive.

China, 7 December 1937. The Japanese launch a general attack on Nanjing; bitter fighting follows.

Java, 10 December 1937. Parts of the skull of one of humankind's ancestors is discovered.

Geneva, 11 December 1937. Italy leaves the League of Nations.

China, 13 December 1937. The Japanese army occupies Nanjing.

Spain, 21 December 1937. Republicans capture Franco's stronghold of Teruel.

Dublin, 29 December 1937. The new constitution comes into force; the republic is called Eire.

London, 6 January 1938. Sigmund Freud arrives in London, fleeing from Nazi persecution.

Rumania, 10 February 1938. King Carol ousts the anti-Semitic prime minister, Octavian Goga, and becomes a dictator.

London, 21 February 1938. Anthony Eden resigns as foreign secretary in protest against Chamberlain's appeasement.

Jewish state is planned for Palestine

Palestine, 7 July 1937

In the face of what they call the "irreconcilable conflict" between Jews and Arabs, the British authorities have succumbed to years of community violence with a plan, finally, to partition Palestine. In a white paper Britain proposes dividing the country into three: two-thirds to remain Arab, the remainder to be the promised national homeland for the Jews. Zionist leaders are unimpressed.

The Holy Cities of Jerusalem, Bethlehem and Nazareth are to be placed under permanent British control. Trans-Jordan will receive a £2 million grant, and Arab landowners will be compensated.

The British lion, in the mud of conflicting promises to Arabs and Jews.

Mexico takes over all US oil firms

Mexico, 18 March 1938

Mexico has today nationalised 17 American and British oil companies, with assets worth $450 million. The seizure follows a government report, bitterly contested by the oil firms, that the companies must pay some $40 million in wages and compensation, as demanded by unions. President Cardenas is a nationalist and trade unionist and his action stems less from a desire to rid Mexico of foreign capitalists than to ensure that those capitalists treat their workers fairly. The oil magnates' refusal to acknowledge the demands of the Syndicate of Petroleum Workers triggered today's move. A last-ditch attempt to compromise with the government failed to halt the expropriation.

Freud is shrunk by female shrink

USA, 1937

The German psychoanalyst Karen Horney has published a strong attack on the founding father of the psychoanalytic movement. In her new book, *The Neurotic Personality of Our Time*, Horney – a leftwing, socially orientated analyst – claims that the industrial civilisation of contemporary America is to blame for the problems and anxieties that beset men, women and children today. This is a direct attack on the orthodox Freudian line that biological givens lie at the core of neuroses. Though Horney trained with the Berlin Psychoanalytic Institute, she began criticising Freud for antifeminism early in her career. This latest book is bound to step up the conflict.

The Spanish painter Pablo Picasso's "Guernica", his angry memorial to the small Basque town destroyed by German bombs in a calculated experiment of terror. Though the town was wrecked, the oak tree, under which the Basque parliament has met since the Middle Ages, has survived.

Japanese seize Nanjing

Nanjing, 13 December 1937
The Japanese marched into Nanjing today and immediately began an orgy of brutality and wanton destruction. Defeated Chinese troops who try to surrender are being slaughtered, women are dragged from their homes to be raped and murdered, the city is being sacked and burnt.

Foreigners gathered in the international safety zone are trying to help the thousands of destitute Chinese who are seeking sanctuary in the zone. Other refugees are trying to flee across the river and many are drowning as the overcrowded junks capsize and sink.

The end in Nanjing was signalled last night when, after months of brave resistance, the Chinese army broke and began to stream in disorder through the city under heavy aerial and artillery bombardment.

All organisation broke down when it became known that General Tang had fled. The soldiers threw away their rifles and there were appalling scenes of panic. Then, at 11 this morning, the Japanese arrived. The planes which had been bombing the city dropped leaflets saying the Japanese were the real friends of the Chinese. And the killing began.

Chinese troops marching towards the front along the Great Wall of China.

"Nylon" points way to tomorrow's world

United States, 1937
It has been a golden year for America's inventors. A former chemistry teacher, Wallace Carothers, has made an artificial silk – superior to cellulose-based rayon – by combining two chemicals. He calls the result "nylon", although it is not yet being marketed. In Chicago, Chester Carlson has developed a system, of dry copying or "herography" which replaces the wet chemical system and will allow machines to do the job at the push of a button. And finally the "Polaroid" camera – the brainchild of Edwin Land – now makes it possible to produce a positive print without taking the negative out of the camera.

The Promenade Deck Cabin Lounge on the "Queen Mary", the most luxurious ship afloat. The flagship of the Cunard Line, the 80,733-ton super liner is taking 1,840 passengers across the Atlantic on each voyage.

The horrors of Guernica

Spain, 27 April 1937
German bombers, sent by Hitler to help Franco's Fascist forces against the Republicans, destroyed the Basque town of Guernica yesterday in one of the most horrific military actions since the 1914-18 war. Thousands of innocent civilians perished.

It was market day in Guernica, and the square was crowded with shoppers when a squadron of Heinkel 1-11 and Junker 52 bombers, escorted by fighter-planes, appeared and jettisoned high explosives on the town.

Incendiary bombs then set it on fire, while the fighters machine-gunned survivors.

Noel Monks, a British reporter, arrived soon after the bombing and helped collect burned bodies. He described the scene: "Some of the soldiers were sobbing like children. There were flames and smoke and grit, and the smell of burning human flesh was nauseating. Houses were collapsing into the inferno. In the Plaza, surrounded almost by a wall of fire, were about 100 refugees. They were weeping and wailing and rocking to and fro."

"It was impossible to go down many of the streets, because they were walls of flame. Debris was piled high. I could see shadowy forms, some large, some just ashes. I moved round to the back of the Plaza among survivors. They had the same story to tell, aeroplanes, bullets, bombs, fire."

Guernica was a communications centre, with a munitions factory. But the bombing was random.

"Hindenburg" explodes in a ball of flame

The "Hindenburg" crashes down in a ball of flame and exploding gas.

New Jersey, 6 May 1937
The *Hindenburg*, the pride of the German airship fleet and veteran of ten successful transatlantic trips, exploded in a ball of flame as she came into land in New Jersey tonight. As horrified crowds watched the mighty *dirigible* was reduced within minutes to a tangle of white-hot metal, a fiery grave for 35 passengers and crew.

The cause of the disaster has yet to be ascertained, but it is thought that static electricity, the product of a thunderstorm that had already held up her landing for 12 hours, somehow ignited the hydrogen gas that kept the airship aloft.

The horror of the explosion was made even more graphic by an eyewitness broadcast by Herb Morrison, a reporter for Chicago's WLS radio. Expecting a routine landing, Morrison, collapsing in tears, told his audience of "smoke and flames, and oh, the humanity ...".

1938 (1938-1939)

Vienna, 11 March 1938. Chancellor Schuschnigg resigns and the pro-Nazi Artur Seyss-Inquart succeeds. German troops invade on his invitation.

Vienna, 13 March 1938. The *Anschluss*, Germany's annexation of Austria, is declared.

Vienna, 14 March 1938. Vienna gives Hitler a tumultuous welcome.

Moscow, 15 March 1938. Another show trial ends in the execution of 18 top-ranking Soviet figures, including Nikolai Bukharin.

London, 24 March 1938. The prime minister, Neville Chamberlain, announces that Britain will fight for France and Belgium.

London, 1 April 1938. Britain and the US abandon the London naval treaty to allow for the building of battleships.

Spain, 3 April 1938. Franco takes Lerida, a major town in Catalonia.

Vienna, 6 April 1938. Leading Jewish figures are sent to Dachau concentration camp.

Vienna, 7 April 1938. The Nazis seize Rothschild's bank; Baron Rothschild is arrested.

China, 7 April 1938. The Chinese claim victory in the battle of Taierzhuang (*Shandong*) against the Japanese.

Austria, 10 April 1938. A plebiscite indicates that 99.75 per cent are in favour of Hitler's annexation of Austria.

Spain, 19 April 1938. After successive victories in Catalonia, Franco broadcasts an appeal for surrender.

Dublin, 21 April 1938. Douglas Hyde is elected Eire's first president.

Eire, 25 April 1938. Under the Anglo-Irish agreement Eire wins big financial and defence concessions.

London, 29 April 1938. Top-level Anglo-French talks end with a vague promise to defend Czechoslovakia.

Rome, 4 May 1938. The Vatican recognises Franco as leader of Spain.

Prague, 20 May 1938. The government orders 400,000 troops to the Austro-German border.

Britain, 1 June 1938. The Bren gun comes into service.

China, 7 June 1938. *Guomindang* (Nationalist) troops burst the dykes of the Yellow River at Huayuankou to prevent the southward move of Japanese forces. The river floods disastrously.

China, 8 June 1938. The Japanese have been bombing Guangzhou (*Canton*) mercilessly for ten days.

Germany, 17 August 1938. Austria's former leaders, including Schuschnigg, are being held in Dachau concentration camp.

Prague, 28 August 1938. The *Sudeten* (Nazi) Party begins talks with President Benes.

Prague, 6 September 1938. Benes offers self-government to the Sudetenland.

Prague, 21 September 1938. The government agrees to Anglo-French plans to cede the Sudetenland to Germany; Czechs protest.

Germany, 30 September 1938. A solution to the Czechoslovakian crisis is announced following talks between Chamberlain, Daladier, Hitler and Mussolini. Sudetenland will be ceded to Germany.

Czechoslovakia, 1 October 1938. German troops march into the Sudetenland as Teschen, in Czech Silesia, is annexed by Poland.

Prague, 5 October 1938. President Benes resigns.

Budapest, 13 October 1938. Tension mounts amid calls for the annexation of southern parts of Czechoslovakia.

London, 19 October 1938. New plans for Palestine abandon the idea of partition.

China, 21 October 1938. Guangzhou falls to the Japanese; fire spreads throughout the entire city.

Budapest, 23 October 1938. Hungary rejects Czech proposals for ceding Czechoslovak areas.

US, 31 October 1938. Orson Welles' vivid radio production *The War of the Worlds* causes widespread panic because of its realism.

Czechoslovakia, 2 November 1938. Following "arbitration" by Hitler, Hungary annexes the southern parts of Slovakia and Ruthenia.

Germany, 9 November 1938. Jews across the country are subjected to violent attacks.

Ankara, 11 November 1938. Ismet Onu succeeds Kemal Ataturk, who died yesterday, as president of Turkey.

Paris, 6 December 1938. France and Germany sign a pact on the inviolability of their present frontiers.

Tokyo, 4 January 1939. The fascist Baron Hiranuma becomes prime minister.

Cairo, 20 January 1939. King Farouk is declared the *caliph* (spiritual leader) of Islam.

Trek is celebrated by the Afrikaners

South Africa, 16 December 1938

On raised ground, near the banks of Blood River, the Afrikaners are celebrating the centenary of the Great *Trek*. No one speaks English; many wear uniforms modelled on Europe's fascist movements. The Great Trek is not the only anniversary today. Five years ago, to the day, South African police used tear-gas for the first time on Blacks. Since 1925, when segregation first became government policy, to protect the wages of "civilised labour", there has been considerable separation of the races – made easier by the disintegration of the main black union, the Industrial and Commercial Workers' Union, in 1928. The Afrikaners at Blood River have a lot to celebrate.

Leading Islamic philosopher dies

Karachi, 21 April 1938

Sir Mohammed Iqbal, the greatest Urdu poet and one of the world's leading Moslem philosophers, is dead. Born at Sialkot in the Punjab in 1873, he studied in Lahore, Cambridge and Germany. Although influenced by Nietzsche and Bergson he never lost his devotion to the great Moslem thinkers. He wrote in Persian as well so that more Moslems could read him.

He emphasised the innate greatness of the human self and argued that this could be best developed if the community were organised on a righteous basis. As president of the All-India League in 1930 he proposed a separate state for the northwestern part of India where Moslems are in a majority.

Britain builds its first "jet" engine

England, 1939

It is ten years since Frank Whittle, a young graduate from the RAF's Cranwell College, suggested that aircraft might be driven not by propellers but by jet propulsion. Only now has he been able to build a prototype of such an engine. Air enters at the front and is compressed and heated up. Then fuel is injected into the compressed air and ignited. The result is a tremendous backward thrust of expanding gases that pushes the whole assembly forwards like a rocket.

Whittle is not the first to apply the jet engine in a real aircraft. The German engineer Dr Hans von Ohain has used one to power a Heinkel He-178.

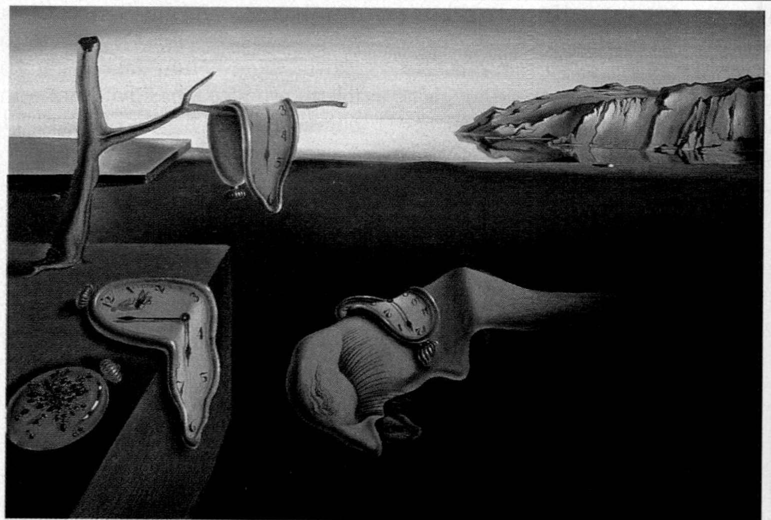

"Persistence of Memory", by Salvador Dali, who was expelled from Europe's Surrealists for his support of Franco in the Spanish Civil War. The accusation was unjust. His instinct was not to support Fascism, but to ignore it – and other forms of uncomfortable reality – and retreat into an inner world. In reaction to the controversy, he has retreated further, producing mannered, almost academic, Surrealism.

Austria joins the Reich

Austria on "Anschluss Day" Viennese women greeting a lost countryman.

Vienna, 14 March 1938
A forest of Nazi salutes stabbed the air as a triumphant Adolf Hitler rode into Vienna today accompanied by goose-stepping soldiers and tanks. Young girls threw flowers into his car, older folk wept with joy and church bells pealed.

At six o'clock he took the salute from the balcony of the Hotel Imperial and withdrew. The crowd continued to cheer with such a frenzy of enthusiasm that he reappeared and cried: "The German nation will never again be rent apart." Thus Hitler returned to his native land and the city where he had lived in poverty and obscurity.

The fall of Austria became inevitable when Hitler persuaded Mussolini to join the Axis pact and abandon support for Vienna. Last February, Hitler took the Austrian Chancellor, Kurt von Schuschnigg, to his Berchtesgaden retreat and shouted and raved at him for hours on end.

Schuschnigg refused to agree to the *Anschluss* (union) Hitler demanded and returned to Vienna to announce a plebiscite on Austrian independence. Hitler demanded Schuschnigg's resignation and the chancellor was replaced by the Austrian Nazi, Artur SeyssInquart, who duly invited German troops to prevent "disorders".

Tonight, Hitler was given an extravagant reception such as few Habsburg emperors can have enjoyed. Nazi supporters were brought in from as far away as Czechoslovakia to swell the crowds. The union of Germany and Austria was forbidden by the peace treaties which Hitler has contemptuously brushed aside. By bluster and bullying he has created a Greater Germany of 74 million people.

Now "the great spring cleaning", as the Nazi newspapers are calling the planned *pogrom*, begins. Jewish judges are marked down for dismissal, Jewish shops will be placarded and theatres and music halls purged of Jews, among them Max Reinhardt and Richard Tauber. Jews are being made to scrub the pavements while Nazis with whips stand over them.

"Planting the Rice", a painting by the Balinese artist G A Oka.

Hitler in Czechoslovakia

Sudetenland: German Czechs also greeting their fellow-countrymen.

Sudetenland, 5 October 1938
"Thus we begin our march into the great German future," Hitler cried as he crossed the frontier to take possession of his latest conquest, the Sudeten border areas of Czechoslovakia, claimed as German-speaking. So they may be, but they also include natural and man-made defences vital for Czechoslovakia's security.

The summer-long crisis, orchestrated by Hitler, with his puppet, Konrad Henlein, in Sudetenland spreading disorder, reached its climax a week ago, when the British and French leaders, Neville Chamberlain and Edouard Daladier, flew to Munich to agree with Hitler and Mussolini on the dismemberment of Czechoslovakia.

Earlier this year, the Czechs were prepared to fight; after all they had a treaty with the French. But the French were defeatist and Chamberlain was ready to make almost any concession to appease Hitler, whom he believed to be a man of his word. The Czechs were pressured into making compromises; but with each step Hitler demanded more.

Chamberlain came home waving a paper bearing Hitler's signature, and saying: "I believe it is peace for our time." He was wildly cheered. Then misgivings began to be felt. A far-away country, as Chamberlain called it, has been sacrificed to a ruthless dictator, whose appetite for conquest seems to grow with each success. Many believe, with Winston Churchill, that Hitler will soon strike again.

Night of violence against Germany's Jews

Germany, 9 November 1938
Exultant Nazis are calling it *Kristallnacht* (Crystal Night), a testimony to the millions of marks worth of broken glass that litter Germany's streets, following the worst outbreak yet of anti-Jewish violence. In a day's orgy of looting, arson and assault, hundreds of synagogues were burnt, shops smashed and thousands of Jews beaten.

According to Dr Goebbels, the minister of propaganda, the outburst came as a spontaneous reaction to the assassination two days ago of a German diplomat in Paris, killed by a young Polish Jew.

Anti-Semitism is a central tenet of Nazi ideology, and under the Nuremberg laws of 1935 the once assimilated Jews, who saw themselves as no less German than their compatriots, have been systematically deprived of their rights and jobs; but today's excesses are quite unprecedented. Nazi storm troopers have always attacked the Jews, but today they were joined by middle-class folk who cheered as "the sub-humans" were beaten.

1939 ⇒

Ireland, 28 January. William Butler Yeats, the poet and playwright, dies aged 73.

Rome, 10 February. Pope Pius XI dies aged 81.

London and Paris, 28 February. The British government recognises Franco's regime in Spain.

Rome, 12 March. Pope Pius XII is consecrated.

Czechoslovakia, 14 March. The Germans march into Bohemia as the Hungarians occupy Ruthenia.

Czechoslovakia, 15 March. Hitler enters Prague.

Lithuania, 21 March. Memel is ceded to the Germans.

Madrid, 28 March. Franco takes Madrid – war is over.

London, 31 March. Chamberlain pledges to defend Poland.

Iraq, 4 April. The king is killed in an accident; four-year-old Faisal succeeds.

London, 6 April. Britain, France and Poland sign a mutual assistance pact.

Albania, 8 April. Italian troops seize the capital, Tirana; King Zog flees the country.

London, 11 May. Chamberlain warns Hitler that the use of force in Danzig will mean war.

Berlin, 22 May. Hitler and Mussolini sign a "pact of steel" – a military alliance.

London, 26 May. The Military Training (Conscription) Act receives Royal Assent.

China, 21 June. The Japanese capture the international treaty port of Shautou (*Swatow*).

Danzig, 20 July. 2,000 Nazi guards arrive in the free city.

Britain, 29 July. A big round-up of IRA suspects begins as new anti-terrorist laws come into force.

China, 20 August. In the battle of Nomonhan Soviet and Mongolian troops win a decisive victory over the Japanese.

Moscow, 23 August. Germany and the USSR sign a non-aggression pact, known as the Hitler-Stalin pact.

Berlin, 26 August. Hitler demands from Poland the port of Danzig (with its mainly German population), a corridor from Germany to Danzig, and the end of the Anglo-French pledge to Poland.

Barcelona is Franco's latest prize

"The Angel of Peace ... of the Fascists!": a Republican poster.

Spanish Republicans behind a barricade in Barcelona, waiting for the Fascists.

Barcelona, 26 January
General Franco's attack on the bastion of Republicanism, Catalonia, has led to another Nationalist triumph. His troops entered Barcelona today and met with only sporadic resistance. Two exhausted Republican armies are crossing into France where they will be interned.

Franco's troops, among them the feared Moors, were greeted by crowds emerging from the underground stations where they sought refuge from bombing raids carried out by the Italian air force. Many of them gave the Fascist salute and carried portraits of the Nationalist leader.

The fundamental weakness and exhaustion, both moral and material, of the Republican forces has been clearly exposed over the last six months. Following the offensive which cut the Republic in two, the Nationalists, heavily reinforced and regularly supplied by Hitler and Mussolini, have won a series of victories. On the other hand a notable weakness of the Republican army has been its inability, from political causes, to launch offensives in the enemy's rear or to organise the type of guerrilla operations which would have held up Franco's troop movements.

The fall of Madrid cannot be delayed for much longer, and with it the Spanish Civil War will be over. At least 300,000 Spaniards have been killed during the hostilities. And Franco's prisons are filling up quickly.

The massive force of atomic fission

Germany
There is colossal power locked in the nucleus of the atom. Now, it seems, it may be possible to release that force by the process of nuclear fission. The German physicists Otto Hahn and Fritz Strassman have bombarded the element uranium with a stream of neutrons. They have found that the element barium is produced.

According to two other scientists, Otto Frisch and Lise Meitner, this means that the uranium atoms' nuclei have been split apart producing new elements with less mass than the original uranium and releasing enormous energy in the process. Properly harnessed, fission could mean energy unlimited.

"Gone with the Wind", the Hollywood box-office success of 1939, in which audiences escaped from the fear of a possible war with the romance of a past one.

Menzies takes over as Australian PM

Canberra, Australia, 24 April
Robert Menzies, a nationalist and an avowedly anti-communist politician, is the new Australian Prime Minister. He is 44. At six foot four inches tall, the United Australia Party leader has a reputation for toughness and has opted to end coalition government by excluding members of the rival Country Party from office.

The main planks of his policy are social insurance and the build-up of defence against Japan's military might. He intends to set up new ministries for both these areas. Bob Menzies has already served as attorney-general and deputy prime minister. He was a barrister before entering politics.

Swastika flies in Prague

German occupation troops on their first day in Prague – very much in control.

Prague, 15 March
The long agony of Czechoslovakia's dying democracy finally ended today when Adolf Hitler entered Prague with detachments of his jackbooted *Wehrmacht*. He was greeted with boos and hisses and tears as he rode up to the Hradzin Castle, the ancient palace of Bohemian kings and latterly the residence of the state president.

Only six months ago, when the Czechs ceded Sudetenland to Germany, Hitler declared he had no further territorial claims; but two days ago he presented Prague with a series of demands:

*Complete independence for Slovakia and Ruthenia;

*Formation of a new Czech government favourable to Germany;

*Payments of gold and foreign exchange to Germany.

The demands were preceded by disorders stage-managed by German agents. German papers carried headlines such as "Bloody Terror of the Czechs against Germans and Czechs creates an Intolerable Situation".

Jews entering Palestine face British curbs

Palestine, July
Europe's Jews are desperate to flee spreading Nazi persecution, but British bureaucrats are equally determined to resist their cries for help. As tens of thousands of Jewish refugees make their way to Palestine, the colonial secretary, Malcolm MacDonald, stated today that from October this year immigration will be suspended for six months. The flood of Jews, he claims, is fanning the flames of Arab revolt and must be suppressed. He denied that the government was indifferent to the refugee situation, saying that 75,000 immigrants would be allowed into Palestine over a five-year period, but stressed that one country could not take in every Jew. He especially condemned organised attempts to outwit the law. Some 8,000 "illegals" have tried to smuggle themselves into Palestine since May. Jewish leaders refuse to bend. In May some 10,000 Jewish women marched through Jerusalem, protesting any limits on immigration and condemning Britain's efforts as "a fatal error" and refusing to accept this "breach of faith".

Gathering war clouds loom over Europe

London, August
Events are unfolding with bewildering speed as Europe races towards a second great war. First there was Ethiopia, of which Mussolini said that with so few Italian casualties "victory had come too cheap". Then there were the Rhineland, Austria, Sudetenland and Czechoslovakia. And all that time Spain was bleeding to death. Now Germany, having made a pact with one dictator, Mussolini, has made a second with Stalin (*see below*).

Signing of the pact has triggered mobilisation orders everywhere. In Poland, men up to the age of 40 have been ordered to report to barracks. France has called up reservists and requisitioned the railways. In Britain, as mobilisation papers went out, the admiralty issued orders closing the Mediterranean and the Baltic to British shipping. Germany has become an armed camp. Troops are everywhere and heavy trucks, motor cycles and civilian aircraft have been requisitioned. In Berlin, Western embassies are destroying secret papers.

Laying the foundations of the state.

Hitler and Stalin in non-aggression pact

Moscow, 23 August
Western hopes that a war in Europe can still be averted were shattered today by the news that Germany and the Soviet Union have signed a non-aggression pact. The treaty between Stalin and Hitler, who have been sworn enemies for the past six years, virtually guarantees Hitler that Germany can now use military force to claim territory from Poland without fear of intervention by Russia.

It is apparent that Stalin has been in secret negotiation with Hitler and his foreign minister, von Ribbentrop, for some time, even though an Anglo-French military mission is about to arrive in Moscow for talks to discourage German aggression against Poland.

The Hitler-Stalin pact comes into force at once and is to be ratified "in the shortest possible time". The two sides agree not to use force against one another or join hostile alliances with other powers. The pact makes German military action more likely, with the army continuing to requisition vehicles.

Jospeh Stalin: doing a deal with his sworn enemy.

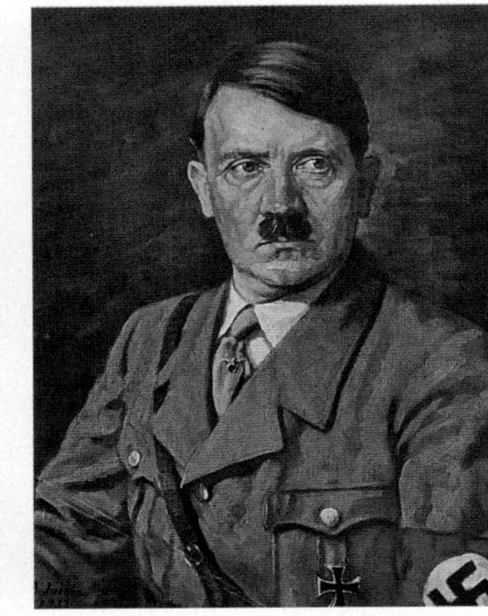
Adolph Hitler: his Soviet pact makes military action more likely.

1939 (1939-1940)

Poland, 1 September 1939. German troops invade at 5.45 am.

London and Paris, 3 September 1939. War is declared.

London, 4 September 1939. Winston Churchill is first lord of the admiralty again.

Germany, 4 September 1939. French troops cross the border into the Saarland.

Washington, DC, 5 September 1939. President Roosevelt declares US neutrality.

Poland, 17 September 1939. Soviet troops invade.

Warsaw, 29 September 1939. Polish troops evacuate as the city surrenders to the *Wehrmacht*.

Moscow, 11 October 1939. The USSR signs a pact ceding the former Polish city of Vilna to Lithuania.

France, 12 October 1939. British troops are now here in strength.

Britain, 16 October 1939. The battleship *Royal Oak* is sunk in her home base of Scapa Flow by a German torpedo.

Ankara, 19 October 1939. Turkey signs a mutual assistance pact with France and Britain.

Berlin, 24 October 1939. Hitler's month-long peace offer to the Allies comes to an end; the fighting continues.

London, 30 October 1939. The government publicises the horrors of Nazi concentration camps.

USA, 4 November 1939. President Roosevelt announces that he will sign the Neutrality Bill, which will allow Britain and France to buy arms from the US.

Germany, 8 November 1939. A bomb goes off shortly after Hitler has made his traditional speech on the anniversary of the abortive 1923 *putsch*.

Britain, 13 November 1939. The first bombs are dropped on British soil, on the Shetlands.

Moscow, 28 November 1939. Stalin renounces the Finno-Soviet non-aggression pact.

Finland, 30 November 1939. Soviet planes bomb Helsinki and Viipuri.

Montevideo, 17 December 1939. The German battleship *Graf Spee* is scuttled after being chased by British warships into the river Plate.

Moscow, 23 December 1939. Stalin sacks General Meretzkov, in charge of the war against Finland, as Finnish successes continue.

London, 1 January 1940. Two million 19- to 27-year-olds are called up.

France, 6 January 1940. The Germans gain ground in a fierce onslaught along a 120-mile front north of Paris.

Finland, 1 February 1940. The Soviet army launches an attack in Karelia.

Britain, 7 February 1940. Two IRA men are hanged.

Britain, 11 February 1940. John Buchan, Lord Tweedsmuir, the governor general of Canada, and author of great adventure stories such as *The Thirty-nine Steps*, dies aged 64.

Finland, 13 February 1940. The biggest battle so far in the winter war between the USSR and Finland is waged. Finland appeals for international aid.

Finland, 16 February 1940. Soviet troops pierce the Mannerheim Line of Finnish defence.

Tibet, 22 February 1940. The new five-year-old Dalai Lama is enthroned.

Norway, 26 February 1940. More than 300 British prisoners of war are rescued from a German tanker hiding in a Norwegian *fjord*.

The Hague, 8 March 1940. Martial law is declared throughout the Netherlands because of the German threat.

Finland, 13 March 1940. Finland signs a peace treaty with the USSR, surrendering a large part of the territory.

USA, 16 March 1940. The mission of Roosevelt's envoy Sumner Welles, to see if peace negotiations in Europe were possible, has ended in failure.

Paris, 22 March 1940. Paul Reynard becomes prime minister following the resignation of Edouard Daladier yesterday.

Poland, 27 March 1940. Heinrich Himmler orders the construction of a concentration camp at Auschwitz, near Cracow.

Holland, 2 April 1940. Dutch troops are put on full alert along the German frontier.

Norway, 9 April 1940. A full-scale German invasion of Norway begins. Denmark has already been overrun.

Norway, 30 April 1940. The Germans claim they have advanced and taken the towns of Dombaas and Stoeren. Meanwhile, British and French troops hit back, particularly in the north.

Norway, 2 May 1940. The Allies withdraw their troops south of Trondheim.

Denmark, 9 May 1940. Britain occupies Iceland and the Faroe islands.

India's Moslems call for separate state

Lahore, India, 23 March 1940

The Moslems of India are opting for a separate state. At the Moslem League conference held here today they accepted the principle of "autonomous and sovereign" Moslem states.

For India's Moslem leader, the brilliant lawyer Mohammed Ali Jinnah, it is a bitter victory. In the 1910s he had been in the Congress Party, an admirer of the moderate Congress leader Gopal Gokhale (who called him a potential ambassador of Hindu-Moslem unity) and a member of the imperial Legislative Council.

But as Congress turned more to mass agitation, and inevitably became more Hindu, he felt alienated. He went into self-imposed exile in England, and has only recently returned – the leader from across the water.

Thousands of Indian Moslems share his sense of alienation. Moslems note with apprehension the steadily increasing communal violence, and the complaints of Moslems in Hindu-dominated areas that provincial Congress governments favour Hindus over Moslems. They resent Congress' assertion that speak it for all Indians.

Mohammed Jinnah, the Indian Moslem barrister from Lincoln's Inn.

"Congress leaders may cry as much as they like that Congress is a national body," said Mr Jinnah. "But I say it is not true. The Congress is nothing but a Hindu body."

Most significant of all, the call for Moslem states is fitting in with the growing aspirations of the people of the north-west and the north-east, where the majority are Moslems opposed to both British rule and Hindu rule, who feel that they have nowhere else to go.

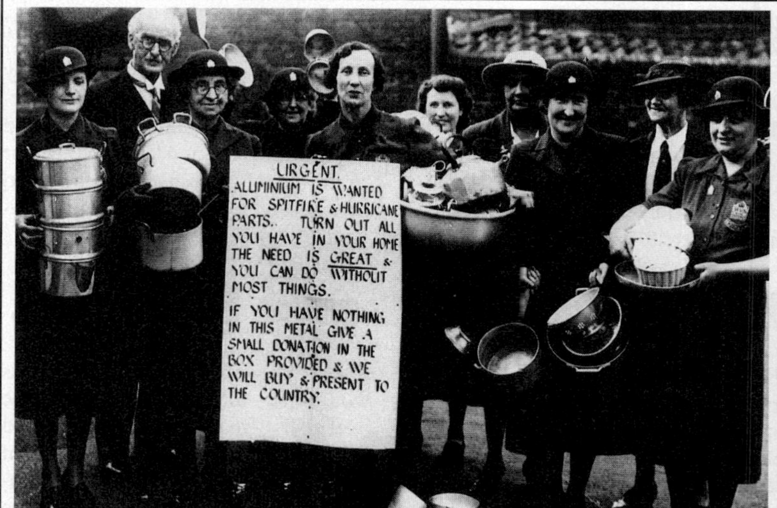

The Home Front: the Women's Voluntary Service, boosting the war economy by collecting pots and pans which the ministry of information in Britain said could be turned into Spitfires and Hurricanes. Critics claim however that the sacrifice will prove useless and that there is easily enough scrap metal without going to the lenghts of depriving housewives of their kitchen equipment. But with individuals reduced to four ounces of butter, 12 ounces of sugar, four ounces of ham and three and a half ounces of bacon, there is not a great deal of use for kitchen equipment – unless you like offal and brawn.

Europe is again at war

London, 30 September 1939
Poland lies shattered, partitioned yet again by her more powerful neighbours. As Polish forces were reeling under the hammer blows of the *Wehrmacht*, Stalin sent Red Army troops to occupy eastern Poland. The treacherous significance of the Nazi-Soviet Pact thus became clear.

Soon after dawn on 1 September, 1.25 million German troops, with six armoured divisions and eight motorised divisions, swept into Poland. The *Luftwaffe* knocked out the Polish railway system and shot the air force out of the sky. By Day Three – when Britain and France declared war – the Germans had cut the Polish Corridor and by Day Eight were at the gates of Warsaw. The city endured two weeks of terror bombing before surrendering.

An estimated 60,000 Poles have been killed, 200,000 wounded and 700,000 taken prisoner. The Polish government has fled to Rumania. Hitler has proved that the static trench warfare of 1914-18 is a thing of the past. The English language has acquired a new and terrifying word – *blitzkrieg,* meaning lightning war. In London, after some uncertainty, the British Government declared war on Sunday, 3 September at 11am. The French followed at 5pm. A joint statement said the two governments would avoid bombing civilians. In Washington, President Roosevelt announced US neutrality, ordering an embargo on the shipment of arms to countries at war.

A stab in the back: Soviet armoured cars invading Poland from the East.

Hitler orders U-boats to hit neutral ships

London, 20 February 1940
Unarmed merchant ships of all nations are potential targets for U-boat torpedoes as a result of Hitler's latest order to his submarine captains to open fire "without question" on neutral shipping in the waters around Britain.

Since war began five months ago most neutral ships passing through the Dover Strait call at British ports for a cargo check. They are granted a certificate stating they are not carrying prohibited cargo to Germany. Hitler wishes to take control of all neutral shipping, forcing uninvolved nations to divert exports from the two Allies, France and Britain, to Germany.

Norway, Sweden, Denmark and the Netherlands are all anxious. Norway's foreign minister recently revealed that 50 Norwegian merchant ships had been sunk since the conflict started, although Norway is not a participant. In every case the attack was made by a German submarine or aircraft. Observers note that no US ship has been hit, perhaps because of memories of the *Lusitania* in May 1915.

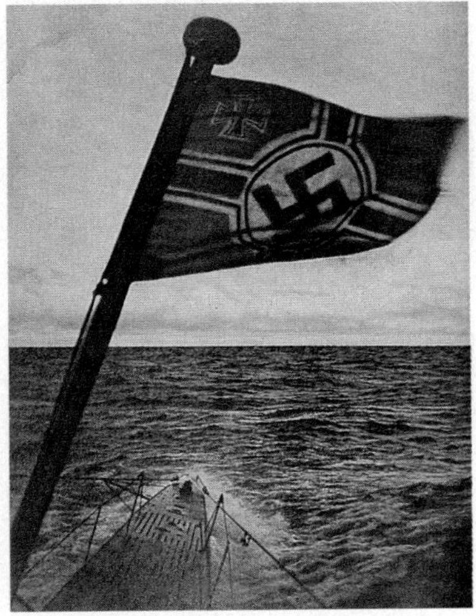
A German U-boat on the hunt for allied shipping in the Atlantic.

Germans overrun Denmark and Norway

German troops landing on the coast in Norway, where they have taken Oslo.

Oslo, 9 April 1940
The Germans have stolen a march on the British in the race to take control of Norwegian home waters. Royal Navy warships were preparing to sow mines in the area, in order to prevent Germany using the ports and fjords, when they ran into a German flotilla. The Germans had already occupied Denmark, with only token resistance from the Royal Guard.

Last night, German warships moved on the Norwegian capital, Oslo, and were attacked by shore batteries. Hitler's newest cruiser, *Blucher*, was sunk, with the loss of 1,000 men. The city was taken by airborne troops. Norway's King Haakon and his government have escaped to a village in the interior. Using a low-powered local radio, the king broadcast mobilisation orders.

Though the Norwegians insist they will put up a determined resistance, the Germans seem already too well established to be dislodged. They successfully put seven divisions ashore within 48 hours and now hold all the main ports. British forces have only a toehold ashore in the far north.

The Germans have installed their puppet in Oslo. Major Vikdun Quisling, a Nazi sympathiser whose name has instantly become a synonym for traitor, made a radio broadcast calling for resistance to Germany to cease.

British troops boost French defences

France, 12 October 1939
The British "Tommy" has returned to France where, like his father in the Great War, he still regards it as effeminate to speak French with a correct accent. Some 158,000 men of the British Expeditionary Force, with 25,000 vehicles, have been ferried across the Channel to take their place alongside the French army under General Gamelin.

The troops' movements are considered a great achievement. A small team of war office planners, helped by just seven clerks and typists, worked out every detail of the complicated movements.

Secret routes were taken across Britain to prevent air attacks on the road convoys. The men moved in small groups, concealed by day and travelling by night. There was not a single casualty.

The RAF, equipped with Blenheim and Battle bombers and Hurricane fighters, has been operating from French airfields for some weeks, carrying out reconnaissance flights over the German lines.

The war secretary, Leslie Hore-Belisha, told the Commons that troops were also being sent to the Near East to reinforce British interests there.

1940 ⇒

London, 10 May. Winston Churchill becomes prime minister.

The Hague, 15 May. German forces occupy the city.

Belgium, 28 May. Belgian troops surrender to the Germans.

London, 31 May. Sir Oswald Mosley, the leader of the British Union of Fascists, is arrested.

France, 4 June. Operation Dynamo evacuates British soldiers from Dunkirk.

France, 10 June. The Germans are 35 miles from Paris; the government moves to Tours.

Italy, 10 June. Italy declares war on Britain and France.

Paris, 14 June. German troops enter Paris.

France, 16 June. Paul Reynaud resigns as prime minister. Marshal Petain takes over and asks the Germans for an armistice.

Britain, 20 June. The first New Zealand and Australian troops arrive.

France, 22 June. The armistice with Germany puts half of France under occupation.

Channel Islands, 1 July. The Germans take the Channel Islands.

Algeria, 3 July. The Royal Navy destroys a large part of the French fleet to prevent it falling into German hands.

France, 11 July. Marshal Henri Petain assumes supreme power in occupied France.

Baltic, 21 July. Lithuania, Latvia and Estonia, occupied by Russian troops in June, vote to become part of the USSR.

Europe, 7 August. Alsace-Lorraine and Luxembourg become part of Germany.

Albania, 12 August. A revolt begins against the Italian occupation.

Britain, 18 August. As *Luftwaffe* pilots home in on southern England, the Battle of Britain begins in earnest.

East Africa, 19 August. British Somaliland falls to the Italians.

China, 20 August. Japanese bombing of Chongqing, China's wartime capital, reaches its climax with raids which destroy most of the city.

London, 25 August. The *Luftwaffe* carries out its first bombing raid on London.

Berlin, 26 August. British planes bomb Berlin.

Low Countries invaded

Amsterdam, 10 May

German forces went into action before dawn today, after heavy bombing of airfields, railways and military strong-points in Holland and Belgium. Along a 150-mile (240-kilometre) front, troops moved forward, seizing key positions before the defenders could react.

In spite of numerous intelligence reports of the presence of at least 28 German divisions in the frontier areas, the Dutch and the Belgians refused to undertake resolute defensive measures, co-ordinated with the Allies, for fear of offending Hitler.

"After our country, with scrupulous conscientiousness, had observed strict neutrality, Germany made a sudden attack on our territory without warning," Holland's Queen Wilhelmina said in a broadcast. She called on her people to fight to the last. Both she and King Leopold of the Belgians are counting on the Allies to come to their aid. Under the Anglo-French contingency plan, a force will advance into Belgium to join up with the Belgians within two days. That may be too late. The Eban Emael fortress on the Liege front has fallen and the Belgian army shows signs of disintegrating. The Dutch are in no better shape. The great port of Rotterdam is about to surrender after a pulverising bombardment killed 800 people.

The remains of a bridge in France, destroyed to delay the Germans.

Stalin strikes at the Baltic republics

Lithuania, 17 June

The Soviet Red Army is marching into neighbouring Baltic republics on the pretext that there is a conspiracy among these tiny countries to attack Russia. No doubt this is part of the same policy which has just defeated Finland, in spite of her gallant resistance.

The first of the little states to come under pressure is Lithuania. More than 200 Soviet tanks crossed the frontier yesterday and soon reached the capital, Kaunas. As Red Army troops seized key points in the city, Russian administrators arrived by air.

The invasion is entirely unopposed. Reports reaching Stockholm suggest that Stalin has committed 500,000 men to the operation. The Lithuanian government accepted an ultimatum alleging a conspiracy before the president, Dr Smetona, with other ministers and their families sought sanctuary in Sweden or Germany.

Now the peoples of Latvia and Estonia wonder how long their freedom will last. The position of German minorities is of special interest. A Nazi-Soviet treaty signed last August makes it unlikely that the Germans will oppose what is happening so long as Hitler's expansion encounters no Soviet opposition. But 35,000 Lithuanian Germans want to go home.

Courageous Finns resisting the USSR: the Baltic republics are next.

Italians advance in British Somaliland

Somaliland, 7 August

Italian troops crossed over the border from Ethiopia into British Somaliland three days ago and are now advancing in three columns. They captured Hargeisa and Zeila despite resistance by the Camel Corps. The Italians have tanks, artillery, machine-guns and aircraft. It was the brutal annexation of Ethiopia in 1936 which first alerted Britain to the danger from Mussolini's Italy. However, the prime minister, Neville Chamberlain, believed that he could reason with the dictator. Two years later he concluded the Anglo-Italian agreement which he said paved the way for future cooperation.

Trotsky killed after ice-pick assault

Mexico City, 21 August

Stalin's rival Leon Trotsky was assassinated today in his closely guarded refuge near Mexico City. The killer, an enigmatic journalist with five aliases, is almost certainly one of a team of assassins who have stalked Trotsky ever since he was sentenced to death in his absence at a Moscow show trial. Last May Trotsky's bodyguard fought off 30 men with machine-guns who missed their target. The latest killer came to consult Trotsky about an article. On a sunny day he carried an ice-axe concealed under a raincoat. The guards did not notice.

Leon Trotsky, a victim of Stalin and martyr for permanant revolution.

British evacuate France

The ones who never made it: British and French troops led to PoW camps.

Dunkirk, 4 June
The beaches of Dunkirk are littered with the wreckage of war and the bodies of those who did not make it to the ships. But 338,226 men of the British Expeditionary Force, together with many French and Belgians, have been brought to England and safety.

When the French front was turned by a German thrust around Sedan, and King Leopold ordered the Belgian army to lay down its weapons, the British position became untenable and Lord Gort, the British commander-in-chief, pulled his men back to Dunkirk under relentless German air attacks and through thousands of fleeing refugees. It was thought at one time that no more than 45,000 could be saved.

As the days passed, the number built up. The Luftwaffe continued the dive-bombing of the beaches, but the German armour which had been pressing forward suddenly stopped outside Dunkirk, apparently unwilling to risk an advance through the coastal marshes.

Lying off Dunkirk was a huge fleet – destroyers, ferries, fishing vessels and even river cruisers. Anyone who had a ship and could cross the Channel was roped in for the great rescue. The troops formed lines from the beach out to sea, where they were hauled on board and taken to south coast ports.

Seven French destroyers went down under Luftwaffe attacks and scores of other ships have been lost. But the Royal Navy continued to shepherd the little ships back and forth. Operation Dynamo, as the heroic rescue operation was called, cannot be presented as a military victory, but it has made sure that the British and their army will live to fight another day.

Germans enter Paris: France humiliated

Paris, 14 June
Victorious German troops are marching up the Champs Elysees less than a month after invading France. The French government, which evacuated Paris four days ago, has moved from Tours to Bordeaux, with little prospect of avoiding total surrender within a matter of days.

Parisians stand on the pavements to drink in their national humiliation. Not since 1871 have they been obliged to bow the knee to German conquerors.

The Germans said they would treat Paris as non-belligerent if it surrendered at once. The French wanted to retain outlying areas, but capitulated when threatened with further bombardment. The first German motor-cyclists rode into the capital soon after 7am, followed by cameramen, radio technicians and announcers, who are now recording the march past in the Place de la Concorde.

Roads to the south are clogged by up to two million refugees pushing carts loaded with their belongings. German dive-bombers are attacking them sporadically, and machine-gunning the columns.

The French High Command says Paris was surrendered for purely military reasons, and still publicly insists that the fight must continue. Germany claims the Armee de Paris has been routed.

While Churchill, the new British leader, has been discussing strategy with General Weygand, the Allied commander-in-chief, French politicians are talking of surrender.

German troops marching in triumph through Place de la Concorde in Paris.

Chinese Communists fight the Japanese

China, 30 August
Mao Zedong's Red Army, striking from its northern vastness at the Japanese, is inflicting heavy casualties and has paralysed their railway communications.

The attack, called the Hundred Regiments campaign, took the Japanese by surprise for, departing from the usual communist practice of waging guerrilla war and avoiding large scale contact, it involves the whole of the Eighth Route Army of nearly half a million men.

These soldiers, trained in the mountains of Shensi, are dedicated fighters, able to exist on a handful of dried rice and, led by peasant guides, can cross difficult terrain at great speed. With no aircraft, little artillery and no mechanical transport, they rely on the local population for food, shelter, and porters. According to Peng Te-huai, "the people are the sea, while the guerrillas are the fish swimming in it".

They fight with rifles, bayonets and grenades, but their main weapon is their determination to defeat the Japanese, a weapon sadly missing from the Nationalist armoury. There are signs, however, that the Japanese are recovering from their surprise and are ready to strike back.

They have already initiated a brutal "Three-all" campaign in which they "kill all, burn all, destroy all". It is being carried out with great cruelty.

1940 (1940-1941)

Bucharest, 6 September 1940. King Carol is made to abdicate in favour of his son Michael after his pro-German prime minister resigns.

Egypt, 12 September 1940. Italian troops advance from Libya.

Japan, 27 September 1940. Japan signs a ten-year pact with Germany and Italy.

London, 30 September 1940. Hitler's long-awaited *blitz* on London has started.

Helsinki, 1 October 1940. Finland signs a military and economic treaty with Germany.

Rumania, 7 October 1940. German and Italian troops invade.

Bucharest, 12 October 1940. The city is occupied by Axis troops.

New York City, 21 October 1940. Ernest Hemingway's novel *For Whom the Bell Tolls* is published.

Spain, 24 October 1940. Hitler fails to persuade Franco or Petain to join the war against Britain.

Greece, 28 October 1940. Italy invades Greece.

USA, 5 November 1940. President Franklin D Roosevelt is re-elected for a record third term.

London, 7 November 1940. Britain, Australia and the US agree on defence co-operation in the Pacific.

Britain, 14 November 1940. Coventry is devastated by the worst air raid of the war.

Warsaw, 15 November 1940. 350,000 Jews are now confined to a ghetto.

Budapest, 20 November 1940. Hungary joins the Axis.

Greece, 22 November 1940. The Greeks put the Italian invaders to flight in a great victory at Koritza.

Bratislava, 24 November 1940. Slovakia joins the Axis.

North Africa, 9 December 1940. British troops launch an attack on Italians in the Western Desert.

London, 29 December 1940. In the biggest air raid of the war, the *Luftwaffe* razed one-third of the City, including the Barbican. St Paul's survives amid the flames.

Libya, 5 January 1941. The Italian garrison of Bardia falls after a two day assault by Commonwealth troops commanded by the brilliant unconventional Irish-born generals, O'Connor and Dorman-Smith.

Britain, 6 January 1941. One of flying's heroines, Amy Johnson, is drowned when her plane ditches in the Thames estuary.

Britain, 8 January 1941. Boy Scouts founder and Boer war hero, Lord Robert Baden-Powell.

Switzerland, 13 January 1941. The Irish author James Joyce dies in Zurich aged 58. His greatest work was undoubtedly the novel *Ulysses*.

Libya, 30 January 1941. Derna falls to General Wavell's troops after a fierce three-day battle.

Libya, 7 February 1941. British and Commonwealth troops take Benghazi.

North Africa, 14 February 1941. The advance guard of Rommel's Afrika Korps arrive in Tripoli.

Sofia, 14 February 1941. Bulgaria accepts German occupation.

Sudan, 16 February 1941. The last Italian troops are expelled.

Sofia, 17 February 1941. Bulgaria and Turkey sign a non-aggression pact under German pressure.

Berlin, 19 February 1941. Hitler warns Greece to end the war with Italy or face Germany fighting with the Italians.

North Africa, 25 February 1941. Mogadishu, the Italian-held port of Somaliland, falls to the British.

Sofia, 1 March 1941. Bulgaria joins the Axis.

Ankara, 4 March 1941. Turkey refuses to join the Axis.

Ethiopia, 6 March 1941. Haile Selassie's troops capture the Italian stronghold of Burye.

Belgrade, 25 March 1941. Prince Paul, the Yugoslav regent, signs a pact with the Axis.

Sofia, 26 March 1941. The pro-German government is ousted.

Britain, 28 March 1941. The novelist Virginia Woolf commits suicide aged 69.

Eritrea, 1 April 1941. Allied troops take the capital Asmara four days after storming Keren.

Libya, 3 April 1941. British-led troops evacuate Benghazi in the face of Rommel's advances.

Iraq, 4 April 1941. The ex-prime minister, Rashid Ali, an Axis supporter, seizes power.

Yugoslavia, 6 April 1941. Axis troops invade.

Ethiopia, 6 April 1941. Allies occupy Addis Ababa, the capital of Ethiopia.

Greenland, 10 April 1941. The US sends forces to Greenland to protect arms supply lines from America to Britain.

USSR, 13 April 1941. Stalin signs a neutrality pact with Japan.

Yugoslavia, 17 April 1941. Yugoslavia falls to German forces.

Athens, 26 April 1941. The Germans march into Athens.

Commonwealth forces capture Tobruk

British Bren-gun carriers advancing into Italian Libya on their way to Tobruk.

Libya, 22 January 1941
The port of Tobruk has fallen to British and Australian forces. General Wavell's Western Desert Force has taken more than 100,000 Italian prisoners, and looks set to advance on Benghazi.

The RAF started bombing Italian bases in Libya three weeks ago, and on 5 January Bardia was captured with 25,000 men and six generals. The Italians have continued to suffer heavy bombardment by land, sea and air. At Tobruk, Italian resistance melted in the face of infantry, tanks and Bren guns. British and Australian forces arrived simultaneously.

Allied armies take Ethiopian capital

Addis Ababa, 6 April 1941
Allied forces including including British, Indian and South African troops and local guerrillas have liberated the Ethiopian capital after a three-month campaign. Plans are now in hand for the Emperor Haile Selassie to re-enter Addis on 5 May, the fifth anniversary of Italy's invasion. Defeat for Italy became certain after British forces took Keren in the north and Harar in the southeast, and converged onto the centre, Addis Ababa.

Britain appeals for more women workers

England, 1941
Womanpower for the war effort – that is now the call from Britain's minister of labour, Ernest Bevin, as he announced the first steps in a massive mobilisation plan. The registration of 20 and 21-year-old women will begin next month with the aim of filling vital jobs in industry and farming together with the auxiliary services.

Women are desperately needed to get shell-filling factories working round the clock and to take over all kinds of other jobs to free men for active service. As yet, married women with young children are exempt, but those who are able do war work locally will be backed up by a huge expansion in day and night nurseries.

Turning ploughshares into swords.

German bombs begin London blitz

London, 30 September 1940
As Britain awaits an invasion, London is now the front line in the war the Britain is fighting virtually alone. Every night for three weeks London has been pounded by bombs, tens of thousands of the population sheltering deep underground in tube stations. The bombs first fell in the Docks and East End, now they are moving westwards. Even Buckingham Palace has been hit. Six days ago King George VI introduced the George Cross, in recognition of the heroism of London's firemen.

In Kent and Sussex, inadequately armed troops and even worse armed "Home Guard" militiamen, can see the fires of London as they prepare to resist invasion. For three months they watched dogfights above them as the RAF and the Luftwaffe fought for control of the skies over southern England. It was not planes that either side were short of, but pilots; and with baled out British pilots returning to their airfields, and baled out Germans going into POW camps, the RAF won the battle.

On 5 September Hitler switched tactics, vowing to turn London into rubble in retaliation for a RAF raid on Berlin. Three days later his bombers came. "Leisurely enormous mushrooms of black and brown smoke shot with crimson climbed into the sunlit sky," a Londoner recalls. "There they hung, and slowly expanded, for there was no wind, and the great fires below fed more smoke into them as the hours passed."

RAF bombing crew: even during the Blitz the RAF was bombing German cities.

The Blitz: London wakes up to the debris of another night's bombing.

Churchill's finest hour: "Let us brace ourselves to our duty."

Japanese join the Nazi-Fascist Axis

Tokyo, 27 September 1940
Although Japan has been politically and militarily linked with Nazi Germany and Fascist Italy for over five years, a formal alliance was signed today which will send tremors through the Soviet Union and the United States.

The wording of the pact tries to assuage the Soviets who are uncomfortably situated between the three powers. For the Americans there is an unmistakable warning that entry into the war on behalf of the Allies will also entail a war in the Pacific.

Britain and USA forge Atlantic Charter

Newfoundland, 14 August 1941
When Britain's newest battleship, the *Prince of Wales*, set sail last week, it was a well-kept secret that Winston Churchill was on board. The purpose of his voyage was to meet Franklin D Roosevelt, ostensibly on a fishing trip, and the outcome is an agreement which brings the United States one step closer to war.

The Atlantic Charter states that neither country has any territorial claims to make and proposes that aggressor nations be disarmed. In the presence of their military chiefs the two leaders discussed Japanese encroachments in the Pacific where both nations have colonies.

The president's support for the Allied cause is no secret. Last December he proudly proclaimed the United States was the "arsenal of democracy". True to his word a "lend-lease" pact was signed this March, deferring British payment for American arms until the end of hostilities.

However, all Roosevelt's efforts at bringing the United States into the war have thus far been thwarted by Congress.

Balkan blitzkrieg smashes Yugoslav and Greek forces

Cairo, 17 April 1941
Late tonight British headquarters here was making no attempt to disguise the seriousness of the situation in the Balkans. Yugoslavia has fallen and Greece is now in grave danger. Just before midnight the German High Command said: "All the Yugoslav armed forces which had not been disarmed before, laid down their arms unconditionally at nine o'clock tonight."

German troops are already crossing the border into Greece to join up with their compatriots who have been pressing hard against the Greek, British and Australian troops. So far the lines are intact, despite very heavy fighting.

The Nazis are clearly throwing their entire weight into the attack. There are at least ten divisions supported by hundreds of Stukas and Messerschmitts which are raining bombs on the allied lines. RAF bombers are pounding the German supply lines. But Greece is now surrounded. German troops are well-established on the Bulgarian frontier and Albania is in the hands of Italy. Now Yugoslavia has fallen, the allied forces have nowhere to retreat except the sea.

Resisting the Nazi occupiers: a wounded Yugoslavian partisan.

1941

Scotland, 10 May. Rudolf Hess lands in a vain attempt to negotiate peace.

Addis Ababa, 20 May. Italian East Africa surrenders to British empire forces.

Crete, 29 May. The Axis forces seize the capital, Canea.

Syria, 21 June. British imperial forces take Damascus.

USSR, 22 June. Germany invades along a 1,800-mile frontier with Finnish, Hungarian and Rumanian allies.

London, 13 July. Britain and the USSR conclude a mutual assistance pact.

USSR, 16 July. German troops advance on Moscow.

Indochina, 27 July. Japanese troops move into Cambodia and Thailand; Saigon falls.

Iran, 25 August. British and Soviet troops move into Iran.

Estonia, 29 August. The Germans capture the capital, Tallin.

Tehran, 16 September. The *shah* of Iran abdicates.

Tehran, 19 September. British and Soviet troops enter the city.

Tehran, 17 September. The new shah, Mohammed Reza Pahlevi, promises to rule as a constitutional monarch.

USSR, 19 September. Kiev falls to the Germans.

Leningrad, 2 October. The Soviet army launches a counter-attack as the winter's first snows begin to fall.

Japan, 17 October. The prime minister, Fumimaro Konoye, and his cabinet resign; General Tojo, a pro-Axis war minister, is appointed.

USSR, 20 October. Stalin declares a state of siege.

Atlantic, 13 November. The Italians sink the aircraft carrier *HMS Ark Royal.*

Hawaii, 7 December. The Japanese bomb the American base at Pearl Harbor.

London, 8 December. Britain declares war on Finland, Rumania and Hungary.

Berlin, 11 December. Hitler and Mussolini declare war on the US.

USSR, 12 December. More than 400 townships have been retaken from the Germans.

Hong Kong, 25 December. Hong Kong surrenders to Japan.

South-East Asia reels under the lightning advance of Japan

Hong Kong, 25 December

Three weeks after the attack on Pearl Harbor (*see right*), Hong Kong fell to Japan today. After a seven-day battle, 6,000 troops will surrender at noon tomorrow.

News of the fall of Hong Kong was announced in a communique that spoke of "a great fight against overwhelming odds", but failed to mention to incompetence of commanders who ignored warnings that the Japanese would swim the straits. It could not have come at a worse time for a British public which was still recovering from the news that Britain's two greatest battleships, the *Repulse* and the *Prince of Wales*, had entered hostile waters without aircraft cover and had been sunk by Japanese dive-bombers in the South China Sea.

In Malaya, crack Japanese divisions have landed and are advancing towards Singapore, where the British are confident they can stop them at their "impregnable" fortress. More are pushing their way northwards and eastwards into Burma, and towards India.

American forces, still shocked by the news from Pearl Harbor, put up fierce resistance before they lost Wake Island and Guam, though the soldiers' courage was ill-served by an inadequate leadership. The Japanese army has landed in strength on the Philippines and are steadily advancing. General Douglas MacArthur, the US commander, is in retreat with 150,000 US and Filipino forces.

Few doubt that the principal Japanese goals are India and Australia, and the creation of a new empire.

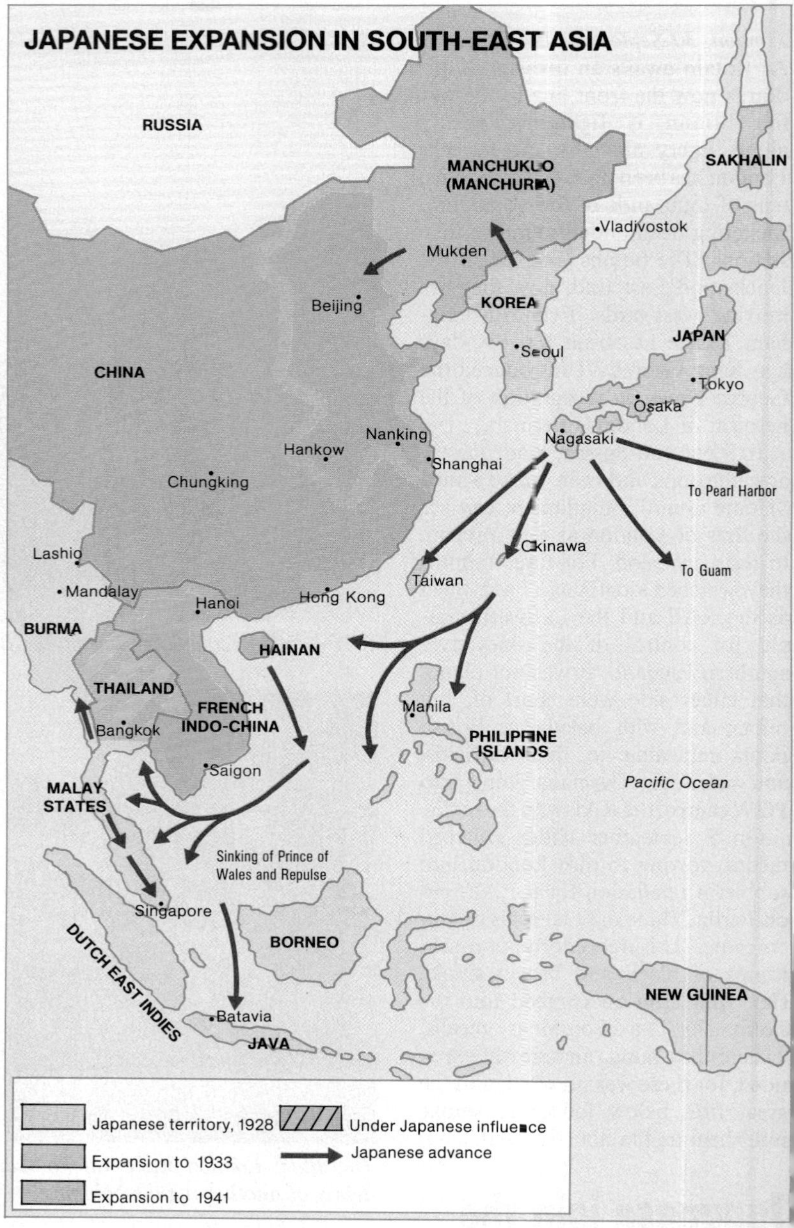

USA takes Iceland

Iceland, 7 July

American forces have landed in Iceland to help Britain prevent it being attacked by the Germans. An independent country, but with no means of defending itself, Iceland was occupied without bloodshed by a British force early last year.

President Roosevelt, announcing the move in Washington today, said that he had sent a marine brigade to Iceland. The marines will release British troops from the 20,000-strong garrison. The British government welcomed the US action.

Allies occupy Iran

Iran, 25 August

British and Soviet troops marched into Iran today, encountering little opposition. The operation, a shameless infringement of Iran's neutrality, claims to have pre-empted a coup by the Germans who had built up a strong Fifth Column. British air troops were dropped on the oilfields to protect Britons and prevent sabotage, while British and Indian troops and armour crossed the border at Khanikin. At the same time Soviet troops moved in from the north capturing Tabriz.

Divers reclaim gold

New Zealand, 8 December

The trans-Pacific liner, *Niagara*, sunk in 70 fathoms by a German mine last year, has yielded her cargo of bullion to the Australian diving brothers J and W Johnstone.

Working at extreme depths in conditions made hazardous by storms and mines which twice threatened to destroy the salvage ship *Claymore*, the Johnstones have raised 555 ingots, valued at £2,379,000 – 94 per cent of the shipment sent by Britain to the USA to pay for American weapons.

Hitler invades the USSR

Russia, 30 June
German *panzers* are smashing into Russia in the greatest blitzkrieg yet seen. Hundreds of tanks supported by clouds of Stukas are rolling across the Russian plains. The Red Army units guarding the frontier have been destroyed. Minsk, over halfway to Moscow, has fallen.

The Germans claim that two Russian armies have been surrounded and "would be forced to capitulate in a few days or be annihilated". The Red Army was clearly caught unprepared by the German onslaught at dawn on 22 June, despite clear indications that Hitler was about to break his infamous non-aggression pact with Stalin.

The Germans had massed 100 divisions and, together with their Finnish and Rumanian allies, rolled over the 1,800-mile (2,880-kilometre) border from the Arctic Circle to the Black Sea.

In Britain Mr Churchill told the Commons: "I gave clear and precise warnings to Stalin of what was coming. I can only hope these warnings did not fall unheeded". He promised Russia "whatever help we can; we have offered any technical or economic assistance in our power". He went on: "We are resolved to destroy Hitler and every vestige of the Nazi regime. From this nothing will turn us. We will never parley, never."

A Cossack tradition, Soviet cavalryman using his dead horse as cover.

Soviets repel Nazi advance on Moscow

Russia, 12 December
The Red Army has turned on the German invaders and inflicted a series of smashing defeats on Hitler's panzers who, unprepared for a winter war, are suffering heavy casualties from "General Frost".

Following the recapture of Rostov in the south, General Zhukov has counter-attacked and routed the Germans halted before Moscow, recapturing Solechnaya Gora, 40 miles (64 kilometres) north-west of the capital, the closest the Nazi spearhead came to Moscow.

According to last night's communique, more than 400 towns and villages have been retaken in five days' fighting. Some 30,000 Germans have been killed and nearly 700 tanks captured or destroyed.

The Russians claim that "German plans for surrounding and capturing Moscow have ended in utter fiasco". Jubilant Russians, warmly clad in white camouflage uniforms are pursuing the frozen Germans through the snow as fresh divisions from Siberia enter the battle. The front has undergone a remarkable change since Marshal Timoshenko's great southern counterstroke a fortnight ago. Now the Red Army holds the initiative everywhere. For the first time the Nazis are on the defensive.

German soldiers, getting their first harsh taste of a Russian winter.

USA joins the Allies

The twisted wreckage of the USS Arizona in Pearl Harbor after the attack.

Pearl Harbor, 7 December
Soon after dawn today, wave after wave of Japanese warplanes began to bomb America's major Pacific base. Pearl Harbor was taken entirely by surprise and within two hours the Japanese had destroyed five battleships, 14 smaller craft and 200 aircraft. At least 2,400 people, many of them civilians, were killed. Although the US Navy has suffered a major disaster, Japan's bombers failed to find and hit America's all-important aircraftcarriers, both of which were away on manoeuvres.

However, Japanese planes have attacked US bases in the Philippines, on Wake Island and Guam in the middle of the Pacific. The Japanese had obviously planned the operation carefully. Twelve days ago, six aircraft-carriers left the Kurile Islands in total secrecy and headed for Honolulu. The first bombs fell even as Japanese diplomats were meeting with the US Government in Washington. Congress will meet to declare war in emergency session tomorrow – to the infinite relief of Britain.

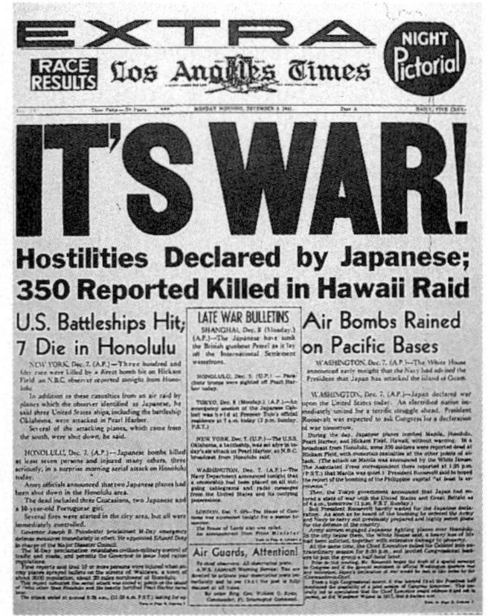
EXTRA

RACE RESULTS — Los Angeles Times — NIGHT Pictorial

IT'S WAR!

Hostilities Declared by Japanese; 350 Reported Killed in Hawaii Raid

U.S. Battleships Hit; 7 Die in Honolulu

LATE WAR BULLETINS

Air Bombs Rained on Pacific Bases

Air Guards, Attention!

How the news broke: Pearl Harbor ends two decades of isolationism.

Bismarck, pride of German fleet, is sunk

Atlantic, 27 May
The Royal Navy avenged *HMS Hood* today and sent the *Bismarck* to the bottom of the sea after a three-day hunt to the death.

The *Bismarck,* reputed to be the world's most powerful warship, broke out from the North Sea to harry the convoy lanes, but was intercepted by the *Hood* and the *Prince of Wales.* One of her shells penetrated the *Hood's* magazine and she blew up.

Bismarck was wounded in the encounter and Swordfish aircraft damaged her steering, enabling the navy to catch her and deluge her with shells and torpedoes.

1942

Philippines, 2 January. Japanese troops take Manila.

India, 15 January. Gandhi names Pandit Nehru as his successor.

Germany, 20 January. Officials learn of Reinhard Heydrich's "final solution" – to exterminate the 11 million Jews in Europe.

Singapore, 31 January. The Japanese lay siege to the island.

Norway, 1 February. Vidkun Quisling is appointed puppet prime minister by the Germans.

Singapore, 9 February. Japanese forces land on the island.

South East Asia, 14 February. The Japanese invade Sumatra.

Singapore, 15 February. Singapore surrenders to the Japanese.

Burma, 22 February. Civilians are evacuated from Rangoon – battles rage 80 miles northeast of the city.

South East Asia, 8 March. Java capitulates to the Japanese.

Germany, 26 March. The Nazis begin the deportation of Jews to Auschwitz concentration camp.

Germany, 28 March. The RAF begins a round-the-clock offensive on German munitions factories.

India, 29 March. The British reveal a plan for Indian independence after the war.

India, 7 April. The Indian National Congress Working Committee rejects British plans for India.

Tokyo, 18 April. US planes bomb Tokyo.

Yugoslavia, 3 May. German reinforcements arrive to fight Tito's partisans.

Libya, 27 May. Rommel's *panzer* divisions launch a long-expected offensive in the desert.

Czechoslovakia, 31 May. Czech partisans assassinate Gestapo leader Heydrich.

Mexico City, 1 June. Mexico declares war on the Axis.

Pacific, 7 June. The Japanese withdraw after four days of serious fighting around Midway Island.

Australia, 8 June. The Japanese shell Sydney and Newcastle.

Libya, 21 June. Tobruk falls to Rommel's troops; 25,000 Allied soldiers are taken prisoner.

USA, 25 June. Major General Dwight Eisenhower is given command of all US forces in Europe.

Egypt, 25 June. Axis forces threaten Cairo.

USSR, 29 June. The Germans launch an offensive at Kursk, south of Moscow.

USSR, 1 July. Sevastopol falls to the Germans after a nine-month siege.

USSR, 6 August. The Germans advance on Stalingrad.

North Africa, 6 August. General Bernard Montgomery becomes commander of the Eighth Army.

Pacific, 7 August. US marines land on the Solomon Islands.

New Delhi, 9 August. Gandhi and other Congress leaders are arrested.

France, 19 August. Allied forces go ashore at Dieppe to gain experience of an amphibious attack against coastal positions.

Brazil, 22 August. Brazil declares war on Germany and Italy.

Egypt, 30 August. Rommel launches a new offensive in Egypt.

Warsaw, 2 September. German SS troops "clear" the Jewish ghetto of 50,000 people.

USSR, 6 September. The Germans take the major Black Sea base of Novorossiisk.

Germany, 10 September. The RAF drop 100,000 bombs on Dusseldorf in under an hour.

USSR, 11 September. The Germans drive a wedge through Soviet positions in Stalingrad.

Madagascar, 23 September. The British capture the island's capital of Antananarivo.

New Guinea, 27 September. The Japanese pull back in the face of the advancing Allies.

Egypt, 30 September. The Eighth Army seizes key German positions near El Alamein in a dawn raid.

Britain, 24 October. A giant task force led by General Eisenhower leaves for North Africa.

Egypt, 30 October. Montgomery is victorious at El Alamein.

Yugoslavia, 3 November. The Bosnian capital of Bihacs falls to Tito's partisans.

North Africa, 7 November. Allied troops land in Vichy-French North Africa.

North Africa, 8 November. Rommel retreats into Libya.

France, 11 November. The Axis invades Vichy France.

USSR, 26 November. Soviet troops smash through German lines in Stalingrad.

France, 27 November. The French fleet is scuttled hours after the Germans move into Toulon.

Burma, 19 December. British troops advance down the Mayu peninsula pushing the Japanese back into Burma.

Chinese peasants beat Japanese veterans

China, January

Nationalist troops have scored a remarkable victory over the Japanese in a bloody ten-day battle for the city of Changsha, the capital of Hunan province. The over-confident Japanese, who had neglected to bring up their heavy guns, were driven off by the raw, young Chinese soldiers – peasants fighting for their own homes and land.

They had waited all winter for the Japanese to attack, planting vegetables in their dug-outs to relieve the boredom. But when the attack came, they fought like veterans under the command of the respected Colonel Li.

His success proves that under efficient officers who care for their men, the Chinese soldier is the equal of any. Certainly these youths in their light-blue padded uniforms inflicted a terrible beating on the Japanese and gave the Nationalist cause a much-needed boost.

Congressmen jailed after Quit India vote

New Delhi, 9 August

Within hours of Mahatma Gandhi and 50 other Congress leaders being arrested by the British authorities, India is experiencing its biggest civil commotions since the Mutiny. The move came only 12 hours after Congress passed a motion demanding Britain "quit India", and launched a mass civil disobedience campaign. It deeply wounded the British psyche. To British administrators and pro-British Indians, particularly those whose soldiers are retreating in the face of Japanese advances in Burma, it is akin to treason. In Bombay, where pro-Congress crowds took over the streets, police fired on rioters, killing five. At Shiva-Ji Park, where Gandhi was to address a meeting, 20,000 people took to the rampage. In Patna and Bihar the administration has completely lost control. Behind the riot is the Indians' disappointment at Sir Stafford Cripps' proposals for self-government. Big expectations were raised, but his proposals were so watered down by Churchill that they were "a postdated cheque on a crashing bank", as Gandhi put it.

Gandhi, the "Mahatma" or Living Soul of India: now confined in jail.

"Casablanca": war means goodbyes for Bogart and Bergman.

The Nazi Spring offensive is blunted

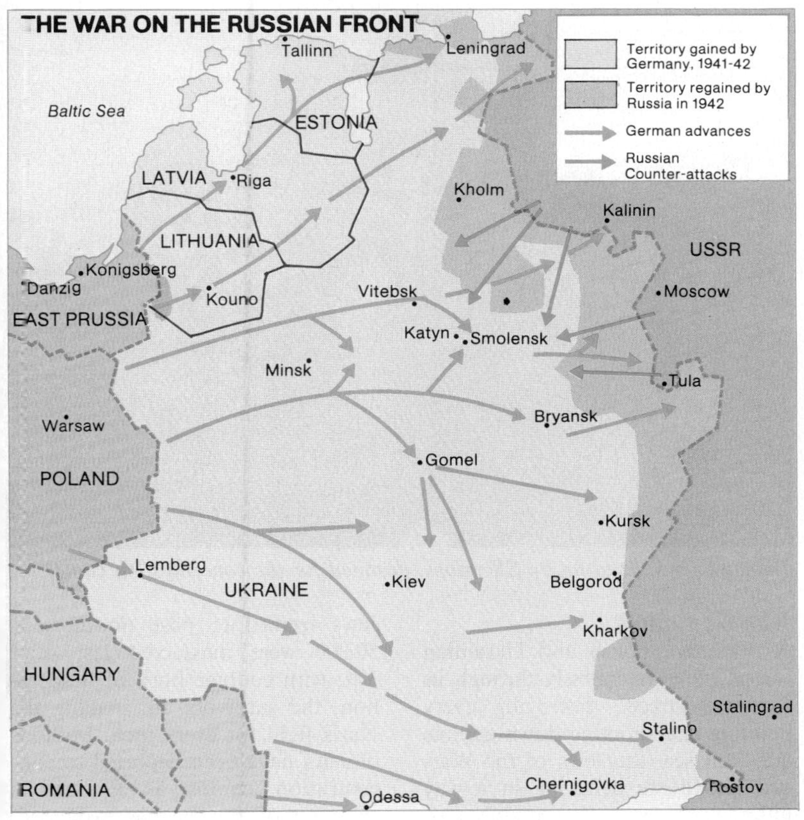

Russia, 31 May

A tremendous battle is raging for the Donetz river crossings south of Kharkov, with the armies of General von Bock and Marshal Timoshenko locked in fierce hand-to-hand fighting. Both sides are pouring in men and tanks and guns. Swirling air battles fill the sky over the front as dive-bombers from both sides pound their enemy.

A Russian dispatch from the Kharkov front speaks of 14 waves of massed German tanks being hurled back. Among the German losses were 500 of their latest tanks. The fighting is part of Hitler's much-talked-about spring offensive which opened on 12 May with an onslaught on the Soviet lines on the Kerch peninsula in the Crimea.

Much of the offensive's impact was blunted, however, when the Russians pre-empted the development of the main German thrust by striking towards Kharkov and inflicting heavy casualties on the Germans still holed up in their winter positions. The battle rages. The outcome is still uncertain.

British put Japanese to flight in Burma

Burma, 19 December

For the first time since Burma was overrun by the Japanese almost a year ago, British and Indian troops are fighting back – and advancing at a remarkable pace through difficult jungle terrain along the Mayu Peninsula on the Bay of Bengal.

First reports suggest that the 14th Indian Division under Major General W L Lloyd are meeting little resistance as they thrust down either side of the Mayu Range of mountains. The little port of Maungdaw has been recaptured and a Punjabi patrol has made contact with the enemy. British generals believe the recapture of Burma is now a distinct possibility.

After the bombing of Pearl Harbor and the fall of Singapore, it is the Japanese who are on the defensive. With massive support from three carriers, the Americans landed successfully on the Solomon Islands and are advancing inland against near-suicidal Japanese resistance.

US Navy trounces Japanese at Midway

The USS Enterprise, waiting to launch its torpedo bombers during the battle.

Pacific, 7 June

In one of the greatest battles ever to be fought at sea, the US Navy wreaked revenge for its Pearl Harbor debacle today, sinking four large Japanese aircraft-carriers, and badly damaging three battleships off Midway Island. As the Japanese Imperial fleet withdraws, American commanders are hoping that the battle will be seen as a turning point in the war.

Unaware that American intelligence had succeeded in "cracking" their battle codes, the Japanese were taken completely by surprise when American dive-bombers flew out of the sun, raining their bombs on carrier decks packed with aircraft. As more dive-bombers savaged the battleships, torpedoes succeeded in turning the carriers into floating infernos.

The significance of Midway has not been lost on either side. It was a battle won by aircraft-carriers. America lost the carrier *Yorktown* and 147 aircraft. The Japanese have only one large carrier left with its others under repair. America has three in service with a further 28 under construction.

El Alamein: Monty hits Germans for six

Egypt, 30 October

The Eighth Army has punched deep into the Afrika Korps positions at El Alamein, in what looks sure to be the crucial battle of the desert war. After ten months in which Rommel's brilliant generalship has won battles against superior numbers, the "Desert Fox" seems at last to be on the run.

The Allied commander General Bernard Montgomery, who promised to hit the Afrika Korps for six, now has a two-to-one advantage in men, and a greater edge in armaments. Although the German lines are five miles deep, and heavily mined, intelligence estimates that they are reduced to a mere 90 tanks against the Eighth Army's 800. Half of Rommel's 100,000 soldiers and 600 planes are Italian, lowly rated by friend and foe alike. Montgomery has about 800 planes. The Axis reserves are now committed to the battle, and against such superior numbers and armaments, they can only postpone defeat.

Monty: leading from the front.

1943

Libya, 7 January. Free French troops take Oum-el-Araneb, the main Axis base in south Libya.

Morocco, 14 January. Churchill and Roosevelt meet in Casablanca to concert a grand strategy.

China, 16 January. Following Commissioner Sheng Shicai's break with the USSR last October, Xinjiang province is officially reincorporated into China.

USSR, 18 January. The Russians break the 16-month siege of Leningrad.

Libya, 23 January. The Allies take Tripoli, Italy's last stronghold in North Africa.

Berlin, 28 January. Hitler orders the mobilisation of the whole population from 16 to 65.

Stalingrad, 31 January. The Germans surrender Stalingrad.

Pacific, 2 February. The Japanese launch a last-ditch effort to regain control of the Solomon Islands.

USSR, 8 February. The Soviet army recaptures Kursk.

Pacific, 9 February. The US navy secretary reports that Japanese resistance in Guadalcanal in the Solomon Islands has ceased.

Germany, 6 March. The RAF pounds the Ruhr city of Essen, in Germany's industrial heartland.

USSR, 14 March. The Germans re-occupy Kharkhov in a counter-offensive against the Russians.

California, 28 March. The Russian composer Sergei Rachmaninov dies here aged 69.

Britain, 7 April. The Keynes Plan for post-war economic recovery is published.

Tunis, 14 April. Rommel evacuates his troops.

Poland, 26 April. The unearthing of a mass grave of 4,000 Polish officers in the Katyn forest causes intense diplomatic friction. Germany accuses Russia of the murders.

Tunis, 7 May. The Allies enter Tunis.

North Africa, 12 May. Resistance by Germans and Italians ceases.

Germany, 18 May. A state of emergency is declared in the Ruhr area following the RAF's "Dambuster" raid yesterday.

Buenos Aires, 5 June. A military *junta* is formed under President Arturo Rawson following yesterday's coup in which President Ramon Castillo was overthrown. The new labour minister is Juan Peron.

Berlin, 19 June. Goebbels declares the city "free of Jews".

France, 8 July. The French Resistance leader, Jean Moulin, dies after torture by the Gestapo.

USSR, 13 July. Germany loses the greatest tank battle in history in the cornlands around Kursk.

Italy, 25 July. Mussolini falls from power.

Poland, 16 August. Jews in the ghetto in Bialystok rise up.

Sicily, 17 August. The island is completely under Allied control.

Bulgaria, 28 August. King Boris III dies from an assassin's bullet.

Poland, 2 September. Inmates of concentration camps are being used for medical experiments.

Rome, 3 September. The prime minister, Badoglio, signs a secret armistice with the Allies.

Rome, 10 September. German troops occupy the city.

Yugoslavia, 14 September. Partisans are advancing along the Dalmatian coast; Allied officers have reached Tito.

Italy, 30 September. The Allies enter Naples.

Corsica, 4 October. Corsica falls to the Allies, the first part of France to be liberated.

Italy, 13 October. Italy declares war on Germany.

Yugoslavia, 19 October. Italian troops aid Tito's partisans in their fight against the Germans.

USSR, 6 November. The Russians retake Kiev.

Lebanon, 11 November. French troops arrest the government after it declares Lebanon independent.

Britain, 20 November. Oswald Mosley, leader of the British Union of Fascists, is released from jail on grounds of ill-health.

Beirut, 21 November. The French release the Lebanese government and reinstate the president.

Cairo, 22 November. Churchill and Roosevelt meet Marshal Chiang Kai-shek.

Tehran, 28 November. Churchill, Roosevelt and Stalin arrive for their first big meeting together.

USA, 15 December. The jazz pianist Thomas "Fats" Waller dies aged 39.

USSR, 19 December. After the first war crimes trial, three Germans are found guilty of atrocities and hanged at Kharkhov.

Britain, 22 December. The author Beatrix Potter dies aged 77.

Europe, 24 December. General Dwight D Eisenhower is to be supreme commander of the Allied invasion of western Europe.

Brutal Nazi pogrom in the Warsaw ghetto

Warsaw Jews, lined up by SS troops, destined for the concentration camps.

Warsaw, 19 April
As German, Polish and Ukrainian troops move relentlessly through its shattered streets, destroying every building and shooting down anyone they can see, the Jews of the Warsaw ghetto are behaving in a way unknown in years of seemingly passive acceptance of Nazi persecution: they are fighting back.

The SS General Jurgen Stroop promised Hitler that the ghetto would be easy to crush. Unarmed, starving, their numbers decimated by years of isolation, Warsaw's Jews seemed to pose no threat – 50,000 were massacred last year. Yet, with courage born of desperation, the survivors are making the Nazis fight for every inch. Millions of Jews have been deported to concentration camps as Germany's conquest of Europe has expanded. For whatever reason, none has resisted. Until now. They will not win, they cannot win, but these "sub-humans and cowards", as the Nazi Stroop dismisses them, are proving a real stumbling block to the "Master Race".

Allies take 110,000 Germans in Africa

North Africa, 12 May
German and Italian resistance is over. Allied forces have taken 110,000 Germans and 40,000 Italians prisoner. It was the arrival of 140,000 American troops last November that clinched the victory.

One by one African landmarks have been falling to a pincer movement by Montgomery's Eighth Army in the south and east, and Eisenhower's forces in the west. Forced back on to the promontory of Tunis, Rommel evacuated four weeks ago, and on 7 May the Allied forces entered Tunis to a rapturous welcome.

General Jurgen von Armin, captured in Cap Bon with his entire staff by a British reconnaissance patrol, signed the surrender.

Communists purify their diluted party

China, 15 August
Cables ordering the screening of *cadres* have today been sent by the Central Committee of the Chinese Communist Party to all party organisations. This is part of the "Rectification Movement" which was started last year in order to cope with the problems caused by the huge expansion of the party.

Many new members have been recruited in the "liberated areas" and there has been some diffusion of the party's ideals. The screening ordered today is designed to stamp out corruption and reinforce the proletarian nature of the party's ideology and political programme.

It will also enable Mao Zedong to strengthen his grip on the party leadership.

Italy is out of the war

Italy, 8 September
A secret meeting between Dwight Eisenhower, the Allied commander, and Marshal Pietro Badoglio, the prime minister of Italy since the fall of Mussolini in July, has resulted in the unconditional surrender of Germany's ally. The news was broadcast this evening by Eisenhower.

Less than an hour earlier, Berlin radio was reporting "solid resistance" by Italian and German troops to the British invasion of southern Italy, and it seems the surrender has taken the Germans by surprise. In Corsica, the Italian garrison is reported to have overpowered its former allies. All ships, trains and vehicles carrying German troops are now liable to be halted on the orders of the Italian government.

Three weeks ago, Messina, the last fortress in Sicily, fell to combined British and American forces after a grim struggle which left the city in ruins. Long-range guns began to pound the mainland, and five days ago the first Allied troops landed opposite Messina. At the same time, Badoglio had embarked on his secret talks with the Allies in Rome. Italians, whose dislike of their German occupiers has become more and more blatant, have been laying down their arms *en masse.* They are now being invited to take them up again – this time against their former allies.

George Patton, the aggressive and charismatic US general, in Sicily.

Russians win Stalingrad

Russia and her ally – snow; sappers clear barbed wire for a Soviet advance.

Russia, 31 January
The Battle of Stalingrad is over. Field-Marshal von Paulus today surrendered the pitiful remains of his once-proud Sixth Army to a Red Army lieutenant in the basement of what had been Stalingrad's largest department store.

The lieutenant told him: "Well, that finishes it". Von Paulus replied with "a miserable look." Fifteen other German generals surrendered at the same time. A small pocket of Germans is still holding out in the northern part of this totally devastated city, but for them, too, the war will soon be over.

Some 300,000 Germans have been killed or died of starvation and cold since the Russians broke the Rumanians and encircled the Sixth Army last November with 100,000 dying in the ferocious hand-to-hand fighting in the city's ruins.

Von Paulus twice refused to surrender although his situation was hopeless. Goering's promises to fly in 500 tons of food, fuel and ammunition a day proved empty. Since December the Germans have been eating what was left of the Rumanian cavalry division's horses. Hitler forbade surrender and made von Paulus a field-marshal because no German marshal had ever surrendered. "Sixth Army will hold its positions to the last man," he ordered. Today the new field-marshal refused to obey his *Fuhrer's* orders any longer.

RAF and US bombs pulverise Hamburg

The aftermath of saturation bombing: the heart of Hamburg lies in ruins.

London, 3 August
Over seven square miles of Hamburg have been "wiped off the map", the British air ministry claimed today, after eight days of round-the-clock bombing with more than 10,000 tons of bombs dropped on Germany's second largest city. The non-stop air raid with the RAF attacking by night and the US Air Force by day is part of new terror-bombing tactics. Civilian casualties are put as high as 200,000 killed. The raids have systematically destroyed the city's factories, shipyards and U-boat bases.

Atlantic war: U-boats are on the run

London, May
The Allies have dramatically turned the tide in the war against U-boats in the Atlantic putting enemy submarines on the run.

Improved submarine detection techniques, including sonar radar, and the deployment of extra escort ships and aircraft-carriers from North Africa have swung the balance in favour of surface vessels with fewer German commanders prepared to venture out into the Atlantic. Last month eight U-boats were sunk in one attack on an Allied convoy.

At the same time Allied losses were down last month to just 18,000 tons of shipping sunk compared with a monthly average loss of 650,000 tons last year.

A German U-boat leaving port to join in the battle of the Atlantic.

1944 ⇒

New York City, 1 January. DNA is discovered by Oswald T Avery.

Berlin, 4 January. Hitler orders the mobilisation of all children over the age of ten.

USSR, 19 January. The Russians smash the German siege of Leningrad.

Italy, 22 January. Allied troops make a surprise landing at Anzio, 30 miles south of Rome.

Pacific, 29 January. The world's biggest warship, the *USS Missouri*, is launched.

France, 1 February. The Forces Francaises de l'Interieur (*FFI*) is created, unifying all Resistance movements.

New York City, 1 February. The Dutch artist Piet Mondrian dies aged 71.

Pacific, 4 February. US warships shell the Japanese home island of Paramishu.

France, 13 February. The Allies drop weapons for the Resistance in Haute-Savoie.

Tokyo, 21 February. Hideki Tojo becomes chief of staff of the Japanese army.

Helsinki, 24 February. The Finnish prime minister announces that his country is ready to make peace.

London, 26 February. The Polish government rejects the Curzon Line, reached by the USSR and Germany in 1939 as its eastern frontier.

Pacific, 29 February. American troops land at Los Negros in the Admiralty Islands in a new assault on Japanese territory.

Britain, 3 March. The RAF admits it is dropping new 12,000-pound bombs in its latest raids on German cities.

Britain, 12 March. All travel between Britain and Ireland is banned to prevent invasion plans from being passed to pro-German spies in Ireland.

Hungary, 18 March. The Germans begin to occupy the country.

Burma, 19 March. It is revealed that Allied troops have been landed by glider 200 miles behind Japanese lines.

Eastern Europe, 22 March. The Germans continue their march into Hungary; German troops cross into Slovakia.

Rumania, 2 April. The Russians cross the Rumanian border.

Hungary, 5 April. The Germans begin deporting Jews.

Berlin, 7 April. Hitler suspends all laws and makes Goebbels dictator of the city.

France, 9 April. General Charles de Gaulle becomes commander-in-chief of the Free French forces.

USSR, 13 April. The Soviet army take Simferopol.

Germany, 20 April. The RAF sets a new record for a single raid, dropping 4,500 tons of bombs for Hitler's 55th birthday.

Paris, 20 April. Petain visits the city for the first time since the fall of France.

Pacific, 24 April. The Japanese evacuate New Guinea as US troops land.

Britain, April. Britain becomes one big armed camp as Eisenhower oversees Allied preparations for the invasion of Europe.

Moscow, 1 May. Stalin tells Bulgaria, Rumania and Hungary to declare war on Germany.

London, 8 May. The exiled Czech government signs a convention to allow the Soviet army to liberate the country.

USSR, 9 May. The Soviet army takes Sevastopol, winning control of the whole Crimea.

France, 15 May. Field-Marshal Erwin Rommel attempts to cut occupied France off from neutral countries to stop information being passed out to the Allies.

Italy, 18 May. British and Polish troops capture Monte Cassino.

Italy, 23 May. The Allies begin an offensive from Anzio.

Yugoslavia, 25 May. Tito escapes to the hills as Germans capture his Bosnian headquarters.

London, 28 May. MPs hear that 47 Allied airmen have been shot in a mass escape bid from *Stalag Luft III* in Silesia.

Eire, 1 June. De Valera's *Fianna Fail* wins an overall majority.

Algiers, 3 June. General de Gaulle announces a provisional French government to take over from Vichy when France is liberated.

Rome, 4 June. The Allies take Rome.

Rome, 5 June. Victor Emmanuel III resigns, Crown Prince Umberto becomes acting head of state.

France, 6 June. Allied forces begin landing in Normandy – the invasion of Europe has begun.

Rome, 9 June. Ex-prime minister, Ivanoe Bonomi, is chosen to head a provisional government.

France, 10 June. German troops obliterate a whole village in reprisal for the killing of an SS officer.

Japan, 15 June. US planes bomb the Japanese mainland.

Allies liberate Rome

US General Mark Clark, commander of the Fifth Army, in St Peter's Square.

Rome, 4 June

Cheering crowds, throwing flowers and handing round bottles of wine, celebrate the arrival of American and British troops as the Allies march into Rome. President Roosevelt declared jubilantly: "The first Axis capital is in our hands. One up and two to go."

Apart from the occasional German sniper, there has been little fighting in Rome itself, and Allied planes command the skies, harassing retreating German columns. The city's historic sites remain undamaged. Hitler's orders to blow up the Tiber bridges were ignored.

But for the Allied victors, it has been a grim struggle since American and British troops landed at Anzio in January. Faced with crack German troops commanding the road to Rome from the fortress of Monte Cassino, they suffered heavy losses before Monte Cassino fell ten days ago, enabling the Anzio forces to link with the Fifth Army, advancing from the south.

British jungle fighters glide into Burma

Burma, 24 March

Britain's "forgotten army" – the "Chindit" jungle fighters who are fighting the Japanese at their own game in Burma – mourned an outstanding leader today. General Orde Wingate, their brilliant yet eccentric commander, has been killed in an air crash. "Gideon" Wingate, a loner who has been compared to Lawrence of Arabia, spurned military orthodoxy, particularly in jungle fighting, and relied on surprise as his principal tactic.

Wingate pioneered the use of gliders to land troops behind the Japanese lines. Five days ago, details of one of the most daring operations of the war were revealed. Gliders landed men, mules and a bulldozer behind the Chin Hills where they built a strategically vital airstrip.

Burma: "the forgotten war".

Allied troops take Normandy beaches

An endless column of US vehicles drives through the village of Isigny on the way to the front at St Lo.

GIs in La Haye du Puits in Normandy, on the sixth day of the invasion.

Normandy, 6 June

In the biggest combined land, sea and air operation of all time, British, American and Canadian forces have landed on the Normandy beaches at more than a dozen points along a hundred miles of coast. The Germans appear to have been caught off their guard. Allied air reconnaissance has shown that the strongest German defences are concentrated in the Pas de Calais, and that a powerful armoured force there has not been moved.

The massive operation began with heavy aerial bombardment of German coastal batteries and the sweeping of mines from the invasion route. A seaborne force of several thousand ships, brought from widely scattered British ports, converged on the invasion coast soon after 5am. Battleships far out to sea and destroyers closer inland pounded the German defences. Engineers demolished beach obstacles and the fighting men came up behind them with tanks and self-propelled artillery.

The question that has yet to be settled is whether the Allies can bring in reinforcements faster by sea than the Germans can by land. The land-based forces would have the advantage, but for the work of the RAF and the US Air Force in knocking out railways, bridges, radar stations and supply columns. Only at night can the Germans risk large-scale movement of men and supplies. In the House of Commons tonight, Mr Churchill told MPs that the invasion "is proceeding in a thoroughly satisfactory manner. Many dangers and difficulties which appeared extremely formidable are now behind us." Shipping losses have been less than feared and the resistance of enemy batteries has been greatly weakened by Allied bombing. At the end of this momentous D-Day, as it was known, Allied forces had penetrated several miles inland.

Japanese launch big attack on China

China, April

The Japanese have opened their first large-scale campaign in China since the end of 1938. In the intervening years an informal truce has been established between units of the Nationalists and the Japanese with much money being made in trade between the two armies.

That cosy arrangement has now been swept away as the Japanese, most of their merchant shipping sunk, attempt to establish a land link with their armies in South-East Asia.

They are also determined to wipe out the airfields from which the Americans have begun bombing the heart of the Japanese war machine. These airfields are poorly protected on the ground and are proving easy targets for the Japanese.

Their assault, codenamed *Ichigo*, has shocked the Chinese. The Nationalist army in Hunan has been routed and the Americans are abandoning their bases, flying their aircraft to safety but destroying huge amounts of equipment.

Russian army drives Germans out of Crimea in bitter attack

Russia, 16 April

The Red Army is sweeping the Germans out of the Crimea. The remnants of nine German and Romanian divisions, once more than 100,000 strong, are being harried through the streets of Sevastopol and in the open country around those other nineteenth century battlefields, Inkerman and Balaclava.

It is only five days since the Russians opened their campaign to recapture the Crimea with three armoured thrusts, their tanks smashing into the German defences across the neck of the peninsula.

The Black Sea port of Odessa fell almost immediately, followed by Kerch, the easternmost town in the Crimea, and the vital railway junction of Dzankhoi. The capture of Odessa was the climax of a 13-mile (21-kilometre) drive which left 5,500 Germans dead and hundreds of tanks destroyed. Now Yalta on the south coast has been taken and the Germans are desperately trying to organise a "Dunkirk" to save their troops pinned against the sea by the Russian tanks and dive-bombers. The Crimean victories are being celebrated with salvoes of gunfire. Stalin has issued an Order of the Day urging the army not to allow any German to escape: "The arrogant invaders run like rats, the ground hot beneath their feet. Destroy their ships. Shoot down their planes. Don't allow a single enemy to escape retribution."

Some 118,000 of the "rats" have already been killed as the Soviets gather for the last push.

The last of the German troops leaving Zhitomir, before the Red Army advance.

1944 (1944-1945)

USSR, 3 July 1944. Minsk, the last big German base on Soviet soil, falls to the Russians.

Lithuania, 13 July 1944. The capital, Vilna, is captured by the Russians as they advance through the Baltic states.

Berlin, 21 July 1944. Troops pour into the city following an attempt on Hitler's life yesterday.

France, 31 July 1944. The pilot and writer Antoine de Saint-Exupery is declared missing.

France, 31 July 1944. The Allies drive the Germans from Normandy.

Berlin, 2 August 1944. Germany breaks off relations with Turkey.

Berlin, 8 August 1944. Officers convicted of attempting to assassinate Hitler are executed by being strangled with piano wire.

France, 15 August 1944. A massive Allied force lands on a coastal strip from Nice to Marseilles.

Germany, 17 August 1944. The Russians reach the East Prussian frontier.

Britain, 19 August 1944. The conductor Sir Henry Wood dies aged 75.

Bucharest, 25 August 1944. Following King Michael's armistice with the USSR on 23 August, Rumania declares war on Germany.

Paris, 25 August 1944. General de Gaulle enters liberated Paris.

Poland, 27 August 1944. Polish and Soviet officials show the Press the Maidenek concentration camp.

Rumania, 31 August 1944. Russians and Rumanians have taken the Ploesti oilfields, which have been supplying Germany with one-third of its military oil.

Belgium, 4 September 1944. The Allies capture Brussels and Antwerp and cross into Holland.

Sofia, 6 September 1944. Bulgaria declares war on Germany.

Germany, 11 September 1944. The US First Army under General Omar Bradley leads the Allies on to German soil.

Helsinki, 19 September 1944. Finland signs an armistice with the USSR.

Estonia, 22 September 1944. The Russians capture the capital, Tallinn.

Athens, 14 October 1944. British troops march into Athens.

Germany, 14 October 1944. Erwin Rommel takes poison rather than be executed for conspiracy against Hitler's life. Hitler had promised him a hero's funeral if he committed suicide.

Czechoslovakia, 18 October 1944. The Russians enter the country.

Germany, 18 October 1944. Hitler orders the formation of a home guard in anticipation of the invasion of Germany.

Philippines, 20 October 1944. General MacArthur lands on the central Philippine island of Leyte.

Germany, 20 October 1944. Aachen surrenders to the Allies.

Belgrade, 20 October 1944. Tito's Partisans and the Red Army take Belgrade.

Paris, 28 October 1944. De Gaulle orders the Resistance to disarm.

Hungary, 5 November 1944. Soviet tanks enter Budapest.

Washington, DC, 7 November 1944. President Franklin Delano Roosevelt wins an unprecedented fourth term in office.

Belgium, 28 November 1944. The first Allied convoy sails into the port of Antwerp.

Hungary, 29 November 1944. The Russians cross the Danube and pierce the German defences in the south of the country.

Germany, 6 December 1944. Twenty million people are reported to be homeless after Allied bombing.

Moscow, 10 December 1944. De Gaulle and Stalin sign a treaty of alliance.

Paris, 13 December 1944. The Russian artist Wassily Kandinsky dies aged 78.

Indochina, 22 December 1944. Vo Nguyen Giap forms the Vietnamese People's Army.

Britain, 1944. The poet T S Eliot completes his *Four Quartets*.

Budapest, 13 January 1945. The city is now in Russian hands.

Warsaw, 17 January 1945. Soviet and Polish troops take the city.

Budapest, 21 January 1945. Hungary declares war on Germany.

Poland, 27 January 1945. The Red Army takes Auschwitz.

Germany, 31 January 1945. Soviet troops cross the river Oder north of Frankfurt, 40 miles from Berlin.

Philippines, 1 February 1945. US troops advance 25 miles into Japanese-held territory and free over 500 prisoners of war.

Philippines, 6 February 1945. MacArthur announces the capture of Manila and the liberation of 5,000 prisoners.

Cairo, 24 February 1945. The prime minister, Ahmed Maher Pasha, is shot dead after reading Egypt's declaration of war on Germany and Japan.

German flying bombs devastate London

London, 19 June 1944

For the past week the Germans' secret weapon, the V1 or "Flying Bomb", has been unleashed on London and its south-east approaches at a rate of 100 a day. The flying bombs, nicknamed "doodlebugs", look like pilotless planes with a primitive rocket engine at the rear and carry nearly a ton of explosive.

Launched from the Pas de Calais with enough petrol to reach London, they stall when the fuel runs out and nose-dive silently for 15 seconds to earth. Their low altitude prevents anti-aircraft guns from ranging on them. Yesterday one hit the Guards Chapel during a service killing 119 people.

RAF fighter pilots are desperately seeking new methods to counter this high-speed menace in what has become known as "bomb alley" over Kent and Sussex.

London's second Blitz: searching for survivors after a "doodlebug" blast.

American warships land in Philippines

Philippines, 21 October 1944

"I shall return", vowed General Douglas MacArthur when Japan ejected him from the Philippines in 1941. He has kept his pledge and strode up a beach at Leyte today to watch his invasion force of 250,000 fighting to retake the islands, while thousands of Japanese reinforcements have been killed in a massive naval battle offshore.

Two divisions of the Japanese navy, including a carrier, several cruisers and destroyers, have been destroyed, and American torpedoes have accounted for numerous troopships. A jubilant MacArthur said: "The Japanese navy has suffered its most crushing defeat of the war."

As American troops fight their way back across the Pacific – island by island – and British and Commonwealth armies are beating the Japanese in jungle warfare, a fearsome new weapon has appeared in the Pacific war: the *kamikaze* (divine wind) bomber. Dressed in ceremonial robes, these pilots fly their aircraft directly at the decks of American ships where their impact bombs do the most damage.

MacArthur: "I have returned."

Paris falls to the Allies

De Gaulle and "la France", marching triumphantly down the Champs Elysees.

Paris, 25 August 1944
Paris was liberated today by the combined efforts of the resistance and the free French forces. By this evening the Germans had capitulated and General de Gaulle himself was able to march down the Champs Elysees and address his countrymen: "I wish simply and from the bottom of my heart to say, *Vive Paris*!"

It was all made possible by General Eisenhower who ordered the Allied armies sweeping through northern France to encircle Paris, not invade it. He then contacted the resistance. Loyal police then took over the Ile de la Cite and the Prefecture and fighting broke out on the streets with the resistance attacking key German positions.

Last night the French Second Armoured Division, under General Jacques Leclerc entered the city. By this morning effective German resistance had collapsed and General Dietrich von Choltitz surrendered, defying an order from Hitler to destroy Paris. Tonight a few Parisians are out for revenge, beating up collaborators and trying to lynch German officers. But most are celebrating, beside themselves with joy now the *swastika* has been hauled down.

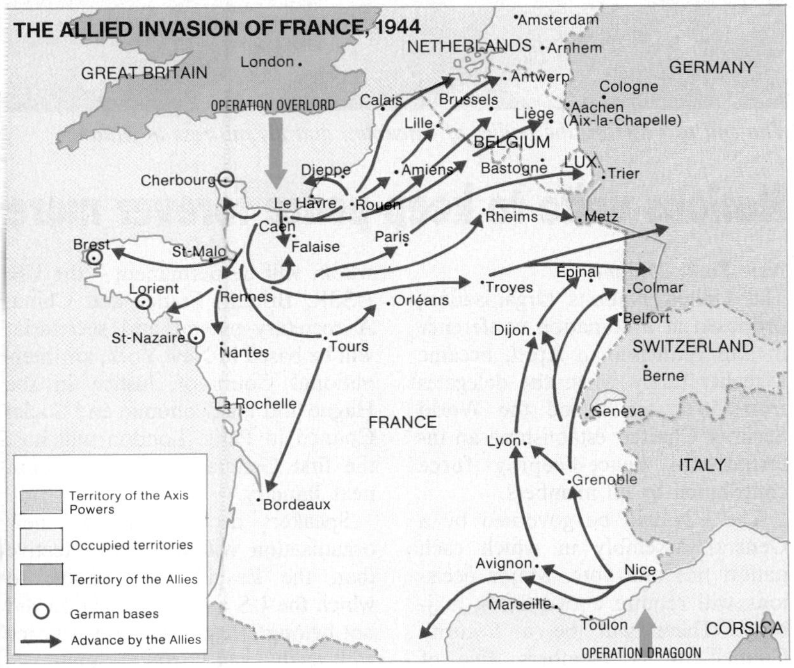

THE ALLIED INVASION OF FRANCE, 1944

Territory of the Axis Powers
Occupied territories
Territory of the Allies
German bases
Advance by the Allies

Allied air raids reduce Dresden to rubble

Dresden, 14 February 1945
The civilian death toll from 24 hours of Allied air raids on Dresden may be as high as 130,000. Total casualties in the devastated city are thought to be 400,000.

The raids by 800 RAF Lancasters and 400 US Air Force heavy bombers have provoked widespread criticism. Dresden, once comparable to Florence for its wealth of fine art and architecture, was thought to be safe from attack, even though it is an industrial centre providing communications for German forces on the Eastern Front. Its population of almost a million is above its peacetime level.

Most of the raids' criticism is aimed at the head of RAF Bomber Command, Air Chief Marshal Sir Arthur Harris. He is accused of clinging to his increasingly controversial theory that terror bombing by itself can destroy the enemy's will to fight. Other senior Allied officers say bomber resources would be better deployed stepping up attacks on enemy communication and oil installations.

Naked city: the remains of Dresden after a firestorm which killed 130,000.

Allies agree shape of post-war world

Yalta, 12 February 1945
Germany is to be forced into unconditional surrender and then partitioned into four zones, according to an agreement revealed here tonight. For the last eight days Churchill, Roosevelt and Stalin have been meeting to plan the final stages of the war and to carve out their post-war areas of influence.

Allied sources are worried that President Roosevelt has been primarily concerned about an invasion plan for Japan. Certainly, Stalin, flushed with recent great Soviet victories, has gone a long way towards winning acceptance for his domination of eastern Europe. And he gets the huge area of eastern Germany, which surrounds Berlin, where a joint control commission is to be established.

Partisans help the British win Athens

Athens, 14 October 1944
The entry of British troops, side by side with Greek Partisans, today brought relief to this strife-torn and poverty-stricken capital. Vast crowds celebrated the end of three and a half years of occupation by the Axis powers.

As the Germans withdrew up the Peloponnese earlier this month, the British landed at Patra on the Gulf of Corinth. Finding little opposition they set their sights for Athens. Colonel Earl Jellicoe headed the motley army's arrival in the city.

They have found a hungry population dispossessed of almost all they had. They are also quite aware that the murderous rivalry of socialist and ultra-right wing resistance groups is not going to disappear with the Nazis' departure.

1945 ⇒

Burma, 5 March. The British take the Japanese base of Meiktila, cutting Burma in two.

Indochina, 10 March. Tran Kim declares the independence of Vietnam.

Indochina, 11 March. Cambodia declares its independence.

Britain, 26 March. The politician and social reformer Lloyd George dies aged 82.

Germany, 30 March. The Russians take Danzig and cross from Hungary into Austria.

Pacific, 7 April. The US Navy sinks Japan's biggest battleship, the *Yamamoto.*

USA, 12 April. The American statesman Franklin Delano Roosevelt, president four times, dies aged 63. Harry S Truman is sworn in as president.

Vienna, 13 April. Vienna is liberated.

Poland, 15 April. Allied troops liberate the concentration camp at Bergen-Belsen.

Germany, 17 April. US troops liberate Buchenwald.

Germany, 20 April. Nuremberg, the scene of huge Nazi rallies, falls to the Allies on Hitler's 56th birthday.

Italy, 28 April. Mussolini is executed.

Germany, 30 April. US troops liberate Dachau.

Berlin, 30 April. Hitler shoots himself.

Europe, 2 May. All the one million German troops in Italy and Austria surrender.

Burma, 3 May. The British 14th Army takes Rangoon.

Berlin, 8 May. Field-Marshal Keitel signs Germany's final act of capitulation.

Prague, 10 May. Prague is the last European capital to be liberated.

Germany, 23 May. Himmler kills himself in British custody.

Britain, 23 May. The Coalition government resigns; there will be a general election on 5 July.

Berlin, 5 June. Allied supreme commanders sign a pact for the occupation of Germany.

USA, 16 July. The first atomic bomb tests take place in the New Mexico desert.

Britain, 26 July. Labour wins a landslide election victory.

Electronic computer sums everything up

Pennsylvania, December

It weighs 30 tons, occupies 1,500 square feet of floor space and contains more than 18,000 thermionic valves. It is the world's first general-purpose computing device.

It was originally intended to calculate gunnery tables, but came too late to contribute to the war effort.

Even so, it can perform 5,000 additions or subtractions in a second and revolutionises computation of all kinds, scientific and commercial. It has a drawback. The valves tend to get very hot, so it cannot work continuously for long periods.

War sparks African nationalist trend

Manchester, 19 October

Here in the unlikely setting of Chorlton town hall, 200 black delegates, representing almost every black colony in the British empire have called for a promise from Britain of eventual independence, as France made at Brazzaville a year ego. From Kenya's Jomo Kenyatta, who opened the Fifth Pan-African Congress's first session, through speakers like Kwame Nkrumah of the Gold Coast, there is a new spirit of optimism. The anti-imperialist USA is the dominant world power. Empire-building is past history – in the west at least.

Britons vote for a socialist future

London, 26 July

Labour has won an historic landslide victory in the British general election. For the first time it has an overall majority with 393 seats compared with 213 for the Conservatives and 34 for others. The party won on a detailed programme of public ownership of key industries and huge social reforms. Winston Churchill, the cigarsmoking wartime leader, has been rejected, even by the armed forces vote. Taking over is the pipesmoking Clement Attlee, who said: "We are facing a new era. We can deliver the goods."

Partisans kill Mussolini and his mistress

Milan, 28 April

The bodies of Benito Mussolini and his mistress, Clara Petacci, hanging upside down in the Piazza Loretto here, provide a grisly monument to European Fascism.

As Italian Partisans were rounding up Nazi sympathisers, the former dictator and a few confederates were discovered hiding in a convoy of eight cars. *Il Duce* emerged from beneath a pile of coats to plead for mercy from his captors.

After a brief trial presided over by the Communist leader Cino Moscatelli, Mussolini and those with him were machine-gunned to death. He had been on the run since his rescue by German parachutists from an Italian prison in September 1943.

Although some of those with him, notably the Fascist bosses Carlo Scorza and Alessandro Pavolini, shouted "Long Live Italy" as they died, Mussolini is said to have gone to death as if in a daze. It was an ignominious end for the man who ruled Italy for more than two decades.

The end of Fascism: the bodies of Mussolini and his mistress in Milan.

Nations unite to keep peace forever more

New York, 26 June

The United Nations Organisation, proposed at a 46-nation conference in San Francisco in April, became a reality today when the delegates from 50 states signed the World Security Charter, establishing an international peace-keeping force contributed by all members.

The UN will be governed by a General Assembly in which each nation has one vote. Major decisions will require a two-thirds majority. There will be a Security Council of 11 members, five of whom will be permanent – the US, USSR, Britain, France and China. A secretary-general and secretariat will be based in New York, an International Court of Justice in the Hague and an Economic and Social Council in Paris. London will host the first General Assembly session next January.

Speakers declare that the new organisation will be more effective than the League of Nations, to which the US and Soviet Union did not belong. "It provides for a peace with teeth," said General Smuts.

Allies march into Berlin

The red flag flies triumphantly over the battered "reichstag" in Berlin.

Berlin, April 30

The Third *Reich* was consumed by the flames of its own mythology today as Red Army tanks and Allied guns pounded Berlin into dust. Below the streets even the architect of the myth of German superiority, Adolf Hitler, was obliged to acknowledge his defeat. In his bunker he dictated a banal message blaming his own army as well as a Jewish-Bolshevik conspiracy for his failure. Then he shot himself.

For other Germans there was no simple, final solution of that sort. With the Russians in control of a third of Berlin, the city was in a state of panic. Soldiers discarded weapons and deserted, only to be shot or hanged on the street by roaming bands of SS fanatics who attached to the bodies the slogan "We betrayed the Fuhrer". Low-flying Russian biplanes machine gunned queues of people desperate for bread. Once-elegant streets were littered with rotting corpses from which anything of value, including boots, were removed. It was not the romantic twilight of the gods described by Goebbels in his address to the party faithful in Berlin, exulting in "total war". Some Berliners believe the Russians have sent a Mongolian horde to exact revenge and now pray they will be defeated by the western allies. Meanwhile, on the Elbe, Russian and American soldiers shook hands.

Mother and child in ruined Berlin.

Russia to occupy half German territory

USSR, 6 June

About half the total territory of Germany is to come under Russian control after the war, according to information published today by Moscow papers.

With the War now over, Russian citizens were treated to a detailed description of the future shape of the map of Germany despite the rule of secrecy adopted by the European Advisory Council responsible for defining the zones of occupation. The Soviet zone will extend far west of its present position. In some areas US troops will have to pull back more than 150 miles (240 kilometres).

The shattered capital, Berlin, will be within the Russian zone, but is to be divided into four parts, occupied separately by Russia, America, France and Britain, with a joint control commission.

In London officials merely commented that current zones of occupation were never expected to be the basis of post-war Europe.

Nazi death camp horror

The horror of it all: corpses of concentration camp victims at Buchenwald.

Buchenwald: the living and dead.

Poland, 30 April

On the day on which Adolf Hitler put paid to his "Thousand Year Reich" with his own suicide, allied troops have begun to uncover the grimmest testimony to the madness of his 12-year rule. Barely able to believe their eyes, soldiers are entering the concentration camps in which millions of Jews, Poles, gypsies, homosexuals, communists and many others have been systematically put to death.

Named after the villages or towns near which they were built – Belsen, Auschwitz, Buchenwald – the camps are 20th-century charnel houses where emaciated, diseased survivors, themselves barely alive, wander between huge piles of naked rotting corpses. Their rescuers are fighting to save them, but their best efforts are often doomed. Of the 40,000 survivors at Belsen, 600 die every day, victims of starvation, typhoid and tuberculosis.

Tales of unimaginable cruelties, of scarcely credible depravity are emerging, but what is most terrifying about the camps is, in some perverse way, their ordinariness. Nazi efficiency permeated the entire war, and these camps are no exception. They are literally factories of death, where the living, brought by cattle truck from every corner of Europe, were transformed, often within hours of their arrival, into corpses to be stripped and burned.

1945

Hiroshima, 6 August. An atomic bomb destroys the city.

Moscow, 8 August. Stalin declares war on Japan.

Nagasaki, 9 August. The city is destroyed by an atomic bomb.

Japan, 14 August. Japan surrenders to the Allies.

Japan, 19 August. The Russians occupy Harbin and Mukden in Manchuria – 100,000 Japanese surrender.

China, 28 August. Mao Zedong and Zhou Enlai discuss peace, democracy and unity with Chiang Kai-shek.

Hong Kong, 1 September. British troops take control.

Tokyo, 3 September. MacArthur formally accepts the Japanese surrender on the aircraft-carrier *Missouri.*

Singapore, 5 September. British troops take the island.

Korea, 8 September. The USA and the USSR divide Korea.

China, 9 September. In Nanjing He Yingqin formally accepts the Japanese surrender.

London, 19 September. The prime minister, Clement Attlee promises India independence.

India, 21 September. The Congress Party calls for the freedom of India, Burma, Malaya and Indochina from colonial rule.

USA, 26 September. The Hungarian composer Bela Bartok dies aged 64.

Indochina, 2 October. A ceasefire is agreed after fighting between Vietnamese insurgents and French troops.

Paris, 9 October. Pierre Laval, prime minister of Vichy France, is sentenced to death.

Norway, 24 October. Vidkun Quisling, prime minster of occupied Norway, is executed.

USSR, 6 November. The USSR says it will make its own atomic bomb.

Yugoslavia, 12 November. Marshal Tito's National Front secures an overwhelming majority in a general election.

France, 13 November. Charles de Gaulle is elected president.

Dutch East Indies, 17 November. The Republic of Indonesia is declared.

Belgrade, 29 November. A federal republic is declared and King Peter is ousted.

Britain. George Orwell publishes *Animal Farm.*

Nazi murderers put on trial by victors at Nuremberg

Nuremberg, 20 November

Hitler's old associates were today brought to the Palace of Justice at Nuremberg, scene of the Fuhrer's rallies, to answer to the world for their crimes before a tribunal of British, American, Russian and French judges.

In the dock are Goering, Hess, Ribbentrop, Keitel, Doenitz, von Papen, Streicher, and a dozen others, men who spread terror through Europe but today are just grey, nerous, nondescript. They are accused of waging a war of aggression, violating the laws and customs of warfare and crimes against humanity.

Justice Jackson, the chief US prosecutor, said that "the wrongs we seek to condemn and punish have been so calculated, so malignant and so devastating that civilisation cannot tolerate them being ignored."

He said the court faced a grave responsibility but that all the evidence of "greed, duplicity and torture" would be taken from "books and records which the defendants kept with their Teutonic passion for thoroughness".

Syria and Lebanon win their freedom

Near East, 13 December

French and British troops are to evacuate Syria and the Lebanon, whose freedom at last seems guaranteed. The Levant states were granted independence by France in 1941, but the British moved in soon afterwards.

Today's agreement, announced in the House of Commons by the foreign secretary, Ernest Bevin, marks the end of three months of negotiations with his opposite number, Georges Bidault. Bevin has had to convince the French that British intervention was aimed purely against the pro-Nazi Vichy government, and not intended to usurp long-standing French influence in the area.

With both countries committed to the United Nations, the principle seems settled. Details will be finalised next week in Beirut.

Colonel takes reins of power in Argentina

Buenos Aires, 17 October

Military leaders here have finally decided to hand over power to the Colonel who has become the idol of the labouring classes, Juan Peron. Only eight days ago they arrested Peron to thwart his ambitions. But the body of union support he built up while secretary of labour and social welfare came to his aid. The so-called "shirtless ones" took to the streets in processions and rioting. Peron is now near his dream of a populist government based on the support of workers, army officers and the police.

The students and teachers will not be pleased. A week ago they were marching on the streets shouting "Death to Peron".

Allied unity lies in tatters after Potsdam

Stalin, Truman and Churchill before the start of the Potsdam conference.

Potsdam, 31 July

The victorious political leaders of the Allies have failed to agree a post-war future for Europe. Meeting at Potsdam, Attlee (who succeeded Churchill after the British general election) and Truman have disagreed with Stalin about where Germany's new frontiers should be drawn. Britain and America object to Poland, with Russian encouragement, seizing huge areas of Germany. Stalin's refusal to accept free elections in eastern European countries or ease restrictions on western officials in those countries has angered the western leaders.

The casualties of war

	Military	Civilian
British Commonwealth	452,000	60,000
China	3,500,000	10,000,000
France	250,000	360,000
Poland	120,000	5,300,000
United States	295,000	
USSR	13,600,000	7,700,000
Other Allies	370,000	1,940,000
Germany	3,250,000	3,810,000
Japan	1,700,000	3,600,000
Other Axis powers	980,000	917,000

The numbers killed in the war: the price of victory and defeat.

Britain pledges independence for India

London, 19 September

India will have its independence, "at the earliest possible date," Mr Attlee broadcast to India today, appealing to Indians to settle their differences and decide their own destiny. In this he has the solid support of his viceroy, Lord Wavell, who released Gandhi from prison in May 1944. Whether Indians will resolve their differences in time is less certain. Moslems and now Sikhs demand states separate from the Hindu majority.

Atom bomb wipes out Japanese city

Hiroshima after the Bomb: survivors spoke of a noiseless flash and a light brighter than a thousand suns.

Japan, 9 August
The people of Hiroshima had been told to expect an air-raid. Many had spent restless nights in shelters; and, as they emerged into the bright sunlight, they watched a small parachute descending from a lone B-29 bomber flying high over the city. For many, it was to be the last thing they saw.

At precisely 8.15 on 6 August, a nuclear chain reaction in the bomb carried by that parachute built up a temperature of several million degrees centigrade. In 0.1 millisecond, a fireball of 300,000 degrees Celsius was created and expanded to 250 yards in diameter one second after the bomb had been detonated. Hiroshima had been the target of the first atomic bomb. And apart from a handful of substantial buildings, a city centre has been wiped from the face of the earth. A third of the population of 300,000 are dead, many of them killed mercifully outright by the blast; more by the firestorm that ripped through the city fanned by fierce man-made winds; and thousands are dying daily from the effects of deadly radiation burns. As stunned survivors stumble hopelessly through the flattened remains of this once-prosperous shipbuilding city, the world has learned of the huge flash – "brighter than the sun", said a US Navy captain who witnessed the bombing from the air – and the mushroom cloud that followed, reaching 23,000 feet into the sky.

The aircraft that dropped the bomb was named *Enola Gay* – after the pilot's mother. The captain, Paul W Tibbets, reported that the blast hurled it around in the air even from a distance of ten miles.

In Washington, President Harry S Truman has demanded the immediate surrender of Japan; and, as though to emphasise the power that the Allies now have, a further bomb was dropped today on Nagasaki killing 40,000 people and creating similar devastation to that of Hiroshima. President Truman has repeated his demand, threatening more A-bombs on a Japan which must be close to collapse.

Mushroom cloud hangs over future

Japan, September
It took two billion dollars, a workforce of 100,000 and several years to develop the atomic bomb. British and American scientists involved in what was code-named the "Manhattan Project" knew they were in a race with German nuclear experts; it was a German who discovered soon before the war that a form of uranium – 235 – could be split into roughly equal halves with the release of energy in a chain reaction. Allied scientists used this knowledge to produce the atomic bombs.

An entire city of 70,000 people was built in the New Mexico Desert around Los Alamos. Most workers did not know what they were making; and the first test bomb was exploded on a pylon so deep in the desert that few were present to assess its power.

The bombs that fell on Japan took less than four seconds to obliterate the hearts of two big cities and kill so many people; but the "mushroom" clouds that followed may kill many more. A new word – "fallout" – has entered the English language; and the radioactivity contained in those clouds will remain in the atmosphere, possibly for years. Scientists have created a monumental force and ended a great war; but they are the first to admit that they do not know a great deal about the effects of "fall-out" on this planet.

VE Day in London, after over 2,000 days of war. By midday Whitehall and the Mall were packed with people chanting "We want the king", while all over Britain people drank, danced and thanked God it was over.

1946

Britain, 1 January. The first civilian flights take off from an airfield to the west of London, known as Heath Row.

Britain, 7 February. A world food shortage as a result of the war forces the government to reintroduce food rationing.

USA, 22 March. First American-built rocket to leave Earth's atmosphere reaches 50-mile (80-kilometre) height.

USA, 18 April. The USA recognises the People's Republic of Yugoslavia, albeit with reservations.

USA, 19 April. President Truman promises a million tons of wheat a month for Europe and Asia.

London, 1 May. The USA and Britain publish a joint plan for the partition of Palestine between Jews and Arabs.

Argentina, 4 June. Juan Peron is installed as the president of Argentina.

Italy, 13 June. King Umberto II abdicates in favour of a republic after only 35 days on the throne.

Britain, 14 June. Television pioneer John Logie Baird dies, aged 57.

Indonesia, 29 June. President Sukarno urges his people to fight for freedom from the Dutch.

Yugoslavia, 17 July. President Tito executes General Mikhailovich, his one-time ally who then fought against the Communists.

Britain, 13 August. Novelist H G Wells dies, aged 79.

Calcutta, 19 August. Over 3,000 people die in Calcutta in three days of intense fighting between Hindus and Moslems over Britain's plans for the future of India.

Switzerland, 19 September. Churchill calls for the speedy formation of a United States of Europe.

Greece, 25 September. Prolonged civil unrest threatens to start a civil war.

USA, 2 October. A scientist claims that smoking could be a cause of lung cancer.

Britain, 22 November. A new type of pen, bearing the surname of its Hungarian inventor, Ladislao Biro, goes on sale.

USA, 25 December. Comedian W C Fields dies, aged 67.

USA, 31 December. President Truman formally ends World War II.

Nuremberg: Nazi war criminals hanged, Goering kills himself

Julius Streicher was found guilty at Nuremberg and hanged.

Nuremberg, 16 October

One by one, the architects of Nazi policy were hanged today in a prison in Nuremberg, Germany. The defendants had been found guilty of war crimes "so calculated, so malignant, and so devastating, that civilisation cannot tolerate their being ignored because it cannot survive their being repeated".

Those executed for war crimes were Joachim von Ribbentrop, Wilhelm Keitel, Julius Streicher, Ernst Kaltenbrunner, Alfred Rosenberg, Hans Frank, Fritz Sauckel, Alfred Jodl and Arthur Seyss-Inquart. None stumbled as they walked to the gallows. Some were defiant; a few begged forgiveness. Streicher shouted "Heil Hitler" as the noose tightened around his neck, while Joachim von Ribbentrop, the foreign minister, said, "My last wish is that German unity be maintained."

One convicted Nazi escaped the hangman's noose. Hermann Goering, for long Hitler's number two, committed suicide only hours before he was to be hanged. Goering was found twitching in his cell just moments after he swallowed cyanide out of view of his guard. It is not clear how the poison made its way to his cell.

The Nuremberg tribunal, however, reserved its harshest criticism for Goering when it found the Nazis guilty two weeks ago. The court called him a "leading war aggressor and creator of the oppressive programme against the Jews". Defiant right up to the end, Goering boasted to his doctor, "In 50 or 60 years, there will be statues of Hermann Goering all over Germany. Little statues, maybe, but one in every German house."

Nazis go on trial at Nuremberg. Goering is at the far end of the front row.

Mao orders all-out war in broadcast

China, 19 August

Communist leader Mao Zedong has ordered a showdown with Chiang Kai-shek and declared all-out war in a national radio broadcast. Peace talks are ruled out by both sides because of the belligerent tone of Chiang's V-J message and the Communist siege of Tatung.

Chinese Communist leader Mao Zedong addresses a crowd.

Churchill's US speech: the Iron Curtain

Fulton, Missouri, 5 March

"From Stettin in the Baltic to Trieste in the Adriatic, an iron curtain has descended across the Continent," Winston Churchill proclaimed today. The former British prime minister, referring to ideological barriers, warned that differences between the Western, capitalist world and the Eastern, Communist world seemed irreconcilable and that the Soviet Union desired "indefinite expansion" of its "power and doctrines". He urged the United States and Great Britain to formulate an alliance to discourage possible Soviet hegemony.

Reaction to the address varied considerably. The London *Times* declared, "while Western democracy and Communism are in many respects opposed, they have much to learn from each other." US senator Petter said Churchill spoke "in his best Marlborough manner for imperialism – but it is always British imperialism".

However, Senator Robertson agreed with the statesman, saying that until Russia "rolls up the iron curtain", close Anglo-American relations are essential.

Churchill delivers his Iron Curtain speech at Fulton, Missouri.

United Nations: first session opened

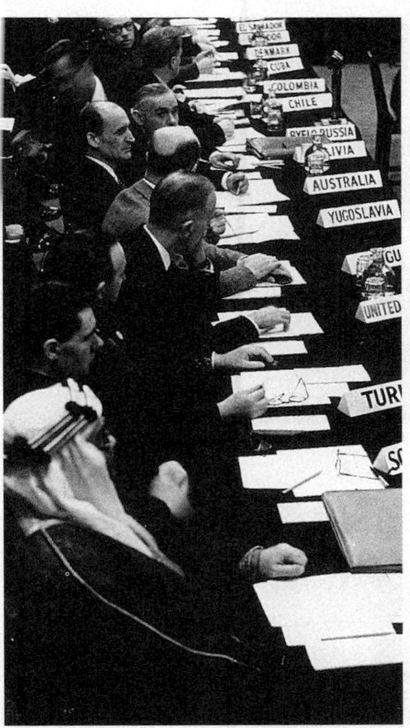

Representatives of 51 nations are in London for the first UN meeting.

London, 10 January
The first session of the United Nations General Assembly opened today at its temporary home of St James's Palace, London. The General Assembly will move to a permanent home in New York later in the year.

The United Nations has been formed to ensure world peace and co-operation, and there is a fervent hope that it will be more successful than the League of Nations, which was created 26 years ago but ultimately proved incapable of preventing conflict.

The British prime minister, Clement Attlee, welcomed the delegates of 51 nations, representing four-fifths of the world's population. Attlee said the new venture into world diplomacy would only succeed if those nations brought "the same sense of urgency, the same self-sacrifice and the same willingness to subordinate self-interests" with which they had won the war.

The UN's first problem concerned the conflict between Iran and the USSR. Iran charged the Soviet Union with interfering in its internal affairs and asked the UN to investigate the matter and take necessary steps. The USSR had authorised its army to stop Iranian troops from occupying the Iranian province of Azerbaijan, in accordance with a treaty signed in 1942 giving Russia the right to send troops into Iran. Iran claimed it threatens her sovereignty and disrupts the flow of oil supplies.

The Security Council of the UN has been called in to supervise the USSR-Iranian negotiations, and has been successful in applying pressure for the Soviets to withdraw. If nothing else, this dispute highlights the tensions beginning to develop between Communism and the nations of the West.

Einstein deplores use of atom bomb

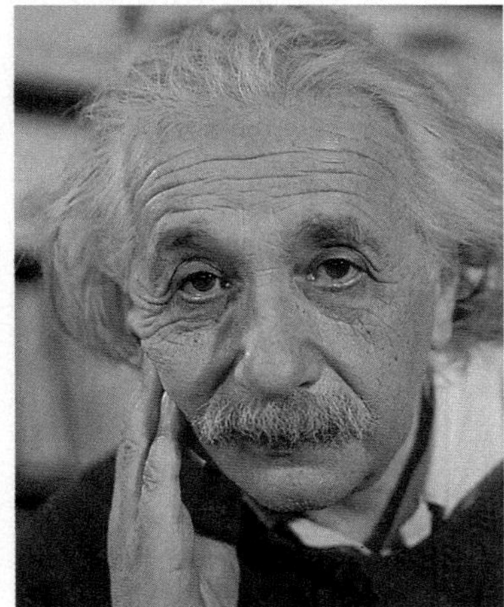

Albert Einstein advised Roosevelt against using bomb on Hiroshima.

United States, 18 August
In an interview with a British journal today, Albert Einstein stated regrets over use of the atom bomb. "A great majority of scientists," he said, "were opposed to the sudden employment of the bomb [on Hiroshima]." Einstein did not think Roosevelt would have used it, as he often counselled the president in nuclear matters. In March 1945, he sent him a memo urging that the bomb not be used on Japan. For reasons unknown, Roosevelt never got that note.

Hirohito declares his divinity a myth

Japan, 1 January
Japanese citizens read this morning's newspapers with shock and consternation as Emperor Hirohito, in an imperial decree, declared his divinity to be a "false conception" founded in fiction.

Since antiquity, emperors have been revered as descendants of Sun Goddess Amaterasu. Debunking this heralds modern government, but tradition dies hard.

Hirohito is received by General MacArthur at the US embassy.

Irgun blasts British offices in Jerusalem

Zionists bomb the King David Hotel, Jerusalem, used as the British HQ.

Jerusalem, 22 July
A powerful explosion has ripped through the southwestern wing of the King David Hotel in Jerusalem, which serves as headquarters for the British government. More than 100 people were killed. Irgun, the Zionist guerrilla band led by Menachem Begin, claimed responsibility for the attack.

US President Truman warned that the bombing might hurt the Zionist cause. The British called it "cold-blooded murder", but Irgun blamed it on the "British tyrants", and Begin said, "The force of the explosion surpassed all our hopes."

Moderate Jews distanced themselves from the attack by branding it a "dastardly crime perpetrated by the gang of desperadoes".

Attacks on the British have risen in protest at their crackdown on the illegal immigration of Jews.

Vietnam sparks war with French

Vietnam, 28 December
France proclaimed martial law in Vietnam tonight. Full-scale war now seems inevitable.

French trucks with loudspeakers patrol Hanoi, demanding that residents lay down their arms. The French warn that they will shoot civilians carrying weapons, search houses not displaying a white flag and attack any house that fires at French troops or civilians.

Tensions increased last week when Hanoi was bombed from the air. French garrisons outside the city were also attacked.

Ho Chi Minh, president of the Vietnamese Democratic Republic, and other officials fled after the attack, which killed French commissioner Roger Santeney.

1947

Britain, 1 January. All of Britain's coal pits come into public ownership.

Britain, 8 January. The army is called in to move food as distribution is frozen by a national road haulage strike.

USA, 25 January. Chicago gangster, Al Capone dies of apoplexy, aged 48.

Britain, 29 January. Freezing weather hits Britain, with temperatures falling as low as -27°C (-16°F).

Washington, 4 February. Thomas Lamont donates $500,000 for restoration of Canterbury Cathedral.

Paris, 12 February. Christian Dior launches the "New Look" in his spring collection, giving women an hour-glass shape.

Palestine, 2 March. Martial law is imposed in five Jewish areas, following attacks on British soldiers and civilians.

Washington, 12 March. President Truman tells Congress that the USA must abandon its traditional isolationism in order to combat Communism.

USA, 7 April. Death of Henry Ford, 83, founder of the huge motor company.

Texas, 19 April. Accidental fire and explosions devastate Texas City, killing 377 people.

Palestine, 4 May. Jewish Irgun guerrillas blast their way into a prison in Acre, releasing 251 inmates.

Britain, 27 August. The government cuts food rations and bans holidays abroad, as Britain faces a foreign exchange crisis.

USA, 29 August. US announces discovery of plutonium fission, suitable for nuclear-power generation.

Budapest, 1 September. Communists win Hungarian governmental elections.

Argentina, 9 September. Women given the vote.

USA, 14 October. Chuck Yeager becomes the first man to travel faster than sound, as his Bell XI rocketplane exceeds 760mph (1,200 km/h).

London, 20 November. Princess Elizabeth, heir to the British throne, marries Prince Philip.

India, 21 December. 400,000 slaughtered during mass migration of Hindus and Moslems into the new states of India and Pakistan.

US House panel claims there are 79 subversives in Hollywood

Washington, 23 October

Actor Ronald Reagan, president of the Screen Actors Guild, testified before the House Committee on Un-American Activities today and said that the guild is not controlled by leftists.

Yesterday, in its third day of hearings on Communism in the film industry, HUAC declared it would present "at least 79" subversives in the coming days. Actor Robert Taylor testified against other stars. His deposition was not as damning as the panel may have hoped; he failed to name any card-carrying Communist infiltrator.

Taylor's arrival at the session was greeted with gasps by women spectators. He took a seat before a microphone and swiftly stated, "I personally believe the Communist Party should be outlawed. If I had my way they'd all be sent back to Russia."

He suspected a few actors, but added sheepishly, "I don't know whether they're Communists." He noted some Screen Actors Guild members "who, if not Communists, are working awfully hard to be so". After 30 minutes of questioning, he retired from the session.

Next week, stars who include Humphrey Bogart, Lauren Bacall, Jane Wyatt, Danny Kaye and Gene Kelly plan to protest at the hearings.

Movie men, Jack Warner, (l) and Louis B. Mayer (r) with attorney Paul McNutt.

Robert Taylor is mobbed by autograph hunters after leaving the Capitol.

Marshall offers US aid plan to Europe

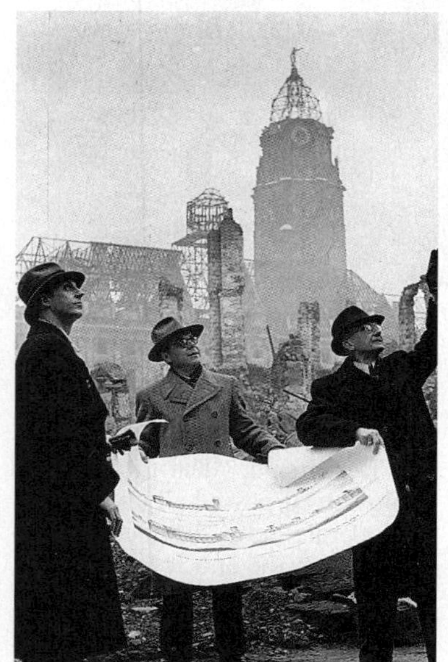

Marshall's economic plan aims to help post-war recovery in Europe.

Harvard, 5 June

Europe's economic recovery is the goal of an ambitious aid plan unveiled by American secretary of state George Marshall in a speech at Harvard University. He warns that Europe "must have substantial additional help or face economic, social and political deterioration of a very grave character".

A special committee established by Marshall concluded that a massive assistance plan would benefit the US, might protect France from Communism and invigorate the French and German economies.

Marshall suggested that the Soviet Union would be eligible to receive help from the new plan. But he pointedly warned that the US would not assist "any government which manoeuvres to block the recovery of other countries".

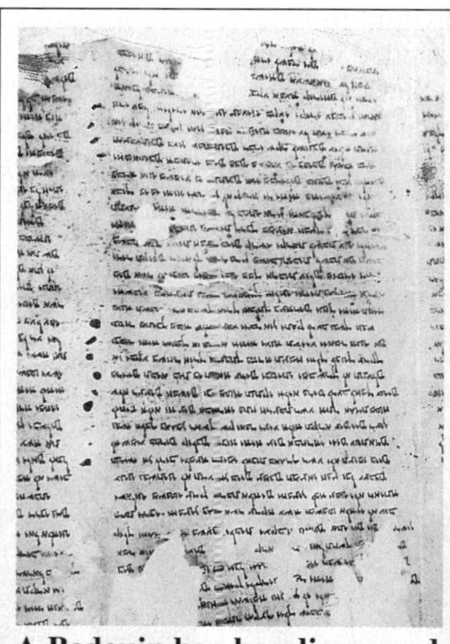

A Bedouin boy has discovered jars housing fragile leather scrolls in a cave by the Dead Sea. They reveal a copy of the Old Testament, dating from 100BC. Detailed translation work continues.

Independence for India and Pakistan

India, 15 August

At the stroke of midnight, India won its long-awaited independence from Britain. And Moslems won a degree of freedom from Hindus. They will have their own separate dominion, Pakistan, in the British Commonwealth.

The division of India into separate states tempered celebrations in New Delhi. Reports from the northern province of Punjab say scores of people have been killed in the past few days in fighting between Hindus and Moslems.

The real hero of India's independence was absent from New Delhi when sovereign power passed to the Indian Assembly. Mohandas Gandhi, longtime leader of the Indian National Congress, was in an ordinary house in Calcutta, trying to restore peace between Hindus and Moslems. He was praised by the president of the assembly, Rajendra Prasad.

Thousands of Indians crowded around the Council of State building as Prasad spoke. Public offices, temples and shopping centres hung the new national flag, coloured saffron, white and dark green.

Pandit Jawaharlal Nehru, the prime minister of the dominion government, then informed Lord Mountbatten, who had ceased to be viceroy at midnight, that he was governor general of India.

Nehru, India's prime minister.

Jinnah, leader of Pakistan.

In Pakistan, Mohammed Ali Jinnah, the Moslem leader, took his oath as governor general of that dominion. The ceremony took place in the capital, Karachi.

The creation of two dominions on the subcontinent is viewed with apprehension in some quarters, including among astrologers, whom many Hindus rely on for guidance about the future.

Nehru spoke of the difficulties facing his country when he praised Gandhi before the assembly, "The ambition of the greatest man of our generation has been to wipe every tear from every eye. That may be beyond us, but so long as there are tears and suffering our work will not be over."

In Punjab tonight, there is more than tears and suffering. The province has been chopped in half and split between India and Pakistan. Moslems are fighting Hindus in the cities and in the country.

India is split into a killing ground

India, 8 September

There has been little time to celebrate independence in India and Pakistan. Large parts of the dominions are paralysed with fear. Mobs run wild as Moslems and Hindus battle to the death and turn streets into rivers of blood.

Indian officials estimate that 150,000 people have been killed in the Punjab, which was partitioned between India and Pakistan, between Hindus and Moslems. The division has created a million refugees. Any one of them unlucky enough to be on the wrong side of the Punjab is a target for murder.

"They got their Pakistan, let them go to it," said one Hindu.

In New Delhi, a curfew goes unobserved, and critics of the Indian army say they are sympathetic to the Hindu killers and looters. At least 50 Moslems were killed by Hindus and Sikhs in the New Delhi railway station. Their bodies were piled on platforms and abandoned.

A victim of intercommunal rioting lies in a New Delhi street.

British intercept Jews on board Exodus at the port of Haifa

The Royal Navy seizes the Jewish immigrant ship "Exodus".

France, 18 July

The ship *President Warfield,* renamed *Exodus* in the hope it would be as successful in crossing the Mediterranean as Moses had been in crossing the Red Sea, has arrived back in French waters.

On board are 4,530 Jews, people without a country. Most are refugees from Germany and left the French port of Sete last week, bound for Palestine. But the British refused to allow them to disembark at Haifa, the official reason being that the Jews are displaced persons and illegal immigrants.

The British threat to send them back to Germany is being criticised in many world capitals. But no other compromise is in sight. The British resolve to bar the Jews from Palestine has been strengthened by the Irgun's violent attacks.

Transistor: a bit of electronic magic

United States

A year ago the US War Department credited vacuum tubes with powering its computer ENIAC. Yet Bell Laboratories has now developed something that may soon make the vacuum tube obsolete: the transistor. A transistor is a solid-state electronic component that is faster, lighter and about one 200th of the size of an early vacuum tube.

1948

Dublin, 18 February. Despite having been returned as leader of the largest party in the general election, Eamon de Valera is voted out of office as prime minister by the *Dail*, the Irish parliament, after 16 years.

London, 16 February. A Royal Navy cruiser is despatched to the Falkland Islands in response to threatening naval manoeuvres by Argentina, which claims the islands for itself.

Prague, 10 March. Jan Masaryk, Czech foreign minister and opponent of the Communist coup, is dead.

USA, 3 May. Pulitzer prizes go to Tennessee Williams for *A Streetcar named Desire* and James Michener for *Tales of the South Pacific.*

South Africa, 28 May. The right-wing Nationalists take over in South African elections, as incumbent prime minister Jan Smuts loses.

London, 7 June. Allies agree to keep troops in Germany until "peace of Europe is secured".

Britain, 5 July. The National Health Service, offering free treatment for the whole nation, is born.

USA, 23 July. Death of D W Griffith, maker of silent film epics, aged 73.

London, 14 August. Cricket's greatest ever batsman, Don Bradman, is out for nought in his final Test innings, needing only four to average 100.

London, 14 August. The first post-war Olympic Games come to a successful conclusion, despite the absence of Germany, Japan and the Soviet Union.

USA, 16 August. Baseball star George Herman "Babe" Ruth dies, aged 53.

North Korea, 9 September. North Korea proclaims independence as the Democratic People's Republic of Korea, under President Kim Il Sung.

Berlin, 18 September. The Allied airlift reaches its peak since the Soviet blockade began three months ago, 895 flights landing in one day.

USA, 3 November. The state of Kansas ends Prohibition after an abstemious 68 years.

New York, 10 December. The United Nations adopts a declaration of human rights.

London, 15 December. Prince Charles, the first child of Princess Elizabeth, is christened.

Mahatma Gandhi shot dead by assassin

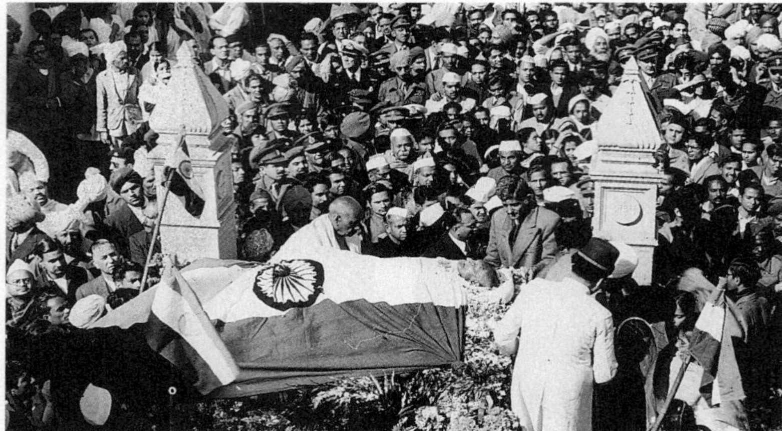

Mahatma Gandhi's body is carried to its traditional Hindu cremation.

New Delhi, 30 January

Mohandas K Gandhi, 78, the spiritual leader of Indian independence, has been shot and killed by a Hindu extremist. Gandhi – the Mahatma, or Great Teacher, to his followers – was shot at point-blank range as he walked through a garden to a pergola where he was to deliver his daily prayer. He died 20 minutes later.

The assassin, who stepped out from a crowd awaiting the prayer meeting, was immediately seized by onlookers. He was identified as Nathuran Vinayak Godse, 36, a Hindu of the Mahratta tribes in Poona, which have been the centre of resistance to the Gandhi message of communal and religious tolerance. Only a few days ago, Gandhi completed a five-day fast to encourage friendship.

The death of Gandhi, who for more than 20 years defied British rule with his programme of civil disobedience, has stunned the newly independent nation that he helped create. In a radio speech to the nation announcing the death, Prime Minister Jawaharlal Nehru, his voice quivering with grief, said, "Gandhi has gone out of our lives and there is darkness everywhere... The father of our nation is no more. No longer will we be able to run to him for advice and solace."

The loss of Gandhi, the strongest voice for peace and unity in a turbulent new nation of 300 million persons, is an incalculable political blow to India. Throughout the nation there is an undercurrent of uncertainty about the political future and a wave of fear that his death will lead to renewed fighting between Hindus and Moslems.

The news of his death set off riots in Bombay and other cities as mobs attacked offices of the Hindu Mahasabha, the extreme anti-Moslem organisation to which the assassin belonged. Nehru has appealed for peace in memory of Gandhi, whose body is to be cremated according to Hindu custom.

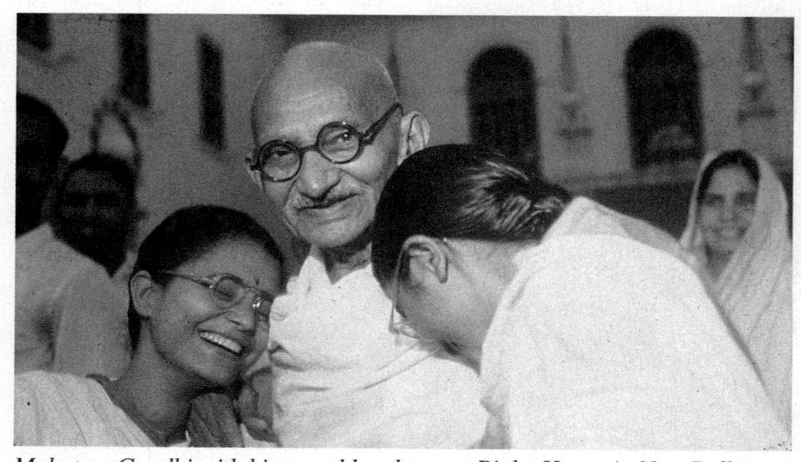

Mahatma Gandhi with his granddaughters at Binka House in New Delhi.

Soviet film genius Eisenstein is dead

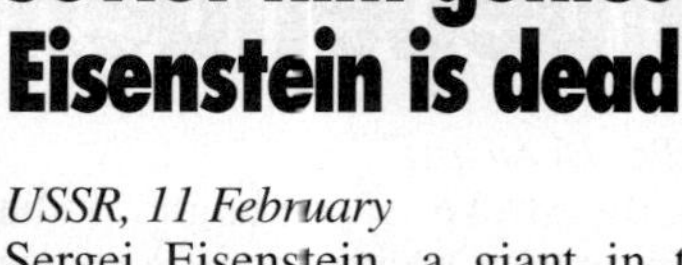

USSR, 11 February

Sergei Eisenstein, a giant in the field of cinema, has died in the Soviet Union. He was 50 years old. Eisenstein directed *The Battleship Potemkin* (1925), *Ten Days That Shook The World* (1928) and the three-part censored epic *Ivan the Terrible*, finally shown in 1947.

Eisenstein was a linguist (Russian, French, English, German and Japanese) who ironically feared the advent of sound. His films often depicted revolution, a natural subject for a revolutionary director.

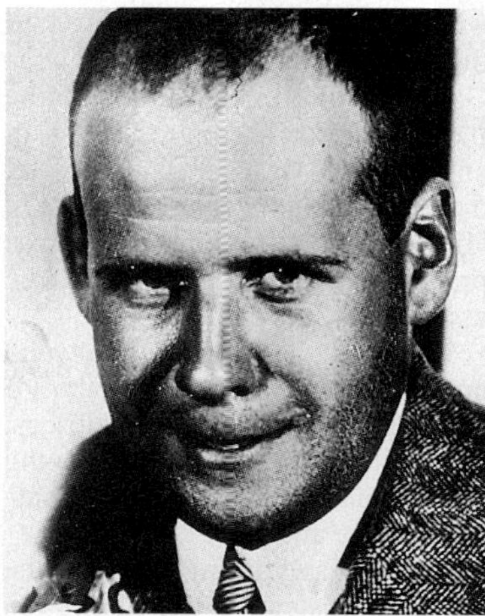

Russian film director Eisenstein.

Tito breaks with Stalin's Russia

Yugoslavia, 4 July

Joseph Stalin may have met his match in Tito, the leader of Yugoslavia. Tito refuses to knuckle under to the Russians, and his independent brand of Communism has led to a break with Moscow. The tensions have been building up between them all year.

Tito charged that Russian agents were trying to topple his government. The Russian-backed Cominform, which has its tentacles spread throughout Europe, accused Tito of deviating from the Communist line and sympathising with the Western imperialists. Tito rejected the criticism, and Russia retaliated by ejecting Yugoslavia from the Cominform and then by moving its headquarters away from Belgrade to Bucharest.

State of Israel attacked

Haganah men keep an eye on an Egyptian plane downed near Tel Aviv.

Middle East, 31 May
The new state of Israel, which is just two weeks old, is under siege and shrinking. It is being attacked from the north, east and south by enemies intent upon forcing it into extinction. The Arab League has rejected an appeal from the United Nations for a cease-fire.

The fighting started as soon as the British mandate expired on the 15th and Israel came into existence. Syria and Lebanon attacked in the north, Transjordan and Iraq moved in from the east, and Egypt invaded from the south.

An Israeli spokesman says the country is ready to respect a cease-fire, "but we have no intention of accepting the condition, suggested in most Arab public statements, that we should abandon the Jewish state. That would be tantamount to political surrender." The Arab states will not negotiate with Israel.

The hostilities in Israel have not stopped Jews from around the world from applying for immigration to Israel. Hundreds of Jews have already arrived from France and Cyprus, where they had been interned by the British.

One of the first actions of the new Israeli government was to open its doors to all Jews. A proclamation invited Jews to join "the struggle for the fulfilment of the dream of generations, the redemption of Israel".

Prime Minister Ben Gurion read the proclamation as the Israeli flag, the Star of David, flew over his head. Dr Chaim Weizmann was elected provisional president.

Truman wins, confounding the prophets

United States, 2 November
President Truman has won a full term in the White House, defeating the Republican favourite, Thomas E Dewey. The Truman victory was one of the major upsets in American political history.

Throughout the night, Truman's political fortunes waxed and waned. While leading at all times in the popular vote, the president trailed at times in the essential electoral vote until just before dawn today when he picked up Illinois and victory was assured.

Truman visits Americans in Brazil.

Communist coup against Czech regime

Czechoslovakia, 29 February
Communist Party leaders in Czechoslovakia moved to seize complete control of the country after toppling the government late last week. Political opponents of Prime Minister Klement Gottwald are being purged. Creation of new political parties has been outlawed.

Last week moderate cabinet members resigned to protest at Communist control over the police. They hoped this would force Gottwald out. The plan backfired, and Gottwald convinced President Benes to allow him to form a "government of the workers". Benes subsequently left Prague and is likely to resign. Masaryk, the populist leader, remains as foreign minister and says democratic institutions won't be harmed.

Gottwald addresses workers.

The Russian command blockades Berlin

Giant American aircraft are on Berlin airlift run to beat the blockade.

Berlin, 25 June
Russian commanders have tightened the blockade on the Allied sectors of Berlin, but the Western powers say they are determined to fly in enough supplies to keep the population from starving. Food supplies will last only one month. The Allies estimate they will have to airlift 2,500 tons of food a day to satisfy requirements in the Western zones. At present, only six tons are flown to Berlin every day.

The Soviet military administration announced today it would ban all food shipments from Soviet areas into Berlin. The Russians also intercepted six barges that were bound for Berlin from Hamburg. This follows blockades of the roads and rail lines. Ten days ago, the Soviets stopped coal shipments. They have also reduced the supply of electricity to the Allied sectors of Berlin.

In response, the Allies have outlawed food shipments to the Russian sector. This is not expected to hurt much, but the Allies believe their interruption of coal and steel shipments will have an effect. Morale in the Western sectors of Berlin remains high. This confidence is reflected in the high-riding Deutschmark, which is still worth 30 of the new Russian marks.

1949

India, 1 January. A UN cease-fire comes into effect to halt fighting between India and Pakistan over the disputed state of Kashmir.

USA, 10 January. Seven-inch vinyl records are launched.

South Africa, 15 January. Three days of race riots in Durban leave 106 dead.

Greece, 24 February. Israel and Egypt sign an armistice.

USA, 1 March. Joe Louis retires, after successfully defending his world heavy-weight title 25 times.

Moscow, 4 March. Vyacheslav Molotov ousted as Soviet foreign minister.

Britain, 1 April. Britain to have its first National Parks.

London, 12 April. The estate of Harry Gordon Selfridge, one-time department store millionaire who died in 1947, is worth only £1,544.

Britain, 24 April. Sweet rationing ends.

Dublin and Delhi, 27 April. India and Ireland are both to become republics.

Berlin, 12 May. The Soviet blockade is lifted.

Bonn, 14 August. Konrad Adenauer wins the West German elections for chancellor.

New York, 25 August. RCA announces invention of system for broadcasting colour television.

Britain, 1 September. The divorce rate has risen tenfold in 12 years.

London, 18 September. The pound is devalued by 30 per cent.

West Germany, 8 September. Composer Richard Strauss dies, aged 85.

San Francisco, 29 September. Wartime propaganda broadcaster "Tokyo Rose" guilty of treason.

East Germany, 12 October. The Communists establish a separate state for eastern Germany.

Greece, 16 October. The civil war ends with the defeat of the Communists.

China, 8 December. Nationalist forces, defeated on the mainland, establish their capital on the island of Formosa.

USA, 31 December. Ladies' Home Journal starts publication of the memoirs of "Crawfie", long-term governess to the British royal family.

Russians have the atomic bomb

United States, 23 September

President Truman told his cabinet this morning, "We have evidence that within recent weeks an atomic explosion occurred in the USSR." This is taken to mean that the Russians have developed an atomic bomb, according to Secretary of State Dean Acheson.

The administration moved fast to prevent a crisis from developing. "The calmer the American people take this the better," General Omar Bradley, chairman of the Joint Chiefs of Staff, said. "We have anticipated it for four years." Truman, who is determined to keep control of the US bomb in civilian hands, repeated his plea for international control of atomic energy.

Pauling describes sickle cell anaemia

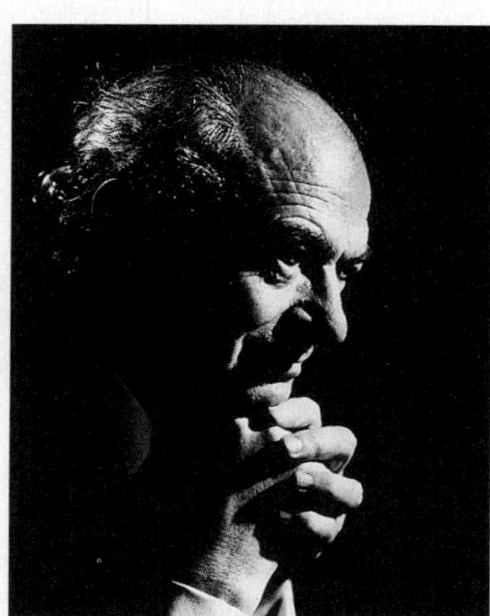

Eminent chemist Dr Linus Pauling.

United States, 1 July

Linus Pauling, the celebrated chemist, reports that he has found the molecular flaw responsible for the debilitating blood disease sickle cell anaemia, which affects black people. The disease gets its name from the observation that it causes blood cells to lose their natural disc-like shape and become sickle-shaped cells that cannot easily pass through the small blood vessels. Pauling's research shows the problem is in haemoglobin, an oxygen-carrying protein made of hundreds of subunits. A change in a single subunit causes the disease.

Allies organise NATO despite opposition

President Truman signs the document formally ratifying the NATO pact.

Washington, 18 March

Is it a legitimate defence treaty or a militaristic plan that will only provoke the USSR? Forceful arguments were made for both viewpoints as the United States and Western Europe unveiled plans for a collective defence alliance they call the North Atlantic Treaty Organisation, or NATO.

The Allies agreed that an armed attack on any one of them would be considered an attack against them all. Their goal is the "preservation of peace and security". They also reaffirmed their support for the United Nations.

Critics say the treaty will turn Europe into an armed camp that will ignite a war with the Russians. Earlier in the month, Belgian Communists adopted a resolution opposing any "war of aggression against the Soviet Union". Strong opposition to the alliance has also surfaced in left-wing circles in Italy and France. A chief backer of the treaty, Secretary of State Dean Acheson, chides critics by saying that only combined strength will preserve the peace.

The US, Canada, Britain, France and the Benelux nations wrote the treaty. Italy, Norway, Denmark, Iceland and Portugal are invited to sign it next month.

Orwell's book foresees a grim 1984

10 June

George Orwell's novel *1984* depicts a familiar future. Censorship, manipulation of historical fact and invasion of privacy reflect totalitarian governments of today. He started writing the book in 1948, reversing the last two digits of the year to set the time. *1984*'s hero is flabby and cowed, as anyone would be in a highly technocratic, highly paranoid society.

Heroes and anti-heroes strode across stages as well as pages this year. "Attention. Attention must be paid," says the wife of Willy Loman, hero of Arthur Miller's *Death of a Salesman*. Willy is trapped in a society fond of a fast buck and friendless handshake.

Carson McCullers' *The Member of the Wedding*, a tender look at race relations, opened on Broadway.

George Orwell, author of "1984".

China establishes People's Republic

China, 1 October
Cheering crowds today hailed the Chinese leader Mao Zedong's proclamation of China's new People's (Communist) Republic and the appointment of Chou En-lai as premier.

The announcement, to a crowd of 200,000 at the Gate of Heavenly Peace, was hailed by a Soviet historian as one of the year's two "stupendous events" – the other being the "failure of US calculations upon atomic monopoly".

Within hours of the news being broken, the USSR recognised the regime and asserted that the Chinese Nationalists led by Chiang Kai-shek now hold no power and that "the victory of the Chinese people deals a cruel blow to the aggressive plans of imperialists in the Pacific region".

Chou En-lai, who is often a representative of the Communists in negotiations with the Nationalists, will also head the foreign ministry, which deals with other nations. The first task ahead of him and Mao Zedong is to gain the world's acceptance.

Mao declared in his speech: "This government is willing to establish diplomatic relations with …any nation willing to observe the principles of equality, mutual respect and territorial sovereignty."

The next step is to ask the United Nations to recognise a Communist Chinese representative as the legitimate delegate for China.

The news of the establishment of a Communist republic in China comes as a setback to the United States and the Western alliance, both of which supported the Nationalists.

Official American comment on the changes is expected to be forthcoming, but so far no statement has been reported.

Mao proclaims People's Republic.

This Chinese poster shows the people celebrating People's Republic Day.

German Federal Republic created

Germany, 23 May
From the ashes of Nazi Germany, a new country is being formed. It will be called the Federal Republic of Germany.

In Bonn, hundreds of people jammed the streets, cheering the news and waving flags coloured red, black and gold, the same colours that festooned the Weimar Republic in the pre-Hitler era.

There was, however, very little cheering in the Russian-controlled sector of Germany. German residents there will not be part of this new country.

Dr Konrad Adenauer, president of the Parliamentary Council, presided over the solemn affair that proclaimed the existence of the new republic.

In a short speech, Adenauer declared, "A new Germany arises." He also said that he hoped a new constitution would reunite all of Germany. But the prospects of that happening appear slim. As evidence of the unlikelihood of this happening, certainly in the foreseeable future, it is reported that once again today, the Western Allies turned down a Russian proposal aimed at reunifying Germany.

This is not, it appears, a new Germany for all.

Truman: US hysteria over Reds

Washington, 30 June
President Truman today assured newsmen that the United States was not going to hell, despite the wave of anti-Communist hysteria now sweeping the country in the wake of all the spy trials and loyalty inquiries.

Responding to questions at his weekly news conference, President Truman likened the national jitters over Reds to the atmosphere that was engendered in the early days of the republic over the Alien and Sedition Acts.

Read your history, the president advised, and it will show that the hysteria over aliens of that earlier period subsided. The country did not go to hell at that time and it isn't going to do so now, he said.

Actor Ronald Reagan earns more than the US president

Bette Davis, top woman earner.

United States, 5 February
The US Internal Revenue Service has released the names of those who earned $75,000 or more last year. President Truman did not make the highest-paid list. Most movie stars did.

Humphrey Bogart led the Hollywood coterie with a salary before taxes of $467,361. Bogart made only three films on his salary in 1947. Lagging behind were Fred MacMurray ($325,000), Errol Flynn ($199,999) and Ronald Reagan ($169,000). Actress Bette Davis led the women with $328,000 from Warner Brothers studios. In fact, she is the highest-paid woman in any profession. Pretty good since she made no film at all in 1947. Other hefty earnings went to Deanna Durbin ($323,477) and Betty Grable ($299,333).

Humphrey Bogart, top-paid star.

1950

London, 21 January. George Orwell, author of *Animal Farm* and *1984*, dies of tuberculosis, aged 46.

London, 3 February. Nuclear scientist Klaus Fuchs is arrested on suspicion of passing atom secrets to the USSR.

Britain, 24 February. The Labour government is re-elected, but with a majority of only six.

Wales, 12 March. Eighty people die in the world's worst air crash to date.

Jordan, 24 April. Jordan annexes Arab Palestine, taking over West Bank territory and East Jerusalem.

Paris, 9 May. The French foreign minister announces the first step towards a possible united Europe.

South Africa, 29 May. Non-whites announce a day of action against the racial legislation.

Chicago, 17 June. A surgeon carries out the first human kidney transplant.

Brazil, 28 June. England's soccer team loses 1-0 to the USA in the World Cup.

Brussels, 1 August. Prince Baudouin is sworn in as prince regent. He will become king on reaching his majority.

Dover, 5 August. American Florence Chadwick swims English Channel in record 13 hours, 23 minutes.

South Africa, 11 September. Jan Smuts, rebel Boer leader then later South African prime minister, dies, aged 80.

Derbyshire, 28 September. Eighty miners die underground in a colliery fire.

Vietnam, 10 October. French troops are overrun by the Viet Minh at Kaobang.

Cairo, 16 November. King Farouk calls on Britain to leave the Suez Canal Zone.

Oslo, 10 December. Bertrand Russell wins the Nobel Prize for Literature.

USA, 19 December. President Harry Truman appoints General Dwight D Eisenhower supreme commander of NATO land forces.

London, 25 December. Scottish Nationalists steal Scotland's ancient Stone of Scone from Westminster Abbey.

Tibet, 25 December. The Dalai Lama is reported to have fled the country, following the Chinese invasion.

Defence against atomic attack

United States, 12 August

A 438-page guide on civilian defence against atomic bomb attack has been released by the US Department of Defense and the Atomic Energy Commission, covering effects of atomic bombs when released high in the air (as over Hiroshima and Nagasaki), low on the ground (as in the test at Alamogordo, New Mexico) and exploded underwater (as at Bikini).

Readers are told that in a high-air burst, danger from radiation is confined to the first minute, and the lethal radius for direct exposure to gamma rays is 4,000 feet (1219.2 metres). A blast wave takes seven seconds to travel two miles (3.32 kilometres).

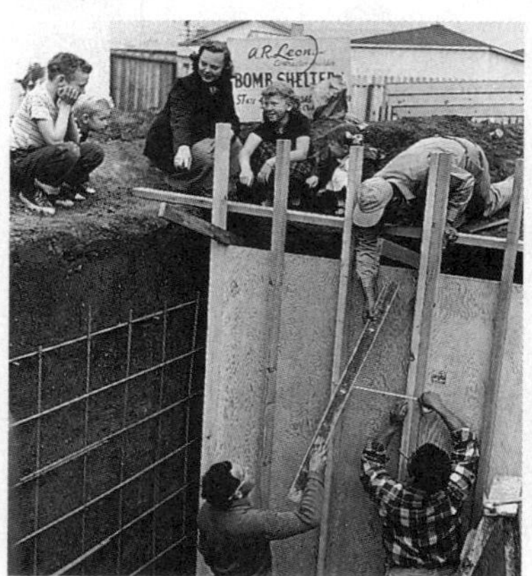

Hollywood's first atomic shelter.

Two Vietnams vie for recognition

Vietnam, 7 February

Two countries with the same name (Vietnam) and borders but different leaders have split the world East by West and are fast becoming a new focus of tensions between the US and the Soviet Union.

The US recognised one of the Vietnams today – that of Emperor Bao Dai. Britain made a similar move earlier in the day; Australia and New Zealand are expected to follow. The other Vietnam, led by the nationalist and Communist Ho Chi Minh, was recognised by the Russians last week. Poland, Czechoslovakia, Bulgaria, Hungary, Romania, Albania and North Korea have also recognised Ho.

Hiss is sentenced to five years in prison

Hiss, former US State Department official, is found guilty of perjury.

New York, 25 January

Alger Hiss, a former top US State Department official, was sentenced today to five years in prison for perjury in denying that he had passed top government secrets to Whittaker Chambers, a one-time agent for the Communists.

The stiff sentence, handed down by Judge Henry W Goddard in New York Federal Court, came four days after a jury of eight women and four men had found Hiss guilty on two counts of perjury. An earlier trial last summer ended in a hung jury.

Throughout the trials, Hiss denied giving secret documents to Chambers in the late 1930s, when he was a top assistant at the State Department, and Chambers was an underground agent for the Communists.

Matisse, fine colourist, wins Venice prize

Venice, 11 June

One of the great French masters of contemporary art, Henri Matisse, was honoured with the grand prize at the Venice Art Festival. Matisse, a brilliant painter and sculptor, asked to share his prize with a colleague and friend, the sculptor Henri Laurens, who has received little public recognition for his work. The selection of the 81-year-old Matisse for the grand prize was applauded in Venice, although a number of artists and critics believe the judges overlooked Marc Chagall.

Matisse has influenced dozens of French painters for the past 50 years. He was considered the prime representative of the Fauvists, but it is also acknowledged that Matisse broke early in his career with all formal schools and styles.

Matisse trained at the *Ecole des Beaux Arts* in Paris under the reclusive Gustave Moreau and had his first exhibition in 1896. At the turn of the century, Matisse drifted away to experiment with his own style and to immerse himself in a new world of bright colours.

Matisse's current project is the decoration of the Chapel of the Rosary at Vence, France.

"The Sadness Of The King" by Matisse, winner at the Venice Festival.

Nijinsky, long ill, succumbs at last

London, 8 April
Vaslav Nijinsky, perhaps the finest male dancer of the century, has died in London. He was 60. Nijinsky was a spectacular dancer and choreographer from 1909 to 1913, but schizophrenia kept him in mental asylums for the last 31 years. Born in Kiev, he joined the Imperial Ballet in 1907 and soon met Diaghilev, the impresario.

The brilliant Nijinsky in "Giselle".

Communists and West fight in Korea

Korea: representatives of four of the nations fighting under the UN banner.

Korea, December
The massive Chinese military intervention in North Korea has repulsed the advance by United Nations forces towards the Yalu River, which marks the border between North Korea and China. Both the American and South Korean armies have suffered extremely heavy casualties and are engaged in a rapid retreat towards the 38th parallel.

Last month UN forces under the command of General Douglas MacArthur seemed on the verge of a brilliant military victory. With a degree of ironic understatement, MacArthur now acknowledged that "we face an entirely new war".

The conflict's see-saw nature has perplexed many commentators, as the forces of the West have experienced both the horrors of defeat and the exhilaration of victory since the fighting started in June. At that time, North Korea launched a surprise attack on its southern neighbour which nearly overran the entire country. The US, however, was quick to come to South Korea's aid. Under the command of General MacArthur, American troops were despatched to defend the beleaguered bridgehead around Pusan. Later, the Americans were joined by other United Nations contingents, including units from Britain and the Commonwealth and Turkey.

In September UN forces struck back and launched a major amphibious assault at Inchon. Supported by more than 200 Allied ships, the invasion was led by the US First Marine Division and the US Army's Seventh Infantry Division. The success of these landings led to the collapse of the North Korean forces and the liberation of the South Korean capital, Seoul, on 26 September.

Subsequently, UN forces were able to drive northwards, capturing the North Korean capital of Pyongyang on 20 October. As the UN advanced towards North Korea's border with China, the Chinese issued warnings that it would come to its Communist ally's aid. But the suddenness of the Chinese response has thrown the UN into confusion.

What seemed a war won, has now taken on a new complexion.

Stalin-Mao treaty has secret clauses

Moscow, 15 February
The Communist leaders of Russia and China shook hands early today in Moscow and told the world they were friends who would fight together if attacked. After two months of difficult negotiations, Joseph Stalin and Mao Zedong signed a mutual defence treaty.

Stalin agreed to return the Manchurian railway, Port Arthur and Dairen to Mao and granted him credits worth US$300 million. In two secret codicils to the treaty, Mao agreed to loan hundreds of thousands of Chinese workers to the Russians and to install Soviet officials in key positions in the army and police. Negotiations took so long, rumours began that Mao had been taken hostage in Moscow.

McCarthy launches US anti-Red crusade

Senator McCarthy in New York.

United States, 20 February
Joseph R McCarthy, an obscure United States senator from Wisconsin, has aroused instantaneous national attention with a crusade against alleged Communism in the federal government. McCarthy entered the Senate in 1946, but he attracted little notice.

His choice of a vehicle to fame was accidental. A Catholic priest told the senator the conflict with Communism was the world's biggest problem. McCarthy arranged to address the Republican Women's Club of Wheeling, West Virginia, on 9 February. The key passage of his speech was, "I have here in my hand a list of 205... members of the Communist Party... still working and shaping policy in the State Department." He offered no proof.

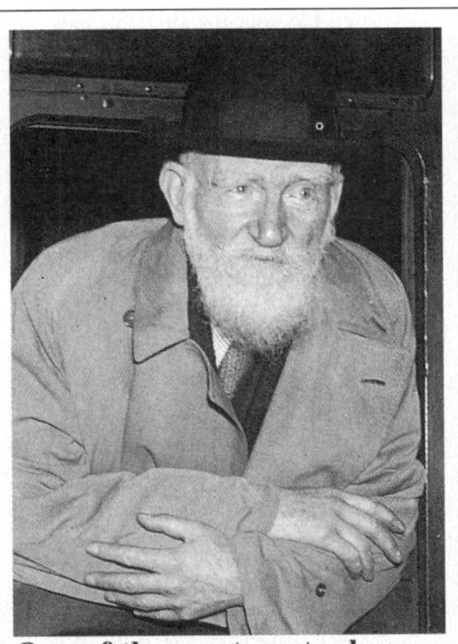
One of the most cantankerous and quotable playwrights of this century, George Bernard Shaw, died at his home at Ayot St Lawrence, England, on 2 November. He was 94 years old and still writing.

1951

Korea, 17 February. UN forces push north attempting to retake Seoul, captured by Communists six weeks ago.

Washington, 26 February. A new amendment to the Constitution limits presidents to two terms of office.

Paris, 19 March. France, West Germany, Italy and the Benelux countries agree to form a European Coal and Steel Community.

London, 22 April. Aneurin Bevan resigns from the government in protest against planned National Health charges.

London, 4 May. Festival of Britain opens on the South Bank of the Thames.

South Africa, 14 May. The government removes the right to vote of "coloured" (mixed race) people.

Dublin, 13 June. Eamon de Valera returns as Irish prime minister.

USA, 14 June. Television broadcasts its first human birth.

Budapest, 28 June. Archbishop Jozsef Groesz is jailed for 15 years for allegedly plotting to bring down the government.

Jerusalem, 20 July. King Abdullah of Jordan is killed by an assassin.

USA, 14 July. A state of emergency is declared in Missouri as floods leave 500,000 homeless.

USA, 14 August. William Randolph Hearst, flamboyant publishing tycoon, aged 88, dies.

USA, 18 August. Figures show average US income in 1950 was $1,436.

Iran, 23 August. British government fails to dissuade the Iranians from taking over the Anglo-Iranian Oil Company's oil fields.

West Germany, 31 August. *Deutsche Grammophon* launches the first 33 rpm "long-playing" record.

USA, 6 October. Breakfast cereal tycoon and statesman William Kellogg, 91, dies.

Egypt, 19 October. British troops occupy the Suez Canal Zone.

Britain, 24 November. The Austin and Morris companies announce a merger, forming the world's largest car company after the US "Big Three".

Libya, 24 December. King Idris el Senussi proclaims independence from Italy.

Tibet submits to Communist China

Tibet, 27 May
Today, the Himalayas looked down on more transient human changes as Communist China "liberated" Tibet. The 16-year-old Dalai Lama, the state's temporal and spiritual leader, sent representatives to Beijing and they signed a 17-point agreement three days ago. The pact allows Tibetans to regulate their internal affairs while relinquishing control of the army and foreign affairs to the Chinese. Tibetans, who surrendered to the Chinese army last October, will be allowed to practise their religion if they sever all "pro-imperialist ties".

Tibetan lamas welcoming Chinese.

USA detonates H-bomb

The world's first thermonuclear device was detonated on Eniwetok today.

Marshall Islands, 12 May
The explosive equivalent of several million tons of TNT was released here today on the tiny atoll of Eniwetok as scientists of the US Atomic Energy Commission detonated the world's first thermonuclear device – the H-bomb.

While most of the details concerning the bomb's design and construction are secret, scientists have long known of the tremendous energy that could be released if the nuclei of heavy hydrogen – deuterium – could be made to combine. This, after all, is the method by which many stars, including the Sun, create their heat. But to make the nuclei react, temperatures of several million degrees would be required.

The only way of achieving such heat on Earth is by nuclear fission, using an atomic bomb of the kind dropped on Hiroshima as a trigger for the hydrogen (fusion) bomb.

Much debate has surrounded the project. Those opposing it included most of the members of the General Advisory Committee of the AEC. But news that the Russians had already begun to test their own atomic weapons late in 1949 tipped the scale, and on 31 January 1950 President Truman gave the go-ahead and approved the project.

Teen spokesman

New York City
Young Americans have found a spokesman in 16-year-old Holden Caulfield, narrator of *The Catcher in the Rye*, the first novel by J D Salinger, 32, and a bestseller. Holden – tall, skinny, hapless and screamingly funny – deplores the "phonys" who rule the roost at Pencey, the high-tone prep school from where he gets the boot. On impulse, he flees to New York City and checks into a flophouse. Holden has become a symbol of plain-talking to a generation of teens. Now, however, some bluenoses are crying "foul language" at the book.

How would Holden respond to this criticism? One can only speculate, but probably with his pet expression: "That kills me."

French break Viet Minh attack on Hanoi

New French commander General de Lattre de Tassigny reviews the troops.

Hanoi, 18 January
French troops, their low morale inflated by their new commander, swung to the offensive and defeated the Viet Minh guerrillas that were threatening to overrun Hanoi. General Giap was forced to retreat, leaving 6,000 Communist soldiers dead. It was the first significant victory for the French after a string of defeats in Tonkin. Credit was given to the new French high commissioner for Indochina, General Jean de Lattre de Tassigny.

Truman recalls MacArthur from Korea

Washington, 11 April
President Truman has stripped General Douglas MacArthur of all his commands in the Far East. With "deep regret" he had concluded that the general "is unable to give his wholehearted support" to the policies of the US government and the United Nations.

The president named Lieutenant General Matthew B Ridgway to head the Far East commands, effective immediately. The dramatic military reshuffling, while a surprise, had been building up for some time. Just last Thursday, the House minority leader, Joseph W Martin Jr, made public a message in which General MacArthur challenged the president's foreign policy. The general urged that the US concentrate on Asia instead of Europe and use Generalissimo Chiang Kai-shek's Formosa-based troops to open a second front on the mainland of China.

General MacArthur has been a man of many titles during the war in Korea, now he loses them all.

The president said that full and vigorous debate on national policies is "a vital element" in any free government. But he added: "It is fundamental, however, that military commanders must be governed by policies and directives issued to them in the manner provided by our laws."

President Truman (left) has relieved General MacArthur of his command.

Winston Churchill, 77, is back in charge

Labour defeat has put Winston Churchill back in power as prime minister.

London, 26 October
Winston Churchill, at the age of 77, has been called upon to form a new government after the Labour Party lost control of parliament in a general election in Britain.

For Churchill, who will succeed Clement Attlee as prime minister, the victory was both a retribution and a challenge. Six years ago, after leading Britain through most of the Second World War, Churchill was ousted from office in a surprise victory by Clement Attlee and his Labour Party.

Now, Churchill takes over once again at a time when Britain faces an economic crisis because of a growing deficit in its trade with the rest of the world.

One of the first tasks of the new Conservative government will be to restore world confidence in the British pound.

Churchill's mandate will be complicated by the fact that the Conservative Party will command a majority of less than 20 seats in parliament. Liberals apparently sided with Conservatives in ousting the Labour government from 10 Downing Street.

Enthusiastic crowds gathered outside Churchill's committee rooms, where he appeared and gave his well-known victory sign.

Rosenbergs get the death penalty

New York City, 5 April
Julius Rosenberg, 32, and his wife, Ethel, 35, convicted of espionage last week, were sentenced today to die in the electric chair for revealing secrets of atomic weapons to the Soviet government. The law under which they were sentenced allows for the death penalty only if the act is committed during wartime, and though the USSR was America's ally at the time, the Rosenberg crime occurred around June 1944. Explaining his sentence today, Judge Irving R Kaufman said, "The nature of Russian terrorism is now self-evident. Idealism as a rationale dissolves." Throughout, the Rosenbergs have protested their innocence.

British diplomats vanish: alleged that they were Soviet spies

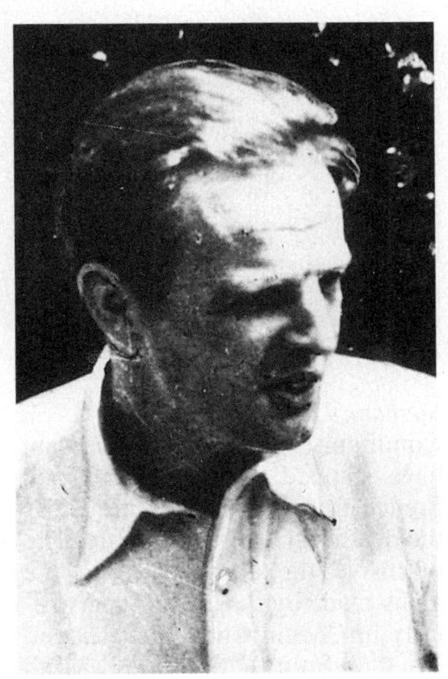

Missing: Donald MacLean.

London, 7 June
Two former top-ranking British diplomats, missing since 25 May, are being sought as alleged spies for the Soviet Union. Donald Duart MacLean and Guy Frances de Moncy Burgess were employees of Great Britain's Foreign Office until 1 June, when British officials suspended them for being absent without leave for a week. It is believed the men went to France, where an investigation is now underway.

Both men had served in the British embassy in Washington. MacLean was believed to have "a thorough knowledge of secret Anglo-American exchanges on such subjects as the North Atlantic pact, the Korean War and the Japanese peace treaty", according to Senator Owen Brewster.

Missing: Guy Burgess.

1952

Paris, 11 January. General Jean de Lattre de Tassigny, former French commander-in-chief in Vietnam, dies, aged 62.

Britain, 6 February. King George VI dies peacefully in his sleep at Sandringham. He is succeeded by Princess Elizabeth, currently on a state visit to Kenya.

London, 26 February. Churchill announces that Britain has developed its own atom bomb.

Gold Coast, 21 March. Dr Kwame Nkrumah is elected the first African prime minister south of the Sahara.

Vietnam, 26 April. French forces launch a major assault on the Viet Minh, north of Saigon.

London, 2 May. A Comet leaves London for Johannesburg on the first scheduled jet-propelled passenger flight.

Greece, 29 May. Women are granted the vote.

London, 15 June. *The Diary of Anne Frank*, describing two years in the life of a Jewish family hiding from the Nazis in an Amsterdam attic, is published in English.

Scotland, 31 July. Two US Air Force Sikorsky H-19s end first helicopter flight over Atlantic.

Helsinki, 3 August. The Olympic Games close. They have been dominated by the Czech Emil Zatopek, who won the 5,000 metres, the 10,000 metres and the marathon.

Bonn, 10 September. West Germany agrees to pay Israel £293 million in restitution for Nazi atrocities.

Washington, 19 September. The actor Charlie Chaplin is investigated for suspected Communist tendencies.

New York, 25 October. The UN refuses Communist China admission for the third year in a row.

India, 29 November. First international organisation for birth control founded in Bombay.

New York, 15 December. The magazine *American Weekly* carries the story of a transsexual. This is the first public admission by someone who has changed their sex.

USA, 20 December. The world's worst air tragedy, in Washington State, claims the lives of 84 servicemen.

Albert Schweitzer gets Peace Prize

Oslo, 10 December

Albert Schweitzer, the Alsatian theologian and musician who gave up a career as organist and Bach expert to establish a hospital in French Equatorial Africa, was awarded the Nobel Peace Prize today. Schweitzer was honoured for setting a living example of "reverence for life", his universal concept of ethics. As well as theological works, Schweitzer is the author of an acclaimed biography of Bach and of a definitive edition of Bach's organ music. Since going to Africa in 1913, he has left only on trips to raise funds for his hospital, which is free to all.

Dr Albert Schweitzer, missionary.

Checkers speech helps Nixon cause

United States, 24 September

On a campaign stop at West Virginia, General Dwight D Eisenhower says his running mate "is completely vindicated as a man of honour", following on from Senator Richard Nixon's explanation on television of his $18,234 "supplementary expense" fund. In Hollywood last night, Nixon said he had never personally used any of his millionaire supporters' fund. He disclosed one gift: a little dog their daughter Trisha had named Checkers. "We're gonna keep it!" Nixon said, adding he's "not quitting". Tonight, Ike read aloud a telegram from Nixon's mother and said her son is all right with him.

Eva Peron dies at 33: Argentina mourns

Argentina, 26 July

"Our spiritual leader is gone!" Those words, broadcast at 9.42 tonight, told Argentinians that Eva Peron, their little Evita, was dead. The president's wife succumbed to ovarian cancer, aged 33.

While the *descamisados*, the "shirtless" poor of Argentina, prepare for a month of mourning, a few members of the middle class and opposition prepare to breathe a sigh of relief. Eva Peron was a charismatic woman, certainly more popular than her husband, Juan Peron. She was also on occasion totally ruthless.

Evita was born Maria Eva Ibaguren at Los Toldos. She was the illegitimate daughter of a cook. When Colonel Peron met her she was a budding 15-year-old singer and actress. He made her his mistress, not an unusual thing for the secretary of labour to do.

What was unusual is that he married her. In October 1945, Peron was arrested on a treason charge. Eva took to the airwaves, beseeching the masses to rally and free him. Panicky higher-ups let him go, and in thanks Peron wed Evita in December. He became president a year later with her by his side.

His mistress, then his wife – Eva had more charisma than Peron.

The *descamisados* could make a lengthy list of Evita's good deeds. She championed women, labour and the poor. She got women the vote and legalised divorce.

Some of her unscrupulous acts were just petty. She kept a tremendous fur collection and practised a little nepotism, getting her widowed sister a rather cosy job as inspector of schools.

Guerrilla actions hit French in Indochina

French and Vietnamese forces in action against the Communists.

Vietnam, 15 January

Communist guerrillas in Vietnam have stepped up their attacks on French troops who are numbed by the death of General de Lattre. The offensive threatens to erode the gains made by the general, particularly in Cochin China and Annam. In the South, the Viet Minh attacked military posts. Cities, especially Saigon, have been disrupted by acts of terrorism. In the North, the guerrillas were checked as they tried to isolate the Hon Binh Basin. The Communists had more success infiltrating the Tonkin delta as they attempted to isolate Hanoi. The son of the late Marshal Jacques Leclerc was wounded in the fighting.

Ike wins: general in the White House

New York City, 5 November
General Dwight D Eisenhower was elected 34th president of the United States today in a Republican landslide that carried both houses of Congress.

Almost-complete vote returns show nearly 34 million for Eisenhower, who campaigned against "Korea, Communism and Corruption", to 27.3 million for his opponent Adlai Stevenson, who said he tried to "talk sense to the American people".

Taking the stump more actively than any other retiring chief executive, President Truman turned out to be a big issue himself.

Republicans say the victory is a repudiation of the Truman Fair Deal. On Communism, the role of the new vice president, Richard M Nixon, in the investigation of Alger Hiss was a major factor, and Eisenhower's pledge to go to Korea is believed to have been decisive.

In the grand ballroom of the Commodore Hotel here, it was 2.05 am when the president-elect, his wife, Mamie, at his side, said he will not give "short weight" to his job.

Meanwhile, loser Stevenson, in Springfield, said he "felt like a little boy who stubbed his toe in the dark. He was too old to cry, but it hurt too much to laugh." After the party, the work will begin.

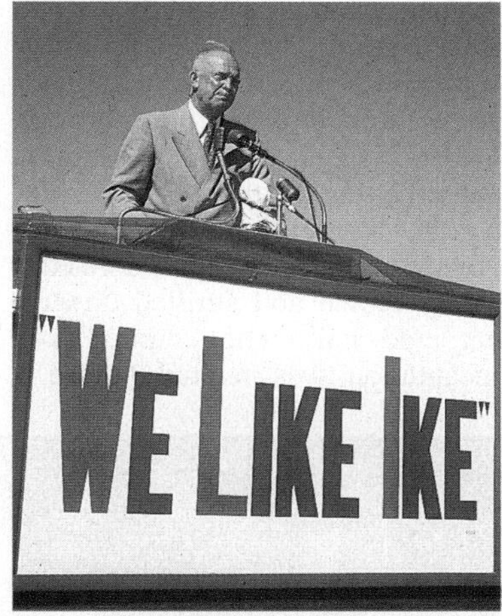

General Dwight Eisenhower became 34th president of the USA.

Lillian Hellman takes her stand

Washington, 20 May
Lillian Hellman, the playwright and activist accused of Communist sympathies, today wrote to John S Wood, chairman of the House Un-American Activities Committee, concerning a subpoena calling for her appearance before the committee tomorrow. She wrote, "I am most willing to answer all questions about myself... But to hurt innocent people whom I knew many years ago in order to save myself is, to me, inhuman and indecent. I cannot and will not cut my conscience to fit this year's fashions." She may reluctantly take the Fifth Amendment.

Hussein to succeed his unstable father

Crown Prince Hussein at Harrow.

Jordan, 11 August
Crown Prince Hussein, going on 17, was today named by Jordan's parliament to succeed his mentally ill father, King Talal. The king's removal followed medical reports that the 41-year-old monarch, who had been treated in Swiss clinics, stood little chance of recovery.

Jordan's action comes a little more than two weeks after another Arab leader, Egypt's King Farouk, was ousted by army leaders in a clean-up campaign against government corruption.

The new king, Hussein I, is a student at Harrow School in England. Fond of horseback riding and driving his own car, he speaks English fluently and hopes to enter England's prestigious military college at Sandhurst after Harrow.

British take action against the Mau Mau

Kenya, 20 October
Responding to actions of the Kenyan anti-white organisation, the Mau Mau, Britain has sent 800 troops to the East African colony. The Mau Mau, dedicated to driving the British out, have set the countryside ablaze with terror and destruction. In recent weeks they have killed 43 people, slaughtered cattle and started dozens of fires.

A battalion of British Lancashire Fusiliers was flown from Middle East stations to Kenya to help enforce the London-declared imposition of martial law. The directive grants the police power to detain suspects without trial. It is believed some 130 suspected Mau-Mau instigators will be arrested immediately.

The movement has the support of over 200,000 Kikuyu tribe members. Its first goal is to oust the 3,000 Britons who monopolise most of the fertile land in the "white highlands" and then to drive out the remaining whites.

The authorities round up Mau Mau suspects for transfer to a camp.

Mechanical heart first used in a human

United States, 8 March
A mechanical heart was used for the first time in a human patient today, officials of Pennsylvania Hospital, Philadelphia, announced. They said the device was successful, although the patient, Peter During, a 41-year-old steel worker from Bethlehem, Pennsylvania, died of causes unrelated to the use of the mechanical heart.

The device was used during an operation to correct a condition that was blocking the flow of blood from During's heart. It sustained him for 80 minutes while surgeons probed to find whether a tumour or a clot was causing the obstruction.

The mechanical heart used today is an improved version of the pump developed in 1932 by Dr Michael de Bakey. Its function is to replace the left ventricle. Successful use of the mechanical heart is regarded as a step toward the long-term goal of a total artificial heart. Several research teams are working to develop such a device.

1953

USA, 1 January. Country-and-western singer Hank Williams dies, aged 29.

USA, 24 January. United Nations figures show that the world has at least 900 cities with 100,000 or more inhabitants.

Yugoslavia, 14 January. Tito is elected president of Yugoslavia.

Britain, 9 February. The death toll from flooding on Britain's east coast rises to 283. Sea defences have collapsed in the face of high tides and gales.

Turkey, 18 March. Earthquake near Gonen kills 1,000 and leaves 50,000 homeless.

Kenya, 8 April. Jomo Kenyatta, leader of the Mau Mau rebels, is jailed for seven years.

New York State, 19 June. Julius and Ethel Rosenberg go to the electric chair in Sing Sing prison.

London, 23 June. Churchill suffers a stroke that partially paralyses his left side.

London, 25 June. John Christie is sentenced to death for the murder of four women, including his wife. He also admits to killing Beryl Evans, whose husband Timothy has already been executed for the crime.

Cuba, 26 July. Government forces capture Communist insurgents, including their leader, Fidel Castro.

France, 13 August. France paralysed by general strike.

Moscow, 21 August. Soviets ban lobotomy as inhumane.

Tehran, 22 August. Shah returns to Iran from exile in Rome.

Moscow, 12 September. Nikita Khrushchev is elected first secretary of the Communist Party.

Rhode Island, 12 September. Aspiring young democrat senator John Kennedy marries Jacqueline Bouvier.

New York, 9 November. Welsh poet Dylan Thomas dies in the Chelsea Hotel, aged 39.

Massachusetts, 11 November. Polio virus definitely identified by scientists and photographed for the first time.

Britain, 21 November. Scientific experiments carried out on its skull reveal "Piltdown Man" as a hoax.

Moscow, 23 December. Lavrenti Beria, Stalin's chief of secret police, is shot after he is found guilty of treason.

Elizabeth II is crowned in spectacular London ceremony

London, 2 June

A young woman who daily drove a truck during wartime was today seated in a gilded carriage. Handsome steeds drew her through London streets while her admirers surged along the thoroughfare. Her coach arrived at Westminster Abbey and she alighted, donned a heavy crown and strolled down a carpeted hall. The centuries-old incantation was recited before a thousand hushed onlookers. Princess Elizabeth was queen.

Although today marks her official debut as monarch, Elizabeth has reigned since the death of her father, George VI, on 6 February 1952. The intervening months allowed Elizabeth to mourn her father, and the nation to prepare a most glorious ceremony.

As a young child Elizabeth never imagined inheriting the throne; her uncle Edward VIII was king, and it seemed likely his children would succeed him. But Edward abdicated when Elizabeth was ten years old and her father, next in line, was made ruler. By the time Elizabeth was a second lieutenant in the Women's Army Corps, repairing and driving trucks, she knew she would be no mechanic but would be a monarch.

That would account for the perfect way she conducted herself on the drive back from Westminster, waving joyously but not indecorously to her subjects. Behind the queen rode premiers of India, Pakistan, Australia, New Zealand and South Africa; sultans from Zanzibar, Brunei, Perak, Lahej and Johore. They were guarded by Canadian Mounties in brilliant red coats and Malayan defence troops in fresh green sarongs.

The queen addressed her empire in a radio speech. She thanked people around the world for their good wishes and said, "I have my husband to support me. He shares my ideals and affection for you."

The queen's children, Prince Charles and Princess Anne, four and two years old, attended part of the ceremony.

The spectacular coronation of Queen Elizabeth II at Westminster Abbey.

Korean armistice after three years

Korea, 28 July

For the first time in three years, the shooting stopped in Korea last night. An armistice took effect, and the two sides counted their losses. Nearly 25,000 US soldiers, more than a million South Koreans and more than a million Communists lost their lives. While the shooting has stopped, the war is not necessarily over. New tensions have seized the Korean peninsula.

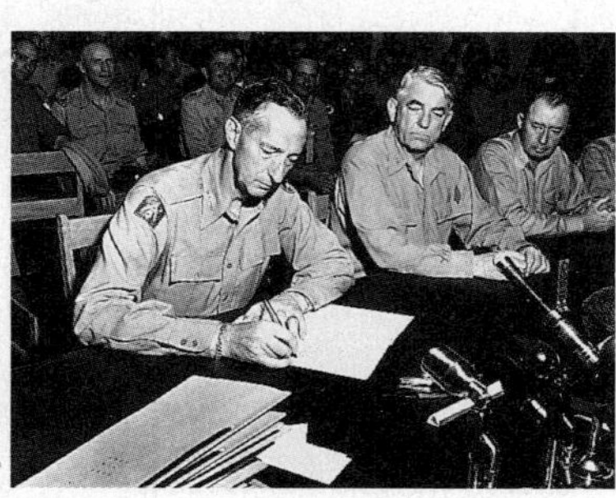

US general Clark signs armistice.

DNA shown as a double not alpha helix

Cambridge, England, 25 April

Writing in the journal *Nature*, Dr James D Watson and Dr Francis H C Crick today suggested a new structure for deoxyribonucleic acid (DNA), known to be the molecular basis of heredity.

The researchers, working at the Cavendish Laboratory in Cambridge, refute American scientist Linus Pauling's idea of an alpha helix structure of DNA and propose a double helix model of the genetic material – that is two spirally wound chains which consist of complementary chemical base pairs – and that the genetic "messages" are stored in coded form as sequences of proteins. These sequences are copied during cell division, when the two strands of the helix separate and acquire new complementary partners.

The new model makes it possible to envisage how genes replicate and carry information.

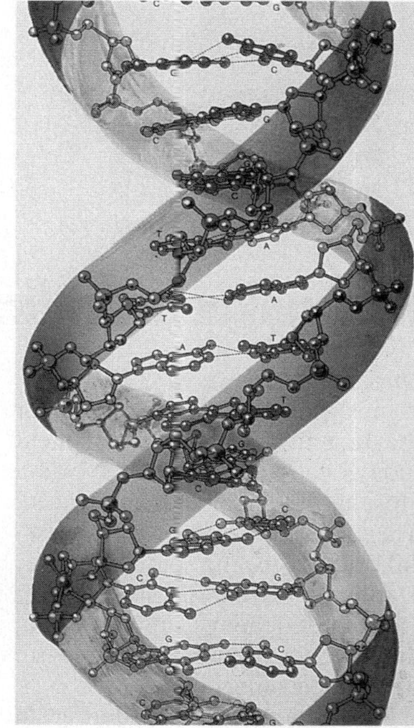

DNA, the genetic blueprint at the heart of life, is a double helix form.

Stalin dies after stroke

Joseph Stalin lies in state in the Kremlin following his death, aged 73.

Moscow, 5 March
Joseph Stalin, 73, the most powerful leader in the history of Russia, died tonight in Moscow. An elite team of Russian doctors, headed by Health Minister Tretyakov, worked around the clock trying to save Stalin's life after he suffered a brain haemorrhage four days ago. He died shortly before 10 am.

News of Stalin's death was withheld for six hours before it was announced on Russian radio and in *Pravda*, the newspaper that Stalin founded more than 40 years ago and later edited with Lenin.

Pravda warned that these are "difficult days" and urged citizens to be wary and vigilant "in the struggle against internal and external foes". A portion of the obituary even read like a Communist manifesto, as *Pravda* announced that Soviet leaders would support "proletarian internationalism". No successor has been announced.

Stalin's body will lie in state for several days in the Kremlin.

Egypt's new rulers proclaim it a republic

Egypt, 18 June
Formalising a situation in existence since King Farouk's exile, Egypt's army junta has decreed the abolition of the monarchy and proclaimed Egypt a republic.

Major General Mohammed Naguib, who led the coup, was named president and premier. The action ends the 148-year-old dynasty of Mohammed Ali, the Albanian adventurer and soldier in the Turkish army who set himself up as viceroy of Egypt under the Ottoman Empire in 1805. Ten of his descendants ruled the country, the last being Farouk.

A statement by the revolutionary council declared that its aim from the start was to annihilate imperialism and its supporters. Citing a series of treacheries against the people "committed by the Ali dynasty", it branded Farouk as a "sinner and oppressor". Among key cabinet changes, Colonel Gamal Abdel Nasser, organiser of the coup and still its dominant figure, was named as the deputy premier and minister of the interior in control of all police forces.

Colonel Gamal Abdel Nasser, Egypt's deputy prime minister.

Hillary scales Everest: world applauds

Nepal, 2 June
Mountaineer Edmund Hillary, 34, of New Zealand and his Nepalese Sherpa guide Tensing have become the first men to conquer Mount Everest, the world's tallest mountain. The two reached the pinnacle of Everest, more than 29,000 feet (8,835 metres) above sea level, at 11.30 am on 29 May, staying for only 15 minutes while Tensing planted the flags of Britain, Nepal, India and the United Nations, and Hillary snapped pictures. Hillary has dedicated his feat to today's coronation of Queen Elizabeth II of England. He has already been knighted by the queen.

The party left England in February and began its assault on Everest in May from a base camp at the 18,000-foot (5,480-metre) level. They went up the south face. The first attempt, on 26 May, failed. A five-hour climb four days ago brought success.

Dr Salk's polio vaccine used successfully

Pittsburgh, 26 March
A vaccine against polio has been tested successfully in 90 adults and children, its developer, Dr Jonas Salk of the University of Pittsburgh, reported today.

The vaccine killed viruses of the kind that cause the dreaded crippling disease. The test shows it provides protection against all three strains of the polio virus. Salk's report, published in the *Journal of the American Medical Association*, called the results "very encouraging" but said they did not indicate that a practical vaccine is at hand. More tests are needed to prove effectiveness.

Soviet tanks crush East Berlin uprising

Soviet tanks rumble through the streets of East Berlin to quell riots.

East Berlin, 21 June
The US, Britain and France sharply condemned the military crackdown by Soviet authorities in East Berlin. But the Soviets shrugged off the criticism and said they would not ease martial law or reopen the city unless the Western powers "guarantee to cease sending provocateurs and other criminal elements" into East Berlin. More than 20 people have been killed and nearly 200 injured in the anti-Communist rioting that began on Tuesday. The strikes started in East Berlin and quickly spread to most of East Germany.

East Berlin police were overwhelmed by the rioters. Soviet troops were called into action and tanks took to the streets to restore calm. The Soviets sealed the border between East and West Berlin and closed a major highway to West Germany. Transportation in East Berlin ground to a halt.

1954

Berlin, 31 January. The USSR and the three Western powers clash over conflicting plans to re-unite Germany.

USA, 23 February. Dr Jonas Salk's polio vaccine is given to children in Pittsburgh.

Japan, 22 March. Fishermen return to port suffering radiation sickness from the American H-bomb test in the Pacific.

USSR, 26 April. Nikita S Khrushchev appeared before the Supreme Soviet this week in a role that observers say was on a par with that of the premier.

New York, 4 April. Arturo Toscanini conducts his last concert before retiring, at Carnegie Hall.

London, 9 April. The government grounds all Comet jet airliners following a third unexplained crash.

Cairo, 18 April. Colonel Nasser emerges triumphant after a power struggle with Egypt's President Naguib.

Kenya, 24 April. Security forces launch a campaign to round up members of the Mau Mau.

USA, 24 May. IBM announces it is to market an electronic calculating machine for businesses.

Cairo, 26 May. Archaeologists find 4,800-year-old Cheops' Ship of the Dead at pyramid.

Britain, 3 July. Rationing finally comes to an end after 14 years of austerity.

Seattle, 15 July. The USA's first passenger jet, the Boeing 707, makes its maiden flight.

North Korea, 12 August. UN leaves North Korea area.

Switzerland, 22 August. Juan Fangio wins the Swiss Grand Prix to clinch the world championship.

Paris, 27 August. Pierre Mendes-France, the French prime minister, announces that Morocco and Tunisia are to be given self-rule, though not total independence.

Algeria, 9 September. An earthquake kills around 1,000 people.

Hanoi, 10 October. Ho Chi Minh returns to Vietnam after France pulls out of the country.

Algeria, 1 November. Nationalists riot in violent protest against French rule.

Stockholm, 10 December. Ernest Hemingway's novel *The Old Man and the Sea* wins him the Nobel Literature prize.

Senate socks McCarthy who is condemned but not censured

Washington, 2 December

The US Senate today voted 67 to 22 to condemn Joseph R McCarthy for conduct unbecoming a senator. The vote – a climax to months of controversy over the tactics of the senator in his investigation of Communists in government – found the Democrats voting solidly for condemnation while Republicans were divided.

The resolution basically censured McCarthy for contemptuous actions against the Senate itself. It condemned him for contempt of a Senate elections subcommittee that investigated his financial affairs, for abuse of its members and for insults to the Senate itself during the lengthy censure proceedings.

Republican senator for Wisconsin McCarthy is condemned by Senate.

A parliamentary manoeuvre allowed the Senate to avoid a direct vote on an amendment that would have censured McCarthy for his denunciation of Brigadier General Ralph W Zwicker as "unfit to wear an army uniform".

The resolution used the word condemn rather than censure to describe the disapproval of the senator's conduct, but the semantic difference did not conceal the fact that he had been subjected to a highly unusual censure. McCarthy said he would resume anti-Communist inquiries in defence plants.

Joe DiMaggio weds Marilyn

Baseball star Joe and movie star Marilyn married in San Francisco.

San Francisco, 14 January

The "Yankee Clipper" has set out on the sea of matrimony with beautiful movie actress Marilyn Monroe. Former centre fielder Joe DiMaggio and Miss Monroe were wed this afternoon in San Francisco City Hall. It is a second marriage for both of them.

Miss Monroe was born in Los Angeles as Norma Jean Baker and has starred in *Niagara* and *How to Marry a Millionaire*. DiMaggio, a San Francisco native, was voted American League Most Valuable Player in 1939, 1941 and 1947. He retired in 1951. The eighth of nine children of a fisherman, he now co-owns an eatery on Fisherman's Wharf. His partner was best man.

Cyprus Greeks riot and British open fire

Cyprus, 18 December

Violence erupted during protest strikes and student demonstrations in the city of Nicosia, Cyprus, earlier today.

Meanwhile, in Limassol, a small, usually sleepy town on the south of the island, British troops fired directly into rioting crowds. They were attempting to restore order in the face of unrest. This was the first such use of firearms in the British Crown Colony.

The wave of protest follows in the wake of the United Nations refusal of Greece's proposal that Cyprus be granted national "self-determination", and the United States delegation's decision to vote with the governments of Great Britain and Turkey against the Greek proposal.

British troops carry out spot checks on civilians in Nicosia's Old Market.

Was the universe made by a Big Bang?

27 December

Observations of 800 galaxies show that the universe was born in a giant cosmic explosion 5.5 billion years ago, astronomers report. Studies with the world's largest telescopes indicate that the universe has been expanding since the original explosion occurred, with countless galaxies receding from each other at speeds proportionate to their distance from one another. Astronomers have so far been able to verify findings up to 1.1 billion light years away. The cause of the giant primeval explosion is a mystery.

Dien Bien Phu falls to Communists

Dien Bien Phu, 8 May
The brutal 55-day-long siege of Dien Bien Phu is over. French resistance collapsed as the Communists slogged through the mud, overran their trenches and captured their airfield. The French lost 4,000 men. They killed 8,000 Viet Minh, but they were all replaced by the Communist juggernaut. The Viet Minh, equipped with modern Chinese and Soviet weapons, prevented any reinforcements and supplies from reaching the beleaguered French. By the end of the struggle, likened by the French to the battle of Verdun, only one French howitzer was working.

Word of the French collapse came in a radio report from General Christian de Castries: "After 20 hours of fighting without respite, including hand-to-hand fighting, the enemy has infiltrated the whole centre. We lack ammunition. The Viet Minh are now within a few metres from the radio transmitter where I am speaking."

Only a few minutes after these words were broadcast, the radio went dead.

The Communists opened a gaping hole in the French defences on Tuesday night southwest of the airfield. Up until then, the sector had been impregnable. The Viet Minh tightened the screws from all directions, pounding the exhausted French with fresh artillery and infiltrating their last lines of defence with rested guerrillas.

General Navarre had invested the national honour of France in the defence of Dien Bien Phu, and his men fought valiantly. They lost more than a battle in the end. They may have lost the war.

French troops are taken prisoner and marched from the battlefield.

Crosswinds of 15 mph (24 km/h) did not prevent Oxford medical student Roger Bannister from breaking the four-minute mile on 6 May. Bannister clocked 3 minutes and 59.4 seconds to shatter a barrier men had been trying to break for 20 years.

Indochina truce signed: imperfect peace

The Cambodian and US delegations at the Geneva conference.

Geneva, 21 July
Admitting that it is not a perfect peace, France signed armistice agreements with the Viet Minh in Geneva early this morning. Vietnam was divided in half along the 17th parallel, with the Communists controlling the north and Emperor Bao Dai controlling the south with French support.

During a ten-month transitional period, French forces will be allowed to remain in the north in the cities of Hanoi and Haiphong, and the Viet Minh may regroup in several areas in the south.

Fighting is halted in Laos, and the Viet Minh recognise the governments of Laos and Cambodia. The agreement will be supervised by a commission composed of India, Canada and Poland.

Haley records "Rock Around the Clock"

United States, 12 April
They're billed as "The Station's Rockingest Rhythm Group", and Bill Haley and the Comets live up to the title with their new record, *(We're Gonna) Rock Around the Clock*. Haley, a 29-year-old former disc jockey and veteran country-and-western singer, is finding a new sound with the Comets by adding a driving rhythm-and-blues dance beat to their music. Their last song, *Crazy, Man, Crazy*, hit number 14 on the pop charts, and *Rock Around the Clock* seems set to take off with a blast.

Bill Haley and the Comets rock their way into the American pop charts.

1955

Kenya, 19 January. The Mau Mau are offered an amnesty, to the fury of whites.

South Africa, 10 February. Armed police start moving 60,000 blacks from a township that has been designated a future whites-only area.

Egypt, 28 February. Israeli forces kill 42 in the Gaza Strip in reprisal for the hanging in Egypt of two Jews accused of spying.

Australia, 2 March. Severe flooding kills 200 people and 300,000 sheep.

Saigon, 29 April. Fighting breaks out between various rival factions struggling for power in South Vietnam.

Yugoslavia, 31 May. Nikita Khrushchev ends a week-long state visit vowing friendship with President Tito.

Britain, 27 May. The Conservative Party, led by Sir Anthony Eden, is re-elected with an increased majority.

France, 11 June. Three cars crash killing 80 spectators during the Le Mans 24-hour race.

15 July. Seven Nobel prize-winners call on all nations to renounce war because of the nuclear threat.

Switzerland, 12 August. Thomas Mann, Germany's greatest novelist, dies in Zurich, aged 80.

India, 15 August. Twelve non-violent marchers, protesting against Portugal's continuing occupation of Goa, are shot while crossing the border into the colony.

Peru, 7 September. Women are given the vote.

Denver, 24 September. President Eisenhower is taken to hospital with a mild heart attack.

New York, 26 September. The Stock Exchange has enormous $44 million one-day loss, the heaviest in history.

London, 31 October. Princess Margaret announces that she will not marry Group Captain Peter Townsend, who is divorced, out of respect for the Church's teaching on marriage.

USSR, 26 November. The Soviets explode their "most powerful" hydrogen bomb. It allegedly contained the equivalent of one million tons of TNT.

London, 14 December. In the wake of Clement Attlee's resignation, Hugh Gaitskell is elected leader of the Labour Party.

The back of the bus no more for Negroes

Alabama, 5 December

When the Cleveland Avenue bus pulled up to a stop on 1 December, Rosa Parks, 43, entered and took a seat at the front. That would not seem to be a particularly remarkable event, except that Rosa Parks is a Negro and, as such, has always been relegated to the rear seats. When Miss Parks refused to give up her seat to a white man, the bus stopped and she was arrested.

That evening, Negro women from Montgomery gathered to call for a boycott of the city buses. Negro leaders met the next day to call for a widespread bus boycott today. The pastor of the Dexter Avenue Baptist Church, the Rev Martin Luther King Jr, was chosen to head the publicity campaign.

Normally, 75 per cent of the bus passengers are Negro and today's boycott was very effective. The demands do not include immediate desegregation, but the boycott will go on until Negroes are treated as equal passengers on the service.

During the boycott a school bus runs with only a few white passengers.

James Dean killed

United States, 30 September

Teen idol James Dean died tonight, killed instantly when his Porsche Spider careered straight off the road between Los Angeles and Salinas. He had been on his way to an auto rally. He was 24 years old.

Indiana-born Dean starred in only three films: *East of Eden*, *Giant* and *Rebel Without a Cause* (the latter two yet to be released). He portrayed restless, inarticulate youth – his mumble was his trademark – and was idolised for *Eden*.

Teen idol screen star James Dean.

Death of humanist Dr Albert Einstein

New Jersey, 18 April

Physicist and humanist Albert Einstein has died in Princeton, New Jersey. His heart, never very strong, failed him. He was 76.

Einstein was born on 14 March 1879, in Ulm, Germany. An unexceptional elementary school student, he made great progress at the University of Zurich, earning a PhD in 1905. That year, he published his *Special Theory of Relativity*, and in 1915 came his *General Theory of Relativity* – ideas that changed the world.

He stayed at German universities until the rise of anti-Semitism drove him out in 1933.

Einstein was an innate pacifist. Fears of German development of a nuclear bomb, however, impelled him to convince the United States to build its own. Later, he urged the weapon never be used.

Peron ousted and exiled by the junta

Argentina, 24 September

Rather than turn former president Juan Peron into a martyr through trial and punishment, Argentina's new military junta recognised "the right of asylum" and used this as a reason to pack him off to Paraguay with the hope of ridding themselves of the dictator. Peron had been hiding out on a Paraguayan gunboat in Buenos Aires harbour since a revolution swept him from office on Monday.

The ten-year regime of Argentinian dictator Juan Peron is overthrown.

The power base for Peron's ten-year-old regime began to crumble when he courted business over labour, stepped up his attacks on the Catholic Church and agreed to let Standard Oil of California develop resources in Argentina. Rebel forces seized control of the army and navy and succeeded in bringing the government to its knees when they threatened the capital with bombardment. News of Peron's downfall brought cheering crowds out into the rain on Monday. Statues of Eva Peron, his late wife, were dragged through the streets. The junta has most of the country in its grasp, but isolated pockets of Peronists continue to fight on.

Algerian rebels launch violent attack

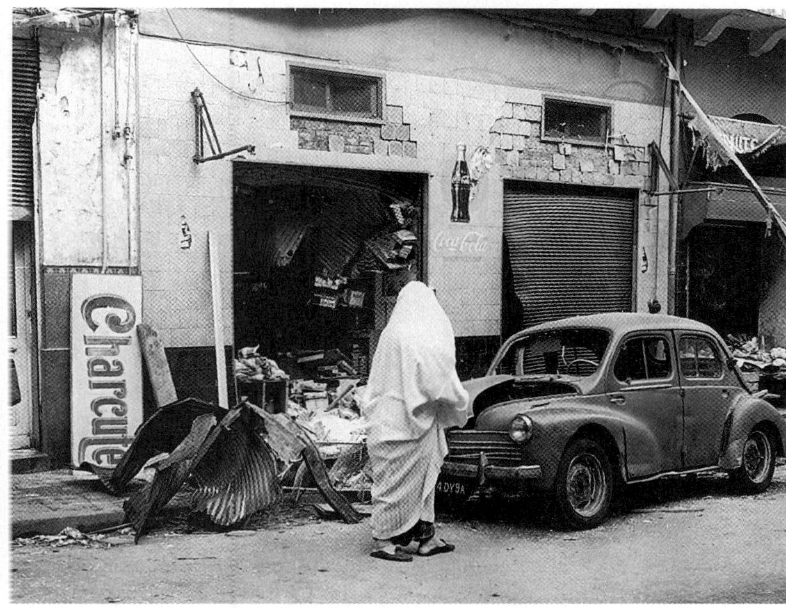

Followers of Zirout Youssef planted bombs in 25 Algerian towns.

Algeria, 20 August
Hundreds of nationalist rebels killed and pillaged in northeastern Algeria today. Their murderous attack was apparently co-ordinated with terrorists in Morocco who massacred dozens of Europeans. The Algerian insurrectionists, led by former town councilman Zirout Youssef, struck in 25 towns, bombing French command posts, police stations, town halls and train stations. At the same time, several thousand men and women from peasant villages attacked the homes of Europeans and massacred the residents. In Philippeville, French Moslems were targeted as 60 people were killed by a mob. French security forces, put on alert yesterday, were quick to strike back and razed entire villages suspected of harbouring the rioters.

Big Four Geneva summit a success

Geneva, 23 July
The Big Four summit meeting has ended in Geneva, with the leaders of the United States, Britain, France and the Soviet Union calling it a success. They did not reach agreement on the future of Germany, European security or disarmament and barely discussed the Far East, but they decided their foreign ministers would discuss most of these problems in October in what might be called the "spirit of Geneva". French prime minister Edgar Faure argued that Germany could be reunited only through the framework of NATO. Soviet premier Nikolai Bulganin replied that the biggest obstacles to reunification were the rearmament of West Germany and the presence of American troops.

Disneyland is a child's dream world

California, 18 July
Disneyland, a steel-and-concrete "Never-Never Land" for youngsters, has come to life at Anaheim, California. Walt Disney, who gave the nation Mickey Mouse, has built a fantastic kingdom on 160 acres (65 hectares), 22 miles (35 kilometres) outside Los Angeles. There a child can drive the car of the future, ride in a Mississippi stern-wheeler or walk down Main Street, USA.

Churchill retires as British premier

London, 5 April
At 80, Sir Winston Churchill gave in to age and resigned as prime minister, a post he held twice, first in war and then in peace. He submitted his resignation in an audience with Queen Elizabeth II at Buckingham Palace. As one of his final official acts, he declined the queen's offer of a dukedom so that he could remain in the House of Commons. Churchill will be succeeded as prime minister by Sir Anthony Eden.

Sir Winston Churchill shakes hands with his successor Sir Anthony Eden.

Eastern bloc signs military compact

Soviet foreign minister Vyacheslav Molotov signs in Prague.

Prague, 14 May
The Warsaw Pact, which will unify the Eastern bloc nations at least militarily, was signed in the Czechoslovak capital this morning, with Soviet marshal Ivan S Konev being named as military commander of all the Communist states.

The alliance resembles that of the North Atlantic Treaty Organisation (NATO) of Western nations and includes the Soviet Union, Poland, Czechoslovakia, Hungary, Rumania, Bulgaria, Albania and East Germany.

The signatories to the treaty agreed to abstain from the use of force in resolving international issues and vowed to collaborate for disarmament and peace. The 20-year treaty also establishes a co-operative army.

1956

Algeria, 6 February. Visiting French prime minister Guy Mollet is hissed, booed, pelted with tomatoes and stones and tear-gassed by French settlers.

Morocco, 2 March. After months of violence French Morocco is finally granted independence.

Cyprus, 9 March. The British deport Archbishop Makarios to the Seychelles, claiming that he has helped foster anti-British terrorism.

Alabama, 22 March. Martin Luther King Jr, on his conviction of organising a bus boycott, vows to use "passive resistance and the weapon of love" in the fight for black rights.

Chicago, 14 April. A machine is demonstrated that records television programmes on magnetic tape and plays them back.

USA, 25 April. Rocky Marciano, world heavyweight champion, announces his retirement, never having been beaten in his 49 professional fights.

London, 29 June. Playwright Arthur Miller and film star Marilyn Monroe marry.

Poland, 29 June. Martial law imposed in Poznan after 38 die when workers' demonstration turns into riot.

Egypt, 26 July. President Gamal Abdel Nasser announces the nationalisation of the Suez Canal Company, formerly under Anglo-French control.

East Berlin, 14 August. Revolutionary playwright Bertolt Brecht dies, aged 58.

Warsaw, 25 October. Thousands of young Poles demonstrate against Russian domination of their country.

Egypt, 29 October. Israeli forces push, unopposed, deep into Egyptian territory, as a warning to Egypt to cease terrorist raids and attacks on Israeli communications.

Hungary, 5 November. Soviet tanks crush the Hungarian uprising. The poorly armed Hungarians are unable to mount effective resistance.

USA, 6 November. President Eisenhower is re-elected with a bigger majority than in 1952.

Egypt, 8 November. The British and French cease military operations at Suez under the terms of a UN cease-fire.

Hungary, 10 December. The country is put under Soviet martial law.

Record viewers for Elvis the Pelvis

United States, 9 September

Elvis Presley gyrated his way into millions of American homes tonight, as his frenetic, hip-shaking performance style captured a record television audience.

Singing over the hysterical shrieks of a mostly teenaged studio audience on Ed Sullivan's *Toast of the Town* show, the 21-year-old rock-and-roller performed *Hound Dog* and *Love Me Tender*, two songs that helped catapult him on his recent meteoric rise to fame. A survey revealed the show was viewed by 82.6 per cent of the total television audience, or an estimated 54 million people.

Presley, who just two years ago drove a truck in Tennessee, scored a string of hits this year, including *Heartbreak Hotel*, *Blue Suede Shoes* and *Don't Be Cruel*. Adult critics have attacked his singing as "hillbilly howling" and called his energetic stage manner "deeply disturbing". But, as tonight's triumph attests, Elvis Presley's hold on the millions of record-buying teenagers appears to be very much intact. As one female fan explained: "He's just one big hunk of forbidden fruit."

Elvis' gyrating made him an extremely popular singer.

UK, France and Israel move on Suez

Port Said burns after latest attacks from Anglo-French forces.

London, 31 October

Britain and France stand isolated tonight following the attack on Egypt by Israeli, French and British forces.

France and Britain fell out with Egypt in late July, when President Nasser announced the nationalisation of the Anglo-French-controlled Suez Canal, a vital conduit for oil supplies to the West. Much diplomatic activity ensued, aimed at establishing some sort of international control of the waterway. Then, two days ago, Israeli forces crossed into Egypt, ostensibly as a reprisal for Arab raids on Israeli territory, and headed for the canal.

With the showdown seeming to threaten canal traffic, Britain and France ordered Egypt and Israel to pull back. Israel agreed, provided that Egypt also complied; Nasser refused. The RAF then started bombing the Canal Zone. An invasion force is also on its way.

There is suspicion that Britain and France may have colluded with Israel to create a pretext for Anglo-French action against Egypt.

British and French troops leave Suez

The first contingent of United Nations troops arrive in Port Said, Egypt.

Egypt, 24 December

Though France and Britain completed their troop withdrawals two days ago, the heavy damage remains. In the United Nations today, Egypt submitted a resolution calling for "adequate compensation". In return for its withdrawal, Britain expects the UN to clear the Suez Canal immediately and support untrammelled traffic. It has also suggested that the Gaza Strip be evacuated by Israeli troops and made a UN responsibility. The salvage operation in the canal, held up by Cairo's previous refusal to permit French and British ships to help out, will begin shortly.

Hungarians fight Reds

Hungary, 30 October
Anti-Soviet protests in Hungary have turned into a full-scale war. On one side are the majority of the Hungarian people. On the other are Soviet troops.

The first shots were fired last week by Hungarian police who were trying to control a crowd outside the Budapest radio building. The students, intellectuals, office workers and even soldiers were demanding the withdrawal of Soviet troops from Hungary and the return to office of Imre Nagy, the pro-consumer former premier forced out by the Soviets.

Budapest radio called the protesters "fascist reactionary elements", and Erno Gero, the chief of the Hungarian Communist Party, charged the demonstrators with trying to replace Communism with a bourgeois system. A new member of the Hungarian *Politburo*, Janos Kadar, accused the protesters of "trying to bring back capitalism".

Other party leaders preferred to compromise with the hundreds of thousands of rebels who were marching through the streets of Budapest. At an all-night meeting on 23 October, they relented and returned Nagy to office.

The new premier was quickly compromised, however, because he did not object as Soviet troops moved in to assist the clearly overwhelmed Hungarian police. Soon, it was Nagy himself who was directing the Soviet troops against his supporters.

Joe Stalin is denounced by Khrushchev

USSR, 5 June
Joseph Stalin was a brutal, psychologically deranged torturer, who committed atrocious acts of mass murder in creating and sustaining his powerful reign of terror.

Westerners, of course, have believed this for years. But now, so do high-ranking Soviet officials, men who were previously forced by fear to praise the mad dictator.

This group had included the Soviet leader Nikita Khrushchev. Until recently, that is. Now even he has denounced Stalin in a long speech to the Twentieth Congress of the Communist Party.

The United States State Department has obtained a copy of Khrushchev's shocking 24 February address to his comrades and has released it for public perusal.

Joseph Stalin: deranged torturer.

Protesters ride through Budapest atop a tank during the demonstrations.

Khrushchev addresses the Soviet Communist Party Congress.

Unit of French soldiers killed in Algeria

Algeria, 18 May
The French government has recoiled in horror at the latest atrocity in Algeria. An entire army unit was wiped out, massacred by rebels. No one survived to describe what happened. And there are no bodies to bury.

The unit of 19 soldiers was based in the mountain village of Beni Amrane. Most of them were inexperienced, having arrived just last week from a barracks outside Paris. Charged with watching the road between Algiers and Constantine, they set out on patrol at 6.25 this morning. By the middle of the day, when nothing was heard from the unit, French authorities became nervous and sent a company out to look for the missing soldiers.

The search party, walking with guns pointed straight ahead, had no luck at first, checking every bush and wall in an isolated area of the Ahmed Mountains. Close to the entrance to a Moslem tent community, the searchers found a pool of blood near a silo. Inside were the bodies. They had been decapitated and hacked into unrecognisable pieces. In remote areas of Algeria, it would seem, there are no limits to the cruelty that can be inflicted.

Prince of Monaco marries Grace Kelly

Grace Kelly weds Prince Rainier.

Monaco, 19 April
Prince Rainier II wed actress Grace Kelly in a Roman Catholic ceremony today in Monaco. Over 1,200 guests attended, including dignitaries from 25 nations. The groom wore a uniform of his own design, a black suit with gold cuffs. The bride wore ivory taffeta and a 125-year-old lace veil. The gown will be sent to the Museum of Art in Philadelphia, the bride's home town. Grace Kelly's career included Hitchcock films such as *To Catch a Thief*, made in Monaco last year. There she met the prince, somehow overlooking Cary Grant.

1957

Hungary, 13 January. Death penalty instituted for strikes and other opposition acts.

USA, 14 January. Actor Humphrey Bogart dies of cancer, aged 57.

Aden, 16 January. Invading Yemeni troops are driven out of Aden by the British army.

Ghana, 6 March. The British colony of the Gold Coast becomes the independent nation of Ghana.

Egypt, 8 March. Sufficient wrecks have been cleared from the Suez Canal to allow small ships through.

Jordan, 14 April. King Hussein successfully faces down an attempted army coup.

China, 24 April. Critics of the government are urged to speak up, as Mao's "let 100 flowers bloom" movement gathers pace.

France, 26 May. Algerian politician killed by Algerian nationalist during soccer game.

Washington, 31 May. Playwright Arthur Miller is convicted of contempt of Congress for refusing to name Communist writers.

Paris, 14 June. Gauguin's *Still Life with Apples* sells for $255,000, the highest amount paid for modern art.

Moscow, 3 July. Khrushchev defeats an attempt to remove him from power by three leading Stalinists.

London, 6 July. US tennis star Althea Gibson becomes the first black player to win a Wimbledon singles title.

Britain, 20 July. Harold Macmillan tells a rally we "have never had it so good".

USA, 7 August. Oliver Hardy, partner of Stan Laurel, dies of a stroke, aged 65.

USA, 29 August. A "drunkometer", which measures the amount of alcohol on the breath, is tested.

London, 4 September. The Wolfenden report says homosexual acts between consenting adults should no longer be illegal.

New York, 1 October. A UN report says that half the world is underfed.

Britain, 17 October. Part of the Windscale nuclear plant is shut down after a fire releases radioactivity into the atmosphere.

Stockholm, 10 December. Frenchman Albert Camus, author of *The Stranger*, is awarded the Nobel Prize for literature.

Troops are sent to Little Rock schools

Governor Faubus uses troops to prevent Negro children entering schools.

Arkansas, 25 September

Arkansas governor Orval Faubus, staunch opponent of racial integration, defied federal law earlier this month when he ordered state militia troops to Little Rock to stop Negro students from entering a white high school. The action has triggered racial violence and forced a showdown with federal officials.

Faubus sent the Arkansas National Guard to Little Rock's Central High School on 2 September to prevent violence and bloodshed, he claimed. The following day, the troops barred nine Negro students from entering the school, while an angry mob of 400 whites yelled, "Go home niggers!" As Faubus declared that the situation was growing "more explosive by the hour", Mayor Woodrow Mann of Little Rock denounced the governor's "interference". Mann said the governor called on troops to "put down trouble where none existed".

He added resentfully: "If any racial trouble does develop the blame rests squarely on the doorstep of the governor's mansion." Trouble did develop, both for Little Rock and the governor.

A federal district court directed Faubus to comply with integration plans, and after meeting with President Eisenhower, the governor reluctantly agreed to observe "the supreme law of the land". Yet, not until Eisenhower angrily threatened to use "whatever force was necessary" to enforce the law, were Negroes able to attend the school.

Despite the court order, and an irate president, violent white agitators continued to gather outside Central High School. Today, federal troops, on orders from Washington, converged on Little Rock, determined to enforce the directive to integrate. With bayonets pointed to deter opposition, they saw to it that Negroes were admitted into the school building; not without incident, however. About 1,500 whites descended on the school. At least seven were arrested and one man was struck down, after trying to wrestle away a soldier's rifle.

After initially berating Eisenhower for having "no guts", jazz great Louis Armstrong praised Ike's show of force in Little Rock. In the meanwhile, Governor Faubus intends to appeal against the federal intervention in Arkansas.

Macmillan replaces Eden as UK premier

Harold Macmillan at Number 10.

London, 10 January

Harold Macmillan, a leader of the right wing of the Conservative Party, was chosen today by Queen Elizabeth II as the new prime minister of Britain.

Macmillan, the 62-year-old former chancellor of the exchequer, will succeed Anthony Eden, who resigned because of ill health.

Sir Winston Churchill, who resigned from the post of prime minister when he was 80, citing old age, was reported to have interceded with the queen to select Macmillan over R A Butler, a spokesman for the moderate and liberal wings of the Conservative Party. One of Macmillan's first tasks will be to restore the traditionally close relationship with the United States that was severely strained by the Suez invasion.

The Soviet Union announced the launching of its second space satellite on 3 November, this one carrying a dog named Laika. It said radio signals indicated the dog was alive and well.

Kerouac draws on the Beat Generation

New York
People hitherto out of step with the Beat Generation are catching up by reading *On the Road* by Jack Kerouac. He writes about a cross-country car trip taken with a buddy named Neal Cassady. Through California and Mexico they meet people, try drugs and talk non-stop.

The beatniks have a lot to say, and they say it with the rhythm and idiom of jazz. They like bongo drums. They don't like the middle-class obsession with conformity; they expand their minds with drugs or religion (often Zen Buddhism). They like New York and San Francisco. They don't like the suburbs.

Kerouac, writer of "On the Road".

Sputnik launching surprises the world

USSR, 4 October
The USSR has announced that it has successfully launched the world's first man-made satellite into orbit. Officials in the United States said they were astonished not only by the Soviet first but also by the size of the satellite, whose weight was given as 184 pounds (84 kilograms) – eight times heavier than the satellite the US plans to launch early next year.

The Soviets said the satellite, a sphere 22 inches (56 centimetres) in diameter, was orbiting the Earth every 95 minutes at a maximum altitude of 560 miles (900 kilometres) and was broadcasting continuous signals on two frequencies. Receiving stations in America and Europe confirmed that they had picked up the signals. The orbit brings the satellite over Moscow twice a day. The Soviets gave no details of the rocket that launched the satellite but said it had left the ground at a speed of five miles (eight kilometres) per second; they said the launch opened the way to interplanetary travel. Like the US satellite programme, it is part of International Geophysical Year, a co-ordinated effort to explore the Earth and its atmosphere. The US said the Soviet satellite had no immediate military applications.

Castro alive and well in the mountains

Cuba, 23 June
Cuban rebel leader Fidel Castro is not only alive but is fighting President Fulgencio Batista's troops with tenacity and strength from a secret jungle outpost.

Last December, President Batista claimed his troops had killed the charismatic revolutionary in a raid on Oriente province. But a *New York Times* correspondent has made exclusive contact with Castro and his men.

According to reporter Herbert Matthews, Castro is waging a successful guerrilla war against the Batista regime and has generated much popular support among his countrymen.

Castro's comrades, which number in the hundreds, are dedicated to ousting Batista: "I'd rather be here fighting for Fidel, than anywhere in the world," said one rebel.

Meanwhile, in Cuba's cities, young revolutionaries have been carrying out carefully planned acts of sabotage. Those caught have been savagely tortured by Batista's police.

French general takes action in Algiers

Algiers, 31 January
The commander of a parachute unit in Algeria, General Massu, has been given extraordinary powers by the French governor general to restore peace to Algiers. Leaders of the separatist National Liberation Front protested the action and called a general strike, but to no avail. Massu's paratroopers, acting like policemen, landed in helicopters at the gates to the Casbah, shot lookouts and fanned out in the old quarter looking for terrorists. Two bombs exploded on Saturday.

General Massu to restore peace.

Smoking is shown to promote cancer

United States, 22 March
Cigarette smoking causes lung cancer, a committee of experts appointed by the American Heart Association, the American Cancer Society and the National Heart and Cancer Institutes reported today.

Their report is the first to state that scientific evidence "establishes beyond reasonable doubt" that there is a direct cause-and-effect relationship between smoking and lung cancer.

The seven-member panel said further research is needed to more fully establish the exact nature of the link, but the evidence they have produced certainly justifies public health measures against smoking as there is now no doubt that such a link does exist.

Major step: European Common Market treaty signed in Rome

A treaty is signed and the European Economic Community established.

Rome, 25 March
The countries of Western Europe took a major step in Rome today to merge into one unified economy. France, West Germany, Italy, Belgium, Luxemburg and the Netherlands signed a treaty setting up the European Economic Community. They signed a separate agreement to establish Euratom, an organisation designed to develop peaceful uses for nuclear energy.

The goal of the economic agreement is to create a "common market" for all products and services, coal and steel in particular. A new international agency, the European Commission, will administer treaty provisions. Eventually, customs barriers among the member countries will be eliminated for most products. Initially, they will adjust their individual import taxes.

1958

Antarctica, 20 January. The Briton, Dr Vivian Fuchs, attempting the first trans-Antarctic crossing, arrives at the South Pole to find New Zealander Sir Edmund Hillary already there.

Venezuela, 23 January. The dictatorship of General Marcos Perez Jimenez is overthrown.

Middle East, 1 February. Egypt and Syria proclaim union as the United Arab Republic.

USA, 1 February. America successfully launches its first space satellite.

Munich, 6 February. A plane crash kills seven of the Manchester United soccer team and seriously injures several more.

Hollywood, 27 March. *The Bridge on the River Kwai* wins three Oscars.

Britain, 7 April. The newly formed Campaign for Nuclear Disarmament completes a protest march from London to Aldermaston.

Hungary, 16 June. Imre Nagy, prime minister at the time of the Hungarian uprising, is hanged by the new regime.

Tokyo, 18 June. Japanese break tradition, letting Prince Akito choose his own bride.

South Africa, 2 September. A hardline supporter of apartheid, Dr Hendrik Verwoerd, takes over as prime minister.

London, 9 September. Race riots flare in the Notting Hill Gate district.

Cuba, 17 September. Fidel Castro leads an offensive against the government of General Batista.

Brussels, 19 October. World's Fair closes with a total of 41 million visitors.

Rome, 28 October. After the death of Pius XII, a liberal cardinal is chosen as the new pope. He will be known as John XXIII.

Chicago, 1 December. A school fire claims 90 lives.

Washington, 5 December. The Democrats win large majorities in both the houses of Congress.

Africa, 18 December. Since the beginning of month, republics have been proclaimed in Central Africa, Niger, Upper Volta, Ivory Coast and Dahomey.

France, 21 December. Charles de Gaulle is elected French president, with an overwhelming majority in the electoral college.

Elvis is now just US 53310761 in army

United States, 24 March

Elvis Presley, 23, traded in his rock-and-roll crown for a set of army fatigues this morning when he reported to Local Draft Board 86 in Memphis, Tennessee.

The star arrived in the drizzling rain at 6.35 am, accompanied by his parents and manager, Colonel Tom Parker. He was met by hordes of press as well as a throng of teenage fans – who were distraught over the prospect of losing their pop and movie idol to the armed forces for the next two years.

Presley's monthly earnings will plummet from more than $100,000 to $83.20. But the star, who sold over 40 million records in the past two years and has just finished his fourth movie, seemed unperturbed. "I'm looking forward to serving in the army," he remarked. "I think it will be a great experience for me."

Elvis swaps suede shoes for boots.

Nixon stoned, spat on and threatened

South America, 14 May

Stoned and shoved in Caracas, booed and spat on in Lima, Vice President Richard M Nixon and his wife landed in San Juan tonight, cutting short a turbulent tour of Latin America.

Holding signs that read "Nixon is a viper!" students at Lima's San Marcos University protested at US economic policies, which threaten to place tariffs on lead and zinc, key exports for Peruvians. The Communist Party is believed to have instigated the demonstrators and their chants of "Death to Yankee imperialism!" Editorials in Lima's *La Tribuna*, official organ of the usually moderate American Popular Revolutionary Alliance, suggest anti-US sentiment is not confined to the Communist faction.

Iraqi coup kills king, prince and premier

Iraq, 31 July

The bloody *coup d'etat* in Iraq has done much more than overturn the pro-Western regime. It unleashed new tensions in the Middle East cauldron and pitted the United States against the Soviet Union.

Baghdad radio announced on the 14th that the Iraqi army had risen against King Faisal. It was subsequently learned that the king, the crown prince and the premier of Iraq had all been executed. The army had opposed Faisal's efforts to help Jordan and Lebanon crush internal rebellions, and the new leaders immediately aligned themselves with the anti-Western, pan-Arab policies of Egypt's Colonel Gamal Abdel Nasser.

President Eisenhower dispatched troop transport planes to Europe. British prime minister Macmillan put troops on alert. Lebanon's President Chamoun appealed to the West to seal his border with Iraq.

King Faisal of Iraq and his uncle the crown prince have been executed.

Drug causes major defects to 7,000

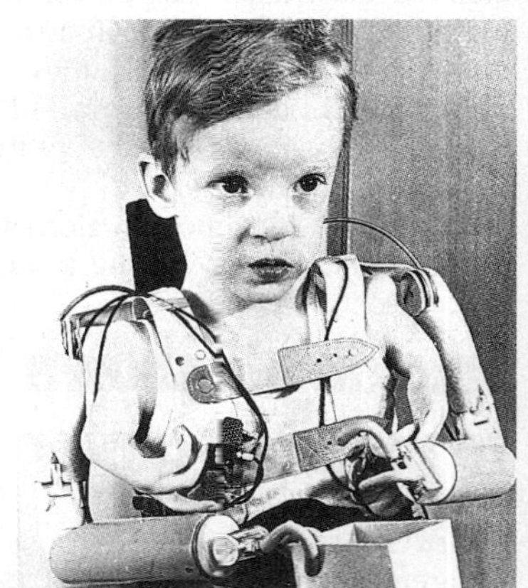

Thalidomide linked to deformities.

Europe, 31 December

An epidemic of severe, deforming birth defects is being linked to thalidomide, a drug sold in Europe as a sleeping pill and treatment for morning sickness during pregnancy. About 7,000 babies have been born with poorly developed limbs and other major deformities because their mothers took thalidomide, officials say. Most births have been in West Germany and England. Thalidomide was kept off the market in the US because Dr Frances Kelsey, a medical officer with the Food and Drug Administration, suspected its safety.

Mobs of Algerian French assault the government

Hundreds of demonstrators storm the prefecture in Oran, Algeria.

Algiers, 13 May
While political pandemonium prevailed in Paris, mobs of Frenchmen took to the streets in Algiers. Concerned that the French cabinet would yield to the demands of Algerian nationalists, protesters seized French government buildings in the city.

Security forces threw a few token tear gas canisters at the rioters. But it was no secret that sympathetic French paratroopers lent the protesters trucks to break down the doors.

Thousands of demonstrators gathered in front of the Algiers post office and yelled abuse at the policies of premier Pierre Pfimlin. Two groups sent telegrams to French president Rene Coty to express a lack of support for the cabinet. A comic-opera atmosphere prevailed in Paris, as the government debated its policy on Algeria. From the left came cries of "Fascism will not prevail." "Algeria is French" was the response from the right.

By nightfall, the French military, given special powers by the government, had control of most of Algiers. Their sympathy was with the demonstrators, and not with Premier Pfimlin. General Raoul Salan broadcast a message saying "the destinies of French Algeria" were in his hands. But the very popular General Jacques Massu said only one man is capable of restoring peace to Algeria and ensuring "the everlastingness of French Algeria, an integral part of France". That man, said Massu, is Charles de Gaulle, and he urged him to come out of seclusion and form a new government.

Most French vote for Fifth Republic

France, 28 September
General Charles de Gaulle was a big winner, and French Communists and Algerians were big losers as an overwhelming majority in France and the overseas territories voted for the new constitution. Nearly 80 per cent of the voters approved the document which establishes the Fifth Republic, enhances the powers of de Gaulle and reduces the authority of the parliament. Communists suffered their worst setback since the Second World War.

Algerians ignored the rebels, who demanded a boycott, and flocked to the polls. Some 96 per cent of the voters approved the constitution. Moslem women voted for the first time, and many said they had "voted for peace".

Khrushchev replaces Bulganin in USSR

Khrushchev is now Soviet premier.

USSR, 27 March
"We shall conquer capitalism with a high level of work and a higher standard of living," promised Nikita Khrushchev, chairman of the USSR Council of Ministers, as he accepted the leadership of the Soviet Union today.

Khrushchev replaces Nikolai Bulganin, who had resigned, as the premier of this nation of 200 million people, while remaining in the post of first secretary of the Communist Party.

Not since Joseph Stalin, now openly discredited as an insane tyrant in the Soviet Union, has a leader of the country held both positions. As yet, it is not known whether most Russians approve of this consolidation of power.

Submarine sails under the polar ice cap

The American nuclear submarine "Nautilus" after its historic voyage.

United States, 27 August
The crew of the nuclear submarine *Nautilus* was honoured by a New York ticker-tape parade today for making history's first undersea voyage across the North Pole. The voyage took place earlier this month, but it has only just been disclosed by the White House.

The *Nautilus* began its historic trip on 23 July at Pearl Harbor, Hawaii, and cruised north through the Bering Strait. It went under the polar ice cap at Point Barrow, Alaska, and remained submerged thereafter, sending its periscope up only once to check its bearings. The *Nautilus* passed beneath the polar ice pack at the North Pole at 11.45 am on 3 August. Its trip across the polar region took four days and ended at Iceland.

1959

USA, 3 January. Having been a US territory since 1912, Alaska becomes the 49th and largest of the United States.

Nyasaland, 20 February. British troops arrive to quell pro-independence riots.

Cyprus, 23 February. A peace deal is signed, guaranteeing independence within a year under a Greek-Cypriot president and a Turkish-Cypriot vice president.

USA, 26 March. Raymond Chandler, author and creator of Philip Marlowe, dies, aged 70.

Tibet, 31 March. The Dalai Lama flees as the Chinese crack down on Tibetan nationalists.

USA, 9 April. NASA names Scott Carpenter, Gordon Cooper, John Glenn, Virgil Grissom, Walter Schirra, Alan Shepard and Donald Slayton as test pilots for their Project Mercury manned space programme.

London, 6 May. Britain protests against Iceland's use of live ammunition in the fishing dispute between the two countries.

USA, 24 May. John Foster Dulles, US secretary of state during the Suez crisis and the Soviet invasion of Hungary, dies.

USA, 28 May. Two monkeys are the first animals to come back alive after being shot into space by the US.

South Africa, 18 June. Over 50,000 black women riot in protest against slum clearances and a ban on home brewing.

Dublin, 25 June. Eamon de Valera ends 21 years as prime minister by taking up the non-political position of president.

Paris, 16 September. President de Gaulle says Algeria can vote for its own future, after four years of peace.

Britain, 9 October. The Conservatives, led by Harold Macmillan, increase their majority in the general election.

Canada, 14 October. Hollywood swashbuckler Errol Flynn dies, aged 50.

Paris, 16 October. Senator Francois Mitterrand escapes with his life after being pursued by would-be assassins.

USSR, 26 October. The Soviet *Lunik III* spacecraft sends back the first-ever views of the dark side of the moon.

Stockholm, 7 November. Seven non-Common Market countries, including Sweden, Britain and Portugal, form the European Free Trade Association.

Three rock'n'rollers die in plane crash

Buddy Holly sold millions of copies of hit records, including "Peggy Sue".

Iowa, 3 February

A small plane carrying rock-and-roll singers Buddy Holly, J P "Big Bopper" Richardson and Richie Valens crashed early today near Mason City, Iowa, killing all three.

The aircraft, headed for Fargo, North Dakota, where the performers were scheduled to appear tonight, took off in light snow at about 1 am. It hit the ground within minutes, also killing the pilot. Authorities blamed weather conditions for the crash.

The singers had each scored million-selling hit records in recent months: Holly, 22, with *Peggy Sue* and *That'll Be the Day*; Richardson, 24, with *Chantilly Lace*; and Valens, 17, with *Donna* and *La Bamba*. Millions of teenage fans have gone into mourning.

Hawaii formally proclaimed 50th state

Washington, 21 August

"The paradise of the Pacific", as Hawaii has been called, became the 50th state of the union today. After White House ceremonies, the new 50-star flag was unfurled, the 20th design since the United States was formed. Both Hawaii and Alaska, which gained statehood in January, were formerly US territories, represented by non-voting delegates in the House of Representatives. Now they will have senators and congressmen.

Epic film producer Cecil B de Mille died in Hollywood on 21 January. One of his great triumphs was the 1959 film "Ben Hur", starring Charlton Heston and featuring a hair-raising chariot race.

Riots in the Congo: Lumumba arrested

Congo, 1 November

Patrice Lumumba, the nationalist leader in the Congo, is under arrest after riots rocked Stanleyville and Mangobo. Lumumba is charged with inciting the violence with public statements he made after a conference of nationalist parties. The conference approved a plan for a boycott of elections, the "immediate liberation" of the Congo and "mobilisation to end Belgian occupation". In a speech afterwards, Lumumba went even further, using violent language as he criticised Belgian authorities and Congolese moderates. He also condemned any collaboration with Belgium.

Congo nationalist Lumumba.

Host of Mafiosi conclave is dead

United States, 17 June

Joseph Barbara, the man whose home played convention centre to the Mafia, slipped away due to natural causes last night. In November 1957, 60 luminaries of the underworld met at Barbara's house in Apalachin, New York. Over 40 of the "delegates" who were arrested by the police claimed they were paying their respects to the ailing Barbara and "just happened" to show up together. Police suspect they met to discuss the assassination of Mafia leader Albert Anastasia. Barbara, who had a drinks company, was suspected of four murders, but his only conviction was for illegally procuring sugar.

Fidel Castro's soldiers conquer Cuba

Rebel leader Fidel Castro parades in victory as Batista is replaced.

Cuba, 16 January
Cuban revolutionaries have completely supplanted the government of Fulgencio Batista, replacing him with rebel leader Fidel Castro's choice of Manuel Urrutia as provisional president. The Cuban leader resigned to "prevent further bloodshed" and has sought refuge in the Dominican Republic. While Castro and his men have seized power, they will remain on a "war footing" until they are sure the remaining members of Batista's junta accept the change of leadership.

When news of the change in power reached the masses, people stormed into the streets to celebrate. The red and black flag of the rebels was displayed on buildings and cars. In some areas, violence broke out, and the office of *El Tiempo*, a newspaper owned by a close friend of Batista, was set ablaze. People in Cuba are both elated and scared by the success of the revolution.

The first official order of the new administration was to lift the suspension of constitutional rights imposed by Batista during the two-year rebellion and to allow freedom of the press.

President Urrutia and Castro, who was named to head the military, also claim that they intend to restore Cuba's economy, refurbish its democracy and oppose dictatorships in Latin America.

The United States government moved swiftly in recognising the new government; within days of Castro's takeover of Havana on 1 January, the State Department sent a note of recognition to President Urrutia.

Normally, America waits for a new nation to become fully established and for several Latin American countries to recognise a new regime first. But upon hearing that the Cuban regime will honour international agreements, United States officials apparently felt no need to delay.

Khrushchev in US

New York City, 27 September
Soviet premier Nikita Khrushchev was a happy man today as he sped to the airport after a 12-day tour of the United States – his first. "Let us have more and more use for the short American word, OK," Khrushchev said after he signed several accords with President Eisenhower at Camp David. The premier had a fine time in Hollywood but was disappointed not to visit *Disneyland* for "security reasons". He spoke of world disarmament at the United Nations General Assembly, toured an IBM plant in San Francisco and ate a hot dog.

Khrushchev with Eisenhower.

Quarrels break out in Castro's regime

Cuba, 30 June
An agrarian reform bill, instituted by Fidel Castro, has ruptured the new government of Cuba. Five cabinet ministers resigned as a result of the new law, which breaks up large landholdings, confiscating thousands of acres from Cuban and foreign property owners.

In Washington, the administration voiced "serious concern" that compensation be paid to Americans who owned lucrative sugar-producing land. Castro claims the policy is at the heart of the revolutionary sentiment.

Castro also asserted the resignations do not splinter his regime. "The revolutionary government is as solid as a rock and is treated with respect by the great and the small," he said.

Cyprus votes for Archbishop Makarios

Cyprus, 14 December
A priest who headed a group at war must now lead a nation to peace. Archbishop Makarios beat his Turkish-Cypriot opponent by a two-to-one margin today to win the presidency of Cyprus.

As head of the Greek Cypriots, Makarios was exiled by the British in 1956. They let him return the following year when *EOKA*, the Greek-Cypriot military organisation, suspended violent attacks. The Greek Cypriots have been agitating for *enosis* or union with Greece while the Turkish Cypriots have favoured partition. Greeks outnumber Turks eight to one. Under an agreement reached by the Turkish and Greek governments with the approval of the British, Cyprus will become a republic in July of 1960. Foremost on Makarios's agenda is a new constitution.

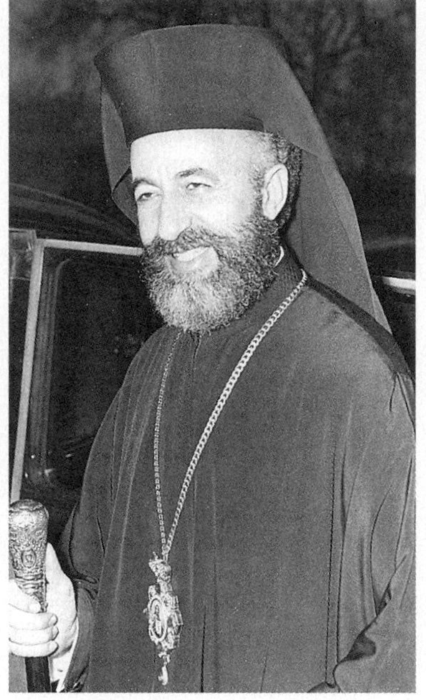

Archbishop Makarios is president.

Producer claims quiz shows fixed

United States, 19 October
Faked emotions, rigged questions and phoney games of chance on television quiz shows were exposed today when producer Dan Enright gave subpoenaed testimony before Congress. Enright, who at one time ran six game shows, said that the purpose of the deception was to increase tensions and boost ratings.

Tactics included giving questions and answers on *Tic Tac Dough* and humming songs before *Name That Tune*. CBS has dropped Enright's shows. These practices apparently ran until a preacher said he "had been fed an answer" on the *$64,000 Question*. A Columbia University professor who won $129,000 on *Twenty-one*, did not respond to the invitation to testify.

1960

Egypt, 10 January. President Nasser lays the foundation stone of the Aswan High Dam.

Paris, 21 January. President de Gaulle sacks popular General Jacques Massu as commander of Central Algerian Region for criticising his Algerian policy. An uprising by European settlers in Algeria results.

Rome, 24 January. The new pope, John XXIII, opens the first synod held in Rome, which is expected to tell Catholics they should not watch "unsafe" films and television programmes.

Cape Town, 3 February. Harold Macmillan tells the South African parliament that "a wind of change" is blowing through the continent.

Israel, 7 February. Biblical scrolls, at least 1,700 years old, have been found in the desert.

Belgian Congo, 11 March. Riot police stand by as fiery nationalist Patrice Lumumba is allowed to speak in public for the first time.

Hollywood, 5 April. *Ben Hur* wins record ten Oscars.

Berlin, 19 April. Over 5,000 people have sought refuge in West Berlin from East Germany over the Easter holiday.

Brazil, 21 April. The new city of Brasilia is inaugurated as capital.

Mississippi, 25 April. Ten blacks are shot in the worst race riot to date after negroes gather on a "whites only" beach.

London, 6 May. Princess Margaret marries Anthony Armstrong-Jones.

Leopoldville, 30 June. King Baudouin presides over ceremony to grant independence to the Belgian Congo, which will now be known as the Congo.

USA, 26 September. Millions watch the first-ever televised debate between presidential candidates, as Richard Nixon and John Kennedy go head to head.

Nigeria, 1 October. Britain's largest colony becomes independent.

London, 2 November. A jury ends a vital censorship trial stating that D H Lawrence's *Lady Chatterley's Lover* is not obscene.

Hollywood, 16 November. Clark Gable, heart-throb and star of 90 films, including *Gone With the Wind*, dies, aged 59.

Britain, 31 December. National Service ends in Britain.

Mobutu leads army coup in Congo

Congo, 14 September
The chief of staff of the Congolese army, Colonel Joseph-Desire Mobutu, marched into a bar in Leopoldville this evening and said he had taken over the country. President Joseph Kasavubu had been sacked, and former premier Patrice Lumumba arrested.

The military takeover is the latest in a series of events that have rocked the Congo since it was granted independence from Belgium on 30 June. Six days after the ceremony, the Congolese army mutinied in protest at senior defence jobs being given to Belgians. Five days later, the copper-rich province of Katanga – the supplier of some 50 per cent of Congolese revenues – declared itself independent under Moise Tshombe, marking the start of a civil war that has yet to be resolved. A UN force was sent to the Congo in a bid to restore, and then maintain, order.

Then, early this month, the Congo was reduced to near-anarchy, when Lumumba launched a military attack on rebel Katanga without consultation. Kasavubu dismissed him and was in turn "sacked" by Lumumba. At this point Mobutu stepped in.

Violent times: Congolese police battle with demonstrators in Leopoldville.

Massacre in Sharpeville: 50 Africans die

Police move among the bodies after the shooting at Sharpeville.

South Africa, 30 March
The South African government declared a state of emergency after demonstrations led to the deaths of more than 50 Africans from police gunfire. The bloodiest incident took place at Sharpeville, where police fired on thousands of Africans demonstrating outside a police station against a government requirement that Africans carry identification passes. A similar clash between protesting Africans and police took place in the non-white town of Langa.

Official reports said 56 Africans had been killed at Sharpeville, where police fired sub-machine guns into the front ranks of the demonstrators, and six at Langa.

South Africa's prime minister, Hendrik Verwoerd, at first relaxed the pass requirement, then proclaimed a national emergency due to the mass demonstrations.

Cuba nationalises US businesses

Cuba, 7 August
American-owned property in Cuba has been seized by Cuban leader Fidel Castro in a dramatic retaliatory move against US "economic aggression". American oil refineries, sugar mills utility plants and other properties worth hundreds of millions of dollars were nationalised with the help of the Cuban military. Castro said the action is justified by recent US economic sanctions against the island-nation.

The expropriated property will be compensated for with bonds over the next 50 years at two per cent interest, according to Castro.

Israelis bring SS head Eichmann to trial

Israel, 23 May
In a daring international operation, Israeli agents have brought one of the most hated Nazis to Israel to stand trial for war crimes.

Adolf Eichmann, who headed the SS Jewish section and allegedly masterminded the extermination of millions of Jews, was discovered living in Argentina under the name of Ricardo Clement. It has been revealed that Israeli agents kidnapped him at work in Buenos Aires, held him under guard in a city suburb and then hid him on a plane that was returning to Israel with a delegation that had attended Argentine independence celebrations. The Argentinian government, which was apparently never asked to extradite Eichmann, has so far not reacted to the unusual methods used.

U-2 spy plane destroys Big 4 summit

Moscow, 26 May

Diplomatic furore over the American spy plane shot down by the Russians has driven East-West relations into a tailspin, broken up the Big Four summit, jeopardised the disarmament conference in Geneva and provoked some dangerously ugly charges at the United Nations. At the Security Council today, Soviet foreign minister Andrei Gromyko charged that the United States could push the world to "the brink of war" by continuing its policy "of military espionage and sabotage against the Soviet Union". US ambassador Henry Cabot Lodge called Gromyko's statement a "fantastic allegation".

When Soviet premier Nikita Khrushchev announced on 5 May that the U-2 reconnaissance plane had been shot down on the 1st, diplomats started scrambling to prevent the disruption of the Big Four summit in Paris. The allies of the United States did not quibble with the plane's mission – taking pictures of Soviet military installations. Getting caught was another story. The Allies viewed it as a diplomatic disaster, which became progressively worse as the United States equivocated on the mission of pilot Francis Gary Powers. The State Department denied at first that Powers was on a spy mission. Then officials conceded that he was, and they ended up by saying the mission was justified. Khrushchev was enraged but by the time he reached Paris on the 14th, his attitude seemed to have cooled. British prime minister Harold Macmillan was appointed as go-between and hopes rose when Eisenhower agreed to the cancellation of future U-2 flights.

Khrushchev shows a photograph of the wrecked U-2 to Soviet parliament.

Doctors introduce an artificial kidney

Washington, 29 January

An artificial kidney that can operate continuously without human monitoring was described today by Dr Belding H Scribner of the University of Washington Medical School. In its first three months the device has helped save the lives of eight people with kidney failure, he said. It prevents the build-up of urea and other waste products, which can be fatal.

The method by which this important breakthrough works was described. Blood flow to the artificial kidney is established by implanting a tube in the patient's arm. The blood flows through a cellophane envelope immersed in a fluid that contains all normal blood chemicals but urea. The urea flows from the blood into the fluid through pores in the cellophane that let urea pass but are too small to allow loss of proteins and other blood elements.

More experiments are needed before an artificial kidney can be built for general use, Scribner said.

Algiers insurgents surrender – for now

Algeria, 10 February

The latest rebellion in Algeria against President de Gaulle's policies is over.

There is, however, likely to be another one in the future. Residents who believe the territory should be French forever are bristling at the president's reforms, which crack down on dissident military elements and tighten de Gaulle's control over Algeria.

Jo Ortiz, the right-wing leader of the French National Front, fled from Algeria as the army crushed the revolt. It's believed he took refuge in Spain. Pierre Lagaillarde, the military official who led the rebellion, was whisked to the airport, where he was saluted as a hero, and flown to Paris, where he was thrown into prison. Also, three generals were stripped of their commands.

De Gaulle abolished the Home Guard and a political and psychological warfare section of the army. Both were accused of participating in the revolt last month.

The president also shook up his cabinet in Paris.

The moves are not sitting well with hard-liners. One ousted cabinet member, Jacques Soustelle, issued a blistering attack on de Gaulle, who responded in equally strong terms by threatening to eject him from the party.

Right-wing Lagaillarde and Ortiz.

JFK wins presidency but by close shave

Washington, 9 November

In one of the closest elections in American history, Senator John F Kennedy has won the presidency by a majority of less than half of 1 per cent, or less than two votes per precinct. The outcome remained uncertain for long hours, and 52 electoral votes remain in doubt, but the Democratic candidate's total now amounts to 300 votes, or 31 more than required. The popular vote was so close that the incumbent vice president, Richard M Nixon, stopped short of conceding at 3.20 this morning, though he told supporters that it looked as though Kennedy had won.

Democrat John F Kennedy became president in a close-run election.

1961

Britain, 8 January. Police arrest five people, including Gordon Lonsdale, a Canadian businessman, on suspicion of spying for the USSR.

Congo, 22 January. Belgian troops fly in to defend Europeans from attacks by supporters of the deposed premier, Patrice Lumumba.

Congo, 13 February. Former premier Lumumba dies in mysterious circumstances.

Washington, 1 March. President Kennedy announces the formation of the Peace Corps.

South Vietnam, 10 April. Anti-Communist Ngo Dinh Diem is re-elected president in a landslide victory.

Paris, 24 April. After a coup in Algeria by senior French army officers, defences are organised to repel a feared airborne invasion by the rebels.

Cape Canaveral, 5 May. Alan Shepard becomes the first American in space.

London, 8 May. Former diplomat George Blake is jailed as spy for 42 years.

Washington, 25 May. President Kennedy says that the USA aims to be first to put a man on the moon.

South Africa, 31 May. Under attack for its apartheid policies, South Africa leaves the British Commonwealth.

London, 31 July. Prime Minister Harold Macmillan announces that Britain is to seek Common Market membership.

USSR, 7 August. A second Russian is put into orbit.

France, 8 September. Raoul Salan, a former French general who served in Algeria, is named as being behind an attempt on General de Gaulle's life.

Congo, 13 September. UN troops ordered into action to suppress breakaway Katanga state.

Northern Rhodesia, 18 September. UN secretary general Dag Hammarskjold dies in an air crash.

Moscow, 30 October. As part of the USSR's de-Stalinisation programme, the late dictator's remains are removed from Lenin's Red Square mausoleum.

New York, 3 November. Burmese diplomat U Thant, 52, is chosen as new secretary general of the UN.

India, 19 December. Indian forces overrun the Portuguese enclave of Goa.

Berlin is split in two by the heavily guarded Communist wall

Berlin, 31 August

A harshly impersonal monument to the Cold War, evidence of the insoluble problems between East and West, slices like a rapier through the heart of Berlin. A wall, constructed with astounding speed from prefabricated blocks of concrete, is the Communists' answer to the Germans who have snubbed their system and fled to the West. It is hard to bypass the wall. East Berliners need a special permit and East German soldiers do not bend the rules for anybody.

Armed East German troops threw barbed wire across the line that divides East and West Berlin early in the morning of the 13th. It was the first step towards sealing the border. The scale of emigration to the West had become embarrassing, with some 2,000 refugees leaving the East every day. The border guards re-inforced the eastern side of the Brandenburg Gate, the main exit point in the flight to freedom, and also stopped the 50,000 East Berliners who were used to earning a pay cheque in West Berlin every week. On top of this, the Communists demanded a stretch of no man's land on the wall's west side, but backed down when Allied troops and tanks appeared inside the zone.

A hastily constructed wall of prefabricated blocks divides East and West.

Freedom Riders beaten in Montgomery

James Davis, Glenda Gaither and Sandra Nixon made first freedom ride.

Alabama, 25 May

"This is an ugly situation," said a Montgomery, Alabama, policeman. The city has erupted in racial violence as Negro and white Freedom Riders, testing segregation policies on state and interstate buses, have been attacked and arrested. Mobs of angry white segregationists, including Ku Klux Klan members, descended on Montgomery. Governor John Patterson imposed martial law in an attempt to quell the riots.

In the most violent outburst, over 1,000 whites attacked a bus load of Freedom Riders last week. At least 20 were hurt as the mob used fists and clubs to beat protesters. The riders were arrested for contempt of an injunction banning this form of protest. The mob also assaulted the press.

Federal marshals were ordered to the city by US attorney general Robert Kennedy to protect a Negro church mass meeting, where integration leader Rev Martin Luther King Jr spoke.

Despite the presence of armed guards, hundreds of whites gathered and shouted obscenities towards the church. Rev King said Negroes would "continue the struggle for freedom".

Death sentence for Adolf Eichmann

Israel, 15 December

There will be no mercy for Adolf Eichmann, an Israeli court decided in Jerusalem today, as the head of the SS Jewish section was sentenced to death by hanging for his role in the extermination of millions of Jews. Eichmann, who was snatched by Israeli agents in Argentina last year, was convicted of "crimes against the Jewish people". Pale but standing straight, he rejected the sentence as unfair. He admitted that Jews were persecuted "with avidity and fervour", but he said he was only following orders.

Nazi Eichmann sentenced to hang.

Disaster of US Bay of Pigs invasion

Washington, 24 April
President Kennedy has accepted full responsibility for the failed Bay of Pigs invasion, even though the plan was hatched under the Eisenhower administration. As Kennedy noted, "There's an old saying that victory has a hundred fathers and defeat is an orphan."

The small force of anti-Castro Cubans, with the support of the United States Central Intelligence Agency, landed a week ago. Within days, Castro's troops had wiped out the rebel beachhead. At the last count, 743 men had been captured.

The action has been condemned worldwide. In Congress, Senator Wayne Morse called the invasion "a colossal mistake". But for the most part, domestic criticism has been scant, pending investigation.

Russia wins space race

Major Yuri Gagarin, in "Vostok", became the first man to orbit the Earth.

USSR, 12 April
The Soviet Union today won the race to place a man in space by sending 27-year-old air force major Yuri Gagarin into orbit and bringing him safely back to Earth.

An announcement by the official press agency, *Tass*, said Gagarin had orbited the Earth in the 10,395-pound (4,725-kilogram) *Vostok*. It said the spacecraft's orbit had a maximum altitude of 187.75 miles (300 kilometres) and a minimum of 109.5 miles (175 kilometres), and that each revolution around the Earth took 89.1 minutes.

The first official word of the flight came when a Moscow radio announcer broke into a programme just before 10 am local time and said emotionally, "Russia has successfully launched a man into space." The announcement was repeated three times.

Gagarin landed less than an hour later in what was described as the "prescribed area" of the USSR. He said after the landing, "Please report to the party and the government, and personally to Nikita Sergeyevich Khrushchev, that the landing was normal. I feel well, have no injuries or bruises." The only statement attributed to him in flight was, "Flight is proceeding normally. I am well."

Bob Dylan plays in Greenwich Village

New York, 28 September
A surprising young talent with a frayed appearance and compelling stage presence is generating the kind of excitement in a Greenwich Village cafe normally reserved for the more grizzled veterans of the folk music scene.

Bob Dylan, 20, who is appearing this week at *Gerde's Folk City*, strikes a vocal blend between the nasal drawl of Depression-era folk-singers and the deep-throated growl of Southern blues. He accompanies himself with a driving guitar and harmonica.

Dylan's repertoire includes a variety of folk styles, and his original material reveals an already-powerful facility with words that may have just started to mature. His stardom seems assured.

Hemingway kills himself with gun

Ernest Hemingway at work.

Idaho, 2 July
The writer Ernest Hemingway was found dead this morning at his home in Ketchum, Idaho. He had been wounded in the head by a shotgun blast.

Bull fighting and the Spanish Civil War, which he covered as a journalist, featured in his books. He was also known for his hard drinking and brawling.

Some friends described Hemingway as despondent; others thought him in good spirits. His wife issued a statement saying he accidentally killed himself while cleaning the firearm.

US helps Vietnam stop infiltration

Vietnam, 28 May
While admitting there is little possibility of preventing outright the use of Laotian bases by subversive Communist forces, the US is undertaking new steps aimed at impeding Communist raids into South Vietnam and Thailand. The South Vietnam army, aided by US military advisers, is setting up a system of village-based operations against Viet Cong moving in from the North via the Laotian corridor. Meanwhile, the US is expanding its Military Advisory Group.

Russian ballet star Nureyev defects

Paris, 16 June
Pleading "Protect me!" Rudolf Nureyev, 23, broke from his Soviet guards this morning and raced towards a group of Paris policemen. The ballet dancer was at Le Bourget Airport ready to board a plane when he made the defection. Asylum will probably be granted.

Nureyev has danced since age 13, joining the Kirov as a soloist in 1958. He was made lead male dancer last year. Arguably the best male dancer in the Soviet Union, he is certainly the best in the West.

President Kennedy inaugural address

Washington, 20 January
President Kennedy stirred the nation and the world today with an inaugural address that is being acclaimed by Democrats and Republicans alike as one of the best in memory. In below-freezing temperatures, the young president addressed a crowd that had braved heavy snow: "Ask not what your country can do for you. Ask what you can do for your country. Let the word go forth from this time and place, to friend and foe alike, that the torch has been passed to a new generation of Americans."

President Kennedy stirs the crowd.

1962

Paris, 15 January. Yves St Laurent, wonder boy of fashion, opens his own couture house.

Paris, 24 January. Ten bombs are exploded by OAS terrorists, fighting against Algerian independence.

Italy, 26 January. "Lucky" Luciano, head of the US Mafia, dies in exile.

Berlin, 10 February. Shot-down US U-2 pilot Francis Gary Powers and Soviet KGB colonel Rudolph Abel are exchanged in "spy swap".

Paris, 23 May. Former OAS chief Raoul Salan is sentenced to life imprisonment.

USA, 24 May. America's second orbital spaceflight ends with the splashdown 250 miles (400 kilometres) off target.

Israel, 31 May. Adolf Eichmann, former SS officer responsible for implementing the "final solution", is hanged.

Italy, 25 June. Sophia Loren faces a bigamy charge for marrying a divorced man. Divorce is not recognised in Italy.

Britain, 20 July. The world's first passenger hovercraft service opens on the Dee estuary.

Ghana, 1 August. President Kwame Nkrumah survives an assassination attempt.

USSR, 12 August. Two cosmonauts orbit the Earth side by side in separate vehicles.

New York, 10 September. In winning the US Open, Rod Laver completes tennis's grand slam.

Britain, 14 September. Distillers, makers of thalidomide, fund research into birth defects allegedly caused by the drug.

Chicago, 25 September. Sonny Liston knocks out the world heavyweight champion Floyd Patterson in the first round.

Mississippi, 30 September. White protesters fail to stop enrolment of the state university's first black student.

London, 22 October. William Vassall is convicted of spying for the USSR.

Himalayas, 26 October. Heavy fighting breaks out on the border between India and China.

Pretoria, 7 November. Black nationalist leader Nelson Mandela is jailed for five years.

Bahamas, 21 December. Agreement is reached for the USA to sell Britain Polaris missiles for its nuclear subs.

UN forces ordered to invade Katanga

Congo, 30 December

For the third time in 16 months, United Nations forces are on the move in Katanga with orders not to stop fighting until they end Katanga's secession from the rest of the Congo. Two previous agreements were later reversed. The Katangese president, Moise Tshombe, who fled to Southern Rhodesia, then accused the UN of forcing its will on Katanga and creating "a new Algeria".

"We have always been prepared to negotiate," Tshombe said, "but if they wish to force a solution on us, all Katangans, including myself, prefer to die."

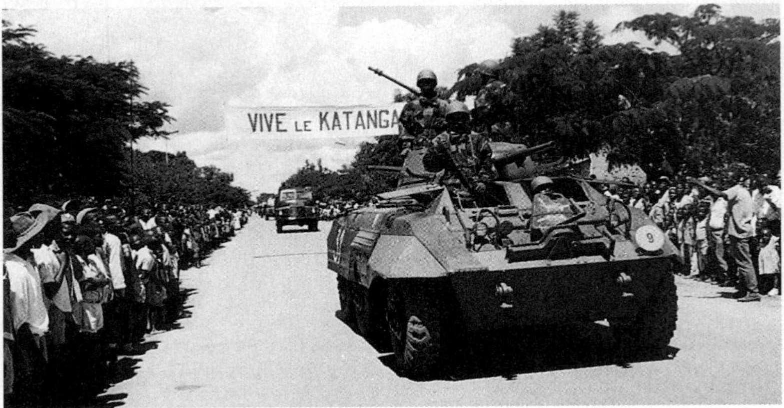

President Tshombe put on a show of strength in April, but has now fled.

Joy as Algeria gets independence

Algiers, 3 July

Thousands of jubilant Algerians filled the streets of Algiers today and welcomed members of their new government at the airport. Premier Benyoussef Ben Khedda flew from Tunisia to Algiers just hours after General de Gaulle proclaimed Algeria's independence from France, ending 132 years of French rule in the North African colony.

Last Sunday, 1 July, the Algerian electorate, numbering some six million, voted for independence nearly unanimously, with the final vote being 99.72 per cent. Once the result was known, de Gaulle took only two days to transfer sovereignty to Algeria.

Ahmed Ben Bella, the new Algerian prime minister's quarrelsome deputy, did not appear at the celebrations, but flew off to Egypt to see his ally, President Nasser.

Teenager killed climbing the Wall

Berlin, 17 August

Peter Fechter, 18, lay in a pool of blood for an hour this afternoon while East German police watched. He was attempting to defect over the six-foot (1.8-metre) Berlin Wall when he was machine-gunned. Helpless West Berlin police could only toss him bandages as he lay dying. His body was finally removed by East Berlin police.

Peter Fechter was shot in the back.

Glenn is first American to orbit Earth

President Kennedy visited Cape Canaveral to praise Glenn's courage.

Washington, 26 February

The US is hailing Lieutenant Colonel John H Glenn Jr as the first American to orbit Earth. In spite of heavy rain, tens of thousands turned out today to cheer Glenn in a parade to the Capitol, where he addressed Congress.

Three days ago, President Kennedy flew to Cape Canaveral to present Glenn with a medal and praise his "unflinching courage" and "extraordinary ability". Glenn's three-orbit flight took place on 20 February, after ten delays caused by bad weather and poor sea conditions in the recovery site area. Glenn's Mercury spacecraft, *Friendship 7*, lifted off from launch complex 14 at Cape Canaveral at 9.47 am, after a last-minute delay caused by a power failure in a computer at Bermuda.

Hundreds of thousands saw it from Florida beaches; millions more watched on television.

Marilyn Monroe is found dead at home

Questions are being raised over the supposed suicide of Marilyn Monroe.

Hollywood, 5 August
The last of the love goddesses is gone. Marilyn Monroe (*nee* Norma Jean Baker) rose from a childhood of deprivation, foster homes and rape to become the world's symbol of the eternal female.

She married at 16 to escape her surroundings. Working as a paint sprayer in a defence plant in 1944, she was discovered by an army photographer and became a pin-up girl and a model. In August 1946, Fox signed her to a contract for $125 a week. From small parts as a dumb blonde, she moved on to starring roles in *Bus Stop* and *Some Like It Hot*. But her health and confidence couldn't stand the strain. In her last movie, *The Misfits*, Clark Gable looks at her and remarks, tenderly: "You're the saddest girl I ever saw." She divorced her third husband, playwright Arthur Miller (her second was baseball hero Joe DiMaggio) last year. In June, she began the movie *Something's Got to Give*, but was fired. This morning, the 36-year-old star was found lifeless in bed. The death was called a suicide, but questions have been raised.

Telstar communications satellite in orbit

Andover, Maine, 11 July
Americans today watched the first transmission of television signals from Earth to a space satellite and back again. The revolutionary Telstar communications satellite, sent into orbit early this morning, received signals from an American Telephone & Telegraph ground station here for 17 minutes and flashed them back to be rebroadcast across the US. Stations in England and France also received the signals. The first broadcasts from Europe to America via Telstar, a $50 million AT&T project, will take place tomorrow.

Telstar communications satellite.

Nuclear conflict avoided

Washington, 28 October
A week of unprecedented worldwide tension that drove the United States and the Soviet Union to the brink of a thermonuclear confrontation ended today. Soviet premier Khrushchev agreed to remove from Cuba missiles that US experts said could have wiped out the nation's defences in 17 minutes. Khrushchev acted after getting a pledge from President Kennedy not to invade Cuba. "I understand very well your anxiety and the anxiety of the people of the United States," he wrote to the president.

Until yesterday, it was not clear that the crisis could be resolved peacefully. The Pentagon reported a U-2 spy plane shot down over Cuba. Thousands of air force reservists were being called up, and Florida looked like a D-Day invasion zone. Khrushchev was offering to withdraw his weapons, but only if the US dismantled missiles in Turkey. "This is the first real, direct confrontation between the superpowers," said a UN aide, "and we all feel pretty powerless."

The president had been aware for weeks that the Soviet Union might be supplying Cuba with mid-range nuclear weapons. He received the evidence he needed to prove his case early on the morning of 16 October. Aerial photographs showing a missile site in Cuba were brought to Kennedy while he was still in bed. An invasion of the island was considered, but it was feared that Khrushchev would retaliate by seizing Berlin.

On Monday, 22 October, Kennedy addressed the nation in a television broadcast. In it he stated that "the greatest danger is to do nothing," and demanded that all offensive weapons be withdrawn from Cuba.

An aerial reconnaissance shot of a missile base at San Cristobal, Cuba.

De Gaulle escapes crossroads assassin

France, 22 August
For the second time in a year, gunmen tried to kill France's president, Charles de Gaulle, after he had left Paris for his country home at Colombey-les-Deux-Eglises. This time, they nearly succeeded. It happened on a road near Versailles. Bullets punctured three of the tyres of de Gaulle's Citroen DS, but his driver plunged his foot on the accelerator and tried to keep going. At the Petit-Clamart crossroads, a car careered into the intersection and sprayed the president's motorcycle escort with machine gun fire. One officer was hit in the helmet. The last assassination attempt was mounted by the OAS, the terrorist group. It's likely this one was too.

1963

Paris, 14 January. French president de Gaulle says that Britain is not qualified to join the Common Market.

Congo, 15 January. Rebel state of Katanga surrenders.

London, 14 February. Harold Wilson is elected leader of the Labour Party.

California, 21 March. The last 27 prisoners leave Alcatraz jail, which is to close.

Belgrade, 7 April. Tito is made president for life.

USA, 10 April. US submarine *Thresher* sinks: 129 feared dead.

Addis Ababa, 25 May. Leaders of 30 African nations found the Organisation of African Unity.

Tehran, 6 June. Rioting breaks out after the arrest of a leading Islamic opponent of the regime, Rouahallah Khomeini.

Saigon, 13 June. A Buddhist monk burns himself to death in the street in protest against the government.

USSR, 16 June. Valentina Tereshkova becomes the first woman in space.

Rome, 21 June. A new pope, Paul VI, is elected 18 days after the death of John XXIII.

Berlin, 26 June. President Kennedy declares "*Ich bin ein Berliner.*"

Yugoslavia, 26 July. Earthquake destroys the city of Skopje, killing over 500.

London, 3 August. Stephen Ward, connected to Christine Keeler, dies after taking a drug overdose during his vice trial.

Moscow, 8 August. The USSR, USA and Britain sign a treaty banning atmospheric tests of nuclear weapons.

Washington, 30 August. A telephone hot line between the Kremlin and the White House goes into operation.

Alabama, 10 September. President Kennedy takes control of the state National Guard after it is used by Governor George Wallace to block school desegregation.

Washington, 27 September. Joseph M Valachi reveals the names of the key figures in organised crime to a Senate committee.

London, 18 October. Eight days after the resignation of Harold Macmillan, Lord Home becomes prime minister.

Hollywood, 22 November. Novelist and mystic Aldous Huxley dies, aged 69.

President Kennedy slain by assassin

President and Jackie Kennedy at the beginning of their motorcade journey.

Dallas, Texas, 22 November
President John F Kennedy was killed today when a sniper fired three rifle shots at the presidential motorcade as it drove along Elm Street in downtown Dallas. Texas governor John B Connally, travelling with his wife and Mrs Kennedy, was seriously wounded in the attack and is at Parkland Memorial Hospital, where he is listed as serious. Mrs Kennedy and Mrs Connally were not wounded.

While the nation was still in shock at the loss of its dynamic and popular president, the momentum of the government continued. Just 98 minutes after the death of President Kennedy, Lyndon Baines Johnson, the 55-year-old vice president who had been in the motorcade several cars behind the president, took the 34-word oath of office aboard *Air Force One*, and became the 36th president of the United States. Jacqueline Kennedy stood beside Johnson while he took the oath, her stockings and shocking pink skirt still spattered with her late husband's blood. She had arrived in the hearse that carried Kennedy's casket to the plane to be taken to Washington for burial.

A few hours after the shooting, the Dallas police arrested Lee Harvey Oswald and later charged him with the murder. Oswald, 24, is a former marine who became a Soviet citizen in 1959 before returning to the US in 1962. He was active in the Fair Play for Cuba Committee. He is believed to have fired at least three rifle shots from the sixth floor of the Texas School Book Depository, where he had been employed as a clerk.

Oswald shot down as TV cameras roll

Dallas, Texas, 24 November
Lee Harvey Oswald, the man accused of killing President Kennedy two days ago, was shot dead today in the basement of a jail as he was being moved to a tighter security prison. Jack Ruby, a Dallas nightclub owner, fired a revolver at point-blank range into Oswald's stomach. Oswald died instantly, in view of 50 reporters, a police escort and millions of television viewers. He died without confessing to the murder. There has been speculation that Ruby killed Oswald to stop him testifying.

Jack Ruby shot Oswald in view of the press, police and television viewers.

JFK laid to rest

John Jr salutes his fallen father.

Washington, 25 November
In a mourning city, silent except for the tap of muffled drums and the tolling of a single bell, America's murdered president, John F Kennedy, was buried today at Arlington National Cemetery. His widow lit an eternal flame alongside his grave.

Six grey horses pulled the gun carriage bearing the coffin to the cemetery. Behind them a soldier led a riderless horse with boots reversed in the stirrups, the symbol of a fallen warrior.

Paris mourns for Piaf and Cocteau

Edith Piaf, the "Little Sparrow".

France, 11 October

"When she sang it was more than a voice, it was like an April nightingale." That is how Jean Cocteau described Edith Piaf this morning, having heard she had passed away. Seven hours later, Cocteau himself died. They were both frail, but that is where their similarities end. He was raised by a wealthy lawyer, was well educated and toured Europe. Edith Piaf, brought up by her grandmother, a brothel keeper, was put on the stage by a gangster.

Sex scandal forces British war minister Profumo to resign

London, 17 June

"Resign!" cry the Labour Party, but British prime minister Harold Macmillan and the Conservatives tenuously hold on to government. Today, his party has a slim majority – 69 votes – in the House of Commons. Macmillan's credibility has crumpled in the wake of the revelations of the Profumo scandal.

Until a few weeks ago, John Dennis Profumo was an illustrious politician. He had been a respected MP who held several prestigious offices, the latest being secretary of state for war. He and his wife often took well-publicised state trips together.

On 5 June, Profumo resigned his office, charged with having sex with Christine Keeler, a prostitute also having an affair with a Soviet naval officer who has now returned to Moscow. Profumo admitted "with deep remorse" that ten weeks before he had lied to the Commons in saying there had been no impropriety in his relationship with Miss Keeler. He reaffirmed, however, that the relationship had involved no breach of security.

The scandal that now threatens the prime minister's position, finally broke when Mr Profumo decided it was time to confess to the government chief whip. Earlier he had persisted in denying impropriety when his original statement to MPs was challenged by Dr Stephen Ward, the West End osteopath at whose flat Mr Profumo met Miss Keeler. Denial became impossible when Dr Ward wrote privately to both the prime minister and Mr Wilson, the leader of the opposition.

Profumo resigned in wake of affair.

Prostitute Christine Keeler, 21, was having an affair with a Soviet officer.

Martin Luther King Jr to 200,000: "I have a dream"

Dr Martin Luther King Jr acknowledges the crowds in Washington.

Washington, 28 August

In the largest civil rights demonstration ever, more than 200,000 non-violent protesters gathered at the foot of the Lincoln Memorial today to hear Dr Martin Luther King Jr, president of the Southern Christian Leadership Conference, describe his vision of the future of race relations in the United States. "I still have a dream," Dr King told the rapt audience. "It is a dream chiefly rooted in the American Dream. I have a dream that one day this nation will rise up and live out the true meaning of its creed: 'We hold these truths to be self-evident, that all men are created equal.'"

As the crowd cheered, King described a land where whites and Negroes would be brothers, and where his people would be "free at last, free at last, thank God Almighty, free at last".

King's speech turned the tone of the event from that of a party into that of a crusade. But, it remains to be seen whether his words will move Congress to action.

Train heist the greatest in history

Police examine the robbed train.

Britain, 14 August

More than a million pounds in cash and jewellery was snatched from a Glasgow to London train this morning. A dozen robbers with guns made off with the booty from the world's greatest heist.

In the early hours, the raiders coshed the driver and told the co-engineer to keep quiet – or else. The engine and front two cars were uncoupled from the rest, taken to a side track and emptied.

1964

Ghana, 2 January. President Kwame Nkrumah escapes fifth assassination attempt.

Jerusalem, 4 January. Pope Paul VI starts a three-day "peace pilgrimage" to the Holy Land.

Dallas, 14 March. Jack Ruby is sentenced to death for the murder of Lee Harvey Oswald.

Cyprus, 19 March. UN forces fly into the island in an attempt to enforce and maintain a cease-fire between warring Greek and Turkish Cypriots.

Peru, 24 May. 300 people die in a riot at a football international against Argentina.

South Africa, 14 June. African nationalist leader Nelson Mandela is sentenced to life on charges of treason.

Washington, 2 July. President Lyndon B Johnson signs Civil Rights Act.

San Francisco, 15 July. The Republican Party chooses right-winger Senator Barry Goldwater as its presidential candidate.

USA, 27 July. New York State governor Nelson Rockefeller calls in the National Guard to quell race riots in Rochester.

Mississippi, 4 August. The bodies are found of three missing civil rights workers.

Zambia, 25 August. Kenneth Kaunda is elected the country's first president.

Malaysia, 3 September. A state of emergency is called after Indonesian troops land.

Washington, 27 September. The Warren Commission reports that there was no conspiracy to kill President Kennedy.

Berlin, 5 October. 57 East Germans escape under the Berlin Wall through a tunnel.

USSR, 13 October. The first ever three-man spacecraft returns after 24 hours in space.

China, 16 October. China explodes her first atomic bomb.

Africa, 24 October. Northern Rhodesia becomes Republic of Zambia, ending 73 years of British rule.

Congo, 26 November. Belgian paratroops swoop on Stanleyville to defend European settlers.

London, 21 December. House of Commons votes to ban the death penalty.

Indian Ocean, 25 December. Hurricane kills 4,000 in Ceylon and 3,000 in Indian province of Madras.

Clay TKOs giant Liston for world title

Miami, 25 February
The brash, cocky kid, incredibly, kept his word. Cassius Clay left a bleeding, wounded Sonny Liston as he ascended to the world heavyweight boxing championship.

Only three of the 46 sports-writers present thought Clay could fell the giant Liston. And yet, after six rounds, Liston was the victim of a 22-year-old upstart who had bragged he would "float like a butterfly, sting like a bee".

It was Liston himself who said he could not come out for the seventh. The state-appointed doctors affirmed that an injury had prevented him defending himself.

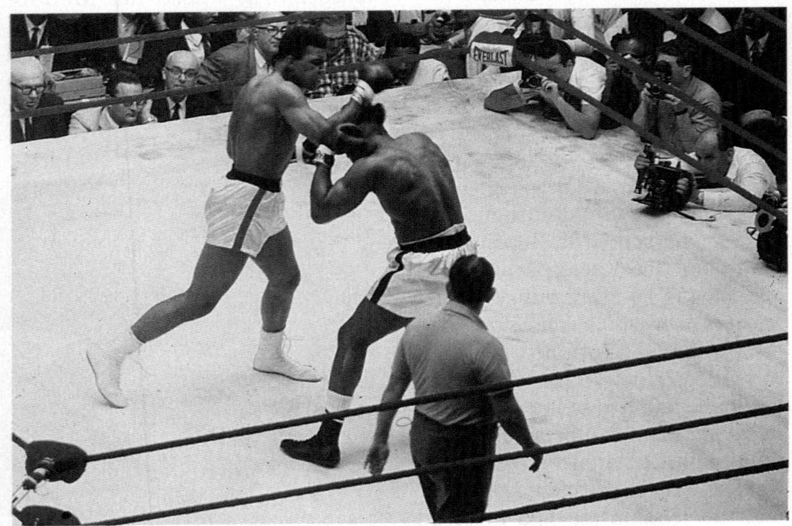

Cassius Clay beats Sonny Liston to win the world heavyweight title.

Beatles frenzy takes over in America

New York City, 12 February
A mass shriek of delight erupted yesterday afternoon at Kennedy Airport the moment the Beatles' plane touched down, and the frenzied adulation from fans never ceased during the Liverpool quartet's first day in America. John Lennon, 23, Paul McCartney, 21, George Harrison, 21, and Ringo Starr, 23, have risen steadily to the peak of pop stardom in Europe over the past year. Their latest record, *I Want to Hold Your Hand*, has now hit number one in the US and, judging from the scene yesterday, it appears Beatlemania has crossed the Atlantic.

Disc jockeys offered constant updates on the flight and played non-stop sets of Beatles music. Police struggled to contain a wild surge in the crowd at 1.20 pm, when the plane landed, and again when the group emerged to wave.

The pandemonium followed the musicians to the Plaza Hotel, where they are staying.

Paul, Ringo, John and George take Beatlemania across the Atlantic.

The beloved Indian leader Nehru dies

India, 28 May
A slow-moving funeral cortege containing the body of Jawaharlal Nehru inched through the streets of New Delhi today. A million and a half Indians lined the route to pay final respects to their beloved leader. Nehru, who died of a heart attack yesterday at 74, had led India since it won its independence from Britain. He suffered a stroke in January, but resumed a full-time schedule against the advice of his doctors. A search for a new prime minister has already begun. Nehru's only daughter, Indira Gandhi, is a leading contender.

In the cortege, Nehru's body was surrounded by flowers and partly covered by the Indian flag. His white, high-collared jacket had the trademark red rose in the buttonhole. The procession moved past the former symbols of British authority, including a palace where the viceroys lived. Nehru refused to tamper with them, saying they were part of Indian history.

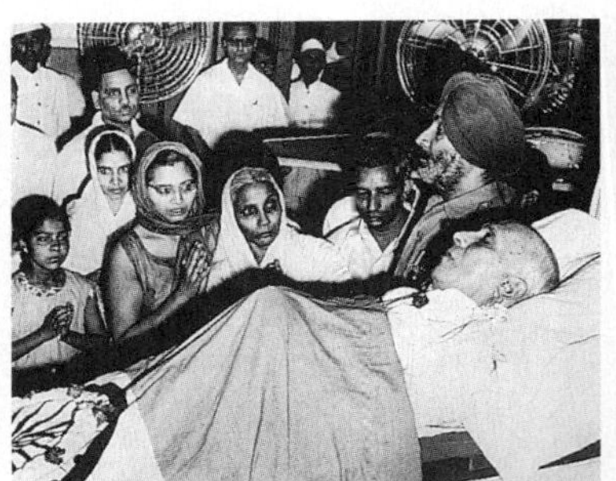

Nehru carried through New Delhi.

Lenny Bruce is on trial for obscenity

New York City, 16 June
Nightclub comedian Lenny Bruce goes on trial today in a New York City court on charges of obscenity. It is not new for Bruce, who faced similar accusations in Chicago and Los Angeles. The cities take exception less to his subject matter than to his vocabulary; he uses expletives to describe everyday occurrences. His lawyer, who successfully defended the novel *Lady Chatterley's Lover*, will hold forth alone. The 37-year-old comic, a known heroin-user, is ill.

Brezhnev replaces deposed Khrushchev

Leonid Brezhnev (right) takes over from Nikita Khrushchev.

USSR, 17 October

Nikita Khrushchev has been ousted by the Soviet Union's Communist Party and replaced by Leonid Brezhnev, who will take over Khrushchev's job as first secretary, and Aleksei Kosygin, who will take over as Soviet premier.

The change in leadership happened quickly, surprising most Western observers.

Initially, spokesmen at the Kremlin said Khrushchev was leaving because of poor health, but today *Pravda*, the official newspaper, ripped into the deposed leader, which clearly indicates he fell from grace in the party.

The paper's report called Khrushchev's leadership one of "harebrained scheming, immature conclusions and hasty decisions and actions divorced from reality".

Pravda's article also suggested that Khrushchev had promoted his own "cult of personality", the very thing for which he himself had criticised Joseph Stalin.

Busy Dr King collects Nobel Peace Prize

Prince Harald and King Olav congratulate Dr Martin Luther King Jr.

Oslo, 10 December

A man J Edgar Hoover once called "the most notorious liar in the country" accepted the Nobel Peace Prize tonight. Dr Martin Luther King Jr, a peaceful warrior for civil rights, took the prize, expressing "abiding faith in America". At 35, the minister is the youngest Nobel recipient. The month has been particularly active for King. On 1 December he met with Hoover, who regretted his earlier outburst and assured King the FBI would get the killers of three civil rights activists in Mississippi. On 6 December the minister preached at St Paul's Cathedral in London.

Congress irate at Tonkin

Washington, 7 August

After reports of two North Vietnamese attacks on American destroyers earlier this week in the Gulf of Tonkin, Congress has overwhelmingly backed President Johnson's request for broad emergency powers. By a unanimous vote in the House of Representatives and an 88 to 2 vote in the Senate, the South-East Asia Resolution (which some legislators call the Gulf of Tonkin Resolution) has become law. The resolution, vaguely worded, says Johnson has full congressional authority "to take all necessary measures to repel any armed attack against the forces of the United States and to prevent further aggression". Thus Congress gave him virtually every power he needs to deal with this growing conflict – except a formal declaration of war.

Aerial view of USS "Ticonderoga".

The Gulf of Tonkin crisis erupted on 2 August when the navy destroyer *Maddox* reported having been attacked by North Vietnamese torpedo boats. The *Maddox* said it returned fire and called in fighter planes from the carrier *Ticonderoga*. The Americans sank two of the three boats and damaged the other. Two days later, the navy said, Communist boats attacked *Maddox* and the destroyer *Turner Joy*, both in international waters. In response to the second attack, which Washington said was unprovoked, the president ordered a retaliatory attack by navy fighter-bombers on the North Vietnamese oil tanks and torpedo boat bases at Vinh. The next day, the president justified the attack, saying, "Aggression unchallenged is aggression unleashed."

After he announced the strike at Vinh, Johnson met with congressional leaders from both parties.

Labour Party leader Wilson is premier

London, 16 October

Harold Wilson is Britain's new prime minister, succeeding Sir Alec Douglas Home. Wilson is confident that his Labour government will be effective in spite of its small majority of four seats in the 630-seat House of Commons. Labour's plans include renationalisation of the steel industry. Labour opposes British participation in West European integration and is against taking part in the US plan for a nuclear fleet.

Harold and Mary Wilson take up residence at 10 Downing Street.

1965

Northern Ireland, 14 January. Premiers of Northern Ireland and the Republic of Ireland meet for the first time.

Spain, 3 February. Franco's "creeping blockade", intended to force Britain to hand over Gibraltar, begins to bite.

Ottawa, 15 February. Canada's distinctive maple leaf flag raised for the first time.

Dominican Republic, 30 April. A military junta seizes power of the country with the apparent backing of the USA.

USA, 3 June. Major Edward White becomes the first American to walk in space, leaving his craft for 14 minutes.

Algeria, 20 June. Defence Minister Houari Boumedienne launches a successful coup against President Ben Bella.

London, 27 July. Five days after the resignation of Sir Alec Douglas Home, Edward Heath becomes the first Conservative leader to be elected by his fellow MPs.

New York, 15 August. Over 55,000 people attend the Beatles' concert in Shea Stadium.

France, 27 August. Le Corbusier, innovative Swiss architect, dies aged 77.

India, 22 September. Pakistani planes attack India as the three-week-old conflict between them over Kashmir becomes more intense.

Japan, 27 September. Launch of a 150,000-ton tanker, the world's largest.

New York, 4 October. Pope Paul VI arrives to address the UN, making him the first pope to set foot in the Americas.

USA, 11 October. A Viking map from the fifteenth century of "Vinland" is published. It appears to show that they discovered North America well before Columbus.

London, 26 October. The Beatles are awarded MBEs at Buckingham Palace.

Britain, 8 November. Capital punishment is abolished.

Rhodesia, 11 November. Prime Minister Ian Smith makes a unilateral declaration of independence from Britain.

Sahara, 26 November. France puts its first satellite into orbit.

New York, 30 November. Throughout this month several anti-Vietnam war protesters have immolated themselves.

Oslo, 10 December. UNICEF is awarded the Nobel Peace Prize.

US goes on the offensive in Vietnam

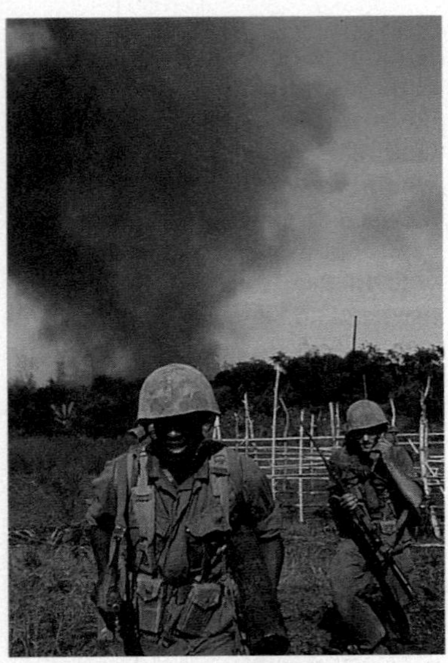

America goes on the offensive.

Vietnam, December

When the history of the Vietnam War is written, 1965 will be seen as the year the United States went from an advisory to a combat role and from a defensive strategy to a full-blown offensive one.

After American bases at Pleiku and Quinhon were attacked in February with significant casualties, President Johnson dramatically escalated the role of the air force. On 13 February, he ordered the air force and navy to commence Operation Rolling Thunder, a vast bombing campaign directed against military targets in North Vietnam. He began a dramatic buildup of combat personnel in March when the first two battalions of marines landed at Danang. American troop strength at the end of 1964 was 23,000; it is now over 154,000.

By last August, the United States had begun regularly engaging the enemy in battalion-sized offensives. On 21 August, marines destroyed a huge Viet Cong force in Quangngai Province during Operation Star Light. By late November, the First Cavalry had sought out and soundly defeated thousands of enemy soldiers who gathered at Iadrang in the Central Highlands to cut South Vietnam in half.

Although the troops of the cavalry achieved a decisive victory, both sides suffered tremendous casualties. The total of American combat deaths this year has passed the 1,500 mark.

Smith to fight for freedom from UK

Rhodesia, 27 October

Police dogs were let loose upon black demonstrators in the Rhodesian capital of Salisbury, as they protested at the attempt of Prime Minister Ian Smith to consolidate his white supremacist government.

Negotiations between British prime minister Harold Wilson and Smith concerning the question of Rhodesian independence broke down on 8 October, when Wilson insisted upon black majority rule in Rhodesia. Smith would not agree to that, and he was quoted as saying that a unilateral declaration of independence from Britain was an imminent possibility.

Prime Minister Ian Smith, no deal.

Sir Winston Churchill passes away at 90

Representatives of 100 nations attended Churchill's state funeral.

London, 30 January

Sir Winston Churchill, who rallied his nation and the world to the cause of freedom in the Second World War, has died at the age of 90. Sir Winston was laid to rest in a small cemetery near his family's ancestral home at Blenheim Palace, following an extraordinary state funeral in London that included representatives of 100 nations. It was the final tribute to a man who stood as a giant among the statesmen of the twentieth century. For Britain, its imperial glories already fading, his death seemed to be the symbolic end of a proud era. For the world as a whole, it was the departure of a brilliant statesman who with his determination and eloquence stood as a symbol of defiance to Hitler.

In 1940, in the darkest hours of the war, it was to Sir Winston that Britain turned as prime minister. Grimly, he told the House of Commons that "I have nothing to offer but blood, toil, tears and sweat." In the months when Britain stood alone, fearing invasion and battered by German bombers, he stood as a symbol of perseverance, a cigar in his mouth and two fingers raised in the signal of victory.

Rendezvous in space for US craft

United States, 15 December
US astronauts today steered two spacecraft to a rendezvous in orbit. The capsules flew side by side only six to ten feet (1.8 to 3 metres) apart for two orbits as high as 195 miles (312 kilometres) above the Earth. The rendezvous was made by Walter P Schirra Jr and Thomas P Stafford aboard *Gemini 6* and Frank Borman and James A Lovell Jr aboard *Gemini 7*.

"Gemini 6" meets "Gemini 7".

Race riots rage in Watts for five days

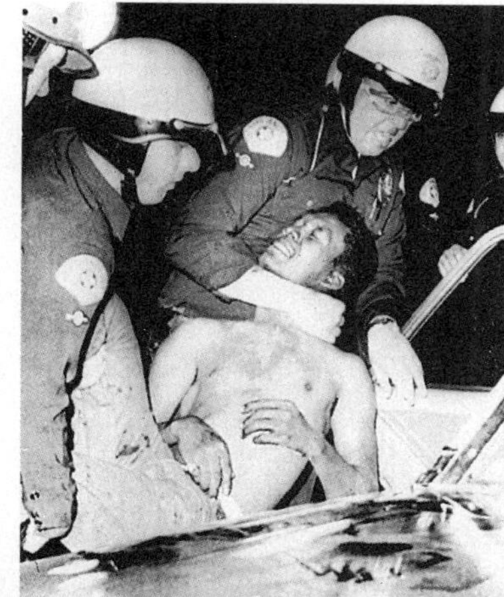

Riots turn LA ghetto into war zone.

Los Angeles, 15 August
The racial tension that has plagued the nation for years exploded in a bloodbath of rioting, looting and arson in the Negro section of Watts in Los Angeles this month. The authorities, with assistance from 20,000 National Guardsmen, finally restored order, but not until five days of violence had left about 30 dead, hundreds injured, over 2,200 arrested and millions of dollars of property damaged. The streets of the LA ghetto now resemble a ravaged war zone.

The arrest of a Negro on drunken driving charges and alleged police brutality triggered the riots.

Johnson installed as US president

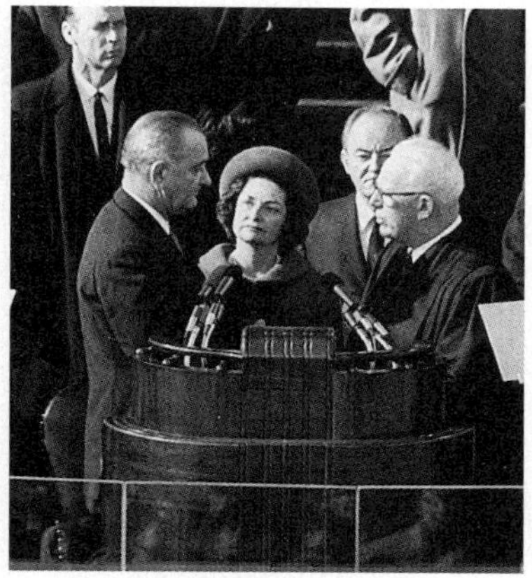

Lyndon Baines Johnson sworn in.

United States, 20 January
Lyndon Baines Johnson officially begins his first full term as president of the United States today. After being sworn in by Chief Justice Earl Warren, LBJ gave a speech, praised by Democrats and Republicans alike, that emphasised his war on poverty and denounced the horrors of racism. He described his notion of a "Great Society".

De Gaulle is re-elected, only after runoff

France, 19 December
Charles de Gaulle has done it again, but it was not so easy this time. The general was re-elected to a seven-year term as president of France, but he needed two rounds at the polls. After the first try, the polls showed a drop in de Gaulle's popularity, but he managed to gather momentum during the second round, as he defeated an old nemesis, Francois Mitterrand, 55 per cent to 45 per cent. Mitterrand headed a coalition which called itself the Federation of the Democratic and Socialist Left.

Stylish start for President Marcos

Philippines, 30 December
With the kind of panache the Filipinos love – strutting horses, blaring bands and the honorific passes of jet fighters – Ferdinand E Marcos was sworn in today as the Philippine republic's sixth president. Marcos, a lawyer who bolted the Liberal Party and won election on a National Party ticket, was inaugurated before an ecstatic crowd of 80,000 in Manila's Luneta Park which borders the bay, providing a spectacular setting.

Men in the crowd were dressed in their best sheer white *barong tagalags* – the country's formal outer shirt – while the women sported brilliantly coloured silk and cotton frocks. Marcos also wore a *barong tagalag*, and when the cheering finally stopped he led the salute to the flag while the national anthem was played.

Waiting in the grandstand was the president's wife, resplendent in a cream-coloured silk dress with butterfly sleeves.

Malcolm X is shot to death in Harlem

New York City, 21 February
In a dramatic shooting in front of a crowd of 400, Negro leader Malcolm X was killed by black assassins. Malcolm X, born Malcolm Little, was for a number of years a minister and one of the principal spokesmen of the Black Muslim organisation led by Elijah Muhammad. Following disagreements with Muhammad, Malcolm split with the Black Muslims and founded his own group, The Organization for Afro-American Unity. The two groups waged a feud which ultimately culminated in the shooting; he was unprepared for the attack which occurred as he was beginning a speech to followers in Harlem, New York City.

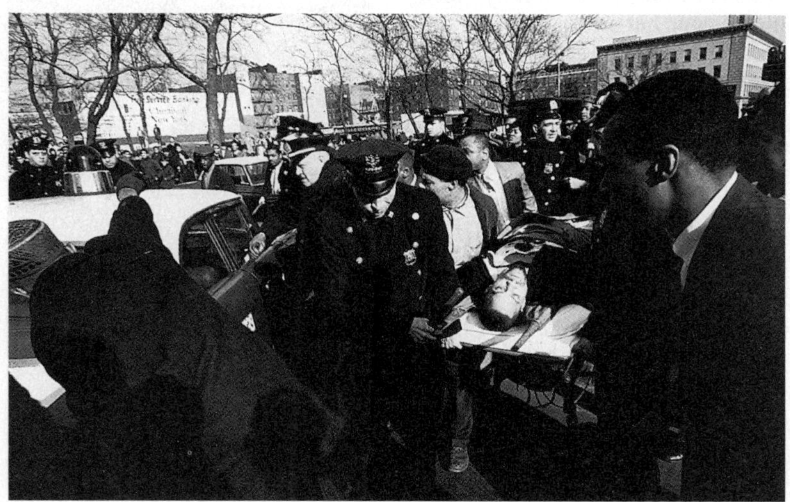

Malcolm X was shot dead in front of 400 supporters at a rally in Harlem.

Americans against Vietnam War

United States, 30 November
What happened in South Vietnam in 1963 is beginning to happen in the United States. It is the ultimate protest against the politics of war. Like the Buddhist monks of Saigon, opponents of the Vietnam War are burning themselves to death in public places.

It started at the beginning of the month when a 32-year-old Quaker, a father of three, set himself on fire in front of a Pentagon entrance. Norman Morrison, of Baltimore, was holding his one-year-old daughter when his clothes caught fire. He dropped her, and she was rescued by a passer-by. Morrison's wife said later he was very upset "over the great loss of life and human suffering" in the war.

A week later, on the 9th, a former seminarian set himself on fire outside the United Nations. Roger Allen LaPorte said it was a protest at "all war". More moderate Americans are also starting to voice protest at the Vietnam War.

1966

Spain, 17 January. A massive search is on for an H-bomb that dropped into the Atlantic when an American B-52 bomber collided with another aircraft.

Tokyo, 3 February. An airliner crashes into Tokyo Bay, killing 133.

France, 8 March. Private art collection of impressionist Claude Monet found.

Indonesia, 13 March. General Suharto orders the military to eradicate all traces of the Communist Party.

Britain, 1 April. Labour secures a majority of 96 in the general election.

Ottawa, 5 April. Canada votes to retain the death penalty.

Switzerland, 14 April. Sandoz corporation suspends distribution of LSD.

USA, 15 April. Paul Parkman and Harry Myer develop rubella vaccine.

Houston, 26 April. American surgeon implants an artificial pump in a human heart.

Alabama, 3 May. Governor Wallace's wife wins the Democratic nomination for state governor.

Britain, 1 June. Philips Petroleum announces the find of the largest North Sea oilfield yet.

Moon, 3 June. An unmanned American spacecraft lands on and then takes off from the moon.

USA, 4 June. 6,400 people sign appeal against Vietnam War, the largest political ad ever published.

Mississippi, 6 June. James Meredith, the first Negro to be admitted to the "Ole Miss" University, shot in the back on a civil rights march.

London, 30 July. England beat West Germany 4-2 to win the soccer World Cup.

Moon, 18 August. First pictures of Earth taken from moon orbit are sent back to USA.

Hollywood, 3 August. Death of the controversial comedian Lenny Bruce from a drugs overdose.

Wales, 21 October. A coal tip slides into a primary school at Aberfan, killing 116 children and 28 adults.

USA, 8 November. Edward W. Brooke is the first Negro to become a Senator.

California, 15 December. Walt Disney dies aged 65.

The Cultural Revolution

Chinese soldiers read Mao's Red Book and are urged to "seize the day".

China, 13 August
"A revolution is not a dinner party, or writing an essay, or painting a picture, or doing embroidery; it cannot be so refined, so leisurely and gentle, so temperate, kind, courteous, restrained and magnanimous. A revolution is an insurrection, an act of violence by which one class overthrows another." So wrote Mao Zedong in 1927 at the start of the Chinese Revolution, words being taken to heart again by the Chinese masses as their "infallible leader" prepares them for what is being called "the great proletarian cultural revolution".

The new campaign, which intends to revive the revolutionary zeal which proved victorious in 1949, takes many forms. Within the Communist Party apparatus, Mao and his followers aim to purge the entrenched power-holders who resist his ideas. In artistic and educational institutions, renewed efforts to "criticise bourgeois reactionary thinking" are under way. In the army, "the chief instrument of the dictatorship of the proletariat in China", a drive to recruit loyal revolutionaries is beginning.

The time has come to act out Mao's latest poem: "Seize the day, seize the hour! Away with all the pests! Our force is irresistible!"

GM apologises to Ralph Nader

Washington, 22 March
The president of General Motors has apologised before a congressional committee for a company-ordered investigation of the private life of Ralph Nader, a crusader for safer cars. James M Roche agreed with Senator Ribicoff that the investigation was "most unworthy of American business". Nader became a target of the auto industry after publishing a book, *Unsafe at Any Speed*, that questioned the safety of US cars. Roche said he knew nothing of private detectives questioning 60 of Nader's friends and relatives about his sex habits, political beliefs and view of Jews.

Nader: questioned safety of cars.

Miniskirt: men can't believe their eyes

London
Take an ineffably skinny teen model, put her in minimum garb, and you have a fashion frenzy. Twiggy, *nee* Lesley Hornby, is popularising the miniskirt. British model Twiggy "rounds out" the look with thick false eyelashes and colourful fishnet stockings.

Fashion observers trace the big mini trend to British designer Mary Quant. But what gave Miss Quant the idea? Perhaps she sees our times as something like the 1920s, when women, free to smoke, drink and curse, did so in flimsy flapper gowns. Today, sure to keep her shape as long as she is on the pill, woman is again feeling free. The mini is complemented by headbands, beads and plastic boots.

Turning heads in trendy London.

LSD advocate Leary held in a drug case

New York, 17 April
Former Harvard psychology professor and self-confessed LSD user, Timothy Leary, 45, was arrested just after midnight on charges of narcotics possession. He was at his Dutchess County, New York, home when police made a raid, finding a small amount of marijuana in a bedroom. Leary said he did not know how it got there.

Police also found about 30 men and women lolling on mattresses in Leary's 64-room mansion. Police seized tapes they were playing and an as yet unidentified substance. Three of Leary's guests were taken into custody, including a 46-year-old Hindu priest and his wife.

Lone sailor makes his longest voyage

Sydney, 12 December
Bruised, emaciated and weary, Francis Chichester was helped ashore in Sydney, Australia, after making the longest solo sea voyage in history – 13,750 miles (22,000 kilometres) in 107 days.

The British adventurer and magazine publisher received a hero's welcome on his arrival from England in his 53-foot (16-metre) ketch, *Gypsy Moth IV*. Sydney was the halfway point of his planned round-the-world voyage.

The lean 65-year-old sailor swigged a glass of English beer on his arrival and vowed: "I shall go on." He has failed in his goal of reaching Sydney in 100 days.

In 1960, he entered the first single-handed race across the Atlantic. At 59, and minus a lung lost to cancer, Chichester not only completed the race but also won it.

Sydney wishes lone sailor "bon voyage" for the homeward leg.

Negroes and police battle in big cities

United States, 31 July
The streets of Chicago, New York and Cleveland are rife with racial unrest this month; many people have been killed and injured in firebomb attacks, sniper gunfire and clashes between white and Negro gangs and police.

Over 4,000 National Guardsmen were called into Chicago to quiet an ongoing war between police and Negro snipers. Two Negroes were killed in the shooting and six policemen were wounded. One community leader expressed the sentiment of many angry ghetto dwellers. "We need jobs," he said. Today, 54 people were hurt when angry whites hurled bricks at civil rights protesters marching through an all-white neighbourhood.

A thousand police were sent to ugly scenes in the east New York section of Brooklyn, where Negroes, whites and Puerto Ricans sparred in the streets for nearly a week, resulting in scores of injuries and at least two deaths.

California elects Reagan governor

California, 8 November
Ronald Reagan, 55, the ruggedly handsome former movie star turned politician, was elected governor of California today, defeating his Democrat opponent, Governor Edmund G "Pat" Brown. A conservative Republican who was once a liberal Democrat, Reagan won in his first bid for public office.

Governor Reagan and wife, Nancy.

Opposition to Vietnam War is growing

Washington, 28 May
On American campuses students picket, march, chant and sometimes riot. On the White House lawn, moderate protesters urge the president to "cool it". In Saigon, Buddhists set themselves ablaze in fiery suicides. At defence contractors' corporate offices, scores denounce the production and use of napalm. Meanwhile record numbers of Americans die in Vietnam.

About 350 students seized control of administration offices at the University of Chicago, protesting against the college's co-operation with the Selective Service. Similar action was taken at City College, New York. Thousands of students are seeking draft deferments.

Vorster replaces slain leader Verwoerd

South Africa, 13 September
Balthazar Vorster has been appointed prime minister one week after Hendrik Verwoerd was stabbed to death by a messenger in the South African parliament. Dimitri Stifianos, the messenger, was a drifter who complained that Verwoerd was helping blacks at the expense of whites. Verwoerd, a pro-Nazi during the Second World War, was the architect of South Africa's apartheid laws. During the war, he railed against "British Jewish liberalism" and protested at Jews being given refuge.

Vorster (left), new prime minister.

Nehru's daughter Indira new premier

Mrs Indira Gandhi at the first meeting of parliament since her election.

India, 19 January
When she became India's third prime minister today, Mrs Indira Gandhi, no relation to Mohandas Gandhi, became only the second woman in modern history to head a government. The other was Mrs Sirimavo Bandaranaike, Ceylon's recently deposed leader.

Though technically her election was only for the leadership of the Congress Parliamentary Party, India's leading party, as leader she is automatically prime minister. At the news conference which followed, the question "How does it feel to be the first woman prime minister in India?" received a cool reply. "I am", she answered, "just an Indian citizen and the first servant of my country." More than 50 women sit in India's parliament.

1967

USA, 3 January. Jack Ruby, the man who shot Lee Harvey Oswald, dies from cancer.

Bahamas, 21 January. First black government takes power.

Britain, 12 February. Rolling Stones Mick Jagger and Keith Richard are arrested at Richard's Sussex home on drugs charges.

Cornwall, 19 March. A huge oil tanker, the *Torrey Canyon*, runs aground off Land's End and starts to spill its cargo.

USA, 3 April. The US State Department alleges that Hanoi may be brainwashing American prisoners.

Bonn, 19 April. West Germany's post-war leader, Konrad Adenauer, dies, aged 91.

Athens, 21 April. A military junta seizes power in Greece and arrests left-wingers.

USSR, 24 April. A Soviet cosmonaut, Vladimir Komarov, dies when his craft crashes on re-entry.

Paris, 16 May. President de Gaulle says that he will block the latest British application to join the Common Market.

Nigeria, 30 May. The Ibo people announce they are breaking away to form the independent state of Biafra.

Britain, 1 June. The Beatles release *Sergeant Pepper's Lonely Hearts Club Band.*

Prague, 28 June. Czech writers sign a petition calling for liberalisation of Communist government.

London, 14 July. A bill to make abortion legal is passed by the House of Commons.

USA, 27 July. Throughout this month race riots have ravaged several US cities, including Detroit, New York and Newark.

USA, 25 August. Founder of the American Nazi Party George Rockwell is shot dead.

USA, 30 August. Thurgood Marshall becomes the first black to get a Supreme Court seat.

Vietnam, 3 September. Military man General Nguyen Van Thieu is elected President of South Vietnam.

Vietnam, 21 November. US bombers intensify their raids on North Vietnam.

Toulouse, 11 December. The prototype is unveiled of Concorde, the first supersonic airliner.

Greece, 13 December. King Constantine flees after leading abortive counter-coup.

Israel smashes Arabs in Six Day War

Jerusalem, 28 June

Israel reaped the reward of victory over its Arab enemies in the Six Day War today. The city of Jerusalem was formally reunited under Israeli control, and Jews streamed into the walled Old City, which was controlled by Jordan before the war. Many of them wept openly, and armed soldiers bent in prayer before the Wailing Wall.

The man who led Israel to victory over Egypt and its Arab allies, Defence Minister Moshe Dayan, told the soldiers, "We have returned to the holiest of our holy places, never to depart from it again."

The biggest loser of this war is Egypt. Its army and air force were humiliated by Israel. Gamal Abdel Nasser gambled and he lost. Even U Thant, the usually neutral secretary general of the United Nations, blamed Egypt for the build-up which led to the outbreak of hostilities on the 5th. Thant stopped short of saying who actually fired the first shot. Israel and Egypt are still blaming each other.

Israel met strong resistance from Egyptian forces in the opening hours of the fighting. The tide turned quickly, however, and within 72 hours it was a rout. Israeli forces swept through Gaza and across the Sinai peninsula all the way to the Suez Canal.

A truck filled with Arab prisoners passes an Israeli army column.

Che Guevara killed by Bolivian forces

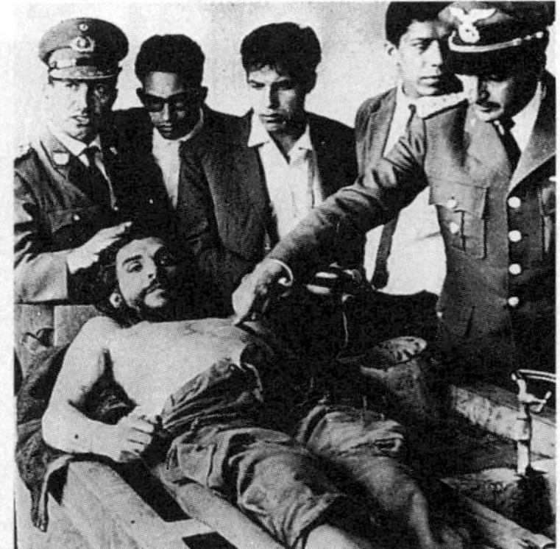

Corpse of Che Guevera displayed.

Bolivia, 10 October

Ernesto Che Guevara, the underground revolutionary leader and hero to popular movements in Central and South America, has been reported dead or captured several times since he disappeared two years ago. Today, military authorities in Bolivia confirmed that Guevara was killed on Sunday, when his guerrilla band was overrun by government forces. Six other guerrillas were also killed, including four Cubans. Guevara's body was displayed at a news conference.

Stalin's daughter defects to the West

New Delhi, 9 March

At first, US officials thought her story was too incredible to be true. A woman walked into the United States embassy in New Delhi, India, and said she was Svetlana Alliluyeva, daughter of the late Soviet dictator, Stalin. After a short conversation, Ambassador Chester Bowles confirmed her identity. She said she wished to defect.

At any other time, the defection of Stalin's daughter would have represented a major propaganda coup for the United States. But the Johnson administration hopes the times are changing.

Svetlana explains her defection.

De Gaulle: "Long live a free Quebec"

Canada, 31 July

France's President de Gaulle is not saying how far he will go, but he is causing quite a controversy on both sides of the Atlantic with his clarion call for the liberation of French Canadians.

The general is not sending in the troops and he says he has no territorial ambitions in Canada. But de Gaulle is promising the support of France to Canadians who, in his view, are short on "liberty, equality and fraternity".

General de Gaulle's statement has further shocked the Ottawa government. Prime Minister Lester Pearson had criticised de Gaulle for saying "Long live a free Quebec" in Montreal last week.

The declaration also created a furore back home in Paris, but it's likely to die down during the traditional August exodus

Ali won't serve, so he loses boxing title

Ali is claiming a draft deferment.

Texas, 30 April
Cassius Clay, who prefers to use the name Muhammad Ali, was stripped of his world heavyweight boxing title today when he refused to be inducted into military service. The 25-year-old boxer baulked at taking the one step forward in Houston that would have constituted induction into the service. The boxing associations took his title and criminal prosecution is expected to follow.

Said Ali: "I have searched my conscience and I find I cannot be true to my belief in my religion by accepting such a call." He has claimed exemption as a minister of a Black Muslim sect. Ali faces a minimum jail term of five years.

Canada's "Expo '67" out of this world

By the end of May, seven million people will have visited Canada's *Expo '67* – and walked on the moon. The US lunar exhibit is one of the most popular displays at the international fair and a 123-foot (40-metre) escalator takes viewers over a simulated lunar landscape. *Expo '67* opened on 27 April in Montreal. The fair covers 700 acres (285 hectares), the largest exhibit being the Canadian complex. The granite, canvas and steel structure borders on La Ronde amusement park, where teens can go-go dance and children can ride tamed zebras.

The first heart transplant patient dies

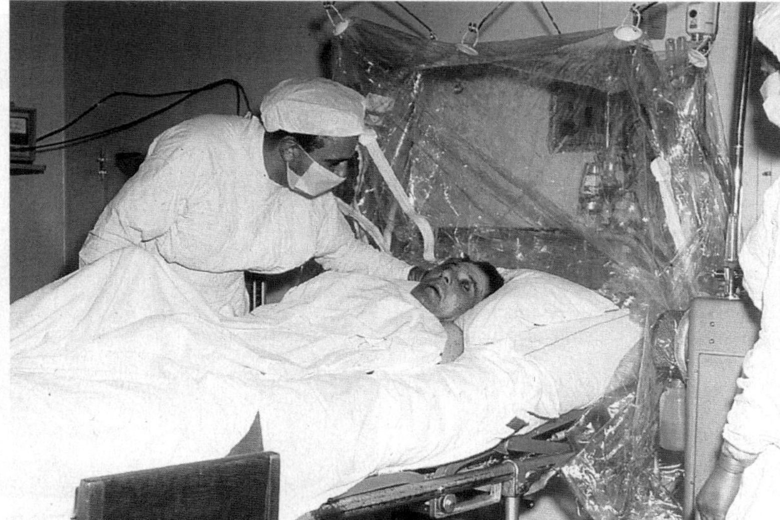
Louis Washkansky was given a woman's heart by Dr Christiaan Barnard.

Cape Town, 21 December
Grocer Louis Washkansky, 53, the world's first heart transplant patient, died in Cape Town, South Africa, today after living for 18 days with the heart of a 25-year-old woman who was killed in a car accident. Doctors at Groote Schuur Hospital said he died after a steady deterioration that began when he developed lung complications a few days ago. The heart continued to beat strongly to the end.

Washkansky's transplant was performed on 3 December by a five-surgeon team headed by Dr Christiaan N Barnard, who trained in the United States and continued animal experiments on heart transplants in South Africa. Washkansky would have lived only a few hours without the transplant.

Three astronauts are killed in flash fire

Florida, 27 January
Astronauts Virgil I Grissom, Edward H White II and Roger B Chaffee were killed tonight in a flash fire that engulfed their *Apollo I* spacecraft. They died on the ground during a full-scale simulation of the scheduled 21 February launching that was to put them in Earth orbit for 14 days.

Officials of the National Aeronautics and Space Administration said an electrical spark must have ignited the pure oxygen inside the cabin. They were seated abreast, as they would have been in a flight.

The charred interior of the Apollo spacecraft where the astronauts died.

Flower children flock to San Francisco

San Francisco
"We want the world, and we want it now," thundered the Doors' lead singer Jim Morrison this year. But many kids figured as long as society was ravaged by war, injustice and materialism, they would do just as well to heed drug guru Timothy Leary's advice and simply drop out. And what better place to do that than in San Francisco, where, as Scott McKenzie warbled in one hit song, everyone was sure to be wearing flowers.

The San Francisco "Summer of Love" began, more or less, in June at the Monterey Pop Festival. With the Beatles' masterpiece *Sergeant Pepper's Lonely Hearts Club Band* as a beacon, the feeling that rock music had come into its own merged with a high-flying counter-culture movement. About 50,000 kids, many with hair even longer than the Beatles' and dressed in a riot of colours, got high on everything from LSD to the communal vibes, and grooved to a fantastic array of artists: the Memphis soul of Otis Redding, the cerebral ragas of Indian sitarist Ravi Shankar and a cavalcade of bands from California, including the Mamas and Papas, Jefferson Airplane, Grateful Dead and Buffalo Springfield.

A summer of love in San Francisco.

1968

Czechoslovakia, 5 January. Liberal Alexander Dubcek, 46, becomes head of the Czechoslovak Communist Party and leader of the country.

London, 22 February. The government announces rushed legislation to stem the rising tide of Kenyan Asian immigrants.

London, 17 March. Anti-Vietnam War demonstrators try to storm the American embassy in Grosvenor Square.

USSR, 27 March. The first man in space, Yuri Gagarin, dies in an air accident.

West Germany, 15 April. The shooting of student leader Rudi Dutschke triggers riots.

Canada, 6 April. Pierre Trudeau becomes prime minister.

USA, 9 April. Within hours of the murder of Dr Martin Luther King Jr, black riots break out in a number of major US cities.

Britain, 21 April. Enoch Powell delivers a speech in which he says immigration into Britain will produce a river "foaming with much blood".

Paris, 13 May. American and North Vietnamese diplomats meet to discuss the setting-up of talks to end the Vietnam War.

Los Angeles, 7 June. Sirhan Sirhan, a young Palestinian Arab immigrant, is charged with murdering Senator Robert Kennedy and assaulting five other people.

London, 8 June. James Earl Ray, 40, wanted by the FBI for the murder of Dr Martin Luther King Jr, is arrested en route for Brussels.

France, 30 June. French voters give huge support to de Gaulle in the presidential election.

Britain, 4 July. Single-handed round-the-world yachtsman Alec Rose is cheered home by 250,000.

Rome, 29 July. Pope Paul VI issues an encyclical, *Humanae Vitae*, condemning birth control.

Mexico, 16 October. Two American athletes give the "Black Power" salute as they collect their Olympic medals.

Washington, 1 November. President Johnson calls off the bombing of North Vietnam in an attempt to stimulate Paris peace talks.

USA, 5 November. Shirley Chisholm becomes first black woman to be elected to the House of Representatives

USA, 27 December. Three astronauts return to Earth after orbiting the moon.

Martin Luther King killed in Memphis

Aides of the stricken King indicate to police where the shot came from.

Memphis, Tennessee, 5 April
The Rev Dr Martin Luther King Jr was fatally shot last night as he leaned over the second-floor balcony railing just outside his room at the Lorraine Motel in Memphis, Tennessee.

The death of the 39-year-old civil rights leader sent shock waves throughout much of the city and the nation. Governor Buford Ellington of Tennessee ordered 4,000 National Guard troops into Memphis to keep order, and a curfew was imposed on residents, 40 per cent of whom are blacks.

The assassin, who managed to escape, is believed to be a white man who was staying in a flophouse about 50 to 100 yards from the motel. Police believe that he fled in a car. A high-powered rifle was found about a block from the scene of the crime.

Police battle anti-Vietnam mobs

Chicago, 29 August
Divisions over the Vietnam War exploded here today as demonstrators were bludgeoned, beaten and maced outside the convention where Hubert Humphrey was nominated as Democrat presidential candidate. Humphrey won on a plank supporting the war, but his candidacy may have been mortally wounded by what Senator Ribicoff called Mayor Daley's "gestapo tactics" against the protesters.

The most violent rioting erupted when hundreds of police charged as organisers tried to lead a march from Grant Park to the convention.

National Guard clears protesters.

Bobby Kennedy is killed with two shots

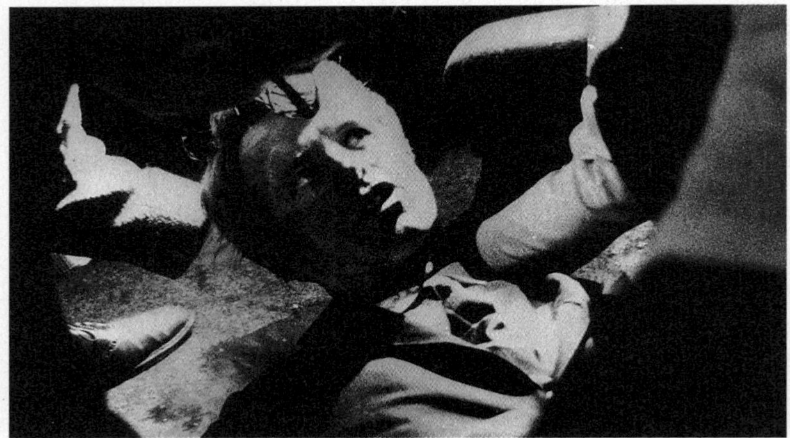

Before losing consciousness Senator Robert Kennedy looks up at helpers.

Los Angeles, 6 June
"Oh God, it can't happen to this family again!" cries a disbelieving bystander in the Embassy Room of the Ambassador Hotel in Los Angeles. Minutes before, Senator Robert F Kennedy had claimed victory in the California primary.

Amid cheers and V-for-victory signs, the New York senator exited into an anteroom. Seconds later, he was lying on the floor of a kitchen corridor. He had been shot twice in the head – once in the forehead and once near the right ear.

Robert Francis Kennedy died at 1.44 am on 6 June, 20 hours after the attack and four and a half years after his brother, President John F Kennedy, was assassinated.

Nixon's close win

Washington, 5 November
Eight years after his defeat by John F Kennedy, Richard M Nixon squeaked past Hubert H Humphrey today to win the presidency in one of the closest votes in history. With 95 per cent counted, Nixon appears to be a minority victor. Following a long, tense night, Nixon held off delivering his victory remarks until 11.35 am, when he thanked supporters. His vice president will be Spiro T Agnew.

Vice President Humphrey, who beat senators Eugene J McCarthy and George McGovern to win the Democratic nomination, entered the presidential race after the shock decision by President Lyndon B Johnson not to run. In a decision in late March that stunned political friends and foes alike, LBJ had announced: "I shall not seek and I will not accept the nomination of my party as your president."

The president said he was withdrawing his stand in the name of national unity.

Reds launch a massive Tet offensive as expected

Washington, 31 January
North Vietnamese and Viet Cong forces have launched a massive offensive throughout South Vietnam, Washington confirmed today. The campaign began yesterday with a series of co-ordinated attacks aimed at American and South Vietnamese troops in the northern and central provinces. In the past 24 hours, an estimated 84,000 Communist combat troops – and an equal number of support forces – have struck at virtually all the provincial capitals and major cities in South Vietnam, including Saigon and Hue.

In Saigon, a North Vietnamese suicide squad blew a hole in the wall of the United States embassy last night, killing two army military policemen. The North Vietnamese occupied the embassy yard for five hours, until they were all killed by other military policemen and marine guards at the embassy this morning. Fighting is continuing on the outskirts of Saigon.

At Khesanh 5,000 US marines are besieged by 20,000 North Vietnamese.

Communist forces have also attacked and captured the port city of Hue. Early word indicates that civilian casualties are extremely high. The Tet offensive has been expected for some time by US military leaders; intelligence officials received word last week of the coming "decisive campaign", a contest that the Viet Cong soldiers were being told would produce the "final victory". Last week, President Johnson was informed by General William Westmoreland, the American commander in Vietnam, that he believed the Communist attack would come just before Tet, the Vietnamese lunar New Year – even though a truce between the two sides was in effect for the holiday period.

With the news that some 5,000 marines are besieged by at least 20,000 North Vietnamese soldiers at Khesanh and with the yearly cost of the war now approaching $25 billion, opposition to America's continuing commitment to the Saigon government is certain to increase. The Tet offensive, if it is successful, may convince many American "doves" that the "light at the end of the tunnel" is now glowing dimmer than ever.

France nearly paralysed by protesters

Students take to the streets of Paris as the country is crippled by strikes.

France, 30 May
The trains are not running in France, and the airports are closed. Millions of workers have barricaded themselves inside factories and offices. Mail is not being delivered, and it is almost impossible to make a telephone call. Universities are closed, and hundreds of thousands of students say they will not open again until their demands are met. A leading politician warns that France is on the brink of civil war.

President Charles de Gaulle, furious at striking workers and students, dissolved the National Assembly today, postponed a national referendum and vowed to use force if necessary to prevent what he called a Communist dictatorship. "I have made my resolutions," de Gaulle said. "I shall not withdraw. I have a mandate from the people. I shall fulfil it."

Many hundreds of thousands of Parisians turned out to support de Gaulle, but his speech was sharply criticised by Francois Mitterrand. The head of the Federation of the Left charged that the president had "committed an action that is a call to civil war".

Soviet tanks invade now defiant Prague

Prague, 22 August
Words could not convince Alexander Dubcek to abandon his liberal experiment in Czechoslovakia. Tonight, Soviet tanks are patrolling Prague, and angry Czechs are fighting back with guns, sticks and even their bare hands. They managed to set some of the Soviet tanks and munitions trucks on fire. Explosions are rattling the previously quiet Czech capital.

Several hundred thousand Soviet troops crossed the border into Czechoslovakia on Tuesday night. Czechs were astounded. The troops, commanded by the Soviet vice minister of defence, General Ivan Pavlovsky, came from the Soviet Union, Poland, Hungary, Bulgaria and East Germany. Weapons and soldiers streamed into Prague in a massive airlift. The skies of the capital were filled with the roar of Soviet planes.

Fighting erupted when the Soviets tried to storm the national radio station in Prague. Thirty Czechs were killed; more than 300 were injured. As the station fell to the Soviets, a Czech announcer urged residents of the city to remain loyal to Communist Party leader Dubcek and President Ludvik Svoboda.

Czech citizens demonstrate against the Russian occupation of Prague.

1969

Kenya, 1 January. The government rescinds Asians' trading licences, triggering another exodus to Britain.

Prague, 19 January. Angry crowds gather after Czech student Jan Palach burns himself to death in protest against the Russian invasion.

Britain, 13 February. Scientists announce they have successfully fertilised human eggs in a test tube.

Tennessee, 11 March. James Earl Ray pleads guilty to killing Martin Luther King and is sentenced to 99 years in prison.

Caribbean, 19 March. British troops put down a rebellion on the tiny island of Anguilla.

Amsterdam, 22 March. Two days after getting married John Lennon and Yoko Ono start a week-long "bed-in" for peace.

USA, 28 March. General Dwight Eisenhower, 34th US president, known to the world as "Ike", dies aged 78.

Northern Ireland, 18 April. Civil rights worker Bernadette Devlin, aged 22, is elected MP for Mid-Ulster.

Los Angeles, 23 April. Sirhan Sirhan is convicted of killing Senator Robert Kennedy last June and is sentenced to death.

France, 28 April. De Gaulle resigns as president when a referendum rejects his proposals for constitutional reform.

Canada, 14 May. Omnibus criminal code bill legalises abortion and homosexuality.

Wales, 1 July. Prince Charles is invested as Prince of Wales at Caernarvon Castle.

Honduras, 13 July. Troops invade from El Salvador, an escalation of conflict provoked by a dispute over a soccer match.

Massachusetts, 20 July. A woman is found drowned in a car abandoned by Senator Edward Kennedy in eight feet (2.5 metres) of water on Chappaquiddick Island.

Northern Ireland, 15 August. British troops are cheered by Catholics as they erect barriers to end a week of sectarian fighting.

Libya, 1 September. A group of army officers led by Colonel Muammar Gaddafi seizes power.

Vietnam, 4 September. Ho Chi Minh, president of North Vietnam, dies aged 79.

Nigeria, 2 November. Biafrans face mass starvation because the Nigerian government will not let the Red Cross in.

Neil Armstrong walks on the moon

Neil Armstrong was watched by 600 million as he took his historic steps.

Houston, 24 July
"Houston, Tranquility base here. The Eagle has landed." As these words crackled 238,000 miles (390,000 kilometres) through the blackness of space four days ago, humanity was awed by the news that two American astronauts, Neil A Armstrong and Edwin E Aldrin Jr, had landed on the moon. Soon after, Armstrong, 38, emerged from the spidery lunar lander. And as a television camera transmitted the otherworldly images to an audience of perhaps 600 million, the astronaut slipped softly onto the bleak, powdery lunar surface at 10.56 pm, delivering the immortal line, "That's one small step for man, one giant step for mankind."

The mission, the culmination of a decade-long effort and an age-old dream, began on 16 July, when *Apollo XI* blasted off from Pad 39-A at Cape Kennedy, Florida. Armstrong said the moon had "a stark beauty all its own".

Concorde maiden flight is a triumph

France, 2 March
"Finally the big bird flies," the pilot said. "And I can say that it flies pretty well." And what a bird! With its sharply pointed beak turned down to give a view of the runway, the aircraft known as Concorde jetted into the air in Toulouse, France, today on its maiden flight. It climbed abruptly as its French and British co-developers crossed their fingers. Some 28 minutes later, the aircraft glided successfully back to Earth.

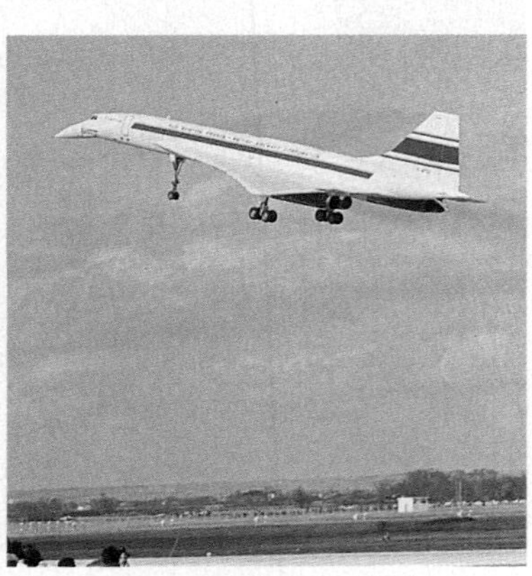

Concorde takes off from Toulouse.

Pregnant Sharon Tate is slain by cult

The cult leader Charles Manson.

Los Angeles, 10 August
The pre-dawn horror of 9 August left five people dead. No weapons were found in the area but the killers wrote the words "HELTER SKELTER" and "PIGS" in blood on the walls. Cult followers with their leader Charles Manson invaded the home of Sharon Tate and her film director husband, Roman Polanski (he was in London at the time), and ritualistically slaughtered the actress, who was eight months pregnant, as well as three guests and a neighbour.

567 massacred at Mylai by US troops

South Vietnam, 30 November
An ugly, 20-month-old story is emerging from a small hamlet in South Vietnam called Mylai. Some 567 residents of the community were reportedly slaughtered by an American platoon. Survivors say many of the victims were women and children as young as two years old. First Lieutenant William Calley, the platoon leader, has been implicated in the murders of more than 100 of the villagers. He will face a general court-martial.

Lieutenant Calley has been accused.

Thousands flock to Woodstock festival

Bethel, New York, 17 August
A massive gathering of young people, estimated at close to 400,000, survived endless traffic jams, food and water shortages and torrential downpours this weekend to proclaim the Woodstock Music and Arts Fair a fantastic success.

The crowd was more than twice as large as anyone had expected. Roads for 20 miles (30 kilometres) around were jammed and thousands walked through the small town of Bethel, New York, near Woodstock, towards the dairy farm site loaned for the event by owner Max Yasgur. The crowd behaved peacefully the entire weekend despite inadequate facilities.

Line-up included Janis Joplin.

Yasir Arafat leads his Palestinian forces

Cairo, 3 February
The trouncing of the Arab world in the Six Day War has not stopped Palestinian terror groups claiming Palestine or attacking Israel.

But their hit-and-run attacks, launched mostly from Syria and Jordan, have not been unified, and the guerrillas lacked political clout. Today, though, they united under the umbrella of the Palestine Liberation Organisation. At a Cairo conference, Yasir Arafat was acknowledged the PLO's leader.

Massive anti-war rallies across USA

Washington, 15 November
The largest anti-war demonstration in the capital's history unfolded peacefully today as 250,000 people marched from the Capitol to the Washington Monument. On the other side of the continent, nearly 200,000 people rallied in San Francisco's Golden Gate Park.

The Washington protest was led by familiar faces in the movement, senators Eugene McCarthy and George McGovern, Coretta King, wife of the slain civil rights leader, Benjamin Spock, childcare expert, and folksinger Arlo Guthrie.

There were tense moments when counter-demonstrators clustered near 12 coffins containing names of American servicemen who had died in Vietnam. They added names of civilians slaughtered by the Viet Cong in the Tet offensive, and the situation was defused.

President Nixon, who vowed to ignore the demonstrations, spent much of the week solidifying support for his Vietnam policy.

Golda Meir is Israel's premier

Golda Meir is sworn in as premier.

Israel, 17 March
Golda Meir, 71, who once taught in a school in Milwaukee, was sworn in as Israel's fourth premier today. In her formal speech, she said she would push for "face-to-face talks" with the Arabs, adding that as long as they thought "there might be a solution without negotiations, the solution is only obstructed".

Communal violence rages in N Ireland

Flames erupt as a petrol bomb explodes on the streets of Belfast.

Belfast, 4 January
Communal violence erupted again in Northern Ireland as Protestant militants stoned and harassed university students marching in support of voting rights for Catholics. As the four-day march from Belfast neared an end in Londonderry, 200 Protestants, wielding sticks and stones, charged the line of about 100 marchers, chasing them into the fields and beating them with sticks. By nightfall, 136 persons, including 26 policemen, had been treated for injuries.

The march, approved by British authorities, was demanding "one man, one vote" in Ulster and abolition of the property qualification for voting. Opposition was led by the Rev Ian Paisley, self-styled Free Presbyterian Church leader.

Nixon begins a "Vietnamisation" plan

With flags flying, American troops march out of Quangtri Combat Base.

Washington, 8 July
In accord with President Nixon's plans for a gradual disengagement from the Vietnam War and for turning over the burden of the fighting to the South Vietnamese, the first American combat unit left Saigon today. A battalion of soldiers from the Ninth Infantry Division was flown out of Tan Son Nhut Airport for its permanent headquarters at Fort Lewis, Washington. The gradual withdrawal of combat forces has been planned since 8 June, when the president announced that 25,000 American troops would be sent home by the end of next month. Administration spokesmen say that even more US soldiers are going to be withdrawn if the South Vietnamese army shows it is capable of containing enemy efforts.

1970

New York, 23 January. The first Boeing 747 "Jumbo" jet flight leaves for London and Frankfurt.

Philippines, 26 January. Two killed as 2,000 storm presidential palace protesting against corruption in Marcos government.

Chicago, 28 February. The Chicago Seven trial ends with five of the defendants found guilty of intending to incite riots while the other two were acquitted.

Laos, 1 March. American planes heavily bomb the Ho Chi Minh trail.

Washington, 10 March. Army accuses five of murder and other crimes at Mylai in 1968.

Pacific Ocean, 17 April. *Apollo XIII* splashes down safely after an explosion in the service module jeopardised the crew's lives and caused the moon landing to be aborted.

Washington, 30 April. President Nixon sends US troops into Cambodia to attack Communist military bases.

Lebanon, 13 May. Israeli troops withdraw after a 32-hour raid; 30 Arabs died.

Britain, 19 June. Edward Heath's Conservatives win a surprise victory in the general election.

New York, 28 June. Thousands of gay men and women protest against laws that make homosexual acts illegal between consenting adults.

Belfast, 3 July. Bombs explode across the city as IRA snipers and the army fight a prolonged gun battle.

Portugal, 27 July. Dictator Antonio d'Oliviera Salazar dies, aged 81.

Jordan, 14 September. Arab terrorists hijack five planes and blow up three in desert, in demand for the release of hundreds of prisoners.

New York, 13 October. Angela Davis, who has been hunted on murder and kidnap charges, is caught by FBI agents.

Pakistan, 20 November. The death toll from a typhoon and tidal wave in the eastern part of the country rises to 150,000.

Canada, 3 December. James Cross, who was kidnapped by the Quebec Liberation Front two months ago, is released.

Poland, 23 December. Riots drive Communist Party chief Gomulka from job.

Anwar Sadat is elected president

Egypt, 5 October

Anwar Sadat, Gamal Abdel Nasser's vice president, has been elected president of the United Arab Republic. Nasser's funeral on the 1st was an extraordinary gathering of dignitaries. And sobbing women cried out, "Gamal, my beloved, what have we done to you to make you leave our house?"

President Sadat succeeds Nasser.

Jordan ends the Palestinian takeover

Cairo, 27 September

Jordan's King Hussein and Palestine Liberation Organisation chief Yasir Arafat both had guns strapped to their waists when they shook hands in Cairo and agreed to stop fighting each other.

The agreement came just 11 days after Hussein proclaimed martial law in Jordan and installed a new military government to fight the Palestinian guerrillas who were threatening to take over the entire country. At one point, the guerrillas had overrun all of northern Jordan and were on the outskirts of Amman. He appealed for help to America, which put forces on alert.

The Jordanian army takes to the streets of the capital, Amman.

Drugs finish Jimi Hendrix, rock star

London, 18 September

Jimi Hendrix, a musician whose searing guitar solos and flamboant, sensual performing style revolutionised rock, died today in London of drug-related causes. He was only 27 years old. Born in Seattle, Hendrix spent years as a sideman before creating an instant stir in England in 1967, with his group, the Jimi Hendrix Experience.

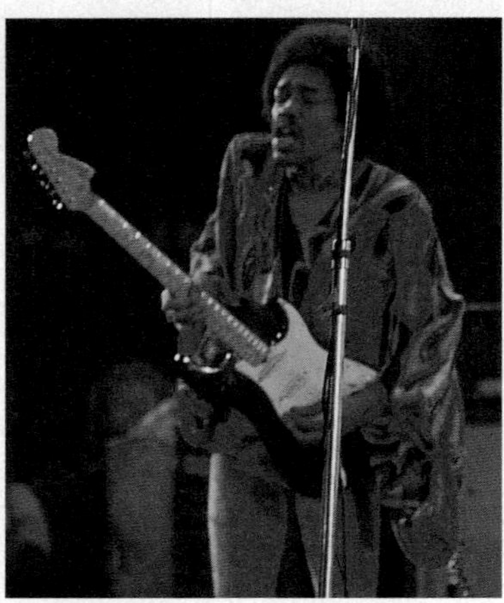

Jimi Hendrix revolutionised rock.

France mourns great leader de Gaulle

France, 12 November

Charles de Gaulle, who represented like no other man the grandeur of France, was buried today in a simple country ceremony near his home in Colombey-les-Deux-Eglises. Kings and heads of state had paid their respects in Paris. De Gaulle had requested that "neither president, nor ministers, nor assembly committees, nor public authorities" come to the funeral. There were no orations, no speeches. But tens of thousands of ordinary Frenchmen did come, squeezing into the square and streets around the church of Notre Dame to catch a glimpse of de Gaulle's coffin as it was driven from his home to the funeral mass in a simple military vehicle.

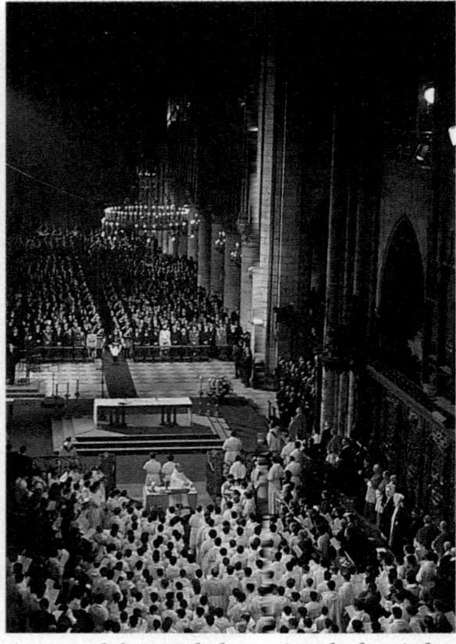

A grand funeral then simple burial.

Twelve boys from the village carried the coffin into the church. Several pews were reserved for veterans of the resistance, including Andre Malraux. The rest of the church was filled by family and villagers. Large wreaths sent by Mao Zedong covered one of the walls. The parish priest, a bishop and de Gaulle's nephew offered the mass and gave communion to the family. The young pall bearers took the casket to be buried next to the grave of Anne, his retarded daughter. "She was not like the others," said a chaplain from the resistance. "And when she was buried there, de Gaulle told his wife, 'Now she is like the others.' Well, now de Gaulle is like the others."

Defenceless Biafra yields to Nigeria

Biafra, 12 January
Biafra, with its last defences crumbling and its supplies of food and ammunition exhausted, capitulated today to the Nigerian government. The flag of independence was first raised on 30 May 1967. On 7 July of that year, the Biafrans were plunged into a brutal, bewildering civil war. Only five nations recognised the secessionist state, for which international groups tried to raise funds. US president Nixon has authorised an additional allocation of $10 million in food and medicine for Biafran relief.

European agencies and governments await authorisation from Nigeria for large-scale relief and seek, with the US, to prevent reprisals against the defeated Ibo.

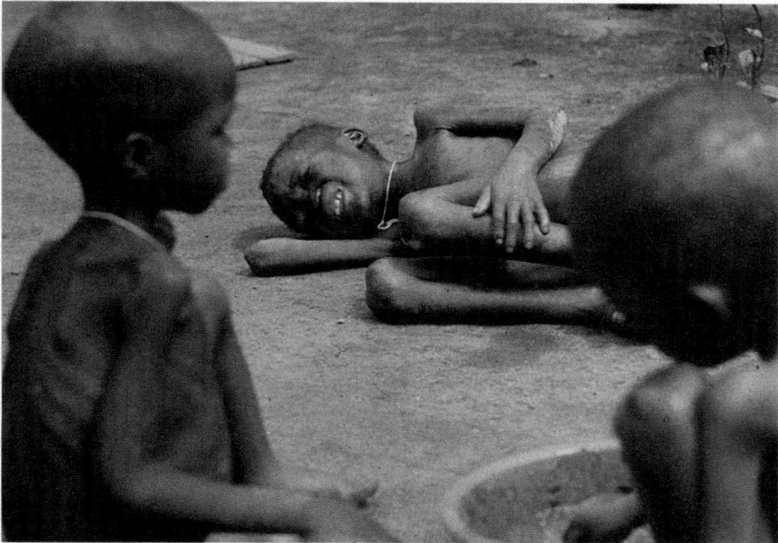

The defeated Ibo people are starving and desperate for help from the West.

Trudeau is firm against Quebec

Canada, 18 October
Canada's prime minister Pierre Trudeau, calling a band of French separatists "insurrectionists", has invoked emergency war powers to quell their rebellion. Hundreds of suspects were rounded up almost immediately in Montreal, Quebec and other cities.

The police crackdown did not come quickly enough to save labour minister Pierre Laporte, who had been kidnapped by French extremists. His body was found crumpled in the boot of a car. Nothing is known of the fate of James Cross, a senior British consular official. He was kidnapped at gunpoint on the 5th by members of the Front for the Liberation of Quebec.

Kent State shootings shock the nation

Ohio, 18 May
National Guardsmen fired into a crowd of Kent State University student protesters, killing four and wounding eight more. The 4 May shootings have created a furore as angry Americans try to comprehend the cause of such a tragedy.

Kent State in Ohio has traditionally been a politically apathetic school. However, as many American campuses have risen up in opposition to the Vietnam War, students here joined in. Expecting trouble from a planned student rally against the US incursion in Cambodia, university officials called in the National Guard, who broke up a demonstration. Some students, enraged over their presence, began yelling and tossing stones at the soldiers. The guardsmen, on previous orders to shoot if attacked, shot at the crowd.

The incident follows statements by politicians on how to control campus unrest, including California governor Ronald Reagan, who said about protesters, "If it takes a bloodbath, then, let's get it over with." Soviet poet Yevgeny Yevtushenko has commemorated one victim, Allison Krause, in a poem published today.

First aid is administered to an injured Kent State University student.

10,000 women march for equal rights

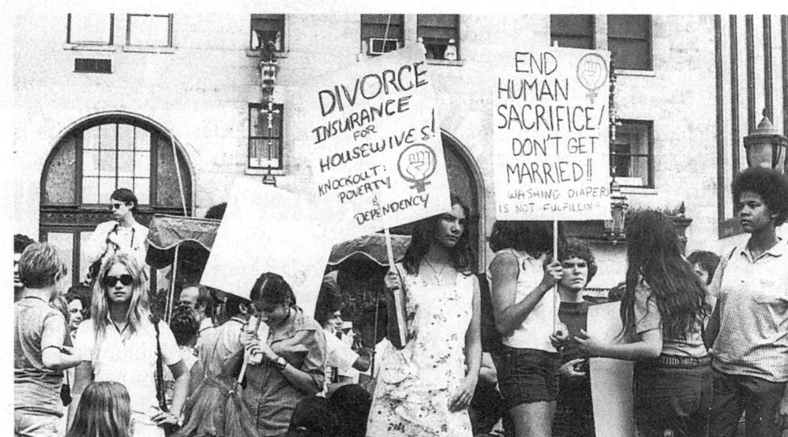

Women's liberation demonstrators rally with their placards in New York.

New York, 26 August
A throng of 10,000 women paraded up New York's Fifth Avenue tonight, celebrating the 50th anniversary of the passing of the 19th Amendment. The march capped a day of activities for the women's movement across the US. Women were demanding passage of the Equal Rights Amendment and other pro-feminist changes.

Betty Friedan, Kate Millett, Bela Abzug and Gloria Steinem spoke out for day-care centres, non-sexist advertising and revision of some social security laws. Members of the National Organisation of Women agitated for equal pay.

McCartney splits, breaking up Beatles

London, 10 April
Paul McCartney marked the end of an era today when he announced he was leaving the Beatles, thereby disbanding the most successful pop group in history. McCartney said the split was the result of "personal differences, business differences, musical differences – but most of all because I have a better time with my family." The Beatles appeared to be drifting apart recently, as members pursued individual projects.

1971

Glasgow, 2 January. Barriers collapse at Ibrox stadium during a Rangers and Celtic soccer match, 66 killed.

London, 14 January. A group calling itself the Angry Brigade admits bombing house of government minister Robert Carr.

Egypt, 15 January. The Aswan High Dam is opened by President Sadat and Soviet president Podgorny.

Los Angeles, 25 January. Charles Manson is found guilty of the Sharon Tate murders.

Switzerland, 7 February. Women are given the vote.

Vietnam, 8 February. South Vietnamese invade Laos with US air support to attack Ho Chi Minh Trail.

Georgia, 29 March. Lieutenant William Calley is found guilty of murdering Vietnamese civilians at Mylai in 1968.

New York, 6 April. Revolutionary composer Igor Stravinsky dies aged 88.

Northern Ireland, 10 April. A more militant, "Provisional", wing splits from the official IRA.

Washington, 2 May. Police eject 3,000 anti-war protesters from the banks of the Potomac.

London, 24 June. Terms are agreed for Britain's entry into the Common Market.

USA, 6 July. Jazz supremo Louis Armstrong dies aged 71.

New York, 1 August. A galaxy of rock stars, led by ex-Beatle George Harrison, perform at Madison Square Garden to raise funds for Bangladesh.

Uruguay, 9 September. Kidnapped British ambassador, Geoffrey Jackson, is released by Tupamaros guerrillas after eight months in captivity.

Moscow, 11 September. Former Soviet leader Nikita Khrushchev dies in obscurity aged 77.

New York State, 12 September. Four-day prison riot at Attica: 32 inmates and 10 warders dead.

Africa, 27 October. Congo renamed Zaire.

London, 31 October. Terrorists explode a bomb in the Post Office tower.

Tokyo, 19 November. 1,785 arrested in demonstrations against US bases in Okinawa.

Rhodesia, 24 November. Britain and Rhodesia sign a deal designed to end UDI.

New York, 21 December. Austrian Kurt Waldheim is chosen as secretary-general of the UN.

Rebel Idi Amin seizes power in Uganda

Uganda, 25 January
President Milton Obote of Uganda was not in the country today when rebels toppled his government. He was lucky. The insurrectionists, led by Major General Idi Amin Dada, left a bloodbath in their wake, murdering all troops and officials who were loyal to Obote. Idi Amin, who rose in the military ranks from private to commander of the army, gave himself dictatorial powers. He declared a night-time curfew, and soldiers in Kampala were shooting into the air tonight to discourage anyone from breaking it. Workers considered to be essential were given military escorts to jobs.

Idi Amin rose from army private to army commander to dictator.

Frazier outpoints Ali to hold on to title

New York, 8 March
A hammer-like left hook in the 15th and final round by Joe Frazier nearly finished off Muhammad Ali and helped to send him to his first defeat. Frazier won the fight on points and retained the heavyweight championship, but that one blow symbolised the crushing humiliation of the once-invincible Cassius Clay. The battle was so exciting that one man in the Madison Square Garden crowd died of a heart attack. Ali was taken to hospital to have his severely swollen jaw X-rayed, but was not kept in.

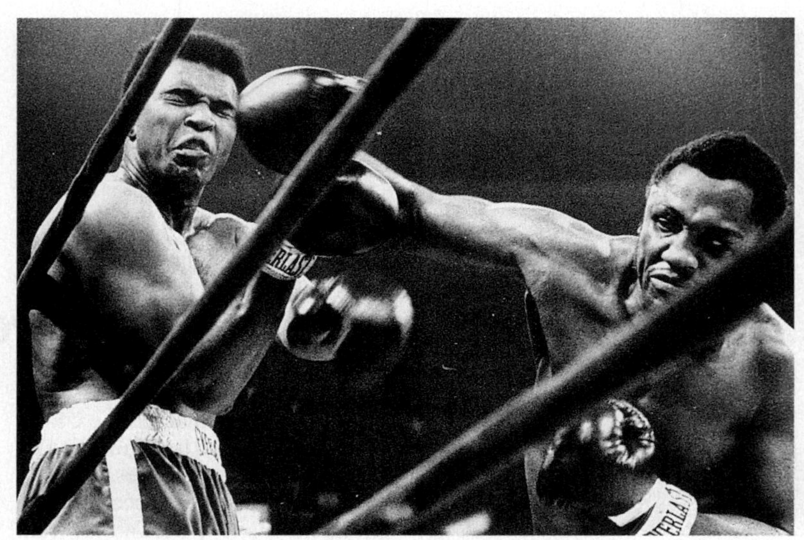

Muhammad Ali, previously Cassius Clay, went 15 rounds with Joe Frazier.

US astronauts take spin on the moon

Moon, 31 July
Apollo 15 astronauts David R Scott and James B Irwin today took mankind's first ride on the moon, steering their four-wheeled moon rover for several miles on the cratered, boulder-strewn lunar surface. They became the seventh and eighth men to walk on the moon; the first to drive a vehicle.

They landed on the moon's Sea of Rains yesterday and left their lunar module at 9.25 am Eastern time today. Minutes later, they detached the rover from the spacecraft and set off on their exploratory trip. The front steering did not function, but the vehicle is designed so that it can be manoeuvred with the rear wheels only.

Astronaut Irwin with moon rover.

China joins the UN

New York, 15 November
The People's Republic of China made its formal entry into the United Nations, with chief delegate Chiao Kuan-hua rebuking its members for allowing the superpowers "to manipulate and monopolise" the international organisation.

The six-member delegation that arrived in New York last Tuesday was the first since 1950, when Peking joined a UN debate on the Korean War. In his welcoming address the US ambassador to the UN, George Bush, said most countries "agreed that the moment has arrived" for China to be in the UN.

Emergency powers in Northern Ireland

Street fighting broke out after army and police patrols seized 300 men.

Belfast, 25 August
Violence has erupted in Northern Ireland after the government invoked emergency powers of preventive detention to arrest suspected leaders of the Irish Republican Army. Northern Ireland prime minister Brian Faulkner, who also imposed a six-month ban on parades, said that the emergency measures were necessary to protect life and property in the province.

The reaction from the Catholic minority was bitter. Hours after 300 men were seized by British army and police patrols, fighting, with guns and bombs, erupted in Belfast and other Northern Ireland cities. Two soldiers and 21 civilians have died in three days.

Britain will join Common Market

London, 28 October
Shouts erupted in the British parliament tonight as the House of Commons ended a 14-year debate and approved membership in the European Common Market.

Polls show that a majority of the country oppose entering the market, but the 356-244 vote was seen as a victory for Prime Minister Heath and his Conservative Party.

Victory for Prime Minister Heath.

Serpico tells all on police payoffs

Detective Frank Serpico testifies.

New York, 14 December
Detective Frank Serpico, deaf in one ear from a bullet wound in the head, told the Knapp Commission of his efforts to tell high-ranking New York City officials of police corruption. For five months, Serpico complained to Jay Kriegel, a close aide to Mayor John Lindsay, and to City Commissioner of Investigation Arnold Fraiman of his fellow officers' dealings in the city's underbelly. They failed to act. Serpico testified to instances of policemen taking "nuts" – payoffs.

Bangladesh established

Pakistan, 25 April
The government of West Pakistan refuses to admit that secessionists even exist in East Pakistan. But they do. They have formed a new cabinet, and given themselves a name: Bangladesh, or Bengal nation. Tajuddin Ahmed, who has acted as deputy to the political leader Sheikh Mujibur Rahman, is the prime minister and minister of defence. Sheikh Rahman has been named president, although it is conceded that he is a prisoner in West Pakistan. You cannot read about any of these developments in West Pakistani papers, and authorities there are reluctant to allow foreign journalists to travel in the East. But reports indicate that troops from the West are using brutal, unrestrained force to eliminate political dissidents in the East. There has been a wholesale slaughter of students and intellectuals. Entire villages suspected of harbouring Rahman's sympathisers have been burned to the ground.

East Pakistan: a suspected Bangladesh guerrilla is found shot dead.

Printing of Pentagon Papers is upheld

Washington, 30 June
The Supreme Court has overruled government attempts to stop the *New York Times* and *Washington Post* from publishing articles based on a secret Pentagon study of the Vietnam War. The government thus failed in the first attempt in US history to stop newspapers publishing facts on the grounds of national security. By a 6-3 vote, the court held that imposing "prior restraint" had "a heavy presumption against its constitutional validity".

Pakistan gives in to India, ending war

Pakistan, 17 December
President Yahya Khan of Pakistan changed his position dramatically today and announced he would accept a cease-fire with India. Only yesterday, after his forces in East Pakistan surrendered unconditionally, Yahya Khan vowed to keep fighting in the West against this political enemy. His reversal today undermines his administration, and there are growing indications he will step down as head of the military government.

Yahya has been criticised for his brutal repression of the Bengali separatists, who have renamed East Pakistan as Bangladesh. India was quick to recognise the rebel government, and the conflict between East and West Pakistan was a major cause of this war. This war has created new frictions between the United States and India.

1972

Bangladesh, 30 January. Sheikh Mujibur Rahman becomes prime minister of newly independent Bangladesh.

Northern Ireland, 30 January. British troops fire on crowd of civil rights protesters in Londonderry, killing 13 and injuring 17.

Dublin, 2 February. The British embassy is destroyed by a crowd protesting at the "Bloody Sunday" shootings of 30 January.

California, 18 January. Californian Supreme Court rules the death penalty unconstitutional.

Britain, 22 February. The IRA bomb a barracks in Aldershot, killing seven.

USA, 2 March. *Pioneer 10* unmanned spacecraft launched on 21-month journey to Jupiter.

Washington, 22 March. The Senate passes the Equal Rights Amendment.

France, 28 May. Duke of Windsor, who abdicated as Britain's King Edward VIII in 1936 to marry divorced American Wallis Simpson, dies, aged 77.

Tel Aviv, 30 May. Japanese Red Army terrorists massacre 25 at the airport.

Washington, 2 May. John Edgar Hoover, former director of the FBI, dies, aged 77.

Hanover, 16 June. West Germany's most wanted terrorist, Ulrike Meinhof, is arrested.

London, 18 July. Reginald Maudling resigns as home secretary because of his connections with John Poulson, an architect on trial for corruption.

Uganda, 6 August. Idi Amin starts expelling 50,000 Asians with British passports.

Vietnam, 11 August. The last US ground forces withdraw from Vietnam.

Munich, 31 August. US swimmer Mark Spitz brings his tally of individual gold medals to four; he also won three relay golds in Munich.

Washington, 3 October. Nixon signs a mutual agreement with the USSR to limit nuclear arms.

Britain, 6 November. Prime Minister Edward Heath imposes a 90-day freeze on wages, prices and rents.

Argentina, 17 November. Juan Peron returns after 17-year exile.

Nicaragua, 25 December. An earthquake hits the capital, Managua, killing 100,000.

Kansas City, 26 December. Former US president Harry S Truman dies, aged 88.

US crash survivors report cannibalism

Chile, 26 December

Survivors of an air crash in the Andes mountains admitted to eating the bodies of other passengers during a 69-day ordeal. Most of the 16 who survived were in Santiago, Chile, yesterday to attend a Christmas mass. On 13 October, their Uruguayan air force plane crashed, and 29 aboard were killed.

Rescue is at hand in the Andes.

Four more join Common Market

Brussels, 22 January

After ten years of difficult negotiations, the European Common Market was enlarged today to include Britain, Ireland, Denmark and Norway. With the signing of the Treaty of Brussels, the ten-nation community becomes, in principle, one of the world's great economic powers with a population greater than the United States or the Soviet Union.

Heath signs for Common Market.

Nixon on visit to China

Shanghai, 28 February

President Nixon is flying home from Shanghai today, convinced that his week-long visit to China has helped build a new "generation of peace". Premier Chou En-lai gave the present secretary of state, William Rogers, and adviser Henry Kissinger a warm farewell, but he refused to characterise his 15 hours of talks with Nixon. Chou said he would let the joint communique "speak for itself".

Throughout Nixon's visit, both sides were aware that American recognition of Taiwan has been a major stumbling block in relations and in the communique, the United States said the problem should be resolved "by the Chinese themselves". Nixon also committed himself to the "ultimate objective of the withdrawal of all United States forces and military installations from Taiwan". Privately, however, administration officials said Nixon has no intention of abandoning Nationalist China. The Americans and Chinese stopped short of saying when they might establish diplomatic relations, but they did promise to increase informal contacts. They also noted their differences on Vietnam and Korea.

Nixon meets with the Chinese Communist premier Chou En-lai in Peking.

It's a victory for Nixon by a landslide

Washington, 8 November

President Richard M Nixon piled up a huge majority yesterday to win a second term in the White House. In the popular vote, the incumbent president lost only Massachusetts and the District of Columbia to Senator George S McGovern, the Democratic candidate, while in the electoral college, Nixon received 520 votes to McGovern's 17.

Nixon's victory was reminiscent of the landslide triumphs of Franklin D Roosevelt in 1936 and Lyndon B Johnson in 1964. Spiro Agnew is once again to be Nixon's vice president.

Seven in Watergate break-in indicted

Washington, 15 September

Two former White House aides, E Howard Hunt and G Gordon Liddy, were among the seven men indicted in Washington today on charges of conspiring to break into the Democratic national headquarters in Washington's Watergate complex three months ago. Liddy is a former presidential assistant on domestic affairs and at the time of the break-in was counsel to the finance committee for re-electing the president. Hunt once served as a White House consultant.

The five others indicted in the US District Court were seized by police during the break-in early on June 17. A spokesman for the White House said there is "absolutely no evidence" that any other people were involved.

Britain imposes direct rule on N Ireland

London, 24 March
Britain's Prime Minister Heath took dramatic steps today to stop the sectarian violence that has flared up again in Northern Ireland. He suspended the provincial government and parliament and established direct rule. William Whitelaw was appointed secretary of state for Northern Ireland. Some 4,000 additional British soldiers were put on standby; 15,000 are already stationed in Northern Ireland. Protestant leaders condemned the moves as surrender to "terrorist violence". Catholics applauded the abolition of the Protestant-dominated provincial government.

Britain has 15,000 troops in Northern Ireland; 4,000 more on standby.

North Vietnamese invade the South

US troops on the Quangtri road.

Vietnam, 30 April
North Vietnamese and Viet Cong troops are tightening the noose around the provincial capital of Quangtri. If the city collapses, Hue and Danang could be next. South Vietnamese forces in the north of the country have been on the run since early this month, when the equivalent of two Communist divisions launched a major attack across the demilitarised zone.

Advancing under heavy cloud cover, the Communist forces have been almost immune from air attacks and managed to seize half of Quangtri Province within just a couple of days.

Americans bomb Hanoi and Haiphong

Washington, 13 May
President Nixon ordered his military commanders to step up B-52 raids around Hanoi and Haiphong as his latest peace proposals were rejected by the Communists in Paris. Soviet-built MiG fighters rose to attack the American planes on Thursday. The Pentagon says ten of the MiGs were shot down. Three American planes were lost, and four crewmen are missing. The communists claim they shot down 16 American planes.

The American command in Vietnam said today that it knocked out a major target, an important bridge, on the bombing raids.

Arabs massacre 11 Israeli Olympians

The wrecked transfer helicopter after the West German rescue attempt.

Lebanon, 8 September
Israeli jets streaked deep into Lebanon and Syria today, bombing and strafing Palestinian guerrilla bases in retaliation for the bloody massacre at the Olympic Games. In Munich, the Games went on without Israeli athletes.

The terrorist assault on the Israeli compound in Munich began early Tuesday morning, the 5th. Black September guerrillas infiltrated the area where 10,000 athletes are staying. At 5 am, the commandos broke into the Israelis' building. A coach managed to sound an alarm, allowing some members of the team to escape. Two Israelis, later identified as Joseph Romano and Moshe Weinberg, were shot dead. Nine more were taken hostage.

The terrorists demanded the release of 200 Palestinians from Israeli jails and safe passage from West Germany. Israel refused to release any prisoners, but just before midnight, the Germans flew the terrorists and hostages by helicopter to a waiting aircraft. An abortive rescue attempt followed, in which all nine hostages died, along with four guerrillas and a German police officer.

Rock samples brought back from moon

Astronaut John Young uses a surface rake to collect rocks on the moon.

Pacific Ocean, 27 April
Apollo 16, carrying more than 200lb (90 kilograms) of rocks from the moon, splashed down today after an 11-day lunar exploration mission. Astronauts John W Young and Charles M Duke Jr spent a record 71 hours on the moon, while the third crew member, Thomas K Mattingly, orbited in the command ship. "You got your money's worth on this one," Young said.

1973

Texas, 22 January. Former US president Lyndon Baines Johnson dies, aged 64.

Northern Ireland, 7 February. A general strike by Unionists cripples the province.

Israel, 22 February. Air force jets shoot down a Libyan Boeing airliner, killing 74.

USA, 27 February. Native Americans seize ten hostages at Wounded Knee in protest at government neglect of their people.

California, 4 March. Scientists report that rings of Saturn are composed of large chunks of solid matter.

Washington, 30 April. The Watergate scandal forces four top White House aides – John Ehrlichman, Bob Haldeman, Richard Kleindienst and John Dean – to resign.

Washington, 11 May. A judge dismisses the charges against Daniel Ellsberg, who leaked Pentagon Papers.

Washington, 17 July. The Senate hears that Nixon regularly bugged his own Oval Office conversations.

Britain, 30 July. An 11-year battle over thalidomide compensation ends with a £20 million court settlement.

Vienna, 28 September. Death of poet and 1930s icon WH Auden, aged 66.

Middle East, 21 October. Arabs put an embargo on oil to the US in protest against the US's support of Israel.

Puerto Rico, 22 October. Pablo Casals, cellist, dies, aged 96.

USA, 23 October. President Nixon, faced with possible impeachment, agrees to hand over key Watergate tapes.

Greece, 25 November, The army seizes power, deposing President Papadopoulos.

Israel, 1 December. David Ben Gurion, modern Israel's first premier and one of its founding fathers, dies from a brain haemorrhage aged 87.

Britain, Ireland, 17 December. Britain and Ireland reach accord; Northern Ireland to get coalition government with Catholic and Protestant politicians.

Britain, 17 December. The government puts the country on a three-day week in response to the hike in oil prices and to industrial disputes in the mines and power stations and on the railways.

Picasso changed our point of view

France, 8 April

The century's greatest artist, Pablo Picasso, has died at his estate in southern France. He was 92 years old. An entire museum could be built around Picasso's work, which was extensive and varied. *Les Demoiselles d'Avignon* (1907) and *Guernica* (1937) are two master works among many.

Picasso: "Portrait of Dora Maar".

The Watergate hearings begin

Washington, 17 May

A Nixon campaign official was the first witness as a special Senate committee opened hearings today into the plot to spy on the Democrats last year and efforts to cover it up. Robert C Odle Jr testified that the file Jeb Stuart Magruder, deputy director of the president's re-election campaign had on his desk, contained "things which have no place in a political campaign".

Robert Odle testifies to the Senate.

Oil embargo brings economic disruption

Britain and USA, 31 December

The Arab oil embargo has led to plans for fuel rationing in the United States, crippling oil price increases for industrialised and Third World countries and a three-day working week in Britain.

The disruption caused by the embargo has led the British government to announce it was shifting from a goal of economic growth to one of survival. It said the oil shortage made the three-day week necessary despite its dire effects on British industry.

In the US, Federal Energy Director William Simon has announced a standby fuel rationing programme that would limit most motorists to about eight gallons (30 litres) a week.

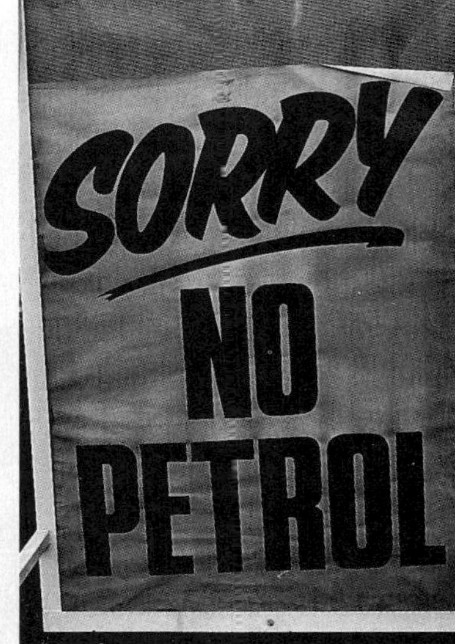

Fuel runs out at filling stations.

Airliner explodes in Paris, killing six

Paris, 3 June

The Soviet Union's Tu-144 supersonic airliner exploded during a flight at the Paris Air Show today, killing its crew of six. The Tu-144 was the first commercial supersonic airliner.

This crash, as well as being a tragic loss of life, is a major blow to Soviet aviation plans.

The Tu-144 came down on Goussainville, near Le Bourget Airport.

Spain's premier a victim of Basque blast

Spain, 29 December

Nine days have passed since the premier of Spain was killed by a powerful bomb explosion in Madrid. No arrests have been made in the case, but the regime of Generalissimo Francisco Franco indicated again today that it will deal harshly with the Basque separatists who have been linked to the murder. Franco appointed the interior minister Carlos Arias Navarro to succeed the late Luis Carrero Blanco as premier. Arias, a former prosecutor and public official, is a strong advocate of law and order.

Franco's government showed in the courts that it will strike back firmly at political dissidents. Ten labour leaders were given prison sentences of up to 20 years. The defendants were accused of running labour commissions that have ties to the Communist Party.

Attack at Yom Kippur

Egypt and Syria launched a surprise attack on Israelis during Yom Kippur.

Middle East, 22 October
The heaviest fighting since 1967 erupted in the Middle East this month, and for a short period of time the Egyptians and Syrians were able to batter the invincible Israeli war machine. They launched a surprise attack on the 6th in the middle of Yom Kippur, the most solemn religious holiday of the Jewish year. Egyptian forces crossed the Suez Canal and quickly controlled most of the eastern bank. Syrian artillery attacked the Golan Heights, and Syria said its forces had recaptured Mount Hermon for the first time since 1967.

Israel acted quickly to mobilise its ground forces, but it was the air force that prevented an Arab rout. Israeli jets struck deep into Syria and Egypt. They scored their biggest successes along the Suez Canal, knocking out nine bridges.

US role in Vietnam War comes to an end

Paris, 27 January
The official cease-fire agreement that effectively ends the American combat role in the Vietnam War was signed here today. According to the statement agreed to by Henry Kissinger and North Vietnamese negotiator Le Duc Tho, the cease-fire order will take effect at 8 am tomorrow (Saigon time). The agreement also stipulates that the North Vietnamese will release all American prisoners of war and that all American troops will be removed from South Vietnam. In addition, it calls for the end to foreign military intervention in Laos and Cambodia and for the establishment of an international force to supervise the truce itself.

Dr Kissinger and Le Duc Tho signed a cease-fire agreement in Paris.

Chile coup: Allende ousted, now dead

Chile, 21 September
Chilean president Salvador Allende Gossens was shot to death in a violent takeover of the government by Chile's armed forces earlier this month, and now the Marxist leader's wife believes the United States sponsored the coup.

Declaring devout dedication to freeing Chile "from the Marxist yoke", a military junta, led by General Augusto Pinochet Ugarte, captured the presidential palace and proclaimed a state of siege. Initial reports indicated Allende committed suicide. Yet, based on new information, Mrs Allende is convinced her husband was murdered, and she feels America financed and helped plan the coup. "We often heard the [US] State Department did not want Allende in power," she said. "Financial interests always predominate." Allende had seized the property of several US corporations who profited in Chile.

Allende (l) shortly before his death.

Military coup in Greece: curfew in effect

Greece, 25 November
President George Papadopoulos of Greece was ousted today in a military coup. The president was put under house arrest and replaced by Lieutenant General Phaidon Gizikis, who was an active participant in the 1967 coup. Premier Spyros Markezinis was dismissed and all the other supporters of Papadopoulos were purged. Leaders of the coup said they had acted to save Greece from "chaos and catastrophe". They are known to believe Papadopoulos was moving too quickly to restore democracy. Military leaders also blamed him for recent violent demonstrations.

Gerald Ford is VP: Agnew has to resign

President Nixon was at Gerald Ford's side when he was sworn into office.

Washington, 6 December
Gerald R Ford has taken the oath as 40th vice president of the United States, replacing Spiro T Agnew, who resigned in disgrace before pleading no contest to a charge of income tax evasion. Chosen according to a new constitutional procedure for replacing a vice president, Ford was sworn in with his wife, Betty, their children and President Nixon at his side.

A veteran of 25 years in Congress, Vice President Ford, aged 60, has been House minority leader since 1965.

1974

USA, 8 February. Skylab astronauts return after 84 days in Earth orbit.

Paris, 3 March. A DC-10 flying to London crashes outside Paris, killing all 344 people aboard.

Washington, 15 March. Federal grand jury has convicted President Nixon as a co-conspirator in the Watergate affair.

Britain, 6 March. After election created by the miners' strike, Harold Wilson forms a minority Labour government.

Paris, 2 April. President Pompidou dies, aged 62.

West Germany, 6 May. Willy Brandt resigns as chancellor after a spy is found working in his office.

Israel, 16 May. Sixteen children die in a gunbattle after being taken hostage by Palestinian terrorists.

France, 19 May. Giscard d'Estaing is elected president with a tiny majority.

Northern Ireland, 17 May. Four car bombs explode on the same day, killing 28.

India, 18 May. India tests its first nuclear bomb.

USA, 24 May. Jazz musician Duke Ellington dies, aged 75.

Northern Ireland, 28 May. General strike by Unionists topples Brain Faulkner's power-sharing executive.

USA, 14 June. Dr Henry Heimlich has developed a special manoeuvre which prevents people from choking to death.

Toronto, 30 June. Mikhail Baryshnikov, leading Soviet ballet star, defects to West.

Washington, 9 August. Presidential aides John Dean and John Ehrlichman sentenced to imprisonment for misconduct.

Washington, 9 August. Gerald Ford is sworn in as president.

Portugal, 30 September. President Spinola resigns warning his country is plunging into chaos.

Britain, 11 October. Labour Party wins power with a tiny majority in the year's second general election.

Britain, 21 November. Seventeen people die in two Birmingham pubs bombed by the IRA.

Pakistan, 29 December. Earthquake kills 4,700 and injures 15,000.

Britain, 31 December. Inflation over the year hits 20 per cent.

Turks invade Cyprus: island cut in two while thousands flee

Cyprus, 16 August

Tens of thousands of refugees clogged the roads of Cyprus today as victorious Turkish invaders split the island in two. The northern third of the island is controlled by some 30,000 Turkish troops who began an all-out offensive against Greek Cypriots on Wednesday. A cease fire went into effect at 6 pm.

The situation on Cyprus has splintered the Atlantic alliance. Greece, complaining that its NATO partners have refused to help in the struggle against Turkey, withdrew its forces from the alliance on Wednesday. Constantine Karamanlis, the premier of Greece, refused an offer from Turkey tonight to resume the Cyprus peace talks in Geneva. He also rejected an invitation from President Ford to visit Washington. Karamanlis said it would be ridiculous for Greece to "negotiate under the pressure of a *fait accompli*". Secretary of State Kissinger said he is willing to visit Cyprus to help arrange a political settlement. Cyprus has been in turmoil since its independence.

A Turkish M-48 tank in Famagusta as Turkish troops occupy the town.

Patty Hearst joins captors' bank raid

Hearst with gun and SLA flag.

San Francisco, 15 April

This morning, Patricia Hearst pointed a rifle not at one of her captors, but at a bank teller. The newspaper heiress assisted the Symbionese Liberation Army in its hold-up of a San Francisco bank. The FBI is not sure if Miss Hearst acted on her own free will or "under duress and coercion". Another SLA member was seen pointing a gun in her direction.

Since her abduction by the SLA on 4 February, Miss Hearst has apparently embraced the group's ideals to "free oppressed people".

Ali KOs Foreman to regain his title

Zaire, 29 October

In an unlikely setting in Zaire, under an African moon a few hours before dawn, Muhammad Ali knocked out George Foreman and became the second man in boxing history to regain the world heavyweight championship. The other was Floyd Patterson. The 32-year-old Ali floored his 25-year-old rival in the eighth round of what was to have been a 15-round bout. "Ali, kill him," most of the 60,000 fans chanted as Ali took Foreman's most powerful punches and came back stronger than ever.

1,000 killed in Irish troubles

Belfast, 20 April

James Corbett, who was a Roman Catholic resident of the city of Belfast, became a grisly statistic today. He was the 1,000th person killed in the terrorist violence that has plagued Northern Ireland since the summer of 1969.

The civil unrest in Ulster which claimed Corbett's life has accelerated since the practice of detention without trial was introduced in the province by the British government in August 1971.

Bloodless coup deposes Selassie

Ethiopia, 12 September

Emperor Haile Selassie, who ruled Ethiopia for 58 years, largely in regal and opulent splendour, was driven away from his palace today in a very unregal Volkswagen. His reign was at an end. The military leaders who ousted Selassie accuse him of tolerating corruption and forcing most of the country to live in abject poverty. The coup was bloodless, and its leaders invited Selassie's son, Crown Prince Asfa Wossen, to return as a figurehead king. The military promise to return land to the people.

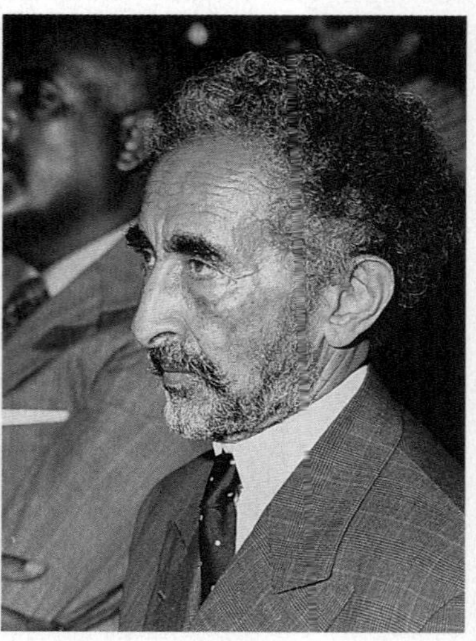

Emperor Haile Selassie dethroned.

Nixon quits, first president to do so

As his family looks on, Richard M Nixon resigns the presidency.

Washington, 8 August
President Nixon, faced with impeachment in Congress, has announced he is resigning, to be succeeded by Vice President Ford.

Less than two years after his landslide re-election victory, Nixon found himself so entangled in the Watergate scandal that he was forced to become the first president in history to resign from office. Only one other president, Andrew Johnson, has faced impeachment; the attempt to remove him in 1868 came to a Senate vote but failed.

Nixon's combative language of the past was gone as he told the nation in a conciliatory speech that he was resigning with the hope that this would start a "process of healing that is so desperately needed in America". Speaking to the nation from the Oval Office, the president, in tones more of sadness than bitterness, expressed regret for any "injuries" caused by his actions and acknowledged that some of his judgements had been wrong.

In describing his personal pain at leaving office, Nixon said, "I have never been a quitter. To leave office before my term is completed is opposed to every instinct in my body." But he had decided to put "the interests of America first".

Only three days before the speech, the president had acknowledged that six days after the Watergate burglary, he had ordered a halt to the investigation of the break-in for political and national security reasons and had withheld the information from his lawyers and the House Judiciary Committee.

Soviets expel Solzhenitsyn

Solzhenitsyn banished for his work.

Switzerland, 15 February
The Soviet author Alexander I Solzhenitsyn arrived in Switzerland today following his expulsion from the USSR two days ago. The Nobel Prize-winner was banished after publication of his new work on the prison system, *The Gulag Archipelago, 1918-1986.*

Ford gives Nixon unconditional pardon

President Ford insisted giving Nixon a full pardon would end the tragedy.

Washington, 16 September
Although mounting evidence indicates former president Nixon may have engaged in criminal acts at the Watergate scandal, he will not be tried on any charges, since President Ford, earlier this month, granted full and unconditional pardon to his predecessor. Today, Ford also granted immunity to Vietnam-era draft evaders.

In his proclamation pardoning Nixon, Ford said the former chief executive, who is in ill health, has already "paid the unprecedented penalty of relinquishing" the presidency. He said the act will spare Nixon and the nation additional grief in this "American tragedy".

The reaction from politicians and citizens has ranged from outright anger to full support of Ford's historic move. Many believe, as Ford enunciated, that the former president has suffered enough and that obtaining a fair trial by jury would be nearly impossible. Others feel it does a disservice to justice.

Portuguese army to end dictatorial rule

Flowers and wine given to troops.

Lisbon, 27 April
When military leaders seize control of a government, they generally suspend the constitution and civil liberties. Just the opposite seems to be happening in Portugal. A seven-man junta has thrown Premier Marcello Caetano out of office and promised to end 40 years of dictatorial rule. Flowers were thrown at soldiers patrolling the streets of Lisbon, and civilians even emerged from liquor stores offering them bottles of wine.

General Antonio de Spinola, leader of the junta, exiled Caetano to Madeira. Spinola promised democratic reform and elections.

Aerosol gases threaten the ozone layer

25 September
Freon gases released from aerosol spray cans are destroying the ozone layer that protects the Earth from lethal ultraviolet radiation, scientists reported today.

Unless use of Freon is reduced, they warn that about 15 per cent of the ozone layer, which is 10 to 15 miles (17 to 25 kilometres) aloft in the Earth's atmosphere, will be destroyed by the year 2000. Writing in the journal *Science,* researchers Michael McElroy and Steven Wofsy claim that the breakdown of the ozone layer could cause a major increase in skin cancer and unpredictable changes in the Earth's weather patterns.

The Freon-using companies have disputed these reports as "largely hypothesis".

1975

Vietnam, 25 March. The South Vietnamese city of Hue, a former imperial capital, falls to the advancing North Vietnamese Army.

Riyadh, 25 March. King Faisal of Saudi Arabia is assassinated by his nephew.

Vietnam, 29 March. Danang, South Vietnam's second-largest city, falls to the North Vietnamese Army.

Formosa, 5 April. Chiang Kaishek, president of Nationalist China and last of the great wartime leaders, dies, aged 87.

USA, 15 May. President Ford announces that US marines have retaken *Mayaguez*, the US merchant ship fired on and seized by Cambodian forces on the 12th.

West Germany, 21 May. The trial begins of the Baader-Meinhof terrorist group.

Britain, 6 June. In a referendum the British vote over 2-1 in favour of staying in the Common Market.

India, 12 June. The prime minister, Mrs Indira Gandhi, is found guilty of electoral corruption.

New York, 24 June. A Boeing 727 crashes at Kennedy Airport, 109 dead.

London, 5 July. Arthur Ashe becomes the first black player to win the Wimbledon men's singles title.

Helsinki, 1 August. 35 nations sign the Helsinki agreement on peace and human rights.

San Francisco, 18 September. Heiress Patty Hearst, seized by the Symbionese Liberation Army 18 months ago, appears in court on a robbery charge.

Scotland, 3 November. The queen opens the first underwater pipeline carrying North Sea oil.

Australia, 11 November. Sir John Kerr, the governor general, dismisses Prime Minister Gough Whitlam.

Angola, 24 November. Some 40,000 people are believed killed in fighting in the two weeks since independence.

London, 12 December. Police successfully arrest four IRA gunmen holding a couple hostage in Marylebone's Balcombe Street.

Vienna, 21 December. Palestinian gunmen, led by infamous terrorist "Carlos", take 11 oil ministers hostage at OPEC headquarters.

Saigon surrenders to Communists

Saigon, 30 April

Shortly after noon today, the Viet Cong flag was raised over the presidential palace in Saigon. Duong Van Minh, president of South Vietnam for only nine days, surrendered unconditionally to the Communists. Saigon was quickly renamed Ho Chi Minh City. American forces were gone, two decades after they had first arrived.

Scores of tanks from North Vietnam and trucks built in China rolled into the capital. Some Saigon residents cheered the arrival of the Viet Cong. Others raced to pillage the American embassy that had propped up former regimes against the Communists. Everything was stolen, and a plaque with the names of five Americans killed at the embassy in 1968 was thrown on the floor.

Thousands of South Vietnamese soldiers, unable to find space on American helicopters, begged for seats on river boats to speed them from Saigon. Many did not make it. As they were rounded up, the Communists cut off communications with the outside world. Speaking in Paris, a representative of the Provisional Revolutionary Government called the collapse of Saigon "a victory of historic significance for the Vietnamese". The departure of the Americans seemed as disorganised as their war effort. The Ford administration was divided in its approach until a few days ago.

Soldiers of the Provisional Revolutionary Government watch their tanks.

Franco's choice Juan Carlos rules Spain

At his proclamation ceremony the king acknowledged need for reforms.

Spain, 22 November

Spain has a new leader today. He has a tough act to follow, and it is not clear how he will proceed. Juan Carlos de Borbon was proclaimed king two days after Generalissimo Francisco Franco died in Madrid. In a posthumous message, Franco appealed for unity in the country and warned that the "enemies of Spain and Christian civilisation are watching". Juan Carlos, who was handpicked by Franco, swore that he would remain faithful to his principles. He also acknowledged, however, the pressure for reform. Without committing himself to change, Juan Carlos said he would encourage "far-reaching improvements". The audience, some in the distinctive blue shirts of the semi-fascist *Falange*, applauded only when he called indirectly for the recapture of Gibraltar.

The Communists capture Cambodia

Cambodia, 17 April

Communist-led forces have seized control of the capital city of Phnom Penh, ending a five-year civil war in Cambodia. The new military government supported by the United States surrendered without a major fight after it became apparent that the Communist-led insurgents were prepared to attack the city. As white flags fluttered over downtown buildings, Communist patrols moved through the city, warning residents to evacuate to the countryside.

As a last-minute gesture, the American embassy had proposed the return from Beijing of Prince Sihanouk, the nominal leader of the insurgents, who was overthrown in 1970 by the US-supported Lon Nol regime. The proposal was rejected by the military leaders who had taken control of the government in recent days. It was not immediately clear what had happened to Premier Long Boret, who was on a Communist list of "traitors", but it was believed he had fled to Thailand.

Portugal grants Angola independence

Angola, 16 January
A nation was born today. After centuries of foreign rule and 13 years of struggle, the people in the Portuguese territory of Angola have gained their sovereignty. The actual date for independence is 11 November, but an agreement signed today seals Angolan liberation. Portugal lost control in what is one of its last colonial territories in Africa, when a coup by the military ousted the authoritarian regime of Dr Caetano in Lisbon last April. Differences were set aside at a banquet for Portuguese and Angolan officials celebrating today's accord.

Crowds celebrate independence from Portugal, in Nova Lisboa, Angola.

China finds 2,000-year-old figures

Funerary figures are unearthed.

China, 11 July
Chinese archaeologists have announced the uncovering of a three-acre (1.2-hectare) burial mound concealing an "army" of funerary figures. *Hsinhua*, the official news agency, states that the site (in Shensi province, north-western China) contains 6,000 clay statues of warriors with regalia.

Tories get first woman leader

London, 11 February
Britain's Conservative Party has elected its first woman leader. Former minister of education Margaret Thatcher defeated former prime minister Edward Heath and four others for the post. "I am very, very thrilled," she said with uncharacteristic ardour. Mrs Thatcher, 49, is the daughter of a grocer. She studied chemistry at Oxford.

Margaret Thatcher to lead Tories.

CIA plotted deaths of foreign leaders

Washington, 20 November
A Senate select committee reported today that American officials plotted to kill, through the Central Intelligence Agency, two foreign leaders and were involved in plots to kill three others. Patrice Lumumba of the Congo (now Zaire) and Cuban premier Fidel Castro were targets in plots originating in Washington. Ngo Dinh Diem of South Vietnam, General Rene Schneider of Chile and Rafael Leonidas Trujillo of the Dominican Republic were killed in plots in which US officials played a part. No evidence directly linked the CIA to the murders.

Beirut torn by Moslems and Christians

The Holiday Inn, Beirut, blazes.

Beirut, 16 September
Civil war is tearing the country of Lebanon apart, turning streets of Beirut into walls of flame and threatening the government. Battles between heavily armed Moslems and Christians have left bodies and debris piled on the sidewalks. The cost of the damage has risen sharply to £8 billion. Foreign capital is fleeing from the once elegant and opulent capital.

Fighting erupted in Tripoli earlier this month. Today, it flared in Beirut. Moslems and Christians battled for control of different neighbourhoods. Shopkeepers and residents ducked for cover.

Americans and Russians meet in space

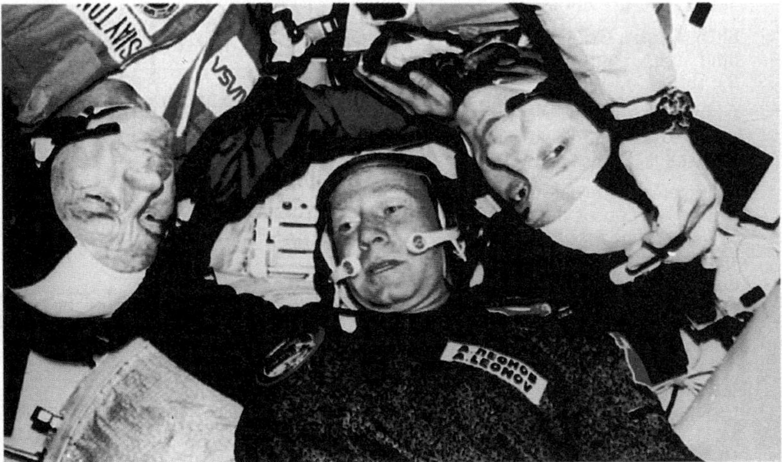

Cosmonaut Leonov greets US astronauts during their historic docking.

19 July
American and Soviet astronauts ended an unprecedented two-day international mission in space today as they undocked their *Apollo* and *Soyuz* spacecraft and went into separate orbits. The Soviets will return to Earth tomorrow; the Americans in five days.

The joint mission began with the two spacecraft, each carrying three astronauts, being launched four days ago. The Soviets broke their habitual secrecy by showing the launch of *Soyuz* live on television. The spacecraft linked together two days ago about 140 miles (225 kilometres) over the Atlantic.

"Glad to see you," Aleksei A Leonov, the Soviet commander, said in English. Thomas B Stafford, the US commander, replied in Russian. They shook hands through the hatches.

1976

China, 22 January. Prime Minister Chou En-lai dies aged 78.

Guatemala, 4 February. A devastating earthquake kills 12,000, and leaves over one million homeless.

Holland, 8 February. An official enquiry is announced into allegations that Prince Bernhard took bribes from the Lockheed aircraft company.

London, 16 March. Harold Wilson unexpectedly resigns as prime minister.

Argentina, 24 March. President Isabel Peron is deposed in a bloodless coup.

London, 5 April. Socialist James Callaghan is sworn in as prime minister.

China, 7 April. Hua Kuo-feng is new prime minister.

Texas, 5 April. Reclusive millionaire Howard Hughes dies, aged 70.

Portugal, 25 April. The first free elections for 50 years in Portugal produce a socialist government.

Southern Italy, 6 May. A severe earthquake kills 95, injures 1,000 and makes 80,000 homeless.

Lebanon, 16 May. Fighting breaks out between Christians and Moslems in Beirut as the 30th cease-fire collapses.

Oslo, 1 June. Britain and Iceland sign an agreement to end the third Cod War.

China, 29 July. The world's worst earthquake for a decade devastates Tangshan.

Montreal, 31 July. A widespread boycott of the Games by African nations protesting against New Zealand's sporting links with South Africa mars the Olympics.

USA, 28 August. Biologists in Massachusetts make the first synthetic gene.

Rhodesia, 24 September. Prime Minister Ian Smith announces transition to majority rule.

Britain, 29 September. A run on the pound drives the government to apply for a $3.9 billion loan from the IMF.

China, 23 October. Mao's widow and three other prominent radicals, dubbed the "Gang of Four", are officially branded as "like dog dung".

Britain, 5 December. Composer Benjamin Britten dies, aged 63.

Daring Israeli raid at Entebbe successful

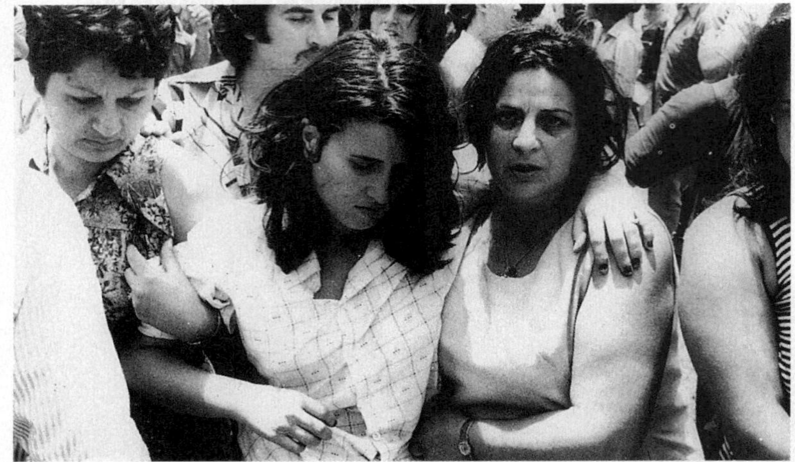

Relatives greet some of the 105 rescued hostages as they arrive in Israel.

Uganda, 4 July

Israeli commandos staged a daring raid last night to free 105 hostages held by pro-Palestinian hijackers at Uganda's Entebbe Airport. The terrorists had threatened to start shooting the mostly Israeli and Jewish hostages later today. They were whisked onto transport planes and flown to Israel. Preliminary reports say at least two hostages may have been killed. All the hijackers were reportedly killed.

The commandos flew more than 2,000 miles (3,200 kilometres) from Israel to Entebbe on three planes. After landing, they set off several explosive devices at one end of the airport to distract Ugandan forces.

Ugandan troops and President Idi Amin had reportedly been cooperating with the hijackers and had even furnished them with fresh weapons. The shoot-out took place in the old passenger terminal where the Arab, Palestinian and German terrorists had been holed up all week with the hostages.

The commando raid came as a surprise to many Israelis, who believed the government was negotiating with the hijackers. After commandeering the Air France jet last Sunday on a flight from Athens to Paris, the guerrillas demanded the release of 53 Palestinian and pro-Palestinian prisoners from jails in Israel and Europe. The Israeli cabinet had offered to release some of the prisoners in response to the demands, and so far no statement has been issued to indicate if this was in fact an attempt to buy time until they were ready to take action.

Patty Hearst is guilty of armed robbery

San Francisco, 20 March

Patricia Hearst, former hostage of the radical group called the Symbionese Liberation Army, has been found guilty of assisting its members in a bank heist.

The jury in the San Francisco courtroom did not sympathise with the arguments of her lawyer, F Lee Bailey, who contended the accused was coerced into taking part in the raid. According to Bailey, Miss Hearst spent weeks locked in closets, bombarded by propaganda. The jury may have sided with the prosecution in part because Miss Hearst often took the Fifth Amendment, refusing to testify.

Patty Hearst on her way to face trial.

Carter credits TV debates for victory

Washington, 2 November

Democrat Jimmy Carter, 52, was elected president today, sweeping his native south and some northern industrial states to defeat President Ford, a Republican, in a close election. Former governor of Georgia, Carter is the first man from the Deep South to be elected president in a century and a quarter. President Ford, the nation's first appointive head of state, is the first incumbent to lose a presidential election since Herbert Hoover in 1932. Carter gave much credit for his win to their televised debates.

The Fords with Jimmy Carter.

Pollution threatens Athens Acropolis

The crumbling ancient Acropolis.

Greece, 10 July

The Acropolis has withstood 24 centuries of wind, rain and military bombardment, but just fifty years of car exhaust fumes and factory fumes are too harsh for the monument to withstand. Today the Director General of UNESCO stood by the pitted edifice in Athens and appealed for donations for a rescue effort. While pollution is the main problem, years of tourists have not helped. Even the English poet Shelley etched his name on a column. More recent souvenir-hunters have been caught pocketing rubble and chipping the walls with chisels.

Violence follows protest in South Africa

Police follow instructions to restore order "at all costs" as black students riot.

Johannesburg, 19 June
The worst racial violence in 15 years has swept through the black townships outside Johannesburg. Police, under orders from Prime Minister John Vorster to restore order "at all costs", refused to release casualty figures. There are unconfirmed reports of at least 100 deaths. A picture on the front page of a South African newspaper this morning showed a 12-year-old girl dead in the street. Police say she had been rioting.

Trouble started on Tuesday when 10,000 black students marched in Soweto to protest at a government order to teach them the Afrikaans language, viewed as a symbol of the white minority government. Police say marchers began to riot. In the confrontations most of the valuable property in Soweto was destroyed leaving only hovels.

Mao Zedong dies at 82

Beijing, 18 September
Eight hundred million Chinese stood silent for three minutes today as the sirens of ships, trains and factories sounded in tribute to Mao Zedong, a giant among the giants of the twentieth century, who died nine days ago at the age of 82.

In Beijing, Hua Kuo-feng saluted Mao as the "founder and wise leader of the Communist Party of China, the Chinese People's Liberation Army and the People's Republic of China."

"It was under Chairman Mao's leadership that the Chinese people, who had long suffered from oppression and exploitation, won emancipation and became masters of the country. It was under Chairman Mao's leadership that the disaster-plagued Chinese nation rose to its feet," the top official said in eulogising the man who led the Communist takeover in 1949 then dominated the nation. Mao guided China from underdevelopment and isolation to the status of nuclear power with an expanding industrial base. He defied Soviet hegemony, purged rivals, opened a relationship with the US and won a seat in the UN. "The Chinese people love, trust and esteem Chairman Mao from the bottom of their hearts."

Eight days of mourning are over, but it may be millennia before China and the world forget Mao.

Chairman Mao Zedong is mourned.

America celebrates its 200th birthday

Streamers and confetti festoon cities all over America as the nation parties.

United States, 4 July
From coast to coast, this has been a day of tall ships, hamburgers and unrestrained fireworks displays. The United States celebrated its 200th birthday today, and millions joined in public festivities. Many more drove to beaches, mountains and parks to spend a peaceful time with their families.

The celebrations started on a mountain in Maine, where dawn first reached the country. Fireworks exploded around the clock from South Carolina to California, and parties were just starting on the American island of Hawaii as the rest of the country was fast asleep.

As part of the festivities over 10,000 people were naturalised in ceremonies in the cities of Chicago, Detroit and Miami.

Beirut factions reach a peace agreement

Beirut, 22 January
A Syrian-drawn peace accord was signed today by both opposing factions in Lebanon's civil war. While details have yet to be released, officials in Beirut announced that "all parties" had accepted "an all-embracing political statement". It seems some Moslem demands for sharing more political power were met while maintaining the rights of the minority Lebanese Christians.

The accord was reached two days after reports indicated Palestine Liberation Organisation troops had crossed the border in Syria to assist the Lebanese Moslems. The inclusion of the PLO in an already violent conflict worried Syria, chief arbitrator in the peace efforts.

Leftist leader Kamal Jumblat, who has fought the Christians on the side of the Moslems, said his faction accepts the accord and expressed gratitude for the "efforts exerted by sister Syria so that we may all get out of this bloodshed and crisis".

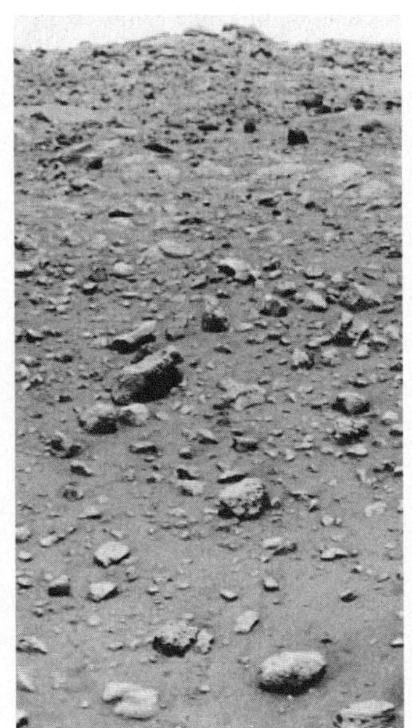

Out of this world is the only way to describe the photographs sent back from *Viking 1* after landing on the planet Mars. Now we on Earth can see the terrain there – with no little green men in sight.

1977

USA 17 January. Gary Gilmore, the convicted killer, is shot by a firing squad in Utah. He is the first man in ten years to be executed.

Ethiopia, 3 February. Chief of state and six other leaders killed in Addis Ababa.

Rhodesia, 6 February. A guerrilla band massacres seven white missionaries.

Uganda, 18 February. Idi Amin's latest wave of terror claims the life of the Archbishop of Uganda.

Congo, 19 March. President Marien Ngouabi killed by suicide commando.

India, 22 March. Mrs Gandhi's Congress Party is routed in the general election.

Britain, 24 March. The Liberal and Labour parties form a pact to keep the Labour government in power.

Canary Islands, 27 March. A KLM Jumbo jet collides with a Pan Am 747 on the ground, killing 574 people.

Holland, 11 June. Marines storm a train in which South Moluccan terrorists have been holding 55 hostages.

Spain, 15 June. Spain goes to the polls for the first time in 41 years. Voters resoundingly voted for the centre-right coalition of Prime Minister Adolfo Suarez.

Alaska, 20 June. Oil starts to flow through the 799-mile (1,280-km) Trans-Alaskan pipeline.

Paris, 17 September. Opera *diva* Maria Callas dies of a heart attack, aged 53.

Somalia, 18 October. West German commandos storm a hijacked jet at Mogadishu.

Philippines, 25 November. Former senator Benigno Aquino sentenced to death on charges including murder.

South Africa, 2 December. Police are cleared of causing the death of black activist Steve Biko while in their custody 12 weeks ago.

USA, 3 December. The State Department proposes admitting 10,000 Vietnamese boat people fleeing from their troubled nation.

Switzerland, 25 December. Cinema's greatest clown, Charlie Chaplin, dies, aged 88.

Space shuttle rides piggyback on 747

California, 18 February

The space shuttle, designed to be America's spaceplane of the 1980s, made its first flight today atop a Boeing 747 Jumbo jet. The flight, made from Edwards Air Force Base in California, was made to test the stability of the 747-shuttle combination, which will be used to transport the shuttle from the landing site to launch areas when it makes its first orbital flights, scheduled for 1979. Ten more 747-shuttle test flights will be performed before the craft is cut free from the jet for the first time, so it can glide back to Earth. The landing will simulate the return to Earth of the shuttle from orbital flights.

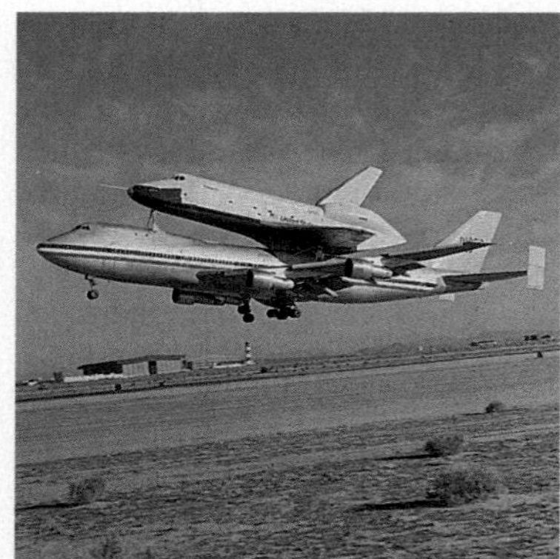

Space shuttle atop a Jumbo jet.

Boat people cannot land

Hong Kong, 23 December

The 2,700 Vietnamese refugees on board the freighter *Huey Pong* are unable to leave the vessel as the Hong Kong government refuses to allow them permission to land.

Emergency arrangements have been made for them by the Hong Kong government over the Christmas holiday period.

These have consisted of food supplies, including tinned meat and fish, rice and sweet biscuits, being flown aboard the ship by helicopter. Blankets were also included in this consignment.

Provisions to cover the Christmas period are stacked aboard "Huey Pong".

Peace Prize for Amnesty International

Oslo, 10 December

For "securing the ground for freedom", as the award committee put it when making the announcement, Amnesty International has been given the Nobel Peace Prize.

The London-based group was established in 1961 by lawyer Peter Benenson, its aim to petition for the freedom of prisoners of conscience. It is their rule that Amnesty International does not assist those who use or have advocated violence.

Begin beats Labour in Israeli elections

Israel, 18 May

Menachem Begin became Israel's new premier yesterday when the Likud Party, which he heads, emerged from 29 years of opposition to hand the hitherto dominant Labour Party, led by Shimon Peres, a surprising defeat. Likud's victory has stunned both foreign and domestic officials because of the party's hawkish stance regarding any compromise solution to the Arab conflict. Begin seems to have already considered this by calling immediately for a unity of "all Zionist parties". The Likud win apparently stems from its strong showing among the Sephardic Jews of North Africa and the Middle East, who now form the bulk of Israel's population.

Elvis Presley, king of rock'n'roll, is gone

Memphis, Tennessee, 16 August

Elvis Presley died at his Graceland mansion today. He was 42. Rock 'n' roll might still be an innocuous hillbilly genre had Elvis Aaron Presley not shown up. Born in Tupelo, Mississippi, to working-class parents, Presley had a voice brushed with a shade of Southern blues. When parents heard his first hit, *Heartbreak Hotel*, in January 1956, they knew they didn't want their teenagers to hear it, and when they saw him gyrating on the *Ed Sullivan Show* in September that year, they didn't want him seen, either. But his songs *Hound Dog*, *Don't Be Cruel*, *Love Me Tender* and *Blue Suede Shoes*, and his films, including *Jailhouse Rock,* had an irresistible appeal to a generation longing to seem a little more dangerous than it really was.

Elvis Presley inspired a generation.

Bokassa's coronation one of contrasts

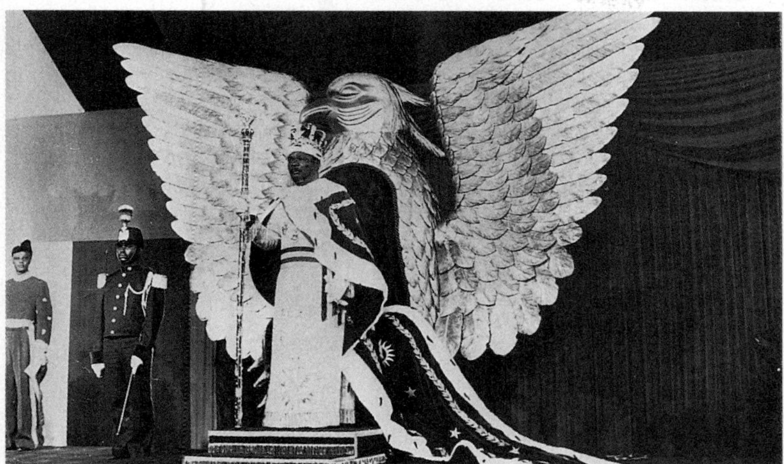

Crowned with 5,000 diamonds but Bokassa's throne is in a sports stadium.

Central Africa, 4 December
Today's coronation of Jean Bedel Bokassa, a former captain in the French colonial army, as emperor of the newly named Central African Empire was full of contradictions. His throne sat in the lap of a bronze eagle and his crown had 5,000 diamonds, but the ceremony was in a sports stadium. Mozart was played with tribal drums in the distance. His party reportedly cost US$30 million, but his country is one of the world's poorest.

Army arrests Bhutto: Zia now in power

Pakistan, 5 July
In a move unconstrained by political lines, the Pakistani army staged an apparently bloodless coup this morning, arresting Prime Minister Ali Bhutto and other prominent officials regardless of their political leanings. Following four months of civil unrest, the coup seems like an effort to stem further violence initially triggered by Bhutto's lopsided victory in last March's national elections.

As Bhutto was charged with fraud and corruption, protest demonstrations led to bloody rioting, with 300 killed. Prime Minister Bhutto arrested most of the opposition leaders and put major cities under martial law.

Bhutto's downfall, after five years in office, was ironic in that he had already admitted to some irregularities, had agreed to new elections and was preparing an election agreement with the opposition. For the army, which ruled Pakistan from 1958 to 1971, his conciliatory posture was apparently too little and too late. It is reported that General Zia ul-Haq will head up the new government.

Zia ul-Haq takes over in Pakistan.

Carter tells US to treat oil crisis like war

Washington, 18 April
President Carter warned tonight that the US faces a national catastrophe unless it responds with a "moral equivalent of war" to dwindling energy supplies. In his televised speech to the nation, the president proposed stringent conservation of fuels, higher energy prices and penalties for waste.

He said the nation would begin to run short of energy supplies in the 1980s unless "wasteful" use of fuels was stopped.

Roots draws record television audiences

United States, 1 February
More Americans watched the final episode of *Roots* tonight than tuned in to the first half of *Gone with the Wind* during its recent airing. The ABC mini-series reached a record 80 million viewers and was shown eight nights in a row, an unprecedented scheduling feat.

Roots, based on the family tree of author Alex Haley, traced the lineage of Kunta Kinte, a West African youth enslaved in America. LeVar Burton, Cicely Tyson and John Amos were among the series' stars. Its gritty, moving plot has all America's interest.

It is ironic that *Roots* should have drawn larger audiences than *Gone with the Wind.* Both are American Civil War tales, but the black experience in the Scarlett O'Hara epic was flatly ignored.

Author Alex Haley used family tree.

Egypt's Sadat addresses Israel's Knesset

In an unprecedented address to the Israeli parliament, Sadat pledged peace.

Israel, 21 November
Egypt's President Anwar Sadat ended an astounding visit to Israel today, joining hands with Prime Minister Menachem Begin and pledging "no more war". Noting that Israel and Egypt are technically still at war, Begin praised Sadat for making "this momentous visit". As he flew back to Cairo, Sadat was escorted part of the way by Israeli jet fighters.

The highlight of Sadat's visit occurred yesterday, when he made an unprecedented address to the Knesset and announced that he accepts the existence of Israel. "If you want to live with us in this part of the world," Sadat told the parliament, "in sincerity I tell you that we welcome you among us with all security and safety." Sadat emphasised, however, that Israel would have to recognise the rights of Palestinians and withdraw from occupied Arab lands. Begin praised his speech, but refused to withdraw from Arab territories.

1978

Belfast, 17 February. A bomb kills 14 in a restaurant.

Nicaragua, 9 March. National Guard chief General Perez Vega assassinated.

Lebanon, 14 March. Israeli troops attack Palestinian camps in reprisal for three bus hijacks.

Pakistan, 18 March. Deposed prime minister Zulfikar Ali Bhutto is sentenced to death.

France, 24 March. Stricken oil tanker the *Amoco Cadiz* splits in two and starts spilling oil onto Brittany beaches.

Afghanistan, 30 April. Soviet-backed army officers take over, assassinating the president.

Southern Zaire, 19 May. French and Belgian forces parachute into Kolwezi to try to free 3,000 foreigners trapped by Communist rebels.

Russia, 14 July. Three Soviet dissidents jailed to widespread protest from Western Europe and the USA.

Nicaragua, 22 August. A hundred rebels, led by Eden Pastora, seize 2,000 hostages in National Palace.

Rome, 26 August. Twenty days after the death of Paul VI, cardinals choose an Italian of peasant origins as Pope John Paul.

Rhodesia, 4 September. Guerrillas shoot down an airliner and open fire on survivors.

Iran, 8 September. Martial law is imposed after mass demonstrations against the shah.

Iran, 16 September. Enormous earthquake kills at least 25,000.

London, 29 September. A Bulgarian defector, Georgi Markov, is killed by a poisoned pellet from an umbrella point.

Rome, 30 September. Pope, John Paul, is found dead after only 33 days in office.

Iraq, 6 October. Iraq expels Iranian Ayatollah Khomeini.

Rome, 16 October. A Polish cardinal, Karol Wojtyla, becomes Pope John Paul II, the first non-Italian pope for over 400 years.

Israel, 8 December. Golda Meir, Israel's first woman prime minister, dies aged 88.

Oslo, 10 December. Israel's Prime Minister Begin and Egypt's President Sadat are jointly awarded the Nobel Peace Prize.

Sadat, Begin, Carter at Camp David

Camp David, 18 September
Israel's Prime Minister Begin and Egypt's President Sadat came down from the mountain last night to announce that they had reached agreement at Camp David. President Carter, who shuttled tirelessly between the two often hostile delegations for 13 days, appeared exhausted but smiling after fashioning two remarkable agreements.

Carter acknowledged that the accords were only a beginning. "There are still great difficulties that remain," he said. Sadat praised Carter, and Begin congratulated him for achieving "a great victory". He said the summit would be called the "Jimmy Carter Conference", and added, "He worked harder than our forefathers did in Egypt building the pyramids."

Sadat and Begin signed two separate documents. The first, *Framework for Peace in the Middle East*, calls for more negotiations to determine the future of the West Bank and the Gaza Strip. Israel agreed to withdraw almost all of its forces from the two areas and not to build any more settlements on the West Bank during the negotiations. The document does not guarantee the creation of a Palestinian state in the area, but one report says Begin did agree to "recognise the legitimate rights of Palestinians".

Whether Jordan's King Hussein will join the future talks between Egypt and Israel remains unclear.

After 13 days of negotiations Carter brings Begin and Sadat to an agreement.

Moro's body is found after eight weeks

The dead body of Aldo Moro was found crumpled in the back of a Renault.

Italy, 13 May
Pope Paul VI presided over a requiem mass today for Aldo Moro, the former prime minister of Italy who was assassinated this week by terrorists. The pope and Moro were friends. This was the first time in history that a pontiff had attended a requiem service for anyone other than a cardinal.

Aldo Moro's body was found crumpled in the back of a small Renault on Tuesday, nearly eight weeks after he was kidnapped in a blaze of gunfire by Red Brigade terrorists. The guerrillas demanded the release of Communist prisoners, but the Italian government refused to negotiate with them. Moro was buried on Wednesday in a small ceremony that was closed to public officials.

Rhodesians agreed on rule by blacks

Rhodesia, 21 March
The first step in Rhodesia's transition to majority rule was taken today when three black nationalists were sworn in as joint leaders of the country's new interim government. The black leaders – Bishop Abel Muzorewa, Rev Ndabaningi Sithole and Chief Jeremiah Chirau – will share executive power with Prime Minister Ian D Smith.

Joshua Nkomo does not back regime.

First test-tube baby is born in London

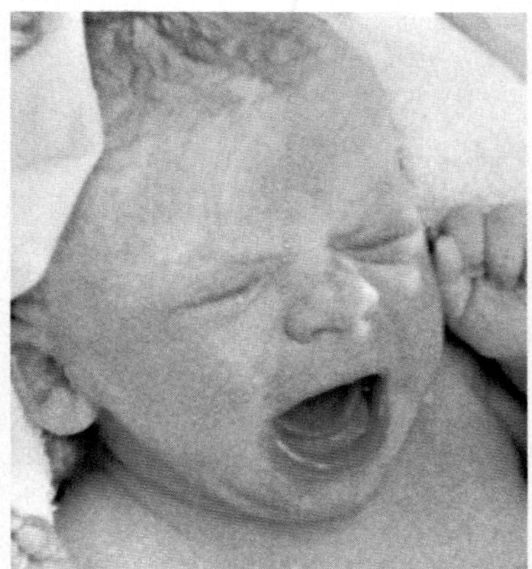

Louise Brown born perfectly healthy.

London, 25 July
The first baby to be conceived outside the human body was born today to a British couple, Lesley Brown and her husband, John. The baby weighed 5lb 12oz (2.6 kilograms) and was delivered by Caesarian section at Oldham General and District Hospital. Named Louise, she is normal and healthy.

Mrs Brown was unable to conceive because of a defect in the fallopian tubes, which carry an egg from the ovaries to the uterus each month. Dr Robert G Edwards and Patrick C Steptoe, the two British researchers who pioneered the so-called test-tube baby technique, removed an egg surgically from an ovary, fertilised it with sperm in a laboratory dish, and implanted the embryo in Lesley Brown's uterus, where it developed normally.

Oldest humanoid footprints are found

Anthropologist, Mary Leakey.

Washington, 24 February
Footprints that appear to be those of a human ancestor who lived 3.5 million years ago have been found at the bottom of an African watering hole, their discoverer, Mary D Leakey, announced today. The prints, which measure 6 inches (15 centimetres) long by 4.5 inches (11 centimetres) wide, were made by a creature about 4 feet (1.2 metres) tall. Studies indicate they were made by a being that moved slowly and took very short steps, Mrs Leakey said, adding that she was "seventy five per cent sure" they were made by an ancestor of the human race.

The trail of prints in Tanzania.

Somoza in struggle to control Nicaragua

Sandinista rebels want Somoza out.

Nicaragua, 29 September
President Anastasio Somoza struggled to put down an insurrection led by the leftist Sandinist National Liberation Front. Since fighting broke out, more than 1,500 people are believed to have been killed, with many casualties among the rebel force that is battling Somoza's National Guard and police force.

The Sandinistas started off as a small Marxist revolutionary group demanding the ousting of Somoza, then gained support as it battled government troops in half a dozen cities. As the fighting expanded, an emissary of President Carter urged Somoza to accept mediation by Latin American states to find a peaceful solution to the crisis.

900 American cultists die in mass suicide

United States, 29 November
Now the last of the bodies have been flown out of Guyana and returned to the United States, legal authorities, diplomats, psychologists and families try to work out why more than 900 American followers of a fanatical Californian committed suicide in the jungle of South America.

The bodies of the cultists, dressed in gaudy clothes, were found sprawled in the grounds of the so-called People's Temple in Jonestown, Guyana. Survivors say temple members took part in a mass suicide rite by swallowing a concoction of Kool-Aid and cyanide. The deadly potion was ladled into the mouths of infants. Small children were ordered to help themselves. Adults swallowed the punch willingly and collapsed in a death embrace, their arms wrapped around other cult members. The body of the leader, James Warren Jones, alias Rev Jim Jones, was found on the altar in the commune, a bullet wound in his head.

One follower said Jones wanted everyone to believe he was God. Others described him as paranoid, sex-crazed and power-hungry. He was apparently infuriated by the visit of California Congressman Leo Ryan to Jonestown.

Bodies found sprawled in the grounds of the People's Temple in Jonestown.

1979

Cambodia, 8 January. Vietnamese forces occupy Cambodia, ousting Pol Pot and the Khmer Rouge.

Vietnam, 17 February. Chinese and Vietnamese troops fight on their common borders in a complex conflict triggered by Vietnam's invasion of Cambodia.

Jupiter, 7 March. *Voyager 1* sends pictures showing Jupiter surrounded by a faint ring.

Britain, 28 March. The Labour government falls, defeated on a vote of confidence.

Uganda, 29 March. Idi Amin flees the country while his capital is under siege by the Tanzanian-backed Uganda Liberation Front.

London, 30 March. A bomb in the House of Commons car park kills Airey Neave, a senior aide to Thatcher.

Pakistan, 5 April. Former prime minister Bhutto hanged on order of President Zia.

South Africa, 4 June. Implication in the so-called "Muldergate" slush fund scandal forces the resignation of President Vorster.

Poland, 10 June. Pope John Paul II says mass to over a million in his native country in the first ever pontifical visit to a Communist country.

USA, 11 June. Hero of many westerns, John Wayne, dies, aged 72.

Vienna, 18 June. Carter and Brezhnev sign the SALT-2 arms limitation treaty.

Nicaragua, 21 August. Sandinistas ban capital punishment and restore human rights laws.

Ireland, 27 August. Lord Mountbatten is killed by an IRA bomb on his boat.

London, 21 November. The Keeper of the Queen's Pictures, Sir Anthony Blunt, is revealed as a Soviet spy.

Seoul, 26 November. President Park Chung Hee assassinated.

Antarctica, 28 November. 257 killed as DC-10 crashes into mountain.

London, 21 December. A deal is signed at Lancaster House to bring an end to the conflict in Rhodesia, which will take the name Zimbabwe.

Afghanistan, 26 December. Soviet troops invade Afghanistan to support the new president, Babrak Karmal.

Iran welcomes Khomeini

Tehran, 26 February

On 30 January the Shah of Iran was forced to leave the country because of the return of the Ayatollah Khomeini. In an emotional leaving speech the shah said, "I hope the government will be able to make amends for the past and also succeed in laying the foundation for the future.

Today the return of the Ayatollah Khomeini from Paris to Iran after 15 years of exile has unleashed a revolutionary fervour that was checked for years by the forces of the departed shah. It has also posed a direct threat to the interests of America. Millions of Shiite Moslems and other followers of the ayatollah jammed the streets of Tehran for his long motorcade at the beginning of the month. Within a matter of days, the new government put in place by the shah before he left was toppled. The US embassy was attacked and scores of Iranians who backed the Pahlavi regime were shot. Every day newspapers carry names of executed officials, many of them members of the secret police, the *Savak*.

Crowds greet Ayatollah Khomeini.

Mother Teresa is given Nobel prize

Mother Teresa: a living saint.

Oslo, 10 December

The Nobel Peace Prize was awarded tonight to Mother Teresa, the founder of a charitable empire now stretching to 700 shelters and clinics. Now frail in body, though not in spirit, she was born in Albania in 1910, and moved to a Calcutta convent at 18. She left its relative comfort in 1946 to pursue more direct work with India's poor.

Iranian militants seize the US embassy

Demonstrators burn the American flag on the roof of the US embassy in Iran.

Tehran, 20 November

A mob of 500 Iranian students seized the United States embassy here on 4 November, taking 90 hostages. The takeover has turned into a diplomatic nightmare, and the situation continues to deteriorate as President Carter begins to hit back. Carter's latest actions have been to freeze all of the considerable Iranian assets in America and to send a naval task force to the Indian Ocean, where carrier-based jets and helicopters would be within easy striking range of Iran.

Meanwhile, US television audiences have been shocked to see blindfolded marines of the US embassy guard, with their hands tied behind their backs, parade before cameras while students chanted "Death to America".

Egypt and Israel sign peace treaty

Middle East, 31 March

Egypt's President Anwar Sadat has made history by signing a peace treaty with Israel. He has also managed to isolate himself in the Arab world. The foreign ministers of 18 Arab countries moved in Baghdad today to cut diplomatic and economic relations with Cairo. Their decision was also approved by the Palestine Liberation Organisation. It calls for the immediate recall of ambassadors from Egypt, a complete termination of diplomatic relations within a month, an end to all financial aid and the imposition of economic sanctions. Egypt receives a billion dollars a year from other Arab countries, mainly Saudi Arabia.

Sadat indicated he was aware of the risks when he signed the peace agreement with Israel's Prime Minister Begin at the White House on Monday. Sadat also recognised its historic importance and he praised President Carter for his role in masterminding the accord.

Carter, who signed the agreement as a witness, said it proved that "peace has come."

Somoza ousted: Nicaragua left in ruins

The victorious Sandinista rebels have driven out General Anastasio Somoza.

Nicaragua, 25 July
Under pressure from guerrillas at home and the United States abroad, General Anastasio Somoza Debayle resigned as president of Nicaragua and flew into exile. Under a plan worked out by the US between the Somoza government and the Sandinista rebels, Somoza, whose family has ruled Nicaragua since 1933, was to be succeeded in power by a five-man junta controlled by the Sandinistas.

A momentary hitch developed in the plan when Francisco Uryco Malianos, the president of the Chamber of Deputies who was to serve as a transitional president, at first declined to surrender power to the junta.

Somoza, who said he had been driven from power by a Communist conspiracy, left behind a nation devastated by civil war, with fighting continuing in several regions of the country. Thousands of people were believed to have been killed in the fighting in the past two months and 500,000 – one fifth of the country's population – have been displaced from their homes.

Within days of the revolutionary junta taking over power, fissures began to develop.

Thatcher is first British woman premier

London, 3 May
Margaret Thatcher became Europe's first woman prime minister as she and her Conservative Party won a decisive victory today in Great Britain's general election.

An Oxford-educated chemist and lawyer, Mrs Thatcher first entered parliament in 1959. In campaigning for prime minister, she promised a government that "would stop trying to step in and make decisions for you that you should be free to take on your own". A dedicated Tory, she has frequently said "free choice is ultimately what life is about".

Thatcher has promised to cut the rate of personal income taxes and to restrain the powers of the trade unions.

Margaret Thatcher wins the election.

Cambodia condemns Pol Pot's atrocities

Pol Pot: finally ousted in January.

Cambodia, 19 August
At the Choeung Ek mass grave site in Cambodia, hundreds of skulls eerily dot the ground as a gruesome reminder of the reign of Pol Pot, the Khmer Rouge and their atrocities. Millions of Cambodians died from 1975, when Pol Pot came to power, to January of this year, when he was finally ousted. The grave site is one of the many trails of genocide left behind by one of the century's most brutal rulers. Pol Pot is now under a death sentence.

US nuclear accident at Three Mile Island

Three Mile Island: scene of the worst ever nuclear accident in America.

United States, 31 March
The worst nuclear accident in American history is being brought under control, federal officials said today, but they added the possibility of a core meltdown at the Three Mile Island nuclear generating plant in Pennsylvania could still not be ruled out. The plant began emitting radiation three days ago when problems with its cooling system exposed part of the core, causing a shutdown.

Evacuation of pregnant women and children within five miles (eight kilometres) of the plant has been advised but a general evacuation has not been called for.

China and Vietnam in border warfare

Beijing, 27 February
Chinese troops, in what Beijing described as a counterattack, struck at Vietnamese positions along the 480-mile (770-kilometre) border. *Hsinhua*, the Chinese news agency, said China did "not want a single inch of Vietnamese territory" and attacked only after Vietnam had "ignored China's repeated warnings" and had "continually sent armed forces to encroach on Chinese territory and attack Chinese frontier guards and inhabitants".

Aside from border incidents, the Chinese invasion seemed designed to serve a warning on Hanoi, which has been taking an increasingly anti-Chinese stance as it consolidates its control over Southeast Asia and made a Soviet pact.

Anti-looting posters go up in Yunnan.

1980

Boston, 16 January. Scientists announce they have successfully synthesised interferon, a naturally occurring virus-fighting agent.

Iran, 29 January. Islamic Conference calls on Soviets to quit Afghanistan.

USSR, 22 January. The USSR's most prominent dissident, Andrei Sakharov, is arrested and exiled to Gorky, a city closed to foreigners.

USA, 21 March. President Carter urges the US Olympic Committee to boycott the Moscow Olympics in protest against the Soviet intervention in Afghanistan.

North Sea, 27 March. An oil platform overturns, killing half of the 100 men on board.

Paris, 15 April. The funeral is held of France's leading philosopher and left-wing thinker, Jean-Paul Sartre.

Hollywood, 29 April. British-born thriller director Alfred Hitchcock dies, aged 80.

Belgrade, 8 May. The world's leaders attend the funeral of President Tito.

East Africa, 12 June. A combination of drought and war threatens ten million people with famine.

New Delhi, 23 June. Mrs Gandhi's younger son and political heir, Sanjay, dies in a plane crash.

Egypt, 27 July. Deposed shah of Iran Mohammed Reza Pahlavi dies in a military hospital aged 60.

Italy, 2 August. A bomb blast at Bologna railway station kills 84. Neo-fascists claim responsibility.

Britain, 27 August. Unemployment tops two million for the first time since 1935.

Turkey, 11 September. The army seizes power in order "to save democracy".

Paraguay, 17 September. Nicaragua's deposed president Somoza is assassinated.

Paris, 3 October. Four people die when a bomb explodes in a synagogue.

Algeria, 11 October. Two earth tremors kill up to 20,000 in the town of El Asnam.

USA, 8 November. NASA says *Voyager 1* has discovered a 15th moon around Saturn.

London, 10 November. Michael Foot is elected leader of the Labour Party after Jim Callaghan steps down.

Archbishop is shot while saying mass

El Salvador, 30 March

Violence has swept El Salvador this week, after human rights advocate Archbishop Oscar Romero was killed while saying mass at a hospital chapel in San Salvador.

Romero, a vocal critic of El Salvador's extremists, and a champion of economic and political reform, was shot on 24 March, during his sermon at a mass in honour of Jorge Pinto, a well-known opposition journalist. The archbishop is believed to be the victim of a right-wing paramilitary group.

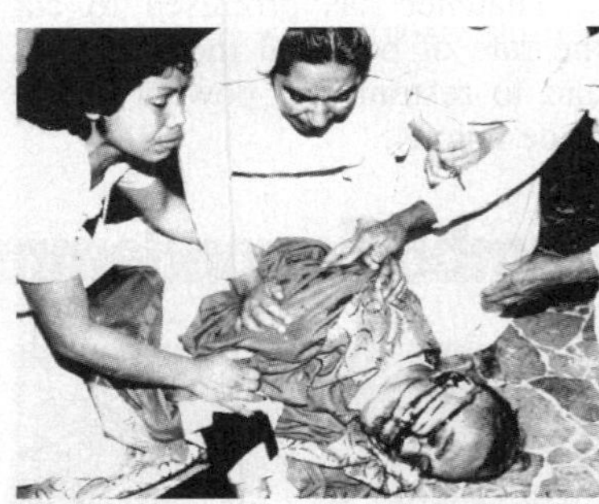

Archbishop Romero is hit by a sniper.

Brezhnev opens the boycotted Olympics

Moscow, 19 July

The Games of the 22nd Olympiad were opened in Moscow, but the usual buoyant spirit of the games was missing as talented athletes of the United States, West Germany and Japan refused to attend.

The boycotting countries were protesting against the military intervention of the Soviet Union in Afghanistan. There was a tightly-controlled approach to the Olympic preparations as the capital was sealed off and traffic barred from the streets hours before the opening ceremony was due to take place.

The Moscow Games opened with ceremony but many top athletes stayed away.

US mission to rescue Iran hostages fails

Iran, 28 April

President Carter's effort to free the American hostages in Tehran collapsed in the Iranian desert on Friday. Today, the president received another jolt. Secretary of State Vance resigned out of disagreement with the rescue mission.

A grim president announced on Friday morning that the mission had failed and eight US servicemen were dead. Carter said that he took full responsibility. Eight helicopters full of commandos had been dispatched to Iran to free the hostages, but they were called back after three had technical failures. The eight servicemen were killed when one of the helicopters collided with a transport plane. Iran had threatened to kill the hostages if military action was taken.

Wreckage of the crashed aircraft following the abortive US rescue mission.

Moslem world torn in Iran-Iraq war

Iran, 30 September

As the war between Iran and Iraq intensifies, Ayatollah Khomeini in a radio broadcast tonight spurned all peace proposals offered by Iraq's President Saddam Hussein. Iran, he said, would carry on and fight "to the end and, God willing, shall be victorious."

As Iraqi jets continued their raids on Abadan, Iran's oil refining centre and one of the world's largest, new fires added to the blanket of smoke over the heavily damaged city. Abadan was also hit by Iraqi ground forces using tanks and other heavy weapons, but early ground victories by the invading Iraqis have stalled before an Iranian resistance stiffer than expected. Meanwhile, Iranian fighter-bombers renewed their attack on Baghdad, the Iraqi capital, striking at, but missing, a nuclear reactor.

Iraq is trying to wrest away the oil-rich province of Khuzistan, jointly run by the two nations under a 1975 treaty.

Reagan: America's 40th president

Washington, 4 November
Ronald Wilson Reagan, promising "to put America back to work again", was elected the 40th president of the United States today with a surprising sweep in the east, south and crucial battlegrounds of the mid-west.

The former California governor, now 69, is the oldest man ever elected to the White House. In a stunning electoral landslide, he wiped out the southern base of President Carter. For Reagan, a former movie star, the win was perhaps all the more sweet in that he had sought nomination in 1976, losing that year to President Ford.

Former film star Ronald Reagan.

Former Beatle John Lennon died on 8 December outside his home in New York City, when David Chapman fired four bullets into his back.

Polish strikers win: unions approved

Union leader Lech Walesa ends the strike with an unprecedented agreement.

Poland, 30 August
Workers in the Gdansk shipyard today won significant concessions from the Polish government, and leaders of the newly formed Solidarity union called an end to a 17-day strike. The unprecedented agreement between government and union recognises the right to form independent unions and to strike. It contains a pledge to restrain state censorship. Union leader Lech Walesa's decision to end the walk-out was prompted by Deputy Minister Mieczyslaw Jagielski's indication that 28 jailed dissidents would be released. The accord is expected to stop slow-downs affecting 300,000 workers.

Mount St Helens spews out steam, small boulders and ash

Washington State, 28 March
Mount St Helens, a volcano in Washington State dormant since 1857, has begun emitting steam, ash and small boulders from a crater and vents on its sides. Scientists from the United States Geological Observatory are monitoring the emissions and have ordered the evacuation of 100 people from areas that could be reached by lava flows or mudslides. It is the first volcanic activity in the continental US since the eruption of Mount Lassen in California in 1917. In 1979, a Geological Survey report described Mount St Helens as "especially dangerous".

Dormant since 1857, Mount St Helens in Washington State is active again.

British storm Iran's embassy, freeing 19

London, 5 May
British commandos and police fought their way into the Iranian embassy in London to free 19 hostages who had been held there for five and a half days. The situation began with gunmen identifying themselves as members of Iran's Arab minority bursting into the embassy. The building was immediately surrounded by police. The gunmen's demands included the release of 91 political prisoners held by the Iranians. Over the next few days, the Arabs released five hostages then announced that they would begin killing captives. They shot two, so a raid was launched.

SAS embassy raid freed captives.

Rhodesia takes name Zimbabwe

Zimbabwe, 18 April
At midnight, Rhodesia became the independent state of Zimbabwe. Prince Charles presented Zimbabwe's new president, the Rev Canaan Banana, with documents signed by Queen Elizabeth II, granting independence to the colony. Blacks celebrated the end of their struggle to obtain majority rule as the new green, yellow, black and red flag replaced the Union Jack.

Former guerrilla leader Robert Mugabe was sworn in as Prime Minister of Zimbabwe's first black majority government.

1981

Northern Ireland, 16 January. Gunmen shoot and wound Bernadette McAliskey, the former nationalist MP Bernadette Devlin.

Tokyo, 16 January. Research study shows that health can be seriously damaged by other people's tobacco smoke.

Poland, 24 January. Millions of workers stay away from their jobs in support of Solidarity's call for a five-day working week

Britain, 25 January. A new political party, the Social Democrats, is founded by four former leading Labour MPs.

Beijing, 25 January. Mao's wife is given a suspended death sentence for "counter-revolutionary crimes".

Poland, 9 February. General Wojciech Jaruzelski replaces Prime Minister Jozef Pinkowski in an attempt to restore order to the country.

Madrid, 23 February. The Spanish king puts down a coup by armed paramilitaries, who occupy the *Cortes*, or parliament, while in session.

London, 3 April. Hundreds of youths riot in the south London suburb of Brixton.

France, 10 May. The Socialist leader, Francois Mitterrand, is elected president.

Miami, 11 May. Reggae star Bob Marley dies of cancer, aged 36.

Israel, 7 June. Israeli planes destroy Iraq's nuclear reactor.

Israel, 24 June. General Moshe Dayan says that Israel has the capacity to make nuclear bombs.

USA, 7 July. First woman, Sandra Day O'Connor, named to Supreme Court.

Nicaragua, 9 July. Eden Pastora steps down as minister to go into self-exile.

Britain, 10 July. Youths, many of them black, riot in several British cities.

Tehran, 30 August. A bomb kills President Mohammed Ali Rajai, Prime Minister Mohammed Javad Bahonar and five others.

Spain, 10 September. Picasso's civil war painting, *Guernica*, is returned after spending the Franco years in New York.

Europe, 24 October. Mass protests are held all across Western Europe against the siting of American nuclear weapons.

An assassin wounds pope at St Peter's

Rome, 13 May
Pope John Paul II was the victim of an assassination attempt today. He was shot twice in the abdomen by an escaped Turkish criminal as he rode in an open car among 10,000 worshippers in St Peter's Square.

He was rushed to Rome's Gemelli hospital. Sections of his intestine were removed during five hours of surgery. A spokesman said that he would recover soon.

The gunman, Mehmet Ali Agca, 23, was arrested. It was reported that he had been convicted of murdering an editor of the newspaper *Milliyet*, in 1979, and had escaped from prison later that year.

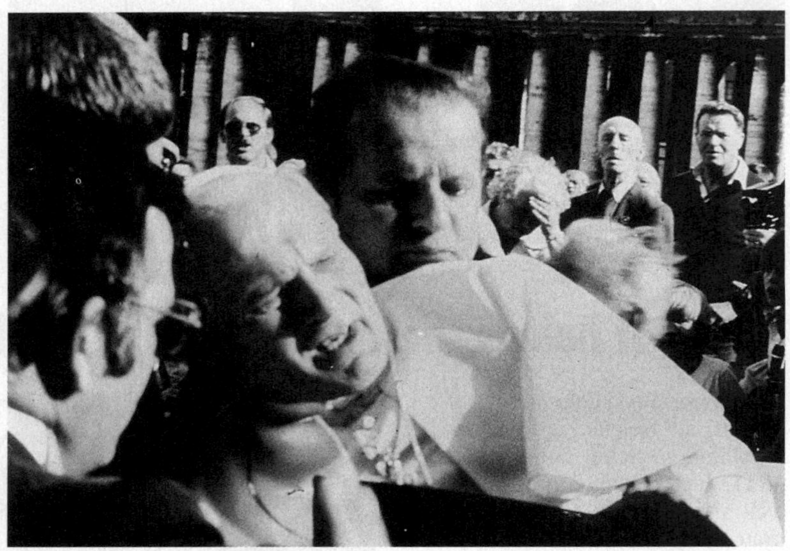

Pope John Paul II is shot in Rome and has to undergo five hours of surgery.

Columbia launched on first shuttle flight

Columbia takes off from Canaveral.

California, 14 April
The space shuttle *Columbia* completed its first orbital flight today when it landed at Edwards Air Force Base in California. The world's first reusable spacecraft orbited the Earth 36 times during a flight of 54 hours and 22 minutes, carrying two astronauts, John W Young and Robert L Crippen. Space agency officials say *Columbia*'s next orbital flight could come in as little as six months, but only if damage to the ceramic tiles of its heat shield is minor.

The major problem of the flight was the discovery that some tiles had been lost during lift-off from Cape Canaveral, but officials say the damage does not appear to be severe. The space shuttle programme, which has cost $10 billion so far, is designed to make orbital flight inexpensive and routine. The goal is to have a shuttle flight every two weeks, with the spacecraft carrying loads up to 65 tons into orbit. Three other orbiters are being built.

AIDS is identified for the first time

Doctors this year identified a disturbing disease that has no known cure. AIDS (Acquired Immune Deficiency Syndrome) destroys the body's immune system. A victim suffers severe weight loss and weakness and eventually succumbs to common infections. Scientists suspect a virus is the cause, perhaps one that infects T-lymphocytes, an integral part of the immune system. At present, the disease mostly affects homosexual men with several partners, Haitians (whose health care system is neglected by their government) and intravenous drug users re-using hypodermic needles.

PC promises to revolutionise office

New York City, August
International Business Machines has introduced its long-awaited version of the personal computer, a move experts say will give new impetus to the revolution in office automation. A first evaluation is that IBM's PC is no great advance over presently available personal computers, but that its arrival is significant in several major ways.

Purchasing agents who have been reluctant to buy personal computers can now say they're going with a PC made by the company that dominates the industry.

President Anwar Sadat, the Egyptian leader who made peace with Israel, was shot dead on 6 October at a military parade in Cairo.

Iran releases hostages

Buses carrying the 52 former hostages are mobbed on Pennsylvania Avenue.

United States, 31 January
From the bridges over the Potomac in Washington to the canyons of Wall Street in New York, Americans welcomed home the 52 former Iran hostages this week with yellow ribbons, thunderous applause and tears. "It's the most emotional experience of our lives," Vice President Bush said. "You could feel it build until the point it hurt inside. It was the greatest event I've ever seen."

It was an event that provided relief to a country and a government that had been paralysed by a crisis that lasted 444 days. The crisis refused to be solved until Jimmy Carter, criticised for his role in the episode, was forced out of power.

Reagan survives attack but is wounded

Washington, 30 March
President Reagan was shot and gravely wounded today as he was leaving the Washington Hilton Hotel after addressing a labour convention. Also wounded were his press secretary, James Brady, and two security officers.

The president was reported to be in "stable" condition tonight after two hours of surgery at George Washington University Hospital, just blocks from the White House.

Minutes after the shooting, officers arrested John W Hinckley Jr, 25, a resident of Colorado, and charged him with having attempted to assassinate the president.

The president is shot by a would-be assassin outside the Washington Hilton.

Charles and Diana marry in splendour

London, 29 July
On the back of the couple's car was a hand-scrawled sign reading "Just Married". Actually, it was not a car but a 70-year-old gilded, horse-drawn carriage. Prince Charles and Lady Diana wed this morning in a splendid ceremony viewed by millions. In St Paul's Cathedral, Charles, supported by his brothers Andrew and Edward, made his vows in the presence of 2,500 guests to Diana, who wore a dress of pale ivory silk.

The couple kiss on the balcony of Buckingham Palace, to the crowd's delight.

Strike crushed in Poland, leaving 7 dead

Poland, 17 December
The Polish government lifted its news blackout long enough tonight to admit that at least seven people were killed resisting the imposition of martial law. The victims were apparently union members on strike at a coal mine in Silesia. More than 300 civilians and police officers were reported injured in clashes that occurred in Gdansk. In the past few days, Polish police have moved to crush strikes in coal mines, shipyards and factories.

Two Irish hunger strikers die in Maze

Belfast, 12 May
Two imprisoned members of the Irish Republican Army have died in Belfast's Maze Prison after long hunger strikes to protest at their treatment by British authorities. Bobby Sands, 27, who was serving a 14-year sentence for possession of firearms, died after 66 days without food. Sands had recently been elected to parliament in a special election to fill a vacancy. A week later, Francis Hughes, 25, died after 59 days of refusing food. Two other fasting Irish nationalists were reported to be nearing death in the prison. The deaths provoked demonstrations in Belfast.

Protests started after the two deaths.

1982

Albania, 11 January. The prime minister is reported killed in a shoot-out involving President Enver Hoxha.

Washington, 13 January. A plane crashes on take-off from National Airport, killing 78.

Britain, 26 January. Unemployment figures pass three million for the first time since the 1930s.

Nicaragua, 25 March. Fearing a US invasion the Sandinista government declares a state of emergency.

Falkland Islands, 2 April. Argentinian forces overrun the islands and capture the few British troops stationed there.

USA, 19 April. Travel to Cuba banned from 15 May.

Egypt, 25 April. The last Israeli troops leave Sinai as the area is returned to Egypt.

Britain, 29 May. The climax of the first papal visit for 450 years is reached as the pope enters Canterbury Cathedral.

New York, 12 June. 800,000 marchers protest against nuclear proliferation.

Falkland Islands, 14 June. The Argentinian invaders surrender to the British task force.

London, 19 June. Roberto Calvi, an Italian banker, is found hanged under Blackfriars Bridge.

Lebanon, 31 August. The PLO is driven out of Beirut by invading Israeli forces.

Australia, 13 September. A mother who claims that a dingo killed her baby goes on trial for murder.

Lebanon, 14 September. President-elect Bashir Gemayel is killed by a bomb.

Monaco, 15 September. Princess Grace dies in a car crash on a mountain road.

West Germany, 1 October. Christian Democrat Helmut Kohl replaces Social Democrat Helmut Schmidt as chancellor.

Spain, 28 October. The Socialist Party of Felipe Gonzalez wins the general election in a landslide.

Poland, 14 November. Lech Walesa returns to Gdansk after 11 months internment.

Britain, 12 December. Over 20,000 women encircle the Greenham airbase in protest at the planned siting of American cruise missiles.

Polish parliament outlaws Solidarity

Poland, 26 October

The Polish parliament approved overwhelmingly a measure outlawing Solidarity, the free trade union that captured the support of millions of Poles but drew the wrath of the Soviet Union.

The new law replaces Solidarity with a set of unions with sharply restricted powers to strike. The move provoked demonstrations and clashes between workers and police in Gdansk, the birthplace of the Solidarity movement, and in the steel-producing suburb of Nowa Huta near Krakow. The government put down a strike in the Gdansk shipyards by using martial law authority to draft the striking workers into military service.

Polish riot police spray a pro-Solidarity rally in Gdansk with tear gas.

Sun Myung Moon is guilty under tax law

New York, 18 May

The Rev Sun Myung Moon, 62, founder and leader of the Unification Church, was convicted in New York yesterday of conspiracy to defraud the federal government and filing false income tax returns. He could face up to five years in prison for conspiracy and three years on each of the three tax counts. One of his top aides, Takeru Kamiyama, was also convicted of conspiracy, perjury and obstructing the investigation that led to the more than eight-week-long trial of the Korean evangelist.

Moon and his wife Hak-ja Han bless the marriage of 35,000 couples in Seoul.

Success of artificial permanent heart

Salt Lake City, 22 December

Barney B Clark, the first recipient of a permanent artificial heart, took his first steps today. The 61-year-old retired dentist from the Seattle area received the implant in a seven-and-a-half-hour operation performed on 2 December by a surgical team headed by Dr William C DeVries at the University of Utah Medical Center in Salt Lake City.

Clark was bedridden and close to death from heart failure when the operation was performed. He is now being kept alive by a Jarvik-7 plastic-and-metal artificial heart.

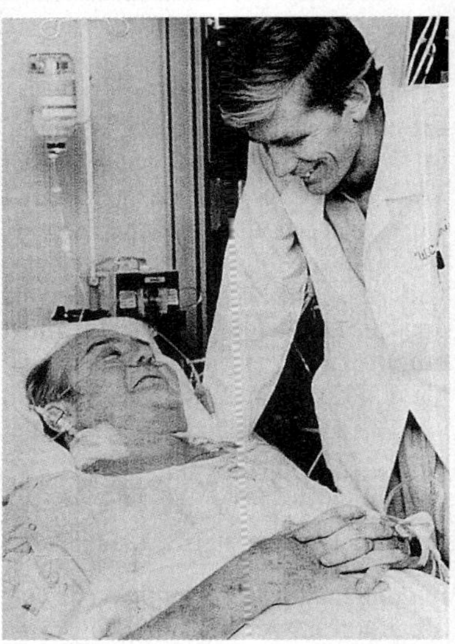

Barney Clark with surgeon DeVries.

Iran scores major victory over Iraq

Tehran, 24 May

Iran is claiming one of its biggest victories in the bloody, two-and-a-half-year war with Iraq. Tehran radio reports that Iranian forces have recaptured the major cargo port city of Khurramshahr. If the report is confirmed, it will mean that Iran has recaptured almost all of the territory it had lost to Iraq.

The Iranian report sent shockwaves through the Arab world, which has divided its loyalties in the war. Saudi Arabia and other major oil producers, fearful that the fundamentalist revolution in Iran might spread, have been financing Iraq. Syria supports Iran which has used Soviet weapons.

Israeli forces successful in Lebanon

Beirut, 29 June
Israeli forces have driven deep into southern Lebanon, battling Palestinian and Syrian forces on the coastal road south of Beirut and trapping the leadership of the Palestine Liberation Organisation in the western half of the capital. East of Beirut, Israeli jets have knocked out Syrian surface-to-air missile batteries in the Bekaa Valley and engaged in vicious dogfights with Syrian pilots flying Soviet-built MiG fighters. Until today, Israel's stated goal was to punish the Palestinian guerrillas and annihilate PLO leaders. Faced with intense international pressure and the threat of Soviet involvement in the fighting, Israel's Prime Minister Begin has backed down.

In an address to the Israeli parliament, Begin offered to let Palestinian guerrillas leave Beirut with their weapons. Just two days ago, the Israeli cabinet was demanding that terrorists hand over their guns.

There seem to be several reasons for the shift in Begin's position. First, US support for the successful Israeli invasion of Lebanon has deteriorated. Begin is also facing increasing anti-war sentiment at home. Opposition leader Shimon Peres warned that Israeli actions are being watched by the world.

Israeli forces drove deep into southern Lebanon in anti-PLO operations.

Christian militiamen kill unarmed Arabs

West Beirut, 18 September
The sickening stench of death rises from Sabra and Shatila, two Palestinian refugee camps in West Beirut. Hundreds of bodies, their faces contorted and bloated, lie in doorways and streets, surrounded by swarms of flies. It is a shocking scene. The shooting started at 6 pm yesterday and carried on through the night. Preliminary reports say the Palestinians were shot by Christian militiamen, but it is not clear who ordered them to shoot.

The sickening scenes of carnage after the massacres in Beirut refugee camps.

Sea battle for Falklands

HMS Sheffield destroyed with loss of 20 lives despite the firefighting attempts.

Falkland Islands, 31 May
Argentinian forces in the Falkland Islands are making their final stand on the ground today after a month-long battle at sea. British forces are advancing through hills 15 miles (24 kilometres) west of Stanley and hope to capture the capital shortly.

Fighting began in earnest at the beginning of the month after General Leopoldo Galtieri, the president of Argentina, charged that Britain had "broken the peace of America and put in danger the security of the world". Argentina's military command said it retaliated against British air strikes on the Falklands by damaging two British frigates and shooting down two Harrier jump-jets. Within 24 hours, however, it was Britain that struck the devastating blow.

On the 3rd, Argentina conceded that its only cruiser, the *General Belgrano*, had been sunk 36 miles (58 kilometres) outside a British exclusion zone by a torpedo fired from a British submarine.

Brezhnev dies at 75, no successor yet

Brezhnev's casket is carried through Moscow to his grave in Red Square.

Moscow, 10 November
Leonid Brezhnev, leader of the Soviet Union for the past 18 years, died this morning in Moscow. Brezhnev, who was 75, had been suffering from heart and lung problems for the past few years, but the official Soviet announcement did not indicate the cause of his death. It is unclear who will succeed him. The leading contenders appear to be Konstantin Chernenko, an aide to Brezhnev, and Yuri Andropov, who headed the KGB for 15 years.

1983

Bolivia, 19 January. Klaus Barbie, the wartime SS "Butcher of Lyons", arrested.

Nigeria, 30 January. A million Ghanaian migrant workers are leaving Nigeria after being expelled by the government.

Australia, 5 March. Robert Hawke and his Labour Party oust eight-year-old Conservative government.

Beirut, 19 April. US embassy bombed, 40 killed.

Washington, 4 May. President Reagan backs Contra guerrillas in Nicaragua in their struggle to overthrow the Marxist Sandinista government.

Bonn, 6 May. Experts declare that the so-called Hitler diaries, authenticated by Lord Dacre and published in *Der Stern* magazine, are fake.

Sicily, 14 May. Explosives are used to divert the lava flow from erupting Mount Etna away from two towns.

Pretoria, 20 May. A car bomb outside the South African air force headquarters kills 16 and injures 190.

Poland, 21 July. Martial law is lifted after 19 months.

Sri Lanka, 27 July. Riots as Sinhalese mobs attack Tamils, claiming over 100 lives.

Northern Ireland, 5 August. Twenty-two IRA men get long prison sentences as the result of the evidence of a "supergrass".

Israel, 2 September. Menachem Begin resigns as leader of the Herut Party and is replaced by Yitzhak Shamir.

Northern Ireland, 25 September. Break-out at the Maze prison by 134 IRA prisoners.

Rhode Island, 26 September. The Australian challenger wins the America's Cup, ending 132 successive years of American victories.

Britain, 2 October. Neil Kinnock, 41, is elected leader of the Labour Party.

Seoul, 9 October. Bomb kills 19, including six top officials.

Washington, 2 November. President Reagan signs bill making Martin Luther King's birthday a national holiday.

Britain, 14 November. First American-made cruise missiles arrive in England.

Oslo, 10 December. Lech Walesa awarded Nobel Peace Prize; his wife accepts award.

Argentina, 20 December. Eight years of army rule ended.

216 marines killed in Beirut bombing

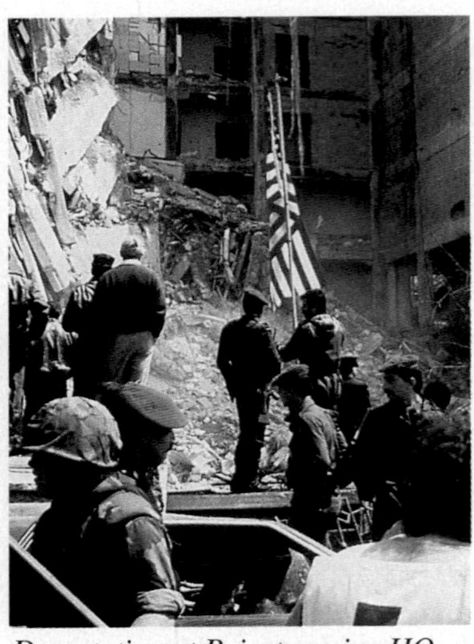
Devastation at Beirut marine HQ.

Beirut, 25 October
General Paul X Kelley, the United States marine commandant, has arrived in Beirut to investigate the terrorist assault on marine headquarters. The marines were in Beirut as part of an international peacekeeping force.

Rescuers have pulled 216 bodies from the charred metal and collapsed cement of the airport complex. New questions were raised about security at the headquarters and about the Reagan administration's involvement in the fragile, volatile politics of Lebanon.

One terrorist is responsible for all the devastation. On Sunday, he drove a truck filled with at least 2,500 pounds (1,140 kilograms) of explosives past sentries and crashed into the building. The vehicle exploded into a fireball and turned four storeys of the structure into burning rubble. "I haven't seen carnage like that since Vietnam," a marine spokesman said. High-rise buildings shuddered with the force of the blast.

Two minutes after the attack, another truck filled with explosives slammed into the compound used by French peacekeeping forces. Fifty-eight people were killed. A telephone caller to *Agence France Presse* said that a group called the Free Islamic Revolution Movement was responsible for it.

Benigno Aquino is gunned down as he arrives back in Manila

Manila, 22 August
Philippine president Ferdinand E Marcos appeared on television tonight to deny rumours that his government was responsible for yesterday's murder of Benigno S Aquino Jr. Aquino was killed by a single shot in the head as he got off a plane at Manila Airport with a military escort, who immediately killed the unidentified assassin. Considered Marcos' main political rival, Aquino had just ended three years of self-exile in the United States to return home.

Benigno Aquino (in white) lies dead while the killer (circled) flees.

Arafat's 4,000 Palestinians quit Tripoli

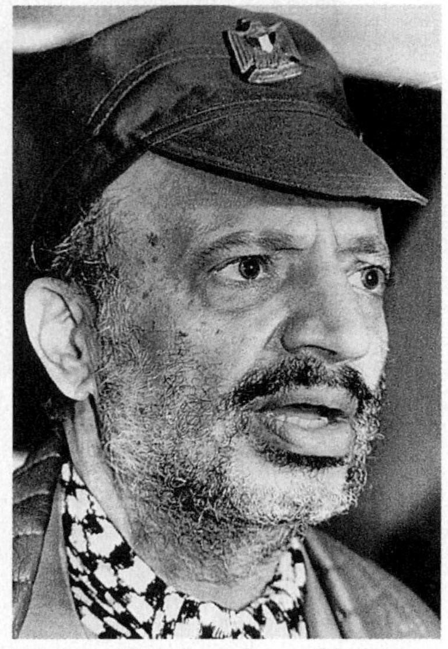
Arafat's PLO forced out of Lebanon.

Tripoli, 20 December
For the second time in 16 months, Yasir Arafat has been forced to evacuate his Palestine Liberation Organisation forces from Lebanon. Today, Arafat and several thousand of his loyalists set sail from Tripoli. They had been completely surrounded there by rival Palestinian factions and Syrian soldiers. The United Nations Security Council arranged the evacuation, and the PLO guerrillas departed on French ships bearing United Nations flags.

It was Israel that forced Arafat to leave Beirut last year, but its role is ambiguous this time, although Arafat's departure from Tripoli was delayed by Israeli bombing raids that were made in retaliation for a terrorist attack in Jerusalem.

The space shuttle *Challenger* landed at Edwards Air Force Base, California, on 24 June after a six-day mission that made Sally K Ride, 32, the first US woman in space.

Mrs Thatcher sweeps to victory in Britain

London, 9 June
The Conservative government of Margaret Thatcher has won a landslide victory by a margin large enough to guarantee Mrs Thatcher a full five-year second term as prime minister of Britain. Although a year ago Thatcher's popularity was at an all-time low, she regained the confidence of her nation when she recaptured the Falkland Islands from Argentina.

Labour Party officials blame their defeat on the Liberal-Social Democratic alliance, which split the anti-Thatcher vote.

Seen as part of a right-wing trend in the West, the election result may encourage America's President Reagan to run for re-election.

Reagan proposes Star Wars defence plan

Washington, 23 March
A plan to use the latest in modern technology to build an invulnerable missile shield for the United States was proposed tonight by President Reagan. In a television address from the White House, Reagan presented "a vision of the future which offers hope" that the US could stop relying on massive retaliation to counter the threat of a Soviet nuclear attack but warned that technological breakthroughs necessary to create a missile shield "may not be accomplished before the end of this century".

Officials said the programme might involve lasers, microwave devices, particle beams and projectile beams from satellites.

Might hostile attacks be intercepted by chemically propelled missiles?

Soviets down Korean jetliner: 269 die

Washington, 15 September
In a unanimous vote, the Senate condemned the USSR's shooting down of Korean Airlines flight 007. The resolution, passed yesterday by the house, calls the destruction of the plane a "brutal massacre" and demands reparations for the victims' families. Some 269 people were aboard the Korean 747 jet when it disappeared from radar screens on the 1st, including 61 Americans, among them Georgia congressman Larry McDonald. The Soviet action has already been denounced by President Reagan as "barbarous". The Soviets claim the plane was on a spying mission for America.

It took almost a week after the plane vanished for the Soviet Union to give an explanation. The plane was on a flight from New York to Seoul when it was reported missing. It disappeared over the highly strategic Sakhalin Island, off Siberia. Little was heard from the Soviets until they held a very unusual, full-blown news conference on the 6th.

Bereaved families weep in front of the altar at a memorial service in Seoul.

Americans take Grenada amidst protest

Grenada, 25 October
A force of American marines and rangers today invaded the tiny island of Grenada, where the United States says a "brutal group of leftist thugs violently seized power". President Reagan said he ordered the attack because he is concerned about the welfare of some 1,100 American citizens on the island. The world press and many Democratic members of Congress reacted negatively to the invasion, which is the first military intervention in the hemisphere by the US since the 1965 invasion of the Dominican Republic.

In the fighting, against inferior Cuban troops, 16 Americans died and 77 were injured.

The Latin American nations call for peace

Washington, 28 July
President Reagan is moving to increase United States military involvement in Nicaragua despite international and domestic opposition. Latin American leaders are calling for the removal of all foreign bases and forces from the area. The House of Representatives voted today to cancel all covert aid to the anti-Sandinista rebels.

The presidents of Mexico, Venezuela, Colombia and Panama released a communique stating "profound concern for the rapid deterioration" of the situation in Central America. Their quickly arranged meeting grew out of an earlier gathering of their foreign ministers, the Contadora Group. The Mexican president made a separate appeal to President Reagan and Fidel Castro to reject the use of force in Central America.

US marines capture People's Revolutionary Army suspects in Georgetown.

1984

Tunisia, 6 January. The death toll reaches 75 after a week of riots over food prices.

Beirut, 26 February. US marines leave as ordered by President Reagan in response to the deteriorating situation.

Canada, 29 February. Prime Minister Trudeau resigns, having been in office almost continuously for 15 years.

Washington, 23 April. The discovery is announced of the virus that causes AIDS.

Britain, 29 May. Police and striking miners clash violently at Orgreave coking plant.

India, 6 June. Troops storm the Sikh Golden Temple at Amritsar to expel armed extremists.

London, 7 July. Martina Navratilova wins her fifth Wimbledon singles title.

USA, 12 July. Democrats pick a woman, Geraldine Ferraro, as Walter Mondale's White House running mate.

California, 18 July. A gunman runs amok in a McDonald's and kills 20 people.

Vermont, 21 July. Jogging guru James F Fixx dies of a heart attack while running.

London, 18 August. Civil servant Clive Ponting is charged with violating the Official Secrets Act by leaking information on the sinking of the *Belgrano*.

Canada, 4 September. Brian Mulroney and his Progressive Conservative Party win in a huge victory.

Beirut, 20 September. A suicide bomber blows up 40 people at the US embassy.

Peking, 26 September. China agrees to let Hong Kong keep its capitalist way of life after sovereignty reverts in 1997.

Britain, 12 October. A massive bomb at the Grand Hotel during the Conservative Party conference in Brighton kills three people and injures several leading Tories. Margaret Thatcher is lucky to escape unharmed.

New Delhi, 1 November. Rajiv Gandhi is sworn in as prime minister.

Oslo, 10 December. Desmond Tutu, the Anglican bishop of Johannesburg, is awarded the Nobel Peace Prize.

Britain, 14 December. A single by leading pop musicians to raise funds for the starving in Ethiopia goes to number one.

China's Communists embrace reforms

Beijing, 28 October

This month the largest celebration ever organised in China marked the nation's 35th year as a Communist state, and today Peking announced plans for economic reforms that will usher in limited capitalist measures and decrease the government's role.

Chinese leader Deng Hsiao-ping watched the 1 October parade from the same balcony at the Gate of Heavenly Peace where Mao Zedong proclaimed the founding of Communist China in 1949. Deng called for a strengthening of national defence in his speech to the festive crowd in the square. It seems an arms build-up has already begun, as the Chinese displayed an impressive arsenal of modern missiles and weapons.

However, the economic reforms announced today may be more explosive than those weapons. They include plans to allow a million state-owned enterprises independence to trigger competition, a programme to leave the pricing of many products to the market forces of supply and demand, a pledge to increase foreign trade and a promise to give industrial plant managers more autonomy from the state bureaucracy.

Adopted by the Communist Party central committee, the reforms are the most significant since 1978. In that year, the government instituted an incentive plan to give China's peasants higher rewards for more production. A dramatic rise in agricultural production resulted, and it is hoped the new measures will bring about a similar increase in industrial productivity and a general boost to the Chinese economy.

Indira Gandhi is murdered by Sikhs

New Delhi, 31 October

Indira Gandhi, India's four-time prime minister, was gunned down today by two members of her personal security guard as she walked from her home to her office in New Delhi. She died after four hours of emergency surgery. The only daughter of former prime minister Nehru was 66.

Both of her attackers were identified as members of the Sikh religion. One was shot dead; the other captured. Sikh extremists have threatened to kill Mrs Gandhi since she ordered the raid on their shrine at Amritsar. Recently, Mrs Gandhi told an interview that she was not intimidated by the threats. "I am not afraid," she said then. "I am frequently attacked."

Indira Gandhi with her son Rajiv.

Libyans gun down London policewoman

Memorial to WPC opposite embassy.

WPC Yvonne Fletcher, 25, shot dead.

London, 22 April

In London, it appears tonight that the gunman who killed a British policewoman in cold blood will be able to leave England scot-free. Constable Yvonne Fletcher was killed on Tuesday when shots were fired from inside the Libyan embassy during a protest outside against Colonel Gaddafi. Ten protesters were wounded, five seriously. Police officers surrounded the building, and Britain tried to convince the Libyan government to allow a search of the embassy for weapons. Gaddafi refused. Tonight, Britain broke diplomatic relations with Libya and gave the occupants of the embassy a week to get out of the country. It was one of those occupants who killed WPC Fletcher.

900,000 Filipinos march against Marcos

Manila, 21 August

One year ago in Manila, government opposition leader Benigno Aquino was assassinated. Today, 900,000 demonstrators filled the streets of the Philippine capital to commemorate Aquino's death and to protest against the government of President Ferdinand Marcos. The main rally was held in Rizal Park where posters read, "Down with the US–Marcos Dictatorship!" Those at the rally who attempted to speak English were booed and forced to speak in Tagalog, the chief native language of Filipinos. In her speech, Aquino's widow called for Marcos to resign.

Reagan and Bush win by 59 per cent

Washington, 6 November
President Reagan swept to victory today, trouncing Walter F Mondale by carrying all but one of the 50 states. The president led in every major block of voters except blacks, Jews and trade unionists.

It was a landslide win for the president, the oldest man ever to occupy the White House, and a very bitter defeat for his Democrat opponent, who once served as vice president. The choice of Geraldine Ferraro, a Roman Catholic woman, made no difference to Mondale's fortunes: Reagan led among both women and Catholics.

President Reagan in landslide win.

Arab League accuses Iran of aggression

Iran, 24 May
Iran ignored a warning from the Arab League today and strafed an oil tanker off the coast of Saudi Arabia. Iraq also struck at other shipping in the Gulf. The new attacks came just four days after the Arab League released an unprecedented statement accusing Iran of aggression in the war against Iraq. A majority of the league's members also warned Iran to stop its attacks on shipping in the international oil lanes of the Gulf. However, the league did not criticise Iraq, which has actually done more damage to oil tankers than Iran has inflicted.

Olympics open like Hollywood spectacle

American sprinter Carl Lewis won the 100-metre final in 9.9 seconds.

Los Angeles, July
The spectacular start of the Los Angeles Olympics was followed closely by some spectacular performances. After a glitzy, splashy opening that was pure Hollywood, the Games settled down to a bright succession of individual triumphs.

The American hero was Carl Lewis, who set an Olympic record in the 200-metre final for his third gold medal. He was also first in the 100 metres and the long jump.

Despite a boycott by the Soviet Union and some other Communist countries, the Olympics attracted more than 7,000 athletes from 140 nations, the largest number in the history of the Games. The closing show was also spectacular.

Fatal gas leak at Bhopal chemical plant

Local residents stand outside the front gates of the Union Carbide factory.

Bhopal, 13 December
The death toll from a toxic gas leak at an insecticide plant at Bhopal, India, is now estimated at 2,100, and tens of thousands of residents fled the city today after it was announced the Union Carbide plant would be started up again to neutralise the remains of the chemical. Warren M Anderson, who is chairman of Union Carbide, was arrested and charged with criminal conspiracy when he flew to Bhopal, but was released on bail.

The gas, methyl isocyanate, escaped from one of three underground storage tanks at the plant early on 3 December. The gas spread over an area inhabited by 200,000 people during the next 40 minutes. Many awoke vomiting and complaining of dizziness, sore throats and burning eyes. Others died where they slept.

Andropov dies: Chernenko succeeds him

Moscow, 13 February
The Soviet Union has a new leader tonight, but it is not clear whether he has the authority or willingness to change the country's domestic or foreign policy.

Konstantin Chernenko was selected to succeed Yuri Andropov as general secretary. Andropov died last Friday after a long fight with kidney disease. Konstantin Chernenko, who is a 72-year-old Bolshevik, was a close associate of former Soviet leader Leonid Brezhnev for 30 years.

In one sense, his reportedly unanimous election by the central committee represents a stunning comeback for him. It could also mean that the same bureaucrats who ruled through the four years when Brezhnev and Andropov were ill will continue to dominate all aspects of policy-making.

Konstantin Chernenko, 72, an associate of Brezhnev, is unanimously elected the new general secretary.

1985

Israel, 3 January. Israel stops bringing Jews from famine-stricken Ethiopia when it is revealed that the airlift has been going on covertly for years.

South Africa, 19 February. Hundreds hurt in police clash with blacks resisting relocation to a black township.

London, 22 February. The pound falls to its lowest ever level, trading at $1.0765.

Britain, 3 March. The National Union of Mineworkers decides to call off its year-long strike.

Sudan, 4 April. A coup ousts President Nimeiry. The new leader is General Dahab.

Beirut, 17 April. The Lebanese cabinet resigns after Shiite Moslems capture West Beirut from the Sunnis.

Britain, 11 May. Over 40 soccer fans die when fire sweeps through a stand at a soccer match in Bradford.

Bangladesh, 25 May. A cyclone and tidal wave devastate the coast, leaving thousands dead.

Brussels, 29 May. Hooligan behaviour by Liverpool soccer fans leads to the death of 41 rival supporters during the European Cup Final at the Heysel Stadium.

Ireland, 23 June. An Air India jet flying from Canada plunges into the sea 120 miles (190 kilometres) off the Irish coast, killing all 325 on board; a terrorist bomb is suspected.

London, 7 July. Boris Becker, aged 17, becomes the first unseeded player to win the Wimbledon men's title.

Auckland, 10 July. *Rainbow Warrior*, a Greenpeace ship in New Zealand in preparation for protests against French nuclear tests, is blown up.

Japan, 22 August. A JAL plane crashes killing 517 people. This latest accident makes 1985 the worst year ever for air disasters.

Colombia, 13 November. A volcano 80 miles (130 kilometres) west of Bogota, erupts, burying two towns and killing around 20,000 people.

Rome and Vienna, 30 December. Palestinian terrorists stage coordinated attacks on check-in counters of the Israeli airline, El Al, at Rome and Vienna airports, killing 14 people.

South African rand at its lowest rate

South Africa, 27 August
The government of South Africa, rocked by new racial violence and unprecedented criticism by black leaders, suspended all trading on its stock and currency markets. The South African currency, the rand, tumbled to 35 cents against the US dollar, its lowest rate ever and a 25 per cent drop since the government imposed a new state of emergency last month. Trading suspensions were announced on the eve of a march on the Cape Town prison where black nationalist Nelson Mandela is being held. Rioting spread to Durban, and security forces rounded up 500 schoolchildren who had boycotted classes.

Bishop Tutu denounces all violence.

Leading man Rock Hudson dies of AIDS

Hudson and co-star Doris Day.

Paris, 2 October
Film star Rock Hudson died this morning, aged 59. He was the first movie star to acknowledge he had AIDS, last month purchasing $10,000 worth of tickets to an AIDS fundraiser.

Hudson, born Ray Schere, shot to stardom with *Magnificent Obsession* (1954), about a cad who blinds a woman and learns eye surgery to make amends. *Giant* (1956) provided him with a bit role, then followed a string of comedies opposite Doris Day, starting with *Pillow Talk* (1959). A recent television show was halted when he had heart surgery.

Earthquake in Mexico kills thousands

Mexico, 21 September
In Mexico City, rescue workers and bereaved family members are using shovels, picks and even their hands to dig through the rubble of Thursday morning's earthquake. Thousands of people are known to be dead. Many more are still trapped under the cement and steel of scores of buildings. Hospitals are "filled to saturation". Entire families are living in the streets. Their homes have disappeared.

The quake was extremely powerful, measuring 7.8 on the Richter scale. The after-shock measured 7.3. The epicentres of both tremors were located about 230 miles (370 kilometres) south-west of Mexico City; the capital took most damage.

Rescue operations in Mexico City.

"Live Aid" world rock festival held for African famine relief

The finale of the London "Live Aid" concert, held at Wembley Stadium.

Philadelphia, 13 July
"Good morning children of the 80s," proclaimed singer Joan Baez to a crowd of 90,000 today in Philadelphia for the "Live Aid" concert for African famine relief. The event coincided with another huge gathering outside London, with a worldwide television simulcast of both concerts. Performers included Paul McCartney, Bob Dylan, Tina Turner, Mick Jagger, Phil Collins, U2, Madonna, Sting, Queen and many others. The massive benefit, organised by Irish singer Bob Geldof, represented the culmination of his previous efforts to raise money through recordings.

American is killed by Arab hijackers

New York, 20 October
The body of Leon Klinghoffer came home to New York City. Wheelchair-bound Klinghoffer was killed by Palestinian hijackers of a Mediterranean cruise ship earlier this month. His wife, Marilyn, who survived the hijacking ordeal, nearly fainted at the airport.

The hijacking of the Italian cruise ship Achille Lauro began on the 7th. Armed guerrillas, believed to be members of the Palestine Liberation Front, took over the ship as it left Alexandria, Egypt, with over 60 Americans on board. The hijackers surrendered on 9 October after Egypt promised them free passage out of the country.

Leon Klinghoffer was shot dead.

Chernenko dies: Gorbachev to lead

New Soviet leader Gorbachev.

Moscow, 13 March
Today saw the third funeral in only two and a half years of a Soviet leader. This time, however, power passed to a new generation.

Konstantin Chernenko, who had been a sick man for most of his time in power, was buried near the Kremlin wall next to predecessors Leonid Brezhnev and Yuri Andropov. The country's new leader, Mikhail Gorbachev, led the funeral procession.

At the agè of 54, Gorbachev is the youngest man to take charge in Moscow since Joseph Stalin.

He called for immediate changes in the Soviet system and said it is time for government to transfer the "economy to the tracks of intensive development". Gorbachev seemed to emphasise economic concerns over military matters by giving military leaders a low profile at the funeral service.

Gorbachev, who was the number two man in the Kremlin under Andropov, also praised *detente* and called for a "real and major reduction in arms stockpiles". US vice president George Bush, who met with Gorbachev for an hour and a half, came away impressed. "If there ever was a time we can move forward with progress, I would say this is a good time for that," Bush said. The vice president gave the Soviet leader a letter that came from President Reagan, urging that they meet in the near future.

Reagan meets Gorbachev for important discussions at Geneva

Geneva, 21 November
President Reagan and Soviet leader Mikhail Gorbachev have proved that showmanship is just as important as diplomacy in two days of remarkable meetings in Geneva. The two men discovered they have sharp differences on most major issues, but they stunned their aides by holding six hours of intensely private discussions with only their interpreters present. The private sessions were the longest in 14 American-Soviet summits, and the two leaders agreed to meet again. Gorbachev is scheduled to visit the United States next year.

Reagan and Gorbachev spent six hours locked in intensely private discussions.

Britain and Ireland ratify the Ulster plan

London, 27 November
A two-day debate ended in the British parliament tonight as the House of Commons voted overwhelmingly for a new agreement with the Irish Republic. The accord allows the Dublin government a new consultative role in Northern Ireland. Prime Minister Thatcher's major opponent in parliament, Labour leader Neil Kinnock urged approval of the agreement. The 15 MPs from Northern Ireland, who are committed to union with Great Britain, opposed the accord and threatened to resign.

Mengele identified and confirmed dead

Brazil, 21 June
Investigators from West Germany, the United States and Brazil are "99 per cent sure" they have found the body of Josef Mengele. Since 6 June, when a corpse was exhumed from a grave outside Sao Paulo, Brazil, countless forensic tests have been conducted. Even Menachem Russek, a Nazi hunter who has encountered more than his share of hoaxes, seems satisfied.

Hijacked hostages freed after 17 days

Captain Testrake freed with others.

Beirut, 30 June
A long hijacking ordeal ended today in the Middle East. Radical Shiites, who are members of *Hezbollah*, or Party of God, released 39 Americans in Beirut, 17 days after the gunmen took over TWA flight 847 on takeoff from Athens. Passengers were beaten and tortured as the aircraft crisscrossed the Mediterranean.

The hostages said they were looking forward to being reunited with their families. One family, however, will not be sharing their joy. Navy diver Robert Stethem was killed by the terrorists on the first day of the drama.

1986

France, 20 January. Mrs Thatcher and President Mitterrand confirm that Britain and France are to build a Channel Tunnel next year.

February. Halley's Comet is visible in the night sky as it passes at its closest to Earth.

Palermo, 10 February. 474 alleged gangsters face court in biggest ever Mafia trial.

Iraq, 19 February. Iranian forces capture the key Iraqi oil port of Al Faw.

Stockholm, 28 February. Swedish prime minister Olaf Palme is shot dead in the street.

West Berlin, 5 April. A bomb explodes in a disco packed with American soldiers.

London, 23 July. Prince Andrew and Sarah Ferguson are married in Westminster Abbey.

Cameroon, 26 August. 1,500 people die when an odourless mixture of carbon dioxide and hydrogen gas escape from a volcanic lake near Wum.

South Africa, 27 August. Twelve people die in clashes between police and demonstrators in Soweto.

Britain, 31 August. Henry Moore, major modern sculptor, dies aged 88.

Turkey, 6 September. Two Arabs kill 21 worshippers in an unprovoked attack on an Istanbul synagogue.

Paris, 17 September. Four die and 44 are injured when an Arab terrorist hurls a bomb into a department store from a passing car.

Iceland, 13 October. President Reagan and Soviet leader Gorbachev blamed each other on their respective national televisions for the failed summit in Reykjavik.

Detroit, 22 October. General Motors becomes the fourth major US company to pull out of South Africa.

Saudi Arabia, 28 October. Sheikh Yamani, Saudi oil minister for 24 years, is sacked by King Fahd.

Britain, 29 December. Harold Macmillan, British prime minister from 1957 to 1963, dies at the age of 92.

Washington, 30 December. Reagan admits mistakes were made in his secret policy initiatives with Iran.

US bombs Libya for its terrorist attack

Washington, 16 April

Last night's surprise American raid on Tripoli has taken the lives of Colonel Muammar Gaddafi's 15-month-old adopted daughter and two American pilots. President Reagan told a meeting of businessmen here today, "We would prefer not to have to repeat the events of last night. What is required is for Libya to end its pursuit of terror for political goals."

The president ordered the attack in retaliation for Libya's "direct" role in the 5 April bombing of a West Berlin disco popular with US servicemen. The 18 bombers striking from a base in England were hampered by France's refusal to let them cross its air space. A further 15 planes took off from US carriers in the Mediterranean.

Sounds of bombs and guns in Tripoli were heard clearly by Americans listening to radio broadcasts live from the scene.

Marcos leaves: Cory Aquino is in office

Philippines, 27 February

Defeated at the polls and renounced by the US, Ferdinand Marcos has fled the Philippines, which he had ruled with increasingly authoritarian control for 20 years. He was succeeded as president by Corazon Aquino, who said, "We are finally free" and "A new life starts for our country".

Marcos had brought the nation to the edge of a military confrontation before he finally agreed to step down. Marcos refused to accept the results of an earlier election that apparently was won by Aquino.

Corazon Aquino poses pre-election before the huge statue of Marcos at Pugo.

Duvalier flees Haiti to shelter in France

"Baby Doc" (l) and "Papa Doc".

Haiti, 10 February

In Haiti, nearly three decades of dictatorship ended as Jean-Claude "Baby Doc" Duvalier, who held the title president-for-life, fled to France. Jubilant Haitians poured into the streets of Port-au-Prince. But the celebrations turned violent when crowds confronted the *Tontons Macoutes*, Duvalier's police.

Possibility of arms-for-hostages dealing

Washington, 30 November

The White House has been plunged into the worst crisis of the Reagan presidency with the disclosure that the administration has been selling arms to Iran and that some of the resulting money had been diverted to the rebels in Nicaragua.

By the end of the month there was a torrent of disclosures, some confusing and contradictory but all politically embarrassing. Reagan found himself confronted with questions of whether his administration had violated its own policy by selling arms to Iran, whether it had been attempting to trade arms for hostages in contravention of its stated policy and whether it had tried to circumvent a congressional ban on aid to the Nicaraguan Contras through diversion of funds.

Colonel North has also been implicated in the Iran-Contra deal.

Colonel Oliver North (right) before the House Foreign Affairs Committee.

Chernobyl releases deadly radiation

Ukraine, 30 April
The Soviet Union acknowledged that a major accident, believed to be the worst in the history of nuclear power, occurred four days ago at a nuclear generating plant at Chernobyl in the Ukraine.

An indication of the nature of the accident came from the Soviet request for West German and Swedish help to fight a fire in a nuclear reactor core. Chernobyl's core contains large amounts of flammable graphite, believed to be burning out of control. But the Soviets have provided no information on the amount of radioactivity released by the accident.

The accident at Chernobyl may be the worst in the history of nuclear power.

Waldheim accused of hiding Nazi past

Austria, 4 March
Former secretary general of the United Nations Kurt Waldheim, now an independent candidate for the presidency of Austria, has just been accused by the World Jewish Congress of serving in a German army command during the Second World War and participating in the torture of Yugoslavian Jews and the deportation of thousands of Greek Jews from Salonika in 1942-43. In a CBS News interview, he responded by saying: "It is true that I served in the German army command in the Balkans, but I never participated in any cruelties."

Kurt Waldheim denies accusations.

Challenger space shuttle explodes as horrified nation watches

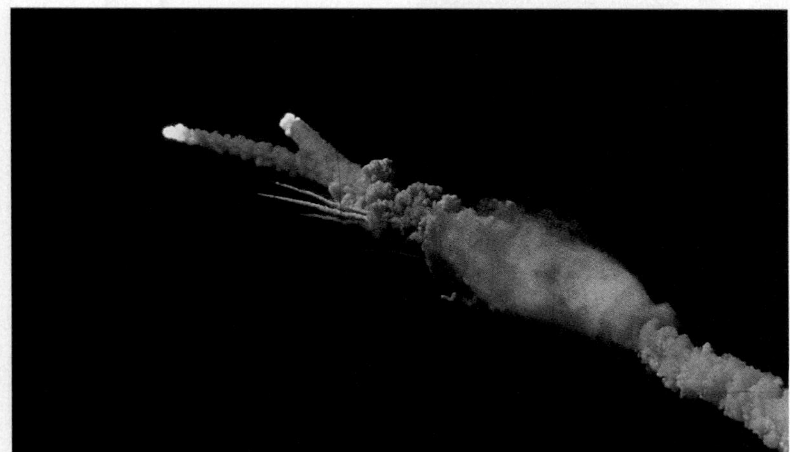

An explosion devastates "Challenger" just after lift-off at Cape Canaveral.

Houston, 31 January
The loss of the American space shuttle *Challenger* and its seven astronauts was mourned at the Johnson Space Center in Houston today, as President Reagan spoke of "our seven *Challenger* heroes" and pledged to honour them with a new national commitment to space exploration. *Challenger* exploded in a ball of fire shortly after it left the launching pad at Cape Canaveral on 28 January, in the worst accident in the history of the US space programme. The disaster was witnessed by thousands of spectators in Florida and by millions of television viewers.

Insider trading scandal hits Wall Street

Ivan Boesky arriving at the court.

New York, 18 November
In the midst of its greatest boom in history, Wall Street has been shaken to its foundations by a major scandal. Ivan Boesky, one of the richest and most famous arbitrageurs in New York's financial district, has pleaded guilty to buying and selling stocks and securities on the strength of illegal secret information. It will cost him dear: $100 million as penalty for his involvement in the insider trading game. Half of that total represents illegal profits, half is a civil penalty. He will also be barred for life from the US securities industry. He said he felt legal reforms should be adopted.

US Congress acclaims President Aquino

Cory Aquino wowed the US.

New York, 19 September
Dressed in her trade-mark yellow attire, Philippine president Corazon Aquino received an ecstatic welcome in Congress on Thursday. New York's Mayor Koch, who greeted Mrs Aquino in Manhattan today, had attended her speech in the House of Representatives. In his nine years in the House, he said, "never did I see anyone take Congress by such a storm as this woman did".

Cheers and applause were not the only things the Filipino leader received. Congress, in a surprise move, has voted to send the Aquino administration $200 million in economic aid.

1987

Beirut, 21 January. While on a church mission the Archbishop of Canterbury's special envoy, Terry Waite, is himself kidnapped trying to negotiate the release of other hostages.

Moscow, 29 January. Mikhail Gorbachev calls for greater democracy, based on *perestroika* (reconstruction) and *glasnost* (openness).

Britain, 26 February. The Synod of the Church of England votes for the ordination of women.

Argentina, 19 April. President Alfonsin personally ends a revolt by senior army officers.

Persian Gulf, 22 May. Iraqi rocket hits the American frigate *Stark*.

Britain, 12 June. Mrs Thatcher is re-elected, with an overall majority of over 100.

USA, 22 June. Fred Astaire, dance king of 1930s and 1940s movies, dies, aged 88.

Lyons, 3 July. Klaus Barbie is found guilty of wartime atrocities.

Washington, 17 July. Lieutenant Colonel Oliver North and Rear Admiral John Poindexter testify to Congress on the "Irangate" scandal.

Greece, 26 July. The government announces a state of emergency as the death toll in the heatwave passes 700.

Mecca, 30 July. Iranian zealots riot during the *Hajj*, the annual holy pilgrimage.

Britain, 20 August. A gunman goes on the rampage in the Wiltshire town of Hungerford, killing 14 and wounding 15.

USA, 28 August. Film director John Huston dies, aged 81.

Montreal, 16 September. More than 70 nations pledge to save the Earth's ozone layer.

Los Angeles, 1 October. An earthquake leaves six dead and 100 injured.

Sri Lanka, 12 October. Indian troops, sent in as peacekeepers, battle Tamil separatists.

Britain, 16 October. The storm of the century batters southern England and northern France with winds up to 110 mph (180 km/h).

Northern Ireland, 8 November. An IRA bomb kills 11 Remembrance Day marchers in Enniskillen.

USA, 18 December. Ivan Boesky, who gained over $80 million through insider trading, is given a three-year sentence.

Hundreds trapped as British ferry sinks

The capsized car ferry is held steady as rescuers search for survivors.

Zeebrugge, 6 March

Rescue divers have pulled some 300 survivors out of the British ferry *Herald of Free Enterprise*, which capsized today on its way from Zeebrugge, Belgium, to Dover, England. At least 26 of her passengers are dead, and up to 200 remain trapped.

Accounts indicate the accident may have been caused when the bow door opened en route, filling the ship with water. Air supplies in the cabin will support those inside, the BBC reports. Two-thirds of the ferry, however, is submerged. And one exhausted rescue diver was a prophet of doom: "I don't think they have a chance," he said.

Divers continue to search, and tugs are pulling the disabled vessel back to Zeebrugge.

Andy Warhol, the high priest of Pop Art, died unexpectedly in New York on 23 February after routine gall bladder surgery. He was 56. Warhol's list of artistic credits included film-making, photography and publishing. But he was best known for turning everyday images into high art through repetitious silk screen reproductions.

German pilot lands plane in Moscow

Moscow, 30 May

Strollers in Moscow's Red Square were amazed when a small plane landed among them yesterday, but Soviet officials were not in the least bit amused.

Marshal Sergei L Sokolov was dismissed as defence minister and military chiefs were rebuked for allowing 19-year-old West German Matthias Rust to fly a rented Cessna 400 miles (640 kilometres) through defended Soviet air space. Rust, who had only 25 hours of flying time to his name, flew in from Helsinki and landed beside the Kremlin wall. He was immediately hustled off for questioning.

Rust touches down in Red Square.

Seoul police lose control of streets

South Korea, 20 June

Ten days of heated protest came to a violent climax today in South Korea as police and student demonstrators clashed in the streets of Seoul. Tens of thousands of rioters ripped through the city, throwing stones, igniting fires and overpowering the police.

South Korea, plagued by years of unrest, seems on the verge of a major political collapse. Tension has mounted ever since President Chun Doo Hwan refused to allow a direct presidential election. There have been protests in 11 cities.

Iran-Contra report blames the president

Washington, 18 November
Seven months after testimonies on the Iran-Contra affair first began, Senate and House panels released a report charging President Reagan with "ultimate responsibility" for the scandal. Signed by Democratic majorities on the panels, the report says that if Reagan did not know funds from the Iran arms sales were diverted to the Contras, "he should have" and the report denounces the administration for allowing "pervasive dishonesty" and "disarray at the highest levels of government".

A minority report, leaked to the press two days earlier, accuses the majority of reaching "hysterical conclusions" and perpetuating "guerrilla warfare" between Congress and the White House. Three of 11 Republicans dissented, siding with the majority.

Colonel North assumed but was not sure the president knew about diversions.

Nuclear treaty is signed

Gorbachev and Reagan sign the arms control agreement at the White House.

Washington, 10 December
History was made two days ago in Washington. Soviet leader Mikhail Gorbachev and President Reagan signed the first treaty to reduce the size of their countries' nuclear arsenals. The treaty allows three years for the dismantling of all 1,752 Soviet and 859 American missiles with ranges of 300 to 3,400 miles (480 to 5,400 kilometres). And it describes in great detail how inspectors from both countries will ensure that the missiles are smashed, exploded, crushed, burned or launched into oblivion. Approval in the Senate is expected, despite the opposition of some conservatives who doubt that Soviet compliance can be verified and fear that removing missiles from Western Europe leaves the area open to attack by superior Soviet conventional forces.

At the summit, talks on strategic long-range weapons yielded a compromise limit of 4,900. The issue of "Star Wars" was shelved.

Israelis quell Arab riots in West Bank

Israel, 25 December
At least 1,000 Palestinians, says the Israeli army, are spending Christmas in jail for their role in recent protests in the West Bank and Gaza. Two weeks of unrest reached a climax on Monday when a general strike spread outside the occupied lands to Arabs with Israeli citizenship.

"This is unprecedented," said one Arab specialist. "It's the first time the Israeli Arabs have chosen to follow Arabs in the territories."

Stock market crash is worse than 1929

New York, 20 October
The bottom fell out of the stock market yesterday, and no one knows for sure what will happen next. Wall Street had its worst day ever, far worse than 1929. The Dow Jones industrial average plummeted a record 508 points, closing at 1,738.74. Volume was an unprecedented 604 million shares, and the ticker fell two hours behind. Shockwaves went around the world. The Tokyo exchange opened down sharply this morning, and the Hong Kong market has closed for a week.

John Phelan Jr, chairman of the New York Stock Exchange, compared the market collapse to a nuclear accident. "It's the nearest thing to a meltdown that I ever want to see." The Dean of the New York University business school said it was "a little like seeing the atom bomb go off. Once you've seen it," Richard West told the *New York Times*, "you know it could happen again."

Hess, last of the Nazi regime, dies in jail

Rudolf Hess, Hitler's deputy, had been in Allied custody since 1941.

West Berlin, 17 August
Alone and sullen – that's how Rudolf Hess, the last of Adolf Hitler's close colleagues, died.

Hess had been sentenced to life imprisonment at West Berlin's Spandau Prison. He tried four times to kill himself. Yesterday he succeeded, by strangulation with an electric cord. He was 93. Hess had been in Allied custody since 1941, after making a desperate attempt to forge peace with Britain. At Nuremberg he was condemned for planning aggressive war. He said then that he had no regrets.

1988

New York City, 13 January. Doctors reveal that one in 61 babies born in the city last month has AIDS.

USSR, 2 March. Russian troops enter mainly Moslem republic of Azerbaijan to quell rioting sparked by Christian Armenia's demand for the return of the enclave of Nagorny Karabakh.

Gibraltar, 6 March. Three IRA terrorists shot by British soldiers in civilian dress.

France, 10 May. Francois Mitterrand re-elected president, defeating Prime Minister Jacques Chirac.

Rangoon, 21 June. Dusk-to-dawn curfew imposed in Burmese capital after student protests in which six people, including five policemen, were killed.

Persian Gulf, 3 July. A US warship shoots down an Iranian airliner, killing 286.

North Sea, 6 July. Over 150 die in an explosion and fire on the *Piper Alpha* oil rig.

Germany, 28 August. 46 people killed and many injured in a terrible airshow accident at an airbase near Frankfurt

Mexico, 16 September. Hurricane Gilbert, the worst storm in the Western world this century, strikes Mexico for the second time in three days.

Seoul, 30 September. Ben Johnson of Canada is stripped of his 100 metres Olympics gold medal after it is discovered he has been taking drugs.

Chile, 6 October. General Pinochet is defeated in the general election.

Britain, 13 October. Carbon-dating tests at Oxford reveal the Turin Shroud to be a medieval fake.

Israel, 2 November. Yitzhak Shamir's right-wing Likud party squeezes home in the general election.

Moscow, 7 December. President Gorbachev announces swingeing cuts in the USSR's armed forces in a speech to the UN General Assembly.

Washington, 14 December. After Yasir Arafat renounces violence the US says it will open a dialogue with the PLO.

Scotland, 22 December. A Pan Am airliner is blown up in mid-air and crashes into Lockerbie, killing all 259 on board and 11 people on the ground.

Reagan visits Russia he dubbed "evil"

Moscow, 31 May

Early in his presidency, Ronald Reagan described the Soviet Union as "the evil empire". Today he appeared before an audience of 600 at Moscow State University – how he and the times have changed.

Reagan's visit is the first of an American chief to the Soviet Union in 14 years. While students and intellectuals greeted him warmly today, Reagan's first day in Moscow on Sunday was tense. He met with Soviet leader Mikhail Gorbachev and assailed the Russians' human rights record. White House chief of staff Howard Baker said the two leaders had not been friendly to begin with, and Reagan's remarks had heated tempers.

Reagan and Gorbachev together during the president's Moscow visit.

Major cities confronting a crack invasion

Detroit

"We're fighting an impossible fight if our city and other cities continue to be inundated by this drug," said Mayor Coleman Young of Detroit, speaking, of course, of the highly potent form of cocaine called crack. A recent State Department report urged that coca production be halted in Bolivia, Colombia and Peru by increasing military and economic aid to the governments of these countries. They could then step up the destruction of crops, processing laboratories and drug shipments. Meanwhile, Detroit, Miami and Washington DC report a surge in drug-related murders.

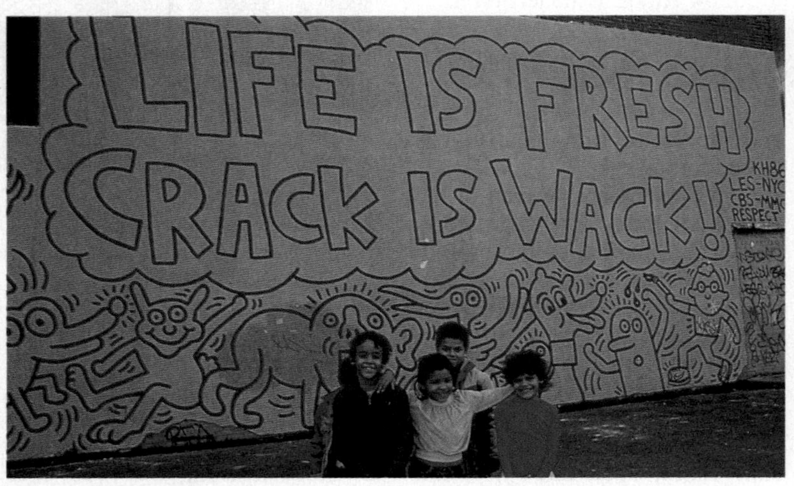

Many murals around America illustrate the deadly effects of crack cocaine.

Bush sweeps to 40-state victory

George Bush is jubilant at results.

Washington, 8 November

George Herbert Walker Bush, a decorated hero of the Second World War, was elected president of the United States today, winning 40 of the 50 states and defeating Governor Michael Dukakis of Massachusetts, his Democratic challenger. The final tally showed Bush with 426 electoral college votes to only 112 for Dukakis.

Iraq admits using chemical weapons

Iraq, 1 July

Iraq's foreign minister, Tariq Aziz, publicly admitted today that his country's planes dropped poison gas bombs during a March attack on the Iraqi town of Halabja, which is in territory occupied by Iran.

Khomeini ends eight-year war

Tehran, 20 July

Ayatollah Khomeini of Iran today proclaimed the end of the eight-year holy war with Iraq. In a radio address, he said Iran would accept the cease-fire plan drafted by the United Nations. He reminded his people that he "had promised to fight to the last drop of my blood", but that the decision to call off the fight comes in the best interests of Iran's Islamic republic. The war has raged since September 1980.

New Arab-Israeli clashes

Palestinians protest outside the Dome of the Rock in East Jerusalem.

Jerusalem, 15 January
Violence erupted today at one of Islam's holiest places, the Dome of the Rock Mosque in Arab East Jerusalem. Palestinians armed with stones sparred with Israeli police after services were held at the mosque for Arab protesters who have died in the recent unrest. The dome is revered as the site where Mohammed ascended to heaven on a white horse. A force of more than 1,000 Israeli police had been ordered to the scene, anticipating trouble. Several hundred young Palestinians excited the volatile crowd by chanting: "There is no God but Allah." The sequence of events that followed is unclear, but the police fired shots and protesters hurled rocks. Several policemen and at least 70 Arabs were injured.

Soviet perestroika is put into effect

Moscow, 1 January
Legislation initiated by Soviet leader Mikhail Gorbachev under his plan for *perestroika*, or restructuring, will transfer a major part of economic responsibility from the government to individual enterprises. However, this plan will also have the effect of removing much of the financial security that Soviet workers have always enjoyed.

Nicaragua gets armistice for May

Nicaragua, 24 March
The bloody six-year war in Nicaragua is over – maybe. The Sandinistas and the Contras have agreed to a cease-fire scheduled to run through May. President Daniel Ortega and Contra leader Adolfo Calera signed an accord, promising to work for protracted peace. It stipulates that the government release prisoners, permit the return of exiled National Guardsmen and guarantee freedom of expression.

Benazir Bhutto wins the election

Pakistan, 14 November
At age 35, she may become the world's youngest prime minister and the first woman to head a Moslem nation in centuries. Benazir Bhutto, who spent months in government jails, has won a seat in Pakistan's parliament. She heads the People's Party, the nation's largest, so she will probably be asked to form a new government.

Bhutto: from prison to parliament.

A huge earthquake devastates Armenia

Armenia, 10 December
An American plane loaded with emergency medical supplies touched down at Leninakan Airport in Armenia late tonight.

The gesture, a sign of improved East-West relations, was one of the few rays of hope in this ravaged area. Early on 7 December, an intense earthquake, 6.9 on the Richter scale, rumbled through Armenia. Leninakan, the republic's second-largest city, was 80 per cent destroyed, with Kirovakan, a city of 150,000, suffering a comparable degree of destruction. Spitak, a town adjacent to the earthquake's epicentre, was completely levelled.

Distraught Armenians in the wake of the massive 7 December earthquake.

Soviets finally pull out of Afghanistan

Russian troops are now moving out of Afghanistan after eight and a half years.

Afghanistan, 16 May
Eight and a half years after Soviet troops arrived, 1,200 of them today began pulling out of Afghanistan. In response to the Geneva agreement reached last month, about 30,000 soldiers are to leave this month; half of the Soviet total of 120,000 are due out by 15 August. Since the Soviet Union first helped the Afghan Communist government fight the Islamic guerrilla forces, some 16,000 Soviet soldiers have been killed.

The Islamic rebels, who have not accepted the Geneva accords, opened a rocket attack on the city of Jalalabad last night. Experts predict they will intensify their drive on Kabul after the August pullout.

1989

Libya, 4 January. US Navy fighter pilots shoot down two Libyan jets.

USA, 5 January. Serious conspiracy charges against Lieutenant Colonel Oliver North are dropped.

Tokyo, 7 January. Hirohito, emperor of Japan for 62 years, dies, aged 87.

Paraguay, 3 February. President Alfredo Stroessner is ousted by General Andres Rodriguez.

Boston, 11 February. The first ever Anglican woman bishop is consecrated in the US Episcopal Church.

USSR, 26 March. In the first free vote in the USSR maverick politican Boris Yeltsin wins an outstanding vote of confidence.

Britain, 15 April. Ninety-four Liverpool soccer fans are killed at Sheffield in a crush during an FA Cup semi-final.

France, 14 July. Celebrations mark the 200th anniversary of the French Revolution.

Beruit, 31 July. American hostage Lt Colonel Higgins hanged by his Shiite Moslem captors.

South Africa, 15 August. F W de Klerk becomes president of South Africa.

USA, 25 August. NASA scientists receive stunning photographs of Neptune and its moons from *Voyager 2*.

USA, 5 September. President Bush goes on television to announce a plan costing $7.86 billion to combat drug abuse.

Hungary, 10 September. Hungary opens its border with Austria as thousands of East Germans flee to a better life in the West.

Cambodia, 26 September. The last Vietnamese troops leave.

East Germany, 18 October. GDR hard-liner Erich Honecker is forced to resign and Egon Krenz is appointed to replace him as East German leader.

London, 20 October. The Guildford Four are freed after 14 years in jail for IRA pub bombings they didn't commit.

Prague, 24 November. The Communist leadership quits in the face of massive public demonstrations.

Malta, 3 December. Presidents Bush and Gorbachev announce an official end to the Cold War.

Massive earthquake rocks San Francisco Bay area, 270 deaths

A building in the Marina District of San Francisco is supported by timber.

California, 21 October
Memories of 1906 were revived at 5.04 pm on Tuesday, when a huge earthquake struck the San Francisco Bay area. The quake lasted 15 seconds and measured 6.9 on the Richter scale.

From the epicentre, 10 miles (16 kilometres) northeast of Santa Cruz along the San Andreas Fault, tremors reached north to Sacramento and south to Los Angeles.

In their wake, a wave of tragedy and devastation was left. There have been an estimated 270 deaths, 3,000 injuries and damage of $1 to $3 billion reported, along with electric power cuts.

US sends troops into Panama

Panama, 29 December
At 1 am on 20 December, Panama City was transformed into a war zone. The Bush administration, embarrassed by impotent attempts to oust General Manuel Noriega, unleashed 24,000 US troops to drive him from office and install the government of Guillermo Endara, elected president by the Panamanian people in a contest voided by Noriega.

After the swearing-in of the Endara government at an American military base, US troops attacked simultaneously at three points in Panama City and gained control of much of the area.

US troops on the streets of Panama.

Vast oil spill poisons the Alaskan shores

Alaska, 30 March
Oil from the biggest tanker spill in United States history has spread over 500 square miles (1,300 square kilometres) of Alaskan waters and coated huge stretches of coastline. A week after the *Exxon Valdez* ran aground with more than a million barrels of crude, the oil is more than a foot (30 centimetres) deep on some beaches. Dead birds, soaked in oil, wash onto the shore; sea otters, blackened by the spill, rub their eyes helplessly as they try to swim home in what used to be a pristine and majestic area.

President Bush today called the spill a "major tragedy", as Exxon admitted it had given up trying to contain the oil. Environmentalists say it will take much longer than the stated two months to clear up.

Animal recovery workers gather up dead sea otters after the oil spill.

Writer condemned to death by Iran

London, 24 February
Iran's Ayatollah Khomeini has declared Salman Rushdie's novel, *The Satanic Verses* blasphemous and has sentenced the author to death. On the 14th, the Ayatollah urged all Moslems to carry out his order, and put a US$1 million bounty on Rushdie, $3 million if the executioner is Iranian.

The author's "criminal" act lies in his portrayal of a worldly businessman-cum-prophet named Mahound, who Moslems claim is a satirical and highly sacrilegious depiction of Mohammed.

East Germany cracks wall to show fall

As the wall falls, Berlin parties.

East Berlin, 10 November
The Berlin Wall has been the most visible symbol of Communist oppression since its creation 28 years ago. Last night on the stroke of midnight, the East German government opened its borders, and the wall – actually two eight-feet (2.4 metre) concrete barriers that slice through Berlin – was transformed into a relic of a Cold War that has passed into history.

Within hours, thousands of East Germans poured across the border, eager to test their freedom and see how the prosperous other half lives. Thousands more spent hours dancing for joy on top of the wall. Some vented years of pent-up anger by taking a pickaxe to the wall. West Germans gave their compatriots a joyful welcome. Speaking outside West Berlin's city hall, Chancellor Helmut Kohl promised, "We're on your side; we are and remain one nation. We belong together."

For many in the West, however, joy was tempered by concern over their ability to handle the flood of refugees – 225,000 from East Germany and 300,000 from the Soviet Union and Poland in this year alone. Said West Berlin's mayor to those considering coming West: "Please do it tomorrow, do it the day after tomorrow. We are having trouble dealing with this."

Solidarity sweeps to power in Poland

Poland, 5 June
In a stunning rebuke to the Communist Party, Polish voters yesterday gave Solidarity candidates a huge victory in Poland's first competitive elections in four decades. "Solidarity has achieved a decisive majority," conceded Communist Party spokesman Jan Bisztyga.

Victory for Solidarity's Walesa.

Revolution in Rumania: dictator Ceausescu and wife executed

Bucharest, 31 December
The Communist dictator Nicolae Ceausescu and his wife Elena, executed on Christmas Day, lie dead while the nation emerges from its bloodsoaked nightmare.

The Rumanian revolution began on 17 December when authorities in the city of Timisoara moved against the Rev Laszlo Toekes, an ethnic Hungarian and vocal supporter of Rumania's two million Hungarians. Within hours up to 10,000 demonstrators were met by tanks and armed security forces. Ceausescu's troops relentlessly mowed down unarmed men, women and children.

A demonstrator mounts the balcony of the central Communist headquarters.

Tiananmen massacre as Chinese soldiers slaughter students

A protester is helped through the crowds, after being bloodied in a clash.

Beijing, 5 June
Fires are still burning in Beijing today and the sounds of automatic weapons can be heard throughout the city as tens of thousands of Chinese soldiers tighten control on pro-democracy demonstrators. The student leaders say more than 2,000 people were killed after the tanks rolled into Tiananmen Square early yesterday morning.

Protest leaders are calling for a general strike, but the hard-liners in control of the government vow to crush the "counter-revolutionary rebellion". Outrage over the massacre spread quickly, and protests are reported in other Chinese cities.

Iran mourns the loss of Khomeini

Tehran, 6 June
Crying, "We have lost our father," three million Iranians today buried Ayatollah Rouahallah Khomeini in Tehran's "martyrs' cemetery". He died on 3 June after a long illness that many surmised to be cancer. He was born in either 1900 or 1902 and had ruled Iran since 1979.

The funeral was a pastiche of bizarre scenes. The anguished mourners, beating their heads in grief, at one point pulled the imam's body from its coffin.

Frantic soldiers finally retrieved the body, battered and stripped by mourners desperate to touch him. When Western journalists turned up, the crowds began shouting, "Death to America".

Americans will best remember the Ayatollah Khomeini as the man whose followers held 52 of their fellow countrymen hostage in Tehran for 444 days.

To these people, however, he is the hero who delivered them from foreign oppression and the shah.

1990

London, 9 January. The British government pledges £2.2 million for research into BSE, or "mad cow disease".

Moscow, 25 February. Hundreds of thousands of demonstrators call for democratic reforms.

Nicaragua, 26 February. President Daniel Ortega suffers shock election defeat at the hands of Violeta Chamorro.

Africa, 21 March. Namibia becomes fully independent.

London, 31 March. A huge march on the eve of the introduction of the poll tax ends in a riot.

Britain, 11 April. Customs seize sections of piping believed to be intended for the construction of an Iraqi "supergun".

USA, 15 April. Actress Greta Garbo dies, aged 84.

USSR, 17 April. Six weeks after Lithuania declares independence, the USSR imposes an economic blockade.

Beirut, 20 April. US hostage Robert Polhill is released after 1,183 days in captivity.

Middle East, 22 May. North and South Yemen merge to become a single state.

Bucharest, 14 June. The government buses in club-wielding miners to tackle opposition demonstrators.

Iran, 22 June. Forty thousand people are feared dead in an earthquake in the north.

Geneva, 27 July. Reports show that AIDS has become the main cause of death for women aged 20 to 40.

Islamabad, 8 August. Prime Minister Benazir Bhutto and her government are sacked by President Gulam Ishaq Khan.

Beirut, 23 August. Irish hostage Brian Keenan is released by *Hezbollah* after 1,597 days in captivity.

Britain, 23 October. Former British prime minister Edward Heath gains the release of some of the hostages held by Saddam Hussein.

Dublin, 9 November. Mary Robinson is elected Ireland's first woman president.

USA, 29 November. President Bush wins UN backing for use of force against Iraq.

Poland, 9 December. Lech Walesa is elected president.

Nelson Mandela is freed

ANC leader Nelson Mandela, with his wife, Winnie, greets supporters.

Cape Town, 11 February

Nelson Mandela, dignified but defiant, left Victor Verster prison near Cape Town this afternoon after 27 years. The African National Congress (ANC) leader was greeted by 2,000 people, but in Cape Town itself 50,000 gathered outside the city hall. A huge banner said it all: "Nelson Mandela – the nation welcomes you home."

Mandela, white-haired and grey-suited, appeared, flanked by his wife, Winnie. His first public words were: "I greet you in the name of peace, democracy and freedom for all." He thanked those who had campaigned for him.

Germans' dream of unity comes true

Berlin, 3 October

Germany is one nation again. Its rebirth was ushered in at the stroke of midnight with a triumphant peal from the Freedom Bell at Berlin's Schöneberg city hall. The Soviet-backed German Democratic Republic (East Germany) no longer exists.

A roar went up from thousands of cheering, weeping people who hugged each other with joy and waved a forest of black, red and gold flags. Germany, divided 45 years ago, after the Second World War, is free and united in liberty.

As fireworks exploded, the people found it hard to believe that it was only eleven months since the hated Wall began to collapse and the Soviets loosened their iron grip on East Germany. They know that the future holds many difficulties but that is for tomorrow. Tonight there is only joy.

Known as the Federal Republic of Germany, the united nation has a total population of 78.5 million people. Its constitution, currency, flag and national anthem are those of what was until tonight West Germany. The single government is headed by Chancellor Helmut Kohl. The new Germany's economy will now have to adjust to the harsh reality of absorbing that of East Germany, which has been in a disastrous state for years. Politicians and economists are already warning affluent West Germans of the consequences of unification.

Celebrations at the Berlin Reichstag.

Iraqi forces seize control of Kuwait

Kuwait, 2 August

Iraqi tanks, aircraft and troops stormed across the Kuwaiti border at dawn and seized control of this tiny oil-rich state on the Persian Gulf. Saddam Hussein, president of Iraq, had massed tanks along the border, but few believed that this was more than a bluff.

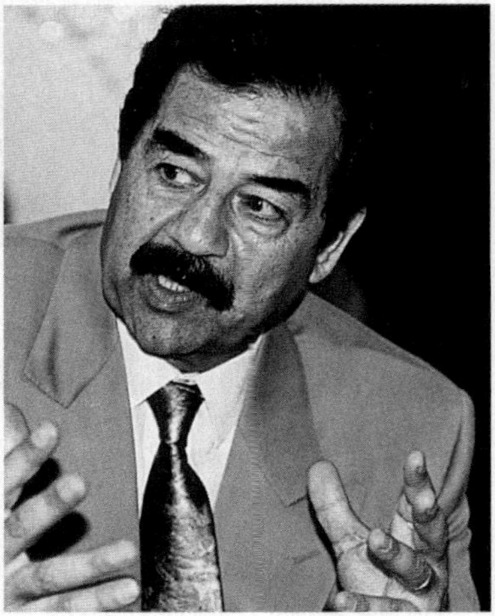

Iraqi president Saddam Hussein.

Noriega flown to Miami and trial

Miami, 4 January

Panama's fallen strongman, Manuel Noriega, stood in a Miami courtroom today charged with drug trafficking. Noriega was arrested when he left the Vatican embassy in Panama City, where he took sanctuary on 24 December following the US invasion of Panama.

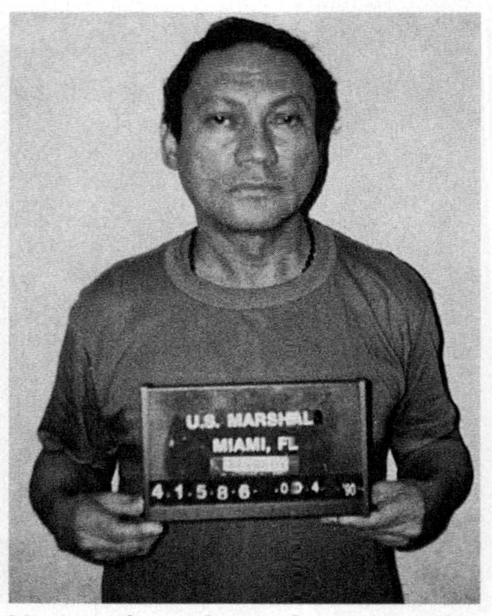

Noriega faces drugs charges in US.

Great Britain no longer an island nation

London, 1 December
Britain's 8,000 years as an island came to an end at 11.15 am today when, to a roar of applause from his assembled colleagues, Graham Fagg's jackhammer broke through the last section of chalk separating France from England.

Through a small hole appeared the head of Philippe Cozette, Fagg's opposite number on the French side of this newly dug service tunnel. English workmen sipped mineral water while the French drank champagne.

The 30.7-mile (49.1-kilometre) Channel Tunnel linking the two countries is due to be open to the public in late 1993. It will have two rail lines so that passengers can travel backwards and forwards beneath the Channel in 30 minutes.

Frenchman Philippe Cozette clutches a piece of Channel Tunnel stone.

Mrs Thatcher, Britain's Iron Lady, quits

London, 27 November
The Thatcher era is over. On 22 November, the prime minister gave up the fight for leadership of the Tory party.

Today she was succeeded by 47-year-old John Major, who had been her chancellor of the exchequer. He was elected by the Conservative Party caucus in the House of Commons.

"It's a funny old world," said Mrs Thatcher when, with eyes moistening, she reflected on the end of the 11-year premiership she had never lost at the polls. She made up her mind to quit less than 24 hours after announcing she would continue her fight to hold on to the position.

"Maggie" (of whom French president Mitterrand said, "she has Marilyn Monroe's mouth and Caligula's eyes") finally threw in the towel after it became clear that most of her cabinet colleagues felt she could no longer beat her chief rival for the Tory party leadership, former defence secretary Michael Heseltine. "I have concluded that the unity of my party and the prospect of victory would be better served if I stood down," she said in explanation for her resignation.

She then went to Westminster where fellow Tories greeted her with cheers, tinged, no doubt, with a little guilt about the nature of the coup which had abruptly ended the reign of Britain's first woman prime minister.

Iron Lady bends to party pressure.

Washington mayor arrested for drugs

Washington DC's Mayor Barry.

Washington, 19 January
Marion Barry, mayor of the capital and one of America's best-known black politicians, was secretly videotaped smoking a pipeful of "crack" – the highly addictive form of cocaine – FBI agents said today.

The filming took place shortly after the mayor had been lured to an hotel room in the city by an ex-girlfriend. FBI agents arrested Barry as he lit up the pipe. The popular mayor now faces a possible prison sentence. Despite his denials, Barry has long been suspected of using illicit drugs.

Russia opts for Yeltsin in third balloting

Boris Yeltsin is adored by the crowds and seen as the radical standard-bearer.

Moscow, 29 May
It has definitely not been a good month for Mikhail Gorbachev. On 1 May the Soviet leader was humiliated by jeering crowds during the May Day celebration in Red Square – that most hallowed of Soviet occasions.

Today, Boris Yeltsin, a popular Soviet politician and his former ally, emerged in triumph as the president of the vast Russian republic. In the third round of the balloting he was elected chairman of the Russian Supreme Soviet. His victory gives him the leadership of more than half the Soviet Union's 280 million people and a formidable power base from which to challenge the Soviet president.

Yeltsin, who is adored by the masses as the standard-bearer for the radicals in the current Soviet parliament, defeated a candidate who was favoured by Gorbachev, Aleksandr Vlasov.

1,400 pilgrims die in disaster at Mecca

Mecca, 2 July
At least 1,400 Moslem pilgrims were crushed to death today in a tunnel leading from the famous *Ka'aba* shrine inside Mecca's Great Mosque to nearby Mount Arafat. In blazing temperatures of up to 110 degrees Fahrenheit (43 degrees Celsius), 5,000 men and women – five times the tunnel's maximum capacity – had poured into the walkway when the air-conditioning failed and panic struck. Over 1,400 of them were suffocated or trampled to death. At least 1.5 million pilgrims have gathered in Mecca and Medina for the beginning of the Moslem feast of *Eid al-Adha*. No one suggests it was not an accident.

1991

Latvia, 15 January. Following their move into Lithuania, Soviet troops also occupy part of the Latvian capital, Riga.

Kuwait, 16 January. Operation "Desert Storm" is launched to drive Iraq out of Kuwait.

Iraq, 18 January. Iraq starts firing Scud missiles at Israeli cities.

South Africa, 1 February. President de Klerk announces the abolition of the last remaining apartheid laws.

London, 7 February. The IRA fires a mortar into the garden of 10 Downing Street.

Thailand, 23 February. A military junta headed by General Sunthorn Kongsompong takes power.

Budapest, 25 February. Leaders of the Warsaw Pact vote to dissolve its military structures by 31 March.

Britain, 14 March. The "Birmingham Six", imprisoned for 16 years for their alleged part in IRA pub bombings, are set free after a court agrees that the police fabricated evidence.

South Africa, 14 May. Winnie Mandela is sentenced to six years in prison for her part in the kidnapping and beating of three black youths and the death of a fourth.

Madras, 21 May. A suicide bomber kills the former prime minister, Rajiv Gandhi.

Milwaukee, 25 July. Police claim that a 31-year-old man cut up 18 victims and ate parts of their bodies.

USSR, 1 October. The city of Leningrad officially changes its name to St Petersburg.

Croatia, 26 October. The historic port of Dubrovnik comes under siege by the Serb-dominated Yugoslav army.

Britain, 19 November. Terry Waite is home after nearly five years in Beirut as a hostage.

USA, 4 December. Pan Am stops flying as a final rescue plan fails.

Lebanon, 4 December. The last American hostages are freed.

Palm Beach, 11 December. William Kennedy Smith, nephew of Senator Edward Kennedy, is acquitted in a rape trial.

Australia, 20 December. Bob Hawke is ousted as prime minister by Paul Keating.

Canary Islands, 5 November. UK publishing tycoon Robert Maxwell, who vanished from his yacht, was found dead in the sea off Tenerife today.

UN allies free Kuwait

Jubilant Kuwaitis celebrate the long-awaited liberation of their country.

Kuwait, 28 February

The Gulf war is over. Yesterday at 9 pm Washington time, President Bush announced on nationwide TV: "Kuwait is liberated. Iraq's army is defeated. I am pleased to announce that at midnight tonight, exactly 100 hours since ground operations began and six weeks since the start of Operation Desert Storm, all United States and coalition forces will suspend offensive combat operations."

Kuwait City, which has endured nearly seven months of occupation, is celebrating wildly. But behind the joy there is anger. The wealthy emirate is in ruins: power is cut, hospitals have been wrecked, banks looted and more than 700 oil wells are spewing flames.

In Saudi Arabia, commanders of the UN alliance are counting the cost of the short, high-tech war. A total of 141 US servicemen were killed, while 472 were wounded. More than 20 of the deaths were in "friendly fire" incidents. US military officials blame the high level of such casualties on the featureless terrain, the long range of modern battlefield weapons and the need to fight in rain and darkness. British land forces lost 18 men, the French two and the Arab contingents 44. But no nation lost more lives than Iraq. The allies estimate that 150,000 Iraqis were killed.

Yugoslavia edges closer to civil war

Tanks are on the streets of Ljubljana.

Yugoslavia, 29 June

Yugoslavia is heading for civil war. In Slovenia and Croatia, constituent republics of Yugoslavia that have declared independence, there is fighting, and airports and borders are closed. An attack on Slovenia by federal forces has claimed 30 lives in two days, and federal tanks are on the streets of the republic's capital, Ljubljana.

Slovenia and Croatia both have democratically elected presidents and enjoy higher standards of living than do the other four republics. Serbia, the most powerful republic, is determined to prevent the break-up of Yugoslavia, and it controls the federal army.

On 30 April, one of the most violent cyclones to hit Bangladesh in two decades came roaring out of the Bay of Bengal. Winds of 145 mph (230 km/h) drove a tidal wave 20ft (6 m) high into the port of Chittagong. An estimated 120,000 people were killed, millions more were made homeless and vast coastal regions were flooded.

Kurdish rebels flee Saddam's troops

Kirkuk, 31 March
Iraqi forces have recaptured the northern oil city of Kirkuk and are pushing back Kurdish guerrillas. Kurdish leaders refuse to admit that they have been defeated. They claim that 1,000 villagers have been massacred by Iraqi soldiers. Thousands of Kurds, terrified by rumours of the massacres, are on the move, fleeing from the Iraqis. Britain and the US are refusing to intervene on the grounds that what happens inside Iraq is a matter for the Iraqis. Saddam is mopping up a Shi'ite revolt in the south. Refugees are fleeing towns along the Euphrates, and Baghdad itself.

Coup fails: Gorbachev survives attack

Tanks on the streets of Moscow after the coup against President Gorbachev.

Moscow, 21 August
Mikhail Gorbachev was restored as Soviet president today as the coup mounted against him by hard-line military and KGB leaders caved in to popular resistance led by the Russian president, Boris Yeltsin.

As some of those responsible for the bungled coup rushed to plead for clemency at the Crimean holiday retreat where Gorbachev had been under house arrest, others went into hiding. Interior Minister Boris Pugo has committed suicide. The coup has unravelled with amazing speed, with thousands in Soviet cities rushing to raise the barricades against tanks and troops ordered in by the conspirators.

Senators home in on sexual harassment

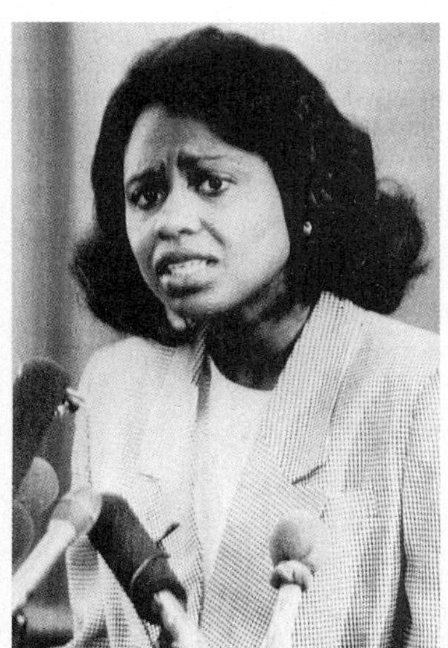
Anita Hill testified against Thomas.

Washington, 15 October
Senate hearings that have thrust sexual harassment to the forefront of American debate ended today. Clarence Thomas, a federal appeals court judge, was confirmed as a Supreme Court justice by a vote of 52-48. Thomas was accused of sexual harassment by Anita Hill, a law professor who had worked for him. Hill said that the judge made lewd suggestions to her, boasted of the size of his penis, and described pornography.

Thomas is a conservative, and President Bush nominated him in order to cement the conservative majority on the court. Liberals tried to stop him, and Hill's allegations were leaked to the media, changing the focus of the hearings.

The US Supreme Court nominee Clarence Thomas denies sexual harassment.

USSR ends, President Gorbachev resigns

Boris Yeltsin (arm raised) will now control the ex-Soviet nuclear arsenal.

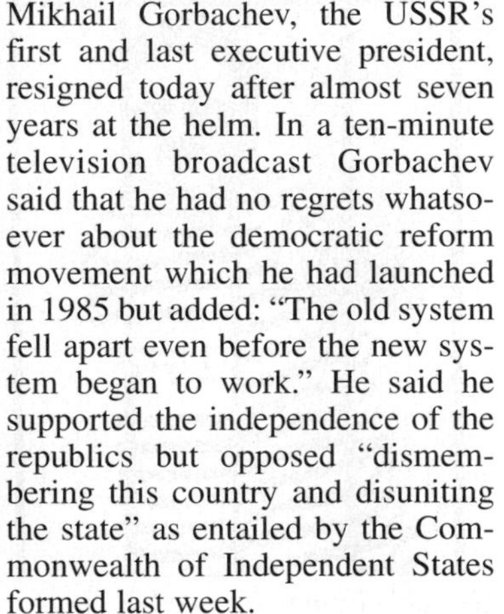

USSR, 25 December
Mikhail Gorbachev, the USSR's first and last executive president, resigned today after almost seven years at the helm. In a ten-minute television broadcast Gorbachev said that he had no regrets whatsoever about the democratic reform movement which he had launched in 1985 but added: "The old system fell apart even before the new system began to work." He said he supported the independence of the republics but opposed "dismembering this country and disuniting the state" as entailed by the Commonwealth of Independent States formed last week.

As Gorbachev spoke, the red flag was lowered over the Kremlin, the ancient fortress which for three-quarters of a century had been the heart of the world's largest Communist empire. The change was more than symbolic: control of the Soviet nuclear arsenal passed to President Boris Yeltsin of Russia.

Gorbachev's fate was sealed four days ago, when the leaders of 11 former Soviet republics formally signed a declaration forming the Commonwealth of Independent States. In doing so, they declared that the Soviet Union no longer existed and abolished Gorbachev's job as president.

1992

Brussels, 15 January. The European Commission recognises Croatia and Slovenia.

Dublin, 30 January. Charles Haughey resigns as the Irish *taoiseach* (prime minister).

Netherlands, 7 February. Two agreements to bring closer European unity are signed in Maastricht.

Detroit, 24 February. Just ten days after Ford posts its biggest-ever loss, General Motors announces a world record deficit of $4.5 billion.

Sarajevo, 1 March. Bosnian Serbs begin sniping, after Croats and Moslems vote for Bosnian independence.

South Africa, 17 March. White South Africans approve constitutional reforms giving legal equality to blacks.

Indianapolis, 26 March. World heavyweight boxing champion Mike Tyson is found guilty of rape.

Britain, 10 April. John Major leads the Conservatives to an unexpected fourth successive general election victory.

Kabul, 28 April. Rebels occupy the Afghan capital.

Algeria, 29 June. President Mohammed Boudiaf is shot dead by a member of the Islamic Salvation Front.

Sarajevo, 2 July. UN troops take control of the airport in Sarajevo, besieged by Bosnian Serbs.

Miami, 10 July. General Manuel Noriega of Panama is sentenced to 40 years in prison for drug trafficking.

Barcelona, 9 August. The Olympic Games close with the former Soviet Union at the top of the medals table.

Northern Ireland, 27 August. A 19-year-old man becomes the 3,000th fatal victim of sectarian violence.

Germany, 29 August. Thousands of people demonstrate against a wave of racist attacks aimed at immigrants.

Canada, 26 October. A national referendum is against giving Quebec special status.

Britain, 11 November. The Church of England votes its final approval for the ordination of women.

India, 7 December. Widespread riots follow the sacking of a mosque by Hindu fanatics in northern town of Ayodhya.

Indonesia, 12 December. An earthquake kills 1,500 people.

Serbian death camps shock the world

Serbian prisoners walk around the yard of a military prison in Sarajevo.

Bosnia, 15 August

The appalling images of emaciated prisoners held in Serbian prison camps in Bosnia have raised the spectre of Nazi camps and shocked the world. Rumours of brutality, murder and rape have now been confirmed by TV pictures seen round the world. Red Cross experts and US officials are denouncing the Serb "ethnic cleansing" policy, removing members of other ethnic communities from the Serbian-dominated areas. A Red Cross report tells of innocent civilians being arrested and subjected to inhumane treatment as part of a policy of forced population transfers carried out on a massive scale.

End of road for the Shining Path head

Lima, 12 September

Peru's most wanted man, Abimael Guzman, 57, was arrested today. The "fourth sword of Marxism," as the former philosophy professor is known by followers, founded the Marxist guerrilla group *Sendero Luminoso*, or Shining Path, in 1970. He faces charges of treason and a life sentence. He had been in hiding since 1980, when Shining Path began its campaign of armed insurgency.

Apprehending Guzman was a main goal of President Alberto Fuji-mori. In April, he suspended parliament and the judiciary to rule the country single-handedly with the backing of the military.

Abimael Guzman arrested in Lima.

Bush collapses during Tokyo state dinner

Tokyo, 8 January

As TV cameras rolled during a state dinner in Tokyo, George Bush turned as white as rice, flopped backward in his chair, vomited on Japanese prime minister Kiichi Miyazawa and finally hit the floor as secret service agents scrambled to assist him. The president regained his composure and excused himself to continue his battle with gastric flu in private.

Bush came to Japan with the heads of top US car manufacturers Ford, General Motors and Chrysler to promote free trade.

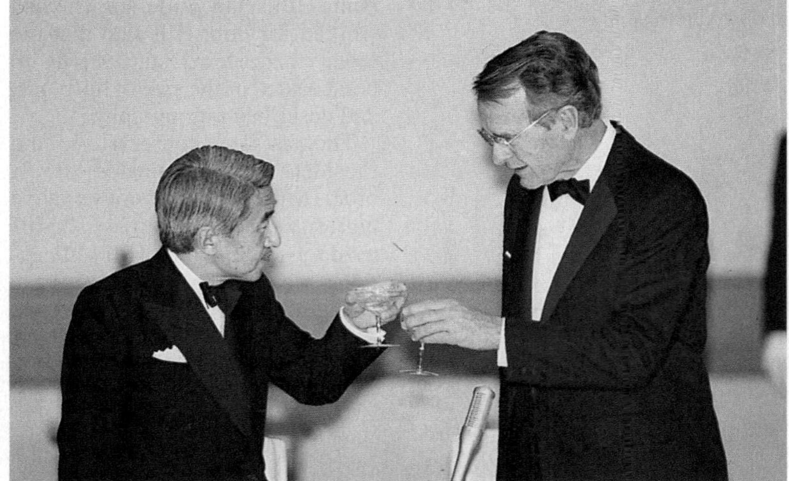

President George Bush drinks a toast before being taken suddenly ill.

World population in 2020 to be 8 billion

London, 21 March

There are 5.4 billion people living on Earth; that is twice as many as in 1952 and in the next 28 years the world's population will grow by a massive 52 per cent.

That means 8.2 billion people will be crammed on to a planet that is already failing to feed itself. That is the alarming conclusion of the UN's Census Bureau's *World Population Profile*.

Worst hit will be Africa; despite having the highest infant death rate, the continent's population is expected to double by 2020.

Bill Clinton beats Bush to White House

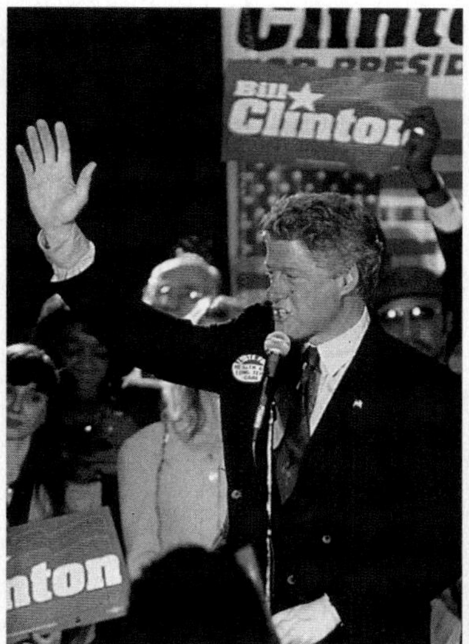

Bill Clinton wins as New Democrat.

Washington, 4 November

Americans have chosen their 42nd president: Bill Clinton. The Arkansas governor is the first Democrat to be elected president since 1976. Clinton campaigned as a "New Democrat", combining the traditionally Democratic liberal social themes with calls for greater fiscal responsibility and closer cooperation with business.

Clinton received 43 per cent of the popular vote, well ahead of President George Bush, who received 38 per cent. A third-party candidate, the Texas billionaire Ross Perot, who ran on a deficit reduction platform, won an unprecedented 19 per cent of the popular vote.

South Africa township massacre kills 39

Johannesburg, 18 June

A gang of 200 men armed with guns and pangas shot and hacked through Biopatong township, 40 miles (64 kilometres) from Johannesburg, and a squatter camp last night, killing 39 people and wounding many more. The African National Congress blamed the Zulu Inkatha Freedom Party for the attack and accused the government of complicity. The government said ANC was at fault for its mass protest campaign. Now the government's plan for negotiations on constitutional reform is put at risk.

Residents of Biopatong township try to carry a wounded friend to safety.

The world's wealthiest trade bloc is born

Washington, 12 August

The US, Canada and Mexico today concluded an historic pact aimed at creating the world's largest and wealthiest trading bloc. It will span a zone from the Yukon to the Yucatan, totalling 360 million people and a $6 trillion economy. The trio have agreed to do away with barriers to the movement of money, goods and services over the next 15 years. President Bush said the accord, known as the North American Free Trade Agreement, or NAFTA, begins "a new era" for economic cooperation.

Los Angeles burns after the King verdict

Videotape taken by a bystander showed Rodney King being beaten by police.

Los Angeles, 2 May

An uneasy calm has returned to a battered Los Angeles after two days of rioting that have left at least 58 dead and thousands injured. Firefighters in bullet-proof vests continue to discover charred bodies in burnt-out buildings.

Barely restrained racial tensions exploded into an orgy of rioting, murder and looting two days ago soon after a jury which included no black members acquitted four white policemen of savagely beating a black motorist, Rodney King. The beating was captured on videotape by a bystander and has been shown on TV news all over the country.

The verdict outraged the city's black community. A few incidents of arson soon grew and spread.

Bush sends marines on Somalia mission

Somalia, 9 December

Heavily armed US marines stormed ashore before dawn today ready to do battle with the Somali gunmen who have been holding the famine-stricken country to ransom. Much to their embarrassment, the marines were instead confronted by the world's press. The plan is to secure the airport and port areas in the capital, Mogadishu, so that food and medicine can be safely airlifted in to the thousands of Somalis dying of starvation. Then, US and UN units will move out to the hinterland to distribute the relief aid and protect supplies from Somalia's warlords.

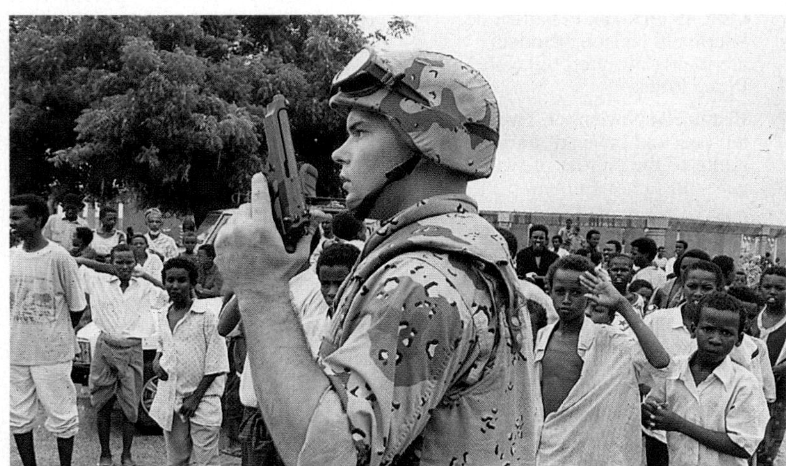

Watched by Somalis, a US marine secures the surrounding of the US embassy.

1993

Europe, 1 January. The Single European Market, encompassing 375 million people, comes into being.

Paris, 6 January. Dancer Rudolph Nureyev dies of AIDS at 54.

New York, 3 February. Black tennis star Arthur Ashe, 49, dies of AIDS, contracted from a blood transfusion.

Britain, 11 February. The queen volunteers to pay income and capital gains tax.

Haiti, 17 February. Up to 1,700 people are feared dead after a ferry sinks.

USA, 14 March. A blizzard sweeps through eastern states leaving 115 dead.

Britain, 20 March. The IRA explode two bombs in a shopping centre in Warrington, killing a four-year-old boy.

France, 29 March. Conservative parties replace socialists as the main force in the National Assembly, with over 80 per cent of the seats.

Texas, 19 April. The FBI ends a 51-day siege by storming the Branch Davidian religious cult headquarters in Waco.

Florence, 27 May. A bomb blast outside the Uffizi kills five people and damages several works of art.

Geneva, 17 June. Lord Owen admits that months of diplomacy have failed to bring about a Bosnian peace plan.

Lebanon, 27 July. Israeli guns and aircraft pound southern Lebanon in reprisal for rocket attacks by *Hezbollah*.

USA, 1 August. Twenty million acres (8,100,000 hectares) of farmland are underwater as the Mississippi and its tributaries burst their banks and cause the worst flooding in US history.

Oslo, 15 October. President de Klerk and Nelson Mandela are jointly awarded the Nobel Peace Prize.

Britain, 24 November. Two ten-year-old boys are found guilty of the murder of two-year-old James Bulger.

Geneva, 15 December. The Uruguay round of the GATT agreement on international trade is signed after seven years of negotiation.

Australia, 22 December. Aborigines celebrate the Native Title Bill, an historic victory over land rights.

Velvet divorce for Czechs and Slovaks

Czechoslovakia, 1 January

Czechoslovakia, born just 74 years ago, ceased to exist at midnight last night. As the new year began, the country's 15.6 million inhabitants became citizens of either Slovakia or the Czech Republic. Unlike Yugoslavia, the split has been a remarkably peaceful one.

Many thousands of Czechs and Slovaks were out today on the streets of Prague and Bratislava, the capitals of Europe's two newest nations, to celebrate what has been dubbed the "velvet divorce".

White rule ends in South Africa

The final whites-only parliament.

South Africa, 22 December

The South African parliament voted itself out of existence by 237 votes to 45 today in a move that will lead to black majority rule after the first all-race election next April. President Frederik de Klerk, the architect of the reforms, told legislators: "By accepting a new constitution, we took South Africa over the threshold of history into a new era, with all its dangers."

President de Klerk added that the next parliament would remove "the albatross of injustice, exclusion and discrimination".

The move was bitterly opposed by the white supremacists, and there are already threats being heard of violence.

Croats destroy Mostar's Ottoman bridge

Mostar, 9 November

The elegant 16th-century bridge built by Sultan Suleiman to link the east and west banks of the Bosnian town of Mostar was sent crashing into the Neretva River by a barrage of shells from Croatian guns today. Moslems who had tried to protect its slender single span with a pathetic barricade of tyres could only weep as the bridge, which has been featured on a million postcards, was destroyed. UN official Jerrie Hulme said the Croats pounded it until there was nothing left. "It was certainly targeted, there's no doubt about it," said Hulme. "It wasn't a symbol of the Moslems or the Croats. It was a symbol of the whole city."

The graceful bridge spanning the Neretva has been destroyed by shell fire.

Yeltsin crushes the hard-liners' rebellion

Moscow, 4 October

The hard-line rebellion against Boris Yeltsin was crushed today when the army swung its might behind the Russian president and in a day-long battle reduced the White House, the besieged parliament building, to a wreck, its white walls holed by tank shells and blackened by the smoke pouring from shattered windows.

Dozens of people are feared dead in the hand-to-hand fighting that raged as Spetsnaz commandos took it over floor by floor. The end came when hundreds of delegates who had barricaded themselves inside the White House emerged under the guns of the soldiers. Some waved white flags, others clasped their hands behind their heads as they walked dejectedly towards buses which carried them off to prison.

Hand-to-hand combat broke out as commandos took over the White House.

Middle East: Shalom, salaam, peace agreed at last

On the lawns of the White House Clinton brings two bitter enemies together.

Washington, 13 September
History was made at 11.47am today on the South Lawn of the White House when two enemies shook hands. Yasir Arafat, the chairman of the PLO, extended his hand to Israeli prime minister Yitzhak Rabin, who hesitated, then took it. Two minutes earlier, on the desk used for the signing of the 1979 Israel-Egypt peace treaty, Shimon Peres, Israel's foreign minister, and the PLO's Mahmoud Abbas signed an agreement providing for limited Palestinian autonomy in the Gaza Strip and the West Bank.

President Bill Clinton, whose foreign policy on Somalia, Bosnia and Haiti has been criticised as unfocused, is reaping the political benefits of today's accord. In his speech, he hailed "the efforts of all who have laboured before us," thanking Norway's government, which brokered the secret talks between Israel and the PLO. The agreement gives the Palestinians a measure of self-rule immediately in Gaza, Jericho and some parts of the West Bank. Israeli withdrawal from Gaza and Jericho is scheduled to begin on 13 December.

The territories will be run by a Palestinian Council which should be elected by 13 July next year. The ultimate objective is a permanent peace accord by December.

Georgia crisis worsens as rebels advance

Abkhazian soldiers fire on Georgia.

Georgia, 6 July
Eduard Shevardnadze, Georgian leader and former Soviet foreign minister, has been given sweeping powers in the face of an onslaught by Abkhazian rebels against the Black Sea resort of Sukhumi, on what was once known as the Soviet Riviera. Shevardnadze narrowly escaped being killed when his car came under fire while visiting troops fighting off the Abkhazian attacks. Russia has called on the Abkhazians, Moslems seeking their own state, and Georgia to sign a peace deal, but the Georgians refuse. They are accusing Moscow of supporting the separatists.

Northern Ireland declaration signed

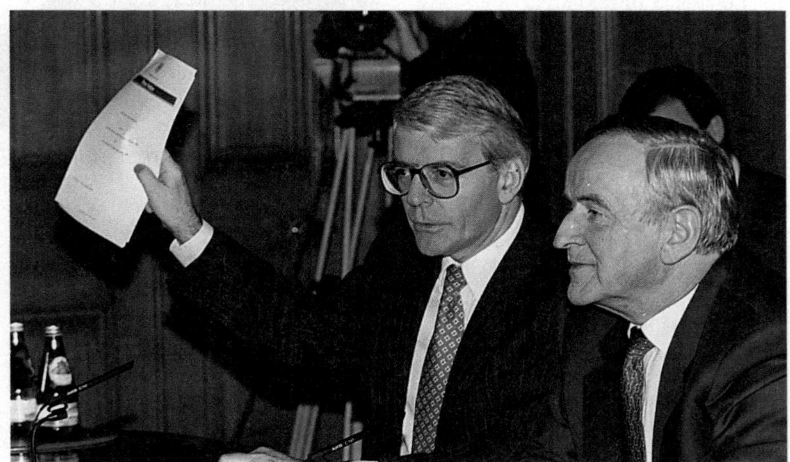
Major and Reynolds sign the historic Irish declaration at Downing Street.

London, 15 December
John Major and Albert Reynolds, prime ministers of Great Britain and Ireland, met in London today and signed an historic declaration to bring peace to Northern Ireland. Standing in front of a Christmas tree in Downing Street, they urged the terrorists on both sides of the conflict in Ulster to grasp the opportunity for peace, saying that another may not come their way. The declaration, agreed after much hard bargaining, holds out the prospect for Sinn Fein to join talks on the future of the province if the IRA renounces violence forever. The gunmen must choose now.

NASA's costly *Mars Observer* goes AWOL

NASA, 24 August
NASA is frantically trying to re-establish contact with *Mars Observer*. The $1 billion craft went missing 72 hours ago. Today it was due to start orbiting Mars, after a space odyssey that has lasted 11 months and covered 450 million miles (720 million km). No one knows what went wrong. The probe may have fired its thrusters on schedule yesterday, it may have been destroyed or it may have flown out of control into space. Glenn Cunningham, the project manager, said if they failed to contact it "it would be a great blow to the planetary science community."

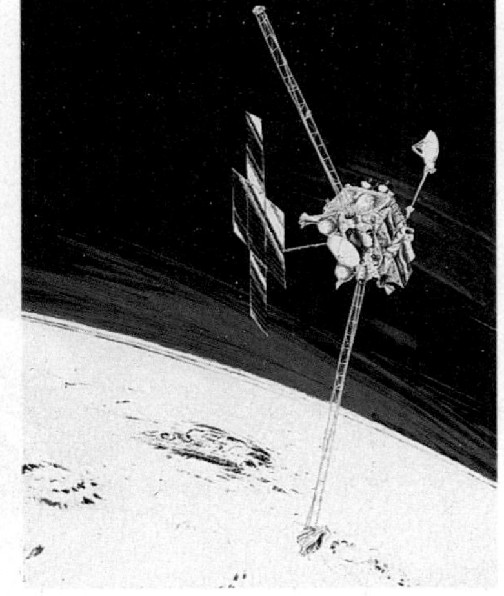
The $1 billion craft missing in space.

Huge bomb rocks the World Trade Center

New York, 26 February
An explosion shook the 110-floor twin towers of New York's World Trade Center today at 12.15 pm. The blast was caused by a bomb in a car park below the towers. Five people were killed and hundreds suffered from smoke inhalation. A crater 100ft (30 m) in diameter was formed, and fire raged through a commuter-train station, sending a pillar of smoke up the stairways. More than 40 phone calls claiming responsibility were received in the hours following the explosion. It is the worst terrorist attack in the US.

1994

London, 1 February. Britain's last major car manufacturer, Rover, is sold to German company BMW.

Israel, 25 February. A Jewish zealot, Dr Baruch Goldstein, shoots 30 Palestinian worshippers in the Ibrahim Mosque, Hebron.

Italy, 28 March. Right-wing media tycoon Silvio Berlusconi wins the general election.

New York, 22 April. The ex-president Richard Nixon dies of a stroke, aged 81.

Japan, 26 April. A China Airlines plane crashes, killing all 262 people aboard.

France, 6 May. Queen Elizabeth and President Mitterrand formally inaugurate the Channel Tunnel.

USA, 17 June. Millions watch on TV as former football star O J Simpson drives across Los Angeles, facing arraignment on murder charges.

London, 3 July. Martina Navratilova is defeated in the final of her last Wimbledon.

Buenos Aires, 18 July. A massive car bomb kills 96 people belonging to Argentinian Jewish organisations.

London, 21 July. Tony Blair is elected leader of the Labour Party, to replace John Smith who died of a heart attack.

India, 27 September. Pneumonic plague breaks out in the western city of Surat.

Baltic Sea, 28 September. The roll-on, roll-off ferry *Estonia* sinks in bad weather with the loss of 912 lives.

Switzerland, 5 October. Police find the charred remains of 23 members of the Order of the Solar Temple in a remote farmhouse, one day after 25 other members are similarly found dead near Montreal, Canada.

Israel, 19 October. A suicide bomber in the centre of Tel Aviv blows up a bus, killing 21 people and wounding 45.

USA, 9 November. The Republicans take control of both houses of Congress for the first time in 40 years.

Britain, 19 November. The first draw is made in the new National Lottery.

Bosnia, 19 December. Former president Jimmy Carter achieves a cease-fire accord.

Italy, 22 December. Silvio Berlusconi's ruling coalition government collapses.

US seizes Haiti without firing single shot

Haiti, 19 September
Heavily armed US troops arrived in Haiti by air and sea today and did not fire a shot.

Haitian and American forces have been spared a bloody invasion thanks to an 11th-hour deal in which the junta's leader, General Raoul Cedras, promised to step down by October 15 so that the island nation's elected leader, exiled President Jean-Bertrand Aristide, can take over and work to restore democracy. Cedras also agreed that his military forces would cooperate with US troops during the transition. The accord was brokered by the former president Jimmy Carter, General Colin Powell and Senator Sam Nunn.

US soldiers from the 10th Mountain Division disembark at Port-au-Prince.

Arafat's exile from Palestine now over

Gaza, 1 July
Yasir Arafat crossed the Egyptian border into the Gaza Strip today, ending 27 years of exile from Palestine. With tears in his eyes, the PLO leader kissed the ground then waved to his supporters. His motorcade hurried on to Gaza City.

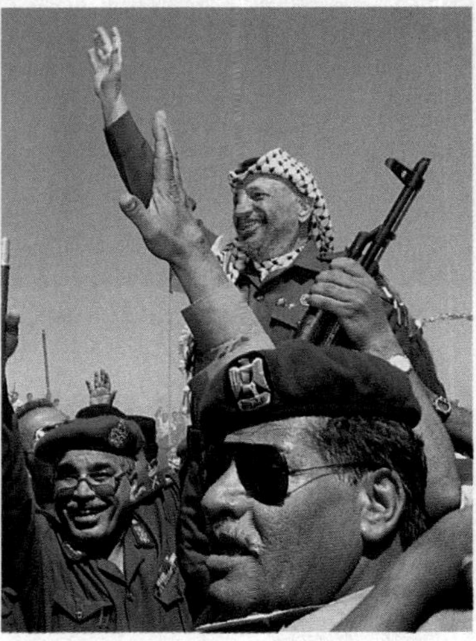

Yasir Arafat and exultant supporters.

IRA cease-fire lifts hopes for peace

Belfast, 31 August
After a quarter of a century of bombing and shooting and the deaths of more than 3,000 people the IRA has announced "complete cessation of military operations". The way now seems open to a political settlement of this savage sectarian conflict.

British soldier on the Shankill Road.

First ever NATO air attack is over Bosnia

Bosnia, 28 February
Four warplanes which had bombed a Bosnian munitions factory at Novi Travnik were shot down today in NATO's first offensive action in its 45-year history.

The Bosnian Serb aircraft had twice ignored warnings to leave the UN no-fly zone and this led to the action being taken. After the warnings US F-16 fighters knocked them out of the sky with their heat-seeking missiles.

Earlier this month, 68 people were killed when a 120mm shell hit Sarajevo's central market and following the attack, NATO issued an ultimatum to the Serbs to remove their heavy artillery from the hills surrounding the city or face air strikes. So far, the Serbs are complying, if reluctantly.

NATO warplanes bombed Serb targets in Bosnia after Serbs defied the UN.

Russian soldiers storm into Chechnya

Russia is attempting to use steamrollering techniques against Chechen rebels.

Chechenia, 11 December
Russian tanks rolled across the Chechen border today after two weeks of bombing had failed to bring the breakaway territory to heel. Boris Yeltsin had made it plain that he would use force when the Chechen leader, General Dzhokar Dudayev, defeated an attempt to topple him by Russian-backed opponents of his rule. Now it seems that the Russian president is following the old Soviet tactic of steamrollering seen in Hungary and Czechoslovakia. He might find himself in difficulties, however, for the Chechens are fierce guerrilla warriors and the Russian army is not the power it was. There are already many reports of evident disaffection among the Russian conscripts sent into Chechenia.

Major earthquake hits LA before dawn

Los Angeles, 18 January
Aftershocks measuring 4.7 on the Richter scale added more damage to the devastation caused by a 6.6-Richter-scale earthquake which struck Los Angeles yesterday at 4.31 am local time.

The earthquake, centred in the suburban San Fernando Valley at the city's northern edge, was the strongest to have hit the city this century. Freeways crumbled, water mains burst and broken gas pipes spread flames throughout the area. The total bill for property damage has been estimated to be in excess of $7 billion, and 34 people have died. It could take this urban region with a population of 9 million, tens of thousands of whom are now homeless, more than a year to repair the damage.

Amongst the devastation left by the earthquake is this collapsed freeway.

Rwanda's killing fields

Rwanda, 21 April
The stench of death pervades the capital of Rwanda. Nothing but decomposing bodies are lying all around because most of the living have fled.

Nuns, priests and aid workers are among the huge toll of victims, which also includes 11 Belgian United Nations soldiers who were killed in a single incident.

The Red Cross has estimated that more than 100,000 people have been killed in two weeks of tribal slaughter following the death of President Habyarimana when his plane crashed – it is believed to have been shot down – but nobody knows the real extent of the killing, which has soaked this lush and verdant land with blood.

Now it is feared that starvation and disease will sweep through the makeshift refugee camps. Drugs, food and, especially, clean water are desperately needed.

Even the small protection that is afforded by the UN force originally deployed to monitor the peace accords made between the Hutu government and the Tutsi rebels will end when, as expected, the Security Council votes to withdraw the force from the area.

A bewildered child wanders among the carnage of Rwanda's civil war.

SA president Nelson Mandela sworn in

South Africa, 10 May
Nelson Mandela, who spent 27 years in jail as a prisoner of the apartheid regime, was inaugurated today as South Africa's first black president in a ceremony attended by the largest assembly of foreign dignitaries ever seen in Africa.

The day, however, belonged to the tens of thousands of ordinary South Africans who danced and sang on the lawn of the Union Buildings in the country's capital, Pretoria, and cheered as their new president said: "Let there be justice for all. Let there be peace for all. Let there be work, bread and salt for all."

F W de Klerk and Nelson Mandela.

1995

Los Angeles, 24 January. The trial of O J Simpson for the murder of his ex-wife and her friend starts.

Belfast, 22 February. John Major and John Bruton present a joint Anglo-Irish framework for the future of Northern Ireland.

London, 27 February. Barings Bank faces insolvency after one of its traders, Nick Leeson, makes spectacular losses in Singapore.

Washington, 16 March. Sinn Fein leader Gerry Adams is received in the White House.

Turkey, 20 March. Turkish forces cross into Iraq in an attempt to crush the Kurdistan Workers Party, which has been raiding Turkey from havens among Kurdish refugees.

France, 7 May. Jacques Chirac is elected president.

Europe, 8 May. Celebrations are held across the continent to mark the 50th anniversary of VE Day.

Italy, 8 June. A downed US pilot returns to safety after being rescued from Bosnia.

Russia, 14 June. Chechen rebels take 2,000 people hostage in a hospital.

London, 4 July. John Major is re-elected leader of the Conservative Party, having resigned to test his support amongst MPs.

Japan, 30 August. Panic sets in in the city of Osaka as Japan's largest credit union collapses.

South Pacific, 5 September. France starts a series of nuclear tests.

USA, 19 September. A manifesto by the Unabomber terrorist, responsible for 16 bombings, is published in the *Washington Post* and the *New York Times*.

Los Angeles, 3 October. O J Simpson is found not guilty.

Washington, 16 October. Louis Farrakhan leads a march of nearly half a million black men on the Mall.

Britain, 22 November. Rosemary West is sentenced to life for the murder of ten girls and young women, including her daughter.

Colombia, 21 December. An American Airlines jet crashes into a Colombian mountainside; 117 killed, but 17 people are taken out alive.

Terror comes to America's heartland

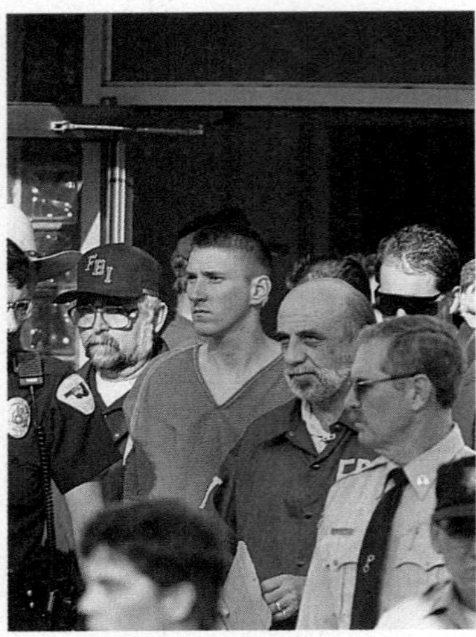
Prime suspect Timothy McVeigh.

Oklahoma City, 21 April

Americans are still in a state of shock today, 48 hours after the worst bomb outrage the nation has ever known. As flags fly at half mast throughout the country, rescue teams search the rubble of the Alfred P Murrah federal building in Oklahoma City, gutted by a huge car bomb. It is feared that more than 100 people have died in the attack, but nearly half of the 550 people who worked in the office building are still unaccounted for. The building housed offices of the Drug Enforcement Administration and the Bureau of Alcohol, Tobacco and Firearms and other federal agencies as well as a child care centre. The victims include 15 children. President Bill Clinton, who spoke just hours after the blast, vowed to swiftly bring the "evil cowards" who carried out the attack, to justice.

The FBI today arrested Timothy McVeigh, a 27-year-old Gulf War veteran with far-right political views, as the prime suspect in the attack. McVeigh has been linked to "patriotic" paramilitary militia groups, which are often anti-Semitic and white-supremacist. The FBI also raided the Michigan home of two brothers, Terry and James Nichols, who both know McVeigh and are linked to far-right militias as well.

Thousands killed by Kobe earthquake

The city of Kobe is reeling after the worst earthquake to hit Japan since 1923.

The devastation was widespread.

Japan, 17 January

A devastating earthquake struck the city of Kobe, in Japan's industrial heartland, early this morning. It is feared that more than 4,000 people are dead. The 20-second shock, which measured 7.2 on the Richter scale, buckled roads and railways. Supposedly earthquake-proof buildings collapsed into mere tangles of concrete and steel rods. Scores of fires, fed by the fractured gas pipes, are raging totally out of control, while the fire-fighters are hampered by blocked roads and broken water mains. After-shocks sent damaged buildings crashing down on people trapped in the ruins of their homes. Whole areas have been reduced to ashes and rubble.

Hutus massacred in refugee camp

Rwanda, 22 April

Rwandan government troops moved in at dawn and opened fire on thousands of Hutu refugees in a camp set up for them at Kibeho. Hundreds of men, women and children died. Most were trampled in the panic that followed the attack.

The Tutsi-dominated army had been ordered by President Pasteur Bizimungu to clear nine camps in south-western Rwanda and force the 250,000 Hutus living there to go home. The government is claiming that Hutu hard-liners at Kibeho opened fire first.

A Rwandan soldier at Kibeho camp.

Israel gives Palestinians autonomy

Crowds cheer Palestinian policemen as they drive through Bethlehem.

Washington, 28 September
An historic agreement giving the Palestinians a degree of self-determination on the West Bank of the Jordan was signed here today. Israeli troops will start withdrawing within ten days and the pullout should be complete in six months.

The agreement was signed by Israeli prime minister Yitzhak Rabin and the PLO's Yasir Arafat. But although peace has been agreed on paper, militant Palestinian groups and Jewish settlers denounce the accords. Both see their leaders as traitors to the cause.

Tokyo on alert after poison-gas horror

Tokyo, 21 March
Police staged a massive raid on the Tokyo headquarters of the *Aum Shinrikyo* (Supreme Truth) religious sect today hunting evidence to link the cult to yesterday's release of the deadly nerve gas Sarin on five trains in the Tokyo subway system.

The gas used in the horrific attack, which has so far killed eight people and affected over 4,000, was developed in Germany during the Second World War. It is fatal within five minutes of a tiny amount being absorbed through the skin or the lungs. Suspicion centres on the *Aum* sect, which is led by Shoko Asahara and has thousands of members in Japan and Russia, following reports of gas releases near its premises. Today, police found the chemical acetonitrile, which can be used to dilute Sarin.

Police moved in to search the premises of the Aum Shinrikyo religious cult.

Rabin assassinated after call for peace

Tel Aviv, 4 November
Israeli prime minister Yitzhak Rabin was shot dead tonight. He had just left the "Peace Yes Violence No" rally called to counter a rising right-wing tide of resentment at the concessions made to Palestinians over self-rule.

The security forces seized the gunman within seconds of the shooting. He was identified as Yigal Amir, a 25-year-old law student at a religious college. Amir told the police, "I acted alone on God's orders and have no regrets." He had also intended to kill Foreign Minister Shimon Peres, but was thwarted when the two politicians left the rally separately. Peres has taken over as interim premier.

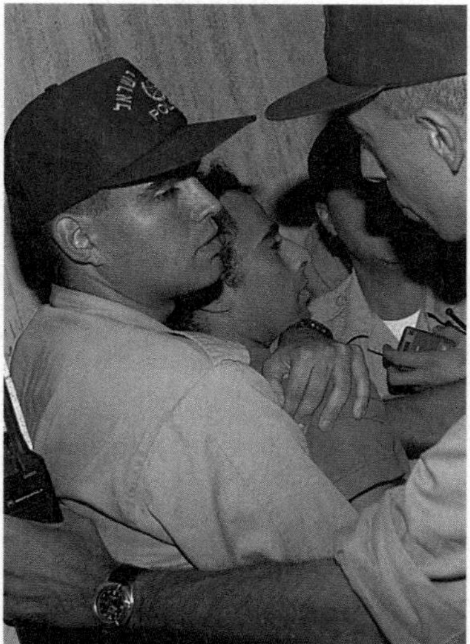
Yigal Amir is hustled away by police.

Yitzhak Rabin (second right) and Shimon Peres (second left) at the peace rally.

Three leaders agree Bosnian peace plan

Dayton, Ohio, 21 November
US negotiator Richard C Holbrooke scored a notable victory here today, when the three main national leaders involved in the conflict accepted a peace agreement that may end the fighting in Bosnia. Slobodan Milosevic of Serbia, Franjo Tudjman of Croatia and Alija Izetbegovic of Bosnia eventually all consented to a formula that ostensibly creates a unified Bosnia, but in fact divides the country along racial lines.

The muscle to make the agreement work will be provided by 60,000 NATO troops, who are to be sent to Bosnia before Christmas. Twenty thousand will be from the US and 13,000 from Britain.

The talks had been going on for 21 days before agreement was reached, and none of the leaders involved is totally satisfied with the outcome. There is to be a unified state called the Union of Bosnia-Herzegovina. This union is to consist of two self-governing parts: a Moslem-Croat federation and a Bosnian Serb republic. International monitors will oversee the first elections; refugees will be allowed to return home; human rights are guaranteed; and war criminals will not be allowed to hold office.

1996

Bosnia, 2 January. US ground forces are taking up their positions in northeastern Bosnia as the NATO peace-keeping force begins in earnest.

France, 8 January. France's former president, François Mitterrand, dies. One of Europe's foremost post-war leaders, he had been president from 1981 to 1995.

Bangladesh, 10 February. A policeman is killed and over 300 injured during a confrontation between protestors and government forces, in the run-up to the election.

USA, 12 February. Chess champion Gary Kasparov scores 1-1 against IBM super-computer Deep Blue.

UK, 28 February. Princess Diana independently announces her willingness to divorce Prince Charles.

UK, 13 March. Sixteen primary school children are massacred along with their teacher in a school in the Scottish town of Dunblane by Thomas Watt Hamilton.

Taiwan, 23 March. Taiwan holds its first democratic presidential election, marking a triumph over intimidation from mainland China, which staged military maneouvres near Taiwan in the election build-up.

Ukraine, 26 April. Another leak is announced at the Chernobyl nuclear plant 10 years after the infamous Chernobyl disaster.

Bahrain, 3 June. Bahrain accuses Iran of trying to overthrow the ruling Al Khalifa family, claiming that it wants Bahrain to have a Shi'ite Muslim government like that of Iran.

Britain, 15 June. A massive IRA bomb devastates the northern England town of Manchester. About 200 people were injured, nine of them seriously.

Belgium, 18 August. Alleged pedophile rapist Marc Dutroux is arrested in connection with the bodies of three girls found in his garden.

USA, 7 September. Hurricane Fran rips through the Carolinas leaving 12 dead and causing millions of dollars' worth of damage.

USA, 2 October. President Clinton's involvement in the Israel-Palestine peace process fails, as Benjamin Netanyahu and Yasir Arafat reach no agreement at the White House.

IRA blast in London ends ceasefire

London, 10 February

A massive explosion last night signalled the end of the fragile IRA ceasefire. For almost 18 months the people of Northern Ireland had enjoyed a life of comparative normality and were cautiously optimistic. Just 80 minutes before the explosion a coded message was received from the Provisional IRA stating that the ceasefire was at an end and that a bomb had been planted at South Quay railway station in London's Docklands. Two people were killed instantly and many more were injured. British Prime Minister John Major vowed to continue the search for peace. He said: "It would be a tragedy if the hopes of the people of Britain and Northern Ireland for a lasting peace were dashed again by the men of violence." Gerry Adams, head of Sinn Fein, the IRA's political wing, seemed genuinely surprised by the attack, although he was unwilling to condemn it outright.

The bomb destruction at South Quay in London's Docklands.

TWA Flight 800 ends in disaster

USA, 18 July

Two hundred and twenty-eight passengers were killed as TWA Flight 800 exploded minutes after leaving New York's JFK International Airport. Everyone on board the Boeing 747 jumbo jet, headed for Paris, died. FBI experts were searching though the wreckage late this evening, looking for evidence of a terrorist attack. Evidence from a pilot who saw the explosion suggested that the disaster may have been caused by a bomb. There were also rumours that the aircraft had been destroyed by a shoulder-fired antiaircraft missile. A veteran TWA pilot spoke volumes when he said: "747s don't just fall out of the sky." As conspiracy theories circulate, the crash investigators are persevering to find the answer to the question: "Did TWA Flight 800 fall or was it pushed?"

Bit by bit, the wreckage of TWA Flight 800 was pieced together.

Chechnya peace deal breaks down

A Grozny resident returns to the rubble.

Chechnya, 2 June

Fighting has broken out once again between Russian and Chechen forces only days after Russian president Boris Yeltsin signed a peace accord in Moscow with the new Chechen leader, Zelimkham Yandarbiyev. The two sides agreed to free prisoners, cease fighting, and demilitarize the republic, but their accord has collapsed. It is thought Yeltsin is pushing for peace to boost his popularity at home in the run-up to forthcoming elections.

The conflict began 18 months ago, when Russia launched an invasion of Chechnya to stop Chechen rebels from forming an independent state. Russian troops almost totally destroyed the Chechen capital, Grozny, before taking control of it three months later.

USA, 2 February. Gene Kelly, star of the 1952 musical "Singin' in the Rain," died today aged 83.

Bomb threatens to wreck Olympics

Spectators tend to shocked victims following the explosion in Atlanta.

Atlanta, 27 July
In July athletes from no fewer than 197 nations converged on Atlanta, Georgia, for the Centennial Olympic Games. The games were deemed an unqualified success until, in the early hours of this morning, their peace and harmony were shattered by a pipe bomb exploding in a crowded Centennial Olympic Park.

The explosion left two people dead and more than 100 injured. It was an act of wanton and random barbarity which sent shock waves around the world. The athletes were united in their determination to continue. "We've got to get on with what we're here to do," said one. The investigation into who committed the outrage has so far not thrown up any leads, and it is even possible that the FBI will never find the culprits.

Mid-air disaster

New Delhi, 12 November
A Saudi Arabian Boeing 747 collided with a Kazakh Airways Ilyushin 76 outside the Indian capital of New Delhi today. All 312 passengers and crew on board the Boeing and 38 people on the Ilyushin are thought to have died – making it the world's third-worst air disaster, and the worst-ever mid-air collision.

A US Air Force cargo plane was flying into New Delhi at the time. The captain described seeing "two fireballs ... diverging from each other" as the planes fell from the sky. Burning wreckage was littered over 6 miles of farmland near the town of Charkhi Dadri.

The jumbo jet was seven minutes out of New Delhi's international airport when the collision occurred. The incoming Kazakh flight was supposed to be flying 1,000 ft above the jumbo.

Refugees stream home to Rwanda

Rwanda, 26 November
Around 500,000 refugees have been returning to their homeland from over the Zairean border in the last 10 days. Most of them fled the bloody ethnic conflict in Rwanda two years ago. Hundreds of thousands remain there without food and basic supplies. Others are hiding in the nearby jungle. Their presence has caused a crisis between the Zairean government and Zairean Tutsis. There has been violence between the Tutsi (who make up 14 percent of the population) and Hutu (85 percent) ethnic groups in Rwanda and surrounding regions since the Tutsis subjugated the Hutus in the 15th century. This worsened when the Belgian colonial authorities favoured the Tutsis. Since Rwandan independence in 1962, there has been frequent bloodshed between the two ethnic groups.

Refugees stream out of refugee camps in Zaire heading for the Rwandan border.

Clinton wins second term as President

President Clinton is sworn in for his second term; his wife and daughter look on.

Washington DC, 6 November
The 1996 presidential election had looked like a one-horse race, and so it proved when Americans went to the polls yesterday. President Clinton became the first Democrat since Franklin D. Roosevelt to win a second term in the White House. A reelected Bill Clinton today called for "humble government" after defeating Republican challenger Bob Dole. He will again face a Republican-dominated Congress, and scandals old and new hang in the air.

Yeltsin wins but fitness still in doubt

Moscow, 4 November
Boris Yeltsin has succeeded in his campaign for reelection as President of Russia. The President adopted a conciliatory tone in his time of triumph. "Let us not divide the country into victors and vanquished," he said. Most observers felt that he was less threatened by the likely problems of the economy than by the deterioration of his own health. It is thought doubtful that his health will hold up for the four-year term of office.

1997

Australia, 9 January. Michael Bullimore is rescued after surviving for four days under his capsized yacht.

Switzerland, 21 January. It is announced that Swiss bankers are to set up a humanitarian fund for Holocaust victims.

USA, 1 February. El Niño sends tornados and floods across the USA, leaving 27 dead and 300 injured.

Boston, USA, 5 February. British au pair Louise Woodward is arrested for assault and battery after admitting shaking a baby in her care.

Washington D.C, 14 February. Astronauts embark on a four-day mission to upgrade the Hubble Space Telescope as it orbits the Earth.

UK, 23 March. The eighth and brightest comet this century, Hale-Bopp, makes its closest pass to Earth, at over 120 million miles away. Astronomers estimate that the two-tailed ball of ice and debris is 25 miles wide and travelling at a speed of 100,000 miles an hour.

USA, 13 April. The 21-year-old American golfing phenomenon Eldrick "Tiger" Woods became the youngest player to win the prestigious US Masters tournament.

USA, 6 May. Chairman of the Orange Literary Prize, Dr Lisa Jardine, refers to British novelists as smug, parochial, and narrow-minded.

Miami, 15 June. Fashion designer Gianni Versace is shot dead outside his home.

USA, 3 July. The US tobacco industry pays $3.4 billion to the state to reimburse money spent on sick smokers, in the first legal settlement of its kind.

India and Pakistan, 15 August. India and Pakistan celebrate 50 years of independence from British rule.

Nevada, 25 September. British RAF pilot Andy Green breaks the world land-speed record at an average of 714 mph—81 mph faster than the previous record.

France, 1 October. The government imposes controls on car use in Paris, as the capital's pollution reaches dangerous levels.

Scotland, 18 December. The Scotland Bill is published, detailing the new independent Scottish parliament due to open in 1999.

OJ Simpson found liable for deaths

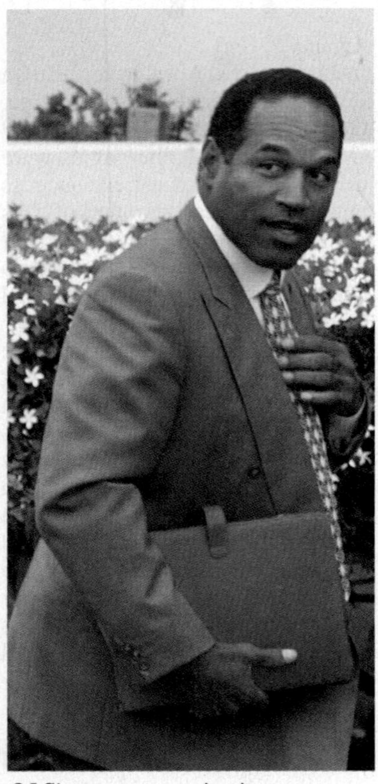

OJ Simpson seen going into court.

Santa Monica, 4 February

The final twist in the 20th-century's most controversial murder case came to an end today. OJ Simpson, 50-year-old former football star turned actor, has today been found liable for the deaths of his former wife, Nicole Brown Simpson, and her friend, Ronald Goldman, who were found with their throats slashed outside Nicole's Los Angeles home in 1994. The jury returned punitive damages that Simpson has to pay to the victims' families: $25 million. Each family was awarded half the money.

In the hugely controversial 1995 trial Simpson was found "not guilty" of the murders. The whole trial had been dominated by the issue of race, centring around Simpson's claim: "I was a victim of racist cops." The families of the two victims immediately filed civil suits against Simpson for wrongful death.

Despite the verdict Simpson is still a free man and, although facing financial ruin, has custody of his two children.

Peruvian hostage crisis finally over

Peruvian president Fujimori leads the hostages away from the Japanese Embassy.

Peru, 21 April

The hostage crisis in the Peruvian capital of Lima is finally over today. On 17 December, 1996, Peru was plunged into an international crisis after the Tupac Amaru left-wing rebels took over the Japanese embassy in Lima, taking over 500 hostages. They announced: "We are here to free our comrades from prison. We are prepared to die and to kill all of you with us."

Today, commandos took up positions and timed explosions allowed them to enter the embassy and release the hostages. All 14 of the guerrillas were killed. As the hostages were led to safety, victorious government troops gathered on the roof of the embassy to the cheers of the crowds below.

New direction for Britain

The Blairs outside 10 Downing Street.

UK, 2 May

Today sees the first change of government in the UK for 18 years. Labour won with a majority of 179 seats, the greatest that any government has had since World War Two. Labour leader Tony Blair became the youngest prime minister the country has had for almost 200 years, at the age of 43. Blair became party leader in 1994 following the sudden death of John Smith. He revolutionized the way the party worked, focusing on a campaign strategy that included advanced media relations techniques, and moving toward the right, away from Labour's trade-union-backed past. The result has become known as "New Labour."

India, 5 September. Mother Teresa, known as the "Saint of the Slums," dies of a heart attack aged 87, having devoted her life to looking after the destitute and dying in Calcutta.

IMF bails out "Tiger economies"

Stockholders demand that the government shut down the Seoul stock exchange.

East Asia, 3 December
The International Monetary Fund (IMF), the lender of last resort, has finalized the third of a series of economic bail-outs for countries in East Asia. The first loan was to Thailand (US$17 billion), the second to Indonesia ($23 billion), and this latest was to South Korea ($57 billion, the highest international bail-out ever).

The bail-outs are intended to redress the economic instability that has swept across Asia in the past year. The Asian economies, known as "Tiger economies," were thought of as miracle money-earners earlier in the 1990s. Investors around the world poured money into their economies, but at the first sign of poor market performance they quickly pulled out, as did local investors, leaving the economies in crisis.

Hong Kong handed over to China

Hong Kong, 1 July
Hong Kong made history today as it was handed back to China after 156 years of British rule. Hong Kong was the last major bastion of British colonialism. During the half-hour ceremony which marked the occasion, the Prince of Wales and Chinese president Jiang Zemin spoke to the 6.3 million residents.

The British agreed to return control to the motherland only if certain conditions were met. The two parties signed the Sino-British Joint Declaration in 1984, pledging that Hong Kong residents would receive the same freedom under Chinese rule that they had under the British.

Prince Charles delivers a speech during the handover ceremony in Hong Kong.

Diana, Princess of Wales, killed in car accident

Paris, 31 August
The world was stunned by the death of Diana, Princess of Wales, in the early hours of this morning, following a car accident last night. Her companion Dodi Fayed and their chauffeur were also killed. It is thought the crash was partly due to the car speeding away from the paparazzi, who were chasing them through an underpass on motorbikes.

The nation awoke to the news this morning, and thousands have begun bringing bouquets of flowers to her London home of Kensington Palace.

Diana Frances Spencer married Charles, Prince of Wales, in 1981 and had two sons by him – William (born in 1982) and Harry (1984). The couple separated at the end of 1992 and finally divorced in 1996 with Diana losing "Her Royal Highness" from her title. Diana was immensely popular internationally; she was known for her beauty and style, her support of humanitarian causes, and, of course, for the traumatic events of her life as a royal princess.

Diana, Princess of Wales.

Foot guards escort the carriage carrying the coffin to Westminster Abbey.

1998

Italy, 3 February. Twenty skiers die after their cable-car crashes into the ground following a collision with an American military aircraft.

Rwanda, 16 March. Mass trials begin in Rwanda for 1994 genocide, with 125,000 suspects for 500,000 murders.

USA, 27 March. Food and Drug Administration approves the prescription drug Viagra, claiming it can help about two-thirds of impotent men.

Cambodia, 16 April. Pol Pot dies.

USA, 14 May. Frank Sinatra dies.

Indonesia, 21 May. President Suharto announces his resignation, ending 32 years of autocratic rule.

Japan, 12 June. Japan's economy is officially in recession, causing financial markets to slump worldwide.

Russia, 20 July. The International Monetary Fund grants a $11.2 billion loan to Russia.

France, 29 July. The Tour de France is shaken by a round of drugs allegations. Cyclists respond angrily, staging strikes and go-slows.

Switzerland, 12 August. Swiss banks agree to pay $1.25 billion as restitution to Holocaust victims.

Bangladesh, 15 September. Bangladesh suffers its most extensive flooding of the century. At least 900 lives are lost and 30 million people are likely to be affected.

USA, 24 September. Hurricane Georges devastates the Florida Keys after killing at least 250 people in the Caribbean.

Northern Ireland, 16 October. Negotiators David Trimble and John Hume receive the Nobel Peace Prize for their part in the Northern Ireland peace accord.

London, 16 October. Former Chilean dictator Augusto Pinochet is detained on behalf of the Spanish Government for the murders, torture and abuses that took place during his regime.

USA, 21 October. The New York Yankees win the baseball World Series, defeating the San Diego Padres 4–0.

USA, 19 December. Democrat President Clinton is impeached by the Republican-controlled House of Representatives on charges of perjury and obstruction of justice.

Clinton shamed over sex scandal

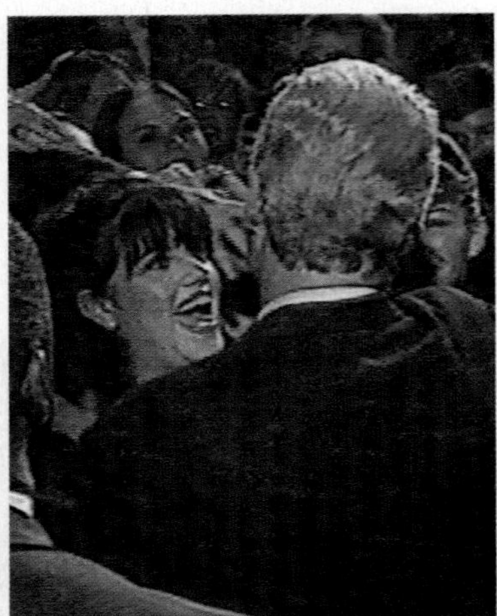

Monica Lewinsky greets President Clinton at an event in October 1996.

Washington DC, 27 January
President Bill Clinton publicly commented today on the scandal that has now engulfed the White House. He forcefully denied any sexual involvement with former young White House intern Monica Lewinsky.

President Clinton denied the allegations of serious misconduct at the end of an event to promote government measures on education. Speaking to the assembled media in the White House, he affirmed: "I want to say one thing to the American people. I want you to listen to me. I did not have sexual relations with that woman, Miss Lewinsky."

President Clinton went on: "I never told anyone to lie, not a single time, never. These allegations are false and I need to go back to work for the American people."

The denials came after days of speculation surrounding President Clinton and Ms Lewinsky. After an initial alert by an internet report, the mainstream media picked up the story as it emerged that Ms Lewinsky's colleague, Linda Tripp, had secretly recorded their conversations about the affair. Extracts from the Tripp tapes indicated that Clinton had lied under oath and had asked Ms Lewinsky to commit perjury by lying about their affair.

Northern Ireland peace settlement

Northern Ireland, 10 April
As Good Friday drew to a close, the political parties involved in the negotiation of a peace settlement for British-ruled Northern Ireland reach an agreement. The historic 32-hour discussions brought together the bitterly divided Unionist and nationalist parties in the hope of ending the 30-year conflict.

A referendum on a devolved Ulster assembly is planned for 22 May. Discussions regarding the early release of prisoners are likely along with the decommissioning of arms and reform of the Royal Ulster Constabulary. British Prime Minister Tony Blair hailed the accord as a triumph of courage.

France, 13 July. France win the 16th soccer World Cup title 3–0, outplaying the favourites, Brazil, in Paris.

Serbs launch major offensive

Serb police take shelter in the Albanian rebel stronghold area of western Kosovo.

Serbia, 25 July
The mainly Serb Yugoslav Army has launched a major offensive against ethnic Albanian rebels in the Serbian-ruled province of Kosovo. The Drenica region of central Kosovo – a heartland of the rebel Kosovo Liberation Army – is under assault from several directions.

Although official information is scant, journalists and other observers have seen tanks and armoured vehicles attacking villages, many of which are on fire. Further south, other observers say the Serbs have launched a series of attacks near other KLA strongholds.

The party of the ethnic Albanian leader, Ibrahim Rugova, called on the United States, NATO, and the European Union to intervene in order to end what it called "outright aggression" as atrocities in the region increasingly come to resemble the "ethnic cleansing" of areas of Bosnia in the recent past.

The Serbian authorities have so far refused to discuss demands for an independent Kosovo with the ethnic Albanian people, who form the majority of Kosovo's population. Serbian police and army checkpoints have now sealed off the area.

US embassies in East Africa bombed

Rescue workers scrambling over the rubble of a collapsed office block in

Nairobi, 7 August
Twin bomb blasts targeting the US embassies in Nairobi and Dar-es-Salaam killed more than 250 people, mostly African civilians.

In total, more than 5,500 people are thought to be injured. Despite the deliberate targeting of US embassies, only 12 Americans are among the dead. Many of the casualties in Nairobi occurred when an office block behind the embassy collapsed in the aftermath of the blast, trapping hundreds of people.

Responsibility for the blasts is still to be determined, but blame is being cast on Islamic extremists, in particular Osama bin Laden, the Saudi head of the terrorist organization al Qaeda. The objective of al Qaeda is to work against perceived enemies in the West, in particular, the United States.

President Bill Clinton described the bombings as "abhorrent" and "inhuman".

Air strikes launched against Iraq

Iraqi officials allege this residential area was damaged by US airstrikes.

Iraq, 17 December
Cruise missiles were fired into Iraq by US forces as a reprisal against the Baghdad Government for obstructing the work of the United Nations weapons inspectors.

President Bill Clinton said the attacks were necessary because the Iraqis had continued to defy the inspectors and placed new restrictions on their work. But Russian Prime Minister Yevgeny Primakov called the strikes "outrageous".

The attack, code-named Operation Desert Fox, began at 22:00 GMT. As well as cruise missile attacks, a senior Pentagon official said Navy EA-6B attack planes struck against Iraqi air-defence radars.

Iraqi doctors in Baghdad say at least five people have been killed and 30 wounded. There is no independent confirmation of this. Four separate raids were counted by witnesses in Baghdad. Reports say several missiles struck the city, one landing near one of the presidential palaces.

Outrage as Omagh bomb kills 28

Northern Ireland, 16 August
Northern Ireland's tenuous state of peace was shattered today when a bomb tore through the quiet town of Omagh. At least 28 people were killed and 100 maimed or injured in the worst paramilitary bombing since the start of the Northern Ireland conflict 30 years ago.

Martin McGuinness, the chief negotiator for Sinn Fein, said: "This appalling act was carried out by those opposed to the peace process."

The bombing is thought to have been carried out by a Republican splinter group calling itself the Real IRA. The group, whose aim is to disrupt the peace process, is responsible for several bombings.

The aftermath in Omagh town centre.

Hurricane Mitch wreaks havoc

Honduras and Nicaragua, 3 November
Large areas of two countries lie in ruins in the wake of Hurricane Mitch. Their fragile economies ruined, Honduras and Nicaragua bore the brunt of horrific deluges and mudslides from a weeklong rampage by Mitch. Gusts were estimated at more than 200 mph (322 km/h) making it the fourth-strongest Caribbean hurricane of the century.

The greatest devastation is reported in Honduras, where an estimated 5,000 people died, and 600,000, nearly 10 per cent of Honduras's population of 6.1 million, were forced to flee their homes after the storm and are now homeless. Countless more were lacking fresh water, food and medicine. Aid workers warn that casualties could rise as a result of disease and starvation.

"The terrible floods and landslides erased from the map many villages and households as well as whole neighbourhoods of cities," Honduran President Carlos Flores Facusse said.

The destruction caused by Mitch makes 1998 the worst hurricane season in the Atlantic Ocean for more than 200 years. The US National Hurricane Center in Miami said if Mitch's feared death toll of 10,000 is confirmed, it will rank as the sixth-most destructive Atlantic storm on record.

Guatemala, pounded on Monday by the tail end of the hurricane, declared a state of emergency, and southern Mexico is bracing itself as heavy rain begins to fall.

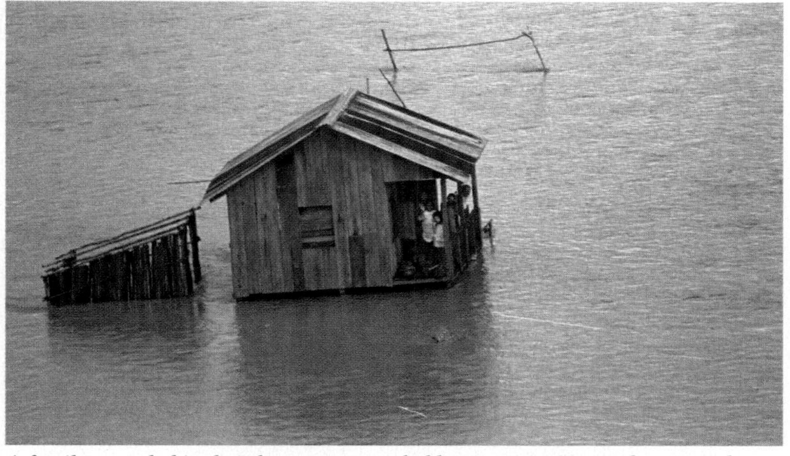

A family stranded in their home, surrounded by water, waiting to be rescued.

1999

France, 12 February. Avalanches in the French Alps near Chamonix kill 18 people. Off-piste skiing is banned as reports indicate that this is the worst avalanche season for 90 years.

Kenya, 16 February. Kurdish separatist leader Abdullah Ocalan is captured and brought to Turkey for trial.

UK, 24 February. The Macpherson report on the killing of black youth Stephen Lawrence is released, alleging the existence of "institutional racism" in the Metropolitan police force.

USA, 25 February. Vocalist Lauryn Hill wins a record-breaking five Grammy awards, including album of the year and best new artist. She is the first rapper to win these major categories.

USA, 8 March. Baseball star Joe DiMaggio, once married to Marilyn Monroe, dies of cancer aged 84.

USA, 9 March. The United States Energy Department fires a computer scientist over the disclosure of sensitive nuclear missile technology to China during the 1980s.

Berlin, March 12. World-class violinist Yehudi Menuhin dies aged 82, He will be remembered not only for his musical prowess, but also for his humanitarian work.

USA, 14 March. The heavy-weight championship of the world ends in a controversial draw between Lennox Lewis and Evander Holyfield.

Belgium, 16 March. President of the European Commission, Jacques Santer, resigns along with the entire executive of the EU after a devastating report into corruption in the commission.

USA, 22 March. *Shakespeare in Love* claims the Oscar for best film. The Elizabethan period drama took seven Academy Awards in total, including best actress, best screenplay, best supporting actress (for Dame Judi Dench), costume, score and art direction.

Kosovo, March 24. NATO launches air strikes on Serbia following President Milosevic's refusal to take part in a peace deal. President Milosevic breaks off diplomatic relations with the USA and UK, and demonstrations are held in defiance of NATO.

Colombia crushed by earthquake

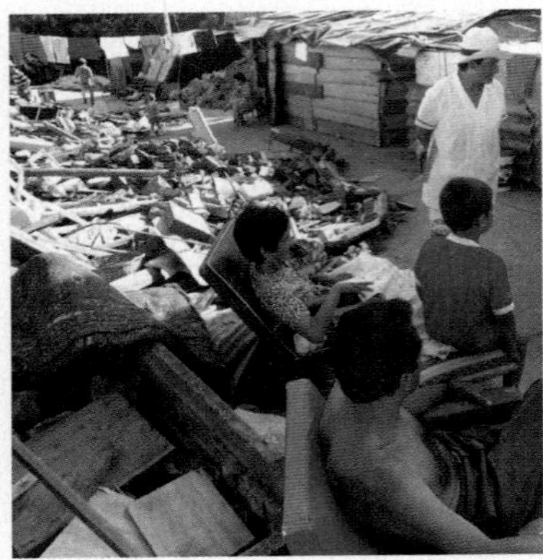

A makeshift home amidst devastation.

Colombia, 2 February
A massive earthquake has killed more than 900 people and injured almost 4,000 across Colombia's western coffee-growing region.

More than 600 people were killed in the state capital, Armenia, a city of 300,000 residents that now is largely in ruins. Calarca, a town 15 minutes from Armenia, had at least 110 deaths in the earthquake and more than 200 people were killed elsewhere in the region.

Emergency food supplies are dangerously low for the more than 200,000 people left homeless by an earlier earthquake only last week. Aid officials are trying to avoid a repetition of the first few days when food shortages were widespread due to the magnitude of the devastation and bureaucratic delays.

It will cost as much as $950 million to rebuild and repair the estimated 35,000 homes rendered uninhabitable by the earthquake.

Clinton survives impeachment

USA, 13 February
President Bill Clinton is keeping a low profile after he was acquitted by the Senate on charges of perjury and obstruction of justice that stemmed from his affair with Monica Lewinsky.

Prosecutors failed to secure the two-thirds majority required to convict the president on either of the two charges brought against him in the Senate trial.

After the Senate voted for acquittal, President Clinton said he was "profoundly sorry for what I said and did to trigger these events". The vote marks an end to the long-running Lewinsky scandal that had threatened to topple the president.

Farewell to the King

Jordan, 7 February
Jordanians are mourning the death of King Hussein two days after he returned to Jordan following unsuccessful treatment for cancer. The king's demise has sparked a nationwide outpouring of grief.

King Hussein became a key force for stability in the turbulent Middle East as ruler of his strategically placed nation. Hussein ruled Jordan for 46 years – longer than any other modern leader in the Middle East. He used his influence to assist the peace process with Israel, helping to move Jordan and its Arab neighbours toward an agreement.

Jordan, a nation of about 4 million people, borders Israel, Iraq, Syria, and Saudi Arabia.

King Hussein will be succeeded by his son, Crown Prince Abdullah.

Jordan's King Hussein in June 1998.

Olympic Committee ethics probe

Geneva, 16 February
Eleven responses have been received by the International Olympic Committee to its request for evidence of corruption in the bidding process to host the Olympic Games since 1996. The IOC said on Tuesday that the replies would be passed to the commission investigating corruption allegations, set up as a result of the scandal surrounding Salt Lake City's successful bid for the 2002 Winter Games.

"Under the procedure followed by the ad hoc commission, its work remains confidential until it has completed its report," the IOC said. Today was the deadline for bidders to respond to 28 letters sent by IOC president Juan Antonio Samaranch asking about corruption.

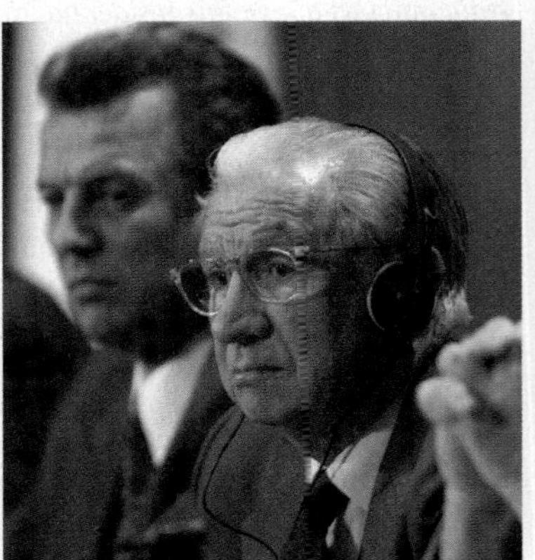

Juan Antonio Samaranch.

Birth of the euro

Europe, 1 January
After much debate, the euro has become the official currency of 11 member states of the European Union: Germany, France, Italy, Spain, Portugal, Finland, Ireland, Belgium, Luxembourg, The Netherlands and Austria. From now on, the value of the euro against the dollar and other currencies, including those of the four member states who have so far opted to stay out of the euro zone – Denmark, Sweden, United Kingdom and Greece – will fluctuate according to market conditions.

Although euro notes and coins will not officially come into general use until 1 January 2002, the new currency can already be used by consumers, retailers, companies of all kinds and public administrations from today in the form of "written money" – that is, by means of cheques, travellers' cheques, bank transfers, credit cards and electronic purses.

The world celebrates

The Millennium Dome in Greenwich, south-east London.

As the dawn of the third millennium approaches, preparations have taken many forms. Many of the world's greatest cities have become the focus for celebrations on a scale never before seen, while more lasting tributes are planned in the form of massive building programmes focused on national monuments.

Each nation's plans reflect in some way the character of the country. In France, for example, the commemorative events have a whimsical flavour: the Eiffel Tower will appear to be laying an egg, and a school of 2,000 luminous plastic fish will be released into the River Seine.

Surprisingly, the United States has not been touched by the architectural millennium fever. There are plans to set up a National Digital Library but there will be no tangible monument to mark the occasion.

Sydney, Australia, won the race to stage the millennium Olympic Games to be held in September/October 2000. The number of overseas visitors is expected to top 1.3 million.

The following are just some of the millennial events around the globe that will attract many millions of people, either for the New Year celebrations or throughout the year:

Earth Day 2000 – 300 million in 150 nations
Expo 2000 – 40 million in Hanover, Germany
March of the Millennium – 30 million in 2,000-plus cities
Holy Year 2000 – 13 million visit Rome
The Millennium Experience – 12 million in Greenwich, UK
Holy Land 2000 – 4 million in Palestine and Israel
Party 2000 – 2.5 million party-goers in Southern California
Times Square 2000 – over a million in Times Square, New York City, and 250 million watching on TV.

Sydney, Australia, will stage the millennium Games in 2000.

Caution over apocalyptic groups

Law enforcement agencies worldwide are preparing for the possibility that religious cults or apocalyptic groups may turn to violence to fulfil their prophecies of Armageddon as the year 2000 approaches.

FBI Director, Louis Freeh, warned recently of such groups at a congressional hearing on counter-terrorism. He cited "rogue terrorists" as probably the most urgent risk to US interests worldwide. But he said the domestic threat could not be ignored as the millennium approaches.

"The possibility of an indigenous group like Aum Supreme Truth cannot be excluded", he said, referring to the cult responsible for the 1995 nerve gas attack in the Tokyo subway system.

Britain's Scotland Yard has launched a massive operation to protect the Greenwich area of London – especially the new Millennium Dome, the focus for Britain's millennium celebrations. Because Greenwich crosses the prime meridian of 0 degrees longitude, it is feared that it might become a target for apocalyptic terrorists.

For some religious groups, however, the certainty of Armageddon is not an occasion for violence, but a reason to stockpile food and emergency supplies in preparation for floods, earthquakes and famine.

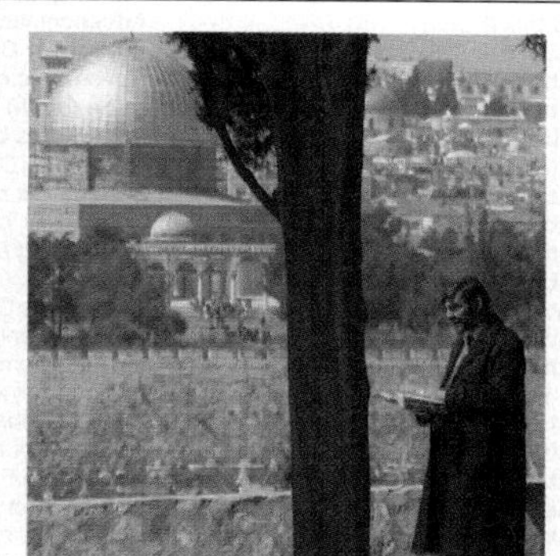
Jerusalem is attracting Christian end-timers as the millennium approaches.

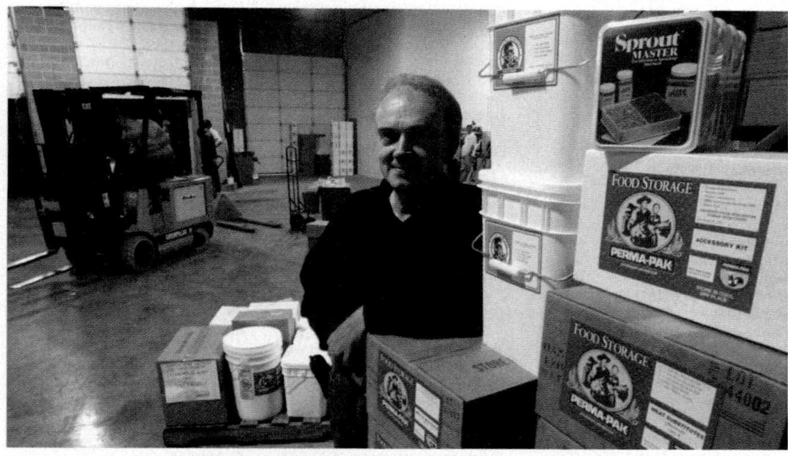

Mormons in Utah are preparing food and emergency supplies for the millennium.

Bug sparks fears of civil unrest

The millennium computer bug could spark civil unrest in Third World countries, a US Senate panel has warned. Utah Republican Senator Robert Bennett, chairman of the Senate's Special Committee on the computer problem, outlined fears of widespread rioting if facilities such as power, telecommunications and the banking system break down.

Other concerns addressed by the committee include the possibility of an accidental nuclear strike against the United States. Although the Committee indicates that this risk is negligible, missile systems and other high-tech weapons in other countries could malfunction.

Senator Bennett also revealed that computer systems at a Pennsylvania nuclear power plant ground to a halt during a test simulating the start of the year 2000.

The Senate's report says that 1 January 2000 should cause no unnecessary alarm for the United States, although the health service, airports and the maritime industry are highlighted for lagging behind with their preparations.

General Index

Page numbers in roman type indicate references in the text, those in *italic* type references in chronologies.

B

C

D

E

F

G

H

I

J

K

M

N

S

U

Photo Credit Index

The position of the pictures is indicated by letters: *B*: Bottom; *T*: Top; *M*: Middle; *L*: Left; *R*: Right; *X*: Middle Left; *Y*: Middle Right; *a*: above; *b*: below. When the pictures are not framed to the usual size, the positions of the pictures are complemented by a number, ie, *BR1, BR2, BR3*.

Every effort has been made to trace the copyright holders. Dorling Kindersley apologises for any unintentional omissions and would be pleased, in such cases, to add an acknowledgement in future editions. The large number of illustrations used in this book regrettably makes it impossible to acknowledge the many museums and art galleries who hold the objects and paintings that appear in the photographs supplied by the agencies and libraries credited on these pages.

Agencies

Some agency names have been abbreviated in this index. The list below provides full names of those picture agencies:

Ann Ronan: Ann Ronan Picture Library; **Art & Architecture**: Ancient Art and Architecture Collection; **Chronique**: Editions Chronique, Paris; **Forman**: Werner Forman Archive; **Granger**: Granger Collection, New York; **Harding**: Robert Harding Picture Library; **Holford**: Michael Holford Photographs; **Hulton**: Hulton Getty Collection; **Mary Evans**: Mary Evans Picture Library; **Newark**: Peter Newark's Pictures; **Popper**: Popperfoto; **Rex**: Rex Features; **Sipa**: Sipa Press; **Syndication**: Syndication International; **Topham**: Topham Picture Library

Cover

Front cover - *TC*: NASA/Finlay-Holiday Films
CR: AKG London/ Museum of Mankind; *BR*: Bridgeman Art Library, London/New York, Giraudon/Musee d'Orsay;
BL: National Railway Museum, York; *CLB*: Bridgeman Art Library, London/New York, Private Collection; *C*: Michael Holford;
CL: 20th Century Fox (courtesy Kobal Collection);
CB: Peter Newark's American Pictures
Back cover - *TR*: Bridgeman Art Library, London/New York, Vatican Museums and Art Galleries, Vatican City, Italy;
TL: Popperfoto; *CL*: American Museum of Natural History;
BR: Novosti (US edition), Rex Features (UK edition);
BL: Rex Features (US edition)
Inside flap - Holiday Film Corp

8 - *TL*: Bridgeman; *MR*: Mary Evans; *MM*: Holford
9 - *TR*: Art & Architecture; *MM, BR*: C M Dixon; *TX*: Forman
10- *TM*: Mary Evans
11 - *MM*: Art & Architecture; *TR*: C M Dixon; *ML*: Popper; *TX*: Forman
12 - *TM*: Chronique; *TR*: Mary Evans; *MY*: Forman
13 - *TY, TR, BR*: Bridgeman; *TL*: Mary Evans; *ML*: Holford
14 - *BR*: Bridgeman; *TY, MY*: Mary Evans
15- *BR*: Bridgeman; *TY*: C M Dixon; *MM*: Chronique; *TX*: E T Archive; *BR*: Mary Evans
16- *MY*: Mary Evans; *TM*: Forman
17 - All pictures from Holford
18 - *BR*: Crown Copyright vested in the control of HMSO/Public Record Office; *TR*: Forman
19- *BY*: Bridgeman; *TM, MM, BL*: C M Dixon
20- *TR*: Art & Architecture; *BR*: Mary Evans
21 - *ML*: Art & Architecture; *MR*: Bridgeman; *TL*: Mary Evans; *TR*: Holford
22 - *MR*: Art & Architecture; *BR*: Mary Evans
23- *ML, BR*: C M Dixon; *TM, TR, BX*: Forman
24 - *BR*: Art & Architecture; *TR, MX*: Mary Evans
25 - *TL, TR*: Art & Architecture; *MR*: C M Dixon; *MX*: Mary Evans
26 - *BR*: Bridgeman; *TM*: C M Dixon
27 - *MM*: The Bodleian Library, Oxford; *TR*: C M Dixon; *TL*: Chronique
28 - *BX, BR*: Popper; *TR*: Top/Ionesco
29- *TL*: Art & Architecture; *MX*: C M Dixon; *MR*: Mary Evans; *TR*: Forman
30 - *TR*: Mary Evans; *BM*: Forman
31 - *TM, MR*: C M Dixon; *MX*: Mary Evans
32 - *BR*: Bridgeman; *TM, MX*: Holford
33 - *TL*: Bridgeman; *MX*: Hulton-Deutsch; *TR*: Holford; *BR*: Forman
34 - *TX*: Art & Architecture; *TR*: Chronique; *MR*: Mary Evans
35 - *TY*: Art & Architecture; *MM, MR*: Mary Evans; *ML, BR*: Forman
36 - *BY*: British Museum; *TM, TR*: Holford; *MR*: Forman
37 - *TY, BM*: Bridgeman; *MX*: Chronique; *TR*: Mary Evans; *TL*: Topham
38 - *TY*: Mary Evans; *BR*: Holford; *MM*: Harding
39 - *TM, BR*: Bridgeman; *BL*: Mary Evans
40 - *TR*: Chronique; *MR*: Mary Evans
41 - *TL1, TX2*: Bridgeman; *TY, MX*: Forman; *TL2*: Hulton - Deutsch; *TX1*: Mary Evans
42 - *MM*: Art & Architecture; *TY*: Holford; *MR*: Forman
43 - *BR*: Chronique; *TL, TX, TR*: Mary Evans; *BL*: Holford
44 - *TM, TR*: Bridgeman; *BR*: Mary Evans
45 - *TM*: Bridgeman; *BM*: Chronique
46 - *MR*: Bridgeman; *TR*: Hulton-Deutsch; *TX*: Mary Evans
47 - *TL*: Art & Architecture; *TM*: Chronique; *MX, BR*: Forman
48 - *BL*: Bridgeman; *TX, MY*: Mary Evans
49 - *ML*: Art & Architecture; *TX*: Bibliotheque Nationale, Paris; *TR*: Bridgeman
50 - *BY*: C M Dixon; *TM, MM, BX, BR*: Holford
51 - *TM*: Forman
52 - *BM*: Artephot/Ogawa; *TY*: Bridgeman; *MR*: Mary Evans
53 - *TM*: Bridgeman; *ML*: Mary Evans; *BR*: Forman
54 - *TM*: Bridgeman; *BR*: C M Dixon
55 - *BR*: Art & Architecture; *TR*: Bridgeman; *TL*: Mary Evans
56 - *MR*: Hulton-Deutsch; *TX*: Mary Evans; *BR*: Forman
57 - *TL*: Chronique; *MR*: Mary Evans
58 - All pictures from Bridgeman
59 - *BL, MR*: Bridgeman; *TR, MY*: Mary Evans
60 - *BM*: Art & Architecture; *TY*: Mary Evans
61 - *TM*: Harding
62 - *TR*: Popper; *BR*: Scala, Florence
63 - *TL*: Art & Architecture; *BL*: Bridgeman; *TR*: E T Archive; *MR*: Holford; *TY, BL*: Forman
64 - *TM*: Hulton-Deutsch; *MR*: Mary Evans
65 - *BY*: Art & Architecture; *TL*: Chronique; *TR*: Mary Evans
66 - *MM*: Bridgeman; *TR*: Mary Evans
67 - *TL*: Bridgeman; *MX*: E T Archive; *TR*: Hulton-Deutsch; *BR*: Popper
68 - *BM*: Chronique; *TR*: Hulton-Deutsch; *TM*: Mary Evans
69 - *TR*: Art & Architecture; *MR*: Hulton-Deutsch; *TL*: Mary Evans
70 - *MR*: Bridgeman; *TY*: Mary Evans
71 - *BL*: Artephot/Phedon Salou; *TL, TR, TX*: Mary Evans
72 - *BX*: E T Archive; *MR*: Mary Evans; *TX*: Holford
73 - *TR*: Bridgeman; *TX, MX*: Mary Evans; *BR*: Shogakukan
74 - *TY*: Art & Architecture; *MY*: Bridgeman
75 - *TM*: Mary Evans; *BR*: Holford; *BL*: Forman
76 - All pictures from Bridgeman
77 - *TR*: Art & Architecture; *MR*: Bridgeman; *TL*: Hulton-Deutsch; *BL*: Forman
78 - *MR*: Bridgeman; *BX, TR*: C M Dixon
79 - *TL*: Chronique; *TR3*: Hulton-Deutsch; *TX, TR1, TR2*: Mary Evans; *BR*: Forman
80 - *TR*: Bridgeman; *MX*: Mary Evans
81 - All pictures from Bridgeman
82 - *TR*: Chronique; *TX*: Mary Evans
83 - *TY*: Art & Architecture; *TL*: Ronald Grant Archive; *TR*: Topham; *BR*: Forman
84 - *MM*: C M Dixon; *TR*: Mary Evans
85 - *MX*: Art & Architecture; *BR*: Bridgeman; *TX*: Hulton-Deutsch; *ML*: Mary Evans; *TR*: Forman
86 - *BR*: C M Dixon; *TR*: Chronique
87 - *TM, TR*: Bridgeman; *MX*: Giraudon, Paris
88 - *BR*: Holford; *TR*: Forman
89 - *TX, TR, BR*: Art & Architecture; *MX, BX*: Holford
90 - *TM*: Bridgeman; *BR*: Harding
91 - All pictures from Mary Evans
92 - *MX*: C M Dixon; *MR*: Mary Evans; *TM*: Popper
93 - *ML*: Bridgeman; *TY*: E T Archive; *TL*: Mary Evans
94 - All pictures from Bridgeman
95 - *MX*: Art & Architecture; *TL, TR*: Bridgeman; *BX*, C M Dixon; *BR*: Holford
96 - *MY*: Mary Evans; *TR*: Holford
97 - *MX*: Bridgeman; *TX, MR, TR*: Mary Evans
98 - *BX*: E T Archive; *TR*: Hulton-Deutsch, Mary Evans; *MR*: Forman
99 - *BR*: Bridgeman; *TL, MR, TX*: Hulton-Deutsch; *BX*: Forman
100 - *MY*: Bridgeman; *TR*: Topham
101 - *TR*: E T Archive; *MX*: Mary Evans; *TX*: Holford
102 - *MM*: Mary Evans
103 - *BR*: Bridgeman; *BL*: E T Archive; *TL, TR*: Scala, Florence
104 - *TX*: Mary Evans; *TR*: Holford; *BR*: Forman
105 - *TL*: Mary Evans; *TM*: Topham; *BL*: Forman
106 - *TR*: Bridgeman; *MM*: Mary Evans
107 - *BR*: Art & Architecture; *TM*: Chronique; *TL*: Hulton-Deutsch; *BL*: Mary Evans
108 - *BR*: Art and Architecture; *TR*: Mary Evans; *BX*: Holford
109 - *TR*: Art & Architecture; *TX*: Mary Evans; *MM*: Holford
110 - *MY*: Bridgeman; *TR*: Mary Evans
111 - *BL, BR*: Bridgeman; *MR*: Mary Evans; *TX*: Scala, Florence
112 - *TX, TR*: Bridgeman; *MM*: Giraudon, Paris
113 - *MX*: Bridgeman; *TL*: Chronique; *BR*: Mary Evans
114 - *MR*: Art and Architecture; *TY*: Bridgeman
115 - *BX, MM*: C M Dixon; *TL*: Forman
116 - *BR*: Art & Architecture; *TM*: Bridgeman; *TY*: Mary Evans
117 - *MY*: Art & Architecture; *ML*: Smeets Offset Archives; *TL, TY, TR, MR*: Bridgeman
118 - All pictures from Mary Evans
119 - *TL, BX*: Bridgeman; *TR, MR*: Mary Evans
120 - *TR, BR*: Bridgeman; *MR*: Mary Evans
121 - *BR*: Artephot/Nimaaatallah; *TL, MX*: Bridgeman; *TL*: Scala, Florence
122 - All pictures from Bridgeman
123 - *BY, MR*: Art & Architecture; *TM*: Bridgeman
124 - *TR*: Art & Architecture; *TM, BR*: Bridgeman
125 - *TX*: Bridgeman; *TY, MM, MR*: Mary Evans
126 - *TM, MY*: Bridgeman; *MR*: Hulton-Deutsch
127 - *MR*: Bridgeman; *TR*: E T Archive; *TX, MX*: Mary Evans
128 - All pictures from Art & Architecture
129 - *TR*: Art & Architecture; *TL*: Bridgeman; *BL*: Giraudon, Paris; *BR*: Mary Evans
130 - *TM*: Bridgeman; *BY*: Hulton-Deutsch
131 - *BR*: Bridgeman; *TM*: Mary Evans
132 - *TY*: Art & Architecture; *MR*: Mary Evans
133 - *BR*: Hulton-Deutsch; *TL, TR, BX*: Holford
134 - *TR*: Art & Architecture; *BR*: Giraudon, Paris; *TM*: Mary Evans
135 - *MR*: Bridgeman; *BL*: E T Archive; *TL*: Hulton-Deutsch; *TR*: Mary Evans
136 - *TY, MR*: Art & Architecture; *BX*: Bridgeman
137 - *BL*: Mary Evans; *TM*: Holford
138 - All pictures from Bridgeman
139 - *BM*: Ann Ronan; *BR*: Bridgeman; *TY*: Chronique; *TL*: Hulton-Deutsch
140 - *TR*: Art & Architecture
141 - *TM, BR*: Bridgeman; *MY*: Mary Evans
142 - *MR*: Bibliotheque Nationale, Paris
143 - *TX, TY*: Barbara Heller Picture Library; *MX*: Hulton-Deutsch; *MR*: Mary Evans
144 - *TR*: Bridgeman; *BR*: Mary Evans
145 - *ML, TR*: Bridgeman; *BR*: Mary Evans
146 - *MR, BM*: Bridgeman; *TR*: Mary Evans
147 - All pictures from Bridgeman
148 - *TR, MR*: Bridgeman; *BX*: Hulton-Deutsch
149 - *BM*: Bridgeman; *TL*: Mary Evans
150 - *MR*: Chronique; *TR, BR*: Mary Evans
151 - *TX, BX*: Bridgeman; *MR*: E T Archive; *TR*: Hulton-Deutsch; *TL*: Mary Evans
152 - *TR*: Bridgeman; *BR*: Holford
153 - All pictures from Bridgeman
154 - *TY*: Hulton-Deutsch; *MR*: Mary Evans
155 - *TL*: Hulton-Deutsch; *MR, TM*: Mary Evans
156 - All pictures from Mary Evans
157 - *TM*: Bridgeman; *TL, BL*: Mary Evans
158 - *TR*: Chronique
159 - *TX*: Belvoir Castle; *TM, BL*: Bridgeman; *MX*: Hulton-Deutsch
160 - *TR*: Wiciwza, Adam
161 - *TR*: Bridgeman; *TL*: Mary Evans
162 - *TR*: Holford
163 - *ML*: Bridgeman; *TX*: Mary Evans; *MR*: Holford
164 - All pictures from Bridgeman
165 - *TX*: Bridgeman; *MR*: E T Archive; *BL*: Holford
166 - *TR*: Holford
167 - *MX, TR*: Bridgeman; *TL*: Chronique; *BL*: Holford
168 - *BR*: E T Archive; *TR*: Holford
169 - *TR*: Bridgeman; *MR*: Erwin Meyer; *MX*: Hulton-Deutsch
170 - *TY*: National Portrait Gallery; *BR*: Topham
171 - *TL*: Bridgeman; *BR*: C M Dixon; *TR*: Mary Evans
172 - *BR*: Bridgeman
173 - *TR*: Bridgeman; *BL*: Chronique; *TL*: Mary Evans
174 - All pictures from Bridgeman
175 - *TL*: E T Archive; *TR*: Mary Evans; *MX*: Popper
176 - *BR*: Mary Evans; *TR*: Forman
177 - *TX*: Art & Architecture; *BR*: Bridgeman; *TR*: Mary Evans
178 - *TR*: Holford
179 - *BR*: Architectural Association; *BX*: Bridgeman; *TR*: Giraudon, Paris; *TL*: Mary Evans
180 - *TR*: Bridgeman
181 - *BX*: E T Archive; *TL*: Mary Evans; *TR*: Holford
182 - All pictures from Mary Evans
183 - *BX*: Barbara Heller Picture Library; *TL, TY, BR*: E T Archive
184 - *MR*: Rapho/Michaud
185 - *BR*: Art & Architecture; *TR*: Holford; *TL*: Scala, Florence
186 - *TR, BR*: Bridgeman
187 - *ML, MR*: Bridgeman; *BR*: Popper
188 - All pictures from Bridgeman
189 - *ML*: Bridgeman; *TR*: Mario Soares; *TL*: Mary Evans
190 - *TL*: Chronique
191 - *BY*: Art & Architecture; *MR*: Mary Evans; *TL, TM*: The Pierpont Morgan Library, New York
192 - *TR*: Hulton-Deutsch; *MR*: Mary Evans
193 - *TR*: Mary Evans; *TX, MR*: Holford
194 - *MR*: Hulton Deutsch
195 - *MM*: Bridgeman; *TL*: E T Archive; *TR, BY*: Mary Evans
196 - *TR*: By kind permission of the Marquis of Tavistock and the Trustees of the Bedford Estate; *BR*: Forman
197 - *MM*: Bridgeman; *TL*: E T Archive
198 - *TR*: Shogakukan
199 - *MR*: Bridgeman; *TX*: Mary Evans; *TR*: Forman
200 - *MR*: Bridgeman
201 - *TX, TY*: Bridgeman; *MM*: Holford
202 - *MR*: Bridgeman
203 - *TR, MR*: Bridgeman; *TX*: E T Archive; *MX*: Holford
204 - *TR*: Bridgeman
205 - *BR*: E T Archive; *TR*: Mary Evans; *ML*: Forman
206 - *TR*: Bridgeman; *MR*: Mary Evans
207 - *TL, MX*: Bridgeman; *MR*: E T Archive; *TR*: Holford
208 - *TR*: Art & Architecture; *MR*: Bridgeman; *BX*: Mary Evans
209 - *TM*: Bridgeman; *BR*: Mary Evans
210 - *TR*: Chronique
211 - *TR*: Chronique; *MR*: Hulton-Deutsch; *MX*: Novosti Press Agency
212 - *TR*: Bridgeman; *TY*: Forman
213 - *BR*: Art & Architecture; *TL, TR*: Bridgeman
214 - *TY, TR, BR*: Bridgeman
215 - *TL*: Bridgeman; *MR*: Hulton-Deutsch; *TR*: Mary Evans
216 - *MR*: Hulton-Deutsch
217 - *TY, BR*: Bridgeman; *ML*: Popper
218 - *TL*: Mary Evans
219 - *TM*: Chronique; *TL*: Holford
220 - All pictures from Mary Evans
221 - *TR, BR*: Bridgeman; *BL*: Scala, Florence
222 - *TR*: Art & Architecture; *MR*: E T Archive
223 - *TR, BR*: Bridgeman; *TX*: Hulton-Deutsch

224 - *TR:* Mary Evans
225 - *TM:* E T Archive; *BR:* Hulton-Deutsch
226 - *BR:* Smeets Offset Archives; *TR:* E T Archive
227 - *MR, BR:* Bridgeman; *TX:* Mary Evans
228 - *MR:* Forman
229 - *TX:* C M Dixon; *MR:* Mary Evans; *BR:* Rights Reserved
230 - *TR:* Mary Evans; *BR:* Forman
231 - *TX, TR:* Mary Evans; *BR:* Bridgeman
232 - *BR:* The Bodleian Library, Oxford; *TR:* Holford
233 - All pictures from Bridgeman
234 - *TR:* Chronique
235 - *TR:* Bridgeman; *BY:* Hulton-Deutsch; *ML:* Mary Evans
236 - *TR:* Bridgeman; *MR:* Mary Evans
237 - *TM, TY, BR:* Bridgeman; *TX:* C M Dixon; *BL, TL:* Mary Evans
238 - *TR:* Art & Architecture
239 - *MX, TR:* Bridgeman; *TL:* Mary Evans
240 - *TR:* Bridgeman
241, 242 - All pictures from Bridgeman
243 - *MR:* Bridgeman; *TL:* C M Dixon; *TR:* Forman
244, 245 - All pictures from Bridgeman
246 - *TR:* Art & Architecture
247 - *MR:* Bridgeman; *ML, TR:* Mary Evans
248 - *TY:* Art & Architecture; *MR:* Bridgeman
249 - *BY:* Bridgeman; *TR:* Mary Evans; *TL, BL:* Holford
250 - *TR:* Mary Evans; *BR:* Holford
251 - *MX:* Ann Ronan; *TL, BL:* Bridgeman; *TR, MR:* Mary Evans
252 - *TR:* Smeets Offset Archives
253 - *TL:* Bridgeman; *MR:* Chronique; *BR, BL:* Mary Evans
254 - *BR:* Smeets Offset Archives; *TR:* Bridgeman
255 - *TX:* Bridgeman; *MX:* Mary Evans ; *MR:* Hubert Josse
256 - *TR:* Mary Evans
257 - *MX:* C M Dixon; *TR:* E T Archive; *BR:* Mary Evans
258 - *TR:* Forman
259 - *TR:* Mary Evans; *TL:* Forman
260, 261 - All pictures from Bridgeman
262 - *TR:* Harenberg Archives; *MR:* Hulton-Deutsch
263 - *BY:* Bridgeman; *TX, BL:* C M Dixon; *TL:* Mary Evans; *MR:* Holford; *TY:* Topham
264 - *TR:* C M Dixon
265 - *MX:* C M Dixon; *TL:* Chronique; *TY:* E T Archive; *MR:* Mary Evans
266 - *BR:* Mary Evans
267 - *TM:* C M Dixon; *MM:* Chronique
268 - *MR:* Forman
269 - *TL, TR:* Mary Evans; *BX:* Holford
270 - *MM:* Bridgeman
271 - *TL:* Bridgeman; *BR:* C M Dixon; *TR:* Hulton-Deutsch
272 - *TR:* Bridgeman; *MR:* Mary Evans
273 - *TM:* Art & Architecture; *ML:* Bridgeman; *BX:* Forman
274 - *BL:* Mary Evans; *TY:* Holford
275 - *ML:* Hulton-Deutsch; *TR, BR:* Holford
276 - *MY:* Mary Evans
277 - *TX, BR:* Bridgeman; *TR:* Mary Evans; *TL, BX:* Holford
278 - *TR:* Chronique; *MR:* Mary Evans
279 - *MY:* Bridgeman; *TM:* E T Archive; *TL:* Harding
280 - *TR:* Bridgeman
281 - *ML:* Bridgeman; *TM:* Mary Evans
282 - *TR:* Holford
283 - *BR:* C M Dixon; *BY:* Holford; *TX, TR:* Scala, Florence
284 - *MY:* Mary Evans
285 - *TL:* Bridgeman; *TM:* Bridgeman, Hulton-Deutsch; *BR:* Larousse; *TM, MR:* Mary Evans; *BX:* Holford
286 - *TR:* E T Archive; *MR:* Mary Evans
287 - *TR, BL:* Bridgeman; *BR:* Hulton-Deutsch
288 - *TR:* Mary Evans; *BR:* Forman
289 - All pictures from Bridgeman
290 - All pictures from Mary Evans
291 - *TR:* Bridgeman; *TX:* Mary Evans; *BR:* Holford
292 - *BR:* Bridgeman
293 - *TX, TR, ML, BY, BR:* Bridgeman; *ML:* E T Archive
294 - *ML:* Mary Evans
295 - *ML:* Bridgeman; *TR, MY:* Hulton-Deutsch; *TX, ML:* Mary Evans
296 - *MM:* Bridgeman; *TR:* Mary Evans
297 - *TR, BM:* Mary Evans; *TX, MX:* Newarks
298 - All pictures from Mary Evans
299 - *BR:* Bridgeman; *BX:* Hulton-Deutsch; *TL:* Mary Evans
300 - *TR:* Bridgeman; *BR:* Hulton-Deutsch
301 - *BR:* Bridgeman; *TR:* Mary Evans
303 - *TM, BR:* Bridgeman; *MY:* Holford
304 - All pictures from Bridgeman
305 - *TR:* Bridgeman; *ML, BY:* Mary Evans
306 - *MR:* Bridgeman; *TR:* Chronique; *BR:* Mary Evans
307 - *MY, BL:* Bridgeman; *BR:* Mary Evans; *TX, TY:* Holford
308 - *MR:* Chronique
309 - *MR:* Smeets Offset Archives; *TM, ML:* Mary Evans
310 - *TR:* E T Archive; *BR:* Hulton-Deutsch
311 - *TR, BR:* Bridgeman; *TL:* Mary Evans
312, 313 - *MR:* Mary Evans
314 - *TR, MY:* Bridgeman
315 - *TL, TR, BR:* Mary Evans; *MX:* Hulton-Deutsch
316 - *BR:* Bridgeman; *TR:* E T Archive
317 - *MR, BL:* Bridgeman; *TM:* Mary Evans
318 - *BR:* Bridgeman; *TY:* Mary Evans
319 - All pictures from Bridgeman
320 - *MR:* Holford; *TR:* Forman
321 - *BR:* Bridgeman; *TM:* Chronique; *BX:* Mary Evans
322 - *BR:* E T Archive; *TR:* Hulton-Deutsch
323 - *MX:* Bridgeman; *BR:* C M Dixon; *TR:* Mary Evans
324 - *BY:* Bridgeman; *MR:* Hulton-Deutsch
325 - *BR:* Art & Architecture; *TL:* Bridgeman; *TR:* Forman
326 - *MR:* Holford; *TR:* Harding
327 - *TX, BR:* Bridgeman; *TR:* Chronique
328 - *TR:* Bridgeman; *BR:* E T Archive
329 - *TM:* Bridgeman; *BR:* Hulton-Deutsch; *BX:* Mary Evans
330 - *TR:* Bridgeman
331 - *TM:* Art & Architecture; *BR:* E T Archive; *ML:* Mary Evans
332 - *MR:* Bildarchiv Preussischer Kurltubesitz
333 - *TL:* Bridgeman; *MR, BR:* E T Archive
334 - R: Holford
335 - *TM, MR:* Bridgeman; *BX:* Mary Evans
336 - *BY:* C M Dixon; *TR:* Holford; *MR:* Forman
337 - *TL, MX:* Bridgeman; *MY, TR:* Mary Evans
338 - *BX:* E T Archive; *TR:* Mary Evans
339 - *TX, TR, ML:* Bridgeman; *MM:* Hulton-Deutsch; *BR:* Harding
340 - *TR:* Bridgeman; *MR:* Holford
341 - *TM:* Granger; *MR:* Hulton-Deutsch; *MY:* Mary Evans; *MR:* Holford
342 - *TR:* Hulton-Deutsch
343 - *MX, MR:* Bridgeman; *ML:* E T Archive; *TR:* Mary Evans
344 - *MY:* Bridgeman; *TR:* Hulton-Deutsch
345 - *BR:* Bridgeman; *TX, TY, TR, ML:* Mary Evans
346 - *MR:* E T Archive
347 - *MM:* Chronique; *TM, BY:* E T Archive; *BR:* Bridgeman
348 - All pictures from Mary Evans
349 - *BR:* Chronique; *MX:* Granger; *TR:* Hulton-Deutsch; *TL:* Holford
350 - *TR:* E T Archive; *BR:* Mary Evans
351 - *ML, TR, BL:* Bridgeman; *TM:* Granger
352 - *TR:* Mary Evans; *MR:* Harding
353 - *MR:* Bridgeman
355 - *TX, MX, MY:* Bridgeman; *TR:* Mary Evans
356 - All pictures from Mary Evans
357 - All pictures from Bridgeman
358 - *BR:* C M Dixon; *TR:* E T Archive
359 - *MR:* Bridgeman; *TL, MM:* Mary Evans
360 - *BY, BR:* Bridgeman; *TR:* Mary Evans
361 - *MR:* Bridgeman; *TL, MX:* Mary Evans
362 - *MR:* Bridgeman; *TR:* Mary Evans
363 - *MR:* Mary Evans; *TL, TX:* Newarks
364 - *BR:* Bridgeman; *TR:* Mary Evans
365 - *BY, BR:* Bridgeman; *TR:* Mary Evans; *TL:* Newarks; *BL:* Forman
366 - *TR:* Hulton-Deutsch
367 - *BR:* E T Archive; *TM, MY:* Newarks
368 - *BR:* Mary Evans; *TR:* Architect of the Capital
369 - *MR:* Bridgeman; *TM:* Holford; *BL:* Harding
370 - All pictures from Mary Evans
371 - *TL:* Chronique; *ML:* E T Archive; *TR:* Mary Evans; *MX:* Holford
372 - *MR:* Bridgeman; *TR:* Mary Evans
373 - *TM:* E T Archive; *TL, MY:* Mary Evans; *BY:* Scala, Florence
374 - All pictures from Mary Evans
375 - *TL, BL:* Bridgeman; *TR:* Mary Evans
376 - All pictures from Bridgeman
377 - *TM:* Chronique; *MM:* John Carter Brown Library; *MR:* Mary Evans
378 - *MR:* Bridgeman; *TR:* Mary Evans
379 - *TR:* Bridgeman; *ML, MX:* Mary Evans
380 - *TR:* E T Archive; *BR:* Mary Evans
381 - *TX:* Art & Architecture; *BX, BR:* Bridgeman; *TR:* Mary Evans
382 - *TR:* Bridgeman
383 - *BR:* Bridgeman; *MX:* Hulton-Deutsch; *TX, TR:* Mary Evans
384 - *TR:* Bridgeman; *MR:* Mary Evans
385 - *MX:* India Office Library; *TL, MR, BR:* Mary Evans
386 - *MR:* Chronique
387 - *TM:* Newarks; *MR:* The Times Archive
388 - *MR:* Bridgeman
389 - *TX:* Hulton-Deutsch; *ML:* Larousse; *TR:* Mansell Collection
390 - *MR:* Bridgeman; *TR:* Hulton-Deutsch
391 - *MR, MX, BR:* Bridgeman; *TR:* Tapabor
392 - *MR:* Bridgeman; *MY:* Mary Evans
393 - *TM:* Bridgeman; *BL:* C M Dixon; *MY:* E T Archive; *BR:* Tapabor
394 - *MR:* Bridgeman, Lauros-Giraudon, Paris
395 - *TX, TR:* Mary Evans; *MX, MY:* The Negroes of Surinam, by J.G.Steadman
396 - *BR:* E T Archive; *TR:* Mary Evans
397 - *ML:* E T Archive; *TR, BR:* Mary Evans
398 - *BR:* Mary Evans; *TY, TR:* Holford
399 - *TL:* Bridgeman; *TR:* Mary Evans
400 - *MR:* Bibliotheque Nationale, Paris; *TR:* Mary Evans
401 - *TM:* Jean-Loup Charmet; *ML:* Mary Evans; *MY:* Scala, Florence
402 - *MR:* Hulton-Deutsch
403 - *MR, MY:* Mary Evans; *TL:* Tapabor
404 - *TR:* C M Dixon; *MR:* Mary Evans
405 - *TM, TR, ML:* Bridgeman; *BX:* Hubert Josse, Paris
406 - *MR:* Mary Evans
407 - *MR, BR:* Bridgeman; *TL:* Mary Evans
408 - *MR:* Hubert Josse, Paris; *TR:* Mary Evans
409 - *TM, BX:* Bridgeman; *MY:* Mary Evans; *MR:* Tapabor
410 - *MR:* Bridgeman
411 - *BL:* Bridgeman; *TL, TR, BR:* E T Archive
412 - *MR:* Hubert Josse, Paris; *TX, TY, TR:* Tapabor
413 - *TR:* Bridgeman; *BR:* Mary Evans; *TX:* Newarks; *BL:* Tapabor
415 - *TR:* Lauros-Giraudon, Paris; *TL, ML, MX:* Mary Evans; *BR:* Tallandier
416 - *TR:* Mary Evans
417 - *BR:* Bridgeman; *TM:* E T Archive; *TR, MX:* Mary Evans
418 - *MR:* Bridgeman; *TR:* Mary Evans
419 - *TL:* Bridgeman; *MY, TR:* Mary Evans
420 - *TR:* Bridgeman; *BR:* Mary Evans
421 - *BY:* Bridgeman; *TM:* Larousse; *ML:* Larousse
422 - *TR:* Hubert Josse, Paris
423 - *TL:* Chronique; *BR:* E T Archive
424 - *BR:* "Travels in the Interior of Africa", by Mungo Park; *TR:* Mary Evans
425 - *TL:* Bridgeman; *MR, BX:* Mary Evans
426 - *TR:* Mary Evans
427 - *BR:* E T Archive; *TR:* Mary Evans; *TX:* Tallandier
428 - *TR, MY:* Mary Evans; *MR:* Tapabor
429 - *TL:* Bridgeman; *TR, BX:* Mary Evans; *MR:* Tapabor
430 - *MR:* Bridgeman; *TR:* E T Archive
431 - *BR:* The Bettmann Archive, New York; *TX:* Bridgeman; *TR:* E T Archive; *ML:* Mary Evans
432 - *BR:* Ann Ronan; *TR:* Bridgeman; *MR:* Mary Evans
433 - *TL, TR:* Mary Evans; *MR:* Harding; *MM:* Topham
434 - *TR:* E T Archive
435 - *TR:* Bridgeman; *ML:* Mary Evans; *BM:* Scala, Florence
436 - *TR:* Mary Evans
437 - *BX:* Bridgeman; *TR:* Mary Evans; *TX:* Newarks; *MX:* Topham
438 - *TR:* Hulton-Deutsch; *TY1, TY2, BR:* Mary Evans
439 - *TL, MX:* Bridgeman; *MR:* Granger
440 - *TR:* Mary Evans; *MR:* Newarks
441 - *MR:* Bridgeman; *BR:* Mary Evans; *TL:* Holford
442 - All pictures from Bridgeman
443 - *TR:* Bridgeman; *BR:* Mary Evans; *TL:* Topham
444 - *TR:* Lauros-Giraudon, Paris; *MR:* Newarks
445 - *ML, MR:* Bridgeman; *TR:* E T Archive
446 - *TR:* Bridgeman
447 - *TL, TR, BL:* Bridgeman; *BR:* Mary Evans
448 - *TR:* Bridgeman; *MR:* Mary Evans
449 - *TR:* Giraudon, Paris; *ML:* Mary Evans
450 - All pictures from Mary Evans
451 - *TR:* E T Archive; *ML:* Granger; *BR:* Mary Evans
452 - All pictures from Mary Evans
453 - *TM, TR:* Mary Evans; *MM:* Holford
454 - *TR1:* Bridgeman; *TR2, TR3, TR4, TR5, TR6, BR:* Mary Evans
455 - *MR:* Bridgeman; *TR:* Mary Evans; *TL:* Forman
456 - *MR:* The Bettmann Archive, New York
457 - *BR:* Ann Ronan; *TL:* E T Archive; *TR:* Mary Evans
458 - *TR:* E T Archive
459 - *MM:* Bridgeman; *TM, BR:* Mary Evans
460 - All pictures from Bridgeman
461 - *TL:* Bridgeman; *TM:* Chronique
462 - *MR:* Bridgeman; *TR:* Mary Evans
463 - *TL, TR:* Bridgeman; *BR:* Mary Evans
464 - *MR:* Bridgeman
465 - *ML:* Bridgeman; *MR:* Mary Evans
466 - *TR, BR:* Bridgeman; *TY:* Holford
467 - *MR:* Bridgeman; *MX:* Mary Evans; *TX:* National Portrait Gallery
468 - *MR:* Bridgeman; *TR:* Chronique
469 - *TR:* Bridgeman; *ML:* Mary Evans
470 - *MR:* E T Archive; *TR:* South American Pictures
471 - *BR:* E T Archive; *TR, ML:* Mary Evans; *TX:* Topham
472 - *TR:* Art & Architecture
473 - *TY, MR:* Hulton-Deutsch; *TL, MY:* Mary Evans
474 - All pictures from Bridgeman
475 - *TR, TX:* Bridgeman; *ML:* Hulton-Deutsch; *MY:* Mary Evans
476 - *MR:* Chronique; *TR:* E T Archive
477 - *MR:* Bridgeman; *TL, MY:* Mary Evans
478 - *TR:* Hulton-Deutsch; *MY:* Mary Evans
479 - *MR:* Bridgeman; *TM, BY:* Mary Evans; *ML:* Holford
480 - *MR:* E T Archive; *TR:* Mary Evans
481 - *MR:* Bridgeman; *TR:* Chronique; *ML:* E T Archive
482, 483 - *BR:* Mary Evans
484 - *TR, BR:* E T Archive
485 - *MR:* Bridgeman; *MY:* E T Archive; *TR, ML, BR:* Mary Evans
486 - *BR:* Bridgeman; *TR, MR:* Mary Evans; *TR:* Newarks
487 - *BR:* E T Archive; *ML:* Mary Evans
488 - *MR:* Mary Evans
489 - *TL:* E T Archive; *TR, MX:* Mary Evans; *MR:* Newarks
490 - All pictures from Mary Evans
491 - *ML:* Bridgeman; *TR:* Holford; *MY:* Harding
492 - All pictures from Bridgeman
493 - *BR:* Bridgeman; *TM:* E T Archive; *MX:* Mary Evans
494 - *MR:* Bridgeman
495 - *TM:* Bridgeman; *BR:* E T Archive; *BL:* Mary Evans
496 - *TR:* Bridgeman
497 - *BX:* Bridgeman; *TM:* Hulton-Deutsch; *ML, BR:* Mary Evans
498 - *MR:* Chronique; *BR:* Mary Evans
499 - *TR:* Ann Ronan; *TL, BX:* Newarks
500 - *BR:* Bridgeman; *TR:* Mary Evans
501 - *BL:* Hulton-Deutsch; *TL:* Mary Evans; *TR:* Newarks
502 - *TR:* E T Archive; *BR:* Holford
503 - *ML, TM:* Mary Evans; *BR:* Newarks
504 - *TR:* E T Archive; *MY:* Harding
505 - All pictures from Hulton-Deutsch
506 - *BR:* Bridgeman; *TY:* E T Archive
507 - *TM, BL:* Bridgeman; *MR:* Harding
508 - All pictures from Bridgeman
509 - All pictures from E T Archive
510 - *BR:* Mary Evans; *TR:* Newarks
511 - *ML-* Bridgeman; *BR:* E T Archive; *BL:* Hulton-Deutsch
512 - *TR:* Bridgeman; *BY:* Mary Evans
513 - *BL:* Mary Evans; *TM:* Holford
514 - *TR:* Bridgeman; *BY:* Mary Evans
515 - *BR, BL:* Mary Evans; *TR:* Holford
516 - *TR:* Bridgeman; *BY:* Mary Evans
517 - *TL, BM:* Bridgeman; *TY:* Mary Evans
518 - *TR:* Bridgeman; *MR:* Mary Evans
519 - *TM:* Bridgeman; *MR:* Hulton-Deutsch; *BL:* Mary Evans
520 - All pctures from Mary Evans
521 - *TR, BR:* Mary Evans; *TL:* Newarks
522 - *TR:* E T Archive
523 - *BY:* Mary Evans; *TM:* Harding
524 - All pictures from Newarks
525 - *BL:* Bridgeman; *TR, TX:* Mary Evans
526 - All pictures from Bridgeman
527 - *TM, BL:* Mary Evans; *BY:* Mary Evans
528 - *TR:* Newarks
529 - *MR:* E T Archive; *TX, TY:* Mary Evans; *BR:* Holford
530 - *MR:* Chronique
531 - *TR:* E T Archive; *MX:* Hulton-Deutsch; *BM:* Holford
532 - All pictures from Mary Evans
533 - *BR:* Ann Ronan; *TM, BL:* Bridgeman
534 - *TR:* Bridgeman; *BR:* E T Archive
535 - *TX:* Bridgeman; *ML:* Mary Evans; *TR:* Popper
536 - All pictures from Bridgeman
537 - *MR:* E T Archive; *TL:* Mary Evans; *BR:* Newarks
538 - *TY:* Mary Evans
539 - *MM, MR:* Bridgeman; *BM:* Chronique; *TM:* Popper
540 - All pictures from Bridgeman
541 - *TM, BY:* E T Archive; *BL:* Newarks
542 - *MR:* Mary Evans
543 - *BR:* Mary Evans; *TL:* Popper; *TR:* Topham
544 - *BR:* Smeets Offset Archives; *TR:* C M Dixon; *MX:* Popper
545 - *TR:* Bridgeman; *BR:* Chronique; *TR:* E T Archive
546 - *TR:* Hulton-Deutsch; *BR:* Holford
547 - *ML, BX:* Mary Evans
548 - Bridgeman; *TR:* Newarks
549 - *TR:* Bridgeman; *MX, MR:* Mary Evans; *ML:* Popper
550 - *MR:* Bridgeman; *TR:* Newarks
551 - *BR:* Chronique; *ML:* E T Archive; *TR:* Forman

Photo Credit Index

552 - MY: Mary Evans; MM: Newarks; MR: Popper
553 - BR: Bridgeman; TL, MX: Mary Evans; TR: Newarks
554 - All pictures from Mary Evans
555 - MR: Popper; TX: Topham
556 - BM: Bridgeman; ML: Hulton-Deutsch; TY: Mary Evans
557 - BR: Mary Evans; TL, TR, ML: Newarks
558 - MR: Bridgeman; TY1, TY2, TY3: Newarks
559 - BR: E T Archive; MR, BL: Holford
560 - TR: Popper
561 - TM: Chronique; MY: Popper; TL: Topham; BR: Forman
562 - TY: Larousse; MR, BY: Mary Evans
563 - MX: Newarks; MR: Popper; TL: Topham
564 - TR: E T Archive; MY: Hulton-Deutsch; BR, BX: Mary Evans
565 - TL: Hulton-Deutsch; MR: Mary Evans
566 - BR: Mary Evans; TR: Popper
567 - MR: E T Archive; TL: Mary Evans
568 - MR: Chronique; BR: Mary Evans
569 - MR: Granger; TR, MX: Mary Evans
570 - TR: Mary Evans
571 - TM: Art & Architecture; BR: Hulton-Deutsch; BX: Mary Evans; MY: Popper
572 - MR: Giraudon, Paris
573 - TL: Art & Architecture; MY: Bridgeman; BR: C M Dixon; MX: Popper
574 - BR, MX: Bridgeman; TM: Mary Evans; TR: Topham
575 - TL: E T Archive; TR, BL: Mary Evans
576 - BR: Bridgeman; MY: Mary Evans
577 - BX: Bridgeman; ML: Chronique; TL, MR: Mary Evans
578 - TM: Mary Evans; MR: Newarks; MY: Popper
579 - MM: Hulton-Deutsch; TM: Topham
580 - BR: Bridgeman; MR: Mary Evans
581 - BR: Bridgeman; MY: E T Archive; BL: Mary Evans; TX: Popper
582 - BR: Mary Evans
583 - TY2, TL3: Bridgeman; TL1, MY, MX: Mary Evans
584 - TR, BR: Bridgeman
585 - ML, BR: Bridgeman; TX: Mary Evans
586 - MR: Popper
587 - MR: Bridgeman; MX: E T Archive; TX: Mary Evans; BR: Popper
588 - All pictures from Mary Evans
589 - TR, BX, MR: Mary Evans; TL, MX: Newarks
590 - BY: Hulton-Deutsch; MR: Mary Evans
591 - TR: Bridgeman; BR1, BR2, BR3: Mary Evans; ML: Popper
592 - MR: Mary Evans
593 - BL, MR: Mary Evans; TL: Popper
594 - TM: Bridgeman; MR: Courtauld Institute Galleries, London; TR, BX: Holford
595 - BX: Bridgeman; TX, TM: Mary Evans; MR: Popper
596 - TR: Mary Evans; BY: Popper
597 - TL: Bridgeman; TR, MR: Newarks
598 - TR, MY, BY: Mary Evans; MR: Newarks
599 - MR: Hulton-Deutsch; TX, MX: Mary Evans
600 - TR: Bridgeman; BY: Mary Evans; TY: Newarks
601 - BL: Bridgeman; TR: Hulton-Deutsch; TL: Topham
602 - MY: Hulton-Deutsch; TR: Mary Evans
603 - ML, MY: Mary Evans; TR, MR: Newarks
604 - All pictures from Mary Evans
605 - BR, BL: Bridgeman; TR: Mary Evans
606 - MR: Popper
607 - TR: Bridgeman; MR: E T Archive; BY: Popper
608 - MR: Bridgeman; TR: E T Archive
609 - TL, MX: Mary Evans; TR, MR: Newarks
610 - MY: Mary Evans
611 - TY: Bridgeman; TL: Mary Evans; MR: Newarks; BL: Photo X
612 - BR: Bridgeman; TY: Popper
613 - MR: Mary Evans; TX, TR, ML: Topham
614 - MR: The Museum of Modern Art, New York, Larry Aldrich Fund
615 - MR: Hulton-Deutsch; TL: Larousse; MX: Popper
616 - TR: Hulton-Deutsch; MR: Newarks
617 - TR: Courtauld Institute Galleries, London; ML: Newarks
618 - TM: Bridgeman; BM: Hulton-Deutsch; MY: Topham
619 - ML: Architectural Association; MY: Bridgeman; MR, BL: Mary Evans; TR: Newarks
620 - MR: Bridgeman; MY: Popper
621 - BL, BR: Bridgeman; TL: Hulton-Deutsch; MX, TR: Mary Evans; TY: Newarks
622 - TY: Ann Ronan; MR: Bridgeman
623 - MR, BY: Bridgeman; TL: Popper
624 - BY: John Hannavy Collection; TR: Mary Evans
625 - TR: Bridgeman; BL, MR: Mary Evans
626 - BY: Bridgeman; TY: Hulton-Deutsch; MR: Topham
627 - All pictures from Mary Evans
628 - All pictures from Bridgeman
629 - TL: Church Missionary Society; TR, BX, MR: Mary Evans
630 - TR: Larousse; BR: Topham
631 - MY, MR, BR: Bridgeman; ML: Chronique; TX: Church Missonary Society
632 - MY: Mary Evans; TM: Newarks
633 - MY: Chronique; TM: E T Archive; MR: Mary Evans; ML: Popper
634 - BY: Bridgeman; TY: C M Dixon
635 - ML: Bridgeman; MX: British Museum; TR: Popper
636 - MM, BR: Mary Evans; TX: Topham
637 - BR: Chronique; MR: Newarks; TL: Popper
638 - MR, BX: Mary Evans; TM: Newarks
639 - TM: Bridgeman; TR: Chronique; BX: Newarks; MR: Popper
640 - MY: Mary Evans; BR: National Film Archive London
641 - TX: Hulton-Deutsch; MX, MR: Mary Evans; ML: Popper
642 - BR: Bridgeman; TY: Mary Evans
643 - TX: E T Archive; BR: Mary Evans; MR, BX: Popper
644 - All pictures from Bridgeman
645 - MX, MR: Mary Evans; TR: Holford; ML: Newarks
646 - TR: Bridgeman (Copyright DACS 1989); MR: Popper
647 - MR: Bridgeman; TL, TR, MX: Mary Evans
648 - BR: Bridgeman
649 - MX: Hulton-Deutsch; MY: Mary Evans; TL, TR: Popper
650 - TR: Popper; MR: Visual Arts (Copyright DACS 1989)
651 - TX: E T Archive; MR, BL: Mary Evans
652 - TR, BY: Mary Evans
653 - BR: Bridgeman; MX: Mary Evans; TL: Newarks
654 - MM: Bridgeman
655 - TY: E T Archive; MR, MX: Mary Evans; TL: Popper
656 - BR: Hulton-Deutsch; TR: Holford
657 - TR: Chronique; MY: E T Archive; ML: Popper; TX: Topham
658 - TR: Hulton-Deutsch
659 - TM: Hulton-Deutsch; BX, BR: Topham
660 - TR: E T Archive; BY: Mary Evans
661 - TM, ML, BY: Hulton-Deutsch
662 - TR: Newarks; BR: Popper
663 - ML: Hulton-Deutsch; TR: Popper; BR: Topham
664 - TR: E T Archive
665 - TL: Chronique; BR: E T Archive; TR: Topham
666 - TR: Hulton-Deutsch; MR: Popper
667 - MM: Chronique; TL: Popper
668 - BR: Aldus Archive; TR: Newarks
669 - TY: Chronique; BM: Popper; TL: Topham
670 - BR: Topham
671 - TM: Popper
672 - BR: Mary Evans; TR: Popper
673 - BR: Hulton-Deutsch; TY: Mary Evans; TL: Popper
674 - MM: Popper; TR: Topham
675 - TM: Hulton-Deutsch; BR, BL: Popper
676 - BR: Chronique; TR: Topham
677 - TR: Trustees of the Imperial War Museum; BR: Chronique
678 - MM: Mary Evans
679 - BR: Mary Evans; TM: Topham
680 - All pictures from Mary Evans
681 - BL: David King Collection; TR: Popper
682 - MR: Popper
683 - TL: Mary Evans; BM: Newarks
684 - TR: Popper
685 - MR, MX: Mary Evans; TM: Popper
686 - BR: Newarks; TR: Popper
687 - BR: Bridgeman (Copyright DACS 1989); BX: Mary Evans; TL: Popper
688 - TR: Popper
689 - BR: Hulton-Deutsch; ML: Popper
690 - MR: Popper
691 - TR1, TR3: Hulton-Deutsch; BR, TR2: Mary Evans; TL: Popper
692 - MY: Hulton-Deutsch; MR: Topham
693 - BM: Bridgeman; TM: Hulton-Deutsch
694 - TR: Kobal Collection
695 - BR: The Bettmann Archive, New York; TR: Hulton-Deutsch; TL: Popper
696 - BR: Kobal Collection; TR: Popper
697 - TL: Chronique; BM: Sygma (L'Illustration)
698 - MR: Hulton-Deutsch; TR: Popper
699 - BX, MR: Mary Evans; TL: Newarks; TM: Popper
700 - TR: Mary Evans; MR, BX: Popper
701 - TX: E T Archive; TR: Hulton-Deutsch; MX: Popper; BR: Ronald Grant Archive
702 - MR: Popper
703 - TL: Hulton-Deutsch; TR: Mary Evans; MY: Popper
704 - BL: Ronald Grant Archive
705 - MR: Chronique; TY: E T Archive; BX: Hulton-Deutsch; TL: Mary Evans; TX: Newarks; TR: Popper
706 - TM, BM: Bridgeman; MR: Newarks
707 - BR: Bridgeman; BY: Hulton-Deutsch; TR: Imperial War Museum; TX: Mary Evans; MX: Topham
708 - All pictures from Popper
709 - BR: Hulton-Deutsch; TR, ML: Popper
710 - TR: Chronique; MR: Popper
711 - BL: Bridgeman; MR: Chronique; TR: Hulton-Deutsch
712 - TY, TR: Mary Evans; BY: Popper
713 - TM, MR: Popper
714 - BR: Bridgeman (Copyright DACS 1989); TR: Mary Evans
715 - TX: Hulton-Deutsch; BL: Mary Evans; MR: Newarks
716 - BR: Bridgeman (Copyright DACS 1989)
717 - BX: Bridgeman; TL, TR: Popper
718 - TR: Hulton-Deutsch; TM: Mary Evans; BY: Ronald Grant Archive
719 - BR: Mary Evans; TL, BY: Popper; TR: Topham
720 - BL: Mary Evans; TR: Popper
721 - TX: Popper; MX: Topham
722 - MY: E T Archive; TY: Hulton-Deutsch; BR: Mary Evans
723 - TL: Hulton-Deutsch; MR: Mary Evans
724 - TR: Popper; BR: Topham
725 - TR, MX, MY: Hulton-Deutsch; TL: Popper
726 - TR: Chronique
727 - TR: Hulton-Deutsch; MM, MX: Newarks; TX: Popper
728 - BR: Kobal Collection; MR: Popper
729 - TL: Chronique; BR: Imperial War Museum; TR: Newarks
730 - TR: Popper
731 - TX: Imperial War Museum; TR, ML: Popper; BR: Topham
732, 733, 734 - All pictures from Popper
735 - BL: Chronique; MR: Imperial War Museum; TL: Topham
736 - MR: Hulton-Deutsch
737 - TL, TR: Hulton-Deutsch; MY: Popper; MX: Topham
738 - BR: Chronique; MR: Hulton-Deutsch
739 - All pictures from Hulton-Deutsch
740 - BL: Hulton; M: TRH; TL, BR: Popper
741 - TL: Hulton; M: TRH; TR, BL: Popper
742 - BL, TR: Hulton; BR, Y: Popper
743 - BL, Y, TM1, TM2: Popper
744 - BL, Y, TL: Popper
745 - BM, Y, TL, T R: Popper
746 - BR: Bertlesmann; X, TR: Popper
747 - TM: Camera Press; M: ET Archive/Sewell; BM, BR: Popper
748 - BR: Bridgeman Art Library/Museé National d'Art Moderne, Paris; X, T M: Popper
749 - BR, BM, X, TM: Popper
750 - BR, X, TR: Popper
751 - BR, BM, X, TR: Popper
752 - X, Y, TR: Popper
753 - X: Hulton; BR, TM: Popper
754 - TM: Hulton; BR: Science Photo Library/Irvine Geis; X: TR Hulton
755 - BM, Y, TL: Popper
756 - X, Y, TM: Popper
757 - TR: Hulton; BR, X, TM: Popper
758 - X, Y, BM: Popper
759 - BL: Hulton; TL, Y: Popper
760 - BM, Y, TR: Popper
761 - TR: Hulton; B, X. Y: Popper
762 - BM, BR, TM: Popper
763 - TM: Bettmann; Y: Hulton; B: Popper
764 - TM, Y, BM: Popper
765 - BL: Hulton; TL, Y: Popper
766 - BM: Kobal Collection; Y, TM: Popper
767 - B, Y: Hulton; TL: Popper
768 - X, Y: Popper
769 - BR: Bettmann; BL: Hulton; M: Popper
770 - BR,X,Y: Popper
771 - X: Bertlesmann; BR: Hulton; TM: Popper
772 - BM, X, Y,: Popper
773 - Y, TL: Bettmann; BM: Popper
774 - Y: Hulton; BM, TM: Popper
775 - BL,TR: Hulton; YB, YT, TL: Popper
776 - BM, Y, X: Popper
777 - Y: Bettmann; TL: Hulton; BR, X: Popper
778 - BL: Hulton; Y, TM: Popper
779 - BM: Bettmann; X,TR: Hulton; TM: Popper
780 - Y: Hulton; BM,TM: Popper
781 - BM: X, YB ,YT: Popper
782 - X,Y,TL: Popper
783 - BL: Hulton; Y, TL, TR: Popper
784 - TL: Associated Press; X, Y: Popper
785 - X: Hulton; BR, TM: Popper
786 - BM, BR, M, TL: Popper
787 - Y,TR: Hulton; X: Popper; TM: Redferns
788 - BL, X, YT ,YB: Popper
789 - X: Hulton; BL, TM: Popper
790 - BM, X: Popper; Y: Syndication
791 - BL: Bettmann; M, Y: Popper; TL: Syndication
792 - BM, X, Y: Popper
793 - XB, BR, TR: Popper; XT: Syndication
794 - X: Bridgeman/Musem Picasso,Paris; BL, Y, TR: Hulton
795 - TR: Bertlesmann; BL: Hulton; TL, BR: Popper
796 - X: Bertlesmann; TR: Popper; BR: Syndication
797 - X: Hulton; Y, TL, TR: Popper
798 - X: Hulton; TR: Popper
799 - YT, X: Hulton; BL, YB, TM: Popper
800 - BM, YT, TM: Hulton; YB: Rex;
801 - TL: Bettmann/UPI; TR: Popper; BL: Rex; BR: TRH
802 - BR: Camera Press; Y: Hulton; X: TRH
803 - BM, YT, TL: Hulton; YB: Popper
804 - BR, X, Y: Bettmann/UPI
805 - TL: Bettmann; BR, Y, TM, TR: Popper
806 - M: Bertlesmann; TM, TR: Bettmann/UPI
807 - TR: Bertlesmann; X, Y, TL: Bettmann/UPI; BR: Hulton
808 - X: Bettmann/UPI; BL, Y: Popper
809 - BL: Bettmann/AFP; Y, TM: Bettmann/UPI; X: Hulton; BM: TRH
810 - X: Hulton; BL: Popper; BM: TRH
811 - BL: Bettmann/UPI; BR, Y, TL: Popper
812 - BM, X, Y: Popper
813 - BL, BR, TR: Popper; X: TRH
814 - BR, TM: TRH; BM, Y: Popper
815 - BR: Bertlemann; X: Popper; Y: TRH
816 - BM: Bettmann/UPI; M: Popper; Y: Syndication
817 - X,TR: Bettmann; TM: Bettmann/UPI; ER: Popper
818 - TM: Bertlesmann; BM: Bettmann/Reuters; X Y: Popper
819 - TM: Bettmann; BM, X, Y: Popper;
820 - BR: Bertlesmann; Y: Bettmann; X: Popper
821 - BR: Bertlesmann; TM: Bettmann; BL, Y: Popper; X: TRH
822 - TM: Bettmann/Reuters; BM,Y: Popper;
823 - X: Bertlesmann; BR: Hulton; TR: Popper
824 - BL, X ,TR: Rex
825 - TL, YT, BL, YB: Rex
826 - BM: Bettmann/Reuters; TM Y: Bettmann/UPI
827 - TL: Bettmann; BL: Bettmann/Reuters; M, Y: Popper
828 - BM,BR: Bertlesmann; TM: Bettmann/Reuters; Y: Popper
829 - TR: Bertlemann; XB, XT, Y: Popper
830 - TM X, BR: Popper; TR: TRH
831 - BL, X, Y, TM: Popper
832 - BM, Y, TM: Popper
833 - BR, X, TL: Popper; TR: Rex
834 - BR: Bertlesmann; X, Y: Popper
835 - TL: Bettmann/Reuters; X, Y: Popper; BM: TRH
836 - Y: Bertlesmann; BM, BR, X: Popper
837 - BL: Bertlesmann; BR ,Y: Bettmann/Reuters; TL: Popper
838 - BR: Popper; TM, M, BM: Rex
839 - Y,TR, TL: Associate Press; BL: Rex
840 - All pictures from Associated Press
841 - T: Asahi Shimbun; MR, B: Associated Press
842 - TL, TR, BL: Associated Press; BR: Bettmann/UPI
843 - All Associated Press
844 - MR, BL, BR: Associated Press; T: CNN;
845 - All Associated Press
846 - All Associated Press
847 - All Associated Press